KEY TO WORLD MAP PAGES

EAN

ASIA 26-27

32-33

34-35

30-31

40-41

42-43

38-39

36-37

PACIFIC OCEAN 64-65

INDIAN OCEAN

59

60-61

62-63

59

AUSTRALIA AND OCEANIA

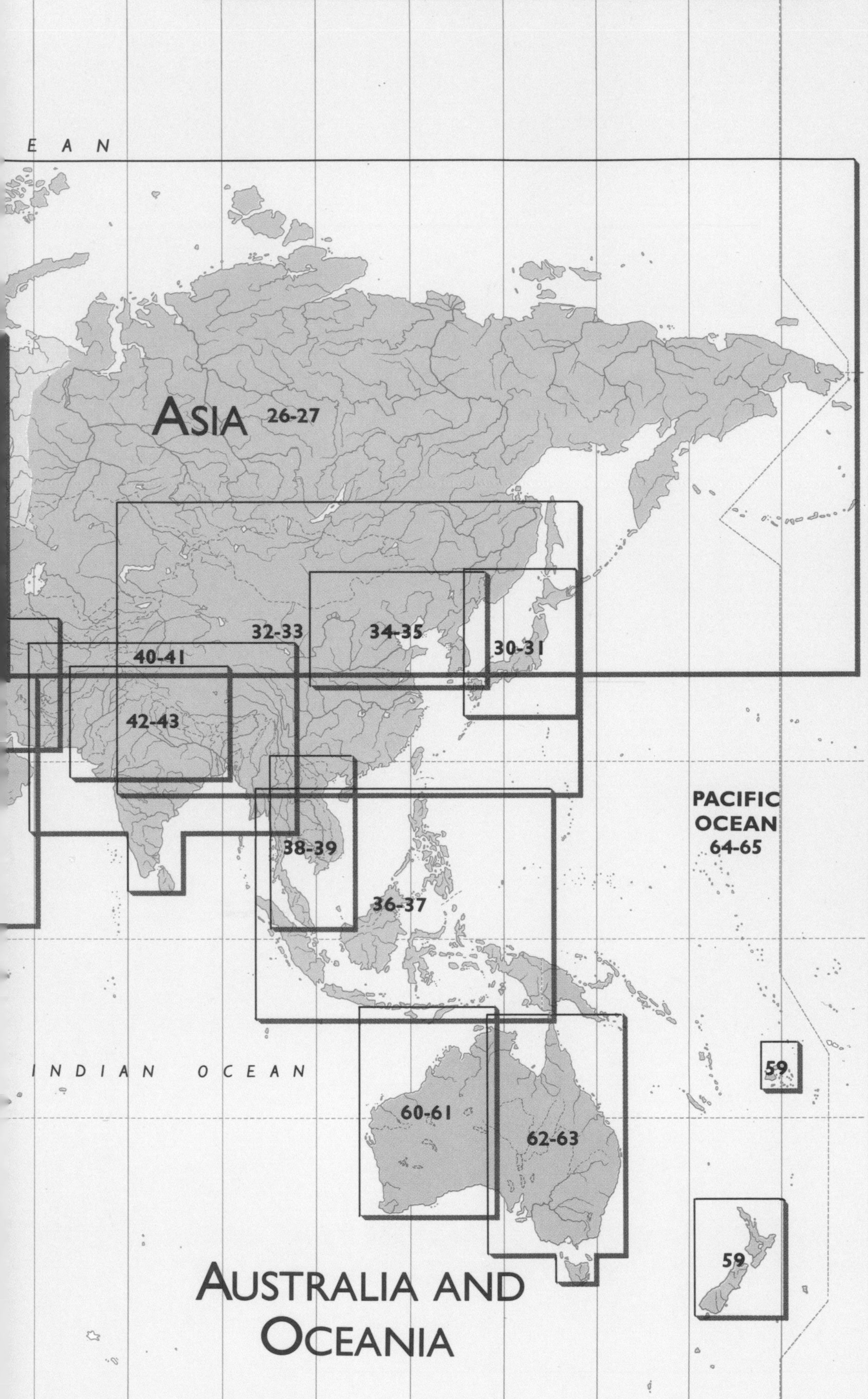

COUNTRY INDEX

Afghanistan 40
Albania 21
Algeria 50
Angola 52–53
Argentina 96
Armenia 25
Australia 60–63
Austria 16
Azerbaijan 25

Bahamas 88–89
Bahrain 45
Bangladesh 41
Barbados 89
Belarus 24
Belgium 15
Belize 88
Benin 50
Bhutan 41
Bolivia 92
Bosnia-Herzegovina 20–21
Botswana 56–57
Brazil 92–96
Brunei 36
Bulgaria 21
Burkina Faso 50
Burma 41
Burundi 54

Cambodia 38–39
Cameroon 52
Canada 68–69
Central African Republic 52
Chad 51
Chile 92–96
China 32–35
Colombia 92
Congo 52
Congo, Dem. Rep. of the 52–53
Costa Rica 88
Croatia 20–21
Cuba 88–89
Cyprus 23
Czech Republic 16–17

Denmark 9
Djibouti 46
Dominican Republic 89

Ecuador 92
Egypt 51
El Salvador 88
England 10–11
Equatorial Guinea 52
Eritrea 46
Estonia 24
Ethiopia 46

Fiji 59
Finland 8–9
France 18
French Guiana 93

Gabon 52
Gambia 50
Georgia 25
Germany 16
Ghana 50
Greece 21
Greenland 4
Guatemala 88
Guinea 50
Guinea-Bissau 50
Guyana 92

Haiti 89
Honduras 88
Hungary 16–17

Iceland 8
India 40–43
Indonesia 36–37
Iran 44–45
Iraq 44–45
Irish Republic 13
Israel 47
Italy 20–21
Ivory Coast 50

Jamaica 88
Japan 30–31
Jordan 47

Kazakstan 26
Kenya 54
Korea, North 35
Korea, South 35
Kuwait 44–45
Kyrgyzstan 26

Laos 38
Latvia 24
Lebanon 47
Lesotho 57
Liberia 50
Libya 51
Lithuania 24
Luxembourg 15

Macedonia 21
Madagascar 57
Malawi 55
Malaysia 36–37
Mali 50
Malta 23
Mauritania 50
Mauritius 49
Mexico 86–87
Moldova 17
Mongolia 32–33
Morocco 50
Mozambique 55, 57

Namibia 56
Nepal 43
Netherlands 15
New Zealand 59
Nicaragua 88
Niger 50–51
Nigeria 50–51
Northern Ireland 13
Norway 8–9

Oman 46

Pakistan 40, 42
Panama 88
Papua New Guinea 64
Paraguay 94–95
Peru 92
Philippines 37
Poland 16–17
Portugal 19
Puerto Rico 89

Qatar 45

Romania 17
Russia 24–27
Rwanda 54

Saudi Arabia 46
Scotland 12
Senegal 50
Sierra Leone 50
Singapore 39
Slovak Republic 16–17
Slovenia 20
Somali Republic 46
South Africa 56–57
Spain 19
Sri Lanka 40
Sudan 51
Surinam 93
Swaziland 57
Sweden 8–9
Switzerland 16
Syria 44

Taiwan 33
Tajikistan 26
Tanzania 54–55
Thailand 38–39
Togo 50
Trinidad and Tobago 89
Tunisia 50–51
Turkey 25
Turkmenistan 26

Uganda 54
Ukraine 24–25
United Arab Emirates 45
United Kingdom 10–14
USA 74–85
Uruguay 94–95
Uzbekistan 26

Venezuela 92
Vietnam 38–39

Wales 10–11

Yemen 46
Yugoslavia 21

Zambia 55
Zimbabwe 55

PHILIP'S

ATLAS
OF THE WORLD

The Gazetteer of Nations
Text Keith Lye

This 1999 edition published
by Chancellor Press,
a division of Octopus Publishing Group Limited,
2–4 Heron Quays, London E14 4JP

Cartography by Philip's

ISBN 0–75370–163–4

A CIP catalogue record for this book is available from the British Library.

Printed in China

Details of other Philip's titles and services can be found on our website at: www.philips-maps.co.uk

PHILIP'S

ATLAS OF THE WORLD

CHANCELLOR PRESS

Contents

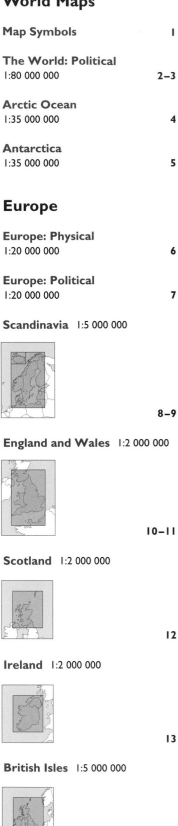

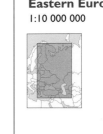

World Statistics

Countries vi

Physical Dimensions vii

Philip's World Maps viii

The Gazetteer of Nations

An A–Z Gazetteer of Countries 1–48

World Maps

Map Symbols 1

The World: Political 1:80 000 000 2–3

Arctic Ocean 1:35 000 000 4

Antarctica 1:35 000 000 5

Europe

Europe: Physical 1:20 000 000 6

Europe: Political 1:20 000 000 7

Scandinavia 1:5 000 000 8–9

England and Wales 1:2 000 000 10–11

Scotland 1:2 000 000 12

Ireland 1:2 000 000 13

British Isles 1:5 000 000 14

Netherlands, Belgium and Luxembourg 1:2 500 000 15

Middle Europe 1:5 000 000 16–17

France 1:5 000 000 18

Spain and Portugal 1:5 000 000 19

Italy and the Balkan States 1:5 000 000 20–21

Balearics, Canaries and Madeira 1:1 000 000 / 1:2 000 000 22

Malta, Crete, Corfu, Rhodes and Cyprus 1:1 000 000 / 1:1 300 000 23

Eastern Europe and Turkey 1:10 000 000 24–25

Asia

Russia and Central Asia 1:20 000 000 26–27

Asia: Physical 1:50 000 000 28

Asia: Political 1:50 000 000 29

Japan 1:5 000 000 30–31

China and Korea 1:15 000 000 32–33

Northern China and Korea 1:6 000 000 34–35

Indonesia and the Philippines 1:12 500 000 36–37

Mainland South-east Asia 1:6 000 000 38–39

South Asia 1:10 000 000 40–41

The Indo-Gangetic Plain
1:6 000 000

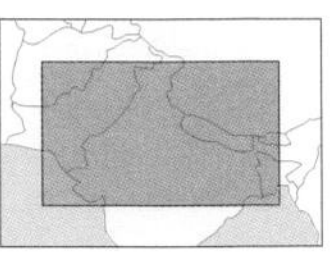

42–43

The Middle East
1:7 000 000

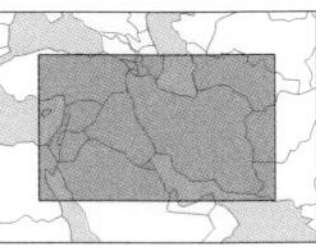

44–45

Arabia and the Horn of Africa 1:15 000 000

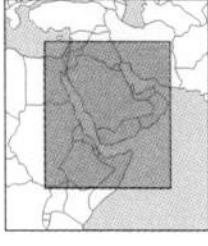

46

The Near East 1:2 500 000

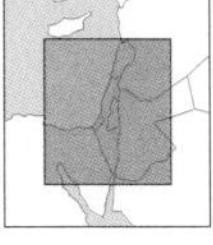

47

Africa

Africa: Physical
1:42 000 000 48

Africa: Political
1:42 000 000 49

Northern Africa
1:15 000 000

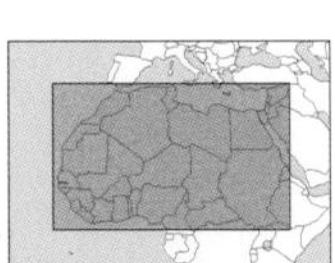

50–51

Central and Southern Africa
1:15 000 000

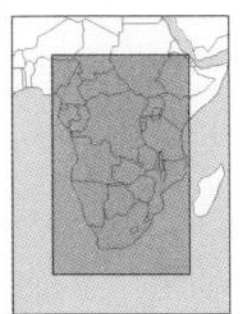

52–53

East Africa 1:8 000 000

54–55

Southern Africa
1:8 000 000
Madagascar 1:8 000 000

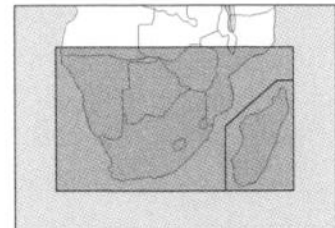

56–57

Australia and Oceania

Australia and Oceania: Physical and Political
1:50 000 000 58

New Zealand 1:6 000 000

59

Western Australia
1:8 000 000

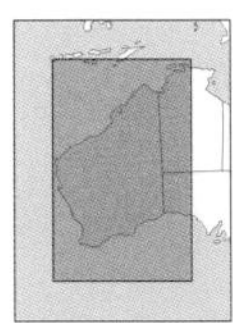

60–61

Eastern Australia
1:8 000 000

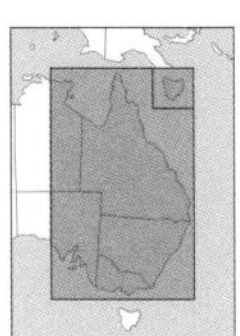

62–63

Pacific Ocean
1:54 000 000 64–65

North America

North America: Physical
1:35 000 000 66

North America: Political
1:35 000 000 67

Canada
1:15 000 000
Alaska 1:30 000 000

68–69

Eastern Canada
1:7 000 000

70–71

Western Canada
1:7 000 000

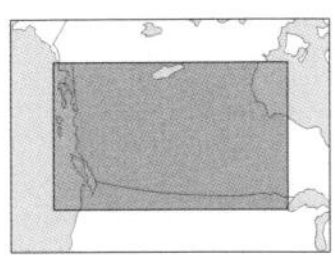

72–73

United States
1:12 000 000
Hawaii 1:10 000 000

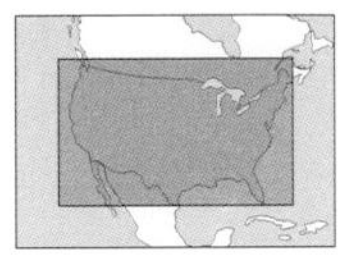

74–75

Eastern United States
1:6 000 000

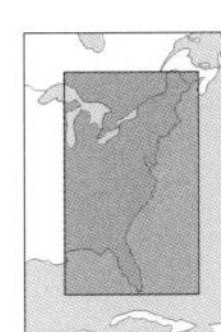

76–77

North-eastern United States
1:2 500 000

78–79

Middle United States
1:6 000 000

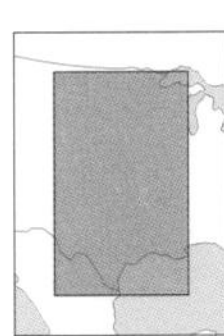

80–81

Western United States
1:6 000 000

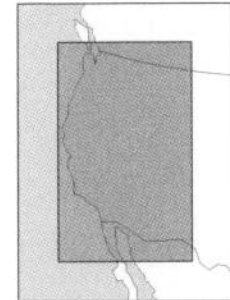

82–83

Central and Southern California and Washington
1:2 500 000

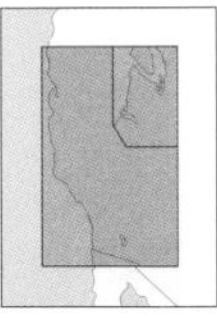

84–85

Mexico 1:8 000 000

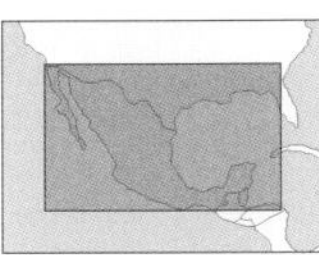

86–87

Central America and the West Indies 1:8 000 000

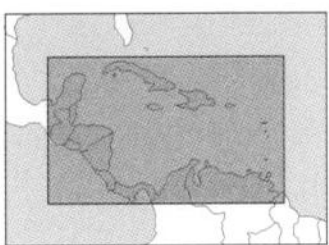

88–89

South America

South America: Physical
1:35 000 000 90

South America: Political
1:35 000 000 91

South America – North
1:16 000 000

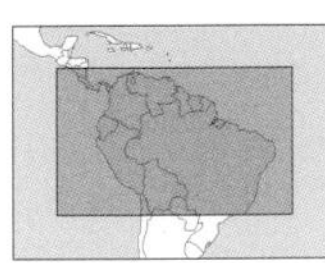

92–93

Central South America
1:8 000 000

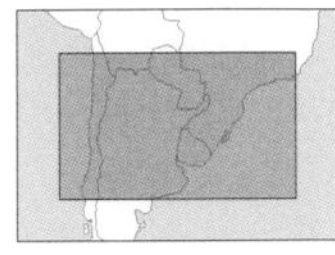

94–95

South America – South
1:16 000 000

96

Index to World Maps
97–176

World: Regions in the News 177

World Statistics: Countries

This alphabetical list includes all the countries and territories of the world. If a territory is not completely independent, then the country it is associated with is named. The area figures give the total area of land, inland water and ice. The population figures are 1998 estimates. The annual income is the Gross National Product per capita in US dollars. The figures are the latest available, usually 1997.

Country/Territory	Area km² Thousands	Area miles² Thousands	Population Thousands	Capital	Annual Income US $
Adélie Land (France)	432	167	0.03	–	–
Afghanistan	652	252	24,792	Kabul	600
Albania	28.8	11.1	3,331	Tirana	750
Algeria	2,382	920	30,481	Algiers	1,490
American Samoa (US)	0.20	0.08	62	Pago Pago	2,600
Andorra	0.45	0.17	75	Andorra La Vella	16,200
Angola	1,247	481	11,200	Luanda	340
Anguilla (UK)	0.1	0.04	11	The Valley	6,800
Antigua & Barbuda	0.44	0.17	64	St John's	7,330
Argentina	2,767	1,068	36,265	Buenos Aires	8,750
Armenia	29.8	11.5	3,422	Yerevan	530
Aruba (Netherlands)	0.19	0.07	69	Oranjestad	15,890
Ascension Is. (UK)	0.09	0.03	1.5	Georgetown	–
Australia	7,687	2,968	18,613	Canberra	20,540
Austria	83.9	32.4	8,134	Vienna	27,980
Azerbaijan	86.6	33.4	7,856	Baku	510
Azores (Portugal)	2.2	0.87	238	Ponta Delgada	–
Bahamas	13.9	5.4	280	Nassau	11,940
Bahrain	0.68	0.26	616	Manama	7,840
Bangladesh	144	56	125,000	Dhaka	270
Barbados	0.43	0.17	259	Bridgetown	6,560
Belarus	207.6	80.1	10,409	Minsk	2,150
Belgium	30.5	11.8	10,175	Brussels	26,420
Belize	23	8.9	230	Belmopan	2,700
Benin	113	43	6,101	Porto-Novo	380
Bermuda (UK)	0.05	0.02	62	Hamilton	31,870
Bhutan	47	18.1	1,908	Thimphu	390
Bolivia	1,099	424	7,826	La Paz/Sucre	950
Bosnia-Herzegovina	51	20	3,366	Sarajevo	300
Botswana	582	225	1,448	Gaborone	4,381
Brazil	8,512	3,286	170,000	Brasília	4,720
British Indian Ocean Terr. (UK)	0.08	0.03	0	–	–
Brunei	5.8	2.2	315	Bandar Seri Begawan	15,800
Bulgaria	111	43	8,240	Sofia	1,140
Burkina Faso	274	106	11,266	Ouagadougou	240
Burma (= Myanmar)	677	261	47,305	Rangoon	1,790
Burundi	27.8	10.7	5,531	Bujumbura	180
Cambodia	181	70	11,340	Phnom Penh	300
Cameroon	475	184	15,029	Yaoundé	650
Canada	9,976	3,852	30,675	Ottawa	19,290
Canary Is. (Spain)	7.3	2.8	1,494	Las Palmas/Santa Cruz	–
Cape Verde Is.	4	1.6	399	Praia	1,010
Cayman Is. (UK)	0.26	0.10	35	George Town	20,000
Central African Republic	623	241	3,376	Bangui	320
Chad	1,284	496	7,360	Ndjaména	240
Chatham Is. (NZ)	0.96	0.37	0.05	Waitangi	–
Chile	757	292	14,788	Santiago	5,020
China	9,597	3,705	1,236,915	Beijing	860
Christmas Is. (Australia)	0.14	0.05	2	The Settlement	–
Cocos (Keeling) Is. (Australia)	0.01	0.005	1	West Island	–
Colombia	1,139	440	38,581	Bogotá	2,280
Comoros	2.2	0.86	545	Moroni	450
Congo	342	132	2,658	Brazzaville	660
Congo (= Zaïre)	2,345	905	49,001	Kinshasa	110
Cook Is. (NZ)	0.24	0.09	20	Avarua	900
Costa Rica	51.1	19.7	3,605	San José	2,640
Croatia	56.5	21.8	4,672	Zagreb	4,610
Cuba	111	43	11,051	Havana	1,300
Cyprus	9.3	3.6	749	Nicosia	13,420
Czech Republic	78.9	30.4	10,286	Prague	5,200
Denmark	43.1	16.6	5,334	Copenhagen	32,500
Djibouti	23.2	9	650	Djibouti	850
Dominica	0.75	0.29	78	Roseau	3,090
Dominican Republic	48.7	18.8	7,999	Santo Domingo	1,670
Ecuador	284	109	12,337	Quito	1,590
Egypt	1,001	387	66,050	Cairo	1,180
El Salvador	21	8.1	5,752	San Salvador	1,810
Equatorial Guinea	28.1	10.8	454	Malabo	530
Eritrea	94	36	3,842	Asmara	570
Estonia	44.7	17.3	1,421	Tallinn	3,330
Ethiopia	1,128	436	58,390	Addis Ababa	110
Falkland Is. (UK)	12.2	4.7	2	Stanley	–
Faroe Is. (Denmark)	1.4	0.54	41	Tórshavn	23,660
Fiji	18.3	7.1	802	Suva	2,470
Finland	338	131	5,149	Helsinki	24,080
France	552	213	58,805	Paris	26,050
French Guiana (France)	90	34.7	162	Cayenne	10,580
French Polynesia (France)	4	1.5	237	Papeete	7,500
Gabon	268	103	1,208	Libreville	4,230
Gambia, The	11.3	4.4	1,292	Banjul	320
Georgia	69.7	26.9	5,109	Tbilisi	840
Germany	357	138	82,079	Berlin/Bonn	28,260
Ghana	239	92	18,497	Accra	370
Gibraltar (UK)	0.007	0.003	29	Gibraltar Town	5,000
Greece	132	51	10,662	Athens	12,010
Greenland (Denmark)	2,176	840	59	Nuuk (Godthåb)	15,500
Grenada	0.34	0.13	96	St George's	2,880
Guadeloupe (France)	1.7	0.66	416	Basse-Terre	9,200
Guam (US)	0.55	0.21	149	Agana	6,000
Guatemala	109	42	12,008	Guatemala City	1,500
Guinea	246	95	7,477	Conakry	570
Guinea-Bissau	36.1	13.9	1,206	Bissau	240
Guyana	215	83	820	Georgetown	690
Haiti	27.8	10.7	6,781	Port-au-Prince	330
Honduras	112	43	5,862	Tegucigalpa	700
Hong Kong (China)	1.1	0.40	6,707	–	22,990
Hungary	93	35.9	10,208	Budapest	4,430
Iceland	103	40	271	Reykjavik	26,580
India	3,288	1,269	984,000	New Delhi	390
Indonesia	1,905	735	212,942	Jakarta	1,110
Iran	1,648	636	64,411	Tehran	4,700
Iraq	438	169	21,722	Baghdad	2,000
Ireland	70.3	27.1	3,619	Dublin	18,280
Israel	27	10.3	5,644	Jerusalem	15,810
Italy	301	116	56,783	Rome	20,120
Ivory Coast (Côte d'Ivoire)	322	125	15,446	Yamoussoukro	690
Jamaica	11	4.2	2,635	Kingston	1,560
Jan Mayen Is. (Norway)	0.38	0.15	1	–	–
Japan	378	146	125,932	Tokyo	37,850
Johnston Is. (US)	0.002	0.0009	1	–	–
Jordan	89.2	34.4	4,435	Amman	1,570
Kazakstan	2,717	1,049	16,847	Astana	1,340
Kenya	580	224	28,337	Nairobi	330
Kerguelen Is. (France)	7.2	2.8	0.7	–	–
Kermadec Is. (NZ)	0.03	0.01	0.1	–	–
Kiribati	0.72	0.28	85	Tarawa	920
Korea, North	121	47	21,234	Pyŏngyang	1,000
Korea, South	99	38.2	46,417	Seoul	10,550
Kuwait	17.8	6.9	1,913	Kuwait City	17,390
Kyrgyzstan	198.5	76.6	4,522	Bishkek	440
Laos	237	91	5,261	Vientiane	400
Latvia	65	25	2,385	Riga	2,430
Lebanon	10.4	4	3,506	Beirut	3,350
Lesotho	30.4	11.7	2,090	Maseru	670
Liberia	111	43	2,772	Monrovia	770
Libya	1,760	679	4,875	Tripoli	6,510
Liechtenstein	0.16	0.06	32	Vaduz	33,000
Lithuania	65.2	25.2	3,600	Vilnius	2,230
Luxembourg	2.6	1	425	Luxembourg	45,360
Macau (China)	0.02	0.006	429	Macau	7,500
Macedonia	25.7	9.9	2,009	Skopje	1,090
Madagascar	587	227	14,463	Antananarivo	250
Madeira (Portugal)	0.81	0.31	253	Funchal	–
Malawi	118	46	9,840	Lilongwe	220
Malaysia	330	127	20,993	Kuala Lumpur	4,680
Maldives	0.30	0.12	290	Malé	1,080
Mali	1,240	479	10,109	Bamako	260
Malta	0.32	0.12	379	Valletta	12,000
Marshall Is.	0.18	0.07	63	Dalap-Uliga-Darrit	1,890
Martinique (France)	1.1	0.42	407	Fort-de-France	10,000
Mauritania	1,030	412	2,511	Nouakchott	450
Mauritius	2.0	0.72	1,168	Port Louis	3,800
Mayotte (France)	0.37	0.14	141	Mamoundzou	1,430
Mexico	1,958	756	98,553	Mexico City	3,680
Micronesia, Fed. States of	0.70	0.27	127	Palikir	2,070
Midway Is. (US)	0.005	0.002	2	–	–
Moldova	33.7	13	4,458	Chişinău	540
Monaco	0.002	0.0001	32	Monaco	25,000
Mongolia	1,567	605	2,579	Ulan Bator	390
Montserrat (UK)	0.10	0.04	12	Plymouth	4,500
Morocco	447	172	29,114	Rabat	1,250
Mozambique	802	309	18,641	Maputo	90
Namibia	825	318	1,622	Windhoek	2,220
Nauru	0.02	0.008	12	Yaren District	10,000
Nepal	141	54	23,698	Katmandu	210
Netherlands	41.5	16	15,731	Amsterdam/The Hague	25,820
Netherlands Antilles (Neths)	0.99	0.38	210	Willemstad	10,400
New Caledonia (France)	18.6	7.2	192	Nouméa	8,000
New Zealand	269	104	3,625	Wellington	16,480
Nicaragua	130	50	4,583	Managua	410
Niger	1,267	489	9,672	Niamey	200
Nigeria	924	357	110,532	Abuja	260
Niue (NZ)	0.26	0.10	2	Alofi	–
Norfolk Is. (Australia)	0.03	0.01	2	Kingston	–
Northern Mariana Is. (US)	0.48	0.18	50	Saipan	11,500
Norway	324	125	4,420	Oslo	36,090
Oman	212	82	2,364	Muscat	4,950
Pakistan	796	307	135,135	Islamabad	490
Palau	0.46	0.18	18	Koror	5,000
Panama	77.1	29.8	2,736	Panama City	3,080
Papua New Guinea	463	179	4,600	Port Moresby	940
Paraguay	407	157	5,291	Asunción	2,010
Peru	1,285	496	26,111	Lima	2,460
Philippines	300	116	77,736	Manila	1,220
Pitcairn Is. (UK)	0.03	0.01	0.05	Adamstown	–
Poland	313	121	38,607	Warsaw	3,590
Portugal	92.4	35.7	9,928	Lisbon	10,450
Puerto Rico (US)	9	3.5	3,860	San Juan	7,800
Qatar	11	4.2	697	Doha	11,600
Queen Maud Land (Norway)	2,800	1,081	0	–	–
Réunion (France)	2.5	0.97	705	Saint-Denis	4,500
Romania	238	92	22,396	Bucharest	1,420
Russia	17,075	6,592	146,861	Moscow	2,740
Rwanda	26.3	10.2	7,956	Kigali	210
St Helena (UK)	0.12	0.05	7	Jamestown	–
St Kitts & Nevis	0.36	0.14	42	Basseterre	5,870
St Lucia	0.62	0.24	150	Castries	3,500
St Pierre & Miquelon (France)	0.24	0.09	7	Saint Pierre	–
St Vincent & Grenadines	0.39	0.15	120	Kingstown	2,370
San Marino	0.06	0.02	25	San Marino	20,000
São Tomé & Príncipe	0.96	0.37	150	São Tomé	330
Saudi Arabia	2,150	830	20,786	Riyadh	6,790
Senegal	197	76	9,723	Dakar	550
Seychelles	0.46	0.18	79	Victoria	6,850
Sierra Leone	71.7	27.7	5,080	Freetown	200
Singapore	0.62	0.24	3,490	Singapore	32,940
Slovak Republic	49	18.9	5,393	Bratislava	3,700
Slovenia	20.3	7.8	1,972	Ljubljana	9,680
Solomon Is.	28.9	11.2	441	Honiara	900
Somalia	638	246	6,842	Mogadishu	500
South Africa	1,220	471	42,835	C. Town/Pretoria/Bloem.	3,400
South Georgia (UK)	3.8	1.4	0.05	–	–
Spain	505	195	39,134	Madrid	14,510
Sri Lanka	65.6	25.3	18,934	Colombo	800
Sudan	2,506	967	33,551	Khartoum	800
Surinam	163	63	427	Paramaribo	1,000
Svalbard (Norway)	62.9	24.3	4	Longyearbyen	–
Swaziland	17.4	6.7	966	Mbabane	1,210
Sweden	450	174	8,887	Stockholm	26,220
Switzerland	41.3	15.9	7,260	Bern	44,220
Syria	185	71	16,673	Damascus	1,150
Taiwan	36	13.9	21,908	Taipei	12,400
Tajikistan	143.1	55.2	6,020	Dushanbe	330
Tanzania	945	365	30,609	Dodoma	210
Thailand	513	198	60,037	Bangkok	2,800
Togo	56.8	21.9	4,906	Lomé	330
Tokelau (NZ)	0.01	0.005	2	Nukunonu	–
Tonga	0.75	0.29	107	Nuku'alofa	1,790
Trinidad & Tobago	5.1	2	1,117	Port of Spain	4,230
Tristan da Cunha (UK)	0.11	0.04	0.33	Edinburgh	–
Tunisia	164	63	9,380	Tunis	2,090
Turkey	779	301	64,568	Ankara	3,130
Turkmenistan	488.1	188.5	4,298	Ashkhabad	630
Turks & Caicos Is. (UK)	0.43	0.17	16	Cockburn Town	5,000
Tuvalu	0.03	0.01	10	Fongafale	600
Uganda	236	91	22,167	Kampala	320
Ukraine	603.7	233.1	50,125	Kiev	1,040
United Arab Emirates	83.6	32.3	2,303	Abu Dhabi	17,360
United Kingdom	243.3	94	58,970	London	20,710
United States of America	9,373	3,619	270,290	Washington, DC	28,740
Uruguay	177	68	3,285	Montevideo	6,020
Uzbekistan	447.4	172.7	23,784	Tashkent	1,010
Vanuatu	12.2	4.7	185	Port-Vila	1,290
Vatican City	0.0004	0.0002	1	–	–
Venezuela	912	352	22,803	Caracas	3,450
Vietnam	332	127	76,236	Hanoi	320
Virgin Is. (UK)	0.15	0.06	13	Road Town	–
Virgin Is. (US)	0.34	0.13	118	Charlotte Amalie	12,000
Wake Is.	0.008	0.003	0.3	–	–
Wallis & Futuna Is. (France)	0.20	0.08	15	Mata-Utu	–
Western Sahara	266	103	280	El Aaiún	300
Western Samoa	2.8	1.1	224	Apia	1,170
Yemen	528	204	16,388	Sana	270
Yugoslavia	102.3	39.5	10,500	Belgrade	2,000
Zambia	753	291	9,461	Lusaka	380
Zimbabwe	391	151	11,044	Harare	750

World Statistics: Physical Dimensions

Each topic list is divided into continents and within a continent the items are listed in order of size. The bottom part of many of the lists is selective in order to give examples from as many different countries as possible. The order of the continents is the same as in the atlas, beginning with Europe and ending with South America. The figures are rounded as appropriate.

World, Continents, Oceans

	km²	miles²	%
The World	509,450,000	196,672,000	–
Land	149,450,000	57,688,000	29.3
Water	360,000,000	138,984,000	70.7
Asia	44,500,000	17,177,000	29.8
Africa	30,302,000	11,697,000	20.3
North America	24,241,000	9,357,000	16.2
South America	17,793,000	6,868,000	11.9
Antarctica	14,100,000	5,443,000	9.4
Europe	9,957,000	3,843,000	6.7
Australia & Oceania	8,557,000	3,303,000	5.7
Pacific Ocean	179,679,000	69,356,000	49.9
Atlantic Ocean	92,373,000	35,657,000	25.7
Indian Ocean	73,917,000	28,532,000	20.5
Arctic Ocean	14,090,000	5,439,000	3.9

Ocean Depths

Atlantic Ocean	m	ft
Puerto Rico (Milwaukee) Deep	9,220	30,249
Cayman Trench	7,680	25,197
Gulf of Mexico	5,203	17,070
Mediterranean Sea	5,121	16,801
Black Sea	2,211	7,254
North Sea	660	2,165
Indian Ocean	m	ft
Java Trench	7,450	24,442
Red Sea	2,635	8,454
Pacific Ocean	m	ft
Mariana Trench	11,022	36,161
Tonga Trench	10,882	35,702
Japan Trench	10,554	34,626
Kuril Trench	10,542	34,587
Arctic Ocean	m	ft
Molloy Deep	5,608	18,399

Mountains

Europe		m	ft
Elbrus	*Russia*	5,642	18,510
Mont Blanc	*France/Italy*	4,807	15,771
Monte Rosa	*Italy/Switzerland*	4,634	15,203
Dom	*Switzerland*	4,545	14,911
Liskamm	*Switzerland*	4,527	14,852
Weisshorn	*Switzerland*	4,505	14,780
Taschorn	*Switzerland*	4,490	14,730
Matterhorn/Cervino	*Italy/Switzerland*	4,478	14,691
Mont Maudit	*France/Italy*	4,465	14,649
Dent Blanche	*Switzerland*	4,356	14,291
Nadelhorn	*Switzerland*	4,327	14,196
Grandes Jorasses	*France/Italy*	4,208	13,806
Jungfrau	*Switzerland*	4,158	13,642
Grossglockner	*Austria*	3,797	12,457
Mulhacén	*Spain*	3,478	11,411
Zugspitze	*Germany*	2,962	9,718
Olympus	*Greece*	2,917	9,570
Triglav	*Slovenia*	2,863	9,393
Gerlachovka	*Slovak Republic*	2,655	8,711
Galdhöpiggen	*Norway*	2,468	8,100
Kebnekaise	*Sweden*	2,117	6,946
Ben Nevis	*UK*	1,343	4,406
Asia		m	ft
Everest	*China/Nepal*	8,848	29,029
K2 (Godwin Austen)	*China/Kashmir*	8,611	28,251
Kanchenjunga	*India/Nepal*	8,598	28,208
Lhotse	*China/Nepal*	8,516	27,939
Makalu	*China/Nepal*	8,481	27,824
Cho Oyu	*China/Nepal*	8,201	26,906
Dhaulagiri	*Nepal*	8,172	26,811
Manaslu	*Nepal*	8,156	26,758
Nanga Parbat	*Kashmir*	8,126	26,660
Annapurna	*Nepal*	8,078	26,502
Gasherbrum	*China/Kashmir*	8,068	26,469
Broad Peak	*China/Kashmir*	8,051	26,414
Xixabangma	*China*	8,012	26,286
Kangbachen	*India/Nepal*	7,902	25,925
Trivor	*Pakistan*	7,720	25,328
Pik Kommunizma	*Tajikistan*	7,495	24,590
Demavend	*Iran*	5,604	18,386
Ararat	*Turkey*	5,165	16,945
Gunong Kinabalu	*Malaysia (Borneo)*	4,101	13,455
Fuji-San	*Japan*	3,776	12,388
Africa		m	ft
Kilimanjaro	*Tanzania*	5,895	19,340
Mt Kenya	*Kenya*	5,199	17,057
Ruwenzori (Margherita)	*Ug./Congo (Z.)*	5,109	16,762
Ras Dashan	*Ethiopia*	4,620	15,157
Meru	*Tanzania*	4,565	14,977
Karisimbi	*Rwanda/Congo (Zaïre)*	4,507	14,787
Mt Elgon	*Kenya/Uganda*	4,321	14,176
Batu	*Ethiopia*	4,307	14,130
Toubkal	*Morocco*	4,165	13,665
Mt Cameroon	*Cameroon*	4,070	13,353
Oceania		m	ft
Puncak Jaya	*Indonesia*	5,029	16,499
Puncak Trikora	*Indonesia*	4,750	15,584
Puncak Mandala	*Indonesia*	4,702	15,427
Mt Wilhelm	*Papua New Guinea*	4,508	14,790
Mauna Kea	*USA (Hawaii)*	4,205	13,796
Mauna Loa	*USA (Hawaii)*	4,170	13,681
Mt Cook (Aoraki)	*New Zealand*	3,753	12,313
Mt Kosciuszko	*Australia*	2,237	7,339
North America		m	ft
Mt McKinley (Denali)	*USA (Alaska)*	6,194	20,321
Mt Logan	*Canada*	5,959	19,551
Citlaltepetl	*Mexico*	5,700	18,701
Mt St Elias	*USA/Canada*	5,489	18,008
Popocatepetl	*Mexico*	5,452	17,887
Mt Foraker	*USA (Alaska)*	5,304	17,401
Ixtaccihuatl	*Mexico*	5,286	17,342
Lucania	*Canada*	5,227	17,149
Mt Steele	*Canada*	5,073	16,644
Mt Bona	*USA (Alaska)*	5,005	16,420
Mt Whitney	*USA*	4,418	14,495
Tajumulco	*Guatemala*	4,220	13,845
Chirripó Grande	*Costa Rica*	3,837	12,589
Pico Duarte	*Dominican Rep.*	3,175	10,417
South America		m	ft
Aconcagua	*Argentina*	6,960	22,834
Bonete	*Argentina*	6,872	22,546
Ojos del Salado	*Argentina/Chile*	6,863	22,516
Pissis	*Argentina*	6,779	22,241
Mercedario	*Argentina/Chile*	6,770	22,211
Huascaran	*Peru*	6,768	22,204
Llullaillaco	*Argentina/Chile*	6,723	22,057
Nudo de Cachi	*Argentina*	6,720	22,047
Yerupaja	*Peru*	6,632	21,758
Sajama	*Bolivia*	6,542	21,463
Chimborazo	*Ecuador*	6,267	20,561
Pico Colon	*Colombia*	5,800	19,029
Pico Bolivar	*Venezuela*	5,007	16,427
Antarctica		m	ft
Vinson Massif		4,897	16,066
Mt Kirkpatrick		4,528	14,855

Rivers

Europe		km	miles
Volga	*Caspian Sea*	3,700	2,300
Danube	*Black Sea*	2,850	1,770
Ural	*Caspian Sea*	2,535	1,575
Dnepr (Dnipro)	*Black Sea*	2,285	1,420
Kama	*Volga*	2,030	1,260
Don	*Black Sea*	1,990	1,240
Petchora	*Arctic Ocean*	1,790	1,110
Oka	*Volga*	1,480	920
Dnister (Dniester)	*Black Sea*	1,400	870
Vyatka	*Kama*	1,370	850
Rhine	*North Sea*	1,320	820
N. Dvina	*Arctic Ocean*	1,290	800
Elbe	*North Sea*	1,145	710
Asia		km	miles
Yangtze	*Pacific Ocean*	6,380	3,960
Yenisey–Angara	*Arctic Ocean*	5,550	3,445
Huang He	*Pacific Ocean*	5,464	3,395
Ob–Irtysh	*Arctic Ocean*	5,410	3,360
Mekong	*Pacific Ocean*	4,500	2,795
Amur	*Pacific Ocean*	4,400	2,730
Lena	*Arctic Ocean*	4,400	2,730
Irtysh	*Ob*	4,250	2,640
Yenisey	*Arctic Ocean*	4,090	2,540
Ob	*Arctic Ocean*	3,680	2,285
Indus	*Indian Ocean*	3,100	1,925
Brahmaputra	*Indian Ocean*	2,900	1,800
Syrdarya	*Aral Sea*	2,860	1,775
Salween	*Indian Ocean*	2,800	1,740
Euphrates	*Indian Ocean*	2,700	1,675
Amudarya	*Aral Sea*	2,540	1,575
Africa		km	miles
Nile	*Mediterranean*	6,670	4,140
Congo	*Atlantic Ocean*	4,670	2,900
Niger	*Atlantic Ocean*	4,180	2,595
Zambezi	*Indian Ocean*	3,540	2,200
Oubangi/Uele	*Congo (Zaïre)*	2,250	1,400
Kasai	*Congo (Zaïre)*	1,950	1,210
Shaballe	*Indian Ocean*	1,930	1,200
Orange	*Atlantic Ocean*	1,860	1,155
Cubango	*Okavango Swamps*	1,800	1,120
Limpopo	*Indian Ocean*	1,600	995
Senegal	*Atlantic Ocean*	1,600	995
Australia		km	miles
Murray–Darling	*Indian Ocean*	3,750	2,330
Darling	*Murray*	3,070	1,905
Murray	*Indian Ocean*	2,575	1,600
Murrumbidgee	*Murray*	1,690	1,050
North America		km	miles
Mississippi–Missouri	*Gulf of Mexico*	6,020	3,740
Mackenzie	*Arctic Ocean*	4,240	2,630
Mississippi	*Gulf of Mexico*	3,780	2,350
Missouri	*Mississippi*	3,780	2,350
Yukon	*Pacific Ocean*	3,185	1,980
Rio Grande	*Gulf of Mexico*	3,030	1,880
Arkansas	*Mississippi*	2,340	1,450
Colorado	*Pacific Ocean*	2,330	1,445
Red	*Mississippi*	2,040	1,270
Columbia	*Pacific Ocean*	1,950	1,210
Saskatchewan	*Lake Winnipeg*	1,940	1,205
South America		km	miles
Amazon	*Atlantic Ocean*	6,450	4,010
Paraná–Plate	*Atlantic Ocean*	4,500	2,800
Purus	*Amazon*	3,350	2,080
Madeira	*Amazon*	3,200	1,990
São Francisco	*Atlantic Ocean*	2,900	1,800
Paraná	*Plate*	2,800	1,740
Tocantins	*Atlantic Ocean*	2,750	1,710
Paraguay	*Paraná*	2,550	1,580
Orinoco	*Atlantic Ocean*	2,500	1,550
Pilcomayo	*Paraná*	2,500	1,550
Araguaia	*Tocantins*	2,250	1,400

Lakes

Europe		km²	miles²
Lake Ladoga	*Russia*	17,700	6,800
Lake Onega	*Russia*	9,700	3,700
Saimaa system	*Finland*	8,000	3,100
Vänern	*Sweden*	5,500	2,100
Asia		km²	miles²
Caspian Sea	*Asia*	371,800	143,550
Lake Baykal	*Russia*	30,500	11,780
Aral Sea	*Kazakstan/Uzbekistan*	28,687	11,086
Tonlé Sap	*Cambodia*	20,000	7,700
Lake Balqash	*Kazakstan*	18,500	7,100
Africa		km²	miles²
Lake Victoria	*East Africa*	68,000	26,000
Lake Tanganyika	*Central Africa*	33,000	13,000
Lake Malawi/Nyasa	*East Africa*	29,600	11,430
Lake Chad	*Central Africa*	25,000	9,700
Lake Turkana	*Ethiopia/Kenya*	8,500	3,300
Lake Volta	*Ghana*	8,500	3,300
Australia		km²	miles²
Lake Eyre	*Australia*	8,900	3,400
Lake Torrens	*Australia*	5,800	2,200
Lake Gairdner	*Australia*	4,800	1,900
North America		km²	miles²
Lake Superior	*Canada/USA*	82,350	31,800
Lake Huron	*Canada/USA*	59,600	23,010
Lake Michigan	*USA*	58,000	22,400
Great Bear Lake	*Canada*	31,800	12,280
Great Slave Lake	*Canada*	28,500	11,000
Lake Erie	*Canada/USA*	25,700	9,900
Lake Winnipeg	*Canada*	24,400	9,400
Lake Ontario	*Canada/USA*	19,500	7,500
Lake Nicaragua	*Nicaragua*	8,200	3,200
South America		km²	miles²
Lake Titicaca	*Bolivia/Peru*	8,300	3,200
Lake Poopo	*Peru*	2,800	1,100

Islands

Europe		km²	miles²
Great Britain	*UK*	229,880	88,700
Iceland	*Atlantic Ocean*	103,000	39,800
Ireland	*Ireland/UK*	84,400	32,600
Novaya Zemlya (N.)	*Russia*	48,200	18,600
Sicily	*Italy*	25,500	9,800
Corsica	*France*	8,700	3,400
Asia		km²	miles²
Borneo	*Southeast Asia*	744,360	287,400
Sumatra	*Indonesia*	473,600	182,860
Honshu	*Japan*	230,500	88,980
Sulawesi (Celebes)	*Indonesia*	189,000	73,000
Java	*Indonesia*	126,700	48,900
Luzon	*Philippines*	104,700	40,400
Hokkaido	*Japan*	78,400	30,300
Africa		km²	miles²
Madagascar	*Indian Ocean*	587,040	226,660
Socotra	*Indian Ocean*	3,600	1,400
Réunion	*Indian Ocean*	2,500	965
Oceania		km²	miles²
New Guinea	*Indonesia/Papua NG*	821,030	317,000
New Zealand (S.)	*Pacific Ocean*	150,500	58,100
New Zealand (N.)	*Pacific Ocean*	114,700	44,300
Tasmania	*Australia*	67,800	26,200
Hawaii	*Pacific Ocean*	10,450	4,000
North America		km²	miles²
Greenland	*Atlantic Ocean*	2,175,600	839,800
Baffin Is.	*Canada*	508,000	196,100
Victoria Is.	*Canada*	212,200	81,900
Ellesmere Is.	*Canada*	212,000	81,800
Cuba	*Caribbean Sea*	110,860	42,800
Hispaniola	*Dominican Rep./Haiti*	76,200	29,400
Jamaica	*Caribbean Sea*	11,400	4,400
Puerto Rico	*Atlantic Ocean*	8,900	3,400
South America		km²	miles²
Tierra del Fuego	*Argentina/Chile*	47,000	18,100
Falkland Is. (E.)	*Atlantic Ocean*	6,800	2,600

Philip's World Maps

The reference maps which form the main body of this atlas have been prepared in accordance with the highest standards of international cartography to provide an accurate and detailed representation of the Earth. The scales and projections used have been carefully chosen to give balanced coverage of the world, while emphasizing the most densely populated and economically significant regions. A hallmark of Philip's mapping is the use of hill shading and relief colouring to create a graphic impression of landforms: this makes the maps exceptionally easy to read. However, knowledge of the key features employed in the construction and presentation of the maps will enable the reader to derive the fullest benefit from the atlas.

Map sequence

The atlas covers the Earth continent by continent: first Europe; then its land neighbour Asia (mapped north before south, in a clockwise sequence), then Africa, Australia and Oceania, North America and South America. This is the classic arrangement adopted by most cartographers since the 16th century. For each continent, there are maps at a variety of scales. First, physical relief and political maps of the whole continent; then a series of larger-scale maps of the regions within the continent, each followed, where required, by still larger-scale maps of the most important or densely populated areas. The governing principle is that by turning the pages of the atlas, the reader moves steadily from north to south through each continent, with each map overlapping its neighbours. A key map showing this sequence, and the area covered by each map, can be found on the endpapers of the atlas.

Map presentation

With very few exceptions (e.g. for the Arctic and Antarctica), the maps are drawn with north at the top, regardless of whether they are presented upright or sideways on the page. In the borders will be found the map title; a locator diagram showing the area covered and the page numbers for maps of adjacent areas; the scale; the projection used; the degrees of latitude and longitude; and the letters and figures used in the index for locating place names and geographical features. Physical relief maps also have a height reference panel identifying the colours used for each layer of contouring.

Map symbols

Each map contains a vast amount of detail which can only be conveyed clearly and accurately by the use of symbols. Points and circles of varying sizes locate and identify the relative importance of towns and cities; different styles of type are employed for administrative, geographical and regional place names. A variety of pictorial symbols denote features such as glaciers and marshes, as well as man-made structures including roads, railways, airports and canals. International borders are shown by red lines. Where neighbouring countries are in dispute, for example in the Middle East, the maps show the *de facto* boundary between nations, regardless of the legal or historical situation. The symbols are explained on the first page of the World Maps section of the atlas.

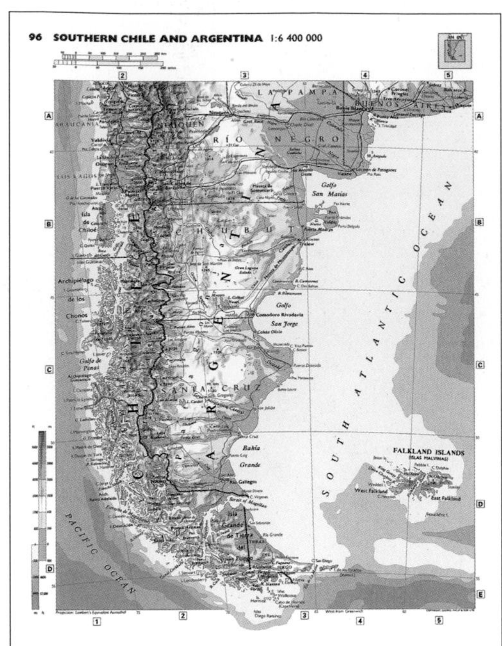
96 SOUTHERN CHILE AND ARGENTINA 1:6 400 000
FALKLAND ISLANDS
SOUTH ATLANTIC OCEAN
PACIFIC OCEAN

Map scales

The scale of each map is given in the numerical form known as the 'representative fraction'. The first figure is always one, signifying one unit of distance on the map; the second figure, usually in millions, is the number by which the map unit must be multiplied to give the equivalent distance on the Earth's surface. Calculations can easily be made in centimetres and kilometres, by dividing the Earth units figure by 100 000 (i.e. deleting the last five 0s). Thus 1:1 000 000 means 1 cm = 10 km. The calculation for inches and miles is more laborious, but 1 000 000 divided by 63 360 (the number of inches in a mile) shows that the ratio 1:1 000 000 means approximately 1 inch = 16 miles. The table below provides distance equivalents for scales down to 1:50 000 000.

LARGE SCALE		
1:1 000 000	1 cm = 10 km	1 inch = 16 miles
1:2 500 000	1 cm = 25 km	1 inch = 39.5 miles
1:5 000 000	1 cm = 50 km	1 inch = 79 miles
1:6 000 000	1 cm = 60 km	1 inch = 95 miles
1:8 000 000	1 cm = 80 km	1 inch = 126 miles
1:10 000 000	1 cm = 100 km	1 inch = 158 miles
1:15 000 000	1 cm = 150 km	1 inch = 237 miles
1:20 000 000	1 cm = 200 km	1 inch = 316 miles
1:50 000 000	1 cm = 500 km	1 inch = 790 miles
SMALL SCALE		

Measuring distances

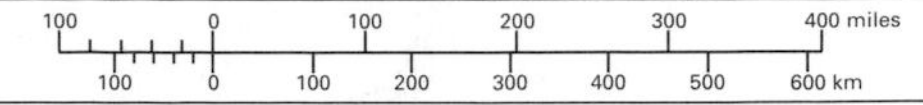
100 0 100 200 300 400 miles
100 0 100 200 300 400 500 600 km

Although each map is accompanied by a scale bar, distances cannot always be measured with confidence because of the distortions involved in portraying the curved surface of the Earth on a flat page. As a general rule, the larger the map scale (i.e. the lower the number of Earth units in the representative fraction), the more accurate and reliable will be the distance measured. On small-scale maps such as those of the world and of entire continents, measurement may only be accurate along the 'standard parallels', or central axes, and should not be attempted without considering the map projection.

Latitude and longitude

Accurate positioning of individual points on the Earth's surface is made possible by reference to the geometrical system of latitude and longitude. Latitude *parallels* are drawn west–east around the Earth and numbered by degrees north and south of the Equator, which is designated 0° of latitude. Longitude *meridians* are drawn north–south and numbered by degrees east and west of the *prime meridian*, 0° of longitude, which passes through Greenwich in England. By referring to these co-ordinates and their subdivisions of minutes (1/60th of a degree) and seconds (1/60th of a minute), any place on Earth can be located to within a few hundred metres. Latitude and longitude are indicated by blue lines on the maps; they are straight or curved according to the projection employed. Reference to these lines is the easiest way of determining the relative positions of places on different maps, and for plotting compass directions.

Name forms

For ease of reference, both English and local name forms appear in the atlas. Oceans, seas and countries are shown in English throughout the atlas; country names may be abbreviated to their commonly accepted form (e.g. Germany, not The Federal Republic of Germany). Conventional English forms are also used for place names on the smaller-scale maps of the continents. However, local name forms are used on all large-scale and regional maps, with the English form given in brackets only for important cities – the large-scale map of Russia and Central Asia thus shows Moskva (Moscow). For countries which do not use a Roman script, place names have been transcribed according to the systems adopted by the British and US Geographic Names Authorities. For China, the Pin Yin system has been used, with some more widely known forms appearing in brackets, as with Beijing (Peking). Both English and local names appear in the index, the English form being cross-referenced to the local form.

The GAZETTEER OF NATIONS

Index to Countries

A
Afghanistan 2
Albania 2
Algeria 2
American Samoa 2
Andorra 2
Angola 2
Anguilla 2
Antigua and Barbuda 3
Argentina 3
Armenia 3
Aruba 3
Australia 3
Austria 3
Azerbaijan 4

B
Bahamas 4
Bahrain 4
Bangladesh 4
Barbados 4
Belarus 4
Belgium 4
Belize 5
Benin 5
Bermuda 5
Bhutan 5
Bolivia 5
Bosnia-Herzegovina 6
Botswana 6
Brazil 6
Brunei 6
Bulgaria 7
Burkina Faso 7
Burma (Myanmar) 7
Burundi 7

C
Cambodia 8
Cameroon 8
Canada 8
Cape Verde 9
Cayman Islands 9
Central African Republic 9
Chad 9
Chile 9
China 10
Colombia 10
Comoros 10
Congo 10
Congo (Zaïre) 11
Costa Rica 11
Croatia 11
Cuba 11
Cyprus 12
Czech Republic 12

D
Denmark 12
Djibouti 13
Dominica 13
Dominican Republic 13

E
Ecuador 13
Egypt 13
El Salvador 14
Equatorial Guinea 14
Eritrea 14
Estonia 14
Ethiopia 15

F
Falkland Islands 15
Faroe Islands 15
Fiji 15
Finland 15
France 15
French Guiana 16
French Polynesia 16

G
Gabon 16
Gambia, The 16
Georgia 17
Germany 17
Ghana 17
Gibraltar 18
Greece 18
Greenland 18
Grenada 18
Guadeloupe 18
Guam 18
Guatemala 18
Guinea 18
Guinea-Bissau 19
Guyana 19

H
Haiti 19
Honduras 19
Hong Kong 20
Hungary 20

I
Iceland 20
India 20
Indonesia 20
Iran 21
Iraq 21
Ireland 21
Israel 22
Italy 22
Ivory Coast 22

J
Jamaica 23
Japan 23
Jordan 23

K
Kazakstan 23
Kenya 24
Kiribati 24
Korea, North 24
Korea, South 25
Kuwait 25
Kyrgyzstan 25

L
Laos 25
Latvia 25
Lebanon 26
Lesotho 26
Liberia 26
Libya 27
Liechtenstein 27
Lithuania 27
Luxembourg 27

M
Macau 27
Macedonia 27
Madagascar 28
Malawi 28
Malaysia 28
Maldives 29
Mali 29
Malta 29
Marshall Islands 29
Martinique 29
Mauritania 29
Mauritius 29
Mexico 30
Micronesia 30
Moldova 30
Monaco 30
Mongolia 30
Montserrat 30
Morocco 31
Mozambique 31

N
Namibia 31
Nauru 31
Nepal 31
Netherlands 32
Netherlands Antilles 32
New Caledonia 32
New Zealand 32
Nicaragua 32
Niger 33

N
Nigeria 33
Northern Mariana Islands 33
Norway 33

O
Oman 33

P
Pakistan 34
Palau 34
Panama 34
Papua New Guinea 34
Paraguay 34
Peru 35
Philippines 35
Pitcairn Islands 35
Poland 35
Portugal 36
Puerto Rico 36

Q
Qatar 36

R
Réunion 36
Romania 36
Russia 36
Rwanda 37

S
St Helena 37
St Kitts and Nevis 37
St Lucia 37
St Vincent and the Grenadines 37
San Marino 37
São Tomé and Príncipe 37
Saudi Arabia 37
Senegal 38
Seychelles 38
Sierra Leone 38
Singapore 38
Slovak Republic 38
Slovenia 39
Solomon Islands 39
Somalia 39
South Africa 40
Spain 40
Sri Lanka 40
Sudan 40
Surinam 41
Swaziland 41
Sweden 41
Switzerland 41
Syria 42

T
Taiwan 42
Tajikistan 42
Tanzania 42
Thailand 43
Togo 43
Tonga 43
Trinidad and Tobago 43
Tunisia 43
Turkey 44
Turkmenistan 44
Turks and Caicos Islands 44
Tuvalu 44

U
Uganda 44
Ukraine 45
United Arab Emirates 45
United Kingdom 45
United States of America 46
Uruguay 46
Uzbekistan 46

V
Vanuatu 46
Vatican City 47
Venezuela 47
Vietnam 47
Virgin Islands, British 47
Virgin Islands, US 47

W
Wallis and Futuna Islands 47
Western Samoa 47

Y
Yemen 47
Yugoslavia (Serbia and Montenegro) 48

Z
Zambia 48
Zimbabwe 48

Notes

The countries are arranged alphabetically, with Afghanistan as the first entry and Zimbabwe as the last. Information is given for all countries and territories, except for some of the smallest and near uninhabited islands. The form of names for all the countries follows the conventions used in all Philip's world atlases.

The statistical data is the latest available, usually for 1997–8. In the statistics boxes: Country area includes inland water and land areas covered in ice, as in Greenland and Canada, for example. City populations are usually those of the 'urban agglomerations' rather than within the legal city boundaries.

AFGHANISTAN

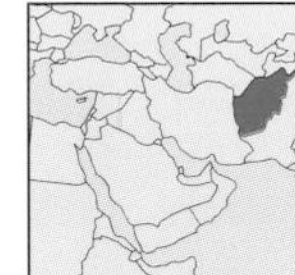

GEOGRAPHY The Republic of Afghanistan is a landlocked, mountainous country in southern Asia. The central highlands reach a height of more than 7,000 m [22,966 ft] in the east and make up nearly three-quarters of Afghanistan. The main range is the Hindu Kush, which is cut by deep, fertile valleys.

The height of the land and the country's remote position have a great effect on the climate. In winter, northerly winds bring cold, snowy weather to the mountains, but summers are hot and dry.

POLITICS & ECONOMY The modern history of Afghanistan began in 1747, when the various tribes in the area united for the first time. In the 19th century, Russia and Britain struggled for control of the country. Following Britain's withdrawal in 1919, Afghanistan became fully independent. Soviet troops invaded Afghanistan in 1979 to support a socialist regime in Kabul, but, facing fierce opposition from Muslim groups, they withdrew in 1989. But Muslim factions continued to fight each other. By early 1999 a group called Taliban ('Islamic students') controlled most of the country apart from the north.

Afghanistan is one of the world's poorest countries. About 60% of the people live by farming. Many people are semi-nomadic herders. Natural gas is produced, together with some coal, copper, gold, precious stones and salt.

AREA 652,090 sq km [251,772 sq mls]
POPULATION 24,792,000
CAPITAL (POPULATION) Kabul (1,565,000)
GOVERNMENT Islamic republic
ETHNIC GROUPS Pashtun ('Pathan') 52%, Tajik 20%, Uzbek 9%, Hazara 9%, Chahar 3%, Turkmen 2%, Baluchi 1%
LANGUAGES Pashto, Dari / Persian (both official), Uzbek
RELIGIONS Islam (Sunni Muslim 74%, Shiite Muslim 25%)
CURRENCY Afghani = 100 puls

ALBANIA

GEOGRAPHY The Republic of Albania lies in the Balkan peninsula, facing the Adriatic Sea. About 70% of the land is mountainous, but most Albanians live in the west on the coastal lowlands.

The coastal areas of Albania have a typical Mediterranean climate, with fairly dry, sunny summers and cool, moist winters. The mountains have a severe climate, with heavy winter snowfalls.

POLITICS & ECONOMY Albania is Europe's poorest country. Formerly a Communist regime, Albania introduced a multiparty system in the early 1990s. The transition to a market economy was traumatic, but, following elections in 1997, a socialist government committed to a market system took office. In 1999, problems arose with the arrival of ethnic Albanian refugees from Kosovo, Yugoslavia, following the NATO offensive against Serbia.

In the early 1990s, agriculture employed 56% of the people. The land was divided into large collective and state farms, but private ownership has been encouraged since 1991. Albania has some minerals and chromite, copper and nickel are exported.

AREA 28,750 sq km [11,100 sq mls]
POPULATION 3,331,000
CAPITAL (POPULATION) Tirana (251,000)
GOVERNMENT Multiparty republic
ETHNIC GROUPS Albanian 98%, Greek 1.8%, Macedonian, Montenegrin, Gypsy
LANGUAGES Albanian (official)
RELIGIONS Many people say they are non-believers; of the believers, 65% follow Islam and 33% follow Christianity (Orthodox 20%, Roman Catholic 13%)
CURRENCY Lek = 100 qindars

ALGERIA

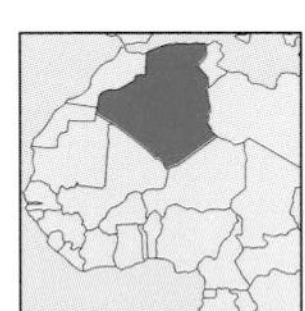

GEOGRAPHY The People's Democratic Republic of Algeria is Africa's second largest country after Sudan. Most Algerians live in the north, on the fertile coastal plains and hill country bordering the Mediterranean Sea. Four-fifths of Algeria is in the Sahara. The coast has a Mediterranean climate, but the arid Sahara is hot by day and cool at night.

POLITICS & ECONOMY France ruled Algeria from 1830 until 1962, when the socialist FLN (National Liberation Front) formed a one-party government. Following the recognition of opposition parties in 1989, a Muslim group, the FIS (Islamic Salvation Front), won an election in 1991. The FLN cancelled the elections and civil conflict broke out. About 75,000 people were killed between 1991 and 1998. Presidential elections in 1999 did little to calm the situation, when the six anti-army candidates withdrew, alleging fraud. This resulted in a hollow victory for Abjulaziz Bouteflika, who was assumed to be the candidate favoured by the army.

Algeria is a developing country, whose chief resources are oil and natural gas. The natural gas reserves are among the world's largest, and gas and oil account for 90% of Algeria's exports. Cement, iron and steel, textiles and vehicles are manufactured.

AREA 2,381,740 sq km [919,590 sq mls]
POPULATION 30,481,000
CAPITAL (POPULATION) Algiers (1,722,000)
GOVERNMENT Socialist republic
ETHNIC GROUPS Arab 83%, Berber 16%
LANGUAGES Arabic (official), Berber, French
RELIGIONS Sunni Muslim 98%
CURRENCY Algerian dinar = 100 centimes

AMERICAN SAMOA

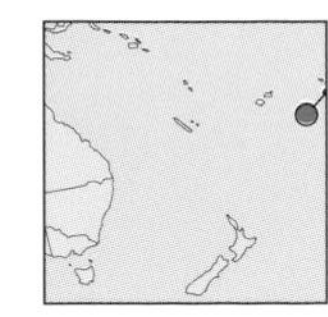

An 'unincorporated territory' of the United States, American Samoa lies in the south-central Pacific Ocean. **AREA** 200 sq km [77 sq mls]; **POPULATION** 62,000; **CAPITAL** Pago Pago.

ANDORRA

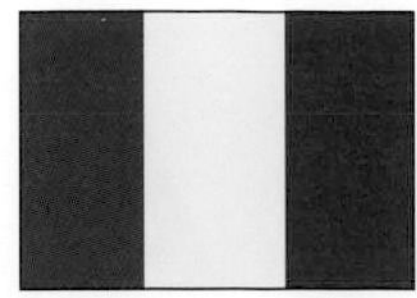
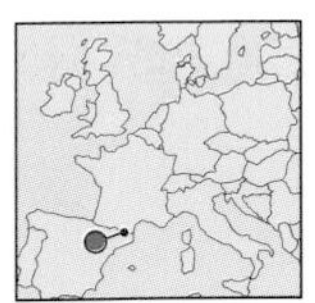

A mini-state situated in the Pyrenees Mountains, Andorra is a co-principality whose main activity is tourism. Most Andorrans live in the six valleys (the Valls) that drain into the River Valira. **AREA** 453 sq km [175 sq mls]; **POPULATION** 75,000; **CAPITAL** Andorra La Vella.

ANGOLA

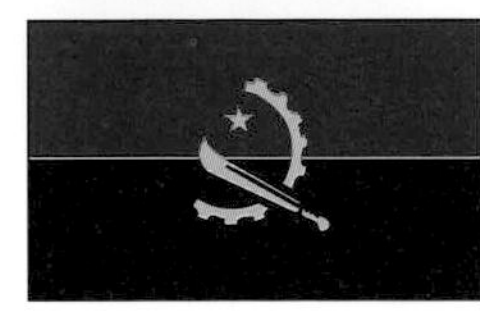
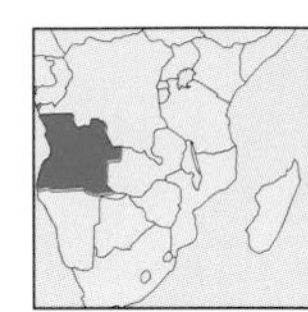

GEOGRAPHY The Republic of Angola is a large country in south-western Africa. Most of the country is part of the plateau that forms most of southern Africa, with a narrow coastal plain in the west.

Angola has a tropical climate, with temperatures of over 20°C [68°F] throughout the year, though the highest areas are cooler. The coastal regions are dry, but the rainfall increases to the north and east.

POLITICS & ECONOMY A former Portuguese colony, Angola gained its independence in 1975, after which rival nationalist forces began a struggle for power. A long-running civil war developed, finally ending with a peace treaty in 1994, which led to a coalition government in 1997. However, civil war again broke out in 1999.

Angola is a developing country, where 70% of the people are poor farmers. The main food crops are cassava and maize. Coffee is exported. Angola has much economic potential. It has oil reserves near Luanda and in the Cabinda enclave, which is separated from Angola by a strip of land belonging to Congo (Zaïre). Oil is the leading export. Angola also produces diamonds and has reserves of copper, manganese and phosphates.

AREA 1,246,700 sq km [481,351 sq mls]
POPULATION 11,200,000
CAPITAL (POPULATION) Luanda (2,250,000)
GOVERNMENT Multiparty republic
ETHNIC GROUPS Ovimbundu 37%, Mbundu 22%, Kongo 13%, Luimbe-Nganguela 5%, Nyaneka-Humbe 5%, Chokwe, Luvale, Luchazi
LANGUAGES Portuguese (official), many others
RELIGIONS Christianity (Roman Catholic 69%, Protestant 20%), traditional beliefs 10%
CURRENCY Kwanza = 100 lwei

ANGUILLA

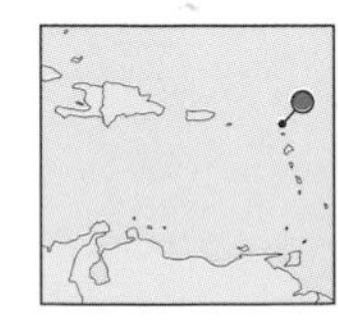

Formerly part of St Kitts and Nevis, Anguilla became a British dependency (now a British overseas territory) in 1980. The main source of revenue is now tourism, although lobster still accounts for half the island's exports. **AREA** 96 sq km [37 sq mls]; **POPULATION** 11,000; **CAPITAL** The Valley.

ANTIGUA AND BARBUDA

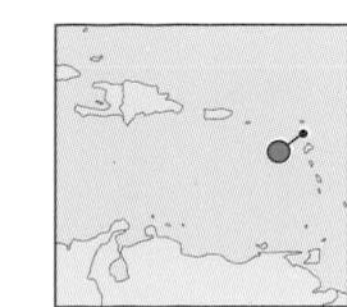

A former British dependency in the Caribbean, Antigua and Barbuda became independent in 1981. Tourism is the main industry. **AREA** 440 sq km [170 sq mls]; **POPULATION** 64,000; **CAPITAL** St John's.

ARGENTINA

GEOGRAPHY The Argentine Republic is South America's second largest and the world's eighth largest country. The high Andes range in the west contains Mount Aconcagua, the highest peak in the Americas. In southern Argentina, the Andes Mountains overlook Patagonia, a plateau region. In east-central Argentina lies a fertile plain called the *pampas*.

The climate varies from subtropical in the north to temperate in the south. Rainfall is abundant in the north-east, but is lower to the west and south. Patagonia is a dry region, crossed by rivers that rise in the Andes.

POLITICS & ECONOMY Argentina became independent from Spain in the early 19th century, but it later suffered from instability and periods of military rule. In 1982, Argentina invaded the Falkland (Malvinas) islands, but Britain regained the islands later in the year. Elections were held in 1983 and constitutional government was restored.

According to the World Bank, Argentina is an 'upper-middle-income' developing country. Large areas are fertile and the main agricultural products are beef, maize and wheat. But about 87% of the people live in cities and towns, where many work in factories that process farm products. Other industries include the manufacture of cars, electrical equipment and textiles. Oil is the leading mineral resource. The leading exports include meat, wheat, maize, vegetable oils, hides and skins, and wool. In 1991, Argentina, Brazil, Paraguay and Uruguay set up Mercosur, an alliance aimed at creating a common market.

AREA 2,766,890 sq km [1,068,296 sq mls]
POPULATION 36,265,000
CAPITAL (POPULATION) Buenos Aires (10,990,000)
GOVERNMENT Federal republic
ETHNIC GROUPS European 85%, Mestizo, Amerindian
LANGUAGES Spanish (official)
RELIGIONS Christianity (Roman Catholic 92%)
CURRENCY Peso = 10,000 australs

ARMENIA

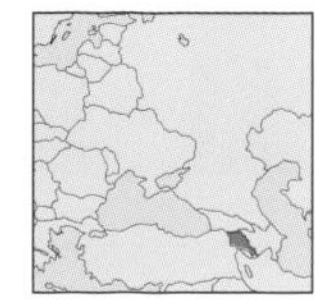

GEOGRAPHY The Republic of Armenia is a landlocked country in south-western Asia. Most of Armenia consists of a rugged plateau, criss-crossed by long faults (cracks). Movements along the faults cause earthquakes. The highest point is Mount Aragats, at 4,090 m [13,419 ft] above sea level.

The height of the land, which averages 1,500 m [4,920 ft] above sea level gives rise to severe winters and cool summers. The highest peaks are snow-capped, but the total yearly rainfall is generally low.

POLITICS & ECONOMY In 1920, Armenia became a Communist republic and, in 1922, it became, with Azerbaijan and Georgia, part of the Transcaucasian Republic within the Soviet Union. But the three territories became separate Soviet Socialist Republics in 1936. After the break-up of the Soviet Union in 1991, Armenia became an independent republic. Fighting broke out over Nagorno-Karabakh, an area enclosed by Azerbaijan where the majority of the people are Armenians. In 1992, Armenia occupied the territory between it and Nagorno-Karabakh. A cease-fire agreed in 1994 left Armenia in control of about 20% of Azerbaijan's land area.

The World Bank classifies Armenia as a 'lower-middle-income economy'. The conflict has badly damaged the economy, but the government has encouraged free enterprise, selling farmland and government-owned businesses.

AREA 29,800 sq km [11,506 sq mls]
POPULATION 3,422,000
CAPITAL (POPULATION) Yerevan (1,226,000)
GOVERNMENT Multiparty republic
ETHNIC GROUPS Armenian 93%, Azerbaijani 3%, Russian, Kurd
LANGUAGES Armenian (official)
RELIGIONS Christianity (Armenian Apostolic)
CURRENCY Dram = 100 couma

ARUBA

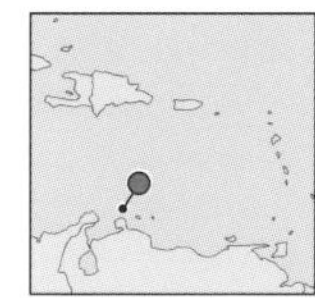

Formerly part of the Netherlands Antilles, Aruba became a separate self-governing Dutch territory in 1986. **AREA** 193 sq km [75 sq mls]; **POPULATION** 69,000; **CAPITAL** Oranjestad.

AUSTRALIA

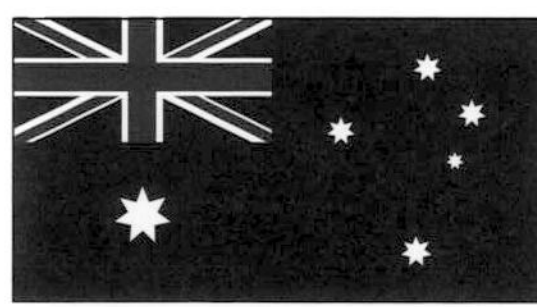

GEOGRAPHY The Commonwealth of Australia, the world's sixth largest country, is also a continent. Australia is the flattest of the continents and the main highland area is in the east. Here the Great Dividing Range separates the eastern coastal plains from the Central Plains. This range extends from the Cape York Peninsula to Victoria in the far south. The longest rivers, the Murray and Darling, drain the south-eastern part of the Central Plains. The Western Plateau makes up two-thirds of Australia. A few mountain ranges break the monotony of the generally flat landscape.

Only 10% of Australia has an average yearly rainfall of more than 1,000 mm [39 in]. These areas include the tropical north, where Darwin is situated, the north-east coast, and the south-east, where Sydney is located. The interior is dry, and water is quickly evaporated in the heat.

POLITICS & ECONOMY The Aboriginal people of Australia entered the continent from South-east Asia more than 50,000 years ago. The first European explorers were Dutch in the 17th century, but they did not settle. In 1770, the British Captain Cook explored the east coast and, in 1788, the first British settlement was established for convicts on the site of what is now Sydney. Australia has strong ties with the British Isles. But in the last 50 years, people from other parts of Europe and, most recently, from Asia have settled in Australia. Ties with Britain were also weakened by Britain's membership of the European Union. Many Australians now believe that they should become more involved with the nations of eastern Asia and the Americas rather than with Europe. By the late 1990s, many people thought that Australia should become a republic, with a president replacing the British monarch as head of state.

Australia is a prosperous country. Crops can be grown on only 6% of the land, though dry pasture covers another 58%. Yet the country remains a major producer and exporter of farm products, particularly cattle, wheat and wool. Grapes grown for wine-making are also important. The country is also rich in natural resources. It is a major producer of minerals, including bauxite, coal, copper, diamonds, gold, iron ore, manganese, nickel, silver, tin, tungsten and zinc. Australia also produces some oil and natural gas. Metals, minerals and farm products account for the bulk of exports. Australia's imports are mostly manufactured products, although the country makes many factory products, especially consumer goods, such as foods and household articles. Major imports include machinery and other goods used by factories.

AREA 7,686,850 sq km [2,967,893 sq mls]
POPULATION 18,613,000
CAPITAL (POPULATION) Canberra (325,000)
GOVERNMENT Federal constitutional monarchy
ETHNIC GROUPS White 95%, Aboriginal 1.5%, Asian 1.3%
LANGUAGES English (official)
RELIGIONS Christianity (Roman Catholic 26%, Anglican 24%, others 20%), Islam, Buddhism, Judaism
CURRENCY Australian dollar = 100 cents

AUSTRIA

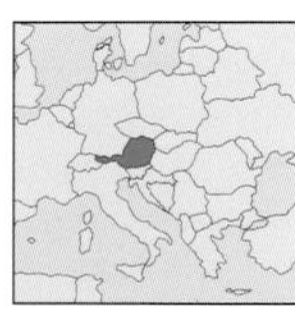

GEOGRAPHY The Republic of Austria is a landlocked country in the heart of Europe. Northern Austria contains the valley of the River Danube, which flows from Germany to the Black Sea, and the Vienna basin – Austria's main farming regions. Southern Austria contains ranges of the Alps, which reach their highest point at Grossglockner, at 3,797 m [12,457 ft] above sea level.

The climate of Austria is influenced both by westerly and easterly winds. The moist westerly winds bring rain and snow. They also moderate the temperatures. But dry easterly winds bring cold weather in winter and hot weather in summer.

POLITICS & ECONOMY Formerly part of the powerful monarchy of Austria-Hungary, which collapsed in 1918, Austria was annexed by Germany in 1938. After World War II, the Allies partitioned and occupied the country until 1955, when Austria became a neutral federal republic. Austria joined the European Union on 1 January 1995.

Austria is a prosperous country. It has plenty of hydroelectric power, as well as some oil, gas and coal reserves. The country's leading economic activity is manufacturing metals and metal products. Crops are grown on 18% of the land and another 24% is pasture. Dairy and livestock farming are the leading activities. Major crops include barley, potatoes, rye, sugar beet and wheat. Tourism is a major activity in this scenic country.

AREA 83,850 sq km [32,374 sq mls]
POPULATION 8,134,000
CAPITAL (POPULATION) Vienna (1,560,000)
GOVERNMENT Federal republic
ETHNIC GROUPS Austrian 93%, Yugoslav 2%, Turkish, German
LANGUAGES German (official)
RELIGIONS Christianity (Roman Catholic 78%, Protestant 6%), Islam
CURRENCY Euro; Schilling = 100 Groschen

AZERBAIJAN

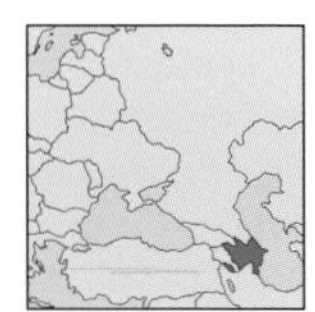

GEOGRAPHY The Azerbaijani Republic is a country in the south-west of Asia, facing the Caspian Sea to the east. It includes an area called the Naxçivan Autonomous Republic, which is completely cut off from the rest of Azerbaijan by Armenian territory. The Caucasus Mountains border Russia in the north.

Azerbaijan has hot summers and cool winters, with low rainfall on the plains and much higher rainfall in the highlands.

POLITICS & ECONOMY After the Russian Revolution of 1917, attempts were made to form a Transcaucasian Federation made up of Armenia, Azerbaijan and Georgia. When this failed, Azerbaijanis set up an independent state. But Russian forces occupied the area in 1920. In 1922, the Communists set up a Transcaucasian Republic consisting of Armenia, Azerbaijan and Georgia under Russian control. In 1936, the three areas became separate Soviet Socialist Republics within the Soviet Union. In 1991, following the break-up of the Soviet Union, Azerbaijan became an independent nation. After independence, the country's economic progress was slow, partly because of the conflict with Armenia over the enclave of Nagorno-Karabakh, a region in Azerbaijan where the majority of people are Armenians. A cease-fire in 1994 left Armenia in control of about 20% of Azerbaijan's area, including Nagorno-Karabakh.

In the mid-1990s, the World Bank classified Azerbaijan as a 'lower-middle-income' economy. Yet by the late 1990s, the enormous oil reserves in the Baku area, on the Caspian Sea and in the sea itself, held out great promise for the future. Oil extraction and manufacturing, including oil refining and the production of chemicals, machinery and textiles, are now the most valuable activities.

AREA 86,600 sq km [33,436 sq mls]
POPULATION 7,856,000
CAPITAL (POPULATION) Baku (1,081,000)
GOVERNMENT Federal multiparty republic
ETHNIC GROUPS Azerbaijani 83%, Russian 6%, Armenian 6%, Lezgin, Avar, Ukrainian, Tatar
LANGUAGES Azerbaijani (official)
RELIGIONS Islam
CURRENCY Manat = 100 gopik

BAHAMAS

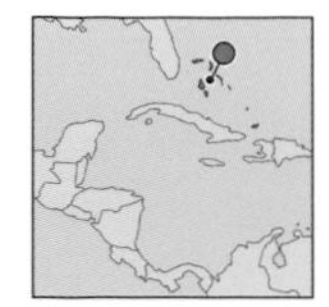

A coral-limestone archipelago off the coast of Florida, the Bahamas became independent from Britain in 1973, and has since developed strong ties with the United States. Tourism and banking are major activities. **AREA** 13,880 sq km [5,359 sq mls]; **POPULATION** 280,000; **CAPITAL** Nassau.

BAHRAIN

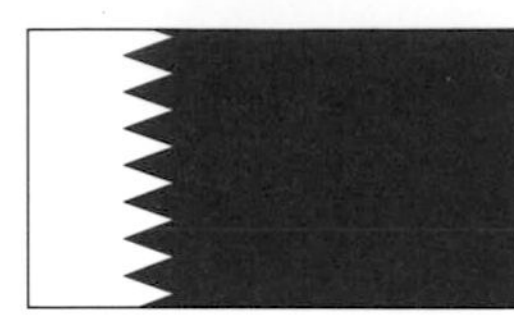

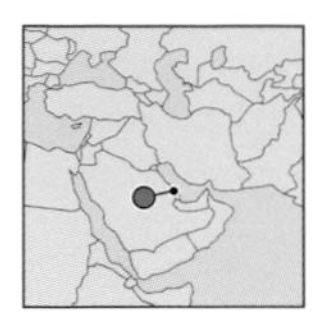

The Emirate of Bahrain, an island nation in the Gulf, became independent from the UK in 1971. Oil accounts for 80% of the country's exports. **AREA** 678 sq km [262 sq mls]; **POPULATION** 616,000; **CAPITAL** Manama.

BANGLADESH

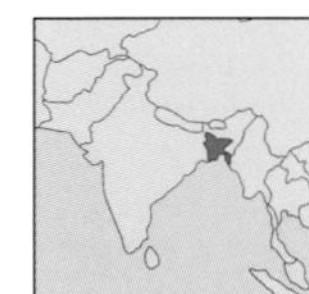

GEOGRAPHY The People's Republic of Bangladesh is one of the world's most densely populated countries. Apart from hilly regions in the far north-east and south-east, most of the land is flat and covered by fertile alluvium spread over the land by the Ganges, Brahmaputra and Meghna rivers. These rivers overflow when they are swollen by the annual monsoon rains. Floods also occur along the coast, 575 km [357 mls] long, when cyclones (hurricanes) drive sea-water inland. Bangladesh has a tropical monsoon climate. Dry northerly winds blow in winter, but, in summer, moist winds from the south bring monsoon rains. Heavy monsoon rains cause floods. In 1998, about two-thirds of the entire country was submerged, causing great suffering.

POLITICS & ECONOMY In 1947, British India was partitioned between the mainly Hindu India and the Muslim Pakistan. Pakistan consisted of two parts, West and East Pakistan, which were separated by about 1,600 km [1,000 mls] of Indian territory. Differences developed between West and East Pakistan. In 1971, the East Pakistanis rebelled. After a nine-month civil war, they declared East Pakistan to be a separate nation named Bangladesh.

Bangladesh is one of the world's poorest countries. Its economy depends mainly on agriculture, which employs over half the population. Bangladesh is the world's fourth largest producer of rice.

AREA 144,000 sq km [55,598 sq mls]
POPULATION 125,000,000
CAPITAL (POPULATION) Dhaka (6,105,000)
GOVERNMENT Multiparty republic
ETHNIC GROUPS Bengali 98%, tribal groups
LANGUAGES Bengali, English (both official)
RELIGIONS Islam 87%, Hinduism 12%, Buddhism, Christianity
CURRENCY Taka = 100 paisas

BARBADOS

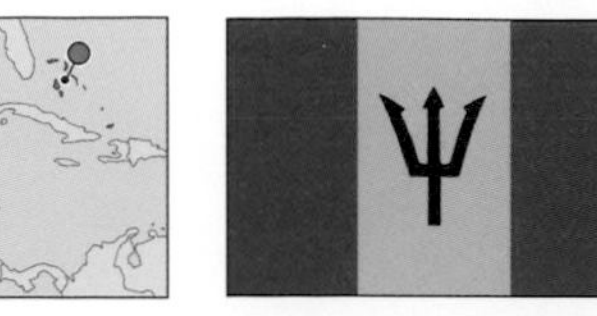

The most easterly Caribbean country, Barbados became independent from the UK in 1960. A densely populated island, Barbados is prosperous by comparison with most Caribbean countries. **AREA** 430 sq km [166 sq mls]; **POPULATION** 259,000; **CAPITAL** Bridgetown.

BELARUS

GEOGRAPHY The Republic of Belarus is a landlocked country in Eastern Europe. The land is low-lying and mostly flat. In the south, much of the land is marshy and this area contains Europe's largest marsh and peat bog, the Pripet Marshes.

The climate of Belarus is affected by both the moderating influence of the Baltic Sea and continental conditions to the east. The winters are cold and the summers warm.

POLITICS & ECONOMY In 1918, Belarus (White Russia) became an independent republic, but Russia invaded the country and, in 1919, a Communist state was set up. In 1922, Belarus became a founder republic of the Soviet Union. In 1991, after the break-up of the Soviet Union, Belarus again became an independent republic, though it retained ties with Russia through an organization called the Commonwealth of Independent States. In 1998, Belarus and Russia set up a 'union state', with plans to have a common currency, a customs union, and common foreign and defence policies. But any surrender of sovereignty was not anticipated.

The World Bank classifies Belarus as an 'upper-middle-income' economy. Like other former republics of the Soviet Union, it faces many problems in turning from Communism to a free-market economy.

AREA 297,600 sq km [80,154 sq mls]
POPULATION 10,409,000
CAPITAL (POPULATION) Minsk (1,700,000)
GOVERNMENT Multiparty republic
ETHNIC GROUPS Belarussian 80%, Russian, Polish
LANGUAGES Belarussian, Russian (both official)
RELIGIONS Christianity (mainly Belarussian Orthodox, with Roman Catholics in the west)
CURRENCY Belarussian rouble = 100 kopecks

BELGIUM

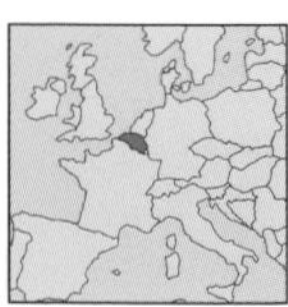

GEOGRAPHY The Kingdom of Belgium is a densely populated country in western Europe. Behind the coastline on the North Sea, which is 63 km [39 mls] long, lie its coastal plains. Central Belgium consists of low plateaux and the only highland region is the Ardennes in the south-east.

Belgium has a cool, temperate climate. Moist winds from the Atlantic Ocean bring fairly heavy rain, especially in the Ardennes. In January and February much snow falls on the Ardennes.

POLITICS & ECONOMY In 1815, Belgium and the Netherlands united as the 'low countries', but Belgium became independent in 1830. Belgium's economy was weakened by the two World Wars, but, from 1945, the country recovered quickly, first through collaboration with the Netherlands and Luxembourg, which formed a customs union called Benelux, and later through its membership of the European Union.

A central political problem in Belgium has been the tension between the Dutch-speaking Flemings and the French-speaking Walloons. In the 1970s, the government divided the country into three economic regions: Dutch-speaking Flanders, French-speaking Wallonia and bilingual Brussels. In 1993, Belgium adopted a federal system of government. Each of the regions now has its own parliament, which is responsible for local matters. Elections under this new system were held in 1995.

Belgium is a major trading nation, with a highly developed economy. Its main products include chemicals, processed food and steel. The textile industry is also important and has existed since medieval times in the Belgium province of Flanders.

Agriculture employs only 3% of the people, but Belgian farmers produce most of the food needed by the people. Barley and wheat are the chief crops, followed by flax, hops, potatoes and sugar beet, but the most valuable activities are dairy farming and livestock rearing.

AREA 30,510 sq km [11,780 sq mls]
POPULATION 10,175,000
CAPITAL (POPULATION) Brussels (952,000)
GOVERNMENT Federal constitutional monarchy
ETHNIC GROUPS Belgian 91% (Fleming 55%, Walloon 32%), Italian, French, Dutch, Turkish, Moroccan
LANGUAGES Dutch, French, German (all official)
RELIGIONS Christianity (Roman Catholic 90%), Islam
CURRENCY Euro; Belgian franc = 100 centimes

BELIZE

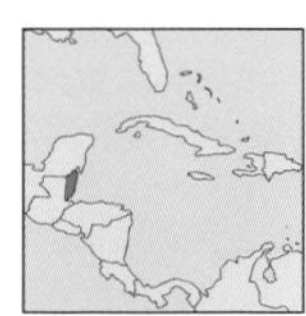

GEOGRAPHY Behind the swampy coastal plain in the south, the land rises to the low Maya Mountains, which reach a height of 1,120 m [3,674 ft] at Victoria Peak. The north is mostly low-lying and swampy.

Belize has a tropical, humid climate. Temperatures are high throughout the year and the average yearly rainfall ranges from 1,300 mm [51 in] in the north to over 3,800 mm [150 in] in the south.

POLITICS & ECONOMY From 1862, Belize (then called British Honduras) was a British colony. Full independence was achieved in 1981, but Guatemala, which had claimed the area since the early 19th century, opposed Belize's independence and British troops remained to prevent a possible invasion. In 1983, Guatemala reduced its claim to the southern fifth of Belize. Improved relations in the early 1990s led Guatemala to recognize Belize's independence and, in 1992, Britain agreed to withdraw its troops from the country.

The World Bank classifies Belize as a 'lower-middle-income' developing country. Its economy is based on agriculture and sugar cane is the chief commercial crop and export. Other crops include bananas, beans, citrus fruits, maize and rice. Forestry, fishing and tourism are other important activities.

AREA 22,960 sq km [8,865 sq mls]
POPULATION 230,000
CAPITAL (POPULATION) Belmopan (44,000)
GOVERNMENT Constitutional monarchy
ETHNIC GROUPS Mestizo (Spanish-Indian) 44%, Creole (mainly African American) 30%, Mayan Indian 11%, Garifuna (Black-Carib Indian) 7%, White 4%, East Indian 3%
LANGUAGES English (official), Creole, Spanish
RELIGIONS Christianity (Roman Catholic 58%, Protestant 29%), Hinduism 2%
CURRENCY Belize dollar = 100 cents

BENIN

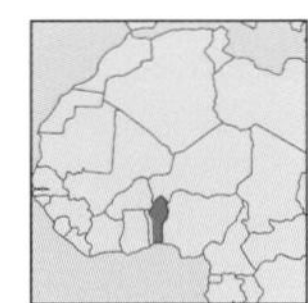

GEOGRAPHY The Republic of Benin is one of Africa's smallest countries. It extends north–south for about 620 km [390 mls]. Lagoons line the short coastline, and the country has no natural harbours.

Benin has a hot, wet climate. The average annual temperature on the coast is about 25°C [77°F], and the average rainfall is about 1,330 mm [52 in]. The inland plains are wetter than the coast.

POLITICS & ECONOMY After slavery was ended in the 19th century, the French began to gain influence in the area. Benin became self-governing in 1958 and fully independent in 1960. After much instability and many changes of government, a military group took over in 1972. The country, renamed Benin in 1975, became a one-party socialist state. Socialism was abandoned in 1989, and multiparty elections were held in 1991 and 1996.

Benin is a developing country. About 70% of the people earn their living by farming, though many remain at subsistence level. The chief exports include cotton, petroleum and palm products.

AREA 112,620 sq km [43,483 sq mls]
POPULATION 6,101,000
CAPITAL (POPULATION) Porto-Novo (179,000)
GOVERNMENT Multiparty republic
ETHNIC GROUPS Fon, Adja, Bariba, Yoruba, Fulani
LANGUAGES French (official), Fon, Adja, Yoruba
RELIGIONS Traditional beliefs 60%, Christianity 23%, Islam 15%
CURRENCY CFA franc = 100 centimes

BERMUDA

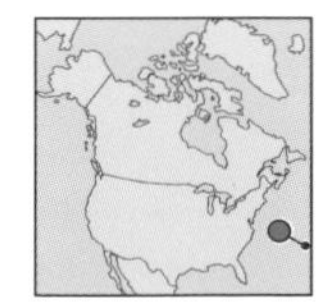

A group of about 150 small islands situated 920 km [570 mls] east of the USA. Bermuda remains Britain's oldest overseas territory, but it has a long tradition of self-government. **AREA** 53 sq km [20 sq mls]; **POPULATION** 62,000; **CAPITAL** Hamilton.

BHUTAN

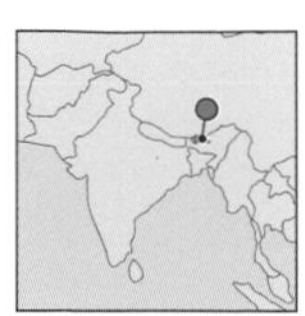

GEOGRAPHY A mountainous, isolated Himalayan country located between India and Tibet. The climate is similar to that of Nepal, being dependent on altitude and affected by monsoonal winds.

POLITICS & ECONOMY The monarch of Bhutan is head of both state and government and this predominantly Buddhist country remains, even in the Asian context, both conservative and poor. Bhutan is the world's most 'rural' country, with over 90% of the population dependent on agriculture and only 6% living in towns.

AREA 47,000 sq km [18,147 sq mls]
POPULATION 1,908,000
CAPITAL (POPULATION) Thimphu [30,000]
GOVERNMENT Constitutional monarchy
ETHNIC GROUPS Bhutanese, Nepali
LANGUAGES Dzongkha (official)
RELIGIONS Buddhism 75%, Hindu
CURRENCY Ngultrum = 100 chetrum

BOLIVIA

GEOGRAPHY The Republic of Bolivia is a land-locked country which straddles the Andes Mountains in central South America. The Andes rise to a height of 6,542 m [21,464 ft] at Nevado Sajama in the west.

About 40% of Bolivians live on a high plateau called the Altiplano in the Andean region, while the sparsely populated east is essentially a vast lowland plain.

The Bolivian climate is greatly affected by altitude, with the Andean peaks permanently snow-covered, while the eastern plains remain hot and humid.

POLITICS & ECONOMY American Indians have lived in Bolivia for at least 10,000 years. The main groups today are the Aymara and Quechua people.

In the last 50 years, Bolivia, an independent country since 1825, has been ruled by a succession of civilian and military governments, which violated human rights. Constitutional government was restored in 1982, but Bolivia faced many problems, including high inflation and poverty.

Bolivia is one of the poorest countries in South America. It has several natural resources, including tin, silver and natural gas, but the chief activity is agriculture, which employs 47% of the people. But experts believe that the main export may be coca, which is used to make the drug cocaine. Coca is exported illegally. The government is trying to stamp out this growing industry.

AREA 1,098,580 sq km [424,162 sq mls]
POPULATION 7,826,000
CAPITAL (POPULATION) La Paz (1,126,000)
GOVERNMENT Multiparty republic
ETHNIC GROUPS Mestizo 31%, Quechua 25%, Aymara 17%, White 15%
LANGUAGES Spanish, Aymara, Quechua (all official)
RELIGIONS Christianity (Roman Catholic 94%)
CURRENCY Boliviano = 100 centavos

BOSNIA-HERZEGOVINA

GEOGRAPHY The Republic of Bosnia-Herzegovina is one of the five republics to emerge from the former Federal People's Republic of Yugoslavia. Much of the country is mountainous or hilly, with an arid limestone plateau in the south-west. The River Sava, which forms most of the northern border with Croatia, is a tributary of the River Danube. Because of the country's odd shape, the coastline is limited to a short stretch of 20 km [13 mls] on the Adriatic coast.

A Mediterranean climate, with dry, sunny summers and moist, mild winters, prevails only near the coast. Inland, the weather becomes more severe, with hot, dry summers and bitterly cold, snowy winters.

POLITICS & ECONOMY In 1918, Bosnia-Herzegovina became part of the Kingdom of the Serbs, Croats and Slovenes, which was renamed Yugoslavia in 1929. Germany occupied the area during World War II (1939–45). From 1945, Communist governments ruled Yugoslavia as a federation containing six republics, one of which was Bosnia-Herzegovina. In the 1980s, the country faced problems as Communist policies proved unsuccessful and differences arose between ethnic groups.

In 1990, free elections were held in Bosnia-Herzegovina and the non-Communists won a majority. A Muslim, Alija Izetbegovic, was elected president. In 1991, Croatia and Slovenia, other parts of the former Yugoslavia, declared themselves independent. In 1992, Bosnia-Herzegovina held a vote on independence. Most Bosnian Serbs boycotted the vote, while the Muslims and Bosnian Croats voted in favour. Many Bosnian Serbs, opposed to independence, started a war against the non-Serbs. They soon occupied more than two-thirds of the land. The Bosnian Serbs were accused of 'ethnic cleansing' – that is, the killing or expulsion of other ethnic groups from Serb-occupied areas. The war was later extended when Croat forces seized other parts of the country.

In 1995, the warring parties agreed to a solution to the conflict. This involved keeping the present boundaries of Bosnia-Herzegovina, but dividing it into two self-governing provinces, one Bosnian Serb and the other Muslim-Croat, under a central, unified, multi-ethnic government. Elections were held in 1996 under this new arrangement.

The economy of Bosnia-Herzegovina, the least developed of the six republics of the former Yugoslavia apart from Macedonia, was shattered by the war in the early 1990s. Before the war, manufactures were the main exports, including electrical equipment, machinery and transport equipment, and textiles. Farm products include fruits, maize, tobacco, vegetables and wheat, but the country has to import food.

AREA 51,129 sq km [19,745 sq mls]
POPULATION 3,366,000
CAPITAL (POPULATION) Sarajevo (526,000)
GOVERNMENT Transitional
ETHNIC GROUPS Muslim 49%, Serb 31%, Croat 17%
LANGUAGES Serbo-Croatian
RELIGIONS Islam 40%, Christianity (Serbian Orthodox 31%, Roman Catholic 15%, Protestant 4%)
CURRENCY Convertible mark = 100 paras

BOTSWANA

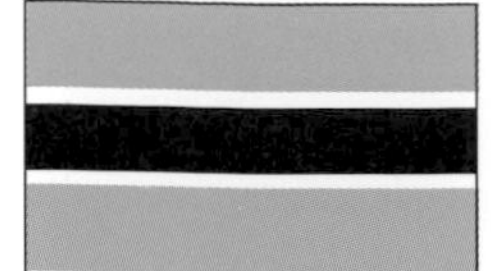

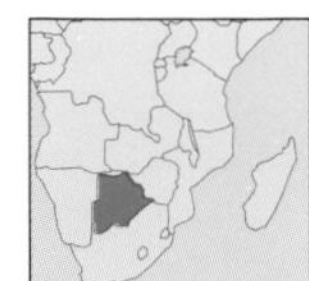

GEOGRAPHY The Republic of Botswana is a landlocked country in southern Africa. The Kalahari, a semi-desert area covered mostly by grasses and thorn scrub, covers much of the country. Most of the south has no permanent streams. But large depressions in the north are inland drainage basins. In one of them, the Okavango River, which rises in Angola, forms a large, swampy delta.

Temperatures are high in the summer months (October to April), but the winter months are much cooler. In winter, night-time temperatures sometimes drop below freezing point. The average annual rainfall ranges from over 400 mm [16 in] in the east to less than 200 mm [8 in] in the south-west.

POLITICS & ECONOMY The earliest inhabitants of the region were the San, who are also called Bushmen. They had a nomadic way of life, hunting wild animals and collecting wild plant foods.

Britain ruled the area as the Bechuanaland Protectorate between 1885 and 1966. When the country became independent, it adopted the name of Botswana. Since then, unlike many African countries, Botswana has been a stable multiparty democracy.

In 1966, Botswana was one of Africa's poorest countries, depending on meat and live cattle for its exports. But the discovery of minerals, including coal, cobalt, copper, diamonds and nickel, has boosted the economy. However, more than 40% of the people still work as farmers, raising cattle and growing crops, such as millet, maize, beans and vegetables. Botswana also has some food-processing plants and factories producing such things as soap and textiles.

AREA 581,730 sq km [224,606 sq mls]
POPULATION 1,448,000
CAPITAL (POPULATION) Gaborone (133,000)
GOVERNMENT Multiparty republic
ETHNIC GROUPS Tswana 75%, Shona 12%, San (Bushmen) 3%
LANGUAGES English (official), Setswana
RELIGIONS Traditional beliefs 49%, Christianity 50%
CURRENCY Pula = 100 thebe

BRAZIL

GEOGRAPHY The Federative Republic of Brazil is the world's fifth largest country. It contains three main regions. The Amazon basin in the north covers more than half of Brazil. The Amazon, the world's second longest river, has a far greater volume than any other river. The second region, the north-east, consists of a coastal plain and the *sertão*, which is the name for the inland plateaux and hill country. The main river in this region is the São Francisco.

The third region is made up of the plateaux in the south-east. This region, which covers about a quarter of the country, is the most developed and densely populated part of Brazil. Its main river is the Paraná, which flows south through Argentina.

Manaus has high temperatures all through the year. The rainfall is heavy, though the period from June to September is drier than the rest of the year. The capital, Brasília, and the city Rio de Janeiro also have tropical climates, with much more marked dry seasons than Manaus. The far south has a temperate climate. The north-eastern interior is the driest region, with an average annual rainfall of only 250 mm [10 in] in places. The rainfall is also unreliable and severe droughts are common in this region.

POLITICS & ECONOMY The Portuguese explorer Pedro Alvarez Cabral claimed Brazil for Portugal in 1500. With Spain occupied in western South America, the Portuguese began to develop their colony, which was more than 90 times as big as Portugal. To do this, they enslaved many local Amerindian people and introduced about 4 million African slaves to work on their plantations and in the mines. Brazil declared itself an independent empire in 1822 and a republic in 1889. From the 1930s, Brazil faced many problems, including corruption and spells of dictatorial military government. Civilian government was restored in 1985 and Brazil adopted a new constitution in 1988.

The United Nations has described Brazil as a 'Rapidly Industrializing Country', or RIC. Its total volume of production is one of the largest in the world. But many people, including poor farmers and residents of the *favelas* (city slums), do not share in the country's fast economic growth. Widespread poverty, together with high inflation and unemployment, cause political problems.

By the early 1990s, industry was the most valuable activity, employing 25% of the people. Brazil is among the world's top producers of bauxite, chrome, diamonds, gold, iron ore, manganese and tin. It is also a major manufacturing country. Its products include aircraft, cars, chemicals, processed food, including raw sugar, iron and steel, paper and textiles.

Brazil is one of the world's leading farming countries and agriculture employs 28% of the people. Coffee is a major export. Other leading products include bananas, citrus fruits, cocoa, maize, rice, soya beans and sugar cane. Brazil is also the top producer of eggs, meat and milk in South America.

Forestry is a major industry, though many people fear that the exploitation of the rainforests, with 1.5% to 4% of Brazil's forest being destroyed every year, is a disaster for the entire world.

AREA 8,511,970 sq km [3,286,472 sq mls]
POPULATION 170,000,000
CAPITAL (POPULATION) Brasília (1,596,000)
GOVERNMENT Federal republic
ETHNIC GROUPS White 53%, Mulatto 22%, Mestizo 12%, African American 11%, Japanese 1%, Amerindian 0.1%
LANGUAGES Portuguese (official)
RELIGIONS Christianity (Roman Catholic 88%)
CURRENCY Real = 100 centavos

BRUNEI

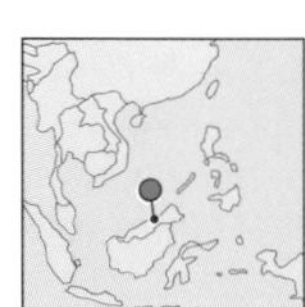

The Islamic Sultanate of Brunei, a British protectorate until 1984, lies on the north coast of Borneo. The climate is tropical and rainforests cover large areas. Brunei is a prosperous country because of its oil and natural gas production, and the Sultan is said to be among the world's richest men. **AREA** 5,770 sq km [2,228 sq mls]; **POPULATION** 315,000; **CAPITAL** Bandar Seri Begawan.

BULGARIA

GEOGRAPHY The Republic of Bulgaria is a country in the Balkan peninsula, facing the Black Sea in the east. The heart of Bulgaria is mountainous. The main ranges are the Balkan Mountains in the centre and the Rhodope (or Rhodopi) Mountains in the south.

Summers are hot and winters are cold, though seldom severe. The rainfall is moderate throughout the year.

POLITICS & ECONOMY Ottoman Turks ruled Bulgaria from 1396 and ethnic Turks still form a sizeable minority in the country. In 1879, Bulgaria became a monarchy, and in 1908 it became fully independent. Bulgaria was an ally of Germany in World War I (1914–18) and again in World War II (1939–45). In 1944, Soviet troops invaded Bulgaria and, after the war, the monarchy was abolished and the country became a Communist ally of the Soviet Union. In the late 1980s, reforms in the Soviet Union led Bulgaria's government to introduce a multiparty system in 1990. A non-Communist government was elected in 1991, the first free elections in 44 years. Since 1991, Bulgaria has faced problems in trying to transform the old Communist economy into a new one based on private enterprise.

According to the World Bank, Bulgaria in the 1990s was a 'lower-middle-income' developing country. Bulgaria has some deposits of minerals, including brown coal, manganese and iron ore. But manufacturing is the leading economic activity, though problems arose in the early 1990s, because much industrial technology is outdated. The main products are chemicals, processed foods, metal products, machinery and textiles. Manufactures are the leading exports. Bulgaria trades mainly with countries in Eastern Europe.

AREA 110,910 sq km [42,822 sq mls]
POPULATION 8,240,000
CAPITAL (POPULATION) Sofia (1,117,000)
GOVERNMENT Multiparty republic
ETHNIC GROUPS Bulgarian 86%, Turkish 10%, Gypsy 3%, Macedonian, Armenian, Romanian, Greek
LANGUAGES Bulgarian (official), Turkish
RELIGIONS Christianity (Eastern Orthodox 87%), Islam 13%
CURRENCY Lev = 100 stotinki

BURKINA FASO

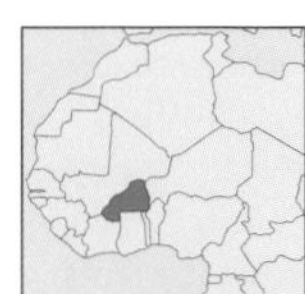

GEOGRAPHY The Democratic People's Republic of Burkina Faso is a landlocked country, a little larger than the United Kingdom, in West Africa. But Burkina Faso has only one-sixth of the population of the UK. The country consists of a plateau, between about 300 m and 700 m [650 ft to 2,300 ft] above sea level. The plateau is cut by several rivers.

The capital city, Ouagadougou, in central Burkina Faso, has high temperatures throughout the year. Most of the rain falls between May and September, but the rainfall is erratic and droughts are common.

POLITICS & ECONOMY The people of Burkina Faso are divided into two main groups. The Voltaic group includes the Mossi, who form the largest single group, and the Bobo. The French conquered the Mossi capital of Ouagadougou in 1897 and they made the area a protectorate. In 1919, the area became a French colony called Upper Volta. After independence in 1960, Upper Volta became a one-party state. But it was unstable – military groups seized power several times and a number of political killings took place.

In 1984, the country's name was changed to Burkina Faso. Elections were held in 1991 – for the first time in more than ten years – but the military kept an important role in the government.

Burkina Faso is one of the world's 20 poorest countries and has become very dependent on foreign aid. Most of Burkina Faso is dry with thin soils. The country's main food crops are beans, maize, millet, rice and sorghum. Cotton, groundnuts and shea nuts, whose seeds produce a fat used to make cooking oil and soap, are grown for sale abroad. Livestock are also an important export.

The country has few resources and manufacturing is on a small scale. There are some deposits of manganese, zinc, lead and nickel in the north of the country, but there is not yet a good enough transport system there. Many young men seek jobs abroad in Ghana and Ivory Coast. The money they send home to their families is important to the country's economy.

AREA 274,200 sq km [105,869 sq mls]
POPULATION 11,266,000
CAPITAL (POPULATION) Ouagadougou (690,000)
GOVERNMENT Multiparty republic
ETHNIC GROUPS Mossi 48%, Mande 9%, Fulani 8%, Bobo 7%
LANGUAGES French (official), Mossi, Fulani
RELIGIONS Traditional beliefs 45%, Islam 43%, Christianity 12%
CURRENCY CFA franc = 100 centimes

BURMA (MYANMAR)

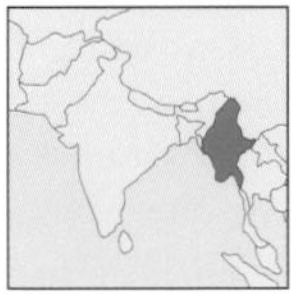

GEOGRAPHY The Union of Burma is now officially known as the Union of Myanmar; its name was changed in 1989. Mountains border the country in the east and west, with the highest mountains in the north. Burma's highest mountain is Hkakabo Razi, which is 5,881 m [19,294 ft] high. Between these ranges is central Burma, which contains the fertile valleys of the Irrawaddy and Sittang rivers. The Irrawaddy delta on the Bay of Bengal is one of the world's leading rice-growing areas. Burma also includes the long Tenasserim coast in the south-east.

Burma has a tropical monsoon climate. There are three seasons. The rainy season runs from late May to mid-October. A cool, dry season follows, between late October and the middle part of February. The hot season lasts from late February to mid-May, though temperatures remain high during the humid rainy season.

POLITICS & ECONOMY Many groups settled in Burma in ancient times. Some, called the hill peoples, live in remote mountain areas where they have retained their own cultures. The ancestors of the country's main ethnic group today, the Burmese, arrived in the 9th century AD.

Britain conquered Burma in the 19th century and made it a province of British India. But, in 1937, the British granted Burma limited self-government. Japan conquered Burma in 1942, but the Japanese were driven out in 1945. Burma became a fully independent country in 1948.

Revolts by Communists and various hill people led to instability in the 1950s. In 1962, Burma became a military dictatorship and, in 1974, a one-party state. Attempts to control minority liberation movements and the opium trade led to repressive rule. The National League for Democracy led by Aung San Suu Kyi won the elections in 1990, but the military ignored the result and continued their repressive rule. They earned Burma the reputation for having one of the world's worst records on human rights. Burma's internal political problems have helped to make it one of the world's poorest countries. Its admission to ASEAN (Association of South-east Asian Nations) in 1997 may have implied regional recognition of the regime, but the European Union continues to voice its concern over human rights abuses.

Agriculture is the main activity, employing 64% of the people. The chief crop is rice. Maize, pulses, oilseeds and sugar cane are other major products. Forestry is important. Teak and rice together make up about two-thirds of the total value of the exports. Burma has many mineral resources, though they are mostly undeveloped, but the country is famous for its precious stones, especially rubies. Manufacturing is mostly on a small scale.

AREA 676,577 sq km [261,228 sq mls]
POPULATION 47,305,000
CAPITAL (POPULATION) Rangoon (2,513,000)
GOVERNMENT Military regime
ETHNIC GROUPS Burman 69%, Shan 9%, Karen 6%, Rakhine 5%, Mon 2%, Kachin 1%
LANGUAGES Burmese (official), Shan, Karen, Rakhine, Mon, Kachin, English, Chin
RELIGIONS Buddhism 89%, Christianity, Islam
CURRENCY Kyat = 100 pyas

BURUNDI

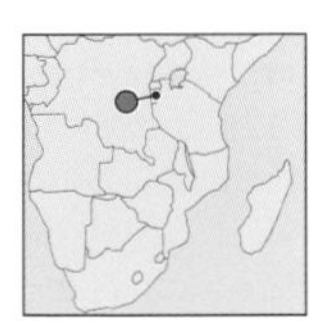

GEOGRAPHY The Republic of Burundi is the fifth smallest country in mainland Africa. It is also the second most densely populated after its northern neighbour, Rwanda. Part of the Great African Rift Valley, which runs throughout eastern Africa into south-western Asia, lies in western Burundi. It includes part of Lake Tanganyika.

Bujumbura, the capital city, lies on the shore of Lake Tanganyika. It has a warm climate. A dry season occurs from June to September, but the other months are fairly rainy. The mountains and plateaux to the east are cooler and wetter, but the rainfall generally decreases to the east.

POLITICS & ECONOMY The Twa, a pygmy people, were the first known inhabitants of Burundi. About 1,000 years ago, the Hutu, a people who speak a Bantu language, gradually began to settle the area, pushing the Twa into remote areas.

From the 15th century, the Tutsi, a cattle-owning people from the north-east, gradually took over the country. The Hutu, although greatly outnumbering the Tutsi, were forced to serve the Tutsi overlords.

Germany conquered the area that is now Burundi and Rwanda in the late 1890s. The area, called

Ruanda-Urundi, was taken by Belgium during World War I (1914–18). In 1961, the people of Urundi voted to become a monarchy, while the people of Ruanda voted to become a republic. The two territories became fully independent as Burundi and Rwanda in 1962. After 1962, the rivalries between the Hutu and Tutsi led to periodic outbreaks of fighting. The Tutsi monarchy was ended in 1966 and Burundi became a republic. Instability continued with coups in 1976, 1987, 1993 and 1996, with periodic massacres of thousands of people as Tutsis and Hutus fought for power.

Burundi is one of the world's ten poorest countries. About 92% of the people are farmers, who mostly grow little more than they need to feed their own families. The main food crops are beans, cassava, maize and sweet potatoes. Cattle, goats and sheep are raised, while fish are an important supplement to people's diets. However, Burundi has to import food.

AREA 27,830 sq km [10,745 sq mls]
POPULATION 5,531,000
CAPITAL (POPULATION) Bujumbura (300,000)
GOVERNMENT Republic
ETHNIC GROUPS Hutu 85%, Tutsi 14%, Twa (pygmy) 1%
LANGUAGES French and Kirundi (both official)
RELIGIONS Christianity 85% (Roman Catholic 78%), traditional beliefs 13%
CURRENCY Burundi franc = 100 centimes

CAMBODIA

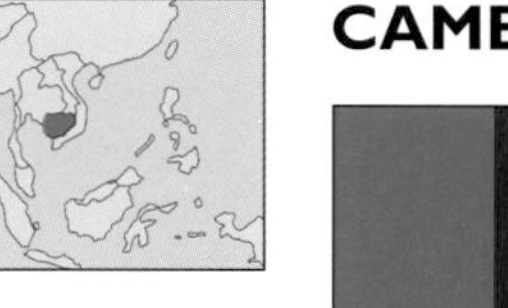

GEOGRAPHY The Kingdom of Cambodia is a country in South-east Asia. Low mountains border the country except in the south-east. But most of Cambodia consists of plains drained by the River Mekong, which enters Cambodia from Laos in the north and exits through Vietnam in the south-east. The north-west contains Tonlé Sap (or Great Lake). In the dry season, this lake drains into the River Mekong. But in the wet season, the level of the Mekong rises and water flows in the opposite direction from the river into Tonlé Sap – the lake then becomes the largest freshwater lake in Asia.

Cambodia has a tropical monsoon climate, with high temperatures all through the year. The dry season, when winds blow from the north or north-east, runs from November to April. During the rainy season, from May to October, moist winds blow from the south or south-east. The high humidity and heat often make conditions unpleasant. The rainfall is heaviest near the coast, and rather lower inland.

POLITICS & ECONOMY From 802 to 1432, the Khmer people ruled a great empire, which reached its peak in the 12th century. The Khmer capital was at Angkor. The Hindu stone temples built there and at nearby Angkor Wat form the world's largest group of religious buildings. France ruled the country between 1863 and 1954, when the country became an independent monarchy. But the monarchy was abolished in 1970 and Cambodia became a republic.

In 1970, US and South Vietnamese troops entered Cambodia but left after destroying North Vietnamese Communist camps in the east. The country became involved in the Vietnamese War, and then in a civil war as Cambodian Communists of the Khmer Rouge organization fought for power. The Khmer Rouge took over Cambodia in 1975 and launched a reign of terror in which between 1 million and 2.5 million people were killed. In 1979, Vietnamese and Cambodian troops overthrew the Khmer Rouge government. But fighting continued between several factions. Vietnam withdrew in 1989, and in 1991 Prince Sihanouk was recognized as head of state. Elections were held in May 1993, and in September 1993 the monarchy was restored. Sihanouk again became king. In 1997, the prime minister, Prince Norodom Ranariddh, was deposed, so ending four years of democratic rule. This led to Cambodia's application to join the Association of South-east Asian Nations to be put on hold.

Cambodia is a poor country whose economy has been wrecked by war. Until the 1970s, the country's farmers produced most of the food needed by the people. But by 1986, it was only able to supply 80% of its needs. Farming is the main activity and rice, rubber and maize are major products. Manufacturing is almost non-existent, apart from rubber processing and a few factories producing items for sale in Cambodia.

AREA 181,040 sq km [69,900 sq mls]
POPULATION 11,340,000
CAPITAL (POPULATION) Phnom Penh (920,000)
GOVERNMENT Constitutional monarchy
ETHNIC GROUPS Khmer 94%, Chinese 3%, Cham 2%, Thai, Lao, Kola, Vietnamese
LANGUAGES Khmer (official)
RELIGIONS Buddhism 88%, Islam 2%
CURRENCY Riel = 100 sen

CAMEROON

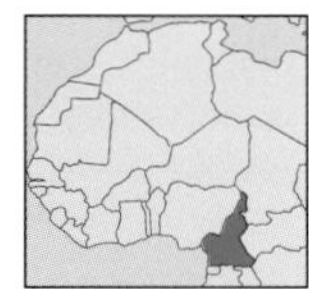

GEOGRAPHY The Republic of Cameroon in West Africa got its name from the Portuguese word *camarões*, or prawns. This name was used by Portuguese explorers who fished for prawns along the coast. Behind the narrow coastal plains on the Gulf of Guinea, the land rises to a series of plateaux, with a mountainous region in the south-west where the volcano Mount Cameroon is situated. In the north, the land slopes down towards the Lake Chad basin.

The rainfall is heavy, especially in the highlands. The rainiest months near the coast are June to September. The rainfall decreases to the north and the far north has a hot, dry climate. Temperatures are high on the coast, whereas the inland plateaux are cooler.

POLITICS & ECONOMY Germany lost Cameroon during World War I (1914–18). The country was then divided into two parts, one ruled by Britain and the other by France. In 1960, French Cameroon became the independent Cameroon Republic. In 1961, after a vote in British Cameroon, part of the territory joined the Cameroon Republic to become the Federal Republic of Cameroon. The other part joined Nigeria. In 1972, Cameroon became a unitary state called the United Republic of Cameroon. It adopted the name Republic of Cameroon in 1984, but the country had two official languages. In 1995, partly to placate English-speaking people, Cameroon became the 52nd member of the Commonwealth.

Like most countries in tropical Africa, Cameroon's economy is based on agriculture, which employs 73% of the people. The chief food crops include cassava, maize, millet, sweet potatoes and yams. The country also has plantations to produce such crops as cocoa and coffee for export.

Cameroon is fortunate in having some oil, the country's chief export, and bauxite. Although Cameroon has few manufacturing and processing industries, its mineral exports and its self-sufficiency in food production make it one of the better-off countries in tropical Africa.

AREA 475,440 sq km [183,567 sq mls]
POPULATION 15,029,000
CAPITAL (POPULATION) Yaoundé (750,000)
GOVERNMENT Multiparty republic
ETHNIC GROUPS Fang 20%, Bamileke and Bamum 19%, Duala, Luanda and Basa 15%, Fulani 10%
LANGUAGES French and English (both official)
RELIGIONS Christianity 53%, traditional beliefs 25%, Islam 22%
CURRENCY CFA franc = 100 centimes

CANADA

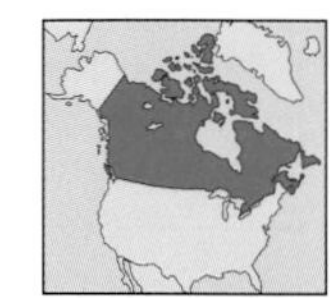

GEOGRAPHY Canada is the world's second largest country after Russia. It is thinly populated, however, with much of the land too cold or too mountainous for human settlement. Most Canadians live within 300 km [186 mls] of the southern border.

Western Canada is rugged. It includes the Pacific ranges and the mighty Rocky Mountains. East of the Rockies are the interior plains. In the north lie the bleak Arctic islands, while to the south lie the densely populated lowlands around lakes Erie and Ontario and in the St Lawrence River valley.

Canada has a cold climate. In winter, temperatures fall below freezing point throughout most of Canada. But the south-western coast has a relatively mild climate. Along the Arctic Circle, mean temperatures are below freezing for seven months a year.

Western and south-eastern Canada experience high rainfall, but the prairies are dry with 250 mm to 500 mm [10 in to 20 in] of rain every year.

POLITICS & ECONOMY Canada's first people, the ancestors of the Native Americans, or Indians, arrived in North America from Asia around 40,000 years ago. Later arrivals were the Inuit (Eskimos), who also came from Asia. Europeans reached the Canadian coast in 1497 and a race began between Britain and France for control of the territory.

France gained an initial advantage, and the French founded Québec in 1608. But the British later occupied eastern Canada. In 1867, Britain passed the British North America Act, which set up the Dominion of Canada, which was made up of Québec, Ontario, Nova Scotia and New Brunswick. Other areas were added, the last being Newfoundland in 1949. Canada fought alongside Britain in both World Wars and many Canadians feel close ties with Britain. Canada is a constitutional monarchy. The head of state is Queen Elizabeth II, though the country is governed by a prime minister, a cabinet and an elected, two-chamber parliament.

Rivalries between French- and English-speaking Canadians continue. In 1995, Québeckers voted against a move to make Québec a sovereign state. The majority was less than 1% and this issue seems unlikely to disappear. Another problem concerns the future of the Native Americans, who would like to have more say in the running of their own affairs. To this end, a new territory, Nunavut, was created for the Inuit population in 1999. It occupies the eastern part of Northern Territories.

Canada is a highly developed and prosperous country. Although farmland covers only 8% of the country, Canadian farms are highly productive. Canada is one of the world's leading producers of barley, wheat, meat and milk. Forestry and fishing are other important industries. It is rich in natural resources, especially oil and natural gas, and is a major exporter of minerals. The country also produces copper, gold, iron ore, uranium and zinc. Manufacturing is highly developed, especially in the cities where 77% of the people live. Canada has many factories that process farm and mineral products. It also produces cars, chemicals, electronic goods, machinery, paper and timber products.

AREA 9,976,140 sq km [3,851,788 sq mls]
POPULATION 30,675,000
CAPITAL (POPULATION) Ottawa (1,010,000)
GOVERNMENT Federal multiparty constitutional monarchy
ETHNIC GROUPS British 34%, French 26%, German 4%, Italian 3%, Ukrainian 2%, Native American (Amerindian/Inuit) 1.5%, Chinese
LANGUAGES English and French (both official)
RELIGIONS Christianity (Roman Catholic 47%, Protestant 41%), Judaism, Islam, Hinduism
CURRENCY Canadian dollar = 100 cents

CAPE VERDE

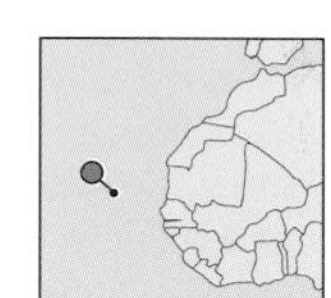

Cape Verde consists of ten large and five small islands, and is situated 560 km [350 mls] west of Dakar in Senegal. The islands have a tropical climate, with high temperatures all year round. Cape Verde became independent from Portugal in 1975 and is rated as a 'low-income' developing country by the World Bank. **AREA** 4,030 sq km [1,556 sq mls]; **POPULATION** 399,000; **CAPITAL** Praia.

CAYMAN ISLANDS

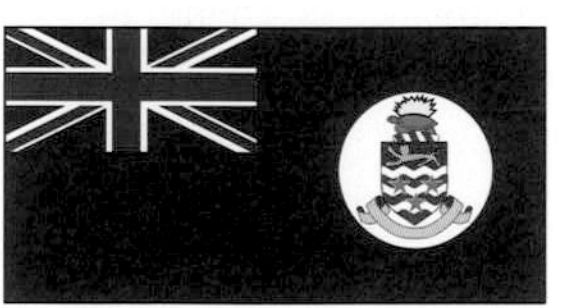

The Cayman Islands are an overseas territory of the UK, consisting of three low-lying islands. Financial services are the main economic activity and the islands offer a secret tax haven to many companies and banks. **AREA** 259 sq km [100 sq mls]; **POPULATION** 35,000; **CAPITAL** George Town.

CENTRAL AFRICAN REPUBLIC

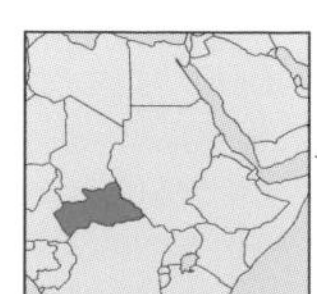

GEOGRAPHY The Central African Republic is a remote, landlocked country in the heart of Africa. It consists mostly of a plateau lying between 600 m and 800 m [1,970 ft to 2,620 ft] above sea level. The Ubangi drains the south, while the Chari (or Shari) River flows from the north to the Lake Chad basin.

Bangui, the capital, lies in the south-west of the country on the Ubangi River. The climate is warm throughout the year, with average yearly rainfall totalling 1,574 mm [62 in]. The north is drier, with an average yearly rainfall of about 800 mm [31 in].

POLITICS & ECONOMY France set up an outpost at Bangui in 1899 and ruled the country as a colony from 1894. Known as Ubangi-Shari, the country was ruled by France as part of French Equatorial Africa until it gained independence in 1960.

Central African Republic became a one-party state in 1962, but army officers seized power in 1966. The head of the army, Jean-Bedel Bokassa, made himself emperor in 1976. The country was renamed the Central African Empire, but after a brutal and tyrannical reign, Bokassa was overthrown by a military group in 1979. As a result, the monarchy was abolished and the country again became a republic.

The country adopted a new, multiparty constitution in 1991. Elections were held in 1993. An army rebellion was put down in 1996 with help from French troops.

The World Bank classifies Central African Republic as a 'low-income' developing country. Over 80% of the people are farmers, and most of them produce little more than they need to feed their families. The main crops are bananas, maize, manioc, millet and yams. Coffee, cotton, timber and tobacco are produced for export, mainly on commercial plantations. The country's development has been impeded by its remote position, its poor transport system and its untrained workforce. The country depends heavily on aid, especially from France.

AREA 622,980 sq km [240,533 sq mls]
POPULATION 3,376,000
CAPITAL (POPULATION) Bangui (706,000)
GOVERNMENT Multiparty republic
ETHNIC GROUPS Banda 29%, Baya 25%, Ngbandi 11%, Azande 10%, Sara 7%, Mbaka 4%
LANGUAGES French and Sango (both official)
RELIGIONS Traditional beliefs 57%, Christianity 35%, Islam 8%
CURRENCY CFA franc = 100 centimes

CHAD

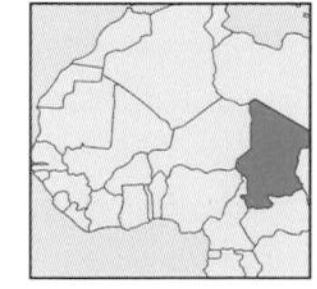

GEOGRAPHY The Republic of Chad is a landlocked country in north-central Africa. It is Africa's fifth largest country and is more than twice as big as France, the country which once ruled it as a colony.

Ndjamena in central Chad has a hot, tropical climate, with a marked dry season from November to April. The south of the country is wetter, with an average yearly rainfall of around 1,000 mm [39 in]. The burning-hot desert in the north has an average yearly rainfall of less than 130 mm [5 in].

POLITICS & ECONOMY Chad straddles two worlds. The north is populated by Muslim Arab and Berber peoples, while black Africans, who follow traditional beliefs or who have converted to Christianity, live in the south.

French explorers were active in the area in the late 19th century. France finally made Chad a colony in 1902. After becoming independent in 1960, Chad has been hit by ethnic conflict. In the 1970s, civil war, frequent coups and intervention in the north by Libya retarded the country's economic development. Chad and Libya agreed a truce in 1987 and, in 1994, the International Court of Justice ruled that Libya had no claim on the Aozou Strip in the far north.

Hit by drought and civil war, Chad is one of the world's poorest countries. Farming, fishing and livestock raising employ 83% of the people. Groundnuts, millet, rice and sorghum are major food crops in the wetter south, but the most valuable crop in export terms is cotton. The country has few natural resources and very few manufacturing industries.

AREA 1,284,000 sq km [495,752 sq mls]
POPULATION 7,360,000
CAPITAL (POPULATION) Ndjaména (530,000)
GOVERNMENT Transitional
ETHNIC GROUPS Bagirmi, Kreish and Sara 31%, Sudanic Arab 26%, Teda 7%, Mbum 6%
LANGUAGES French and Arabic (both official)
RELIGIONS Islam 40%, Christianity 33%, traditional beliefs 27%
CURRENCY CFA franc = 100 centimes

CHILE

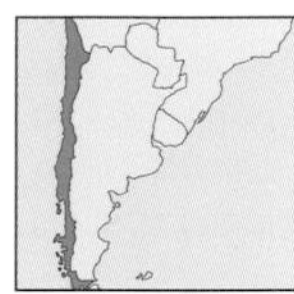

GEOGRAPHY The Republic of Chile stretches about 4,260 km [2,650 mls] from north to south, although the maximum east–west distance is only about 430 km [267 mls]. The high Andes Mountains form Chile's eastern borders with Argentina and Bolivia. To the west are basins and valleys, with coastal uplands overlooking the shore. Most people live in the central valley, where Santiago is situated.

Santiago, Chile's capital, has a Mediterranean climate, with hot, dry summers from November to March and mild, moist winters from April to October. However, the Atacama Desert in the north is one of the world's driest places, while southern Chile is cold and stormy.

POLITICS & ECONOMY Amerindian people reached the southern tip of South America at least 8,000 years ago. In 1520, the Portuguese navigator Ferdinand Magellan became the first European to sight Chile, but the country became a Spanish colony in the 1540s. Chile became independent in 1818 and, during a war (1879–83), it gained mineral-rich areas from Peru and Bolivia.

In 1970, Salvador Allende became the first Communist leader ever to be elected democratically. He was overthrown in 1973 by army officers, who were supported by the CIA. General Augusto Pinochet then ruled as a dictator. A new constitution was introduced in 1981 and elections were held in 1989.

The World Bank classifies Chile as a 'lower-middle-income' developing country. Mining is important, especially copper production. Minerals dominate Chile's exports. But the most valuable activity is manufacturing; products include processed foods, metals, iron and steel, wood products, transport equipment and textiles.

AREA 756,950 sq km [292,258 sq mls]
POPULATION 14,788,000
CAPITAL (POPULATION) Santiago (5,077,000)
GOVERNMENT Multiparty republic
ETHNIC GROUPS Mestizo 92%, Amerindian 7%
LANGUAGES Spanish (official)
RELIGIONS Christianity (Roman Catholic 81%)
CURRENCY Peso = 100 centavos

CHINA

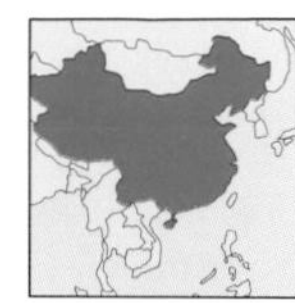

GEOGRAPHY The People's Republic of China is the world's third largest country. It is also the only country with more than 1,000 million people. Most people live in the east – on the coastal plains or in the fertile valleys of the Huang He (Hwang Ho or Yellow River), the Chang Jiang (Yangtze Kiang), which is Asia's longest river at 6,380 km [3,960 mls], and the Xi Jiang (Si Kiang).

Western China is thinly populated. It includes the bleak Tibetan plateau which is bounded by the Himalaya, the world's highest mountain range. Other ranges include the Kunlun Shan, the Altun Shan and the Tian Shan. Deserts include the Gobi desert along the Mongolian border and the Taklimakan desert in the far west.

Beijing in north-eastern China has cold winters and warm summers, with a moderate rainfall. Shanghai, in the east-central region of China, has milder winters and more rain. The south-east has a wet, subtropical climate. In the west, the climate is severe. Lhasa has very cold winters and a low rainfall.

POLITICS & ECONOMY China is one of the world's oldest civilizations, going back 3,500 years. Under the Han dynasty (202 BC to AD 220), the Chinese empire was as large as the Roman empire. Mongols conquered China in the 13th century, but Chinese rule was restored in 1368. The Manchu people of Mongolia ruled the country from 1644 to 1912, when the country became a republic.

War with Japan (1937–45) was followed by civil war between the nationalists and the Communists. The Communists triumphed in 1949, setting up the People's Republic of China.

In the 1980s, following the death of the revolutionary leader Mao Zedong (Mao Tse-tung) in 1976, China introduced reforms. It encouraged private enterprise and foreign investment, formerly forbidden policies. But the Communist leaders have not permitted political freedom. Opponents of the regime continue to be harshly treated, while attempts to negotiate some degree of autonomy for Tibet were firmly rejected in 1998.

China's economy, which is one of the world's largest, has expanded rapidly since the late 1970s. This is partly the result of the gradual abandonment of some fundamental Communist policies, including the setting up of many private manufacturing industries in the east. China's sheer size, combined with its rapid economic growth, have led to predictions that China will soon become a superpower. It was forecast in 1996 that China would become the world's biggest economy 'within a generation'. This was made more likely by the return of Hong Kong in July 1997 and, to a much lesser extent, by the return of Macau in December 1999.

In the early 1990s, agriculture employed about 70% of the people, although only 10% of the land is used for crops. Major products include rice, sweet potatoes, tea and wheat, together with many fruits and vegetables. Livestock farming is also important. Pork is a popular meat and China has more than a third of the world's pigs.

China's resources include coal, oil, iron ore and various other metals. China has huge steel industries and manufactures include cement, chemicals, fertilizers, machinery, telecommunications and recording equipment, and textiles. Consumer goods, such as bicycles and radios, are becoming increasingly important.

AREA 9,596,960 sq km [3,705,386 sq mls]
POPULATION 1,236,915,000
CAPITAL (POPULATION) Beijing (12,362,000)
GOVERNMENT Single-party Communist republic
ETHNIC GROUPS Han Chinese 92%, 55 minority groups
LANGUAGES Mandarin Chinese (official)
RELIGIONS Atheist 50%, Confucian 20%
CURRENCY Renminbi yuan = 10 jiao = 100 fen

COLOMBIA

GEOGRAPHY The Republic of Colombia, in north-eastern South America, is the only country in the continent to have coastlines on both the Pacific and the Caribbean Sea. Colombia also contains the northernmost ranges of the Andes Mountains.

There is a tropical climate in the lowlands. But the altitude greatly affects the climate of the Andes. The capital, Bogotá, which stands on a plateau in the eastern Andes at about 2,800 m [9,200 ft] above sea level, has mild temperatures throughout the year. The rainfall is heavy, especially on the Pacific coast

POLITICS & ECONOMY Amerindian people have lived in Colombia for thousands of years. But today, only a small proportion of the people are of unmixed Amerindian ancestry. Mestizos (people of mixed white and Amerindian ancestry) form the largest group, followed by whites and mulattos (people of mixed European and African ancestry).

Spaniards opened up the area in the early 16th century and they set up a territory known as the Viceroyalty of the New Kingdom of Granada, which included Colombia, Ecuador, Panama and Venezuela. In 1819, the area became independent, but Ecuador and Venezuela soon split away, followed by Panama in 1903. Colombia's recent history has been very unstable. Rivalries between the main political parties led to civil wars in 1899–1902 and 1949–57, when the parties agreed to form a coalition. The coalition government ended in 1986 when the Liberal Party was elected. Colombia faces many economic problems, as well as the difficulty of controlling a large illicit drug industry run by violent dealers. Colombia exports coal and oil, and it also produces emeralds and gold.

AREA 1,138,910 sq km [439,733 sq mls]
POPULATION 38,581,000
CAPITAL (POPULATION) Bogotá (5,026,000)
GOVERNMENT Multiparty republic
ETHNIC GROUPS Mestizo 58%, White 20%, Mulatto 14%, Black 4%
LANGUAGES Spanish (official)
RELIGIONS Christianity (Roman Catholic 93%)
CURRENCY Peso = 100 centavos

COMOROS

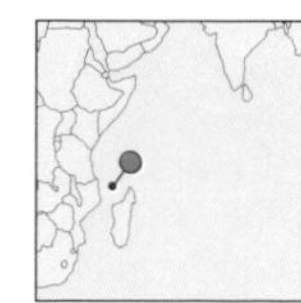

The Federal Islamic Republic of the Comoros consists of three large islands and some smaller ones, lying at the north end of the Mozambique Channel in the Indian Ocean. The country became independent from France in 1974, but the people on a fourth island, Mayotte, voted to remain French. In 1997, secessionists on the island of Anjouan, who favoured a return to French rule, defeated forces from Grand Comore and, in 1998, they voted overwhelmingly to break away from the Comoros. Most people are subsistence farmers, although cash crops such as coconuts, coffee, cocoa and spices are also produced. The main exports are cloves, perfume oils and vanilla. **AREA** 2,230 sq km [115 sq mls]; **POPULATION** 545,000; **CAPITAL** Moroni.

CONGO

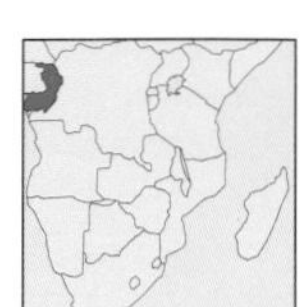

GEOGRAPHY The Republic of Congo is a country on the River Congo in west-central Africa. The Equator runs through the centre of the country. Congo has a narrow coastal plain on which its main port, Pointe Noire, stands. Behind the plain are uplands through which the River Niari has carved a fertile valley. Central Congo consists of high plains. The north contains large swampy areas in the valleys of rivers that flow into the River Congo and its large tributary, the Oubangi.

Congo has a hot, wet equatorial climate. Brazzaville and its environs experience a dry season between June and September. The coastal plain is drier and cooler than the rest of the country because a cold ocean current, the Benguela, flows northwards along the coast.

POLITICS & ECONOMY Part of the huge Kongo kingdom between the 15th and 18th centuries, the coast of the Congo later became a centre of the European slave trade. The area came under French protection in 1880. It was later governed as part of a larger region called French Equatorial Africa. The country remained under French control until 1960.

Congo became a one-party state in 1964 and a military group took over the government in 1968. In 1970, Congo declared itself a Communist country, though it continued to seek aid from Western countries. The government officially abandoned its Communist policies in 1990. Multiparty elections were held in 1992, but the elected president, Pascal Lissouba, was overthrown in 1997 by former president, Denis Sassou-Nguesso.

The World Bank classifies Congo as a 'lower-middle-income' developing country. Agriculture is the most important activity, employing more than 60% of the people. But many farmers produce little more than they need to feed their families. Major food crops include bananas, cassava, maize and rice, while the leading cash crops are coffee and cocoa. Congo's main exports are oil (which makes up 70% of the total) and timber. Manufacturing is relatively unimportant at the moment, still hampered by poor transport links, but it is gradually being developed.

AREA 342,000 sq km [132,046 sq mls]
POPULATION 2,658,000
CAPITAL (POPULATION) Brazzaville (938,000)
GOVERNMENT Military regime
ETHNIC GROUPS Kongo 52%, Teke 17%, Mboshi 12%, Mbete 5%
LANGUAGES French (official), Kongo, Teke
RELIGIONS Christianity (Roman Catholic 54%, Protestant 25%, African Christians 14%
CURRENCY CFA franc = 100 centimes

CONGO (ZAÏRE)

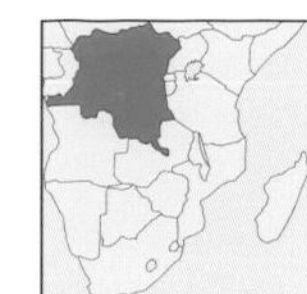

GEOGRAPHY The Democratic Republic of the Congo, formerly known as Zaïre, is the world's 12th largest country. Much of the country lies within the drainage basin of the huge River Congo. The river reaches the sea along the country's coastline, which is 40 km [25 mls] long. Mountains rise in the east, where the country's borders run through lakes Tanganyika, Kivu, Edward and Albert. These lakes lie on the floor of an arm of the Great Rift Valley.

The equatorial region has high temperatures and heavy rainfall throughout the year. In the subtropical south, where the town of Lubumbashi is situated, there is a marked wet and dry season.

POLITICS & ECONOMY Pygmies were the first inhabitants of the region, with Portuguese navigators not reaching the coast until 1482, but the interior was not explored until the late 19th century. In 1885, the country, called Congo Free State, became the personal property of King Léopold II of Belgium. In 1908, the country became a Belgian colony.

The Belgian Congo became independent in 1960 and was renamed Zaïre in 1971. Ethnic rivalries caused instability until 1965, when the country became a one-party state, ruled by President Mobutu. The government allowed the formation of political parties in 1990, but elections were repeatedly postponed. In 1996, fighting broke out in eastern Zaïre, as the Tutsi–Hutu conflict in Burundi and Rwanda spilled over. The rebel leader Laurent Kabila took power in 1997, ousting Mobutu and renaming the country. A rebellion against Kabila broke out in 1998. Rwanda and Uganda supported the rebels, while Angola, Chad, Namibia and Zimbabwe sent troops to assist Kabila.

The World Bank classifies the Democratic Republic of the Congo as a 'low-income' developing country, despite its reserves of copper, the main export, and other minerals. Agriculture, mainly at subsistence level, employs 71% of the people.

AREA 2,344,885 sq km [905,365 sq mls]
POPULATION 49,001,000
CAPITAL (POPULATION) Kinshasa (3,804,000)
GOVERNMENT Single-party republic
ETHNIC GROUPS Luba 18%, Kongo 16%, Mongo 14%, Rwanda 10%, Azande 6%, Bandi and Ngale 6%, Rundi 4%, Teke, Boa, Chokwe, Lugbara, Banda
LANGUAGES French (official), tribal languages
RELIGIONS Christianity (Roman Catholic 48%, Protestant 29%, indigenous Christian churches 17%), traditional beliefs 3%, Islam 1%
CURRENCY Congolese franc

COSTA RICA

GEOGRAPHY The Republic of Costa Rica in Central America has coastlines on both the Pacific Ocean and also on the Caribbean Sea. Central Costa Rica consists of mountain ranges and plateaux with many volcanoes.

The coolest months are December and January. The north-east trade winds bring heavy rain to the Caribbean coast. There is less rainfall in the highlands and on the Pacific coastlands.

POLITICS & ECONOMY Christopher Columbus reached the Caribbean coast in 1502 and rumours of treasure soon attracted many Spaniards to settle in the country. Spain ruled the country until 1821, when Spain's Central American colonies broke away to join Mexico in 1822. In 1823, the Central American states broke with Mexico and set up the Central American Federation. Later, this large union broke up and Costa Rica became fully independent in 1838. From the late 19th century, Costa Rica experienced a number of revolutions, with periods of dictatorship and periods of democracy. In 1948, following a revolt, the armed forces were abolished. Since 1948, Costa Rica has enjoyed a long period of stable democracy, which many in Latin America admire and envy.

Costa Rica is classified by the World Bank as a 'lower-middle-income' developing country and one of the most prosperous countries in Central America. There are high educational standards and a high life expectancy (to an average of 73.5 years). Agriculture employs 24% of the people.

The country's resources include its forests, but it lacks minerals apart from some bauxite and manganese. Manufacturing is increasing. The United States is Costa Rica's chief trading partner. Tourism is a growing industry.

AREA 51,100 sq km [19,730 sq mls]
POPULATION 3,605,000
CAPITAL (POPULATION) San José (1,186,000)
GOVERNMENT Multiparty republic
ETHNIC GROUPS White 85%, Mestizo 8%, Black and Mulatto 3%, East Asian (mostly Chinese) 3%
LANGUAGES Spanish (official)
RELIGIONS Christianity (Roman Catholic 81%)
CURRENCY Colón = 100 céntimos

CROATIA

GEOGRAPHY The Republic of Croatia was one of the six republics that made up the former Communist country of Yugoslavia until it became independent in 1991. The region bordering the Adriatic Sea is called Dalmatia. It includes the coastal ranges, which contain large areas of bare limestone. Most of the rest of the country consists of the fertile Pannonian plains.

The coastal area has a typical Mediterranean climate, with hot, dry summers and mild, moist winters. Inland, the climate becomes more continental. Winters are cold, while temperatures often soar to 38°C [100°F] in the summer months.

POLITICS & ECONOMY Slav people settled in the area around 1,400 years ago. In 803, Croatia became part of the Holy Roman Empire and the Croats soon adopted Christianity. Croatia was an independent kingdom in the 10th and 11th centuries. In 1102, the king of Hungary also became king of Croatia, creating a union that lasted 800 years. In 1526, part of Croatia came under the Turkish Ottoman empire, while the rest came under the Austrian Habsburgs.

After Austria-Hungary was defeated in World War I (1914–18), Croatia became part of the new Kingdom of the Serbs, Croats and Slovenes. This kingdom was renamed Yugoslavia in 1929. Germany occupied Yugoslavia during World War II (1939–45). Croatia was proclaimed independent, but it was really ruled by the invaders.

After the war, Communists took power with Josip Broz Tito as the country's leader. Despite ethnic differences between the people, Tito held Yugoslavia together until his death in 1980. In the 1980s, economic and ethnic problems, including a deterioration in relations with Serbia, threatened stability. In the 1990s, Yugoslavia split into five nations, one of which was Croatia, which declared itself independent in 1991.

After Serbia supplied arms to Serbs living in Croatia, war broke out between the two republics, causing great damage. Croatia lost more than 30% of its territory. But in 1992, the United Nations sent a peacekeeping force to Croatia, which effectively ended the war with Serbia.

In 1992, when war broke out in Bosnia-Herzegovina, Bosnian Croats occupied parts of the country. But in 1994, Croatia helped to end Croat–Muslim conflict in Bosnia-Herzegovina and, in 1995, after retaking some areas occupied by Serbs, it helped to draw up the Dayton Peace Accord which ended the civil war there.

The wars of the early 1990s disrupted Croatia's economy, which had been quite prosperous before the disturbances. Tourism on the Dalmatian coast had been a major industry. Croatia also had major manufacturing industries, and manufactures remain the chief exports.

AREA 56,538 sq km [21,824 sq mls]
POPULATION 4,672,000
CAPITAL (POPULATION) Zagreb (931,000)
GOVERNMENT Multiparty republic
ETHNIC GROUPS Croat 78%, Serb 12%, Bosnian
LANGUAGES Serbo-Croatian
RELIGIONS Christianity (Roman Catholic 77%, Eastern Orthodox 11%), Islam 1%
CURRENCY Kuna = 100 lipas

CUBA

GEOGRAPHY The Republic of Cuba is the largest island country in the Caribbean Sea. It consists of one large island, Cuba, the Isle of Youth (Isla de la Juventud) and about 1,600 small islets. Mountains and hills cover about a quarter of Cuba. The highest mountain range, the Sierra Maestra in the south-east, reaches 2,000 m [6,562 ft] above sea level. The rest of the land consists of gently rolling country or coastal plains, crossed by fertile valleys carved by the short, mostly shallow and narrow rivers.

Cuba lies in the tropics. But sea breezes moderate the temperature, warming the land in winter and cooling it in summer.

POLITICS & ECONOMY Christopher Columbus discovered the island in 1492 and Spaniards began to settle there from 1511. Spanish rule ended in 1898, when the United States defeated Spain in the Spanish-American War. American influence in Cuba remained strong until 1959, when revolutionary forces under Fidel Castro overthrew the dictatorial government of Fulgencio Batista.

The United States opposed Castro's policies, when he turned to the Soviet Union for assistance. In 1961, Cuban exiles attempting an invasion were defeated. In 1962, the US learned that nuclear missile bases armed by the Soviet Union had been established in Cuba. The US ordered the Soviet Union to remove the missiles and bases and, after a few days, when many people feared that a world war might break out, the Soviet Union agreed to the American demands.

Cuba's relations with the Soviet Union remained strong until 1991, when the Soviet Union was broken up. The loss of Soviet aid greatly damaged Cuba's economy, but Castro continued the country's left-wing policies. Elections in February 1993 showed a continuing high level of support from the people for Castro.

The government runs Cuba's economy and owns 70% of the farmland. Agriculture is important and sugar is the chief export, followed by refined nickel ore. Other exports include cigars, citrus fruits, fish, medical products and rum.

Before 1959, US companies owned most of Cuba's manufacturing industries. But under Fidel Castro, they became government property. After the collapse of Communist governments in the Soviet Union and its allies, Cuba worked to increase its trade with Latin America and China.

AREA 110,860 sq km [42,803 sq mls]
POPULATION 11,051,000
CAPITAL (POPULATION) Havana (2,241,000)
GOVERNMENT Socialist republic
ETHNIC GROUPS White 66%, Mulatto 22%, Black 12%
LANGUAGES Spanish (official)
RELIGIONS Christianity (Roman Catholic 40%, Protestant 3%)
CURRENCY Cuban peso = 100 centavos

CYPRUS

GEOGRAPHY The Republic of Cyprus is an island nation in the north-eastern Mediterranean Sea. Geographers regard it as part of Asia, but it resembles southern Europe in many ways.

Cyprus has scenic mountain ranges, including the Kyrenia range in the north and the Troodos Mountains in the south, which rise to 1,951 m [6,401 ft] at Mount Olympus. The island also contains several fertile lowlands, including the broad Mesaoria plain between the Kyrenia and Troodos mountains.

Cyprus has a Mediterranean climate, with hot, dry summers and mild, moist winters. But the summers are hotter than in the western Mediterranean lands; this is because Cyprus lies close to the hot mainland of south-western Asia.

POLITICS & ECONOMY Greeks settled on Cyprus around 3,200 years ago. From AD 330, the island was part of the Byzantine empire. In the 1570s, Cyprus became part of the Turkish Ottoman empire. Turkish rule continued until 1878 when Cyprus was leased to Britain. Britain annexed the island in 1914 and proclaimed it a colony in 1925.

In the 1950s, Greek Cypriots, who made up four-fifths of the population, began a campaign for enosis (union) with Greece. Their leader was the Greek Orthodox Archbishop Makarios. A secret guerrilla force called EOKA attacked the British, who exiled Makarios. Cyprus became an independent country in 1960, although Britain retained two military bases. Independent Cyprus had a constitution which provided for power-sharing between the Greek and Turkish Cypriots. But the constitution proved unworkable and fighting broke out between the two communities. In 1964, the United Nations sent in a peacekeeping force. Communal clashes recurred in 1967.

In 1974, Cypriot forces led by Greek officers overthrew Makarios. This led Turkey to invade northern Cyprus, a territory occupying about 40% of the island. Many Greek Cypriots fled from the Turkish-occupied area, which, in 1979, was proclaimed to be a self-governing region. In 1983, the Turkish Cypriots declared the north to be an independent state called the Turkish Republic of Northern Cyprus. But only Turkey recognizes this state. The UN regards Cyprus as a single nation under the Greek Cypriot government in the south.

Cyprus got its name from the Greek word *kypros*, meaning copper. But little copper remains and the chief minerals today are asbestos and chromium. However, the most valuable activity in Cyprus is tourism. In the early 1990s, the United Nations reclassified Cyprus as a developed rather than a developing country. But the economy of the Turkish-Cypriot north lags behind that of the more prosperous Greek-Cypriot south.

AREA 9,250 sq km [3,571 sq mls]
POPULATION 749,000
CAPITAL (POPULATION) Nicosia (189,000)
GOVERNMENT Multiparty republic
ETHNIC GROUPS Greek Cypriot 81%, Turkish Cypriot 19%
LANGUAGES Greek and Turkish (both official)
RELIGIONS Christianity (Greek Orthodox), Islam
CURRENCY Cyprus pound = 100 cents

CZECH REPUBLIC

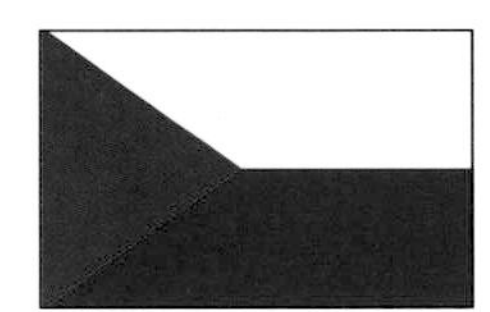

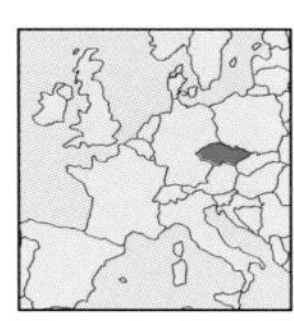

GEOGRAPHY The Czech Republic is the western three-fifths of the former country of Czechoslovakia. It contains two regions: Bohemia in the west and Moravia in the east. Mountains border much of the country in the west. The Bohemian basin in the north-centre is a fertile lowland region, with Prague, the capital city, as its main centre. Highlands cover much of the centre of the country, with lowlands in the south-east.

The climate is influenced by its landlocked position in east-central Europe. Prague has warm, sunny summers and cold winters. The average rainfall is moderate, with 500 mm to 750 mm [20 in to 30 in] every year in lowland areas.

POLITICS & ECONOMY After World War I (1914–18), Czechoslovakia was created. Germany seized the country in World War II (1939–45). In 1948, Communist leaders took power and Czechoslovakia was allied to the Soviet Union. When democratic reforms were introduced in the Soviet Union in the late 1980s, the Czechs also demanded reforms. Free elections were held in 1990, but differences between the Czechs and Slovaks and a resurgence of Slovak nationalism led the government to agree in 1992 to the partitioning of the country on 1 January 1993. The break was peaceful. In 1999, the Czech Republic became a member of NATO.

Under Communist rule the Czech Republic became one of the most industrialized parts of Eastern Europe. The country has deposits of coal, uranium, iron ore, magnesite, tin and zinc. Manufacturing employs about 40% of the Czech Republic's entire workforce. Farming is also important. Under Communism, the government owned the land, but private ownership is now being restored. The country was admitted into the OECD in 1995.

AREA 78,864 sq km [30,449 sq mls]
POPULATION 10,286,000
CAPITAL (POPULATION) Prague (1,213,000)
GOVERNMENT Multiparty republic
ETHNIC GROUPS Czech 81%, Moravian 13%, Slovak 3%, Polish, German, Silesian, Gypsy, Hungarian, Ukrainian
LANGUAGES Czech (official), Moravian
RELIGIONS Christianity (Roman Catholic 39%, Protestant 4%)
CURRENCY Czech koruna = 100 haler

DENMARK

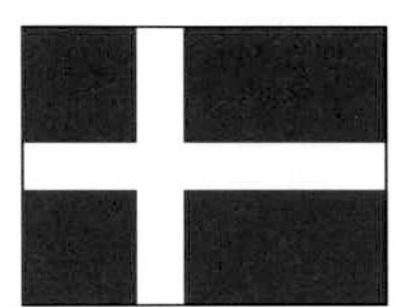

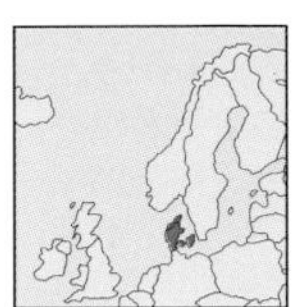

GEOGRAPHY The Kingdom of Denmark is the smallest country in Scandinavia. It consists of a peninsula, called Jutland (or Jylland), which is joined to Germany, and more than 400 islands, 89 of which are inhabited.

The land is flat and mostly covered by rocks dropped there by huge ice-sheets during the last Ice Age. The highest point in Denmark is on Jutland. It is only 173 m [568 ft] above sea level.

Denmark has a cool but pleasant climate, except during cold spells in the winter when The Sound between Sjælland and Sweden may freeze over. Summers are warm. Rainfall occurs all through the year.

POLITICS & ECONOMY Danish Vikings terrorized much of Western Europe for about 300 years after AD 800. Danish kings ruled England in the 11th century. In the late 14th century, Denmark formed a union with Norway and Sweden (which included Finland). Sweden broke away in 1523, while Denmark lost Norway to Sweden in 1814.

After 1945, Denmark played an important part in European affairs, becoming a member of the North Atlantic Treaty Organization (NATO). In 1973, Denmark joined the European Union, although it remains one of its least enthusiastic members. The Danes now enjoy some of the world's highest living standards, although the extensive social welfare provisions exert a considerable cost.

Denmark has few natural resources apart from some oil and gas from wells deep under the North Sea. But the economy is highly developed. Manufacturing industries, which employ about 27% of all workers, produce a wide variety of products, including furniture, processed food, machinery, television sets and textiles. Farms cover about three-quarters of the land. Farming employs only 4% of the workers, but it is highly scientific and productive. Meat and dairy farming are the chief activities.

AREA 43,070 sq km [16,629 sq mls]
POPULATION 5,334,000
CAPITAL (POPULATION) Copenhagen (1,353,000)
GOVERNMENT Parliamentary monarchy
ETHNIC GROUPS Danish 97%
LANGUAGES Danish (official)
RELIGIONS Christianity (Lutheran 91%, Roman Catholic 1%)
CURRENCY Krone = 100 øre

DJIBOUTI

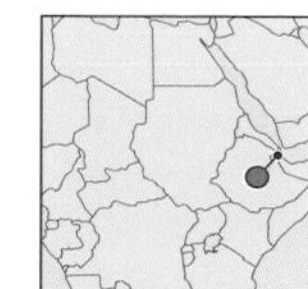

GEOGRAPHY The Republic of Djibouti is a small country in eastern Africa which occupies a strategic position where the Red Sea meets the Gulf of Aden. Behind the coastal plain on the northern side of the Gulf of Tadjoura is a highland region, the Mabla Mountains, rising to 1,783 m [5,850 ft] above sea level. Djibouti also contains Lake Assal, the lowest point on land in Africa.

Djibouti has one of the world's hottest and driest climates. Summer days are very hot with recorded temperatures of more than 44°C [112°F]. On average, it rains on only 26 days every year.

POLITICS & ECONOMY Islam was introduced into the area which is now Djibouti in the 9th century AD. The conversion of the Afars led to conflict between them and the Christian Ethiopians who lived in the interior. By the 19th century, the Issas, who are Somalis, had moved north and occupied much of the traditional grazing land of the Afars. France gained influence in the area in the second half of the 19th century and, in 1888, they set up a territory called French Somaliland. The capital of the territory, Djibouti, became important when the Ethiopian emperor, Menelik II, decided to build a railway to it from Addis Ababa, thus making it the main port handling Ethiopian trade.

In 1967, the people voted to retain their links with France, though most of the Issas favoured independence. The country was renamed the French Territory of the Afars and Issas, but it was named Djibouti when it became fully independent in 1977.

Djibouti became a one-party state in 1981, but a new constitution was introduced in 1992, permitting four parties which must maintain a balance between the ethnic groups in the country. However, in 1992 and 1993, tensions between the Afars and Issas flared up when Afars launched an uprising which was put down by government troops.

Djibouti is a poor country. Its economy is based mainly on money it gets for use of its port and the railway that links it to Addis Ababa. Most of the food the country needs has to be imported.

AREA 23,200 sq km [8,958 sq mls]
POPULATION 650,000
CAPITAL (POPULATION) Djibouti (383,000)
GOVERNMENT Multiparty republic
ETHNIC GROUPS Issa 47%, Afar 37%, Arab 6%
LANGUAGES Arabic and French (both official)
RELIGIONS Islam 96%, Christianity 4%
CURRENCY Djibouti franc = 100 centimes

DOMINICA

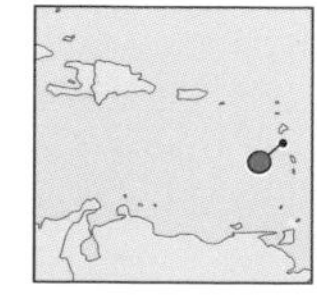

The Commonwealth of Dominica, a former British colony, became independent in 1978. The island has a mountainous spine and less than 10% of the land is cultivated. Yet agriculture employs more than 60% of the people. Manufacturing, mining and tourism are other minor activities. **AREA** 751 sq km [290 sq mls]; **POPULATION** 78,000; **CAPITAL** Roseau.

DOMINICAN REPUBLIC

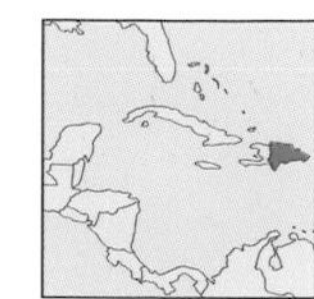

GEOGRAPHY Second largest of the Caribbean nations in both area and population, the Dominican Republic shares the island of Hispaniola with Haiti. The country is mountainous, and the generally hot and humid climate eases with altitude.

POLITICS & ECONOMY The Dominican Republic has chaotic origins, having been held by Spain, France, Haiti and the USA at various times. Civil war broke out in 1966 but soon ended after US intervention. Joaquín Balaguer, elected president in 1966 under a new constitution, stood down in 1996 and was replaced by Leonel Fernández.

AREA 48,730 sq km [18,815 sq mls]
POPULATION 7,999,000
CAPITAL (POPULATION) Santo Domingo (2,135,000)
GOVERNMENT Multiparty republic
ETHNIC GROUPS Mulatto 73%, White 16%, Black 11%
LANGUAGES Spanish (official)
RELIGIONS Roman Catholic 93%
CURRENCY Peso = 100 centavos

ECUADOR

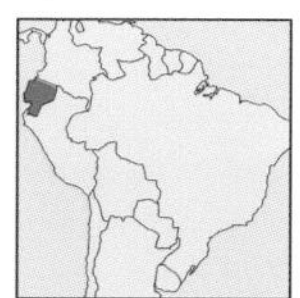

GEOGRAPHY The Republic of Ecuador straddles the Equator on the west coast of South America. Three ranges of the high Andes Mountains form the backbone of the country. Between the towering, snow-capped peaks of the mountains, some of which are volcanoes, lie a series of high plateaux, or basins. Nearly half of Ecuador's population lives on these plateaux.

The climate in Ecuador depends on the height above sea level. Though the coastline is cooled by the cold Peruvian Current, temperatures are between 23°C and 25°C [73°F to 77°F] all through the year. In Quito, at 2,500 m [8,200 ft] above sea level, temperatures are 14°C to 15°C [57°F to 59°F], though the city is just south of the Equator.

POLITICS & ECONOMY The Inca people of Peru conquered much of what is now Ecuador in the late 15th century. They introduced their language, Quechua, which is widely spoken today. Spanish forces defeated the Incas in 1533 and took control of Ecuador. The country became independent in 1822, following the defeat of a Spanish force in a battle near Quito. In the 19th and 20th centuries, Ecuador suffered from political instability, while successive governments failed to tackle the country's social and economic problems. A war with Peru in 1941 led to a loss of territory, and border disputes continued, with the most recent conflict occurring in 1995. An agreement was eventually signed in January 1998. Civilian governments have ruled Ecuador since multiparty elections took place in 1979.

The World Bank classifies Ecuador as a 'lower-middle-income' developing country. Agriculture employs 30% of the people and bananas, cocoa and coffee are all important crops. Fishing, forestry, mining and manufacturing are other activities.

AREA 283,560 sq km [109,483 sq mls]
POPULATION 12,337,000
CAPITAL (POPULATION) Quito (1,101,000)
GOVERNMENT Multiparty republic
ETHNIC GROUPS Mestizo (mixed White and Amerindian) 40%, Amerindian 40%, White 15%, Black 5%
LANGUAGES Spanish (official), Quechua
RELIGIONS Christianity (Roman Catholic 92%)
CURRENCY Sucre = 100 centavos

EGYPT

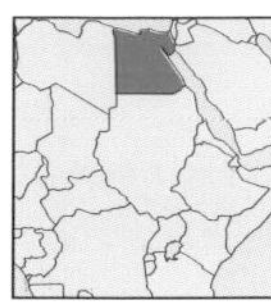

GEOGRAPHY The Arab Republic of Egypt is Africa's second largest country by population after Nigeria, though it ranks 13th in area. Most of Egypt is desert. Almost all the people live either in the Nile Valley and its fertile delta or along the Suez Canal, the artificial waterway between the Mediterranean and Red seas. This canal shortens the sea journey between the United Kingdom and India by 9,700 km [6,027 mls]. Recent attempts have been made to irrigate parts of the western desert and thus redistribute the rapidly growing Egyptian population into previously uninhabited regions.

Apart from the Nile Valley, Egypt has three other main regions. The Western and Eastern deserts are parts of the Sahara. The Sinai peninsula (Es Sina), to the east of the Suez Canal, is a mountainous desert region, geographically within Asia. It contains Egypt's highest peak, Gebel Katherina (2,637 m [8,650 ft]); few people live in this area.

Egypt is a dry country. The low rainfall occurs, if at all, in winter and the country is one of the sunniest places on Earth.

POLITICS & ECONOMY Ancient Egypt, which was founded about 5,000 years ago, was one of the great early civilizations. Throughout the country, pyramids, temples and richly decorated tombs are memorials to its great achievements.

After Ancient Egypt declined, the country came under successive foreign rulers. Arabs occupied Egypt in AD 639–42. They introduced the Arabic language and Islam. Their influence was so great that most Egyptians now regard themselves as Arabs.

Egypt came under British rule in 1882, but it gained partial independence in 1922, becoming a monarchy. The monarchy was abolished in 1952, when Egypt became a republic. The creation of Israel in 1948 led Egypt into a series of wars in 1948–9, 1956, 1967 and 1973. Since the late 1970s, Egypt has sought for peace. In 1979, Egypt signed a peace treaty with Israel and regained the Sinai region which it had lost in a war in 1967. Extremists opposed contacts with Israel and, in 1981, President Sadat, who had signed the treaty, was assassinated.

While Egypt is important in foreign affairs, most people are poor. Some groups within the country dislike Western influences on their way of life and favour a return to the fundamental principles of Islam. In the 1990s, attacks on foreign visitors caused a decline in the valuable tourist industry. In 1997, 62 people, mostly foreign tourists, were killed by Islamic terrorists near Luxor.

Egypt is Africa's second most industrialized country after South Africa, but it remains a developing country and income levels remain low for the vast majority of Egyptian people. Oil and textiles are the chief exports.

AREA 1,001,450 sq km [386,660 sq mls]
POPULATION 66,050,000
CAPITAL (POPULATION) Cairo (9,656,000)
GOVERNMENT Republic
ETHNIC GROUPS Egyptian 99%
LANGUAGES Arabic (official), French, English
RELIGIONS Islam (Sunni Muslim 94%), Christianity (mainly Coptic Christian 6%)
CURRENCY Pound = 100 piastres

EL SALVADOR

GEOGRAPHY The Republic of El Salvador is the only country in Central America which does not have a coast on the Caribbean Sea. El Salvador has a narrow coastal plain along the Pacific Ocean. Behind the coastal plain, the coastal range is a zone of rugged mountains, including volcanoes, which overlooks a densely populated inland plateau. Beyond the plateau, the land rises to the sparsely populated interior highlands.

The coast has a hot, tropical climate. Inland, the climate is moderated by the altitude. Rain falls on practically every afternoon between May and October.

POLITICS & ECONOMY Amerindians have lived in El Salvador for thousands of years. The ruins of Mayan pyramids built between AD 100 and 1000 are still found in the western part of the country. Spanish soldiers conquered the area in 1524 and 1525, and Spain ruled until 1821. In 1823, all the Central American countries, except for Panama, set up a Central American Federation. But El Salvador withdrew in 1840 and declared its independence in 1841. El Salvador suffered from instability throughout the 19th century. The 20th century saw a more stable government, but from 1931 military dictatorships alternated with elected governments and the country remained poor.

In the 1970s, El Salvador was plagued by conflict as protesters demanded that the government introduce reforms to help the poor. Kidnappings and murders committed by left- and right-wing groups caused instability. A civil war broke out in 1979 between the US-backed, right-wing government forces and left-wing guerrillas in the FMLN (Farabundo Marti National Liberation Front). In 12 years, more than 750,000 people died and hundreds of thousands were made homeless. A cease-fire was agreed on 1 February 1992 and elections were held in 1994. With its economy shattered by war, El Salvador remains a 'lower-middle-income' economy, according to the World Bank. Farmland and pasture cover about three-quarters of the country. Coffee, grown in the highlands, is the main export, followed by sugar and cotton, which grow on the coastal lowlands. Fishing for lobsters and shrimps is important, but manufacturing is on a small scale.

AREA 21,040 sq km [8,124 sq mls]
POPULATION 5,752,000
CAPITAL (POPULATION) San Salvador (1,522,000)
GOVERNMENT Republic
ETHNIC GROUPS Mestizo (mixed White and Amerindian) 89%, Amerindian 10%, White 1%
LANGUAGES Spanish (official)
RELIGIONS Christianity (Roman Catholic 94%)
CURRENCY Colón = 100 centavos

EQUATORIAL GUINEA

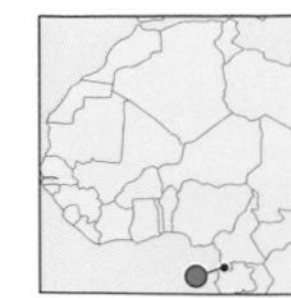

GEOGRAPHY The Republic of Equatorial Guinea is a small republic in west-central Africa. It consists of a mainland territory which makes up 90% of the land area, called Mbini (or Rio Muni), between Cameroon and Gabon, and five offshore islands in the Bight of Bonny, the largest of which is Bioko. The island of Annobon lies 560 km [350 mls] south-west of Mbini. Mbini consists mainly of hills and plateaux behind the coastal plains.

The climate is hot and humid. Bioko is mountainous, with the land rising to 3,008 m [9,869 ft], and hence it is particularly rainy. But there is a marked dry season between the months of December and February. Mainland Mbini has a similar climate, though the rainfall diminishes inland.

POLITICS & ECONOMY Portuguese navigators reached the area in 1471. In 1778, Portugal granted Bioko, together with rights over Mbini, to Spain.

In 1959, Spain made Bioko and Mbini provinces of overseas Spain and, in 1963, it gave the provinces a degree of self-government. Equatorial Guinea became independent in 1968.

The first president of Equatorial Guinea, Francisco Macias Nguema, proved to be a tyrant. He was overthrown in 1979 and a group of officers, led by Lt.-Col. Teodoro Obiang Nguema Mbasogo, set up a Supreme Military Council to rule the country. In 1991, the people voted to set up a multiparty democracy. Elections were held in 1993 and 1996, amid many allegations of intimidation and fraud.

Equatorial Guinea is a poor country. Agriculture employs up to 66% of the people. The main food crops are bananas, cassava and sweet potatoes, but the most valuable crop is cocoa, grown on Bioko.

AREA 28,050 sq km [10,830 sq mls]
POPULATION 454,000
CAPITAL (POPULATION) Malabo (35,000)
GOVERNMENT Multiparty republic (transitional)
ETHNIC GROUPS Fang 83%, Bubi 10%, Ndowe 4%
LANGUAGES Spanish (official), Fang, Bubi
RELIGIONS Christianity 89%, traditional beliefs 5%
CURRENCY CFA franc = 100 centimes

ERITREA

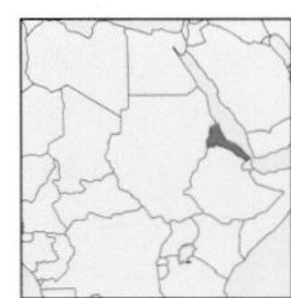

GEOGRAPHY The State of Eritrea consists of a hot, dry coastal plain facing the Red Sea, with a fairly mountainous area in the centre. Most people live in the cooler highland area.

POLITICS & ECONOMY Eritrea, which was an Italian colony from the 1880s, was part of Ethiopia from 1952 until 1993, when it became a fully independent nation. National reconstruction was hampered by conflict with Yemen over three islands in the Red Sea, while in 1998 and 1999, clashes with Ethiopia flared up along the countries' borders.

Farming and nomadic livestock rearing are the main activities in this poor, war-ravaged territory. Eritrea has a few manufacturing industries, based mainly in Asmara.

AREA 94,000 sq km [36,293 sq mls]
POPULATION 3,842,000
CAPITAL (POPULATION) Asmara (367,500)
GOVERNMENT Transitional government
ETHNIC GROUPS Tigrinya 49%, Tigre 32%, Afar 4%, Beja 3%, Saho 3%, Kunama 3%, Nara 2%
LANGUAGES Arabic, English, Tigrinya, Tigre, Saho
RELIGIONS Coptic Christian 50%, Muslim 50%
CURRENCY Nakfa

ESTONIA

GEOGRAPHY The Republic of Estonia is the smallest of the three states on the Baltic Sea, which were formerly part of the Soviet Union, but which became independent in the early 1990s. Estonia consists of a generally flat plain which was covered by ice-sheets during the Ice Age. The land is strewn with moraine (rocks deposited by the ice).

The country is dotted with more than 1,500 small lakes, and water, including the large Lake Peipus (Chudskoye Ozero) and the River Narva, makes up much of Estonia's eastern border with Russia. Estonia has more than 800 islands, which together make up about a tenth of the country. The largest island is Saaremaa (Sarema).

Despite its northerly position, Estonia has a fairly mild climate because of its nearness to the sea. This is because sea winds tend to warm the land in winter and cool it in summer.

POLITICS & ECONOMY The ancestors of the Estonians, who are related to the Finns, settled in the area several thousand years ago. German crusaders, known as the Teutonic Knights, introduced Christianity in the early 13th century. By the 16th century, German noblemen owned much of the land in Estonia. In 1561, Sweden took the northern part of the country and Poland the south. From 1625, Sweden controlled the entire country until Sweden handed it over to Russia in 1721.

Estonian nationalists campaigned for their independence from around the mid-19th century. Finally, Estonia was proclaimed independent in 1918. In 1919, the government began to break up the large estates and distribute land among the peasants.

In 1939, Germany and the Soviet Union agreed to take over parts of Eastern Europe. In 1940, Soviet forces occupied Estonia, but they were driven out by the Germans in 1941. Soviet troops returned in 1944 and Estonia became one of the 15 Soviet Socialist Republics of the Soviet Union. The Estonians strongly opposed Soviet rule. Many of them were deported to Siberia.

Political changes in the Soviet Union in the late 1980s led to renewed demands for freedom. In 1990, the Estonian government declared the country independent and, finally, the Soviet Union recognized this act in September 1991, shortly before the Soviet Union was dissolved. Estonia adopted a new constitution in 1992, when multiparty elections were held for a new national assembly. In 1993, Estonia negotiated an agreement with Russia to withdraw its troops.

Under Soviet rule, Estonia was the most prosperous of the three Baltic states. Since 1988, Estonia has begun to change its government-dominated economy to one based on private enterprise, and the country has started to strengthen its links with the rest of Europe. Estonia's resources include oil shale and its forests. Industries produce fertilizers, machinery, petrochemical products, machinery, processed food, wood products and textiles. Agriculture and fishing are also important.

AREA 44,700 sq km [17,300 sq mls]
POPULATION 1,421,000
CAPITAL (POPULATION) Tallinn (435,000)
GOVERNMENT Multiparty republic
ETHNIC GROUPS Estonian 62%, Russian 30%, Ukrainian 3%, Belarussian 2%, Finnish 1%
LANGUAGES Estonian (official), Russian
RELIGIONS Christianity (Lutheran, with Orthodox and Baptist minorities)
CURRENCY Kroon = 100 sents

ETHIOPIA

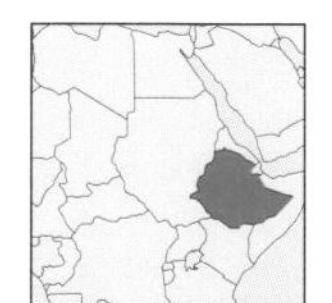

GEOGRAPHY Ethiopia is a landlocked country in north-eastern Africa. The land is mainly mountainous, though there are extensive plains in the east, bordering southern Eritrea, and in the south, bordering Somalia. The highlands are divided into two blocks by an arm of the Great Rift Valley which runs throughout eastern Africa. North of the Rift Valley, the land is especially rugged, rising to 4,620 m [15,157 ft] at Ras Dashen. South-east of Ras Dashen is Lake Tana, source of the River Abay (Blue Nile).

The climate in Ethiopia is greatly affected by the altitude. Addis Ababa, at 2,450 m [8,000 ft], has an average yearly temperature of 20°C [68°F]. The rainfall is generally more than 1,000 mm [39 in]. But the lowlands bordering the Eritrean coast are hot.

POLITICS & ECONOMY Ethiopia was the home of an ancient monarchy, which became Christian in the 4th century. In the 7th century, Muslims gained control of the lowlands, but Christianity survived in the highlands. In the 19th century, Ethiopia resisted attempts to colonize it. Italy invaded Ethiopia in 1935, but Ethiopian and British troops defeated the Italians in 1941.

In 1952, Eritrea, on the Red Sea coast, was federated with Ethiopia. But in 1961, Eritrean nationalists demanded their freedom and began a struggle that ended in their independence in 1993. Relations with Eritrea gradually soured and border clashes occurred in 1998 and 1999. Ethnic diversity in Ethiopia has led to demands by several minorities for self-government. As a result, in 1995, Ethiopia was divided into nine provinces, each province with its own regional assembly.

Ethiopia is one of the world's poorest countries, particularly in the 1970s and 1980s when it was plagued by civil war and famine caused partly by long droughts. Many richer countries have sent aid (money and food) to help the Ethiopian people. Agriculture remains the leading activity.

AREA 1,128,000 sq km [435,521 sq mls]
POPULATION 58,390,000
CAPITAL (POPULATION) Addis Ababa (2,316,000)
GOVERNMENT Federation of nine provinces
ETHNIC GROUPS Amharic 38%, Galla 35%, Tigrinya 9%, Guage 3%, 60 others
LANGUAGES Amharic (official), 280 others
RELIGIONS Ethiopian Orthodox 53%, Sunni Muslim 31%, animist beliefs 11%
CURRENCY Birr = 100 cents

FALKLAND ISLANDS

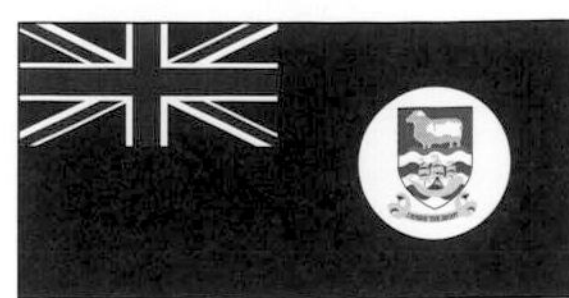

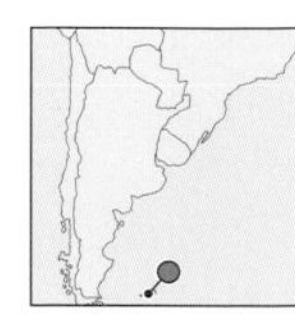

Comprising two main islands and over 200 small islands, the Falkland Islands lie 480 km [300 mls] from South America. Sheep farming is the main activity, though the search for oil and diamonds holds out hope for the future of this harsh and virtually treeless environment. **AREA** 12,170 sq km [4,699 sq mls]; **POPULATION** 2,000; **CAPITAL** Stanley.

FAROE ISLANDS

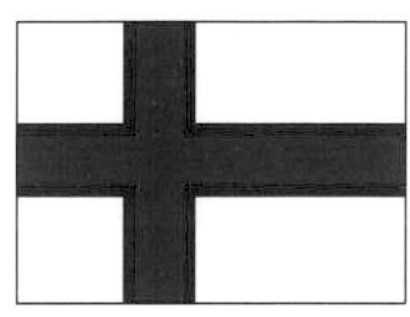

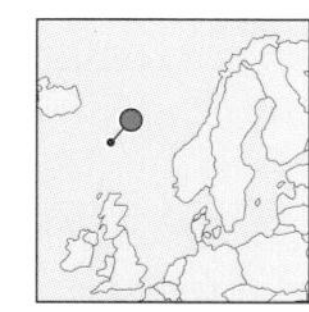

The Faroe Islands are a group of 18 volcanic islands and some reefs in the North Atlantic Ocean. The islands have been Danish since the 1380s, but they became largely self-governing in 1948. In 1998, the government of the Faroes announced its intention to become independent of Denmark. **AREA** 1,400 sq km [541 sq mls]; **POPULATION** 41,000; **CAPITAL** Torshávn.

FIJI

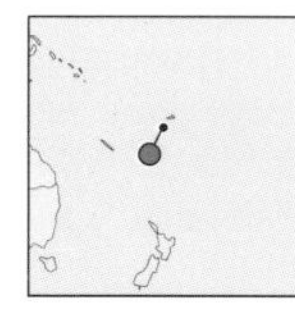

The Republic of Fiji comprises more than 800 Melanesian islands, the biggest being Viti Levu and Vanua Levu. The climate is tropical, with south-east trade winds blowing throughout the year. A former British colony, Fiji became independent in 1970. Its membership of the Commonwealth lapsed in 1987 after the enactment of discriminatory legislation against the country's Indian population. Fiji rejoined the Commonwealth in 1997 following changes in the constitution. **AREA** 18,270 sq km [7,054 sq mls]; **POPULATION** 802,000; **CAPITAL** Suva.

FINLAND

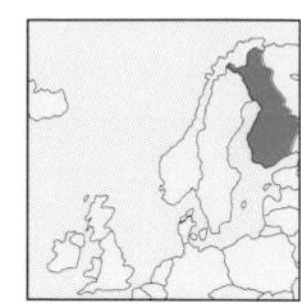

GEOGRAPHY The Republic of Finland is a beautiful country in northern Europe. In the south, behind the coastal lowlands where most Finns live, lies a region of sparkling lakes worn out by ice-sheets in the Ice Age. The thinly populated northern uplands cover about two-fifths of the country.

Helsinki, the capital city, has warm summers, but the average temperatures between the months of December and March are below freezing point. Snow covers the land in winter. The north has less precipitation than the south, but it is much colder.

POLITICS & ECONOMY Between 1150 and 1809, Finland was under Swedish rule. The close links between the countries continue today. Swedish remains an official language in Finland and many towns have Swedish as well as Finnish names.

In 1809, Finland became a grand duchy of the Russian empire. It finally declared itself independent in 1917, after the Russian Revolution and the collapse of the Russian empire. But during World War II (1939–45), the Soviet Union declared war on Finland and took part of Finland's territory. Finland allied itself with Germany, but it lost more land to the Soviet Union at the end of the war.

After World War II, Finland became a neutral country and negotiated peace treaties with the Soviet Union. Finland also strengthened its relations with other northern European countries and became an associate member of the European Free Trade Association (EFTA) in 1961. Finland became a full member of EFTA in 1986, but in 1992, along with most of its fellow EFTA members, it applied for membership of the European Union. In 1994, the Finnish people voted in favour of membership of the EU. Finland officially joined on 1 January 1995.

Forests are Finland's most valuable resource, and forestry accounts for about 35% of the country's exports. The chief manufactures are wood products, pulp and paper. Since World War II, Finland has set up many other industries, producing such things as machinery and transport equipment. Its economy has expanded rapidly, but there has been a large increase in the number of unemployed people.

AREA 338,130 sq km [130,552 sq mls]
POPULATION 5,149,000
CAPITAL (POPULATION) Helsinki (525,000)
GOVERNMENT Multiparty republic
ETHNIC GROUPS Finnish 93%, Swedish 6%
LANGUAGES Finnish and Swedish (both official)
RELIGIONS Christianity (Evangelical Lutheran 88%)
CURRENCY Euro; Markka = 100 penniä

FRANCE

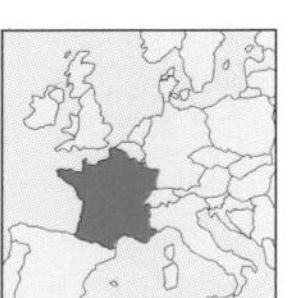

GEOGRAPHY The Republic of France is the largest country in Western Europe. The scenery is extremely varied. The Vosges Mountains overlook the Rhine valley in the north-east, the Jura Mountains and the Alps form the borders with Switzerland and Italy in the south-east, while the Pyrenees straddle France's border with Spain. The only large highland area entirely within France is the Massif Central in southern France.

Brittany (Bretagne) and Normandy (Normande) form a scenic hill region. Fertile lowlands cover most of northern France, including the densely populated Paris basin. Another major lowland area, the Aquitanian basin, is in the south-west, while the Rhône-Saône valley and the Mediterranean lowlands are in the south-east.

The climate of France varies from west to east and from north to south. The west comes under the moderating influence of the Atlantic Ocean, giving generally mild weather. To the east, summers are warmer and winters colder. The climate also becomes warmer as one travels from north to south. The Mediterranean Sea coast has hot, dry summers and mild, moist winters. The Alps, Jura and Pyrenees mountains have snowy winters. Winter sports centres are found in all three areas. Large glaciers occupy high valleys in the Alps.

POLITICS & ECONOMY The Romans conquered France (then called Gaul) in the 50s BC. Roman rule began to decline in the fifth century AD and, in 486, the Frankish realm (as France was called) became independent under a Christian king, Clovis. In 800, Charlemagne, who had been king since 768, became emperor of the Romans. He extended France's boundaries, but, in 843, his empire was divided into three parts and the area of France contracted. After the Norman invasion of England in 1066, large areas of France came under English rule, but this was finally ended in 1453.

France later became a powerful monarchy. But the French Revolution (1789–99) ended absolute rule by French kings. In 1799, Napoleon Bonaparte took power and fought a series of brilliant military campaigns before his final defeat in 1815. The monarchy was restored until 1848, when the Second Republic was founded. In 1852, Napoleon's nephew became Napoleon III, but the Third Republic was established in 1875. France was the scene of much fighting during World War I (1914–18) and World War II (1939–45), causing great loss of life and much damage to the economy.

In 1946, France adopted a new constitution, establishing the Fourth Republic. But political instability and costly colonial wars slowed France's post-war recovery. In 1958, Charles de Gaulle was elected president and he introduced a new constitution, giving the president extra powers and inaugurating the Fifth Republic.

Since the 1960s, France has made rapid economic progress, becoming one of the most prosperous nations in the European Union. But France's government faced a number of problems, including unemployment, pollution and the growing number of elderly people, who find it difficult to live when inflation rates are high. One social problem concerns the presence in France of large numbers of immigrants from Africa and southern Europe, many of whom live in poor areas.

A socialist government under Lionel Jospin was elected in June 1997. Jospin pledged to take France into the European single currency, but also increased the minimum wage and shortened the working week. The French system of high social security taxes and inflexible labour laws seems set to continue, although the economy continues to develop, with exports booming and inflation negligible.

France is one of the world's most developed countries. Its natural resources include its fertile soil, together with deposits of bauxite, coal, iron ore, oil and natural gas, and potash. France is also one of the world's top manufacturing nations, and it has often innovated in bold and imaginative ways. The TGV, Concorde and hypermarkets are all typical examples. Paris is a world centre of fashion industries, but France has many other industrial towns and cities. Major manufactures include aircraft, cars, chemicals, electronic products, machinery, metal products, processed food, steel and textiles.

Agriculture employs about 7% of the people, but France is the largest producer of farm products in Western Europe, producing most of the food it needs. Wheat is the leading crop and livestock farming is of major importance. Fishing and forestry are leading industries, while tourism is a major activity.

AREA 551,500 sq km [212,934 sq mls]
POPULATION 58,805,000
CAPITAL (POPULATION) Paris (9,469,000)
GOVERNMENT Multiparty republic
ETHNIC GROUPS French 93%, Arab, German
LANGUAGES French (official), Breton, Occitan
RELIGIONS Roman Catholic 86%, Islam 3%
CURRENCY Euro; Franc = 100 centimes

FRENCH GUIANA

GEOGRAPHY French Guiana is the smallest country in mainland South America. The coastal plain is swampy in places, but some dry areas are cultivated. Inland lies a plateau, with the low Tumachumac Mountains in the south. Most of the rivers run north towards the Atlantic Ocean.

French Guiana has a hot, equatorial climate, with high temperatures throughout the year. The rainfall is heavy, especially between December and June, but it is dry between August and October. The north-east trade winds blow constantly across the country.

POLITICS & ECONOMY The first people to live in what is now French Guiana were Amerindians. Today, only a few of them survive in the interior. The first Europeans to explore the coast arrived in 1500, and they were followed by adventurers seeking El Dorado, the mythical city of gold. Cayenne was founded in 1637 by a group of French merchants. The area became a French colony in the late 17th century.

France used the colony as a penal settlement for political prisoners from the times of the French Revolution in the 1790s. From the 1850s to 1945, the country became notorious as a place where prisoners were harshly treated. Many of them died, unable to survive in the tropical conditions.

In 1946, French Guiana became an overseas department of France, and in 1974 it also became an administrative region. An independence movement developed in the 1980s, but most people want to retain their links with France and continue to obtain financial aid to develop their territory.

Although it has rich forest and mineral resources, such as bauxite (aluminium ore), French Guiana is a developing country. It depends greatly on France for money to run its services and the government is the country's biggest employer. Since 1968, Kourou in French Guiana, the European Space Agency's rocket-launching site, has earned money for France by sending communications satellites into space.

AREA 90,000 sq km [34,749 sq mls]
POPULATION 162,000
CAPITAL (POPULATION) Cayenne (42,000)
GOVERNMENT Overseas department of France
ETHNIC GROUPS Creole 42%, Chinese 14%, French 10%, Haitian 7%
LANGUAGES French (official)
RELIGIONS Christianity (Roman Catholic 80%, Protestant 4%)
CURRENCY French franc = 100 centimes

FRENCH POLYNESIA

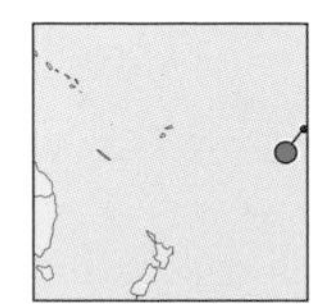

French Polynesia consists of 130 islands, scattered over 4 million sq km [1.5 million sq mls] of the Pacific Ocean. Tribal chiefs in the area agreed to a French protectorate in 1843. They gained increased autonomy in 1984, but the links with France ensure a high standard of living. **AREA** 3,941 sq km [1,520 sq mls]; **POPULATION** 237,000; **CAPITAL** Papeete.

GABON

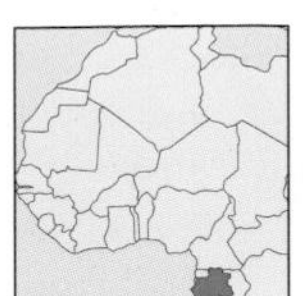

GEOGRAPHY The Gabonese Republic lies on the Equator in west-central Africa. In area, it is a little larger than the United Kingdom, with a coastline 800 km [500 mls] long. Behind the narrow, partly lagoon-lined coastal plain, the land rises to hills, plateaux and mountains divided by deep valleys carved by the River Ogooué and its tributaries.

Most of Gabon has an equatorial climate, with high temperatures and humidity throughout the year. The rainfall is heavy and the skies are often cloudy.

POLITICS & ECONOMY Gabon became a French colony in the 1880s, but it achieved full independence in 1960. In 1964, an attempted coup was put down when French troops intervened and crushed the revolt. Gabon became a one-party state in 1968. Opposition parties were legalized in 1990 and elections took place amid allegations of fraud. The Gabonese Democratic Party, formerly the only party, won a majority in the National Assembly.

Gabon's abundant natural resources include its forests, oil and gas deposits near Port Gentil, together with manganese and uranium. These mineral deposits make Gabon one of Africa's better-off countries. But agriculture still employs about 75% of the population and many farmers produce little more than they need to support their families.

AREA 267,670 sq km [103,347 sq mls]
POPULATION 1,208,000
CAPITAL (POPULATION) Libreville (418,000)
GOVERNMENT Multiparty republic
ETHNIC GROUPS Fang 36%, Mpongwe 15%, Mbete 14%, Punu 12%
LANGUAGES French (official), Bantu languages
RELIGIONS Christianity (Roman Catholic 65%, Protestant 19%, African churches 12%), traditional beliefs 3%, Islam 2%
CURRENCY CFA franc = 100 centimes

GAMBIA, THE

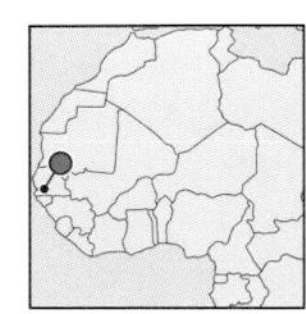

GEOGRAPHY The Republic of The Gambia is the smallest country in mainland Africa. It consists of a narrow strip of land bordering the River Gambia. The Gambia is almost entirely enclosed by Senegal, except along the short Atlantic coastline.

The Gambia has hot and humid summers, but the winter temperatures (November to May) drop to around 16°C [61°F]. In the summer, moist south-westerlies bring rain, which is heaviest on the coast.

POLITICS & ECONOMY English traders bought rights to trade on the River Gambia in 1588, and in 1664 the English established a settlement on an island in the river estuary. In 1765, the British founded a colony called Senegambia, which included parts of The Gambia and Senegal. In 1783, Britain handed this colony over to France.

In the 1860s and 1870s, Britain and France discussed the exchange of The Gambia for some other French territory. But no agreement was reached and Britain made The Gambia a British colony in 1888. It remained under British rule until it achieved full independence in 1965. In 1970, The Gambia became a republic. Relations between the English-speaking Gambians and the French-speaking Senegalese form a major political issue. In 1981, an attempted coup in The Gambia was put down with the help of Senegalese troops. In 1982, The Gambia and Senegal set up a defence alliance, called the Confederation of Senegambia. But this alliance was dissolved in 1989. In July 1994, a military group overthrew the president, Sir Dawda Jawara, who fled into exile. Captain Yahya Jammeh, who took power, was elected president in 1996.

Agriculture employs more than 80% of the people. The main food crops include cassava, millet and sorghum, but groundnuts and groundnut products are the chief exports. Tourism is a growing industry.

AREA 11,300 sq km [4,363 sq mls]
POPULATION 1,292,000
CAPITAL (POPULATION) Banjul (171,000)
GOVERNMENT Military regime
ETHNIC GROUPS Mandinka (also called Mandingo or Malinke) 40%, Fulani (also called Peul) 19%, Wolof 15%, Dyola 10%, Soninke 8%
LANGUAGES English (official), Mandinka, Fula
RELIGIONS Islam 95%, Christianity 4%, traditional beliefs 1%
CURRENCY Dalasi = 100 butut

GEORGIA

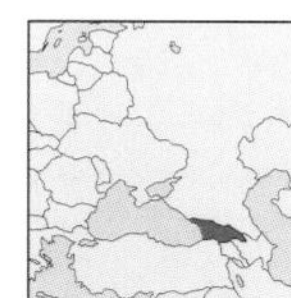

GEOGRAPHY Georgia is a country on the borders of Europe and Asia, facing the Black Sea. The land is rugged with the Caucasus Mountains forming its northern border. The highest mountain in this range, Mount Elbrus (5,633 m [18,481 ft]), lies over the border in Russia.

The Black Sea plains have hot summers and mild winters, when the temperatures seldom drop below freezing point. The rainfall is heavy, but inland Tbilisi has moderate rainfall, with the heaviest rains in the spring and early summer.

POLITICS & ECONOMY The first Georgian state was set up nearly 2,500 years ago. But for much of its history, the area was ruled by various conquerors. Christianity was introduced in AD 330. Georgia freed itself of foreign rule in the 11th and 12th centuries, but Mongol armies attacked in the 13th century. From the 16th to the 18th centuries, Iran and the Turkish Ottoman empire struggled for control of the area, and in the late 18th century Georgia sought the protection of Russia and, by the early 19th century, Georgia was part of the Russian empire. After the Russian Revolution of 1917, Georgia declared itself independent and was recognized by the League of Nations. But Russian troops invaded and made Georgia part of the Soviet regime.

In 1991, following reforms in the Soviet Union, Georgia declared itself independent. It became a separate country when the Soviet Union was dissolved in December 1991.

Georgia contains three regions containing minority peoples: Abkhazia in the north-west, South Ossetia in north-central Georgia, and Adjaria (also spelled Adzharia) in the south-west. Communal conflict in the early 1990s led to outbreaks of civil war in South Ossetia and Abkhazia, where the people expressed the wish to set up their own independent countries.

Georgia is a developing country. Agriculture is important. Major products include barley, citrus fruits, grapes for wine-making, maize, tea, tobacco and vegetables. Food processing and silk and perfume-making are other important activities. Sheep and cattle are reared.

AREA 69,700 sq km [26,910 sq mls]
POPULATION 5,109,000
CAPITAL (POPULATION) Tbilisi (1,279,000)
GOVERNMENT Multiparty republic
ETHNIC GROUPS Georgian 70%, Armenian 8%, Russian 6%, Azerbaijani 6%, Ossetes 3%, Greek 2%, Abkhazian 2%, others 3%
LANGUAGES Georgian (official)
RELIGIONS Christianity (Georgian Orthodox 65%, Russian Orthodox 10%, Armenian Orthodox 8%), Islam 11%
CURRENCY Lari

GERMANY

GEOGRAPHY The Federal Republic of Germany is the fourth largest country in Western Europe, after France, Spain and Sweden. The North German plain borders the North Sea in the north-west and the Baltic Sea in the north-east. Major rivers draining the plain include the Weser, Elbe and Oder.

The central highlands contain plateaux and highlands, including the Harz Mountains, the Thuringian Forest (Thüringer Wald), the Ore Mountains (Erzgebirge), and the Bohemian Forest (Böhmerwald) on the Czech border. South Germany is largely hilly, but the land rises in the south to the Bavarian Alps, which contain Germany's highest peak, Zugspitze, at 2,963 m [9,721 ft] above sea level. The scenic Black Forest (Scharzwald) overlooks the River Rhine, which flows through a rift valley in the south-west. The Black Forest contains the source of the River Danube.

North-western Germany has a mild climate, but the Baltic coastlands are cooler. To the south, the climate becomes more continental, especially in the highlands. The precipitation is greatest on the uplands, many of which are snow-capped in winter.

POLITICS & ECONOMY Germany and its allies were defeated in World War I (1914–18) and the country became a republic. Adolf Hitler came to power in 1933 and ruled as a dictator. His order to invade Poland led to the start of World War II (1939–45), which ended with Germany in ruins.

In 1945, Germany was divided into four military zones. In 1949, the American, British and French zones were amalgamated to form the Federal Republic of Germany (West Germany), while the Soviet zone became the German Democratic Republic (East Germany), a Communist state. Berlin, which had also been partitioned, became a divided city. West Berlin was part of West Germany, while East Berlin became the capital of East Germany. Bonn was the capital of West Germany.

Tension between East and West mounted during the Cold War, but West Germany rebuilt its economy quickly. In East Germany, the recovery was less rapid. In the late 1980s, reforms in the Soviet Union led to unrest in East Germany. Free elections were held in East Germany in 1990 and, on 3 October 1990, Germany was reunited.

The united Germany adopted West Germany's official name, the Federal Republic of Germany. Elections in December 1990 returned Helmut Kohl, West Germany's Chancellor (head of government) since 1982, to power. His government faced many problems, especially the restructuring of the economy of the former East Germany. Kohl was defeated in elections in 1998 and was succeeded as Chancellor by Social Democrat Gerhard Schröder. In 1999, Germany's parliament moved from Bonn to the reconstructed Reichstag building in Berlin.

West Germany's 'economic miracle' after the destruction of World War II was greatly helped by foreign aid. Today, despite all the problems caused by reunification, Germany is one of the world's greatest economic and trading nations.

Manufacturing is the most valuable part of Germany's economy and manufactured goods make up the bulk of the country's exports. Cars and other vehicles, cement, chemicals, computers, electrical equipment, processed food, machinery, scientific instruments, ships, steel, textiles and tools are among the leading manufactures. Germany has some coal, lignite, potash and rock salt deposits. But it imports many of the raw materials needed by its industries.

Germany also imports food. Major agricultural products include fruits, grapes for wine-making, potatoes, sugar beet and vegetables. Beef and dairy cattle are raised, together with many other livestock.

AREA 356,910 sq km [137,803 sq mls]
POPULATION 82,079,000
CAPITAL (POPULATION) Berlin (3,472,000) / Bonn (293,000)
GOVERNMENT Federal multiparty republic
ETHNIC GROUPS German 93%, Turkish 2%, Yugoslav 1%, Italian 1%, Greek, Polish, Spanish
LANGUAGES German (official)
RELIGIONS Christianity (Protestant, mainly Lutheran 45%, Roman Catholic 37%), Islam 2%
CURRENCY Euro; Deutschmark = 100 Pfennig

GHANA

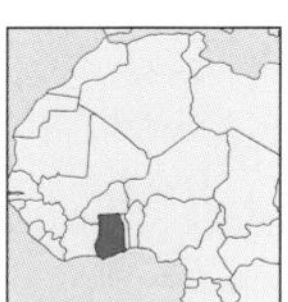

GEOGRAPHY The Republic of Ghana faces the Gulf of Guinea in West Africa. This hot country, just north of the Equator, was formerly called the Gold Coast. Behind the thickly populated southern coastal plains, which are lined with lagoons, lies a plateau region in the south-west.

Accra has a hot, tropical climate. Rain occurs all through the year, though Accra is drier than areas inland.

POLITICS & ECONOMY Portuguese explorers reached the area in 1471 and named it the Gold Coast. The area became a centre of the slave trade in the 17th century. The slave trade was ended in the 1860s and, gradually, the British took control of the area. After independence in 1957, attempts were made to develop the economy by creating large state-owned manufacturing industries. But debt and corruption, together with falls in the price of cocoa, the chief export, caused economic problems. This led to instability and frequent coups. In 1981, power was invested in a Provisional National Defence Council, led by Flight-Lieutenant Jerry Rawlings.

The government steadied the economy and introduced several new policies, including the relaxation of government controls. In 1992, the government introduced a new constitution, which allowed for multiparty election, and Rawlings was re-elected later that year.

The World Bank classifies Ghana as a 'low-income' developing country. Most people are poor and farming employs 59% of the population.

AREA 238,540 sq km [92,100 sq mls]
POPULATION 18,497,000
CAPITAL (POPULATION) Accra (1,781,000)
GOVERNMENT Republic
ETHNIC GROUPS Akan 54%, Mossi 16%, Ewe 12%, Ga-Adangame 8%, Gurma 3%
LANGUAGES English (official), Akan, Mossi
RELIGIONS Christianity 62%, traditional beliefs 21%, Islam 16%
CURRENCY Cedi = 100 pesewas

GIBRALTAR

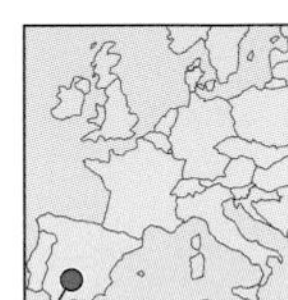

Gibraltar occupies a strategic position on the south coast of Spain where the Mediterranean meets the Atlantic. It was recognized as a British possession in 1713 and, despite Spanish claims, its population has consistently voted to retain its contacts with Britain. **AREA** 6.5 sq km [2.5 sq mls]; **POPULATION** 29,000; **CAPITAL** Gibraltar Town.

GREECE

GEOGRAPHY The Hellenic Republic, as Greece is officially called, is a rugged country situated at the southern end of the Balkan peninsula. Olympus, at 2,917 m [9,570 ft] is the highest peak. Islands make up about a fifth of the land.

Low-lying areas in Greece have mild, moist winters and hot, dry summers. The east coast has more than 2,700 hours of sunshine a year and only about half of the rainfall of the west. The mountains have a much more severe climate, with snow on the higher slopes in winter.

POLITICS & ECONOMY After World War II (1939–45), when Germany had occupied Greece, a civil war broke out between Communist and nationalist forces. This war ended in 1949. A military dictatorship took power in 1967. The monarchy was abolished in 1973 and democratic government was restored in 1974. Greece joined the European Community in 1981. But despite efforts to develop the economy, Greece remains one of the poorest nations in the European Union and, in 1998, it failed to qualify for the adoption of the euro.

Manufacturing is important. Products include processed food, cement, chemicals, metal products, textiles and tobacco. Greece also mines lignite (brown coal), bauxite and chromite.

Farmland covers about a third of the country, and grazing land another 40%. Major crops include barley, grapes for wine-making, dried fruits, olives, potatoes, sugar beet and wheat. Poultry, sheep, goats, pigs and cattle are raised. Greece's beaches and ancient ruins make it a major tourist destination.

AREA 131,990 sq km [50,961 sq mls]
POPULATION 10,662,000
CAPITAL (POPULATION) Athens (3,097,000)
GOVERNMENT Multiparty republic
ETHNIC GROUPS Greek 96%, Macedonian 2%, Turkish 1%, Albanian, Slav
LANGUAGES Greek (official)
RELIGIONS Christianity (Eastern Orthodox 97%)
CURRENCY Drachma = 100 lepta

GREENLAND

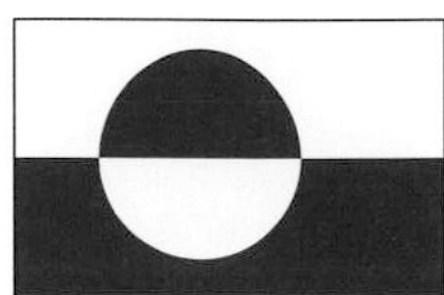

Greenland is the world's largest island. Settlements are confined to the coast, because an ice-sheet covers four-fifths of the land. Greenland became a Danish possession in 1380. Full internal self-government was granted in 1981 and, in 1997, Danish place names were superseded by Inuit forms. However, Greenland remains heavily dependent on Danish subsidies. **AREA** 2,175,600 sq km [838,999 sq mls]; **POPULATION** 59,000; **CAPITAL** Nuuk (Godthaab).

GRENADA

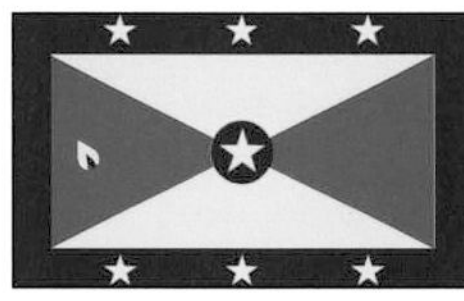

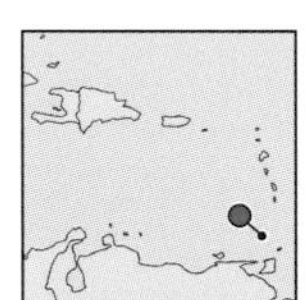

The most southerly of the Windward Islands in the Caribbean Sea, Grenada became independent from the UK in 1974. A military group seized power in 1983, when the prime minister was killed. US troops intervened and restored order and constitutional government. **AREA** 344 sq km [133 sq mls]; **POPULATION** 96,000; **CAPITAL** St George's.

GUADELOUPE

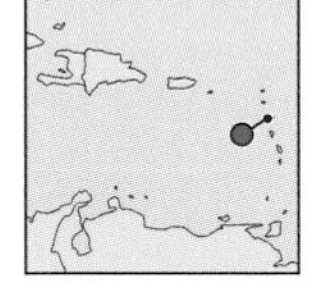

Guadeloupe is a French overseas department which includes seven Caribbean islands, the largest of which is Basse-Terre. French aid has helped to mantain a reasonable standard of living for the people. **AREA** 1,710 sq km [660 sq mls]; **POPULATION** 416,000; **CAPITAL** Basse-Terre.

GUAM

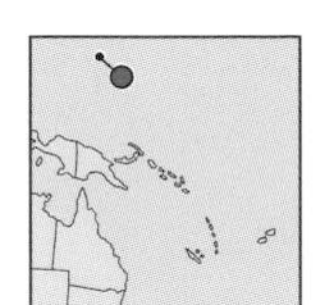

Guam, a strategically important 'unincorporated territory' of the USA, is the largest of the Mariana Islands in the Pacific Ocean. It is composed of a coralline limestone plateau. **AREA** 541 sq km [209 sq mls]; **POPULATION** 149,000; **CAPITAL** Agana.

GUATEMALA

GEOGRAPHY The Republic of Guatemala in Central America contains a thickly populated mountain region, with fertile soils. The mountains, which run in an east–west direction, contain many volcanoes, some of which are active. Volcanic eruptions and earthquakes are common in the highlands. South of the mountains lie the thinly populated Pacific coastlands, while a large inland plain occupies the north.

Guatemala lies in the tropics. The lowlands are hot and rainy. But the central mountain region is cooler and drier. Guatemala City, at about 1,500 m [5,000 ft] above sea level, has a pleasant, warm climate, with a marked dry season between November and April.

POLITICS & ECONOMY In 1823, Guatemala joined the Central American Federation. But it became fully independent in 1839. Since independence, Guatemala has been plagued by instability and periodic violence.

Guatemala has a long-standing claim over Belize, but this was reduced in 1983 to the southern fifth of the country. Violence became widespread in Guatemala from the early 1960s, because of conflict between left-wing groups, including many Amerindians, and government forces. Talks were held to end the war in 1993, but by then the conflict had claimed an estimated 100,000 lives.

The World Bank classifies Guatemala as a 'lower-middle-income' developing country. Agriculture employs nearly half of the population and coffee, sugar, bananas and beef are the leading exports. Other important crops include the spice cardamom and cotton, while maize is the chief food crop. But Guatemala still has to import food to feed the people.

AREA 108,890 sq km [42,042 sq mls]
POPULATION 12,008,000
CAPITAL (POPULATION) Guatemala City (1,814,000)
GOVERNMENT Republic
ETHNIC GROUPS Amerindian 45%, Ladino (mixed Hispanic and Amerindian) 45%, White 5%, Black 2%, others including Chinese 3%
LANGUAGES Spanish (official), Mayan languages
RELIGIONS Christianity (Roman Catholic 75%, Protestant 25%)
CURRENCY Guatemalan quetzal = 100 centavos

GUINEA

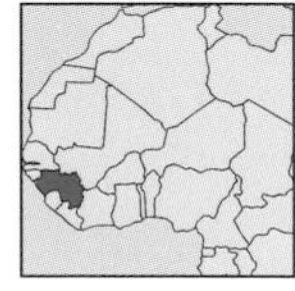

GEOGRAPHY The Republic of Guinea faces the Atlantic Ocean in West Africa. A flat, swampy plain borders the coast. Behind this plain, the land rises to a plateau region called Fouta Djalon. The Upper Niger plains, named after one of Africa's longest rivers, the Niger, which rises there, are in the north-east.

Guinea has a tropical climate and Conakry, on the coast, has heavy rains between May and November. This is also the coolest period in the year. During the dry season, hot, dry harmattan winds blow south-westwards from the Sahara Desert.

POLITICS & ECONOMY Guinea became independent in 1958. The first president, Sékou Touré, followed socialist policies, but most people remained poor and Touré had to introduce repressive policies to hold on to power. After his death in 1984, military leaders took over. Colonel Lansana Conté became president and his government introduced free enterprise policies. In 1993, Conté won a presidential election.

The World Bank classifies Guinea as a 'low-income' developing country. It has several natural resources, including bauxite (aluminium ore), diamonds, gold, iron ore and uranium. Bauxite and alumina (processed bauxite) account for 90% of the value of the exports. Agriculture, however, employs 78% of the people, many of whom produce little more than they need for their own families. Guinea has some manufacturing industries. Products include alumina, processed food and textiles.

AREA 245,860 sq km [94,927 sq mls]
POPULATION 7,477,000
CAPITAL (POPULATION) Conakry (1,508,000)
GOVERNMENT Multiparty republic
ETHNIC GROUPS Fulani 40%, Malinke 26%, Susu 11%, Kissi 7%, Kpelle 5%
LANGUAGES French (official), Fulani, Malinke
RELIGIONS Islam 85%, traditional beliefs 5%
CURRENCY Guinean franc = 100 cauris

GUINEA-BISSAU

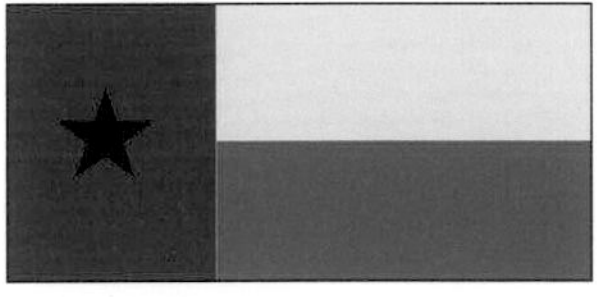
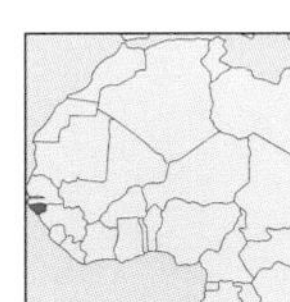

GEOGRAPHY The Republic of Guinea-Bissau, formerly known as Portuguese Guinea, is a small country in West Africa. The land is mostly low-lying, with a broad, swampy coastal plain and many flat offshore islands, including the Bijagós Archipelago.

The country has a tropical climate, with one dry season (December to May) and a rainy season from June to November.

POLITICS & ECONOMY Portugal appointed a governor to administer Guinea-Bissau and the Cape Verde Islands in 1836, but in 1879 the two territories were separated and Guinea-Bissau became a colony, then called Portuguese Guinea. But development was slow, partly because the territory did not attract settlers on the same scale as Portugal's much healthier African colonies of Angola and Mozambique.

In 1956, African nationalists in Portuguese Guinea and Cape Verde founded the African Party for the Independence of Guinea and Cape Verde (PAIGC). Because Portugal seemed determined to hang on to its overseas territories, the PAIGC began a guerrilla war in 1963. By 1968, it held two-thirds of the country. In 1972, a rebel National Assembly, elected by the people in the PAIGC-controlled area, voted to make the country independent as Guinea-Bissau.

In 1974, newly independent Guinea-Bissau faced many problems arising from its under-developed economy and its lack of trained people to work in the administration. One objective of the leaders of Guinea-Bissau was to unite their country with Cape Verde. But, in 1980, army leaders overthrew Guinea-Bissau's government. The Revolutionary Council, which took over, opposed unification with Cape Verde. Guinea-Bissau ceased to be a one-party state in 1991 and multiparty elections were held in 1994. However, a government of national unity was set up after a short civil war in 1998.

Guinea-Bissau is a poor country. Agriculture employs more than 80% of the people, but most farming is at subsistence level. Major crops include beans, coconuts, groundnuts, maize, palm kernels and rice, the staple food.

AREA 36,120 sq km [13,946 sq mls]
POPULATION 1,206,000
CAPITAL (POPULATION) Bissau (145,000)
GOVERNMENT Multiparty republic
ETHNIC GROUPS Balante 27%, Fulani (or Peul) 23%, Malinke 12%, Mandyako 11%, Pepel 10%
LANGUAGES Portuguese (official), Crioulo
RELIGIONS Traditional beliefs 54%, Islam 38%
CURRENCY CFA franc = 100 centimes

GUYANA

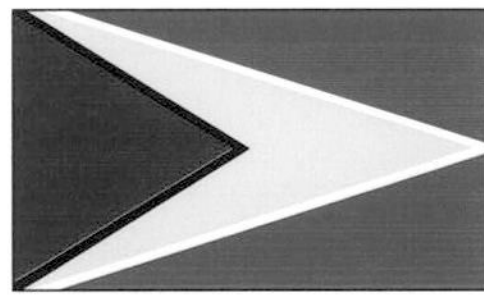
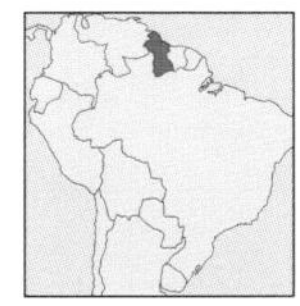

GEOGRAPHY The Co-operative Republic of Guyana is a country facing the Atlantic Ocean in north-eastern South America. The coastal plain is flat and much of it is below sea level.

The climate is hot and humid, though the interior highlands are cooler than the coast. The rainfall is heavy, occurring on more than 200 days a year.

POLITICS & ECONOMY British Guiana became independent in 1966. A black lawyer, Forbes Burnham, became the first prime minister. Under a new constitution adopted in 1980, the powers of the president were increased. Burnham became president until his death in 1985. He was succeeded by Hugh Desmond Hoyte. Hoyte was defeated in presidential elections in 1993 by Cheddli Jagan. Following Jagan's death in 1997, his wife Janet was elected president.

Guyana is a poor, developing country. Its resources include gold, bauxite (aluminium ore) and other minerals, and its forests and fertile soils. Agriculture employs 27% of the people. Sugar cane and rice are the leading crops. Electric power is in short supply, although the country has great potential for producing hydroelectricity from its many rivers.

AREA 214,970 sq km [83,000 sq mls]
POPULATION 820,000
CAPITAL (POPULATION) Georgetown (200,000)
GOVERNMENT Multiparty republic
ETHNIC GROUPS Asian Indian 49%, Black 36%, Mixed 7%, Amerindian 7%, Portuguese, Chinese
LANGUAGES English (official)
RELIGIONS Christianity (Protestant 34%, Roman Catholic 18%), Hinduism 34%, Islam 9%
CURRENCY Guyana dollar = 100 cents

HAITI

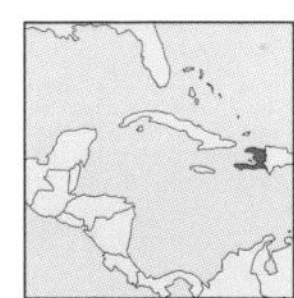

GEOGRAPHY The Republic of Haiti occupies the western third of Hispaniola in the Caribbean. The land is mainly mountainous. The climate is hot and humid, though the northern highlands, with about 200 mm [79 in], have more than twice as much rainfall as the southern coast.

POLITICS & ECONOMY Visited by Christopher Columbus in 1492, Haiti was later developed by the French to become the richest territory in the Caribbean region. The African slaves revolted in 1791 and the country became independent in 1804. Since independence, Haiti has suffered from instability, violence and dictatorial governments. Elections in 1990 returned Jean-Bertrand Aristide as president. But he was overthrown in 1991. Following US intervention, Aristide returned in 1994. In 1995, René Preval was elected president.

AREA 27,750 sq km [10,714 sq mls]
POPULATION 6,781,000
CAPITAL (POPULATION) Port-au-Prince (1,402,000)
GOVERNMENT Multiparty republic
ETHNIC GROUPS Black 95%, Mulatto 5%
LANGUAGES French (official), Creole
RELIGIONS Roman Catholic 80%, Voodoo
CURRENCY Gourde = 100 centimes

HONDURAS

GEOGRAPHY The Republic of Honduras is the second largest country in Central America. The northern coast on the Caribbean Sea extends more than 600 km [373 mls], but the Pacific coast in the south-east is only about 80 km [50 mls] long.

Honduras has a tropical climate, but the highlands, where the capital Tegucigalpa is situated, have a cooler climate than the hot coastal plains. The months between May and November are the rainiest and the north coast is sometimes hit by fierce hurricanes that cause great damage.

POLITICS & ECONOMY In the 1890s, American companies developed plantations in Honduras to grow bananas, which soon became the country's chief source of income. The companies exerted great political influence in Honduras and the country became known as a 'banana republic', a name that was later applied to several other Latin American nations. Instability has continued to mar the country's progress. In 1969, Honduras fought the short 'Soccer War' with El Salvador. The war was sparked off by the treatment of fans during a World Cup soccer series. But the real reason was that Honduras had forced Salvadoreans in Honduras to give up their land. In 1980, the countries signed a peace agreement.

Honduras is a developing country – one of the poorest in the Americas. It has few resources besides some silver, lead and zinc, and agriculture dominates the economy. Bananas and coffee are the leading exports, and maize is the main food crop.

Honduras is the least industrialized country in Central America. Manufactures include processed food, textiles, and a wide variety of wood products.

AREA 112,090 sq km [43,278 sq mls]
POPULATION 5,862,000
CAPITAL (POPULATION) Tegucigalpa (739,000)
GOVERNMENT Republic
ETHNIC GROUPS Mestizo 90%, Amerindian 7%, Black (including Black Carib) 2%, White 1%
LANGUAGES Spanish (official)
RELIGIONS Christianity (Roman Catholic 85%)
CURRENCY Honduran lempira = 100 centavos

HONG KONG

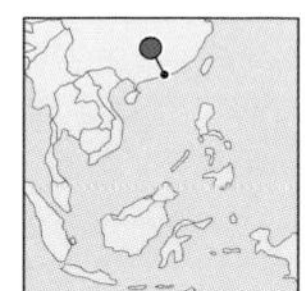

Hong Kong, or Xianggang as it is known in Chinese, was a British dependency until 1 July 1997. It is now a Special Administrative Region of China. It consists of 236 islands, part of the mainland, and is home to over six million people. Hong Kong is a major financial and industrial centre, the world's biggest container port, and a major producer of textiles. **AREA** 1,071 sq km [413 sq mls]; **POPULATION** 6,707,000.

HUNGARY

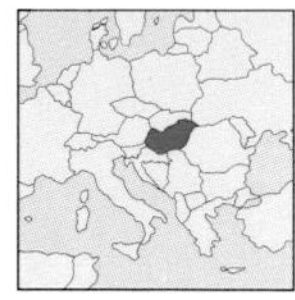

GEOGRAPHY The Hungarian Republic is a landlocked country in central Europe. The land is mostly low-lying and drained by the Danube (Duna) and its tributary, the Tisza. Most of the land east of the Danube belongs to a region called the Great Plain (Nagyalföld), which covers about half of Hungary.

Hungary lies far from the moderating influence of the sea. As a result, summers are warmer and sunnier, and the winters colder than in Western Europe.

POLITICS & ECONOMY Hungary entered World War II (1939–45) in 1941, as an ally of Germany, but the Germans occupied the country in 1944. The Soviet Union invaded Hungary in 1944 and, in 1946, the country became a republic. The Communists gradually took over the government, taking complete control in 1949. From 1949, Hungary was an ally of the Soviet Union. In 1956, Soviet troops crushed an anti-Communist revolt. But in the 1980s, reforms in the Soviet Union led to the growth of anti-Communist groups in Hungary.

In 1989, Hungary adopted a new constitution making it a multiparty state. Elections held in 1990 led to a victory for the non-Communist Democratic Forum. In 1994, the Hungarian Socialist Party, composed of ex-Communists who had renounced Communism, won a majority in new elections and, in 1999, Hungary became a member of NATO.

Before World War II, Hungary's economy was based mainly on agriculture. But the Communists set up many manufacturing industries. The new factories were owned by the government, as also was most of the land. However, from the late 1980s, the government has worked to increase private ownership. This change of policy caused many problems, including inflation and high rates of unemployment. Manufacturing is the chief activity. Major products include aluminium, chemicals, and electrical and electronic goods.

AREA 93,030 sq km [35,919 sq mls]
POPULATION 10,208,000
CAPITAL (POPULATION) Budapest (1,909,000)
GOVERNMENT Multiparty republic
ETHNIC GROUPS Magyar (Hungarian) 98%, Gypsy, German, Croat, Romanian, Slovak
LANGUAGES Hungarian (official)
RELIGIONS Christianity (Roman Catholic 64%, Protestant 23%, Orthodox 1%), Judaism 1%
CURRENCY Forint = 100 fillér

ICELAND

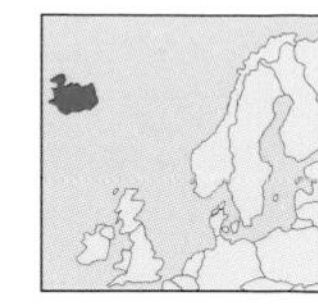

GEOGRAPHY The Republic of Iceland, in the North Atlantic Ocean, is closer to Greenland than Scotland. Iceland sits astride the Mid-Atlantic Ridge. It is slowly getting wider as the ocean is being stretched apart by continental drift.

Iceland has around 200 volcanoes and eruptions are frequent. An eruption under the Vatnajökull icecap in 1996 created a subglacial lake which subsequently burst, causing severe flooding. Geysers and hot springs are other common volcanic features. Icecaps and glaciers cover about an eighth of the land. The only habitable regions are the coastal lowlands.

Although it lies far to the north, Iceland's climate is moderated by the warm waters of the Gulf Stream. The port of Reykjavik is ice-free all the year round.

POLITICS & ECONOMY Norwegian Vikings colonized Iceland in AD 874, and in 930 the settlers founded the world's oldest parliament, the Althing.

Iceland united with Norway in 1262. But when Norway united with Denmark in 1380, Iceland came under Danish rule. Iceland became a self-governing kingdom, united with Denmark, in 1918. It became a fully independent republic in 1944, following a referendum in which 97% of the people voted to break their country's ties with Denmark.

Iceland has played an important part in European affairs. It is a member of the North Atlantic Treaty Organization, though it has been involved in disputes with the United Kingdom over fishing rights. In 1977, the UK agreed not to fish within Iceland's 370 km [200 nautical mls] fishing limits.

Iceland has few resources besides the fishing grounds which surround it. Fishing and fish processing are major industries which dominate Iceland's overseas trade. Barely 1% of the land is used to grow crops, mainly root vegetables and fodder for livestock. But 23% of the country is used for grazing sheep and cattle.

AREA 103,000 sq km [39,768 sq mls]
POPULATION 271,000
CAPITAL (POPULATION) Reykjavik (103,000)
GOVERNMENT Multiparty republic
ETHNIC GROUPS Icelandic 97%, Danish 1%
LANGUAGES Icelandic (official)
RELIGIONS Christianity (Evangelical Lutheran 92%, other Lutheran 3%, Roman Catholic 1%)
CURRENCY Króna = 100 aurar

INDIA

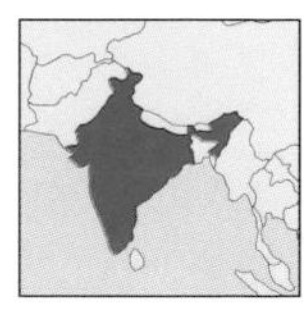

GEOGRAPHY The Republic of India is the world's seventh largest country. In population, it ranks second only to China. The north is mountainous, with mountains and foothills of the Himalayan range. Rivers, such as the Brahmaputra and Ganges (Ganga), rise in the Himalaya and flow across the fertile northern plains. Southern India consists of a large plateau, called the Deccan. The Deccan is bordered by two mountain ranges, the Western Ghats and the Eastern Ghats.

India has three main seasons. The cool season runs from October to February. The hot season runs from March to June. The rainy monsoon season starts in the middle of June and continues into September. Delhi has a moderate rainfall, with about 640 mm [25 in] a year. The south-western coast and the north-east have far more rain. Darjeeling in the north-east has an average annual rainfall of 3,040 mm [120 in]. But parts of the Thar Desert in the north-west have only 50 mm [2 in] of rain per year.

POLITICS & ECONOMY In southern India, most people are descendants of the dark-skinned Dravidians, who were among India's earliest people. Most northerners are descendants of lighter-skinned Aryans who arrived around 3,500 years ago.

India was the birthplace of several major religions, including Hinduism, Buddhism and Sikhism. Islam was introduced from about AD 1000. The Muslim Mughal empire was founded in 1526. From the 17th century, Britain began to gain influence. From 1858 to 1947, India was ruled as part of the British Empire. Independence in 1947 led to the break-up of British India into India and Muslim Pakistan.

Although India has 15 major languages and hundreds of minor ones, together with many religions, the country remains the world's largest democracy. It has faced many problems, especially with Pakistan, over the disputed territory of Jammu and Kashmir. Tension arose again in 1998 when both India and Pakistan tested nuclear devices.

Economic development has been a major problem and, according to the World Bank, India is a 'low-income' developing country. Socialist policies have failed to raise the living standards of the poor and, in the early 1990s, the government introduced private enterprise policies to stimulate growth.

Farming employs more than 60% of the people. The main food crops are rice, wheat, millet and sorghum, together with beans and peas. India has more cattle than any other country. These animals provide milk, but Hindus do not eat beef. India's large mineral reserves include coal, iron ore and oil, and manufacturing has expanded greatly since 1947. Products include iron and steel, machinery, refined petroleum, textiles and transport equipment.

AREA 3,287,590 sq km [1,269,338 sq mls]
POPULATION 984,000,000
CAPITAL (POPULATION) New Delhi (part of Delhi, 301,000)
GOVERNMENT Multiparty federal republic
ETHNIC GROUPS Indo-Aryan (Caucasoid) 72%, Dravidian (Aboriginal) 25%, other (mainly Mongoloid) 3%
LANGUAGES Hindi 30% and English (both official), Telugu 8%, Bengali 8%, Marati 8%, Urdu 5%, Tamil, many local languages
RELIGIONS Hinduism 83%, Islam (Sunni Muslim) 11%, Christianity 2%, Sikhism 2%, Buddhism 1%
CURRENCY Rupee = 100 paisa

INDONESIA

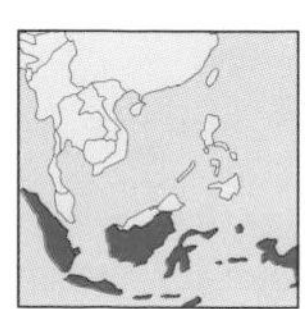

GEOGRAPHY The Republic of Indonesia is an island nation in South-east Asia. In all, Indonesia contains about 13,600 islands, less than 6,000 of which are inhabited. Three-quarters of the country is made up of five main areas: the islands of Sumatra, Java and Sulawesi (Celebes), together with

Kalimantan (southern Borneo) and Irian Jaya (western New Guinea). The islands are generally mountainous and Indonesia has more active volcanoes than any other country. The larger islands have extensive coastal lowlands.

Indonesia lies on the Equator and temperatures are high throughout the year. The climate is also humid. The rainfall is generally heavy, and only Java and the Sunda Islands have a relatively dry season. The highlands are cooler than the lowlands.

POLITICS & ECONOMY Indonesia is the world's most populous Muslim nation, though Islam was introduced as recently as the 15th century. The Dutch became active in the area in the early 17th century and Indonesia became a Dutch colony in 1799. After a long struggle, the Netherlands recognized Indonesia's independence in 1949. Despite instability, the economy has expanded, although a general depression hit the economies of most nations in eastern Asia in 1997. The removal from office of the autocratic President Suharto in 1998 held out hopes for a more democratic system and the resolution of the disputed status of East (formerly Portuguese) Timor, which Indonesia had annexed in 1976.

Indonesia is a developing country. Its resources include oil, natural gas, tin and other minerals, its fertile volcanic soils and its forests. Oil and gas are major exports. Timber, textiles, rubber, coffee and tea are also exported. The chief food crop is rice. Manufacturing is increasing, especially on Java.

AREA 1,904,570 sq km [735,354 sq mls]
POPULATION 212,942,000
CAPITAL (POPULATION) Jakarta (11,500,000)
GOVERNMENT Multiparty republic
ETHNIC GROUPS Javanese 39%, Sundanese 16%, Indonesian (Malay) 12%, Madurese 4%, more than 300 others
LANGUAGES Bahasa Indonesian (official), others
RELIGIONS Islam 87%, Christianity 10% (Roman Catholic 6%), Hinduism 2%, Buddhism 1%
CURRENCY Indonesian rupiah = 100 sen

IRAN

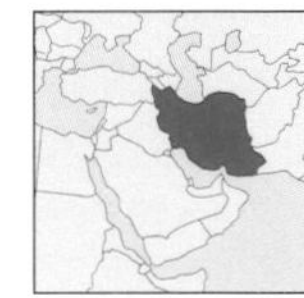

GEOGRAPHY The Republic of Iran contains a barren central plateau which covers about half of the country. It includes the Dasht-e-Kavir (Great Salt Desert) and the Dasht-e-Lut (Great Sand Desert). The Elburz Mountains north of the plateau contain Iran's highest peak, Damavand, while narrow lowlands lie between the mountains and the Caspian Sea. West of the plateau are the Zagros Mountains, beyond which the land descends to the plains bordering the Gulf.

Much of Iran has a severe, dry climate, with hot summers and cold winters. In Tehran, rain falls on only about 30 days in the year and the annual temperature range is more than 25°C [45°F]. The climate in the lowlands, however, is generally milder.

POLITICS & ECONOMY Iran was called Persia until 1935. The empire of Ancient Persia flourished between 550 and 350 BC, when it fell to Alexander the Great. Islam was introduced in AD 641.

Britain and Russia competed for influence in the area in the 19th century, and in the early 20th century the British began to develop the country's oil resources. In 1925, the Pahlavi family took power. Reza Khan became shah (king) and worked to modernize the country. The Pahlavi dynasty was ended in 1979 when a religious leader, Ayatollah Ruhollah Khomeini, made Iran an Islamic republic. In 1980–8, Iran and Iraq fought a war over disputed borders. Khomeini died in 1989, but his fundamentalist views and anti-Western attitudes continued to influence many Muslims around the world. In 1995, Iran's alleged support for such terrorist groups as the Palestinian Hamas led the United States to impose trade sanctions.

Iran's prosperity is based on its oil production and oil accounts for 95% of the country's exports. However, the economy was severely damaged by the Iran–Iraq war in the 1980s. Oil revenues have been used to develop a growing manufacturing sector. Agriculture is important even though farms cover only a tenth of the land. The main crops are wheat and barley. Livestock farming and fishing are other important activities, although Iran has to import much of the food it needs.

AREA 1,648,000 sq km [636,293 sq mls]
POPULATION 64,411,000
CAPITAL (POPULATION) Tehran (6,750,000)
GOVERNMENT Islamic republic
ETHNIC GROUPS Persian 46%, Azerbaijani 17%, Kurdish 9%, Gilaki 5%, Luri, Mazandarani, Baluchi, Arab
LANGUAGES Farsi/Persian (official), Kurdish
RELIGIONS Islam 99%
CURRENCY Rial = 100 dinars

IRAQ

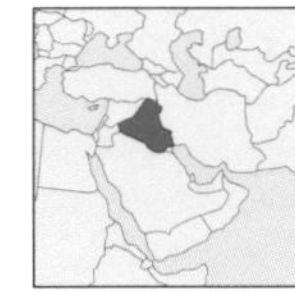

GEOGRAPHY The Republic of Iraq is a south-west Asian country at the head of The Gulf. Rolling deserts cover western and south-western Iraq, with mountains in the north-east. The northern plains, across which flow the rivers Euphrates (Nahr al Furat) and Tigris (Nahr Dijlah), are dry. But the southern plains, including Mesopotamia, and the delta of the Shatt al Arab, the river formed south of Al Qurnah by the combined Euphrates and Tigris, contain irrigated farmland, together with marshes.

The climate of Iraq varies from temperate in the north to subtropical in the south and east. Baghdad, in central Iraq, has cool winters, with occasional frosts, and hot summers. The rainfall is generally low.

POLITICS & ECONOMY Mesopotamia was the home of several great civilizations, including Sumer, Babylon and Assyria. It later became part of the Persian empire. Islam was introduced in AD 637 and Baghdad became the brilliant capital of the powerful Arab empire. But Mesopotamia declined after the Mongols invaded it in 1258. From 1534, Mesopotamia became part of the Turkish Ottoman empire. Britain invaded the area in 1916. In 1921, Britain renamed the country Iraq and set up an Arab monarchy. Iraq finally became independent in 1932.

By the 1950s, oil dominated Iraq's economy. In 1952, Iraq agreed to take 50% of the profits of the foreign oil companies. This revenue enabled the government to pay for welfare services and development projects. But many Iraqis felt that they should benefit more from their oil.

Since 1958, when army officers killed the king and made Iraq a republic, the country has undergone turbulent times. In the 1960s, the Kurds, who live in northern Iraq and also in Iran, Turkey, Syria and Armenia, asked for self-rule. The government rejected their demands and war broke out. A peace treaty was signed in 1975, but conflict has continued.

In 1979, Saddam Hussein became Iraq's president. Under his leadership, Iraq invaded Iran in 1980, starting an eight-year war. During this war, Iraqi Kurds supported Iran and the Iraqi government attacked Kurdish villages with poison gas.

In 1990, Iraqi troops occupied Kuwait but an international force drove them out in 1991. Since 1991, Iraqi troops have attacked Shiite Marsh Arabs and Kurds. In 1996, the government aided the forces of the Kurdish Democratic Party in an offensive against the Patriotic Union of Kurdistan, a rival Kurdish faction. In 1998, Iraq's failure to permit UNSCOM, the UN body charged with disposing of Iraq's deadliest weapons, access to all suspect sites led to Western bombardment of military sites.

Civil war, war damage, UN sanctions and economic mismanagement have all contributed to economic chaos in the 1990s. Oil remains Iraq's main resource, but a UN trade embargo in 1990 halted oil exports. Farmland, including pasture, covers about a fifth of the land. Products include barley, cotton, dates, fruit, livestock, wheat and wool, but Iraq still has to import food. Industries include oil refining and the manufacture of petrochemicals and consumer goods.

AREA 438,320 sq km [169,235 sq mls]
POPULATION 21,722,000
CAPITAL (POPULATION) Baghdad (3,841,000)
GOVERNMENT Republic
ETHNIC GROUPS Arab 77%, Kurdish 19%, Turkmen, Persian, Assyrian
LANGUAGES Arabic (official), Kurdish (official in Kurdish areas)
RELIGIONS Islam 96%, Christianity 4%
CURRENCY Iraqi dinar = 20 dirhams = 1,000 fils

IRELAND

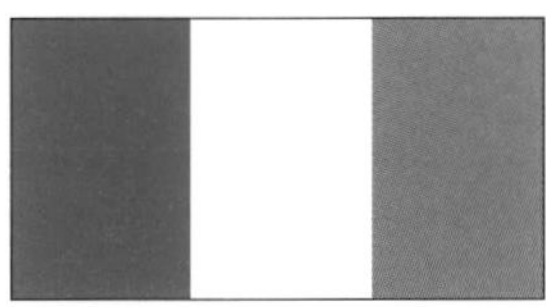

GEOGRAPHY The Republic of Ireland occupies five-sixths of the island of Ireland. The country consists of a large lowland region surrounded by a broken rim of low mountains. The uplands include the Mountains of Kerry where Carrauntoohill, Ireland's highest peak at 1,041 m [3,415 ft], is situated. The River Shannon is the longest in the British Isles. It flows through three large lakes, loughs Allen, Ree and Derg.

Ireland has a mild, damp climate greatly influenced by the warm Gulf Stream current that washes its shores. The effects of the Gulf Stream are greatest in the west. Dublin in the east is cooler than places on the west coast. Rain occurs throughout the year.

POLITICS & ECONOMY In 1801, the Act of Union created the United Kingdom of Great Britain and Ireland. But Irish discontent intensified in the 1840s when a potato blight caused a famine in which a million people died and nearly a million emigrated. Britain was blamed for not having done enough to help. In 1916, an uprising in Dublin was crushed, but between 1919 and 1922 civil war occurred. In 1922, the Irish Free State was created as a Dominion in the British Commonwealth. But Northern Ireland remained part of the UK.

Ireland became a republic in 1949. Since then, Irish governments have sought to develop the economy, and it was for this reason that Ireland joined the European Community in 1973. In 1998, Ireland took part in the negotiations to produce a constitutional settlement in Northern Ireland. As part of the agreement, Ireland agreed to give up its constitutional claim on Northern Ireland.

Major farm products in Ireland include barley, cattle and dairy products, pigs, potatoes, poultry, sheep, sugar beet and wheat, while fishing provides another valuable source of food. Farming is now profitable, aided by European Union grants, but manufacturing is the leading economic sector. Many factories produce food and beverages. Chemicals and pharmaceuticals, electronic equipment, machinery, paper and textiles are also important.

AREA 70,280 sq km [27,135 sq mls]
POPULATION 3,619,000
CAPITAL (POPULATION) Dublin (1,024,000)
GOVERNMENT Multiparty republic
ETHNIC GROUPS Irish 94%
LANGUAGES Irish and English (both official)
RELIGIONS Christianity (Roman Catholic 93%, Protestant 3%)
CURRENCY Euro; Irish pound = 100 new pence

ISRAEL

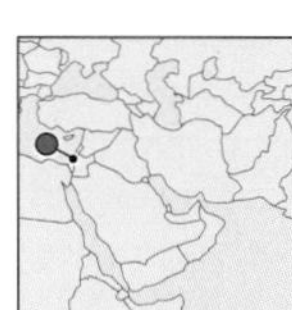

GEOGRAPHY The State of Israel is a small country in the eastern Mediterranean. It includes a fertile coastal plain, where Israel's main industrial cities, Haifa (Hefa) and Tel Aviv–Jaffa are situated. Inland lie the Judaeo-Galilean highlands, which run from northern Israel to the northern tip of the Negev Desert in the south. To the east lies part of the Great Rift Valley which runs through East Africa into Asia. In Israel, the Rift Valley contains the River Jordan, the Sea of Galilee and the Dead Sea.

Israel has hot, dry, sunny summers. Winters are mild and moist on the coast, but the total rainfall decreases from west to east and also from north to south, where the Dead Sea region has only 70 mm [2.5 in] a year.

POLITICS & ECONOMY Israel is part of a region called Palestine. Some Jews have always lived in the area, though most modern Israelis are descendants of immigrants who began to settle there from the 1880s. Britain ruled Palestine from 1917. Large numbers of Jews escaping Nazi persecution arrived in the 1930s, provoking an Arab uprising against British rule. In 1947, the UN agreed to partition Palestine into an Arab and a Jewish state. Fighting broke out after Arabs rejected the plan. The State of Israel came into being in May 1948, but fighting continued into 1949. Other Arab–Israeli wars in 1956, 1967 and 1973 led to land gains for Israel.

In 1978, Israel signed a treaty with Egypt which led to the return of the occupied Sinai peninsula to Egypt in 1979. But conflict continued between Israel and the PLO (Palestine Liberation Organization). In 1993, the PLO and Israel agreed to establish Palestinian self-rule in two areas: the occupied Gaza Strip, and in the town of Jericho in the occupied West Bank. The agreement was extended in 1995 to include more than 30% of the West Bank. Israel's prime minister, Yitzhak Rabin, was assassinated in 1995 and his successor, Simon Peres, was narrowly defeated in elections in 1996. His right-wing successor, Benjamin Netanyahu, who resigned in 1999, favoured a more hardline policy towards Palestinians and the peace process became stalled. His successor, the left-wing challenger, Ehud Barak, vows to continue the peace process.

Israel's most valuable activity is manufacturing and the country's products include chemicals, electronic equipment, fertilizers, military equipment, plastics, processed food, scientific instruments and textiles. Fruits and vegetables are leading exports.

AREA 26,650 sq km [10,290 sq mls]
POPULATION 5,644,000
CAPITAL (POPULATION) Jerusalem (591,000)
GOVERNMENT Multiparty republic
ETHNIC GROUPS Jewish 82%, Arab and others 18%
LANGUAGES Hebrew and Arabic (both official)
RELIGIONS Judaism 82%, Islam 14%, Christianity 2%, Druse and others 2%
CURRENCY New Israeli sheqel = 100 agorat

ITALY

GEOGRAPHY The Republic of Italy is famous for its history and traditions, its art and culture, and its beautiful scenery. Northern Italy is bordered in the north by the high Alps, with their many climbing and skiing resorts. The Alps overlook the northern plains – Italy's most fertile and densely populated region – drained by the River Po. The rugged Apennines form the backbone of southern Italy. Bordering the range are scenic hilly areas and coastal plains.

Southern Italy contains a string of volcanoes, stretching from Vesuvius, near Naples (Nápoli), through the Lipari Islands, to Mount Etna on Sicily. Sicily is the largest island in the Mediterranean. Sardinia is also part of Italy.

Milan (Milano), in the north, has cold, often snowy winters. But the summer months are warm and sunny. Rainfall is plentiful, with brief but powerful thunderstorms in summer. Southern Italy has mild, moist winters and warm, dry summers.

POLITICS & ECONOMY Magnificent ruins throughout Italy testify to the glories of the ancient Roman Empire, which was founded, according to legend, in 753 BC. It reached its peak in the AD 100s. It finally collapsed in the 400s, although the Eastern Roman Empire, also called the Byzantine Empire, survived for another 1,000 years.

In the Middle Ages, Italy was split into many tiny states. But they made a great contribution to the revival of art and learning, called the Renaissance, in the 14th to 16th centuries. Beautiful cities, such as Florence (Firenze) and Venice (Venézia), testify to the artistic achievements of this period.

Italy finally became a united kingdom in 1861, although the Papal Territories (a large area ruled by the Roman Catholic Church) was not added until 1870. The Pope and his successors disputed the takeover of the Papal Territories. The dispute was finally resolved in 1929, when the Vatican City was set up in Rome as a fully independent state.

Italy fought in World War I (1914–18) alongside the Allies – Britain, France and Russia. In 1922, the dictator Benito Mussolini, leader of the Fascist party, took power. Under Mussolini, Italy conquered Ethiopia. During World War II (1939–45), Italy at first fought on Germany's side against the Allies. But in late 1943, Italy declared war on Germany. Italy became a republic in 1946. It has played an important part in European affairs. It was a founder member of the North Atlantic Treaty Organization (NATO) in 1949 and also of what has now become the European Union in 1958.

After the setting up of the European Union, Italy's economy developed quickly. But the country faced many problems. For example, much of the economic development was in the north. This forced many people to leave the poor south to find jobs in the north or abroad. Social problems, corruption at high levels of society, and a succession of weak coalition governments all contributed to instability. Elections in 1996 were won by the left-wing Olive Tree alliance led by Romano Prodi. After losing a confidence vote in October 1998, Prodi was replaced as prime minister by an ex-Communist, Massimo D'Alema.

Only 50 years ago, Italy was a mainly agricultural society. But today it is a leading industrial power. It lacks mineral resources, and imports most of the raw materials used in industry. Manufactures include textiles and clothing, processed food, machinery, cars and chemicals.The chief industrial region is in the north-west.

Farmland covers around 42% of the land, pasture 17%, and forest and woodland 22%. Major crops include citrus fruits, grapes which are used to make wine, olive oil, sugar beet and vegetables. Livestock farming is important, though meat is imported.

AREA 301,270 sq km [116,320 sq mls]
POPULATION 56,783,000
CAPITAL (POPULATION) Rome (2,688,000)
GOVERNMENT Multiparty republic
ETHNIC GROUPS Italian 94%, German, French, Albanian, Ladino, Slovenian, Greek
LANGUAGES Italian 94% (official)
RELIGIONS Christianity (Roman Catholic) 83%
CURRENCY Euro; Lira = 100 centesimi

IVORY COAST

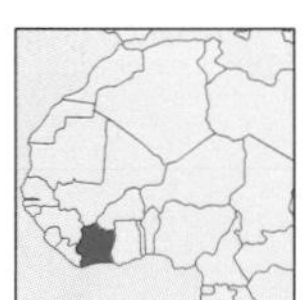

GEOGRAPHY The Republic of the Ivory Coast, in West Africa, is officially known as Côte d'Ivoire. The south-east coast is bordered by sand bars that enclose lagoons, on one of which the former capital and chief port of Abidjan is situated. But the south-western coast is lined by rocky cliffs.

Ivory Coast has a hot and humid tropical climate, with high temperatures throughout the year. The south of the country has two distinct rainy seasons: between May and July, and from October to November. Inland, the rainfall decreases and the north has one dry and one rainy season.

POLITICS & ECONOMY From 1895, Ivory Coast was governed as part of French West Africa, a massive union which also included what are now Benin, Burkina Faso, Guinea, Mali, Mauritania, Niger and Senegal. In 1946, Ivory Coast became a territory in the French Union.

Ivory Coast became fully independent in 1960 and its first president, Félix Houphouët-Boigny, became the longest serving head of state in Africa with an uninterrupted period in office which ended with his death in 1993. Houphouët-Boigny was a paternalistic, pro-Western leader, who made his country a one-party state. In 1983, the National Assembly agreed to move the capital from Abidjan to Yamoussoukro, the president's birthplace.

Agriculture employs about two-thirds of the people,

and farm products, notably cocoa beans, coffee, cotton and cotton cloth, make up nearly half of the value of the exports. Manufacturing has grown in importance since 1960; products include fertilizers, processed food, refined oil, textiles and timber.

AREA 322,460 sq km [124,502 sq mls]
POPULATION 15,446,000
CAPITAL (POPULATION) Yamoussoukro (120,000)
GOVERNMENT Multiparty republic
ETHNIC GROUPS Akan 41%, Kru 17%, Voltaic 16%, Malinke 15%, Southern Mande 10%
LANGUAGES French (official), Akan, Voltaic
RELIGIONS Islam 38%, Christianity 28%, traditional beliefs 17%
CURRENCY CFA franc = 100 centimes

JAMAICA

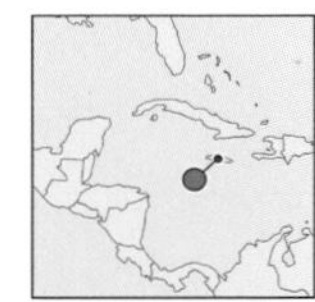

GEOGRAPHY Third largest of the Caribbean islands, half of Jamaica lies above 300 m [1,000 ft] and moist south-east trade winds bring rain to the central mountain range.

The 'cockpit country' in the north-west of the island is an inaccessible limestone area of steep broken ridges and isolated basins.

POLITICS & ECONOMY Britain took Jamaica from Spain in the 17th century, and the island did not gain its independence until 1962. Some economic progress was made by the socialist government in the 1980s, but migration and unemployment remain high. Farming is the leading activity and sugar cane is the main crop, though bauxite production provides much of the country's income. Jamaica has some industries and tourism is a major industry.

AREA 10,990 sq km [4,243 sq mls]
POPULATION 2,635,000
CAPITAL (POPULATION) Kingston (644,000)
GOVERNMENT Constitutional monarchy
ETHNIC GROUPS Black 76%, Afro-European 15%, East Indian 3%, White 3%
LANGUAGES English (official), Creole, Hindi, Spanish, Chinese
RELIGIONS Protestant 70%, Roman Catholic 8%
CURRENCY Dollar = 100 cents

JAPAN

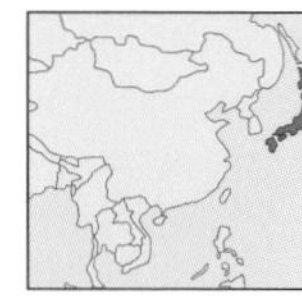

GEOGRAPHY Japan's four largest islands – Honshu, Hokkaido, Kyushu and Shikoku – make up 98% of the country. But Japan contains thousands of small islands. The four largest islands are mainly mountainous, while many of the small islands are the tips of volcanoes. Japan has more than 150 volcanoes, about 60 of which are active. Volcanic eruptions, earthquakes and tsunamis (destructive sea waves triggered by underwater earthquakes and eruptions) are common because the islands lie in an unstable part of our planet, where continental plates are always on the move. One powerful recent earthquake killed more than 5,000 people in Kobe in 1995.

The climate of Japan varies greatly from north to south. Hokkaido in the north has cold, snowy winters. At Sapporo, temperatures below –20°C [4°F] have been recorded between December and March. But summers are warm, with temperatures sometimes exceeding 30°C [86°F]. Rain falls throughout the year, though Hokkaido is one of the driest parts of Japan.

Tokyo has higher rainfall and temperatures, though frosts may occur as late as April when north-westerly winds are blowing. The southern islands of Shikoku and Kyushu have warm temperate climates. Summers are long and hot. Winters are mild.

POLITICS & ECONOMY In the late 19th century, Japan began a programme of modernization. Under its new imperial leaders, it began to look for lands to conquer. In 1894–5, it fought a war with China and, in 1904–5, it defeated Russia. Soon its overseas empire included Korea and Taiwan. In 1930, Japan invaded Manchuria (north-east China) and, in 1937, it began a war against China. In 1941, Japan launched an attack on the US base at Pearl Harbor in Hawaii. This drew both Japan and the United States into World War II.

Japan surrendered in 1945 when the Americans dropped atomic bombs on two cities, Hiroshima and Nagasaki. The United States occupied Japan until 1952. During this period, Japan adopted a democratic constitution. The emperor, who had previously been regarded as a god, became a constitutional monarch. Power was vested in the prime minister and cabinet, who are chosen from the Diet (elected parliament).

From the 1960s, Japan experienced many changes as the country rapidly built up new industries. By the early 1990s, Japan had become the world's second richest economic power after the US. But economic success has brought problems. For example, the rapid growth of cities has led to housing shortages and pollution. Another problem is that the proportion of people over 65 years of age is steadily increasing.

Japan has the world's second highest gross domestic product (GDP) after the United States. [The GDP is the total value of all goods and services produced in a country in one year.] The most important sector of the economy is industry. Yet Japan has to import most of the raw materials and fuels it needs for its industries. Its success is based on its use of the latest technology, its skilled and hard-working labour force, its vigorous export policies and its comparatively small government spending on defence. Manufactures dominate its exports, which include machinery, electrical and electronic equipment, vehicles and transport equipment, iron and steel, chemicals, textiles and ships.

Japan is one of the world's top fishing nations and fish is an important source of protein. Because the land is so rugged, only 15% of the country can be farmed. Yet Japan produces about 70% of the food it needs. Rice is the chief crop, taking up about half of the total farmland. Other major products include fruits, sugar beet, tea and vegetables. Livestock farming has increased since the 1950s.

AREA 377,800 sq km [145,869 sq mls]
POPULATION 125,932,000
CAPITAL (POPULATION) Tokyo (26,836,000)
GOVERNMENT Constitutional monarchy
ETHNIC GROUPS Japanese 99%, Chinese, Korean, Ainu
LANGUAGES Japanese (official)
RELIGIONS Shintoism 93%, Buddhism 74%, Christianity 1% (most Japanese consider themselves to be both Shinto and Buddhist)
CURRENCY Yen = 100 sen

JORDAN

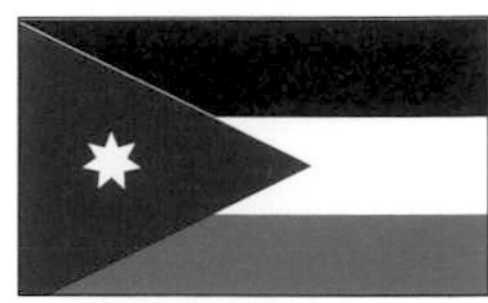

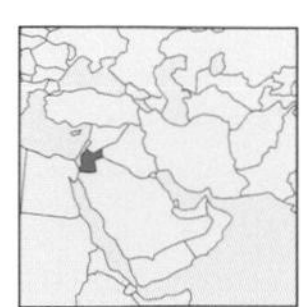

GEOGRAPHY The Hashemite Kingdom of Jordan is an Arab country in south-western Asia. The Great Rift Valley in the west contains the River Jordan and the Dead Sea, which Jordan shares with Israel. East of the Rift Valley is the Transjordan plateau, where most Jordanians live. To the east and south lie vast areas of desert.

Amman has a much lower rainfall and longer dry season than the Mediterranean lands to the west. The Transjordan plateau, on which Amman stands, is a transition zone between the Mediterranean climate zone to the west and the desert climate to the east.

POLITICS & ECONOMY In 1921, Britain created a territory called Transjordan east of the River Jordan. In 1923, Transjordan became self-governing, but Britain retained control of its defences, finances and foreign affairs. This territory became fully independent as Jordan in 1946.

Jordan has suffered from instability arising from the Arab–Israeli conflict since the creation of the State of Israel in 1948. After the first Arab–Israeli War in 1948–9, Jordan acquired East Jerusalem and a fertile area called the West Bank. In 1967, Israel occupied this area. In Jordan, the presence of Palestinian refugees led to civil war in 1970–1.

In 1974, Arab leaders declared that the PLO (Palestine Liberation Organization) was the sole representative of the Palestinian people. In 1988, King Hussein of Jordan renounced his country's claims to the West Bank and passed responsibility for it to the PLO. In 1991, opposition parties were legalized and multiparty elections were held in 1993.

In October 1994, Jordan and Israel signed a peace treaty ending a state of war which had been going on for over 40 years. Jordan's King Hussein continued to command respect by playing an important role in Middle Eastern affairs until his death in 1999.

Jordan lacks natural resources, apart from phosphates and potash, and the country's economy depends substantially on aid. The World Bank classifies Jordan as a 'lower-middle-income' developing country. Less than 6% of the land is farmed or used as pasture. Jordan has an oil refinery and manufactures include cement, pharmaceuticals, processed food, fertilizers and textiles.

AREA 89,210 sq km [34,444 sq mls]
POPULATION 4,435,000
CAPITAL (POPULATION) Amman (1,300,000)
GOVERNMENT Constitutional monarchy
ETHNIC GROUPS Arab 99%, of which Palestinians make up roughly half
LANGUAGES Arabic (official)
RELIGIONS Islam 93%, Christianity 5%
CURRENCY Jordan dinar = 1,000 fils

KAZAKSTAN

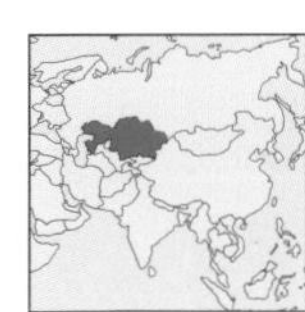

GEOGRAPHY Kazakstan is a large country in west-central Asia. In the west, the Caspian Sea lowlands include the Karagiye depression, which reaches 132 m [433 ft] below sea level. The lowlands extend eastwards through the Aral Sea area. The north contains high plains, but the highest land is along the eastern and southern borders. These areas include parts of the Altai and Tian Shan mountain ranges.

Eastern Kazakstan contains several freshwater lakes, the largest of which is Lake Balkhash. The water in the rivers has been used for irrigation, causing ecological problems. For example, the Aral Sea, deprived of water, shrank from 66,900 sq km [25,830 sq mls] in 1960 to 33,642 sq km [12,989 sq mls] in 1993. Areas which once provided fish have dried up and are now barren desert.

The climate reflects Kazakstan's position in the heart of Asia, far from the moderating influence of the oceans. Winters are cold and snow covers the land for about 100 days, on average, at Almaty. The rainfall is generally low.

POLITICS & ECONOMY After the Russian Revolution of 1917, many Kazaks wanted to make their country independent. But the Communists prevailed and in 1936 Kazakstan became a republic of the Soviet Union, called the Kazak Soviet Socialist Republic. During World War II and also after the war, the Soviet government moved many people from the west into Kazakstan. From the 1950s, people were encouraged to work on a 'Virgin Lands' project, which involved bringing large areas of grassland under cultivation.

Reforms in the Soviet Union in the 1980s led to the break-up of the country in December 1991. Kazakstan kept contacts with Russia and most of the other republics in the former Soviet Union by joining the Commonwealth of Independent States (CIS), and in 1995 Kazakstan announced that its army would unite with that of Russia. In December 1997, the government moved the capital from Almaty to Aqmola (later renamed Astana), a town in the Russian-dominated north. It was hoped that this move would bring some Kazak identity to the area.

The World Bank classifies Kazakstan as a 'lower-middle-income' developing country. Livestock farming, especially sheep and cattle, is an important activity, and major crops include barley, cotton, rice and wheat. The country is rich in mineral resources, including coal and oil reserves, together with bauxite, copper, lead, tungsten and zinc. Manufactures include chemicals, food products, machinery and textiles. Oil is exported via a pipeline through Russia, though, to reduce dependence on Russia, Kazakstan signed an agreement in 1997 to build a new pipeline to China. Other exports include metals, chemicals, grain, wool and meat.

AREA 2,717,300 sq km [1,049,150 sq mls]
POPULATION 16,847,000
CAPITAL (POPULATION) Astana (280,000)
GOVERNMENT Multiparty republic
ETHNIC GROUPS Kazak 40%, Russian 38%, German 6%, Ukrainian 5%, Uzbek, Tatar
LANGUAGES Kazak (official); Russian, the former official language, is widely spoken
RELIGIONS Mainly Islam, with a Christian minority
CURRENCY Tenge

KENYA

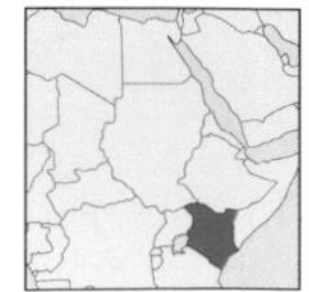

GEOGRAPHY The Republic of Kenya is a country in East Africa which straddles the Equator. It is slightly larger in area than France. Behind the narrow coastal plain on the Indian Ocean, the land rises to high plains and highlands, broken by volcanic mountains, including Mount Kenya, the country's highest peak at 5,199 m [17,057 ft]. Crossing the country is an arm of the Great Rift Valley, on the floor of which are several lakes, including Baringo, Magadi, Naivasha, Nakuru and, on the northern frontier, Lake Turkana (formerly Lake Rudolf).

Mombasa on the coast is hot and humid. But inland, the climate is moderated by the height of the land. As a result, Nairobi, in the thickly populated south-western highlands, has summer temperatures which are 10°C [18°F] lower than Mombasa. Nights can be cool, but temperatures do not fall below freezing. Nairobi's main rainy season is from April to May, with 'little rains' in November and December. However, only about 15% of the country has a reliable rainfall of 800 mm [31 in].

POLITICS & ECONOMY The Kenyan coast has been a trading centre for more than 2,000 years. Britain took over the coast in 1895 and soon extended its influence inland. In the 1950s, a secret movement, called Mau Mau, launched an armed struggle against British rule. Although Mau Mau was eventually defeated, Kenya became independent in 1963.

Many Kenyan leaders felt that the division of the population into 40 ethnic groups might lead to instability. They argued that Kenya should have a strong central government and it was a one-party state for much of the time since independence. Multiparty democracy was restored in the early 1990s and elections were held in 1992 and 1997, each resulting in a victory for the ruling president Daniel Arap Moi.

According to the United Nations, Kenya is a 'low-income' developing country. Agriculture employs about 80% of the people, but many Kenyans are subsistence farmers, growing little more than they need to support their families. The chief food crop is maize. The main cash crops and leading exports are coffee and tea. Manufactures include chemicals, leather and footwear, processed food, petroleum products and textiles.

AREA 580,370 sq km [224,081 sq mls]
POPULATION 28,337,000
CAPITAL (POPULATION) Nairobi (2,000,000)
GOVERNMENT Multiparty republic
ETHNIC GROUPS Kikuyu 21%, Luhya 14%, Luo 13%, Kamba 11%, Kalenjin 11%
LANGUAGES Swahili and English (both official)
RELIGIONS Christianity (Roman Catholic 27%, Protestant 19%, others 27%), traditional beliefs 19%, Islam 6%
CURRENCY Kenya shilling = 100 cents

KIRIBATI

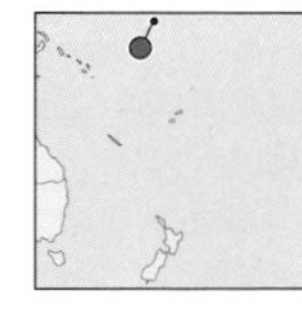

The Republic of Kiribati comprises three groups of corall atolls scattered over about 5 million sq km [2 million sq mls]. Kiribati straddles the equator and temperatures are high and the rainfall is abundant.

Formerly part of the British Gilbert and Ellice Islands, Kiribati became independent in 1979. The main export is copra and the country depends heavily on foreign aid. **AREA** 728 sq km [281 sq mls]; **POPULATION** 85,000; **CAPITAL** Tarawa.

KOREA, NORTH

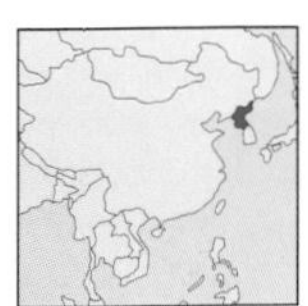

GEOGRAPHY The Democratic People's Republic of Korea occupies the northern part of the Korean peninsula which extends south from north-eastern China. Mountains form the heart of the country, with the highest peak, Paektu-san, reaching 2,744 m [9,003 ft] on the northern border.

North Korea has a fairly severe climate, with bitterly cold winters when winds blow from across central Asia, bringing snow and freezing conditions. In summer, moist winds from the oceans bring rain.

POLITICS & ECONOMY North Korea was created in 1945, when the peninsula, a Japanese colony since 1910, was divided into two parts. Soviet forces occupied the north, with US forces in the south. Soviet occupation led to a Communist government being established in 1948 under the leadership of Kim Il Sung. He initiated a Stalinist regime in which he assumed the role of dictator, and a personality cult developed around him. He was to become the world's most durable Communist leader.

The Korean War began in June 1950 when North Korean troops invaded the south. North Korea, aided by China and the Soviet Union, fought with South Korea, which was supported by troops from the United States and other UN members. The war ended in July 1953. An armistice was signed but no permanent peace treaty was agreed. After the war, North Korea adopted a hostile policy towards South Korea in pursuit of its policy of reunification. At times, the situation grew so tense that it became a matter of international concern.

The ending of the Cold War in the late 1980s eased the situation and both North and South Korea joined the United Nations in 1991. The two countries made several agreements, including one in which they agreed not to use force against each other.

As Communism collapsed in the Soviet Union, however, North Korea remained as isolated as ever, pursuing the overriding principle of self-reliance.

In 1993, North Korea began a new international crisis by announcing that it was withdrawing from the Nuclear Non-Proliferation Treaty. This led to suspicions that North Korea, which had signed the Treaty in 1985, was developing its own nuclear weapons. Kim Il Sung, who had ruled as a virtual dictator from 1948 until his death in 1994, was succeeded by his son, Kim Jong Il.

North Korea has considerable resources, including coal, copper, iron ore, lead, tin, tungsten and zinc. Under Communism, North Korea has concentrated on developing heavy, state-owned industries. Manufactures include chemicals, iron and steel, machinery, processed food and textiles. Agriculture employs about a third of the people of North Korea and rice is the leading crop. Economic decline and mismanagement, aggravated by three successive crop failures caused by floods in 1995 and 1996 and a drought in 1997, led to famine on a large scale.

AREA 120,540 sq km [46,540 sq mls]
POPULATION 21,234,000
CAPITAL (POPULATION) Pyŏngyang (2,639,000)
GOVERNMENT Single-party people's republic
ETHNIC GROUPS Korean 99%
LANGUAGES Korean (official)
RELIGIONS Traditional beliefs 16%, Chondogyo 14%, Buddhism 2%, Christianity 1%
CURRENCY North Korean won = 100 chon

KOREA, SOUTH

GEOGRAPHY The Republic of Korea, as South Korea is officially known, occupies the southern part of the Korean peninsula. Mountains cover much of the country. The southern and western coasts are major farming regions. Many islands are found along the west and south coasts. The largest is Cheju-do, which contains South Korea's highest peak, which rises to 1,950 m [6,398 ft].

Like North Korea, South Korea is chilled in winter by cold, dry winds blowing from central Asia. Snow often covers the mountains in the east. The summers are hot and wet, especially in July and August.

POLITICS & ECONOMY After Japan's defeat in World War II (1939–45), North Korea was occupied by troops from the Soviet Union, while South Korea was occupied by United States forces. Attempts to reunify Korea failed and, in 1948, a National Assembly was elected in South Korea. This Assembly created the Republic of Korea, while North Korea became a Communist state. North Korean troops invaded the South in June 1950, sparking off the Korean War (1950–3).

In the 1950s, South Korea had a weak economy, which had been further damaged by the destruction caused by the Korean War. From the 1960s to the 1980s, South Korean governments worked to industrialize the economy. The governments were dominated by military leaders, who often used authoritarian methods, imprisoning opponents and restricting freedom of speech. In 1987, a new constitution was approved, enabling presidential elections to be held every five years.

In 1991, both South and North Korea became members of the United Nations. The two countries signed several agreements, including one in which they agreed not to use force against each other. But tensions between them continued.

The World Bank classifies South Korea as an 'upper-middle-income' developing country. It is also one of the world's fastest growing industrial economies. The country's resources include coal and tungsten, and its main manufactures are processed food and textiles. Since partition, heavy industries have been built up, making chemicals, fertilizers, iron and steel, and ships. South Korea has also developed the production of such things as computers, cars and television sets. In late 1997, however, the dramatic expansion of the economy was halted by a market crash which affected many of the booming economies of Asia. In an effort to negate the economic and social turmoil that resulted, tough reforms were demanded by the International Monetary Fund and an agreement was reached to restructure much of the short-term debt faced by the government.

Farming remains important in South Korea. Rice is the chief crop, together with fruit, grains and vegetables, while fishing provides a major source of protein.

AREA 99,020 sq km [38,232 sq mls]
POPULATION 46,417,000
CAPITAL (POPULATION) Seoul (11,641,000)
GOVERNMENT Multiparty republic
ETHNIC GROUPS Korean 99%
LANGUAGES Korean (official)
RELIGIONS Buddhism 28%, Christianity (Protestant 19%, Roman Catholic 6%)
CURRENCY South Korean won = 100 chon

KUWAIT

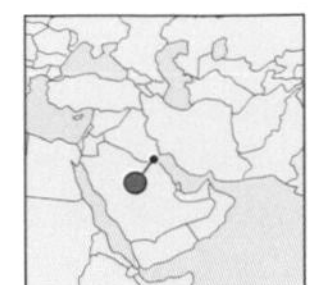

The State of Kuwait at the north end of the Gulf is largely made up of desert. Temperatures are high and the rainfall low. Kuwait became independent from Britain in 1961 and revenues from its oil wells have made it highly prosperous. Iraq invaded Kuwait in 1990 and much damage was inflicted in the ensuing conflict in 1991 when Kuwait was liberated. **AREA** 17,820 sq km [6,880 sq mls]; **POPULATION** 1,913,000; **CAPITAL** Kuwait City.

KYRGYZSTAN

GEOGRAPHY The Republic of Kyrgyzstan is a landlocked country between China, Tajikistan, Uzbekistan and Kazakstan. The country is mountainous, with spectacular scenery. The highest mountain, Pik Pobedy in the Tian Shan range, reaches 7,439 m [24,406 ft] in the east.

The lowlands of Kyrgyzstan have warm summers and cold winters. But the altitude influences the climate in the mountains, where the January temperatures plummet to –28°C [–18°F]. Far from any sea, Kyrgyzstan has a low annual rainfall.

POLITICS & ECONOMY In 1876, Kyrgyzstan became a province of Russia and Russian settlement in the area began. In 1916, Russia crushed a rebellion among the Kyrgyz, and many subsequently fled to China. In 1922, the area became an autonomous *oblast* (self-governing region) of the newly formed Soviet Union but, in 1936, it became one of the Soviet Socialist Republics. Under Communist rule, nomads were forced to work on government-run farms, while local customs and religious worship were suppressed. However, there were concurrent improvements in education and health.

In 1991, Kyrgyzstan became an independent country following the break-up of the Soviet Union. The Communist party was dissolved, but the country maintained ties with Russia through an organization called the Commonwealth of Independent States. Kyrgyzstan adopted a new constitution in 1994 and parliamentary elections were held in 1995.

In the early 1990s, when Kyrgyzstan was working to reform its economy, the World Bank classified it as a 'lower-middle-income' developing country. Agriculture, especially livestock rearing, is the chief activity. The chief products include cotton, eggs, fruits, grain, tobacco, vegetables and wool. But food must be imported. Industries are mainly concentrated around the capital Bishkek.

AREA 198,500 sq km [76,640 sq mls]
POPULATION 4,522,000
CAPITAL (POPULATION) Bishkek (584,000)
GOVERNMENT Multiparty republic
ETHNIC GROUPS Kyrgyz 52%, Russian 22%, Uzbek 13%, Ukrainian 3%, German 2%, Tatar 2%
LANGUAGES Kyrgyz (official), Russian, Uzbek
RELIGIONS Islam
CURRENCY Som = 100 tyiyn

LAOS

GEOGRAPHY The Lao People's Democratic Republic is a landlocked country in South-east Asia. Mountains and plateaux cover much of the country.

Most people live on the plains bordering the River Mekong and its tributaries. This river, one of Asia's longest, forms much of the country's north-western and south-western borders.

Laos has a tropical monsoon climate. Winters are dry and sunny, with winds blowing in from the north-east. The temperatures rise until April, when the wind directions are reversed and moist south-westerly winds reach Laos, heralding the start of the wet monsoon season.

POLITICS & ECONOMY France made Laos a protectorate in the late 19th century and ruled it as part of French Indo-China, a region which also included Cambodia and Vietnam. Laos became a member of the French Union in 1948 and an independent kingdom in 1954.

After independence, Laos suffered from instability caused by a long power struggle between royalist government forces and a pro-Communist group called the Pathet Lao. A civil war broke out in 1960 and continued into the 1970s. The Pathet Lao took control in 1975 and the king abdicated. Laos then came under the influence of Communist Vietnam, which had used Laos as a supply base during the Vietnam War (1957–75). However, from the late 1980s, Laos began to introduce economic reforms, including the encouragement of private enterprise.

Laos is one of the world's poorest countries. Agriculture employs about 76% of the people, as compared with 7% in industry and 17% in services. Rice is the main crop, and timber and coffee are both exported. But the most valuable export is electricity, which is produced at hydroelectric power stations on the River Mekong and is exported to Thailand. Laos also produces opium. In the early 1990s, Laos was thought to be the world's third biggest source of this illegal drug.

AREA 236,800 sq km [91,428 sq mls]
POPULATION 5,261,000
CAPITAL (POPULATION) Vientiane (449,000)
GOVERNMENT Single-party republic
ETHNIC GROUPS Lao 67%, Mon-Khmer 17%, Tai 8%
LANGUAGES Lao (official), Khmer, Tai, Miao
RELIGIONS Buddhism 58%, traditional beliefs 34%, Christianity 2%, Islam 1%
CURRENCY Kip = 100 at

LATVIA

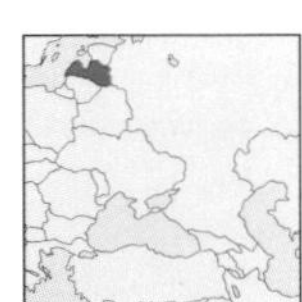

GEOGRAPHY The Republic of Latvia is one of three states on the south-eastern corner of the Baltic Sea which were ruled as parts of the Soviet Union between 1940 and 1991. Latvia consists mainly of flat plains separated by low hills, composed of moraine (ice-worn rocks).

Riga has warm summers, but the winter months

(from December to March) are subzero. In the winter, the sea often freezes over. The rainfall is moderate and it occurs throughout the year, with light snow in winter.

POLITICS & ECONOMY In 1800, Russia was in control of Latvia, but Latvians declared their independence after World War I. In 1940, under a German-Soviet pact, Soviet troops occupied Latvia, but they were driven out by the Germans in 1941. Soviet troops returned in 1944 and Latvia became part of the Soviet Union. Under Soviet rule, many Russian immigrants settled in Latvia and many Latvians feared that the Russians would become the dominant ethnic group.

In the late 1980s, when reforms were being introduced in the Soviet Union, Latvia's government ended absolute Communist rule and made Latvian the official language. In 1990, it declared the country to be independent, an act which was finally recognized by the Soviet Union in September 1991.

Latvia held its first free elections to its parliament (the Saeima) in 1993. Voting was limited only to citizens of Latvia on 17 June 1940 and their descendants. This meant that about 34% of Latvian residents were unable to vote. In 1994, Latvia restricted the naturalization of non-Latvians, including many Russian settlers, who were not allowed to vote or own land. However, in 1998, the government agreed that all children born since independence should have automatic citizenship regardless of the status of their parents.

The World Bank classifies Latvia as a 'lower-middle-income' country and, in the 1990s, it faced many problems in turning its economy into a free-market system. Products include electronic goods, farm machinery, fertilizers, processed food, plastics, radios and vehicles. Latvia produces only about a tenth of the electricity it needs. It imports the rest from Belarus, Russia and Ukraine.

AREA 64,589 sq km [24,938 sq mls]
POPULATION 2,385,000
CAPITAL (POPULATION) Riga (840,000)
GOVERNMENT Multiparty republic
ETHNIC GROUPS Latvian 53%, Russian 34%, Belarussian 4%, Ukrainian 3%, Polish 2%, Lithuanian, Jewish
LANGUAGES Latvian (official), Russian
RELIGIONS Christianity (including Lutheran, Russian Orthodox and Roman Catholic)
CURRENCY Lats = 10 santimi

LEBANON

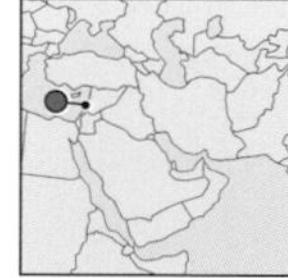

GEOGRAPHY The Republic of Lebanon is a country on the eastern shores of the Mediterranean Sea. Behind the coastal plain are the rugged Lebanon Mountains (Jabal Lubnan), which rise to 3,088 m [10,131 ft]. Another range, the Anti-Lebanon Mountains (Al Jabal Ash Sharqi), form the eastern border with Syria. Between the two ranges is the Bekaa (Beqaa) Valley, a fertile farming region.

The Lebanese coast has the hot, dry summers and mild, wet winters that are typical of many Mediterranean lands. Inland, onshore winds bring heavy rain to the western slopes of the mountains in the winter months, with snow at the higher altitudes.

POLITICS & ECONOMY Lebanon was ruled by Turkey from 1516 until World War I. France ruled the country from 1923, but Lebanon became independent in 1946. After independence, the Muslims and Christians agreed to share power, and Lebanon made rapid economic progress. But from the late 1950s, development was slowed by periodic conflict between Sunni and Shia Muslims, Druze and Christians. The situation was further complicated by the presence of Palestinian refugees who used bases in Lebanon to attack Israel.

In 1975, civil war broke out as private armies representing the many factions struggled for power. This led to intervention by Israel in the south and Syria in the north. UN peacekeeping forces arrived in 1978, but bombings, assassinations and kidnappings became almost everyday events in the 1980s. From 1991, Lebanon enjoyed an uneasy peace. However, Israel continued to occupy an area in the south and, periodically, Israel launched attacks on pro-Iranian (Shia) Hezbollah guerrilla bases in Lebanon.

Lebanon's civil war almost destroyed the valuable trade and financial services which had been Lebanon's chief source of income, together with tourism. The manufacturing industry, formerly another major activity, was also badly hit and many factories were damaged.

AREA 10,400 sq km [4,015 sq mls]
POPULATION 3,506,000
CAPITAL (POPULATION) Beirut (1,500,000)
GOVERNMENT Multiparty republic
ETHNIC GROUPS Arab (Lebanese 80%, Palestinian 12%), Armenian 5%, Syrian, Kurdish
LANGUAGES Arabic (official)
RELIGIONS Islam 58%, Christianity 27%, Druse
CURRENCY Lebanese pound = 100 piastres

LESOTHO

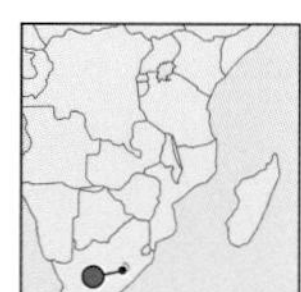

GEOGRAPHY The Kingdom of Lesotho is a landlocked country, completely enclosed by South Africa. The land is mountainous, rising to 3,482 m [11,424 ft] on the north-eastern border. The Drakensberg range covers most of the country.

The climate of Lesotho is greatly affected by the altitude, because most of the country lies above 1,500 m [4,921 ft]. Maseru has warm summers, but the temperatures fall below freezing in the winter. The mountains are colder. The rainfall varies, averaging around 700 mm [28 in].

POLITICS & ECONOMY The Basotho nation was founded in the 1820s by King Moshoeshoe I, who united various groups fleeing from tribal wars in southern Africa. Britain made the area a protectorate in 1868 and, in 1971, placed it under the British Cape Colony in South Africa. But in 1884, Basutoland, as the area was called, was reconstituted as a British protectorate, where whites were not allowed to own land.

The country finally became independent in 1966 as the Kingdom of Lesotho, with Moshoeshoe II, great-grandson of Moshoeshoe I, as its king. Since independence, Lesotho has suffered instability. The military seized power in 1986 and stripped Moshoeshoe II of his powers in 1990, installing his son, Letsie III, as monarch. After elections in 1993, Moshoeshoe II was restored to office in 1995. But after his death in a car crash in 1996, Letsie III again became king. In 1998, an army revolt, following an election in which the ruling party won 79 out of the 80 seats, caused much damage to the economy, despite the intervention of a South African force intended to maintain order.

Lesotho is a 'low-income' developing country. It lacks natural resources. Agriculture, mainly at subsistence level, light manufacturing and money sent home by Basotho working abroad are the main sources of income.

AREA 30,350 sq km [11,718 sq mls]
POPULATION 2,090,000
CAPITAL (POPULATION) Maseru (130,000)
GOVERNMENT Constitutional monarchy
ETHNIC GROUPS Sotho 99%
LANGUAGES Sesotho and English (both official)
RELIGIONS Christianity 93% (Roman Catholic 44%), traditional beliefs 6%
CURRENCY Loti = 100 lisente

LIBERIA

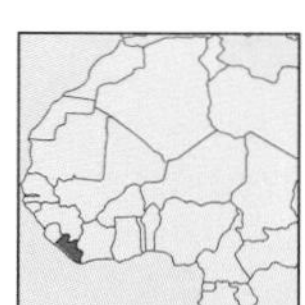

GEOGRAPHY The Republic of Liberia is a country in West Africa. Behind the coastline, 500 km [311 mls] long, lies a narrow coastal plain. Beyond, the land rises to a plateau region, with the highest land along the border with Guinea.

Liberia has a tropical climate with high temperatures and high humidity all through the year. The rainfall is abundant all year round, but there is a particularly wet period from June to November. The rainfall generally increases from east to west.

POLITICS & ECONOMY In the late 18th century, some white Americans in the United States wanted to help freed black slaves to return to Africa. In 1816, they set up the American Colonization Society, which bought land in what is now Liberia.

In 1822, the Society landed former slaves at a settlement on the coast which they named Monrovia. In 1847, Liberia became a fully independent republic with a constitution much like that of the United States. For many years, the Americo-Liberians controlled the country's government. US influence remained strong and the American Firestone Company, which ran Liberia's rubber plantations, was especially influential. Foreign companies were also involved in exploiting Liberia's mineral resources, including its huge iron-ore deposits.

In 1980, a military group composed of people from the local population killed the Americo-Liberian president, William R. Tolbert. An army sergeant, Samuel K. Doe, was made president of Liberia. Elections held in 1985 resulted in victory for Doe.

From 1989, the country was plunged into civil war between various ethnic groups. Doe was assassinated in 1990, but his successor, Amos Sawyer, continued to struggle with rebel groups. Peacekeeping forces from other West African countries arrived in Liberia, but the fighting continued. In 1995, a cease-fire was agreed and a council of state, composed of former warlords, was set up. In 1997, one of the warlords, Charles Taylor, was elected president.

Liberia's civil war devastated its economy. Three out of every four people depend on agriculture, though many of them grow little more than they need to feed their families. The chief food crops include cassava, rice and sugar cane, while rubber, cocoa and coffee are grown for export. But the most valuable export is iron ore.

Liberia also obtains revenue from its 'flag of

convenience', which is used by about one-sixth of the world's commercial shipping, exploiting low taxes.

AREA 111,370 sq km [43,000 sq mls]
POPULATION 2,772,000
CAPITAL (POPULATION) Monrovia (490,000)
GOVERNMENT Multiparty republic
ETHNIC GROUPS Kpelle 19%, Bassa 14%, Grebo 9%, Gio 8%, Kru 7%, Mano 7%
LANGUAGES English (official), Mande, Mel, Kwa
RELIGIONS Christianity 68%, Islam 14%, traditional beliefs and others 18%
CURRENCY Liberian dollar = 100 cents

LIBYA

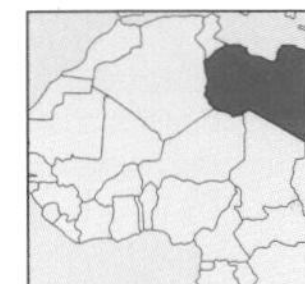

GEOGRAPHY The Socialist People's Libyan Arab Jamahiriya, as Libya is officially called, is a large country in North Africa. Most people live on the coastal plains in the north-east and north-west. The Sahara, the world's largest desert which occupies 95% of Libya, reaches the Mediterranean coast along the Gulf of Sidra (Khalij Surt).

The coastal plains in the north-east and north-west of the country have Mediterranean climates, with hot, dry summers and mild winters, with some rain in the winter months. Inland, the average yearly rainfall drops to 100 mm [4 in] or less.

POLITICS & ECONOMY Italy took over Libya in 1911, but lost it during World War II. Britain and France then jointly ruled Libya until 1951, when the country became an independent kingdom.

In 1969, a military group headed by Colonel Muammar Gaddafi deposed the king and set up a military government. Under Gaddafi, the government took control of the economy and used money from oil exports to finance welfare services and development projects. Gaddafi has attracted international criticism for his support for radical movements, such as the PLO (Palestine Liberation Organization) and various terrorist groups. In 1986, his policies led the United States to bomb installations in the capital. Libya has disputes with its neighbours, including Chad, where it sent troops to intervene in a civil war. In 1994, the International Court of Justice ruled against Libya's claim for territory in the Aozou Strip in northern Chad.

The discovery of oil and natural gas in 1959 led to the transformation of Libya's economy. Formerly one of the world's poorest countries, it has become Africa's richest in terms of its per capita income. But it remains a developing country because of its dependence on oil, which accounts for nearly all of its export revenues.

Agriculture is important, although Libya has to import food. Crops include barley, citrus fruits, dates, olives, potatoes and wheat. Cattle, sheep and poultry are raised. Libya has oil refineries and petrochemical plants. Other manufactures include cement and steel.

AREA 1,759,540 sq km [679,358 sq mls]
POPULATION 4,875,000
CAPITAL (POPULATION) Tripoli (960,000)
GOVERNMENT Single-party socialist state
ETHNIC GROUPS Libyan Arab and Berber 89%
LANGUAGES Arabic (official), Berber
RELIGIONS Islam
CURRENCY Libyan dinar = 1,000 dirhams

LIECHTENSTEIN

The tiny Principality of Liechtenstein is sandwiched between Switzerland and Austria. The River Rhine flows along its western border, while Alpine peaks rise in the east and south. The climate is relatively mild. Since 1924, Liechtenstein has been in a customs union with Switzerland and, like its neighbour, it is extremely prosperous. Taxation is low and, as a result, the country has become a haven for international companies. **AREA** 157 sq km [61 sq mls]; **POPULATION** 32,000; **CAPITAL** Vaduz.

LITHUANIA

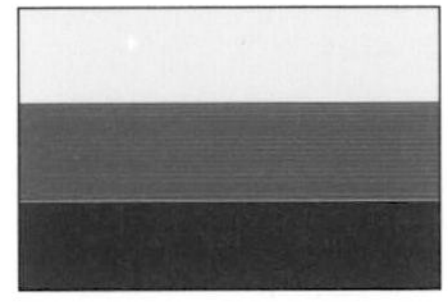
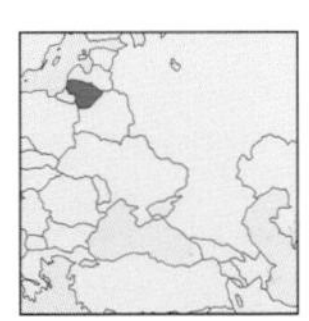

GEOGRAPHY The Republic of Lithuania is the southernmost of the three Baltic states which were ruled as part of the Soviet Union between 1940 and 1991. Much of the land is flat or gently rolling, with the highest land in the south-east.

Winters are cold. January's temperatures average –3°C [27°F] in the west and –6°C [21°F] in the east. Summers are warm, with average temperatures in July of 17°C [63°F]. The average rainfall in the west is about 630 mm [25 in]. Inland areas are drier.

POLITICS & ECONOMY The Lithuanian people were united into a single nation in the 12th century, and later joined a union with Poland. In 1795, Lithuania came under Russian rule. After World War I (1914–18), Lithuania declared itself independent, and in 1920 it signed a peace treaty with the Russians, though Poland held Vilnius until 1939. In 1940, the Soviet Union occupied Lithuania, but the Germans invaded in 1941. Soviet forces returned in 1944, and Lithuania was integrated into the Soviet Union. In 1988, when the Soviet Union was introducing reforms, the Lithuanians demanded independence. Their language is one of the oldest in the world, and the country was always the most homogenous of the Baltic states, staunchly Catholic and resistant of attempts to suppress their culture. Pro-independence groups won the national elections in 1990 and, in 1991, the Soviet Union recognized Lithuania's independence.

After independence, Lithuania faced many problems as it sought to reform its economy and introduce a private enterprise system. In 1998, Valdas Adamkus, a Lithuanian-American who had fled the country in 1944, was elected president.

The World Bank classifies Lithuania as a 'lower-middle-income' developing country. Lithuania lacks natural resources, but manufacturing, based on imported materials, is the most valuable activity.

AREA 65,200 sq km [25,200 sq mls]
POPULATION 3,600,000
CAPITAL (POPULATION) Vilnius (576,000)
GOVERNMENT Multiparty republic
ETHNIC GROUPS Lithuanian 80%, Russian 9%, Polish 7%, Belarussian 2%
LANGUAGES Lithuanian (official), Russian, Polish
RELIGIONS Christianity (mainly Roman Catholic)
CURRENCY Litas = 100 centai

LUXEMBOURG

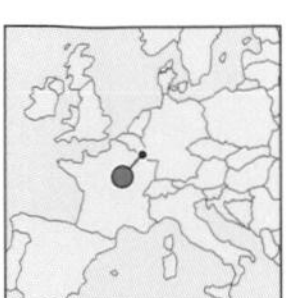

GEOGRAPHY The Grand Duchy of Luxembourg is one of the smallest and oldest countries in Europe. The north belongs to an upland region which includes the Ardenne in Belgium and Luxembourg, and the Eifel highlands in Germany.

Luxembourg has a temperate climate. The south has warm summers and autumns, when grapes ripen in sheltered south-eastern valleys. Winters are sometimes severe, especially in upland areas.

POLITICS & ECONOMY Germany occupied Luxembourg in World Wars I and II. In 1944–5, northern Luxembourg was the scene of the famous Battle of the Bulge. In 1948, Luxembourg joined Belgium and the Netherlands in a union called Benelux and, in the 1950s, it was one of the six founders of what is now the European Union. Luxembourg has played a major role in Europe. Its capital contains the headquarters of several international agencies, including the European Coal and Steel Community and the European Court of Justice. The city is also a major financial centre.

Luxembourg has iron-ore reserves and is a major steel producer. It also has many high-technology industries, producing electronic goods and computers. Steel and other manufactures, including chemicals, rubber products, glass and aluminium, dominate the country's exports. Other major activities include tourism and financial services.

AREA 2,590 sq km [1,000 sq mls]
POPULATION 425,000
CAPITAL (POPULATION) Luxembourg (76,000)
GOVERNMENT Constitutional monarchy (Grand Duchy)
ETHNIC GROUPS Luxembourger 71%, Portuguese 10%, Italian 5%, French 3%, Belgian 3%
LANGUAGES Letzeburgish/Luxembourgian (official), French, German
RELIGIONS Christianity (Roman Catholic 95%)
CURRENCY Euro; Luxem. franc = 100 centimes

MACAU

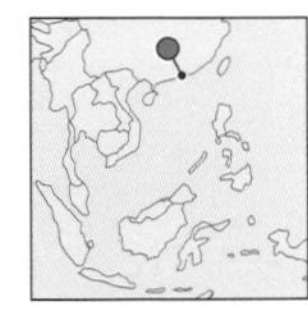

Macau is a small peninsula at the head of the Zhu Jiang (Pearl) River, west of Hong Kong. A Portuguese colony since 1557, Macau was returned to China in 1999. Its main industries are textiles, gambling and tourism. **AREA** 16 sq km [6 sq mls]; **POPULATION** 429,000; **CAPITAL** Macau.

MACEDONIA

GEOGRAPHY The Republic of Macedonia is a country in south-eastern Europe, which was once one of the six republics that made up the former Federal People's Republic of Yugoslavia. This landlocked country is largely mountainous or hilly.

Macedonia has hot summers, though highland areas are cooler. Winters are cold and snowfalls are often heavy. The climate is fairly continental in character and rain occurs throughout the year.

POLITICS & ECONOMY Between 1912 and 1913, the area called Macedonia was divided between Serbia, Bulgaria, which took a small area in the east, and Greece, which gained the south. At the end of World War I, Serbian Macedonia became part of the Kingdom of the Serbs, Croats and Slovenes, which was renamed Yugoslavia in 1929. After World War II, Yugoslavia became a Communist regime.

Tito died in 1980 and, in the early 1990s, the country broke up into five separate republics. Macedonia declared its independence in September 1991. Greece objected to this territory using the name Macedonia, which it considered to be a Greek name. It also objected to a symbol on Macedonia's flag and a reference in the constitution to the desire to reunite the three parts of the old Macedonia.

Macedonia adopted a new clause in its constitution rejecting any Macedonian claims on Greek territory and, in 1993, the United Nations accepted the new republic as a member under the name of The Former Yugoslav Republic of Macedonia (FYROM).

By the end of 1993, all the countries of the European Union, except Greece, were establishing diplomatic relations with the FYROM. Greece barred Macedonian trade in 1994, but lifted the ban in 1995 when Macedonia agreed to redesign its flag and remove all territorial claims from its constitution.

In 1999, Macedonia faced new problems caused by the influx of ethnic Albanian refugees from neighbouring Kosovo, Yugoslavia.

The World Bank describes Macedonia as a 'lower-middle-income' developing country. Manufactures dominate the country's exports. Macedonia mines coal, but imports all its oil and natural gas. The country is self-sufficient in its basic food needs.

AREA 25,710 sq km [9,927 sq mls]
POPULATION 2,009,000
CAPITAL (POPULATION) Skopje (541,000)
GOVERNMENT Multiparty republic
ETHNIC GROUPS Macedonian 65%, Albanian 21%, Turkish 5%, Romanian 3%, Serb 2%
LANGUAGES Macedonian (official), Albanian
RELIGIONS Christianity (mainly Eastern Orthodox, with Macedonian Orthodox and Roman Catholic communities), Islam
CURRENCY Dinar = 100 paras

MADAGASCAR

GEOGRAPHY The Democratic Republic of Madagascar, in south-eastern Africa, is an island nation, which has a larger area than France. Behind the narrow coastal plains in the east lies a highland zone, mostly between 610 m and 1,220 m [2,000 ft to 4,000 ft] above sea level. Broad plains border the Mozambique Channel in the west.

Temperatures in the highlands are moderated by the altitude. The winters (from April to September) are dry, but heavy rains occur in summer. The eastern coastlands are warm and humid. The west is drier and the south and south-west are hot and dry.

POLITICS & ECONOMY People from South-east Asia began to settle on Madagascar around 2,000 years ago. Subsequent influxes from Africa and Arabia added to the island's diverse heritage, culture and language.

French troops defeated a Malagasy army in 1895 and Madagascar became a French colony. In 1960, it achieved full independence as the Malagasy Republic. In 1972, army officers seized control and, in 1975, under the leadership of Lt-Commander Didier Ratsiraka, the country was renamed Madagascar. Parliamentary elections were held in 1977, but Ratsiraka remained president of a one-party socialist state. The government resigned in 1991 following huge demonstrations. In 1992–3, Ratsiraka was defeated by opposition leader, Albert Zafy. But Ratsiraka returned to power following presidential elections in 1996.

Madagascar is one of the world's poorest countries. The land has been badly eroded because of the cutting down of the forests and overgrazing of the grasslands. Farming, fishing and forestry employ about 80% of the people. The country's food crops include bananas, cassava, rice and sweet potatoes. Coffee is the leading export.

AREA 587,040 sq km [226,656 sq mls]
POPULATION 14,463,000
CAPITAL (POPULATION) Antananarivo (1,053,000)
GOVERNMENT Republic
ETHNIC GROUPS Merina 27%, Betsimisaraka 15%, Betsileo 11%, Tsimihety 7%, Sakalava 6%
LANGUAGES Malagasy, French (both official)
RELIGIONS Christianity 51%, traditional beliefs 47%, Islam 2%
CURRENCY Malagasy franc = 100 centimes

MALAWI

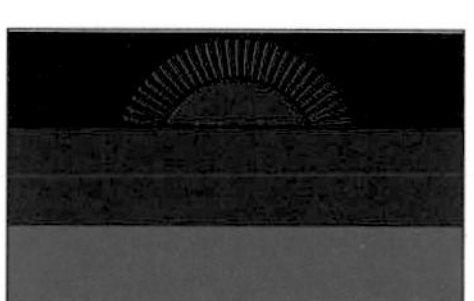

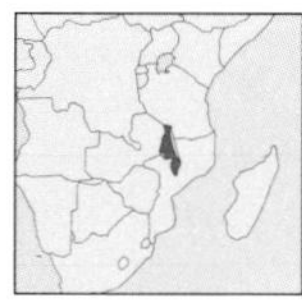

GEOGRAPHY The Republic of Malawi includes part of Lake Malawi, which is drained by the River Shire, a tributary of the River Zambezi. The land is mostly mountainous. The highest peak, Mulanje, reaches 3,000 m [9,843 ft] in the south-east.

While the low-lying areas of Malawi are hot and humid all year round, the uplands have a pleasant climate. Lilongwe, at about 1,100 m [3,609 ft] above sea level, has a warm and sunny climate. Frosts sometimes occur in July and August, in the middle of the long dry season.

POLITICS & ECONOMY Malawi, then called Nyasaland, became a British protectorate in 1891. In 1953, Britain established the Federation of Rhodesia and Nyasaland, which also included what are now Zambia and Zimbabwe. Black African opposition, led in Nyasaland by Dr Hastings Kamuzu Banda, led to the dissolution of the federation in 1963. In 1964, Nyasaland became independent as Malawi, with Banda as prime minister. Banda became president when the country became a republic in 1966 and, in 1971, he was made president for life. Banda ruled autocratically through the only party, the Malawi Congress Party. However, a multiparty system was restored in 1993, and in elections in 1994, Banda and his party were defeated and Bakili Muluzi became president. Banda died in 1997.

Malawi is one of the world's poorest countries. More than 80% of the people are farmers, but many grow little more than they need to feed their families.

AREA 118,480 sq km [45,745 sq mls]
POPULATION 9,840,000
CAPITAL (POPULATION) Lilongwe (395,000)
GOVERNMENT Multiparty republic
ETHNIC GROUPS Maravi (Chewa, Nyanja, Tonga, Tumbuka) 58%, Lomwe 18%, Yao 13%, Ngoni 7%
LANGUAGES Chichewa and English (both official)
RELIGIONS Christianity (Protestant 34%, Roman Catholic 28%), traditional beliefs 21%, Islam 16%
CURRENCY Kwacha = 100 tambala

MALAYSIA

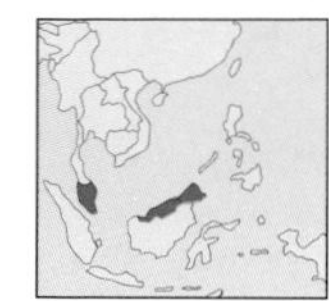

GEOGRAPHY The Federation of Malaysia consists of two main parts. Peninsular Malaysia, which is joined to mainland Asia, contains about 80% of the population. The other main regions, Sabah and Sarawak, are in northern Borneo, an island which Malaysia shares with Indonesia. Much of the land is mountainous, with coastal lowlands bordering the rugged interior. The highest peak, Kinabalu, reaches 4,101 m [13,455 ft] in Sabah.

Malaysia has a hot equatorial climate. The temperatures are high all through the year, though the mountains are much cooler than the lowland areas. The rainfall is heavy throughout the year.

POLITICS & ECONOMY Japan occupied what is now Malaysia during World War II, but British rule was re-established in 1945. In the 1940s and 1950s, British troops fought a war against Communist guerrillas, but Peninsular Malaysia (then called Malaya) became independent in 1957. Malaysia was created in 1963, when Malaya, Singapore, Sabah and Sarawak agreed to unite, but Singapore withdrew in 1965.

From the 1970s, Malaysia achieved rapid economic progress and, by the mid-1990s, it was playing a major part in regional affairs, especially through its membership of ASEAN (Association of South-east Asian Nations). However, together with several other countries in eastern Asia, Malaysia was hit by economic recession in 1997, including a major fall in stock market values. In response to the crisis, the government ordered the repatriation of many temporary foreign workers and initiated a series of austerity measures aimed at restoring confidence and avoiding the chronic debt problems affecting some other Asian countries.

The World Bank classifies Malaysia as an 'upper-middle-income' developing country. Malaysia is a leading producer of palm oil, rubber and tin.

Manufacturing now plays a major part in the economy. Manufactures are diverse, including cars, chemicals, a wide range of electronic goods, plastics, textiles, rubber and wood products.

AREA 329,750 sq km [127,316 sq mls]
POPULATION 20,993,000
CAPITAL (POPULATION) Kuala Lumpur (1,145,000)
GOVERNMENT Federal constitutional monarchy
ETHNIC GROUPS Malay and other indigenous groups 62%, Chinese 30%, Indian 8%
LANGUAGES Malay (official), Chinese, Iban
RELIGIONS Islam 53%, Buddhism 17%, Chinese folk religionist 12%, Hinduism 7%, Christianity 6%
CURRENCY Ringgit (Malaysian dollar) = 100 cents

MALDIVES

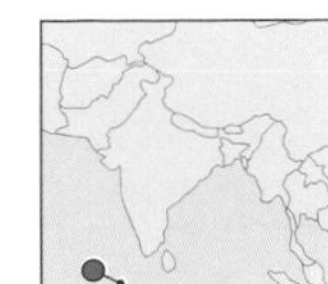

The Republic of the Maldives consists of about 1,200 low-lying coral islands, south of India. The highest point is 24 m [79 ft], but most of the land is only 1.8 m [6 ft] above sea level. The islands became a British territory in 1887 and independence was achieved in 1965. Tourism and fishing are the main industries. **AREA** 298 sq km [115 sq mls]; **POPULATION** 290,000; **CAPITAL** Malé.

MALI

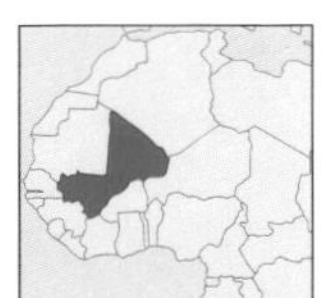

GEOGRAPHY The Republic of Mali is a landlocked country in northern Africa. The land is generally flat, with the highest land in the Adrar des Iforhas on the border with Algeria.

Northern Mali is part of the Sahara, with a hot, practically rainless climate. But the south has enough rain for farming.

POLITICS & ECONOMY France ruled the area, then known as French Sudan, from 1893 until the country became independent as Mali in 1960.

The first socialist government was overthrown in 1968 by an army group led by Moussa Traoré, but he was ousted in 1991. Multiparty democracy was restored in 1992 and Alpha Oumar Konaré was elected president. The new government agreed a pact providing for a special administration for the Tuareg minority in the north.

Mali is one of the world's poorest countries and 70% of the land is desert or semi-desert. Only about 2% of the land is used for growing crops, while 25% is used for grazing animals. Despite this, agriculture employs more than 80% of the people, many of whom still subsist by nomadic livestock rearing.

AREA 1,240,190 sq km [478,837 sq mls]
POPULATION 10,109,000
CAPITAL (POPULATION) Bamako (746,000)
GOVERNMENT Multiparty republic
ETHNIC GROUPS Bambara 32%, Fulani (or Peul) 14%, Senufo 12%, Soninke 9%, Tuareg 7%, Songhai 7%, Malinke (Mandingo or Mandinke) 7%
LANGUAGES French (official), Voltaic languages
RELIGIONS Islam 90%, traditional beliefs 9%, Christianity 1%
CURRENCY CFA franc = 100 centimes

MALTA

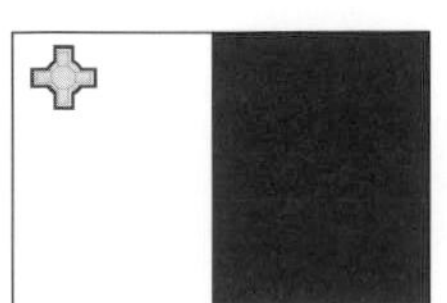
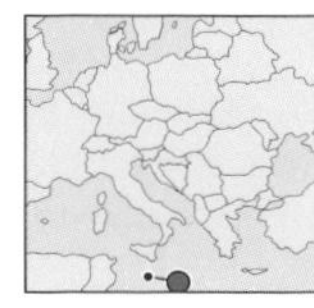

GEOGRAPHY The Republic of Malta consists of two main islands, Malta and Gozo, a third, much smaller island called Comino lying between the two large islands, and two tiny islets.

Malta's climate is typically Mediterranean, with hot and dry summers and mild and wet winters. The sirocco, a hot wind that blows from North Africa, may raise temperatures considerably during the spring.

POLITICS & ECONOMY During World War I (1914–18) Malta was an important naval base. In World War II (1939–45), Italian and German aircraft bombed the islands. In recognition of the bravery of the Maltese, the British King George VI awarded the George Cross to Malta in 1942. In 1953, Malta became a base for NATO (North Atlantic Treaty Organization). Malta became independent in 1964, and in 1974 it became a republic. In 1979, Britain's military agreement with Malta expired, and Malta ceased to be a military base when all the British forces withdrew. In the 1980s, the people declared Malta a neutral country. In the 1990s, Malta applied to join the European Union. The application was scrapped when the Labour Party won the elections in 1996, but, following the Labour Party's defeat in elections in 1998, the situation changed yet again.

The World Bank classifies Malta as an 'upper-middle-income' developing country. It lacks natural resources, and most people work in the former naval dockyards, which are now used for commercial shipbuilding and repair, in manufacturing industries and in the tourist industry.

Manufactures include chemicals, processed food and chemicals. Farming is difficult, because of the rocky soils. Crops include barley, fruits, potatoes and wheat. Malta also has a small fishing industry.

AREA 316 sq km [122 sq mls]
POPULATION 379,000
CAPITAL (POPULATION) Valletta (102,000)
GOVERNMENT Multiparty republic
ETHNIC GROUPS Maltese 96%, British 2%
LANGUAGES Maltese and English (both official)
RELIGIONS Christianity (Roman Catholic 99%)
CURRENCY Maltese lira = 100 cents

MARSHALL ISLANDS

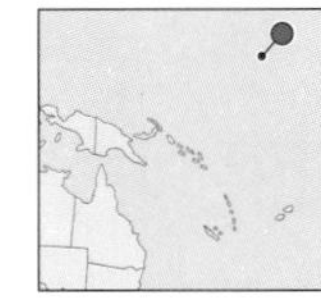

The Republic of the Marshall Islands, a former US territory, became fully independent in 1991. This island nation, lying north of Kiribati in a region known as Micronesia, is heavily dependent on US aid. The main activities are agriculture and tourism. **AREA** 181 sq km [70 sq mls]; **POPULATION** 63,000; **CAPITAL** Dalap-Uliga-Darrit, on Majuro island.

MARTINIQUE

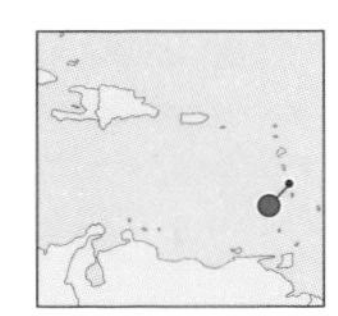

Martinique, a volcanic island nation in the Caribbean, was colonized by France in 1635. It became a French overseas department in 1946. Tourism and agriculture are major activities. About 70% of Martinique's Gross Domestic Product is provided by the French government, allowing for a good standard of living. **AREA** 1,100 sq km [425 sq mls]; **POPULATION** 407,000; **CAPITAL** Fort-de-France.

MAURITANIA

GEOGRAPHY The Islamic Republic of Mauritania in north-western Africa is nearly twice the size of France. But France has more than 26 times as many people. Part of the world's largest desert, the Sahara, covers northern Mauritania and most Mauritanians live in the south-west.

The amount of rainfall and the length of the rainy season increase from north to south. Much of the land is desert, with dry north-east and easterly winds throughout the year. But south-westerly winds bring summer rain to the south.

POLITICS & ECONOMY Originally part of the great African empires of Ghana and Mali, France set up a protectorate in Mauritania in 1903, attempting to exploit the trade in gum arabic. The country became a territory of French West Africa and a French colony in 1920. French West Africa was a huge territory, which included present-day Benin, Burkina Faso, Guinea, Ivory Coast, Mali, Niger and Senegal, as well as Mauritania. In 1958, Mauritania became a self-governing territory in the French Union and it became fully independent in 1960.

In 1976, Spain withdrew from Spanish (now Western) Sahara, a territory bordering Mauritania to the north. Morocco occupied the northern two-thirds of this territory, while Mauritania took the rest. But Saharan guerrillas belonging to POLISARIO (the Popular Front for the Liberation of Saharan Territories) began an armed struggle for independence. In 1979, Mauritania withdrew from the southern part of Western Sahara, which was then occupied by Morocco. In 1991, the country adopted a new constitution when the people voted to create a multiparty government. Multiparty elections were held in 1992 and 1996-7.

The World Bank classifies Mauritania as a 'low-income' developing country. Agriculture employs 69% of the people. Some are herders who move around with herds of cattle and sheep, though recent droughts forced many farmers to seek aid in the cities.

AREA 1,030,700 sq km [397,953 sq mls]
POPULATION 2,511,000
CAPITAL (POPULATION) Nouakchott (600,000)
GOVERNMENT Multiparty Islamic republic
ETHNIC GROUPS Moor (Arab-Berber) 70%, Wolof 7%, Tukulor 5%, Soninke 3%, Fulani 1%
LANGUAGES Arabic (official), Wolof, French
RELIGIONS Islam 99%
CURRENCY Ouguiya = 5 khoums

MAURITIUS

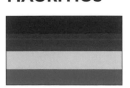

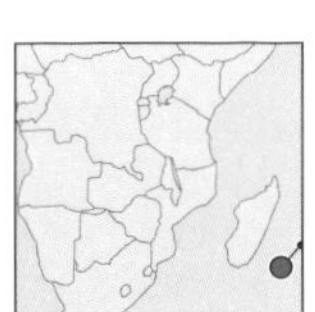

The Republic of Mauritius, an Indian Ocean nation lying east of Madagascar, was previously ruled by France and Britain until it achieved independence in 1968. It became a republic in 1992. Sugar is the main export, but tourism is now vital to the economy. **AREA** 1,860 sq km [718 sq mls]; **POPULATION** 1,168,000; **CAPITAL** Port Louis.

MEXICO

GEOGRAPHY The United Mexican States, as Mexico is officially named, is the world's most populous Spanish-speaking country. Much of the land is mountainous, although most people live on the central plateau. Mexico contains two large peninsulas, Lower (or Baja) California in the north-west and the flat Yucatán peninsula in the south-east.

The climate varies according to the altitude. The resort of Acapulco on the south-west coast has a dry and sunny climate. Mexico City, at about 2,300 m [7,546 ft] above sea level, is much cooler. Most rain occurs between June and September. The rainfall decreases north of Mexico City and northern Mexico is mainly arid.

POLITICS & ECONOMY In the mid-19th century, Mexico lost land to the United States, and between 1910 and 1921 violent revolutions created chaos.

Reforms were introduced in the 1920s and, in 1929, the Institutional Revolutionary Party (PRI) was formed. The PRI dominated Mexican politics, though it lost its overall majority in the Chamber of Deputies in 1997. Mexico faces many problems, including unemployment and rapid urbanization especially around Mexico City, demands for indigenous rights by Amerindian groups, and illegal emigration to the USA.

The World Bank classifies Mexico as an 'upper-middle-income' developing country. Agriculture is important. Food crops include beans, maize, rice and wheat, while cash crops include coffee, cotton, fruits and vegetables. Beef cattle, dairy cattle and other livestock are raised and fishing is also important.

But oil and oil products are the chief exports, while manufacturing is the most valuable activity. Many factories near the northern border assemble goods, such as car parts and electrical products, for US companies. These factories are called *maquiladoras*. Hope for the future lies in increasing economic co-operation with the USA and Canada through NAFTA (North American Free Trade Association), which came into being on 1 January 1994.

AREA 1,958,200 sq km [756,061 sq mls]
POPULATION 98,553,000
CAPITAL (POPULATION) Mexico City (15,643,000)
GOVERNMENT Federal republic
ETHNIC GROUPS Mestizo 60%, Amerindian 30%, European 9%
LANGUAGES Spanish (official)
RELIGIONS Christianity (Roman Catholic 90%, Protestant 5%)
CURRENCY New peso = 100 centavos

MICRONESIA

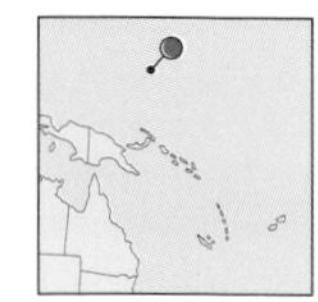

The Federated States of Micronesia, a former US territory covering a vast area in the western Pacific Ocean, became fully independent in 1991. The main export is copra. Fishing and tourism are also important. **AREA** 705 sq km [272 sq mls]; **POPULATION** 127,000; **CAPITAL** Palikir.

MOLDOVA

GEOGRAPHY The Republic of Moldova is a small country sandwiched between Ukraine and Romania. It was formerly one of the 15 republics that made up the Soviet Union. Much of the land is hilly and the highest areas are near the centre of the country.

Moldova has a moderately continental climate, with warm summers and fairly cold winters when temperatures dip below freezing point. Most of the rain comes in the warmer months.

POLITICS & ECONOMY In the 14th century, the Moldavians formed a state called Moldavia. It included part of Romania and Bessarabia (now the modern country of Moldova). The Ottoman Turks took the area in the 16th century, but in 1812 Russia took over Bessarabia. In 1861, Moldavia and Walachia united to form Romania. Russia retook southern Bessarabia in 1878.

After World War I (1914–18), all of Bessarabia was returned to Romania, but the Soviet Union did not recognize this act. From 1944, the Moldovan Soviet Socialist Republic was part of the Soviet Union.

In 1989, the Moldovans asserted their independence and ethnicity by making Romanian the official language and, at the end of 1991, Moldova became an independent country. In 1992, fighting occurred between Moldovans and Russians in Trans-Dniester, a mainly Russian-speaking area east of the River Dniester. This region was given a special status within Moldova in 1996. The first multiparty elections were held in 1994, when a proposal to unite with Romania was decisively rejected.

Moldova is a fertile country in which agriculture remains central to the economy. Major products include fruits, maize, tobacco and wine.

There are few natural resources within Moldova, and the government imports materials and fuels for its industries. Light industries, such as food processing and the manufacturing of household appliances, are gradually expanding.

AREA 33,700 sq km [13,010 sq mls]
POPULATION 4,458,000
CAPITAL (POPULATION) Chisinau (700,000)
GOVERNMENT Multiparty republic
ETHNIC GROUPS Moldovan 65%, Ukrainian 14%, Russian 13%, Gagauz 4%, Jewish 2%, Bulgarian
LANGUAGES Moldovan/Romanian (official)
RELIGIONS Christianity (Eastern Orthodox)
CURRENCY Leu = 100 bani

MONACO

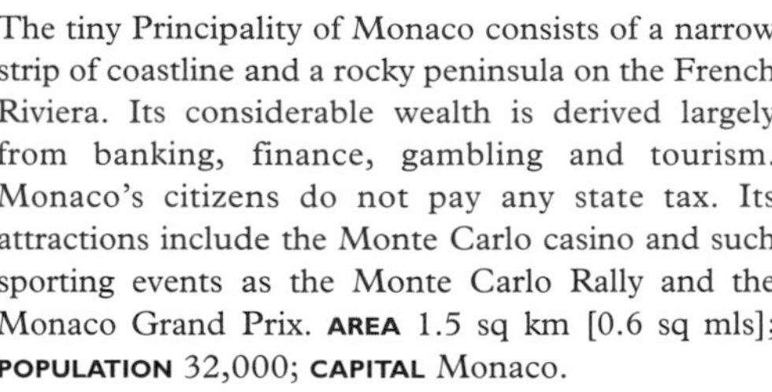

The tiny Principality of Monaco consists of a narrow strip of coastline and a rocky peninsula on the French Riviera. Its considerable wealth is derived largely from banking, finance, gambling and tourism. Monaco's citizens do not pay any state tax. Its attractions include the Monte Carlo casino and such sporting events as the Monte Carlo Rally and the Monaco Grand Prix. **AREA** 1.5 sq km [0.6 sq mls]; **POPULATION** 32,000; **CAPITAL** Monaco.

MONGOLIA

GEOGRAPHY The State of Mongolia is the world's largest landlocked country. It consists mainly of high plateaux, with the Gobi desert in the south-east.

Ulan Bator lies on the northern edge of a desert plateau in the heart of Asia. It has bitterly cold winters. In the summer months, the temperatures are moderated by the height of the land.

POLITICS & ECONOMY In the 13th century, Genghis Khan united the Mongolian peoples and built up a great empire. Under his grandson, Kublai Khan, the Mongol empire extended from Korea and China to eastern Europe and present-day Iraq.

The Mongol empire broke up in the late 14th century. In the early 17th century, Inner Mongolia came under Chinese control, and by the late 17th century Outer Mongolia had become a Chinese province. In 1911, the Mongolians drove the Chinese out of Outer Mongolia and made the area a Buddhist kingdom. But in 1924, under Russian influence, the Communist Mongolian People's Republic was set up. From the 1950s, Mongolia supported the Soviet Union in its disputes with China. In 1990, the people demonstrated for more freedom and free elections in June 1990 resulted in victory for the Mongolian People's Revolutionary Party, which was composed of Communists. But Communist rule finally ended in 1996 when the elections were won by the opposition Democratic Union coalition.

The World Bank classifies Mongolia as a 'lower-middle-income' developing country. Most people were once nomads, who moved around with their herds of sheep, cattle, goats and horses. Under Communist rule, most people were moved into permanent homes on government-owned farms. But livestock and animal products remain leading exports. The Communists also developed industry, especially the mining of coal, copper, gold, molybdenum, tin and tungsten, and manufacturing. Minerals and fuels now account for around half of Mongolia's exports.

AREA 1,566,500 sq km [604,826 sq mls]
POPULATION 2,579,000
CAPITAL (POPULATION) Ulan Bator (619,000)
GOVERNMENT Multiparty republic
ETHNIC GROUPS Khalkha Mongol 79%, Kazak 6%
LANGUAGES Khalkha Mongolian (official), Kazak
RELIGIONS Tibetan Buddhist (Lamaist)
CURRENCY Tugrik = 100 möngös

MONTSERRAT

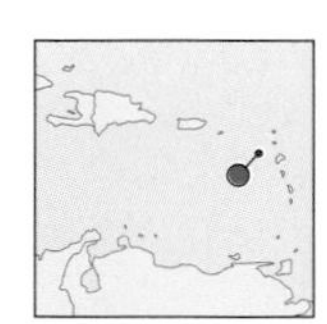

Monserrat is a British overseas territory in the Caribbean Sea. The climate is tropical and hurricanes often cause much damage. Intermittent eruptions of the Soufrière Hills volcano between 1995 and 1998 led to the emigration of many of the inhabitants and the virtual destruction of Plymouth, the capital, in the southern part of the island. **AREA** 1,100 sq km [39 sq mls]; **POPULATION** (prior to the volcanic activity) 12,000; **CAPITAL** Plymouth.

MOROCCO

GEOGRAPHY The Kingdom of Morocco lies in north-western Africa. Its name comes from the Arabic Maghreb-el-Aksa, meaning 'the farthest west'. Behind the western coastal plain the land rises to a broad plateau and ranges of the Atlas Mountains. The High (Haut) Atlas contains the highest peak, Djebel Toubkal, at 4,165 m [13,665 ft]. East of the mountains, the land descends to the arid Sahara.

The Atlantic coast of Morocco is cooled by the Canaries Current. Inland, summers are hot and dry. The winters are mild. In winter, between October and April, south-westerly winds from the Atlantic Ocean bring moderate rainfall, and snow often falls on the High Atlas Mountains.

POLITICS & ECONOMY The original people of Morocco were the Berbers. But in the 680s, Arab invaders introduced Islam and the Arabic language. By the early 20th century, France and Spain controlled Morocco, but Morocco became an independent kingdom in 1956. Although Morocco is a constitutional monarchy, King Hassan II has ruled the country in a generally authoritarian way since coming to the throne in 1961. Since 1979, Morocco has occupied the whole of Western (formerly Spanish) Sahara. UN attempts to hold a referendum on the territory's future have failed because of the difficulty of drawing up an agreed voters' register.

Morocco is classified as a 'lower-middle-income' developing country. It is the world's third largest producer of phosphate rock, which is used to make fertilizer. One reason why Morocco wants to keep Western Sahara is that it, too, has large phosphate reserves. Farming employs 44% of Moroccans. Tourism is also important.

AREA 446,550 sq km [172,413 sq mls]
POPULATION 29,114,000
CAPITAL (POPULATION) Rabat (1,220,000)
GOVERNMENT Constitutional monarchy
ETHNIC GROUPS Arab 70%, Berber 30%
LANGUAGES Arabic (official), Berber, French
RELIGIONS Islam 99%, Christianity 1%
CURRENCY Moroccan dirham = 100 centimes

MOZAMBIQUE

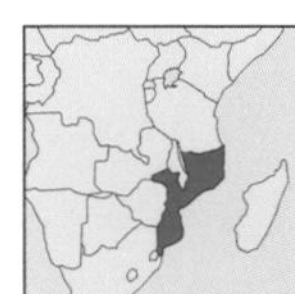

GEOGRAPHY The Republic of Mozambique borders the Indian Ocean in south-eastern Africa. The coastal plains are narrow in the north but broaden in the south. Inland lie plateaux and hills, which make up another two-fifths of Mozambique.

Mozambique has a mostly tropical climate. The capital Maputo, which lies outside the tropics, has hot and humid summers, though the winters are mild and fairly dry.

POLITICS & ECONOMY In 1885, when the European powers divided Africa, Mozambique was recognized as a Portuguese colony. But black African opposition to European rule gradually increased. In 1961, the Front for the Liberation of Mozambique (FRELIMO) was founded to oppose Portuguese rule. In 1964, FRELIMO launched a guerrilla war, which continued for ten years. Mozambique became independent in 1975.

After independence, Mozambique became a one-party state. Its government aided African nationalists in Rhodesia (now Zimbabwe) and South Africa. But the white governments of these countries helped an opposition group, the Mozambique National Resistance Movement (RENAMO) to lead an armed struggle against Mozambique's government. The civil war, combined with severe droughts, caused much human suffering in the 1980s. In 1989, FRELIMO declared that it had dropped its Communist policies and ended one-party rule. The war officially ended in 1992 and multiparty elections in 1994 heralded more stable conditions. In 1995 Mozambique became the 53rd member of the Commonwealth, joining its English-speaking allies in southern Africa.

According to the World Bank, Mozambique is one of the world's five poorest countries. Agriculture employs 85% of the people, though many farmers grow little more than they need to feed their families. Crops include cassava, cotton, cashew nuts, fruits, maize, rice, sugar cane and tea.

AREA 801,590 sq km [309,494 sq mls]
POPULATION 18,641,000
CAPITAL (POPULATION) Maputo (2,000,000)
GOVERNMENT Multiparty republic
ETHNIC GROUPS Makua 47%, Tsonga 23%, Malawi 12%, Shona 11%, Yao 4%, Swahili 1%, Makonde 1%
LANGUAGES Portuguese (official), many others
RELIGIONS Traditional beliefs 48%, Christianity (Roman Catholic 31%, others 9%), Islam 13%
CURRENCY Metical = 100 centavos

NAMIBIA

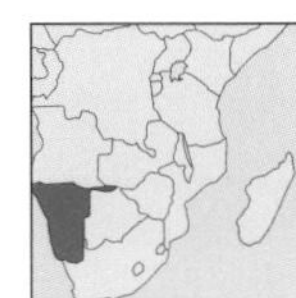

GEOGRAPHY The Republic of Namibia was formerly ruled by South Africa, who called it South West Africa. The country became independent in 1990. The coastal region contains the arid Namib Desert, which is virtually uninhabited. Inland is a central plateau, bordered by a rugged spine of mountains stretching north–south. Eastern Namibia contains part of the Kalahari desert.

Namibia is a warm and mostly arid country. Lying at 1,700 m [5,500 ft] above sea level, Windhoek has an average annual rainfall of about 370 mm [15 in], often occurring during thunderstorms in the hot summer months.

POLITICS & ECONOMY During World War I, South African troops defeated the Germans who ruled what is now Namibia. After World War II, many people challenged South Africa's right to govern the territory and a civil war began in the 1960s between African guerrillas and South African troops. A cease-fire was agreed in 1989 and the country became independent in 1990. After winning independence, the government pursued a successful policy of 'national reconciliation'. A small area on Namibia's coast, called Walvis Bay (Walvisbaai), remained part of South Africa until 1994, when South Africa transferred it to Namibia.

Namibia is rich in mineral reserves, including diamonds, uranium, zinc and copper. Minerals make up 90% of the exports. But farming employs about two out of every five Namibians. Sea fishing is also important, though overfishing has reduced the yields of the country's fishing fleet. The country has few industries, but tourism is increasing.

AREA 825,414 sq km [318,434 sq mls], including Walvis Bay, a former South African territory
POPULATION 1,622,000
CAPITAL (POPULATION) Windhoek (126,000)
GOVERNMENT Multiparty republic
ETHNIC GROUPS Ovambo 50%, Kavango 9%, Herero 7%, Damara 7%, White 6%, Nama 5%
LANGUAGES English (official), Ovambo
RELIGIONS Christianity 90% (Lutheran 51%)
CURRENCY Namibian dollar = 100 cents

NAURU

Nauru is the world's smallest republic, located in the western Pacific Ocean, close to the equator. Independent since 1968, Nauru's prosperity is based on phosphate mining, but the reserves are running out. **AREA** 21 sq km [8 sq mls]; **POPULATION** 12,000; **CAPITAL** Yaren.

NEPAL

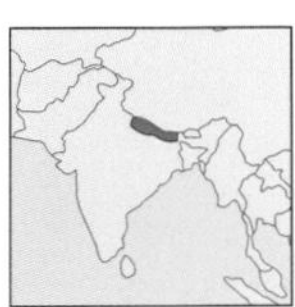

GEOGRAPHY Over three-quarters of Nepal lies in the Himalayan mountain heartland, culminating in the world's highest peak (Mount Everest, or Chomolongma in Nepali) at 8,848 m [29,029 ft]. The far lower Siwalik Range overlooks the Ganges plain.

As a result, there is a wide range of climatic conditions from tropical forest to the permanently glaciated landscape of the high Himalaya.

POLITICS & ECONOMY Nepal was united in the late 18th century, although its complex topography has ensured that it remains a diverse patchwork of peoples. From the mid-19th century to 1951, power was held by the royal Rana family. Attempts to introduce a democratic system in the 1950s failed and political parties were banned in 1962. The first democratic elections for 32 years were held in 1991.

Agriculture remains the chief activity in this overwhelmingly rural country and the government is heavily dependent on aid. Tourism, centred around the high Himalaya, grows in importance year by year, although Nepal was closed to foreigners until 1951. There are also ambitious plans to exploit the hydroelectric potential offered by the ferocious Himalayan rivers.

AREA 140,880 sq km [54,363 sq mls]
POPULATION 23,698,000
CAPITAL (POPULATION) Katmandu (535,000)
GOVERNMENT Constitutional monarchy
ETHNIC GROUPS Nepalese 53%, Bihari 18%, Tharu 5%, Tamang 5%, Newar 3%
LANGUAGES Nepali (official), local languages
RELIGIONS Hindu 86%, Buddhist 8%, Muslim 4%
CURRENCY Nepalese rupee = 100 paisa

NETHERLANDS

GEOGRAPHY The Netherlands lies at the western end of the North European Plain, which extends to the Ural Mountains in Russia. Except for the far south-eastern corner, the Netherlands is flat and about 40% lies below sea level at high tide. To prevent flooding, the Dutch have built dykes (sea walls) to hold back the waves. Large areas which were once under the sea, but which have been reclaimed, are called polders.

Because of its position on the North Sea, the Netherlands has a temperate climate. The winters are mild, with rain coming from the Atlantic depressions which pass over the country.

POLITICS & ECONOMY Before the 16th century, the area that is now the Netherlands was under a succession of foreign rulers, including the Romans, the Germanic Franks, the French and the Spanish. The Dutch declared their independence from Spain in 1581 and their status was finally recognized by Spain in 1648. In the 17th century, the Dutch built up a great overseas empire, especially in South-east Asia. But in the early 18th century, the Dutch lost control of the seas to England.

France controlled the Netherlands from 1795 to 1813. In 1815, the Netherlands, then containing Belgium and Luxembourg, became an independent kingdom. Belgium broke away in 1830 and Luxembourg followed in 1890.

The Netherlands was neutral in World War I (1914–18), but was occupied by Germany in World War II (1939–45). After the war, the Netherlands Indies became independent as Indonesia. The Netherlands became active in West European affairs. With Belgium and Luxembourg, it formed a customs union called Benelux in 1948. In 1949, it joined NATO (the North Atlantic Treaty Organization), and the European Coal and Steel Community (ECSC) in 1953. In 1957, it became a founder member of the European Economic Community (now the European Union), and its economy prospered. Although the economy was based on private enterprise, the government introduced many social welfare programmes.

The Netherlands is a highly industrialized country and industry and commerce are the most valuable activities. Its resources include natural gas, some oil, salt and china clay. But the Netherlands imports many of the materials needed by its industries and it is, therefore, a major trading country. Industrial products are wide-ranging, including aircraft, chemicals, electronic equipment, machinery, textiles and vehicles. Agriculture employs only 5% of the people, but scientific methods are used and yields are high. Dairy farming is the leading farming activity. Major products include barley, flowers and bulbs, potatoes, sugar beet and wheat.

AREA 41,526 sq km [16,033 sq mls]
POPULATION 15,731,000
CAPITAL (POPULATION) Amsterdam (1,100,000)
GOVERNMENT Constitutional monarchy
ETHNIC GROUPS Netherlander 95%, Indonesian, Turkish, Moroccan, German
LANGUAGES Dutch (official), Frisian
RELIGIONS Christianity (Roman Catholic 34%, Dutch Reformed Church 17%, Calvinist 8%), Islam 3%
CURRENCY Euro; Guilder = 100 cents

NETHERLANDS ANTILLES

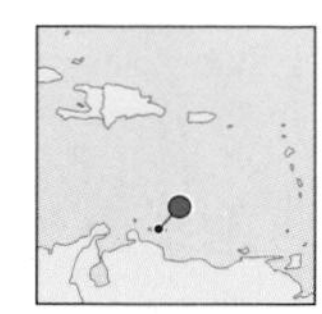

The Netherlands Antilles consists of two different island groups; one off the coast of Venezuela, and the other at the northern end of the Leeward Islands, some 800 km [500 mls] away. They remain a self-governing Dutch territory. The island of Aruba was once part of the territory, but it broke away in 1986. Oil refining and tourism are important activities. **AREA** 993 sq km [383 sq mls]; **POPULATION** 210,000; **CAPITAL** Willemstad.

NEW CALEDONIA

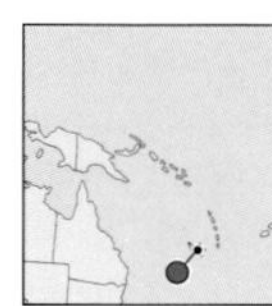

New Caledonia is the most southerly of the Melanesian countries in the Pacific. A French possession since 1853 and an Overseas Territory since 1958. In 1998, France announced an agreement with local Melanesians that a vote on independence would be postponed for 15 years. The country is rich in mineral resources, especially nickel. **AREA** 18,580 sq km [7,174 sq mls]; **POPULATION** 192,000; **CAPITAL** Nouméa.

NEW ZEALAND

GEOGRAPHY New Zealand lies about 1,600 km [994 mls] south-east of Australia. It consists of two main islands and several other small ones. Much of North Island is volcanic. Active volcanoes include Ngauruhoe and Ruapehu. Hot springs and geysers are common, and steam from the ground is used to produce electricity. The Southern Alps, which contain the country's highest peak Mount Cook (Aoraki), at 3,753 m [12,313 ft] form the backbone of South Island. The island also has some large, fertile plains.

Auckland in the north has a warm, humid climate throughout the year. Wellington has cooler summers, while in Dunedin, in the south-east, temperatures sometimes dip below freezing in winter. The rainfall is heaviest on the western highlands.

POLITICS & ECONOMY Evidence suggests that early Maori settlers arrived in New Zealand more than 1,000 years ago. The Dutch navigator Abel Tasman reached New Zealand in 1642, but his discovery was not followed up. In 1769, the British Captain James Cook rediscovered the islands. In the early 19th century, British settlers arrived and, in 1840, under the Treaty of Waitangi, Britain took possession of the islands. Clashes occurred with the Maoris in the 1860s but, from the 1870s, the Maoris were gradually integrated into society.

In 1907, New Zealand became a self-governing dominion in the British Commonwealth. The country's economy developed quickly and the people became increasingly prosperous. However, after Britain joined the European Economic Community in 1973, New Zealand's exports to Britain shrank and the country had to reassess its economic and defence strategies and seek new markets. The world economic recession also led the government to cut back on its spending on welfare services in the 1990s. Maori rights and the preservation of Maori culture are other major political issues.

New Zealand's economy has traditionally depended on agriculture, but manufacturing now employs twice as many people as agriculture. Meat and dairy products are the most valuable items produced on farms. The country has more than 48 million sheep, 4 million dairy cattle and 5 million beef cattle.

AREA 268,680 sq km [103,737 sq mls]
POPULATION 3,625,000
CAPITAL (POPULATION) Wellington (329,000)
GOVERNMENT Constitutional monarchy
ETHNIC GROUPS New Zealand European 74%, New Zealand Maori 10%, Polynesian 4%
LANGUAGES English and Maori (both official)
RELIGIONS Christianity (Anglican 21%, Presbyterian 16%, Roman Catholic 15%)
CURRENCY New Zealand dollar = 100 cents

NICARAGUA

GEOGRAPHY The Republic of Nicaragua is the second largest country in Central America. In the east is a broad plain bordering the Caribbean Sea. The plain is drained by rivers that flow from the Central Highlands. The fertile western Pacific region contains about 40 volcanoes, many of which are active, and earthquakes are common.

Nicaragua has a tropical climate. Managua is hot throughout the year and there is a marked rainy season from May to October. The Central Highlands and Caribbean region are cooler and wetter. The wettest region is the humid Caribbean plain.

POLITICS & ECONOMY In 1502, Christopher Colombus claimed the area for Spain, which ruled Nicaragua until 1821. By the early 20th century, the United States had considerable influence in the country and, in 1912, US forces entered Nicaragua to protect US interests. From 1927 to 1933, rebels under General Augusto César Sandino, tried to drive US forces out of the country. In 1933, US marines set up a Nicaraguan army, the National Guard, to help to defeat the rebels. Its leader, Anastasio Somoza Garcia, had Sandino murdered in 1934 and, from 1937, Somoza ruled as a dictator.

In the mid-1970s, many people began to protest against Somoza's rule. Many joined a guerrilla force, called the Sandinista National Liberation Front, named after General Sandino. The rebels defeated the Somoza regime in 1979. In the 1980s, the US-supported forces, called the 'Contras', launched a campaign against the Sandinista government. The US government opposed the Sandinista regime, under Daniel José Ortega Saavedra, claiming that it was a Communist dictatorship. A coalition, the National Opposition Union, defeated the Sandinistas in elections in 1990. In 1996, the Sandinistas were again defeated and Arnoldo Alemán, leader of the Liberal Alliance Party, became president.

In the early 1990s, Nicaragua faced many problems in rebuilding its shattered economy. Agriculture is the main activity, employing nearly half of the people.

Coffee, cotton, sugar and bananas are grown for export, while rice is the main food crop.

AREA 130,000 sq km [50,193 sq mls]
POPULATION 4,583,000
CAPITAL (POPULATION) Managua (974,000)
GOVERNMENT Multiparty republic
ETHNIC GROUPS Mestizo 77%, White 10%, Black 9%, Amerindian 4%
LANGUAGES Spanish (official), Misumalpan
RELIGIONS Christianity (Roman Catholic 91%, others 9%)
CURRENCY Córdoba oro (gold córdoba) = 100 centavos

NIGER

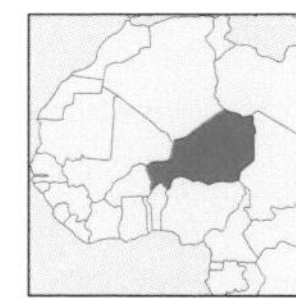

GEOGRAPHY The Republic of Niger is a landlocked nation in north-central Africa. The northern plateaux lie in the Sahara Desert, while Central Niger contains the rugged Aïr Mountains, but the most fertile and densely populated region is the narrow Niger valley in the south-west.

Niger has a tropical climate and the south has a rainy season between June and September. The hot harmattan wind blows from the Sahara between March and May. The north is practically rainless.

POLITICS & ECONOMY Since independence in 1960, Niger, a French territory from 1900, has suffered severe droughts. Food shortages and the collapse of the traditional nomadic way of life of some of Niger's people have caused political instability. After a period of military rule, a multiparty constitution was adopted in 1992, but the military again seized power in 1996. Later that year, the coup leader Col. Ibrahim Barre Mainassara, was elected president.

Niger's chief resource is uranium and it is the fourth largest producer in the world. Some tin and tungsten are also mined, though other mineral resources are largely untouched.

Despite its resources, Niger is one of the world's poorest countries. Farming employs 85% of the population, though only 3% of the land can be used for crops and 7% for grazing.

AREA 1,267,000 sq km [489,189 sq mls]
POPULATION 9,672,000
CAPITAL (POPULATION) Niamey (398,000)
GOVERNMENT Multiparty republic
ETHNIC GROUPS Hausa 53%, Zerma-Songhai 21%, Tuareg 11%, Fulani (or Peul) 10%
LANGUAGES French (official), Hausa, Songhai
RELIGIONS Islam 98%
CURRENCY CFA franc = 100 centimes

NIGERIA

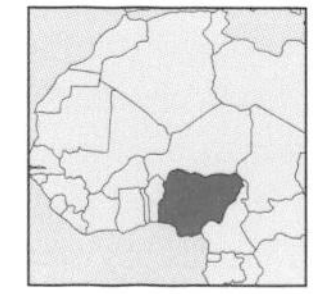

GEOGRAPHY The Federal Republic of Nigeria is the most populous nation in Africa. The country's main rivers are the Niger and Benue, which meet in central Nigeria. North of the two river valleys are high plains and plateaux. The Lake Chad basin is in the north-east, with the Sokoto plains in the north-west. Southern Nigeria contains hilly uplands and broad coastal plains, including the swampy Niger delta.

The south has high temperatures and rain throughout the year. The north is drier and often hotter than the south.

POLITICS & ECONOMY Nigeria has a long artistic tradition. Major cultures include the Nok (500 BC to AD 200), Ife, which developed about 1,000 years ago, and Benin, which flourished between the 15th and 17th centuries. Britain gradually extended its influence over the area in the second half of the 19th century. Nigeria became independent in 1960 and a federal republic in 1963. A federal constitution dividing the country into regions was necessary because Nigeria contains more than 250 ethnic and linguistic groups, as well as several religious ones. Local rivalries have long been a threat to national unity, and six new states were created in 1996 in an attempt to overcome this. Civil war occurred between 1967 and 1970, when the people of the south-east attempted unsuccessfully to secede during the Biafran War. Between 1960 and 1998, Nigeria had only nine years of civilian government. However, in 1998-9, Nigeria held elections at state and national level aimed at restoring civilian rule. The former general, Olusegun Obasanjo, was elected president.

Nigeria is a developing country, with great economic potential. Its greatest natural resource is oil, which accounts for the bulk of its exports. But agriculture employs 43% of the people. The country is a major producer of cocoa, palm oil and palm kernels, groundnuts and rubber.

AREA 923,770 sq km [356,668 sq mls]
POPULATION 110,532,000
CAPITAL (POPULATION) Abuja (339,000)
GOVERNMENT Federal republic
ETHNIC GROUPS Hausa 21%, Yoruba 21%, Ibo (or Igbo) 19%, Fulani 11%, Ibibio 6%
LANGUAGES English (official), Hausa, Yoruba, Ibo
RELIGIONS Christianity (Protestant 26%, Roman Catholic 12%, others 11%), Islam 45%
CURRENCY Naira = 100 kobo

NORTHERN MARIANA ISLANDS

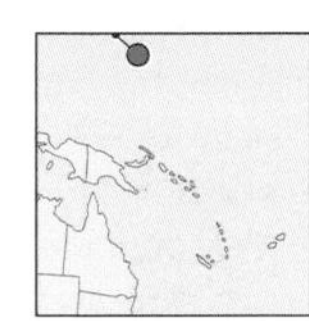

The Commonwealth of the Northern Mariana Islands contains 16 mountainous islands north of Guam in the western Pacific Ocean. In a 1975 plebiscite, the islanders voted for Commonwealth status in union with the USA and, in 1986, they were granted US citizenship. **AREA** 477 sq km [184 sq mls]; **POPULATION** 50,000; **CAPITAL** Saipan.

NORWAY

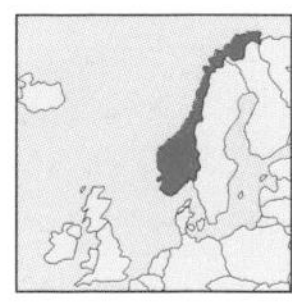

GEOGRAPHY The Kingdom of Norway forms the western part of the rugged Scandinavian peninsula. The deep inlets along the highly indented coastline were worn out by glaciers during the Ice Age.

The warm North Atlantic Drift off the coast of Norway moderates the climate, with mild winters and cool summers. Nearly all the ports are ice-free throughout the year. Inland, winters are colder and snow cover lasts for at least three months a year.

POLITICS & ECONOMY Under a treaty in 1814, Denmark handed Norway over to Sweden, but it kept Norway's colonies – Greenland, Iceland and the Faroe Islands. Norway briefly became independent, but Swedish forces defeated the Norwegians and Norway had to accept Sweden's king as its ruler.

The union between Norway and Sweden ended in 1903. During World War II (1939–45), Germany occupied Norway. Norway's economy developed quickly after the war and the country now enjoys one of the world's highest standards of living. In 1960, Norway, together with six other countries, formed the European Free Trade Association (EFTA). In 1994, the Norwegians voted against joining the EU.

Norway's chief resources and exports are oil and natural gas which come from wells under the North Sea. Farmland covers only 3% of the land. Dairy farming and meat production are important, but Norway has to import food. Norway has many industries powered by cheap hydroelectricity.

AREA 323,900 sq km [125,050 sq mls]
POPULATION 4,420,000
CAPITAL (POPULATION) Oslo (714,000)
GOVERNMENT Constitutional monarchy
ETHNIC GROUPS Norwegian 97%
LANGUAGES Norwegian (official), Lappish, Finnish
RELIGIONS Christianity (Lutheran 88%)
CURRENCY Krone = 100 ore

OMAN

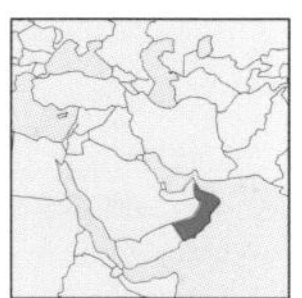

GEOGRAPHY The Sultanate of Oman occupies the south-eastern corner of the Arabian peninsula. It also includes the tip of the Musandam peninsula, overlooking the strategic Strait of Hormuz.

Oman has a hot tropical climate. In Muscat, temperatures may reach 47°C [117°F] in summer.

POLITICS & ECONOMY British influence in Oman dates back to the end of the 18th century, but the country became fully independent in 1971. Since then, using revenue from oil, which was discovered in 1964, the government has sought to modernize and develop the country.

The World Bank classifies Oman as an 'upper-middle-income' developing country. Its economy is based on oil production and oil accounts for more than 90% of Oman's export revenues. But agriculture still provides a living for half of the people. Major crops include alfalfa, bananas, coconuts, dates, limes, tobacco, vegetables and wheat. Some farmers raise cattle, and fishing, especially for sardines, is also important, though Oman still has to import food.

AREA 212,460 sq km [82,031 sq mls]
POPULATION 2,364,000
CAPITAL (POPULATION) Muscat (350,000)
GOVERNMENT Monarchy with consultative council
ETHNIC GROUPS Omani Arab 74%, Pakistani 21%
LANGUAGES Arabic (official), Baluchi, English
RELIGIONS Islam (Ibadiyah) 86%, Hinduism 13%
CURRENCY Omani rial = 100 baizas

PAKISTAN

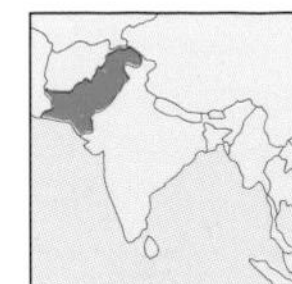

GEOGRAPHY The Islamic Republic of Pakistan contains high mountains, fertile plains and rocky deserts. The Karakoram range, which contains K2, the world's second highest peak, lies in the northern part of Jammu and Kashmir, which is occupied by Pakistan but claimed by India. Other mountains rise in the west. Plains, drained by the River Indus and its tributaries, occupy much of eastern Pakistan. The Thar Desert is in the south-east and the dry Baluchistan plateau is in the south-west.

The mountains have cold, snowy winters. But most of Pakistan has hot summers and cool winters. The rainfall is sparse throughout much of the country. Most of it comes between July and September, when south-west monsoon winds blow.

POLITICS & ECONOMY Pakistan was the site of the Indus Valley civilization which developed about 4,500 years ago. But Pakistan's modern history dates from 1947, when British India was divided into India and Pakistan. Muslim Pakistan was divided into two parts: East and West Pakistan, but East Pakistan broke away in 1971 to become Bangladesh. In 1948–9, 1965 and 1971, Pakistan and India clashed over the disputed territory of Kashmir. In 1998, Pakistan responded in kind to a series of Indian nuclear weapon tests, provoking global controversy.

Pakistan has been subject to several periods of military rule, but elections held in 1988 led to Benazir Bhutto, daughter of a former prime minister and president, Zulfikar Ali Bhutto, becoming prime minister. Benazir Bhutto was removed from office in 1990 but she again became prime minister in 1993, until she was dismissed in 1996. Following elections in 1997, Nawaz Sharif became prime minister.

According to the World Bank, Pakistan is a 'low-income' developing country. The economy is based on farming or rearing goats and sheep. Agriculture employs nearly half the people. Major crops, grown mainly on irrigated land, include cotton, fruits, rice, sugar cane and, most important of all, wheat.

AREA 796,100 sq km [307,374 sq mls]
POPULATION 135,135,000
CAPITAL (POPULATION) Islamabad (204,000)
GOVERNMENT Federal republic
ETHNIC GROUPS Punjabi 60%, Sindhi 12%, Pushtun 13%, Baluch, Muhajir
LANGUAGES Urdu (official), many others
RELIGIONS Islam 97%, Christianity, Hinduism
CURRENCY Pakistan rupee = 100 paisa

PALAU

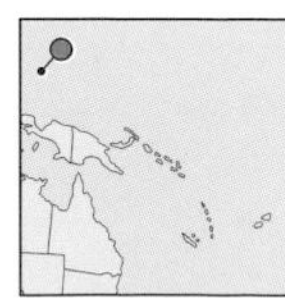

The Republic of Palau became fully independent in 1994, after the USA refused to accede to a 1979 referendum that declared this island nation a nuclear-free zone. The economy relies on US aid, tourism, fishing and subsistence agriculture. The main crops include cassava, coconuts and copra. **AREA** 458 sq km [177 sq mls]; **POPULATION** 18,000; **CAPITAL** Koror.

PANAMA

GEOGRAPHY The Republic of Panama forms an isthmus linking Central America to South America. The Panama Canal, which is 81.6 km [50.7 mls] long, cuts across the isthmus. It has made the country a major transport centre.

Panama has a tropical climate. Temperatures are high, though the mountains are much cooler than the coastal plains. The main rainy season is between May and December.

POLITICS & ECONOMY Christopher Columbus landed in Panama in 1502 and Spain soon took control of the area. In 1821, Panama became independent from Spain and a province of Colombia.

In 1903, Colombia refused a request by the United States to build a canal. Panama then revolted against Colombia, and became independent. The United States then began to build the canal, which was opened in 1914. The United States administered the Panama Canal Zone, a strip of land along the canal. But many Panamanians resented US influence and, in 1979, the Canal Zone was returned to Panama. The USA also agreed to hand over control of the Canal to Panama on 31 December 1999.

Panama's government has changed many times since independence, and there have been periods of military dictatorships. In 1983, General Manuel Antonio Noriega became Panama's leader. In 1988, two US grand juries in Florida indicted Noriega on charges of drug trafficking. In 1989, Noriega was apparently defeated in a presidential election, but the government declared the election invalid. After the killing of a US marine, US troops entered Panama and arrested Noriega, who was convicted by a Miami court of drug offences in 1992. Elections in 1994 were won the Democratic Revolutionary Party, led by Ernesto Pérez Balladares.

The World Bank classifies Panama as a 'lower-middle-income' developing country. The Panama Canal is an important source of revenue and it generates many jobs in commerce, trade, manufacturing and transport. Away from the Canal, the main activity is agriculture, which employs 27% of the people.

AREA 77,080 sq km [29,761 sq mls]
POPULATION 2,736,000
CAPITAL (POPULATION) Panama City (452,000)
GOVERNMENT Multiparty republic
ETHNIC GROUPS Mestizo 60%, Black and Mulatto 20%, White 10%, Amerindian 8%, Asian 2%
LANGUAGES Spanish (official)
RELIGIONS Christianity (Roman Catholic 84%, Protestant 5%), Islam 5%
CURRENCY Balboa = 100 centésimos

PAPUA NEW GUINEA

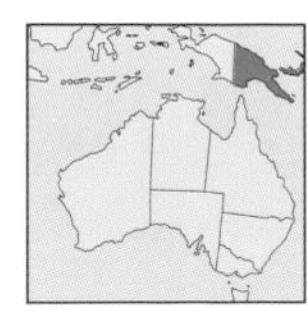

GEOGRAPHY Papua New Guinea is an independent country in the Pacific Ocean, north of Australia. It is part of a Pacific island region called Melanesia. Papua New Guinea includes the eastern part of New Guinea, the Bismarck Archipelago, the northern Solomon Islands, the D'Entrecasteaux Islands and the Louisiade Archipelago. The land is largely mountainous.

Papua New Guinea has a tropical climate, with high temperatures throughout the year. Most of the rain occurs during the monsoon season (from December to April), when the north-westerly winds blow. Winds blow from the south-east during the dry season.

POLITICS & ECONOMY The Dutch took western New Guinea (now part of Indonesia) in 1828, but it was not until 1884 that Germany took north-eastern New Guinea and Britain the south-east. In 1906, Britain handed the south-east over to Australia. It then became known as the Territory of Papua. When World War I broke out in 1914, Australia took German New Guinea and, in 1921, the League of Nations gave Australia a mandate to rule the area, which was named the Territory of New Guinea.

Japan invaded New Guinea in 1942, but the Allies reconquered the area in 1944. In 1949, Papua and New Guinea were combined into the Territory of Papua and New Guinea. Papua New Guinea became fully independent in 1975.

Since independence, the government of Papua New Guinea has worked to develop its mineral reserves. One of the most valuable mines was on Bougainville, in the northern Solomon Islands. But the people of Bougainville demanded a larger share in the profits of the mine. Conflict broke out, the mine was closed and the Bougainville Revolutionary Army proclaimed the island independent. But their attempted secession was not recognized internationally. An agreement to end the conflict was finally signed in New Zealand in January 1998.

The World Bank classifies Papua New Guinea as a 'lower-middle-income' developing country. Agriculture employs three out of every four people, many of whom produce little more than they need to feed their families. But minerals, notably copper and gold, are the most valuable exports.

AREA 462,840 sq km [178,703 sq mls]
POPULATION 4,600,000
CAPITAL (POPULATION) Port Moresby (174,000)
GOVERNMENT Constitutional monarchy
ETHNIC GROUPS Papuan 84%, Melanesian 1%
LANGUAGES English (official), about 800 others
RELIGIONS Christianity (Protestant 58%, Roman Catholic 33%, Anglican 5%), traditional beliefs 3%
CURRENCY Kina = 100 toea

PARAGUAY

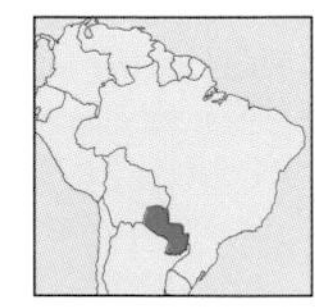

GEOGRAPHY The Republic of Paraguay is a land-locked country and rivers, notably the Paraná, Pilcomayo (Brazo Sur) and Paraguay, form most of its borders. A flat region called the Gran Chaco lies in the north-west, while the south-east contains plains, hills and plateaux.

Northern Paraguay lies in the tropics, while the south is subtropical. Most of the country has a warm, humid climate.

POLITICS & ECONOMY In 1776, Paraguay became part of a large colony called the Vice-royalty of La Plata, with Buenos Aires as the capital. Paraguayans opposed this move and the country declared its independence in 1811.

For many years, Paraguay was torn by internal strife and conflict with its neighbours. A war against Brazil, Argentina and Uruguay (1865–70) led to the deaths of more than half of Paraguay's population, and a great loss of territory.

General Alfredo Stroessner took power in 1954 and ruled as a dictator. His government imprisoned many opponents. Stroessner was overthrown in 1989. Free multiparty elections were held in 1993 and 1998. However, the return of democracy frequently seemed precarious because of rivalries between politicians and army leaders.

The World Bank classifies Paraguay as a 'lower-middle-income' developing country. Agriculture and forestry are the leading activities, employing 48% of the population. The country has abundant hydroelectricity and it exports power to Argentina and Brazil.

AREA 406,750 sq km [157,046 sq mls]
POPULATION 5,291,000
CAPITAL (POPULATION) Asunción (945,000)
GOVERNMENT Multiparty republic
ETHNIC GROUPS Mestizo 90%, Amerindian 3%
LANGUAGES Spanish and Guaraní (both official)
RELIGIONS Christianity (Roman Catholic 96%, Protestant 2%)
CURRENCY Guaraní = 100 céntimos

PERU

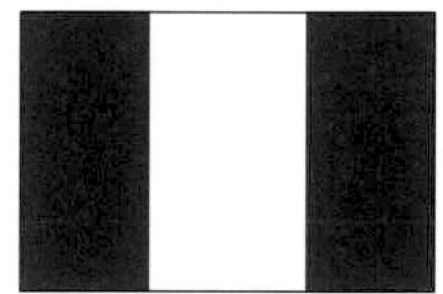

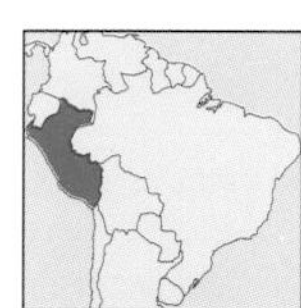

GEOGRAPHY The Republic of Peru lies in the tropics in western South America. A narrow coastal plain borders the Pacific Ocean in the west. Inland are ranges of the Andes Mountains, which rise to 6,768 m [22,205 ft] at Mount Huascarán, an extinct volcano. East of the Andes, the land descends to the Amazon basin.

Lima, on the coastal plain, has an arid climate. The coastal region is chilled by the cold, offshore Humboldt Current. The rainfall increases inland and many mountains in the high Andes are snow-capped.
POLITICS & ECONOMY Spanish conquistadors conquered Peru in the 1530s. In 1820, an Argentinian, José de San Martín, led an army into Peru and declared it independent. But Spain still held large areas. In 1823, the Venezuelan Simon Bolívar led another army into Peru and, in 1824, one of his generals defeated the Spaniards at Ayacucho. The Spaniards surrendered in 1826. Peru suffered much instability throughout the 19th century.

Instability continued in the 20th century. In 1980, when civilian rule was restored, a left-wing group called the Sendero Luminoso, or the 'Shining Path', began guerrilla warfare against the government. In 1990, Alberto Fujimori, son of Japanese immigrants, became president. In 1992, he suspended the constitution and dismissed the legislature. The guerrilla leader, Abimael Guzmán, was arrested in 1992, but instability continued. A new constitution was introduced in 1993, giving increased power to the president, who faced many problems in rebuilding the shattered economy.

The World Bank classifies Peru as a 'lower-middle-income' developing country. Agriculture employs 35% of the people and major food crops include beans, maize, potatoes and rice. Fish products are exported, but the most valuable export is copper. Peru also produces lead, silver, zinc and iron ore.

AREA 1,285,220 sq km [496,223 sq mls]
POPULATION 26,111,000
CAPITAL (POPULATION) Lima (Lima-Callao, 6,601,000)
GOVERNMENT Transitional republic
ETHNIC GROUPS Quechua 47%, Mestizo 32%, White 12%, Aymara 5%
LANGUAGES Spanish and Quechua (both official), Aymara
RELIGIONS Christianity (Roman Catholic 93%, Protestant 6%)
CURRENCY New sol = 100 centavos

PHILIPPINES

GEOGRAPHY The Republic of the Philippines is an island country in south-eastern Asia. It includes about 7,100 islands, of which 2,770 are named and about 1,000 are inhabited. Luzon and Mindanao, the two largest islands, make up more than two-thirds of the country. The land is mainly mountainous and lacks large lowlands.

The country has a tropical climate, with high temperatures all through the year. The dry season runs from December to April. The rest of the year is wet. The high rainfall is associated with typhoons which periodically strike the east coast.
POLITICS & ECONOMY The first European to reach the Philippines was the Portuguese navigator Ferdinand Magellan in 1521. Spanish explorers claimed the region in 1565 when they established a settlement on Cebu. The Spaniards ruled the country until 1898, when the United States took over at the end of the Spanish–American War. Japan invaded the Philippines in 1941, but US forces returned in 1944. The country became fully independent as the Republic of the Philippines in 1946.

Since independence, the country's problems have included armed uprisings by left-wing guerrillas demanding land reform, and Muslim separatist groups, crime, corruption and unemployment. The dominant figure in recent times was Ferdinand Marcos, who ruled in a dictatorial manner from 1965 to 1986. His successor was Corazon Aquino, widow of an assassinated opponent of Marcos. Aquino did not stand in the presidential elections in 1992. Her successor was General Fidel Ramos.

The Philippines is a developing country with a lower-middle-income economy. Agriculture employs 45% of the people. The main foods are rice and maize, while such crops as bananas, cocoa, coconuts, coffee, sugar cane and tobacco are grown commercially. Manufacturing now plays an increasingly important role in the economy.

AREA 300,000 sq km [115,300 sq mls]
POPULATION 77,736,000
CAPITAL (POPULATION) Manila (Metro Manila, 9,280,000)
GOVERNMENT Multiparty republic
ETHNIC GROUPS Tagalog 30%, Cebuano 24%, Ilocano 10%, Hiligaynon Ilongo 9%, Bicol 6%
LANGUAGES Pilipino (Tagalog) and English (both official), Spanish, many others
RELIGIONS Christianity (Roman Catholic 84%, Philippine Independent Church or Aglipayan 6%, Protestant 4%), Islam 4%
CURRENCY Philippine peso = 100 centavos

PITCAIRN ISLANDS

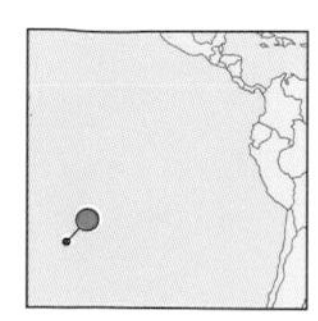

Pitcairn Island is a British overseas territory in the Pacific Ocean. Its inhabitants are descendants of the original settlers – nine mutineers from *HMS Bounty* and 18 Tahitians who arrived in 1790. **AREA** 48 sq km [19 sq mls]; **POPULATION** 60; **CAPITAL** Adamstown.

POLAND

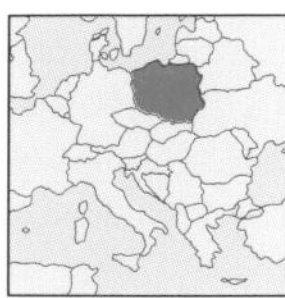

GEOGRAPHY The Republic of Poland faces the Baltic Sea and, behind its lagoon-fringed coast, lies a broad plain. The land rises to a plateau region in the south-east, while the Sudeten Highlands straddle part of the border with the Czech Republic. Part of the Carpathian range (the Tatra) lies on the south-eastern border with the Slovak Republic.

Poland's climate is influenced by its position in Europe. Warm, moist air masses come from the west, while cold air masses come from the north and east. Summers are warm, but winters are cold and snowy.
POLITICS & ECONOMY Poland's boundaries have changed several times in the last 200 years, partly as a result of its geographical location between the powers of Germany and Russia. It disappeared from the map in the late 18th century, when a Polish state called the Grand Duchy of Warsaw was set up. But in 1815, the country was partitioned, between Austria, Prussia and Russia. Poland became independent in 1918, but in 1939 it was divided between Germany and the Soviet Union. The country again became independent in 1945, when it lost land to Russia but gained some from Germany. Communists took power in 1948, but opposition mounted and eventually became focused through an organization called Solidarity.

Solidarity was led by a trade unionist, Lech Walesa. A coalition government was formed between Solidarity and the Communists in 1989. In 1990, the Communist party was dissolved and Walesa became president. But Walesa faced many problems in turning Poland towards a market economy. In presidential elections in 1995, Walesa was defeated by ex-Communist Aleksander Kwasniewski. However, Kwasniewski continued to follow westward-looking policies and, in 1999, it joined NATO. Poland seemed likely to be among the first eastern European countries to join an expanded EU.

Poland has large reserves of coal and deposits of various minerals which are used in its factories. Manufactures include chemicals, processed food, machinery, ships, steel and textiles.

AREA 312,680 sq km [120,726 sq mls]
POPULATION 38,607,000
CAPITAL (POPULATION) Warsaw (1,638,000)
GOVERNMENT Multiparty republic
ETHNIC GROUPS Polish 98%, Ukrainian 1%, German 1%
LANGUAGES Polish (official)
RELIGIONS Christianity (Roman Catholic 94%, Orthodox 2%)
CURRENCY Zloty = 100 groszy

PORTUGAL

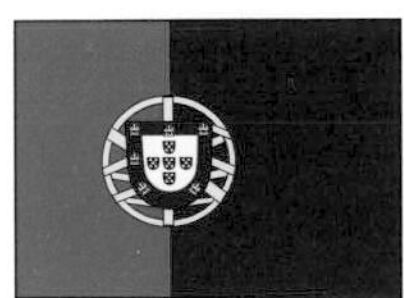

GEOGRAPHY The Republic of Portugal is the most westerly of Europe's mainland countries. The land rises from the coastal plains on the Atlantic Ocean to the western edge of the huge plateau, or Meseta, which occupies most of the Iberian peninsula. Portugal also contains two autonomous regions, the Azores and Madeira island groups.

The climate is moderated by winds blowing from the Atlantic Ocean. Summers are cooler and winters are milder than in other Mediterranean lands.

POLITICS & ECONOMY Portugal became a separate country, independent of Spain, in 1143. In the 15th century, Portugal led the 'Age of European Exploration'. This led to the growth of a large Portuguese empire, with colonies in Africa, Asia and, most valuable of all, Brazil in South America. Portuguese power began to decline in the 16th century and, between 1580 and 1640, Portugal was ruled by Spain. Portugal lost Brazil in 1822 and, in 1910, Portugal became a republic. Instability hampered progress and army officers seized power in 1926. In 1928, they chose Antonio de Salazar to be minister of finance. He became prime minister in 1932 and ruled as a dictator from 1933.

Salazar ruled until 1968, but his successor, Marcello Caetano, was overthrown in 1974 by a group of army officers. The new government made most of Portugal's remaining colonies independent. Free elections were held in 1978. Portugal joined the European Community (now the European Union) in 1986. But despite great efforts to increase economic growth, Portugal remains one of its poorest members.

Agriculture and fishing were the mainstays of the economy until the mid-20th century. But manufacturing is now the most valuable sector.

AREA 92,390 sq km [35,670 sq mls]
POPULATION 9,928,000
CAPITAL (POPULATION) Lisbon (2,561,000)
GOVERNMENT Multiparty republic
ETHNIC GROUPS Portuguese 99%, Cape Verdean, Brazilian, Spanish, British
LANGUAGES Portuguese (official)
RELIGIONS Christianity (Roman Catholic 95%, other Christians 2%)
CURRENCY Euro; Escudo = 100 centavos

PUERTO RICO

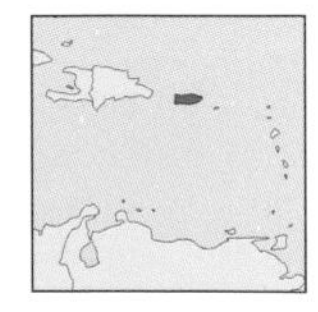

The Commonwealth of Puerto Rico, a mainly mountainous island, is the easternmost of the Greater Antilles chain. The climate is hot and wet. Puerto Rico is a dependent territory of the USA and the people are US citizens. In 1998, 50.2% of the population voted in a referendum on possible statehood to maintain the status quo. Puerto Rico is the most industrialized country in the Caribbean. Tax exemptions attract US companies to the island and manufacturing is expanding. **AREA** 8,900 sq km [3,436 sq km]; **POPULATION** 3,860,000; **CAPITAL** San Juan.

QATAR

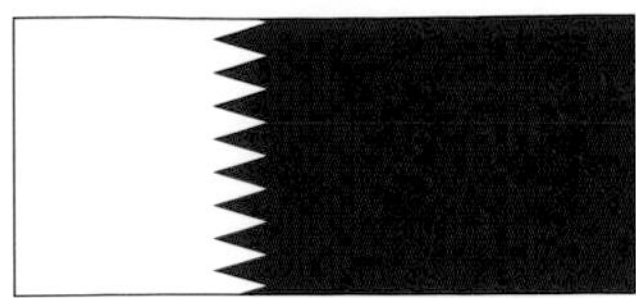

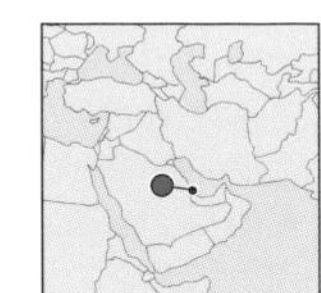

The State of Qatar occupies a low, barren peninsula that extends northwards from the Arabian peninsula into the Gulf. The climate is hot and dry. Qatar became a British protectorate in 1916, but it became fully independent in 1971. Oil, first discovered in 1939, is the mainstay of the economy of this prosperous nation. **AREA** 11,000 sq km [4,247 sq mls]; **POPULATION** 697,000; **CAPITAL** Doha.

RÉUNION

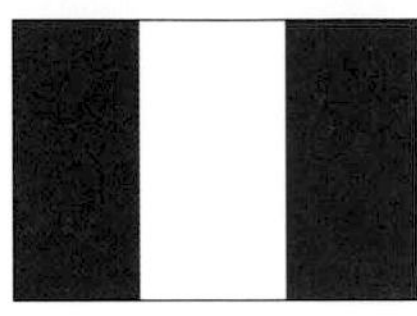

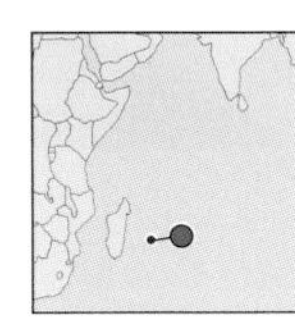

Réunion is a French overseas department in the Indian Ocean. The land is mainly mountainous, though the lowlands are intensely cultivated. Sugar and sugar products are the main exports, but French aid, given to the island in return for its use as a military base, is important to the economy. **AREA** 2,510 sq km [969 sq mls]; **POPULATION** 705,000; **CAPITAL** Saint-Denis.

ROMANIA

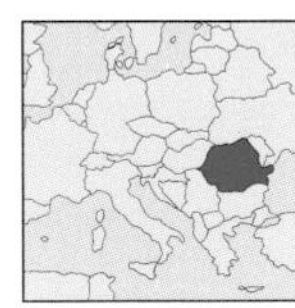

GEOGRAPHY Romania is a country on the Black Sea in eastern Europe. Eastern and southern Romania form part of the Danube river basin. The delta region, near the mouths of the Danube, where the river flows into the Black Sea, is one of Europe's finest wetlands. The southern part of the coast contains several resorts. The heart of the country is called Transylvania. It is ringed in the east, south and west by scenic mountains which are part of the Carpathian mountain system.

Romania has hot summers and cold winters. The rainfall is heaviest in spring and early summer, when thundery showers are common.

POLITICS & ECONOMY From the late 18th century, the Turkish empire began to break up. The modern history of Romania began in 1861 when Walachia and Moldavia united. After World War I (1914–18), Romania, which had fought on the side of the victorious Allies, obtained large areas, including Transylvania, where most people were Romanians. This almost doubled the country's size and population. In 1939, Romania lost territory to Bulgaria, Hungary and the Soviet Union. Romania fought alongside Germany in World War II, and Soviet troops occupied the country in 1944. Hungary returned northern Transylvania to Romania in 1945, but Bulgaria and the Soviet Union kept former Romanian territory. In 1947, Romania officially became a Communist country.

In 1990, Romania held its first free elections since the end of World War II. The National Salvation Front, led by Ion Iliescu and containing many former Communist leaders, won a large majority. A new constitution, approved in 1991, made the country a democratic republic. Elections held under this constitution in 1992 again resulted in victory for Ion Iliescu, whose party was renamed the Party of Social Democracy (PDSR) in 1993. But the government faced many problems as it tried to reform the economy. In 1996, the PDSR was defeated in elections by the centre-right Democratic Convention led by Emil Constantinescu.

According to the World Bank, Romania is a 'lower-middle-income' economy. Under Communist rule, industry, including mining and manufacturing, became more important than agriculture.

AREA 237,500 sq km [91,699 sq mls]
POPULATION 22,396,000
CAPITAL (POPULATION) Bucharest (2,061,000)
GOVERNMENT Multiparty republic
ETHNIC GROUPS Romanian 89%, Hungarian 7%, Gypsy 2%
LANGUAGES Romanian (official), Hungarian
RELIGIONS Christianity (Romanian Orthodox 87%, Roman Catholic 5%, Greek Orthodox 4%)
CURRENCY Romanian leu = 100 bani

RUSSIA

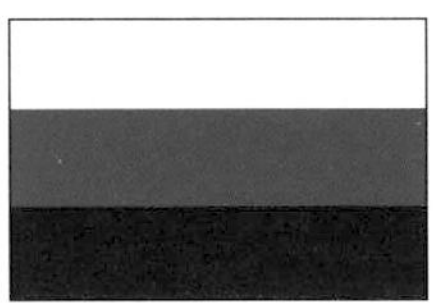

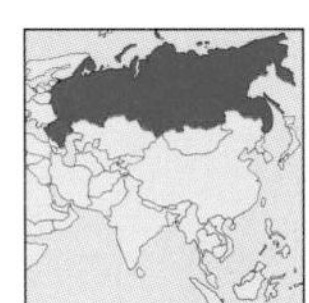

GEOGRAPHY Russia is the world's largest country. About 25% lies west of the Ural Mountains in European Russia, where 80% of the population lives. It is mostly flat or undulating, but the land rises to the Caucasus Mountains in the south, where Russia's highest peak, Elbrus, at 5,633 m [18,481 ft], is found. Asian Russia, or Siberia, contains vast plains and plateaux, with mountains in the east and south. The Kamchatka peninsula in the far east has many active volcanoes. Russia contains many of the world's longest rivers, including the Yenisey-Angara and the Ob-Irtysh. It also includes part of the world's largest inland body of water, the Caspian Sea, and Lake Baikal, the world's deepest lake.

Moscow has a continental climate with cold and snowy winters and warm summers. Krasnoyarsk in south-central Siberia has a harsher, drier climate, but it is not as severe as parts of northern Siberia.

POLITICS & ECONOMY In the 9th century AD, a state called Kievan Rus was formed by a group of people called the East Slavs. Kiev, now capital of Ukraine, became a major trading centre, but, in 1237, Mongol armies conquered Russia and destroyed Kiev. Russia was part of the Mongol empire until the late 15th century. Under Mongol rule, Moscow became the leading Russian city.

In the 16th century, Moscow's grand prince was retitled 'tsar'. The first tsar, Ivan the Terrible, expanded Russian territory. In 1613, after a period of civil war, Michael Romanov became tsar, founding a dynasty which ruled until 1917. In the early 18th century, Tsar Peter the Great began to westernize Russia and, by 1812, when Napoleon failed to conquer the country, Russia was a major European power. But during the 19th century, many Russians demanded reforms and discontent was widespread.

In World War I (1914–18), the Russian people suffered great hardships and, in 1917, Tsar Nicholas II was forced to abdicate. In November 1917, the Bolsheviks seized power under Vladimir Lenin. In 1922, the Bolsheviks set up a new nation, the Union of Soviet Socialist Republics (also called the USSR or the Soviet Union).

From 1924, Joseph Stalin introduced a socialist economic programme, suppressing all opposition. In 1939, the Soviet Union and Germany signed a non-aggression pact, but Germany invaded the Soviet Union in 1941. Soviet forces pushed the Germans back, occupying eastern Europe. They reached Berlin in May 1945. From the late 1940s, tension between the Soviet Union and its allies and Western nations developed into a 'Cold War'. This continued until 1991, when the Soviet Union was dissolved.

The Soviet Union collapsed because of the failure of its economic policies. From 1991, its new leader, Boris Yeltsin, worked to develop democratic systems, reform the economy and increase private ownership. Russia kept contacts with 11 of the republics in the former Soviet Union through the Commonwealth of Independent States. But fighting in Chechenia in the 1990s showed that Russia's diverse population makes national unity difficult to achieve.

Russia's economy was thrown into disarray after the collapse of the Soviet Union, and in the early 1990s the World Bank described Russia as a 'lower-middle-income' economy. Russia was admitted to the Council of Europe in 1997, essentially to discourage instability in the Caucasus. More significantly still, Boris Yeltsin was invited to attend the G7 summit in Denver in 1997. The summit became known as 'the Summit of the Eight' and it appeared that Russia will now be included in future meetings of the world's most powerful economies. Industry is the most valuable activity, though, under Communist rule, manufacturing was less efficient than in the West and the emphasis was on heavy industry. Today, light industries producing consumer goods are becoming important. Russia's adundant resources include oil and natural gas, coal, timber, metal ores and hydroelectric power.

Most farmland is still government-owned or run as collectives. Russia is a major producer of farm products, though it imports grains. Major crops include barley, flax, fruits, oats, rye, potatoes, sugar beet, sunflower seeds, vegetables and wheat. Livestock farming is also important.

AREA 17,075,000 sq km [6,592,800 sq mls]
POPULATION 146,861,000
CAPITAL (POPULATION) Moscow (9,233,000)
GOVERNMENT Federal multiparty republic
ETHNIC GROUPS Russian 82%, Tatar 4%, Ukrainian 3%, Chuvash 1%, more than 100 other nationalities
LANGUAGES Russian (official), many others
RELIGIONS Christianity (mainly Russian Orthodox, with Roman Catholic and Protestant minorities), Islam, Judaism
CURRENCY Russian rouble = 100 kopeks

RWANDA

R

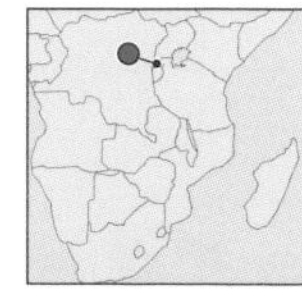

GEOGRAPHY The Republic of Rwanda is a small, landlocked country in east-central Africa. Lake Kivu and the River Ruzizi in the Great African Rift Valley form the country's western border.

Kigali stands on the central plateau of Rwanda. Here, temperatures are moderated by the altitude. The rainfall is abundant, but much heavier rain falls on the western mountains.

POLITICS & ECONOMY Germany conquered the area, called Ruanda-Urundi, in the 1890s. But Belgium occupied the region during World War I (1914–18) and ruled it until 1961, when the people of Ruanda voted for their country to become a republic, called Rwanda. This decision followed a rebellion by the majority Hutu people against the Tutsi monarchy. About 150,000 deaths resulted from this conflict. Many Tutsis fled to Uganda, where they formed a rebel army. Burundi became independent as a monarchy, though it became a republic in 1966. Relations between Hutus and Tutsis continued to cause friction. Civil war broke out in 1994 and in 1996 the conflict spilled over into Congo (then Zaïre), where Tutsis clashes with government troops.

According to the World Bank, Rwanda is a 'low-income' developing country. Most people are poor farmers, who produce little more than they need to feed their families. Food crops include bananas, beans, cassava and sorghum. Some cattle are raised.

AREA 26,340 sq km [10,170 sq mls]
POPULATION 7,956,000
CAPITAL (POPULATION) Kigali (235,000)
GOVERNMENT Republic
ETHNIC GROUPS Hutu 90%, Tutsi 9%, Twa 1%
LANGUAGES French, English and Kinyarwanda (all official)
RELIGIONS Christianity 74% (Roman Catholic 65%), traditional beliefs 17%, Islam 9%
CURRENCY Rwanda franc = 100 centimes

ST HELENA

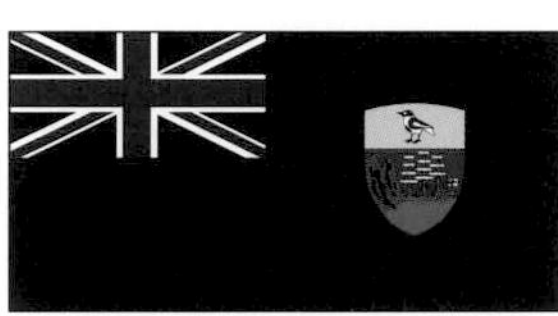

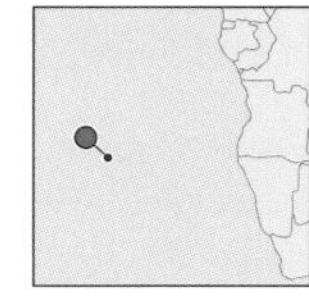

St Helena, which became a British colony in 1834, is an isolated volcanic island in the south Atlantic Ocean. Now a British overseas territory, it is also the administrative centre of Ascension and Tristan da Cunha. **AREA** 122 sq km [47 sq mls]; **POPULATION** 8,200; **CAPITAL** Jamestown.

ST KITTS AND NEVIS

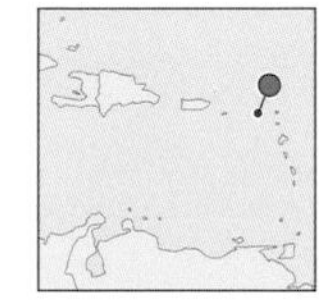

The Federation of St Kitts and Nevis became independent from Britain in 1983. In 1998, a vote for the secession of Nevis fell short of the two-thirds required. **AREA** 360 sq km [139 sq mls]; **POPULATION** 42,000; **CAPITAL** Basseterre.

ST LUCIA

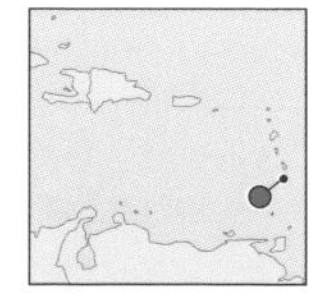

St Lucia, which became independent from Britain in 1979, is a mountainous, forested island of extinct volcanoes. It exports bananas and coconuts, and now attracts many tourists. **AREA** 610 sq km [236 sq mls]; **POPULATION** 150,000; **CAPITAL** Castries.

ST VINCENT AND THE GRENADINES

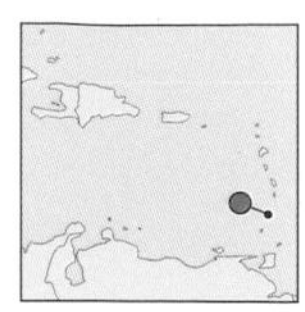

St Vincent and the Grenadines achieved its independence from Britain in 1979. Tourism is growing, but the territory is less prosperous than its neighbours. **AREA** 388 sq km [150 sq mls]; **POPULATION** 120,000; **CAPITAL** Kingstown.

SAN MARINO

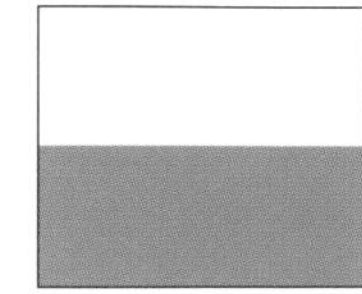

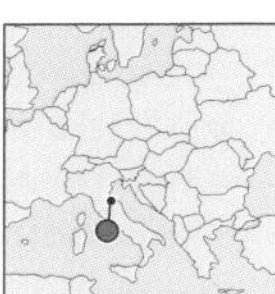

The 'Most Serene Republic of San Marino', as this tiny state in northern Italy is officially called, has been independent since 885 and a republic since the 14th century. This makes it the world's oldest republic. **AREA** 61 sq km [24 sq mls]; **POPULATION** 25,000; **CAPITAL** San Marino

SÃO TOMÉ AND PRÍNCIPE

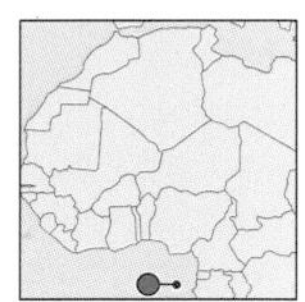

The Democratic Republic of São Tomé and Príncipe, a mountainous island territory west of Gabon, became a Portuguese colony in 1522. Following independence in 1975, the islands became a one-party Marxist state, but multiparty elections were held in 1991. Cocoa is the main product. **AREA** 964 sq km [372 sq mls]; **POPULATION** 150,000; **CAPITAL** Sao Tome.

SAUDI ARABIA

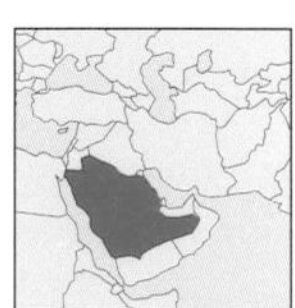

GEOGRAPHY The Kingdom of Saudi Arabia occupies about three-quarters of the Arabian peninsula in south-west Asia. Deserts cover most of the land. Mountains border the Red Sea plains in the west. In the north is the sandy Nafud Desert (An Nafud). In the south is the Rub' al Khali (the 'Empty Quarter'), one of the world's bleakest deserts.

Saudi Arabia has a hot, dry climate. In the summer months, the temperatures in Riyadh often exceed 40°C [104°F], though the nights are cool.

POLITICS & ECONOMY Saudi Arabia contains the two holiest places in Islam – Mecca (or Makka), the birthplace of the Prophet Muhammad in AD 570, and Medina (Al Madinah) where Muhammad went in 622. These places are visited by many pilgrims.

Saudi Arabia was poor until the oil industry began to operate on the eastern plains in 1933. Oil revenues have been used to develop the country and Saudi Arabia has given aid to poorer Arab nations. The monarch has supreme authority and Saudi Arabia has no formal constitution. In the first Gulf War (1980-88), Saudi Arabia supported Iraq against Iran. But when Iraq invaded Kuwait in 1990, it joined the international alliance to drive Iraq's forces out of Kuwait in 1991.

Saudi Arabia has about 25% of the world's known oil reserves, and oil and oil products make up 85% of its exports. But agriculture still employs 48% of the people, including nomadic herders who rear cattle, goats, sheep, and other animals. Crops grown in the south-western highlands and at oases include dates and other fruits, vegetables and wheat. Modern irrigation and desalination schemes have greatly increased crop production in recent years. The government continues to encourage the development of modern agriculture and new industries as a method of diversifying the economy.

AREA 2,149,690 sq km [829,995 sq mls]
POPULATION 20,786,000
CAPITAL (POPULATION) Riyadh (2,000,000)
GOVERNMENT Absolute monarchy with consultative assembly
ETHNIC GROUPS Arab (Saudi 82%, Yemeni 10%, other Arab 3%)
LANGUAGES Arabic (official)
RELIGIONS Islam 99%, Christianity 1%
CURRENCY Saudi riyal = 100 halalas

SENEGAL

GEOGRAPHY The Republic of Senegal is on the north-west coast of Africa. The volcanic Cape Verde (Cap Vert), on which Dakar stands, is the most westerly point in Africa. Plains cover most of Senegal, though the land rises gently in the south-east.

Dakar has a tropical climate, with a short rainy season between July and October when moist winds blow from the south-west.

POLITICS & ECONOMY In 1882, Senegal became a French colony, and from 1895 it was ruled as part of French West Africa, the capital of which, Dakar, developed as a major port and city.

In 1959, Senegal joined French Sudan (now Mali) to form the Federation of Mali. But Senegal withdrew in 1960 and became the separate Republic of Senegal. Its first president, Léopold Sédar Senghor, was a noted African poet. He continued in office until 1981, when he was succeeded by the prime minister, Abdou Diouf.

Senegal and The Gambia have always enjoyed close relations despite their differing French and British traditions. In 1981, Senegalese troops put down an attempted coup in The Gambia and, in 1982, the two countries set up a defence alliance, called the Confederation of Senegambia. But this confederation was dissolved in 1989.

According to the World Bank, Senegal is a 'lower-middle-income' developing country. It was badly hit in the 1960s and 1970s by droughts, which caused starvation. Agriculture still employs 81% of the population though many farmers produce little more than they need to feed their families. Food crops include groundnuts, millet and rice. Phosphates are the country's chief resource, but Senegal also refines oil which it imports from Gabon and Nigeria. Dakar is a busy port and has many industries.

Senegal exports fish products, groundnuts, oil products and phosphates.

AREA 196,720 sq km [75,954 sq mls]
POPULATION 9,723,000
CAPITAL (POPULATION) Dakar (1,729,000)
GOVERNMENT Multiparty republic
ETHNIC GROUPS Wolof 44%, Fulani-Tukulor 24%, Serer 15%
LANGUAGES French (official), tribal languages
RELIGIONS Islam 94%, Christianity (mainly Roman Catholic) 5%, traditional beliefs and others 1%
CURRENCY CFA franc = 100 centimes

SEYCHELLES

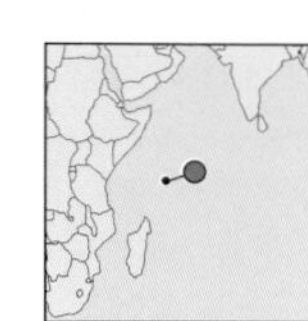

The Republic of Seychelles in the western Indian Ocean achieved independence from Britain in 1976. Coconuts are the main cash crop and fishing and tourism are important. **AREA** 455 sq km [176 sq mls]; **POPULATION** 79,000; **CAPITAL** Victoria.

SIERRA LEONE

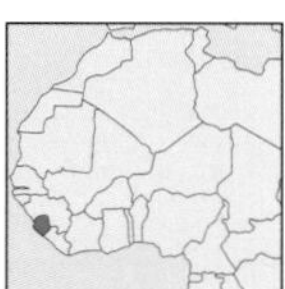

GEOGRAPHY The Republic of Sierra Leone in West Africa is about the same size as the Republic of Ireland. The coast contains several deep estuaries in the north, with lagoons in the south. The most prominent feature is the mountainous Freetown (or Sierra Leone) peninsula. North of the peninsula is the River Rokel estuary, West Africa's best natural harbour.

Sierra Leone has a tropical climate, with heavy rainfall between April and November.

POLITICS & ECONOMY After independence, Sierra Leone became a monarchy. Its head of state was the British monarch, who was represented in the country by a governor-general. But after a military government took power in 1968, Sierra Leone became a republic in 1971 and a one-party state in 1978. In 1991, a majority of the people voted for the restoration of democracy but, in 1992, a military group seized power. In 1994 and 1995, civil war caused a collapse of law and order in some areas. Elections were held in 1996, but another military coup occurred in 1997. In 1998, the West Africa Peace Force restored the elected President Ahmed Tejan Kabbah to power, but conflict continued.

The World Bank classifies Sierra Leone among the 'low-income' economies. Agriculture provides a living for 70% of the people, though farming is mainly at subsistence level. The most valuable exports are minerals, including diamonds, bauxite and rutile (titanium ore). The country has few manufacturing industries.

AREA 71,740 sq km [27,699 sq mls]
POPULATION 5,080,000
CAPITAL (POPULATION) Freetown (505,000)
GOVERNMENT Single-party republic
ETHNIC GROUPS Mende 35%, Temne 37%
LANGUAGES English (official), Mande, Temne
RELIGIONS Traditional beliefs 51%, Islam 39%
CURRENCY Leone = 100 cents

SINGAPORE

GEOGRAPHY The Republic of Singapore is an island country at the southern tip of the Malay peninsula. It consists of the large Singapore Island and 58 small islands, 20 of which are inhabited.

Singapore has a hot and humid climate, typical of places near the Equator. The temperatures are high and the rainfall is heavy throughout the year.

POLITICS & ECONOMY Singapore's modern history began in 1819 when Sir Thomas Stamford Raffles (1781–1826), agent of the British East India Company, made a treaty with the Sultan of Johor. This treaty allowed the British to build a settlement on Singapore Island. Singapore soon became the leading British trading centre in South-east Asia and it later became a naval base. Japanese forces seized the island in 1942, but British rule was restored in 1945.

In 1963, Singapore became part of the Federation of Malaysia, which also included Malaya and the territories of Sabah and Sarawak on the island of Borneo. But, in 1965, Singapore broke away from the Federation and became an independent country.

The People's Action Party (PAP) has ruled Singapore since 1959. Its leader, Lee Kuan Yew, served as prime minister from 1959 until 1990, when he resigned and was succeeded by Goh Chok Tong. Under the PAP, the economy has expanded rapidly, though some people consider that the PAP's rule has been rather dictatorial and oversensitive to criticism.

The World Bank classifies Singapore as a 'high-income' economy. Its highly skilled workforce has created one of the world's fastest growing economies, though the recession in East Asia in 1997–8 was a setback. Trade and finance are leading activities and manufactures include chemicals, electronic products, machinery, metal products, paper, scientific instruments, ships and textiles. Singapore has a large oil refinery and petroleum products and manufactures are the main exports.

AREA 618 sq km [239 sq mls]
POPULATION 3,490,000
CAPITAL (POPULATION) Singapore City (2,874,000)
GOVERNMENT Multiparty republic
ETHNIC GROUPS Chinese 78%, Malay 14%, Indian 7%
LANGUAGES Chinese, Malay, Tamil and English (all official)
RELIGIONS Buddhism, Taoism and other traditional beliefs 54%, Islam 15%, Christianity 13%, Hinduism 4%
CURRENCY Singapore dollar = 100 cents

SLOVAK REPUBLIC

GEOGRAPHY The Slovak Republic is a predominantly mountainous country, consisting of part of the Carpathian range. The highest peak is Gerlachovka in the Tatra Mountains, which reaches 2,655 m [8,711 ft]. The south is a fertile lowland drained by the River Danube.

The Slovak Republic has cold winters and warm summers. Kosice, in the east, has average temperatures ranging from –3°C [27°F] in January to 20°C [68°F] in July. The highland areas are much colder. Snow or rain falls throughout the year. Kosice has an average annual rainfall of 600 mm [24 in], the wettest months being July and August.

POLITICS & ECONOMY Slavic peoples settled in the region in the 5th century AD. They were subsequently conquered by Hungary; the beginning of a millennium of Hungarian rule and concurrent suppression of Slovak culture.

In 1867, Hungary and Austria united to form Austria-Hungary, of which the present-day Slovak Republic was a part. Austria-Hungary collapsed at the end of World War I (1914–18). The Czech and Slovak people then united to form a new nation, Czechoslovakia, but Czech domination of the union led to resentment by many Slovaks. In 1939, the Slovak Republic declared itself independent, but Germany occupied the entire country. At the end of World War II, the Slovak Republic again became part of Czechoslovakia.

The Communist party took control in 1948. In the 1960s, many Czechs and Slovaks sought to reform the Communist system, but the Russians crushed the reformers. However, in the late 1980s, demands for democracy mounted as Soviet reformers began to question Communist policies. Elections in Czechoslovakia in 1992 led to victory for the Movement for a Democratic Slovakia, led by a former Communist and nationalist, Vladimir Meciar. In September 1992, the Slovak National Council voted to create a separate, independent Slovak Republic on 1 January 1994.

After independence, the Slovaks maintained close relations with the Czech Republic, although occasional diplomatic spats occurred. Relations with Hungary were damaged in 1996 when the Slovak government initiated eight new administrative regions which the Hungarian minority claimed under-represented them politically. In addition, a law was convened to make Slovak the only official language.

Before 1948, the Slovak Republic's economy was based on farming, but Communist governments developed manufacturing industries, producing such things as chemicals, machinery, steel and weapons. Since the late 1980s, many state-run businesses have been handed over to private owners.

AREA 49,035 sq km [18,932 sq mls]
POPULATION 5,393,000
CAPITAL (POPULATION) Bratislava (451,000)
GOVERNMENT Multiparty republic
ETHNIC GROUPS Slovak, Hungarian, with small groups of Czechs, Germans, Gypsies, Poles, Russians and Ukrainians
LANGUAGES Slovak (official), Hungarian
RELIGIONS Christianity (Roman Catholic 60%, Protestant 6%, Orthodox 3%)
CURRENCY Koruna = 100 halierov

SLOVENIA

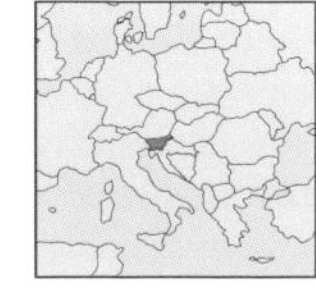

GEOGRAPHY The Republic of Slovenia was one of the six republics which made up the former Yugoslavia. Much of the land is mountainous, rising to 2,863 m [9,393 ft] at Mount Triglav in the Julian Alps (Julijske Alpe) in the north-west. Central Slovenia contains the limestone Karst region. The Postojna caves near Ljubljana are among the largest in Europe.

The coast has a mild Mediterranean climate, but inland the climate is more continental. The mountains are snow-capped in winter.

POLITICS & ECONOMY In the last 2,000 years, the Slovene people have been independent as a nation for less than 50 years. The Austrian Habsburgs ruled over the region from the 13th century until World War I. Slovenia became part of the Kingdom of the Serbs, Croats and Slovenes (later called Yugoslavia) in 1918. During World War II, Slovenia was invaded and partitioned between Italy, Germany and Hungary but, after the war, Slovenia again became part of Yugoslavia.

From the late 1960s, some Slovenes demanded independence, but the central government opposed the break-up of the country. In 1990, when Communist governments had collapsed throughout Eastern Europe, elections were held and a non-Communist coalition government was set up. Slovenia then declared itself independent. This led to fighting between Slovenes and the federal army, but Slovenia did not become a battlefield like other parts of the former Yugoslavia. The European Community recognized Slovenia's independence in 1992 and elections were held. A coalition government led by the Liberal Democrats was set up.

The reform of the economy, formerly run by the government, and the fighting in areas to the south have caused problems for Slovenia, although it remains one of the fastest growing economies in Europe. In 1992, the World Bank classified Slovenia as an 'upper-middle-income' developing country, and it is expected to be among the first countries to join an expanded European Union.

Manufacturing is the leading activity and manufactures are the principal exports. Manufactures include chemicals, machinery and transport equipment, metal goods and textiles. Agriculture employs 8% of the people. Fruits, maize, potatoes and wheat are major crops, while many farmers raise cattle, pigs and sheep.

AREA 20,251 sq km [7,817 sq mls]
POPULATION 1,972,000
CAPITAL (POPULATION) Ljubljana (280,000)
GOVERNMENT Multiparty republic
ETHNIC GROUPS Slovene 88%, Croat 3%, Serb 2%, Bosnian 1%
LANGUAGES Slovene (official), Serbo-Croat
RELIGIONS Christianity (mainly Roman Catholic)
CURRENCY Tolar = 100 stotin

SOLOMON ISLANDS

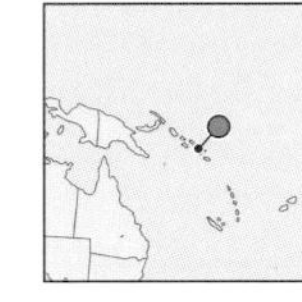

The Solomon Islands, a chain of mainly volcanic islands south of the equator in the Pacific Ocean, were a British territory territory between 1893 and 1978. The chain extends for some 2,250 km [1,400 mls]. They were the scene of fierce fighting during World War II. Most people are Melanesians, and the islands have a very young population profile, with half the people aged under 20. Fish, coconuts and cocoa are leading products, although development is hampered by the mountainous, densely forested terrain. **AREA** 29,900 sq km [11,158 sq mls]; **POPULATION** 441,000; **CAPITAL** Honiara.

SOMALIA

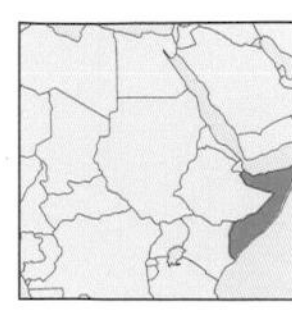

GEOGRAPHY The Somali Democratic Republic, or Somalia, is in a region known as the 'Horn of Africa'. It is more than twice the size of Italy, the country which once ruled the southern part of Somalia. The most mountainous part of the country is in the north, behind the narrow coastal plains that border the Gulf of Aden.

Rainfall is light throughout Somalia. The wettest regions are the south and the northern mountains, but droughts often occur. Temperatures are high on the low plateaux and plains.

POLITICS & ECONOMY European powers became interested in the Horn of Africa in the 19th century. In 1884, Britain made the northern part of what is now Somalia a protectorate, while Italy took the south in 1905. The new boundaries divided the Somalis into five areas: the two Somalilands, Djibouti (which was taken by France in the 1880s), Ethiopia and Kenya. Since then, many Somalis have longed for reunification in a Greater Somalia.

Italy entered World War II in 1940 and invaded British Somaliland. But British forces conquered the region in 1941 and ruled both Somalilands until 1950, when the United Nations asked Italy to take over the former Italian Somaliland for ten years. In 1960, both Somalilands became independent and united to become Somalia.

Somalia has faced many problems since independence. Economic problems led a military group to seize power in 1969. In the 1970s, Somalia supported an uprising of Somali-speaking people in the Ogaden region of Ethiopia. But Ethiopian forces prevailed and, in 1988, Somalia signed a peace treaty with Ethiopia. The cost of the fighting weakened Somalia's economy.

Further problems occurred when people in the north fought to secede from Somalia. In 1991, they set up the 'Somaliland Republic', with its capital at Hargeisa. But the new state was recognized neither internationally nor by Somalia's government. Fighting continued and US troops sent by the UN in 1993 had to withdraw in 1994. By 1995, Somalia was divided into three main regions – the north, the north-east and the south. The country had no effective national government.

Somalia is a developing country, whose economy has been shattered by drought and war. Catastrophic flooding in late 1997 displaced tens of thousands of people, further damaging the country's infrastrucure and destroying the slender hope of an economic recovery.

Many Somalis are nomads who raise livestock. Live animals, meat and hides and skins are major exports, followed by bananas grown in the wetter south. Other crops include citrus fruits, cotton, maize and sugar cane. Mining and manufacturing remain relatively unimportant in the economy.

AREA 637,660 sq km [246,201 sq mls]
POPULATION 6,842,000
CAPITAL (POPULATION) Mogadishu (1,000,000)
GOVERNMENT Single-party republic, military dominated
ETHNIC GROUPS Somali 98%, Arab 1%
LANGUAGES Somali and Arabic (both official), English, Italian
RELIGIONS Islam 99%
CURRENCY Somali shilling = 100 cents

SOUTH AFRICA

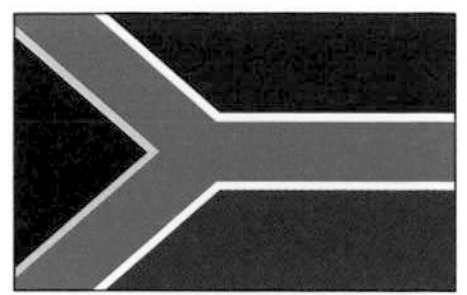

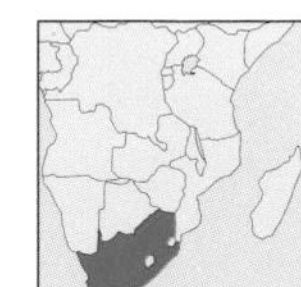

GEOGRAPHY The Republic of South Africa is made up largely of the southern part of the huge plateau which makes up most of southern Africa. The highest peaks are in the Drakensberg range, which is formed by the uptilted rim of the plateau. In the south-west lie the folded Cape Mountain ranges. The coastal plains are mostly narrow. The Namib Desert is in the north-west.

Most of South Africa has a mild, sunny climate. Much of the coastal strip, including the city of Cape Town, has warm, dry summers and mild, rainy winters, just like the Mediterranean lands in northern Africa. Inland, large areas are arid.

POLITICS & ECONOMY Early inhabitants in South Africa were the Khoisan. In the last 2,000 years, Bantu-speaking people moved into the area. Their descendants include the Zulu, Xhosa, Sotho and Tswana. The Dutch founded a settlement at the Cape in 1652, but Britain took over in the early 19th century, making the area a colony. The Dutch, called Boers or Afrikaners, resented British rule and moved inland. Rivalry between the groups led to Anglo-Boer Wars in 1880–1 and 1899–1902.

In 1910, the country was united as the Union of South Africa. In 1948, the National Party won power and introduced a policy known as apartheid, under which non-whites had no votes and their human rights were strictly limited. In 1990, Nelson Mandela, leader of the banned African National Congress (ANC), was released after serving 28 years as a political prisoner. Under a new constitution, multiracial elections were held in 1994. They resulted in victory for the ANC and Mandela became president. A new constitution was adopted in 1996.

South Africa is Africa's most developed country. But most of the black people are poor, with low standards of living. Natural resources include diamonds, gold and many other metals. Mining and manufacturing are the most valuable activities.

AREA 1,219,916 sq km [470,566 sq mls]
POPULATION 42,835,000
CAPITAL (POPULATION) Cape Town (legislative, 2,350,000); Pretoria (administrative, 1,080,000); Bloemfontein (judiciary, 300,000)
GOVERNMENT Multiparty republic
ETHNIC GROUPS Black 76%, White 13%, Coloured 9%, Asian 2%
LANGUAGES Afrikaans, English, Ndebele, North Sotho, South Sotho, Swazi, Tsonga, Tswana, Venda, Xhosa, Zulu (all official)
RELIGIONS Christianity 68%, Hinduism 1%, Islam 1%
CURRENCY Rand = 100 cents

SPAIN

GEOGRAPHY The Kingdom of Spain is the second largest country in Western Europe after France. It shares the Iberian peninsula with Portugal. A large plateau, called the Meseta, covers most of Spain. Much of the Meseta is flat, but it is crossed by several mountain ranges, called sierras.

The northern highlands include the Cantabrian Mountains (Cordillera Cantabrica) and the high Pyrenees, which form Spain's border with France. But Mulhacén, the highest peak on the Spanish mainland, is in the Sierra Nevada in the south-east. Spain also contains fertile coastal plains. Other major lowlands are the Ebro river basin in the north-east and the Guadalquivir river basin in the south-west. Spain also includes the Balearic Islands in the Mediterranean Sea and the Canary Islands off the north-west coast of Africa.

The Meseta has a continental climate, with hot summers and cold winters, when temperatures often fall below freezing point. Snow often covers the mountain ranges on the Meseta. The Mediterranean coastal regions also have hot, dry summers, but the winters are mild.

POLITICS & ECONOMY In the 16th century, Spain became a world power. At its peak, it controlled much of Central and South America, parts of Africa and the Philippines in Asia. Spain began to decline in the late 16th century. Its sea power was destroyed by a British fleet in the Battle of Trafalgar (1805). By the 20th century, it was a poor country.

Spain became a republic in 1931, but the republicans were defeated in the Spanish Civil War (1936–9). General Francisco Franco (1892–1975) became the country's dictator, though, technically, it was a monarchy. When Franco died, the monarchy was restored. Prince Juan Carlos became king.

Spain has several groups with their own languages and cultures. Some of these people want to run their own regional affairs. In the northern Basque region, some nationalists have waged a terrorist campaign, though a truce was declared in September 1998.

Since the late 1970s, a regional parliament with a considerable degree of autonomy has been set up in the Basque Country (called Euskadi in the indigenous tongue and Pais Vasco in Spanish). Similar parliaments have been initiated in Catalonia in the north-east and Galicia in the north-west. All these regions have their own languages.

The revival of Spain's economy, which was shattered by the Civil War, began in the 1950s and 1960s, especially through the growth of tourism and manufacturing. Since the 1950s, Spain has changed from a poor country, dependent on agriculture, to a fairly prosperous industrial nation.

By the early 1990s, agriculture employed 10% of the people, as compared with industry 35% and services, including tourism, 55%. Farmland, including pasture, makes up about two-thirds of the land, with forest making up most of the rest. Major crops include barley, citrus fruits, grapes for wine-making, olives, potatoes and wheat. Sheep are the leading livestock.

Spain has some high-grade iron ore in the north, though otherwise it lacks natural resources. But it has many manufacturing industries. Manufactures include cars, chemicals, clothing, electronics, processed food, metal goods, steel and textiles. The leading manufacturing centres are Barcelona, Bilbao and Madrid.

AREA 504,780 sq km [194,896 sq mls]
POPULATION 39,134,000
CAPITAL (POPULATION) Madrid (3,041,000)
GOVERNMENT Constitutional monarchy
ETHNIC GROUPS Castilian Spanish 72%, Catalan 16%, Galician 8%, Basque 2%
LANGUAGES Castilian Spanish (official), Catalan, Galician, Basque
RELIGIONS Christianity (Roman Catholic 97%)
CURRENCY Euro; Peseta = 100 céntimos

SRI LANKA

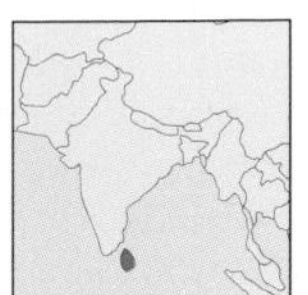

GEOGRAPHY The Democratic Socialist Republic of Sri Lanka is an island nation, separated from the south-east coast of India by the Palk Strait. The land is mostly low-lying, but a mountain region dominates the south-central part of the country.

The western part of Sri Lanka has a wet equatorial climate. Temperatures are high and the rainfall is heavy. Eastern Sri Lanka is drier than the west.

POLITICS & ECONOMY From the early 16th century, Ceylon (as Sri Lanka was then known) was ruled successively by the Portuguese, Dutch and British. Independence was achieved in 1948 and the country was renamed Sri Lanka in 1972.

After independence, rivalries between the two main ethnic groups, the Sinhalese and Tamils, marred progress. In the 1950s, the government made Sinhala the official language. Following protests, the prime minister made provisions for Tamil to be used in some areas. In 1959, the prime minister was assassinated by a Sinhalese extremist and he was succeeded by Sirimavo Bandanaraike, who became the world's first woman prime minister.

Conflict between Tamils and Sinhalese continued in the 1970s and 1980s. In 1987, India helped to engineer a cease-fire. Indian troops arrived to enforce the agreement, but withdrew in 1990 after failing to subdue the main guerrilla group, the Tamil Tigers, who wanted to set up an independent Tamil homeland in northern Sri Lanka. In 1993, the country's president was assassinated by a suspected Tamil separatist. Offensives against the Tamil Tigers continued through the 1990s.

The World Bank classifies Sri Lanka as a 'low-income' developing country. Agriculture employs half of the workforce and coconuts, rubber and tea are exported.

AREA 65,610 sq km [25,332 sq mls]
POPULATION 18,934,000
CAPITAL (POPULATION) Colombo (1,863,000)
GOVERNMENT Multiparty republic
ETHNIC GROUPS Sinhalese 74%, Tamil 18%, Sri Lankan Moor 7%
LANGUAGES Sinhala and Tamil (both official)
RELIGIONS Buddhism 69%, Hinduism 16%, Islam 8%, Christianity 7%
CURRENCY Sri Lankan rupee = 100 cents

SUDAN

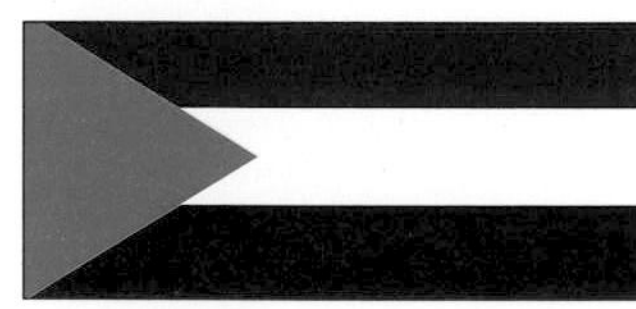

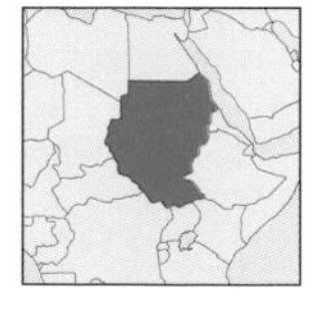

GEOGRAPHY The Republic of Sudan is the largest country in Africa. From north to south, it spans a vast area extending from the arid Sahara in the north to the wet equatorial region in the south. The land is mostly flat, with the highest mountains in the far south. The main physical feature is the River Nile.

The climate of Khartoum represents a transition between the virtually rainless northern deserts and the equatorial lands in the south. Some rain falls in Khartoum in summer.

POLITICS & ECONOMY In the 19th century, Egypt

gradually took over Sudan. In 1881, a Muslim religious teacher, the Mahdi ('divinely appointed guide'), led an uprising. Britain and Egypt put the rebellion down in 1898. In 1899, they agreed to rule Sudan jointly as a condominium.

After independence in 1952, the black Africans in the south, who were either Christians or followers of traditional beliefs, feared domination by the Muslim northerners. For example, they objected to the government declaring that Arabic was the only official language. In 1964, civil war broke out and continued until 1972, when the south was given regional self-government, though executive power was still vested in the military government in Khartoum.

In 1983, the government established Islamic law throughout the country. This sparked off further conflict when the Sudan People's Liberation Army in the south launched attacks on government installations. Despite attempts to restore order, the fighting continued into the late 1990s. The problems of food shortages and the displacement of people who became refugees added to Sudan's difficulties. By 1998, the situation had become critical. Widespread famine in southern Sudan attracted global attention and humanitarian aid.

AREA 2,505,810 sq km [967,493 sq mls]
POPULATION 33,551,000
CAPITAL (POPULATION) Khartoum (925,000)
GOVERNMENT Military regime
ETHNIC GROUPS Sudanese Arab 49%, Dinka 12%, Nuba 8%, Beja 6%, Nuer 5%, Azande 3%
LANGUAGES Arabic (official), Nubian, Dinka
RELIGIONS Islam 73%, traditional beliefs 17%, Christianity (Roman Catholic 4%, Protestant 2%)
CURRENCY Dinar = 10 Sudanese pounds

SURINAM

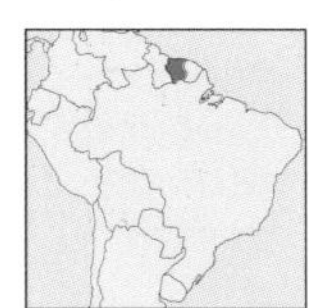

GEOGRAPHY The Republic of Surinam is sandwiched between French Guiana and Guyana in north-eastern South America. The narrow coastal plain was once swampy, but it has been drained and now consists mainly of farmland. Inland lie hills and low mountains, which rise to 1,280 m [4,199 ft].

Surinam has a hot, wet and humid climate. Temperatures are high throughout the year.

POLITICS & ECONOMY In 1667, the British handed Surinam to the Dutch in return for New Amsterdam, an area that is now the state of New York. Slave revolts and Dutch neglect hampered development. In the early 19th century, Britain and the Netherlands disputed the ownership of the area. The British gave up their claims in 1813. Slavery was abolished in 1863 and, soon afterwards, Indian and Indonesian labourers were introduced to work on the plantations. Surinam became fully independent in 1975, but the economy was weakened when thousands of skilled people emigrated from Surinam to the Netherlands.

In 1992, the government negotiated a peace agreement with the *boschneger*, descendants of African slaves, who had launched a struggle against the government in 1986. This rebellion had disrupted the area where bauxite, the main export, was mined. But instability continued, especially among the military. In 1993, the Netherlands stopped financial aid after an EC report stated that Surinam had failed to reform the economy and control inflation.

The World Bank classifies Surinam as an 'upper-middle-income' developing country. Its economy is based on mining and metal processing. Surinam is a leading producer of bauxite, from which the metal aluminium is made.

AREA 163,270 sq km [63,039 sq mls]
POPULATION 427,000
CAPITAL (POPULATION) Paramaribo (201,000)
GOVERNMENT Multiparty republic
ETHNIC GROUPS Asian Indian 37%, Creole (mixed White and Black), 31%, Indonesian 14%, Black 9%, Amerindian 3%, Chinese 3%, Dutch 1%
LANGUAGES Dutch (official), Sranantonga
RELIGIONS Christianity (Roman Catholic 23%, Protestant 19%), Hinduism 27%, Islam 20%
CURRENCY Surinam guilder = 100 cents

SWAZILAND

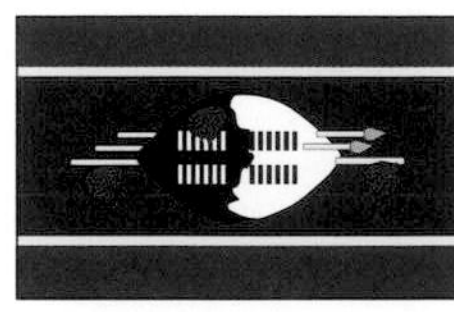

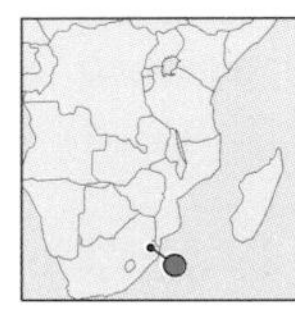

GEOGRAPHY The Kingdom of Swaziland is a small, landlocked country in southern Africa. The country has four regions which run north-south. In the west, the Highveld, with an average height of 1,200 m [3,937 ft], makes up 30% of Swaziland. The Middleveld, between 350 m and 1,000 m [1,148 ft to 3,281 ft], covers 28% of the country. The Lowveld, with an average height of 270 m [886 ft], covers another 33%. Finally, the Lebombo Mountains reach 800 m [2,600 ft] along the eastern border.

The Lowveld is almost tropical, with an average temperature of 22°C [72°F] and low rainfall. The altitude moderates the climate in the west of the country. Mbabane has a climate typical of the Highveld with warm summers and cool winters.

POLITICS & ECONOMY In 1894, Britain and the Boers of South Africa agreed to put Swaziland under the control of the South African Republic (the Transvaal). But at the end of the Anglo-Boer War (1899–1902), Britain took control of the country. In 1968, when Swaziland became fully independent as a constitutional monarchy, the head of state was King Sobhuza II. Sobhuza died in 1982 after a reign of 82 years. In 1983, one of his sons, Prince Makhosetive (born 1968), was chosen as his heir. In 1986, he was installed as King Mswati III. In 1993, Swaziland held its first-ever multiparty elections.

The World Bank classifies Swaziland as a 'lower-middle-income' developing country. Agriculture employs 74% of the people, and farm products and processed foods, including soft drink concentrates, sugar, wood pulp, citrus fruits and canned fruit, are the leading exports. Many farmers live at subsistence level, producing little more than they need to feed their own families. Swaziland is heavily dependent on South Africa and the two countries are linked through a customs union.

AREA 17,360 sq km [6,703 sq mls]
POPULATION 966,000
CAPITAL (POPULATION) Mbabane (42,000)
GOVERNMENT Monarchy
ETHNIC GROUPS Swazi 84%, Zulu 10%, Tsonga 2%
LANGUAGES Siswati and English (both official)
RELIGIONS Christianity 77%, traditional beliefs
CURRENCY Lilangeni = 100 cents

SWEDEN

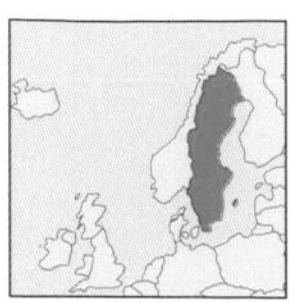

GEOGRAPHY The Kingdom of Sweden is the largest of the countries of Scandinavia in both area and population. It shares the Scandinavian peninsula with Norway. The western part of the country, along the border with Norway, is mountainous. The highest point is Kebnekaise, which reaches 2,117 m [6,946 ft] in the north-west.

The climate of Sweden becomes more severe from south to north. Stockholm has cold winters and cool summers. The far south is much milder.

POLITICS & ECONOMY Swedish Vikings plundered areas to the south and east between the 9th and 11th centuries. Sweden, Denmark and Norway were united in 1397, but Sweden regained its independence in 1523. In 1809, Sweden lost Finland to Russia, but, in 1814, it gained Norway from Denmark. The union between Sweden and Norway was dissolved in 1905. Sweden was neutral in World Wars I and II. Since 1945, Sweden has become a prosperous country. It was a founder member of the European Free Trade Association, but in 1994 the people voted to join the European Union on 1 January 1995.

Sweden has wide-ranging welfare services. But many people are concerned about the high cost of these services and the high taxes they must pay. In 1991, the Social Democrats, who had built up the welfare state, were defeated by a coalition of centre and right-wing parties, though a minority Social Democrat government took office in 1994.

Sweden is a highly developed industrial country. Major products include steel and steel goods. Steel is used in the engineering industry to manufacture aircraft, cars, machinery and ships. Sweden has some of the world's richest iron ore deposits. They are located near Kiruna in the far north. But most of this ore is exported, and Sweden imports most of the materials needed by its industries. In 1996, a decision was taken to decommission all of Sweden's nuclear power stations. This is said to be one of the boldest and most expensive environmental pledges ever made by a government.

AREA 449,960 sq km [173,730 sq mls]
POPULATION 8,887,000
CAPITAL (POPULATION) Stockholm (1,553,000)
GOVERNMENT Constitutional monarchy
ETHNIC GROUPS Swedish 91%, Finnish 3%
LANGUAGES Swedish (official), Finnish
RELIGIONS Christianity (Lutheran 89%, Roman Catholic 2%)
CURRENCY Swedish krona = 100 öre

SWITZERLAND

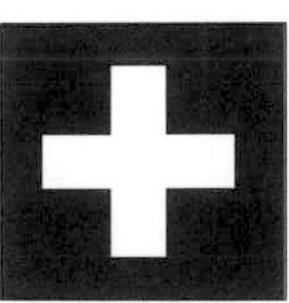

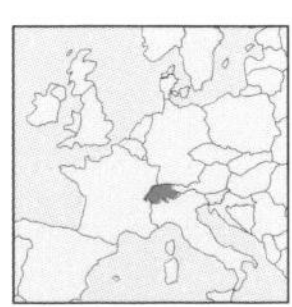

GEOGRAPHY The Swiss Confederation is a landlocked country in Western Europe. Much of the land is mountainous. The Jura Mountains lie along Switzerland's western border with France, while the Swiss Alps make up about 60% of the country in the south and east. Four-fifths of the people of

Switzerland live on the fertile Swiss plateau, which contains most of Switzerland's large cities.

The climate of Switzerland varies greatly according to the height of the land. The plateau region has a central European climate with warm summers, but cold and snowy winters. Rain occurs all through the year. The rainiest months are in summer.

POLITICS & ECONOMY In 1291, three small cantons (states) united to defend their freedom against the Habsburg rulers of the Holy Roman Empire. They were Schwyz, Uri and Unterwalden, and they called the confederation they formed 'Switzerland'. Switzerland expanded and, in the 14th century, defeated Austria in three wars of independence. After a defeat by the French in 1515, the Swiss adopted a policy of neutrality, which they still follow. In 1815, the Congress of Vienna expanded Switzerland to 22 cantons and guaranteed its neutrality. Switzerland's 23rd canton, Jura, was created in 1979 from part of Bern. Neutrality combined with the vigour and independence of its people have made Switzerland prosperous. In 1993, the Swiss people voted against joining the European Union.

Although lacking in natural resources, Switzerland is a wealthy, industrialized country. Many workers are highly skilled. Major products include chemicals, electrical equipment, machinery and machine tools, precision instruments, processed food, watches and textiles. Farmers produce about three-fifths of the country's food – the rest is imported. Livestock raising, especially dairy farming, is the chief agricultural activity. Crops include fruits, potatoes and wheat. Tourism and banking are also important. Swiss banks attract investors from all over the world.

AREA 41,290 sq km [15,942 sq mls]
POPULATION 7,260,000
CAPITAL (POPULATION) Bern (324,000)
GOVERNMENT Federal republic
ETHNIC GROUPS German 64%, French 19%, Italian 8%, Yugoslav 3%, Spanish 2%, Romansch 1%
LANGUAGES French, German, Italian, Romansch (all official)
RELIGIONS Christianity (Roman Catholic 46%, Protestant 40%)
CURRENCY Swiss franc = 100 centimes

SYRIA

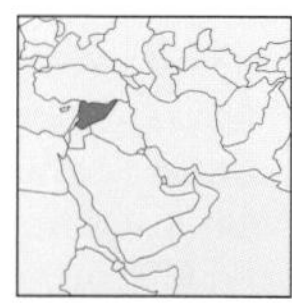

GEOGRAPHY The Syrian Arab Republic is a country in south-western Asia. The narrow coastal plain is overlooked by a low mountain range which runs north–south. Another range, the Jabal ash Sharqi, runs along the border with Lebanon. South of this range is the Golan Heights, which Israel has occupied since 1967.

The coast has a Mediterranean climate, with dry, warm summers and wet, mild winters. The low mountains cut off Damascus from the sea. It has less rainfall than the coastal areas. To the east, the land becomes drier.

POLITICS & ECONOMY After the collapse of the Turkish Ottoman empire in World War I, Syria was ruled by France. Since independence in 1946, Syria has been involved in the Arab–Israeli wars and, in 1967, it lost a strategic border area, the Golan Heights, to Israel. In 1970, Lieutenant-General Hafez al-Assad took power, establishing a stable but repressive regime which attracted international criticism. In the mid-1990s, Syria had talks with Israel over the future of the Golan Heights, but the negotiations were suspended after the election of Benjamin Netanyahu's right-wing government in Israel in 1996.

The World Bank classifies Syria as a 'lower-middle-income' developing country. But it has great potential for development. Its main resources are oil, hydro-electricity from the dam at Lake Assad, and fertile land. Oil is the main export; farm products, textiles and phosphates are also important. Agriculture employs about 26% of the workforce.

AREA 185,180 sq km [71,498 sq mls]
POPULATION 16,673,000
CAPITAL (POPULATION) Damascus (2,230,000)
GOVERNMENT Multiparty republic
ETHNIC GROUPS Arab 89%, Kurd 6%
LANGUAGES Arabic (official)
RELIGIONS Islam 90%, Christianity 9%
CURRENCY Syrian pound = 100 piastres

TAIWAN

GEOGRAPHY High mountain ranges run down the length of the island, with dense forest in many areas.

The climate is warm, moist and suitable for agriculture.

POLITICS & ECONOMY Chinese settlers occupied Taiwan from the 7th century. In 1895, Japan seized the territory from the Portuguese, who had named it Isla Formosa, or 'beautiful island'. China regained the island after World War II. In 1949, it became the refuge of the Nationalists who had been driven out of China by the Communists. They set up the Republic of China, which, with US help, launched an ambitious programme of economic development. Today, it produces a wide range of manufactured goods. Mainland China regards Taiwan as one of its provinces, though reunification seems unlikely in the foreseeable future.

AREA 36,000 sq km [13,900 sq mls]
POPULATION 21,908,000
CAPITAL (population) Taipei (2,653,000)
GOVERNMENT Unitary multiparty republic
ETHNIC GROUPS Taiwanese (Han Chinese) 84%, mainland Chinese 14%
LANGUAGES Mandarin (official), Min, Hakka
RELIGIONS Buddhist 43%, Taoist & Confucian 49%
CURRENCY New Taiwan dollar = 100 cents

TAJIKISTAN

GEOGRAPHY The Republic of Tajikistan is one of the five central Asian republics that formed part of the former Soviet Union. Only 7% of the land is below 1,000 m [3,280 ft], while almost all of eastern Tajikistan is above 3,000 m [9,840 ft]. The highest point is Communism Peak (Pik Kommunizma), which reaches 7,495 m [24,590 ft].

Tajikistan has a severe continental climate. Summers are hot and dry in the lower valleys, and winters are long and bitterly cold in the mountains.

POLITICS & ECONOMY Russia conquered parts of Tajikistan in the late 19th century and, by 1920, Russia took complete control. In 1924, Tajikistan became part of the Uzbek Soviet Socialist Republic, but, in 1929, it was expanded, taking in some areas populated by Uzbeks, becoming the Tajik Soviet Socialist Republic.

While the Soviet Union began to introduce reforms in the 1980s, many Tajiks demanded freedom. In 1989, the Tajik government made Tajik the official language instead of Russian and, in 1990, it stated that its local laws overruled Soviet laws. Tajikistan became fully independent in 1991, following the break-up of the Soviet Union. As the poorest of the ex-Soviet republics, Tajikistan faced many problems in trying to introduce a free-market system.

In 1992, civil war broke out between the government, which was run by former Communists, and an alliance of democrats and Islamic forces. The government maintained control, but it relied heavily on aid from the Commonwealth of Independent States, the organization through which most of the former republics of the Soviet Union kept in contact.

The World Bank classifies Tajikistan as a 'low-income' developing country. Agriculture, mainly on irrigated land, is the main activity and cotton is the chief product. Other crops include fruits, grains and vegetables. The country has large hydroelectric power resources and it produces aluminium.

AREA 143,100 sq km [55,520 sq mls]
POPULATION 6,020,000
CAPITAL (POPULATION) Dushanbe (524,000)
GOVERNMENT Transitional democracy
ETHNIC GROUPS Tajik 62%, Uzbek 24%, Russian 8%, Tatar, Kyrgyz, Ukrainian, German
LANGUAGES Tajik (official), Uzbek, Russian
RELIGIONS Islam
CURRENCY Tajik rouble = 100 tanga

TANZANIA

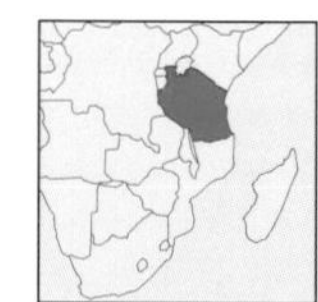

GEOGRAPHY The United Republic of Tanzania consists of the former mainland country of Tanganyika and the island nation of Zanzibar, which also includes the island of Pemba. Behind a narrow coastal plain, most of Tanzania is a plateau, which is broken by arms of the Great African Rift Valley. In the west, this valley contains lakes Nyasa and Tanganyika. The highest peak is Kilimanjaro, Africa's tallest mountain.

The coast has a hot and humid climate, with the greatest rainfall in April and May. The inland plateaux and mountains are cooler and less humid.

POLITICS & ECONOMY Mainland Tanganyika became a German territory in the 1880s, while Zanzibar and Pemba became a British protectorate in 1890. Following Germany's defeat in World War I, Britain took over Tanganyika, which remained a British territory until its independence in 1961. In 1964, Tanganyika and Zanzibar united to form the United Republic of Tanzania. The country's president, Julius Nyerere, pursued socialist policies of self-help (*ujamaa*) and egalitarianism. Many of its social reforms were successful, but the country failed to make economic progress. Nyerere resigned as president in 1985 and his successors introduced more liberal economic policies.

Tanzania is one of the world's poorest countries. Although crops are grown on only 5% of the land, agriculture employs 85% of the people. Most farmers grow only enough to feed their families. Food crops include bananas, cassava, maize, millet, rice and vegetables.

AREA 945,090 sq km [364,899 sq mls]
POPULATION 30,609,000
CAPITAL (POPULATION) Dodoma (204,000)
GOVERNMENT Multiparty republic
ETHNIC GROUPS Nyamwezi and Sukuma 21%, Swahili 9%, Hehet and Bena 7%, Makonde 6%, Haya 6%
LANGUAGES Swahili and English (both official)
RELIGIONS Christianity (mostly Roman Catholic) 34%, Islam 33% (99% in Zanzibar), traditional beliefs and others 33%
CURRENCY Tanzanian shilling = 100 cents

THAILAND

GEOGRAPHY The Kingdom of Thailand is one of the ten countries in South-east Asia. The highest land is in the north, where Doi Inthanon, the highest peak, reaches 2,595 m [8,514 ft]. The Khorat Plateau, in the north-east, makes up about 30% of the country and is the most heavily populated part of Thailand. In the south, Thailand shares the finger-like Malay Peninsula with Burma and Malaysia.

Thailand has a tropical climate. Monsoon winds from the south-west bring heavy rains between the months of May and October. The rainfall in Bangkok is lower than in many other parts of South-east Asia, because mountains shelter the central plains from the rain-bearing winds.

POLITICS & ECONOMY The first Thai state was set up in the 13th century. By 1350, it included most of what is now Thailand. European contact began in the early 16th century. But, in the late 17th century, the Thais, fearing interference in their affairs, forced all Europeans to leave. This policy continued for 150 years. In 1782, a Thai General, Chao Phraya Chakkri, became king, founding a dynasty which continues today. The country became known as Siam, and Bangkok became its capital. From the mid-19th century, contacts with the West were restored. In World War I, Siam supported the Allies against Germany and Austria-Hungary. But in 1941, the country was conquered by Japan and became its ally. But, after the end of World War II, it became an ally of the United States.

Since 1967, when Thailand became a member of ASEAN (the Association of South-east Asian Nations), its economy has grown, especially its manufacturing and service industries. However, in 1997, it suffered recession along with other eastern Asian countries. Despite its rapid progress, the World Bank classifies the country as a 'lower-middle-income' developing country. Manufactures, including food products, machinery, timber products and textiles, are exported, but agriculture still employs two-thirds of the people. Rice is the main food, while other major crops include cassava, cotton, maize, pineapples, rubber, sugar cane and tobacco. Thailand also mines tin and other minerals, and tourism is a major source of income.

AREA 513,120 sq km [198,116 sq mls]
POPULATION 60,037,000
CAPITAL (POPULATION) Bangkok (5,876,000)
GOVERNMENT Constitutional monarchy
ETHNIC GROUPS Thai 80%, Chinese 12%, Malay 4%, Khmer 3%
LANGUAGES Thai (official), Chinese, Malay
RELIGIONS Buddhism 94%, Islam 4%, Christianity 1%
CURRENCY Thai baht = 100 satang

TOGO

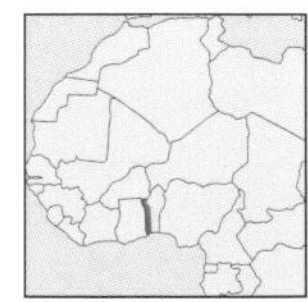

GEOGRAPHY The Republic of Togo is a long, narrow country in West Africa. From north to south, it extends about 500 km [311 mls]. Its coastline on the Gulf of Guinea is only 64 km [40 mls] long and it is only 145 km [90 mls] at its widest point.

Togo has high temperatures all through the year. The main wet season is from March to July, with a minor wet season in October and November.

POLITICS & ECONOMY Togo became a German protectorate in 1884 but, in 1919, Britain took over the western third of the territory, while France took over the eastern two-thirds. In 1956, the people of British Togoland voted to join Ghana, while French Togoland became an independent republic in 1960.

Local rivalries, especially between the northerners and southerners, are important political factors, and, in 1963, a group of army officers from the north assassinated the president, a southerner. In 1967, Gnassingbé Eyadéma, one of the officers responsible for the 1963 coup, took power and suspended the constitution. Constitutional government was restored in 1980 and multiparty elections were held in 1994.

Togo is a poor developing country. Farming employs 65% of the people, but most farmers grow little more than they need to feed their families. Major food crops include cassava, maize, millet and yams. The leading export is phosphate rock, which is used to make fertilizers.

AREA 56,790 sq km [21,927 sq mls]
POPULATION 4,906,000
CAPITAL (POPULATION) Lomé (590,000)
CAPITAL Multiparty republic
ETHNIC GROUPS Ewe-Adja 43%, Tem-Kabre 26%, Gurma 16%
LANGUAGES French (official), Ewe, Kabiye
RELIGIONS Traditional beliefs 50%, Christianity 35%, Islam 15%
CURRENCY CFA franc = 100 centimes

TONGA

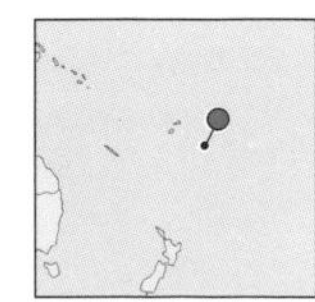

The Kingdom of Tonga, a former British protectorate, became independent in 1970. Situated in the South Pacific Ocean, it contains more than 170 islands, 36 of which are inhabited. Agriculture is the main activity; coconuts, copra, fruits and fish are leading products. **AREA** 75 sq km [290 sq mls]; **POPULATION** 107,000; **CAPITAL** Nuku'alofa.

TRINIDAD AND TOBAGO

The Republic of Trinidad and Tobago became independent from Britain in 1962. These tropical islands, populated by people of African, Asian (mainly Indian) and European origin, are hilly and forested, though there are some fertile plains. Oil production is the main sector of the economy. **AREA** 5,130 sq km [1,981 sq mls]; **POPULATION** 1,117,000; **CAPITAL** Port-of-Spain.

TUNISIA

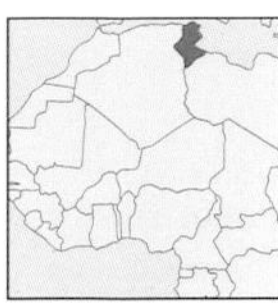

GEOGRAPHY The Republic of Tunisia is the smallest country in North Africa. The mountains in the north are an eastwards and comparatively low extension of the Atlas Mountains. To the north and east of the mountains lie fertile plains, especially between Sfax, Tunis and Bizerte. In the south, low-lying regions contain a vast salt pan, called the Chott Djerid, and part of the Sahara Desert.

Northern Tunisia has a Mediterranean climate, with dry, sunny summers, and mild winters with a moderate rainfall. The average yearly rainfall decreases towards the south.

POLITICS & ECONOMY In 1881, France established a protectorate over Tunisia and ruled the country until 1956. The new parliament abolished the monarchy and declared Tunisia to be a republic in 1957, with the nationalist leader, Habib Bourguiba, as president. His government introduced many reforms, including votes for women, but various problems arose, including unemployment among the middle class and fears that Western values introduced by tourists might undermine Muslim values. In 1987, the prime minister Zine el Abidine Ben Ali removed Bourguiba from office and succeeded him as president. He was elected in 1989 and again in 1994.

The World Bank classifies Tunisia as a 'middle-income' developing country. The main resources and chief exports are phosphates and oil. Most industries are concerned with food processing. Agriculture employs 22% of the people; major crops being barley, dates, grapes, olives and wheat. Fishing is important, as is tourism. Almost four million tourists visited Tunisia in 1994.

AREA 163,610 sq km [63,170 sq mls]
POPULATION 9,380,000
CAPITAL (POPULATION) Tunis (1,827,000)
CAPITAL Multiparty republic
ETHNIC GROUPS Arab 98%, Berber 1%, French
LANGUAGES Arabic (official), French
RELIGIONS Islam 99%
CURRENCY Dinar = 1,000 millimes

TURKEY

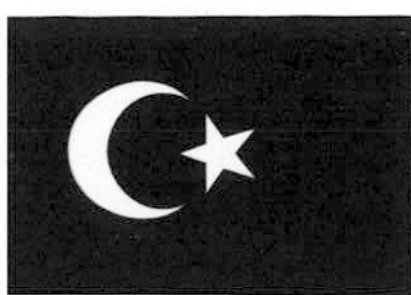

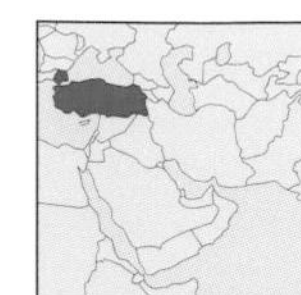

GEOGRAPHY The Republic of Turkey lies in two continents. The European section lies west of a waterway between the Black and Mediterranean seas. European Turkey, also called Thrace, is a fertile, hilly region. Most of the Asian part of Turkey consists of plateaux and mountains, which rise to 5,165 m [16,945 ft] at Mount Ararat (Agri Dagi) near the border with Armenia.

Central Turkey has a dry climate, with hot, sunny summers and cold winters. The driest part of the central plateau lies south of the city of Ankara, around Lake Tuz. Western Turkey has a Mediterranean climate, while the Black Sea coast has cooler summers.

POLITICS & ECONOMY In AD 330, the Roman empire moved its capital to Byzantium, which it renamed Constantinople. Constantinople became capital of the East Roman (or Byzantine) empire in 395. Muslim Seljuk Turks from central Asia invaded Anatolia in the 11th century. In the 14th century, another group of Turks, the Ottomans, conquered the area. In 1435, the Ottoman Turks took Constantinople, which they called Istanbul.

The Ottoman Turks built up a large empire which finally collapsed during World War I (1914–18). In 1923, Turkey became a republic. Its leader Mustafa Kemal, or Atatürk ('father of the Turks'), launched policies to modernize and secularize the country.

Since the 1940s, Turkey has sought to strengthen its ties with Western powers. It joined NATO (North Atlantic Treaty Organization) in 1951 and it applied to join the European Economic Community in 1987. But Turkey's conflict with Greece, together with its invasion of northern Cyprus in 1974, have led many Europeans to treat Turkey's aspirations with caution. Political instability, military coups, conflict with Kurdish nationalists in eastern Turkey and concern about the country's record on human rights are other problems. Turkey has enjoyed democracy since 1983, though, in 1998, the government banned the Islamist Welfare Party, which it accused of violating secular principles. In 1999, the Muslim Virtue Party (successor to Islamist Welfare Party) lost ground. The largest numbers of parliamentary seats were won by the ruling Democratic Left Party and the far-right National Action Party.

The World Bank classifies Turkey as a 'lower-middle-income' developing country. Agriculture employs 47% of the people, and barley, cotton, fruits, maize, tobacco and wheat are major crops. Livestock farming is important and wool is a leading product.

Turkey produces chromium, but manufacturing is the chief activity. Manufactures include processed farm products and textiles, cars, fertilizers, iron and steel, machinery, metal products and paper products. Over nine million tourists visited Turkey in 1998. But, in 1999, tourism was threatened by Kurdish bombings in Ankara and Istanbul.

AREA 779,450 sq km [300,946 sq mls]
POPULATION 64,568,000
CAPITAL (POPULATION) Ankara (3,028,000)
GOVERNMENT Multiparty republic
ETHNIC GROUPS Turkish 86%, Kurdish 11%, Arab 2%
LANGUAGES Turkish (official), Kurdish
RELIGIONS Islam 99%
CURRENCY Turkish lira = 100 kurus

TURKMENISTAN

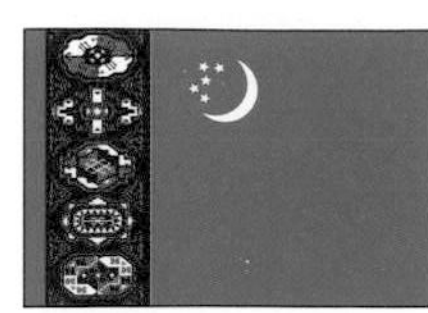

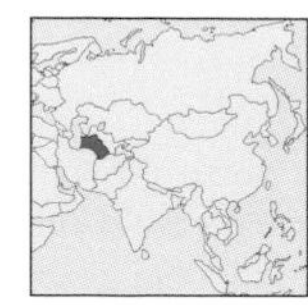

GEOGRAPHY The Republic of Turkmenistan is one of the five central Asian republics which once formed part of the former Soviet Union. Most of the land is low-lying, with mountains lying on the southern and south-western borders. In the west lies the salty Caspian Sea. Most of Turkmenistan is arid and the Garagum, Asia's largest sand desert, covers about 80% of the country. Turkmenistan has a continental climate, with average annual rainfall varying from 80 mm [3 in] in the desert to 300 mm [12 in] in the mountains. Summer months are hot but winter temperatures drop well below freezing point.

POLITICS & ECONOMY Just over 1,000 years ago, Turkic people settled in the lands east of the Caspian Sea and the name 'Turkmen' comes from this time. Mongol armies conquered the area in the 13th century and Islam was introduced in the 14th century. Russia took over the area in the 1870s and 1880s. After the Russian Revolution of 1917, the area came under Communist rule and, in 1924, it became the Turkmen Soviet Socialist Republic. The Communists strictly controlled all aspects of life and, in particular, they discouraged religious worship. But they also improved such services as education, health, housing and transport.

In the 1980s, when the Soviet Union began to introduce reforms, the Turkmen began to demand more freedom. In 1990, the Turkmen government stated that its laws overruled Soviet laws. In 1991, Turkmenistan became fully independent after the break-up of the Soviet Union. But the country kept ties with Russia through the Commonwealth of Independent States (CIS).

In 1992, Turkmenistan adopted a new constitution, allowing for the setting up of political parties, providing that they were not ethnic or religious in character. But, effectively, Turkmenistan remained a one-party state and, in 1992, Saparmurad Niyazov, the former Communist and now Democratic party leader, was the only candidate. In 1994, 99.5% of the voters in a referendum were in favour of prolonging Niyazov's term of office to 2002.

Faced with many economic problems, Turkmenistan began to look south rather than to the CIS for support. As part of this policy, it joined the Economic Co-operation Organization which had been set up in 1985 by Iran, Pakistan and Turkey. In 1996, the completion of a rail link from Turkmenistan to the Iranian coast was seen both as a revival of the traditions of the ancient silk road, and as a highly significant step for the future economic development of Central Asia.

Turkmenistan's chief resources are oil and natural gas, but the main activity is agriculture, with cotton, grown on irrigated land, as the main crop. Grain and vegetables are also important. Manufactures include cement, glass, petrochemicals and textiles.

AREA 488,100 sq km [188,450 sq mls]
POPULATION 4,298,000
CAPITAL (POPULATION) Ashgabat (407,000)
GOVERNMENT Single-party republic
ETHNIC GROUPS Turkmen 72%, Russian 10%, Uzbek 9%, Kazak 3%, Tatar
LANGUAGES Turkmen (official), Russian, Uzbek, Kazak
RELIGIONS Islam
CURRENCY Manat = 100 tenesi

TURKS AND CAICOS ISLANDS

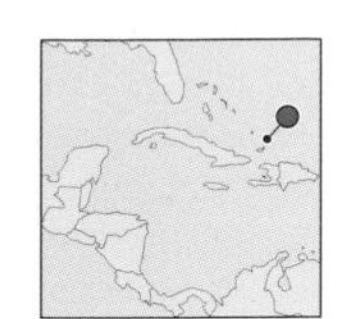

The Turks and Caicos Islands, a British territory in the Caribbean since 1776, are a group of about 30 islands. Fishing and tourism are major activities. **AREA** 430 sq km [166 sq mls]; **POPULATION** 16,000; **CAPITAL** Cockburn Town.

TUVALU

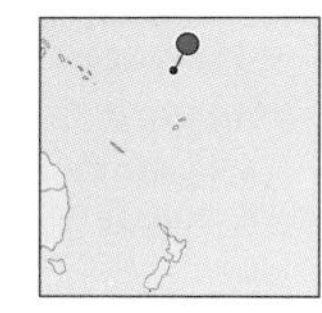

Tuvalu, formerly called the Ellice Islands, was a British territory from the 1890s until it became independent in 1978. It consists of nine low-lying coral atolls in the southern Pacific Ocean. Copra is the chief export. **AREA** 24 sq km [9 sq mls]; **POPULATION** 10,000; **CAPITAL** Fongafale.

UGANDA

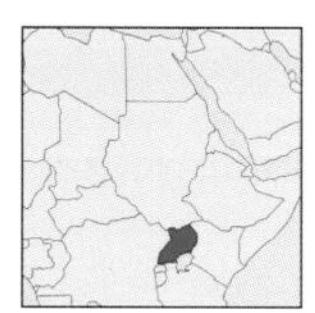

GEOGRAPHY The Republic of Uganda is a landlocked country on the East African plateau. It contains part of Lake Victoria, Africa's largest lake and a source of the River Nile, which occupies a shallow depression in the plateau.

The equator runs through Uganda and the country is warm throughout the year, though the high altitude moderates the temperature. The wettest regions are the lands to the north of Lake Victoria, where Kampala is situated, and the western mountains, especially the high Ruwenzori range.

POLITICS & ECONOMY Little is known of the early history of Uganda. When Europeans first reached the area in the 19th century, many of the people were organized in kingdoms, the most powerful of which was Buganda, the home of the Baganda people. Britain took over the country between 1894 and 1914, and ruled it until independence in 1962.

In 1967, Uganda became a republic and Buganda's Kabaka (king), Sir Edward Mutesa II, was made president. But tensions between the Kabaka and the prime minister, Apollo Milton Obote, led to the dismissal of the Kabaka in 1966. Obote also abolished the traditional kingdoms, including Buganda. Obote was overthrown in 1971 by an army group led by General Idi Amin Dada. Amin ruled as a dictator. He forced most of the Asians who lived in Uganda to leave the country and had many of his opponents killed.

In 1978, a border dispute between Uganda and Tanzania led Tanzanian troops to enter Uganda. With help from Ugandan opponents of Amin, they overthrew Amin's government. In 1980, Obote led his party to victory in national elections. But after charges of fraud, Obote's opponents began guerrilla warfare. A military group overthrew Obote in 1985, but strife continued until 1986, when Yoweri

Museveni's National Resistance Movement seized power. In 1993, Museveni restored the traditional kingdoms, including Buganda where a new Kabaka was crowned. Museveni also held national elections in 1994 but political parties were not permitted. Museveni was elected president in 1996.

The strife in Uganda since the 1960s has greatly damaged the economy. By 1991 Uganda was, according to the World Bank, among the world's five poorest countries. Agriculture dominates the economy, employing 86% of the people. The chief export is coffee.

AREA 235,880 sq km [91,073 sq mls]
POPULATION 22,167,000
CAPITAL (POPULATION) Kampala (773,000)
GOVERNMENT Republic in transition
ETHNIC GROUPS Baganda 18%, Banyoro 14%, Teso 9%, Banyan 8%, Basoga 8%, Bagisu 7%, Bachiga 7%, Lango 6%, Acholi 5%
LANGUAGES English and Swahili (both official)
RELIGIONS Christianity (Roman Catholic 40%, Protestant 29%), traditional beliefs 18%, Islam 7%
CURRENCY Uganda shilling = 100 cent

UKRAINE

GEOGRAPHY Ukraine is the second largest country in Europe after Russia. It was formerly part of the Soviet Union, which split apart in 1991. This mostly flat country faces the Black Sea in the south. The Crimean peninsula includes a highland region overlooking Yalta.

Ukraine has warm summers, but the winters are cold, becoming more severe from west to east. In the summer, the east of the country is often warmer than the west. The heaviest rainfall occurs in the summer.

POLITICS & ECONOMY Kiev was the original capital of the early Slavic civilization known as Kievan Rus. In the 17th and 18th centuries, parts of Ukraine came under Polish and Russian rule. But Russia gained most of Ukraine in the late 18th century. In 1918, Ukraine became independent, but in 1922 it became part of the Soviet Union. Millions of people died in the 1930s as the result of Soviet policies, while millions more died during the Nazi occupation (1941–4).

In the 1980s, Ukrainian people demanded more say over their affairs. The country finally became independent when the Soviet Union broke up in 1991. Ukraine continued to work with Russia through the Commonwealth of Independent States. But Ukraine differed with Russia on some issues, including control over Crimea. In 1999, a treaty ratifying Ukraine's present boundaries failed to get the approval of Russia's upper house.

The World Bank classifies Ukraine as a 'lower-middle-income' economy. Agriculture is important. Crops include wheat and sugar beet, which are the major exports, together with barley, maize, potatoes, sunflowers and tobacco. Livestock rearing and fishing are also important industries.

Manufacturing is the chief economic activity. Major manufactures include iron and steel, machinery and vehicles. The country has large coalfields. The country imports oil and natural gas, but it has hydro-electric and nuclear power stations. In 1986, an accident at the Chernobyl nuclear power plant caused widespread nuclear radiation.

AREA 603,700 sq km [233,100 sq mls]
POPULATION 50,125,000
CAPITAL (POPULATION) Kiev (2,630,000)
GOVERNMENT Multiparty republic
ETHNIC GROUPS Ukrainian 73%, Russian 22%, Jewish 1%, Belarussian 1%, Moldovan, Bulgarian, Polish
LANGUAGES Ukrainian (official), Russian
RELIGIONS Christianity (mostly Ukrainian Orthodox)
CURRENCY Hryvna

UNITED ARAB EMIRATES

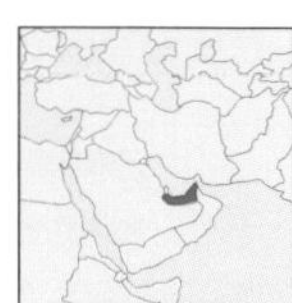

The United Arab Emirates were formed in 1971 when the seven Trucial States of the Gulf (Abu Dhabi, Dubai, Sharjah, Ajman, Umm al Qawayn, Ra's al Khaymah and Al Fujayrah) opted to join together and form an independent country. The economy of this hot and dry country depends on oil production, and oil revenues give the United Arab Emirates one of the highest per capita GNPs in Asia. **AREA** 83,600 sq km [32,278 sq mls]; **POPULATION** 2,303,000; **CAPITAL** Abu Dhabi.

UNITED KINGDOM

GEOGRAPHY The United Kingdom (or UK) is a union of four countries. Three of them – England, Scotland and Wales – make up Great Britain. The fourth country is Northern Ireland. The Isle of Man and the Channel Islands, including Jersey and Guernsey, are not part of the UK. They are self-governing British dependencies.

The land is highly varied. Much of Scotland and Wales is mountainous, and the highest peak is Scotland's Ben Nevis at 1,343 m [4,406 ft]. England has some highland areas, including the Cumbrian Mountains (or Lake District) and the Pennine range in the north. But England also has large areas of fertile lowland. Northern Ireland is also a mixture of lowlands and uplands. It contains the UK's largest lake, Lough Neagh.

The UK has a mild climate, influenced by the warm Gulf Stream which flows across the Atlantic from the Gulf of Mexico, then past the British Isles. Moist winds from the south-west bring rain, but the rainfall decreases from west to east. Winds from the east and north bring cold weather in winter.

POLITICS & ECONOMY In ancient times, Britain was invaded by many peoples, including Iberians, Celts, Romans, Angles, Saxons, Jutes, Norsemen, Danes, and Normans, who arrived in 1066. The evolution of the United Kingdom spanned hundreds of years. The Normans finally overcame Welsh resistance in 1282, when King Edward I annexed Wales and united it with England. Union with Scotland was achieved by the Act of Union of 1707. This created a country known as the United Kingdom of Great Britain.

Ireland came under Norman rule in the 11th century, and much of its later history was concerned with a struggle against English domination. In 1801, Ireland became part of the United Kingdom of Great Britain and Ireland. But in 1921, southern Ireland broke away to become the Irish Free State. Most of the people in the Irish Free State were Roman Catholics. In Northern Ireland, where the majority of the people were Protestants, most people wanted to remain citizens of the United Kingdom. As a result, the country's official name changed to the United Kingdom of Great Britain and Northern Ireland.

The modern history of the UK began in the 18th century when the British empire began to develop, despite the loss in 1783 of its 13 North American colonies which became the core of the modern United States. The other major event occurred in the late 18th century, when the UK became the first country to industrialize its economy.

The British empire broke up after World War II (1939–45), though the UK still administers many small, mainly island, territories around the world. The empire was transformed into the Commonwealth of Nations, a free association of independent countries which numbered 54 in 1999.

But while the UK retained a world role through the Commonwealth and the United Nations, it recognized that its economic future lay within Europe. As a result, it became a member of the European Economic Community (now the European Union) in 1973. In the 1990s, most people accepted the importance of the European Union to the UK's economic future. But some feared a loss of British identity should the European Union evolve into a political federation. In 1999, the UK began to decentralize power away from London as people in Scotland and Wales elected regional assemblies, while referendums on city mayors were planned.

The UK is a major industrial and trading nation. It lacks natural resources apart from coal, iron ore, oil and natural gas, and has to import most of the materials it needs for its industries. The UK also has to import food, because it produces only about two-thirds of the food it needs.

In the first half of the 20th century, the UK became known for exporting such products as cars, ships, steel and textiles. However, many traditional industries have suffered from increased competition from other countries, whose lower labour costs enable them to produce goods more cheaply. Today, a growing number of industries use sophisticated high-technology in order to compete on the world market.

The UK is one of the world's most urbanized countries, and agriculture employs only 2% of the people. Yet production is high because farms use scientific methods and modern machinery. Major crops include barley, potatoes, sugar beet and wheat. Sheep are the leading livestock, but beef cattle, dairy cattle, pigs and poultry are also important. Fishing is another major activity.

Service industries play a major part in the UK's economy. Financial and insurance services bring in much-needed foreign exchange, while tourism has become a major earner.

AREA 243,368 sq km [94,202 sq mls]
POPULATION 58,970,000
CAPITAL (POPULATION) London (8,089,000)
GOVERNMENT Constitutional monarchy
ETHNIC GROUPS White 94%, Asian Indian 1%, Pakistani 1%, West Indian 1%
LANGUAGES English (official), Welsh, Gaelic
RELIGIONS Christianity (Anglican 57%, Roman Catholic 13%, Presbyterian 7%, Methodist 4%, Baptist 1%), Islam 1%, Judaism, Hinduism, Sikhism
CURRENCY Pound sterling = 100 pence

UNITED STATES OF AMERICA

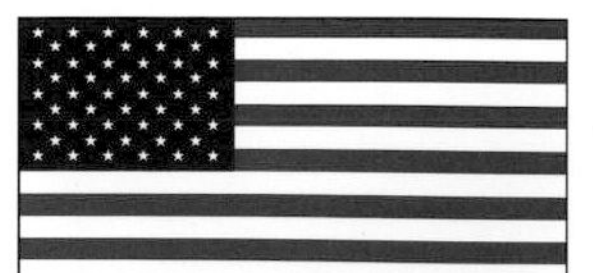

GEOGRAPHY The United States of America is the world's fourth largest country in area and the third largest in population. It contains 50 states, 48 of which lie between Canada and Mexico, plus Alaska in north-western North America, and Hawaii, a group of volcanic islands in the North Pacific Ocean. Densely populated coastal plains lie to the east and south of the Appalachian Mountains. The central lowlands drained by the Mississippi–Missouri rivers stretch from the Appalachians to the Rocky Mountains in the west. The Pacific region contains fertile valleys, separated by mountain ranges.

The climate varies greatly, ranging from the Arctic cold of Alaska to the intense heat of Death Valley, a bleak desert in California. Of the 48 states between Canada and Mexico, winters are cold and snowy in the north, but mild in the south, a region which is often called the 'Sun Belt'.

POLITICS & ECONOMY The first people in North America, the ancestors of the Native Americans (or American Indians) arrived perhaps 40,000 years ago from Asia. Although Vikings probably reached North America 1,000 years ago, European exploration proper did not begin until the late 15th century.

The first Europeans to settle in large numbers were the British, who founded settlements on the eastern coast in the early 17th century. British rule ended in the War of Independence (1775–83). The country expanded in 1803 when a vast territory in the south and west was acquired through the Louisiana Purchase, while the border with Mexico was fixed in the mid-19th century.

The Civil War (1861–5) ended the threat that the nation might split in two parts. It also ended slavery for the country's many African Americans. In the late 19th century, the West was opened up, while immigrants flooded in from Europe and elsewhere.

During the late 19th and early 20th centuries, industrialization led to the United States becoming the world's leading economic superpower and a pioneer in science and technology. Because of its economic strength, it has been able to take on the mantle of the champion of the Western world and of democratic government. The fall of Communism and the subsequent break-up of the Soviet Union left the US as the world's only real superpower. While this supremacy may well be challenged by China in time, the USA remains the most powerful voice in global politics.

The United States has the world's largest economy in terms of the total value of its production. Although agriculture employs only 2% of the people, farming is highly mechanized and scientific, and the United States leads the world in farm production. Major products include beef and dairy cattle, together with such crops as cotton, fruits, groundnuts, maize, potatoes, soya beans, tobacco and wheat.

The country's natural resources include oil, natural gas and coal. There are also a wide range of metal ores which are used in manufacturing industries, together with timber, especially from the forests of the Pacific north-west. Manufacturing is the single most important activity, employing about 17% of the population. Major products include vehicles, food products, chemicals, machinery, printed goods, metal products and scientific instruments. California is now the leading manufacturing state. Many southern states, petroleum rich and climatically favoured, have also become highly prosperous in recent years.

AREA 9,372,610 sq km [3,618,765 sq mls]
POPULATION 270,290,000
CAPITAL (POPULATION) Washington, D.C. (4,466,000)
GOVERNMENT Federal republic
ETHNIC GROUPS White 80%, African American 12%, other races 8%
LANGUAGES English (official), Spanish, more than 30 others
RELIGIONS Christianity (Protestant 53%, Roman Catholic 26%, other Christian 8%), Islam 2%, Judaism 2%
CURRENCY US dollar = 100 cents

URUGUAY

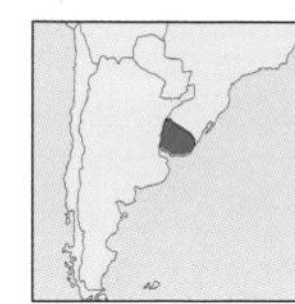

GEOGRAPHY Uruguay is South America's second smallest independent country after Surinam. The land consists mainly of flat plains and hills. The River Uruguay, which forms the country's western border, flows into the Río de la Plata, a large estuary which leads into the South Atlantic Ocean.

Uruguay has a mild climate, with rain in every month, though droughts sometimes occur. Summers are pleasantly warm, especially near the coast. The weather remains relatively mild throughout the winter.

POLITICS & ECONOMY In 1726, Spanish settlers founded Montevideo in order to halt the Portuguese gaining influence in the area. By the late 18th century, Spaniards had settled in most of the country. Uruguay became part of a colony called the Viceroyalty of La Plata, which also included Argentina, Paraguay, and parts of Bolivia, Brazil and Chile. In 1820 Brazil annexed Uruguay, ending Spanish rule. In 1825, Uruguayans, supported by Argentina, began a struggle for independence. Finally, in 1828, Brazil and Argentina recognized Uruguay as an independent republic. Social and economic developments were slow in the 19th century, but, from 1903, governments made Uruguay a democratic and stable country.

From the 1950s, economic problems caused unrest. Terrorist groups, notably the Tupumaros, carried out murders and kidnappings. The army crushed the Tupumaros in 1972, but the army took over the government in 1973. Military rule continued until 1984 when elections were held. Julio Maria Sanguinetti, who led Uruguay back to civilian rule, was re-elected president in 1994.

The World Bank classifies Uruguay as an 'upper-middle-income' developing country. Agriculture employs only 5% of the people, but farm products, notably hides and leather goods, beef and wool, are the leading exports, while the leading manufacturing industries process farm products. The main crops include maize, potatoes, wheat and sugar beet.

AREA 177,410 sq km [68,498 sq mls]
POPULATION 3,285,000
CAPITAL (POPULATION) Montevideo (1,326,000)
GOVERNMENT Multiparty republic
ETHNIC GROUPS White 86%, Mestizo 8%, Mulatto or Black 6%
LANGUAGES Spanish (official)
RELIGIONS Christianity (Roman Catholic 66%, Protestant 2%), Judaism 1%
CURRENCY Uruguay peso = 100 centésimos

UZBEKISTAN

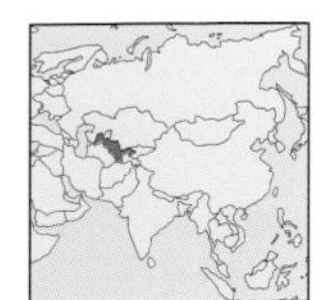

GEOGRAPHY The Republic of Uzbekistan is one of the five republics in Central Asia which were once part of the Soviet Union. Plains cover most of western Uzbekistan, with highlands in the east. The main rivers, the Amu (or Amu Darya) and Syr (or Syr Darya), drain into the Aral Sea. So much water has been taken from these rivers to irrigate the land that the Aral Sea shrank from 66,900 sq km [25,830 sq mls] in 1960 to 33,642 sq km [12,989 sq mls] in 1993. The dried-up lake area has become desert, like much of the rest of the country.

Uzbekistan has a continental climate. The winters are cold, but the temperatures soar in the summer months. The west is extremely arid, with an average annual rainfall of about 200 mm [8 in].

POLITICS & ECONOMY Russia took the area in the 19th century. After the Russian Revolution of 1917, the Communists took over and, in 1924, they set up the Uzbek Soviet Socialist Republic. Under Communism, all aspects of Uzbek life were controlled and religious worship was discouraged. But education, health, housing and transport were improved. In the late 1980s, the people demanded more freedom and, in 1990, the government stated that its laws overruled those of the Soviet Union. Uzbekistan became independent in 1991 when the Soviet Union broke up, but it retained links with Russia through the Commonwealth of Independent States. Islam Karimov, leader of the People's Democratic Party (formerly the Communist Party), was elected president in December 1991. In 1992–3, many opposition leaders were arrested because the government said that they threatened national stability. In 1994–5, the PDP won sweeping victories in national elections and, in 1995, a referendum extended Karimov's term in office until 2000.

The World Bank classifies Uzbekistan as a 'lower-middle-income' developing country and the government still controls most economic activity. The country produces coal, copper, gold, oil and natural gas.

AREA 447,400 sq km [172,740 sq mls]
POPULATION 23,784,000
CAPITAL (POPULATION) Tashkent (2,106,000)
GOVERNMENT Socialist republic
ETHNIC GROUPS Uzbek 71%, Russian 8%, Tajik 5%, Kazak 4%, Tatar 2%, Kara-Kalpak 2%
LANGUAGES Uzbek (official), several others
RELIGIONS Islam
CURRENCY Som = 100 tyiyn

VANUATU

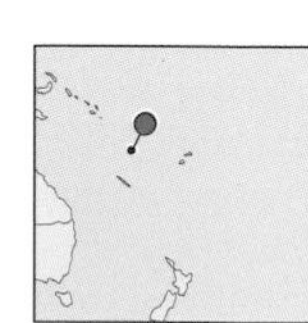

The Republic of Vanuatu, formerly the Anglo-French Condominium of the New Hebrides, became independent in 1980. It consists of a chain of 80 islands in the South Pacific Ocean. Its economy is based on agriculture and it exports copra, beef and veal, timber and cocoa. **AREA** 12,190 sq km [4,707 sq mls]; **POPULATION** 185,000; **CAPITAL** Port-Vila.

VATICAN CITY

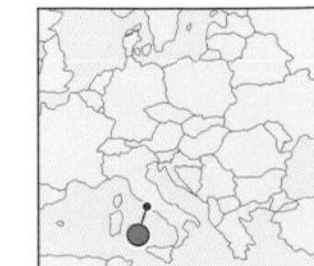

Vatican City State, the world's smallest independent nation, is an enclave on the west bank of the River Tiber in Rome. It forms an independent base for the Holy See, the governing body of the Roman Catholic Church. **AREA** 0.44 sq km [0.17 sq mls]; **POPULATION** about 1,000.

VENEZUELA

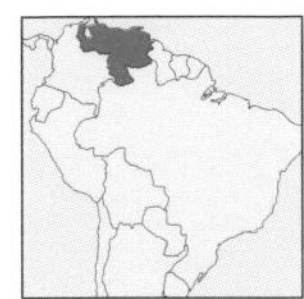

GEOGRAPHY The Republic of Venezuela, in northern South America, contains the Maracaibo lowlands around the oil-rich Lake Maracaibo in the west. Andean ranges enclose the lowlands and extend across most of northern Venezuela. The Orinoco river basin, containing tropical grasslands called *llanos*, lies between the northern highlands and the Guiana Highlands in the south-east.

Venezuela has a tropical climate. Temperatures are high throughout the year on the lowlands, though the mountains are much cooler. The rainfall is heaviest in the mountains. But much of the country has a marked dry season between December and April.

POLITICS & ECONOMY In the early 19th century, Venezuelans, such as Simón Bolívar and Francisco de Miranda, began a struggle against Spanish rule. Venezuela declared its independence in 1811. But it only become truly independent in 1821, when the Spanish were defeated in a battle near Valencia.

The development of Venezuela in the 19th and the first half of the 20th centuries was marred by instability, violence and periods of harsh dictatorial rule. But the country has had elected governments since 1958. The country has greatly benefited from its oil resources which were first exploited in 1917. In 1960, Venezuela helped to form OPEC (the Organization of Petroleum Exporting Countries) and, in 1976, the government of Venezuela took control of the entire oil industry. Money from oil exports has helped Venezuela to raise living standards and diversify the economy.

The World Bank classifies Venezuela as an 'upper-middle-income' developing country. Oil accounts for 80% of the exports. Other exports include bauxite and aluminium, iron ore and farm products. Agriculture employs 13% of the people and cattle ranching is important. The chief industry is petroleum refining. Other manufactures include aluminium, cement, processed food, steel and textiles. The main manufacturing centres include Caracas, Ciudad Guayana (aluminium and steel) and Maracaibo (oil refineries).

AREA 912,050 sq km [352,143 sq mls]
POPULATION 22,803,000
CAPITAL (POPULATION) Caracas (2,784,000)
GOVERNMENT Federal republic
ETHNIC GROUPS Mestizo 67%, White 21%, Black 10%, Amerindian 2%
LANGUAGES Spanish (official), Goajiro
RELIGIONS Christianity (Roman Catholic 94%)
CURRENCY Bolívar = 100 céntimos

VIETNAM

GEOGRAPHY The Socialist Republic of Vietnam occupies an S-shaped strip of land facing the South China Sea in South-east Asia. The coastal plains include two densely populated, fertile delta regions: the Red (Hong) delta facing the Gulf of Tonkin in the north, and the Mekong delta in the south.

Vietnam has a tropical climate, though the driest months of January to March are a little cooler than the wet, hot summer months, when monsoon winds blow from the south-west. Typhoons (cyclones) sometimes hit the coast, causing much damage.

POLITICS & ECONOMY China dominated Vietnam for a thousand years before AD 939, when a Vietnamese state was founded. The French took over the area between the 1850s and 1880s. They ruled Vietnam as part of French Indo-China, which also included Cambodia and Laos.

Japan conquered Vietnam during World War II (1939–45). In 1946, war broke out between a nationalist group, called the Vietminh, and the French colonial government. France withdrew in 1954 and Vietnam was divided into a Communist North Vietnam, led by the Vietminh leader, Ho Chi Minh, and a non-Communist South.

A force called the Viet Cong rebelled against South Vietnam's government in 1957 and a war began, which gradually increased in intensity. The United States aided the South, but after it withdrew in 1975, South Vietnam surrendered. In 1976, the united Vietnam became a Socialist Republic.

Vietnamese troops intervened in Cambodia in 1978 to defeat the Communist Khmer Rouge government, but it withdrew its troops in 1989. In the 1990s, Vietnam began to introduce reforms. In 1995, relations with the US were normalized when the US opened an embassy in Hanoi.

The World Bank classifies Vietnam as a 'low-income' developing country and agriculture employs 67% of the population. The main food crop is rice. The country also produces chromium, oil (which was discovered off the south coast in 1986), phosphates and tin.

AREA 331,689 sq km [128,065 sq mls]
POPULATION 76,236,000
CAPITAL (POPULATION) Hanoi (3,056,000)
GOVERNMENT Socialist republic
ETHNIC GROUPS Vietnamese 87%, Tho (Tay), Chinese (Hoa), Tai, Khmer, Muong, Nung
LANGUAGES Vietnamese (official), Chinese
RELIGIONS Buddhism 55%, Christianity (Roman Catholic 7%)
CURRENCY Dong = 10 hao = 100 xu

VIRGIN ISLANDS, BRITISH

VIGILATE
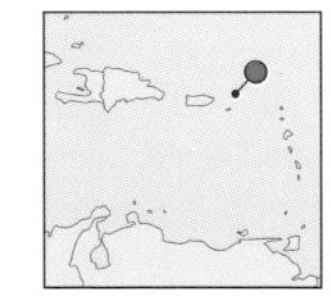

The British Virgin Islands, the most northerly of the Lesser Antilles, are a British overseas territory, with a substantial measure of self-government. **AREA** 153 sq km [59 sq mls]; **POPULATION** 13,000; **CAPITAL** Road Town.

VIRGIN ISLANDS, US

V
I
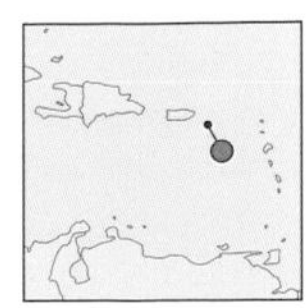

The Virgin Islands of the United States, a group of three islands and 65 small islets, are a self-governing US territory. Purchased from Denmark in 1917, its residents are US citizens and they elect a non-voting delegate to the US House of Representatives. **AREA** 340 sq km [130 sq mls]; **POPULATION** 118,000; **CAPITAL** Charlotte Amalie.

WALLIS AND FUTUNA

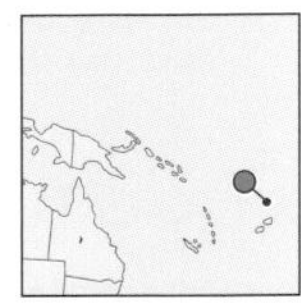

Wallis and Futuna, in the South Pacific Ocean, is the smallest and the poorest of France's overseas territories. **AREA** 200 sq km [77 sq mls]; **POPULATION** 15,000; **CAPITAL** Mata-Utu.

WESTERN SAMOA

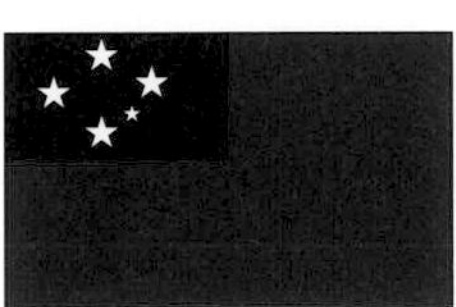
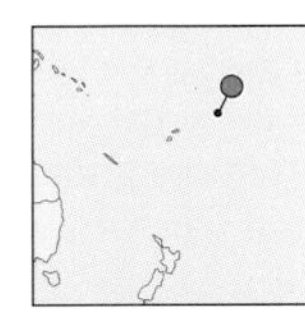

The Independent State of Western Samoa comprises two islands in the South Pacific Ocean. Governed by New Zealand from 1920, the territory became independent in 1962. Exports include taro, coconut cream and beer. **AREA** 2,840 sq km [1,097 sq mls]; **POPULATION** 224,000; **CAPITAL** Apia.

YEMEN

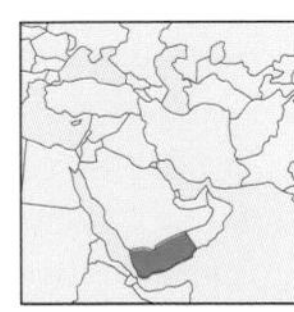

GEOGRAPHY The Republic of Yemen faces the Red Sea and the Gulf of Aden in the south-western corner of the Arabian peninsula. Behind the narrow coastal plain along the Red Sea, the land rises to a mountain region called High Yemen.

The climate ranges from hot and often humid conditions on the coast to the cooler highlands. Most of the country is arid.

POLITICS & ECONOMY After World War I, northern Yemen, which had been ruled by Turkey, began to evolve into a separate state from the south, where Britain was in control. Britain withdrew in 1967 and a left-wing government took power in the south. In North Yemen, the monarchy was abolished in 1962 and the country became a republic.

Clashes occurred between the traditionalist Yemen Arab Republic in the north and the formerly British Marxist People's Democratic Republic of Yemen but, in 1990, the two Yemens merged to form a single country. Since then, the union has held together, despite a two-month civil war in 1994.

The World Bank classifies Yemen as a 'low-income'

developing country. Agriculture employs up to 63% of the people. Herders raise sheep and other animals, while farmers grow such crops as barley, fruits, wheat and vegetables in highland valleys and around oases. Cash crops include coffee and cotton.

Imported oil is refined at Aden and petroleum extraction began in the north-west in the 1980s. Handicrafts, leather goods and textiles are manufactured. Remittances from Yemenis abroad are a major source of revenue.

AREA 527,970 sq km [203,849 sq mls]
POPULATION 16,388,000
CAPITAL (POPULATION) San'a (972,000)
GOVERNMENT Multiparty republic
ETHNIC GROUPS Arab 96%, Somali 1%
LANGUAGES Arabic (official)
RELIGIONS Islam
CURRENCY Rial = 100 fils

YUGOSLAVIA

GEOGRAPHY The Federal Republic of Yugoslavia consists of Serbia and Montenegro, two of the six republics which made up the former country of Yugoslavia until it broke up in 1991 and 1992. Behind the short coastline along the Adriatic Sea lies a mountainous region, including the Dinaric Alps and part of the Balkan Mountains. The Pannonian Plains make up northern Yugoslavia.

The coast has a Mediterranean climate. The highlands have cold winters and cool summers.

POLITICS & ECONOMY People who became known as the South Slavs began to move into the region around 1,500 years ago. Each group, including the Serbs and Croats, founded its own state. But, by the 15th century, foreign countries controlled the region. Serbia and Montenegro were under the Turkish Ottoman empire.

In the 19th century, many Slavs worked for independence and Slavic unity. In 1914, Austria-Hungary declared war on Serbia, blaming it for the assassination of Archduke Francis Ferdinand of Austria-Hungary. This led to World War I and the defeat of Austria-Hungary. In 1918, the South Slavs united in the Kingdom of the Serbs, Croats and Slovenes, which consisted of Bosnia-Herzegovina, Croatia, Dalmatia, Montenegro, Serbia and Slovenia. The country was renamed Yugoslavia in 1929. Germany occupied Yugoslavia during World War II, but partisans, including a Communist force led by Josip Broz Tito, fought the invaders.

From 1945, the Communists controlled the country, which was called the Federal People's Republic of Yugoslavia. But after Tito's death in 1980, the country faced many problems. In 1990, non-Communist parties were permitted and non-Communists won majorities in elections in all but Serbia and Montenegro, where Socialists (former Communists) won control. Yugoslavia split apart in 1991–2 with Bosnia-Herzegovina, Croatia, Macedonia and Slovenia proclaiming their independence. The two remaining republics of Serbia and Montenegro became the new Yugoslavia.

Fighting broke out in Croatia and Bosnia-Herzegovina as rival groups struggled for power. In 1992, the United Nations withdrew recognition of Yugoslavia because of its failure to halt atrocities committed by Serbs living in Croatia and Bosnia. In 1995, Yugoslavia was involved in the talks that led to the Dayton Peace Accord, which brought peace to Bosnia-Herzegovina. But the issue of Yugoslav repression of minorities flared up again in 1998 in Kosovo, a province where the majority are ethnic Albanians. In response to a developing conflict between Kosovar nationalism and Serb ethnic cleansing, NATO forces launched an aerial offensive against Yugoslavia in March 1999. This accelerated the flight of ethnic Albanians from Kosovo.

Under Communist rule, manufacturing became increasingly important in Yugoslavia. But in the early 1990s, the World Bank classified Yugoslavia as a 'lower-middle-income' economy. Its resources include bauxite, coal, copper and other metals, together with oil and natural gas. Manufactures include aluminium, machinery, plastics, steel, textiles and vehicles. The chief exports are manufactures, but agriculture remains important. Crops include fruits, maize, potatoes, tobacco and wheat. Cattle, pigs and sheep are reared.

AREA 102,170 sq km [39,449 sq mls]
POPULATION 10,500,000
CAPITAL (POPULATION) Belgrade (1,137,000)
GOVERNMENT Federal republic
ETHNIC GROUPS Serb 62%, Albanian 17%, Montenegrin 5%, Hungarian, Muslim, Croat
LANGUAGES Serbo-Croat (official), Albanian
RELIGIONS Christianity (mainly Serbian Orthodox), Islam
CURRENCY Yugoslav new dinar = 100 paras

ZAMBIA

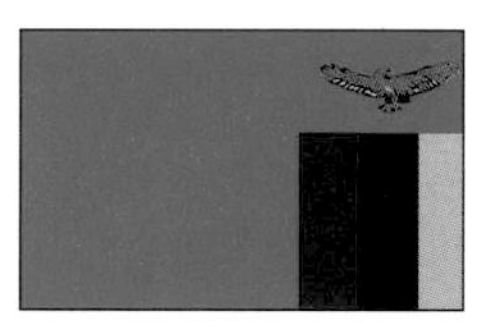

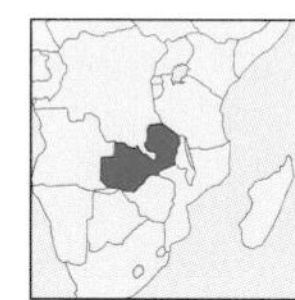

GEOGRAPHY The Republic of Zambia is a landlocked country in southern Africa. Zambia lies on the plateau that makes up most of southern Africa. Much of the land is between 900 m and 1,500 m [2,950 ft to 4,920 ft] above sea level. The Muchinga Mountains in the north-east rise above this flat land.

Zambia lies in the tropics, but temperatures are moderated by the altitude. The rainy season runs from November to March.

POLITICS & ECONOMY European contact with Zambia began in the 19th century, when the explorer David Livingstone crossed the River Zambezi. In the 1890s, the British South Africa Company, set up by Cecil Rhodes (1853–1902), the British financier and statesman, made treaties with local chiefs and gradually took over the area. In 1911, the Company named the area Northern Rhodesia. In 1924, Britain took over the government of the country.

In 1953, Britain formed a federation of Northern Rhodesia, Southern Rhodesia (now Zimbabwe) and Nyasaland (now Malawi). Because of African opposition, the federation was dissolved in 1963 and Northern Rhodesia became independent as Zambia in 1964. Kenneth Kaunda became president and one-party rule was introduced in 1972. However, a new constitution was adopted in 1990 and, in 1991, Kaunda's party was defeated and Frederick Chiluba became president.

Copper is the leading export, accounting for 90% of Zambia's total exports in 1990. Zambia also produces cobalt, lead, zinc and various gemstones. Agriculture accounts for 75% of the workers, as compared with 8% in industry, including mining. Maize is the chief crop. Other crops include cassava, coffee and millet.

AREA 752,614 sq km [290,586 sq mls]
POPULATION 9,461,000
CAPITAL (POPULATION) Lusaka (982,000)
GOVERNMENT Multiparty republic
ETHNIC GROUPS Bemba 36%, Maravi (Nyanja) 18%, Tonga 15%
LANGUAGES English (official), Bemba, Nyanja
RELIGIONS Christianity 68%, traditional beliefs 27%
CURRENCY Kwacha = 100 ngwee

ZIMBABWE

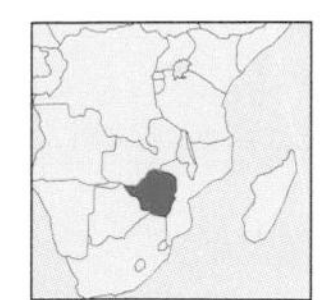

GEOGRAPHY The Republic of Zimbabwe is a landlocked country in southern Africa. Most of the country lies on a high plateau between the Zambezi and Limpopo rivers between 900 m and 1,500 m [2,950 ft to 4,920 ft] above sea level. The highest land is in the east near the Mozambique border.

In the summer, between October and March, the weather is hot and wet. But in the winter, daily temperatures can vary greatly. Frosts have been recorded between June and August. The climate varies according to the altitude.

POLITICS & ECONOMY The Shona people became dominant in the region about 1,000 years ago. They built the impressive Great Zimbabwe, a city of stone buildings. The British South Africa Company, under the statesman Cecil Rhodes (1853–1902), occupied the area in the 1890s, after obtaining mineral rights from local chiefs. The area was named Rhodesia and later Southern Rhodesia. It became a self-governing British colony in 1923. Between 1953 and 1963, Southern and Northern Rhodesia (now Zambia) were joined to Nyasaland (Malawi) in the Central African Federation.

In 1965, the European government of Southern Rhodesia (then called Rhodesia) declared their country independent. But Britain refused to accept Rhodesia's independence. Finally, after a civil war, the country became legally independent in 1980. After independence, rivalries between the Shona and Ndebele people threatened its stability. But order was restored when the Shona prime minister, Robert Mugabe, brought his Ndebele rivals into his government. In 1987, Mugabe became the country's executive president and, in 1991, the government renounced its Marxist ideology. Mugabe was re-elected president in 1990 and 1996.

The World Bank classifies Zimbabwe as a 'low-income' developing country. The country has valuable mineral resources and mining accounts for a fifth of the country's exports. Gold, asbestos, chromium and nickel are all mined. Zimbabwe also has some coal and iron ore, and some metal and food-processing industries. But agriculture employs 68% of working people. Maize is the chief food crop, while export crops include tobacco, cotton and sugar.

AREA 390,579 sq km [150,873 sq mls]
POPULATION 11,044,000
CAPITAL (POPULATION) Harare (1,189,000)
GOVERNMENT Multiparty republic
ETHNIC GROUPS Shona 71%, Ndebele 16%, other Bantu-speaking Africans 11%, White 2%
LANGUAGES English (official), Shona, Ndebele, Nyanja
RELIGIONS Christianity 45%, traditional beliefs 40%
CURRENCY Zimbabwe dollar = 100 cents

WORLD MAPS

SETTLEMENTS

▣ PARIS ▣ Berne ⦿ Livorno ⦿ Brugge ◎ Algeciras ○ *Frejus* ○ *Oberammergau* ○ *Thira*

Settlement symbols and type styles vary according to the scale of each map and indicate the importance of towns on the map rather than specific population figures

∴ Ruins or Archæological Sites

Wells in Desert

ADMINISTRATION

International Boundaries

International Boundaries (Undefined or Disputed)

Internal Boundaries

National Parks

Country Names

NICARAGUA

Administrative Area Names

KENT

CALABRIA

International boundaries show the *de facto* situation where there are rival claims to territory

COMMUNICATIONS

Principal Roads

Other Roads

Road Tunnels

Passes

Airfields

Principal Railways

Railways Under Construction

Other Railways

Railway Tunnels

Principal Canals

PHYSICAL FEATURES

Perennial Streams

Intermittent Streams

Perennial Lakes

Intermittent Lakes

Swamps and Marshes

Permanent Ice and Glaciers

▲ 8848 Elevations in metres

▼ 8500 Sea Depths in metres

1134 Height of Lake Surface Above Sea Level in metres

Beaufort Sea
Banks I.
Queen Elizabeth Is.
Devon I.
Ellesmere I.
Victoria I.
Baffin Bay
Baffin I.
GREENLAND (Denmark)
Bering Strait
ALASKA (U.S.A.)
Fairbanks
Anchorage
G. of Alaska
Kodiak I.
Aleutian Is. (U.S.A.)
Yellowknife
Great Slave L.
Hudson Bay
Churchill
Davis Str.
Nuuk
Denmark Str.
Reykjavik
ICELAND
Faroe Is. (Den.)
UNITED KINGDOM
Glasgow
Dublin
IRELAND
Queen Charlotte Is.
CANADA
Edmonton
Calgary
Winnipeg
Schefferville
Vancouver
Vancouver I.
Seattle
Portland
Newfoundland
St. John's
UNITED STATES OF AMERICA
Minneapolis
Milwaukee
Detroit
Ottawa
Montreal
Québec
Toronto
Halifax
Boston
CHICAGO
Cleveland
NEW YORK
PHILADELPHIA
Pittsburgh
Baltimore
Washington D.C.
Salt Lake City
Denver
SAN FRANCISCO
Sacramento
Kansas City
St. Louis
Cincinnati
LOS ANGELES
San Diego
Phoenix
Memphis
Atlanta
El Paso
Dallas
Ciudad Juárez
Houston
New Orleans
Jacksonville
Bermuda (U.K.)
NORTH ATLANTIC OCEAN
Azores (Port.)
PORTUGAL
Lisbon
Tangier
Rabat
Casablanca
Marrakesh
MOROCCO
Madeira (Port.)
Canary Is. (Sp.)
El Aaiun
WESTERN SAHARA
Midway Is.
International Date Line
Hawaiian Is. (U.S.A.)
Honolulu
Oahu
Hawaii
Guadalupe I. (Mexico)
Tropic of Cancer
G. of California
Monterrey
MEXICO
Gulf of Mexico
Miami
BAHAMAS
Havana
CUBA
Turks & Caicos Is. (U.K.)
Guadalajara
León
MÉXICO
Puebla
Revilla Gigedo Is. (Mexico)
Cayman Is. (U.K.)
JAMAICA
Kingston
HAITI
Port-au-Prince
DOMINICAN REP.
Santo Domingo
PUERTO RICO
Virgin Is. (U.S.A.)&(U.K.)
ANTIGUA & BARBUDA
ST. KITTS & NEVIS
GUADELOUPE (Fr.)
DOMINICA
MARTINIQUE (Fr.)
ST. LUCIA
ST. VINCENT & THE GRENADINES
BARBADOS
GRENADA
TRINIDAD & TOBAGO
NETH. ANTILLES
Belmopan
BELIZE
GUATEMALA
Guatemala
HONDURAS
Tegucigalpa
San Salvador
EL SALVADOR
NICARAGUA
Managua
Caribbean Sea
Barranquilla
San José
COSTA RICA
Panamá
PANAMA
Clipperton I. (Fr.)
Caracas
VENEZUELA
Georgetown
GUYANA
Paramaribo
SURINAM
Cayenne
FRENCH GUIANA
Nouakchott
MAURITANIA
Timbuktu
CAPE VERDE IS.
Dakar
SENEGAL
GAMBIA
GUINEA-BISSAU
Bissau
Bamako
GUINEA
Conakry
Freetown
SIERRA LEONE
Monrovia
LIBERIA
Yamoussoukro
IVORY COAST
Abidjan
Ouagadougou
PACIFIC OCEAN
Palmyra Is. (U.S.A.)
Kiritimati
Howland I. (U.S.A.)
Baker I. (U.S.A.)
Jarvis I. (U.S.A.)
Equator
Coco I. (C.Rica)
Malpelo (Colombia)
Medellín
Cali
BOGOTÁ
COLOMBIA
São Paulo (Brazil)
Gulf
Abariringa
KIRIBATI
Phoenix Is.
Malden I.
Starbuck I.
Galápagos (Ecuador)
Quito
ECUADOR
Guayaquil
Iquitos
Manaus
Amazon
Belém
Fortaleza
Fernando de Noronha (Brazil)
Natal
Recife
Tokelau Is. (N.Z.)
Penrhyn Is.
Marquesas Is.
Ascension I. (U.K.)
BRAZIL
PERU
LIMA
Callao
Salvador
WESTERN SAMOA
Wallis & Futuna (Fr.)
AMERICAN SAMOA
Manihiki
Flint I.
FRENCH POLYNESIA
Tuamotu Is.
Society Is.
Tahiti
Cook Is. (N.Z.)
FIJI
TONGA
Niue (N.Z.)
Brasília
Arequipa
L. Titicaca
La Paz
BOLIVIA
Sucre
St. Helena (U.K.)
SOUTH ATLANTIC OCEAN
Belo Horizonte
Trindade (Brazil)
SÃO PAULO
RIO DE JANEIRO
Antofagasta
PARAGUAY
Asunción
Santos
Curitiba
Tropic of Capricorn
Tubuai Is.
Pitcairn I. (U.K.)
Ducie I.
Rapa
Easter I. (Chile)
Sala-y-Gómez (Chile)
San Felix (Chile)
San Ambrosio (Chile)
Tucumán
Pôrto Alegre
Córdoba
Rosario
Paraná
Rio Grande
URUGUAY
Montevideo
Valparaíso
SANTIAGO
BUENOS AIRES
ARGENTINA
Juan Fernández (Chile)
Talcahuano
CHILE
Bahía Blanca
Kermadec Is. (N.Z.)
Tristan da Cunha (U.K.)
Gough I. (U.K.)
Chiloé I.
Chatham Is. (N.Z.)
Falkland Is. (U.K.)
Punta Arenas
Tierra del Fuego
C. Horn
Scotia Sea
South Georgia (U.K.)
South Sandwich Is. (U.K.)
Drake Passage
South Orkney Is.
South Shetland Is.
Bellingshausen Sea
Antarctic Circle
Weddell Sea
Amundsen Sea
Antarctica
West from Greenwich
A
B
C
D
E
F
G
H
1
2
3
4
5
6
7
8
9

Projection: *Hammer Equal Area*

A R C T I C O C E A N
Novaya Zemlya
Severnaya Zemlya
Barents Sea
Kara Sea
Laptev Sea
New Siberian Is.
East Siberian Sea
Wrangel I.
Arctic Circle
Murmansk
Arkhangelsk
Norilsk
Verkhoyansk
Salekhard
R U S S I A
Yakutsk
Magadan
Okhotsk
Sea of Okhotsk
Bering Sea
Petropavlovsk-Kamchatskiy
International Date Line
FINLAND
Helsinki
ST.PETERSBURG
SWEDEN
Stockholm
Oslo
Copenhagen
Perm
Yekaterinburg
Kazan
Volga
MOSCOW
Omsk
Novosibirsk
Tomsk
Krasnoyarsk
L. Baikal
Irkutsk
Ulan Ude
Barnaul
Samara
Chelyabinsk
Astana
Saratov
Qaraghandy
Minsk
Berlin
Prague
Warsaw
Kiev
Brussels
UKRAINE
Volgograd
K A Z A K S T A N
Sakhalin
Komsomolsk
Khabarovsk
Amur
Kuril Is.
Ulan Bator
M O N G O L I A
Harbin
Changchun
Vladivostok
Sapporo
Odessa
Astrakhan
L. Balkhash
Vienna
Budapest
ROMANIA
Bucharest
Black Sea
Caspian Sea
Almaty
Bishkek
KYRGYZSTAN
Ürümqi
SHENYANG
BEIJING
TIANJIN
NORTH KOREA
Pyongyang
SEOUL
SOUTH KOREA
Dalian
JAPAN
TÔKYÔ
Ôsaka
Kitakyushu
P A C I F I C
O C E A N
Milan
ITALY
Rome
Naples
BULGARIA
Sofia
ISTANBUL
Ankara
TURKEY
GEORGIA
Tbilisi
Yerevan
Baku
UZBEKISTAN
Tashkent
Samarkand
TURKMENISTAN
Ashkhabad
Dushanbe
TAJIKISTAN
C H I N A
Lanzhou
Taiyuan
Xi'an
Nanjing
SHANGHAI
East China Sea
Athens
Izmir
Tabriz
Mediterranean Sea
Tunis
TUNISIA
MALTA
Tripoli
CYPRUS
Beirut
SYRIA
Damascus
Jerusalem
Ammân
JORDAN
Baghdâd
TEHRÂN
Mashhad
IRAQ
IRAN
Esfahân
Shirâz
Kâbul
AFGHANISTAN
Islamabad
Lahore
T I B E T
Chengdu
CHONGQING
Wuhan
Lhasa
Katmandu
NEPAL
Benghazi
Alexandria
CAIRO
L I B Y A
EGYPT
Aswân
KUWAIT
The Gulf
BAHRAIN
QATAR
Riyadh
Abu Dhabi
U.A.E.
Muscat
OMAN
S A U D I A R A B I A
Mecca
Red Sea
PAKISTAN
KARACHI
DELHI
New Delhi
Kanpur
I N D I A
CALCUTTA
DACCA
BANGLADESH
BURMA (MYANMAR)
Ahmadabad
Nagpur
Arabian Sea
MUMBAI (Bombay)
Bay of Bengal
Kunming
GUANGZHOU
HONG KONG
Fuzhou
Taipei
TAIWAN
Ryukyu Is.
Hanoi
Hainan
South China Sea
Bonin Is. (Japan)
Volcano Is. (Japan)
Marcus I. (Japan)
Tropic of Cancer
Wake I. (U.S.A.)
NORTHERN MARIANAS (U.S.A.)
GUAM (U.S.A.)
NIGER
Niamey
CHAD
L. Chad
Ndjamena
Kano
NIGERIA
Abuja
Ibadan
Lagos
Omdurmân
Khartoum
SUDAN
White Nile
Blue Nile
Asmara
ERITREA
DJIBOUTI
Sana
YEMEN
Aden
G. of Aden
Socotra (Yemen)
Addis Ababa
ETHIOPIA
SOMALI REP.
Hyderabad
CHENNAI (Madras)
Bangalore
Lakshadweep Is. (India)
Andaman Is. (India)
Rangoon
Vientiane
THAILAND
BANGKOK
CAMBODIA
Phnom Penh
VIET-NAM
Ho Chi Minh City
MANILA
PHILIPPINES
Yap
PALAU
FEDERATED STATES OF MICRONESIA
Truk
Pohnpei
Caroline Is.
MARSHALL IS.
CAMEROON
Douala
Yaoundé
CENTRAL AFRICAN REP.
Bangui
EQUATORIAL GUINEA
SAO TOMÉ & PRINCIPE
Libreville
GABON
Kisangani
UGANDA
Kampala
L. Turkana
KENYA
Nairobi
Mogadishu
SRI LANKA
Colombo
Nicobar Is. (India)
MALDIVES
Medan
M A L A Y S I A
Kuala Lumpur
PEN. MALAYSIA
SABAH
BRUNEI
SARAWAK
SINGAPORE
Sumatra
Borneo
Equator
Gilbert Is.
NAURU
KIRIBATI
CONGO
CONGO (DEM. REP. OF THE)
Brazzaville
Kinshasa
CABINDA (Angola)
Zaire
L. Victoria
RWANDA
BURUNDI
Kigali
Bujumbura
Dodoma
L. Tanganyika
Kananga
TANZANIA
Mombasa
Zanzibar
Dar es Salaam
SEYCHELLES
Amirante Is.
Diego Garcia
Chagos Arch. (U.K.)
I N D I A N
O C E A N
Palembang
Banjarmasin
JAKARTA
Bandung
Surabaya
Java
I N D O N E S I A
Ujung Pandang
IRIAN JAYA
PAPUA NEW GUINEA
Port Moresby
New Ireland
New Britain
SOLOMON IS.
TUVALU
Luanda
ANGOLA
Benguela
Lubumbashi
ZAMBIA
Lusaka
Malawi
Lilongwe
MALAWI
Aldabra Is.
COMOROS
Mayotte (Fr.)
Agalega Is.
Cocos Is. (Austral.)
Christmas I. (Austral.)
Timor
Arafura Sea
C. York
Santa Cruz I.
Darwin
Cairns
Townsville
VANUATU
FIJI
Suva
Harare
ZIMBABWE
MOZAMBIQUE
Mozambique Channel
MADAGASCAR
Antananarivo
Cargados Carajos
Rodriguez
MAURITIUS
RÉUNION (Fr.)
NAMIBIA
Windhoek
BOTSWANA
Bulawayo
Gaborone
Pretoria
Johannesburg
Maputo
SWAZILAND
LESOTHO
SOUTH AFRICA
Durban
Cape Town
C. of Good Hope
Port Elizabeth
Tropic of Capricorn
Port Hedland
Alice Springs
A U S T R A L I A
Rockhampton
NEW CALEDONIA (Fr.)
Geraldton
Kalgoorlie-Boulder
Perth
Fremantle
Brisbane
Great Australian Bight
Adelaide
Darling
Newcastle
Sydney
Canberra
Lord Howe I. (Austral.)
Norfolk I. (Austral.)
Melbourne
Tasman Sea
Tasmania
Hobart
Auckland
North I.
NEW ZEALAND
Wellington
Christchurch
South I.
Stewart I.
Dunedin
Amsterdam I. (Fr.)
St.Paul (Fr.)
Prince Edward Is. (S.Africa)
Crozet Is. (Fr.)
Kerguelen (Fr.)
McDonald Is. (Austral.)
Heard I. (Austral.)
Bounty Is. (N.Z.)
Antipodes Is.
Auckland Is. (N.Z.)
Campbell I. (N.Z.)
Macquarie Is. (Austral.)
Bouvet I. (Norw.)
S O U T H E R N O C E A N
Antarctic Circle
A n t a r c t i c a
Ross Sea
East from Greenwich
10 11 12 13 14 15 16 17 18
A B C D E F G H

Hanoi ● Capital Cities

ARCTIC OCEAN 1:35 000 000

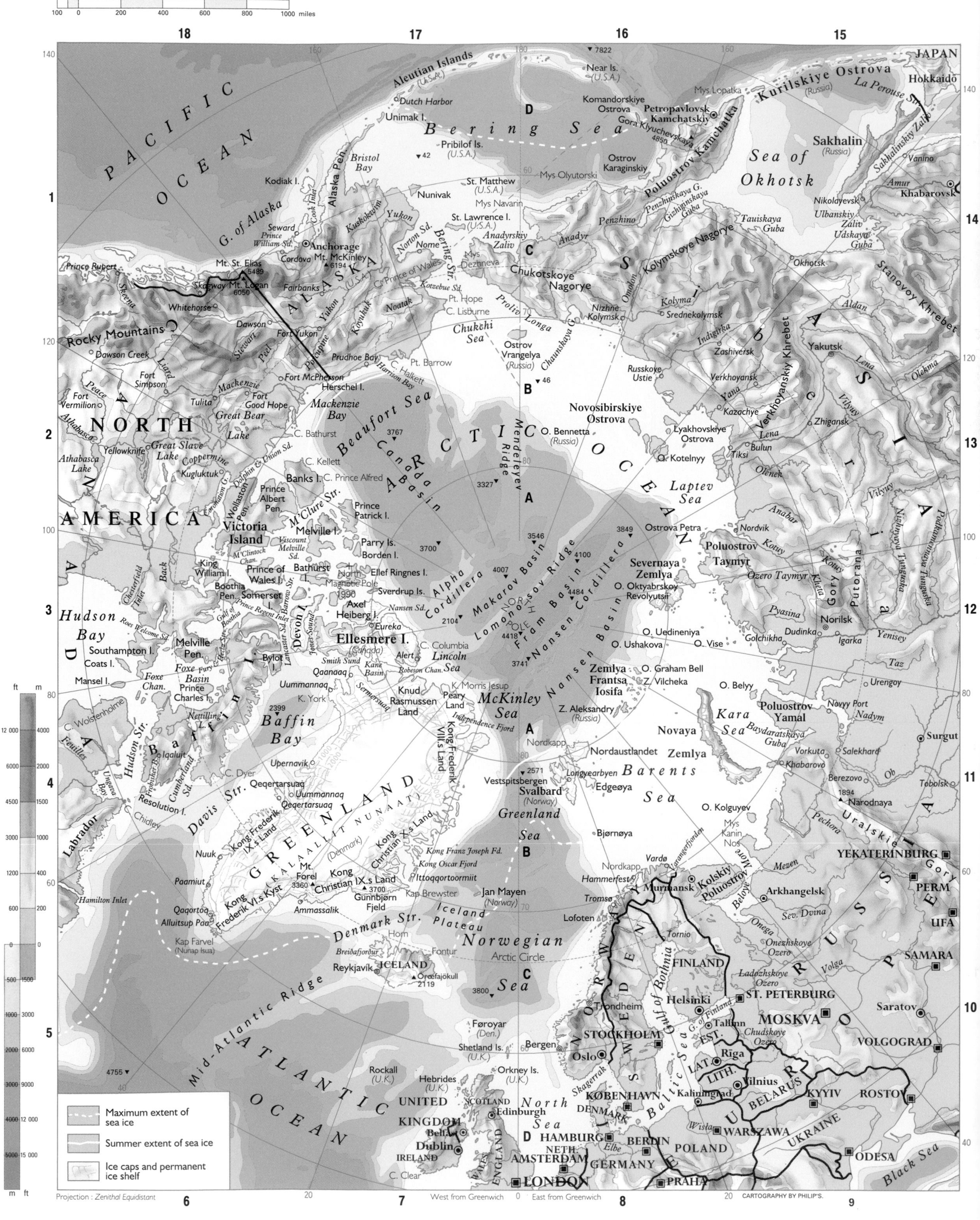
100 0 200 400 600 800 1000 1200 1400 km
100 0 200 400 600 800 1000 miles
Maximum extent of sea ice
Summer extent of sea ice
Ice caps and permanent ice shelf
PACIFIC OCEAN
ARCTIC OCEAN
ATLANTIC OCEAN
NORTH AMERICA
GREENLAND
Bering Sea
Sea of Okhotsk
Beaufort Sea
Baffin Bay
Hudson Bay
Greenland Sea
Norwegian Sea
Barents Sea
Kara Sea
Laptev Sea
North Sea
Projection : Zenithal Equidistant
West from Greenwich
East from Greenwich
CARTOGRAPHY BY PHILIP'S.

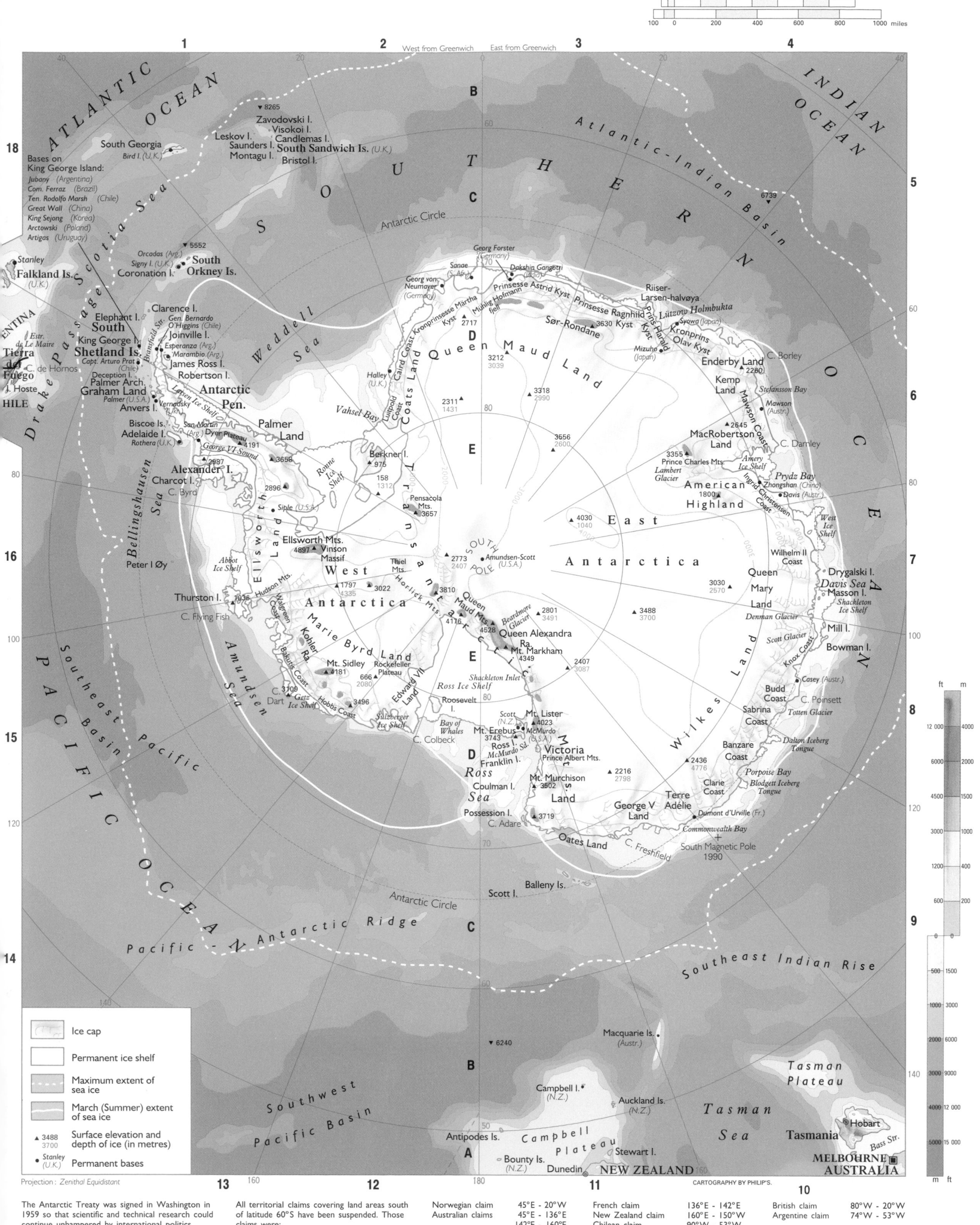
100 0 200 400 600 800 1000 1200 1400 km
100 0 200 400 600 800 1000 miles
West from Greenwich
East from Greenwich
ATLANTIC OCEAN
INDIAN OCEAN
SOUTHERN OCEAN
PACIFIC OCEAN
Atlantic-Indian Basin
South Georgia
Bird I. (U.K.)
Bases on King George Island:
Jubany (Argentina)
Com. Ferraz (Brazil)
Ten. Rodolfo Marsh (Chile)
Great Wall (China)
King Sejong (Korea)
Arctowski (Poland)
Artigas (Uruguay)
8265
Zavodovski I.
Visokoi I.
Leskov I.
Candlemas I.
Saunders I.
South Sandwich Is. (U.K.)
Montagu I.
Bristol I.
Scotia Sea
Stanley
Falkland Is. (U.K.)
5552
Orcadas (Arg.)
Signy I. (U.K.)
Coronation I.
South Orkney Is.
Weddell Sea
Drake Passage
Clarence I.
Elephant I.
Gen. Bernardo O'Higgins (Chile)
South Shetland Is.
King George I.
Joinville I.
Esperanza (Arg.)
Marambio (Arg.)
Capt. Arturo Prat (Chile)
James Ross I.
Robertson I.
Deception I.
Palmer Arch.
Graham Land
Palmer (U.S.A.)
Anvers I.
Antarctic Pen.
Larsen Ice Shelf
Vernadsky (Ukr.)
Tierra del Fuego
C. de Hornos
Estr. de Le Maire
I. Hoste
Bransfield Str.
Biscoe Is.
Adelaide I.
Rothera (U.K.)
San Martín (Arg.)
Dyer Plateau
4191
George VI Sound
2987
Alexander I.
Charcot I.
C. Byrd
Palmer Land
Bellingshausen Sea
Peter I Øy
Antarctic Circle
Georg Forster (Germany)
Sanae (S. Afr.)
Dakshin Gangotri (India)
Georg von Neumayer (Germany)
Prinsesse Astrid Kyst
Prinsesse Ragnhild Kyst
Prins Harald Kyst
Riiser-Larsen-halvøya
Lützow Holmbukta
Syowa (Japan)
Kronprinsesse Märtha Kyst
Mühlig Hofmann fjell
Sør-Rondane
3630
Kronprins Olav Kyst
Mizuho (Japan)
Queen Maud Land
2717
3212
3039
Halley (U.K.)
Caird Coast
Luitpold Coast
Coats Land
Vahsel Bay
2311
1431
3318
2990
Enderby Land
2280
C. Borley
Kemp Land
Stefansson Bay
Mawson (Austr.)
Mawson Coast
2645
MacRobertson Land
C. Darnley
3355
Prince Charles Mts.
Lambert Glacier
Amery Ice Shelf
Prydz Bay
Zhongshan (China)
Davis (Austr.)
Ingrid Christensen Coast
American Highland
1800
3656
2600
Berkner I.
975
Ronne Ice Shelf
158
1312
3658
2896
Pensacola Mts.
3657
Siple (U.S.A.)
Transantarctic Mts.
Ellsworth Land
Ellsworth Mts.
4897
Vinson Massif
Abbot Ice Shelf
Hudson Mts.
Thurston I.
C. Flying Fish
Walgreen Coast
West Antarctica
Thiel Mts.
1797
4335
3022
Horlick Mts.
2773
2407
Amundsen-Scott (U.S.A.)
SOUTH POLE
4030
1040
East Antarctica
West Ice Shelf
Wilhelm II Coast
Queen Mary Land
3030
2570
Drygalski I.
Davis Sea
Masson I.
Shackleton Ice Shelf
Denman Glacier
3810
Queen Maud Mts.
4176
Beardmore Glacier
4528
2801
3491
Queen Alexandra Ra.
Mt. Markham
4349
3488
3700
Mill I.
Bowman I.
Scott Glacier
Knox Coast
Marie Byrd Land
Kohler Ra.
Mt. Sidley
4181
Rockefeller Plateau
666
2080
Edward VII Land
Shackleton Inlet
Ross Ice Shelf
2407
3087
Wilkes Land
Casey (Austr.)
Budd Coast
C. Poinsett
Totten Glacier
Amundsen Sea
Bakutis Coast
C. Dart
3109
Getz Ice Shelf
Hobbs Coast
3496
Sulzberger Ice Shelf
Roosevelt I.
Bay of Whales
C. Colbeck
Scott (N.Z.)
Mt. Lister
4023
Mt. Erebus
3743
McMurdo (U.S.A.)
Ross I.
McMurdo Sd.
Franklin I.
Victoria Land
Prince Albert Mts.
2216
2798
Sabrina Coast
Dalton Iceberg Tongue
Banzare Coast
2436
4776
Porpoise Bay
Blodgett Iceberg Tongue
Clarie Coast
Ross Sea
Coulman I.
Mt. Murchison
3502
Terre Adélie
George V Land
Possession I.
C. Adare
3719
Dumont d'Urville (Fr.)
Commonwealth Bay
Oates Land
C. Freshfield
South Magnetic Pole 1990
Southeast Pacific Basin
Balleny Is.
Scott I.
Antarctic Circle
Pacific-Antarctic Ridge
Southeast Indian Rise
Ice cap
Permanent ice shelf
Maximum extent of sea ice
March (Summer) extent of sea ice
3488 3700 Surface elevation and depth of ice (in metres)
Stanley (U.K.) Permanent bases
6240
Macquarie Is. (Austr.)
Tasman Plateau
Campbell I. (N.Z.)
Auckland Is. (N.Z.)
Southwest Pacific Basin
Tasman Sea
Antipodes Is.
Campbell Plateau
Tasmania
Hobart
Bass Str.
Bounty Is. (N.Z.)
Stewart I.
Dunedin
NEW ZEALAND
MELBOURNE
AUSTRALIA
Projection: Zenithal Equidistant
CARTOGRAPHY BY PHILIP'S

The Antarctic Treaty was signed in Washington in 1959 so that scientific and technical research could continue unhampered by international politics.

All territorial claims covering land areas south of latitude 60°S have been suspended. Those claims were:

Norwegian claim	45°E - 20°W	French claim	136°E - 142°E	British claim	80°W - 20°W
Australian claims	45°E - 136°E	New Zealand claim	160°E - 150°W	Argentine claim	74°W - 53°W
	142°E - 160°E	Chilean claim	90°W - 53°W		

EUROPE : Physical 1:20 000 000

100 0 100 200 300 400 500 600 700 800 km
100 0 100 200 300 400 500 miles
Norwegian Sea
North Sea
ATLANTIC OCEAN
Bay of Biscay
English Channel
Celtic Sea
Irish Sea
Baltic Sea
G. of Bothnia
G. of Finland
G. of Riga
White Sea
Caspian Sea
Caspian Depression
Black Sea
Sea of Azov
Adriatic Sea
Tyrrhenian Sea
Ionian Sea
Ligurian Sea
Aegean Sea
Mediterranean Sea
Sea of Marmara
Str. of Gibraltar
Str. of Otranto
Str. of Bonifacio
Str. of Messina
Str. of Kerch
G. of Lions
Skagerrak
Kattegat
Iceland
Faroe Is.
Shetland Is.
Orkney Is.
Hebrides
British Isles
Great Britain
Ireland
Channel Is.
Brittany
Rockall
Lofoten
Vesterålen
North Cape
Nordkinn
Lapland
Scandinavia
Finland
Kola Pen.
Kanin Pen.
Jutland
Lindesnes
Helgoland
Bornholm
Öland
Gotland
Saaremaa
Åland
Ural Mountains
Obshchi Syrt
Volga Hts.
Central Russian Uplands
European Plain
Ukraine
Caucasus
Carpathians
Transylvanian Alps
Wallachia
Balkans
Rhodope
Pindus
Morea
Dinaric Alps
Apennines
Alps
Jura
Vosges
Black Forest
Ardennes
Hunsrück
Taunus
Westerwald
Harz
Erzgebirge
Bohemian Forest
Moravian Hts.
Sudeten
Plain of Hungary
Bakony Forest
Massif Central
Cévennes
Pyrenees
Cantabrian Mts.
Iberian Peninsula
Old Castile
New Castile
Sierra Morena
Sierra Nevada
Andalusia
Balearic Is.
Majorca
Minorca
Ibiza
Corsica
Sardinia
Sicily
Malta
Pantelleria
Calabria
Crete
Rhodes
Cyprus
Crimea
Anatolia (Asia Minor)
Pontine Mts.
Taurus Mts.
Armenia
Kurdistan
Asia
Mesopotamia
Africa
Er Rif
Plateau of the Shotts
Volga
Don
Dnieper
Dniester
Danube
Prut
Bug
Pripet
Oka
Kama
Pechora
Mezen
N. Dvina
Onega
W. Dvina
Niemen
Vistula
Oder
Elbe
Weser
Rhine
Meuse
Seine
Loire
Garonne
Gironde
Rhône
Ebro
Douro
Tagus
Guadiana
Guadalquivir
Po
Tiber
Tisza
Drava
Sava
Mureș
Inn
Ural
Terek
Kuban
Kura
Manych
Donets
Thames
Ob
Tigris
Euphrates
Neva
Svir
Torne
Ume
Indals
Aras
L. Ladoga
L. Onega
L. Chudskoye
Inari
Rybinsk Res.
Tsimlyansk Res.
Vänern
Vättern
Mälaren
L. Van
L. Urmia
L. Tuz
Mont Blanc 4807
Elbrus 5642
Ararat 5165
Etna 3340
Vesuvius 1277
Olympus 2917
Mt. Ida 1766
Tatra 2655
Galdhøpiggen 2469
Kebnekaise 2117
Ben Nevis 1347
Snowdon 1085
Pico de Aneto 3404
Puy de Sancy 1886
Mulhacén 3478
Gran Sasso d'Italia 2914
Hekla 1491
Öræfajökull 2119
Narodnaya 1894
Telpos Iz 1617
Erciyas Dağı 3770
Land's End
Ushant
C. Clear
C. Finisterre
C. da Roca
C. de São Vicente
C. Trafalgar
C. Matapan
C. Bon
C. Blanc
Arctic Circle
Bosporus
Dardanelles
Kizil Irmak
2211
4070
4817
2851
15
-28
Projection: Bonne
West from Greenwich 0 East from Greenwich
CARTOGRAPHY BY PHILIP'S
m ft
5000 15 000
4000 12 000
2000 6000
1000 3000
400 1200
200 600
0 0
200 600
1000 3000
2000 6000
4000 12 000

100 0 100 200 300 400 500 600 700 800 km
100 0 100 200 300 400 500 miles
Arctic Circle
ICELAND
Reykjavik
Norwegian Sea
Faroe Is. (Den.)
Shetland Is.
Orkney Is.
Hebrides
NORWAY
SWEDEN
FINLAND
G. of Bothnia
White Sea
L. Onega
L. Ladoga
RUSSIA
ESTONIA
LATVIA
LITHUANIA
BELARUS
UKRAINE
POLAND
GERMANY
DENMARK
NETHER-LANDS
BELGIUM
LUX.
UNITED KINGDOM
SCOTLAND
ENGLAND
WALES
N. IRELAND
IRELAND
FRANCE
SPAIN
PORTUGAL
ANDORRA
MONACO
ITALY
SAN MARINO
SWITZERLAND
LIECH.
CZECH REP.
SLOVAK REP.
AUSTRIA
HUNGARY
SLOVENIA
CROATIA
BOSNIA-HERZ.
YUGOSLAVIA
SERBIA
MONTENEGRO
ROMANIA
MOLDOVA
BULGARIA
MACEDONIA
ALBANIA
GREECE
TURKEY
GEORGIA
ARMENIA
AZERBAIJAN
KAZAKSTAN
IRAN
IRAQ
SYRIA
CYPRUS
MALTA
TUNISIA
ALGERIA
MOROCCO
Africa
ATLANTIC OCEAN
North Sea
Skagerrak
Kattegat
Baltic Sea
English Channel
Bay of Biscay
Black Sea
Crimea
Bosporus
Caspian Sea
Mediterranean Sea
Adriatic Sea
Tyrrhenian Sea
Ionian Sea
Ægean Sea
Str. of Gibraltar
Corsica
Sardinia
Sicily
Crete
Balearic Is.
MOSCOW
ST. PETERSBURG
LONDON
PARIS
■ LONDON Capital Cities
Projection: Bonne
West from Greenwich
East from Greenwich
CARTOGRAPHY BY PHILIPS.

SCANDINAVIA 1:5 000 000

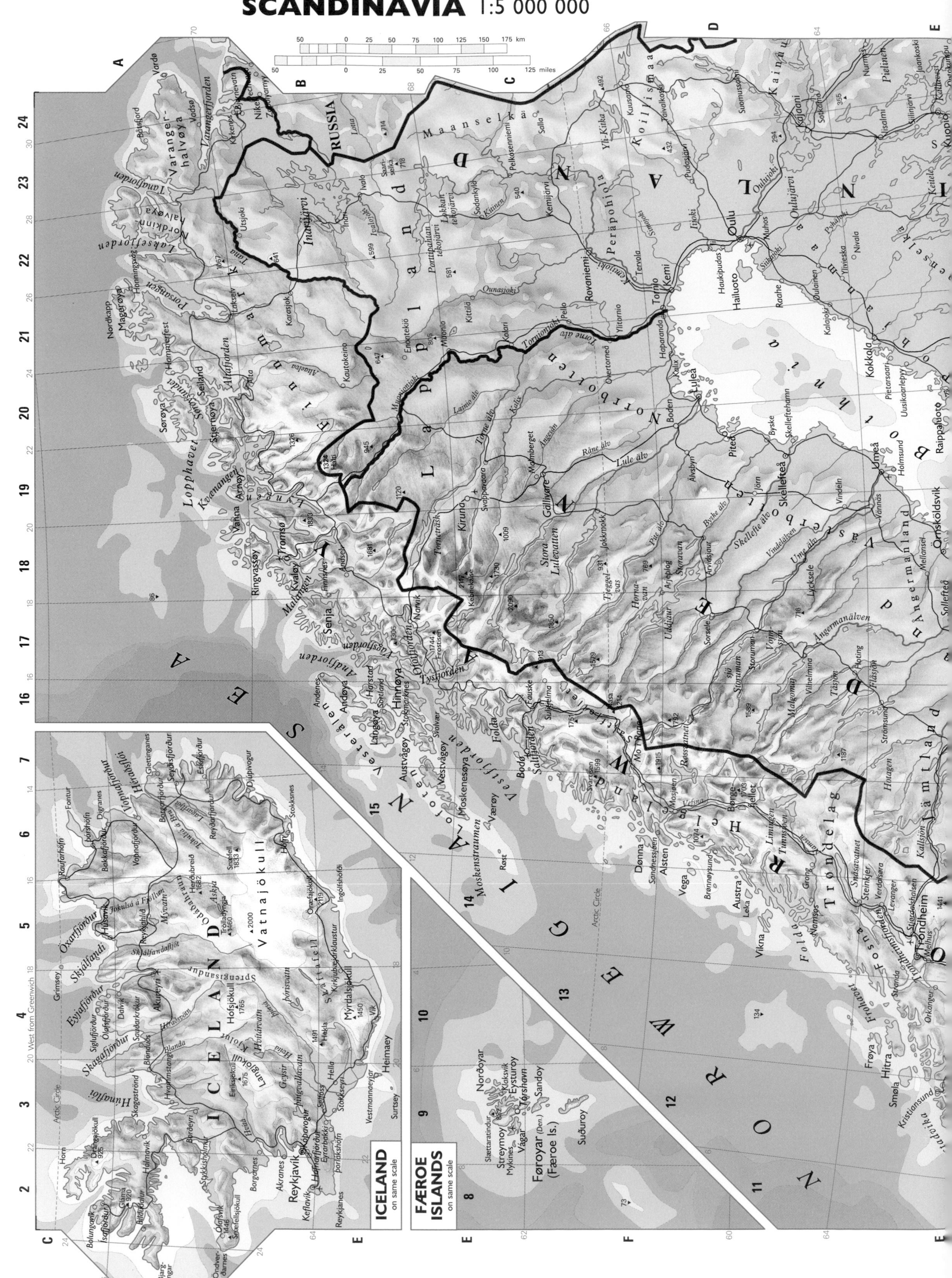

50 0 25 50 75 100 125 150 175 km
50 0 25 50 75 100 125 miles
ICELAND
on same scale
FÆROE ISLANDS
on same scale
RUSSIA
Finnmark
Lappland
Norrbotten
Västerbotten
Ångermanland
Jämtland
Trøndelag
NORWEGIAN SEA
Gulf of Bothnia
Vatnajökull
Tromsø
Narvik
Bodø
Trondheim
Luleå
Oulu
Kemi
Tornio
Haparanda
Kiruna
Gällivare
Umeå
Skellefteå
Piteå
Kokkola
Reykjavík
Akureyri
Tórshavn
Føroyar (Færoe Is.)

BALTIC SEA
Gulf of Finland
Gulf of Riga
Gulf of Bothnia
Ålands hav
Skagerrak
Kattegat
NORWAY
SWEDEN
FINLAND
ESTONIA
LATVIA
LITHUANIA
BELARUS
POLAND
GERMANY
DENMARK
Svealand
Götaland
Norrland
STOCKHOLM
Oslo
Helsinki (Helsingfors)
Tallinn
Riga
Vilnius
KØBENHAVN (Copenhagen)
Göteborg (Gothenburg)
Kaliningrad (Russia)
Gotland
Öland
Bornholm
Saaremaa (Ösel)
Hiiumaa (Dagö)
Åland (Ahvenanmaa)

ft	m
6000	2000
4500	1500
3000	1000
1500	500
600	200
0	0
150	50
300	100
600	200
1500	500
3000	1000
6000	2000

Projection: Conical with two standard parallels
East from Greenwich

ENGLAND AND WALES 1:2 000 000

10 0 10 20 30 40 50 60 70 80 km
10 0 10 20 30 40 50 miles
Key to English unitary authorities on map.
25. HARTLEPOOL
26. DARLINGTON
27. STOCKTON-ON-TEES
28. MIDDLESBROUGH
29. REDCAR AND CLEVELAND
30. BLACKPOOL
31. BLACKBURN WITH DARWEN
32. HALTON
33. WARRINGTON
34. KINGSTON UPON HULL
35. NORTH EAST LINCOLNSHIRE
36. STOKE-ON-TRENT
37. TELFORD AND WREKIN
38. DERBY CITY
39. CITY OF NOTTINGHAM
40. LEICESTER CITY
41. RUTLAND
42. PETERBOROUGH
43. MILTON KEYNES
44. LUTON
45. NORTH SOMERSET
46. CITY OF BRISTOL
47. BATH AND NORTH EAST SOMERSET
48. SWINDON
49. READING
50. WOKINGHAM
51. WINDSOR AND MAIDENHEAD
52. SLOUGH
53. BRACKNELL FOREST
54. THURROCK
55. SOUTHEND-ON-SEA
56. MEDWAY TOWNS
57. PLYMOUTH
58. TORBAY
59. POOLE
60. BOURNEMOUTH
61. SOUTHAMPTON
62. PORTSMOUTH
63. BRIGHTON AND HOVE
Key to Welsh unitary authorities on map.
15. SWANSEA
16. NEATH PORT TALBOT
17. BRIDGEND
18. RHONDDA CYNON TAFF
19. MERTHYR TYDFIL
20. CAERPHILLY
21. BLAENAU GWENT
22. TORFAEN
23. CARDIFF
24. NEWPORT
NORTH SEA
IRISH SEA
North Channel
NORTHERN IRELAND
ISLE OF MAN
SCOTLAND

Cardigan Bay

Bristol Channel

ENGLISH CHANNEL

Strait of Dover

Thames Estuary

Lyme Bay

Bridgwater Bay

Carmarthen Bay

Baie de la Seine

Baie de la Somme

WALES

ENGLAND

FRANCE

CHANNEL ISLANDS (U.K.)

CORNWALL

DEVON

SOMERSET

DORSET

WILTSHIRE

HANTS

SUSSEX

KENT

ESSEX

SUFFOLK

NORFOLK

CAMBRIDGE

NORTHAMPTON

WARWICK

WORCESTER

HEREFORD

GLOUCS

OXFORD

BUCKS

BEDFORD

HERTS

SURREY

GREATER LONDON

SHROPSHIRE

POWYS

CEREDIGION

PEMBROKESHIRE

CARMARTHENSHIRE

SEINE-MARITIME

HAUTE-NORMANDIE

CALVADOS

MANCHE

Isles of Scilly
On same scale

Tresco
Isles of Scilly
St. Mary's
Camborne
St. Ives
Hayle
Penzance
Newlyn
Land's End

ft	m
3000	1000
1500	500
600	200
300	100
0	0
150	50
300	100
600	200
ft	m

Projection : *Lambert's Conformal Conic*

West from Greenwich

East from Greenwich

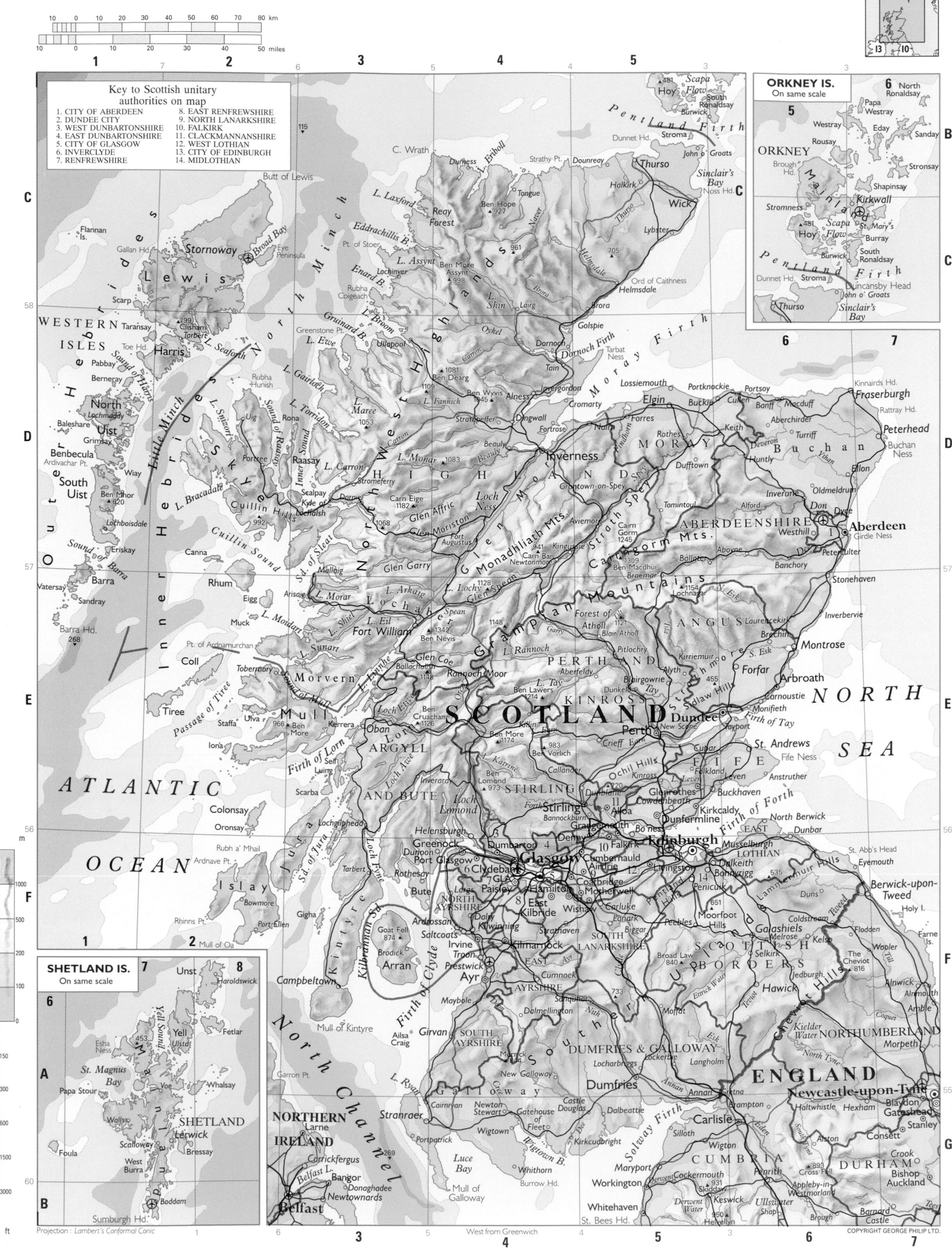
Key to Scottish unitary authorities on map
1. CITY OF ABERDEEN
2. DUNDEE CITY
3. WEST DUNBARTONSHIRE
4. EAST DUNBARTONSHIRE
5. CITY OF GLASGOW
6. INVERCLYDE
7. RENFREWSHIRE
8. EAST RENFREWSHIRE
9. NORTH LANARKSHIRE
10. FALKIRK
11. CLACKMANNANSHIRE
12. WEST LOTHIAN
13. CITY OF EDINBURGH
14. MIDLOTHIAN
ORKNEY IS.
On same scale
SHETLAND IS.
On same scale
SCOTLAND
ENGLAND
NORTHERN IRELAND
ATLANTIC OCEAN
NORTH SEA
North Channel
Pentland Firth
Moray Firth
Firth of Forth
Firth of Clyde
Solway Firth
WESTERN ISLES
Outer Hebrides
Inner Hebrides
Lewis
Harris
Skye
Mull
Islay
Jura
Arran
Kintyre
Stornoway
Inverness
Aberdeen
Dundee
Perth
Stirling
Edinburgh
Glasgow
Fort William
Oban
Ayr
Dumfries
Carlisle
Newcastle-upon-Tyne
Belfast
Kirkwall
Lerwick
Thurso
Wick
Grampian Mountains
Cairngorm Mts.
Monadhliath Mts.
Southern Uplands
Cheviot Hills
Ben Nevis
1343
Projection: Lambert's Conformal Conic
West from Greenwich
COPYRIGHT GEORGE PHILIP LTD.

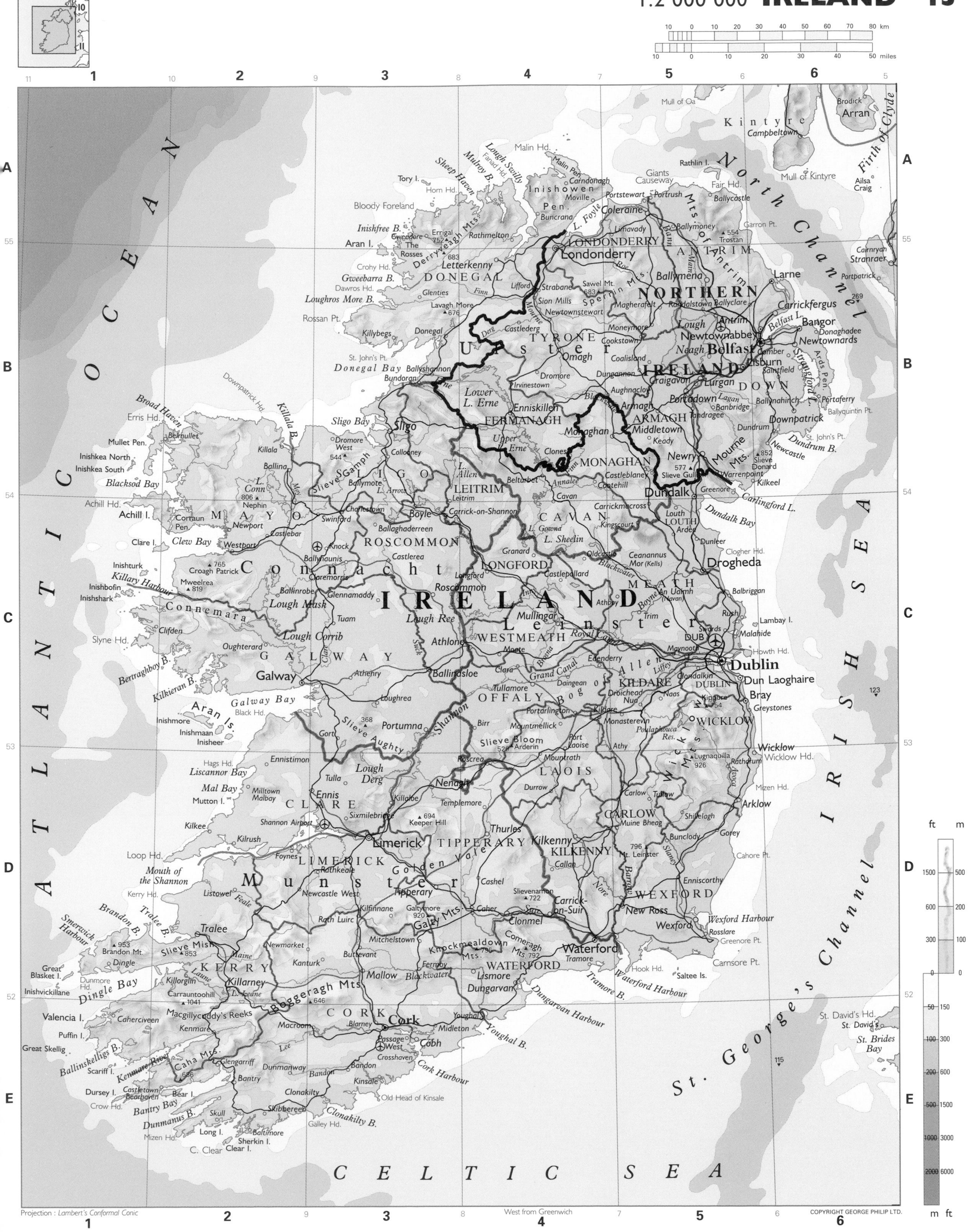

10 0 10 20 30 40 50 60 70 80 km
10 0 10 20 30 40 50 miles
ATLANTIC OCEAN
North Channel
IRISH SEA
St. George's Channel
CELTIC SEA
NORTHERN IRELAND
IRELAND
Ulster
Connacht
Leinster
Munster
Kintyre
Campbeltown
Mull of Oa
Brodick
Arran
Firth of Clyde
Mull of Kintyre
Ailsa Craig
Rathlin I.
Fair Hd.
Ballycastle
Giants Causeway
Portrush
Portstewart
Coleraine
Malin Hd.
Malin Pen.
Carndonagh
Moville
Inishowen Pen.
Buncrana
L. Foyle
Lough Swilly
Fanad Hd.
Mulroy B.
Sheep Haven
Tory I.
Horn Hd.
Bloody Foreland
Inishfree B.
Gweedore
The Rosses
Errigal 752
Derryveagh Mts.
683
Rathmelton
Aran I.
Crohy Hd.
Gweebarra B.
Dawros Hd.
Letterkenny
DONEGAL
Glenties
Lavagh More 676
Loughros More B.
Rossan Pt.
Killybegs
Donegal
Lifford
Strabane
Finn
Sion Mills
Newtownstewart
Castlederg
Derg
Mourne
LONDONDERRY
Londonderry
Limavady
Roe
Sawel Mt. 683
Sperrin Mts.
Magherafelt
Mts. of Antrim
Ballymoney
Ballymena
Main
Trostan 554
ANTRIM
Garron Pt.
Cairnryan
Stranraer
Portpatrick
Larne
Randalstown
Ballyclare
Carrickfergus
269
Antrim
Lough Neagh
Newtownabbey
Belfast L.
Bangor
Donaghadee
Newtownards
Belfast
Comber
Lisburn
Saintfield
Strangford L.
Ards Pen.
Portaferry
Ballyquintin Pt.
TYRONE
Moneymore
Cookstown
Coalisland
Omagh
Dungannon
Craigavon
Lurgan
DOWN
Portadown
Lagan
Banbridge
Ballynahinch
Downpatrick
St. John's Pt.
Dundrum B.
Dundrum
Dromore
Irvinestown
Aughnacloy
Armagh
ARMAGH
Tandragee
Middletown
Keady
Blackwater
Newry
Mourne Mts.
Slieve Donard 852
Newcastle
Slieve Gullion 577
Warrenpoint
Kilkeel
Greenore
Carlingford L.
Dundalk
Dundalk Bay
Lower L. Erne
Enniskillen
FERMANAGH
Upper L. Erne
Monaghan
Clones
MONAGHAN
Castleblaney
Cootehill
St. John's Pt.
Donegal Bay
Ballyshannon
Bundoran
Erne
Downpatrick Hd.
Broad Haven
Erris Hd.
Belmullet
Mullet Pen.
Inishkea North
Inishkea South
Blacksod Bay
Killala B.
Killala
Ballina
Moy
L. Conn
Nephin 806
Sligo Bay
Sligo
Dromore West 544
Slieve Gamph
SLIGO
Collooney
Ballymote
L. Arrow
L. Allen
LEITRIM
Leitrim
Carrick-on-Shannon
Boyle
Achill Hd.
Achill I.
Corraun Pen.
MAYO
Newport
Charlestown
Swinford
Ballaghaderreen
Clare I.
Clew Bay
Westport
Castlebar
Knock
ROSCOMMON
Castlerea
Ballyhaunis
Inishturk
Croagh Patrick 765
Killary Harbour
Inishbofin
Mweelrea 819
Inishshark
Claremorris
Ballinrobe
Glennamaddy
Lough Mask
Roscommon
Longford
LONGFORD
Granard
L. Gowna
CAVAN
L. Sheelin
Cavan
Belturbet
Annalee
Carrickmacross
Kingscourt
Louth
LOUTH
Ardee
Dunleer
Clogher Hd.
Drogheda
Oldcastle
Ceanannus Mor (Kells)
Castlepollard
Blackwater
MEATH
Boyne
An Uaimh (Navan)
Balbriggan
Athboy
Trim
Connemara
Clifden
Slyne Hd.
Tuam
Lough Corrib
Lough Ree
Inny
Mullingar
WESTMEATH
Royal Canal
Rush
Lambay I.
Malahide
Swords
DUB
Howth Hd.
Dublin
DUBLIN
Dun Laoghaire
Bray
Greystones
123
Maynooth
Oughterard
GALWAY
Athlone
Moate
Clare
Suck
Bertraghboy B.
Kilkieran B.
Galway
Galway Bay
Athenry
Ballinasloe
Clara
Brosna
Grand Canal
Edenderry
Bog of Allen
Liffey
Clondalkin
KILDARE
Naas
Kippure 754
Tullamore
Daingean
Droichead Nua
OFFALY
Loughrea
Aran Is.
Black Hd.
Inishmore
Inishmaan
Inisheer
Slieve Aughty
368
Portumna
Gort
Shannon
Birr
Portarlington
Kildare
Monasterevin
Poulaphouca Res.
WICKLOW
Mountmellick
Slieve Bloom 528
Arderin
Port Laoise
Athy
Wicklow Mts.
Lugnaquilla 926
Wicklow
Wicklow Hd.
Rathdrum
Avoca
Hags Hd.
Liscannor Bay
Ennistimon
Lough Derg
Tulla
Roscrea
Mountrath
LAOIS
Mal Bay
Milltown Malbay
Mutton I.
Ennis
CLARE
Nenagh
Killaloe
Templemore
Durrow
Carlow
Tullow
Mizen Hd.
Arklow
Kilkee
Shannon Airport
Sixmilebridge
Keeper Hill 694
Thurles
CARLOW
Muine Bheag
Shillelagh
Gorey
Kilrush
Limerick
TIPPERARY
Kilkenny
KILKENNY
Bunclody
Loop Hd.
Foynes
LIMERICK
Golden Vale
Callan
796 Mt. Leinster
Slaney
Cahore Pt.
Mouth of the Shannon
Rathkeale
Barrow
Nore
Enniscorthy
Kerry Hd.
Listowel
Newcastle West
Tipperary
Cashel
Slievenamon 722
WEXFORD
Feale
Carrick-on-Suir
New Ross
Brandon B.
Tralee B.
Smerwick Harbour
Kilfinnane
Galtymore 920
Galty Mts.
Cahir
Clonmel
Wexford
Wexford Harbour
Rosslare
Greenore Pt.
Tralee
Rath Luirc
Mitchelstown
Comeragh Mts. 792
Waterford
Tramore
Carnsore Pt.
953 Brandon Mt.
Slieve Mish 853
Newmarket
Buttevant
Knockmealdown Mts. 795
Dingle
Maine
KERRY
Kanturk
Fermoy
WATERFORD
Hook Hd.
Saltee Is.
Great Blasket I.
Dunmore Hd.
Killorglin
Laune
Killarney
Mallow
Blackwater
Lismore
Waterford Harbour
Tramore B.
Inishvickillane
Dingle Bay
Carrauntoohill 1041
L. Leane
Boggeragh Mts.
646
Dungarvan
Dungarvan Harbour
Valencia I.
Caherciveen
Macgillycuddy's Reeks
CORK
Youghal
St. David's Hd.
St. David's
Puffin I.
Kenmare
Macroom
Blarney
Cork
Midleton
St. Brides Bay
Great Skellig
Ballinskelligs B.
Kenmare River
Caha Mts. 686
Glengarriff
Lee
Passage West
Cobh
Youghal B.
115
Scariff I.
Dunmanway
Crosshaven
Cork Harbour
Bandon
Bantry
Kinsale
Dursey I.
Castletown Bearhaven
Bear I.
Clonakilty
Old Head of Kinsale
Crow Hd.
Bantry Bay
Dunmanus B.
Skull
Skibbereen
Clonakilty B.
Long I.
Baltimore
Galley Hd.
Mizen Hd.
Sherkin I.
C. Clear
Clear I.
ft m
1500 500
600 200
300 100
0 0
50 150
100 300
200 600
500 1500
1000 3000
2000 6000
m ft
Projection : Lambert's Conformal Conic
West from Greenwich
COPYRIGHT GEORGE PHILIP LTD.

ATLANTIC OCEAN
NORTH SEA
IRISH SEA
CELTIC SEA
English Channel
St. George's Channel
Bristol Channel
North Channel
Firth of Clyde
Moray Firth
Pentland Firth
North Minch
The Wash
Str. of Dover
Shetland Is.
Yell
Unst
Fetlar
Mainland
Lerwick
Foula
Fair Isle
Orkney Is.
Westray
Sanday
Stronsay
Mainland
Kirkwall
Hoy
South Ronaldsay
C. Wrath
Thurso
Wick
Helmsdale
Outer Hebrides
Lewis
Stornoway
Harris
St. Kilda
North Uist
Benbecula
South Uist
Barra
Inner Hebrides
Skye
Portree
Rhum
Eigg
Mallaig
Coll
Tiree
Mull
Tobermory
Oban
Colonsay
Jura
Islay
Arran
North West Highlands
Ullapool
Lairg
Golspie
Tain
Invergordon
Dingwall
Nairn
Inverness
Elgin
Buckie
Banff
Fraserburgh
Peterhead
Huntly
Inverurie
Aberdeen
Stonehaven
L. Ness
Aviemore
Spey
Don
Dee
Ballater
SCOTLAND
Grampian Mts.
Ben Nevis
1342
Fort William
1214
Tay
Forfar
Montrose
Arbroath
Dundee
Perth
St. Andrews
Glenrothes
Kirkcaldy
Dunbar
L. Lomond
Stirling
Dunfermline
Edinburgh
Greenock
Paisley
Glasgow
East Kilbride
Hamilton
Irvine
Kilmarnock
Ayr
Campbeltown
Girvan
Stranraer
Mull of Galloway
Kirkcudbright
Dumfries
Southern Uplands
Jedburgh
Galashiels
Hawick
Cheviot Hills
Berwick-upon-Tweed
Alnwick
Newcastle-upon-Tyne
South Shields
Sunderland
Gateshead
Hexham
Durham
Hartlepool
Redcar
Middlesbrough
Darlington
Stockton-on-Tees
Scarborough
Carlisle
Workington
Whitehaven
Cumbrian Mts.
Pennines
Barrow-in-Furness
Lancaster
Harrogate
York
Bridlington
Beverley
Kingston upon Hull
Humber
Scunthorpe
Grimsby
Leeds
Bradford
Keighley
Huddersfield
Barnsley
Doncaster
Rotherham
Sheffield
Halifax
Blackpool
Preston
Burnley
Blackburn
Bolton
Manchester
Oldham
Stockport
Liverpool
Warrington
Chester
Crewe
Chesterfield
Mansfield
Lincoln
Louth
Skegness
Boston
Nottingham
Derby
Stoke on Trent
Stafford
Grantham
King's Lynn
Cromer
Norwich
Great Yarmouth
Lowestoft
Peterborough
Leicester
Nuneaton
Coventry
Corby
Thetford
Telford
Shrewsbury
Wolverhampton
BIRMINGHAM
Redditch
Worcester
Royal Leamington Spa
Rugby
Northampton
Bedford
Cambridge
Ely
Bury St. Edmunds
Ipswich
Felixstowe
Harwich
Colchester
Chelmsford
Milton Keynes
Stevenage
Luton
Harlow
Hemel Hempstead
Oxford
High Wycombe
Watford
Basildon
Southend-on-Sea
LONDON
Slough
Reading
Swindon
Newbury
Basingstoke
Guildford
Reigate
Crawley
Maidstone
Chatham
Margate
Canterbury
Dover
Ashford
Folkestone
Hastings
Eastbourne
Brighton
Worthing
Portsmouth
Havant
Fareham
Winchester
Southampton
Salisbury
Isle of Wight
Newport
Bournemouth
Poole
Weymouth
Yeovil
Taunton
Exmoor
Weston-super-Mare
Bath
Bristol
Cheltenham
Gloucester
Hereford
Cotswold Hills
ENGLAND
WALES
Anglesey
Holyhead
Bangor
Colwyn Bay
Snowdon
1085
Wrexham
Pwllheli
Cardigan Bay
Aberystwyth
Cambrian Mts.
Welshpool
Brecon
886
Carmarthen
Fishguard
Haverfordwest
Milford Haven
Pembroke
Llanelli
Swansea
Neath
Port Talbot
Rhondda
Barry
Cardiff
Cwmbran
Newport
Merthyr Tydfil
Barnstaple
Bude
Exeter
Dartmoor
618
Exmouth
Torbay
Plymouth
Newquay
Truro
St. Austell
Falmouth
Penzance
Land's End
Isles of Scilly
UNITED KINGDOM
I. of Man
Douglas
NORTHERN IRELAND
Ulster
Malin Hd.
Buncrana
Coleraine
Letterkenny
Londonderry
Ballymena
Larne
Lifford
Antrim
Bangor
Lough Neagh
Belfast
Omagh
Portadown
Lisburn
Lurgan
Armagh
Newry
Enniskillen
Lower L. Erne
Donegal
Aran I.
Bundoran
Sligo
Ballina
Achill I.
L. Conn
Castlebar
Westport
Connacht
Roscommon
Leitrim
Cavan
Clones
Dundalk
Drogheda
Ceanannus Mor
Longford
Mullingar
Lough Ree
Boyne
Lough Mask
Lough Corrib
Connemara
Athlone
Galway
Galway B.
Aran Is.
Ballinasloe
Tullamore
Liffey
Dublin
Dun Laoghaire
Bray
Wicklow Mts.
926
IRELAND
Leinster
Birr
Port Laoise
Athy
Lough Derg
Ennis
Nenagh
Carlow
Kilkenny
Limerick
Thurles
Kilrush
Shannon
Listowel
Tipperary
Tralee
Munster
Clonmel
Carrick-on-Suir
Wexford
Rosslare
Arklow
Dingle
Carrauntoohill
1041
Macgillycuddy's Reeks
Killarney
Mallow
Blackwater
Waterford
Dungarvan
Valencia I.
Cork
Cobh
Youghal
Bandon
Kinsale
Bantry
C. Clear
Channel Is. (U.K.)
Alderney
Guernsey
St. Peter Port
Sark
Jersey
St. Helier
C. de la Hague
Cotentin
Pte. de Barfleur
Cherbourg
Valognes
Bayeux
Caen
Trouville-sur-Mer
Lisieux
Le Havre
Bolbec
Fécamp
Pays de Caux
Seine
Rouen
Elbeuf
Dieppe
Le Tréport
Abbeville
Somme
Amiens
Picardie
St-Quentin
FRANCE
Le Touquet-Paris-Plage
Boulogne-sur-Mer
Calais
C. Gris Nez
Dunkerque
St-Omer
Béthune
Bruyay-la-Buissière
Lens
Lille
Valenciennes
Cambrai
Tourcoing
Tournai
BELGIUM
Brugge
Gent
Oostende
Zeebrugge
Antwerpen
Vlissingen
NETHERLANDS
's-Gravenhage (Den Haag)
Hoek van Holland
ROTTERDAM
Dordrecht
Haarlem
Alkmaar
Den Helder
NORWAY
Bergen
Askøy
Osøyro
Stord
Bømlo
Haugesund
Kopervik
Åkrahamn
Bokna
Stavanger
Sandnes
Bryne
Nærbø
1224
316
789
238
16
36
33
99
Projection: Conical with two standard parallels
East from Greenwich
West from Greenwich
COPYRIGHT GEORGE PHILIP LTD.
ft m
3000 1000
1500 500
600 200
0 0
50 150
100 300
200 600
500 1500
1000 3000
2000 6000
m ft

10 0 10 20 30 40 50 60 70 80 90 km

10 0 10 20 30 40 50 60 miles

Projection : Lambert's Conformal Conic

East from Greenwich

Underlined towns give their name to the administrative area in which they stand.

MIDDLE EUROPE 1:5 000 000

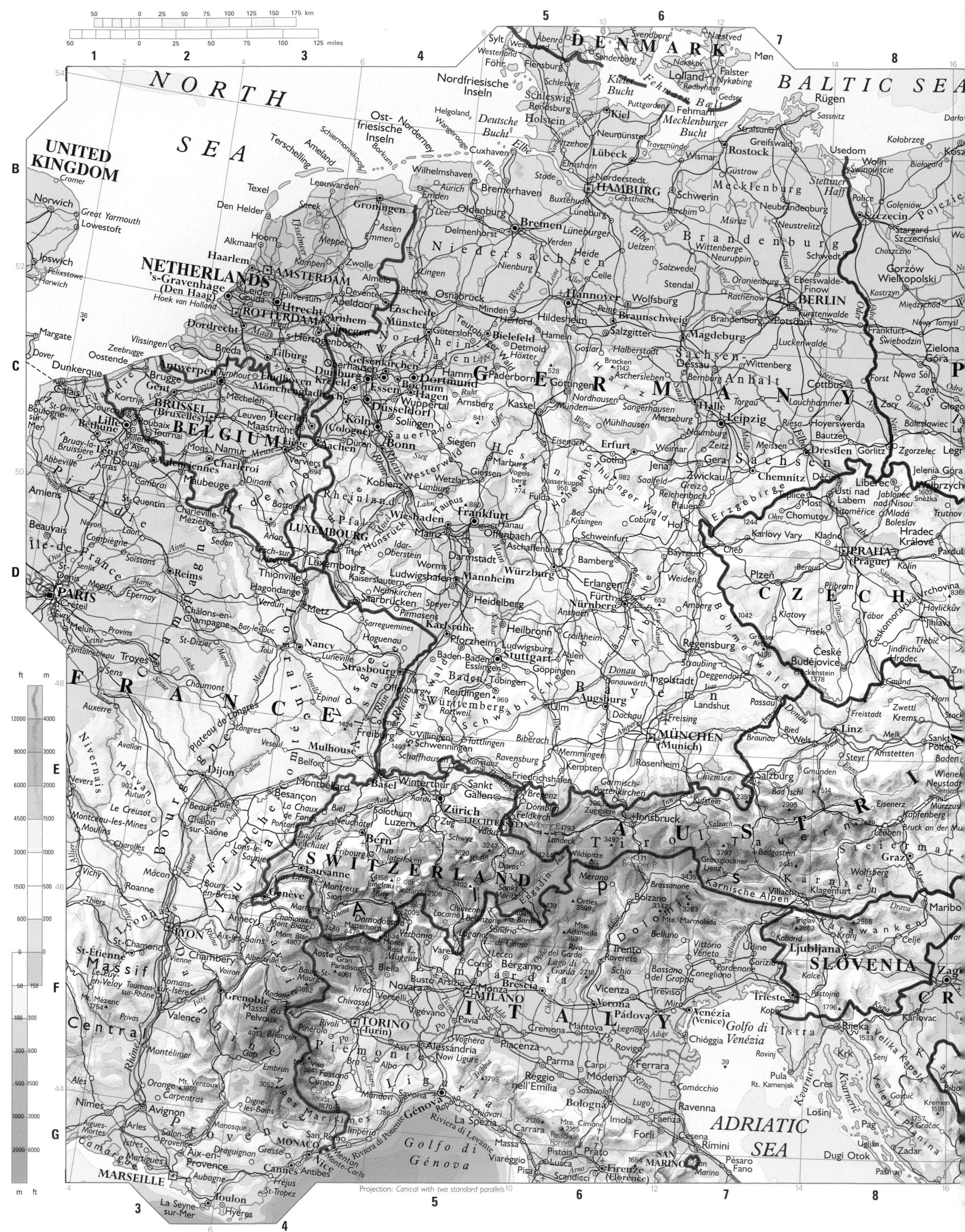

NORTH SEA
BALTIC SEA
ADRIATIC SEA
UNITED KINGDOM
NETHERLANDS
BELGIUM
LUXEMBOURG
GERMANY
DENMARK
FRANCE
SWITZERLAND
LIECHTENSTEIN
AUSTRIA
CZECH
SLOVENIA
ITALY
MONACO
SAN MARINO
BERLIN
PRAHA (Prague)
PARIS
AMSTERDAM
BRUSSEL (Bruxelles)
HAMBURG
MÜNCHEN (Munich)
MILANO
TORINO (Turin)
LYON
MARSEILLE
Ljubljana
Golfo di Génova
Golfo di Venézia
Projection: Conical with two standard parallels

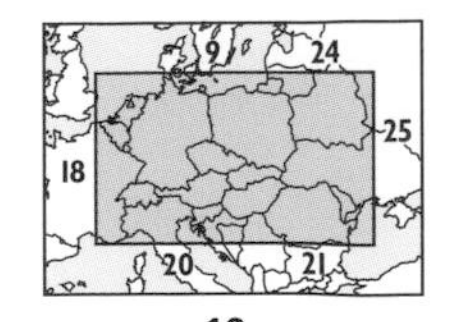

9
24
25
18
20
21

9 10 11 12 13 14 15 16

18 20 22 24 26 28 30

LITHUANIA

BELARUS

POLAND

UKRAINE

SLOVAK REP.

HUNGARY

ROMANIA

MOLDOVA

YUGOSLAVIA

BOSNIA-HERZEGOVINA

BULGARIA

Zatoka Gdańska

Kaliningrad (Russia)

Gdynia

Sopot

Gdańsk

Elbląg

Olsztyn

Pojezierze Mazurskie

Suwałki

Vilnius

Hrodna

Minsk

Mahilyow

Homyel

Babruysk

Baranavichy

Białystok

Bydgoszcz

Toruń

Włocławek

Płock

WARSZAWA (Warsaw)

Siedlce

Biała Podlaska

Brest

Pinsk

Mazyr

Pripet Marshes

Poznań

Łódź

Radom

Lublin

Chełm

Kovel

Lutsk

Rivne

Zhytomyr

KYYIV (Kiev)

Wrocław

Opole

Częstochowa

Kielce

Katowice

Kraków

Tarnów

Rzeszów

Przemyśl

Lviv (Lvov)

Ternopil

Khmelnytskyy

Vinnytsya

Bila Tserkva

Uman

Ostrava

Bielsko-Biała

Nowy Sącz

Karpaty

Vychodné Beskydy

Zakopane

Žilina

Poprad

Prešov

Košice

Uzhhorod

Ivano-Frankivsk

Chernivtsi

Kamyanets-Podilskyy

Bratislava

Nitra

Banská Bystrica

Nízke Tatry

Miskolc

Nyíregyháza

Debrecen

Eger

Győr

BUDAPEST

Székesfehérvár

Balaton

Kecskemét

Szeged

Pécs

Oradea

Cluj-Napoca

Satu Mare

Baia Mare

Suceava

Botoşani

Iaşi

Chişinău

Tiraspol

Bacău

Braşov

Sibiu

Arad

Timişoara

Transilvania

Carpaţi Meridionali

Galaţi

Brăila

Constanţa

Ploieşti

BUCUREŞTI (Bucharest)

Craiova

Pitești

Dunărea (Danube)

Subotica

Novi Sad

Vojvodina

BEOGRAD (Belgrade)

Osijek

Sarajevo

Ruse

Varna

Dobrich

Sava

Dunav

Tisza

Dniester

Prut

Wisła (Vistula)

East from Greenwich

9 10 11 12 13 14 15

COPYRIGHT GEORGE PHILIP LTD.

FRANCE 1:5 000 000

50 0 25 50 75 100 125 150 175 km

50 0 25 50 75 100 125 miles

m ft

4000 12000

3000 9000

2000 6000

1500 4500

1000 3000

500 1500

200 600

0 0

50 150

100 300

200 600

500 1500

1000 3000

2000 6000

3000 9000

4000 12000

m ft

Projection: Conical with two standard parallels

West from Greenwich 0 East from Greenwich

Corse (Corsica)

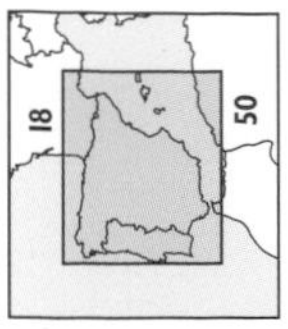

50 0 25 50 75 100 125 150 175 km

50 0 25 50 75 100 125 miles

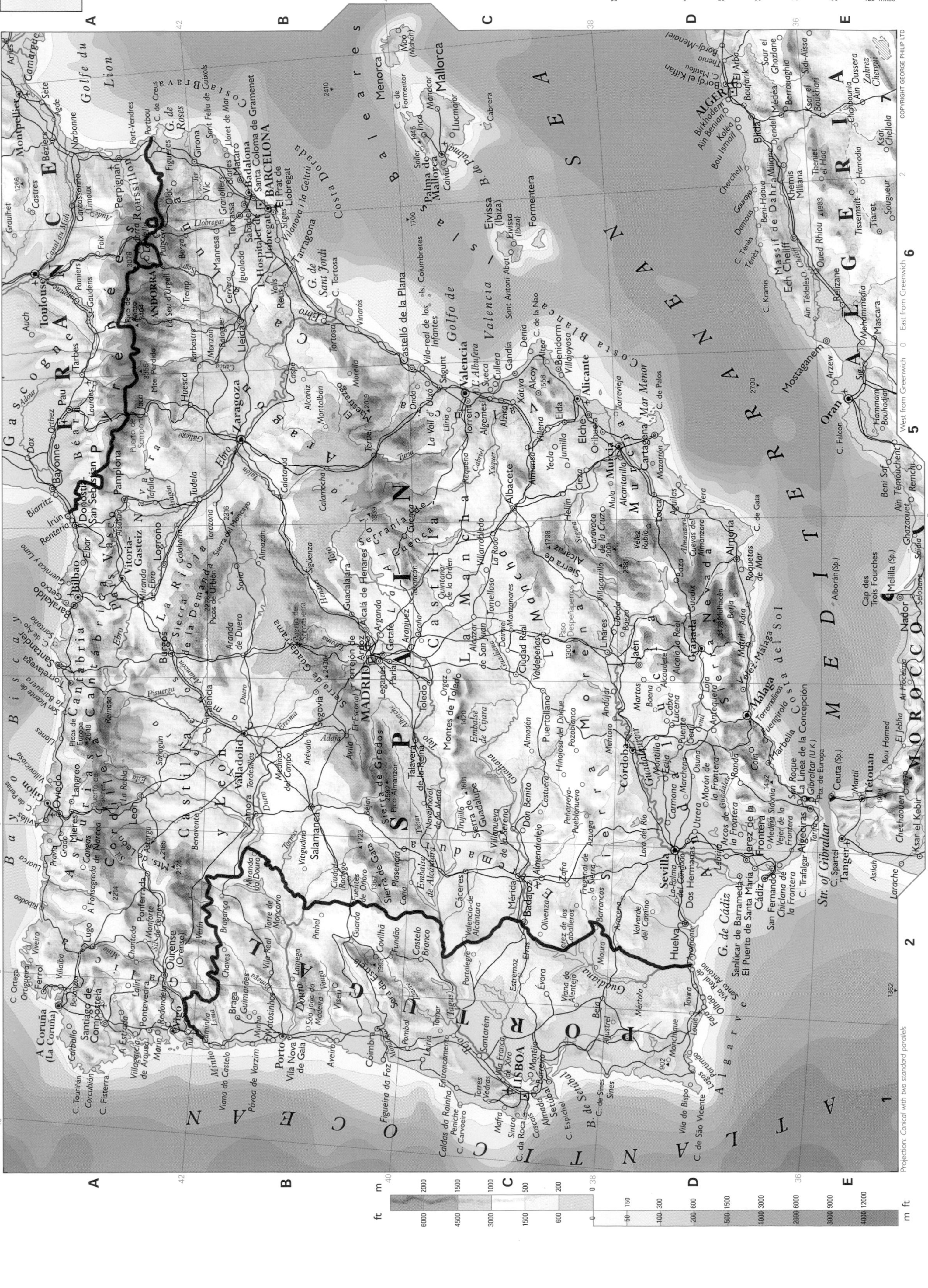

m 2000 1500 1000 500 200 0 50 150 300 600 1500 3000 6000 9000 12000 ft

ft 6000 4500 3000 1500 600 0 50 100 200 500 1000 2000 3000 4000 m

Projection: Conical with two standard parallels

West from Greenwich 0 East from Greenwich

SWITZERLAND
AUSTRIA
SLOVENIA
CROAT
FRANCE
MONACO
SAN MARINO
VATICAN CITY
ALGERIA
TUNISIA
MALTA
LIGURIAN SEA
TYRRHENIAN SEA
ADRIATIC SEA
MEDITER
Golfo di Génova
Golfo di Venézia
Golfo di Tunis
Golfe de Hammamet
Corse
Sardegna
Elba
Ísole Eólie
Ísole Égadi
Ísole Pelagie (Italy)
Ísole Ponziane
ROMA
MILANO
TORINO (Turin)
NÁPOLI
Firenze (Florence)
Venézia (Venice)
Génova
Bologna
Palermo
Catánia
Messina
Bari
Cágliari
Tunis
Ljubljana
Zagreb
Trieste
MARSEILLE
Lyon
Grenoble
Nice
Toulon
Avignon
Ajaccio
Bastia
Sassari
Ancona
Pescara
Livorno
Pisa
Perúgia
Verona
Pádova
Brescia
Bergamo
Parma
Módena
Ravenna
Rímini
Foggia
Taranto
Cosenza
Catanzaro
Siracusa
Reggio di Calábria
Valletta
Constantine
Annaba
Bizerte
Sousse
Kairouan
Projection: Conical with two standard parallels

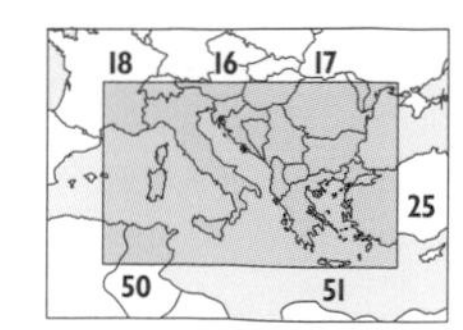
18
16
17
25
50
51

8 9 10 11 12 13

HUNGARY

ROMANIA

UKRAINE

YUGOSLAVIA

SERBIA

MONTENEGRO

BOSNIA-HERZEGOVINA

ALBANIA

MACEDONIA

BULGARIA

GREECE

TURKEY

BLACK SEA

ÆGEAN SEA

IONIAN SEA

MEDITERRANEAN SEA

Marmara Denizi (Sea of Marmara)

Str. of Otranto

Transilvania

Carpaţii Meridionali

Walachia

Dobruja

Vojvodina

Kosovo

Stara Planina

Rhodopi Planina

Thrace

Makedhonía

Pindhos

Pelopónnisos

Kikládhes

Dhodhekánisos

Kríti

Mysia

Lydia

Caria

BUCUREŞTI (Bucharest)

BEOGRAD (Belgrade)

SOFIYA

Skopje

Tiranë

ATHÍNAI (Athens)

İSTANBUL

Thessaloníki

İzmir (Smyrna)

Sarajevo

Podgorica

Constanţa

Varna

Burgas

Plovdiv

Craiova

Timişoara

Brăila

Galaţi

Ploieşti

Braşov

Sibiu

Novi Sad

Niš

Bursa

Balıkesir

Manisa

Pátrai

Lárisa

Iráklion

Ródhos (Rhodes)

Kérkira (Corfu)

B C D E F G

East from Greenwich

18 20 22 24 26 28 30

44 42 40 38 36

8 9 10 11 12 13

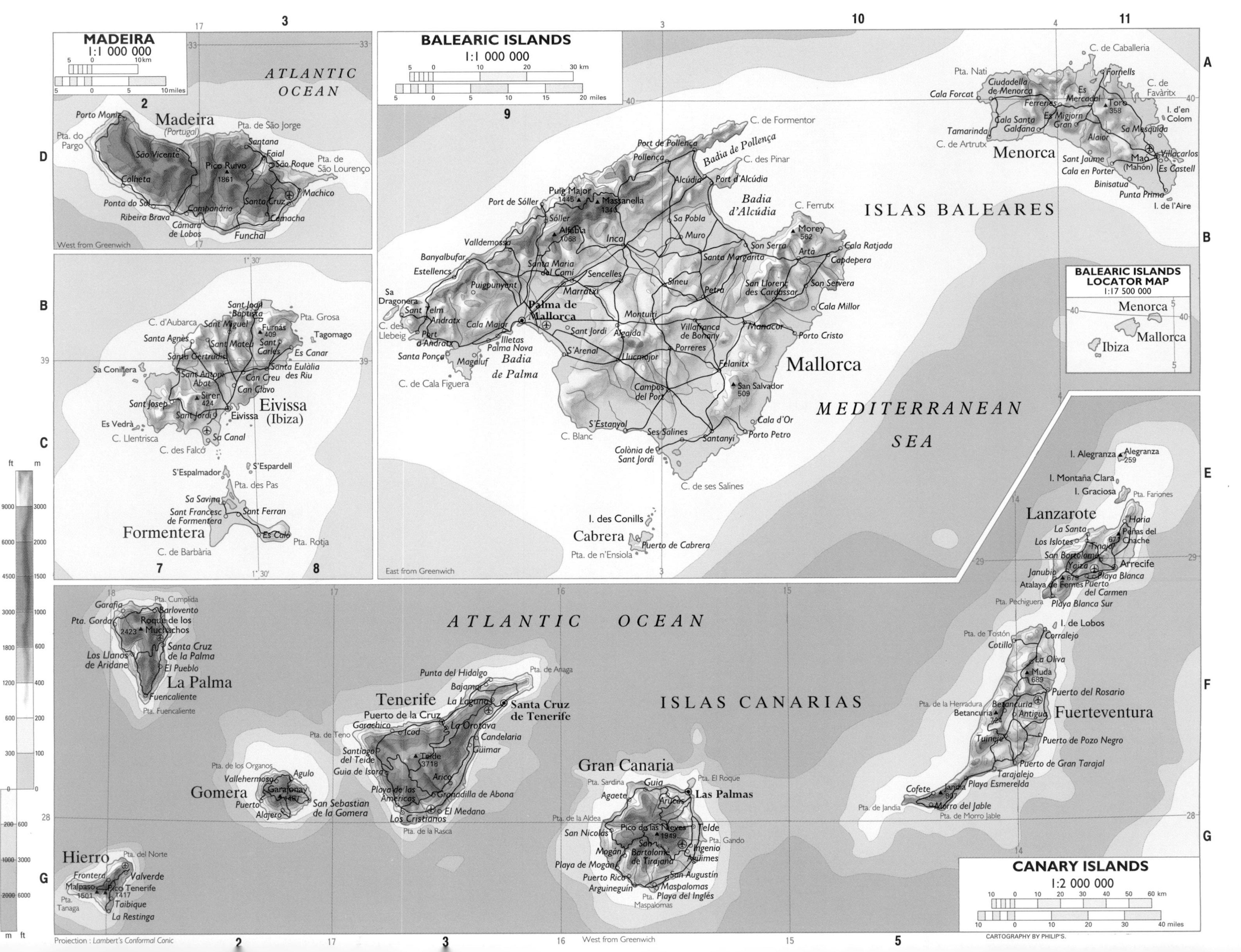
MADEIRA
1:1 000 000
ATLANTIC OCEAN
Madeira
(Portugal)
Pico Ruivo 1861
Funchal
BALEARIC ISLANDS
1:1 000 000
BALEARIC ISLANDS LOCATOR MAP
1:17 500 000
Menorca
Mallorca
Ibiza
ISLAS BALEARES
MEDITERRANEAN SEA
Mallorca
Palma de Mallorca
Badia de Palma
Badia d'Alcúdia
Badia de Pollença
Menorca
Cabrera
Eivissa (Ibiza)
Formentera
CANARY ISLANDS
1:2 000 000
ATLANTIC OCEAN
ISLAS CANARIAS
Lanzarote
Fuerteventura
Gran Canaria
Las Palmas
Tenerife
Santa Cruz de Tenerife
Teide 3718
La Palma
Gomera
Hierro
East from Greenwich
West from Greenwich
Projection : Lambert's Conformal Conic
CARTOGRAPHY BY PHILIP'S.

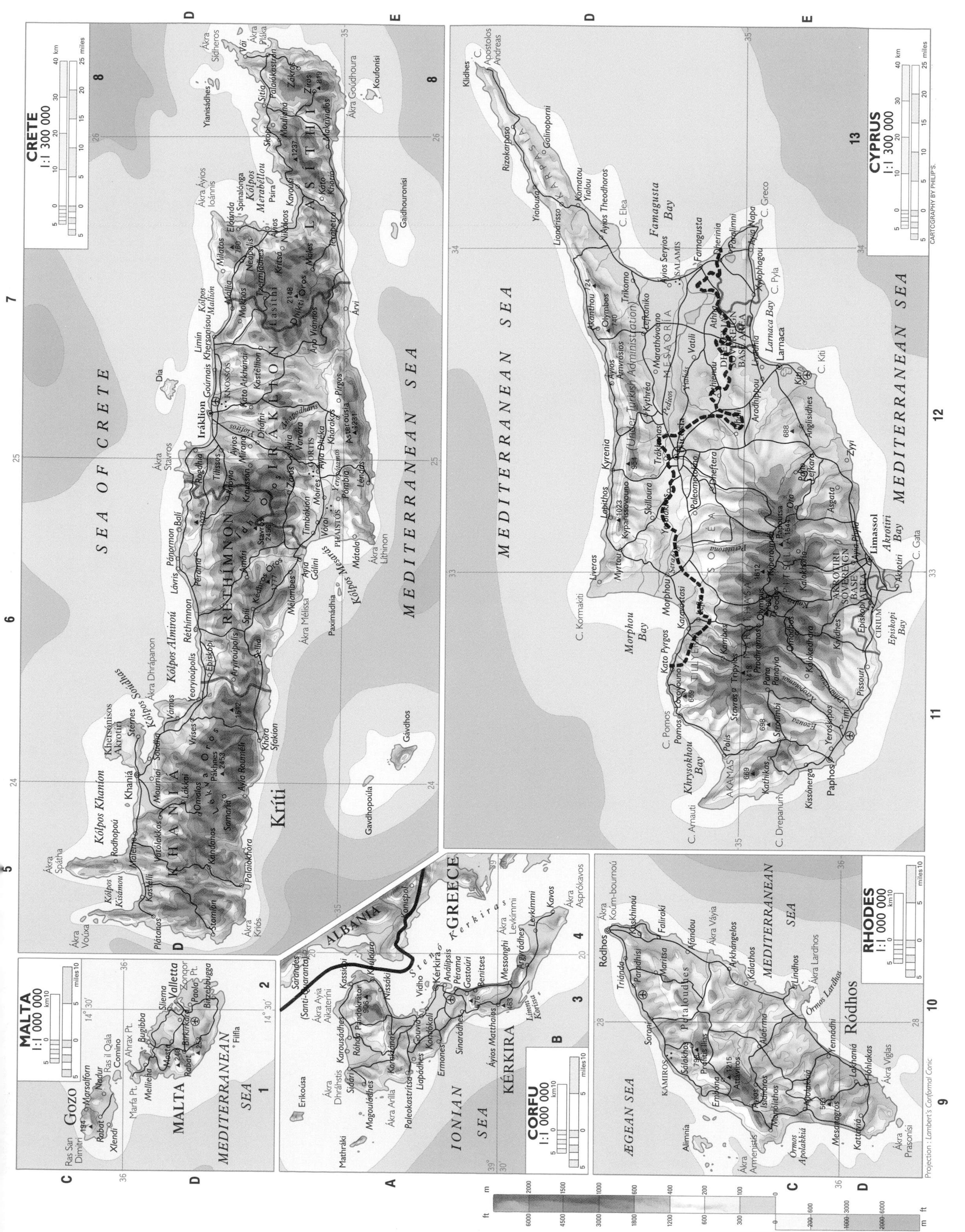
CRETE
1:1 300 000
SEA OF CRETE
MEDITERRANEAN SEA
Kríti
Iráklion
Khaniá
Réthimnon
Gávdhos
CYPRUS
1:1 300 000
MEDITERRANEAN SEA
Famagusta Bay
Morphou Bay
Larnaca Bay
Nicosia
Limassol
Larnaca
Paphos
Kyrenia
Famagusta
MALTA
1:1 000 000
Gozo
MALTA
Valletta
MEDITERRANEAN SEA
CORFU
1:1 000 000
KÉRKIRA
IONIAN SEA
ALBANIA
GREECE
Kérkira
RHODES
1:1 000 000
Ródhos
ÆGEAN SEA
MEDITERRANEAN SEA
CARTOGRAPHY BY PHILIP'S
Projection : Lambert's Conformal Conic

 1:10 000 000

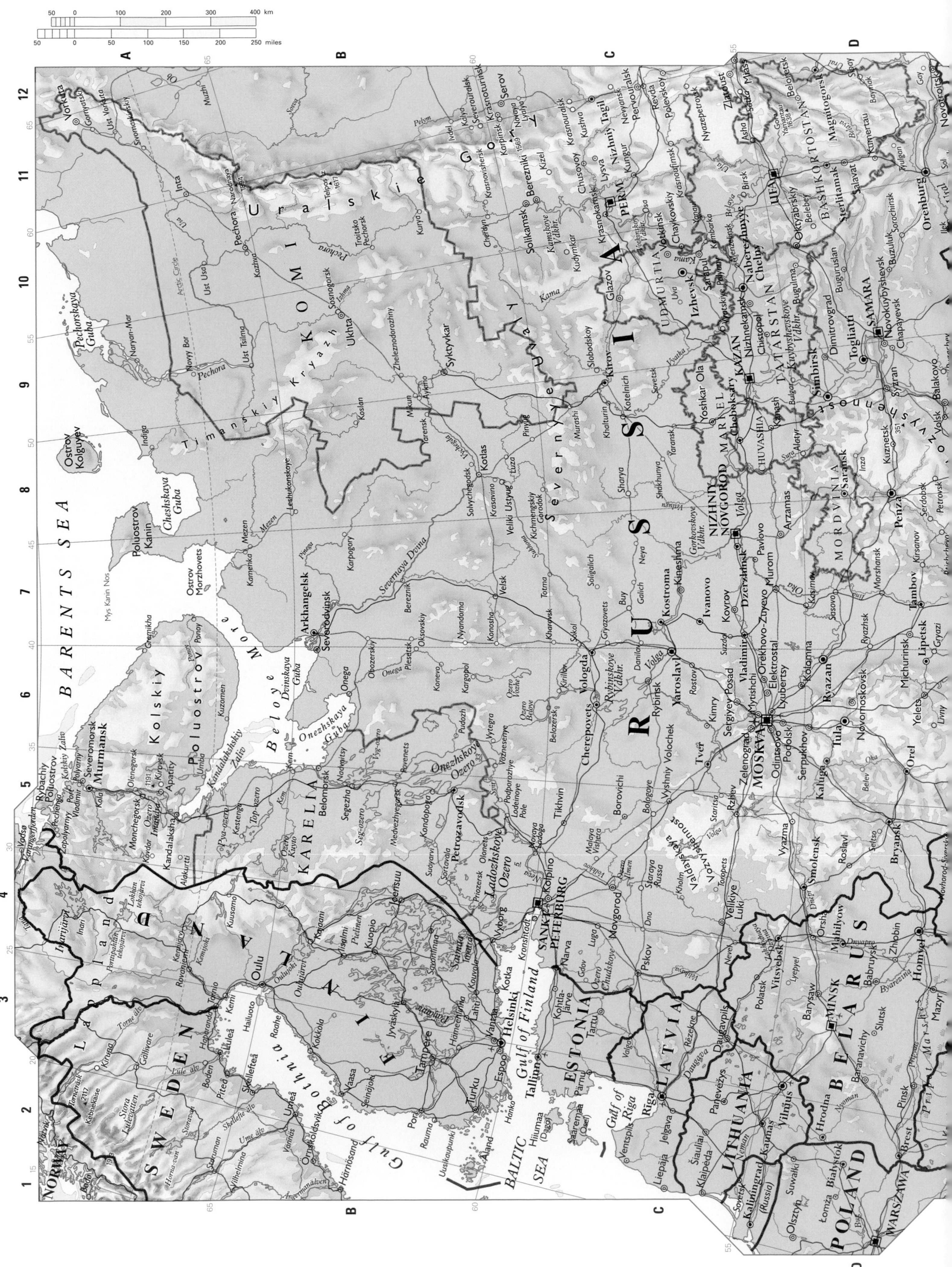

50 0 100 200 300 400 km
50 0 50 100 150 200 250 miles
BARENTS SEA
Beloye More
Gulf of Bothnia
Gulf of Finland
Gulf of Riga
BALTIC SEA
NORWAY
SWEDEN
FINLAND
ESTONIA
LATVIA
LITHUANIA
BELARUS
POLAND
RUSSIA
KOMI
KARELIA
UDMURTIA
TATARSTAN
CHUVASHIA
MARI EL
MORDVINIA
BASHKORTOSTAN
Lappland
Kolskiy Poluostrov
Timanskiy Kryazh
Uralskie Gory
Severnyye Uvaly
Ladozhskoye Ozero
Onezhskoye Ozero
MOSKVA
SANKT PETERBURG
Helsinki
Tallinn
Riga
Vilnius
MINSK
WARSZAWA
Arkhangelsk
Murmansk
NIZHNIY NOVGOROD
KAZAN
SAMARA
PERM
UFA
Orenburg
Kaliningrad (Russia)

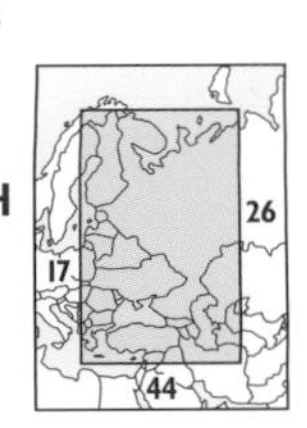

ft	m
12 000	4000
9000	3000
6000	2000
4500	1500
3000	1000
1500	500
600	200
0	0
600	200
1500	500
3000	1000
6000	2000
ft	m

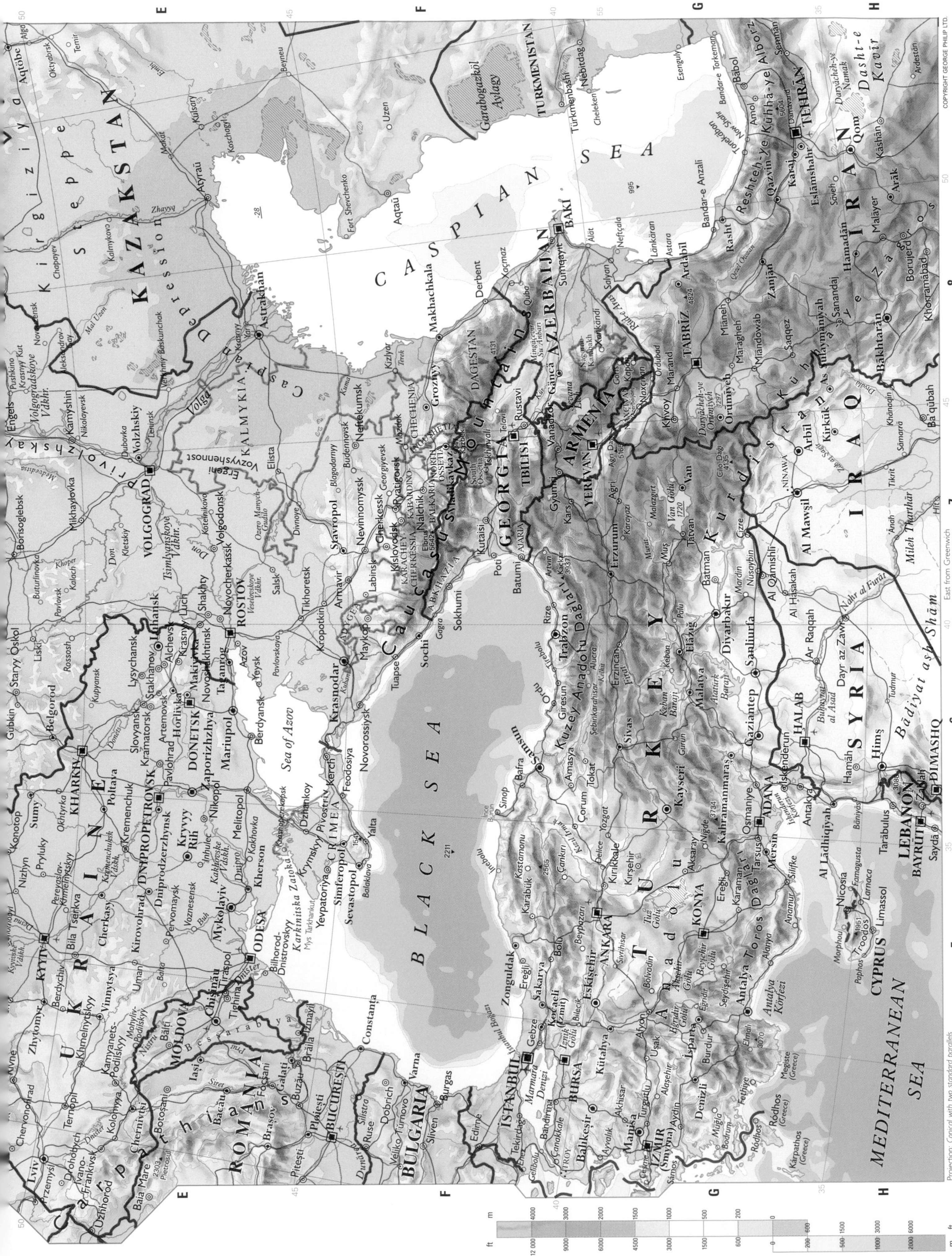

Projection: Conical with two standard parallels

East from Greenwich

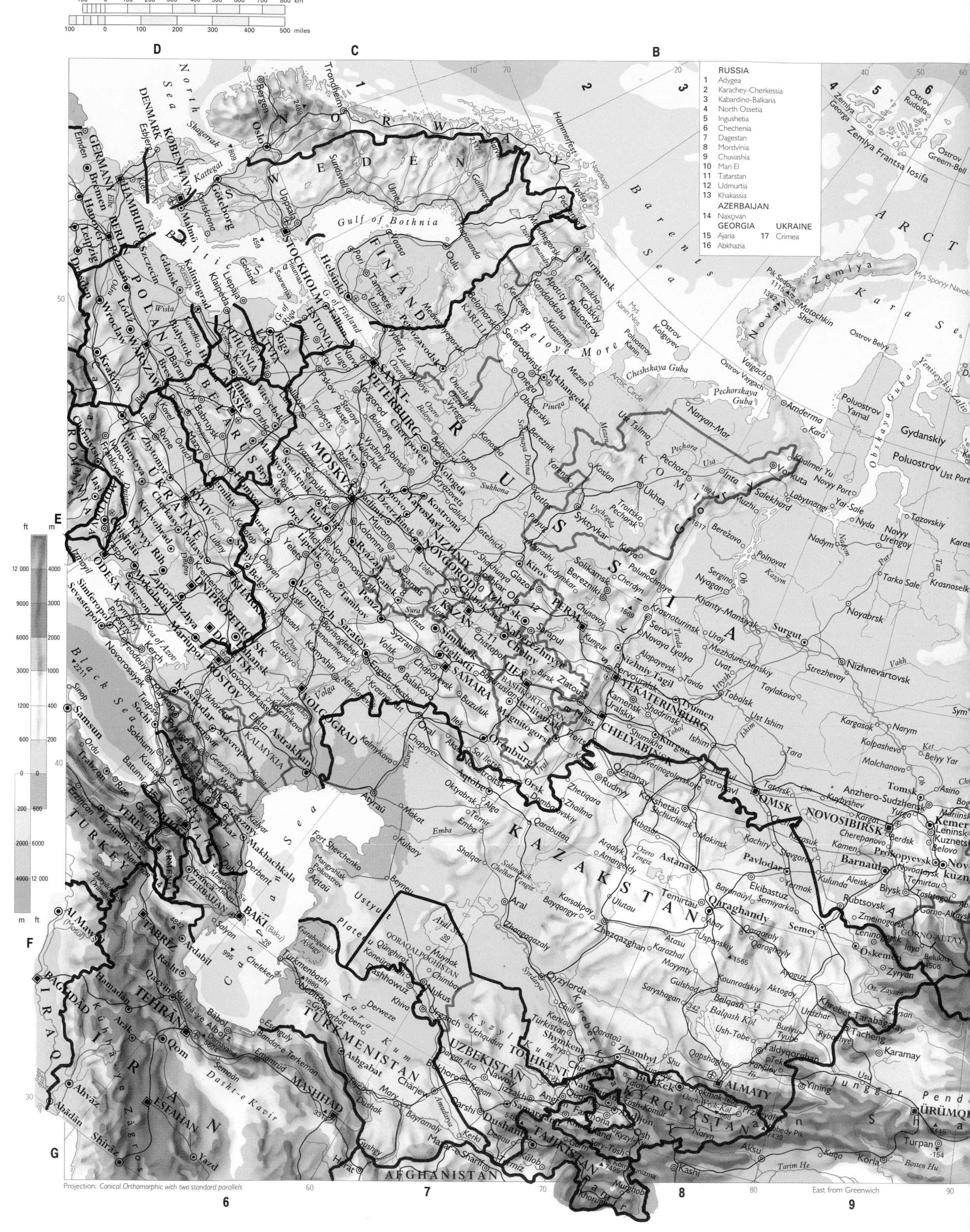
100 0 100 200 300 400 500 600 700 800 km
100 0 100 200 300 400 500 miles
RUSSIA
1 Adygea
2 Karachey-Cherkessia
3 Kabardino-Balkaria
4 North Ossetia
5 Ingushetia
6 Chechenia
7 Dagestan
8 Mordvinia
9 Chuvashia
10 Mari El
11 Tatarstan
12 Udmurtia
13 Khakassia
AZERBAIJAN
14 Naxçıvan
GEORGIA
15 Ajaria
16 Abkhazia
UKRAINE
17 Crimea
ft m
12 000 4000
9000 3000
6000 2000
3000 1000
1200 400
600 200
200 600
2000 6000
4000 12 000
m ft
D C B E F G
6 7 8 9
Projection: Conical Orthomorphic with two standard parallels
East from Greenwich
Barents Sea
Kara Sea
Gulf of Bothnia
Baltic Sea
Black Sea
Caspian Sea
Beloye More
North Sea
Zemlya Frantsa Iosifa
Novaya Zemlya
RUSSIA
KAZAKSTAN
UZBEKISTAN
TURKMENISTAN
KYRGYZSTAN
TAJIKISTAN
AFGHANISTAN
IRAN
IRAQ
TURKEY
GEORGIA
ARMENIA
AZERBAIJAN
UKRAINE
BELARUS
POLAND
LITHUANIA
LATVIA
ESTONIA
FINLAND
SWEDEN
NORWAY
DENMARK
GERMANY
ROMANIA
MOLDOVA
MOSKVA
SANKT-PETERBURG
KYYIV
MINSK
TEHRAN
TASHKENT
ALMATY
ASTANA
BAKI
NOVOSIBIRSK
OMSK
YEKATERINBURG
CHELYABINSK
VOLGOGRAD
ROSTOV
SAMARA
KAZAN
NIZHNIY NOVGOROD
PERM
UFA
ODESA
DNIPROPETROVSK
DONETSK
KHARKIV
STOCKHOLM
HELSINKI
TALLINN
RIGA
VILNIUS
WARSZAWA
BERLIN
HAMBURG
KØBENHAVN
Murmansk
Arkhangelsk
Vorkuta
Surgut
Tyumen
Orenburg
Astrakhan
Ashgabat
Dushanbe
Bishkek
Ürümqi
Tomsk
Barnaul
Semey
Qaraghandy
Pavlodar
Aral Sea
Ural
Volga
Ob
Irtysh
Pechora
Kyzyl Kum
Kara Kum
Ustyurt Plateau

Sea of Okhotsk
Sea of Japan
East Siberian Sea
Laptev Sea
Bering Sea
Sakhalin
Hokkaidō
Honshū
JAPAN
MONGOLIA
CHINA
RUSSIA
NORTH KOREA
SOUTH KOREA
BEIJING
SAPPORO
Khabarovsk
Vladivostok
Magadan
Yakutsk
Irkutsk
Ulaanbaatar
COPYRIGHT GEORGE PHILIP LTD.

500 0 250 500 750 1000 1250 1500 1750 km

500 0 250 500 750 1000 1250 miles

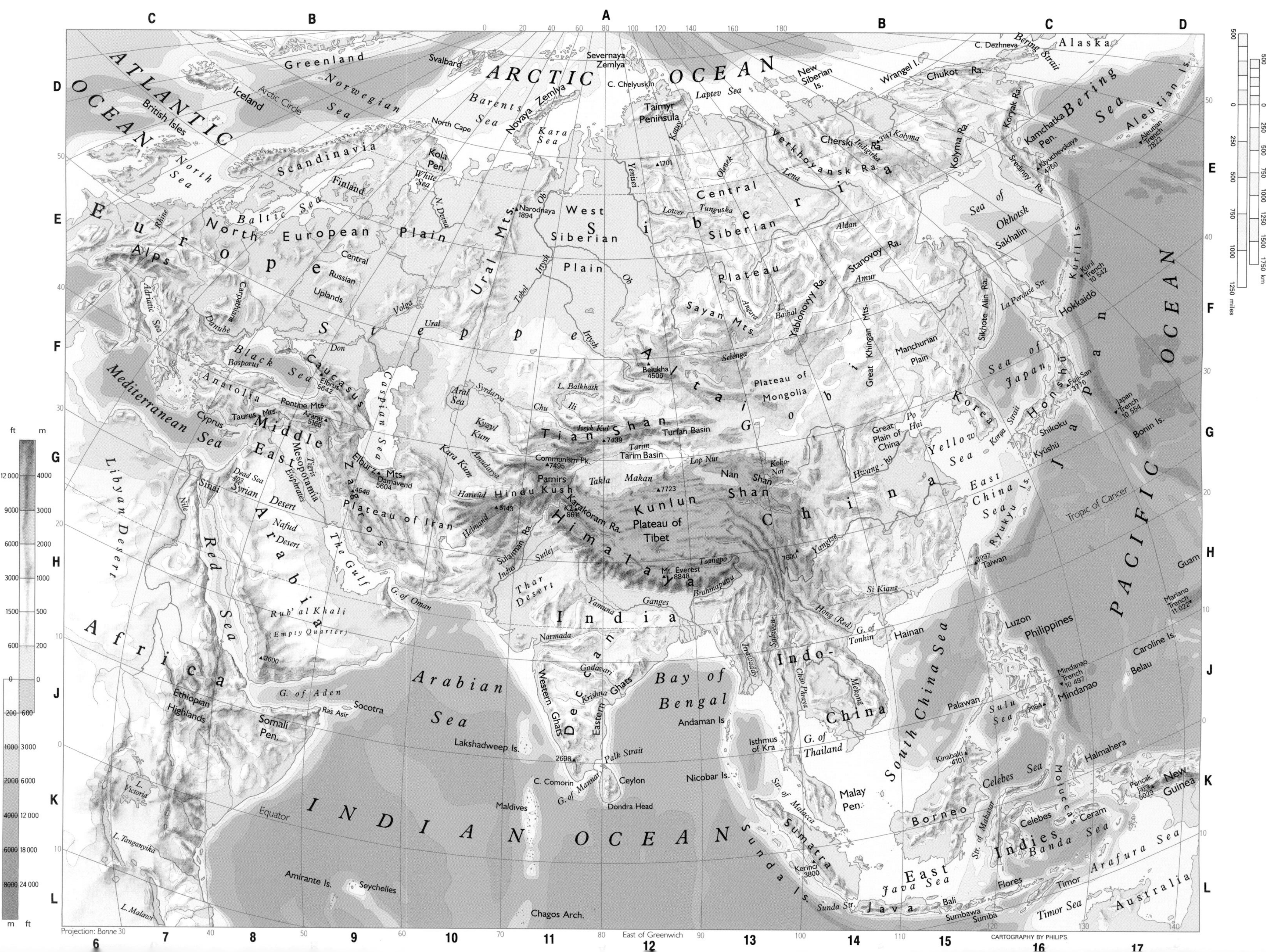

ARCTIC OCEAN
PACIFIC OCEAN
INDIAN OCEAN
ATLANTIC OCEAN
Europe
Siberia
Steppes
Altai
Gobi
China
Japan
Tibet
India
Deccan
Arabia
Africa
Indo-China
East Indies
Bay of Bengal
Arabian Sea
South China Sea
Sea of Japan
Sea of Okhotsk
Bering Sea
Caspian Sea
Black Sea
Mediterranean Sea
Red Sea
Laptev Sea
Kara Sea
Barents Sea
Norwegian Sea
North Sea
Baltic Sea
White Sea
Adriatic Sea
Yellow Sea
East China Sea
Java Sea
Timor Sea
Arafura Sea
Banda Sea
Celebes Sea
Sulu Sea
Molucca Sea
The Gulf
G. of Aden
G. of Oman
G. of Thailand
G. of Tonkin
G. of Mannar
Himalaya
Hindu Kush
Karakoram Ra.
Kunlun Shan
Tian Shan
Nan Shan
Ural Mts.
Caucasus
Alps
Carpathians
Pontine Mts.
Taurus Mts.
Zagros
Elburz Mts.
Sulaiman Ra.
Sayan Mts.
Yablonovy Ra.
Stanovoy Ra.
Verkhoyansk Ra.
Cherski Ra.
Kolyma Ra.
Chukot Ra.
Koryak Ra.
Sredinny Ra.
Sikhote Alin Ra.
Great Khingan Mts.
Western Ghats
Eastern Ghats
Plateau of Tibet
Plateau of Iran
Plateau of Mongolia
Central Siberian Plateau
West Siberian Plain
North European Plain
Central Russian Uplands
Manchurian Plain
Great Plain of China
Tarim Basin
Turfan Basin
Takla Makan
Kara Kum
Kyzyl Kum
Thar Desert
Syrian Desert
Nafud Desert
Rub' al Khali (Empty Quarter)
Libyan Desert
Ethiopian Highlands
Mesopotamia
Middle East
Anatolia
Pamirs
Mt. Everest 8848
K2 8611
Communism Pk. 7495
Damavend 5604
Ararat 5165
Elbrus 5642
Belukha 4506
Fuji-San 3776
Kinabalu 4101
Kerinci 3800
Puncak Jaya 5029
Narodnaya 1894
Klyuchevskaya 4750
Dead Sea 403
Scandinavia
Finland
Iceland
Greenland
Svalbard
Novaya Zemlya
Severnaya Zemlya
New Siberian Is.
Wrangel I.
Kamchatka Pen.
Sakhalin
Hokkaido
Honshu
Kyushu
Shikoku
Korea
Taiwan
Hainan
Luzon
Mindanao
Philippines
Borneo
Sumatra
Java
Celebes
New Guinea
Ceylon
Maldives
Malay Pen.
Kola Pen.
Taimyr Peninsula
Somali Pen.
Socotra
Ras Asir
Seychelles
Andaman Is.
Nicobar Is.
Lakshadweep Is.
Chagos Arch.
Amirante Is.
Cyprus
British Isles
Alaska
Australia
Bering Strait
Aleutian Is.
Aleutian Trench 7822
Kuril Is.
Kuril Trench 10 542
Japan Trench 10 554
Mariano Trench 11 022
Mindanao Trench 10 497
Bonin Is.
Ryukyu Is.
Caroline Is.
Belau
Guam
Halmahera
Ceram
Timor
Flores
Sumba
Bali
Sumbawa
Palawan
Sunda Is.
Irtysh
Ob
Tobol
Yenisei
Lower Tunguska
Olenek
Lena
Aldan
Indigirka
Kolyma
Amur
Selenga
Angara
Hwang-Ho
Yangtze
Si Kiang
Hong (Red)
Mekong
Irrawaddy
Salween
Chao Phraya
Tsangpo
Brahmaputra
Ganges
Yamuna
Indus
Sutlej
Narmada
Godavari
Krishna
Helmand
Harirud
Tigris
Euphrates
Nile
Volga
Ural
Don
Danube
Rhine
Amudarya
Syrdarya
Chu
Ili
Aral Sea
L. Balkhash
Issyk Kul
L. Baikal
Lop Nur
Koko Nor
Po Hai
L. Victoria
L. Tanganyika
L. Malawi
Tropic of Cancer
Arctic Circle
Equator
C. Chelyuskin
C. Dezhneva
C. Comorin
Dondra Head
North Cape
La Perouse Str.
Korea Strait
Str. of Malacca
Str. of Makasar
Sunda Str.
Palk Strait
Isthmus of Kra
Bosporus
Sinai
Projection: Bonne
East of Greenwich
CARTOGRAPHY BY PHILIPS

m	4000	3000	2000	1000	500	200	0
ft	12 000	9000	6000	3000	1500	600	0

m	200	1000	2000	4000	6000	8000
ft	600	3000	6000	12 000	18 000	24 000

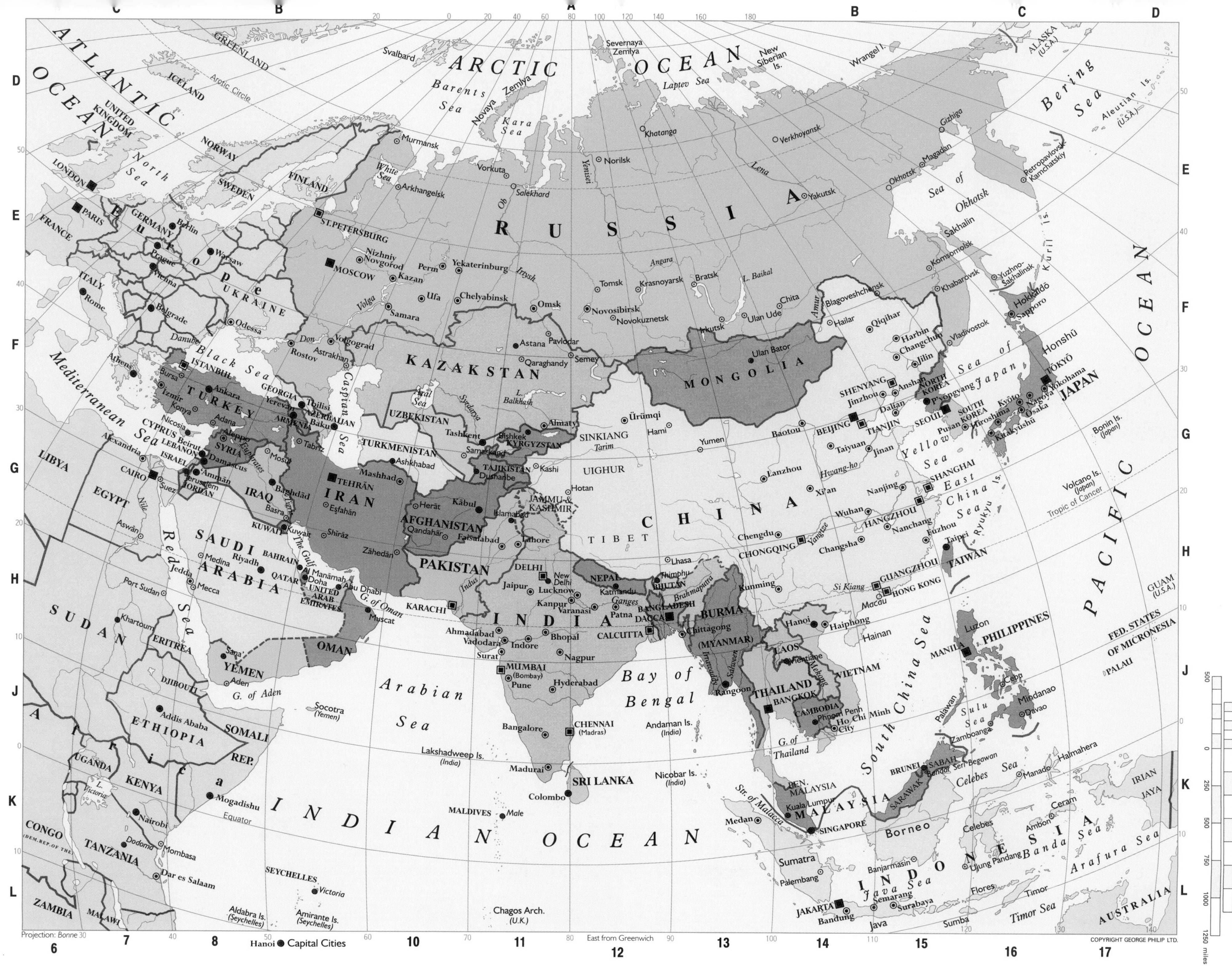

500 0 250 500 750 1000 1250 1500 1750 km
500 0 250 500 750 1000 1250 miles
ARCTIC OCEAN
PACIFIC OCEAN
INDIAN OCEAN
ATLANTIC OCEAN
RUSSIA
CHINA
MONGOLIA
KAZAKSTAN
INDIA
PAKISTAN
AFGHANISTAN
IRAN
IRAQ
SAUDI ARABIA
TURKEY
SYRIA
JORDAN
ISRAEL
LEBANON
YEMEN
OMAN
KUWAIT
QATAR
BAHRAIN
UZBEKISTAN
TURKMENISTAN
TAJIKISTAN
KYRGYZSTAN
GEORGIA
ARMENIA
AZERBAIJAN
NEPAL
BHUTAN
BANGLADESH
BURMA (MYANMAR)
THAILAND
LAOS
VIETNAM
CAMBODIA
MALAYSIA
SINGAPORE
BRUNEI
INDONESIA
PHILIPPINES
TAIWAN
JAPAN
NORTH KOREA
SOUTH KOREA
SRI LANKA
MALDIVES
CYPRUS
EGYPT
SUDAN
ETHIOPIA
ERITREA
DJIBOUTI
SOMALI REP.
KENYA
UGANDA
TANZANIA
LIBYA
FINLAND
SWEDEN
NORWAY
UKRAINE
GERMANY
FRANCE
ITALY
UNITED KINGDOM
ICELAND
GREENLAND
Caspian Sea
Black Sea
Mediterranean Sea
Red Sea
Arabian Sea
Bay of Bengal
South China Sea
East China Sea
Yellow Sea
Sea of Japan
Sea of Okhotsk
Bering Sea
Laptev Sea
Kara Sea
Barents Sea
Arctic Circle
Tropic of Cancer
Equator
Hanoi ● Capital Cities
East from Greenwich
Projection: Bonne
COPYRIGHT GEORGE PHILIP LTD.

JAPAN 1:5 000 000

50 0 25 50 75 100 125 150 175 km
50 0 25 50 75 100 125 miles
SEA OF JAPAN
SEA OF OKHOTSK
La Perouse Strait (Sōya-Kaikyō)
Sakhalin (Russia)
HOKKAIDO
Hokkaidō
SAPPORO
Asahikawa
Kushiro
Obihiro
Hakodate
Muroran
Otaru
Wakkanai
Abashiri
Nemuro
Rebun-Tō
Rishiri-Tō
Okushiri-Tō
Ishikari-Wan (Otaru-Wan)
Uchiura-Wan
Tsugaru-Kaikyō
TŌHOKU
Aomori
Hachinohe
Morioka
Akita
Sendai
Sendai-Wan
Yamagata
Niigata
Sado
Fukushima
Miyako
Kamaishi
Hirosaki
Noshiro
Sakata
Tsuruoka
Ishinomaki
Kitakami
Mutsu-Wan
RUSSIA
CHINA
NORTH KOREA
HEILONGJIANG
JILIN
Khrebet Sikhote Alin
Vladivostok
Nakhodka
Ussuriysk
Lake Khanka
Zaliv Petra Velikogo
Dalnegorsk
Jiamusi
Chŏngjin
Najin
Khasan
Ostrov Kunashir

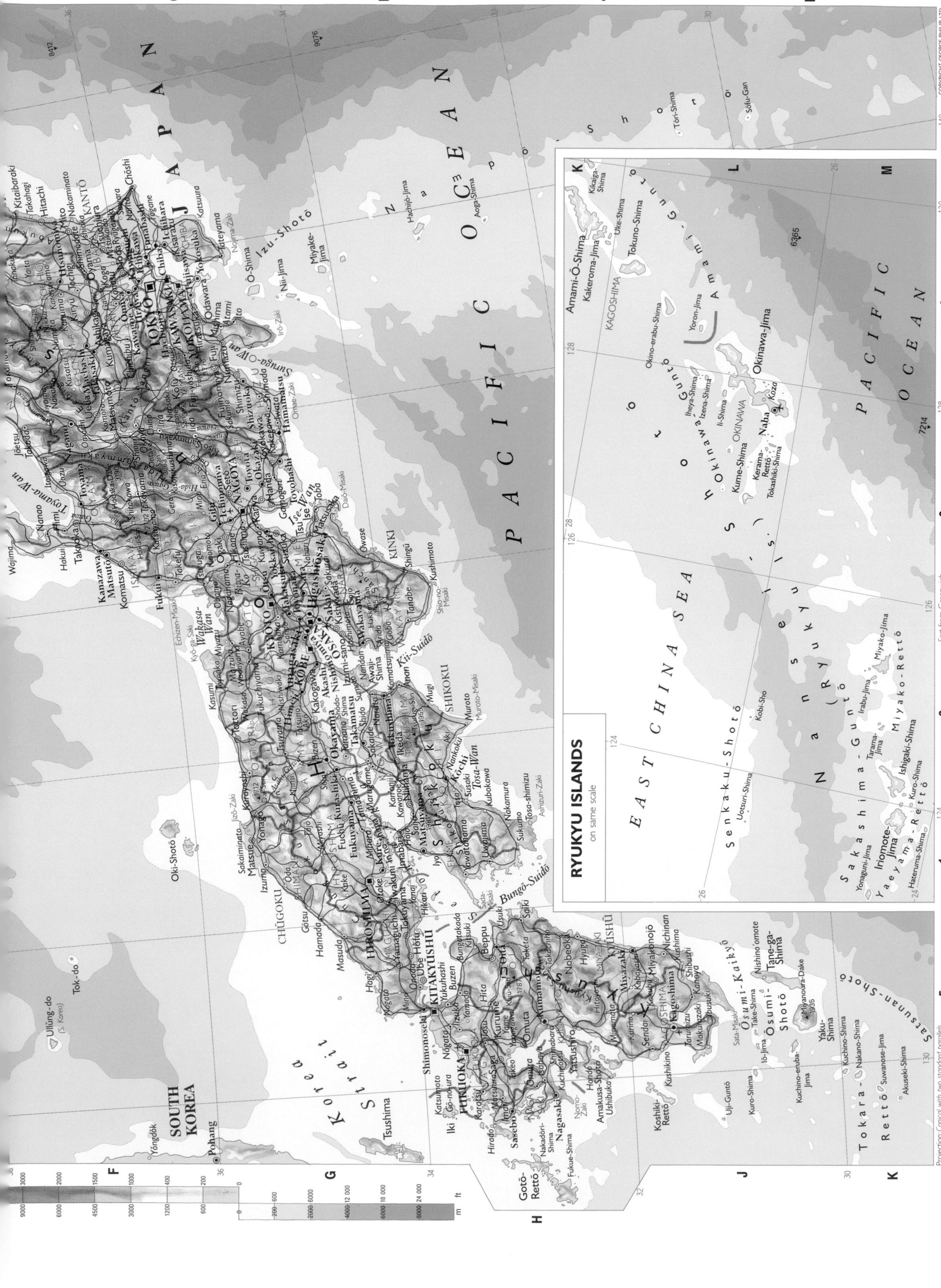

JAPAN

SOUTH KOREA

Korea Strait

PACIFIC OCEAN

RYUKYU ISLANDS

on same scale

EAST CHINA SEA

Nansei-Shotō (Ryukyu Is.)

PACIFIC OCEAN

Projection: Conical with two standard parallels

East from Greenwich

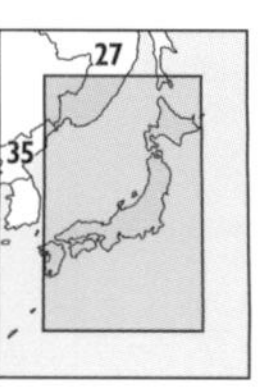
27
35

m	ft
9000	3000
6000	2000
4500	1500
3000	1000
1200	400
600	200
0	0
200	600
2000	6000
4000	12 000
6000	18 000
8000	24 000

CHINA AND KOREA 1:15 000 000

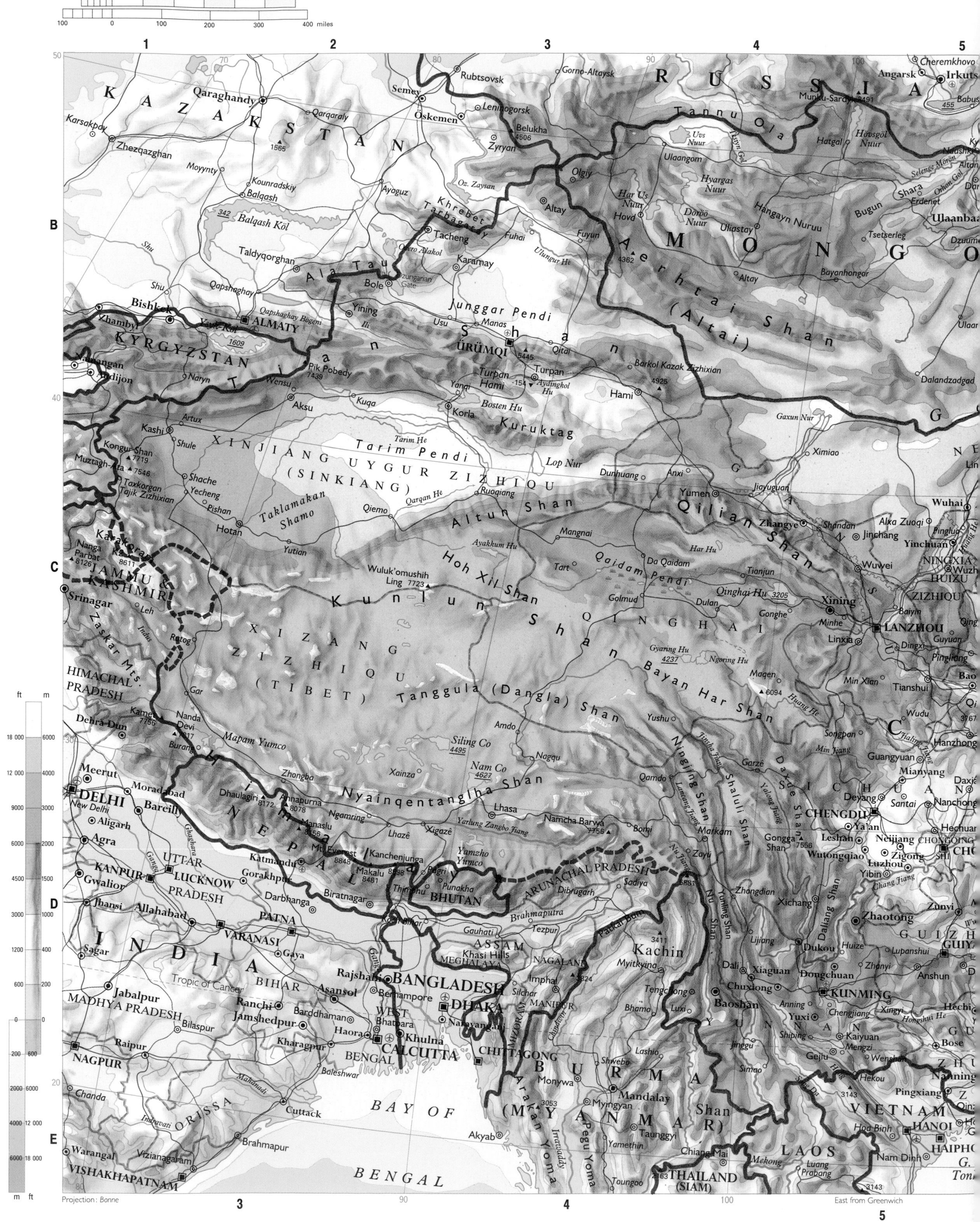
100 0 100 200 300 400 500 600 km
100 0 100 200 300 400 miles
1
2
3
4
5
B
C
D
E
KAZAKSTAN
RUSSIA
MONGOLIA
KYRGYZSTAN
XINJIANG UYGUR ZIZHIQU (SINKIANG)
XIZANG ZIZHIQU (TIBET)
QINGHAI
SICHUAN
YUNNAN
NEPAL
BHUTAN
BANGLADESH
INDIA
BURMA (MYANMAR)
LAOS
VIETNAM
THAILAND (SIAM)
JAMMU & KASHMIR
HIMACHAL PRADESH
UTTAR PRADESH
ARUNACHAL PRADESH
ASSAM
MEGHALAYA
NAGALAND
MANIPUR
MIZORAM
BIHAR
WEST BENGAL
MADHYA PRADESH
ORISSA
NINGXIA HUIZU ZIZHIQU
Qaraghandy
Karsakpay
Zhezqazghan
Qarqaraly
Semey
Rubtsovsk
Gorno-Altaysk
Leninogorsk
Öskemen
Zyryan
Belukha 4506
Moyynty
Kounradskiy
Balqash
Balqash Köl
Ayoguz
Oz. Zaysan
Khrebet Tarbagatay
Tacheng
Ozero Alakol
Karamay
Fuhai
Altay
Fuyun
Olgiy
Hovd
Har Us Nuur
Dörgön Nuur
Uliastay
Hyargas Nuur
Ulaangom
Uvs Nuur
Tannu Ola
Hatgal
Hövsgöl Nuur
Munku-Sardyk 3491
Angarsk
Irkutsk
Cheremkhovo
Babushkin
Bugun
Shara
Erdenet
Ulaanbaatar
Tsetserleg
Hangayn Nuruu
Bayanhongor
Altay
Aerhtai Shan (Altai)
Ulungur He
Taldyqorghan
Shu
Qapshaghay
Ala Tau
Zungarian Gate
Bole
Bishkek
Zhambyl
ALMATY
Qapshaghay Bögeni
Yining
Ili
Usu
Manas
Junggar Pendi
ÜRÜMQI
Qitai
Tian Shan
Barkol Kazak Zizhixian
Turpan
Turpan Hami
Aydingkol Hu
Hami
Namangan
Andijon
Naryn
Pik Pobedy 7439
Wensu
Aksu
Kuqa
Yanqi
Korla
Bosten Hu
Kuruktag
Gaxun Nur
Dalandzadgad
Kashi
Artux
Shule
Kongur Shan 7719
Muztagh-Ata 7546
Taxkorgan Tajik Zizhixian
Shache
Yecheng
Pishan
Hotan
Tarim He
Tarim Pendi
Taklamakan Shamo
Qiemo
Qarqan He
Ruoqiang
Lop Nur
Dunhuang
Anxi
Yumen
Jiayuguan
Ximiao
Altun Shan
Qilian Shan
Zhangye
Shandan
Jinchang
Wuwei
Alxa Zuoqi
Yinchuan
Wuhai
Mangnai
Har Hu
Tianjun
Ayakkum Hu
Qaidam Pendi
Da Qaidam
Tart
Golmud
Dulan
Qinghai Hu 3205
Xining
Gonghe
Minhe
LANZHOU
Linxia
Dingxi
Baiyin
Guyuan
Pingliang
Yutian
Wuluk'omushih Ling 7723
Hoh Xil Shan
Kunlun Shan
Karakoram
Nanga Parbat 8126
8611
Srinagar
Leh
Indus
Rutog
Zaskar Mts.
Gyaring Hu 4237
Ngoring Hu
Maqen
6094
Bayan Har Shan
Min Xian
Tianshui
Gar
Kamet 7756
Nanda Devi 7817
Burang
Dehra Dun
Tanggula (Dangla) Shan
Amdo
Yushu
Siling Co 4495
Mapam Yumco
Nam Co 4627
Nagqu
Qamdo
Songpan
Wudu
Min Jiang
Guangyuan
Hanzhong
Mianyang
Meerut
Moradabad
Bareilly
DELHI
New Delhi
Aligarh
Agra
Dhaulagiri 8172
Annapurna 8078
Manaslu 8156
Zhongba
Xainza
Nyainqentanglha Shan
Lhasa
Ngamring
Xigazê
Yarlung Zangbo Jiang
Lhazê
Namcha Barwa 7756
Bomi
Ningjing Shan
Shaluli Shan
Jinsha Jiang
Lancang Jiang
Yalong Jiang
Daxue Shan
Garzê
Markam
Zayü
Deyang
CHENGDU
Santai
Nanchong
Ya'an
Leshan
Gongga Shan 7556
Neijiang
Zigong
Luzhou
Wutongqiao
Yibin
Chang Jiang
CHONGQING
Mt Everest 8848
Kanchenjunga 8598
Makalu 8481
Katmandu
Gorakhpur
Yamzho Yumco
Punakha
Thimphu
Biratnagar
Darbhanga
Dibrugarh
Sadiya
5881
Nu Jiang
Yunling Shan
Zhongdian
Xichang
Daliang Shan
Zhaotong
Zunyi
KANPUR
LUCKNOW
Gwalior
Jhansi
Allahabad
VARANASI
PATNA
Gaya
Ganges
Ghaghara
Cooch Behar
Gauhati
Tezpur
Brahmaputra
Khasi Hills
Patkai Bum
3411
Kachin
Myitkyina
Lijiang
Dukou
Huize
Lupanshui
GUIYANG
Sagar
Tropic of Cancer
Rajshahi
Asansol
Berhampore
DHAKA
Imphal
3824
Silchar
Dali
Xiaguan
Dongchuan
Zhanyi
Anshun
Chuxiong
KUNMING
Jabalpur
Ranchi
Barddhaman
Jamshedpur
Bilaspur
Bhatpara
Haora
Kharagpur
Khulna
CALCUTTA
Narayanganj
Tengchong
Luxi
Bhamo
Baoshan
Anning
Yuxi
Chengjiang
Xingyi
Hechi
Shiping
Kaiyuan
Mengzi
Nagpur
Raipur
Mahanadi
Baleshwar
CHITTAGONG
Chindwin
Lashio
Jinggu
Simao
Gejiu
Wenshan
Bose
Nanning
Hekou
3143
Pingxiang
Chanda
Indravati
Cuttack
BAY OF BENGAL
Akyab
3053
Arakan Yoma
Irrawaddy
Pegu Yoma
Shwebo
Monywa
Mandalay
Myingyan
Taunggyi
Yamethin
Shan
Hoa Binh
HANOI
HAIPHONG
Nam Dinh
Warangal
Vizianagaram
Brahmapur
VISHAKHAPATNAM
Chiang Mai
Mekong
Luang Prabang
Toungoo
2163
3143
Projection: Bonne
East from Greenwich
50
40
30
20
70
80
90
100
ft m
18 000 6000
12 000 4000
9000 3000
6000 2000
4500 1500
3000 1000
1200 400
600 200
0 0
200 600
2000 6000
4000 12 000
6000 18 000
m ft

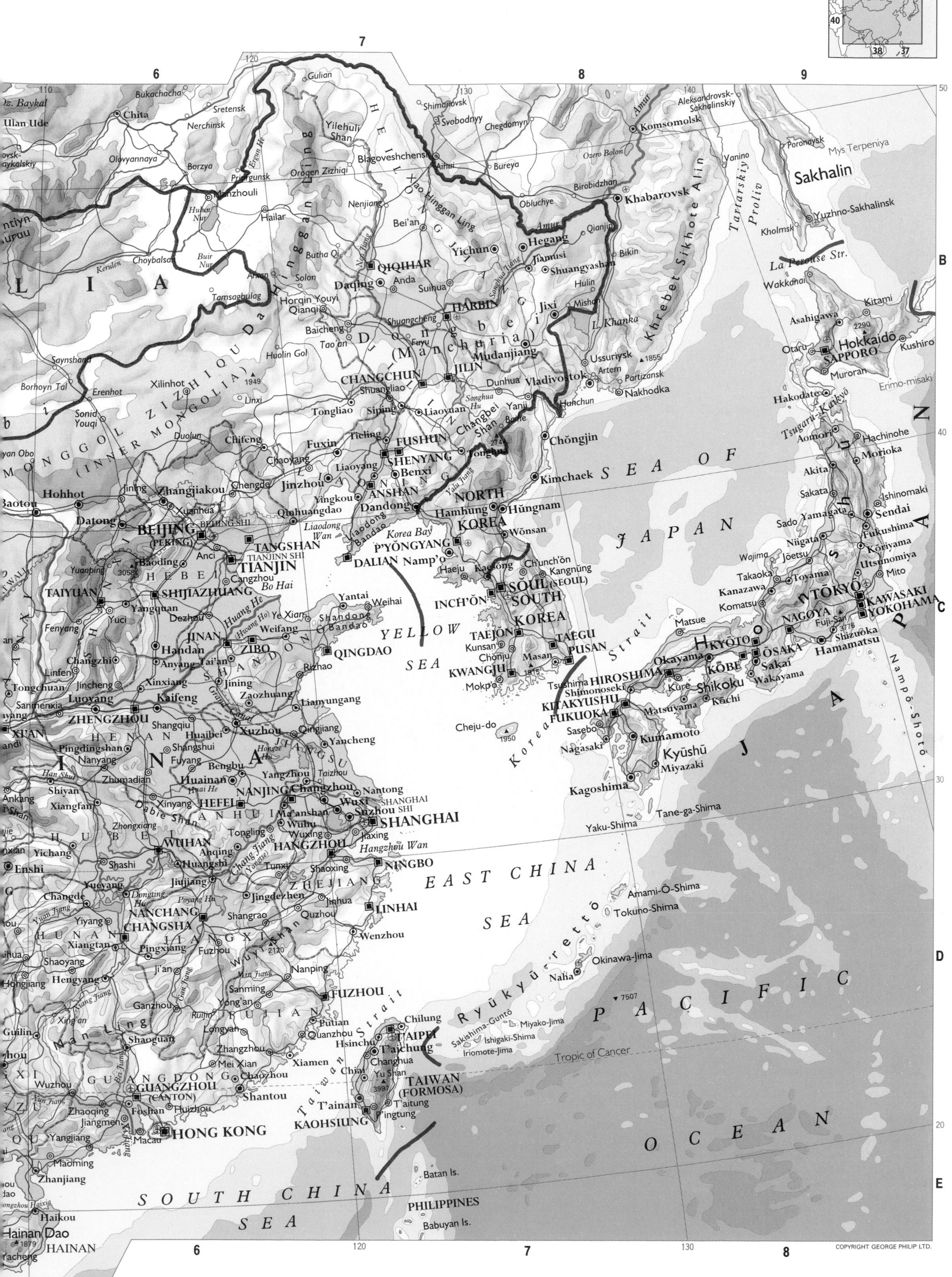

SEA OF JAPAN
YELLOW SEA
EAST CHINA SEA
SOUTH CHINA SEA
PACIFIC OCEAN
JAPAN
NORTH KOREA
SOUTH KOREA
TAIWAN (FORMOSA)
PHILIPPINES
Sakhalin
Hokkaidō
Honshū
Shikoku
Kyūshū
Hainan Dao
HAINAN
Korea Bay
Bo Hai
Liaodong Wan
Hangzhou Wan
Korea Strait
Taiwan Strait
La Pérouse Str.
Tatarskiy Proliv
Tsugaru-Kaikyō
Ryūkyū-rettō
Nampō-Shotō
Tropic of Cancer
Cheju-do
Yaku-Shima
Tane-ga-Shima
Amami-Ō-Shima
Tokuno-Shima
Okinawa-Jima
Miyako-Jima
Ishigaki-Shima
Iriomote-Jima
Sakishima-Guntō
Batan Is.
Babuyan Is.
Mys Terpeniya
Erimo-misaki
Khrebet Sikhote Alin
Da Hinggan Ling
Xiao Hinggan Ling
Changbai Shan
Yilehuli Shan
HEILONGJIANG
JILIN
LIAONING
NEI MONGGOL ZIZHIQU (INNER MONGOLIA)
HEBEI
SHANDONG
HENAN
JIANGSU
ANHUI
HUBEI
ZHEJIANG
HUNAN
JIANGXI
FUJIAN
GUANGDONG
Dongbei (Manchuria)
Oz. Baykal
Ulan Ude
Chita
Sretensk
Nerchinsk
Bukachacha
Olovyannaya
Borzya
Priargunsk
Manzhouli
Hailar
Choybalsan
Blagoveshchensk
Svobodnyy
Shimanovsk
Chegdomyn
Bureya
Komsomolsk
Aleksandrovsk-Sakhalinskiy
Khabarovsk
Birobidzhan
Obluchye
Amur
Yuzhno-Sakhalinsk
Kholmsk
Poronaysk
Vanino
Bikin
Hulin
Mishan
Jixi
L. Khanka
Ussuriysk
Artem
Partizansk
Nakhodka
Vladivostok
Hunchun
QIQIHAR
Daqing
HARBIN
Jiamusi
Hegang
Yichun
Shuangyashan
Mudanjiang
CHANGCHUN
JILIN
Siping
Liaoyuan
Tonghua
SHENYANG
FUSHUN
Benxi
ANSHAN
Dandong
Yingkou
DALIAN
Jinzhou
Fuxin
Chifeng
Chengde
Zhangjiakou
Hohhot
Datong
Baotou
BEIJING (PEKING)
TIANJIN
TANGSHAN
Qinhuangdao
Baoding
SHIJIAZHUANG
TAIYUAN
Handan
JINAN
ZIBO
QINGDAO
Yantai
Weihai
Weifang
Rizhao
Lianyungang
Xuzhou
ZHENGZHOU
Luoyang
Kaifeng
XI'AN
NANJING
HEFEI
SHANGHAI
Suzhou
Wuxi
Changzhou
HANGZHOU
NINGBO
WUHAN
Nanchang
CHANGSHA
Wenzhou
FUZHOU
Xiamen
Shantou
GUANGZHOU (CANTON)
HONG KONG
Macau
Zhanjiang
Haikou
TAIPEI
Chilung
Hsinchu
T'aichung
Changhua
Chiai
T'ainan
KAOHSIUNG
P'ingtung
T'aitung
Yu Shan
P'YŎNGYANG
Nampo
Hamhung
Hŭngnam
Wŏnsan
Chŏngjin
Kimchaek
Kaesŏng
Haeju
SŎUL (SEOUL)
INCH'ŎN
Ch'unch'ŏn
Kangnŭng
TAEJŎN
TAEGU
PUSAN
KWANGJU
Chŏnju
Kunsan
Mokp'o
Masan
Sapporo
Otaru
Muroran
Hakodate
Kushiro
Asahigawa
Kitami
Wakkanai
Aomori
Hachinohe
Morioka
Akita
Sakata
Ishinomaki
Sendai
Yamagata
Fukushima
Niigata
Kōriyama
Utsunomiya
Mito
Sado
Jōetsu
Toyama
Takaoka
Kanazawa
Komatsu
Wajima
TŌKYŌ
KAWASAKI
YOKOHAMA
Fuji-San
Shizuoka
Hamamatsu
NAGOYA
KYŌTO
ŌSAKA
KŌBE
Sakai
Wakayama
Okayama
HIROSHIMA
Kure
Matsue
Matsuyama
Kōchi
Shimonoseki
KITAKYUSHU
FUKUOKA
Sasebo
Nagasaki
Kumamoto
Miyazaki
Kagoshima
Tsushima

50 0 50 100 150 200 km

50 0 50 100 150 miles

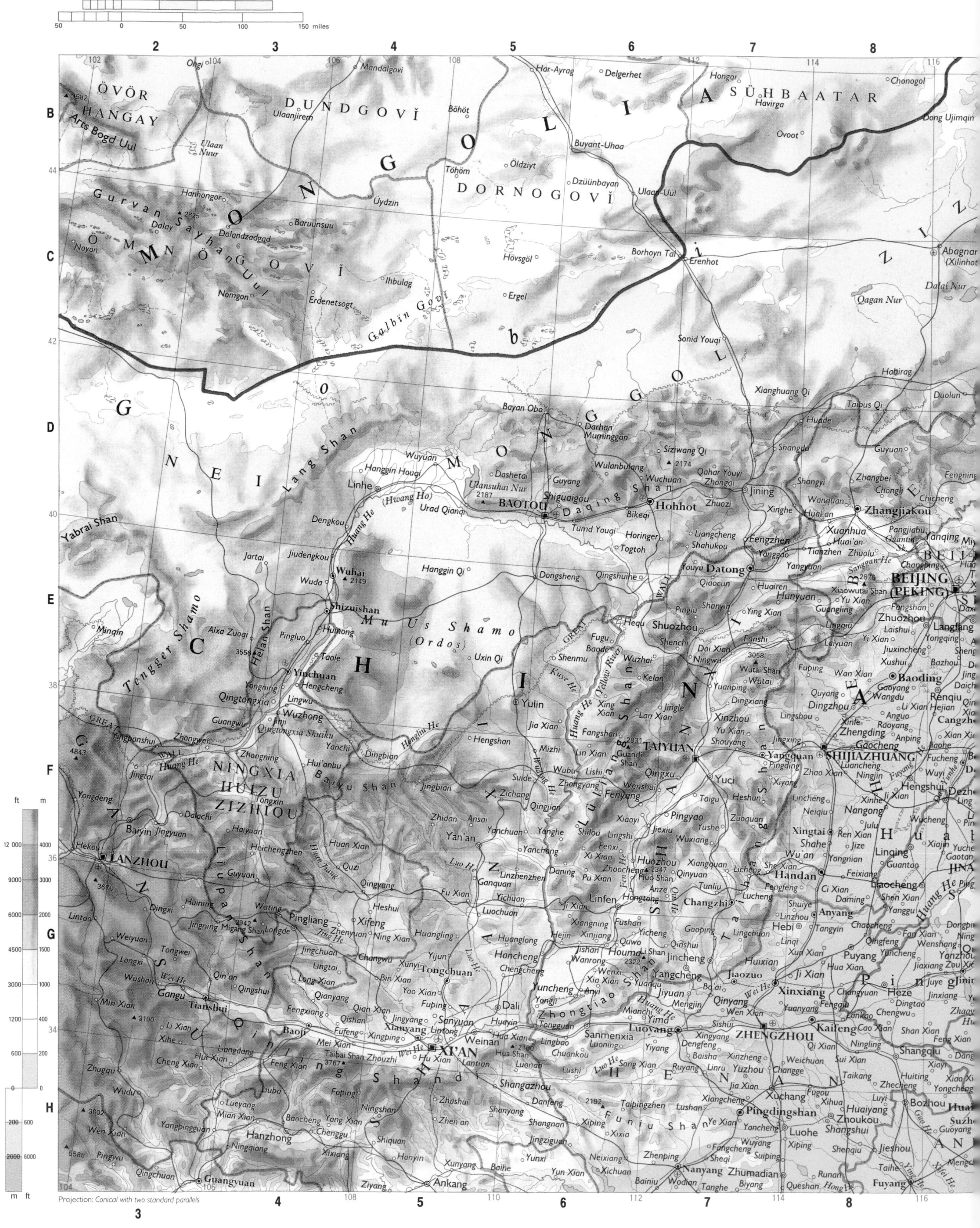

ÖVÖR HANGAY
Arts Bogd Uul
DUNDGOVĬ
Mandalgovi
Ulaanjirem
Ongi
Böhöt
Har-Ayrag
Delgerhet
Hongor
SÜHBAATAR
Havirga
Chonogol
Dong Ujimqin
Ovoot
Ulaan Nuur
MONGOLIA
Buyant-Uhaa
Töhöm
Öldziyt
Dzüünbayan
DORNOGOVĬ
Ulaan-Uul
Hanhongor
Gurvan Sayhan Uul
Dalay
Dalandzadgad
Baruunsuu
Üydzin
ÖMNÖGOVĬ
Noyon
Ihbulag
Erdenetsogt
Nomgon
Galbin Govi
Gobi
Hövsgöl
Ergel
Borhoyn Tal
Erenhot
Abagnar (Xilinhot)
Dalai Nur
Qagan Nur
Sonid Youqi
Habirag
Xianghuang Qi
Taibus Qi
Duolun
NEI MONGOL
Bayan Obo
Darhan Muminggan
Huade
Shangdu
Guyuan
Lang Shan
Wuyuan
Hanggin Houqi
Dashetai
Ulansuhai Nur
Linhe
Siziwang Qi
Wulanbulang
Qahar Youyi Zhongqi
Guyang
Wuchuan
Jining
Shangyi
Zhangbei
Chongli
Fengning
Chicheng
Yabrai Shan
Huang He (Hwang Ho)
Urad Qianqi
BAOTOU
Shiguaigou
Daqing Shan
Hohhot
Zhuozi
Xinghe
Wanquan
Zhangjiakou
Xuanhua
Dengkou
Tumd Youqi
Horinger
Liangcheng
Shahukou
Fengzhen
Yanggao
Tianzhen
Yanqing
Togtoh
Jartai
Jiudengkou
Wuhai
Hanggin Qi
Dongsheng
Qingshuihe
Youyu
Datong
Qiaocun
Huairen
Hunyuan
BEIJING (PEKING)
Wuda
Shizuishan
Mu Us Shamo (Ordos)
Tengger Shamo
Minqin
Alxa Zuoqi
Helan Shan
Huinong
Pingluo
Taole
Uxin Qi
Fugu
Baode
Shenmu
Hequ
Shuozhou
Pinglu
Shanyin
Ying Xian
Guangling
Zhuozhou
Laishui
Yi Xian
Yinchuan
Hengcheng
Yongning
Qingtongxia
Lingwu
Wuzhong
Guangwu
Zhongwei
Yulin
Jia Xian
Kuye He
Wuzhai
Kelan
Shenchi
Dai Xian
Ningwu
Wutai Shan
Fuping
Wan Xian
Baoding
Dingzhou
Quyang
Renqiu
Jiuxincheng
Xushui
Xing Xian
Lan Xian
Jingle
Xinzhou
Yu Xian
Shouyang
Lingshou
Zhengding
SHIJIAZHUANG
Hengshan
Fangshan
TAIYUAN
Yangquan
Pingding
Zhao Xian
Luancheng
Ningjin
Jingbian
Hengshui
Hangliu He
Dingbian
Yanchi
Hui'anbu
Baiyu Shan
NINGXIA HUIZU ZIZHIQU
Zhongning
Jingtai
Yongdeng
Tongxin
Dalachi
Baiyin
Jingyuan
Haiyuan
Heichengzhen
Huan Xian
Quzi
Hekou
LANZHOU
Guyuan
Liupan Shan
Huining
Dingxi
Lintao
Weiyuan
Tongwei
Longxi
Wushan
Wei He
Gangu
Tianshui
Min Xian
Li Xian
Xihe
Qin'an
Qingshui
Zhuanglang
Jingning
Migang Shan
Longde
Pingliang
Jingchuan
Zhenyuan
Xifeng
Heshui
Ning Xian
Qingyang
Suide
Zichang
Qingjian
Mizhi
Wubu
Lin Xian
Lishi
Zhongyang
Wenshui
Fenyang
Qingxu
Yuci
Taigu
Heshun
Xiyang
Lüliang Shan
Zhidan
Ansai
Yan'an
Yanchuan
Yanghe
Yanchang
Xiaoyi
Jiexiu
Pingyao
Yushe
Zuoquan
Shilou
Lingshi
Wuxiang
Fenxi
Xi Xian
Huozhou
Zhaocheng
Huo Shan
Pu Xian
Daning
Qinyuan
Xiangyuan
Licheng
Linzhenzhen
Ganquan
Luo He
Fu Xian
Yichuan
Luochuan
Huangling
Ji Xian
Linfen
Hongtong
Anze
Tunliu
Changzhi
Lucheng
Xiangning
Fushan
Yicheng
Jincheng
Gaoping
Lingchuan
Huanglong
Hancheng
Chengcheng
Hejin
Jishan
Xinjiang
Quwo
Houma
Qinshui
Wanrong
Wenxi
Xia Xian
Yangcheng
Jiaozuo
Huixian
Yuncheng
Yongji
Zhongtiao Shan
Anyi
Yuanqu
Jiyuan
Mengjin
Qinyang
Wen Xian
Tongchuan
Yijun
Xunyi
Changwu
Lingtai
Bin Xian
Long Xian
Qianyang
Yao Xian
Fuping
Fengxiang
Qishan
Qian Xian
Jingyang
Sanyuan
Dali
Huayin
Tongguan
Lingbao
Sanmenxia
Luoning
Chuankou
Luoyang
Yiyang
Xingyang
ZHENGZHOU
Kaifeng
Dengfeng
Baoji
Fufeng
Xingping
Xianyang
Lintong
Weinan
Hua Xian
Hua Shan
Luonan
Lushi
Mei Xian
Taibai Shan
Zhouzhi
Hu Xian
XI'AN
Lantian
Shangzhou
Qinling Shandi
Feng Xian
Cheng Xian
Hui Xian
Liangdang
Zhugqu
Wudu
Liuba
Foping
Ningshan
Zhashui
Shanyang
Danfeng
Xichuan
Funiu Shan
Lueyang
Mian Xian
Baocheng
Yang Xian
Chenggu
Hanzhong
Ningqiang
Xixiang
Shiquan
Hanyin
Zhen'an
Xunyang
Baihe
Ankang
Yunxi
Yun Xian
Neixiang
Zhenping
Nanyang
Tanghe
Biyang
Zhumadian
Qingchuan
Guangyuan
Pingwu
Wen Xian
Yangpingguan
Ziyang
Xiping
Xixia
Jingziguan
Shangnan
Bainiu
Wodian
Taipingzhen
Lushan
Ye Xian
Pingdingshan
Xiangcheng
Yancheng
Luohe
Wuyang
Fangcheng
Sheqi
Suiping
Xiping
Shangshui
Zhoukou
Huaiyang
Jieshou
Runan
Queshan
Fuyang
Taihe
Xuchang
Fugou
Xihua
Jia Xian
Yuzhou
Ruyang
Linru
Xinzheng
Weichuan
Changge
Baisha
Song Xian
HENAN
Taikang
Zhecheng
Huiting
Luyi
Bozhou
Shangqiu
Sui Xian
Ningling
Qi Xian
Cao Xian
Shan Xian
Lankao
Dingtao
Heze
Juye
Jinxiang
Chengwu
Xinxiang
Yuanyang
Fengqiu
Hua Xian
Ji Xian
Changyuan
Puyang
Qingfeng
Wenshang
Nanle
Handan
Ci Xian
Feixiang
Daming
Guantao
Linqing
Anyang
Tangyin
Hebi
Linzhou
Shuiye
Fengfeng
She Xian
Wu'an
Yongnian
Shahe
Xingtai
Ren Xian
Jize
Nangong
Neiqiu
Lincheng
Xinhe
Ji Xian
Wucheng
Julu
Taihang Shan
SHANXI
SHAANXI
GANSU
HEBEI
Huang He
Sanggan He
Yellow River
Fen He
Qin He
Jing He
Wei He
Great Wall
102
104
106
108
110
112
114
116
44
42
40
38
36
34
2582
2825
2187
2149
3556
4843
3670
2942
3100
3767
2160
3002
5588
2174
2870
3058
2831
2347
2322
2192

2 3 4 5 6 7 8

B C D E F G H

ft m

12 000 4000
9000 3000
6000 2000
4500 1500
3000 1000
1200 400
600 200
0 0
200 600
2000 6000
m ft

Projection: *Conical with two standard parallels*

3 4 5 6 7 8

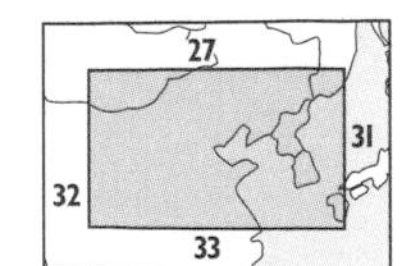

27
31
32
33

9 10 11 12 13 14 15 16

B C D E F G H

HARBIN
CHANGCHUN
JILIN
SHENYANG
FUSHUN
ANSHAN
DALIAN
Vladivostok
Ussuriysk
Mudanjiang
Jixi
Qiqihar
Baicheng
Taonan
Tongliao
Siping
Liaoyuan
Tonghua
Dandong
Sinŭiju
Chongjin
Hamhung
P'YŎNGYANG
Nampo
Kaesŏng
SOUL
INCH'ON
TAEJŎN
TAEGU
KWANGJU
PUSAN
Ulsan
P'ohang
Chŏnju
Mokp'o
Yŏsu
Cheju
Cheju-do
Halla-san 1950
Sasebo
Nagasaki
Tsushima
Iki
Karatsu

HEILONGJIANG
JILIN
LIAONING
NORTH KOREA
SOUTH KOREA
JAPAN
RUSSIA

Liaodong Wan
Bo Hai
Korea Bay
Tongjosŏn Man
SEA OF JAPAN
HUANG HAI
(Yellow Sea)
Korea Strait
Shandong Bandao
Laizhou Wan
QINGDAO
Yantai
Weihai
Weifang
ZIBO
Linyi
Lianyungang
Xuzhou
Huai'an
Yancheng
TIANJIN
TIANJIN SHI
Tanggu
Qinhuangdao
Jinzhou
Huludao
Yingkou
Fuxin
Chaoyang
Chifeng

East from Greenwich

9 10 11 12 13 14 15

BURMA (MYANMAR)
RANGOON (YANGON)
THAILAND
BANGKOK
LAOS
VIETNAM
CAMBODIA
Phnom Penh (Phnum Penh)
THANH PHO HO CHI MINH
Gulf of Thailand
ANDAMAN SEA
SOUTH CHINA SEA
MALAYSIA
PENINSULAR MALAYSIA
KUALA LUMPUR
SINGAPORE
Strait of Malacca
BRUNEI
SARAWAK
SABAH
Borneo
KALIMANTAN
INDONESIA
Sumatera
Greater Sunda Islands
JAVA SEA
Jawa (Java)
JAKARTA
INDIAN OCEAN
Java Trench
Paracel Is.
Spratly Is.
Projection: Mercator
East from Greenwich

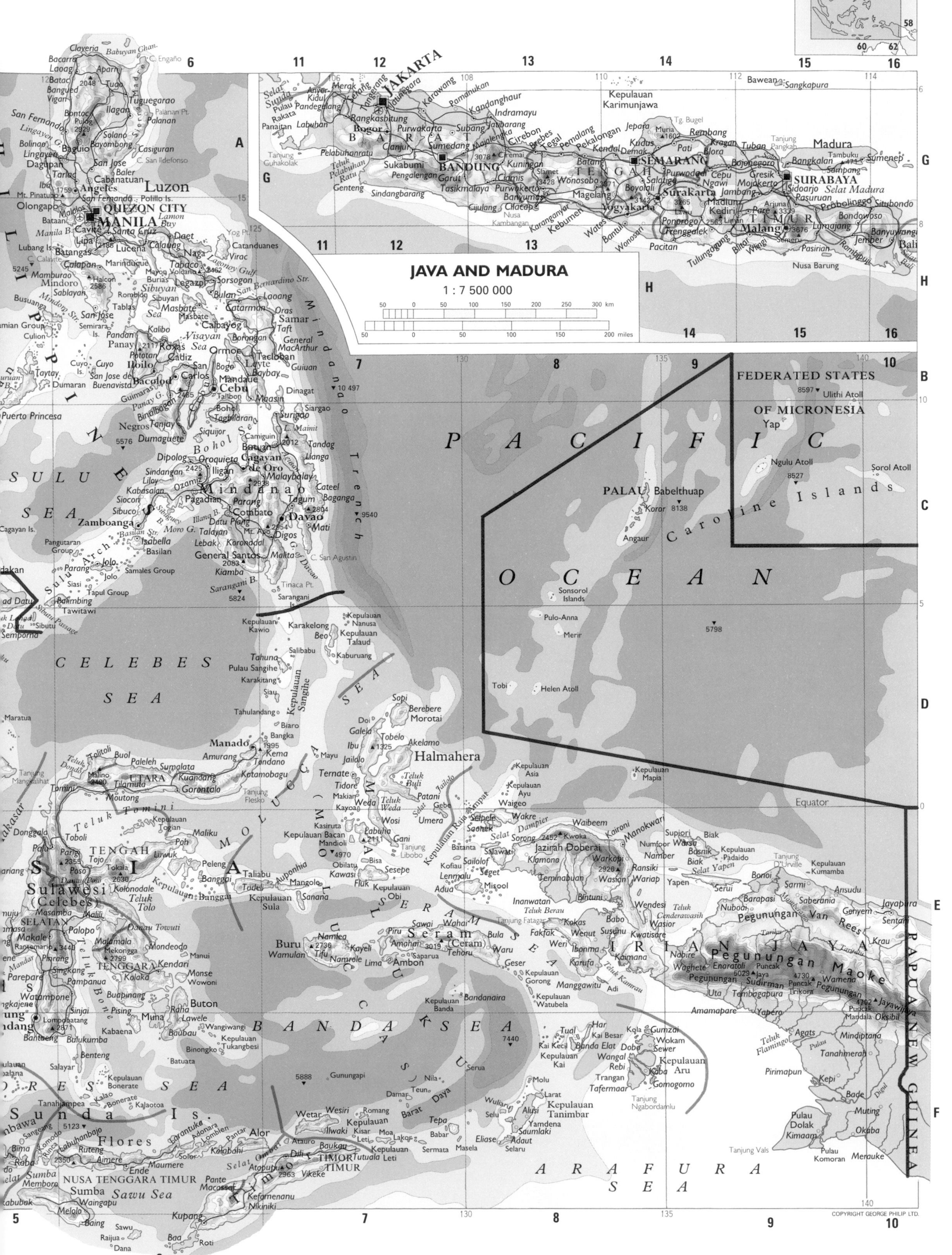
JAVA AND MADURA
1 : 7 500 000
JAKARTA
Bogor
BANDUNG
SEMARANG
SURAKARTA
Yogyakarta
SURABAYA
Malang
Madura
Kepulauan Karimunjawa
Bawean
Luzon
QUEZON CITY
MANILA
Mindoro
Panay
Negros
Cebu
Samar
Leyte
Mindanao
Davao
Zamboanga
General Santos
SULU SEA
CELEBES SEA
PACIFIC OCEAN
FEDERATED STATES OF MICRONESIA
Yap
Ulithi Atoll
Ngulu Atoll
Sorol Atoll
Caroline Islands
PALAU
Babelthuap
Koror
Angaur
Sonsorol Islands
Pulo-Anna
Merir
Tobi
Helen Atoll
Equator
Halmahera
Morotai
Ternate
Tidore
MOLUCCA SEA
Manado
Gorontalo
Sulawesi (Celebes)
Teluk Tomini
Kendari
Buton
Muna
Buru
Seram (Ceram)
Ambon
BANDA SEA
SERAM SEA
Jazirah Doberai
Manokwari
Sorong
IRIAN JAYA
Pegunungan Maoke
Puncak Jaya
Jayapura
Merauke
Kepulauan Aru
Kepulauan Tanimbar
Kepulauan Kai
ARAFURA SEA
Timor
Kupang
Flores
Sumba
Sawu Sea
Alor
Sunda Is.
NUSA TENGGARA TIMUR
PAPUA NEW GUINEA
COPYRIGHT GEORGE PHILIP LTD.

MAINLAND SOUTH-EAST ASIA 1:6 000 000

50 0 50 100 150 200 km

50 0 50 100 150 miles

BURMA
(MYANMAR)
SHAN
KAYAH
KAWTHULE
TENASSERIM
YUNNAN
CHINA
GUANGXI ZHUANGZU ZIZHIQU
GUANGDONG
LAOS
THAILAND
CAMBODIA
VIETNAM
HAINAN
G. of Tonkin
Qiongzhou Haixia
Leizhou Wan
Mandalay
RANGOON
Moulmein
G. of Martaban
Moscos Islands
HANOI
Haiphong
Vientiane
BANGKOK
Thon Buri
Hue
Da Nang
Haikou
Zhanjiang
Nanning
Luang Prabang
Tran Ninh
Cao Nguyen Khorat
Cao Nguyen Boloven
Phnom Dangrek
Thiu Khao Phetchabun
Chao Phraya Lowlands
Annamitique
Bac Phan
Hoang Lien Son
Tonle Sap
ANGKOR
Mekong
Salween
Lancang Jiang
Sittang Myit
Tanen Tong Dan
Dawna Range
Mui Falaise
Mui Doc
Col Barthélemy
Deo Keo Neua

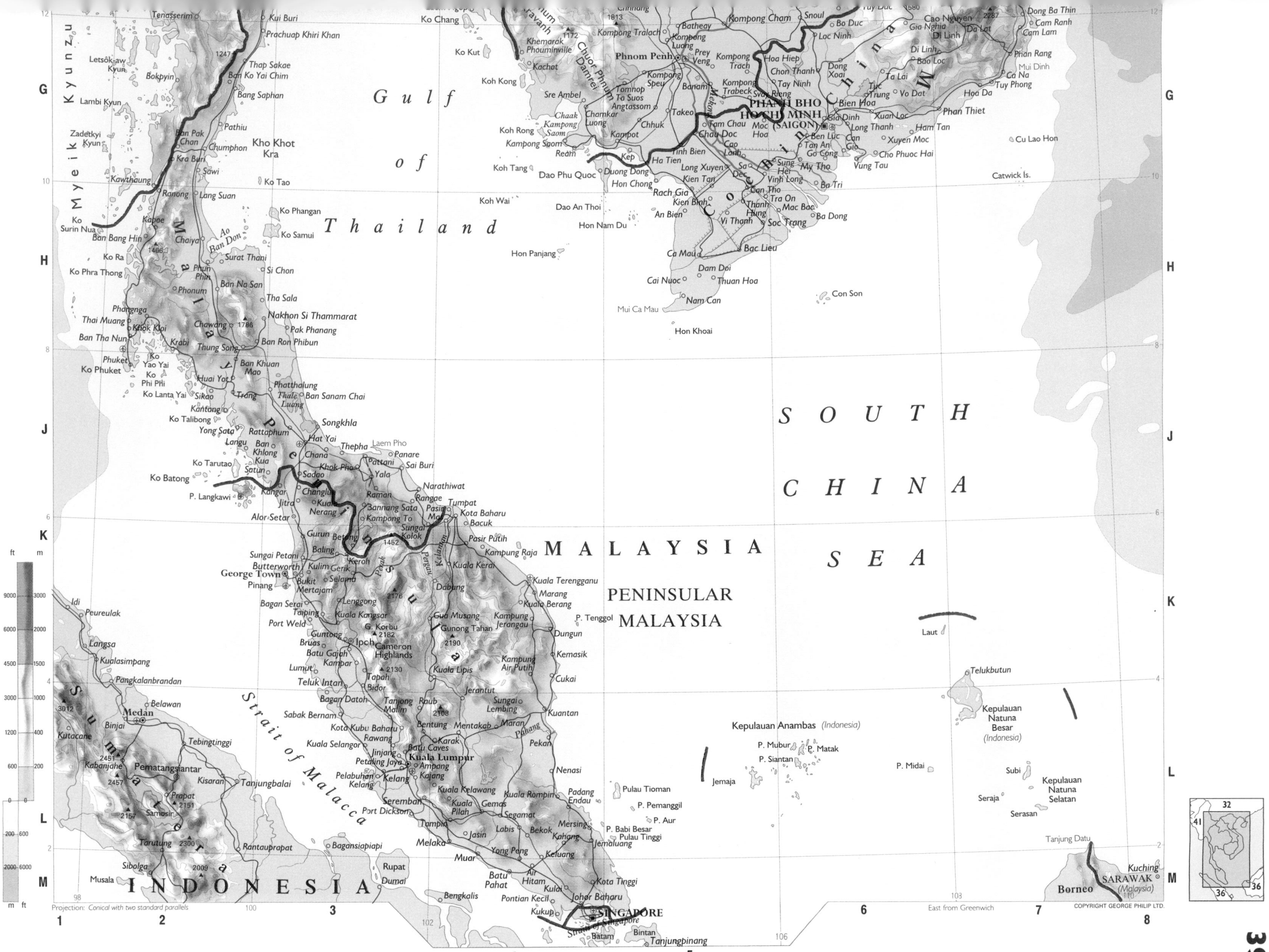

Gulf of Thailand

SOUTH CHINA SEA

MALAYSIA

PENINSULAR MALAYSIA

INDONESIA

Strait of Malacca

Malay Peninsula

Sumatera

Cochin China

Myeik Kyunzu

Tenasserim
Kui Buri
Prachuap Khiri Khan
Letsôk-aw Kyun
Bokpyin
Thap Sakae
Ban Ko Yai Chim
Bang Saphan
Lambi Kyun
Zadetkyi Kyun
Ban Pak Chan
Pathiu
Chumphon
Kho Khot Kra
Kra Buri
Sawi
Kawthaung
Ranong
Lang Suan
Ko Tao
Ko Phangan
Ko Samui
Ko Surin Nua
Kapoe
Ban Bang Hin
Chaiya
Ao Ban Don
Surat Thani
Ko Ra
Ko Phra Thong
Phun Phin
Si Chon
Phonum
Ban Na San
Tha Sala
Phangnga
Thai Muang
Khok Kloi
Chawang
Nakhon Si Thammarat
Pak Phanang
Ban Tha Nun
Krabi
Thung Song
Ban Ron Phibun
Phuket
Ko Phuket
Ko Yao Yai
Ko Phi Phi
Ko Lanta Yai
Huai Yot
Ban Khuan Mao
Sikao
Trang
Phatthalung
Thale Luang
Ban Sanam Chai
Kantang
Ko Talibong
Songkhla
Yong Sata
Rattaphum
Hat Yai
Langu
Ban Khlong Kua
Chana
Thepha
Laem Pho
Ko Tarutao
Satun
Pattani
Panare
Sai Buri
Ko Batong
Sadao
Khok Pho
Yala
P. Langkawi
Kangar
Changlun
Raman
Narathiwat
Jitra
Kuala Nerang
Sannang Sata
Rangae
Pasir Mas
Tumpat
Kota Baharu
Alor Setar
Kampong To
Sungai Kolok
Bacuk
Gurun
Betong
1452
Pasir Putih
Sungai Petani
Baling
Keroh
Kampung Raja
Butterworth
Kulim
Gerik
Kuala Kerai
George Town
Pinang
Bukit Mertajam
Selama
Dabong
Kuala Terengganu
Marang
Kuala Berang
Bagan Serai
Lenggong
Taiping
Kuala Kangsar
Gua Musang
Kampung Jerangau
P. Tenggol
Port Weld
G. Korbu 2182
Gunong Tahan 2190
Dungun
Gunong
Bruas
Ipoh
Cameron Highlands
Batu Gajah
Kampar
2130
Kampung Air Putih
Kemasik
Lumut
Kuala Lipis
Teluk Intan
Tapah
Bidor
Cukai
Jerantut
Bagan Datoh
Tanjong Malim
Raub
2108
Sungai Lembing
Kuantan
Sabak Bernam
Bentung
Mentakab
Maran
Pahang
Kota Kubu Baharu
Rawang
Karak
Batu Caves
Kuala Selangor
Jinjang
Petaling Jaya
Kuala Lumpur
Ampang
Kajang
Pekan
Pelabuhan Kelang
Kelang
Nenasi
Kuala Kelawang
Kuala Rompin
Padang Endau
Seremban
Kuala Pilah
Gemas
Port Dickson
Segamat
Tampin
Jasin
Labis
Bekok
Mersing
Kahang
Melaka
Yong Peng
Keluang
Jemaluang
Muar
Batu Pahat
Air Hitam
Kulai
Kota Tinggi
Bengkalis
Pontian Kecil
Johor Baharu
Kukup
SINGAPORE
Singapore
Strait of Singapore
Batam
Bintan
Tanjungpinang
Rupat
Dumai
Bagansiapiapi
Rantauprapat
Tanjungbalai
Kisaran
Tebingtinggi
Pematangsiantar
Prapat 2151
Samosir
Tarutung
2300
2009
Sibolga
Musala
Kabanjahe
2451
2457
2157
Binjai
Medan
Belawan
Kutacane
3012
Pangkalanbrandan
Kualasimpang
Langsa
Peureulak
Idi

Ko Chang
Ko Kut
Koh Kong
Koh Rong
Kampong Saom
Koh Tang
Koh Wai
Dao Phu Quoc
Dao An Thoi
Hon Nam Du
Hon Panjang
Khemarak Phouminville
Kachot
Sre Ambel
Chaak
Kampong Saom
Ream
Chuor Phnum Damrei
1172
1813
Kompong Tralach
Phnom Penh
Tomnop Ta Suos
Angtassom
Chamkar Luong
Kampot
Kep
Ha Tien
Duong Dong
Hon Chong
Rach Gia
Kien Binh
An Bien
Ca Mau
Cai Nuoc
Dam Doi
Thuan Hoa
Nam Can
Mui Ca Mau
Hon Khoai
Con Son
Batheay
Kompong Luong
Prey Veng
Kompong Trach
Kompong Speu
Banam
Kompong Trabeck
Mekong
Takeo
Chhuk
Tinh Bien
Tam Chau
Chau Doc
Cao Lanh
Long Xuyen
Kien Tan
Sa Dec
Can Tho
Vinh Long
Tra On
Thanh Hung
Vi Thanh
Soc Trang
Mac Bac
Bac Lieu
Ba Dong
Ba Tri
My Tho
Sung Hieu
Go Cong
Tan An
Can Gio
Ben Luc
Moc Hoa
Kompong Cham
Snoul
Hoa Hiep
Chon Thanh
Svay Rieng
Tay Ninh
PHANH BHO HO CHI MINH (SAIGON)
Gia Dinh
Bien Hoa
Dong Xoai
Bo Duc
Loc Ninh
Tuc Trung
Ta Lai
Vo Dat
Long Thanh
Xuan Loc
Xuyen Moc
Cho Phuoc Hai
Vung Tau
Ham Tan
Phan Thiet
Hoa Da
Tuy Phong
Ca Na
Mui Dinh
Phan Rang
Cam Lam
Cam Ranh
Dong Ba Thin
Da Lat
2287
Cao Nguyen Gia Nghia
Di Linh
Bao Loc
Cu Lao Hon
Catwick Is.

Laut
Telukbutun
Kepulauan Natuna Besar (Indonesia)
Kepulauan Anambas (Indonesia)
P. Mubur
P. Matak
P. Siantan
Jemaja
P. Midai
Subi
Seraja
Serasan
Kepulauan Natuna Selatan
Pulau Tioman
P. Pemanggil
P. Aur
P. Babi Besar
Pulau Tinggi
Tanjung Datu
Kuching
SARAWAK (Malaysia)
Borneo

East from Greenwich

Projection: Conical with two standard parallels

ft	m
9000	3000
6000	2000
4500	1500
3000	1000
1200	400
600	200
0	0
200	600
2000	6000
m	ft

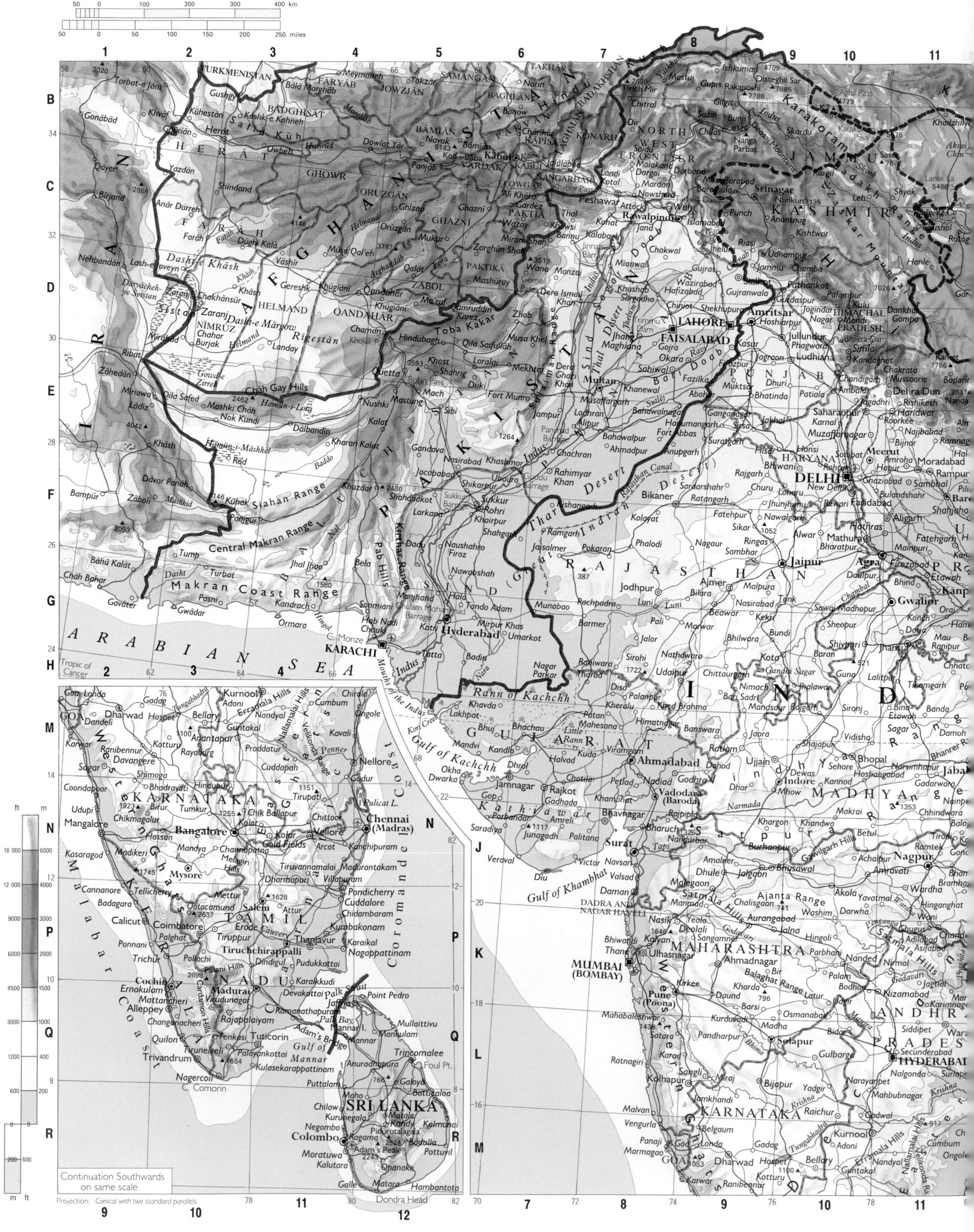

50 0 100 200 300 400 km
50 0 50 100 150 200 250 miles
TURKMENISTAN
IRAN
AFGHANISTAN
PAKISTAN
INDIA
SRI LANKA
ARABIAN SEA
Gulf of Kachchh
Gulf of Khambhat
Gulf of Mannar
Palk Strait
Adam's Bridge
Tropic of Cancer
Rann of Kachchh
Mouths of the Indus
Thar Desert
Great Indian Desert
Makran Coast Range
Central Makran Range
Siahan Range
Chāh Gay Hills
Rigestān
Dasht-e Khāsh
Dasht-e Mārgow
Safīd Kūh
Hindu Kush
Karakoram Range
Ladakh Range
Zaskar Mountains
Toba Kakar
Sulaiman Range
Kirthar Range
Pab Hills
Salt Range
Vindhya Range
Satpura Range
Satmala Hills
Ajanta Range
Balaghat Range
Western Ghats
Eastern Ghats
Nallamalai Hills
Erramala Hills
Cardamon Hills
Palani Hills
Malabar Coast
Coromandel Coast
Indus
Helmand
Sutlej
Ravi
Chenab
Jhelum
Narmada
Tapi
Godavari
Krishna
Kaveri
HERAT
FARAH
NĪMRŪZ
HELMAND
QANDAHAR
ORUZGĀN
GHOWR
BĀMIĀN
BADGHĪS
FĀRYĀB
JOWZJĀN
SAMANGAN
BAGHLĀN
TAKHĀR
PARVĀN
KĀPĪSĀ
KABUL
VARDAK
LOWGAR
PAKTĪĀ
PAKTĪKĀ
GHAZNĪ
ZĀBOL
NANGARHĀR
LAGHMĀN
KONARHĀ
BADAKHSHĀN
NORTH WEST FRONTIER
BALUCHISTAN
PUNJAB
SIND
JAMMU & KASHMIR
HIMACHAL PRADESH
HARYANA
RAJASTHAN
GUJARAT
MADHYA PRADESH
MAHARASHTRA
ANDHRA PRADESH
KARNATAKA
KERALA
TAMIL NADU
GOA
DADRA AND NAGAR HAVELI
Kābul
Herāt
Qandahār
Quetta
KARACHI
Hyderabad
Islāmābād
Rawalpindi
Peshawar
LAHORE
FAISALABAD
Multan
Amritsar
Srinagar
DELHI
New Delhi
Jaipur
Agra
Gwalior
Ahmadabad
Vadodara (Baroda)
Surat
MUMBAI (BOMBAY)
Pune (Poona)
Nagpur
Bhopal
Indore
HYDERABAD
Bangalore
Chennai (Madras)
Mysore
Coimbatore
Madurai
Tiruchchirappalli
Cochin
Trivandrum
Colombo
Jaffna
Kandy
Trincomalee
C. Comorin
Dondra Head
Point Pedro
Continuation Southwards on same scale
Projection: Conical with two standard parallels

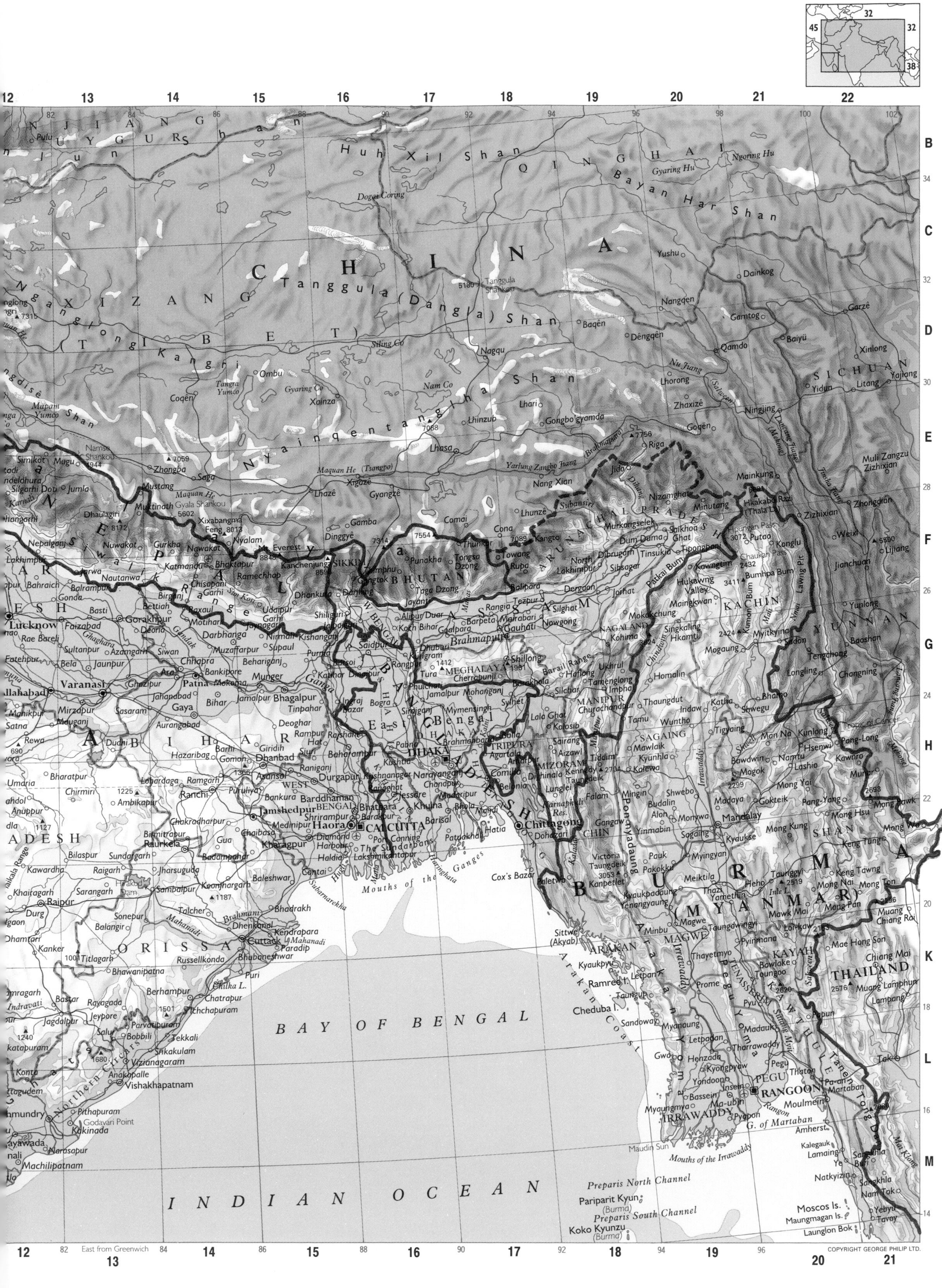

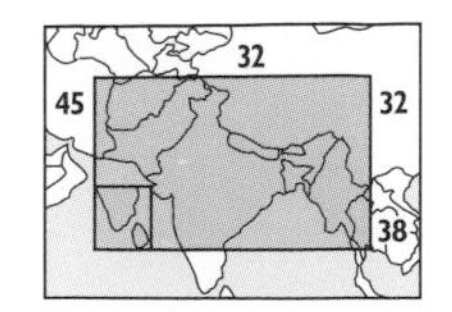
32
45
32
38

12 13 14 15 16 17 18 19 20 21 22

B C D E F G H J K L M

CHINA
XIZANG
(TIBET)
QINGHAI
SICHUAN
YUNNAN
NEPAL
BHUTAN
SIKKIM
BANGLADESH
East Bengal
ARUNACHAL PRADESH
ASSAM
MEGHALAYA
NAGALAND
MANIPUR
MIZORAM
TRIPURA
BIHAR
ORISSA
WEST BENGAL
BURMA
(MYANMAR)
KACHIN
SAGAING
CHIN
MAGWE
ARAKAN
SHAN
KAYAH
PEGU
IRRAWADDY
TENASSERIM
THAILAND

Huh Xil Shan
Bayan Har Shan
Tanggula (Dangla) Shan
Nyainqentanglha Shan
Gangdisê Shan
Siwalik Range
Arakan Yoma
Pegu Yoma
Tanen Taunggyi
Dawna

Lhasa
Xigazê
Qamdo
Kathmandu
Everest 8848
Kanchenjunga 8598
Thimphu
Lucknow
Varanasi
Allahabad
Patna
Gaya
Ranchi
Jamshedpur
Dhanbad
Calcutta
Haora
Dhaka
Chittagong
Cox's Bazar
Shillong
Gauhati
Imphal
Kohima
Agartala
Mandalay
Sittwe (Akyab)
Rangoon
Pegu
Bassein
Moulmein
Cuttack
Bhubaneshwar
Puri
Berhampur
Vishakhapatnam
Kakinada

Brahmaputra
Ganga
Mouths of the Ganges
The Sundarbans
Irrawaddy
Mouths of the Irrawaddy
Chindwin
Salween
Sittang Myit
Mahanadi

BAY OF BENGAL
INDIAN OCEAN
G. of Martaban
Preparis North Channel
Preparis South Channel
Paripart Kyun (Burma)
Koko Kyunzu (Burma)
Moscos Is.
Cheduba I.
Ramree I.

82 84 86 88 90 92 94 96 98 100 102
East from Greenwich
34 32 30 28 26 24 22 20 18 16 14

THE INDO-GANGETIC PLAIN 1:6 000 000

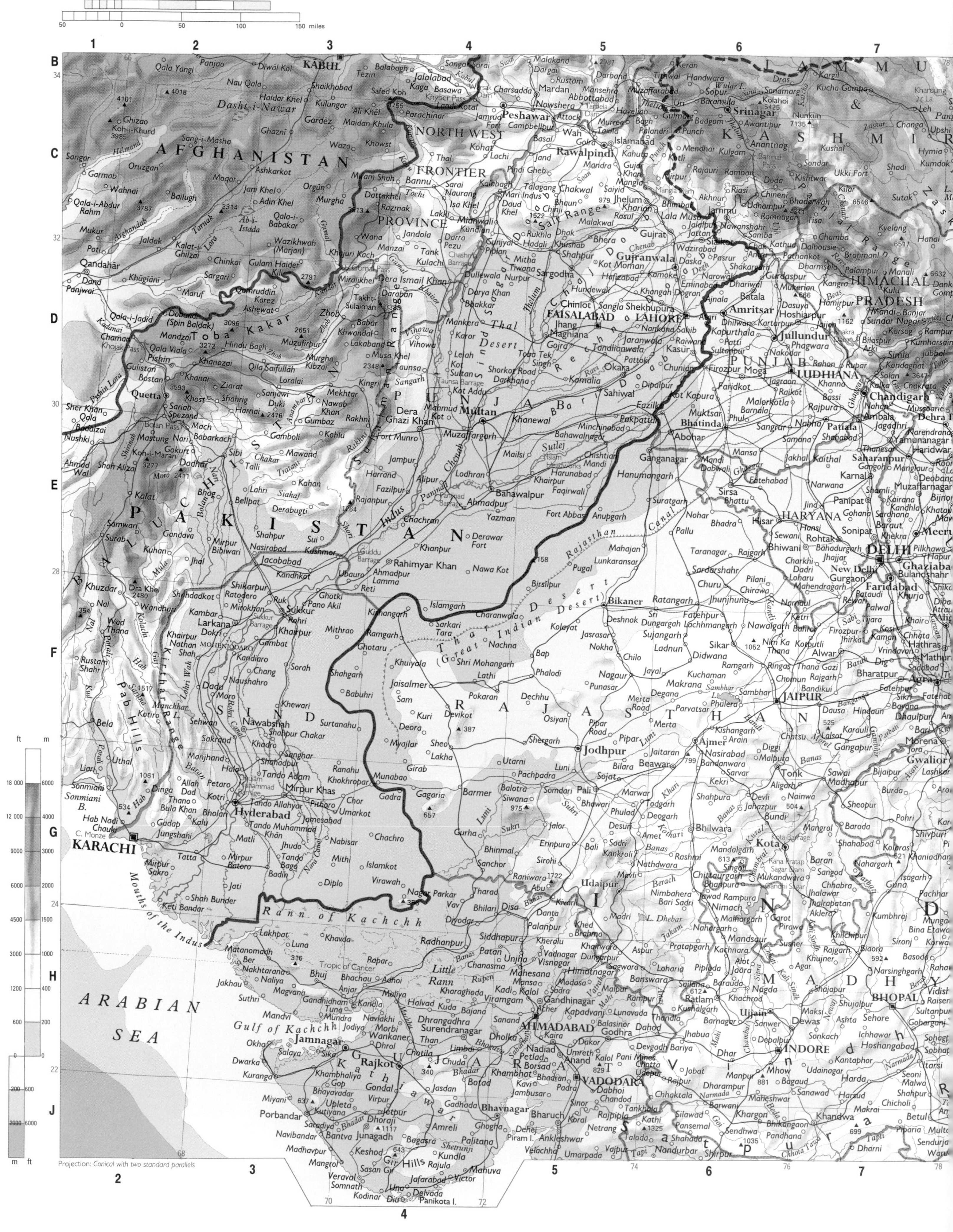
50 0 50 100 150 200 km
50 0 50 100 150 miles
1 2 3 4 5 6 7
B C D E F G H J
AFGHANISTAN
PAKISTAN
BALUCHISTAN
SIND
PUNJAB
NORTH WEST FRONTIER PROVINCE
KASHMIR
JAMMU & KASHMIR
HIMACHAL PRADESH
PUNJAB
HARYANA
RAJASTHAN
GUJARAT
MADHYA PRADESH
INDIA
ARABIAN SEA
Gulf of Kachchh
Rann of Kachchh
Little Rann
Mouths of the Indus
Thar Desert (Great Indian Desert)
Thal Desert
Dasht-i-Nawar
Toba Kakar
Sulaiman Range
Kirthar Range
Pab Hills
Salt Range
Pir Panjal Range
Kathiawar
Satpura Range
Tropic of Cancer
Rajasthan Canal
KABUL
Jalalabad
Peshawar
Rawalpindi
Islamabad
Srinagar
Jammu
Qandahar
Quetta
Zhob
Dera Ismail Khan
Dera Ghazi Khan
Multan
Faisalabad
Lahore
Gujranwala
Sialkot
Sargodha
Bahawalpur
Rahimyar Khan
Sukkur
Larkana
Jacobabad
Nawabshah
Hyderabad
KARACHI
Amritsar
Jullundur
Ludhiana
Chandigarh
Patiala
Bhatinda
Ambala
Saharanpur
Meerut
DELHI
New Delhi
Hisar
Rohtak
Bikaner
Jaisalmer
Jodhpur
Ajmer
JAIPUR
Alwar
Agra
Gwalior
Udaipur
Kota
Bhilwara
Ujjain
INDORE
BHOPAL
AHMADABAD
VADODARA
Gandhinagar
Rajkot
Jamnagar
Bhavnagar
Junagadh
Porbandar
Bhuj
Diu
Ratlam
Mhow
Barmer
Pali
Abu
Projection: Conical with two standard parallels
ft m
18 000 6000
12 000 4000
9000 3000
6000 2000
4500 1500
3000 1000
1200 400
600 200
0 0
200 600
2000 6000
m ft

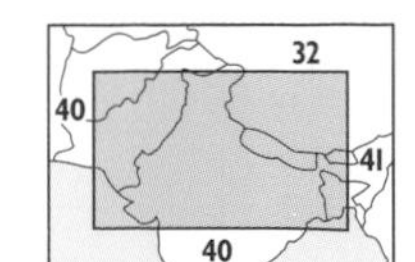
32
40
41
40

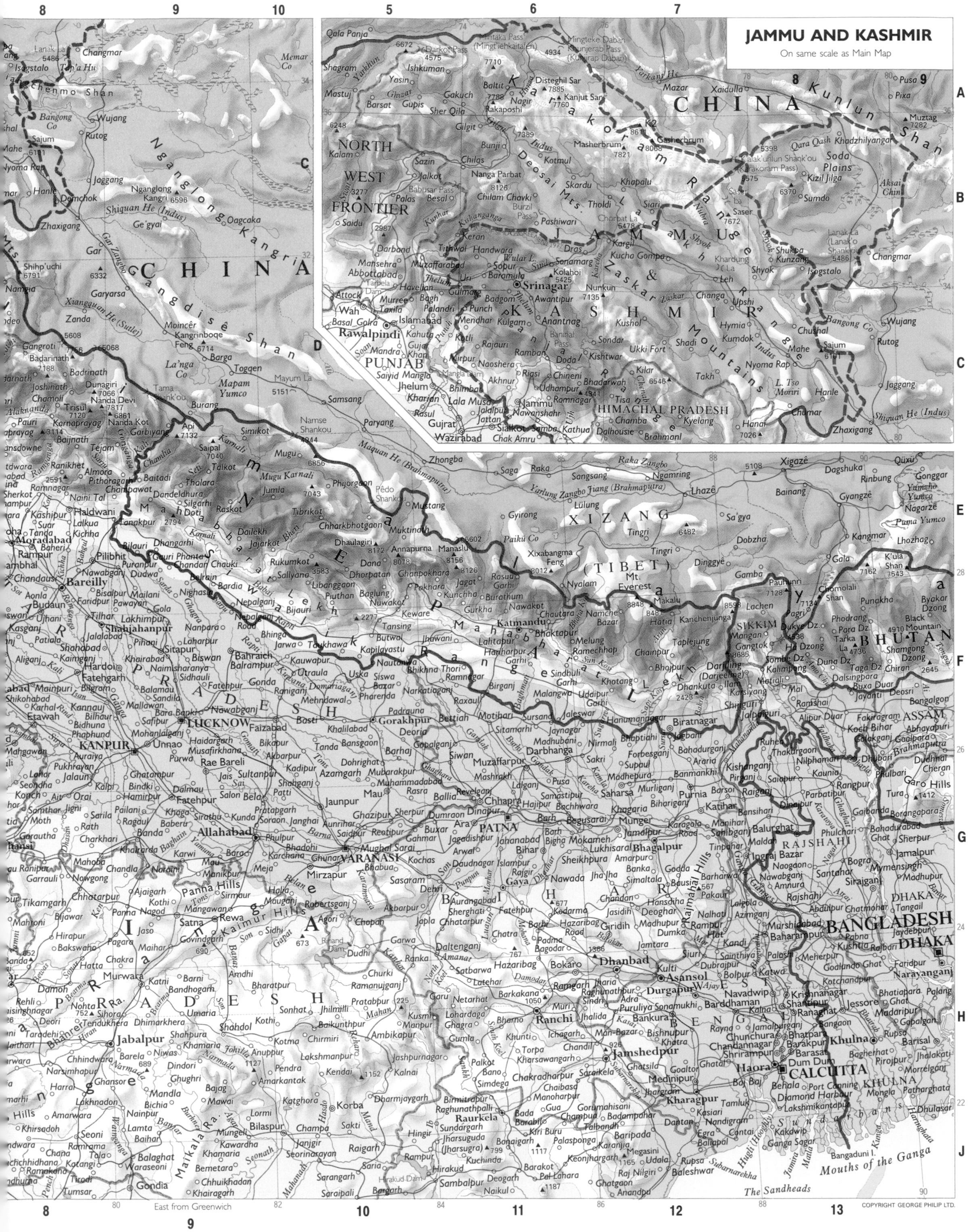

JAMMU AND KASHMIR

On same scale as Main Map

8 9 10 5 6 7

A B C D E F G H J

8 80 East from Greenwich 9 82 10 84 11 86 12 88 13 90

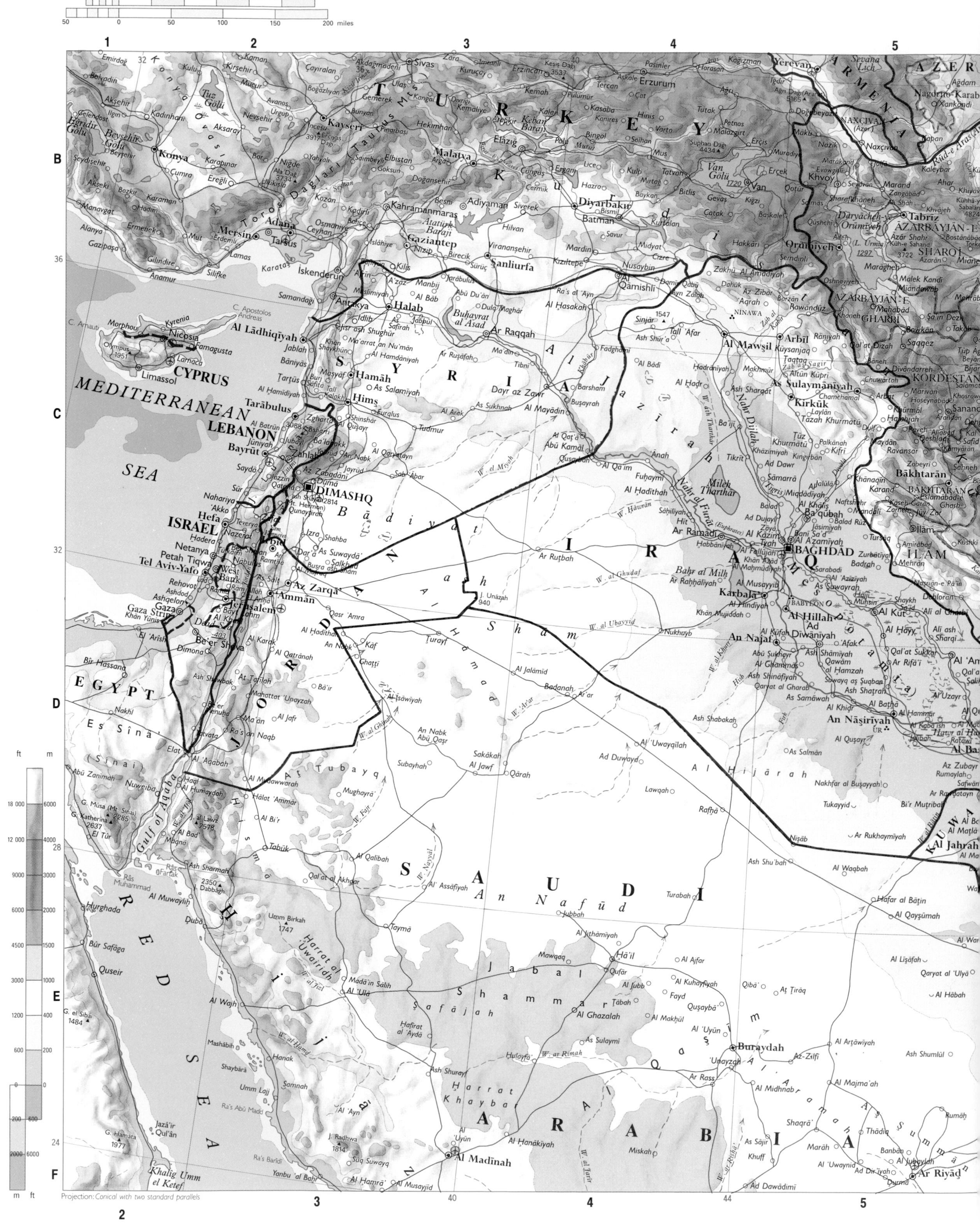
50 0 50 100 150 200 250 300 km
50 0 50 100 150 200 miles
TURKEY
ARMENIA
AZER
CYPRUS
Nicosia
Limassol
MEDITERRANEAN SEA
LEBANON
Bayrūt
SYRIA
DIMASHQ
Ḥalab
Ḥims
Ḥamāh
Al Lādhiqīyah
Dayr az Zawr
Ar Raqqah
ISRAEL
Tel Aviv-Yafo
Ḥefa
Jerusalem
Gaza
JORDAN
'Ammān
Az Zarqā'
Al 'Aqabah
IRAQ
BAGHDĀD
Al Mawṣil
Arbīl
Kirkūk
As Sulaymānīyah
Karbalā'
An Najaf
Al Ḥillah
An Nāṣirīyah
EGYPT
Es Sînâ'
Gulf of Aqaba
RED SEA
SAUDI ARABIA
An Nafūd
Jabal Shammar
Ḥā'il
Buraydah
Al Madīnah
Ar Riyāḍ
Tabūk
Al Jawf
KUWAIT
Al Jahrah
Erzurum
Kayseri
Konya
Adana
Mersin
Malatya
Diyarbakır
Gaziantep
Şanlıurfa
Kahramanmaraş
Sivas
Yerevan
Tabrīz
Orūmīyeh
Bākhtarān
ft m
18 000 6000
12 000 4000
9000 3000
6000 2000
4500 1500
3000 1000
1200 400
600 200
0 0
200 600
2000 6000
m ft
Projection: Conical with two standard parallels

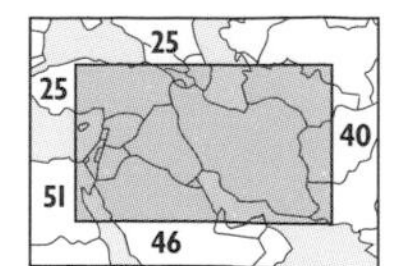
25
25
40
51
46

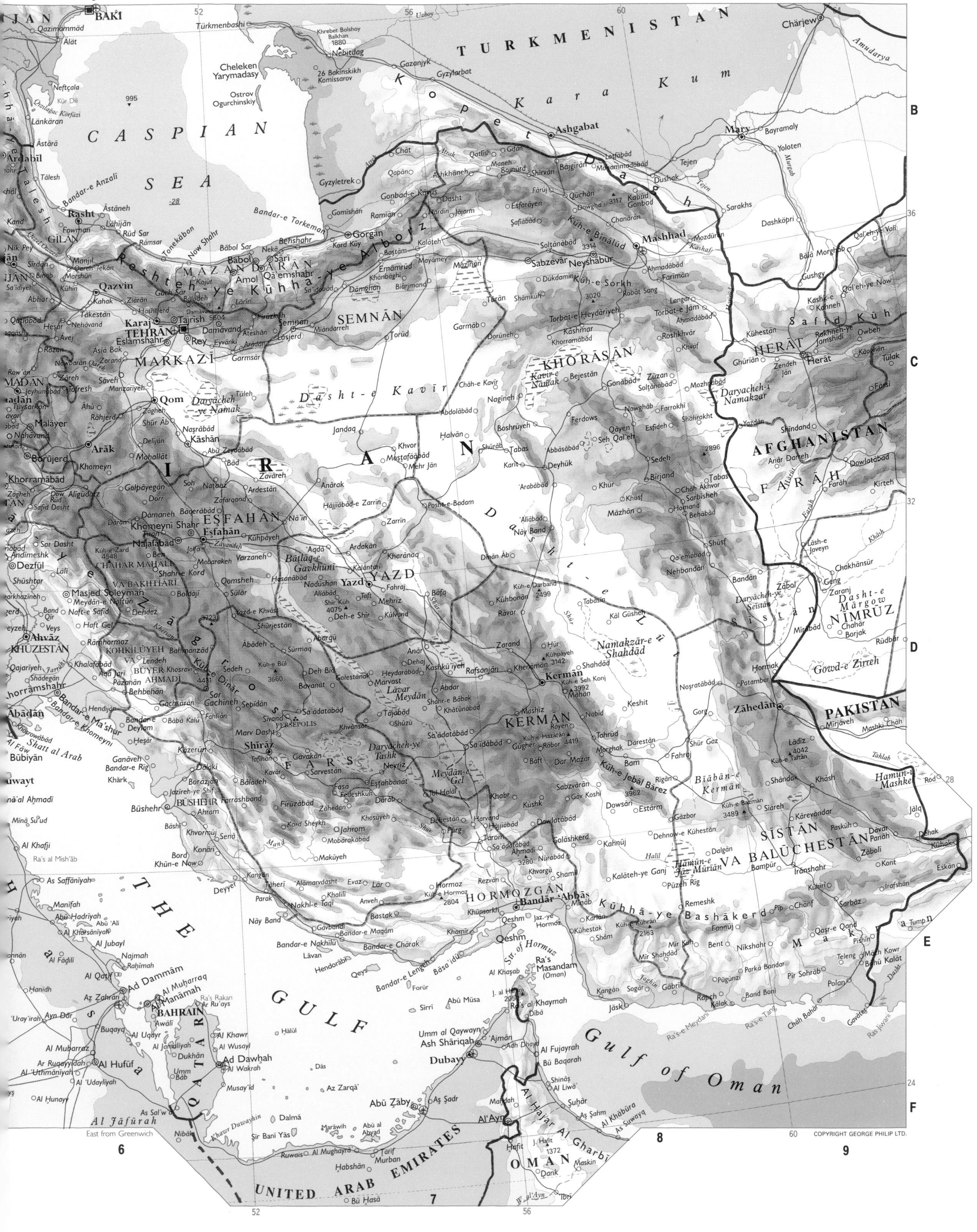

6 7 8 9 10

B C D E F

East from Greenwich

ARABIA AND THE HORN OF AFRICA 1:15 000 000

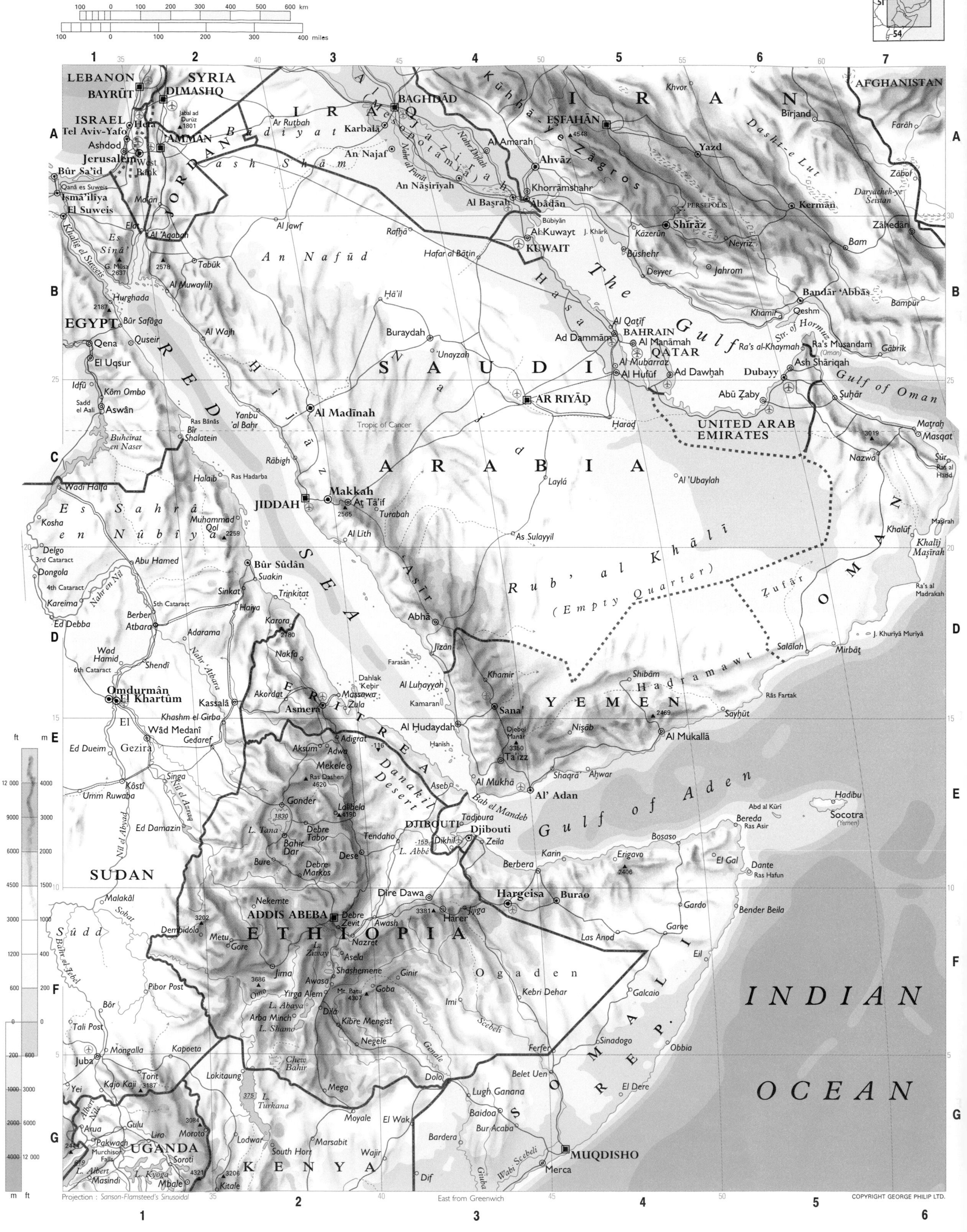
LEBANON
BAYRŪT
SYRIA
DIMASHQ
ISRAEL
Tel Aviv-Yafo
JORDAN
'AMMĀN
Jerusalem
BAGHDĀD
IRAQ
IRAN
ESFAHĀN
AFGHANISTAN
KUWAIT
BAHRAIN
QATAR
Ad Dawḩah
AR RIYĀD
SAUDI ARABIA
UNITED ARAB EMIRATES
Abū Ẓaby
Dubayy
Masqat
OMAN
YEMEN
Sana'
Al' Adan
Al Mukallā
Socotra
ERITREA
Asmera
DJIBOUTI
Djibouti
ETHIOPIA
ADDIS ABEBA
SOMALI REP.
MUQDISHO
Hargeisa
SUDAN
Omdurmân
El Khartûm
EGYPT
UGANDA
KENYA
RED SEA
The Gulf
Gulf of Oman
Gulf of Aden
INDIAN OCEAN
Rub' al Khālī (Empty Quarter)
An Nafūd
Es Sahrâ en Nûbîya
Danakil Desert
Ogaden
Tropic of Cancer
Al Madīnah
Makkah
JIDDAH
Yazd
Shīrāz
Kermān
Bandar 'Abbās
Al Başrah
Abādān
Ahvāz
Ta'izz
Berbera
Dire Dawa
Harer
Kassalā
Port Sudan
Bûr Sûdân
Aswân
Kisumu
Juba
Projection : Sanson-Flamsteed's Sinusoidal
East from Greenwich

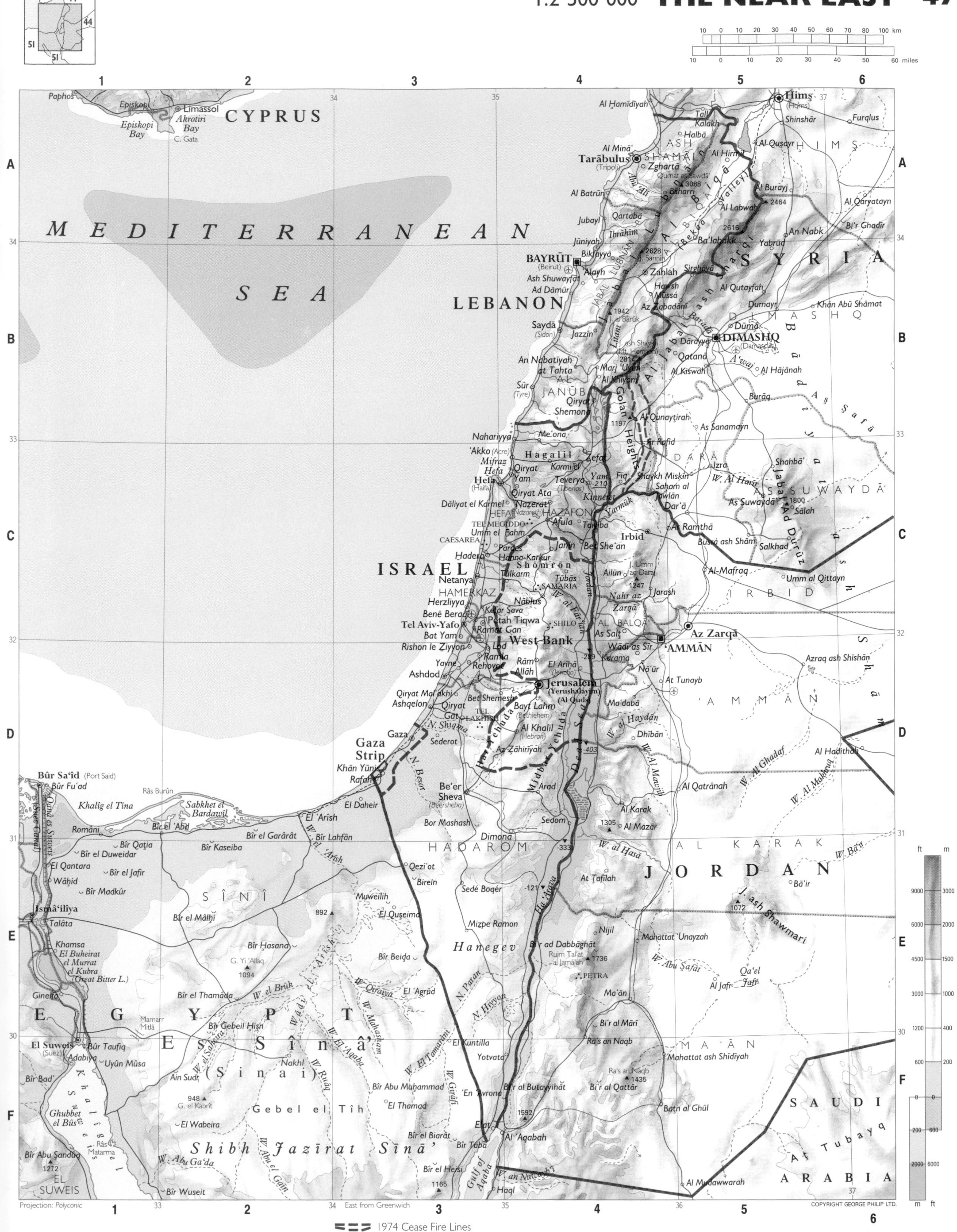
CYPRUS
MEDITERRANEAN SEA
LEBANON
SYRIA
ISRAEL
JORDAN
EGYPT
SAUDI ARABIA
BAYRŪT (Beirut)
DIMASHQ (Damascus)
Jerusalem (Yerushalayim) (Al Quds)
AMMĀN
Tel Aviv-Yafo
Gaza Strip
West Bank
Golan Heights
Es Sînâ' (Sinai)
Hanegev
Projection: Polyconic
East from Greenwich
COPYRIGHT GEORGE PHILIP LTD.

1974 Cease Fire Lines

AFRICA : Physical 1:42 000 000

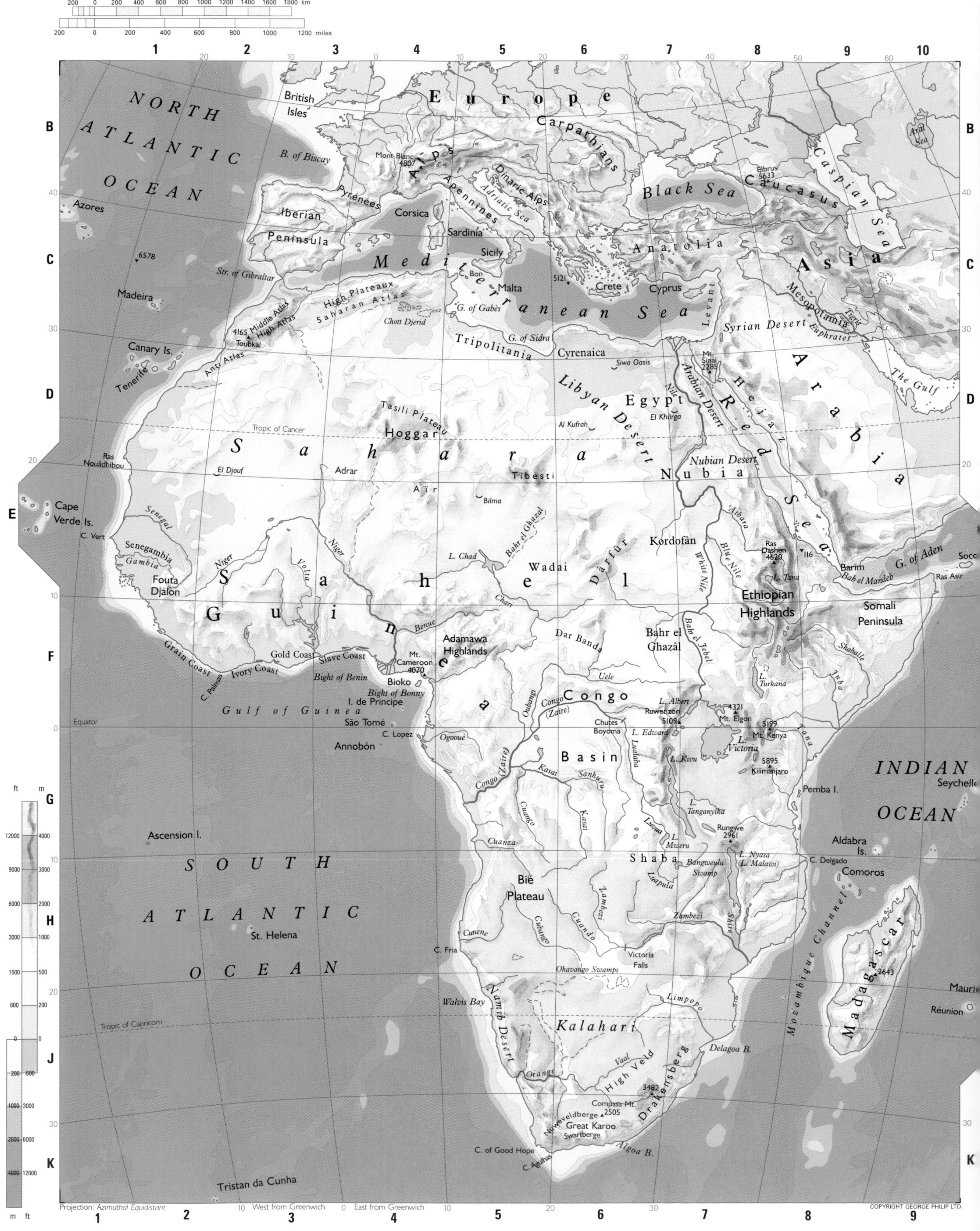

NORTH ATLANTIC OCEAN
Azores
Madeira
Canary Is.
Tenerife
Cape Verde Is.
C. Vert
British Isles
B. of Biscay
Europe
Carpathians
Mont Blanc 4807
Alps
Apennines
Dinaric Alps
Adriatic Sea
Black Sea
Elbrus 5633
Caucasus
Caspian Sea
Aral Sea
Pyrénées
Iberian Peninsula
Corsica
Sardinia
Sicily
Anatolia
Asia
Str. of Gibraltar
Mediterranean Sea
C. Bon
Malta
Crete
Cyprus
Levant
Mesopotamia
Tigris
Euphrates
Syrian Desert
High Plateaux
Saharan Atlas
Middle Atlas
High Atlas
4165 Toubkal
Anti Atlas
Chott Djerid
G. of Gabès
G. of Sidra
Tripolitania
Cyrenaica
Siwa Oasis
Mt. Sinai 2285
Arabian Desert
Hejaz
Arabia
The Gulf
Libyan Desert
Egypt
Nile
El Khârga
Al Kufrah
Red Sea
Tasili Plateau
Hoggar
Tropic of Cancer
Sahara
Ras Nouâdhibou
El Djouf
Adrar
Tibesti
Nubian Desert
Nubia
Aïr
Bilma
Atbara
Senegal
Senegambia
Gambia
Niger
Volta
L. Chad
Bahr el Ghazal
Wadai
Darfur
Kordofân
White Nile
Blue Nile
Ras Dashen 4620
116
L. Tana
Barim
Bab el Mandeb
G. of Aden
Ras Asir
Fouta Djalon
Sahel
Ethiopian Highlands
Somali Peninsula
Chari
Benue
Guinea
Dar Banda
Bahr el Ghazâl
Bahr el Jebel
Adamawa Highlands
Shaballe
Juba
Grain Coast
Ivory Coast
Gold Coast
Slave Coast
C. Palmas
Mt. Cameroon 4070
Bight of Benin
Bioko
Bight of Bonny
I. de Principe
Gulf of Guinea
São Tomé
Equator
C. Lopez
Annobón
Ogooué
Oubangi
Uele
Congo
Congo (Zaïre)
L. Albert
Ruwenzori 5109
Chutes Boyoma
L. Edward
L. Turkana
4321 Mt. Elgon
5199 Mt. Kenya
L. Victoria
Tana
Basin
Lualaba
L. Kivu
5895 Kilimanjaro
INDIAN OCEAN
Seychelles
Kasai
Sankuru
Cuango
Pemba I.
L. Tanganyika
Luvua
L. Mweru
Rungwe 2961
Ascension I.
Cuanza
Shaba
Bangweulu Swamp
L. Nyasa (L. Malawi)
Luapula
C. Delgado
Aldabra Is.
Comoros
SOUTH ATLANTIC OCEAN
Bié Plateau
Lungwebungu
Zambezi
Cuando
Shire
Mozambique Channel
Madagascar
2643
St. Helena
Cunene
Cubango
C. Fria
Victoria Falls
Okavango Swamps
Mauritius
Réunion
Walvis Bay
Namib Desert
Limpopo
Tropic of Capricorn
Kalahari
Delagoa B.
Vaal
High Veld
Orange
Drakensberg
3482
Compass Mt. 2505
Nuweveldberge
Great Karoo
Swartberge
C. of Good Hope
C. Agulhas
Algoa B.
Tristan da Cunha
Projection: Azimuthal Equidistant
West from Greenwich
East from Greenwich
COPYRIGHT GEORGE PHILIP LTD.

NORTH ATLANTIC OCEAN
SOUTH ATLANTIC OCEAN
INDIAN OCEAN
Mediterranean Sea
Black Sea
Caspian Sea
Red Sea
Sahara
ALGERIA
LIBYA
EGYPT
MOROCCO
TUNISIA
WESTERN SAHARA
MAURITANIA
MALI
NIGER
CHAD
SUDAN
SENEGAL
GAMBIA
GUINEA-BISSAU
GUINEA
SIERRA LEONE
LIBERIA
IVORY COAST
GHANA
TOGO
BENIN
BURKINA FASO
NIGERIA
CAMEROON
CENTRAL AFRICAN REP.
ETHIOPIA
ERITREA
DJIBOUTI
SOMALI REP.
KENYA
UGANDA
RWANDA
BURUNDI
TANZANIA
GABON
CONGO
CONGO (DEM. REP. OF THE)
EQUATORIAL GUINEA
SÃO TOMÉ & PRINCIPE
ANGOLA
ZAMBIA
MALAWI
MOZAMBIQUE
ZIMBABWE
NAMIBIA
BOTSWANA
SOUTH AFRICA
LESOTHO
SWAZ.
MADAGASCAR
COMOROS
SEYCHELLES
MAURITIUS
SAUDI ARABIA
YEMEN
IRAN
IRAQ
SYRIA
TURKEY
SPAIN
PORTUGAL
FRANCE
ITALY
RUSSIA
KAZAKSTAN
UKRAINE
Dakar Capital Cities
Projection: Azimuthal Equidistant
West from Greenwich
East from Greenwich
Tropic of Cancer
Equator
Tropic of Capricorn
COPYRIGHT GEORGE PHILIP LTD.

NORTHERN AFRICA

1:15 000 000

ATLANTIC OCEAN
Azores (Port.)
Madeira (Port.)
Funchal
Porto Santo
Islas Canarias (Sp.)
Santa Cruz de Tenerife
Las Palmas
SPAIN
Málaga
Almería
Cádiz
Gibraltar (U.K.)
Str. of Gibraltar
Tanger
Ceuta (Sp.)
Tétouan
Al Hoceima
Melilla (Sp.)
Nador
Oujda
ALGER
Oran
MOROCCO
Rabat
Salé
Kenitra
CASABLANCA
Mohammedia
Fès
Meknès
Marrakech
Agadir
Safi
El Jadida
Essaouira
Ouarzazate
Taroudannt
Anti Atlas
Haut Atlas
Moyen Atlas
Dj. Toubkal 4165
WESTERN SAHARA
El Aaiún
Tarfaya
Dakhla
Smara
ALGERIA
Tindouf
Béchar
Ghardaïa
Ouargla
El Goléa
In Salah
Tamanrasset
Ahaggar
Tassili n Ajjer
Grand Erg Occidental
Grand Erg Oriental
Plateau du Tademaït
Erg Iguidi
Erg Chech
Tanezrouft
Sahara
El Djouf
Tropic of Cancer
MAURITANIA
Nouâdhibou
Nouakchott
Atâr
Chinguetti
Akjoujt
Rosso
Kiffa
Aoukâr
MALI
Tombouctou
Gao
Mopti
Ségou
Bamako
Kidal
Adrar des Iforas
Taoudenni
Niger
SENEGAL
DAKAR
St. Louis
Thiès
Kaolack
Tambacounda
GAMBIA
Banjul
GUINEA-BISSAU
Bissau
Ziguinchor
GUINEA
Conakry
Fouta Djalon
Kankan
SIERRA LEONE
Freetown
LIBERIA
Monrovia
IVORY COAST
ABIDJAN
Yamoussoukro
Bouaké
BURKINA FASO
Ouagadougou
Bobo-Dioulasso
GHANA
Accra
Kumasi
Tamale
Lake Volta
TOGO
Lomé
BENIN
Porto-Novo
Cotonou
NIGER
Niamey
Agadez
Aïr
Zinder
Maradi
NIGERIA
LAGOS
IBADAN
Abuja
Kano
Kaduna
Zaria
Port Harcourt
Bioko
Gulf of Guinea
Slave Coast
Bight of Benin
Gold Coast
Ivory Coast
Grain Coast
Projection : Sanson-Flamsteed's Sinusoidal
West from Greenwich 0 East from Greenwich

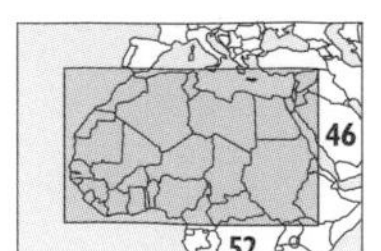
46
52

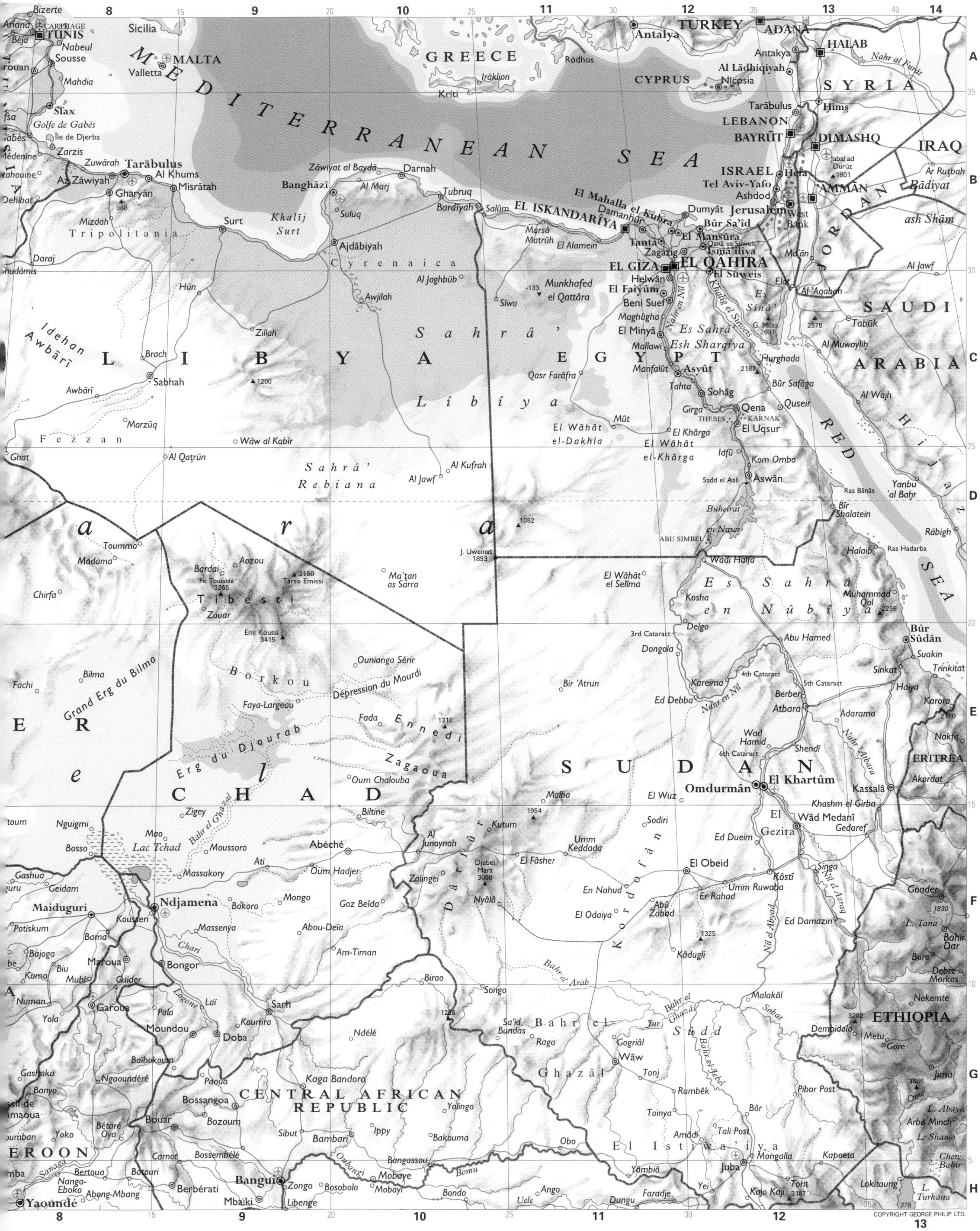

8 15 9 20 10 25 11 30 12 35 13 40 14

A B C D E F G H

Bizerte
Ariana CARTHAGE
TUNIS
Béja
Nabeul
Sousse
Mahdia
Sfax
Golfe de Gabès
Île de Djerba
Zarzis
Médenine
Zuwārah
Tarābulus
Al Khums
Az Zāwiyah
Gharyān
968
Misrātah
Mizdah
Tripolitania
Daraj
Sicilia
MALTA
Valletta
MEDITERRANEAN SEA
GREECE
Iráklion
Kríti
Ródhos
Antalya
TURKEY
ADANA
Antakya
HALAB
Nahr al Furat
Al Lādhiqīyah
Nicosia
CYPRUS
SYRIA
Tarābulus
Hims
LEBANON
BAYRŪT
DIMASHQ
IRAQ
Jabal ad Durūz
1801
ISRAEL
Hefa
Tel Aviv-Yafo
Ashdod
Jerusalem
West Bank
'AMMĀN
Ar Rutbah
Bādiyat ash Shām
JORDAN
Ma'ān
Al Jawf
Zāwiyat al Baydā
Darnah
Banghāzī
Al Marj
Tubruq
Bardīyah
Salûm
Suluq
Surt
Khalīj Surt
Ajdābiyah
Cyrenaica
Al Jaghbūb
Awjilah
Hūn
Zillah
Idehan Awbārī
Brach
LIBYA
Sabhah
1200
Awbārī
Marzūq
Fezzan
Wāw al Kabīr
Ghat
Al Qatrūn
Sahrâ' Rebiana
Al Jawf
Al Kufrah
EL ISKANDARÎYA
El Mahalla el Kubra
Damanhûr
Dumyât
Bûr Sa'îd
El Mansûra
Marsā Matrûh
El Alamein
Tanta
Zagazig
Ismâ'ilîya
Qanâ es Suweis
EL GÎZA
EL QAHIRA
Helwân
El Suweis
El Faiyûm
Siwa
-133
Munkhafed el Qattâra
Beni Suef
Maghâgha
El Minyâ
Mallawi
Nahr en Nil
Khalîg el Suweis
Es Sînâ'
G. Mûsa 2637
Elat
Al 'Aqabah
2578
SAUDI ARABIA
Tabūk
Al Muwaylih
Es Sahrâ Esh Sharqîya
Sahrâ' Lîbîya
EGYPT
Manfalût
Asyût
Hurghada
2187
Qasr Farâfra
Tahta
Sohâg
Bûr Safâga
Al Wajh
Girga
Qena
Quseir
THEBES
KARNAK
El Uqsur
Mût
El Khârga
El Wâhât el-Dakhla
El Wâhât el-Khârga
Idfû
Kom Ombo
RED SEA
Hijaz
Sadd el Aali
Aswân
Yanbu 'al Bahr
Ras Bânâs
Bîr Shalatein
Râbigh
Buheirat en Nasser
ABU SIMBEL
1082
J. Uweinat 1893
Sahara
Toummo
Madama
Aozou
Bardai
Pic Toussidé 3265
3150 Tarso Emissi
Tibesti
Zouar
Emi Koussi 3415
Chirfa
Ma'tan as Sarra
El Wâhât el Selîma
Wadi Halfa
Halaib
Ras Hadarba
Es Sahrâ en Nûbîya
Kosha
Muhammad Qol
2259
Delgo
3rd Cataract
Dongola
Abu Hamed
Bûr Sûdân
Suakin
Trinkitat
Ounianga Sérir
Bilma
Grand Erg du Bilma
Fachi
Borkou
Dépression du Mourdi
Faya-Largeau
Bir 'Atrun
Kareima
4th Cataract
5th Cataract
Sinkat
Hâiya
Berber
Atbara
Karora
2780
Ed Debba
Nahr en Nil
Adarama
Nakfa
Fada
Ennedi
1310
Erg du Djourab
Zagaoua
Oum Chalouba
Wad Hamid
6th Cataract
Shendî
Nahr Atbara
ERITREA
Akordat
CHAD
SUDAN
Omdurmân
El Khartûm
Kassalâ
Malha
El Wuz
Khashm el Girba
Zigey
Biltine
1954
Kutum
Sodiri
El Gezira
Wâd Medanî
Gedaref
toum
Nguigmi
Mao
Lac Tchad
Bahr el Ghazal
Moussoro
Abéché
Al Junaynah
Umm Keddada
Ed Dueim
Bosso
Ati
Oum Hadjer
Djebel Mara 3088
El Fâsher
Kordofân
El Obeid
Singa
Gashua
Geidam
Massakory
Zalingei
Dârfûr
Kôstî
Gonder
1830
Maiduguri
Ndjamena
Bokoro
Mongo
Goz Beïda
Nyâlâ
En Nahud
Umm Ruwaba
Er Rahad
Nil el Azraq
Potiskum
Kousseri
Massenya
Abou-Deïa
El Odaiya
Abû Zabad
Ed Damazin
L. Tana
Bahir Dar
Bama
Chari
Am-Timan
1325
Nil el Abyad
Bajoga
Maroua
Biu
Mubi
Bongor
Kâdugli
Bure
Kumo
Guider
Debre Markos
Numan
Garoua
Logone
Birao
Bahr el Arab
Songa
Malakâl
Yola
Pala
Laï
Sarh
Koumra
1216
Bahr el Jur
Sobat
Nekemte
Moundou
Doba
Ndélé
Sa'id Bundas
Bahr el Ghazâl
Raga
Sudd
Bahr el Jebel
Dempidolo
3202
ETHIOPIA
Metu
Gore
Baibokoum
Gogriâl
Wâw
Tonj
Gashaka
Ngaoundéré
Kaga Bandoro
Rumbêk
Pibor Post
Jima
3686
Omo
Banyo
CENTRAL AFRICAN REPUBLIC
Bossangoa
Yalinga
Toinya
Bôr
L. Abaya
Adamaoua
Bouar
Bozoum
Bétaré Oya
Sibut
Ippy
Bakouma
Amadi
Tali Post
Arba Minch
L. Shamo
Yoko
CAMEROON
Carnot
Bossembélé
Bambari
Obo
El Istiwa'iya
Mongalla
Kapoeta
Chew Bahir
Sanaga
Bertoua
Baboua
Bangassou
Oubangi
Mobaye
Bomu
Yambiô
Juba
Nanga-Eboko
Abong-Mbang
Berbérati
Bangui
Zongo
Bosobolo
Mobayi
Bondo
Ango
Uele
Yei
Kajo Kaji
Torit
3187
Lokitaung
L. Turkana
Yaoundé
Mbaïki
Libenge
Dungu
Faradje
375

8 15 9 20 10 25 11 30 12 35 13

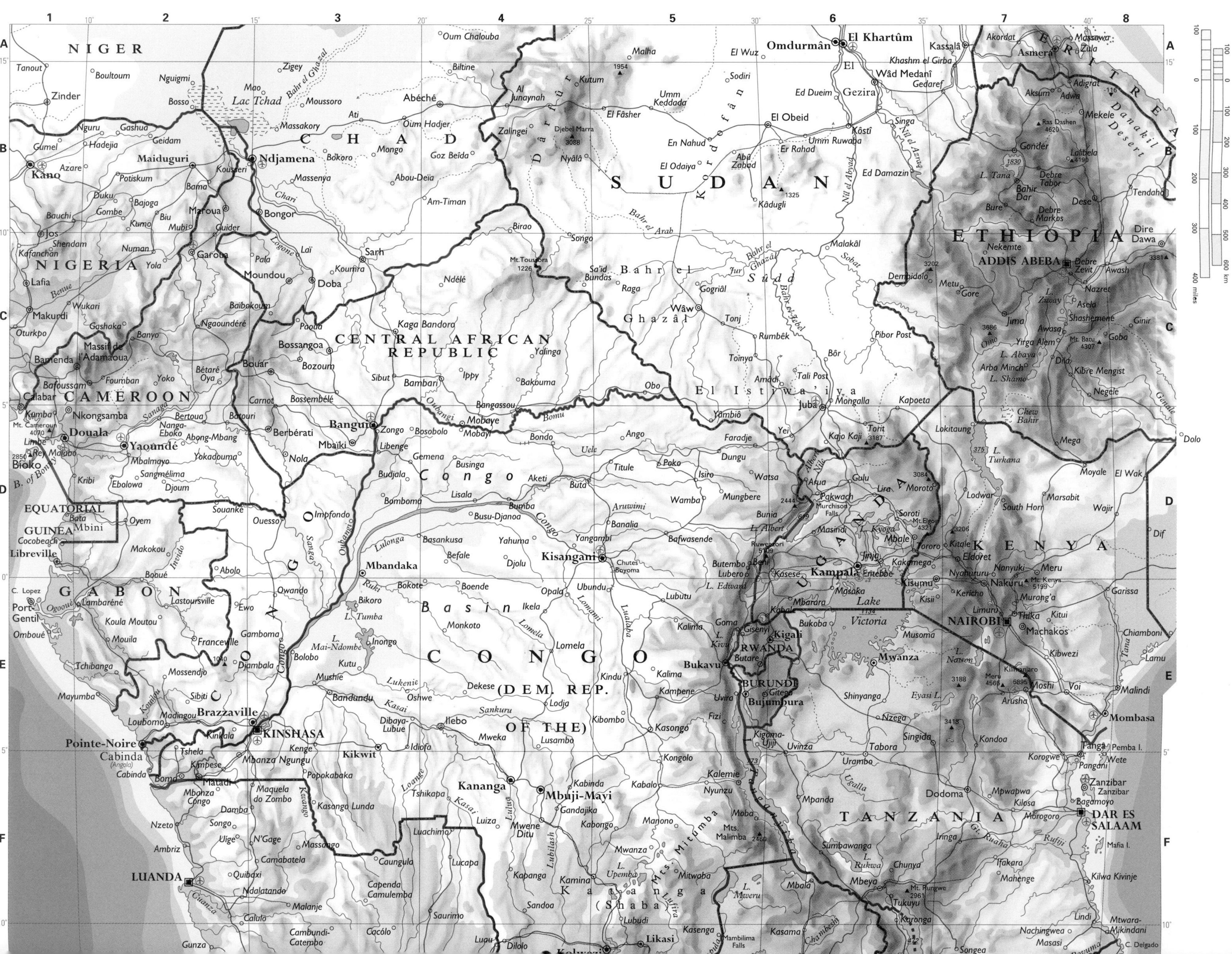
100 0 100 200 300 400 500 600 km
100 0 100 200 300 400 miles
NIGER
NIGERIA
CHAD
SUDAN
ETHIOPIA
ERITREA
KENYA
UGANDA
RWANDA
BURUNDI
TANZANIA
CENTRAL AFRICAN REPUBLIC
CAMEROON
EQUATORIAL GUINEA
GABON
CONGO
CONGO (DEM. REP. OF THE)
ADDIS ABEBA
NAIROBI
Kampala
Kigali
Bujumbura
DAR ES SALAAM
El Khartûm
Omdurmân
Ndjamena
Bangui
Yaoundé
Libreville
Brazzaville
KINSHASA
LUANDA
Kisangani
Mombasa
Asmera
Douala
Pointe-Noire
Kano
Maiduguri
Lake Victoria
Lac Tchad
Congo Basin
Danakil Desert
Sudd
Bahr el Ghazâl
Mts. Mitumba
Katanga (Shaba)

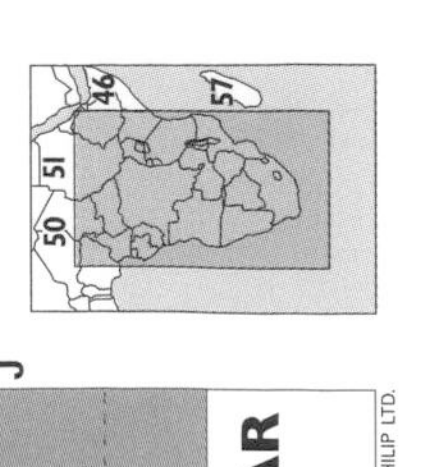
46
57
50
51

MADAGASCAR

On same scale as General Map

INDIAN OCEAN

ATLANTIC OCEAN

SOUTH AFRICA

NAMIBIA

BOTSWANA

ZIMBABWE

ZAMBIA

MOZAMBIQUE

East from Greenwich

Tropic of Capricorn

Projection: Sanson-Flamsteed's Sinusoidal

m	ft
4000	12 000
3000	9000
2000	6000
1500	4500
1000	3000
400	1200
200	600
0	0
200	600
1000	3000
2000	6000
4000	12 000

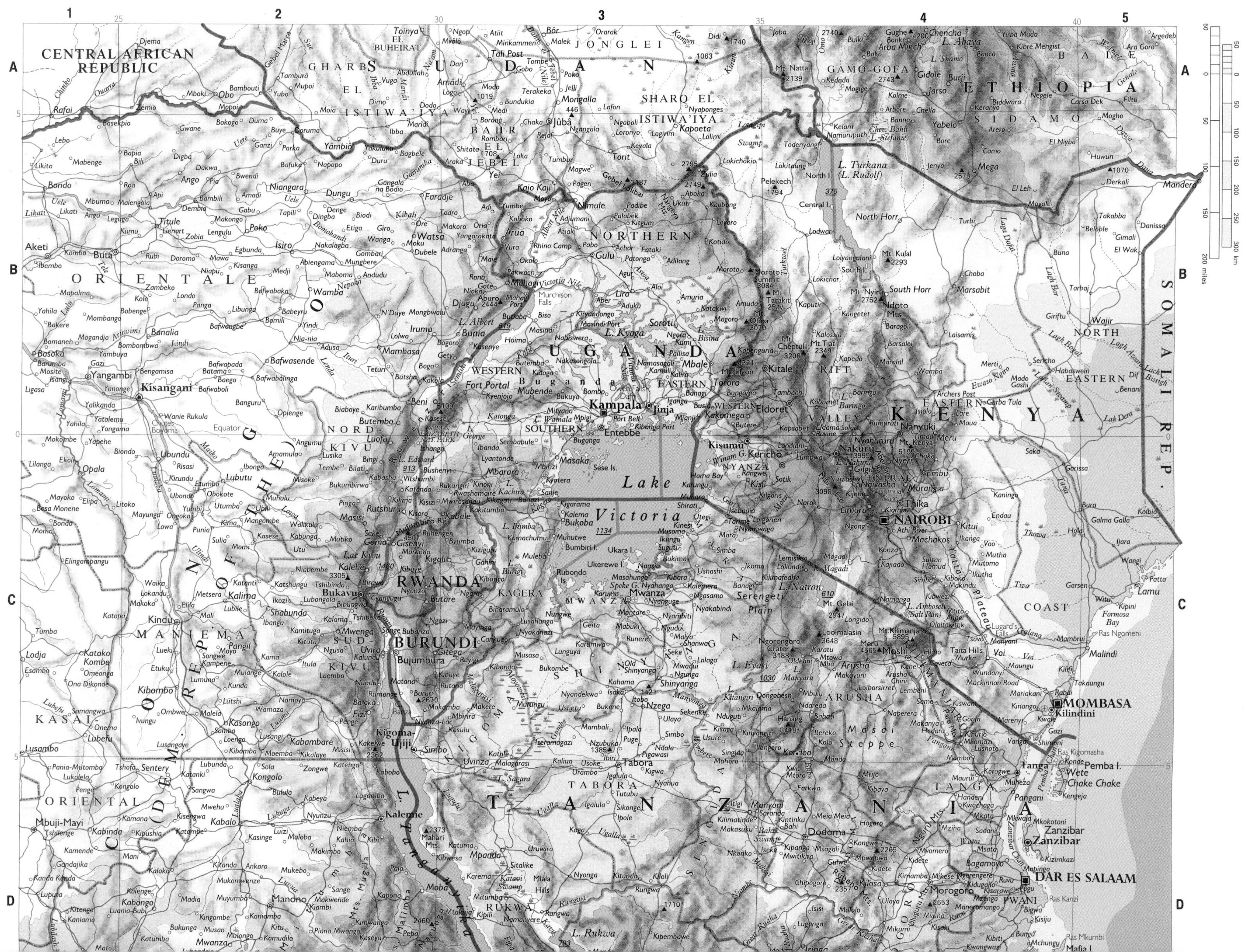

50 0 50 100 150 200 250 300 km
50 0 50 100 150 200 miles
A
B
C
D
1
2
3
4
5
CENTRAL AFRICAN REPUBLIC
SUDAN
ETHIOPIA
SOMALI REP.
KENYA
UGANDA
TANZANIA
RWANDA
BURUNDI
ORIENTALE
NORTHERN
WESTERN
EASTERN
SOUTHERN
NORTH EASTERN
RIFT VALLEY
NYANZA
COAST
KAGERA
TABORA
ARUSHA
RUKWA
Lake Victoria
L. Turkana (L. Rudolf)
L. Albert
L. Edward
L. Kyoga
L. Tanganyika
L. Rukwa
Masai Steppe
Serengeti Plain
Yatta Plateau
Equator
NAIROBI
MOMBASA
DAR ES SALAAM
Zanzibar
Kampala
Entebbe
Jinja
Kisumu
Nakuru
Eldoret
Kitale
Kericho
Mwanza
Tabora
Dodoma
Arusha
Moshi
Tanga
Morogoro
Kigoma-Ujiji
Bujumbura
Kigali
Bukavu
Goma
Kisangani
Juba
Gulu
Lamu
Malindi
Marsabit
Moyale
Mandera
Wajir
Garissa
Pemba I.
Kilindini

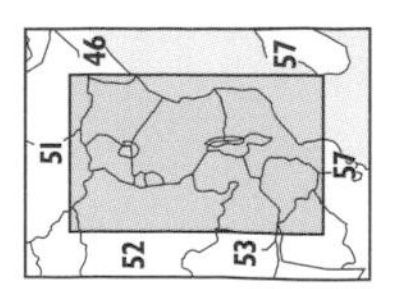

46
51
57
52
53
57

ZAMBIA
MALAWI
MOZAMBIQUE
ZIMBABWE
BOTSWANA
SOUTH AFRICA
NAMIBIA
ANGOLA
INDIAN OCEAN
L. Nyasa (L. Malawi)
Lake Kariba
L. de Cahora Bassa
LUSAKA
HARARE
BULAWAYO
Lilongwe
Blantyre
Zomba
Beira
Moçambique
Ndola
Kitwe
Lubumbashi
Livingstone
Victoria Falls
Mutare
Masvingo
Gweru

Projection: Lambert's Equivalent Azimuthal

East from Greenwich

m	ft
6000	18 000
4000	12 000
3000	9000
2000	6000
1500	4500
1000	3000
400	1200
200	600
0	0
200	600
2000	6000

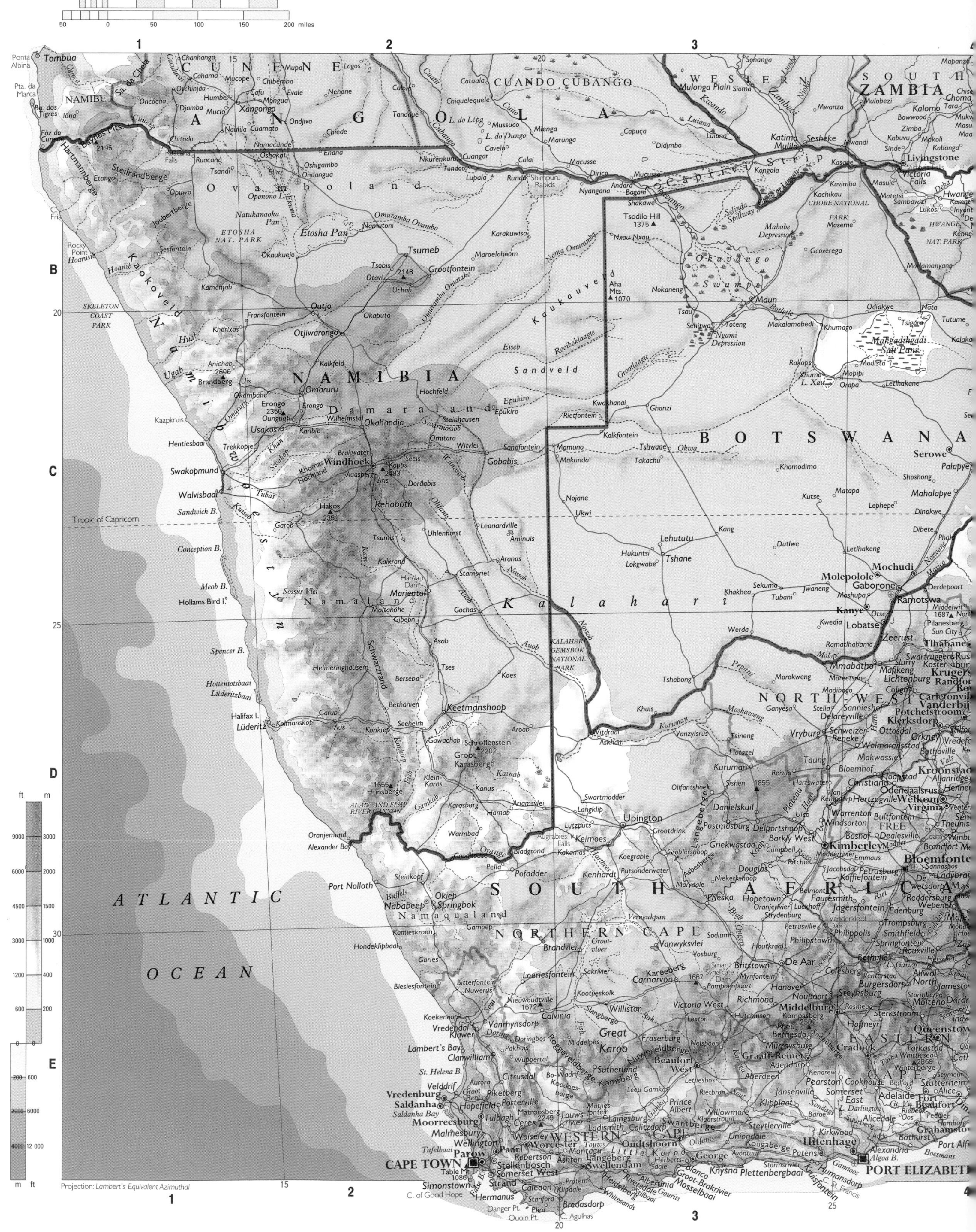

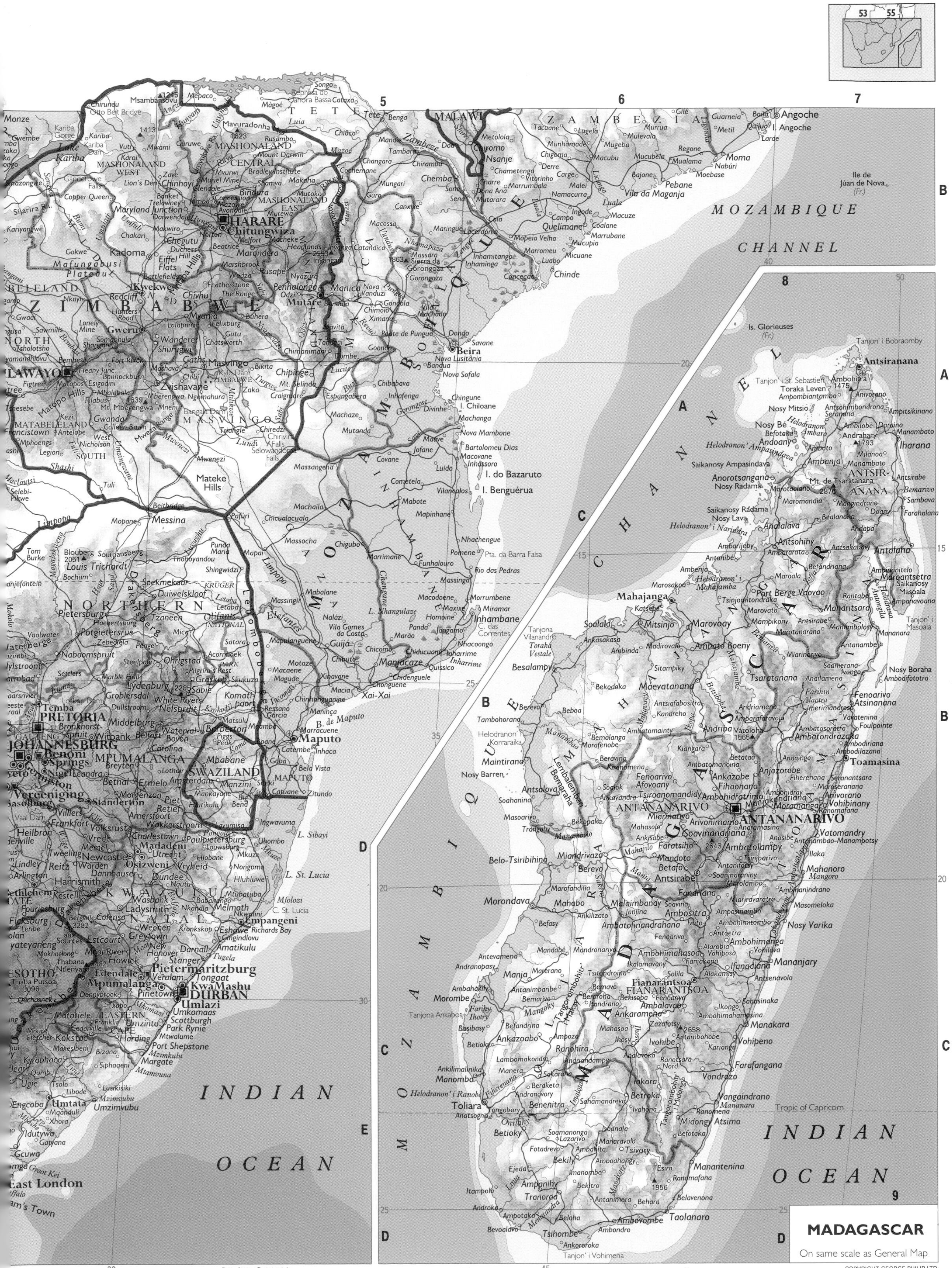

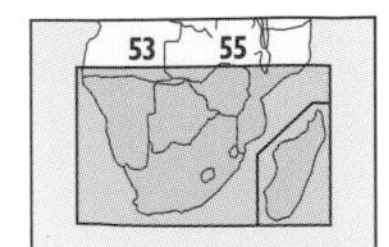

53
55

ZIMBABWE

MOZAMBIQUE

MALAWI

ZAMBEZIA

MASHONALAND CENTRAL

MASHONALAND WEST

MASHONALAND EAST

MANICA

MASVINGO

MATABELELAND SOUTH

NORTHERN

MPUMALANGA

GAUTENG

KWAZULU NATAL

SWAZILAND

LESOTHO

EASTERN CAPE

INHAMBANE

GAZA

MAPUTO

MOZAMBIQUE CHANNEL

INDIAN OCEAN

MADAGASCAR

ANTANANARIVO

FIANARANTSOA

TOLIARA

MAHAJANGA

TOAMASINA

ANTSIRANANA

Tropic of Capricorn

5 6 7 8 9

A B C D E

MADAGASCAR

On same scale as General Map

East from Greenwich

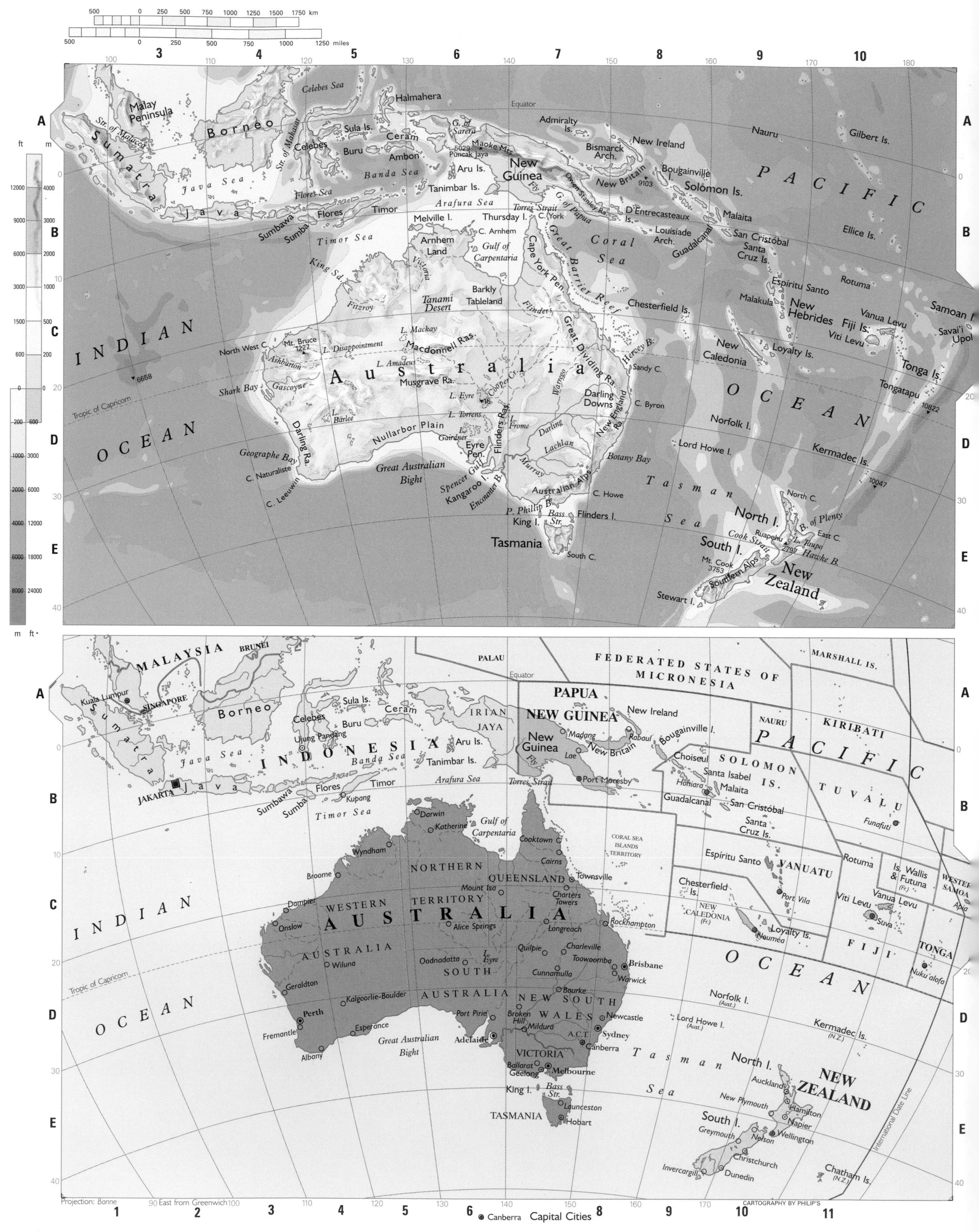

Malay Peninsula
Borneo
Sumatra
Celebes Sea
Halmahera
Celebes
Sula Is.
Ceram
Buru
Ambon
Banda Sea
Java Sea
Java
Flores Sea
Sumbawa
Sumba
Flores
Timor
Timor Sea
Aru Is.
Tanimbar Is.
Arafura Sea
Puncak Jaya
5029
Maoke Mts.
New Guinea
Admiralty Is.
Bismarck Arch.
New Ireland
New Britain
Bougainville I.
Solomon Is.
Nauru
Gilbert Is.
PACIFIC
OCEAN
Torres Strait
Thursday I.
C. York
G. of Papua
D'Entrecasteaux Is.
Louisiade Arch.
Guadalcanal
Malaita
San Cristóbal
Santa Cruz Is.
Ellice Is.
Melville I.
C. Arnhem
Arnhem Land
Gulf of Carpentaria
Cape York Pen.
Coral Sea
Great Barrier Reef
Espíritu Santo
Rotuma
Malakula
New Hebrides
Fiji Is.
Vanua Levu
Viti Levu
Samoan Is.
Savai'i
Upolu
Chesterfield Is.
King Sd.
Fitzroy
Tanami Desert
Barkly Tableland
Flinders
INDIAN OCEAN
6668
North West C.
Mt. Bruce 1227
L. Disappointment
L. Mackay
Macdonnell Ras.
L. Amadeus
Ashburton
Gascoyne
Shark Bay
Australia
Musgrave Ra.
L. Eyre
Great Dividing Ra.
Hervey B.
Sandy C.
New Caledonia
Loyalty Is.
Tonga Is.
Tongatapu
10822
Tropic of Capricorn
Darling Downs
C. Byron
L. Barlee
L. Torrens
L. Frome
Nullarbor Plain
Norfolk I.
Kermadec Is.
Darling Ra.
Geographe Bay
C. Naturaliste
C. Leeuwin
Gairdner
Eyre Pen.
Flinders Ras.
Darling
Lachlan
Murray
Botany Bay
Lord Howe I.
Great Australian Bight
Spencer Gulf
Kangaroo I.
Encounter B.
Australian Alps
C. Howe
Tasman Sea
10047
North C.
North I.
B. of Plenty
East C.
P. Phillip B.
King I.
Bass Str.
Flinders I.
Tasmania
South C.
Cook Strait
Ruapehu 2797
L. Taupo
Hawke B.
South I.
Mt. Cook 3753
Southern Alps
New Zealand
Stewart I.
Equator
MALAYSIA
BRUNEI
PALAU
FEDERATED STATES OF MICRONESIA
MARSHALL IS.
Kuala Lumpur
SINGAPORE
PAPUA NEW GUINEA
IRIAN JAYA
INDONESIA
Ujung Pandang
Madang
Rabaul
Lae
Port Moresby
NAURU
KIRIBATI
JAKARTA
Kupang
Choiseul
Santa Isabel
SOLOMON IS.
Honiara
TUVALU
Funafuti
Darwin
Katherine
Cooktown
Cairns
CORAL SEA ISLANDS TERRITORY
Wyndham
Broome
NORTHERN TERRITORY
QUEENSLAND
Mount Isa
Townsville
Charters Towers
VANUATU
Port Vila
Is. Wallis & Futuna (Fr.)
WESTERN SAMOA
Apia
Dampier
Onslow
WESTERN AUSTRALIA
AUSTRALIA
Alice Springs
Longreach
Rockhampton
NEW CALEDONIA (Fr.)
Nouméa
Suva
FIJI
TONGA
Nuku'alofa
Wiluna
Oodnadatta
SOUTH AUSTRALIA
Quilpie
Charleville
Toowoomba
Brisbane
Warwick
Cunnamulla
Geraldton
Kalgoorlie-Boulder
Bourke
NEW SOUTH WALES
Newcastle
Sydney
Norfolk I. (Aust.)
Lord Howe I. (Aust.)
Kermadec Is. (N.Z.)
Perth
Fremantle
Esperance
Albany
Port Pirie
Broken Hill
Mildura
Adelaide
A.C.T.
Canberra
VICTORIA
Ballarat
Geelong
Melbourne
Launceston
Hobart
TASMANIA
NEW ZEALAND
Auckland
New Plymouth
Hamilton
Napier
Wellington
Nelson
Greymouth
Christchurch
Dunedin
Invercargill
Chatham Is. (N.Z.)
International Date Line
Projection: Bonne
East from Greenwich
Capital Cities
CARTOGRAPHY BY PHILIP'S

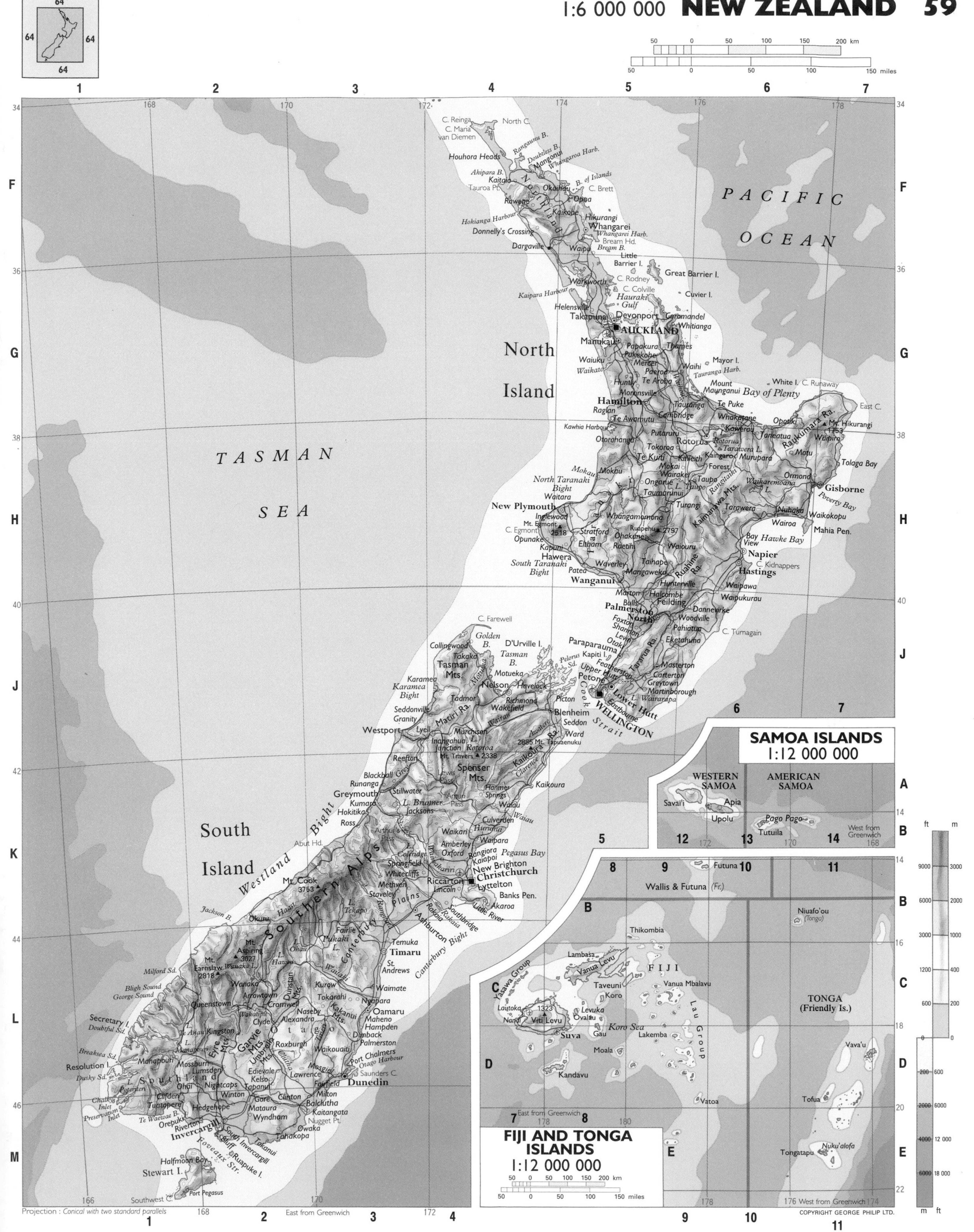
PACIFIC OCEAN
TASMAN SEA
North Island
South Island
AUCKLAND
WELLINGTON
Hamilton
Christchurch
Dunedin
Invercargill
Napier
Hastings
Gisborne
Wanganui
New Plymouth
Palmerston North
Nelson
Timaru
Greymouth
Westport
Blenheim
Whangarei
Rotorua
Tauranga
Bay of Plenty
Hawke Bay
Cook Strait
Foveaux Str.
Stewart I.
Southern Alps
Mt. Cook 3753
Canterbury Plains
Westland Bight
Canterbury Bight
Great Barrier I.
SAMOA ISLANDS
1:12 000 000
WESTERN SAMOA
AMERICAN SAMOA
Savai'i
Upolu
Apia
Pago Pago
Tutuila
FIJI AND TONGA ISLANDS
1:12 000 000
FIJI
TONGA (Friendly Is.)
Viti Levu
Vanua Levu
Suva
Kandavu
Wallis & Futuna (Fr.)
Tongatapu
Nuku'alofa
Vava'u
Projection : Conical with two standard parallels
East from Greenwich
COPYRIGHT GEORGE PHILIP LTD.

WESTERN AUSTRALIA 1:8 000 000

50 0 50 100 150 200 250 300 km
50 0 50 100 150 200 miles
INDONESIA
TIMOR SEA
INDIAN OCEAN
NORTHERN TERRITORY
Great Sandy Desert
Gibson Desert
Tanami Desert
Kimberley
King Leopold Ranges
Hamersley Range
Bonaparte Archipelago
Joseph Bonaparte Gulf
Eighty Mile Beach
Exmouth Gulf
Timor
Kupang
Roti
Sawu
Sumba
Waingapu
Waikabubak
Sumbawa
Lombok
Bali
Melville I.
Bathurst I.
Darwin
Katherine
Kununurra
Wyndham
Derby
Broome
Port Hedland
Karratha
Dampier
Newman
Onslow
Exmouth
Fitzroy Crossing
Halls Creek
Lake Mackay
Lake Disappointment
Ashmore Reef
Cartier I.
Scott Reef
Rowley Shoals
Barrow I.
Monte Bello Is.
Tropic of Capricorn

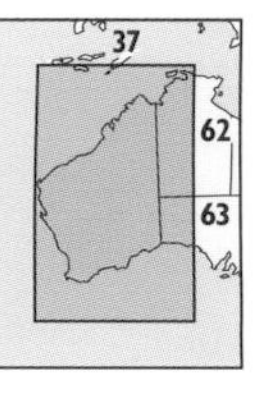
37
62
63

WESTERN AUSTRALIA

SOUTH AUSTRALIA

Great Victoria Desert

Nullarbor Plain

Hampton Tableland

Great Australian Bight

INDIAN OCEAN

SOUTHERN OCEAN

Carnarvon
Geraldton
PERTH
Fremantle
Kwinana
Rockingham
Mandurah
Bunbury
Busselton
Albany
Esperance
Kalgoorlie-Boulder
Norseman
Merredin
Northam
Katanning
Wiluna
Meekatharra
Cue
Mount Magnet
Leonora
Laverton
Menzies
Southern Cross
Ravensthorpe
Hopetoun
Balladonia
Cocklebiddy
Madura
Mundrabilla
Eucla
Nullarbor
Forrest
Cook
Ooldea
Maralinga
Warburton
Ayers Rock 868
Mt. Olga 1069
Yulara
ULURU NAT. PARK
Docker River
Petermann Ranges
Musgrave Ranges
Mt. Woodroffe 1440
Everard Ranges
Mt. Augustus 1105
Mt. Essendon 906
Mt. Fraser 799
Mt. Eureka 499
Mt. Redcliffe 576
Mt. Burges 554
Peak Eleanora 503
Mt. Ragged 585
Archipelago of the Recherche
Shark Bay
Dirk Hartog I.
Houtman Abrolhos
L. Carnegie
L. Wells
L. Carey
L. Austin
L. Moore
L. Barlee
L. Ballard
L. Cowan
L. Dundas
L. Lefroy
L. Throssell
L. Mackay

▼ 5632

Projection: Bonne

East from Greenwich

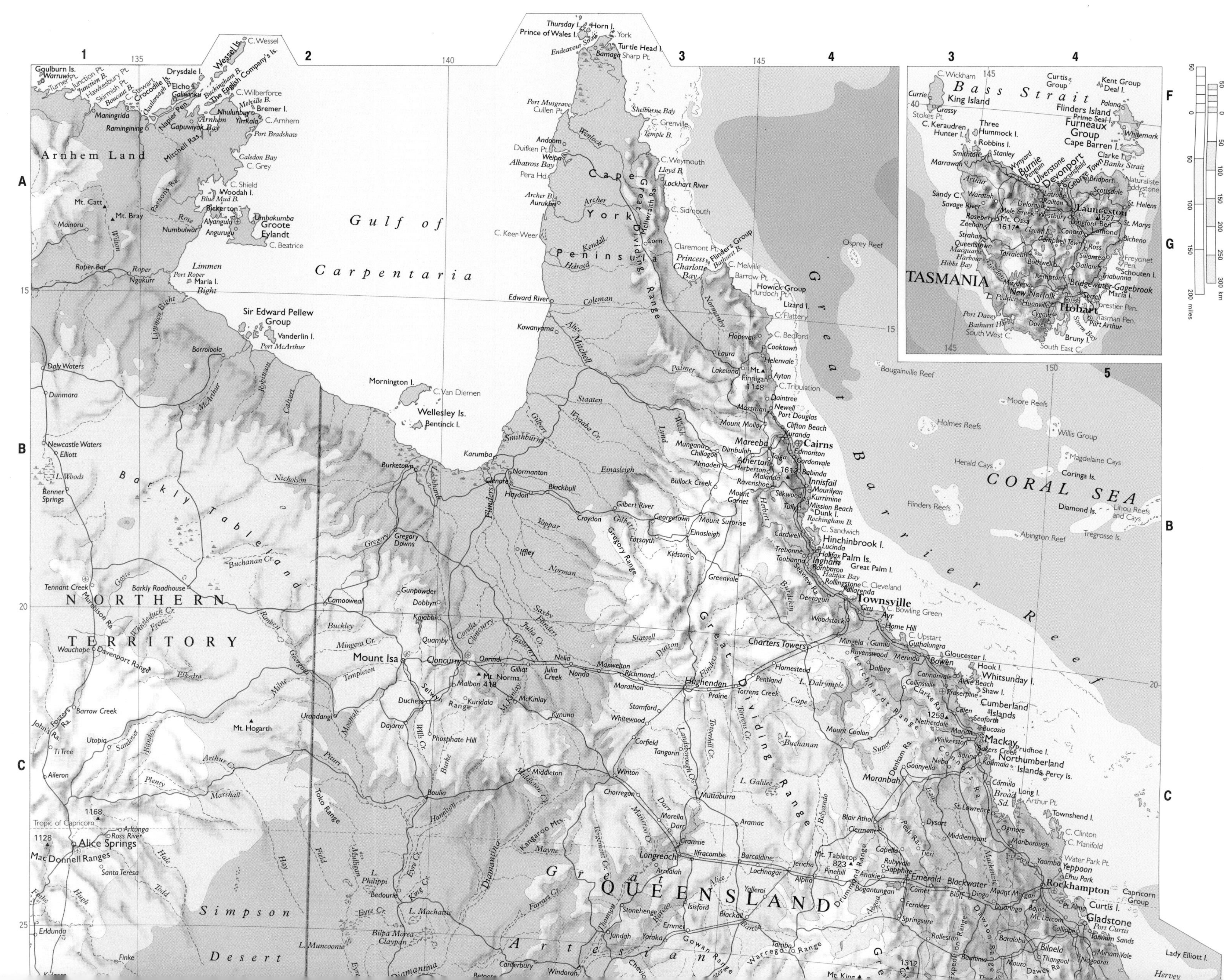

50 0 50 100 150 200 250 300 km
50 0 50 100 150 200 miles
TASMANIA
Bass Strait
King Island
Flinders Island
Furneaux Group
Cape Barren I.
Kent Group
Launceston
Devonport
Burnie
Hobart
CORAL SEA
Great Barrier Reef
Gulf of Carpentaria
Cape York Peninsula
Great Dividing Range
Arnhem Land
NORTHERN TERRITORY
QUEENSLAND
Barkly Tableland
Simpson Desert
Great Artesian Basin
Groote Eylandt
Wellesley Is.
Mornington I.
Sir Edward Pellew Group
Cairns
Townsville
Mackay
Rockhampton
Gladstone
Mount Isa
Cloncurry
Longreach
Charters Towers
Hughenden
Alice Springs
Tennant Creek
MacDonnell Ranges
Thursday I.
Prince of Wales I.
Cooktown
Bowen
Emerald
Winton
Normanton
Karumba
Burketown
Camooweal
Tropic of Capricorn

SOUTH AUSTRALIA
NEW SOUTH WALES
VICTORIA
TASMAN SEA
SOUTHERN OCEAN
Bass Strait
SYDNEY
MELBOURNE
ADELAIDE
CANBERRA
BRISBANE
Gold Coast
Tweed Heads
Newcastle
Wollongong
Geelong
Ballarat
Bendigo
Albury-Wodonga
Wagga Wagga
Dubbo
Tamworth
Armidale
Orange
Bathurst
Goulburn
Broken Hill
Mildura
Mount Gambier
Port Augusta
Port Pirie
Whyalla
Port Lincoln
Kangaroo I.
King Island
Flinders Island
Furneaux Group
Cape Barren I.
Lake Eyre (North)
Lake Eyre (South)
Lake Torrens
Lake Gairdner
Lake Frome
Toowoomba
Ipswich
Coffs Harbour
Port Macquarie
Lismore
Grafton
Gympie
Maryborough
Hervey Bay
Warrnambool
Portland
Shepparton
Horsham
Mornington
Dandenong
Cobar
Bourke
Charleville
Cunnamulla
Roma
Moree
St. George
Coober Pedy
Ceduna
Griffith
Leeton
Murray Bridge
Gawler
Elizabeth
Darling Downs
Grey Range
Spencer Gulf
Eyre Peninsula
Wilsons Promontory
Mt. Kosciuszko 2230
Snowy Mts.
(COMMONWEALTH TERRITORY)
Projection: Bonne
East from Greenwich
COPYRIGHT, GEORGE PHILIP LTD.
ft
m
4500
3000
1200
600
0
200
2000
4000
1500
1000
400
200
0
600
6000
12 000

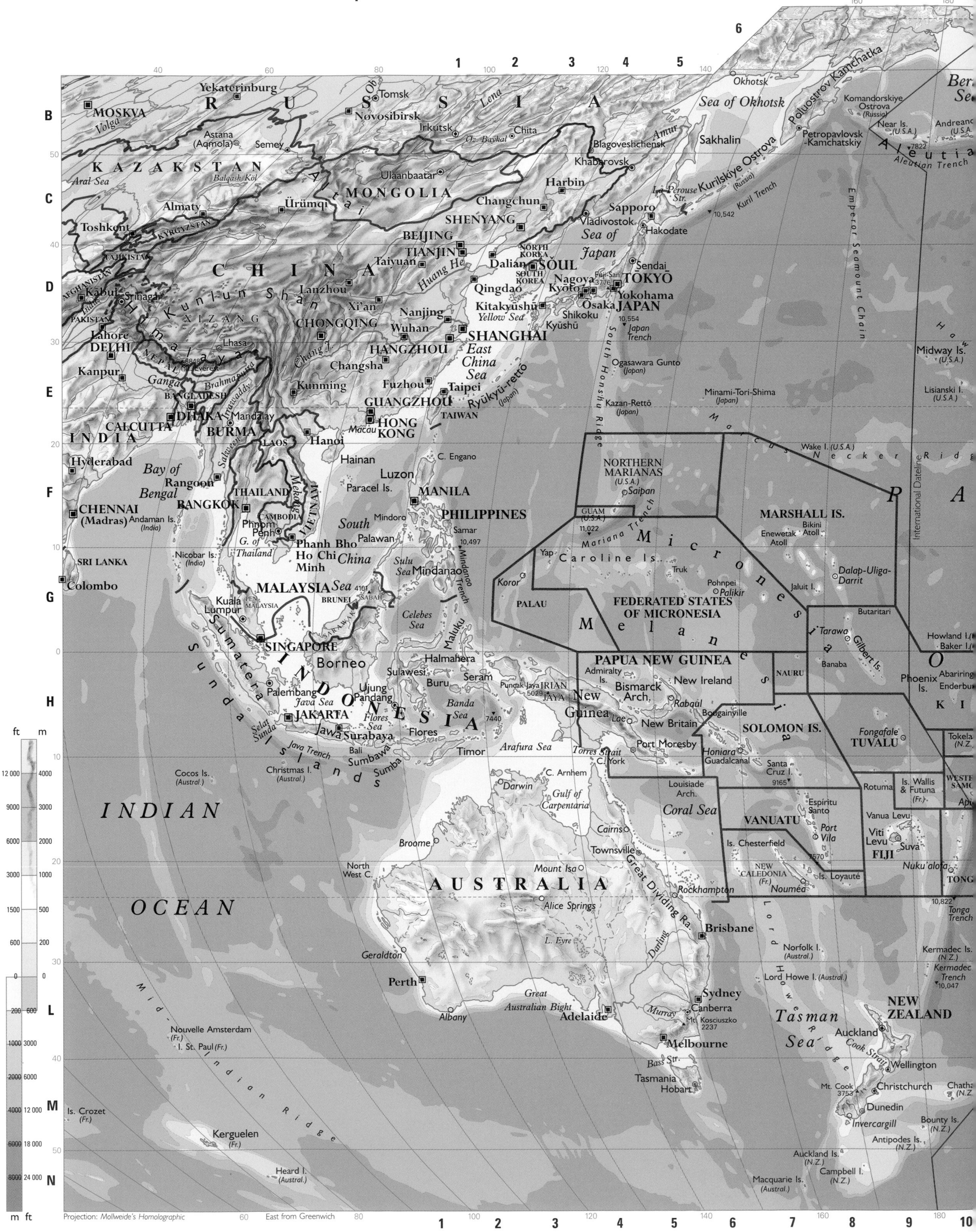

Equatorial Scale 1:54 000 000

RUSSIA
MOSKVA
Volga
Yekaterinburg
Tomsk
Ob
Novosibirsk
Lena
Irkutsk
Oz. Baykal
Chita
Astana (Aqmola)
Semey
KAZAKSTAN
Aral Sea
Balqash Köl
Ulaanbaatar
MONGOLIA
Altai
Amur
Blagoveshchensk
Khabarovsk
Harbin
Sea of Okhotsk
Okhotsk
Sakhalin
Poluostrov Kamchatka
Petropavlovsk-Kamchatskiy
Komandorskiye Ostrova (Russia)
Near Is. (U.S.A.)
Andreanof Is. (U.S.A.)
Bering Sea
Aleutian Is.
Aleutian Trench
7822
La Pérouse Str.
Kurilskiye Ostrova (Russia)
Kuril Trench
10,542
Emperor Seamount Chain
Almaty
KYRGYZSTAN
Toshkent
TAJIKISTAN
AFGHANISTAN
Kabul
PAKISTAN
Srinagar
Ürümqi
Changchun
SHENYANG
Sapporo
Vladivostok
Hakodate
Sea of Japan
BEIJING
TIANJIN
Taiyuan
Huang He
Dalian
NORTH KOREA
SOUTH KOREA
SÕUL
Sendai
TOKYO
Fuji-San 3776
Nagoya
Kyoto
Osaka
Yokohama
JAPAN
Shikoku
Kyūshū
Kitakyūshū
Qingdao
Yellow Sea
CHINA
Lanzhou
Xi'an
Kunlun Shan
XIZANG
Himalaya
Nanjing
CHONGQING
Wuhan
SHANGHAI
Lahore
DELHI
NEPAL
Lhasa
Mt. Everest 8848
Chang Jiang
HANGZHOU
East China Sea
10,554
Japan Trench
Changsha
Kanpur
Ganga
Brahmaputra
Irrawaddy
Kunming
Fuzhou
Taipei
Ryukyu-retto (Japan)
South Honshu Ridge
Ogasawara Gunto (Japan)
Kazan-Retto (Japan)
Minami-Tori-Shima (Japan)
BANGLADESH
DHAKA
CALCUTTA
INDIA
Mandalay
BURMA
Salween
GUANGZHOU
HONG KONG
Macau
TAIWAN
Marcus Necker Ridge
Wake I. (U.S.A.)
Midway Is. (U.S.A.)
Lisianski I. (U.S.A.)
Hawaiian Ridge
LAOS
Hanoi
Hainan
Hyderabad
Bay of Bengal
Rangoon
Mekong
THAILAND
VIETNAM
Luzon
C. Engano
Paracel Is.
MANILA
PHILIPPINES
NORTHERN MARIANAS (U.S.A.)
Saipan
GUAM (U.S.A.)
11,022
Mariana Trench
CHENNAI (Madras)
Andaman Is. (India)
BANGKOK
CAMBODIA
Phnom Penh
South China Sea
Mindoro
Samar
10,497
Palawan
G. of Thailand
Phanh Bho Ho Chi Minh
Nicobar Is. (India)
SRI LANKA
Colombo
Sulu Sea
Mindanao
Mindanao Trench
Yap
Caroline Is.
Micronesia
Truk
Pohnpei
Palikir
MARSHALL IS.
Bikini Atoll
Enewetak Atoll
Jaluit I.
Dalap-Uliga-Darrit
International Dateline
PACIFIC
Koror
PALAU
FEDERATED STATES OF MICRONESIA
MALAYSIA
4101
SABAH
BRUNEI
SARAWAK
Kuala Lumpur
PEN. MALAYSIA
Celebes Sea
Maluku
Butaritari
Tarawa
Gilbert Is.
Banaba
Howland I.
Baker I.
SINGAPORE
Sumatera
Borneo
Halmahera
INDONESIA
Melanesia
PAPUA NEW GUINEA
Admiralty Is.
Bismarck Arch.
New Ireland
NAURU
Phoenix Is.
Abariringa
Enderbury
KIRIBATI
OCEANIA
Sunda Islands
Palembang
Java Sea
Sulawesi
Ujung Pandang
Buru
Seram
Puncak Jaya 5029
IRIAN JAYA
New Guinea
Lae
Rabaul
Bougainville
New Britain
SOLOMON IS.
JAKARTA
Banda Sea
7440
Flores Sea
Selat Sunda
Jawa
Surabaya
Flores
Timor
Arafura Sea
Torres Strait
C. York
Port Moresby
Honiara
Guadalcanal
Fongafale
TUVALU
Tokelau (N.Z.)
Java Trench
Bali
Sumbawa
Sumba
Cocos Is. (Austral.)
Christmas I. (Austral.)
C. Arnhem
Darwin
Gulf of Carpentaria
Louisiade Arch.
Santa Cruz I. 9165
Rotuma
Is. Wallis & Futuna (Fr.)
WESTERN SAMOA
Apia
INDIAN OCEAN
Coral Sea
Espíritu Santo
VANUATU
Port Vila
Vanua Levu
Viti Levu
Suva
FIJI
Cairns
Broome
Townsville
Is. Chesterfield
7570
North West C.
Mount Isa
Great Dividing Ra.
NEW CALEDONIA (Fr.)
Nouméa
Is. Loyauté
Nuku'alofa
TONGA
AUSTRALIA
Rockhampton
Alice Springs
10,822
Tonga Trench
Lord Howe Rise
Brisbane
L. Eyre
Darling
Norfolk I. (Austral.)
Kermadec Is. (N.Z.)
Kermadec Trench
10,047
Geraldton
Perth
Lord Howe I. (Austral.)
Great Australian Bight
Adelaide
Murray
Sydney
Canberra
Mt. Kosciuszko 2237
Tasman Sea
NEW ZEALAND
Albany
Mid-Indian Ridge
Nouvelle Amsterdam (Fr.)
I. St. Paul (Fr.)
Melbourne
Bass Str.
Tasmania
Hobart
Auckland
Cook Strait
Wellington
Mt. Cook 3753
Christchurch
Chatham Is. (N.Z.)
Dunedin
Invercargill
Bounty Is. (N.Z.)
Antipodes Is. (N.Z.)
Is. Crozet (Fr.)
Kerguelen (Fr.)
Heard I. (Austral.)
Auckland Is. (N.Z.)
Campbell I. (N.Z.)
Macquarie Is. (Austral.)

ft	m
12 000	4000
9000	3000
6000	2000
3000	1000
1500	500
600	200
0	0
600	200
3000	1000
6000	2000
12 000	4000
18 000	6000
24 000	8000

Projection: *Mollweide's Homolographic*

East from Greenwich

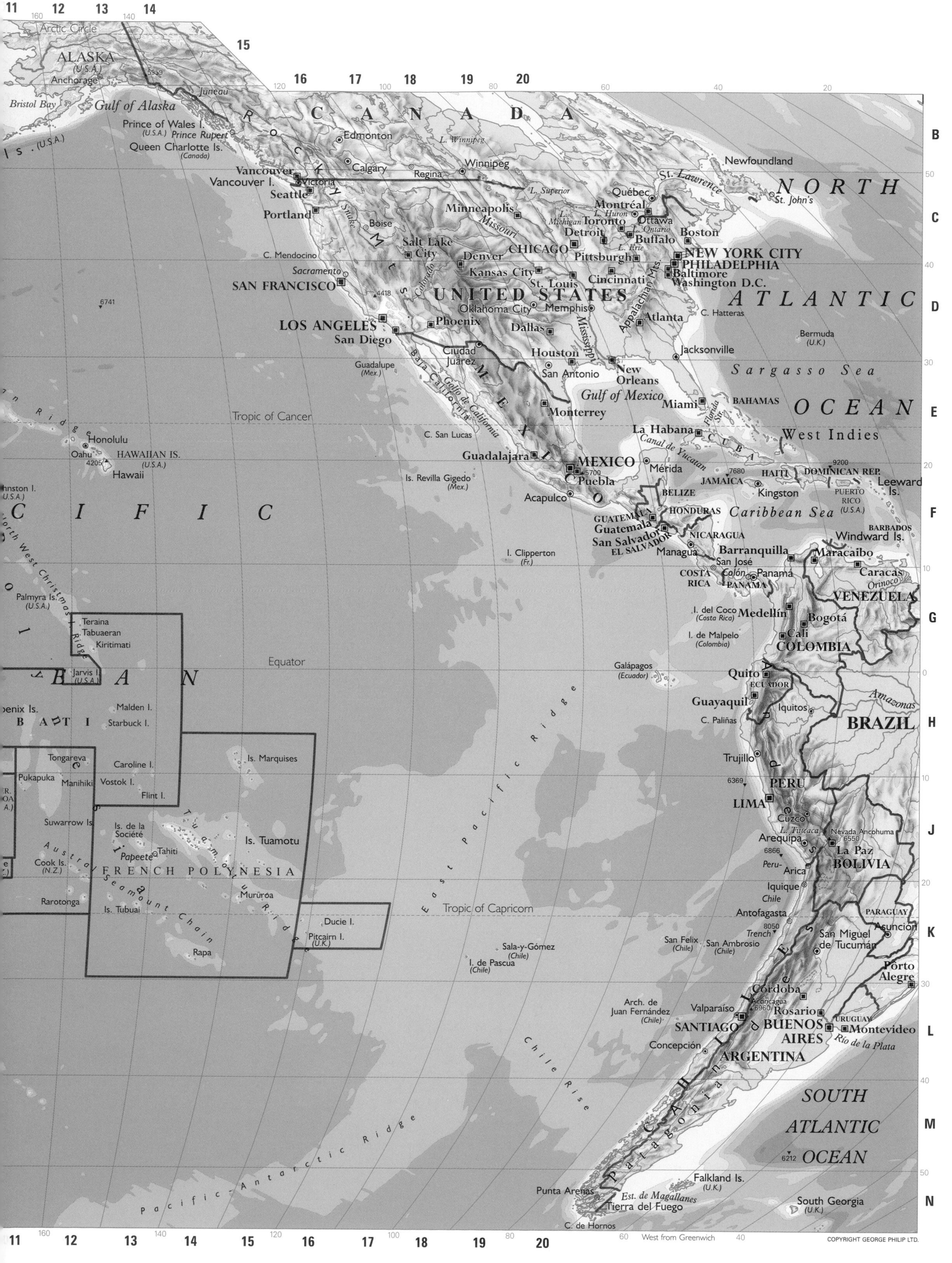
ALASKA
(U.S.A.)
Anchorage
Arctic Circle
Bristol Bay
Gulf of Alaska
Juneau
Prince of Wales I.
Prince Rupert
Queen Charlotte Is.
(Canada)
CANADA
Edmonton
Calgary
Regina
Winnipeg
L. Winnipeg
Vancouver
Vancouver I.
Victoria
Seattle
Portland
Boise
Salt Lake City
Denver
Minneapolis
Missouri
CHICAGO
Detroit
Toronto
Ottawa
Montréal
Québec
Buffalo
Boston
NEW YORK CITY
PHILADELPHIA
Baltimore
Washington D.C.
Pittsburgh
Cincinnati
Kansas City
St. Louis
UNITED STATES
Oklahoma City
Memphis
Atlanta
Dallas
Phoenix
LOS ANGELES
San Diego
SAN FRANCISCO
Sacramento
C. Mendocino
Houston
San Antonio
New Orleans
Jacksonville
Miami
C. Hatteras
Newfoundland
St. John's
St. Lawrence
L. Superior
L. Huron
L. Michigan
L. Ontario
L. Erie
Appalachian Mts.
Mississippi
NORTH
ATLANTIC
OCEAN
Bermuda
(U.K.)
Sargasso Sea
Gulf of Mexico
BAHAMAS
West Indies
Ciudad Juárez
Guadalupe
(Mex.)
Baja California
Golfo de California
Monterrey
C. San Lucas
Guadalajara
MEXICO
Puebla
Acapulco
Mérida
Is. Revilla Gigedo
(Mex.)
La Habana
CUBA
Canal de Yucatan
HAITI
DOMINICAN REP.
JAMAICA
Kingston
PUERTO RICO
(U.S.A.)
Leeward Is.
BELIZE
HONDURAS
GUATEMALA
Guatemala
San Salvador
EL SALVADOR
NICARAGUA
Managua
Caribbean Sea
BARBADOS
Windward Is.
Barranquilla
Maracaibo
Caracas
San José
COSTA RICA
Colón
Panamá
PANAMA
VENEZUELA
Orinoco
I. Clipperton
(Fr.)
I. del Coco
(Costa Rica)
Medellín
Bogotá
Cali
COLOMBIA
I. de Malpelo
(Colombia)
Galápagos
(Ecuador)
Quito
ECUADOR
Guayaquil
C. Paliñas
Iquitos
Amazonas
BRAZIL
Trujillo
PERU
LIMA
Cuzco
L. Titicaca
Nevada Ancohuma
6550
Arequipa
La Paz
BOLIVIA
Peru-Chile Trench
Arica
Iquique
Antofagasta
8050
Trench
PARAGUAY
Asunción
San Miguel de Tucumán
San Felix
(Chile)
San Ambrosio
(Chile)
Córdoba
Aconcagua
6960
Rosario
Porto Alegre
Valparaíso
SANTIAGO
BUENOS AIRES
URUGUAY
Montevideo
Río de la Plata
Concepción
ARGENTINA
Andes
Patagonia
SOUTH ATLANTIC OCEAN
6212
Falkland Is.
(U.K.)
Punta Arenas
Est. de Magallanes
Tierra del Fuego
C. de Hornos
South Georgia
(U.K.)
Arch. de Juan Fernández
(Chile)
Sala-y-Gómez
(Chile)
I. de Pascua
(Chile)
Chile Rise
East Pacific Ridge
Pacific-Antarctic Ridge
Tropic of Cancer
Tropic of Capricorn
Equator
PACIFIC OCEAN
Honolulu
Oahu
4205
HAWAIIAN IS.
(U.S.A.)
Hawaii
Johnston I.
(U.S.A.)
Palmyra Is.
(U.S.A.)
Teraina
Tabuaeran
Kiritimati
Jarvis I.
(U.S.A.)
Phoenix Is.
Malden I.
Starbuck I.
Tongareva
Pukapuka
Manihiki
Caroline I.
Vostok I.
Flint I.
Suwarrow Is.
Cook Is.
(N.Z.)
Rarotonga
Is. de la Société
Papeete
Tahiti
FRENCH POLYNESIA
Is. Marquises
Is. Tuamotu
Tuamotu Ridge
Mururoa
Is. Tubuai
Rapa
Austral Seamount Chain
Ducie I.
Pitcairn I.
(U.K.)
6741
4418
5700
7680
9200
6369
6866
West from Greenwich

NORTH AMERICA : Physical 1:35 000 000

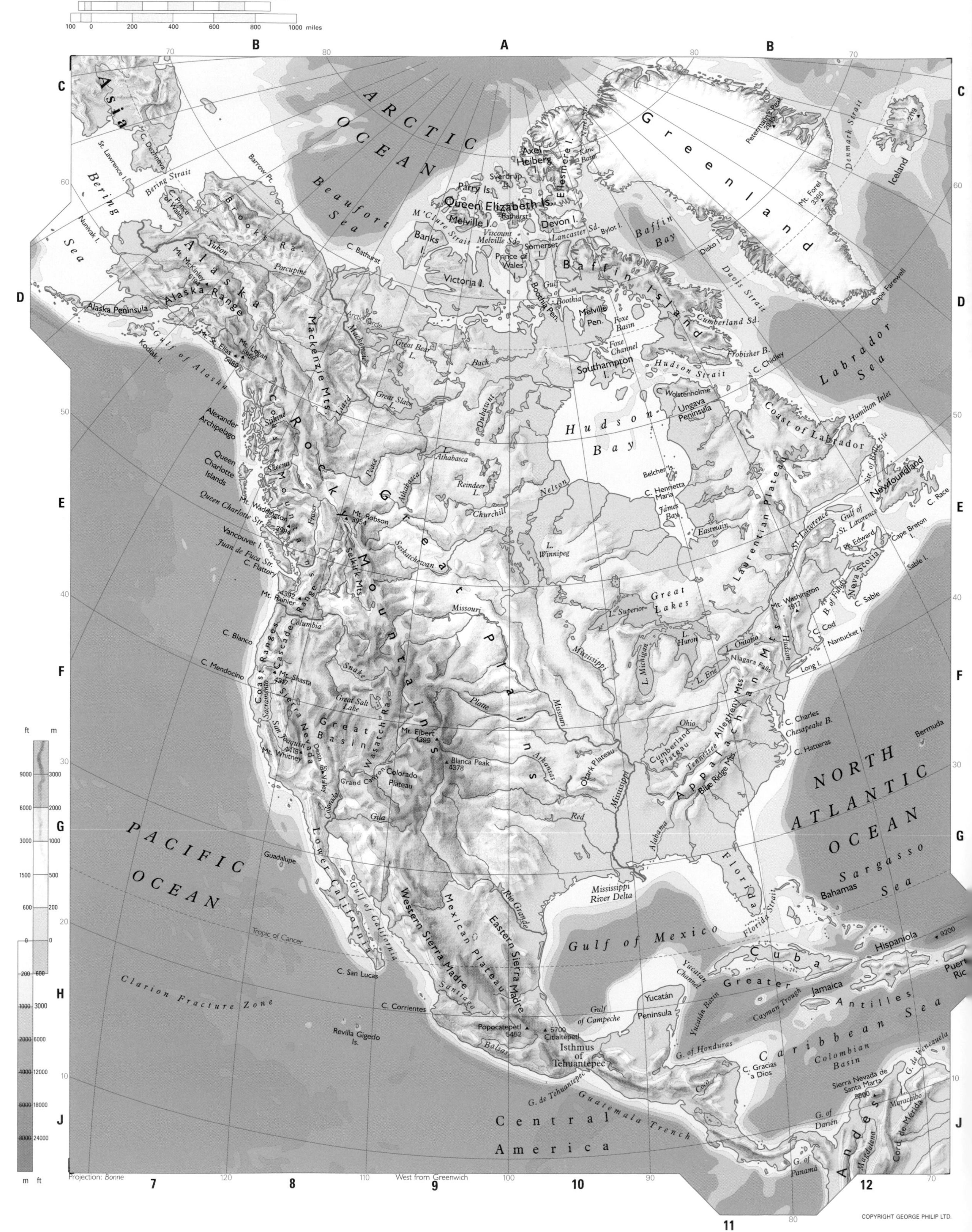
ARCTIC OCEAN
Beaufort Sea
Greenland
Baffin Bay
Hudson Bay
Labrador Sea
Great Lakes
Rocky Mountains
Great Plains
Gulf of Mexico
Caribbean Sea
NORTH ATLANTIC OCEAN
PACIFIC OCEAN
Central America
Alaska Range
Alaska Peninsula
Gulf of Alaska
Bering Sea
Bering Strait
Mt. McKinley 6194
Mt. Logan 5959
Mt. St. Elias 5489
Mackenzie Mts.
Queen Elizabeth Is.
Victoria I.
Banks I.
Baffin Island
Southampton I.
Hudson Strait
Ungava Peninsula
Coast of Labrador
Laurentian Plateau
Newfoundland
Gulf of St. Lawrence
Nova Scotia
Appalachian Mts.
Mississippi
Missouri
Great Basin
Colorado Plateau
Sierra Nevada
Cascade Range
Coast Ranges
Mt. Whitney 4418
Mt. Elbert 4399
Mt. Rainier 4392
Mt. Shasta 4317
Mt. Robson 3954
Mt. Waddington 3994
Western Sierra Madre
Eastern Sierra Madre
Mexican Plateau
Yucatán Peninsula
Isthmus of Tehuantepec
Popocatepetl 5452
Citlaltépetl 5700
Cuba
Hispaniola
Jamaica
Greater Antilles
Bahamas
Sargasso Sea
Bermuda
Clarion Fracture Zone
Tropic of Cancer
Andes
Projection: Bonne
West from Greenwich

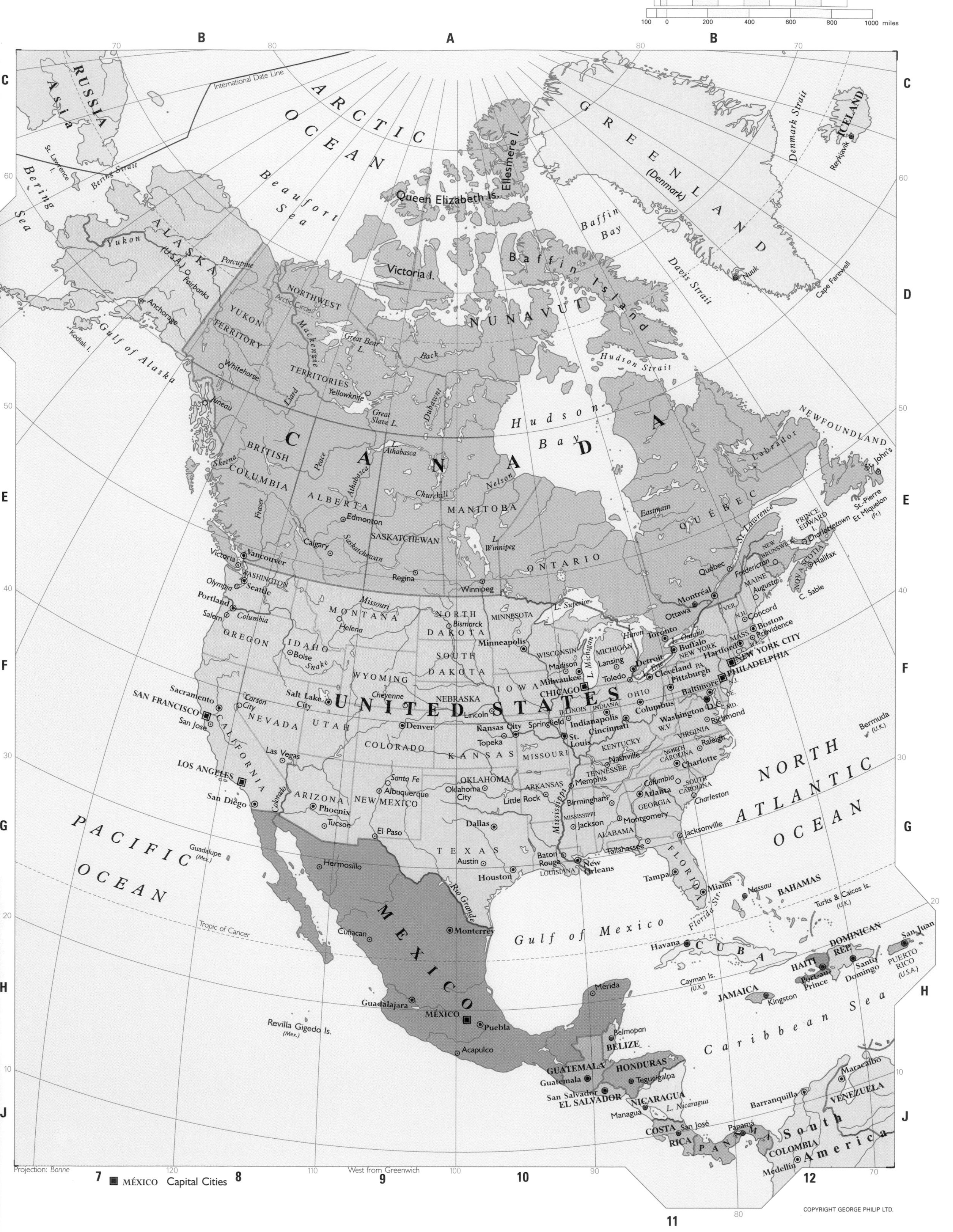
ARCTIC OCEAN
Beaufort Sea
Queen Elizabeth Is.
Ellesmere I.
GREENLAND (Denmark)
Baffin Bay
Baffin Island
Victoria I.
NUNAVUT
ICELAND
Reykjavik
Denmark Strait
Davis Strait
Nuuk
Cape Farewell
RUSSIA
Asia
Bering Strait
Bering Sea
St. Lawrence I.
ALASKA (U.S.A.)
Yukon
Porcupine
Fairbanks
Anchorage
Kodiak I.
Gulf of Alaska
NORTHWEST TERRITORIES
YUKON TERRITORY
Whitehorse
Juneau
Great Bear L.
Great Slave L.
Yellowknife
Hudson Strait
Hudson Bay
CANADA
BRITISH COLUMBIA
ALBERTA
SASKATCHEWAN
MANITOBA
ONTARIO
QUÉBEC
NEWFOUNDLAND
Labrador
St. John's
NEW BRUNSWICK
PRINCE EDWARD I.
NOVA SCOTIA
Halifax
Charlottetown
Fredericton
St.-Pierre Et Miquelon (Fr.)
Edmonton
Calgary
Regina
Winnipeg
Vancouver
Victoria
Québec
Montréal
Ottawa
Toronto
UNITED STATES
NORTH ATLANTIC OCEAN
PACIFIC OCEAN
Gulf of Mexico
MEXICO
MÉXICO
Guadalajara
Puebla
Acapulco
Monterrey
Culiacan
Hermosillo
Mérida
Revilla Gigedo Is. (Mex.)
Guadalupe (Mex.)
Tropic of Cancer
CUBA
Havana
BAHAMAS
Nassau
Turks & Caicos Is. (U.K.)
Cayman Is. (U.K.)
JAMAICA
Kingston
HAITI
Port-au-Prince
DOMINICAN REP.
Santo Domingo
PUERTO RICO (U.S.A.)
San Juan
Bermuda (U.K.)
Caribbean Sea
BELIZE
Belmopan
GUATEMALA
Guatemala
HONDURAS
Tegucigalpa
EL SALVADOR
San Salvador
NICARAGUA
Managua
L. Nicaragua
COSTA RICA
San José
PANAMA
Panamá
COLOMBIA
Barranquilla
Medellín
VENEZUELA
Maracaibo
South America
Projection: Bonne
West from Greenwich
■ MÉXICO Capital Cities
COPYRIGHT GEORGE PHILIP LTD.

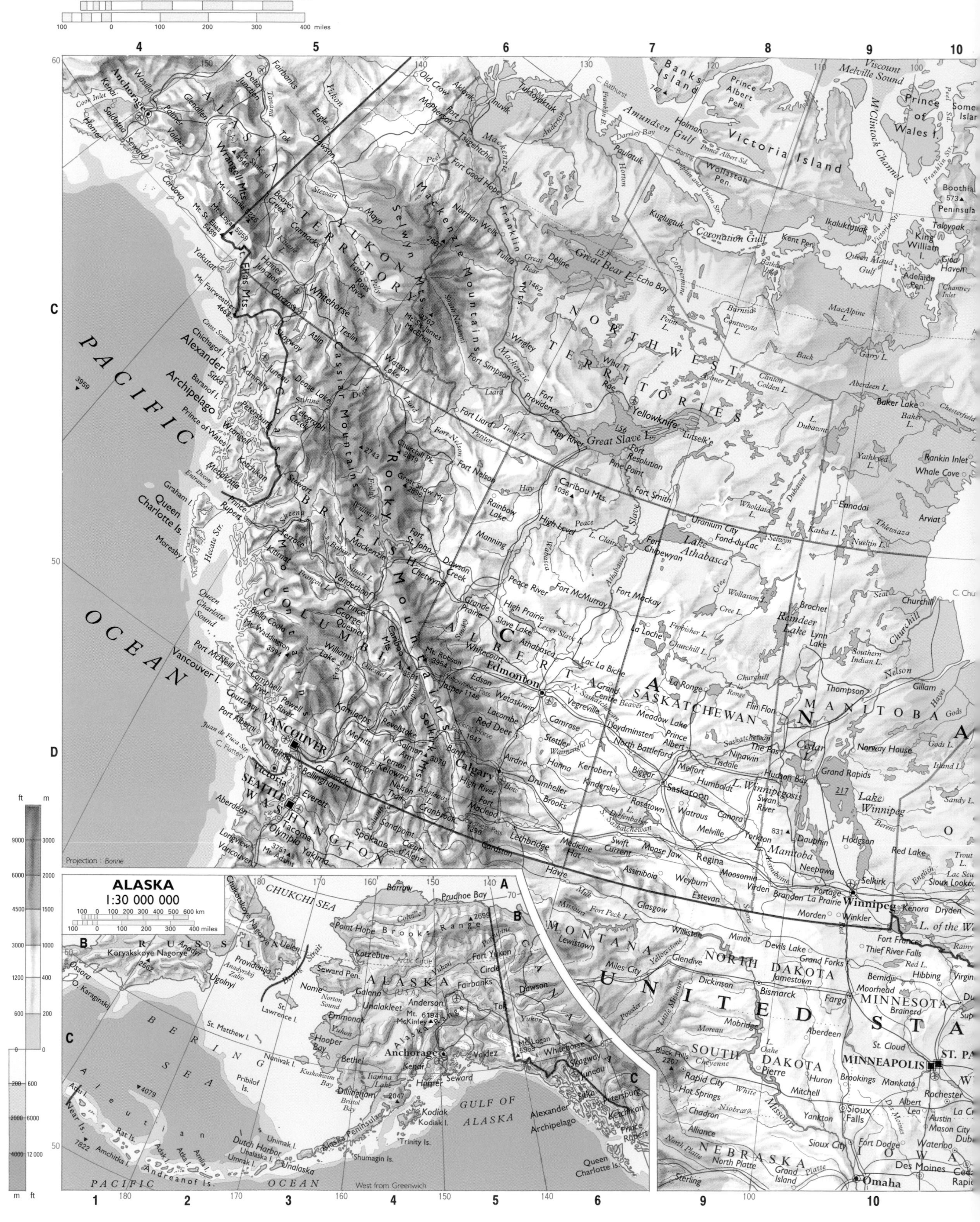
PACIFIC OCEAN
YUKON TERRITORY
NORTHWEST TERRITORIES
BRITISH COLUMBIA
ALBERTA
SASKATCHEWAN
MANITOBA
MONTANA
NORTH DAKOTA
SOUTH DAKOTA
MINNESOTA
NEBRASKA
IOWA
WASHINGTON
UNITED STATES
Victoria Island
Banks Island
Great Bear L.
Great Slave L.
Lake Athabasca
Lake Winnipeg
Rocky Mountains
Mackenzie Mountains
Coast Mountains
Cassiar Mountains
Selkirk Mts.
Edmonton
Calgary
Vancouver
Seattle
Winnipeg
Regina
Saskatoon
Yellowknife
Whitehorse
Anchorage
Projection : Bonne
ALASKA
1:30 000 000
CHUKCHI SEA
BERING SEA
GULF OF ALASKA
PACIFIC OCEAN
Brooks Range
Aleutian Is.
West from Greenwich

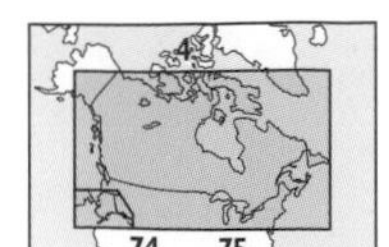
74
75

11 12 13 14 15 16

Devon I.
Lancaster Sound
Arctic Bay
Bylot I.
Borden Pen.
Pond Inlet
Brodeur Peninsula
Baffin Bay
C. Adair
Clyde River
C. Raper
Home B.
B a f f i n I s l a n d
Fury and Hecla Str.
Igloolik
Sanirajak
Simpson Pen.
Pelly Bay
Committee B.
Melville Peninsula
Foxe
Prince Charles I.
Air Force I.
Cumberland Peninsula
C. Dyer
Pangnirtung
Hoare B.
Mercy C.
Cumberland Sd.
Nettilling L.
Basin
Rae Isthmus
Repulse Bay
N U N A V U T
C. Dorchester
Amadjuak L.
Wager B.
Roes Welcome Sd.
Foxe Channel
Foxe Pen.
Iqaluit
Hall Peninsula
Meta
Cape Dorset
Incognita
Kimmirut
Frobisher Bay
Southampton I.
Sallig
Bell Pen.
Salisbury I.
Peninsula
Resolution I.
Nottingham I.
Hudson Strait
C. Chidley
Coats I.
Ivujivik
Salluit
Quaqtaq
Akpatok I.
Mansel I.
Kangiqsujuaq
Péninsule
Kangirsuk
Ungava Bay
Puvirnituq
Arnaud
L. Payne
d'Ungava
Kangiqsualujjuaq
Hebron
H u d s o n
Ottawa Is.
Kuujjuaq
George
Baleine
Feuilles
Koksoak
Nain
Inukjuak
Caniapiscau
Mélèzes
L. Minto
B a y
Sleeper Is.
King George Is.
Baker's Dozen Is.
Belcher Is.
L. à l'Eau Claire
Kuujjuarapik
Grande Baleine
L. Bienville
Schefferville
Petitsikapau
Smallwood Res.
Labrador
North West River
Happy Valley-Goose Bay
Churchill Falls
Churchill
Esker
Hopedale
C. Harrison
Rigolet
Cartwright
Port Hope Simpson
Belle Isle
C. Bauld
St. Anthony
N E W F O U N D L A N D
C. Henrietta Maria
Peawanuck
Winisk
Pte. Louis XIV
Chisasibi
Kanaaupscow
La Grande
Rés. de Caniapiscau
Labrador City
Fermont
Ashuanipi
Natashquan
Romaine
St-Augustin
Str. of Belle Isle
Notre Dame B.
Baie Verte
Lewisporte
Gander
Bonavista
Grand Falls
Deer Lake
Corner Brook
Newfoundland
Carbonear
St. John's
Trinity B.
Placentia
Marystown
Stephenville
Channel-Port aux Basques
C. Race
Big Trout L.
James Bay
Akimiski I.
Wemindji
Eastmain
Attawapiskat
Charlton I.
Fort Albany
Waskaganish
Rupert
Moosonee
Albany
Q U É B E C
Gagnon
Rés. Manicouagan
Moisie
Havre-St-Pierre
I. d'Anticosti
Sept-Îles
Port-Cartier
Gulf of St. Lawrence
Cabot Str.
ST.-PIERRE et MIQUELON (Fr.)
North C.
Cape Breton I.
Glace Bay
Sydney
Port Hawkesbury
Antigonish
New Glasgow
Truro
Dartmouth
Halifax
Bridgewater
Liverpool
Yarmouth
C. Sable
Sable I. (Nova Scotia)
NOVA SCOTIA
Digby
Kentville
Amherst
Moncton
Charlottetown
Summerside
PR. EDWARD I.
Northumberland Str.
Îs. de la Madeleine
Gaspé
Pén. de Gaspé
Matane
Campbellton
Bathurst
Miramichi
NEW BRUNSWICK
Fredericton
Saint John
B. of Fundy
Woodstock
Edmundston
Rivière-du-Loup
Rimouski
Baie Comeau
St. Lawrence
L. Mistassini
L. Albanel
Chibougamau
Péribonca
Manicouagan
Nottaway
Harricana
Missinaibi
Kenogami
Nakina
St. Joseph
O N T A R I O
L. Matagami
Matagami
Rés. Gouin
Roberval
St-Jean
Dolbeau
Chicoutimi
Jonquière
Hearst
Cochrane
Abitibi L.
Amos
Kapuskasing
Geraldton
L. Nipigon
Nipigon
Marathon
Oba
Mattagami
Timmins
Val-d'Or
Rouyn-Noranda
Kirkland Lake
New Liskeard
La Tuque
Québec
Lévis
Thetford Mines
Grand Falls
Thunder Bay
Lake Superior
Chapleau
Wawa
Rés. Cabonga
Mont-Laurier
Shawinigan
Trois-Rivières
Joliette
St-Hyacinthe
Sherbrooke
M A I N E
Bangor
Augusta
Lewiston
Portland
Houghton
Marquette
Sault Ste. Marie
Elliot Lake
Sudbury
L. Nipissing
North Bay
Outaouais
MONTRÉAL
Hull
Ottawa
Granby
Pembroke
Parry Sound
Manitoulin I.
Georgian Bay
Huntsville
Cornwall
Burlington
L. Champlain
Montpelier
VERMONT
NEW HAMPSHIRE
Concord
Manchester
MASS.
BOSTON
C. Cod
Providence
R.I.
Springfield
New Haven
CONN.
HARTFORD
Albany
Syracuse
Kingston
Belleville
Peterborough
Barrie
Oshawa
TORONTO
Kitchener
Hamilton
L. Ontario
Niagara Falls
Rochester
BUFFALO
NEW YORK
Elmira
Binghamton
Jamestown
Scranton
Bridgeport
NEW YORK
Newark
N.J.
Allentown
Trenton
PENNSYLVANIA
Erie
L. Erie
CLEVELAND
Toledo
OHIO
Windsor
DETROIT
London
Sarnia
Flint
Saginaw
Lake Huron
Owen Sound
Manistique
Escanaba
Menominee
Petoskey
Traverse City
Cadillac
Green Bay
Grand Rapids
Lansing
L. Michigan
M I C H I G A N
Wausau
Sheboygan
MILWAUKEE
Racine
Kenosha
CHICAGO
Gary
South Bend
INDIANA
G R E E N L A N D
(KALAALLIT NUNAAT)
(Denmark)
Nunavik
Uummannaq
Ilulissat
Qasigiannguit
Qeqertarsuaq
Kangerlussuaq
Sisimiut
Maniitsoq
Nuuk
Davis Strait
Paamiut
Arsuk
Qaqortoq
Nanortalik
Alluitsup Paa
Qeqertarsuatsiaat
Uummannarsuaq
Kong Frederik VI's Kyst
Ammassalik
Labrador Sea
A T L A N T I C
O C E A N
2136
1890
2591
2850
3809
1652
257
1135
1190
814
183
174
6309

B C D E

60 50 40 30
80 70 60

West from Greenwich

11 12 13 14

EASTERN CANADA 1:7 000 000

50 0 50 100 150 200 250 300 km

50 0 50 100 150 200 miles

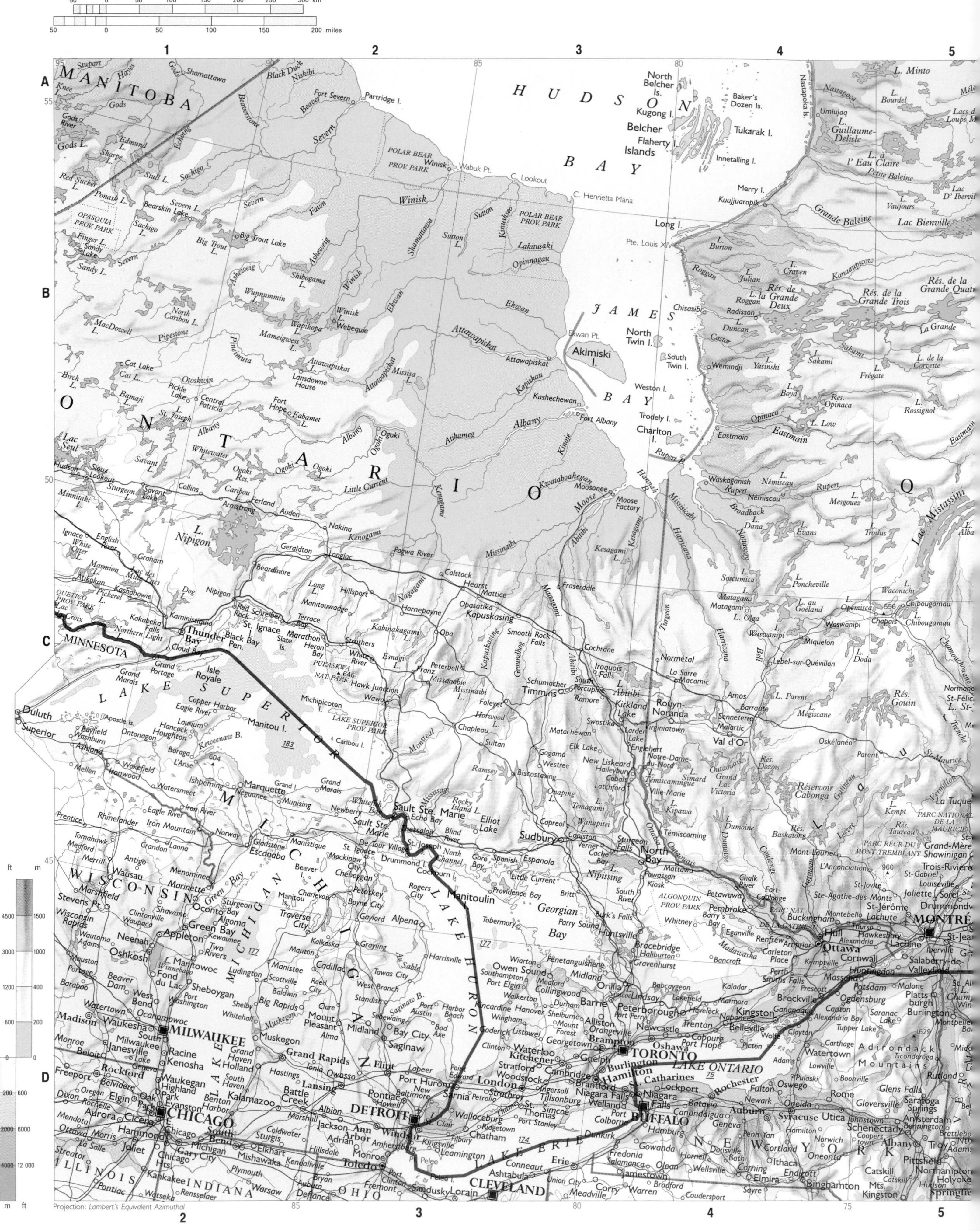
1 2 3 4 5
A B C D
HUDSON BAY
JAMES BAY
MANITOBA
ONTARIO
MINNESOTA
WISCONSIN
MICHIGAN
ILLINOIS
INDIANA
OHIO
NEW YORK
LAKE SUPERIOR
LAKE MICHIGAN
LAKE HURON
LAKE ERIE
LAKE ONTARIO
Georgian Bay
Belcher Islands
Akimiski I.
L. Nipigon
L. Mistassini
Manitoulin
Isle Royale
POLAR BEAR PROV. PARK
QUETICO PROV. PARK
PURASKWA NAT. PARK
LAKE SUPERIOR PROV. PARK
ALGONQUIN PROV. PARK
OPASQUIA PROV. PARK
Thunder Bay
Sault Ste. Marie
Sudbury
North Bay
Timmins
Kapuskasing
Moosonee
Rouyn-Noranda
Val d'Or
Ottawa
MONTRÉAL
TORONTO
Hamilton
London
Kingston
DETROIT
Windsor
CHICAGO
MILWAUKEE
CLEVELAND
BUFFALO
Duluth
Green Bay
Grand Rapids
Toledo
Rochester
Syracuse
Adirondack Mountains
Projection: Lambert's Equivalent Azimuthal

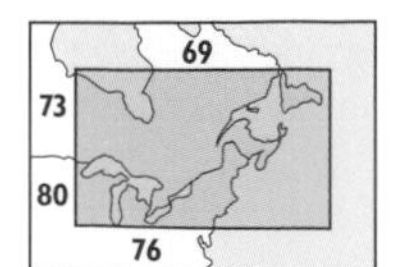
69
73
80
76

6 7 8 9

A B C D

LABRADOR SEA

NEWFOUNDLAND

Labrador

QUÉBEC

Newfoundland

GULF OF ST. LAWRENCE

ATLANTIC OCEAN

UNITED STATES

MAINE

NEW BRUNSWICK

NOVA SCOTIA

PRINCE EDWARD ISLAND

Cape Breton Island

ST.-PIERRE ET MIQUELON (France)

NEW HAMPSHIRE

MASS.

South Aulatsivik I.
Nain
Paul I.
Voisey B.
Tuhungayualok I.
Nunaksaluk I.
Davis Inlet
Big Bay
Hopedale
Kogaluk
Mistastin L.
Fraser
L. de la Hutte Sauvage
George
L. le Moyne
L. Nachicapau
L. Chakonipau
L. Otelnuk
Wheeler
L. Champdoré
610
L. Tudor
L. Mistinibi
L. Whitegull
Harp L.
Postville
Kaipokok B.
Aillik
Makkovik
Adlavik Is.
C. Harrison
Holton
Indian Harbour
Groswater B.
Rigolet
Hamilton Inlet
Cartwright
Table B.
Black Tickle
Island of Ponds
North River
Sandwich B.
Mealy Mts.
1128
Paradise River
Eagle
Melville
Nipishish L.
Seal L.
Kanairiktok
Naskaupi
Grand L.
North West River
Goose
Happy Valley-Goose Bay
Churchill
Churchill Falls
Twin Falls
Smallwood Reservoir
Attikamagen L.
Schefferville
Menihek
Menihek Lakes
Esker
Petitsikapau L.
Ossokmanuan L.
Winokapau L.
Minipi L.
Atikonak L.
Natashquan
Little Mecatina
Burnt L.
Ashuanipi L.
Wabush
Labrador City
Fermont
L. Joseph
Shabogamo L.
L. Opiscoteo
Charlottetown
Square Islands
Williams harbour
Alexis
Port Hope Simpson
Battle Harbour
Lodge Bay
Mary's Harbour
St. Lewis
Red Bay
Belle Isle
L'Anse au Loup
L'Anse aux Meadows
St. Anthony
Str. of Belle Isle
Forteau
Blanc-Sablon
Rivière St-Paul
St-Paul
St-Augustin
Hare B.
Groais I.
Bell I.
St. Barbe
Roddickton
Englee
Port au Choix
Hawke's Bay
Harbour Deep
White B.
Horse Is.
C. St. John
La Scie
Notre Dame B.
Baie Verte
Fogo
Fogo I.
Musgrave Harbour
Twillingate
C. Freels
Jackson's Arm
Springdale
Lewisporte
Wesleyville
Bonavista B.
C. Bonavista
Bonavista
Catalina
Long Range Mts.
Daniel's Harbour
GROS MORNE NAT. PARK
Rocky Harbour
Norris Point
Trout River
Deer Lake
South Brook
Botwood
Bishop's Falls
Glenwood
Gander
Gambo
Glovertown
TERRA NOVA NAT. PARK
Trinity
Trinity B.
Old Perlican
Conception B.
Port Blandford
Clarenville
Heart's Content
Carbonear
Wabana
Torbay
St. John's
Mt. Pearl
Bay Roberts
Whitless Bay
Holyrood
Avalon Peninsula
Ferryland
Trepassey
C. Race
C. Pine
St. Mary's B.
St. Bride's
Placentia B.
C. St. Mary's
Argentia
Placentia
Terrenceville
Fortune B.
Marystown
Burin
St. Lawrence
Grand Bank
Fortune
Miquelon
Langlade
St.-Pierre
Belleoram
Harbour Breton
St. Alban's
Jeddore L.
Grey
Granite L.
François
Burgeo
Red Indian L.
Maelpaeg Res.
Victoria L.
Buchans
Badger
Grand Falls-Windsor
B. of Islands
Pasadena
Corner Brook
Humber
814
Port au Port B.
Stephenville
Petit Jardin
C. St. George
St. George's B.
St. David's
South Branch
Great Codroy
St. Andrew's
C. Ray
Channel-Port aux Basques
Rose Blanche
Isle aux Morts
Cabot Strait
St. Paul I.
Cape North
Ingonish
St. Ann's B.
Sydney Mines
New Waterford
Glace Bay
North Sydney
Sydney
Louisbourg
Bras d'Or L.
St. Peters
I. Madame
Chedabucto B.
Canso
Port Hawkesbury
Port Hood
Chéticamp
Inverness
CAPE BRETON HIGHLANDS NAT. PARK
532
Pleasant Bay
Mulgrave
Antigonish
Sherbrooke
Pictou
New Glasgow
Stellarton
Truro
Stewiacke
Upper Musquodoboit
Sheet Harbour
Musquodoboit Harbour
Enfield
Dartmouth
Halifax
Windsor
Kentville
Minas Basin
Parrsboro
Springhill
Amherst
Sackville
Moncton
Shediac
Cape Tormentine
Northumberland Str.
Summerside
Borden
Kensington
Charlottetown
St. Peters
Souris
East Pt.
Montague
Georgetown
Murray Hr.
North Cape
Tignish
Alberton
Îs. de la Madeleine (Québec)
Grande-Entrée
Fatima
Cap-aux-Meules
Havre-Aubert
Î. Brion
Sable I. (Nova Scotia)
Middleton
Annapolis Royal
Bridgetown
Digby
KEJIMKUJIK NAT. PARK
Middle Sackville
Mahone Bay
Lunenburg
Bridgewater
Liverpool
Milton
Weymouth
L. Rossignol
Shelburne
Lockeport
Yarmouth
Wedgeport
St. Mary's Bay
Clark's Harbour
C. Sable
Bay of Fundy
Saint John
Chignecto B.
Sussex
Hampton
Rothesay
St. George
St. Stephen
Blacks Hr.
Grand Manan I.
Eastport
Calais
Machias
Fredericton
Fredericton Junc.
Oromocto
Grand L.
Minto
Chipman
Petitcodiac
Doaktown
Buctouche
St. Antoine
Richibucto
Rogersville
Newcastle
Miramichi
Miramichi B.
Neguac
Bathurst
Caraquet
Lamèque
Shippegan
Tracadie-Sheila
Chaleur Bay
Campbellton
Dalhousie
Atholville
Kedgwick
St. Quentin
Mt. Carleton
820
Edmundston
St. Leonard
Grand Falls
Plaster Rock
Perth-Andover
Hartland
Woodstock
St. John
Houlton
Caribou
Presque Isle
Ashland
Eagle Lake
Van Buren
Fort Kent
Allagash
Chamberlain L.
Chesuncook L.
1606
Patten
Millinocket
Moosehead L.
Greenville
Jackman
Lincoln
Dover-Foxcroft
Old Town
Brewer
Bangor
Bingham
Mooselookmeguntic L.
Skowhegan
Waterville
Belfast
Ellsworth
Bar Harbor
Mount Desert I.
Camden
Rockland
Augusta
Brunswick
Bath
Rumford
Norway
Auburn
Lewiston
Portland
Saco
Biddeford
Sebago L.
Conway
Berlin
Island Pond
St. Johnsbury
Newport
Hanover
Laconia
Sanford
Rochester
Concord
Dover
Portsmouth
Manchester
Nashua
Haverhill
Lawrence
Gloucester
Lowell
Lynn
Newton
BOSTON
Quincy
Brockton
Woonsocket
Worcester
C. Cod
Sherbrooke
Magog
Coaticook
East Angus
Lac-Mégantic
Thetford Mines
Asbestos
Victoriaville
Plessisville
Ste-Marie
St-Georges
Beauceville
Deschaillons
Charny
Lévis
Québec
Î. d'Orléans
Montmagny
St-Pamphile
St-Jean-Port-Joli
La Pocatière
Beaupré
PARC PROV. DE LA JACQUES-CARTIER
1190
PARC PROV. DES GRANDS JARDINS
Baie-St-Paul
La Malbaie
St-Siméon
Petite Saguenay
Tadoussac
La Baie
Jonquière
Chicoutimi
Saguenay
Alma
Les Escoumins
Forestville
Betsiamites
Chute-aux-Outardes
Baie Comeau
Godbout
Baie Trinité
Pte. des Monts
Cap-Chat
Ste-Anne-des-Monts
Mont-Louis
1268
Mt. Jacques-Cartier
PARC DE CONSERVATION DE LA GASPÉSIE
Chic-Chocs Mts.
Pén. de Gaspé
Gaspé
Percé
Grande-Rivière
Chandler
Bonaventure
New Richmond
Paspébiac
Miscou I.
Matane
Mont-Joli
Sayabec
Amqui
Causapscal
Matapédia
Rimouski
Trois-Pistoles
Rivière-du-Loup
Cabano
Dégelis
St. Pascal
St. Lawrence
Rivière-au-Renard
C. de Gaspé
Grande-Vallée
Dét. d'Honguedo
Pte. du Sud-Ouest
Port-Menier
Pte. de l'Ouest
Î. d'Anticosti
Dét. de Jacques-Cartier
Pte. Heath
Pte. du Sud
572
Sept-Îles
Moisie
Port-Cartier
Rivière-Pentecôte
Sainte-Anne
Clarke City
Sheldrake
Mingan
Havre-St-Pierre
Natashquan
Kegaska
Romaine
Musquaro
Olomane
Aguanus
Nabisipi
Romaine
St-Jean
Magpie
L. Magpie
1048
L. Manitou
L. Walker
Moisie
Ste-Marguerite
Manicouagan
Rés. Manicouagan
Gagnon
Petit Lac Manicouagan
Outardes
Betsiamites
Rés. Pipmuacan
L. Manouane
Manouane
Péribonca
L. Péribonca
L. Plétipi
1135
Mistassibi
Mistassini
Rés. de Caniapiscau
Caniapiscau
Delay
L. Chateauguay
Sérigny
Sable
L. Wakuach
L. Néret
L. Bermen
L. Damas
Nitchequon
L. Nichicun
L. Naococane
I. du Petit Mécatina
Harrington Harbour
Petit Mécatina
St-Augustin
Baleine

55 50 45

70 65 60 55 50

West from Greenwich

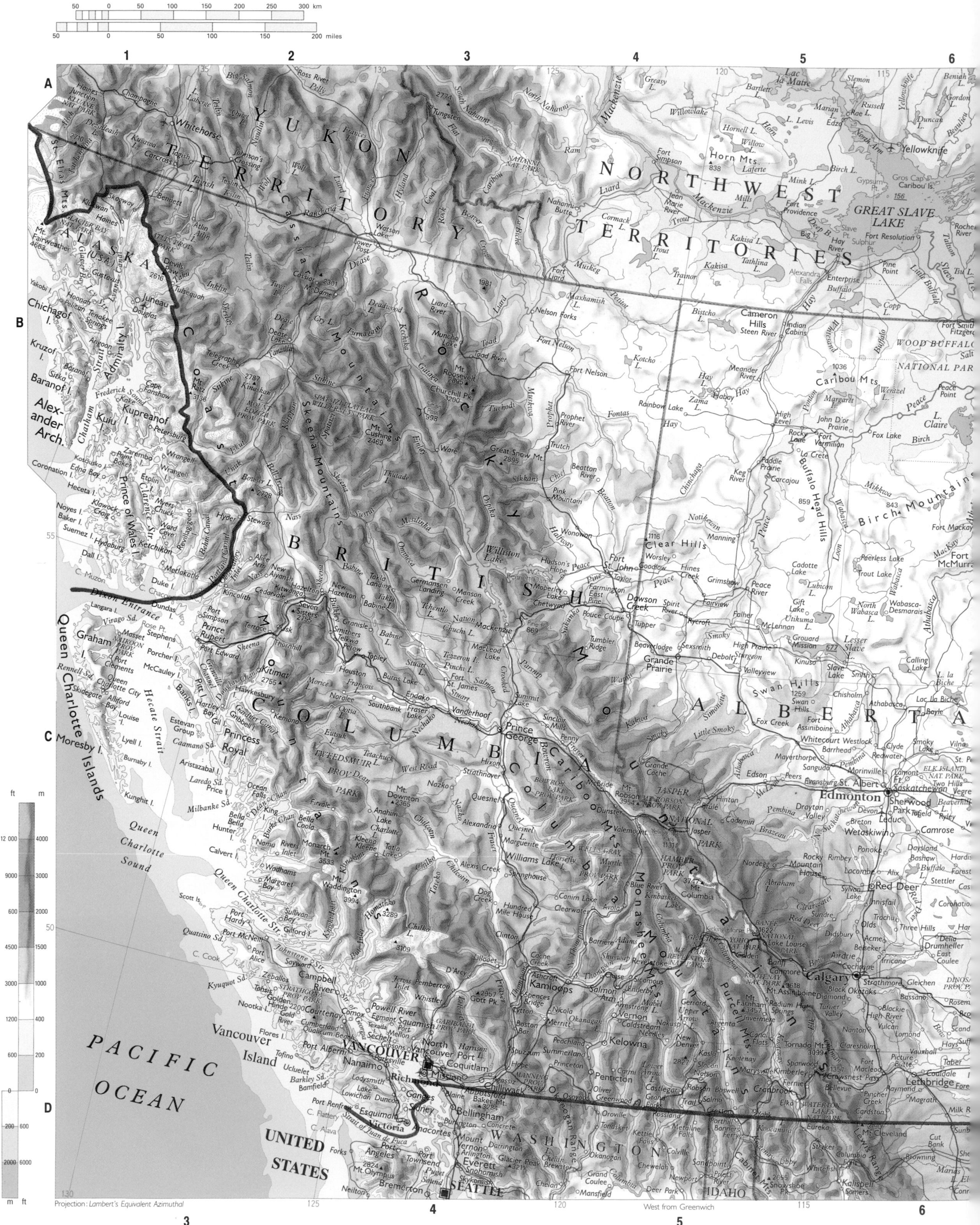

50 0 50 100 150 200 250 300 km
50 0 50 100 150 200 miles
YUKON TERRITORY
NORTHWEST TERRITORIES
BRITISH COLUMBIA
ALBERTA
ALASKA (USA)
WASHINGTON
IDAHO
UNITED STATES
PACIFIC OCEAN
GREAT SLAVE LAKE
Coast Mountains
Rocky Mountains
Skeena Mountains
Cariboo Mts
Columbia Mts
Monashee Mts
Purcell Mts
Birch Mountains
Swan Hills
Caribou Mts
Clear Hills
Horn Mts.
Cameron Hills
Buffalo Head Hills
Queen Charlotte Islands
Queen Charlotte Sound
Hecate Strait
Dixon Entrance
Vancouver Island
Alexander Arch.
Prince of Wales I.
Graham I.
Moresby I.
Whitehorse
Yellowknife
Juneau
Prince Rupert
Prince George
Kamloops
Kelowna
Vancouver
Victoria
Nanaimo
Seattle
Edmonton
Calgary
Red Deer
Lethbridge
Fort Nelson
Fort St. John
Dawson Creek
Grande Prairie
Peace River
Fort McMurray
Jasper
Banff
Hay River
Fort Simpson
Fort Providence
Fort Resolution
Projection: Lambert's Equivalent Azimuthal
West from Greenwich

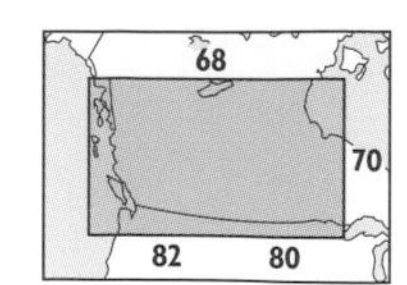
68
70
82
80

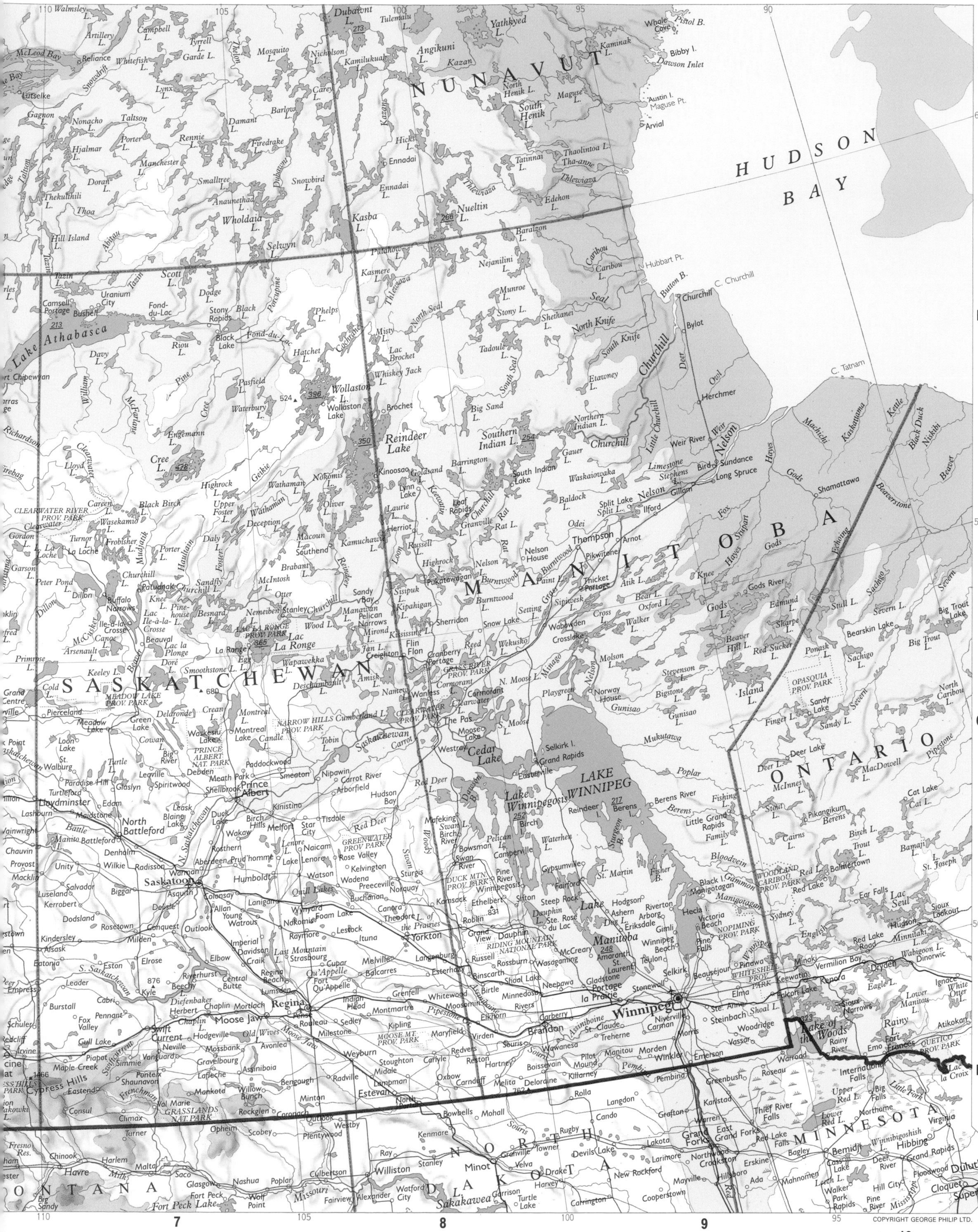

NUNAVUT

HUDSON BAY

SASKATCHEWAN

MANITOBA

ONTARIO

LAKE WINNIPEG

NORTH DAKOTA

MINNESOTA

UNITED STATES 1:12 000 000

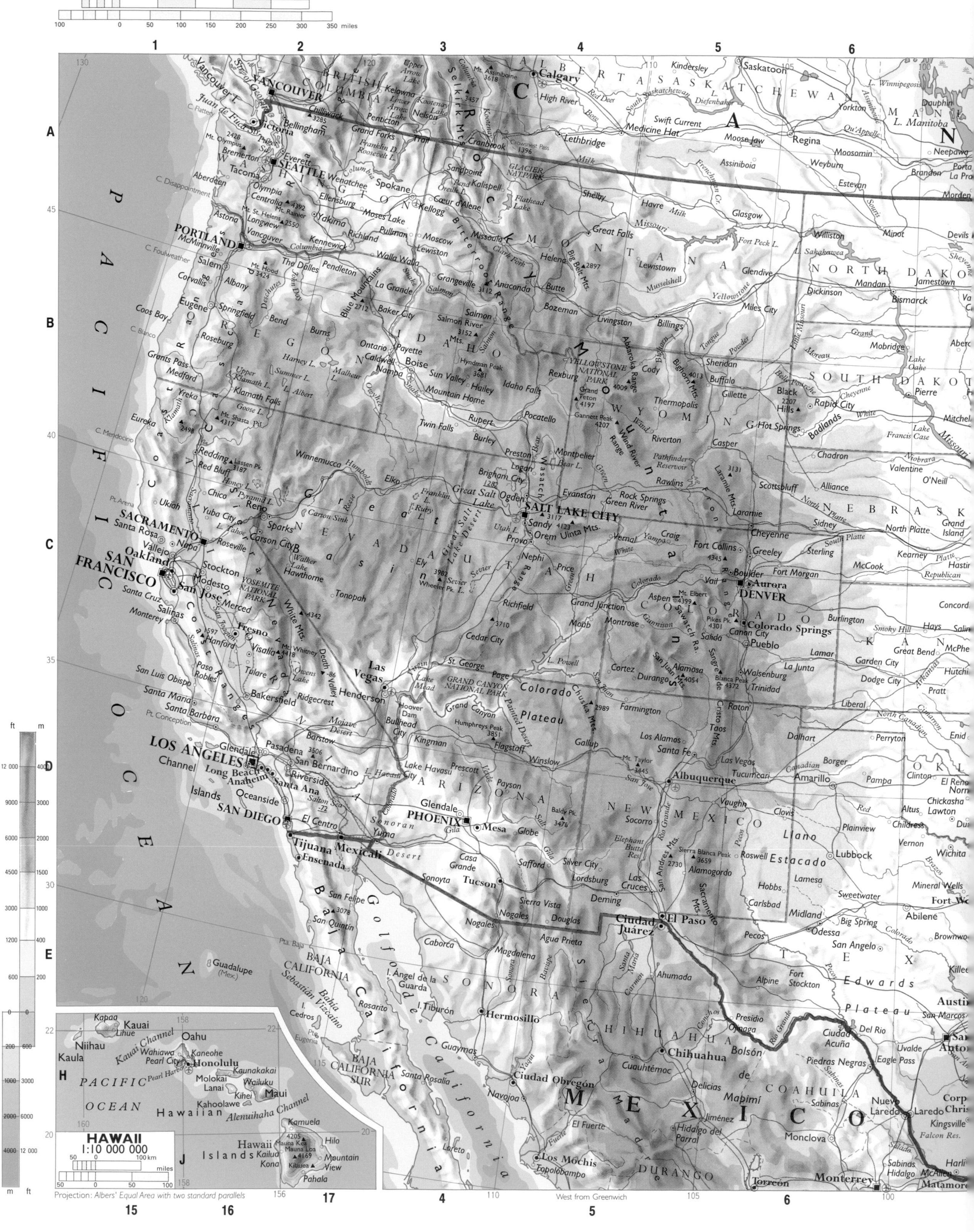

100 0 100 200 300 400 500 km
100 0 50 100 150 200 250 300 350 miles
1 2 3 4 5 6
A B C D E H J
PACIFIC OCEAN
CANADA
BRITISH COLUMBIA
ALBERTA
SASKATCHEWAN
MANITOBA
WASHINGTON
OREGON
IDAHO
MONTANA
WYOMING
NORTH DAKOTA
SOUTH DAKOTA
NEBRASKA
KANSAS
OKLAHOMA
TEXAS
NEW MEXICO
COLORADO
UTAH
NEVADA
ARIZONA
CALIFORNIA
MEXICO
BAJA CALIFORNIA
BAJA CALIFORNIA SUR
SONORA
CHIHUAHUA
COAHUILA
DURANGO
Rocky Mountains
Great Basin
Sierra Nevada
Coast Ranges
Colorado Plateau
Llano Estacado
Edwards Plateau
Gulf of California
Baja California
Sebastián Vizcaíno
Mojave Desert
Sonoran Desert
Bolsón de Mapimí
Sierra Madre
VANCOUVER
Victoria
Calgary
Saskatoon
Regina
Lethbridge
Medicine Hat
Swift Current
Moose Jaw
SEATTLE
Tacoma
Olympia
Spokane
Yakima
PORTLAND
Salem
Eugene
Boise
Missoula
Helena
Great Falls
Billings
Butte
Bozeman
Idaho Falls
Pocatello
Twin Falls
Casper
Cheyenne
Laramie
Rapid City
Pierre
Bismarck
SALT LAKE CITY
Ogden
Provo
Great Salt Lake
Reno
Carson City
Las Vegas
Henderson
SACRAMENTO
SAN FRANCISCO
Oakland
San Jose
Fresno
Bakersfield
LOS ANGELES
Long Beach
Anaheim
Santa Ana
SAN DIEGO
Tijuana
Mexicali
Ensenada
PHOENIX
Mesa
Tucson
Flagstaff
Albuquerque
Santa Fe
El Paso
Ciudad Juárez
DENVER
Aurora
Colorado Springs
Pueblo
Amarillo
Lubbock
Midland
Odessa
San Angelo
Abilene
Chihuahua
Hermosillo
Ciudad Obregón
Los Mochis
Torreón
Monterrey
Nuevo Laredo
Laredo
YELLOWSTONE NATIONAL PARK
GLACIER NATL PARK
YOSEMITE NATIONAL PARK
GRAND CANYON NATIONAL PARK
Mt. Rainier 4392
Mt. Whitney 4418
Mt. Elbert 4399
Mt. Shasta 4317
Death Valley -86
Salton Sea -72
HAWAII
1:10 000 000
Kauai
Oahu
Honolulu
Molokai
Lanai
Maui
Kahoolawe
Hawaii
Hilo
Mauna Kea
Mauna Loa
PACIFIC OCEAN
Hawaiian Islands
ft m
12 000 4000
9000 3000
6000 2000
4500 1500
3000 1000
1200 400
600 200
0 0
200 600
1000 3000
2000 6000
4000 12 000
Projection: Albers' Equal Area with two standard parallels
West from Greenwich
15 16 17 4 5 6

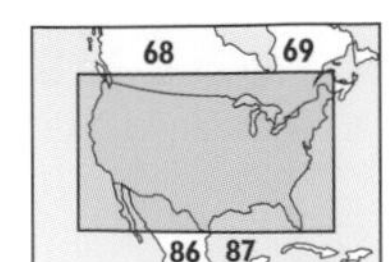
68
69
86
87

8 9 10 11 12 13

A B C D E F

CANADA

ATLANTIC OCEAN

GULF OF MEXICO

BAHAMAS

Lake Superior

Lake Michigan

Lake Huron

Lake Ontario

Lake Erie

MINNESOTA

WISCONSIN

IOWA

MISSOURI

ILLINOIS

INDIANA

OHIO

KENTUCKY

TENNESSEE

WEST VIRGINIA

PENNSYLVANIA

NEW YORK

VERMONT

NEW HAMPSHIRE

MAINE

NEW BRUNSWICK

ARKANSAS

MISSISSIPPI

ALABAMA

GEORGIA

SOUTH CAROLINA

NORTH CAROLINA

LOUISIANA

FLORIDA

MINNEAPOLIS

ST. PAUL

MILWAUKEE

CHICAGO

DETROIT

TORONTO

CLEVELAND

BUFFALO

MONTREAL

BOSTON

HARTFORD

NEW YORK

PHILADELPHIA

BALTIMORE

WASHINGTON D.C.

PITTSBURGH

COLUMBUS

INDIANAPOLIS

CINCINNATI

KANSAS CITY

ST. LOUIS

Nashville

CHARLOTTE

Memphis

ATLANTA

DALLAS

HOUSTON

NEW ORLEANS

TAMPA

MIAMI

Jacksonville

Québec

Ottawa

95 90 85 80

EASTERN UNITED STATES 1:6 000 000

50 0 50 100 150 200 km
50 0 50 100 150 miles
LAKE SUPERIOR
LAKE MICHIGAN
LAKE HURON
LAKE ERIE
LAKE ONTARIO
Georgian Bay
ONTARIO
QUEBEC
CANADA
WISCONSIN
MICHIGAN
ILLINOIS
INDIANA
OHIO
KENTUCKY
WEST VIRGINIA
VIRGINIA
PENNSYLVANIA
NEW YORK
NEW JERSEY
DELAWARE
MARYLAND
VERMONT
NEW HAMPSHIRE
MASS.
R.I.
CONN.
NEW YORK CITY
BOSTON
MONTREAL
Québec
Ottawa
TORONTO
BUFFALO
CLEVELAND
DETROIT
CHICAGO
MILWAUKEE
INDIANAPOLIS
COLUMBUS
CINCINNATI
PITTSBURGH
PHILADELPHIA
BALTIMORE
WASHINGTON D.C.
HARTFORD
Chesapeake Bay
Delaware Bay

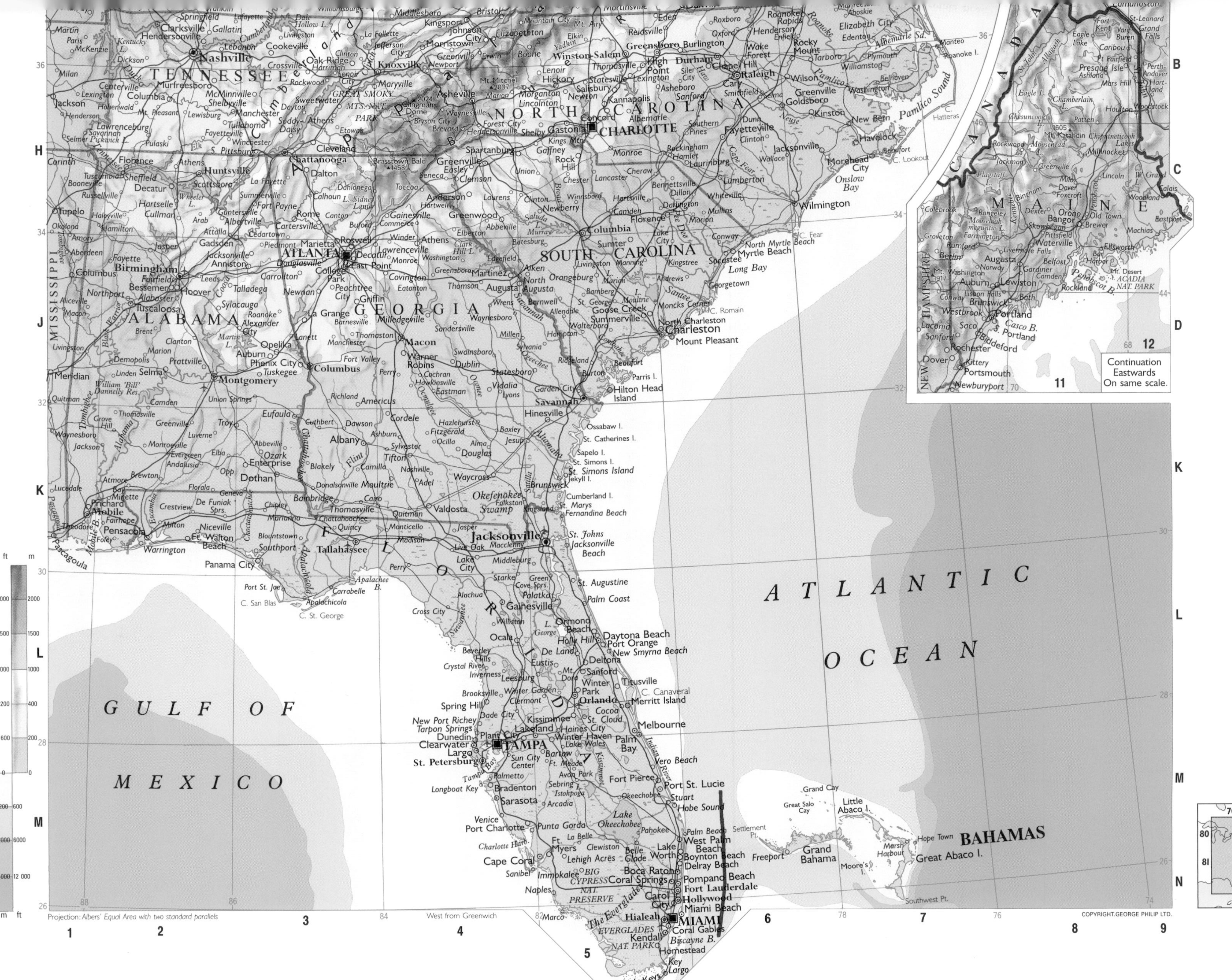
ATLANTIC OCEAN
GULF OF MEXICO
BAHAMAS
TENNESSEE
NORTH CAROLINA
SOUTH CAROLINA
GEORGIA
ALABAMA
FLORIDA
MISSISSIPPI
MAINE
NEW HAMPSHIRE
CANADA
Continuation Eastwards On same scale.
Nashville
Knoxville
Chattanooga
Birmingham
Montgomery
Mobile
Pensacola
Tallahassee
Jacksonville
Savannah
Charleston
Columbia
CHARLOTTE
ATLANTA
Augusta
Macon
Columbus
Raleigh
Durham
Greensboro
Winston-Salem
Wilmington
Orlando
TAMPA
St. Petersburg
Clearwater
Daytona Beach
Melbourne
Fort Lauderdale
MIAMI
Hialeah
Key Largo
Grand Bahama
Great Abaco I.
Freeport
Portland
Augusta
Bangor
Portsmouth
Projection: Albers' Equal Area with two standard parallels
West from Greenwich
COPYRIGHT GEORGE PHILIP LTD.

NORTH-EASTERN UNITED STATES 1:2 500 000

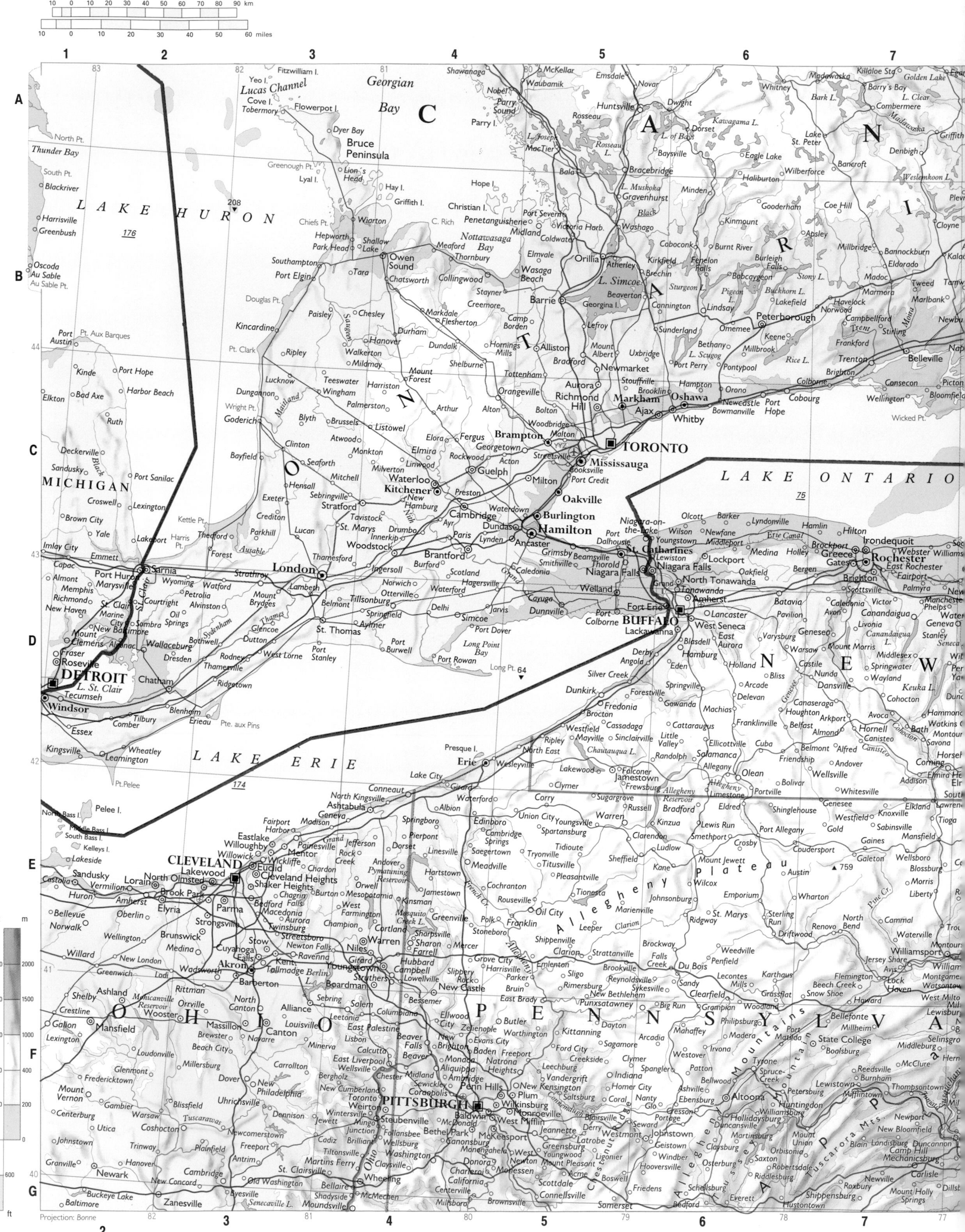
LAKE HURON
LAKE ONTARIO
LAKE ERIE
Georgian Bay
MICHIGAN
OHIO
PENNSYLVANIA
NEW YORK
ONTARIO
CANADA
DETROIT
CLEVELAND
TORONTO
BUFFALO
PITTSBURGH
Rochester
Hamilton
London
Mississauga
Projection: Bonne

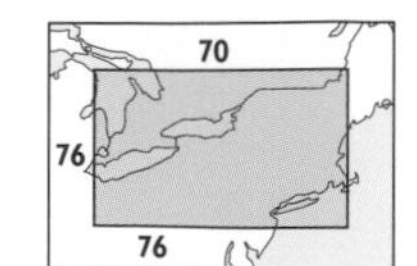

70
76
76

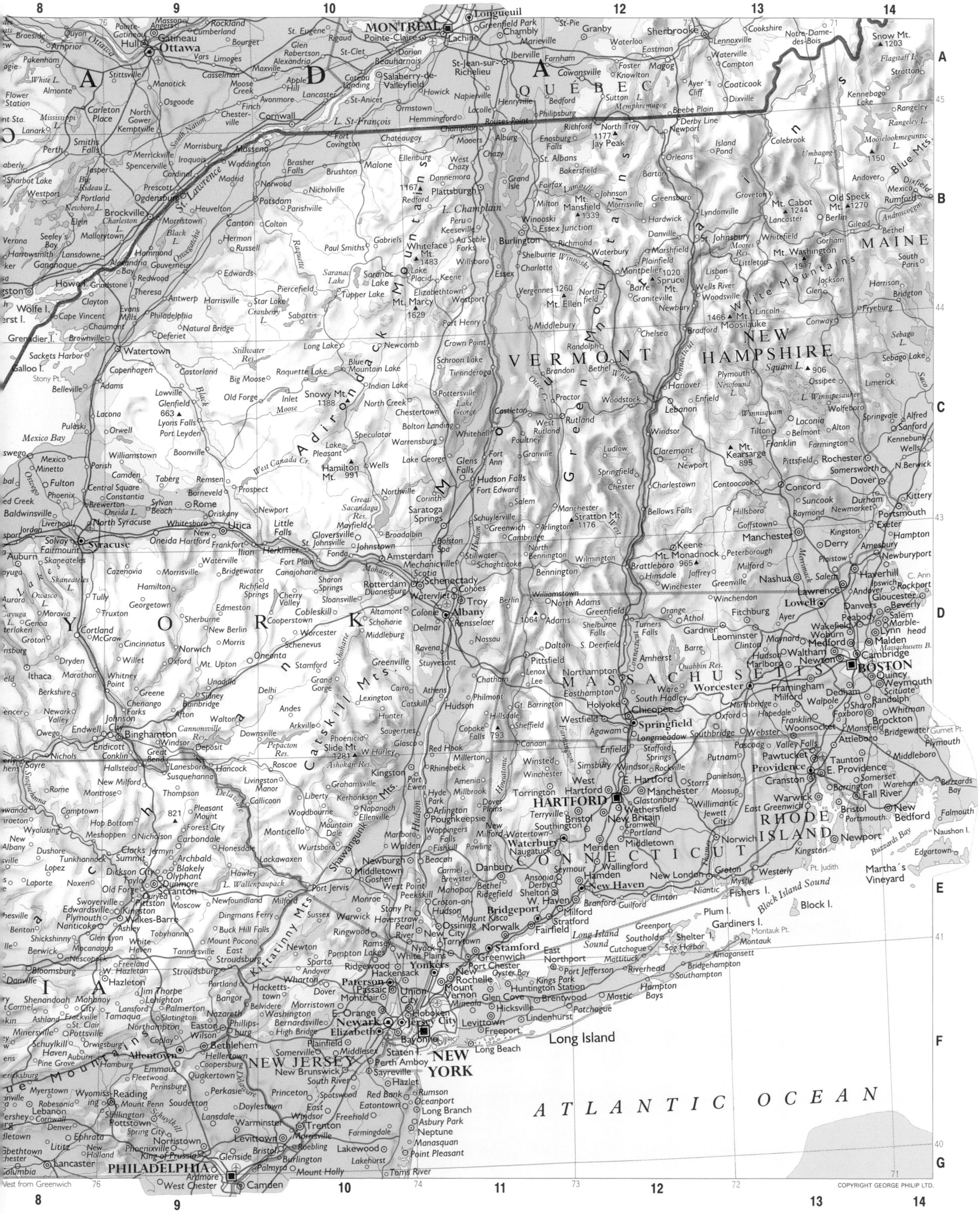

8 9 10 11 12 13 14

A B C D E F G

CANADA
QUÉBEC
NEW YORK
VERMONT
NEW HAMPSHIRE
MAINE
MASSACHUSETTS
CONNECTICUT
RHODE ISLAND
NEW JERSEY
PENNSYLVANIA

MONTREAL
Ottawa
Sherbrooke
Burlington
Syracuse
Utica
Albany
Schenectady
Binghamton
Scranton
Allentown
PHILADELPHIA
Trenton
Newark
NEW YORK
Yonkers
Stamford
Bridgeport
New Haven
HARTFORD
Springfield
Worcester
BOSTON
Providence
Manchester
Concord
Portsmouth

Adirondack Mountains
Green Mountains
White Mountains
Catskill Mts.
Kittatinny Mts.
Blue Mts.
L. Champlain
Long Island
Long Island Sound
Block Island Sound
Martha´s Vineyard
ATLANTIC OCEAN

West from Greenwich 76 74 73 72 71

MIDDLE UNITED STATES 1:6 000 000

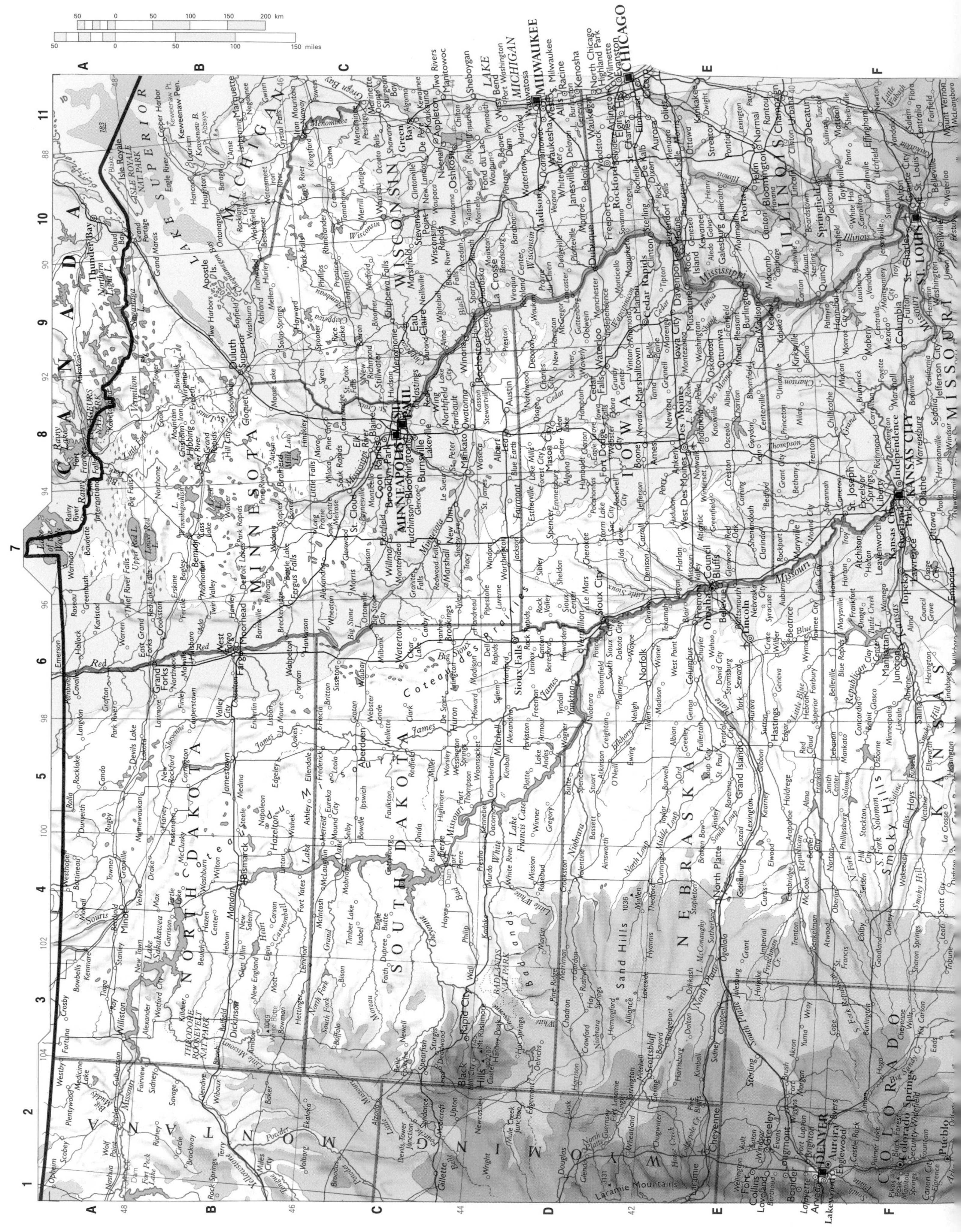

50 0 50 100 150 200 km
50 0 50 100 150 miles
CANADA
NORTH DAKOTA
SOUTH DAKOTA
NEBRASKA
KANSAS
MINNESOTA
IOWA
MISSOURI
WISCONSIN
ILLINOIS
MICHIGAN
COLORADO
WYOMING
MONTANA
LAKE SUPERIOR
LAKE MICHIGAN
MINNEAPOLIS
ST. PAUL
MILWAUKEE
CHICAGO
ST. LOUIS
KANSAS CITY
DENVER
Des Moines
Omaha
Lincoln
Sioux Falls
Bismarck
Sand Hills
Smoky Hills
Laramie Mountains

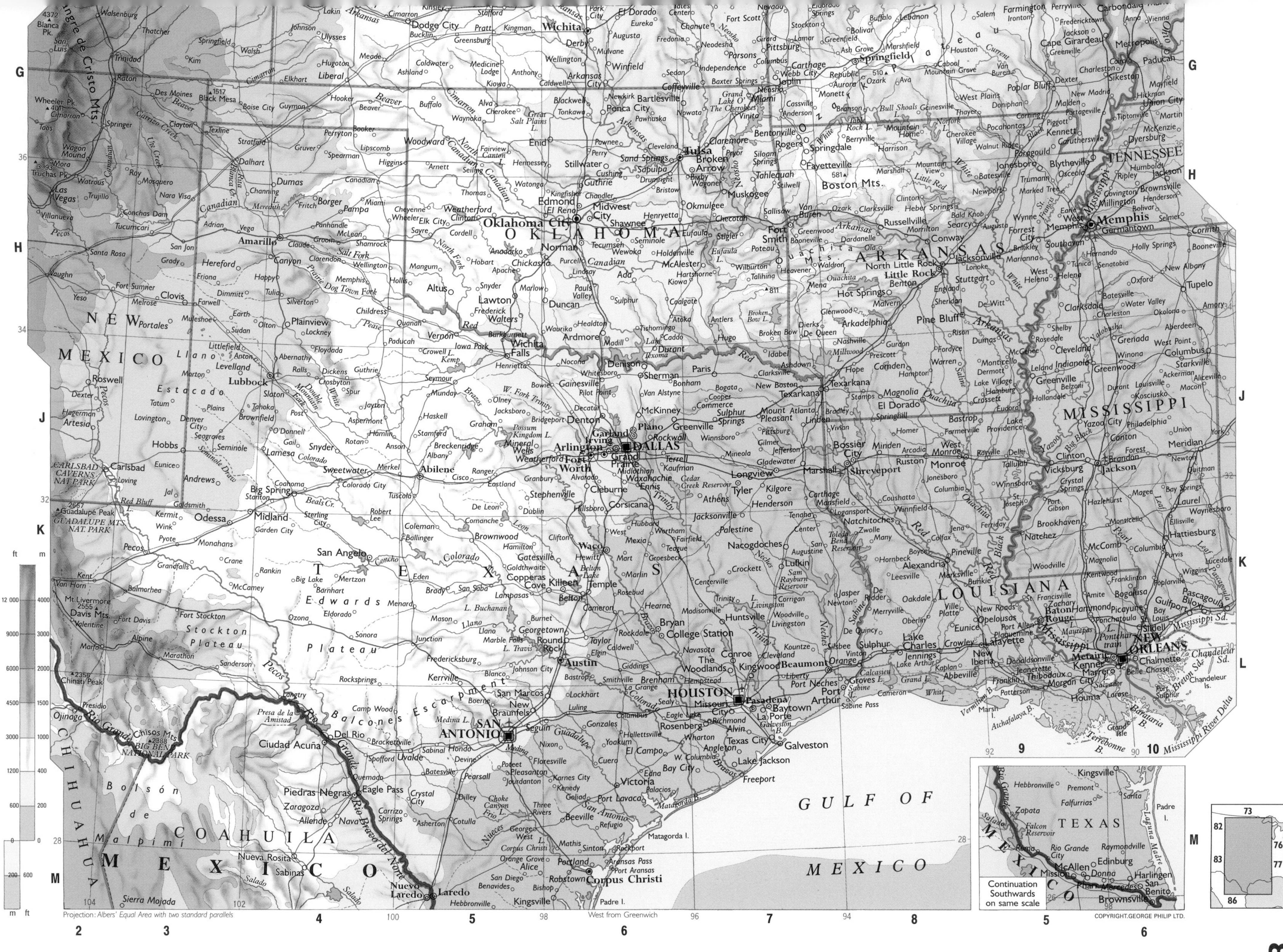
OKLAHOMA
ARKANSAS
TENNESSEE
MISSISSIPPI
LOUISIANA
TEXAS
NEW MEXICO
MEXICO
COAHUILA
CHIHUAHUA
GULF OF MEXICO
Oklahoma City
Tulsa
Wichita
Dallas
Fort Worth
Arlington
Houston
San Antonio
Austin
El Paso
Memphis
Little Rock
Shreveport
Jackson
New Orleans
Baton Rouge
Corpus Christi
Galveston
Beaumont
Lubbock
Amarillo
Abilene
Midland
Odessa
Laredo
Nuevo Laredo
Brownsville
Springfield
Sangre de Cristo Mts.
Boston Mts.
Ouachita Mts.
Ozark Plateau
Llano Estacado
Edwards Plateau
Stockton Plateau
Balcones Escarpment
Bolsón de Mapimí
CARLSBAD CAVERNS NAT. PARK
GUADALUPE MTS. NAT. PARK
BIG BEND NATIONAL PARK
Rio Grande
Red
Arkansas
Canadian
Mississippi
Brazos
Colorado
Pecos
Trinity
Sabine
Mississippi River Delta
Continuation Southwards on same scale
Projection: Albers' Equal Area with two standard parallels
West from Greenwich
COPYRIGHT GEORGE PHILIP LTD.
ft
m
12 000
9000
6000
4500
3000
1200
600
0
200
4000
3000
2000
1500
1000
400
200
600

WESTERN UNITED STATES 1:6 000 000

50 0 50 100 150 200 km
50 0 50 100 150 miles
CANADA
BRITISH COLUMBIA
ALBERTA
SASKATCHEWAN
WASHINGTON
OREGON
IDAHO
MONTANA
WYOMING
NEVADA
VANCOUVER
SEATTLE
PORTLAND
SACRAMENTO
SALT LAKE CITY
Great Salt Lake
Great Salt Lake Desert
Columbia Plateau
Snake River Plain
Salmon River Mountains
Bitterroot Range
Bighorn Mountains
Absaroka Range
Wind River Range
Uinta Mountains
Cascade Range
Coast Ranges
Blue Mountains
Harney Basin
Columbia Basin

PACIFIC
OCEAN
NEW MEXICO
ARIZONA
COLORADO
TEXAS
CHIHUAHUA
SONORA
MEXICO
BAJA CALIFORNIA
Golfo de California
Colorado Plateau
Mojave Desert
Sonoran Desert
Desierto de Altar
Sangre de Cristo Mts.
San Juan Mts.
Sacramento Mts.
Chocolate Mts.
Sierra de Juárez
Sierra de San Pedro Mártir
Channel Is.
Isla Guadalupe (Mexico)
LOS ANGELES
SAN DIEGO
PHOENIX
Tijuana
Mexicali
Tucson
Albuquerque
Santa Fe
El Paso
Ciudad Juárez
Chihuahua
Hermosillo
Las Vegas
Flagstaff
Yuma
Ensenada
Bakersfield
Fresno
San Jose
Death Valley
Grand Canyon
Rio Grande
Projection: Albers' Equal Area with two standard parallels
West from Greenwich
COPYRIGHT GEORGE PHILIP LTD.

CENTRAL AND SOUTHERN CALIFORNIA AND WESTERN WASHINGTON 1:2 500 000

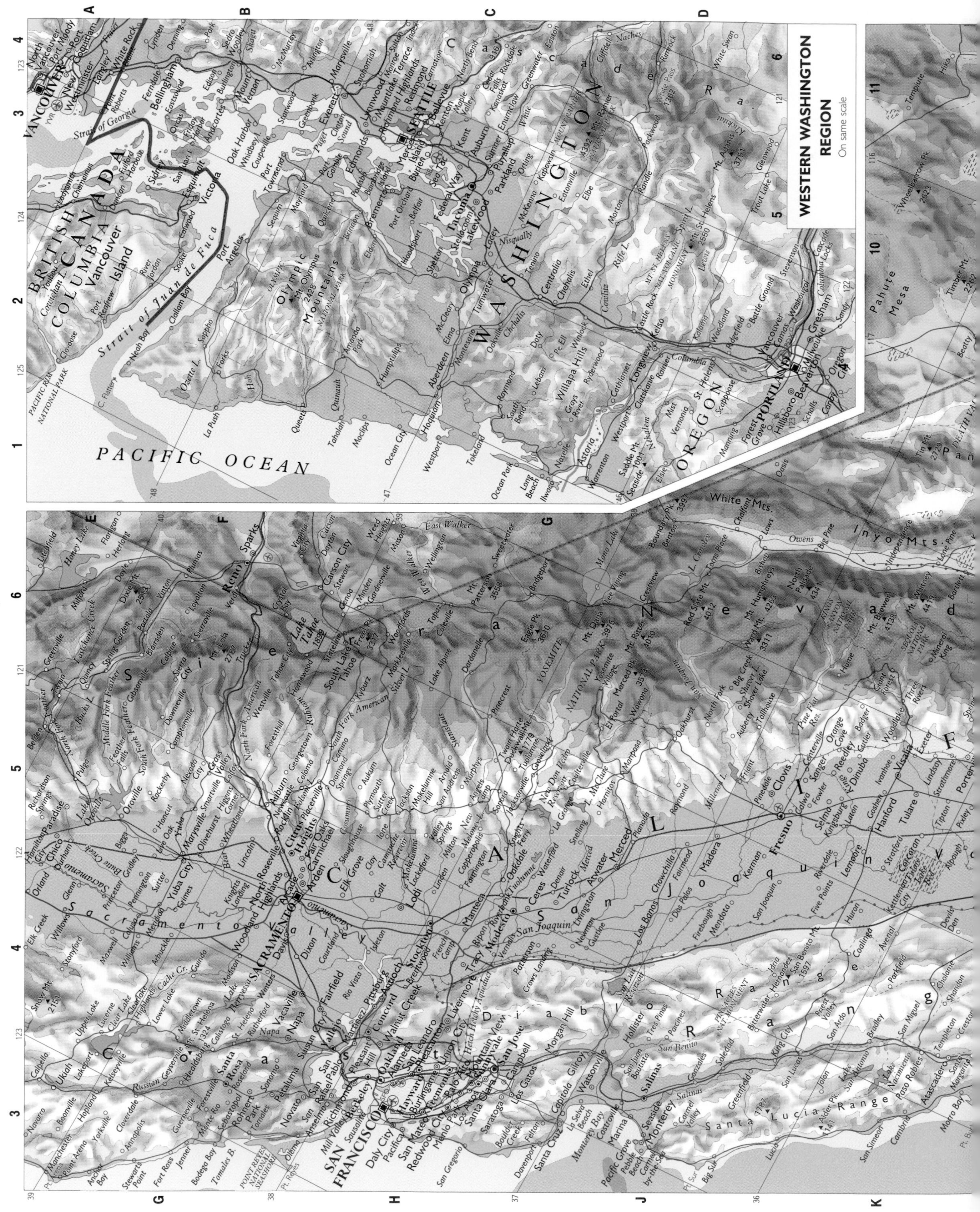

WESTERN WASHINGTON REGION
On same scale
PACIFIC OCEAN
BRITISH COLUMBIA
CANADA
WASHINGTON
OREGON
VANCOUVER
SEATTLE
Tacoma
Olympia
Vancouver Island
Strait of Juan de Fuca
Olympic Mountains
PORTLAND
SACRAMENTO
SAN FRANCISCO
Oakland
San Jose
Stockton
Modesto
Fresno
Reno
Lake Tahoe
Sierra Nevada
San Joaquin
Santa Lucia Range
Monterey
White Mts.
Inyo Mts.
Pahute Mesa

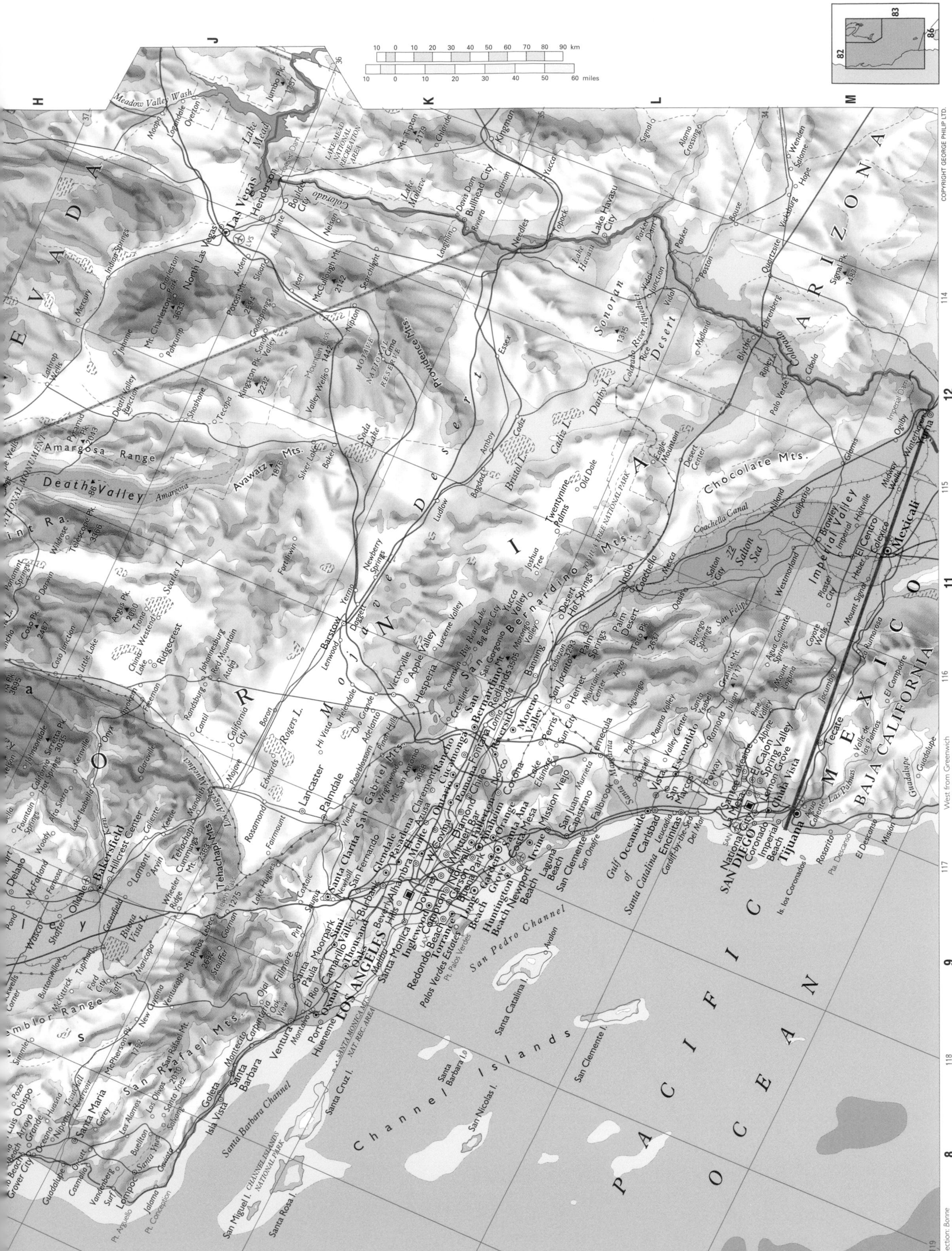

10 0 10 20 30 40 50 60 70 80 90 km

10 0 10 20 30 40 50 60 miles

Projection: Bonne

West from Greenwich

m	4000	3000	2000	1500	1000	400	200	0
ft	12 000	9000	6000	4500	3000	1200	600	0

m	0	200	2000
ft	0	600	6000

MEXICO 1:8 000 000

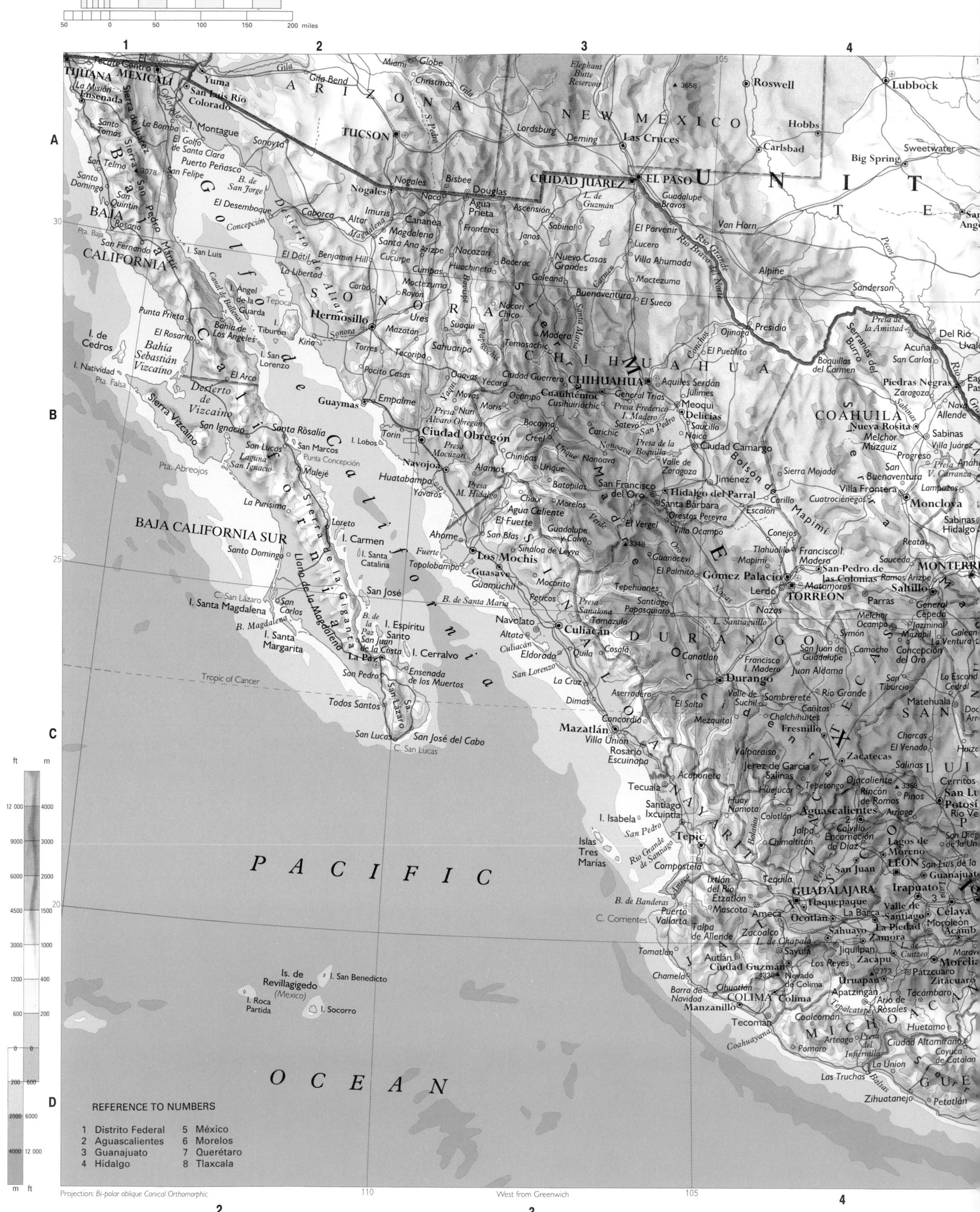
50 0 50 100 150 200 250 300 km
50 0 50 100 150 200 miles
PACIFIC
OCEAN
Golfo de California
BAJA CALIFORNIA
BAJA CALIFORNIA SUR
SONORA
CHIHUAHUA
SINALOA
DURANGO
COAHUILA
NAYARIT
ZACATECAS
JALISCO
MICHOACÁN
ARIZONA
NEW MEXICO
TIJUANA
MEXICALI
Yuma
San Luis Río Colorado
Ensenada
TUCSON
Nogales
Douglas
Agua Prieta
CIUDAD JUÁREZ
EL PASO
Las Cruces
Roswell
Lubbock
Carlsbad
Hobbs
Big Spring
Caborca
Hermosillo
Guaymas
Empalme
Ciudad Obregón
Navojoa
Huatabampo
Los Mochis
Topolobampo
Culiacán
Mazatlán
CHIHUAHUA
Cuauhtémoc
Delicias
Ciudad Camargo
Hidalgo del Parral
Ojinaga
Presidio
Gómez Palacio
TORREÓN
Durango
Monclova
Piedras Negras
Saltillo
MONTERREY
Fresnillo
Zacatecas
Tepic
Aguascalientes
GUADALAJARA
Tlaquepaque
Puerto Vallarta
Manzanillo
COLIMA
Colima
Uruapan
Morelia
Irapuato
Celaya
LEÓN
Guanajuato
San Luis Potosí
Santa Rosalía
Loreto
La Paz
Todos Santos
San José del Cabo
San Lucas
C. San Lucas
Bahía Sebastián Vizcaíno
I. de Cedros
Desierto de Vizcaíno
Sierra Madre Occidental
Tropic of Cancer
Islas Tres Marías
Is. de Revillagigedo (Mexico)
I. San Benedicto
I. Socorro
I. Roca Partida
Río Bravo del Norte
Rio Grande
Bolsón de Mapimí
L. de Chapala
Zihuatanejo
Petatlán
REFERENCE TO NUMBERS
1 Distrito Federal
2 Aguascalientes
3 Guanajuato
4 Hidalgo
5 México
6 Morelos
7 Querétaro
8 Tlaxcala
Projection: Bi-polar oblique Conical Orthomorphic
West from Greenwich
110
105

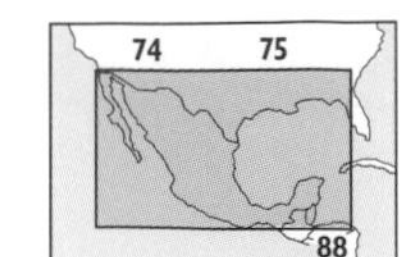
74
75
88

5 6 7 8

A B C D E

ARKANSAS
MISSISSIPPI
ALABAMA
GEORGIA
LOUISIANA
FLORIDA
TEXAS
UNITED STATES

Wichita Falls
Denison
Sherman
Paris
Hope
Camden
Greenville
Tuscaloosa
Opelika
Columbus
McRae
Texarkana
El Dorado
Phenix City
Possum Kingdom Res.
Denton
Greenville
Meridian
Selma
Montgomery
Americus
Cordele
Tifton
Monroe
Vicksburg
Troy
DALLAS
FORT WORTH
Marshall
Tallulah
Jackson
Albany
Ranger
Longview
Shreveport
Waycross
Abilene
Cleburne
Tyler
Toledo Bend Res.
Laurel
Dothan
Valdosta
Hillsboro
Corsicana
Natchez
Hattiesburg
Jim Woodruff Res.
Chattahoochee
Palestine
Nacogdoches
Flomaton
Tallahassee
Brownwood
Waco
Lufkin
Sam Rayburn Reservoir
Alexandria
McComb
Jewett
Bogalusa
MOBILE
Pensacola
Panama City
Lake City
Temple
Baton Rouge
Hammond
Biloxi
Huntsville
Gulfport
Apalachee Bay
Bryan
L. Pontchartrain
Lake Charles
C. San Blas
Navasota
Lafayette
NEW ORLEANS
Austin
Beaumont
Breton Sd.
Suwannee
Port Arthur
HOUSTON
Atchafalaya Bay
Terrebonne Bay
Mississippi River Delta
Rosenberg
Galveston
Clearwater
SAN ANTONIO
Victoria
Dilley
Nueces
Alice
Corpus Christi
Laredo
Kingsville
Nuevo Laredo
Zapata
Laguna Madre
Camargo
McAllen
Harlingen
Brownsville
Reynosa
Matamoros
Presa M. R. Gómez
China
Valle Hermoso
Santa Teresa
Montemorelos
Mendez
Laguna Madre
San Fernando
Linares
Villagrán
Hidalgo
Santander Jiménez
Zaragoza
La Pesca
Soto la Marina
Ciudad Victoria
Sierra de Tamaulipas
Llera
Aldama
Pta. Jerez
Ocampo
Ciudad Mante
Ciudad Madero
Altamira
Tampico
Ciudad de Valles
Cárdenas
Pánuco
Ozuluama
L. de Tamiahua
Tempoal
Magozal
C. Rojo
Tantoyuca
Tamazunchale
Chicontepec
Tuxpan
Zimapán
Zacualtipán
Poza Rica
Papantla
San Juan del Río
Huichapan
Nautla
Pachuca
Huauchinango
Misantla
Tulancingo
Jalapa Enríquez
Tula
Zumpango
Teziutlán
MÉXICO
ZEMPOALA
Apizaco
Tlaxcala
Coatepec
Veracruz
Toluca
Amecameca
Citlaltépetl
PUEBLA
5700
Tenango
5452
Popocatépetl
Córdoba
Alvarado
Tlacotalpan
Cuernavaca
Orizaba
San Andrés Tuxtla
PUEBLA
Tehuacán
Cosamaloapan
1879
Coatzacoalcos
Jojutla
Izúcar de Matamoros
Chilac
Ajalpan
Tres Valles
Acayucan
Minatitlán
Iguala
Chiautla
Acatlán
Huautla de Jiménez
Presa Miguel Alemán
LA VENTA
Cárdenas
San Juan Bautista Valle Nacional
Istmo de Tehuantepec
Huajuapan de León
Asunción Nochixtlán
Jesús Carranza
Presa Netzahualcóyotl
Chilapa
Silacayoapan
Chilpancingo
Tlaxiaco
Oaxaca
Tehuantepec
Tierra Colorada
Tlacolula
MONTE ALBAN
Ayutla
Ometepec
Ocotlán
San Jerónimo Táviche
Matías Romero
Ixtepec
Acapulco
Ejutla
Tehuantepec
Juchitán
Pinotepa Nacional
Miahuatlán
Jamiltepec
Tututepec
San Pedro Mixtepec
3750
Salina Cruz
Punta Maldonado
Pochutla
Puerto Escondido
Puerto Ángel
Golfo de Tehuantepec
Verde
GUERRERO
OAXACA
Sierra Madre del Sur

GULF OF MEXICO
Golfo de Campeche
Tropic of Cancer
I. Desterrada
I. Pérez (Mexico)

Canal de Yucatán
La Esperanza
CUBA
Guane
La Fé
C. San Antonio
C. Corrientes
C. Catoche
Pta. Yalkubul
Río Lagartos
Dzilam de Bravo
El Cuyo
Cancún
Puerto Juárez
Progreso
Motul
Temax
Tizimín
DZIBILCHALTUN
Izamal
Espita
Puerto Morelos
Mérida
YUCATÁN
CHICHEN ITZA
Valladolid
Cozumel
Isla Cozumel
Maxcanú
MAYAPAN
Sotuta
Ticul
UXMAL
Peto
Tekax
Tenabo
Bolonchenticul
Vigía Chico
B. de la Ascensión
Campeche
Hopelchén
Felipe Carrillo Puerto
B. del Espíritu Santo
EDZNA
Champotón
QUINTANA ROO
Chenkán
Bacalar
Banco Chinchorro
Chetumal
B. de Chetumal
Ciudad del Carmen
L. de Términos
Matamoros
Corozal
Ambergris Cay
Frontera
CAMPECHE
Paraíso
Orange Walk
Comalcalco
Palizada
Concepción
Hondo
TABASCO
Villahermosa
Balancán
Turneffe Is.
Macuspana
Tenosique
Uaxactún
San Ignacio
Belize City
BELIZE
Teapa
Belmopan
Raudales de Malpaso
Simojovel
PALENQUE
TIKAL
Benque Viejo
Dangriga
Is. de la Bahía
Copainalá
Ocosingo
Usumacinta
L. Petén Itzá
Flores
Golfo de Honduras
Roatán
Puerto Castilla
Tuxtla Gutiérrez
Chiapa de Corzo
San Cristóbal de las Casas
La Libertad
Maya Mts.
Monkey River
Trujillo
Iriona
La Independencia
San Luis
San Antonio
Comitán
Punta Gorda
Puerto Barrios
Tela
Balfate
CHIAPAS
Livingston
San Pedro Sula
Savá
Olanchito
Arriaga
Tonalá
La Concordia
Sebol
El Progreso
Arenal
GUATEMALA
L. de Izabal
HONDURAS
Sierra Madre
Cuchumatanes
Cobán
Yoro
Puerto Arista
3993
Sierra de los Cuchumatanes
Catacamas
Pijijiapan
Motozintla
Cuilco
Huehuetenango
Sierra de las Minas
Gualán
Santa Bárbara
Juticalpa
Mapastepec
4220
Zacapa
L. de Yojoa
Patuca
Huixtla
San Marcos
Totonicapán
COPÁN
Santa Rosa de Copán
Comayagua
Sololá
Jalapa
Chiquimula
Tegucigalpa
Tapachula
Antigua
Coatepeque
Mazatenango
GUATEMALA
Amatitlán
La Esperanza
La Paz
Retalhuleu
Yuscarán
Danlí

95 90 30 25 20 15

CENTRAL AMERICA AND THE WEST INDIES

1:8 000 000

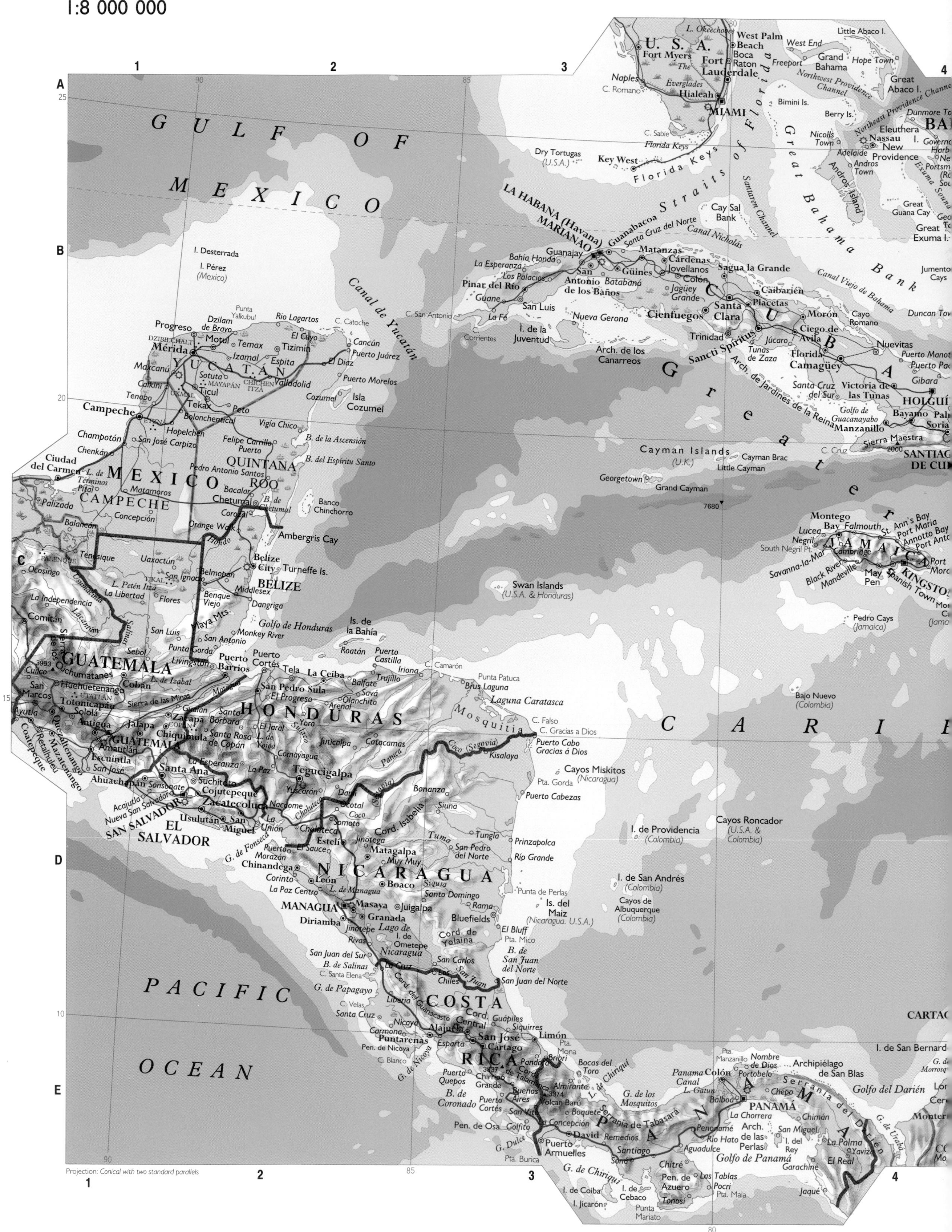

GULF OF MEXICO
PACIFIC OCEAN
C A R I B
Great Bahama Bank
Straits of Florida
Canal de Yucatán
Florida Keys
U. S. A.
Fort Myers
The Everglades
Naples
C. Romano
Hialeah
MIAMI
West Palm Beach
Boca Raton
Fort Lauderdale
L. Okeechobee
C. Sable
Key West
Dry Tortugas
(U.S.A.)
West End
Freeport
Grand Bahama
Little Abaco I.
Hope Town
Great Abaco I.
Northwest Providence Channel
Northeast Providence Channel
Bimini Is.
Berry Is.
Nicolls Town
Nassau
New Providence
Adelaide
Andros Town
Andros Island
Eleuthera
Exuma Sound
Great Guana Cay
Great Exuma I.
Jumento Cays
Duncan Town
Cay Sal Bank
Santaren Channel
Canal Nicholás
Canal Viejo de Bahama
LA HABANA (Havana)
MARIANAO
Guanabacoa
Santa Cruz del Norte
Matanzas
Cárdenas
Jovellanos
Colón
Güines
Guanajay
Bahía Honda
La Esperanza
Los Palacios
San Antonio de los Baños
Batabanó
Pinar del Río
Guane
San Luis
La Fé
C. San Antonio
C. Corrientes
I. de la Juventud
Nueva Gerona
Arch. de los Canarreos
Jagüey Grande
Sagua la Grande
Caibarién
Placetas
Santa Clara
Cienfuegos
Trinidad
Sancti Spíritus
Júcaro
Tunas de Zaza
Morón
Cayo Romano
Ciego de Avila
Florida
Camagüey
Nuevitas
Puerto Manatí
Puerto Padre
Gibara
Santa Cruz del Sur
Victoria de las Tunas
HOLGUÍN
Bayamo
Manzanillo
Golfo de Guacanayabo
Arch. de Jardines de la Reina
Sierra Maestra
2000
C. Cruz
SANTIAGO DE CUBA
C U B A
Greater
Cayman Islands
(U.K.)
Cayman Brac
Little Cayman
Georgetown
Grand Cayman
7680
Montego Bay
Falmouth
St. Ann's Bay
Port Maria
Annotto Bay
Lucea
Negril
South Negril Pt.
Savanna-la-Mar
Black River
Mandeville
May Pen
Spanish Town
KINGSTON
J A M A I C A
Pedro Cays
(Jamaica)
Swan Islands
(U.S.A. & Honduras)
Bajo Nuevo
(Colombia)
I. Desterrada
I. Pérez
(Mexico)
Punta Yalkubul
Rio Lagartos
C. Catoche
El Cuyo
Cancún
Puerto Juárez
El Diaz
Puerto Morelos
Isla Cozumel
Cozumel
Progreso
Dzilam de Bravo
DZIBILCHALTÚN
Motul
Temax
Tizimín
Izamal
Espita
Mérida
Maxcanú
Valladolid
Y U C A T Á N
CHICHEN ITZÁ
MAYAPÁN
UXMAL
Sotuta
Calkini
Ticul
Tenabo
Tekax
Peto
Campeche
Bolonchenticul
Hopelchen
Vigía Chico
Champotón
San José Carpizo
Chenkán
Felipe Carrillo Puerto
B. de la Ascensión
B. del Espíritu Santo
QUINTANA ROO
Ciudad del Carmen
L. de Términos
M E X I C O
Pedro Antonio Santos
Bacalar
Chetumal
B. de Chetumal
Banco Chinchorro
Matamoros
Pital
Palizada
CAMPECHE
Concepción
Balancán
Corozal
Orange Walk
Hondo
Ambergris Cay
PALENQUE
Tenosique
Uaxactún
Ocosingo
TIKAL
San Ignacio
L. Petén Itzá
La Libertad
Flores
Belmopan
Belize City
Turneffe Is.
BELIZE
Middlesex
Benque Viejo
Dangriga
La Independencia
Comitán
Maya Mts.
San Luis
Golfo de Honduras
Monkey River
San Antonio
Punta Gorda
Is. de la Bahía
Roatán
Sebol
Livingston
Puerto Barrios
Puerto Cortés
Tela
La Ceiba
Trujillo
Iriona
C. Camarón
Puerto Castilla
Balfate
Punta Patuca
Brus Laguna
Laguna Caratasca
Mosquitia
C. Falso
C. Gracias a Dios
Puerto Cabo Gracias á Dios
Kisalaya
GUATEMALA
3993
Cuchumatanes
Cobán
L. de Izabal
Huehuetenango
San Marcos
UTATLÁN
Totonicapán
Sololá
Sierra de las Minas
Ayutla
Coatepeque
Retalhuleu
Mazatenango
Quezaltenango
Antigua
Amatitlán
Escuintla
San José
Jalapa
Zacapa
Chiquimula
GUATEMALA
Santa Rosa de Copán
Santa Bárbara
San Pedro Sula
El Progreso
Savá
Olanchito
Arenal
H O N D U R A S
Yoro
El Jaral
L. de Yojoa
Sulaco
Juticalpa
Catacamas
Comayagua
Patuca
Coco (Segovia)
La Esperanza
La Paz
Tegucigalpa
Yuscarán
Danlí
Ahuachapán
Sonsonate
Santa Ana
Suchitoto
Cojutepeque
Acajutla
Nueva San Salvador
SAN SALVADOR
Zacatecoluca
Usulután
San Miguel
La Unión
EL SALVADOR
Nacaome
Choluteca
Ocotal
Somoto
Bonanza
Siuna
Cayos Miskitos
(Nicaragua)
Pta. Gorda
Puerto Cabezas
G. de Fonseca
Puerto Morazán
El Sauce
Estelí
Jinotega
Cord. Isabelia
Tuma
Tungla
San Pedro del Norte
Prinzapolca
Río Grande
Matagalpa
Muy Muy
Chinandega
Corinto
León
La Paz Centro
L. de Managua
N I C A R A G U A
Boaco
Siquia
Santo Domingo
Punta de Perlas
MANAGUA
Masaya
Juigalpa
Rama
Granada
Diriamba
Jinotepe
Lago de Nicaragua
Rivas
I. de Ometepe
Bluefields
Is. del Maiz
(Nicaragua. U.S.A.)
Cord. de Yolaina
El Bluff
Pta. Mico
B. de San Juan del Norte
San Juan del Sur
B. de Salinas
C. Santa Elena
La Cruz
San Carlos
Los Chiles
San Juan
San Juan del Norte
G. de Papagayo
C. Velas
Santa Cruz
Liberia
Cord. del Guanacaste
COSTA RICA
Cord. Central
Guápiles
Siquirres
Limón
Nicoya
Carmona
Alajuela
Puntarenas
Pen. de Nicoya
Esparta
San José
Cartago
Pta. Mona
C. Blanco
G. de Nicoya
Puerto Quepos
Chirripó Grande
3837
Cord. de Talamanca
Bribri
Bocas del Toro
Almirante
L. de Chiriquí
B. de Coronado
Puerto Cortés
Buenos Aires
San Vito
Volcán Barú
3374
Boquete
Concepción
David
Pen. de Osa
Golfito
G. Dulce
Puerto Armuelles
Pta. Burica
G. de Chiriquí
I. de Coiba
I. Jicarón
I. de Cebaco
Punta Mariato
G. de los Mosquitos
Serranía de Tabasará
Remedios
Santiago
Soná
Chitré
Pen. de Azuero
Tonosí
Las Tablas
Pocri
Pta. Mala
Penonomé
Río Hato
Aguadulce
Pta. Manzanillo
Nombre de Dios
Portobelo
Colón
Panama Canal
L. Gatún
Balboa
PANAMÁ
Chepo
La Chorrera
Chimán
Arch. de las Perlas
San Miguel
I. del Rey
Golfo de Panamá
Garachiné
La Palma
Yaviza
El Real
Jaqué
Archipiélago de San Blas
Serranía del Darién
Golfo del Darién
G. de Urabá
P A N A M A
I. de Providencia
(Colombia)
Cayos Roncador
(U.S.A. & Colombia)
I. de San Andrés
(Colombia)
Cayos de Albuquerque
(Colombia)
CARTAGENA
I. de San Bernardo
Projection: Conical with two standard parallels

ATLANTIC OCEAN
Tropic of Cancer
Puerto Rico Trench
Milwaukee Deep 9200
Turks & Caicos (U.K.)
Caicos Is.
Turks Is.
Great Inagua I.
Little Inagua I.
Mayaguana I.
Crooked I.
Acklins I.
Long I.
Cat I.
San Salvador I.
Conception I.
Rum Cay
Samana Cay
Plana Cays
Caicos Passage
Turks Island Passage
Crooked I. Passage
Baracoa
Paso de los Vientos (Windward Passage)
Î. de la Tortue
Monte Cristi
Cap-Haïtien
Port-de-Paix
Gonaïves
Hinche
St-Marc
HAITI
PORT-AU-PRINCE
Jérémie
Les Cayes
Massif de la Hotte
Jacmel
DOMINICAN REP.
Santiago de los Caballeros
San Francisco de Macorís
Puerto Plata
La Vega
Nagua
Samana
Sánchez
Sabana de la Mar
Hato Mayor
San Pedro de Macorís
Higüey
La Romana
SANTO DOMINGO
San Cristóbal
Baní
Barahona
Pedernales
C. Engaño
I. Saona
Isla Mona (U.S.A.)
Hispaniola
I. Beata
C. Beata
Antilles
Aguadilla
Arecibo
Bayamón
SAN JUAN
Carolina
Fajardo
Mayagüez
Ponce
Caguas
Guayama
PUERTO RICO (U.S.A.)
Virgin Is. (U.K.)
Anegada
Road Town
Tortola
Charlotte Amalie
Virgin Is. (U.S.A.)
Christiansted
Frederiksted
St. Croix
Sombrero (U.K.)
Anguilla (U.K.)
St.-Martin (Fr.)
St. Maarten (Neth.)
St.-Barthélemy (Fr.)
Saba (Neth.)
St. Eustatius (Neth.)
ST. KITTS & NEVIS
Basseterre
Nevis
Barbuda
ANTIGUA & BARBUDA
St. John's
Antigua
Redonda
Montserrat (U.K.)
Guadeloupe Passage
GUADELOUPE (Fr.)
Pointe-à-Pitre
Basse-Terre
La Désirade
Marie-Galante (Fr.)
Grand-Bourg
Dominica Passage
DOMINICA
Portsmouth
Roseau
Martinique Passage
Mt. Pelée 1397
Fort-de-France
MARTINIQUE (Fr.)
St. Lucia Channel
Castries
ST. LUCIA
Soufrière
St. Vincent Passage
ST. VINCENT & THE GRENADINES
Kingstown
BARBADOS
Bridgetown
Speightstown
GRENADINES
GRENADA
St. George's
Leeward Islands
Windward Islands
Lesser Antilles
I. de Aves (Venezuela)
CARIBBEAN SEA
Aruba (Neth.)
Curaçao
Bonaire
NETH. ANTILLES
Willemstad
Pta. Gallinas
Pen. de la Guajira
Pen. de Paraguaná
Punto Fijo
Golfo de Venezuela
Riohacha
SANTA MARTA
Ciénaga
Barranquilla
Valledupar
MARACAIBO
Lago de Maracaibo
Cabimas
Coro
FALCÓN
ZULIA
LARA
Barquisimeto
Puerto Cabello
Valencia
Maracay
CARACAS
La Guaira
I. Orchila (Ven.)
Is. Los Roques (Ven.)
Is. Las Aves (Ven.)
I. Blanquilla (Ven.)
Is. Los Hermanos (Ven.)
Is. Los Testigos (Ven.)
I. de Margarita
I. La Tortuga (Ven.)
NUEVA ESPARTA
Porlamar
Cumaná
Carúpano
Barcelona
Puerto La Cruz
SUCRE
MONAGAS
Maturín
Trinidad
Port of Spain
Tobago
Scarborough
TRINIDAD & TOBAGO
San Fernando
Dragon's Mouth
Serpent's Mouth
G. de Paria
DELTA AMACURO
Tucupita
Ciudad Guayana
Ciudad Bolívar
ANZOÁTEGUI
GUÁRICO
Calabozo
San Fernando de Apure
BARINAS
Barinas
Mérida
MÉRIDA
TRUJILLO
PORTUGUESA
Guanare
COJEDES
San Carlos
TÁCHIRA
San Cristóbal
Cúcuta
VENEZUELA
Orinoco
Apure
West from Greenwich
COPYRIGHT GEORGE PHILIP LTD

SOUTH AMERICA : Physical 1:35 000 000

NORTH ATLANTIC OCEAN
SOUTH ATLANTIC OCEAN
PACIFIC OCEAN
Caribbean Sea
Greater Antilles
Lesser Antilles
Cuba
Hispaniola
Jamaica
Puerto Rico
Turks & Caicos Is.
Guadeloupe
Dominica
Martinique
St. Lucia
St. Vincent
Barbados
Grenada
Tobago
Trinidad
I. Margarita
Yucatan Channel
Gulf of Campeche
Yucatán Peninsula
Isthmus of Tehuantepec
G. de Honduras
C. Gracias a Dios
Coco
L. Nicaragua
Guatemala Trench
Panama Canal
G. of Darién
Gulf of Panama
C. de la Aguja
Sierra Nevada de Santa Marta
L. Maracaibo
Magdalena
Cordillera Occidental
Cordillera Central
Cordillera Oriental
Cord. de Mérida
Llanos
Orinoco
Meta
Guaviare
Guiana Highlands
Mt. Roraima
Sierra Pacaraima
Serra Tumucumaque
Essequibo
Courantyne
Branco
Negro
C. Orange
Marajó I.
Amazon
Caquetá
Japurá
Putumayo
Napo
Marañón
Ucayali
Juruá
Purus
Madeira
Aripuanã
Roosevelt
Tapajós
Teles Pires
Xingu
Araguaia
Tocantins
Parnaíba
Selvas
C. de San Francisco
Cotopaxi
Chimborazo
Galapagos Is.
G. of Guayaquil
Pta. Pariñas
Pta. Negra
Huascarán
Chile Peru Trench
Madre de Dios
Guaporé
Mamoré
Arinos
Chincha Alta
L. Titicaca
Nevada Ancohuma
L. de Poopó
Bolivian Plateau
Plateau of Mato Grosso
Brazilian Highlands
Plat. of Borborema
C. de São Roque
São Francisco
Abrolhos Bank
Serra da Mantiqueira
Pico da Bandeira
C. Frio
Paraná
Paraguay
Gran Chaco
Pilcomayo
Iguaçu Falls
Uruguay
Serra do Mar
Atacama Desert
Cerro Ojos del Salado
San Félix
San Ambrosio
Salado
Salinas Grandes
Entre Ríos
Sierra de Córdoba
L. Mar Chiquita
L. dos Patos
Mt. Aconcagua
Arch. de Juan Fernández
Andes
Pampas
Río de la Plata
Colorado
Bahía Blanca
Negro
G. San Matías
Valdés Peninsula
Chile Rise
Chiloé I.
Chonos Archipelago
Chubut
Patagonia
Mte. San Valentín
Taitao Peninsula
Gulf of Penas
Gulf of San Jorge
Argentine Basin
Wellington I.
Madre de Dios I.
Magellan's Str.
West Falkland
Falkland Is.
East Falkland
Santa Inés I.
Tierra del Fuego
Staten I.
Canal Cockburn
Canal Beagle
C. Horn
South Georgia
Tropic of Cancer
Tropic of Capricorn
Equator
Projection: Lambert's Azimuthal Equal Area
West from Greenwich
CARTOGRAPHY BY PHILIP'S.

NORTH ATLANTIC OCEAN
Caribbean Sea
PACIFIC OCEAN
SOUTH ATLANTIC OCEAN
MEXICO
BELIZE
GUATEMALA
HONDURAS
EL SALVADOR
NICARAGUA
COSTA RICA
PANAMA
CUBA
BAHAMAS
HAITI
DOMINICAN REP.
JAMAICA
PUERTO RICO (U.S.A.)
COLOMBIA
VENEZUELA
GUYANA
SURINAM
FRENCH GUIANA
ECUADOR
PERU
BOLIVIA
BRAZIL
PARAGUAY
CHILE
ARGENTINA
URUGUAY
FALKLAND IS. (U.K.)
South Georgia (U.K.)
Galapagos Is. (Ecuador)
Tropic of Cancer
Equator
Tropic of Capricorn
LIMA Capital Cities
Projection: Lambert's Azimuthal Equal Area
CARTOGRAPHY BY PHILIP'S.
West from Greenwich

SOUTH AMERICA-NORTH 1:16 000 000

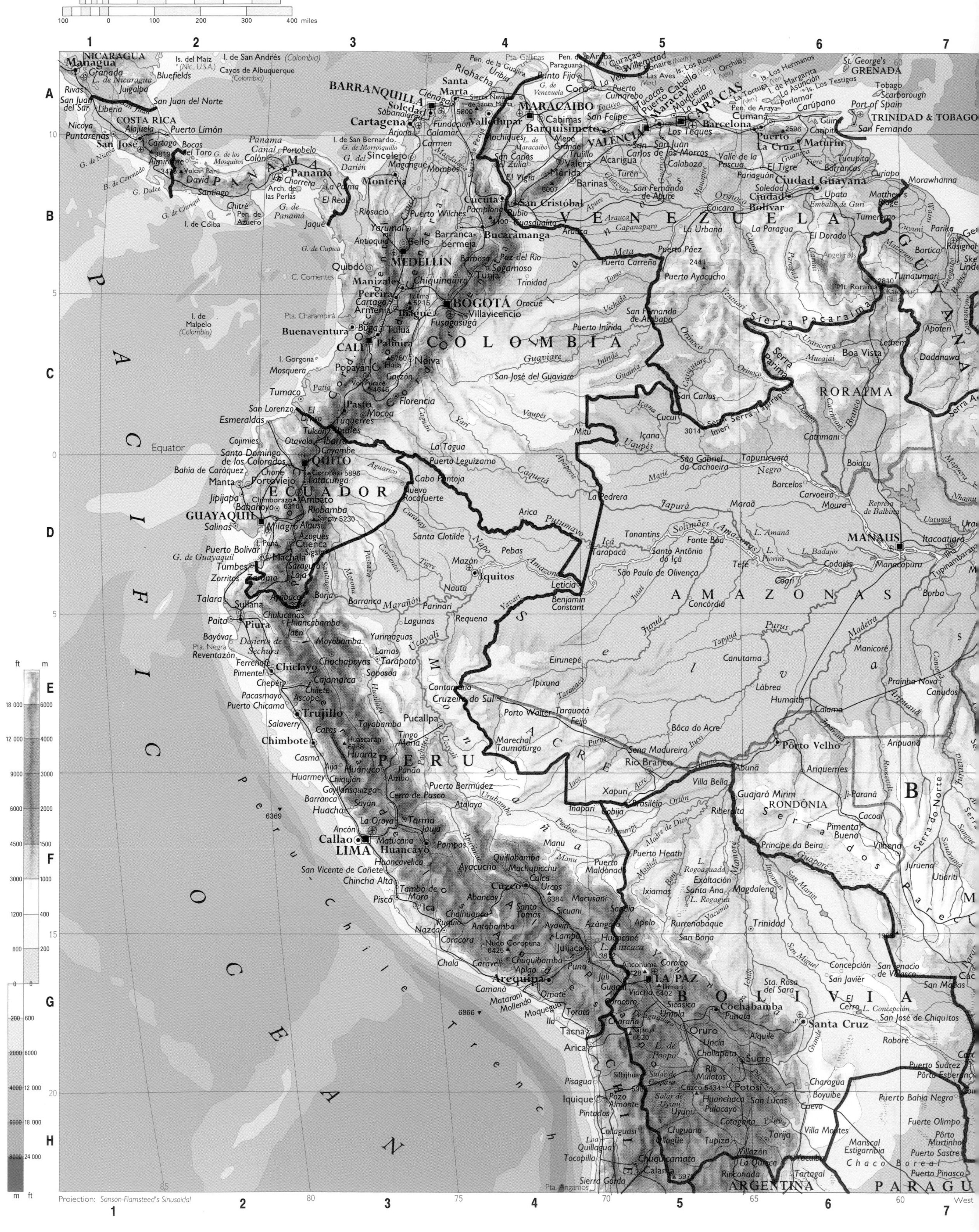

100 0 100 200 300 400 500 km
100 0 100 200 300 400 miles
1 2 3 4 5 6 7
A B C D E F G H
PACIFIC OCEAN
Peru-Chile Trench
Equator
NICARAGUA
Managua
Granada
L. de Nicaragua
Juigalpa
Bluefields
Is. del Maiz (Nic. U.S.A.)
I. de San Andrés (Colombia)
Cayos de Albuquerque (Colombia)
Rivas
San Juan del Sur
Liberia
San Juan del Norte
COSTA RICA
Nicoya
Puntarenas
Alajuela
Puerto Limón
San José
Cartago
Bocas del Toro
G. de los Mosquitos
Panama Canal
Portobelo
Colón
PANAMA
Panamá
Chorrera
David
Santiago
Chitré
I. de Coiba
Arch. de las Perlas
G. de Panamá
La Palma
El Real
Jaqué
BARRANQUILLA
Santa Marta
Ciénaga
Soledad
Cartagena
Sincelejo
Montería
Magangué
Mompós
Valledupar
Riohacha
Pen. de la Guajira
MARACAIBO
Cabimas
Barquisimeto
Punto Fijo
Coro
Aruba
Curaçao
Willemstad
Bonaire (Neth)
Puerto Cabello
Maracay
VALENCIA
CARACAS
Los Teques
Barcelona
Cumaná
Carúpano
Maturín
Puerto La Cruz
I. de Margarita
Port of Spain
TRINIDAD & TOBAGO
San Fernando
St. George's
GRENADA
Tobago
Scarborough
Mérida
Valera
Barinas
Acarigua
San Carlos
Calabozo
Valle de la Pascua
El Tigre
Ciudad Guayana
Ciudad Bolívar
Upata
Tumeremo
San Fernando de Apure
Cúcuta
San Cristóbal
Bucaramanga
Barrancabermeja
VENEZUELA
La Urbana
La Paragua
El Dorado
Angel Falls
Mt. Roraima 2810
Puerto Páez
Puerto Carreño
Puerto Ayacucho
San Fernando de Atabapo
Sierra Pacaraima
Serra Parima
GUYANA
Lethem
Boa Vista
RORAIMA
MEDELLÍN
Quibdó
Manizales
Pereira
Armenia
Ibagué
BOGOTÁ
Villavicencio
Tunja
Sogamoso
Trinidad
Buenaventura
CALI
Palmira
Tuluá
Popayán
Neiva
Pasto
Florencia
Mocoa
I. de Malpelo (Colombia)
I. Gorgona
Tumaco
COLOMBIA
Puerto Inírida
San José del Guaviare
Mitú
Esmeraldas
San Lorenzo
Ibarra
Tulcán
QUITO
Santo Domingo de los Colorados
Manta
Portoviejo
Latacunga
Ambato
Riobamba
ECUADOR
GUAYAQUIL
Salinas
Milagro
Machala
Cuenca
Loja
Tumbes
Talara
Sullana
Piura
Paita
Chiclayo
Cajamarca
Chachapoyas
Moyobamba
Tarapoto
Trujillo
Chimbote
Huaraz
Huánuco
Cerro de Pasco
Tingo María
Pucallpa
Callao
LIMA
Huancayo
Huancavelica
Ayacucho
Ica
Pisco
Nazca
Cuzco
Abancay
Machupicchu
Arequipa
Moquegua
Tacna
Arica
Juliaca
Puno
L. Titicaca
PERU
Iquitos
Nauta
Leticia
Benjamin Constant
Tabatinga
Iça
Putumayo
Amazonas
Marañón
Ucayali
Tefé
Coari
Codajás
Manacapuru
MANAUS
Itacoatiara
AMAZONAS
Purus
Juruá
Madeira
Humaitá
Porto Velho
Lábrea
Eirunepé
Cruzeiro do Sul
Tarauacá
Feijó
Sena Madureira
Rio Branco
ACRE
Xapuri
Brasiléia
Cobija
RONDÔNIA
Guajará Mirim
Ariquemes
Ji-Paraná
Vilhena
Riberalta
Puerto Heath
Puerto Maldonado
Trinidad
Santa Ana
Magdalena
Rurrenabaque
San Borja
LA PAZ
Cochabamba
Oruro
Potosí
Sucre
Santa Cruz
Uyuni
Tupiza
Tarija
Villa Montes
BOLIVIA
Concepción
San Javier
San José de Chiquitos
Roboré
Puerto Suárez
Iquique
Pisagua
Tocopilla
Calama
Chuquicamata
ARGENTINA
PARAGU
Puerto Bahía Negra
Fuerte Olimpo
Mariscal Estigarribia
Chaco Boreal
Puerto Pinasco
Projection: Sanson-Flamsteed's Sinusoidal
West

ATLANTIC
OCEAN
Equator
FRENCH GUIANA
AMAPÁ
PARÁ
MARANHÃO
PIAUÍ
CEARÁ
RIO GRANDE DO NORTE
PARAÍBA
PERNAMBUCO
ALAGOAS
SERGIPE
BAHIA
TOCANTINS
GOIÁS
MINAS GERAIS
ESPÍRITO SANTO
SÃO PAULO
RIO DE JANEIRO
DIST. FED.
MATO GROSSO
MATO GROSSO DO SUL
Planalto do Mato Grosso
Paramaribo
Nieuw Amsterdam
Moengo
Albina
St-Laurent
Iracoubo
Sinnamary
Kourou
Cayenne
Kaw
St-Georges
Oiapoque
C. Orange
Camopi
Amapá
I. de Maracá
Serra Tumucumaque
Merirumã
Serra do Navio
Macapá
I. Caviana
I. Mexiana
Mazagão
Chaves
C. Maguarinho
Soure
I. de Marajó
Curuçá
Salinópolis
Bragança
Vigia
BELÉM
Castanhal
Abaetetuba
Breves
Afuá
Gurupá
I. Grande de Gurupá
Almeirim
Prainha
Monte Alegre
Óbidos
Alenquer
Juruti
Santarém
Belterra
Aveiro
Brasília Legal
Altamira
Itaituba
Pôrto de Moz
Curralinho
Cametá
Baião
Tucuruí
Represa de Tucuruí
Amazonas (Amazon)
Xingu
Iriri
Tocantins
Araguaia
Viseu
Turiaçu
Cururupu
B. de São Marcos
São Luís
Alcântara
Pinheiro
Barreirinhas
Tutóia
Luís Correia
Camocim
Parnaíba
Rosário
Itapecuru-Mirim
Viana
Santa Inês
Bacabal
Brejo
Coroatá
Codó
Caxias
Piripiri
Piracuruca
Granja
Itapipoca
Caucaia
FORTALEZA
Sobral
Maranguape
Cascavel
Baturité
Aracati
Russas
Quixadá
Ipu
Campo Maior
Oiticica
Crateús
Senador Pompeu
Pedreiras
Açailândia
Marabá
São João do Araguaia
Imperatriz
Barra do Corda
Carajás
Serra dos Carajás
Tocantinópolis
Grajaú
Pôrto Franco
Estreito
Carolina
Colinas
Teresina
Amarante
Floriano
Valença do Piauí
Oeiras
Picos
Iguatu
Cedro
Crato
Juàzeiro do Norte
Cajàzeiras
Sousa
Patos
Caraúbas
Mossoró
Areia Branca
Macau
Ceará Mirim
C. de São Roque
Natal
Currais Novos
Canguaretama
Mamanguape
Alagoa Grande
Cabedelo
João Pessoa
Campina Grande
Caruaru
Olinda
RECIFE
Jaboatão
Vitória de Santo Antão
Garanhuns
Palmares
Palmeira dos Índios
Arapiraca
Rio Largo
Maceió
Penedo
Propriá
Capela
Aracaju
São Cristóvão
Estância
Pesqueira
Salgueiro
Ouricuri
Paulistana
Chapada do Araripe
Loreto
Nova Iorque
Uruçuí
Riachão
Araguaína
Conceição do Araguaia
Araguacema
Pedro Afonso
São João do Piauí
Santa Filomena
Caracol
Novo Remanso
Sa. Dois Irmãos
Petrolina
Juàzeiro
Nova Casa Nova
Paulo Afonso
Represa de Sobradinho
Senhor-do-Bonfim
Jacobina
Queimadas
Serrinha
Alagoinhas
Feira de Santana
Cachoeira
Santo Amaro
SALVADOR
B. de Todos os Santos
Nazaré
Valença
Castro Alves
Jequié
Itaberaba
Ibotirama
Barreiras
Barra
Xique-Xique
Mundo Novo
Parnaguá
Palmas
Pôrto Nacional
Gurupi
Peixe
Paranã
Campos Belos
São Domingos
Serra Geral de Goiás
Serra do Roncador
Serra Formosa
I. do Bananal
Santa Isabel do Morro
Bom Jesus da Lapa
Santa Maria da Vitória
Serra do Sincorá
Posse
Caetité
Carinhanha
Brumado
Vitória da Conquista
Ubaitaba
Itabuna
Ilhéus
Canavieiras
Belmonte
Pôrto Seguro
Itamaraju
Prado
Caravelas
Mucuri
Nanuque
Conceição da Barra
São Mateus
Linhares
Niquelândia
Uruaçu
Aruanã
Formosa
BRASÍLIA
Taguatinga
Luziânia
Anápolis
Goiânia
Goiás
Barra do Garças
Rondonópolis
Santo Antônio
Alto Araguaia
Jataí
Rio Verde
Quirinópolis
Itumbiara
Morrinhos
Catalão
Araguari
Uberlândia
Uberaba
Ituiutaba
Paracatu
Patos de Minas
Januária
Monte Azul
São Francisco
Janaúba
Montes Claros
Pirapora
Salinas
Araçuaí
Pedra Azul
Jequitinhonha
Teófilo Otoni
Diamantina
Governador Valadares
Nova Venécia
Colatina
Curvelo
Sete Lagoas
Ipatinga
Itabira
Caratinga
BELO HORIZONTE
Sabará
Divinópolis
Nova Lima
Ponte Nova
Ouro Prêto
Conselheiro Lafaiete
São João del Rei
Ubá
Barbacena
Juiz de Fora
Cariacica
Vitória
Vila Velha
Cachoeiro de Itapemirim
Campos
Itaperuna
Nova Friburgo
Petrópolis
Três Rios
Volta Redonda
Niterói
RIO DE JANEIRO
Cabo Frio
Campo Grande
Coxim
Paranaíba
Santa Fé do Sul
Três Lagoas
São José do Rio Prêto
Araçatuba
Catanduva
Ribeirão Preto
Franca
Araraquara
Poços de Caldas
São Carlos
Jaú
Bauru
Marília
Presidente Prudente
Presidente Epitácio
Penápolis
Assis
Botucatu
Piracicaba
Limeira
Campinas
Mogi-Mirim
Dourados
Ponta Porã
Rocas
Fernando de Noronha (Braz.)
São Paulo (Braz.)
Trindade (Braz.)
8
9
10
11
12
13
A
B
C
D
E
F
G
H
55
50
45
40
35
30
10
5
0
15
20

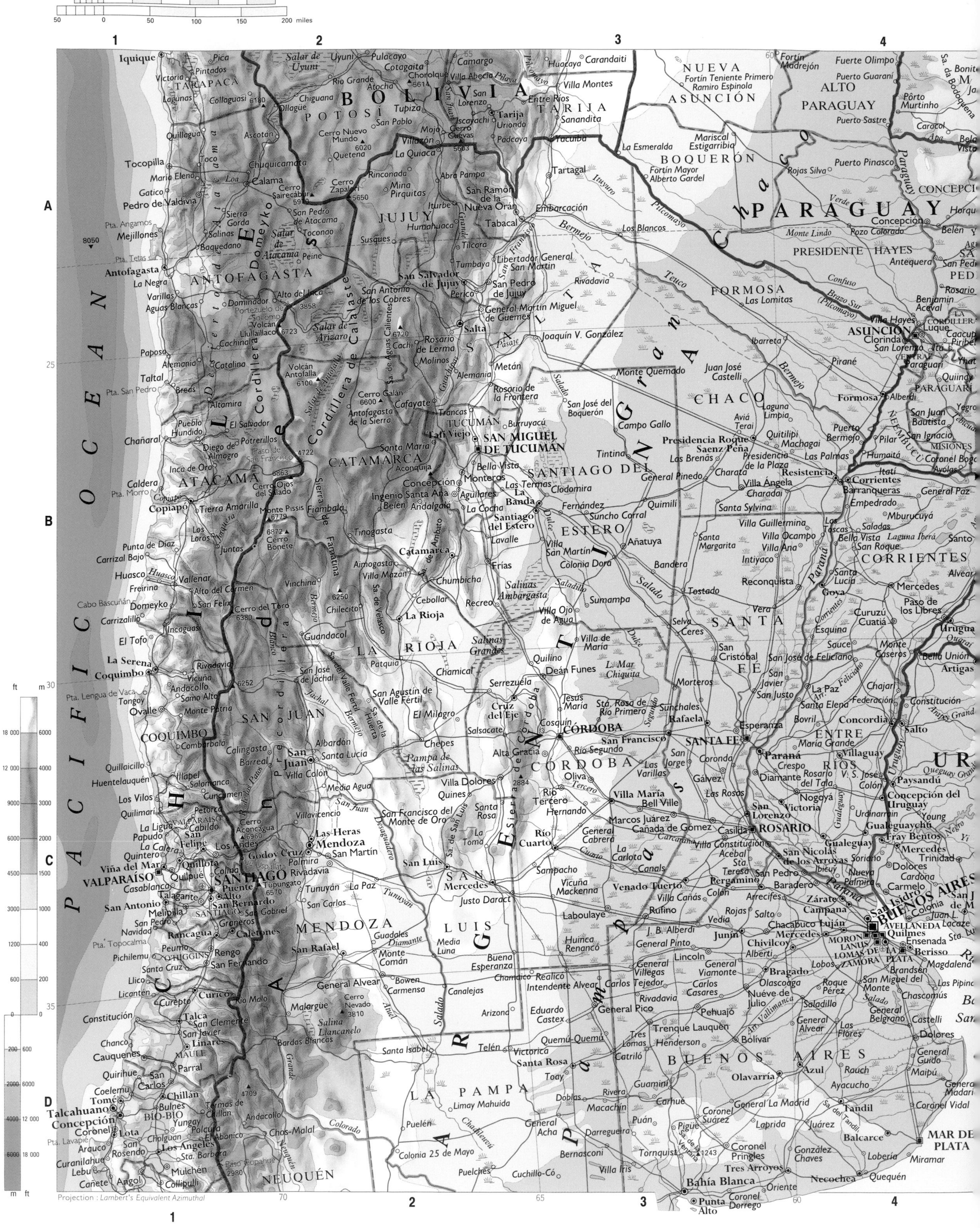

50 0 50 100 150 200 250 300 km
50 0 50 100 150 200 miles
1
2
3
4
A
B
C
D
PACIFIC OCEAN
BOLIVIA
POTOSÍ
TARIJA
NUEVA ASUNCIÓN
ALTO PARAGUAY
BOQUERÓN
PARAGUAY
PRESIDENTE HAYES
CONCEPCIÓN
Gran Chaco
TARAPACÁ
ANTOFAGASTA
ATACAMA
COQUIMBO
VALPARAÍSO
SANTIAGO
O'HIGGINS
MAULE
BÍO-BÍO
CHILE
Cordillera Domeyko
Desierto de Atacama
Cordillera de Calalaste
JUJUY
SALTA
CATAMARCA
TUCUMÁN
SANTIAGO DEL ESTERO
FORMOSA
CHACO
CORRIENTES
MISIONES
SANTA FE
ENTRE RÍOS
LA RIOJA
SAN JUAN
CÓRDOBA
SAN LUIS
MENDOZA
LA PAMPA
NEUQUÉN
BUENOS AIRES
ARGENTINA
Pampas
Andes
URUGUAY
Iquique
Pica
Pintados
Victoria
Lagunas
Collaguasi
Tocopilla
María Elena
Gatico
Pedro de Valdivia
Calama
Chuquicamata
Mejillones
Baquedano
Antofagasta
La Negra
Taltal
Chañaral
Diego de Almagro
El Salvador
Caldera
Copiapó
Tierra Amarilla
Huasco
Vallenar
Freirina
La Serena
Coquimbo
Vicuña
Andacollo
Ovalle
Tongoy
Combarbalá
Illapel
Los Vilos
Quillota
Viña del Mar
VALPARAÍSO
SANTIAGO
San Antonio
Rancagua
San Fernando
Curicó
Talca
Linares
Constitución
Cauquenes
Chillán
Talcahuano
Concepción
Coronel
Lota
Los Angeles
Angol
Cañete
Lebu
Uyuni
Salar de Uyuni
Pulacayo
Cotagaita
Atocha
Tupiza
Villazón
La Quiaca
Camargo
Tarija
Villa Montes
Yacuiba
Tartagal
Embarcación
San Ramón de la Nueva Orán
Humahuaca
Tilcara
San Salvador de Jujuy
Salta
Metán
Joaquín V. González
San Pedro de Atacama
Tocanao
Cafayate
SAN MIGUEL DE TUCUMÁN
Tafí Viejo
Santiago del Estero
La Banda
Catamarca
La Rioja
Chilecito
Belén
Tinogasta
Fiambalá
San José de Jáchal
San Juan
Mendoza
San Martín
San Rafael
Malargüe
General Alvear
San Luis
Villa Mercedes
Río Cuarto
CÓRDOBA
Villa María
Bell Ville
Cruz del Eje
Deán Funes
Jesús María
San Francisco
Rafaela
SANTA FE
Paraná
ROSARIO
San Nicolás de los Arroyos
Pergamino
Venado Tuerto
Junín
BUENOS AIRES
Quilmes
La Plata
Luján
Zárate
Campana
Chivilcoy
Bragado
Nueve de Julio
Olavarría
Azul
Tandil
Bahía Blanca
Punta Alto
Tres Arroyos
Necochea
MAR DEL PLATA
Santa Rosa
General Pico
General Acha
Presidencia Roque Sáenz Peña
Resistencia
Corrientes
Formosa
Clorinda
ASUNCIÓN
Concepción
Reconquista
Goya
Paso de los Libres
Concordia
Salto
Paysandú
Gualeguaychú
Fray Bentos
Mercedes
Villaguay
Victoria
Gualeguay
Colón
Pilcomayo
Bermejo
Salado
Río Dulce
Paraná
Uruguay
Colorado
Desaguadero
Salinas Grandes
Mar Chiquita
Laguna Iberá
Salar de Atacama
Salar de Arizaro
Ojos del Salado 6863
Llullaillaco 6723
Cerro Aconcagua 6960
Tupungato 6570
Cerro Bonete 6872
Monte Pissis 6779
Cerro Nevado 3810
Nevado del Famatina 6250
Cerro Zapaleri 5650
Projection : Lambert's Equivalent Azimuthal

BELO HORIZONTE
SÃO PAULO
RIO DE JANEIRO
CURITIBA
PÔRTO ALEGRE
Florianópolis
CAMPINAS
SANTOS
NITERÓI
CAMPOS
Vitória
Londrina
Maringá
Ponta Grossa
Joinville
Blumenau
Pelotas
Rio Grande
Caxias do Sul
B R A Z I L
PARANÁ
SANTA CATARINA
RIO GRANDE DO SUL
SÃO PAULO
RIO DE JANEIRO
MISIONES
Tropic of Capricorn
A T L A N T I C
O C E A N
West from Greenwich

94 95
100 0 100 200 300 400 500 km
100 0 100 200 300 400 miles
2 3 4 5 6 7 8
A B C D E F G H
SOUTH ATLANTIC OCEAN
PACIFIC OCEAN
Peru-Chile Trench
Tropic of Capricorn
PARAGUAY
URUGUAY
BRAZIL
CHILE
ARGENTINA
PATAGONIA
Chaco Boreal
Chaco Central
Chaco Austral
Puna de Atacama
Desierto de Atacama
Salar de Atacama
Pampas
Lagunas
Collaguasi
Chiguana
Uyuni
Tupiza
Tarija
Villa Montes
Mariscal Estigarribia
Fuerte Olimpo
Puerto Sastre
Pôrto Murtinho
Bela Vista
Pedro Juan Caballero
Ponta Porã
Dourados
Presidente Epitácio
Presidente Prudente
Panorama
Araçatuba
Penápolis
Marília
Bauru
Catanduva
Araraquara
Ribeirão Prêto
São Carlos
Jaú
Rio Claro
Piracicaba
Campinas
Jundiaí
Sorocaba
SÃO PAULO
Santos
São Bernardo do Campo
Moji das Cruzes
Taubaté
RIO DE JANEIRO
NOVA IGUAÇU
Poços de Caldas
Três Corações
São Lourenço
Londrina
Maringá
Arapongas
Apucarana
Umuarama
Cianorte
Goio-Erê
Cascavel
Guarapuava
Ponta Grossa
CURITIBA
Paranaguá
Registro
Foz do Iguaçu
Ciudad del Este
Asunción
Concepción
Horqueta
Villa Hayes
Coronel Oviedo
Villarrica
Paraguarí
Pilar
San Pedro del Paraná
Encarnación
Posadas
Resistencia
Corrientes
Formosa
Presidencia Roque Saenz Peña
Chuquicamata
Calama
Tocopilla
Mejillones
Antofagasta
Taltal
Chañaral
Caldera
Copiapó
Vallenar
Huasco
La Serena
Coquimbo
Ovalle
Illapel
Los Vilos
Viña del Mar
Valparaíso
SANTIAGO
San Antonio
San Bernardo
Rancagua
Pichilemu
Curicó
Talca
Linares
Constitución
Cauquenes
Chillán
Talcahuano
Concepción
Coronel
Lota
Los Angeles
Temuco
Valdivia
Osorno
Puerto Montt
Ancud
Castro
Quellón
I. de Chiloé
Is. Guaitecas
Arch. de los Chonos
Puerto Aisén
Coihaique
Pen. de Taitao
Pen. Tres Montes
G. de Penas
Cochrane
I. Campana
I. Wellington
I. Mornington
I. Madre de Dios
I. Hanover
Puerto Natales
Arch. Reina Adelaida
Estrecho de Magallanes
Punta Arenas
Porvenir
I. Desolación
I. Santa Inés
Tierra del Fuego
Isla Grande de Tierra del Fuego
Ushuaia
I. Navarino
I. Hoste
Is. Wollaston
C. de Hornos (C. Horn)
I. de los Estados (Staten I.)
Río Grande
San Sebastián
Río Gallegos
C. Virgenes
Puerto Santa Cruz
Puerto San Julián
Puerto Deseado
Comodoro Rivadavia
Golfo San Jorge
Sarmiento
Perito Moreno
Camarones
Rawson
Trelew
Puerto Madryn
Pen. Valdés
Golfo San Matías
Viedma
Carmen de Patagones
San Antonio Oeste
Esquel
San Carlos de Bariloche
Neuquén
Zapala
General Roca
Bahía Blanca
Punta Alta
Tres Arroyos
Necochea
Mar del Plata
Tandil
Azul
Olavarría
La Plata
BUENOS AIRES
Avellaneda
Mercedes
Junín
Pergamino
San Nicolás
ROSARIO
Santa Fe
Paraná
Rafaela
Concordia
Concepción del Uruguay
Gualeguaychú
Río Cuarto
Villa María
CÓRDOBA
San Luis
Mendoza
San Rafael
San Juan
La Rioja
Catamarca
Santiago del Estero
San Miguel de Tucumán
Salta
San Salvador de Jujuy
Santa Rosa
Paysandú
Salto
Rivera
Tacuarembó
Mercedes
Fray Bentos
Durazno
Florida
Minas
Maldonado
Rocha
MONTEVIDEO
San José de Mayo
Río de la Plata
Treinta y Tres
Melo
Pelotas
Rio Grande
Bagé
Santana do Livramento
Alegrete
Uruguaiana
Santa Maria
Cachoeira do Sul
PORTO ALEGRE
Canoas
Novo Hamburgo
São Leopoldo
Caxias do Sul
Passo Fundo
Santo Ângelo
Erechim
Chapecó
Joaçaba
Lajes
Criciúma
Tubarão
Laguna
Florianópolis
Blumenau
Itajaí
Joinville
São Francisco do Sul
RIO GRANDE DO SUL
SANTA CATARINA
PARANÁ
SÃO PAULO
Lagoa dos Patos
L. Mirim
L. da Mangueira
Santa Vitória do Palmar
FALKLAND ISLANDS (U.K.) (ISLAS MALVINAS)
West Falkland
East Falkland
Stanley
Port Darwin
South Georgia (U.K.)
Cerro Aconcagua 6960
5830
Projection: Sanson-Flamsteed's Sinusoidal
60 West from Greenwich 55
1 2 3 4 5 6 7 8 9

INDEX

The index contains the names of all the principal places and features shown on the World Maps. Each name is followed by an additional entry in italics giving the country or region within which it is located. The alphabetical order of names composed of two or more words is governed primarily by the first word and then by the second. This is an example of the rule:

Mīr Kūh, *Iran*	**45 E8**	26 22N	58 55 E
Mīr Shahdād, *Iran*	**45 E8**	26 15N	58 29 E
Mira, *Italy*	**20 B5**	45 26N	12 8 E
Mira por vos Cay, *Bahamas*	**89 B5**	22 9N	74 30W
Miraj, *India*	**40 L9**	16 50N	74 45 E

Physical features composed of a proper name (Erie) and a description (Lake) are positioned alphabetically by the proper name. The description is positioned after the proper name and is usually abbreviated:

Erie, L., *N. Amer.*	**78 D4**	42 15N	81 0W

Where a description forms part of a settlement or administrative name however, it is always written in full and put in its true alphabetic position:

Mount Morris, *U.S.A.*	**78 D7**	42 44N	77 52W

Names beginning with M' and Mc are indexed as if they were spelled Mac. Names beginning St. are alphabetised under Saint, but Sankt, Sint, Sant', Santa and San are all spelt in full and are alphabetised accordingly. If the same place name occurs two or more times in the index and all are in the same country, each is followed by the name of the administrative subdivision in which it is located. The names are placed in the alphabetical order of the subdivisions. For example:

Jackson, *Ky., U.S.A.*	**76 G4**	37 33N	83 23W
Jackson, *Mich., U.S.A.*	**76 D3**	42 15N	84 24W
Jackson, *Minn., U.S.A.*	**80 D7**	43 37N	95 1W

The number in bold type which follows each name in the index refers to the number of the map page where that feature or place will be found. This is usually the largest scale at which the place or feature appears.

The letter and figure which are in bold type immediately after the page number give the grid square on the map page, within which the feature is situated. The letter represents the latitude and the figure the longitude.

In some cases the feature itself may fall within the specified square, while the name is outside. This is usually the case only with features which are larger than a grid square.

For a more precise location the geographical coordinates which follow the letter/figure references give the latitude and the longitude of each place. The first set of figures represent the latitude which is the distance north or south of the Equator measured as an angle at the centre of the earth. The Equator is latitude 0°, the North Pole is 90°N, and the South Pole 90°S.

The second set of figures represent the longitude, which is the distance East or West of the prime meridian, which runs through Greenwich, England. Longitude is also measured as an angle at the centre of the earth and is given East or West of the prime meridian, from 0° to 180° in either direction.

The unit of measurement for latitude and longitude is the degree, which is subdivided into 60 minutes. Each index entry states the position of a place in degrees and minutes, a space being left between the degrees and the minutes.

The latitude is followed by N(orth) or S(outh) and the longitude by E(ast) or W(est).

Rivers are indexed to their mouths or confluences, and carry the symbol → after their names. A solid square ■ follows the name of a country, while an open square □ refers to a first order administrative area.

Abbreviations used in the index

A.C.T. – Australian Capital Territory
Afghan. – Afghanistan
Ala. – Alabama
Alta. – Alberta
Amer. – America(n)
Arch. – Archipelago
Ariz. – Arizona
Ark. – Arkansas
Atl. Oc. – Atlantic Ocean
B. – Baie, Bahía, Bay, Bucht, Bugt
B.C. – British Columbia
Bangla. – Bangladesh
Barr. – Barrage
Bos.-H. – Bosnia-Herzegovina
C. – Cabo, Cap, Cape, Coast
C.A.R. – Central African Republic
C. Prov. – Cape Province
Calif. – California
Cent. – Central
Chan. – Channel
Colo. – Colorado
Conn. – Connecticut
Cord. – Cordillera
Cr. – Creek
Czech. – Czech Republic
D.C. – District of Columbia
Del. – Delaware
Dep. – Dependency
Des. – Desert
Dist. – District
Dj. – Djebel
Domin. – Dominica
Dom. Rep. – Dominican Republic
E. – East
E. Salv. – El Salvador
Eq. Guin. – Equatorial Guinea
Fla. – Florida
Falk. Is. – Falkland Is.
G. – Golfe, Golfo, Gulf, Guba, Gebel
Ga. – Georgia
Gt. – Great, Greater
Guinea-Biss. – Guinea-Bissau
H.K. – Hong Kong
H.P. – Himachal Pradesh
Hants. – Hampshire
Harb. – Harbor, Harbour
Hd. – Head
Hts. – Heights
I.(s). – Île, Ilha, Insel, Isla, Island, Isle
Ill. – Illinois
Ind. – Indiana
Ind. Oc. – Indian Ocean
Ivory C. – Ivory Coast
J. – Jabal, Jebel, Jazira
Junc. – Junction
K. – Kap, Kapp
Kans. – Kansas
Kep. – Kepulauan
Ky. – Kentucky
L. – Lac, Lacul, Lago, Lagoa, Lake, Limni, Loch, Lough
La. – Louisiana
Liech. – Liechtenstein
Lux. – Luxembourg
Mad. P. – Madhya Pradesh
Madag. – Madagascar
Man. – Manitoba
Mass. – Massachusetts
Md. – Maryland
Me. – Maine
Medit. S. – Mediterranean Sea
Mich. – Michigan
Minn. – Minnesota
Miss. – Mississippi
Mo. – Missouri
Mont. – Montana
Mozam. – Mozambique
Mt.(e) – Mont, Monte, Monti, Montaña, Mountain
N. – Nord, Norte, North, Northern, Nouveau
N.B. – New Brunswick
N.C. – North Carolina
N. Cal. – New Caledonia
N. Dak. – North Dakota
N.H. – New Hampshire
N.I. – North Island
N.J. – New Jersey
N. Mex. – New Mexico
N.S. – Nova Scotia
N.S.W. – New South Wales
N.W.T. – North West Territory
N.Y. – New York
N.Z. – New Zealand
Nebr. – Nebraska
Neths. – Netherlands
Nev. – Nevada
Nfld. – Newfoundland
Nic. – Nicaragua
O. – Oued, Ouadi
Occ. – Occidentale
Okla. – Oklahoma
Ont. – Ontario
Or. – Orientale
Oreg. – Oregon
Os. – Ostrov
Oz. – Ozero
P. – Pass, Passo, Pasul, Pulau
P.E.I. – Prince Edward Island
Pa. – Pennsylvania
Pac. Oc. – Pacific Ocean
Papua N.G. – Papua New Guinea
Pass. – Passage
Pen. – Peninsula, Péninsule
Phil. – Philippines
Pk. – Park, Peak
Plat. – Plateau
Prov. – Province, Provincial
Pt. – Point
Pta. – Ponta, Punta
Pte. – Pointe
Qué. – Québec
Queens. – Queensland
R. – Rio, River
R.I. – Rhode Island
Ra.(s). – Range(s)
Raj. – Rajasthan
Reg. – Region
Rep. – Republic
Res. – Reserve, Reservoir
S. – San, South, Sea
Si. Arabia – Saudi Arabia
S.C. – South Carolina
S. Dak. – South Dakota
S.I. – South Island
S. Leone – Sierra Leone
Sa. – Serra, Sierra
Sask. – Saskatchewan
Scot. – Scotland
Sd. – Sound
Sev. – Severnaya
Sib. – Siberia
Sprs. – Springs
St. – Saint
Sta. – Santa, Station
Ste. – Sainte
Sto. – Santo
Str. – Strait, Stretto
Switz. – Switzerland
Tas. – Tasmania
Tenn. – Tennessee
Tex. – Texas
Tg. – Tanjung
Trin. & Tob. – Trinidad & Tobago
U.A.E. – United Arab Emirates
U.K. – United Kingdom
U.S.A. – United States of America
Ut. P. – Uttar Pradesh
Va. – Virginia
Vdkhr. – Vodokhranilishche
Vf. – Vírful
Vic. – Victoria
Vol. – Volcano
Vt. – Vermont
W. – Wadi, West
W. Va. – West Virginia
Wash. – Washington
Wis. – Wisconsin
Wlkp. – Wielkopolski
Wyo. – Wyoming
Yorks. – Yorkshire
Yug. – Yugoslavia

A

A Coruña, Spain 19 A1 43 20N 8 25W
A Estrada, Spain 19 A1 42 43N 8 27W
A Fonsagrada, Spain 19 A2 43 8N 7 4W
Aachen, Germany 16 C4 50 45N 6 6 E
Aalborg = Ålborg, Denmark 9 H13 57 2N 9 54 E
Aalen, Germany 16 D6 48 51N 10 6 E
Aalst, Belgium 15 D4 50 56N 4 2 E
Aalten, Neths. 15 C6 51 56N 6 35 E
Aalter, Belgium 15 C3 51 5N 3 28 E
Äänekoski, Finland 9 E21 62 36N 25 44 E
Aarau, Switz. 18 C8 47 23N 8 4 E
Aare →, Switz. 18 C8 47 33N 8 14 E
Aarhus = Århus, Denmark 9 H14 56 8N 10 11 E
Aarschot, Belgium 15 D4 50 59N 4 49 E
Aba,
Dem. Rep. of the Congo 54 B3 3 58N 30 17 E
Aba, Nigeria 50 G7 5 10N 7 19 E
Ābādān, Iran 45 D6 30 22N 48 20 E
Ābādeh, Iran 45 D7 31 8N 52 40 E
Abadla, Algeria 50 B5 31 2N 2 45W
Abaetetuba, Brazil 93 D9 1 40S 48 50W
Abagnar Qi, China 34 C9 43 52N 116 2 E
Abai, Paraguay 95 B4 25 58S 55 54W
Abakan, Russia 27 D10 53 40N 91 10 E
Abancay, Peru 92 F4 13 35S 72 55W
Abariringa, Kiribati 64 H10 2 50S 171 40W
Abarqū, Iran 45 D7 31 10N 53 20 E
Abashiri, Japan 30 C12 44 0N 144 15 E
Abashiri-Wan, Japan 30 C12 44 0N 144 30 E
Abay, Kazakstan 26 E8 49 38N 72 53 E
Abaya, L., Ethiopia 46 F2 6 30N 37 50 E
Abaza, Russia 26 D10 52 39N 90 6 E
'Abbāsābād, Iran 45 C8 33 34N 58 23 E
Abbay = Nîl el Azraq →,
Sudan 51 E12 15 38N 32 31 E
Abbaye, Pt., U.S.A. 76 B1 46 58N 88 8W
Abbé, L., Ethiopia 46 E3 11 8N 41 47 E
Abbeville, France 18 A4 50 6N 1 49 E
Abbeville, Ala., U.S.A. 77 K3 31 34N 85 15W
Abbeville, La., U.S.A. 81 L8 29 58N 92 8W
Abbeville, S.C., U.S.A. 77 H4 34 11N 82 23W
Abbot Ice Shelf, Antarctica 5 D16 73 0S 92 0W
Abbottabad, Pakistan 42 B5 34 10N 73 15 E
Abd al Kūrī, Ind. Oc. 46 E5 12 5N 52 20 E
Ābdar, Iran 45 D7 30 16N 55 19 E
'Abdolābād, Iran 45 C8 34 12N 56 30 E
Abdulpur, Bangla. 43 G13 24 15N 88 59 E
Abéché, Chad 51 F10 13 50N 20 35 E
Abengourou, Ivory C. 50 G5 6 42N 3 27W
Åbenrå, Denmark 9 J13 55 3N 9 25 E
Abeokuta, Nigeria 50 G6 7 3N 3 19 E
Aber, Uganda 54 B3 2 12N 32 25 E
Aberaeron, U.K. 11 E3 52 15N 4 15W
Aberayron = Aberaeron,
U.K. 11 E3 52 15N 4 15W
Aberchirder, U.K. 12 D6 57 34N 2 37W
Abercorn = Mbala, Zambia 55 D3 8 46S 31 24 E
Abercorn, Australia 63 D5 25 12S 151 5 E
Aberdare, U.K. 11 F4 51 43N 3 27W
Aberdare Ra., Kenya 54 C4 0 15S 36 50 E
Aberdeen, Australia 63 E5 32 9S 150 56 E
Aberdeen, Canada 73 C7 52 20N 106 8W
Aberdeen, S. Africa 56 E3 32 28S 24 2 E
Aberdeen, U.K. 12 D6 57 9N 2 5W
Aberdeen, Ala., U.S.A. 77 J1 33 49N 88 33W
Aberdeen, Idaho, U.S.A. 82 E7 42 57N 112 50W
Aberdeen, Md., U.S.A. 76 F7 39 31N 76 10W
Aberdeen, S. Dak., U.S.A. 80 C5 45 28N 98 29W
Aberdeen, Wash., U.S.A. 84 D3 46 59N 123 50W
Aberdeen, City of □, U.K. 12 D6 57 10N 2 10W
Aberdeenshire □, U.K. 12 D6 57 17N 2 36W
Aberdovey = Aberdyfi, U.K. 11 E3 52 33N 4 3W
Aberdyfi, U.K. 11 E3 52 33N 4 3W
Aberfeldy, U.K. 12 E5 56 37N 3 51W
Abergavenny, U.K. 11 F4 51 49N 3 1W
Abergele, U.K. 10 D4 53 17N 3 35W
Abernathy, U.S.A. 81 J4 33 50N 101 51W
Abert, L., U.S.A. 82 E3 42 38N 120 14W
Aberystwyth, U.K. 11 E3 52 25N 4 5W
Abhā, Si. Arabia 46 D3 18 0N 42 34 E
Abhar, Iran 45 B6 36 9N 49 13 E
Abhayapuri, India 43 F14 26 24N 90 38 E
Abidjan, Ivory C. 50 G5 5 26N 3 58W
Abilene, Kans., U.S.A. 80 F6 38 55N 97 13W
Abilene, Tex., U.S.A. 81 J5 32 28N 99 43W
Abingdon, U.K. 11 F6 51 40N 1 17W
Abingdon, U.S.A. 77 G5 36 43N 81 59W
Abington Reef, Australia 62 B4 18 0S 149 35 E
Abitau →, Canada 73 B7 59 53N 109 3W
Abitibi →, Canada 70 B3 51 3N 80 55W
Abitibi, L., Canada 70 C4 48 40N 79 40W
Abkhaz Republic =
Abkhazia □, Georgia 25 F7 43 12N 41 5 E
Abkhazia □, Georgia 25 F7 43 12N 41 5 E
Abminga, Australia 63 D1 26 8S 134 51 E
Åbo = Turku, Finland 9 F20 60 30N 22 19 E
Abohar, India 42 D6 30 10N 74 10 E
Abolo, Congo 52 D2 0 8N 14 16 E
Abomey, Benin 50 G6 7 10N 2 5 E
Abong-Mbang, Cameroon 52 D2 4 0N 13 8 E
Abou-Deïa, Chad 51 F9 11 20N 19 20 E
Aboyne, U.K. 12 D6 57 4N 2 47W
Abra Pampa, Argentina 94 A2 22 43S 65 42W
Abraham L., Canada 72 C5 52 15N 116 35W
Abreojos, Pta., Mexico 86 B2 26 50N 113 40W
Abrud, Romania 17 E12 46 19N 23 5 E
Absaroka Range, U.S.A. 82 D9 44 45N 109 50W
Abu, India 42 G5 24 41N 72 50 E
Abū al Abyad, U.A.E. 45 E7 24 11N 53 50 E
Abū al Khaşīb, Iraq 45 D6 30 25N 48 0 E
Abū 'Alī, Si. Arabia 45 E6 27 20N 49 27 E
Abū 'Alī →, Lebanon 47 A4 34 25N 35 50 E
Abu Dhabi = Abū Ẓāby,
U.A.E. 45 E7 24 28N 54 22 E
Abū Du'ān, Syria 44 B3 36 25N 38 15 E
Abu el Gairi, W. →, Egypt 47 F2 29 35N 33 30 E
Abu Ga'da, W. →, Egypt 47 F1 29 15N 32 53 E
Abū Ḥadrīyah, Si. Arabia 45 E6 27 20N 48 58 E
Abu Hamed, Sudan 51 E12 19 32N 33 13 E
Abū Kamāl, Syria 44 C4 34 30N 41 0 E
Abū Madd, Ra's, Si. Arabia 44 E3 24 50N 37 7 E
Abū Mūsā, U.A.E. 45 E7 25 52N 55 3 E
Abu Şafāt, W. →, Jordan 47 E5 30 24N 36 7 E
Abu Simbel, Egypt 51 D12 22 18N 31 40 E
Abū Şukhayr, Iraq 44 D5 31 54N 44 30 E
Abū Zabad, Sudan 51 F11 12 25N 29 10 E
Abū Ẓāby, U.A.E. 45 E7 24 28N 54 22 E
Abū Zeydābād, Iran 45 C6 33 54N 51 45 E
Abuja, Nigeria 50 G7 9 16N 7 2 E
Abukuma-Gawa →, Japan 30 E10 38 6N 140 52 E
Abukuma-Sammyaku, Japan 30 F10 37 30N 140 45 E
Abunã, Brazil 92 E5 9 40S 65 20W
Abunã →, Brazil 92 E5 9 41S 65 20W
Aburo,
Dem. Rep. of the Congo 54 B3 2 4N 30 53 E
Abut Hd., N.Z. 59 K3 43 7S 170 15 E
Acadia National Park, U.S.A. 77 C11 44 20N 68 13W
Açailândia, Brazil 93 D9 4 57S 47 0W
Acajutla, El Salv. 88 D2 13 36N 89 50W
Acámbaro, Mexico 86 D4 20 0N 100 40W
Acaponeta, Mexico 86 C3 22 30N 105 20W
Acapulco, Mexico 87 D5 16 51N 99 56W
Acarai, Serra, Brazil 92 C7 1 50N 57 50W
Acarigua, Venezuela 92 B5 9 33N 69 12W
Acatlán, Mexico 87 D5 18 10N 98 3W
Acayucan, Mexico 87 D6 17 59N 94 58W
Accomac, U.S.A. 76 G8 37 43N 75 40W
Accra, Ghana 50 G5 5 35N 0 6W
Accrington, U.K. 10 D5 53 45N 2 22W
Acebal, Argentina 94 C3 33 20S 60 50W
Aceh □, Indonesia 36 D1 4 15N 97 30 E
Achalpur, India 40 J10 21 22N 77 32 E
Acheng, China 35 B14 45 30N 126 58 E
Acher, India 42 H5 23 10N 72 32 E
Achill Hd., Ireland 13 C1 53 58N 10 15W
Achill I., Ireland 13 C1 53 58N 10 1W
Achinsk, Russia 27 D10 56 20N 90 20 E
Acireale, Italy 20 F6 37 37N 15 10 E
Ackerman, U.S.A. 81 J10 33 19N 89 11W
Acklins I., Bahamas 89 B5 22 30N 74 0W
Acme, Canada 72 C6 51 33N 113 30W
Acme, U.S.A. 78 F5 40 8N 79 26W
Aconcagua, Cerro,
Argentina 94 C2 32 39S 70 0W
Aconquija, Mt., Argentina 94 B2 27 0S 66 0W
Açores, Is. dos = Azores,
Atl. Oc. 50 A1 38 44N 29 0W
Acraman, L., Australia 63 E2 32 2S 135 23 E
Acre = 'Akko, Israel 47 C4 32 55N 35 4 E
Acre □, Brazil 92 E4 9 1S 71 0W
Acre →, Brazil 92 E5 8 45S 67 22W
Acton, Canada 78 C4 43 38N 80 3W
Acuña, Mexico 86 B4 29 18N 100 55W
Ad Dammām, Si. Arabia 45 E6 26 20N 50 5 E
Ad Dāmūr, Lebanon 47 B4 33 44N 35 27 E
Ad Dawādimī, Si. Arabia 44 E5 24 35N 44 15 E
Ad Dawḥah, Qatar 45 E6 25 15N 51 35 E
Ad Dawr, Iraq 44 C4 34 27N 43 47 E
Ad Dir'īyah, Si. Arabia 44 E5 24 44N 46 35 E
Ad Dīwānīyah, Iraq 44 D5 32 0N 45 0 E
Ad Dujayl, Iraq 44 C5 33 51N 44 14 E
Ad Duwayd, Si. Arabia 44 D4 30 15N 42 17 E
Ada, Minn., U.S.A. 80 B6 47 18N 96 31W
Ada, Okla., U.S.A. 81 H6 34 46N 96 41W
Adabiya, Egypt 47 F1 29 53N 32 28 E
Adair, C., Canada 69 A12 71 31N 71 24W
Adaja →, Spain 19 B3 41 32N 4 52W
Adak I., U.S.A. 68 C2 51 45N 176 45W
Adamaoua, Massif de l',
Cameroon 52 C2 7 20N 12 20 E
Adamawa Highlands =
Adamaoua, Massif de l',
Cameroon 52 C2 7 20N 12 20 E
Adamello, Mte., Italy 18 C9 46 9N 10 30 E
Adaminaby, Australia 63 F4 36 0S 148 45 E
Adams, Mass., U.S.A. 79 D11 42 38N 73 7W
Adams, N.Y., U.S.A. 79 C8 43 49N 76 1W
Adams, Wis., U.S.A. 80 D10 43 57N 89 49W
Adam's Bridge, Sri Lanka 40 Q11 9 15N 79 40 E
Adams L., Canada 72 C5 51 10N 119 40W
Adams Mt., U.S.A. 84 D5 46 12N 121 30W
Adam's Peak, Sri Lanka 40 R12 6 48N 80 30 E
Adana, Turkey 25 G6 37 0N 35 16 E
Adapazarı = Sakarya,
Turkey 25 F5 40 48N 30 25 E
Adarama, Sudan 51 E12 17 10N 34 52 E
Adare, C., Antarctica 5 D11 71 0S 171 0 E
Adaut, Indonesia 37 F8 8 8S 131 7 E
Adavale, Australia 63 D3 25 52S 144 32 E
Adda →, Italy 18 D8 45 8N 9 53 E
Addis Ababa = Addis
Abeba, Ethiopia 46 F2 9 2N 38 42 E
Addis Abeba, Ethiopia 46 F2 9 2N 38 42 E
Addison, U.S.A. 78 D7 42 1N 77 14W
Addo, S. Africa 56 E4 33 32S 25 45 E
Ādeh, Iran 44 B5 37 42N 45 11 E
Adel, U.S.A. 77 K4 31 8N 83 25W
Adelaide, Australia 63 E2 34 52S 138 30 E
Adelaide, Bahamas 88 A4 25 4N 77 31W
Adelaide, S. Africa 56 E4 32 42S 26 20 E
Adelaide I., Antarctica 5 C17 67 15S 68 30W
Adelaide Pen., Canada 68 B10 68 15N 97 30W
Adelaide River, Australia 60 B5 13 15S 131 7 E
Adelanto, U.S.A. 85 L9 34 35N 117 22W
Adele I., Australia 60 C3 15 32S 123 9 E
Adélie, Terre, Antarctica 5 C10 68 0S 140 0 E
Adélie Land = Adélie, Terre,
Antarctica 5 C10 68 0S 140 0 E
Aden = Al 'Adan, Yemen 46 E4 12 45N 45 0 E
Aden, G. of, Asia 46 E4 12 30N 47 30 E
Adendorp, S. Africa 56 E3 32 15S 24 30 E
Adh Dhayd, U.A.E. 45 E7 25 17N 55 53 E
Adhoi, India 42 H4 23 26N 70 32 E
Adi, Indonesia 37 E8 4 15S 133 30 E
Adieu, C., Australia 61 F5 32 0S 132 10 E
Adieu Pt., Australia 60 C3 15 14S 124 35 E
Adige →, Italy 20 B5 45 9N 12 20 E
Adigrat, Ethiopia 46 E2 14 20N 39 26 E
Adilabad, India 40 K11 19 33N 78 20 E
Adin Khel, Afghan. 40 C6 32 45N 68 5 E
Adirondack Mts., U.S.A. 79 C10 44 0N 74 0W
Adjumani, Uganda 54 B3 3 20N 31 50 E
Adlavik Is., Canada 71 A8 55 2N 57 45W
Admiralty G., Australia 60 B4 14 20S 125 55 E
Admiralty I., U.S.A. 72 B2 57 30N 134 30W
Admiralty Is., Papua N. G. 64 H6 2 0S 147 0 E
Adonara, Indonesia 37 F6 8 15S 123 5 E
Adoni, India 40 M10 15 33N 77 18 E
Adour →, France 18 E3 43 32N 1 32W
Adra, India 43 H12 23 30N 86 42 E
Adra, Spain 19 D4 36 43N 3 3W
Adrano, Italy 20 F6 37 40N 14 50 E
Adrar, Algeria 50 C5 27 51N 0 11 E
Adrar, Mauritania 50 D3 20 30N 7 30 E
Adrian, Mich., U.S.A. 76 E3 41 54N 84 2W
Adrian, Tex., U.S.A. 81 H3 35 16N 102 40W
Adriatic Sea, Medit. S. 20 C6 43 0N 16 0 E
Adua, Indonesia 37 E7 1 45S 129 50 E
Adwa, Ethiopia 46 E2 14 15N 38 52 E
Adygea □, Russia 25 F7 45 0N 40 0 E
Adzhar Republic = Ajaria □,
Georgia 25 F7 41 30N 42 0 E
Adzopé, Ivory C. 50 G5 6 7N 3 49W
Ægean Sea, Medit. S. 21 E11 38 30N 25 0 E
Aerhtai Shan, Mongolia 32 B4 46 40N 92 45 E
'Afak, Iraq 44 C5 32 4N 45 15 E
Afándou, Greece 23 C10 36 18N 28 12 E
Afghanistan ■, Asia 40 C4 33 0N 65 0 E
Aflou, Algeria 50 B6 34 7N 2 3 E
Africa 48 E6 10 0N 20 0 E
'Afrīn, Syria 44 B3 36 32N 36 50 E
Afton, N.Y., U.S.A. 79 D9 42 14N 75 32W
Afton, Wyo., U.S.A. 82 E8 42 44N 110 56W
Afuá, Brazil 93 D8 0 15S 50 20W
'Afula, Israel 47 C4 32 37N 35 17 E
Afyon, Turkey 25 G5 38 45N 30 33 E
Afyonkarahisar = Afyon,
Turkey 25 G5 38 45N 30 33 E
Agadès = Agadez, Niger 50 E7 16 58N 7 59 E
Agadez, Niger 50 E7 16 58N 7 59 E
Agadir, Morocco 50 B4 30 28N 9 55W
Agaete, Canary Is. 22 F4 28 6N 15 43W
Agar, India 42 H7 23 40N 76 2 E
Agartala, India 41 H17 23 50N 91 23 E
Agassiz, Canada 72 D4 49 14N 121 46W
Agats, Indonesia 37 F9 5 33S 138 0 E
Agawam, U.S.A. 79 D12 42 5N 72 37W
Agboville, Ivory C. 50 G5 5 55N 4 15W
Ağdam, Azerbaijan 44 B5 40 0N 46 58 E
Agde, France 18 E5 43 19N 3 28 E
Agen, France 18 D4 44 12N 0 38 E
Āgh Kand, Iran 45 B6 37 15N 48 4 E
Aginskoye, Russia 27 D12 51 6N 114 32 E
Agnew, Australia 61 E3 28 1S 120 31 E
Agori, India 43 G10 24 33N 82 57 E
Agra, India 42 F7 27 17N 77 58 E
Ağrı, Turkey 25 G7 39 44N 43 3 E
Agri →, Italy 20 D7 40 13N 16 44 E
Ağrı Dağı, Turkey 25 G7 39 50N 44 15 E
Ağrı Karakose = Ağrı,
Turkey 25 G7 39 44N 43 3 E
Agrigento, Italy 20 F5 37 19N 13 34 E
Agrinion, Greece 21 E9 38 37N 21 27 E
Agua Caliente, Baja Calif.,
Mexico 85 N10 32 29N 116 59W
Agua Caliente, Sinaloa,
Mexico 86 B3 26 30N 108 20W
Agua Caliente Springs,
U.S.A. 85 N10 32 56N 116 19W
Água Clara, Brazil 93 H8 20 25S 52 45W
Agua Hechicero, Mexico 85 N10 32 26N 116 14W
Agua Prieta, Mexico 86 A3 31 20N 109 32W
Aguadilla, Puerto Rico 89 C6 18 26N 67 10W
Aguadulce, Panama 88 E3 8 15N 80 32W
Aguanga, U.S.A. 85 M10 33 27N 116 51W
Aguanish, Canada 71 B7 50 14N 62 2W
Aguanus →, Canada 71 B7 50 13N 62 5W
Aguapey →, Argentina 94 B4 29 7S 56 36W
Aguaray Guazú →,
Paraguay 94 A4 24 47S 57 19W
Aguarico →, Ecuador 92 D3 0 59S 75 11W
Aguas Blancas, Chile 94 A2 24 15S 69 55W
Aguas Calientes, Sierra de,
Argentina 94 B2 25 26S 66 40W
Aguascalientes, Mexico 86 C4 21 53N 102 12W
Aguascalientes □, Mexico 86 C4 22 0N 102 20W
Aguilares, Argentina 94 B2 27 26S 65 35W
Aguilas, Spain 19 D5 37 23N 1 35W
Agüimes, Canary Is. 22 G4 27 58N 15 27W
Aguja, C. de la, Colombia 90 B3 11 18N 74 12W
Agulhas, C., S. Africa 56 E3 34 52S 20 0 E
Agulo, Canary Is. 22 F2 28 11N 17 12W
Agung, Indonesia 36 F5 8 20S 115 28 E
Agur, Uganda 54 B3 2 28N 32 55 E
Agusan →, Phil. 37 C7 9 0N 125 30 E
Aha Mts., Botswana 56 B3 19 45S 21 0 E
Ahaggar, Algeria 50 D7 23 0N 6 30 E
Ahar, Iran 44 B5 38 35N 47 0 E
Ahipara B., N.Z. 59 F4 35 5S 173 5 E
Ahiri, India 40 K12 19 30N 80 0 E
Ahmad Wal, Pakistan 42 E1 29 18N 65 58 E
Ahmadabad, India 42 H5 23 0N 72 40 E
Aḥmadābād, Khorāsān, Iran 45 C9 35 3N 60 50 E
Aḥmadābād, Khorāsān, Iran 45 C8 35 49N 59 42 E
Aḥmadī, Iran 45 E8 27 56N 56 42 E
Ahmadnagar, India 40 K9 19 7N 74 46 E
Ahmadpur, Pakistan 42 E4 29 12N 71 10 E
Ahmadpur Lamma, Pakistan 42 E4 28 19N 70 3 E
Ahmedabad = Ahmadabad,
India 42 H5 23 0N 72 40 E
Ahmednagar =
Ahmadnagar, India 40 K9 19 7N 74 46 E
Ahome, Mexico 86 B3 25 55N 109 11W
Ahoskie, U.S.A. 77 G7 36 17N 76 59W
Ahram, Iran 45 D6 28 52N 51 16 E
Ahrax Pt., Malta 23 D1 35 59N 14 22 E
Āhū, Iran 45 C6 34 33N 50 2 E
Ahuachapán, El Salv. 88 D2 13 54N 89 52W
Ahvāz, Iran 45 D6 31 20N 48 40 E
Ahvenanmaa = Åland,
Finland 9 F19 60 15N 20 0 E
Aḥwar, Yemen 46 E4 13 30N 46 40 E
Ai →, India 43 F14 26 26N 90 44 E
Aichi □, Japan 31 G8 35 0N 137 15 E
Aigua, Uruguay 95 C5 34 13S 54 46W
Aigues-Mortes, France 18 E6 43 35N 4 12 E
Aihui, China 33 A7 50 10N 127 30 E
Aija, Peru 92 E3 9 50S 77 45W
Aikawa, Japan 30 E9 38 2N 138 15 E
Aiken, U.S.A. 77 J5 33 34N 81 43W
Aileron, Australia 62 C1 22 39S 133 20 E
Aillik, Canada 71 A8 55 11N 59 18W
Ailsa Craig, U.K. 12 F3 55 15N 5 6W
'Ailūn, Jordan 47 C4 32 18N 35 47 E
Aim, Russia 27 D14 59 0N 133 55 E
Aimere, Indonesia 37 F6 8 45S 121 3 E
Aimogasta, Argentina 94 B2 28 33S 66 50W
Aïn Ben Tili, Mauritania 50 C4 25 59N 9 27W
Aïn-Sefra, Algeria 50 B5 32 47N 0 37W
'Ain Sudr, Egypt 47 F2 29 50N 33 6 E
Ainaži, Latvia 9 H21 57 50N 24 24 E
Ainsworth, U.S.A. 80 D5 42 33N 99 52W
Aiquile, Bolivia 92 G5 18 10S 65 10W
Aïr, Niger 50 E7 18 30N 8 0 E
Air Force I., Canada 69 B12 67 58N 74 5W
Air Hitam, Malaysia 39 M4 1 55N 103 11 E
Airdrie, Canada 72 C6 51 18N 114 2W
Airdrie, U.K. 12 F5 55 52N 3 57W
Aire →, U.K. 10 D7 53 43N 0 55W
Aire, I. de l', Spain 22 B11 39 48N 4 16 E
Airlie Beach, Australia 62 C4 20 16S 148 43 E
Aisne →, France 18 B5 49 26N 2 50 E
Ait, India 43 G8 25 54N 79 14 E
Aitkin, U.S.A. 80 B8 46 32N 93 42W
Aiud, Romania 17 E12 46 19N 23 44 E
Aix-en-Provence, France 18 E6 43 32N 5 27 E
Aix-la-Chapelle = Aachen,
Germany 16 C4 50 45N 6 6 E
Aix-les-Bains, France 18 D6 45 41N 5 53 E
Aíyion, Greece 21 E10 38 15N 22 5 E
Aizawl, India 41 H18 23 40N 92 44 E
Aizkraukle, Latvia 9 H21 56 36N 25 11 E
Aizpute, Latvia 9 H19 56 43N 21 40 E
Aizuwakamatsu, Japan 30 F9 37 30N 139 56 E
Ajaccio, France 18 F8 41 55N 8 40 E
Ajaigarh, India 43 G9 24 52N 80 16 E
Ajalpan, Mexico 87 D5 18 22N 97 15W
Ajanta Ra., India 40 J9 20 28N 75 50 E
Ajari Rep. = Ajaria □,
Georgia 25 F7 41 30N 42 0 E
Ajaria □, Georgia 25 F7 41 30N 42 0 E
Ajax, Canada 78 C5 43 50N 79 1W
Ajdābiyah, Libya 51 B10 30 54N 20 4 E
Ajka, Hungary 17 E9 47 4N 17 31 E
'Ajmān, U.A.E. 45 E7 25 25N 55 30 E
Ajmer, India 42 F6 26 28N 74 37 E
Ajnala, India 42 D6 31 50N 74 48 E
Ajo, U.S.A. 83 K7 32 22N 112 52W
Ajo, C. de, Spain 19 A4 43 31N 3 35W
Akabira, Japan 30 C11 43 33N 142 5 E
Akamas □, Cyprus 23 D11 35 3N 32 18 E
Akanthou, Cyprus 23 D12 35 22N 33 45 E
Akaroa, N.Z. 59 K4 43 49S 172 59 E
Akashi, Japan 31 G7 34 45N 134 58 E
Akbarpur, Bihar, India 43 G10 24 39N 83 58 E
Akbarpur, Ut. P., India 43 F10 26 25N 82 32 E
Akelamo, Indonesia 37 D7 1 35N 129 40 E
Aketi,
Dem. Rep. of the Congo 52 D4 2 38N 23 47 E
Akharnaí, Greece 21 E10 38 5N 23 44 E
Akhelóös →, Greece 21 E9 38 19N 21 7 E
Akhisar, Turkey 21 E12 38 56N 27 48 E
Akhnur, India 43 C6 32 52N 74 45 E
Akhtyrka = Okhtyrka,
Ukraine 25 D5 50 25N 35 0 E
Aki, Japan 31 H6 33 30N 133 54 E
Akimiski I., Canada 70 B3 52 50N 81 30W
Akita, Japan 30 E10 39 45N 140 7 E
Akita □, Japan 30 E10 39 40N 140 30 E
Akjoujt, Mauritania 50 E3 19 45N 14 15W
Akkeshi, Japan 30 C12 43 2N 144 51 E
'Akko, Israel 47 C4 32 55N 35 4 E
Aklavik, Canada 68 B6 68 12N 135 0W
Aklera, India 42 G7 24 26N 76 32 E
Akmolinsk = Astana,
Kazakstan 26 D8 51 10N 71 30 E
Akō, Japan 31 G7 34 45N 134 24 E
Akola, India 40 J10 20 42N 77 2 E
Akordat, Eritrea 46 D2 15 30N 37 40 E
Akpatok I., Canada 69 B13 60 25N 68 8W
Åkrahamn, Norway 9 G11 59 15N 5 10 E
Akranes, Iceland 8 D2 64 19N 22 5W
Akron, Colo., U.S.A. 80 E3 40 10N 103 13W
Akron, Ohio, U.S.A. 78 E3 41 5N 81 31W
Akrotiri, Cyprus 23 E11 34 36N 32 57 E
Akrotiri Bay, Cyprus 23 E12 34 35N 33 10 E
Aksai Chin, India 43 B8 35 15N 79 55 E
Aksaray, Turkey 25 G5 38 25N 34 2 E
Aksay, Kazakstan 25 D9 51 11N 53 0 E
Akşehir, Turkey 44 B1 38 18N 31 30 E
Akşehir Gölü, Turkey 25 G5 38 30N 31 25 E
Aksu, China 32 B3 41 5N 80 10 E
Aksum, Ethiopia 46 E2 14 5N 38 40 E
Aktogay, Kazakstan 26 E8 46 57N 79 40 E
Aktsyabrski, Belarus 17 B15 52 38N 28 53 E
Aktyubinsk = Aqtöbe,
Kazakstan 25 D10 50 17N 57 10 E
Akure, Nigeria 50 G7 7 15N 5 5 E
Akureyri, Iceland 8 D4 65 40N 18 6W
Akuseki-Shima, Japan 31 K4 29 27N 129 37 E
Akyab = Sittwe, Burma 41 J18 20 18N 92 45 E
Al 'Adan, Yemen 46 E4 12 45N 45 0 E
Al Aḥsā = Hasa □,
Si. Arabia 45 E6 25 50N 49 0 E
Al Ajfar, Si. Arabia 44 E4 27 26N 43 0 E
Al Amādīyah, Iraq 44 B4 37 5N 43 30 E
Al 'Amārah, Iraq 44 D5 31 55N 47 15 E
Al 'Aqabah, Jordan 47 F4 29 31N 35 0 E
Al Arak, Syria 44 C3 34 38N 38 35 E
Al 'Aramah, Si. Arabia 44 E5 25 30N 46 0 E
Al Arṭāwīyah, Si. Arabia 44 E5 26 31N 45 20 E
Al 'Āṣimah = 'Ammān □,
Jordan 47 D5 31 40N 36 30 E
Al 'Assāfīyah, Si. Arabia 44 D3 28 17N 38 59 E
Al 'Ayn, Oman 45 E7 24 15N 55 45 E
Al 'Ayn, Si. Arabia 44 E3 25 4N 38 6 E
Al 'Aẓamīyah, Iraq 44 C5 33 22N 44 22 E
Al 'Azīzīyah, Iraq 44 C5 32 54N 45 4 E
Al Bāb, Syria 44 B3 36 23N 37 29 E
Al Bad', Si. Arabia 44 D2 28 28N 35 1 E
Al Bādī, Iraq 44 C4 35 56N 41 32 E
Al Baḥrah, Kuwait 44 D5 29 40N 47 52 E
Al Baḥral Mayyit = Dead
Sea, Asia 47 D4 31 30N 35 30 E
Al Balqā' □, Jordan 47 C4 32 5N 35 45 E
Al Bārūk, J., Lebanon 47 B4 33 39N 35 40 E
Al Başrah, Iraq 44 D5 30 30N 47 50 E
Al Baṭḥā, Iraq 44 D5 31 6N 45 53 E
Al Batrūn, Lebanon 47 A4 34 15N 35 40 E
Al Bayḍā, Libya 51 B10 32 50N 21 44 E
Al Biqā, Lebanon 47 A5 34 10N 36 10 E
Al Bi'r, Si. Arabia 44 D3 28 51N 36 16 E
Al Burayj, Syria 47 A5 34 15N 36 46 E
Al Faḍilī, Si. Arabia 45 E6 26 58N 49 10 E

Al Fallūjah, *Iraq* **44 C4** 33 20N 43 55 E
Al Fāw, *Iraq* **45 D6** 30 0N 48 30 E
Al Fujayrah, *U.A.E.* **45 E8** 25 7N 56 18 E
Al Ghadaf, W. →, *Jordan* **47 D5** 31 26N 36 43 E
Al Ghammās, *Iraq* **44 D5** 31 45N 44 37 E
Al Ghazālah, *Si. Arabia* **44 E4** 26 48N 41 19 E
Al Hābah, *Si. Arabia* **44 E5** 27 10N 47 0 E
Al Ḥadīthah, *Iraq* **44 C4** 34 0N 41 13 E
Al Ḥadīthah, *Si. Arabia* **47 D6** 31 28N 37 8 E
Al Ḥaḍr, *Iraq* **44 C4** 35 35N 42 44 E
Al Hājānah, *Syria* **47 B5** 33 20N 36 33 E
Al Hajar al Gharbi, *Oman* **45 E8** 24 10N 56 15 E
Al Hāmad, *Si. Arabia* **44 D3** 31 30N 39 30 E
Al Hamdānīyah, *Syria* **44 C3** 35 25N 36 50 E
Al Ḥamīdīyah, *Syria* **47 A4** 34 42N 35 57 E
Al Ḥammār, *Iraq* **44 D5** 30 57N 46 51 E
Al Ḥamrā', *Si. Arabia* **44 E3** 24 2N 38 55 E
Al Ḥanākīyah, *Si. Arabia* **44 E4** 24 51N 40 31 E
Al Harīr, W. →, *Syria* **47 C4** 32 44N 35 59 E
Al Ḥasā, W. →, *Jordan* **47 D4** 31 4N 35 29 E
Al Ḥasakah, *Syria* **44 B4** 36 35N 40 45 E
Al Haydān, W. →, *Jordan* **47 D4** 31 29N 35 34 E
Al Ḥayy, *Iraq* **44 C5** 32 5N 46 5 E
Al Ḥijarah, *Asia* **44 D4** 30 0N 44 0 E
Al Ḥillah, *Iraq* **44 C5** 32 30N 44 25 E
Al Hindīyah, *Iraq* **44 C5** 32 30N 44 10 E
Al Hirmil, *Lebanon* **47 A5** 34 26N 36 24 E
Al Hoceïma, *Morocco* **50 A5** 35 8N 3 58W
Al Ḥudaydah, *Yemen* **46 E3** 14 50N 43 0 E
Al Hufūf, *Si. Arabia* **45 E6** 25 25N 49 45 E
Al Ḥumayḍah, *Si. Arabia* **44 D2** 29 14N 34 56 E
Al Ḥunayy, *Si. Arabia* **45 E6** 25 58N 48 45 E
Al Īsāwīyah, *Si. Arabia* **44 D3** 30 43N 37 59 E
Al Jafr, *Jordan* **47 E5** 30 18N 36 14 E
Al Jāfūrah, *Si. Arabia* **45 E7** 25 0N 50 15 E
Al Jaghbūb, *Libya* **51 C10** 29 42N 24 38 E
Al Jahrah, *Kuwait* **44 D5** 29 25N 47 40 E
Al Jalāmīd, *Si. Arabia* **44 D3** 31 20N 40 6 E
Al Jamalīyah, *Qatar* **45 E6** 25 37N 51 5 E
Al Janūb □, *Lebanon* **47 B4** 33 20N 35 20 E
Al Jawf, *Libya* **51 D10** 24 10N 23 24 E
Al Jawf, *Si. Arabia* **44 D3** 29 55N 39 40 E
Al Jazirah, *Iraq* **44 C5** 33 30N 44 0 E
Al Jithāmīyah, *Si. Arabia* **44 E4** 27 41N 41 43 E
Al Jubayl, *Si. Arabia* **45 E6** 27 0N 49 50 E
Al Jubaylah, *Si. Arabia* **44 E5** 24 55N 46 25 E
Al Jubb, *Si. Arabia* **44 E4** 27 11N 42 17 E
Al Junaynah, *Sudan* **51 F10** 13 27N 22 45 E
Al Kabā'ish, *Iraq* **44 D5** 30 58N 47 0 E
Al Karak, *Jordan* **47 D4** 31 11N 35 42 E
Al Karak □, *Jordan* **47 E5** 31 0N 36 0 E
Al Kāzim Tyah, *Iraq* **44 C5** 33 22N 44 12 E
Al Khābūra, *Oman* **45 F8** 23 57N 57 5 E
Al Khafji, *Si. Arabia* **45 E6** 28 24N 48 29 E
Al Khalīl, *West Bank* **47 D4** 31 32N 35 6 E
Al Khāliş, *Iraq* **44 C5** 33 49N 44 32 E
Al Kharsānīyah, *Si. Arabia* **45 E6** 27 13N 49 18 E
Al Khaṣab, *Oman* **45 E8** 26 14N 56 15 E
Al Khawr, *Qatar* **45 E6** 25 41N 51 30 E
Al Khiḍr, *Iraq* **44 D5** 31 12N 45 33 E
Al Khiyām, *Lebanon* **47 B4** 33 20N 35 36 E
Al Khums, *Libya* **51 B8** 32 40N 14 17 E
Al Kiswah, *Syria* **47 B5** 33 23N 36 14 E
Al Kūfah, *Iraq* **44 C5** 32 2N 44 24 E
Al Kufrah, *Libya* **51 D10** 24 17N 23 15 E
Al Kuhayfiyah, *Si. Arabia* **44 E4** 27 12N 43 3 E
Al Kūt, *Iraq* **44 C5** 32 30N 46 0 E
Al Kuwayt, *Kuwait* **44 D5** 29 30N 48 0 E
Al Labwah, *Lebanon* **47 A5** 34 11N 36 20 E
Al Lādhiqīyah, *Syria* **44 C2** 35 30N 35 45 E
Al Līth, *Si. Arabia* **46 C3** 20 9N 40 15 E
Al Liwā', *Oman* **45 E8** 24 31N 56 36 E
Al Luḥayyah, *Yemen* **46 D3** 15 45N 42 40 E
Al Madīnah, *Iraq* **44 D5** 30 57N 47 16 E
Al Madīnah, *Si. Arabia* **46 C2** 24 35N 39 52 E
Al Mafraq, *Jordan* **47 C5** 32 17N 36 14 E
Al Maḥmūdīyah, *Iraq* **44 C5** 33 3N 44 21 E
Al Majma'ah, *Si. Arabia* **44 E5** 25 57N 45 22 E
Al Makhruq, W. →, *Jordan* **47 D6** 31 28N 37 0 E
Al Makḥūl, *Si. Arabia* **44 E4** 26 37N 42 39 E
Al Manāmah, *Bahrain* **45 E6** 26 10N 50 30 E
Al Maqwa', *Kuwait* **44 D5** 29 10N 47 59 E
Al Marj, *Libya* **51 B10** 32 25N 20 30 E
Al Maṭlā, *Kuwait* **44 D5** 29 24N 47 40 E
Al Mawjib, W. →, *Jordan* **47 D4** 31 28N 35 36 E
Al Mawṣil, *Iraq* **44 B4** 36 15N 43 5 E
Al Mayādin, *Syria* **44 C4** 35 1N 40 27 E
Al Mazār, *Jordan* **47 D4** 31 4N 35 41 E
Al Midhnab, *Si. Arabia* **44 E5** 25 50N 44 18 E
Al Minā', *Lebanon* **47 A4** 34 24N 35 49 E
Al Miqdādīyah, *Iraq* **44 C5** 34 0N 45 0 E
Al Mubarraz, *Si. Arabia* **45 E6** 25 30N 49 40 E
Al Mudawwarah, *Jordan* **47 F5** 29 19N 36 0 E
Al Mughayrā', *U.A.E.* **45 E7** 24 5N 53 32 E
Al Muḥarraq, *Bahrain* **45 E6** 26 15N 50 40 E
Al Mukallā, *Yemen* **46 E4** 14 33N 49 2 E
Al Mukhā, *Yemen* **46 E3** 13 18N 43 15 E
Al Musayjīd, *Si. Arabia* **44 E3** 24 5N 39 5 E
Al Musayyib, *Iraq* **44 C5** 32 49N 44 20 E
Al Muwayliḥ, *Si. Arabia* **44 E2** 27 40N 35 30 E
Al Qā'im, *Iraq* **44 C4** 34 21N 41 7 E
Al Qalībah, *Si. Arabia* **44 D3** 28 24N 37 42 E
Al Qāmishli, *Syria* **44 B4** 37 10N 41 10 E
Al Qaryatayn, *Syria* **47 A6** 34 12N 37 13 E
Al Qaşim, *Si. Arabia* **44 E4** 26 0N 43 0 E
Al Qaṭ'ā, *Syria* **44 C4** 34 40N 40 48 E
Al Qaṭīf, *Si. Arabia* **45 E6** 26 35N 50 0 E
Al Qatrānah, *Jordan* **47 D5** 31 12N 36 6 E
Al Qaṭrūn, *Libya* **51 D9** 24 56N 15 3 E
Al Qayṣūmah, *Si. Arabia* **44 D5** 28 20N 46 7 E
Al Quds = Jerusalem, *Israel* **47 D4** 31 47N 35 10 E
Al Qunayṭirah, *Syria* **47 C4** 32 55N 35 45 E
Al Qurnah, *Iraq* **44 D5** 31 1N 47 25 E
Al Quşayr, *Iraq* **44 D5** 30 39N 45 50 E
Al Quşayr, *Syria* **47 A5** 34 31N 36 34 E
Al Qutayfah, *Syria* **47 B5** 33 44N 36 36 E
Al 'Ubaylah, *Si. Arabia* **46 C5** 21 59N 50 57 E
Al 'Uḍaylīyah, *Si. Arabia* **45 E6** 25 8N 49 18 E
Al 'Ulā, *Si. Arabia* **44 E3** 26 35N 38 0 E
Al 'Uqayr, *Si. Arabia* **45 E6** 25 40N 50 15 E
Al 'Uthmānīyah, *Si. Arabia* **45 E6** 25 5N 49 22 E
Al 'Uwaynid, *Si. Arabia* **44 E5** 24 50N 46 0 E
Al 'Uwayqilah, *Si. Arabia* **44 D4** 30 30N 42 10 E
Al 'Uyūn, *Ḥijāz, Si. Arabia* **44 E3** 24 33N 39 35 E
Al 'Uyūn, *Najd, Si. Arabia* **44 E4** 26 30N 43 50 E
Al 'Uzayr, *Iraq* **44 D5** 31 19N 47 25 E
Al Wajh, *Si. Arabia* **44 E3** 26 10N 36 30 E
Al Wakrah, *Qatar* **45 E6** 25 10N 51 40 E
Al Wannān, *Si. Arabia* **45 E6** 26 55N 48 24 E
Al Waqbah, *Si. Arabia* **44 D5** 28 48N 45 33 E
Al Wari'āh, *Si. Arabia* **44 E5** 27 51N 47 25 E
Al Wusayl, *Qatar* **45 E6** 25 29N 51 29 E
Ala Dağ, *Turkey* **44 B2** 37 44N 35 9 E
Ala Tau Shankou = Dzungarian Gates, *Kazakstan* **32 B3** 45 0N 82 0 E
Alabama □, *U.S.A.* **77 J2** 33 0N 87 0W
Alabama →, *U.S.A.* **77 K2** 31 8N 87 57W
Alabaster, *U.S.A.* **77 J2** 33 15N 86 49W
Alaçam Dağları, *Turkey* **21 E13** 39 18N 28 49 E
Alachua, *U.S.A.* **77 L4** 29 47N 82 30W
Alaérma, *Greece* **23 C9** 36 9N 27 57 E
Alagoa Grande, *Brazil* **93 E11** 7 3S 35 35W
Alagoas □, *Brazil* **93 E11** 9 0S 36 0W
Alagoinhas, *Brazil* **93 F11** 12 7S 38 20W
Alaior, *Spain* **22 B11** 39 57N 4 8 E
Alajero, *Canary Is.* **22 F2** 28 3N 17 13W
Alajuela, *Costa Rica* **88 D3** 10 2N 84 8W
Alakamisy, *Madag.* **57 C8** 21 19S 47 14 E
Alaknanda →, *India* **43 D8** 30 8N 78 36 E
Alakurtti, *Russia* **24 A5** 67 0N 30 30 E
Alamarvdasht, *Iran* **45 E7** 27 37N 52 59 E
Alameda, *Calif., U.S.A.* **84 H4** 37 46N 122 15W
Alameda, *N. Mex., U.S.A.* **83 J10** 35 11N 106 37W
Alamo, *U.S.A.* **85 J11** 37 22N 115 10W
Alamo Crossing, *U.S.A.* **85 L13** 34 16N 113 33W
Alamogordo, *U.S.A.* **83 K11** 32 54N 105 57W
Alamos, *Mexico* **86 B3** 27 0N 109 0W
Alamosa, *U.S.A.* **83 H11** 37 28N 105 52W
Åland, *Finland* **9 F19** 60 15N 20 0 E
Ålands hav, *Sweden* **9 F18** 60 0N 19 30 E
Alandur, *India* **40 N12** 13 0N 80 15 E
Alania = North Ossetia □, *Russia* **25 F7** 43 30N 44 30 E
Alanya, *Turkey* **25 G5** 36 38N 32 0 E
Alaotra, Farihin', *Madag.* **57 B8** 17 30S 48 30 E
Alapayevsk, *Russia* **26 D7** 57 52N 61 42 E
Alaşehir, *Turkey* **21 E13** 38 23N 28 30 E
Alaska □, *U.S.A.* **68 B5** 64 0N 154 0W
Alaska, G. of, *Pac. Oc.* **68 C5** 58 0N 145 0W
Alaska Peninsula, *U.S.A.* **68 C4** 56 0N 159 0W
Alaska Range, *U.S.A.* **68 B4** 62 50N 151 0W
Älät, *Azerbaijan* **25 G8** 39 58N 49 25 E
Alatyr, *Russia* **24 D8** 54 55N 46 35 E
Alausi, *Ecuador* **92 D3** 2 0S 78 50W
Alava, C., *U.S.A.* **82 B1** 48 10N 124 44W
Alavus, *Finland* **9 E20** 62 35N 23 36 E
Alawoona, *Australia* **63 E3** 34 45S 140 30 E
'Alayh, *Lebanon* **47 B4** 33 46N 35 33 E
Alba, *Italy* **18 D8** 44 42N 8 2 E
Alba-Iulia, *Romania* **17 E12** 46 8N 23 39 E
Albacete, *Spain* **19 C5** 39 0N 1 50W
Albacutya, L., *Australia* **63 F3** 35 45S 141 58 E
Albanel, L., *Canada* **70 B5** 50 55N 73 12W
Albania ■, *Europe* **21 D9** 41 0N 20 0 E
Albany, *Australia* **61 G2** 35 1S 117 58 E
Albany, *Ga., U.S.A.* **77 K3** 31 35N 84 10W
Albany, *N.Y., U.S.A.* **79 D11** 42 39N 73 45W
Albany, *Oreg., U.S.A.* **82 D2** 44 38N 123 6W
Albany, *Tex., U.S.A.* **81 J5** 32 44N 99 18W
Albany →, *Canada* **70 B3** 52 17N 81 31W
Albardón, *Argentina* **94 C2** 31 20S 68 30W
Albatross B., *Australia* **62 A3** 12 45S 141 30 E
Albemarle, *U.S.A.* **77 H5** 35 21N 80 11W
Albemarle Sd., *U.S.A.* **77 H7** 36 5N 76 0W
Alberche →, *Spain* **19 C3** 39 58N 4 46W
Alberdi, *Paraguay* **94 B4** 26 14S 58 20W
Albert, L., *Australia* **63 F2** 35 30S 139 10 E
Albert Edward Ra., *Australia* **60 C4** 18 17S 127 57 E
Albert L., *Africa* **54 B3** 1 30N 31 0 E
Albert Lea, *U.S.A.* **80 D8** 43 39N 93 22W
Albert Nile →, *Uganda* **54 B3** 3 36N 32 2 E
Albert Town, *Bahamas* **89 B5** 22 37N 74 33W
Alberta □, *Canada* **72 C6** 54 40N 115 0W
Alberti, *Argentina* **94 D3** 35 1S 60 16W
Albertinia, *S. Africa* **56 E3** 34 11S 21 34 E
Alberton, *Canada* **71 C7** 46 50N 64 0W
Albertville = Kalemie, *Dem. Rep. of the Congo* **54 D2** 5 55S 29 9 E
Albertville, *France* **18 D7** 45 40N 6 22 E
Albertville, *U.S.A.* **77 H2** 34 16N 86 13W
Albi, *France* **18 E5** 43 56N 2 9 E
Albia, *U.S.A.* **80 E8** 41 2N 92 48W
Albina, *Surinam* **93 B8** 5 37N 54 15W
Albina, Ponta, *Angola* **56 B1** 15 52S 11 44 E
Albion, *Mich., U.S.A.* **76 D3** 42 15N 84 45W
Albion, *Nebr., U.S.A.* **80 E6** 41 42N 98 0W
Albion, *Pa., U.S.A.* **78 E4** 41 53N 80 22W
Alborán, *Medit. S.* **19 E4** 35 57N 3 0W
Ålborg, *Denmark* **9 H13** 57 2N 9 54 E
Alborz, Reshteh-ye Kūhhā-ye, *Iran* **45 C7** 36 0N 52 0 E
Albuquerque, *U.S.A.* **83 J10** 35 5N 106 39W
Albuquerque, Cayos de, *Caribbean* **88 D3** 12 10N 81 50W
Alburg, *U.S.A.* **79 B11** 44 59N 73 18W
Albury-Wodonga, *Australia* **63 F4** 36 3S 146 56 E
Alcalá de Henares, *Spain* **19 B4** 40 28N 3 22W
Alcalá la Real, *Spain* **19 D4** 37 27N 3 57W
Álcamo, *Italy* **20 F5** 37 59N 12 55 E
Alcañiz, *Spain* **19 B5** 41 2N 0 8W
Alcântara, *Brazil* **93 D10** 2 20S 44 30W
Alcántara, Embalse de, *Spain* **19 C2** 39 44N 6 50W
Alcantarilla, *Spain* **19 D5** 37 59N 1 12W
Alcaraz, Sierra de, *Spain* **19 C4** 38 40N 2 20W
Alcaudete, *Spain* **19 D3** 37 35N 4 5W
Alcázar de San Juan, *Spain* **19 C4** 39 24N 3 12W
Alchevsk, *Ukraine* **25 E6** 48 30N 38 45 E
Alcira = Alzira, *Spain* **19 C5** 39 9N 0 30W
Alcova, *U.S.A.* **82 E10** 42 34N 106 43W
Alcoy, *Spain* **19 C5** 38 43N 0 30W
Alcúdia, *Spain* **22 B10** 39 51N 3 7 E
Alcúdia, B. d', *Spain* **22 B10** 39 47N 3 15 E
Aldabra Is., *Seychelles* **49 G8** 9 22S 46 28 E
Aldama, *Mexico* **87 C5** 23 0N 98 4W
Aldan, *Russia* **27 D13** 58 40N 125 30 E
Aldan →, *Russia* **27 C13** 63 28N 129 35 E
Aldea, Pta. de la, *Canary Is.* **22 G4** 28 0N 15 50W
Aldeburgh, *U.K.* **11 E9** 52 10N 1 37 E
Alder Pk., *U.S.A.* **84 K5** 35 53N 121 22W
Alderney, *U.K.* **11 H5** 49 42N 2 11W
Aldershot, *U.K.* **11 F7** 51 15N 0 44W
Aledo, *U.S.A.* **80 E9** 41 12N 90 45W
Aleg, *Mauritania* **50 E3** 17 3N 13 55W
Alegranza, *Canary Is.* **22 E6** 29 23N 13 32W
Alegranza, I., *Canary Is.* **22 E6** 29 23N 13 32W
Alegre, *Brazil* **95 A7** 20 50S 41 30W
Alegrete, *Brazil* **95 B4** 29 40S 56 0W
Aleisk, *Russia* **26 D9** 52 40N 83 0 E
Aleksandriya = Oleksandriya, *Ukraine* **17 C14** 50 37N 26 19 E
Aleksandrov Gay, *Russia* **25 D8** 50 9N 48 34 E
Aleksandrovsk-Sakhalinskiy, *Russia* **27 D15** 50 50N 142 20 E
Além Paraíba, *Brazil* **95 A7** 21 52S 42 41W
Alemania, *Argentina* **94 B2** 25 40S 65 30W
Alemania, *Chile* **94 B2** 25 10S 69 55W
Alençon, *France* **18 B4** 48 27N 0 4 E
Alenquer, *Brazil* **93 D8** 1 56S 54 46W
Alenuihaha Channel, *U.S.A.* **74 H17** 20 30N 156 0W
Aleppo = Ḥalab, *Syria* **44 B3** 36 10N 37 15 E
Alès, *France* **18 D6** 44 9N 4 5 E
Alessándria, *Italy* **18 D8** 44 54N 8 37 E
Ålesund, *Norway* **9 E12** 62 28N 6 12 E
Aleutian Is., *Pac. Oc.* **68 C2** 52 0N 175 0W
Aleutian Trench, *Pac. Oc.* **64 C10** 48 0N 180 0 E
Alexander, *U.S.A.* **80 B3** 47 51N 103 39W
Alexander, Mt., *Australia* **61 E3** 28 58S 120 16 E
Alexander Arch., *U.S.A.* **68 C6** 56 0N 136 0W
Alexander Bay, *S. Africa* **56 D2** 28 40S 16 30 E
Alexander City, *U.S.A.* **77 J3** 32 56N 85 58W
Alexander I., *Antarctica* **5 C17** 69 0S 70 0W
Alexandra, *Australia* **63 F4** 37 8S 145 40 E
Alexandra, *N.Z.* **59 L2** 45 14S 169 25 E
Alexandra Falls, *Canada* **72 A5** 60 29N 116 18W
Alexandria = El Iskandarîya, *Egypt* **51 B11** 31 13N 29 58 E
Alexandria, *B.C., Canada* **72 C4** 52 35N 122 27W
Alexandria, *Ont., Canada* **79 A10** 45 19N 74 38W
Alexandria, *Romania* **17 G13** 43 57N 25 24 E
Alexandria, *S. Africa* **56 E4** 33 38S 26 28 E
Alexandria, *U.K.* **12 F4** 55 59N 4 35W
Alexandria, *La., U.S.A.* **81 K8** 31 18N 92 27W
Alexandria, *Minn., U.S.A.* **80 C7** 45 53N 95 22W
Alexandria, *S. Dak., U.S.A.* **80 D6** 43 39N 97 47W
Alexandria, *Va., U.S.A.* **76 F7** 38 48N 77 3W
Alexandria Bay, *U.S.A.* **79 B9** 44 20N 75 55W
Alexandrina, L., *Australia* **63 F2** 35 25S 139 10 E
Alexandroúpolis, *Greece* **21 D11** 40 50N 25 54 E
Alexis →, *Canada* **71 B8** 52 33N 56 8W
Alexis Creek, *Canada* **72 C4** 52 10N 123 20W
Alfabia, *Spain* **22 B9** 39 44N 2 44 E
Alfenas, *Brazil* **95 A6** 21 20S 46 10W
Alford, *Aberds., U.K.* **12 D6** 57 14N 2 41W
Alford, *Lincs., U.K.* **10 D8** 53 15N 0 10 E
Alfred, *Maine, U.S.A.* **79 C14** 43 29N 70 43W
Alfred, *N.Y., U.S.A.* **78 D7** 42 16N 77 48W
Alfreton, *U.K.* **10 D6** 53 6N 1 24W
Alga, *Kazakstan* **25 E10** 49 53N 57 20 E
Algaida, *Spain* **22 B9** 39 33N 2 53 E
Ålgård, *Norway* **9 G11** 58 46N 5 53 E
Algarve, *Portugal* **19 D1** 36 58N 8 20W
Algeciras, *Spain* **19 D3** 36 9N 5 28W
Algemesí, *Spain* **19 C5** 39 11N 0 27W
Alger, *Algeria* **50 A6** 36 42N 3 8 E
Algeria ■, *Africa* **50 C6** 28 30N 2 0 E
Alghero, *Italy* **20 D3** 40 33N 8 19 E
Algiers = Alger, *Algeria* **50 A6** 36 42N 3 8 E
Algoa B., *S. Africa* **56 E4** 33 50S 25 45 E
Algoma, *U.S.A.* **76 C2** 44 36N 87 26W
Algona, *U.S.A.* **80 D7** 43 4N 94 14W
Algonac, *U.S.A.* **78 D2** 42 37N 82 32W
Algonquin Prov. Park, *Canada* **70 C4** 45 50N 78 30W
Algorta, *Uruguay* **96 C5** 32 25S 57 23W
Alhambra, *U.S.A.* **85 L8** 34 8N 118 6W
Alhucemas = Al Hoceïma, *Morocco* **50 A5** 35 8N 3 58W
'Alī al Gharbī, *Iraq* **44 C5** 32 30N 46 45 E
'Alī ash Sharqī, *Iraq* **44 C5** 32 7N 46 44 E
'Alī Khēl, *Afghan.* **42 C3** 33 57N 69 43 E
'Alī Shāh, *Iran* **44 B5** 38 9N 45 50 E
'Alīābād, *Khorāsān, Iran* **45 C8** 32 30N 57 30 E
'Alīābād, *Kordestān, Iran* **44 C5** 35 4N 46 58 E
'Alīābād, *Yazd, Iran* **45 D7** 31 41N 53 49 E
Aliağa, *Turkey* **21 E12** 38 47N 26 59 E
Aliákmon →, *Greece* **21 D10** 40 30N 22 36 E
Alicante, *Spain* **19 C5** 38 23N 0 30W
Alice, *S. Africa* **56 E4** 32 48S 26 55 E
Alice, *U.S.A.* **81 M5** 27 45N 98 5W
Alice →, *Queens., Australia* **62 C3** 24 2S 144 50 E
Alice →, *Queens., Australia* **62 B3** 15 35S 142 20 E
Alice Arm, *Canada* **72 B3** 55 29N 129 31W
Alice Springs, *Australia* **62 C1** 23 40S 133 50 E
Alicedale, *S. Africa* **56 E4** 33 15S 26 4 E
Aliceville, *U.S.A.* **77 J1** 33 8N 88 9W
Aliganj, *India* **43 F8** 27 30N 79 10 E
Aligarh, *Raj., India* **42 G7** 25 55N 76 15 E
Aligarh, *Ut. P., India* **42 F8** 27 55N 78 10 E
Alīgūdarz, *Iran* **45 C6** 33 25N 49 45 E
Alimnía, *Greece* **23 C9** 36 16N 27 43 E
Alingsås, *Sweden* **9 H15** 57 56N 12 31 E
Alipur, *Pakistan* **42 E4** 29 25N 70 55 E
Alipur Duar, *India* **41 F16** 26 30N 89 35 E
Aliquippa, *U.S.A.* **78 F4** 40 37N 80 15W
Alitus = Alytus, *Lithuania* **9 J21** 54 24N 24 3 E
Aliwal North, *S. Africa* **56 E4** 30 45S 26 45 E
Alix, *Canada* **72 C6** 52 24N 113 11W
Aljustrel, *Portugal* **19 D1** 37 55N 8 10W
Alkmaar, *Neths.* **15 B4** 52 37N 4 45 E
All American Canal, *U.S.A.* **83 K6** 32 45N 115 15W
Allagash →, *U.S.A.* **77 B11** 47 5N 69 3W
Allah Dad, *Pakistan* **42 G2** 25 38N 67 34 E
Allahabad, *India* **43 G9** 25 25N 81 58 E
Allan, *Canada* **73 C7** 51 53N 106 4W
Allanmyo, *Burma* **41 K19** 19 30N 95 17 E
Allanridge, *S. Africa* **56 D4** 27 45S 26 40 E
Allegany, *U.S.A.* **78 D6** 42 6N 78 30W
Allegheny →, *U.S.A.* **78 F5** 40 27N 80 1W
Allegheny Mts., *U.S.A.* **76 G6** 38 15N 80 10W
Allegheny Reservoir, *U.S.A.* **78 E6** 41 50N 79 0W
Allen, Bog of, *Ireland* **13 C5** 53 15N 7 0W
Allen, L., *Ireland* **13 B3** 54 8N 8 4W
Allendale, *U.S.A.* **77 J5** 33 1N 81 18W
Allende, *Mexico* **86 B4** 28 20N 100 50W
Allentown, *U.S.A.* **79 F9** 40 37N 75 29W
Alleppey, *India* **40 Q10** 9 30N 76 28 E
Aller →, *Germany* **16 B5** 52 56N 9 12 E
Alliance, *Nebr., U.S.A.* **80 D3** 42 6N 102 52W
Alliance, *Ohio, U.S.A.* **78 F3** 40 55N 81 6W
Allier →, *France* **18 C5** 46 57N 3 4 E
Alliford Bay, *Canada* **72 C2** 53 12N 131 58W
Alliston, *Canada* **78 B5** 44 9N 79 52W
Alloa, *U.K.* **12 E5** 56 7N 3 47W
Allora, *Australia* **63 D5** 28 2S 152 0 E
Alluitsup Paa = Sydprøven, *Greenland* **4 C5** 60 30N 45 35W
Alma, *Canada* **71 C5** 48 35N 71 40W
Alma, *Ga., U.S.A.* **77 K4** 31 33N 82 28W
Alma, *Kans., U.S.A.* **80 F6** 39 1N 96 17W
Alma, *Mich., U.S.A.* **76 D3** 43 23N 84 39W
Alma, *Nebr., U.S.A.* **80 E5** 40 6N 99 22W
Alma Ata = Almaty, *Kazakstan* **26 E8** 43 15N 76 57 E
Almada, *Portugal* **19 C1** 38 40N 9 9W
Almaden, *Australia* **62 B3** 17 22S 144 40 E
Almadén, *Spain* **19 C3** 38 49N 4 52W
Almanor, L., *U.S.A.* **82 F3** 40 14N 121 9W
Almansa, *Spain* **19 C5** 38 51N 1 5W
Almanzor, Pico, *Spain* **19 B3** 40 15N 5 18W
Almanzora →, *Spain* **19 D5** 37 14N 1 46W
Almaty, *Kazakstan* **26 E8** 43 15N 76 57 E
Almazán, *Spain* **19 B4** 41 30N 2 30W
Almeirim, *Brazil* **93 D8** 1 30S 52 34W
Almelo, *Neths.* **15 B6** 52 22N 6 42 E
Almendralejo, *Spain* **19 C2** 38 41N 6 26W
Almere-Stad, *Neths.* **15 B5** 52 20N 5 15 E
Almería, *Spain* **19 D4** 36 52N 2 27W
Almirante, *Panama* **88 E3** 9 10N 82 30W
Almiroú, Kólpos, *Greece* **23 D6** 35 23N 24 20 E
Almond, *U.S.A.* **78 D7** 42 19N 77 44W
Almont, *U.S.A.* **78 D1** 42 55N 83 3W
Almonte, *Canada* **79 A8** 45 14N 76 12W
Almora, *India* **43 E8** 29 38N 79 40 E
Alness, *U.K.* **12 D4** 57 41N 4 16W
Alnmouth, *U.K.* **10 B6** 55 24N 1 37W
Alnwick, *U.K.* **10 B6** 55 24N 1 42W
Aloi, *Uganda* **54 B3** 2 16N 33 10 E
Alon, *Burma* **41 H19** 22 12N 95 5 E
Alor, *Indonesia* **37 F6** 8 15S 124 30 E
Alor Setar, *Malaysia* **39 J3** 6 7N 100 22 E
Alot, *India* **42 H6** 23 56N 75 40 E
Aloysius, Mt., *Australia* **61 E4** 26 0S 128 38 E
Alpaugh, *U.S.A.* **84 K7** 35 53N 119 29W
Alpena, *U.S.A.* **76 C4** 45 4N 83 27W
Alpha, *Australia* **62 C4** 23 39S 146 37 E
Alphen aan den Rijn, *Neths.* **15 B4** 52 7N 4 40 E
Alpine, *Ariz., U.S.A.* **83 K9** 33 51N 109 9W
Alpine, *Calif., U.S.A.* **85 N10** 32 50N 116 46W
Alpine, *Tex., U.S.A.* **81 K3** 30 22N 103 40W
Alps, *Europe* **18 C8** 46 30N 9 30 E
Alsace, *France* **18 B7** 48 15N 7 25 E
Alsask, *Canada* **73 C7** 51 21N 109 59W
Alsasua, *Spain* **19 A4** 42 54N 2 10W
Alsek →, *U.S.A.* **72 B1** 59 10N 138 12W
Alsten, *Norway* **8 D15** 65 58N 12 40 E
Alston, *U.K.* **10 C5** 54 49N 2 25W
Alta, *Norway* **8 B20** 69 57N 23 10 E
Alta Gracia, *Argentina* **94 C3** 31 40S 64 30W
Alta Sierra, *U.S.A.* **85 K8** 35 42N 118 33W
Altaelva →, *Norway* **8 B20** 69 54N 23 17 E
Altafjorden, *Norway* **8 A20** 70 5N 23 5 E
Altai = Aerhtai Shan, *Mongolia* **32 B4** 46 40N 92 45 E
Altamaha →, *U.S.A.* **77 K5** 31 20N 81 20W
Altamira, *Brazil* **93 D8** 3 12S 52 10W
Altamira, *Chile* **94 B2** 25 47S 69 51W
Altamira, *Mexico* **87 C5** 22 24N 97 55W
Altamont, *U.S.A.* **79 D10** 42 43N 74 3W
Altamura, *Italy* **20 D7** 40 49N 16 33 E
Altanbulag, *Mongolia* **32 A5** 50 16N 106 30 E
Altar, *Mexico* **86 A2** 30 40N 111 50W
Altar, Desierto de, *Mexico* **86 B2** 30 10N 112 0W
Altata, *Mexico* **86 C3** 24 30N 108 0W
Altavista, *U.S.A.* **76 G6** 37 6N 79 17W
Altay, *China* **32 B3** 47 48N 88 10 E
Altea, *Spain* **19 C5** 38 38N 0 2W
Altiplano = Bolivian Plateau, *S. Amer.* **90 E4** 20 0S 67 30W
Alto Araguaia, *Brazil* **93 G8** 17 15S 53 20W
Alto Cuchumatanes = Cuchumatanes, Sierra de los, *Guatemala* **88 C1** 15 35N 91 25W
Alto del Carmen, *Chile* **94 B1** 28 46S 70 30W
Alto del Inca, *Chile* **94 A2** 24 10S 68 10W
Alto Ligonha, *Mozam.* **55 F4** 15 30S 38 11 E
Alto Molocue, *Mozam.* **55 F4** 15 50S 37 35 E
Alto Paraguay □, *Paraguay* **94 A4** 21 0S 58 30W
Alto Paraná □, *Paraguay* **95 B5** 25 30S 54 50W
Alton, *Canada* **78 C4** 43 54N 80 5W
Alton, *U.K.* **11 F7** 51 9N 0 59W
Alton, *Ill., U.S.A.* **80 F9** 38 53N 90 11W
Alton, *N.H., U.S.A.* **79 C13** 43 27N 71 13W
Altoona, *U.S.A.* **78 F6** 40 31N 78 24W
Altūn Kūprī, *Iraq* **44 C5** 35 45N 44 9 E
Altun Shan, *China* **32 C3** 38 30N 88 0 E
Alturas, *U.S.A.* **82 F3** 41 29N 120 32W
Altus, *U.S.A.* **81 H5** 34 38N 99 20W
Alucra, *Turkey* **25 F6** 40 22N 38 47 E
Alūksne, *Latvia* **9 H22** 57 24N 27 3 E
Alunite, *U.S.A.* **85 K12** 35 59N 114 55W
Alusi, *Indonesia* **37 F8** 7 35S 131 40 E
Alva, *U.S.A.* **81 G5** 36 48N 98 40W
Alvarado, *Mexico* **87 D5** 18 40N 95 50W
Alvarado, *U.S.A.* **81 J6** 32 24N 97 13W
Alvaro Obregón, Presa, *Mexico* **86 B3** 27 55N 109 52W
Alvear, *Argentina* **94 B4** 29 5S 56 30W
Alvesta, *Sweden* **9 H16** 56 54N 14 35 E
Alvin, *U.S.A.* **81 L7** 29 26N 95 15W
Alvinston, *Canada* **78 D3** 42 49N 81 52W
Älvkarleby, *Sweden* **9 F17** 60 34N 17 26 E
Alvord Desert, *U.S.A.* **82 E4** 42 30N 118 25W
Älvsbyn, *Sweden* **8 D19** 65 40N 21 0 E
Alwar, *India* **42 F7** 27 38N 76 34 E
Alxa Zuoqi, *China* **34 E3** 38 50N 105 40 E
Alyangula, *Australia* **62 A2** 13 55S 136 30 E
Alyata = Älät, *Azerbaijan* **25 G8** 39 58N 49 25 E
Alyth, *U.K.* **12 E5** 56 38N 3 13W
Alytus, *Lithuania* **9 J21** 54 24N 24 3 E
Alzada, *U.S.A.* **80 C2** 45 2N 104 25W
Alzira, *Spain* **19 C5** 39 9N 0 30W
Am-Timan, *Chad* **51 F10** 11 0N 20 10 E
Amadeus, L., *Australia* **61 D5** 24 54S 131 0 E

Amadi, Dem. Rep. of the Congo 54 B2 3 40N 26 40 E
Amâdi, Sudan 51 G12 5 29N 30 25 E
Amadjuak L., Canada 69 B12 65 0N 71 8W
Amagansett, U.S.A. 79 F12 40 59N 72 9W
Amagasaki, Japan 31 G7 34 42N 135 20 E
Amahai, Indonesia 37 E7 3 20S 128 55 E
Amakusa-Shotō, Japan 31 H5 32 15N 130 10 E
Åmål, Sweden 9 G15 59 3N 12 42 E
Amaliás, Greece 21 F9 37 47N 21 22 E
Amalner, India 40 J9 21 5N 75 5 E
Amamapare, Indonesia 37 E9 4 53S 136 38 E
Amambaí, Brazil 95 A4 23 5S 55 13W
Amambaí →, Brazil 95 A5 23 22S 53 56W
Amambay □, Paraguay 95 A4 23 0S 56 0W
Amambay, Cordillera de, S. Amer. 95 A4 23 0S 55 45W
Amami-Guntō, Japan 31 L4 27 16N 129 21 E
Amami-Ō-Shima, Japan 31 L4 28 0N 129 0 E
Amaná, L., Brazil 92 D6 2 35S 64 40W
Amanat →, India 43 G11 24 7N 84 4 E
Amanda Park, U.S.A. 84 C3 47 28N 123 55W
Amangeldy, Kazakstan 26 D7 50 10N 65 10 E
Amapá, Brazil 93 C8 2 5N 50 50W
Amapá □, Brazil 93 C8 1 40N 52 0W
Amarante, Brazil 93 E10 6 14S 42 50W
Amaranth, Canada 73 C9 50 36N 98 43W
Amargosa →, U.S.A. 85 J10 36 14N 116 51W
Amargosa Range, U.S.A. 85 J10 36 20N 116 45W
Amári, Greece 23 D6 35 13N 24 40 E
Amarillo, U.S.A. 81 H4 35 13N 101 50W
Amarkantak, India 43 H9 22 40N 81 45 E
Amaro, Mte., Italy 20 C6 42 5N 14 5 E
Amarpur, India 43 G12 25 5N 87 0 E
Amarwara, India 43 H8 22 18N 79 10 E
Amasya □, Turkey 25 F6 40 40N 35 50 E
Amata, Australia 61 E5 26 9S 131 9 E
Amatikulu, S. Africa 57 D5 29 3S 31 33 E
Amatitlán, Guatemala 88 D1 14 29N 90 38W
Amay, Belgium 15 D5 50 33N 5 19 E
Amazon = Amazonas →, S. Amer. 93 D9 0 5S 50 0W
Amazonas □, Brazil 92 E6 5 0S 65 0W
Amazonas →, S. Amer. 93 D9 0 5S 50 0W
Ambah, India 42 F8 26 43N 78 13 E
Ambahakily, Madag. 57 C7 21 36S 43 41 E
Ambala, India 42 D7 30 23N 76 56 E
Ambalavao, Madag. 57 C8 21 50S 46 56 E
Ambanja, Madag. 57 A8 13 40S 48 27 E
Ambarchik, Russia 27 C17 69 40N 162 20 E
Ambarijeby, Madag. 57 A8 14 56S 47 41 E
Ambaro, Helodranon', Madag. 57 A8 13 23S 48 38 E
Ambato, Ecuador 92 D3 1 5S 78 42W
Ambato, Sierra de, Argentina 94 B2 28 25S 66 10W
Ambato Boeny, Madag. 57 B8 16 28S 46 43 E
Ambatofinandrahana, Madag. 57 C8 20 33S 46 48 E
Ambatolampy, Madag. 57 B8 19 20S 47 35 E
Ambatondrazaka, Madag. 57 B8 17 55S 48 28 E
Ambatosoratra, Madag. 57 B8 17 37S 48 31 E
Ambenja, Madag. 57 B8 15 17S 46 58 E
Amberg, Germany 16 D6 49 26N 11 52 E
Ambergris Cay, Belize 87 D7 18 0N 88 0W
Amberley, N.Z. 59 K4 43 9S 172 44 E
Ambikapur, India 43 H10 23 15N 83 15 E
Ambilobé, Madag. 57 A8 13 10S 49 3 E
Ambinanindrano, Madag. 57 C8 20 5S 48 23 E
Amble, U.K. 10 B6 55 20N 1 36W
Ambleside, U.K. 10 C5 54 26N 2 58W
Ambo, Peru 92 F3 10 5S 76 10W
Ambodifototra, Madag. 57 B8 16 59S 49 52 E
Ambodilazana, Madag. 57 B8 18 6S 49 10 E
Ambohimahasoa, Madag. 57 C8 21 7S 47 13 E
Ambohimanga, Madag. 57 C8 20 52S 47 36 E
Ambohitra, Madag. 57 A8 12 30S 49 10 E
Amboise, France 18 C4 47 24N 1 2 E
Ambon, Indonesia 37 E7 3 35S 128 20 E
Amboseli, L., Kenya 54 C4 2 40S 37 10 E
Ambositra, Madag. 57 C8 20 31S 47 25 E
Ambovombe, Madag. 57 D8 25 11S 46 5 E
Amboy, U.S.A. 85 L11 34 33N 115 45W
Amboyna Cay, S. China Sea 36 C4 7 50N 112 50 E
Ambridge, U.S.A. 78 F4 40 36N 80 14W
Ambriz, Angola 52 F2 7 48S 13 8 E
Amchitka I., U.S.A. 68 C1 51 32N 179 0 E
Amderma, Russia 26 C7 69 45N 61 30 E
Amdhi, India 43 H9 23 51N 81 27 E
Ameca, Mexico 86 C4 20 30N 104 0W
Ameca →, Mexico 86 C3 20 40N 105 15W
Amecameca, Mexico 87 D5 19 7N 98 46W
Ameland, Neths. 15 A5 53 27N 5 45 E
Amenia, U.S.A. 79 E11 41 51N 73 33W
American Falls, U.S.A. 82 E7 42 47N 112 51W
American Falls Reservoir, U.S.A. 82 E7 42 47N 112 52W
American Fork, U.S.A. 82 F8 40 23N 111 48W
American Highland, Antarctica 5 D6 73 0S 75 0 E
American Samoa ■, Pac. Oc. 59 B13 14 20S 170 40W
Americana, Brazil 95 A6 22 45S 47 20W
Americus, U.S.A. 77 K3 32 4N 84 14W
Amersfoort, Neths. 15 B5 52 9N 5 23 E
Amersfoort, S. Africa 57 D4 26 59S 29 53 E
Amery Ice Shelf, Antarctica 5 C6 69 30S 72 0 E
Ames, U.S.A. 80 E8 42 2N 93 37W
Amesbury, U.S.A. 79 D14 42 51N 70 56W
Amet, India 42 G5 25 18N 73 56 E
Amga, Russia 27 C14 60 50N 132 0 E
Amga →, Russia 27 C14 62 38N 134 32 E
Amgu, Russia 27 E14 45 45N 137 15 E
Amgun →, Russia 27 D14 52 56N 139 38 E
Amherst, Burma 41 L20 16 2N 97 20 E
Amherst, Canada 71 C7 45 48N 64 8W
Amherst, Mass., U.S.A. 79 D12 42 23N 72 31W
Amherst, N.Y., U.S.A. 78 D6 42 59N 78 48W
Amherst, Ohio, U.S.A. 78 E2 41 24N 82 14W
Amherst I., Canada 79 B8 44 8N 76 43W
Amherstburg, Canada 70 D3 42 6N 83 6W
Amiata, Mte., Italy 20 C4 42 53N 11 37 E
Amidon, U.S.A. 80 B3 46 29N 103 19W
Amiens, France 18 B5 49 54N 2 16 E
Amīrābād, Iran 44 C5 33 20N 46 16 E
Amirante Is., Seychelles 28 K9 6 0S 53 0 E
Amisk L., Canada 73 C8 54 35N 102 15W
Amistad, Presa de la, Mexico 86 B4 29 24N 101 0W
Amite, U.S.A. 81 K9 30 44N 90 30W
Amla, India 42 J8 21 56N 78 7 E
Amlia I., U.S.A. 68 C2 52 4N 173 30W
Amlwch, U.K. 10 D3 53 24N 4 20W
'Ammān, Jordan 47 D4 31 57N 35 52 E
'Ammān □, Jordan 47 D5 31 40N 36 30 E
Ammanford, U.K. 11 F4 51 48N 3 59W
Ammassalik = Angmagssalik, Greenland 4 C6 65 40N 37 20W
Ammon, U.S.A. 82 E8 43 28N 111 58W
Amnat Charoen, Thailand 38 E5 15 51N 104 38 E
Amnura, Bangla. 43 G13 24 37N 88 25 E
Āmol, Iran 45 B7 36 23N 52 20 E
Amorgós, Greece 21 F11 36 50N 25 57 E
Amory, U.S.A. 77 J1 33 59N 88 29W
Amos, Canada 70 C4 48 35N 78 5W
Åmot, Norway 9 G13 59 57N 9 54 E
Amoy = Xiamen, China 33 D6 24 25N 118 4 E
Ampang, Malaysia 39 L3 3 8N 101 45 E
Ampanihy, Madag. 57 C7 24 40S 44 45 E
Ampasindava, Helodranon', Madag. 57 A8 13 40S 48 15 E
Ampasindava, Saikanosy, Madag. 57 A8 13 42S 47 55 E
Ampenan, Indonesia 36 F5 8 35S 116 13 E
Amper →, Germany 16 D6 48 29N 11 55 E
Ampotaka, Madag. 57 D7 25 3S 44 41 E
Ampoza, Madag. 57 C7 22 20S 44 44 E
Amqui, Canada 71 C6 48 28N 67 27W
Amravati, India 40 J10 20 55N 77 45 E
Amreli, India 42 J4 21 35N 71 17 E
Amritsar, India 42 D6 31 35N 74 57 E
Amroha, India 43 E8 28 53N 78 30 E
Amsterdam, Neths. 15 B4 52 23N 4 54 E
Amsterdam, U.S.A. 79 D10 42 56N 74 11W
Amsterdam, I., Ind. Oc. 3 F13 38 30S 77 30 E
Amstetten, Austria 16 D8 48 7N 14 51 E
Amudarya →, Uzbekistan 26 E6 43 58N 59 34 E
Amundsen Gulf, Canada 68 A7 71 0N 124 0W
Amundsen Sea, Antarctica 5 D15 72 0S 115 0W
Amuntai, Indonesia 36 E5 2 28S 115 25 E
Amur →, Russia 27 D15 52 56N 141 10 E
Amurang, Indonesia 37 D6 1 5N 124 40 E
Amuri Pass, N.Z. 59 K4 42 31S 172 11 E
Amursk, Russia 27 D14 50 14N 136 54 E
Amyderya = Amudarya →, Uzbekistan 26 E6 43 58N 59 34 E
An Bien, Vietnam 39 H5 9 45N 105 0 E
An Hoa, Vietnam 38 E7 15 40N 108 5 E
An Nabatīyah at Tahta, Lebanon 47 B4 33 23N 35 27 E
An Nabk, Si. Arabia 44 D3 31 20N 37 20 E
An Nabk, Syria 47 A5 34 2N 36 44 E
An Nabk Abū Qaşr, Si. Arabia 44 D3 30 21N 38 34 E
An Nafūd, Si. Arabia 44 D4 28 15N 41 0 E
An Najaf, Iraq 44 C5 32 3N 44 15 E
An Nāşirīyah, Iraq 44 D5 31 0N 46 15 E
An Nhon, Vietnam 38 F7 13 55N 109 7 E
An Nu'ayrīyah, Si. Arabia 45 E6 27 30N 48 30 E
An Nuwayb'ī, W. →, Si. Arabia 47 F3 29 18N 34 57 E
An Thoi, Dao, Vietnam 39 H5 9 58N 104 0 E
An Uaimh, Ireland 13 C5 53 39N 6 41W
Anabar →, Russia 27 B12 73 8N 113 36 E
'Anabtā, West Bank 47 C4 32 19N 35 7 E
Anaconda, U.S.A. 82 C7 46 8N 112 57W
Anacortes, U.S.A. 84 B4 48 30N 122 37W
Anadarko, U.S.A. 81 H5 35 4N 98 15W
Anadolu, Turkey 25 G5 39 0N 30 0 E
Anadyr, Russia 27 C18 64 35N 177 20 E
Anadyr →, Russia 27 C18 64 55N 176 5 E
Anadyrskiy Zaliv, Russia 27 C19 64 0N 180 0 E
Anaga, Pta. de, Canary Is. 22 F3 28 34N 16 9W
'Ānah, Iraq 44 C4 34 25N 42 0 E
Anaheim, U.S.A. 85 M9 33 50N 117 55W
Anahim Lake, Canada 72 C3 52 28N 125 18W
Anáhuac, Mexico 86 B4 27 14N 100 9W
Anakapalle, India 41 L13 17 42N 83 6 E
Anakie, Australia 62 C4 23 32S 147 45 E
Analalava, Madag. 57 A8 14 35S 48 0 E
Análipsis, Greece 23 A3 39 36N 19 55 E
Anambar →, Pakistan 42 D3 30 15N 68 50 E
Anambas, Kepulauan, Indonesia 39 L6 3 20N 106 30 E
Anambas Is. = Anambas, Kepulauan, Indonesia 39 L6 3 20N 106 30 E
Anamosa, U.S.A. 80 D9 42 7N 91 17W
Anamur, Turkey 25 G5 36 8N 32 58 E
Anan, Japan 31 H7 33 54N 134 40 E
Anand, India 42 H5 22 32N 72 59 E
Anantnag, India 43 C6 33 45N 75 10 E
Ananyiv, Ukraine 17 E15 47 44N 29 58 E
Anapodháris →, Greece 23 E7 34 59N 25 20 E
Anápolis, Brazil 93 G9 16 15S 48 50W
Anapu →, Brazil 93 D8 1 53S 50 53W
Anār, Iran 45 D7 30 55N 55 13 E
Anārak, Iran 45 C7 33 25N 53 40 E
Anas →, India 42 H5 23 26N 74 0 E
Anatolia = Anadolu, Turkey 25 G5 39 0N 30 0 E
Anatsogno, Madag. 57 C7 23 33S 43 46 E
Añatuya, Argentina 94 B3 28 20S 62 50W
Anaunethad L., Canada 73 A8 60 55N 104 25W
Anbyŏn, N. Korea 35 E14 39 1N 127 35 E
Ancaster, Canada 78 C5 43 13N 79 59W
Anchor Bay, U.S.A. 84 G3 38 48N 123 34W
Anchorage, U.S.A. 68 B5 61 13N 149 54W
Anci, China 34 E9 39 20N 116 40 E
Ancohuma, Nevada, Bolivia 92 G5 16 0S 68 50W
Ancón, Peru 92 F3 11 50S 77 10W
Ancona, Italy 20 C5 43 38N 13 30 E
Ancud, Chile 96 E2 42 0S 73 50W
Ancud, G. de, Chile 96 E2 42 0S 73 0W
Anda, China 33 B7 46 24N 125 19 E
Andacollo, Argentina 94 D1 37 10S 70 42W
Andacollo, Chile 94 C1 30 14S 71 6W
Andalgalá, Argentina 94 B2 27 40S 66 30W
Åndalsnes, Norway 9 E12 62 35N 7 43 E
Andalucía □, Spain 19 D3 37 35N 5 0W
Andalusia = Andalucía □, Spain 19 D3 37 35N 5 0W
Andalusia, U.S.A. 77 K2 31 18N 86 29W
Andaman Is., Ind. Oc. 28 H13 12 30N 92 30 E
Andaman Sea, Ind. Oc. 36 B1 13 0N 96 0 E
Andamooka Opal Fields, Australia 63 E2 30 27S 137 9 E
Andapa, Madag. 53 G9 14 39S 49 39 E
Andara, Namibia 56 B3 18 2S 21 9 E
Andenes, Norway 8 B17 69 19N 16 18 E
Andenne, Belgium 15 D5 50 28N 5 5 E
Anderson, Alaska, U.S.A. 68 B5 64 25N 149 15W
Anderson, Calif., U.S.A. 82 F2 40 27N 122 18W
Anderson, Ind., U.S.A. 76 E3 40 10N 85 41W
Anderson, Mo., U.S.A. 81 G7 36 39N 94 27W
Anderson, S.C., U.S.A. 77 H4 34 31N 82 39W
Anderson →, Canada 68 B7 69 42N 129 0W
Andes, U.S.A. 79 D10 42 12N 74 47W
Andes, Cord. de los, S. Amer. 92 H5 20 0S 68 0W
Andfjorden, Norway 8 B17 69 10N 16 20 E
Andhra Pradesh □, India 40 L11 18 0N 79 0 E
Andijon, Uzbekistan 26 E8 41 10N 72 15 E
Andikíthira, Greece 21 G10 35 52N 23 15 E
Andīmeshk, Iran 45 C6 32 27N 48 21 E
Andizhan = Andijon, Uzbekistan 26 E8 41 10N 72 15 E
Andoany, Madag. 57 A8 13 25S 48 16 E
Andong, S. Korea 35 F15 36 40N 128 43 E
Andongwei, China 35 G10 35 6N 119 20 E
Andoom, Australia 62 A3 12 25S 141 53 E
Andorra ■, Europe 18 E4 42 30N 1 30 E
Andorra La Vella, Andorra 18 E4 42 31N 1 32 E
Andover, U.K. 11 F6 51 12N 1 29W
Andover, Maine, U.S.A. 79 B14 44 38N 70 45W
Andover, Mass., U.S.A. 79 D13 42 40N 71 8W
Andover, N.J., U.S.A. 79 F10 40 59N 74 45W
Andover, N.Y., U.S.A. 78 D7 42 10N 77 48W
Andover, Ohio, U.S.A. 78 E4 41 36N 80 34W
Andøya, Norway 8 B16 69 10N 15 50 E
Andradina, Brazil 93 H8 20 54S 51 23W
Andrahary, Mt., Madag. 57 A8 13 37S 49 17 E
Andramasina, Madag. 57 B8 19 11S 47 35 E
Andranopasy, Madag. 57 C7 21 17S 43 44 E
Andratx, Spain 22 B9 39 39N 2 25 E
Andreanof Is., U.S.A. 68 C2 51 30N 176 0W
Andrews, S.C., U.S.A. 77 J6 33 27N 79 34W
Andrews, Tex., U.S.A. 81 J3 32 19N 102 33W
Ándria, Italy 20 D7 41 13N 16 17 E
Andriba, Madag. 57 B8 17 30S 46 58 E
Androka, Madag. 57 C7 24 58S 44 2 E
Andropov = Rybinsk, Russia 24 C6 58 5N 38 50 E
Ándros, Greece 21 F11 37 50N 24 57 E
Andros I., Bahamas 88 B4 24 30N 78 0W
Andros Town, Bahamas 88 B4 24 43N 77 47W
Androscoggin →, U.S.A. 79 C14 43 58N 70 0W
Andselv, Norway 8 B18 69 4N 18 34 E
Andújar, Spain 19 C3 38 3N 4 5W
Andulo, Angola 52 G3 11 25S 16 45 E
Anegada I., Virgin Is. 89 C7 18 45N 64 20W
Anegada Passage, W. Indies 89 C7 18 15N 63 45W
Aneto, Pico de, Spain 19 A6 42 37N 0 40 E
Ang Thong, Thailand 38 E3 14 35N 100 31 E
Angamos, Punta, Chile 94 A1 23 1S 70 32W
Angara →, Russia 27 D10 58 5N 94 20 E
Angarsk, Russia 27 D11 52 30N 104 0 E
Angas Hills, Australia 60 D4 23 0S 127 50 E
Angaston, Australia 63 E2 34 30S 139 8 E
Angaur I., Pac. Oc. 37 C8 6 54N 134 9 E
Ånge, Sweden 9 E16 62 31N 15 35 E
Ángel, Salto = Angel Falls, Venezuela 92 B6 5 57N 62 30W
Ángel de la Guarda, I., Mexico 86 B2 29 30N 113 30W
Angel Falls, Venezuela 92 B6 5 57N 62 30W
Angeles, Phil. 37 A6 15 9N 120 33 E
Ängelholm, Sweden 9 H15 56 15N 12 58 E
Angels Camp, U.S.A. 84 G6 38 4N 120 32W
Ångermanälven →, Sweden 8 E17 62 40N 18 0 E
Ångermanland, Sweden 8 E18 63 36N 17 45 E
Angers, Canada 79 A9 45 31N 75 29W
Angers, France 18 C3 47 30N 0 35W
Ängesån →, Sweden 8 C20 66 16N 22 47 E
Angikuni L., Canada 73 A9 62 0N 100 0W
Angkor, Cambodia 38 F4 13 22N 103 50 E
Anglesey, U.K. 10 D3 53 17N 4 20W
Anglesey, Isle of □, U.K. 10 D3 53 16N 4 18W
Angleton, U.S.A. 81 L7 29 10N 95 26W
Anglisidhes, Cyprus 23 E12 34 51N 33 27 E
Angmagssalik, Greenland 4 C6 65 40N 37 20W
Ango, Dem. Rep. of the Congo 54 B2 4 10N 26 5 E
Angoche, Mozam. 55 F4 16 8S 39 55 E
Angoche, I., Mozam. 55 F4 16 20S 39 50 E
Angol, Chile 94 D1 37 56S 72 45W
Angola, Ind., U.S.A. 76 E3 41 38N 85 0W
Angola, N.Y., U.S.A. 78 D5 42 38N 79 2W
Angola ■, Africa 53 G3 12 0S 18 0 E
Angoulême, France 18 D4 45 39N 0 10 E
Angoumois, France 18 D3 45 50N 0 25 E
Angra dos Reis, Brazil 95 A7 23 0S 44 10W
Angren, Uzbekistan 26 E8 41 1N 70 12 E
Angtassom, Cambodia 39 G5 11 1N 104 41 E
Angu, Dem. Rep. of the Congo 54 B1 3 25N 24 28 E
Anguang, China 35 B12 45 15N 123 45 E
Anguilla ■, W. Indies 89 C7 18 14N 63 5W
Anguo, China 34 E8 38 28N 115 15 E
Angurugu, Australia 62 A2 14 0S 136 25 E
Angus □, U.K. 12 E6 56 46N 2 56W
Anhanduí →, Brazil 95 A5 21 46S 52 9W
Anholt, Denmark 9 H14 56 42N 11 33 E
Anhui □, China 33 C6 32 0N 117 0 E
Anhwei = Anhui □, China 33 C6 32 0N 117 0 E
Anichab, Namibia 56 C1 21 0S 14 46 E
Animas →, U.S.A. 83 H9 36 43N 108 13W
Anivorano, Madag. 57 B8 18 44S 48 58 E
Anjalankoski, Finland 9 F22 60 45N 26 51 E
Anjar, India 42 H4 23 6N 70 10 E
Anjidiv I., India 40 M9 14 40N 74 10 E
Anjou, France 18 C3 47 20N 0 15W
Anjozorobe, Madag. 57 B8 18 22S 47 52 E
Anju, N. Korea 35 E13 39 36N 125 40 E
Ankaboa, Tanjon, Madag. 57 C7 21 58S 43 20 E
Ankang, China 34 H5 32 40N 109 1 E
Ankara, Turkey 25 G5 39 57N 32 54 E
Ankaramena, Madag. 57 C8 21 57S 46 39 E
Ankaratra, Madag. 53 H9 19 25S 47 12 E
Ankazoabo, Madag. 57 C7 22 18S 44 31 E
Ankazobe, Madag. 57 B8 18 20S 47 10 E
Ankeny, U.S.A. 80 E8 41 44N 93 36W
Ankisabe, Madag. 57 B8 19 17S 46 29 E
Ankoro, Dem. Rep. of the Congo 54 D2 6 45S 26 55 E
Anmyŏn-do, S. Korea 35 F14 36 25N 126 25 E
Ann, C., U.S.A. 79 D14 42 38N 70 35W
Ann Arbor, U.S.A. 76 D4 42 17N 83 45W
Anna, U.S.A. 81 G10 37 28N 89 15W
Annaba, Algeria 50 A7 36 50N 7 46 E
Annalee →, Ireland 13 B4 54 2N 7 24W
Annam, Vietnam 38 E7 16 0N 108 0 E
Annamitique, Chaîne, Asia 38 D6 17 0N 106 0 E
Annan, U.K. 12 G5 54 59N 3 16W
Annan →, U.K. 12 G5 54 58N 3 16W
Annapolis, U.S.A. 76 F7 38 59N 76 30W
Annapolis Royal, Canada 71 D6 44 44N 65 32W
Annapurna, Nepal 43 E10 28 34N 83 50 E
Annean, L., Australia 61 E2 26 54S 118 14 E
Annecy, France 18 D7 45 55N 6 8 E
Anning, China 32 D5 24 55N 102 26 E
Anniston, U.S.A. 77 J3 33 39N 85 50W
Annobón, Atl. Oc. 49 G4 1 25S 5 36 E
Annotto Bay, Jamaica 88 C4 18 17N 76 45W
Annville, U.S.A. 79 F8 40 20N 76 31W
Áno Viánnos, Greece 23 D7 35 2N 25 21 E
Anorotsangana, Madag. 57 A8 13 56S 47 55 E
Anóyia, Greece 23 D6 35 16N 24 52 E
Anping, Hebei, China 34 E8 38 15N 115 30 E
Anping, Liaoning, China 35 D12 41 5N 123 30 E
Anqing, China 33 C6 30 30N 117 3 E
Anqiu, China 35 F10 36 25N 119 10 E
Ansai, China 34 F5 36 50N 109 20 E
Ansbach, Germany 16 D6 49 28N 10 34 E
Anshan, China 35 D12 41 5N 122 58 E
Anshun, China 32 D5 26 18N 105 57 E
Ansley, U.S.A. 80 E5 41 18N 99 23W
Anson, U.S.A. 81 J5 32 45N 99 54W
Anson B., Australia 60 B5 13 20S 130 6 E
Ansongo, Mali 50 E6 15 25N 0 35 E
Ansonia, U.S.A. 79 E11 41 21N 73 5W
Anstruther, U.K. 12 E6 56 14N 2 41W
Ansudu, Indonesia 37 E9 2 11S 139 22 E
Antabamba, Peru 92 F4 14 40S 73 0W
Antakya, Turkey 25 G6 36 14N 36 10 E
Antalaha, Madag. 57 A9 14 57S 50 20 E
Antalya, Turkey 25 G5 36 52N 30 45 E
Antalya Körfezi, Turkey 25 G5 36 15N 31 30 E
Antananarivo, Madag. 57 B8 18 55S 47 31 E
Antananarivo □, Madag. 57 B8 19 0S 47 0 E
Antanimbaribe, Madag. 57 C7 21 30S 44 48 E
Antarctic Pen., Antarctica 5 C18 67 0S 60 0W
Antarctica 5 E3 90 0S 0 0 E
Antelope, Zimbabwe 55 G2 21 2S 28 31 E
Antequera, Paraguay 94 A4 24 8S 57 7W
Antequera, Spain 19 D3 37 5N 4 33W
Antero, Mt., U.S.A. 83 G10 38 41N 106 15W
Anthony, Kans., U.S.A. 81 G5 37 9N 98 2W
Anthony, N. Mex., U.S.A. 83 K10 32 0N 106 36W
Anti Atlas, Morocco 50 C4 30 0N 8 30W
Anti-Lebanon = Ash Sharqi, Al Jabal, Lebanon 47 B5 33 40N 36 10 E
Antibes, France 18 E7 43 34N 7 6 E
Anticosti, Î. d', Canada 71 C7 49 30N 63 0W
Antigo, U.S.A. 80 C10 45 9N 89 9W
Antigonish, Canada 71 C7 45 38N 61 58W
Antigua, Canary Is. 22 F5 28 24N 14 1W
Antigua, W. Indies 89 C7 17 0N 61 50W
Antigua & Barbuda ■, W. Indies 89 C7 17 20N 61 48W
Antigua Guatemala, Guatemala 88 D1 14 34N 90 41W
Antilla, Cuba 88 B4 20 40N 75 50W
Antilles = West Indies, Cent. Amer. 89 D7 15 0N 65 0W
Antioch, U.S.A. 84 G5 38 1N 121 48W
Antioquia, Colombia 92 B3 6 40N 75 55W
Antipodes Is., Pac. Oc. 64 M9 49 45S 178 40 E
Antlers, U.S.A. 81 H7 34 14N 95 37W
Antofagasta, Chile 94 A1 23 50S 70 30W
Antofagasta □, Chile 94 A2 24 0S 69 0W
Antofagasta de la Sierra, Argentina 94 B2 26 5S 67 20W
Antofalla, Argentina 94 B2 25 30S 68 5W
Antofalla, Salar de, Argentina 94 B2 25 40S 67 45W
Anton, U.S.A. 81 J3 33 49N 102 10W
Antongila, Helodrano, Madag. 57 B8 15 30S 49 50 E
Antonibé, Madag. 57 B8 15 7S 47 24 E
Antonibé, Presqu'île d', Madag. 57 A8 14 55S 47 20 E
Antonina, Brazil 95 B6 25 26S 48 42W
Antrim, U.K. 13 B5 54 43N 6 14W
Antrim, U.S.A. 78 F3 40 7N 81 21W
Antrim □, U.K. 13 B5 54 56N 6 25W
Antrim, Mts. of, U.K. 13 A5 55 3N 6 14W
Antrim Plateau, Australia 60 C4 18 8S 128 20 E
Antsalova, Madag. 57 B7 18 40S 44 37 E
Antsirabe, Madag. 57 B8 19 55S 47 2 E
Antsiranana, Madag. 57 A8 12 25S 49 20 E
Antsohihy, Madag. 57 A8 14 50S 47 59 E
Antsohimbondrona Seranana, Madag. 57 A8 13 7S 48 48 E
Antu, China 35 C15 42 30N 128 20 E
Antwerp = Antwerpen, Belgium 15 C4 51 13N 4 25 E
Antwerp, U.S.A. 79 B9 44 12N 75 37W
Antwerpen, Belgium 15 C4 51 13N 4 25 E
Antwerpen □, Belgium 15 C4 51 15N 4 40 E
Anupgarh, India 42 E5 29 10N 73 10 E
Anuppur, India 43 H9 23 6N 81 41 E
Anuradhapura, Sri Lanka 40 Q12 8 22N 80 28 E
Anveh, Iran 45 E7 27 23N 54 11 E
Anvers = Antwerpen, Belgium 15 C4 51 13N 4 25 E
Anvers I., Antarctica 5 C17 64 30S 63 40W
Anxi, China 32 B4 40 30N 95 43 E
Anxious B., Australia 63 E1 33 24S 134 45 E
Anyang, China 34 F8 36 5N 114 21 E
Anyer-Kidul, Indonesia 37 G11 6 4S 105 53 E
Anyi, China 34 G6 35 2N 111 2 E
Anza, U.S.A. 85 M10 33 35N 116 39W
Anze, China 34 F7 36 10N 112 12 E
Anzhero-Sudzhensk, Russia 26 D9 56 10N 86 0 E
Ánzio, Italy 20 D5 41 27N 12 37 E
Aoga-Shima, Japan 31 H9 32 28N 139 46 E
Aomen = Macau, China 33 D6 22 16N 113 35 E
Aomori, Japan 30 D10 40 45N 140 45 E

Aomori □, *Japan* **30 D10** 40 45N 140 40 E
Aonla, *India* **43 E8** 28 16N 79 11 E
Aosta, *Italy* **18 D7** 45 45N 7 20 E
Aouker, *Mauritania* **50 E4** 17 40N 10 0W
Aozou, *Chad* **51 D9** 21 45N 17 28 E
Apa —►, *S. Amer.* **94 A4** 22 6S 58 2W
Apache, *U.S.A.* **81 H5** 34 54N 98 22W
Apache Junction, *U.S.A.* **83 K8** 33 25N 111 33W
Apalachee B., *U.S.A.* **77 L4** 30 0N 84 0W
Apalachicola, *U.S.A.* **77 L3** 29 43N 84 59W
Apalachicola —►, *U.S.A.* **77 L3** 29 43N 84 58W
Apaporis —►, *Colombia* **92 D5** 1 23S 69 25W
Aparri, *Phil.* **37 A6** 18 22N 121 38 E
Apatity, *Russia* **24 A5** 67 34N 33 22 E
Apatzingán, *Mexico* **86 D4** 19 0N 102 20W
Apeldoorn, *Neths.* **15 B5** 52 13N 5 57 E
Apennines = Appennini, *Italy* **20 B4** 44 0N 10 0 E
Apia, *W. Samoa* **59 A13** 13 50S 171 50W
Apiacás, Serra dos, *Brazil* **92 E7** 9 50S 57 0W
Apizaco, *Mexico* **87 D5** 19 26N 98 9W
Aplao, *Peru* **92 G4** 16 0S 72 40W
Apo, Mt., *Phil.* **37 C7** 6 53N 125 14 E
Apolakkiá, *Greece* **23 C9** 36 5N 27 48 E
Apolakkiá, Órmos, *Greece* **23 C9** 36 5N 27 45 E
Apollo Bay, *Australia* **63 F3** 38 45S 143 40 E
Apolo, *Bolivia* **92 F5** 14 30S 68 30W
Aporé —►, *Brazil* **93 G8** 19 27S 50 57W
Apostle Is., *U.S.A.* **80 B9** 47 0N 90 40W
Apóstoles, *Argentina* **95 B4** 28 0S 56 0W
Apostolos Andreas, C., *Cyprus* **23 D13** 35 42N 34 35 E
Apoteri, *Guyana* **92 C7** 4 2N 58 32W
Appalachian Mts., *U.S.A.* **76 G6** 38 0N 80 0W
Appennini, *Italy* **20 B4** 44 0N 10 0 E
Apple Hill, *Canada* **79 A10** 45 13N 74 46W
Apple Valley, *U.S.A.* **85 L9** 34 32N 117 14W
Appleby-in-Westmorland, *U.K.* **10 C5** 54 35N 2 29W
Appleton, *U.S.A.* **76 C1** 44 16N 88 25W
Approuague —►, *Fr. Guiana* **93 C8** 4 30N 51 57W
Aprília, *Italy* **20 D5** 41 36N 12 39 E
Apsley, *Canada* **78 B6** 44 45N 78 6W
Apucarana, *Brazil* **95 A5** 23 55S 51 33W
Apure —►, *Venezuela* **92 B5** 7 37N 66 25W
Apurimac —►, *Peru* **92 F4** 12 17S 73 56W
Āqā Jarī, *Iran* **45 D6** 30 42N 49 50 E
Aqaba = Al 'Aqabah, *Jordan* **47 F4** 29 31N 35 0 E
Aqaba, G. of, *Red Sea* **44 D2** 28 15N 33 20 E
'Aqabah, Khalīj al = Aqaba, G. of, *Red Sea* **44 D2** 28 15N 33 20 E
'Aqdā, *Iran* **45 C7** 32 26N 53 37 E
Aqmola = Astana, *Kazakstan* **26 D8** 51 10N 71 30 E
Aqrah, *Iraq* **44 B4** 36 46N 43 45 E
Aqtaū, *Kazakstan* **26 E6** 43 39N 51 12 E
Aqtöbe, *Kazakstan* **25 D10** 50 17N 57 10 E
Aquidauana, *Brazil* **93 H7** 20 30S 55 50W
Aquiles Serdán, *Mexico* **86 B3** 28 37N 105 54W
Aquin, *Haiti* **89 C5** 18 16N 73 24W
Aquitain, Bassin, *France* **18 D3** 44 0N 0 30W
Ar Rachidiya, *Morocco* **50 B5** 31 58N 4 20W
Ar Rafīd, *Syria* **47 C4** 32 57N 35 52 E
Ar Raḩḩālīyah, *Iraq* **44 C4** 32 44N 43 23 E
Ar Ramādī, *Iraq* **44 C4** 33 25N 43 20 E
Ar Ramthā, *Jordan* **47 C5** 32 34N 36 0 E
Ar Raqqah, *Syria* **44 C3** 35 59N 39 8 E
Ar Rass, *Si. Arabia* **44 E4** 25 50N 43 40 E
Ar Rifā'ī, *Iraq* **44 D5** 31 50N 46 10 E
Ar Riyāḑ, *Si. Arabia* **46 C4** 24 41N 46 42 E
Ar Ru'ays, *Qatar* **45 E6** 26 8N 51 12 E
Ar Rukhaymīyah, *Iraq* **44 D5** 29 22N 45 38 E
Ar Ruqayyidah, *Si. Arabia* **45 E6** 25 21N 49 34 E
Ar Ruşāfah, *Syria* **44 C3** 35 45N 38 49 E
Ar Ruţbah, *Iraq* **44 C4** 33 0N 40 15 E
Ara, *India* **43 G11** 25 35N 84 32 E
Arab, *U.S.A.* **77 H2** 34 19N 86 30W
'Arab, Bahr el —►, *Sudan* **51 G11** 9 0N 29 30 E
'Arabābād, *Iran* **45 C8** 33 2N 57 41 E
Arabia, *Asia* **28 G8** 25 0N 45 0 E
Arabian Desert = Es Sahrâ' Esh Sharqîya, *Egypt* **51 C12** 27 30N 32 30 E
Arabian Gulf = Gulf, The, *Asia* **45 E6** 27 0N 50 0 E
Arabian Sea, *Ind. Oc.* **29 H10** 16 0N 65 0 E
Aracaju, *Brazil* **93 F11** 10 55S 37 4W
Aracati, *Brazil* **93 D11** 4 30S 37 44W
Araçatuba, *Brazil* **95 A5** 21 10S 50 30W
Aracena, *Spain* **19 D2** 37 53N 6 38W
Araçuaí, *Brazil* **93 G10** 16 52S 42 4W
'Arad, *Israel* **47 D4** 31 15N 35 12 E
Arad, *Romania* **17 E11** 46 10N 21 20 E
Arādān, *Iran* **45 C7** 35 21N 52 30 E
Aradhippou, *Cyprus* **23 E12** 34 57N 33 36 E
Arafura Sea, *E. Indies* **37 F9** 9 0S 135 0 E
Aragón □, *Spain* **19 B5** 41 25N 0 40W
Aragón —►, *Spain* **19 A5** 42 13N 1 44W
Araguacema, *Brazil* **93 E9** 8 50S 49 20W
Araguaia —►, *Brazil* **93 E9** 5 21S 48 41W
Araguaína, *Brazil* **93 E9** 7 12S 48 12W
Araguari, *Brazil* **93 G9** 18 38S 48 11W
Araguari —►, *Brazil* **93 C9** 1 15N 49 55W
Arain, *India* **42 F6** 26 27N 75 2 E
Arak, *Algeria* **50 C6** 25 20N 3 45 E
Arāk, *Iran* **45 C6** 34 0N 49 40 E
Arakan Coast, *Burma* **41 K19** 19 0N 94 0 E
Arakan Yoma, *Burma* **41 K19** 20 0N 94 40 E
Araks = Aras, Rūd-e —►, *Azerbaijan* **44 B5** 40 5N 48 29 E
Aral, *Kazakstan* **26 E7** 46 41N 61 45 E
Aral Sea, *Asia* **26 E7** 44 30N 60 0 E
Aral Tengizi = Aral Sea, *Asia* **26 E7** 44 30N 60 0 E
Aralsk = Aral, *Kazakstan* **26 E7** 46 41N 61 45 E
Aralskoye More = Aral Sea, *Asia* **26 E7** 44 30N 60 0 E
Aramac, *Australia* **62 C4** 22 58S 145 14 E
Aran I., *Ireland* **13 A3** 55 0N 8 30W
Aran Is., *Ireland* **13 C2** 53 6N 9 38W
Aranda de Duero, *Spain* **19 B4** 41 39N 3 42W
Arandān, *Iran* **44 C5** 35 23N 46 55 E
Aranjuez, *Spain* **19 B4** 40 1N 3 40W
Aranos, *Namibia* **56 C2** 24 9S 19 7 E
Aransas Pass, *U.S.A.* **81 M6** 27 55N 97 9W
Aranyaprathet, *Thailand* **38 F4** 13 41N 102 30 E
Arapahoe, *U.S.A.* **80 E5** 40 18N 99 54W
Arapey Grande —►, *Uruguay* **94 C4** 30 55S 57 49W
Arapgir, *Turkey* **44 B3** 39 5N 38 30 E
Arapiraca, *Brazil* **93 E11** 9 45S 36 39W
Arapongas, *Brazil* **95 A5** 23 29S 51 28W
Ar'ar, *Si. Arabia* **44 D4** 30 59N 41 2 E
Araranguá, *Brazil* **95 B6** 29 0S 49 30W
Araraquara, *Brazil* **93 H9** 21 50S 48 0W
Ararás, Serra das, *Brazil* **95 B5** 25 0S 53 10W
Ararat, *Australia* **63 F3** 37 16S 143 0 E
Ararat, Mt. = Ağrı Dağı, *Turkey* **25 G7** 39 50N 44 15 E
Araria, *India* **43 F12** 26 9N 87 33 E
Araripe, Chapada do, *Brazil* **93 E11** 7 20S 40 0W
Araruama, L. de, *Brazil* **95 A7** 22 53S 42 12W
Aras, Rūd-e —►, *Azerbaijan* **44 B5** 40 5N 48 29 E
Arauca, *Colombia* **92 B4** 7 0N 70 40W
Arauca —►, *Venezuela* **92 B5** 7 24N 66 35W
Arauco, *Chile* **94 D1** 37 16S 73 25W
Araxá, *Brazil* **93 G9** 19 35S 46 55W
Araya, Pen. de, *Venezuela* **92 A6** 10 40N 64 0W
Arba Minch, *Ethiopia* **46 F2** 6 0N 37 30 E
Arbat, *Iraq* **44 C5** 35 25N 45 35 E
Árbatax, *Italy* **20 E3** 39 56N 9 42 E
Arbīl, *Iraq* **44 B5** 36 15N 44 5 E
Arborfield, *Canada* **73 C8** 53 6N 103 39W
Arborg, *Canada* **73 C9** 50 54N 97 13W
Arbroath, *U.K.* **12 E6** 56 34N 2 35W
Arbuckle, *U.S.A.* **84 F4** 39 1N 122 3W
Arcachon, *France* **18 D3** 44 40N 1 10W
Arcade, *Calif., U.S.A.* **85 L8** 34 2N 118 15W
Arcade, *N.Y., U.S.A.* **78 D6** 42 32N 78 25W
Arcadia, *Fla., U.S.A.* **77 M5** 27 13N 81 52W
Arcadia, *La., U.S.A.* **81 J8** 32 33N 92 55W
Arcadia, *Pa., U.S.A.* **78 F6** 40 47N 78 51W
Arcata, *U.S.A.* **82 F1** 40 52N 124 5W
Archangel = Arkhangelsk, *Russia* **24 B7** 64 38N 40 36 E
Archbald, *U.S.A.* **79 E9** 41 30N 75 32W
Archer —►, *Australia* **62 A3** 13 28S 141 41 E
Archer B., *Australia* **62 A3** 13 20S 141 30 E
Archers Post, *Kenya* **54 B4** 0 35N 37 35 E
Arches National Park, *U.S.A.* **83 G9** 38 45N 109 25W
Arckaringa Cr. —►, *Australia* **63 D2** 28 10S 135 22 E
Arco, *U.S.A.* **82 E7** 43 38N 113 18W
Arcos de la Frontera, *Spain* **19 D3** 36 45N 5 49W
Arcot, *India* **40 N11** 12 53N 79 20 E
Arctic Bay, *Canada* **69 A11** 73 1N 85 7W
Arctic Ocean, *Arctic* **4 B18** 78 0N 160 0W
Arctic Red River = Tsiigehtchic, *Canada* **68 B6** 67 15N 134 0W
Arda —►, *Bulgaria* **21 D12** 41 40N 26 30 E
Ardabīl, *Iran* **45 B6** 38 15N 48 18 E
Ardakān = Sepīdān, *Iran* **45 D7** 30 20N 52 5 E
Ardakān, *Iran* **45 C7** 32 19N 53 59 E
Ardee, *Ireland* **13 C5** 53 52N 6 33W
Arden, *Canada* **78 B8** 44 43N 76 56W
Arden, *Calif., U.S.A.* **84 G5** 38 36N 121 33W
Arden, *Nev., U.S.A.* **85 J11** 36 1N 115 14W
Ardenne, *Belgium* **16 D3** 49 50N 5 5 E
Ardennes = Ardenne, *Belgium* **16 D3** 49 50N 5 5 E
Arderin, *Ireland* **13 C4** 53 2N 7 39W
Ardestān, *Iran* **45 C7** 33 20N 52 25 E
Ardivachar Pt., *U.K.* **12 D1** 57 23N 7 26W
Ardlethan, *Australia* **63 E4** 34 22S 146 53 E
Ardmore, *Okla., U.S.A.* **81 H6** 34 10N 97 8W
Ardmore, *Pa., U.S.A.* **79 G9** 39 58N 75 18W
Ardnamurchan, Pt. of, *U.K.* **12 E2** 56 43N 6 14W
Ardnave Pt., *U.K.* **12 F2** 55 53N 6 20W
Ardrossan, *Australia* **63 E2** 34 26S 137 53 E
Ardrossan, *U.K.* **12 F4** 55 39N 4 49W
Ards Pen., *U.K.* **13 B6** 54 33N 5 34W
Arecibo, *Puerto Rico* **89 C6** 18 29N 66 43W
Areia Branca, *Brazil* **93 E11** 5 0S 37 0W
Arena, Pt., *U.S.A.* **84 G3** 38 57N 123 44W
Arenal, *Honduras* **88 C2** 15 21N 86 50W
Arendal, *Norway* **9 G13** 58 28N 8 46 E
Arequipa, *Peru* **92 G4** 16 20S 71 30W
Arévalo, *Spain* **19 B3** 41 3N 4 43W
Arezzo, *Italy* **20 C4** 43 25N 11 53 E
Arga, *Turkey* **44 B3** 38 21N 37 59 E
Arganda, *Spain* **19 B4** 40 19N 3 26W
Argenta, *Canada* **72 C5** 50 11N 116 56W
Argentan, *France* **18 B3** 48 45N 0 1W
Argentário, Mte., *Italy* **20 C4** 42 24N 11 9 E
Argentia, *Canada* **71 C9** 47 18N 53 58W
Argentina ■, *S. Amer.* **96 D3** 35 0S 66 0W
Argentina Is., *Antarctica* **5 C17** 66 0S 64 0W
Argentino, L., *Argentina* **96 G2** 50 10S 73 0W
Argeş —►, *Romania* **17 F14** 44 5N 26 38 E
Arghandab —►, *Afghan.* **42 D1** 31 30N 64 15 E
Argolikós Kólpos, *Greece* **21 F10** 37 20N 22 52 E
Árgos, *Greece* **21 F10** 37 40N 22 43 E
Argostólion, *Greece* **21 E9** 38 12N 20 33 E
Arguello, Pt., *U.S.A.* **85 L6** 34 35N 120 39W
Arguineguín, *Canary Is.* **22 G4** 27 46N 15 41W
Argun —►, *Russia* **27 D13** 53 20N 121 28 E
Argus Pk., *U.S.A.* **85 K9** 35 52N 117 26W
Argyle, L., *Australia* **60 C4** 16 20S 128 40 E
Argyll & Bute □, *U.K.* **12 E3** 56 13N 5 28W
Århus, *Denmark* **9 H14** 56 8N 10 11 E
Ariadnoye, *Russia* **30 B7** 45 8N 134 25 E
Ariamsvlei, *Namibia* **56 D2** 28 9S 19 51 E
Ariana, *Tunisia* **51 A7** 36 52N 10 12 E
Arica, *Chile* **92 G4** 18 32S 70 20W
Arica, *Colombia* **92 D4** 2 0S 71 50W
Arico, *Canary Is.* **22 F3** 28 9N 16 29W
Arid, C., *Australia* **61 F3** 34 1S 123 10 E
Arida, *Japan* **31 G7** 34 5N 135 8 E
Arílla, Ákra, *Greece* **23 A3** 39 43N 19 39 E
Arima, *Trin. & Tob.* **89 D7** 10 38N 61 17W
Arinos —►, *Brazil* **92 F7** 10 25S 58 20W
Ario de Rosales, *Mexico* **86 D4** 19 12N 102 0W
Aripuanã, *Brazil* **92 E6** 9 25S 60 30W
Aripuanã —►, *Brazil* **92 E6** 5 7S 60 25W
Ariquemes, *Brazil* **92 E6** 9 55S 63 6W
Arisaig, *U.K.* **12 E3** 56 55N 5 51W
Aristazabal I., *Canada* **72 C3** 52 40N 129 10W
Arivonimamo, *Madag.* **57 B8** 19 1S 47 11 E
Arizaro, Salar de, *Argentina* **94 A2** 24 40S 67 50W
Arizona, *Argentina* **94 D2** 35 45S 65 25W
Arizona □, *U.S.A.* **83 J8** 34 0N 112 0W
Arizpe, *Mexico* **86 A2** 30 20N 110 11W
Arjeplog, *Sweden* **8 D18** 66 3N 18 2 E
Arjona, *Colombia* **92 A3** 10 14N 75 22W
Arjuna, *Indonesia* **37 G15** 7 49S 112 34 E
Arka, *Russia* **27 C15** 60 15N 142 0 E
Arkadelphia, *U.S.A.* **81 H8** 34 7N 93 4W
Arkaig, L., *U.K.* **12 E3** 56 59N 5 10W
Arkalyk = Arqalyk, *Kazakstan* **26 D7** 50 13N 66 50 E
Arkansas □, *U.S.A.* **81 H8** 35 0N 92 30W
Arkansas —►, *U.S.A.* **81 J9** 33 47N 91 4W
Arkansas City, *U.S.A.* **81 G6** 37 4N 97 2W
Arkaroola, *Australia* **63 E2** 30 20S 139 22 E
Arkhángelos, *Greece* **23 C10** 36 13N 28 7 E
Arkhangelsk, *Russia* **24 B7** 64 38N 40 36 E
Arki, *India* **42 D7** 31 9N 76 58 E
Arklow, *Ireland* **13 D5** 52 48N 6 10W
Arkport, *U.S.A.* **78 D7** 42 24N 77 42W
Arkticheskiy, Mys, *Russia* **27 A10** 81 10N 95 0 E
Arkville, *U.S.A.* **79 D10** 42 9N 74 37W
Arlanzón —►, *Spain* **19 A3** 42 3N 4 17W
Arlbergpass, *Austria* **16 E6** 47 9N 10 12 E
Arles, *France* **18 E6** 43 41N 4 40 E
Arlington, *S. Africa* **57 D4** 28 1S 27 53 E
Arlington, *N.Y., U.S.A.* **79 E11** 41 42N 73 54W
Arlington, *Oreg., U.S.A.* **82 D3** 45 43N 120 12W
Arlington, *S. Dak., U.S.A.* **80 C6** 44 22N 97 8W
Arlington, *Tex., U.S.A.* **81 J6** 32 44N 97 7W
Arlington, *Va., U.S.A.* **76 F7** 38 53N 77 7W
Arlington, *Vt., U.S.A.* **79 C11** 43 5N 73 9W
Arlington, *Wash., U.S.A.* **84 B4** 48 12N 122 8W
Arlington Heights, *U.S.A.* **76 D2** 42 5N 87 59W
Arlit, *Niger* **50 E7** 19 0N 7 38 E
Arlon, *Belgium* **15 E5** 49 42N 5 49 E
Arltunga, *Australia* **62 C1** 23 26S 134 41 E
Armagh, *U.K.* **13 B5** 54 21N 6 39W
Armagh □, *U.K.* **13 B5** 54 18N 6 37W
Armavir, *Russia* **25 E7** 45 2N 41 7 E
Armenia, *Colombia* **92 C3** 4 35N 75 45W
Armenia ■, *Asia* **25 F7** 40 20N 45 0 E
Armenistís, Ákra, *Greece* **23 C9** 36 8N 27 42 E
Armidale, *Australia* **63 E5** 30 30S 151 40 E
Armour, *U.S.A.* **80 D5** 43 19N 98 21W
Armstrong, *B.C., Canada* **72 C5** 50 25N 119 10W
Armstrong, *Ont., Canada* **70 B2** 50 18N 89 4W
Arnarfjörður, *Iceland* **8 D2** 65 48N 23 40W
Arnaud —►, *Canada* **69 C13** 60 0N 70 0W
Arnauti, C., *Cyprus* **23 D11** 35 6N 32 17 E
Arnett, *U.S.A.* **81 G5** 36 8N 99 46W
Arnhem, *Neths.* **15 C5** 51 58N 5 55 E
Arnhem, C., *Australia* **62 A2** 12 20S 137 30 E
Arnhem B., *Australia* **62 A2** 12 20S 136 10 E
Arnhem Land, *Australia* **62 A1** 13 10S 134 30 E
Arno —►, *Italy* **20 C4** 43 41N 10 17 E
Arno Bay, *Australia* **63 E2** 33 54S 136 34 E
Arnold, *U.K.* **10 D6** 53 1N 1 7W
Arnold, *U.S.A.* **84 G6** 38 15N 120 20W
Arnot, *Canada* **73 B9** 55 56N 96 41W
Arnøy, *Norway* **8 A19** 70 9N 20 40 E
Arnprior, *Canada* **79 A8** 45 26N 76 21W
Arnsberg, *Germany* **16 C5** 51 24N 8 5 E
Aroab, *Namibia* **56 D2** 26 41S 19 39 E
Aron, *India* **42 G6** 25 57N 77 56 E
Arqalyk, *Kazakstan* **26 D7** 50 13N 66 50 E
Arrah = Ara, *India* **43 G11** 25 35N 84 32 E
Arran, *U.K.* **12 F3** 55 34N 5 12W
Arras, *France* **18 A5** 50 17N 2 46 E
Arrecife, *Canary Is.* **22 F6** 28 57N 13 37W
Arrecifes, *Argentina* **94 C3** 34 6S 60 9W
Arrée, Mts. d', *France* **18 B2** 48 26N 3 55W
Arriaga, *Chiapas, Mexico* **87 D6** 16 15N 93 52W
Arriaga, *San Luis Potosí, Mexico* **86 C4** 21 55N 101 23W
Arrilalah, *Australia* **62 C3** 23 43S 143 54 E
Arrino, *Australia* **61 E2** 29 30S 115 40 E
Arrow, L., *Ireland* **13 B3** 54 3N 8 19W
Arrowhead, L., *U.S.A.* **85 L9** 34 16N 117 10W
Arrowtown, *N.Z.* **59 L2** 44 57S 168 50 E
Arroyo Grande, *U.S.A.* **85 K6** 35 7N 120 35W
Ars, *Iran* **44 B5** 37 9N 47 46 E
Arsenault L., *Canada* **73 B7** 55 6N 108 32W
Arsenev, *Russia* **30 B6** 44 10N 133 15 E
Árta, *Greece* **21 E9** 39 8N 21 2 E
Artà, *Spain* **22 B10** 39 41N 3 21 E
Arteaga, *Mexico* **86 D4** 18 50N 102 20W
Artem, *Russia* **30 C6** 43 22N 132 13 E
Artemovsk, *Russia* **27 D10** 54 45N 93 35 E
Artemovsk, *Ukraine* **25 E6** 48 35N 38 0 E
Artesia = Mosomane, *Botswana* **56 C4** 24 2S 26 19 E
Artesia, *U.S.A.* **81 J2** 32 51N 104 24W
Arthur, *Canada* **78 C4** 43 50N 80 32W
Arthur —►, *Australia* **62 G3** 41 2S 144 40 E
Arthur Cr. —►, *Australia* **62 C2** 22 30S 136 25 E
Arthur Pt., *Australia* **62 C5** 22 7S 150 3 E
Arthur River, *Australia* **61 F2** 33 20S 117 2 E
Arthur's Pass, *N.Z.* **59 K3** 42 54S 171 35 E
Arthur's Town, *Bahamas* **89 B4** 24 38N 75 42W
Artigas, *Uruguay* **94 C4** 30 20S 56 30W
Artillery L., *Canada* **73 A7** 63 9N 107 52W
Artois, *France* **18 A5** 50 20N 2 30 E
Artrutx, C. de, *Spain* **22 B10** 39 55N 3 49 E
Artsyz, *Ukraine* **17 E15** 46 4N 29 26 E
Artvin, *Turkey* **25 F7** 41 14N 41 44 E
Aru, Kepulauan, *Indonesia* **37 F8** 6 0S 134 30 E
Aru Is. = Aru, Kepulauan, *Indonesia* **37 F8** 6 0S 134 30 E
Arua, *Uganda* **54 B3** 3 1N 30 58 E
Aruanã, *Brazil* **93 F8** 14 54S 51 10W
Aruba ■, *W. Indies* **89 D6** 12 30N 70 0W
Arucas, *Canary Is.* **22 F4** 28 7N 15 32W
Arun —►, *Nepal* **43 F12** 26 55N 87 10 E
Arun —►, *U.K.* **11 G7** 50 49N 0 33W
Arunachal Pradesh □, *India* **41 F19** 28 0N 95 0 E
Arusha, *Tanzania* **54 C4** 3 20S 36 40 E
Arusha □, *Tanzania* **54 C4** 4 0S 36 30 E
Arusha Chini, *Tanzania* **54 C4** 3 32S 37 20 E
Aruwimi —►, *Dem. Rep. of the Congo* **54 B1** 1 13N 23 36 E
Arvada, *Colo., U.S.A.* **80 F2** 39 48N 105 5W
Arvada, *Wyo., U.S.A.* **82 D10** 44 39N 106 8W
Árvi, *Greece* **23 E7** 34 59N 25 28 E
Arviat, *Canada* **73 A10** 61 6N 93 59W
Arvidsjaur, *Sweden* **8 D18** 65 35N 19 10 E
Arvika, *Sweden* **9 G15** 59 40N 12 36 E
Arvin, *U.S.A.* **85 K8** 35 12N 118 50W
Arwal, *India* **43 G11** 25 15N 84 41 E
Arxan, *China* **33 B6** 47 11N 119 57 E
Aryirádhes, *Greece* **23 B3** 39 27N 19 58 E
Aryiroúpolis, *Greece* **23 D6** 35 17N 24 20 E
Arys, *Kazakstan* **26 E7** 42 26N 68 48 E
Arzamas, *Russia* **24 C7** 55 27N 43 55 E
Aş Şadr, *U.A.E.* **45 E7** 24 40N 54 41 E
Aş Şafā, *Syria* **47 B6** 33 10N 37 0 E
As Saffānīyah, *Si. Arabia* **45 E6** 27 55N 48 50 E
As Safīrah, *Syria* **44 B3** 36 5N 37 21 E
Aş Şahm, *Oman* **45 E8** 24 10N 56 53 E
As Sājir, *Si. Arabia* **44 E5** 25 11N 44 36 E
As Salamīyah, *Syria* **44 C3** 35 1N 37 2 E
As Salmān, *Iraq* **44 D5** 30 30N 44 32 E
As Salţ, *Jordan* **47 C4** 32 2N 35 43 E
As Sal'w'a, *Qatar* **45 E6** 24 23N 50 50 E
As Samāwah, *Iraq* **44 D5** 31 15N 45 15 E
As Sanamayn, *Syria* **47 B5** 33 3N 36 10 E
As Sohar = Şuḩār, *Oman* **45 E8** 24 20N 56 40 E
As Sukhnah, *Syria* **44 C3** 34 52N 38 52 E
As Sulaymānīyah, *Iraq* **44 C5** 35 35N 45 29 E
As Sulaymī, *Si. Arabia* **44 E4** 26 17N 41 21 E
As Sulayyil, *Si. Arabia* **46 C4** 20 27N 45 34 E
As Summān, *Si. Arabia* **44 E5** 25 0N 47 0 E
As Suwaydā', *Syria* **47 C5** 32 40N 36 30 E
As Suwaydā' □, *Syria* **47 C5** 32 45N 36 45 E
As Suwayq, *Oman* **45 F8** 23 51N 57 26 E
As Şuwayrah, *Iraq* **44 C5** 32 55N 45 0 E
Asab, *Namibia* **56 D2** 25 30S 18 0 E
Asad, Buḩayrat al, *Syria* **44 C3** 36 0N 38 15 E
Asahi-Gawa —►, *Japan* **31 G6** 34 36N 133 58 E
Asahigawa, *Japan* **30 C11** 43 46N 142 22 E
Asamankese, *Ghana* **50 G5** 5 50N 0 40W
Asan —►, *India* **43 F8** 26 37N 78 24 E
Asansol, *India* **43 H12** 23 40N 87 1 E
Asbesberge, *S. Africa* **56 D3** 29 0S 23 0 E
Asbestos, *Canada* **71 C5** 45 47N 71 58W
Asbury Park, *U.S.A.* **79 F10** 40 13N 74 1W
Ascensión, *Mexico* **86 A3** 31 6N 107 59W
Ascensión, B. de la, *Mexico* **87 D7** 19 50N 87 20W
Ascension I., *Atl. Oc.* **49 G2** 8 0S 14 15W
Aschaffenburg, *Germany* **16 D5** 49 58N 9 6 E
Aschersleben, *Germany* **16 C6** 51 45N 11 29 E
Áscoli Piceno, *Italy* **20 C5** 42 51N 13 34 E
Ascope, *Peru* **92 E3** 7 46S 79 8W
Ascotán, *Chile* **94 A2** 21 45S 68 17W
Aseb, *Eritrea* **46 E3** 13 0N 42 40 E
Asela, *Ethiopia* **46 F2** 8 0N 39 0 E
Asenovgrad, *Bulgaria* **21 C11** 42 1N 24 51 E
Aserradero, *Mexico* **86 C3** 23 40N 105 43W
Asgata, *Cyprus* **23 E12** 34 46N 33 15 E
Ash Fork, *U.S.A.* **83 J7** 35 13N 112 29W
Ash Grove, *U.S.A.* **81 G8** 37 19N 93 35W
Ash Shabakah, *Iraq* **44 D4** 30 49N 43 39 E
Ash Shamāl □, *Lebanon* **47 A5** 34 25N 36 0 E
Ash Shāmīyah, *Iraq* **44 D5** 31 55N 44 35 E
Ash Shāriqah, *U.A.E.* **45 E7** 25 23N 55 26 E
Ash Sharmah, *Si. Arabia* **44 D2** 28 1N 35 16 E
Ash Sharqāt, *Iraq* **44 C4** 35 27N 43 16 E
Ash Sharqi, Al Jabal, *Lebanon* **47 B5** 33 40N 36 10 E
Ash Shaţrah, *Iraq* **44 D5** 31 30N 46 10 E
Ash Shawbak, *Jordan* **44 D2** 30 32N 35 34 E
Ash Shawmari, J., *Jordan* **47 E5** 30 35N 36 35 E
Ash Shināfīyah, *Iraq* **44 D5** 31 35N 44 39 E
Ash Shu'bah, *Si. Arabia* **44 D5** 28 54N 44 44 E
Ash Shumlūl, *Si. Arabia* **44 E5** 26 31N 47 20 E
Ash Shūr'a, *Iraq* **44 C4** 35 58N 43 13 E
Ash Shurayf, *Si. Arabia* **44 E3** 25 43N 39 14 E
Ash Shuwayfāt, *Lebanon* **47 B4** 33 45N 35 30 E
Asha, *Russia* **24 D10** 55 0N 57 16 E
Ashau, *Vietnam* **38 D6** 16 6N 107 22 E
Ashbourne, *U.K.* **10 D6** 53 2N 1 43W
Ashburn, *U.S.A.* **77 K4** 31 43N 83 39W
Ashburton, *N.Z.* **59 K3** 43 53S 171 48 E
Ashburton —►, *Australia* **60 D1** 21 40S 114 56 E
Ashcroft, *Canada* **72 C4** 50 40N 121 20W
Ashdod, *Israel* **47 D3** 31 49N 34 35 E
Ashdown, *U.S.A.* **81 J7** 33 40N 94 8W
Asheboro, *U.S.A.* **77 H6** 35 43N 79 49W
Ashern, *Canada* **73 C9** 51 11N 98 21W
Asherton, *U.S.A.* **81 L5** 28 27N 99 46W
Asheville, *U.S.A.* **77 H4** 35 36N 82 33W
Ashewat, *Pakistan* **42 D3** 31 22N 68 32 E
Asheweig —►, *Canada* **70 B2** 54 17N 87 12W
Ashford, *Australia* **63 D5** 29 15S 151 3 E
Ashford, *U.K.* **11 F8** 51 8N 0 53 E
Ashgabat, *Turkmenistan* **26 F6** 38 0N 57 50 E
Ashibetsu, *Japan* **30 C11** 43 31N 142 11 E
Ashikaga, *Japan* **31 F9** 36 28N 139 29 E
Ashington, *U.K.* **10 B6** 55 11N 1 33W
Ashizuri-Zaki, *Japan* **31 H6** 32 44N 133 0 E
Ashkarkot, *Afghan.* **42 C2** 33 3N 67 58 E
Ashkhabad = Ashgabat, *Turkmenistan* **26 F6** 38 0N 57 50 E
Āshkhāneh, *Iran* **45 B8** 37 26N 56 55 E
Ashland, *Kans., U.S.A.* **81 G5** 37 11N 99 46W
Ashland, *Ky., U.S.A.* **76 F4** 38 28N 82 38W
Ashland, *Mont., U.S.A.* **82 D10** 45 36N 106 16W
Ashland, *Ohio, U.S.A.* **78 F2** 40 52N 82 19W
Ashland, *Oreg., U.S.A.* **82 E2** 42 12N 122 43W
Ashland, *Pa., U.S.A.* **79 F8** 40 45N 76 22W
Ashland, *Va., U.S.A.* **76 G7** 37 46N 77 29W
Ashland, *Wis., U.S.A.* **80 B9** 46 35N 90 53W
Ashley, *N. Dak., U.S.A.* **80 B5** 46 2N 99 22W
Ashley, *Pa., U.S.A.* **79 E9** 41 12N 75 55W
Ashmore Reef, *Australia* **60 B3** 12 14S 123 5 E
Ashmyany, *Belarus* **9 J21** 54 26N 25 52 E
Ashokan Reservoir, *U.S.A.* **79 E10** 41 56N 74 13W
Ashqelon, *Israel* **47 D3** 31 42N 34 35 E
Ashta, *India* **42 H7** 23 1N 76 43 E
Ashtabula, *U.S.A.* **78 E4** 41 52N 80 47W
Ashton, *S. Africa* **56 E3** 33 50S 20 5 E
Ashton, *U.S.A.* **82 D8** 44 4N 111 27W
Ashuanipi, L., *Canada* **71 B6** 52 45N 66 15W
Ashville, *U.S.A.* **78 F6** 40 34N 78 33W
Asia **28 E11** 45 0N 75 0 E
Asia, Kepulauan, *Indonesia* **37 D8** 1 0N 131 13 E
Āsīā Bak, *Iran* **45 C6** 35 19N 50 30 E
Asifabad, *India* **40 K11** 19 20N 79 24 E
Asinara, *Italy* **20 D3** 41 4N 8 16 E
Asinara, G. dell', *Italy* **20 D3** 41 0N 8 30 E
Asino, *Russia* **26 D9** 57 0N 86 0 E
Asipovichy, *Belarus* **17 B15** 53 19N 28 33 E
'Asīr □, *Si. Arabia* **46 D3** 18 40N 42 30 E
Asir, Ras, *Somali Rep.* **46 E5** 11 55N 51 10 E
Askersund, *Sweden* **9 G16** 58 53N 14 55 E
Askham, *S. Africa* **56 D3** 26 59S 20 47 E
Askim, *Norway* **9 G14** 59 35N 11 10 E
Askja, *Iceland* **8 D5** 65 3N 16 48W
Askøy, *Norway* **9 F11** 60 29N 5 10 E
Asmara = Asmera, *Eritrea* **46 D2** 15 19N 38 55 E

Asmera, *Eritrea* **46 D2** 15 19N 38 55 E
Åsnen, *Sweden* **9 H16** 56 37N 14 45 E
Aspen, *U.S.A.* **83 G10** 39 11N 106 49W
Aspermont, *U.S.A.* **81 J4** 33 8N 100 14W
Aspiring, Mt., *N.Z.* **59 L2** 44 23S 168 46 E
Asprókavos, Ákra, *Greece* **23 B4** 39 21N 20 6 E
Aspur, *India* **42 H6** 23 58N 74 7 E
Asquith, *Canada* **73 C7** 52 8N 107 13W
Assam □, *India* **41 G18** 26 0N 93 0 E
Asse, *Belgium* **15 D4** 50 24N 4 10 E
Assen, *Neths.* **15 A6** 53 0N 6 35 E
Assiniboia, *Canada* **73 D7** 49 40N 105 59W
Assiniboine →, *Canada* **73 D9** 49 53N 97 8W
Assiniboine, Mt., *Canada* **72 C5** 50 52N 115 39W
Assis, *Brazil* **95 A5** 22 40S 50 20W
Assisi, *Italy* **20 C5** 43 4N 12 37 E
Assynt, L., *U.K.* **12 C3** 58 10N 5 3W
Astana, *Kazakstan* **26 D8** 51 10N 71 30 E
Āstāneh, *Iran* **45 B6** 37 17N 49 59 E
Astara, *Azerbaijan* **25 G8** 38 30N 48 50 E
Asteroúsia, *Greece* **23 E7** 34 59N 25 3 E
Asti, *Italy* **18 D8** 44 54N 8 12 E
Astipálaia, *Greece* **21 F12** 36 32N 26 22 E
Astorga, *Spain* **19 A2** 42 29N 6 8W
Astoria, *U.S.A.* **84 D3** 46 11N 123 50W
Astrakhan, *Russia* **25 E8** 46 25N 48 5 E
Asturias □, *Spain* **19 A3** 43 15N 6 0W
Asunción, *Paraguay* **94 B4** 25 10S 57 30W
Asunción Nochixtlán, *Mexico* **87 D5** 17 28N 97 14W
Aswa →, *Uganda* **54 B3** 3 43N 31 55 E
Aswân, *Egypt* **51 D12** 24 4N 32 57 E
Aswân High Dam = Sadd el Aali, *Egypt* **51 D12** 23 54N 32 54 E
Asyût, *Egypt* **51 C12** 27 11N 31 4 E
At Tafilah, *Jordan* **47 E4** 30 45N 35 30 E
At Tā'if, *Si. Arabia* **46 C3** 21 5N 40 27 E
At Tirāq, *Si. Arabia* **44 E5** 27 19N 44 33 E
At Tubayq, *Si. Arabia* **44 D3** 29 30N 37 0 E
Atacama □, *Chile* **94 B2** 27 30S 70 0W
Atacama, Desierto de, *Chile* **94 A2** 24 0S 69 20W
Atacama, Salar de, *Chile* **94 A2** 23 30S 68 20W
Atalaya, *Peru* **92 F4** 10 45S 73 50W
Atalaya de Femes, *Canary Is.* **22 F6** 28 56N 13 47W
Atami, *Japan* **31 G9** 35 5N 139 4 E
Atapupu, *Indonesia* **37 F6** 9 0S 124 51 E
Atâr, *Mauritania* **50 D3** 20 30N 13 5W
Atari, *Pakistan* **42 D6** 30 56N 74 2 E
Atascadero, *U.S.A.* **84 K6** 35 29N 120 40W
Atasu, *Kazakstan* **26 E8** 48 30N 71 0 E
Atatürk Barajı, *Turkey* **25 G6** 37 28N 38 30 E
Atauro, *Indonesia* **37 F7** 8 10S 125 30 E
Atbara, *Sudan* **51 E12** 17 42N 33 59 E
'Atbara →, *Sudan* **51 E12** 17 40N 33 56 E
Atbasar, *Kazakstan* **26 D7** 51 48N 68 20 E
Atchafalaya B., *U.S.A.* **81 L9** 29 25N 91 25W
Atchison, *U.S.A.* **80 F7** 39 34N 95 7W
Āteshān, *Iran* **45 C7** 35 35N 52 37 E
Ath, *Belgium* **15 D3** 50 38N 3 47 E
Athabasca, *Canada* **72 C6** 54 45N 113 20W
Athabasca →, *Canada* **73 B6** 58 40N 110 50W
Athabasca, L., *Canada* **73 B7** 59 15N 109 15W
Athboy, *Ireland* **13 C5** 53 37N 6 56W
Athenry, *Ireland* **13 C3** 53 18N 8 44W
Athens = Athinai, *Greece* **21 F10** 37 58N 23 46 E
Athens, *Ala., U.S.A.* **77 H2** 34 48N 86 58W
Athens, *Ga., U.S.A.* **77 J4** 33 57N 83 23W
Athens, *N.Y., U.S.A.* **79 D11** 42 16N 73 49W
Athens, *Ohio, U.S.A.* **76 F4** 39 20N 82 6W
Athens, *Pa., U.S.A.* **79 E8** 41 57N 76 31W
Athens, *Tenn., U.S.A.* **77 H3** 35 27N 84 36W
Athens, *Tex., U.S.A.* **81 J7** 32 12N 95 51W
Atherley, *Canada* **78 B5** 44 37N 79 20W
Atherton, *Australia* **62 B4** 17 17S 145 30 E
Athienou, *Cyprus* **23 D12** 35 3N 33 32 E
Athínai, *Greece* **21 F10** 37 58N 23 46 E
Athlone, *Ireland* **13 C4** 53 25N 7 56W
Athna, *Cyprus* **23 D12** 35 3N 33 47 E
Athol, *U.S.A.* **79 D12** 42 36N 72 14W
Atholl, Forest of, *U.K.* **12 E5** 56 51N 3 50W
Atholville, *Canada* **71 C6** 47 59N 66 43W
Áthos, *Greece* **21 D11** 40 9N 24 22 E
Athy, *Ireland* **13 C5** 53 0N 7 0W
Ati, *Chad* **51 F9** 13 13N 18 20 E
Atiak, *Uganda* **54 B3** 3 12N 32 2 E
Atik L., *Canada* **73 B9** 55 15N 96 0W
Atikameg →, *Canada* **70 B3** 52 30N 82 46W
Atikokan, *Canada* **70 C1** 48 45N 91 37W
Atikonak L., *Canada* **71 B7** 52 40N 64 32W
Atka, *Russia* **27 C16** 60 50N 151 48 E
Atka I., *U.S.A.* **68 C2** 52 7N 174 30W
Atkinson, *U.S.A.* **80 D5** 42 32N 98 59W
Atlanta, *Ga., U.S.A.* **77 J3** 33 45N 84 23W
Atlanta, *Tex., U.S.A.* **81 J7** 33 7N 94 10W
Atlantic, *U.S.A.* **80 E7** 41 24N 95 1W
Atlantic City, *U.S.A.* **76 F8** 39 21N 74 27W
Atlantic Ocean **2 E9** 0 0 20 0W
Atlas Mts. = Haut Atlas, *Morocco* **50 B4** 32 30N 5 0W
Atlin, *Canada* **72 B2** 59 31N 133 41W
Atlin, L., *Canada* **72 B2** 59 26N 133 45W
Atlin Prov. Park, *Canada* **72 B2** 59 10N 134 30W
Atmore, *U.S.A.* **77 K2** 31 2N 87 29W
Atoka, *U.S.A.* **81 H6** 34 23N 96 8W
Atolia, *U.S.A.* **85 K9** 35 19N 117 37W
Atrai →, *Bangla.* **43 G13** 24 7N 89 22 E
Atrak = Atrek →, *Turkmenistan* **45 B8** 37 35N 53 58 E
Atrauli, *India* **42 E8** 28 2N 78 20 E
Atrek →, *Turkmenistan* **45 B8** 37 35N 53 58 E
Atsuta, *Japan* **30 C10** 43 24N 141 26 E
Attalla, *U.S.A.* **77 H2** 34 1N 86 6W
Attapu, *Laos* **38 E6** 14 48N 106 50 E
Attáviros, *Greece* **23 C9** 36 12N 27 50 E
Attawapiskat, *Canada* **70 B3** 52 56N 82 24W
Attawapiskat →, *Canada* **70 B3** 52 57N 82 18W
Attawapiskat L., *Canada* **70 B2** 52 18N 87 54W
Attica, *Ind., U.S.A.* **76 E2** 40 18N 87 15W
Attica, *Ohio, U.S.A.* **78 E2** 41 4N 82 53W
Attikamagen L., *Canada* **71 B6** 55 0N 66 30W
Attleboro, *U.S.A.* **79 E13** 41 57N 71 17W
Attock, *Pakistan* **42 C5** 33 52N 72 20 E
Attopeu = Attapu, *Laos* **38 E6** 14 48N 106 50 E
Attu I., *U.S.A.* **68 C1** 52 55N 172 55 E
Attur, *India* **40 P11** 11 35N 78 30 E
Atuel →, *Argentina* **94 D2** 36 17S 66 50W
Åtvidaberg, *Sweden* **9 G17** 58 12N 16 0 E
Atwater, *U.S.A.* **84 H6** 37 21N 120 37W
Atwood, *Canada* **78 C3** 43 40N 81 1W
Atwood, *U.S.A.* **80 F4** 39 48N 101 3W
Atyraū, *Kazakstan* **25 E9** 47 5N 52 0 E
Au Sable, *U.S.A.* **78 B1** 44 25N 83 20W
Au Sable →, *U.S.A.* **76 C4** 44 25N 83 20W
Au Sable Forks, *U.S.A.* **79 B11** 44 27N 73 41W
Au Sable Pt., *U.S.A.* **78 B1** 44 20N 83 20W
Aubagne, *France* **18 E6** 43 17N 5 37 E
Aubarca, C. d', *Spain* **22 B7** 39 4N 1 22 E
Aube →, *France* **18 B5** 48 34N 3 43 E
Auberry, *U.S.A.* **84 H7** 37 7N 119 29W
Auburn, *Ala., U.S.A.* **77 J3** 32 36N 85 29W
Auburn, *Calif., U.S.A.* **84 G5** 38 54N 121 4W
Auburn, *Ind., U.S.A.* **76 E3** 41 22N 85 4W
Auburn, *Maine, U.S.A.* **77 C10** 44 6N 70 14W
Auburn, *N.Y., U.S.A.* **79 D8** 42 56N 76 34W
Auburn, *Nebr., U.S.A.* **80 E7** 40 23N 95 51W
Auburn, *Pa., U.S.A.* **79 F8** 40 36N 76 6W
Auburn, *Wash., U.S.A.* **84 C4** 47 18N 122 14W
Auburn Ra., *Australia* **63 D5** 25 15S 150 30 E
Aubusson, *France* **18 D5** 45 57N 2 11 E
Auch, *France* **18 E4** 43 39N 0 36 E
Auckland, *N.Z.* **59 G5** 36 52S 174 46 E
Auckland Is., *Pac. Oc.* **64 N8** 50 40S 166 5 E
Aude →, *France* **18 E5** 43 13N 3 14 E
Auden, *Canada* **70 B2** 50 14N 87 53W
Audubon, *U.S.A.* **80 E7** 41 43N 94 56W
Augathella, *Australia* **63 D4** 25 48S 146 35 E
Aughnacloy, *U.K.* **13 B5** 54 25N 6 59W
Augrabies Falls, *S. Africa* **56 D3** 28 35S 20 20 E
Augsburg, *Germany* **16 D6** 48 25N 10 52 E
Augusta, *Australia* **61 F2** 34 19S 115 9 E
Augusta, *Italy* **20 F6** 37 13N 15 13 E
Augusta, *Ark., U.S.A.* **81 H9** 35 17N 91 22W
Augusta, *Ga., U.S.A.* **77 J5** 33 28N 81 58W
Augusta, *Kans., U.S.A.* **81 G6** 37 41N 96 59W
Augusta, *Maine, U.S.A.* **69 D13** 44 19N 69 47W
Augusta, *Mont., U.S.A.* **82 C7** 47 30N 112 24W
Augustów, *Poland* **17 B12** 53 51N 23 0 E
Augustus, Mt., *Australia* **61 D2** 24 20S 116 50 E
Augustus I., *Australia* **60 C3** 15 20S 124 30 E
Aukum, *U.S.A.* **84 G6** 38 34N 120 43W
Auld, L., *Australia* **60 D3** 22 25S 123 50 E
Ault, *U.S.A.* **80 E2** 40 35N 104 44W
Aunis, *France* **18 C3** 46 5N 0 50W
Auponhia, *Indonesia* **37 E7** 1 58S 125 27 E
Aur, Pulau, *Malaysia* **39 L5** 2 35N 104 10 E
Auraiya, *India* **43 F8** 26 28N 79 33 E
Aurangabad, *Bihar, India* **43 G11** 24 45N 84 18 E
Aurangabad, *Maharashtra, India* **40 K9** 19 50N 75 23 E
Aurich, *Germany* **16 B4** 53 28N 7 28 E
Aurillac, *France* **18 D5** 44 55N 2 26 E
Aurora, *Canada* **78 C5** 44 0N 79 28W
Aurora, *S. Africa* **56 E2** 32 40S 18 29 E
Aurora, *Colo., U.S.A.* **80 F2** 39 44N 104 52W
Aurora, *Ill., U.S.A.* **76 E1** 41 45N 88 19W
Aurora, *Mo., U.S.A.* **81 G8** 36 58N 93 43W
Aurora, *N.Y., U.S.A.* **79 D8** 42 45N 76 42W
Aurora, *Nebr., U.S.A.* **80 E6** 40 52N 98 0W
Aurora, *Ohio, U.S.A.* **78 E3** 41 21N 81 20W
Aurukun, *Australia* **62 A3** 13 20S 141 45 E
Aus, *Namibia* **56 D2** 26 35S 16 12 E
Ausable →, *Canada* **78 C3** 43 19N 81 46W
Auschwitz = Oświęcim, *Poland* **17 C10** 50 2N 19 11 E
Austin, *Minn., U.S.A.* **80 D8** 43 40N 92 58W
Austin, *Nev., U.S.A.* **82 G5** 39 30N 117 4W
Austin, *Pa., U.S.A.* **78 E6** 41 38N 78 6W
Austin, *Tex., U.S.A.* **81 K6** 30 17N 97 45W
Austin, L., *Australia* **61 E2** 27 40S 118 0 E
Austin I., *Canada* **73 A10** 61 10N 94 0W
Austra, *Norway* **8 D14** 65 8N 11 55 E
Austral Is. = Tubuai Is., *Pac. Oc.* **65 K13** 25 0S 150 0W
Austral Seamount Chain, *Pac. Oc.* **65 K13** 24 0S 150 0W
Australia ■, *Oceania* **64 K5** 23 0S 135 0 E
Australian Capital Territory □, *Australia* **63 F4** 35 30S 149 0 E
Australind, *Australia* **61 F2** 33 17S 115 42 E
Austria ■, *Europe* **16 E8** 47 0N 14 0 E
Austvågøy, *Norway* **8 B16** 68 20N 14 40 E
Autlán, *Mexico* **86 D4** 19 40N 104 30W
Autun, *France* **18 C6** 46 58N 4 17 E
Auvergne, *France* **18 D5** 45 20N 3 15 E
Auvergne, Mts. d', *France* **18 D5** 45 20N 2 55 E
Auxerre, *France* **18 C5** 47 48N 3 32 E
Ava, *U.S.A.* **81 G8** 36 57N 92 40W
Avallon, *France* **18 C5** 47 30N 3 53 E
Avalon, *U.S.A.* **85 M8** 33 21N 118 20W
Avalon Pen., *Canada* **71 C9** 47 30N 53 20W
Avanos, *Turkey* **44 B2** 38 43N 34 51 E
Avaré, *Brazil* **95 A6** 23 4S 48 58W
Avawatz Mts., *U.S.A.* **85 K10** 35 40N 116 30W
Aveiro, *Brazil* **93 D7** 3 10S 55 5W
Aveiro, *Portugal* **19 B1** 40 37N 8 38W
Āvej, *Iran* **45 C6** 35 40N 49 15 E
Avellaneda, *Argentina* **94 C4** 34 50S 58 10W
Avellino, *Italy* **20 D6** 40 54N 14 47 E
Avenal, *U.S.A.* **84 K6** 36 0N 120 8W
Aversa, *Italy* **20 D6** 40 58N 14 12 E
Avery, *U.S.A.* **82 C6** 47 15N 115 49W
Aves, Is. las, *Venezuela* **89 D6** 12 0N 67 30W
Avesta, *Sweden* **9 F17** 60 9N 16 10 E
Avezzano, *Italy* **20 C5** 42 2N 13 25 E
Aviá Terai, *Argentina* **94 B3** 26 45S 60 50W
Aviemore, *U.K.* **12 D5** 57 12N 3 50W
Avignon, *France* **18 E6** 43 57N 4 50 E
Ávila, *Spain* **19 B3** 40 39N 4 43W
Avila Beach, *U.S.A.* **85 K6** 35 11N 120 44W
Avilés, *Spain* **19 A3** 43 35N 5 57W
Avis, *U.S.A.* **78 E7** 41 11N 77 19W
Avoca, *U.S.A.* **78 D7** 42 25N 77 25W
Avoca →, *Australia* **63 F3** 35 40S 143 43 E
Avoca →, *Ireland* **13 D5** 52 48N 6 10W
Avola, *Canada* **72 C5** 51 45N 119 19W
Avola, *Italy* **20 F6** 36 56N 15 7 E
Avon, *U.S.A.* **78 D7** 42 55N 77 45W
Avon →, *Australia* **61 F2** 31 40S 116 7 E
Avon →, *Bristol, U.K.* **11 F5** 51 29N 2 41W
Avon →, *Dorset, U.K.* **11 G6** 50 44N 1 46W
Avon →, *Warks., U.K.* **11 E5** 52 0N 2 8W
Avon Park, *U.S.A.* **77 M5** 27 36N 81 31W
Avondale, *Zimbabwe* **55 F3** 17 43S 30 58 E
Avonlea, *Canada* **73 D8** 50 0N 105 0W
Avonmore, *Canada* **79 A10** 45 10N 74 58W
Avranches, *France* **18 B3** 48 40N 1 20W
A'waj →, *Syria* **47 B5** 33 23N 36 20 E
Awaji-Shima, *Japan* **31 G7** 34 30N 134 50 E
'Awālī, *Bahrain* **45 E6** 26 0N 50 30 E
Awantipur, *India* **43 C6** 33 55N 75 3 E
Awasa, *Ethiopia* **46 F2** 7 3N 38 28 E
Awash, *Ethiopia* **46 F3** 9 1N 40 10 E
Awatere →, *N.Z.* **59 J5** 41 37S 174 10 E
Awbārī, *Libya* **51 C8** 26 46N 12 57 E
Awe, L., *U.K.* **12 E3** 56 17N 5 16W
Awjilah, *Libya* **51 C10** 29 8N 21 7 E
Axe →, *U.K.* **11 F5** 50 42N 3 4W
Axel Heiberg I., *Canada* **4 B3** 80 0N 90 0W
Axim, *Ghana* **50 H5** 4 51N 2 15W
Axiós →, *Greece* **21 D10** 40 57N 22 35 E
Axminster, *U.K.* **11 G4** 50 46N 3 0W
Ayabaca, *Peru* **92 D3** 4 40S 79 53W
Ayabe, *Japan* **31 G7** 35 20N 135 20 E
Ayacucho, *Argentina* **94 D4** 37 5S 58 20W
Ayacucho, *Peru* **92 F4** 13 0S 74 0W
Ayaguz, *Kazakstan* **26 E9** 48 10N 80 10 E
Ayamonte, *Spain* **19 D2** 37 12N 7 24W
Ayan, *Russia* **27 D14** 56 30N 138 16 E
Ayaviri, *Peru* **92 F4** 14 50S 70 35W
Aydın, *Turkey* **21 F12** 37 51N 27 51 E
Aydin □, *Turkey* **25 G4** 37 50N 28 0 E
Ayer, *U.S.A.* **79 D13** 42 34N 71 35W
Ayer's Cliff, *Canada* **79 A12** 45 10N 72 3W
Ayers Rock, *Australia* **61 E5** 25 23S 131 5 E
Ayia Aikateríni, Ákra, *Greece* **23 A3** 39 50N 19 50 E
Ayia Dhéka, *Greece* **23 D6** 35 3N 24 58 E
Ayia Gálini, *Greece* **23 D6** 35 6N 24 41 E
Ayia Napa, *Cyprus* **23 E13** 34 59N 34 0 E
Ayia Phyla, *Cyprus* **23 E12** 34 43N 33 1 E
Ayia Varvára, *Greece* **23 D7** 35 8N 25 1 E
Áyios Amvrósios, *Cyprus* **23 D12** 35 20N 33 35 E
Áyios Evstrátios, *Greece* **21 E11** 39 34N 24 58 E
Áyios Ioánnis, Ákra, *Greece* **23 D7** 35 20N 25 40 E
Áyios Isídhoros, *Greece* **23 C9** 36 9N 27 51 E
Áyios Matthaíos, *Greece* **23 B3** 39 30N 19 47 E
Áyios Nikólaos, *Greece* **23 D7** 35 11N 25 41 E
Áyios Seryios, *Cyprus* **23 D12** 35 12N 33 53 E
Ayios Theodhoros, *Cyprus* **23 D13** 35 22N 34 1 E
Aykino, *Russia* **24 B8** 62 15N 49 56 E
Aylesbury, *U.K.* **11 F7** 51 49N 0 49W
Aylmer, *Canada* **78 D4** 42 46N 80 59W
Aylmer, L., *Canada* **68 B8** 64 0N 110 8W
'Ayn, Wādī al, *Oman* **45 F7** 22 15N 55 28 E
Ayn Dār, *Si. Arabia* **45 E7** 25 55N 49 10 E
Ayn Zālah, *Iraq* **44 B4** 36 45N 42 35 E
Ayolas, *Paraguay* **94 B4** 27 10S 56 59W
Ayon, Ostrov, *Russia* **27 C17** 69 50N 169 0 E
'Ayoûn el 'Atroûs, *Mauritania* **50 E4** 16 40N 9 37W
Ayr, *Australia* **62 B4** 19 35S 147 25 E
Ayr, *Canada* **78 C4** 43 17N 80 27W
Ayr, *U.K.* **12 F4** 55 28N 4 38W
Ayr →, *U.K.* **12 F4** 55 28N 4 38W
Ayre, Pt. of, *U.K.* **10 C3** 54 25N 4 21W
Ayton, *Australia* **62 B4** 15 56S 145 22 E
Aytos, *Bulgaria* **21 C12** 42 42N 27 16 E
Ayu, Kepulauan, *Indonesia* **37 D8** 0 35N 131 5 E
Ayutla, *Guatemala* **88 D1** 14 40N 92 10W
Ayutla, *Mexico* **87 D5** 16 58N 99 17W
Ayvacık, *Turkey* **21 E12** 39 36N 26 24 E
Ayvalık, *Turkey* **21 E12** 39 20N 26 46 E
Az Zabadānī, *Syria* **47 B5** 33 43N 36 5 E
Az Zāhirīyah, *West Bank* **47 D3** 31 25N 34 58 E
Az Zahrān, *Si. Arabia* **45 E6** 26 10N 50 7 E
Az Zarqā, *Jordan* **47 C5** 32 5N 36 4 E
Az Zarqā', *U.A.E.* **45 E7** 24 53N 53 4 E
Az Zāwiyah, *Libya* **51 B8** 32 52N 12 56 E
Az Zībār, *Iraq* **44 B5** 36 52N 44 4 E
Az-Zilfī, *Si. Arabia* **44 E5** 26 12N 44 52 E
Az Zubayr, *Iraq* **44 D5** 30 26N 47 40 E
Azamgarh, *India* **43 F10** 26 5N 83 13 E
Azangaro, *Peru* **92 F4** 14 55S 70 13W
Āzār Shahr, *Iran* **44 B5** 37 45N 45 59 E
Azarān, *Iran* **44 B5** 37 25N 47 16 E
Azärbayjan = Azerbaijan ■, *Asia* **25 F8** 40 20N 48 0 E
Āzarbāyjān-e Gharbī □, *Iran* **44 B5** 37 0N 44 30 E
Āzarbāyjān-e Sharqī □, *Iran* **44 B5** 37 20N 47 0 E
Azare, *Nigeria* **50 F8** 11 55N 10 10 E
A'zāz, *Syria* **44 B3** 36 36N 37 4 E
Azbine = Aïr, *Niger* **50 E7** 18 30N 8 0 E
Azerbaijan ■, *Asia* **25 F8** 40 20N 48 0 E
Azerbaijchan = Azerbaijan ■, *Asia* **25 F8** 40 20N 48 0 E
Azimganj, *India* **43 G13** 24 14N 88 16 E
Azogues, *Ecuador* **92 D3** 2 35S 78 0W
Azores, *Atl. Oc.* **50 A1** 38 44N 29 0W
Azov, *Russia* **25 E6** 47 3N 39 25 E
Azov, Sea of, *Europe* **25 E6** 46 0N 36 30 E
Azovskoye More = Azov, Sea of, *Europe* **25 E6** 46 0N 36 30 E
Azraq ash Shīshān, *Jordan* **47 D5** 31 50N 36 49 E
Aztec, *U.S.A.* **83 H10** 36 49N 107 59W
Azúa de Compostela, *Dom. Rep.* **89 C5** 18 25N 70 44W
Azuaga, *Spain* **19 C3** 38 16N 5 39W
Azuero, Pen. de, *Panama* **88 E3** 7 30N 80 30W
Azul, *Argentina* **94 D4** 36 42S 59 43W
Azusa, *U.S.A.* **85 L9** 34 8N 117 52W

B

Ba Don, *Vietnam* **38 D6** 17 45N 106 26 E
Ba Dong, *Vietnam* **39 H6** 9 40N 106 33 E
Ba Ngoi = Cam Lam, *Vietnam* **39 G7** 11 54N 109 10 E
Ba Tri, *Vietnam* **39 G6** 10 2N 106 36 E
Ba Xian = Bazhou, *China* **34 E9** 39 8N 116 22 E
Baa, *Indonesia* **37 F6** 10 50S 123 0 E
Baarle-Nassau, *Belgium* **15 C4** 51 27N 4 56 E
Bab el Mandeb, *Red Sea* **46 E3** 12 35N 43 25 E
Baba Burnu, *Turkey* **21 E12** 39 29N 26 2 E
Bābā Kalū, *Iran* **45 D6** 30 7N 50 49 E
Babadag, *Romania* **17 F15** 44 53N 28 44 E
Babadayhan, *Turkmenistan* **26 F7** 37 42N 60 23 E
Babaeski, *Turkey* **21 D12** 41 26N 27 6 E
Babahoyo, *Ecuador* **92 D3** 1 40S 79 30W
Babai = Sarju →, *India* **43 F9** 27 21N 81 23 E
Babar, *Indonesia* **37 F7** 8 0S 129 30 E
Babar, *Pakistan* **42 D3** 31 7N 69 32 E
Babarkach, *Pakistan* **42 E3** 29 45N 68 0 E
Babb, *U.S.A.* **82 B7** 48 51N 113 27W
Babelthuap, *Pac. Oc.* **37 C8** 7 30N 134 30 E
Baberu, *India* **43 G9** 25 33N 80 43 E
Babi Besar, Pulau, *Malaysia* **39 L4** 2 25N 103 59 E
Babinda, *Australia* **62 B4** 17 20S 145 56 E
Babine, *Canada* **72 B3** 55 22N 126 37W
Babine →, *Canada* **72 B3** 55 45N 127 44W
Babine L., *Canada* **72 C3** 54 48N 126 0W
Babo, *Indonesia* **37 E8** 2 30S 133 30 E
Bābol, *Iran* **45 B7** 36 40N 52 50 E
Bābol Sar, *Iran* **45 B7** 36 45N 52 45 E
Babruysk, *Belarus* **17 B15** 53 10N 29 15 E
Babuhri, *India* **42 F3** 26 49N 69 43 E
Babusar Pass, *Pakistan* **43 B5** 35 12N 73 59 E
Babuyan Chan., *Phil.* **37 A6** 18 40N 121 30 E
Babylon, *Iraq* **44 C5** 32 34N 44 22 E
Bac Lieu, *Vietnam* **39 H5** 9 17N 105 43 E
Bac Phan, *Vietnam* **38 B5** 22 0N 105 0 E
Bacabal, *Brazil* **93 D10** 4 15S 44 45W
Bacalar, *Mexico* **87 D7** 18 50N 87 27W
Bacan, Kepulauan, *Indonesia* **37 E7** 0 35S 127 30 E
Bacarra, *Phil.* **37 A6** 18 15N 120 37 E
Bacău, *Romania* **17 E14** 46 35N 26 55 E
Bacerac, *Mexico* **86 A3** 30 18N 108 50W
Bach Long Vi, Dao, *Vietnam* **38 B6** 20 10N 107 40 E
Bachelina, *Russia* **26 D7** 57 45N 67 20 E
Bachhwara, *India* **43 G11** 25 35N 85 54 E
Back →, *Canada* **68 B9** 65 10N 104 0W
Bacolod, *Phil.* **37 B6** 10 40N 122 57 E
Bacuk, *Malaysia* **39 J4** 6 4N 102 25 E
Bād, *Iran* **45 C7** 33 41N 52 1 E
Bad →, *U.S.A.* **80 C4** 44 21N 100 22W
Bad Axe, *U.S.A.* **78 C2** 43 48N 83 0W
Bad Ischl, *Austria* **16 E7** 47 44N 13 38 E
Bad Kissingen, *Germany* **16 C6** 50 11N 10 4 E
Bad Lands, *U.S.A.* **80 D3** 43 40N 102 10W
Bada Barabil, *India* **43 H11** 22 7N 85 24 E
Badagara, *India* **40 P9** 11 35N 75 40 E
Badajós, L., *Brazil* **92 D6** 3 15S 62 50W
Badajoz, *Spain* **19 C2** 38 50N 6 59W
Badalona, *Spain* **19 B7** 41 26N 2 15 E
Badalzai, *Afghan.* **42 E1** 29 50N 65 35 E
Badampahar, *India* **41 H15** 22 10N 86 10 E
Badanah, *Si. Arabia* **44 D4** 30 58N 41 30 E
Badarinath, *India* **43 D8** 30 45N 79 30 E
Badas, Kepulauan, *Indonesia* **36 D3** 0 45N 107 5 E
Baddo →, *Pakistan* **40 F4** 28 0N 64 20 E
Bade, *Indonesia* **37 F9** 7 10S 139 35 E
Baden, *Austria* **16 D9** 48 1N 16 13 E
Baden, *U.S.A.* **78 F4** 40 38N 80 14W
Baden-Baden, *Germany* **16 D5** 48 44N 8 13 E
Baden-Württemberg □, *Germany* **16 D5** 48 20N 8 40 E
Badgastein, *Austria* **16 E7** 47 7N 13 9 E
Badger, *Canada* **71 C8** 49 0N 56 4W
Badger, *U.S.A.* **84 J7** 36 38N 119 1W
Bādghīsāt □, *Afghan.* **40 B3** 35 0N 63 0 E
Badgom, *India* **43 B6** 34 1N 74 45 E
Badin, *Pakistan* **42 G3** 24 38N 68 54 E
Badlands National Park, *U.S.A.* **80 D3** 43 38N 102 56W
Badrah, *Iraq* **44 C5** 33 6N 45 58 E
Badrinath, *India* **43 D8** 30 44N 79 29 E
Badulla, *Sri Lanka* **40 R12** 7 1N 81 7 E
Baena, *Spain* **19 D3** 37 37N 4 20W
Baeza, *Spain* **19 D4** 37 57N 3 25W
Baffin B., *Canada* **4 B4** 72 0N 64 0W
Baffin I., *Canada* **69 B12** 68 0N 75 0W
Bafing →, *Mali* **50 F3** 13 49N 10 50W
Bafliyūn, *Syria* **44 B3** 36 37N 36 59 E
Bafoulabé, *Mali* **50 F3** 13 50N 10 55W
Bafoussam, *Cameroon* **52 C2** 5 28N 10 25 E
Bāfq, *Iran* **45 D7** 31 40N 55 25 E
Bafra, *Turkey* **25 F6** 41 34N 35 54 E
Bāft, *Iran* **45 D8** 29 15N 56 38 E
Bafwasende, *Dem. Rep. of the Congo* **54 B2** 1 3N 27 5 E
Bagamoyo, *Tanzania* **54 D4** 6 28S 38 55 E
Bagan Datoh, *Malaysia* **39 L3** 3 59N 100 47 E
Bagan Serai, *Malaysia* **39 K3** 5 1N 100 32 E
Baganga, *Phil.* **37 C7** 7 34N 126 33 E
Bagani, *Namibia* **56 B3** 18 7S 21 41 E
Bagansiapiapi, *Indonesia* **36 D2** 2 12N 100 50 E
Bagasra, *India* **42 J4** 21 30N 71 0 E
Bagaud, *India* **42 H6** 22 19N 75 53 E
Bagdad, *U.S.A.* **85 L11** 34 35N 115 53W
Bagdarin, *Russia* **27 D12** 54 26N 113 36 E
Bagé, *Brazil* **95 C5** 31 20S 54 15W
Bagenalstown = Muine Bheag, *Ireland* **13 D5** 52 42N 6 58W
Baggs, *U.S.A.* **82 F10** 41 2N 107 39W
Bagh, *Pakistan* **43 C5** 33 59N 73 45 E
Baghain →, *India* **43 G9** 25 32N 81 1 E
Baghdād, *Iraq* **44 C5** 33 20N 44 30 E
Bagheria, *Italy* **20 E5** 38 5N 13 30 E
Baghlān, *Afghan.* **40 A6** 36 12N 69 0 E
Bagley, *U.S.A.* **80 B7** 47 32N 95 24W
Bagodar, *India* **43 G11** 24 5N 85 52 E
Bagrationovsk, *Russia* **9 J19** 54 23N 20 39 E
Baguio, *Phil.* **37 A6** 16 26N 120 34 E
Bah, *India* **43 F8** 26 53N 78 36 E
Bahadurganj, *India* **43 F12** 26 16N 87 49 E
Bahadurgarh, *India* **42 E7** 28 40N 76 57 E
Bahama, Canal Viejo de, *W. Indies* **88 B4** 22 10N 77 30W
Bahamas ■, *N. Amer.* **89 B5** 24 0N 75 0W
Baharampur, *India* **43 G13** 24 2N 88 27 E
Bahawalnagar, *Pakistan* **42 E5** 30 0N 73 15 E
Bahawalpur, *Pakistan* **42 E4** 29 24N 71 40 E
Baheri, *India* **43 E8** 28 45N 79 34 E
Bahgul →, *India* **43 F8** 27 45N 79 36 E
Bahi, *Tanzania* **54 D4** 5 58S 35 21 E
Bahi Swamp, *Tanzania* **54 D4** 6 10S 35 0 E
Bahía = Salvador, *Brazil* **93 F11** 13 0S 38 30W
Bahía □, *Brazil* **93 F10** 12 0S 42 0W
Bahía, Is. de la, *Honduras* **88 C2** 16 45N 86 15W
Bahía Blanca, *Argentina* **94 D3** 38 35S 62 13W
Bahía de Caráquez, *Ecuador* **92 D2** 0 40S 80 27W
Bahía Honda, *Cuba* **88 B3** 22 54N 83 10W
Bahía Laura, *Argentina* **96 F3** 48 10S 66 30W
Bahía Negra, *Paraguay* **92 H7** 20 5S 58 5W

Bahir Dar, Ethiopia 46 E2 11 37N 37 10 E
Bahmanzād, Iran 45 D6 31 15N 51 47 E
Bahr el Ghazâl □, Sudan 51 G11 7 0N 28 0 E
Bahraich, India 43 F9 27 38N 81 37 E
Bahrain ■, Asia 45 E6 26 0N 50 35 E
Bahror, India 42 F7 27 51N 76 20 E
Bāhū Kalāt, Iran 45 E9 25 43N 61 25 E
Bai Bung, Mui = Ca Mau, Mui, Vietnam 39 H5 8 38N 104 44 E
Bai Duc, Vietnam 38 C5 18 3N 105 49 E
Bai Thuong, Vietnam 38 C5 19 54N 105 23 E
Baia Mare, Romania 17 E12 47 40N 23 35 E
Baião, Brazil 93 D9 2 40S 49 40W
Baïbokoum, Chad 51 G9 7 46N 15 43 E
Baicheng, China 35 B12 45 38N 122 42 E
Baidoa, Somali Rep. 46 G3 3 8N 43 30 E
Baie Comeau, Canada 71 C6 49 12N 68 10W
Baie-St-Paul, Canada 71 C5 47 28N 70 32W
Baie Trinité, Canada 71 C6 49 25N 67 20W
Baie Verte, Canada 71 C8 49 55N 56 12W
Baihar, India 43 H9 22 6N 80 33 E
Baihe, China 34 H6 32 50N 110 5 E
Ba'ījī, Iraq 44 C4 35 0N 43 30 E
Baijnath, India 43 E8 29 55N 79 37 E
Baikal, L. = Baykal, Oz., Russia 27 D11 53 0N 108 0 E
Baikunthpur, India 43 H10 23 15N 82 33 E
Baile Atha Cliath = Dublin, Ireland 13 C5 53 21N 6 15W
Băileşti, Romania 17 F12 44 1N 23 20 E
Bainbridge, Ga., U.S.A. 77 K3 30 55N 84 35W
Bainbridge, N.Y., U.S.A. 79 D9 42 18N 75 29W
Baing, Indonesia 37 F6 10 14S 120 34 E
Bainiu, China 34 H7 32 50N 112 15 E
Bā'ir, Jordan 47 E5 30 45N 36 55 E
Bairin Youqi, China 35 C10 43 30N 118 35 E
Bairin Zuoqi, China 35 C10 43 58N 119 15 E
Bairnsdale, Australia 63 F4 37 48S 147 36 E
Baisha, China 34 G7 34 20N 112 32 E
Baitadi, Nepal 43 E9 29 35N 80 25 E
Baiyin, China 34 F3 36 45N 104 14 E
Baiyu Shan, China 34 F4 37 15N 107 30 E
Baj Baj, India 43 H13 22 30N 88 5 E
Baja, Hungary 17 E10 46 12N 18 59 E
Baja, Pta., Mexico 86 B1 29 50N 116 0W
Baja California, Mexico 86 A1 31 10N 115 12W
Baja California □, Mexico 86 B2 30 0N 115 0W
Baja California Sur □, Mexico 86 B2 25 50N 111 50W
Bajag, India 43 H9 22 40N 81 21 E
Bajamar, Canary Is. 22 F3 28 33N 16 20W
Bajana, India 42 H4 23 7N 71 49 E
Bājgīrān, Iran 45 B8 37 36N 58 24 E
Bajimba, Mt., Australia 63 D5 29 17S 152 6 E
Bajo Nuevo, Caribbean 88 C4 15 40N 78 50W
Bajoga, Nigeria 51 F8 10 57N 11 20 E
Bajool, Australia 62 C5 23 40S 150 35 E
Bakel, Senegal 50 F3 14 56N 12 20W
Baker, Calif., U.S.A. 85 K10 35 16N 116 4W
Baker, Mont., U.S.A. 80 B2 46 22N 104 17W
Baker, L., Canada 68 B10 64 0N 96 0W
Baker City, U.S.A. 82 D5 44 47N 117 50W
Baker I., Pac. Oc. 64 G10 0 10N 176 35W
Baker I., U.S.A. 72 B2 55 20N 133 40W
Baker L., Australia 61 E4 26 54S 126 5 E
Baker Lake, Canada 68 B10 64 20N 96 3W
Baker Mt., U.S.A. 82 B3 48 50N 121 49W
Bakers Creek, Australia 62 C4 21 13S 149 7 E
Baker's Dozen Is., Canada 70 A4 56 45N 78 45W
Bakersfield, Calif., U.S.A. 85 K8 35 23N 119 1W
Bakersfield, Vt., U.S.A. 79 B12 44 45N 72 48W
Bākhtarān, Iran 44 C5 34 23N 47 0 E
Bākhtarān □, Iran 44 C5 34 0N 46 30 E
Bakı, Azerbaijan 25 F8 40 29N 49 56 E
Bakkafjörður, Iceland 8 C6 66 2N 14 48W
Bakony, Hungary 17 E9 47 10N 17 30 E
Bakony Forest = Bakony, Hungary 17 E9 47 10N 17 30 E
Bakouma, C.A.R. 52 C4 5 40N 22 56 E
Bakswaho, India 43 G8 24 15N 79 18 E
Baku = Bakı, Azerbaijan 25 F8 40 29N 49 56 E
Bakutis Coast, Antarctica 5 D15 74 0S 120 0W
Baky = Bakı, Azerbaijan 25 F8 40 29N 49 56 E
Bala, Canada 78 A5 45 1N 79 37W
Bala, U.K. 10 E4 52 54N 3 36W
Bala, L., U.K. 10 E4 52 53N 3 37W
Balabac I., Phil. 36 C5 8 0N 117 0 E
Balabac Str., E. Indies 36 C5 7 53N 117 5 E
Balabagh, Afghan. 42 B4 34 25N 70 12 E
Ba'labakk, Lebanon 47 B5 34 0N 36 10 E
Balabalangan, Kepulauan, Indonesia 36 E5 2 20S 117 30 E
Balad, Iraq 44 C5 34 1N 44 9 E
Balad Rūz, Iraq 44 C5 33 42N 45 5 E
Bālādeh, Fārs, Iran 45 D6 29 17N 51 56 E
Bālādeh, Māzandaran, Iran 45 B6 36 12N 51 48 E
Balaghat, India 40 J12 21 49N 80 12 E
Balaghat Ra., India 40 K10 18 50N 76 30 E
Balaguer, Spain 19 B6 41 50N 0 50 E
Balaklava, Ukraine 25 F5 44 30N 33 30 E
Balakovo, Russia 24 D8 52 4N 47 55 E
Balamau, India 43 F9 27 10N 80 21 E
Balancán, Mexico 87 D6 17 48N 91 32W
Balashov, Russia 25 D7 51 30N 43 10 E
Balasinor, India 42 H5 22 57N 73 23 E
Balasore = Baleshwar, India 41 J15 21 35N 87 3 E
Balaton, Hungary 17 E9 46 50N 17 40 E
Balbina, Reprêsa de, Brazil 92 D7 2 0S 59 30W
Balboa, Panama 88 E4 8 57N 79 34W
Balbriggan, Ireland 13 C5 53 37N 6 11W
Balcarce, Argentina 94 D4 38 0S 58 10W
Balcarres, Canada 73 C8 50 50N 103 35W
Balchik, Bulgaria 21 C13 43 28N 28 11 E
Balclutha, N.Z. 59 M2 46 15S 169 45 E
Balcones Escarpment, U.S.A. 81 L5 29 30N 99 15W
Bald Hd., Australia 61 G2 35 6S 118 1 E
Bald I., Australia 61 F2 34 57S 118 27 E
Bald Knob, U.S.A. 81 H9 35 19N 91 34W
Baldock L., Canada 73 B9 56 33N 97 57W
Baldwin, Mich., U.S.A. 76 D3 43 54N 85 51W
Baldwin, Pa., U.S.A. 78 F5 40 23N 79 59W
Baldwinsville, U.S.A. 79 C8 43 10N 76 20W
Baldy Mt., U.S.A. 82 B9 48 9N 109 39W
Baldy Peak, U.S.A. 83 K9 33 54N 109 34W
Baleares, Is., Spain 22 B10 39 30N 3 0 E
Balearic Is. = Baleares, Is., Spain 22 B10 39 30N 3 0 E
Baleine = Whale →, Canada 71 A6 58 15N 67 40W
Baler, Phil. 37 A6 15 46N 121 34 E
Baleshare, U.K. 12 D1 57 31N 7 22W
Baleshwar, India 41 J15 21 35N 87 3 E
Balfate, Honduras 88 C2 15 48N 86 25W
Balí, Greece 23 D6 35 25N 24 47 E
Bali, India 42 G5 25 11N 73 17 E
Bali □, Indonesia 36 F5 8 20S 115 0 E
Bali, Selat, Indonesia 37 H16 8 18S 114 25 E
Baliapal, India 43 J12 21 40N 87 17 E
Balikeşir, Turkey 21 E12 39 39N 27 53 E
Balikpapan, Indonesia 36 E5 1 10S 116 55 E
Balimbing, Phil. 37 C5 5 5N 119 58 E
Baling, Malaysia 39 K3 5 41N 100 55 E
Balipara, India 41 F18 26 50N 92 45 E
Balkan Mts. = Stara Planina, Bulgaria 21 C10 43 15N 23 0 E
Balkhash = Balqash, Kazakstan 26 E8 46 50N 74 50 E
Balkhash, Ozero = Balqash Köl, Kazakstan 26 E8 46 0N 74 50 E
Balla, Bangla. 41 G17 24 10N 91 35 E
Ballachulish, U.K. 12 E3 56 41N 5 8W
Balladonia, Australia 61 F3 32 27S 123 51 E
Ballaghaderreen, Ireland 13 C3 53 55N 8 34W
Ballarat, Australia 63 F3 37 33S 143 50 E
Ballard, L., Australia 61 E3 29 20S 120 40 E
Ballater, U.K. 12 D5 57 3N 3 3W
Ballenas, Canal de, Mexico 86 B2 29 10N 113 45W
Balleny Is., Antarctica 5 C11 66 30S 163 0 E
Ballia, India 43 G11 25 46N 84 12 E
Ballina, Australia 63 D5 28 50S 153 31 E
Ballina, Ireland 13 B2 54 7N 9 9W
Ballinasloe, Ireland 13 C3 53 20N 8 13W
Ballinger, U.S.A. 81 K5 31 45N 99 57W
Ballinrobe, Ireland 13 C2 53 38N 9 13W
Ballinskelligs B., Ireland 13 E1 51 48N 10 13W
Ballston Spa, U.S.A. 79 D11 43 0N 73 51W
Ballycastle, U.K. 13 A5 55 12N 6 15W
Ballyclare, U.K. 13 B5 54 46N 6 0W
Ballyhaunis, Ireland 13 C3 53 46N 8 46W
Ballymena, U.K. 13 B5 54 52N 6 17W
Ballymoney, U.K. 13 A5 55 5N 6 31W
Ballymote, Ireland 13 B3 54 5N 8 31W
Ballynahinch, U.K. 13 B6 54 24N 5 54W
Ballyquintin Pt., U.K. 13 B6 54 20N 5 30W
Ballyshannon, Ireland 13 B3 54 30N 8 11W
Balmaceda, Chile 96 F2 46 0S 71 50W
Balmertown, Canada 73 C10 51 4N 93 41W
Balmoral, Australia 63 F3 37 15S 141 48 E
Balmorhea, U.S.A. 81 K3 30 59N 103 45W
Balonne →, Australia 63 D4 28 47S 147 56 E
Balotra, India 42 G5 25 50N 72 14 E
Balqash, Kazakstan 26 E8 46 50N 74 50 E
Balqash Köl, Kazakstan 26 E8 46 0N 74 50 E
Balrampur, India 43 F10 27 30N 82 20 E
Balranald, Australia 63 E3 34 38S 143 33 E
Balsas, Mexico 87 D5 18 0N 99 40W
Balsas →, Brazil 93 E9 7 15S 44 35W
Balsas →, Mexico 86 D4 17 55N 102 10W
Balston Spa, U.S.A. 79 D11 43 0N 73 52W
Balta, Ukraine 17 D15 48 2N 29 45 E
Bălţi, Moldova 17 E14 47 48N 27 58 E
Baltic Sea, Europe 9 H18 57 0N 19 0 E
Baltimore, Ireland 13 E2 51 29N 9 22W
Baltimore, Md., U.S.A. 76 F7 39 17N 76 37W
Baltimore, Ohio, U.S.A. 78 G2 39 51N 82 36W
Baltit, Pakistan 43 A6 36 15N 74 40 E
Baltiysk, Russia 9 J18 54 41N 19 58 E
Baluchistan □, Pakistan 40 F4 27 30N 65 0 E
Balurghat, India 43 G13 25 15N 88 44 E
Balvi, Latvia 9 H22 57 8N 27 15 E
Balya, Turkey 21 E12 39 44N 27 35 E
Bam, Iran 45 D8 29 7N 58 14 E
Bama, Nigeria 51 F8 11 33N 13 41 E
Bamaga, Australia 62 A3 10 50S 142 25 E
Bamaji L., Canada 70 B1 51 9N 91 25W
Bamako, Mali 50 F4 12 34N 7 55W
Bambari, C.A.R. 52 C4 5 40N 20 35 E
Bambaroo, Australia 62 B4 18 50S 146 10 E
Bamberg, Germany 16 D6 49 54N 10 54 E
Bamberg, U.S.A. 77 J5 33 18N 81 2W
Bambili, Dem. Rep. of the Congo 54 B2 3 40N 26 0 E
Bamenda, Cameroon 52 C1 5 57N 10 11 E
Bamfield, Canada 72 D3 48 45N 125 10W
Bāmīān □, Afghan. 40 B5 35 0N 67 0 E
Bamiancheng, China 35 C13 43 15N 124 2 E
Bampūr, Iran 45 E9 27 15N 60 21 E
Ban Ban, Laos 38 C4 19 31N 103 30 E
Ban Bang Hin, Thailand 39 H2 9 32N 98 35 E
Ban Chiang Klang, Thailand 38 C3 19 25N 100 55 E
Ban Chik, Laos 38 D4 17 15N 102 22 E
Ban Choho, Thailand 38 E4 15 2N 102 9 E
Ban Dan Lan Hoi, Thailand 38 D2 17 0N 99 35 E
Ban Don = Surat Thani, Thailand 39 H2 9 6N 99 20 E
Ban Don, Vietnam 38 F6 12 53N 107 48 E
Ban Don, Ao →, Thailand 39 H2 9 20N 99 25 E
Ban Dong, Thailand 38 C3 19 30N 100 59 E
Ban Hong, Thailand 38 C2 18 18N 98 50 E
Ban Kaeng, Thailand 38 D3 17 29N 100 7 E
Ban Kantang, Thailand 39 J2 7 25N 99 31 E
Ban Keun, Laos 38 C4 18 22N 102 35 E
Ban Khai, Thailand 38 F3 12 46N 101 18 E
Ban Kheun, Laos 38 B3 20 13N 101 7 E
Ban Khlong Kua, Thailand 39 J3 6 57N 100 8 E
Ban Khuan Mao, Thailand 39 J2 7 50N 99 37 E
Ban Ko Yai Chim, Thailand 39 G2 11 17N 99 26 E
Ban Kok, Thailand 38 D4 16 40N 103 40 E
Ban Laem, Thailand 38 F2 13 13N 99 59 E
Ban Lao Ngam, Laos 38 E6 15 28N 106 10 E
Ban Le Kathe, Thailand 38 E2 15 49N 98 53 E
Ban Mae Chedi, Thailand 38 C2 19 11N 99 31 E
Ban Mae Laeng, Thailand 38 B2 20 1N 99 17 E
Ban Mae Sariang, Thailand 38 C1 18 10N 97 56 E
Ban Mê Thuôt = Buon Ma Thuot, Vietnam 38 F7 12 40N 108 3 E
Ban Mi, Thailand 38 E3 15 3N 100 32 E
Ban Muong Mo, Laos 38 C4 19 4N 103 58 E
Ban Na Mo, Laos 38 D5 17 7N 105 40 E
Ban Na San, Thailand 39 H2 8 53N 99 52 E
Ban Na Tong, Laos 38 B3 20 56N 101 47 E
Ban Nam Bac, Laos 38 B4 20 38N 102 20 E
Ban Nam Ma, Laos 38 A3 22 2N 101 37 E
Ban Ngang, Laos 38 E6 15 59N 106 11 E
Ban Nong Bok, Laos 38 D5 17 5N 104 48 E
Ban Nong Boua, Laos 38 E6 15 40N 106 33 E
Ban Nong Pling, Thailand 38 E3 15 40N 100 10 E
Ban Pak Chan, Thailand 39 G2 10 32N 98 51 E
Ban Phai, Thailand 38 D4 16 4N 102 44 E
Ban Pong, Thailand 38 F2 13 50N 99 55 E
Ban Ron Phibun, Thailand 39 H2 8 9N 99 51 E
Ban Sanam Chai, Thailand 39 J3 7 33N 100 25 E
Ban Sangkha, Thailand 38 E4 14 37N 103 52 E
Ban Tak, Thailand 38 D2 17 2N 99 4 E
Ban Tako, Thailand 38 E4 14 5N 102 40 E
Ban Tha Dua, Thailand 38 D2 17 59N 98 39 E
Ban Tha Li, Thailand 38 D3 17 37N 101 25 E
Ban Tha Nun, Thailand 39 H2 8 12N 98 18 E
Ban Thahine, Laos 38 E5 14 12N 105 33 E
Ban Xien Kok, Laos 38 B3 20 54N 100 39 E
Ban Yen Nhan, Vietnam 38 B6 20 57N 106 2 E
Banaba, Kiribati 64 H8 0 45S 169 50 E
Banalia, Dem. Rep. of the Congo 54 B2 1 32N 25 5 E
Banam, Cambodia 39 G5 11 20N 105 17 E
Bananal, I. do, Brazil 93 F8 11 30S 50 30W
Banaras = Varanasi, India 43 G10 25 22N 83 0 E
Banas →, Gujarat, India 42 H4 23 45N 71 25 E
Banas →, Mad. P., India 43 G9 24 15N 81 30 E
Bânâs, Ras, Egypt 51 D13 23 57N 35 59 E
Banbān, Si. Arabia 44 E5 25 1N 46 35 E
Banbridge, U.K. 13 B5 54 22N 6 16W
Banbury, U.K. 11 E6 52 4N 1 20W
Banchory, U.K. 12 D6 57 3N 2 29W
Bancroft, Canada 78 A7 45 3N 77 51W
Band Bonī, Iran 45 E8 25 30N 59 33 E
Band Qīr, Iran 45 D6 31 39N 48 53 E
Banda, India 43 G9 25 30N 80 26 E
Banda, Mad. P., India 43 G8 24 3N 78 57 E
Banda, Kepulauan, Indonesia 37 E7 4 37S 129 50 E
Banda Aceh, Indonesia 36 C1 5 35N 95 20 E
Banda Banda, Mt., Australia 63 E5 31 10S 152 28 E
Banda Elat, Indonesia 37 F8 5 40S 133 5 E
Banda Is. = Banda, Kepulauan, Indonesia 37 E7 4 37S 129 50 E
Banda Sea, Indonesia 37 F8 6 0S 130 0 E
Bandai-San, Japan 30 F10 37 36N 140 4 E
Bandān, Iran 45 D9 31 23N 60 44 E
Bandanaira, Indonesia 37 E7 4 32S 129 54 E
Bandanwara, India 42 F6 26 9N 74 38 E
Bandar = Machilipatnam, India 41 L12 16 12N 81 8 E
Bandār 'Abbās, Iran 45 E8 27 15N 56 15 E
Bandar-e Anzalī, Iran 45 B6 37 30N 49 30 E
Bandar-e Bushehr = Būshehr, Iran 45 D6 28 55N 50 55 E
Bandar-e Chārak, Iran 45 E7 26 45N 54 20 E
Bandar-e Deylam, Iran 45 D6 30 5N 50 10 E
Bandar-e Khomeynı, Iran 45 D6 30 30N 49 5 E
Bandar-e Lengeh, Iran 45 E7 26 35N 54 58 E
Bandar-e Maqām, Iran 45 E7 26 56N 53 29 E
Bandar-e Ma'shur, Iran 45 D6 30 35N 49 10 E
Bandar-e Nakhīlū, Iran 45 E7 26 58N 53 30 E
Bandar-e Rīg, Iran 45 D6 29 29N 50 38 E
Bandar-e Torkeman, Iran 45 B7 37 0N 54 10 E
Bandar Maharani = Muar, Malaysia 39 L4 2 3N 102 34 E
Bandar Penggaram = Batu Pahat, Malaysia 39 M4 1 50N 102 56 E
Bandar Seri Begawan, Brunei 36 D5 4 52N 115 0 E
Bandar Sri Aman, Malaysia 36 D4 1 15N 111 32 E
Bandawe, Malawi 55 E3 11 58S 34 5 E
Bandeira, Pico da, Brazil 95 A7 20 26S 41 47W
Bandera, Argentina 94 B3 28 55S 62 20W
Banderas, B. de, Mexico 86 C3 20 40N 105 30W
Bandhogarh, India 43 H9 23 40N 81 2 E
Bandi →, India 42 F6 26 12N 75 47 E
Bandikui, India 42 F7 27 3N 76 34 E
Bandırma, Turkey 21 D13 40 20N 28 0 E
Bandon, Ireland 13 E3 51 44N 8 44W
Bandon →, Ireland 13 E3 51 43N 8 37W
Bandula, Mozam. 55 F3 19 0S 33 7 E
Bandundu, Dem. Rep. of the Congo 52 E3 3 15S 17 22 E
Bandung, Indonesia 37 G12 6 54S 107 36 E
Bāneh, Iran 44 C5 35 59N 45 53 E
Banes, Cuba 89 B4 21 0N 75 42W
Banff, Canada 72 C5 51 10N 115 34W
Banff, U.K. 12 D6 57 40N 2 33W
Banff Nat. Park, Canada 72 C5 51 30N 116 15W
Bang Fai →, Laos 38 D5 16 57N 104 45 E
Bang Hieng →, Laos 38 D5 16 10N 105 10 E
Bang Krathum, Thailand 38 D3 16 34N 100 18 E
Bang Lamung, Thailand 38 F3 13 3N 100 56 E
Bang Mun Nak, Thailand 38 D3 16 2N 100 23 E
Bang Pa In, Thailand 38 E3 14 14N 100 35 E
Bang Rakam, Thailand 38 D3 16 45N 100 7 E
Bang Saphan, Thailand 39 G2 11 14N 99 28 E
Bangaduni I., India 43 J13 21 34N 88 52 E
Bangala Dam, Zimbabwe 55 G3 21 7S 31 25 E
Bangalore, India 40 N10 12 59N 77 40 E
Banganga →, India 42 F6 27 6N 77 25 E
Bangaon, India 43 H13 23 0N 88 47 E
Bangassou, C.A.R. 52 D4 4 55N 23 7 E
Banggai, Indonesia 37 E6 1 34S 123 30 E
Banggai, Kepulauan, Indonesia 37 E6 1 40S 123 30 E
Banggai Arch. = Banggai, Kepulauan, Indonesia 37 E6 1 40S 123 30 E
Banggi, Malaysia 36 C5 7 17N 117 12 E
Banghāzī, Libya 51 B10 32 11N 20 3 E
Bangka, Sulawesi, Indonesia 37 D7 1 50N 125 5 E
Bangka, Sumatera, Indonesia 36 E3 2 0S 105 50 E
Bangka, Selat, Indonesia 36 E3 2 30S 105 30 E
Bangkalan, Indonesia 37 G15 7 2S 112 46 E
Bangkinang, Indonesia 36 D2 0 18N 101 5 E
Bangko, Indonesia 36 E2 2 5S 102 9 E
Bangkok, Thailand 38 F3 13 45N 100 35 E
Bangladesh ■, Asia 41 H17 24 0N 90 0 E
Bangong Co, India 43 B8 35 50N 79 20 E
Bangor, Down, U.K. 13 B6 54 40N 5 40W
Bangor, Gwynedd, U.K. 10 D3 53 14N 4 8W
Bangor, Maine, U.S.A. 69 D13 44 48N 68 46W
Bangor, Pa., U.S.A. 79 F9 40 52N 75 13W
Bangued, Phil. 37 A6 17 40N 120 37 E
Bangui, C.A.R. 52 D3 4 23N 18 35 E
Banguru, Dem. Rep. of the Congo 54 B2 0 30N 27 10 E
Bangweulu, L., Zambia 55 E3 11 0S 30 0 E
Bangweulu Swamp, Zambia 55 E3 11 20S 30 15 E
Bani, Dom. Rep. 89 C5 18 16N 70 22W
Banī Sa'd, Iraq 44 C5 33 34N 44 32 E
Banihal Pass, India 43 C6 33 30N 75 12 E
Bāniyās, Syria 44 C3 35 10N 36 0 E
Banja Luka, Bos.-H. 20 B7 44 49N 17 11 E
Banjar, India 42 D7 31 38N 77 21 E
Banjar →, India 43 H9 22 36N 80 22 E
Banjarmasin, Indonesia 36 E4 3 20S 114 35 E
Banjul, Gambia 50 F2 13 28N 16 40W
Banka, India 43 G12 24 53N 86 55 E
Banket, Zimbabwe 55 F3 17 27S 30 19 E
Bankipore, India 41 G14 25 35N 85 10 E
Banks I., B.C., Canada 72 C3 53 20N 130 0W
Banks I., N.W.T., Canada 68 A7 73 15N 121 30W
Banks Pen., N.Z. 59 K4 43 45S 173 15 E
Banks Str., Australia 62 G4 40 40S 148 10 E
Bankura, India 43 H12 23 11N 87 18 E
Banmankhi, India 43 G12 25 53N 87 11 E
Bann →, Arm., U.K. 13 B5 54 30N 6 31W
Bann →, L'derry., U.K. 13 A5 55 8N 6 41W
Bannang Sata, Thailand 39 J3 6 16N 101 16 E
Banning, U.S.A. 85 M10 33 56N 116 53W
Banningville = Bandundu, Dem. Rep. of the Congo 52 E3 3 15S 17 22 E
Bannockburn, Canada 78 B7 44 39N 77 33W
Bannockburn, U.K. 12 E5 56 5N 3 55W
Bannockburn, Zimbabwe 55 G2 20 17S 29 48 E
Bannu, Pakistan 40 C7 33 0N 70 18 E
Bano, India 43 H11 22 40N 84 55 E
Bansgaon, India 43 F10 26 33N 83 21 E
Banská Bystrica, Slovak Rep. 17 D10 48 46N 19 14 E
Banswara, India 42 H6 23 32N 74 24 E
Bantaeng, Indonesia 37 F5 5 32S 119 56 E
Bantry, Ireland 13 E2 51 41N 9 27W
Bantry B., Ireland 13 E2 51 37N 9 44W
Bantul, Indonesia 37 G14 7 55S 110 19 E
Bantva, India 42 J4 21 29N 70 12 E
Banu, Afghan. 40 B6 35 35N 69 5 E
Banyak, Kepulauan, Indonesia 36 D1 2 10N 97 10 E
Banyalbufar, Spain 22 B9 39 42N 2 31 E
Banyo, Cameroon 52 C2 6 52N 11 45 E
Banyumas, Indonesia 37 G13 7 32S 109 18 E
Banyuwangi, Indonesia 37 H16 8 13S 114 21 E
Banzare Coast, Antarctica 5 C9 68 0S 125 0 E
Banzyville = Mobayi, Dem. Rep. of the Congo 52 D4 4 15N 21 8 E
Bao Lac, Vietnam 38 A5 22 57N 105 40 E
Bao Loc, Vietnam 39 G6 11 32N 107 48 E
Baocheng, China 34 H4 33 12N 106 56 E
Baode, China 34 E6 39 1N 111 5 E
Baodi, China 35 E9 39 38N 117 20 E
Baoding, China 34 E8 38 50N 115 28 E
Baoji, China 34 G4 34 20N 107 5 E
Baoshan, China 32 D4 25 10N 99 5 E
Baotou, China 34 D6 40 32N 110 2 E
Baoying, China 35 H10 33 17N 119 20 E
Bap, India 42 F5 27 23N 72 18 E
Bapatla, India 41 M12 15 55N 80 30 E
Bāqerābād, Iran 45 C6 33 2N 51 58 E
Ba'qūbah, Iraq 44 C5 33 45N 44 50 E
Baquedano, Chile 94 A2 23 20S 69 52W
Bar, Montenegro, Yug. 21 C8 42 8N 19 6 E
Bar, Ukraine 17 D14 49 4N 27 40 E
Bar Bigha, India 43 G11 25 21N 85 47 E
Bar Harbor, U.S.A. 77 C11 44 23N 68 13W
Bar-le-Duc, France 18 B6 48 47N 5 10 E
Bara, India 43 G9 25 16N 81 43 E
Bara Banki, India 43 F9 26 55N 81 12 E
Barabai, Indonesia 36 E5 2 32S 115 34 E
Baraboo, U.S.A. 80 D10 43 28N 89 45W
Baracoa, Cuba 89 B5 20 20N 74 30W
Baradā →, Syria 47 B5 33 33N 36 34 E
Baradero, Argentina 94 C4 33 52S 59 29W
Baradine, Australia 63 E4 30 56S 149 4 E
Baraga, U.S.A. 80 B10 46 47N 88 30W
Barah →, India 42 F6 27 42N 77 5 E
Barahona, Dom. Rep. 89 C5 18 13N 71 7W
Barail Range, India 41 G18 25 15N 93 20 E
Barakaldo, Spain 19 A4 43 18N 2 59W
Barakar →, India 43 G12 24 7N 86 14 E
Barakhola, India 41 G18 25 0N 92 45 E
Barakot, India 43 J11 21 33N 84 59 E
Barakpur, India 43 H13 22 44N 88 30 E
Baralaba, Australia 62 C4 24 13S 149 50 E
Baralzon L., Canada 73 B9 60 0N 98 3W
Baramula, India 43 B6 34 15N 74 20 E
Baran, India 42 G7 25 9N 76 40 E
Baran →, Pakistan 42 G3 25 13N 68 17 E
Baranavichy, Belarus 17 B14 53 10N 26 0 E
Baranof, U.S.A. 72 B2 57 5N 134 50W
Baranof I., U.S.A. 68 C6 57 0N 135 0W
Barapasi, Indonesia 37 E9 2 15S 137 5 E
Barasat, India 43 H13 22 46N 88 31 E
Barat Daya, Kepulauan, Indonesia 37 F7 7 30S 128 0 E
Barataria B., U.S.A. 81 L10 29 20N 89 55W
Barauda, India 42 H6 23 33N 75 15 E
Baraut, India 42 E7 29 13N 77 7 E
Barbacena, Brazil 95 A7 21 15S 43 56W
Barbados ■, W. Indies 89 D8 13 10N 59 30W
Barbària, C. de, Spain 22 C7 38 39N 1 24 E
Barbastro, Spain 19 A6 42 2N 0 5 E
Barberton, S. Africa 57 D5 25 42S 31 2 E
Barberton, U.S.A. 78 E3 41 0N 81 39W
Barbosa, Colombia 92 B4 5 57N 73 37W
Barbourville, U.S.A. 77 G4 36 52N 83 53W
Barbuda, W. Indies 89 C7 17 30N 61 40W
Barcaldine, Australia 62 C4 23 43S 145 6 E
Barcellona Pozzo di Gotto, Italy 20 E6 38 9N 15 13 E
Barcelona, Spain 19 B7 41 21N 2 10 E
Barcelona, Venezuela 92 A6 10 10N 64 40W
Barcelos, Brazil 92 D6 1 0S 63 0W
Barcoo →, Australia 62 D3 25 30S 142 50 E
Bardaï, Chad 51 D9 21 25N 17 0 E
Bardas Blancas, Argentina 94 D2 35 49S 69 45W
Barddhaman, India 43 H12 23 14N 87 39 E
Bardejov, Slovak Rep. 17 D11 49 18N 21 15 E
Bardera, Somali Rep. 46 G3 2 20N 42 27 E
Bardīyah, Libya 51 B10 31 45N 25 5 E
Bardsey I., U.K. 10 E3 52 45N 4 47W
Bardstown, U.S.A. 76 G3 37 49N 85 28W

Bareilly, India 43 E8 28 22N 79 27 E
Barela, India 43 H9 23 6N 80 3 E
Barents Sea, Arctic 4 B9 73 0N 39 0 E
Barfleur, Pte. de, France 18 B3 49 42N 1 16W
Bargara, Australia 62 C5 24 50S 152 25 E
Barguzin, Russia 27 D11 53 37N 109 37 E
Barh, India 43 G11 25 29N 85 46 E
Barhaj, India 43 F10 26 18N 83 44 E
Barham, Australia 63 F3 35 36S 144 8 E
Barharwa, India 43 G12 24 52N 87 47 E
Barhi, India 43 G11 24 15N 85 25 E
Bari, India 42 F7 26 39N 77 39 E
Bari, Italy 20 D7 41 8N 16 51 E
Bari Doab, Pakistan 42 D5 30 20N 73 0 E
Bari Sadri, India 42 G6 24 28N 74 30 E
Barīdī, Ra's, Si. Arabia 44 E3 24 17N 37 31 E
Barīm, Yemen 48 E8 12 39N 43 25 E
Barinas, Venezuela 92 B4 8 36N 70 15W
Baring, C., Canada 68 B8 70 0N 117 30W
Baringo, Kenya 54 B4 0 47N 36 16 E
Baringo, L., Kenya 54 B4 0 47N 36 16 E
Barisal, Bangla. 41 H17 22 45N 90 20 E
Barisan, Bukit, Indonesia 36 E2 3 30S 102 15 E
Barito →, Indonesia 36 E4 4 0S 114 50 E
Bark L., Canada 78 A7 45 27N 77 51W
Barkakana, India 43 H11 23 37N 85 29 E
Barker, U.S.A. 78 C6 43 20N 78 33W
Barkley, L., U.S.A. 77 G2 37 1N 88 14W
Barkley Sound, Canada 72 D3 48 50N 125 10W
Barkly East, S. Africa 56 E4 30 58S 27 33 E
Barkly Roadhouse, Australia 62 B2 19 52S 135 50 E
Barkly Tableland, Australia 62 B2 17 50S 136 40 E
Barkly West, S. Africa 56 D3 28 5S 24 31 E
Barkol Kazak Zizhixian, China 32 B4 43 37N 93 2 E
Bârlad, Romania 17 E14 46 15N 27 38 E
Bârlad →, Romania 17 F14 45 38N 27 32 E
Barlee, L., Australia 61 E2 29 15S 119 30 E
Barlee, Mt., Australia 61 D4 24 38S 128 13 E
Barletta, Italy 20 D7 41 19N 16 17 E
Barlovento, Canary Is. 22 F2 28 48N 17 48W
Barlow L., Canada 73 A8 62 0N 103 0W
Barmedman, Australia 63 E4 34 9S 147 21 E
Barmer, India 42 G4 25 45N 71 20 E
Barmera, Australia 63 E3 34 15S 140 28 E
Barmouth, U.K. 10 E3 52 44N 4 4W
Barna →, India 43 G10 25 21N 83 3 E
Barnagar, India 42 H6 23 7N 75 19 E
Barnala, India 42 D6 30 23N 75 33 E
Barnard Castle, U.K. 10 C6 54 33N 1 55W
Barnaul, Russia 26 D9 53 20N 83 40 E
Barnesville, U.S.A. 77 J3 33 3N 84 9W
Barnet, U.K. 11 F7 51 38N 0 9W
Barneveld, Neths. 15 B5 52 7N 5 36 E
Barneveld, U.S.A. 79 C9 43 16N 75 14W
Barnhart, U.S.A. 81 K4 31 8N 101 10W
Barnsley, U.K. 10 D6 53 34N 1 27W
Barnstaple, U.K. 11 F3 51 5N 4 4W
Barnstaple Bay = Bideford Bay, U.K. 11 F3 51 5N 4 20W
Barnsville, U.S.A. 80 B6 46 43N 96 28W
Barnwell, U.S.A. 77 J5 33 15N 81 23W
Baro, Nigeria 50 G7 8 35N 6 18 E
Baroda = Vadodara, India 42 H5 22 20N 73 10 E
Baroda, India 42 G7 25 29N 76 35 E
Baroe, S. Africa 56 E3 33 13S 24 33 E
Baron Ra., Australia 60 D4 23 30S 127 45 E
Barotseland, Zambia 53 H4 15 0S 24 0 E
Barpeta, India 41 F17 26 20N 91 10 E
Barques, Pt. Aux, U.S.A. 78 B2 44 4N 82 58W
Barquísimeto, Venezuela 92 A5 10 4N 69 19W
Barr Smith Range, Australia 61 E3 27 4S 120 20 E
Barra, Brazil 93 F10 11 5S 43 10W
Barra, U.K. 12 E1 57 0N 7 29W
Barra, Sd. of, U.K. 12 D1 57 4N 7 25W
Barra de Navidad, Mexico 86 D4 19 12N 104 41W
Barra do Corda, Brazil 93 E9 5 30S 45 10W
Barra do Piraí, Brazil 95 A7 22 30S 43 50W
Barra Falsa, Pta. da, Mozam. 57 C6 22 58S 35 37 E
Barra Hd., U.K. 12 E1 56 47N 7 40W
Barra Mansa, Brazil 95 A7 22 35S 44 12W
Barraba, Australia 63 E5 30 21S 150 35 E
Barrackpur = Barakpur, India 43 H13 22 44N 88 30 E
Barradale Roadhouse, Australia 60 D1 22 42S 114 58 E
Barraigh = Barra, U.K. 12 E1 57 0N 7 29W
Barranca, Lima, Peru 92 F3 10 45S 77 50W
Barranca, Loreto, Peru 92 D3 4 50S 76 50W
Barrancabermeja, Colombia 92 B4 7 0N 73 50W
Barrancas, Venezuela 92 B6 8 55N 62 5W
Barrancos, Portugal 19 C2 38 10N 6 58W
Barranqueras, Argentina 94 B4 27 30S 59 0W
Barranquilla, Colombia 92 A4 11 0N 74 50W
Barraute, Canada 70 C4 48 26N 77 38W
Barre, Mass., U.S.A. 79 D12 42 25N 72 6W
Barre, Vt., U.S.A. 79 B12 44 12N 72 30W
Barreal, Argentina 94 C2 31 33S 69 28W
Barreiras, Brazil 93 F10 12 8S 45 0W
Barreirinhas, Brazil 93 D10 2 30S 42 50W
Barreiro, Portugal 19 C1 38 40N 9 6W
Barren, Nosy, Madag. 57 B7 18 25S 43 40 E
Barretos, Brazil 93 H9 20 30S 48 35W
Barrhead, Canada 72 C6 54 10N 114 24W
Barrie, Canada 78 B5 44 24N 79 40W
Barrier Ra., Australia 63 E3 31 0S 141 30 E
Barrière, Canada 72 C4 51 12N 120 7W
Barrington, U.S.A. 79 E13 41 44N 71 18W
Barrington L., Canada 73 B8 56 55N 100 15W
Barrington Tops, Australia 63 E5 32 6S 151 28 E
Barringun, Australia 63 D4 29 1S 145 41 E
Barro do Garças, Brazil 93 G8 15 54S 52 16W
Barron, U.S.A. 80 C9 45 24N 91 51W
Barrow, U.S.A. 68 A4 71 18N 156 47W
Barrow →, Ireland 13 D5 52 25N 6 58W
Barrow Creek, Australia 62 C1 21 30S 133 55 E
Barrow I., Australia 60 D2 20 45S 115 20 E
Barrow-in-Furness, U.K. 10 C4 54 7N 3 14W
Barrow Pt., Australia 62 A3 14 20S 144 40 E
Barrow Pt., U.S.A. 66 B4 71 24N 156 29W
Barrow Ra., Australia 61 E4 26 0S 127 40 E
Barrow Str., Canada 4 B3 74 20N 95 0W
Barry, U.K. 11 F4 51 24N 3 16W
Barry's Bay, Canada 78 A7 45 29N 77 41W
Barsat, Pakistan 43 A5 36 10N 72 45 E
Barsham, Syria 44 C4 35 21N 40 33 E
Barsi, India 40 K9 18 10N 75 50 E
Barsoi, India 41 G15 25 48N 87 57 E
Barstow, U.S.A. 85 L9 34 54N 117 1W
Barthélemy, Col, Vietnam 38 C5 19 26N 104 6 E
Bartica, Guyana 92 B7 6 25N 58 40W
Bartlesville, U.S.A. 81 G7 36 45N 95 59W
Bartlett, U.S.A. 84 J8 36 29N 118 2W
Bartlett, L., Canada 72 A5 63 5N 118 20W
Bartolomeu Dias, Mozam. 55 G4 21 10S 35 8 E
Barton, U.S.A. 79 B12 44 45N 72 11W
Barton upon Humber, U.K. 10 D7 53 41N 0 25W
Bartow, U.S.A. 77 M5 27 54N 81 50W
Barú, Volcan, Panama 88 E3 8 55N 82 35W
Barumba, Dem. Rep. of the Congo 54 B1 1 3N 23 37 E
Baruunsuu, Mongolia 34 C3 43 43N 105 35 E
Barwani, India 42 H6 22 2N 74 57 E
Barysaw, Belarus 17 A15 54 17N 28 28 E
Barzān, Iraq 44 B5 36 55N 44 3 E
Bāsa'idū, Iran 45 E7 26 35N 55 20 E
Basal, Pakistan 42 C5 33 33N 72 13 E
Basankusa, Dem. Rep. of the Congo 52 D3 1 5N 19 50 E
Basarabeasca, Moldova 17 E15 46 21N 28 58 E
Basawa, Afghan. 42 B4 34 15N 70 50 E
Bascuñán, C., Chile 94 B1 28 52S 71 35W
Basel, Switz. 18 C7 47 35N 7 35 E
Bashākerd, Kūhhā-ye, Iran 45 E8 26 42N 58 35 E
Bashaw, Canada 72 C6 52 35N 112 58W
Bāshī, Iran 45 D6 28 41N 51 4 E
Bashkir Republic = Bashkortostan □, Russia 24 D10 54 0N 57 0 E
Bashkortostan □, Russia 24 D10 54 0N 57 0 E
Basilan, Phil. 37 C6 6 35N 122 0 E
Basilan Str., Phil. 37 C6 6 50N 122 0 E
Basildon, U.K. 11 F8 51 34N 0 28 E
Basim = Washim, India 40 J10 20 3N 77 0 E
Basin, U.S.A. 82 D9 44 23N 108 2W
Basingstoke, U.K. 11 F6 51 15N 1 5W
Baskatong, Rés., Canada 70 C4 46 46N 75 50W
Basle = Basel, Switz. 18 C7 47 35N 7 35 E
Basoda, India 42 H7 23 52N 77 54 E
Basoka, Dem. Rep. of the Congo 54 B1 1 16N 23 40 E
Basque Provinces = País Vasco □, Spain 19 A4 42 50N 2 45W
Basra = Al Başrah, Iraq 44 D5 30 30N 47 50 E
Bass Str., Australia 62 F4 39 15S 146 30 E
Bassano, Canada 72 C6 50 48N 112 20W
Bassano del Grappa, Italy 20 B4 45 46N 11 44 E
Bassas da India, Ind. Oc. 53 J7 22 0S 39 0 E
Basse-Terre, Guadeloupe 89 C7 16 0N 61 44W
Bassein, Burma 41 L19 16 45N 94 30 E
Basseterre, St. Kitts & Nevis 89 C7 17 17N 62 43W
Bassett, U.S.A. 80 D5 42 35N 99 32W
Bassi, India 42 D7 30 44N 76 21 E
Bastak, Iran 45 E7 27 15N 54 25 E
Baştām, Iran 45 B7 36 29N 55 4 E
Bastar, India 41 K12 19 15N 81 40 E
Basti, India 43 F10 26 52N 82 55 E
Bastia, France 18 E8 42 40N 9 30 E
Bastogne, Belgium 15 D5 50 1N 5 43 E
Bastrop, La., U.S.A. 81 J9 32 47N 91 55W
Bastrop, Tex., U.S.A. 81 K6 30 7N 97 19W
Bat Yam, Israel 47 C3 32 2N 34 44 E
Bata, Eq. Guin. 52 D1 1 57N 9 50 E
Bataan, Phil. 37 B6 14 40N 120 25 E
Batabanó, Cuba 88 B3 22 40N 82 20W
Batabanó, G. de, Cuba 88 B3 22 30N 82 30W
Batac, Phil. 37 A6 18 3N 120 34 E
Batagai, Russia 27 C14 67 38N 134 38 E
Batala, India 42 D6 31 48N 75 12 E
Batama, Dem. Rep. of the Congo 54 B2 0 58N 26 33 E
Batamay, Russia 27 C13 63 30N 129 15 E
Batang, Indonesia 37 G13 6 55S 109 45 E
Batangas, Phil. 37 B6 13 35N 121 10 E
Batanta, Indonesia 37 E8 0 55S 130 40 E
Batatais, Brazil 95 A6 20 54S 47 37W
Batavia, U.S.A. 78 D6 43 0N 78 11W
Batchelor, Australia 60 B5 13 4S 131 1 E
Batdambang, Cambodia 38 F4 13 7N 103 12 E
Bateman's B., Australia 63 F5 35 40S 150 12 E
Batemans Bay, Australia 63 F5 35 44S 150 11 E
Bates Ra., Australia 61 E3 27 27S 121 5 E
Batesburg, U.S.A. 77 J5 33 54N 81 33W
Batesville, Ark., U.S.A. 81 H9 35 46N 91 39W
Batesville, Miss., U.S.A. 81 H10 34 19N 89 57W
Batesville, Tex., U.S.A. 81 L5 28 58N 99 37W
Bath, Canada 79 B8 44 11N 76 47W
Bath, U.K. 11 F5 51 23N 2 22W
Bath, Maine, U.S.A. 77 D11 43 55N 69 49W
Bath, N.Y., U.S.A. 78 D7 42 20N 77 19W
Bath & North East Somerset □, U.K. 11 F5 51 21N 2 27W
Batheay, Cambodia 39 G5 11 59N 104 57 E
Bathurst = Banjul, Gambia 50 F2 13 28N 16 40W
Bathurst, Australia 63 E4 33 25S 149 31 E
Bathurst, Canada 71 C6 47 37N 65 43W
Bathurst, S. Africa 56 E4 33 30S 26 50 E
Bathurst, C., Canada 68 A7 70 34N 128 0W
Bathurst B., Australia 62 A3 14 16S 144 25 E
Bathurst Harb., Australia 62 G4 43 15S 146 10 E
Bathurst I., Australia 60 B5 11 30S 130 10 E
Bathurst I., Canada 4 B2 76 0N 100 30W
Bathurst Inlet, Canada 68 B9 66 50N 108 1W
Batlow, Australia 63 F4 35 31S 148 9 E
Batman, Turkey 25 G7 37 55N 41 5 E
Baṭn al Ghūl, Jordan 47 F4 29 36N 35 56 E
Batna, Algeria 50 A7 35 34N 6 15 E
Batoka, Zambia 55 F2 16 45S 27 15 E
Baton Rouge, U.S.A. 81 K9 30 27N 91 11W
Batong, Ko, Thailand 39 J2 6 32N 99 12 E
Batopilas, Mexico 86 B3 27 0N 107 45W
Batouri, Cameroon 52 D2 4 30N 14 25 E
Båtsfjord, Norway 8 A23 70 38N 29 39 E
Battambang = Batdambang, Cambodia 38 F4 13 7N 103 12 E
Batticaloa, Sri Lanka 40 R12 7 43N 81 45 E
Battipáglia, Italy 20 D6 40 37N 14 58 E
Battle, U.K. 11 G8 50 55N 0 30 E
Battle →, Canada 73 C7 52 43N 108 15W
Battle Creek, U.S.A. 76 D3 42 19N 85 11W
Battle Ground, U.S.A. 84 E4 45 47N 122 32W
Battle Harbour, Canada 71 B8 52 16N 55 35W
Battle Lake, U.S.A. 80 B7 46 17N 95 43W
Battle Mountain, U.S.A. 82 F5 40 38N 116 56W
Battlefields, Zimbabwe 55 F2 18 37S 29 47 E
Battleford, Canada 73 C7 52 45N 108 15W
Batu, Kepulauan, Indonesia 36 E1 0 30S 98 25 E
Batu, Mt., Ethiopia 46 F2 6 55N 39 45 E
Batu Caves, Malaysia 39 L3 3 15N 101 40 E
Batu Gajah, Malaysia 39 K3 4 28N 101 3 E
Batu Is. = Batu, Kepulauan, Indonesia 36 E1 0 30S 98 25 E
Batu Pahat, Malaysia 39 M4 1 50N 102 56 E
Batuata, Indonesia 37 F6 6 12S 122 42 E
Batumi, Georgia 25 F7 41 39N 41 44 E
Baturaja, Indonesia 36 E2 4 11S 104 15 E
Baturité, Brazil 93 D11 4 28S 38 45W
Bau, Malaysia 36 D4 1 25N 110 9 E
Baubau, Indonesia 37 F6 5 25S 122 38 E
Bauchi, Nigeria 50 F7 10 22N 9 48 E
Baudette, U.S.A. 80 A7 48 43N 94 36W
Bauer, C., Australia 63 E1 32 44S 134 4 E
Bauhinia, Australia 62 C4 24 35S 149 18 E
Baukau, Indonesia 37 F7 8 27S 126 27 E
Bauld, C., Canada 69 C14 51 38N 55 26W
Bauru, Brazil 95 A6 22 10S 49 0W
Bausi, India 43 G12 24 48N 87 1 E
Bauska, Latvia 9 H21 56 24N 24 15 E
Bautzen, Germany 16 C8 51 10N 14 26 E
Bavānāt, Iran 45 D7 30 28N 53 27 E
Bavaria = Bayern □, Germany 16 D6 48 50N 12 0 E
Bavispe →, Mexico 86 B3 29 30N 109 11W
Bawdwin, Burma 41 H20 23 5N 97 20 E
Bawean, Indonesia 36 F4 5 46S 112 35 E
Bawku, Ghana 50 F5 11 3N 0 19W
Bawlake, Burma 41 K20 19 11N 97 21 E
Baxley, U.S.A. 77 K4 31 47N 82 21W
Baxter, U.S.A. 80 B7 46 21N 94 17W
Baxter Springs, U.S.A. 81 G7 37 2N 94 44W
Bay City, Mich., U.S.A. 76 D4 43 36N 83 54W
Bay City, Tex., U.S.A. 81 L7 28 59N 95 58W
Bay Minette, U.S.A. 77 K2 30 53N 87 46W
Bay Roberts, Canada 71 C9 47 36N 53 16W
Bay St. Louis, U.S.A. 81 K10 30 19N 89 20W
Bay Springs, U.S.A. 81 K10 31 59N 89 17W
Bay View, N.Z. 59 H6 39 25S 176 50 E
Baya, Dem. Rep. of the Congo 55 E2 11 53S 27 25 E
Bayamo, Cuba 88 B4 20 20N 76 40W
Bayamón, Puerto Rico 89 C6 18 24N 66 10W
Bayan Har Shan, China 32 C4 34 0N 98 0 E
Bayan Hot = Alxa Zuoqi, China 34 E3 38 50N 105 40 E
Bayan Obo, China 34 D5 41 52N 109 59 E
Bayan-Ovoo = Erdenetsogt, Mongolia 34 C4 42 55N 106 5 E
Bayana, India 42 F7 26 55N 77 18 E
Bayanaūyl, Kazakstan 26 D8 50 45N 75 45 E
Bayandalay, Mongolia 34 C2 43 30N 103 29 E
Bayanhongor, Mongolia 32 B5 46 8N 102 43 E
Bayard, N. Mex., U.S.A. 83 K9 32 46N 108 8W
Bayard, Nebr., U.S.A. 80 E3 41 45N 103 20W
Baybay, Phil. 37 B6 10 40N 124 55 E
Bayern □, Germany 16 D6 48 50N 12 0 E
Bayeux, France 18 B3 49 17N 0 42W
Bayfield, Canada 78 C3 43 34N 81 42W
Bayfield, U.S.A. 80 B9 46 49N 90 49W
Bayındır, Turkey 21 E12 38 13N 27 39 E
Baykal, Oz., Russia 27 D11 53 0N 108 0 E
Baykan, Turkey 44 B4 38 7N 41 44 E
Baykonur = Bayqongyr, Kazakstan 26 E7 47 48N 65 50 E
Baymak, Russia 24 D10 52 36N 58 19 E
Baynes Mts., Namibia 56 B1 17 15S 13 0 E
Bayombong, Phil. 37 A6 16 30N 121 10 E
Bayonne, France 18 E3 43 30N 1 28W
Bayonne, U.S.A. 79 F10 40 40N 74 7W
Bayovar, Peru 92 E2 5 50S 81 0W
Bayqongyr, Kazakstan 26 E7 47 48N 65 50 E
Bayram-Ali = Bayramaly, Turkmenistan 26 F7 37 37N 62 10 E
Bayramaly, Turkmenistan 26 F7 37 37N 62 10 E
Bayramiç, Turkey 21 E12 39 48N 26 36 E
Bayreuth, Germany 16 D6 49 56N 11 35 E
Bayrūt, Lebanon 47 B4 33 53N 35 31 E
Bays, L. of, Canada 78 A5 45 15N 79 4W
Baysville, Canada 78 A5 45 9N 79 7W
Bayt Lahm, West Bank 47 D4 31 43N 35 12 E
Baytown, U.S.A. 81 L7 29 43N 94 59W
Baza, Spain 19 D4 37 30N 2 47W
Bazaruto, I. do, Mozam. 57 C6 21 40S 35 28 E
Bazhou, China 34 E9 39 8N 116 22 E
Bazmān, Kūh-e, Iran 45 D9 28 4N 60 1 E
Beach, U.S.A. 80 B3 46 58N 104 0W
Beach City, U.S.A. 78 F3 40 39N 81 35W
Beachport, Australia 63 F3 37 29S 140 0 E
Beachy Hd., U.K. 11 G8 50 44N 0 15 E
Beacon, Australia 61 F2 30 26S 117 52 E
Beacon, U.S.A. 79 E11 41 30N 73 58W
Beaconsfield, Australia 62 G4 41 11S 146 48 E
Beagle, Canal, S. Amer. 96 H3 55 0S 68 30W
Beagle Bay, Australia 60 C3 16 58S 122 40 E
Bealanana, Madag. 57 A8 14 33S 48 44 E
Beals Cr. →, U.S.A. 81 J4 32 10N 100 51W
Beamsville, Canada 78 C5 43 12N 79 28W
Bear →, Calif., U.S.A. 84 G5 38 56N 121 36W
Bear →, Utah, U.S.A. 74 B4 41 30N 112 8W
Bear I., Ireland 13 E2 51 38N 9 50W
Bear L., Canada 73 B9 55 8N 96 0W
Bear L., U.S.A. 82 F8 41 59N 111 21W
Beardmore, Canada 70 C2 49 36N 87 57W
Beardmore Glacier, Antarctica 5 E11 84 30S 170 0 E
Beardstown, U.S.A. 80 F9 40 1N 90 26W
Bearma →, India 43 G8 24 20N 79 51 E
Béarn, France 18 E3 43 20N 0 30W
Bearpaw Mts., U.S.A. 82 B9 48 12N 109 30W
Bearskin Lake, Canada 70 B1 53 58N 91 2W
Beas →, India 42 D6 31 10N 74 59 E
Beata, C., Dom. Rep. 89 C5 17 40N 71 30W
Beata, I., Dom. Rep. 89 C5 17 34N 71 31W
Beatrice, U.S.A. 80 E6 40 16N 96 45W
Beatrice, Zimbabwe 55 F3 18 15S 30 55 E
Beatrice, C., Australia 62 A2 14 20S 136 55 E
Beatton →, Canada 72 B4 56 15N 120 45W
Beatton River, Canada 72 B4 57 26N 121 20W
Beatty, U.S.A. 84 J10 36 54N 116 46W
Beauce, Plaine de la, France 18 B4 48 10N 1 45 E
Beauceville, Canada 71 C5 46 13N 70 46W
Beaudesert, Australia 63 D5 27 59S 153 0 E
Beaufort, Malaysia 36 C5 5 30N 115 40 E
Beaufort, N.C., U.S.A. 77 H7 34 43N 76 40W
Beaufort, S.C., U.S.A. 77 J5 32 26N 80 40W
Beaufort Sea, Arctic 4 B1 72 0N 140 0W
Beaufort West, S. Africa 56 E3 32 18S 22 36 E
Beauharnois, Canada 79 A11 45 20N 73 52W
Beaulieu →, Canada 72 A6 62 3N 113 11W
Beauly, U.K. 12 D4 57 30N 4 28W
Beauly →, U.K. 12 D4 57 29N 4 27W
Beaumaris, U.K. 10 D3 53 16N 4 6W
Beaumont, Belgium 15 D4 50 15N 4 14 E
Beaumont, U.S.A. 81 K7 30 5N 94 6W
Beaune, France 18 C6 47 2N 4 50 E
Beaupré, Canada 71 C5 47 3N 70 54W
Beauraing, Belgium 15 D4 50 7N 4 57 E
Beauséjour, Canada 73 C9 50 5N 96 35W
Beauvais, France 18 B5 49 25N 2 8 E
Beauval, Canada 73 B7 55 9N 107 37W
Beaver, Okla., U.S.A. 81 G4 36 49N 100 31W
Beaver, Pa., U.S.A. 78 F4 40 42N 80 19W
Beaver, Utah, U.S.A. 83 G7 38 17N 112 38W
Beaver →, B.C., Canada 72 B4 59 52N 124 20W
Beaver →, Ont., Canada 70 A2 55 55N 87 48W
Beaver →, Sask., Canada 73 B7 55 26N 107 45W
Beaver →, U.S.A. 81 G5 36 35N 99 30W
Beaver City, U.S.A. 80 E5 40 8N 99 50W
Beaver Creek, Canada 68 B5 63 0N 141 0W
Beaver Dam, U.S.A. 80 D10 43 28N 88 50W
Beaver Falls, U.S.A. 78 F4 40 46N 80 20W
Beaver Hill L., Canada 73 C10 54 5N 94 50W
Beaver I., U.S.A. 76 C3 45 40N 85 33W
Beaverhill L., Canada 72 C6 53 27N 112 32W
Beaverlodge, Canada 72 B5 55 11N 119 29W
Beaverstone →, Canada 70 B2 54 59N 89 25W
Beaverton, Canada 78 B5 44 26N 79 9W
Beaverton, U.S.A. 84 E4 45 29N 122 48W
Beawar, India 42 F6 26 3N 74 18 E
Bebedouro, Brazil 95 A6 21 0S 48 25W
Beboa, Madag. 57 B7 17 22S 44 33 E
Beccles, U.K. 11 E9 52 27N 1 35 E
Bečej, Serbia, Yug. 21 B9 45 36N 20 3 E
Béchar, Algeria 50 B5 31 38N 2 18W
Beckley, U.S.A. 76 G5 37 47N 81 11W
Beddouza, Ras, Morocco 50 B4 32 33N 9 9W
Bedford, Canada 79 A12 45 7N 72 59W
Bedford, S. Africa 56 E4 32 40S 26 10 E
Bedford, U.K. 11 E7 52 8N 0 28W
Bedford, Ind., U.S.A. 76 F2 38 52N 86 29W
Bedford, Iowa, U.S.A. 80 E7 40 40N 94 44W
Bedford, Ohio, U.S.A. 78 E3 41 23N 81 32W
Bedford, Pa., U.S.A. 78 F6 40 1N 78 30W
Bedford, Va., U.S.A. 76 G6 37 20N 79 31W
Bedford, C., Australia 62 B4 15 14S 145 21 E
Bedfordshire □, U.K. 11 E7 52 4N 0 28W
Bedourie, Australia 62 C2 24 30S 139 30 E
Bedum, Neths. 15 A6 53 18N 6 36 E
Beebe Plain, Canada 79 A12 45 1N 72 9W
Beech Creek, U.S.A. 78 E7 41 5N 77 36W
Beenleigh, Australia 63 D5 27 43S 153 10 E
Be'er Menuha, Israel 44 D2 30 19N 35 8 E
Be'er Sheva, Israel 47 D3 31 15N 34 48 E
Beersheba = Be'er Sheva, Israel 47 D3 31 15N 34 48 E
Beeston, U.K. 10 E6 52 56N 1 14W
Beeville, U.S.A. 81 L6 28 24N 97 45W
Befale, Dem. Rep. of the Congo 52 D4 0 25N 20 45 E
Befandriana, Madag. 57 C7 21 55S 44 0 E
Befotaka, Madag. 57 C8 23 49S 47 0 E
Bega, Australia 63 F4 36 41S 149 51 E
Begusarai, India 43 G12 25 24N 86 9 E
Behābād, Iran 45 C8 32 24N 59 47 E
Behala, India 43 H13 22 30N 88 20 E
Behara, Madag. 57 C8 24 55S 46 20 E
Behbehān, Iran 45 D6 30 30N 50 15 E
Behm Canal, U.S.A. 72 B2 55 10N 131 0W
Behshahr, Iran 45 B7 36 45N 53 35 E
Bei Jiang →, China 33 D6 23 2N 112 58 E
Bei'an, China 33 B7 48 10N 126 20 E
Beihai, China 33 D5 21 28N 109 6 E
Beijing, China 34 E9 39 55N 116 20 E
Beijing □, China 34 E9 39 55N 116 20 E
Beilen, Neths. 15 B6 52 52N 6 27 E
Beilpajah, Australia 63 E3 32 54S 143 52 E
Beinn na Faoghla = Benbecula, U.K. 12 D1 57 26N 7 21W
Beipiao, China 35 D11 41 52N 120 32 E
Beira, Mozam. 55 F3 19 50S 34 52 E
Beirut = Bayrūt, Lebanon 47 B4 33 53N 35 31 E
Beiseker, Canada 72 C6 51 23N 113 32W
Beitaolaizhao, China 35 B13 44 58N 125 58 E
Beitbridge, Zimbabwe 55 G3 22 12S 30 0 E
Beizhen = Binzhou, China 35 F10 37 20N 118 2 E
Beizhen, China 35 D11 41 38N 121 54 E
Beizhengzhen, China 35 B12 44 31N 123 30 E
Beja, Portugal 19 C2 38 2N 7 53W
Béja, Tunisia 51 A7 36 43N 9 12 E
Bejaia, Algeria 50 A7 36 42N 5 2 E
Béjar, Spain 19 B3 40 23N 5 46W
Bejestān, Iran 45 C8 34 30N 58 5 E
Békéscsaba, Hungary 17 E11 46 40N 21 5 E
Bekily, Madag. 57 C8 24 13S 45 19 E
Bekok, Malaysia 39 L4 2 20N 103 7 E
Bela, India 43 G10 25 50N 82 0 E
Bela, Pakistan 42 F2 26 12N 66 20 E
Bela Crkva, Serbia, Yug. 21 B9 44 55N 21 27 E
Bela Vista, Brazil 94 A4 22 12S 56 20W
Bela Vista, Mozam. 57 D5 26 10S 32 44 E
Belan →, India 43 G9 24 2N 81 45 E
Belarus ■, Europe 17 B14 53 30N 27 0 E
Belau = Palau ■, Pac. Oc. 28 J17 7 30N 134 30 E
Belavenona, Madag. 57 C8 24 50S 47 4 E
Belawan, Indonesia 36 D1 3 33N 98 32 E
Belaya →, Russia 24 C9 54 40N 56 0 E
Belaya Tserkov = Bila Tserkva, Ukraine 17 D16 49 45N 30 10 E
Belcher Is., Canada 70 A3 56 15N 78 45W
Belden, U.S.A. 84 E5 40 2N 121 17W
Belebey, Russia 24 D9 54 7N 54 7 E
Belém, Brazil 93 D9 1 20S 48 30W
Belén, Argentina 94 B2 27 40S 67 5W
Belén, Paraguay 94 A4 23 30S 57 6W
Belen, U.S.A. 83 J10 34 40N 106 46W
Belet Uen, Somali Rep. 46 G4 4 30N 45 5 E
Belev, Russia 24 D6 53 50N 36 5 E
Belfair, U.S.A. 84 C4 47 27N 122 50W
Belfast, S. Africa 57 D5 25 42S 30 2 E
Belfast, U.K. 13 B6 54 37N 5 56W

Belfast, *Maine, U.S.A.* **77 C11** 44 26N 69 1W
Belfast, *N.Y., U.S.A.* **78 D6** 42 21N 78 7W
Belfast L., *U.K.* **13 B6** 54 40N 5 50W
Belfield, *U.S.A.* **80 B3** 46 53N 103 12W
Belfort, *France* **18 C7** 47 38N 6 50 E
Belfry, *U.S.A.* **82 D9** 45 9N 109 1W
Belgaum, *India* **40 M9** 15 55N 74 35 E
Belgium ■, *Europe* **15 D4** 50 30N 5 0 E
Belgorod, *Russia* **25 D6** 50 35N 36 35 E
Belgorod-Dnestrovskiy = Bilhorod-Dnistrovskyy, *Ukraine* **25 E5** 46 11N 30 23 E
Belgrade = Beograd, *Serbia, Yug.* **21 B9** 44 50N 20 37 E
Belgrade, *U.S.A.* **82 D8** 45 47N 111 11W
Belhaven, *U.S.A.* **77 H7** 35 33N 76 37W
Beli Drim →, *Europe* **21 C9** 42 6N 20 25 E
Belinyu, *Indonesia* **36 E3** 1 35S 105 50 E
Beliton Is. = Belitung, *Indonesia* **36 E3** 3 10S 107 50 E
Belitung, *Indonesia* **36 E3** 3 10S 107 50 E
Belize ■, *Cent. Amer.* **87 D7** 17 0N 88 30W
Belize City, *Belize* **87 D7** 17 25N 88 0W
Belkovskiy, Ostrov, *Russia* **27 B14** 75 32N 135 44 E
Bell →, *Canada* **70 C4** 49 48N 77 38W
Bell I., *Canada* **71 B8** 50 46N 55 35W
Bell-Irving →, *Canada* **72 B3** 56 12N 129 5W
Bell Peninsula, *Canada* **69 B11** 63 50N 82 0W
Bell Ville, *Argentina* **94 C3** 32 40S 62 40W
Bella Bella, *Canada* **72 C3** 52 10N 128 10W
Bella Coola, *Canada* **72 C3** 52 25N 126 40W
Bella Unión, *Uruguay* **94 C4** 30 15S 57 40W
Bella Vista, *Corrientes, Argentina* **94 B4** 28 33S 59 0W
Bella Vista, *Tucuman, Argentina* **94 B2** 27 10S 65 25W
Bellaire, *U.S.A.* **78 F4** 40 1N 80 45W
Bellary, *India* **40 M10** 15 10N 76 56 E
Bellata, *Australia* **63 D4** 29 53S 149 46 E
Belle-Chasse, *U.S.A.* **81 L10** 29 51N 89 59W
Belle Fourche, *U.S.A.* **80 C3** 44 40N 103 51W
Belle Fourche →, *U.S.A.* **80 C3** 44 26N 102 18W
Belle Glade, *U.S.A.* **77 M5** 26 41N 80 40W
Belle-Île, *France* **18 C2** 47 20N 3 10W
Belle Isle, *Canada* **71 B8** 51 57N 55 25W
Belle Isle, Str. of, *Canada* **71 B8** 51 30N 56 30W
Belle Plaine, *U.S.A.* **80 E8** 41 54N 92 17W
Bellefontaine, *U.S.A.* **76 E4** 40 22N 83 46W
Bellefonte, *U.S.A.* **78 F7** 40 55N 77 47W
Belleoram, *Canada* **71 C8** 47 31N 55 25W
Belleville, *Canada* **78 B7** 44 10N 77 23W
Belleville, *Ill., U.S.A.* **80 F10** 38 31N 89 59W
Belleville, *Kans., U.S.A.* **80 F6** 39 50N 97 38W
Belleville, *N.Y., U.S.A.* **79 C8** 43 46N 76 10W
Bellevue, *Canada* **72 D6** 49 35N 114 22W
Bellevue, *Idaho, U.S.A.* **82 E6** 43 28N 114 16W
Bellevue, *Nebr., U.S.A.* **80 E7** 41 8N 95 53W
Bellevue, *Ohio, U.S.A.* **78 E2** 41 17N 82 51W
Bellevue, *Wash., U.S.A.* **84 C4** 47 37N 122 12W
Bellin = Kangirsuk, *Canada* **69 C13** 60 0N 70 0W
Bellingen, *Australia* **63 E5** 30 25S 152 50 E
Bellingham, *U.S.A.* **68 D7** 48 46N 122 29W
Bellingshausen Sea, *Antarctica* **5 C17** 66 0S 80 0W
Bellinzona, *Switz.* **18 C8** 46 11N 9 1 E
Bello, *Colombia* **92 B3** 6 20N 75 33W
Bellows Falls, *U.S.A.* **79 C12** 43 8N 72 27W
Bellpat, *Pakistan* **42 E3** 29 0N 68 5 E
Belluno, *Italy* **20 A5** 46 9N 12 13 E
Bellwood, *U.S.A.* **78 F6** 40 36N 78 20W
Belmont, *Canada* **78 D3** 42 53N 81 5W
Belmont, *S. Africa* **56 D3** 29 28S 24 22 E
Belmont, *U.S.A.* **78 D6** 42 14N 78 2W
Belmonte, *Brazil* **93 G11** 16 0S 39 0W
Belmopan, *Belize* **87 D7** 17 18N 88 30W
Belmullet, *Ireland* **13 B2** 54 14N 9 58W
Belo Horizonte, *Brazil* **93 G10** 19 55S 43 56W
Belo-sur-Mer, *Madag.* **57 C7** 20 42S 44 0 E
Belo-Tsiribihina, *Madag.* **57 B7** 19 40S 44 30 E
Belogorsk, *Russia* **27 D13** 51 0N 128 20 E
Beloha, *Madag.* **57 D8** 25 10S 45 3 E
Beloit, *Kans., U.S.A.* **80 F5** 39 28N 98 6W
Beloit, *Wis., U.S.A.* **80 D10** 42 31N 89 2W
Belokorovichi, *Ukraine* **17 C15** 51 7N 28 2 E
Belomorsk, *Russia* **24 B5** 64 35N 34 54 E
Belonia, *India* **41 H17** 23 15N 91 30 E
Beloretsk, *Russia* **24 D10** 53 58N 58 24 E
Belorussia = Belarus ■, *Europe* **17 B14** 53 30N 27 0 E
Belovo, *Russia* **26 D9** 54 30N 86 0 E
Beloye, Ozero, *Russia* **24 B6** 60 10N 37 35 E
Beloye More, *Russia* **24 A6** 66 30N 38 0 E
Belozersk, *Russia* **24 B6** 60 1N 37 45 E
Belpre, *U.S.A.* **76 F5** 39 17N 81 34W
Belrain, *India* **43 E9** 28 23N 80 55 E
Belt, *U.S.A.* **82 C8** 47 23N 110 55W
Beltana, *Australia* **63 E2** 30 48S 138 25 E
Belterra, *Brazil* **93 D8** 2 45S 55 0W
Belton, *U.S.A.* **81 K6** 31 3N 97 28W
Belton L., *U.S.A.* **81 K6** 31 8N 97 32W
Beltsy = Bălţi, *Moldova* **17 E14** 47 48N 27 58 E
Belturbet, *Ireland* **13 B4** 54 6N 7 26W
Belukha, *Russia* **26 E9** 49 50N 86 50 E
Beluran, *Malaysia* **36 C5** 5 48N 117 35 E
Belvidere, *Ill., U.S.A.* **80 D10** 42 15N 88 50W
Belvidere, *N.J., U.S.A.* **79 F9** 40 50N 75 5W
Belyando →, *Australia* **62 C4** 21 38S 146 50 E
Belyy, Ostrov, *Russia* **26 B8** 73 30N 71 0 E
Belyy Yar, *Russia* **26 D9** 58 26N 84 39 E
Belzoni, *U.S.A.* **81 J9** 33 11N 90 29W
Bemaraha, Lembalemban' i, *Madag.* **57 B7** 18 40S 44 45 E
Bemarivo, *Madag.* **57 C7** 21 45S 44 45 E
Bemarivo →, *Madag.* **57 B8** 15 27S 47 40 E
Bemavo, *Madag.* **57 C8** 21 33S 45 25 E
Bembéréke, *Benin* **50 F6** 10 11N 2 43 E
Bembesi, *Zimbabwe* **55 G2** 20 0S 28 58 E
Bembesi →, *Zimbabwe* **55 F2** 18 57S 27 47 E
Bemetara, *India* **43 J9** 21 42N 81 32 E
Bemidji, *U.S.A.* **80 B7** 47 28N 94 53W
Ben, *Iran* **45 C6** 32 32N 50 45 E
Ben Cruachan, *U.K.* **12 E3** 56 26N 5 8W
Ben Dearg, *U.K.* **12 D4** 57 47N 4 56W
Ben Hope, *U.K.* **12 C4** 58 25N 4 36W
Ben Lawers, *U.K.* **12 E4** 56 32N 4 14W
Ben Lomond, *N.S.W., Australia* **63 E5** 30 1S 151 43 E
Ben Lomond, *Tas., Australia* **62 G4** 41 38S 147 42 E
Ben Lomond, *U.K.* **12 E4** 56 11N 4 38W
Ben Luc, *Vietnam* **39 G6** 10 39N 106 29 E
Ben Macdhui, *U.K.* **12 D5** 57 4N 3 40W
Ben Mhor, *U.K.* **12 D1** 57 15N 7 18W
Ben More, *Arg. & Bute, U.K.* **12 E2** 56 26N 6 1W
Ben More, *Stirl., U.K.* **12 E4** 56 23N 4 32W
Ben More Assynt, *U.K.* **12 C4** 58 8N 4 52W
Ben Nevis, *U.K.* **12 E3** 56 48N 5 1W
Ben Quang, *Vietnam* **38 D6** 17 3N 106 55 E
Ben Vorlich, *U.K.* **12 E4** 56 21N 4 14W
Ben Wyvis, *U.K.* **12 D4** 57 40N 4 35W
Bena, *Nigeria* **50 F7** 11 20N 5 50 E
Benalla, *Australia* **63 F4** 36 30S 146 0 E
Benares = Varanasi, *India* **43 G10** 25 22N 83 0 E
Benavente, *Spain* **19 A3** 42 2N 5 43W
Benavides, *U.S.A.* **81 M5** 27 36N 98 25W
Benbecula, *U.K.* **12 D1** 57 26N 7 21W
Benbonyathe, *Australia* **63 E2** 30 25S 139 11 E
Bend, *U.S.A.* **82 D3** 44 4N 121 19W
Bendemeer, *Australia* **63 E5** 30 53S 151 8 E
Bender Beila, *Somali Rep.* **46 F5** 9 30N 50 48 E
Bendery = Tighina, *Moldova* **17 E15** 46 50N 29 30 E
Bendigo, *Australia* **63 F3** 36 40S 144 15 E
Benē Beraq, *Israel* **47 C3** 32 6N 34 51 E
Benenitra, *Madag.* **57 C8** 23 27S 45 5 E
Benevento, *Italy* **20 D6** 41 8N 14 45 E
Benga, *Mozam.* **55 F3** 16 11S 33 40 E
Bengal, Bay of, *Ind. Oc.* **41 M17** 15 0N 90 0 E
Bengbu, *China* **35 H9** 32 58N 117 20 E
Benghazi = Banghāzī, *Libya* **51 B10** 32 11N 20 3 E
Bengkalis, *Indonesia* **36 D2** 1 30N 102 10 E
Bengkulu, *Indonesia* **36 E2** 3 50S 102 12 E
Bengkulu □, *Indonesia* **36 E2** 3 48S 102 16 E
Bengough, *Canada* **73 D7** 49 25N 105 10W
Benguela, *Angola* **53 G2** 12 37S 13 25 E
Benguérua, I., *Mozam.* **57 C6** 21 58S 35 28 E
Beni, *Dem. Rep. of the Congo* **54 B2** 0 30N 29 27 E
Beni →, *Bolivia* **92 F5** 10 23S 65 24W
Beni Mellal, *Morocco* **50 B4** 32 21N 6 21W
Beni Suef, *Egypt* **51 C12** 29 5N 31 6 E
Beniah L., *Canada* **72 A6** 63 23N 112 17W
Benicia, *U.S.A.* **84 G4** 38 3N 122 9W
Benidorm, *Spain* **19 C5** 38 33N 0 9W
Benin ■, *Africa* **50 G6** 10 0N 2 0 E
Benin, Bight of, *W. Afr.* **50 H6** 5 0N 3 0 E
Benin City, *Nigeria* **50 G7** 6 20N 5 31 E
Benitses, *Greece* **23 A3** 39 32N 19 55 E
Benjamin Aceval, *Paraguay* **94 A4** 24 58S 57 34W
Benjamin Constant, *Brazil* **92 D4** 4 40S 70 15W
Benjamin Hill, *Mexico* **86 A2** 30 10N 111 10W
Benkelman, *U.S.A.* **80 E4** 40 3N 101 32W
Bennett, *Canada* **72 B2** 59 56N 134 53W
Bennett, L., *Australia* **60 D5** 22 50S 131 2 E
Bennetta, Ostrov, *Russia* **27 B15** 76 21N 148 56 E
Bennettsville, *U.S.A.* **77 H6** 34 37N 79 41W
Bennington, *N.H., U.S.A.* **79 D11** 43 0N 71 55W
Bennington, *Vt., U.S.A.* **79 D11** 42 53N 73 12W
Benoni, *S. Africa* **57 D4** 26 11S 28 18 E
Benque Viejo, *Belize* **87 D7** 17 5N 89 8W
Benson, *Ariz., U.S.A.* **83 L8** 31 58N 110 18W
Benson, *Minn., U.S.A.* **80 C7** 45 19N 95 36W
Bent, *Iran* **45 E8** 26 20N 59 31 E
Benteng, *Indonesia* **37 F6** 6 10S 120 30 E
Bentinck I., *Australia* **62 B2** 17 3S 139 35 E
Bento Gonçalves, *Brazil* **95 B5** 29 10S 51 31W
Benton, *Ark., U.S.A.* **81 H8** 34 34N 92 35W
Benton, *Calif., U.S.A.* **84 H8** 37 48N 118 32W
Benton, *Ill., U.S.A.* **80 G10** 38 0N 88 55W
Benton, *Pa., U.S.A.* **79 E8** 41 12N 76 23W
Benton Harbor, *U.S.A.* **76 D2** 42 6N 86 27W
Bentonville, *U.S.A.* **81 G7** 36 22N 94 13W
Bentung, *Malaysia* **39 L3** 3 31N 101 55 E
Benue →, *Nigeria* **50 G7** 7 48N 6 46 E
Benxi, *China* **35 D12** 41 20N 123 48 E
Beo, *Indonesia* **37 D7** 4 25N 126 50 E
Beograd, *Serbia, Yug.* **21 B9** 44 50N 20 37 E
Beppu, *Japan* **31 H5** 33 15N 131 30 E
Beqaa Valley = Al Biqā, *Lebanon* **47 A5** 34 10N 36 10 E
Ber Mota, *India* **42 H3** 23 27N 68 34 E
Berach →, *India* **42 G6** 25 15N 75 2 E
Berati, *Albania* **21 D8** 40 43N 19 59 E
Berau, Teluk, *Indonesia* **37 E8** 2 30S 132 30 E
Berber, *Sudan* **51 E12** 18 0N 34 0 E
Berbera, *Somali Rep.* **46 E4** 10 30N 45 2 E
Berbérati, *C.A.R.* **52 D3** 4 15N 15 40 E
Berbice →, *Guyana* **92 B7** 6 20N 57 32W
Berdichev = Berdychiv, *Ukraine* **17 D15** 49 57N 28 30 E
Berdsk, *Russia* **26 D9** 54 47N 83 2 E
Berdyansk, *Ukraine* **25 E6** 46 45N 36 50 E
Berdychiv, *Ukraine* **17 D15** 49 57N 28 30 E
Berea, *U.S.A.* **76 G3** 37 34N 84 17W
Berebere, *Indonesia* **37 D7** 2 25N 128 45 E
Bereda, *Somali Rep.* **46 E5** 11 45N 51 0 E
Berehove, *Ukraine* **17 D12** 48 15N 22 35 E
Berekum, *Ghana* **50 G5** 7 29N 2 34W
Berens →, *Canada* **73 C9** 52 25N 97 2W
Berens I., *Canada* **73 C9** 52 18N 97 18W
Berens River, *Canada* **73 C9** 52 25N 97 0W
Beresford, *U.S.A.* **80 D6** 43 5N 96 47W
Berestechko, *Ukraine* **17 C13** 50 22N 25 5 E
Berevo, *Mahajanga, Madag.* **57 B7** 17 14S 44 17 E
Berevo, *Toliara, Madag.* **57 B7** 19 44S 44 58 E
Bereza, *Belarus* **17 B13** 52 31N 24 51 E
Berezhany, *Ukraine* **17 D13** 49 26N 24 58 E
Berezina = Byarezina →, *Belarus* **17 B16** 52 33N 30 14 E
Bereznik, *Russia* **24 B7** 62 51N 42 40 E
Berezniki, *Russia* **24 C10** 59 24N 56 46 E
Berezovo, *Russia* **26 C7** 64 0N 65 0 E
Berga, *Spain* **19 A6** 42 6N 1 48 E
Bergama, *Turkey* **21 E12** 39 8N 27 11 E
Bérgamo, *Italy* **18 D8** 45 41N 9 43 E
Bergen, *Neths.* **15 B4** 52 40N 4 43 E
Bergen, *Norway* **9 F11** 60 20N 5 20 E
Bergen, *U.S.A.* **78 C7** 43 5N 77 57W
Bergen op Zoom, *Neths.* **15 C4** 51 28N 4 18 E
Bergerac, *France* **18 D4** 44 51N 0 30 E
Bergholz, *U.S.A.* **78 F4** 40 31N 80 53W
Bergisch Gladbach, *Germany* **15 D7** 50 59N 7 8 E
Bergville, *S. Africa* **57 D4** 28 52S 29 18 E
Berhala, Selat, *Indonesia* **36 E2** 1 0S 104 15 E
Berhampore = Baharampur, *India* **43 G13** 24 2N 88 27 E
Berhampur = Brahmapur, *India* **41 K14** 19 15N 84 54 E
Bering Sea, *Pac. Oc.* **68 C1** 58 0N 171 0 E
Bering Strait, *Pac. Oc.* **68 B3** 65 30N 169 0W
Beringovskiy, *Russia* **27 C18** 63 3N 179 19 E
Berisso, *Argentina* **94 C4** 34 56S 57 50W
Berja, *Spain* **19 D4** 36 50N 2 56W
Berkeley, *U.S.A.* **84 H4** 37 52N 122 16W
Berkner I., *Antarctica* **5 D18** 79 30S 50 0W
Berkshire, *U.S.A.* **79 D8** 42 19N 76 11W
Berkshire Downs, *U.K.* **11 F6** 51 33N 1 29W
Berlin, *Germany* **16 B7** 52 30N 13 25 E
Berlin, *Md., U.S.A.* **76 F8** 38 20N 75 13W
Berlin, *N.H., U.S.A.* **79 B13** 44 28N 71 11W
Berlin, *N.Y., U.S.A.* **79 D11** 42 42N 73 23W
Berlin, *Wis., U.S.A.* **76 D1** 43 58N 88 57W
Berlin L., *U.S.A.* **78 E4** 41 3N 81 0W
Bermejo →, *Formosa, Argentina* **94 B4** 26 51S 58 23W
Bermejo →, *San Juan, Argentina* **94 C2** 32 30S 67 30W
Bermen, L., *Canada* **71 B6** 53 35N 68 55W
Bermuda ■, *Atl. Oc.* **66 F13** 32 45N 65 0W
Bern, *Switz.* **18 C7** 46 57N 7 28 E
Bernalillo, *U.S.A.* **83 J10** 35 18N 106 33W
Bernardo de Irigoyen, *Argentina* **95 B5** 26 15S 53 40W
Bernardo O'Higgins □, *Chile* **94 C1** 34 15S 70 45W
Bernardsville, *U.S.A.* **79 F10** 40 43N 74 34W
Bernasconi, *Argentina* **94 D3** 37 55S 63 44W
Bernburg, *Germany* **16 C6** 51 47N 11 44 E
Berne = Bern, *Switz.* **18 C7** 46 57N 7 28 E
Berneray, *U.K.* **12 D1** 57 43N 7 11W
Bernier I., *Australia* **61 D1** 24 50S 113 12 E
Bernina, Piz, *Switz.* **18 C8** 46 20N 9 54 E
Beroroha, *Madag.* **57 C8** 21 40S 45 10 E
Beroun, *Czech Rep.* **16 D8** 49 57N 14 5 E
Berri, *Australia* **63 E3** 34 14S 140 35 E
Berriane, *Algeria* **50 B6** 32 50N 3 46 E
Berrigan, *Australia* **63 F4** 35 38S 145 49 E
Berry, *Australia* **63 E5** 34 46S 150 43 E
Berry, *France* **18 C5** 46 50N 2 0 E
Berry Is., *Bahamas* **88 A4** 25 40N 77 50W
Berryessa L., *U.S.A.* **84 G4** 38 31N 122 6W
Berryville, *U.S.A.* **81 G8** 36 22N 93 34W
Bershad, *Ukraine* **17 D15** 48 22N 29 31 E
Berthold, *U.S.A.* **80 A4** 48 19N 101 44W
Berthoud, *U.S.A.* **80 E2** 40 19N 105 5W
Bertoua, *Cameroon* **52 D2** 4 30N 13 45 E
Bertraghboy B., *Ireland* **13 C2** 53 22N 9 54W
Berwick, *U.S.A.* **79 E8** 41 3N 76 14W
Berwick-upon-Tweed, *U.K.* **10 B6** 55 46N 2 0W
Berwyn Mts., *U.K.* **10 E4** 52 54N 3 26W
Besal, *Pakistan* **43 B5** 35 4N 73 56 E
Besalampy, *Madag.* **57 B7** 16 43S 44 29 E
Besançon, *France* **18 C7** 47 15N 6 2 E
Besar, *Indonesia* **36 E5** 2 40S 116 0 E
Besnard L., *Canada* **73 B7** 55 25N 106 0W
Besni, *Turkey* **44 B3** 37 41N 37 52 E
Besor, N. →, *Egypt* **47 D3** 31 28N 34 22 E
Bessarabiya, *Moldova* **17 E15** 47 0N 28 10 E
Bessarabka = Basarabeasca, *Moldova* **17 E15** 46 21N 28 58 E
Bessemer, *Ala., U.S.A.* **77 J2** 33 24N 86 58W
Bessemer, *Mich., U.S.A.* **80 B9** 46 29N 90 3W
Bessemer, *Pa., U.S.A.* **78 F4** 40 59N 80 30W
Beswick, *Australia* **60 B5** 14 34S 132 53 E
Bet She'an, *Israel* **47 C4** 32 30N 35 30 E
Bet Shemesh, *Israel* **47 D4** 31 44N 35 0 E
Betafo, *Madag.* **57 B8** 19 50S 46 51 E
Betancuria, *Canary Is.* **22 F5** 28 25N 14 3W
Betanzos, *Spain* **19 A1** 43 15N 8 12W
Bétaré Oya, *Cameroon* **52 C2** 5 40N 14 5 E
Bethal, *S. Africa* **57 D4** 26 27S 29 28 E
Bethanien, *Namibia* **56 D2** 26 31S 17 8 E
Bethany, *Canada* **78 B6** 44 11N 78 34W
Bethany, *U.S.A.* **80 E7** 40 16N 94 2W
Bethel, *Alaska, U.S.A.* **68 B3** 60 48N 161 45W
Bethel, *Conn., U.S.A.* **79 E11** 41 22N 73 25W
Bethel, *Maine, U.S.A.* **79 B14** 44 25N 70 47W
Bethel, *Vt., U.S.A.* **79 C12** 43 50N 72 38W
Bethel Park, *U.S.A.* **78 F4** 40 20N 80 1W
Bethlehem = Bayt Lahm, *West Bank* **47 D4** 31 43N 35 12 E
Bethlehem, *S. Africa* **57 D4** 28 14S 28 18 E
Bethlehem, *U.S.A.* **79 F9** 40 37N 75 23W
Bethulie, *S. Africa* **56 E4** 30 30S 25 59 E
Béthune, *France* **18 A5** 50 30N 2 38 E
Betioky, *Madag.* **57 C7** 23 48S 44 20 E
Betong, *Thailand* **39 K3** 5 45N 101 5 E
Betoota, *Australia* **62 D3** 25 45S 140 42 E
Betroka, *Madag.* **57 C8** 23 16S 46 0 E
Betsiamites, *Canada* **71 C6** 48 56N 68 40W
Betsiamites →, *Canada* **71 C6** 48 56N 68 38W
Betsiboka →, *Madag.* **57 B8** 16 3S 46 36 E
Bettendorf, *U.S.A.* **80 E9** 41 32N 90 30W
Bettiah, *India* **43 F11** 26 48N 84 33 E
Betul, *India* **40 J10** 21 58N 77 59 E
Betung, *Malaysia* **36 D4** 1 24N 111 31 E
Betws-y-Coed, *U.K.* **10 D4** 53 5N 3 48W
Beulah, *Mich., U.S.A.* **76 C2** 44 38N 86 6W
Beulah, *N. Dak., U.S.A.* **80 B4** 47 16N 101 47W
Beveren, *Belgium* **15 C4** 51 12N 4 16 E
Beverley, *Australia* **61 F2** 32 9S 116 56 E
Beverley, *U.K.* **10 D7** 53 51N 0 26W
Beverley Hills, *U.S.A.* **77 L4** 28 56N 82 28W
Beverly, *U.S.A.* **79 D14** 42 33N 70 53W
Beverly Hills, *U.S.A.* **85 L8** 34 4N 118 25W
Bewas →, *India* **43 H8** 23 59N 79 21 E
Bexhill, *U.K.* **11 G8** 50 51N 0 29 E
Beyānlū, *Iran* **44 C5** 36 0N 47 51 E
Beyneu, *Kazakstan* **25 E10** 45 18N 55 9 E
Beypazarı, *Turkey* **25 F5** 40 10N 31 56 E
Beyşehir Gölü, *Turkey* **25 G5** 37 41N 31 33 E
Béziers, *France* **18 E5** 43 20N 3 12 E
Bezwada = Vijayawada, *India* **41 L12** 16 31N 80 39 E
Bhabua, *India* **43 G10** 25 3N 83 37 E
Bhachau, *India* **40 H7** 23 20N 70 16 E
Bhadar →, *Gujarat, India* **43 J4** 22 17N 72 20 E
Bhadar →, *Gujarat, India* **42 J3** 21 27N 69 47 E
Bhadarwah, *India* **43 C6** 32 58N 75 46 E
Bhadohi, *India* **43 G10** 25 25N 82 34 E
Bhadra, *India* **42 E6** 29 8N 75 14 E
Bhadrakh, *India* **41 J15** 21 10N 86 30 E
Bhadran, *India* **42 H5** 22 19N 72 6 E
Bhadravati, *India* **40 N9** 13 49N 75 40 E
Bhag, *Pakistan* **42 E2** 29 2N 67 49 E
Bhagalpur, *India* **43 G12** 25 10N 87 0 E
Bhagirathi →, *Ut. P., India* **43 D8** 30 8N 78 35 E
Bhagirathi →, *W. Bengal, India* **43 H13** 23 25N 88 23 E
Bhakkar, *Pakistan* **42 D4** 31 40N 71 5 E
Bhakra Dam, *India* **42 D7** 31 30N 76 45 E
Bhamo, *Burma* **41 G20** 24 15N 97 15 E
Bhandara, *India* **40 J11** 21 5N 79 42 E
Bhanpura, *India* **42 G6** 24 31N 75 44 E
Bhanrer Ra., *India* **43 H8** 23 40N 79 45 E
Bhaptiahi, *India* **43 F12** 26 19N 86 44 E
Bharat = India ■, *Asia* **40 K11** 20 0N 78 0 E
Bharatpur, *Mad. P., India* **43 H9** 23 44N 81 46 E
Bharatpur, *Raj., India* **42 F7** 27 15N 77 30 E
Bharno, *India* **43 H11** 23 14N 84 53 E
Bhatinda, *India* **42 D6** 30 15N 74 57 E
Bhatpara, *India* **43 H13** 22 50N 88 25 E
Bhattu, *India* **42 E6** 29 36N 75 19 E
Bhaun, *Pakistan* **42 C5** 32 55N 72 40 E
Bhaunagar = Bhavnagar, *India* **40 J8** 21 45N 72 10 E
Bhavnagar, *India* **40 J8** 21 45N 72 10 E
Bhawanipatna, *India* **41 K12** 19 55N 80 10 E
Bhawari, *India* **42 G5** 25 42N 73 4 E
Bhayavadar, *India* **42 J4** 21 51N 70 15 E
Bhera, *Pakistan* **42 C5** 32 29N 72 57 E
Bhikangaon, *India* **42 J6** 21 52N 75 57 E
Bhilsa = Vidisha, *India* **42 H7** 23 28N 77 53 E
Bhilwara, *India* **42 G6** 25 25N 74 38 E
Bhima →, *India* **40 L10** 16 25N 77 17 E
Bhimavaram, *India* **41 L12** 16 30N 81 30 E
Bhimbar, *Pakistan* **43 C6** 32 59N 74 3 E
Bhind, *India* **43 F8** 26 30N 78 46 E
Bhinga, *India* **43 F9** 27 43N 81 56 E
Bhinmal, *India* **42 G5** 25 0N 72 15 E
Bhiwandi, *India* **40 K8** 19 20N 73 0 E
Bhiwani, *India* **42 E7** 28 50N 76 9 E
Bhogava →, *India* **42 H5** 22 26N 72 20 E
Bhola, *Bangla.* **41 H17** 22 45N 90 35 E
Bholari, *Pakistan* **42 G3** 25 19N 68 13 E
Bhopal, *India* **42 H7** 23 20N 77 30 E
Bhubaneshwar, *India* **41 J14** 20 15N 85 50 E
Bhuj, *India* **42 H3** 23 15N 69 49 E
Bhusaval, *India* **40 J9** 21 3N 75 46 E
Bhutan ■, *Asia* **41 F17** 27 25N 90 30 E
Biafra, B. of = Bonny, Bight of, *Africa* **52 D1** 3 30N 9 20 E
Biak, *Indonesia* **37 E9** 1 10S 136 6 E
Biała Podlaska, *Poland* **17 B12** 52 4N 23 6 E
Białogard, *Poland* **16 A8** 54 2N 15 58 E
Białystok, *Poland* **17 B12** 53 10N 23 10 E
Biaora, *India* **42 H7** 23 56N 76 56 E
Bīārjmand, *Iran* **45 B7** 36 6N 55 53 E
Biaro, *Indonesia* **37 D7** 2 5N 125 26 E
Biarritz, *France* **18 E3** 43 29N 1 33W
Bibai, *Japan* **30 C10** 43 19N 141 52 E
Bibby I., *Canada* **73 A10** 61 55N 93 0W
Biberach, *Germany* **16 D5** 48 5N 9 47 E
Bibungwa, *Dem. Rep. of the Congo* **54 C2** 2 40S 28 15 E
Bic, *Canada* **71 C6** 48 20N 68 41W
Bicester, *U.K.* **11 F6** 51 54N 1 9W
Bicheno, *Australia* **62 G4** 41 52S 148 18 E
Bichia, *India* **43 H9** 22 27N 80 42 E
Bickerton I., *Australia* **62 A2** 13 45S 136 10 E
Bida, *Nigeria* **50 G7** 9 3N 5 58 E
Bidar, *India* **40 L10** 17 55N 77 35 E
Biddeford, *U.S.A.* **77 D10** 43 30N 70 28W
Bideford, *U.K.* **11 F3** 51 1N 4 13W
Bideford Bay, *U.K.* **11 F3** 51 5N 4 20W
Bidhuna, *India* **43 F8** 26 49N 79 31 E
Bidor, *Malaysia* **39 K3** 4 6N 101 15 E
Bié, Planalto de, *Angola* **53 G3** 12 0S 16 0 E
Bieber, *U.S.A.* **82 F3** 41 7N 121 8W
Biel, *Switz.* **18 C7** 47 8N 7 14 E
Bielefeld, *Germany* **16 B5** 52 1N 8 33 E
Biella, *Italy* **18 D8** 45 34N 8 3 E
Bielsk Podlaski, *Poland* **17 B12** 52 47N 23 12 E
Bielsko-Biała, *Poland* **17 D10** 49 50N 19 2 E
Bien Hoa, *Vietnam* **39 G6** 10 57N 106 49 E
Bienne = Biel, *Switz.* **18 C7** 47 8N 7 14 E
Bienville, L., *Canada* **70 A5** 55 5N 72 40W
Biesiesfontein, *S. Africa* **56 E2** 30 57S 17 58 E
Big →, *Canada* **71 B8** 54 50N 58 55W
Big B., *Canada* **71 A7** 55 43N 60 35W
Big Bear City, *U.S.A.* **85 L10** 34 16N 116 51W
Big Bear Lake, *U.S.A.* **85 L10** 34 15N 116 56W
Big Belt Mts., *U.S.A.* **82 C8** 46 30N 111 25W
Big Bend, *Swaziland* **57 D5** 26 50S 31 58 E
Big Bend National Park, *U.S.A.* **81 L3** 29 20N 103 5W
Big Black →, *U.S.A.* **81 K9** 32 3N 91 4W
Big Blue →, *U.S.A.* **80 F6** 39 35N 96 34W
Big Creek, *U.S.A.* **84 H7** 37 11N 119 14W
Big Cypress National Preserve, *U.S.A.* **77 M5** 26 0N 81 10W
Big Cypress Swamp, *U.S.A.* **77 M5** 26 12N 81 10W
Big Falls, *U.S.A.* **80 A8** 48 12N 93 48W
Big Fork →, *U.S.A.* **80 A8** 48 31N 93 43W
Big Horn Mts. = Bighorn Mts., *U.S.A.* **82 D10** 44 30N 107 30W
Big I., *Canada* **72 A5** 61 7N 116 45W
Big Lake, *U.S.A.* **81 K4** 31 12N 101 28W
Big Moose, *U.S.A.* **79 C10** 43 49N 74 58W
Big Muddy Cr. →, *U.S.A.* **80 A2** 48 8N 104 36W
Big Pine, *U.S.A.* **84 H8** 37 10N 118 17W
Big Piney, *U.S.A.* **82 E8** 42 32N 110 7W
Big Rapids, *U.S.A.* **76 D3** 43 42N 85 29W
Big Rideau L., *Canada* **79 B8** 44 40N 76 15W
Big River, *Canada* **73 C7** 53 50N 107 0W
Big Run, *U.S.A.* **78 F6** 40 57N 78 55W
Big Sable Pt., *U.S.A.* **76 C2** 44 3N 86 1W
Big Salmon →, *Canada* **72 A2** 61 52N 134 55W
Big Sand L., *Canada* **73 B9** 57 45N 99 45W
Big Sandy, *U.S.A.* **82 B8** 48 11N 110 7W
Big Sandy →, *U.S.A.* **76 F4** 38 25N 82 36W
Big Sandy Cr. →, *U.S.A.* **80 F3** 38 7N 102 29W
Big Sioux →, *U.S.A.* **80 D6** 42 29N 96 27W
Big Spring, *U.S.A.* **81 J4** 32 15N 101 28W
Big Stone City, *U.S.A.* **80 C6** 45 18N 96 28W
Big Stone Gap, *U.S.A.* **77 G4** 36 52N 82 47W
Big Stone L., *U.S.A.* **80 C6** 45 30N 96 35W
Big Sur, *U.S.A.* **84 J5** 36 15N 121 48W
Big Timber, *U.S.A.* **82 D9** 45 50N 109 57W

Big Trout L., *Canada* **70 B2** 53 40N 90 0W
Big Trout Lake, *Canada* **70 B2** 53 45N 90 0W
Biğa, *Turkey* **21 D12** 40 13N 27 14 E
Bigadiç, *Turkey* **21 E13** 39 22N 28 7 E
Biggar, *Canada* **73 C7** 52 4N 108 0W
Biggar, *U.K.* **12 F5** 55 38N 3 32W
Bigge I., *Australia* **60 B4** 14 35S 125 10 E
Biggenden, *Australia* **63 D5** 25 31S 152 4 E
Biggleswade, *U.K.* **11 E7** 52 5N 0 14W
Biggs, *U.S.A.* **84 F5** 39 25N 121 43W
Bighorn, *U.S.A.* **82 C10** 46 10N 107 27W
Bighorn →, *U.S.A.* **82 C10** 46 10N 107 28W
Bighorn L., *U.S.A.* **82 D9** 44 55N 108 15W
Bighorn Mts., *U.S.A.* **82 D10** 44 30N 107 30W
Bigstone L., *Canada* **73 C9** 53 42N 95 44W
Bigwa, *Tanzania* **54 D4** 7 10S 39 10 E
Bihać, *Bos.-H.* **16 F8** 44 49N 15 57 E
Bihar, *India* **43 G11** 25 5N 85 40 E
Bihar □, *India* **43 G12** 25 0N 86 0 E
Biharamulo, *Tanzania* **54 C3** 2 25S 31 25 E
Bihariganj, *India* **43 G12** 25 44N 86 59 E
Bihor, Munţii, *Romania* **17 E12** 46 29N 22 47 E
Bijagós, Arquipélago dos, *Guinea-Biss.* **50 F2** 11 15N 16 10W
Bijaipur, *India* **42 F7** 26 2N 77 20 E
Bijapur, *Karnataka, India* **40 L9** 16 50N 75 55 E
Bijapur, *Mad. P., India* **41 K12** 18 50N 80 50 E
Bījār, *Iran* **44 C5** 35 52N 47 35 E
Bijawar, *India* **43 G8** 24 38N 79 30 E
Bijeljina, *Bos.-H.* **21 B8** 44 46N 19 14 E
Bijnor, *India* **42 E8** 29 27N 78 11 E
Bikaner, *India* **42 E5** 28 2N 73 18 E
Bikapur, *India* **43 F10** 26 30N 82 7 E
Bikeqi, *China* **34 D6** 40 43N 111 20 E
Bikfayyā, *Lebanon* **47 B4** 33 55N 35 41 E
Bikin, *Russia* **27 E14** 46 50N 134 20 E
Bikin →, *Russia* **30 A7** 46 51N 134 2 E
Bikini Atoll, *Marshall Is.* **64 F8** 12 0N 167 30 E
Bikoro, *Dem. Rep. of the Congo* **52 E3** 0 48S 18 15 E
Bila Tserkva, *Ukraine* **17 D16** 49 45N 30 10 E
Bilara, *India* **42 F5** 26 14N 73 53 E
Bilaspur, *Mad. P., India* **43 H10** 22 2N 82 15 E
Bilaspur, *Punjab, India* **42 D7** 31 19N 76 50 E
Bilauk Taungdan, *Thailand* **38 F2** 13 0N 99 0 E
Bilbao, *Spain* **19 A4** 43 16N 2 56W
Bilbo = Bilbao, *Spain* **19 A4** 43 16N 2 56W
Bíldudalur, *Iceland* **8 D2** 65 41N 23 36W
Bílé Karpaty, *Europe* **17 D9** 49 5N 18 0 E
Bilecik, *Turkey* **25 F5** 40 5N 30 5 E
Bilgram, *India* **43 F9** 27 11N 80 2 E
Bilhaur, *India* **43 F9** 26 51N 80 5 E
Bilhorod-Dnistrovskyy, *Ukraine* **25 E5** 46 11N 30 23 E
Bilibino, *Russia* **27 C17** 68 3N 166 20 E
Bilibiza, *Mozam.* **55 E5** 12 30S 40 20 E
Billabalong Roadhouse, *Australia* **61 E2** 27 25S 115 49 E
Billiluna, *Australia* **60 C4** 19 37S 127 41 E
Billings, *U.S.A.* **82 D9** 45 47N 108 30W
Billiton Is. = Belitung, *Indonesia* **36 E3** 3 10S 107 50 E
Bilma, *Niger* **51 E8** 18 50N 13 30 E
Biloela, *Australia* **62 C5** 24 24S 150 31 E
Biloxi, *U.S.A.* **81 K10** 30 24N 88 53W
Bilpa Morea Claypan, *Australia* **62 D3** 25 0S 140 0 E
Biltine, *Chad* **51 F10** 14 40N 20 50 E
Bima, *Indonesia* **37 F5** 8 22S 118 49 E
Bimini Is., *Bahamas* **88 A4** 25 42N 79 25W
Bin Xian, *Heilongjiang, China* **35 B14** 45 42N 127 32 E
Bin Xian, *Shaanxi, China* **34 G5** 35 2N 108 4 E
Bina-Etawah, *India* **42 G8** 24 13N 78 14 E
Bināb, *Iran* **45 B6** 36 35N 48 41 E
Binalbagan, *Phil.* **37 B6** 10 12N 122 50 E
Binalong, *Australia* **63 E4** 34 40S 148 39 E
Bīnālūd, Kūh-e, *Iran* **45 B8** 36 30N 58 30 E
Binatang = Bintangor, *Malaysia* **36 D4** 2 10N 111 40 E
Binche, *Belgium* **15 D4** 50 26N 4 10 E
Bindki, *India* **43 F9** 26 2N 80 36 E
Bindura, *Zimbabwe* **55 F3** 17 18S 31 18 E
Bingara, *Australia* **63 D5** 29 52S 150 36 E
Bingham, *U.S.A.* **77 C11** 45 3N 69 53W
Binghamton, *U.S.A.* **79 D9** 42 6N 75 55W
Bingöl, *Turkey* **44 B4** 38 53N 40 29 E
Binh Dinh = An Nhon, *Vietnam* **38 F7** 13 55N 109 7 E
Binh Khe, *Vietnam* **38 F7** 13 57N 108 51 E
Binh Son, *Vietnam* **38 E7** 15 20N 108 40 E
Binhai, *China* **35 G10** 34 2N 119 49 E
Binisatua, *Spain* **22 B11** 39 50N 4 11 E
Binjai, *Indonesia* **36 D1** 3 20N 98 30 E
Binnaway, *Australia* **63 E4** 31 28S 149 24 E
Binongko, *Indonesia* **37 F6** 5 55S 123 55 E
Binscarth, *Canada* **73 C8** 50 37N 101 17W
Bintan, *Indonesia* **36 D2** 1 0N 104 0 E
Bintangor, *Malaysia* **36 D4** 2 10N 111 40 E
Bintulu, *Malaysia* **36 D4** 3 10N 113 0 E
Bintuni, *Indonesia* **37 E8** 2 7S 133 32 E
Binzert = Bizerte, *Tunisia* **51 A7** 37 15N 9 50 E
Binzhou, *China* **35 F10** 37 20N 118 2 E
Bío Bío □, *Chile* **94 D1** 37 35S 72 0W
Bioko, *Eq. Guin.* **52 D1** 3 30N 8 40 E
Bir, *India* **40 K9** 19 0N 75 54 E
Bîr Abu Muḩammad, *Egypt* **47 F3** 29 44N 34 14 E
Bi'r ad Dabbāghāt, *Jordan* **47 E4** 30 26N 35 32 E
Bi'r al Butayyihāt, *Jordan* **47 F4** 29 47N 35 20 E
Bi'r al Mārī, *Jordan* **47 E4** 30 4N 35 33 E
Bi'r al Qattār, *Jordan* **47 F4** 29 47N 35 32 E
Bir 'Atrun, *Sudan* **51 E11** 18 15N 26 40 E
Bîr Beiḍa, *Egypt* **47 E3** 30 25N 34 29 E
Bîr el 'Abd, *Egypt* **47 D2** 31 2N 33 0 E
Bîr el Biarât, *Egypt* **47 F3** 29 30N 34 43 E
Bîr el Duweidar, *Egypt* **47 E1** 30 56N 32 32 E
Bîr el Garârât, *Egypt* **47 D2** 31 3N 33 34 E
Bîr el Heisi, *Egypt* **47 F3** 29 22N 34 36 E
Bîr el Jafir, *Egypt* **47 E1** 30 50N 32 41 E
Bîr el Mâlḥi, *Egypt* **47 E2** 30 38N 33 19 E
Bîr el Thamâda, *Egypt* **47 E2** 30 12N 33 27 E
Bîr Gebeil Ḥiṣn, *Egypt* **47 E2** 30 2N 33 18 E
Bi'r Ghadīr, *Syria* **47 A6** 34 6N 37 3 E
Bîr Ḥasana, *Egypt* **47 E2** 30 29N 33 46 E
Bîr Kaseiba, *Egypt* **47 E2** 31 0N 33 17 E
Bîr Lahfân, *Egypt* **47 E2** 31 0N 33 51 E
Bîr Madkûr, *Egypt* **47 E1** 30 44N 32 33 E
Bîr Mogreïn, *Mauritania* **50 C3** 25 10N 11 25W
Bi'r Muṭribah, *Kuwait* **44 D5** 29 54N 47 17 E
Bîr Qaṭia, *Egypt* **47 E1** 30 58N 32 45 E
Bîr Shalatein, *Egypt* **51 D13** 23 5N 35 25 E
Biratnagar, *Nepal* **43 F12** 26 27N 87 17 E
Birawa, *Dem. Rep. of the Congo* **54 C2** 2 20S 28 48 E
Birch →, *Canada* **72 B6** 58 28N 112 17W
Birch Hills, *Canada* **73 C7** 52 59N 105 25W
Birch I., *Canada* **73 C9** 52 26N 99 54W
Birch L., *N.W.T., Canada* **72 A5** 62 4N 116 33W
Birch L., *Ont., Canada* **70 B1** 51 23N 92 18W
Birch Mts., *Canada* **72 B6** 57 30N 113 10W
Birch River, *Canada* **73 C8** 52 24N 101 6W
Birchip, *Australia* **63 F3** 35 56S 142 55 E
Bird, *Canada* **73 B10** 56 30N 94 13W
Bird I. = Las Aves, Is., *W. Indies* **89 C7** 15 45N 63 55W
Birdsville, *Australia* **62 D2** 25 51S 139 20 E
Birdum Cr., *Australia* **60 C5** 15 14S 133 0 E
Birecik, *Turkey* **44 B3** 37 2N 38 0 E
Birein, *Israel* **47 E3** 30 50N 34 28 E
Bireuen, *Indonesia* **36 C1** 5 14N 96 39 E
Birigui, *Brazil* **95 A5** 21 18S 50 16W
Birjand, *Iran* **45 C8** 32 53N 59 13 E
Birkenhead, *U.K.* **10 D4** 53 23N 3 2W
Bîrlad = Bârlad, *Romania* **17 E14** 46 15N 27 38 E
Birmingham, *U.K.* **11 E6** 52 29N 1 52W
Birmingham, *U.S.A.* **77 J2** 33 31N 86 48W
Birmitrapur, *India* **41 H14** 22 24N 84 46 E
Birni Nkonni, *Niger* **50 F7** 13 55N 5 15 E
Birnin Kebbi, *Nigeria* **50 F6** 12 32N 4 12 E
Birobidzhan, *Russia* **27 E14** 48 50N 132 50 E
Birr, *Ireland* **13 C4** 53 6N 7 54W
Birrie →, *Australia* **63 D4** 29 43S 146 37 E
Birsilpur, *India* **42 E5** 28 11N 72 15 E
Birsk, *Russia* **24 C10** 55 25N 55 30 E
Birtle, *Canada* **73 C8** 50 30N 101 5W
Birur, *India* **40 N9** 13 30N 75 55 E
Biržai, *Lithuania* **9 H21** 56 11N 24 45 E
Birzebbugga, *Malta* **23 D2** 35 49N 14 32 E
Bisa, *Indonesia* **37 E7** 1 15S 127 28 E
Bisalpur, *India* **43 E8** 28 14N 79 48 E
Bisbee, *U.S.A.* **83 L9** 31 27N 109 55W
Biscay, B. of, *Atl. Oc.* **18 D1** 45 0N 2 0W
Biscayne B., *U.S.A.* **77 N5** 25 40N 80 12W
Biscoe Bay, *Antarctica* **5 D13** 77 0S 152 0W
Biscoe Is., *Antarctica* **5 C17** 66 0S 67 0W
Biscostasing, *Canada* **70 C3** 47 18N 82 9W
Bishkek, *Kyrgyzstan* **26 E8** 42 54N 74 46 E
Bishnupur, *India* **43 H12** 23 8N 87 20 E
Bisho, *S. Africa* **57 E4** 32 50S 27 23 E
Bishop, *Calif., U.S.A.* **84 H8** 37 22N 118 24W
Bishop, *Tex., U.S.A.* **81 M6** 27 35N 97 48W
Bishop Auckland, *U.K.* **10 C6** 54 39N 1 40W
Bishop's Falls, *Canada* **71 C8** 49 2N 55 30W
Bishop's Stortford, *U.K.* **11 F8** 51 52N 0 10 E
Bisina, L., *Uganda* **54 B3** 1 38N 33 56 E
Biskra, *Algeria* **50 B7** 34 50N 5 44 E
Bismarck, *U.S.A.* **80 B4** 46 48N 100 47W
Bismarck Arch., *Papua N. G.* **64 H7** 2 30S 150 0 E
Biso, *Uganda* **54 B3** 1 44N 31 26 E
Bison, *U.S.A.* **80 C3** 45 31N 102 28W
Bīsotūn, *Iran* **44 C5** 34 23N 47 26 E
Bissagos = Bijagós, Arquipélago dos, *Guinea-Biss.* **50 F2** 11 15N 16 10W
Bissau, *Guinea-Biss.* **50 F2** 11 45N 15 45W
Bistcho L., *Canada* **72 B5** 59 45N 118 50W
Bistriţa, *Romania* **17 E13** 47 9N 24 35 E
Bistriţa →, *Romania* **17 E14** 46 30N 26 57 E
Biswan, *India* **43 F9** 27 29N 81 2 E
Bitola, *Macedonia* **21 D9** 41 1N 21 20 E
Bitolj = Bitola, *Macedonia* **21 D9** 41 1N 21 20 E
Bitter Creek, *U.S.A.* **82 F9** 41 33N 108 33W
Bitterfontein, *S. Africa* **56 E2** 31 1S 18 32 E
Bitterroot →, *U.S.A.* **82 C6** 46 52N 114 7W
Bitterroot Range, *U.S.A.* **82 D6** 46 0N 114 20W
Bitterwater, *U.S.A.* **84 J6** 36 23N 121 0W
Biu, *Nigeria* **51 F8** 10 40N 12 3 E
Biwa-Ko, *Japan* **31 G8** 35 15N 136 10 E
Biwabik, *U.S.A.* **80 B8** 47 32N 92 21W
Bixby, *U.S.A.* **81 H7** 35 57N 95 53W
Biyang, *China* **34 H7** 32 38N 113 21 E
Biysk, *Russia* **26 D9** 52 40N 85 0 E
Bizana, *S. Africa* **57 E4** 30 50S 29 52 E
Bizen, *Japan* **31 G7** 34 43N 134 8 E
Bizerte, *Tunisia* **51 A7** 37 15N 9 50 E
Bjargtangar, *Iceland* **8 D1** 65 30N 24 30W
Bjelovar, *Croatia* **20 B7** 45 56N 16 49 E
Bjørnevatn, *Norway* **8 B23** 69 40N 30 0 E
Bjørnøya, *Arctic* **4 B8** 74 30N 19 0 E
Black →, *Canada* **78 B5** 44 42N 79 19W
Black →, *Ariz., U.S.A.* **83 K8** 33 44N 110 13W
Black →, *Ark., U.S.A.* **81 H9** 35 38N 91 20W
Black →, *Mich., U.S.A.* **78 D2** 42 59N 82 27W
Black →, *N.Y., U.S.A.* **79 C8** 43 59N 76 4W
Black →, *Wis., U.S.A.* **80 D9** 43 57N 91 22W
Black Bay Pen., *Canada* **70 C2** 48 38N 88 21W
Black Birch L., *Canada* **73 B7** 56 53N 107 45W
Black Diamond, *Canada* **72 C6** 50 45N 114 14W
Black Duck →, *Canada* **70 A2** 56 51N 89 2W
Black Forest = Schwarzwald, *Germany* **16 D5** 48 30N 8 20 E
Black Forest, *U.S.A.* **80 F2** 39 0N 104 43W
Black Hd., *Ireland* **13 C2** 53 9N 9 16W
Black Hills, *U.S.A.* **80 D3** 44 0N 103 45W
Black I., *Canada* **73 C9** 51 12N 96 30W
Black L., *Canada* **73 B7** 59 12N 105 15W
Black L., *Mich., U.S.A.* **76 C3** 45 28N 84 16W
Black L., *N.Y., U.S.A.* **79 B9** 44 31N 75 36W
Black Lake, *Canada* **73 B7** 59 11N 105 20W
Black Mesa, *U.S.A.* **81 G3** 36 58N 102 58W
Black Mt. = Mynydd Du, *U.K.* **11 F4** 51 52N 3 50W
Black Mts., *U.K.* **11 F4** 51 55N 3 7W
Black Range, *U.S.A.* **83 K10** 33 15N 107 50W
Black River, *Jamaica* **88 C4** 18 0N 77 50W
Black River Falls, *U.S.A.* **80 C9** 44 18N 90 51W
Black Sea, *Eurasia* **25 F6** 43 30N 35 0 E
Black Tickle, *Canada* **71 B8** 53 28N 55 45W
Black Volta →, *Africa* **50 G5** 8 41N 1 33W
Black Warrior →, *U.S.A.* **77 J2** 32 32N 87 51W
Blackall, *Australia* **62 C4** 24 25S 145 45 E
Blackball, *N.Z.* **59 K3** 42 22S 171 26 E
Blackbull, *Australia* **62 B3** 17 55S 141 45 E
Blackburn, *U.K.* **10 D5** 53 45N 2 29W
Blackburn with Darwen □, *U.K.* **10 D5** 53 45N 2 29W
Blackfoot, *U.S.A.* **82 E7** 43 11N 112 21W
Blackfoot →, *U.S.A.* **82 C7** 46 52N 113 53W
Blackfoot River Reservoir, *U.S.A.* **82 E8** 43 0N 111 43W
Blackie, *Canada* **72 C6** 50 36N 113 37W
Blackpool, *U.K.* **10 D4** 53 49N 3 3W
Blackpool □, *U.K.* **10 D4** 53 49N 3 3W
Blackriver, *U.S.A.* **78 B1** 44 46N 83 17W
Blacks Harbour, *Canada* **71 C6** 45 3N 66 49W
Blacksburg, *U.S.A.* **76 G5** 37 14N 80 25W
Blacksod B., *Ireland* **13 B1** 54 6N 10 0W
Blackstone, *U.S.A.* **76 G7** 37 4N 78 0W
Blackstone Ra., *Australia* **61 E4** 26 0S 128 30 E
Blackwater, *Australia* **62 C4** 23 35S 148 53 E
Blackwater →, *Meath, Ireland* **13 C4** 53 39N 6 41W
Blackwater →, *Waterford, Ireland* **13 D4** 52 4N 7 52W
Blackwater →, *U.K.* **13 B5** 54 31N 6 35W
Blackwell, *U.S.A.* **81 G6** 36 48N 97 17W
Blackwells Corner, *U.S.A.* **85 K7** 35 37N 119 47W
Blaenau Ffestiniog, *U.K.* **10 E4** 53 0N 3 56W
Blaenau Gwent □, *U.K.* **11 F4** 51 48N 3 12W
Blagodarnoye = Blagodarnyy, *Russia* **25 E7** 45 7N 43 37 E
Blagodarnyy, *Russia* **25 E7** 45 7N 43 37 E
Blagoevgrad, *Bulgaria* **21 C10** 42 2N 23 5 E
Blagoveshchensk, *Russia* **27 D13** 50 20N 127 30 E
Blain, *U.S.A.* **78 F7** 40 20N 77 31W
Blaine, *Minn., U.S.A.* **80 C8** 45 10N 93 13W
Blaine, *Wash., U.S.A.* **84 B4** 48 59N 122 45W
Blaine Lake, *Canada* **73 C7** 52 51N 106 52W
Blair, *U.S.A.* **80 E6** 41 33N 96 8W
Blair Athol, *Australia* **62 C4** 22 42S 147 31 E
Blair Atholl, *U.K.* **12 E5** 56 46N 3 50W
Blairgowrie, *U.K.* **12 E5** 56 35N 3 21W
Blairsden, *U.S.A.* **84 F6** 39 47N 120 37W
Blairsville, *U.S.A.* **78 F5** 40 26N 79 16W
Blake Pt., *U.S.A.* **80 A10** 48 11N 88 25W
Blakely, *Ga., U.S.A.* **77 K3** 31 23N 84 56W
Blakely, *Pa., U.S.A.* **79 E9** 41 28N 75 37W
Blanc, C., *Spain* **22 B9** 39 21N 2 51 E
Blanc, Mont, *Alps* **18 D7** 45 48N 6 50 E
Blanc-Sablon, *Canada* **71 B8** 51 24N 57 12W
Blanca, B., *Argentina* **96 D4** 39 10S 61 30W
Blanca Peak, *U.S.A.* **83 H11** 37 35N 105 29W
Blanche, C., *Australia* **63 E1** 33 1S 134 9 E
Blanche, L., *S. Austral., Australia* **63 D2** 29 15S 139 40 E
Blanche, L., *W. Austral., Australia* **60 D3** 22 25S 123 17 E
Blanco, *S. Africa* **56 E3** 33 55S 22 23 E
Blanco, *U.S.A.* **81 K5** 30 6N 98 25W
Blanco →, *Argentina* **94 C2** 30 20S 68 42W
Blanco, C., *Costa Rica* **88 E2** 9 34N 85 8W
Blanco, C., *U.S.A.* **82 E1** 42 51N 124 34W
Blanda →, *Iceland* **8 D3** 65 37N 20 9W
Blandford Forum, *U.K.* **11 G5** 50 51N 2 9W
Blanding, *U.S.A.* **83 H9** 37 37N 109 29W
Blanes, *Spain* **19 B7** 41 40N 2 48 E
Blankenberge, *Belgium* **15 C3** 51 20N 3 9 E
Blanquilla, I., *Venezuela* **89 D7** 11 51N 64 37W
Blanquillo, *Uruguay* **95 C4** 32 53S 55 37W
Blantyre, *Malawi* **55 F4** 15 45S 35 0 E
Blarney, *Ireland* **13 E3** 51 56N 8 33W
Blasdell, *U.S.A.* **78 D6** 42 48N 78 50W
Blåvands Huk, *Denmark* **9 J13** 55 33N 8 4 E
Blaydon, *U.K.* **10 C6** 54 58N 1 42W
Blayney, *Australia* **63 E4** 33 32S 149 14 E
Blaze, Pt., *Australia* **60 B5** 12 56S 130 11 E
Blekinge, *Sweden* **9 H16** 56 25N 15 20 E
Blenheim, *Canada* **78 D3** 42 20N 82 0W
Blenheim, *N.Z.* **59 J4** 41 38S 173 57 E
Bletchley, *U.K.* **11 F7** 51 59N 0 44W
Blida, *Algeria* **50 A6** 36 30N 2 49 E
Bligh Sound, *N.Z.* **59 L1** 44 47S 167 32 E
Blind River, *Canada* **70 C3** 46 10N 82 58W
Bliss, *Idaho, U.S.A.* **82 E6** 42 56N 114 57W
Bliss, *N.Y., U.S.A.* **78 D6** 42 34N 78 15W
Blissfield, *U.S.A.* **78 F3** 40 24N 81 58W
Blitar, *Indonesia* **37 H15** 8 5S 112 11 E
Block I., *U.S.A.* **79 E13** 41 11N 71 35W
Block Island Sd., *U.S.A.* **79 E13** 41 15N 71 40W
Blodgett Iceberg Tongue, *Antarctica* **5 C9** 66 8S 130 35 E
Bloemfontein, *S. Africa* **56 D4** 29 6S 26 7 E
Bloemhof, *S. Africa* **56 D4** 27 38S 25 32 E
Blois, *France* **18 C4** 47 35N 1 20 E
Blönduós, *Iceland* **8 D3** 65 40N 20 12W
Bloodvein →, *Canada* **73 C9** 51 47N 96 43W
Bloody Foreland, *Ireland* **13 A3** 55 10N 8 17W
Bloomer, *U.S.A.* **80 C9** 45 6N 91 29W
Bloomfield, *Canada* **78 C7** 43 59N 77 14W
Bloomfield, *Iowa, U.S.A.* **80 E8** 40 45N 92 25W
Bloomfield, *N. Mex., U.S.A.* **83 H10** 36 43N 107 59W
Bloomfield, *Nebr., U.S.A.* **80 D6** 42 36N 97 39W
Bloomington, *Ill., U.S.A.* **80 E10** 40 28N 89 0W
Bloomington, *Ind., U.S.A.* **76 F2** 39 10N 86 32W
Bloomington, *Minn., U.S.A.* **80 C8** 44 50N 93 17W
Bloomsburg, *U.S.A.* **79 F8** 41 0N 76 27W
Blora, *Indonesia* **37 G14** 6 57S 111 25 E
Blossburg, *U.S.A.* **78 E7** 41 41N 77 4W
Blouberg, *S. Africa* **57 C4** 23 8S 28 59 E
Blountstown, *U.S.A.* **77 K3** 30 27N 85 3W
Blue Earth, *U.S.A.* **80 D8** 43 38N 94 6W
Blue Mesa Reservoir, *U.S.A.* **83 G10** 38 28N 107 20W
Blue Mountain Lake, *U.S.A.* **79 C10** 43 52N 74 30W
Blue Mts., *Maine, U.S.A.* **79 B14** 44 50N 70 35W
Blue Mts., *Oreg., U.S.A.* **82 D4** 45 15N 119 0W
Blue Mts., *Pa., U.S.A.* **79 F8** 40 30N 76 30W
Blue Mud B., *Australia* **62 A2** 13 30S 136 0 E
Blue Nile = Nîl el Azraq →, *Sudan* **51 E12** 15 38N 32 31 E
Blue Rapids, *U.S.A.* **80 F6** 39 41N 96 39W
Blue Ridge Mts., *U.S.A.* **77 G5** 36 30N 80 15W
Blue River, *Canada* **72 C5** 52 6N 119 18W
Bluefield, *U.S.A.* **76 G5** 37 15N 81 17W
Bluefields, *Nic.* **88 D3** 12 20N 83 50W
Bluff, *Australia* **62 C4** 23 35S 149 4 E
Bluff, *N.Z.* **59 M2** 46 37S 168 20 E
Bluff, *U.S.A.* **83 H9** 37 17N 109 33W
Bluff Knoll, *Australia* **61 F2** 34 24S 118 15 E
Bluff Pt., *Australia* **61 E1** 27 50S 114 5 E
Bluffton, *U.S.A.* **76 E3** 40 44N 85 11W
Blumenau, *Brazil* **95 B6** 27 0S 49 0W
Blunt, *U.S.A.* **80 C5** 44 31N 99 59W
Bly, *U.S.A.* **82 E3** 42 24N 121 3W
Blyth, *Canada* **78 C3** 43 44N 81 26W
Blyth, *U.K.* **10 B6** 55 8N 1 31W
Blythe, *U.S.A.* **85 M12** 33 37N 114 36W
Blytheville, *U.S.A.* **81 H10** 35 56N 89 55W
Bo, *S. Leone* **50 G3** 7 55N 11 50W
Bo Duc, *Vietnam* **39 G6** 11 58N 106 50 E
Bo Hai, *China* **35 E10** 39 0N 119 0 E
Bo Xian = Bozhou, *China* **34 H8** 33 55N 115 41 E
Boa Vista, *Brazil* **92 C6** 2 48N 60 30W
Boaco, *Nic.* **88 D2** 12 29N 85 35W
Bo'ai, *China* **34 G7** 35 10N 113 3 E
Boalsburg, *U.S.A.* **78 F7** 40 46N 77 47W
Boardman, *U.S.A.* **78 E4** 41 2N 80 40W
Bobadah, *Australia* **63 E4** 32 19S 146 41 E
Bobbili, *India* **41 K13** 18 35N 83 30 E
Bobcaygeon, *Canada* **78 B6** 44 33N 78 33W
Bobo-Dioulasso, *Burkina Faso* **50 F5** 11 8N 4 13W
Bóbr →, *Poland* **16 B8** 52 4N 15 4 E
Bobraomby, Tanjon' i, *Madag.* **57 A8** 12 40S 49 10 E
Bobruysk = Babruysk, *Belarus* **17 B15** 53 10N 29 15 E
Boby, Pic, *Madag.* **53 J9** 22 12S 46 55 E
Bôca do Acre, *Brazil* **92 E5** 8 50S 67 27W
Boca Raton, *U.S.A.* **77 M5** 26 21N 80 5W
Bocas del Toro, *Panama* **88 E3** 9 15N 82 20W
Bochnia, *Poland* **17 D11** 49 58N 20 27 E
Bochum, *Germany* **16 C4** 51 28N 7 13 E
Bocoyna, *Mexico* **86 B3** 27 52N 107 35W
Bodaybo, *Russia* **27 D12** 57 50N 114 0 E
Boddam, *U.K.* **12 B7** 59 56N 1 17W
Boddington, *Australia* **61 F2** 32 50S 116 30 E
Bodega Bay, *U.S.A.* **84 G3** 38 20N 123 3W
Boden, *Sweden* **8 D19** 65 50N 21 42 E
Bodensee, *Europe* **18 C8** 47 35N 9 25 E
Bodhan, *India* **40 K10** 18 40N 77 44 E
Bodmin, *U.K.* **11 G3** 50 28N 4 43W
Bodmin Moor, *U.K.* **11 G3** 50 33N 4 36W
Bodø, *Norway* **8 C16** 67 17N 14 24 E
Bodrog →, *Hungary* **17 D11** 48 11N 21 22 E
Bodrum, *Turkey* **21 F12** 37 3N 27 30 E
Boende, *Dem. Rep. of the Congo* **52 E4** 0 24S 21 12 E
Boerne, *U.S.A.* **81 L5** 29 47N 98 44W
Bogalusa, *U.S.A.* **81 K10** 30 47N 89 52W
Bogan →, *Australia* **63 D4** 29 59S 146 17 E
Bogan Gate, *Australia* **63 E4** 33 7S 147 49 E
Bogantungan, *Australia* **62 C4** 23 41S 147 17 E
Bogata, *U.S.A.* **81 J7** 33 28N 95 13W
Boggabilla, *Australia* **63 D5** 28 36S 150 24 E
Boggabri, *Australia* **63 E5** 30 45S 150 5 E
Boggeragh Mts., *Ireland* **13 D3** 52 2N 8 55W
Boglan = Solhan, *Turkey* **44 B4** 38 57N 41 3 E
Bognor Regis, *U.K.* **11 G7** 50 47N 0 40W
Bogo, *Phil.* **37 B6** 11 3N 124 0 E
Bogong, Mt., *Australia* **63 F4** 36 47S 147 17 E
Bogor, *Indonesia* **37 G12** 6 36S 106 48 E
Bogotá, *Colombia* **92 C4** 4 34N 74 0W
Bogotol, *Russia* **26 D9** 56 15N 89 50 E
Bogra, *Bangla.* **41 G16** 24 51N 89 22 E
Boguchany, *Russia* **27 D10** 58 40N 97 30 E
Bohemian Forest = Böhmerwald, *Germany* **16 D7** 49 8N 13 14 E
Böhmerwald, *Germany* **16 D7** 49 8N 13 14 E
Bohol, *Phil.* **37 C6** 9 50N 124 10 E
Bohol Sea, *Phil.* **37 C6** 9 0N 124 0 E
Bohuslän, *Sweden* **9 G14** 58 25N 12 0 E
Boi, Pta. de, *Brazil* **95 A6** 23 55S 45 15W
Boiaçu, *Brazil* **92 D6** 0 27S 61 46W
Boileau, C., *Australia* **60 C3** 17 40S 122 7 E
Boise, *U.S.A.* **82 E5** 43 37N 116 13W
Boise City, *U.S.A.* **81 G3** 36 44N 102 31W
Boissevain, *Canada* **73 D8** 49 15N 100 5W
Bojador C., *W. Sahara* **50 C3** 26 0N 14 30W
Bojana →, *Albania* **21 D8** 41 52N 19 22 E
Bojnūrd, *Iran* **45 B8** 37 30N 57 20 E
Bojonegoro, *Indonesia* **37 G14** 7 11S 111 54 E
Bokaro, *India* **43 H11** 23 46N 85 55 E
Bokhara →, *Australia* **63 D4** 29 55S 146 42 E
Boknafjorden, *Norway* **9 G11** 59 14N 5 40 E
Bokoro, *Chad* **51 F9** 12 25N 17 14 E
Bokote, *Dem. Rep. of the Congo* **52 E4** 0 12S 21 8 E
Bokpyin, *Burma* **39 G2** 11 18N 98 42 E
Bolan →, *Pakistan* **42 E2** 28 38N 67 42 E
Bolan Pass, *Pakistan* **40 E5** 29 50N 67 20 E
Bolaños →, *Mexico* **86 C4** 21 14N 104 8W
Bolbec, *France* **18 B4** 49 30N 0 30 E
Boldājī, *Iran* **45 D6** 31 56N 51 3 E
Bole, *China* **32 B3** 45 11N 81 37 E
Bolekhiv, *Ukraine* **17 D12** 49 0N 23 57 E
Bolesławiec, *Poland* **16 C8** 51 17N 15 37 E
Bolgrad = Bolhrad, *Ukraine* **17 F15** 45 40N 28 32 E
Bolhrad, *Ukraine* **17 F15** 45 40N 28 32 E
Bolívar, *Argentina* **94 D3** 36 15S 60 53W
Bolivar, *Mo., U.S.A.* **81 G8** 37 37N 93 25W
Bolivar, *N.Y., U.S.A.* **78 D6** 42 4N 78 10W
Bolivar, *Tenn., U.S.A.* **81 H10** 35 12N 89 0W
Bolivia ■, *S. Amer.* **92 G6** 17 6S 64 0W
Bolivian Plateau, *S. Amer.* **90 E4** 20 0S 67 30W
Bollnäs, *Sweden* **9 F17** 61 21N 16 24 E
Bollon, *Australia* **63 D4** 28 2S 147 29 E
Bolmen, *Sweden* **9 H15** 56 55N 13 40 E
Bolobo, *Dem. Rep. of the Congo* **52 E3** 2 6S 16 20 E
Bologna, *Italy* **20 B4** 44 29N 11 20 E
Bologoye, *Russia* **24 C5** 57 55N 34 5 E
Bolonchenticul, *Mexico* **87 D7** 20 0N 89 49W
Boloven, Cao Nguyen, *Laos* **38 E6** 15 10N 106 30 E
Bolpur, *India* **43 H12** 23 40N 87 45 E
Bolsena, L. di, *Italy* **20 C4** 42 36N 11 56 E
Bolshevik, Ostrov, *Russia* **27 B11** 78 30N 102 0 E
Bolshoi Kavkas = Caucasus Mountains, *Eurasia* **25 F7** 42 50N 44 0 E
Bolshoy Anyuy →, *Russia* **27 C17** 68 30N 160 49 E
Bolshoy Begichev, Ostrov, *Russia* **27 B12** 74 20N 112 30 E
Bolshoy Lyakhovskiy, Ostrov, *Russia* **27 B15** 73 35N 142 0 E
Bolshoy Tyuters, Ostrov, *Russia* **9 G22** 59 51N 27 13 E
Bolsward, *Neths.* **15 A5** 53 3N 5 32 E
Bolt Head, *U.K.* **11 G4** 50 12N 3 48W
Bolton, *Canada* **78 C5** 43 54N 79 45W

Bolton, *U.K.* **10 D5** 53 35N 2 26W
Bolton Landing, *U.S.A.* **79 C11** 43 32N 73 35W
Bolu, *Turkey* **25 F5** 40 45N 31 35 E
Bolungavík, *Iceland* **8 C2** 66 9N 23 15W
Bolvadin, *Turkey* **25 G5** 38 45N 31 4 E
Bolzano, *Italy* **20 A4** 46 31N 11 22 E
Bom Jesus da Lapa, *Brazil* **93 F10** 13 15S 43 25W
Boma,
Dem. Rep. of the Congo **52 F2** 5 50S 13 4 E
Bombala, *Australia* **63 F4** 36 56S 149 15 E
Bombay = Mumbai, *India* **40 K8** 18 55N 72 50 E
Bomboma,
Dem. Rep. of the Congo **52 D3** 2 25N 18 55 E
Bombombwa,
Dem. Rep. of the Congo **54 B2** 1 40N 25 40 E
Bomili,
Dem. Rep. of the Congo **54 B2** 1 45N 27 5 E
Bømlo, *Norway* **9 G11** 59 37N 5 13 E
Bomokandi →,
Dem. Rep. of the Congo **54 B2** 3 39N 26 8 E
Bomu →, *C.A.R.* **52 D4** 4 40N 22 30 E
Bon, C., *Tunisia* **48 C5** 37 1N 11 2 E
Bon Sar Pa, *Vietnam* **38 F6** 12 24N 107 35 E
Bonaigarh, *India* **43 J11** 21 50N 84 57 E
Bonaire, *Neth. Ant.* **89 D6** 12 10N 68 15W
Bonang, *Australia* **63 F4** 37 11S 148 41 E
Bonanza, *Nic.* **88 D3** 13 54N 84 35W
Bonaparte Arch., *Australia* **60 B3** 14 0S 124 30 E
Bonaventure, *Canada* **71 C6** 48 5N 65 32W
Bonavista, *Canada* **71 C9** 48 40N 53 5W
Bonavista, C., *Canada* **71 C9** 48 42N 53 5W
Bonavista B., *Canada* **71 C9** 48 45N 53 25W
Bondo,
Dem. Rep. of the Congo **54 B1** 3 55N 23 53 E
Bondoukou, *Ivory C.* **50 G5** 8 2N 2 47W
Bondowoso, *Indonesia* **37 G15** 7 55S 113 49 E
Bone, Teluk, *Indonesia* **37 E6** 4 10S 120 50 E
Bonerate, *Indonesia* **37 F6** 7 25S 121 5 E
Bonerate, Kepulauan,
Indonesia **37 F6** 6 30S 121 10 E
Bo'ness, *U.K.* **12 E5** 56 1N 3 37W
Bonete, Cerro, *Argentina* **94 B2** 27 55S 68 40W
Bong Son = Hoai Nhon,
Vietnam **38 E7** 14 28N 109 1 E
Bongor, *Chad* **51 F9** 10 35N 15 20 E
Bonham, *U.S.A.* **81 J6** 33 35N 96 11W
Bonifacio, *France* **18 F8** 41 24N 9 10 E
Bonifacio, Bouches de,
Medit. S. **20 D3** 41 12N 9 15 E
Bonin Is. = Ogasawara
Gunto, *Pac. Oc.* **28 G18** 27 0N 142 0 E
Bonn, *Germany* **16 C4** 50 46N 7 6 E
Bonne Terre, *U.S.A.* **81 G9** 37 55N 90 33W
Bonners Ferry, *U.S.A.* **82 B5** 48 42N 116 19W
Bonney, L., *Australia* **63 F3** 37 50S 140 20 E
Bonnie Rock, *Australia* **61 F2** 30 29S 118 22 E
Bonny, Bight of, *Africa* **52 D1** 3 30N 9 20 E
Bonnyrigg, *U.K.* **12 F5** 55 53N 3 6W
Bonnyville, *Canada* **73 C6** 54 20N 110 45W
Bonoi, *Indonesia* **37 E9** 1 45S 137 41 E
Bonsall, *U.S.A.* **85 M9** 33 16N 117 14W
Bontang, *Indonesia* **36 D5** 0 10N 117 30 E
Bonthe, *S. Leone* **50 G3** 7 30N 12 33W
Bontoc, *Phil.* **37 A6** 17 7N 120 58 E
Bonython Ra., *Australia* **60 D4** 23 40S 128 45 E
Bookabie, *Australia* **61 F5** 31 50S 132 41 E
Booker, *U.S.A.* **81 G4** 36 27N 100 32W
Booligal, *Australia* **63 E3** 33 58S 144 53 E
Boonah, *Australia* **63 D5** 27 58S 152 41 E
Boone, *Iowa, U.S.A.* **80 D8** 42 4N 93 53W
Boone, *N.C., U.S.A.* **77 G5** 36 13N 81 41W
Booneville, *Ark., U.S.A.* **81 H8** 35 8N 93 55W
Booneville, *Miss., U.S.A.* **77 H1** 34 39N 88 34W
Boonville, *Calif., U.S.A.* **84 F3** 39 1N 123 22W
Boonville, *Ind., U.S.A.* **76 F2** 38 3N 87 16W
Boonville, *Mo., U.S.A.* **80 F8** 38 58N 92 44W
Boonville, *N.Y., U.S.A.* **79 C9** 43 29N 75 20W
Boorindal, *Australia* **63 E4** 30 22S 146 11 E
Boorowa, *Australia* **63 E4** 34 28S 148 44 E
Boothia, Gulf of, *Canada* **69 A11** 71 0N 90 0W
Boothia Pen., *Canada* **68 A10** 71 0N 94 0W
Bootle, *U.K.* **10 D4** 53 28N 3 1W
Booué, *Gabon* **52 E2** 0 5S 11 55 E
Boquete, *Panama* **88 E3** 8 46N 82 27W
Boquilla, Presa de la,
Mexico **86 B3** 27 40N 105 30W
Boquillas del Carmen,
Mexico **86 B4** 29 17N 102 53W
Bor, *Serbia, Yug.* **21 B10** 44 5N 22 7 E
Bôr, *Sudan* **51 G12** 6 10N 31 40 E
Bor Mashash, *Israel* **47 D3** 31 7N 34 50 E
Borah Peak, *U.S.A.* **82 D7** 44 8N 113 47W
Borås, *Sweden* **9 H15** 57 43N 12 56 E
Borāzjān, *Iran* **45 D6** 29 22N 51 10 E
Borba, *Brazil* **92 D7** 4 12S 59 34W
Borborema, Planalto da,
Brazil **90 D7** 7 0S 37 0W
Bord Khūn-e Now, *Iran* **45 D6** 28 3N 51 28 E
Borda, C., *Australia* **63 F2** 35 45S 136 34 E
Bordeaux, *France* **18 D3** 44 50N 0 36W
Borden, *Australia* **61 F2** 34 3S 118 12 E
Borden, *Canada* **71 C7** 46 18N 63 47W
Borden I., *Canada* **4 B2** 78 30N 111 30W
Borden Pen., *Canada* **69 A11** 73 0N 83 0W
Borders = Scottish
Borders □, *U.K.* **12 F6** 55 35N 2 50W
Bordertown, *Australia* **63 F3** 36 19S 140 45 E
Borðeyri, *Iceland* **8 D3** 65 12N 21 6W
Bordj Fly Ste. Marie, *Algeria* **50 C5** 27 19N 2 32W
Bordj-in-Eker, *Algeria* **50 D7** 24 9N 5 3 E
Bordj Omar Driss, *Algeria* **50 C7** 28 10N 6 40 E
Borehamwood, *U.K.* **11 F7** 51 40N 0 15W
Borgå = Porvoo, *Finland* **9 F21** 60 24N 25 40 E
Borgarfjörður, *Iceland* **8 D7** 65 31N 13 49W
Borgarnes, *Iceland* **8 D3** 64 32N 21 55W
Børgefjellet, *Norway* **8 D15** 65 20N 13 45 E
Borger, *Neths.* **15 B6** 52 54N 6 44 E
Borger, *U.S.A.* **81 H4** 35 39N 101 24W
Borgholm, *Sweden* **9 H17** 56 52N 16 39 E
Borhoyn Tal, *Mongolia* **34 C6** 43 50N 111 58 E
Borikhane, *Laos* **38 C4** 18 33N 103 43 E
Borisoglebsk, *Russia* **25 D7** 51 27N 42 5 E
Borisov = Barysaw, *Belarus* **17 A15** 54 17N 28 28 E
Borja, *Peru* **92 D3** 4 20S 77 40W
Borkou, *Chad* **51 E9** 18 15N 18 50 E
Borkum, *Germany* **16 B4** 53 34N 6 40 E
Borlänge, *Sweden* **9 F16** 60 29N 15 26 E
Borley, C., *Antarctica* **5 C5** 66 15S 52 30 E
Borneo, *E. Indies* **36 D5** 1 0N 115 0 E
Bornholm, *Denmark* **9 J16** 55 10N 15 0 E
Borogontsy, *Russia* **27 C14** 62 42N 131 8 E
Boron, *U.S.A.* **85 L9** 35 0N 117 39W
Borongan, *Phil.* **37 B7** 11 37N 125 26 E
Borovichi, *Russia* **24 C5** 58 25N 33 55 E
Borrego Springs, *U.S.A.* **85 M10** 33 15N 116 23W
Borroloola, *Australia* **62 B2** 16 4S 136 17 E
Borşa, *Romania* **17 E13** 47 41N 24 50 E
Borsad, *India* **42 H5** 22 25N 72 54 E
Borth, *U.K.* **11 E3** 52 29N 4 2W
Borūjerd, *Iran* **45 C6** 33 55N 48 50 E
Boryslav, *Ukraine* **17 D12** 49 18N 23 28 E
Borzya, *Russia* **27 D12** 50 24N 116 31 E
Bosa, *Italy* **20 D3** 40 18N 8 30 E
Bosanska Gradiška, *Bos.-H.* **20 B7** 45 10N 17 15 E
Bosaso, *Somali Rep.* **46 E4** 11 12N 49 18 E
Boscastle, *U.K.* **11 G3** 50 41N 4 42W
Boshan, *China* **35 F9** 36 28N 117 49 E
Boshof, *S. Africa* **56 D4** 28 31S 25 13 E
Boshrūyeh, *Iran* **45 C8** 33 50N 57 30 E
Bosna →, *Bos.-H.* **21 B8** 45 4N 18 29 E
Bosna i Hercegovina =
Bosnia-Herzegovina ■,
Europe **20 B7** 44 0N 18 0 E
Bosnia-Herzegovina ■,
Europe **20 B7** 44 0N 18 0 E
Bosnik, *Indonesia* **37 E9** 1 5S 136 10 E
Bosobolo,
Dem. Rep. of the Congo **52 D3** 4 15N 19 50 E
Bosporus = İstanbul Boğazı,
Turkey **21 D13** 41 10N 29 10 E
Bosque Farms, *U.S.A.* **83 J10** 34 53N 106 40W
Bossangoa, *C.A.R.* **52 C3** 6 35N 17 30 E
Bossier City, *U.S.A.* **81 J8** 32 31N 93 44W
Bosso, *Niger* **51 F8** 13 43N 13 19 E
Bostan, *Pakistan* **42 D2** 30 26N 67 2 E
Bostānābād, *Iran* **44 B5** 37 50N 46 50 E
Bosten Hu, *China* **32 B3** 41 55N 87 40 E
Boston, *U.K.* **10 E7** 52 59N 0 2W
Boston, *U.S.A.* **79 D13** 42 22N 71 4W
Boston Bar, *Canada* **72 D4** 49 52N 121 30W
Boston Mts., *U.S.A.* **81 H8** 35 42N 93 15W
Boswell, *Canada* **72 D5** 49 28N 116 45W
Boswell, *U.S.A.* **78 F5** 40 10N 79 2W
Botad, *India* **42 H4** 22 15N 71 40 E
Botene, *Laos* **38 D3** 17 35N 101 12 E
Bothaville, *S. Africa* **56 D4** 27 23S 26 34 E
Bothnia, G. of, *Europe* **8 E19** 63 0N 20 15 E
Bothwell, *Australia* **62 G4** 42 20S 147 1 E
Bothwell, *Canada* **78 D3** 42 38N 81 52W
Botletle →, *Botswana* **56 C3** 20 10S 23 15 E
Botoşani, *Romania* **17 E14** 47 42N 26 41 E
Botou, *Burkina Faso* **50 F6** 12 40N 2 3 E
Botswana ■, *Africa* **56 C3** 22 0S 24 0 E
Bottineau, *U.S.A.* **80 A4** 48 50N 100 27W
Bottrop, *Germany* **15 C6** 51 31N 6 58 E
Botucatu, *Brazil* **95 A6** 22 55S 48 30W
Botwood, *Canada* **71 C8** 49 6N 55 23W
Bouaflé, *Ivory C.* **50 G4** 7 1N 5 47W
Bouaké, *Ivory C.* **50 G4** 7 40N 5 2W
Bouar, *C.A.R.* **52 C3** 6 0N 15 40 E
Bouârfa, *Morocco* **50 B5** 32 32N 1 58W
Boucaut B., *Australia* **62 A1** 12 0S 134 25 E
Bougainville, C., *Australia* **60 B4** 13 57S 126 4 E
Bougainville I., *Papua N. G.* **64 H7** 6 0S 155 0 E
Bougainville Reef, *Australia* **62 B4** 15 30S 147 5 E
Bougie = Bejaia, *Algeria* **50 A7** 36 42N 5 2 E
Bougouni, *Mali* **50 F4** 11 30N 7 20W
Bouillon, *Belgium* **15 E5** 49 44N 5 3 E
Boulder, *Colo., U.S.A.* **80 E2** 40 1N 105 17W
Boulder, *Mont., U.S.A.* **82 C7** 46 14N 112 7W
Boulder City, *U.S.A.* **85 K12** 35 59N 114 50W
Boulder Creek, *U.S.A.* **84 H4** 37 7N 122 7W
Boulder Dam = Hoover
Dam, *U.S.A.* **85 K12** 36 1N 114 44W
Boulia, *Australia* **62 C2** 22 52S 139 51 E
Boulogne-sur-Mer, *France* **18 A4** 50 42N 1 36 E
Boultoum, *Niger* **51 F8** 14 45N 10 25 E
Boun Neua, *Laos* **38 B3** 21 38N 101 54 E
Boun Tai, *Laos* **38 B3** 21 23N 101 58 E
Bouna, *Ivory C.* **50 G5** 9 10N 3 0W
Boundary Peak, *U.S.A.* **84 H8** 37 51N 118 21W
Boundiali, *Ivory C.* **50 G4** 9 30N 6 20W
Bountiful, *U.S.A.* **82 F8** 40 53N 111 53W
Bounty Is., *Pac. Oc.* **64 M9** 48 0S 178 30 E
Bourbonnais, *France* **18 C5** 46 28N 3 0 E
Bourdel L., *Canada* **70 A5** 56 43N 74 10W
Bourem, *Mali* **50 E5** 17 0N 0 24W
Bourg-en-Bresse, *France* **18 C6** 46 13N 5 12 E
Bourg-St-Maurice, *France* **18 D7** 45 35N 6 46 E
Bourges, *France* **18 C5** 47 9N 2 25 E
Bourget, *Canada* **79 A9** 45 26N 75 9W
Bourgogne, *France* **18 C6** 47 0N 4 50 E
Bourke, *Australia* **63 E4** 30 8S 145 55 E
Bourne, *U.K.* **10 E7** 52 47N 0 22W
Bournemouth, *U.K.* **11 G6** 50 43N 1 52W
Bournemouth □, *U.K.* **11 G6** 50 43N 1 52W
Bouse, *U.S.A.* **85 M13** 33 56N 114 0W
Bouvet I. = Bouvetøya,
Antarctica **3 G10** 54 26S 3 24 E
Bouvetøya, *Antarctica* **3 G10** 54 26S 3 24 E
Bovill, *U.S.A.* **82 C5** 46 51N 116 24W
Bovril, *Argentina* **94 C4** 31 21S 59 26W
Bow →, *Canada* **72 C6** 49 57N 111 41W
Bow Island, *Canada* **72 D6** 49 50N 111 23W
Bowbells, *U.S.A.* **80 A3** 48 48N 102 15W
Bowdle, *U.S.A.* **80 C5** 45 27N 99 39W
Bowelling, *Australia* **61 F2** 33 25S 116 30 E
Bowen, *Argentina* **94 D2** 35 0S 67 31W
Bowen, *Australia* **62 C4** 20 0S 148 16 E
Bowen Mts., *Australia* **63 F4** 37 0S 147 50 E
Bowie, *Ariz., U.S.A.* **83 K9** 32 19N 109 29W
Bowie, *Tex., U.S.A.* **81 J6** 33 34N 97 51W
Bowkān, *Iran* **44 B5** 36 31N 46 12 E
Bowland, Forest of, *U.K.* **10 D5** 54 0N 2 30W
Bowling Green, *Ky., U.S.A.* **76 G2** 36 59N 86 27W
Bowling Green, *Ohio, U.S.A.* **76 E4** 41 23N 83 39W
Bowling Green, C., *Australia* **62 B4** 19 19S 147 25 E
Bowman, *U.S.A.* **80 B3** 46 11N 103 24W
Bowman I., *Antarctica* **5 C8** 65 0S 104 0 E
Bowmanville, *Canada* **78 C6** 43 55N 78 41W
Bowmore, *U.K.* **12 F2** 55 45N 6 17W
Bowral, *Australia* **63 E5** 34 26S 150 27 E
Bowraville, *Australia* **63 E5** 30 37S 152 52 E
Bowron →, *Canada* **72 C4** 54 3N 121 50W
Bowron Lake Prov. Park,
Canada **72 C4** 53 10N 121 5W
Bowser L., *Canada* **72 B3** 56 30N 129 30W
Bowsman, *Canada* **73 C8** 52 14N 101 12W
Bowwood, *Zambia* **55 F2** 17 5S 26 20 E
Box Cr. →, *Australia* **63 E3** 34 10S 143 50 E
Boxmeer, *Neths.* **15 C5** 51 38N 5 56 E
Boxtel, *Neths.* **15 C5** 51 36N 5 20 E
Boyce, *U.S.A.* **81 K8** 31 23N 92 40W
Boyd L., *Canada* **70 B4** 52 46N 76 42W
Boyle, *Canada* **72 C6** 54 35N 112 49W
Boyle, *Ireland* **13 C3** 53 59N 8 18W
Boyne →, *Ireland* **13 C5** 53 43N 6 15W
Boyne City, *U.S.A.* **76 C3** 45 13N 85 1W
Boynton Beach, *U.S.A.* **77 M5** 26 32N 80 4W
Boyolali, *Indonesia* **37 G14** 7 32S 110 35 E
Boyoma, Chutes,
Dem. Rep. of the Congo **54 B2** 0 35N 25 23 E
Boysen Reservoir, *U.S.A.* **82 E9** 43 25N 108 11W
Boyuibe, *Bolivia* **92 G6** 20 25S 63 17W
Boyup Brook, *Australia* **61 F2** 33 50S 116 23 E
Boz Dağları, *Turkey* **21 E13** 38 20N 28 0 E
Bozburun, *Turkey* **21 F13** 36 43N 28 4 E
Bozcaada, *Turkey* **21 E12** 39 49N 26 3 E
Bozdoğan, *Turkey* **21 F13** 37 40N 28 17 E
Bozeman, *U.S.A.* **82 D8** 45 41N 111 2W
Bozen = Bolzano, *Italy* **20 A4** 46 31N 11 22 E
Bozhou, *China* **34 H8** 33 55N 115 41 E
Bozoum, *C.A.R.* **52 C3** 6 25N 16 35 E
Bra, *Italy* **18 D7** 44 42N 7 51 E
Brabant □, *Belgium* **15 D4** 50 46N 4 30 E
Brabant L., *Canada* **73 B8** 55 58N 103 43W
Brač, *Croatia* **20 C7** 43 20N 16 40 E
Bracadale, L., *U.K.* **12 D2** 57 20N 6 30W
Bracciano, L. di, *Italy* **20 C5** 42 7N 12 14 E
Bracebridge, *Canada* **78 A5** 45 2N 79 19W
Brach, *Libya* **51 C8** 27 31N 14 20 E
Bräcke, *Sweden* **9 E16** 62 45N 15 26 E
Brackettville, *U.S.A.* **81 L4** 29 19N 100 25W
Bracknell, *U.K.* **11 F7** 51 25N 0 43W
Bracknell Forest □, *U.K.* **11 F7** 51 25N 0 44W
Brad, *Romania* **17 E12** 46 10N 22 50 E
Bradenton, *U.S.A.* **77 M4** 27 30N 82 34W
Bradford, *Canada* **78 B5** 44 7N 79 34W
Bradford, *U.K.* **10 D6** 53 47N 1 45W
Bradford, *Pa., U.S.A.* **78 E6** 41 58N 78 38W
Bradford, *Vt., U.S.A.* **79 C12** 43 59N 72 9W
Bradley, *Ark., U.S.A.* **81 J8** 33 6N 93 39W
Bradley, *Calif., U.S.A.* **84 K6** 35 52N 120 48W
Bradley Institute, *Zimbabwe* **55 F3** 17 7S 31 25 E
Brady, *U.S.A.* **81 K5** 31 9N 99 20W
Braemar, *U.K.* **12 D5** 57 0N 3 23W
Braeside, *Canada* **79 A8** 45 28N 76 24W
Braga, *Portugal* **19 B1** 41 35N 8 25W
Bragado, *Argentina* **94 D3** 35 2S 60 27W
Bragança, *Brazil* **93 D9** 1 0S 47 2W
Bragança, *Portugal* **19 B2** 41 48N 6 50W
Bragança Paulista, *Brazil* **95 A6** 22 55S 46 32W
Brahmanbaria, *Bangla.* **41 H17** 23 58N 91 15 E
Brahmani →, *India* **41 J15** 20 39N 86 46 E
Brahmapur, *India* **41 K14** 19 15N 84 54 E
Brahmaputra →, *India* **43 H13** 23 58N 89 50 E
Braich-y-pwll, *U.K.* **10 E3** 52 47N 4 46W
Braidwood, *Australia* **63 F4** 35 27S 149 49 E
Brăila, *Romania* **17 F14** 45 19N 27 59 E
Brainerd, *U.S.A.* **80 B7** 46 22N 94 12W
Braintree, *U.K.* **11 F8** 51 53N 0 34 E
Braintree, *U.S.A.* **79 D14** 42 13N 71 0W
Brak →, *S. Africa* **56 D3** 29 35S 22 55 E
Brakwater, *Namibia* **56 C2** 22 28S 17 3 E
Brampton, *Canada* **78 C5** 43 45N 79 45W
Brampton, *U.K.* **10 C5** 54 57N 2 44W
Branco →, *Brazil* **92 D6** 1 20S 61 50W
Brandenburg =
Neubrandenburg,
Germany **16 B7** 53 33N 13 15 E
Brandenburg, *Germany* **16 B7** 52 25N 12 33 E
Brandenburg □, *Germany* **16 B6** 52 50N 13 0 E
Brandfort, *S. Africa* **56 D4** 28 40S 26 30 E
Brandon, *Canada* **73 D9** 49 50N 99 57W
Brandon, *U.S.A.* **79 C11** 43 48N 73 4W
Brandon B., *Ireland* **13 D1** 52 17N 10 8W
Brandon Mt., *Ireland* **13 D1** 52 15N 10 15W
Brandsen, *Argentina* **94 D4** 35 10S 58 15W
Brandvlei, *S. Africa* **56 E3** 30 25S 20 30 E
Branford, *U.S.A.* **79 E12** 41 17N 72 49W
Braniewo, *Poland* **17 A10** 54 25N 19 50 E
Bransfield Str., *Antarctica* **5 C18** 63 0S 59 0W
Branson, *U.S.A.* **81 G8** 36 39N 93 13W
Brantford, *Canada* **78 C4** 43 10N 80 15W
Bras d'Or L., *Canada* **71 C7** 45 50N 60 50W
Brasher Falls, *U.S.A.* **79 B10** 44 49N 74 47W
Brasil, Planalto, *Brazil* **90 E6** 18 0S 46 30W
Brasiléia, *Brazil* **92 F5** 11 0S 68 45W
Brasília, *Brazil* **93 G9** 15 47S 47 55W
Brasília Legal, *Brazil* **93 D7** 3 49S 55 36W
Braslaw, *Belarus* **9 J22** 55 38N 27 0 E
Braşov, *Romania* **17 F13** 45 38N 25 35 E
Brasschaat, *Belgium* **15 C4** 51 19N 4 27 E
Brassey, Banjaran, *Malaysia* **36 D5** 5 0N 117 15 E
Brassey Ra., *Australia* **61 E3** 25 8S 122 15 E
Brasstown Bald, *U.S.A.* **77 H4** 34 53N 83 49W
Brastad, *Sweden* **9 G14** 58 23N 11 30 E
Bratislava, *Slovak Rep.* **17 D9** 48 10N 17 7 E
Bratsk, *Russia* **27 D11** 56 10N 101 30 E
Brattleboro, *U.S.A.* **79 D12** 42 51N 72 34W
Braunau, *Austria* **16 D7** 48 15N 13 3 E
Braunschweig, *Germany* **16 B6** 52 15N 10 31 E
Braunton, *U.K.* **11 F3** 51 7N 4 10W
Bravo del Norte, Rio =
Grande, Rio →, *U.S.A.* **81 N6** 25 58N 97 9W
Brawley, *U.S.A.* **85 N11** 32 59N 115 31W
Bray, *Ireland* **13 C5** 53 13N 6 7W
Bray, Mt., *Australia* **62 A1** 14 0S 134 30 E
Bray, Pays de, *France* **18 B4** 49 46N 1 26 E
Brazeau →, *Canada* **72 C5** 52 55N 115 14W
Brazil, *U.S.A.* **76 F2** 39 32N 87 8W
Brazil ■, *S. Amer.* **93 F9** 12 0S 50 0W
Brazilian Highlands = Brasil,
Planalto, *Brazil* **90 E6** 18 0S 46 30W
Brazo Sur →, *S. Amer.* **94 B4** 25 21S 57 42W
Brazos →, *U.S.A.* **81 L7** 28 53N 95 23W
Brazzaville, *Congo* **52 E3** 4 9S 15 12 E
Brčko, *Bos.-H.* **21 B8** 44 54N 18 46 E
Breaden, L., *Australia* **61 E4** 25 51S 125 28 E
Breaksea Sd., *N.Z.* **59 L1** 45 35S 166 35 E
Bream B., *N.Z.* **59 F5** 35 56S 174 28 E
Bream Hd., *N.Z.* **59 F5** 35 51S 174 36 E
Breas, *Chile* **94 B1** 25 29S 70 24W
Brebes, *Indonesia* **37 G13** 6 52S 109 3 E
Brechin, *Canada* **78 B5** 44 32N 79 10W
Brechin, *U.K.* **12 E6** 56 44N 2 39W
Brecht, *Belgium* **15 C4** 51 21N 4 38 E
Breckenridge, *Colo., U.S.A.* **82 G10** 39 29N 106 3W
Breckenridge, *Minn., U.S.A.* **80 B6** 46 16N 96 35W
Breckenridge, *Tex., U.S.A.* **81 J5** 32 45N 98 54W
Breckland, *U.K.* **11 E8** 52 30N 0 40 E
Brecon, *U.K.* **11 F4** 51 57N 3 23W
Brecon Beacons, *U.K.* **11 F4** 51 53N 3 26W
Breda, *Neths.* **15 C4** 51 35N 4 45 E
Bredasdorp, *S. Africa* **56 E3** 34 33S 20 2 E
Bree, *Belgium* **15 C5** 51 8N 5 35 E
Bregenz, *Austria* **16 E5** 47 30N 9 45 E
Breiðafjörður, *Iceland* **8 D2** 65 15N 23 15W
Brejo, *Brazil* **93 D10** 3 41S 42 47W
Bremen, *Germany* **16 B5** 53 4N 8 47 E
Bremer Bay, *Australia* **61 F2** 34 21S 119 20 E
Bremer I., *Australia* **62 A2** 12 5S 136 45 E
Bremerhaven, *Germany* **16 B5** 53 33N 8 36 E
Bremerton, *U.S.A.* **84 C4** 47 34N 122 38W
Brenham, *U.S.A.* **81 K6** 30 10N 96 24W
Brennerpass, *Austria* **16 E6** 47 2N 11 30 E
Brent, *U.S.A.* **77 J2** 32 56N 87 10W
Brentwood, *U.K.* **11 F8** 51 37N 0 19 E
Brentwood, *Calif., U.S.A.* **84 H5** 37 56N 121 42W
Brentwood, *N.Y., U.S.A.* **79 F11** 40 47N 73 15W
Bréscia, *Italy* **18 D9** 45 33N 10 15 E
Breskens, *Neths.* **15 C3** 51 23N 3 33 E
Breslau = Wrocław, *Poland* **17 C9** 51 5N 17 5 E
Bressanone, *Italy* **20 A4** 46 43N 11 39 E
Bressay, *U.K.* **12 A7** 60 9N 1 6W
Brest, *Belarus* **17 B12** 52 10N 23 40 E
Brest, *France* **18 B1** 48 24N 4 31W
Brest-Litovsk = Brest,
Belarus **17 B12** 52 10N 23 40 E
Bretagne, *France* **18 B2** 48 10N 3 0W
Breton, *Canada* **72 C6** 53 7N 114 28W
Breton Sd., *U.S.A.* **81 L10** 29 35N 89 15W
Brett, C., *N.Z.* **59 F5** 35 10S 174 20 E
Brevard, *U.S.A.* **77 H4** 35 14N 82 44W
Breves, *Brazil* **93 D8** 1 40S 50 29W
Brewarrina, *Australia* **63 E4** 30 0S 146 51 E
Brewer, *U.S.A.* **77 C11** 44 48N 68 46W
Brewer, Mt., *U.S.A.* **84 J8** 36 44N 118 28W
Brewster, *N.Y., U.S.A.* **79 E11** 41 23N 73 37W
Brewster, *Ohio, U.S.A.* **78 F3** 40 43N 81 36W
Brewster, *Wash., U.S.A.* **82 B4** 48 6N 119 47W
Brewster, Kap, *Greenland* **4 B6** 70 7N 22 0W
Brewton, *U.S.A.* **77 K2** 31 7N 87 4W
Breyten, *S. Africa* **57 D5** 26 16S 30 0 E
Brezhnev = Naberezhnyye
Chelny, *Russia* **24 C9** 55 42N 52 19 E
Briançon, *France* **18 D7** 44 54N 6 39 E
Bribie I., *Australia* **63 D5** 27 0S 153 10 E
Bribri, *Costa Rica* **88 E3** 9 38N 82 50W
Bridgehampton, *U.S.A.* **79 F12** 40 56N 72 19W
Bridgend, *U.K.* **11 F4** 51 30N 3 34W
Bridgend □, *U.K.* **11 F4** 51 36N 3 36W
Bridgeport, *Calif., U.S.A.* **84 G7** 38 15N 119 14W
Bridgeport, *Conn., U.S.A.* **79 E11** 41 11N 73 12W
Bridgeport, *Nebr., U.S.A.* **80 E3** 41 40N 103 6W
Bridgeport, *Tex., U.S.A.* **81 J6** 33 13N 97 45W
Bridger, *U.S.A.* **82 D9** 45 18N 108 55W
Bridgeton, *U.S.A.* **76 F8** 39 26N 75 14W
Bridgetown, *Australia* **61 F2** 33 58S 116 7 E
Bridgetown, *Barbados* **89 D8** 13 5N 59 30W
Bridgetown, *Canada* **71 D6** 44 55N 65 18W
Bridgewater, *Canada* **71 D7** 44 25N 64 31W
Bridgewater, *Mass., U.S.A.* **79 E14** 41 59N 70 58W
Bridgewater, *N.Y., U.S.A.* **79 D9** 42 53N 75 15W
Bridgewater, C., *Australia* **63 F3** 38 23S 141 23 E
Bridgewater-Gagebrook,
Australia **62 G4** 42 44S 147 14 E
Bridgnorth, *U.K.* **11 E5** 52 32N 2 25W
Bridgton, *U.S.A.* **79 B14** 44 3N 70 42W
Bridgwater, *U.K.* **11 F5** 51 8N 2 59W
Bridgwater B., *U.K.* **11 F4** 51 15N 3 15W
Bridlington, *U.K.* **10 C7** 54 5N 0 12W
Bridlington B., *U.K.* **10 C7** 54 4N 0 10W
Bridport, *Australia* **62 G4** 40 59S 147 23 E
Bridport, *U.K.* **11 G5** 50 44N 2 45W
Brig, *Switz.* **18 C7** 46 18N 7 59 E
Brigg, *U.K.* **10 D7** 53 34N 0 28W
Brigham City, *U.S.A.* **82 F7** 41 31N 112 1W
Bright, *Australia* **63 F4** 36 42S 146 56 E
Brighton, *Australia* **63 F2** 35 5S 138 30 E
Brighton, *Canada* **78 B7** 44 2N 77 44W
Brighton, *U.K.* **11 G7** 50 49N 0 7W
Brighton, *Colo., U.S.A.* **80 F2** 39 59N 104 49W
Brighton, *N.Y., U.S.A.* **78 C7** 43 8N 77 34W
Brilliant, *U.S.A.* **78 F4** 40 15N 80 39W
Bríndisi, *Italy* **21 D7** 40 39N 17 55 E
Brinkley, *U.S.A.* **81 H9** 34 53N 91 12W
Brinnon, *U.S.A.* **84 C4** 47 41N 122 54W
Brion, I., *Canada* **71 C7** 47 46N 61 26W
Brisbane, *Australia* **63 D5** 27 25S 153 2 E
Brisbane →, *Australia* **63 D5** 27 24S 153 9 E
Bristol, *U.K.* **11 F5** 51 26N 2 35W
Bristol, *Conn., U.S.A.* **79 E12** 41 40N 72 57W
Bristol, *Pa., U.S.A.* **79 F10** 40 6N 74 51W
Bristol, *R.I., U.S.A.* **79 E13** 41 40N 71 16W
Bristol, *Tenn., U.S.A.* **77 G4** 36 36N 82 11W
Bristol, City of □, *U.K.* **11 F5** 51 27N 2 36W
Bristol B., *U.S.A.* **68 C4** 58 0N 160 0W
Bristol Channel, *U.K.* **11 F3** 51 18N 4 30W
Bristol I., *Antarctica* **5 B1** 58 45S 28 0W
Bristol L., *U.S.A.* **83 J5** 34 23N 116 50W
Bristow, *U.S.A.* **81 H6** 35 50N 96 23W
Britain = Great Britain,
Europe **6 E5** 54 0N 2 15W
British Columbia □, *Canada* **72 C3** 55 0N 125 15W
British Indian Ocean Terr. =
Chagos Arch., *Ind. Oc.* **29 K11** 6 0S 72 0 E
British Isles, *Europe* **6 E5** 54 0N 4 0W
Brits, *S. Africa* **57 D4** 25 37S 27 48 E
Britstown, *S. Africa* **56 E3** 30 37S 23 30 E
Britt, *Canada* **70 C3** 45 46N 80 34W
Brittany = Bretagne, *France* **18 B2** 48 10N 3 0W
Britton, *U.S.A.* **80 C6** 45 48N 97 45W
Brive-la-Gaillarde, *France* **18 D4** 45 10N 1 32 E
Brixen = Bressanone, *Italy* **20 A4** 46 43N 11 39 E
Brixham, *U.K.* **11 G4** 50 23N 3 31W
Brno, *Czech Rep.* **17 D9** 49 10N 16 35 E
Broad →, *U.S.A.* **77 J5** 34 1N 81 4W

Broad Arrow, *Australia* **61 F3** 30 23S 121 15 E
Broad B., *U.K.* **12 C2** 58 14N 6 18W
Broad Haven, *Ireland* **13 B2** 54 20N 9 55W
Broad Law, *U.K.* **12 F5** 55 30N 3 21W
Broad Sd., *Australia* **62 C4** 22 0S 149 45 E
Broadalbin, *U.S.A.* **79 C10** 43 4N 74 12W
Broadback →, *Canada* **70 B4** 51 21N 78 52W
Broadford, *Australia* **63 F4** 37 14S 145 4 E
Broadhurst Ra., *Australia* **60 D3** 22 30S 122 30 E
Broads, The, *U.K.* **10 E9** 52 45N 1 30 E
Broadus, *U.S.A.* **80 C2** 45 27N 105 25W
Brochet, *Canada* **73 B8** 57 53N 101 40W
Brochet, L., *Canada* **73 B8** 58 36N 101 35W
Brocken, *Germany* **16 C6** 51 47N 10 37 E
Brockport, *U.S.A.* **78 C7** 43 13N 77 56W
Brockton, *U.S.A.* **79 D13** 42 5N 71 1W
Brockville, *Canada* **79 B9** 44 35N 75 41W
Brockway, *Mont., U.S.A.* **80 B2** 47 18N 105 45W
Brockway, *Pa., U.S.A.* **78 E6** 41 15N 78 47W
Brocton, *U.S.A.* **78 D5** 42 23N 79 26W
Brodeur Pen., *Canada* **69 A11** 72 30N 88 10W
Brodhead, Mt., *U.S.A.* **78 E7** 41 39N 77 47W
Brodick, *U.K.* **12 F3** 55 35N 5 9W
Brodnica, *Poland* **17 B10** 53 15N 19 25 E
Brody, *Ukraine* **17 C13** 50 5N 25 10 E
Brogan, *U.S.A.* **82 D5** 44 15N 117 31W
Broken Arrow, *U.S.A.* **81 G7** 36 3N 95 48W
Broken Bow, *Nebr., U.S.A.* **80 E5** 41 24N 99 38W
Broken Bow, *Okla., U.S.A.* **81 H7** 34 2N 94 44W
Broken Bow Lake, *U.S.A.* **81 H7** 34 9N 94 40W
Broken Hill = Kabwe, *Zambia* **55 E2** 14 30S 28 29 E
Broken Hill, *Australia* **63 E3** 31 58S 141 29 E
Bromley, *U.K.* **11 F8** 51 24N 0 2 E
Bromsgrove, *U.K.* **11 E5** 52 21N 2 2W
Brønderslev, *Denmark* **9 H13** 57 16N 9 57 E
Bronkhorstspruit, *S. Africa* **57 D4** 25 46S 28 45 E
Brønnøysund, *Norway* **8 D15** 65 28N 12 14 E
Brook Park, *U.S.A.* **78 E4** 41 24N 81 51W
Brookhaven, *U.S.A.* **81 K9** 31 35N 90 26W
Brookings, *Oreg., U.S.A.* **82 E1** 42 3N 124 17W
Brookings, *S. Dak., U.S.A.* **80 C6** 44 19N 96 48W
Brooklin, *Canada* **78 C6** 43 55N 78 55W
Brooklyn Park, *U.S.A.* **80 C8** 45 6N 93 23W
Brooks, *Canada* **72 C6** 50 35N 111 55W
Brooks Range, *U.S.A.* **68 B5** 68 0N 152 0W
Brooksville, *U.S.A.* **77 L4** 28 33N 82 23W
Brookton, *Australia* **61 F2** 32 22S 117 0 E
Brookville, *U.S.A.* **78 E5** 41 10N 79 5W
Broom, L., *U.K.* **12 D3** 57 55N 5 15W
Broome, *Australia* **60 C3** 18 0S 122 15 E
Brora, *U.K.* **12 C5** 58 0N 3 52W
Brora →, *U.K.* **12 C5** 58 0N 3 51W
Brosna →, *Ireland* **13 C4** 53 14N 7 58W
Brothers, *U.S.A.* **82 E3** 43 49N 120 36W
Brough, *U.K.* **10 C5** 54 32N 2 18W
Brough Hd., *U.K.* **12 B5** 59 8N 3 20W
Broughton Island = Qikiqtarjuaq, *Canada* **69 B13** 67 33N 63 0W
Brown, L., *Australia* **61 F2** 31 5S 118 15 E
Brown, Pt., *Australia* **63 E1** 32 32S 133 50 E
Brown City, *U.S.A.* **78 C2** 43 13N 82 59W
Brown Willy, *U.K.* **11 G3** 50 35N 4 37W
Brownfield, *U.S.A.* **81 J3** 33 11N 102 17W
Browning, *U.S.A.* **82 B7** 48 34N 113 1W
Brownsville, *Oreg., U.S.A.* **82 D2** 44 24N 122 59W
Brownsville, *Pa., U.S.A.* **78 F5** 40 1N 79 53W
Brownsville, *Tenn., U.S.A.* **81 H10** 35 36N 89 16W
Brownsville, *Tex., U.S.A.* **81 N6** 25 54N 97 30W
Brownville, *U.S.A.* **79 C9** 44 0N 75 59W
Brownwood, *U.S.A.* **81 K5** 31 43N 98 59W
Browse I., *Australia* **60 B3** 14 7S 123 33 E
Bruas, *Malaysia* **39 K3** 4 30N 100 47 E
Bruay-la-Buissière, *France* **18 A5** 50 29N 2 33 E
Bruce, Mt., *Australia* **60 D2** 22 37S 118 8 E
Bruce Pen., *Canada* **78 B3** 45 0N 81 30W
Bruce Rock, *Australia* **61 F2** 31 52S 118 8 E
Bruck an der Leitha, *Austria* **17 D9** 48 1N 16 47 E
Bruck an der Mur, *Austria* **16 E8** 47 24N 15 16 E
Brue →, *U.K.* **11 F5** 51 13N 2 59W
Bruges = Brugge, *Belgium* **15 C3** 51 13N 3 13 E
Brugge, *Belgium* **15 C3** 51 13N 3 13 E
Bruin, *U.S.A.* **78 E5** 41 3N 79 43W
Brûlé, *Canada* **72 C5** 53 15N 117 58W
Brumado, *Brazil* **93 F10** 14 14S 41 40W
Brumunddal, *Norway* **9 F14** 60 53N 10 56 E
Bruneau, *U.S.A.* **82 E6** 42 53N 115 48W
Bruneau →, *U.S.A.* **82 E6** 42 56N 115 57W
Brunei = Bandar Seri Begawan, *Brunei* **36 D5** 4 52N 115 0 E
Brunei ■, *Asia* **36 D5** 4 50N 115 0 E
Brunner, L., *N.Z.* **59 K3** 42 37S 171 27 E
Brunssum, *Neths.* **15 D5** 50 57N 5 59 E
Brunswick = Braunschweig, *Germany* **16 B6** 52 15N 10 31 E
Brunswick, *Ga., U.S.A.* **77 K5** 31 10N 81 30W
Brunswick, *Maine, U.S.A.* **77 D11** 43 55N 69 58W
Brunswick, *Md., U.S.A.* **76 F7** 39 19N 77 38W
Brunswick, *Mo., U.S.A.* **80 F8** 39 26N 93 8W
Brunswick, *Ohio, U.S.A.* **78 E3** 41 14N 81 51W
Brunswick, Pen. de, *Chile* **96 G2** 53 30S 71 30W
Brunswick B., *Australia* **60 C3** 15 15S 124 50 E
Brunswick Junction, *Australia* **61 F2** 33 15S 115 50 E
Bruny I., *Australia* **62 G4** 43 20S 147 15 E
Brus Laguna, *Honduras* **88 C3** 15 47N 84 35W
Brush, *U.S.A.* **80 E3** 40 15N 103 37W
Brushton, *U.S.A.* **79 B10** 44 50N 74 31W
Brusque, *Brazil* **95 B6** 27 5S 49 0W
Brussel, *Belgium* **15 D4** 50 51N 4 21 E
Brussels = Brussel, *Belgium* **15 D4** 50 51N 4 21 E
Brussels, *Canada* **78 C3** 43 44N 81 15W
Bruthen, *Australia* **63 F4** 37 42S 147 50 E
Bruxelles = Brussel, *Belgium* **15 D4** 50 51N 4 21 E
Bryan, *Ohio, U.S.A.* **76 E3** 41 28N 84 33W
Bryan, *Tex., U.S.A.* **81 K6** 30 40N 96 22W
Bryan, Mt., *Australia* **63 E2** 33 30S 139 0 E
Bryansk, *Russia* **24 D5** 53 13N 34 25 E
Bryce Canyon National Park, *U.S.A.* **83 H7** 37 30N 112 10W
Bryne, *Norway* **9 G11** 58 44N 5 38 E
Bryson City, *U.S.A.* **77 H4** 35 26N 83 27W
Bsharri, *Lebanon* **47 A5** 34 15N 36 0 E
Bū Baqarah, *U.A.E.* **45 E8** 25 35N 56 25 E
Bu Craa, *W. Sahara* **50 C3** 26 45N 12 50W
Bū Ḩasā, *U.A.E.* **45 F7** 23 30N 53 20 E
Bua Yai, *Thailand* **38 E4** 15 33N 102 26 E
Buapinang, *Indonesia* **37 E6** 4 40S 121 30 E
Bubanza, *Burundi* **54 C2** 3 6S 29 23 E
Būbiyān, *Kuwait* **45 D6** 29 45N 48 15 E
Bucaramanga, *Colombia* **92 B4** 7 0N 73 0W
Bucasia, *Australia* **62 C4** 21 2S 149 10 E
Buccaneer Arch., *Australia* **60 C3** 16 7S 123 20 E
Buchach, *Ukraine* **17 D13** 49 5N 25 25 E
Buchan, *U.K.* **12 D6** 57 32N 2 21W
Buchan Ness, *U.K.* **12 D7** 57 29N 1 46W
Buchanan, *Canada* **73 C8** 51 40N 102 45W
Buchanan, *Liberia* **50 G3** 5 57N 10 2W
Buchanan, L., *Queens., Australia* **62 C4** 21 35S 145 52 E
Buchanan, L., *W. Austral., Australia* **61 E3** 25 33S 123 2 E
Buchanan, L., *U.S.A.* **81 K5** 30 45N 98 25W
Buchanan Cr. →, *Australia* **62 B2** 19 13S 136 33 E
Buchans, *Canada* **71 C8** 48 50N 56 52W
Bucharest = Bucureşti, *Romania* **17 F14** 44 27N 26 10 E
Buchon, Pt., *U.S.A.* **84 K6** 35 15N 120 54W
Buck Hill Falls, *U.S.A.* **79 E9** 41 11N 75 16W
Buckeye, *U.S.A.* **83 K7** 33 22N 112 35W
Buckeye Lake, *U.S.A.* **78 G2** 39 55N 82 29W
Buckhannon, *U.S.A.* **76 F5** 39 0N 80 8W
Buckhaven, *U.K.* **12 E5** 56 11N 3 3W
Buckhorn L., *Canada* **78 B6** 44 29N 78 23W
Buckie, *U.K.* **12 D6** 57 41N 2 58W
Buckingham, *Canada* **70 C4** 45 37N 75 24W
Buckingham, *U.K.* **11 F7** 51 59N 0 57W
Buckingham B., *Australia* **62 A2** 12 10S 135 40 E
Buckinghamshire □, *U.K.* **11 F7** 51 53N 0 55W
Buckle Hd., *Australia* **60 B4** 14 26S 127 52 E
Buckleboo, *Australia* **63 E2** 32 54S 136 12 E
Buckley, *U.K.* **10 D4** 53 10N 3 5W
Buckley →, *Australia* **62 C2** 20 10S 138 49 E
Bucklin, *U.S.A.* **81 G5** 37 33N 99 38W
Bucks L., *U.S.A.* **84 F5** 39 54N 121 12W
Buctouche, *Canada* **71 C7** 46 30N 64 45W
Bucureşti, *Romania* **17 F14** 44 27N 26 10 E
Bucyrus, *U.S.A.* **76 E4** 40 48N 82 59W
Budalin, *Burma* **41 H19** 22 20N 95 10 E
Budapest, *Hungary* **17 E10** 47 29N 19 5 E
Budaun, *India* **43 E8** 28 5N 79 10 E
Budd Coast, *Antarctica* **5 C8** 68 0S 112 0 E
Bude, *U.K.* **11 G3** 50 49N 4 34W
Budennovsk, *Russia* **25 F7** 44 50N 44 10 E
Budge Budge = Baj Baj, *India* **43 H13** 22 30N 88 5 E
Budgewoi, *Australia* **63 E5** 33 13S 151 34 E
Budjala, *Dem. Rep. of the Congo* **52 D3** 2 50N 19 40 E
Buellton, *U.S.A.* **85 L6** 34 37N 120 12W
Buena Esperanza, *Argentina* **94 C2** 34 45S 65 15W
Buena Park, *U.S.A.* **85 M9** 33 52N 117 59W
Buena Vista, *Colo., U.S.A.* **83 G10** 38 51N 106 8W
Buena Vista, *Va., U.S.A.* **76 G6** 37 44N 79 21W
Buena Vista Lake Bed, *U.S.A.* **85 K7** 35 12N 119 18W
Buenaventura, *Colombia* **92 C3** 3 53N 77 4W
Buenaventura, *Mexico* **86 B3** 29 50N 107 30W
Buenos Aires, *Argentina* **94 C4** 34 30S 58 20W
Buenos Aires, *Costa Rica* **88 E3** 9 10N 83 20W
Buenos Aires □, *Argentina* **94 D4** 36 30S 60 0W
Buenos Aires, L., *Chile* **96 F2** 46 35S 72 30W
Buffalo, *Mo., U.S.A.* **81 G8** 37 39N 93 6W
Buffalo, *N.Y., U.S.A.* **78 D6** 42 53N 78 53W
Buffalo, *Okla., U.S.A.* **81 G5** 36 50N 99 38W
Buffalo, *S. Dak., U.S.A.* **80 C3** 45 35N 103 33W
Buffalo, *Wyo., U.S.A.* **82 D10** 44 21N 106 42W
Buffalo →, *Canada* **72 A5** 60 5N 115 5W
Buffalo Head Hills, *Canada* **72 B5** 57 25N 115 55W
Buffalo L., *Canada* **72 A5** 60 12N 115 25W
Buffalo L., *Alta., Canada* **72 C6** 52 27N 112 54W
Buffalo Narrows, *Canada* **73 B7** 55 51N 108 29W
Buffels →, *S. Africa* **56 D2** 29 36S 17 3 E
Buford, *U.S.A.* **77 H4** 34 10N 84 0W
Bug = Buh →, *Ukraine* **25 E5** 46 59N 31 58 E
Bug →, *Poland* **17 B11** 52 31N 21 5 E
Buga, *Colombia* **92 C3** 4 0N 76 15W
Buganda, *Uganda* **54 C3** 0 0 31 30 E
Buganga, *Uganda* **54 C3** 0 3S 32 0 E
Bugel, Tanjung, *Indonesia* **37 G14** 6 26S 111 3 E
Bugibba, *Malta* **23 D1** 35 57N 14 25 E
Bugsuk, *Phil.* **36 C5** 8 15N 117 15 E
Bugulma, *Russia* **24 D9** 54 33N 52 48 E
Bugun Shara, *Mongolia* **32 B5** 49 0N 104 0 E
Buguruslan, *Russia* **24 D9** 53 39N 52 26 E
Buh →, *Ukraine* **25 E5** 46 59N 31 58 E
Buhl, *U.S.A.* **82 E6** 42 36N 114 46W
Builth Wells, *U.K.* **11 E4** 52 9N 3 25W
Buir Nur, *Mongolia* **33 B6** 47 50N 117 42 E
Bujumbura, *Burundi* **54 C2** 3 16S 29 18 E
Bukachacha, *Russia* **27 D12** 52 55N 116 50 E
Bukama, *Dem. Rep. of the Congo* **55 D2** 9 10S 25 50 E
Bukavu, *Dem. Rep. of the Congo* **54 C2** 2 20S 28 52 E
Bukene, *Tanzania* **54 C3** 4 15S 32 48 E
Bukhara = Bukhoro, *Uzbekistan* **26 F7** 39 48N 64 25 E
Bukhoro, *Uzbekistan* **26 F7** 39 48N 64 25 E
Bukima, *Tanzania* **54 C3** 1 50S 33 25 E
Bukit Mertajam, *Malaysia* **39 K3** 5 22N 100 28 E
Bukittinggi, *Indonesia* **36 E2** 0 20S 100 20 E
Bukoba, *Tanzania* **54 C3** 1 20S 31 49 E
Bukuya, *Uganda* **54 B3** 0 40N 31 52 E
Būl, Kuh-e, *Iran* **45 D7** 30 48N 52 45 E
Bula, *Indonesia* **37 E8** 3 6S 130 30 E
Bulahdelah, *Australia* **63 E5** 32 23S 152 13 E
Bulan, *Phil.* **37 B6** 12 40N 123 52 E
Bulandshahr, *India* **42 E7** 28 28N 77 51 E
Bulawayo, *Zimbabwe* **55 G2** 20 7S 28 32 E
Buldan, *Turkey* **21 E13** 38 2N 28 50 E
Bulgar, *Russia* **24 D8** 54 57N 49 4 E
Bulgaria ■, *Europe* **21 C11** 42 35N 25 30 E
Buli, Teluk, *Indonesia* **37 D7** 1 5N 128 25 E
Buliluyan, C., *Phil.* **36 C5** 8 20N 117 15 E
Bulkley →, *Canada* **72 B3** 55 15N 127 40W
Bull Shoals L., *U.S.A.* **81 G8** 36 22N 92 35W
Bullhead City, *U.S.A.* **85 K12** 35 8N 114 32W
Büllingen, *Belgium* **15 D6** 50 25N 6 16 E
Bullock Creek, *Australia* **62 B3** 17 43S 144 31 E
Bulloo →, *Australia* **63 D3** 28 43S 142 30 E
Bulloo L., *Australia* **63 D3** 28 43S 142 25 E
Bulls, *N.Z.* **59 J5** 40 10S 175 24 E
Bulnes, *Chile* **94 D1** 36 42S 72 19W
Bulsar = Valsad, *India* **40 J8** 20 40N 72 58 E
Bultfontein, *S. Africa* **56 D4** 28 18S 26 10 E
Bulukumba, *Indonesia* **37 F6** 5 33S 120 11 E
Bulun, *Russia* **27 B13** 70 37N 127 30 E
Bumba, *Dem. Rep. of the Congo* **52 D4** 2 13N 22 30 E
Bumbiri I., *Tanzania* **54 C3** 1 40S 31 55 E
Bumhpa Bum, *Burma* **41 F20** 26 51N 97 14 E
Bumi →, *Zimbabwe* **55 F2** 17 0S 28 20 E
Buna, *Kenya* **54 B4** 2 58N 39 30 E
Bunazi, *Tanzania* **54 C3** 1 3S 31 23 E
Bunbury, *Australia* **61 F2** 33 20S 115 35 E
Bunclody, *Ireland* **13 D5** 52 39N 6 40W
Buncrana, *Ireland* **13 A4** 55 8N 7 27W
Bundaberg, *Australia* **63 C5** 24 54S 152 22 E
Bundey →, *Australia* **62 C2** 21 46S 135 37 E
Bundi, *India* **42 G6** 25 30N 75 35 E
Bundoran, *Ireland* **13 B3** 54 28N 8 16W
Bung Kan, *Thailand* **38 C4** 18 23N 103 37 E
Bungatakada, *Japan* **31 H5** 33 35N 131 25 E
Bungay, *U.K.* **11 E9** 52 27N 1 28 E
Bungil Cr. →, *Australia* **63 D4** 27 5S 149 5 E
Bungo-Suidō, *Japan* **31 H6** 33 0N 132 15 E
Bungoma, *Kenya* **54 B3** 0 34N 34 34 E
Bungu, *Tanzania* **54 D4** 7 35S 39 0 E
Bunia, *Dem. Rep. of the Congo* **54 B3** 1 35N 30 20 E
Bunji, *Pakistan* **43 B6** 35 45N 74 40 E
Bunkie, *U.S.A.* **81 K8** 30 57N 92 11W
Buntok, *Indonesia* **36 E4** 1 40S 114 58 E
Bunyu, *Indonesia* **36 D5** 3 35N 117 50 E
Buol, *Indonesia* **37 D6** 1 15N 121 32 E
Buon Brieng, *Vietnam* **38 F7** 13 9N 108 12 E
Buon Ma Thuot, *Vietnam* **38 F7** 12 40N 108 3 E
Buong Long, *Cambodia* **38 F6** 13 44N 106 59 E
Buorkhaya, Mys, *Russia* **27 B14** 71 50N 132 40 E
Buqayq, *Si. Arabia* **45 E6** 26 0N 49 45 E
Bur Acaba, *Somali Rep.* **46 G3** 3 12N 44 20 E
Bûr Safâga, *Egypt* **44 E2** 26 43N 33 57 E
Bûr Sa'îd, *Egypt* **51 B12** 31 16N 32 18 E
Bûr Sûdân, *Sudan* **51 E13** 19 32N 37 9 E
Bura, *Kenya* **54 C4** 1 4S 39 58 E
Burakin, *Australia* **61 F2** 30 31S 117 10 E
Burao, *Somali Rep.* **46 F4** 9 32N 45 32 E
Burāq, *Syria* **47 B5** 33 11N 36 29 E
Buraydah, *Si. Arabia* **44 E5** 26 20N 44 8 E
Burbank, *U.S.A.* **85 L8** 34 11N 118 19W
Burda, *India* **42 G6** 25 50N 77 35 E
Burdekin →, *Australia* **62 B4** 19 38S 147 25 E
Burdur, *Turkey* **25 G5** 37 45N 30 17 E
Burdwan = Barddhaman, *India* **43 H12** 23 14N 87 39 E
Bure, *Ethiopia* **46 E2** 10 40N 37 4 E
Bure →, *U.K.* **10 E9** 52 38N 1 43 E
Bureya →, *Russia* **27 E13** 49 27N 129 30 E
Burford, *Canada* **78 C4** 43 7N 80 27W
Burgas, *Bulgaria* **21 C12** 42 33N 27 29 E
Burgeo, *Canada* **71 C8** 47 37N 57 38W
Burgersdorp, *S. Africa* **56 E4** 31 0S 26 20 E
Burges, Mt., *Australia* **61 F3** 30 50S 121 5 E
Burgos, *Spain* **19 A4** 42 21N 3 41W
Burgsvik, *Sweden* **9 H18** 57 3N 18 19 E
Burgundy = Bourgogne, *France* **18 C6** 47 0N 4 50 E
Burhaniye, *Turkey* **21 E12** 39 30N 26 58 E
Burhanpur, *India* **40 J10** 21 18N 76 14 E
Burhi Gandak →, *India* **43 G12** 25 20N 86 37 E
Burhner →, *India* **43 H9** 22 43N 80 31 E
Burias, *Phil.* **37 B6** 12 55N 123 5 E
Burica, Pta., *Costa Rica* **88 E3** 8 3N 82 51W
Burien, *U.S.A.* **84 C4** 47 28N 122 21W
Burigi, L., *Tanzania* **54 C3** 2 2S 31 22 E
Burin, *Canada* **71 C8** 47 1N 55 14W
Buriram, *Thailand* **38 E4** 15 0N 103 0 E
Burj Sāfitā, *Syria* **44 C3** 34 48N 36 7 E
Burkburnett, *U.S.A.* **81 H5** 34 6N 98 34W
Burke →, *Australia* **62 C2** 23 12S 139 33 E
Burke Chan., *Canada* **72 C3** 52 10N 127 30W
Burketown, *Australia* **62 B2** 17 45S 139 33 E
Burkina Faso ■, *Africa* **50 F5** 12 0N 1 0W
Burk's Falls, *Canada* **70 C4** 45 37N 79 24W
Burleigh Falls, *Canada* **78 B6** 44 33N 78 12W
Burley, *U.S.A.* **82 E7** 42 32N 113 48W
Burlingame, *U.S.A.* **84 H4** 37 35N 122 21W
Burlington, *Canada* **78 C5** 43 18N 79 45W
Burlington, *Colo., U.S.A.* **80 F3** 39 18N 102 16W
Burlington, *Iowa, U.S.A.* **80 E9** 40 49N 91 14W
Burlington, *Kans., U.S.A.* **80 F7** 38 12N 95 45W
Burlington, *N.C., U.S.A.* **77 G6** 36 6N 79 26W
Burlington, *N.J., U.S.A.* **79 F10** 40 4N 74 51W
Burlington, *Vt., U.S.A.* **79 B11** 44 29N 73 12W
Burlington, *Wash., U.S.A.* **84 B4** 48 28N 122 20W
Burlington, *Wis., U.S.A.* **76 D1** 42 41N 88 17W
Burlyu-Tyube, *Kazakstan* **26 E8** 46 30N 79 10 E
Burma ■, *Asia* **41 J20** 21 0N 96 30 E
Burnaby I., *Canada* **72 C2** 52 25N 131 19W
Burnet, *U.S.A.* **81 K5** 30 45N 98 14W
Burney, *U.S.A.* **82 F3** 40 53N 121 40W
Burnham, *U.S.A.* **78 F7** 40 38N 77 34W
Burnham-on-Sea, *U.K.* **11 F5** 51 14N 3 0W
Burnie, *Australia* **62 G4** 41 4S 145 56 E
Burnley, *U.K.* **10 D5** 53 47N 2 14W
Burns, *U.S.A.* **82 E4** 43 35N 119 3W
Burns Lake, *Canada* **72 C3** 54 20N 125 45W
Burnside →, *Canada* **68 B9** 66 51N 108 4W
Burnside, L., *Australia* **61 E3** 25 22S 123 0 E
Burnsville, *U.S.A.* **80 C8** 44 47N 93 17W
Burnt L., *Canada* **71 B7** 53 35N 64 4W
Burnt River, *Canada* **78 B6** 44 41N 78 42W
Burntwood →, *Canada* **73 B9** 56 8N 96 34W
Burntwood L., *Canada* **73 B8** 55 22N 100 26W
Burqān, *Kuwait* **44 D5** 29 0N 47 57 E
Burra, *Australia* **63 E2** 33 40S 138 55 E
Burray, *U.K.* **12 C6** 58 51N 2 54W
Burren Junction, *Australia* **63 E4** 30 7S 148 59 E
Burrinjuck Res., *Australia* **63 F4** 35 0S 148 36 E
Burro, Serranías del, *Mexico* **86 B4** 29 0N 102 0W
Burrow Hd., *U.K.* **12 G4** 54 41N 4 24W
Burruyacú, *Argentina* **94 B3** 26 30S 64 40W
Burry Port, *U.K.* **11 F3** 51 41N 4 15W
Bursa, *Turkey* **21 D13** 40 15N 29 5 E
Burstall, *Canada* **73 C7** 50 39N 109 54W
Burton, *Ohio, U.S.A.* **78 E3** 41 28N 81 8W
Burton, *S.C., U.S.A.* **77 J5** 32 25N 80 45W
Burton, L., *Canada* **70 B4** 54 45N 78 20W
Burton upon Trent, *U.K.* **10 E6** 52 48N 1 38W
Buru, *Indonesia* **37 E7** 3 30S 126 30 E
Burûn, Râs, *Egypt* **47 D2** 31 14N 33 7 E
Burundi ■, *Africa* **54 C3** 3 15S 30 0 E
Bururi, *Burundi* **54 C2** 3 57S 29 37 E
Burutu, *Nigeria* **50 G7** 5 20N 5 29 E
Burwell, *U.S.A.* **80 E5** 41 47N 99 8W
Burwick, *U.K.* **12 C5** 58 45N 2 58W
Bury, *U.K.* **10 D5** 53 35N 2 17W
Bury St. Edmunds, *U.K.* **11 E8** 52 15N 0 43 E
Buryatia □, *Russia* **27 D12** 53 0N 110 0 E
Busango Swamp, *Zambia* **55 E2** 14 15S 25 45 E
Buşayrah, *Syria* **44 C4** 35 9N 40 26 E
Būshehr, *Iran* **45 D6** 28 55N 50 55 E
Būshehr □, *Iran* **45 D6** 28 20N 51 45 E
Bushell, *Canada* **73 B7** 59 31N 108 45W
Bushenyi, *Uganda* **54 C3** 0 35S 30 10 E
Bushire = Būshehr, *Iran* **45 D6** 28 55N 50 55 E
Businga, *Dem. Rep. of the Congo* **52 D4** 3 16N 20 59 E
Buşra ash Shām, *Syria* **47 C5** 32 30N 36 25 E
Busselton, *Australia* **61 F2** 33 42S 115 15 E
Bussum, *Neths.* **15 B5** 52 16N 5 10 E
Busto Arsízio, *Italy* **18 D8** 45 37N 8 51 E
Busu-Djanoa, *Dem. Rep. of the Congo* **52 D4** 1 43N 21 23 E
Busuanga, *Phil.* **37 B6** 12 10N 120 0 E
Buta, *Dem. Rep. of the Congo* **54 B1** 2 50N 24 53 E
Butare, *Rwanda* **54 C2** 2 31S 29 52 E
Butaritari, *Kiribati* **64 G9** 3 30N 174 0 E
Bute, *U.K.* **12 F3** 55 48N 5 2W
Bute Inlet, *Canada* **72 C4** 50 40N 124 53W
Butemba, *Uganda* **54 B3** 1 9N 31 37 E
Butembo, *Dem. Rep. of the Congo* **54 B2** 0 9N 29 18 E
Butha Qi, *China* **33 B7** 48 0N 122 32 E
Butiaba, *Uganda* **54 B3** 1 50N 31 20 E
Butler, *Mo., U.S.A.* **80 F7** 38 16N 94 20W
Butler, *Pa., U.S.A.* **78 F5** 40 52N 79 54W
Buton, *Indonesia* **37 F6** 5 0S 122 45 E
Butte, *Mont., U.S.A.* **82 C7** 46 0N 112 32W
Butte, *Nebr., U.S.A.* **80 D5** 42 58N 98 51W
Butte Creek →, *U.S.A.* **84 F5** 39 12N 121 56W
Butterworth = Gcuwa, *S. Africa* **57 E4** 32 20S 28 11 E
Butterworth, *Malaysia* **39 K3** 5 24N 100 23 E
Buttevant, *Ireland* **13 D3** 52 14N 8 40W
Buttfield, Mt., *Australia* **61 D4** 24 45S 128 9 E
Button B., *Canada* **73 B10** 58 45N 94 23W
Buttonwillow, *U.S.A.* **85 K7** 35 24N 119 28W
Butty Hd., *Australia* **61 F3** 33 54S 121 39 E
Butuan, *Phil.* **37 C7** 8 57N 125 33 E
Butung = Buton, *Indonesia* **37 F6** 5 0S 122 45 E
Buturlinovka, *Russia* **25 D7** 50 50N 40 35 E
Buxa Duar, *India* **43 F13** 27 45N 89 35 E
Buxar, *India* **43 G10** 25 34N 83 58 E
Buxtehude, *Germany* **16 B5** 53 28N 9 39 E
Buxton, *U.K.* **10 D6** 53 16N 1 54W
Buy, *Russia* **24 C7** 58 28N 41 28 E
Büyük Menderes →, *Turkey* **21 F12** 37 28N 27 11 E
Büyükçekmece, *Turkey* **21 D13** 41 2N 28 35 E
Buzău, *Romania* **17 F14** 45 10N 26 50 E
Buzău →, *Romania* **17 F14** 45 26N 27 44 E
Buzen, *Japan* **31 H5** 33 35N 131 5 E
Buzi →, *Mozam.* **55 F3** 19 50S 34 43 E
Buzuluk, *Russia* **24 D9** 52 48N 52 12 E
Buzzards B., *U.S.A.* **79 E14** 41 45N 70 37W
Buzzards Bay, *U.S.A.* **79 E14** 41 44N 70 37W
Bwana Mkubwe, *Dem. Rep. of the Congo* **55 E2** 13 8S 28 38 E
Byarezina →, *Belarus* **17 B16** 52 33N 30 14 E
Bydgoszcz, *Poland* **17 B9** 53 10N 18 0 E
Byelarus = Belarus ■, *Europe* **17 B14** 53 30N 27 0 E
Byelorussia = Belarus ■, *Europe* **17 B14** 53 30N 27 0 E
Byers, *U.S.A.* **80 F2** 39 43N 104 14W
Byesville, *U.S.A.* **78 G3** 39 58N 81 32W
Byford, *Australia* **61 F2** 32 15S 116 0 E
Bykhaw, *Belarus* **17 B16** 53 31N 30 14 E
Bykhov = Bykhaw, *Belarus* **17 B16** 53 31N 30 14 E
Bylas, *U.S.A.* **83 K8** 33 8N 110 7W
Bylot, *Canada* **73 B10** 58 25N 94 8W
Bylot I., *Canada* **69 A12** 73 13N 78 34W
Byrd, C., *Antarctica* **5 C17** 69 38S 76 7W
Byrock, *Australia* **63 E4** 30 40S 146 27 E
Byron Bay, *Australia* **63 D5** 28 43S 153 37 E
Byrranga, Gory, *Russia* **27 B11** 75 0N 100 0 E
Byrranga Mts. = Byrranga, Gory, *Russia* **27 B11** 75 0N 100 0 E
Byske, *Sweden* **8 D19** 64 57N 21 11 E
Byske älv →, *Sweden* **8 D19** 64 57N 21 13 E
Bytom, *Poland* **17 C10** 50 25N 18 54 E
Bytów, *Poland* **17 A9** 54 10N 17 30 E
Byumba, *Rwanda* **54 C3** 1 35S 30 4 E

C

Ca →, *Vietnam* **38 C5** 18 45N 105 45 E
Ca Mau, *Vietnam* **39 H5** 9 7N 105 8 E
Ca Mau, Mui, *Vietnam* **39 H5** 8 38N 104 44 E
Ca Na, *Vietnam* **39 G7** 11 20N 108 54 E
Caacupé, *Paraguay* **94 B4** 25 23S 57 5W
Caála, *Angola* **53 G3** 12 46S 15 30 E
Caamano Sd., *Canada* **72 C3** 52 55N 129 25W
Caazapá, *Paraguay* **94 B4** 26 8S 56 19W
Caazapá □, *Paraguay* **95 B4** 26 10S 56 0W
Cabanatuan, *Phil.* **37 A6** 15 30N 120 58 E
Cabano, *Canada* **71 C6** 47 40N 68 56W
Cabazon, *U.S.A.* **85 M10** 33 55N 116 47W
Cabedelo, *Brazil* **93 E12** 7 0S 34 50W
Cabildo, *Chile* **94 C1** 32 30S 71 5W
Cabimas, *Venezuela* **92 A4** 10 23N 71 25W
Cabinda, *Angola* **52 F2** 5 33S 12 11 E
Cabinda □, *Angola* **52 F2** 5 0S 12 30 E
Cabinet Mts., *U.S.A.* **82 C6** 48 0N 115 30W
Cabo Blanco, *Argentina* **96 F3** 47 15S 65 47W
Cabo Frio, *Brazil* **95 A7** 22 51S 42 3W
Cabo Pantoja, *Peru* **92 D3** 1 0S 75 10W
Cabonga, Réservoir, *Canada* **70 C4** 47 20N 76 40W
Cabool, *U.S.A.* **81 G8** 37 7N 92 6W
Caboolture, *Australia* **63 D5** 27 5S 152 58 E

Cabora Bassa Dam =
Cahora Bassa, Reprêsa de,
Mozam. **55 F3** 15 20S 32 50 E
Caborca, *Mexico* **86 A2** 30 40N 112 10W
Cabot, Mt., *U.S.A.* **79 B13** 44 30N 71 25W
Cabot Hd., *Canada* **78 A3** 45 14N 81 17W
Cabot Str., *Canada* **71 C8** 47 15N 59 40W
Cabra, *Spain* **19 D3** 37 30N 4 28W
Cabrera, *Spain* **22 B9** 39 8N 2 57 E
Cabri, *Canada* **73 C7** 50 35N 108 25W
Cabriel →, *Spain* **19 C5** 39 14N 1 3W
Caçador, *Brazil* **95 B5** 26 47S 51 0W
Čačak, *Serbia, Yug.* **21 C9** 43 54N 20 20 E
Caçapava do Sul, *Brazil* **95 C5** 30 30S 53 30W
Cáceres, *Brazil* **92 G7** 16 5S 57 40W
Cáceres, *Spain* **19 C2** 39 26N 6 23W
Cache Bay, *Canada* **70 C4** 46 22N 80 0W
Cache Cr. →, *U.S.A.* **84 G5** 38 42N 121 42W
Cache Creek, *Canada* **72 C4** 50 48N 121 19W
Cachi, *Argentina* **94 B2** 25 5S 66 10W
Cachimbo, Serra do, *Brazil* **93 E7** 9 30S 55 30W
Cachinal de la Sierra, *Chile* **94 A2** 24 58S 69 32W
Cachoeira, *Brazil* **93 F11** 12 30S 39 0W
Cachoeira de Itapemirim,
Brazil **95 A7** 20 51S 41 7W
Cachoeira do Sul, *Brazil* **95 C5** 30 3S 52 53W
Cacoal, *Brazil* **92 F6** 11 32S 61 18W
Cacólo, *Angola* **52 G3** 10 9S 19 21 E
Caconda, *Angola* **53 G3** 13 48S 15 8 E
Caddo, *U.S.A.* **81 H6** 34 7N 96 16W
Cader Idris, *U.K.* **11 E4** 52 42N 3 53W
Cadereyta, *Mexico* **86 B5** 25 36N 100 0W
Cadibarrawirracanna, L.,
Australia **63 D2** 28 52S 135 27 E
Cadillac, *U.S.A.* **76 C3** 44 15N 85 24W
Cadiz, *Phil.* **37 B6** 10 57N 123 15 E
Cádiz, *Spain* **19 D2** 36 30N 6 20W
Cadiz, *Calif., U.S.A.* **85 L11** 34 30N 115 28W
Cadiz, *Ohio, U.S.A.* **78 F4** 40 22N 81 0W
Cádiz, G. de, *Spain* **19 D2** 36 40N 7 0W
Cadiz L., *U.S.A.* **83 J6** 34 18N 115 24W
Cadney Park, *Australia* **63 D1** 27 55S 134 3 E
Cadomin, *Canada* **72 C5** 53 2N 117 20W
Cadotte Lake, *Canada* **72 B5** 56 26N 116 23W
Cadoux, *Australia* **61 F2** 30 46S 117 7 E
Caen, *France* **18 B3** 49 10N 0 22W
Caernarfon, *U.K.* **10 D3** 53 8N 4 16W
Caernarfon B., *U.K.* **10 D3** 53 4N 4 40W
Caernarvon = Caernarfon,
U.K. **10 D3** 53 8N 4 16W
Caerphilly, *U.K.* **11 F4** 51 35N 3 13W
Caerphilly □, *U.K.* **11 F4** 51 37N 3 12W
Caesarea, *Israel* **47 C3** 32 30N 34 53 E
Caetité, *Brazil* **93 F10** 13 50S 42 32W
Cafayate, *Argentina* **94 B2** 26 2S 66 0W
Cafu, *Angola* **56 B2** 16 30S 15 8 E
Cagayan de Oro, *Phil.* **37 C6** 8 30N 124 40 E
Cagayan Is., *Phil.* **37 C5** 9 40N 121 16 E
Cágliari, *Italy* **20 E3** 39 13N 9 7 E
Cágliari, G. di, *Italy* **20 E3** 39 8N 9 11 E
Caguán →, *Colombia* **92 D4** 0 8S 74 18W
Caguas, *Puerto Rico* **89 C6** 18 14N 66 2W
Caha Mts., *Ireland* **13 E2** 51 45N 9 40W
Cahama, *Angola* **56 B1** 16 17S 14 19 E
Caher, *Ireland* **13 D4** 52 22N 7 56W
Caherciveen, *Ireland* **13 E1** 51 56N 10 14W
Cahora Bassa, Reprêsa de,
Mozam. **55 F3** 15 20S 32 50 E
Cahore Pt., *Ireland* **13 D5** 52 33N 6 12W
Cahors, *France* **18 D4** 44 27N 1 27 E
Cahul, *Moldova* **17 F15** 45 50N 28 15 E
Cai Nuoc, *Vietnam* **39 H5** 8 56N 105 1 E
Caia, *Mozam.* **55 F4** 17 51S 35 24 E
Caianda, *Angola* **55 E1** 11 2S 23 31 E
Caibarién, *Cuba* **88 B4** 22 30N 79 30W
Caicara, *Venezuela* **92 B5** 7 38N 66 10W
Caicó, *Brazil* **93 E11** 6 20S 37 0W
Caicos Is., *W. Indies* **89 B5** 21 40N 71 40W
Caicos Passage, *W. Indies* **89 B5** 22 45N 72 45W
Caird Coast, *Antarctica* **5 D1** 75 0S 25 0W
Cairn Gorm, *U.K.* **12 D5** 57 7N 3 39W
Cairngorm Mts., *U.K.* **12 D5** 57 6N 3 42W
Cairnryan, *U.K.* **12 G3** 54 59N 5 1W
Cairns, *Australia* **62 B4** 16 57S 145 45 E
Cairns L., *Canada* **73 C10** 51 42N 94 30W
Cairo = El Qâhira, *Egypt* **51 B12** 30 1N 31 14 E
Cairo, *Ga., U.S.A.* **77 K3** 30 52N 84 13W
Cairo, *Ill., U.S.A.* **81 G10** 37 0N 89 11W
Cairo, *N.Y., U.S.A.* **79 D11** 42 18N 74 0W
Caithness, Ord of, *U.K.* **12 C5** 58 8N 3 36W
Cajamarca, *Peru* **92 E3** 7 5S 78 28W
Cajàzeiras, *Brazil* **93 E11** 6 52S 38 30W
Cala d'Or, *Spain* **22 B10** 39 23N 3 14 E
Cala en Porter, *Spain* **22 B11** 39 52N 4 8 E
Cala Figuera, C. de, *Spain* **22 B9** 39 27N 2 31 E
Cala Forcat, *Spain* **22 B10** 40 0N 3 47 E
Cala Major, *Spain* **22 B9** 39 33N 2 37 E
Cala Mezquida = Sa
Mesquida, *Spain* **22 B11** 39 55N 4 16 E
Cala Millor, *Spain* **22 B10** 39 35N 3 22 E
Cala Ratjada, *Spain* **22 B10** 39 43N 3 27 E
Cala Santa Galdana, *Spain* **22 B10** 39 56N 3 58 E
Calabar, *Nigeria* **50 H7** 4 57N 8 20 E
Calabogie, *Canada* **79 A8** 45 18N 76 43W
Calabozo, *Venezuela* **92 B5** 9 0N 67 28W
Calábria □, *Italy* **20 E7** 39 0N 16 30 E
Calafate, *Argentina* **96 G2** 50 19S 72 15W
Calahorra, *Spain* **19 A5** 42 18N 1 59W
Calais, *France* **18 A4** 50 57N 1 56 E
Calais, *U.S.A.* **77 C12** 45 11N 67 17W
Calalaste, Cord. de,
Argentina **94 B2** 25 0S 67 0W
Calama, *Brazil* **92 E6** 8 0S 62 50W
Calama, *Chile* **94 A2** 22 30S 68 55W
Calamar, *Colombia* **92 A4** 10 15N 74 55W
Calamian Group, *Phil.* **37 B5** 11 50N 119 55 E
Calamocha, *Spain* **19 B5** 40 50N 1 17W
Calang, *Indonesia* **36 D1** 4 37N 95 37 E
Calapan, *Phil.* **37 B6** 13 25N 121 7 E
Călăraşi, *Romania* **17 F14** 44 12N 27 20 E
Calatayud, *Spain* **19 B5** 41 20N 1 40W
Calauag, *Phil.* **37 B6** 13 55N 122 15 E
Calavite, C., *Phil.* **37 B6** 13 26N 120 20 E
Calbayog, *Phil.* **37 B6** 12 4N 124 38 E
Calca, *Peru* **92 F4** 13 22S 72 0W
Calcasieu L., *U.S.A.* **81 L8** 29 55N 93 18W
Calcutta, *India* **43 H13** 22 36N 88 24 E
Calcutta, *U.S.A.* **78 F4** 40 40N 80 34W
Caldas da Rainha, *Portugal* **19 C1** 39 24N 9 8W
Calder →, *U.K.* **10 D6** 53 44N 1 22W
Caldera, *Chile* **94 B1** 27 5S 70 55W
Caldwell, *Idaho, U.S.A.* **82 E5** 43 40N 116 41W
Caldwell, *Kans., U.S.A.* **81 G6** 37 2N 97 37W
Caldwell, *Tex., U.S.A.* **81 K6** 30 32N 96 42W
Caledon, *S. Africa* **56 E2** 34 14S 19 26 E
Caledon →, *S. Africa* **56 E4** 30 31S 26 5 E
Caledon B., *Australia* **62 A2** 12 45S 137 0 E
Caledonia, *Canada* **78 C5** 43 7N 79 58W
Caledonia, *U.S.A.* **78 D7** 42 58N 77 51W
Calemba, *Angola* **56 B2** 16 0S 15 44 E
Calen, *Australia* **62 C4** 20 56S 148 48 E
Caletones, *Chile* **94 C1** 34 6S 70 27W
Calexico, *U.S.A.* **85 N11** 32 40N 115 30W
Calf of Man, *U.K.* **10 C3** 54 3N 4 48W
Calgary, *Canada* **72 C6** 51 0N 114 10W
Calheta, *Madeira* **22 D2** 32 44N 17 11W
Calhoun, *U.S.A.* **77 H3** 34 30N 84 57W
Cali, *Colombia* **92 C3** 3 25N 76 35W
Calicut, *India* **40 P9** 11 15N 75 43 E
Caliente, *U.S.A.* **83 H6** 37 37N 114 31W
California, *Mo., U.S.A.* **80 F8** 38 38N 92 34W
California, *Pa., U.S.A.* **78 F5** 40 4N 79 54W
California □, *U.S.A.* **84 H7** 37 30N 119 30W
California, Baja, *Mexico* **86 A1** 32 10N 115 12W
California, Baja, T.N. = Baja
California □, *Mexico* **86 B2** 30 0N 115 0W
California, Baja, T.S. = Baja
California Sur □, *Mexico* **86 B2** 25 50N 111 50W
California, G. de, *Mexico* **86 B2** 27 0N 111 0W
California City, *U.S.A.* **85 K9** 35 10N 117 55W
California Hot Springs,
U.S.A. **85 K8** 35 51N 118 41W
Calingasta, *Argentina* **94 C2** 31 15S 69 30W
Calipatria, *U.S.A.* **85 M11** 33 8N 115 31W
Calistoga, *U.S.A.* **84 G4** 38 35N 122 35W
Calitzdorp, *S. Africa* **56 E3** 33 33S 21 42 E
Callabonna, L., *Australia* **63 D3** 29 40S 140 5 E
Callan, *Ireland* **13 D4** 52 32N 7 24W
Callander, *U.K.* **12 E4** 56 15N 4 13W
Callao, *Peru* **92 F3** 12 0S 77 0W
Calles, *Mexico* **87 C5** 23 2N 98 42W
Callicoon, *U.S.A.* **79 E9** 41 46N 75 3W
Calling Lake, *Canada* **72 B6** 55 15N 113 12W
Calliope, *Australia* **62 C5** 24 0S 151 16 E
Calne, *U.K.* **11 F6** 51 26N 2 0W
Calola, *Angola* **56 B2** 16 25S 17 48 E
Caloundra, *Australia* **63 D5** 26 45S 153 10 E
Calpella, *U.S.A.* **84 F3** 39 14N 123 12W
Calpine, *U.S.A.* **84 F6** 39 40N 120 27W
Calstock, *Canada* **70 C3** 49 47N 84 9W
Caltagirone, *Italy* **20 F6** 37 14N 14 31 E
Caltanissetta, *Italy* **20 F6** 37 29N 14 4 E
Calulo, *Angola* **52 G2** 10 1S 14 56 E
Caluquembe, *Angola* **53 G2** 13 47S 14 44 E
Calvert →, *Australia* **62 B2** 16 17S 137 44 E
Calvert I., *Canada* **72 C3** 51 30N 128 0W
Calvert Ra., *Australia* **60 D3** 24 0S 122 30 E
Calvi, *France* **18 E8** 42 34N 8 45 E
Calviá, *Spain* **22 B9** 39 34N 2 31 E
Calvillo, *Mexico* **86 C4** 21 51N 102 43W
Calvinia, *S. Africa* **56 E2** 31 28S 19 45 E
Calwa, *U.S.A.* **84 J7** 36 42N 119 46W
Cam →, *U.K.* **11 E8** 52 21N 0 16 E
Cam Lam, *Vietnam* **39 G7** 11 54N 109 10 E
Cam Ranh, *Vietnam* **39 G7** 11 54N 109 12 E
Cam Xuyen, *Vietnam* **38 C6** 18 15N 106 0 E
Camabatela, *Angola* **52 F3** 8 20S 15 26 E
Camacha, *Madeira* **22 D3** 32 41N 16 49W
Camacho, *Mexico* **86 C4** 24 25N 102 18W
Camacupa, *Angola* **53 G3** 11 58S 17 22 E
Camagüey, *Cuba* **88 B4** 21 20N 78 0W
Camaná, *Peru* **92 G4** 16 30S 72 50W
Camanche Reservoir, *U.S.A.* **84 G6** 38 14N 121 1W
Camaquã, *Brazil* **95 C5** 30 51S 51 49W
Camaquã →, *Brazil* **95 C5** 31 17S 51 47W
Câmara de Lobos, *Madeira* **22 D3** 32 39N 16 59W
Camargo, *Mexico* **87 B5** 26 19N 98 50W
Camargue, *France* **18 E6** 43 34N 4 34 E
Camarillo, *U.S.A.* **85 L7** 34 13N 119 2W
Camarón, C., *Honduras* **88 C2** 16 0N 85 5W
Camarones, *Argentina* **96 E3** 44 50S 65 40W
Camas, *U.S.A.* **84 E4** 45 35N 122 24W
Camas Valley, *U.S.A.* **82 E2** 43 2N 123 40W
Camballin, *Australia* **60 C3** 17 59S 124 12 E
Cambará, *Brazil* **95 A5** 23 2S 50 5W
Cambay = Khambhat, *India* **42 H5** 22 23N 72 33 E
Cambay, G. of = Khambhat,
G. of, *India* **40 J8** 20 45N 72 30 E
Cambodia ■, *Asia* **38 F5** 12 15N 105 0 E
Camborne, *U.K.* **11 G2** 50 12N 5 19W
Cambrai, *France* **18 A5** 50 11N 3 14 E
Cambria, *U.S.A.* **84 K5** 35 34N 121 5W
Cambrian Mts., *U.K.* **11 E4** 52 3N 3 57W
Cambridge, *Canada* **78 C4** 43 23N 80 15W
Cambridge, *Jamaica* **88 C4** 18 18N 77 54W
Cambridge, *N.Z.* **59 G5** 37 54S 175 29 E
Cambridge, *U.K.* **11 E8** 52 12N 0 8 E
Cambridge, *Mass., U.S.A.* **79 D13** 42 22N 71 6W
Cambridge, *Md., U.S.A.* **75 C11** 38 34N 76 5W
Cambridge, *Minn., U.S.A.* **80 C8** 45 34N 93 13W
Cambridge, *N.Y., U.S.A.* **79 C11** 43 2N 73 22W
Cambridge, *Nebr., U.S.A.* **80 E4** 40 17N 100 10W
Cambridge, *Ohio, U.S.A.* **78 F3** 40 2N 81 35W
Cambridge Bay =
Ikaluktutiak, *Canada* **68 B9** 69 10N 105 0W
Cambridge G., *Australia* **60 B4** 14 55S 128 15 E
Cambridge Springs, *U.S.A.* **78 E4** 41 48N 80 4W
Cambridgeshire □, *U.K.* **11 E7** 52 25N 0 7W
Cambuci, *Brazil* **95 A7** 21 35S 41 55W
Cambundi-Catembo, *Angola* **52 G3** 10 10S 17 35 E
Camden, *Ala., U.S.A.* **77 K2** 31 59N 87 17W
Camden, *Ark., U.S.A.* **81 J8** 33 35N 92 50W
Camden, *Maine, U.S.A.* **77 C11** 44 13N 69 4W
Camden, *N.J., U.S.A.* **79 G9** 39 56N 75 7W
Camden, *N.Y., U.S.A.* **79 C9** 43 20N 75 45W
Camden, *S.C., U.S.A.* **77 H5** 34 16N 80 36W
Camden Sd., *Australia* **60 C3** 15 27S 124 25 E
Camdenton, *U.S.A.* **81 F8** 38 1N 92 45W
Cameron, *Ariz., U.S.A.* **83 J8** 35 53N 111 25W
Cameron, *La., U.S.A.* **81 L8** 29 48N 93 20W
Cameron, *Mo., U.S.A.* **80 F7** 39 44N 94 14W
Cameron, *Tex., U.S.A.* **81 K6** 30 51N 96 59W
Cameron Highlands,
Malaysia **39 K3** 4 27N 101 22 E
Cameron Hills, *Canada* **72 B5** 59 48N 118 0W
Cameroon ■, *Africa* **52 C2** 6 0N 12 30 E
Cameroun, Mt., *Cameroon* **52 D1** 4 13N 9 10 E
Cametá, *Brazil* **93 D9** 2 12S 49 30W
Camiguin I., *Phil.* **37 C6** 18 56N 121 55 E
Camilla, *U.S.A.* **77 K3** 31 14N 84 12W
Caminha, *Portugal* **19 B1** 41 50N 8 50W
Camino, *U.S.A.* **84 G6** 38 44N 120 41W
Camira Creek, *Australia* **63 D5** 29 15S 152 58 E
Cammal, *U.S.A.* **78 E7** 41 24N 77 28W
Camocim, *Brazil* **93 D10** 2 55S 40 50W
Camooweal, *Australia* **62 B2** 19 56S 138 7 E
Camopi, *Fr. Guiana* **93 C8** 3 12N 52 17W
Camp Borden, *Canada* **78 B5** 44 18N 79 56W
Camp Hill, *U.S.A.* **78 F8** 40 14N 76 55W
Camp Nelson, *U.S.A.* **85 J8** 36 8N 118 39W
Camp Pendleton, *U.S.A.* **85 M9** 33 16N 117 23W
Camp Verde, *U.S.A.* **83 J8** 34 34N 111 51W
Camp Wood, *U.S.A.* **81 L5** 29 40N 100 1W
Campana, *Argentina* **94 C4** 34 10S 58 55W
Campana, I., *Chile* **96 F1** 48 20S 75 20W
Campanário, *Madeira* **22 D2** 32 39N 17 2W
Campânia □, *Italy* **20 D6** 41 0N 14 30 E
Campbell, *S. Africa* **56 D3** 28 48S 23 44 E
Campbell, *Calif., U.S.A.* **84 H5** 37 17N 121 57W
Campbell, *Ohio, U.S.A.* **78 E4** 41 5N 80 37W
Campbell I., *Pac. Oc.* **64 N8** 52 30S 169 0 E
Campbell L., *Canada* **73 A7** 63 14N 106 55W
Campbell River, *Canada* **72 C3** 50 5N 125 20W
Campbell Town, *Australia* **62 G4** 41 52S 147 30 E
Campbellford, *Canada* **78 B7** 44 18N 77 48W
Campbellpur, *Pakistan* **42 C5** 33 46N 72 26 E
Campbellsville, *U.S.A.* **76 G3** 37 21N 85 20W
Campbellton, *Canada* **71 C6** 47 57N 66 43W
Campbelltown, *Australia* **63 E5** 34 4S 150 49 E
Campbeltown, *U.K.* **12 F3** 55 26N 5 36W
Campeche, *Mexico* **87 D6** 19 50N 90 32W
Campeche □, *Mexico* **87 D6** 19 50N 90 32W
Campeche, Golfo de,
Mexico **87 D6** 19 30N 93 0W
Camperdown, *Australia* **63 F3** 38 14S 143 9 E
Camperville, *Canada* **73 C8** 51 59N 100 9W
Câmpina, *Romania* **17 F13** 45 10N 25 45 E
Campina Grande, *Brazil* **93 E11** 7 20S 35 47W
Campinas, *Brazil* **95 A6** 22 50S 47 0W
Campo Grande, *Brazil* **93 H8** 20 25S 54 40W
Campo Maíor, *Brazil* **93 D10** 4 50S 42 12W
Campo Mourão, *Brazil* **95 A5** 24 3S 52 22W
Campobasso, *Italy* **20 D6** 41 34N 14 39 E
Campos, *Brazil* **95 A7** 21 50S 41 20W
Campos Belos, *Brazil* **93 F9** 13 10S 47 3W
Campos del Puerto, *Spain* **22 B10** 39 26N 3 1 E
Campos Novos, *Brazil* **95 B5** 27 21S 51 50W
Camptonville, *U.S.A.* **84 F5** 39 27N 121 3W
Camptown, *U.S.A.* **79 E8** 41 44N 76 14W
Câmpulung, *Romania* **17 F13** 45 17N 25 3 E
Camrose, *Canada* **72 C6** 53 0N 112 50W
Camsell Portage, *Canada* **73 B7** 59 37N 109 15W
Çan, *Turkey* **21 D12** 40 2N 27 3 E
Can Clavo, *Spain* **22 C7** 38 57N 1 27 E
Can Creu, *Spain* **22 C7** 38 58N 1 28 E
Can Gio, *Vietnam* **39 G6** 10 25N 106 58 E
Can Tho, *Vietnam* **39 G5** 10 2N 105 46 E
Canaan, *U.S.A.* **79 D11** 42 2N 73 20W
Canada ■, *N. Amer.* **68 C10** 60 0N 100 0W
Cañada de Gómez,
Argentina **94 C3** 32 40S 61 30W
Canadian, *U.S.A.* **81 H4** 35 55N 100 23W
Canadian →, *U.S.A.* **81 H7** 35 28N 95 3W
Canajoharie, *U.S.A.* **79 D10** 42 54N 74 35W
Çanakkale, *Turkey* **21 D12** 40 8N 26 24 E
Çanakkale Boğazı, *Turkey* **21 D12** 40 17N 26 32 E
Canal Flats, *Canada* **72 C5** 50 10N 115 48W
Canalejas, *Argentina* **94 D2** 35 15S 66 34W
Canals, *Argentina* **94 C3** 33 35S 62 53W
Canandaigua, *U.S.A.* **78 D7** 42 54N 77 17W
Canandaigua L., *U.S.A.* **78 D7** 42 47N 77 19W
Cananea, *Mexico* **86 A2** 31 0N 110 20W
Canarias, Is., *Atl. Oc.* **22 F4** 28 30N 16 0W
Canarreos, Arch. de los,
Cuba **88 B3** 21 35N 81 40W
Canary Is. = Canarias, Is.,
Atl. Oc. **22 F4** 28 30N 16 0W
Canaseraga, *U.S.A.* **78 D7** 42 27N 77 45W
Canatlán, *Mexico* **86 C4** 24 31N 104 47W
Canaveral, C., *U.S.A.* **77 L5** 28 27N 80 32W
Canavieiras, *Brazil* **93 G11** 15 39S 39 0W
Canberra, *Australia* **63 F4** 35 15S 149 8 E
Canby, *Calif., U.S.A.* **82 F3** 41 27N 120 52W
Canby, *Minn., U.S.A.* **80 C6** 44 43N 96 16W
Canby, *Oreg., U.S.A.* **84 E4** 45 16N 122 42W
Cancún, *Mexico* **87 C7** 21 8N 86 44W
Candelaria, *Argentina* **95 B4** 27 29S 55 44W
Candelaria, *Canary Is.* **22 F3** 28 22N 16 22W
Candelo, *Australia* **63 F4** 36 47S 149 43 E
Candia = Iráklion, *Greece* **23 D7** 35 20N 25 12 E
Candle L., *Canada* **73 C7** 53 50N 105 18W
Candlemas I., *Antarctica* **5 B1** 57 3S 26 40W
Cando, *U.S.A.* **80 A5** 48 32N 99 12W
Canea = Khaniá, *Greece* **23 D6** 35 30N 24 4 E
Canelones, *Uruguay* **95 C4** 34 32S 56 17W
Cañete, *Chile* **94 D1** 37 50S 73 30W
Cañete, *Peru* **92 F3** 13 8S 76 30W
Cangas de Narcea, *Spain* **19 A2** 43 10N 6 32W
Canguaretama, *Brazil* **93 E11** 6 20S 35 5W
Canguçu, *Brazil* **95 C5** 31 22S 52 43W
Canguçu, Serra do, *Brazil* **95 C5** 31 20S 52 40W
Cangzhou, *China* **34 E9** 38 19N 116 52 E
Caniapiscau →, *Canada* **71 A6** 56 40N 69 30W
Caniapiscau Rés. de, *Canada* **71 B6** 54 10N 69 55W
Canicattì, *Italy* **20 F5** 37 21N 13 51 E
Canim Lake, *Canada* **72 C4** 51 47N 120 54W
Canindeyu □, *Paraguay* **95 A5** 24 10S 55 0W
Canisteo, *U.S.A.* **78 D7** 42 16N 77 36W
Canisteo →, *U.S.A.* **78 D7** 42 7N 77 8W
Cañitas, *Mexico* **86 C4** 23 36N 102 43W
Çankırı, *Turkey* **25 F5** 40 40N 33 37 E
Cankuzo, *Burundi* **54 C3** 3 10S 30 31 E
Canmore, *Canada* **72 C5** 51 7N 115 18W
Cann River, *Australia* **63 F4** 37 35S 149 7 E
Canna, *U.K.* **12 D2** 57 3N 6 33W
Cannanore, *India* **40 P9** 11 53N 75 27 E
Cannes, *France* **18 E7** 43 32N 7 1 E
Canning Town = Port
Canning, *India* **43 H13** 22 23N 88 40 E
Cannington, *Canada* **78 B5** 44 20N 79 2W
Cannock, *U.K.* **11 E5** 52 41N 2 1W
Cannon Ball →, *U.S.A.* **80 B4** 46 20N 100 38W
Cannondale Mt., *Australia* **62 D4** 25 13S 148 57 E
Cannonsville Reservoir,
U.S.A. **79 D9** 42 4N 75 22W
Cannonvale, *Australia* **62 C4** 20 17S 148 43 E
Canoas, *Brazil* **95 B5** 29 56S 51 11W
Canoe L., *Canada* **73 B7** 55 10N 108 15W
Canon City, *U.S.A.* **80 F2** 38 27N 105 14W
Canora, *Canada* **73 C8** 51 40N 102 30W
Canowindra, *Australia* **63 E4** 33 35S 148 38 E
Canso, *Canada* **71 C7** 45 20N 61 0W
Cantabria □, *Spain* **19 A4** 43 10N 4 0W
Cantabrian Mts. =
Cantábrica, Cordillera,
Spain **19 A3** 43 0N 5 10W
Cantábrica, Cordillera, *Spain* **19 A3** 43 0N 5 10W
Cantal, Plomb du, *France* **18 D5** 45 3N 2 45 E
Canterbury, *Australia* **62 D3** 25 23S 141 53 E
Canterbury, *U.K.* **11 F9** 51 16N 1 6 E
Canterbury □, *N.Z.* **59 K3** 43 45S 171 19 E
Canterbury Bight, *N.Z.* **59 L3** 44 16S 171 55 E
Canterbury Plains, *N.Z.* **59 K3** 43 55S 171 22 E
Cantil, *U.S.A.* **85 K9** 35 18N 117 58W
Canton = Guangzhou, *China* **33 D6** 23 5N 113 10 E
Canton, *Ga., U.S.A.* **77 H3** 34 14N 84 29W
Canton, *Ill., U.S.A.* **80 E9** 40 33N 90 2W
Canton, *Miss., U.S.A.* **81 J9** 32 37N 90 2W
Canton, *Mo., U.S.A.* **80 E9** 40 8N 91 32W
Canton, *N.Y., U.S.A.* **79 B9** 44 36N 75 10W
Canton, *Ohio, U.S.A.* **78 F3** 40 48N 81 23W
Canton, *Pa., U.S.A.* **78 E8** 41 39N 76 51W
Canton, *S. Dak., U.S.A.* **80 D6** 43 18N 96 35W
Canton L., *U.S.A.* **81 G5** 36 6N 98 35W
Canudos, *Brazil* **92 E7** 7 13S 58 5W
Canumã →, *Brazil* **92 D7** 3 55S 59 10W
Canutama, *Brazil* **92 E6** 6 30S 64 20W
Canutillo, *U.S.A.* **83 L10** 31 55N 106 36W
Canvey, *U.K.* **11 F8** 51 31N 0 37 E
Canyon, *U.S.A.* **81 H4** 34 59N 101 55W
Canyonlands National Park,
U.S.A. **83 G9** 38 15N 110 0W
Canyonville, *U.S.A.* **82 E2** 42 56N 123 17W
Cao He →, *China* **35 D13** 40 10N 124 32 E
Cao Lanh, *Vietnam* **39 G5** 10 27N 105 38 E
Cao Xian, *China* **34 G8** 34 50N 115 35 E
Cap-aux-Meules, *Canada* **71 C7** 47 23N 61 52W
Cap-Chat, *Canada* **71 C6** 49 6N 66 40W
Cap-de-la-Madeleine,
Canada **70 C5** 46 22N 72 31W
Cap-Haïtien, *Haiti* **89 C5** 19 40N 72 20W
Capac, *U.S.A.* **78 C2** 43 1N 82 56W
Capanaparo →, *Venezuela* **92 B5** 7 1N 67 7W
Cape →, *Australia* **62 C4** 20 59S 146 51 E
Cape Barren I., *Australia* **62 G4** 40 25S 148 15 E
Cape Breton Highlands Nat.
Park, *Canada* **71 C7** 46 50N 60 40W
Cape Breton I., *Canada* **71 C7** 46 0N 60 30W
Cape Charles, *U.S.A.* **76 G8** 37 16N 76 1W
Cape Coast, *Ghana* **50 G5** 5 5N 1 15W
Cape Coral, *U.S.A.* **77 M5** 26 33N 81 57W
Cape Dorset, *Canada* **69 B12** 64 14N 76 32W
Cape Fear →, *U.S.A.* **77 H6** 33 53N 78 1W
Cape Girardeau, *U.S.A.* **81 G10** 37 19N 89 32W
Cape May, *U.S.A.* **76 F8** 38 56N 74 56W
Cape May Point, *U.S.A.* **75 C12** 38 56N 74 58W
Cape Province □, *S. Africa* **53 L3** 32 0S 23 0 E
Cape Tormentine, *Canada* **71 C7** 46 8N 63 47W
Cape Town, *S. Africa* **56 E2** 33 55S 18 22 E
Cape Verde Is. ■, *Atl. Oc.* **49 E1** 17 10N 25 20W
Cape Vincent, *U.S.A.* **79 B8** 44 8N 76 20W
Cape York Peninsula,
Australia **62 A3** 12 0S 142 30 E
Capela, *Brazil* **93 F11** 10 30S 37 0W
Capella, *Australia* **62 C4** 23 2S 148 1 E
Capenda Camulemba,
Angola **52 F3** 9 24S 18 27 E
Capim →, *Brazil* **93 D9** 1 40S 47 47W
Capitan, *U.S.A.* **83 K11** 33 35N 105 35W
Capitol Reef National Park,
U.S.A. **83 G8** 38 15N 111 10W
Capitola, *U.S.A.* **84 J5** 36 59N 121 57W
Capoche →, *Mozam.* **55 F3** 15 35S 33 0 E
Capraia, *Italy* **18 E8** 43 2N 9 50 E
Capreol, *Canada* **70 C3** 46 43N 80 56W
Capri, *Italy* **20 D6** 40 33N 14 14 E
Capricorn Group, *Australia* **62 C5** 23 30S 151 55 E
Capricorn Ra., *Australia* **60 D2** 23 20S 116 50 E
Caprivi Strip, *Namibia* **56 B3** 18 0S 23 0 E
Captain's Flat, *Australia* **63 F4** 35 35S 149 27 E
Caquetá →, *Colombia* **92 D5** 1 15S 69 15W
Caracal, *Romania* **17 F13** 44 8N 24 22 E
Caracas, *Venezuela* **92 A5** 10 30N 66 55W
Caracol, *Brazil* **94 A4** 22 18S 57 1W
Caracol, *Piauí, Brazil* **93 E10** 9 15S 43 22W
Carajas, *Brazil* **93 E8** 6 5S 50 23W
Carajás, Serra dos, *Brazil* **93 E8** 6 0S 51 30W
Carangola, *Brazil* **95 A7** 20 44S 42 5W
Caransebeş, *Romania* **17 F12** 45 28N 22 18 E
Caraquet, *Canada* **71 C6** 47 48N 64 57W
Caras, *Peru* **92 E3** 9 3S 77 47W
Caratasca, L., *Honduras* **88 C3** 15 20N 83 40W
Caratinga, *Brazil* **93 G10** 19 50S 42 10W
Caraúbas, *Brazil* **93 E11** 5 43S 37 33W
Caravaca = Caravaca de la
Cruz, *Spain* **19 C5** 38 8N 1 52W
Caravaca de la Cruz, *Spain* **19 C5** 38 8N 1 52W
Caravelas, *Brazil* **93 G11** 17 45S 39 15W
Caraveli, *Peru* **92 G4** 15 45S 73 25W
Caràzinho, *Brazil* **95 B5** 28 16S 52 46W
Carballo, *Spain* **19 A1** 43 13N 8 41W
Carberry, *Canada* **73 D9** 49 50N 99 25W
Carbó, *Mexico* **86 B2** 29 42N 110 58W
Carbonara, C., *Italy* **20 E3** 39 6N 9 31 E
Carbondale, *Colo., U.S.A.* **82 G10** 39 24N 107 13W
Carbondale, *Ill., U.S.A.* **81 G10** 37 44N 89 13W
Carbondale, *Pa., U.S.A.* **79 E9** 41 35N 75 30W
Carbonear, *Canada* **71 C9** 47 42N 53 13W
Carbónia, *Italy* **20 E3** 39 10N 8 30 E
Carcajou, *Canada* **72 B5** 57 47N 117 6W
Carcarana →, *Argentina* **94 C3** 32 27S 60 48W
Carcasse, C., *Haiti* **89 C5** 18 30N 74 28W
Carcassonne, *France* **18 E5** 43 13N 2 20 E
Carcross, *Canada* **72 A2** 60 13N 134 45W
Cardamon Hills, *India* **40 Q10** 9 30N 77 15 E
Cárdenas, *Cuba* **88 B3** 23 0N 81 30W
Cárdenas, *San Luis Potosí,*
Mexico **87 C5** 22 0N 99 41W

Cárdenas, Tabasco, Mexico 87 D6 17 59N 93 21W
Cardiff, U.K. 11 F4 51 29N 3 10W
Cardiff □, U.K. 11 F4 51 31N 3 12W
Cardiff-by-the-Sea, U.S.A. 85 M9 33 1N 117 17W
Cardigan, U.K. 11 E3 52 5N 4 40W
Cardigan B., U.K. 11 E3 52 30N 4 30W
Cardinal, Canada 79 B9 44 47N 75 23W
Cardona, Uruguay 94 C4 33 53S 57 18W
Cardoso, Ilha do, Brazil 95 B5 25 8S 47 58W
Cardston, Canada 72 D6 49 15N 113 20W
Cardwell, Australia 62 B4 18 14S 146 2 E
Careen L., Canada 73 B7 57 0N 108 11W
Carei, Romania 17 E12 47 40N 22 29 E
Careme = Ciremai, Indonesia 37 G13 6 55S 108 27 E
Carey, U.S.A. 82 E7 43 19N 113 57W
Carey, L., Australia 61 E3 29 0S 122 15 E
Carey L., Canada 73 A8 62 12N 102 55W
Carhué, Argentina 94 D3 37 10S 62 50W
Caria, Turkey 21 F13 37 20N 28 10 E
Cariacica, Brazil 93 H10 20 16S 40 25W
Caribbean Sea, W. Indies 89 D5 15 0N 75 0W
Cariboo Mts., Canada 72 C4 53 0N 121 0W
Caribou, U.S.A. 77 B12 46 52N 68 1W
Caribou →, Man., Canada 73 B10 59 20N 94 44W
Caribou →, N.W.T., Canada 72 A3 61 27N 125 45W
Caribou I., Canada 70 C2 47 22N 85 49W
Caribou Is., Canada 72 A6 61 55N 113 15W
Caribou L., Man., Canada 73 B9 59 21N 96 10W
Caribou L., Ont., Canada 70 B2 50 25N 89 5W
Caribou Mts., Canada 72 B5 59 12N 115 40W
Carichic, Mexico 86 B3 27 56N 107 3W
Carillo, Mexico 86 B4 26 50N 103 55W
Carinda, Australia 63 E4 30 28S 147 41 E
Carinhanha, Brazil 93 F10 14 15S 44 46W
Carinhanha →, Brazil 93 F10 14 20S 43 47W
Carinthia = Kärnten □, Austria 16 E8 46 52N 13 30 E
Caripito, Venezuela 92 A6 10 8N 63 6W
Carleton, Mt., Canada 71 C6 47 23N 66 53W
Carleton Place, Canada 79 A8 45 8N 76 9W
Carletonville, S. Africa 56 D4 26 23S 27 22 E
Carlin, U.S.A. 82 F5 40 43N 116 7W
Carlingford L., U.K. 13 B5 54 3N 6 9W
Carlinville, U.S.A. 80 F10 39 17N 89 53W
Carlisle, U.K. 10 C5 54 54N 2 56W
Carlisle, U.S.A. 78 F7 40 12N 77 12W
Carlos Casares, Argentina 94 D3 35 32S 61 20W
Carlos Tejedor, Argentina 94 D3 35 25S 62 25W
Carlow, Ireland 13 D5 52 50N 6 56W
Carlow □, Ireland 13 D5 52 43N 6 50W
Carlsbad, Calif., U.S.A. 85 M9 33 10N 117 21W
Carlsbad, N. Mex., U.S.A. 81 J2 32 25N 104 14W
Carlsbad Caverns National Park, U.S.A. 81 J2 32 10N 104 35W
Carluke, U.K. 12 F5 55 45N 3 50W
Carlyle, Canada 73 D8 49 40N 102 20W
Carmacks, Canada 68 B6 62 5N 136 16W
Carman, Canada 73 D9 49 30N 98 0W
Carmarthen, U.K. 11 F3 51 52N 4 19W
Carmarthen B., U.K. 11 F3 51 40N 4 30W
Carmarthenshire □, U.K. 11 F3 51 55N 4 13W
Carmaux, France 18 D5 44 3N 2 10 E
Carmel, U.S.A. 79 E11 41 26N 73 41W
Carmel-by-the-Sea, U.S.A. 84 J5 36 33N 121 55W
Carmel Valley, U.S.A. 84 J5 36 29N 121 43W
Carmelo, Uruguay 94 C4 34 0S 58 20W
Carmen, Colombia 92 B3 9 43N 75 8W
Carmen, Paraguay 95 B4 27 13S 56 12W
Carmen →, Mexico 86 A3 30 42N 106 29W
Carmen, I., Mexico 86 B2 26 0N 111 20W
Carmen de Patagones, Argentina 96 E4 40 50S 63 0W
Carmensa, Argentina 94 D2 35 15S 67 40W
Carmi, Canada 72 D5 49 36N 119 8W
Carmi, U.S.A. 76 F1 38 5N 88 10W
Carmichael, U.S.A. 84 G5 38 38N 121 19W
Carmila, Australia 62 C4 21 55S 149 24 E
Carmona, Costa Rica 88 E2 10 0N 85 15W
Carmona, Spain 19 D3 37 28N 5 42W
Carn Ban, U.K. 12 D4 57 7N 4 15W
Carn Eige, U.K. 12 D3 57 17N 5 8W
Carnac, France 18 C2 47 35N 3 6W
Carnamah, Australia 61 E2 29 41S 115 53 E
Carnarvon, Australia 61 D1 24 51S 113 42 E
Carnarvon, S. Africa 56 E3 30 56S 22 8 E
Carnarvon Ra., Queens., Australia 62 D4 25 15S 148 30 E
Carnarvon Ra., W. Austral., Australia 61 E3 25 20S 120 45 E
Carnation, U.S.A. 84 C5 47 39N 121 55W
Carndonagh, Ireland 13 A4 55 16N 7 15W
Carnduff, Canada 73 D8 49 10N 101 50W
Carnegie, U.S.A. 78 F4 40 24N 80 5W
Carnegie, L., Australia 61 E3 26 5S 122 30 E
Carnic Alps = Karnische Alpen, Europe 16 E7 46 36N 13 0 E
Carniche Alpi = Karnische Alpen, Europe 16 E7 46 36N 13 0 E
Carnot, C.A.R. 52 D3 4 59N 15 56 E
Carnot, C., Australia 63 E2 34 57S 135 38 E
Carnot B., Australia 60 C3 17 20S 122 15 E
Carnoustie, U.K. 12 E6 56 30N 2 42W
Carnsore Pt., Ireland 13 D5 52 10N 6 22W
Caro, U.S.A. 76 D4 43 29N 83 24W
Carol City, U.S.A. 77 N5 25 56N 80 16W
Carolina, Brazil 93 E9 7 10S 47 30W
Carolina, Puerto Rico 89 C6 18 23N 65 58W
Carolina, S. Africa 57 D5 26 5S 30 6 E
Caroline I., Kiribati 65 H12 9 15S 150 3W
Caroline Is., Micronesia 28 J17 8 0N 150 0 E
Caroni →, Venezuela 92 B6 8 21N 62 43W
Caronie = Nébrodi, Monti, Italy 20 F6 37 54N 14 35 E
Caroona, Australia 63 E5 31 24S 150 26 E
Carpathians, Europe 17 D11 49 30N 21 0 E
Carpații Meridionali, Romania 17 F13 45 30N 25 0 E
Carpentaria, G. of, Australia 62 A2 14 0S 139 0 E
Carpentras, France 18 D6 44 3N 5 2 E
Carpi, Italy 20 B4 44 47N 10 53 E
Carpinteria, U.S.A. 85 L7 34 24N 119 31W
Carr Boyd Ra., Australia 60 C4 16 15S 128 35 E
Carrabelle, U.S.A. 77 L3 29 51N 84 40W
Carranza, Presa V., Mexico 86 B4 27 20N 100 50W
Carrara, Italy 18 D9 44 5N 10 6 E
Carrauntoohill, Ireland 13 D2 52 0N 9 45W
Carrick-on-Shannon, Ireland 13 C3 53 57N 8 5W
Carrick-on-Suir, Ireland 13 D4 52 21N 7 24W
Carrickfergus, U.K. 13 B6 54 43N 5 49W
Carrickmacross, Ireland 13 C5 53 59N 6 43W
Carrieton, Australia 63 E2 32 25S 138 31 E
Carrington, U.S.A. 80 B5 47 27N 99 8W
Carrizal Bajo, Chile 94 B1 28 5S 71 20W
Carrizalillo, Chile 94 B1 29 5S 71 30W
Carrizo Cr. →, U.S.A. 81 G3 36 55N 103 55W
Carrizo Springs, U.S.A. 81 L5 28 31N 99 52W
Carrizozo, U.S.A. 83 K11 33 38N 105 53W
Carroll, U.S.A. 80 D7 42 4N 94 52W
Carrollton, Ga., U.S.A. 77 J3 33 35N 85 5W
Carrollton, Ill., U.S.A. 80 F9 39 18N 90 24W
Carrollton, Ky., U.S.A. 76 F3 38 41N 85 11W
Carrollton, Mo., U.S.A. 80 F8 39 22N 93 30W
Carrollton, Ohio, U.S.A. 78 F3 40 34N 81 5W
Carron →, U.K. 12 D4 57 53N 4 22W
Carron, L., U.K. 12 D3 57 22N 5 35W
Carrot →, Canada 73 C8 53 50N 101 17W
Carrot River, Canada 73 C8 53 17N 103 35W
Carruthers, Canada 73 C7 52 52N 109 16W
Carson, Calif., U.S.A. 85 M8 33 48N 118 17W
Carson, N. Dak., U.S.A. 80 B4 46 25N 101 34W
Carson →, U.S.A. 84 F8 39 45N 118 40W
Carson City, U.S.A. 84 F7 39 10N 119 46W
Carson Sink, U.S.A. 82 G4 39 50N 118 25W
Cartagena, Colombia 92 A3 10 25N 75 33W
Cartagena, Spain 19 D5 37 38N 0 59W
Cartago, Colombia 92 C3 4 45N 75 55W
Cartago, Costa Rica 88 E3 9 50N 83 55W
Cartersville, U.S.A. 77 H3 34 10N 84 48W
Carterton, N.Z. 59 J5 41 2S 175 31 E
Carthage, Tunisia 51 A8 36 50N 10 21 E
Carthage, Ill., U.S.A. 80 E9 40 25N 91 8W
Carthage, Mo., U.S.A. 81 G7 37 11N 94 19W
Carthage, N.Y., U.S.A. 76 D8 43 59N 75 37W
Carthage, Tex., U.S.A. 81 J7 32 9N 94 20W
Cartier I., Australia 60 B3 12 31S 123 29 E
Cartwright, Canada 71 B8 53 41N 56 58W
Caruaru, Brazil 93 E11 8 15S 35 55W
Carúpano, Venezuela 92 A6 10 39N 63 15W
Caruthersville, U.S.A. 81 G10 36 11N 89 39W
Carvoeiro, Brazil 92 D6 1 30S 61 59W
Carvoeiro, C., Portugal 19 C1 39 21N 9 24W
Cary, U.S.A. 77 H6 35 47N 78 46W
Casa Grande, U.S.A. 83 K8 32 53N 111 45W
Casablanca, Chile 94 C1 33 20S 71 25W
Casablanca, Morocco 50 B4 33 36N 7 36W
Cascade, Idaho, U.S.A. 82 D5 44 31N 116 2W
Cascade, Mont., U.S.A. 82 C8 47 16N 111 42W
Cascade Locks, U.S.A. 84 E5 45 40N 121 54W
Cascade Ra., U.S.A. 84 D5 47 0N 121 30W
Cascade Reservoir, U.S.A. 82 D5 44 32N 116 3W
Cascais, Portugal 19 C1 38 41N 9 25W
Cascavel, Brazil 95 A5 24 57S 53 28W
Cáscina, Italy 20 C4 43 41N 10 33 E
Casco B., U.S.A. 77 D10 43 45N 70 0W
Caserta, Italy 20 D6 41 4N 14 20 E
Cashel, Ireland 13 D4 52 30N 7 53W
Casiguran, Phil. 37 A6 16 22N 122 7 E
Casilda, Argentina 94 C3 33 10S 61 10W
Casino, Australia 63 D5 28 52S 153 3 E
Casiquiare →, Venezuela 92 C5 2 1N 67 7W
Casma, Peru 92 E3 9 30S 78 20W
Casmalia, U.S.A. 85 L6 34 50N 120 32W
Caspe, Spain 19 B5 41 14N 0 1W
Casper, U.S.A. 82 E10 42 51N 106 19W
Caspian Depression, Eurasia 25 E8 47 0N 48 0 E
Caspian Sea, Eurasia 25 F9 43 0N 50 0 E
Cass Lake, U.S.A. 80 B7 47 23N 94 37W
Cassadaga, U.S.A. 78 D5 42 20N 79 19W
Casselman, Canada 79 A9 45 19N 75 5W
Casselton, U.S.A. 80 B6 46 54N 97 13W
Cassiar, Canada 72 B3 59 16N 129 40W
Cassiar Mts., Canada 72 B2 59 30N 130 30W
Cassino, Italy 20 D5 41 30N 13 49 E
Cassville, U.S.A. 81 G8 36 41N 93 52W
Castaic, U.S.A. 85 L8 34 30N 118 38W
Castalia, U.S.A. 78 E2 41 24N 82 49W
Castanhal, Brazil 93 D9 1 18S 47 55W
Castellammare di Stábia, Italy 20 D6 40 42N 14 29 E
Castelli, Argentina 94 D4 36 7S 57 47W
Castelló de la Plana, Spain 19 C5 39 58N 0 3W
Castelo, Brazil 95 A7 20 33S 41 14W
Castelo Branco, Portugal 19 C2 39 50N 7 31W
Castelsarrasin, France 18 E4 44 2N 1 7 E
Castelvetrano, Italy 20 F5 37 41N 12 47 E
Casterton, Australia 63 F3 37 30S 141 30 E
Castile, U.S.A. 78 D6 42 38N 78 3W
Castilla-La Mancha □, Spain 19 C4 39 30N 3 30W
Castilla y Leon □, Spain 19 B3 42 0N 5 0W
Castillos, Uruguay 95 C5 34 12S 53 52W
Castle Dale, U.S.A. 82 G8 39 13N 111 1W
Castle Douglas, U.K. 12 G5 54 56N 3 56W
Castle Rock, Colo., U.S.A. 80 F2 39 22N 104 51W
Castle Rock, Wash., U.S.A. 84 D4 46 17N 122 54W
Castlebar, Ireland 13 C2 53 52N 9 18W
Castleblaney, Ireland 13 B5 54 7N 6 44W
Castlederg, U.K. 13 B4 54 42N 7 35W
Castleford, U.K. 10 D6 53 43N 1 21W
Castlegar, Canada 72 D5 49 20N 117 40W
Castlemaine, Australia 63 F3 37 2S 144 12 E
Castlepollard, Ireland 13 C4 53 41N 7 19W
Castlerea, Ireland 13 C3 53 46N 8 29W
Castlereagh →, Australia 63 E4 30 12S 147 32 E
Castlereagh B., Australia 62 A2 12 10S 135 10 E
Castleton, U.S.A. 79 C11 43 37N 73 11W
Castletown, U.K. 10 C3 54 5N 4 38W
Castletown Bearhaven, Ireland 13 E2 51 39N 9 55W
Castor, Canada 72 C6 52 15N 111 50W
Castor →, Canada 70 B4 53 24N 78 58W
Castorland, U.S.A. 79 C9 43 53N 75 31W
Castres, France 18 E5 43 37N 2 13 E
Castricum, Neths. 15 B4 52 33N 4 40 E
Castries, St. Lucia 89 D7 14 2N 60 58W
Castro, Brazil 95 A6 24 45S 50 0W
Castro, Chile 96 E2 42 30S 73 50W
Castro Alves, Brazil 93 F11 12 46S 39 33W
Castroville, U.S.A. 84 J5 36 46N 121 45W
Castuera, Spain 19 C3 38 43N 5 37W
Cat Ba, Dao, Vietnam 38 B6 20 50N 107 0 E
Cat I., Bahamas 89 B4 24 30N 75 30W
Cat L., Canada 70 B1 51 40N 91 50W
Cat Lake, Canada 70 B1 51 40N 91 50W
Catacamas, Honduras 88 D2 14 54N 85 56W
Cataguases, Brazil 95 A7 21 23S 42 39W
Catalão, Brazil 93 G9 18 10S 47 57W
Çatalca, Turkey 21 D13 41 8N 28 27 E
Catalina, Canada 71 C9 48 31N 53 4W
Catalina, Chile 94 B2 25 13S 69 43W
Catalina, U.S.A. 83 K8 32 30N 110 50W
Catalonia = Cataluña □, Spain 19 B6 41 40N 1 15 E
Cataluña □, Spain 19 B6 41 40N 1 15 E
Catamarca, Argentina 94 B2 28 30S 65 50W
Catamarca □, Argentina 94 B2 27 0S 65 50W
Catanduanes, Phil. 37 B6 13 50N 124 20 E
Catanduva, Brazil 95 A6 21 5S 48 58W
Catánia, Italy 20 F6 37 30N 15 6 E
Catanzaro, Italy 20 E7 38 54N 16 35 E
Catarman, Phil. 37 B6 12 28N 124 35 E
Cateel, Phil. 37 C7 7 47N 126 24 E
Caterham, U.K. 11 F7 51 15N 0 4W
Cathcart, S. Africa 56 E4 32 18S 27 10 E
Cathlamet, U.S.A. 84 D3 46 12N 123 23W
Catlettsburg, U.S.A. 76 F4 38 25N 82 36W
Catoche, C., Mexico 87 C7 21 40N 87 8W
Catriló, Argentina 94 D3 36 26S 63 24W
Catrimani, Brazil 92 C6 0 27N 61 41W
Catrimani →, Brazil 92 C6 0 28N 61 44W
Catskill, U.S.A. 79 D11 42 14N 73 52W
Catskill Mts., U.S.A. 79 D10 42 10N 74 25W
Catt, Mt., Australia 62 A1 13 49S 134 23 E
Cattaraugus, U.S.A. 78 D6 42 22N 78 52W
Catuala, Angola 56 B2 16 25S 19 2 E
Catur, Mozam. 55 E4 13 45S 35 30 E
Catwick Is., Vietnam 39 H7 10 0N 109 0 E
Cauca →, Colombia 92 B4 8 54N 74 28W
Caucaia, Brazil 93 D11 3 40S 38 35W
Caucasus Mountains, Eurasia 25 F7 42 50N 44 0 E
Caungula, Angola 52 F3 8 26S 18 38 E
Cauquenes, Chile 94 D1 36 0S 72 22W
Caura →, Venezuela 92 B6 7 38N 64 53W
Cauresi →, Mozam. 55 F3 17 8S 33 0 E
Causapscal, Canada 71 C6 48 19N 67 12W
Cauvery →, India 40 P11 11 9N 78 52 E
Caux, Pays de, France 18 B4 49 38N 0 35 E
Cavalier, U.S.A. 80 A6 48 48N 97 37W
Cavalleria, C. de, Spain 22 A11 40 5N 4 5 E
Cavan, Ireland 13 B4 54 0N 7 22W
Cavan □, Ireland 13 C4 54 1N 7 16W
Cave Creek, U.S.A. 83 K7 33 50N 111 57W
Cavenagh Ra., Australia 61 E4 26 12S 127 55 E
Cavendish, Australia 63 F3 37 31S 142 2 E
Caviana, I., Brazil 93 C8 0 10N 50 10W
Cavite, Phil. 37 B6 14 29N 120 55 E
Cawndilla L., Australia 63 E3 32 30S 142 15 E
Cawnpore = Kanpur, India 43 F9 26 28N 80 20 E
Caxias, Brazil 93 D10 4 55S 43 20W
Caxias do Sul, Brazil 95 B5 29 10S 51 10W
Cay Sal Bank, Bahamas 88 B4 23 45N 80 0W
Cayambe, Ecuador 92 C3 0 3N 78 8W
Cayenne, Fr. Guiana 93 B8 5 5N 52 18W
Cayman Brac, Cayman Is. 88 C4 19 43N 79 49W
Cayman Is. ■, W. Indies 88 C3 19 40N 80 30W
Cayo Romano, Cuba 88 B4 22 0N 78 0W
Cayuga, Canada 78 D5 42 59N 79 50W
Cayuga, U.S.A. 79 D8 42 54N 76 44W
Cayuga L., U.S.A. 79 D8 42 41N 76 41W
Cazenovia, U.S.A. 79 D9 42 56N 75 51W
Cazombo, Angola 53 G4 11 54S 22 56 E
Ceanannus Mor, Ireland 13 C5 53 44N 6 53W
Ceará = Fortaleza, Brazil 93 D11 3 45S 38 35W
Ceará □, Brazil 93 E11 5 0S 40 0W
Ceará Mirim, Brazil 93 E11 5 38S 35 25W
Cebaco, I. de, Panama 88 E3 7 33N 81 9W
Cebollar, Argentina 94 B2 29 10S 66 35W
Cebu, Phil. 37 B6 10 18N 123 54 E
Cecil Plains, Australia 63 D5 27 30S 151 11 E
Cedar →, U.S.A. 80 E9 41 17N 91 21W
Cedar City, U.S.A. 83 H7 37 41N 113 4W
Cedar Creek Reservoir, U.S.A. 81 J6 32 11N 96 4W
Cedar Falls, Iowa, U.S.A. 80 D8 42 32N 92 27W
Cedar Falls, Wash., U.S.A. 84 C5 47 25N 121 45W
Cedar L., Canada 73 C9 53 10N 100 0W
Cedar Rapids, U.S.A. 80 E9 41 59N 91 40W
Cedartown, U.S.A. 77 H3 34 1N 85 15W
Cedarvale, Canada 72 B3 55 1N 128 22W
Cedarville, S. Africa 57 E4 30 23S 29 3 E
Cedral, Mexico 86 C4 23 50N 100 42W
Cedro, Brazil 93 E11 6 34S 39 3W
Cedros, I. de, Mexico 86 B1 28 10N 115 20W
Ceduna, Australia 63 E1 32 7S 133 46 E
Cefalù, Italy 20 E6 38 2N 14 1 E
Cegléd, Hungary 17 E10 47 11N 19 47 E
Celaya, Mexico 86 C4 20 31N 100 37W
Celebes = Sulawesi □, Indonesia 37 E6 2 0S 120 0 E
Celebes Sea, Indonesia 37 D6 3 0N 123 0 E
Celina, U.S.A. 76 E3 40 33N 84 35W
Celje, Slovenia 16 E8 46 16N 15 18 E
Celle, Germany 16 B6 52 37N 10 4 E
Cenderwasih, Teluk, Indonesia 37 E9 3 0S 135 20 E
Center, N. Dak., U.S.A. 80 B4 47 7N 101 18W
Center, Tex., U.S.A. 81 K7 31 48N 94 11W
Centerburg, U.S.A. 78 F2 40 18N 82 42W
Centerville, Calif., U.S.A. 84 J7 36 44N 119 30W
Centerville, Iowa, U.S.A. 80 E8 40 44N 92 52W
Centerville, Pa., U.S.A. 78 F5 40 3N 79 59W
Centerville, Tenn., U.S.A. 77 H2 35 47N 87 28W
Centerville, Tex., U.S.A. 81 K7 31 16N 95 59W
Central □, Kenya 54 C4 0 30S 37 30 E
Central □, Malawi 55 E3 13 30S 33 30 E
Central □, Zambia 55 E2 14 25S 28 50 E
Central, Cordillera, Colombia 92 C4 5 0N 75 0W
Central, Cordillera, Costa Rica 88 D3 10 10N 84 5W
Central, Cordillera, Dom. Rep. 89 C5 19 15N 71 0W
Central African Rep. ■, Africa 52 C4 7 0N 20 0 E
Central America, America 66 H11 12 0N 85 0W
Central Butte, Canada 73 C7 50 48N 106 31W
Central City, Colo., U.S.A. 82 G11 39 48N 105 31W
Central City, Ky., U.S.A. 76 G2 37 18N 87 7W
Central City, Nebr., U.S.A. 80 E6 41 7N 98 0W
Central I., Kenya 54 B4 3 30N 36 0 E
Central Makran Range, Pakistan 40 F4 26 30N 64 15 E
Central Patricia, Canada 70 B1 51 30N 90 9W
Central Point, U.S.A. 82 E2 42 23N 122 55W
Central Russian Uplands, Europe 6 E13 54 0N 36 0 E
Central Siberian Plateau, Russia 28 C14 65 0N 105 0 E
Central Square, U.S.A. 79 C8 43 17N 76 9W
Centralia, Ill., U.S.A. 80 F10 38 32N 89 8W
Centralia, Mo., U.S.A. 80 F8 39 13N 92 8W
Centralia, Wash., U.S.A. 84 D4 46 43N 122 58W
Cephalonia = Kefallinía, Greece 21 E9 38 20N 20 30 E
Cepu, Indonesia 37 G14 7 9S 111 35 E
Ceram = Seram, Indonesia 37 E7 3 10S 129 0 E
Ceram Sea = Seram Sea, Indonesia 37 E7 2 30S 128 30 E
Ceredigion □, U.K. 11 E3 52 16N 4 15W
Ceres, Argentina 94 B3 29 55S 61 55W
Ceres, S. Africa 56 E2 33 21S 19 18 E
Ceres, U.S.A. 84 H6 37 35N 120 57W
Cerignola, Italy 20 D6 41 17N 15 53 E
Cerigo = Kíthira, Greece 21 F10 36 8N 23 0 E
Çerkezköy, Turkey 21 D12 41 17N 28 0 E
Cerralvo, I., Mexico 86 C3 24 20N 109 45W
Cerritos, Mexico 86 C4 22 27N 100 20W
Cerro Chato, Uruguay 95 C4 33 6S 55 8W
Cervantes, Australia 61 F2 30 31S 115 3 E
Cervera, Spain 19 B6 41 40N 1 16 E
Cesena, Italy 20 B5 44 8N 12 15 E
Cēsis, Latvia 9 H21 57 18N 25 15 E
České Budějovice, Czech Rep. 16 D8 48 55N 14 25 E
Českomoravská Vrchovina, Czech Rep. 16 D8 49 30N 15 40 E
Çeşme, Turkey 21 E12 38 20N 26 23 E
Cessnock, Australia 63 E5 32 50S 151 21 E
Cetinje, Montenegro, Yug. 21 C8 42 23N 18 59 E
Cetraro, Italy 20 E6 39 31N 15 55 E
Ceuta, N. Afr. 19 E3 35 52N 5 18W
Cévennes, France 18 D5 44 10N 3 50 E
Ceyhan, Turkey 44 B2 37 4N 35 47 E
Ceylon = Sri Lanka ■, Asia 40 R12 7 30N 80 50 E
Cha-am, Thailand 38 F2 12 48N 99 58 E
Cha Pa, Vietnam 38 A4 22 20N 103 47 E
Chacabuco, Argentina 94 C3 34 40S 60 27W
Chachapoyas, Peru 92 E3 6 15S 77 50W
Chachoengsao, Thailand 38 F3 13 42N 101 5 E
Chachran, Pakistan 40 E7 28 55N 70 30 E
Chachro, Pakistan 42 G4 25 5N 70 15 E
Chaco □, Argentina 94 B3 26 30S 61 0W
Chaco □, Paraguay 94 B4 26 0S 60 0W
Chaco →, U.S.A. 83 H9 36 46N 108 39W
Chaco Austral, S. Amer. 96 B4 27 0S 61 30W
Chaco Boreal, S. Amer. 92 H6 22 0S 60 0W
Chaco Central, S. Amer. 96 A4 24 0S 61 0W
Chacon, C., U.S.A. 72 C2 54 42N 132 0W
Chad ■, Africa 51 F8 15 0N 17 15 E
Chad, L. = Tchad, L., Chad 51 F8 13 30N 14 30 E
Chadan, Russia 27 D10 51 17N 91 35 E
Chadileuvú →, Argentina 94 D2 37 46S 66 0W
Chadiza, Zambia 55 E3 14 45S 32 27 E
Chadron, U.S.A. 80 D3 42 50N 103 0W
Chadyr-Lunga = Ciadâr-Lunga, Moldova 17 E15 46 3N 28 51 E
Chae Hom, Thailand 38 C2 18 43N 99 35 E
Chaem →, Thailand 38 C2 18 11N 98 38 E
Chaeryŏng, N. Korea 35 E13 38 24N 125 36 E
Chagai Hills, Afghan. 40 E3 29 30N 63 0 E
Chagda, Russia 27 D14 58 45N 130 38 E
Chagos Arch., Ind. Oc. 29 K11 6 0S 72 0 E
Chagrin Falls, U.S.A. 78 E3 41 26N 81 24W
Chāh Ākhvor, Iran 45 C8 32 41N 59 40 E
Chāh Bahār, Iran 45 E9 25 20N 60 40 E
Chāh-e Kavīr, Iran 45 C8 34 29N 56 52 E
Chahar Burjak, Afghan. 40 D3 30 15N 62 0 E
Chahār Mahāll va Bakhtīarī □, Iran 45 C6 32 0N 49 0 E
Chaibasa, India 41 H14 22 42N 85 49 E
Chainat, Thailand 38 E3 15 11N 100 8 E
Chaiya, Thailand 39 H2 9 23N 99 14 E
Chaj Doab, Pakistan 42 C5 32 15N 73 0 E
Chajari, Argentina 94 C4 30 42S 58 0W
Chak Amru, Pakistan 42 C6 32 22N 75 11 E
Chakar →, Pakistan 42 E3 29 29N 68 2 E
Chake Chake, Tanzania 54 D4 5 15S 39 45 E
Chakhānsūr, Afghan. 40 D3 31 10N 62 0 E
Chakonipau, L., Canada 71 A6 56 18N 68 30W
Chakradharpur, India 43 H11 22 45N 85 40 E
Chakrata, India 42 D7 30 42N 77 51 E
Chakwal, Pakistan 42 C5 32 56N 72 53 E
Chala, Peru 92 G4 15 48S 74 20W
Chalchihuites, Mexico 86 C4 23 29N 103 53W
Chalcis = Khalkís, Greece 21 E10 38 27N 23 42 E
Chaleur B., Canada 71 C6 47 55N 65 30W
Chalfant, U.S.A. 84 H8 37 32N 118 21W
Chalhuanca, Peru 92 F4 14 15S 73 15W
Chalisgaon, India 40 J9 20 30N 75 10 E
Chalk River, Canada 70 C4 46 1N 77 27W
Chalky Inlet, N.Z. 59 M1 46 3S 166 31 E
Challapata, Bolivia 92 G5 18 53S 66 50W
Challis, U.S.A. 82 D6 44 30N 114 14W
Chalmette, U.S.A. 81 L10 29 56N 89 58W
Chalon-sur-Saône, France 18 C6 46 48N 4 50 E
Châlons-en-Champagne, France 18 B6 48 58N 4 20 E
Chalyaphum, Thailand 38 E4 15 48N 102 2 E
Cham, Cu Lao, Vietnam 38 E7 15 57N 108 30 E
Chama, U.S.A. 83 H10 36 54N 106 35W
Chamaicó, Argentina 94 D3 35 3S 64 58W
Chaman, Pakistan 40 D5 30 58N 66 25 E
Chamba, India 42 C7 32 35N 76 10 E
Chamba, Tanzania 55 E4 11 37S 37 0 E
Chambal →, India 43 F8 26 29N 79 15 E
Chamberlain, U.S.A. 80 D5 43 49N 99 20W
Chamberlain →, Australia 60 C4 15 30S 127 54 E
Chamberlain L., U.S.A. 77 B11 46 14N 69 19W
Chambers, U.S.A. 83 J9 35 11N 109 26W
Chambersburg, U.S.A. 76 F7 39 56N 77 40W
Chambéry, France 18 D6 45 34N 5 55 E
Chambeshi →, Zambia 52 G6 11 53S 29 48 E
Chambly, Canada 79 A11 45 27N 73 17W
Chambord, Canada 71 C5 48 25N 72 6W
Chamchamal, Iraq 44 C5 35 32N 44 50 E
Chamela, Mexico 86 D3 19 32N 105 5W

Chamical, Argentina 94 C2 30 22S 66 27W
Chamkar Luong, Cambodia 39 G4 11 0N 103 45 E
Chamoli, India 43 D8 30 24N 79 21 E
Chamonix-Mont Blanc, France 18 D7 45 55N 6 51 E
Chamouchouane →, Canada 70 C5 48 37N 72 20W
Champa, India 43 H10 22 2N 82 43 E
Champagne, Canada 72 A1 60 49N 136 30W
Champagne, France 18 B6 48 40N 4 20 E
Champaign, U.S.A. 76 E1 40 7N 88 15W
Champassak, Laos 38 E5 14 53N 105 52 E
Champawat, India 43 E9 29 20N 80 6 E
Champdoré, L., Canada 71 A6 55 55N 65 49W
Champion, U.S.A. 78 E4 41 19N 80 51W
Champlain, U.S.A. 79 B11 44 59N 73 27W
Champlain, L., U.S.A. 79 B11 44 40N 73 20W
Champotón, Mexico 87 D6 19 20N 90 50W
Champua, India 43 H11 22 5N 85 40 E
Chana, Thailand 39 J3 6 55N 100 44 E
Chañaral, Chile 94 B1 26 23S 70 40W
Chanārān, Iran 45 B8 36 39N 59 6 E
Chanasma, India 42 H5 23 44N 72 5 E
Chanco, Chile 94 D1 35 44S 72 32W
Chand, India 43 J8 21 57N 79 7 E
Chandan, India 43 G12 24 38N 86 40 E
Chandan Chauki, India 43 E9 28 33N 80 47 E
Chandannagar, India 43 H13 22 52N 88 24 E
Chandausi, India 43 E8 28 27N 78 49 E
Chandeleur Is., U.S.A. 81 L10 29 55N 88 57W
Chandeleur Sd., U.S.A. 81 L10 29 55N 89 0W
Chandigarh, India 42 D7 30 43N 76 47 E
Chandil, India 43 H12 22 58N 86 3 E
Chandler, Australia 63 D1 27 0S 133 19 E
Chandler, Canada 71 C7 48 18N 64 46W
Chandler, Ariz., U.S.A. 83 K8 33 18N 111 50W
Chandler, Okla., U.S.A. 81 H6 35 42N 96 53W
Chandod, India 42 J5 21 59N 73 28 E
Chandpur, Bangla. 41 H17 23 8N 90 45 E
Chandrapur, India 40 K11 19 57N 79 25 E
Chānf, Iran 45 E9 26 38N 60 29 E
Chang, Pakistan 42 F3 26 59N 68 30 E
Chang, Ko, Thailand 39 G4 12 0N 102 23 E
Ch'ang Chiang = Chang Jiang →, China 33 C7 31 48N 121 10 E
Chang Jiang →, China 33 C7 31 48N 121 10 E
Changa, India 43 C7 33 53N 77 35 E
Changanacheri, India 40 Q10 9 25N 76 31 E
Changane →, Mozam. 57 C5 24 30S 33 30 E
Changbai, China 35 D15 41 25N 128 5 E
Changbai Shan, China 35 C15 42 20N 129 0 E
Changchiak'ou = Zhangjiakou, China 34 D8 40 48N 114 55 E
Ch'angchou = Changzhou, China 33 C6 31 47N 119 58 E
Changchun, China 35 C13 43 57N 125 17 E
Changchunling, China 35 B13 45 18N 125 27 E
Changde, China 33 D6 29 4N 111 35 E
Changdo-ri, N. Korea 35 E14 38 30N 127 40 E
Changhai = Shanghai, China 33 C7 31 15N 121 26 E
Changhua, Taiwan 33 D7 24 2N 120 30 E
Changhŭng, S. Korea 35 G14 34 41N 126 52 E
Changhŭngni, N. Korea 35 D15 40 24N 128 19 E
Changjiang, China 38 C7 19 20N 108 55 E
Changjin, N. Korea 35 D14 40 23N 127 15 E
Changjin-chŏsuji, N. Korea 35 D14 40 30N 127 15 E
Changli, China 35 E10 39 40N 119 13 E
Changling, China 35 B12 44 20N 123 58 E
Changlun, Malaysia 39 J3 6 25N 100 26 E
Changping, China 34 D9 40 14N 116 12 E
Changsha, China 33 D6 28 12N 113 0 E
Changwu, China 34 G4 35 10N 107 45 E
Changyi, China 35 F10 36 40N 119 30 E
Changyŏn, N. Korea 35 E13 38 15N 125 6 E
Changyuan, China 34 G8 35 15N 114 42 E
Changzhi, China 34 F7 36 10N 113 6 E
Changzhou, China 33 C6 31 47N 119 58 E
Chanhanga, Angola 56 B1 16 0S 14 8 E
Channapatna, India 40 N10 12 40N 77 15 E
Channel Is., U.K. 11 H5 49 19N 2 24W
Channel Is., U.S.A. 85 M7 33 40N 119 15W
Channel Islands National Park, U.S.A. 85 M8 33 30N 119 0W
Channel-Port aux Basques, Canada 71 C8 47 30N 59 9W
Channel Tunnel, Europe 11 F9 51 0N 1 30 E
Channing, U.S.A. 81 H3 35 41N 102 20W
Chantada, Spain 19 A2 42 36N 7 46W
Chanthaburi, Thailand 38 F4 12 38N 102 12 E
Chantrey Inlet, Canada 68 B10 67 48N 96 20W
Chanute, U.S.A. 81 G7 37 41N 95 27W
Chao Phraya →, Thailand 38 F3 13 32N 100 36 E
Chao Phraya Lowlands, Thailand 38 E3 15 30N 100 0 E
Chaocheng, China 34 F8 36 4N 115 37 E
Chaoyang, China 35 D11 41 35N 120 22 E
Chaozhou, China 33 D6 23 42N 116 32 E
Chapais, Canada 70 C5 49 47N 74 51W
Chapala, Mozam. 55 F4 15 50S 37 35 E
Chapala, L. de, Mexico 86 C4 20 10N 103 20W
Chapayev, Kazakstan 25 D9 50 25N 51 10 E
Chapayevsk, Russia 24 D8 53 0N 49 40 E
Chapecó, Brazil 95 B5 27 14S 52 41W
Chapel Hill, U.S.A. 77 H6 35 55N 79 4W
Chapleau, Canada 70 C3 47 50N 83 24W
Chaplin, Canada 73 C7 50 28N 106 40W
Chaplin L., Canada 73 C7 50 22N 106 36W
Chappell, U.S.A. 80 E3 41 6N 102 28W
Chapra = Chhapra, India 43 G11 25 48N 84 44 E
Chara, Russia 27 D12 56 54N 118 20 E
Charadai, Argentina 94 B4 27 35S 59 55W
Charagua, Bolivia 92 G6 19 45S 63 10W
Charambirá, Punta, Colombia 92 C3 4 16N 77 32W
Charaña, Bolivia 92 G5 17 30S 69 25W
Charanwala, India 42 F5 27 51N 72 10 E
Charata, Argentina 94 B3 27 13S 61 14W
Charcas, Mexico 86 C4 23 10N 101 20W
Chard, U.K. 11 G5 50 52N 2 58W
Chardon, U.S.A. 78 E3 41 35N 81 12W
Chardzhou = Chärjew, Turkmenistan 26 F7 39 6N 63 34 E
Charente →, France 18 D3 45 57N 1 5W
Chari →, Chad 51 F8 12 58N 14 31 E
Chārīkār, Afghan. 40 B6 35 0N 69 10 E
Chariton →, U.S.A. 80 F8 39 19N 92 58W
Chärjew, Turkmenistan 26 F7 39 6N 63 34 E
Charkhari, India 43 G8 25 24N 79 45 E
Charkhi Dadri, India 42 E7 28 37N 76 17 E
Charleroi, Belgium 15 D4 50 24N 4 27 E
Charleroi, U.S.A. 78 F5 40 9N 79 57W
Charles, C., U.S.A. 76 G8 37 7N 75 58W
Charles City, U.S.A. 80 D8 43 4N 92 41W
Charles L., Canada 73 B6 59 50N 110 33W
Charles Town, U.S.A. 76 F7 39 17N 77 52W
Charleston, Ill., U.S.A. 76 F1 39 30N 88 10W
Charleston, Miss., U.S.A. 81 H9 34 1N 90 4W
Charleston, Mo., U.S.A. 81 G10 36 55N 89 21W
Charleston, S.C., U.S.A. 77 J6 32 46N 79 56W
Charleston, W. Va., U.S.A. 76 F5 38 21N 81 38W
Charleston L., Canada 79 B9 44 32N 76 0W
Charleston Peak, U.S.A. 85 J11 36 16N 115 42W
Charlestown, Ireland 13 C3 53 58N 8 48W
Charlestown, S. Africa 57 D4 27 26S 29 53 E
Charlestown, Ind., U.S.A. 76 F3 38 27N 85 40W
Charlestown, N.H., U.S.A. 79 C12 43 14N 72 25W
Charleville = Rath Luirc, Ireland 13 D3 52 21N 8 40W
Charleville, Australia 63 D4 26 24S 146 15 E
Charleville-Mézières, France 18 B6 49 44N 4 40 E
Charlevoix, U.S.A. 76 C3 45 19N 85 16W
Charlotte, Mich., U.S.A. 76 D3 42 34N 84 50W
Charlotte, N.C., U.S.A. 77 H5 35 13N 80 51W
Charlotte, Vt., U.S.A. 79 B11 44 19N 73 14W
Charlotte Amalie, Virgin Is. 89 C7 18 21N 64 56W
Charlotte Harbor, U.S.A. 77 M4 26 50N 82 10W
Charlotte L., Canada 72 C3 52 12N 125 19W
Charlottesville, U.S.A. 76 F6 38 2N 78 30W
Charlottetown, Nfld., Canada 71 B8 52 46N 56 7W
Charlottetown, P.E.I., Canada 71 C7 46 14N 63 8W
Charlton, Australia 63 F3 36 16S 143 24 E
Charlton, U.S.A. 80 E8 40 59N 93 20W
Charlton I., Canada 70 B4 52 0N 79 20W
Charny, Canada 71 C5 46 43N 71 15W
Charolles, France 18 C6 46 27N 4 16 E
Charre, Mozam. 55 F4 17 13S 35 10 E
Charsadda, Pakistan 42 B4 34 7N 71 45 E
Charters Towers, Australia 62 C4 20 5S 146 13 E
Chartres, France 18 B4 48 29N 1 30 E
Chascomús, Argentina 94 D4 35 30S 58 0W
Chasefu, Zambia 55 E3 11 55S 33 8 E
Chashma Barrage, Pakistan 42 C4 32 27N 71 20 E
Chāt, Iran 45 B7 37 59N 55 16 E
Châteaubriant, France 18 C3 47 43N 1 23W
Chateaugay, U.S.A. 79 B10 44 56N 74 5W
Châteauguay, L., Canada 71 A5 56 26N 70 3W
Châteaulin, France 18 B1 48 11N 4 8W
Châteauroux, France 18 C4 46 50N 1 40 E
Châtellerault, France 18 C4 46 50N 0 30 E
Chatham = Miramichi, Canada 71 C6 47 2N 65 28W
Chatham, Canada 78 D2 42 24N 82 11W
Chatham, U.K. 11 F8 51 22N 0 32 E
Chatham, U.S.A. 79 D11 42 21N 73 36W
Chatham Is., Pac. Oc. 64 M10 44 0S 176 40W
Chatmohar, Bangla. 43 G13 24 15N 89 15 E
Chatra, India 43 G11 24 12N 84 56 E
Chatrapur, India 41 K14 19 22N 85 2 E
Chats, L. des, Canada 79 A8 45 30N 76 20W
Chatsu, India 42 F6 26 36N 75 57 E
Chatsworth, Canada 78 B4 44 27N 80 54W
Chatsworth, Zimbabwe 55 F3 19 38S 31 13 E
Chattahoochee, U.S.A. 77 K3 30 42N 84 51W
Chattahoochee →, U.S.A. 77 K3 30 54N 84 57W
Chattanooga, U.S.A. 77 H3 35 3N 85 19W
Chatteris, U.K. 11 E8 52 28N 0 2 E
Chaturat, Thailand 38 E3 15 40N 101 51 E
Chau Doc, Vietnam 39 G5 10 42N 105 7 E
Chauk, Burma 41 J19 20 53N 94 49 E
Chaukan La, Burma 41 F20 27 0N 97 15 E
Chaumont, France 18 B6 48 7N 5 8 E
Chaumont, U.S.A. 79 B8 44 4N 76 8W
Chautauqua L., U.S.A. 78 D5 42 10N 79 24W
Chauvin, Canada 73 C6 52 45N 110 10W
Chaves, Brazil 93 D9 0 15S 49 55W
Chaves, Portugal 19 B2 41 45N 7 32W
Chawang, Thailand 39 H2 8 25N 99 30 E
Chaykovskiy, Russia 24 C9 56 47N 54 9 E
Chazy, U.S.A. 79 B11 44 53N 73 26W
Cheb, Czech Rep. 16 C7 50 9N 12 28 E
Cheboksary, Russia 24 C8 56 8N 47 12 E
Cheboygan, U.S.A. 76 C3 45 39N 84 29W
Chech, Erg, Africa 50 D5 25 0N 2 15W
Chechenia □, Russia 25 F8 43 30N 45 29 E
Checheno-Ingush Republic = Chechenia □, Russia 25 F8 43 30N 45 29 E
Chechnya = Chechenia □, Russia 25 F8 43 30N 45 29 E
Chech'ŏn, S. Korea 35 F15 37 8N 128 12 E
Checotah, U.S.A. 81 H7 35 28N 95 31W
Chedabucto B., Canada 71 C7 45 25N 61 8W
Cheduba I., Burma 41 K18 18 45N 93 40 E
Cheepie, Australia 63 D4 26 33S 145 1 E
Chegdomyn, Russia 27 D14 51 7N 133 1 E
Chegga, Mauritania 50 C4 25 27N 5 40W
Chegutu, Zimbabwe 55 F3 18 10S 30 14 E
Chehalis, U.S.A. 84 D4 46 40N 122 58W
Chehalis →, U.S.A. 84 D3 46 57N 123 50W
Cheju do, S. Korea 35 H14 33 29N 126 34 E
Chekiang = Zhejiang □, China 33 D7 29 0N 120 0 E
Chela, Sa. da, Angola 56 B1 16 20S 13 20 E
Chelan, U.S.A. 82 C4 47 51N 120 1W
Chelan, L., U.S.A. 82 B3 48 11N 120 30W
Cheleken, Turkmenistan 25 G9 39 34N 53 16 E
Cheleken Yarymadasy, Turkmenistan 45 B7 39 30N 53 15 E
Chelforó, Argentina 96 D3 39 0S 66 33W
Chelkar = Shalqar, Kazakstan 26 E6 47 48N 59 39 E
Chelkar Tengiz, Solonchak, Kazakstan 26 E7 48 5N 63 7 E
Chełm, Poland 17 C12 51 8N 23 30 E
Chełmno, Poland 17 B10 53 20N 18 30 E
Chelmsford, U.K. 11 F8 51 44N 0 29 E
Chelsea, U.S.A. 79 C12 43 59N 72 27W
Cheltenham, U.K. 11 F5 51 54N 2 4W
Chelyabinsk, Russia 26 D7 55 10N 61 24 E
Chelyuskin, C., Russia 28 B14 77 30N 103 0 E
Chemainus, Canada 84 B3 48 55N 123 42W
Chemba, Mozam. 53 H6 17 9S 34 53 E
Chemnitz, Germany 16 C7 50 51N 12 54 E
Chemult, U.S.A. 82 E3 43 14N 121 47W
Chen, Gora, Russia 27 C15 65 16N 141 50 E
Chenab →, Pakistan 42 D4 30 23N 71 2 E
Chenango Forks, U.S.A. 79 D9 42 15N 75 51W
Cheney, U.S.A. 82 C5 47 30N 117 35W
Cheng Xian, China 34 H3 33 43N 105 42 E
Chengcheng, China 34 G5 35 8N 109 56 E
Chengchou = Zhengzhou, China 34 G7 34 45N 113 34 E
Chengde, China 35 D9 40 59N 117 58 E
Chengdu, China 32 C5 30 38N 104 2 E
Chenggu, China 34 H4 33 10N 107 21 E
Chengjiang, China 32 D5 24 39N 103 0 E
Ch'engmai, China 38 C7 19 50N 109 58 E
Ch'engtu = Chengdu, China 32 C5 30 38N 104 2 E
Chengwu, China 34 G8 34 58N 115 50 E
Chengyang, China 35 F11 36 18N 120 21 E
Chenjiagang, China 35 G10 34 23N 119 47 E
Chenkán, Mexico 87 D6 19 8N 90 58W
Chennai, India 40 N12 13 8N 80 19 E
Cheo Reo, Vietnam 36 B3 13 25N 108 28 E
Cheom Ksan, Cambodia 38 E5 14 13N 104 56 E
Chepén, Peru 92 E3 7 15S 79 23W
Chepes, Argentina 94 C2 31 20S 66 35W
Chepo, Panama 88 E4 9 10N 79 6W
Chepstow, U.K. 11 F5 51 38N 2 41W
Cheptulil, Mt., Kenya 54 B4 1 25N 35 35 E
Chequamegon B., U.S.A. 80 B9 46 40N 90 30W
Cher →, France 18 C4 47 21N 0 29 E
Cheraw, U.S.A. 77 H6 34 42N 79 53W
Cherbourg, France 18 B3 49 39N 1 40W
Cherdyn, Russia 24 B10 60 24N 56 29 E
Cheremkhovo, Russia 27 D11 53 8N 103 1 E
Cherepanovo, Russia 26 D9 54 15N 83 30 E
Cherepovets, Russia 24 C6 59 5N 37 55 E
Chergui, Chott ech, Algeria 50 B6 34 21N 0 25 E
Cherikov = Cherykaw, Belarus 17 B16 53 32N 31 20 E
Cherkasy, Ukraine 25 E5 49 27N 32 4 E
Cherkessk, Russia 25 F7 44 15N 42 5 E
Cherlak, Russia 26 D8 54 15N 74 55 E
Chernaya, Russia 27 B9 70 30N 89 10 E
Chernigov = Chernihiv, Ukraine 24 D5 51 28N 31 20 E
Chernihiv, Ukraine 24 D5 51 28N 31 20 E
Chernivtsi, Ukraine 17 D13 48 15N 25 52 E
Chernobyl = Chornobyl, Ukraine 17 C16 51 20N 30 15 E
Chernogorsk, Russia 27 D10 53 49N 91 18 E
Chernovtsy = Chernivtsi, Ukraine 17 D13 48 15N 25 52 E
Chernyakhovsk, Russia 9 J19 54 36N 21 48 E
Chernysheyskiy, Russia 27 C12 63 0N 112 30 E
Cherokee, Iowa, U.S.A. 80 D7 42 45N 95 33W
Cherokee, Okla., U.S.A. 81 G5 36 45N 98 21W
Cherokee Village, U.S.A. 81 G9 36 17N 91 30W
Cherokees, Grand Lake O' The, U.S.A. 81 G7 36 28N 95 2W
Cherrapunji, India 41 G17 25 17N 91 47 E
Cherry Valley, Calif., U.S.A. 85 M10 33 59N 116 57W
Cherry Valley, N.Y., U.S.A. 79 D10 42 48N 74 45W
Cherskiy, Russia 27 C17 68 45N 161 18 E
Cherskogo Khrebet, Russia 27 C15 65 0N 143 0 E
Cherven, Belarus 17 B15 53 45N 28 28 E
Chervonohrad, Ukraine 17 C13 50 25N 24 10 E
Cherwell →, U.K. 11 F6 51 44N 1 14W
Cherykaw, Belarus 17 B16 53 32N 31 20 E
Chesapeake, U.S.A. 76 G7 36 50N 76 17W
Chesapeake B., U.S.A. 76 G7 38 0N 76 10W
Cheshire □, U.K. 10 D5 53 14N 2 30W
Cheshskaya Guba, Russia 24 A8 67 20N 47 0 E
Cheshunt, U.K. 11 F7 51 43N 0 1W
Chesil Beach, U.K. 11 G5 50 37N 2 33W
Chesley, Canada 78 B3 44 17N 81 5W
Chester, U.K. 10 D5 53 12N 2 53W
Chester, Calif., U.S.A. 82 F3 40 19N 121 14W
Chester, Ill., U.S.A. 81 G10 37 55N 89 49W
Chester, Mont., U.S.A. 82 B8 48 31N 110 58W
Chester, Pa., U.S.A. 76 F8 39 51N 75 22W
Chester, S.C., U.S.A. 77 H5 34 43N 81 12W
Chester, Vt., U.S.A. 79 C12 43 16N 72 36W
Chester, W. Va., U.S.A. 78 F4 40 37N 80 34W
Chester-le-Street, U.K. 10 C6 54 51N 1 34W
Chesterfield, U.K. 10 D6 53 15N 1 25W
Chesterfield, Is., N. Cal. 64 J7 19 52S 158 15 E
Chesterfield Inlet, Canada 68 B10 63 30N 90 45W
Chesterton Ra., Australia 63 D4 25 30S 147 27 E
Chestertown, U.S.A. 79 C11 43 40N 73 48W
Chesterville, Canada 79 A9 45 6N 75 14W
Chestnut Ridge, U.S.A. 78 F5 40 20N 79 10W
Chesuncook L., U.S.A. 77 C11 46 0N 69 21W
Chéticamp, Canada 71 C7 46 37N 60 59W
Chetumal, Mexico 87 D7 18 30N 88 20W
Chetumal, B. de, Mexico 87 D7 18 40N 88 10W
Chetwynd, Canada 72 B4 55 45N 121 36W
Cheviot, The, U.K. 10 B5 55 29N 2 9W
Cheviot Hills, U.K. 10 B5 55 20N 2 30W
Cheviot Ra., Australia 62 D3 25 20S 143 45 E
Chew Bahir, Ethiopia 46 G2 4 40N 36 50 E
Chewelah, U.S.A. 82 B5 48 17N 117 43W
Cheyenne, Okla., U.S.A. 81 H5 35 37N 99 40W
Cheyenne, Wyo., U.S.A. 80 E2 41 8N 104 49W
Cheyenne →, U.S.A. 80 C4 44 41N 101 18W
Cheyenne Wells, U.S.A. 80 F3 38 49N 102 21W
Cheyne B., Australia 61 F2 34 35S 118 50 E
Chhabra, India 42 G7 24 40N 76 54 E
Chhaktala, India 42 H6 22 6N 74 11 E
Chhapra, India 43 G11 25 48N 84 44 E
Chhata, India 42 F7 27 42N 77 30 E
Chhatarpur, Bihar, India 43 G11 24 23N 84 11 E
Chhatarpur, Mad. P., India 43 G8 24 55N 79 35 E
Chhep, Cambodia 38 F5 13 45N 105 24 E
Chhindwara, Mad. P., India 43 H8 23 3N 79 29 E
Chhindwara, Mad. P., India 43 H8 22 2N 78 59 E
Chhlong, Cambodia 39 F5 12 15N 105 58 E
Chhota Tawa →, India 42 H7 22 14N 76 36 E
Chhoti Kali Sindh →, India 42 G6 24 2N 75 31 E
Chhuikhadan, India 43 J9 21 32N 80 59 E
Chhuk, Cambodia 39 G5 10 46N 104 28 E
Chi →, Thailand 38 E5 15 11N 104 43 E
Chiai, Taiwan 33 D7 23 29N 120 25 E
Chiamboni, Somali Rep. 52 E8 1 39S 41 35 E
Chiamussu = Jiamusi, China 33 B8 46 40N 130 26 E
Chiang Dao, Thailand 38 C2 19 22N 98 58 E
Chiang Kham, Thailand 38 C3 19 32N 100 18 E
Chiang Khan, Thailand 38 D3 17 52N 101 36 E
Chiang Mai, Thailand 38 C2 18 47N 98 59 E
Chiang Rai, Thailand 38 C2 19 52N 99 50 E
Chiapa →, Mexico 87 D6 16 42N 93 0W
Chiapa de Corzo, Mexico 87 D6 16 42N 93 0W
Chiapas □, Mexico 87 D6 17 0N 92 45W
Chiautla, Mexico 87 D5 18 18N 98 34W
Chiávari, Italy 18 D8 44 19N 9 19 E
Chiavenna, Italy 18 C8 46 19N 9 24 E
Chiba, Japan 31 G10 35 30N 140 7 E
Chiba □, Japan 31 G10 35 30N 140 20 E
Chibabava, Mozam. 57 C5 20 17S 33 35 E
Chibemba, Cunene, Angola 53 H2 15 48S 14 8 E
Chibemba, Huila, Angola 56 B2 16 20S 15 20 E
Chibia, Angola 53 H2 15 10S 13 42 E
Chibougamau, Canada 70 C5 49 56N 74 24W
Chibougamau, L., Canada 70 C5 49 50N 74 20W
Chic-Chocs, Mts., Canada 71 C6 48 55N 66 0W
Chicacole = Srikakulam, India 41 K13 18 14N 83 58 E
Chicago, U.S.A. 76 E2 41 53N 87 38W
Chicago Heights, U.S.A. 76 E2 41 30N 87 38W
Chichagof I., U.S.A. 68 C6 57 30N 135 30W
Chichén-Itzá, Mexico 87 C7 20 40N 88 36W
Chicheng, China 34 D8 40 55N 115 55 E
Chichester, U.K. 11 G7 50 50N 0 47W
Chichester Ra., Australia 60 D2 22 12S 119 15 E
Chichibu, Japan 31 F9 36 5N 139 10 E
Ch'ich'ihaerh = Qiqihar, China 27 E13 47 26N 124 0 E
Chicholi, India 42 H8 22 1N 77 40 E
Chickasha, U.S.A. 81 H6 35 3N 97 58W
Chiclana de la Frontera, Spain 19 D2 36 26N 6 9W
Chiclayo, Peru 92 E3 6 42S 79 50W
Chico, U.S.A. 84 F5 39 44N 121 50W
Chico →, Chubut, Argentina 96 E3 44 0S 67 0W
Chico →, Santa Cruz, Argentina 96 G3 50 0S 68 30W
Chicomo, Mozam. 57 C5 24 31S 34 6 E
Chicontepec, Mexico 87 C5 20 58N 98 10W
Chicopee, U.S.A. 79 D12 42 9N 72 37W
Chicoutimi, Canada 71 C5 48 28N 71 5W
Chicualacuala, Mozam. 57 C5 22 6S 31 42 E
Chidambaram, India 40 P11 11 20N 79 45 E
Chidenguele, Mozam. 57 C5 24 55S 34 11 E
Chidley, C., Canada 69 B13 60 23N 64 26W
Chiede, Angola 56 B2 17 15S 16 22 E
Chiefs Pt., Canada 78 B3 44 41N 81 18W
Chiem Hoa, Vietnam 38 A5 22 12N 105 17 E
Chiemsee, Germany 16 E7 47 53N 12 28 E
Chiengi, Zambia 55 D2 8 45S 29 10 E
Chiengmai = Chiang Mai, Thailand 38 C2 18 47N 98 59 E
Chiese →, Italy 18 D9 45 8N 10 25 E
Chieti, Italy 20 C6 42 21N 14 10 E
Chifeng, China 35 C10 42 18N 118 58 E
Chignecto B., Canada 71 C7 45 30N 64 40W
Chiguana, Bolivia 94 A2 21 0S 67 58W
Chigwell, U.K. 11 F8 51 37N 0 5 E
Chiha-ri, N. Korea 35 E14 38 40N 126 30 E
Chihli, G. of = Bo Hai, China 35 E10 39 0N 119 0 E
Chihuahua, Mexico 86 B3 28 40N 106 3W
Chihuahua □, Mexico 86 B3 28 40N 106 3W
Chiili, Kazakstan 26 E7 44 20N 66 15 E
Chik Bollapur, India 40 N10 13 25N 77 45 E
Chikmagalur, India 40 N9 13 15N 75 45 E
Chikwawa, Malawi 55 F3 16 2S 34 50 E
Chilac, Mexico 87 D5 18 20N 97 24W
Chilam Chavki, Pakistan 43 B6 35 5N 75 5 E
Chilanga, Zambia 55 F2 15 33S 28 16 E
Chilapa, Mexico 87 D5 17 40N 99 11W
Chilas, Pakistan 43 B6 35 25N 74 5 E
Chilaw, Sri Lanka 40 R11 7 30N 79 50 E
Chilcotin →, Canada 72 C4 51 44N 122 23W
Childers, Australia 63 D5 25 15S 152 17 E
Childress, U.S.A. 81 H4 34 25N 100 13W
Chile ■, S. Amer. 96 D2 35 0S 72 0W
Chile Rise, Pac. Oc. 65 L18 38 0S 92 0W
Chilecito, Argentina 94 B2 29 10S 67 30W
Chilete, Peru 92 E3 7 10S 78 50W
Chililabombwe, Zambia 55 E2 12 18S 27 43 E
Chilin = Jilin, China 35 C14 43 44N 126 30 E
Chilka L., India 41 K14 19 40N 85 25 E
Chilko →, Canada 72 C4 52 0N 123 40W
Chilko L., Canada 72 C4 51 20N 124 10W
Chillagoe, Australia 62 B3 17 7S 144 33 E
Chillán, Chile 94 D1 36 40S 72 10W
Chillicothe, Ill., U.S.A. 80 E10 40 55N 89 29W
Chillicothe, Mo., U.S.A. 80 F8 39 48N 93 33W
Chillicothe, Ohio, U.S.A. 76 F4 39 20N 82 59W
Chilliwack, Canada 72 D4 49 10N 121 54W
Chilo, India 42 F5 27 25N 73 32 E
Chiloane, I., Mozam. 57 C5 20 40S 34 55 E
Chiloé, I. de, Chile 96 E2 42 30S 73 50W
Chilpancingo, Mexico 87 D5 17 30N 99 30W
Chiltern Hills, U.K. 11 F7 51 40N 0 53W
Chilton, U.S.A. 76 C1 44 2N 88 10W
Chilubi, Zambia 55 E2 11 5S 29 58 E
Chilubula, Zambia 55 E3 10 14S 30 51 E
Chilumba, Malawi 55 E3 10 28S 34 12 E
Chilung, Taiwan 33 D7 25 3N 121 45 E
Chilwa, L., Malawi 55 F4 15 15S 35 40 E
Chimaltitán, Mexico 86 C4 21 46N 103 50W
Chimán, Panama 88 E4 8 45N 78 40W
Chimay, Belgium 15 D4 50 3N 4 20 E
Chimayo, U.S.A. 83 H11 36 0N 105 56W
Chimbay, Uzbekistan 26 E6 42 57N 59 47 E
Chimborazo, Ecuador 92 D3 1 29S 78 55W
Chimbote, Peru 92 E3 9 0S 78 35W
Chimkent = Shymkent, Kazakstan 26 E7 42 18N 69 36 E
Chimoio, Mozam. 55 F3 19 4S 33 30 E
Chimpembe, Zambia 55 D2 9 31S 29 33 E
Chin □, Burma 41 J18 22 0N 93 0 E
Chin Ling Shan = Qinling Shandi, China 34 H5 33 50N 108 10 E
China, Mexico 87 B5 25 40N 99 20W
China ■, Asia 33 D6 30 0N 110 0 E
China Lake, U.S.A. 85 K9 35 44N 117 37W
Chinan = Jinan, China 34 F9 36 38N 117 1 E
Chinandega, Nic. 88 D2 12 35N 87 12W
Chinati Peak, U.S.A. 81 L2 29 57N 104 29W
Chincha Alta, Peru 92 F3 13 25S 76 7W
Chinchaga →, Canada 72 B5 58 53N 118 20W
Chinchilla, Australia 63 D5 26 45S 150 38 E

Chinchorro, Banco, *Mexico* **87 D7** 18 35N 87 20W
Chinchou = Jinzhou, *China* **35 D11** 41 5N 121 3 E
Chincoteague, *U.S.A.* **76 G8** 37 56N 75 23W
Chinde, *Mozam.* **55 F4** 18 35S 36 30 E
Chindo, *S. Korea* **35 G14** 34 28N 126 15 E
Chindwin →, *Burma* **41 J19** 21 26N 95 15 E
Chineni, *India* **43 C6** 33 2N 75 15 E
Chinga, *Mozam.* **55 F4** 15 13S 38 35 E
Chingola, *Zambia* **55 E2** 12 31S 27 53 E
Chingole, *Malawi* **55 E3** 13 4S 34 17 E
Ch'ingtao = Qingdao, *China* **35 F11** 36 5N 120 20 E
Chinguar, *Angola* **53 G3** 12 25S 16 45 E
Chinguetti, *Mauritania* **50 D3** 20 25N 12 24W
Chingune, *Mozam.* **57 C5** 20 33S 34 58 E
Chinhae, *S. Korea* **35 G15** 35 9N 128 47 E
Chinhanguanine, *Mozam.* **57 D5** 25 21S 32 30 E
Chinhoyi, *Zimbabwe* **55 F3** 17 20S 30 8 E
Chini, *India* **42 D8** 31 32N 78 15 E
Chiniot, *Pakistan* **42 D5** 31 45N 73 0 E
Chínipas, *Mexico* **86 B3** 27 22N 108 32W
Chinji, *Pakistan* **42 C5** 32 42N 72 22 E
Chinju, *S. Korea* **35 G15** 35 12N 128 2 E
Chinle, *U.S.A.* **83 H9** 36 9N 109 33W
Chinnampo = Namp'o, *N. Korea* **35 E13** 38 52N 125 10 E
Chino, *Japan* **31 G9** 35 59N 138 9 E
Chino, *U.S.A.* **85 L9** 34 1N 117 41W
Chino Valley, *U.S.A.* **83 J7** 34 45N 112 27W
Chinon, *France* **18 C4** 47 10N 0 15 E
Chinook, *U.S.A.* **82 B9** 48 35N 109 14W
Chinsali, *Zambia* **55 E3** 10 30S 32 2 E
Chióggia, *Italy* **20 B5** 45 13N 12 17 E
Chíos = Khíos, *Greece* **21 E12** 38 27N 26 9 E
Chipata, *Zambia* **55 E3** 13 38S 32 28 E
Chipinge, *Zimbabwe* **55 G3** 20 13S 32 28 E
Chipley, *U.S.A.* **77 K3** 30 47N 85 32W
Chipman, *Canada* **71 C6** 46 6N 65 53W
Chipoka, *Malawi* **55 E3** 13 57S 34 28 E
Chippenham, *U.K.* **11 F5** 51 27N 2 6W
Chippewa →, *U.S.A.* **80 C8** 44 25N 92 5W
Chippewa Falls, *U.S.A.* **80 C9** 44 56N 91 24W
Chipping Norton, *U.K.* **11 F6** 51 56N 1 32W
Chiputneticook Lakes, *U.S.A.* **77 C11** 45 35N 67 35W
Chiquián, *Peru* **92 F3** 10 10S 77 0W
Chiquimula, *Guatemala* **88 D2** 14 51N 89 37W
Chiquinquira, *Colombia* **92 B4** 5 37N 73 50W
Chirala, *India* **40 M12** 15 50N 80 26 E
Chiramba, *Mozam.* **55 F3** 16 55S 34 39 E
Chirawa, *India* **42 E6** 28 14N 75 42 E
Chirchiq, *Uzbekistan* **26 E7** 41 29N 69 35 E
Chiredzi, *Zimbabwe* **57 C5** 21 0S 31 38 E
Chirfa, *Niger* **51 D8** 20 55N 12 22 E
Chiricahua Peak, *U.S.A.* **83 L9** 31 51N 109 18W
Chiriquí, G. de, *Panama* **88 E3** 8 0N 82 10W
Chiriquí, L. de, *Panama* **88 E3** 9 10N 82 0W
Chirivira Falls, *Zimbabwe* **55 G3** 21 10S 32 12 E
Chirmiri, *India* **41 H13** 23 15N 82 20 E
Chirripó Grande, Cerro, *Costa Rica* **88 E3** 9 29N 83 29W
Chisamba, *Zambia* **55 E2** 14 55S 28 20 E
Chisapani Garhi, *Nepal* **41 F14** 27 30N 84 2 E
Chisasibi, *Canada* **70 B4** 53 50N 79 0W
Chisholm, *Canada* **72 C6** 54 55N 114 10W
Chisholm, *U.S.A.* **80 B8** 47 29N 92 53W
Chishtian Mandi, *Pakistan* **42 E5** 29 50N 72 55 E
Chisimaio, *Somali Rep.* **49 G8** 0 22S 42 32 E
Chisimba Falls, *Zambia* **55 E3** 10 12S 30 56 E
Chişinău, *Moldova* **17 E15** 47 2N 28 50 E
Chisos Mts., *U.S.A.* **81 L3** 29 5N 103 15W
Chistopol, *Russia* **24 C9** 55 25N 50 38 E
Chita, *Russia* **27 D12** 52 0N 113 35 E
Chitipa, *Malawi* **55 D3** 9 41S 33 19 E
Chitose, *Japan* **30 C10** 42 49N 141 39 E
Chitral, *Pakistan* **40 B7** 35 50N 71 56 E
Chitré, *Panama* **88 E3** 7 59N 80 27W
Chittagong, *Bangla.* **41 H17** 22 19N 91 48 E
Chittagong □, *Bangla.* **41 G17** 24 5N 91 0 E
Chittaurgarh, *India* **42 G6** 24 52N 74 38 E
Chittoor, *India* **40 N11** 13 15N 79 5 E
Chitungwiza, *Zimbabwe* **55 F3** 18 0S 31 6 E
Chiusi, *Italy* **20 C4** 43 1N 11 57 E
Chivasso, *Italy* **18 D7** 45 11N 7 53 E
Chivhu, *Zimbabwe* **55 F3** 19 2S 30 52 E
Chivilcoy, *Argentina* **94 C4** 34 55S 60 0W
Chiwanda, *Tanzania* **55 E3** 11 23S 34 55 E
Chizera, *Zambia* **55 E2** 13 10S 25 0 E
Chkalov = Orenburg, *Russia* **24 D10** 51 45N 55 6 E
Chloride, *U.S.A.* **85 K12** 35 25N 114 12W
Cho-do, *N. Korea* **35 E13** 38 30N 124 40 E
Cho Phuoc Hai, *Vietnam* **39 G6** 10 26N 107 18 E
Choba, *Kenya* **54 B4** 2 30N 38 5 E
Chobe National Park, *Botswana* **56 B4** 18 0S 25 0 E
Choch'iwŏn, *S. Korea* **35 F14** 36 37N 127 18 E
Chocolate Mts., *U.S.A.* **85 M11** 33 15N 115 15W
Choctawatchee →, *U.S.A.* **77 K3** 30 25N 86 8W
Choctawhatchee B., *U.S.A.* **75 D9** 30 20N 86 20W
Choele Choel, *Argentina* **96 D3** 39 11S 65 40W
Choix, *Mexico* **86 B3** 26 40N 108 23W
Chojnice, *Poland* **17 B9** 53 42N 17 32 E
Chōkai-San, *Japan* **30 E10** 39 6N 140 3 E
Choke Canyon L., *U.S.A.* **81 L5** 28 30N 98 20W
Chokurdakh, *Russia* **27 B15** 70 38N 147 55 E
Cholame, *U.S.A.* **84 K6** 35 44N 120 18W
Cholet, *France* **18 C3** 47 4N 0 52W
Cholguan, *Chile* **94 D1** 37 10S 72 3W
Choluteca, *Honduras* **88 D2** 13 20N 87 14W
Choluteca →, *Honduras* **88 D2** 13 0N 87 20W
Chom Bung, *Thailand* **38 F2** 13 37N 99 36 E
Chom Thong, *Thailand* **38 C2** 18 25N 98 41 E
Choma, *Zambia* **55 F2** 16 48S 26 59 E
Chomun, *India* **42 F6** 27 15N 75 40 E
Chomutov, *Czech Rep.* **16 C7** 50 28N 13 23 E
Chon Buri, *Thailand* **38 F3** 13 21N 101 1 E
Chon Thanh, *Vietnam* **39 G6** 11 24N 106 36 E
Ch'onan, *S. Korea* **35 F14** 36 48N 127 9 E
Chone, *Ecuador* **92 D3** 0 40S 80 0W
Chong Kai, *Cambodia* **38 F4** 13 57N 103 35 E
Chong Mek, *Thailand* **38 E5** 15 10N 105 27 E
Chŏngdo, *S. Korea* **35 G15** 35 38N 128 42 E
Chŏngha, *S. Korea* **35 F15** 36 12N 129 21 E
Chŏngjin, *N. Korea* **35 D15** 41 47N 129 50 E
Chŏngjiu, *S. Korea* **35 F14** 36 39N 127 27 E
Chŏngju, *N. Korea* **35 E13** 39 40N 125 5 E
Chongli, *China* **34 D8** 40 58N 115 15 E
Chongqing, *China* **32 D5** 29 35N 106 25 E
Chongqing □, *China* **32 C5** 30 0N 108 0 E
Chŏngŭp, *S. Korea* **35 G14** 35 35N 126 50 E
Chŏnju, *S. Korea* **35 G14** 35 50N 127 4 E
Chonos, Arch. de los, *Chile* **96 F2** 45 0S 75 0W
Chop, *Ukraine* **17 D12** 48 26N 22 12 E
Chopim →, *Brazil* **95 B5** 25 35S 53 5W
Chor, *Pakistan* **42 G3** 25 31N 69 46 E
Chorbat La, *India* **43 B7** 34 42N 76 37 E
Chorley, *U.K.* **10 D5** 53 39N 2 38W
Chornobyl, *Ukraine* **17 C16** 51 20N 30 15 E
Chorolque, Cerro, *Bolivia* **94 A2** 20 59S 66 5W
Chorregon, *Australia* **62 C3** 22 40S 143 32 E
Chortkiv, *Ukraine* **17 D13** 49 2N 25 46 E
Ch'ŏrwon, *S. Korea* **35 E14** 38 15N 127 10 E
Chorzów, *Poland* **17 C10** 50 18N 18 57 E
Chos-Malal, *Argentina* **94 D1** 37 20S 70 15W
Ch'osan, *N. Korea* **35 D13** 40 50N 125 47 E
Choszczno, *Poland* **16 B8** 53 7N 15 25 E
Choteau, *U.S.A.* **82 C7** 47 49N 112 11W
Chotila, *India* **42 H4** 22 23N 71 15 E
Chotta Udepur, *India* **42 H6** 22 19N 74 1 E
Chowchilla, *U.S.A.* **84 H6** 37 7N 120 16W
Choybalsan, *Mongolia* **33 B6** 48 4N 114 30 E
Christchurch, *N.Z.* **59 K4** 43 33S 172 47 E
Christchurch, *U.K.* **11 G6** 50 44N 1 47W
Christian I., *Canada* **78 B4** 44 50N 80 12W
Christiana, *S. Africa* **56 D4** 27 52S 25 8 E
Christiansted, *Virgin Is.* **89 C7** 17 45N 64 42W
Christie B., *Canada* **73 A6** 62 32N 111 10W
Christina →, *Canada* **73 B6** 56 40N 111 3W
Christmas Cr. →, *Australia* **60 C4** 18 29S 125 23 E
Christmas I. = Kiritimati, *Kiribati* **65 G12** 1 58N 157 27W
Christmas I., *Ind. Oc.* **64 J2** 10 30S 105 40 E
Christopher L., *Australia* **61 D4** 24 49S 127 42 E
Chtimba, *Malawi* **55 E3** 10 35S 34 13 E
Chu = Shu, *Kazakstan* **26 E8** 43 36N 73 42 E
Chu = Shu →, *Kazakstan* **28 E10** 45 0N 67 44 E
Chu →, *Vietnam* **38 C5** 19 53N 105 45 E
Chu Lai, *Vietnam* **38 E7** 15 28N 108 45 E
Ch'uanchou = Quanzhou, *China* **33 D6** 24 55N 118 34 E
Chuankou, *China* **34 G6** 34 20N 110 59 E
Chubbuck, *U.S.A.* **82 E7** 42 55N 112 28W
Chūbu □, *Japan* **31 F8** 36 45N 137 30 E
Chubut →, *Argentina* **96 E3** 43 20S 65 5W
Chuchi L., *Canada* **72 B4** 55 12N 124 30W
Chuda, *India* **42 H4** 22 29N 71 41 E
Chudskoye, Ozero, *Russia* **9 G22** 58 13N 27 30 E
Chūgoku □, *Japan* **31 G6** 35 0N 133 0 E
Chūgoku-Sanchi, *Japan* **31 G6** 35 0N 133 0 E
Chugwater, *U.S.A.* **80 E2** 41 46N 104 50W
Chukchi Sea, *Russia* **27 C19** 68 0N 175 0W
Chukotskoye Nagorye, *Russia* **27 C18** 68 0N 175 0 E
Chula Vista, *U.S.A.* **85 N9** 32 39N 117 5W
Chulucanas, *Peru* **92 E2** 5 8S 80 10W
Chulym →, *Russia* **26 D9** 57 43N 83 51 E
Chum Phae, *Thailand* **38 D4** 16 40N 102 6 E
Chum Saeng, *Thailand* **38 E3** 15 55N 100 15 E
Chumar, *India* **43 C8** 32 40N 78 35 E
Chumbicha, *Argentina* **94 B2** 29 0S 66 10W
Chumikan, *Russia* **27 D14** 54 40N 135 10 E
Chumphon, *Thailand* **39 G2** 10 35N 99 14 E
Chumuare, *Mozam.* **55 E3** 14 31S 31 50 E
Chumunjin, *S. Korea* **35 F15** 37 55N 128 54 E
Chuna →, *Russia* **27 D10** 57 47N 94 37 E
Ch'unch'ŏn, *S. Korea* **35 F14** 37 58N 127 44 E
Chunchura, *India* **43 H13** 22 53N 88 27 E
Chunga, *Zambia* **55 F2** 15 0S 26 2 E
Chunggang-ŭp, *N. Korea* **35 D14** 41 48N 126 48 E
Chunghwa, *N. Korea* **35 E13** 38 52N 125 47 E
Ch'ungju, *S. Korea* **35 F14** 36 58N 127 58 E
Chungking = Chongqing, *China* **32 D5** 29 35N 106 25 E
Ch'ungmu, *S. Korea* **35 G15** 34 50N 128 20 E
Chungt'iaoshan = Zhongtiao Shan, *China* **34 G6** 35 0N 111 10 E
Chunian, *Pakistan* **42 D6** 30 57N 74 0 E
Chunya, *Tanzania* **55 D3** 8 30S 33 27 E
Chunyang, *China* **35 C15** 43 38N 129 23 E
Chuquibamba, *Peru* **92 G4** 15 47S 72 44W
Chuquicamata, *Chile* **94 A2** 22 15S 69 0W
Chur, *Switz.* **18 C8** 46 52N 9 32 E
Churachandpur, *India* **41 G18** 24 20N 93 40 E
Churchill, *Canada* **73 B10** 58 47N 94 11W
Churchill →, *Man., Canada* **73 B10** 58 47N 94 12W
Churchill →, *Nfld., Canada* **71 B7** 53 19N 60 10W
Churchill, C., *Canada* **73 B10** 58 46N 93 12W
Churchill Falls, *Canada* **71 B7** 53 36N 64 19W
Churchill L., *Canada* **73 B7** 55 55N 108 20W
Churchill Pk., *Canada* **72 B3** 58 10N 125 10W
Churki, *India* **43 H10** 23 50N 83 12 E
Churu, *India* **42 E6** 28 20N 74 50 E
Churún Merú = Angel Falls, *Venezuela* **92 B6** 5 57N 62 30W
Chushal, *India* **43 C8** 33 40N 78 40 E
Chuska Mts., *U.S.A.* **83 H9** 36 15N 108 50W
Chusovoy, *Russia* **24 C10** 58 22N 57 50 E
Chute-aux-Outardes, *Canada* **71 C6** 49 7N 68 24W
Chuuronjang, *N. Korea* **35 D15** 41 35N 129 40 E
Chuvash Republic = Chuvashia □, *Russia* **24 C8** 55 30N 47 0 E
Chuvashia □, *Russia* **24 C8** 55 30N 47 0 E
Chuwārtah, *Iraq* **44 C5** 35 43N 45 34 E
Chuy, *Uruguay* **95 C5** 33 41S 53 27W
Ci Xian, *China* **34 F8** 36 20N 114 25 E
Ciadâr-Lunga, *Moldova* **17 E15** 46 3N 28 51 E
Ciamis, *Indonesia* **37 G13** 7 20S 108 21 E
Cianjur, *Indonesia* **37 G12** 6 49S 107 8 E
Cianorte, *Brazil* **95 A5** 23 37S 52 37W
Cibola, *U.S.A.* **85 M12** 33 17N 114 42W
Cicero, *U.S.A.* **76 E2** 41 48N 87 48W
Ciechanów, *Poland* **17 B11** 52 52N 20 38 E
Ciego de Avila, *Cuba* **88 B4** 21 50N 78 50W
Ciénaga, *Colombia* **92 A4** 11 1N 74 15W
Cienfuegos, *Cuba* **88 B3** 22 10N 80 30W
Cieszyn, *Poland* **17 D10** 49 45N 18 35 E
Cieza, *Spain* **19 C5** 38 17N 1 23W
Cihuatlán, *Mexico* **86 D4** 19 14N 104 35W
Cijara, Embalse de, *Spain* **19 C3** 39 18N 4 52W
Cijulang, *Indonesia* **37 G13** 7 42S 108 27 E
Cilacap, *Indonesia* **37 G13** 7 43S 109 0 E
Cill Chainnigh = Kilkenny, *Ireland* **13 D4** 52 39N 7 15W
Cilo Dağı, *Turkey* **25 G7** 37 28N 43 55 E
Cima, *U.S.A.* **85 K11** 35 14N 115 30W
Cimarron, *Kans., U.S.A.* **81 G4** 37 48N 100 21W
Cimarron, *N. Mex., U.S.A.* **81 G2** 36 31N 104 55W
Cimarron →, *U.S.A.* **81 G6** 36 10N 96 17W
Cimişlia, *Moldova* **17 E15** 46 34N 28 44 E
Cimone, Mte., *Italy* **20 B4** 44 12N 10 42 E
Cinca →, *Spain* **19 B6** 41 26N 0 21 E
Cincar, *Bos.-H.* **20 C7** 43 55N 17 5 E
Cincinnati, *U.S.A.* **76 F3** 39 6N 84 31W
Cincinnatus, *U.S.A.* **79 D9** 42 33N 75 54W
Çine, *Turkey* **21 F13** 37 37N 28 2 E
Ciney, *Belgium* **15 D5** 50 18N 5 5 E
Cinto, Mte., *France* **18 E8** 42 24N 8 54 E
Circle, *Alaska, U.S.A.* **68 B5** 65 50N 144 4W
Circle, *Mont., U.S.A.* **80 B2** 47 25N 105 35W
Circleville, *U.S.A.* **76 F4** 39 36N 82 57W
Cirebon, *Indonesia* **37 G13** 6 45S 108 32 E
Ciremai, *Indonesia* **37 G13** 6 55S 108 27 E
Cirencester, *U.K.* **11 F6** 51 43N 1 57W
Cirium, *Cyprus* **23 E11** 34 40N 32 53 E
Cisco, *U.S.A.* **81 J5** 32 23N 98 59W
Citlaltépetl, *Mexico* **87 D5** 19 0N 97 20W
Citrus Heights, *U.S.A.* **84 G5** 38 42N 121 17W
Citrusdal, *S. Africa* **56 E2** 32 35S 19 0 E
Città di Castello, *Italy* **20 C5** 43 27N 12 14 E
City of Edinburgh □, *U.K.* **12 F5** 55 57N 3 17W
City of Glasgow □, *U.K.* **12 F4** 55 51N 4 12W
Ciudad Altamirano, *Mexico* **86 D4** 18 20N 100 40W
Ciudad Bolívar, *Venezuela* **92 B6** 8 5N 63 36W
Ciudad Camargo, *Mexico* **86 B3** 27 41N 105 10W
Ciudad de Valles, *Mexico* **87 C5** 22 0N 99 0W
Ciudad del Carmen, *Mexico* **87 D6** 18 38N 91 50W
Ciudad del Este, *Paraguay* **95 B5** 25 30S 54 50W
Ciudad Delicias = Delicias, *Mexico* **86 B3** 28 10N 105 30W
Ciudad Guayana, *Venezuela* **92 B6** 8 0N 62 30W
Ciudad Guerrero, *Mexico* **86 B3** 28 33N 107 28W
Ciudad Guzmán, *Mexico* **86 D4** 19 40N 103 30W
Ciudad Juárez, *Mexico* **86 A3** 31 40N 106 28W
Ciudad Madero, *Mexico* **87 C5** 22 19N 97 50W
Ciudad Mante, *Mexico* **87 C5** 22 50N 99 0W
Ciudad Obregón, *Mexico* **86 B3** 27 28N 109 59W
Ciudad Real, *Spain* **19 C4** 38 59N 3 55W
Ciudad Rodrigo, *Spain* **19 B2** 40 35N 6 32W
Ciudad Trujillo = Santo Domingo, *Dom. Rep.* **89 C6** 18 30N 69 59W
Ciudad Victoria, *Mexico* **87 C5** 23 41N 99 9W
Ciudadela, *Spain* **22 B10** 40 0N 3 50 E
Civitanova Marche, *Italy* **20 C5** 43 18N 13 44 E
Civitavécchia, *Italy* **20 C4** 42 6N 11 48 E
Cizre, *Turkey* **25 G7** 37 19N 42 10 E
Clackmannanshire □, *U.K.* **12 E5** 56 10N 3 43W
Clacton-on-Sea, *U.K.* **11 F9** 51 47N 1 11 E
Claire, L., *Canada* **72 B6** 58 35N 112 5W
Clairton, *U.S.A.* **78 F5** 40 18N 79 53W
Clallam Bay, *U.S.A.* **84 B2** 48 15N 124 16W
Clanton, *U.S.A.* **77 J2** 32 51N 86 38W
Clanwilliam, *S. Africa* **56 E2** 32 11S 18 52 E
Clara, *Ireland* **13 C4** 53 21N 7 37W
Claraville, *U.S.A.* **85 K8** 35 24N 118 20W
Clare, *Australia* **63 E2** 33 50S 138 37 E
Clare, *U.S.A.* **76 D3** 43 49N 84 46W
Clare □, *Ireland* **13 D3** 52 45N 9 0W
Clare →, *Ireland* **13 C2** 53 20N 9 2W
Clare I., *Ireland* **13 C1** 53 49N 10 0W
Claremont, *Calif., U.S.A.* **85 L9** 34 6N 117 43W
Claremont, *N.H., U.S.A.* **79 C12** 43 23N 72 20W
Claremont Pt., *Australia* **62 A3** 14 1S 143 41 E
Claremore, *U.S.A.* **81 G7** 36 19N 95 36W
Claremorris, *Ireland* **13 C3** 53 45N 9 0W
Clarence →, *Australia* **63 D5** 29 25S 153 22 E
Clarence →, *N.Z.* **59 K4** 42 10S 173 56 E
Clarence, I., *Chile* **96 G2** 54 0S 72 0W
Clarence I., *Antarctica* **5 C18** 61 10S 54 0W
Clarence Str., *Australia* **60 B5** 12 0S 131 0 E
Clarence Town, *Bahamas* **89 B5** 23 6N 74 59W
Clarendon, *Pa., U.S.A.* **78 E5** 41 47N 79 6W
Clarendon, *Tex., U.S.A.* **81 H4** 34 56N 100 53W
Clarenville, *Canada* **71 C9** 48 10N 54 1W
Claresholm, *Canada* **72 D6** 50 0N 113 33W
Clarie Coast, *Antarctica* **5 C9** 68 0S 135 0 E
Clarinda, *U.S.A.* **80 E7** 40 44N 95 2W
Clarion, *Iowa, U.S.A.* **80 D8** 42 44N 93 44W
Clarion, *Pa., U.S.A.* **78 E5** 41 13N 79 23W
Clarion →, *U.S.A.* **78 E5** 41 7N 79 41W
Clark, *U.S.A.* **80 C6** 44 53N 97 44W
Clark, Pt., *Canada* **78 B3** 44 4N 81 45W
Clark Fork, *U.S.A.* **82 B5** 48 9N 116 11W
Clark Fork →, *U.S.A.* **82 B5** 48 9N 116 15W
Clark Hill L., *U.S.A.* **77 J4** 33 40N 82 12W
Clarkdale, *U.S.A.* **83 J7** 34 46N 112 3W
Clarke City, *Canada* **71 B6** 50 12N 66 38W
Clarke I., *Australia* **62 G4** 40 32S 148 10 E
Clarke Ra., *Australia* **62 C4** 20 40S 148 30 E
Clark's Fork →, *U.S.A.* **82 D9** 45 39N 108 43W
Clark's Harbour, *Canada* **71 D6** 43 25N 65 38W
Clarks Summit, *U.S.A.* **79 E9** 41 30N 75 42W
Clarksburg, *U.S.A.* **76 F5** 39 17N 80 30W
Clarksdale, *U.S.A.* **81 H9** 34 12N 90 35W
Clarksville, *Ark., U.S.A.* **81 H8** 35 28N 93 28W
Clarksville, *Tenn., U.S.A.* **77 G2** 36 32N 87 21W
Clarksville, *Tex., U.S.A.* **81 J7** 33 37N 95 3W
Clatskanie, *U.S.A.* **84 D3** 46 6N 123 12W
Claude, *U.S.A.* **81 H4** 35 7N 101 22W
Claveria, *Phil.* **37 A6** 18 37N 121 4 E
Clay, *U.S.A.* **84 G5** 38 17N 121 10W
Clay Center, *U.S.A.* **80 F6** 39 23N 97 8W
Claypool, *U.S.A.* **83 K8** 33 25N 110 51W
Claysburg, *U.S.A.* **78 F6** 40 17N 78 27W
Claysville, *U.S.A.* **78 F4** 40 7N 80 25W
Clayton, *N. Mex., U.S.A.* **81 G3** 36 27N 103 11W
Clayton, *N.Y., U.S.A.* **79 B8** 44 14N 76 5W
Clear, C., *Ireland* **13 E2** 51 25N 9 32W
Clear, L., *Canada* **78 A7** 45 26N 77 12W
Clear Hills, *Canada* **72 B5** 56 40N 119 30W
Clear I., *Ireland* **13 E2** 51 26N 9 30W
Clear L., *U.S.A.* **84 F4** 39 2N 122 47W
Clear Lake, *Iowa, U.S.A.* **80 D8** 43 8N 93 23W
Clear Lake, *S. Dak., U.S.A.* **80 C6** 44 45N 96 41W
Clear Lake Reservoir, *U.S.A.* **82 F3** 41 56N 121 5W
Clearfield, *Pa., U.S.A.* **78 E6** 41 2N 78 27W
Clearfield, *Utah, U.S.A.* **82 F8** 41 7N 112 2W
Clearlake, *U.S.A.* **82 G2** 38 57N 122 38W
Clearlake Highlands, *U.S.A.* **84 G4** 38 57N 122 38W
Clearwater, *Canada* **72 C4** 51 38N 120 2W
Clearwater, *U.S.A.* **77 M4** 27 58N 82 48W
Clearwater →, *Alta., Canada* **72 C6** 52 22N 114 57W
Clearwater →, *Alta., Canada* **73 B6** 56 44N 111 23W
Clearwater L., *Canada* **73 C9** 53 34N 99 49W
Clearwater Mts., *U.S.A.* **82 C6** 46 5N 115 20W
Clearwater Prov. Park, *Canada* **73 C8** 54 0N 101 0W
Clearwater River Prov. Park, *Canada* **73 B7** 56 55N 109 10W
Cleburne, *U.S.A.* **81 J6** 32 21N 97 23W
Clee Hills, *U.K.* **11 E5** 52 26N 2 35W
Cleethorpes, *U.K.* **10 D7** 53 33N 0 3W
Cleeve Cloud, *U.K.* **11 F6** 51 56N 2 0W
Clemson, *U.S.A.* **77 H4** 34 41N 82 50W
Clerke Reef, *Australia* **60 C2** 17 22S 119 20 E
Clermont, *Australia* **62 C4** 22 49S 147 39 E
Clermont, *U.S.A.* **77 L5** 28 33N 81 46W
Clermont-Ferrand, *France* **18 D5** 45 46N 3 4 E
Clervaux, *Lux.* **15 D6** 50 4N 6 2 E
Cleve, *Australia* **63 E2** 33 43S 136 30 E
Clevedon, *U.K.* **11 F5** 51 26N 2 52W
Cleveland, *Miss., U.S.A.* **81 J9** 33 45N 90 43W
Cleveland, *Ohio, U.S.A.* **78 E3** 41 30N 81 42W
Cleveland, *Okla., U.S.A.* **81 G6** 36 19N 96 28W
Cleveland, *Tenn., U.S.A.* **77 H3** 35 10N 84 53W
Cleveland, *Tex., U.S.A.* **81 K7** 30 21N 95 5W
Cleveland, C., *Australia* **62 B4** 19 11S 147 1 E
Cleveland, Mt., *U.S.A.* **82 B7** 48 56N 113 51W
Cleveland Heights, *U.S.A.* **78 E3** 41 30N 81 34W
Clevelândia, *Brazil* **95 B5** 26 24S 52 23W
Clew B., *Ireland* **13 C2** 53 50N 9 49W
Clewiston, *U.S.A.* **77 M5** 26 45N 80 56W
Clifden, *Ireland* **13 C1** 53 29N 10 1W
Clifden, *N.Z.* **59 M1** 46 1S 167 42 E
Cliffdell, *U.S.A.* **84 D5** 46 56N 121 5W
Cliffy Hd., *Australia* **61 G2** 35 1S 116 29 E
Clifton, *Australia* **63 D5** 27 59S 151 53 E
Clifton, *Ariz., U.S.A.* **83 K9** 33 3N 109 18W
Clifton, *Colo., U.S.A.* **83 G9** 39 7N 108 25W
Clifton, *Tex., U.S.A.* **81 K6** 31 47N 97 35W
Clifton Beach, *Australia* **62 B4** 16 46S 145 39 E
Climax, *Canada* **73 D7** 49 10N 108 20W
Clinch →, *U.S.A.* **77 H3** 35 53N 84 29W
Clingmans Dome, *U.S.A.* **77 H4** 35 34N 83 30W
Clint, *U.S.A.* **83 L10** 31 35N 106 14W
Clinton, *B.C., Canada* **72 C4** 51 6N 121 35W
Clinton, *Ont., Canada* **78 C3** 43 37N 81 32W
Clinton, *N.Z.* **59 M2** 46 12S 169 23 E
Clinton, *Ark., U.S.A.* **81 H8** 35 36N 92 28W
Clinton, *Conn., U.S.A.* **79 E12** 41 17N 72 32W
Clinton, *Ill., U.S.A.* **80 E10** 40 9N 88 57W
Clinton, *Ind., U.S.A.* **76 F2** 39 40N 87 24W
Clinton, *Iowa, U.S.A.* **80 E9** 41 51N 90 12W
Clinton, *Mass., U.S.A.* **79 D13** 42 25N 71 41W
Clinton, *Miss., U.S.A.* **81 J9** 32 20N 90 20W
Clinton, *Mo., U.S.A.* **80 F8** 38 22N 93 46W
Clinton, *N.C., U.S.A.* **77 H6** 35 0N 78 22W
Clinton, *Okla., U.S.A.* **81 H5** 35 31N 98 58W
Clinton, *S.C., U.S.A.* **77 H5** 34 29N 81 53W
Clinton, *Tenn., U.S.A.* **77 G3** 36 6N 84 8W
Clinton, *Wash., U.S.A.* **84 C4** 47 59N 122 21W
Clinton C., *Australia* **62 C5** 22 30S 150 45 E
Clinton Colden L., *Canada* **68 B9** 63 58N 107 27W
Clintonville, *U.S.A.* **80 C10** 44 37N 88 46W
Clipperton, I., *Pac. Oc.* **65 F17** 10 18N 109 13W
Clisham, *U.K.* **12 D2** 57 57N 6 49W
Clitheroe, *U.K.* **10 D5** 53 53N 2 22W
Clo-oose, *Canada* **84 B2** 48 39N 124 49W
Cloates, Pt., *Australia* **60 D1** 22 43S 113 40 E
Clocolan, *S. Africa* **57 D4** 28 55S 27 34 E
Clodomira, *Argentina* **94 B3** 27 35S 64 14W
Clogher Hd., *Ireland* **13 C5** 53 48N 6 14W
Clonakilty, *Ireland* **13 E3** 51 37N 8 53W
Clonakilty B., *Ireland* **13 E3** 51 35N 8 51W
Cloncurry, *Australia* **62 C3** 20 40S 140 28 E
Cloncurry →, *Australia* **62 B3** 18 37S 140 40 E
Clondalkin, *Ireland* **13 C5** 53 19N 6 25W
Clones, *Ireland* **13 B4** 54 11N 7 15W
Clonmel, *Ireland* **13 D4** 52 21N 7 42W
Cloquet, *U.S.A.* **80 B8** 46 43N 92 28W
Clorinda, *Argentina* **94 B4** 25 16S 57 45W
Cloud Bay, *Canada* **70 C2** 48 5N 89 26W
Cloud Peak, *U.S.A.* **82 D10** 44 23N 107 11W
Cloudcroft, *U.S.A.* **83 K11** 32 58N 105 45W
Cloverdale, *U.S.A.* **84 G4** 38 48N 123 1W
Clovis, *Calif., U.S.A.* **84 J7** 36 49N 119 42W
Clovis, *N. Mex., U.S.A.* **81 H3** 34 24N 103 12W
Cloyne, *Canada* **78 B7** 44 49N 77 11W
Cluj-Napoca, *Romania* **17 E12** 46 47N 23 38 E
Clunes, *Australia* **63 F3** 37 20S 143 45 E
Clutha →, *N.Z.* **59 M2** 46 20S 169 49 E
Clwyd →, *U.K.* **10 D4** 53 19N 3 31W
Clyde, *Canada* **72 C6** 54 9N 113 39W
Clyde, *N.Z.* **59 L2** 45 12S 169 20 E
Clyde, *U.S.A.* **78 C8** 43 5N 76 52W
Clyde →, *U.K.* **12 F4** 55 55N 4 30W
Clyde, Firth of, *U.K.* **12 F3** 55 22N 5 1W
Clyde River, *Canada* **69 A13** 70 30N 68 30W
Clydebank, *U.K.* **12 F4** 55 54N 4 23W
Clymer, *N.Y., U.S.A.* **78 D5** 42 1N 79 37W
Clymer, *Pa., U.S.A.* **78 D5** 40 40N 79 1W
Coachella, *U.S.A.* **85 M10** 33 41N 116 10W
Coachella Canal, *U.S.A.* **85 N12** 32 43N 114 57W
Coahoma, *U.S.A.* **81 J4** 32 18N 101 18W
Coahuayana →, *Mexico* **86 D4** 18 41N 103 45W
Coahuila □, *Mexico* **86 B4** 27 0N 103 0W
Coal →, *Canada* **72 B3** 59 39N 126 57W
Coalane, *Mozam.* **55 F4** 17 48S 37 2 E
Coalcomán, *Mexico* **86 D4** 18 40N 103 10W
Coaldale, *Canada* **72 D6** 49 45N 112 35W
Coalgate, *U.S.A.* **81 H6** 34 32N 96 13W
Coalinga, *U.S.A.* **84 J6** 36 9N 120 21W
Coalisland, *U.K.* **13 B5** 54 33N 6 42W
Coalville, *U.K.* **10 E6** 52 44N 1 23W
Coalville, *U.S.A.* **82 F8** 40 55N 111 24W
Coari, *Brazil* **92 D6** 4 8S 63 7W
Coast □, *Kenya* **54 C4** 2 40S 39 45 E
Coast Mts., *Canada* **72 C3** 55 0N 129 20W
Coast Ranges, *U.S.A.* **84 G4** 39 0N 123 0W
Coatbridge, *U.K.* **12 F4** 55 52N 4 6W
Coatepec, *Mexico* **87 D5** 19 27N 96 58W
Coatepeque, *Guatemala* **88 D1** 14 46N 91 55W
Coatesville, *U.S.A.* **76 F8** 39 59N 75 50W
Coaticook, *Canada* **79 A13** 45 10N 71 46W
Coats I., *Canada* **69 B11** 62 30N 83 0W
Coats Land, *Antarctica* **5 D1** 77 0S 25 0W
Coatzacoalcos, *Mexico* **87 D6** 18 7N 94 25W
Cobalt, *Canada* **70 C4** 47 25N 79 42W

Cobán, *Guatemala* **88 C1** 15 30N 90 21W
Cobar, *Australia* **63 E4** 31 27S 145 48 E
Cobargo, *Australia* **63 F4** 36 20S 149 55 E
Cóbh, *Ireland* **13 E3** 51 51N 8 17W
Cobija, *Bolivia* **92 F5** 11 0S 68 50W
Cobleskill, *U.S.A.* **79 D10** 42 41N 74 29W
Coboconk, *Canada* **78 B6** 44 39N 78 48W
Cobourg, *Canada* **78 C6** 43 58N 78 10W
Cobourg Pen., *Australia* **60 B5** 11 20S 132 15 E
Cobram, *Australia* **63 F4** 35 54S 145 40 E
Cóbué, *Mozam.* **55 E3** 12 0S 34 58 E
Coburg, *Germany* **16 C6** 50 15N 10 58 E
Cocanada = Kakinada, *India* **41 L13** 16 57N 82 11 E
Cochabamba, *Bolivia* **92 G5** 17 26S 66 10W
Cochemane, *Mozam.* **55 F3** 17 0S 32 54 E
Cochin, *India* **40 Q10** 9 59N 76 22 E
Cochin China, *Vietnam* **39 G6** 10 30N 106 0 E
Cochran, *U.S.A.* **77 J4** 32 23N 83 21W
Cochrane, *Alta., Canada* **72 C6** 51 11N 114 30W
Cochrane, *Ont., Canada* **70 C3** 49 0N 81 0W
Cochrane, *Chile* **96 F2** 47 15S 72 33W
Cochrane →, *Canada* **73 B8** 59 0N 103 40W
Cochrane, L., *Chile* **96 F2** 47 10S 72 0W
Cochranton, *U.S.A.* **78 E4** 41 31N 80 3W
Cockburn, *Australia* **63 E3** 32 5S 141 0 E
Cockburn, Canal, *Chile* **96 G2** 54 30S 72 0W
Cockburn I., *Canada* **70 C3** 45 55N 83 22W
Cockburn Ra., *Australia* **60 C4** 15 46S 128 0 E
Cockermouth, *U.K.* **10 C4** 54 40N 3 22W
Cocklebiddy, *Australia* **61 F4** 32 0S 126 3 E
Coco →, *Cent. Amer.* **88 D3** 15 0N 83 8W
Coco, I. del, *Pac. Oc.* **65 G19** 5 25N 87 55W
Cocoa, *U.S.A.* **77 L5** 28 21N 80 44W
Cocobeach, *Gabon* **52 D1** 0 59N 9 34 E
Cocos Is., *Ind. Oc.* **64 J1** 12 10S 96 55 E
Cod, C., *U.S.A.* **76 D10** 42 5N 70 10W
Codajás, *Brazil* **92 D6** 3 55S 62 0W
Codó, *Brazil* **93 D10** 4 30S 43 55W
Cody, *U.S.A.* **82 D9** 44 32N 109 3W
Coe Hill, *Canada* **78 B7** 44 52N 77 50W
Coelemu, *Chile* **94 D1** 36 30S 72 48W
Coen, *Australia* **62 A3** 13 52S 143 12 E
Cœur d'Alene, *U.S.A.* **82 C5** 47 45N 116 51W
Cœur d'Alene L., *U.S.A.* **82 C5** 47 32N 116 48W
Coevorden, *Neths.* **15 B6** 52 40N 6 44 E
Cofete, *Canary Is.* **22 F5** 28 6N 14 23W
Coffeyville, *U.S.A.* **81 G7** 37 2N 95 37W
Coffin B., *Australia* **63 E2** 34 38S 135 28 E
Coffin Bay, *Australia* **63 E2** 34 37S 135 29 E
Coffin Bay Peninsula, *Australia* **63 E2** 34 32S 135 15 E
Coffs Harbour, *Australia* **63 E5** 30 16S 153 5 E
Cognac, *France* **18 D3** 45 41N 0 20W
Cohocton, *U.S.A.* **78 D7** 42 30N 77 30W
Cohocton →, *U.S.A.* **78 D7** 42 9N 77 6W
Cohoes, *U.S.A.* **79 D11** 42 46N 73 42W
Cohuna, *Australia* **63 F3** 35 45S 144 15 E
Coiba, I., *Panama* **88 E3** 7 30N 81 40W
Coig →, *Argentina* **96 G3** 51 0S 69 10W
Coigeach, Rubha, *U.K.* **12 C3** 58 6N 5 26W
Coihaique, *Chile* **96 F2** 45 30S 71 45W
Coimbatore, *India* **40 P10** 11 2N 76 59 E
Coimbra, *Brazil* **92 G7** 19 55S 57 48W
Coimbra, *Portugal* **19 B1** 40 15N 8 27W
Coín, *Spain* **19 D3** 36 40N 4 48W
Coipasa, Salar de, *Bolivia* **92 G5** 19 26S 68 9W
Cojimies, *Ecuador* **92 C3** 0 20N 80 0W
Cojutepequé, *El Salv.* **88 D2** 13 41N 88 54W
Cokeville, *U.S.A.* **82 E8** 42 5N 110 57W
Colac, *Australia* **63 F3** 38 21S 143 35 E
Colatina, *Brazil* **93 G10** 19 32S 40 37W
Colbeck, C., *Antarctica* **5 D13** 77 6S 157 48W
Colborne, *Canada* **78 C7** 44 0N 77 53W
Colby, *U.S.A.* **80 F4** 39 24N 101 3W
Colchester, *U.K.* **11 F8** 51 54N 0 55 E
Cold L., *Canada* **73 C7** 54 33N 110 5W
Coldstream, *Canada* **72 C5** 50 13N 119 11W
Coldstream, *U.K.* **12 F6** 55 39N 2 15W
Coldwater, *Canada* **78 B5** 44 42N 79 40W
Coldwater, *Kans., U.S.A.* **81 G5** 37 16N 99 20W
Coldwater, *Mich., U.S.A.* **76 E3** 41 57N 85 0W
Coleambally, *Australia* **63 E4** 34 49S 145 52 E
Colebrook, *U.S.A.* **79 B13** 44 54N 71 30W
Coleman, *U.S.A.* **81 K5** 31 50N 99 26W
Coleman →, *Australia* **62 B3** 15 6S 141 38 E
Colenso, *S. Africa* **57 D4** 28 44S 29 50 E
Coleraine, *Australia* **63 F3** 37 36S 141 40 E
Coleraine, *U.K.* **13 A5** 55 8N 6 41W
Coleridge, L., *N.Z.* **59 K3** 43 17S 171 30 E
Colesberg, *S. Africa* **56 E4** 30 45S 25 5 E
Coleville, *U.S.A.* **84 G7** 38 34N 119 30W
Colfax, *Calif., U.S.A.* **84 F6** 39 6N 120 57W
Colfax, *La., U.S.A.* **81 K8** 31 31N 92 42W
Colfax, *Wash., U.S.A.* **82 C5** 46 53N 117 22W
Colhué Huapi, L., *Argentina* **96 F3** 45 30S 69 0W
Coligny, *S. Africa* **57 D4** 26 17S 26 15 E
Colima, *Mexico* **86 D4** 19 14N 103 43W
Colima □, *Mexico* **86 D4** 19 10N 103 40W
Colima, Nevado de, *Mexico* **86 D4** 19 35N 103 45W
Colina, *Chile* **94 C1** 33 13S 70 45W
Colinas, *Brazil* **93 E10** 6 0S 44 10W
Coll, *U.K.* **12 E2** 56 39N 6 34W
Collaguasi, *Chile* **94 A2** 21 5S 68 45W
Collarenebri, *Australia* **63 D4** 29 33S 148 34 E
Colleen Bawn, *Zimbabwe* **55 G2** 21 0S 29 12 E
College Park, *U.S.A.* **77 J3** 33 40N 84 27W
College Station, *U.S.A.* **81 K6** 30 37N 96 21W
Collie, *Australia* **61 F2** 33 22S 116 8 E
Collier B., *Australia* **60 C3** 16 10S 124 15 E
Collier Ra., *Australia* **61 D2** 24 45S 119 10 E
Collina, Passo di, *Italy* **20 B4** 44 2N 10 56 E
Collingwood, *Canada* **78 B4** 44 29N 80 13W
Collingwood, *N.Z.* **59 J4** 40 41S 172 40 E
Collins, *Canada* **70 B2** 50 17N 89 27W
Collinsville, *Australia* **62 C4** 20 30S 147 56 E
Collipulli, *Chile* **94 D1** 37 55S 72 30W
Collooney, *Ireland* **13 B3** 54 11N 8 29W
Colmar, *France* **18 B7** 48 5N 7 20 E
Colo →, *Australia* **63 E5** 33 25S 150 52 E
Cologne = Köln, *Germany* **16 C4** 50 56N 6 57 E
Colom, I. d'en, *Spain* **22 B11** 39 58N 4 16 E
Coloma, *U.S.A.* **84 G6** 38 48N 120 53W
Colomb-Béchar = Béchar, *Algeria* **50 B5** 31 38N 2 18W
Colombia ■, *S. Amer.* **92 C4** 3 45N 73 0W
Colombian Basin, *S. Amer.* **66 H12** 14 0N 76 0W
Colombo, *Sri Lanka* **40 R11** 6 56N 79 58 E
Colón, *Buenos Aires, Argentina* **94 C3** 33 53S 61 7W
Colón, *Entre Ríos, Argentina* **94 C4** 32 12S 58 10W
Colón, *Cuba* **88 B3** 22 42N 80 54W
Colón, *Panama* **88 E4** 9 20N 79 54W
Colonia de Sant Jordi, *Spain* **22 B9** 39 19N 2 59 E
Colonia del Sacramento, *Uruguay* **94 C4** 34 25S 57 50W
Colonia Dora, *Argentina* **94 B3** 28 34S 62 59W
Colonial Beach, *U.S.A.* **76 F7** 38 15N 76 58W
Colonie, *U.S.A.* **79 D11** 42 43N 73 50W
Colonsay, *Canada* **73 C7** 51 59N 105 52W
Colonsay, *U.K.* **12 E2** 56 5N 6 12W
Colorado □, *U.S.A.* **83 G10** 39 30N 105 30W
Colorado →, *Argentina* **96 D4** 39 50S 62 8W
Colorado →, *N. Amer.* **83 L6** 31 45N 114 40W
Colorado →, *U.S.A.* **81 L7** 28 36N 95 59W
Colorado City, *U.S.A.* **81 J4** 32 24N 100 52W
Colorado Desert, *U.S.A.* **74 D3** 34 20N 116 0W
Colorado Plateau, *U.S.A.* **83 H8** 37 0N 111 0W
Colorado River Aqueduct, *U.S.A.* **85 L12** 34 17N 114 10W
Colorado Springs, *U.S.A.* **80 F2** 38 50N 104 49W
Colotlán, *Mexico* **86 C4** 22 6N 103 16W
Colstrip, *U.S.A.* **82 D10** 45 53N 106 38W
Colton, *U.S.A.* **79 B10** 44 33N 74 56W
Columbia, *Ky., U.S.A.* **76 G3** 37 6N 85 18W
Columbia, *La., U.S.A.* **81 J8** 32 6N 92 5W
Columbia, *Miss., U.S.A.* **81 K10** 31 15N 89 50W
Columbia, *Mo., U.S.A.* **80 F8** 38 57N 92 20W
Columbia, *Pa., U.S.A.* **79 F8** 40 2N 76 30W
Columbia, *S.C., U.S.A.* **77 J5** 34 0N 81 2W
Columbia, *Tenn., U.S.A.* **77 H2** 35 37N 87 2W
Columbia →, *N. Amer.* **84 D2** 46 15N 124 5W
Columbia, C., *Canada* **4 A4** 83 0N 70 0W
Columbia, District of □, *U.S.A.* **76 F7** 38 55N 77 0W
Columbia, Mt., *Canada* **72 C5** 52 8N 117 20W
Columbia Basin, *U.S.A.* **82 C4** 46 45N 119 5W
Columbia Falls, *U.S.A.* **82 B6** 48 23N 114 11W
Columbia Mts., *Canada* **72 C5** 52 0N 119 0W
Columbia Plateau, *U.S.A.* **82 D5** 44 0N 117 30W
Columbiana, *U.S.A.* **78 F4** 40 53N 80 42W
Columbretes, Is., *Spain* **19 C6** 39 50N 0 50 E
Columbus, *Ga., U.S.A.* **77 J3** 32 28N 84 59W
Columbus, *Ind., U.S.A.* **76 F3** 39 13N 85 55W
Columbus, *Kans., U.S.A.* **81 G7** 37 10N 94 50W
Columbus, *Miss., U.S.A.* **77 J1** 33 30N 88 25W
Columbus, *Mont., U.S.A.* **82 D9** 45 38N 109 15W
Columbus, *N. Mex., U.S.A.* **83 L10** 31 50N 107 38W
Columbus, *Nebr., U.S.A.* **80 E6** 41 26N 97 22W
Columbus, *Ohio, U.S.A.* **76 F4** 39 58N 83 0W
Columbus, *Tex., U.S.A.* **81 L6** 29 42N 96 33W
Colusa, *U.S.A.* **84 F4** 39 13N 122 1W
Colville, *U.S.A.* **82 B5** 48 33N 117 54W
Colville →, *U.S.A.* **68 A4** 70 25N 150 30W
Colville, C., *N.Z.* **59 G5** 36 29S 175 21 E
Colwood, *Canada* **84 B3** 48 26N 123 29W
Colwyn Bay, *U.K.* **10 D4** 53 18N 3 44W
Comácchio, *Italy* **20 B5** 44 42N 12 11 E
Comalcalco, *Mexico* **87 D6** 18 16N 93 13W
Comallo, *Argentina* **96 E2** 41 0S 70 5W
Comanche, *U.S.A.* **81 K5** 31 54N 98 36W
Comayagua, *Honduras* **88 D2** 14 25N 87 37W
Combahee →, *U.S.A.* **77 J5** 32 30N 80 31W
Combarbalá, *Chile* **94 C1** 31 11S 71 2W
Comber, *Canada* **78 D2** 42 14N 82 33W
Comber, *U.K.* **13 B6** 54 33N 5 45W
Combermere, *Canada* **78 A7** 45 22N 77 37W
Comblain-au-Pont, *Belgium* **15 D5** 50 29N 5 35 E
Comeragh Mts., *Ireland* **13 D4** 52 18N 7 34W
Comet, *Australia* **62 C4** 23 36S 148 38 E
Comilla, *Bangla.* **41 H17** 23 28N 91 10 E
Comino, *Malta* **23 C1** 36 2N 14 20 E
Comino, C., *Italy* **20 D3** 40 32N 9 49 E
Comitán, *Mexico* **87 D6** 16 18N 92 9W
Commerce, *Ga., U.S.A.* **77 H4** 34 12N 83 28W
Commerce, *Tex., U.S.A.* **81 J7** 33 15N 95 54W
Committee B., *Canada* **69 B11** 68 30N 86 30W
Commonwealth B., *Antarctica* **5 C10** 67 0S 144 0 E
Commoron Cr. →, *Australia* **63 D5** 28 22S 150 8 E
Communism Pk. = Kommunizma, Pik, *Tajikistan* **26 F8** 39 0N 72 2 E
Como, *Italy* **18 D8** 45 47N 9 5 E
Como, Lago di, *Italy* **18 D8** 46 0N 9 11 E
Comodoro Rivadavia, *Argentina* **96 F3** 45 50S 67 40W
Comorin, C., *India* **40 Q10** 8 3N 77 40 E
Comoro Is. = Comoros ■, *Ind. Oc.* **49 H8** 12 10S 44 15 E
Comoros ■, *Ind. Oc.* **49 H8** 12 10S 44 15 E
Comox, *Canada* **72 D4** 49 42N 124 55W
Compiègne, *France* **18 B5** 49 24N 2 50 E
Compostela, *Mexico* **86 C4** 21 15N 104 53W
Comprida, I., *Brazil* **95 A6** 24 50S 47 42W
Compton, *Canada* **79 A13** 45 14N 71 49W
Compton, *U.S.A.* **85 M8** 33 54N 118 13W
Comrat, *Moldova* **17 E15** 46 18N 28 40 E
Con Cuong, *Vietnam* **38 C5** 19 2N 104 54 E
Con Son, *Vietnam* **39 H6** 8 41N 106 37 E
Conakry, *Guinea* **50 G3** 9 29N 13 49W
Conara, *Australia* **62 G4** 41 50S 147 26 E
Concarneau, *France* **18 C2** 47 52N 3 56W
Conceição, *Mozam.* **55 F4** 18 47S 36 7 E
Conceição da Barra, *Brazil* **93 G11** 18 35S 39 45W
Conceição do Araguaia, *Brazil* **93 E9** 8 0S 49 2W
Concepción, *Argentina* **94 B2** 27 20S 65 35W
Concepción, *Bolivia* **92 G6** 16 15S 62 8W
Concepción, *Chile* **94 D1** 36 50S 73 0W
Concepción, *Mexico* **87 D6** 18 15N 90 5W
Concepción, *Paraguay* **94 A4** 23 22S 57 26W
Concepción □, *Chile* **94 D1** 37 0S 72 30W
Concepción →, *Mexico* **86 A2** 30 32N 113 2W
Concepción, Est. de, *Chile* **96 G2** 50 30S 74 55W
Concepción, L., *Bolivia* **92 G6** 17 20S 61 20W
Concepción, Punta, *Mexico* **86 B2** 26 55N 111 59W
Concepción del Oro, *Mexico* **86 C4** 24 40N 101 30W
Concepción del Uruguay, *Argentina* **94 C4** 32 35S 58 20W
Conception, Pt., *U.S.A.* **85 L6** 34 27N 120 28W
Conception B., *Canada* **71 C9** 47 45N 53 0W
Conception B., *Namibia* **56 C1** 23 55S 14 22 E
Conception I., *Bahamas* **89 B4** 23 52N 75 9W
Concession, *Zimbabwe* **55 F3** 17 27S 30 56 E
Conchas Dam, *U.S.A.* **81 H2** 35 22N 104 11W
Concho, *U.S.A.* **83 J9** 34 28N 109 36W
Concho →, *U.S.A.* **81 K5** 31 34N 99 43W
Conchos →, *Chihuahua, Mexico* **86 B4** 29 32N 105 0W
Conchos →, *Tamaulipas, Mexico* **87 B5** 25 9N 98 35W
Concord, *Calif., U.S.A.* **84 H4** 37 59N 122 2W
Concord, *N.C., U.S.A.* **77 H5** 35 25N 80 35W
Concord, *N.H., U.S.A.* **79 C13** 43 12N 71 32W
Concordia, *Argentina* **94 C4** 31 20S 58 2W
Concórdia, *Brazil* **92 D5** 4 36S 66 36W
Concordia, *Mexico* **86 C3** 23 18N 106 2W
Concordia, *U.S.A.* **80 F6** 39 34N 97 40W
Concrete, *U.S.A.* **82 B3** 48 32N 121 45W
Condamine, *Australia* **63 D5** 26 56S 150 9 E
Conde, *U.S.A.* **80 C5** 45 9N 98 6W
Condeúba, *Brazil* **93 F10** 14 52S 42 0W
Condobolin, *Australia* **63 E4** 33 4S 147 6 E
Condon, *U.S.A.* **82 D3** 45 14N 120 11W
Conegliano, *Italy* **20 B5** 45 53N 12 18 E
Conejera, I. = Conills, I. des, *Spain* **22 B9** 39 11N 2 58 E
Conejos, *Mexico* **86 B4** 26 14N 103 53W
Confuso →, *Paraguay* **94 B4** 25 9S 57 34W
Congleton, *U.K.* **10 D5** 53 10N 2 13W
Congo (Kinshasa) = Congo, Dem. Rep. of the ■, *Africa* **52 E4** 3 0S 23 0 E
Congo ■, *Africa* **52 E3** 1 0S 16 0 E
Congo →, *Africa* **52 F2** 6 4S 12 24 E
Congo, Dem. Rep. of the ■, *Africa* **52 E4** 3 0S 23 0 E
Congo Basin, *Africa* **52 E4** 0 10S 24 30 E
Congonhas, *Brazil* **95 A7** 20 30S 43 52W
Congress, *U.S.A.* **83 J7** 34 9N 112 51W
Conills, I. des, *Spain* **22 B9** 39 11N 2 58 E
Coniston, *Canada* **70 C3** 46 29N 80 51W
Conjeeveram = Kanchipuram, *India* **40 N11** 12 52N 79 45 E
Conklin, *Canada* **73 B6** 55 38N 111 5W
Conklin, *U.S.A.* **79 D9** 42 2N 75 49W
Conn, L., *Ireland* **13 B2** 54 3N 9 15W
Connacht □, *Ireland* **13 C2** 53 43N 9 12W
Conneaut, *U.S.A.* **78 E4** 41 57N 80 34W
Connecticut □, *U.S.A.* **79 E12** 41 30N 72 45W
Connecticut →, *U.S.A.* **79 E12** 41 16N 72 20W
Connell, *U.S.A.* **82 C4** 46 40N 118 52W
Connellsville, *U.S.A.* **78 F5** 40 1N 79 35W
Connemara, *Ireland* **13 C2** 53 29N 9 45W
Connemaugh →, *U.S.A.* **78 F5** 40 28N 79 19W
Connersville, *U.S.A.* **76 F3** 39 39N 85 8W
Connors Ra., *Australia* **62 C4** 21 40S 149 10 E
Conquest, *Canada* **73 C7** 51 32N 107 14W
Conrad, *U.S.A.* **82 B8** 48 10N 111 57W
Conran, C., *Australia* **63 F4** 37 49S 148 44 E
Conroe, *U.S.A.* **81 K7** 30 19N 95 27W
Consecon, *Canada* **78 C7** 44 0N 77 31W
Conselheiro Lafaiete, *Brazil* **95 A7** 20 40S 43 48W
Consett, *U.K.* **10 C6** 54 51N 1 50W
Consort, *Canada* **73 C6** 52 1N 110 46W
Constance = Konstanz, *Germany* **16 E5** 47 40N 9 10 E
Constance, L. = Bodensee, *Europe* **18 C8** 47 35N 9 25 E
Constanța, *Romania* **17 F15** 44 14N 28 38 E
Constantia, *U.S.A.* **79 C8** 43 15N 76 1W
Constantine, *Algeria* **50 A7** 36 25N 6 42 E
Constitución, *Chile* **94 D1** 35 20S 72 30W
Constitución, *Uruguay* **94 C4** 31 0S 57 50W
Consul, *Canada* **73 D7** 49 20N 109 30W
Contact, *U.S.A.* **82 F6** 41 46N 114 45W
Contai, *India* **43 J12** 21 54N 87 46 E
Contamana, *Peru* **92 E4** 7 19S 74 55W
Contas →, *Brazil* **93 F11** 14 17S 39 1W
Contoocook, *U.S.A.* **79 C13** 43 13N 71 45W
Contra Costa, *Mozam.* **57 D5** 25 9S 33 30 E
Contwoyto L., *Canada* **68 B8** 65 42N 110 50W
Conway = Conwy, *U.K.* **10 D4** 53 17N 3 50W
Conway = Conwy →, *U.K.* **10 D4** 53 17N 3 50W
Conway, *Ark., U.S.A.* **81 H8** 35 5N 92 26W
Conway, *N.H., U.S.A.* **79 C13** 43 59N 71 7W
Conway, *S.C., U.S.A.* **77 J6** 33 51N 79 3W
Conway, L., *Australia* **63 D2** 28 17S 135 35 E
Conwy, *U.K.* **10 D4** 53 17N 3 50W
Conwy □, *U.K.* **10 D4** 53 10N 3 44W
Conwy →, *U.K.* **10 D4** 53 17N 3 50W
Coober Pedy, *Australia* **63 D1** 29 1S 134 43 E
Cooch Behar = Koch Bihar, *India* **41 F16** 26 22N 89 29 E
Cooinda, *Australia* **60 B5** 13 15S 130 5 E
Cook, *Australia* **61 F5** 30 37S 130 25 E
Cook, *U.S.A.* **80 B8** 47 49N 92 39W
Cook, B., *Chile* **96 H3** 55 10S 70 0W
Cook, C., *Canada* **72 C3** 50 8N 127 55W
Cook, Mt., *N.Z.* **59 K3** 43 36S 170 9 E
Cook Inlet, *U.S.A.* **68 C4** 60 0N 152 0W
Cook Is., *Pac. Oc.* **65 J12** 17 0S 160 0W
Cook Strait, *N.Z.* **59 J5** 41 15S 174 29 E
Cookeville, *U.S.A.* **77 G3** 36 10N 85 30W
Cookhouse, *S. Africa* **56 E4** 32 44S 25 47 E
Cookshire, *Canada* **79 A13** 45 25N 71 38W
Cookstown, *U.K.* **13 B5** 54 39N 6 45W
Cooksville, *Canada* **78 C5** 43 36N 79 35W
Cooktown, *Australia* **62 B4** 15 30S 145 16 E
Coolabah, *Australia* **63 E4** 31 1S 146 43 E
Cooladdi, *Australia* **63 D4** 26 37S 145 23 E
Coolah, *Australia* **63 E4** 31 48S 149 41 E
Coolamon, *Australia* **63 E4** 34 46S 147 8 E
Coolgardie, *Australia* **61 F3** 30 55S 121 8 E
Coolidge, *U.S.A.* **83 K8** 32 59N 111 31W
Coolidge Dam, *U.S.A.* **83 K8** 33 0N 110 20W
Cooma, *Australia* **63 F4** 36 12S 149 8 E
Coon Rapids, *U.S.A.* **80 C8** 45 9N 93 19W
Coonabarabran, *Australia* **63 E4** 31 14S 149 18 E
Coonalpyn, *Australia* **63 F2** 35 43S 139 52 E
Coonamble, *Australia* **63 E4** 30 56S 148 27 E
Coonana, *Australia* **61 F3** 31 0S 123 0 E
Coondapoor, *India* **40 N9** 13 42N 74 40 E
Cooninie, L., *Australia* **63 D2** 26 4S 139 59 E
Cooper, *U.S.A.* **81 J7** 33 23N 95 42W
Cooper Cr. →, *Australia* **63 D2** 28 29S 137 46 E
Cooperstown, *N. Dak., U.S.A.* **80 B5** 47 27N 98 8W
Cooperstown, *N.Y., U.S.A.* **79 D10** 42 42N 74 56W
Coorabie, *Australia* **61 F5** 31 54S 132 18 E
Coorow, *Australia* **61 E2** 29 53S 116 2 E
Cooroy, *Australia* **63 D5** 26 22S 152 54 E
Coos Bay, *U.S.A.* **82 E1** 43 22N 124 13W
Coosa →, *U.S.A.* **77 J2** 32 30N 86 16W
Cootamundra, *Australia* **63 E4** 34 36S 148 1 E
Cootehill, *Ireland* **13 B4** 54 4N 7 5W
Copahue Paso, *Argentina* **94 D1** 37 49S 71 8W
Copainalá, *Mexico* **87 D6** 17 8N 93 11W
Copake Falls, *U.S.A.* **79 D11** 42 7N 73 31W
Copán, *Honduras* **88 D2** 14 50N 89 9W
Cope, *U.S.A.* **80 F3** 39 40N 102 51W
Copenhagen = København, *Denmark* **9 J15** 55 41N 12 34 E
Copenhagen, *U.S.A.* **79 C9** 43 54N 75 41W
Copiapó, *Chile* **94 B1** 27 30S 70 20W
Copiapó →, *Chile* **94 B1** 27 19S 70 56W
Coplay, *U.S.A.* **79 F9** 40 44N 75 29W
Copp L., *Canada* **72 A6** 60 14N 114 40W
Coppename →, *Surinam* **93 B7** 5 48N 55 55W
Copper Harbor, *U.S.A.* **76 B2** 47 28N 87 53W
Copper Queen, *Zimbabwe* **55 F2** 17 29S 29 18 E
Copperas Cove, *U.S.A.* **81 K6** 31 8N 97 54W
Copperbelt □, *Zambia* **55 E2** 13 15S 27 30 E
Coppermine = Kugluktuk, *Canada* **68 B8** 67 50N 115 5W
Coppermine →, *Canada* **68 B8** 67 49N 116 4W
Copperopolis, *U.S.A.* **84 H6** 37 58N 120 38W
Coquet →, *U.K.* **10 B6** 55 20N 1 32W
Coquilhatville = Mbandaka, *Dem. Rep. of the Congo* **52 D3** 0 1N 18 18 E
Coquille, *U.S.A.* **82 E1** 43 11N 124 11W
Coquimbo, *Chile* **94 C1** 30 0S 71 20W
Coquimbo □, *Chile* **94 C1** 31 0S 71 0W
Corabia, *Romania* **17 G13** 43 48N 24 30 E
Coracora, *Peru* **92 G4** 15 5S 73 45W
Coraki, *Australia* **63 D5** 28 59S 153 17 E
Coral, *U.S.A.* **78 F5** 40 29N 79 10W
Coral Gables, *U.S.A.* **77 N5** 25 45N 80 16W
Coral Harbour = Salliq, *Canada* **69 B11** 64 8N 83 10W
Coral Sea, *Pac. Oc.* **64 J7** 15 0S 150 0 E
Coral Springs, *U.S.A.* **77 M5** 26 16N 80 13W
Coraopolis, *U.S.A.* **78 F4** 40 31N 80 10W
Corato, *Italy* **20 D7** 41 9N 16 25 E
Corbin, *U.S.A.* **76 G3** 36 57N 84 6W
Corby, *U.K.* **11 E7** 52 30N 0 41W
Corcaigh = Cork, *Ireland* **13 E3** 51 54N 8 29W
Corcoran, *U.S.A.* **84 J7** 36 6N 119 33W
Corcubión, *Spain* **19 A1** 42 56N 9 12W
Cordele, *U.S.A.* **77 K4** 31 58N 83 47W
Cordell, *U.S.A.* **81 H5** 35 17N 98 59W
Córdoba, *Argentina* **94 C3** 31 20S 64 10W
Córdoba, *Mexico* **87 D5** 18 50N 97 0W
Córdoba, *Spain* **19 D3** 37 50N 4 50W
Córdoba □, *Argentina* **94 C3** 31 22S 64 15W
Córdoba, Sierra de, *Argentina* **94 C3** 31 10S 64 25W
Cordova, *U.S.A.* **68 B5** 60 33N 145 45W
Corella →, *Australia* **62 B3** 19 34S 140 47 E
Corfield, *Australia* **62 C3** 21 40S 143 21 E
Corfu = Kérkira, *Greece* **23 A3** 39 38N 19 50 E
Corfu, Str. of, *Greece* **23 A4** 39 34N 20 0 E
Coria, *Spain* **19 C2** 39 58N 6 33W
Corigliano Cálabro, *Italy* **20 E7** 39 36N 16 31 E
Coringa Is., *Australia* **62 B4** 16 58S 149 58 E
Corinth = Kórinthos, *Greece* **21 F10** 37 56N 22 55 E
Corinth, *Miss., U.S.A.* **77 H1** 34 56N 88 31W
Corinth, *N.Y., U.S.A.* **79 C11** 43 14N 73 49W
Corinth, *N.Y., U.S.A.* **79 C11** 43 15N 73 49W
Corinth, G. of = Korinthiakós Kólpos, *Greece* **21 E10** 38 16N 22 30 E
Corinto, *Brazil* **93 G10** 18 20S 44 30W
Corinto, *Nic.* **88 D2** 12 30N 87 10W
Cork, *Ireland* **13 E3** 51 54N 8 29W
Cork □, *Ireland* **13 E3** 51 57N 8 40W
Cork Harbour, *Ireland* **13 E3** 51 47N 8 16W
Çorlu, *Turkey* **21 D12** 41 11N 27 49 E
Cormack L., *Canada* **72 A4** 60 56N 121 37W
Cormorant, *Canada* **73 C8** 54 14N 100 35W
Cormorant L., *Canada* **73 C8** 54 15N 100 50W
Corn Is. = Maíz, Is. del, *Nic.* **88 D3** 12 15N 83 4W
Cornélio Procópio, *Brazil* **95 A5** 23 7S 50 40W
Corner Brook, *Canada* **71 C8** 48 57N 57 58W
Cornești, *Moldova* **17 E15** 47 21N 28 1 E
Corning, *Ark., U.S.A.* **81 G9** 36 25N 90 35W
Corning, *Calif., U.S.A.* **82 G2** 39 56N 122 11W
Corning, *Iowa, U.S.A.* **80 E7** 40 59N 94 44W
Corning, *N.Y., U.S.A.* **78 D7** 42 9N 77 3W
Cornwall, *Canada* **79 A10** 45 2N 74 44W
Cornwall, *U.S.A.* **79 F8** 40 17N 76 25W
Cornwall □, *U.K.* **11 G3** 50 26N 4 40W
Corny Pt., *Australia* **63 E2** 34 55S 137 0 E
Coro, *Venezuela* **92 A5** 11 25N 69 41W
Coroatá, *Brazil* **93 D10** 4 8S 44 0W
Corocoro, *Bolivia* **92 G5** 17 15S 68 28W
Coroico, *Bolivia* **92 G5** 16 0S 67 50W
Coromandel, *N.Z.* **59 G5** 36 45S 175 31 E
Coromandel Coast, *India* **40 N12** 12 30N 81 0 E
Corona, *Calif., U.S.A.* **85 M9** 33 53N 117 34W
Corona, *N. Mex., U.S.A.* **83 J11** 34 15N 105 36W
Coronach, *Canada* **73 D7** 49 7N 105 31W
Coronado, *U.S.A.* **85 N9** 32 41N 117 11W
Coronado, B. de, *Costa Rica* **88 E3** 9 0N 83 40W
Coronados, Is. los, *U.S.A.* **85 N9** 32 25N 117 15W
Coronation, *Canada* **72 C6** 52 5N 111 27W
Coronation Gulf, *Canada* **68 B9** 68 25N 110 0W
Coronation I., *Antarctica* **5 C18** 60 45S 46 0W
Coronation Is., *Australia* **60 B3** 14 57S 124 55 E
Coronda, *Argentina* **94 C3** 31 58S 60 56W
Coronel, *Chile* **94 D1** 37 0S 73 10W
Coronel Bogado, *Paraguay* **94 B4** 27 11S 56 18W
Coronel Dorrego, *Argentina* **94 D3** 38 40S 61 10W
Coronel Oviedo, *Paraguay* **94 B4** 25 24S 56 30W
Coronel Pringles, *Argentina* **94 D3** 38 0S 61 30W
Coronel Suárez, *Argentina* **94 D3** 37 30S 61 52W
Coronel Vidal, *Argentina* **94 D4** 37 28S 57 45W
Coropuna, Nevado, *Peru* **92 G4** 15 30S 72 41W
Corowa, *Australia* **63 F4** 35 58S 146 21 E
Corozal, *Belize* **87 D7** 18 23N 88 23W
Corpus, *Argentina* **95 B4** 27 10S 55 30W
Corpus Christi, *U.S.A.* **81 M6** 27 47N 97 24W
Corpus Christi, L., *U.S.A.* **81 L6** 28 2N 97 52W
Corralejo, *Canary Is.* **22 F6** 28 43N 13 53W
Corraun Pen., *Ireland* **13 C2** 53 54N 9 54W
Correntes, C. das, *Mozam.* **57 C6** 24 6S 35 34 E
Corrib, L., *Ireland* **13 C2** 53 27N 9 16W
Corrientes, *Argentina* **94 B4** 27 30S 58 45W

Corrientes □, Argentina 94 B4 28 0S 57 0W
Corrientes →, Argentina 94 C4 30 42S 59 38W
Corrientes →, Peru 92 D4 3 43S 74 35W
Corrientes, C., Colombia 92 B3 5 30N 77 34W
Corrientes, C., Cuba 88 B3 21 43N 84 30W
Corrientes, C., Mexico 86 C3 20 25N 105 42W
Corrigan, U.S.A. 81 K7 31 0N 94 52W
Corrigin, Australia 61 F2 32 20S 117 53 E
Corry, U.S.A. 78 E5 41 55N 79 39W
Corryong, Australia 63 F4 36 12S 147 53 E
Corse, France 18 F8 42 0N 9 0 E
Corse, C., France 18 E8 43 1N 9 25 E
Corsica = Corse, France 18 F8 42 0N 9 0 E
Corsicana, U.S.A. 81 J6 32 6N 96 28W
Corte, France 18 E8 42 19N 9 11 E
Cortez, U.S.A. 83 H9 37 21N 108 35W
Cortland, N.Y., U.S.A. 79 D8 42 36N 76 11W
Cortland, Ohio, U.S.A. 78 E4 41 20N 80 44W
Çorum, Turkey 25 F5 40 30N 34 57 E
Corumbá, Brazil 92 G7 19 0S 57 30W
Corunna = A Coruña, Spain 19 A1 43 20N 8 25W
Corvallis, U.S.A. 82 D2 44 34N 123 16W
Corvette, L. de la, Canada 70 B5 53 25N 74 3W
Corydon, U.S.A. 80 E8 40 46N 93 19W
Cosalá, Mexico 86 C3 24 28N 106 40W
Cosamaloapan, Mexico 87 D5 18 23N 95 50W
Cosenza, Italy 20 E7 39 18N 16 15 E
Coshocton, U.S.A. 78 F3 40 16N 81 51W
Cosmo Newberry, Australia 61 E3 28 0S 122 54 E
Coso Junction, U.S.A. 85 J9 36 3N 117 57W
Coso Pk., U.S.A. 85 J9 36 13N 117 44W
Cosquín, Argentina 94 C3 31 15S 64 30W
Costa Blanca, Spain 19 C5 38 25N 0 10W
Costa Brava, Spain 19 B7 41 30N 3 0 E
Costa del Sol, Spain 19 D3 36 30N 4 30W
Costa Dorada, Spain 19 B6 41 12N 1 15 E
Costa Mesa, U.S.A. 85 M9 33 38N 117 55W
Costa Rica ■, Cent. Amer. 88 E3 10 0N 84 0W
Cosumnes →, U.S.A. 84 G5 38 16N 121 26W
Cotabato, Phil. 37 C6 7 14N 124 15 E
Cotagaita, Bolivia 94 A2 20 45S 65 40W
Côte d'Azur, France 18 E7 43 25N 7 10 E
Côte-d'Ivoire = Ivory Coast ■, Africa 50 G4 7 30N 5 0W
Coteau des Prairies, U.S.A. 80 C6 45 20N 97 50W
Coteau du Missouri, U.S.A. 80 B4 47 0N 100 0W
Coteau Landing, Canada 79 A10 45 15N 74 13W
Cotentin, France 18 B3 49 15N 1 30W
Cotillo, Canary Is. 22 F5 28 41N 14 1W
Cotonou, Benin 50 G6 6 20N 2 25 E
Cotopaxi, Ecuador 92 D3 0 40S 78 30W
Cotswold Hills, U.K. 11 F5 51 42N 2 10W
Cottage Grove, U.S.A. 82 E2 43 48N 123 3W
Cottbus, Germany 16 C8 51 45N 14 20 E
Cottonwood, U.S.A. 83 J7 34 45N 112 1W
Cotulla, U.S.A. 81 L5 28 26N 99 14W
Coudersport, U.S.A. 78 E6 41 46N 78 1W
Couedic, C. du, Australia 63 F2 36 5S 136 40 E
Coulee City, U.S.A. 82 C4 47 37N 119 17W
Coulman I., Antarctica 5 D11 73 35S 170 0 E
Coulonge →, Canada 70 C4 45 52N 76 46W
Coulterville, U.S.A. 84 H6 37 43N 120 12W
Council, U.S.A. 82 D5 44 44N 116 26W
Council Bluffs, U.S.A. 80 E7 41 16N 95 52W
Council Grove, U.S.A. 80 F6 38 40N 96 29W
Coupeville, U.S.A. 84 B4 48 13N 122 41W
Courantyne →, S. Amer. 92 B7 5 55N 57 5W
Courcelles, Belgium 15 D4 50 28N 4 22 E
Courtenay, Canada 72 D4 49 45N 125 0W
Courtland, U.S.A. 84 G5 38 20N 121 34W
Courtrai = Kortrijk, Belgium 15 D3 50 50N 3 17 E
Courtright, Canada 78 D2 42 49N 82 28W
Coushatta, U.S.A. 81 J8 32 1N 93 21W
Coutts Crossing, Australia 63 D5 29 49S 152 55 E
Couvin, Belgium 15 D4 50 3N 4 29 E
Cove I., Canada 78 A3 45 17N 81 44W
Coventry, U.K. 11 E6 52 25N 1 28W
Covilhã, Portugal 19 B2 40 17N 7 31W
Covington, Ga., U.S.A. 77 J4 33 36N 83 51W
Covington, Ky., U.S.A. 76 F3 39 5N 84 31W
Covington, Okla., U.S.A. 81 G6 36 18N 97 35W
Covington, Tenn., U.S.A. 81 H10 35 34N 89 39W
Covington, Va., U.S.A. 76 G5 37 47N 79 59W
Cowal, L., Australia 63 E4 33 40S 147 25 E
Cowan, L., Australia 61 F3 31 45S 121 45 E
Cowan L., Canada 73 C7 54 0N 107 15W
Cowangie, Australia 63 F3 35 12S 141 26 E
Cowansville, Canada 79 A12 45 14N 72 46W
Coward Springs, Australia 63 D2 29 24S 136 49 E
Cowcowing Lakes, Australia 61 F2 30 55S 117 20 E
Cowdenbeath, U.K. 12 E5 56 7N 3 21W
Cowell, Australia 63 E2 33 39S 136 56 E
Cowes, U.K. 11 G6 50 45N 1 18W
Cowichan L., Canada 84 B2 48 53N 124 17W
Cowlitz →, U.S.A. 84 D4 46 6N 122 55W
Cowra, Australia 63 E4 33 49S 148 42 E
Coxilha Grande, Brazil 95 B5 28 18S 51 30W
Coxim, Brazil 93 G8 18 30S 54 55W
Cox's Bazar, Bangla. 41 J17 21 26N 91 59 E
Coyote Wells, U.S.A. 85 N11 32 44N 115 58W
Coyuca de Benítez, Mexico 87 D4 17 1N 100 8W
Coyuca de Catalan, Mexico 86 D4 18 18N 100 41W
Cozad, U.S.A. 80 E5 40 52N 99 59W
Cozumel, Mexico 87 C7 20 31N 86 55W
Cozumel, Isla, Mexico 87 C7 20 30N 86 40W
Cracow = Kraków, Poland 17 C10 50 4N 19 57 E
Cracow, Australia 63 D5 25 17S 150 17 E
Cradock, Australia 63 E2 32 6S 138 31 E
Cradock, S. Africa 56 E4 32 8S 25 36 E
Craig, U.S.A. 82 F10 40 31N 107 33W
Craigavon, U.K. 13 B5 54 27N 6 23W
Craigmore, Zimbabwe 55 G3 20 28S 32 50 E
Craik, Canada 73 C7 51 3N 105 49W
Crailsheim, Germany 16 D6 49 8N 10 5 E
Craiova, Romania 17 F12 44 21N 23 48 E
Cramsie, Australia 62 C3 23 20S 144 15 E
Cranberry L., U.S.A. 79 B10 44 11N 74 50W
Cranberry Portage, Canada 73 C8 54 35N 101 23W
Cranbrook, Australia 61 F2 34 18S 117 33 E
Cranbrook, Canada 72 D5 49 30N 115 46W
Crandon, U.S.A. 80 C10 45 34N 88 54W
Crane, Oreg., U.S.A. 82 E4 43 25N 118 35W
Crane, Tex., U.S.A. 81 K3 31 24N 102 21W
Cranston, U.S.A. 79 E13 41 47N 71 26W
Crater L., U.S.A. 82 E2 42 56N 122 6W
Crater Lake National Park, U.S.A. 82 E2 42 55N 122 10W
Crateús, Brazil 93 E10 5 10S 40 39W
Crato, Brazil 93 E11 7 10S 39 25W
Craven, L., Canada 70 B4 54 20N 76 56W
Crawford, U.S.A. 80 D3 42 41N 103 25W
Crawfordsville, U.S.A. 76 E2 40 2N 86 54W
Crawley, U.K. 11 F7 51 7N 0 11W
Crazy Mts., U.S.A. 82 C8 46 12N 110 20W
Crean L., Canada 73 C7 54 5N 106 9W
Crediton, Canada 78 C3 43 17N 81 33W
Cree →, Canada 73 B7 58 57N 105 47W
Cree →, U.K. 12 G4 54 55N 4 25W
Cree L., Canada 73 B7 57 30N 106 30W
Creede, U.S.A. 83 H10 37 51N 106 56W
Creekside, U.S.A. 78 F5 40 40N 79 11W
Creel, Mexico 86 B3 27 45N 107 38W
Creemore, Canada 78 B4 44 19N 80 6W
Creighton, Canada 73 C8 54 45N 101 54W
Creighton, U.S.A. 80 D6 42 28N 97 54W
Crema, Italy 18 D8 45 22N 9 41 E
Cremona, Italy 18 D9 45 7N 10 2 E
Cres, Croatia 16 F8 44 58N 14 25 E
Crescent City, U.S.A. 82 F1 41 45N 124 12W
Crespo, Argentina 94 C3 32 2S 60 19W
Cresson, U.S.A. 78 F6 40 28N 78 36W
Crestline, Calif., U.S.A. 85 L9 34 14N 117 18W
Crestline, Ohio, U.S.A. 78 F2 40 47N 82 44W
Creston, Canada 72 D5 49 10N 116 31W
Creston, Calif., U.S.A. 84 K6 35 32N 120 33W
Creston, Iowa, U.S.A. 80 E7 41 4N 94 22W
Crestview, Calif., U.S.A. 84 H8 37 46N 118 58W
Crestview, Fla., U.S.A. 77 K2 30 46N 86 34W
Crete = Kríti, Greece 23 D7 35 15N 25 0 E
Crete, U.S.A. 80 E6 40 38N 96 58W
Créteil, France 18 B5 48 47N 2 28 E
Creus, C. de, Spain 19 A7 42 20N 3 19 E
Creuse →, France 18 C4 47 0N 0 34 E
Crewe, U.K. 10 D5 53 6N 2 26W
Crewkerne, U.K. 11 G5 50 53N 2 48W
Criciúma, Brazil 95 B6 28 40S 49 23W
Crieff, U.K. 12 E5 56 22N 3 50W
Crimea □, Ukraine 25 E5 45 30N 33 10 E
Crimean Pen. = Krymskyy Pivostriv, Ukraine 25 F5 45 0N 34 0 E
Crişul Alb →, Romania 17 E11 46 42N 21 17 E
Crişul Negru →, Romania 17 E11 46 42N 21 16 E
Crna →, Macedonia 21 D9 41 33N 21 59 E
Crna Gora = Montenegro □, Yugoslavia 21 C8 42 40N 19 20 E
Crna Gora, Macedonia 21 C9 42 10N 21 30 E
Crna Reka = Crna →, Macedonia 21 D9 41 33N 21 59 E
Croagh Patrick, Ireland 13 C2 53 46N 9 40W
Croatia ■, Europe 16 F9 45 20N 16 0 E
Crocker, Banjaran, Malaysia 36 C5 5 40N 116 30 E
Crockett, U.S.A. 81 K7 31 19N 95 27W
Crocodile = Krokodil →, Mozam. 57 D5 25 14S 32 18 E
Crocodile Is., Australia 62 A1 12 3S 134 58 E
Crohy Hd., Ireland 13 B3 54 55N 8 26W
Croix, L. La, Canada 70 C1 48 20N 92 15W
Croker, C., Australia 60 B5 10 58S 132 35 E
Croker, C., Canada 78 B4 44 58N 80 59W
Croker I., Australia 60 B5 11 12S 132 32 E
Cromarty, U.K. 12 D4 57 40N 4 2W
Cromer, U.K. 10 E9 52 56N 1 17 E
Cromwell, N.Z. 59 L2 45 3S 169 14 E
Cromwell, U.S.A. 79 E12 41 36N 72 39W
Crook, U.K. 10 C6 54 43N 1 45W
Crooked →, Canada 72 C4 54 50N 122 54W
Crooked →, U.S.A. 82 D3 44 32N 121 16W
Crooked I., Bahamas 89 B5 22 50N 74 10W
Crooked Island Passage, Bahamas 89 B5 23 0N 74 30W
Crookston, Minn., U.S.A. 80 B6 47 47N 96 37W
Crookston, Nebr., U.S.A. 80 D4 42 56N 100 45W
Crookwell, Australia 63 E4 34 28S 149 24 E
Crosby, U.K. 10 D4 53 30N 3 3W
Crosby, U.S.A. 78 E6 41 45N 78 23W
Crosbyton, U.S.A. 81 J4 33 40N 101 14W
Cross City, U.S.A. 77 L4 29 38N 83 7W
Cross Fell, U.K. 10 C5 54 43N 2 28W
Cross L., Canada 73 C9 54 45N 97 30W
Cross Lake, Canada 73 C9 54 37N 97 47W
Cross Sound, U.S.A. 68 C6 58 0N 135 0W
Crossett, U.S.A. 81 J9 33 8N 91 58W
Crosshaven, Ireland 13 E3 51 47N 8 17W
Crossville, U.S.A. 77 G3 35 57N 85 2W
Croswell, U.S.A. 78 C2 43 16N 82 37W
Croton-on-Hudson, U.S.A. 79 E11 41 12N 73 55W
Crotone, Italy 20 E7 39 5N 17 8 E
Crow →, Canada 72 B4 59 41N 124 20W
Crow Agency, U.S.A. 82 D10 45 36N 107 28W
Crow Hd., Ireland 13 E1 51 35N 10 9W
Crowell, U.S.A. 81 J5 33 59N 99 43W
Crowley, U.S.A. 81 K8 30 13N 92 22W
Crowley, L., U.S.A. 84 H8 37 35N 118 42W
Crown Point, Ind., U.S.A. 76 E2 41 25N 87 22W
Crown Point, N.Y., U.S.A. 79 C11 43 57N 73 26W
Crownpoint, U.S.A. 83 J9 35 41N 108 9W
Crows Landing, U.S.A. 84 H5 37 23N 121 6W
Crows Nest, Australia 63 D5 27 16S 152 4 E
Crowsnest Pass, Canada 72 D6 49 40N 114 40W
Croydon, Australia 62 B3 18 13S 142 14 E
Croydon, U.K. 11 F7 51 22N 0 5W
Crozet Is., Ind. Oc. 3 G12 46 27S 52 0 E
Cruz, C., Cuba 88 C4 19 50N 77 50W
Cruz Alta, Brazil 95 B5 28 45S 53 40W
Cruz del Eje, Argentina 94 C3 30 45S 64 50W
Cruzeiro, Brazil 95 A7 22 33S 45 0W
Cruzeiro do Oeste, Brazil 95 A5 23 46S 53 4W
Cruzeiro do Sul, Brazil 92 E4 7 35S 72 35W
Cry L., Canada 72 B3 58 45N 129 0W
Crystal Bay, U.S.A. 84 F7 39 15N 120 0W
Crystal Brook, Australia 63 E2 33 21S 138 12 E
Crystal City, U.S.A. 81 L5 28 41N 99 50W
Crystal Falls, U.S.A. 76 B1 46 5N 88 20W
Crystal River, U.S.A. 77 L4 28 54N 82 35W
Crystal Springs, U.S.A. 81 K9 31 59N 90 21W
Csongrád, Hungary 17 E11 46 43N 20 12 E
Cu Lao Hon, Vietnam 39 G7 10 54N 108 18 E
Cua Rao, Vietnam 38 C5 19 16N 104 27 E
Cuácua →, Mozam. 55 F4 17 54S 37 0 E
Cuamato, Angola 56 B2 17 2S 15 7 E
Cuamba, Mozam. 55 E4 14 45S 36 22 E
Cuando →, Angola 53 H4 17 30S 23 15 E
Cuando Cubango □, Angola 56 B3 16 25S 20 0 E
Cuangar, Angola 56 B2 17 36S 18 39 E
Cuanza →, Angola 52 F2 9 2S 13 30 E
Cuarto →, Argentina 94 C3 33 25S 63 2W
Cuatrociénegas, Mexico 86 B4 26 59N 102 5W
Cuauhtémoc, Mexico 86 B3 28 25N 106 52W
Cuba, N. Mex., U.S.A. 83 J10 36 1N 107 4W
Cuba, N.Y., U.S.A. 78 D6 42 13N 78 17W
Cuba ■, W. Indies 88 B4 22 0N 79 0W
Cubal, Angola 53 G2 12 26S 14 3 E
Cubango →, Africa 56 B3 18 50S 22 25 E
Cuchumatanes, Sierra de los, Guatemala 88 C1 15 35N 91 25W
Cuckfield, U.K. 11 F7 51 1N 0 8W
Cucuí, Brazil 92 C5 1 12N 66 50W
Cucurpe, Mexico 86 A2 30 20N 110 43W
Cúcuta, Colombia 92 B4 7 54N 72 31W
Cuddalore, India 40 P11 11 46N 79 45 E
Cuddapah, India 40 M11 14 30N 78 47 E
Cuddapan, L., Australia 62 D3 25 45S 141 26 E
Cue, Australia 61 E2 27 25S 117 54 E
Cuenca, Ecuador 92 D3 2 50S 79 9W
Cuenca, Spain 19 B4 40 5N 2 10W
Cuenca, Serranía de, Spain 19 C5 39 55N 1 50W
Cuernavaca, Mexico 87 D5 18 55N 99 15W
Cuero, U.S.A. 81 L6 29 6N 97 17W
Cuevas del Almanzora, Spain 19 D5 37 18N 1 58W
Cuevo, Bolivia 92 H6 20 15S 63 30W
Cuiabá, Brazil 93 G7 15 30S 56 0W
Cuiabá →, Brazil 93 G7 17 5S 56 36W
Cuijk, Neths. 15 C5 51 44N 5 50 E
Cuilco, Guatemala 88 C1 15 24N 91 58W
Cuillin Hills, U.K. 12 D2 57 13N 6 15W
Cuillin Sd., U.K. 12 D2 57 4N 6 20W
Cuito →, Angola 56 B3 18 1S 20 48 E
Cuitzeo, L. de, Mexico 86 D4 19 55N 101 5W
Cukai, Malaysia 39 K4 4 13N 103 25 E
Culbertson, U.S.A. 80 A2 48 9N 104 31W
Culcairn, Australia 63 F4 35 41S 147 3 E
Culgoa →, Australia 63 D4 29 56S 146 20 E
Culiacán, Mexico 86 C3 24 50N 107 23W
Culiacán →, Mexico 86 C3 24 30N 107 42W
Culion, Phil. 37 B6 11 54N 119 58 E
Cullarin Ra., Australia 63 E4 34 30S 149 30 E
Cullen, U.K. 12 D6 57 42N 2 49W
Cullen Pt., Australia 62 A3 11 57S 141 54 E
Cullera, Spain 19 C5 39 9N 0 17W
Cullman, U.S.A. 77 H2 34 11N 86 51W
Culpeper, U.S.A. 76 F7 38 30N 78 0W
Culuene →, Brazil 93 F8 12 56S 52 51W
Culver, Pt., Australia 61 F3 32 54S 124 43 E
Culverden, N.Z. 59 K4 42 47S 172 49 E
Cumaná, Venezuela 92 A6 10 30N 64 5W
Cumberland, B.C., Canada 72 D4 49 40N 125 0W
Cumberland, Ont., Canada 79 A9 45 29N 75 24W
Cumberland, U.S.A. 76 F6 39 39N 78 46W
Cumberland →, U.S.A. 77 G2 36 15N 87 0W
Cumberland, L., U.S.A. 77 G3 36 57N 84 55W
Cumberland I., U.S.A. 77 K5 30 50N 81 25W
Cumberland Is., Australia 62 C4 20 35S 149 10 E
Cumberland L., Canada 73 C8 54 3N 102 18W
Cumberland Pen., Canada 69 B13 67 0N 64 0W
Cumberland Plateau, U.S.A. 77 H3 36 0N 85 0W
Cumberland Sd., Canada 69 B13 65 30N 66 0W
Cumbernauld, U.K. 12 F5 55 57N 3 58W
Cumborah, Australia 63 D4 29 40S 147 45 E
Cumbria □, U.K. 10 C5 54 42N 2 52W
Cumbrian Mts., U.K. 10 C5 54 30N 3 0W
Cumbum, India 40 M11 15 40N 79 10 E
Cuminá →, Brazil 93 D7 1 30S 56 0W
Cummings Mt., U.S.A. 85 K8 35 2N 118 34W
Cummins, Australia 63 E2 34 16S 135 43 E
Cumnock, Australia 63 E4 32 59S 148 46 E
Cumnock, U.K. 12 F4 55 28N 4 17W
Cumpas, Mexico 86 B3 30 0N 109 48W
Cumplida, Pta., Canary Is. 22 F2 28 50N 17 48W
Cunco, Chile 96 D2 38 55S 72 2W
Cuncumén, Chile 94 C1 31 53S 70 38W
Cunderdin, Australia 61 F2 31 37S 117 12 E
Cunene →, Angola 56 B1 17 20S 11 50 E
Cúneo, Italy 18 D7 44 23N 7 32 E
Çüngüş, Turkey 44 B3 38 13N 39 17 E
Cunillera, I. = Sa Conillera, Spain 22 C7 38 59N 1 13 E
Cunnamulla, Australia 63 D4 28 2S 145 38 E
Cupar, Canada 73 C8 50 57N 104 10W
Cupar, U.K. 12 E5 56 19N 3 1W
Cupica, G. de, Colombia 92 B3 6 25N 77 30W
Curaçao, Neth. Ant. 89 D6 12 10N 69 0W
Curanilahue, Chile 94 D1 37 29S 73 28W
Curaray →, Peru 92 D4 2 20S 74 5W
Curepto, Chile 94 D1 35 8S 72 1W
Curiapo, Venezuela 92 B6 8 33N 61 5W
Curicó, Chile 94 C1 34 55S 71 20W
Curitiba, Brazil 95 B6 25 20S 49 10W
Curitibanos, Brazil 95 B5 27 18S 50 36W
Currabubula, Australia 63 E5 31 16S 150 44 E
Currais Novos, Brazil 93 E11 6 13S 36 30W
Curralinho, Brazil 93 D9 1 45S 49 46W
Currant, U.S.A. 82 G6 38 51N 115 32W
Current →, U.S.A. 81 G9 36 15N 90 55W
Currie, Australia 62 F3 39 56S 143 53 E
Currie, U.S.A. 82 F6 40 16N 114 45W
Curtea de Argeş, Romania 17 F13 45 12N 24 42 E
Curtis, U.S.A. 80 E4 40 38N 100 31W
Curtis Group, Australia 62 F4 39 30S 146 37 E
Curtis I., Australia 62 C5 23 35S 151 10 E
Curuápanema →, Brazil 93 D7 2 25S 55 2W
Curuçá, Brazil 93 D9 0 43S 47 50W
Curuguaty, Paraguay 95 A4 24 31S 55 42W
Curup, Indonesia 36 E2 4 26S 102 13 E
Cururupu, Brazil 93 D10 1 50S 44 50W
Curuzú Cuatiá, Argentina 94 B4 29 50S 58 5W
Curvelo, Brazil 93 G10 18 45S 44 27W
Cushing, U.S.A. 81 H6 35 59N 96 46W
Cushing, Mt., Canada 72 B3 57 35N 126 57W
Cusihuiriáchic, Mexico 86 B3 28 10N 106 50W
Custer, U.S.A. 80 D3 43 46N 103 36W
Cut Bank, U.S.A. 82 B7 48 38N 112 20W
Cutchogue, U.S.A. 79 E12 41 1N 72 30W
Cuthbert, U.S.A. 77 K3 31 46N 84 48W
Cutler, U.S.A. 84 J7 36 31N 119 17W
Cuttaburra →, Australia 63 D3 29 43S 144 22 E
Cuttack, India 41 J14 20 25N 85 57 E
Cuvier, C., Australia 61 D1 23 14S 113 22 E
Cuvier I., N.Z. 59 G5 36 27S 175 50 E
Cuxhaven, Germany 16 B5 53 51N 8 41 E
Cuyahoga Falls, U.S.A. 78 E3 41 8N 81 29W
Cuyo, Phil. 37 B6 10 50N 121 5 E
Cuyuni →, Guyana 92 B7 6 23N 58 41W
Cuzco, Bolivia 92 H5 20 0S 66 50W
Cuzco, Peru 92 F4 13 32S 72 0W
Cwmbran, U.K. 11 F4 51 39N 3 2W
Cyangugu, Rwanda 54 C2 2 29S 28 54 E
Cyclades = Kikládhes, Greece 21 F11 37 0N 24 30 E
Cygnet, Australia 62 G4 43 8S 147 1 E
Cynthiana, U.S.A. 76 F3 38 23N 84 18W
Cypress Hills, Canada 73 D7 49 40N 109 30W
Cypress Hills Prov. Park, Canada 73 D7 49 40N 109 30W
Cyprus ■, Asia 23 E12 35 0N 33 0 E
Cyrenaica, Libya 51 C10 27 0N 23 0 E
Czar, Canada 73 C6 52 27N 110 50W
Czech Rep. ■, Europe 16 D8 50 0N 15 0 E
Częstochowa, Poland 17 C10 50 49N 19 7 E

D

Da Hinggan Ling, China 33 B7 48 0N 121 0 E
Da Lat, Vietnam 39 G7 11 56N 108 25 E
Da Nang, Vietnam 38 D7 16 4N 108 13 E
Da Qaidam, China 32 C4 37 50N 95 15 E
Da Yunhe →, China 35 G11 34 25N 120 5 E
Da'an, China 35 B13 45 30N 124 7 E
Daba Shan, China 33 C5 32 0N 109 0 E
Dabbagh, Jabal, Si. Arabia 44 E2 27 52N 35 45 E
Dabhoi, India 42 H5 22 10N 73 20 E
Dabo = Pasirkuning, Indonesia 36 E2 0 30S 104 33 E
Dabola, Guinea 50 F3 10 50N 11 5W
Dabung, Malaysia 39 K4 5 23N 102 1 E
Dacca = Dhaka, Bangla. 43 H14 23 43N 90 26 E
Dacca = Dhaka □, Bangla. 43 G14 24 25N 90 25 E
Dachau, Germany 16 D6 48 15N 11 26 E
Dadanawa, Guyana 92 C7 2 50N 59 30W
Dade City, U.S.A. 77 L4 28 22N 82 11W
Dadhar, Pakistan 42 E2 29 28N 67 39 E
Dadra & Nagar Haveli □, India 40 J8 20 5N 73 0 E
Dadri = Charkhi Dadri, India 42 E7 28 37N 76 17 E
Dadu, Pakistan 42 F2 26 45N 67 45 E
Daet, Phil. 37 B6 14 2N 122 55 E
Dagana, Senegal 50 E2 16 30N 15 35W
Dagestan □, Russia 25 F8 42 30N 47 0 E
Daggett, U.S.A. 85 L10 34 52N 116 52W
Daghestan Republic = Dagestan □, Russia 25 F8 42 30N 47 0 E
Dağlıq Qarabağ = Nagorno-Karabakh, Azerbaijan 25 F8 39 55N 46 45 E
Dagö = Hiiumaa, Estonia 9 G20 58 50N 22 45 E
Dagu, China 35 E9 38 59N 117 40 E
Dagupan, Phil. 37 A6 16 3N 120 20 E
Daguragu, Australia 60 C5 17 33S 130 30 E
Dahlak Kebir, Eritrea 46 D3 15 50N 40 10 E
Dahlonega, U.S.A. 77 H4 34 32N 83 59W
Dahod, India 42 H6 22 50N 74 15 E
Dahomey = Benin ■, Africa 50 G6 10 0N 2 0 E
Dahūk, Iraq 44 B3 36 50N 43 1 E
Dai Hao, Vietnam 38 C6 18 1N 106 25 E
Dai-Sen, Japan 31 G6 35 22N 133 32 E
Dai Xian, China 34 E7 39 4N 112 58 E
Daicheng, China 34 E9 38 42N 116 38 E
Daingean, Ireland 13 C4 53 18N 7 17W
Daintree, Australia 62 B4 16 20S 145 20 E
Daiō-Misaki, Japan 31 G8 34 15N 136 45 E
Daisetsu-Zan, Japan 30 C11 43 30N 142 57 E
Dajarra, Australia 62 C2 21 42S 139 30 E
Dak Dam, Cambodia 38 F6 12 20N 107 21 E
Dak Nhe, Vietnam 38 E6 15 28N 107 48 E
Dak Pek, Vietnam 38 E6 15 4N 107 44 E
Dak Song, Vietnam 39 F6 12 19N 107 35 E
Dak Sui, Vietnam 38 E6 14 55N 107 43 E
Dakar, Senegal 50 F2 14 34N 17 29W
Dakhla, W. Sahara 50 D2 23 50N 15 53W
Dakhla, El Wâhât el-, Egypt 51 C11 25 30N 28 50 E
Dakor, India 42 H5 22 45N 73 11 E
Dakota City, U.S.A. 80 D6 42 25N 96 25W
Đakovica, Yugoslavia 21 C9 42 22N 20 26 E
Dalachi, China 34 F3 36 48N 105 0 E
Dalai Nur, China 34 C9 43 20N 116 45 E
Dālaki, Iran 45 D6 29 26N 51 17 E
Dalälven, Sweden 9 F17 60 12N 16 43 E
Dalaman →, Turkey 21 F13 36 41N 28 43 E
Dalandzadgad, Mongolia 34 C3 43 27N 104 30 E
Dalap-Uliga-Darrit, Marshall Is. 64 G9 7 7N 171 24 E
Dalarna, Sweden 9 F16 61 0N 14 0 E
Dālbandīn, Pakistan 40 E4 29 0N 64 23 E
Dalbeattie, U.K. 12 G5 54 56N 3 50W
Dalbeg, Australia 62 C4 20 16S 147 18 E
Dalby, Australia 63 D5 27 10S 151 17 E
Dale City, U.S.A. 76 F7 38 38N 77 18W
Dale Hollow L., U.S.A. 77 G3 36 32N 85 27W
Dalgān, Iran 45 E8 27 31N 59 19 E
Dalhart, U.S.A. 81 G3 36 4N 102 31W
Dalhousie, Canada 71 C6 48 5N 66 26W
Dalhousie, India 42 C6 32 38N 75 58 E
Dali, Shaanxi, China 34 G5 34 48N 109 58 E
Dali, Yunnan, China 32 D5 25 40N 100 10 E
Dalian, China 35 E11 38 50N 121 40 E
Daliang Shan, China 32 D5 28 0N 102 45 E
Daling He →, China 35 D11 40 55N 121 40 E
Dāliyat el Karmel, Israel 47 C4 32 43N 35 2 E
Dalkeith, U.K. 12 F5 55 54N 3 4W
Dallas, Oreg., U.S.A. 82 D2 44 55N 123 19W
Dallas, Tex., U.S.A. 81 J6 32 47N 96 49W
Dalmā, U.A.E. 45 E7 24 30N 52 20 E
Dalmacija, Croatia 20 C7 43 20N 17 0 E
Dalmas, L., Canada 71 B5 53 30N 71 50W
Dalmatia = Dalmacija, Croatia 20 C7 43 20N 17 0 E
Dalmau, India 43 F9 26 4N 81 2 E
Dalmellington, U.K. 12 F4 55 19N 4 23W
Dalnegorsk, Russia 27 E14 44 32N 135 33 E
Dalnerechensk, Russia 27 E14 45 50N 133 40 E
Daloa, Ivory C. 50 G4 7 0N 6 30W
Dalry, U.K. 12 F4 55 42N 4 43W
Dalrymple, L., Australia 62 C4 20 40S 147 0 E
Dalsland, Sweden 9 G14 58 50N 12 15 E
Daltenganj, India 43 H11 24 0N 84 5 E
Dalton, Ga., U.S.A. 77 H3 34 46N 84 58W

Dalton, *Mass., U.S.A.* **79 D11** 42 28N 73 11W
Dalton, *Nebr., U.S.A.* **80 E3** 41 25N 102 58W
Dalton Iceberg Tongue, *Antarctica* **5 C9** 66 15S 121 30 E
Dalton-in-Furness, *U.K.* **10 C4** 54 10N 3 11W
Dalvík, *Iceland* **8 D4** 65 58N 18 32W
Dalwallinu, *Australia* **61 F2** 30 17S 116 40 E
Daly →, *Australia* **60 B5** 13 35S 130 19 E
Daly City, *U.S.A.* **84 H4** 37 42N 122 28W
Daly L., *Canada* **73 B7** 56 32N 105 39W
Daly River, *Australia* **60 B5** 13 46S 130 42 E
Daly Waters, *Australia* **62 B1** 16 15S 133 24 E
Dam Doi, *Vietnam* **39 H5** 8 50N 105 12 E
Dam Ha, *Vietnam* **38 B6** 21 21N 107 36 E
Daman, *India* **40 J8** 20 25N 72 57 E
Dāmaneh, *Iran* **45 C6** 33 1N 50 29 E
Damanhûr, *Egypt* **51 B12** 31 0N 30 30 E
Damant L., *Canada* **73 A7** 61 45N 105 5W
Damanzhuang, *China* **34 E9** 38 5N 116 35 E
Damar, *Indonesia* **37 F7** 7 7S 128 40 E
Damaraland, *Namibia* **56 C2** 20 0S 15 0 E
Damascus = Dimashq, *Syria* **47 B5** 33 30N 36 18 E
Damāvand, *Iran* **45 C7** 35 47N 52 0 E
Damāvand, Qolleh-ye, *Iran* **45 C7** 35 56N 52 10 E
Damba, *Angola* **52 F3** 6 44S 15 20 E
Dâmboviţa →, *Romania* **17 F14** 44 12N 26 26 E
Dame Marie, *Haiti* **89 C5** 18 36N 74 26W
Dāmghān, *Iran* **45 B7** 36 10N 54 17 E
Damiel, *Spain* **19 C4** 39 4N 3 37W
Damietta = Dumyât, *Egypt* **51 B12** 31 24N 31 48 E
Daming, *China* **34 F8** 36 15N 115 6 E
Damīr Qābū, *Syria* **44 B4** 36 58N 41 51 E
Dammam = Ad Dammām, *Si. Arabia* **45 E6** 26 20N 50 5 E
Damodar →, *India* **43 H12** 23 17N 87 35 E
Damoh, *India* **43 H8** 23 50N 79 28 E
Dampier, *Australia* **60 D2** 20 41S 116 42 E
Dampier, Selat, *Indonesia* **37 E8** 0 40S 131 0 E
Dampier Arch., *Australia* **60 D2** 20 38S 116 32 E
Damrei, Chuor Phnum, *Cambodia* **39 G4** 11 30N 103 0 E
Dan Xian, *China* **38 C7** 19 31N 109 33 E
Dana, *Indonesia* **37 F6** 11 0S 122 52 E
Dana, L., *Canada* **70 B4** 50 53N 77 20W
Dana, Mt., *U.S.A.* **84 H7** 37 54N 119 12W
Danakil Depression, *Ethiopia* **46 E3** 12 45N 41 0 E
Danané, *Ivory C.* **50 G4** 7 16N 8 9W
Danau Poso, *Indonesia* **37 E6** 1 52S 120 35 E
Danbury, *U.S.A.* **79 E11** 41 24N 73 28W
Danby L., *U.S.A.* **83 J6** 34 13N 115 5W
Dand, *Afghan.* **42 D1** 31 28N 65 32 E
Dandeldhura, *Nepal* **43 E9** 29 20N 80 35 E
Dandeli, *India* **40 M9** 15 5N 74 30 E
Dandenong, *Australia* **63 F4** 38 0S 145 15 E
Dandong, *China* **35 D13** 40 10N 124 20 E
Danfeng, *China* **34 H6** 33 45N 110 25 E
Danger Is. = Pukapuka, *Cook Is.* **65 J11** 10 53S 165 49W
Danger Pt., *S. Africa* **56 E2** 34 40S 19 17 E
Dangla Shan = Tanggula Shan, *China* **32 C4** 32 40N 92 10 E
Dangrek, Phnom, *Thailand* **38 E5** 14 15N 105 0 E
Dangriga, *Belize* **87 D7** 17 0N 88 13W
Dangshan, *China* **34 G9** 34 27N 116 22 E
Daniel, *U.S.A.* **82 E8** 42 52N 110 4W
Daniel's Harbour, *Canada* **71 B8** 50 13N 57 35W
Danielskuil, *S. Africa* **56 D3** 28 11S 23 33 E
Danielson, *U.S.A.* **79 E13** 41 48N 71 53W
Danilov, *Russia* **24 C7** 58 16N 40 13 E
Daning, *China* **34 F6** 36 28N 110 45 E
Danissa, *Kenya* **54 B5** 3 15N 40 58 E
Ḑank, *Oman* **45 F8** 23 33N 56 16 E
Dankhar Gompa, *India* **40 C11** 32 10N 78 10 E
Danlí, *Honduras* **88 D2** 14 4N 86 35W
Dannemora, *U.S.A.* **79 B11** 44 43N 73 44W
Dannevirke, *N.Z.* **59 J6** 40 12S 176 8 E
Dannhauser, *S. Africa* **57 D5** 28 0S 30 3 E
Dansville, *U.S.A.* **78 D7** 42 34N 77 42W
Danta, *India* **42 G5** 24 11N 72 46 E
Dantan, *India* **43 J12** 21 57N 87 20 E
Dante, *Somali Rep.* **46 E5** 10 25N 51 16 E
Danube = Dunărea →, *Europe* **17 F15** 45 20N 29 40 E
Danvers, *U.S.A.* **79 D14** 42 34N 70 56W
Danville, *Ill., U.S.A.* **76 E2** 40 8N 87 37W
Danville, *Ky., U.S.A.* **76 G3** 37 39N 84 46W
Danville, *Pa., U.S.A.* **79 F8** 40 58N 76 37W
Danville, *Va., U.S.A.* **77 G6** 36 36N 79 23W
Danville, *Vt., U.S.A.* **79 B12** 44 25N 72 9W
Danzig = Gdańsk, *Poland* **17 A10** 54 22N 18 40 E
Dapaong, *Togo* **50 F6** 10 55N 0 16 E
Daqing Shan, *China* **34 D6** 40 40N 111 0 E
Dar Banda, *Africa* **48 F6** 8 0N 23 0 E
Dar el Beida = Casablanca, *Morocco* **50 B4** 33 36N 7 36W
Dar es Salaam, *Tanzania* **54 D4** 6 50S 39 12 E
Dar Mazār, *Iran* **45 D8** 29 14N 57 20 E
Dar'ā, *Syria* **47 C5** 32 36N 36 7 E
Dar'ā □, *Syria* **47 C5** 32 55N 36 10 E
Dārāb, *Iran* **45 D7** 28 50N 54 30 E
Daraban, *Pakistan* **42 D4** 31 44N 70 20 E
Daraj, *Libya* **51 B8** 30 10N 10 28 E
Dārān, *Iran* **45 C6** 32 59N 50 24 E
Dārayyā, *Syria* **47 B5** 33 28N 36 15 E
Darband, *Pakistan* **42 B5** 34 20N 72 50 E
Darband, Kūh-e, *Iran* **45 D8** 31 34N 57 8 E
Darbhanga, *India* **43 F11** 26 15N 85 55 E
D'Arcy, *Canada* **72 C4** 50 27N 122 35W
Dardanelle, *Ark., U.S.A.* **81 H8** 35 13N 93 9W
Dardanelle, *Calif., U.S.A.* **84 G7** 38 20N 119 50W
Dardanelles = Çanakkale Boğazı, *Turkey* **21 D12** 40 17N 26 32 E
Dārestān, *Iran* **45 D8** 29 9N 58 42 E
Dârfûr, *Sudan* **51 F10** 13 40N 24 0 E
Dargai, *Pakistan* **42 B4** 34 25N 71 55 E
Dargan Ata, *Uzbekistan* **26 E7** 40 29N 62 10 E
Dargaville, *N.Z.* **59 F4** 35 57S 173 52 E
Darhan, *Mongolia* **32 B5** 49 37N 106 21 E
Darhan Muminggan Lianheqi, *China* **34 D6** 41 40N 110 28 E
Darıca, *Turkey* **21 D13** 40 45N 29 23 E
Darién, G. del, *Colombia* **92 B3** 9 0N 77 0W
Dariganga = Ovoot, *Mongolia* **34 B7** 45 21N 113 45 E
Darjeeling = Darjiling, *India* **43 F13** 27 3N 88 18 E
Darjiling, *India* **43 F13** 27 3N 88 18 E
Darkan, *Australia* **61 F2** 33 20S 116 43 E
Darkhana, *Pakistan* **42 D5** 30 39N 72 11 E
Darkhazīneh, *Iran* **45 D6** 31 54N 48 39 E
Darkot Pass, *Pakistan* **43 A5** 36 45N 73 26 E
Darling →, *Australia* **63 E3** 34 4S 141 54 E
Darling Downs, *Australia* **63 D5** 27 30S 150 30 E
Darling Ra., *Australia* **61 F2** 32 30S 116 0 E
Darlington, *U.K.* **10 C6** 54 32N 1 33W
Darlington, *U.S.A.* **77 H6** 34 18N 79 52W
Darlington □, *U.K.* **10 C6** 54 32N 1 33W
Darlington, L., *S. Africa* **56 E4** 33 10S 25 9 E
Darlington Point, *Australia* **63 E4** 34 37S 146 1 E
Darlot, L., *Australia* **61 E3** 27 48S 121 35 E
Darłowo, *Poland* **16 A9** 54 25N 16 25 E
Darmstadt, *Germany* **16 D5** 49 51N 8 39 E
Darnah, *Libya* **51 B10** 32 45N 22 45 E
Darnall, *S. Africa* **57 D5** 29 23S 31 18 E
Darnley, C., *Antarctica* **5 C6** 68 0S 69 0 E
Darnley B., *Canada* **68 B7** 69 30N 123 30W
Darr →, *Australia* **62 C3** 23 39S 143 50 E
Darra Pezu, *Pakistan* **42 C4** 32 19N 70 44 E
Darrequeira, *Argentina* **94 D3** 37 42S 63 10W
Darrington, *U.S.A.* **82 B3** 48 15N 121 36W
Dart →, *U.K.* **11 G4** 50 24N 3 39W
Dart, C., *Antarctica* **5 D14** 73 6S 126 20W
Dartford, *U.K.* **11 F8** 51 26N 0 13 E
Dartmoor, *U.K.* **11 G4** 50 38N 3 57W
Dartmouth, *Canada* **71 D7** 44 40N 63 30W
Dartmouth, *U.K.* **11 G4** 50 21N 3 36W
Dartmouth, L., *Australia* **63 D4** 26 4S 145 18 E
Dartuch, C. = Artrutx, C. de, *Spain* **22 B10** 39 55N 3 49 E
Darvaza, *Turkmenistan* **26 E6** 40 11N 58 24 E
Darvel, Teluk = Lahad Datu, Teluk, *Malaysia* **37 D5** 4 50N 118 20 E
Darwen, *U.K.* **10 D5** 53 42N 2 29W
Darwha, *India* **40 J10** 20 15N 77 45 E
Darwin, *Australia* **60 B5** 12 25S 130 51 E
Darwin, *U.S.A.* **85 J9** 36 15N 117 35W
Darya Khan, *Pakistan* **42 D4** 31 48N 71 6 E
Daryoi Amu = Amudarya →, *Uzbekistan* **26 E6** 43 58N 59 34 E
Dās, *U.A.E.* **45 E7** 25 20N 53 30 E
Dashetai, *China* **34 D5** 41 0N 109 5 E
Dashhowuz, *Turkmenistan* **26 E6** 41 49N 59 58 E
Dashköpri, *Turkmenistan* **45 B9** 36 16N 62 8 E
Dasht, *Iran* **45 B8** 37 17N 56 7 E
Dasht →, *Pakistan* **40 G2** 25 10N 61 40 E
Dasht-e Mārgow, *Afghan.* **40 D3** 30 40N 62 30 E
Dasht-i-Nawar, *Afghan.* **42 C3** 33 52N 68 0 E
Daska, *Pakistan* **42 C6** 32 20N 74 20 E
Dasuya, *India* **42 D6** 31 49N 75 38 E
Datça, *Turkey* **21 F12** 36 46N 27 40 E
Datia, *India* **43 G8** 25 39N 78 27 E
Datong, *China* **34 D7** 40 6N 113 18 E
Dattakhel, *Pakistan* **42 C3** 32 54N 69 46 E
Datu, Tanjung, *Indonesia* **36 D3** 2 5N 109 39 E
Datu Piang, *Phil.* **37 C6** 7 2N 124 30 E
Daud Khel, *Pakistan* **42 C4** 32 53N 71 34 E
Daudnagar, *India* **43 G11** 25 2N 84 24 E
Daugava →, *Latvia* **9 H21** 57 4N 24 3 E
Daugavpils, *Latvia* **9 J22** 55 53N 26 32 E
Daulpur, *India* **42 F7** 26 45N 77 59 E
Dauphin, *Canada* **73 C8** 51 9N 100 5W
Dauphin, *U.S.A.* **78 F8** 40 22N 76 56W
Dauphin L., *Canada* **73 C9** 51 20N 99 45W
Dauphiné, *France* **18 D6** 45 15N 5 25 E
Dausa, *India* **42 F7** 26 52N 76 20 E
Davangere, *India* **40 M9** 14 25N 75 55 E
Davao, *Phil.* **37 C7** 7 0N 125 40 E
Davao, G. of, *Phil.* **37 C7** 6 30N 125 48 E
Dāvar Panāh, *Iran* **45 E9** 27 25N 62 15 E
Davenport, *Calif., U.S.A.* **84 H4** 37 1N 122 12W
Davenport, *Iowa, U.S.A.* **80 E9** 41 32N 90 35W
Davenport, *Wash., U.S.A.* **82 C4** 47 39N 118 9W
Davenport Ra., *Australia* **62 C1** 20 28S 134 0 E
Daventry, *U.K.* **11 E6** 52 16N 1 10W
David, *Panama* **88 E3** 8 30N 82 30W
David City, *U.S.A.* **80 E6** 41 15N 97 8W
David Gorodok = Davyd Haradok, *Belarus* **17 B14** 52 4N 27 8 E
Davidson, *Canada* **73 C7** 51 16N 105 59W
Davis, *U.S.A.* **84 G5** 38 33N 121 44W
Davis Dam, *U.S.A.* **85 K12** 35 11N 114 34W
Davis Inlet, *Canada* **71 A7** 55 50N 60 59W
Davis Mts., *U.S.A.* **81 K2** 30 50N 103 55W
Davis Sea, *Antarctica* **5 C7** 66 0S 92 0 E
Davis Str., *N. Amer.* **69 B14** 65 0N 58 0W
Davos, *Switz.* **18 C8** 46 48N 9 49 E
Davy L., *Canada* **73 B7** 58 53N 108 18W
Davyd Haradok, *Belarus* **17 B14** 52 4N 27 8 E
Dawei, *Burma* **38 E2** 14 2N 98 12 E
Dawes Ra., *Australia* **62 C5** 24 40S 150 40 E
Dawlish, *U.K.* **11 G4** 50 35N 3 28W
Dawros Hd., *Ireland* **13 B3** 54 50N 8 33W
Dawson, *Canada* **68 B6** 64 10N 139 30W
Dawson, *U.S.A.* **77 K3** 31 46N 84 27W
Dawson, I., *Chile* **96 G2** 53 50S 70 50W
Dawson B., *Canada* **73 C8** 52 53N 100 49W
Dawson Creek, *Canada* **72 B4** 55 45N 120 15W
Dawson Inlet, *Canada* **73 A10** 61 50N 93 25W
Dawson Ra., *Australia* **62 C4** 24 30S 149 48 E
Dax, *France* **18 E3** 43 44N 1 3W
Daxian, *China* **32 C5** 31 15N 107 23 E
Daxindian, *China* **35 F11** 37 30N 120 50 E
Daxinggou, *China* **35 C15** 43 25N 129 40 E
Daxue Shan, *China* **32 C5** 30 30N 101 30 E
Daylesford, *Australia* **63 F3** 37 21S 144 9 E
Dayr az Zawr, *Syria* **44 C4** 35 20N 40 5 E
Daysland, *Canada* **72 C6** 52 50N 112 20W
Dayton, *Nev., U.S.A.* **84 F7** 39 14N 119 36W
Dayton, *Ohio, U.S.A.* **76 F3** 39 45N 84 12W
Dayton, *Pa., U.S.A.* **78 F5** 40 53N 79 15W
Dayton, *Tenn., U.S.A.* **77 H3** 35 30N 85 1W
Dayton, *Wash., U.S.A.* **82 C4** 46 19N 117 59W
Dayton, *Wyo., U.S.A.* **82 D10** 44 53N 107 16W
Daytona Beach, *U.S.A.* **77 L5** 29 13N 81 1W
Dayville, *U.S.A.* **82 D4** 44 28N 119 32W
De Aar, *S. Africa* **56 E3** 30 39S 24 0 E
De Funiak Springs, *U.S.A.* **77 K2** 30 43N 86 7W
De Grey →, *Australia* **60 D2** 20 12S 119 13 E
De Haan, *Belgium* **15 C3** 51 16N 3 2 E
De Kalb, *U.S.A.* **80 E10** 41 56N 88 46W
De Land, *U.S.A.* **77 L5** 29 2N 81 18W
De Leon, *U.S.A.* **81 J5** 32 7N 98 32W
De Panne, *Belgium* **15 C2** 51 6N 2 34 E
De Pere, *U.S.A.* **76 C1** 44 27N 88 4W
De Queen, *U.S.A.* **81 H7** 34 2N 94 21W
De Quincy, *U.S.A.* **81 K8** 30 27N 93 26W
De Ridder, *U.S.A.* **81 K8** 30 51N 93 17W
De Smet, *U.S.A.* **80 C6** 44 23N 97 33W
De Soto, *U.S.A.* **80 F9** 38 8N 90 34W
De Tour Village, *U.S.A.* **76 C4** 46 0N 83 56W
De Witt, *U.S.A.* **81 H9** 34 18N 91 20W
Dead Sea, *Asia* **47 D4** 31 30N 35 30 E
Deadwood, *U.S.A.* **80 C3** 44 23N 103 44W
Deadwood L., *Canada* **72 B3** 59 10N 128 30W
Deal, *U.K.* **11 F9** 51 13N 1 25 E
Deal I., *Australia* **62 F4** 39 30S 147 20 E
Dealesville, *S. Africa* **56 D4** 28 41S 25 44 E
Dean →, *Canada* **72 C3** 52 49N 126 58W
Dean, Forest of, *U.K.* **11 F5** 51 45N 2 33W
Dean Chan., *Canada* **72 C3** 52 30N 127 15W
Deán Funes, *Argentina* **94 C3** 30 20S 64 20W
Dease →, *Canada* **72 B3** 59 56N 128 32W
Dease L., *Canada* **72 B2** 58 40N 130 5W
Dease Lake, *Canada* **72 B2** 58 25N 130 6W
Death Valley, *U.S.A.* **85 J10** 36 15N 116 50W
Death Valley Junction, *U.S.A.* **85 J10** 36 20N 116 25W
Death Valley National Park, *U.S.A.* **85 J10** 36 45N 117 15W
Debar, *Macedonia* **21 D9** 41 31N 20 30 E
Debden, *Canada* **73 C7** 53 30N 106 50W
Dębica, *Poland* **17 C11** 50 2N 21 25 E
Debolt, *Canada* **72 B5** 55 12N 118 1W
Deborah East, L., *Australia* **61 F2** 30 45S 119 0 E
Deborah West, L., *Australia* **61 F2** 30 45S 118 50 E
Debre Markos, *Ethiopia* **46 E2** 10 20N 37 40 E
Debre Tabor, *Ethiopia* **46 E2** 11 50N 38 26 E
Debre Zeyit, *Ethiopia* **46 F2** 11 48N 38 30 E
Debrecen, *Hungary* **17 E11** 47 33N 21 42 E
Decatur, *Ala., U.S.A.* **77 H2** 34 36N 86 59W
Decatur, *Ga., U.S.A.* **77 J3** 33 47N 84 18W
Decatur, *Ill., U.S.A.* **80 F10** 39 51N 88 57W
Decatur, *Ind., U.S.A.* **76 E3** 40 50N 84 56W
Decatur, *Tex., U.S.A.* **81 J6** 33 14N 97 35W
Deccan, *India* **40 L11** 18 0N 79 0 E
Deception Bay, *Australia* **63 D5** 27 10S 153 5 E
Deception L., *Canada* **73 B8** 56 33N 104 13W
Dechhu, *India* **42 F5** 26 46N 72 20 E
Děčín, *Czech Rep.* **16 C8** 50 47N 14 12 E
Deckerville, *U.S.A.* **78 C2** 43 32N 82 44W
Decorah, *U.S.A.* **80 D9** 43 18N 91 48W
Dedéagach = Alexandroúpolis, *Greece* **21 D11** 40 50N 25 54 E
Dedham, *U.S.A.* **79 D13** 42 15N 71 10W
Dedza, *Malawi* **55 E3** 14 20S 34 20 E
Dee →, *Aberds., U.K.* **12 D6** 57 9N 2 5W
Dee →, *Dumf. & Gall., U.K.* **12 G4** 54 51N 4 3W
Dee →, *Wales, U.K.* **10 D4** 53 22N 3 17W
Deep B., *Canada* **72 A5** 61 15N 116 35W
Deepwater, *Australia* **63 D5** 29 25S 151 51 E
Deer →, *Canada* **73 B10** 58 23N 94 13W
Deer L., *Canada* **73 C10** 52 40N 94 20W
Deer Lake, *Nfld., Canada* **71 C8** 49 11N 57 27W
Deer Lake, *Ont., Canada* **73 C10** 52 36N 94 20W
Deer Lodge, *U.S.A.* **82 C7** 46 24N 112 44W
Deer Park, *U.S.A.* **82 C5** 47 57N 117 28W
Deer River, *U.S.A.* **80 B8** 47 20N 93 48W
Deeragun, *Australia* **62 B4** 19 16S 146 33 E
Deerdepoort, *S. Africa* **56 C4** 24 37S 26 27 E
Defiance, *U.S.A.* **79 B9** 44 2N 75 41W
Defiance, *U.S.A.* **76 E3** 41 17N 84 22W
Degana, *India* **42 F6** 26 50N 74 20 E
Dégelis, *Canada* **71 C6** 47 30N 68 35W
Deggendorf, *Germany* **16 D7** 48 50N 12 57 E
Degh →, *Pakistan* **42 D5** 31 3N 73 21 E
Deh Bīd, *Iran* **45 D7** 30 39N 53 11 E
Deh-e Shīr, *Iran* **45 D7** 31 29N 53 45 E
Dehaj, *Iran* **45 D7** 30 42N 54 53 E
Dehak, *Iran* **45 E9** 27 11N 62 37 E
Dehdez, *Iran* **45 D6** 31 43N 50 17 E
Dehej, *India* **42 J5** 21 44N 72 40 E
Dehestān, *Iran* **45 D7** 28 30N 55 35 E
Dehgolān, *Iran* **44 C5** 35 17N 47 25 E
Dehi Titan, *Afghan.* **40 C3** 33 45N 63 50 E
Dehibat, *Tunisia* **51 B8** 32 0N 10 47 E
Dehlorān, *Iran* **44 C5** 32 41N 47 16 E
Dehnow-e Kūhestān, *Iran* **45 E8** 27 58N 58 32 E
Dehra Dun, *India* **42 D8** 30 20N 78 4 E
Dehri, *India* **43 G11** 24 50N 84 15 E
Dehui, *China* **35 B13** 44 30N 125 40 E
Deinze, *Belgium* **15 D3** 50 59N 3 32 E
Dej, *Romania* **17 E12** 47 10N 23 52 E
Dekese, *Dem. Rep. of the Congo* **52 E4** 3 24S 21 24 E
Del Mar, *U.S.A.* **85 N9** 32 58N 117 16W
Del Norte, *U.S.A.* **83 H10** 37 41N 106 21W
Del Rio, *U.S.A.* **81 L4** 29 22N 100 54W
Delambre I., *Australia* **60 D2** 20 26S 117 5 E
Delano, *U.S.A.* **85 K7** 35 46N 119 15W
Delano Peak, *U.S.A.* **83 G7** 38 22N 112 22W
Delareyville, *S. Africa* **56 D4** 26 41S 25 26 E
Delaronde L., *Canada* **73 C7** 54 3N 107 3W
Delavan, *U.S.A.* **80 D10** 42 38N 88 39W
Delaware, *U.S.A.* **76 E4** 40 18N 83 4W
Delaware □, *U.S.A.* **76 F8** 39 0N 75 20W
Delaware →, *U.S.A.* **79 G9** 39 15N 75 20W
Delaware B., *U.S.A.* **76 F8** 39 0N 75 10W
Delay →, *Canada* **71 A5** 56 56N 71 28W
Delegate, *Australia* **63 F4** 37 4S 148 56 E
Delevan, *U.S.A.* **78 D6** 42 29N 78 29W
Delft, *Neths.* **15 B4** 52 1N 4 22 E
Delfzijl, *Neths.* **15 A6** 53 20N 6 55 E
Delgado, C., *Mozam.* **55 E5** 10 45S 40 40 E
Delgerhet, *Mongolia* **34 B6** 45 50N 110 30 E
Delgo, *Sudan* **51 D12** 20 6N 30 40 E
Delhi, *Canada* **78 D4** 42 51N 80 30W
Delhi, *India* **42 E7** 28 38N 77 17 E
Delhi, *La., U.S.A.* **81 J9** 32 28N 91 30W
Delhi, *N.Y., U.S.A.* **79 D10** 42 17N 74 55W
Delia, *Canada* **72 C6** 51 38N 112 23W
Delice, *Turkey* **25 G5** 39 54N 34 2 E
Delicias, *Mexico* **86 B3** 28 10N 105 30W
Delījān, *Iran* **45 C6** 33 59N 50 40 E
Déline, *Canada* **68 B7** 65 10N 123 30W
Delisle, *Canada* **73 C7** 51 55N 107 8W
Dell City, *U.S.A.* **83 L11** 31 56N 105 12W
Dell Rapids, *U.S.A.* **80 D6** 43 50N 96 43W
Delmar, *U.S.A.* **79 D11** 42 37N 73 47W
Delmenhorst, *Germany* **16 B5** 53 3N 8 37 E
Delong, Ostrova, *Russia* **27 B15** 76 40N 149 20 E
Deloraine, *Australia* **62 G4** 41 30S 146 40 E
Deloraine, *Canada* **73 D8** 49 15N 100 29W
Delphi, *U.S.A.* **76 E2** 40 36N 86 41W
Delphos, *U.S.A.* **76 E3** 40 51N 84 21W
Delportshoop, *S. Africa* **56 D3** 28 22S 24 20 E
Delray Beach, *U.S.A.* **77 M5** 26 28N 80 4W
Delta, *Colo., U.S.A.* **83 G9** 38 44N 108 4W
Delta, *Utah, U.S.A.* **82 G7** 39 21N 112 35W
Delta Junction, *U.S.A.* **68 B5** 64 2N 145 44W
Deltona, *U.S.A.* **77 L5** 28 54N 81 16W
Delungra, *Australia* **63 D5** 29 39S 150 51 E
Delvada, *India* **42 J4** 20 46N 71 2 E
Delvinë, *Albania* **21 E9** 39 59N 20 6 E
Demak, *Indonesia* **37 G14** 6 53S 110 38 E
Demanda, Sierra de la, *Spain* **19 A4** 42 15N 3 0W
Demavand = Damāvand, *Iran* **45 C7** 35 47N 52 0 E
Dembia, *Dem. Rep. of the Congo* **54 B2** 3 33N 25 48 E
Dembidolo, *Ethiopia* **46 F1** 8 34N 34 50 E
Demchok, *India* **43 C8** 32 42N 79 29 E
Demer →, *Belgium* **15 D4** 50 57N 4 42 E
Deming, *N. Mex., U.S.A.* **83 K10** 32 16N 107 46W
Deming, *Wash., U.S.A.* **84 B4** 48 50N 122 13W
Demini →, *Brazil* **92 D6** 0 46S 62 56W
Demirci, *Turkey* **21 E13** 39 2N 28 38 E
Demirköy, *Turkey* **21 D12** 41 49N 27 45 E
Demopolis, *U.S.A.* **77 J2** 32 31N 87 50W
Dempo, *Indonesia* **36 E2** 4 2S 103 15 E
Den Burg, *Neths.* **15 A4** 53 3N 4 47 E
Den Chai, *Thailand* **38 D3** 17 59N 100 4 E
Den Haag = 's-Gravenhage, *Neths.* **15 B4** 52 7N 4 17 E
Den Helder, *Neths.* **15 B4** 52 57N 4 45 E
Den Oever, *Neths.* **15 B5** 52 56N 5 2 E
Denair, *U.S.A.* **84 H6** 37 32N 120 48W
Denau, *Uzbekistan* **26 F7** 38 16N 67 54 E
Denbigh, *Canada* **78 A7** 45 8N 77 15W
Denbigh, *U.K.* **10 D4** 53 12N 3 25W
Denbighshire □, *U.K.* **10 D4** 53 8N 3 22W
Dendang, *Indonesia* **36 E3** 3 7S 107 56 E
Dendermonde, *Belgium* **15 C4** 51 2N 4 5 E
Dengfeng, *China* **34 G7** 34 25N 113 2 E
Dengkou, *China* **34 D4** 40 18N 106 55 E
Denham, *Australia* **61 E1** 25 56S 113 31 E
Denham Ra., *Australia* **62 C4** 21 55S 147 46 E
Denham Sd., *Australia* **61 E1** 25 45S 113 15 E
Denholm, *Canada* **73 C7** 52 39N 108 1W
Denia, *Spain* **19 C6** 38 49N 0 8 E
Denial B., *Australia* **63 E1** 32 14S 133 32 E
Deniliquin, *Australia* **63 F3** 35 30S 144 58 E
Denison, *Iowa, U.S.A.* **80 E7** 42 1N 95 21W
Denison, *Tex., U.S.A.* **81 J6** 33 45N 96 33W
Denison Plains, *Australia* **60 C4** 18 35S 128 0 E
Denizli, *Turkey* **25 G4** 37 42N 29 2 E
Denman Glacier, *Antarctica* **5 C7** 66 45S 99 25 E
Denmark, *Australia* **61 F2** 34 59S 117 25 E
Denmark ■, *Europe* **9 J13** 55 45N 10 0 E
Denmark Str., *Atl. Oc.* **4 C6** 66 0N 30 0W
Dennison, *U.S.A.* **78 F3** 40 24N 81 19W
Denny, *U.K.* **12 E5** 56 1N 3 55W
Denpasar, *Indonesia* **36 F5** 8 45S 115 14 E
Denton, *Mont., U.S.A.* **82 C9** 47 19N 109 57W
Denton, *Tex., U.S.A.* **81 J6** 33 13N 97 8W
D'Entrecasteaux, Pt., *Australia* **61 F2** 34 50S 115 57 E
Denver, *Colo., U.S.A.* **80 F2** 39 44N 104 59W
Denver, *Pa., U.S.A.* **79 F8** 40 14N 76 8W
Denver City, *U.S.A.* **81 J3** 32 58N 102 50W
Deoband, *India* **42 E7** 29 42N 77 43 E
Deogarh, *India* **42 G5** 25 32N 73 54 E
Deoghar, *India* **43 G12** 24 30N 86 42 E
Deolali, *India* **40 K8** 19 58N 73 50 E
Deoli = Devli, *India* **42 G6** 25 50N 75 20 E
Deora, *India* **42 F4** 26 22N 70 55 E
Deori, *India* **43 H8** 23 24N 79 1 E
Deoria, *India* **43 F10** 26 31N 83 48 E
Deosai Mts., *Pakistan* **43 B6** 35 40N 75 0 E
Deosri, *India* **43 F14** 26 46N 90 29 E
Depalpur, *India* **42 H6** 22 51N 75 33 E
Deping, *China* **35 F9** 37 25N 116 58 E
Deposit, *U.S.A.* **79 D9** 42 4N 75 25W
Depuch I., *Australia* **60 D2** 20 37S 117 44 E
Deputatskiy, *Russia* **27 C14** 69 18N 139 54 E
Dera Ghazi Khan, *Pakistan* **42 D4** 30 5N 70 43 E
Dera Ismail Khan, *Pakistan* **42 D4** 31 50N 70 50 E
Derabugti, *Pakistan* **42 E3** 29 2N 69 9 E
Derawar Fort, *Pakistan* **42 E4** 28 46N 71 20 E
Derbent, *Russia* **25 F8** 42 5N 48 15 E
Derby, *Australia* **60 C3** 17 18S 123 38 E
Derby, *U.K.* **10 E6** 52 56N 1 28W
Derby, *Conn., U.S.A.* **79 E11** 41 19N 73 5W
Derby, *Kans., U.S.A.* **81 G6** 37 33N 97 16W
Derby, *N.Y., U.S.A.* **78 D6** 42 41N 78 58W
Derby City □, *U.K.* **10 E6** 52 56N 1 28W
Derby Line, *U.S.A.* **79 B12** 45 0N 72 6W
Derbyshire □, *U.K.* **10 D6** 53 11N 1 38W
Derg →, *U.K.* **13 B4** 54 44N 7 26W
Derg, L., *Ireland* **13 D3** 53 0N 8 20W
Dergaon, *India* **41 F19** 26 45N 94 0 E
Dermott, *U.S.A.* **81 J9** 33 32N 91 26W
Derry = Londonderry, *U.K.* **13 B4** 55 0N 7 20W
Derry = Londonderry □, *U.K.* **13 B4** 55 0N 7 20W
Derry, *N.H., U.S.A.* **79 D13** 42 53N 71 19W
Derry, *Pa., U.S.A.* **78 F5** 40 20N 79 18W
Derryveagh Mts., *Ireland* **13 B3** 54 56N 8 11W
Derwent →, *Cumb., U.K.* **10 C4** 54 39N 3 33W
Derwent →, *Derby, U.K.* **10 E6** 52 57N 1 28W
Derwent →, *N. Yorks., U.K.* **10 D7** 53 45N 0 58W
Derwent Water, *U.K.* **10 C4** 54 35N 3 9W
Des Moines, *Iowa, U.S.A.* **80 E8** 41 35N 93 37W
Des Moines, *N. Mex., U.S.A.* **81 G3** 36 46N 103 50W
Des Moines →, *U.S.A.* **80 E9** 40 23N 91 25W
Desaguadero →, *Argentina* **94 C2** 34 30S 66 46W
Desaguadero →, *Bolivia* **92 G5** 16 35S 69 5W
Descanso, Pta., *Mexico* **85 N9** 32 21N 117 3W
Deschaillons, *Canada* **71 C5** 46 32N 72 7W
Deschambault L., *Canada* **73 C8** 54 50N 103 30W
Deschutes →, *U.S.A.* **82 D3** 45 38N 120 55W
Dese, *Ethiopia* **46 E2** 11 5N 39 40 E
Deseado →, *Argentina* **96 F3** 47 45S 65 54W
Desert Center, *U.S.A.* **85 M11** 33 43N 115 24W
Desert Hot Springs, *U.S.A.* **85 M10** 33 58N 116 30W
Deshnok, *India* **42 F5** 27 48N 73 21 E
Desna →, *Ukraine* **17 C16** 50 33N 30 32 E
Desolación, I., *Chile* **96 G2** 53 0S 74 0W

Despeñaperros, Paso, *Spain* **19 C4** 38 24N 3 30W
Dessau, *Germany* **16 C7** 51 51N 12 14 E
Dessye = Dese, *Ethiopia* **46 E2** 11 5N 39 40 E
D'Estrees B., *Australia* **63 F2** 35 55S 137 45 E
Desuri, *India* **42 G5** 25 18N 73 35 E
Det Udom, *Thailand* **38 E5** 14 54N 105 5 E
Dete, *Zimbabwe* **55 F2** 18 38S 26 50 E
Detmold, *Germany* **16 C5** 51 56N 8 52 E
Detour, Pt., *U.S.A.* **76 C2** 45 40N 86 40W
Detroit, *U.S.A.* **78 D1** 42 20N 83 3W
Detroit Lakes, *U.S.A.* **80 B7** 46 49N 95 51W
Deurne, *Neths.* **15 C5** 51 27N 5 49 E
Deutsche Bucht, *Germany* **16 A5** 54 15N 8 0 E
Deva, *Romania* **17 F12** 45 53N 22 55 E
Devakottai, *India* **40 Q11** 9 55N 78 45 E
Devaprayag, *India* **43 D8** 30 13N 78 35 E
Deventer, *Neths.* **15 B6** 52 15N 6 10 E
Deveron →, *U.K.* **12 D6** 57 41N 2 32W
Devgadh Bariya, *India* **42 H5** 22 40N 73 55 E
Devikot, *India* **42 F4** 26 42N 71 12 E
Devils Den, *U.S.A.* **84 K7** 35 46N 119 58W
Devils Lake, *U.S.A.* **80 A5** 48 7N 98 52W
Devils Paw, *Canada* **72 B2** 58 47N 134 0W
Devils Tower Junction, *U.S.A.* **80 C2** 44 31N 104 57W
Devine, *U.S.A.* **81 L5** 29 8N 98 54W
Devizes, *U.K.* **11 F6** 51 22N 1 58W
Devli, *India* **42 G6** 25 50N 75 20 E
Devon, *Canada* **72 C6** 53 24N 113 44W
Devon □, *U.K.* **11 G4** 50 50N 3 40W
Devon I., *Canada* **4 B3** 75 10N 85 0W
Devonport, *Australia* **62 G4** 41 10S 146 22 E
Devonport, *N.Z.* **59 G5** 36 49S 174 49 E
Dewas, *India* **42 H7** 22 59N 76 3 E
Dewetsdorp, *S. Africa* **56 D4** 29 33S 26 39 E
Dexter, *Maine, U.S.A.* **77 C11** 45 1N 69 18W
Dexter, *Mo., U.S.A.* **81 G10** 36 48N 89 57W
Dexter, *N. Mex., U.S.A.* **81 J2** 33 12N 104 22W
Dey-Dey, L., *Australia* **61 E5** 29 12S 131 4 E
Deyhūk, *Iran* **45 C8** 33 15N 57 30 E
Deyyer, *Iran* **45 E6** 27 55N 51 55 E
Dezadeash L., *Canada* **72 A1** 60 28N 136 58W
Dezfūl, *Iran* **45 C6** 32 20N 48 30 E
Dezhneva, Mys, *Russia* **27 C19** 66 5N 169 40W
Dezhou, *China* **34 F9** 37 26N 116 18 E
Dhadhar →, *India* **43 G11** 24 56N 85 24 E
Dháfni, *Greece* **23 D7** 35 13N 25 3 E
Dhahiriya = Az Zāhirīyah, *West Bank* **47 D3** 31 25N 34 58 E
Dhahran = Az Zahrān, *Si. Arabia* **45 E6** 26 10N 50 7 E
Dhak, *Pakistan* **42 C5** 32 25N 72 33 E
Dhaka, *Bangla.* **43 H14** 23 43N 90 26 E
Dhaka □, *Bangla.* **43 G14** 24 25N 90 25 E
Dhali, *Cyprus* **23 D12** 35 1N 33 25 E
Dhampur, *India* **43 E8** 29 19N 78 33 E
Dhamtari, *India* **41 J12** 20 42N 81 35 E
Dhanbad, *India* **43 H12** 23 50N 86 30 E
Dhangarhi, *Nepal* **41 E12** 28 55N 80 40 E
Dhankuta, *Nepal* **43 F12** 26 55N 87 40 E
Dhar, *India* **42 H6** 22 35N 75 26 E
Dharampur, *India* **42 H6** 22 13N 75 18 E
Dharamsala = Dharmsala, *India* **42 C7** 32 16N 76 23 E
Dhariwal, *India* **42 D6** 31 57N 75 19 E
Dharla →, *Bangla.* **43 G13** 25 46N 89 42 E
Dharmapuri, *India* **40 N11** 12 10N 78 10 E
Dharmjaygarh, *India* **43 H10** 22 28N 83 13 E
Dharmsala, *India* **42 C7** 32 16N 76 23 E
Dharni, *India* **42 J7** 21 33N 76 53 E
Dhasan →, *India* **43 G8** 25 48N 79 24 E
Dhaulagiri, *Nepal* **43 E10** 28 39N 83 28 E
Dhebar, L., *India* **42 G6** 24 10N 74 0 E
Dheftera, *Cyprus* **23 D12** 35 5N 33 16 E
Dhenkanal, *India* **41 J14** 20 45N 85 35 E
Dherinia, *Cyprus* **23 D12** 35 3N 33 57 E
Dhiarrizos →, *Cyprus* **23 E11** 34 41N 32 34 E
Dhībān, *Jordan* **47 D4** 31 30N 35 46 E
Dhíkti Óros, *Greece* **23 D7** 35 8N 25 30 E
Dhilwan, *India* **42 D6** 31 31N 75 21 E
Dhimarkhera, *India* **43 H9** 23 28N 80 22 E
Dhírfis = Dhírfis Óros, *Greece* **21 E10** 38 40N 23 54 E
Dhírfis Óros, *Greece* **21 E10** 38 40N 23 54 E
Dhodhekánisos, *Greece* **21 F12** 36 35N 27 0 E
Dholka, *India* **42 H5** 22 44N 72 29 E
Dhoraji, *India* **42 J4** 21 45N 70 37 E
Dhráhstis, Ákra, *Greece* **23 A3** 39 48N 19 40 E
Dhrangadhra, *India* **42 H4** 22 59N 71 31 E
Dhrápanon, Ákra, *Greece* **23 D6** 35 28N 24 14 E
Dhrol, *India* **42 H4** 22 33N 70 25 E
Dhuburi, *India* **41 F16** 26 2N 89 59 E
Dhule, *India* **40 J9** 20 58N 74 50 E
Di Linh, *Vietnam* **39 G7** 11 35N 108 4 E
Di Linh, Cao Nguyen, *Vietnam* **39 G7** 11 30N 108 0 E
Día, *Greece* **23 D7** 35 28N 25 14 E
Diablo, Mt., *U.S.A.* **84 H5** 37 53N 121 56W
Diablo Range, *U.S.A.* **84 J5** 37 20N 121 25W
Diafarabé, *Mali* **50 F5** 14 9N 4 57W
Diamante, *Argentina* **94 C3** 32 5S 60 40W
Diamante →, *Argentina* **94 C2** 34 30S 66 46W
Diamantina, *Brazil* **93 G10** 18 17S 43 40W
Diamantina →, *Australia* **63 D2** 26 45S 139 10 E
Diamantino, *Brazil* **93 F7** 14 30S 56 30W
Diamond Bar, *U.S.A.* **85 L9** 34 1N 117 48W
Diamond Harbour, *India* **43 H13** 22 11N 88 14 E
Diamond Is., *Australia* **62 B5** 17 25S 151 5 E
Diamond Mts., *U.S.A.* **82 G6** 39 50N 115 30W
Diamond Springs, *U.S.A.* **84 G6** 38 42N 120 49W
Dībā, *Oman* **45 E8** 25 45N 56 16 E
Dibai, *India* **42 E8** 28 13N 78 15 E
Dibaya-Lubue, *Dem. Rep. of the Congo* **52 E3** 4 12S 19 54 E
Dibete, *Botswana* **56 C4** 23 45S 26 32 E
Dibrugarh, *India* **41 F19** 27 29N 94 55 E
Dickens, *U.S.A.* **81 J4** 33 37N 100 50W
Dickinson, *U.S.A.* **80 B3** 46 53N 102 47W
Dickson = Dikson, *Russia* **26 B9** 73 40N 80 5 E
Dickson, *U.S.A.* **77 G2** 36 5N 87 23W
Dickson City, *U.S.A.* **79 E9** 41 29N 75 40W
Didiéni, *Mali* **50 F4** 13 53N 8 6W
Didsbury, *Canada* **72 C6** 51 35N 114 10W
Didwana, *India* **42 F6** 27 23N 74 36 E
Diefenbaker, L., *Canada* **73 C7** 51 0N 106 55W
Diego de Almagro, *Chile* **94 B1** 26 22S 70 3W
Diego Garcia, *Ind. Oc.* **3 E13** 7 50S 72 50 E
Diekirch, *Lux.* **15 E6** 49 52N 6 10 E
Dien Ban, *Vietnam* **38 E7** 15 53N 108 16 E
Dien Khanh, *Vietnam* **39 F7** 12 15N 109 6 E
Dieppe, *France* **18 B4** 49 54N 1 4 E
Dierks, *U.S.A.* **81 H8** 34 7N 94 1W
Diest, *Belgium* **15 D5** 50 58N 5 4 E
Dif, *Somali Rep.* **46 G3** 0 59N 0 56 E
Differdange, *Lux.* **15 E5** 49 31N 5 54 E
Dig, *India* **42 F7** 27 28N 77 20 E
Digba, *Dem. Rep. of the Congo* **54 B2** 4 25N 25 48 E
Digby, *Canada* **71 D6** 44 38N 65 50W
Diggi, *India* **42 F6** 26 22N 75 26 E
Dighinala, *Bangla.* **41 H18** 23 15N 92 5 E
Dighton, *U.S.A.* **80 F4** 38 29N 100 28W
Digne-les-Bains, *France* **18 D7** 44 5N 6 12 E
Digos, *Phil.* **37 C7** 6 45N 125 20 E
Digranes, *Iceland* **8 C6** 66 4N 14 44W
Digul →, *Indonesia* **37 F9** 7 7S 138 42 E
Dihang →, *India* **41 F19** 27 48N 95 30 E
Dijlah, Nahr →, *Asia* **44 D5** 31 0N 47 25 E
Dijon, *France* **18 C6** 47 20N 5 3 E
Dikkil, *Djibouti* **46 E3** 11 8N 42 20 E
Dikomu di Kai, *Botswana* **56 C3** 24 58S 24 36 E
Diksmuide, *Belgium* **15 C2** 51 2N 2 52 E
Dikson, *Russia* **26 B9** 73 40N 80 5 E
Dila, *Ethiopia* **46 F2** 6 21N 38 22 E
Dili, *Indonesia* **37 F7** 8 39S 125 34 E
Dilley, *U.S.A.* **81 L5** 28 40N 99 10W
Dillingham, *U.S.A.* **68 C4** 59 3N 158 28W
Dillon, *Canada* **73 B7** 55 56N 108 35W
Dillon, *Mont., U.S.A.* **82 D7** 45 13N 112 38W
Dillon, *S.C., U.S.A.* **77 H6** 34 25N 79 22W
Dillon →, *Canada* **73 B7** 55 56N 108 56W
Dillsburg, *U.S.A.* **78 F7** 40 7N 77 2W
Dilolo, *Dem. Rep. of the Congo* **52 G4** 10 28S 22 18 E
Dimas, *Mexico* **86 C3** 23 43N 106 47W
Dimashq, *Syria* **47 B5** 33 30N 36 18 E
Dimashq □, *Syria* **47 B5** 33 30N 36 30 E
Dimbaza, *S. Africa* **57 E4** 32 50S 27 14 E
Dimboola, *Australia* **63 F3** 36 28S 142 7 E
Dîmboviţa = Dâmboviţa →, *Romania* **17 F14** 44 12N 26 26 E
Dimbulah, *Australia* **62 B4** 17 8S 145 4 E
Dimitrovgrad, *Bulgaria* **21 C11** 42 5N 25 35 E
Dimitrovgrad, *Russia* **24 D8** 54 14N 49 39 E
Dimitrovo = Pernik, *Bulgaria* **21 C10** 42 35N 23 2 E
Dimmitt, *U.S.A.* **81 H3** 34 33N 102 19W
Dimona, *Israel* **47 D4** 31 2N 35 1 E
Dinagat, *Phil.* **37 B7** 10 10N 125 40 E
Dinajpur, *Bangla.* **41 G16** 25 33N 88 43 E
Dinan, *France* **18 B2** 48 28N 2 2W
Dīnān Āb, *Iran* **45 C8** 32 4N 56 49 E
Dinant, *Belgium* **15 D4** 50 16N 4 55 E
Dinapur, *India* **43 G11** 25 38N 85 5 E
Dīnār, Kūh-e, *Iran* **45 D6** 30 42N 51 46 E
Dinara Planina, *Croatia* **20 C7** 44 0N 16 30 E
Dinard, *France* **18 B2** 48 38N 2 6W
Dinaric Alps = Dinara Planina, *Croatia* **20 C7** 44 0N 16 30 E
Dindigul, *India* **40 P11** 10 25N 78 0 E
Dindori, *India* **43 H9** 22 57N 81 5 E
Ding Xian = Dingzhou, *China* **34 E8** 38 30N 114 59 E
Dinga, *Pakistan* **42 G2** 25 26N 67 10 E
Dingbian, *China* **34 F4** 37 35N 107 32 E
Dingle, *Ireland* **13 D1** 52 9N 10 17W
Dingle B., *Ireland* **13 D1** 52 3N 10 20W
Dingmans Ferry, *U.S.A.* **79 E10** 41 13N 74 55W
Dingo, *Australia* **62 C4** 23 38S 149 19 E
Dingtao, *China* **34 G8** 35 5N 115 35 E
Dingwall, *U.K.* **12 D4** 57 36N 4 26W
Dingxi, *China* **34 G3** 35 30N 104 33 E
Dingxiang, *China* **34 E7** 38 30N 112 58 E
Dingzhou, *China* **34 E8** 38 30N 114 59 E
Dinh, Mui, *Vietnam* **39 G7** 11 22N 109 1 E
Dinokwe, *Botswana* **56 C4** 23 29S 26 37 E
Dinorwic, *Canada* **73 D10** 49 41N 92 30W
Dinosaur National Monument, *U.S.A.* **82 F9** 40 30N 108 45W
Dinosaur Prov. Park, *Canada* **72 C6** 50 47N 111 30W
Dinuba, *U.S.A.* **84 J7** 36 32N 119 23W
Dipalpur, *Pakistan* **42 D5** 30 40N 73 39 E
Diplo, *Pakistan* **42 G3** 24 35N 69 35 E
Dipolog, *Phil.* **37 C6** 8 36N 123 20 E
Dir, *Pakistan* **40 B7** 35 8N 71 59 E
Dire Dawa, *Ethiopia* **46 F3** 9 35N 41 45 E
Diriamba, *Nic.* **88 D2** 11 51N 86 19W
Dirk Hartog I., *Australia* **61 E1** 25 50S 113 5 E
Dirranbandi, *Australia* **63 D4** 28 33S 148 17 E
Disa, *India* **42 G5** 24 18N 72 10 E
Disappointment, C., *U.S.A.* **82 C2** 46 18N 124 5W
Disappointment, L., *Australia* **60 D3** 23 20S 122 40 E
Disaster B., *Australia* **63 F4** 37 15S 149 58 E
Discovery B., *Australia* **63 F3** 38 10S 140 40 E
Disko, *Greenland* **4 C5** 69 45N 53 30W
Disko Bugt, *Greenland* **4 C5** 69 10N 52 0W
Diss, *U.K.* **11 E9** 52 23N 1 7 E
Disteghil Sar, *Pakistan* **43 A6** 36 20N 75 12 E
Distrito Federal □, *Brazil* **93 G9** 15 45S 47 45W
Distrito Federal □, *Mexico* **87 D5** 19 15N 99 10W
Diu, *India* **42 J4** 20 45N 70 58 E
Dīvāndarreh, *Iran* **44 C5** 35 55N 47 2 E
Divide, *U.S.A.* **82 D7** 45 45N 112 45W
Dividing Ra., *Australia* **61 E2** 27 45S 116 0 E
Divinópolis, *Brazil* **93 H10** 20 10S 44 54W
Divnoye, *Russia* **25 E7** 45 55N 43 21 E
Divo, *Ivory C.* **50 G4** 5 48N 5 15W
Dīwāl Kol, *Afghan.* **42 B2** 34 23N 67 52 E
Dixie Mt., *U.S.A.* **84 F6** 39 55N 120 16W
Dixon, *Calif., U.S.A.* **84 G5** 38 27N 121 49W
Dixon, *Ill., U.S.A.* **80 E10** 41 50N 89 29W
Dixon Entrance, *U.S.A.* **68 C6** 54 30N 132 0W
Dixville, *Canada* **79 A13** 45 4N 71 46W
Diyālā →, *Iraq* **44 C5** 33 14N 44 31 E
Diyarbakır, *Turkey* **25 G7** 37 55N 40 18 E
Diyodar, *India* **42 G4** 24 8N 71 50 E
Djakarta = Jakarta, *Indonesia* **37 G12** 6 9S 106 49 E
Djamba, *Angola* **56 B1** 16 45S 13 58 E
Djambala, *Congo* **52 E2** 2 32S 14 30 E
Djanet, *Algeria* **50 D7** 24 35N 9 32 E
Djawa = Jawa, *Indonesia* **37 G14** 7 0S 110 0 E
Djelfa, *Algeria* **50 B6** 34 40N 3 15 E
Djema, *C.A.R.* **54 A2** 6 3N 25 15 E
Djerba, I. de, *Tunisia* **51 B8** 33 50N 10 48 E
Djerid, Chott, *Tunisia* **50 B7** 33 42N 8 30 E
Djibouti, *Djibouti* **46 E3** 11 30N 43 5 E
Djibouti ■, *Africa* **46 E3** 12 0N 43 0 E
Djolu, *Dem. Rep. of the Congo* **52 D4** 0 35N 22 5 E
Djoum, *Cameroon* **52 D2** 2 41N 12 35 E
Djourab, Erg du, *Chad* **51 E9** 16 40N 18 50 E
Djugu, *Dem. Rep. of the Congo* **54 B3** 1 55N 30 35 E
Djúpivogur, *Iceland* **8 D6** 64 39N 14 17W
Dmitriya Lapteva, Proliv, *Russia* **27 B15** 73 0N 140 0 E
Dnepr = Dnipro →, *Ukraine* **25 E5** 46 30N 32 18 E
Dneprodzerzhinsk = Dniprodzerzhynsk, *Ukraine* **25 E5** 48 32N 34 37 E
Dnepropetrovsk = Dnipropetrovsk, *Ukraine* **25 E6** 48 30N 35 0 E
Dnestr = Dnister →, *Europe* **17 E16** 46 18N 30 17 E
Dnestrovski = Belgorod, *Russia* **25 D6** 50 35N 36 35 E
Dnieper = Dnipro →, *Ukraine* **25 E5** 46 30N 32 18 E
Dniester = Dnister →, *Europe* **17 E16** 46 18N 30 17 E
Dnipro →, *Ukraine* **25 E5** 46 30N 32 18 E
Dniprodzerzhynsk, *Ukraine* **25 E5** 48 32N 34 37 E
Dnipropetrovsk, *Ukraine* **25 E6** 48 30N 35 0 E
Dnister →, *Europe* **17 E16** 46 18N 30 17 E
Dnistrovskyy Lyman, *Ukraine* **17 E16** 46 15N 30 17 E
Dno, *Russia* **24 C4** 57 50N 29 58 E
Dnyapro = Dnipro →, *Ukraine* **25 E5** 46 30N 32 18 E
Doaktown, *Canada* **71 C6** 46 33N 66 8W
Doba, *Chad* **51 G9** 8 40N 16 50 E
Dobandi, *Pakistan* **42 D2** 31 13N 66 50 E
Dobbyn, *Australia* **62 B3** 19 44S 140 2 E
Dobele, *Latvia* **9 H20** 56 37N 23 16 E
Doberai, Jazirah, *Indonesia* **37 E8** 1 25S 133 0 E
Doblas, *Argentina* **94 D3** 37 5S 64 0W
Dobo, *Indonesia* **37 F8** 5 45S 134 15 E
Doboj, *Bos.-H.* **21 B8** 44 46N 18 4 E
Dobreta-Turnu Severin, *Romania* **17 F12** 44 39N 22 41 E
Dobrich, *Bulgaria* **21 C12** 43 37N 27 49 E
Dobruja, *Europe* **17 F15** 44 30N 28 15 E
Dobrush, *Belarus* **17 B16** 52 25N 31 22 E
Docea, Mui, *Vietnam* **38 D6** 17 58N 106 30 E
Docker River, *Australia* **61 D4** 24 52S 129 5 E
Doctor Arroyo, *Mexico* **86 C4** 23 40N 100 11W
Doda, *India* **43 C6** 33 10N 75 34 E
Doda, L., *Canada* **70 C4** 49 25N 75 13W
Dodecanese = Dhodhekánisos, *Greece* **21 F12** 36 35N 27 0 E
Dodge City, *U.S.A.* **81 G5** 37 45N 100 1W
Dodge L., *Canada* **73 B7** 59 50N 105 36W
Dodgeville, *U.S.A.* **80 D9** 42 58N 90 8W
Dodoma, *Tanzania* **54 D4** 6 8S 35 45 E
Dodoma □, *Tanzania* **54 D4** 6 0S 36 0 E
Dodsland, *Canada* **73 C7** 51 50N 108 45W
Dodson, *U.S.A.* **82 B9** 48 24N 108 15W
Doesburg, *Neths.* **15 B6** 52 1N 6 9 E
Doetinchem, *Neths.* **15 C6** 51 59N 6 18 E
Dog Creek, *Canada* **72 C4** 51 35N 122 14W
Dog L., *Man., Canada* **73 C9** 51 2N 98 31W
Dog L., *Ont., Canada* **70 C2** 48 48N 89 30W
Dogi, *Afghan.* **40 C3** 32 20N 62 50 E
Dogran, *Pakistan* **42 D5** 31 48N 73 35 E
Doğubayazıt, *Turkey* **44 B5** 39 31N 44 5 E
Doha = Ad Dawḩah, *Qatar* **45 E6** 25 15N 51 35 E
Dohazari, *Bangla.* **41 H18** 22 10N 92 5 E
Dohrighat, *India* **43 F10** 26 16N 83 31 E
Doi, *Indonesia* **37 D7** 2 14N 127 49 E
Doi Luang, *Thailand* **38 C3** 18 30N 101 0 E
Doi Saket, *Thailand* **38 C2** 18 52N 99 9 E
Dois Irmãos, Sa., *Brazil* **93 E10** 9 0S 42 30W
Dokkum, *Neths.* **15 A5** 53 20N 5 59 E
Dokri, *Pakistan* **42 F3** 27 25N 68 7 E
Dolak, Pulau, *Indonesia* **37 F9** 8 0S 138 30 E
Dolbeau, *Canada* **71 C5** 48 53N 72 18W
Dole, *France* **18 C6** 47 7N 5 31 E
Dolgellau, *U.K.* **10 E4** 52 45N 3 53W
Dolgelley = Dolgellau, *U.K.* **10 E4** 52 45N 3 53W
Dollard, *Neths.* **15 A7** 53 20N 7 10 E
Dolo, *Ethiopia* **46 G3** 4 11N 42 3 E
Dolomites = Dolomiti, *Italy* **20 A4** 46 23N 11 51 E
Dolomiti, *Italy* **20 A4** 46 23N 11 51 E
Dolores, *Argentina* **94 D4** 36 20S 57 40W
Dolores, *Uruguay* **94 C4** 33 34S 58 15W
Dolores, *U.S.A.* **83 H9** 37 28N 108 30W
Dolores →, *U.S.A.* **83 G9** 38 49N 109 17W
Dolphin, C., *Falk. Is.* **96 G5** 51 10S 59 0W
Dolphin and Union Str., *Canada* **68 B8** 69 5N 114 45W
Dom Pedrito, *Brazil* **95 C5** 31 0S 54 40W
Domariaganj →, *India* **43 F10** 26 17N 83 44 E
Domasi, *Malawi* **55 F4** 15 15S 35 22 E
Dombarovskiy, *Russia* **26 D6** 50 46N 59 32 E
Dombås, *Norway* **9 E13** 62 4N 9 8 E
Domel I. = Letsôk-aw Kyun, *Burma* **39 G2** 11 30N 98 25 E
Domeyko, *Chile* **94 B1** 29 0S 71 0W
Domeyko, Cordillera, *Chile* **94 A2** 24 30S 69 0W
Dominador, *Chile* **94 A2** 24 21S 69 20W
Dominica ■, *W. Indies* **89 C7** 15 20N 61 20W
Dominica Passage, *W. Indies* **89 C7** 15 10N 61 20W
Dominican Rep. ■, *W. Indies* **89 C5** 19 0N 70 30W
Domodóssola, *Italy* **18 C8** 46 7N 8 17 E
Domville, Mt., *Australia* **63 D5** 28 1S 151 15 E
Don →, *Russia* **25 E6** 47 4N 39 18 E
Don →, *Aberds., U.K.* **12 D6** 57 11N 2 5W
Don →, *S. Yorks., U.K.* **10 D7** 53 41N 0 52W
Don, C., *Australia* **60 B5** 11 18S 131 46 E
Don Benito, *Spain* **19 C3** 38 53N 5 51W
Dona Ana = Nhamaabué, *Mozam.* **55 F4** 17 25S 35 5 E
Donaghadee, *U.K.* **13 B6** 54 39N 5 33W
Donald, *Australia* **63 F3** 36 23S 143 0 E
Donaldsonville, *U.S.A.* **81 K9** 30 6N 90 59W
Donalsonville, *U.S.A.* **77 K3** 31 3N 84 53W
Donau = Dunărea →, *Europe* **17 F15** 45 20N 29 40 E
Donau →, *Austria* **15 D3** 48 10N 17 0 E
Donauwörth, *Germany* **16 D6** 48 43N 10 47 E
Doncaster, *U.K.* **10 D6** 53 32N 1 6W
Dondo, *Mozam.* **55 F3** 19 33S 34 46 E
Dondo, Teluk, *Indonesia* **37 D6** 0 50N 120 30 E
Dondra Head, *Sri Lanka* **40 S12** 5 55N 80 40 E
Donegal, *Ireland* **13 B3** 54 39N 8 5W
Donegal □, *Ireland* **13 B4** 54 53N 8 0W
Donegal B., *Ireland* **13 B3** 54 31N 8 49W
Donets →, *Russia* **25 E7** 47 33N 40 55 E
Donetsk, *Ukraine* **25 E6** 48 0N 37 45 E
Dong Ba Thin, *Vietnam* **39 F7** 12 8N 109 13 E
Dong Giam, *Vietnam* **38 C5** 19 25N 105 31 E
Dong Ha, *Vietnam* **38 D6** 16 55N 107 8 E
Dong Hene, *Laos* **38 D5** 16 40N 105 18 E
Dong Hoi, *Vietnam* **38 D6** 17 29N 106 36 E
Dong Khe, *Vietnam* **38 A6** 22 26N 106 27 E
Dong Ujimqin Qi, *China* **34 B9** 45 32N 116 55 E
Dong Van, *Vietnam* **38 A5** 23 16N 105 22 E
Dong Xoai, *Vietnam* **39 G6** 11 32N 106 55 E
Dongara, *Australia* **61 E1** 29 14S 114 57 E
Dongbei, *China* **35 D13** 45 0N 125 0 E
Dongchuan, *China* **32 D5** 26 8N 103 1 E
Dongfang, *China* **38 C7** 18 50N 108 33 E
Dongfeng, *China* **35 C13** 42 40N 125 34 E
Donggala, *Indonesia* **37 E5** 0 30S 119 40 E
Donggou, *China* **35 E13** 39 52N 124 10 E
Dongguang, *China* **34 F9** 37 50N 116 30 E
Dongjingcheng, *China* **35 B15** 44 5N 129 10 E
Dongning, *China* **35 B16** 44 2N 131 5 E
Dongola, *Sudan* **51 E12** 19 9N 30 22 E
Dongping, *China* **34 G9** 35 55N 116 20 E
Dongsheng, *China* **34 E6** 39 50N 110 0 E
Dongtai, *China* **35 H11** 32 51N 120 21 E
Dongting Hu, *China* **33 D6** 29 18N 112 45 E
Donington, C., *Australia* **63 E2** 34 45S 136 0 E
Doniphan, *U.S.A.* **81 G9** 36 37N 90 50W
Dønna, *Norway* **8 C15** 66 6N 12 30 E
Donna, *U.S.A.* **81 M5** 26 9N 98 4W
Donnaconna, *Canada* **71 C5** 46 41N 71 41W
Donnelly's Crossing, *N.Z.* **59 F4** 35 42S 173 38 E
Donnybrook, *Australia* **61 F2** 33 34S 115 48 E
Donnybrook, *S. Africa* **57 D4** 29 59S 29 48 E
Donora, *U.S.A.* **78 F5** 40 11N 79 52W
Donostia = Donostia-San Sebastián, *Spain* **19 A5** 43 17N 1 58W
Donostia-San Sebastián, *Spain* **19 A5** 43 17N 1 58W
Doon →, *U.K.* **12 F4** 55 27N 4 39W
Dora, L., *Australia* **60 D3** 22 0S 123 0 E
Dora Báltea →, *Italy* **18 D8** 45 11N 8 3 E
Doran L., *Canada* **73 A7** 61 13N 108 6W
Dorchester, *U.K.* **11 G5** 50 42N 2 27W
Dorchester, C., *Canada* **69 B12** 65 27N 77 27W
Dordogne →, *France* **18 D3** 45 2N 0 36W
Dordrecht, *Neths.* **15 C4** 51 48N 4 39 E
Dordrecht, *S. Africa* **56 E4** 31 20S 27 3 E
Doré L., *Canada* **73 C7** 54 46N 107 17W
Doré Lake, *Canada* **73 C7** 54 38N 107 36W
Dori, *Burkina Faso* **50 F5** 14 3N 0 2W
Doring →, *S. Africa* **56 E2** 31 54S 18 39 E
Doringbos, *S. Africa* **56 E2** 31 59S 19 16 E
Dorion, *Canada* **79 A10** 45 23N 74 3W
Dornbirn, *Austria* **16 E5** 47 25N 9 45 E
Dornie, *U.K.* **12 D3** 57 17N 5 31W
Dornoch, *U.K.* **12 D4** 57 53N 4 2W
Dornoch Firth, *U.K.* **12 D4** 57 51N 4 4W
Dornogovĭ □, *Mongolia* **34 C6** 44 0N 110 0 E
Dorohoi, *Romania* **17 E14** 47 56N 26 23 E
Döröö Nuur, *Mongolia* **32 B4** 48 0N 93 0 E
Dorr, *Iran* **45 C6** 33 17N 50 38 E
Dorre I., *Australia* **61 E1** 25 13S 113 12 E
Dorrigo, *Australia* **63 E5** 30 20S 152 44 E
Dorris, *U.S.A.* **82 F3** 41 58N 121 55W
Dorset, *Canada* **78 A6** 45 14N 78 54W
Dorset, *U.S.A.* **78 E4** 41 40N 80 40W
Dorset □, *U.K.* **11 G5** 50 45N 2 26W
Dortmund, *Germany* **16 C4** 51 30N 7 28 E
Doruma, *Dem. Rep. of the Congo* **54 B2** 4 42N 27 33 E
Dorūneh, *Iran* **45 C8** 35 10N 57 18 E
Dos Bahias, C., *Argentina* **96 E3** 44 58S 65 32W
Dos Hermanas, *Spain* **19 D3** 37 16N 5 55W
Dos Palos, *U.S.A.* **84 J6** 36 59N 120 37W
Dosso, *Niger* **50 F6** 13 0N 3 13 E
Dothan, *U.S.A.* **77 K3** 31 13N 85 24W
Doty, *U.S.A.* **84 D3** 46 38N 123 17W
Douai, *France* **18 A5** 50 21N 3 4 E
Douala, *Cameroon* **52 D1** 4 0N 9 45 E
Douarnenez, *France* **18 B1** 48 6N 4 21W
Double Island Pt., *Australia* **63 D5** 25 56S 153 11 E
Double Mountain Fork →, *U.S.A.* **81 J4** 33 16N 100 0W
Doubs →, *France* **18 C6** 46 53N 5 1 E
Doubtful Sd., *N.Z.* **59 L1** 45 20S 166 49 E
Doubtless B., *N.Z.* **59 F4** 34 55S 173 26 E
Douglas, *S. Africa* **56 D3** 29 4S 23 46 E
Douglas, *U.K.* **10 C3** 54 10N 4 28W
Douglas, *Ariz., U.S.A.* **83 L9** 31 21N 109 33W
Douglas, *Ga., U.S.A.* **77 K4** 31 31N 82 51W
Douglas, *Wyo., U.S.A.* **80 D2** 42 45N 105 24W
Douglas Chan., *Canada* **72 C3** 53 40N 129 20W
Douglas Pt., *Canada* **78 B3** 44 19N 81 37W
Douglasville, *U.S.A.* **77 J3** 33 45N 84 45W
Dounreay, *U.K.* **12 C5** 58 35N 3 44W
Dourada, Serra, *Brazil* **93 F9** 13 10S 48 45W
Dourados, *Brazil* **95 A5** 22 9S 54 50W
Dourados →, *Brazil* **95 A5** 21 58S 54 18W
Dourados, Serra dos, *Brazil* **95 A5** 23 30S 53 30W
Douro →, *Europe* **19 B1** 41 8N 8 40W
Dove →, *U.K.* **10 E6** 52 51N 1 36W
Dove Creek, *U.S.A.* **83 H9** 37 46N 108 54W
Dover, *Australia* **62 G4** 43 18S 147 2 E
Dover, *U.K.* **11 F9** 51 7N 1 19 E
Dover, *Del., U.S.A.* **76 F8** 39 10N 75 32W
Dover, *N.H., U.S.A.* **79 C14** 43 12N 70 56W
Dover, *N.J., U.S.A.* **79 F10** 40 53N 74 34W
Dover, *Ohio, U.S.A.* **78 F3** 40 32N 81 29W
Dover, Pt., *Australia* **61 F4** 32 32S 125 32 E
Dover, Str. of, *Europe* **11 G9** 51 0N 1 30 E
Dover-Foxcroft, *U.S.A.* **77 C11** 45 11N 69 13W
Dover Plains, *U.S.A.* **79 E11** 41 43N 73 35W
Dovey = Dyfi →, *U.K.* **11 E3** 52 32N 4 3W
Dovrefjell, *Norway* **9 E13** 62 15N 9 33 E
Dow Rūd, *Iran* **45 C6** 33 28N 49 4 E
Dowa, *Malawi* **55 E3** 13 38S 33 58 E
Dowagiac, *U.S.A.* **76 E2** 41 59N 86 6W

Dowerin, Australia 61 F2 31 12S 117 2 E
Dowgha'i, Iran 45 B8 36 54N 58 32 E
Dowlatābād, Iran 45 D8 28 20N 56 40 E
Down □, U.K. 13 B5 54 23N 6 2W
Downey, Calif., U.S.A. 85 M8 33 56N 118 7W
Downey, Idaho, U.S.A. 82 E7 42 26N 112 7W
Downham Market, U.K. 11 E8 52 37N 0 23 E
Downieville, U.S.A. 84 F6 39 34N 120 50W
Downpatrick, U.K. 13 B6 54 20N 5 43W
Downpatrick Hd., Ireland 13 B2 54 20N 9 21W
Downsville, U.S.A. 79 D10 42 5N 74 50W
Downton, Mt., Canada 72 C4 52 42N 124 52W
Dowsārī, Iran 45 D8 28 25N 57 59 E
Doyle, U.S.A. 84 E6 40 2N 120 6W
Doylestown, U.S.A. 79 F9 40 21N 75 10W
Dozois, Rés., Canada 70 C4 47 30N 77 5W
Dra Khel, Pakistan 42 F2 27 58N 66 45 E
Drachten, Neths. 15 A6 53 7N 6 5 E
Drăgăşani, Romania 17 F13 44 39N 24 17 E
Dragichyn, Belarus 17 B13 52 15N 25 8 E
Dragoman, Prokhod, Bulgaria 21 C10 42 58N 22 53 E
Draguignan, France 18 E7 43 32N 6 27 E
Drain, U.S.A. 82 E2 43 40N 123 19W
Drake, U.S.A. 80 B4 47 55N 100 23W
Drake Passage, S. Ocean 5 B17 58 0S 68 0W
Drakensberg, S. Africa 57 E4 31 0S 28 0 E
Dráma, Greece 21 D11 41 9N 24 10 E
Drammen, Norway 9 G14 59 42N 10 12 E
Drangajökull, Iceland 8 C2 66 9N 22 15W
Dras, India 43 B6 34 25N 75 48 E
Drau = Drava →, Croatia 21 B8 45 33N 18 55 E
Drava →, Croatia 21 B8 45 33N 18 55 E
Drayton Valley, Canada 72 C6 53 12N 114 58W
Drenthe □, Neths. 15 B6 52 52N 6 40 E
Drepanum, C., Cyprus 23 E11 34 54N 32 19 E
Dresden, Canada 78 D2 42 35N 82 11W
Dresden, Germany 16 C7 51 3N 13 44 E
Dreux, France 18 B4 48 44N 1 23 E
Driffield, U.K. 10 C7 54 0N 0 26W
Driftwood, U.S.A. 78 E6 41 20N 78 8W
Driggs, U.S.A. 82 E8 43 44N 111 6W
Drina →, Bos.-H. 21 B8 44 53N 19 21 E
Drini →, Albania 21 C8 42 1N 19 38 E
Drøbak, Norway 9 G14 59 39N 10 39 E
Drochia, Moldova 17 D14 48 2N 27 48 E
Drogheda, Ireland 13 C5 53 43N 6 22W
Drogichin = Dragichyn, Belarus 17 B13 52 15N 25 8 E
Drogobych = Drohobych, Ukraine 17 D12 49 20N 23 30 E
Drohobych, Ukraine 17 D12 49 20N 23 30 E
Droichead Atha = Drogheda, Ireland 13 C5 53 43N 6 22W
Droichead Nua, Ireland 13 C5 53 11N 6 48W
Droitwich, U.K. 11 E5 52 16N 2 8W
Dromedary, C., Australia 63 F5 36 17S 150 10 E
Dromore, U.K. 13 B4 54 31N 7 28W
Dromore West, Ireland 13 B3 54 15N 8 52W
Dronfield, U.K. 10 D6 53 19N 1 27W
Dronten, Neths. 15 B5 52 32N 5 43 E
Drumbo, Canada 78 C4 43 16N 80 35W
Drumheller, Canada 72 C6 51 25N 112 40W
Drummond, U.S.A. 82 C7 46 40N 113 9W
Drummond I., U.S.A. 76 C4 46 1N 83 39W
Drummond Pt., Australia 63 E2 34 9S 135 16 E
Drummond Ra., Australia 62 C4 23 45S 147 10 E
Drummondville, Canada 70 C5 45 55N 72 25W
Drumright, U.S.A. 81 H6 35 59N 96 36W
Druskininkai, Lithuania 9 J20 54 3N 23 58 E
Drut →, Belarus 17 B16 53 8N 30 5 E
Druzhina, Russia 27 C15 68 14N 145 18 E
Dry Tortugas, U.S.A. 88 B3 24 38N 82 55W
Dryden, Canada 73 D10 49 47N 92 50W
Dryden, U.S.A. 79 D8 42 30N 76 18W
Drygalski I., Antarctica 5 C7 66 0S 92 0 E
Drysdale →, Australia 60 B4 13 59S 126 51 E
Drysdale I., Australia 62 A2 11 41S 136 0 E
Du Bois, U.S.A. 78 E6 41 8N 78 46W
Du Gué →, Canada 70 A5 57 21N 70 45W
Du Quoin, U.S.A. 80 G10 38 1N 89 14W
Duanesburg, U.S.A. 79 D10 42 45N 74 11W
Duaringa, Australia 62 C4 23 42S 149 42 E
Ḑubā, Si. Arabia 44 E2 27 10N 35 40 E
Dubai = Dubayy, U.A.E. 45 E7 25 18N 55 20 E
Dubăsari, Moldova 17 E15 47 15N 29 10 E
Dubăsari Vdkhr., Moldova 17 E15 47 30N 29 0 E
Dubawnt →, Canada 73 A8 64 33N 100 6W
Dubawnt, L., Canada 73 A8 63 4N 101 42W
Dubayy, U.A.E. 45 E7 25 18N 55 20 E
Dubbo, Australia 63 E4 32 11S 148 35 E
Dubele, Dem. Rep. of the Congo 54 B2 2 56N 29 35 E
Dublin, Ireland 13 C5 53 21N 6 15W
Dublin, Ga., U.S.A. 77 J4 32 32N 82 54W
Dublin, Tex., U.S.A. 81 J5 32 5N 98 21W
Dublin □, Ireland 13 C5 53 24N 6 20W
Dubno, Ukraine 17 C13 50 25N 25 45 E
Dubois, U.S.A. 82 D7 44 10N 112 14W
Dubossary = Dubăsari, Moldova 17 E15 47 15N 29 10 E
Dubossary Vdkhr. = Dubăsari Vdkhr., Moldova 17 E15 47 30N 29 0 E
Dubovka, Russia 25 E7 49 5N 44 50 E
Dubrajpur, India 43 H12 23 48N 87 25 E
Dubréka, Guinea 50 G3 9 46N 13 31W
Dubrovitsa = Dubrovytsya, Ukraine 17 C14 51 31N 26 35 E
Dubrovnik, Croatia 21 C8 42 39N 18 6 E
Dubrovytsya, Ukraine 17 C14 51 31N 26 35 E
Dubuque, U.S.A. 80 D9 42 30N 90 41W
Duchesne, U.S.A. 82 F8 40 10N 110 24W
Duchess, Australia 62 C2 21 20S 139 50 E
Ducie I., Pac. Oc. 65 K15 24 40S 124 48W
Duck →, U.S.A. 77 G2 36 2N 87 52W
Duck Cr. →, Australia 60 D2 22 37S 116 53 E
Duck Lake, Canada 73 C7 52 50N 106 16W
Duck Mountain Prov. Park, Canada 73 C8 51 45N 101 0W
Duckwall, Mt., U.S.A. 84 H6 37 58N 120 7W
Dudhi, India 41 G13 24 15N 83 10 E
Dudinka, Russia 27 C9 69 30N 86 13 E
Dudley, U.K. 11 E5 52 31N 2 5W
Dudwa, India 43 E9 28 30N 80 41 E
Duero = Douro →, Europe 19 B1 41 8N 8 40W
Dufftown, U.K. 12 D5 57 27N 3 8W
Dugi Otok, Croatia 16 G8 44 0N 15 3 E
Duifken Pt., Australia 62 A3 12 33S 141 38 E
Duisburg, Germany 16 C4 51 26N 6 45 E
Duiwelskloof, S. Africa 57 C5 23 42S 30 10 E
Dūkdamīn, Iran 45 C8 35 59N 57 43 E
Dukelský Průsmyk, Slovak Rep. 17 D11 49 25N 21 42 E
Dukhān, Qatar 45 E6 25 25N 50 50 E
Duki, Pakistan 40 D6 30 14N 68 25 E
Duku, Nigeria 51 F8 10 43N 10 43 E
Dulce, U.S.A. 83 H10 36 56N 107 0W
Dulce →, Argentina 94 C3 30 32S 62 33W
Dulce, G., Costa Rica 88 E3 8 40N 83 20W
Dulf, Iraq 44 C5 35 7N 45 51 E
Dulit, Banjaran, Malaysia 36 D4 3 15N 114 30 E
Duliu, China 34 E9 39 2N 116 55 E
Dullewala, Pakistan 42 D4 31 50N 71 25 E
Dulq Maghār, Syria 44 B3 36 22N 38 39 E
Duluth, U.S.A. 80 B8 46 47N 92 6W
Dum Dum, India 43 H13 22 39N 88 33 E
Dum Duma, India 41 F19 27 40N 95 40 E
Dūmā, Syria 47 B5 33 34N 36 24 E
Dumaguete, Phil. 37 C6 9 17N 123 15 E
Dumai, Indonesia 36 D2 1 35N 101 28 E
Dumaran, Phil. 37 B5 10 33N 119 50 E
Dumas, Ark., U.S.A. 81 J9 33 53N 91 29W
Dumas, Tex., U.S.A. 81 H4 35 52N 101 58W
Ḑumayr, Syria 47 B5 33 39N 36 42 E
Dumbarton, U.K. 12 F4 55 57N 4 33W
Dumbleyung, Australia 61 F2 33 17S 117 42 E
Dumfries, U.K. 12 F5 55 4N 3 37W
Dumfries & Galloway □, U.K. 12 F5 55 9N 3 58W
Dumka, India 43 G12 24 12N 87 15 E
Dumoine →, Canada 70 C4 46 13N 77 51W
Dumoine, L., Canada 70 C4 46 55N 77 55W
Dumraon, India 43 G11 25 33N 84 8 E
Dumyât, Egypt 51 B12 31 24N 31 48 E
Dún Dealgan = Dundalk, Ireland 13 B5 54 1N 6 24W
Dun Laoghaire, Ireland 13 C5 53 17N 6 8W
Duna = Dunărea →, Europe 17 F15 45 20N 29 40 E
Dunagiri, India 43 D8 30 31N 79 52 E
Dunaj = Dunărea →, Europe 17 F15 45 20N 29 40 E
Dunakeszi, Hungary 17 E10 47 37N 19 8 E
Dunărea →, Europe 17 F15 45 20N 29 40 E
Dunaújváros, Hungary 17 E10 46 58N 18 57 E
Dunav = Dunărea →, Europe 17 F15 45 20N 29 40 E
Dunay, Russia 30 C6 42 52N 132 22 E
Dunback, N.Z. 59 L3 45 23S 170 36 E
Dunbar, U.K. 12 E6 56 0N 2 31W
Dunblane, U.K. 12 E5 56 11N 3 58W
Duncan, Canada 72 D4 48 45N 123 40W
Duncan, Ariz., U.S.A. 83 K9 32 43N 109 6W
Duncan, Okla., U.S.A. 81 H6 34 30N 97 57W
Duncan, L., Canada 70 B4 53 29N 77 58W
Duncan L., Canada 72 A6 62 51N 113 58W
Duncan Town, Bahamas 88 B4 22 15N 75 45W
Duncannon, U.S.A. 78 F7 40 23N 77 2W
Duncansby Head, U.K. 12 C5 58 38N 3 1W
Duncansville, U.S.A. 78 F6 40 25N 78 26W
Dundalk, Canada 78 B4 44 10N 80 24W
Dundalk, Ireland 13 B5 54 1N 6 24W
Dundalk, U.S.A. 76 F7 39 16N 76 32W
Dundalk Bay, Ireland 13 C5 53 55N 6 15W
Dundas, Canada 78 C5 43 17N 79 59W
Dundas, L., Australia 61 F3 32 35S 121 50 E
Dundas I., Canada 72 C2 54 30N 130 50W
Dundas Str., Australia 60 B5 11 15S 131 35 E
Dundee, S. Africa 57 D5 28 11S 30 15 E
Dundee, U.K. 12 E6 56 28N 2 59W
Dundee, U.S.A. 78 D8 42 32N 76 59W
Dundee City □, U.K. 12 E6 56 30N 2 58W
Dundgovĭ □, Mongolia 34 B4 45 10N 106 0 E
Dundrum, U.K. 13 B6 54 16N 5 52W
Dundrum B., U.K. 13 B6 54 13N 5 47W
Dunedin, N.Z. 59 L3 45 50S 170 33 E
Dunedin, U.S.A. 77 L4 28 1N 82 47W
Dunedoo, Australia 63 E4 32 0S 149 25 E
Dunfermline, U.K. 12 E5 56 5N 3 27W
Dungannon, Canada 78 C3 43 51N 81 36W
Dungannon, U.K. 13 B5 54 31N 6 46W
Dungarpur, India 42 H5 23 52N 73 45 E
Dungarvan, Ireland 13 D4 52 5N 7 37W
Dungarvan Harbour, Ireland 13 D4 52 4N 7 35W
Dungeness, U.K. 11 G8 50 54N 0 59 E
Dungo, L. do, Angola 56 B2 17 15S 19 0 E
Dungog, Australia 63 E5 32 22S 151 46 E
Dungu, Dem. Rep. of the Congo 54 B2 3 40N 28 32 E
Dungun, Malaysia 39 K4 4 45N 103 25 E
Dunhua, China 35 C15 43 20N 128 14 E
Dunhuang, China 32 B4 40 8N 94 36 E
Dunk I., Australia 62 B4 17 59S 146 29 E
Dunkeld, Australia 63 E4 33 25S 149 29 E
Dunkeld, U.K. 12 E5 56 34N 3 35W
Dunkerque, France 18 A5 51 2N 2 20 E
Dunkery Beacon, U.K. 11 F4 51 9N 3 36W
Dunkirk = Dunkerque, France 18 A5 51 2N 2 20 E
Dunkirk, U.S.A. 78 D5 42 29N 79 20W
Dúnleary = Dun Laoghaire, Ireland 13 C5 53 17N 6 8W
Dunleer, Ireland 13 C5 53 50N 6 24W
Dunmanus B., Ireland 13 E2 51 31N 9 50W
Dunmanway, Ireland 13 E2 51 43N 9 6W
Dunmara, Australia 62 B1 16 42S 133 25 E
Dunmore, U.S.A. 79 E9 41 25N 75 38W
Dunmore Hd., Ireland 13 D1 52 10N 10 35W
Dunmore Town, Bahamas 88 A4 25 30N 76 39W
Dunn, U.S.A. 77 H6 35 19N 78 37W
Dunnet Hd., U.K. 12 C5 58 40N 3 21W
Dunning, U.S.A. 80 E4 41 50N 100 6W
Dunnville, Canada 78 D5 42 54N 79 36W
Dunolly, Australia 63 F3 36 51S 143 44 E
Dunoon, U.K. 12 F4 55 57N 4 56W
Dunphy, U.S.A. 82 F5 40 42N 116 31W
Duns, U.K. 12 F6 55 47N 2 20W
Dunseith, U.S.A. 80 A4 48 50N 100 3W
Dunsmuir, U.S.A. 82 F2 41 13N 122 16W
Dunstable, U.K. 11 F7 51 53N 0 32W
Dunstan Mts., N.Z. 59 L2 44 53S 169 35 E
Dunster, Canada 72 C5 53 8N 119 50W
Dunvegan L., Canada 73 A7 60 8N 107 10W
Duolun, China 34 C9 42 12N 116 28 E
Duong Dong, Vietnam 39 G4 10 13N 103 58 E
Dupree, U.S.A. 80 C4 45 4N 101 35W
Dupuyer, U.S.A. 82 B7 48 13N 112 30W
Duque de Caxias, Brazil 95 A7 22 45S 43 19W
Durack →, Australia 60 C4 15 33S 127 52 E
Durack Ra., Australia 60 C4 16 50S 127 40 E
Durance →, France 18 E6 43 55N 4 45 E
Durand, U.S.A. 80 C9 44 38N 91 58W
Durango, Mexico 86 C4 24 3N 104 39W
Durango, U.S.A. 83 H10 37 16N 107 53W
Durango □, Mexico 86 C4 25 0N 105 0W
Durant, Miss., U.S.A. 81 J10 33 4N 89 51W
Durant, Okla., U.S.A. 81 J6 33 59N 96 25W
Durazno, Uruguay 94 C4 33 25S 56 31W
Durazzo = Durrësi, Albania 21 D8 41 19N 19 28 E
Durban, S. Africa 57 D5 29 49S 31 1 E
Durbuy, Belgium 15 D5 50 21N 5 28 E
Düren, Germany 16 C4 50 48N 6 29 E
Durg, India 41 J12 21 15N 81 22 E
Durgapur, India 43 H12 23 30N 87 20 E
Durham, Canada 78 B4 44 10N 80 49W
Durham, U.K. 10 C6 54 47N 1 34W
Durham, Calif., U.S.A. 84 F5 39 39N 121 48W
Durham, N.C., U.S.A. 77 H6 35 59N 78 54W
Durham, N.H., U.S.A. 79 C14 43 8N 70 56W
Durham □, U.K. 10 C6 54 42N 1 45W
Ḑurmā, Si. Arabia 44 E5 24 37N 46 8 E
Durmitor, Montenegro, Yug. 21 C8 43 10N 19 0 E
Durness, U.K. 12 C4 58 34N 4 45W
Durrësi, Albania 21 D8 41 19N 19 28 E
Durrow, Ireland 13 D4 52 51N 7 24W
Dursey I., Ireland 13 E1 51 36N 10 12W
Dursunbey, Turkey 21 E13 39 35N 28 37 E
Duru, Dem. Rep. of the Congo 54 B2 4 14N 28 50 E
Durūz, Jabal ad, Jordan 47 C5 32 35N 36 40 E
D'Urville, Tanjung, Indonesia 37 E9 1 28S 137 54 E
D'Urville I., N.Z. 59 J4 40 50S 173 55 E
Duryea, U.S.A. 79 E9 41 20N 75 45W
Dushak, Turkmenistan 26 F7 37 13N 60 1 E
Dushanbe, Tajikistan 26 F7 38 33N 68 48 E
Dushore, U.S.A. 79 E8 41 31N 76 24W
Dusky Sd., N.Z. 59 L1 45 47S 166 30 E
Dussejour, C., Australia 60 B4 14 45S 128 13 E
Düsseldorf, Germany 16 C4 51 14N 6 47 E
Dutch Harbor, U.S.A. 68 C3 53 53N 166 32W
Dutlwe, Botswana 56 C3 23 58S 23 46 E
Dutton, Canada 78 D3 42 39N 81 30W
Dutton →, Australia 62 C3 20 44S 143 10 E
Duwayhin, Khawr, U.A.E. 45 E6 24 20N 51 25 E
Duyun, China 32 D5 26 18N 107 29 E
Duzdab = Zāhedān, Iran 45 D9 29 30N 60 50 E
Dvina, Severnaya →, Russia 24 B7 64 32N 40 30 E
Dvinsk = Daugavpils, Latvia 9 J22 55 53N 26 32 E
Dvinskaya Guba, Russia 24 B6 65 0N 39 0 E
Dwarka, India 42 H3 22 18N 69 8 E
Dwellingup, Australia 61 F2 32 43S 116 4 E
Dwight, Canada 78 A5 45 20N 79 1W
Dwight, U.S.A. 76 E1 41 5N 88 26W
Dyatlovo = Dzyatlava, Belarus 17 B13 53 28N 25 28 E
Dyce, U.K. 12 D6 57 13N 2 12W
Dyer, C., Canada 69 B13 66 40N 61 0W
Dyer Bay, Canada 78 A3 45 10N 81 20W
Dyer Plateau, Antarctica 5 D17 70 45S 65 30W
Dyersburg, U.S.A. 81 G10 36 3N 89 23W
Dyfi →, U.K. 11 E3 52 32N 4 3W
Dymer, Ukraine 17 C16 50 47N 30 18 E
Dysart, Australia 62 C4 22 32S 148 23 E
Dzamin Üüd = Borhoyn Tal, Mongolia 34 C6 43 50N 111 58 E
Dzerzhinsk, Russia 24 C7 56 14N 43 30 E
Dzhalinda, Russia 27 D13 53 26N 124 0 E
Dzhambul = Zhambyl, Kazakstan 26 E8 42 54N 71 22 E
Dzhankoy, Ukraine 25 E5 45 40N 34 20 E
Dzhezkazgan = Zhezqazghan, Kazakstan 26 E7 47 44N 67 40 E
Dzhizak = Jizzakh, Uzbekistan 26 E7 40 6N 67 50 E
Dzhugdzur, Khrebet, Russia 27 D14 57 30N 138 0 E
Dzhungarskiye Vorota = Dzungarian Gates, Kazakstan 32 B3 45 0N 82 0 E
Działdowo, Poland 17 B11 53 15N 20 15 E
Dzibilchaltun, Mexico 87 C7 21 5N 89 36W
Dzierzoniów, Poland 17 C9 50 45N 16 39 E
Dzilam de Bravo, Mexico 87 C7 21 24N 88 53W
Dzungaria = Junggar Pendi, China 32 B3 44 30N 86 0 E
Dzungarian Gates, Kazakstan 32 B3 45 0N 82 0 E
Dzuumod, Mongolia 32 B5 47 45N 106 58 E
Dzyarzhynsk, Belarus 17 B14 53 40N 27 1 E
Dzyatlava, Belarus 17 B13 53 28N 25 28 E

E

Eabamet L., Canada 70 B2 51 30N 87 46W
Eads, U.S.A. 80 F3 38 29N 102 47W
Eagar, U.S.A. 83 J9 34 6N 109 17W
Eagle, Alaska, U.S.A. 68 B5 64 47N 141 12W
Eagle, Colo., U.S.A. 82 G10 39 39N 106 50W
Eagle →, Canada 71 B8 53 36N 57 26W
Eagle Butte, U.S.A. 80 C4 45 0N 101 10W
Eagle Grove, U.S.A. 80 D8 42 40N 93 54W
Eagle L., Canada 73 D10 49 42N 93 13W
Eagle L., Calif., U.S.A. 82 F3 40 39N 120 45W
Eagle L., Maine, U.S.A. 77 B11 46 20N 69 22W
Eagle Lake, Canada 78 A6 45 8N 78 29W
Eagle Lake, Maine, U.S.A. 77 B11 47 3N 68 36W
Eagle Lake, Tex., U.S.A. 81 L6 29 35N 96 20W
Eagle Mountain, U.S.A. 85 M11 33 49N 115 27W
Eagle Nest, U.S.A. 83 H11 36 33N 105 16W
Eagle Pass, U.S.A. 81 L4 28 43N 100 30W
Eagle Pk., U.S.A. 84 G7 38 10N 119 25W
Eagle Pt., Australia 60 C3 16 11S 124 23 E
Eagle River, Mich., U.S.A. 76 B1 47 24N 88 18W
Eagle River, Wis., U.S.A. 80 C10 45 55N 89 15W
Eaglehawk, Australia 63 F3 36 44S 144 15 E
Eagles Mere, U.S.A. 79 E8 41 25N 76 33W
Ealing, U.K. 11 F7 51 31N 0 20W
Ear Falls, Canada 73 C10 50 38N 93 13W
Earle, U.S.A. 81 H9 35 16N 90 28W
Earlimart, U.S.A. 85 K7 35 53N 119 16W
Earn →, U.K. 12 E5 56 21N 3 18W
Earn, L., U.K. 12 E4 56 23N 4 13W
Earnslaw, Mt., N.Z. 59 L2 44 32S 168 27 E
Earth, U.S.A. 81 H3 34 14N 102 24W
Easley, U.S.A. 77 H4 34 50N 82 36W
East Anglia, U.K. 10 E9 52 30N 1 0 E
East Angus, Canada 71 C5 45 30N 71 40W
East Aurora, U.S.A. 78 D6 42 46N 78 37W
East Ayrshire □, U.K. 12 F4 55 26N 4 11W
East Bengal, Bangla. 41 H17 24 0N 90 0 E
East Beskids = Vychodné Beskydy, Europe 17 D11 49 20N 22 0 E
East Brady, U.S.A. 78 F5 40 59N 79 36W
East C., N.Z. 59 G7 37 42S 178 35 E
East Chicago, U.S.A. 76 E2 41 38N 87 27W
East China Sea, Asia 33 D7 30 0N 126 0 E
East Coulee, Canada 72 C6 51 23N 112 27W
East Dereham, U.K. 11 E8 52 41N 0 57 E
East Dunbartonshire □, U.K. 12 F4 55 57N 4 13W
East Falkland, Falk. Is. 96 G5 51 30S 58 30W
East Grand Forks, U.S.A. 80 B6 47 56N 97 1W
East Greenwich, U.S.A. 79 E13 41 40N 71 27W
East Grinstead, U.K. 11 F8 51 7N 0 0 E
East Hartford, U.S.A. 79 E12 41 46N 72 39W
East Helena, U.S.A. 82 C8 46 35N 111 56W
East Indies, Asia 28 K15 0 0 120 0 E
East Kilbride, U.K. 12 F4 55 47N 4 11W
East Lansing, U.S.A. 76 D3 42 44N 84 29W
East Liverpool, U.S.A. 78 F4 40 37N 80 35W
East London, S. Africa 57 E4 33 0S 27 55 E
East Lothian □, U.K. 12 F6 55 58N 2 44W
East Main = Eastmain, Canada 70 B4 52 10N 78 30W
East Northport, U.S.A. 79 F11 40 53N 73 20W
East Orange, U.S.A. 79 F10 40 46N 74 13W
East Pacific Ridge, Pac. Oc. 65 J17 15 0S 110 0W
East Palestine, U.S.A. 78 F4 40 50N 80 33W
East Pine, Canada 72 B4 55 48N 120 12W
East Point, U.S.A. 77 J3 33 41N 84 27W
East Providence, U.S.A. 79 E13 41 49N 71 23W
East Pt., Canada 71 C7 46 27N 61 58W
East Renfrewshire □, U.K. 12 F4 55 46N 4 21W
East Retford = Retford, U.K. 10 D7 53 19N 0 56W
East Riding of Yorkshire □, U.K. 10 D7 53 55N 0 30W
East Rochester, U.S.A. 78 C7 43 7N 77 29W
East St. Louis, U.S.A. 80 F9 38 37N 90 9W
East Schelde = Oosterschelde →, Neths. 15 C4 51 33N 4 0 E
East Siberian Sea, Russia 27 B17 73 0N 160 0 E
East Stroudsburg, U.S.A. 79 E9 41 1N 75 11W
East Sussex □, U.K. 11 G8 50 56N 0 19 E
East Tawas, U.S.A. 76 C4 44 17N 83 29W
East Timor = Timor Timur □, Indonesia 37 F7 9 0S 125 0 E
East Toorale, Australia 63 E4 30 27S 145 28 E
East Walker →, U.S.A. 84 G7 38 52N 119 10W
East Windsor, U.S.A. 79 F10 40 17N 74 34W
Eastbourne, N.Z. 59 J5 41 19S 174 55 E
Eastbourne, U.K. 11 G8 50 46N 0 18 E
Eastend, Canada 73 D7 49 32N 108 50W
Easter I. = Pascua, I. de, Pac. Oc. 65 K17 27 0S 109 0W
Eastern □, Kenya 54 C4 0 0 38 30 E
Eastern □, Uganda 54 B3 1 50N 33 45 E
Eastern Cape □, S. Africa 56 E4 32 0S 26 0 E
Eastern Cr. →, Australia 62 C3 20 40S 141 35 E
Eastern Ghats, India 40 N11 14 0N 78 50 E
Eastern Group = Lau Group, Fiji 59 C9 17 0S 178 30W
Eastern Group, Australia 61 F3 33 30S 124 30 E
Eastern Transvaal = Mpumalanga □, S. Africa 57 B5 26 0S 30 0 E
Easterville, Canada 73 C9 53 8N 99 49W
Easthampton, U.S.A. 79 D12 42 16N 72 40W
Eastlake, U.S.A. 78 E3 41 40N 81 26W
Eastland, U.S.A. 81 J5 32 24N 98 49W
Eastleigh, U.K. 11 G6 50 58N 1 21W
Eastmain, Canada 70 B4 52 10N 78 30W
Eastmain →, Canada 70 B4 52 27N 78 26W
Eastman, Canada 79 A12 45 18N 72 19W
Eastman, U.S.A. 77 J4 32 12N 83 11W
Easton, Md., U.S.A. 76 F7 38 47N 76 5W
Easton, Pa., U.S.A. 79 F9 40 41N 75 13W
Easton, Wash., U.S.A. 84 C5 47 14N 121 11W
Eastpointe, U.S.A. 78 D2 42 27N 82 56W
Eastport, U.S.A. 77 C12 44 56N 67 0W
Eastsound, U.S.A. 84 B4 48 42N 122 55W
Eaton, U.S.A. 80 E2 40 32N 104 42W
Eatonia, Canada 73 C7 51 13N 109 25W
Eatonton, U.S.A. 77 J4 33 20N 83 23W
Eatontown, U.S.A. 79 F10 40 19N 74 4W
Eatonville, U.S.A. 84 D4 46 52N 122 16W
Eau Claire, U.S.A. 80 C9 44 49N 91 30W
Eau Claire, L. à l', Canada 70 A5 56 10N 74 25W
Ebbw Vale, U.K. 11 F4 51 46N 3 12W
Ebeltoft, Denmark 9 H14 56 12N 10 41 E
Ebensburg, U.S.A. 78 F6 40 29N 78 44W
Eberswalde-Finow, Germany 16 B7 52 50N 13 49 E
Ebetsu, Japan 30 C10 43 7N 141 34 E
Ebolowa, Cameroon 52 D2 2 55N 11 10 E
Ebro →, Spain 19 B6 40 43N 0 54 E
Eceabat, Turkey 21 D12 40 11N 26 21 E
Ech Cheliff, Algeria 50 A6 36 10N 1 20 E
Echigo-Sammyaku, Japan 31 F9 36 50N 139 50 E
Echizen-Misaki, Japan 31 G7 35 59N 135 57 E
Echo Bay, N.W.T., Canada 68 B8 66 5N 117 55W
Echo Bay, Ont., Canada 70 C3 46 29N 84 4W
Echoing →, Canada 70 B1 55 51N 92 5W
Echternach, Lux. 15 E6 49 49N 6 25 E
Echuca, Australia 63 F3 36 10S 144 20 E
Ecija, Spain 19 D3 37 30N 5 10W
Eclipse Is., Australia 60 B4 13 54S 126 19 E
Eclipse Sd., Canada 69 A11 72 38N 79 0W
Ecuador ■, S. Amer. 92 D3 2 0S 78 0W
Ed Damazin, Sudan 51 F12 11 46N 34 21 E
Ed Debba, Sudan 51 E12 18 0N 30 51 E
Ed Dueim, Sudan 51 F12 14 0N 32 10 E
Edam, Canada 73 C7 53 11N 108 46W
Edam, Neths. 15 B5 52 31N 5 3 E
Eday, U.K. 12 B6 59 11N 2 47W
Eddrachillis B., U.K. 12 C3 58 17N 5 14W
Eddystone Pt., Australia 62 G4 40 59S 148 20 E

Ede, Neths. 15 B5 52 4N 5 40 E
Edehon L., Canada 73 A9 60 25N 97 15W
Eden, Australia 63 F4 37 3S 149 55 E
Eden, N.C., U.S.A. 77 G6 36 29N 79 53W
Eden, N.Y., U.S.A. 78 D6 42 39N 78 55W
Eden, Tex., U.S.A. 81 K5 31 13N 99 51W
Eden →, U.K. 10 C4 54 57N 3 1W
Edenburg, S. Africa 56 D4 29 43S 25 58 E
Edendale, S. Africa 57 D5 29 39S 30 18 E
Edenderry, Ireland 13 C4 53 21N 7 4W
Edenhope, Australia 63 F3 37 4S 141 19 E
Edenton, U.S.A. 77 G7 36 4N 76 39W
Edenville, S. Africa 57 D4 27 37S 27 34 E
Eder →, Germany 16 C5 51 12N 9 28 E
Edgar, U.S.A. 80 E6 40 22N 97 58W
Edgartown, U.S.A. 79 E14 41 23N 70 31W
Edge Hill, U.K. 11 E6 52 8N 1 26W
Edgefield, U.S.A. 77 J5 33 47N 81 56W
Edgeley, U.S.A. 80 B5 46 22N 98 43W
Edgemont, U.S.A. 80 D3 43 18N 103 50W
Edgeøya, Svalbard 4 B9 77 45N 22 30 E
Édhessa, Greece 21 D10 40 48N 22 5 E
Edievale, N.Z. 59 L2 45 49S 169 22 E
Edina, U.S.A. 80 E8 40 10N 92 11W
Edinboro, U.S.A. 78 E4 41 52N 80 8W
Edinburg, U.S.A. 81 M5 26 18N 98 10W
Edinburgh, U.K. 12 F5 55 57N 3 13W
Edineţ, Moldova 17 D14 48 9N 27 18 E
Edirne, Turkey 21 D12 41 40N 26 34 E
Edison, U.S.A. 84 B4 48 33N 122 27W
Edithburgh, Australia 63 F2 35 5S 137 43 E
Edmeston, U.S.A. 79 D9 42 42N 75 15W
Edmond, U.S.A. 81 H6 35 39N 97 29W
Edmonds, U.S.A. 84 C4 47 49N 122 23W
Edmonton, Australia 62 B4 17 2S 145 46 E
Edmonton, Canada 72 C6 53 30N 113 30W
Edmund L., Canada 70 B1 54 45N 93 17W
Edmundston, Canada 71 C6 47 23N 68 20W
Edna, U.S.A. 81 L6 28 59N 96 39W
Edremit, Turkey 21 E12 39 34N 27 0 E
Edremit Körfezi, Turkey 21 E12 39 30N 26 45 E
Edson, Canada 72 C5 53 35N 116 28W
Eduardo Castex, Argentina 94 D3 35 50S 64 18W
Edward →, Australia 63 F3 35 5S 143 30 E
Edward, L., Africa 54 C2 0 25S 29 40 E
Edward River, Australia 62 A3 14 59S 141 26 E
Edward VII Land, Antarctica 5 E13 80 0S 150 0W
Edwards, Calif., U.S.A. 85 L9 34 55N 117 51W
Edwards, N.Y., U.S.A. 79 B9 44 20N 75 15W
Edwards Air Force Base, U.S.A. 85 L9 34 50N 117 40W
Edwards Plateau, U.S.A. 81 K4 30 45N 101 20W
Edwardsville, U.S.A. 79 E9 41 15N 75 56W
Edzo, Canada 72 A5 62 49N 116 4W
Eeklo, Belgium 15 C3 51 11N 3 33 E
Effingham, U.S.A. 76 F1 39 7N 88 33W
Égadi, Ísole, Italy 20 F5 37 55N 12 16 E
Egan Range, U.S.A. 82 G6 39 35N 114 55W
Eganville, Canada 78 A7 45 32N 77 5W
Eger = Cheb, Czech Rep. 16 C7 50 9N 12 28 E
Eger, Hungary 17 E11 47 53N 20 27 E
Egersund, Norway 9 G12 58 26N 6 1 E
Egg L., Canada 73 B7 55 5N 105 30W
Éghezée, Belgium 15 D4 50 35N 4 55 E
Egmont, Canada 72 D4 49 45N 123 56W
Egmont, C., N.Z. 59 H4 39 16S 173 45 E
Egmont, Mt., N.Z. 59 H5 39 17S 174 5 E
Egra, India 43 J12 21 54N 87 32 E
Eğridir, Turkey 25 G5 37 52N 30 51 E
Eğridir Gölü, Turkey 25 G5 37 53N 30 50 E
Egvekinot, Russia 27 C19 66 19N 179 50W
Egypt ■, Africa 51 C12 28 0N 31 0 E
Ehime □, Japan 31 H6 33 30N 132 40 E
Ehrenberg, U.S.A. 85 M12 33 36N 114 31W
Eibar, Spain 19 A4 43 11N 2 28W
Eidsvold, Australia 63 D5 25 25S 151 12 E
Eidsvoll, Norway 9 F14 60 19N 11 14 E
Eifel, Germany 16 C4 50 15N 6 50 E
Eiffel Flats, Zimbabwe 55 F3 18 20S 30 0 E
Eigg, U.K. 12 E2 56 54N 6 10W
Eighty Mile Beach, Australia 60 C3 19 30S 120 40 E
Eil, Somali Rep. 46 F4 8 0N 49 50 E
Eil, L., U.K. 12 E3 56 51N 5 16W
Eildon, Australia 63 F4 37 14S 145 55 E
Eildon, L., Australia 63 F4 37 10S 146 0 E
Einasleigh, Australia 62 B3 18 32S 144 5 E
Einasleigh →, Australia 62 B3 17 30S 142 17 E
Eindhoven, Neths. 15 C5 51 26N 5 28 E
Eire = Ireland ■, Europe 13 C4 53 50N 7 52W
Eiríksjökull, Iceland 8 D3 64 46N 20 24W
Eirunepé, Brazil 92 E5 6 35S 69 53W
Eisenach, Germany 16 C6 50 58N 10 19 E
Eisenerz, Austria 16 E8 47 32N 14 54 E
Eivissa, Spain 22 C7 38 54N 1 26 E
Ejutla, Mexico 87 D5 16 34N 96 44W
Ekalaka, U.S.A. 80 C2 45 53N 104 33W
Eketahuna, N.Z. 59 J5 40 38S 175 43 E
Ekibastuz, Kazakstan 26 D8 51 50N 75 10 E
Ekoli, Dem. Rep. of the Congo 54 C1 0 23S 24 13 E
Eksjö, Sweden 9 H16 57 40N 14 58 E
Ekwan →, Canada 70 B3 53 12N 82 15W
Ekwan Pt., Canada 70 B3 53 16N 82 7W
El Aaiún, W. Sahara 50 C3 27 9N 13 12W
El Abanico, Chile 94 D1 37 20S 71 31W
El 'Agrûd, Egypt 47 E3 30 14N 34 24 E
El Alamein, Egypt 51 B11 30 48N 28 58 E
El 'Aqaba, W. →, Egypt 47 E2 30 7N 33 54 E
El Arīḥā, West Bank 47 D4 31 52N 35 27 E
El 'Arîsh, Egypt 47 D2 31 8N 33 50 E
El 'Arîsh, W. →, Egypt 47 D2 31 8N 33 47 E
El Asnam = Ech Cheliff, Algeria 50 A6 36 10N 1 20 E
El Bayadh, Algeria 50 B6 33 40N 1 1 E
El Bluff, Nic. 88 D3 11 59N 83 40W
El Brûk, W. →, Egypt 47 E2 30 15N 33 50 E
El Cajon, U.S.A. 85 N10 32 48N 116 58W
El Campo, U.S.A. 81 L6 29 12N 96 16W
El Centro, U.S.A. 85 N11 32 48N 115 34W
El Cerro, Bolivia 92 G6 17 30S 61 40W
El Compadre, Mexico 85 N10 32 20N 116 14W
El Cuy, Argentina 96 D3 39 55S 68 25W
El Cuyo, Mexico 87 C7 21 30N 87 40W
El Daheir, Egypt 47 D3 31 13N 34 10 E
El Dátil, Mexico 86 B2 30 7N 112 15W
El Dere, Somali Rep. 46 G4 3 50N 47 8 E
El Descanso, Mexico 85 N10 32 12N 116 58W
El Desemboque, Mexico 86 A2 30 30N 112 57W
El Diviso, Colombia 92 C3 1 22N 78 14W
El Djouf, Mauritania 50 D4 20 0N 9 0W
El Dorado, Ark., U.S.A. 81 J8 33 12N 92 40W
El Dorado, Kans., U.S.A. 81 G6 37 49N 96 52W
El Dorado, Venezuela 92 B6 6 55N 61 37W
El Escorial, Spain 19 B3 40 35N 4 7W
El Faiyûm, Egypt 51 C12 29 19N 30 50 E
El Fâsher, Sudan 51 F11 13 33N 25 26 E
El Ferrol = Ferrol, Spain 19 A1 43 29N 8 15W
El Fuerte, Mexico 86 B3 26 30N 108 40W
El Gal, Somali Rep. 46 E5 10 58N 50 20 E
El Geneina = Al Junaynah, Sudan 51 F10 13 27N 22 45 E
El Gîza, Egypt 51 C12 30 0N 31 10 E
El Goléa, Algeria 50 B6 30 30N 2 50 E
El Iskandarîya, Egypt 51 B11 31 13N 29 58 E
El Istiwa'iya, Sudan 51 G11 5 0N 28 0 E
El Jadida, Morocco 50 B4 33 11N 8 17W
El Jardal, Honduras 88 D2 14 54N 88 50W
El Kabrît, G., Egypt 47 F2 29 42N 33 16 E
El Khârga, Egypt 51 C12 25 30N 30 33 E
El Khartûm, Sudan 51 E12 15 31N 32 35 E
El Kuntilla, Egypt 47 E3 30 1N 34 45 E
El Maestrazgo, Spain 19 B5 40 30N 0 25W
El Mahalla el Kubra, Egypt 51 B12 31 0N 31 0 E
El Mansûra, Egypt 51 B12 31 0N 31 19 E
El Medano, Canary Is. 22 F3 28 3N 16 32W
El Milagro, Argentina 94 C2 30 59S 65 59W
El Minyâ, Egypt 51 C12 28 7N 30 33 E
El Monte, U.S.A. 85 L8 34 4N 118 1W
El Obeid, Sudan 51 F12 13 8N 30 10 E
El Odaiya, Sudan 51 F11 12 8N 28 12 E
El Oro, Mexico 87 D4 19 48N 100 8W
El Oued, Algeria 50 B7 33 20N 6 58 E
El Palmito, Presa, Mexico 86 B3 25 40N 105 30W
El Paso, U.S.A. 83 L10 31 45N 106 29W
El Paso Robles, U.S.A. 84 K6 35 38N 120 41W
El Portal, U.S.A. 84 H7 37 41N 119 47W
El Porvenir, Mexico 86 A3 31 15N 105 51W
El Prat de Llobregat, Spain 19 B7 41 18N 2 3 E
El Progreso, Honduras 88 C2 15 26N 87 51W
El Pueblito, Mexico 86 B3 29 3N 105 4W
El Pueblo, Canary Is. 22 F2 28 36N 17 47W
El Puerto de Santa María, Spain 19 D2 36 36N 6 13W
El Qâhira, Egypt 51 B12 30 1N 31 14 E
El Qantara, Egypt 47 E1 30 51N 32 20 E
El Quseima, Egypt 47 E3 30 40N 34 15 E
El Real, Panama 92 B3 8 0N 77 40W
El Reno, U.S.A. 81 H6 35 32N 97 57W
El Rio, U.S.A. 85 L7 34 14N 119 10W
El Roque, Pta., Canary Is. 22 F4 28 10N 15 25W
El Rosarito, Mexico 86 B2 28 38N 114 4W
El Saheira, W. →, Egypt 47 E2 30 5N 33 25 E
El Salto, Mexico 86 C3 23 47N 105 22W
El Salvador ■, Cent. Amer. 88 D2 13 50N 89 0W
El Sauce, Nic. 88 D2 13 0N 86 40W
El Sueco, Mexico 86 B3 29 54N 106 24W
El Suweis, Egypt 51 C12 29 58N 32 31 E
El Tamarâni, W. →, Egypt 47 E3 30 7N 34 43 E
El Thamad, Egypt 47 F3 29 40N 34 28 E
El Tigre, Venezuela 92 B6 8 44N 64 15W
El Tîh, Gebal, Egypt 47 F2 29 40N 33 50 E
El Tîna, Khalîg, Egypt 47 D1 31 10N 32 40 E
El Tofo, Chile 94 B1 29 22S 71 18W
El Tránsito, Chile 94 B1 28 52S 70 17W
El Tûr, Egypt 44 D2 28 14N 33 36 E
El Turbio, Argentina 96 G2 51 45S 72 5W
El Uqsur, Egypt 51 C12 25 41N 32 38 E
El Venado, Mexico 86 C4 22 56N 101 10W
El Vergel, Mexico 86 B3 26 28N 106 22W
El Vigía, Venezuela 92 B4 8 38N 71 39W
El Wabeira, Egypt 47 F2 29 34N 33 6 E
El Wak, Kenya 54 B5 2 49N 40 56 E
El Wuz, Sudan 51 E12 15 5N 30 7 E
Elat, Israel 47 F3 29 30N 34 56 E
Elâzığ, Turkey 25 G6 38 37N 39 14 E
Elba, Italy 20 C4 42 46N 10 17 E
Elba, U.S.A. 77 K2 31 25N 86 4W
Elbasani, Albania 21 D9 41 9N 20 9 E
Elbe, U.S.A. 84 D4 46 45N 122 10W
Elbe →, Europe 16 B5 53 50N 9 0 E
Elbert, Mt., U.S.A. 83 G10 39 7N 106 27W
Elberton, U.S.A. 77 H4 34 7N 82 52W
Elbeuf, France 18 B4 49 17N 1 2 E
Elbidtan, Turkey 44 B3 38 13N 37 12 E
Elbing = Elbląg, Poland 17 A10 54 10N 19 25 E
Elbląg, Poland 17 A10 54 10N 19 25 E
Elbow, Canada 73 C7 51 7N 106 35W
Elbrus, Asia 25 F7 43 21N 42 30 E
Elburz Mts. = Alborz, Reshteh-ye Kūhhā-ye, Iran 45 C7 36 0N 52 0 E
Elche, Spain 19 C5 38 15N 0 42W
Elcho I., Australia 62 A2 11 55S 135 45 E
Elda, Spain 19 C5 38 29N 0 47W
Elde →, Germany 16 B6 53 7N 11 15 E
Eldon, Mo., U.S.A. 80 F8 38 21N 92 35W
Eldon, Wash., U.S.A. 84 C3 47 33N 123 3W
Eldora, U.S.A. 80 D8 42 22N 93 5W
Eldorado, Argentina 95 B5 26 28S 54 43W
Eldorado, Canada 78 B7 44 35N 77 31W
Eldorado, Mexico 86 C3 24 20N 107 22W
Eldorado, Ill., U.S.A. 76 G1 37 49N 88 26W
Eldorado, Tex., U.S.A. 81 K4 30 52N 100 36W
Eldorado Springs, U.S.A. 81 G8 37 52N 94 1W
Eldoret, Kenya 54 B4 0 30N 35 17 E
Eldred, U.S.A. 78 E6 41 58N 78 23W
Elea, C., Cyprus 23 D13 35 19N 34 4 E
Eleanora, Pk., Australia 61 F3 32 57S 121 9 E
Electra, U.S.A. 74 D7 34 2N 98 55W
Elefantes →, Mozam. 57 C5 24 10S 32 40 E
Elektrostal, Russia 24 C6 55 41N 38 32 E
Elephant Butte Reservoir, U.S.A. 83 K10 33 9N 107 11W
Elephant I., Antarctica 5 C18 61 0S 55 0W
Eleuthera, Bahamas 88 B4 25 0N 76 20W
Elgin, Canada 79 B8 44 36N 76 13W
Elgin, U.K. 12 D5 57 39N 3 19W
Elgin, Ill., U.S.A. 76 D1 42 2N 88 17W
Elgin, N. Dak., U.S.A. 80 B4 46 24N 101 51W
Elgin, Oreg., U.S.A. 82 D5 45 34N 117 55W
Elgin, Tex., U.S.A. 81 K6 30 21N 97 22W
Elgon, Mt., Africa 54 B3 1 10N 34 30 E
Eliase, Indonesia 37 F8 8 21S 130 48 E
Elim, S. Africa 56 E2 34 35S 19 45 E
Elisabethville = Lubumbashi, Dem. Rep. of the Congo 55 E2 11 40S 27 28 E
Elista, Russia 25 E7 46 16N 44 14 E
Elizabeth, Australia 63 E2 34 42S 138 41 E
Elizabeth, N.J., U.S.A. 79 F10 40 39N 74 13W
Elizabeth, N.J., U.S.A. 79 F10 40 40N 74 13W
Elizabeth City, U.S.A. 77 G7 36 18N 76 14W
Elizabethton, U.S.A. 77 G4 36 21N 82 13W
Elizabethtown, Ky., U.S.A. 76 G3 37 42N 85 52W
Elizabethtown, N.Y., U.S.A. 79 B11 44 13N 73 36W
Elizabethtown, Pa., U.S.A. 79 F8 40 9N 76 36W
Ełk, Poland 17 B12 53 50N 22 21 E
Elk →, Canada 72 C5 49 11N 115 14W
Elk →, U.S.A. 77 H2 34 46N 87 16W
Elk City, U.S.A. 81 H5 35 25N 99 25W
Elk Creek, U.S.A. 84 F4 39 36N 122 32W
Elk Grove, U.S.A. 84 G5 38 25N 121 22W
Elk Island Nat. Park, Canada 72 C6 53 35N 112 59W
Elk Lake, Canada 70 C3 47 40N 80 25W
Elk Point, Canada 73 C6 53 54N 110 55W
Elk River, Idaho, U.S.A. 82 C5 46 47N 116 11W
Elk River, Minn., U.S.A. 80 C8 45 18N 93 35W
Elkedra →, Australia 62 C2 21 8S 136 22 E
Elkhart, Ind., U.S.A. 76 E3 41 41N 85 58W
Elkhart, Kans., U.S.A. 81 G4 37 0N 101 54W
Elkhorn, Canada 73 D8 49 59N 101 14W
Elkhorn →, U.S.A. 80 E6 41 8N 96 19W
Elkhovo, Bulgaria 21 C12 42 10N 26 35 E
Elkin, U.S.A. 77 G5 36 15N 80 51W
Elkins, U.S.A. 76 F6 38 55N 79 51W
Elkland, U.S.A. 78 E7 41 59N 77 19W
Elko, Canada 72 D5 49 20N 115 10W
Elko, U.S.A. 82 F6 40 50N 115 46W
Elkton, U.S.A. 78 C1 43 49N 83 11W
Ell, L., Australia 61 E4 29 13S 127 46 E
Ellef Ringnes I., Canada 4 B2 78 30N 102 2W
Ellen, Mt., U.S.A. 79 B12 44 9N 72 56W
Ellenburg, U.S.A. 79 B11 44 54N 73 48W
Ellendale, U.S.A. 80 B5 46 0N 98 32W
Ellensburg, U.S.A. 82 C3 46 59N 120 34W
Ellenville, U.S.A. 79 E10 41 43N 74 24W
Ellery, Mt., Australia 63 F4 37 28S 148 47 E
Ellesmere, L., N.Z. 59 M4 47 47S 172 28 E
Ellesmere I., Canada 4 B4 79 30N 80 0W
Ellesmere Port, U.K. 10 D5 53 17N 2 54W
Ellice Is. = Tuvalu ■, Pac. Oc. 64 H9 8 0S 178 0 E
Ellicottville, U.S.A. 78 D6 42 17N 78 40W
Elliot, Australia 62 B1 17 33S 133 32 E
Elliot, S. Africa 57 E4 31 22S 27 48 E
Elliot Lake, Canada 70 C3 46 25N 82 35W
Elliotdale = Xhora, S. Africa 57 E4 31 55S 28 38 E
Ellis, U.S.A. 80 F5 38 56N 99 34W
Elliston, Australia 63 E1 33 39S 134 53 E
Ellisville, U.S.A. 81 K10 31 36N 89 12W
Ellon, U.K. 12 D6 57 22N 2 4W
Ellore = Eluru, India 41 L12 16 48N 81 8 E
Ellsworth, Kans., U.S.A. 80 F5 38 44N 98 14W
Ellsworth, Maine, U.S.A. 77 C11 44 33N 68 25W
Ellsworth Land, Antarctica 5 D16 76 0S 89 0W
Ellsworth Mts., Antarctica 5 D16 78 30S 85 0W
Ellwood City, U.S.A. 78 F4 40 52N 80 17W
Elma, Canada 73 D9 49 52N 95 55W
Elma, U.S.A. 84 D3 47 0N 123 25W
Elmalı, Turkey 25 G4 36 44N 29 56 E
Elmhurst, U.S.A. 76 E2 41 53N 87 56W
Elmira, Canada 78 C4 43 36N 80 33W
Elmira, U.S.A. 78 D8 42 6N 76 48W
Elmira Heights, U.S.A. 78 D8 42 8N 76 50W
Elmore, Australia 63 F3 36 30S 144 37 E
Elmore, U.S.A. 85 M11 33 7N 115 49W
Elmshorn, Germany 16 B5 53 43N 9 40 E
Elmvale, Canada 78 B5 44 35N 79 52W
Elora, Canada 78 C4 43 41N 80 26W
Eloúnda, Greece 23 D7 35 16N 25 42 E
Eloy, U.S.A. 83 K8 32 45N 111 33W
Elrose, Canada 73 C7 51 12N 108 0W
Elsie, U.S.A. 84 E3 45 52N 123 36W
Elsinore = Helsingør, Denmark 9 H15 56 2N 12 35 E
Eltham, N.Z. 59 H5 39 26S 174 19 E
Eluru, India 41 L12 16 48N 81 8 E
Elvas, Portugal 19 C2 38 50N 7 10W
Elverum, Norway 9 F14 60 53N 11 34 E
Elvire →, Australia 60 C4 17 51S 128 11 E
Elvire, Mt., Australia 61 E2 29 22S 119 36 E
Elwell, L., U.S.A. 82 B8 48 22N 111 17W
Elwood, Ind., U.S.A. 76 E3 40 17N 85 50W
Elwood, Nebr., U.S.A. 80 E5 40 36N 99 52W
Elx = Elche, Spain 19 C5 38 15N 0 42W
Ely, U.K. 11 E8 52 24N 0 16 E
Ely, Minn., U.S.A. 80 B9 47 55N 91 51W
Ely, Nev., U.S.A. 82 G6 39 15N 114 54W
Elyria, U.S.A. 78 E2 41 22N 82 7W
Emāmrūd, Iran 45 B7 36 30N 55 0 E
Emba, Kazakstan 26 E6 48 50N 58 8 E
Emba →, Kazakstan 25 E9 46 55N 53 28 E
Embarcación, Argentina 94 A3 23 10S 64 0W
Embarras Portage, Canada 73 B6 58 27N 111 28W
Embetsu, Japan 30 B10 44 44N 141 47 E
Embi = Emba, Kazakstan 26 E6 48 50N 58 8 E
Embi = Emba →, Kazakstan 25 E9 46 55N 53 28 E
Embóna, Greece 23 C9 36 13N 27 51 E
Embrun, France 18 D7 44 34N 6 30 E
Embu, Kenya 54 C4 0 32S 37 38 E
Emden, Germany 16 B4 53 21N 7 12 E
Emerald, Australia 62 C4 23 32S 148 10 E
Emerson, Canada 73 D9 49 0N 97 10W
Emet, Turkey 21 E13 39 20N 29 15 E
Emi Koussi, Chad 51 E9 19 45N 18 55 E
Eminabad, Pakistan 42 C6 32 2N 74 8 E
Emine, Nos, Bulgaria 21 C12 42 40N 27 56 E
Emlenton, U.S.A. 78 E5 41 11N 79 43W
Emmaus, U.S.A. 79 F9 40 32N 75 30W
Emmeloord, Neths. 15 B5 52 44N 5 46 E
Emmen, Neths. 15 B6 52 48N 6 57 E
Emmet, Australia 62 C3 24 45S 144 30 E
Emmetsburg, U.S.A. 80 D7 43 7N 94 41W
Emmett, Idaho, U.S.A. 82 E5 43 52N 116 30W
Emmett, Mich., U.S.A. 78 D2 42 59N 82 46W
Emmonak, U.S.A. 68 B3 62 46N 164 30W
Emo, Canada 73 D10 48 38N 93 50W
Empalme, Mexico 86 B2 28 1N 110 49W
Empangeni, S. Africa 57 D5 28 50S 31 52 E
Empedrado, Argentina 94 B4 28 0S 58 46W
Emperor Seamount Chain, Pac. Oc. 64 D9 40 0N 170 0 E
Emporia, Kans., U.S.A. 80 F6 38 25N 96 11W
Emporia, Va., U.S.A. 77 G7 36 42N 77 32W
Emporium, U.S.A. 78 E6 41 31N 78 14W
Empress, Canada 73 C7 50 57N 110 0W
Empty Quarter = Rub' al Khālī, Si. Arabia 46 D4 18 0N 48 0 E
Ems →, Germany 16 B4 53 20N 7 12 E
Emsdale, Canada 78 A5 45 32N 79 19W
Emu, China 35 C15 43 40N 128 6 E
Emu Park, Australia 62 C5 23 13S 150 50 E
'En 'Avrona, Israel 47 F4 29 43N 35 0 E
En Nahud, Sudan 51 F11 12 45N 28 25 E
Ena, Japan 31 G8 35 25N 137 25 E
Enana, Namibia 56 B2 17 30S 16 23 E
Enaratoli, Indonesia 37 E9 3 55S 136 21 E
Enard B., U.K. 12 C3 58 5N 5 20W
Enare = Inarijärvi, Finland 8 B22 69 0N 28 0 E
Encampment, U.S.A. 82 F10 41 12N 106 47W
Encantadas, Serra, Brazil 95 C5 30 40S 53 0W
Encarnación, Paraguay 95 B4 27 15S 55 50W
Encarnación de Diaz, Mexico 86 C4 21 30N 102 13W
Encinitas, U.S.A. 85 M9 33 3N 117 17W
Encino, U.S.A. 83 J11 34 39N 105 28W
Encounter B., Australia 63 F2 35 45S 138 45 E
Endako, Canada 72 C3 54 6N 125 2W
Ende, Indonesia 37 F6 8 45S 121 40 E
Endeavour Str., Australia 62 A3 10 45S 142 0 E
Enderbury I., Kiribati 64 H10 3 8S 171 5W
Enderby, Canada 72 C5 50 35N 119 10W
Enderby I., Australia 60 D2 20 35S 116 30 E
Enderby Land, Antarctica 5 C5 66 0S 53 0 E
Enderlin, U.S.A. 80 B6 46 38N 97 36W
Endicott, U.S.A. 79 D8 42 6N 76 4W
Endwell, U.S.A. 79 D8 42 6N 76 2W
Endyalgout I., Australia 60 B5 11 40S 132 35 E
Eneabba, Australia 61 E2 29 49S 115 16 E
Enewetak Atoll, Marshall Is. 64 F8 11 30N 162 15 E
Enez, Turkey 21 D12 40 45N 26 5 E
Enfield, Canada 71 D7 44 56N 63 32W
Enfield, Conn., U.S.A. 79 E12 41 58N 72 36W
Enfield, N.H., U.S.A. 79 C12 43 39N 72 9W
Engadin, Switz. 18 C9 46 45N 10 10 E
Engaño, C., Dom. Rep. 89 C6 18 30N 68 20W
Engaño, C., Phil. 37 A6 18 35N 122 23 E
Engaru, Japan 30 B11 44 3N 143 31 E
Engcobo, S. Africa 57 E4 31 37S 28 0 E
Engels, Russia 25 D8 51 28N 46 6 E
Engemann L., Canada 73 B7 58 0N 106 55W
Enggano, Indonesia 36 F2 5 20S 102 40 E
England, U.S.A. 81 H9 34 33N 91 58W
England □, U.K. 10 D7 53 0N 2 0W
Englee, Canada 71 B8 50 45N 56 5W
Englehart, Canada 70 C4 47 49N 79 52W
Englewood, U.S.A. 80 F2 39 39N 104 59W
English →, Canada 73 C10 50 35N 93 30W
English Bazar = Ingraj Bazar, India 43 G13 24 58N 88 10 E
English Channel, Europe 11 G6 50 0N 2 0W
English River, Canada 70 C1 49 14N 91 0W
Enid, U.S.A. 81 G6 36 24N 97 53W
Enkhuizen, Neths. 15 B5 52 42N 5 17 E
Enna, Italy 20 F6 37 34N 14 16 E
Ennadai, Canada 73 A8 61 8N 100 53W
Ennadai L., Canada 73 A8 61 0N 101 0W
Ennedi, Chad 51 E10 17 15N 22 0 E
Enngonia, Australia 63 D4 29 21S 145 50 E
Ennis, Ireland 13 D3 52 51N 8 59W
Ennis, Mont., U.S.A. 82 D8 45 21N 111 44W
Ennis, Tex., U.S.A. 81 J6 32 20N 96 38W
Enniscorthy, Ireland 13 D5 52 30N 6 34W
Enniskillen, U.K. 13 B4 54 21N 7 39W
Ennistimon, Ireland 13 D2 52 57N 9 17W
Enns →, Austria 16 D8 48 14N 14 32 E
Enontekiö, Finland 8 B20 68 23N 23 37 E
Enosburg Falls, U.S.A. 79 B12 44 55N 72 48W
Enriquillo, L., Dom. Rep. 89 C5 18 20N 72 5W
Enschede, Neths. 15 B6 52 13N 6 53 E
Ensenada, Argentina 94 C4 34 55S 57 55W
Ensenada, Mexico 86 A1 31 50N 116 50W
Ensenada de los Muertos, Mexico 86 C2 23 59N 109 50W
Ensiola, Pta. de n', Spain 22 B9 39 7N 2 55 E
Entebbe, Uganda 54 B3 0 4N 32 28 E
Enterprise, Canada 72 A5 60 47N 115 45W
Enterprise, Ala., U.S.A. 77 K3 31 19N 85 51W
Enterprise, Oreg., U.S.A. 82 D5 45 25N 117 17W
Entre Ríos, Bolivia 94 A3 21 30S 64 25W
Entre Ríos □, Argentina 94 C4 30 30S 58 30W
Entroncamento, Portugal 19 C1 39 28N 8 28W
Enugu, Nigeria 50 G7 6 20N 7 30 E
Enumclaw, U.S.A. 84 C5 47 12N 121 59W
Eólie, Ís., Italy 20 E6 38 30N 14 57 E
Epe, Neths. 15 B5 52 21N 5 59 E
Épernay, France 18 B5 49 3N 3 56 E
Ephesus, Turkey 21 F12 37 55N 27 22 E
Ephraim, U.S.A. 82 G8 39 22N 111 35W
Ephrata, Pa., U.S.A. 79 F8 40 11N 76 11W
Ephrata, Wash., U.S.A. 82 C4 47 19N 119 33W
Épinal, France 18 B7 48 10N 6 27 E
Episkopi, Cyprus 23 E11 34 40N 32 54 E
Episkopi, Greece 23 D6 35 20N 24 20 E
Episkopi Bay, Cyprus 23 E11 34 35N 32 50 E
Epsom, U.K. 11 F7 51 19N 0 16W
Epukiro, Namibia 56 C2 21 40S 19 9 E
Equatorial Guinea ■, Africa 52 D1 2 0N 8 0 E
Er Rahad, Sudan 51 F12 12 45N 30 32 E
Er Rif, Morocco 50 A5 35 1N 4 1W
Erāwadī Myit = Irrawaddy →, Burma 41 M19 15 50N 95 6 E
Erbil = Arbīl, Iraq 44 B5 36 15N 44 5 E
Erçek, Turkey 44 B4 38 39N 43 36 E
Erciyaş Dağı, Turkey 25 G6 38 30N 35 30 E
Érd, Hungary 17 E10 47 22N 18 56 E
Erdao Jiang →, China 35 C14 43 0N 127 0 E
Erdek, Turkey 21 D12 40 23N 27 47 E
Erdene = Ulaan-Uul, Mongolia 34 B6 44 13N 111 10 E
Erdenetsogt, Mongolia 34 C4 42 55N 106 5 E
Erebus, Mt., Antarctica 5 D11 77 35S 167 0 E
Erechim, Brazil 95 B5 27 35S 52 15W
Ereğli, Konya, Turkey 25 G5 37 31N 34 4 E
Ereğli, Zonguldak, Turkey 25 F5 41 15N 31 24 E
Erenhot, China 34 C7 43 48N 112 2 E
Eresma →, Spain 19 B3 41 26N 4 45W
Erewadi Myitwanya, Burma 41 M19 15 30N 95 0 E

Erfenisdam, S. Africa 56 D4 28 30S 26 50 E
Erfurt, Germany 16 C6 50 58N 11 2 E
Erg Iguidi, Africa 50 C4 27 0N 7 0 E
Ergani, Turkey 44 B3 38 17N 39 49 E
Ergel, Mongolia 34 C5 43 8N 109 5 E
Ergeni Vozvyshennost, Russia 25 E7 47 0N 44 0 E
Ērgli, Latvia 9 H21 56 54N 25 38 E
Eriboll, L., U.K. 12 C4 58 30N 4 42W
Érice, Italy 20 E5 38 2N 12 35 E
Erie, U.S.A. 78 D4 42 8N 80 5W
Erie, L., N. Amer. 78 D4 42 15N 81 0W
Erie Canal, U.S.A. 78 C7 43 5N 78 43W
Erieau, Canada 78 D3 42 16N 81 57W
Erigavo, Somali Rep. 46 E4 10 35N 47 20 E
Erikoúsa, Greece 23 A3 39 53N 19 34 E
Eriksdale, Canada 73 C9 50 52N 98 7W
Erímanthos, Greece 21 F9 37 57N 21 50 E
Erimo-misaki, Japan 30 D11 41 50N 143 15 E
Erinpura, India 42 G5 25 9N 73 3 E
Eriskay, U.K. 12 D1 57 4N 7 18W
Eritrea ■, Africa 46 D2 14 0N 38 30 E
Erlangen, Germany 16 D6 49 36N 11 0 E
Erldunda, Australia 62 D1 25 14S 133 12 E
Ermelo, Neths. 15 B5 52 18N 5 35 E
Ermelo, S. Africa 57 D4 26 31S 29 59 E
Ermenek, Turkey 44 B2 36 38N 33 0 E
Ermones, Greece 23 A3 39 37N 19 46 E
Ermoúpolis = Síros, Greece 21 F11 37 28N 24 57 E
Ernakulam = Cochin, India 40 Q10 9 59N 76 22 E
Erne →, Ireland 13 B3 54 30N 8 16W
Erne, Lower L., U.K. 13 B4 54 28N 7 47W
Erne, Upper L., U.K. 13 B4 54 14N 7 32W
Ernest Giles Ra., Australia 61 E3 27 0S 123 45 E
Erode, India 40 P10 11 24N 77 45 E
Eromanga, Australia 63 D3 26 40S 143 11 E
Erongo, Namibia 56 C2 21 39S 15 58 E
Erramala Hills, India 40 M11 15 30N 78 15 E
Errigal, Ireland 13 A3 55 2N 8 6W
Erris Hd., Ireland 13 B1 54 19N 10 0W
Erskine, U.S.A. 80 B7 47 40N 96 0W
Ertis = Irtysh →, Russia 26 C7 61 4N 68 52 E
Erwin, U.S.A. 77 G4 36 9N 82 25W
Erzgebirge, Germany 16 C7 50 27N 12 55 E
Erzin, Russia 27 D10 50 15N 95 10 E
Erzincan, Turkey 25 G6 39 46N 39 30 E
Erzurum, Turkey 25 G7 39 57N 41 15 E
Es Caló, Spain 22 C8 38 40N 1 30 E
Es Canar, Spain 22 B8 39 2N 1 36 E
Es Mercadal, Spain 22 B11 39 59N 4 5 E
Es Migjorn Gran, Spain 22 B11 39 57N 4 3 E
Es Sahrâ' Esh Sharqîya, Egypt 51 C12 27 30N 32 30 E
Es Sînâ', Egypt 47 F3 29 0N 34 0 E
Es Vedrà, Spain 22 C7 38 52N 1 12 E
Esambo, Dem. Rep. of the Congo 54 C1 3 48S 23 30 E
Esan-Misaki, Japan 30 D10 41 40N 141 10 E
Esashi, Hokkaidō, Japan 30 B11 44 56N 142 35 E
Esashi, Hokkaidō, Japan 30 D10 41 52N 140 7 E
Esbjerg, Denmark 9 J13 55 29N 8 29 E
Escalante, U.S.A. 83 H8 37 47N 111 36W
Escalante →, U.S.A. 83 H8 37 24N 110 57W
Escalón, Mexico 86 B4 26 46N 104 20W
Escambia →, U.S.A. 77 K2 30 32N 87 11W
Escanaba, U.S.A. 76 C2 45 45N 87 4W
Esch-sur-Alzette, Lux. 18 B6 49 32N 6 0 E
Escondido, U.S.A. 85 M9 33 7N 117 5W
Escuinapa, Mexico 86 C3 22 50N 105 50W
Escuintla, Guatemala 88 D1 14 20N 90 48W
Esenguly, Turkmenistan 26 F6 37 37N 53 59 E
Eşfahān, Iran 45 C6 32 39N 51 43 E
Eşfahān □, Iran 45 C6 32 50N 51 50 E
Esfarāyen, Iran 45 B8 37 4N 57 30 E
Esfideh, Iran 45 C8 33 39N 59 46 E
Esh Sham = Dimashq, Syria 47 B5 33 30N 36 18 E
Esha Ness, U.K. 12 A7 60 29N 1 38W
Esher, U.K. 11 F7 51 21N 0 20W
Eshowe, S. Africa 57 D5 28 50S 31 30 E
Esil = Ishim →, Russia 26 D8 57 45N 71 10 E
Esk →, Cumb., U.K. 12 G5 54 58N 3 2W
Esk →, N. Yorks., U.K. 10 C7 54 30N 0 37W
Eskān, Iran 45 E9 26 48N 63 9 E
Esker, Canada 71 B6 53 53N 66 25W
Eskifjörður, Iceland 8 D7 65 3N 13 55W
Eskilstuna, Sweden 9 G17 59 22N 16 32 E
Eskimo Pt., Canada 68 B10 61 10N 94 15W
Eskişehir, Turkey 25 G5 39 50N 30 30 E
Esla →, Spain 19 B2 41 29N 6 3W
Eslāmābād-e Gharb, Iran 44 C5 34 10N 46 30 E
Eslāmshahr, Iran 45 C6 35 40N 51 10 E
Eşme, Turkey 21 E13 38 23N 28 58 E
Esmeraldas, Ecuador 92 C3 1 0N 79 40W
Esnagi L., Canada 70 C3 48 36N 84 33W
Espanola, Canada 70 C3 46 15N 81 46W
Espanola, U.S.A. 83 H10 35 59N 106 5W
Esparta, Costa Rica 88 E3 9 59N 84 40W
Esperance, Australia 61 F3 33 45S 121 55 E
Esperance B., Australia 61 F3 33 48S 121 55 E
Esperanza, Argentina 94 C3 31 29S 61 3W
Espichel, C., Portugal 19 C1 38 22N 9 16W
Espigão, Serra do, Brazil 95 B5 26 35S 50 30W
Espinazo, Sierra del = Espinhaço, Serra do, Brazil 93 G10 17 30S 43 30W
Espinhaço, Serra do, Brazil 93 G10 17 30S 43 30W
Espinilho, Serra do, Brazil 95 B5 28 30S 55 0W
Espírito Santo □, Brazil 93 H10 20 0S 40 45W
Espíritu Santo, Vanuatu 64 J8 15 15S 166 50 E
Espíritu Santo, B. del, Mexico 87 D7 19 15N 87 0W
Espíritu Santo, I., Mexico 86 C2 24 30N 110 23W
Espita, Mexico 87 C7 21 1N 88 19W
Espoo, Finland 9 F21 60 12N 24 40 E
Espungabera, Mozam. 57 C5 20 29S 32 45 E
Esquel, Argentina 96 E2 42 55S 71 20W
Esquimalt, Canada 72 D4 48 26N 123 25W
Esquina, Argentina 94 C4 30 0S 59 30W
Essaouira, Morocco 50 B4 31 32N 9 42W
Essebie, Dem. Rep. of the Congo 54 B3 2 58N 30 40 E
Essen, Belgium 15 C4 51 28N 4 28 E
Essen, Germany 16 C4 51 28N 7 2 E
Essendon, Mt., Australia 61 E3 25 0S 120 29 E
Essequibo →, Guyana 92 B7 6 50N 58 30W
Essex, Canada 78 D2 42 10N 82 49W
Essex, Calif., U.S.A. 85 L11 34 44N 115 15W
Essex, N.Y., U.S.A. 79 B11 44 19N 73 21W
Essex □, U.K. 11 F8 51 54N 0 27 E
Essex Junction, U.S.A. 79 B11 44 29N 73 7W
Esslingen, Germany 16 D5 48 44N 9 18 E
Estados, I. de Los, Argentina 96 G4 54 40S 64 30W
Eşţahbānāt, Iran 45 D7 29 8N 54 4 E
Estância, Brazil 93 F11 11 16S 37 26W
Estancia, U.S.A. 83 J10 34 46N 106 4W
Estārm, Iran 45 D8 28 21N 58 21 E
Estcourt, S. Africa 57 D4 29 0S 29 53 E
Estelí, Nic. 88 D2 13 9N 86 22W
Estellencs, Spain 22 B9 39 39N 2 29 E
Esterhazy, Canada 73 C8 50 37N 102 5W
Estevan, Canada 73 D8 49 10N 102 59W
Estevan Group, Canada 72 C3 53 3N 129 38W
Estherville, U.S.A. 80 D7 43 24N 94 50W
Eston, Canada 73 C7 51 8N 108 40W
Estonia ■, Europe 9 G21 58 30N 25 30 E
Estreito, Brazil 93 E9 6 32S 47 25W
Estrela, Serra da, Portugal 19 B2 40 10N 7 45W
Estremoz, Portugal 19 C2 38 51N 7 39W
Estrondo, Serra do, Brazil 93 E9 7 20S 48 0W
Esztergom, Hungary 17 E10 47 47N 18 44 E
Etah, India 43 F8 27 35N 78 40 E
Étampes, France 18 B5 48 26N 2 10 E
Etanga, Namibia 56 B1 17 55S 13 0 E
Etawah, India 43 F8 26 48N 79 6 E
Etawney L., Canada 73 B9 57 50N 96 50W
Ethel, U.S.A. 84 D4 46 32N 122 46W
Ethelbert, Canada 73 C8 51 32N 100 25W
Ethiopia ■, Africa 46 F3 8 0N 40 0 E
Ethiopian Highlands, Ethiopia 28 J7 10 0N 37 0 E
Etive, L., U.K. 12 E3 56 29N 5 10W
Etna, Italy 20 F6 37 50N 14 55 E
Etoile, Dem. Rep. of the Congo 55 E2 11 33S 27 30 E
Etosha Pan, Namibia 56 B2 18 40S 16 30 E
Etowah, U.S.A. 77 H3 35 20N 84 32W
Ettelbruck, Lux. 15 E6 49 51N 6 5 E
Ettrick Water →, U.K. 12 F6 55 31N 2 55W
Etuku, Dem. Rep. of the Congo 54 C2 3 42S 25 45 E
Etzatlán, Mexico 86 C4 20 48N 104 5W
Etzná, Mexico 87 D6 19 35N 90 15W
Euboea = Évvoia, Greece 21 E11 38 30N 24 0 E
Eucla, Australia 61 F4 31 41S 128 52 E
Euclid, U.S.A. 78 E3 41 34N 81 32W
Eucumbene, L., Australia 63 F4 36 2S 148 40 E
Eudora, U.S.A. 81 J9 33 7N 91 16W
Eufaula, Ala., U.S.A. 77 K3 31 54N 85 9W
Eufaula, Okla., U.S.A. 81 H7 35 17N 95 35W
Eufaula L., U.S.A. 81 H7 35 18N 95 21W
Eugene, U.S.A. 82 E2 44 5N 123 4W
Eugowra, Australia 63 E4 33 22S 148 24 E
Eulo, Australia 63 D4 28 10S 145 3 E
Eunice, La., U.S.A. 81 K8 30 30N 92 25W
Eunice, N. Mex., U.S.A. 81 J3 32 26N 103 10W
Eupen, Belgium 15 D6 50 37N 6 3 E
Euphrates = Furāt, Nahr al →, Asia 44 D5 31 0N 47 25 E
Eureka, Canada 4 B3 80 0N 85 56W
Eureka, Calif., U.S.A. 82 F1 40 47N 124 9W
Eureka, Kans., U.S.A. 81 G6 37 49N 96 17W
Eureka, Mont., U.S.A. 82 B6 48 53N 115 3W
Eureka, Nev., U.S.A. 82 G5 39 31N 115 58W
Eureka, S. Dak., U.S.A. 80 C5 45 46N 99 38W
Eureka, Mt., Australia 61 E3 26 35S 121 35 E
Euroa, Australia 63 F4 36 44S 145 35 E
Europa, Île, Ind. Oc. 53 J8 22 20S 40 22 E
Europa, Picos de, Spain 19 A3 43 10N 4 49W
Europa, Pta. de, Gib. 19 D3 36 3N 5 21W
Europe 6 E10 50 0N 20 0 E
Europoort, Neths. 15 C4 51 57N 4 10 E
Eustis, U.S.A. 77 L5 28 51N 81 41W
Euston, Australia 63 E3 34 30S 142 46 E
Eutsuk L., Canada 72 C3 53 20N 126 45W
Evale, Angola 56 B2 16 33S 15 44 E
Evans, U.S.A. 80 E2 40 23N 104 41W
Evans, L., Canada 70 B4 50 50N 77 0W
Evans City, U.S.A. 78 F4 40 46N 80 4W
Evans Head, Australia 63 D5 29 7S 153 27 E
Evans Mills, U.S.A. 79 B9 44 6N 75 48W
Evansburg, Canada 72 C5 53 36N 114 59W
Evanston, Ill., U.S.A. 76 E2 42 3N 87 41W
Evanston, Wyo., U.S.A. 82 F8 41 16N 110 58W
Evansville, U.S.A. 76 G2 37 58N 87 35W
Evaz, Iran 45 E7 27 46N 53 59 E
Eveleth, U.S.A. 80 B8 47 28N 92 32W
Evensk, Russia 27 C16 62 12N 159 30 E
Everard, L., Australia 63 E2 31 30S 135 0 E
Everard Ranges, Australia 61 E5 27 5S 132 28 E
Everest, Mt., Nepal 43 E12 28 5N 86 58 E
Everett, Pa., U.S.A. 78 F6 40 1N 78 23W
Everett, Wash., U.S.A. 84 C4 47 59N 122 12W
Everglades, The, U.S.A. 77 N5 25 50N 81 0W
Everglades National Park, U.S.A. 77 N5 25 30N 81 0W
Evergreen, Ala., U.S.A. 77 K2 31 26N 86 57W
Evergreen, Mont., U.S.A. 82 B6 48 9N 114 13W
Evesham, U.K. 11 E6 52 6N 1 56W
Evje, Norway 9 G12 58 36N 7 51 E
Évora, Portugal 19 C2 38 33N 7 57W
Evowghlī, Iran 44 B5 38 43N 45 13 E
Évreux, France 18 B4 49 3N 1 8 E
Évros →, Bulgaria 21 D12 41 40N 26 34 E
Évry, France 18 B5 48 38N 2 27 E
Évvoia, Greece 21 E11 38 30N 24 0 E
Ewe, L., U.K. 12 D3 57 49N 5 38W
Ewing, U.S.A. 80 D5 42 16N 98 21W
Ewo, Congo 52 E2 0 48S 14 45 E
Exaltación, Bolivia 92 F5 13 10S 65 20W
Excelsior Springs, U.S.A. 80 F7 39 20N 94 13W
Exe →, U.K. 11 G4 50 41N 3 29W
Exeter, Canada 78 C3 43 21N 81 29W
Exeter, U.K. 11 G4 50 43N 3 31W
Exeter, Calif., U.S.A. 84 J7 36 18N 119 9W
Exeter, N.H., U.S.A. 79 D14 42 59N 70 57W
Exmoor, U.K. 11 F4 51 12N 3 45W
Exmouth, Australia 60 D1 21 54S 114 10 E
Exmouth, U.K. 11 G4 50 37N 3 25W
Exmouth G., Australia 60 D1 22 15S 114 15 E
Expedition Ra., Australia 62 C4 24 30S 149 12 E
Extremadura □, Spain 19 C2 39 30N 6 5W
Exuma Sound, Bahamas 88 B4 24 30N 76 20W
Eyasi, L., Tanzania 54 C4 3 30S 35 0 E
Eye Pen., U.K. 12 C2 58 13N 6 10W
Eyemouth, U.K. 12 F6 55 52N 2 5W
Eyjafjörður, Iceland 8 C4 66 15N 18 30W
Eyre (North), L., Australia 63 D2 28 30S 137 20 E
Eyre (South), L., Australia 63 D2 29 18S 137 25 E
Eyre Mts., N.Z. 59 L2 45 25S 168 25 E
Eyre Pen., Australia 63 E2 33 30S 136 17 E
Eysturoy, Færoe Is. 8 E9 62 13N 6 54W
Eyvānkī, Iran 45 C6 35 24N 51 56 E
Ezine, Turkey 21 E12 39 48N 26 20 E
Ezouza →, Cyprus 23 E11 34 44N 32 27 E

F

F.Y.R.O.M. = Macedonia ■, Europe 21 D9 41 53N 21 40 E
Fabala, Guinea 50 G4 9 44N 9 5W
Fabens, U.S.A. 83 L10 31 30N 106 10W
Fabriano, Italy 20 C5 43 20N 12 54 E
Fachi, Niger 51 E8 18 6N 11 34 E
Fada, Chad 51 E10 17 13N 21 34 E
Fada-n-Gourma, Burkina Faso 50 F6 12 10N 0 30 E
Faddeyevskiy, Ostrov, Russia 27 B15 76 0N 144 0 E
Fadghāmī, Syria 44 C4 35 53N 40 52 E
Faenza, Italy 20 B4 44 17N 11 53 E
Færoe Is. = Føroyar, Atl. Oc. 8 F9 62 0N 7 0W
Făgăraş, Romania 17 F13 45 48N 24 58 E
Fagersta, Sweden 9 F16 60 1N 15 46 E
Fagnano, L., Argentina 96 G3 54 30S 68 0W
Fahliān, Iran 45 D6 30 11N 51 28 E
Fahraj, Kermān, Iran 45 D8 29 0N 59 0 E
Fahraj, Yazd, Iran 45 D7 31 46N 54 36 E
Faial, Madeira 22 D3 32 47N 16 53W
Fair Haven, U.S.A. 76 D9 43 36N 73 16W
Fair Hd., U.K. 13 A5 55 14N 6 9W
Fair Oaks, U.S.A. 84 G5 38 39N 121 16W
Fairbanks, U.S.A. 68 B5 64 51N 147 43W
Fairbury, U.S.A. 80 E6 40 8N 97 11W
Fairfax, U.S.A. 79 B11 44 40N 73 1W
Fairfield, Ala., U.S.A. 77 J2 33 29N 86 55W
Fairfield, Calif., U.S.A. 84 G4 38 15N 122 3W
Fairfield, Conn., U.S.A. 79 E11 41 9N 73 16W
Fairfield, Idaho, U.S.A. 82 E6 43 21N 114 44W
Fairfield, Ill., U.S.A. 76 F1 38 23N 88 22W
Fairfield, Iowa, U.S.A. 80 E9 40 56N 91 57W
Fairfield, Tex., U.S.A. 81 K7 31 44N 96 10W
Fairford, Canada 73 C9 51 37N 98 38W
Fairhope, U.S.A. 77 K2 30 31N 87 54W
Fairlie, N.Z. 59 L3 44 5S 170 49 E
Fairmead, U.S.A. 84 H6 37 5N 120 10W
Fairmont, Minn., U.S.A. 80 D7 43 39N 94 28W
Fairmont, W. Va., U.S.A. 76 F5 39 29N 80 9W
Fairmount, Calif., U.S.A. 85 L8 34 45N 118 26W
Fairmount, N.Y., U.S.A. 79 C8 43 5N 76 12W
Fairplay, U.S.A. 83 G11 39 15N 106 2W
Fairport, U.S.A. 78 C7 43 6N 77 27W
Fairport Harbor, U.S.A. 78 E3 41 45N 81 17W
Fairview, Canada 72 B5 56 5N 118 25W
Fairview, Mont., U.S.A. 80 B2 47 51N 104 3W
Fairview, Okla., U.S.A. 81 G5 36 16N 98 29W
Fairweather, Mt., U.S.A. 72 B1 58 55N 137 32W
Faisalabad, Pakistan 42 D5 31 30N 73 5 E
Faith, U.S.A. 80 C3 45 2N 102 2W
Faizabad, India 43 F10 26 45N 82 10 E
Fajardo, Puerto Rico 89 C6 18 20N 65 39W
Fajr, Wādī, Si. Arabia 44 D3 29 10N 38 10 E
Fakenham, U.K. 10 E8 52 51N 0 51 E
Fakfak, Indonesia 37 E8 3 0S 132 15 E
Faku, China 35 C12 42 32N 123 21 E
Falaise, France 18 B3 48 54N 0 12W
Falaise, Mui, Vietnam 38 C5 19 6N 105 45 E
Falam, Burma 41 H18 23 0N 93 45 E
Falcó, C. des, Spain 22 C7 38 50N 1 23 E
Falcón, Presa, Mexico 87 B5 26 35N 99 10W
Falcon Lake, Canada 73 D9 49 42N 95 15W
Falcon Reservoir, U.S.A. 81 M5 26 34N 99 10W
Falconara Marittima, Italy 20 C5 43 37N 13 24 E
Falcone, C. del, Italy 20 D3 40 58N 8 12 E
Falconer, U.S.A. 78 D5 42 7N 79 13W
Faleshty = Făleşti, Moldova 17 E14 47 32N 27 44 E
Făleşti, Moldova 17 E14 47 32N 27 44 E
Falfurrias, U.S.A. 81 M5 27 14N 98 9W
Falher, Canada 72 B5 55 44N 117 15W
Falirakí, Greece 23 C10 36 22N 28 12 E
Falkenberg, Sweden 9 H15 56 54N 12 30 E
Falkirk, U.K. 12 F5 56 0N 3 47W
Falkirk □, U.K. 12 F5 55 58N 3 49W
Falkland, U.K. 12 E5 56 16N 3 12W
Falkland Is. □, Atl. Oc. 96 G5 51 30S 59 0W
Falkland Sd., Falk. Is. 96 G5 52 0S 60 0W
Falköping, Sweden 9 G15 58 12N 13 33 E
Fall River, U.S.A. 79 E13 41 43N 71 10W
Fallbrook, U.S.A. 85 M9 33 23N 117 15W
Fallon, U.S.A. 82 G4 39 28N 118 47W
Falls City, U.S.A. 80 E7 40 3N 95 36W
Falls Creek, U.S.A. 78 E6 41 9N 78 48W
Falmouth, Jamaica 88 C4 18 30N 77 40W
Falmouth, U.K. 11 G2 50 9N 5 5W
Falmouth, U.S.A. 79 E14 41 33N 70 37W
Falsa, Pta., Mexico 86 B1 27 51N 115 3W
False B., S. Africa 56 E2 34 15S 18 40 E
Falso, C., Honduras 88 C3 15 12N 83 21W
Falster, Denmark 9 J14 54 45N 11 55 E
Falsterbo, Sweden 9 J15 55 23N 12 50 E
Fălticeni, Romania 17 E14 47 21N 26 20 E
Falun, Sweden 9 F16 60 37N 15 37 E
Famagusta, Cyprus 23 D12 35 8N 33 55 E
Famagusta Bay, Cyprus 23 D13 35 15N 34 0 E
Famalé, Niger 50 F6 14 33N 1 5 E
Famatina, Sierra de, Argentina 94 B2 27 30S 68 0W
Family L., Canada 73 C9 51 54N 95 27W
Famoso, U.S.A. 85 K7 35 37N 119 12W
Fan Xian, China 34 G8 35 55N 115 38 E
Fanad Hd., Ireland 13 A4 55 17N 7 38W
Fandriana, Madag. 57 C8 20 14S 47 21 E
Fangcheng, China 34 H7 33 18N 112 59 E
Fangshan, China 34 E6 38 3N 111 25 E
Fangzi, China 35 F10 36 33N 119 10 E
Fanjiatun, China 35 C13 43 40N 125 15 E
Fannich, L., U.K. 12 D4 57 38N 4 59W
Fannūj, Iran 45 E8 26 35N 59 38 E
Fanø, Denmark 9 J13 55 25N 8 25 E
Fano, Italy 20 C5 43 50N 13 1 E
Fanshi, China 34 E7 39 12N 113 20 E
Fao = Al Fāw, Iraq 45 D6 30 0N 48 30 E
Faqirwali, Pakistan 42 E5 29 27N 73 0 E
Faradje, Dem. Rep. of the Congo 54 B2 3 50N 29 45 E
Farafangana, Madag. 57 C8 22 49S 47 50 E
Farāh, Afghan. 40 C3 32 20N 62 7 E
Farāh □, Afghan. 40 C3 32 25N 62 10 E
Farahalana, Madag. 57 A9 14 26S 50 10 E
Faranah, Guinea 50 F3 10 3N 10 45W
Farasān, Jazā'ir, Si. Arabia 46 D3 16 45N 41 55 E
Farasan Is. = Farasān, Jazā'ir, Si. Arabia 46 D3 16 45N 41 55 E
Faratsiho, Madag. 57 B8 19 24S 46 57 E
Fareham, U.K. 11 G6 50 51N 1 11W
Farewell, C., N.Z. 59 J4 40 29S 172 43 E
Farewell C. = Farvel, Kap, Greenland 4 D5 59 48N 43 55W
Farghona, Uzbekistan 26 E8 40 23N 71 19 E
Fargo, U.S.A. 80 B6 46 53N 96 48W
Fār'iah, W. al →, West Bank 47 C4 32 12N 35 27 E
Faribault, U.S.A. 80 C8 44 18N 93 16W
Faridabad, India 42 E6 28 26N 77 19 E
Faridkot, India 42 D6 30 44N 74 45 E
Faridpur, Bangla. 43 H13 23 15N 89 55 E
Faridpur, India 43 E8 28 13N 79 33 E
Farīmān, Iran 45 C8 35 40N 59 49 E
Farina, Australia 63 E2 30 3S 138 15 E
Fariones, Pta., Canary Is. 22 E6 29 13N 13 28W
Farmerville, U.S.A. 81 J8 32 47N 92 24W
Farmingdale, U.S.A. 79 F10 40 12N 74 10W
Farmington, Canada 72 B4 55 54N 120 30W
Farmington, Calif., U.S.A. 84 H6 37 55N 120 59W
Farmington, Maine, U.S.A. 77 C10 44 40N 70 9W
Farmington, Mo., U.S.A. 81 G9 37 47N 90 25W
Farmington, N.H., U.S.A. 79 C13 43 24N 71 4W
Farmington, N. Mex., U.S.A. 83 H9 36 44N 108 12W
Farmington, Utah, U.S.A. 82 F8 41 0N 111 12W
Farmington →, U.S.A. 79 E12 41 51N 72 38W
Farmville, U.S.A. 76 G6 37 18N 78 24W
Farne Is., U.K. 10 B6 55 38N 1 37W
Farnham, Canada 79 A12 45 17N 72 59W
Farnham, Mt., Canada 72 C5 50 29N 116 30W
Faro, Brazil 93 D7 2 10S 56 39W
Faro, Canada 68 B6 62 11N 133 22W
Faro, Portugal 19 D2 37 2N 7 55W
Fårö, Sweden 9 H18 57 55N 19 5 E
Farquhar, C., Australia 61 D1 23 50S 113 36 E
Farrars Cr. →, Australia 62 D3 25 35S 140 43 E
Farrāshband, Iran 45 D7 28 57N 52 5 E
Farrell, U.S.A. 78 E4 41 13N 80 30W
Farrokhī, Iran 45 C8 33 50N 59 31 E
Farruch, C. = Ferrutx, C., Spain 22 B10 39 47N 3 21 E
Farrukhabad-cum-Fatehgarh, India 40 F11 27 30N 79 32 E
Fārs □, Iran 45 D7 29 30N 55 0 E
Fársala, Greece 21 E10 39 17N 22 23 E
Farson, U.S.A. 82 E9 42 6N 109 27W
Farsund, Norway 9 G12 58 5N 6 55 E
Fartak, Râs, Si. Arabia 44 D2 28 5N 34 34 E
Fartak, Ra's, Yemen 46 D5 15 38N 52 15 E
Fartura, Serra da, Brazil 95 B5 26 21S 52 52W
Fārūj, Iran 45 B8 37 14N 58 14 E
Farvel, Kap, Greenland 4 D5 59 48N 43 55W
Farwell, U.S.A. 81 H3 34 23N 103 2W
Fasā, Iran 45 D7 29 0N 53 39 E
Fasano, Italy 20 D7 40 50N 17 22 E
Fastiv, Ukraine 17 C15 50 7N 29 57 E
Fastov = Fastiv, Ukraine 17 C15 50 7N 29 57 E
Fatagar, Tanjung, Indonesia 37 E8 2 46S 131 57 E
Fatehabad, Haryana, India 42 E6 29 31N 75 27 E
Fatehabad, Ut. P., India 42 F8 27 1N 78 19 E
Fatehgarh, India 43 F8 27 25N 79 35 E
Fatehpur, Bihar, India 43 G11 24 38N 85 14 E
Fatehpur, Raj., India 42 F6 28 0N 74 40 E
Fatehpur, Ut. P., India 43 G9 25 56N 81 13 E
Fatehpur, Ut. P., India 43 F9 27 10N 81 13 E
Fatehpur Sikri, India 42 F6 27 6N 77 40 E
Fatima, Canada 71 C7 47 24N 61 53W
Faulkton, U.S.A. 80 C5 45 2N 99 8W
Faure I., Australia 61 E1 25 52S 113 50 E
Fauresmith, S. Africa 56 D4 29 44S 25 17 E
Fauske, Norway 8 C16 67 17N 15 25 E
Favara, Italy 20 F5 37 19N 13 39 E
Favàritx, C. de, Spain 22 B11 40 0N 4 15 E
Favignana, Italy 20 F5 37 56N 12 20 E
Fawcett, Pt., Australia 60 B5 11 46S 130 2 E
Fawn →, Canada 70 A2 55 20N 87 35W
Fawnskin, U.S.A. 85 L10 34 16N 116 56W
Faxaflói, Iceland 8 D2 64 29N 23 0W
Faya-Largeau, Chad 51 E9 17 58N 19 6 E
Fayd, Si. Arabia 44 E4 27 1N 42 52 E
Fayette, Ala., U.S.A. 77 J2 33 41N 87 50W
Fayette, Mo., U.S.A. 80 F8 39 9N 92 41W
Fayetteville, Ark., U.S.A. 81 G7 36 4N 94 10W
Fayetteville, N.C., U.S.A. 77 H6 35 3N 78 53W
Fayetteville, Tenn., U.S.A. 77 H2 35 9N 86 34W
Fazilka, India 42 D6 30 27N 74 2 E
Fazilpur, Pakistan 42 E4 29 18N 70 29 E
Fdérik, Mauritania 50 D3 22 40N 12 45W
Feale →, Ireland 13 D2 52 27N 9 37W
Fear, C., U.S.A. 77 J7 33 50N 77 58W
Feather →, U.S.A. 82 G3 38 47N 121 36W
Feather Falls, U.S.A. 84 F5 39 36N 121 16W
Featherston, N.Z. 59 J5 41 6S 175 20 E
Featherstone, Zimbabwe 55 F3 18 42S 30 55 E
Fécamp, France 18 B4 49 45N 0 22 E
Fedala = Mohammedia, Morocco 50 B4 33 44N 7 21W
Federación, Argentina 94 C4 31 0S 57 55W
Féderal, Argentina 96 C5 30 57S 58 48W
Federal Way, U.S.A. 84 C4 47 18N 122 19W
Fedeshkūh, Iran 45 D7 28 49N 53 50 E
Fehmarn, Germany 16 A6 54 27N 11 7 E
Fehmarn Bælt, Europe 9 J14 54 35N 11 20 E
Fehmarn Belt = Fehmarn Bælt, Europe 9 J14 54 35N 11 20 E
Fei Xian, China 35 G9 35 18N 117 59 E
Feijó, Brazil 92 E4 8 9S 70 21W
Feilding, N.Z. 59 J5 40 13S 175 35 E
Feira de Santana, Brazil 93 F11 12 15S 38 57W
Feixiang, China 34 F8 36 30N 114 45 E
Felanitx, Spain 22 B10 39 28N 3 9 E
Feldkirch, Austria 16 E5 47 15N 9 37 E

Felipe Carrillo Puerto, *Mexico* **87 D7** 19 38N 88 3W
Felixstowe, *U.K.* **11 F9** 51 58N 1 23 E
Felton, *U.S.A.* **84 H4** 37 3N 122 4W
Femer Bælt = Fehmarn Bælt, *Europe* **9 J14** 54 35N 11 20 E
Femunden, *Norway* **9 E14** 62 10N 11 53 E
Fen He →, *China* **34 G6** 35 36N 110 42 E
Fenelon Falls, *Canada* **78 B6** 44 32N 78 45W
Feng Xian, *Jiangsu, China* **34 G9** 34 43N 116 35 E
Feng Xian, *Shaanxi, China* **34 H4** 33 54N 106 40 E
Fengcheng, *China* **35 D13** 40 28N 124 5 E
Fengfeng, *China* **34 F8** 36 28N 114 8 E
Fengjie, *China* **33 C5** 31 5N 109 36 E
Fengning, *China* **34 D9** 41 10N 116 33 E
Fengqiu, *China* **34 G8** 35 2N 114 25 E
Fengrun, *China* **35 E10** 39 48N 118 8 E
Fengtai, *China* **34 E9** 39 50N 116 18 E
Fengxiang, *China* **34 G4** 34 29N 107 25 E
Fengyang, *China* **35 H9** 32 51N 117 29 E
Fengzhen, *China* **34 D7** 40 25N 113 2 E
Fenoarivo Afovoany, *Madag.* **57 B8** 18 26S 46 34 E
Fenoarivo Atsinanana, *Madag.* **57 B8** 17 22S 49 25 E
Fens, The, *U.K.* **10 E7** 52 38N 0 2W
Fenton, *U.S.A.* **76 D4** 42 48N 83 42W
Fenxi, *China* **34 F6** 36 40N 111 31 E
Fenyang, *China* **34 F6** 37 18N 111 48 E
Feodosiya, *Ukraine* **25 E6** 45 2N 35 16 E
Ferdows, *Iran* **45 C8** 33 58N 58 2 E
Ferfer, *Somali Rep.* **46 F4** 5 4N 45 9 E
Fergana = Farghona, *Uzbekistan* **26 E8** 40 23N 71 19 E
Fergus, *Canada* **78 C4** 43 43N 80 24W
Fergus Falls, *U.S.A.* **80 B6** 46 17N 96 4W
Ferkéssédougou, *Ivory C.* **50 G4** 9 35N 5 6W
Ferland, *Canada* **70 B2** 50 19N 88 27W
Fermanagh □, *U.K.* **13 B4** 54 21N 7 40W
Fermo, *Italy* **20 C5** 43 9N 13 43 E
Fermont, *Canada* **71 B6** 52 47N 67 5W
Fermont, *Qué., Canada* **69 C13** 50 28N 67 29W
Fermoy, *Ireland* **13 D3** 52 9N 8 16W
Fernández, *Argentina* **94 B3** 27 55S 63 50W
Fernandina Beach, *U.S.A.* **77 K5** 30 40N 81 27W
Fernando de Noronha, *Brazil* **93 D12** 4 0S 33 10W
Fernando Póo = Bioko, *Eq. Guin.* **52 D1** 3 30N 8 40 E
Ferndale, *U.S.A.* **84 B4** 48 51N 122 36W
Fernie, *Canada* **72 D5** 49 30N 115 5W
Fernlees, *Australia* **62 C4** 23 51S 148 7 E
Fernley, *U.S.A.* **82 G4** 39 36N 119 15W
Ferozepore = Firozpur, *India* **42 D6** 30 55N 74 40 E
Ferrara, *Italy* **20 B4** 44 50N 11 35 E
Ferreñafe, *Peru* **92 E3** 6 42S 79 50W
Ferrerías, *Spain* **22 B11** 39 59N 4 1 E
Ferret, C., *France* **18 D3** 44 38N 1 15W
Ferriday, *U.S.A.* **81 K9** 31 38N 91 33W
Ferrol, *Spain* **19 A1** 43 29N 8 15W
Ferron, *U.S.A.* **83 G8** 39 5N 111 8W
Ferrutx, C., *Spain* **22 B10** 39 47N 3 21 E
Ferryland, *Canada* **71 C9** 47 2N 52 53W
Fertile, *U.S.A.* **80 B6** 47 32N 96 17W
Fès, *Morocco* **50 B5** 34 0N 5 0W
Fessenden, *U.S.A.* **80 B5** 47 39N 99 38W
Festus, *U.S.A.* **80 F9** 38 13N 90 24W
Feteşti, *Romania* **17 F14** 44 22N 27 51 E
Fethiye, *Turkey* **25 G4** 36 36N 29 6 E
Fetlar, *U.K.* **12 A8** 60 36N 0 52W
Feuilles →, *Canada* **69 C12** 58 47N 70 4W
Fez = Fès, *Morocco* **50 B5** 34 0N 5 0W
Fezzan, *Libya* **51 C8** 27 0N 13 0 E
Fiambalá, *Argentina* **94 B2** 27 45S 67 37W
Fianarantsoa, *Madag.* **57 C8** 21 26S 47 5 E
Fianarantsoa □, *Madag.* **57 B8** 19 30S 47 0 E
Ficksburg, *S. Africa* **57 D4** 28 51S 27 53 E
Field →, *Australia* **62 C2** 23 48S 138 0 E
Field I., *Australia* **60 B5** 12 5S 132 23 E
Fieri, *Albania* **21 D8** 40 43N 19 33 E
Fife □, *U.K.* **12 E5** 56 16N 3 1W
Fife Ness, *U.K.* **12 E6** 56 17N 2 35W
Fifth Cataract, *Sudan* **51 E12** 18 23N 33 47 E
Figeac, *France* **18 D5** 44 37N 2 2 E
Figtree, *Zimbabwe* **55 G2** 20 22S 28 20 E
Figueira da Foz, *Portugal* **19 B1** 40 7N 8 54W
Figueres, *Spain* **19 A7** 42 18N 2 58 E
Figuig, *Morocco* **50 B5** 32 5N 1 11W
Fihaonana, *Madag.* **57 B8** 18 36S 47 12 E
Fiherenana, *Madag.* **57 B8** 18 29S 48 24 E
Fiherenana →, *Madag.* **57 C7** 23 19S 43 37 E
Fiji ■, *Pac. Oc.* **59 C8** 17 20S 179 0 E
Filey, *U.K.* **10 C7** 54 12N 0 18W
Filey B., *U.K.* **10 C7** 54 12N 0 15W
Filfla, *Malta* **23 D1** 35 47N 14 24 E
Filiatrá, *Greece* **21 F9** 37 9N 21 35 E
Filingué, *Niger* **50 F6** 14 21N 3 22 E
Filipstad, *Sweden* **9 G16** 59 43N 14 9 E
Fillmore, *Calif., U.S.A.* **85 L8** 34 24N 118 55W
Fillmore, *Utah, U.S.A.* **83 G7** 38 58N 112 20W
Finch, *Canada* **79 A9** 45 11N 75 7W
Findhorn →, *U.K.* **12 D5** 57 38N 3 38W
Findlay, *U.S.A.* **76 E4** 41 2N 83 39W
Finger L., *Canada* **70 B1** 53 33N 93 30W
Finger Lakes, *U.S.A.* **79 D8** 42 40N 76 30W
Fingoè, *Mozam.* **55 E3** 14 55S 31 50 E
Finisterre, C. = Fisterra, C., *Spain* **19 A1** 42 50N 9 19W
Finke, *Australia* **62 D1** 25 34S 134 35 E
Finland ■, *Europe* **8 E22** 63 0N 27 0 E
Finland, G. of, *Europe* **9 G21** 60 0N 26 0 E
Finlay →, *Canada* **72 B3** 57 0N 125 10W
Finley, *Australia* **63 F4** 35 38S 145 35 E
Finley, *U.S.A.* **80 B6** 47 31N 97 50W
Finn →, *Ireland* **13 B4** 54 51N 7 28W
Finnigan, Mt., *Australia* **62 B4** 15 49S 145 17 E
Finniss, C., *Australia* **63 E1** 33 8S 134 51 E
Finnmark, *Norway* **8 B20** 69 37N 23 57 E
Finnsnes, *Norway* **8 B18** 69 14N 18 0 E
Finspång, *Sweden* **9 G16** 58 43N 15 47 E
Fiora →, *Italy* **20 C4** 42 20N 11 34 E
Fiq, *Syria* **47 C4** 32 46N 35 41 E
Firat = Furāt, Nahr al →, *Asia* **44 D5** 31 0N 47 25 E
Firebag →, *Canada* **73 B6** 57 45N 111 21W
Firebaugh, *U.S.A.* **84 J6** 36 52N 120 27W
Firedrake L., *Canada* **73 A8** 61 25N 104 30W
Firenze, *Italy* **20 C4** 43 46N 11 15 E
Firk →, *Iraq* **44 D5** 30 59N 44 34 E
Firozabad, *India* **43 F8** 27 10N 78 25 E
Firozpur, *India* **42 D6** 30 55N 74 40 E
Firozpur-Jhirka, *India* **42 F7** 27 48N 76 57 E
Fīrūzābād, *Iran* **45 D7** 28 52N 52 35 E
Fīrūzkūh, *Iran* **45 C7** 35 50N 52 50 E
Firvale, *Canada* **72 C3** 52 27N 126 13W
Fish →, *Namibia* **56 D2** 28 7S 17 10 E
Fish →, *S. Africa* **56 E3** 31 30S 20 16 E
Fisher, *Australia* **61 F5** 30 30S 131 0 E
Fisher B., *Canada* **73 C9** 51 35N 97 13W
Fishers I., *U.S.A.* **79 E13** 41 15N 72 0W
Fishguard, *U.K.* **11 E3** 52 0N 4 58W
Fishing L., *Canada* **73 C9** 52 10N 95 24W
Fishkill, *U.S.A.* **79 E11** 41 32N 73 53W
Fisterra, C., *Spain* **19 A1** 42 50N 9 19W
Fitchburg, *U.S.A.* **79 D13** 42 35N 71 48W
Fitz Roy, *Argentina* **96 F3** 47 0S 67 0W
Fitzgerald, *Canada* **72 B6** 59 51N 111 36W
Fitzgerald, *U.S.A.* **77 K4** 31 43N 83 15W
Fitzmaurice →, *Australia* **60 B5** 14 45S 130 5 E
Fitzroy →, *Queens., Australia* **62 C5** 23 32S 150 52 E
Fitzroy →, *W. Austral., Australia* **60 C3** 17 31S 123 35 E
Fitzroy, Mte., *Argentina* **96 F2** 49 17S 73 5W
Fitzroy Crossing, *Australia* **60 C4** 18 9S 125 38 E
Fitzwilliam I., *Canada* **78 A3** 45 30N 81 45W
Fiume = Rijeka, *Croatia* **16 F8** 45 20N 14 21 E
Five Points, *U.S.A.* **84 J6** 36 26N 120 6W
Fizi, *Dem. Rep. of the Congo* **54 C2** 4 17S 28 55 E
Flagstaff, *U.S.A.* **83 J8** 35 12N 111 39W
Flagstaff L., *Maine, U.S.A.* **77 C10** 45 12N 70 19W
Flagstaff L., *Maine, U.S.A.* **79 A14** 45 12N 70 18W
Flaherty I., *Canada* **70 A4** 56 15N 79 15W
Flåm, *Norway* **9 F12** 60 50N 7 7 E
Flambeau →, *U.S.A.* **80 C9** 45 18N 91 14W
Flamborough Hd., *U.K.* **10 C7** 54 7N 0 5W
Flaming Gorge Reservoir, *U.S.A.* **82 F9** 41 10N 109 25W
Flamingo, Teluk, *Indonesia* **37 F9** 5 30S 138 0 E
Flanders = Flandre, *Europe* **18 A5** 50 50N 2 30 E
Flandre, *Europe* **18 A5** 50 50N 2 30 E
Flandre Occidentale = West-Vlaanderen □, *Belgium* **15 D2** 51 0N 3 0 E
Flandre Orientale = Oost-Vlaanderen □, *Belgium* **15 C3** 51 5N 3 50 E
Flandreau, *U.S.A.* **80 C6** 44 3N 96 36W
Flanigan, *U.S.A.* **84 E7** 40 10N 119 53W
Flannan Is., *U.K.* **12 C1** 58 9N 7 52W
Flåsjön, *Sweden* **8 D16** 64 5N 15 40 E
Flat →, *Canada* **72 A3** 61 33N 125 18W
Flathead L., *U.S.A.* **82 C7** 47 51N 114 8W
Flattery, C., *Australia* **62 A4** 14 58S 145 21 E
Flattery, C., *U.S.A.* **84 B2** 48 23N 124 29W
Flatwoods, *U.S.A.* **76 F4** 38 31N 82 43W
Fleetwood, *U.K.* **10 D4** 53 55N 3 1W
Fleetwood, *U.S.A.* **79 F9** 40 27N 75 49W
Flekkefjord, *Norway* **9 G12** 58 18N 6 39 E
Flemington, *U.S.A.* **78 E7** 41 7N 77 28W
Flensburg, *Germany* **16 A5** 54 47N 9 27 E
Flers, *France* **18 B3** 48 47N 0 33W
Flesherton, *Canada* **78 B4** 44 16N 80 33W
Flesko, Tanjung, *Indonesia* **37 D6** 0 29N 124 30 E
Fleurieu Pen., *Australia* **63 F2** 35 40S 138 5 E
Flevoland □, *Neths.* **15 B5** 52 30N 5 30 E
Flin Flon, *Canada* **73 C8** 54 46N 101 53W
Flinders →, *Australia* **62 B3** 17 36S 140 36 E
Flinders B., *Australia* **61 F2** 34 19S 115 19 E
Flinders Group, *Australia* **62 A3** 14 11S 144 15 E
Flinders I., *S. Austral., Australia* **63 E1** 33 44S 134 41 E
Flinders I., *Tas., Australia* **62 G4** 40 0S 148 0 E
Flinders Ranges, *Australia* **63 E2** 31 30S 138 30 E
Flinders Reefs, *Australia* **62 B4** 17 37S 148 31 E
Flint, *U.K.* **10 D4** 53 15N 3 8W
Flint, *U.S.A.* **76 D4** 43 1N 83 41W
Flint →, *U.S.A.* **77 K3** 30 57N 84 34W
Flint I., *Kiribati* **65 J12** 11 26S 151 48W
Flintshire □, *U.K.* **10 D4** 53 17N 3 17W
Flodden, *U.K.* **10 B5** 55 37N 2 8W
Floodwood, *U.S.A.* **80 B8** 46 55N 92 55W
Flora, *U.S.A.* **76 F1** 38 40N 88 29W
Florala, *U.S.A.* **77 K2** 31 0N 86 20W
Florence = Firenze, *Italy* **20 C4** 43 46N 11 15 E
Florence, *Ala., U.S.A.* **77 H2** 34 48N 87 41W
Florence, *Ariz., U.S.A.* **83 K8** 33 2N 111 23W
Florence, *Colo., U.S.A.* **80 F2** 38 23N 105 8W
Florence, *Oreg., U.S.A.* **82 E1** 43 58N 124 7W
Florence, *S.C., U.S.A.* **77 H6** 34 12N 79 46W
Florence, L., *Australia* **63 D2** 28 53S 138 9 E
Florencia, *Colombia* **92** 1 36N 75 36W
Florennes, *Belgium* **15 D4** 50 15N 4 35 E
Florenville, *Belgium* **15 E5** 49 40N 5 19 E
Flores, *Guatemala* **88 C2** 16 59N 89 50W
Flores, *Indonesia* **37 F6** 8 35S 121 0 E
Flores I., *Canada* **72 D3** 49 20N 126 10W
Flores Sea, *Indonesia* **37 F6** 6 30S 120 0 E
Floreşti, *Moldova* **17 E15** 47 53N 28 17 E
Floresville, *U.S.A.* **81 L5** 29 8N 98 10W
Floriano, *Brazil* **93 E10** 6 50S 43 0W
Florianópolis, *Brazil* **95 B6** 27 30S 48 30W
Florida, *Cuba* **88 B4** 21 32N 78 14W
Florida, *Uruguay* **95 C4** 34 7S 56 10W
Florida □, *U.S.A.* **77 L5** 28 0N 82 0W
Florida, Straits of, *U.S.A.* **88 B4** 25 0N 80 0W
Florida B., *U.S.A.* **88 B3** 25 0N 80 45W
Florida Keys, *U.S.A.* **77 N5** 24 40N 81 0W
Flórina, *Greece* **21 D9** 40 48N 21 26 E
Florø, *Norway* **9 F11** 61 35N 5 1 E
Flower Station, *Canada* **79 A8** 45 10N 76 41W
Flowerpot I., *Canada* **78 A3** 45 18N 81 38W
Floydada, *U.S.A.* **81 J4** 33 59N 101 20W
Fluk, *Indonesia* **37 E7** 1 42S 127 44 E
Flushing = Vlissingen, *Neths.* **15 C3** 51 26N 3 34 E
Flying Fish, C., *Antarctica* **5 D15** 72 6S 102 29W
Foam Lake, *Canada* **73 C8** 51 40N 103 32W
Foça, *Turkey* **21 E12** 38 39N 26 46 E
Focşani, *Romania* **17 F14** 45 41N 27 15 E
Fóggia, *Italy* **20 D6** 41 27N 15 34 E
Fogo, *Canada* **71 C9** 49 43N 54 17W
Fogo I., *Canada* **71 C9** 49 40N 54 5W
Föhr, *Germany* **16 A5** 54 43N 8 30 E
Foix, *France* **18 E4** 42 58N 1 38 E
Folda, *Nord-Trøndelag, Norway* **8 D14** 64 32N 10 30 E
Folda, *Nordland, Norway* **8 C16** 67 38N 14 50 E
Foley, *U.S.A.* **77 K2** 30 24N 87 41W
Foleyet, *Canada* **70 C3** 48 15N 82 25W
Folgefonni, *Norway* **9 F12** 60 3N 6 23 E
Foligno, *Italy* **20 C5** 42 57N 12 42 E
Folkestone, *U.K.* **11 F9** 51 5N 1 12 E
Folkston, *U.S.A.* **77 K5** 30 50N 82 0W
Follansbee, *U.S.A.* **78 F4** 40 19N 80 35W
Folsom L., *U.S.A.* **84 G5** 38 42N 121 9W
Fond-du-Lac, *Canada* **73 B7** 59 19N 107 12W
Fond du Lac, *U.S.A.* **80 D10** 43 47N 88 27W
Fond-du-Lac →, *Canada* **73 B7** 59 17N 106 0W
Fonda, *U.S.A.* **79 D10** 42 57N 74 22W
Fondi, *Italy* **20 D5** 41 21N 13 25 E
Fongafale, *Tuvalu* **64 H9** 8 31S 179 13 E
Fonsagrada = A Fonsagrada, *Spain* **19 A2** 43 8N 7 4W
Fonseca, G. de, *Cent. Amer.* **88 D2** 13 10N 87 40W
Fontainebleau, *France* **18 B5** 48 24N 2 40 E
Fontana, *U.S.A.* **85 L9** 34 6N 117 26W
Fontas →, *Canada* **72 B4** 58 14N 121 48W
Fonte Boa, *Brazil* **92 D5** 2 33S 66 0W
Fontenay-le-Comte, *France* **18 C3** 46 28N 0 48W
Fontenelle Reservoir, *U.S.A.* **82 E8** 42 1N 110 3W
Fontur, *Iceland* **8 C6** 66 23N 14 32W
Foochow = Fuzhou, *China* **33 D6** 26 5N 119 16 E
Foping, *China* **34 H5** 33 41N 108 0 E
Forbes, *Australia* **63 E4** 33 22S 148 0 E
Forbesganj, *India* **43 F12** 26 17N 87 18 E
Ford City, *Calif., U.S.A.* **85 K7** 35 9N 119 27W
Ford City, *Pa., U.S.A.* **78 F5** 40 46N 79 32W
Førde, *Norway* **9 F11** 61 27N 5 53 E
Ford's Bridge, *Australia* **63 D4** 29 41S 145 29 E
Fordyce, *U.S.A.* **81 J8** 33 49N 92 25W
Forel, Mt., *Greenland* **4 C6** 66 52N 36 55W
Foremost, *Canada* **72 D6** 49 26N 111 34W
Forest, *Canada* **78 C3** 43 6N 82 0W
Forest, *U.S.A.* **81 J10** 32 22N 89 29W
Forest City, *Iowa, U.S.A.* **80 D8** 43 16N 93 39W
Forest City, *N.C., U.S.A.* **77 H5** 35 20N 81 52W
Forest City, *Pa., U.S.A.* **79 E9** 41 39N 75 28W
Forest Grove, *U.S.A.* **84 E3** 45 31N 123 7W
Forestburg, *Canada* **72 C6** 52 35N 112 1W
Foresthill, *U.S.A.* **84 F6** 39 1N 120 49W
Forestier Pen., *Australia* **62 G4** 43 0S 148 0 E
Forestville, *Canada* **71 C6** 48 48N 69 2W
Forestville, *Calif., U.S.A.* **84 G4** 38 28N 122 54W
Forestville, *N.Y., U.S.A.* **78 D5** 42 28N 79 10W
Forfar, *U.K.* **12 E6** 56 39N 2 53W
Forks, *U.S.A.* **84 C2** 47 57N 124 23W
Forksville, *U.S.A.* **79 E8** 41 29N 76 35W
Forlì, *Italy* **20 B5** 44 13N 12 3 E
Forman, *U.S.A.* **80 B6** 46 7N 97 38W
Formby Pt., *U.K.* **10 D4** 53 33N 3 6W
Formentera, *Spain* **22 C7** 38 43N 1 27 E
Formentor, C. de, *Spain* **22 B10** 39 58N 3 13 E
Former Yugoslav Republic of Macedonia = Macedonia ■, *Europe* **21 D9** 41 53N 21 40 E
Fórmia, *Italy* **20 D5** 41 15N 13 37 E
Formosa = Taiwan ■, *Asia* **33 D7** 23 30N 121 0 E
Formosa, *Argentina* **94 B4** 26 15S 58 10W
Formosa, *Brazil* **93 G9** 15 32S 47 20W
Formosa □, *Argentina* **94 B4** 25 0S 60 0W
Formosa, Serra, *Brazil* **93 F8** 12 0S 55 0W
Formosa Bay, *Kenya* **54 C5** 2 40S 40 20 E
Fornells, *Spain* **22 A11** 40 3N 4 7 E
Føroyar, *Atl. Oc.* **8 F9** 62 0N 7 0W
Forres, *U.K.* **12 D5** 57 37N 3 37W
Forrest, *Australia* **61 F4** 30 51S 128 6 E
Forrest, Mt., *Australia* **61 D4** 24 48S 127 45 E
Forrest City, *U.S.A.* **81 H9** 35 1N 90 47W
Forsayth, *Australia* **62 B3** 18 33S 143 34 E
Forssa, *Finland* **9 F20** 60 49N 23 38 E
Forst, *Germany* **16 C8** 51 45N 14 37 E
Forsyth, *U.S.A.* **82 C10** 46 16N 106 41W
Fort Abbas, *Pakistan* **42 E5** 29 12N 72 52 E
Fort Albany, *Canada* **70 B3** 52 15N 81 35W
Fort Ann, *U.S.A.* **79 C11** 43 25N 73 30W
Fort Assiniboine, *Canada* **72 C6** 54 20N 114 45W
Fort Augustus, *U.K.* **12 D4** 57 9N 4 42W
Fort Beaufort, *S. Africa* **56 E4** 32 46S 26 40 E
Fort Benton, *U.S.A.* **82 C8** 47 49N 110 40W
Fort Bragg, *U.S.A.* **82 G2** 39 26N 123 48W
Fort Bridger, *U.S.A.* **82 F8** 41 19N 110 23W
Fort Chipewyan, *Canada* **73 B6** 58 42N 111 8W
Fort Collins, *U.S.A.* **80 E2** 40 35N 105 5W
Fort-Coulonge, *Canada* **70 C4** 45 50N 76 45W
Fort Covington, *U.S.A.* **79 B10** 44 59N 74 29W
Fort Davis, *U.S.A.* **81 K3** 30 35N 103 54W
Fort-de-France, *Martinique* **89 D7** 14 36N 61 2W
Fort Defiance, *U.S.A.* **83 J9** 35 45N 109 5W
Fort Dodge, *U.S.A.* **80 D7** 42 30N 94 11W
Fort Edward, *U.S.A.* **79 C11** 43 16N 73 35W
Fort Erie, *Canada* **78 D6** 42 54N 78 56W
Fort Fairfield, *U.S.A.* **77 B12** 46 46N 67 50W
Fort Frances, *Canada* **73 D10** 48 36N 93 24W
Fort Garland, *U.S.A.* **83 H11** 37 26N 105 26W
Fort George = Chisasibi, *Canada* **70 B4** 53 50N 79 0W
Fort Good-Hope, *Canada* **68 B7** 66 14N 128 40W
Fort Hancock, *U.S.A.* **83 L11** 31 18N 105 51W
Fort Hertz = Putao, *Burma* **41 F20** 27 28N 97 30 E
Fort Hope, *Canada* **70 B2** 51 30N 88 0W
Fort Irwin, *U.S.A.* **85 K10** 35 16N 116 34W
Fort Jameson = Chipata, *Zambia* **55 E3** 13 38S 32 28 E
Fort Kent, *U.S.A.* **77 B11** 47 15N 68 36W
Fort Klamath, *U.S.A.* **82 E3** 42 42N 122 0W
Fort-Lamy = Ndjamena, *Chad* **51 F8** 12 10N 14 59 E
Fort Laramie, *U.S.A.* **80 D2** 42 13N 104 31W
Fort Lauderdale, *U.S.A.* **77 M5** 26 7N 80 8W
Fort Liard, *Canada* **72 A4** 60 14N 123 30W
Fort Liberté, *Haiti* **89 C5** 19 42N 71 51W
Fort Lupton, *U.S.A.* **80 E2** 40 5N 104 49W
Fort Mackay, *Canada* **72 B6** 57 12N 111 41W
Fort Macleod, *Canada* **72 D6** 49 45N 113 30W
Fort McMurray, *Canada* **72 B6** 56 44N 111 7W
Fort McPherson, *Canada* **68 B6** 67 30N 134 55W
Fort Madison, *U.S.A.* **80 E9** 40 38N 91 27W
Fort Meade, *U.S.A.* **77 M5** 27 45N 81 48W
Fort Morgan, *U.S.A.* **80 E3** 40 15N 103 48W
Fort Munro, *Pakistan* **42 E3** 29 54N 69 58 E
Fort Myers, *U.S.A.* **77 M5** 26 39N 81 52W
Fort Nelson, *Canada* **72 B4** 58 50N 122 44W
Fort Nelson →, *Canada* **72 B4** 59 32N 124 0W
Fort Norman = Tulita, *Canada* **68 B7** 64 57N 125 30W
Fort Payne, *U.S.A.* **77 H3** 34 26N 85 43W
Fort Peck, *U.S.A.* **82 B10** 48 1N 106 27W
Fort Peck Dam, *U.S.A.* **82 C10** 48 0N 106 26W
Fort Peck L., *U.S.A.* **82 C10** 48 0N 106 26W
Fort Pierce, *U.S.A.* **77 M5** 27 27N 80 20W
Fort Pierre, *U.S.A.* **80 C4** 44 21N 100 22W
Fort Plain, *U.S.A.* **79 D10** 42 56N 74 37W
Fort Portal, *Uganda* **54 B3** 0 40N 30 20 E
Fort Providence, *Canada* **72 A5** 61 3N 117 40W
Fort Qu'Appelle, *Canada* **73 C8** 50 45N 103 50W
Fort Resolution, *Canada* **72 A6** 61 10N 113 40W
Fort Rixon, *Zimbabwe* **55 G2** 20 2S 29 17 E
Fort Rosebery = Mansa, *Zambia* **55 E2** 11 13S 28 55 E
Fort Ross, *U.S.A.* **84 G3** 38 32N 123 13W
Fort Rousset = Owando, *Congo* **52 E3** 0 29S 15 55 E
Fort Rupert = Waskaganish, *Canada* **70 B4** 51 30N 78 40W
Fort St. James, *Canada* **72 C4** 54 30N 124 10W
Fort St. John, *Canada* **72 B4** 56 15N 120 50W
Fort Sandeman = Zhob, *Pakistan* **42 D3** 31 20N 69 31 E
Fort Saskatchewan, *Canada* **72 C6** 53 40N 113 15W
Fort Scott, *U.S.A.* **81 G7** 37 50N 94 42W
Fort Severn, *Canada* **70 A2** 56 0N 87 40W
Fort Shevchenko, *Kazakstan* **25 F9** 44 35N 50 23 E
Fort Simpson, *Canada* **72 A4** 61 45N 121 15W
Fort Smith, *Canada* **72 B6** 60 0N 111 51W
Fort Smith, *U.S.A.* **81 H7** 35 23N 94 25W
Fort Stockton, *U.S.A.* **81 K3** 30 53N 102 53W
Fort Sumner, *U.S.A.* **81 H2** 34 28N 104 15W
Fort Thompson, *U.S.A.* **80 C5** 44 3N 99 26W
Fort Trinquet = Bir Mogreïn, *Mauritania* **50 C3** 25 10N 11 25W
Fort Valley, *U.S.A.* **77 J4** 32 33N 83 53W
Fort Vermilion, *Canada* **72 B5** 58 24N 116 0W
Fort Walton Beach, *U.S.A.* **77 K2** 30 25N 86 36W
Fort Wayne, *U.S.A.* **76 E3** 41 4N 85 9W
Fort William, *U.K.* **12 E3** 56 49N 5 7W
Fort Worth, *U.S.A.* **81 J6** 32 45N 97 18W
Fort Yates, *U.S.A.* **80 B4** 46 5N 100 38W
Fort Yukon, *U.S.A.* **68 B5** 66 34N 145 16W
Fortaleza, *Brazil* **93 D11** 3 45S 38 35W
Forteau, *Canada* **71 B8** 51 28N 56 58W
Fortescue →, *Australia* **60 D2** 21 0S 116 4 E
Forth →, *U.K.* **12 E5** 56 9N 3 50W
Forth, Firth of, *U.K.* **12 E6** 56 5N 2 55W
Fortrose, *U.K.* **12 D4** 57 35N 4 9W
Fortuna, *Calif., U.S.A.* **82 F1** 40 36N 124 9W
Fortuna, *N. Dak., U.S.A.* **80 A3** 48 55N 103 47W
Fortune, *Canada* **71 C8** 47 4N 55 50W
Fortune B., *Canada* **71 C8** 47 30N 55 22W
Forūr, *Iran* **45 E7** 26 17N 54 32 E
Foshan, *China* **33 D6** 23 4N 113 5 E
Fosna, *Norway* **8 E14** 63 50N 10 20 E
Fosnavåg, *Norway* **9 E11** 62 22N 5 38 E
Fossano, *Italy* **18 D7** 44 33N 7 43 E
Fossil, *U.S.A.* **82 D3** 45 0N 120 9W
Foster, *Australia* **63 F4** 38 40S 146 15 E
Foster, *Canada* **79 A12** 45 17N 72 30W
Foster →, *Canada* **73 B7** 55 47N 105 49W
Fosters Ra., *Australia* **62 C1** 21 35S 133 48 E
Fostoria, *U.S.A.* **76 E4** 41 10N 83 25W
Fougères, *France* **18 B3** 48 21N 1 14W
Foul Pt., *Sri Lanka* **40 Q12** 8 35N 81 18 E
Foula, *U.K.* **12 A6** 60 10N 2 5W
Foulness I., *U.K.* **11 F8** 51 36N 0 55 E
Foulpointe, *Madag.* **57 B8** 17 41S 49 31 E
Foulweather, C., *U.S.A.* **74 B2** 44 50N 124 5W
Foumban, *Cameroon* **52 C2** 5 45N 10 50 E
Fountain, *U.S.A.* **80 F2** 38 41N 104 42W
Fountain Springs, *U.S.A.* **85 K8** 35 54N 118 51W
Fouriesburg, *S. Africa* **56 D4** 28 38S 28 14 E
Foúrnoi, *Greece* **21 F12** 37 36N 26 32 E
Fourth Cataract, *Sudan* **51 E12** 18 47N 32 3 E
Fouta Djalon, *Guinea* **50 F3** 11 20N 12 10W
Foux, Cap-à-, *Haiti* **89 C5** 19 43N 73 27W
Foveaux Str., *N.Z.* **59 M2** 46 42S 168 10 E
Fowey, *U.K.* **11 G3** 50 20N 4 39W
Fowler, *Calif., U.S.A.* **84 J7** 36 38N 119 41W
Fowler, *Colo., U.S.A.* **80 F3** 38 8N 104 2W
Fowlers B., *Australia* **61 F5** 31 59S 132 34 E
Fowman, *Iran* **45 B6** 37 13N 49 19 E
Fox →, *Canada* **73 B10** 56 3N 93 18W
Fox Creek, *Canada* **72 C5** 54 24N 116 48W
Fox Lake, *Canada* **72 B6** 58 28N 114 31W
Fox Valley, *Canada* **73 C7** 50 30N 109 25W
Foxboro, *U.S.A.* **79 D13** 42 4N 71 16W
Foxe Basin, *Canada* **69 B12** 66 0N 77 0W
Foxe Chan., *Canada* **69 B12** 65 0N 80 0W
Foxe Pen., *Canada* **69 B12** 65 0N 76 0W
Foxton, *N.Z.* **59 J5** 40 29S 175 18 E
Foyle, Lough, *U.K.* **13 A4** 55 7N 7 4W
Foynes, *Ireland* **13 D2** 52 37N 9 7W
Fóz do Cunene, *Angola* **56 B1** 17 15S 11 48 E
Foz do Iguaçu, *Brazil* **95 B5** 25 30S 54 30W
Frackville, *U.S.A.* **79 F8** 40 47N 76 14W
Fraile Muerto, *Uruguay* **95 C5** 32 31S 54 32W
Framingham, *U.S.A.* **79 D13** 42 17N 71 25W
Franca, *Brazil* **93 H9** 20 33S 47 30W
Francavilla Fontana, *Italy* **21 D7** 40 32N 17 35 E
France ■, *Europe* **18 C5** 47 0N 3 0 E
Frances, *Australia* **63 F3** 36 41S 140 55 E
Frances →, *Canada* **72 A3** 60 16N 129 10W
Frances L., *Canada* **72 A3** 61 23N 129 30W
Franceville, *Gabon* **52 E2** 1 40S 13 32 E
Franche-Comté, *France* **18 C6** 46 50N 5 55 E
Francis Case, L., *U.S.A.* **80 D5** 43 4N 98 34W
Francisco Beltrão, *Brazil* **95 B5** 26 5S 53 4W
Francisco I. Madero, *Coahuila, Mexico* **86 B4** 25 48N 103 18W
Francisco I. Madero, *Durango, Mexico* **86 C4** 24 32N 104 22W
Francistown, *Botswana* **57 C4** 21 7S 27 33 E
François, *Canada* **71 C8** 47 35N 56 45W
François L., *Canada* **72 C3** 54 0N 125 30W
Franeker, *Neths.* **15 A5** 53 12N 5 33 E
Frankford, *Canada* **78 B7** 44 12N 77 36W
Frankfort, *S. Africa* **57 D4** 27 17S 28 30 E
Frankfort, *Ind., U.S.A.* **76 E2** 40 17N 86 31W
Frankfort, *Kans., U.S.A.* **80 F6** 39 42N 96 25W
Frankfort, *Ky., U.S.A.* **76 F3** 38 12N 84 52W
Frankfort, *N.Y., U.S.A.* **79 C9** 43 2N 75 4W

Frankfurt, *Brandenburg, Germany* . . . . **16 B8** 52 20N 14 32 E
Frankfurt, *Hessen, Germany* **16 C5** 50 7N 8 41 E
Fränkische Alb, *Germany* . . **16 D6** 49 10N 11 23 E
Frankland →, *Australia* . . **61 G2** 35 0S 116 48 E
Franklin, *Ky., U.S.A.* **77 G2** 36 43N 86 35W
Franklin, *La., U.S.A.* **81 L9** 29 48N 91 30W
Franklin, *Mass., U.S.A.* **79 D13** 42 5N 71 24W
Franklin, *N.H., U.S.A.* **79 C13** 43 27N 71 39W
Franklin, *Nebr., U.S.A.* **80 E5** 40 6N 98 57W
Franklin, *Pa., U.S.A.* **78 E5** 41 24N 79 50W
Franklin, *Va., U.S.A.* **77 G7** 36 41N 76 56W
Franklin, *W. Va., U.S.A.* . . . **76 F6** 38 39N 79 20W
Franklin B., *Canada* **68 B7** 69 45N 126 0W
Franklin D. Roosevelt L., *U.S.A.* **82 B4** 48 18N 118 9W
Franklin I., *Antarctica* . . . . . **5 D11** 76 10S 168 30 E
Franklin L., *U.S.A.* **82 F6** 40 25N 115 22W
Franklin Mts., *Canada* **68 B7** 65 0N 125 0W
Franklin Str., *Canada* **68 A10** 72 0N 96 0W
Franklinton, *U.S.A.* **81 K9** 30 51N 90 9W
Franklinville, *U.S.A.* **78 D6** 42 20N 78 27W
Franks Pk., *U.S.A.* **82 E9** 43 58N 109 18W
Frankston, *Australia* . . . . . . **63 F4** 38 8S 145 8 E
Frantsa Iosifa, Zemlya, *Russia* . . . . **26 A6** 82 0N 55 0 E
Franz, *Canada* **70 C3** 48 25N 84 30W
Franz Josef Land = Frantsa Iosifa, Zemlya, *Russia* . . . **26 A6** 82 0N 55 0 E
Fraser, *U.S.A.* **78 D2** 42 32N 82 57W
Fraser →, *B.C., Canada* . . **72 D4** 49 7N 123 11W
Fraser →, *Nfld., Canada* . . **71 A7** 56 39N 62 10W
Fraser, Mt., *Australia* . . . . . **61 E2** 25 35S 118 20 E
Fraser I., *Australia* . . . . **63 D5** 25 15S 153 10 E
Fraser Lake, *Canada* **72 C4** 54 0N 124 50W
Fraserburg, *S. Africa* . . . . . **56 E3** 31 55S 21 30 E
Fraserburgh, *U.K.* **12 D6** 57 42N 2 1W
Fraserdale, *Canada* **70 C3** 49 55N 81 37W
Fray Bentos, *Uruguay* **94 C4** 33 10S 58 15W
Fredericia, *Denmark* . . . . . . **9 J13** 55 34N 9 45 E
Frederick, *Md., U.S.A.* **76 F7** 39 25N 77 25W
Frederick, *Okla., U.S.A.* **81 H5** 34 23N 99 1W
Frederick, *S. Dak., U.S.A.* . . **80 C5** 45 50N 98 31W
Fredericksburg, *Pa., U.S.A.* **79 F8** 40 27N 76 26W
Fredericksburg, *Tex., U.S.A.* **81 K5** 30 16N 98 52W
Fredericksburg, *Va., U.S.A.* **76 F7** 38 18N 77 28W
Fredericktown, *Mo., U.S.A.* **81 G9** 37 34N 90 18W
Fredericktown, *Ohio, U.S.A.* **78 F2** 40 29N 82 33W
Frederico I. Madero, Presa, *Mexico* **86 B3** 28 7N 105 40W
Frederico Westphalen, *Brazil* **95 B5** 27 22S 53 24W
Fredericton, *Canada* **71 C6** 45 57N 66 40W
Fredericton Junction, *Canada* **71 C6** 45 41N 66 40W
Frederikshåb, *Greenland* . . **4 C5** 62 0N 49 43W
Frederikshavn, *Denmark* . . **9 H14** 57 28N 10 31 E
Frederiksted, *Virgin Is.* **89 C7** 17 43N 64 53W
Fredonia, *Ariz., U.S.A.* **83 H7** 36 57N 112 32W
Fredonia, *Kans., U.S.A.* **81 G7** 37 32N 95 49W
Fredonia, *N.Y., U.S.A.* **78 D5** 42 26N 79 20W
Fredrikstad, *Norway* . . . . . . **9 G14** 59 13N 10 57 E
Free State □, *S. Africa* . . . . **56 D4** 28 30S 27 0 E
Freehold, *U.S.A.* **79 F10** 40 16N 74 17W
Freel Peak, *U.S.A.* **84 G7** 38 52N 119 54W
Freeland, *U.S.A.* **79 E9** 41 1N 75 54W
Freels, C., *Canada* **71 C9** 49 15N 53 30W
Freeman, *Calif., U.S.A.* **85 K9** 35 35N 117 53W
Freeman, *S. Dak., U.S.A.* . . **80 D6** 43 21N 97 26W
Freeport, *Bahamas* **88 A4** 26 30N 78 47W
Freeport, *Ill., U.S.A.* **80 D10** 42 17N 89 36W
Freeport, *N.Y., U.S.A.* **79 F11** 40 39N 73 35W
Freeport, *Ohio, U.S.A.* **78 F3** 40 12N 81 15W
Freeport, *Pa., U.S.A.* **78 F5** 40 41N 79 41W
Freeport, *Tex., U.S.A.* **81 L7** 28 57N 95 21W
Freetown, *S. Leone* **50 G3** 8 30N 13 17W
Frégate, L., *Canada* **70 B5** 53 15N 74 45W
Fregenal de la Sierra, *Spain* **19 C2** 38 10N 6 39W
Freibourg = Fribourg, *Switz.* **18 C7** 46 49N 7 9 E
Freiburg, *Germany* . . . . **16 E4** 47 59N 7 51 E
Freire, *Chile* **96 D2** 38 54S 72 38W
Freirina, *Chile* **94 B1** 28 30S 71 10W
Freising, *Germany* . . . . **16 D6** 48 24N 11 45 E
Freistadt, *Austria* . . . . **16 D8** 48 30N 14 30 E
Fréjus, *France* . . . . **18 E7** 43 25N 6 44 E
Fremantle, *Australia* . . . . . . **61 F2** 32 7S 115 47 E
Fremont, *Calif., U.S.A.* **84 H4** 37 32N 121 57W
Fremont, *Mich., U.S.A.* **76 D3** 43 28N 85 57W
Fremont, *Nebr., U.S.A.* **80 E6** 41 26N 96 30W
Fremont, *Ohio, U.S.A.* **76 E4** 41 21N 83 7W
Fremont →, *U.S.A.* **83 G8** 38 24N 110 42W
French Camp, *U.S.A.* **84 H5** 37 53N 121 16W
French Creek →, *U.S.A.* . . **78 E5** 41 24N 79 50W
French Guiana ■, *S. Amer.* **93 C8** 4 0N 53 0W
French Pass, *N.Z.* . . . . **59 J4** 40 55S 173 55 E
French Polynesia ■, *Pac. Oc.* **65 K13** 20 0S 145 0W
Frenchman Cr. →, *N. Amer.* **82 B10** 48 31N 107 10W
Frenchman Cr. →, *U.S.A.* . **80 E4** 40 14N 100 50W
Fresco →, *Brazil* **93 E8** 7 15S 51 30W
Freshfield, C., *Antarctica* . . **5 C10** 68 25S 151 10 E
Fresnillo, *Mexico* **86 C4** 23 10N 103 0W
Fresno, *U.S.A.* **84 J7** 36 44N 119 47W
Fresno Reservoir, *U.S.A.* . . **82 B9** 48 36N 109 57W
Frew →, *Australia* . . . . **62 C2** 20 0S 135 38 E
Frewsburg, *U.S.A.* **78 D5** 42 3N 79 10W
Freycinet Pen., *Australia* . . **62 G4** 42 10S 148 25 E
Fria, C., *Namibia* . . . . **56 B1** 18 0S 12 0 E
Friant, *U.S.A.* **84 J7** 36 59N 119 43W
Frías, *Argentina* **94 B2** 28 40S 65 5W
Fribourg, *Switz.* . . . . **18 C7** 46 49N 7 9 E
Friday Harbor, *U.S.A.* **84 B3** 48 32N 123 1W
Friedens, *U.S.A.* **78 F6** 40 3N 78 59W
Friedrichshafen, *Germany* . **16 E5** 47 39N 9 30 E
Friendly Is. = Tonga ■, *Pac. Oc.* **59 D11** 19 50S 174 30W
Friendship, *U.S.A.* **78 D6** 42 12N 78 8W
Friesland □, *Neths.* . . . . **15 A5** 53 5N 5 50 E
Frio →, *U.S.A.* **81 L5** 28 26N 98 11W
Frio, C., *Brazil* **90 F6** 22 50S 41 50W
Friona, *U.S.A.* **81 H3** 34 38N 102 43W
Fritch, *U.S.A.* **81 H4** 35 38N 101 36W
Frobisher B., *Canada* **69 B13** 62 30N 66 0W
Frobisher Bay = Iqaluit, *Canada* **69 B13** 63 44N 68 31W
Frobisher L., *Canada* **73 B7** 56 20N 108 15W
Frohavet, *Norway* . . . . **8 E13** 64 0N 9 30 E
Frome, *U.K.* **11 F5** 51 14N 2 19W
Frome →, *U.K.* **11 G5** 50 41N 2 6W
Frome, L., *Australia* . . . . . . **63 E2** 30 45S 139 45 E
Front Range, *U.S.A.* **74 C5** 40 25N 105 45W
Front Royal, *U.S.A.* **76 F6** 38 55N 78 12W
Frontera, *Canary Is.* **22 G2** 27 47N 17 59W
Frontera, *Mexico* **87 D6** 18 30N 92 40W
Fronteras, *Mexico* **86 A3** 30 56N 109 31W
Frosinone, *Italy* . . . . **20 D5** 41 38N 13 19 E
Frostburg, *U.S.A.* **76 F6** 39 39N 78 56W
Frostisen, *Norway* . . . . **8 B17** 68 14N 17 10 E
Frøya, *Norway* . . . . **8 E13** 63 43N 8 40 E
Frunze = Bishkek, *Kyrgyzstan* . . . . **26 E8** 42 54N 74 46 E
Frutal, *Brazil* **93 H9** 20 0S 49 0W
Frýdek-Místek, *Czech Rep.* . **17 D10** 49 40N 18 20 E
Fryeburg, *U.S.A.* **79 B14** 44 1N 70 59W
Fu Xian = Wafangdian, *China* . . . . **35 E11** 39 38N 121 58 E
Fu Xian, *China* . . . . **34 G5** 36 0N 109 20 E
Fucheng, *China* . . . . **34 F9** 37 50N 116 10 E
Fuchou = Fuzhou, *China* . . . **33 D6** 26 5N 119 16 E
Fuchū, *Japan* . . . . **31 G6** 34 34N 133 14 E
Fuencaliente, *Canary Is.* . . . **22 F2** 28 28N 17 50W
Fuencaliente, Pta., *Canary Is.* **22 F2** 28 27N 17 51W
Fuengirola, *Spain* **19 D3** 36 32N 4 41W
Fuentes de Oñoro, *Spain* . . **19 B2** 40 33N 6 52W
Fuerte →, *Mexico* **86 B3** 25 50N 109 25W
Fuerte Olimpo, *Paraguay* . . **94 A4** 21 0S 57 51W
Fuerteventura, *Canary Is.* . . **22 F6** 28 30N 14 0W
Fufeng, *China* . . . . **34 G5** 34 22N 108 0 E
Fugou, *China* . . . . **34 G8** 34 3N 114 25 E
Fugu, *China* . . . . **34 E6** 39 2N 111 3 E
Fuhai, *China* . . . . **32 B3** 47 2N 87 25 E
Fuḩaymī, *Iraq* . . . . **44 C4** 34 16N 42 10 E
Fuji, *Japan* . . . . **31 G9** 35 9N 138 39 E
Fuji-San, *Japan* . . . . **31 G9** 35 22N 138 44 E
Fuji-yoshida, *Japan* . . . . **31 G9** 35 30N 138 46 E
Fujian □, *China* . . . . **33 D6** 26 0N 118 0 E
Fujinomiya, *Japan* . . . . **31 G9** 35 10N 138 40 E
Fujisawa, *Japan* . . . . **31 G9** 35 22N 139 29 E
Fujiyama, Mt. = Fuji-San, *Japan* . . . . **31 G9** 35 22N 138 44 E
Fukien = Fujian □, *China* . . . **33 D6** 26 0N 118 0 E
Fukuchiyama, *Japan* . . . . . . **31 G7** 35 19N 135 9 E
Fukue-Shima, *Japan* . . . . . . **31 H4** 32 40N 128 45 E
Fukui, *Japan* . . . . **31 F8** 36 5N 136 10 E
Fukui □, *Japan* . . . . **31 G8** 36 0N 136 12 E
Fukuoka, *Japan* . . . . **31 H5** 33 39N 130 21 E
Fukuoka □, *Japan* . . . . **31 H5** 33 30N 131 0 E
Fukushima, *Japan* . . . . **30 F10** 37 44N 140 28 E
Fukushima □, *Japan* . . . . . . **30 F10** 37 30N 140 15 E
Fukuyama, *Japan* . . . . **31 G6** 34 35N 133 20 E
Fulda, *Germany* . . . . **16 C5** 50 32N 9 40 E
Fulda →, *Germany* . . . . **16 C5** 51 25N 9 39 E
Fulford Harbour, *Canada* . . **84 B3** 48 47N 123 27W
Fullerton, *Calif., U.S.A.* **85 M9** 33 53N 117 56W
Fullerton, *Nebr., U.S.A.* **80 E6** 41 22N 97 58W
Fulongquan, *China* . . . . **35 B13** 44 20N 124 42 E
Fulton, *Mo., U.S.A.* **80 F9** 38 52N 91 57W
Fulton, *N.Y., U.S.A.* **79 C8** 43 19N 76 25W
Funabashi, *Japan* . . . . **31 G10** 35 45N 140 0 E
Funchal, *Madeira* **22 D3** 32 38N 16 54W
Fundación, *Colombia* **92 A4** 10 31N 74 11W
Fundão, *Portugal* **19 B2** 40 8N 7 30W
Fundy, B. of, *Canada* **71 D6** 45 0N 66 0W
Funing, *Hebei, China* . . . . . . **35 E10** 39 53N 119 12 E
Funing, *Jiangsu, China* . . . . **35 H10** 33 45N 119 50 E
Funiu Shan, *China* . . . . **34 H7** 33 30N 112 20 E
Funtua, *Nigeria* . . . . **50 F7** 11 30N 7 18 E
Fuping, *Hebei, China* . . . . . . **34 E8** 38 48N 114 12 E
Fuping, *Shaanxi, China* . . . . **34 G5** 34 42N 109 10 E
Furano, *Japan* . . . . **30 C11** 43 21N 142 23 E
Furāt, Nahr al →, *Asia* . . . **44 D5** 31 0N 47 25 E
Fūrg, *Iran* . . . . **45 D7** 28 18N 55 13 E
Furnás, *Spain* . . . . **22 B8** 39 3N 1 32 E
Furnas, Reprêsa de, *Brazil* . **95 A6** 20 50S 45 30W
Furneaux Group, *Australia* . **62 G4** 40 10S 147 50 E
Furqlus, *Syria* . . . . **47 A6** 34 36N 37 8 E
Fürstenwalde, *Germany* . . . **16 B8** 52 22N 14 3 E
Fürth, *Germany* . . . . **16 D6** 49 28N 10 59 E
Furukawa, *Japan* . . . . **30 E10** 38 34N 140 58 E
Fury and Hecla Str., *Canada* **69 B11** 69 56N 84 0W
Fusagasuga, *Colombia* **92 C4** 4 21N 74 22W
Fushan, *Shandong, China* . . **35 F11** 37 30N 121 15 E
Fushan, *Shanxi, China* . . . . **34 G6** 35 58N 111 51 E
Fushun, *China* . . . . **35 D12** 41 50N 123 56 E
Fusong, *China* . . . . **35 C14** 42 20N 127 15 E
Futuna, *Wall. & F. Is.* . . . . . **59 B8** 14 25S 178 20 E
Fuxin, *China* . . . . **35 C11** 42 5N 121 48 E
Fuyang, *China* . . . . **34 H8** 33 0N 115 48 E
Fuyang He →, *China* . . . . . **34 E9** 38 12N 117 0 E
Fuyu, *China* . . . . **35 B13** 45 12N 124 43 E
Fuzhou, *China* . . . . **33 D6** 26 5N 119 16 E
Fylde, *U.K.* **10 D5** 53 50N 2 58W
Fyn, *Denmark* . . . . **9 J14** 55 20N 10 30 E
Fyne, L., *U.K.* **12 F3** 55 59N 5 23W

G

Gabela, *Angola* . . . . **52 G2** 11 0S 14 24 E
Gabès, *Tunisia* . . . . **51 B8** 33 53N 10 2 E
Gabès, G. de, *Tunisia* . . . . . **51 B8** 34 0N 10 30 E
Gabon ■, *Africa* . . . . **52 E2** 0 10S 10 0 E
Gaborone, *Botswana* . . . . . . **56 C4** 24 45S 25 57 E
Gabriels, *U.S.A.* **79 B10** 44 26N 74 12W
Gābrīk, *Iran* . . . . **45 E8** 25 44N 58 28 E
Gabrovo, *Bulgaria* . . . . **21 C11** 42 52N 25 19 E
Gāch Sār, *Iran* . . . . **45 B6** 36 7N 51 19 E
Gachsārān, *Iran* . . . . **45 D6** 30 15N 50 45 E
Gadag, *India* . . . . **40 M9** 15 30N 75 45 E
Gadap, *Pakistan* . . . . **42 G2** 25 5N 67 28 E
Gadarwara, *India* . . . . **43 H8** 22 50N 78 50 E
Gadhada, *India* . . . . **42 J4** 22 0N 71 35 E
Gadra, *Pakistan* . . . . **42 G4** 25 40N 70 38 E
Gadsden, *U.S.A.* **77 H3** 34 1N 86 1W
Gadwal, *India* . . . . **40 L10** 16 10N 77 50 E
Gaffney, *U.S.A.* **77 H5** 35 5N 81 39W
Gafsa, *Tunisia* . . . . **50 B7** 34 24N 8 43 E
Gagaria, *India* . . . . **42 G4** 25 43N 70 46 E
Gagnoa, *Ivory C.* **50 G4** 6 56N 5 16W
Gagnon, *Canada* **71 B6** 51 50N 68 5W
Gagnon, L., *Canada* **73 A6** 62 3N 110 27W
Gahini, *Rwanda* . . . . **54 C3** 1 50S 30 30 E
Gahmar, *India* . . . . **43 G10** 25 27N 83 49 E
Gai Xian = Gaizhou, *China* **35 D12** 40 22N 122 20 E
Gaïdhouronísi, *Greece* . . . . **23 E7** 34 53N 25 41 E
Gail, *U.S.A.* **81 J4** 32 46N 101 27W
Gaillimh = Galway, *Ireland* **13 C2** 53 17N 9 3W
Gaines, *U.S.A.* **78 E7** 41 46N 77 35W
Gainesville, *Fla., U.S.A.* . . . **77 L4** 29 40N 82 20W
Gainesville, *Ga., U.S.A.* . . . **77 H4** 34 18N 83 50W
Gainesville, *Mo., U.S.A.* . . . **81 G8** 36 36N 92 26W
Gainesville, *Tex., U.S.A.* . . . **81 J6** 33 38N 97 8W
Gainsborough, *U.K.* **10 D7** 53 24N 0 46W
Gairdner, L., *Australia* . . . . **63 E2** 31 30S 136 0 E
Gairloch, L., *U.K.* **12 D3** 57 43N 5 45W
Gaizhou, *China* . . . . **35 D12** 40 22N 122 20 E
Gaj →, *Pakistan* . . . . **42 F2** 26 26N 67 21 E
Gakuch, *Pakistan* . . . . **43 A5** 36 7N 73 45 E
Galán, Cerro, *Argentina* . . . **94 B2** 25 55S 66 52W
Galana →, *Kenya* . . . . **54 C5** 3 9S 40 8 E
Galápagos, *Pac. Oc.* **90 D1** 0 0 91 0W
Galashiels, *U.K.* **12 F6** 55 37N 2 49W
Galaţi, *Romania* . . . . **17 F15** 45 27N 28 2 E
Galatina, *Italy* . . . . **21 D8** 40 10N 18 10 E
Galax, *U.S.A.* **77 G5** 36 40N 80 56W
Galcaio, *Somali Rep.* . . . . . **46 F4** 6 30N 47 30 E
Galdhøpiggen, *Norway* . . . **9 F12** 61 38N 8 18 E
Galeana, *Mexico* **86 C4** 24 50N 100 4W
Galeana, *Nuevo León, Mexico* **86 A3** 24 50N 100 4W
Galela, *Indonesia* . . . . **37 D7** 1 50N 127 49 E
Galena, *U.S.A.* **68 B4** 64 44N 156 56W
Galera Point, *Trin. & Tob.* . **89 D7** 10 8N 61 0W
Galesburg, *U.S.A.* **80 E9** 40 57N 90 22W
Galeton, *U.S.A.* **78 E7** 41 44N 77 39W
Galich, *Russia* . . . . **24 C7** 58 22N 42 24 E
Galicia □, *Spain* **19 A2** 42 43N 7 45W
Galilee = Hagalil, *Israel* . . . **47 C4** 32 53N 35 18 E
Galilee, L., *Australia* . . . . . **62 C4** 22 20S 145 50 E
Galilee, Sea of = Yam Kinneret, *Israel* . . . . **47 C4** 32 45N 35 35 E
Galinoporni, *Cyprus* . . . . . . **23 D13** 35 31N 34 18 E
Galion, *U.S.A.* **78 F2** 40 44N 82 47W
Galiuro Mts., *U.S.A.* **83 K8** 32 30N 110 20W
Galiwinku, *Australia* . . . . . . **62 A2** 12 2S 135 34 E
Gallan Hd., *U.K.* **12 C1** 58 15N 7 2W
Gallatin, *U.S.A.* **77 G2** 36 24N 86 27W
Galle, *Sri Lanka* . . . . **40 R12** 6 5N 80 10 E
Gállego →, *Spain* **19 B5** 41 39N 0 51W
Gallegos →, *Argentina* . . . **96 G3** 51 35S 69 0W
Galley Hd., *Ireland* **13 E3** 51 32N 8 55W
Gallinas, Pta., *Colombia* . . **92 A4** 12 28N 71 40W
Gallipoli = Gelibolu, *Turkey* **21 D12** 40 28N 26 43 E
Gallípoli, *Italy* . . . . **21 D8** 40 3N 17 58 E
Gallipolis, *U.S.A.* **76 F4** 38 49N 82 12W
Gällivare, *Sweden* . . . . **8 C19** 67 9N 20 40 E
Galloo I., *U.S.A.* **79 C8** 43 55N 76 25W
Galloway, *U.K.* **12 F4** 55 1N 4 29W
Galloway, Mull of, *U.K.* **12 G4** 54 39N 4 52W
Gallup, *U.S.A.* **83 J9** 35 32N 108 45W
Galoya, *Sri Lanka* . . . . **40 Q12** 8 10N 80 55 E
Galt, *U.S.A.* **84 G5** 38 15N 121 18W
Galty Mts., *Ireland* **13 D3** 52 22N 8 10W
Galtymore, *Ireland* **13 D3** 52 21N 8 11W
Galva, *U.S.A.* **80 E9** 41 10N 90 3W
Galveston, *U.S.A.* **81 L7** 29 18N 94 48W
Galveston B., *U.S.A.* **81 L7** 29 36N 94 50W
Gálvez, *Argentina* **94 C3** 32 0S 61 14W
Galway, *Ireland* **13 C2** 53 17N 9 3W
Galway □, *Ireland* **13 C2** 53 22N 9 1W
Galway B., *Ireland* **13 C2** 53 13N 9 10W
Gam →, *Vietnam* . . . . **38 B5** 21 55N 105 12 E
Gamagori, *Japan* . . . . **31 G8** 34 50N 137 14 E
Gambat, *Pakistan* . . . . **42 F3** 27 17N 68 26 E
Gambhir →, *India* . . . . **42 F6** 26 58N 77 27 E
Gambia ■, *W. Afr.* **50 F2** 13 25N 16 0W
Gambia →, *W. Afr.* **50 F2** 13 28N 16 34W
Gambier, *U.S.A.* **78 F2** 40 22N 82 23W
Gambier, C., *Australia* . . . . **60 B5** 11 56S 130 57 E
Gambier Is., *Australia* . . . . **63 F2** 35 3S 136 30 E
Gambo, *Canada* **71 C9** 48 47N 54 13W
Gamboli, *Pakistan* . . . . **42 E3** 29 53N 68 24 E
Gamboma, *Congo* . . . . **52 E3** 1 55S 15 52 E
Gamlakarleby = Kokkola, *Finland* . . . . **8 E20** 63 50N 23 8 E
Gammon →, *Canada* **73 C9** 51 24N 95 44W
Gan Jiang →, *China* . . . . . **33 D6** 29 15N 116 0 E
Ganado, *U.S.A.* **83 J9** 35 43N 109 33W
Gananoque, *Canada* **79 B8** 44 20N 76 10W
Ganāveh, *Iran* . . . . **45 D6** 29 35N 50 35 E
Gäncä, *Azerbaijan* . . . . **25 F8** 40 45N 46 20 E
Gancheng, *China* . . . . **38 C7** 18 51N 108 37 E
Gand = Gent, *Belgium* . . . . **15 C3** 51 2N 3 42 E
Ganda, *Angola* . . . . **53 G2** 13 3S 14 35 E
Gandajika, *Dem. Rep. of the Congo* . **52 F4** 6 45S 23 57 E
Gandak →, *India* . . . . **43 G11** 25 39N 85 13 E
Gandava, *Pakistan* . . . . **42 E2** 28 32N 67 32 E
Gander, *Canada* **71 C9** 48 58N 54 35W
Gander L., *Canada* **71 C9** 48 58N 54 35W
Ganderowe Falls, *Zimbabwe* **55 F2** 17 20S 29 10 E
Gandhi Sagar, *India* . . . . . . **42 G6** 24 40N 75 40 E
Gandhinagar, *India* . . . . **42 H5** 23 15N 72 45 E
Gandía, *Spain* **19 C5** 38 58N 0 9W
Gando, Pta., *Canary Is.* . . . **22 G4** 27 55N 15 22W
Ganedidalem = Gani, *Indonesia* . . . . **37 E7** 0 48S 128 14 E
Ganga →, *India* . . . . **43 H14** 23 20N 90 30 E
Ganga Sagar, *India* . . . . **43 J13** 21 38N 88 5 E
Gangan →, *India* . . . . **43 E8** 28 38N 78 58 E
Ganganagar, *India* . . . . **42 E5** 29 56N 73 56 E
Gangapur, *India* . . . . **42 F7** 26 32N 76 49 E
Gangaw, *Burma* . . . . **41 H19** 22 5N 94 5 E
Gangdisê Shan, *China* . . . . **41 D12** 31 20N 81 0 E
Ganges = Ganga →, *India* **43 H14** 23 20N 90 30 E
Ganges, *Canada* **72 D4** 48 51N 123 31W
Ganges, Mouths of the, *India* . . . . **43 J14** 21 30N 90 0 E
Gangoh, *India* . . . . **42 E7** 29 46N 77 18 E
Gangroti, *India* . . . . **43 D8** 30 50N 79 10 E
Gangtok, *India* . . . . **41 F16** 27 20N 88 37 E
Gangu, *China* . . . . **34 G3** 34 40N 105 15 E
Gangyao, *China* . . . . **35 B14** 44 12N 126 37 E
Gani, *Indonesia* . . . . **37 E7** 0 48S 128 14 E
Ganj, *India* . . . . **43 F8** 27 45N 78 57 E
Gannett Peak, *U.S.A.* **82 E9** 43 11N 109 39W
Ganquan, *China* . . . . **34 F5** 36 20N 109 20 E
Gansu □, *China* . . . . **34 G3** 36 0N 104 0 E
Ganta, *Liberia* **50 G4** 7 15N 8 59W
Gantheaume, C., *Australia* . **63 F2** 36 4S 137 32 E
Gantheaume B., *Australia* . **61 E1** 27 40S 114 10 E
Gantsevichi = Hantsavichy, *Belarus* . . . . **17 B14** 52 49N 26 30 E
Ganyem = Genyem, *Indonesia* . . . . **37 E10** 2 46S 140 12 E
Ganyu, *China* . . . . **35 G10** 34 50N 119 8 E
Ganzhou, *China* . . . . **33 D6** 25 51N 114 56 E
Gao, *Mali* **50 E5** 16 15N 0 5W
Gaomi, *China* . . . . **35 F10** 36 20N 119 42 E
Gaoping, *China* . . . . **34 G7** 35 45N 112 55 E
Gaotang, *China* . . . . **34 F9** 36 50N 116 15 E
Gaoua, *Burkina Faso* **50 F5** 10 20N 3 8W
Gaoual, *Guinea* **50 F3** 11 45N 13 25W
Gaoxiong = Kaohsiung, *Taiwan* . . . . **33 D7** 22 35N 120 16 E
Gaoyang, *China* . . . . **34 E8** 38 40N 115 45 E
Gaoyou Hu, *China* . . . . **35 H10** 32 45N 119 20 E
Gaoyuan, *China* . . . . **35 F9** 37 8N 117 58 E
Gap, *France* . . . . **18 D7** 44 33N 6 5 E
Gapat →, *India* . . . . **43 G10** 24 30N 82 28 E
Gapuwiyak, *Australia* . . . . . **62 A2** 12 25S 135 43 E
Gar, *China* . . . . **32 C2** 32 10N 79 58 E
Garabogazköl Aylagy, *Turkmenistan* . . . . **25 F9** 41 0N 53 30 E
Garachico, *Canary Is.* **22 F3** 28 22N 16 46W
Garachiné, *Panama* **88 E4** 8 0N 78 12W
Garafia, *Canary Is.* **22 F2** 28 48N 17 57W
Garah, *Australia* . . . . **63 D4** 29 5S 149 38 E
Garajonay, *Canary Is.* **22 F2** 28 7N 17 14W
Garanhuns, *Brazil* **93 E11** 8 50S 36 30W
Garautha, *India* . . . . **43 G8** 25 34N 79 18 E
Garba Tula, *Kenya* . . . . **54 B4** 0 30N 38 32 E
Garberville, *U.S.A.* **82 F2** 40 6N 123 48W
Garbiyang, *India* . . . . **43 D9** 30 8N 80 54 E
Garda, L. di, *Italy* . . . . **20 B4** 45 40N 10 41 E
Garde L., *Canada* **73 A7** 62 50N 106 13W
Garden City, *Ga., U.S.A.* . . . **77 J5** 32 6N 81 9W
Garden City, *Kans., U.S.A.* . . **81 G4** 37 58N 100 53W
Garden City, *Tex., U.S.A.* . . . **81 K4** 31 52N 101 29W
Garden Grove, *U.S.A.* **85 M9** 33 47N 117 55W
Gardēz, *Afghan.* . . . . **42 C3** 33 37N 69 9 E
Gardiner, *Maine, U.S.A.* . . . **77 C11** 44 14N 69 47W
Gardiner, *Mont., U.S.A.* **82 D8** 45 2N 110 22W
Gardiners I., *U.S.A.* **79 E12** 41 6N 72 6W
Gardner, *U.S.A.* **79 D13** 42 34N 71 59W
Gardner Canal, *Canada* . . . **72 C3** 53 27N 128 8W
Gardnerville, *U.S.A.* **84 G7** 38 56N 119 45W
Gardo, *Somali Rep.* . . . . **46 F4** 9 30N 49 6 E
Garey, *U.S.A.* **85 L6** 34 53N 120 19W
Garfield, *U.S.A.* **82 C5** 47 1N 117 9W
Garforth, *U.K.* **10 D6** 53 47N 1 24W
Gargano, Mte., *Italy* . . . . . . **20 D6** 41 43N 15 43 E
Garibaldi Prov. Park, *Canada* **72 D4** 49 50N 122 40W
Garies, *S. Africa* . . . . **56 E2** 30 32S 17 59 E
Garigliano →, *Italy* . . . . . . **20 D5** 41 13N 13 45 E
Garissa, *Kenya* . . . . **54 C4** 0 25S 39 40 E
Garland, *Tex., U.S.A.* **81 J6** 32 55N 96 38W
Garland, *Utah, U.S.A.* **82 F7** 41 47N 112 10W
Garm, *Tajikistan* . . . . **26 F8** 39 0N 70 20 E
Garmāb, *Iran* . . . . **45 C8** 35 25N 56 45 E
Garmisch-Partenkirchen, *Germany* . . . . **16 E6** 47 30N 11 6 E
Garmsār, *Iran* . . . . **45 C7** 35 20N 52 25 E
Garner, *U.S.A.* **80 D8** 43 6N 93 36W
Garnett, *U.S.A.* **80 F7** 38 17N 95 14W
Garo Hills, *India* . . . . **43 G14** 25 30N 90 30 E
Garoe, *Somali Rep.* . . . . **46 F4** 8 25N 48 33 E
Garonne →, *France* **18 D3** 45 2N 0 36W
Garot, *India* . . . . **42 G6** 24 19N 75 41 E
Garoua, *Cameroon* . . . . **51 G8** 9 19N 13 21 E
Garrauli, *India* . . . . **43 G8** 25 5N 79 22 E
Garrison, *Mont., U.S.A.* **82 C7** 46 31N 112 49W
Garrison, *N. Dak., U.S.A.* . . **80 B4** 47 40N 101 25W
Garrison Res. = Sakakawea, L., *U.S.A.* **80 B4** 47 30N 101 25W
Garron Pt., *U.K.* **13 A6** 55 3N 5 59W
Garry →, *U.K.* **12 E5** 56 44N 3 47W
Garry, L., *Canada* **68 B9** 65 58N 100 18W
Garsen, *Kenya* . . . . **54 C5** 2 20S 40 5 E
Garson L., *Canada* **73 B6** 56 19N 110 2W
Garu, *India* . . . . **43 H11** 23 40N 84 14 E
Garub, *Namibia* . . . . **56 D2** 26 37S 16 0 E
Garut, *Indonesia* . . . . **37 G12** 7 14S 107 53 E
Garvie Mts., *N.Z.* . . . . **59 L2** 45 30S 168 50 E
Garwa = Garoua, *Cameroon* **51 G8** 9 19N 13 21 E
Garwa, *India* . . . . **43 G10** 24 11N 83 47 E
Gary, *U.S.A.* **76 E2** 41 36N 87 20W
Garzê, *China* . . . . **32 C5** 31 38N 100 1 E
Garzón, *Colombia* **92 C3** 2 10N 75 40W
Gas-San, *Japan* . . . . **30 E10** 38 32N 140 1 E
Gasan Kuli = Esenguly, *Turkmenistan* . . . . **26 F6** 37 37N 53 59 E
Gascogne, *France* . . . . **18 E4** 43 45N 0 20 E
Gascogne, G. de, *Europe* . . **18 D2** 44 0N 2 0W
Gascony = Gascogne, *France* . . . . **18 E4** 43 45N 0 20 E
Gascoyne →, *Australia* . . **61 D1** 24 52S 113 37 E
Gascoyne Junction, *Australia* . . . . **61 E2** 25 2S 115 17 E
Gashaka, *Nigeria* . . . . **51 G8** 7 20N 11 29 E
Gasherbrum, *Pakistan* . . . . **43 B7** 35 40N 76 40 E
Gashua, *Nigeria* . . . . **51 F8** 12 54N 11 0 E
Gaspé, *Canada* **71 C7** 48 52N 64 30W
Gaspé, C. de, *Canada* **71 C7** 48 48N 64 7W
Gaspé, Pén. de, *Canada* . . . **71 C6** 48 45N 65 40W
Gaspésie, Parc de Conservation de la, *Canada* **71 C6** 48 55N 65 50W
Gasteiz = Vitoria-Gasteiz, *Spain* **19 A4** 42 50N 2 41W
Gastonia, *U.S.A.* **77 H5** 35 16N 81 11W
Gastre, *Argentina* **96 E3** 42 20S 69 15W
Gata, C., *Cyprus* . . . . **23 E12** 34 34N 33 2 E
Gata, C. de, *Spain* **19 D4** 36 41N 2 13W
Gata, Sierra de, *Spain* **19 B2** 40 20N 6 45W
Gataga →, *Canada* **72 B3** 58 35N 126 59W
Gatehouse of Fleet, *U.K.* . . **12 G4** 54 53N 4 12W
Gates, *U.S.A.* **78 C7** 43 9N 77 42W
Gateshead, *U.K.* **10 C6** 54 57N 1 35W
Gatesville, *U.S.A.* **81 K6** 31 26N 97 45W
Gaths, *Zimbabwe* . . . . **55 G3** 20 2S 30 32 E
Gatico, *Chile* **94 A1** 22 29S 70 20W
Gatineau, *Canada* **79 A9** 45 29N 75 38W
Gatineau →, *Canada* **70 C4** 45 27N 75 42W
Gatineau, Parc Nat. de la, *Canada* **70 C4** 45 40N 76 0W
Gatton, *Australia* . . . . **63 D5** 27 32S 152 17 E

Gatun, L., *Panama* **88 E4** 9 7N 79 56W
Gatyana, *S. Africa* **57 E4** 32 16S 28 31 E
Gau, *Fiji* **59 D8** 18 2S 179 18 E
Gauer L., *Canada* **73 B9** 57 0N 97 50W
Gauhati, *India* **41 F17** 26 10N 91 45 E
Gauja —►, *Latvia* **9 H21** 57 10N 24 16 E
Gaula —►, *Norway* **8 E14** 63 21N 10 14 E
Gauri Phanta, *India* **43 E9** 28 41N 80 36 E
Gausta, *Norway* **9 G13** 59 48N 8 40 E
Gauteng □, *S. Africa* **57 D4** 26 0S 28 0 E
Gāv Koshī, *Iran* **45 D8** 28 38N 57 12 E
Gāvakān, *Iran* **45 D7** 29 37N 53 10 E
Gavāter, *Iran* **45 E9** 25 10N 61 31 E
Gāvbandī, *Iran* **45 E7** 27 12N 53 4 E
Gavdhopoúla, *Greece* **23 E6** 34 56N 24 0 E
Gávdhos, *Greece* **23 E6** 34 50N 24 5 E
Gaviota, *U.S.A.* **85 L6** 34 29N 120 13W
Gāvkhūnī, Bāţlāq-e, *Iran* **45 C7** 32 6N 52 52 E
Gävle, *Sweden* **9 F17** 60 40N 17 9 E
Gawachab, *Namibia* **56 D2** 27 4S 17 55 E
Gawilgarh Hills, *India* **40 J10** 21 15N 76 45 E
Gawler, *Australia* **63 E2** 34 30S 138 42 E
Gaxun Nur, *China* **32 B5** 42 22N 100 30 E
Gay, *Russia* **24 D10** 51 27N 58 27 E
Gaya, *India* **43 G11** 24 47N 85 4 E
Gaya, *Niger* **50 F6** 11 52N 3 28 E
Gaylord, *U.S.A.* **76 C3** 45 2N 84 41W
Gayndah, *Australia* **63 D5** 25 35S 151 32 E
Gaysin = Haysyn, *Ukraine* **17 D15** 48 57N 29 25 E
Gayvoron = Hayvoron, *Ukraine* **17 D15** 48 22N 29 52 E
Gaza, *Gaza Strip* **47 D3** 31 30N 34 28 E
Gaza □, *Mozam.* **57 C5** 23 10S 32 45 E
Gaza Strip □, *Asia* **47 D3** 31 29N 34 25 E
Gazanjyk, *Turkmenistan* **45 B7** 39 16N 55 32 E
Gāzbor, *Iran* **45 D8** 28 5N 58 51 E
Gazi, *Dem. Rep. of the Congo* **54 B1** 1 3N 24 30 E
Gaziantep, *Turkey* **25 G6** 37 6N 37 23 E
Gcuwa, *S. Africa* **57 E4** 32 20S 28 11 E
Gdańsk, *Poland* **17 A10** 54 22N 18 40 E
Gdańska, Zatoka, *Poland* **17 A10** 54 30N 19 20 E
Gdov, *Russia* **9 G22** 58 48N 27 55 E
Gdynia, *Poland* **17 A10** 54 35N 18 33 E
Gebe, *Indonesia* **37 D7** 0 5N 129 25 E
Gebze, *Turkey* **21 D13** 40 47N 29 25 E
Gedaref, *Sudan* **51 F13** 14 2N 35 28 E
Gediz —►, *Turkey* **21 E12** 38 35N 26 48 E
Gedser, *Denmark* **9 J14** 54 35N 11 55 E
Geegully Cr. —►, *Australia* **60 C3** 18 32S 123 41 E
Geel, *Belgium* **15 C4** 51 10N 4 59 E
Geelong, *Australia* **63 F3** 38 10S 144 22 E
Geelvink B. = Cenderwasih, Teluk, *Indonesia* **37 E9** 3 0S 135 20 E
Geelvink Chan., *Australia* **61 E1** 28 30S 114 0 E
Geesthacht, *Germany* **16 B6** 53 26N 10 22 E
Geidam, *Nigeria* **51 F8** 12 57N 11 57 E
Geikie —►, *Canada* **73 B8** 57 45N 103 52W
Geistown, *U.S.A.* **78 F6** 40 18N 78 52W
Geita, *Tanzania* **54 C3** 2 48S 32 12 E
Gejiu, *China* **32 D5** 23 20N 103 10 E
Gel, Meydān-e, *Iran* **45 D7** 29 4N 54 50 E
Gela, *Italy* **20 F6** 37 4N 14 15 E
Gelderland □, *Neths.* **15 B6** 52 5N 6 10 E
Geldrop, *Neths.* **15 C5** 51 25N 5 32 E
Geleen, *Neths.* **15 D5** 50 57N 5 49 E
Gelibolu, *Turkey* **21 D12** 40 28N 26 43 E
Gelsenkirchen, *Germany* **16 C4** 51 32N 7 6 E
Gemas, *Malaysia* **39 L4** 2 37N 102 36 E
Gembloux, *Belgium* **15 D4** 50 34N 4 43 E
Gemena, *Dem. Rep. of the Congo* **52 D3** 3 13N 19 48 E
Gemerek, *Turkey* **44 B3** 39 15N 36 10 E
Gemlik, *Turkey* **21 D13** 40 26N 29 9 E
Genale, *Ethiopia* **46 F2** 6 0N 39 30 E
General Acha, *Argentina* **94 D3** 37 20S 64 38W
General Alvear, *Buenos Aires, Argentina* **94 D4** 36 0S 60 0W
General Alvear, *Mendoza, Argentina* **94 D2** 35 0S 67 40W
General Artigas, *Paraguay* **94 B4** 26 52S 56 16W
General Belgrano, *Argentina* **94 D4** 36 35S 58 47W
General Cabrera, *Argentina* **94 C3** 32 53S 63 52W
General Cepeda, *Mexico* **86 B4** 25 23N 101 27W
General Guido, *Argentina* **94 D4** 36 40S 57 50W
General Juan Madariaga, *Argentina* **94 D4** 37 0S 57 0W
General La Madrid, *Argentina* **94 D3** 37 17S 61 20W
General MacArthur, *Phil.* **37 B7** 11 18N 125 28 E
General Martin Miguel de Güemes, *Argentina* **94 A3** 24 50S 65 0W
General Paz, *Argentina* **94 B4** 27 45S 57 36W
General Pico, *Argentina* **94 D3** 35 45S 63 50W
General Pinedo, *Argentina* **94 B3** 27 15S 61 20W
General Pinto, *Argentina* **94 C3** 34 45S 61 50W
General Roca, *Argentina* **96 D3** 39 2S 67 35W
General Santos, *Phil.* **37 C7** 6 5N 125 14 E
General Trevino, *Mexico* **87 B5** 26 14N 99 29W
General Trías, *Mexico* **86 B3** 28 21N 106 22W
General Viamonte, *Argentina* **94 D3** 35 1S 61 3W
General Villegas, *Argentina* **94 D3** 35 5S 63 0W
Genesee, *Idaho, U.S.A.* **82 C5** 46 33N 116 56W
Genesee, *Pa., U.S.A.* **78 E7** 41 59N 77 54W
Genesee —►, *U.S.A.* **78 C7** 43 16N 77 36W
Geneseo, *Ill., U.S.A.* **80 E9** 41 27N 90 9W
Geneseo, *N.Y., U.S.A.* **78 D7** 42 48N 77 49W
Geneva = Genève, *Switz.* **18 C7** 46 12N 6 9 E
Geneva, *Ala., U.S.A.* **77 K3** 31 2N 85 52W
Geneva, *N.Y., U.S.A.* **78 D8** 42 52N 76 59W
Geneva, *Nebr., U.S.A.* **80 E6** 40 32N 97 36W
Geneva, *Ohio, U.S.A.* **78 E4** 41 48N 80 57W
Geneva, L. = Léman, L., *Europe* **18 C7** 46 26N 6 30 E
Geneva, L., *U.S.A.* **76 D1** 42 38N 88 30W
Genève, *Switz.* **18 C7** 46 12N 6 9 E
Genil —►, *Spain* **19 D3** 37 42N 5 19W
Genk, *Belgium* **15 D5** 50 58N 5 32 E
Gennargentu, Mti. del, *Italy* **20 D3** 40 1N 9 19 E
Genoa = Génova, *Italy* **18 D8** 44 25N 8 57 E
Genoa, *Australia* **63 F4** 37 29S 149 35 E
Genoa, *N.Y., U.S.A.* **79 D8** 42 40N 76 32W
Genoa, *Nebr., U.S.A.* **80 E6** 41 27N 97 44W
Genoa, *Nev., U.S.A.* **84 F7** 39 2N 119 50W
Génova, *Italy* **18 D8** 44 25N 8 57 E
Génova, G. di, *Italy* **20 C3** 44 0N 9 0 E
Genriyetty, Ostrov, *Russia* **27 B16** 77 6N 156 30 E
Gent, *Belgium* **15 C3** 51 2N 3 42 E
Genteng, *Indonesia* **37 G12** 7 22S 106 24 E
Genyem, *Indonesia* **37 E10** 2 46S 140 12 E
Geographe B., *Australia* **61 F2** 33 30S 115 15 E
Geographe Chan., *Australia* **61 D1** 24 30S 113 0 E
Georga, Zemlya, *Russia* **26 A5** 80 30N 49 0 E
George, *S. Africa* **56 E3** 33 58S 22 29 E
George —►, *Canada* **71 A6** 58 49N 66 10W
George, L., *N.S.W., Australia* **63 F4** 35 10S 149 25 E
George, L., *S. Austral., Australia* **63 F3** 37 25S 140 0 E
George, L., *W. Austral., Australia* **60 D3** 22 45S 123 40 E
George, L., *Uganda* **54 B3** 0 5N 30 10 E
George, L., *Fla., U.S.A.* **77 L5** 29 17N 81 36W
George, L., *N.Y., U.S.A.* **79 C11** 43 37N 73 33W
George Gill Ra., *Australia* **60 D5** 24 22S 131 45 E
George River = Kangiqsualujjuaq, *Canada* **69 C13** 58 30N 65 59W
George Sound, *N.Z.* **59 L1** 44 52S 167 25 E
George Town, *Australia* **62 G4** 41 6S 146 49 E
George Town, *Bahamas* **88 B4** 23 33N 75 47W
George Town, *Malaysia* **39 K3** 5 25N 100 15 E
George V Land, *Antarctica* **5 C10** 69 0S 148 0 E
George VI Sound, *Antarctica* **5 D17** 71 0S 68 0W
George West, *U.S.A.* **81 L5** 28 20N 98 7W
Georgetown, *Australia* **62 B3** 18 17S 143 33 E
Georgetown, *Ont., Canada* **78 C5** 43 40N 79 56W
Georgetown, *P.E.I., Canada* **71 C7** 46 13N 62 24W
Georgetown, *Cayman Is.* **88 C3** 19 20N 81 24W
Georgetown, *Gambia* **50 F3** 13 30N 14 47W
Georgetown, *Guyana* **92 B7** 6 50N 58 12W
Georgetown, *Calif., U.S.A.* **84 G6** 38 54N 120 50W
Georgetown, *Colo., U.S.A.* **82 G11** 39 42N 105 42W
Georgetown, *Ky., U.S.A.* **76 F3** 38 13N 84 33W
Georgetown, *N.Y., U.S.A.* **79 D9** 42 46N 75 44W
Georgetown, *Ohio, U.S.A.* **76 F4** 38 52N 83 54W
Georgetown, *S.C., U.S.A.* **77 J6** 33 23N 79 17W
Georgetown, *Tex., U.S.A.* **81 K6** 30 38N 97 41W
Georgia □, *U.S.A.* **77 K5** 32 50N 83 15W
Georgia ■, *Asia* **25 F7** 42 0N 43 0 E
Georgia, Str. of, *Canada* **72 D4** 49 25N 124 0W
Georgian B., *Canada* **78 A4** 45 15N 81 0W
Georgina —►, *Australia* **62 C2** 23 30S 139 47 E
Georgina I., *Canada* **78 B5** 44 22N 79 17W
Georgiu-Dezh = Liski, *Russia* **25 D6** 51 3N 39 30 E
Georgiyevsk, *Russia* **25 F7** 44 12N 43 28 E
Gera, *Germany* **16 C7** 50 53N 12 4 E
Geraardsbergen, *Belgium* **15 D3** 50 45N 3 53 E
Geral, Serra, *Brazil* **95 B6** 26 25S 50 0W
Geral de Goiás, Serra, *Brazil* **93 F9** 12 0S 46 0W
Geraldine, *U.S.A.* **82 C8** 47 36N 110 16W
Geraldton, *Australia* **61 E1** 28 48S 114 32 E
Geraldton, *Canada* **70 C2** 49 44N 86 59W
Gereshk, *Afghan.* **40 D4** 31 47N 64 35 E
Gerik, *Malaysia* **39 K3** 5 50N 101 15 E
Gering, *U.S.A.* **80 E3** 41 50N 103 40W
Gerlach, *U.S.A.* **82 F4** 40 39N 119 21W
Germansen Landing, *Canada* **72 B4** 55 43N 124 40W
Germantown, *U.S.A.* **81 M10** 35 5N 89 49W
Germany ■, *Europe* **16 C6** 51 0N 10 0 E
Germī, *Iran* **45 B6** 39 1N 48 3 E
Germiston, *S. Africa* **57 D4** 26 15S 28 10 E
Gernika-Lumo, *Spain* **19 A4** 43 19N 2 40W
Gero, *Japan* **31 G8** 35 48N 137 14 E
Gerona = Girona, *Spain* **19 B7** 41 58N 2 46 E
Gerrard, *Canada* **72 C5** 50 30N 117 17W
Geser, *Indonesia* **37 E8** 3 50S 130 54 E
Getafe, *Spain* **19 B4** 40 18N 3 44W
Gettysburg, *Pa., U.S.A.* **76 F7** 39 50N 77 14W
Gettysburg, *S. Dak., U.S.A.* **80 C5** 45 1N 99 57W
Getxo, *Spain* **19 A4** 43 21N 2 59W
Getz Ice Shelf, *Antarctica* **5 D14** 75 0S 130 0W
Geyser, *U.S.A.* **82 C8** 47 16N 110 30W
Geyserville, *U.S.A.* **84 G4** 38 42N 122 54W
Ghaggar —►, *India* **42 E6** 29 30N 74 53 E
Ghaghara —►, *India* **43 G11** 25 45N 84 40 E
Ghaghat —►, *Bangla.* **43 G13** 25 19N 89 38 E
Ghagra, *India* **43 H11** 23 17N 84 33 E
Ghagra —►, *India* **43 F9** 27 29N 81 9 E
Ghana ■, *W. Afr.* **50 G5** 8 0N 1 0W
Ghansor, *India* **43 H9** 22 39N 80 1 E
Ghanzi, *Botswana* **56 C3** 21 50S 21 34 E
Ghanzi □, *Botswana* **56 C3** 21 50S 21 45 E
Ghardaïa, *Algeria* **50 B6** 32 20N 3 37 E
Gharyān, *Libya* **51 B8** 32 10N 13 0 E
Ghat, *Libya* **51 D8** 24 59N 10 11 E
Ghatal, *India* **43 H12** 22 40N 87 46 E
Ghatampur, *India* **43 F9** 26 8N 80 13 E
Ghatsila, *India* **43 H12** 22 36N 86 29 E
Ghaţţī, *Si. Arabia* **44 D3** 31 16N 37 31 E
Ghawdex = Gozo, *Malta* **23 C1** 36 3N 14 13 E
Ghazal, Bahr el —►, *Chad* **51 F9** 13 0N 15 47 E
Ghazâl, Bahr el —►, *Sudan* **51 G12** 9 31N 30 25 E
Ghaziabad, *India* **42 E7** 28 42N 77 26 E
Ghazipur, *India* **43 G10** 25 38N 83 35 E
Ghaznī, *Afghan.* **42 C3** 33 30N 68 28 E
Ghaznī □, *Afghan.* **40 C6** 32 10N 68 20 E
Ghent = Gent, *Belgium* **15 C3** 51 2N 3 42 E
Ghīnah, Wādī al, *Si. Arabia* **44 D3** 30 27N 38 14 E
Ghizao, *Afghan.* **42 C1** 33 20N 65 44 E
Ghizar —►, *Pakistan* **43 A5** 36 15N 73 43 E
Ghotaru, *India* **42 F4** 27 20N 70 1 E
Ghotki, *Pakistan* **42 E3** 28 5N 69 21 E
Ghowr □, *Afghan.* **40 C4** 34 0N 64 20 E
Ghudaf, W. al —►, *Iraq* **44 C4** 32 56N 43 30 E
Ghudāmis, *Libya* **51 B7** 30 11N 9 29 E
Ghughri, *India* **43 H9** 22 39N 80 41 E
Ghugus, *India* **40 K11** 19 58N 79 12 E
Ghulam Mohammad Barrage, *Pakistan* **42 G3** 25 30N 68 20 E
Ghūriān, *Afghan.* **40 B2** 34 17N 61 25 E
Gia Dinh, *Vietnam* **39 G6** 10 49N 106 42 E
Gia Lai = Plei Ku, *Vietnam* **38 F7** 13 57N 108 0 E
Gia Nghia, *Vietnam* **39 G6** 11 58N 107 42 E
Gia Ngoc, *Vietnam* **38 E7** 14 50N 108 58 E
Gia Vuc, *Vietnam* **38 E7** 14 42N 108 34 E
Giant Forest, *U.S.A.* **84 J8** 36 36N 118 43W
Giants Causeway, *U.K.* **13 A5** 55 16N 6 29W
Giarabub = Al Jaghbūb, *Libya* **51 C10** 29 42N 24 38 E
Giarre, *Italy* **20 F6** 37 43N 15 11 E
Gibara, *Cuba* **88 B4** 21 9N 76 11W
Gibb River, *Australia* **60 C4** 16 26S 126 26 E
Gibbon, *U.S.A.* **80 E5** 40 45N 98 51W
Gibeon, *Namibia* **53 K3** 25 7S 17 40 E
Gibraltar ■, *Europe* **19 D3** 36 7N 5 22W
Gibraltar, Str. of, *Medit. S.* **19 E3** 35 55N 5 40W
Gibson Desert, *Australia* **60 D4** 24 0S 126 0 E
Gibsons, *Canada* **72 D4** 49 24N 123 32W
Gibsonville, *U.S.A.* **84 F6** 39 46N 120 54W
Giddings, *U.S.A.* **81 K6** 30 11N 96 56W
Giessen, *Germany* **16 C5** 50 34N 8 41 E
Gīfān, *Iran* **45 B8** 37 54N 57 28 E
Gift Lake, *Canada* **72 B5** 55 53N 115 49W
Gifu, *Japan* **31 G8** 35 30N 136 45 E
Gifu □, *Japan* **31 G8** 35 40N 137 0 E
Giganta, Sa. de la, *Mexico* **86 B2** 25 30N 111 30W
Gigha, *U.K.* **12 F3** 55 42N 5 44W
Giglio, *Italy* **20 C4** 42 20N 10 52 E
Gijón, *Spain* **19 A3** 43 32N 5 42W
Gil I., *Canada* **72 C3** 53 12N 129 15W
Gila —►, *U.S.A.* **83 K6** 32 43N 114 33W
Gila Bend, *U.S.A.* **83 K7** 32 57N 112 43W
Gila Bend Mts., *U.S.A.* **83 K7** 33 10N 113 0W
Gīlān □, *Iran* **45 B6** 37 0N 50 0 E
Gilbert —►, *Australia* **62 B3** 16 35S 141 15 E
Gilbert Is., *Kiribati* **64 G9** 1 0N 172 0 E
Gilbert River, *Australia* **62 B3** 18 9S 142 52 E
Gilead, *U.S.A.* **79 B14** 44 24N 70 59W
Gilford I., *Canada* **72 C3** 50 40N 126 30W
Gilgandra, *Australia* **63 E4** 31 43S 148 39 E
Gilgil, *Kenya* **54 C4** 0 30S 36 20 E
Gilgit, *India* **43 B6** 35 50N 74 15 E
Gilgit —►, *Pakistan* **43 B6** 35 44N 74 37 E
Gilgunnia, *Australia* **63 E4** 32 26S 146 2 E
Gillam, *Canada* **73 B10** 56 20N 94 40W
Gillen, L., *Australia* **61 E3** 26 11S 124 38 E
Gilles, L., *Australia* **63 E2** 32 50S 136 45 E
Gillette, *U.S.A.* **80 C2** 44 18N 105 30W
Gilliat, *Australia* **62 C3** 20 40S 141 28 E
Gillingham, *U.K.* **11 F8** 51 23N 0 33 E
Gilmer, *U.S.A.* **81 J7** 32 44N 94 57W
Gilmore, L., *Australia* **61 F3** 32 29S 121 37 E
Gilroy, *U.S.A.* **84 H5** 37 1N 121 34W
Gimli, *Canada* **73 C9** 50 40N 97 0W
Gin Gin, *Australia* **63 D5** 25 0S 151 58 E
Gingin, *Australia* **61 F2** 31 22S 115 54 E
Ginir, *Ethiopia* **46 F3** 7 6N 40 40 E
Gióna, Óros, *Greece* **21 E10** 38 38N 22 14 E
Gippsland, *Australia* **63 F4** 37 52S 147 0 E
Gir Hills, *India* **42 J4** 21 0N 71 0 E
Girab, *India* **42 F4** 26 2N 70 38 E
Girâfi, W. —►, *Egypt* **47 F3** 29 58N 34 39 E
Girard, *Kans., U.S.A.* **81 G7** 37 31N 94 51W
Girard, *Ohio, U.S.A.* **78 E4** 41 9N 80 42W
Girard, *Pa., U.S.A.* **78 D4** 42 0N 80 19W
Girard, *Pa., U.S.A.* **78 E4** 42 0N 80 19W
Girdle Ness, *U.K.* **12 D6** 57 9N 2 3W
Giresun, *Turkey* **25 F6** 40 55N 38 30 E
Girga, *Egypt* **51 C12** 26 17N 31 55 E
Giri —►, *India* **42 D7** 30 28N 77 41 E
Giridih, *India* **43 G12** 24 10N 86 21 E
Girne = Kyrenia, *Cyprus* **23 D12** 35 20N 33 20 E
Girona, *Spain* **19 B7** 41 58N 2 46 E
Gironde —►, *France* **18 D3** 45 32N 1 7W
Giru, *Australia* **62 B4** 19 30S 147 5 E
Girvan, *U.K.* **12 F4** 55 14N 4 51W
Gisborne, *N.Z.* **59 H7** 38 39S 178 5 E
Gisenyi, *Rwanda* **54 C2** 1 41S 29 15 E
Gislaved, *Sweden* **9 H15** 57 19N 13 32 E
Gitega, *Burundi* **54 C2** 3 26S 29 56 E
Giuba —►, *Somali Rep.* **46 G3** 1 30N 42 35 E
Giurgiu, *Romania* **17 G13** 43 52N 25 57 E
Giza = El Gîza, *Egypt* **51 C12** 30 0N 31 10 E
Gizhiga, *Russia* **27 C17** 62 3N 160 30 E
Gizhiginskaya Guba, *Russia* **27 C16** 61 0N 158 0 E
Giżycko, *Poland* **17 A11** 54 2N 21 48 E
Gjirokastra, *Albania* **21 D9** 40 7N 20 10 E
Gjoa Haven, *Canada* **68 B10** 68 20N 96 8W
Gjøvik, *Norway* **9 F14** 60 47N 10 43 E
Glace Bay, *Canada* **71 C8** 46 11N 59 58W
Glacier Bay National Park and Preserve, *U.S.A.* **72 B1** 58 45N 136 30W
Glacier National Park, *Canada* **72 C5** 51 15N 117 30W
Glacier National Park, *U.S.A.* **82 B7** 48 30N 113 18W
Glacier Peak, *U.S.A.* **82 B3** 48 7N 121 7W
Gladewater, *U.S.A.* **81 J7** 32 33N 94 56W
Gladstone, *Queens., Australia* **62 C5** 23 52S 151 16 E
Gladstone, *S. Austral., Australia* **63 E2** 33 15S 138 22 E
Gladstone, *Canada* **73 C9** 50 13N 98 57W
Gladstone, *U.S.A.* **76 C2** 45 51N 87 1W
Gladwin, *U.S.A.* **76 D3** 43 59N 84 29W
Glåma = Glomma —►, *Norway* **9 G14** 59 12N 10 57 E
Gláma, *Iceland* **8 D2** 65 48N 23 0W
Glamis, *U.S.A.* **85 N11** 32 55N 115 5W
Glasco, *Kans., U.S.A.* **80 F6** 39 22N 97 50W
Glasco, *N.Y., U.S.A.* **79 D11** 42 3N 73 57W
Glasgow, *U.K.* **12 F4** 55 51N 4 15W
Glasgow, *Ky., U.S.A.* **76 G3** 37 0N 85 55W
Glasgow, *Mont., U.S.A.* **82 B10** 48 12N 106 38W
Glaslyn, *Canada* **73 C7** 53 22N 108 21W
Glastonbury, *U.K.* **11 F5** 51 9N 2 43W
Glastonbury, *U.S.A.* **79 E12** 41 43N 72 37W
Glazov, *Russia* **24 C9** 58 9N 52 40 E
Gleichen, *Canada* **72 C6** 50 52N 113 3W
Gleiwitz = Gliwice, *Poland* **17 C10** 50 22N 18 41 E
Glen, *U.S.A.* **79 B13** 44 7N 71 11W
Glen Affric, *U.K.* **12 D3** 57 17N 5 1W
Glen Canyon, *U.S.A.* **83 H8** 37 30N 110 40W
Glen Canyon Dam, *U.S.A.* **83 H8** 36 57N 111 29W
Glen Canyon National Recreation Area, *U.S.A.* **83 H8** 37 15N 111 0W
Glen Coe, *U.K.* **12 E3** 56 40N 5 0W
Glen Cove, *U.S.A.* **79 F11** 40 52N 73 38W
Glen Garry, *U.K.* **12 D3** 57 3N 5 7W
Glen Innes, *Australia* **63 D5** 29 44S 151 44 E
Glen Lyon, *U.S.A.* **79 E8** 41 10N 76 5W
Glen Mor, *U.K.* **12 D4** 57 9N 4 37W
Glen Moriston, *U.K.* **12 D4** 57 11N 4 52W
Glen Robertson, *Canada* **79 A10** 45 22N 74 30W
Glen Spean, *U.K.* **12 E4** 56 53N 4 40W
Glen Ullin, *U.S.A.* **80 B4** 46 49N 101 50W
Glencoe, *Canada* **78 D3** 42 45N 81 43W
Glencoe, *S. Africa* **57 D5** 28 11S 30 11 E
Glencoe, *U.S.A.* **80 C7** 44 46N 94 9W
Glendale, *Ariz., U.S.A.* **83 K7** 33 32N 112 11W
Glendale, *Calif., U.S.A.* **85 L8** 34 9N 118 15W
Glendale, *Zimbabwe* **55 F3** 17 22S 31 5 E
Glendive, *U.S.A.* **80 B2** 47 7N 104 43W
Glendo, *U.S.A.* **80 D2** 42 30N 105 2W
Glenelg —►, *Australia* **63 F3** 38 4S 140 59 E
Glenfield, *U.S.A.* **79 C9** 43 43N 75 24W
Glengarriff, *Ireland* **13 E2** 51 45N 9 34W
Glenmont, *U.S.A.* **78 F2** 40 31N 82 6W
Glenmorgan, *Australia* **63 D4** 27 14S 149 42 E
Glenn, *U.S.A.* **84 F4** 39 31N 122 1W
Glennallen, *U.S.A.* **68 B5** 62 0N 145 50W
Glennamaddy, *Ireland* **13 C3** 53 37N 8 33W
Glenns Ferry, *U.S.A.* **82 E6** 42 57N 115 18W
Glenore, *Australia* **62 B3** 17 50S 141 12 E
Glenreagh, *Australia* **63 E5** 30 2S 153 1 E
Glenrock, *U.S.A.* **82 E11** 42 52N 105 52W
Glenrothes, *U.K.* **12 E5** 56 12N 3 10W
Glens Falls, *U.S.A.* **79 C11** 43 19N 73 39W
Glenside, *U.S.A.* **79 F9** 40 6N 75 9W
Glenties, *Ireland* **13 B3** 54 49N 8 16W
Glenville, *U.S.A.* **76 F5** 38 56N 80 50W
Glenwood, *Canada* **71 C9** 49 0N 54 58W
Glenwood, *Ark., U.S.A.* **81 H8** 34 20N 93 33W
Glenwood, *Hawaii, U.S.A.* **74 J17** 19 29N 155 9W
Glenwood, *Iowa, U.S.A.* **80 E7** 41 3N 95 45W
Glenwood, *Minn., U.S.A.* **80 C7** 45 39N 95 23W
Glenwood, *Wash., U.S.A.* **84 D5** 46 1N 121 17W
Glenwood Springs, *U.S.A.* **82 G10** 39 33N 107 19W
Glettinganes, *Iceland* **8 D7** 65 30N 13 37W
Gliwice, *Poland* **17 C10** 50 22N 18 41 E
Globe, *U.S.A.* **83 K8** 33 24N 110 47W
Głogów, *Poland* **16 C9** 51 37N 16 5 E
Glomma —►, *Norway* **9 G14** 59 12N 10 57 E
Glorieuses, Is., *Ind. Oc.* **57 A8** 11 30S 47 20 E
Glossop, *U.K.* **10 D6** 53 27N 1 56W
Gloucester, *Australia* **63 E5** 32 0S 151 59 E
Gloucester, *U.K.* **11 F5** 51 53N 2 15W
Gloucester, *U.S.A.* **79 D14** 42 37N 70 40W
Gloucester I., *Australia* **62 C4** 20 0S 148 30 E
Gloucester Point, *U.S.A.* **76 G7** 37 15N 76 29W
Gloucestershire □, *U.K.* **11 F5** 51 46N 2 15W
Gloversville, *U.S.A.* **79 C10** 43 3N 74 21W
Glovertown, *Canada* **71 C9** 48 40N 54 3W
Glusk, *Belarus* **17 B15** 52 53N 28 41 E
Gmünd, *Austria* **16 D8** 48 45N 15 0 E
Gmunden, *Austria* **16 E7** 47 55N 13 48 E
Gniezno, *Poland* **17 B9** 52 30N 17 35 E
Gnowangerup, *Australia* **61 F2** 33 58S 117 59 E
Go Cong, *Vietnam* **39 G6** 10 22N 106 40 E
Gō-no-ura, *Japan* **31 H4** 33 44N 129 40 E
Goa, *India* **40 M8** 15 33N 73 59 E
Goa □, *India* **40 M8** 15 33N 73 59 E
Goalen Hd., *Australia* **63 F5** 36 33S 150 4 E
Goalpara, *India* **41 F17** 26 10N 90 40 E
Goaltor, *India* **43 H12** 22 43N 87 10 E
Goalundo Ghat, *Bangla.* **43 H13** 23 50N 89 47 E
Goat Fell, *U.K.* **12 F3** 55 38N 5 11W
Goba, *Ethiopia* **46 F2** 7 1N 39 59 E
Goba, *Mozam.* **57 D5** 26 15S 32 13 E
Gobabis, *Namibia* **56 C2** 22 30S 19 0 E
Gobi, *Asia* **34 C6** 44 0N 110 0 E
Gobō, *Japan* **31 H7** 33 53N 135 10 E
Gochas, *Namibia* **56 C2** 24 59S 18 55 E
Godavari —►, *India* **41 L13** 16 25N 82 18 E
Godavari Pt., *India* **41 L13** 17 0N 82 20 E
Godbout, *Canada* **71 C6** 49 20N 67 38W
Godda, *India* **43 G12** 24 50N 87 13 E
Goderich, *Canada* **78 C3** 43 45N 81 41W
Godfrey Ra., *Australia* **61 D2** 24 0S 117 0 E
Godhavn, *Greenland* **4 C5** 69 15N 53 38W
Godhra, *India* **42 H5** 22 49N 73 40 E
Godoy Cruz, *Argentina* **94 C2** 32 56S 68 52W
Gods —►, *Canada* **70 A1** 56 22N 92 51W
Gods L., *Canada* **70 B1** 54 40N 94 15W
Gods River, *Canada* **73 C10** 54 50N 94 5W
Godthåb = Nuuk, *Greenland* **69 B14** 64 10N 51 35W
Godwin Austen = K2, *Pakistan* **43 B7** 35 58N 76 32 E
Goeie Hoop, Kaap die = Good Hope, C. of, *S. Africa* **56 E2** 34 24S 18 30 E
Goéland, L. au, *Canada* **70 C4** 49 50N 76 48W
Goeree, *Neths.* **15 C3** 51 50N 4 0 E
Goes, *Neths.* **15 C3** 51 30N 3 55 E
Goffstown, *U.S.A.* **79 C13** 43 1N 71 36W
Gogama, *Canada* **70 C3** 47 35N 81 43W
Gogebic, L., *U.S.A.* **80 B10** 46 30N 89 35W
Gogra = Ghaghara —►, *India* **43 G11** 25 45N 84 40 E
Gogriâl, *Sudan* **51 G11** 8 30N 28 8 E
Gohana, *India* **42 E7** 29 8N 76 42 E
Goharganj, *India* **42 H7** 23 1N 77 41 E
Goi —►, *India* **42 H6** 22 4N 74 46 E
Goiânia, *Brazil* **93 G9** 16 43S 49 20W
Goiás, *Brazil* **93 G8** 15 55S 50 10W
Goiás □, *Brazil* **93 F9** 12 10S 48 0W
Goio-Ere, *Brazil* **95 A5** 24 12S 53 1W
Gojō, *Japan* **31 G7** 34 21N 135 42 E
Gojra, *Pakistan* **42 D5** 31 10N 72 40 E
Gökçeada, *Turkey* **21 D11** 40 10N 25 50 E
Gökova Körfezi, *Turkey* **21 F12** 36 55N 27 50 E
Gokteik, *Burma* **41 H20** 22 26N 97 0 E
Gokurt, *Pakistan* **42 E2** 29 40N 67 26 E
Gol Gol, *Australia* **63 E3** 34 12S 142 14 E
Gola, *India* **43 E9** 28 3N 80 32 E
Golakganj, *India* **43 F13** 26 8N 89 52 E
Golan Heights = Hagolan, *Syria* **47 C4** 33 0N 35 45 E
Golāshkerd, *Iran* **45 E8** 27 59N 57 16 E
Golchikha, *Russia* **4 B12** 71 45N 83 30 E
Golconda, *U.S.A.* **82 F5** 40 58N 117 30W
Gold, *U.S.A.* **78 E7** 41 52N 77 50W
Gold Beach, *U.S.A.* **82 E1** 42 25N 124 25W
Gold Coast, *W. Afr.* **50 H5** 4 0N 1 40W
Gold Hill, *U.S.A.* **82 E2** 42 26N 123 3W
Gold River, *Canada* **72 D3** 49 46N 126 3W
Golden, *Canada* **72 C5** 51 20N 116 59W
Golden B., *N.Z.* **59 J4** 40 40S 172 50 E
Golden Gate, *U.S.A.* **82 H2** 37 54N 122 30W
Golden Hinde, *Canada* **72 D3** 49 40N 125 44W
Golden Lake, *Canada* **78 A7** 45 34N 77 21W
Golden Vale, *Ireland* **13 D3** 52 33N 8 17W
Goldendale, *U.S.A.* **82 D3** 45 49N 120 50W
Goldfield, *U.S.A.* **83 H5** 37 42N 117 14W
Goldsand L., *Canada* **73 B8** 57 2N 101 8W
Goldsboro, *U.S.A.* **77 H7** 35 23N 77 59W
Goldsmith, *U.S.A.* **81 K3** 31 59N 102 37W

Goldsworthy, *Australia* **60 D2** 20 21S 119 30 E
Goldthwaite, *U.S.A.* **81 K5** 31 27N 98 34W
Goleniów, *Poland* **16 B8** 53 35N 14 50 E
Golestānak, *Iran* **45 D7** 30 36N 54 14 E
Goleta, *U.S.A.* **85 L7** 34 27N 119 50W
Golfito, *Costa Rica* **88 E3** 8 41N 83 5W
Golfo Aranci, *Italy* **20 D3** 40 59N 9 38 E
Goliad, *U.S.A.* **81 L6** 28 40N 97 23W
Golpāyegān, *Iran* **45 C6** 33 27N 50 18 E
Golra, *Pakistan* **42 C5** 33 37N 72 56 E
Golspie, *U.K.* **12 D5** 57 58N 3 59W
Goma, *Dem. Rep. of the Congo* **54 C2** 1 37S 29 10 E
Gomal Pass, *Pakistan* **42 D3** 31 56N 69 20 E
Gomati →, *India* **43 G10** 25 32N 83 11 E
Gombari, *Dem. Rep. of the Congo* **54 B2** 2 45N 29 3 E
Gombe, *Nigeria* **51 F8** 10 19N 11 2 E
Gombe →, *Tanzania* **54 C3** 4 38S 31 40 E
Gomel = Homyel, *Belarus* **17 B16** 52 28N 31 0 E
Gomera, *Canary Is.* **22 F2** 28 7N 17 14W
Gómez Palacio, *Mexico* **86 B4** 25 40N 104 0W
Gomīshān, *Iran* **45 B7** 37 4N 54 6 E
Gomogomo, *Indonesia* **37 F8** 6 39S 134 43 E
Gomoh, *India* **41 H15** 23 52N 86 10 E
Gompa = Ganta, *Liberia* **50 G4** 7 15N 8 59W
Gonābād, *Iran* **45 C8** 34 15N 58 45 E
Gonaïves, *Haiti* **89 C5** 19 20N 72 42W
Gonâve, G. de la, *Haiti* **89 C5** 19 29N 72 42W
Gonâve, I. de la, *Haiti* **89 C5** 18 45N 73 0W
Gonbad-e Kāvūs, *Iran* **45 B7** 37 20N 55 25 E
Gonda, *India* **43 F9** 27 9N 81 58 E
Gondal, *India* **42 J4** 21 58N 70 52 E
Gonder, *Ethiopia* **46 E2** 12 39N 37 30 E
Gondia, *India* **40 J12** 21 23N 80 10 E
Gondola, *Mozam.* **55 F3** 19 10S 33 37 E
Gönen, *Turkey* **21 D12** 40 6N 27 39 E
Gonghe, *China* **32 C5** 36 18N 100 32 E
Gongolgon, *Australia* **63 E4** 30 21S 146 54 E
Gongzhuling, *China* **35 C13** 43 30N 124 40 E
Gonzales, *Calif., U.S.A.* **84 J5** 36 30N 121 26W
Gonzales, *Tex., U.S.A.* **81 L6** 29 30N 97 27W
González Chaves, *Argentina* **94 D3** 38 2S 60 5W
Good Hope, C. of, *S. Africa* **56 E2** 34 24S 18 30 E
Gooderham, *Canada* **78 B6** 44 54N 78 21W
Gooding, *U.S.A.* **82 E6** 42 56N 114 43W
Goodland, *U.S.A.* **80 F4** 39 21N 101 43W
Goodlow, *Canada* **72 B4** 56 20N 120 8W
Goodooga, *Australia* **63 D4** 29 3S 147 28 E
Goodsprings, *U.S.A.* **85 K11** 35 49N 115 27W
Goole, *U.K.* **10 D7** 53 42N 0 53W
Goolgowi, *Australia* **63 E4** 33 58S 145 41 E
Goolwa, *Australia* **63 F2** 35 30S 138 47 E
Goomalling, *Australia* **61 F2** 31 15S 116 49 E
Goomeri, *Australia* **63 D5** 26 12S 152 6 E
Goonda, *Mozam.* **55 F3** 19 48S 33 57 E
Goondiwindi, *Australia* **63 D5** 28 30S 150 21 E
Goongarrie, L., *Australia* **61 F3** 30 3S 121 9 E
Goonyella, *Australia* **62 C4** 21 47S 147 58 E
Goose →, *Canada* **71 B7** 53 20N 60 35W
Goose Creek, *U.S.A.* **77 J5** 32 59N 80 2W
Goose L., *U.S.A.* **82 F3** 41 56N 120 26W
Gop, *India* **40 H6** 22 5N 69 50 E
Gopalganj, *India* **43 F11** 26 28N 84 30 E
Göppingen, *Germany* **16 D5** 48 42N 9 39 E
Gorakhpur, *India* **43 F10** 26 47N 83 23 E
Goražde, *Bos.-H.* **21 C8** 43 38N 18 58 E
Gorda, *U.S.A.* **84 K5** 35 53N 121 26W
Gorda, Pta., *Canary Is.* **22 F2** 28 45N 18 0W
Gorda, Pta., *Nic.* **88 D3** 14 20N 83 10W
Gordan B., *Australia* **60 B5** 11 35S 130 10 E
Gordon, *U.S.A.* **80 D3** 42 48N 102 12W
Gordon →, *Australia* **62 G4** 42 27S 145 30 E
Gordon L., *Alta., Canada* **73 B6** 56 30N 110 25W
Gordon L., *N.W.T., Canada* **72 A6** 63 5N 113 11W
Gordonvale, *Australia* **62 B4** 17 5S 145 50 E
Gore, *Ethiopia* **46 F2** 8 12N 35 32 E
Gore, *N.Z.* **59 M2** 46 5S 168 58 E
Gore Bay, *Canada* **70 C3** 45 57N 82 28W
Gorey, *Ireland* **13 D5** 52 41N 6 18W
Gorg, *Iran* **45 D8** 29 29N 59 43 E
Gorgān, *Iran* **45 B7** 36 50N 54 29 E
Gorgona, I., *Colombia* **92 C3** 3 0N 78 10W
Gorham, *U.S.A.* **79 B13** 44 23N 71 10W
Goriganga →, *India* **43 E9** 29 45N 80 23 E
Gorinchem, *Neths.* **15 C4** 51 50N 4 59 E
Goris, *Armenia* **25 G8** 39 31N 46 22 E
Gorízia, *Italy* **20 B5** 45 56N 13 37 E
Gorki = Nizhniy Novgorod, *Russia* **24 C7** 56 20N 44 0 E
Gorkiy = Nizhniy Novgorod, *Russia* **24 C7** 56 20N 44 0 E
Gorkovskoye Vdkhr., *Russia* **24 C7** 57 2N 43 4 E
Görlitz, *Germany* **16 C8** 51 9N 14 58 E
Gorlovka = Horlivka, *Ukraine* **25 E6** 48 19N 38 5 E
Gorman, *U.S.A.* **85 L8** 34 47N 118 51W
Gorna Dzhumayo = Blagoevgrad, *Bulgaria* **21 C10** 42 2N 23 5 E
Gorna Oryakhovitsa, *Bulgaria* **21 C11** 43 7N 25 40 E
Gorno-Altay □, *Russia* **26 D9** 51 0N 86 0 E
Gorno-Altaysk, *Russia* **26 D9** 51 50N 86 5 E
Gornyatski, *Russia* **24 A11** 67 32N 64 3 E
Gornyy, *Russia* **30 B6** 44 57N 133 59 E
Gorodenka = Horodenka, *Ukraine* **17 D13** 48 41N 25 29 E
Gorodok = Horodok, *Ukraine* **17 D12** 49 46N 23 32 E
Gorokhov = Horokhiv, *Ukraine* **17 C13** 50 30N 24 45 E
Goromonzi, *Zimbabwe* **55 F3** 17 52S 31 22 E
Gorong, Kepulauan, *Indonesia* **37 E8** 3 59S 131 25 E
Gorongose →, *Mozam.* **57 C5** 20 30S 34 40 E
Gorongoza, *Mozam.* **55 F3** 18 44S 34 2 E
Gorongoza, Sa. da, *Mozam.* **55 F3** 18 27S 34 2 E
Gorontalo, *Indonesia* **37 D6** 0 35N 123 5 E
Gort, *Ireland* **13 C3** 53 3N 8 49W
Gortis, *Greece* **23 D6** 35 4N 24 58 E
Gorzów Wielkopolski, *Poland* **16 B8** 52 43N 15 15 E
Gosford, *Australia* **63 E5** 33 23S 151 18 E
Goshen, *Calif., U.S.A.* **84 J7** 36 21N 119 25W
Goshen, *Ind., U.S.A.* **76 E3** 41 35N 85 50W
Goshen, *N.Y., U.S.A.* **79 E10** 41 24N 74 20W
Goshogawara, *Japan* **30 D10** 40 48N 140 27 E
Goslar, *Germany* **16 C6** 51 54N 10 25 E
Gospič, *Croatia* **16 F8** 44 35N 15 23 E
Gosport, *U.K.* **11 G6** 50 48N 1 9W
Gosse →, *Australia* **62 B1** 19 32S 134 37 E
Göta älv →, *Sweden* **9 H14** 57 42N 11 54 E
Göta kanal, *Sweden* **9 G16** 58 30N 15 58 E
Götaland, *Sweden* **9 G15** 57 30N 14 30 E
Göteborg, *Sweden* **9 H14** 57 43N 11 59 E
Gotha, *Germany* **16 C6** 50 56N 10 42 E
Gothenburg = Göteborg, *Sweden* **9 H14** 57 43N 11 59 E
Gothenburg, *U.S.A.* **80 E4** 40 56N 100 10W
Gotland, *Sweden* **9 H18** 57 30N 18 33 E
Gotō-Rettō, *Japan* **31 H4** 32 55N 129 5 E
Gotska Sandön, *Sweden* **9 G18** 58 24N 19 15 E
Gōtsu, *Japan* **31 G6** 35 0N 132 14 E
Gott Pk., *Canada* **72 C4** 50 18N 122 16W
Göttingen, *Germany* **16 C5** 51 31N 9 55 E
Gottwaldov = Zlín, *Czech Rep.* **17 D9** 49 14N 17 40 E
Goubangzi, *China* **35 D11** 41 20N 121 52 E
Gouda, *Neths.* **15 B4** 52 1N 4 42 E
Goúdhoura, Ákra, *Greece* **23 E8** 34 59N 26 6 E
Gough I., *Atl. Oc.* **2 G9** 40 10S 9 45W
Gouin, Rés., *Canada* **70 C5** 48 35N 74 40W
Goulburn, *Australia* **63 E4** 34 44S 149 44 E
Goulburn Is., *Australia* **62 A1** 11 40S 133 20 E
Goulimine, *Morocco* **50 C3** 28 56N 10 0W
Gourits →, *S. Africa* **56 E3** 34 21S 21 52 E
Goúrnais, *Greece* **23 D7** 35 19N 25 16 E
Gouverneur, *U.S.A.* **79 B9** 44 20N 75 28W
Gouviá, *Greece* **23 A3** 39 39N 19 50 E
Governador Valadares, *Brazil* **93 G10** 18 15S 41 57W
Governor's Harbour, *Bahamas* **88 A4** 25 10N 76 14W
Govindgarh, *India* **43 G9** 24 23N 81 18 E
Gowan Ra., *Australia* **62 D4** 25 0S 145 0 E
Gowanda, *U.S.A.* **78 D6** 42 28N 78 56W
Gowd-e Zirreh, *Afghan.* **40 E3** 29 45N 62 0 E
Gower, *U.K.* **11 F3** 51 35N 4 10W
Gowna, L., *Ireland* **13 C4** 53 51N 7 34W
Goya, *Argentina* **94 B4** 29 10S 59 10W
Goyder Lagoon, *Australia* **63 D2** 27 3S 138 58 E
Goyllarisquisga, *Peru* **92 F3** 10 31S 76 24W
Goz Beïda, *Chad* **51 F10** 12 10N 21 20 E
Gozo, *Malta* **23 C1** 36 3N 14 13 E
Graaff-Reinet, *S. Africa* **56 E3** 32 13S 24 32 E
Gračac, *Croatia* **16 F8** 44 18N 15 57 E
Gracias a Dios, C., *Honduras* **88 D3** 15 0N 83 10W
Graciosa, I., *Canary Is.* **22 E6** 29 15N 13 32W
Grado, *Spain* **19 A2** 43 23N 6 4W
Grady, *U.S.A.* **81 H3** 34 49N 103 19W
Grafham Water, *U.K.* **11 E7** 52 19N 0 18W
Grafton, *Australia* **63 D5** 29 38S 152 58 E
Grafton, *N. Dak., U.S.A.* **80 A6** 48 25N 97 25W
Grafton, *W. Va., U.S.A.* **76 F5** 39 21N 80 2W
Graham, *Canada* **70 C1** 49 20N 90 30W
Graham, *U.S.A.* **81 J5** 33 6N 98 35W
Graham, Mt., *U.S.A.* **83 K9** 32 42N 109 52W
Graham Bell, Ostrov = Greem-Bell, Ostrov, *Russia* **26 A7** 81 0N 62 0 E
Graham I., *B.C., Canada* **72 C2** 53 40N 132 30W
Graham I., *N.W.T., Canada* **68 C6** 77 25N 90 30W
Graham Land, *Antarctica* **5 C17** 65 0S 64 0W
Grahamstown, *S. Africa* **56 E4** 33 19S 26 31 E
Grahamsville, *U.S.A.* **79 E10** 41 51N 74 33W
Grain Coast, *W. Afr.* **50 H3** 4 20N 10 0W
Grajaú, *Brazil* **93 E9** 5 50S 46 4W
Grajaú →, *Brazil* **93 D10** 3 41S 44 48W
Grampian, *U.S.A.* **78 F6** 40 58N 78 37W
Grampian Highlands = Grampian Mts., *U.K.* **12 E5** 56 50N 4 0W
Grampian Mts., *U.K.* **12 E5** 56 50N 4 0W
Grampians, The, *Australia* **63 F3** 37 0S 142 20 E
Gran Canaria, *Canary Is.* **22 G4** 27 55N 15 35W
Gran Chaco, *S. Amer.* **94 B3** 25 0S 61 0W
Gran Paradiso, *Italy* **18 D7** 45 33N 7 17 E
Gran Sasso d'Itália, *Italy* **20 C5** 42 27N 13 42 E
Granada, *Nic.* **88 D2** 11 58N 86 0W
Granada, *Spain* **19 D4** 37 10N 3 35W
Granada, *U.S.A.* **81 F3** 38 4N 102 19W
Granadilla de Abona, *Canary Is.* **22 F3** 28 7N 16 33W
Granard, *Ireland* **13 C4** 53 47N 7 30W
Granbury, *U.S.A.* **81 J6** 32 27N 97 47W
Granby, *Canada* **79 A12** 45 25N 72 45W
Granby, *U.S.A.* **82 F11** 40 5N 105 56W
Grand →, *Canada* **78 D5** 42 51N 79 34W
Grand →, *Mo., U.S.A.* **80 F8** 39 23N 93 7W
Grand →, *S. Dak., U.S.A.* **80 C4** 45 40N 100 45W
Grand Bahama, *Bahamas* **88 A4** 26 40N 78 30W
Grand Bank, *Canada* **71 C8** 47 6N 55 48W
Grand Bassam, *Ivory C.* **50 G5** 5 10N 3 49W
Grand-Bourg, *Guadeloupe* **89 C7** 15 53N 61 19W
Grand Canal = Yun Ho →, *China* **35 E9** 39 10N 117 10 E
Grand Canyon, *U.S.A.* **83 H7** 36 3N 112 9W
Grand Canyon National Park, *U.S.A.* **83 H7** 36 15N 112 30W
Grand Cayman, *Cayman Is.* **88 C3** 19 20N 81 20W
Grand Centre, *Canada* **73 C6** 54 25N 110 13W
Grand Coulee, *U.S.A.* **82 C4** 47 57N 119 0W
Grand Coulee Dam, *U.S.A.* **82 C4** 47 57N 118 59W
Grand Erg du Bilma, *Niger* **51 E8** 18 30N 14 0 E
Grand Erg Occidental, *Algeria* **50 B6** 30 20N 1 0 E
Grand Erg Oriental, *Algeria* **50 B7** 30 0N 6 30 E
Grand Falls, *Canada* **71 C6** 47 3N 67 44W
Grand Falls-Windsor, *Canada* **71 C8** 48 56N 55 40W
Grand Forks, *Canada* **72 D5** 49 0N 118 30W
Grand Forks, *U.S.A.* **80 B6** 47 55N 97 3W
Grand Gorge, *U.S.A.* **79 D10** 42 21N 74 29W
Grand Haven, *U.S.A.* **76 D2** 43 4N 86 13W
Grand I., *Mich., U.S.A.* **76 B2** 46 31N 86 40W
Grand I., *N.Y., U.S.A.* **78 D6** 43 0N 78 58W
Grand Island, *U.S.A.* **80 E5** 40 55N 98 21W
Grand Isle, *La., U.S.A.* **81 L9** 29 14N 90 0W
Grand Isle, *Vt., U.S.A.* **79 B11** 44 43N 73 18W
Grand Junction, *U.S.A.* **83 G9** 39 4N 108 33W
Grand L., *N.B., Canada* **71 C6** 45 57N 66 7W
Grand L., *Nfld., Canada* **71 C8** 49 0N 57 30W
Grand L., *Nfld., Canada* **71 B7** 53 40N 60 30W
Grand L., *U.S.A.* **81 L8** 29 55N 92 47W
Grand Lake, *U.S.A.* **82 F11** 40 15N 105 49W
Grand Manan I., *Canada* **71 D6** 44 45N 66 52W
Grand Marais, *Canada* **80 B9** 47 45N 90 25W
Grand Marais, *U.S.A.* **76 B3** 46 40N 85 59W
Grand-Mère, *Canada* **70 C5** 46 36N 72 40W
Grand Prairie, *U.S.A.* **81 J6** 32 47N 97 0W
Grand Rapids, *Canada* **73 C9** 53 12N 99 19W
Grand Rapids, *Mich., U.S.A.* **76 D2** 42 58N 85 40W
Grand Rapids, *Minn., U.S.A.* **80 B8** 47 14N 93 31W
Grand St-Bernard, Col du, *Europe* **18 D7** 45 50N 7 10 E
Grand Teton, *U.S.A.* **82 E8** 43 54N 111 50W
Grand Teton National Park, *U.S.A.* **82 D8** 43 50N 110 50W
Grand Union Canal, *U.K.* **11 E7** 52 7N 0 53W
Grand View, *Canada* **73 C8** 51 10N 100 42W
Grande →, *Jujuy, Argentina* **94 A2** 24 20S 65 2W
Grande →, *Mendoza, Argentina* **94 D2** 36 52S 69 45W
Grande →, *Bolivia* **92 G6** 15 51S 64 39W
Grande →, *Bahia, Brazil* **93 F10** 11 30S 44 30W
Grande →, *Minas Gerais, Brazil* **93 H8** 20 6S 51 4W
Grande, B., *Argentina* **96 G3** 50 30S 68 20W
Grande, Rio →, *U.S.A.* **81 N6** 25 58N 97 9W
Grande Baleine, R. de la →, *Canada* **70 A4** 55 16N 77 47W
Grande Cache, *Canada* **72 C5** 53 53N 119 8W
Grande-Entrée, *Canada* **71 C7** 47 30N 61 40W
Grande Prairie, *Canada* **72 B5** 55 10N 118 50W
Grande-Rivière, *Canada* **71 C7** 48 26N 64 30W
Grande-Vallée, *Canada* **71 C6** 49 14N 65 8W
Grandfalls, *U.S.A.* **81 K3** 31 20N 102 51W
Grandview, *U.S.A.* **82 C4** 46 15N 119 54W
Graneros, *Chile* **94 C1** 34 5S 70 45W
Grangemouth, *U.K.* **12 E5** 56 1N 3 42W
Granger, *U.S.A.* **82 F9** 41 35N 109 58W
Grangeville, *U.S.A.* **82 D5** 45 56N 116 7W
Granisle, *Canada* **72 C3** 54 53N 126 13W
Granite City, *U.S.A.* **80 F9** 38 42N 90 9W
Granite Falls, *U.S.A.* **80 C7** 44 49N 95 33W
Granite L., *Canada* **71 C8** 48 8N 57 5W
Granite Mt., *U.S.A.* **85 M10** 33 5N 116 28W
Granite Pk., *U.S.A.* **82 D9** 45 10N 109 48W
Graniteville, *U.S.A.* **79 B12** 44 8N 72 29W
Granity, *N.Z.* **59 J3** 41 39S 171 51 E
Granja, *Brazil* **93 D10** 3 7S 40 50W
Granollers, *Spain* **19 B7** 41 39N 2 18 E
Grant, *U.S.A.* **80 E4** 40 53N 101 42W
Grant, Mt., *U.S.A.* **82 G4** 38 34N 118 48W
Grant City, *U.S.A.* **80 E7** 40 29N 94 25W
Grant I., *Australia* **60 B5** 11 10S 132 52 E
Grant Range, *U.S.A.* **83 G6** 38 30N 115 25W
Grantham, *U.K.* **10 E7** 52 55N 0 38W
Grantown-on-Spey, *U.K.* **12 D5** 57 20N 3 36W
Grants, *U.S.A.* **83 J10** 35 9N 107 52W
Grants Pass, *U.S.A.* **82 E2** 42 26N 123 19W
Grantsville, *U.S.A.* **82 F7** 40 36N 112 28W
Granville, *France* **18 B3** 48 50N 1 35W
Granville, *N. Dak., U.S.A.* **80 A4** 48 16N 100 47W
Granville, *N.Y., U.S.A.* **79 C11** 43 24N 73 16W
Granville, *Ohio, U.S.A.* **78 F2** 40 4N 82 31W
Granville L., *Canada* **73 B8** 56 18N 100 30W
Graskop, *S. Africa* **57 C5** 24 56S 30 49 E
Grass →, *Canada* **73 B9** 56 3N 96 33W
Grass Range, *U.S.A.* **82 C9** 47 0N 109 0W
Grass River Prov. Park, *Canada* **73 C8** 54 40N 100 50W
Grass Valley, *Calif., U.S.A.* **84 F6** 39 13N 121 4W
Grass Valley, *Oreg., U.S.A.* **82 D3** 45 22N 120 47W
Grasse, *France* **18 E7** 43 38N 6 56 E
Grassflat, *U.S.A.* **78 F6** 41 0N 78 6W
Grasslands Nat. Park, *Canada* **73 D7** 49 11N 107 38W
Grassy, *Australia* **62 G3** 40 3S 144 5 E
Graulhet, *France* **18 E4** 43 45N 1 59 E
Gravelbourg, *Canada* **73 D7** 49 50N 106 35W
's-Gravenhage, *Neths.* **15 B4** 52 7N 4 17 E
Gravenhurst, *Canada* **78 B5** 44 52N 79 20W
Gravesend, *Australia* **63 D5** 29 35S 150 20 E
Gravesend, *U.K.* **11 F8** 51 26N 0 22 E
Gravois, Pointe-à-, *Haiti* **89 C5** 18 15N 73 56W
Grayling, *U.S.A.* **76 C3** 44 40N 84 43W
Grays Harbor, *U.S.A.* **82 C1** 46 59N 124 1W
Grays L., *U.S.A.* **82 E8** 43 4N 111 26W
Grays River, *U.S.A.* **84 D3** 46 21N 123 37W
Graz, *Austria* **16 E8** 47 4N 15 27 E
Greasy L., *Canada* **72 A4** 62 55N 122 12W
Great Abaco I., *Bahamas* **88 A4** 26 25N 77 10W
Great Artesian Basin, *Australia* **62 C3** 23 0S 144 0 E
Great Australian Bight, *Australia* **61 F5** 33 30S 130 0 E
Great Bahama Bank, *Bahamas* **88 B4** 23 15N 78 0W
Great Barrier I., *N.Z.* **59 G5** 36 11S 175 25 E
Great Barrier Reef, *Australia* **62 B4** 18 0S 146 50 E
Great Barrington, *U.S.A.* **79 D11** 42 12N 73 22W
Great Basin, *U.S.A.* **82 G5** 40 0N 117 0W
Great Basin Nat. Park, *U.S.A.* **82 G6** 38 55N 114 14W
Great Bear →, *Canada* **68 B7** 65 0N 124 0W
Great Bear L., *Canada* **68 B8** 65 30N 120 0W
Great Belt = Store Bælt, *Denmark* **9 J14** 55 20N 11 0 E
Great Bend, *Kans., U.S.A.* **80 F5** 38 22N 98 46W
Great Bend, *Pa., U.S.A.* **79 E9** 41 58N 75 45W
Great Blasket I., *Ireland* **13 D1** 52 6N 10 32W
Great Britain, *Europe* **6 E5** 54 0N 2 15W
Great Codroy, *Canada* **71 C8** 47 51N 59 16W
Great Dividing Ra., *Australia* **62 C4** 23 0S 146 0 E
Great Driffield = Driffield, *U.K.* **10 C7** 54 0N 0 26W
Great Exuma I., *Bahamas* **88 B4** 23 30N 75 50W
Great Falls, *U.S.A.* **82 C8** 47 30N 111 17W
Great Fish = Groot Vis →, *S. Africa* **56 E4** 33 28S 27 5 E
Great Guana Cay, *Bahamas* **88 B4** 24 0N 76 20W
Great Inagua I., *Bahamas* **89 B5** 21 0N 73 20W
Great Indian Desert = Thar Desert, *India* **42 F5** 28 0N 72 0 E
Great Karoo, *S. Africa* **56 E3** 31 55S 21 0 E
Great Lake, *Australia* **62 G4** 41 50S 146 40 E
Great Lakes, *N. Amer.* **66 E11** 46 0N 84 0W
Great Malvern, *U.K.* **11 E5** 52 7N 2 18W
Great Miami →, *U.S.A.* **76 F3** 39 20N 84 40W
Great Ormes Head, *U.K.* **10 D4** 53 20N 3 52W
Great Ouse →, *U.K.* **10 E8** 52 48N 0 21 E
Great Palm I., *Australia* **62 B4** 18 45S 146 40 E
Great Plains, *N. Amer.* **74 A6** 47 0N 105 0W
Great Ruaha →, *Tanzania* **54 D4** 7 56S 37 52 E
Great Sacandaga Res., *U.S.A.* **79 C10** 43 6N 74 16W
Great Saint Bernard Pass = Grand St-Bernard, Col du, *Europe* **18 D7** 45 50N 7 10 E
Great Salt L., *U.S.A.* **82 F7** 41 15N 112 40W
Great Salt Lake Desert, *U.S.A.* **82 F7** 40 50N 113 30W
Great Salt Plains L., *U.S.A.* **81 G5** 36 45N 98 8W
Great Sandy Desert, *Australia* **60 D3** 21 0S 124 0 E
Great Sangi = Sangihe, Pulau, *Indonesia* **37 D7** 3 45N 125 30 E
Great Skellig, *Ireland* **13 E1** 51 47N 10 33W
Great Slave L., *Canada* **72 A5** 61 23N 115 38W
Great Smoky Mts. Nat. Park, *U.S.A.* **77 H4** 35 40N 83 40W
Great Snow Mt., *Canada* **72 B4** 57 26N 124 0W
Great Stour = Stour →, *U.K.* **11 F9** 51 18N 1 22 E
Great Victoria Desert, *Australia* **61 E4** 29 30S 126 30 E
Great Wall, *China* **34 E5** 38 30N 109 30 E
Great Whernside, *U.K.* **10 C6** 54 10N 1 58W
Great Yarmouth, *U.K.* **11 E9** 52 37N 1 44 E
Greater Antilles, *W. Indies* **89 C5** 17 40N 74 0W
Greater London □, *U.K.* **11 F7** 51 31N 0 6W
Greater Manchester □, *U.K.* **10 D5** 53 30N 2 15W
Greater Sunda Is., *Indonesia* **36 F4** 7 0S 112 0 E
Greco, C., *Cyprus* **23 E13** 34 57N 34 5 E
Gredos, Sierra de, *Spain* **19 B3** 40 20N 5 0W
Greece, *U.S.A.* **78 C7** 43 13N 77 41W
Greece ■, *Europe* **21 E9** 40 0N 23 0 E
Greeley, *Colo., U.S.A.* **80 E2** 40 25N 104 42W
Greeley, *Nebr., U.S.A.* **80 E5** 41 33N 98 32W
Greem-Bell, Ostrov, *Russia* **26 A7** 81 0N 62 0 E
Green, *U.S.A.* **82 E2** 43 9N 123 22W
Green →, *Ky., U.S.A.* **76 G2** 37 54N 87 30W
Green →, *Utah, U.S.A.* **83 G9** 38 11N 109 53W
Green B., *U.S.A.* **76 C2** 45 0N 87 30W
Green Bay, *U.S.A.* **76 C2** 44 31N 88 0W
Green C., *Australia* **63 F5** 37 13S 150 1 E
Green Cove Springs, *U.S.A.* **77 L5** 29 59N 81 42W
Green Lake, *Canada* **73 C7** 54 17N 107 47W
Green Mts., *U.S.A.* **79 C12** 43 45N 72 45W
Green River, *Utah, U.S.A.* **83 G8** 38 59N 110 10W
Green River, *Wyo., U.S.A.* **82 F9** 41 32N 109 28W
Green Valley, *U.S.A.* **83 L8** 31 52N 110 56W
Greenbank, *U.S.A.* **84 B4** 48 6N 122 34W
Greenbush, *Mich., U.S.A.* **78 B1** 44 35N 83 19W
Greenbush, *Minn., U.S.A.* **80 A6** 48 42N 96 11W
Greencastle, *U.S.A.* **76 F2** 39 38N 86 52W
Greene, *U.S.A.* **79 D9** 42 20N 75 46W
Greenfield, *Calif., U.S.A.* **84 J5** 36 19N 121 15W
Greenfield, *Calif., U.S.A.* **85 K8** 35 15N 119 0W
Greenfield, *Ind., U.S.A.* **76 F3** 39 47N 85 46W
Greenfield, *Iowa, U.S.A.* **80 E7** 41 18N 94 28W
Greenfield, *Mass., U.S.A.* **79 D12** 42 35N 72 36W
Greenfield, *Mo., U.S.A.* **81 G8** 37 25N 93 51W
Greenfield Park, *Canada* **79 A11** 45 29N 73 29W
Greenland ■, *N. Amer.* **4 C5** 66 0N 45 0W
Greenland Sea, *Arctic* **4 B7** 73 0N 10 0W
Greenock, *U.K.* **12 F4** 55 57N 4 46W
Greenore, *Ireland* **13 B5** 54 2N 6 8W
Greenore Pt., *Ireland* **13 D5** 52 14N 6 19W
Greenough, *Australia* **61 E1** 28 58S 114 43 E
Greenough →, *Australia* **61 E1** 28 51S 114 38 E
Greenough Pt., *Canada* **78 B3** 44 58N 81 26W
Greenport, *U.S.A.* **79 E12** 41 6N 72 22W
Greensboro, *Ga., U.S.A.* **77 J4** 33 35N 83 11W
Greensboro, *N.C., U.S.A.* **77 G6** 36 4N 79 48W
Greensboro, *Vt., U.S.A.* **79 B12** 44 36N 72 18W
Greensburg, *Ind., U.S.A.* **76 F3** 39 20N 85 29W
Greensburg, *Kans., U.S.A.* **81 G5** 37 36N 99 18W
Greensburg, *Pa., U.S.A.* **78 F5** 40 18N 79 33W
Greenstone Pt., *U.K.* **12 D3** 57 55N 5 37W
Greenvale, *Australia* **62 B4** 18 59S 145 7 E
Greenville, *Ala., U.S.A.* **77 K2** 31 50N 86 38W
Greenville, *Calif., U.S.A.* **84 E6** 40 8N 120 57W
Greenville, *Maine, U.S.A.* **77 C11** 45 28N 69 35W
Greenville, *Mich., U.S.A.* **76 D3** 43 11N 85 15W
Greenville, *Miss., U.S.A.* **81 J9** 33 24N 91 4W
Greenville, *Mo., U.S.A.* **81 G9** 37 8N 90 27W
Greenville, *N.C., U.S.A.* **77 H7** 35 37N 77 23W
Greenville, *N.H., U.S.A.* **79 D13** 42 46N 71 49W
Greenville, *N.Y., U.S.A.* **79 D10** 42 25N 74 1W
Greenville, *Ohio, U.S.A.* **76 E3** 40 6N 84 38W
Greenville, *Pa., U.S.A.* **78 E4** 41 24N 80 23W
Greenville, *S.C., U.S.A.* **77 H4** 34 51N 82 24W
Greenville, *Tenn., U.S.A.* **77 G4** 36 13N 82 51W
Greenville, *Tex., U.S.A.* **81 J6** 33 8N 96 7W
Greenwater Lake Prov. Park, *Canada* **73 C8** 52 32N 103 30W
Greenwich, *U.K.* **11 F8** 51 29N 0 1 E
Greenwich, *Conn., U.S.A.* **79 E11** 41 2N 73 38W
Greenwich, *N.Y., U.S.A.* **79 C11** 43 5N 73 30W
Greenwich, *Ohio, U.S.A.* **78 E2** 41 2N 82 31W
Greenwood, *Canada* **72 D5** 49 10N 118 40W
Greenwood, *Ark., U.S.A.* **81 H7** 35 13N 94 16W
Greenwood, *Ind., U.S.A.* **76 F2** 39 37N 86 7W
Greenwood, *Miss., U.S.A.* **81 J9** 33 31N 90 11W
Greenwood, *S.C., U.S.A.* **77 H4** 34 12N 82 10W
Greenwood, Mt., *Australia* **60 B5** 13 48S 130 4 E
Gregory, *U.S.A.* **80 D5** 43 14N 99 20W
Gregory →, *Australia* **62 B2** 17 53S 139 17 E
Gregory, L., *S. Austral., Australia* **63 D2** 28 55S 139 0 E
Gregory, L., *W. Austral., Australia* **61 E2** 25 38S 119 58 E
Gregory Downs, *Australia* **62 B2** 18 35S 138 45 E
Gregory L., *Australia* **60 D4** 20 0S 127 40 E
Gregory Ra., *Queens., Australia* **62 B3** 19 30S 143 40 E
Gregory Ra., *W. Austral., Australia* **60 D3** 21 20S 121 12 E
Greifswald, *Germany* **16 A7** 54 5N 13 23 E
Greiz, *Germany* **16 C7** 50 39N 12 10 E
Gremikha, *Russia* **24 A6** 67 59N 39 47 E
Grenå, *Denmark* **9 H14** 56 25N 10 53 E
Grenada, *U.S.A.* **81 J10** 33 47N 89 49W
Grenada ■, *W. Indies* **89 D7** 12 10N 61 40W
Grenadier I., *U.S.A.* **79 B8** 44 3N 76 22W
Grenadines, *W. Indies* **89 D7** 12 40N 61 20W

Grenen, Denmark 9 H14 57 44N 10 40 E
Grenfell, Australia 63 E4 33 52S 148 8 E
Grenfell, Canada 73 C8 50 30N 102 56W
Grenoble, France 18 D6 45 12N 5 42 E
Grenville, C., Australia 62 A3 12 0S 143 13 E
Grenville Chan., Canada 72 C3 53 40N 129 46W
Gresham, U.S.A. 84 E4 45 30N 122 26W
Gresik, Indonesia 37 G15 7 13S 112 38 E
Gretna, U.K. 12 F5 55 0N 3 3W
Grevenmacher, Lux. 15 E6 49 41N 6 26 E
Grey →, Canada 71 C8 47 34N 57 6W
Grey →, N.Z. 59 K3 42 27S 171 12 E
Grey, C., Australia 62 A2 13 0S 136 35 E
Grey Ra., Australia 63 D3 27 0S 143 30 E
Greybull, U.S.A. 82 D9 44 30N 108 3W
Greymouth, N.Z. 59 K3 42 29S 171 13 E
Greystones, Ireland 13 C5 53 9N 6 5W
Greytown, N.Z. 59 J5 41 5S 175 29 E
Greytown, S. Africa 57 D5 29 1S 30 36 E
Gribbell I., Canada 72 C3 53 23N 129 0W
Gridley, U.S.A. 84 F5 39 22N 121 42W
Griekwastad, S. Africa 56 D3 28 49S 23 15 E
Griffin, U.S.A. 77 J3 33 15N 84 16W
Griffith, Australia 63 E4 34 18S 146 2 E
Griffith, Canada 78 A7 45 15N 77 10W
Griffith I., Canada 78 B4 44 50N 80 55W
Grimaylov = Hrymayliv, Ukraine 17 D14 49 20N 26 5 E
Grimes, U.S.A. 84 F5 39 4N 121 54W
Grimsay, U.K. 12 D1 57 29N 7 14W
Grimsby, Canada 78 C5 43 12N 79 34W
Grimsby, U.K. 10 D7 53 34N 0 5W
Grímsey, Iceland 8 C5 66 33N 17 58W
Grimshaw, Canada 72 B5 56 10N 117 40W
Grimstad, Norway 9 G13 58 20N 8 35 E
Grindstone I., Canada 79 B8 44 43N 76 14W
Grinnell, U.S.A. 80 E8 41 45N 92 43W
Gris-Nez, C., France 18 A4 50 52N 1 35 E
Groais I., Canada 71 B8 50 55N 55 35W
Groblersdal, S. Africa 57 D4 25 15S 29 25 E
Grodno = Hrodna, Belarus 17 B12 53 42N 23 52 E
Grodzyanka = Hrodzyanka, Belarus 17 B15 53 31N 28 42 E
Groesbeck, U.S.A. 81 K6 31 31N 96 31W
Grójec, Poland 17 C11 51 50N 20 58 E
Grong, Norway 8 D15 64 25N 12 8 E
Groningen, Neths. 15 A6 53 15N 6 35 E
Groningen □, Neths. 15 A6 53 16N 6 40 E
Groom, U.S.A. 81 H4 35 12N 101 6W
Groot →, S. Africa 56 E3 33 45S 24 36 E
Groot Berg →, S. Africa 56 E2 32 47S 18 8 E
Groot-Brakrivier, S. Africa 56 E3 34 2S 22 18 E
Groot-Kei →, S. Africa 57 E4 32 41S 28 22 E
Groot Vis →, S. Africa 56 E4 33 28S 27 5 E
Groote Eylandt, Australia 62 A2 14 0S 136 40 E
Grootfontein, Namibia 56 B2 19 31S 18 6 E
Grootlaagte →, Africa 56 C3 20 55S 21 27 E
Grootvloer, S. Africa 56 E3 30 0S 20 40 E
Gros C., Canada 72 A6 61 59N 113 32W
Gros Morne Nat. Park, Canada 71 C8 49 40N 57 50W
Grossa, Pta., Spain 22 B8 39 6N 1 36 E
Grosser Arber, Germany 16 D7 49 6N 13 8 E
Grosseto, Italy 20 C4 42 46N 11 8 E
Grossglockner, Austria 16 E7 47 5N 12 40 E
Groswater B., Canada 71 B8 54 20N 57 40W
Groton, Conn., U.S.A. 79 E12 41 21N 72 5W
Groton, N.Y., U.S.A. 79 D8 42 36N 76 22W
Groton, S. Dak., U.S.A. 80 C5 45 27N 98 6W
Grouard Mission, Canada 72 B5 55 33N 116 9W
Groundhog →, Canada 70 C3 48 45N 82 58W
Grouw, Neths. 15 A5 53 5N 5 51 E
Grove City, U.S.A. 78 E4 41 10N 80 5W
Grove Hill, U.S.A. 77 K2 31 42N 87 47W
Groveland, U.S.A. 84 H6 37 50N 120 14W
Grover City, U.S.A. 85 K6 35 7N 120 37W
Groves, U.S.A. 81 L8 29 57N 93 54W
Groveton, U.S.A. 79 B13 44 36N 71 31W
Groznyy, Russia 25 F8 43 20N 45 45 E
Grudziądz, Poland 17 B10 53 30N 18 47 E
Gruinard B., U.K. 12 D3 57 56N 5 35W
Grundy Center, U.S.A. 80 D8 42 22N 92 47W
Gruver, U.S.A. 81 G4 36 16N 101 24W
Gryazi, Russia 24 D6 52 30N 39 58 E
Gryazovets, Russia 24 C7 58 50N 40 10 E
Gua, India 41 H14 22 18N 85 20 E
Gua Musang, Malaysia 39 K3 4 53N 101 58 E
Guacanayabo, G. de, Cuba 88 B4 20 40N 77 20W
Guachípas →, Argentina 94 B2 25 40S 65 30W
Guadalajara, Mexico 86 C4 20 40N 103 20W
Guadalajara, Spain 19 B4 40 37N 3 12W
Guadalcanal, Solomon Is. 64 H8 9 32S 160 12 E
Guadales, Argentina 94 C2 34 30S 67 55W
Guadalete →, Spain 19 D2 36 35N 6 13W
Guadalquivir →, Spain 19 D2 36 47N 6 22W
Guadalupe = Guadeloupe ■, W. Indies 89 C7 16 20N 61 40W
Guadalupe, Mexico 85 N10 32 4N 116 32W
Guadalupe, U.S.A. 85 L6 34 59N 120 33W
Guadalupe →, Mexico 85 N10 32 6N 116 51W
Guadalupe →, U.S.A. 81 L6 28 27N 96 47W
Guadalupe, Sierra de, Spain 19 C3 39 28N 5 30W
Guadalupe Bravos, Mexico 86 A3 31 20N 106 10W
Guadalupe I., Pac. Oc. 66 G8 29 0N 118 50W
Guadalupe Mts. Nat. Park, U.S.A. 81 K2 32 0N 104 30W
Guadalupe Peak, U.S.A. 81 K2 31 50N 104 52W
Guadalupe y Calvo, Mexico 86 B3 26 6N 106 58W
Guadarrama, Sierra de, Spain 19 B4 41 0N 4 0W
Guadeloupe ■, W. Indies 89 C7 16 20N 61 40W
Guadeloupe Passage, W. Indies 89 C7 16 50N 62 15W
Guadiana →, Portugal 19 D2 37 14N 7 22W
Guadix, Spain 19 D4 37 18N 3 11W
Guafo, Boca del, Chile 96 E2 43 35S 74 0W
Guainía →, Colombia 92 C5 2 1N 67 7W
Guaíra, Brazil 95 A5 24 5S 54 10W
Guaíra □, Paraguay 94 B4 25 45S 56 30W
Guaitecas, Is., Chile 96 E2 44 0S 74 30W
Guajará-Mirim, Brazil 92 F5 10 50S 65 20W
Guajira, Pen. de la, Colombia 92 A4 12 0N 72 0W
Gualán, Guatemala 88 C2 15 8N 89 22W
Gualeguay, Argentina 94 C4 33 10S 59 14W
Gualeguaychú, Argentina 94 C4 33 3S 59 31W
Gualequay →, Argentina 94 C4 33 19S 59 39W
Guam ■, Pac. Oc. 64 F6 13 27N 144 45 E
Guaminí, Argentina 94 D3 37 1S 62 28W
Guamúchil, Mexico 86 B3 25 25N 108 3W
Guanabacoa, Cuba 88 B3 23 8N 82 18W
Guanacaste, Cordillera del, Costa Rica 88 D2 10 40N 85 4W
Guanacevi, Mexico 86 B3 25 40N 106 0W
Guanahani = San Salvador I., Bahamas 89 B5 24 0N 74 40W
Guanajay, Cuba 88 B3 22 56N 82 42W
Guanajuato, Mexico 86 C4 21 0N 101 20W
Guanajuato □, Mexico 86 C4 20 40N 101 20W
Guandacol, Argentina 94 B2 29 30S 68 40W
Guane, Cuba 88 B3 22 10N 84 7W
Guangdong □, China 33 D6 23 0N 113 0 E
Guangling, China 34 E8 39 47N 114 22 E
Guangrao, China 35 F10 37 5N 118 25 E
Guangwu, China 34 F3 37 48N 105 57 E
Guangxi Zhuangzu Zizhiqu □, China 33 D5 24 0N 109 0 E
Guangzhou, China 33 D6 23 5N 113 10 E
Guanipa →, Venezuela 92 B6 9 56N 62 26W
Guannan, China 35 G10 34 8N 119 21 E
Guantánamo, Cuba 89 B4 20 10N 75 14W
Guantao, China 34 F8 36 42N 115 25 E
Guanyun, China 35 G10 34 20N 119 18 E
Guápiles, Costa Rica 88 D3 10 10N 83 46W
Guaporé, Brazil 95 B5 28 51S 51 54W
Guaporé →, Brazil 92 F5 11 55S 65 4W
Guaqui, Bolivia 92 G5 16 41S 68 54W
Guarapari, Brazil 95 A7 20 40S 40 30W
Guarapuava, Brazil 95 B5 25 20S 51 30W
Guaratinguetá, Brazil 95 A6 22 49S 45 9W
Guaratuba, Brazil 95 B6 25 53S 48 38W
Guarda, Portugal 19 B2 40 32N 7 20W
Guardafui, C. = Asir, Ras, Somali Rep. 46 E5 11 55N 51 10 E
Guárico □, Venezuela 92 B5 8 40N 66 35W
Guarujá, Brazil 95 A6 24 2S 46 25W
Guarus, Brazil 95 A7 21 44S 41 20W
Guasave, Mexico 86 B3 25 34N 108 27W
Guasdualito, Venezuela 92 B4 7 15N 70 44W
Guatemala, Guatemala 88 D1 14 40N 90 22W
Guatemala ■, Cent. Amer. 88 C1 15 40N 90 30W
Guaviare →, Colombia 92 C5 4 3N 67 44W
Guaxupé, Brazil 95 A6 21 10S 47 5W
Guayama, Puerto Rico 89 C6 17 59N 66 7W
Guayaquil, Ecuador 92 D3 2 15S 79 52W
Guayaquil, G. de, Ecuador 92 D2 3 10S 81 0W
Guaymas, Mexico 86 B2 27 59N 110 54W
Guba, Dem. Rep. of the Congo 55 E2 10 38S 26 27 E
Gubkin, Russia 25 D6 51 17N 37 32 E
Gudbrandsdalen, Norway 9 F14 61 33N 10 10 E
Guddu Barrage, Pakistan 40 E6 28 30N 69 50 E
Gudivada, India 41 L12 16 30N 81 3 E
Gudur, India 40 M11 14 12N 79 55 E
Guecho = Getxo, Spain 19 A4 43 21N 2 59W
Guelph, Canada 78 C4 43 35N 80 20W
Guéret, France 18 C4 46 11N 1 51 E
Guerneville, U.S.A. 84 G4 38 30N 123 0W
Guernica = Gernika-Lumo, Spain 19 A4 43 19N 2 40W
Guernsey, U.K. 11 H5 49 26N 2 35W
Guernsey, U.S.A. 80 D2 42 19N 104 45W
Guerrero □, Mexico 87 D5 17 30N 100 0W
Gügher, Iran 45 D8 29 28N 56 27 E
Guhakolak, Tanjung, Indonesia 37 G11 6 50S 105 14 E
Guia, Canary Is. 22 F4 28 8N 15 38W
Guia de Isora, Canary Is. 22 F3 28 12N 16 46W
Guia Lopes da Laguna, Brazil 95 A4 21 26S 56 7W
Guiana, S. Amer. 90 C4 5 10N 60 40W
Guider, Cameroon 51 G8 9 56N 13 57 E
Guidónia-Montecélio, Italy 20 C5 42 1N 12 45 E
Guijá, Mozam. 57 C5 24 27S 33 0 E
Guildford, U.K. 11 F7 51 14N 0 34W
Guilford, U.S.A. 79 E12 41 17N 72 41W
Guilin, China 33 D6 25 18N 110 15 E
Guillaume-Delisle L., Canada 70 A4 56 15N 76 17W
Güímar, Canary Is. 22 F3 28 18N 16 24W
Guimarães, Portugal 19 B1 41 28N 8 24W
Guimaras, Phil. 37 B6 10 35N 122 37 E
Guinda, U.S.A. 84 G4 38 50N 122 12W
Guinea, Africa 48 F4 8 0N 8 0 E
Guinea ■, W. Afr. 50 F3 10 20N 11 30W
Guinea, Gulf of, Atl. Oc. 48 F4 3 0N 2 30 E
Guinea-Bissau ■, Africa 50 F3 12 0N 15 0W
Güines, Cuba 88 B3 22 50N 82 0W
Guingamp, France 18 B2 48 34N 3 10W
Güiria, Venezuela 92 A6 10 32N 62 18W
Guiuan, Phil. 37 B7 11 5N 125 55 E
Guiyang, China 32 D5 26 32N 106 40 E
Guizhou □, China 32 D5 27 0N 107 0 E
Gujar Khan, Pakistan 42 C5 33 16N 73 19 E
Gujarat □, India 42 H4 23 20N 71 0 E
Gujranwala, Pakistan 42 C6 32 10N 74 12 E
Gujrat, Pakistan 42 C6 32 40N 74 2 E
Gulargambone, Australia 63 E4 31 20S 148 30 E
Gulbarga, India 40 L10 17 20N 76 50 E
Gulbene, Latvia 9 H22 57 8N 26 52 E
Gulf, The, Asia 45 E6 27 0N 50 0 E
Gulfport, U.S.A. 81 K10 30 22N 89 6W
Gulgong, Australia 63 E4 32 20S 149 49 E
Gulistan, Pakistan 42 D2 30 30N 66 35 E
Gull Lake, Canada 73 C7 50 10N 108 29W
Güllük, Turkey 21 F12 37 14N 27 35 E
Gulmarg, India 43 B6 34 3N 74 25 E
Gulshad, Kazakstan 26 E8 46 45N 74 25 E
Gulu, Uganda 54 B3 2 48N 32 17 E
Gulwe, Tanzania 54 D4 6 30S 36 25 E
Gumal →, Pakistan 42 D4 31 40N 71 50 E
Gumbaz, Pakistan 42 D3 30 2N 69 0 E
Gumel, Nigeria 50 F7 12 39N 9 22 E
Gumla, India 43 H11 23 3N 84 33 E
Gumlu, Australia 62 B4 19 53S 147 41 E
Gumma □, Japan 31 F9 36 30N 138 20 E
Gumzai, Indonesia 37 F8 5 28S 134 42 E
Guna, India 42 G7 24 40N 77 19 E
Gunisao →, Canada 73 C9 53 56N 97 53W
Gunisao L., Canada 73 C9 53 33N 96 15W
Gunjyal, Pakistan 42 C4 32 20N 71 55 E
Gunnbjørn Fjeld, Greenland 4 C6 68 55N 29 47W
Gunnedah, Australia 63 E5 30 59S 150 15 E
Gunnewin, Australia 63 D4 25 59S 148 33 E
Gunningbar Cr. →, Australia 63 E4 31 14S 147 6 E
Gunnison, Colo., U.S.A. 83 G10 38 33N 106 56W
Gunnison, Utah, U.S.A. 82 G8 39 9N 111 49W
Gunnison →, U.S.A. 83 G9 39 4N 108 35W
Gunpowder, Australia 62 B2 19 42S 139 22 E
Guntakal, India 40 M10 15 11N 77 27 E
Guntersville, U.S.A. 77 H2 34 21N 86 18W
Guntong, Malaysia 39 K3 4 36N 101 3 E
Guntur, India 41 L12 16 23N 80 30 E
Gunungapi, Indonesia 37 F7 6 45S 126 30 E
Gunungsitoli, Indonesia 36 D1 1 15N 97 30 E
Gunza, Angola 52 G2 10 50S 13 50 E
Guo He →, China 35 H9 32 59N 117 10 E
Guoyang, China 34 H9 33 32N 116 12 E
Gupis, Pakistan 43 A5 36 15N 73 20 E
Gurdaspur, India 42 C6 32 5N 75 31 E
Gurdon, U.S.A. 81 J8 33 55N 93 9W
Gurgaon, India 42 E7 28 27N 77 1 E
Gurgueia →, Brazil 93 E10 6 50S 43 24W
Gurha, India 42 G4 25 12N 71 39 E
Guri, Embalse de, Venezuela 92 B6 7 50N 62 52W
Gurkha, Nepal 43 E11 28 5N 84 40 E
Gurley, Australia 63 D4 29 45S 149 48 E
Gurnet Point, U.S.A. 79 D14 42 1N 70 34W
Gurué, Mozam. 55 F4 15 25S 36 58 E
Gurun, Malaysia 39 K3 5 49N 100 27 E
Gürün, Turkey 25 G6 38 43N 37 15 E
Gurupá, Brazil 93 D8 1 25S 51 35W
Gurupá, I. Grande de, Brazil 93 D8 1 25S 51 45W
Gurupi, Brazil 93 F9 11 43S 49 4W
Gurupi →, Brazil 93 D9 1 13S 46 6W
Guryev = Atyraū, Kazakstan 25 E9 47 5N 52 0 E
Gusau, Nigeria 50 F7 12 12N 6 40 E
Gusev, Russia 9 J20 54 35N 22 10 E
Gushan, China 35 E12 39 50N 123 35 E
Gushgy, Turkmenistan 26 F7 35 20N 62 18 E
Gusinoozersk, Russia 27 D11 51 16N 106 27 E
Gustavus, U.S.A. 72 B1 58 25N 135 44W
Gustine, U.S.A. 84 H6 37 16N 121 0W
Güstrow, Germany 16 B7 53 47N 12 10 E
Gütersloh, Germany 16 C5 51 54N 8 24 E
Gutha, Australia 61 E2 28 58S 115 55 E
Guthalungra, Australia 62 B4 19 52S 147 50 E
Guthrie, Okla., U.S.A. 81 H6 35 53N 97 25W
Guthrie, Tex., U.S.A. 81 J4 33 37N 100 19W
Guttenberg, U.S.A. 80 D9 42 47N 91 6W
Guyana ■, S. Amer. 92 C7 5 0N 59 0W
Guyane française = French Guiana ■, S. Amer. 93 C8 4 0N 53 0W
Guyang, China 34 D6 41 0N 110 5 E
Guyenne, France 18 D4 44 30N 0 40 E
Guymon, U.S.A. 81 G4 36 41N 101 29W
Guyra, Australia 63 E5 30 15S 151 40 E
Guyuan, Hebei, China 34 D8 41 37N 115 40 E
Guyuan, Ningxia Huizu, China 34 G4 36 0N 106 20 E
Guzhen, China 35 H9 33 22N 117 18 E
Guzmán, L. de, Mexico 86 A3 31 25N 107 25W
Gvardeysk, Russia 9 J19 54 39N 21 5 E
Gwa, Burma 41 L19 17 36N 94 34 E
Gwaai, Zimbabwe 55 F2 19 15S 27 45 E
Gwabegar, Australia 63 E4 30 31S 149 0 E
Gwādar, Pakistan 40 G3 25 10N 62 18 E
Gwalior, India 42 F8 26 12N 78 10 E
Gwanda, Zimbabwe 55 G2 20 55S 29 0 E
Gwane, Dem. Rep. of the Congo 54 B2 4 45N 25 48 E
Gweebarra B., Ireland 13 B3 54 51N 8 23W
Gweedore, Ireland 13 A3 55 3N 8 13W
Gweru, Zimbabwe 55 F2 19 28S 29 45 E
Gwinn, U.S.A. 76 B2 46 19N 87 27W
Gwydir →, Australia 63 D4 29 27S 149 48 E
Gwynedd □, U.K. 10 E3 52 52N 4 10W
Gyandzha = Gäncä, Azerbaijan 25 F8 40 45N 46 20 E
Gyaring Hu, China 32 C4 34 50N 97 40 E
Gydanskiy Poluostrov, Russia 26 C8 70 0N 78 0 E
Gympie, Australia 63 D5 26 11S 152 38 E
Gyöngyös, Hungary 17 E10 47 48N 19 56 E
Győr, Hungary 17 E9 47 41N 17 40 E
Gypsum Pt., Canada 72 A6 61 53N 114 35W
Gypsumville, Canada 73 C9 51 45N 98 40W
Gyula, Hungary 17 E11 46 38N 21 17 E
Gyumri, Armenia 25 F7 40 47N 43 50 E
Gyzylarbat, Turkmenistan 26 F6 39 4N 56 23 E
Gyzyletrek, Turkmenistan 45 B7 37 36N 54 46 E

H

Ha 'Arava →, Israel 47 E4 30 50N 35 20 E
Ha Tien, Vietnam 39 G5 10 23N 104 29 E
Ha Tinh, Vietnam 38 C5 18 20N 105 54 E
Ha Trung, Vietnam 38 C5 19 58N 105 50 E
Haaksbergen, Neths. 15 B6 52 9N 6 45 E
Haapsalu, Estonia 9 G20 58 56N 23 30 E
Haarlem, Neths. 15 B4 52 23N 4 39 E
Haast →, N.Z. 59 K2 43 50S 169 2 E
Haast Bluff, Australia 60 D5 23 22S 132 0 E
Hab →, Pakistan 42 G3 24 53N 66 41 E
Hab Nadi Chauki, Pakistan 42 G2 25 0N 66 50 E
Habaswein, Kenya 54 B4 1 2N 39 30 E
Habay, Canada 72 B5 58 50N 118 44W
Ḩabbānīyah, Iraq 44 C4 33 17N 43 29 E
Haboro, Japan 30 B10 44 22N 141 42 E
Ḩabshān, U.A.E. 45 F7 23 50N 53 37 E
Hachijō-Jima, Japan 31 H9 33 5N 139 45 E
Hachinohe, Japan 30 D10 40 30N 141 29 E
Hachiōji, Japan 31 G9 35 40N 139 20 E
Hachŏn, N. Korea 35 D15 41 29N 129 2 E
Hackensack, U.S.A. 79 F10 40 53N 74 3W
Hackettstown, U.S.A. 79 F10 40 51N 74 50W
Hadali, Pakistan 42 C5 32 16N 72 11 E
Hadarba, Ras, Sudan 51 D13 22 4N 36 51 E
Hadarom □, Israel 47 E4 31 0N 35 0 E
Hadd, Ra's al, Oman 46 C6 22 35N 59 50 E
Hadejia, Nigeria 50 F7 12 30N 10 5 E
Ḩadera, Israel 47 C3 32 27N 34 55 E
Ḩadera, N. →, Israel 47 C3 32 28N 34 52 E
Haderslev, Denmark 9 J13 55 15N 9 30 E
Hadhramaut = Ḩaḑramawt, Yemen 46 D4 15 30N 49 30 E
Hadibu, Yemen 46 E5 12 39N 54 2 E
Hadong, S. Korea 35 G14 35 5N 127 44 E
Ḩaḑramawt, Yemen 46 D4 15 30N 49 30 E
Ḩadrānīyah, Iraq 44 C4 35 38N 43 14 E
Hadrian's Wall, U.K. 10 B5 55 0N 2 30W
Haeju, N. Korea 35 E13 38 3N 125 45 E
Haenam, S. Korea 35 G14 34 34N 126 35 E
Haerhpin = Harbin, China 35 B14 45 48N 126 40 E
Hafar al Bāţin, Si. Arabia 44 D5 28 32N 45 52 E
Ḩafirat al 'Aydā, Si. Arabia 44 E3 26 26N 39 12 E
Ḩafit, Oman 45 F7 23 59N 55 49 E
Ḩafit, Jabal, Oman 45 E7 24 3N 55 46 E
Hafizabad, Pakistan 42 C5 32 5N 73 40 E
Haflong, India 41 G18 25 10N 93 5 E
Hafnarfjörður, Iceland 8 D3 64 4N 21 57W
Haft Gel, Iran 45 D6 31 30N 49 32 E
Hafun, Ras, Somali Rep. 46 E5 10 29N 51 30 E
Hagalil, Israel 47 C4 32 53N 35 18 E
Hagen, Germany 16 C4 51 21N 7 27 E
Hagerman, U.S.A. 81 J2 33 7N 104 20W
Hagerstown, U.S.A. 76 F7 39 39N 77 43W
Hagersville, Canada 78 D4 42 58N 80 3W
Hagfors, Sweden 9 F15 60 3N 13 45 E
Hagi, Japan 31 G5 34 30N 131 22 E
Hagolan, Syria 47 C4 33 0N 35 45 E
Hagondange, France 18 B7 49 16N 6 11 E
Hags Hd., Ireland 13 D2 52 57N 9 28W
Hague, C. de la, France 18 B3 49 44N 1 56W
Hague, The = 's-Gravenhage, Neths. 15 B4 52 7N 4 17 E
Haguenau, France 18 B7 48 49N 7 47 E
Haicheng, China 35 D12 40 50N 122 45 E
Haidar Khel, Afghan. 42 C3 33 58N 68 38 E
Haidargarh, India 43 F9 26 37N 81 22 E
Haifa = Ḩefa, Israel 47 C4 32 46N 35 0 E
Haikou, China 33 D6 20 1N 110 16 E
Ḩā'il, Si. Arabia 44 E4 27 28N 41 45 E
Hailar, China 33 B6 49 10N 119 38 E
Hailey, U.S.A. 82 E6 43 31N 114 19W
Haileybury, Canada 70 C4 47 30N 79 38W
Hailin, China 35 B15 44 37N 129 30 E
Hailong, China 35 C13 42 32N 125 40 E
Hailuoto, Finland 8 D21 65 3N 24 45 E
Hainan □, China 33 E5 19 0N 109 30 E
Hainaut □, Belgium 15 D4 50 30N 4 0 E
Haines, Alaska, U.S.A. 72 B1 59 14N 135 26W
Haines, Oreg., U.S.A. 82 D5 44 55N 117 56W
Haines City, U.S.A. 77 L5 28 7N 81 38W
Haines Junction, Canada 72 A1 60 45N 137 30W
Haiphong, Vietnam 32 D5 20 47N 106 41 E
Haiti ■, W. Indies 89 C5 19 0N 72 30W
Haiya, Sudan 51 E13 18 20N 36 21 E
Haiyang, China 35 F11 36 47N 121 9 E
Haiyuan, China 34 F3 36 35N 105 52 E
Haizhou, China 35 G10 34 37N 119 7 E
Haizhou Wan, China 35 G10 34 50N 119 20 E
Hajdúböszörmény, Hungary 17 E11 47 40N 21 30 E
Hajipur, India 43 G11 25 45N 85 13 E
Ḩājjī Muḩsin, Iraq 44 C5 32 35N 45 29 E
Ḩājjīābād, Iran 45 D7 28 19N 55 55 E
Ḩājjīābād-e Zarrīn, Iran 45 C7 33 9N 54 51 E
Hajnówka, Poland 17 B12 52 47N 23 35 E
Hakansson, Mts., Dem. Rep. of the Congo 55 D2 8 40S 25 45 E
Hakkâri, Turkey 44 B4 37 34N 43 44 E
Hakken-Zan, Japan 31 G7 34 10N 135 54 E
Hakodate, Japan 30 D10 41 45N 140 44 E
Haku-San, Japan 31 F8 36 9N 136 46 E
Hakui, Japan 31 F8 36 53N 136 47 E
Hala, Pakistan 40 G6 25 43N 68 20 E
Ḩalab, Syria 44 B3 36 10N 37 15 E
Ḩalabjah, Iraq 44 C5 35 10N 45 58 E
Halaib, Sudan 51 D13 22 12N 36 30 E
Hālat 'Ammār, Si. Arabia 44 D3 29 10N 36 4 E
Halbā, Lebanon 47 A5 34 34N 36 6 E
Halberstadt, Germany 16 C6 51 54N 11 3 E
Halcombe, N.Z. 59 J5 40 8S 175 30 E
Halcon, Phil. 37 B6 13 0N 121 30 E
Halden, Norway 9 G14 59 9N 11 23 E
Haldia, India 41 H16 22 5N 88 3 E
Haldwani, India 43 E8 29 31N 79 30 E
Hale →, Australia 62 C2 24 56S 135 53 E
Haleakala Crater, U.S.A. 74 H16 20 43N 156 16W
Halesowen, U.K. 11 E5 52 27N 2 3W
Haleyville, U.S.A. 77 H2 34 14N 87 37W
Halfway →, Canada 72 B4 56 12N 121 32W
Halia, India 43 G10 24 50N 82 19 E
Haliburton, Canada 78 A6 45 3N 78 30W
Halifax, Australia 62 B4 18 32S 146 22 E
Halifax, Canada 71 D7 44 38N 63 35W
Halifax, U.K. 10 D6 53 43N 1 52W
Halifax, U.S.A. 78 F8 40 25N 76 55W
Halifax B., Australia 62 B4 18 50S 147 0 E
Halifax I., Namibia 56 D2 26 38S 15 4 E
Halīl →, Iran 45 E8 27 40N 58 30 E
Halkirk, U.K. 12 C5 58 30N 3 29W
Hall Beach = Sanirajak, Canada 69 B11 68 46N 81 12W
Hall Pen., Canada 69 B13 63 30N 66 0W
Hall Pt., Australia 60 C3 15 40S 124 23 E
Halland, Sweden 9 H15 57 8N 12 47 E
Halle, Belgium 15 D4 50 44N 4 13 E
Halle, Germany 16 C6 51 30N 11 56 E
Hällefors, Sweden 9 G16 59 47N 14 31 E
Hallett, Australia 63 E2 33 25S 138 55 E
Hallettsville, U.S.A. 81 L6 29 27N 96 57W
Hallim, S. Korea 35 H14 33 24N 126 15 E
Hallingdalselvi →, Norway 9 F13 60 23N 9 35 E
Halls Creek, Australia 60 C4 18 16S 127 38 E
Hallsberg, Sweden 9 G16 59 5N 15 7 E
Hallstead, U.S.A. 79 E9 41 58N 75 45W
Halmahera, Indonesia 37 D7 0 40N 128 0 E
Halmstad, Sweden 9 H15 56 41N 12 52 E
Hälsingborg = Helsingborg, Sweden 9 H15 56 3N 12 42 E
Hälsingland, Sweden 9 F16 61 40N 16 5 E
Halstead, U.K. 11 F8 51 57N 0 40 E
Haltiatunturi, Finland 8 B19 69 17N 21 18 E
Halton □, U.K. 10 D5 53 22N 2 45W
Haltwhistle, U.K. 10 C5 54 58N 2 26W
Ḩalul, Qatar 45 E7 25 40N 52 40 E
Halvad, India 42 H4 23 1N 71 11 E
Ḩalvān, Iran 45 C8 33 57N 56 15 E
Ham Tan, Vietnam 39 G6 10 40N 107 45 E
Ham Yen, Vietnam 38 A5 22 4N 105 3 E
Hamab, Namibia 56 D2 28 7S 19 16 E
Hamada, Japan 31 G6 34 56N 132 4 E
Hamadān, Iran 45 C6 34 52N 48 32 E

Hamadān □, Iran 45 C6 35 0N 49 0 E
Hamāh, Syria 44 C3 35 5N 36 40 E
Hamamatsu, Japan 31 G8 34 45N 137 45 E
Hamar, Norway 9 F14 60 48N 11 7 E
Hamâta, Gebel, Egypt 44 E2 24 17N 35 0 E
Hambantota, Sri Lanka 40 R12 6 10N 81 10 E
Hamber Prov. Park, Canada 72 C5 52 20N 118 0W
Hamburg, Germany 16 B5 53 33N 9 59 E
Hamburg, Ark., U.S.A. 81 J9 33 14N 91 48W
Hamburg, N.Y., U.S.A. 78 D6 42 43N 78 50W
Hamburg, Pa., U.S.A. 79 F9 40 33N 75 59W
Ḥamḍ, W. al →, Si. Arabia 44 E3 24 55N 36 20 E
Hamden, U.S.A. 79 E12 41 23N 72 54W
Häme, Finland 9 F20 61 38N 25 10 E
Hämeenlinna, Finland 9 F21 61 0N 24 28 E
Hamelin Pool, Australia 61 E1 26 22S 114 20 E
Hameln, Germany 16 B5 52 6N 9 21 E
Hamerkaz □, Israel 47 C3 32 15N 34 55 E
Hamersley Ra., Australia 60 D2 22 0S 117 45 E
Hamhung, N. Korea 35 E14 39 54N 127 30 E
Hami, China 32 B4 42 55N 93 25 E
Hamilton, Australia 63 F3 37 45S 142 2 E
Hamilton, Canada 78 C5 43 15N 79 50W
Hamilton, N.Z. 59 G5 37 47S 175 19 E
Hamilton, U.K. 12 F4 55 46N 4 2W
Hamilton, Ala., U.S.A. 77 H1 34 9N 87 59W
Hamilton, Mont., U.S.A. 82 C6 46 15N 114 10W
Hamilton, N.Y., U.S.A. 79 D9 42 50N 75 33W
Hamilton, Ohio, U.S.A. 76 F3 39 24N 84 34W
Hamilton, Tex., U.S.A. 81 K5 31 42N 98 7W
Hamilton →, Australia 62 C2 23 30S 139 47 E
Hamilton City, U.S.A. 84 F4 39 45N 122 1W
Hamilton Inlet, Canada 71 B8 54 0N 57 30W
Hamilton Mt., U.S.A. 79 C10 43 25N 74 22W
Hamina, Finland 9 F22 60 34N 27 12 E
Hamirpur, H.P., India 42 D7 31 41N 76 31 E
Hamirpur, Ut. P., India 43 G9 25 57N 80 9 E
Hamlet, U.S.A. 77 H6 34 53N 79 42W
Hamley Bridge, Australia 63 E2 34 17S 138 35 E
Hamlin = Hameln, Germany 16 B5 52 6N 9 21 E
Hamlin, N.Y., U.S.A. 78 C7 43 17N 77 55W
Hamlin, Tex., U.S.A. 81 J4 32 53N 100 8W
Hamm, Germany 16 C4 51 40N 7 50 E
Ḥammār, Hawr al, Iraq 44 D5 30 50N 47 10 E
Hammerfest, Norway 8 A20 70 39N 23 41 E
Hammond, Ind., U.S.A. 76 E2 41 38N 87 30W
Hammond, La., U.S.A. 81 K9 30 30N 90 28W
Hammond, N.Y., U.S.A. 79 B9 44 27N 75 42W
Hammondsport, U.S.A. 78 D7 42 25N 77 13W
Hammonton, U.S.A. 76 F8 39 39N 74 48W
Hampden, N.Z. 59 L3 45 18S 170 50 E
Hampshire □, U.K. 11 F6 51 7N 1 23W
Hampshire Downs, U.K. 11 F6 51 15N 1 10W
Hampton, N.B., Canada 71 C6 45 32N 65 51W
Hampton, Ont., Canada 78 C6 43 58N 78 45W
Hampton, Ark., U.S.A. 81 J8 33 32N 92 28W
Hampton, Iowa, U.S.A. 80 D8 42 45N 93 13W
Hampton, N.H., U.S.A. 79 D14 42 57N 70 50W
Hampton, S.C., U.S.A. 77 J5 32 52N 81 7W
Hampton, Va., U.S.A. 76 G7 37 2N 76 21W
Hampton Bays, U.S.A. 79 F12 40 53N 72 30W
Hampton Tableland, Australia 61 F4 32 0S 127 0 E
Hamyang, S. Korea 35 G14 35 32N 127 42 E
Han Pijesak, Bos.-H. 21 B8 44 5N 18 57 E
Hana, U.S.A. 74 H17 20 45N 155 59W
Hanak, Si. Arabia 44 E3 25 32N 37 0 E
Hanamaki, Japan 30 E10 39 23N 141 7 E
Hanang, Tanzania 54 C4 4 30S 35 25 E
Hanau, Germany 16 C5 50 7N 8 56 E
Hanbogd = Ihbulag, Mongolia 34 C4 43 11N 107 10 E
Hancheng, China 34 G6 35 31N 110 25 E
Hancock, Mich., U.S.A. 80 B10 47 8N 88 35W
Hancock, N.Y., U.S.A. 79 E9 41 57N 75 17W
Handa, Japan 31 G8 34 53N 136 55 E
Handan, China 34 F8 36 35N 114 28 E
Handeni, Tanzania 54 D4 5 25S 38 2 E
Handwara, India 43 B6 34 21N 74 20 E
Hanegev, Israel 47 E4 30 50N 35 0 E
Hanford, U.S.A. 84 J7 36 20N 119 39W
Hang Chat, Thailand 38 C2 18 20N 99 21 E
Hang Dong, Thailand 38 C2 18 41N 98 55 E
Hangang →, S. Korea 35 F14 37 50N 126 30 E
Hangayn Nuruu, Mongolia 32 B4 47 30N 99 0 E
Hangchou = Hangzhou, China 33 C7 30 18N 120 11 E
Hanggin Houqi, China 34 D4 40 58N 107 4 E
Hanggin Qi, China 34 E5 39 52N 108 50 E
Hangu, China 35 E9 39 18N 117 53 E
Hangzhou, China 33 C7 30 18N 120 11 E
Hangzhou Wan, China 33 C7 30 15N 120 45 E
Hanhongor, Mongolia 34 C3 43 55N 104 28 E
Ḥanīdh, Si. Arabia 45 E6 26 35N 48 38 E
Ḥanīsh, Yemen 46 E3 13 45N 42 46 E
Hankinson, U.S.A. 80 B6 46 4N 96 54W
Hanko, Finland 9 G20 59 50N 22 57 E
Hanksville, U.S.A. 83 G8 38 22N 110 43W
Hanle, India 43 C8 32 42N 79 4 E
Hanmer Springs, N.Z. 59 K4 42 32S 172 50 E
Hann →, Australia 60 C4 17 26S 126 17 E
Hann, Mt., Australia 60 C4 15 45S 126 0 E
Hanna, Canada 72 C6 51 40N 111 54W
Hanna, U.S.A. 82 F10 41 52N 106 34W
Hannah B., Canada 70 B4 51 40N 80 0W
Hannibal, Mo., U.S.A. 80 F9 39 42N 91 22W
Hannibal, N.Y., U.S.A. 79 C8 43 19N 76 35W
Hannover, Germany 16 B5 52 22N 9 46 E
Hanoi, Vietnam 32 D5 21 5N 105 55 E
Hanover = Hannover, Germany 16 B5 52 22N 9 46 E
Hanover, Canada 78 B3 44 9N 81 2W
Hanover, S. Africa 56 E3 31 4S 24 29 E
Hanover, N.H., U.S.A. 79 C12 43 42N 72 17W
Hanover, Ohio, U.S.A. 78 F2 40 4N 82 16W
Hanover, Pa., U.S.A. 76 F7 39 48N 76 59W
Hanover, I., Chile 96 G2 51 0S 74 50W
Hansdiha, India 43 G12 24 36N 87 5 E
Hansi, India 42 E6 29 10N 75 57 E
Hanson, L., Australia 63 E2 31 0S 136 15 E
Hantsavichy, Belarus 17 B14 52 49N 26 30 E
Hanumangarh, India 42 E6 29 35N 74 19 E
Hanzhong, China 34 H4 33 10N 107 1 E
Hanzhuang, China 35 G9 34 33N 117 23 E
Haora, India 43 H13 22 37N 88 20 E
Haparanda, Sweden 8 D21 65 52N 24 8 E
Happy, U.S.A. 81 H4 34 45N 101 52W
Happy Camp, U.S.A. 82 F2 41 48N 123 23W
Happy Valley-Goose Bay, Canada 71 B7 53 15N 60 20W
Hapsu, N. Korea 35 D15 41 13N 128 51 E
Hapur, India 42 E7 28 45N 77 45 E
Ḥaql, Si. Arabia 47 F3 29 10N 34 58 E
Har, Indonesia 37 F8 5 16S 133 14 E
Har-Ayrag, Mongolia 34 B5 45 47N 109 16 E
Har Hu, China 32 C4 38 20N 97 38 E
Har Us Nuur, Mongolia 32 B4 48 0N 92 0 E
Har Yehuda, Israel 47 D3 31 35N 34 57 E
Ḥaraḍ, Si. Arabia 46 C4 24 22N 49 0 E
Haranomachi, Japan 30 F10 37 38N 140 58 E
Harare, Zimbabwe 55 F3 17 43S 31 2 E
Harbin, China 35 B14 45 48N 126 40 E
Harbor Beach, U.S.A. 78 C2 43 51N 82 39W
Harbour Breton, Canada 71 C8 47 29N 55 50W
Harbour Deep, Canada 71 B8 50 25N 56 32W
Harda, India 42 H7 22 27N 77 5 E
Hardangerfjorden, Norway 9 F12 60 5N 6 0 E
Hardangervidda, Norway 9 F12 60 7N 7 20 E
Hardap Dam, Namibia 56 C2 24 32S 17 50 E
Hardenberg, Neths. 15 B6 52 34N 6 37 E
Harderwijk, Neths. 15 B5 52 21N 5 38 E
Hardey →, Australia 60 D2 22 45S 116 8 E
Hardin, U.S.A. 82 D10 45 44N 107 37W
Harding, S. Africa 57 E4 30 35S 29 55 E
Harding Ra., Australia 60 C3 16 17S 124 55 E
Hardisty, Canada 72 C6 52 40N 111 18W
Hardoi, India 43 F9 27 26N 80 6 E
Hardwar = Haridwar, India 42 E8 29 58N 78 9 E
Hardwick, U.S.A. 79 B12 44 30N 72 22W
Hardy, Pen., Chile 96 H3 55 30S 68 20W
Hare B., Canada 71 B8 51 15N 55 45W
Hareid, Norway 9 E12 62 22N 6 1 E
Harer, Ethiopia 46 F3 9 20N 42 8 E
Hargeisa, Somali Rep. 46 F3 9 30N 44 2 E
Hari →, Indonesia 36 E2 1 16S 104 5 E
Haria, Canary Is. 22 E6 29 8N 13 32W
Haridwar, India 42 E8 29 58N 78 9 E
Harim, Jabal al, Oman 45 E8 25 58N 56 14 E
Haringhata →, Bangla. 41 J16 22 0N 89 58 E
Harīrūd →, Asia 40 A2 37 24N 60 38 E
Härjedalen, Sweden 9 E15 62 22N 13 5 E
Harlan, Iowa, U.S.A. 80 E7 41 39N 95 19W
Harlan, Ky., U.S.A. 77 G4 36 51N 83 19W
Harlech, U.K. 10 E3 52 52N 4 6W
Harlem, U.S.A. 82 B9 48 32N 108 47W
Harlingen, Neths. 15 A5 53 11N 5 25 E
Harlingen, U.S.A. 81 M6 26 12N 97 42W
Harlow, U.K. 11 F8 51 46N 0 8 E
Harlowton, U.S.A. 82 C9 46 26N 109 50W
Harnai, Pakistan 42 D2 30 6N 67 56 E
Harney Basin, U.S.A. 82 E4 43 30N 119 0W
Harney L., U.S.A. 82 E4 43 14N 119 8W
Harney Peak, U.S.A. 80 D3 43 52N 103 32W
Härnösand, Sweden 9 E17 62 38N 17 55 E
Haroldswick, U.K. 12 A8 60 48N 0 50W
Harp L., Canada 71 A7 55 5N 61 50W
Harper, Liberia 50 H4 4 25N 7 43W
Harrai, India 43 H8 22 37N 79 13 E
Harrand, Pakistan 42 E4 29 28N 70 3 E
Harricana →, Canada 70 B4 50 56N 79 32W
Harriman, U.S.A. 77 H3 35 56N 84 33W
Harrington Harbour, Canada 71 B8 50 31N 59 30W
Harris, U.K. 12 D2 57 50N 6 55W
Harris, Sd. of, U.K. 12 D1 57 44N 7 6W
Harris L., Australia 63 E2 31 10S 135 10 E
Harris Pt., Canada 78 C2 43 6N 82 9W
Harrisburg, Ill., U.S.A. 81 G10 37 44N 88 32W
Harrisburg, Nebr., U.S.A. 80 E3 41 33N 103 44W
Harrisburg, Pa., U.S.A. 78 F8 40 16N 76 53W
Harrismith, S. Africa 57 D4 28 15S 29 8 E
Harrison, Ark., U.S.A. 81 G8 36 14N 93 7W
Harrison, Maine, U.S.A. 79 B14 44 7N 70 39W
Harrison, Nebr., U.S.A. 80 D3 42 41N 103 53W
Harrison, C., Canada 71 B8 54 55N 57 55W
Harrison L., Canada 72 D4 49 33N 121 50W
Harrisonburg, U.S.A. 76 F6 38 27N 78 52W
Harrisonville, U.S.A. 80 F7 38 39N 94 21W
Harriston, Canada 78 C4 43 57N 80 53W
Harrisville, Mich., U.S.A. 78 B1 44 39N 83 17W
Harrisville, N.Y., U.S.A. 79 B9 44 9N 75 19W
Harrisville, Pa., U.S.A. 78 E5 41 8N 80 0W
Harrodsburg, U.S.A. 76 G3 37 46N 84 51W
Harrogate, U.K. 10 C6 54 0N 1 33W
Harrow, U.K. 11 F7 51 35N 0 21W
Harrowsmith, Canada 79 B8 44 24N 76 40W
Harry S. Truman Reservoir, U.S.A. 80 F7 38 16N 93 24W
Harsīn, Iran 44 C5 34 18N 47 33 E
Harstad, Norway 8 B17 68 48N 16 30 E
Harsud, India 42 H7 22 6N 76 44 E
Hart, U.S.A. 76 D2 43 42N 86 22W
Hart, L., Australia 63 E2 31 10S 136 25 E
Hartbees →, S. Africa 56 D3 28 45S 20 32 E
Hartford, Conn., U.S.A. 79 E12 41 46N 72 41W
Hartford, Ky., U.S.A. 76 G2 37 27N 86 55W
Hartford, S. Dak., U.S.A. 80 D6 43 38N 96 57W
Hartford, Wis., U.S.A. 80 D10 43 19N 88 22W
Hartford City, U.S.A. 76 E3 40 27N 85 22W
Hartland, Canada 71 C6 46 20N 67 32W
Hartland Pt., U.K. 11 F3 51 1N 4 32W
Hartlepool, U.K. 10 C6 54 42N 1 13W
Hartlepool □, U.K. 10 C6 54 42N 1 17W
Hartley Bay, Canada 72 C3 53 25N 129 15W
Hartmannberge, Namibia 56 B1 17 0S 13 0 E
Hartney, Canada 73 D8 49 30N 100 35W
Harts →, S. Africa 56 D3 28 24S 24 17 E
Hartselle, U.S.A. 77 H2 34 27N 86 56W
Hartshorne, U.S.A. 81 H7 34 51N 95 34W
Hartstown, U.S.A. 78 E4 41 33N 80 23W
Hartsville, U.S.A. 77 H5 34 23N 80 4W
Hartwell, U.S.A. 77 H4 34 21N 82 56W
Harunabad, Pakistan 42 E5 29 35N 73 8 E
Harvand, Iran 45 D7 28 25N 55 43 E
Harvey, Australia 61 F2 33 5S 115 54 E
Harvey, Ill., U.S.A. 76 E2 41 36N 87 50W
Harvey, N. Dak., U.S.A. 80 B5 47 47N 99 56W
Harwich, U.K. 11 F9 51 56N 1 17 E
Haryana □, India 42 E7 29 0N 76 10 E
Haryn →, Belarus 17 B14 52 7N 27 17 E
Harz, Germany 16 C6 51 38N 10 44 E
Hasa □, Si. Arabia 45 E6 25 50N 49 0 E
Ḥasanābād, Iran 45 C7 32 8N 52 44 E
Hasdo →, India 43 J10 21 44N 82 44 E
Hashimoto, Japan 31 G7 34 19N 135 37 E
Hashtjerd, Iran 45 C6 35 52N 50 40 E
Haskell, U.S.A. 81 J5 33 10N 99 44W
Haslemere, U.K. 11 F7 51 5N 0 43W
Hasselt, Belgium 15 D5 50 56N 5 21 E
Hassi Messaoud, Algeria 50 B7 31 51N 6 1 E
Hässleholm, Sweden 9 H15 56 10N 13 46 E
Hastings, N.Z. 59 H6 39 39S 176 52 E
Hastings, U.K. 11 G8 50 51N 0 35 E
Hastings, Mich., U.S.A. 76 D3 42 39N 85 17W
Hastings, Minn., U.S.A. 80 C8 44 44N 92 51W
Hastings, Nebr., U.S.A. 80 E5 40 35N 98 23W
Hastings Ra., Australia 63 E5 31 15S 152 14 E
Hat Yai, Thailand 39 J3 7 1N 100 27 E
Hatanbulag = Ergel, Mongolia 34 C5 43 8N 109 5 E
Hatay = Antalya, Turkey 25 G5 36 52N 30 45 E
Hatch, U.S.A. 83 K10 32 40N 107 9W
Hatchet L., Canada 73 B8 58 36N 103 40W
Hateruma-Shima, Japan 31 M1 24 3N 123 47 E
Hatfield P.O., Australia 63 E3 33 54S 143 49 E
Hatgal, Mongolia 32 A5 50 26N 100 9 E
Hathras, India 42 F8 27 36N 78 6 E
Hatia, Bangla. 41 H17 22 30N 91 5 E
Hato Mayor, Dom. Rep. 89 C6 18 46N 69 15W
Hatta, India 43 G8 24 7N 79 36 E
Hattah, Australia 63 E3 34 48S 142 17 E
Hatteras, C., U.S.A. 77 H8 35 14N 75 32W
Hattiesburg, U.S.A. 81 K10 31 20N 89 17W
Hatvan, Hungary 17 E10 47 40N 19 45 E
Hau Bon = Cheo Reo, Vietnam 36 B3 13 25N 108 28 E
Hau Duc, Vietnam 38 E7 15 20N 108 13 E
Haugesund, Norway 9 G11 59 23N 5 13 E
Haukipudas, Finland 8 D21 65 12N 25 20 E
Haultain →, Canada 73 B7 55 51N 106 46W
Hauraki G., N.Z. 59 G5 36 35S 175 5 E
Haut Atlas, Morocco 50 B4 32 30N 5 0W
Haut-Zaïre = Orientale □, Dem. Rep. of the Congo 54 B2 2 20N 26 0 E
Hautes Fagnes = Hohe Venn, Belgium 15 D6 50 30N 6 5 E
Hauts Plateaux, Algeria 48 C4 35 0N 1 0 E
Havana = La Habana, Cuba 88 B3 23 8N 82 22W
Havana, U.S.A. 80 E9 40 18N 90 4W
Havant, U.K. 11 G7 50 51N 0 58W
Havasu, L., U.S.A. 85 L12 34 18N 114 28W
Havel →, Germany 16 B7 52 50N 12 3 E
Havelian, Pakistan 42 B5 34 2N 73 10 E
Havelock, Canada 78 B7 44 26N 77 53W
Havelock, N.Z. 59 J4 41 17S 173 48 E
Havelock, U.S.A. 77 H7 34 53N 76 54W
Haverfordwest, U.K. 11 F3 51 48N 4 58W
Haverhill, U.S.A. 79 D13 42 47N 71 5W
Haverstraw, U.S.A. 79 E11 41 12N 73 58W
Havirga, Mongolia 34 B7 45 41N 113 5 E
Havířov, Czech. 17 D10 49 46N 18 20 E
Havlíčkův Brod, Czech Rep. 16 D8 49 36N 15 33 E
Havre, U.S.A. 82 B9 48 33N 109 41W
Havre-Aubert, Canada 71 C7 47 12N 61 56W
Havre-St.-Pierre, Canada 71 B7 50 18N 63 33W
Haw →, U.S.A. 77 H6 35 36N 79 3W
Hawaii □, U.S.A. 74 H16 19 30N 156 30W
Hawaii I., Pac. Oc. 74 J17 20 0N 155 0W
Hawaiian Is., Pac. Oc. 74 H17 20 30N 156 0W
Hawaiian Ridge, Pac. Oc. 65 E11 24 0N 165 0W
Hawarden, U.S.A. 80 D6 43 0N 96 29W
Hawea, L., N.Z. 59 L2 44 28S 169 19 E
Hawera, N.Z. 59 H5 39 35S 174 19 E
Hawick, U.K. 12 F6 55 26N 2 47W
Hawk Junction, Canada 70 C3 48 5N 84 38W
Hawke B., N.Z. 59 H6 39 25S 177 20 E
Hawker, Australia 63 E2 31 59S 138 22 E
Hawkesbury, Canada 70 C5 45 37N 74 37W
Hawkesbury I., Canada 72 C3 53 37N 129 3W
Hawkesbury Pt., Australia 62 A1 11 55S 134 5 E
Hawkinsville, U.S.A. 77 J4 32 17N 83 28W
Hawley, Minn., U.S.A. 80 B6 46 53N 96 19W
Hawley, Pa., U.S.A. 79 E9 41 28N 75 11W
Ḥawrān, W. →, Iraq 44 C4 33 58N 42 34 E
Hawsh Müssá, Lebanon 47 B4 33 45N 35 55 E
Hawthorne, U.S.A. 82 G4 38 32N 118 38W
Hay, Australia 63 E3 34 30S 144 51 E
Hay →, Australia 62 C2 24 50S 138 0 E
Hay →, Canada 72 A5 60 50N 116 26W
Hay, C., Australia 60 B4 14 5S 129 29 E
Hay I., Canada 78 B4 44 53N 80 58W
Hay L., Canada 72 B5 58 50N 118 50W
Hay-on-Wye, U.K. 11 E4 52 5N 3 8W
Hay River, Canada 72 A5 60 51N 115 44W
Hay Springs, U.S.A. 80 D3 42 41N 102 41W
Haya = Tehoru, Indonesia 37 E7 3 19S 129 37 E
Hayachine-San, Japan 30 E10 39 34N 141 29 E
Hayden, U.S.A. 82 F10 40 30N 107 16W
Haydon, Australia 62 B3 18 0S 141 30 E
Hayes, U.S.A. 80 C4 44 23N 101 1W
Hayes →, Canada 70 A1 57 3N 92 12W
Hayes Creek, Australia 60 B5 13 43S 131 22 E
Hayle, U.K. 11 G2 50 11N 5 26W
Hayling I., U.K. 11 G7 50 48N 0 59W
Hayrabolu, Turkey 21 D12 41 12N 27 5 E
Hays, Canada 72 C6 50 6N 111 48W
Hays, U.S.A. 80 F5 38 53N 99 20W
Haysyn, Ukraine 17 D15 48 57N 29 25 E
Hayvoron, Ukraine 17 D15 48 22N 29 52 E
Hayward, Calif., U.S.A. 84 H4 37 40N 122 5W
Hayward, Wis., U.S.A. 80 B9 46 1N 91 29W
Haywards Heath, U.K. 11 G7 51 0N 0 5W
Hazafon □, Israel 47 C4 32 40N 35 20 E
Hazārān, Kūh-e, Iran 45 D8 29 35N 57 20 E
Hazard, U.S.A. 76 G4 37 15N 83 12W
Hazaribag, India 43 H11 23 58N 85 26 E
Hazaribag Road, India 43 G11 24 12N 85 57 E
Hazelton, Canada 72 B3 55 20N 127 42W
Hazelton, U.S.A. 80 B4 46 29N 100 17W
Hazen, U.S.A. 80 B4 47 18N 101 38W
Hazlehurst, Ga., U.S.A. 77 K4 31 52N 82 36W
Hazlehurst, Miss., U.S.A. 81 K9 31 52N 90 24W
Hazlet, U.S.A. 79 F10 40 25N 74 12W
Hazleton, U.S.A. 79 F9 40 57N 75 59W
Hazlett, L., Australia 60 D4 21 30S 128 48 E
Hazro, Turkey 44 B4 38 15N 40 47 E
Head of Bight, Australia 61 F5 31 30S 131 25 E
Headlands, Zimbabwe 55 F3 18 15S 32 2 E
Healdsburg, U.S.A. 84 G4 38 37N 122 52W
Healdton, U.S.A. 81 H6 34 14N 97 29W
Healesville, Australia 63 F4 37 35S 145 30 E
Heard I., Ind. Oc. 3 G13 53 0S 74 0 E
Hearne, U.S.A. 81 K6 30 53N 96 36W
Hearst, Canada 70 C3 49 40N 83 41W
Heart →, U.S.A. 80 B4 46 46N 100 50W
Heart's Content, Canada 71 C9 47 54N 53 27W
Heath Pt., Canada 71 C7 49 8N 61 40W
Heavener, U.S.A. 81 H7 34 53N 94 36W
Hebbronville, U.S.A. 81 M5 27 18N 98 41W
Hebei □, China 34 E9 39 0N 116 0 E
Hebel, Australia 63 D4 28 58S 147 47 E
Heber, U.S.A. 85 N11 32 44N 115 32W
Heber City, U.S.A. 82 F8 40 31N 111 25W
Heber Springs, U.S.A. 81 H9 35 30N 92 2W
Hebert, Canada 73 C7 50 30N 107 10W
Hebgen L., U.S.A. 82 D8 44 52N 111 20W
Hebi, China 34 G8 35 57N 114 7 E
Hebrides, U.K. 6 D4 57 30N 7 0W
Hebron = Al Khalīl, West Bank 47 D4 31 32N 35 6 E
Hebron, Canada 69 C13 58 5N 62 30W
Hebron, N. Dak., U.S.A. 80 B3 46 54N 102 3W
Hebron, Nebr., U.S.A. 80 E6 40 10N 97 35W
Hecate Str., Canada 72 C2 53 10N 130 30W
Heceta I., U.S.A. 72 B2 55 46N 133 40W
Hechi, China 32 D5 24 40N 108 2 E
Hechuan, China 32 C5 30 2N 106 12 E
Hecla, U.S.A. 80 C5 45 53N 98 9W
Hecla I., Canada 73 C9 51 10N 96 43W
Hede, Sweden 9 E15 62 23N 13 30 E
Hedemora, Sweden 9 F16 60 18N 15 58 E
Heerde, Neths. 15 B6 52 24N 6 2 E
Heerenveen, Neths. 15 B5 52 57N 5 55 E
Heerhugowaard, Neths. 15 B4 52 40N 4 51 E
Heerlen, Neths. 18 A6 50 55N 5 58 E
Ḥefa, Israel 47 C4 32 46N 35 0 E
Ḥefa □, Israel 47 C4 32 40N 35 0 E
Hefei, China 33 C6 31 52N 117 18 E
Hegang, China 33 B8 47 20N 130 19 E
Heichengzhen, China 34 F4 36 24N 106 3 E
Heidelberg, Germany 16 D5 49 24N 8 42 E
Heidelberg, S. Africa 56 E3 34 6S 20 59 E
Heilbron, S. Africa 57 D4 27 16S 27 59 E
Heilbronn, Germany 16 D5 49 9N 9 13 E
Heilongjiang □, China 33 B7 48 0N 126 0 E
Heilunkiang = Heilongjiang □, China 33 B7 48 0N 126 0 E
Heimaey, Iceland 8 E3 63 26N 20 17W
Heinola, Finland 9 F22 61 13N 26 2 E
Heinze Is., Burma 41 M20 14 25N 97 45 E
Heishan, China 35 D12 41 40N 122 5 E
Heishui, China 35 C10 42 8N 119 30 E
Hejaz = Ḥijāz □, Si. Arabia 46 C3 24 0N 40 0 E
Hejian, China 34 E9 38 25N 116 5 E
Hejin, China 34 G6 35 35N 110 42 E
Hekımhan, Turkey 44 B3 38 50N 37 55 E
Hekla, Iceland 8 E4 63 56N 19 35W
Hekou, China 32 D5 22 30N 103 59 E
Helan Shan, China 34 E3 38 30N 105 55 E
Helen Atoll, Pac. Oc. 37 D8 2 40N 132 0 E
Helena, Ark., U.S.A. 81 H9 34 32N 90 36W
Helena, Mont., U.S.A. 82 C7 46 36N 112 2W
Helendale, U.S.A. 85 L9 34 44N 117 19W
Helensburgh, U.K. 12 E4 56 1N 4 43W
Helensville, N.Z. 59 G5 36 41S 174 29 E
Helenvale, Australia 62 B4 15 43S 145 14 E
Helgeland, Norway 8 C15 66 7N 13 29 E
Helgoland, Germany 16 A4 54 10N 7 53 E
Heligoland = Helgoland, Germany 16 A4 54 10N 7 53 E
Heligoland B. = Deutsche Bucht, Germany 16 A5 54 15N 8 0 E
Hella, Iceland 8 E3 63 50N 20 24W
Hellertown, U.S.A. 79 F9 40 35N 75 21W
Hellespont = Çanakkale Boğazı, Turkey 21 D12 40 17N 26 32 E
Hellevoetsluis, Neths. 15 C4 51 50N 4 8 E
Hellín, Spain 19 C5 38 31N 1 40W
Helmand □, Afghan. 40 D4 31 20N 64 0 E
Helmand →, Afghan. 40 D2 31 12N 61 34 E
Helmond, Neths. 15 C5 51 29N 5 41 E
Helmsdale, U.K. 12 C5 58 7N 3 39W
Helmsdale →, U.K. 12 C5 58 7N 3 40W
Helong, China 35 C15 42 40N 129 0 E
Helper, U.S.A. 82 G8 39 41N 110 51W
Helsingborg, Sweden 9 H15 56 3N 12 42 E
Helsingfors = Helsinki, Finland 9 F21 60 15N 25 3 E
Helsingør, Denmark 9 H15 56 2N 12 35 E
Helsinki, Finland 9 F21 60 15N 25 3 E
Helston, U.K. 11 G2 50 6N 5 17W
Helvellyn, U.K. 10 C4 54 32N 3 1W
Helwân, Egypt 51 C12 29 50N 31 20 E
Hemel Hempstead, U.K. 11 F7 51 44N 0 28W
Hemet, U.S.A. 85 M10 33 45N 116 58W
Hemingford, U.S.A. 80 D3 42 19N 103 4W
Hemmingford, Canada 79 A11 45 3N 73 35W
Hempstead, U.S.A. 81 K6 30 6N 96 5W
Hemse, Sweden 9 H18 57 15N 18 22 E
Henan □, China 34 H8 34 0N 114 0 E
Henares →, Spain 19 B4 40 24N 3 30W
Henashi-Misaki, Japan 30 D9 40 37N 139 51 E
Henderson, Argentina 94 D3 36 18S 61 43W
Henderson, Ky., U.S.A. 76 G2 37 50N 87 35W
Henderson, N.C., U.S.A. 77 G6 36 20N 78 25W
Henderson, Nev., U.S.A. 85 J12 36 2N 114 59W
Henderson, Tenn., U.S.A. 77 H1 35 26N 88 38W
Henderson, Tex., U.S.A. 81 J7 32 9N 94 48W
Hendersonville, N.C., U.S.A. 77 H4 35 19N 82 28W
Hendersonville, Tenn., U.S.A. 77 G2 36 18N 86 37W
Hendījān, Iran 45 D6 30 14N 49 43 E
Hendorābī, Iran 45 E7 26 40N 53 37 E
Hengcheng, China 34 E4 38 18N 106 28 E
Hengdaohezi, China 35 B15 44 52N 129 0 E
Hengelo, Neths. 15 B6 52 16N 6 48 E
Hengshan, China 34 F5 37 58N 109 5 E
Hengshui, China 34 F8 37 41N 115 40 E
Hengyang, China 33 D6 26 52N 112 33 E
Henlopen, C., U.S.A. 76 F8 38 48N 75 6W
Hennenman, S. Africa 56 D4 27 59S 27 1 E
Hennessey, U.S.A. 81 G6 36 6N 97 54W
Henrietta, U.S.A. 81 J5 33 49N 98 12W
Henrietta, Ostrov = Genriyetty, Ostrov, Russia 27 B16 77 6N 156 30 E
Henrietta Maria, C., Canada 70 A3 55 9N 82 20W
Henry, U.S.A. 80 E10 41 7N 89 22W
Henryetta, U.S.A. 81 H7 35 27N 95 59W
Henryville, Canada 79 A11 45 8N 73 11W

Hensall, *Canada* **78 C3** 43 26N 81 30W
Hentiyn Nuruu, *Mongolia* . **33 B5** 48 30N 108 30 E
Henty, *Australia* . . . . **63 F4** 35 30S 147 0 E
Henzada, *Burma* . . . . **41 L19** 17 38N 95 26 E
Heppner, *U.S.A.* **82 D4** 45 21N 119 33W
Hepworth, *Canada* **78 B3** 44 37N 81 9W
Hequ, *China* . . . . **34 E6** 39 20N 111 15 E
Héraðsflói, *Iceland* **8 D6** 65 42N 14 12W
Héraðsvötn →, *Iceland* . . . **8 D4** 65 45N 19 25W
Herald Cays, *Australia* . . . . **62 B4** 16 58S 149 9 E
Herāt, *Afghan.* . . . . **40 B3** 34 20N 62 7 E
Herāt □, *Afghan.* . . . . **40 B3** 35 0N 62 0 E
Herbert →, *Australia* . . . . **62 B4** 18 31S 146 17 E
Herberton, *Australia* . . . . . **62 B4** 17 20S 145 25 E
Herceg-Novi, *Montenegro, Yug.* . . . . . . **21 C8** 42 30N 18 33 E
Herchmer, *Canada* **73 B10** 57 22N 94 10W
Herðubreið, *Iceland* **8 D5** 65 11N 16 21W
Hereford, *U.K.* **11 E5** 52 4N 2 43W
Hereford, *U.S.A.* **81 H3** 34 49N 102 24W
Herefordshire □, *U.K.* **11 E5** 52 8N 2 40W
Herentals, *Belgium* . . . . **15 C4** 51 12N 4 51 E
Herford, *Germany* . . . . **16 B5** 52 7N 8 39 E
Herington, *U.S.A.* **80 F6** 38 40N 96 57W
Herkimer, *U.S.A.* **79 D10** 43 0N 74 59W
Herlong, *U.S.A.* **84 E6** 40 8N 120 8W
Herm, *U.K.* **11 H5** 49 30N 2 28W
Hermann, *U.S.A.* **80 F9** 38 42N 91 27W
Hermannsburg, *Australia* . . **60 D5** 23 57S 132 45 E
Hermanus, *S. Africa* . . . . . . **56 E2** 34 27S 19 12 E
Hermidale, *Australia* . . . . . . **63 E4** 31 30S 146 42 E
Hermiston, *U.S.A.* **82 D4** 45 51N 119 17W
Hermitage, *N.Z.* . . . . **59 K3** 43 44S 170 5 E
Hermite, I., *Chile* **96 H3** 55 50S 68 0W
Hermon, *U.S.A.* **79 B9** 44 28N 75 14W
Hermon, Mt. = Shaykh, J. ash, *Lebanon* . . . . **47 B4** 33 25N 35 50 E
Hermosillo, *Mexico* **86 B2** 29 10N 111 0W
Hernád →, *Hungary* . . . . . **17 D11** 47 56N 21 8 E
Hernandarias, *Paraguay* . . . **95 B5** 25 20S 54 40W
Hernandez, *U.S.A.* **84 J6** 36 24N 120 46W
Hernando, *Argentina* **94 C3** 32 28S 63 40W
Hernando, *U.S.A.* **81 H10** 34 50N 90 0W
Herndon, *U.S.A.* **78 F8** 40 43N 76 51W
Herne, *Germany* . . . . **15 C7** 51 32N 7 14 E
Herne Bay, *U.K.* . . . . **11 F9** 51 21N 1 8 E
Herning, *Denmark* . . . . **9 H13** 56 8N 8 58 E
Heroica = Caborca, *Mexico* **86 A2** 30 40N 112 10W
Heroica Nogales = Nogales, *Mexico* **86 A2** 31 20N 110 56W
Heron Bay, *Canada* **70 C2** 48 40N 86 25W
Herradura, Pta. de la, *Canary Is.* **22 F5** 28 26N 14 8W
Herreid, *U.S.A.* **80 C4** 45 50N 100 4W
Herrin, *U.S.A.* **81 G10** 37 48N 89 2W
Herriot, *Canada* **73 B8** 56 22N 101 16W
Hershey, *U.S.A.* **79 F8** 40 17N 76 39W
Hersonissos, *Greece* . . . . . . **23 D7** 35 18N 25 22 E
Herstal, *Belgium* . . . . **15 D5** 50 40N 5 38 E
Hertford, *U.K.* **11 F7** 51 48N 0 4W
Hertfordshire □, *U.K.* **11 F7** 51 51N 0 5W
's-Hertogenbosch, *Neths.* . . **15 C5** 51 42N 5 17 E
Hertzogville, *S. Africa* . . . . . **56 D4** 28 9S 25 30 E
Hervey B., *Australia* . . . . . . **62 C5** 25 0S 152 52 E
Herzliyya, *Israel* . . . . **47 C3** 32 10N 34 50 E
Ḥeşār, *Fārs, Iran* . . . . **45 D6** 29 52N 50 16 E
Ḥeşār, *Markazī, Iran* . . . . . **45 C6** 35 50N 49 12 E
Heshui, *China* . . . . **34 G5** 35 48N 108 0 E
Heshun, *China* . . . . **34 F7** 37 22N 113 32 E
Hesperia, *U.S.A.* **85 L9** 34 25N 117 18W
Hesse = Hessen □, *Germany* . . . . **16 C5** 50 30N 9 0 E
Hessen □, *Germany* . . . . . . **16 C5** 50 30N 9 0 E
Hetch Hetchy Aqueduct, *U.S.A.* **84 H5** 37 29N 122 19W
Hettinger, *U.S.A.* **80 C3** 46 0N 102 42W
Heuvelton, *U.S.A.* **79 B9** 44 37N 75 25W
Hewitt, *U.S.A.* **81 K6** 31 27N 97 11W
Hexham, *U.K.* **10 C5** 54 58N 2 4W
Hexigten Qi, *China* . . . . **35 C9** 43 18N 117 30 E
Ḥeydarābād, *Iran* . . . . **45 D7** 30 33N 55 38 E
Heysham, *U.K.* **10 C5** 54 3N 2 53W
Heywood, *Australia* . . . . **63 F3** 38 8S 141 37 E
Heze, *China* . . . . **34 G8** 35 14N 115 20 E
Hi Vista, *U.S.A.* **85 L9** 34 45N 117 46W
Hialeah, *U.S.A.* **77 N5** 25 50N 80 17W
Hiawatha, *U.S.A.* **80 F7** 39 51N 95 32W
Hibbing, *U.S.A.* **80 B8** 47 25N 92 56W
Hibbs B., *Australia* . . . . **62 G4** 42 35S 145 15 E
Hibernia Reef, *Australia* . . . **60 B3** 12 0S 123 23 E
Hickman, *U.S.A.* **81 G10** 36 34N 89 11W
Hickory, *U.S.A.* **77 H5** 35 44N 81 21W
Hicks, Pt., *Australia* . . . . . . **63 F4** 37 49S 149 17 E
Hicks L., *Canada* **73 A9** 61 25N 100 0W
Hicksville, *U.S.A.* **79 F11** 40 46N 73 32W
Hida-Gawa →, *Japan* . . . . **31 G8** 35 26N 137 3 E
Hida-Sammyaku, *Japan* . . . **31 F8** 36 30N 137 40 E
Hidaka-Sammyaku, *Japan* . **30 C11** 42 35N 142 45 E
Hidalgo, *Mexico* **87 C5** 24 15N 99 26W
Hidalgo □, *Mexico* **87 C5** 20 30N 99 10W
Hidalgo, Presa M., *Mexico* . **86 B3** 26 30N 108 35W
Hidalgo, Pta. del, *Canary Is.* **22 F3** 28 33N 16 19W
Hidalgo del Parral, *Mexico* . **86 B3** 26 58N 105 40W
Hierro, *Canary Is.* **22 G1** 27 44N 18 0W
Higashiajima-San, *Japan* . . **30 F10** 37 40N 140 10 E
Higashiōsaka, *Japan* . . . . . **31 G7** 34 40N 135 37 E
Higgins, *U.S.A.* **81 G4** 36 7N 100 2W
Higgins Corner, *U.S.A.* **84 F5** 39 2N 121 5W
High Atlas = Haut Atlas, *Morocco* **50 B4** 32 30N 5 0W
High Bridge, *U.S.A.* **79 F10** 40 40N 74 54W
High Level, *Canada* **72 B5** 58 31N 117 8W
High Point, *U.S.A.* **77 H6** 35 57N 80 0W
High Prairie, *Canada* **72 B5** 55 30N 116 30W
High River, *Canada* **72 C6** 50 30N 113 50W
High Tatra = Tatry, *Slovak Rep.* . . . . **17 D11** 49 20N 20 0 E
High Veld, *Africa* . . . . **48 J6** 27 0S 27 0 E
High Wycombe, *U.K.* **11 F7** 51 37N 0 45W
Highland □, *U.K.* **12 D4** 57 17N 4 21W
Highland Park, *U.S.A.* **76 D2** 42 11N 87 48W
Highmore, *U.S.A.* **80 C5** 44 31N 99 27W
Highrock L., *Canada* **73 B8** 55 45N 100 30W
Highrock L., *Sask., Canada* . **73 B7** 57 5N 105 32W
Higüey, *Dom. Rep.* **89 C6** 18 37N 68 42W
Hiiumaa, *Estonia* . . . . **9 G20** 58 50N 22 45 E
Ḥijāz □, *Si. Arabia* . . . . **46 C3** 24 0N 40 0 E
Hijo = Tagum, *Phil.* . . . . . . **37 C7** 7 33N 125 53 E
Hikari, *Japan* . . . . **31 H5** 33 58N 131 58 E
Hiko, *U.S.A.* **84 H11** 37 32N 115 14W
Hikone, *Japan* . . . . **31 G8** 35 15N 136 10 E
Hikurangi, *N.Z.* . . . . **59 F5** 35 36S 174 17 E
Hikurangi, Mt., *N.Z.* . . . . **59 H6** 38 21S 176 52 E
Hildesheim, *Germany* . . . . . **16 B5** 52 9N 9 56 E
Hill →, *Australia* . . . . **61 F2** 30 23S 115 3 E
Hill City, *Idaho, U.S.A.* **82 E6** 43 18N 115 3W
Hill City, *Kans., U.S.A.* **80 F5** 39 22N 99 51W
Hill City, *S. Dak., U.S.A.* . . . **80 D3** 43 56N 103 35W
Hill Island L., *Canada* **73 A7** 60 30N 109 50W
Hillcrest Center, *U.S.A.* **85 K8** 35 23N 118 57W
Hillegom, *Neths.* . . . . **15 B4** 52 18N 4 35 E
Hillerød, *Denmark* . . . . **9 J15** 55 56N 12 19 E
Hillsboro, *Kans., U.S.A.* . . . **80 F6** 38 21N 97 12W
Hillsboro, *N. Dak., U.S.A.* . . **80 B6** 47 26N 97 3W
Hillsboro, *N.H., U.S.A.* **79 C13** 43 7N 71 54W
Hillsboro, *Ohio, U.S.A.* **76 F4** 39 12N 83 37W
Hillsboro, *Oreg., U.S.A.* **84 E4** 45 31N 122 59W
Hillsboro, *Tex., U.S.A.* **81 J6** 32 1N 97 8W
Hillsborough, *Grenada* **89 D7** 12 28N 61 28W
Hillsdale, *Mich., U.S.A.* **76 E3** 41 56N 84 38W
Hillsdale, *N.Y., U.S.A.* **79 D11** 42 11N 73 30W
Hillsport, *Canada* **70 C2** 49 27N 85 34W
Hillston, *Australia* . . . . **63 E4** 33 30S 145 31 E
Hilo, *U.S.A.* **74 J17** 19 44N 155 5W
Hilton, *U.S.A.* **78 C7** 43 17N 77 48W
Hilton Head Island, *U.S.A.* . . **77 J5** 32 13N 80 45W
Hilversum, *Neths.* . . . . **15 B5** 52 14N 5 10 E
Himachal Pradesh □, *India* **42 D7** 31 30N 77 0 E
Himalaya, *Asia* . . . . **43 E11** 29 0N 84 0 E
Himatnagar, *India* . . . . **40 H8** 23 37N 72 57 E
Himeji, *Japan* . . . . **31 G7** 34 50N 134 40 E
Himi, *Japan* . . . . **31 F8** 36 50N 136 55 E
Ḥimş, *Syria* . . . . **47 A5** 34 40N 36 45 E
Ḥimş □, *Syria* . . . . **47 A6** 34 30N 37 0 E
Hinche, *Haiti* **89 C5** 19 9N 72 1W
Hinchinbrook I., *Australia* . . **62 B4** 18 20S 146 15 E
Hinckley, *U.K.* **11 E6** 52 33N 1 22W
Hinckley, *U.S.A.* **80 B8** 46 1N 92 56W
Hindaun, *India* . . . . **42 F7** 26 44N 77 5 E
Hindmarsh, L., *Australia* . . . **63 F3** 36 5S 141 55 E
Hindu Bagh, *Pakistan* . . . . . **42 D2** 30 56N 67 50 E
Hindu Kush, *Asia* . . . . **40 B7** 36 0N 71 0 E
Hindubagh, *Pakistan* . . . . . . **40 D5** 30 56N 67 57 E
Hindupur, *India* . . . . **40 N10** 13 49N 77 32 E
Hines Creek, *Canada* **72 B5** 56 20N 118 40W
Hinesville, *U.S.A.* **77 K5** 31 51N 81 36W
Hinganghat, *India* . . . . **40 J11** 20 30N 78 52 E
Hingham, *U.S.A.* **82 B8** 48 33N 110 25W
Hingir, *India* . . . . **43 J10** 21 57N 83 41 E
Hingoli, *India* . . . . **40 K10** 19 41N 77 15 E
Hinna = Imi, *Ethiopia* . . . . . **46 F3** 6 28N 42 10 E
Hinnøya, *Norway* . . . . **8 B16** 68 35N 15 50 E
Hinojosa del Duque, *Spain* **19 C3** 38 30N 5 9W
Hinsdale, *U.S.A.* **79 D12** 42 47N 72 29W
Hinton, *Canada* **72 C5** 53 26N 117 34W
Hinton, *U.S.A.* **76 G5** 37 40N 80 54W
Hirado, *Japan* . . . . **31 H4** 33 22N 129 33 E
Hirakud Dam, *India* . . . . **41 J13** 21 32N 83 45 E
Hiran →, *India* . . . . **43 H8** 23 6N 79 21 E
Hirapur, *India* . . . . **43 G8** 24 22N 79 13 E
Hiratsuka, *Japan* . . . . **31 G9** 35 19N 139 21 E
Hiroo, *Japan* . . . . **30 C11** 42 17N 143 19 E
Hirosaki, *Japan* . . . . **30 D10** 40 34N 140 28 E
Hiroshima, *Japan* . . . . **31 G6** 34 24N 132 30 E
Hiroshima □, *Japan* . . . . **31 G6** 34 50N 133 0 E
Hisar, *India* . . . . **42 E6** 29 12N 75 45 E
Hisb →, *Iraq* . . . . **44 D5** 31 45N 44 17 E
Ḥismá, *Si. Arabia* . . . . **44 D3** 28 30N 36 0 E
Hispaniola, *W. Indies* **89 C5** 19 0N 71 0W
Hīt, *Iraq* . . . . **44 C4** 33 38N 42 49 E
Hita, *Japan* . . . . **31 H5** 33 20N 130 58 E
Hitachi, *Japan* . . . . **31 F10** 36 36N 140 39 E
Hitchin, *U.K.* **11 F7** 51 58N 0 16W
Hitoyoshi, *Japan* . . . . **31 H5** 32 13N 130 45 E
Hitra, *Norway* . . . . **8 E13** 63 30N 8 45 E
Hixon, *Canada* **72 C4** 53 25N 122 35W
Ḥiyyon, N. →, *Israel* . . . . . **47 E4** 30 25N 35 10 E
Hjalmar L., *Canada* **73 A7** 61 33N 109 25W
Hjälmaren, *Sweden* . . . . **9 G16** 59 18N 15 40 E
Hjørring, *Denmark* . . . . **9 H13** 57 29N 9 59 E
Hluhluwe, *S. Africa* . . . . **57 D5** 28 1S 32 15 E
Hlyboka, *Ukraine* . . . . **17 D13** 48 5N 25 56 E
Ho Chi Minh City = Phanh Bho Ho Chi Minh, *Vietnam* . . . . **39 G6** 10 58N 106 40 E
Ho Thuong, *Vietnam* . . . . . . **38 C5** 19 32N 105 48 E
Hoa Da, *Vietnam* . . . . **39 G7** 11 16N 108 40 E
Hoa Hiep, *Vietnam* . . . . **39 G5** 11 34N 105 51 E
Hoai Nhon, *Vietnam* . . . . . . **38 E7** 14 28N 109 1 E
Hoang Lien Son, *Vietnam* . . **38 A4** 22 0N 104 0 E
Hoare B., *Canada* **69 B13** 65 17N 62 30W
Hobart, *Australia* . . . . **62 G4** 42 50S 147 21 E
Hobart, *U.S.A.* **81 H5** 35 1N 99 6W
Hobbs, *U.S.A.* **81 J3** 32 42N 103 8W
Hobbs Coast, *Antarctica* . . . **5 D14** 74 50S 131 0W
Hobe Sound, *U.S.A.* **77 M5** 27 4N 80 8W
Hoboken, *U.S.A.* **79 F10** 40 45N 74 4W
Hobro, *Denmark* . . . . **9 H13** 56 39N 9 46 E
Hoburgen, *Sweden* . . . . **9 H18** 56 55N 18 7 E
Hodaka-Dake, *Japan* . . . . . . **31 F8** 36 17N 137 39 E
Hodgeville, *Canada* **73 C7** 50 7N 106 58W
Hodgson, *Canada* **73 C9** 51 13N 97 36W
Hódmezővásárhely, *Hungary* **17 E11** 46 28N 20 22 E
Hodna, Chott el, *Algeria* . . . **50 A6** 35 26N 4 43 E
Hodonín, *Czech Rep.* . . . . . . **17 D9** 48 50N 17 10 E
Hoeamdong, *N. Korea* . . . . . **35 C16** 42 30N 130 16 E
Hoek van Holland, *Neths.* . . **15 C4** 52 0N 4 7 E
Hoengsŏng, *S. Korea* . . . . . . **35 F14** 37 29N 127 59 E
Hoeryong, *N. Korea* . . . . **35 C15** 42 30N 129 45 E
Hoeyang, *N. Korea* . . . . **35 E14** 38 43N 127 36 E
Hof, *Germany* . . . . **16 C6** 50 19N 11 55 E
Hofmeyr, *S. Africa* . . . . **56 E4** 31 39S 25 50 E
Höfn, *Iceland* **8 D6** 64 15N 15 13W
Hofors, *Sweden* . . . . **9 F17** 60 31N 16 15 E
Hofsjökull, *Iceland* **8 D4** 64 49N 18 48W
Hōfu, *Japan* . . . . **31 G5** 34 3N 131 34 E
Hogan Group, *Australia* . . . . **63 F4** 39 13S 147 1 E
Hogarth, Mt., *Australia* . . . . **62 C2** 21 48S 136 58 E
Hoggar = Ahaggar, *Algeria* **50 D7** 23 0N 6 30 E
Hogsty Reef, *Bahamas* **89 B5** 21 41N 73 48W
Hoh →, *U.S.A.* **84 C2** 47 45N 124 29W
Hohe Venn, *Belgium* . . . . **15 D6** 50 30N 6 5 E
Hohenwald, *U.S.A.* **77 H2** 35 33N 87 33W
Hohhot, *China* . . . . **34 D6** 40 52N 111 40 E
Hóhlakas, *Greece* . . . . **23 D9** 35 57N 27 53 E
Hoi An, *Vietnam* . . . . **38 E7** 15 30N 108 19 E
Hoisington, *U.S.A.* **80 F5** 38 31N 98 47W
Hōjō, *Japan* . . . . **31 H6** 33 58N 132 46 E
Hokianga Harbour, *N.Z.* . . . **59 F4** 35 31S 173 22 E
Hokitika, *N.Z.* . . . . **59 K3** 42 42S 171 0 E
Hokkaidō □, *Japan* . . . . **30 C11** 43 30N 143 0 E
Holbrook, *Australia* . . . . **63 F4** 35 42S 147 18 E
Holbrook, *U.S.A.* **83 J8** 34 54N 110 10W
Holden, *U.S.A.* **82 G7** 39 6N 112 16W
Holdenville, *U.S.A.* **81 H6** 35 5N 96 24W
Holdrege, *U.S.A.* **80 E5** 40 26N 99 23W
Holguín, *Cuba* **88 B4** 20 50N 76 20W
Hollams Bird I., *Namibia* . . **56 C1** 24 40S 14 30 E
Holland, *Mich., U.S.A.* **76 D2** 42 47N 86 7W
Holland, *N.Y., U.S.A.* **78 D6** 42 38N 78 32W
Hollandale, *U.S.A.* **81 J9** 33 10N 90 51W
Hollandia = Jayapura, *Indonesia* . . . . **37 E10** 2 28S 140 38 E
Holley, *U.S.A.* **78 C6** 43 14N 78 2W
Hollidaysburg, *U.S.A.* **78 F6** 40 26N 78 24W
Hollis, *U.S.A.* **81 H5** 34 41N 99 55W
Hollister, *Calif., U.S.A.* **84 J5** 36 51N 121 24W
Hollister, *Idaho, U.S.A.* **82 E6** 42 21N 114 35W
Holly Hill, *U.S.A.* **77 L5** 29 16N 81 3W
Holly Springs, *U.S.A.* **81 H10** 34 46N 89 27W
Hollywood, *Calif., U.S.A.* . . . **74 D3** 34 7N 118 25W
Hollywood, *Fla., U.S.A.* **77 N5** 26 1N 80 9W
Holman, *Canada* **68 A8** 70 42N 117 41W
Holman, *N.W.T., Canada* . . . **68 A8** 70 44N 117 44W
Hólmavík, *Iceland* **8 D3** 65 42N 21 40W
Holmen, *U.S.A.* **80 D9** 43 58N 91 15W
Holmes Reefs, *Australia* . . . **62 B4** 16 27S 148 0 E
Holmsund, *Sweden* . . . . **8 E19** 63 41N 20 20 E
Holroyd →, *Australia* . . . . . **62 A3** 14 10S 141 36 E
Holstebro, *Denmark* . . . . . . **9 H13** 56 22N 8 37 E
Holsworthy, *U.K.* **11 G3** 50 48N 4 22W
Holton, *Canada* **71 B8** 54 31N 57 12W
Holton, *U.S.A.* **80 F7** 39 28N 95 44W
Holtville, *U.S.A.* **85 N11** 32 49N 115 23W
Holwerd, *Neths.* . . . . **15 A5** 53 22N 5 54 E
Holy I., *Angl., U.K.* **10 D3** 53 17N 4 37W
Holy I., *Northumb., U.K.* . . . **10 B6** 55 40N 1 47W
Holyhead, *U.K.* **10 D3** 53 18N 4 38W
Holyoke, *Colo., U.S.A.* **80 E3** 40 35N 102 18W
Holyoke, *Mass., U.S.A.* **79 D12** 42 12N 72 37W
Holyrood, *Canada* **71 C9** 47 27N 53 8W
Homa Bay, *Kenya* . . . . **54 C3** 0 36S 34 30 E
Homalin, *Burma* . . . . **41 G19** 24 55N 95 0 E
Homand, *Iran* . . . . **45 C8** 32 28N 59 37 E
Homathko →, *Canada* **72 C4** 51 0N 124 56W
Hombori, *Mali* **50 E5** 15 20N 1 38W
Home B., *Canada* **69 B13** 68 40N 67 10W
Home Hill, *Australia* . . . . . . **62 B4** 19 43S 147 25 E
Homedale, *U.S.A.* **82 E5** 43 37N 116 56W
Homer, *Alaska, U.S.A.* **68 C4** 59 39N 151 33W
Homer, *La., U.S.A.* **81 J8** 32 48N 93 4W
Homer City, *U.S.A.* **78 F5** 40 32N 79 10W
Homestead, *Australia* . . . . . **62 C4** 20 20S 145 40 E
Homestead, *U.S.A.* **77 N5** 25 28N 80 29W
Homewood, *U.S.A.* **84 F6** 39 4N 120 8W
Homoine, *Mozam.* . . . . **57 C6** 23 55S 35 8 E
Homs = Ḥimş, *Syria* . . . . . . **47 A5** 34 40N 36 45 E
Homyel, *Belarus* . . . . **17 B16** 52 28N 31 0 E
Hon Chong, *Vietnam* . . . . . . **39 G5** 10 25N 104 30 E
Hon Me, *Vietnam* . . . . **38 C5** 19 23N 105 56 E
Honan = Henan □, *China* . . **34 H8** 34 0N 114 0 E
Honbetsu, *Japan* . . . . **30 C11** 43 7N 143 37 E
Honcut, *U.S.A.* **84 F5** 39 20N 121 32W
Hondeklipbaai, *S. Africa* . . . **56 E2** 30 19S 17 17 E
Hondo, *Japan* . . . . **31 H5** 32 27N 130 12 E
Hondo, *U.S.A.* **81 L5** 29 21N 99 9W
Hondo →, *Belize* **87 D7** 18 25N 88 21W
Honduras ■, *Cent. Amer.* . . **88 D2** 14 40N 86 30W
Honduras, G. de, *Caribbean* **88 C2** 16 50N 87 0W
Hønefoss, *Norway* . . . . **9 F14** 60 10N 10 18 E
Honesdale, *U.S.A.* **79 E9** 41 34N 75 16W
Honey L., *U.S.A.* **84 E6** 40 15N 120 19W
Honfleur, *France* . . . . **18 B4** 49 25N 0 13 E
Hong →, *Vietnam* . . . . **32 D5** 22 0N 104 0 E
Hong He →, *China* . . . . **34 H8** 32 25N 115 35 E
Hong Kong □, *China* . . . . . . **33 D6** 22 11N 114 14 E
Hongch'ŏn, *S. Korea* . . . . . . **35 F14** 37 44N 127 53 E
Hongjiang, *China* . . . . **33 D5** 27 7N 109 59 E
Hongliu He →, *China* . . . . . **34 F5** 38 0N 109 50 E
Hongor, *Mongolia* . . . . **34 B7** 45 45N 112 50 E
Hongsa, *Laos* . . . . **38 C3** 19 43N 101 20 E
Hongshui He →, *China* . . . . **33 D5** 23 48N 109 30 E
Hongsŏng, *S. Korea* . . . . . . **35 F14** 36 37N 126 38 E
Hongtong, *China* . . . . **34 F6** 36 16N 111 40 E
Honguedo, Détroit d', *Canada* **71 C7** 49 15N 64 0W
Hongwon, *N. Korea* . . . . **35 E14** 40 0N 127 56 E
Hongze Hu, *China* . . . . **35 H10** 33 15N 118 35 E
Honiara, *Solomon Is.* . . . . . **64 H7** 9 27S 159 57 E
Honiton, *U.K.* **11 G4** 50 47N 3 11W
Honjō, *Japan* . . . . **30 E10** 39 23N 140 3 E
Honningsvåg, *Norway* . . . . . **8 A21** 70 59N 25 59 E
Honolulu, *U.S.A.* **74 H16** 21 19N 157 52W
Honshū, *Japan* . . . . **31 G9** 36 0N 138 0 E
Hood, Mt., *U.S.A.* **82 D3** 45 23N 121 42W
Hood, Pt., *Australia* . . . . . . **61 F2** 34 23S 119 34 E
Hood River, *U.S.A.* **82 D3** 45 43N 121 31W
Hoodsport, *U.S.A.* **84 C3** 47 24N 123 9W
Hoogeveen, *Neths.* . . . . **15 B6** 52 44N 6 28 E
Hoogezand-Sappemeer, *Neths.* . . . . **15 A6** 53 9N 6 45 E
Hooghly = Hugli →, *India* **43 J13** 21 56N 88 4 E
Hooghly-Chinsura = Chunchura, *India* . . . . . **43 H13** 22 53N 88 27 E
Hook Hd., *Ireland* **13 D5** 52 7N 6 56W
Hook I., *Australia* . . . . **62 C4** 20 4S 149 0 E
Hook of Holland = Hoek van Holland, *Neths.* . . . . **15 C4** 52 0N 4 7 E
Hooker, *U.S.A.* **81 G4** 36 52N 101 13W
Hooker Creek, *Australia* . . . **60 C5** 18 23S 130 38 E
Hoonah, *U.S.A.* **72 B1** 58 7N 135 27W
Hooper Bay, *U.S.A.* **68 B3** 61 32N 166 6W
Hoopeston, *U.S.A.* **76 E2** 40 28N 87 40W
Hoopstad, *S. Africa* . . . . **56 D4** 27 50S 25 55 E
Hoorn, *Neths.* . . . . **15 B5** 52 38N 5 4 E
Hoover, *U.S.A.* **77 J2** 33 20N 86 11W
Hoover Dam, *U.S.A.* **85 K12** 36 1N 114 44W
Hooversville, *U.S.A.* **78 F6** 40 9N 78 55W
Hop Bottom, *U.S.A.* **79 E9** 41 42N 75 46W
Hope, *Canada* **72 D4** 49 25N 121 25W
Hope, *Ariz., U.S.A.* **85 M13** 33 43N 113 42W
Hope, *Ark., U.S.A.* **81 J8** 33 40N 93 36W
Hope, L., *S. Austral., Australia* . . . . **63 D2** 28 24S 139 18 E
Hope, L., *W. Austral., Australia* . . . . **61 F3** 32 35S 120 15 E
Hope I., *Canada* **78 B4** 44 55N 80 11W
Hope Town, *Bahamas* **88 A4** 26 35N 76 57W
Hopedale, *Canada* **71 A7** 55 28N 60 13W
Hopedale, *U.S.A.* **79 D13** 42 8N 71 33W
Hopefield, *S. Africa* . . . . **56 E2** 33 3S 18 22 E
Hopei = Hebei □, *China* . . . **34 E9** 39 0N 116 0 E
Hopelchén, *Mexico* **87 D7** 19 46N 89 50W
Hopetoun, *Vic., Australia* . . **63 F3** 35 42S 142 22 E
Hopetoun, *W. Austral., Australia* . . . . **61 F3** 33 57S 120 7 E
Hopetown, *S. Africa* . . . . **56 D3** 29 34S 24 3 E
Hopevale, *Australia* . . . . **62 B4** 15 16S 145 20 E
Hopewell, *U.S.A.* **76 G7** 37 18N 77 17W
Hopkins, L., *Australia* . . . . . **60 D4** 24 15S 128 35 E
Hopkinsville, *U.S.A.* **77 G2** 36 52N 87 29W
Hopland, *U.S.A.* **84 G3** 38 58N 123 7W
Hoquiam, *U.S.A.* **84 D3** 46 59N 123 53W
Horden Hills, *Australia* . . . . **60 D5** 20 15S 130 0 E
Horinger, *China* . . . . **34 D6** 40 28N 111 48 E
Horlick Mts., *Antarctica* . . . **5 E15** 84 0S 102 0W
Horlivka, *Ukraine* . . . . **25 E6** 48 19N 38 5 E
Hormak, *Iran* . . . . **45 D9** 29 58N 60 51 E
Hormoz, *Iran* . . . . **45 E7** 27 35N 55 0 E
Hormoz, Jaz.-ye, *Iran* . . . . . **45 E8** 27 8N 56 28 E
Hormozgān □, *Iran* . . . . **45 E8** 27 30N 56 0 E
Hormuz, Kūh-e, *Iran* . . . . . . **45 E7** 27 27N 55 10 E
Hormuz, Str. of, *The Gulf* . . **45 E8** 26 30N 56 30 E
Horn, *Austria* . . . . **16 D8** 48 39N 15 40 E
Horn, *Iceland* **8 C2** 66 28N 22 28W
Horn →, *Canada* **72 A5** 61 30N 118 1W
Horn, Cape = Hornos, C. de, *Chile* **96 H3** 55 50S 67 30W
Horn Head, *Ireland* **13 A3** 55 14N 8 0W
Horn I., *Australia* . . . . **62 A3** 10 37S 142 17 E
Horn Mts., *Canada* **72 A5** 62 15N 119 15W
Hornavan, *Sweden* . . . . **8 C17** 66 15N 17 30 E
Hornbeck, *U.S.A.* **81 K8** 31 20N 93 24W
Hornbrook, *U.S.A.* **82 F2** 41 55N 122 33W
Horncastle, *U.K.* **10 D7** 53 13N 0 7W
Hornell, *U.S.A.* **78 D7** 42 20N 77 40W
Hornell L., *Canada* **72 A5** 62 20N 119 25W
Hornepayne, *Canada* **70 C3** 49 14N 84 48W
Hornings Mills, *Canada* **78 B4** 44 9N 80 12W
Hornitos, *U.S.A.* **84 H6** 37 30N 120 14W
Hornos, C. de, *Chile* **96 H3** 55 50S 67 30W
Hornsea, *U.K.* **10 D7** 53 55N 0 11W
Horobetsu, *Japan* . . . . **30 C10** 42 24N 141 6 E
Horodenka, *Ukraine* . . . . **17 D13** 48 41N 25 29 E
Horodok, *Khmelnytskyy, Ukraine* . . . . **17 D14** 49 10N 26 34 E
Horodok, *Lviv, Ukraine* . . . . **17 D12** 49 46N 23 32 E
Horokhiv, *Ukraine* . . . . **17 C13** 50 30N 24 45 E
Horqin Youyi Qianqi, *China* **35 A12** 46 5N 122 3 E
Horqueta, *Paraguay* **94 A4** 23 15S 56 55W
Horse Creek, *U.S.A.* **80 E3** 41 57N 105 10W
Horse Is., *Canada* **71 B8** 50 15N 55 50W
Horsefly L., *Canada* **72 C4** 52 25N 121 0W
Horseheads, *U.S.A.* **78 D8** 42 10N 76 49W
Horsens, *Denmark* . . . . **9 J13** 55 52N 9 51 E
Horsham, *Australia* . . . . **63 F3** 36 44S 142 13 E
Horsham, *U.K.* **11 F7** 51 4N 0 20W
Horten, *Norway* . . . . **9 G14** 59 25N 10 32 E
Horton, *U.S.A.* **80 F7** 39 40N 95 32W
Horton →, *Canada* **68 B7** 69 56N 126 52W
Horwood L., *Canada* **70 C3** 48 5N 82 20W
Hose, Gunung-Gunung, *Malaysia* . . . . **36 D4** 2 5N 114 6 E
Ḥoseynābād, *Khuzestān, Iran* . . . . **45 C6** 32 45N 48 20 E
Ḥoseynābād, *Kordestān, Iran* . . . . **44 C5** 35 33N 47 8 E
Hoshangabad, *India* . . . . **42 H7** 22 45N 77 45 E
Hoshiarpur, *India* . . . . **42 D6** 31 30N 75 58 E
Hospet, *India* . . . . **40 M10** 15 15N 76 20 E
Hoste, I., *Chile* **96 H3** 55 0S 69 0W
Hot, *Thailand* . . . . **38 C2** 18 8N 98 29 E
Hot Creek Range, *U.S.A.* . . . **82 G6** 38 40N 116 20W
Hot Springs, *Ark., U.S.A.* . . . **81 H8** 34 31N 93 3W
Hot Springs, *S. Dak., U.S.A.* **80 D3** 43 26N 103 29W
Hotagen, *Sweden* . . . . **8 E16** 63 50N 14 30 E
Hotan, *China* . . . . **32 C2** 37 25N 79 55 E
Hotazel, *S. Africa* . . . . **56 D3** 27 17S 22 58 E
Hotchkiss, *U.S.A.* **83 G10** 38 48N 107 43W
Hotham, C., *Australia* . . . . . **60 B5** 12 2S 131 18 E
Hoting, *Sweden* . . . . **8 D17** 64 8N 16 15 E
Hotte, Massif de la, *Haiti* . . **89 C5** 18 30N 73 45W
Hottentotsbaai, *Namibia* . . . **56 D1** 26 8S 14 59 E
Houffalize, *Belgium* . . . . **15 D5** 50 8N 5 48 E
Houghton, *Mich., U.S.A.* . . . **80 B10** 47 7N 88 34W
Houghton, *N.Y., U.S.A.* **78 D6** 42 25N 78 10W
Houghton L., *U.S.A.* **76 C3** 44 21N 84 44W
Houhora Heads, *N.Z.* . . . . . . **59 F4** 34 49S 173 9 E
Houlton, *U.S.A.* **77 B12** 46 8N 67 51W
Houma, *U.S.A.* **81 L9** 29 36N 90 43W
Housatonic →, *U.S.A.* **79 E11** 41 10N 73 7W
Houston, *Canada* **72 C3** 54 25N 126 39W
Houston, *Mo., U.S.A.* **81 G9** 37 22N 91 58W
Houston, *Tex., U.S.A.* **81 L7** 29 46N 95 22W
Houtman Abrolhos, *Australia* . . . . **61 E1** 28 43S 113 48 E
Hovd, *Mongolia* . . . . **32 B4** 48 2N 91 37 E
Hove, *U.K.* **11 G7** 50 50N 0 10W
Hoveyzeh, *Iran* . . . . **45 D6** 31 27N 48 4 E
Hövsgöl, *Mongolia* . . . . **34 C5** 43 37N 109 39 E
Hövsgöl Nuur, *Mongolia* . . . **32 A5** 51 0N 100 30 E
Howard, *Australia* . . . . **63 D5** 25 16S 152 32 E
Howard, *Pa., U.S.A.* **78 F7** 41 1N 77 40W
Howard, *S. Dak., U.S.A.* . . . **80 C6** 44 1N 97 32W
Howe, *U.S.A.* **82 E7** 43 48N 113 0W
Howe, C., *Australia* . . . . **63 F5** 37 30S 150 0 E
Howe I., *Canada* **79 B8** 44 16N 76 17W
Howell, *U.S.A.* **76 D4** 42 36N 83 56W
Howick, *Canada* **79 A11** 45 11N 73 51W
Howick, *S. Africa* . . . . **57 D5** 29 28S 30 14 E
Howick Group, *Australia* . . . **62 A4** 14 20S 145 30 E
Howitt, L., *Australia* . . . . . . **63 D2** 27 40S 138 40 E
Howland I., *Pac. Oc.* **64 G10** 0 48N 176 38W
Howrah = Haora, *India* . . . . **43 H13** 22 37N 88 20 E
Howth Hd., *Ireland* **13 C5** 53 22N 6 3W
Höxter, *Germany* . . . . **16 C5** 51 46N 9 22 E
Hoy, *U.K.* **12 C5** 58 50N 3 15W
Høyanger, *Norway* . . . . **9 F12** 61 13N 6 4 E

Hoyerswerda, Germany 16 C8 51 26N 14 14 E
Hoylake, U.K. 10 D4 53 24N 3 10W
Hpungan Pass, Burma 41 F20 27 30N 96 55 E
Hradec Králové, Czech Rep. 16 C8 50 15N 15 50 E
Hrodna, Belarus 17 B12 53 42N 23 52 E
Hrodzyanka, Belarus 17 B15 53 31N 28 42 E
Hron →, Slovak Rep. 17 E10 47 49N 18 45 E
Hrvatska = Croatia ■, Europe 16 F9 45 20N 16 0 E
Hrymayliv, Ukraine 17 D14 49 20N 26 5 E
Hsenwi, Burma 41 H20 23 22N 97 55 E
Hsiamen = Xiamen, China 33 D6 24 25N 118 4 E
Hsian = Xi'an, China 34 G5 34 15N 109 0 E
Hsinchu, Taiwan 33 D7 24 48N 120 58 E
Hsinhailien = Lianyungang, China 35 G10 34 40N 119 11 E
Hsüchou = Xuzhou, China 35 G9 34 18N 117 10 E
Hu Xian, China 34 G5 34 8N 108 42 E
Hua Hin, Thailand 38 F2 12 34N 99 58 E
Hua Xian, Henan, China 34 G8 35 30N 114 30 E
Hua Xian, Shaanxi, China 34 G5 34 30N 109 48 E
Huachinera, Mexico 86 A3 30 9N 108 55W
Huacho, Peru 92 F3 11 10S 77 35W
Huade, China 34 D7 41 55N 113 59 E
Huadian, China 35 C14 43 0N 126 40 E
Huai He →, China 33 C6 33 0N 118 30 E
Huai Yot, Thailand 39 J2 7 45N 99 37 E
Huai'an, Hebei, China 34 D8 40 30N 114 20 E
Huai'an, Jiangsu, China 35 H10 33 30N 119 10 E
Huaibei, China 34 G9 34 0N 116 48 E
Huaide = Gongzhuling, China 35 C13 43 30N 124 40 E
Huaidezhen, China 35 C13 43 48N 124 50 E
Huainan, China 33 C6 32 38N 116 58 E
Huairen, China 34 E7 39 48N 113 20 E
Huairou, China 34 D9 40 20N 116 35 E
Huaiyang, China 34 H8 33 40N 114 52 E
Huaiyin, China 35 H10 33 30N 119 2 E
Huaiyuan, China 35 H9 32 55N 117 10 E
Huajianzi, China 35 D13 41 23N 125 20 E
Huajuapan de Leon, Mexico 87 D5 17 50N 97 48W
Hualapai Peak, U.S.A. 83 J7 35 5N 113 54W
Huallaga →, Peru 92 E3 5 15S 75 30W
Huambo, Angola 53 G3 12 42S 15 54 E
Huan Jiang →, China 34 G5 34 28N 109 0 E
Huan Xian, China 34 F4 36 33N 107 7 E
Huancabamba, Peru 92 E3 5 10S 79 15W
Huancane, Peru 92 G5 15 10S 69 44W
Huancavelica, Peru 92 F3 12 50S 75 5W
Huancayo, Peru 92 F3 12 5S 75 12W
Huanchaca, Bolivia 92 H5 20 15S 66 40W
Huang Hai = Yellow Sea, China 35 G12 35 0N 123 0 E
Huang He →, China 35 F10 37 55N 118 50 E
Huang Xian, China 35 F11 37 38N 120 30 E
Huangling, China 34 G5 35 34N 109 15 E
Huanglong, China 34 G5 35 30N 109 59 E
Huangshan, China 33 D6 29 42N 118 25 E
Huangshi, China 33 C6 30 10N 115 3 E
Huangsongdian, China 35 C14 43 45N 127 25 E
Huantai, China 35 F9 36 58N 117 56 E
Huánuco, Peru 92 E3 9 55S 76 15W
Huaraz, Peru 92 E3 9 30S 77 32W
Huarmey, Peru 92 F3 10 5S 78 5W
Huascarán, Peru 92 E3 9 8S 77 36W
Huasco, Chile 94 B1 28 30S 71 15W
Huasco →, Chile 94 B1 28 27S 71 13W
Huasna, U.S.A. 85 K6 35 6N 120 24W
Huatabampo, Mexico 86 B3 26 50N 109 50W
Huauchinango, Mexico 87 C5 20 11N 98 3W
Huautla de Jiménez, Mexico 87 D5 18 8N 96 51W
Huay Namota, Mexico 86 C4 21 56N 104 30W
Huayin, China 34 G6 34 35N 110 5 E
Hubbard, Ohio, U.S.A. 78 E4 41 9N 80 34W
Hubbard, Tex., U.S.A. 81 K6 31 51N 96 48W
Hubbart Pt., Canada 73 B10 59 21N 94 41W
Hubei □, China 33 C6 31 0N 112 0 E
Hubli, India 40 M9 15 22N 75 15 E
Huch'ang, N. Korea 35 D14 41 25N 127 2 E
Hucknall, U.K. 10 D6 53 3N 1 13W
Huddersfield, U.K. 10 D6 53 39N 1 47W
Hudiksvall, Sweden 9 F17 61 43N 17 10 E
Hudson, Canada 70 B1 50 6N 92 9W
Hudson, Mass., U.S.A. 79 D13 42 23N 71 34W
Hudson, N.Y., U.S.A. 79 D11 42 15N 73 46W
Hudson, Wis., U.S.A. 80 C8 44 58N 92 45W
Hudson, Wyo., U.S.A. 82 E9 42 54N 108 35W
Hudson →, U.S.A. 79 F10 40 42N 74 2W
Hudson Bay, N.W.T., Canada 69 C11 60 0N 86 0W
Hudson Bay, Sask., Canada 73 C8 52 51N 102 23W
Hudson Falls, U.S.A. 79 C11 43 18N 73 35W
Hudson Mts., Antarctica 5 D16 74 32S 99 20W
Hudson Str., Canada 69 B13 62 0N 70 0W
Hudson's Hope, Canada 72 B4 56 0N 121 54W
Hue, Vietnam 38 D6 16 30N 107 35 E
Huehuetenango, Guatemala 88 C1 15 20N 91 28W
Huejúcar, Mexico 86 C4 22 21N 103 13W
Huelva, Spain 19 D2 37 18N 6 57W
Huentelauquén, Chile 94 C1 31 38S 71 33W
Huerta, Sa. de la, Argentina 94 C2 31 10S 67 30W
Huesca, Spain 19 A5 42 8N 0 25W
Huetamo, Mexico 86 D4 18 36N 100 54W
Hugh →, Australia 62 D1 25 1S 134 1 E
Hughenden, Australia 62 C3 20 52S 144 10 E
Hughes, Australia 61 F4 30 42S 129 31 E
Hughesville, U.S.A. 79 E8 41 14N 76 44W
Hugli →, India 43 J13 21 56N 88 4 E
Hugo, Colo., U.S.A. 80 F3 39 8N 103 28W
Hugo, Okla., U.S.A. 81 H7 34 1N 95 31W
Hugoton, U.S.A. 81 G4 37 11N 101 21W
Hui Xian = Huixian, China 34 G7 35 27N 113 12 E
Hui Xian, China 34 H4 33 50N 106 4 E
Hui'anbu, China 34 F4 37 28N 106 38 E
Huichapán, Mexico 87 C5 20 24N 99 40W
Huifa He →, China 35 C14 43 0N 127 50 E
Huila, Nevado del, Colombia 92 C3 3 0N 76 0W
Huimin, China 35 F9 37 27N 117 28 E
Huinan, China 35 C14 42 40N 126 2 E
Huinca Renancó, Argentina 94 C3 34 51S 64 22W
Huining, China 34 G3 35 38N 105 0 E
Huinong, China 34 E4 39 5N 106 35 E
Huisache, Mexico 86 C4 22 55N 100 25W
Huiting, China 34 G9 34 5N 116 5 E
Huixian, China 34 G7 35 27N 113 12 E
Huixtla, Mexico 87 D6 15 9N 92 28W
Huize, China 32 D5 26 24N 103 15 E
Hukawng Valley, Burma 41 F20 26 30N 96 30 E
Hukuntsi, Botswana 56 C3 23 58S 21 45 E
Ḩulayfā', Si. Arabia 44 E4 25 58N 40 45 E
Huld = Ulaanjirem, Mongolia 34 B3 45 5N 105 30 E
Hulin He →, China 35 B12 45 0N 122 10 E
Hull = Kingston upon Hull, U.K. 10 D7 53 45N 0 21W
Hull, Canada 79 A9 45 25N 75 44W
Hull →, U.K. 10 D7 53 44N 0 20W
Hulst, Neths. 15 C4 51 17N 4 2 E
Hulun Nur, China 33 B6 49 0N 117 30 E
Humahuaca, Argentina 94 A2 23 10S 65 25W
Humaitá, Brazil 92 E6 7 35S 63 1W
Humaitá, Paraguay 94 B4 27 2S 58 31W
Humansdorp, S. Africa 56 E3 34 2S 24 46 E
Humbe, Angola 56 B1 16 40S 14 55 E
Humber →, U.K. 10 D7 53 42N 0 27W
Humboldt, Canada 73 C7 52 15N 105 9W
Humboldt, Iowa, U.S.A. 80 D7 42 44N 94 13W
Humboldt, Tenn., U.S.A. 81 H10 35 50N 88 55W
Humboldt →, U.S.A. 82 F4 39 59N 118 36W
Humboldt Gletscher, Greenland 4 B4 79 30N 62 0W
Hume, U.S.A. 84 J8 36 48N 118 54W
Hume, L., Australia 63 F4 36 0S 147 5 E
Humenné, Slovak Rep. 17 D11 48 55N 21 50 E
Humphreys, Mt., U.S.A. 84 H8 37 17N 118 40W
Humphreys Peak, U.S.A. 83 J8 35 21N 111 41W
Humptulips, U.S.A. 84 C3 47 14N 123 57W
Hūn, Libya 51 C9 29 2N 16 0 E
Hun Jiang →, China 35 D13 40 50N 125 38 E
Húnaflói, Iceland 8 D3 65 50N 20 50W
Hunan □, China 33 D6 27 30N 112 0 E
Hunchun, China 35 C16 42 52N 130 28 E
Hundewali, Pakistan 42 D5 31 55N 72 38 E
Hundred Mile House, Canada 72 C4 51 38N 121 18W
Hunedoara, Romania 17 F12 45 40N 22 50 E
Hungary ■, Europe 17 E10 47 20N 19 20 E
Hungary, Plain of, Europe 6 F10 47 0N 20 0 E
Hungerford, Australia 63 D3 28 58S 144 24 E
Hŭngnam, N. Korea 35 E14 39 49N 127 45 E
Hunsberge, Namibia 56 D2 27 45S 17 12 E
Hunsrück, Germany 16 D4 49 56N 7 27 E
Hunstanton, U.K. 10 E8 52 56N 0 29 E
Hunter, U.S.A. 79 D10 42 13N 74 13W
Hunter I., Australia 62 G3 40 30S 144 45 E
Hunter I., Canada 72 C3 51 55N 128 0W
Hunter Ra., Australia 63 E5 32 45S 150 15 E
Hunters Road, Zimbabwe 55 F2 19 9S 29 49 E
Hunterville, N.Z. 59 H5 39 56S 175 35 E
Huntingburg, U.S.A. 76 F2 38 18N 86 57W
Huntingdon, Canada 70 C5 45 6N 74 10W
Huntingdon, U.K. 11 E7 52 20N 0 11W
Huntingdon, U.S.A. 78 F6 40 30N 78 1W
Huntington, Ind., U.S.A. 76 E3 40 53N 85 30W
Huntington, Oreg., U.S.A. 82 D5 44 21N 117 16W
Huntington, Utah, U.S.A. 82 G8 39 20N 110 58W
Huntington, W. Va., U.S.A. 76 F4 38 25N 82 27W
Huntington Beach, U.S.A. 85 M9 33 40N 118 5W
Huntington Station, U.S.A. 79 F11 40 52N 73 26W
Huntly, N.Z. 59 G5 37 34S 175 11 E
Huntly, U.K. 12 D6 57 27N 2 47W
Huntsville, Canada 78 A5 45 20N 79 14W
Huntsville, Ala., U.S.A. 77 H2 34 44N 86 35W
Huntsville, Tex., U.S.A. 81 K7 30 43N 95 33W
Hunyani →, Zimbabwe 55 F3 15 57S 30 39 E
Hunyuan, China 34 E7 39 42N 113 42 E
Hunza →, India 43 B6 35 54N 74 20 E
Huo Xian = Huozhou, China 34 F6 36 36N 111 42 E
Huong Hoa, Vietnam 38 D6 16 37N 106 45 E
Huong Khe, Vietnam 38 C5 18 13N 105 41 E
Huonville, Australia 62 G4 43 0S 147 5 E
Huozhou, China 34 F6 36 36N 111 42 E
Hupeh = Hubei □, China 33 C6 31 0N 112 0 E
Ḩūr, Iran 45 D8 30 50N 57 7 E
Hurd, C., Canada 78 A3 45 13N 81 44W
Hure Qi, China 35 C11 42 45N 121 45 E
Hurghada, Egypt 51 C12 27 15N 33 50 E
Hurley, N. Mex., U.S.A. 83 K9 32 42N 108 8W
Hurley, Wis., U.S.A. 80 B9 46 27N 90 11W
Huron, Calif., U.S.A. 84 J6 36 12N 120 6W
Huron, Ohio, U.S.A. 78 E2 41 24N 82 33W
Huron, S. Dak., U.S.A. 80 C5 44 22N 98 13W
Huron, L., U.S.A. 78 B2 44 30N 82 40W
Hurricane, U.S.A. 83 H7 37 11N 113 17W
Hurunui →, N.Z. 59 K4 42 54S 173 18 E
Húsavík, Iceland 8 C5 66 3N 17 21W
Huşi, Romania 17 E15 46 41N 28 7 E
Huskvarna, Sweden 9 H16 57 47N 14 15 E
Hustadvika, Norway 8 E12 63 0N 7 0 E
Hustontown, U.S.A. 78 F6 40 3N 78 2W
Hutchinson, Kans., U.S.A. 81 F6 38 5N 97 56W
Hutchinson, Minn., U.S.A. 80 C7 44 54N 94 22W
Hutte Sauvage, L. de la, Canada 71 A7 56 15N 64 45W
Hutton, Mt., Australia 63 D4 25 51S 148 20 E
Huy, Belgium 15 D5 50 31N 5 15 E
Huzhou, China 33 C7 30 51N 120 8 E
Hvammstangi, Iceland 8 D3 65 24N 20 57W
Hvar, Croatia 20 C7 43 11N 16 28 E
Hvítá →, Iceland 8 D3 64 30N 21 58W
Hwachŏn-chŏsuji, S. Korea 35 E14 38 5N 127 50 E
Hwang Ho = Huang He →, China 35 F10 37 55N 118 50 E
Hwange, Zimbabwe 55 F2 18 18S 26 30 E
Hwange Nat. Park, Zimbabwe 56 B4 19 0S 26 30 E
Hyannis, Mass., U.S.A. 76 E10 41 39N 70 17W
Hyannis, Nebr., U.S.A. 80 E4 42 0N 101 46W
Hyargas Nuur, Mongolia 32 B4 49 0N 93 0 E
Hydaburg, U.S.A. 72 B2 55 15N 132 50W
Hyde Park, U.S.A. 79 E11 41 47N 73 56W
Hyden, Australia 61 F2 32 24S 118 53 E
Hyder, U.S.A. 72 B2 55 55N 130 5W
Hyderabad, India 40 L11 17 22N 78 29 E
Hyderabad, Pakistan 42 G3 25 23N 68 24 E
Hyères, France 18 E7 43 8N 6 9 E
Hyères, Îs. d', France 18 E7 43 0N 6 20 E
Hyesan, N. Korea 35 D15 41 20N 128 10 E
Hyland →, Canada 72 B3 59 52N 128 12W
Hymia, India 43 C8 33 40N 78 2 E
Hyndman Peak, U.S.A. 82 E6 43 45N 114 8W
Hyōgo □, Japan 31 G7 35 15N 134 50 E
Hyrum, U.S.A. 82 F8 41 38N 111 51W
Hysham, U.S.A. 82 C10 46 18N 107 14W
Hythe, U.K. 11 F9 51 4N 1 5 E
Hyūga, Japan 31 H5 32 25N 131 35 E
Hyvinge = Hyvinkää, Finland 9 F21 60 38N 24 50 E
Hyvinkää, Finland 9 F21 60 38N 24 50 E

I

I-n-Gall, Niger 50 E7 16 51N 7 1 E
Iaco →, Brazil 92 E5 9 3S 68 34W
Iakora, Madag. 57 C8 23 6S 46 40 E
Ialomiţa →, Romania 17 F14 44 42N 27 51 E
Iaşi, Romania 17 E14 47 10N 27 40 E
Ib →, India 43 J10 21 34N 83 48 E
Iba, Phil. 37 A6 15 22N 120 0 E
Ibadan, Nigeria 50 G6 7 22N 3 58 E
Ibagué, Colombia 92 C3 4 20N 75 20W
Ibar →, Serbia, Yug. 21 C9 43 43N 20 45 E
Ibaraki □, Japan 31 F10 36 10N 140 10 E
Ibarra, Ecuador 92 C3 0 21N 78 7W
Ibembo, Dem. Rep. of the Congo 54 B1 2 35N 23 35 E
Ibera, L., Argentina 94 B4 28 30S 57 9W
Iberian Peninsula, Europe 6 H5 40 0N 5 0W
Iberville, Canada 79 A11 45 19N 73 17W
Iberville, Lac d', Canada 70 A5 55 55N 73 15W
Ibiá, Brazil 93 G9 19 30S 46 30W
Ibicuí →, Brazil 95 B4 29 25S 56 47W
Ibicuy, Argentina 94 C4 33 55S 59 10W
Ibioapaba, Sa. da, Brazil 93 D10 4 0S 41 30W
Ibiza = Eivissa, Spain 22 C7 38 54N 1 26 E
Ibo, Mozam. 55 E5 12 22S 40 40 E
Ibonma, Indonesia 37 E8 3 29S 133 31 E
Ibotirama, Brazil 93 F10 12 13S 43 12W
Ibrāhīm →, Lebanon 47 A4 34 4N 35 38 E
'Ibrī, Oman 45 F8 23 14N 56 30 E
Ibu, Indonesia 37 D7 1 35N 127 33 E
Ibusuki, Japan 31 J5 31 12N 130 40 E
Ica, Peru 92 F3 14 0S 75 48W
Iça →, Brazil 92 D5 2 55S 67 58W
Içana, Brazil 92 C5 0 21N 67 19W
Içana →, Brazil 92 C5 0 26N 67 19W
Içel = Mersin, Turkey 25 G5 36 51N 34 36 E
Iceland ■, Europe 8 D4 64 45N 19 0W
Ich'ang = Yichang, China 33 C6 30 40N 111 20 E
Ichchapuram, India 41 K14 19 10N 84 40 E
Ichhawar, India 42 H7 23 1N 77 1 E
Ichihara, Japan 31 G10 35 28N 140 5 E
Ichikawa, Japan 31 G9 35 44N 139 55 E
Ichilo →, Bolivia 92 G6 15 57S 64 50W
Ichinohe, Japan 30 D10 40 13N 141 17 E
Ichinomiya, Japan 31 G8 35 18N 136 48 E
Ichinoseki, Japan 30 E10 38 55N 141 8 E
Ichŏn, S. Korea 35 F14 37 17N 127 27 E
Icod, Canary Is. 22 F3 28 22N 16 43W
Ida Grove, U.S.A. 80 D7 42 21N 95 28W
Idabel, U.S.A. 81 J7 33 54N 94 50W
Idaho □, U.S.A. 82 D7 45 0N 115 0W
Idaho City, U.S.A. 82 E6 43 50N 115 50W
Idaho Falls, U.S.A. 82 E7 43 30N 112 2W
Idar-Oberstein, Germany 16 D4 49 43N 7 16 E
Idfû, Egypt 51 D12 24 55N 32 49 E
Ídhi Óros, Greece 23 D6 35 15N 24 45 E
Ídhra, Greece 21 F10 37 20N 23 28 E
Idi, Indonesia 36 C1 5 2N 97 37 E
Idiofa, Dem. Rep. of the Congo 52 E3 4 55S 19 42 E
Idlib, Syria 44 C3 35 55N 36 36 E
Idria, U.S.A. 84 J6 36 25N 120 41W
Idutywa, S. Africa 57 E4 32 8S 28 18 E
Ieper, Belgium 15 D2 50 51N 2 53 E
Ierápetra, Greece 23 E7 35 1N 25 44 E
Iesi, Italy 20 C5 43 31N 13 14 E
Ifakara, Tanzania 52 F7 8 8S 36 41 E
'Ifāl, W. al →, Si. Arabia 44 D2 28 7N 35 3 E
Ifanadiana, Madag. 57 C8 21 19S 47 39 E
Ife, Nigeria 50 G6 7 30N 4 31 E
Iférouâne, Niger 50 E7 19 5N 8 24 E
Iffley, Australia 62 B3 18 53S 141 12 E
Ifni, Morocco 50 C3 29 29N 10 12W
Iforas, Adrar des, Mali 50 E6 19 40N 1 40 E
Ifould, L., Australia 61 F5 30 52S 132 6 E
Iganga, Uganda 54 B3 0 37N 33 28 E
Igarapava, Brazil 93 H9 20 3S 47 47W
Igarka, Russia 26 C9 67 30N 86 33 E
Igatimi, Paraguay 95 A4 24 5S 55 40W
Iggesund, Sweden 9 F17 61 39N 17 10 E
Iglésias, Italy 20 E3 39 19N 8 32 E
Igloolik, Canada 69 B11 69 20N 81 49W
Igluligaarjuk, Canada 69 B10 63 21N 90 42W
Ignace, Canada 70 C1 49 30N 91 40W
İğneada Burnu, Turkey 21 D13 41 53N 28 2 E
Igoumenítsa, Greece 21 E9 39 32N 20 18 E
Iguaçu →, Brazil 95 B5 25 36S 54 36W
Iguaçu, Cat. del, Brazil 95 B5 25 41S 54 26W
Iguaçu Falls = Iguaçu, Cat. del, Brazil 95 B5 25 41S 54 26W
Iguala, Mexico 87 D5 18 20N 99 40W
Igualada, Spain 19 B6 41 37N 1 37 E
Iguassu = Iguaçu →, Brazil 95 B5 25 36S 54 36W
Iguatu, Brazil 93 E11 6 20S 39 18W
Iharana, Madag. 57 A9 13 25S 50 0 E
Ihbulag, Mongolia 34 C4 43 11N 107 10 E
Iheya-Shima, Japan 31 L3 27 4N 127 58 E
Ihosy, Madag. 57 C8 22 24S 46 8 E
Ihotry, L., Madag. 57 C7 21 56S 43 41 E
Ii, Finland 8 D21 65 19N 25 22 E
Ii-Shima, Japan 31 L3 26 43N 127 47 E
Iida, Japan 31 G8 35 35N 137 50 E
Iijoki →, Finland 8 D21 65 20N 25 20 E
Iisalmi, Finland 8 E22 63 32N 27 10 E
Iiyama, Japan 31 F9 36 51N 138 22 E
Iizuka, Japan 31 H5 33 38N 130 42 E
Ijebu-Ode, Nigeria 50 G6 6 47N 3 58 E
IJmuiden, Neths. 15 B4 52 28N 4 35 E
IJssel →, Neths. 15 B5 52 35N 5 50 E
IJsselmeer, Neths. 15 B5 52 45N 5 20 E
Ijuí, Brazil 95 B5 28 23S 53 55W
Ijuí →, Brazil 95 B4 27 58S 55 20W
Ikaluktutiak, Canada 68 B9 69 10N 105 0W
Ikare, Nigeria 50 G7 7 32N 5 40 E
Ikaría, Greece 21 F12 37 35N 26 10 E
Ikeda, Japan 31 G6 34 1N 133 48 E
Ikela, Dem. Rep. of the Congo 52 E4 1 6S 23 6 E
Iki, Japan 31 H4 33 45N 129 42 E
Ikimba L., Tanzania 54 C3 1 30S 31 20 E
Ikopa →, Madag. 57 B8 16 45S 46 40 E
Ikungu, Tanzania 54 C3 1 33S 33 42 E
Ilagan, Phil. 37 A6 17 7N 121 53 E
Īlām, Iran 44 C5 33 36N 46 36 E
Ilam, Nepal 43 F12 26 58N 87 58 E
Ilam □, Iran 44 C5 33 0N 47 0 E
Ilanskiy, Russia 27 D10 56 14N 96 3 E
Iława, Poland 17 B10 53 36N 19 34 E
Ile-à-la-Crosse, Canada 73 B7 55 27N 107 53W
Ile-à-la-Crosse, Lac, Canada 73 B7 55 40N 107 45W
Île-de-France □, France 18 B5 49 0N 2 20 E
Ilebo, Dem. Rep. of the Congo 52 E4 4 17S 20 55 E
Ilek, Russia 26 D6 51 32N 53 21 E
Ilek →, Russia 24 D9 51 30N 53 22 E
Ilesha, Nigeria 50 G6 7 37N 4 40 E
Ilford, Canada 73 B9 56 4N 95 35W
Ilfracombe, Australia 62 C3 23 30S 144 30 E
Ilfracombe, U.K. 11 F3 51 12N 4 8W
Ilhéus, Brazil 93 F11 14 49S 39 2W
Ili →, Kazakstan 26 E8 45 53N 77 10 E
Iliamna L., U.S.A. 68 C4 59 30N 155 0W
Iligan, Phil. 37 C6 8 12N 124 13 E
Ilion, U.S.A. 79 D9 43 1N 75 2W
Ilkeston, U.K. 10 E6 52 58N 1 19W
Ilkley, U.K. 10 D6 53 56N 1 48W
Illampu = Ancohuma, Nevada, Bolivia 92 G5 16 0S 68 50W
Illana B., Phil. 37 C6 7 35N 123 45 E
Illapel, Chile 94 C1 32 0S 71 10W
Iller →, Germany 16 D6 48 23N 9 58 E
Illetas, Spain 22 B9 39 32N 2 35 E
Illimani, Nevado, Bolivia 92 G5 16 30S 67 50W
Illinois □, U.S.A. 80 E10 40 15N 89 30W
Illinois →, U.S.A. 75 C8 38 58N 90 28W
Illium = Troy, Turkey 21 E12 39 57N 26 12 E
Illizi, Algeria 50 C7 26 31N 8 32 E
Ilmajoki, Finland 9 E20 62 44N 22 34 E
Ilmen, Ozero, Russia 24 C5 58 15N 31 10 E
Ilo, Peru 92 G4 17 40S 71 20W
Iloilo, Phil. 37 B6 10 45N 122 33 E
Ilorin, Nigeria 50 G6 8 30N 4 35 E
Ilwaco, U.S.A. 84 D2 46 19N 124 3W
Ilwaki, Indonesia 37 F7 7 55S 126 30 E
Imabari, Japan 31 G6 34 4N 133 0 E
Imaloto →, Madag. 57 C8 23 27S 45 13 E
Imandra, Ozero, Russia 24 A5 67 30N 33 0 E
Imari, Japan 31 H4 33 15N 129 52 E
Imatra, Finland 24 B4 61 12N 28 48 E
Imbil, Australia 63 D5 26 22S 152 32 E
imeni 26 Bakinskikh Komissarov = Neftçala, Azerbaijan 25 G8 39 19N 49 12 E
Imeri, Serra, Brazil 92 C5 0 50N 65 25W
Imerimandroso, Madag. 57 B8 17 26S 48 35 E
Imi, Ethiopia 46 F3 6 28N 42 10 E
Imlay, U.S.A. 82 F4 40 40N 118 9W
Imlay City, U.S.A. 78 D1 43 2N 83 5W
Immingham, U.K. 10 D7 53 37N 0 13W
Immokalee, U.S.A. 77 M5 26 25N 81 25W
Ímola, Italy 20 B4 44 20N 11 42 E
Imperatriz, Brazil 93 E9 5 30S 47 29W
Impéria, Italy 18 E8 43 53N 8 3 E
Imperial, Canada 73 C7 51 21N 105 28W
Imperial, Calif., U.S.A. 85 N11 32 51N 115 34W
Imperial, Nebr., U.S.A. 80 E4 40 31N 101 39W
Imperial Beach, U.S.A. 85 N9 32 35N 117 8W
Imperial Dam, U.S.A. 85 N12 32 55N 114 25W
Imperial Reservoir, U.S.A. 85 N12 32 53N 114 28W
Imperial Valley, U.S.A. 85 N11 33 0N 115 30W
Imperieuse Reef, Australia 60 C2 17 36S 118 50 E
Impfondo, Congo 52 D3 1 40N 18 0 E
Imphal, India 41 G18 24 48N 93 56 E
İmroz = Gökçeada, Turkey 21 D11 40 10N 25 50 E
Imuris, Mexico 86 A2 30 47N 110 52W
Imuruan B., Phil. 37 B5 10 40N 119 10 E
In Salah, Algeria 50 C6 27 10N 2 32 E
Ina, Japan 31 G8 35 50N 137 55 E
Inangahua Junction, N.Z. 59 J3 41 52S 171 59 E
Inanwatan, Indonesia 37 E8 2 10S 132 14 E
Iñapari, Peru 92 F5 11 0S 69 40W
Inari, Finland 8 B22 68 54N 27 5 E
Inarijärvi, Finland 8 B22 69 0N 28 0 E
Inawashiro-Ko, Japan 30 F10 37 29N 140 6 E
Inca, Spain 22 B9 39 43N 2 54 E
Inca de Oro, Chile 94 B2 26 45S 69 54W
Incaguasi, Chile 94 B1 29 12S 71 5W
İnce Burun, Turkey 25 F5 42 7N 34 56 E
İncesu, Turkey 44 B2 38 38N 35 11 E
Inch'ŏn, S. Korea 35 F14 37 27N 126 40 E
İncirliova, Turkey 21 F12 37 50N 27 41 E
Incline Village, U.S.A. 82 G4 39 10N 119 58W
Incomáti →, Mozam. 57 D5 25 46S 32 43 E
Indalsälven →, Sweden 9 E17 62 36N 17 30 E
Indaw, Burma 41 G20 24 15N 96 5 E
Independence, Calif., U.S.A. 84 J8 36 48N 118 12W
Independence, Iowa, U.S.A. 80 D9 42 28N 91 54W
Independence, Kans., U.S.A. 81 G7 37 14N 95 42W
Independence, Ky., U.S.A. 76 F3 38 57N 84 33W
Independence, Mo., U.S.A. 80 F7 39 6N 94 25W
Independence Fjord, Greenland 4 A6 82 10N 29 0W
Independence Mts., U.S.A. 82 F5 41 20N 116 0W
Index, U.S.A. 84 C5 47 50N 121 33W
India ■, Asia 40 K11 20 0N 78 0 E
Indian →, U.S.A. 77 M5 27 59N 80 34W
Indian Cabins, Canada 72 B5 59 52N 117 40W
Indian Harbour, Canada 71 B8 54 27N 57 13W
Indian Head, Canada 73 C8 50 30N 103 41W
Indian Lake, U.S.A. 79 C10 43 47N 74 16W
Indian Ocean 28 K11 5 0S 75 0 E
Indian Springs, U.S.A. 85 J11 36 35N 115 40W
Indiana, U.S.A. 78 F5 40 37N 79 9W
Indiana □, U.S.A. 76 F3 40 0N 86 0W
Indianapolis, U.S.A. 76 F2 39 46N 86 9W
Indianola, Iowa, U.S.A. 80 E8 41 22N 93 34W
Indianola, Miss., U.S.A. 81 J9 33 27N 90 39W
Indiga, Russia 24 A8 67 38N 49 9 E
Indigirka →, Russia 27 B15 70 48N 148 54 E
Indio, U.S.A. 85 M10 33 43N 116 13W
Indo-China, Asia 28 H14 15 0N 102 0 E
Indonesia ■, Asia 36 F5 5 0S 115 0 E

Indore, *India* **42 H6** 22 42N 75 53 E
Indramayu, *Indonesia* **37 G13** 6 20S 108 19 E
Indravati →, *India* **41 K12** 19 20N 80 20 E
Indre →, *France* **18 C4** 47 16N 0 11 E
Indulkana, *Australia* **63 D1** 26 58S 133 5 E
Indus →, *Pakistan* **42 G2** 24 20N 67 47 E
Indus, Mouth of the, *Pakistan* **42 H3** 24 0N 68 0 E
İnebolu, *Turkey* **25 F5** 41 55N 33 40 E
Infiernillo, Presa del, *Mexico* **86 D4** 18 9N 102 0W
Ingenio, *Canary Is.* **22 G4** 27 55N 15 26W
Ingenio Santa Ana, *Argentina* **94 B2** 27 25S 65 40W
Ingersoll, *Canada* **78 C4** 43 4N 80 55W
Ingham, *Australia* **62 B4** 18 43S 146 10 E
Ingleborough, *U.K.* **10 C5** 54 10N 2 22W
Inglewood, *Queens., Australia* **63 D5** 28 25S 151 2 E
Inglewood, *Vic., Australia* **63 F3** 36 29S 143 53 E
Inglewood, *N.Z.* **59 H5** 39 9S 174 14 E
Inglewood, *U.S.A.* **85 M8** 33 58N 118 21W
Ingólfshöfði, *Iceland* **8 E5** 63 48N 16 39W
Ingolstadt, *Germany* **16 D6** 48 46N 11 26 E
Ingomar, *U.S.A.* **82 C10** 46 35N 107 23W
Ingonish, *Canada* **71 C7** 46 42N 60 18W
Ingraj Bazar, *India* **43 G13** 24 58N 88 10 E
Ingrid Christensen Coast, *Antarctica* **5 C6** 69 30S 76 0 E
Ingulec = Inhulec, *Ukraine* **25 E5** 47 42N 33 14 E
Ingushetia □, *Russia* **25 E8** 43 20N 44 50 E
Ingwavuma, *S. Africa* **57 D5** 27 9S 31 59 E
Inhaca, I., *Mozam.* **57 D5** 26 1S 32 57 E
Inhafenga, *Mozam.* **57 C5** 20 36S 33 53 E
Inhambane, *Mozam.* **57 C6** 23 54S 35 30 E
Inhambane □, *Mozam.* **57 C5** 22 30S 34 20 E
Inhaminga, *Mozam.* **55 F4** 18 26S 35 0 E
Inharrime, *Mozam.* **57 C6** 24 30S 35 0 E
Inharrime →, *Mozam.* **57 C6** 24 30S 35 0 E
Inhulec, *Ukraine* **25 E5** 47 42N 33 14 E
Ining = Yining, *China* **26 E9** 43 58N 81 10 E
Inírida →, *Colombia* **92 C5** 3 55N 67 52W
Inishbofin, *Ireland* **13 C1** 53 37N 10 13W
Inisheer, *Ireland* **13 C2** 53 3N 9 32W
Inishfree B., *Ireland* **13 A3** 55 4N 8 23W
Inishkea North, *Ireland* **13 B1** 54 9N 10 11W
Inishkea South, *Ireland* **13 B1** 54 7N 10 12W
Inishmaan, *Ireland* **13 C2** 53 5N 9 35W
Inishmore, *Ireland* **13 C2** 53 8N 9 45W
Inishowen Pen., *Ireland* **13 A4** 55 14N 7 15W
Inishshark, *Ireland* **13 C1** 53 37N 10 16W
Inishturk, *Ireland* **13 C1** 53 42N 10 7W
Inishvickillane, *Ireland* **13 D1** 52 3N 10 37W
Injune, *Australia* **63 D4** 25 53S 148 32 E
Inklin →, *Canada* **72 B2** 58 50N 133 10W
Inle L., *Burma* **41 J20** 20 30N 96 58 E
Inlet, *U.S.A.* **79 C10** 43 45N 74 48W
Inn →, *Austria* **16 D7** 48 35N 13 28 E
Innamincka, *Australia* **63 D3** 27 44S 140 46 E
Inner Hebrides, *U.K.* **12 E2** 57 0N 6 30W
Inner Mongolia = Nei Monggol Zizhiqu □, *China* **34 D7** 42 0N 112 0 E
Inner Sound, *U.K.* **12 D3** 57 30N 5 55W
Innerkip, *Canada* **78 C4** 43 13N 80 42W
Innetalling I., *Canada* **70 A4** 56 0N 79 0W
Innisfail, *Australia* **62 B4** 17 33S 146 5 E
Innisfail, *Canada* **72 C6** 52 0N 113 57W
In'no-shima, *Japan* **31 G6** 34 19N 133 10 E
Innsbruck, *Austria* **16 E6** 47 16N 11 23 E
Inny →, *Ireland* **13 C4** 53 30N 7 50W
Inongo, *Dem. Rep. of the Congo* **52 E3** 1 55S 18 30 E
Inoucdjouac = Inukjuak, *Canada* **69 C12** 58 25N 78 15W
Inowrocław, *Poland* **17 B10** 52 50N 18 12 E
Inpundong, *N. Korea* **35 D14** 41 25N 126 34 E
Inscription, C., *Australia* **61 E1** 25 29S 112 59 E
Insein, *Burma* **41 L20** 16 50N 96 5 E
Inta, *Russia* **24 A11** 66 5N 60 8 E
Intendente Alvear, *Argentina* **94 D3** 35 12S 63 32W
Interlaken, *Switz.* **18 C7** 46 41N 7 50 E
Interlaken, *U.S.A.* **79 D8** 42 37N 76 44W
International Falls, *U.S.A.* **80 A8** 48 36N 93 25W
Intiyaco, *Argentina* **94 B3** 28 43S 60 5W
Inukjuak, *Canada* **69 C12** 58 25N 78 15W
Inútil, B., *Chile* **96 G2** 53 30S 70 15W
Inuvik, *Canada* **68 B6** 68 16N 133 40W
Inveraray, *U.K.* **12 E3** 56 14N 5 5W
Inverbervie, *U.K.* **12 E6** 56 51N 2 17W
Invercargill, *N.Z.* **59 M2** 46 24S 168 24 E
Inverclyde □, *U.K.* **12 F4** 55 55N 4 49W
Inverell, *Australia* **63 D5** 29 45S 151 8 E
Invergordon, *U.K.* **12 D4** 57 41N 4 10W
Inverloch, *Australia* **63 F4** 38 38S 145 45 E
Invermere, *Canada* **72 C5** 50 30N 116 2W
Inverness, *Canada* **71 C7** 46 15N 61 19W
Inverness, *U.K.* **12 D4** 57 29N 4 13W
Inverness, *U.S.A.* **77 L4** 28 50N 82 20W
Inverurie, *U.K.* **12 D6** 57 17N 2 23W
Investigator Group, *Australia* **63 E1** 34 45S 134 20 E
Investigator Str., *Australia* **63 F2** 35 30S 137 0 E
Inya, *Russia* **26 D9** 50 28N 86 37 E
Inyanga, *Zimbabwe* **55 F3** 18 12S 32 40 E
Inyangani, *Zimbabwe* **55 F3** 18 5S 32 50 E
Inyantue, *Zimbabwe* **55 F2** 18 30S 26 40 E
Inyo Mts., *U.S.A.* **84 J9** 36 40N 118 0W
Inyokern, *U.S.A.* **85 K9** 35 39N 117 49W
Inza, *Russia* **24 D8** 53 55N 46 25 E
Iō-Jima, *Japan* **31 J5** 30 48N 130 18 E
Ioánnina, *Greece* **21 E9** 39 42N 20 47 E
Iola, *U.S.A.* **81 G7** 37 55N 95 24W
Iona, *U.K.* **12 E2** 56 20N 6 25W
Ione, *U.S.A.* **84 G6** 38 21N 120 56W
Ionia, *U.S.A.* **76 D3** 42 59N 85 4W
Ionian Is. = Iónioi Nísoi, *Greece* **21 E9** 38 40N 20 0 E
Ionian Sea, *Medit. S.* **21 E7** 37 30N 17 30 E
Iónioi Nísoi, *Greece* **21 E9** 38 40N 20 0 E
Íos, *Greece* **21 F11** 36 41N 25 20 E
Iowa □, *U.S.A.* **80 D8** 42 18N 93 30W
Iowa →, *U.S.A.* **80 E9** 41 10N 91 1W
Iowa City, *U.S.A.* **80 E9** 41 40N 91 32W
Iowa Falls, *U.S.A.* **80 D8** 42 31N 93 16W
Iowa Park, *U.S.A.* **81 J5** 33 57N 98 40W
Ipala, *Tanzania* **54 C3** 4 30S 32 52 E
Ipameri, *Brazil* **93 G9** 17 44S 48 9W
Ipatinga, *Brazil* **93 G10** 19 32S 42 30W
Ipiales, *Colombia* **92 C3** 0 50N 77 37W
Ipin = Yibin, *China* **32 D5** 28 45N 104 32 E
Ipixuna, *Brazil* **92 E4** 7 0S 71 40W
Ipoh, *Malaysia* **39 K3** 4 35N 101 5 E
Ippy, *C.A.R.* **52 C4** 6 5N 21 7 E
İpsala, *Turkey* **21 D12** 40 55N 26 23 E
Ipswich, *Australia* **63 D5** 27 35S 152 40 E
Ipswich, *U.K.* **11 E9** 52 4N 1 10 E
Ipswich, *Mass., U.S.A.* **79 D14** 42 41N 70 50W
Ipswich, *S. Dak., U.S.A.* **80 C5** 45 27N 99 2W
Ipu, *Brazil* **93 D10** 4 23S 40 44W
Iqaluit, *Canada* **69 B13** 63 44N 68 31W
Iquique, *Chile* **92 H4** 20 19S 70 5W
Iquitos, *Peru* **92 D4** 3 45S 73 10W
Irabu-Jima, *Japan* **31 M2** 24 50N 125 10 E
Iracoubo, *Fr. Guiana* **93 B8** 5 30N 53 10W
Īrafshān, *Iran* **45 E9** 26 42N 61 56 E
Iráklion, *Greece* **23 D7** 35 20N 25 12 E
Iráklion □, *Greece* **23 D7** 35 10N 25 10 E
Irala, *Paraguay* **95 B5** 25 55S 54 35W
Iran ■, *Asia* **45 C7** 33 0N 53 0 E
Iran, Gunung-Gunung, *Malaysia* **36 D4** 2 20N 114 50 E
Iran, Plateau of, *Asia* **28 F9** 32 0N 55 0 E
Iran Ra. = Iran, Gunung-Gunung, *Malaysia* **36 D4** 2 20N 114 50 E
Īrānshahr, *Iran* **45 E9** 27 15N 60 40 E
Irapuato, *Mexico* **86 C4** 20 40N 101 30W
Iraq ■, *Asia* **44 C5** 33 0N 44 0 E
Irati, *Brazil* **95 B5** 25 25S 50 38W
Irbid, *Jordan* **47 C4** 32 35N 35 48 E
Irbid □, *Jordan* **47 C5** 32 15N 36 35 E
Ireland ■, *Europe* **13 C4** 53 50N 7 52W
Irhyangdong, *N. Korea* **35 D15** 41 15N 129 30 E
Iri, *S. Korea* **35 G14** 35 59N 127 0 E
Irian Jaya □, *Indonesia* **37 E9** 4 0S 137 0 E
Iringa, *Tanzania* **54 D4** 7 48S 35 43 E
Iringa □, *Tanzania* **54 D4** 7 48S 35 43 E
Iriomote-Jima, *Japan* **31 M1** 24 19N 123 48 E
Iriona, *Honduras* **88 C2** 15 57N 85 11W
Iriri →, *Brazil* **93 D8** 3 52S 52 37W
Irish Republic ■, *Europe* **13 C3** 53 0N 8 0W
Irish Sea, *U.K.* **10 D3** 53 38N 4 48W
Irkutsk, *Russia* **27 D11** 52 18N 104 20 E
Irma, *Canada* **73 C6** 52 55N 111 14W
Irō-Zaki, *Japan* **31 G9** 34 36N 138 51 E
Iron Baron, *Australia* **63 E2** 32 58S 137 11 E
Iron Gate = Portile de Fier, *Europe* **17 F12** 44 44N 22 30 E
Iron Knob, *Australia* **63 E2** 32 46S 137 8 E
Iron Mountain, *U.S.A.* **76 C1** 45 49N 88 4W
Iron River, *U.S.A.* **80 B10** 46 6N 88 39W
Irondequoit, *U.S.A.* **78 C7** 43 13N 77 35W
Ironstone Kopje, *Botswana* **56 D3** 25 17S 24 5 E
Ironton, *Mo., U.S.A.* **81 G9** 37 36N 90 38W
Ironton, *Ohio, U.S.A.* **76 F4** 38 32N 82 41W
Ironwood, *U.S.A.* **80 B9** 46 27N 90 9W
Iroquois, *Canada* **79 B9** 44 51N 75 19W
Iroquois Falls, *Canada* **70 C3** 48 46N 80 41W
Irpin, *Ukraine* **17 C16** 50 30N 30 15 E
Irrara Cr. →, *Australia* **63 D4** 29 35S 145 31 E
Irrawaddy □, *Burma* **41 L19** 17 0N 95 0 E
Irrawaddy →, *Burma* **41 M19** 15 50N 95 6 E
Irricana, *Canada* **72 C6** 51 19N 113 37W
Irtysh →, *Russia* **26 C7** 61 4N 68 52 E
Irumu, *Dem. Rep. of the Congo* **54 B2** 1 32N 29 53 E
Irún, *Spain* **19 A5** 43 20N 1 52W
Irunea = Pamplona, *Spain* **19 A5** 42 48N 1 38W
Irvine, *Canada* **73 D6** 49 57N 110 16W
Irvine, *U.K.* **12 F4** 55 37N 4 41W
Irvine, *Calif., U.S.A.* **85 M9** 33 41N 117 46W
Irvine, *Ky., U.S.A.* **76 G4** 37 42N 83 58W
Irvinestown, *U.K.* **13 B4** 54 28N 7 39W
Irving, *U.S.A.* **81 J6** 32 49N 96 56W
Irvona, *U.S.A.* **78 F6** 40 46N 78 33W
Irwin →, *Australia* **61 E1** 29 15S 114 54 E
Irymple, *Australia* **63 E3** 34 14S 142 8 E
Isa Khel, *Pakistan* **42 C4** 32 41N 71 17 E
Isaac →, *Australia* **62 C4** 22 55S 149 20 E
Isabel, *U.S.A.* **80 C4** 45 24N 101 26W
Isabela, I., *Mexico* **86 C3** 21 51N 105 55W
Isabelia, Cord., *Nic.* **88 D2** 13 30N 85 25W
Isabella, *Phil.* **37 C6** 6 40N 122 10 E
Isabella Ra., *Australia* **60 D3** 21 0S 121 4 E
Ísafjarðardjúp, *Iceland* **8 C2** 66 10N 23 0W
Ísafjörður, *Iceland* **8 C2** 66 5N 23 9W
Isagarh, *India* **42 G7** 24 48N 77 51 E
Isahaya, *Japan* **31 H5** 32 52N 130 2 E
Isaka, *Tanzania* **54 C3** 3 56S 32 59 E
Isan →, *India* **43 F9** 26 51N 80 7 E
Isana = Içana →, *Brazil* **92 C5** 0 26N 67 19W
Isar →, *Germany* **16 D7** 48 48N 12 57 E
Íschia, *Italy* **20 D5** 40 44N 13 57 E
Isdell →, *Australia* **60 C3** 16 27S 124 51 E
Ise, *Japan* **31 G8** 34 25N 136 45 E
Ise-Wan, *Japan* **31 G8** 34 43N 136 43 E
Iseramagazi, *Tanzania* **54 C3** 4 37S 32 10 E
Isère →, *France* **18 D6** 44 59N 4 51 E
Isérnia, *Italy* **20 D6** 41 36N 14 14 E
Isfahan = Eşfahān, *Iran* **45 C6** 32 39N 51 43 E
Ishigaki-Shima, *Japan* **31 M2** 24 20N 124 10 E
Ishikari-Gawa →, *Japan* **30 C10** 43 15N 141 23 E
Ishikari-Sammyaku, *Japan* **30 C11** 43 30N 143 0 E
Ishikari-Wan, *Japan* **30 C10** 43 25N 141 1 E
Ishikawa □, *Japan* **31 F8** 36 30N 136 30 E
Ishim, *Russia* **26 D7** 56 10N 69 30 E
Ishim →, *Russia* **26 D8** 57 45N 71 10 E
Ishinomaki, *Japan* **30 E10** 38 32N 141 20 E
Ishioka, *Japan* **31 F10** 36 11N 140 16 E
Ishkuman, *Pakistan* **43 A5** 36 30N 73 50 E
Ishpeming, *U.S.A.* **76 B2** 46 29N 87 40W
Isil Kul, *Russia* **26 D8** 54 55N 71 16 E
Isiolo, *Kenya* **54 B4** 0 24N 37 33 E
Isiro, *Dem. Rep. of the Congo* **54 B2** 2 53N 27 40 E
Isisford, *Australia* **62 C3** 24 15S 144 21 E
İskenderun, *Turkey* **25 G6** 36 32N 36 10 E
İskenderun Körfezi, *Turkey* **25 G6** 36 40N 35 50 E
Iskŭr →, *Bulgaria* **21 C11** 43 45N 24 25 E
Iskut →, *Canada* **72 B2** 56 45N 131 49W
Isla →, *U.K.* **12 E5** 56 32N 3 20W
Isla Vista, *U.S.A.* **85 L7** 34 25N 119 53W
Islam Headworks, *Pakistan* **42 E5** 29 49N 72 33 E
Islamabad, *Pakistan* **42 C5** 33 40N 73 10 E
Islamgarh, *Pakistan* **42 F4** 27 51N 70 48 E
Islamkot, *Pakistan* **42 G4** 24 42N 70 13 E
Islampur, *India* **43 G11** 25 9N 85 12 E
Island L., *Canada* **73 C10** 53 47N 94 25W
Island Lagoon, *Australia* **63 E2** 31 30S 136 40 E
Island Pond, *U.S.A.* **79 B13** 44 49N 71 53W
Islands, B. of, *Canada* **71 C8** 49 11N 58 15W
Islay, *U.K.* **12 F2** 55 46N 6 10W
Isle →, *France* **18 D3** 44 55N 0 15W
Isle aux Morts, *Canada* **71 C8** 47 35N 59 0W
Isle of Wight □, *U.K.* **11 G6** 50 41N 1 17W
Isle Royale, *U.S.A.* **80 B10** 48 0N 88 54W
Isle Royale National Park, *U.S.A.* **80 B10** 48 0N 88 55W
Isleton, *U.S.A.* **84 G5** 38 10N 121 37W
Ismail = Izmayil, *Ukraine* **17 F15** 45 22N 28 46 E
Ismâ'ilîya, *Egypt* **51 B12** 30 37N 32 18 E
Isogstalo, *India* **43 B8** 34 15N 78 46 E
Isparta, *Turkey* **25 G5** 37 47N 30 30 E
Ispica, *Italy* **20 F6** 36 47N 14 55 E
Israel ■, *Asia* **47 D3** 32 0N 34 50 E
Issoire, *France* **18 D5** 45 32N 3 15 E
Issyk-Kul = Ysyk-Köl, *Kyrgyzstan* **28 E11** 42 26N 76 12 E
Issyk-Kul, Ozero = Ysyk-Köl, Ozero, *Kyrgyzstan* **26 E8** 42 25N 77 15 E
İstanbul, *Turkey* **21 D13** 41 0N 29 0 E
İstanbul Boğazı, *Turkey* **21 D13** 41 10N 29 10 E
Istiaía, *Greece* **21 E10** 38 57N 23 9 E
Istokpoga, L., *U.S.A.* **77 M5** 27 23N 81 17W
Istra, *Croatia* **16 F7** 45 10N 14 0 E
Istres, *France* **18 E6** 43 31N 4 59 E
Istria = Istra, *Croatia* **16 F7** 45 10N 14 0 E
Itá, *Paraguay* **94 B4** 25 29S 57 21W
Itaberaba, *Brazil* **93 F10** 12 32S 40 18W
Itabira, *Brazil* **93 G10** 19 37S 43 13W
Itabirito, *Brazil* **95 A7** 20 15S 43 48W
Itabuna, *Brazil* **93 F11** 14 48S 39 16W
Itacaunas →, *Brazil* **93 E9** 5 21S 49 8W
Itacoatiara, *Brazil* **92 D7** 3 8S 58 25W
Itaipú, Represa de, *Brazil* **95 B5** 25 30S 54 30W
Itaituba, *Brazil* **93 D7** 4 10S 55 50W
Itajaí, *Brazil* **95 B6** 27 50S 48 39W
Itajubá, *Brazil* **95 A6** 22 24S 45 30W
Itaka, *Tanzania* **55 D3** 8 50S 32 49 E
Italy ■, *Europe* **20 C5** 42 0N 13 0 E
Itamaraju, *Brazil* **93 G11** 17 5S 39 31W
Itampolo, *Madag.* **57 C7** 24 41S 43 57 E
Itapecuru-Mirim, *Brazil* **93 D10** 3 24S 44 20W
Itaperuna, *Brazil* **95 A7** 21 10S 41 54W
Itapetininga, *Brazil* **95 A6** 23 36S 48 7W
Itapeva, *Brazil* **95 A6** 23 59S 48 59W
Itapicuru →, *Bahia, Brazil* **93 F11** 11 47S 37 32W
Itapicuru →, *Maranhão, Brazil* **93 D10** 2 52S 44 12W
Itapipoca, *Brazil* **93 D11** 3 30S 39 35W
Itapuá □, *Paraguay* **95 B4** 26 40S 55 40W
Itaquari, *Brazil* **95 A7** 20 20S 40 25W
Itaquí, *Brazil* **94 B4** 29 8S 56 30W
Itararé, *Brazil* **95 A6** 24 6S 49 23W
Itarsi, *India* **42 H7** 22 36N 77 51 E
Itatí, *Argentina* **94 B4** 27 16S 58 15W
Itchen →, *U.K.* **11 G6** 50 55N 1 22W
Itezhi Tezhi, L., *Zambia* **55 F2** 15 30S 25 30 E
Ithaca = Itháki, *Greece* **21 E9** 38 25N 20 40 E
Ithaca, *U.S.A.* **79 D8** 42 27N 76 30W
Itháki, *Greece* **21 E9** 38 25N 20 40 E
Itiquira →, *Brazil* **93 G7** 17 18S 56 44W
Ito, *Japan* **31 G9** 34 58N 139 5 E
Ito Aba I., *S. China Sea* **36 B4** 10 23N 114 21 E
Itoigawa, *Japan* **31 F8** 37 2N 137 51 E
Itonamas →, *Bolivia* **92 F6** 12 28S 64 24W
Ittoqqortoormiit = Scoresbysund, *Greenland* **4 B6** 70 20N 23 0W
Itu, *Brazil* **95 A6** 23 17S 47 15W
Ituiutaba, *Brazil* **93 G9** 19 0S 49 25W
Itumbiara, *Brazil* **93 G9** 18 20S 49 10W
Ituna, *Canada* **73 C8** 51 10N 103 24W
Itunge Port, *Tanzania* **55 D3** 9 40S 33 55 E
Iturbe, *Argentina* **94 A2** 23 0S 65 25W
Ituri →, *Dem. Rep. of the Congo* **54 B2** 1 40N 27 1 E
Iturup, Ostrov, *Russia* **27 E15** 45 0N 148 0 E
Ituxi →, *Brazil* **92 E6** 7 18S 64 51W
Ituyuro →, *Argentina* **94 A3** 22 40S 63 50W
Itzehoe, *Germany* **16 B5** 53 55N 9 31 E
Ivaí →, *Brazil* **95 A5** 23 18S 53 42W
Ivalo, *Finland* **8 B22** 68 38N 27 35 E
Ivalojoki →, *Finland* **8 B22** 68 40N 27 40 E
Ivanava, *Belarus* **17 B13** 52 7N 25 29 E
Ivanhoe, *Australia* **63 E3** 32 56S 144 20 E
Ivanhoe, *Calif., U.S.A.* **84 J7** 36 23N 119 13W
Ivanhoe, *Minn., U.S.A.* **80 C6** 44 28N 96 15W
Ivano-Frankivsk, *Ukraine* **17 D13** 48 40N 24 40 E
Ivano-Frankovsk = Ivano-Frankivsk, *Ukraine* **17 D13** 48 40N 24 40 E
Ivanovo = Ivanava, *Belarus* **17 B13** 52 7N 25 29 E
Ivanovo, *Russia* **24 C7** 57 5N 41 0 E
Ivato, *Madag.* **57 C8** 20 37S 47 10 E
Ivatsevichy, *Belarus* **17 B13** 52 43N 25 21 E
Ivdel, *Russia* **24 B11** 60 42N 60 24 E
Ivindo →, *Gabon* **52 D2** 0 9S 12 9 E
Ivinheima →, *Brazil* **95 A5** 23 14S 53 42W
Ivinhema, *Brazil* **95 A5** 22 10S 53 37W
Ivohibe, *Madag.* **57 C8** 22 31S 46 57 E
Ivory Coast, *Africa* **50 H4** 5 0N 5 0W
Ivory Coast ■, *Africa* **50 G4** 7 30N 5 0W
Ivrea, *Italy* **18 D7** 45 28N 7 52 E
Ivujivik, *Canada* **69 B12** 62 24N 77 55W
Ivybridge, *U.K.* **11 G4** 50 23N 3 56W
Iwaizumi, *Japan* **30 E10** 39 50N 141 45 E
Iwaki, *Japan* **31 F10** 37 3N 140 55 E
Iwakuni, *Japan* **31 G6** 34 15N 132 8 E
Iwamizawa, *Japan* **30 C10** 43 12N 141 46 E
Iwanai, *Japan* **30 C10** 42 58N 140 30 E
Iwata, *Japan* **31 G8** 34 42N 137 51 E
Iwate □, *Japan* **30 E10** 39 30N 141 30 E
Iwate-San, *Japan* **30 E10** 39 51N 141 0 E
Iwo, *Nigeria* **50 G6** 7 39N 4 9 E
Ixiamas, *Bolivia* **92 F5** 13 50S 68 5W
Ixopo, *S. Africa* **57 E5** 30 11S 30 5 E
Ixtepec, *Mexico* **87 D5** 16 32N 95 10W
Ixtlán del Río, *Mexico* **86 C4** 21 5N 104 21W
Iyo, *Japan* **31 H6** 33 45N 132 45 E
Izabal, L. de, *Guatemala* **88 C2** 15 30N 89 10W
Izamal, *Mexico* **87 C7** 20 56N 89 1W
Izena-Shima, *Japan* **31 L3** 26 56N 127 56 E
Izhevsk, *Russia* **24 C9** 56 51N 53 14 E
Izhma →, *Russia* **24 A9** 65 19N 52 54 E
Izmayil, *Ukraine* **17 F15** 45 22N 28 46 E
İzmir, *Turkey* **21 E12** 38 25N 27 8 E
İzmit = Kocaeli, *Turkey* **25 F4** 40 45N 29 50 E
İznik Gölü, *Turkey* **21 D13** 40 27N 29 30 E
Izra, *Syria* **47 C5** 32 51N 36 15 E
Izu-Shotō, *Japan* **31 G10** 34 30N 140 0 E
Izúcar de Matamoros, *Mexico* **87 D5** 18 36N 98 28W
Izumi-sano, *Japan* **31 G7** 34 23N 135 18 E
Izumo, *Japan* **31 G6** 35 20N 132 46 E
Izyaslav, *Ukraine* **17 C14** 50 5N 26 50 E

J

Jabalpur, *India* **43 H8** 23 9N 79 58 E
Jabbūl, *Syria* **44 B3** 36 4N 37 30 E
Jabiru, *Australia* **60 B5** 12 40S 132 53 E
Jablah, *Syria* **44 C3** 35 20N 36 0 E
Jablonec nad Nisou, *Czech Rep.* **16 C8** 50 43N 15 10 E
Jaboatão, *Brazil* **93 E11** 8 7S 35 1W
Jaboticabal, *Brazil* **95 A6** 21 15S 48 17W
Jaca, *Spain* **19 A5** 42 35N 0 33W
Jacareí, *Brazil* **95 A6** 23 20S 46 0W
Jacarèzinho, *Brazil* **95 A6** 23 5S 49 58W
Jackman, *U.S.A.* **77 C10** 45 35N 70 17W
Jacksboro, *U.S.A.* **81 J5** 33 14N 98 15W
Jackson, *Ala., U.S.A.* **77 K2** 31 31N 87 53W
Jackson, *Calif., U.S.A.* **84 G6** 38 21N 120 46W
Jackson, *Ky., U.S.A.* **76 G4** 37 33N 83 23W
Jackson, *Mich., U.S.A.* **76 D3** 42 15N 84 24W
Jackson, *Minn., U.S.A.* **80 D7** 43 37N 95 1W
Jackson, *Miss., U.S.A.* **81 J9** 32 18N 90 12W
Jackson, *Mo., U.S.A.* **81 G10** 37 23N 89 40W
Jackson, *N.H., U.S.A.* **79 B13** 44 10N 71 11W
Jackson, *Ohio, U.S.A.* **76 F4** 39 3N 82 39W
Jackson, *Tenn., U.S.A.* **77 H1** 35 37N 88 49W
Jackson, *Wyo., U.S.A.* **82 E8** 43 29N 110 46W
Jackson B., *N.Z.* **59 K2** 43 58S 168 42 E
Jackson L., *U.S.A.* **82 E8** 43 52N 110 36W
Jacksons, *N.Z.* **59 K3** 42 46S 171 32 E
Jackson's Arm, *Canada* **71 C8** 49 52N 56 47W
Jacksonville, *Ala., U.S.A.* **77 J3** 33 49N 85 46W
Jacksonville, *Ark., U.S.A.* **81 H8** 34 52N 92 7W
Jacksonville, *Calif., U.S.A.* **84 H6** 37 52N 120 24W
Jacksonville, *Fla., U.S.A.* **77 K5** 30 20N 81 39W
Jacksonville, *Ill., U.S.A.* **80 F9** 39 44N 90 14W
Jacksonville, *N.C., U.S.A.* **77 H7** 34 45N 77 26W
Jacksonville, *Tex., U.S.A.* **81 K7** 31 58N 95 17W
Jacksonville Beach, *U.S.A.* **77 K5** 30 17N 81 24W
Jacmel, *Haiti* **89 C5** 18 14N 72 32W
Jacob Lake, *U.S.A.* **83 H7** 36 43N 112 13W
Jacobabad, *Pakistan* **42 E3** 28 20N 68 29 E
Jacobina, *Brazil* **93 F10** 11 11S 40 30W
Jacques Cartier, Dét. de, *Canada* **71 C7** 50 0N 63 30W
Jacques-Cartier, Mt., *Canada* **71 C6** 48 57N 66 0W
Jacques Cartier, Parc Prov., *Canada* **71 C5** 47 15N 71 33W
Jacuí →, *Brazil* **95 C5** 30 2S 51 15W
Jacumba, *U.S.A.* **85 N10** 32 37N 116 11W
Jacundá →, *Brazil* **93 D8** 1 57S 50 26W
Jadotville = Likasi, *Dem. Rep. of the Congo* **55 E2** 10 55S 26 48 E
Jaén, *Peru* **92 E3** 5 25S 78 40W
Jaén, *Spain* **19 D4** 37 44N 3 43W
Jafarabad, *India* **42 J4** 20 52N 71 22 E
Jaffa = Tel Aviv-Yafo, *Israel* **47 C3** 32 4N 34 48 E
Jaffa, C., *Australia* **63 F2** 36 58S 139 40 E
Jaffna, *Sri Lanka* **40 Q12** 9 45N 80 2 E
Jaffrey, *U.S.A.* **79 D12** 42 49N 72 2W
Jagadhri, *India* **42 D7** 30 10N 77 20 E
Jagadishpur, *India* **43 G11** 25 30N 84 21 E
Jagdalpur, *India* **41 K13** 19 3N 82 0 E
Jagersfontein, *S. Africa* **56 D4** 29 44S 25 27 E
Jaghīn →, *Iran* **45 E8** 27 17N 57 13 E
Jagodina, *Serbia, Yug.* **21 C9** 44 5N 21 15 E
Jagraon, *India* **40 D9** 30 50N 75 25 E
Jagtial, *India* **40 K11** 18 50N 79 0 E
Jaguariaíva, *Brazil* **95 A6** 24 10S 49 50W
Jaguaribe →, *Brazil* **93 D11** 4 25S 37 45W
Jagüey Grande, *Cuba* **88 B3** 22 35N 81 7W
Jahanabad, *India* **43 G11** 25 13N 84 59 E
Jahazpur, *India* **42 G6** 25 37N 75 17 E
Jahrom, *Iran* **45 D7** 28 30N 53 31 E
Jaijon, *India* **42 D7** 31 21N 76 9 E
Jailolo, *Indonesia* **37 D7** 1 5N 127 30 E
Jailolo, Selat, *Indonesia* **37 D7** 0 5N 129 5 E
Jaipur, *India* **42 F6** 27 0N 75 50 E
Jais, *India* **43 F9** 26 15N 81 32 E
Jaisalmer, *India* **42 F4** 26 55N 70 54 E
Jaisinghnagar, *India* **43 H8** 23 38N 78 34 E
Jaitaran, *India* **42 F5** 26 12N 73 56 E
Jaithari, *India* **43 H8** 23 14N 78 37 E
Jājarm, *Iran* **45 B8** 36 58N 56 27 E
Jakam →, *India* **42 H6** 23 54N 74 13 E
Jakarta, *Indonesia* **37 G12** 6 9S 106 49 E
Jakhal, *India* **42 E6** 29 48N 75 50 E
Jakhau, *India* **42 H3** 23 13N 68 43 E
Jakobstad = Pietarsaari, *Finland* **8 E20** 63 40N 22 43 E
Jal, *U.S.A.* **81 J3** 32 7N 103 12W
Jalalabad, *Afghan.* **42 B4** 34 30N 70 29 E
Jalalabad, *India* **43 F8** 27 41N 79 42 E
Jalalpur Jattan, *Pakistan* **42 C6** 32 38N 74 11 E
Jalama, *U.S.A.* **85 L6** 34 29N 120 29W
Jalapa, *Guatemala* **88 D2** 14 39N 89 59W
Jalapa Enríquez, *Mexico* **87 D5** 19 32N 96 55W
Jalasjärvi, *Finland* **9 E20** 62 29N 22 47 E
Jalaun, *India* **43 F8** 26 8N 79 25 E
Jaldhaka →, *Bangla.* **43 F13** 26 16N 89 16 E
Jalesar, *India* **42 F8** 27 29N 78 19 E
Jaleswar, *Nepal* **43 F11** 26 38N 85 48 E
Jalgaon, *Maharashtra, India* **40 J10** 21 2N 76 31 E
Jalgaon, *Maharashtra, India* **40 J9** 21 0N 75 42 E
Jalībah, *Iraq* **44 D5** 30 35N 46 32 E
Jalisco □, *Mexico* **86 D4** 20 0N 104 0W
Jalkot, *Pakistan* **43 B5** 35 14N 73 24 E
Jalna, *India* **40 K9** 19 48N 75 38 E
Jalón →, *Spain* **19 B5** 41 47N 1 4W
Jalor, *India* **42 G5** 25 21N 72 37 E
Jalpa, *Mexico* **86 C4** 21 38N 102 58W
Jalpaiguri, *India* **41 F16** 26 32N 88 46 E
Jaluit I., *Marshall Is.* **64 G8** 6 0N 169 30 E

Jalūlā, *Iraq* **44 C5** 34 16N 45 10 E
Jamaica ■, *W. Indies* **88 C4** 18 10N 77 30W
Jamalpur, *Bangla.* **41 G16** 24 52N 89 56 E
Jamalpur, *India* **43 G12** 25 18N 86 28 E
Jamalpurganj, *India* **43 H13** 23 2N 87 59 E
Jamanxim →, *Brazil* **93 D7** 4 43S 56 18W
Jambi, *Indonesia* **36 E2** 1 38S 103 30 E
Jambi □, *Indonesia* **36 E2** 1 30S 102 30 E
Jambusar, *India* **42 H5** 22 3N 72 51 E
James →, *S. Dak., U.S.A.* **80 D6** 42 52N 97 18W
James →, *Va., U.S.A.* **76 G7** 36 56N 76 27W
James B., *Canada* **70 B3** 54 0N 80 0W
James Ranges, *Australia* **60 D5** 24 10S 132 30 E
James Ross I., *Antarctica* **5 C18** 63 58S 57 50W
Jamesabad, *Pakistan* **42 G3** 25 17N 69 15 E
Jamestown, *Australia* **63 E2** 33 10S 138 32 E
Jamestown, *S. Africa* **56 E4** 31 6S 26 45 E
Jamestown, *N. Dak., U.S.A.* **80 B5** 46 54N 98 42W
Jamestown, *N.Y., U.S.A.* **78 D5** 42 6N 79 14W
Jamestown, *Pa., U.S.A.* **78 E4** 41 29N 80 27W
Jamīlābād, *Iran* **45 C6** 34 24N 48 28 E
Jamiltepec, *Mexico* **87 D5** 16 17N 97 49W
Jamira →, *India* **43 J13** 21 35N 88 28 E
Jamkhandi, *India* **40 L9** 16 30N 75 15 E
Jammu, *India* **42 C6** 32 43N 74 54 E
Jammu & Kashmir □, *India* **43 B7** 34 25N 77 0 E
Jamnagar, *India* **42 H4** 22 30N 70 6 E
Jamni →, *India* **43 G8** 25 13N 78 35 E
Jampur, *Pakistan* **42 E4** 29 39N 70 40 E
Jamrud, *Pakistan* **42 C4** 33 59N 71 24 E
Jämsä, *Finland* **9 F21** 61 53N 25 10 E
Jamshedpur, *India* **43 H12** 22 44N 86 12 E
Jamtara, *India* **43 H12** 23 59N 86 49 E
Jämtland, *Sweden* **8 E15** 63 31N 14 0 E
Jan L., *Canada* **73 C8** 54 56N 102 55W
Jan Mayen, *Arctic* **4 B7** 71 0N 9 0W
Janakkala, *Finland* **9 F21** 60 54N 24 36 E
Janaúba, *Brazil* **93 G10** 15 48S 43 19W
Jand, *Pakistan* **42 C5** 33 30N 72 6 E
Jandaq, *Iran* **45 C7** 34 3N 54 22 E
Jandia, *Canary Is.* **22 F5** 28 6N 14 21W
Jandia, Pta. de, *Canary Is.* **22 F5** 28 3N 14 31W
Jandola, *Pakistan* **42 C4** 32 20N 70 9 E
Jandowae, *Australia* **63 D5** 26 45S 151 7 E
Janesville, *U.S.A.* **80 D10** 42 41N 89 1W
Janghai, *India* **43 G10** 25 33N 82 19 E
Janīn, *West Bank* **47 C4** 32 28N 35 18 E
Janjgir, *India* **43 J10** 22 1N 82 34 E
Janos, *Mexico* **86 A3** 30 45N 108 10W
Januária, *Brazil* **93 G10** 15 25S 44 25W
Janubio, *Canary Is.* **22 F6** 28 56N 13 50W
Jaora, *India* **42 H6** 23 40N 75 10 E
Japan ■, *Asia* **31 G8** 36 0N 136 0 E
Japan, Sea of, *Asia* **30 E7** 40 0N 135 0 E
Japan Trench, *Pac. Oc.* **28 F18** 32 0N 142 0 E
Japen = Yapen, *Indonesia* **37 E9** 1 50S 136 0 E
Japla, *India* **43 G11** 24 33N 84 1 E
Japurá →, *Brazil* **92 D5** 3 8S 65 46W
Jaquarão, *Brazil* **95 C5** 32 34S 53 23W
Jaqué, *Panama* **88 E4** 7 27N 78 8W
Jarābulus, *Syria* **44 B3** 36 49N 38 1 E
Jarama →, *Spain* **19 B4** 40 24N 3 32W
Jaranwala, *Pakistan* **42 D5** 31 15N 73 26 E
Jarash, *Jordan* **47 C4** 32 17N 35 54 E
Jardim, *Brazil* **94 A4** 21 28S 56 2W
Jardines de la Reina, Arch. de los, *Cuba* **88 B4** 20 50N 78 50W
Jargalang, *China* **35 C12** 43 5N 122 55 E
Jargalant = Hovd, *Mongolia* **32 B4** 48 2N 91 37 E
Jari →, *Brazil* **93 D8** 1 9S 51 54W
Jarīr, W. al →, *Si. Arabia* **44 E4** 25 38N 42 30 E
Jarosław, *Poland* **17 C12** 50 2N 22 42 E
Jarrahdale, *Australia* **61 F2** 32 24S 116 5 E
Jarrahi →, *Iran* **45 D6** 30 49N 48 48 E
Jarres, Plaine des, *Laos* **38 C4** 19 27N 103 10 E
Jartai, *China* **34 E3** 39 45N 105 48 E
Jarud Qi, *China* **35 B11** 44 28N 120 50 E
Järvenpää, *Finland* **9 F21** 60 29N 25 5 E
Jarvis, *Canada* **78 D4** 42 53N 80 6W
Jarvis I., *Pac. Oc.* **65 H12** 0 15S 159 55W
Jarwa, *India* **43 F10** 27 38N 82 30 E
Jasdan, *India* **42 H4** 22 2N 71 12 E
Jashpurnagar, *India* **43 H11** 22 54N 84 9 E
Jasidih, *India* **43 G12** 24 31N 86 39 E
Jāsimīyah, *Iraq* **44 C5** 33 45N 44 41 E
Jasin, *Malaysia* **39 L4** 2 20N 102 26 E
Jāsk, *Iran* **45 E8** 25 38N 57 45 E
Jasło, *Poland* **17 D11** 49 45N 21 30 E
Jaso, *India* **43 G9** 24 30N 80 29 E
Jasper, *Alta., Canada* **72 C5** 52 55N 118 5W
Jasper, *Ont., Canada* **79 B9** 44 52N 75 57W
Jasper, *Ala., U.S.A.* **77 J2** 33 50N 87 17W
Jasper, *Fla., U.S.A.* **77 K4** 30 31N 82 57W
Jasper, *Ind., U.S.A.* **76 F2** 38 24N 86 56W
Jasper, *Tex., U.S.A.* **81 K8** 30 56N 94 1W
Jasper Nat. Park, *Canada* **72 C5** 52 50N 118 8W
Jasrasar, *India* **42 F5** 27 43N 73 49 E
Jászberény, *Hungary* **17 E10** 47 30N 19 55 E
Jataí, *Brazil* **93 G8** 17 58S 51 48W
Jati, *Pakistan* **42 G3** 24 20N 68 19 E
Jatibarang, *Indonesia* **37 G13** 6 28S 108 18 E
Jatinegara, *Indonesia* **37 G12** 6 13S 106 52 E
Játiva = Xátiva, *Spain* **19 C5** 38 59N 0 32W
Jaú, *Brazil* **95 A6** 22 10S 48 30W
Jauja, *Peru* **92 F3** 11 45S 75 15W
Jaunpur, *India* **43 G10** 25 46N 82 44 E
Java = Jawa, *Indonesia* **37 G14** 7 0S 110 0 E
Java Barat □, *Indonesia* **37 G12** 7 0S 107 0 E
Java Sea, *Indonesia* **36 E3** 4 35S 107 15 E
Java Tengah □, *Indonesia* **37 G14** 7 0S 110 0 E
Java Timur □, *Indonesia* **37 G15** 8 0S 113 0 E
Java Trench, *Ind. Oc.* **36 F3** 9 0S 105 0 E
Javhlant = Uliastay, *Mongolia* **32 B4** 47 56N 97 28 E
Jawa, *Indonesia* **37 G14** 7 0S 110 0 E
Jawad, *India* **42 G6** 24 36N 74 51 E
Jay Peak, *U.S.A.* **79 B12** 44 55N 72 32W
Jaya, Puncak, *Indonesia* **37 E9** 3 57S 137 17 E
Jayanti, *India* **41 F16** 26 45N 89 40 E
Jayapura, *Indonesia* **37 E10** 2 28S 140 38 E
Jayawijaya, Pegunungan, *Indonesia* **37 F9** 5 0S 139 0 E
Jaynagar, *India* **41 F15** 26 43N 86 9 E
Jayrūd, *Syria* **44 C3** 33 49N 36 44 E
Jayton, *U.S.A.* **81 J4** 33 15N 100 34W
Jāz Mūrīān, Hāmūn-e, *Iran* **45 E8** 27 20N 58 55 E
Jazīreh-ye Shīf, *Iran* **45 D6** 29 4N 50 54 E
Jazminal, *Mexico* **86 C4** 24 56N 101 25W
Jazzīn, *Lebanon* **47 B4** 33 31N 35 35 E
Jean, *U.S.A.* **85 K11** 35 47N 115 20W
Jean Marie River, *Canada* **72 A4** 61 32N 120 38W
Jean Rabel, *Haiti* **89 C5** 19 50N 73 5W
Jeanerette, *U.S.A.* **81 L9** 29 55N 91 40W
Jeanette, Ostrov = Zhannetty, Ostrov, *Russia* **27 B16** 76 43N 158 0 E
Jeannette, *U.S.A.* **78 F5** 40 20N 79 36W
Jebāl Bārez, Kūh-e, *Iran* **45 D8** 28 30N 58 20 E
Jebel, Bahr el →, *Sudan* **51 G12** 9 30N 30 25 E
Jedburgh, *U.K.* **12 F6** 55 29N 2 33W
Jedda = Jiddah, *Si. Arabia* **46 C2** 21 29N 39 10 E
Jeddore L., *Canada* **71 C8** 48 3N 55 55W
Jędrzejów, *Poland* **17 C11** 50 35N 20 15 E
Jefferson, *Iowa, U.S.A.* **80 D7** 42 1N 94 23W
Jefferson, *Ohio, U.S.A.* **78 E4** 41 44N 80 46W
Jefferson, *Tex., U.S.A.* **81 J7** 32 46N 94 21W
Jefferson, Mt., *Nev., U.S.A.* **82 G5** 38 51N 117 0W
Jefferson, Mt., *Oreg., U.S.A.* **82 D3** 44 41N 121 48W
Jefferson City, *Mo., U.S.A.* **80 F8** 38 34N 92 10W
Jefferson City, *Tenn., U.S.A.* **77 G4** 36 7N 83 30W
Jeffersontown, *U.S.A.* **76 F3** 38 12N 85 35W
Jeffersonville, *U.S.A.* **76 F3** 38 17N 85 44W
Jeffrey City, *U.S.A.* **82 E10** 42 30N 107 49W
Jega, *Nigeria* **50 F6** 12 15N 4 23 E
Jēkabpils, *Latvia* **9 H21** 56 29N 25 57 E
Jekyll I., *U.S.A.* **77 K5** 31 4N 81 25W
Jelenia Góra, *Poland* **16 C8** 50 50N 15 45 E
Jelgava, *Latvia* **9 H20** 56 41N 23 49 E
Jemaja, *Indonesia* **39 L5** 3 5N 105 45 E
Jemaluang, *Malaysia* **39 L4** 2 16N 103 52 E
Jember, *Indonesia* **37 H15** 8 11S 113 41 E
Jembongan, *Malaysia* **36 C5** 6 45N 117 20 E
Jena, *Germany* **16 C6** 50 54N 11 35 E
Jena, *U.S.A.* **81 K8** 31 41N 92 8W
Jenkins, *U.S.A.* **76 G4** 37 10N 82 38W
Jenner, *U.S.A.* **84 G3** 38 27N 123 7W
Jennings, *U.S.A.* **81 K8** 30 13N 92 40W
Jepara, *Indonesia* **37 G14** 7 40S 109 14 E
Jeparit, *Australia* **63 F3** 36 8S 142 1 E
Jequié, *Brazil* **93 F10** 13 51S 40 5W
Jequitinhonha, *Brazil* **93 G10** 16 30S 41 0W
Jequitinhonha →, *Brazil* **93 G11** 15 51S 38 53W
Jerantut, *Malaysia* **39 L4** 3 56N 102 22 E
Jérémie, *Haiti* **89 C5** 18 40N 74 10W
Jerez, Punta, *Mexico* **87 C5** 22 58N 97 40W
Jerez de García Salinas, *Mexico* **86 C4** 22 39N 103 0W
Jerez de la Frontera, *Spain* **19 D2** 36 41N 6 7W
Jerez de los Caballeros, *Spain* **19 C2** 38 20N 6 45W
Jericho = El Arīḥā, *West Bank* **47 D4** 31 52N 35 27 E
Jericho, *Australia* **62 C4** 23 38S 146 6 E
Jerilderie, *Australia* **63 F4** 35 20S 145 41 E
Jermyn, *U.S.A.* **79 E9** 41 31N 75 31W
Jerome, *U.S.A.* **82 E6** 42 44N 114 31W
Jerramungup, *Australia* **61 F2** 33 55S 118 55 E
Jersey, *U.K.* **11 H5** 49 11N 2 7W
Jersey City, *U.S.A.* **79 F10** 40 44N 74 4W
Jersey Shore, *U.S.A.* **78 E7** 41 12N 77 15W
Jerseyville, *U.S.A.* **80 F9** 39 7N 90 20W
Jerusalem, *Israel* **47 D4** 31 47N 35 10 E
Jervis B., *Australia* **63 F5** 35 8S 150 46 E
Jervis Inlet, *Canada* **72 C4** 50 0N 123 57W
Jesselton = Kota Kinabalu, *Malaysia* **36 C5** 6 0N 116 4 E
Jessore, *Bangla.* **41 H16** 23 10N 89 10 E
Jesup, *U.S.A.* **77 K5** 31 36N 81 53W
Jesús Carranza, *Mexico* **87 D5** 17 28N 95 1W
Jesús María, *Argentina* **94 C3** 30 59S 64 5W
Jetmore, *U.S.A.* **81 F5** 38 4N 99 54W
Jetpur, *India* **42 J4** 21 45N 70 10 E
Jevnaker, *Norway* **9 F14** 60 15N 10 26 E
Jewett, *U.S.A.* **78 F3** 40 22N 81 2W
Jewett City, *U.S.A.* **79 E13** 41 36N 72 0W
Jeyḥūnābād, *Iran* **45 C6** 34 58N 48 59 E
Jeypore, *India* **41 K13** 18 50N 82 38 E
Jha Jha, *India* **43 G12** 24 46N 86 22 E
Jhabua, *India* **42 H6** 22 46N 74 36 E
Jhajjar, *India* **42 E7** 28 37N 76 42 E
Jhal, *Pakistan* **42 E2** 28 17N 67 27 E
Jhal Jhao, *Pakistan* **40 F4** 26 20N 65 35 E
Jhalawar, *India* **42 G7** 24 40N 76 10 E
Jhalida, *India* **43 H11** 23 22N 85 58 E
Jhalrapatan, *India* **42 G7** 24 33N 76 10 E
Jhang Maghiana, *Pakistan* **42 D5** 31 15N 72 22 E
Jhansi, *India* **43 G8** 25 30N 78 36 E
Jhargram, *India* **43 H12** 22 27N 86 59 E
Jharia, *India* **43 H12** 23 45N 86 26 E
Jharsuguda, *India* **41 J14** 21 56N 84 5 E
Jhelum, *Pakistan* **42 C5** 33 0N 73 45 E
Jhelum →, *Pakistan* **42 D5** 31 20N 72 10 E
Jhilmilli, *India* **43 H10** 23 24N 82 51 E
Jhudo, *Pakistan* **42 G3** 24 58N 69 18 E
Jhunjhunu, *India* **42 E6** 28 10N 75 30 E
Ji-Paraná, *Brazil* **92 F6** 10 52S 62 57W
Ji Xian, *Hebei, China* **34 F8** 37 35N 115 30 E
Ji Xian, *Henan, China* **34 G8** 35 22N 114 5 E
Ji Xian, *Shanxi, China* **34 F6** 36 7N 110 40 E
Jia Xian, *Henan, China* **34 H7** 33 59N 113 12 E
Jia Xian, *Shaanxi, China* **34 E6** 38 12N 110 28 E
Jiamusi, *China* **33 B8** 46 40N 130 26 E
Ji'an, *Jiangxi, China* **33 D6** 27 6N 114 59 E
Ji'an, *Jilin, China* **35 D14** 41 5N 126 10 E
Jianchang, *China* **35 D11** 40 55N 120 35 E
Jianchangying, *China* **35 D10** 40 10N 118 50 E
Jiangcheng, *China* **32 D5** 22 36N 101 52 E
Jiangmen, *China* **33 D6** 22 32N 113 0 E
Jiangsu □, *China* **35 H11** 33 0N 120 0 E
Jiangxi □, *China* **33 D6** 27 30N 116 0 E
Jiao Xian = Jiaozhou, *China* **35 F11** 36 18N 120 1 E
Jiaohe, *Hebei, China* **34 E9** 38 2N 116 20 E
Jiaohe, *Jilin, China* **35 C14** 43 40N 127 22 E
Jiaozhou, *China* **35 F11** 36 18N 120 1 E
Jiaozhou Wan, *China* **35 F11** 36 5N 120 10 E
Jiaozuo, *China* **34 G7** 35 16N 113 12 E
Jiawang, *China* **35 G9** 34 28N 117 26 E
Jiaxiang, *China* **34 G9** 35 25N 116 20 E
Jiaxing, *China* **33 C7** 30 49N 120 45 E
Jiayi = Chiai, *Taiwan* **33 D7** 23 29N 120 25 E
Jibuti = Djibouti ■, *Africa* **46 E3** 12 0N 43 0 E
Jicarón, I., *Panama* **88 E3** 7 10N 81 50W
Jiddah, *Si. Arabia* **46 C2** 21 29N 39 10 E
Jido, *India* **41 E19** 29 2N 94 58 E
Jieshou, *China* **34 H8** 33 18N 115 22 E
Jiexiu, *China* **34 F6** 37 2N 111 55 E
Jiggalong, *Australia* **60 D3** 23 21S 120 47 E
Jigni, *India* **43 G8** 25 45N 79 25 E
Jihlava, *Czech Rep.* **16 D8** 49 28N 15 35 E
Jihlava →, *Czech Rep.* **17 D9** 48 55N 16 36 E
Jijiga, *Ethiopia* **46 F3** 9 20N 42 50 E
Jilin, *China* **35 C14** 43 44N 126 30 E
Jilin □, *China* **35 C14** 44 0N 127 0 E
Jilong = Chilung, *Taiwan* **33 D7** 25 3N 121 45 E
Jim Thorpe, *U.S.A.* **79 F9** 40 52N 75 44W
Jima, *Ethiopia* **46 F2** 7 40N 36 47 E
Jiménez, *Mexico* **86 B4** 27 10N 104 54W
Jimo, *China* **35 F11** 36 23N 120 30 E
Jin Xian = Jinzhou, *China* **34 E8** 38 2N 115 2 E
Jin Xian, *China* **35 E11** 38 55N 121 42 E
Jinan, *China* **34 F9** 36 38N 117 1 E
Jincheng, *China* **34 G7** 35 29N 112 50 E
Jind, *India* **42 E7** 29 19N 76 22 E
Jindabyne, *Australia* **63 F4** 36 25S 148 35 E
Jindřichův Hradec, *Czech Rep.* **16 D8** 49 10N 15 2 E
Jing He →, *China* **34 G5** 34 27N 109 4 E
Jingbian, *China* **34 F5** 37 20N 108 30 E
Jingchuan, *China* **34 G4** 35 20N 107 20 E
Jingdezhen, *China* **33 D6** 29 20N 117 11 E
Jinggu, *China* **32 D5** 23 35N 100 41 E
Jinghai, *China* **34 E9** 38 55N 116 55 E
Jingle, *China* **34 E6** 38 20N 111 55 E
Jingning, *China* **34 G3** 35 30N 105 43 E
Jingpo Hu, *China* **35 C15** 43 55N 128 55 E
Jingtai, *China* **34 F3** 37 10N 104 6 E
Jingxing, *China* **34 E8** 38 2N 114 8 E
Jingyang, *China* **34 G5** 34 30N 108 50 E
Jingyu, *China* **35 C14** 42 25N 126 45 E
Jingyuan, *China* **34 F3** 36 30N 104 40 E
Jingziguan, *China* **34 H6** 33 15N 111 0 E
Jinhua, *China* **33 D6** 29 8N 119 38 E
Jining, *Nei Mongol Zizhiqu, China* **34 D7** 41 5N 113 0 E
Jining, *Shandong, China* **34 G9** 35 22N 116 34 E
Jinja, *Uganda* **54 B3** 0 25N 33 12 E
Jinjang, *Malaysia* **39 L3** 3 13N 101 39 E
Jinji, *China* **34 F4** 37 58N 106 8 E
Jinnah Barrage, *Pakistan* **40 C7** 32 58N 71 33 E
Jinotega, *Nic.* **88 D2** 13 6N 85 59W
Jinotepe, *Nic.* **88 D2** 11 50N 86 10W
Jinsha Jiang →, *China* **32 D5** 28 50N 104 36 E
Jinxi, *China* **35 D11** 40 52N 120 50 E
Jinxiang, *China* **34 G9** 35 5N 116 22 E
Jinzhou, *Hebei, China* **34 E8** 38 2N 115 2 E
Jinzhou, *Liaoning, China* **35 D11** 41 5N 121 3 E
Jiparaná →, *Brazil* **92 E6** 8 3S 62 52W
Jipijapa, *Ecuador* **92 D2** 1 0S 80 40W
Jiquilpan, *Mexico* **86 D4** 19 57N 102 42W
Jishan, *China* **34 G6** 35 34N 110 58 E
Jisr ash Shughūr, *Syria* **44 C3** 35 49N 36 18 E
Jitarning, *Australia* **61 F2** 32 48S 117 57 E
Jitra, *Malaysia* **39 J3** 6 16N 100 25 E
Jiu →, *Romania* **17 F12** 43 47N 23 48 E
Jiudengkou, *China* **34 E4** 39 56N 106 40 E
Jiujiang, *China* **33 D6** 29 42N 115 58 E
Jiutai, *China* **35 B13** 44 10N 125 50 E
Jiuxiangcheng, *China* **34 H8** 33 12N 114 50 E
Jiuxincheng, *China* **34 E8** 39 17N 115 59 E
Jixi, *China* **35 B16** 45 20N 130 50 E
Jiyang, *China* **35 F9** 37 0N 117 12 E
Jiyuan, *China* **34 G7** 35 7N 112 57 E
Jīzān, *Si. Arabia* **46 D3** 17 0N 42 20 E
Jize, *China* **34 F8** 36 54N 114 56 E
Jizl, Wādī al, *Si. Arabia* **44 E3** 25 39N 38 25 E
Jizō-Zaki, *Japan* **31 G6** 35 34N 133 20 E
Jizzakh, *Uzbekistan* **26 E7** 40 6N 67 50 E
Joaçaba, *Brazil* **95 B5** 27 5S 51 31W
João Pessoa, *Brazil* **93 E12** 7 10S 34 52W
Joaquín V. González, *Argentina* **94 B3** 25 10S 64 0W
Jobat, *India* **42 H6** 22 25N 74 34 E
Jodhpur, *India* **42 F5** 26 23N 73 8 E
Jodiya, *India* **42 H4** 22 42N 70 18 E
Joensuu, *Finland* **24 B4** 62 37N 29 49 E
Jōetsu, *Japan* **31 F9** 37 12N 138 10 E
Jofane, *Mozam.* **57 C5** 21 15S 34 18 E
Jogbani, *India* **43 F12** 26 25N 87 15 E
Jõgeva, *Estonia* **9 G22** 58 45N 26 24 E
Jogjakarta = Yogyakarta, *Indonesia* **37 G14** 7 49S 110 22 E
Johannesburg, *S. Africa* **57 D4** 26 10S 28 2 E
Johannesburg, *U.S.A.* **85 K9** 35 22N 117 38W
Johilla →, *India* **43 H9** 23 37N 81 14 E
John Day, *U.S.A.* **82 D4** 44 25N 118 57W
John Day →, *U.S.A.* **82 D3** 45 44N 120 39W
John D'Or Prairie, *Canada* **72 B5** 58 30N 115 8W
John H. Kerr Reservoir, *U.S.A.* **77 G6** 36 36N 78 18W
John o' Groats, *U.K.* **12 C5** 58 38N 3 4W
Johnnie, *U.S.A.* **85 J10** 36 25N 116 5W
John's Ra., *Australia* **62 C1** 21 55S 133 23 E
Johnson, *Kans., U.S.A.* **81 G4** 37 34N 101 45W
Johnson, *Vt., U.S.A.* **79 B12** 44 38N 72 41W
Johnson City, *N.Y., U.S.A.* **79 D9** 42 7N 75 58W
Johnson City, *Tenn., U.S.A.* **77 G4** 36 19N 82 21W
Johnson City, *Tex., U.S.A.* **81 K5** 30 17N 98 25W
Johnsonburg, *U.S.A.* **78 E6** 41 29N 78 41W
Johnsondale, *U.S.A.* **85 K8** 35 58N 118 32W
Johnson's Crossing, *Canada* **72 A2** 60 29N 133 18W
Johnston, L., *Australia* **61 F3** 32 25S 120 30 E
Johnston Falls = Mambilima Falls, *Zambia* **55 E2** 10 31S 28 45 E
Johnston I., *Pac. Oc.* **65 F11** 17 10N 169 8W
Johnstone Str., *Canada* **72 C3** 50 28N 126 0W
Johnstown, *N.Y., U.S.A.* **79 C10** 43 0N 74 22W
Johnstown, *Ohio, U.S.A.* **78 F2** 40 9N 82 41W
Johnstown, *Pa., U.S.A.* **78 F6** 40 20N 78 55W
Johor Baharu, *Malaysia* **39 M4** 1 28N 103 46 E
Jõhvi, *Estonia* **9 G22** 59 22N 27 27 E
Joinville, *Brazil* **95 B6** 26 15S 48 55W
Joinville I., *Antarctica* **5 C18** 65 0S 55 30W
Jojutla, *Mexico* **87 D5** 18 37N 99 11W
Jokkmokk, *Sweden* **8 C18** 66 35N 19 50 E
Jökulsá á Bru →, *Iceland* **8 D6** 65 40N 14 16W
Jökulsá á Fjöllum →, *Iceland* **8 C5** 66 10N 16 30W
Jolfā, *Āzarbājān-e Sharqī, Iran* **44 B5** 38 57N 45 38 E
Jolfā, *Eşfahan, Iran* **45 C6** 32 58N 51 37 E
Joliet, *U.S.A.* **76 E1** 41 32N 88 5W
Joliette, *Canada* **70 C5** 46 3N 73 24W
Jolo, *Phil.* **37 C6** 6 0N 121 0 E
Jolon, *U.S.A.* **84 K5** 35 58N 121 9W
Jombang, *Indonesia* **37 G15** 7 33S 112 14 E
Jonava, *Lithuania* **9 J21** 55 8N 24 12 E
Jones Sound, *Canada* **4 B3** 76 0N 85 0W
Jonesboro, *Ark., U.S.A.* **81 H9** 35 50N 90 42W
Jonesboro, *La., U.S.A.* **81 J8** 32 15N 92 43W
Joniškis, *Lithuania* **9 H20** 56 13N 23 35 E
Jönköping, *Sweden* **9 H16** 57 45N 14 8 E
Jonquière, *Canada* **71 C5** 48 27N 71 14W
Joplin, *U.S.A.* **81 G7** 37 6N 94 31W
Jora, *India* **42 F6** 26 20N 77 49 E
Jordan, *Mont., U.S.A.* **82 C10** 47 19N 106 55W
Jordan, *N.Y., U.S.A.* **79 C8** 43 4N 76 29W
Jordan ■, *Asia* **47 E5** 31 0N 36 0 E
Jordan →, *Asia* **47 D4** 31 48N 35 32 E
Jordan Valley, *U.S.A.* **82 E5** 42 59N 117 3W
Jorhat, *India* **41 F19** 26 45N 94 12 E
Jörn, *Sweden* **8 D19** 65 4N 20 1 E
Jorong, *Indonesia* **36 E4** 3 58S 114 56 E
Jørpeland, *Norway* **9 G11** 59 3N 6 1 E
Jorquera →, *Chile* **94 B2** 28 3S 69 58W
Jos, *Nigeria* **50 G7** 9 53N 8 51 E
José Batlle y Ordóñez, *Uruguay* **95 C4** 33 20S 55 10W
Joseph, L., *Nfld., Canada* **71 B6** 52 45N 65 18W
Joseph, L., *Ont., Canada* **78 A5** 45 10N 79 44W
Joseph Bonaparte G., *Australia* **60 B4** 14 35S 128 50 E
Joshinath, *India* **43 D8** 30 34N 79 34 E
Joshua Tree, *U.S.A.* **85 L10** 34 8N 116 19W
Joshua Tree National Park, *U.S.A.* **85 M10** 33 55N 116 0W
Jostedalsbreen, *Norway* **9 F12** 61 40N 6 59 E
Jotunheimen, *Norway* **9 F13** 61 35N 8 25 E
Jourdanton, *U.S.A.* **81 L5** 28 55N 98 33W
Jovellanos, *Cuba* **88 B3** 22 40N 81 10W
Ju Xian, *China* **35 F10** 36 35N 118 20 E
Juan Aldama, *Mexico* **86 C4** 24 20N 103 23W
Juan Bautista Alberdi, *Argentina* **94 C3** 34 26S 61 48W
Juan de Fuca Str., *Canada* **84 B3** 48 15N 124 0W
Juan de Nova, *Ind. Oc.* **57 B7** 17 3S 43 45 E
Juan Fernández, Arch. de, *Pac. Oc.* **90 G2** 33 50S 80 0W
Juan José Castelli, *Argentina* **94 B3** 25 27S 60 57W
Juan L. Lacaze, *Uruguay* **94 C4** 34 26S 57 25W
Juankoski, *Finland* **8 E23** 63 3N 28 19 E
Juárez, *Argentina* **94 D4** 37 40S 59 43W
Juárez, *Mexico* **85 N11** 32 20N 115 57W
Juárez, Sierra de, *Mexico* **86 A1** 32 0N 116 0W
Juàzeiro, *Brazil* **93 E10** 9 30S 40 30W
Juàzeiro do Norte, *Brazil* **93 E11** 7 10S 39 18W
Juba, *Sudan* **51 H12** 4 50N 31 35 E
Jubayl, *Lebanon* **47 A4** 34 5N 35 39 E
Jubbah, *Si. Arabia* **44 D4** 28 2N 40 56 E
Jubbal, *India* **42 D7** 31 5N 77 40 E
Jubbulpore = Jabalpur, *India* **43 H8** 23 9N 79 58 E
Jubilee L., *Australia* **61 E4** 29 0S 126 50 E
Juby, C., *Morocco* **50 C3** 28 0N 12 59W
Júcar = Xúquer →, *Spain* **19 C5** 39 5N 0 10W
Júcaro, *Cuba* **88 B4** 21 37N 78 51W
Juchitán, *Mexico* **87 D5** 16 27N 95 5W
Judaea = Har Yehuda, *Israel* **47 D3** 31 35N 34 57 E
Judith →, *U.S.A.* **82 C9** 47 44N 109 39W
Judith, Pt., *U.S.A.* **79 E13** 41 22N 71 29W
Judith Gap, *U.S.A.* **82 C9** 46 41N 109 45W
Jugoslavia = Yugoslavia ■, *Europe* **21 B9** 43 20N 20 0 E
Juigalpa, *Nic.* **88 D2** 12 6N 85 26W
Juiz de Fora, *Brazil* **95 A7** 21 43S 43 19W
Jujuy □, *Argentina* **94 A2** 23 20S 65 40W
Julesburg, *U.S.A.* **80 E3** 40 59N 102 16W
Juli, *Peru* **92 G5** 16 10S 69 25W
Julia Cr. →, *Australia* **62 C3** 20 0S 141 11 E
Julia Creek, *Australia* **62 C3** 20 39S 141 44 E
Juliaca, *Peru* **92 G4** 15 25S 70 10W
Julian, *U.S.A.* **85 M10** 33 4N 116 38W
Julian L., *Canada* **70 B4** 54 25N 77 57W
Julianatop, *Surinam* **93 C7** 3 40N 56 30W
Julianehåb, *Greenland* **4 C5** 60 43N 46 0W
Julimes, *Mexico* **86 B3** 28 25N 105 27W
Jullundur, *India* **42 D6** 31 20N 75 40 E
Julu, *China* **34 F8** 37 15N 115 2 E
Jumbo, *Zimbabwe* **55 F3** 17 30S 30 58 E
Jumbo Pk., *U.S.A.* **85 J12** 36 12N 114 11W
Jumentos Cays, *Bahamas* **88 B4** 23 0N 75 40W
Jumilla, *Spain* **19 C5** 38 28N 1 19W
Jumla, *Nepal* **43 E10** 29 15N 82 13 E
Jumna = Yamuna →, *India* **43 G9** 25 30N 81 53 E
Junagadh, *India* **42 J4** 21 30N 70 30 E
Junction, *Tex., U.S.A.* **81 K5** 30 29N 99 46W
Junction, *Utah, U.S.A.* **83 G7** 38 14N 112 13W
Junction B., *Australia* **62 A1** 11 52S 133 55 E
Junction City, *Kans., U.S.A.* **80 F6** 39 2N 96 50W
Junction City, *Oreg., U.S.A.* **82 D2** 44 13N 123 12W
Junction Pt., *Australia* **62 A1** 11 45S 133 50 E
Jundah, *Australia* **62 C3** 24 46S 143 2 E
Jundiaí, *Brazil* **95 A6** 24 30S 47 0W
Juneau, *U.S.A.* **72 B2** 58 18N 134 25W
Junee, *Australia* **63 E4** 34 53S 147 35 E
Jungfrau, *Switz.* **18 C7** 46 32N 7 58 E
Junggar Pendi, *China* **32 B3** 44 30N 86 0 E
Jungshahi, *Pakistan* **42 G2** 24 52N 67 44 E
Juniata →, *U.S.A.* **78 F7** 40 30N 77 40W
Junín, *Argentina* **94 C3** 34 33S 60 57W
Junín de los Andes, *Argentina* **96 D2** 39 45S 71 0W
Jūniyah, *Lebanon* **47 B4** 33 59N 35 38 E
Juntas, *Chile* **94 B2** 28 24S 69 58W
Juntura, *U.S.A.* **82 E4** 43 45N 118 5W
Jur, Nahr el →, *Sudan* **51 G11** 8 45N 29 15 E
Jura = Jura, Mts. du, *Europe* **18 C7** 46 40N 6 5 E
Jura = Schwäbische Alb, *Germany* **16 D5** 48 20N 9 30 E
Jura, *U.K.* **12 F3** 56 0N 5 50W
Jura, Mts. du, *Europe* **18 C7** 46 40N 6 5 E
Jura, Sd. of, *U.K.* **12 F3** 55 57N 5 45W
Jurbarkas, *Lithuania* **9 J20** 55 4N 22 46 E
Jurien, *Australia* **61 F2** 30 18S 115 2 E
Jūrmala, *Latvia* **9 H20** 56 58N 23 34 E
Juruá →, *Brazil* **92 D5** 2 37S 65 44W
Juruena, *Brazil* **92 F7** 13 0S 58 10W

Juruena →, *Brazil* **92 E7** 7 20S 58 3W
Juruti, *Brazil* **93 D7** 2 9S 56 4W
Justo Daract, *Argentina* **94 C2** 33 52S 65 12W
Jutaí →, *Brazil* **92 D5** 2 43S 66 57W
Juticalpa, *Honduras* **88 D2** 14 40N 86 12W
Jutland = Jylland, *Denmark* **9 H13** 56 25N 9 30 E
Juventud, I. de la, *Cuba* **88 B3** 21 40N 82 40W
Juwain, *Afghan.* **40 D2** 31 45N 61 30 E
Jūy Zar, *Iran* **44 C5** 33 50N 46 18 E
Juye, *China* **34 G9** 35 22N 116 5 E
Jwaneng, *Botswana* **53 J4** 24 45S 24 50 E
Jylland, *Denmark* **9 H13** 56 25N 9 30 E
Jyväskylä, *Finland* **9 E21** 62 14N 25 50 E

K

K2, *Pakistan* **43 B7** 35 58N 76 32 E
Kaap Plateau, *S. Africa* **56 D3** 28 30S 24 0 E
Kaapkruis, *Namibia* **56 C1** 21 55S 13 57 E
Kaapstad = Cape Town, *S. Africa* **56 E2** 33 55S 18 22 E
Kabaena, *Indonesia* **37 F6** 5 15S 122 0 E
Kabala, *S. Leone* **50 G3** 9 38N 11 37W
Kabale, *Uganda* **54 C3** 1 15S 30 0 E
Kabalo, *Dem. Rep. of the Congo* **54 D2** 6 0S 27 0 E
Kabambare, *Dem. Rep. of the Congo* **54 C2** 4 41S 27 39 E
Kabango, *Dem. Rep. of the Congo* **55 D2** 8 35S 28 30 E
Kabanjahe, *Indonesia* **36 D1** 3 6N 98 30 E
Kabardino-Balkar Republic = Kabardino-Balkaria □, *Russia* **25 F7** 43 30N 43 30 E
Kabardino-Balkaria □, *Russia* **25 F7** 43 30N 43 30 E
Kabarega Falls = Murchison Falls, *Uganda* **54 B3** 2 15N 31 30 E
Kabasalan, *Phil.* **37 C6** 7 47N 122 44 E
Kabetogama, *U.S.A.* **80 A8** 48 28N 92 59W
Kabin Buri, *Thailand* **38 F3** 13 57N 101 43 E
Kabinakagami L., *Canada* **70 C3** 48 54N 84 25W
Kabinda, *Dem. Rep. of the Congo* **52 F4** 6 19S 24 20 E
Kabompo, *Zambia* **55 E1** 13 36S 24 14 E
Kabompo →, *Zambia* **53 G4** 14 10S 23 11 E
Kabondo, *Dem. Rep. of the Congo* **55 D2** 8 58S 25 40 E
Kabongo, *Dem. Rep. of the Congo* **54 D2** 7 22S 25 33 E
Kabūd Gonbad, *Iran* **45 B8** 37 5N 59 45 E
Kābul, *Afghan.* **42 B3** 34 28N 69 11 E
Kābul □, *Afghan.* **40 B6** 34 30N 69 0 E
Kabul →, *Pakistan* **42 C5** 33 55N 72 14 E
Kabunga, *Dem. Rep. of the Congo* **54 C2** 1 38S 28 3 E
Kaburuang, *Indonesia* **37 D7** 3 50N 126 30 E
Kabwe, *Zambia* **55 E2** 14 30S 28 29 E
Kachchh, Gulf of, *India* **42 H3** 22 50N 69 15 E
Kachchh, Rann of, *India* **42 H4** 24 0N 70 0 E
Kachchhidhana, *India* **43 J8** 21 44N 78 46 E
Kachebera, *Zambia* **55 E3** 13 50S 32 50 E
Kachin □, *Burma* **41 G20** 26 0N 97 30 E
Kachira, L., *Uganda* **54 C3** 0 40S 31 7 E
Kachiry, *Kazakstan* **26 D8** 53 10N 75 50 E
Kachnara, *India* **42 H6** 23 50N 75 6 E
Kachot, *Cambodia* **39 G4** 11 30N 103 3 E
Kaçkar, *Turkey* **25 F7** 40 45N 41 10 E
Kadan Kyun, *Burma* **38 F2** 12 30N 98 20 E
Kadanai →, *Afghan.* **42 D1** 31 22N 65 45 E
Kadi, *India* **42 H5** 23 18N 72 23 E
Kadina, *Australia* **63 E2** 33 55S 137 43 E
Kadipur, *India* **43 F10** 26 10N 82 23 E
Kadirli, *Turkey* **44 B3** 37 23N 36 5 E
Kadiyevka = Stakhanov, *Ukraine* **25 E6** 48 35N 38 40 E
Kadoka, *U.S.A.* **80 D4** 43 50N 101 31W
Kadoma, *Zimbabwe* **55 F2** 18 20S 29 52 E
Kâdugli, *Sudan* **51 F11** 11 0N 29 45 E
Kaduna, *Nigeria* **50 F7** 10 30N 7 21 E
Kaédi, *Mauritania* **50 E3** 16 9N 13 28W
Kaeng Khoï, *Thailand* **38 E3** 14 35N 101 0 E
Kaesŏng, *N. Korea* **35 F14** 37 58N 126 35 E
Kāf, *Si. Arabia* **44 D3** 31 25N 37 29 E
Kafan = Kapan, *Armenia* **25 G8** 39 18N 46 27 E
Kafanchan, *Nigeria* **50 G7** 9 40N 8 20 E
Kafinda, *Zambia* **55 E3** 12 32S 30 20 E
Kafirévs, Ákra, *Greece* **21 E11** 38 9N 24 38 E
Kafue, *Zambia* **55 F2** 15 46S 28 9 E
Kafue →, *Zambia* **53 H5** 15 30S 29 0 E
Kafue Flats, *Zambia* **55 F2** 15 40S 27 25 E
Kafue Nat. Park, *Zambia* **55 F2** 15 0S 25 30 E
Kafulwe, *Zambia* **55 D2** 9 0S 29 1 E
Kaga, *Afghan.* **42 B4** 34 14N 70 10 E
Kaga Bandoro, *C.A.R.* **52 C3** 7 0N 19 10 E
Kagan, *Uzbekistan* **26 F7** 39 43N 64 33 E
Kagawa □, *Japan* **31 G7** 34 15N 134 0 E
Kagera □, *Tanzania* **54 C3** 2 0S 31 30 E
Kagera →, *Uganda* **54 C3** 0 57S 31 47 E
Kağızman, *Turkey* **44 A4** 40 5N 43 10 E
Kagoshima, *Japan* **31 J5** 31 35N 130 33 E
Kagoshima □, *Japan* **31 J5** 31 30N 130 30 E
Kagul = Cahul, *Moldova* **17 F15** 45 50N 28 15 E
Kahak, *Iran* **45 B6** 36 6N 49 46 E
Kahama, *Tanzania* **54 C3** 4 8S 32 30 E
Kahan, *Pakistan* **42 E3** 29 18N 68 54 E
Kahang, *Malaysia* **39 L4** 2 12N 103 32 E
Kahayan →, *Indonesia* **36 E4** 3 40S 114 0 E
Kahe, *Tanzania* **54 C4** 3 30S 37 25 E
Kahnūj, *Iran* **45 E8** 27 55N 57 40 E
Kahoka, *U.S.A.* **80 E9** 40 25N 91 44W
Kahoolawe, *U.S.A.* **74 H16** 20 33N 156 37W
Kahramanmaraş, *Turkey* **25 G6** 37 37N 36 53 E
Kahuta, *Pakistan* **42 C5** 33 35N 73 24 E
Kai, Kepulauan, *Indonesia* **37 F8** 5 55S 132 45 E
Kai Besar, *Indonesia* **37 F8** 5 35S 133 0 E
Kai Is. = Kai, Kepulauan, *Indonesia* **37 F8** 5 55S 132 45 E
Kai Kecil, *Indonesia* **37 F8** 5 45S 132 40 E
Kaiapoi, *N.Z.* **59 K4** 43 24S 172 40 E
Kaieteur Falls, *Guyana* **92 B7** 5 1N 59 10W
Kaifeng, *China* **34 G8** 34 48N 114 21 E
Kaikohe, *N.Z.* **59 F4** 35 25S 173 49 E
Kaikoura, *N.Z.* **59 K4** 42 25S 173 43 E
Kaikoura Ra., *N.Z.* **59 J4** 41 59S 173 41 E
Kailu, *China* **35 C11** 43 38N 121 18 E
Kailua Kona, *U.S.A.* **74 J17** 19 39N 155 59W
Kaimana, *Indonesia* **37 E8** 3 39S 133 45 E
Kaimanawa Mts., *N.Z.* **59 H5** 39 15S 175 56 E
Kaimganj, *India* **43 F8** 27 33N 79 24 E
Kaimur Hills, *India* **43 G10** 24 30N 82 0 E
Kaingaroa Forest, *N.Z.* **59 H6** 38 24S 176 30 E
Kainji Res., *Nigeria* **50 F6** 10 1N 4 40 E
Kainuu, *Finland* **8 D23** 64 30N 29 7 E
Kaipara Harbour, *N.Z.* **59 G5** 36 25S 174 14 E
Kaipokok B., *Canada* **71 B8** 54 54N 59 47W
Kaira, *India* **42 H5** 22 45N 72 50 E
Kairana, *India* **42 E7** 29 24N 77 15 E
Kaironi, *Indonesia* **37 E8** 0 47S 133 40 E
Kairouan, *Tunisia* **51 A8** 35 45N 10 5 E
Kaiserslautern, *Germany* **16 D4** 49 26N 7 45 E
Kaitaia, *N.Z.* **59 F4** 35 8S 173 17 E
Kaitangata, *N.Z.* **59 M2** 46 17S 169 51 E
Kaithal, *India* **42 E7** 29 48N 76 26 E
Kaitu →, *Pakistan* **42 C4** 33 10N 70 30 E
Kaiwi Channel, *U.S.A.* **74 H16** 21 15N 157 30W
Kaiyuan, *China* **35 C13** 42 28N 124 1 E
Kajaani, *Finland* **8 D22** 64 17N 27 46 E
Kajabbi, *Australia* **62 C3** 20 0S 140 1 E
Kajana = Kajaani, *Finland* **8 D22** 64 17N 27 46 E
Kajang, *Malaysia* **39 L3** 2 59N 101 48 E
Kajiado, *Kenya* **54 C4** 1 53S 36 48 E
Kajo Kaji, *Sudan* **51 H12** 3 58N 31 40 E
Kakabeka Falls, *Canada* **70 C2** 48 24N 89 37W
Kakadu Nat. Park, *Australia* **60 B5** 12 30S 132 5 E
Kakamas, *S. Africa* **56 D3** 28 45S 20 33 E
Kakamega, *Kenya* **54 B3** 0 20N 34 46 E
Kakanui Mts., *N.Z.* **59 L3** 45 10S 170 30 E
Kakdwip, *India* **43 J13** 21 53N 88 11 E
Kake, *Japan* **31 G6** 34 36N 132 19 E
Kake, *U.S.A.* **72 B2** 56 59N 133 57W
Kakegawa, *Japan* **31 G9** 34 45N 138 1 E
Kakeroma-Jima, *Japan* **31 K4** 28 8N 129 14 E
Kakhovka, *Ukraine* **25 E5** 46 45N 33 30 E
Kakhovske Vdskh., *Ukraine* **25 E5** 47 5N 34 0 E
Kakinada, *India* **41 L13** 16 57N 82 11 E
Kakisa →, *Canada* **72 A5** 61 3N 118 10W
Kakisa L., *Canada* **72 A5** 60 56N 117 43W
Kakogawa, *Japan* **31 G7** 34 46N 134 51 E
Kakwa →, *Canada* **72 C5** 54 37N 118 28W
Kāl Güsheh, *Iran* **45 D8** 30 59N 58 12 E
Kal Safīd, *Iran* **44 C5** 34 52N 47 23 E
Kalabagh, *Pakistan* **42 C4** 33 0N 71 28 E
Kalabahi, *Indonesia* **37 F6** 8 13S 124 31 E
Kalach, *Russia* **25 D7** 50 22N 41 0 E
Kaladan →, *Burma* **41 J18** 20 20N 93 5 E
Kaladar, *Canada* **78 B7** 44 37N 77 5W
Kalahari, *Africa* **56 C3** 24 0S 21 30 E
Kalahari Gemsbok Nat. Park, *S. Africa* **56 D3** 25 30S 20 30 E
Kalajoki, *Finland* **8 D20** 64 12N 24 10 E
Kālak, *Iran* **45 E8** 25 29N 59 22 E
Kalakamati, *Botswana* **57 C4** 20 40S 27 25 E
Kalakan, *Russia* **27 D12** 55 15N 116 45 E
K'alak'unlun Shank'ou, *Pakistan* **43 B7** 35 33N 77 46 E
Kalam, *Pakistan* **43 B5** 35 34N 72 30 E
Kalama, *Dem. Rep. of the Congo* **54 C2** 2 52S 28 35 E
Kalama, *U.S.A.* **84 E4** 46 1N 122 51W
Kalámai, *Greece* **21 F10** 37 3N 22 10 E
Kalamata = Kalámai, *Greece* **21 F10** 37 3N 22 10 E
Kalamazoo, *U.S.A.* **76 D3** 42 17N 85 35W
Kalamazoo →, *U.S.A.* **76 D2** 42 40N 86 10W
Kalambo Falls, *Tanzania* **55 D3** 8 37S 31 35 E
Kalan, *Turkey* **44 B3** 39 7N 39 32 E
Kalannie, *Australia* **61 F2** 30 22S 117 5 E
Kalāntarī, *Iran* **45 C7** 32 10N 54 8 E
Kalao, *Indonesia* **37 F6** 7 21S 121 0 E
Kalaotoa, *Indonesia* **37 F6** 7 20S 121 50 E
Kalasin, *Thailand* **38 D4** 16 26N 103 30 E
Kalat, *Pakistan* **40 E5** 29 8N 66 31 E
Kalāteh, *Iran* **45 B7** 36 33N 55 41 E
Kalāteh-ye Ganj, *Iran* **45 E8** 27 31N 57 55 E
Kalbarri, *Australia* **61 E1** 27 40S 114 10 E
Kalce, *Slovenia* **16 F8** 45 54N 14 13 E
Kale, *Turkey* **21 F13** 37 27N 28 49 E
Kalegauk Kyun, *Burma* **41 M20** 15 33N 97 35 E
Kalehe, *Dem. Rep. of the Congo* **54 C2** 2 6S 28 50 E
Kalema, *Tanzania* **54 C3** 1 12S 31 55 E
Kalemie, *Dem. Rep. of the Congo* **54 D2** 5 55S 29 9 E
Kalewa, *Burma* **41 H19** 23 10N 94 15 E
Kaleybar, *Iran* **44 B5** 38 47N 47 2 E
Kalgan = Zhangjiakou, *China* **34 D8** 40 48N 114 55 E
Kalgoorlie-Boulder, *Australia* **61 F3** 30 40S 121 22 E
Kali →, *India* **43 F8** 27 6N 79 55 E
Kali Sindh →, *India* **42 G6** 25 32N 76 17 E
Kaliakra, Nos, *Bulgaria* **21 C13** 43 21N 28 30 E
Kalianda, *Indonesia* **36 F3** 5 50S 105 45 E
Kalibo, *Phil.* **37 B6** 11 43N 122 22 E
Kalima, *Dem. Rep. of the Congo* **54 C2** 2 33S 26 32 E
Kalimantan □, *Indonesia* **36 E4** 0 0 114 0 E
Kalimantan Barat □, *Indonesia* **36 E4** 0 0 110 30 E
Kalimantan Selatan □, *Indonesia* **36 E5** 2 30S 115 30 E
Kalimantan Tengah □, *Indonesia* **36 E4** 2 0S 113 30 E
Kalimantan Timur □, *Indonesia* **36 D5** 1 30N 116 30 E
Kálimnos, *Greece* **21 F12** 37 0N 27 0 E
Kalimpong, *India* **43 F13** 27 4N 88 35 E
Kalinin = Tver, *Russia* **24 C6** 56 55N 35 55 E
Kaliningrad, *Russia* **9 J19** 54 42N 20 32 E
Kalinkavichy, *Belarus* **17 B15** 52 12N 29 20 E
Kalinkovichi = Kalinkavichy, *Belarus* **17 B15** 52 12N 29 20 E
Kaliro, *Uganda* **54 B3** 0 56N 33 30 E
Kalispell, *U.S.A.* **82 B6** 48 12N 114 19W
Kalisz, *Poland* **17 C10** 51 45N 18 8 E
Kaliua, *Tanzania* **54 D3** 5 5S 31 48 E
Kalix, *Sweden* **8 D20** 65 53N 23 12 E
Kalix →, *Sweden* **8 D20** 65 50N 23 11 E
Kalka, *India* **42 D7** 30 46N 76 57 E
Kalkarindji, *Australia* **60 C5** 17 30S 130 47 E
Kalkaska, *U.S.A.* **76 C3** 44 44N 85 11W
Kalkfeld, *Namibia* **56 C2** 20 57S 16 14 E
Kalkfontein, *Botswana* **56 C3** 22 4S 20 57 E
Kalkrand, *Namibia* **56 C2** 24 1S 17 35 E
Kallavesi, *Finland* **8 E22** 62 58N 27 30 E
Kallsjön, *Sweden* **8 E15** 63 38N 13 0 E
Kalmar, *Sweden* **9 H17** 56 40N 16 20 E
Kalmyk Republic = Kalmykia □, *Russia* **25 E8** 46 5N 46 1 E
Kalmykia □, *Russia* **25 E8** 46 5N 46 1 E
Kalmykovo, *Kazakstan* **25 E9** 49 0N 51 47 E
Kalna, *India* **43 H13** 23 13N 88 25 E
Kalnai, *India* **43 H10** 22 46N 83 30 E
Kalocsa, *Hungary* **17 E10** 46 32N 19 0 E
Kalokhorio, *Cyprus* **23 E12** 34 51N 33 2 E
Kaloko, *Dem. Rep. of the Congo* **54 D2** 6 47S 25 48 E
Kalol, *Gujarat, India* **42 H5** 22 37N 73 31 E
Kalol, *Gujarat, India* **42 H5** 23 15N 72 33 E
Kalomo, *Zambia* **55 F2** 17 0S 26 30 E
Kalpi, *India* **43 F8** 26 8N 79 47 E
Kalu, *Pakistan* **42 G2** 25 5N 67 39 E
Kaluga, *Russia* **24 D6** 54 35N 36 10 E
Kalulushi, *Zambia* **55 E2** 12 50S 28 3 E
Kalundborg, *Denmark* **9 J14** 55 41N 11 5 E
Kalush, *Ukraine* **17 D13** 49 3N 24 23 E
Kalutara, *Sri Lanka* **40 R12** 6 35N 80 0 E
Kalya, *Russia* **24 B10** 60 15N 59 59 E
Kama, *Dem. Rep. of the Congo* **54 C2** 3 30S 27 5 E
Kama →, *Russia* **24 C9** 55 45N 52 0 E
Kamachumu, *Tanzania* **54 C3** 1 37S 31 37 E
Kamaishi, *Japan* **30 E10** 39 16N 141 53 E
Kamalia, *Pakistan* **42 D5** 30 44N 72 42 E
Kaman, *India* **42 F6** 27 39N 77 16 E
Kamapanda, *Zambia* **55 E1** 12 5S 24 0 E
Kamaran, *Yemen* **46 D3** 15 21N 42 35 E
Kamativi, *Zimbabwe* **55 F2** 18 15S 27 27 E
Kambalda, *Australia* **61 F3** 31 10S 121 37 E
Kambar, *Pakistan* **42 F3** 27 37N 68 1 E
Kambarka, *Russia* **24 C9** 56 15N 54 11 E
Kambolé, *Zambia* **55 D3** 8 47S 30 48 E
Kambos, *Cyprus* **23 D11** 35 2N 32 44 E
Kambove, *Dem. Rep. of the Congo* **55 E2** 10 51S 26 33 E
Kamchatka, Poluostrov, *Russia* **27 D17** 57 0N 160 0 E
Kamchatka Pen. = Kamchatka, Poluostrov, *Russia* **27 D17** 57 0N 160 0 E
Kamchiya →, *Bulgaria* **21 C12** 43 4N 27 44 E
Kamen, *Russia* **26 D9** 53 50N 81 30 E
Kamen-Rybolov, *Russia* **30 B6** 44 46N 132 2 E
Kamenjak, Rt., *Croatia* **16 F7** 44 47N 13 55 E
Kamenka, *Russia* **24 A7** 65 58N 44 0 E
Kamenka Bugskaya = Kamyanka-Buzka, *Ukraine* **17 C13** 50 8N 24 16 E
Kamensk Uralskiy, *Russia* **26 D7** 56 25N 62 2 E
Kamenskoye, *Russia* **27 C17** 62 45N 165 30 E
Kameoka, *Japan* **31 G7** 35 0N 135 35 E
Kamiah, *U.S.A.* **82 C5** 46 14N 116 2W
Kamieskroon, *S. Africa* **56 E2** 30 9S 17 56 E
Kamilukuak, L., *Canada* **73 A8** 62 22N 101 40W
Kamin-Kashyrskyy, *Ukraine* **17 C13** 51 39N 24 56 E
Kamina, *Dem. Rep. of the Congo* **55 D2** 8 45S 25 0 E
Kaminak L., *Canada* **73 A10** 62 10N 95 0W
Kaministiquia, *Canada* **70 C1** 48 32N 89 35W
Kaminoyama, *Japan* **30 E10** 38 9N 140 17 E
Kamiros, *Greece* **23 C9** 36 20N 27 56 E
Kamituga, *Dem. Rep. of the Congo* **54 C2** 3 2S 28 10 E
Kamla →, *India* **43 G12** 25 35N 86 36 E
Kamloops, *Canada* **72 C4** 50 40N 120 20W
Kamo, *Japan* **30 F9** 37 39N 139 3 E
Kamoke, *Pakistan* **42 C6** 32 4N 74 4 E
Kampala, *Uganda* **54 B3** 0 20N 32 30 E
Kampang Chhnang, *Cambodia* **39 F5** 12 20N 104 35 E
Kampar, *Malaysia* **39 K3** 4 18N 101 9 E
Kampar →, *Indonesia* **36 D2** 0 30N 103 8 E
Kampen, *Neths.* **15 B5** 52 33N 5 53 E
Kampene, *Dem. Rep. of the Congo* **52 E5** 3 36S 26 40 E
Kamphaeng Phet, *Thailand* **38 D2** 16 28N 99 30 E
Kampolombo, L., *Zambia* **55 E2** 11 37S 29 42 E
Kampong Saom, *Cambodia* **39 G4** 10 38N 103 30 E
Kampong Saom, Chaak, *Cambodia* **36 B2** 10 45N 103 30 E
Kampong Saom, Chaak, *Cambodia* **39 G4** 10 50N 103 32 E
Kampong To, *Thailand* **39 J3** 6 3N 101 13 E
Kampot, *Cambodia* **39 G5** 10 36N 104 10 E
Kampuchea = Cambodia ■, *Asia* **38 F5** 12 15N 105 0 E
Kampung Air Putih, *Malaysia* **39 K4** 4 15N 103 10 E
Kampung Jerangau, *Malaysia* **39 K4** 4 50N 103 10 E
Kampung Raja, *Malaysia* **39 K4** 5 45N 102 35 E
Kampungbaru = Tolitoli, *Indonesia* **37 D6** 1 5N 120 50 E
Kamrau, Teluk, *Indonesia* **37 E8** 3 30S 133 36 E
Kamsack, *Canada* **73 C8** 51 34N 101 54W
Kamskoye Vdkhr., *Russia* **24 C10** 58 41N 56 7 E
Kamuchawie L., *Canada* **73 B8** 56 18N 101 59W
Kamuela, *U.S.A.* **74 H17** 20 1N 155 41W
Kamui-Misaki, *Japan* **30 C10** 43 20N 140 21 E
Kamyanets-Podilskyy, *Ukraine* **17 D14** 48 45N 26 40 E
Kamyanka-Buzka, *Ukraine* **17 C13** 50 8N 24 16 E
Kāmyārān, *Iran* **44 C5** 34 47N 46 56 E
Kamyshin, *Russia* **25 D8** 50 10N 45 24 E
Kanaaupscow, *Canada* **70 B4** 54 2N 76 30W
Kanaaupscow →, *Canada* **69 C12** 53 39N 77 9W
Kanab, *U.S.A.* **83 H7** 37 3N 112 32W
Kanab →, *U.S.A.* **83 H7** 36 24N 112 38W
Kanagi, *Japan* **30 D10** 40 54N 140 27 E
Kanairiktok →, *Canada* **71 A7** 55 2N 60 18W
Kananga, *Dem. Rep. of the Congo* **52 F4** 5 55S 22 18 E
Kanash, *Russia* **24 C8** 55 30N 47 32 E
Kanaskat, *U.S.A.* **84 C5** 47 19N 121 54W
Kanastraíon, Ákra = Palioúrion, Ákra, *Greece* **21 E10** 39 57N 23 45 E
Kanawha →, *U.S.A.* **76 F4** 38 50N 82 9W
Kanazawa, *Japan* **31 F8** 36 30N 136 38 E
Kanchanaburi, *Thailand* **38 E2** 14 2N 99 31 E
Kanchenjunga, *Nepal* **43 F13** 27 50N 88 10 E
Kanchipuram, *India* **40 N11** 12 52N 79 45 E
Kandaghat, *India* **42 D7** 30 59N 77 7 E
Kandahar = Qandahār, *Afghan.* **40 D4** 31 32N 65 30 E
Kandalaksha, *Russia* **24 A5** 67 9N 32 30 E
Kandalakshkiy Zaliv, *Russia* **24 A6** 66 0N 35 0 E
Kandalu, *Afghan.* **40 E3** 29 55N 63 20 E
Kandangan, *Indonesia* **36 E5** 2 50S 115 20 E
Kandanghaur, *Indonesia* **37 G13** 6 21S 108 6 E
Kandanos, *Greece* **23 D5** 35 19N 23 44 E
Kandhkot, *Pakistan* **42 E3** 28 16N 69 8 E
Kandhla, *India* **42 E7** 29 18N 77 19 E
Kandi, *Benin* **50 F6** 11 7N 2 55 E
Kandi, *India* **43 H13** 23 58N 88 5 E
Kandiaro, *Pakistan* **42 F3** 27 4N 68 13 E
Kandla, *India* **42 H4** 23 0N 70 10 E
Kandos, *Australia* **63 E4** 32 45S 149 58 E
Kandy, *Sri Lanka* **40 R12** 7 18N 80 43 E
Kane, *U.S.A.* **78 E6** 41 40N 78 49W
Kane Basin, *Greenland* **4 B4** 79 1N 70 0W
Kaneohe, *U.S.A.* **74 H16** 21 25N 157 48W
Kangān, *Fārs, Iran* **45 E7** 27 50N 52 3 E
Kangān, *Hormozgān, Iran* **45 E8** 25 48N 57 28 E
Kangar, *Malaysia* **39 J3** 6 27N 100 12 E
Kangaroo I., *Australia* **63 F2** 35 45S 137 0 E
Kangaroo Mts., *Australia* **62 C3** 23 29S 141 51 E
Kangasala, *Finland* **9 F21** 61 28N 24 4 E
Kangāvar, *Iran* **45 C6** 34 40N 48 0 E
Kangdong, *N. Korea* **35 E14** 39 9N 126 5 E
Kangean, Kepulauan, *Indonesia* **36 F5** 6 55S 115 23 E
Kangean Is. = Kangean, Kepulauan, *Indonesia* **36 F5** 6 55S 115 23 E
Kanggye, *N. Korea* **35 D14** 41 0N 126 35 E
Kanggyŏng, *S. Korea* **35 F14** 36 10N 127 0 E
Kanghwa, *S. Korea* **35 F14** 37 45N 126 30 E
Kangiqsualujjuaq, *Canada* **69 C13** 58 30N 65 59W
Kangiqsujuaq, *Canada* **69 B12** 61 30N 72 0W
Kangirsuk, *Canada* **69 C13** 60 0N 70 0W
Kangnŭng, *S. Korea* **35 F15** 37 45N 128 54 E
Kangping, *China* **35 C12** 42 43N 123 18 E
Kangra, *India* **42 C7** 32 6N 76 16 E
Kangto, *India* **41 F18** 27 50N 92 35 E
Kanhar →, *India* **43 G10** 24 28N 83 8 E
Kaniama, *Dem. Rep. of the Congo* **54 D1** 7 30S 24 12 E
Kaniapiskau = Caniapiscau →, *Canada* **71 A6** 56 40N 69 30W
Kaniapiskau, Res. = Caniapiscau Rés. de, *Canada* **71 B6** 54 10N 69 55W
Kanin, Poluostrov, *Russia* **24 A8** 68 0N 45 0 E
Kanin Nos, Mys, *Russia* **24 A7** 68 39N 43 32 E
Kanin Pen. = Kanin, Poluostrov, *Russia* **24 A8** 68 0N 45 0 E
Kaniva, *Australia* **63 F3** 36 22S 141 18 E
Kanjut Sar, *Pakistan* **43 A6** 36 7N 75 25 E
Kankaanpää, *Finland* **9 F20** 61 44N 22 50 E
Kankakee, *U.S.A.* **76 E2** 41 7N 87 52W
Kankakee →, *U.S.A.* **76 E1** 41 23N 88 15W
Kankan, *Guinea* **50 F4** 10 23N 9 15W
Kankendy = Xankändi, *Azerbaijan* **25 G8** 39 52N 46 49 E
Kanker, *India* **41 J12** 20 10N 81 40 E
Kankroli, *India* **42 G5** 25 4N 73 53 E
Kannapolis, *U.S.A.* **77 H5** 35 30N 80 37W
Kannauj, *India* **43 F8** 27 3N 79 56 E
Kannod, *India* **40 H10** 22 45N 76 40 E
Kano, *Nigeria* **50 F7** 12 2N 8 30 E
Kan'onji, *Japan* **31 G6** 34 7N 133 39 E
Kanowit, *Malaysia* **36 D4** 2 14N 112 20 E
Kanoya, *Japan* **31 J5** 31 25N 130 50 E
Kanpetlet, *Burma* **41 J18** 21 10N 93 59 E
Kanpur, *India* **43 F9** 26 28N 80 20 E
Kansas □, *U.S.A.* **80 F6** 38 30N 99 0W
Kansas →, *U.S.A.* **80 F7** 39 7N 94 37W
Kansas City, *Kans., U.S.A.* **80 F7** 39 7N 94 38W
Kansas City, *Mo., U.S.A.* **80 F7** 39 6N 94 35W
Kansenia, *Dem. Rep. of the Congo* **55 E2** 10 20S 26 0 E
Kansk, *Russia* **27 D10** 56 20N 95 37 E
Kansŏng, *S. Korea* **35 E15** 38 24N 128 30 E
Kansu = Gansu □, *China* **34 G3** 36 0N 104 0 E
Kantaphor, *India* **42 H7** 22 35N 76 34 E
Kantharalak, *Thailand* **38 E5** 14 39N 104 39 E
Kantli →, *India* **42 E6** 28 20N 75 30 E
Kantō □, *Japan* **31 F9** 36 15N 139 30 E
Kantō-Sanchi, *Japan* **31 G9** 35 59N 138 50 E
Kanturk, *Ireland* **13 D3** 52 11N 8 54W
Kanuma, *Japan* **31 F9** 36 34N 139 42 E
Kanus, *Namibia* **56 D2** 27 50S 18 39 E
Kanye, *Botswana* **56 C4** 24 55S 25 28 E
Kanzenze, *Dem. Rep. of the Congo* **55 E2** 10 30S 25 12 E
Kanzi, Ras, *Tanzania* **54 D4** 7 1S 39 33 E
Kaohsiung, *Taiwan* **33 D7** 22 35N 120 16 E
Kaokoveld, *Namibia* **56 B1** 19 15S 14 30 E
Kaolack, *Senegal* **50 F2** 14 5N 16 8W
Kaoshan, *China* **35 B13** 44 38N 124 50 E
Kapaa, *U.S.A.* **74 G15** 22 5N 159 19W
Kapadvanj, *India* **42 H5** 23 5N 73 0 E
Kapan, *Armenia* **25 G8** 39 18N 46 27 E
Kapanga, *Dem. Rep. of the Congo* **52 F4** 8 30S 22 40 E
Kapchagai = Qapshaghay, *Kazakstan* **26 E8** 43 51N 77 14 E
Kapela = Velika Kapela, *Croatia* **16 F8** 45 10N 15 5 E
Kapema, *Dem. Rep. of the Congo* **55 E2** 10 45S 28 22 E
Kapfenberg, *Austria* **16 E8** 47 26N 15 18 E
Kapiri Mposhi, *Zambia* **55 E2** 13 59S 28 43 E
Kapiskau →, *Canada* **70 B3** 52 47N 81 55W
Kapit, *Malaysia* **36 D4** 2 0N 112 55 E
Kapiti I., *N.Z.* **59 J5** 40 50S 174 56 E
Kaplan, *U.S.A.* **81 K8** 30 0N 92 17W
Kapoe, *Thailand* **39 H2** 9 34N 98 32 E
Kapoeta, *Sudan* **51 H12** 4 50N 33 35 E
Kaposvár, *Hungary* **17 E9** 46 25N 17 47 E
Kapowsin, *U.S.A.* **84 D4** 46 59N 122 13W
Kapps, *Namibia* **56 C2** 22 32S 17 18 E
Kapsan, *N. Korea* **35 D15** 41 4N 128 19 E
Kapsukas = Marijampole, *Lithuania* **9 J20** 54 33N 23 19 E
Kapuas →, *Indonesia* **36 E3** 0 25S 109 20 E
Kapuas Hulu, Pegunungan, *Malaysia* **36 D4** 1 30N 113 30 E

Kapuas Hulu Ra. = Kapuas Hulu, Pegunungan, Malaysia 36 D4 1 30N 113 30 E
Kapulo, Dem. Rep. of the Congo 55 D2 8 18S 29 15 E
Kapunda, Australia 63 E2 34 20S 138 56 E
Kapuni, N.Z. 59 H5 39 29S 174 8 E
Kapurthala, India 42 D6 31 23N 75 25 E
Kapuskasing, Canada 70 C3 49 25N 82 30W
Kapuskasing →, Canada 70 C3 49 49N 82 0W
Kaputar, Australia 63 E5 30 15S 150 10 E
Kaputir, Kenya 54 B4 2 5N 35 28 E
Kara, Russia 26 C7 69 10N 65 0 E
Kara Bogaz Gol, Zaliv = Garabogazköl Aylagy, Turkmenistan 25 F9 41 0N 53 30 E
Kara Kalpak Republic = Karakalpakstan □, Uzbekistan 26 E6 43 0N 58 0 E
Kara Kum, Turkmenistan 26 F7 39 30N 60 0 E
Kara Sea, Russia 26 B8 75 0N 70 0 E
Karabiğa, Turkey 21 D12 40 23N 27 17 E
Karabük, Turkey 25 F5 41 12N 32 37 E
Karaburun, Turkey 21 E12 38 41N 26 28 E
Karabutak = Qarabutaq, Kazakstan 26 E7 49 59N 60 14 E
Karacabey, Turkey 21 D13 40 12N 28 21 E
Karacasu, Turkey 21 F13 37 43N 28 35 E
Karachey-Cherkessia □, Russia 25 F7 43 40N 41 30 E
Karachi, Pakistan 42 G2 24 53N 67 0 E
Karad, India 40 L9 17 15N 74 10 E
Karaganda = Qaraghandy, Kazakstan 26 E8 49 50N 73 10 E
Karagayly, Kazakstan 26 E8 49 26N 76 0 E
Karaginskiy, Ostrov, Russia 27 D17 58 45N 164 0 E
Karagiye, Vpadina, Kazakstan 25 F9 43 27N 51 45 E
Karagiye Depression = Karagiye, Vpadina, Kazakstan 25 F9 43 27N 51 45 E
Karagola Road, India 43 G12 25 29N 87 23 E
Karaikal, India 40 P11 10 59N 79 50 E
Karaikkudi, India 40 P11 10 5N 78 45 E
Karaj, Iran 45 C6 35 48N 51 0 E
Karak, Malaysia 39 L4 3 25N 102 2 E
Karakalpakstan □, Uzbekistan 26 E6 43 0N 58 0 E
Karakelong, Indonesia 37 D7 4 35N 126 50 E
Karakitang, Indonesia 37 D7 3 14N 125 28 E
Karaklis = Vanadzor, Armenia 25 F7 40 48N 44 30 E
Karakoram Pass, Pakistan 43 B7 35 33N 77 50 E
Karakoram Ra., Pakistan 43 B7 35 30N 77 0 E
Karalon, Russia 27 D12 57 5N 115 50 E
Karama, Jordan 47 D4 31 57N 35 35 E
Karaman, Turkey 25 G5 37 14N 33 13 E
Karamay, China 32 B3 45 30N 84 58 E
Karambu, Indonesia 36 E5 3 53S 116 6 E
Karamea Bight, N.Z. 59 J3 41 22S 171 40 E
Karamnasa →, India 43 G10 25 31N 83 52 E
Karand, Iran 44 C5 34 16N 46 15 E
Karanganyar, Indonesia 37 G13 7 38S 109 37 E
Karanjia, India 43 J11 21 47N 85 58 E
Karasburg, Namibia 56 D2 28 0S 18 44 E
Karasino, Russia 26 C9 66 50N 86 50 E
Karasjok, Norway 8 B21 69 27N 25 30 E
Karasuk, Russia 26 D8 53 44N 78 2 E
Karasuyama, Japan 31 F10 36 39N 140 9 E
Karatau = Qarataū, Kazakstan 26 E8 43 10N 70 28 E
Karatau, Khrebet, Kazakstan 26 E7 43 30N 69 30 E
Karatsu, Japan 31 H5 33 26N 129 58 E
Karaul, Russia 26 B9 70 6N 82 15 E
Karauli, India 42 F7 26 30N 77 4 E
Karavostasi, Cyprus 23 D11 35 8N 32 50 E
Karawang, Indonesia 37 G12 6 30S 107 15 E
Karawanken, Europe 16 E8 46 30N 14 40 E
Karayazı, Turkey 25 G7 39 41N 42 9 E
Karazhal, Kazakstan 26 E8 48 2N 70 49 E
Karbalā', Iraq 44 C5 32 36N 44 3 E
Karcag, Hungary 17 E11 47 19N 20 57 E
Karcha →, Pakistan 43 B7 34 45N 76 10 E
Karchana, India 43 G9 25 17N 81 56 E
Kardhítsa, Greece 21 E9 39 23N 21 54 E
Kärdla, Estonia 9 G20 58 50N 22 40 E
Kareeberge, S. Africa 56 E3 30 59S 21 50 E
Kareha →, India 43 G12 25 44N 86 21 E
Kareima, Sudan 51 E12 18 30N 31 49 E
Karelia □, Russia 24 A5 65 30N 32 30 E
Karelian Republic = Karelia □, Russia 24 A5 65 30N 32 30 E
Karera, India 42 G8 25 32N 78 9 E
Kārevāndar, Iran 45 E9 27 53N 60 44 E
Kargasok, Russia 26 D9 59 3N 80 53 E
Kargat, Russia 26 D9 55 10N 80 15 E
Kargil, India 43 B7 34 32N 76 12 E
Kargopol, Russia 24 B6 61 30N 38 58 E
Karhal, India 43 F8 27 1N 78 57 E
Karīān, Iran 45 E8 26 57N 57 14 E
Kariba, Zimbabwe 55 F2 16 28S 28 50 E
Kariba, L., Zimbabwe 55 F2 16 40S 28 25 E
Kariba Dam, Zimbabwe 55 F2 16 30S 28 35 E
Kariba Gorge, Zambia 55 F2 16 30S 28 50 E
Karibib, Namibia 56 C2 22 0S 15 56 E
Karimata, Kepulauan, Indonesia 36 E3 1 25S 109 0 E
Karimata, Selat, Indonesia 36 E3 2 0S 108 40 E
Karimata Is. = Karimata, Kepulauan, Indonesia 36 E3 1 25S 109 0 E
Karimnagar, India 40 K11 18 26N 79 10 E
Karimunjawa, Kepulauan, Indonesia 36 F4 5 50S 110 30 E
Karin, Somali Rep. 46 E4 10 50N 45 52 E
Karīt, Iran 45 C8 33 29N 56 55 E
Kariya, Japan 31 G8 34 58N 137 1 E
Karkaralinsk = Qarqaraly, Kazakstan 26 E8 49 26N 75 30 E
Karkheh →, Iran 44 D5 31 2N 47 29 E
Karkinitska Zatoka, Ukraine 25 E5 45 56N 33 0 E
Karkinitskiy Zaliv = Karkinitska Zatoka, Ukraine 25 E5 45 56N 33 0 E
Karl-Marx-Stadt = Chemnitz, Germany 16 C7 50 51N 12 54 E
Karlovac, Croatia 16 F8 45 31N 15 36 E
Karlovo, Bulgaria 21 C11 42 38N 24 47 E
Karlovy Vary, Czech Rep. 16 C7 50 13N 12 51 E
Karlsbad = Karlovy Vary, Czech Rep. 16 C7 50 13N 12 51 E
Karlsborg, Sweden 9 G16 58 33N 14 33 E
Karlshamn, Sweden 9 H16 56 10N 14 51 E
Karlskoga, Sweden 9 G16 59 28N 14 33 E
Karlskrona, Sweden 9 H16 56 10N 15 35 E
Karlsruhe, Germany 16 D5 49 0N 8 23 E
Karlstad, Sweden 9 G15 59 23N 13 30 E
Karlstad, U.S.A. 80 A6 48 35N 96 31W
Karmi'el, Israel 47 C4 32 55N 35 18 E
Karnak, Egypt 51 C12 25 43N 32 39 E
Karnal, India 42 E7 29 42N 77 2 E
Karnali →, Nepal 43 E9 28 45N 81 16 E
Karnaphuli Res., Bangla. 41 H18 22 40N 92 20 E
Karnaprayag, India 43 D8 30 16N 79 15 E
Karnataka □, India 40 N10 13 15N 77 0 E
Karnes City, U.S.A. 81 L6 28 53N 97 54W
Karnische Alpen, Europe 16 E7 46 36N 13 0 E
Kärnten □, Austria 16 E8 46 52N 13 30 E
Karoi, Zimbabwe 55 F2 16 48S 29 45 E
Karonga, Malawi 55 D3 9 57S 33 55 E
Karoonda, Australia 63 F2 35 1S 139 59 E
Karor, Pakistan 42 D4 31 15N 70 59 E
Karora, Sudan 51 E13 17 44N 38 15 E
Karpasia □, Cyprus 23 D13 35 32N 34 15 E
Kárpathos, Greece 21 G12 35 37N 27 10 E
Karpinsk, Russia 24 C11 59 45N 60 1 E
Karpogory, Russia 24 B7 64 0N 44 27 E
Karpuz Burnu = Apostolos Andreas, C., Cyprus 23 D13 35 42N 34 35 E
Karratha, Australia 60 D2 20 53S 116 40 E
Kars, Turkey 25 F7 40 40N 43 5 E
Karsakpay, Kazakstan 26 E7 47 55N 66 40 E
Karshi = Qarshi, Uzbekistan 26 F7 38 53N 65 48 E
Karsiyang, India 43 F13 26 56N 88 18 E
Karsog, India 42 D7 31 23N 77 12 E
Kartaly, Russia 26 D7 53 3N 60 40 E
Kartapur, India 42 D6 31 27N 75 32 E
Karthaus, U.S.A. 78 E6 41 8N 78 9W
Karufa, Indonesia 37 E8 3 50S 133 20 E
Karumba, Australia 62 B3 17 31S 140 50 E
Karumo, Tanzania 54 C3 2 25S 32 50 E
Karumwa, Tanzania 54 C3 3 12S 32 38 E
Kārūn →, Iran 45 D6 30 26N 48 10 E
Karungu, Kenya 54 C3 0 50S 34 10 E
Karviná, Czech Rep. 17 D10 49 53N 18 31 E
Karwan →, India 42 F8 27 26N 78 4 E
Karwar, India 40 M9 14 55N 74 13 E
Karwi, India 43 G9 25 12N 80 57 E
Kasache, Malawi 55 E3 13 25S 34 20 E
Kasai →, Dem. Rep. of the Congo 52 E3 3 30S 16 10 E
Kasaï-Oriental □, Dem. Rep. of the Congo 54 D1 5 0S 24 30 E
Kasaji, Dem. Rep. of the Congo 55 E1 10 25S 23 27 E
Kasama, Zambia 55 E3 10 16S 31 9 E
Kasan-dong, N. Korea 35 D14 41 18N 126 55 E
Kasane, Namibia 56 B3 17 34S 24 50 E
Kasanga, Tanzania 55 D3 8 30S 31 10 E
Kasaragod, India 40 N9 12 30N 74 58 E
Kasba L., Canada 73 A8 60 20N 102 10W
Kāseh Garān, Iran 44 C5 34 5N 46 2 E
Kasempa, Zambia 55 E2 13 30S 25 44 E
Kasenga, Dem. Rep. of the Congo 55 E2 10 20S 28 45 E
Kasese, Uganda 54 B3 0 13N 30 3 E
Kasewa, Zambia 55 E2 14 28S 28 53 E
Kasganj, India 43 F8 27 48N 78 42 E
Kashabowie, Canada 70 C1 48 40N 90 26W
Kashaf, Iran 45 C9 35 58N 61 7 E
Kāshān, Iran 45 C6 34 5N 51 30 E
Kashechewan, Canada 70 B3 52 18N 81 37W
Kashi, China 32 C2 39 30N 76 2 E
Kashimbo, Dem. Rep. of the Congo 55 E2 11 12S 26 19 E
Kashipur, India 43 E8 29 15N 79 0 E
Kashiwazaki, Japan 31 F9 37 22N 138 33 E
Kashk-e Kohneh, Afghan. 40 B3 34 55N 62 30 E
Kashkū'īyeh, Iran 45 D7 30 31N 55 40 E
Kāshmar, Iran 45 C8 35 16N 58 26 E
Kashmir, Asia 43 C7 34 0N 76 0 E
Kashmor, Pakistan 42 E3 28 28N 69 32 E
Kashun Noerh = Gaxun Nur, China 32 B5 42 22N 100 30 E
Kasiari, India 43 H12 22 8N 87 14 E
Kasimov, Russia 24 D7 54 55N 41 20 E
Kasinge, Dem. Rep. of the Congo 54 D2 6 15S 26 58 E
Kasiruta, Indonesia 37 E7 0 25S 127 12 E
Kaskaskia →, U.S.A. 80 G10 37 58N 89 57W
Kaskattama →, Canada 73 B10 57 3N 90 4W
Kaskinen, Finland 9 E19 62 22N 21 15 E
Kaslo, Canada 72 D5 49 55N 116 55W
Kasmere L., Canada 73 B8 59 34N 101 10W
Kasongo, Dem. Rep. of the Congo 54 C2 4 30S 26 33 E
Kasongo Lunda, Dem. Rep. of the Congo 52 F3 6 35S 16 49 E
Kásos, Greece 21 G12 35 20N 26 55 E
Kassalâ, Sudan 51 E13 15 30N 36 0 E
Kassel, Germany 16 C5 51 18N 9 26 E
Kassiópi, Greece 23 A3 39 48N 19 53 E
Kasson, U.S.A. 80 C8 44 2N 92 45W
Kastamonu, Turkey 25 F5 41 25N 33 43 E
Kastélli, Greece 23 D5 35 29N 23 38 E
Kastéllion, Greece 23 D7 35 12N 25 20 E
Kasterlee, Belgium 15 C4 51 15N 4 59 E
Kastoría, Greece 21 D9 40 30N 21 19 E
Kasulu, Tanzania 54 C3 4 37S 30 5 E
Kasumi, Japan 31 G7 35 38N 134 38 E
Kasungu, Malawi 55 E3 13 0S 33 29 E
Kasur, Pakistan 42 D6 31 5N 74 25 E
Kataba, Zambia 55 F2 16 5S 25 10 E
Katahdin, Mt., U.S.A. 77 C11 45 54N 68 56W
Katako Kombe, Dem. Rep. of the Congo 54 C1 3 25S 24 20 E
Katale, Tanzania 54 C3 4 52S 31 7 E
Katanda, Katanga, Dem. Rep. of the Congo 54 D1 7 52S 24 13 E
Katanda, Nord-Kivu, Dem. Rep. of the Congo 54 C2 0 55S 29 21 E
Katanga □, Dem. Rep. of the Congo 54 D2 8 0S 25 0 E
Katangi, India 40 J11 21 56N 79 50 E
Katanning, Australia 61 F2 33 40S 117 33 E
Katavi Swamp, Tanzania 54 D3 6 50S 31 10 E
Kateríni, Greece 21 D10 40 18N 22 37 E
Katghora, India 43 H10 22 30N 82 33 E
Katha, Burma 41 G20 24 10N 96 30 E
Katherîna, Gebel, Egypt 44 D2 28 30N 33 57 E
Katherine, Australia 60 B5 14 27S 132 20 E
Katherine Gorge, Australia 60 B5 14 18S 132 28 E
Kathi, India 42 J6 21 47N 74 3 E
Kathiawar, India 42 H4 22 20N 71 0 E
Kathikas, Cyprus 23 E11 34 55N 32 25 E
Kathua, India 42 C6 32 23N 75 34 E
Katihar, India 43 G12 25 34N 87 36 E
Katima Mulilo, Zambia 56 B3 17 28S 24 13 E
Katimbira, Malawi 55 E3 12 40S 34 0 E
Katingan = Mendawai →, Indonesia 36 E4 3 30S 113 0 E
Katiola, Ivory C. 50 G4 8 10N 5 10W
Katmandu, Nepal 43 F11 27 45N 85 20 E
Katni, India 43 H9 23 51N 80 24 E
Káto Arkhánai, Greece 23 D7 35 15N 25 10 E
Káto Khorió, Greece 23 D7 35 3N 25 47 E
Kato Pyrgos, Cyprus 23 D11 35 11N 32 41 E
Katompe, Dem. Rep. of the Congo 54 D2 6 2S 26 23 E
Katonga →, Uganda 54 B3 0 34N 31 50 E
Katoomba, Australia 63 E5 33 41S 150 19 E
Katowice, Poland 17 C10 50 17N 19 5 E
Katrine, L., U.K. 12 E4 56 15N 4 30W
Katrineholm, Sweden 9 G17 59 9N 16 12 E
Katsepe, Madag. 57 B8 15 45S 46 15 E
Katsina, Nigeria 50 F7 13 0N 7 32 E
Katsumoto, Japan 31 H4 33 51N 129 42 E
Katsuura, Japan 31 G10 35 10N 140 20 E
Katsuyama, Japan 31 F8 36 3N 136 30 E
Kattaviá, Greece 23 D9 35 57N 27 46 E
Kattegat, Denmark 9 H14 56 40N 11 20 E
Katumba, Dem. Rep. of the Congo 54 D2 7 40S 25 17 E
Katungu, Kenya 54 C5 2 55S 40 3 E
Katwa, India 43 H13 23 30N 88 5 E
Katwijk, Neths. 15 B4 52 12N 4 24 E
Kauai, U.S.A. 74 H15 22 3N 159 30W
Kauai Channel, U.S.A. 74 H15 21 45N 158 50W
Kaufman, U.S.A. 81 J6 32 35N 96 19W
Kauhajoki, Finland 9 E20 62 25N 22 10 E
Kaukauna, U.S.A. 76 C1 44 17N 88 17W
Kaukauveld, Namibia 56 C3 20 0S 20 15 E
Kaunakakai, U.S.A. 74 H16 21 6N 157 1W
Kaunas, Lithuania 9 J20 54 54N 23 54 E
Kaunia, Bangla. 43 G13 25 46N 89 26 E
Kautokeino, Norway 8 B20 69 0N 23 4 E
Kauwapur, India 43 F10 27 31N 82 18 E
Kavacha, Russia 27 C17 60 16N 169 51 E
Kavalerovo, Russia 30 B7 44 15N 135 4 E
Kavali, India 40 M12 14 55N 80 1 E
Kavála, Greece 21 D11 40 57N 24 28 E
Kavār, Iran 45 D7 29 11N 52 44 E
Kavi, India 42 H5 22 12N 72 38 E
Kavīr, Dasht-e, Iran 45 C7 34 30N 55 0 E
Kavos, Greece 23 B4 39 23N 20 3 E
Kaw, Fr. Guiana 93 C8 4 30N 52 15W
Kawagama L., Canada 78 A6 45 18N 78 45W
Kawagoe, Japan 31 G9 35 55N 139 29 E
Kawaguchi, Japan 31 G9 35 52N 139 45 E
Kawaihae, U.S.A. 74 H17 20 3N 155 50W
Kawambwa, Zambia 55 D2 9 48S 29 3 E
Kawanoe, Japan 31 G6 34 1N 133 34 E
Kawardha, India 43 J9 22 0N 81 17 E
Kawasaki, Japan 31 G9 35 35N 139 42 E
Kawasi, Indonesia 37 E7 1 38S 127 28 E
Kawerau, N.Z. 59 H6 38 7S 176 42 E
Kawhia Harbour, N.Z. 59 H5 38 5S 174 51 E
Kawio, Kepulauan, Indonesia 37 D7 4 30N 125 30 E
Kawnro, Burma 41 H21 22 48N 99 8 E
Kawthaung, Burma 39 H2 10 5N 98 36 E
Kawthoolei = Kawthule □, Burma 41 L20 18 0N 97 30 E
Kawthule □, Burma 41 L20 18 0N 97 30 E
Kaya, Burkina Faso 50 F5 13 4N 1 10W
Kayah □, Burma 41 K20 19 15N 97 15 E
Kayan →, Indonesia 36 D5 2 55N 117 35 E
Kaycee, U.S.A. 82 E10 43 43N 106 38W
Kayeli, Indonesia 37 E7 3 20S 127 10 E
Kayenta, U.S.A. 83 H8 36 44N 110 15W
Kayes, Mali 50 F3 14 25N 11 30W
Kayin = Kawthule □, Burma 41 L20 18 0N 97 30 E
Kayoa, Indonesia 37 D7 0 1N 127 28 E
Kayomba, Zambia 55 E1 13 11S 24 2 E
Kayseri, Turkey 25 G6 38 45N 35 30 E
Kaysville, U.S.A. 82 F8 41 2N 111 56W
Kazachye, Russia 27 B14 70 52N 135 58 E
Kazakstan ■, Asia 26 E8 50 0N 70 0 E
Kazan, Russia 24 C8 55 50N 49 10 E
Kazan →, Canada 73 A9 64 3N 95 35W
Kazan-Rettō, Pac. Oc. 64 E6 25 0N 141 0 E
Kazanlŭk, Bulgaria 21 C11 42 38N 25 20 E
Kazatin = Kozyatyn, Ukraine 17 D15 49 45N 28 50 E
Kāzerūn, Iran 45 D6 29 38N 51 40 E
Kazi Magomed = Qazimämmäd, Azerbaijan 45 A6 40 3N 49 0 E
Kazuno, Japan 30 D10 40 10N 140 45 E
Kazym →, Russia 26 C7 63 54N 65 50 E
Kéa, Greece 21 F11 37 35N 24 22 E
Keady, U.K. 13 B5 54 15N 6 42W
Kearney, U.S.A. 80 E5 40 42N 99 5W
Kearny, U.S.A. 83 K8 33 3N 110 55W
Kearsarge, Mt., U.S.A. 79 C13 43 22N 71 50W
Keban, Turkey 25 G6 38 50N 38 50 E
Keban Baraji, Turkey 25 G6 38 41N 38 33 E
Kebnekaise, Sweden 8 C18 67 53N 18 33 E
Kebri Dehar, Ethiopia 46 F3 6 45N 44 17 E
Kebumen, Indonesia 37 G13 7 42S 109 40 E
Kechika →, Canada 72 B3 59 41N 127 12W
Kecskemét, Hungary 17 E10 46 57N 19 42 E
Kėdainiai, Lithuania 9 J21 55 15N 24 2 E
Kedarnath, India 43 D8 30 44N 79 4 E
Kedgwick, Canada 71 C6 47 40N 67 20W
Kédhros Óros, Greece 23 D6 35 11N 24 37 E
Kedia Hill, Botswana 56 C3 21 28S 24 37 E
Kediri, Indonesia 37 G15 7 51S 112 1 E
Keeler, U.S.A. 84 J9 36 29N 117 52W
Keeley L., Canada 73 C7 54 54N 108 8W
Keeling Is. = Cocos Is., Ind. Oc. 64 J1 12 10S 96 55 E
Keelung = Chilung, Taiwan 33 D7 25 3N 121 45 E
Keene, Canada 78 B6 44 15N 78 10W
Keene, Calif., U.S.A. 85 K8 35 13N 118 33W
Keene, N.H., U.S.A. 79 D12 42 56N 72 17W
Keene, N.Y., U.S.A. 79 B11 44 16N 73 46W
Keeper Hill, Ireland 13 D3 52 45N 8 16W
Keer-Weer, C., Australia 62 A3 14 0S 141 32 E
Keeseville, U.S.A. 79 B11 44 29N 73 30W
Keetmanshoop, Namibia 56 D2 26 35S 18 8 E
Keewatin, Canada 73 D10 49 46N 94 34W
Keewatin →, Canada 73 B8 56 29N 100 46W
Kefallinía, Greece 21 E9 38 20N 20 30 E
Kefamenanu, Indonesia 37 F6 9 28S 124 29 E
Kefar Sava, Israel 47 C3 32 11N 34 54 E
Keffi, Nigeria 50 G7 8 55N 7 43 E
Keflavík, Iceland 8 D2 64 2N 22 35W
Keg River, Canada 72 B5 57 54N 117 55W
Kegaska, Canada 71 B7 50 9N 61 18W
Keighley, U.K. 10 D6 53 52N 1 54W
Keila, Estonia 9 G21 59 18N 24 25 E
Keimoes, S. Africa 56 D3 28 41S 20 59 E
Keitele, Finland 8 E22 63 10N 26 20 E
Keith, Australia 63 F3 36 6S 140 20 E
Keith, U.K. 12 D6 57 32N 2 57W
Keizer, U.S.A. 82 D2 44 57N 123 1W
Kejimkujik Nat. Park, Canada 71 D6 44 25N 65 25W
Kejser Franz Joseph Fjord = Kong Franz Joseph Fd., Greenland 4 B6 73 30N 24 30W
Kekri, India 42 G6 26 0N 75 10 E
Kelan, China 34 E6 38 43N 111 31 E
Kelang, Malaysia 39 L3 3 2N 101 26 E
Kelantan →, Malaysia 39 J4 6 13N 102 14 E
Kelkit →, Turkey 25 F6 40 45N 36 32 E
Kellerberrin, Australia 61 F2 31 36S 117 38 E
Kellett, C., Canada 4 B1 72 0N 126 0W
Kelleys I., U.S.A. 78 E2 41 36N 82 42W
Kellogg, U.S.A. 82 C5 47 32N 116 7W
Kells = Ceanannus Mor, Ireland 13 C5 53 44N 6 53W
Kelokedhara, Cyprus 23 E11 34 48N 32 39 E
Kelowna, Canada 72 D5 49 50N 119 25W
Kelseyville, U.S.A. 84 G4 38 59N 122 50W
Kelso, N.Z. 59 L2 45 54S 169 15 E
Kelso, U.K. 12 F6 55 36N 2 26W
Kelso, U.S.A. 84 D4 46 9N 122 54W
Keluang, Malaysia 39 L4 2 3N 103 18 E
Kelvington, Canada 73 C8 52 10N 103 30W
Kem, Russia 24 B5 65 0N 34 38 E
Kem →, Russia 24 B5 64 57N 34 41 E
Kema, Indonesia 37 D7 1 22N 125 8 E
Kemah, Turkey 44 B3 39 32N 39 5 E
Kemaman, Malaysia 36 D2 4 12N 103 18 E
Kemano, Canada 72 C3 53 35N 128 0W
Kemasik, Malaysia 39 K4 4 25N 103 27 E
Kemerovo, Russia 26 D9 55 20N 86 5 E
Kemi, Finland 8 D21 65 44N 24 34 E
Kemi älv = Kemijoki →, Finland 8 D21 65 47N 24 32 E
Kemijärvi, Finland 8 C22 66 43N 27 22 E
Kemijoki →, Finland 8 D21 65 47N 24 32 E
Kemmerer, U.S.A. 82 F8 41 48N 110 32W
Kemmuna = Comino, Malta 23 C1 36 2N 14 20 E
Kemp, L., U.S.A. 81 J5 33 46N 99 9W
Kemp Land, Antarctica 5 C5 69 0S 55 0 E
Kempsey, Australia 63 E5 31 1S 152 50 E
Kempt, L., Canada 70 C5 47 25N 74 22W
Kempten, Germany 16 E6 47 45N 10 17 E
Kempton, Australia 62 G4 42 31S 147 12 E
Kemptville, Canada 79 B9 45 0N 75 38W
Ken →, India 43 G9 25 13N 80 27 E
Kenai, U.S.A. 68 B4 60 33N 151 16W
Kendai, India 43 H10 22 45N 82 37 E
Kendal, Indonesia 37 G14 6 56S 110 14 E
Kendal, U.K. 10 C5 54 20N 2 44W
Kendall, Australia 63 E5 31 35S 152 44 E
Kendall, U.S.A. 77 N5 25 41N 80 19W
Kendall →, Australia 62 A3 14 4S 141 35 E
Kendallville, U.S.A. 76 E3 41 27N 85 16W
Kendari, Indonesia 37 E6 3 50S 122 30 E
Kendawangan, Indonesia 36 E4 2 32S 110 17 E
Kendrapara, India 41 J15 20 35N 86 30 E
Kendrew, S. Africa 56 E3 32 32S 24 30 E
Kene Thao, Laos 38 D3 17 44N 101 10 E
Kenedy, U.S.A. 81 L6 28 49N 97 51W
Kenema, S. Leone 50 G3 7 50N 11 14W
Keng Kok, Laos 38 D5 16 26N 105 12 E
Keng Tawng, Burma 41 J21 20 45N 98 18 E
Keng Tung, Burma 41 J21 21 0N 99 30 E
Kenge, Dem. Rep. of the Congo 52 E3 4 50S 17 4 E
Kengeja, Tanzania 54 D4 5 26S 39 45 E
Kenhardt, S. Africa 56 D3 29 19S 21 12 E
Kenitra, Morocco 50 B4 34 15N 6 40W
Kenli, China 35 F10 37 30N 118 20 E
Kenmare, Ireland 13 E2 51 53N 9 36W
Kenmare, U.S.A. 80 A3 48 41N 102 5W
Kenmare River, Ireland 13 E2 51 48N 9 51W
Kennebago Lake, U.S.A. 79 A14 45 4N 70 40W
Kennebec, U.S.A. 80 D5 43 54N 99 52W
Kennebec →, U.S.A. 77 D11 43 45N 69 46W
Kennebunk, U.S.A. 79 C14 43 23N 70 33W
Kennedy, Zimbabwe 55 F2 18 52S 27 10 E
Kennedy Ra., Australia 61 D2 24 45S 115 10 E
Kennedy Taungdeik, Burma 41 H18 23 15N 93 45 E
Kenner, U.S.A. 81 L9 29 59N 90 15W
Kennet →, U.K. 11 F7 51 27N 0 57W
Kenneth Ra., Australia 61 D2 23 50S 117 8 E
Kennett, U.S.A. 81 G9 36 14N 90 3W
Kennewick, U.S.A. 82 C4 46 12N 119 7W
Kenogami →, Canada 70 B3 51 6N 84 28W
Kenora, Canada 73 D10 49 47N 94 29W
Kenosha, U.S.A. 76 D2 42 35N 87 49W
Kensington, Canada 71 C7 46 28N 63 34W
Kent, Ohio, U.S.A. 78 E3 41 9N 81 22W
Kent, Tex., U.S.A. 81 K2 31 4N 104 13W
Kent, Wash., U.S.A. 84 C4 47 23N 122 14W
Kent □, U.K. 11 F8 51 12N 0 40 E
Kent Group, Australia 62 F4 39 30S 147 20 E
Kent Pen., Canada 68 B9 68 30N 107 0W
Kentau, Kazakstan 26 E7 43 32N 68 36 E
Kentland, U.S.A. 76 E2 40 46N 87 27W
Kenton, U.S.A. 76 E4 40 39N 83 37W
Kentucky □, U.S.A. 76 G3 37 0N 84 0W
Kentucky →, U.S.A. 76 F3 38 41N 85 11W
Kentucky L., U.S.A. 77 G2 37 1N 88 16W

Kentville, *Canada* **71 C7** 45 6N 64 29W
Kentwood, *U.S.A.* **81 K9** 30 56N 90 31W
Kenya ■, *Africa* .... **54 B4** 1 0N 38 0 E
Kenya, Mt., *Kenya* .... **54 C4** 0 10S 37 18 E
Keo Neua, Deo, *Vietnam* .. **38 C5** 18 23N 105 10 E
Keokuk, *U.S.A.* **80 E9** 40 24N 91 24W
Keonjhargarh, *India* ...... **43 J11** 21 28N 85 35 E
Kep, *Cambodia* .... **39 G5** 10 29N 104 19 E
Kep, *Vietnam* .... **38 B6** 21 24N 106 16 E
Kepi, *Indonesia* .... **37 F9** 6 32S 139 19 E
Kerala □, *India* .... **40 P10** 11 0N 76 15 E
Kerama-Rettō, *Japan* ..... **31 L3** 26 5N 127 15 E
Keran, *Pakistan* .... **43 B5** 34 35N 73 59 E
Kerang, *Australia* .... **63 F3** 35 40S 143 55 E
Keraudren, C., *Australia* ... **60 C2** 19 58S 119 45 E
Kerava, *Finland* .... **9 F21** 60 25N 25 5 E
Kerch, *Ukraine* .... **25 E6** 45 20N 36 20 E
Kerguelen, *Ind. Oc.* .... **3 G13** 49 15S 69 10 E
Kericho, *Kenya* .... **54 C4** 0 22S 35 15 E
Kerinci, *Indonesia* .... **36 E2** 1 40S 101 15 E
Kerki, *Turkmenistan* ...... **26 F7** 37 50N 65 12 E
Kérkira, *Greece* .... **23 A3** 39 38N 19 50 E
Kerkrade, *Neths.* .... **15 D6** 50 53N 6 4 E
Kermadec Is., *Pac. Oc.* **64 L10** 30 0S 178 15W
Kermadec Trench, *Pac. Oc.* **64 L10** 30 30S 176 0W
Kermān, *Iran* .... **45 D8** 30 15N 57 1 E
Kerman, *U.S.A.* **84 J6** 36 43N 120 4W
Kermān □, *Iran* .... **45 D8** 30 0N 57 0 E
Kermān, Bīābān-e, *Iran* .... **45 D8** 28 45N 59 45 E
Kermānshāh = Bākhtarān,
Iran .... **44 C5** 34 23N 47 0 E
Kermit, *U.S.A.* **81 K3** 31 52N 103 6W
Kern →, *U.S.A.* **85 K7** 35 16N 119 18W
Kernville, *U.S.A.* **85 K8** 35 45N 118 26W
Keroh, *Malaysia* .... **39 K3** 5 43N 101 1 E
Kerrera, *U.K.* **12 E3** 56 24N 5 33W
Kerrobert, *Canada* **73 C7** 51 56N 109 8W
Kerrville, *U.S.A.* **81 K5** 30 3N 99 8W
Kerry □, *Ireland* **13 D2** 52 7N 9 35W
Kerry Hd., *Ireland* **13 D2** 52 25N 9 56W
Kerulen →, *Asia* .... **33 B6** 48 48N 117 0 E
Kerzaz, *Algeria* **50 C5** 29 29N 1 37W
Kesagami →, *Canada* **70 B4** 51 40N 79 45W
Kesagami L., *Canada* **70 B3** 50 23N 80 15W
Keşan, *Turkey* .... **21 D12** 40 49N 26 38 E
Kesennuma, *Japan* .... **30 E10** 38 54N 141 35 E
Keshit, *Iran* .... **45 D8** 29 43N 58 17 E
Kestell, *S. Africa* .... **57 D4** 28 17S 28 42 E
Kestenga, *Russia* .... **24 A5** 65 50N 31 45 E
Keswick, *U.K.* **10 C4** 54 36N 3 8W
Ket →, *Russia* .... **26 D9** 58 55N 81 32 E
Ketapang, *Indonesia* ...... **36 E4** 1 55S 110 0 E
Ketchikan, *U.S.A.* **72 B2** 55 21N 131 39W
Ketchum, *U.S.A.* **82 E6** 43 41N 114 22W
Ketef, Khalîg Umm el, *Egypt* **44 F2** 23 40N 35 35 E
Keti Bandar, *Pakistan* ..... **42 G2** 24 8N 67 27 E
Ketri, *India* .... **42 E6** 28 1N 75 50 E
Kętrzyn, *Poland* .... **17 A11** 54 7N 21 22 E
Kettering, *U.K.* **11 E7** 52 24N 0 43W
Kettering, *U.S.A.* **76 F3** 39 41N 84 10W
Kettle →, *Canada* **73 B11** 56 40N 89 34W
Kettle Falls, *U.S.A.* **82 B4** 48 37N 118 3W
Kettle Pt., *Canada* **78 C2** 43 13N 82 1W
Kettleman City, *U.S.A.* **84 J7** 36 1N 119 58W
Keuka L., *U.S.A.* **78 D7** 42 30N 77 9W
Keuruu, *Finland* .... **9 E21** 62 16N 24 41 E
Kewanee, *U.S.A.* **80 E10** 41 14N 89 56W
Kewaunee, *U.S.A.* **76 C2** 44 27N 87 31W
Keweenaw B., *U.S.A.* **76 B1** 47 0N 88 15W
Keweenaw Pen., *U.S.A.* ... **76 B2** 47 30N 88 0W
Keweenaw Pt., *U.S.A.* **76 B2** 47 25N 87 43W
Key Largo, *U.S.A.* **77 N5** 25 5N 80 27W
Key West, *U.S.A.* **75 F10** 24 33N 81 48W
Keynsham, *U.K.* **11 F5** 51 24N 2 29W
Keyser, *U.S.A.* **76 F6** 39 26N 78 59W
Kezhma, *Russia* .... **27 D11** 58 59N 101 9 E
Khabarovsk, *Russia* ...... **27 E14** 48 30N 135 5 E
Khabr, *Iran* .... **45 D8** 28 51N 56 22 E
Khābūr →, *Syria* .... **44 C4** 35 17N 40 35 E
Khachmas = Xaçmaz,
Azerbaijan .... **25 F8** 41 31N 48 42 E
Khachrod, *India* .... **42 H6** 23 25N 75 20 E
Khadro, *Pakistan* .... **42 F3** 26 11N 68 50 E
Khadzhilyangar, *India* ..... **43 B8** 35 45N 79 20 E
Khaga, *India* .... **43 G9** 25 47N 81 7 E
Khagaria, *India* .... **43 G12** 25 30N 86 32 E
Khaipur, *Pakistan* .... **42 E5** 29 34N 72 17 E
Khair, *India* .... **42 F7** 27 57N 77 46 E
Khairabad, *India* .... **43 F9** 27 33N 80 47 E
Khairagarh, *India* .... **43 J9** 21 27N 81 2 E
Khairpur, *Pakistan* .... **40 F6** 27 32N 68 49 E
Khairpur, *Hyderabad,*
Pakistan .... **42 F3** 27 32N 68 49 E
Khairpur Nathan Shah,
Pakistan .... **42 F2** 27 6N 67 44 E
Khairwara, *India* .... **42 H5** 23 58N 73 38 E
Khaisor →, *Pakistan* ..... **42 D3** 31 17N 68 59 E
Khajuri Kach, *Pakistan* .... **42 C3** 32 4N 69 51 E
Khakassia □, *Russia* ...... **26 D9** 53 0N 90 0 E
Khakhea, *Botswana* ...... **56 C3** 24 48S 23 22 E
Khalafābād, *Iran* .... **45 D6** 30 54N 49 24 E
Khalilabad, *India* .... **43 F10** 26 48N 83 5 E
Khalīlī, *Iran* .... **45 E7** 27 38N 53 17 E
Khalkhāl, *Iran* .... **45 B6** 37 37N 48 32 E
Khalkís, *Greece* .... **21 E10** 38 27N 23 42 E
Khalmer-Sede = Tazovskiy,
Russia .... **26 C8** 67 30N 78 44 E
Khalmer Yu, *Russia* ...... **26 C7** 67 58N 65 1 E
Khalturin, *Russia* .... **24 C8** 58 40N 48 50 E
Khalūf, *Oman* .... **46 C6** 20 30N 58 13 E
Kham Keut, *Laos* .... **38 C5** 18 15N 104 43 E
Khamaria, *India* .... **43 H9** 23 5N 80 48 E
Khamas Country, *Botswana* **56 C4** 21 45S 26 30 E
Khambhaliya, *India* .... **42 H3** 22 14N 69 41 E
Khambhat, *India* .... **42 H5** 22 23N 72 33 E
Khambhat, G. of, *India* .... **40 J8** 20 45N 72 30 E
Khamīr, *Iran* .... **45 E7** 26 57N 55 36 E
Khamir, *Yemen* .... **46 D3** 16 2N 44 0 E
Khamsa, *Egypt* .... **47 E1** 30 27N 32 23 E
Khān Abū Shāmat, *Syria* .. **47 B5** 33 39N 36 53 E
Khān Azād, *Iraq* .... **44 C5** 33 7N 44 22 E
Khān Mujiddah, *Iraq* ...... **44 C4** 32 21N 43 48 E
Khān Shaykhūn, *Syria* .... **44 C3** 35 26N 36 38 E
Khān Yūnis, *Gaza Strip* ... **47 D3** 31 21N 34 18 E
Khanai, *Pakistan* .... **42 D2** 30 30N 67 8 E
Khānaqīn, *Iraq* .... **44 C5** 34 23N 45 25 E
Khānbāghī, *Iran* .... **45 B7** 36 10N 55 25 E
Khandwa, *India* .... **40 J10** 21 49N 76 22 E
Khandyga, *Russia* .... **27 C14** 62 42N 135 35 E
Khāneh, *Iran* .... **44 B5** 36 41N 45 8 E
Khanewal, *Pakistan* ...... **42 D4** 30 20N 71 55 E
Khangah Dogran, *Pakistan* . **42 D5** 31 50N 73 37 E
Khanh Duong, *Vietnam* ... **38 F7** 12 44N 108 44 E
Khaniá, *Greece* .... **23 D6** 35 30N 24 4 E
Khaniá □, *Greece* .... **23 D6** 35 30N 24 0 E
Khaniadhana, *India* .... **42 G8** 25 1N 78 8 E
Khaníon, Kólpos, *Greece* .. **23 D5** 35 33N 23 55 E
Khanka, L., *Asia* .... **27 E14** 45 0N 132 24 E
Khankendy = Xankändi,
Azerbaijan .... **25 G8** 39 52N 46 49 E
Khanna, *India* .... **42 D7** 30 42N 76 16 E
Khanozai, *Pakistan* .... **42 D2** 30 37N 67 19 E
Khanpur, *Pakistan* .... **42 E4** 28 42N 70 35 E
Khanty-Mansiysk, *Russia* .. **26 C7** 61 0N 69 0 E
Khapalu, *Pakistan* .... **43 B7** 35 10N 76 20 E
Khapcheranga, *Russia* .... **27 E12** 49 42N 112 24 E
Kharaghoda, *India* .... **42 H4** 23 11N 71 46 E
Kharagpur, *India* .... **43 H12** 22 20N 87 25 E
Khárakas, *Greece* .... **23 D7** 35 1N 25 7 E
Kharan Kalat, *Pakistan* .... **40 E4** 28 34N 65 21 E
Kharānaq, *Iran* .... **45 C7** 32 20N 54 45 E
Kharda, *India* .... **40 K9** 18 40N 75 34 E
Khardung La, *India* .... **43 B7** 34 20N 77 43 E
Khârga, El Wâhât el, *Egypt* **51 C12** 25 10N 30 35 E
Khargon, *India* .... **40 J9** 21 45N 75 40 E
Khari →, *India* .... **42 G6** 25 54N 74 31 E
Kharian, *Pakistan* .... **42 C5** 32 49N 73 52 E
Khārk, Jazīreh-ye, *Iran* .... **45 D6** 29 15N 50 28 E
Kharkiv, *Ukraine* .... **25 E6** 49 58N 36 20 E
Kharkov = Kharkiv, *Ukraine* **25 E6** 49 58N 36 20 E
Kharovsk, *Russia* .... **24 C7** 59 56N 40 13 E
Kharsawangarh, *India* .... **43 H11** 22 48N 85 50 E
Kharta, *Turkey* .... **21 D13** 40 55N 29 7 E
Khartoum = El Khartûm,
Sudan .... **51 E12** 15 31N 32 35 E
Khasan, *Russia* .... **30 C5** 42 25N 130 40 E
Khāsh, *Iran* .... **40 E2** 28 15N 61 15 E
Khashm el Girba, *Sudan* .. **51 F13** 14 59N 35 58 E
Khaskovo, *Bulgaria* .... **21 D11** 41 56N 25 30 E
Khatanga, *Russia* .... **27 B11** 72 0N 102 20 E
Khatanga →, *Russia* ...... **27 B11** 72 55N 106 0 E
Khatauli, *India* .... **42 E7** 29 17N 77 43 E
Khatra, *India* .... **43 H12** 22 59N 86 51 E
Khātūnābād, *Iran* .... **45 D7** 30 1N 55 25 E
Khatyrka, *Russia* .... **27 C18** 62 3N 175 15 E
Khavda, *India* .... **42 H3** 23 51N 69 43 E
Khaybar, Harrat, *Si. Arabia* **44 E4** 25 45N 40 0 E
Khayelitsha, *S. Africa* ..... **53 L3** 34 5S 18 42 E
Khāzimiyah, *Iraq* .... **44 C4** 34 46N 43 37 E
Khe Bo, *Vietnam* .... **38 C5** 19 8N 104 41 E
Khe Long, *Vietnam* .... **38 B5** 21 29N 104 46 E
Khed Brahma, *India* ...... **40 G8** 24 7N 73 5 E
Khekra, *India* .... **42 E7** 28 52N 77 20 E
Khemarak Phouminville,
Cambodia .... **39 G4** 11 37N 102 59 E
Khemisset, *Morocco* **50 B4** 33 50N 6 1W
Khemmarat, *Thailand* ..... **38 D5** 16 10N 105 15 E
Khenāmān, *Iran* .... **45 D8** 30 27N 56 29 E
Khenchela, *Algeria* .... **50 A7** 35 28N 7 11 E
Khersān →, *Iran* .... **45 D6** 31 33N 50 22 E
Kherson, *Ukraine* .... **25 E5** 46 35N 32 35 E
Khersónisos Akrotíri, *Greece* **23 D6** 35 30N 24 10 E
Kheta →, *Russia* .... **27 B11** 71 54N 102 6 E
Khewari, *Pakistan* .... **42 F3** 26 36N 68 52 E
Khilchipur, *India* .... **42 G7** 24 2N 76 34 E
Khilok, *Russia* .... **27 D12** 51 30N 110 45 E
Khíos, *Greece* .... **21 E12** 38 27N 26 9 E
Khirsadoh, *India* .... **43 H8** 22 11N 78 47 E
Khiuma = Hiiumaa, *Estonia* **9 G20** 58 50N 22 45 E
Khiva, *Uzbekistan* .... **26 E7** 41 30N 60 18 E
Khīyāv, *Iran* .... **44 B5** 38 30N 47 45 E
Khlong Khlung, *Thailand* .. **38 D2** 16 12N 99 43 E
Khmelnik, *Ukraine* .... **17 D14** 49 33N 27 58 E
Khmelnitskiy =
Khmelnytskyy, *Ukraine* .. **17 D14** 49 23N 27 0 E
Khmelnytskyy, *Ukraine* ... **17 D14** 49 23N 27 0 E
Khmer Rep. = Cambodia ■,
Asia .... **38 F5** 12 15N 105 0 E
Khoai, Hon, *Vietnam* ...... **39 H5** 8 26N 104 50 E
Khodoriv, *Ukraine* .... **17 D13** 49 24N 24 19 E
Khodzent = Khudzhand,
Tajikistan .... **26 E7** 40 17N 69 37 E
Khojak Pass, *Afghan.* ..... **42 D2** 30 51N 66 34 E
Khok Kloi, *Thailand* ...... **39 H2** 8 17N 98 19 E
Khok Pho, *Thailand* ...... **39 J3** 6 43N 101 6 E
Kholm, *Russia* .... **24 C5** 57 10N 31 15 E
Kholmsk, *Russia* .... **27 E15** 47 40N 142 5 E
Khomas Hochland, *Namibia* **56 C2** 22 40S 16 0 E
Khomeyn, *Iran* .... **45 C6** 33 40N 50 7 E
Khomeynī Shahr, *Iran* .... **45 C6** 32 41N 51 31 E
Khon Kaen, *Thailand* ..... **38 D4** 16 30N 102 47 E
Khong →, *Cambodia* ..... **38 F5** 13 32N 105 58 E
Khong Sedone, *Laos* ..... **38 E5** 15 34N 105 49 E
Khonuu, *Russia* .... **27 C15** 66 30N 143 12 E
Khoper →, *Russia* .... **25 D6** 49 30N 42 20 E
Khóra Sfakíon, *Greece* ... **23 D6** 35 15N 24 9 E
Khorāsān □, *Iran* .... **45 C8** 34 0N 58 0 E
Khorat = Nakhon
Ratchasima, *Thailand* ... **38 E4** 14 59N 102 12 E
Khorat, Cao Nguyen,
Thailand .... **38 E4** 15 30N 102 50 E
Khorixas, *Namibia* .... **56 C1** 20 16S 14 59 E
Khorramābād, *Khorāsān,*
Iran .... **45 C8** 35 6N 57 57 E
Khorramābād, *Lorestān, Iran* **45 C6** 33 30N 48 25 E
Khorrāmshahr, *Iran* ...... **45 D6** 30 29N 48 15 E
Khorugh, *Tajikistan* ...... **26 F8** 37 30N 71 36 E
Khosravī, *Iran* .... **45 D6** 30 48N 51 28 E
Khosrowābād, *Khuzestān,*
Iran .... **45 D6** 30 10N 48 25 E
Khosrowābād, *Kordestān,*
Iran .... **44 C5** 35 31N 47 38 E
Khost, *Pakistan* .... **42 D2** 30 13N 67 35 E
Khosūyeh, *Iran* .... **45 D7** 28 32N 54 26 E
Khotyn, *Ukraine* .... **17 D14** 48 31N 26 27 E
Khouribga, *Morocco* **50 B4** 32 58N 6 57W
Khowai, *Bangla.* .... **41 G17** 24 5N 91 40 E
Khowst, *Afghan.* .... **42 C3** 33 22N 69 58 E
Khoyniki, *Belarus* .... **17 C15** 51 54N 29 55 E
Khrysokhou B., *Cyprus* ... **23 D11** 35 6N 32 25 E
Khu Khan, *Thailand* ...... **38 E5** 14 42N 104 12 E
Khudzhand, *Tajikistan* .... **26 E7** 40 17N 69 37 E
Khuff, *Si. Arabia* .... **44 E5** 24 55N 44 53 E
Khūgīānī, *Afghan.* .... **42 D1** 31 28N 65 14 E
Khuiyala, *India* .... **42 F4** 27 9N 70 25 E
Khujner, *India* .... **42 H7** 23 47N 76 36 E
Khulna, *Bangla.* .... **41 H16** 22 45N 89 34 E
Khulna □, *Bangla.* .... **41 H16** 22 25N 89 35 E
Khumago, *Botswana* ...... **56 C3** 20 26S 24 32 E
Khūnsorkh, *Iran* .... **45 E8** 27 9N 56 7 E
Khunti, *India* .... **43 H11** 23 5N 85 17 E
Khūr, *Iran* .... **45 C8** 32 55N 58 18 E
Khurai, *India* .... **42 G8** 24 3N 78 23 E
Khurayş, *Si. Arabia* .... **45 E6** 25 6N 48 2 E
Khurīyā Murīyā, Jazā 'ir,
Oman .... **46 D6** 17 30N 55 58 E
Khurja, *India* .... **42 E7** 28 15N 77 58 E
Khūrmāl, *Iraq* .... **44 C5** 35 18N 46 2 E
Khurr, Wādī al, *Iraq* ...... **44 C4** 32 3N 43 52 E
Khūsf, *Iran* .... **45 C8** 32 46N 58 53 E
Khush, *Afghan.* .... **40 C3** 32 55N 62 10 E
Khushab, *Pakistan* .... **42 C5** 32 20N 72 20 E
Khust, *Ukraine* .... **17 D12** 48 10N 23 18 E
Khuzdar, *Pakistan* .... **42 F2** 27 52N 66 30 E
Khūzestān □, *Iran* .... **45 D6** 31 0N 49 0 E
Khvāf, *Iran* .... **45 C9** 34 33N 60 8 E
Khvājeh, *Iran* .... **44 B5** 38 9N 46 35 E
Khvānsār, *Iran* .... **45 D7** 29 56N 54 8 E
Khvor, *Iran* .... **45 C7** 33 45N 55 0 E
Khvorgū, *Iran* .... **45 E8** 27 34N 56 27 E
Khvormūj, *Iran* .... **45 D6** 28 40N 51 30 E
Khvoy, *Iran* .... **44 B5** 38 35N 45 0 E
Khyber Pass, *Afghan.* ..... **42 B4** 34 10N 71 8 E
Kiabukwa,
Dem. Rep. of the Congo . **55 D1** 8 40S 24 48 E
Kiama, *Australia* .... **63 E5** 34 40S 150 50 E
Kiamba, *Phil.* .... **37 C6** 6 2N 124 46 E
Kiambi,
Dem. Rep. of the Congo . **54 D2** 7 15S 28 0 E
Kiambu, *Kenya* .... **54 C4** 1 8S 36 50 E
Kiangsi = Jiangxi □, *China* **33 D6** 27 30N 116 0 E
Kiangsu = Jiangsu □, *China* **35 H11** 33 0N 120 0 E
Kibanga Port, *Uganda* .... **54 B3** 0 10N 32 58 E
Kibara, *Tanzania* .... **54 C3** 2 8S 33 30 E
Kibare, Mts.,
Dem. Rep. of the Congo . **54 D2** 8 25S 27 10 E
Kibombo,
Dem. Rep. of the Congo . **54 C2** 3 57S 25 53 E
Kibondo, *Tanzania* .... **54 C3** 3 35S 30 45 E
Kibre Mengist, *Ethiopia* ... **46 F2** 5 53N 38 59 E
Kibumbu, *Burundi* .... **54 C2** 3 32S 29 45 E
Kibungo, *Rwanda* .... **54 C3** 2 10S 30 32 E
Kibuye, *Burundi* .... **54 C2** 3 39S 29 59 E
Kibuye, *Rwanda* .... **54 C2** 2 3S 29 21 E
Kibwesa, *Tanzania* .... **54 D2** 6 30S 29 58 E
Kibwezi, *Kenya* .... **54 C4** 2 27S 37 57 E
Kichha, *India* .... **43 E8** 28 53N 79 30 E
Kichha →, *India* .... **43 E8** 28 41N 79 18 E
Kichmengskiy Gorodok,
Russia .... **24 B8** 59 59N 45 48 E
Kicking Horse Pass, *Canada* **72 C5** 51 28N 116 16W
Kidal, *Mali* .... **50 E6** 18 26N 1 22 E
Kidderminster, *U.K.* **11 E5** 52 24N 2 15W
Kidete, *Tanzania* .... **54 D4** 6 25S 37 17 E
Kidnappers, C., *N.Z.* ..... **59 H6** 39 38S 177 5 E
Kidsgrove, *U.K.* **10 D5** 53 5N 2 14W
Kidston, *Australia* .... **62 B3** 18 52S 144 8 E
Kidugallo, *Tanzania* ...... **54 D4** 6 49S 38 15 E
Kiel, *Germany* .... **16 A6** 54 19N 10 8 E
Kiel Canal = Nord-Ostsee-
Kanal, *Germany* .... **16 A5** 54 12N 9 32 E
Kielce, *Poland* .... **17 C11** 50 52N 20 42 E
Kielder Water, *U.K.* **10 B5** 55 11N 2 31W
Kieler Bucht, *Germany* .... **16 A6** 54 35N 10 25 E
Kien Binh, *Vietnam* .... **39 H5** 9 55N 105 19 E
Kien Tan, *Vietnam* .... **39 G5** 10 7N 105 17 E
Kienge,
Dem. Rep. of the Congo . **55 E2** 10 30S 27 30 E
Kiev = Kyyiv, *Ukraine* .... **17 C16** 50 30N 30 28 E
Kiffa, *Mauritania* **50 E3** 16 37N 11 24W
Kifrī, *Iraq* .... **44 C5** 34 45N 45 0 E
Kigali, *Rwanda* .... **54 C3** 1 59S 30 4 E
Kigarama, *Tanzania* ...... **54 C3** 1 1S 31 50 E
Kigoma □, *Tanzania* ...... **54 D3** 5 0S 30 0 E
Kigoma-Ujiji, *Tanzania* ... **54 C2** 4 55S 29 36 E
Kigomasha, Ras, *Tanzania* . **54 C4** 4 58S 38 58 E
Kığızı, *Turkey* .... **44 B4** 38 18N 43 25 E
Kihei, *U.S.A.* **74 H16** 20 47N 156 28W
Kihnu, *Estonia* .... **9 G21** 58 9N 24 1 E
Kii-Sanchi, *Japan* .... **31 G8** 34 20N 136 0 E
Kii-Suidō, *Japan* .... **31 H7** 33 40N 134 45 E
Kikaiga-Shima, *Japan* .... **31 K4** 28 19N 129 59 E
Kikinda, *Serbia, Yug.* ..... **21 B9** 45 50N 20 30 E
Kikládhes, *Greece* .... **21 F11** 37 0N 24 30 E
Kikwit,
Dem. Rep. of the Congo . **52 F3** 5 0S 18 45 E
Kilar, *India* .... **42 C7** 33 6N 76 25 E
Kilauea, *U.S.A.* **74 J14** 22 13N 159 25W
Kilauea Crater, *U.S.A.* **74 J17** 19 25N 155 17W
Kilbrannan Sd., *U.K.* **12 F3** 55 37N 5 26W
Kilchu, *N. Korea* .... **35 D15** 40 57N 129 25 E
Kilcoy, *Australia* .... **63 D5** 26 59S 152 30 E
Kildare, *Ireland* **13 C5** 53 9N 6 55W
Kildare □, *Ireland* **13 C5** 53 10N 6 50W
Kilfinnane, *Ireland* **13 D3** 52 21N 8 28W
Kilgore, *U.S.A.* **81 J7** 32 23N 94 53W
Kilifi, *Kenya* .... **54 C4** 3 40S 39 48 E
Kilimanjaro, *Tanzania* .... **54 C4** 3 7S 37 20 E
Kilimanjaro □, *Tanzania* .. **54 C4** 4 0S 38 0 E
Kilindini, *Kenya* .... **54 C4** 4 4S 39 40 E
Kilis, *Turkey* .... **44 B3** 36 42N 37 6 E
Kiliya, *Ukraine* .... **17 F15** 45 28N 29 16 E
Kilkee, *Ireland* **13 D2** 52 41N 9 39W
Kilkeel, *U.K.* **13 B5** 54 4N 6 0W
Kilkenny, *Ireland* **13 D4** 52 39N 7 15W
Kilkenny □, *Ireland* **13 D4** 52 35N 7 15W
Kilkieran B., *Ireland* **13 C2** 53 20N 9 41W
Kilkís, *Greece* .... **21 D10** 40 58N 22 57 E
Killala, *Ireland* **13 B2** 54 13N 9 12W
Killala B., *Ireland* **13 B2** 54 16N 9 8W
Killaloe, *Ireland* **13 D3** 52 48N 8 28W
Killaloe Sta., *Canada* **78 A7** 45 33N 77 25W
Killarney, *Australia* ...... **63 D5** 28 20S 152 18 E
Killarney, *Canada* **73 D9** 49 10N 99 40W
Killarney, *Ireland* **13 D2** 52 4N 9 30W
Killary Harbour, *Ireland* .. **13 C2** 53 38N 9 52W
Killdeer, *U.S.A.* **80 B3** 47 26N 102 48W
Killeen, *U.S.A.* **81 K6** 31 7N 97 44W
Killin, *U.K.* **12 E4** 56 28N 4 19W
Killíni, *Greece* .... **21 F10** 37 54N 22 25 E
Killorglin, *Ireland* **13 D2** 52 6N 9 47W
Killybegs, *Ireland* **13 B3** 54 38N 8 26W
Kilmarnock, *U.K.* **12 F4** 55 37N 4 29W
Kilmore, *Australia* .... **63 F3** 37 25S 144 53 E
Kilondo, *Tanzania* .... **55 D3** 9 45S 34 20 E
Kilosa, *Tanzania* .... **54 D4** 6 48S 37 0 E
Kilrush, *Ireland* **13 D2** 52 38N 9 29W
Kilwa Kisiwani, *Tanzania* .. **55 D4** 8 58S 39 32 E
Kilwa Kivinje, *Tanzania* ... **55 D4** 8 45S 39 25 E
Kilwa Masoko, *Tanzania* .. **55 D4** 8 55S 39 30 E
Kilwinning, *U.K.* **12 F4** 55 39N 4 43W
Kim, *U.S.A.* **81 G3** 37 15N 103 21W
Kimaam, *Indonesia* ...... **37 F9** 7 58S 138 53 E
Kimamba, *Tanzania* ...... **54 D4** 6 45S 37 10 E
Kimba, *Australia* .... **63 E2** 33 8S 136 23 E
Kimball, *Nebr., U.S.A.* **80 E3** 41 14N 103 40W
Kimball, *S. Dak., U.S.A.* ... **80 D5** 43 45N 98 57W
Kimberley, *Australia* ..... **60 C4** 16 20S 127 0 E
Kimberley, *Canada* **72 D5** 49 40N 115 59W
Kimberley, *S. Africa* ..... **56 D3** 28 43S 24 46 E
Kimberly, *U.S.A.* **82 E6** 42 32N 114 22W
Kimch'aek, *N. Korea* ..... **35 D15** 40 40N 129 10 E
Kimch'ŏn, *S. Korea* ...... **35 F15** 36 11N 128 4 E
Kimje, *S. Korea* .... **35 G14** 35 48N 126 45 E
Kimmirut, *Canada* **69 B13** 62 50N 69 50W
Kimpese,
Dem. Rep. of the Congo . **52 F2** 5 35S 14 26 E
Kimry, *Russia* .... **24 C6** 56 55N 37 15 E
Kinabalu, Gunong, *Malaysia* **36 C5** 6 3N 116 14 E
Kinaskan L., *Canada* **72 B2** 57 38N 130 8W
Kinbasket L., *Canada* **72 C5** 52 0N 118 10W
Kincardine, *Canada* **78 B3** 44 10N 81 40W
Kincolith, *Canada* **72 B3** 55 0N 129 57W
Kinda,
Dem. Rep. of the Congo . **55 D2** 9 18S 25 4 E
Kinde, *U.S.A.* **78 C2** 43 56N 83 0W
Kinder Scout, *U.K.* **10 D6** 53 24N 1 52W
Kindersley, *Canada* **73 C7** 51 30N 109 10W
Kindia, *Guinea* **50 F3** 10 0N 12 52W
Kindu,
Dem. Rep. of the Congo . **54 C2** 2 55S 25 50 E
Kineshma, *Russia* .... **24 C7** 57 30N 42 5 E
Kinesi, *Tanzania* .... **54 C3** 1 25S 33 50 E
King, L., *Australia* .... **61 F2** 33 10S 119 35 E
King, Mt., *Australia* ...... **62 D4** 25 10S 147 30 E
King City, *U.S.A.* **84 J5** 36 13N 121 8W
King Cr. →, *Australia* .... **62 C2** 24 35S 139 30 E
King Edward →, *Australia* **60 B4** 14 14S 126 35 E
King Frederick VI Land =
Kong Frederik VI.s Kyst,
Greenland **4 C5** 63 0N 43 0W
King George B., *Falk. Is.* ... **96 G4** 51 30S 60 30W
King George I., *Antarctica* . **5 C18** 60 0S 60 0W
King George Is., *Canada* .. **69 C11** 57 20N 80 30W
King I. = Kadan Kyun,
Burma .... **38 F2** 12 30N 98 20 E
King I., *Australia* .... **62 F3** 39 50S 144 0 E
King I., *Canada* **72 C3** 52 10N 127 40W
King Leopold Ranges,
Australia .... **60 C4** 17 30S 125 45 E
King of Prussia, *U.S.A.* ... **79 F9** 40 5N 75 23W
King Sd., *Australia* ...... **60 C3** 16 50S 123 20 E
King William I., *Canada* ... **68 B10** 69 10N 97 25W
King William's Town,
S. Africa .... **56 E4** 32 51S 27 22 E
Kingaroy, *Australia* ...... **63 D5** 26 32S 151 51 E
Kingfisher, *U.S.A.* **81 H6** 35 52N 97 56W
Kingirbān, *Iraq* .... **44 C5** 34 40N 44 54 E
Kingisepp = Kuressaare,
Estonia .... **9 G20** 58 15N 22 30 E
Kingman, *Ariz., U.S.A.* ... **85 K12** 35 12N 114 4W
Kingman, *Kans., U.S.A.* ... **81 G5** 37 39N 98 7W
Kingoonya, *Australia* .... **63 E2** 30 55S 135 19 E
Kingri, *Pakistan* .... **42 D3** 30 27N 69 49 E
Kings →, *U.S.A.* **84 J7** 36 3N 119 50W
Kings Canyon National Park,
U.S.A. **84 J8** 36 50N 118 40W
King's Lynn, *U.K.* .... **10 E8** 52 45N 0 24 E
Kings Mountain, *U.S.A.* ... **77 H5** 35 15N 81 20W
Kings Park, *U.S.A.* **79 F11** 40 53N 73 16W
King's Peak, *U.S.A.* **82 F8** 40 46N 110 27W
Kingsbridge, *U.K.* **11 G4** 50 17N 3 47W
Kingsburg, *U.S.A.* **84 J7** 36 31N 119 33W
Kingscote, *Australia* ..... **63 F2** 35 40S 137 38 E
Kingscourt, *Ireland* **13 C5** 53 55N 6 48W
Kingsford, *U.S.A.* **76 C1** 45 48N 88 4W
Kingsland, *U.S.A.* **77 K5** 30 48N 81 41W
Kingsley, *U.S.A.* **80 D7** 42 35N 95 58W
Kingsport, *U.S.A.* **77 G4** 36 33N 82 33W
Kingston, *Canada* **79 B8** 44 14N 76 30W
Kingston, *Jamaica* **88 C4** 18 0N 76 50W
Kingston, *N.Z.* .... **59 L2** 45 20S 168 43 E
Kingston, *N.H., U.S.A.* ... **79 D13** 42 56N 71 3W
Kingston, *N.Y., U.S.A.* ... **79 E11** 41 56N 73 59W
Kingston, *Pa., U.S.A.* **79 E9** 41 16N 75 54W
Kingston, *R.I., U.S.A.* **79 E13** 41 29N 71 30W
Kingston Pk., *U.S.A.* **85 K11** 35 44N 115 25W
Kingston South East,
Australia .... **63 F2** 36 51S 139 55 E
Kingston upon Hull, *U.K.* .. **10 D7** 53 45N 0 21W
Kingston upon Hull □, *U.K.* **10 D7** 53 45N 0 21W
Kingston-upon-Thames, *U.K.* **11 F7** 51 24N 0 17W
Kingstown, *St. Vincent* ... **89 D7** 13 10N 61 10W
Kingstree, *U.S.A.* **77 J6** 33 40N 79 50W
Kingsville, *Canada* **78 D2** 42 2N 82 45W
Kingsville, *U.S.A.* **81 M6** 27 31N 97 52W
Kingussie, *U.K.* **12 D4** 57 6N 4 2W
Kingwood, *U.S.A.* **81 K7** 29 54N 95 18W
Kınık, *Turkey* .... **21 E12** 39 6N 27 24 E
Kinistino, *Canada* **73 C7** 52 57N 105 2W
Kinkala, *Congo* .... **52 E2** 4 18S 14 49 E
Kinki □, *Japan* .... **31 H8** 33 45N 136 0 E
Kinleith, *N.Z.* .... **59 H5** 38 20S 175 56 E
Kinmount, *Canada* **78 B6** 44 48N 78 45W
Kinna, *Sweden* .... **9 H15** 57 32N 12 42 E
Kinnairds Hd., *U.K.* **12 D6** 57 43N 2 1W
Kinnarodden, *Norway* .... **6 A11** 71 8N 27 40 E
Kino, *Mexico* **86 B2** 28 45N 111 59W
Kinoje →, *Canada* **70 B3** 52 8N 81 25W
Kinomoto, *Japan* .... **31 G8** 35 30N 136 13 E
Kinoni, *Uganda* .... **54 C3** 0 41S 30 28 E
Kinoosao, *Canada* **73 B8** 57 5N 102 1W
Kinross, *U.K.* **12 E5** 56 13N 3 25W
Kinsale, *Ireland* **13 E3** 51 42N 8 31W

Kinsale, Old Hd. of, Ireland 13 E3 51 37N 8 33W
Kinsha = Chang Jiang →, China 33 C7 31 48N 121 10 E
Kinshasa, Dem. Rep. of the Congo 52 E3 4 20S 15 15 E
Kinsley, U.S.A. 81 G5 37 55N 99 25W
Kinsman, U.S.A. 78 E4 41 26N 80 35W
Kinston, U.S.A. 77 H7 35 16N 77 35W
Kintore Ra., Australia 60 D4 23 15S 128 47 E
Kintyre, U.K. 12 F3 55 30N 5 35W
Kintyre, Mull of, U.K. 12 F3 55 17N 5 47W
Kinushseo →, Canada 70 A3 55 15N 83 45W
Kinuso, Canada 72 B5 55 20N 115 25W
Kinyangiri, Tanzania 54 C3 4 25S 34 37 E
Kinzua, U.S.A. 78 E6 41 52N 78 58W
Kinzua Dam, U.S.A. 78 E6 41 53N 79 0W
Kiosk, Canada 70 C4 46 6N 78 53W
Kiowa, Kans., U.S.A. 81 G5 37 1N 98 29W
Kiowa, Okla., U.S.A. 81 H7 34 43N 95 54W
Kipahigan L., Canada 73 B8 55 20N 101 55W
Kipanga, Tanzania 54 D4 6 15S 35 20 E
Kiparissía, Greece 21 F9 37 15N 21 40 E
Kiparissiakós Kólpos, Greece 21 F9 37 25N 21 25 E
Kipawa, L., Canada 70 C4 46 50N 79 0W
Kipembawe, Tanzania 54 D3 7 38S 33 27 E
Kipengere Ra., Tanzania 55 D3 9 12S 34 15 E
Kipili, Tanzania 54 D3 7 28S 30 32 E
Kipini, Kenya 54 C5 2 30S 40 32 E
Kipling, Canada 73 C8 50 6N 102 38W
Kippure, Ireland 13 C5 53 11N 6 21W
Kipushi, Dem. Rep. of the Congo 55 E2 11 48S 27 12 E
Kirensk, Russia 27 D11 57 50N 107 55 E
Kirghizia = Kyrgyzstan ■, Asia 26 E8 42 0N 75 0 E
Kirghizstan = Kyrgyzstan ■, Asia 26 E8 42 0N 75 0 E
Kirgiziya Steppe, Eurasia 25 E10 50 0N 55 0 E
Kiribati ■, Pac. Oc. 64 H10 5 0S 180 0 E
Kırıkkale, Turkey 25 G5 39 51N 33 32 E
Kirillov, Russia 24 C6 59 49N 38 24 E
Kirin = Jilin, China 35 C14 43 44N 126 30 E
Kiritimati, Kiribati 65 G12 1 58N 157 27W
Kirkby, U.K. 10 D5 53 30N 2 54W
Kirkby Lonsdale, U.K. 10 C5 54 12N 2 36W
Kirkcaldy, U.K. 12 E5 56 7N 3 9W
Kirkcudbright, U.K. 12 G4 54 50N 4 2W
Kirkee, India 40 K8 18 34N 73 56 E
Kirkenes, Norway 8 B23 69 40N 30 5 E
Kirkfield, Canada 78 B6 44 34N 78 59W
Kirkjubæjarklaustur, Iceland 8 E4 63 47N 18 4W
Kirkkonummi, Finland 9 F21 60 8N 24 26 E
Kirkland Lake, Canada 70 C3 48 9N 80 2W
Kırklareli, Turkey 21 D12 41 44N 27 15 E
Kirksville, U.S.A. 80 E8 40 12N 92 35W
Kirkūk, Iraq 44 C5 35 30N 44 21 E
Kirkwall, U.K. 12 C6 58 59N 2 58W
Kirkwood, S. Africa 56 E4 33 22S 25 15 E
Kirov, Russia 24 C8 58 35N 49 40 E
Kirovabad = Gäncä, Azerbaijan 25 F8 40 45N 46 20 E
Kirovakan = Vanadzor, Armenia 25 F7 40 48N 44 30 E
Kirovograd = Kirovohrad, Ukraine 25 E5 48 35N 32 20 E
Kirovohrad, Ukraine 25 E5 48 35N 32 20 E
Kirovsk = Babadayhan, Turkmenistan 26 F7 37 42N 60 23 E
Kirovsk, Russia 24 A5 67 32N 33 41 E
Kirovskiy, Kamchatka, Russia 27 D16 54 27N 155 42 E
Kirovskiy, Primorsk, Russia 30 B6 45 7N 133 30 E
Kirriemuir, U.K. 12 E5 56 41N 3 1W
Kirsanov, Russia 24 D7 52 35N 42 40 E
Kırşehir, Turkey 25 G5 39 14N 34 5 E
Kirthar Range, Pakistan 42 F2 27 0N 67 0 E
Kirtland, U.S.A. 83 H9 36 44N 108 21W
Kiruna, Sweden 8 C19 67 52N 20 15 E
Kirundu, Dem. Rep. of the Congo 54 C2 0 50S 25 35 E
Kiryū, Japan 31 F9 36 24N 139 20 E
Kisaga, Tanzania 54 C3 4 30S 34 23 E
Kisalaya, Nic. 88 D3 14 40N 84 3W
Kisámou, Kólpos, Greece 23 D5 35 30N 23 38 E
Kisanga, Dem. Rep. of the Congo 54 B2 2 30N 26 35 E
Kisangani, Dem. Rep. of the Congo 54 B2 0 35N 25 15 E
Kisar, Indonesia 37 F7 8 5S 127 10 E
Kisarawe, Tanzania 54 D4 6 53S 39 0 E
Kisarazu, Japan 31 G9 35 23N 139 55 E
Kishanganga →, Pakistan 43 B5 34 18N 73 28 E
Kishanganj, India 43 F13 26 3N 88 14 E
Kishangarh, Raj., India 42 F6 26 34N 74 52 E
Kishangarh, Raj., India 42 F4 27 50N 70 30 E
Kishinev = Chişinău, Moldova 17 E15 47 2N 28 50 E
Kishiwada, Japan 31 G7 34 28N 135 22 E
Kishtwar, India 43 C6 33 20N 75 48 E
Kisii, Kenya 54 C3 0 40S 34 45 E
Kisiju, Tanzania 54 D4 7 23S 39 19 E
Kisizi, Uganda 54 C2 1 0S 29 58 E
Kiskőrös, Hungary 17 E10 46 37N 19 20 E
Kiskunfélegyháza, Hungary 17 E10 46 42N 19 53 E
Kiskunhalas, Hungary 17 E10 46 28N 19 37 E
Kislovodsk, Russia 25 F7 43 50N 42 45 E
Kismayu = Chisimaio, Somali Rep. 49 G8 0 22S 42 32 E
Kiso-Gawa →, Japan 31 G8 35 20N 136 45 E
Kiso-Sammyaku, Japan 31 G8 35 45N 137 45 E
Kisofukushima, Japan 31 G8 35 52N 137 43 E
Kisoro, Uganda 54 C2 1 17S 29 48 E
Kissidougou, Guinea 50 G3 9 5N 10 5W
Kissimmee, U.S.A. 77 L5 28 18N 81 24W
Kissimmee →, U.S.A. 77 M5 27 9N 80 52W
Kississing L., Canada 73 B8 55 10N 101 20W
Kissónerga, Cyprus 23 E11 34 49N 32 24 E
Kisumu, Kenya 54 C3 0 3S 34 45 E
Kiswani, Tanzania 54 C4 4 5S 37 57 E
Kiswere, Tanzania 55 D4 9 27S 39 30 E
Kit Carson, U.S.A. 80 F3 38 46N 102 48W
Kita, Mali 50 F4 13 5N 9 25W
Kitaibaraki, Japan 31 F10 36 50N 140 45 E
Kitakami, Japan 30 E10 39 20N 141 10 E
Kitakami-Gawa →, Japan 30 E10 38 25N 141 19 E
Kitakami-Sammyaku, Japan 30 E10 39 30N 141 30 E
Kitakata, Japan 30 F9 37 39N 139 52 E
Kitakyūshū, Japan 31 H5 33 50N 130 50 E
Kitale, Kenya 54 B4 1 0N 35 0 E
Kitami, Japan 30 C11 43 48N 143 54 E
Kitami-Sammyaku, Japan 30 B11 44 22N 142 43 E
Kitangiri, L., Tanzania 54 C3 4 5S 34 20 E
Kitaya, Tanzania 55 E5 10 38S 40 8 E
Kitchener, Canada 78 C4 43 27N 80 29W
Kitega = Gitega, Burundi 54 C2 3 26S 29 56 E
Kitengo, Dem. Rep. of the Congo 54 D1 7 26S 24 8 E
Kitgum, Uganda 54 B3 3 17N 32 52 E
Kíthira, Greece 21 F10 36 8N 23 0 E
Kíthnos, Greece 21 F11 37 26N 24 27 E
Kiti, Cyprus 23 E12 34 50N 33 34 E
Kiti, C., Cyprus 23 E12 34 48N 33 36 E
Kitimat, Canada 72 C3 54 3N 128 38W
Kitinen →, Finland 8 C22 67 14N 27 27 E
Kitsuki, Japan 31 H5 33 25N 131 37 E
Kittakittaooloo, L., Australia 63 D2 28 3S 138 14 E
Kittanning, U.S.A. 78 F5 40 49N 79 31W
Kittatinny Mts., U.S.A. 79 F10 41 0N 75 0W
Kittery, U.S.A. 77 D10 43 5N 70 45W
Kittilä, Finland 8 C21 67 40N 24 51 E
Kitui, Kenya 54 C4 1 17S 38 0 E
Kitwanga, Canada 72 B3 55 6N 128 4W
Kitwe, Zambia 55 E2 12 54S 28 13 E
Kivarli, India 42 G5 24 33N 72 46 E
Kivertsi, Ukraine 17 C13 50 50N 25 28 E
Kividhes, Cyprus 23 E11 34 46N 32 51 E
Kivu, L., Dem. Rep. of the Congo 54 C2 1 48S 29 0 E
Kiyev = Kyyiv, Ukraine 17 C16 50 30N 30 28 E
Kiyevskoye Vdkhr. = Kyyivske Vdskh., Ukraine 17 C16 51 0N 30 25 E
Kizel, Russia 24 C10 59 3N 57 40 E
Kiziguru, Rwanda 54 C3 1 46S 30 23 E
Kızıl Irmak →, Turkey 25 F6 41 44N 35 58 E
Kizil Jilga, India 43 B8 35 26N 78 50 E
Kızıltepe, Turkey 44 B4 37 12N 40 35 E
Kizimkazi, Tanzania 54 D4 6 28S 39 30 E
Kizlyar, Russia 25 F8 43 51N 46 40 E
Kizyl-Arvat = Gyzylarbat, Turkmenistan 26 F6 39 4N 56 23 E
Kjölur, Iceland 8 D4 64 50N 19 25W
Kladno, Czech Rep. 16 C8 50 10N 14 7 E
Klaeng, Thailand 38 F3 12 47N 101 39 E
Klagenfurt, Austria 16 E8 46 38N 14 20 E
Klaipėda, Lithuania 9 J19 55 43N 21 10 E
Klaksvík, Færoe Is. 8 E9 62 14N 6 35W
Klamath →, U.S.A. 82 F1 41 33N 124 5W
Klamath Falls, U.S.A. 82 E3 42 13N 121 46W
Klamath Mts., U.S.A. 82 F2 41 20N 123 0W
Klamono, Indonesia 37 E8 1 8S 131 30 E
Klappan →, Canada 72 B3 58 0N 129 43W
Klarälven →, Sweden 9 G15 59 23N 13 32 E
Klatovy, Czech Rep. 16 D7 49 23N 13 18 E
Klawer, S. Africa 56 E2 31 44S 18 36 E
Klazienaveen, Neths. 15 B6 52 44N 7 0 E
Kleena Kleene, Canada 72 C4 52 0N 124 59W
Klein-Karas, Namibia 56 D2 27 33S 18 7 E
Klerksdorp, S. Africa 56 D4 26 53S 26 38 E
Kletsk = Klyetsk, Belarus 17 B14 53 5N 26 45 E
Kletskiy, Russia 25 E7 49 16N 43 11 E
Klickitat, U.S.A. 82 D3 45 49N 121 9W
Klickitat →, U.S.A. 84 E5 45 42N 121 17W
Klidhes, Cyprus 23 D13 35 42N 34 36 E
Klinaklini →, Canada 72 C3 51 21N 125 40W
Klipdale, S. Africa 56 E2 34 19S 19 57 E
Klipplaat, S. Africa 56 E3 33 1S 24 22 E
Kłodzko, Poland 17 C9 50 28N 16 38 E
Klouto, Togo 50 G6 6 57N 0 44 E
Kluane L., Canada 68 B6 61 15N 138 40W
Kluane Nat. Park, Canada 72 A1 60 45N 139 30W
Kluczbork, Poland 17 C10 50 58N 18 12 E
Klukwan, U.S.A. 72 B1 59 24N 135 54W
Klyetsk, Belarus 17 B14 53 5N 26 45 E
Klyuchevskaya, Gora, Russia 27 D17 55 50N 160 30 E
Knaresborough, U.K. 10 C6 54 1N 1 28W
Knee L., Man., Canada 70 A1 55 3N 94 45W
Knee L., Sask., Canada 73 B7 55 51N 107 0W
Knight Inlet, Canada 72 C3 50 45N 125 40W
Knighton, U.K. 11 E4 52 21N 3 3W
Knights Ferry, U.S.A. 84 H6 37 50N 120 40W
Knights Landing, U.S.A. 84 G5 38 48N 121 43W
Knob, C., Australia 61 F2 34 32S 119 16 E
Knock, Ireland 13 C3 53 48N 8 55W
Knockmealdown Mts., Ireland 13 D4 52 14N 7 56W
Knokke-Heist, Belgium 15 C3 51 21N 3 17 E
Knossós, Greece 23 D7 35 16N 25 10 E
Knowlton, Canada 79 A12 45 13N 72 31W
Knox, U.S.A. 76 E2 41 18N 86 37W
Knox Coast, Antarctica 5 C8 66 30S 108 0 E
Knoxville, Iowa, U.S.A. 80 E8 41 19N 93 6W
Knoxville, Pa., U.S.A. 78 E7 41 57N 77 27W
Knoxville, Tenn., U.S.A. 77 H4 35 58N 83 55W
Knysna, S. Africa 56 E3 34 2S 23 2 E
Ko Kha, Thailand 38 C2 18 11N 99 24 E
Koartac = Quaqtaq, Canada 69 B13 60 55N 69 40W
Koba, Indonesia 37 F8 6 37S 134 37 E
Kobarid, Slovenia 16 E7 46 15N 13 30 E
Kobayashi, Japan 31 J5 31 56N 130 59 E
Kobdo = Hovd, Mongolia 32 B4 48 2N 91 37 E
Kōbe, Japan 31 G7 34 45N 135 10 E
København, Denmark 9 J15 55 41N 12 34 E
Kōbi-Sho, Japan 31 M1 25 56N 123 41 E
Koblenz, Germany 16 C4 50 21N 7 36 E
Kobryn, Belarus 17 B13 52 15N 24 22 E
Kocaeli, Turkey 25 F4 40 45N 29 50 E
Kočani, Macedonia 21 D10 41 55N 22 25 E
Koch Bihar, India 41 F16 26 22N 89 29 E
Kochang, S. Korea 35 G14 35 41N 127 55 E
Kochas, India 43 G10 25 15N 83 56 E
Kōchi, Japan 31 H6 33 30N 133 35 E
Kōchi □, Japan 31 H6 33 40N 133 30 E
Kochiu = Gejiu, China 32 D5 23 20N 103 10 E
Kodarma, India 43 G11 24 28N 85 36 E
Kodiak, U.S.A. 68 C4 57 47N 152 24W
Kodiak I., U.S.A. 68 C4 57 30N 152 45W
Kodinar, India 42 J4 20 46N 70 46 E
Koes, Namibia 56 D2 26 0S 19 15 E
Koffiefontein, S. Africa 56 D4 29 30S 25 0 E
Kofiau, Indonesia 37 E7 1 11S 129 50 E
Koforidua, Ghana 50 G5 6 3N 0 17W
Kōfu, Japan 31 G9 35 40N 138 30 E
Koga, Japan 31 F9 36 11N 139 43 E
Kogaluk →, Canada 71 A7 56 12N 61 44W
Køge, Denmark 9 J15 55 27N 12 11 E
Koh-i-Bābā, Afghan. 40 B5 34 30N 67 0 E
Koh-i-Khurd, Afghan. 42 C1 33 30N 65 59 E
Koh-i-Maran, Pakistan 42 E2 29 18N 66 50 E
Kohat, Pakistan 42 C4 33 40N 71 29 E
Kohima, India 41 G19 25 35N 94 10 E
Kohkīlūyeh va Būyer Aḩmadi □, Iran 45 D6 31 30N 50 30 E
Kohler Ra., Antarctica 5 D15 77 0S 110 0W
Kohlu, Pakistan 42 E3 29 54N 69 15 E
Kohtla-Järve, Estonia 9 G22 59 20N 27 20 E
Koillismaa, Finland 8 D23 65 44N 28 36 E
Koin-dong, N. Korea 35 D14 40 28N 126 18 E
Kojō, N. Korea 35 E14 38 58N 127 58 E
Kojonup, Australia 61 F2 33 48S 117 10 E
Kojūr, Iran 45 B6 36 23N 51 43 E
Kokand = Qŭqon, Uzbekistan 26 E8 40 30N 70 57 E
Kokas, Indonesia 37 E8 2 42S 132 26 E
Kokchetav = Kökshetaū, Kazakstan 26 D7 53 20N 69 25 E
Kokemäenjoki →, Finland 9 F19 61 32N 21 44 E
Kokkola, Finland 8 E20 63 50N 23 8 E
Koko Kyunzu, Burma 41 M18 14 10N 93 25 E
Kokomo, U.S.A. 76 E2 40 29N 86 8W
Koksan, N. Korea 35 E14 38 46N 126 40 E
Kökshetaū, Kazakstan 26 D7 53 20N 69 25 E
Koksoak →, Canada 69 C13 58 30N 68 10W
Kokstad, S. Africa 57 E4 30 32S 29 29 E
Kokubu, Japan 31 J5 31 44N 130 46 E
Kola, Indonesia 37 F8 5 35S 134 30 E
Kola, Russia 24 A5 68 45N 33 8 E
Kola Pen. = Kolskiy Poluostrov, Russia 24 A6 67 30N 38 0 E
Kolachi →, Pakistan 42 F2 27 8N 67 2 E
Kolahoi, India 43 B6 34 12N 75 22 E
Kolaka, Indonesia 37 E6 4 3S 121 46 E
Kolar, India 40 N11 13 12N 78 15 E
Kolar Gold Fields, India 40 N11 12 58N 78 16 E
Kolaras, India 42 G6 25 14N 77 36 E
Kolari, Finland 8 C20 67 20N 23 48 E
Kolayat, India 40 F8 27 50N 72 50 E
Kolchugino = Leninsk-Kuznetskiy, Russia 26 D9 54 44N 86 10 E
Kolding, Denmark 9 J13 55 30N 9 29 E
Kolepom = Dolak, Pulau, Indonesia 37 F9 8 0S 138 30 E
Kolguyev, Ostrov, Russia 24 A8 69 20N 48 30 E
Kolhapur, India 40 L9 16 43N 74 15 E
Kolín, Czech Rep. 16 C8 50 2N 15 9 E
Kolkas rags, Latvia 9 H20 57 46N 22 37 E
Kollum, Neths. 15 A6 53 17N 6 10 E
Kolmanskop, Namibia 56 D2 26 45S 15 14 E
Köln, Germany 16 C4 50 56N 6 57 E
Koło, Poland 17 B10 52 14N 18 40 E
Kołobrzeg, Poland 16 A8 54 10N 15 35 E
Kolomna, Russia 24 C6 55 8N 38 45 E
Kolomyya, Ukraine 17 D13 48 31N 25 2 E
Kolonodale, Indonesia 37 E6 2 3S 121 25 E
Kolosib, India 41 G18 24 15N 92 45 E
Kolpashevo, Russia 26 D9 58 20N 83 5 E
Kolpino, Russia 24 C5 59 44N 30 39 E
Kolskiy Poluostrov, Russia 24 A6 67 30N 38 0 E
Kolskiy Zaliv, Russia 24 A5 69 23N 34 0 E
Kolwezi, Dem. Rep. of the Congo 55 E2 10 40S 25 25 E
Kolyma →, Russia 27 C17 69 30N 161 0 E
Kolymskoye Nagorye, Russia 27 C16 63 0N 157 0 E
Kôm Ombo, Egypt 51 D12 24 25N 32 52 E
Komandorskiye Is. = Komandorskiye Ostrova, Russia 27 D17 55 0N 167 0 E
Komandorskiye Ostrova, Russia 27 D17 55 0N 167 0 E
Komárno, Slovak Rep. 17 E10 47 49N 18 5 E
Komatipoort, S. Africa 57 D5 25 25S 31 55 E
Komatou Yialou, Cyprus 23 D13 35 25N 34 8 E
Komatsu, Japan 31 F8 36 25N 136 30 E
Komatsujima, Japan 31 H7 34 0N 134 35 E
Komi □, Russia 24 B10 64 0N 55 0 E
Kommunarsk = Alchevsk, Ukraine 25 E6 48 30N 38 45 E
Kommunizma, Pik, Tajikistan 26 F8 39 0N 72 2 E
Komodo, Indonesia 37 F5 8 37S 119 20 E
Komoran, Pulau, Indonesia 37 F9 8 18S 138 45 E
Komoro, Japan 31 F9 36 19N 138 26 E
Komotini, Greece 21 D11 41 9N 25 26 E
Kompasberg, S. Africa 56 E3 31 45S 24 32 E
Kompong Bang, Cambodia 39 F5 12 24N 104 40 E
Kompong Cham, Cambodia 39 G5 12 0N 105 30 E
Kompong Chhnang = Kampang Chhnang, Cambodia 39 F5 12 20N 104 35 E
Kompong Chikreng, Cambodia 38 F5 13 5N 104 18 E
Kompong Kleang, Cambodia 38 F5 13 6N 104 8 E
Kompong Luong, Cambodia 39 G5 11 49N 104 48 E
Kompong Pranak, Cambodia 38 F5 13 35N 104 55 E
Kompong Som = Kampong Saom, Cambodia 39 G4 10 38N 103 30 E
Kompong Som, Chhung = Kampong Saom, Chaak, Cambodia 39 G4 10 50N 103 32 E
Kompong Speu, Cambodia 39 G5 11 26N 104 32 E
Kompong Sralao, Cambodia 38 E5 14 5N 105 46 E
Kompong Thom, Cambodia 38 F5 12 35N 104 51 E
Kompong Trabeck, Cambodia 38 F5 13 6N 105 14 E
Kompong Trabeck, Cambodia 39 G5 11 9N 105 28 E
Kompong Trach, Cambodia 39 G5 11 25N 105 48 E
Kompong Tralach, Cambodia 39 G5 11 54N 104 47 E
Komrat = Comrat, Moldova 17 E15 46 18N 28 40 E
Komsberg, S. Africa 56 E3 32 40S 20 45 E
Komsomolets, Ostrov, Russia 27 A10 80 30N 95 0 E
Komsomolsk, Russia 27 D14 50 30N 137 0 E
Kon Tum, Vietnam 38 E7 14 24N 108 0 E
Kon Tum, Plateau du, Vietnam 38 E7 14 30N 108 30 E
Konarhā □, Afghan. 40 B7 35 30N 71 3 E
Konārī, Iran 45 D6 28 13N 51 36 E
Konch, India 43 G8 26 0N 79 10 E
Konde, Tanzania 54 C4 4 57S 39 45 E
Kondinin, Australia 61 F2 32 34S 118 8 E
Kondoa, Tanzania 54 C4 4 55S 35 50 E
Kondókali, Greece 23 A3 39 38N 19 51 E
Kondopaga, Russia 24 B5 62 12N 34 17 E
Kondratyevo, Russia 27 D10 57 22N 98 15 E
Köneürgench, Turkmenistan 26 E6 42 19N 59 10 E
Konevo, Russia 24 B6 62 8N 39 20 E
Kong = Khong →, Cambodia 38 F5 13 32N 105 58 E
Kong, Ivory C. 50 G5 8 54N 4 36W
Kong, Koh, Cambodia 39 G4 11 20N 103 0 E
Kong Christian IX.s Land, Greenland 4 C6 68 0N 36 0W
Kong Christian X.s Land, Greenland 4 B6 74 0N 29 0W
Kong Franz Joseph Fd., Greenland 4 B6 73 30N 24 30W
Kong Frederik IX.s Land, Greenland 4 C5 67 0N 52 0W
Kong Frederik VI.s Kyst, Greenland 4 C5 63 0N 43 0W
Kong Frederik VIII.s Land, Greenland 4 B6 78 30N 26 0W
Kong Oscar Fjord, Greenland 4 B6 72 20N 24 0W
Kongju, S. Korea 35 F14 36 30N 127 0 E
Konglu, Burma 41 F20 27 13N 97 57 E
Kongolo, Kasai-Or., Dem. Rep. of the Congo 54 D1 5 26S 24 49 E
Kongolo, Katanga, Dem. Rep. of the Congo 54 D2 5 22S 27 0 E
Kongsberg, Norway 9 G13 59 39N 9 39 E
Kongsvinger, Norway 9 F15 60 12N 12 2 E
Kongwa, Tanzania 54 D4 6 11S 36 26 E
Koni, Dem. Rep. of the Congo 55 E2 10 40S 27 11 E
Koni, Mts., Dem. Rep. of the Congo 55 E2 10 36S 27 10 E
Königsberg = Kaliningrad, Russia 9 J19 54 42N 20 32 E
Konin, Poland 17 B10 52 12N 18 15 E
Konjic, Bos.-H. 21 C7 43 42N 17 58 E
Konkiep, Namibia 56 D2 26 49S 17 15 E
Konosha, Russia 24 B7 61 0N 40 5 E
Kōnosu, Japan 31 F9 36 3N 139 31 E
Konotop, Ukraine 25 D5 51 12N 33 7 E
Końskie, Poland 17 C11 51 15N 20 23 E
Konstanz, Germany 16 E5 47 40N 9 10 E
Kont, Iran 45 E9 26 55N 61 50 E
Kontagora, Nigeria 50 F7 10 23N 5 27 E
Konya, Turkey 25 G5 37 52N 32 35 E
Konza, Kenya 54 C4 1 45S 37 7 E
Koocanusa, L., Canada 82 B6 49 20N 115 15W
Kookynie, Australia 61 E3 29 17S 121 22 E
Koolyanobbing, Australia 61 F2 30 48S 119 36 E
Koonibba, Australia 63 E1 31 54S 133 25 E
Koorawatha, Australia 63 E4 34 2S 148 33 E
Koorda, Australia 61 F2 30 48S 117 35 E
Kooskia, U.S.A. 82 C6 46 9N 115 59W
Kootenay →, U.S.A. 72 D5 49 19N 117 39W
Kootenay L., Canada 72 D5 49 45N 116 50W
Kootenay Nat. Park, Canada 72 C5 51 0N 116 0W
Kootjieskolk, S. Africa 56 E3 31 15S 20 21 E
Kopaonik, Serbia, Yug. 21 C9 43 10N 20 50 E
Kópavogur, Iceland 8 D3 64 6N 21 55W
Koper, Slovenia 16 F7 45 31N 13 44 E
Kopervik, Norway 9 G11 59 17N 5 17 E
Kopet Dagh, Asia 45 B8 38 0N 58 0 E
Kopi, Australia 63 E2 33 24S 135 40 E
Köping, Sweden 9 G17 59 31N 16 3 E
Koppeh Dāgh = Kopet Dagh, Asia 45 B8 38 0N 58 0 E
Koppies, S. Africa 57 D4 27 20S 27 30 E
Koprivnica, Croatia 20 A7 46 12N 16 45 E
Kopychyntsi, Ukraine 17 D13 49 7N 25 58 E
Korab, Macedonia 21 D9 41 44N 20 40 E
Korakiána, Greece 23 A3 39 42N 19 45 E
Koral, India 42 J5 21 50N 73 12 E
Korba, India 43 H10 22 20N 82 45 E
Korbu, G., Malaysia 39 K3 4 41N 101 18 E
Korça, Albania 21 D9 40 37N 20 50 E
Korce = Korça, Albania 21 D9 40 37N 20 50 E
Korčula, Croatia 20 C7 42 56N 16 57 E
Kord Kūy, Iran 45 B7 36 48N 54 7 E
Kord Sheykh, Iran 45 D7 28 31N 52 53 E
Kordestān □, Iran 44 C5 36 0N 47 0 E
Kordofân, Sudan 51 F11 13 0N 29 0 E
Korea, North ■, Asia 35 E14 40 0N 127 0 E
Korea, South ■, Asia 35 G15 36 0N 128 0 E
Korea Bay, Korea 35 E13 39 0N 124 0 E
Korea Strait, Asia 35 H15 34 0N 129 30 E
Korets, Ukraine 17 C14 50 40N 27 5 E
Korhogo, Ivory C. 50 G4 9 29N 5 28W
Korinthiakós Kólpos, Greece 21 E10 38 16N 22 30 E
Kórinthos, Greece 21 F10 37 56N 22 55 E
Koríssa, Límni, Greece 23 B3 39 27N 19 53 E
Kōriyama, Japan 30 F10 37 24N 140 23 E
Korla, China 32 B3 41 45N 86 4 E
Kormakiti, C., Cyprus 23 D11 35 23N 32 56 E
Korneshty = Corneşti, Moldova 17 E15 47 21N 28 1 E
Koro, Fiji 59 C8 17 19S 179 23 E
Koro, Ivory C. 50 G4 8 32N 7 30W
Koro Sea, Fiji 59 C9 17 30S 179 45W
Korogwe, Tanzania 54 D4 5 5S 38 25 E
Koronadal, Phil. 37 C6 6 12N 125 1 E
Koror, Palau 37 C8 7 20N 134 28 E
Körös →, Hungary 17 E11 46 43N 20 12 E
Korosten, Ukraine 17 C15 50 54N 28 36 E
Korostyshev, Ukraine 17 C15 50 19N 29 4 E
Korraraika, Helodranon' i, Madag. 57 B7 17 45S 43 57 E
Korsakov, Russia 27 E15 46 36N 142 42 E
Korshunovo, Russia 27 D12 58 37N 110 10 E
Korsør, Denmark 9 J14 55 20N 11 9 E
Kortrijk, Belgium 15 D3 50 50N 3 17 E
Korwai, India 42 G8 24 7N 78 5 E
Koryakskoye Nagorye, Russia 27 C18 61 0N 171 0 E
Koryŏng, S. Korea 35 G15 35 44N 128 15 E
Kos, Greece 21 F12 36 50N 27 15 E
Koschagyl, Kazakstan 25 E9 46 40N 54 0 E
Kościan, Poland 17 B9 52 5N 16 40 E

Kosciusko, U.S.A. 81 J10 33 4N 89 35W
Kosciuszko, Mt., Australia 63 F4 36 27S 148 16 E
Kosha, Sudan 51 D12 20 50N 30 30 E
K'oshih = Kashi, China 32 C2 39 30N 76 2 E
Koshiki-Rettō, Japan 31 J4 31 45N 129 49 E
Kosi, India 42 F7 27 48N 77 29 E
Kosi →, India 43 E8 28 41N 78 57 E
Košice, Slovak Rep. 17 D11 48 42N 21 15 E
Koskhinoú, Greece 23 C10 36 23N 28 13 E
Koslan, Russia 24 B8 63 34N 49 14 E
Kosŏng, N. Korea 35 E15 38 40N 128 22 E
Kosovo □, Yugoslavia 21 C9 42 30N 21 0 E
Kosovska Mitrovica, Yugoslavia 21 C9 42 54N 20 52 E
Kossou, L. de, Ivory C. 50 G4 6 59N 5 31W
Koster, S. Africa 56 D4 25 52S 26 54 E
Kôstî, Sudan 51 F12 13 8N 32 43 E
Kostopil, Ukraine 17 C14 50 51N 26 22 E
Kostroma, Russia 24 C7 57 50N 40 58 E
Kostrzyn, Poland 16 B8 52 35N 14 39 E
Koszalin, Poland 16 A9 54 11N 16 8 E
Kot Addu, Pakistan 42 D4 30 30N 71 0 E
Kot Kapura, India 42 D6 30 35N 74 50 E
Kot Moman, Pakistan 42 C5 32 13N 73 0 E
Kot Sultan, Pakistan 42 D4 30 46N 70 56 E
Kota, India 42 G6 25 14N 75 49 E
Kota Baharu, Malaysia 39 J4 6 7N 102 14 E
Kota Barrage, India 42 G6 25 6N 75 51 E
Kota Belud, Malaysia 36 C5 6 21N 116 26 E
Kota Kinabalu, Malaysia 36 C5 6 0N 116 4 E
Kota Kubu Baharu, Malaysia 39 L3 3 34N 101 39 E
Kota Tinggi, Malaysia 39 M4 1 44N 103 53 E
Kotaagung, Indonesia 36 F2 5 38S 104 29 E
Kotabaru, Indonesia 36 E5 3 20S 116 20 E
Kotabumi, Indonesia 36 E2 4 49S 104 54 E
Kotamobagu, Indonesia 37 D6 0 57N 124 31 E
Kotcho L., Canada 72 B4 59 7N 121 12W
Kotdwara, India 43 E8 29 45N 78 32 E
Kotelnich, Russia 24 C8 58 22N 48 24 E
Kotelnikovo, Russia 25 E7 47 38N 43 8 E
Kotelnyy, Ostrov, Russia 27 B14 75 10N 139 0 E
Kothari →, India 42 G6 25 20N 75 4 E
Kothi, Mad. P., India 43 H10 23 21N 82 3 E
Kothi, Mad. P., India 43 G9 24 45N 80 40 E
Kotiro, Pakistan 42 F2 26 17N 67 13 E
Kotka, Finland 9 F22 60 28N 26 58 E
Kotlas, Russia 24 B8 61 17N 46 43 E
Kotli, Pakistan 42 C5 33 30N 73 55 E
Kotma, India 43 H9 23 12N 81 58 E
Kotmul, Pakistan 43 B6 35 32N 75 10 E
Kotor, Montenegro, Yug. 21 C8 42 25N 18 47 E
Kotovsk, Ukraine 17 E15 47 45N 29 35 E
Kotputli, India 42 F7 27 43N 76 12 E
Kotri, Pakistan 42 G3 25 22N 68 22 E
Kottayam, India 40 Q10 9 35N 76 33 E
Kotturu, India 40 M10 14 45N 76 10 E
Kotuy →, Russia 27 B11 71 54N 102 6 E
Kotzebue, U.S.A. 68 B3 66 53N 162 39W
Koudougou, Burkina Faso 50 F5 12 10N 2 20W
Koufonísi, Greece 23 E8 34 56N 26 8 E
Kougaberge, S. Africa 56 E3 33 48S 23 50 E
Kouilou →, Congo 52 E2 4 10S 12 5 E
Koula Moutou, Gabon 52 E2 1 15S 12 25 E
Koulen = Kulen, Cambodia 38 F5 13 50N 104 40 E
Kouloúra, Greece 23 A3 39 42N 19 54 E
Koúm-bournoú, Ákra, Greece 23 C10 36 15N 28 11 E
Koumala, Australia 62 C4 21 38S 149 15 E
Koumra, Chad 51 G9 8 50N 17 35 E
Kounradskiy, Kazakstan 26 E8 46 59N 75 0 E
Kountze, U.S.A. 81 K7 30 22N 94 19W
Kouris →, Cyprus 23 E11 34 38N 32 54 E
Kourou, Fr. Guiana 93 B8 5 9N 52 39W
Kousseri, Cameroon 51 F8 12 0N 14 55 E
Kouvola, Finland 9 F22 60 52N 26 43 E
Kovdor, Russia 24 A5 67 34N 30 24 E
Kovel, Ukraine 17 C13 51 11N 24 38 E
Kovrov, Russia 24 C7 56 25N 41 25 E
Kowanyama, Australia 62 B3 15 29S 141 44 E
Kowŏn, N. Korea 35 E14 39 26N 127 14 E
Köyceğiz, Turkey 21 F13 36 57N 28 40 E
Koza, Japan 31 L3 26 19N 127 46 E
Kozan, Turkey 44 B2 37 26N 35 50 E
Kozáni, Greece 21 D9 40 19N 21 47 E
Kozhikode = Calicut, India 40 P9 11 15N 75 43 E
Kozhva, Russia 24 A10 65 10N 57 0 E
Kozyatyn, Ukraine 17 D15 49 45N 28 50 E
Kra, Isthmus of = Kra, Kho Khot, Thailand 39 G2 10 15N 99 30 E
Kra, Kho Khot, Thailand 39 G2 10 15N 99 30 E
Kra Buri, Thailand 39 G2 10 22N 98 46 E
Krabi, Thailand 39 H2 8 4N 98 55 E
Kracheh, Cambodia 38 F6 12 32N 106 10 E
Kragan, Indonesia 37 G14 6 43S 111 38 E
Kragerø, Norway 9 G13 58 52N 9 25 E
Kragujevac, Serbia, Yug. 21 B9 44 2N 20 56 E
Krajina, Bos.-H. 20 B7 44 45N 16 35 E
Krakatau = Rakata, Pulau, Indonesia 36 F3 6 10S 105 20 E
Krakatoa = Rakata, Pulau, Indonesia 36 F3 6 10S 105 20 E
Krakor, Cambodia 38 F5 12 32N 104 12 E
Kraków, Poland 17 C10 50 4N 19 57 E
Kralanh, Cambodia 38 F4 13 35N 103 25 E
Kraljevo, Serbia, Yug. 21 C9 43 44N 20 41 E
Kramatorsk, Ukraine 25 E6 48 50N 37 30 E
Kramfors, Sweden 9 E17 62 55N 17 48 E
Kranj, Slovenia 16 E8 46 16N 14 22 E
Krankskop, S. Africa 57 D5 28 0S 30 47 E
Krasavino, Russia 24 B8 60 58N 46 29 E
Kraskino, Russia 27 E14 42 44N 130 48 E
Kraśnik, Poland 17 C12 50 55N 22 15 E
Krasnoarmeysk, Russia 26 D5 51 0N 45 42 E
Krasnodar, Russia 25 E6 45 5N 39 0 E
Krasnokamsk, Russia 24 C10 58 4N 55 48 E
Krasnoperekopsk, Ukraine 25 E5 46 0N 33 54 E
Krasnorechenskiy, Russia 30 B7 44 41N 135 14 E
Krasnoselkup, Russia 26 C9 65 20N 82 10 E
Krasnoturinsk, Russia 24 C11 59 46N 60 12 E
Krasnoufimsk, Russia 24 C10 56 36N 57 38 E
Krasnouralsk, Russia 24 C11 58 21N 60 3 E
Krasnovishersk, Russia 24 B10 60 23N 57 3 E
Krasnovodsk = Türkmenbashi, Turkmenistan 25 G9 40 5N 53 5 E
Krasnoyarsk, Russia 27 D10 56 8N 93 0 E
Krasnyy Kut, Russia 25 D8 50 50N 47 0 E
Krasnyy Luch, Ukraine 25 E6 48 13N 39 0 E
Krasnyy Yar, Russia 25 E8 46 43N 48 23 E
Kratie = Kracheh, Cambodia 38 F6 12 32N 106 10 E
Krau, Indonesia 37 E10 3 19S 140 5 E
Kravanh, Chuor Phnum, Cambodia 39 G4 12 0N 103 32 E
Krefeld, Germany 16 C4 51 20N 6 33 E
Kremen, Croatia 16 F8 44 28N 15 53 E
Kremenchug = Kremenchuk, Ukraine 25 E5 49 5N 33 25 E
Kremenchuk, Ukraine 25 E5 49 5N 33 25 E
Kremenchuksk Vdskh., Ukraine 25 E5 49 20N 32 30 E
Kremenets, Ukraine 17 C13 50 8N 25 43 E
Kremmling, U.S.A. 82 F10 40 4N 106 24W
Krems, Austria 16 D8 48 25N 15 36 E
Kretinga, Lithuania 9 J19 55 53N 21 15 E
Kribi, Cameroon 52 D1 2 57N 9 56 E
Krichev = Krychaw, Belarus 17 B16 53 40N 31 41 E
Kriós, Ákra, Greece 23 D5 35 13N 23 34 E
Krishna →, India 41 M12 15 57N 80 59 E
Krishnanagar, India 43 H13 23 24N 88 33 E
Kristiansand, Norway 9 G13 58 8N 8 1 E
Kristianstad, Sweden 9 H16 56 2N 14 9 E
Kristiansund, Norway 8 E12 63 7N 7 45 E
Kristiinankaupunki, Finland 9 E19 62 16N 21 21 E
Kristinehamn, Sweden 9 G16 59 18N 14 7 E
Kristinestad = Kristiinankaupunki, Finland 9 E19 62 16N 21 21 E
Kríti, Greece 23 D7 35 15N 25 0 E
Kritsá, Greece 23 D7 35 10N 25 41 E
Krivoy Rog = Kryvyy Rih, Ukraine 25 E5 47 51N 33 20 E
Krk, Croatia 16 F8 45 8N 14 40 E
Krokodil →, Mozam. 57 D5 25 14S 32 18 E
Krong Kaoh Kong, Cambodia 36 B2 11 35N 103 0 E
Kronprins Olav Kyst, Antarctica 5 C5 69 0S 42 0 E
Kronshtadt, Russia 24 B4 59 57N 29 51 E
Kroonstad, S. Africa 56 D4 27 43S 27 19 E
Kropotkin, Russia 25 E7 45 28N 40 28 E
Krosno, Poland 17 D11 49 42N 21 46 E
Krotoszyn, Poland 17 C9 51 42N 17 23 E
Kroussón, Greece 23 D6 35 13N 24 59 E
Kruger Nat. Park, S. Africa 57 C5 23 30S 31 40 E
Krugersdorp, S. Africa 57 D4 26 5S 27 46 E
Kruisfontein, S. Africa 56 E3 33 59S 24 43 E
Krung Thep = Bangkok, Thailand 38 F3 13 45N 100 35 E
Krupki, Belarus 17 A15 54 19N 29 8 E
Kruševac, Serbia, Yug. 21 C9 43 35N 21 28 E
Krychaw, Belarus 17 B16 53 40N 31 41 E
Krymskiy Poluostrov = Krymskyy Pivostriv, Ukraine 25 F5 45 0N 34 0 E
Krymskyy Pivostriv, Ukraine 25 F5 45 0N 34 0 E
Kryvyy Rih, Ukraine 25 E5 47 51N 33 20 E
Ksar el Kebir, Morocco 50 B4 35 0N 6 0W
Ksar es Souk = Ar Rachidiya, Morocco 50 B5 31 58N 4 20W
Kuala Belait, Malaysia 36 D4 4 35N 114 11 E
Kuala Berang, Malaysia 39 K4 5 5N 103 1 E
Kuala Dungun = Dungun, Malaysia 39 K4 4 45N 103 25 E
Kuala Kangsar, Malaysia 39 K3 4 46N 100 56 E
Kuala Kelawang, Malaysia 39 L4 2 56N 102 5 E
Kuala Kerai, Malaysia 39 K4 5 30N 102 12 E
Kuala Lipis, Malaysia 39 K4 4 10N 102 3 E
Kuala Lumpur, Malaysia 39 L3 3 9N 101 41 E
Kuala Nerang, Malaysia 39 J3 6 16N 100 37 E
Kuala Pilah, Malaysia 39 L4 2 45N 102 15 E
Kuala Rompin, Malaysia 39 L4 2 49N 103 29 E
Kuala Selangor, Malaysia 39 L3 3 20N 101 15 E
Kuala Sepetang, Malaysia 39 K3 4 49N 100 28 E
Kuala Terengganu, Malaysia 39 K4 5 20N 103 8 E
Kualajelai, Indonesia 36 E4 2 58S 110 46 E
Kualakapuas, Indonesia 36 E4 2 55S 114 20 E
Kualakurun, Indonesia 36 E4 1 10S 113 50 E
Kualapembuang, Indonesia 36 E4 3 14S 112 38 E
Kualasimpang, Indonesia 36 D1 4 17N 98 3 E
Kuancheng, China 35 D10 40 37N 118 30 E
Kuandang, Indonesia 37 D6 0 56N 123 1 E
Kuandian, China 35 D13 40 45N 124 45 E
Kuangchou = Guangzhou, China 33 D6 23 5N 113 10 E
Kuantan, Malaysia 39 L4 3 49N 103 20 E
Kuba = Quba, Azerbaijan 25 F8 41 21N 48 32 E
Kuban →, Russia 25 E6 45 20N 37 30 E
Kubokawa, Japan 31 H6 33 12N 133 8 E
Kucha Gompa, India 43 B7 34 25N 76 56 E
Kuchaman, India 42 F6 27 13N 74 47 E
Kuchinda, India 43 J11 21 44N 84 21 E
Kuching, Malaysia 36 D4 1 33N 110 25 E
Kuchino-eruba-Jima, Japan 31 J5 30 28N 130 12 E
Kuchino-Shima, Japan 31 K4 29 57N 129 55 E
Kuchinotsu, Japan 31 H5 32 36N 130 11 E
Kucing = Kuching, Malaysia 36 D4 1 33N 110 25 E
Kud →, Pakistan 42 F2 26 5N 66 20 E
Kuda, India 40 H7 23 10N 71 15 E
Kudat, Malaysia 36 C5 6 55N 116 55 E
Kudus, Indonesia 37 G14 6 48S 110 51 E
Kudymkar, Russia 24 C9 59 1N 54 39 E
Kueiyang = Guiyang, China 32 D5 26 32N 106 40 E
Kufra Oasis = Al Kufrah, Libya 51 D10 24 17N 23 15 E
Kufstein, Austria 16 E7 47 35N 12 11 E
Kugluktuk, Canada 68 B8 67 50N 115 5W
Kugong I., Canada 70 A4 56 18N 79 50W
Kūhak, Iran 40 F3 27 12N 63 10 E
Kuhan, Pakistan 42 E2 28 19N 67 14 E
Kūhbonān, Iran 45 D8 31 23N 56 19 E
Kūhestak, Iran 45 E8 26 47N 57 2 E
Kuhin, Iran 45 B6 36 22N 49 40 E
Kūhīrī, Iran 45 E9 26 55N 61 2 E
Kūhpāyeh, Eşfahan, Iran 45 C7 32 44N 52 20 E
Kūhpāyeh, Kermān, Iran 45 D8 30 35N 57 15 E
Kūhrān, Kūh-e, Iran 45 E8 26 46N 58 12 E
Kui Buri, Thailand 39 F2 12 3N 99 52 E
Kuito, Angola 53 G3 12 22S 16 55 E
Kuiu I., U.S.A. 72 B2 57 45N 134 10W
Kujang, N. Korea 35 E14 39 57N 126 1 E
Kuji, Japan 30 D10 40 11N 141 46 E
Kujū-San, Japan 31 H5 33 5N 131 15 E
Kukësi, Albania 21 C9 42 5N 20 27 E
Kukup, Malaysia 39 M4 1 20N 103 27 E
Kula, Turkey 21 E13 38 32N 28 40 E
Kulachi, Pakistan 42 D4 31 56N 70 27 E
Kulai, Malaysia 39 M4 1 44N 103 35 E
Kulal, Mt., Kenya 54 B4 2 42N 36 57 E
Kulasekarappattinam, India 40 Q11 8 20N 78 5 E
Kuldīga, Latvia 9 H19 56 58N 21 59 E
Kuldja = Yining, China 26 E9 43 58N 81 10 E
Kulen, Cambodia 38 F5 13 50N 104 40 E
Kulgam, India 43 C6 33 36N 75 2 E
Kulgera, Australia 62 D1 25 50S 133 18 E
Kulim, Malaysia 39 K3 5 22N 100 34 E
Kulin, Australia 61 F2 32 40S 118 2 E
Kŭlob, Tajikistan 26 F7 37 55N 69 50 E
Kulsary, Kazakstan 25 E9 46 59N 54 1 E
Kulti, India 43 H12 23 43N 86 50 E
Kulu, India 42 D7 31 58N 77 6 E
Kulumbura, Australia 60 B4 13 55S 126 35 E
Kulunda, Russia 26 D8 52 35N 78 57 E
Kulungar, Afghan. 42 C3 34 0N 69 2 E
Kūlvand, Iran 45 D7 31 21N 54 35 E
Kulwin, Australia 63 F3 35 0S 142 42 E
Kulyab = Kŭlob, Tajikistan 26 F7 37 55N 69 50 E
Kuma →, Russia 25 F8 44 55N 47 0 E
Kumagaya, Japan 31 F9 36 9N 139 22 E
Kumai, Indonesia 36 E4 2 44S 111 43 E
Kumamba, Kepulauan, Indonesia 37 E9 1 36S 138 45 E
Kumamoto, Japan 31 H5 32 45N 130 45 E
Kumamoto □, Japan 31 H5 32 55N 130 55 E
Kumanovo, Macedonia 21 C9 42 9N 21 42 E
Kumara, N.Z. 59 K3 42 37S 171 12 E
Kumarina, Australia 61 D2 24 41S 119 32 E
Kumasi, Ghana 50 G5 6 41N 1 38W
Kumayri = Gyumri, Armenia 25 F7 40 47N 43 50 E
Kumba, Cameroon 52 D1 4 36N 9 24 E
Kumbakonam, India 40 P11 10 58N 79 25 E
Kumbarilla, Australia 63 D5 27 15S 150 55 E
Kumbhraj, India 42 G7 24 22N 77 3 E
Kumbia, Australia 63 D5 26 41S 151 39 E
Kŭmch'ŏn, N. Korea 35 E14 38 10N 126 29 E
Kumdok, India 43 C8 33 32N 78 10 E
Kume-Shima, Japan 31 L3 26 20N 126 47 E
Kumertau, Russia 24 D10 52 45N 55 57 E
Kumharsain, India 42 D7 31 19N 77 27 E
Kŭmhwa, S. Korea 35 E14 38 17N 127 28 E
Kumi, Uganda 54 B3 1 30N 33 58 E
Kumla, Sweden 9 G16 59 8N 15 10 E
Kumo, Nigeria 51 F8 10 1N 11 12 E
Kumon Bum, Burma 41 F20 26 30N 97 15 E
Kunashir, Ostrov, Russia 27 E15 44 0N 146 0 E
Kunda, Estonia 9 G22 59 30N 26 34 E
Kunda, India 43 G9 25 43N 81 31 E
Kundar →, Pakistan 42 D3 31 56N 69 19 E
Kundian, Pakistan 42 C4 32 27N 71 28 E
Kundla, India 42 J4 21 21N 71 25 E
Kunga →, Bangla. 43 J13 21 46N 89 30 E
Kunghit I., Canada 72 C2 52 6N 131 3W
Kungrad = Qŭnghirot, Uzbekistan 26 E6 43 6N 58 54 E
Kungsbacka, Sweden 9 H15 57 30N 12 5 E
Kungur, Russia 24 C10 57 25N 56 57 E
Kunhar →, Pakistan 43 B5 34 20N 73 30 E
Kuningan, Indonesia 37 G13 6 59S 108 29 E
Kunlong, Burma 41 H21 23 20N 98 50 E
Kunlun Shan, Asia 32 C3 36 0N 86 30 E
Kunming, China 32 D5 25 1N 102 41 E
Kunsan, S. Korea 35 G14 35 59N 126 45 E
Kununurra, Australia 60 C4 15 40S 128 50 E
Kunwari →, India 43 F8 26 26N 79 11 E
Kunya-Urgench = Köneürgench, Turkmenistan 26 E6 42 19N 59 10 E
Kuopio, Finland 8 E22 62 53N 27 35 E
Kupa →, Croatia 16 F9 45 28N 16 24 E
Kupang, Indonesia 37 F6 10 19S 123 39 E
Kupreanof I., U.S.A. 72 B2 56 50N 133 30W
Kupyansk-Uzlovoi, Ukraine 25 E6 49 40N 37 43 E
Kuqa, China 32 B3 41 35N 82 30 E
Kür →, Azerbaijan 25 G8 39 29N 49 15 E
Kür Dili, Azerbaijan 45 B6 39 3N 49 13 E
Kura = Kür →, Azerbaijan 25 G8 39 29N 49 15 E
Kuranda, Australia 62 B4 16 48S 145 35 E
Kuranga, India 42 H3 22 4N 69 10 E
Kurashiki, Japan 31 G6 34 40N 133 50 E
Kurayoshi, Japan 31 G6 35 26N 133 50 E
Kŭrdzhali, Bulgaria 21 D11 41 38N 25 21 E
Kure, Japan 31 G6 34 14N 132 32 E
Kuressaare, Estonia 9 G20 58 15N 22 30 E
Kurgan, Russia 26 D7 55 26N 65 18 E
Kuri, India 42 F4 26 37N 70 43 E
Kuria Maria Is. = Khurīyā Murīyā, Jazā 'ir, Oman 46 D6 17 30N 55 58 E
Kuridala, Australia 62 C3 21 16S 140 29 E
Kurigram, Bangla. 41 G16 25 49N 89 39 E
Kurikka, Finland 9 E20 62 36N 22 24 E
Kuril Is. = Kurilskiye Ostrova, Russia 27 E16 45 0N 150 0 E
Kuril Trench, Pac. Oc. 28 E19 44 0N 153 0 E
Kurilsk, Russia 27 E15 45 14N 147 53 E
Kurilskiye Ostrova, Russia 27 E16 45 0N 150 0 E
Kurino, Japan 31 J5 31 57N 130 43 E
Kurinskaya Kosa = Kür Dili, Azerbaijan 45 B6 39 3N 49 13 E
Kurnool, India 40 M11 15 45N 78 0 E
Kuro-Shima, Kagoshima, Japan 31 J4 30 50N 129 57 E
Kuro-Shima, Okinawa, Japan 31 M2 24 14N 124 1 E
Kurow, N.Z. 59 L3 44 44S 170 29 E
Kurram →, Pakistan 42 C4 32 36N 71 20 E
Kurri Kurri, Australia 63 E5 32 50S 151 28 E
Kurrimine, Australia 62 B4 17 47S 146 6 E
Kurshskiy Zaliv, Russia 9 J19 55 9N 21 6 E
Kursk, Russia 24 D6 51 42N 36 11 E
Kuruçay, Turkey 44 B3 39 39N 38 29 E
Kuruktag, China 32 B3 41 0N 89 0 E
Kuruman, S. Africa 56 D3 27 28S 23 28 E
Kuruman →, S. Africa 56 D3 26 56S 20 39 E
Kurume, Japan 31 H5 33 15N 130 30 E
Kurunegala, Sri Lanka 40 R12 7 30N 80 23 E
Kurya, Russia 24 B10 61 42N 57 9 E
Kus Gölü, Turkey 21 D12 40 10N 27 55 E
Kuşadası, Turkey 21 F12 37 52N 27 15 E
Kusatsu, Japan 31 F9 36 37N 138 36 E
Kusawa L., Canada 72 A1 60 20N 136 13W
Kushalgarh, India 42 H6 23 10N 74 27 E
Kushikino, Japan 31 J5 31 44N 130 16 E
Kushima, Japan 31 J5 31 29N 131 14 E
Kushimoto, Japan 31 H7 33 28N 135 47 E
Kushiro, Japan 30 C12 43 0N 144 25 E
Kushiro-Gawa →, Japan 30 C12 42 59N 144 23 E
Kūshk, Iran 45 D8 28 46N 56 51 E
Kushka = Gushgy, Turkmenistan 26 F7 35 20N 62 18 E
Kūshkī, Iran 44 C5 33 31N 47 13 E
Kushol, India 43 C7 33 40N 76 36 E
Kushtia, Bangla. 41 H16 23 55N 89 5 E
Kushva, Russia 24 C10 58 18N 59 45 E
Kuskokwim B., U.S.A. 68 C3 59 45N 162 25W
Kusmi, India 43 H10 23 17N 83 55 E
Kussharo-Ko, Japan 30 C12 43 38N 144 21 E
Kustanay = Qostanay, Kazakstan 26 D7 53 10N 63 35 E
Kut, Ko, Thailand 39 G4 11 40N 102 35 E
Kütahya, Turkey 25 G5 39 30N 30 2 E
Kutaisi, Georgia 25 F7 42 19N 42 40 E
Kutaraja = Banda Aceh, Indonesia 36 C1 5 35N 95 20 E
Kutch, Gulf of = Kachchh, Gulf of, India 42 H3 22 50N 69 15 E
Kutch, Rann of = Kachchh, Rann of, India 42 H4 24 0N 70 0 E
Kutiyana, India 42 J4 21 36N 70 2 E
Kutno, Poland 17 B10 52 15N 19 23 E
Kutu, Dem. Rep. of the Congo 52 E3 2 40S 18 11 E
Kutum, Sudan 51 F10 14 10N 24 40 E
Kuujjuaq, Canada 69 C13 58 6N 68 15W
Kuujjuarapik, Canada 70 A4 55 20N 77 35W
Kuŭp-tong, N. Korea 35 D14 40 45N 126 1 E
Kuusamo, Finland 8 D23 65 57N 29 8 E
Kuusankoski, Finland 9 F22 60 55N 26 38 E
Kuvango, Angola 53 G3 14 28S 16 20 E
Kuwait = Al Kuwayt, Kuwait 44 D5 29 30N 48 0 E
Kuwait ■, Asia 44 D5 29 30N 47 30 E
Kuwana, Japan 31 G8 35 5N 136 43 E
Kuwana →, India 43 F10 26 25N 83 15 E
Kuybyshev = Samara, Russia 24 D9 53 8N 50 6 E
Kuybyshev, Russia 26 D8 55 27N 78 19 E
Kuybyshevskoye Vdkhr., Russia 24 C8 55 2N 49 30 E
Kuye He →, China 34 E6 38 23N 110 46 E
Kūyeh, Iran 44 B5 38 45N 47 57 E
Kūysanjaq, Iraq 44 B5 36 5N 44 38 E
Kuyto, Ozero, Russia 24 B5 65 6N 31 20 E
Kuyumba, Russia 27 C10 60 58N 96 59 E
Kuzey Anadolu Dağlan, Turkey 25 F6 41 30N 35 0 E
Kuznetsk, Russia 24 D8 53 12N 46 40 E
Kuzomen, Russia 24 A6 66 22N 36 50 E
Kvænangen, Norway 8 A19 70 5N 21 15 E
Kvaløy, Norway 8 B18 69 40N 18 30 E
Kvarner, Croatia 16 F8 44 50N 14 10 E
Kvarnerič, Croatia 16 F8 44 43N 14 37 E
Kwa-Nobuhle, S. Africa 53 L5 33 50S 25 22 E
Kwabhaca, S. Africa 57 E4 30 51S 29 0 E
Kwakhanai, Botswana 56 C3 21 39S 21 16 E
Kwakoegron, Surinam 93 B7 5 12N 55 25W
Kwale, Kenya 54 C4 4 15S 39 31 E
KwaMashu, S. Africa 57 D5 29 45S 30 58 E
Kwando →, Africa 56 B3 18 27S 23 32 E
Kwangdaeri, N. Korea 35 D14 40 31N 127 32 E
Kwangju, S. Korea 35 G14 35 9N 126 54 E
Kwango →, Dem. Rep. of the Congo 52 E3 3 14S 17 22 E
Kwangsi-Chuang = Guangxi Zhuangzu Zizhiqu □, China 33 D5 24 0N 109 0 E
Kwangtung = Guangdong □, China 33 D6 23 0N 113 0 E
Kwataboahegan →, Canada 70 B3 51 9N 80 50W
Kwatisore, Indonesia 37 E8 3 18S 134 50 E
KwaZulu Natal □, S. Africa 57 D5 29 0S 30 0 E
Kweichow = Guizhou □, China 32 D5 27 0N 107 0 E
Kwekwe, Zimbabwe 55 F2 18 58S 29 48 E
Kwidzyn, Poland 17 B10 53 44N 18 55 E
Kwinana New Town, Australia 61 F2 32 15S 115 47 E
Kwoka, Indonesia 37 E8 0 31S 132 27 E
Kyabra Cr. →, Australia 63 D3 25 36S 142 55 E
Kyabram, Australia 63 F4 36 19S 145 4 E
Kyaikto, Burma 38 D1 17 20N 97 3 E
Kyakhta, Russia 27 D11 50 30N 106 25 E
Kyancutta, Australia 63 E2 33 8S 135 33 E
Kyangin, Burma 41 K19 18 20N 95 20 E
Kyaukpadaung, Burma 41 J19 20 52N 95 8 E
Kyaukpyu, Burma 41 K18 19 28N 93 30 E
Kyaukse, Burma 41 J20 21 36N 96 10 E
Kyburz, U.S.A. 84 G6 38 47N 120 18W
Kyelang, India 42 C7 32 35N 77 2 E
Kyenjojo, Uganda 54 B3 0 40N 30 37 E
Kyle, Canada 73 C7 50 50N 108 2W
Kyle Dam, Zimbabwe 55 G3 20 15S 31 0 E
Kyle of Lochalsh, U.K. 12 D3 57 17N 5 44W
Kymijoki →, Finland 9 F22 60 30N 26 55 E
Kyneton, Australia 63 F3 37 10S 144 29 E
Kynuna, Australia 62 C3 21 37S 141 55 E
Kyō-ga-Saki, Japan 31 G7 35 45N 135 15 E
Kyoga, L., Uganda 54 B3 1 35N 33 0 E
Kyogle, Australia 63 D5 28 40S 153 0 E
Kyongju, S. Korea 35 G15 35 51N 129 14 E
Kyongpyaw, Burma 41 L19 17 12N 95 10 E
Kyŏngsŏng, N. Korea 35 D15 41 35N 129 36 E
Kyōto, Japan 31 G7 35 0N 135 45 E
Kyōto □, Japan 31 G7 35 15N 135 45 E
Kyparissovouno, Cyprus 23 D12 35 19N 33 10 E
Kyperounda, Cyprus 23 E11 34 56N 32 58 E
Kyrenia, Cyprus 23 D12 35 20N 33 20 E
Kyrgyzstan ■, Asia 26 E8 42 0N 75 0 E
Kyrönjoki →, Finland 8 E19 63 14N 21 45 E
Kystatyam, Russia 27 C13 67 20N 123 10 E
Kythréa, Cyprus 23 D12 35 15N 33 29 E
Kyunhla, Burma 41 H19 23 25N 95 15 E
Kyuquot Sound, Canada 72 D3 50 2N 127 22W
Kyūshū, Japan 31 H5 33 0N 131 0 E
Kyūshū □, Japan 31 H5 33 0N 131 0 E
Kyūshū-Sanchi, Japan 31 H5 32 35N 131 17 E

Kyustendil, Bulgaria 21 C10 42 16N 22 41 E
Kyusyur, Russia 27 B13 70 19N 127 30 E
Kyyiv, Ukraine 17 C16 50 30N 30 28 E
Kyyivske Vdskh., Ukraine 17 C16 51 0N 30 25 E
Kyzyl, Russia 27 D10 51 50N 94 30 E
Kyzyl Kum, Uzbekistan 26 E7 42 30N 65 0 E
Kyzyl-Kyya, Kyrgyzstan 26 E8 40 16N 72 8 E
Kzyl-Orda = Qyzylorda, Kazakstan 26 E7 44 48N 65 28 E

L

La Alcarria, Spain 19 B4 40 31N 2 45W
La Asunción, Venezuela 92 A6 11 2N 63 53W
La Baie, Canada 71 C5 48 19N 70 53W
La Banda, Argentina 94 B3 27 45S 64 10W
La Barca, Mexico 86 C4 20 20N 102 40W
La Barge, U.S.A. 82 E8 42 16N 110 12W
La Belle, U.S.A. 77 M5 26 46N 81 26W
La Biche →, Canada 72 B4 59 57N 123 50W
La Biche, L., Canada 72 C6 54 50N 112 5W
La Bomba, Mexico 86 A1 31 53N 115 2W
La Calera, Chile 94 C1 32 50S 71 10W
La Canal = Sa Canal, Spain 22 C7 38 51N 1 23 E
La Carlota, Argentina 94 C3 33 30S 63 20W
La Ceiba, Honduras 88 C2 15 40N 86 50W
La Chaux-de-Fonds, Switz. 18 C7 47 7N 6 50 E
La Chorrera, Panama 88 E4 8 53N 79 47W
La Cocha, Argentina 94 B2 27 50S 65 40W
La Concepción, Panama 88 E3 8 31N 82 37W
La Concordia, Mexico 87 D6 16 8N 92 38W
La Coruña = A Coruña, Spain 19 A1 43 20N 8 25W
La Crescent, U.S.A. 80 D9 43 50N 91 18W
La Crete, Canada 72 B5 58 11N 116 24W
La Crosse, Kans., U.S.A. 80 F5 38 32N 99 18W
La Crosse, Wis., U.S.A. 80 D9 43 48N 91 15W
La Cruz, Costa Rica 88 D2 11 4N 85 39W
La Cruz, Mexico 86 C3 23 55N 106 54W
La Désirade, Guadeloupe 89 C7 16 18N 61 3W
La Escondida, Mexico 86 C5 24 6N 99 55W
La Esmeralda, Paraguay 94 A3 22 16S 62 33W
La Esperanza, Cuba 88 B3 22 46N 83 44W
La Esperanza, Honduras 88 D2 14 15N 88 10W
La Estrada = A Estrada, Spain 19 A1 42 43N 8 27W
La Fayette, U.S.A. 77 H3 34 42N 85 17W
La Fé, Cuba 88 B3 22 2N 84 15W
La Follette, U.S.A. 77 G3 36 23N 84 7W
La Grande, U.S.A. 82 D4 45 20N 118 5W
La Grande →, Canada 70 B5 53 50N 79 0W
La Grande Deux, Rés., Canada 70 B4 53 40N 76 55W
La Grande Quatre, Rés., Canada 70 B5 54 0N 73 15W
La Grande Trois, Rés., Canada 70 B4 53 40N 75 10W
La Grange, Calif., U.S.A. 84 H6 37 42N 120 27W
La Grange, Ga., U.S.A. 77 J3 33 2N 85 2W
La Grange, Ky., U.S.A. 76 F3 38 25N 85 23W
La Grange, Tex., U.S.A. 81 L6 29 54N 96 52W
La Guaira, Venezuela 92 A5 10 36N 66 56W
La Habana, Cuba 88 B3 23 8N 82 22W
La Independencia, Mexico 87 D6 16 31N 91 47W
La Isabela, Dom. Rep. 89 C5 19 58N 71 2W
La Junta, U.S.A. 81 F3 37 59N 103 33W
La Laguna, Canary Is. 22 F3 28 28N 16 18W
La Libertad, Guatemala 88 C1 16 47N 90 7W
La Libertad, Mexico 86 B2 29 55N 112 41W
La Ligua, Chile 94 C1 32 30S 71 16W
La Línea de la Concepción, Spain 19 D3 36 15N 5 23W
La Loche, Canada 73 B7 56 29N 109 26W
La Louvière, Belgium 15 D4 50 27N 4 10 E
La Malbaie, Canada 71 C5 47 40N 70 10W
La Mancha, Spain 19 C4 39 10N 2 54W
La Martre, L., Canada 72 A5 63 15N 117 55W
La Mesa, U.S.A. 85 N9 32 46N 117 3W
La Misión, Mexico 86 A1 32 5N 116 50W
La Moure, U.S.A. 80 B5 46 21N 98 18W
La Negra, Chile 94 A1 23 46S 70 18W
La Oliva, Canary Is. 22 F6 28 36N 13 57W
La Orotava, Canary Is. 22 F3 28 22N 16 31W
La Oroya, Peru 92 11 32S 75 54W
La Palma, Canary Is. 22 F2 28 40N 17 50W
La Palma, Panama 88 E4 8 15N 78 0W
La Palma del Condado, Spain 19 D2 37 21N 6 38W
La Paloma, Chile 94 C1 30 35S 71 0W
La Pampa □, Argentina 94 D2 36 50S 66 0W
La Paragua, Venezuela 92 B6 6 50N 63 20W
La Paz, Entre Ríos, Argentina 94 C4 30 50S 59 45W
La Paz, San Luis, Argentina 94 C2 33 30S 67 20W
La Paz, Bolivia 92 G5 16 20S 68 10W
La Paz, Honduras 88 D2 14 20N 87 47W
La Paz, Mexico 86 C2 24 10N 110 20W
La Paz Centro, Nic. 88 D2 12 20N 86 41W
La Pedrera, Colombia 92 D5 1 18S 69 43W
La Pérade, Canada 71 C5 46 35N 72 12W
La Perouse Str., Asia 30 B11 45 40N 142 0 E
La Pesca, Mexico 87 C5 23 46N 97 47W
La Piedad, Mexico 86 C4 20 20N 102 1W
La Pine, U.S.A. 82 E3 43 40N 121 30W
La Plata, Argentina 94 D4 35 0S 57 55W
La Pocatière, Canada 71 C5 47 22N 70 2W
La Porte, Ind., U.S.A. 76 E2 41 36N 86 43W
La Porte, Tex., U.S.A. 81 L7 29 39N 95 1W
La Purísima, Mexico 86 B2 26 10N 112 4W
La Push, U.S.A. 84 C2 47 55N 124 38W
La Quiaca, Argentina 94 A2 22 5S 65 35W
La Restinga, Canary Is. 22 G2 27 38N 17 59W
La Rioja, Argentina 94 B2 29 20S 67 0W
La Rioja □, Argentina 94 B2 29 30S 67 0W
La Rioja □, Spain 19 A4 42 20N 2 20W
La Robla, Spain 19 A3 42 50N 5 41W
La Roche-en-Ardenne, Belgium 15 D5 50 11N 5 35 E
La Roche-sur-Yon, France 18 C3 46 40N 1 25W
La Rochelle, France 18 C3 46 10N 1 9W
La Roda, Spain 19 C4 39 13N 2 15W
La Romana, Dom. Rep. 89 C6 18 27N 68 57W
La Ronge, Canada 73 B7 55 5N 105 20W
La Rumorosa, Mexico 85 N10 32 33N 116 4W
La Sabina = Sa Savina, Spain 22 C7 38 44N 1 25 E
La Salle, U.S.A. 80 E10 41 20N 89 6W
La Santa, Canary Is. 22 E6 29 5N 13 40W
La Sarre, Canada 70 C4 48 45N 79 15W
La Scie, Canada 71 C8 49 57N 55 36W
La Selva Beach, U.S.A. 84 J5 36 56N 121 51W
La Serena, Chile 94 B1 29 55S 71 10W
La Seu d'Urgell, Spain 19 A6 42 22N 1 23 E
La Seyne-sur-Mer, France 18 E6 43 7N 5 52 E
La Soufrière, St. Vincent 89 D7 13 20N 61 11W
La Spézia, Italy 18 D8 44 7N 9 50 E
La Tagua, Colombia 92 C4 0 3N 74 40W
La Tortuga, Venezuela 89 D6 11 0N 65 22W
La Tuque, Canada 70 C5 47 30N 72 50W
La Unión, Chile 96 E2 40 10S 73 0W
La Unión, El Salv. 88 D2 13 20N 87 50W
La Unión, Mexico 86 D4 17 58N 101 49W
La Urbana, Venezuela 92 B5 7 8N 66 56W
La Vall d'Uixó, Spain 19 C5 39 49N 0 15W
La Vega, Dom. Rep. 89 C5 19 20N 70 30W
La Vela de Coro, Venezuela 92 A5 11 27N 69 34W
La Venta, Mexico 87 D6 18 8N 94 3W
La Ventura, Mexico 86 C4 24 38N 100 54W
Labe = Elbe →, Europe 16 B5 53 50N 9 0 E
Labé, Guinea 50 F3 11 24N 12 16W
Laberge, L., Canada 72 A1 61 11N 135 12W
Labinsk, Russia 25 F7 44 40N 40 48 E
Labis, Malaysia 39 L4 2 22N 103 2 E
Laboulaye, Argentina 94 C3 34 10S 63 30W
Labrador, Canada 71 B7 53 20N 61 0W
Labrador City, Canada 71 B6 52 57N 66 55W
Labrador Sea, Atl. Oc. 69 C14 57 0N 54 0W
Lábrea, Brazil 92 E6 7 15S 64 51W
Labuan, Malaysia 36 C5 5 20N 115 14 E
Labuan, Pulau, Malaysia 36 C5 5 21N 115 13 E
Labuha, Indonesia 37 E7 0 30S 127 30 E
Labuhan, Indonesia 37 G11 6 22S 105 50 E
Labuhanbajo, Indonesia 37 F6 8 28S 120 1 E
Labuk, Telok, Malaysia 36 C5 6 10N 117 50 E
Labyrinth, L., Australia 63 E2 30 40S 135 11 E
Labytnangi, Russia 26 C7 66 39N 66 21 E
Lac Bouchette, Canada 71 C5 48 16N 72 11W
Lac Édouard, Canada 70 C5 47 40N 72 16W
Lac La Biche, Canada 72 C6 54 45N 111 58W
Lac la Martre = Wha Ti, Canada 68 B8 63 8N 117 16W
Lac La Ronge Prov. Park, Canada 73 B7 55 9N 104 41W
Lac-Mégantic, Canada 71 C5 45 35N 70 53W
Lac Seul, Res., Canada 70 B1 50 25N 92 30W
Lac Thien, Vietnam 38 F7 12 25N 108 11 E
Lacanau, France 18 D3 44 58N 1 5W
Lacantúm →, Mexico 87 D6 16 36N 90 40W
Laccadive Is. = Lakshadweep Is., Ind. Oc. 28 H11 10 0N 72 30 E
Lacepede B., Australia 63 F2 36 40S 139 40 E
Lacepede Is., Australia 60 C3 16 55S 122 0 E
Lacerdónia, Mozam. 55 F4 18 3S 35 35 E
Lacey, U.S.A. 84 C4 47 7N 122 49W
Lachhmangarh, India 42 F6 27 50N 75 4 E
Lachi, Pakistan 42 C4 33 25N 71 20 E
Lachine, Canada 79 A11 45 30N 73 40W
Lachlan →, Australia 63 E3 34 22S 143 55 E
Lachute, Canada 70 C5 45 39N 74 21W
Lackawanna, U.S.A. 78 D6 42 50N 78 50W
Lackawaxen, U.S.A. 79 E10 41 29N 74 59W
Lacolle, Canada 79 A11 45 5N 73 22W
Lacombe, Canada 72 C6 52 30N 113 44W
Lacona, U.S.A. 79 C8 43 39N 76 10W
Laconia, U.S.A. 79 C13 43 32N 71 28W
Ladakh Ra., India 43 C8 34 0N 78 0 E
Ladismith, S. Africa 56 E3 33 28S 21 15 E
Ladnun, India 42 F6 27 38N 74 25 E
Ladoga, L. = Ladozhskoye Ozero, Russia 24 B5 61 15N 30 30 E
Ladozhskoye Ozero, Russia 24 B5 61 15N 30 30 E
Lady Elliott I., Australia 62 C5 24 7S 152 42 E
Lady Grey, S. Africa 56 E4 30 43S 27 13 E
Ladybrand, S. Africa 56 D4 29 9S 27 29 E
Ladysmith, Canada 72 D4 49 0N 123 49W
Ladysmith, S. Africa 57 D4 28 32S 29 46 E
Ladysmith, U.S.A. 80 C9 45 28N 91 12W
Lae, Papua N. G. 64 H6 6 40S 147 2 E
Laem Ngop, Thailand 39 F4 12 10N 102 26 E
Laem Pho, Thailand 39 J3 6 55N 101 19 E
Læsø, Denmark 9 H14 57 15N 11 5 E
Lafayette, Colo., U.S.A. 80 F2 39 58N 105 12W
Lafayette, Ind., U.S.A. 76 E2 40 25N 86 54W
Lafayette, La., U.S.A. 81 K9 30 14N 92 1W
Lafayette, Tenn., U.S.A. 77 G2 36 31N 86 2W
Laferte →, Canada 72 A5 61 53N 117 44W
Lafia, Nigeria 50 G7 8 30N 8 34 E
Lafleche, Canada 73 D7 49 45N 106 40W
Lagan →, U.K. 13 B6 54 36N 5 55W
Lagarfljót →, Iceland 8 D6 65 40N 14 18W
Lågen →, Oppland, Norway 9 F14 61 8N 10 25 E
Lågen →, Vestfold, Norway 9 G14 59 3N 10 3 E
Laghouat, Algeria 50 B6 33 50N 2 59 E
Lagoa Vermelha, Brazil 95 B5 28 13S 51 32W
Lagonoy G., Phil. 37 B6 13 50N 123 50 E
Lagos, Nigeria 50 G6 6 25N 3 27 E
Lagos, Portugal 19 D1 37 5N 8 41W
Lagos de Moreno, Mexico 86 C4 21 21N 101 55W
Lagrange, Australia 60 C3 18 45S 121 43 E
Lagrange B., Australia 60 C3 18 38S 121 42 E
Laguna, Brazil 95 B6 28 30S 48 50W
Laguna, U.S.A. 83 J10 35 2N 107 25W
Laguna Beach, U.S.A. 85 M9 33 33N 117 47W
Laguna Limpia, Argentina 94 B4 26 32S 59 45W
Laguna Madre, U.S.A. 87 B5 27 0N 97 20W
Lagunas, Chile 94 A2 21 0S 69 45W
Lagunas, Peru 92 E3 5 10S 75 35W
Lahad Datu, Malaysia 37 D5 5 0N 118 20 E
Lahad Datu, Teluk, Malaysia 37 D5 4 50N 118 20 E
Lahan Sai, Thailand 38 E4 14 25N 102 52 E
Lahanam, Laos 38 D5 16 16N 105 16 E
Lahar, India 43 F8 26 12N 78 57 E
Laharpur, India 43 F9 27 43N 80 56 E
Lahat, Indonesia 36 E2 3 45S 103 30 E
Lahewa, Indonesia 36 D1 1 22N 97 12 E
Lāhījān, Iran 45 B6 37 10N 50 6 E
Lahn →, Germany 16 C4 50 19N 7 37 E
Laholm, Sweden 9 H15 56 30N 13 2 E
Lahore, Pakistan 42 D6 31 32N 74 22 E
Lahri, Pakistan 42 E3 29 11N 68 13 E
Lahti, Finland 9 F21 60 58N 25 40 E
Lahtis = Lahti, Finland 9 F21 60 58N 25 40 E
Laï, Chad 51 G9 9 25N 16 18 E
Laila = Laylá, Si. Arabia 46 C4 22 10N 46 40 E
Laingsburg, S. Africa 56 E3 33 9S 20 52 E
Lainio älv →, Sweden 8 C20 67 35N 22 40 E
Lairg, U.K. 12 C4 58 2N 4 24W
Laishui, China 34 E8 39 23N 115 45 E
Laiwu, China 35 F9 36 15N 117 40 E
Laixi, China 35 F11 36 50N 120 31 E
Laiyang, China 35 F11 36 59N 120 45 E
Laiyuan, China 34 E8 39 20N 114 40 E
Laizhou, China 35 F10 37 8N 119 57 E
Laizhou Wan, China 35 F10 37 30N 119 30 E
Laja →, Mexico 86 C4 20 55N 100 46W
Lajes, Brazil 95 B5 27 48S 50 20W
Lak Sao, Laos 38 C5 18 11N 104 59 E
Lakaband, Pakistan 42 D3 31 2N 69 15 E
Lake Alpine, U.S.A. 84 G7 38 29N 120 0W
Lake Andes, U.S.A. 80 D5 43 9N 98 32W
Lake Arthur, U.S.A. 81 K8 30 5N 92 41W
Lake Cargelligo, Australia 63 E4 33 15S 146 22 E
Lake Charles, U.S.A. 81 K8 30 14N 93 13W
Lake City, Colo., U.S.A. 83 G10 38 2N 107 19W
Lake City, Fla., U.S.A. 77 K4 30 11N 82 38W
Lake City, Mich., U.S.A. 76 C3 44 20N 85 13W
Lake City, Minn., U.S.A. 80 C8 44 27N 92 16W
Lake City, Pa., U.S.A. 78 D4 42 1N 80 21W
Lake City, S.C., U.S.A. 77 J6 33 52N 79 45W
Lake Cowichan, Canada 72 D4 48 49N 124 3W
Lake District, U.K. 10 C4 54 35N 3 20 E
Lake Elsinore, U.S.A. 85 M9 33 38N 117 20W
Lake George, U.S.A. 79 C11 43 26N 73 43W
Lake Grace, Australia 61 F2 33 7S 118 28 E
Lake Harbour = Kimmirut, Canada 69 B13 62 50N 69 50W
Lake Havasu City, U.S.A. 85 L12 34 27N 114 22W
Lake Hughes, U.S.A. 85 L8 34 41N 118 26W
Lake Isabella, U.S.A. 85 K8 35 38N 118 28W
Lake Jackson, U.S.A. 81 L7 29 3N 95 27W
Lake Junction, U.S.A. 82 D8 44 35N 110 28W
Lake King, Australia 61 F2 33 5S 119 45 E
Lake Lenore, Canada 73 C8 52 24N 104 59W
Lake Louise, Canada 72 C5 51 30N 116 10W
Lake Mead National Recreation Area, U.S.A. 85 K12 36 15N 114 30W
Lake Mills, U.S.A. 80 D8 43 25N 93 32W
Lake Placid, U.S.A. 79 B11 44 17N 73 59W
Lake Pleasant, U.S.A. 79 C10 43 28N 74 25W
Lake Providence, U.S.A. 81 J9 32 48N 91 10W
Lake St. Peter, Canada 78 A6 45 18N 78 2W
Lake Superior Prov. Park, Canada 70 C3 47 45N 84 45W
Lake Village, U.S.A. 81 J9 33 20N 91 17W
Lake Wales, U.S.A. 77 M5 27 54N 81 35W
Lake Worth, U.S.A. 77 M5 26 37N 80 3W
Lakefield, Canada 78 B6 44 25N 78 16W
Lakehurst, U.S.A. 79 F10 40 1N 74 19W
Lakeland, Australia 62 B3 15 49S 144 57 E
Lakeland, U.S.A. 77 M5 28 3N 81 57W
Lakemba, Fiji 59 D9 18 13S 178 47W
Lakeport, Calif., U.S.A. 84 F4 39 3N 122 55W
Lakeport, Mich., U.S.A. 78 C2 43 7N 82 30W
Lakes Entrance, Australia 63 F4 37 50S 148 0 E
Lakeside, Ariz., U.S.A. 83 J9 34 9N 109 58W
Lakeside, Calif., U.S.A. 85 N10 32 52N 116 55W
Lakeside, Nebr., U.S.A. 80 D3 42 3N 102 26W
Lakeside, Ohio, U.S.A. 78 E2 41 32N 82 46W
Lakeview, U.S.A. 82 E3 42 11N 120 21W
Lakeville, U.S.A. 80 C8 44 39N 93 14W
Lakewood, Colo., U.S.A. 80 F2 39 44N 105 5W
Lakewood, N.J., U.S.A. 79 F10 40 6N 74 13W
Lakewood, N.Y., U.S.A. 78 D5 42 6N 79 19W
Lakewood, Ohio, U.S.A. 78 E3 41 29N 81 48W
Lakewood, Wash., U.S.A. 84 C4 47 11N 122 32W
Lakha, India 42 F4 26 9N 70 54 E
Lakhaniá, Greece 23 D9 35 58N 27 54 E
Lakhimpur, India 43 F9 27 57N 80 46 E
Lakhnadon, India 43 H8 22 36N 79 36 E
Lakhonpheng, Laos 38 E5 15 54N 105 34 E
Lakhpat, India 42 H3 23 48N 68 47 E
Lakin, U.S.A. 81 G4 37 57N 101 15W
Lakitusaki →, Canada 70 B3 54 21N 82 25W
Lakki, Pakistan 42 C4 32 36N 70 55 E
Lákkoi, Greece 23 D5 35 24N 23 57 E
Lakonikós Kólpos, Greece 21 F10 36 40N 22 40 E
Lakor, Indonesia 37 F7 8 15S 128 17 E
Lakota, Ivory C. 50 G4 5 50N 5 30W
Lakota, U.S.A. 80 A5 48 2N 98 21W
Laksar, India 42 E8 29 46N 78 3 E
Lakselfjorden, Norway 8 A22 70 45N 26 50 E
Lakselv, Norway 8 A21 70 2N 25 0 E
Lakshadweep Is., Ind. Oc. 28 H11 10 0N 72 30 E
Lakshmanpur, India 43 H10 22 58N 83 3 E
Lakshmikantapur, India 43 H13 22 5N 88 20 E
Lala Ghat, India 41 G18 24 30N 92 40 E
Lala Musa, Pakistan 42 C5 32 40N 73 57 E
Lalago, Tanzania 54 C3 3 28S 33 58 E
Lalapanzi, Zimbabwe 55 F3 19 20S 30 15 E
L'Albufera, Spain 19 C5 39 20N 0 27W
Lalganj, India 43 G11 25 52N 85 13 E
Lalgola, India 43 G13 24 25N 88 15 E
Lālī, Iran 45 C6 32 21N 49 6 E
Lalibela, Ethiopia 46 E2 12 2N 39 2 E
Lalin, China 35 B14 45 12N 127 0 E
Lalín, Spain 19 A1 42 40N 8 5W
Lalin He →, China 35 B13 45 32N 125 40 E
Lalitapur = Patan, Nepal 41 F14 27 40N 85 20 E
Lalitpur, India 43 G8 24 42N 78 28 E
Lalkua, India 43 E8 29 5N 79 31 E
Lalsot, India 42 F7 26 34N 76 20 E
Lam, Vietnam 38 B6 21 21N 106 31 E
Lam Pao Res., Thailand 38 D4 16 50N 103 15 E
Lamaing, Burma 41 M20 15 25N 97 53 E
Lamar, Colo., U.S.A. 80 F3 38 5N 102 37W
Lamar, Mo., U.S.A. 81 G7 37 30N 94 16W
Lamas, Peru 92 E3 6 28S 76 31W
Lambaréné, Gabon 52 E2 0 41S 10 12 E
Lambasa, Fiji 59 C8 16 30S 179 10 E
Lambay I., Ireland 13 C5 53 29N 6 1W
Lambert Glacier, Antarctica 5 D6 71 0S 70 0 E
Lamberts Bay, S. Africa 56 E2 32 5S 18 17 E
Lambeth, Canada 78 D3 42 54N 81 18W
Lambi Kyun, Burma 39 G2 10 50N 98 20 E
Lame Deer, U.S.A. 82 D10 45 37N 106 40W
Lamego, Portugal 19 B2 41 5N 7 52W
Lamèque, Canada 71 C7 47 45N 64 38W
Lameroo, Australia 63 F3 35 19S 140 33 E
Lamesa, U.S.A. 81 J4 32 44N 101 58W
Lamía, Greece 21 E10 38 55N 22 26 E
Lammermuir Hills, U.K. 12 F6 55 50N 2 40W
Lamoille →, U.S.A. 79 B11 44 38N 73 13W
Lamon B., Phil. 37 B6 14 30N 122 20 E
Lamont, Canada 72 C6 53 46N 112 50W
Lamont, Calif., U.S.A. 85 K8 35 15N 118 55W
Lamont, Wyo., U.S.A. 82 E10 42 13N 107 29W
Lampa, Peru 92 G4 15 22S 70 22W
Lampang, Thailand 38 C2 18 16N 99 32 E
Lampasas, U.S.A. 81 K5 31 4N 98 11W
Lampazos de Naranjo, Mexico 86 B4 27 2N 100 32W
Lampedusa, Medit. S. 20 G5 35 36N 12 40 E
Lampeter, U.K. 11 E3 52 7N 4 4W
Lampione, Medit. S. 20 G5 35 33N 12 20 E
Lampman, Canada 73 D8 49 25N 102 50W
Lampung □, Indonesia 36 F2 5 30S 104 30 E
Lamta, India 43 H9 22 8N 80 7 E
Lamu, Kenya 54 C5 2 16S 40 55 E
Lamy, U.S.A. 83 J11 35 29N 105 53W
Lan Xian, China 34 E6 38 15N 111 35 E
Lanai, U.S.A. 74 H16 20 50N 156 55W
Lanak La, India 43 B8 34 27N 79 32 E
Lanak'o Shank'ou = Lanak La, India 43 B8 34 27N 79 32 E
Lanark, Canada 79 A8 45 1N 76 22W
Lanark, U.K. 12 F5 55 40N 3 47W
Lancang Jiang →, China 32 D5 21 40N 101 10 E
Lancashire □, U.K. 10 D5 53 50N 2 48W
Lancaster, Canada 79 A10 45 10N 74 30W
Lancaster, U.K. 10 C5 54 3N 2 48W
Lancaster, Calif., U.S.A. 85 L8 34 42N 118 8W
Lancaster, Ky., U.S.A. 76 G3 37 37N 84 35W
Lancaster, N.H., U.S.A. 79 B13 44 29N 71 34W
Lancaster, N.Y., U.S.A. 78 D6 42 54N 78 40W
Lancaster, Ohio, U.S.A. 76 F4 39 43N 82 36W
Lancaster, Pa., U.S.A. 79 F8 40 2N 76 19W
Lancaster, S.C., U.S.A. 77 H5 34 43N 80 46W
Lancaster, Wis., U.S.A. 80 D9 42 51N 90 43W
Lancaster Sd., Canada 69 A11 74 13N 84 0W
Lancelin, Australia 61 F2 31 0S 115 18 E
Lanchow = Lanzhou, China 34 F2 36 1N 103 52 E
Lanciano, Italy 20 C6 42 14N 14 23 E
Lancun, China 35 F11 36 25N 120 10 E
Landeck, Austria 16 E6 47 9N 10 34 E
Lander, U.S.A. 82 E9 42 50N 108 44W
Lander →, Australia 60 D5 22 0S 132 0 E
Landes, France 18 D3 44 0N 1 0W
Landi Kotal, Pakistan 42 B4 34 7N 71 6 E
Landisburg, U.S.A. 78 F7 40 21N 77 19W
Land's End, U.K. 11 G2 50 4N 5 44W
Landsborough Cr. →, Australia 62 C3 22 28S 144 35 E
Landshut, Germany 16 D7 48 34N 12 8 E
Landskrona, Sweden 9 J15 55 53N 12 50 E
Lanesboro, U.S.A. 79 E9 41 57N 75 34W
Lanett, U.S.A. 77 J3 32 52N 85 12W
Lang Qua, Vietnam 38 A5 22 16N 104 27 E
Lang Shan, China 34 D4 41 0N 106 30 E
Lang Suan, Thailand 39 H2 9 57N 99 4 E
La'nga Co, China 41 D12 30 45N 81 15 E
Langar, Iran 45 C9 35 23N 60 25 E
Langara I., Canada 72 C2 54 14N 133 1W
Langdon, U.S.A. 80 A5 48 45N 98 22W
Langeberg, S. Africa 56 E3 33 55S 21 0 E
Langeberge, S. Africa 56 D3 28 15S 22 33 E
Langeland, Denmark 9 J14 54 56N 10 48 E
Langenburg, Canada 73 C8 50 51N 101 43W
Langholm, U.K. 12 F5 55 9N 3 0W
Langjökull, Iceland 8 D3 64 39N 20 12W
Langkawi, Pulau, Malaysia 39 J2 6 25N 99 45 E
Langklip, S. Africa 56 D3 28 12S 20 20 E
Langkon, Malaysia 36 C5 6 30N 116 40 E
Langlade, St- P. & M. 71 C8 46 50N 56 20W
Langley, Canada 84 A4 49 7N 122 39W
Langøya, Norway 8 B16 68 45N 14 50 E
Langreo, Spain 19 A3 43 18N 5 40W
Langres, France 18 C6 47 52N 5 20 E
Langres, Plateau de, France 18 C6 47 45N 5 3 E
Langsa, Indonesia 36 D1 4 30N 97 57 E
Langtry, U.S.A. 81 L4 29 49N 101 34W
Langu, Thailand 39 J2 6 53N 99 47 E
Languedoc, France 18 E5 43 58N 3 55 E
Langxiangzhen, China 34 E9 39 43N 116 8 E
Lanigan, Canada 73 C7 51 51N 105 2W
Lankao, China 34 G8 34 48N 114 50 E
Länkäran, Azerbaijan 25 G8 38 48N 48 52 E
Lannion, France 18 B2 48 46N 3 29W
L'Annonciation, Canada 70 C5 46 25N 74 55W
Lansdale, U.S.A. 79 F9 40 14N 75 17W
Lansdowne, Australia 63 E5 31 48S 152 30 E
Lansdowne, Canada 79 B8 44 24N 76 1W
Lansdowne, India 43 E8 29 50N 78 41 E
Lansdowne House, Canada 70 B2 52 14N 87 53W
L'Anse, Mich., U.S.A. 76 B1 46 42N 88 25W
L'Anse, Mich., U.S.A. 80 B10 46 45N 88 27W
L'Anse au Loup, Canada 71 B8 51 32N 56 50W
L'Anse aux Meadows, Canada 71 B8 51 36N 55 32W
Lansford, U.S.A. 79 F9 40 50N 75 53W
Lansing, U.S.A. 76 D3 42 44N 84 33W
Lanta Yai, Ko, Thailand 39 J2 7 35N 99 3 E
Lantian, China 34 G5 34 11N 109 20 E
Lanus, Argentina 94 C4 34 44S 58 27W
Lanusei, Italy 20 E3 39 52N 9 34 E
Lanzarote, Canary Is. 22 F6 29 0N 13 40W
Lanzhou, China 34 F2 36 1N 103 52 E
Lao Bao, Laos 38 D6 16 35N 106 30 E
Laoag, Phil. 37 A6 18 7N 120 34 E
Laoang, Phil. 37 B7 12 32N 125 8 E
Laoha He →, China 35 C11 43 25N 120 35 E
Laois □, Ireland 13 D4 52 57N 7 36W
Laon, France 18 B5 49 33N 3 35 E
Laona, U.S.A. 76 C1 45 34N 88 40W
Laos ■, Asia 38 D5 17 45N 105 0 E
Lapa, Brazil 95 B6 25 46S 49 44W
Lapeer, U.S.A. 76 D4 43 3N 83 19W
Lapithos, Cyprus 23 D12 35 21N 33 11 E
Lapland = Lappland, Europe 8 B21 68 7N 24 0 E
Laporte, U.S.A. 79 E8 41 25N 76 30W

Lappeenranta, Finland 9 F23 61 3N 28 12 E
Lappland, Europe 8 B21 68 7N 24 0 E
Laprida, Argentina 94 D3 37 34S 60 45W
Lapseki, Turkey 21 D12 40 20N 26 41 E
Laptev Sea, Russia 27 B13 76 0N 125 0 E
Lapua, Finland 8 E20 62 58N 23 0 E
L'Áquila, Italy 20 C5 42 22N 13 22 E
Lār, Āzarbājān-e Sharqī, Iran 44 B5 38 30N 47 52 E
Lār, Fārs, Iran 45 E7 27 40N 54 14 E
Laramie, U.S.A. 80 E2 41 19N 105 35W
Laramie →, U.S.A. 82 F11 42 13N 104 33W
Laramie Mts., U.S.A. 80 E2 42 0N 105 30W
Laranjeiras do Sul, Brazil 95 B5 25 23S 52 23W
Larantuka, Indonesia 37 F6 8 21S 122 55 E
Larat, Indonesia 37 F8 7 0S 132 0 E
Larde, Mozam. 55 F4 16 28S 39 43 E
Larder Lake, Canada 70 C4 48 5N 79 40W
Lardhos, Ákra = Líndhos, Ákra, Greece 23 C10 36 4N 28 10 E
Lardhos, Órmos, Greece 23 C10 36 4N 28 2 E
Laredo, U.S.A. 81 M5 27 30N 99 30W
Laredo Sd., Canada 72 C3 52 30N 128 53W
Largo, U.S.A. 77 M4 27 55N 82 47W
Largs, U.K. 12 F4 55 47N 4 52W
Lariang, Indonesia 37 E5 1 26S 119 17 E
Larimore, U.S.A. 80 B6 47 54N 97 38W
Lārīn, Iran 45 C7 35 55N 52 19 E
Lárisa, Greece 21 E10 39 36N 22 27 E
Larkana, Pakistan 42 F3 27 32N 68 18 E
Larnaca, Cyprus 23 E12 34 55N 33 38 E
Larnaca Bay, Cyprus 23 E12 34 53N 33 45 E
Larne, U.K. 13 B6 54 51N 5 51W
Larned, U.S.A. 80 F5 38 11N 99 6W
Larose, U.S.A. 81 L9 29 34N 90 23W
Larrimah, Australia 60 C5 15 35S 133 12 E
Larsen Ice Shelf, Antarctica 5 C17 67 0S 62 0W
Larvik, Norway 9 G14 59 4N 10 2 E
Las Animas, U.S.A. 80 F3 38 4N 103 13W
Las Anod, Somali Rep. 46 F4 8 26N 47 19 E
Las Aves, Is., W. Indies 89 C7 15 45N 63 55W
Las Brenãs, Argentina 94 B3 27 5S 61 7W
Las Cejas, Argentina 96 B4 26 53S 64 44W
Las Chimeneas, Mexico 85 N10 32 8N 116 5W
Las Cruces, U.S.A. 83 K10 32 19N 106 47W
Las Flores, Argentina 94 D4 36 10S 59 7W
Las Heras, Argentina 94 C2 32 51S 68 49W
Las Lajas, Argentina 96 D2 38 30S 70 25W
Las Lomitas, Argentina 94 A3 24 43S 60 35W
Las Palmas, Argentina 94 B4 27 8S 58 45W
Las Palmas, Canary Is. 22 F4 28 7N 15 26W
Las Palmas →, Mexico 85 N10 32 26N 116 54W
Las Piedras, Uruguay 95 C4 34 44S 56 14W
Las Pipinas, Argentina 94 D4 35 30S 57 19W
Las Plumas, Argentina 96 E3 43 40S 67 15W
Las Rosas, Argentina 94 C3 32 30S 61 35W
Las Tablas, Panama 88 E3 7 49N 80 14W
Las Termas, Argentina 94 B3 27 29S 64 52W
Las Toscas, Argentina 94 B4 28 21S 59 18W
Las Truchas, Mexico 86 D4 17 57N 102 13W
Las Varillas, Argentina 94 C3 31 50S 62 50W
Las Vegas, N. Mex., U.S.A. 83 J11 35 36N 105 13W
Las Vegas, Nev., U.S.A. 85 J11 36 10N 115 9W
Lascano, Uruguay 95 C5 33 35S 54 12W
Lashburn, Canada 73 C7 53 10N 109 40W
Lashio, Burma 41 H20 22 56N 97 45 E
Lashkar, India 42 F8 26 10N 78 10 E
Lasíthi, Greece 23 D7 35 11N 25 31 E
Lasíthi □, Greece 23 D7 35 5N 25 50 E
Lāsjerd, Iran 45 C7 35 24N 53 4 E
Lassen Pk., U.S.A. 82 F3 40 29N 121 31W
Lassen Volcanic National Park, U.S.A. 82 F3 40 30N 121 20W
Last Mountain L., Canada 73 C7 51 5N 105 14W
Lastchance Cr. →, U.S.A. 84 E5 40 2N 121 15W
Lastoursville, Gabon 52 E2 0 55S 12 38 E
Lastovo, Croatia 20 C7 42 46N 16 55 E
Lat Yao, Thailand 38 E2 15 45N 99 48 E
Latacunga, Ecuador 92 D3 0 50S 78 35W
Latakia = Al Lādhiqīyah, Syria 44 C2 35 30N 35 45 E
Latchford, Canada 70 C4 47 20N 79 50W
Latehar, India 43 H11 23 45N 84 30 E
Latham, Australia 61 E2 29 44S 116 20 E
Lathi, India 42 F4 27 43N 71 23 E
Lathrop Wells, U.S.A. 85 J10 36 39N 116 24W
Latina, Italy 20 D5 41 28N 12 52 E
Latium = Lazio □, Italy 20 C5 42 10N 12 30 E
Laton, U.S.A. 84 J7 36 26N 119 41W
Latouche Treville, C., Australia 60 C3 18 27S 121 49 E
Latrobe, Australia 62 G4 41 14S 146 30 E
Latrobe, U.S.A. 78 F5 40 19N 79 23W
Latvia ■, Europe 9 H20 56 50N 24 0 E
Lau Group, Fiji 59 C9 17 0S 178 30W
Lauchhammer, Germany 16 C7 51 29N 13 47 E
Laughlin, U.S.A. 83 J6 35 8N 114 35W
Laukaa, Finland 9 E21 62 24N 25 56 E
Launceston, Australia 62 G4 41 24S 147 8 E
Launceston, U.K. 11 G3 50 38N 4 22W
Laune →, Ireland 13 D2 52 7N 9 47W
Launglon Bok, Burma 38 F1 13 50N 97 54 E
Laura, Australia 62 B3 15 32S 144 32 E
Laurel, Miss., U.S.A. 81 K10 31 41N 89 8W
Laurel, Mont., U.S.A. 82 D9 45 40N 108 46W
Laurencekirk, U.K. 12 E6 56 50N 2 28W
Laurens, U.S.A. 77 H4 34 30N 82 1W
Laurentian Plateau, Canada 71 B6 52 0N 70 0W
Lauria, Italy 20 E6 40 2N 15 50 E
Laurie L., Canada 73 B8 56 35N 101 57W
Laurinburg, U.S.A. 77 H6 34 47N 79 28W
Laurium, U.S.A. 76 B1 47 14N 88 27W
Lausanne, Switz. 18 C7 46 32N 6 38 E
Laut, Indonesia 39 K6 4 45N 108 0 E
Laut, Pulau, Indonesia 36 E5 3 40S 116 10 E
Laut Kecil, Kepulauan, Indonesia 36 E5 4 45S 115 40 E
Lautoka, Fiji 59 C7 17 37S 177 27 E
Lavagh More, Ireland 13 B3 54 46N 8 6W
Laval, France 18 B3 48 4N 0 48W
Lavalle, Argentina 94 B2 28 15S 65 15W
Lavant Station, Canada 79 A8 45 3N 76 42W
Lāvar Meydān, Iran 45 D7 30 20N 54 30 E
Laverton, Australia 61 E3 28 44S 122 29 E
Lavras, Brazil 95 A7 21 20S 45 0W
Lávrion, Greece 21 F11 37 40N 24 4 E
Lávris, Greece 23 D6 35 25N 24 40 E
Lavumisa, Swaziland 57 D5 27 20S 31 55 E
Lawas, Malaysia 36 D5 4 55N 115 25 E
Lawele, Indonesia 37 F6 5 16S 123 3 E
Lawng Pit, Burma 41 G20 25 30N 97 25 E
Lawqah, Si. Arabia 44 D4 29 49N 42 45 E
Lawrence, N.Z. 59 L2 45 55S 169 41 E
Lawrence, Kans., U.S.A. 80 F7 38 58N 95 14W
Lawrence, Mass., U.S.A. 79 D13 42 43N 71 10W
Lawrenceburg, Ind., U.S.A. 76 F3 39 6N 84 52W
Lawrenceburg, Tenn., U.S.A. 77 H2 35 14N 87 20W
Lawrenceville, Ga., U.S.A. 77 J4 33 57N 83 59W
Lawrenceville, Pa., U.S.A. 78 E7 41 59N 77 8W
Laws, U.S.A. 84 H8 37 24N 118 20W
Lawton, U.S.A. 81 H5 34 37N 98 25W
Lawu, Indonesia 37 G14 7 40S 111 13 E
Laxford, L., U.K. 12 C3 58 24N 5 6W
Laylá, Si. Arabia 46 C4 22 10N 46 40 E
Laylān, Iraq 44 C5 35 18N 44 31 E
Layton, U.S.A. 82 F7 41 4N 111 58W
Laytonville, U.S.A. 82 G2 39 41N 123 29W
Lazio □, Italy 20 C5 42 10N 12 30 E
Lazo, Russia 30 C6 43 25N 133 55 E
Le Creusot, France 18 C6 46 48N 4 24 E
Le François, Martinique 89 D7 14 38N 60 57W
Le Havre, France 18 B4 49 30N 0 5 E
Le Mans, France 18 C4 48 0N 0 10 E
Le Mars, U.S.A. 80 D6 42 47N 96 10W
Le Mont-St-Michel, France 18 B3 48 40N 1 30W
Le Moule, Guadeloupe 89 C7 16 20N 61 22W
Le Puy-en-Velay, France 18 D5 45 3N 3 52 E
Le Sueur, U.S.A. 80 C8 44 28N 93 55W
Le Thuy, Vietnam 38 D6 17 14N 106 49 E
Le Touquet-Paris-Plage, France 18 A4 50 30N 1 36 E
Le Tréport, France 18 A4 50 3N 1 20 E
Le Verdon-sur-Mer, France 18 D3 45 33N 1 4W
Lea →, U.K. 11 F8 51 31N 0 1 E
Leach, Cambodia 39 F4 12 21N 103 46 E
Lead, U.S.A. 80 C3 44 21N 103 46W
Leader, Canada 73 C7 50 50N 109 30W
Leadville, U.S.A. 83 G10 39 15N 106 18W
Leaf →, U.S.A. 81 K10 30 59N 88 44W
Leaf Rapids, Canada 73 B9 56 30N 99 59W
Leamington, Canada 78 D2 42 3N 82 36W
Leamington, U.S.A. 82 G7 39 32N 112 17W
Leamington Spa = Royal Leamington Spa, U.K. 11 E6 52 18N 1 31W
Leandro Norte Alem, Argentina 95 B4 27 34S 55 15W
Leane, L., Ireland 13 D2 52 2N 9 32W
Learmonth, Australia 60 D1 22 13S 114 10 E
Leask, Canada 73 C7 53 5N 106 45W
Leatherhead, U.K. 11 F7 51 18N 0 20W
Leavenworth, Kans., U.S.A. 80 F7 39 19N 94 55W
Leavenworth, Wash., U.S.A. 82 C3 47 36N 120 40W
Lebak, Phil. 37 C6 6 32N 124 5 E
Lebam, U.S.A. 84 D3 46 34N 123 33W
Lebanon, Ind., U.S.A. 76 E2 40 3N 86 28W
Lebanon, Kans., U.S.A. 80 F5 39 49N 98 33W
Lebanon, Ky., U.S.A. 76 G3 37 34N 85 15W
Lebanon, Mo., U.S.A. 81 G8 37 41N 92 40W
Lebanon, N.H., U.S.A. 79 C12 43 39N 72 15W
Lebanon, Oreg., U.S.A. 82 D2 44 32N 122 55W
Lebanon, Pa., U.S.A. 79 F8 40 20N 76 26W
Lebanon, Tenn., U.S.A. 77 G2 36 12N 86 18W
Lebanon ■, Asia 47 B5 34 0N 36 0 E
Lebec, U.S.A. 85 L8 34 50N 118 52W
Lebel-sur-Quévillon, Canada 70 C4 49 3N 76 59W
Lebomboberge, S. Africa 57 C5 24 30S 32 0 E
Lębork, Poland 17 A9 54 33N 17 46 E
Lebrija, Spain 19 D2 36 53N 6 5W
Lebu, Chile 94 D1 37 40S 73 47W
Lecce, Italy 21 D8 40 23N 18 11 E
Lecco, Italy 18 D8 45 51N 9 23 E
Lech →, Germany 16 D6 48 43N 10 56 E
Lecontes Mills, U.S.A. 78 E6 41 5N 78 17W
Łęczyca, Poland 17 B10 52 5N 19 15 E
Ledong, China 38 C7 18 41N 109 5 E
Leduc, Canada 72 C6 53 15N 113 30W
Lee, U.S.A. 79 D11 42 19N 73 15W
Lee →, Ireland 13 E3 51 53N 8 56W
Lee Vining, U.S.A. 84 H7 37 58N 119 7W
Leech L., U.S.A. 80 B7 47 10N 94 24W
Leechburg, U.S.A. 78 F5 40 37N 79 36W
Leeds, U.K. 10 D6 53 48N 1 33W
Leeds, U.S.A. 77 J2 33 33N 86 33W
Leek, Neths. 15 A6 53 10N 6 24 E
Leek, U.K. 10 D5 53 7N 2 1W
Leeman, Australia 61 E1 29 57S 114 58 E
Leeper, U.S.A. 78 E5 41 22N 79 18W
Leer, Germany 16 B4 53 13N 7 26 E
Leesburg, U.S.A. 77 L5 28 49N 81 53W
Leesville, U.S.A. 81 K8 31 9N 93 16W
Leeton, Australia 63 E4 34 33S 146 23 E
Leetonia, U.S.A. 78 F4 40 53N 80 45W
Leeu Gamka, S. Africa 56 E3 32 47S 21 59 E
Leeuwarden, Neths. 15 A5 53 15N 5 48 E
Leeuwin, C., Australia 61 F2 34 20S 115 9 E
Leeward Is., Atl. Oc. 89 C7 16 30N 63 30W
Lefka, Cyprus 23 D11 35 6N 32 51 E
Lefkoniko, Cyprus 23 D12 35 18N 33 44 E
Lefroy, Canada 78 B5 44 16N 79 34W
Lefroy, L., Australia 61 F3 31 21S 121 40 E
Leganés, Spain 19 B4 40 19N 3 45W
Legazpi, Phil. 37 B6 13 10N 123 45 E
Legendre I., Australia 60 D2 20 22S 116 55 E
Leghorn = Livorno, Italy 20 C4 43 33N 10 19 E
Legionowo, Poland 17 B11 52 25N 20 50 E
Legnago, Italy 20 B4 45 11N 11 18 E
Legnica, Poland 16 C9 51 12N 16 10 E
Leh, India 43 B7 34 9N 77 35 E
Lehigh Acres, U.S.A. 77 M5 26 36N 81 39W
Lehighton, U.S.A. 79 F9 40 50N 75 43W
Lehututu, Botswana 56 C3 23 54S 21 55 E
Leiah, Pakistan 42 D4 30 58N 70 58 E
Leicester, U.K. 11 E6 52 38N 1 8W
Leicester City □, U.K. 11 E6 52 38N 1 8W
Leicestershire □, U.K. 11 E6 52 41N 1 17W
Leichhardt →, Australia 62 B2 17 35S 139 48 E
Leichhardt Ra., Australia 62 C4 20 46S 147 40 E
Leiden, Neths. 15 B4 52 9N 4 30 E
Leie →, Belgium 15 C3 51 2N 3 45 E
Leigh Creek, Australia 63 E2 30 38S 138 26 E
Leine →, Germany 16 B5 52 43N 9 36 E
Leinster, Australia 61 E3 27 51S 120 36 E
Leinster □, Ireland 13 C4 53 3N 7 8W
Leinster, Mt., Ireland 13 D5 52 37N 6 46W
Leipzig, Germany 16 C7 51 18N 12 22 E
Leiria, Portugal 19 C1 39 46N 8 53W
Leirvik, Norway 9 G11 59 47N 5 28 E
Leisler, Mt., Australia 60 D4 23 23S 129 20 E
Leith, U.K. 12 F5 55 59N 3 11W
Leith Hill, U.K. 11 F7 51 11N 0 22W
Leitrim, Ireland 13 B3 54 0N 8 5W
Leitrim □, Ireland 13 B4 54 8N 8 0W
Leizhou Bandao, China 33 D6 21 0N 110 0 E
Lek →, Neths. 15 C4 51 54N 4 35 E
Leka, Norway 8 D14 65 5N 11 35 E
Lékva Óros, Greece 23 D6 35 18N 24 3 E
Leland, Mich., U.S.A. 76 C3 45 1N 85 45W
Leland, Miss., U.S.A. 81 J9 33 24N 90 54W
Leleque, Argentina 96 E2 42 28S 71 0W
Lelystad, Neths. 15 B5 52 30N 5 25 E
Léman, L., Europe 18 C7 46 26N 6 30 E
Lemera, Dem. Rep. of the Congo 54 C2 3 0S 28 55 E
Lemhi Ra., U.S.A. 82 D7 44 30N 113 30W
Lemmer, Neths. 15 B5 52 51N 5 43 E
Lemmon, U.S.A. 80 C3 45 57N 102 10W
Lemon Grove, U.S.A. 85 N9 32 45N 117 2W
Lemoore, U.S.A. 84 J7 36 18N 119 46W
Lemvig, Denmark 9 H13 56 33N 8 20 E
Lena →, Russia 27 B13 72 52N 126 40 E
Léndas, Greece 23 E6 34 56N 24 56 E
Lendeh, Iran 45 D6 30 58N 50 25 E
Lenggong, Malaysia 39 K3 5 6N 100 58 E
Lengua de Vaca, Pta., Chile 94 C1 30 14S 71 38W
Leninabad = Khudzhand, Tajikistan 26 E7 40 17N 69 37 E
Leninakan = Gyumri, Armenia 25 F7 40 47N 43 50 E
Leningrad = Sankt-Peterburg, Russia 24 C5 59 55N 30 20 E
Leninogorsk, Kazakstan 26 D9 50 20N 83 30 E
Leninsk, Russia 25 E8 48 40N 45 15 E
Leninsk-Kuznetskiy, Russia 26 D9 54 44N 86 10 E
Lenkoran = Länkäran, Azerbaijan 25 G8 38 48N 48 52 E
Lenmalu, Indonesia 37 E8 1 45S 130 15 E
Lennox, U.S.A. 80 D6 43 21N 96 53W
Lennoxville, Canada 79 A13 45 22N 71 51W
Lenoir, U.S.A. 77 H5 35 55N 81 32W
Lenoir City, U.S.A. 77 H3 35 48N 84 16W
Lenore L., Canada 73 C8 52 30N 104 59W
Lenox, U.S.A. 79 D11 42 22N 73 17W
Lens, France 18 A5 50 26N 2 50 E
Lensk, Russia 27 C12 60 48N 114 55 E
Lentini, Italy 20 F6 37 17N 15 0 E
Lenwood, U.S.A. 85 L9 34 53N 117 7W
Lenya, Burma 36 B1 11 33N 98 57 E
Leoben, Austria 16 E8 47 22N 15 5 E
Leodhas = Lewis, U.K. 12 C2 58 9N 6 40W
Leola, U.S.A. 80 C5 45 43N 98 56W
Leominster, U.K. 11 E5 52 14N 2 43W
Leominster, U.S.A. 79 D13 42 32N 71 46W
León, Mexico 86 C4 21 7N 101 40W
León, Nic. 88 D2 12 20N 86 51W
León, Spain 19 A3 42 38N 5 34W
Leon, U.S.A. 80 E8 40 44N 93 45W
Leon →, U.S.A. 81 K6 31 14N 97 28W
León, Montes de, Spain 19 A2 42 30N 6 18W
Leonardtown, U.S.A. 76 F7 38 17N 76 38W
Leongatha, Australia 63 F4 38 30S 145 58 E
Leonora, Australia 61 E3 28 49S 121 19 E
Léopold II, Lac = Mai-Ndombe, L., Dem. Rep. of the Congo 52 E3 2 0S 18 20 E
Leopoldina, Brazil 95 A7 21 28S 42 40W
Leopoldsburg, Belgium 15 C5 51 7N 5 13 E
Léopoldville = Kinshasa, Dem. Rep. of the Congo 52 E3 4 20S 15 15 E
Leoti, U.S.A. 80 F4 38 29N 101 21W
Leova, Moldova 17 E15 46 28N 28 15 E
Leoville, Canada 73 C7 53 39N 107 33W
Lepel = Lyepyel, Belarus 24 D4 54 50N 28 40 E
Lépo, L. do, Angola 56 B2 17 0S 19 0 E
Leppävirta, Finland 9 E22 62 29N 27 46 E
Lerdo, Mexico 86 B4 25 32N 103 32W
Leribe, Lesotho 57 D4 28 51S 28 3 E
Lérida = Lleida, Spain 19 B6 41 37N 0 39 E
Lerwick, U.K. 12 A7 60 9N 1 9W
Les Cayes, Haiti 89 C5 18 15N 73 46W
Les Sables-d'Olonne, France 18 C3 46 30N 1 45W
Lesbos = Lésvos, Greece 21 E12 39 10N 26 20 E
Leshan, China 32 D5 29 33N 103 41 E
Leshukonskoye, Russia 24 B8 64 54N 45 46 E
Leskov I., Antarctica 5 B1 56 0S 28 0W
Leskovac, Serbia, Yug. 21 C9 43 0N 21 58 E
Lesopilnoye, Russia 30 A7 46 44N 134 20 E
Lesotho ■, Africa 57 D4 29 40S 28 0 E
Lesozavodsk, Russia 27 E14 45 30N 133 29 E
Lesse →, Belgium 15 D4 50 15N 4 54 E
Lesser Antilles, W. Indies 89 D7 15 0N 61 0W
Lesser Slave L., Canada 72 B5 55 30N 115 25W
Lesser Sunda Is., Indonesia 37 F6 7 0S 120 0 E
Lessines, Belgium 15 D3 50 42N 3 50 E
Lester, U.S.A. 84 C5 47 12N 121 29W
Lestock, Canada 73 C8 51 19N 103 59W
Lesuer I., Australia 60 B4 13 50S 127 17 E
Lésvos, Greece 21 E12 39 10N 26 20 E
Leszno, Poland 17 C9 51 50N 16 30 E
Letchworth, U.K. 11 F7 51 59N 0 13W
Lethbridge, Canada 72 D6 49 45N 112 45W
Lethem, Guyana 92 C7 3 20N 59 50W
Leti, Kepulauan, Indonesia 37 F7 8 10S 128 0 E
Leti Is. = Leti, Kepulauan, Indonesia 37 F7 8 10S 128 0 E
Letiahau →, Botswana 56 C3 21 16S 24 0 E
Leticia, Colombia 92 D5 4 9S 70 0W
Leting, China 35 E10 39 23N 118 55 E
Letjiesbos, S. Africa 56 E3 32 34S 22 16 E
Letlhakeng, Botswana 56 C3 24 0S 24 59 E
Letong, Indonesia 36 D3 2 58N 105 42 E
Letpadan, Burma 41 L19 17 45N 95 45 E
Letpan, Burma 41 K19 19 28N 94 10 E
Letsôk-aw Kyun, Burma 39 G2 11 30N 98 25 E
Letterkenny, Ireland 13 B4 54 57N 7 45W
Leucadia, U.S.A. 85 M9 33 4N 117 18W
Leuser, G., Indonesia 36 D1 3 46N 97 12 E
Leuven, Belgium 15 D4 50 52N 4 42 E
Leuze-en-Hainaut, Belgium 15 D3 50 36N 3 37 E
Levádhia, Greece 21 E10 38 27N 22 54 E
Levanger, Norway 8 E14 63 45N 11 19 E
Levelland, U.S.A. 81 J3 33 35N 102 23W
Leven, U.K. 12 E6 56 12N 3 0W
Leven, L., U.K. 12 E5 56 12N 3 22W
Leven, Toraka, Madag. 57 A8 12 30S 47 45 E
Leveque C., Australia 60 C3 16 20S 123 0 E
Levice, Slovak Rep. 17 D10 48 13N 18 35 E
Levin, N.Z. 59 J5 40 37S 175 18 E
Lévis, Canada 71 C5 46 48N 71 9W
Levis, L., Canada 72 A5 62 37N 117 58W
Levittown, N.Y., U.S.A. 79 F11 40 44N 73 31W
Levittown, Pa., U.S.A. 79 F10 40 9N 74 51W
Levkás, Greece 21 E9 38 40N 20 43 E
Levkímmi, Greece 23 B4 39 25N 20 3 E
Levkímmi, Ákra, Greece 23 B4 39 29N 20 4 E
Levkôsia = Nicosia, Cyprus 23 D12 35 10N 33 25 E
Levskigrad = Karlovo, Bulgaria 21 C11 42 38N 24 47 E
Lewes, U.K. 11 G8 50 52N 0 1 E
Lewes, U.S.A. 76 F8 38 46N 75 9W
Lewis, U.K. 12 C2 58 9N 6 40W
Lewis →, U.S.A. 84 E4 45 51N 122 48W
Lewis, Butt of, U.K. 12 C2 58 31N 6 16W
Lewis Ra., Australia 60 D4 20 3S 128 50 E
Lewis Range, U.S.A. 82 C7 48 5N 113 5W
Lewis Run, U.S.A. 78 E6 41 52N 78 40W
Lewisburg, Pa., U.S.A. 78 F8 40 58N 76 54W
Lewisburg, Tenn., U.S.A. 77 H2 35 27N 86 48W
Lewisburg, W. Va., U.S.A. 76 G5 37 48N 80 27W
Lewisporte, Canada 71 C8 49 15N 55 3W
Lewiston, Idaho, U.S.A. 82 C5 46 25N 117 1W
Lewiston, Maine, U.S.A. 77 C11 44 6N 70 13W
Lewiston, N.Y., U.S.A. 78 C5 43 11N 79 3W
Lewistown, Mont., U.S.A. 82 C9 47 4N 109 26W
Lewistown, Pa., U.S.A. 78 F7 40 36N 77 34W
Lexington, Ill., U.S.A. 80 E10 40 39N 88 47W
Lexington, Ky., U.S.A. 76 F3 38 3N 84 30W
Lexington, Mich., U.S.A. 78 C2 43 16N 82 32W
Lexington, Mo., U.S.A. 80 F8 39 11N 93 52W
Lexington, N.C., U.S.A. 77 H5 35 49N 80 15W
Lexington, N.Y., U.S.A. 79 D10 42 15N 74 22W
Lexington, Nebr., U.S.A. 80 E5 40 47N 99 45W
Lexington, Ohio, U.S.A. 78 F2 40 41N 82 35W
Lexington, Tenn., U.S.A. 77 H1 35 39N 88 24W
Lexington, Va., U.S.A. 76 G6 37 47N 79 27W
Lexington Park, U.S.A. 76 F7 38 16N 76 27W
Leyburn, U.K. 10 C6 54 19N 1 48W
Leyland, U.K. 10 D5 53 42N 2 43W
Leyte, Phil. 37 B7 11 0N 125 0 E
Lezha, Albania 21 D8 41 47N 19 39 E
Lhasa, China 32 D4 29 25N 90 58 E
Lhazê, China 32 D3 29 5N 87 38 E
Lhokkruet, Indonesia 36 D1 4 55N 95 24 E
Lhokseumawe, Indonesia 36 C1 5 10N 97 10 E
L'Hospitalet de Llobregat, Spain 19 B7 41 21N 2 6 E
Lhuntsi Dzong, India 41 F17 27 39N 91 10 E
Li, Thailand 38 D2 17 48N 98 57 E
Li Xian, Gansu, China 34 G3 34 10N 105 5 E
Li Xian, Hebei, China 34 E8 38 30N 115 35 E
Lianga, Phil. 37 C7 8 38N 126 6 E
Liangcheng, Nei Mongol Zizhiqu, China 34 D7 40 28N 112 25 E
Liangcheng, Shandong, China 35 G10 35 32N 119 37 E
Liangdang, China 34 H4 33 56N 106 18 E
Liangpran, Indonesia 36 D4 1 4N 114 23 E
Lianshanguan, China 35 D12 40 53N 123 43 E
Lianshui, China 35 H10 33 42N 119 20 E
Lianyungang, China 35 G10 34 40N 119 11 E
Liao He →, China 35 D11 41 0N 121 50 E
Liaocheng, China 34 F8 36 28N 115 58 E
Liaodong Bandao, China 35 E12 40 0N 122 30 E
Liaodong Wan, China 35 D11 40 20N 121 10 E
Liaoning □, China 35 D12 41 40N 122 30 E
Liaoyang, China 35 D12 41 15N 122 58 E
Liaoyuan, China 35 C13 42 58N 125 2 E
Liaozhong, China 35 D12 41 23N 122 50 E
Liard →, Canada 72 A4 61 51N 121 18W
Liard River, Canada 72 B3 59 25N 126 5W
Liari, Pakistan 42 G2 25 37N 66 30 E
Libau = Liepāja, Latvia 9 H19 56 30N 21 0 E
Libby, U.S.A. 82 B6 48 23N 115 33W
Libenge, Dem. Rep. of the Congo 52 D3 3 40N 18 55 E
Liberal, U.S.A. 81 G4 37 3N 100 55W
Liberec, Czech Rep. 16 C8 50 47N 15 7 E
Liberia, Costa Rica 88 D2 10 40N 85 30W
Liberia ■, W. Afr. 50 G4 6 30N 9 30W
Liberty, Mo., U.S.A. 80 F7 39 15N 94 25W
Liberty, N.Y., U.S.A. 79 E10 41 48N 74 45W
Liberty, Pa., U.S.A. 78 E7 41 34N 77 6W
Liberty, Tex., U.S.A. 81 K7 30 3N 94 48W
Lîbîya, Sahrâ', Africa 51 C10 25 0N 25 0 E
Libobo, Tanjung, Indonesia 37 E7 0 54S 128 28 E
Libode, S. Africa 57 E4 31 33S 29 2 E
Libourne, France 18 D3 44 55N 0 14W
Libramont, Belgium 15 E5 49 55N 5 23 E
Libreville, Gabon 52 D1 0 25N 9 26 E
Libya ■, N. Afr. 51 C9 27 0N 17 0 E
Libyan Desert = Lîbîya, Sahrâ', Africa 51 C10 25 0N 25 0 E
Licantén, Chile 94 D1 35 55S 72 0W
Licata, Italy 20 F5 37 6N 13 56 E
Licheng, China 34 F7 36 28N 113 20 E
Lichfield, U.K. 11 E6 52 41N 1 49W
Lichinga, Mozam. 55 E4 13 13S 35 11 E
Lichtenburg, S. Africa 56 D4 26 8S 26 8 E
Licking →, U.S.A. 76 F3 39 6N 84 30W
Lida, Belarus 9 K21 53 53N 25 15 E
Lidköping, Sweden 9 G15 58 31N 13 7 E
Liebig, Mt., Australia 60 D5 23 18S 131 22 E
Liechtenstein ■, Europe 18 C8 47 8N 9 35 E
Liège, Belgium 15 D5 50 38N 5 35 E
Liège □, Belgium 15 D5 50 32N 5 35 E
Liegnitz = Legnica, Poland 16 C9 51 12N 16 10 E
Lienart, Dem. Rep. of the Congo 54 B2 3 3N 25 31 E
Lienyünchiangshih = Lianyungang, China 35 G10 34 40N 119 11 E
Lienz, Austria 16 E7 46 50N 12 46 E
Liepāja, Latvia 9 H19 56 30N 21 0 E
Lier, Belgium 15 C4 51 7N 4 34 E
Lièvre →, Canada 70 C4 45 31N 75 26W
Liffey →, Ireland 13 C5 53 21N 6 13W
Lifford, Ireland 13 B4 54 51N 7 29W

Lifudzin, Russia 30 B7 44 21N 134 58 E
Lightning Ridge, Australia 63 D4 29 22S 148 0 E
Ligonier, U.S.A. 78 F5 40 15N 79 14W
Liguria □, Italy 18 D8 44 30N 8 50 E
Ligurian Sea, Medit. S. 20 C3 43 20N 9 0 E
Lihou Reefs and Cays, Australia 62 B5 17 25S 151 40 E
Lihue, U.S.A. 74 H15 21 59N 159 23W
Lijiang, China 32 D5 26 55N 100 20 E
Likasi, Dem. Rep. of the Congo 55 E2 10 55S 26 48 E
Likoma I., Malawi 55 E3 12 3S 34 45 E
Likumburu, Tanzania 55 D4 9 43S 35 8 E
Lille, France 18 A5 50 38N 3 3 E
Lille Bælt, Denmark 9 J13 55 20N 9 45 E
Lillehammer, Norway 9 F14 61 8N 10 30 E
Lillesand, Norway 9 G13 58 15N 8 23 E
Lillian Pt., Australia 61 E4 27 40S 126 6 E
Lillooet, Canada 72 C4 50 44N 121 57W
Lillooet →, Canada 72 D4 49 15N 121 57W
Lilongwe, Malawi 55 E3 14 0S 33 48 E
Liloy, Phil. 37 C6 8 4N 122 39 E
Lim →, Bos.-H. 21 C8 43 45N 19 15 E
Lima, Indonesia 37 E7 3 37S 128 4 E
Lima, Peru 92 F3 12 0S 77 0W
Lima, Mont., U.S.A. 82 D7 44 38N 112 36W
Lima, Ohio, U.S.A. 76 E3 40 44N 84 6W
Lima →, Portugal 19 B1 41 41N 8 50W
Liman, Indonesia 37 G14 7 48S 111 45 E
Limassol, Cyprus 23 E12 34 42N 33 1 E
Limavady, U.K. 13 A5 55 3N 6 56W
Limay →, Argentina 96 D3 39 0S 68 0W
Limay Mahuida, Argentina 94 D2 37 10S 66 45W
Limbang, Brunei 36 D5 4 42N 115 6 E
Limbaži, Latvia 9 H21 57 31N 24 42 E
Limbdi, India 42 H4 22 34N 71 51 E
Limbe, Cameroon 52 D1 4 1N 9 10 E
Limburg, Germany 16 C5 50 22N 8 4 E
Limburg □, Belgium 15 C5 51 2N 5 25 E
Limburg □, Neths. 15 C5 51 20N 5 55 E
Limeira, Brazil 95 A6 22 35S 47 28W
Limerick, Ireland 13 D3 52 40N 8 37W
Limerick, U.S.A. 79 C14 43 41N 70 48W
Limerick □, Ireland 13 D3 52 30N 8 50W
Limestone, U.S.A. 78 D6 42 2N 78 38W
Limestone →, Canada 73 B10 56 31N 94 7W
Limfjorden, Denmark 9 H13 56 55N 9 0 E
Limia = Lima →, Portugal 19 B1 41 41N 8 50W
Limingen, Norway 8 D15 64 48N 13 35 E
Limmen Bight, Australia 62 A2 14 40S 135 35 E
Limmen Bight →, Australia 62 B2 15 7S 135 44 E
Límnos, Greece 21 E11 39 50N 25 5 E
Limoges, Canada 79 A9 45 20N 75 16W
Limoges, France 18 D4 45 50N 1 15 E
Limón, Costa Rica 88 E3 10 0N 83 2W
Limon, U.S.A. 80 F3 39 16N 103 41W
Limousin, France 18 D4 45 30N 1 30 E
Limoux, France 18 E5 43 4N 2 12 E
Limpopo →, Africa 57 D5 25 5S 33 30 E
Limuru, Kenya 54 C4 1 2S 36 35 E
Lin Xian, China 34 F6 37 57N 110 58 E
Linares, Chile 94 D1 35 50S 71 40W
Linares, Mexico 87 C5 24 50N 99 40W
Linares, Spain 19 C4 38 10N 3 40W
Lincheng, China 34 F8 37 25N 114 30 E
Lincoln, Argentina 94 C3 34 55S 61 30W
Lincoln, N.Z. 59 K4 43 38S 172 30 E
Lincoln, U.K. 10 D7 53 14N 0 32W
Lincoln, Calif., U.S.A. 84 G5 38 54N 121 17W
Lincoln, Ill., U.S.A. 80 E10 40 9N 89 22W
Lincoln, Kans., U.S.A. 80 F5 39 3N 98 9W
Lincoln, Maine, U.S.A. 77 C11 45 22N 68 30W
Lincoln, N.H., U.S.A. 79 B13 44 3N 71 40W
Lincoln, N. Mex., U.S.A. 83 K11 33 30N 105 23W
Lincoln, Nebr., U.S.A. 80 E6 40 49N 96 41W
Lincoln City, U.S.A. 82 D1 44 57N 124 1W
Lincoln Hav = Lincoln Sea, Arctic 4 A5 84 0N 55 0W
Lincoln Sea, Arctic 4 A5 84 0N 55 0W
Lincolnshire □, U.K. 10 D7 53 14N 0 32W
Lincolnshire Wolds, U.K. 10 D7 53 26N 0 13W
Lincolnton, U.S.A. 77 H5 35 29N 81 16W
Lind, U.S.A. 82 C4 46 58N 118 37W
Linda, U.S.A. 84 F5 39 8N 121 34W
Linden, Guyana 92 B7 6 0N 58 10W
Linden, Ala., U.S.A. 77 J2 32 18N 87 48W
Linden, Calif., U.S.A. 84 G5 38 1N 121 5W
Linden, Tex., U.S.A. 81 J7 33 1N 94 22W
Lindenhurst, U.S.A. 79 F11 40 41N 73 23W
Lindesnes, Norway 9 H12 57 58N 7 3 E
Líndhos, Greece 23 C10 36 6N 28 4 E
Líndhos, Ákra, Greece 23 C10 36 4N 28 10 E
Lindi, Tanzania 55 D4 9 58S 39 38 E
Lindi □, Tanzania 55 D4 9 40S 38 30 E
Lindi →, Dem. Rep. of the Congo 54 B2 0 33N 25 5 E
Lindsay, Canada 78 B6 44 22N 78 43W
Lindsay, Calif., U.S.A. 84 J7 36 12N 119 5W
Lindsay, Okla., U.S.A. 81 H6 34 50N 97 38W
Lindsborg, U.S.A. 80 F6 38 35N 97 40W
Linesville, U.S.A. 78 E4 41 39N 80 26W
Linfen, China 34 F6 36 3N 111 30 E
Ling Xian, China 34 F9 37 22N 116 30 E
Lingao, China 38 C7 19 56N 109 42 E
Lingayen, Phil. 37 A6 16 1N 120 14 E
Lingayen G., Phil. 37 A6 16 10N 120 15 E
Lingbi, China 35 H9 33 33N 117 33 E
Lingchuan, China 34 G7 35 45N 113 12 E
Lingen, Germany 16 B4 52 31N 7 19 E
Lingga, Indonesia 36 E2 0 12S 104 37 E
Lingga, Kepulauan, Indonesia 36 E2 0 10S 104 30 E
Lingga Arch. = Lingga, Kepulauan, Indonesia 36 E2 0 10S 104 30 E
Lingle, U.S.A. 80 D2 42 8N 104 21W
Lingqiu, China 34 E8 39 28N 114 22 E
Lingshi, China 34 F6 36 48N 111 48 E
Lingshou, China 34 E8 38 20N 114 20 E
Lingshui, China 38 C8 18 27N 110 0 E
Lingtai, China 34 G4 35 0N 107 40 E
Linguère, Senegal 50 E2 15 25N 15 5W
Lingwu, China 34 E4 38 6N 106 20 E
Lingyuan, China 35 D10 41 10N 119 15 E
Linhai, China 33 D7 28 50N 121 8 E
Linhares, Brazil 93 G10 19 25S 40 4W
Linhe, China 34 D4 40 48N 107 20 E
Linjiang, China 35 D14 41 50N 127 0 E
Linköping, Sweden 9 G16 58 28N 15 36 E
Linkou, China 35 B16 45 15N 130 18 E
Linnhe, L., U.K. 12 E3 56 36N 5 25W
Linosa, I., Medit. S. 20 G5 35 51N 12 50 E
Linqi, China 34 G7 35 45N 113 52 E
Linqing, China 34 F8 36 50N 115 42 E
Linqu, China 35 F10 36 25N 118 30 E
Linru, China 34 G7 34 11N 112 52 E
Lins, Brazil 95 A6 21 40S 49 44W
Linton, Ind., U.S.A. 76 F2 39 2N 87 10W
Linton, N. Dak., U.S.A. 80 B4 46 16N 100 14W
Lintong, China 34 G5 34 20N 109 10 E
Linwood, Canada 78 C4 43 35N 80 43W
Linxi, China 35 C10 43 36N 118 2 E
Linxia, China 32 C5 35 36N 103 10 E
Linyanti →, Africa 56 B4 17 50S 25 5 E
Linyi, China 35 G10 35 5N 118 21 E
Linz, Austria 16 D8 48 18N 14 18 E
Linzhenzhen, China 34 F5 36 30N 109 59 E
Linzi, China 35 F10 36 50N 118 20 E
Lion, G. du, France 18 E6 43 10N 4 0 E
Lionárisso, Cyprus 23 D13 35 28N 34 8 E
Lions, G. of = Lion, G. du, France 18 E6 43 10N 4 0 E
Lion's Den, Zimbabwe 55 F3 17 15S 30 5 E
Lion's Head, Canada 78 B3 44 58N 81 15W
Lipa, Phil. 37 B6 13 57N 121 10 E
Lipali, Mozam. 55 F4 15 50S 35 50 E
Lipari, Italy 20 E6 38 26N 14 58 E
Lipari, Is. = Eólie, Ís., Italy 20 E6 38 30N 14 57 E
Lipcani, Moldova 17 D14 48 14N 26 48 E
Lipetsk, Russia 24 D6 52 37N 39 35 E
Lipkany = Lipcani, Moldova 17 D14 48 14N 26 48 E
Lipovcy Manzovka, Russia 30 B6 44 12N 132 26 E
Lipovets, Ukraine 17 D15 49 12N 29 1 E
Lippe →, Germany 16 C4 51 39N 6 36 E
Lipscomb, U.S.A. 81 G4 36 14N 100 16W
Liptrap C., Australia 63 F4 38 50S 145 55 E
Lira, Uganda 54 B3 2 17N 32 57 E
Liria = Lliria, Spain 19 C5 39 37N 0 35W
Lisala, Dem. Rep. of the Congo 52 D4 2 12N 21 38 E
Lisboa, Portugal 19 C1 38 42N 9 10W
Lisbon = Lisboa, Portugal 19 C1 38 42N 9 10W
Lisbon, N. Dak., U.S.A. 80 B6 46 27N 97 41W
Lisbon, N.H., U.S.A. 79 B13 44 13N 71 55W
Lisbon, Ohio, U.S.A. 78 F4 40 46N 80 46W
Lisbon Falls, U.S.A. 77 D10 44 0N 70 4W
Lisburn, U.K. 13 B5 54 31N 6 3W
Liscannor B., Ireland 13 D2 52 55N 9 24W
Lishi, China 34 F6 37 31N 111 8 E
Lishu, China 35 C13 43 20N 124 18 E
Lisianski I., Pac. Oc. 64 E10 26 2N 174 0W
Lisichansk = Lysychansk, Ukraine 25 E6 48 55N 38 30 E
Lisieux, France 18 B4 49 10N 0 12 E
Liski, Russia 25 D6 51 3N 39 30 E
Lismore, Australia 63 D5 28 44S 153 21 E
Lismore, Ireland 13 D4 52 8N 7 55W
Lista, Norway 9 G12 58 7N 6 39 E
Lister, Mt., Antarctica 5 D11 78 0S 162 0 E
Liston, Australia 63 D5 28 39S 152 6 E
Listowel, Canada 78 C4 43 44N 80 58W
Listowel, Ireland 13 D2 52 27N 9 29W
Litani →, Lebanon 47 B4 33 20N 35 15 E
Litchfield, Calif., U.S.A. 84 E6 40 24N 120 23W
Litchfield, Conn., U.S.A. 79 E11 41 45N 73 11W
Litchfield, Ill., U.S.A. 80 F10 39 11N 89 39W
Litchfield, Minn., U.S.A. 80 C7 45 8N 94 32W
Lithgow, Australia 63 E5 33 25S 150 8 E
Lithinon, Ákra, Greece 23 E6 34 55N 24 44 E
Lithuania ■, Europe 9 J20 55 30N 24 0 E
Lititz, U.S.A. 79 F8 40 9N 76 18W
Litoměřice, Czech Rep. 16 C8 50 33N 14 10 E
Little Abaco I., Bahamas 88 A4 26 50N 77 30W
Little Barrier I., N.Z. 59 G5 36 12S 175 8 E
Little Belt Mts., U.S.A. 82 C8 46 40N 110 45W
Little Blue →, U.S.A. 80 F6 39 42N 96 41W
Little Buffalo →, Canada 72 A6 61 0N 113 46W
Little Cayman, I., Cayman Is. 88 C3 19 41N 80 3W
Little Churchill →, Canada 73 B9 57 30N 95 22W
Little Colorado →, U.S.A. 83 H8 36 12N 111 48W
Little Current, Canada 70 C3 45 55N 82 0W
Little Current →, Canada 70 B3 50 57N 84 36W
Little Falls, Minn., U.S.A. 80 C7 45 59N 94 22W
Little Falls, N.Y., U.S.A. 79 C10 43 3N 74 51W
Little Fork →, U.S.A. 80 A8 48 31N 93 35W
Little Grand Rapids, Canada 73 C9 52 0N 95 29W
Little Humboldt →, U.S.A. 82 F5 41 1N 117 43W
Little Inagua I., Bahamas 89 B5 21 40N 73 50W
Little Karoo, S. Africa 56 E3 33 45S 21 0 E
Little Lake, U.S.A. 85 K9 35 56N 117 55W
Little Laut Is. = Laut Kecil, Kepulauan, Indonesia 36 E5 4 45S 115 40 E
Little-Mecatina = Petit-Mécatina →, Canada 71 B8 50 40N 59 30W
Little Minch, U.K. 12 D2 57 35N 6 45W
Little Missouri →, U.S.A. 80 B3 47 36N 102 25W
Little Ouse →, U.K. 11 E9 52 22N 1 12 E
Little Rann, India 42 H4 23 25N 71 25 E
Little Red →, U.S.A. 81 H9 35 11N 91 27W
Little River, N.Z. 59 K4 43 45S 172 49 E
Little Rock, U.S.A. 81 H8 34 45N 92 17W
Little Ruaha →, Tanzania 54 D4 7 57S 37 53 E
Little Sable Pt., U.S.A. 76 D2 43 38N 86 33W
Little Sioux →, U.S.A. 80 E6 41 48N 96 4W
Little Smoky →, Canada 72 C5 54 44N 117 11W
Little Snake →, U.S.A. 82 F9 40 27N 108 26W
Little Valley, U.S.A. 78 D6 42 15N 78 48W
Little Wabash →, U.S.A. 76 G1 37 55N 88 5W
Little White →, U.S.A. 80 D4 43 40N 100 40W
Littlefield, U.S.A. 81 J3 33 55N 102 20W
Littlehampton, U.K. 11 G7 50 49N 0 32W
Littleton, U.S.A. 79 B13 44 18N 71 46W
Liu He →, China 35 D11 40 55N 121 35 E
Liuba, China 34 H4 33 38N 106 55 E
Liugou, China 35 D10 40 57N 118 15 E
Liuhe, China 35 C13 42 17N 125 43 E
Liukang Tenggaja = Sabalana, Kepulauan, Indonesia 37 F5 6 45S 118 50 E
Liuli, Tanzania 55 E3 11 3S 34 38 E
Liuwa Plain, Zambia 53 G4 14 20S 22 30 E
Liuzhou, China 33 D5 24 22N 109 22 E
Liuzhuang, China 35 H11 33 12N 120 18 E
Livadhia, Cyprus 23 E12 34 57N 33 38 E
Live Oak, Calif., U.S.A. 84 F5 39 17N 121 40W
Live Oak, Fla., U.S.A. 77 K4 30 18N 82 59W
Liveras, Cyprus 23 D11 35 23N 32 57 E
Livermore, U.S.A. 84 H5 37 41N 121 47W
Livermore, Mt., U.S.A. 81 K2 30 38N 104 11W
Livermore Falls, U.S.A. 77 C11 44 29N 70 11W
Liverpool, Canada 71 D7 44 5N 64 41W
Liverpool, U.K. 10 D4 53 25N 3 0W
Liverpool, U.S.A. 79 C8 43 6N 76 13W
Liverpool Bay, U.K. 10 D4 53 30N 3 20W
Liverpool Plains, Australia 63 E5 31 15S 150 15 E
Liverpool Ra., Australia 63 E5 31 50S 150 30 E
Livingston, Guatemala 88 C2 15 50N 88 50W
Livingston, U.K. 12 F5 55 54N 3 30W
Livingston, Ala., U.S.A. 77 J1 32 35N 88 11W
Livingston, Calif., U.S.A. 84 H6 37 23N 120 43W
Livingston, Mont., U.S.A. 82 D8 45 40N 110 34W
Livingston, S.C., U.S.A. 77 J5 33 32N 80 53W
Livingston, Tenn., U.S.A. 77 G3 36 23N 85 19W
Livingston, Tex., U.S.A. 81 K7 30 43N 94 56W
Livingston, L., U.S.A. 81 K7 30 50N 95 10W
Livingston Manor, U.S.A. 79 E10 41 54N 74 50W
Livingstone, Zambia 55 F2 17 46S 25 52 E
Livingstone Mts., Tanzania 55 D3 9 40S 34 20 E
Livingstonia, Malawi 55 E3 10 38S 34 5 E
Livny, Russia 24 D6 52 30N 37 30 E
Livonia, Mich., U.S.A. 76 D4 42 23N 83 23W
Livonia, N.Y., U.S.A. 78 D7 42 49N 77 40W
Livorno, Italy 20 C4 43 33N 10 19 E
Livramento, Brazil 95 C4 30 55S 55 30W
Liwale, Tanzania 55 D4 9 48S 37 58 E
Lizard I., Australia 62 A4 14 42S 145 30 E
Lizard Pt., U.K. 11 H2 49 57N 5 13W
Ljubljana, Slovenia 16 E8 46 4N 14 33 E
Ljungan →, Sweden 9 E17 62 18N 17 23 E
Ljungby, Sweden 9 H15 56 49N 13 55 E
Ljusdal, Sweden 9 F17 61 46N 16 3 E
Ljusnan →, Sweden 9 F17 61 12N 17 8 E
Ljusne, Sweden 9 F17 61 13N 17 7 E
Llancanelo, Salina, Argentina 94 D2 35 40S 69 8W
Llandeilo, U.K. 11 F4 51 53N 3 59W
Llandovery, U.K. 11 F4 51 59N 3 48W
Llandrindod Wells, U.K. 11 E4 52 14N 3 22W
Llandudno, U.K. 10 D4 53 19N 3 50W
Llanelli, U.K. 11 F3 51 41N 4 10W
Llanes, Spain 19 A3 43 25N 4 50W
Llangollen, U.K. 10 E4 52 58N 3 11W
Llanidloes, U.K. 11 E4 52 27N 3 31W
Llano, U.S.A. 81 K5 30 45N 98 41W
Llano →, U.S.A. 81 K5 30 39N 98 26W
Llano Estacado, U.S.A. 81 J3 33 30N 103 0W
Llanos, S. Amer. 92 C4 5 0N 71 35W
Llanquihue, L., Chile 96 E1 41 10S 75 50W
Llanwrtyd Wells, U.K. 11 E4 52 7N 3 38W
Llebeig, C. des, Spain 22 B9 39 33N 2 18 E
Lleida, Spain 19 B6 41 37N 0 39 E
Llentrisca, C., Spain 22 C7 38 52N 1 15 E
Llera, Mexico 87 C5 23 19N 99 1W
Lleyn Peninsula, U.K. 10 E3 52 51N 4 36W
Llico, Chile 94 C1 34 46S 72 5W
Llíria, Spain 19 C5 39 37N 0 35W
Llobregat →, Spain 19 B7 41 19N 2 9 E
Lloret de Mar, Spain 19 B7 41 41N 2 53 E
Lloyd B., Australia 62 A3 12 45S 143 27 E
Lloyd L., Canada 73 B7 57 22N 108 57W
Lloydminster, Canada 73 C7 53 17N 110 0W
Llucmajor, Spain 22 B9 39 29N 2 53 E
Llullaillaco, Volcán, S. Amer. 94 A2 24 43S 68 30W
Lo →, Vietnam 38 B5 21 18N 105 25 E
Loa, U.S.A. 83 G8 38 24N 111 39W
Loa →, Chile 94 A1 21 26S 70 41W
Loaita I., S. China Sea 36 B4 10 41N 114 25 E
Loange →, Dem. Rep. of the Congo 52 E4 4 17S 20 2 E
Lobatse, Botswana 56 D4 25 12S 25 40 E
Lobería, Argentina 94 D4 38 10S 58 40W
Lobito, Angola 53 G2 12 18S 13 35 E
Lobos, Argentina 94 D4 35 10S 59 0W
Lobos, I., Mexico 86 B2 27 15N 110 30W
Lobos, I. de, Canary Is. 22 F6 28 45N 13 50W
Loc Binh, Vietnam 38 B6 21 46N 106 54 E
Loc Ninh, Vietnam 39 G6 11 50N 106 34 E
Locarno, Switz. 18 C8 46 10N 8 47 E
Loch Baghasdail = Lochboisdale, U.K. 12 D1 57 9N 7 20W
Loch Garman = Wexford, Ireland 13 D5 52 20N 6 28W
Loch Nam Madadh = Lochmaddy, U.K. 12 D1 57 36N 7 10W
Lochaber, U.K. 12 E3 56 59N 5 1W
Locharbriggs, U.K. 12 F5 55 7N 3 35W
Lochboisdale, U.K. 12 D1 57 9N 7 20W
Loche, L. La, Canada 73 B7 56 30N 109 30W
Lochem, Neths. 15 B6 52 9N 6 26 E
Loches, France 18 C4 47 7N 1 0 E
Lochgilphead, U.K. 12 E3 56 2N 5 26W
Lochinver, U.K. 12 C3 58 9N 5 14W
Lochmaddy, U.K. 12 D1 57 36N 7 10W
Lochnagar, Australia 62 C4 23 33S 145 38 E
Lochnagar, U.K. 12 E5 56 57N 3 15W
Lochy, L., U.K. 12 E4 57 0N 4 53W
Lock, Australia 63 E2 33 34S 135 46 E
Lock Haven, U.S.A. 78 E7 41 8N 77 28W
Lockeford, U.S.A. 84 G5 38 10N 121 9W
Lockeport, Canada 71 D6 43 47N 65 4W
Lockerbie, U.K. 12 F5 55 7N 3 21W
Lockhart, Australia 63 F4 35 14S 146 40 E
Lockhart, U.S.A. 81 L6 29 53N 97 40W
Lockhart, L., Australia 61 F2 33 15S 119 3 E
Lockhart River, Australia 62 A3 12 58S 143 30 E
Lockney, U.S.A. 81 H4 34 7N 101 27W
Lockport, U.S.A. 78 C6 43 10N 78 42W
Lod, Israel 47 D3 31 57N 34 54 E
Lodeinoye Pole, Russia 24 B5 60 44N 33 33 E
Lodge Bay, Canada 71 B8 52 14N 55 51W
Lodge Grass, U.S.A. 82 D10 45 19N 107 22W
Lodgepole Cr. →, U.S.A. 80 E2 41 20N 104 30W
Lodhran, Pakistan 42 E4 29 32N 71 30 E
Lodi, Italy 18 D8 45 19N 9 30 E
Lodi, Calif., U.S.A. 84 G5 38 8N 121 16W
Lodi, Ohio, U.S.A. 78 E3 41 2N 82 0W
Lodja, Dem. Rep. of the Congo 54 C1 3 30S 23 23 E
Lodwar, Kenya 54 B4 3 10N 35 40 E
Łódź, Poland 17 C10 51 45N 19 27 E
Loei, Thailand 38 D3 17 29N 101 35 E
Loengo, Dem. Rep. of the Congo 54 C2 4 48S 26 30 E
Loeriesfontein, S. Africa 56 E2 31 0S 19 26 E
Lofoten, Norway 8 B15 68 30N 14 0 E
Logan, Iowa, U.S.A. 80 E7 41 39N 95 47W
Logan, Ohio, U.S.A. 76 F4 39 32N 82 25W
Logan, Utah, U.S.A. 82 F8 41 44N 111 50W
Logan, W. Va., U.S.A. 76 G5 37 51N 81 59W
Logan, Mt., Canada 68 B5 60 31N 140 22W
Logandale, U.S.A. 85 J12 36 36N 114 29W
Logansport, Ind., U.S.A. 76 E2 40 45N 86 22W
Logansport, La., U.S.A. 81 K8 31 58N 94 0W
Logone →, Chad 51 F9 12 6N 15 2 E
Logroño, Spain 19 A4 42 28N 2 27W
Lohardaga, India 43 H11 23 27N 84 45 E
Loharia, India 42 H6 23 45N 74 14 E
Loharu, India 42 E6 28 27N 75 49 E
Lohja, Finland 9 F21 60 12N 24 5 E
Lohri Wah →, Pakistan 42 F2 27 27N 67 37 E
Loi-kaw, Burma 41 K20 19 40N 97 17 E
Loimaa, Finland 9 F20 60 50N 23 5 E
Loir →, France 18 C3 47 33N 0 32W
Loire →, France 18 C2 47 16N 2 10W
Loja, Ecuador 92 D3 3 59S 79 16W
Loja, Spain 19 D3 37 10N 4 10W
Loji = Kawasi, Indonesia 37 E7 1 38S 127 28 E
Lokandu, Dem. Rep. of the Congo 54 C2 2 30S 25 45 E
Lokeren, Belgium 15 C3 51 6N 3 59 E
Lokichokio, Kenya 54 B3 4 19N 34 13 E
Lokitaung, Kenya 54 B4 4 12N 35 48 E
Lokkan tekojärvi, Finland 8 C22 67 55N 27 35 E
Lokoja, Nigeria 50 G7 7 47N 6 45 E
Lola, Mt., U.S.A. 84 F6 39 26N 120 22W
Loliondo, Tanzania 54 C4 2 2S 35 39 E
Lolland, Denmark 9 J14 54 45N 11 30 E
Lolo, U.S.A. 82 C6 46 45N 114 5W
Lom, Bulgaria 21 C10 43 48N 23 12 E
Lom Kao, Thailand 38 D3 16 53N 101 14 E
Lom Sak, Thailand 38 D3 16 47N 101 15 E
Loma, U.S.A. 82 C8 47 56N 110 30W
Loma Linda, U.S.A. 85 L9 34 3N 117 16W
Lomami →, Dem. Rep. of the Congo 54 B1 0 46N 24 16 E
Lomas de Zamóra, Argentina 94 C4 34 45S 58 25W
Lombadina, Australia 60 C3 16 31S 122 54 E
Lombárdia □, Italy 18 D8 45 40N 9 30 E
Lombardy = Lombárdia □, Italy 18 D8 45 40N 9 30 E
Lomblen, Indonesia 37 F6 8 30S 123 32 E
Lombok, Indonesia 36 F5 8 45S 116 30 E
Lomé, Togo 50 G6 6 9N 1 20 E
Lomela, Dem. Rep. of the Congo 52 E4 2 19S 23 15 E
Lomela →, Dem. Rep. of the Congo 52 E4 0 15S 20 40 E
Lommel, Belgium 15 C5 51 14N 5 19 E
Lomond, Canada 72 C6 50 24N 112 36W
Lomond, L., U.K. 12 E4 56 8N 4 38W
Lomphat, Cambodia 38 F6 13 30N 106 59 E
Lompobatang, Indonesia 37 F5 5 24S 119 56 E
Lompoc, U.S.A. 85 L6 34 38N 120 28W
Łomża, Poland 17 B12 53 10N 22 2 E
Loncoche, Chile 96 D2 39 20S 72 50W
Londa, India 40 M9 15 30N 74 30 E
Londiani, Kenya 54 C4 0 10S 35 33 E
London, Canada 78 D3 42 59N 81 15W
London, U.K. 11 F7 51 30N 0 3W
London, Ky., U.S.A. 76 G3 37 8N 84 5W
London, Ohio, U.S.A. 76 F4 39 53N 83 27W
London, Greater □, U.K. 11 F7 51 36N 0 5W
Londonderry, U.K. 13 B4 55 0N 7 20W
Londonderry □, U.K. 13 B4 55 0N 7 20W
Londonderry, C., Australia 60 B4 13 45S 126 55 E
Londonderry, I., Chile 96 H2 55 0S 71 0W
Londres, Argentina 96 B3 27 43S 67 7W
Londrina, Brazil 95 A5 23 18S 51 10W
Lone Pine, U.S.A. 84 J8 36 36N 118 4W
Long B., U.S.A. 77 J6 33 35N 78 45W
Long Beach, Calif., U.S.A. 85 M8 33 47N 118 11W
Long Beach, N.Y., U.S.A. 79 F11 40 35N 73 39W
Long Beach, Wash., U.S.A. 84 D2 46 21N 124 3W
Long Branch, U.S.A. 79 F11 40 18N 74 0W
Long Creek, U.S.A. 82 D4 44 43N 119 6W
Long Eaton, U.K. 10 E6 52 53N 1 15W
Long I., Australia 62 C4 22 8S 149 53 E
Long I., Bahamas 89 B4 23 20N 75 10W
Long I., Canada 70 B4 54 50N 79 20W
Long I., Ireland 13 E2 51 30N 9 34W
Long I., U.S.A. 79 F11 40 45N 73 30W
Long Island Sd., U.S.A. 79 E12 41 10N 73 0W
Long L., Canada 70 C2 49 30N 86 50W
Long Lake, U.S.A. 79 C10 43 58N 74 25W
Long Point B., Canada 78 D4 42 40N 80 10W
Long Prairie →, U.S.A. 80 C7 46 20N 94 36W
Long Pt., Canada 78 D4 42 35N 80 2W
Long Range Mts., Canada 71 C8 49 30N 57 30W
Long Reef, Australia 60 B4 14 1S 125 48 E
Long Spruce, Canada 73 B10 56 24N 94 21W
Long Str. = Longa, Proliv, Russia 4 C16 70 0N 175 0 E
Long Thanh, Vietnam 39 G6 10 47N 106 57 E
Long Xian, China 34 G4 34 55N 106 55 E
Long Xuyen, Vietnam 39 G5 10 19N 105 28 E
Longa, Proliv, Russia 4 C16 70 0N 175 0 E
Longbenton, U.K. 10 B6 55 1N 1 31W
Longboat Key, U.S.A. 77 M4 27 23N 82 39W
Longde, China 34 G4 35 30N 106 20 E
Longford, Australia 62 G4 41 32S 147 3 E
Longford, Ireland 13 C4 53 43N 7 49W
Longford □, Ireland 13 C4 53 42N 7 45W
Longguan, China 34 D8 40 45N 115 30 E
Longhua, China 35 D9 41 18N 117 45 E
Longido, Tanzania 54 C4 2 43S 36 42 E
Longiram, Indonesia 36 E5 0 5S 115 45 E
Longkou, China 35 F11 37 40N 120 18 E
Longlac, Canada 70 C2 49 45N 86 25W
Longmeadow, U.S.A. 79 D12 42 3N 72 34W
Longmont, U.S.A. 80 E2 40 10N 105 6W
Longnawan, Indonesia 36 D4 1 51N 114 55 E
Longreach, Australia 62 C3 23 28S 144 14 E
Longueuil, Canada 79 A11 45 32N 73 28W
Longview, Tex., U.S.A. 81 J7 32 30N 94 44W

Longview, *Wash., U.S.A.* **84 D4** 46 8N 122 57W
Longxi, *China* **34 G3** 34 53N 104 40 E
Lonoke, *U.S.A.* **81 H9** 34 47N 91 54W
Lonquimay, *Chile* **96 D2** 38 26S 71 14W
Lons-le-Saunier, *France* **18 C6** 46 40N 5 31 E
Looe, *U.K.* **11 G3** 50 22N 4 28W
Lookout, C., *Canada* **70 A3** 55 18N 83 56W
Lookout, C., *U.S.A.* **77 H7** 34 35N 76 32W
Loolmalasin, *Tanzania* **54 C4** 3 0S 35 53 E
Loon →, *Alta., Canada* **72 B5** 57 8N 115 3W
Loon →, *Man., Canada* **73 B8** 55 53N 101 59W
Loon Lake, *Canada* **73 C7** 54 2N 109 10W
Loongana, *Australia* **61 F4** 30 52S 127 5 E
Loop Hd., *Ireland* **13 D2** 52 34N 9 56W
Lop Buri, *Thailand* **38 E3** 14 48N 100 37 E
Lop Nor = Lop Nur, *China* **32 B4** 40 20N 90 10 E
Lop Nur, *China* **32 B4** 40 20N 90 10 E
Lopatina, Gora, *Russia* **27 D15** 50 47N 143 10 E
Lopez, *U.S.A.* **79 E8** 41 27N 76 20W
Lopez, C., *Gabon* **52 E1** 0 47S 8 40 E
Lopphavet, *Norway* **8 A19** 70 27N 21 15 E
Lora →, *Afghan.* **40 D4** 31 35N 65 50 E
Lora, Hamun-i-, *Pakistan* **40 E4** 29 38N 64 58 E
Lora Cr. →, *Australia* **63 D2** 28 10S 135 22 E
Lora del Río, *Spain* **19 D3** 37 39N 5 33W
Lorain, *U.S.A.* **78 E2** 41 28N 82 11W
Loralai, *Pakistan* **42 D3** 30 20N 68 41 E
Lorca, *Spain* **19 D5** 37 41N 1 42W
Lord Howe I., *Pac. Oc.* **64 L7** 31 33S 159 6 E
Lord Howe Ridge, *Pac. Oc.* **64 L8** 30 0S 162 30 E
Lordsburg, *U.S.A.* **83 K9** 32 21N 108 43W
Lorestan □, *Iran* **45 C6** 33 30N 48 40 E
Loreto, *Brazil* **93 E9** 7 5S 45 10W
Loreto, *Mexico* **86 B2** 26 1N 111 21W
Lorient, *France* **18 C2** 47 45N 3 23W
Lormi, *India* **43 H9** 22 17N 81 41 E
Lorn, *U.K.* **12 E3** 56 26N 5 10W
Lorn, Firth of, *U.K.* **12 E3** 56 20N 5 40W
Lorne, *Australia* **63 F3** 38 33S 143 59 E
Lorovouno, *Cyprus* **23 D11** 35 8N 32 36 E
Lorraine □, *France* **18 B7** 48 53N 6 0 E
Los Alamos, *Calif., U.S.A.* **85 L6** 34 44N 120 17W
Los Alamos, *N. Mex., U.S.A.* **83 J10** 35 53N 106 19W
Los Altos, *U.S.A.* **84 H4** 37 23N 122 7W
Los Andes, *Chile* **94 C1** 32 50S 70 40W
Los Angeles, *Chile* **94 D1** 37 28S 72 23W
Los Angeles, *U.S.A.* **85 M8** 34 4N 118 15W
Los Angeles, Bahia de, *Mexico* **86 B2** 28 56N 113 34W
Los Angeles Aqueduct, *U.S.A.* **85 K9** 35 22N 118 5W
Los Banos, *U.S.A.* **84 H6** 37 4N 120 51W
Los Blancos, *Argentina* **94 A3** 23 40S 62 30W
Los Chiles, *Costa Rica* **88 D3** 11 2N 84 43W
Los Cristianos, *Canary Is.* **22 F3** 28 3N 16 42W
Los Gatos, *U.S.A.* **84 H5** 37 14N 121 59W
Los Hermanos, I., *Venezuela* **89 D7** 11 45N 64 25W
Los Islotes, *Canary Is.* **22 E6** 29 4N 13 44W
Los Llanos de Aridane, *Canary Is.* **22 F2** 28 38N 17 54W
Los Loros, *Chile* **94 B1** 27 50S 70 6W
Los Lunas, *U.S.A.* **83 J10** 34 48N 106 44W
Los Mochis, *Mexico* **86 B3** 25 45N 108 57W
Los Olivos, *U.S.A.* **85 L6** 34 40N 120 7W
Los Palacios, *Cuba* **88 B3** 22 35N 83 15W
Los Reyes, *Mexico* **86 D4** 19 34N 102 30W
Los Roques Is., *Venezuela* **89 D6** 11 50N 66 45W
Los Teques, *Venezuela* **92 A5** 10 21N 67 2W
Los Testigos, Is., *Venezuela* **92 A6** 11 23N 63 6W
Los Vilos, *Chile* **94 C1** 32 10S 71 30W
Lošinj, *Croatia* **16 F8** 44 30N 14 30 E
Lossiemouth, *U.K.* **12 D5** 57 42N 3 17W
Lostwithiel, *U.K.* **11 G3** 50 24N 4 41W
Lot →, *France* **18 D4** 44 18N 0 20 E
Lota, *Chile* **94 D1** 37 5S 73 10W
Loṭfābād, *Iran* **45 B8** 37 32N 59 20 E
Lothair, *S. Africa* **57 D5** 26 22S 30 27 E
Loubomo, *Congo* **52 E2** 4 9S 12 47 E
Loudonville, *U.S.A.* **78 F2** 40 38N 82 14W
Louga, *Senegal* **50 E2** 15 45N 16 5W
Loughborough, *U.K.* **10 E6** 52 47N 1 11W
Loughrea, *Ireland* **13 C3** 53 12N 8 33W
Loughros More B., *Ireland* **13 B3** 54 48N 8 32W
Louis Trichardt, *S. Africa* **57 C4** 23 1S 29 43 E
Louis XIV, Pte., *Canada* **70 B4** 54 37N 79 45W
Louisa, *U.S.A.* **76 F4** 38 7N 82 36W
Louisbourg, *Canada* **71 C8** 45 55N 60 0W
Louise I., *Canada* **72 C2** 52 55N 131 50W
Louiseville, *Canada* **70 C5** 46 20N 72 56W
Louisiade Arch., *Papua N. G.* **64 J7** 11 10S 153 0 E
Louisiana, *U.S.A.* **80 F9** 39 27N 91 3W
Louisiana □, *U.S.A.* **81 K9** 30 50N 92 0W
Louisville, *Ky., U.S.A.* **76 F3** 38 15N 85 46W
Louisville, *Miss., U.S.A.* **81 J10** 33 7N 89 3W
Louisville, *Ohio, U.S.A.* **78 F3** 40 50N 81 16W
Loulé, *Portugal* **19 D1** 37 9N 8 0W
Loup City, *U.S.A.* **80 E5** 41 17N 98 58W
Loups Marins, Lacs des, *Canada* **70 A5** 56 30N 73 45W
Lourdes, *France* **18 E3** 43 6N 0 3W
Lourenço-Marques = Maputo, *Mozam.* **57 D5** 25 58S 32 32 E
Louth, *Australia* **63 E4** 30 30S 145 8 E
Louth, *Ireland* **13 C5** 53 58N 6 32W
Louth, *U.K.* **10 D7** 53 22N 0 1W
Louth □, *Ireland* **13 C5** 53 56N 6 34W
Louvain = Leuven, *Belgium* **15 D4** 50 52N 4 42 E
Louwsburg, *S. Africa* **57 D5** 27 37S 31 7 E
Lovech, *Bulgaria* **21 C11** 43 8N 24 42 E
Loveland, *U.S.A.* **80 E2** 40 24N 105 5W
Lovell, *U.S.A.* **82 D9** 44 50N 108 24W
Lovelock, *U.S.A.* **82 F4** 40 11N 118 28W
Loviisa, *Finland* **9 F22** 60 28N 26 12 E
Loving, *U.S.A.* **81 J2** 32 17N 104 6W
Lovington, *U.S.A.* **81 J3** 32 57N 103 21W
Lovisa = Loviisa, *Finland* **9 F22** 60 28N 26 12 E
Low, L., *Canada* **70 B4** 52 29N 76 17W
Low Pt., *Australia* **61 F4** 32 25S 127 25 E
Low Tatra = Nízké Tatry, *Slovak Rep.* **17 D10** 48 55N 19 30 E
Lowa, *Dem. Rep. of the Congo* **54 C2** 1 25S 25 47 E
Lowa →, *Dem. Rep. of the Congo* **54 C2** 1 24S 25 51 E
Lowell, *U.S.A.* **79 D13** 42 38N 71 19W
Lowellville, *U.S.A.* **78 E4** 41 2N 80 32W
Lower Alkali L., *U.S.A.* **82 F3** 41 16N 120 2W
Lower Arrow L., *Canada* **72 D5** 49 40N 118 5W
Lower California = Baja California, *Mexico* **86 A1** 31 10N 115 12W
Lower Hutt, *N.Z.* **59 J5** 41 10S 174 55 E
Lower Lake, *U.S.A.* **84 G4** 38 55N 122 37W
Lower Manitou L., *Canada* **73 D10** 49 15N 93 0W
Lower Post, *Canada* **72 B3** 59 58N 128 30W
Lower Red L., *U.S.A.* **80 B7** 47 58N 95 0W
Lower Saxony = Niedersachsen □, *Germany* **16 B5** 52 50N 9 0 E
Lower Tunguska = Tunguska, Nizhnyaya →, *Russia* **27 C9** 65 48N 88 4 E
Lowestoft, *U.K.* **11 E9** 52 29N 1 45 E
Łowicz, *Poland* **17 B10** 52 6N 19 55 E
Lowville, *U.S.A.* **79 C9** 43 47N 75 29W
Loxton, *Australia* **63 E3** 34 28S 140 31 E
Loxton, *S. Africa* **56 E3** 31 30S 22 22 E
Loyalton, *U.S.A.* **84 F6** 39 41N 120 14W
Loyalty Is. = Loyauté, Is., *N. Cal.* **64 K8** 20 50S 166 30 E
Loyang = Luoyang, *China* **34 G7** 34 40N 112 26 E
Loyauté, Is., *N. Cal.* **64 K8** 20 50S 166 30 E
Loyev = Loyew, *Belarus* **17 C16** 51 56N 30 46 E
Loyew, *Belarus* **17 C16** 51 56N 30 46 E
Loyoro, *Uganda* **54 B3** 3 22N 34 14 E
Luachimo, *Angola* **52 F4** 7 23S 20 48 E
Luajan →, *India* **43 G11** 24 44N 85 1 E
Lualaba →, *Dem. Rep. of the Congo* **54 B2** 0 26N 25 20 E
Luampa, *Zambia* **55 F1** 15 4S 24 20 E
Luan He →, *China* **35 E10** 39 20N 119 5 E
Luan Xian, *China* **35 E10** 39 40N 118 40 E
Luancheng, *China* **34 F8** 37 53N 114 40 E
Luanda, *Angola* **52 F2** 8 50S 13 15 E
Luang, Thale, *Thailand* **39 J3** 7 30N 100 15 E
Luangwa, *Zambia* **55 F3** 15 35S 30 16 E
Luangwa →, *Zambia* **55 E3** 14 25S 30 25 E
Luangwa Valley, *Zambia* **55 E3** 13 30S 31 30 E
Luanne, *China* **35 D9** 40 55N 117 40 E
Luanping, *China* **35 D9** 40 53N 117 23 E
Luanshya, *Zambia* **55 E2** 13 3S 28 28 E
Luapula □, *Zambia* **55 E2** 11 0S 29 0 E
Luapula →, *Africa* **55 D2** 9 26S 28 33 E
Luarca, *Spain* **19 A2** 43 32N 6 32W
Luashi, *Dem. Rep. of the Congo* **55 E1** 10 50S 23 36 E
Luau, *Angola* **52 G4** 10 40S 22 10 E
Lubana, Ozero = Lubānas Ezers, *Latvia* **9 H22** 56 45N 27 0 E
Lubānas Ezers, *Latvia* **9 H22** 56 45N 27 0 E
Lubang Is., *Phil.* **37 B6** 13 50N 120 12 E
Lubango, *Angola* **53 G2** 14 55S 13 30 E
Lubbock, *U.S.A.* **81 J4** 33 35N 101 51W
Lübeck, *Germany* **16 B6** 53 52N 10 40 E
Lubefu, *Dem. Rep. of the Congo* **54 C1** 4 47S 24 27 E
Lubefu →, *Dem. Rep. of the Congo* **54 C1** 4 10S 23 0 E
Lubero = Luofu, *Dem. Rep. of the Congo* **54 C2** 0 10S 29 15 E
Lubicon L., *Canada* **72 B5** 56 23N 115 56W
Lubilash →, *Dem. Rep. of the Congo* **52 F4** 6 2S 23 45 E
Lubin, *Poland* **16 C9** 51 24N 16 11 E
Lublin, *Poland* **17 C12** 51 12N 22 38 E
Lubnān, Jabal, *Lebanon* **47 B4** 33 45N 35 40 E
Lubny, *Ukraine* **26 D4** 50 3N 32 58 E
Lubongola, *Dem. Rep. of the Congo* **54 C2** 2 35S 27 50 E
Lubudi, *Dem. Rep. of the Congo* **52 F5** 9 57S 25 58 E
Lubudi →, *Dem. Rep. of the Congo* **55 D2** 9 0S 25 35 E
Lubuklinggau, *Indonesia* **36 E2** 3 15S 102 55 E
Lubuksikaping, *Indonesia* **36 D2** 0 10N 100 15 E
Lubumbashi, *Dem. Rep. of the Congo* **55 E2** 11 40S 27 28 E
Lubunda, *Dem. Rep. of the Congo* **54 D2** 5 12S 26 41 E
Lubungu, *Zambia* **55 E2** 14 35S 26 24 E
Lubutu, *Dem. Rep. of the Congo* **54 C2** 0 45S 26 30 E
Luc An Chau, *Vietnam* **38 A5** 22 6N 104 43 E
Lucan, *Canada* **78 C3** 43 11N 81 24W
Lucania, Mt., *Canada* **68 B5** 61 1N 140 29W
Lucapa, *Angola* **52 F4** 8 25S 20 45 E
Lucas Channel, *Canada* **78 A3** 45 21N 81 45W
Lucca, *Italy* **20 C4** 43 50N 10 29 E
Luce Bay, *U.K.* **12 G4** 54 45N 4 48W
Lucea, *Jamaica* **88 C4** 18 25N 78 10W
Lucedale, *U.S.A.* **77 K1** 30 56N 88 35W
Lucena, *Phil.* **37 B6** 13 56N 121 37 E
Lucena, *Spain* **19 D3** 37 27N 4 31W
Lučenec, *Slovak Rep.* **17 D10** 48 18N 19 42 E
Lucerne = Luzern, *Switz.* **18 C8** 47 3N 8 18 E
Lucerne, *U.S.A.* **84 F4** 39 6N 122 48W
Lucerne Valley, *U.S.A.* **85 L10** 34 27N 116 57W
Lucero, *Mexico* **86 A3** 30 49N 106 30W
Lucheng, *China* **34 F7** 36 20N 113 11 E
Lucheringo →, *Mozam.* **55 E4** 11 43S 36 17 E
Lucia, *U.S.A.* **84 J5** 36 2N 121 33W
Lucinda, *Australia* **62 B4** 18 32S 146 20 E
Lucindale, *Australia* **63 F3** 36 58S 140 26 E
Luckenwalde, *Germany* **16 B7** 52 5N 13 10 E
Lucknow, *Canada* **78 C3** 43 57N 81 31W
Lucknow, *India* **43 F9** 26 50N 81 0 E
Lüda = Dalian, *China* **35 E11** 38 50N 121 40 E
Lüderitz, *Namibia* **56 D2** 26 41S 15 8 E
Ludhiana, *India* **42 D6** 30 57N 75 56 E
Ludington, *U.S.A.* **76 D2** 43 57N 86 27W
Ludlow, *U.K.* **11 E5** 52 22N 2 42W
Ludlow, *Calif., U.S.A.* **85 L10** 34 43N 116 10W
Ludlow, *Pa., U.S.A.* **78 E6** 41 43N 78 56W
Ludlow, *Vt., U.S.A.* **79 C12** 43 24N 72 42W
Ludvika, *Sweden* **9 F16** 60 8N 15 14 E
Ludwigsburg, *Germany* **16 D5** 48 53N 9 11 E
Ludwigshafen, *Germany* **16 D5** 49 29N 8 26 E
Lueki, *Dem. Rep. of the Congo* **54 C2** 3 20S 25 48 E
Luena, *Angola* **53 G3** 12 13S 19 51 E
Luena, *Dem. Rep. of the Congo* **55 D2** 9 28S 25 43 E
Luena, *Zambia* **55 E3** 10 40S 30 25 E
Lüeyang, *China* **34 H4** 33 22N 106 10 E
Lufira →, *Dem. Rep. of the Congo* **55 D2** 9 30S 27 0 E
Lufkin, *U.S.A.* **81 K7** 31 21N 94 44W
Lufupa, *Dem. Rep. of the Congo* **55 E1** 10 37S 24 56 E
Luga, *Russia* **24 C4** 58 40N 29 55 E
Lugano, *Switz.* **18 C8** 46 1N 8 57 E
Lugansk = Luhansk, *Ukraine* **25 E6** 48 38N 39 15 E
Lugard's Falls, *Kenya* **54 C4** 3 6S 38 41 E
Lugela, *Mozam.* **55 F4** 16 25S 36 43 E
Lugenda →, *Mozam.* **55 E4** 11 25S 38 33 E
Lugh Ganana, *Somali Rep.* **46 G3** 3 48N 42 34 E
Lugnaquilla, *Ireland* **13 D5** 52 58N 6 28W
Lugo, *Italy* **20 B4** 44 25N 11 54 E
Lugo, *Spain* **19 A2** 43 2N 7 35W
Lugoj, *Romania* **17 F11** 45 42N 21 57 E
Lugovoy, *Kazakstan* **26 E8** 42 55N 72 43 E
Luhansk, *Ukraine* **25 E6** 48 38N 39 15 E
Luiana, *Angola* **56 B3** 17 25S 22 59 E
Luimneach = Limerick, *Ireland* **13 D3** 52 40N 8 37W
Luing, *U.K.* **12 E3** 56 14N 5 39W
Luís Correia, *Brazil* **93 D10** 3 0S 41 35W
Luitpold Coast, *Antarctica* **5 D1** 78 30S 32 0W
Luiza, *Dem. Rep. of the Congo* **52 F4** 7 40S 22 30 E
Luizi, *Dem. Rep. of the Congo* **54 D2** 6 0S 27 25 E
Luján, *Argentina* **94 C4** 34 45S 59 5W
Lukanga Swamp, *Zambia* **55 E2** 14 30S 27 40 E
Lukenie →, *Dem. Rep. of the Congo* **52 E3** 3 0S 18 50 E
Lukhisaral, *India* **43 G12** 25 11N 86 5 E
Lukolela, *Dem. Rep. of the Congo* **54 D1** 5 23S 24 32 E
Lukosi, *Zimbabwe* **55 F2** 18 30S 26 30 E
Łuków, *Poland* **17 C12** 51 55N 22 23 E
Lule älv →, *Sweden* **8 D19** 65 35N 22 10 E
Luleå, *Sweden* **8 D20** 65 35N 22 10 E
Lüleburgaz, *Turkey* **21 D12** 41 23N 27 22 E
Luling, *U.S.A.* **81 L6** 29 41N 97 39W
Lulong, *China* **35 E10** 39 53N 118 51 E
Lulonga →, *Dem. Rep. of the Congo* **52 D3** 1 0N 18 10 E
Lulua →, *Dem. Rep. of the Congo* **52 E4** 4 30S 20 30 E
Luluabourg = Kananga, *Dem. Rep. of the Congo* **52 F4** 5 55S 22 18 E
Lumajang, *Indonesia* **37 H15** 8 8S 113 13 E
Lumbala N'guimbo, *Angola* **53 G4** 14 18S 21 18 E
Lumberton, *U.S.A.* **77 H6** 34 37N 79 0W
Lumbwa, *Kenya* **54 C4** 0 12S 35 28 E
Lumsden, *Canada* **73 C8** 50 39N 104 52W
Lumsden, *N.Z.* **59 L2** 45 44S 168 27 E
Lumut, *Malaysia* **39 K3** 4 13N 100 37 E
Lumut, Tanjung, *Indonesia* **36 E3** 3 50S 105 58 E
Luna, *India* **42 H3** 23 43N 69 16 E
Lunavada, *India* **42 H5** 23 8N 73 37 E
Lund, *Sweden* **9 J15** 55 44N 13 12 E
Lundazi, *Zambia* **55 E3** 12 20S 33 7 E
Lundi →, *Zimbabwe* **55 G3** 21 43S 32 34 E
Lundu, *Malaysia* **36 D3** 1 40N 109 50 E
Lundy, *U.K.* **11 F3** 51 10N 4 41W
Lune →, *U.K.* **10 C5** 54 0N 2 51W
Lüneburg, *Germany* **16 B6** 53 15N 10 24 E
Lüneburg Heath = Lüneburger Heide, *Germany* **16 B6** 53 10N 10 12 E
Lüneburger Heide, *Germany* **16 B6** 53 10N 10 12 E
Lunenburg, *Canada* **71 D7** 44 22N 64 18W
Lunéville, *France* **18 B7** 48 36N 6 30 E
Lunga →, *Zambia* **55 E2** 14 34S 26 25 E
Lunglei, *India* **41 H18** 22 55N 92 45 E
Luni, *India* **42 G5** 26 0N 73 6 E
Luni →, *India* **42 G4** 24 41N 71 14 E
Luninets = Luninyets, *Belarus* **17 B14** 52 15N 26 50 E
Luning, *U.S.A.* **82 G4** 38 30N 118 11W
Luninyets, *Belarus* **17 B14** 52 15N 26 50 E
Lunkaransar, *India* **42 E5** 28 29N 73 44 E
Lunsemfwa →, *Zambia* **55 E3** 14 54S 30 12 E
Lunsemfwa Falls, *Zambia* **55 E2** 14 30S 29 6 E
Luo He →, *China* **34 G6** 34 35N 110 20 E
Luochuan, *China* **34 G5** 35 45N 109 26 E
Luofu, *Dem. Rep. of the Congo* **54 C2** 0 10S 29 15 E
Luohe, *China* **34 H8** 33 32N 114 2 E
Luonan, *China* **34 G6** 34 5N 110 10 E
Luoning, *China* **34 G6** 34 35N 111 40 E
Luoyang, *China* **34 G7** 34 40N 112 26 E
Luozigou, *China* **35 C16** 43 42N 130 18 E
Lupanshui, *China* **32 D5** 26 38N 104 48 E
Lupilichi, *Mozam.* **55 E4** 11 47S 35 13 E
Luque, *Paraguay* **94 B4** 25 19S 57 25W
Luray, *U.S.A.* **76 F6** 38 40N 78 28W
Lurgan, *U.K.* **13 B5** 54 28N 6 19W
Lusaka, *Zambia* **55 F2** 15 28S 28 16 E
Lusambo, *Dem. Rep. of the Congo* **54 C1** 4 58S 23 28 E
Lusangaye, *Dem. Rep. of the Congo* **54 C2** 4 54S 26 0 E
Luseland, *Canada* **73 C7** 52 5N 109 24W
Lushan, *China* **34 H7** 33 45N 112 55 E
Lushi, *China* **34 G6** 34 3N 111 3 E
Lushnja, *Albania* **21 D8** 40 55N 19 41 E
Lushoto, *Tanzania* **54 C4** 4 47S 38 20 E
Lüshun, *China* **35 E11** 38 45N 121 15 E
Lusk, *U.S.A.* **80 D2** 42 46N 104 27W
Lūt, Dasht-e, *Iran* **45 D8** 31 30N 58 0 E
Luta = Dalian, *China* **35 E11** 38 50N 121 40 E
Lutherstadt Wittenberg, *Germany* **16 C7** 51 53N 12 39 E
Luton, *U.K.* **11 F7** 51 53N 0 24W
Luton □, *U.K.* **11 F7** 51 53N 0 24W
Lutselke, *Canada* **73 A6** 62 24N 110 44W
Lutsk, *Ukraine* **17 C13** 50 50N 25 15 E
Lützow Holmbukta, *Antarctica* **5 C4** 69 10S 37 30 E
Lutzputs, *S. Africa* **56 D3** 28 3S 20 40 E
Luverne, *Ala., U.S.A.* **77 K2** 31 43N 86 16W
Luverne, *Minn., U.S.A.* **80 D6** 43 39N 96 13W
Luvua, *Dem. Rep. of the Congo* **55 D2** 8 48S 25 17 E
Luvua →, *Dem. Rep. of the Congo* **54 D2** 6 50S 27 30 E
Luwegu →, *Tanzania* **55 D4** 8 31S 37 23 E
Luwuk, *Indonesia* **37 E6** 0 56S 122 47 E
Luxembourg, *Lux.* **18 B7** 49 37N 6 9 E
Luxembourg □, *Belgium* **15 E5** 49 58N 5 30 E
Luxembourg ■, *Europe* **18 B7** 49 45N 6 0 E
Luxi, *China* **32 D4** 24 27N 98 36 E
Luxor = El Uqsur, *Egypt* **51 C12** 25 41N 32 38 E
Luyi, *China* **34 H8** 33 50N 115 35 E
Luza, *Russia* **24 B8** 60 39N 47 10 E
Luzern, *Switz.* **18 C8** 47 3N 8 18 E
Luzhou, *China* **32 D5** 28 52N 105 20 E
Luziânia, *Brazil* **93 G9** 16 20S 48 0W
Luzon, *Phil.* **37 A6** 16 0N 121 0 E
Lviv, *Ukraine* **17 D13** 49 50N 24 0 E
Lvov = Lviv, *Ukraine* **17 D13** 49 50N 24 0 E
Lyakhavichy, *Belarus* **17 B14** 53 2N 26 32 E
Lyakhovskiye, Ostrova, *Russia* **27 B15** 73 40N 141 0 E
Lyal I., *Canada* **78 B3** 44 57N 81 24W
Lyallpur = Faisalabad, *Pakistan* **42 D5** 31 30N 73 5 E
Lybster, *U.K.* **12 C5** 58 18N 3 15W
Lycksele, *Sweden* **8 D18** 64 38N 18 40 E
Lydda = Lod, *Israel* **47 D3** 31 57N 34 54 E
Lydenburg, *S. Africa* **57 D5** 25 10S 30 29 E
Lydia, *Turkey* **21 E13** 38 48N 28 19 E
Lyell, *N.Z.* **59 J4** 41 48S 172 4 E
Lyell I., *Canada* **72 C2** 52 40N 131 35W
Lyepyel, *Belarus* **24 D4** 54 50N 28 40 E
Lykens, *U.S.A.* **79 F8** 40 34N 76 42W
Lyman, *U.S.A.* **82 F8** 41 20N 110 18W
Lyme B., *U.K.* **11 G4** 50 42N 2 53W
Lyme Regis, *U.K.* **11 G5** 50 43N 2 57W
Lymington, *U.K.* **11 G6** 50 45N 1 32W
Łyna →, *Poland* **9 J19** 54 37N 21 14 E
Lynchburg, *U.S.A.* **76 G6** 37 25N 79 9W
Lynd →, *Australia* **62 B3** 16 28S 143 18 E
Lynd Ra., *Australia* **63 D4** 25 30S 149 20 E
Lynden, *Canada* **78 C4** 43 14N 80 9W
Lynden, *U.S.A.* **84 B4** 48 57N 122 27W
Lyndhurst, *Australia* **63 E2** 30 15S 138 18 E
Lyndon →, *Australia* **61 D1** 23 29S 114 6 E
Lyndonville, *N.Y., U.S.A.* **78 C6** 43 20N 78 23W
Lyndonville, *Vt., U.S.A.* **79 B12** 44 31N 72 1W
Lyngen, *Norway* **8 B19** 69 45N 20 30 E
Lynher Reef, *Australia* **60 C3** 15 27S 121 55 E
Lynn, *U.S.A.* **79 D14** 42 28N 70 57W
Lynn Lake, *Canada* **73 B8** 56 51N 101 3W
Lynnwood, *U.S.A.* **84 C4** 47 49N 122 19W
Lynton, *U.K.* **11 F4** 51 13N 3 50W
Lyntupy, *Belarus* **9 J22** 55 4N 26 23 E
Lynx L., *Canada* **73 A7** 62 25N 106 15W
Lyon, *France* **18 D6** 45 46N 4 50 E
Lyonnais, *France* **18 D6** 45 45N 4 15 E
Lyons = Lyon, *France* **18 D6** 45 46N 4 50 E
Lyons, *Ga., U.S.A.* **77 J4** 32 12N 82 19W
Lyons, *Kans., U.S.A.* **80 F5** 38 21N 98 12W
Lyons, *N.Y., U.S.A.* **78 C8** 43 5N 77 0W
Lyons →, *Australia* **61 E2** 25 2S 115 9 E
Lyons Falls, *U.S.A.* **79 C9** 43 37N 75 22W
Lys = Leie →, *Belgium* **15 C3** 51 2N 3 45 E
Lysva, *Russia* **24 C10** 58 7N 57 49 E
Lysychansk, *Ukraine* **25 E6** 48 55N 38 30 E
Lytham St. Anne's, *U.K.* **10 D4** 53 45N 3 0W
Lyttelton, *N.Z.* **59 K4** 43 35S 172 44 E
Lytton, *Canada* **72 C4** 50 13N 121 31W
Lyubertsy, *Russia* **24 C6** 55 39N 37 50 E
Lyuboml, *Ukraine* **17 C13** 51 11N 24 4 E

M

M.R. Gomez, Presa, *Mexico* **87 B5** 26 10N 99 0W
Ma →, *Vietnam* **38 C5** 19 47N 105 56 E
Ma'adaba, *Jordan* **47 E4** 30 43N 35 47 E
Maamba, *Zambia* **56 B4** 17 17S 26 28 E
Ma'ān, *Jordan* **47 E4** 30 12N 35 44 E
Ma'ān □, *Jordan* **47 F5** 30 0N 36 0 E
Maanselkä, *Finland* **8 C23** 63 52N 28 32 E
Ma'anshan, *China* **33 C6** 31 44N 118 29 E
Maarianhamina, *Finland* **9 F18** 60 5N 19 55 E
Ma'arrat an Nu'mān, *Syria* **44 C3** 35 43N 36 43 E
Maas →, *Neths.* **15 C4** 51 45N 4 32 E
Maaseik, *Belgium* **15 C5** 51 6N 5 45 E
Maasin, *Phil.* **37 B6** 10 8N 124 50 E
Maastricht, *Neths.* **18 A6** 50 50N 5 40 E
Maave, *Mozam.* **57 C5** 21 4S 34 47 E
Mabel L., *Canada* **72 C5** 50 35N 118 43W
Mabenge, *Dem. Rep. of the Congo* **54 B1** 4 15N 24 12 E
Maberly, *Canada* **79 B8** 44 50N 76 32W
Mablethorpe, *U.K.* **10 D8** 53 20N 0 15 E
Maboma, *Dem. Rep. of the Congo* **54 B2** 2 30N 28 10 E
Mac Bac, *Vietnam* **39 H6** 9 46N 106 7 E
Macachín, *Argentina* **94 D3** 37 10S 63 43W
Macaé, *Brazil* **95 A7** 22 20S 41 43W
McAlester, *U.S.A.* **81 H7** 34 56N 95 46W
McAllen, *U.S.A.* **81 M5** 26 12N 98 14W
MacAlpine L., *Canada* **68 B9** 66 40N 102 50W
Macamic, *Canada* **70 C4** 48 45N 79 0W
Macao = Macau, *China* **33 D6** 22 16N 113 35 E
Macapá, *Brazil* **93 C8** 0 5N 51 4W
McArthur →, *Australia* **62 B2** 15 54S 136 40 E
McArthur, Port, *Australia* **62 B2** 16 4S 136 23 E
Macau, *Brazil* **93 E11** 5 15S 36 40W
Macau, *China* **33 D6** 22 16N 113 35 E
McBride, *Canada* **72 C4** 53 20N 120 19W
McCall, *U.S.A.* **82 D5** 44 55N 116 6W
McCamey, *U.S.A.* **81 K3** 31 8N 102 14W
McCammon, *U.S.A.* **82 E7** 42 39N 112 12W
McCauley I., *Canada* **72 C2** 53 40N 130 15W
McCleary, *U.S.A.* **84 C3** 47 3N 123 16W
Macclenny, *U.S.A.* **77 K4** 30 17N 82 7W
Macclesfield, *U.K.* **10 D5** 53 15N 2 8W
M'Clintock Chan., *Canada* **68 A9** 72 0N 102 0W
McClintock Ra., *Australia* **60 C4** 18 44S 127 38 E
McCloud, *U.S.A.* **82 F2** 41 15N 122 8W
McCluer I., *Australia* **60 B5** 11 5S 133 0 E
McClure, *U.S.A.* **78 F7** 40 42N 77 19W
McClure, L., *U.S.A.* **84 H6** 37 35N 120 16W
M'Clure Str., *Canada* **4 B2** 75 0N 119 0W
McClusky, *U.S.A.* **80 B4** 47 29N 100 27W
McComb, *U.S.A.* **81 K9** 31 15N 90 27W

McConaughy, L., *U.S.A.* **80 E4** 41 14N 101 40W
McCook, *U.S.A.* **80 E4** 40 12N 100 38W
McCreary, *Canada* **73 C9** 50 47N 99 29W
McCullough Mt., *U.S.A.* **85 K11** 35 35N 115 13W
McCusker —►, *Canada* **73 B7** 55 32N 108 39W
McDame, *Canada* **72 B3** 59 44N 128 59W
McDermitt, *U.S.A.* **82 F5** 41 59N 117 43W
McDonald, *U.S.A.* **78 F4** 40 22N 80 14W
Macdonald, L., *Australia* **60 D4** 23 30S 129 0 E
McDonald Is., *Ind. Oc.* **3 G13** 53 0S 73 0 E
MacDonnell Ranges, *Australia* **60 D5** 23 40S 133 0 E
MacDowell L., *Canada* **70 B1** 52 15N 92 45W
Macduff, *U.K.* **12 D6** 57 40N 2 31W
Macedonia = Makedhonía □, *Greece* **21 D10** 40 39N 22 0 E
Macedonia, *U.S.A.* **78 E3** 41 19N 81 31W
Macedonia ■, *Europe* **21 D9** 41 53N 21 40 E
Maceió, *Brazil* **93 E11** 9 40S 35 41W
Macerata, *Italy* **20 C5** 43 18N 13 27 E
McFarland, *U.S.A.* **85 K7** 35 41N 119 14W
McFarlane —►, *Canada* **73 B7** 59 12N 107 58W
Macfarlane, L., *Australia* **63 E2** 32 0S 136 40 E
McGehee, *U.S.A.* **81 J9** 33 38N 91 24W
McGill, *U.S.A.* **82 G6** 39 23N 114 47W
Macgillycuddy's Reeks, *Ireland* **13 E2** 51 58N 9 45W
McGraw, *U.S.A.* **79 D8** 42 36N 76 8W
McGregor, *U.S.A.* **80 D9** 43 1N 91 11W
McGregor Ra., *Australia* **63 D3** 27 0S 142 45 E
Mach, *Pakistan* **40 E5** 29 50N 67 20 E
Māch Kowr, *Iran* **45 E9** 25 48N 61 28 E
Machado = Jiparaná —►, *Brazil* **92 E6** 8 3S 62 52W
Machagai, *Argentina* **94 B3** 26 56S 60 2W
Machakos, *Kenya* **54 C4** 1 30S 37 15 E
Machala, *Ecuador* **92 D3** 3 20S 79 57W
Machanga, *Mozam.* **57 C6** 20 59S 35 0 E
Machattie, L., *Australia* **62 C2** 24 50S 139 48 E
Machava, *Mozam.* **57 D5** 25 54S 32 28 E
Machece, *Mozam.* **55 F4** 19 15S 35 32 E
Machhu —►, *India* **42 H4** 23 6N 70 46 E
Machias, *Maine, U.S.A.* **77 C12** 44 43N 67 28W
Machias, *N.Y., U.S.A.* **78 D6** 42 25N 78 30W
Machichi —►, *Canada* **73 B10** 57 3N 92 6W
Machico, *Madeira* **22 D3** 32 43N 16 44W
Machilipatnam, *India* **41 L12** 16 12N 81 8 E
Machiques, *Venezuela* **92 A4** 10 4N 72 34W
Machupicchu, *Peru* **92 F4** 13 8S 72 30W
Machynlleth, *U.K.* **11 E4** 52 35N 3 50W
McIlwraith Ra., *Australia* **62 A3** 13 50S 143 20 E
McInnes L., *Canada* **73 C10** 52 13N 93 45W
McIntosh, *U.S.A.* **80 C4** 45 55N 101 21W
McIntosh L., *Canada* **73 B8** 55 45N 105 0W
Macintosh Ra., *Australia* **61 E4** 27 39S 125 32 E
Macintyre —►, *Australia* **63 D5** 28 37S 150 47 E
Mackay, *Australia* **62 C4** 21 8S 149 11 E
Mackay, *U.S.A.* **82 E7** 43 55N 113 37W
MacKay —►, *Canada* **72 B6** 57 10N 111 38W
Mackay, L., *Australia* **60 D4** 22 30S 129 0 E
McKay Ra., *Australia* **60 D3** 23 0S 122 30 E
McKeesport, *U.S.A.* **78 F5** 40 21N 79 52W
McKellar, *Canada* **78 A5** 45 30N 79 55W
McKenna, *U.S.A.* **84 D4** 46 56N 122 33W
Mackenzie, *Canada* **72 B4** 55 20N 123 5W
McKenzie, *U.S.A.* **77 G1** 36 8N 88 31W
Mackenzie —►, *Australia* **62 C4** 23 38S 149 46 E
Mackenzie —►, *Canada* **68 B6** 69 10N 134 20W
McKenzie —►, *U.S.A.* **82 D2** 44 7N 123 6W
Mackenzie Bay, *Canada* **4 B1** 69 0N 137 30W
Mackenzie City = Linden, *Guyana* **92 B7** 6 0N 58 10W
Mackenzie Mts., *Canada* **68 B7** 64 0N 130 0W
Mackinaw City, *U.S.A.* **76 C3** 45 47N 84 44W
McKinlay, *Australia* **62 C3** 21 16S 141 18 E
McKinlay —►, *Australia* **62 C3** 20 50S 141 28 E
McKinley, Mt., *U.S.A.* **68 B4** 63 4N 151 0W
McKinley Sea, *Arctic* **4 A7** 82 0N 0 0 E
McKinney, *U.S.A.* **81 J6** 33 12N 96 37W
Mackinnon Road, *Kenya* **54 C4** 3 40S 39 1 E
McKittrick, *U.S.A.* **85 K7** 35 18N 119 37W
Macklin, *Canada* **73 C7** 52 20N 109 56W
Macksville, *Australia* **63 E5** 30 40S 152 56 E
McLaughlin, *U.S.A.* **80 C4** 45 49N 100 49W
Maclean, *Australia* **63 D5** 29 26S 153 16 E
McLean, *U.S.A.* **81 H4** 35 14N 100 36W
McLeansboro, *U.S.A.* **80 F10** 38 6N 88 32W
Maclear, *S. Africa* **57 E4** 31 2S 28 23 E
Macleay —►, *Australia* **63 E5** 30 56S 153 0 E
McLennan, *Canada* **72 B5** 55 42N 116 50W
McLeod —►, *Canada* **72 C5** 54 9N 115 44W
MacLeod, B., *Canada* **73 A7** 62 53N 110 0W
McLeod, L., *Australia* **61 D1** 24 9S 113 47 E
MacLeod Lake, *Canada* **72 C4** 54 58N 123 0W
McLoughlin, Mt., *U.S.A.* **82 E2** 42 27N 122 19W
McMechen, *U.S.A.* **78 G4** 39 57N 80 44W
McMinnville, *Oreg., U.S.A.* **82 D2** 45 13N 123 12W
McMinnville, *Tenn., U.S.A.* **77 H3** 35 41N 85 46W
McMurdo Sd., *Antarctica* **5 D11** 77 0S 170 0 E
McMurray = Fort McMurray, *Canada* **72 B6** 56 44N 111 7W
McMurray, *U.S.A.* **84 B4** 48 19N 122 14W
Macodoene, *Mozam.* **57 C6** 23 32S 35 5 E
Macomb, *U.S.A.* **80 E9** 40 27N 90 40W
Mâcon, *France* **18 C6** 46 19N 4 50 E
Macon, *Ga., U.S.A.* **77 J4** 32 51N 83 38W
Macon, *Miss., U.S.A.* **77 J1** 33 7N 88 34W
Macon, *Mo., U.S.A.* **80 F8** 39 44N 92 28W
Macossa, *Mozam.* **55 F3** 17 55S 33 56 E
Macoun L., *Canada* **73 B8** 56 32N 103 40W
Macovane, *Mozam.* **57 C6** 21 30S 35 2 E
McPherson, *U.S.A.* **80 F6** 38 22N 97 40W
McPherson Pk., *U.S.A.* **85 L7** 34 53N 119 53W
McPherson Ra., *Australia* **63 D5** 28 15S 153 15 E
Macquarie —►, *Australia* **63 E4** 30 5S 147 30 E
Macquarie Harbour, *Australia* **62 G4** 42 15S 145 23 E
Macquarie Is., *Pac. Oc.* **64 N7** 54 36S 158 55 E
MacRobertson Land, *Antarctica* **5 D6** 71 0S 64 0 E
Macroom, *Ireland* **13 E3** 51 54N 8 57W
MacTier, *Canada* **78 A5** 45 9N 79 46W
Macubela, *Mozam.* **55 F4** 16 53S 37 49 E
Macuiza, *Mozam.* **55 F3** 18 7S 34 29 E
Macusani, *Peru* **92 F4** 14 4S 70 29W
Macuse, *Mozam.* **55 F4** 17 45S 37 10 E
Macuspana, *Mexico* **87 D6** 17 46N 92 36W
Macusse, *Angola* **56 B3** 17 48S 20 23 E
Madadeni, *S. Africa* **57 D5** 27 43S 30 3 E
Madagascar ■, *Africa* **57 C8** 20 0S 47 0 E
Madā'in Sālih, *Si. Arabia* **44 E3** 26 46N 37 57 E
Madama, *Niger* **51 D8** 22 0N 13 40 E
Madame I., *Canada* **71 C7** 45 30N 60 58W
Madaripur, *Bangla.* **41 H17** 23 19N 90 15 E
Madauk, *Burma* **41 L20** 17 56N 96 52 E
Madawaska, *Canada* **78 A7** 45 30N 78 0W
Madawaska —►, *Canada* **78 A8** 45 27N 76 21W
Madaya, *Burma* **41 H20** 22 12N 96 10 E
Maddalena, *Italy* **20 D3** 41 16N 9 23 E
Madeira, *Atl. Oc.* **22 D3** 32 50N 17 0W
Madeira —►, *Brazil* **92 D7** 3 22S 58 45W
Madeleine, Îs. de la, *Canada* **71 C7** 47 30N 61 40W
Madera, *Mexico* **86 B3** 29 12N 108 7W
Madera, *Calif., U.S.A.* **84 J6** 36 57N 120 3W
Madera, *Pa., U.S.A.* **78 F6** 40 49N 78 26W
Madha, *India* **40 L9** 18 0N 75 30 E
Madhavpur, *India* **42 J3** 21 15N 69 58 E
Madhepura, *India* **43 F12** 26 11N 86 23 E
Madhubani, *India* **43 F12** 26 21N 86 7 E
Madhupur, *India* **43 G12** 24 16N 86 39 E
Madhya Pradesh □, *India* **42 J8** 22 50N 78 0 E
Madidi —►, *Bolivia* **92 F5** 12 32S 66 52W
Madikeri, *India* **40 N9** 12 30N 75 45 E
Madill, *U.S.A.* **81 H6** 34 6N 96 46W
Madimba, *Dem. Rep. of the Congo* **52 E3** 4 58S 15 5 E
Ma'din, *Syria* **44 C3** 35 45N 39 36 E
Madingou, *Congo* **52 E2** 4 10S 13 33 E
Madirovalo, *Madag.* **57 B8** 16 26S 46 32 E
Madison, *Calif., U.S.A.* **84 G5** 38 41N 121 59W
Madison, *Fla., U.S.A.* **77 K4** 30 28N 83 25W
Madison, *Ind., U.S.A.* **76 F3** 38 44N 85 23W
Madison, *Nebr., U.S.A.* **80 E6** 41 50N 97 27W
Madison, *Ohio, U.S.A.* **78 E3** 41 46N 81 3W
Madison, *S. Dak., U.S.A.* **80 D6** 44 0N 97 7W
Madison, *Wis., U.S.A.* **80 D10** 43 4N 89 24W
Madison —►, *U.S.A.* **82 D8** 45 56N 111 31W
Madison Heights, *U.S.A.* **76 G6** 37 25N 79 8W
Madisonville, *Ky., U.S.A.* **76 G2** 37 20N 87 30W
Madisonville, *Tex., U.S.A.* **81 K7** 30 57N 95 55W
Madista, *Botswana* **56 C4** 21 15S 25 6 E
Madiun, *Indonesia* **37 G14** 7 38S 111 32 E
Madoc, *Canada* **78 B7** 44 30N 77 28W
Madona, *Latvia* **9 H22** 56 53N 26 5 E
Madrakah, Ra's al, *Oman* **46 D6** 19 0N 57 50 E
Madras = Chennai, *India* **40 N12** 13 8N 80 19 E
Madras = Tamil Nadu □, *India* **40 P10** 11 0N 77 0 E
Madras, *U.S.A.* **82 D3** 44 38N 121 8W
Madre, L., *Mexico* **87 C5** 25 0N 97 30W
Madre, Laguna, *U.S.A.* **81 M6** 27 0N 97 30W
Madre, Sierra, *Phil.* **37 A6** 17 0N 122 0 E
Madre de Dios —►, *Bolivia* **92 F5** 10 59S 66 8W
Madre de Dios, I., *Chile* **96 G1** 50 20S 75 10W
Madre del Sur, Sierra, *Mexico* **87 D5** 17 30N 100 0W
Madre Occidental, Sierra, *Mexico* **86 B3** 27 0N 107 0W
Madre Oriental, Sierra, *Mexico* **86 C5** 25 0N 100 0W
Madri, *India* **42 G5** 24 16N 73 32 E
Madrid, *Spain* **19 B4** 40 25N 3 45W
Madrid, *U.S.A.* **79 B9** 44 45N 75 8W
Madura, *Australia* **61 F4** 31 55S 127 0 E
Madura, *Indonesia* **37 G15** 7 30S 114 0 E
Madura, Selat, *Indonesia* **37 G15** 7 30S 113 20 E
Madurai, *India* **40 Q11** 9 55N 78 10 E
Madurantakam, *India* **40 N11** 12 30N 79 50 E
Mae Chan, *Thailand* **38 B2** 20 9N 99 52 E
Mae Hong Son, *Thailand* **38 C2** 19 16N 97 56 E
Mae Khlong —►, *Thailand* **38 F3** 13 24N 100 0 E
Mae Phrik, *Thailand* **38 D2** 17 27N 99 7 E
Mae Ramat, *Thailand* **38 D2** 16 58N 98 31 E
Mae Rim, *Thailand* **38 C2** 18 54N 98 57 E
Mae Sot, *Thailand* **38 D2** 16 43N 98 34 E
Mae Suai, *Thailand* **38 C2** 19 39N 99 33 E
Mae Tha, *Thailand* **38 C2** 18 28N 99 8 E
Maebashi, *Japan* **31 F9** 36 24N 139 4 E
Maesteg, *U.K.* **11 F4** 51 36N 3 40W
Maestra, Sierra, *Cuba* **88 B4** 20 15N 77 0W
Maevatanana, *Madag.* **57 B8** 16 56S 46 49 E
Mafeking = Mafikeng, *S. Africa* **56 D4** 25 50S 25 38 E
Mafeking, *Canada* **73 C8** 52 40N 101 10W
Mafeteng, *Lesotho* **56 D4** 29 51S 27 15 E
Maffra, *Australia* **63 F4** 37 53S 146 58 E
Mafia I., *Tanzania* **54 D4** 7 45S 39 50 E
Mafikeng, *S. Africa* **56 D4** 25 50S 25 38 E
Mafra, *Brazil* **95 B6** 26 10S 49 55W
Mafra, *Portugal* **19 C1** 38 55N 9 20W
Mafungabusi Plateau, *Zimbabwe* **55 F2** 18 30S 29 8 E
Magadan, *Russia* **27 D16** 59 38N 150 50 E
Magadi, *Kenya* **54 C4** 1 54S 36 19 E
Magadi, L., *Kenya* **54 C4** 1 54S 36 19 E
Magaliesburg, *S. Africa* **57 D4** 26 0S 27 32 E
Magallanes, Estrecho de, *Chile* **96 G2** 52 30S 75 0W
Magangué, *Colombia* **92 B4** 9 14N 74 45W
Magdalen Is. = Madeleine, Îs. de la, *Canada* **71 C7** 47 30N 61 40W
Magdalena, *Argentina* **94 D4** 35 5S 57 30W
Magdalena, *Bolivia* **92 F6** 13 13S 63 57W
Magdalena, *Mexico* **86 A2** 30 50N 112 0W
Magdalena, *U.S.A.* **83 J10** 34 7N 107 15W
Magdalena —►, *Colombia* **92 A4** 11 6N 74 51W
Magdalena —►, *Mexico* **86 A2** 30 40N 112 25W
Magdalena, B., *Mexico* **86 C2** 24 30N 112 10W
Magdalena, Llano de la, *Mexico* **86 C2** 25 0N 111 30W
Magdeburg, *Germany* **16 B6** 52 7N 11 38 E
Magdelaine Cays, *Australia* **62 B5** 16 33S 150 18 E
Magee, *U.S.A.* **81 K10** 31 52N 89 44W
Magelang, *Indonesia* **37 G14** 7 29S 110 13 E
Magellan's Str. = Magallanes, Estrecho de, *Chile* **96 G2** 52 30S 75 0W
Magenta, L., *Australia* **61 F2** 33 30S 119 2 E
Magerøya, *Norway* **8 A21** 71 3N 25 40 E
Maggiore, Lago, *Italy* **18 D8** 45 57N 8 39 E
Maghâgha, *Egypt* **51 C12** 28 38N 30 50 E
Magherafelt, *U.K.* **13 B5** 54 45N 6 37W
Maghreb, *N. Afr.* **50 B5** 32 0N 4 0W
Magistralnyy, *Russia* **27 D11** 56 16N 107 36 E
Magnetic Pole (North) = North Magnetic Pole, *Canada* **4 B2** 77 58N 102 8W
Magnetic Pole (South) = South Magnetic Pole, *Antarctica* **5 C9** 64 8S 138 8 E
Magnitogorsk, *Russia* **24 D10** 53 27N 59 4 E
Magnolia, *Ark., U.S.A.* **81 J8** 33 16N 93 14W
Magnolia, *Miss., U.S.A.* **81 K9** 31 9N 90 28W
Magog, *Canada* **79 A12** 45 18N 72 9W
Magoro, *Uganda* **54 B3** 1 45N 34 12 E
Magosa = Famagusta, *Cyprus* **23 D12** 35 8N 33 55 E
Magouládhes, *Greece* **23 A3** 39 45N 19 42 E
Magoye, *Zambia* **55 F2** 16 1S 27 30 E
Magozal, *Mexico* **87 C5** 21 34N 97 59W
Magpie, L., *Canada* **71 B7** 51 0N 64 41W
Magrath, *Canada* **72 D6** 49 25N 112 50W
Maguarinho, C., *Brazil* **93 D9** 0 15S 48 30W
Mağusa = Famagusta, *Cyprus* **23 D12** 35 8N 33 55 E
Maguse L., *Canada* **73 A9** 61 40N 95 10W
Maguse Pt., *Canada* **73 A10** 61 20N 93 50W
Magvana, *India* **42 H3** 23 13N 69 22 E
Magwe, *Burma* **41 J19** 20 10N 95 0 E
Maha Sarakham, *Thailand* **38 D4** 16 12N 103 16 E
Mahābād, *Iran* **44 B5** 36 50N 45 45 E
Mahabharat Lekh, *Nepal* **43 E10** 28 30N 82 0 E
Mahabo, *Madag.* **57 C7** 20 23S 44 40 E
Mahadeo Hills, *India* **43 H8** 22 20N 78 30 E
Mahaffey, *U.S.A.* **78 F6** 40 53N 78 44W
Mahagi, *Dem. Rep. of the Congo* **54 B3** 2 20N 31 0 E
Mahajamba —►, *Madag.* **57 B8** 15 33S 47 8 E
Mahajamba, Helodranon' i, *Madag.* **57 B8** 15 24S 47 5 E
Mahajan, *India* **42 E5** 28 48N 73 56 E
Mahajanga, *Madag.* **57 B8** 15 40S 46 25 E
Mahajanga □, *Madag.* **57 B8** 17 0S 47 0 E
Mahajilo —►, *Madag.* **57 B8** 19 42S 45 22 E
Mahakam —►, *Indonesia* **36 E5** 0 35S 117 17 E
Mahalapye, *Botswana* **56 C4** 23 1S 26 51 E
Maḩallāt, *Iran* **45 C6** 33 55N 50 30 E
Māhān, *Iran* **45 D8** 30 5N 57 18 E
Mahan —►, *India* **43 H10** 23 30N 82 50 E
Mahanadi —►, *India* **41 J15** 20 20N 86 25 E
Mahananda —►, *India* **43 G12** 25 12N 87 52 E
Mahanoro, *Madag.* **57 B8** 19 54S 48 48 E
Mahanoy City, *U.S.A.* **79 F8** 40 49N 76 9W
Maharashtra □, *India* **40 J9** 20 30N 75 30 E
Mahari Mts., *Tanzania* **54 D3** 6 20S 30 0 E
Mahasham, W. —►, *Egypt* **47 E3** 30 15N 34 10 E
Mahasolo, *Madag.* **57 B8** 19 7S 46 22 E
Mahattat ash Shīdīyah, *Jordan* **47 F4** 29 55N 35 55 E
Mahattat 'Unayzah, *Jordan* **47 E4** 30 30N 35 47 E
Mahaxay, *Laos* **38 D5** 17 22N 105 12 E
Mahbubnagar, *India* **40 L10** 16 45N 77 59 E
Maḩḑah, *Oman* **45 E7** 24 24N 55 59 E
Mahdia, *Tunisia* **51 A8** 35 28N 11 0 E
Mahe, *India* **43 C8** 33 10N 78 32 E
Mahendragarh, *India* **42 E7** 28 17N 76 14 E
Mahenge, *Tanzania* **55 D4** 8 45S 36 41 E
Maheno, *N.Z.* **59 L3** 45 10S 170 50 E
Mahesana, *India* **42 H5** 23 39N 72 26 E
Maheshwar, *India* **42 H6** 22 11N 75 35 E
Mahgawan, *India* **43 F8** 26 29N 78 37 E
Mahi —►, *India* **42 H5** 22 15N 72 55 E
Mahia Pen., *N.Z.* **59 H6** 39 9S 177 55 E
Mahilyow, *Belarus* **17 B16** 53 55N 30 18 E
Mahmud Kot, *Pakistan* **42 D4** 30 16N 71 0 E
Mahnomen, *U.S.A.* **80 B7** 47 19N 95 58W
Mahoba, *India* **43 G8** 25 15N 79 55 E
Mahón = Maó, *Spain* **22 B11** 39 53N 4 16 E
Mahone Bay, *Canada* **71 D7** 44 30N 64 20W
Mahopac, *U.S.A.* **79 E11** 41 22N 73 45W
Mahuva, *India* **42 J4** 21 5N 71 48 E
Mai-Ndombe, L., *Dem. Rep. of the Congo* **52 E3** 2 0S 18 20 E
Mai-Sai, *Thailand* **38 B2** 20 20N 99 55 E
Maicurú —►, *Brazil* **93 D8** 2 14S 54 17W
Maidan Khula, *Afghan.* **42 C3** 33 36N 69 50 E
Maidenhead, *U.K.* **11 F7** 51 31N 0 42W
Maidstone, *Canada* **73 C7** 53 5N 109 20W
Maidstone, *U.K.* **11 F8** 51 16N 0 32 E
Maiduguri, *Nigeria* **51 F8** 12 0N 13 20 E
Maihar, *India* **43 G9** 24 16N 80 45 E
Maijdi, *Bangla.* **41 H17** 22 48N 91 10 E
Maikala Ra., *India* **41 J12** 22 0N 81 0 E
Mailani, *India* **43 E9** 28 17N 80 21 E
Mailsi, *Pakistan* **42 E5** 29 48N 72 15 E
Main —►, *Germany* **16 C5** 50 0N 8 18 E
Main —►, *U.K.* **13 B5** 54 48N 6 18W
Maine, *France* **18 C3** 48 20N 0 15W
Maine □, *U.S.A.* **77 C11** 45 20N 69 0W
Maine —►, *Ireland* **13 D2** 52 9N 9 45W
Maingkwan, *Burma* **41 F20** 26 15N 96 37 E
Mainit, L., *Phil.* **37 C7** 9 31N 125 30 E
Mainland, *Orkney, U.K.* **12 C5** 58 59N 3 8W
Mainland, *Shet., U.K.* **12 A7** 60 15N 1 22W
Mainoru, *Australia* **62 A1** 14 0S 134 6 E
Mainpuri, *India* **43 F8** 27 18N 79 4 E
Maintirano, *Madag.* **57 B7** 18 3S 44 1 E
Mainz, *Germany* **16 C5** 50 1N 8 14 E
Maipú, *Argentina* **94 D4** 36 52S 57 50W
Maiquetía, *Venezuela* **92 A5** 10 36N 66 57W
Mairabari, *India* **41 F18** 26 30N 92 22 E
Maisí, *Cuba* **89 B5** 20 17N 74 9W
Maisí, Pta. de, *Cuba* **89 B5** 20 10N 74 10W
Maitland, *N.S.W., Australia* **63 E5** 32 33S 151 36 E
Maitland, *S. Austral., Australia* **63 E2** 34 23S 137 40 E
Maitland —►, *Canada* **78 C3** 43 45N 81 43W
Maiz, Is. del, *Nic.* **88 D3** 12 15N 83 4W
Maizuru, *Japan* **31 G7** 35 25N 135 22 E
Majalengka, *Indonesia* **37 G13** 6 50S 108 13 E
Majene, *Indonesia* **37 E5** 3 38S 118 57 E
Majorca = Mallorca, *Spain* **22 B10** 39 30N 3 0 E
Makale, *Indonesia* **37 E5** 3 6S 119 51 E
Makamba, *Burundi* **54 C2** 4 8S 29 49 E
Makarikari = Makgadikgadi Salt Pans, *Botswana* **56 C4** 20 40S 25 45 E
Makarovo, *Russia* **27 D11** 57 40N 107 45 E
Makasar = Ujung Pandang, *Indonesia* **37 F5** 5 10S 119 20 E
Makasar, Selat, *Indonesia* **37 E5** 1 0S 118 20 E
Makasar, Str. of = Makasar, Selat, *Indonesia* **37 E5** 1 0S 118 20 E
Makat, *Kazakstan* **25 E9** 47 39N 53 19 E
Makedhonía □, *Greece* **21 D10** 40 39N 22 0 E
Makedonija = Macedonia ■, *Europe* **21 D9** 41 53N 21 40 E
Makena, *U.S.A.* **74 H16** 20 39N 156 27W
Makeyevka = Makiyivka, *Ukraine* **25 E6** 48 0N 38 0 E
Makgadikgadi Salt Pans, *Botswana* **56 C4** 20 40S 25 45 E
Makhachkala, *Russia* **25 F8** 43 0N 47 30 E
Makhmūr, *Iraq* **44 C4** 35 46N 43 35 E
Makian, *Indonesia* **37 D7** 0 20N 127 20 E
Makindu, *Kenya* **54 C4** 2 18S 37 50 E
Makinsk, *Kazakstan* **26 D8** 52 37N 70 26 E
Makiyivka, *Ukraine* **25 E6** 48 0N 38 0 E
Makkah, *Si. Arabia* **46 C2** 21 30N 39 54 E
Makkovik, *Canada* **71 A8** 55 10N 59 10W
Makó, *Hungary* **17 E11** 46 14N 20 33 E
Makokou, *Gabon* **52 D2** 0 40N 12 50 E
Makongo, *Dem. Rep. of the Congo* **54 B2** 3 25N 26 17 E
Makoro, *Dem. Rep. of the Congo* **54 B2** 3 10N 29 59 E
Makrai, *India* **40 H10** 22 2N 77 0 E
Makran Coast Range, *Pakistan* **40 G4** 25 40N 64 0 E
Makrana, *India* **42 F6** 27 2N 74 46 E
Makriyialos, *Greece* **23 D7** 35 2N 25 59 E
Mākū, *Iran* **44 B5** 39 15N 44 31 E
Makunda, *Botswana* **56 C3** 22 30S 20 7 E
Makurazaki, *Japan* **31 J5** 31 15N 130 20 E
Makurdi, *Nigeria* **50 G7** 7 43N 8 35 E
Makūyeh, *Iran* **45 D7** 28 7N 53 9 E
Makwassie, *S. Africa* **56 D4** 27 17S 26 0 E
Mal B., *Ireland* **13 D2** 52 50N 9 30W
Mala, Pta., *Panama* **88 E3** 7 28N 80 2W
Malabar Coast, *India* **40 P9** 11 0N 75 0 E
Malabo = Rey Malabo, *Eq. Guin.* **52 D1** 3 45N 8 50 E
Malacca, Str. of, *Indonesia* **39 L3** 3 0N 101 0 E
Malad City, *U.S.A.* **82 E7** 42 12N 112 15W
Maladzyechna, *Belarus* **17 A14** 54 20N 26 50 E
Málaga, *Spain* **19 D3** 36 43N 4 23W
Malagarasi, *Tanzania* **54 D3** 5 5S 30 50 E
Malagarasi —►, *Tanzania* **54 D2** 5 12S 29 47 E
Malagasy Rep. = Madagascar ■, *Africa* **57 C8** 20 0S 47 0 E
Malahide, *Ireland* **13 C5** 53 26N 6 9W
Malaimbandy, *Madag.* **57 C8** 20 20S 45 36 E
Malakâl, *Sudan* **51 G12** 9 33N 31 40 E
Malakand, *Pakistan* **42 B4** 34 40N 71 55 E
Malakwal, *Pakistan* **42 C5** 32 34N 73 13 E
Malamala, *Indonesia* **37 E6** 3 21S 120 55 E
Malanda, *Australia* **62 B4** 17 22S 145 35 E
Malang, *Indonesia* **37 G15** 7 59S 112 45 E
Malangen, *Norway* **8 B18** 69 24N 18 37 E
Malanje, *Angola* **52 F3** 9 36S 16 17 E
Mälaren, *Sweden* **9 G17** 59 30N 17 10 E
Malargüe, *Argentina* **94 D2** 35 32S 69 30W
Malartic, *Canada* **70 C4** 48 9N 78 9W
Malaryta, *Belarus* **17 C13** 51 50N 24 3 E
Malatya, *Turkey* **25 G6** 38 25N 38 20 E
Malawi ■, *Africa* **55 E3** 11 55S 34 0 E
Malawi, L. = Nyasa, L., *Africa* **55 E3** 12 30S 34 30 E
Malay Pen., *Asia* **39 J3** 7 25N 100 0 E
Malaya Vishera, *Russia* **24 C5** 58 55N 32 25 E
Malaybalay, *Phil.* **37 C7** 8 5N 125 7 E
Malāyer, *Iran* **45 C6** 34 19N 48 51 E
Malaysia ■, *Asia* **39 K4** 5 0N 110 0 E
Malazgirt, *Turkey* **25 G7** 39 10N 42 33 E
Malbon, *Australia* **62 C3** 21 5S 140 17 E
Malbooma, *Australia* **63 E1** 30 41S 134 11 E
Malbork, *Poland* **17 B10** 54 3N 19 1 E
Malcolm, *Australia* **61 E3** 28 51S 121 25 E
Malcolm, Pt., *Australia* **61 F3** 33 48S 123 45 E
Maldah, *India* **43 G13** 25 2N 88 9 E
Maldegem, *Belgium* **15 C3** 51 14N 3 26 E
Malden, *Mass., U.S.A.* **79 D13** 42 26N 71 4W
Malden, *Mo., U.S.A.* **81 G10** 36 34N 89 57W
Malden I., *Kiribati* **65 H12** 4 3S 155 1W
Maldives ■, *Ind. Oc.* **29 J11** 5 0N 73 0 E
Maldonado, *Uruguay* **95 C5** 34 59S 55 0W
Maldonado, Punta, *Mexico* **87 D5** 16 19N 98 35W
Malé, *Maldives* **29 J11** 4 0N 73 28 E
Malé Karpaty, *Slovak Rep.* **17 D9** 48 30N 17 20 E
Maléa, Ákra, *Greece* **21 F10** 36 28N 23 7 E
Malegaon, *India* **40 J9** 20 30N 74 38 E
Malei, *Mozam.* **55 F4** 17 12S 36 58 E
Malek Kandī, *Iran* **44 B5** 37 9N 46 6 E
Malela, *Dem. Rep. of the Congo* **54 C2** 4 22S 26 8 E
Malema, *Mozam.* **55 E4** 14 57S 37 20 E
Máleme, *Greece* **23 D5** 35 31N 23 49 E
Maleny, *Australia* **63 D5** 26 45S 152 52 E
Malerkotla, *India* **42 D6** 30 32N 75 58 E
Máles, *Greece* **23 D7** 35 6N 25 35 E
Malgomaj, *Sweden* **8 D17** 64 40N 16 30 E
Malha, *Sudan* **51 E11** 15 8N 25 10 E
Malhargarh, *India* **42 G6** 24 17N 74 59 E
Malheur —►, *U.S.A.* **82 D5** 44 4N 116 59W
Malheur L., *U.S.A.* **82 E4** 43 20N 118 48W
Mali ■, *Africa* **50 E5** 17 0N 3 0W
Mali —►, *Burma* **41 G20** 25 40N 97 40 E
Mali Kyun, *Burma* **38 F2** 13 0N 98 20 E
Malibu, *U.S.A.* **85 L8** 34 2N 118 41W
Maliku, *Indonesia* **37 E6** 0 39S 123 16 E
Malili, *Indonesia* **37 E6** 2 42S 121 6 E
Malimba, Mts., *Dem. Rep. of the Congo* **54 D2** 7 30S 29 30 E
Malin Hd., *Ireland* **13 A4** 55 23N 7 23W
Malin Pen., *Ireland* **13 A4** 55 20N 7 17W
Malindi, *Kenya* **54 C5** 3 12S 40 5 E
Malines = Mechelen, *Belgium* **15 C4** 51 2N 4 29 E
Malino, *Indonesia* **37 D6** 1 0N 121 0 E
Malinyi, *Tanzania* **55 D4** 8 56S 36 0 E
Malita, *Phil.* **37 C7** 6 19N 125 39 E
Maliwun, *Burma* **36 B1** 10 17N 98 40 E
Maliya, *India* **42 H4** 23 5N 70 46 E
Malkara, *Turkey* **21 D12** 40 53N 26 53 E
Mallacoota Inlet, *Australia* **63 F4** 37 34S 149 40 E
Mallaig, *U.K.* **12 D3** 57 0N 5 50W

Mallawan, India 43 F9 27 4N 80 12 E
Mallawi, Egypt 51 C12 27 44N 30 44 E
Mállia, Greece 23 D7 35 17N 25 32 E
Mallión, Kólpos, Greece 23 D7 35 19N 25 27 E
Mallorca, Spain 22 B10 39 30N 3 0 E
Mallorytown, Canada 79 B9 44 29N 75 53W
Mallow, Ireland 13 D3 52 8N 8 39W
Malmberget, Sweden 8 C19 67 11N 20 40 E
Malmédy, Belgium 15 D6 50 25N 6 2 E
Malmesbury, S. Africa 56 E2 33 28S 18 41 E
Malmö, Sweden 9 J15 55 36N 12 59 E
Malolos, Phil. 37 B6 14 50N 120 49 E
Malombe L., Malawi 55 E4 14 40S 35 15 E
Malone, U.S.A. 79 B10 44 51N 74 18W
Måløy, Norway 9 F11 61 57N 5 6 E
Malpaso, Canary Is. 22 G1 27 43N 18 3W
Malpelo, I. de, Colombia 92 C2 4 3N 81 35W
Malpur, India 42 H5 23 21N 73 27 E
Malpura, India 42 F6 26 17N 75 23 E
Malta, Idaho, U.S.A. 82 E7 42 18N 113 22W
Malta, Mont., U.S.A. 82 B10 48 21N 107 52W
Malta ■, Europe 23 D2 35 50N 14 30 E
Maltahöhe, Namibia 56 C2 24 55S 17 0 E
Malton, Canada 78 C5 43 42N 79 38W
Malton, U.K. 10 C7 54 8N 0 49W
Maluku, Indonesia 37 E7 1 0S 127 0 E
Maluku □, Indonesia 37 E7 3 0S 128 0 E
Maluku Sea = Molucca Sea, Indonesia 37 E6 2 0S 124 0 E
Malvan, India 40 L8 16 2N 73 30 E
Malvern, U.S.A. 81 H8 34 22N 92 49W
Malvern Hills, U.K. 11 E5 52 0N 2 19W
Malvinas, Is. = Falkland Is. □, Atl. Oc. 96 G5 51 30S 59 0W
Malya, Tanzania 54 C3 3 5S 33 38 E
Malyn, Ukraine 17 C15 50 46N 29 3 E
Malyy Lyakhovskiy, Ostrov, Russia 27 B15 74 7N 140 36 E
Mama, Russia 27 D12 58 18N 112 54 E
Mamanguape, Brazil 93 E11 6 50S 35 4W
Mamarr Mitlā, Egypt 47 E1 30 2N 32 54 E
Mamasa, Indonesia 37 E5 2 55S 119 20 E
Mambasa, Dem. Rep. of the Congo 54 B2 1 22N 29 3 E
Mamberamo →, Indonesia 37 E9 2 0S 137 50 E
Mambilima Falls, Zambia 55 E2 10 31S 28 45 E
Mambirima, Dem. Rep. of the Congo 55 E2 11 25S 27 33 E
Mambo, Tanzania 54 C4 4 52S 38 22 E
Mambrui, Kenya 54 C5 3 5S 40 5 E
Mamburao, Phil. 37 B6 13 13N 120 39 E
Mameigwess L., Canada 70 B2 52 35N 87 50W
Mammoth, U.S.A. 83 K8 32 43N 110 39W
Mammoth Cave National Park, U.S.A. 76 G3 37 8N 86 13W
Mamoré →, Bolivia 92 F5 10 23S 65 53W
Mamou, Guinea 50 F3 10 15N 12 0W
Mamuju, Indonesia 37 E5 2 41S 118 50 E
Man, Ivory C. 50 G4 7 30N 7 40W
Man, I. of, U.K. 10 C3 54 15N 4 30W
Man-Bazar, India 43 H12 23 4N 86 39 E
Man Na, Burma 41 H20 23 27N 97 19 E
Mana →, Fr. Guiana 93 B8 5 45N 53 55W
Manaar, G. of = Mannar, G. of, Asia 40 Q11 8 30N 79 0 E
Manacapuru, Brazil 92 D6 3 16S 60 37W
Manacor, Spain 22 B10 39 34N 3 13 E
Manado, Indonesia 37 D6 1 29N 124 51 E
Managua, Nic. 88 D2 12 6N 86 20W
Managua, L. de, Nic. 88 D2 12 20N 86 30W
Manakara, Madag. 57 C8 22 8S 48 1 E
Manali, India 42 C7 32 16N 77 10 E
Manama = Al Manāmah, Bahrain 45 E6 26 10N 50 30 E
Manambao →, Madag. 57 B7 17 35S 44 0 E
Manambato, Madag. 57 A8 13 43S 49 7 E
Manambolo →, Madag. 57 B7 19 18S 44 22 E
Manambolosy, Madag. 57 B8 16 2S 49 40 E
Mananara, Madag. 57 B8 16 10S 49 46 E
Mananara →, Madag. 57 C8 23 21S 47 42 E
Mananjary, Madag. 57 C8 21 13S 48 20 E
Manantenina, Madag. 57 C8 24 17S 47 19 E
Manaos = Manaus, Brazil 92 D7 3 0S 60 0W
Manapire →, Venezuela 92 B5 7 42N 66 7W
Manapouri, N.Z. 59 L1 45 34S 167 39 E
Manapouri, L., N.Z. 59 L1 45 32S 167 32 E
Manār, Jabal, Yemen 46 E3 14 2N 44 17 E
Manas, China 32 B3 44 17N 85 56 E
Manas →, India 41 F17 26 12N 90 40 E
Manaslu, Nepal 43 E11 28 33N 84 33 E
Manasquan, U.S.A. 79 F10 40 8N 74 3W
Manassa, U.S.A. 83 H11 37 11N 105 56W
Manaung, Burma 41 K18 18 45N 93 40 E
Manaus, Brazil 92 D7 3 0S 60 0W
Manawan L., Canada 73 B8 55 24N 103 14W
Manbij, Syria 44 B3 36 31N 37 57 E
Manchegorsk, Russia 26 C4 67 54N 32 58 E
Manchester, U.K. 10 D5 53 29N 2 12W
Manchester, Calif., U.S.A. 84 G3 38 58N 123 41W
Manchester, Conn., U.S.A. 79 E12 41 47N 72 31W
Manchester, Ga., U.S.A. 77 J3 32 51N 84 37W
Manchester, Iowa, U.S.A. 80 D9 42 29N 91 27W
Manchester, Ky., U.S.A. 76 G4 37 9N 83 46W
Manchester, N.H., U.S.A. 79 D13 42 59N 71 28W
Manchester, N.Y., U.S.A. 78 D7 42 56N 77 16W
Manchester, Pa., U.S.A. 79 F8 40 4N 76 43W
Manchester, Tenn., U.S.A. 77 H2 35 29N 86 5W
Manchester, Vt., U.S.A. 79 C11 43 10N 73 5W
Manchester L., Canada 73 A7 61 28N 107 29W
Manchhar L., Pakistan 42 F2 26 25N 67 39 E
Manchuria = Dongbei, China 35 D13 45 0N 125 0 E
Manchurian Plain, China 28 E16 47 0N 124 0 E
Mand →, India 43 J10 21 42N 83 15 E
Mand →, Iran 45 D7 28 20N 52 30 E
Manda, Chunya, Tanzania 54 D3 6 51S 32 29 E
Manda, Ludewe, Tanzania 55 E3 10 30S 34 40 E
Mandabé, Madag. 57 C7 21 0S 44 55 E
Mandaguari, Brazil 95 A5 23 32S 51 42W
Mandah = Töhöm, Mongolia 34 B5 44 27N 108 2 E
Mandal, Norway 9 G12 58 2N 7 25 E
Mandala, Puncak, Indonesia 37 E10 4 44S 140 20 E
Mandalay, Burma 41 J20 22 0N 96 4 E
Mandale = Mandalay, Burma 41 J20 22 0N 96 4 E
Mandalgarh, India 42 G6 25 12N 75 6 E
Mandalgovi, Mongolia 34 B4 45 45N 106 10 E
Mandalī, Iraq 44 C5 33 43N 45 28 E
Mandan, U.S.A. 80 B4 46 50N 100 54W
Mandar, Teluk, Indonesia 37 E5 3 35S 119 15 E
Mandaue, Phil. 37 B6 10 20N 123 56 E
Mandera, Kenya 54 B5 3 55N 41 53 E
Mandi, India 42 D7 31 39N 76 58 E
Mandi Dabwali, India 42 E6 29 58N 74 42 E
Mandimba, Mozam. 55 E4 14 20S 35 40 E
Mandioli, Indonesia 37 E7 0 40S 127 20 E
Mandla, India 43 H9 22 39N 80 30 E
Mandorah, Australia 60 B5 12 32S 130 42 E
Mandoto, Madag. 57 B8 19 34S 46 17 E
Mandra, Pakistan 42 C5 33 23N 73 12 E
Mandrare →, Madag. 57 D8 25 10S 46 30 E
Mandritsara, Madag. 57 B8 15 50S 48 49 E
Mandsaur, India 42 G6 24 3N 75 8 E
Mandurah, Australia 61 F2 32 36S 115 48 E
Mandvi, India 42 H3 22 51N 69 22 E
Mandya, India 40 N10 12 30N 77 0 E
Mandzai, Pakistan 42 D2 30 55N 67 6 E
Maneh, Iran 45 B8 37 39N 57 7 E
Maneroo Cr. →, Australia 62 C3 23 21S 143 53 E
Manfalût, Egypt 51 C12 27 20N 30 52 E
Manfredónia, Italy 20 D6 41 38N 15 55 E
Mangabeiras, Chapada das, Brazil 93 F9 10 0S 46 30W
Mangalia, Romania 17 G15 43 50N 28 35 E
Mangalore, India 40 N9 12 55N 74 47 E
Mangan, India 43 F13 27 31N 88 32 E
Mangaung, S. Africa 53 K5 29 10S 26 25 E
Mangawan, India 43 G9 24 41N 81 33 E
Mangaweka, N.Z. 59 H5 39 48S 175 47 E
Manggar, Indonesia 36 E3 2 50S 108 10 E
Manggawitu, Indonesia 37 E8 4 8S 133 32 E
Mangkalihat, Tanjung, Indonesia 37 D5 1 2N 118 59 E
Mangla, Pakistan 42 C5 33 7N 73 39 E
Mangla Dam, Pakistan 43 C5 33 9N 73 44 E
Manglaur, India 42 E7 29 44N 77 49 E
Mangnai, China 32 C4 37 52N 91 43 E
Mango, Togo 50 F6 10 20N 0 30 E
Mangoche, Malawi 55 E4 14 25S 35 16 E
Mangoky →, Madag. 57 C7 21 29S 43 41 E
Mangole, Indonesia 37 E6 1 50S 125 55 E
Mangombe, Dem. Rep. of the Congo 54 C2 1 20S 26 48 E
Mangonui, N.Z. 59 F4 35 1S 173 32 E
Mangrol, Mad. P., India 42 J4 21 7N 70 7 E
Mangrol, Raj., India 42 G6 25 20N 76 31 E
Mangueira, L. da, Brazil 95 C5 33 0S 52 50W
Mangum, U.S.A. 81 H5 34 53N 99 30W
Mangyshlak Poluostrov, Kazakstan 26 E6 44 30N 52 30 E
Manhattan, U.S.A. 80 F6 39 11N 96 35W
Manhiça, Mozam. 57 D5 25 23S 32 49 E
Mania →, Madag. 57 B8 19 42S 45 22 E
Manica, Mozam. 57 B5 18 58S 32 59 E
Manica e Sofala □, Mozam. 57 B5 19 10S 33 45 E
Manicaland □, Zimbabwe 55 F3 19 0S 32 30 E
Manicoré, Brazil 92 E6 5 48S 61 16W
Manicouagan →, Canada 71 C6 49 30N 68 30W
Manicouagan, Rés., Canada 71 B6 51 5N 68 40W
Maniema □, Dem. Rep. of the Congo 54 C2 3 0S 26 0 E
Manīfah, Si. Arabia 45 E6 27 44N 49 0 E
Manifold, C., Australia 62 C5 22 41S 150 50 E
Manigotagan, Canada 73 C9 51 6N 96 18W
Manigotagan →, Canada 73 C9 51 7N 96 20W
Manihari, India 43 G12 25 21N 87 38 E
Manihiki, Cook Is. 65 J11 10 24S 161 1W
Manika, Plateau de la, Dem. Rep. of the Congo 55 E2 10 0S 25 5 E
Manikpur, India 43 G9 25 4N 81 7 E
Manila, Phil. 37 B6 14 40N 121 3 E
Manila, U.S.A. 82 F9 40 59N 109 43W
Manila B., Phil. 37 B6 14 40N 120 35 E
Manilla, Australia 63 E5 30 45S 150 43 E
Maningrida, Australia 62 A1 12 3S 134 13 E
Manipur □, India 41 G19 25 0N 94 0 E
Manipur →, Burma 41 H19 23 45N 94 20 E
Manisa, Turkey 21 E12 38 38N 27 30 E
Manistee, U.S.A. 76 C2 44 15N 86 19W
Manistee →, U.S.A. 76 C2 44 15N 86 21W
Manistique, U.S.A. 76 C2 45 57N 86 15W
Manito L., Canada 73 C7 52 43N 109 43W
Manitoba □, Canada 73 B9 55 30N 97 0W
Manitoba, L., Canada 73 C9 51 0N 98 45W
Manitou, Canada 73 D9 49 15N 98 32W
Manitou, L., Canada 71 B6 50 55N 65 17W
Manitou Is., U.S.A. 76 C3 45 8N 86 0W
Manitou Springs, U.S.A. 80 F2 38 52N 104 55W
Manitoulin I., Canada 70 C3 45 40N 82 30W
Manitouwadge, Canada 70 C2 49 8N 85 48W
Manitowoc, U.S.A. 76 C2 44 5N 87 40W
Manizales, Colombia 92 B3 5 5N 75 32W
Manja, Madag. 57 C7 21 26S 44 20 E
Manjacaze, Mozam. 57 C5 24 45S 34 0 E
Manjakandriana, Madag. 57 B8 18 55S 47 47 E
Manjhand, Pakistan 42 G3 25 50N 68 10 E
Manjil, Iran 45 B6 36 46N 49 30 E
Manjimup, Australia 61 F2 34 15S 116 6 E
Manjra →, India 40 K10 18 49N 77 52 E
Mankato, Kans., U.S.A. 80 F5 39 47N 98 13W
Mankato, Minn., U.S.A. 80 C8 44 10N 94 0W
Mankayane, Swaziland 57 D5 26 40S 31 4 E
Mankera, Pakistan 42 D4 31 23N 71 26 E
Mankota, Canada 73 D7 49 25N 107 5W
Manlay = Üydzin, Mongolia 34 B4 44 9N 107 0 E
Manmad, India 40 J9 20 18N 74 28 E
Mann Ranges, Australia 61 E5 26 6S 130 5 E
Manna, Indonesia 36 E2 4 25S 102 55 E
Mannahill, Australia 63 E3 32 25S 140 0 E
Mannar, Sri Lanka 40 Q11 9 1N 79 54 E
Mannar, G. of, Asia 40 Q11 8 30N 79 0 E
Mannar I., Sri Lanka 40 Q11 9 5N 79 45 E
Mannheim, Germany 16 D5 49 29N 8 29 E
Manning, Canada 72 B5 56 53N 117 39W
Manning, Oreg., U.S.A. 84 E3 45 45N 123 13W
Manning, S.C., U.S.A. 77 J5 33 42N 80 13W
Manning Prov. Park, Canada 72 D4 49 5N 120 45W
Mannum, Australia 63 E2 34 50S 139 20 E
Manoharpur, India 43 H11 22 23N 85 12 E
Manokwari, Indonesia 37 E8 0 54S 134 0 E
Manombo, Madag. 57 C7 22 57S 43 28 E
Manono, Dem. Rep. of the Congo 54 D2 7 15S 27 25 E
Manosque, France 18 E6 43 49N 5 47 E
Manotick, Canada 79 A9 45 13N 75 41W
Manouane →, Canada 71 C5 49 30N 71 10W
Manouane, L., Canada 71 B5 50 45N 70 45W
Manp'o, N. Korea 35 D14 41 6N 126 24 E
Manpojin = Manp'o, N. Korea 35 D14 41 6N 126 24 E
Manpur, Mad. P., India 42 H6 22 26N 75 37 E
Manpur, Mad. P., India 43 H10 23 17N 83 35 E
Manresa, Spain 19 B6 41 48N 1 50 E
Mansa, Gujarat, India 42 H5 23 27N 72 45 E
Mansa, Punjab, India 42 E6 30 0N 75 27 E
Mansa, Zambia 55 E2 11 13S 28 55 E
Mansehra, Pakistan 42 B5 34 20N 73 15 E
Mansel I., Canada 69 B12 62 0N 80 0W
Mansfield, Australia 63 F4 37 4S 146 6 E
Mansfield, U.K. 10 D6 53 9N 1 11W
Mansfield, La., U.S.A. 81 J8 32 2N 93 43W
Mansfield, Mass., U.S.A. 79 D13 42 2N 71 13W
Mansfield, Ohio, U.S.A. 78 F2 40 45N 82 31W
Mansfield, Pa., U.S.A. 78 E7 41 48N 77 5W
Mansfield, Mt., U.S.A. 79 B12 44 33N 72 49W
Manson Creek, Canada 72 B4 55 37N 124 32W
Manta, Ecuador 92 D2 1 0S 80 40W
Mantalingajan, Mt., Phil. 36 C5 8 55N 117 45 E
Mantare, Tanzania 54 C3 2 42S 33 13 E
Manteca, U.S.A. 84 H5 37 48N 121 13W
Manteo, U.S.A. 77 H8 35 55N 75 40W
Mantes-la-Jolie, France 18 B4 48 58N 1 41 E
Manthani, India 40 K11 18 40N 79 35 E
Manti, U.S.A. 82 G8 39 16N 111 38W
Mantiqueira, Serra da, Brazil 95 A7 22 0S 44 0W
Manton, U.S.A. 76 C3 44 25N 85 24W
Mántova, Italy 20 B4 45 9N 10 48 E
Mänttä, Finland 9 E21 62 0N 24 40 E
Mantua = Mántova, Italy 20 B4 45 9N 10 48 E
Manu, Peru 92 F4 12 10S 70 51W
Manu →, Peru 92 F4 12 16S 70 55W
Manua Is., Amer. Samoa 59 B14 14 13S 169 35W
Manuel Alves →, Brazil 93 F9 11 19S 48 28W
Manui, Indonesia 37 E6 3 35S 123 5 E
Manuripi →, Bolivia 92 F5 11 6S 67 36W
Many, U.S.A. 81 K8 31 34N 93 29W
Manyara, L., Tanzania 54 C4 3 40S 35 50 E
Manych-Gudilo, Ozero, Russia 25 E7 46 24N 42 38 E
Manyonga →, Tanzania 54 C3 4 10S 34 15 E
Manyoni, Tanzania 54 D3 5 45S 34 55 E
Manzai, Pakistan 42 C4 32 12N 70 15 E
Manzanares, Spain 19 C4 39 2N 3 22W
Manzanillo, Cuba 88 B4 20 20N 77 31W
Manzanillo, Mexico 86 D4 19 0N 104 20W
Manzanillo, Pta., Panama 88 E4 9 30N 79 40W
Manzano Mts., U.S.A. 83 J10 34 40N 106 20W
Manzarīyeh, Iran 45 C6 34 53N 50 50 E
Manzhouli, China 33 B6 49 35N 117 25 E
Manzini, Swaziland 57 D5 26 30S 31 25 E
Mao, Chad 51 F9 14 4N 15 19 E
Maó, Spain 22 B11 39 53N 4 16 E
Maoke, Pegunungan, Indonesia 37 E9 3 40S 137 30 E
Maolin, China 35 C12 43 58N 123 30 E
Maoming, China 33 D6 21 50N 110 54 E
Maoxing, China 35 B13 45 28N 124 40 E
Mapam Yumco, China 32 C3 30 45N 81 28 E
Mapastepec, Mexico 87 D6 15 26N 92 54W
Mapia, Kepulauan, Indonesia 37 D8 0 50N 134 20 E
Mapimí, Mexico 86 B4 25 50N 103 50W
Mapimí, Bolsón de, Mexico 86 B4 27 30N 104 15W
Mapinga, Tanzania 54 D4 6 40S 39 12 E
Mapinhane, Mozam. 57 C6 22 20S 35 0 E
Maple Creek, Canada 73 D7 49 55N 109 29W
Maple Valley, U.S.A. 84 C4 47 25N 122 3W
Mapleton, U.S.A. 82 D2 44 2N 123 52W
Mapuera →, Brazil 92 D7 1 5S 57 2W
Maputo, Mozam. 57 D5 25 58S 32 32 E
Maputo, B. de, Mozam. 57 D5 25 50S 32 45 E
Maqiaohe, China 35 B16 44 40N 130 30 E
Maqnā, Si. Arabia 44 D2 28 25N 34 50 E
Maquela do Zombo, Angola 52 F3 6 0S 15 15 E
Maquinchao, Argentina 96 E3 41 15S 68 50W
Maquoketa, U.S.A. 80 D9 42 4N 90 40W
Mar, Serra do, Brazil 95 B6 25 30S 49 0W
Mar Chiquita, L., Argentina 94 C3 30 40S 62 50W
Mar del Plata, Argentina 94 D4 38 0S 57 30W
Mar Menor, Spain 19 D5 37 40N 0 45W
Mara, Tanzania 54 C3 1 30S 34 32 E
Mara □, Tanzania 54 C3 1 45S 34 20 E
Maraã, Brazil 92 D5 1 52S 65 25W
Marabá, Brazil 93 E9 5 20S 49 5W
Maracá, I. de, Brazil 93 C8 2 10N 50 30W
Maracaibo, Venezuela 92 A4 10 40N 71 37W
Maracaibo, L. de, Venezuela 92 B4 9 40N 71 30W
Maracaju, Brazil 95 A4 21 38S 55 9W
Maracay, Venezuela 92 A5 10 15N 67 28W
Maradi, Niger 50 F7 13 29N 7 20 E
Marāgheh, Iran 44 B5 37 30N 46 12 E
Marāh, Si. Arabia 44 E5 25 0N 45 35 E
Marajó, I. de, Brazil 93 D9 1 0S 49 30W
Marākand, Iran 44 B5 38 51N 45 16 E
Maralal, Kenya 54 B4 1 0N 36 38 E
Maralinga, Australia 61 F5 30 13S 131 32 E
Maran, Malaysia 39 L4 3 35N 102 45 E
Marana, U.S.A. 83 K8 32 27N 111 13W
Maranboy, Australia 60 B5 14 40S 132 39 E
Marand, Iran 44 B5 38 30N 45 45 E
Marang, Malaysia 39 K4 5 12N 103 13 E
Maranguape, Brazil 93 D11 3 55S 38 50W
Maranhão = São Luís, Brazil 93 D10 2 39S 44 15W
Maranhão □, Brazil 93 E9 5 0S 46 0W
Maranoa →, Australia 63 D4 27 50S 148 37 E
Marañón →, Peru 92 D4 4 30S 73 35W
Marão, Mozam. 57 C5 24 18S 34 2 E
Maraş = Kahramanmaraş, Turkey 25 G6 37 37N 36 53 E
Marathasa □, Cyprus 23 E11 34 59N 32 51 E
Marathon, Australia 62 C3 20 51S 143 32 E
Marathon, Canada 70 C2 48 44N 86 23W
Marathon, N.Y., U.S.A. 79 D8 42 26N 76 2W
Marathon, N.Y., U.S.A. 79 D8 42 27N 76 2W
Marathon, Tex., U.S.A. 81 K3 30 12N 103 15W
Marathóvouno, Cyprus 23 D12 35 13N 33 37 E
Maratua, Indonesia 37 D5 2 10N 118 35 E
Maravatío, Mexico 86 D4 19 51N 100 25W
Marāwih, U.A.E. 45 E7 24 18N 53 18 E
Marbella, Spain 19 D3 36 30N 4 57W
Marble Bar, Australia 60 D2 21 9S 119 44 E
Marble Falls, U.S.A. 81 K5 30 35N 98 16W
Marblehead, U.S.A. 79 D14 42 30N 70 51W
Marburg, Germany 16 C5 50 47N 8 46 E
March, U.K. 11 E8 52 33N 0 5 E
Marche, France 18 C4 46 5N 1 20 E
Marche-en-Famenne, Belgium 15 D5 50 14N 5 19 E
Marchena, Spain 19 D3 37 18N 5 23W
Marco, U.S.A. 77 N5 25 58N 81 44W
Marcos Juárez, Argentina 94 C3 32 42S 62 5W
Marcus I. = Minami-Tori-Shima, Pac. Oc. 64 E7 24 20N 153 58 E
Marcus Necker Ridge, Pac. Oc. 64 F9 20 0N 175 0 E
Marcy, Mt., U.S.A. 79 B11 44 7N 73 56W
Mardan, Pakistan 42 B5 34 20N 72 0 E
Mardin, Turkey 25 G7 37 20N 40 43 E
Maree, L., U.K. 12 D3 57 40N 5 26W
Mareeba, Australia 62 B4 16 59S 145 28 E
Marek = Stanke Dimitrov, Bulgaria 21 C10 42 17N 23 9 E
Marengo, U.S.A. 80 E8 41 48N 92 4W
Marenyi, Kenya 54 C4 4 22S 39 8 E
Marerano, Madag. 57 C7 21 23S 44 52 E
Marfa, U.S.A. 81 K2 30 19N 104 1W
Marfa Pt., Malta 23 D1 35 59N 14 19 E
Margaret →, Australia 60 C4 18 9S 125 41 E
Margaret Bay, Canada 72 C3 51 20N 127 35W
Margaret L., Canada 72 B5 58 56N 115 25W
Margaret River, Australia 61 F2 33 57S 115 4 E
Margarita, I. de, Venezuela 92 A6 11 0N 64 0W
Margaritovo, Russia 30 C7 43 25N 134 45 E
Margate, S. Africa 57 E5 30 50S 30 20 E
Margate, U.K. 11 F9 51 23N 1 23 E
Marguerite, Canada 72 C4 52 30N 122 25W
Mari El □, Russia 24 C8 56 30N 48 0 E
Mari Indus, Pakistan 42 C4 32 57N 71 34 E
Mari Republic = Mari El □, Russia 24 C8 56 30N 48 0 E
María Elena, Chile 94 A2 22 18S 69 40W
María Grande, Argentina 94 C4 31 45S 59 55W
Maria I., N. Terr., Australia 62 A2 14 52S 135 45 E
Maria I., Tas., Australia 62 G4 42 35S 148 0 E
Maria van Diemen, C., N.Z. 59 F4 34 29S 172 40 E
Mariakani, Kenya 54 C4 3 50S 39 27 E
Marian, Australia 62 C4 21 9S 148 57 E
Marian L., Canada 72 A5 63 0N 116 15W
Mariana Trench, Pac. Oc. 28 H18 13 0N 145 0 E
Marianao, Cuba 88 B3 23 8N 82 24W
Marianna, Ark., U.S.A. 81 H9 34 46N 90 46W
Marianna, Fla., U.S.A. 77 K3 30 46N 85 14W
Marias →, U.S.A. 82 C8 47 56N 110 30W
Mariato, Punta, Panama 88 E3 7 12N 80 52W
Maribor, Slovenia 16 E8 46 36N 15 40 E
Marico →, Africa 56 C4 23 35S 26 57 E
Maricopa, Ariz., U.S.A. 83 K7 33 4N 112 3W
Maricopa, Calif., U.S.A. 85 K7 35 4N 119 24W
Marié →, Brazil 92 D5 0 27S 66 26W
Marie Byrd Land, Antarctica 5 D14 79 30S 125 0W
Marie-Galante, Guadeloupe 89 C7 15 56N 61 16W
Mariecourt = Kangiqsujuaq, Canada 69 B12 61 30N 72 0W
Mariembourg, Belgium 15 D4 50 6N 4 31 E
Mariental, Namibia 56 C2 24 36S 18 0 E
Marienville, U.S.A. 78 E5 41 28N 79 8W
Mariestad, Sweden 9 G15 58 43N 13 50 E
Marietta, Ga., U.S.A. 77 J3 33 57N 84 33W
Marietta, Ohio, U.S.A. 76 F5 39 25N 81 27W
Marieville, Canada 79 A11 45 26N 73 10W
Mariinsk, Russia 26 D9 56 10N 87 20 E
Marijampole, Lithuania 9 J20 54 33N 23 19 E
Marília, Brazil 95 A6 22 13S 50 0W
Marín, Spain 19 A1 42 23N 8 42W
Marina, U.S.A. 84 J5 36 41N 121 48W
Marinduque, Phil. 37 B6 13 25N 122 0 E
Marinette, U.S.A. 76 C2 45 6N 87 38W
Maringá, Brazil 95 A5 23 26S 52 2W
Marion, Ala., U.S.A. 77 J2 32 38N 87 19W
Marion, Ill., U.S.A. 81 G10 37 44N 88 56W
Marion, Ind., U.S.A. 76 E3 40 32N 85 40W
Marion, Iowa, U.S.A. 80 D9 42 2N 91 36W
Marion, Kans., U.S.A. 80 F6 38 21N 97 1W
Marion, N.C., U.S.A. 77 H5 35 41N 82 1W
Marion, Ohio, U.S.A. 76 E4 40 35N 83 8W
Marion, S.C., U.S.A. 77 H6 34 11N 79 24W
Marion, Va., U.S.A. 77 G5 36 50N 81 31W
Marion, L., U.S.A. 77 J5 33 28N 80 10W
Mariposa, U.S.A. 84 H7 37 29N 119 58W
Mariscal Estigarribia, Paraguay 94 A3 22 3S 60 40W
Maritime Alps = Maritimes, Alpes, Europe 18 D7 44 10N 7 10 E
Maritimes, Alpes, Europe 18 D7 44 10N 7 10 E
Maritsa = Évros →, Bulgaria 21 D12 41 40N 26 34 E
Maritsá, Greece 23 C10 36 22N 28 8 E
Mariupol, Ukraine 25 E6 47 5N 37 31 E
Marīvān, Iran 44 C5 35 30N 46 25 E
Marj 'Uyūn, Lebanon 47 B4 33 20N 35 35 E
Markazī □, Iran 45 C6 35 0N 49 30 E
Markdale, Canada 78 B4 44 19N 80 39W
Marked Tree, U.S.A. 81 H9 35 32N 90 25W
Market Drayton, U.K. 10 E5 52 54N 2 29W
Market Harborough, U.K. 11 E7 52 29N 0 55W
Market Rasen, U.K. 10 D7 53 24N 0 20W
Markham, Canada 78 C5 43 52N 79 16W
Markham, Mt., Antarctica 5 E11 83 0S 164 0 E
Markleeville, U.S.A. 84 G7 38 42N 119 47W
Markovo, Russia 27 C17 64 40N 170 24 E
Marks, Russia 24 D8 51 45N 46 50 E
Marksville, U.S.A. 81 K8 31 8N 92 4W
Marla, Australia 63 D1 27 19S 133 33 E
Marlbank, Canada 78 B7 44 26N 77 6W
Marlboro, Mass., U.S.A. 79 D13 42 19N 71 33W
Marlboro, N.Y., U.S.A. 79 E11 41 36N 73 59W
Marlborough, Australia 62 C4 22 46S 149 52 E
Marlborough, U.K. 11 F6 51 25N 1 43W
Marlborough Downs, U.K. 11 F6 51 27N 1 53W
Marlin, U.S.A. 81 K6 31 18N 96 54W
Marlow, U.S.A. 81 H6 34 39N 97 58W
Marmagao, India 40 M8 15 25N 73 56 E
Marmara, Turkey 21 D12 40 35N 27 38 E

Marmara, Sea of = Marmara Denizi, Turkey **21 D13** 40 45N 28 15 E
Marmara Denizi, Turkey **21 D13** 40 45N 28 15 E
Marmaris, Turkey **21 F13** 36 50N 28 14 E
Marmion, Mt., Australia **61 E2** 29 16S 119 50 E
Marmion L., Canada **70 C1** 48 55N 91 20W
Marmolada, Mte., Italy **20 A4** 46 26N 11 51 E
Marmora, Canada **78 B7** 44 28N 77 41W
Marne →, France **18 B5** 48 48N 2 24 E
Maroala, Madag. **57 B8** 15 23S 47 59 E
Maroantsetra, Madag. **57 B8** 15 26S 49 44 E
Maromandia, Madag. **57 A8** 14 13S 48 5 E
Marondera, Zimbabwe **55 F3** 18 5S 31 42 E
Maroni →, Fr. Guiana **93 B8** 5 30N 54 0W
Maroochydore, Australia **63 D5** 26 29S 153 5 E
Maroona, Australia **63 F3** 37 27S 142 54 E
Marosakoa, Madag. **57 B8** 15 26S 46 38 E
Maroua, Cameroon **51 F8** 10 40N 14 20 E
Marovoay, Madag. **57 B8** 16 6S 46 39 E
Marquard, S. Africa **56 D4** 28 40S 27 28 E
Marquesas Is. = Marquises, Is., Pac. Oc. **65 H14** 9 30S 140 0W
Marquette, U.S.A. **76 B2** 46 33N 87 24W
Marquises, Is., Pac. Oc. **65 H14** 9 30S 140 0W
Marra, Djebel, Sudan **51 F10** 13 10N 24 22 E
Marracuene, Mozam. **57 D5** 25 45S 32 35 E
Marrakech, Morocco **50 B4** 31 9N 8 0W
Marrawah, Australia **62 G3** 40 55S 144 42 E
Marree, Australia **63 D2** 29 39S 138 1 E
Marrero, U.S.A. **81 L9** 29 54N 90 6W
Marrimane, Mozam. **57 C5** 22 58S 33 34 E
Marromeu, Mozam. **57 B6** 18 15S 36 25 E
Marrowie Cr. →, Australia **63 E4** 33 23S 145 40 E
Marrubane, Mozam. **55 F4** 18 0S 37 0 E
Marrupa, Mozam. **55 E4** 13 8S 37 30 E
Mars Hill, U.S.A. **77 B12** 46 31N 67 52W
Marsá Matrûh, Egypt **51 B11** 31 19N 27 9 E
Marsabit, Kenya **54 B4** 2 18N 38 0 E
Marsala, Italy **20 F5** 37 48N 12 26 E
Marsalforn, Malta **23 C1** 36 4N 14 15 E
Marsden, Australia **63 E4** 33 47S 147 32 E
Marseille, France **18 E6** 43 18N 5 23 E
Marseilles = Marseille, France **18 E6** 43 18N 5 23 E
Marsh I., U.S.A. **81 L9** 29 34N 91 53W
Marshall, Ark., U.S.A. **81 H8** 35 55N 92 38W
Marshall, Mich., U.S.A. **76 D3** 42 16N 84 58W
Marshall, Minn., U.S.A. **80 C7** 44 25N 95 45W
Marshall, Mo., U.S.A. **80 F8** 39 7N 93 12W
Marshall, Tex., U.S.A. **81 J7** 32 33N 94 23W
Marshall →, Australia **62 C2** 22 59S 136 59 E
Marshall Is. ■, Pac. Oc. **64 G9** 9 0N 171 0 E
Marshalltown, U.S.A. **80 D8** 42 3N 92 55W
Marshfield, Mo., U.S.A. **81 G8** 37 15N 92 54W
Marshfield, Vt., U.S.A. **79 B12** 44 20N 72 20W
Marshfield, Wis., U.S.A. **80 C9** 44 40N 90 10W
Marshūn, Iran **45 B6** 36 19N 49 23 E
Märsta, Sweden **9 G17** 59 37N 17 52 E
Mart, U.S.A. **81 K6** 31 33N 96 50W
Martaban, Burma **41 L20** 16 30N 97 35 E
Martaban, G. of, Burma **41 L20** 16 5N 96 30 E
Martapura, Kalimantan, Indonesia **36 E4** 3 22S 114 47 E
Martapura, Sumatera, Indonesia **36 E2** 4 19S 104 22 E
Martelange, Belgium **15 E5** 49 49N 5 43 E
Martha's Vineyard, U.S.A. **79 E14** 41 25N 70 38W
Martigny, Switz. **18 C7** 46 6N 7 3 E
Martigues, France **18 E6** 43 24N 5 4 E
Martin, Slovak Rep. **17 D10** 49 6N 18 58 E
Martin, S. Dak., U.S.A. **80 D4** 43 11N 101 44W
Martin, Tenn., U.S.A. **81 G10** 36 21N 88 51W
Martin L., U.S.A. **77 J3** 32 41N 85 55W
Martina Franca, Italy **20 D7** 40 42N 17 20 E
Martinborough, N.Z. **59 J5** 41 14S 175 29 E
Martinez, Calif., U.S.A. **84 G4** 38 1N 122 8W
Martinez, Ga., U.S.A. **77 J4** 33 31N 82 4W
Martinique ■, W. Indies **89 D7** 14 40N 61 0W
Martinique Passage, W. Indies **89 C7** 15 15N 61 0W
Martinópolis, Brazil **95 A5** 22 11S 51 12W
Martins Ferry, U.S.A. **78 F4** 40 6N 80 44W
Martinsburg, Pa., U.S.A. **78 F6** 40 19N 78 20W
Martinsburg, W. Va., U.S.A. **76 F7** 39 27N 77 58W
Martinsville, Ind., U.S.A. **76 F2** 39 26N 86 25W
Martinsville, Va., U.S.A. **77 G6** 36 41N 79 52W
Marton, N.Z. **59 J5** 40 4S 175 23 E
Martos, Spain **19 D4** 37 44N 3 58W
Marudi, Malaysia **36 D4** 4 11N 114 19 E
Ma'ruf, Afghan. **40 D5** 31 30N 67 6 E
Marugame, Japan **31 G6** 34 15N 133 40 E
Marunga, Angola **56 B3** 17 28S 20 2 E
Marungu, Mts., Dem. Rep. of the Congo **54 D3** 7 30S 30 0 E
Marv Dasht, Iran **45 D7** 29 50N 52 40 E
Marvast, Iran **45 D7** 30 30N 54 15 E
Marvel Loch, Australia **61 F2** 31 28S 119 29 E
Marwar, India **42 G5** 25 43N 73 45 E
Mary, Turkmenistan **26 F7** 37 40N 61 50 E
Maryborough = Port Laoise, Ireland **13 C4** 53 2N 7 18W
Maryborough, Queens., Australia **63 D5** 25 31S 152 37 E
Maryborough, Vic., Australia **63 F3** 37 0S 143 44 E
Maryfield, Canada **73 D8** 49 50N 101 35W
Maryland □, U.S.A. **76 F7** 39 0N 76 30W
Maryland Junction, Zimbabwe **55 F3** 17 45S 30 31 E
Maryport, U.K. **10 C4** 54 44N 3 28W
Mary's Harbour, Canada **71 B8** 52 18N 55 51W
Marystown, Canada **71 C8** 47 10N 55 10W
Marysville, Canada **72 D5** 49 35N 116 0W
Marysville, Calif., U.S.A. **84 F5** 39 9N 121 35W
Marysville, Kans., U.S.A. **80 F6** 39 51N 96 39W
Marysville, Mich., U.S.A. **78 D2** 42 54N 82 29W
Marysville, Ohio, U.S.A. **76 E4** 40 14N 83 22W
Marysville, Wash., U.S.A. **84 B4** 48 3N 122 11W
Maryville, Mo., U.S.A. **80 E7** 40 21N 94 52W
Maryville, Tenn., U.S.A. **77 H4** 35 46N 83 58W
Marzūq, Libya **51 C8** 25 53N 13 57 E
Masahunga, Tanzania **54 C3** 2 6S 33 18 E
Masai Steppe, Tanzania **54 C4** 4 30S 36 30 E
Masaka, Uganda **54 C3** 0 21S 31 45 E
Masalembo, Kepulauan, Indonesia **36 F4** 5 35S 114 30 E
Masalima, Kepulauan, Indonesia **36 F5** 5 4S 117 5 E
Masamba, Indonesia **37 E6** 2 30S 120 15 E
Masan, S. Korea **35 G15** 35 11N 128 32 E
Masandam, Ra's, Oman **45 E8** 26 30N 56 30 E
Masasi, Tanzania **55 E4** 10 45S 38 52 E
Masaya, Nic. **88 D2** 12 0N 86 7W
Masbate, Phil. **37 B6** 12 21N 123 36 E
Mascara, Algeria **50 A6** 35 26N 0 6 E
Mascota, Mexico **86 C4** 20 30N 104 50W
Masela, Indonesia **37 F7** 8 9S 129 51 E
Maseru, Lesotho **56 D4** 29 18S 27 30 E
Mashaba, Zimbabwe **55 G3** 20 2S 30 29 E
Mashābih, Si. Arabia **44 E3** 25 35N 36 30 E
Masherbrum, Pakistan **43 B7** 35 38N 76 18 E
Mashhad, Iran **45 B8** 36 20N 59 35 E
Mashīz, Iran **45 D8** 29 56N 56 37 E
Mashkel, Hamun-i, Pakistan **40 E3** 28 20N 62 56 E
Mashki Chāh, Pakistan **40 E3** 29 5N 62 30 E
Mashonaland, Zimbabwe **53 H6** 16 30S 31 0 E
Mashonaland Central □, Zimbabwe **57 B5** 17 30S 31 0 E
Mashonaland East □, Zimbabwe **57 B5** 18 0S 32 0 E
Mashonaland West □, Zimbabwe **57 B4** 17 30S 29 30 E
Mashrakh, India **43 F11** 26 7N 84 48 E
Masindi, Uganda **54 B3** 1 40N 31 43 E
Masindi Port, Uganda **54 B3** 1 43N 32 2 E
Maşīrah, Oman **46 C6** 21 0N 58 50 E
Maşīrah, Khalīj, Oman **46 C6** 20 10N 58 10 E
Masisi, Dem. Rep. of the Congo **54 C2** 1 23S 28 49 E
Masjed Soleyman, Iran **45 D6** 31 55N 49 18 E
Mask, L., Ireland **13 C2** 53 36N 9 22W
Maskin, Oman **45 F8** 23 30N 56 50 E
Masoala, Tanjon' i, Madag. **57 B9** 15 59S 50 13 E
Masoarivo, Madag. **57 B7** 19 3S 44 19 E
Masohi = Amahai, Indonesia **37 E7** 3 20S 128 55 E
Masomeloka, Madag. **57 C8** 20 17S 48 37 E
Mason, Nev., U.S.A. **84 G7** 38 56N 119 8W
Mason, Tex., U.S.A. **81 K5** 30 45N 99 14W
Mason City, U.S.A. **80 D8** 43 9N 93 12W
Maspalomas, Canary Is. **22 G4** 27 46N 15 35W
Maspalomas, Pta., Canary Is. **22 G4** 27 43N 15 36W
Masqat, Oman **46 C6** 23 37N 58 36 E
Massa, Italy **18 D9** 44 1N 10 9 E
Massachusetts □, U.S.A. **79 D13** 42 30N 72 0W
Massachusetts B., U.S.A. **79 D14** 42 20N 70 50W
Massakory, Chad **51 F9** 13 0N 15 49 E
Massanella, Spain **22 B9** 39 48N 2 51 E
Massangena, Mozam. **57 C5** 21 34S 33 0 E
Massango, Angola **52 F3** 8 2S 16 21 E
Massawa = Mitsiwa, Eritrea **46 D2** 15 35N 39 25 E
Massena, U.S.A. **79 B10** 44 56N 74 54W
Massénya, Chad **51 F9** 11 21N 16 9 E
Masset, Canada **72 C2** 54 2N 132 10W
Massif Central, France **18 D5** 44 55N 3 0 E
Massillon, U.S.A. **78 F3** 40 48N 81 32W
Massinga, Mozam. **57 C6** 23 15S 35 22 E
Masson, Canada **79 A9** 45 32N 75 25W
Masson I., Antarctica **5 C7** 66 10S 93 20 E
Mastanli = Momchilgrad, Bulgaria **21 D11** 41 33N 25 23 E
Masterton, N.Z. **59 J5** 40 56S 175 39 E
Mastic, U.S.A. **79 F12** 40 47N 72 54W
Mastuj, Pakistan **43 A5** 36 20N 72 36 E
Mastung, Pakistan **40 E5** 29 50N 66 56 E
Masty, Belarus **17 B13** 53 27N 24 38 E
Masuda, Japan **31 G5** 34 40N 131 51 E
Masvingo, Zimbabwe **55 G3** 20 8S 30 49 E
Masvingo □, Zimbabwe **55 G3** 21 0S 31 30 E
Maşyāf, Syria **44 C3** 35 4N 36 20 E
Matabeleland, Zimbabwe **53 H5** 18 0S 27 0 E
Matabeleland North □, Zimbabwe **55 F2** 19 0S 28 0 E
Matabeleland South □, Zimbabwe **55 G2** 21 0S 29 0 E
Matachewan, Canada **70 C3** 47 56N 80 39W
Matadi, Dem. Rep. of the Congo **52 F2** 5 52S 13 31 E
Matagalpa, Nic. **88 D2** 13 0N 85 58W
Matagami, Canada **70 C4** 49 45N 77 34W
Matagami, L., Canada **70 C4** 49 50N 77 40W
Matagorda B., U.S.A. **81 L6** 28 40N 96 0W
Matagorda I., U.S.A. **81 L6** 28 15N 96 30W
Matak, Indonesia **39 L6** 3 18N 106 16 E
Mátala, Greece **23 E6** 34 59N 24 45 E
Matam, Senegal **50 E3** 15 34N 13 17W
Matamoros, Campeche, Mexico **87 D6** 18 50N 90 50W
Matamoros, Coahuila, Mexico **86 B4** 25 33N 103 15W
Matamoros, Tamaulipas, Mexico **87 B5** 25 50N 97 30W
Ma'ţan as Sarra, Libya **51 D10** 21 45N 22 0 E
Matandu →, Tanzania **55 D3** 8 45S 34 19 E
Matane, Canada **71 C6** 48 50N 67 33W
Matanomadh, India **42 H3** 23 33N 68 57 E
Matanzas, Cuba **88 B3** 23 0N 81 40W
Matapan, C. = Taínaron, Ákra, Greece **21 F10** 36 22N 22 27 E
Matapédia, Canada **71 C6** 48 0N 66 59W
Matara, Sri Lanka **40 S12** 5 58N 80 30 E
Mataram, Indonesia **36 F5** 8 41S 116 10 E
Matarani, Peru **92 G4** 17 0S 72 10W
Mataranka, Australia **60 B5** 14 55S 133 4 E
Matarma, Râs, Egypt **47 E1** 30 27N 32 44 E
Mataró, Spain **19 B7** 41 32N 2 29 E
Matatiele, S. Africa **57 E4** 30 20S 28 49 E
Mataura, N.Z. **59 M2** 46 11S 168 51 E
Matehuala, Mexico **86 C4** 23 40N 100 40W
Mateke Hills, Zimbabwe **55 G3** 21 48S 31 0 E
Matera, Italy **20 D7** 40 40N 16 36 E
Matetsi, Zimbabwe **55 F2** 18 12S 26 0 E
Mathis, U.S.A. **81 L6** 28 6N 97 50W
Mathráki, Greece **23 A3** 39 48N 19 31 E
Mathura, India **42 F7** 27 30N 77 40 E
Mati, Phil. **37 C7** 6 55N 126 15 E
Matiali, India **43 F13** 26 56N 88 49 E
Matías Romero, Mexico **87 D5** 16 53N 95 2W
Matibane, Mozam. **55 E5** 14 49S 40 45 E
Matima, Botswana **56 C3** 20 15S 24 26 E
Matiri Ra., N.Z. **59 J4** 41 38S 172 20 E
Matla →, India **43 J13** 21 40N 88 40 E
Matli, Pakistan **42 G3** 25 2N 68 39 E
Matlock, U.K. **10 D6** 53 9N 1 33W
Mato Grosso □, Brazil **93 F8** 14 0S 55 0W
Mato Grosso, Planalto do, Brazil **93 G8** 15 0S 55 0W
Mato Grosso do Sul □, Brazil **93 G8** 18 0S 55 0W
Matochkin Shar, Russia **26 B6** 73 10N 56 40 E
Matopo Hills, Zimbabwe **55 G2** 20 36S 28 20 E
Matopos, Zimbabwe **55 G2** 20 20S 28 29 E
Matosinhos, Portugal **19 B1** 41 11N 8 42W
Maţraḩ, Oman **46 C6** 23 37N 58 30 E
Matsue, Japan **31 G6** 35 25N 133 10 E
Matsumae, Japan **30 D10** 41 26N 140 7 E
Matsumoto, Japan **31 F9** 36 15N 138 0 E
Matsusaka, Japan **31 G8** 34 34N 136 32 E
Matsutō, Japan **31 F8** 36 31N 136 34 E
Matsuura, Japan **31 H4** 33 20N 129 49 E
Matsuyama, Japan **31 H6** 33 45N 132 45 E
Mattagami →, Canada **70 B3** 50 43N 81 29W
Mattancheri, India **40 Q10** 9 50N 76 15 E
Mattawa, Canada **70 C4** 46 20N 78 45W
Matterhorn, Switz. **18 D7** 45 58N 7 39 E
Matthew Town, Bahamas **89 B5** 20 57N 73 40W
Matthew's Ridge, Guyana **92 B6** 7 37N 60 10W
Mattice, Canada **70 C3** 49 40N 83 20W
Mattituck, U.S.A. **79 F12** 40 59N 72 32W
Mattoon, U.S.A. **76 F1** 39 29N 88 23W
Matuba, Mozam. **57 C5** 24 28S 32 49 E
Matucana, Peru **92 F3** 11 55S 76 25W
Matūn = Khowst, Afghan. **42 C3** 33 22N 69 58 E
Maturín, Venezuela **92 B6** 9 45N 63 11W
Mau, India **43 G10** 25 56N 83 33 E
Mau, Mad. P., India **43 F8** 26 17N 78 41 E
Mau, Ut. P., India **43 G9** 25 17N 81 23 E
Mau Escarpment, Kenya **54 C4** 0 40S 36 0 E
Mau Ranipur, India **43 G8** 25 16N 79 8 E
Maubeuge, France **18 A6** 50 17N 3 57 E
Maud, Pt., Australia **60 D1** 23 6S 113 45 E
Maude, Australia **63 E3** 34 29S 144 18 E
Maudin Sun, Burma **41 M19** 16 0N 94 30 E
Maués, Brazil **92 D7** 3 20S 57 45W
Mauganj, India **41 G12** 24 50N 81 55 E
Maughold Hd., U.K. **10 C3** 54 18N 4 18W
Maui, U.S.A. **74 H16** 20 48N 156 20W
Maulamyaing = Moulmein, Burma **41 L20** 16 30N 97 40 E
Maule □, Chile **94 D1** 36 5S 72 30W
Maumee, U.S.A. **76 E4** 41 34N 83 39W
Maumee →, U.S.A. **76 E4** 41 42N 83 28W
Maumere, Indonesia **37 F6** 8 38S 122 13 E
Maun, Botswana **56 C3** 20 0S 23 26 E
Mauna Kea, U.S.A. **74 J17** 19 50N 155 28W
Mauna Loa, U.S.A. **74 J17** 19 30N 155 35W
Maungmagan Is., Burma **38 F1** 14 0N 97 30 E
Maungmagan Kyunzu, Burma **41 N20** 14 0N 97 48 E
Maupin, U.S.A. **82 D3** 45 11N 121 5W
Maurepas, L., U.S.A. **81 K9** 30 15N 90 30W
Maurice, L., Australia **61 E5** 29 30S 131 0 E
Mauricie, Parc Nat. de la, Canada **70 C5** 46 45N 73 0W
Mauritania ■, Africa **50 E3** 20 50N 10 0W
Mauritius ■, Ind. Oc. **49 J9** 20 0S 57 0 E
Mauston, U.S.A. **80 D9** 43 48N 90 5W
Mavli, India **42 G5** 24 45N 73 55 E
Mavuradonha Mts., Zimbabwe **55 F3** 16 30S 31 30 E
Mawa, Dem. Rep. of the Congo **54 B2** 2 45N 26 40 E
Mawai, India **43 H9** 22 30N 81 4 E
Mawana, India **42 E7** 29 6N 77 58 E
Mawand, Pakistan **42 E3** 29 33N 68 38 E
Mawk Mai, Burma **41 J20** 20 14N 97 37 E
Mawlaik, Burma **41 H19** 23 40N 94 26 E
Mawqaq, Si. Arabia **44 E4** 27 25N 41 8 E
Mawson Coast, Antarctica **5 C6** 68 30S 63 0 E
Max, U.S.A. **80 B4** 47 49N 101 18W
Maxcanú, Mexico **87 C6** 20 40N 92 0W
Maxesibeni, S. Africa **57 E4** 30 49S 29 23 E
Maxhamish L., Canada **72 B4** 59 50N 123 17W
Maxixe, Mozam. **57 C6** 23 54S 35 17 E
Maxville, Canada **79 A10** 45 17N 74 51W
Maxwell, U.S.A. **84 F4** 39 17N 122 11W
Maxwelton, Australia **62 C3** 20 43S 142 41 E
May, C., U.S.A. **76 F8** 38 56N 74 58W
May Pen, Jamaica **88 C4** 17 58N 77 15W
Maya →, Russia **27 D14** 60 28N 134 28 E
Maya Mts., Belize **87 D7** 16 30N 89 0W
Mayaguana, Bahamas **89 B5** 22 30N 72 44W
Mayagüez, Puerto Rico **89 C6** 18 12N 67 9W
Mayāmey, Iran **45 B7** 36 24N 55 42 E
Mayanup, Australia **61 F2** 33 57S 116 27 E
Mayapan, Mexico **87 C7** 20 30N 89 25W
Mayarí, Cuba **89 B4** 20 40N 75 41W
Maybell, U.S.A. **82 F9** 40 31N 108 5W
Maybole, U.K. **12 F4** 55 21N 4 42W
Maydān, Iraq **44 C5** 34 55N 45 37 E
Maydena, Australia **62 G4** 42 45S 146 30 E
Mayenne →, France **18 C3** 47 30N 0 32W
Mayer, U.S.A. **83 J7** 34 24N 112 14W
Mayerthorpe, Canada **72 C5** 53 57N 115 8W
Mayfield, Ky., U.S.A. **77 G1** 36 44N 88 38W
Mayfield, N.Y., U.S.A. **79 C10** 43 6N 74 16W
Mayhill, U.S.A. **83 K11** 32 53N 105 29W
Maykop, Russia **25 F7** 44 35N 40 10 E
Maymyo, Burma **38 A1** 22 2N 96 28 E
Maynard, Mass., U.S.A. **79 D13** 42 26N 71 27W
Maynard, Wash., U.S.A. **84 C4** 47 59N 122 55W
Maynard Hills, Australia **61 E2** 28 28S 119 49 E
Mayne →, Australia **62 C3** 23 40S 141 55 E
Maynooth, Ireland **13 C5** 53 23N 6 34W
Mayo, Canada **68 B6** 63 38N 135 57W
Mayo □, Ireland **13 C2** 53 53N 9 3W
Mayon Volcano, Phil. **37 B6** 13 15N 123 41 E
Mayor I., N.Z. **59 G6** 37 16S 176 17 E
Mayotte, I., Mayotte **53 G9** 12 50S 45 10 E
Maysville, U.S.A. **76 F4** 38 39N 83 46W
Mayu, Indonesia **37 D7** 1 30N 126 30 E
Mayumba, Gabon **52 E2** 3 25S 10 39 E
Mayville, N. Dak., U.S.A. **80 B6** 47 30N 97 20W
Mayville, N.Y., U.S.A. **78 D5** 42 15N 79 30W
Mayya, Russia **27 C14** 61 44N 130 18 E
Mazabuka, Zambia **55 F2** 15 52S 27 44 E
Mazagán = El Jadida, Morocco **50 B4** 33 11N 8 17W
Mazagão, Brazil **93 D8** 0 7S 51 16W
Mazán, Peru **92 D4** 3 30S 73 0W
Māzandarān □, Iran **45 B7** 36 30N 52 0 E
Mazapil, Mexico **86 C4** 24 38N 101 34W
Mazara del Vallo, Italy **20 F5** 37 39N 12 35 E
Mazarrón, Spain **19 D5** 37 38N 1 19W
Mazaruni →, Guyana **92 B7** 6 25N 58 35W
Mazatán, Mexico **86 B2** 29 0N 110 8W
Mazatenango, Guatemala **88 D1** 14 35N 91 30W
Mazatlán, Mexico **86 C3** 23 13N 106 25W
Mažeikiai, Lithuania **9 H20** 56 20N 22 20 E
Māzhān, Iran **45 C8** 32 30N 59 0 E
Mazīnān, Iran **45 B8** 36 19N 56 56 E
Mazoe, Mozam. **55 F3** 16 42S 33 7 E
Mazoe →, Mozam. **55 F3** 16 20S 33 30 E
Mazowe, Zimbabwe **55 F3** 17 28S 30 58 E
Mazurian Lakes = Mazurski, Pojezierze, Poland **17 B11** 53 50N 21 0 E
Mazurski, Pojezierze, Poland **17 B11** 53 50N 21 0 E
Mazyr, Belarus **17 B15** 51 59N 29 15 E
Mbabane, Swaziland **57 D5** 26 18S 31 6 E
Mbaïki, C.A.R. **52 D3** 3 53N 18 1 E
Mbala, Zambia **55 D3** 8 46S 31 24 E
Mbale, Uganda **54 B3** 1 8N 34 12 E
Mbalmayo, Cameroon **52 D2** 3 33N 11 33 E
Mbamba Bay, Tanzania **55 E3** 11 13S 34 49 E
Mbandaka, Dem. Rep. of the Congo **52 D3** 0 1N 18 18 E
Mbanza Congo, Angola **52 F2** 6 18S 14 16 E
Mbanza Ngungu, Dem. Rep. of the Congo **52 F2** 5 12S 14 53 E
Mbarara, Uganda **54 C3** 0 35S 30 40 E
Mbashe →, S. Africa **57 E4** 32 15S 28 54 E
Mbenkuru →, Tanzania **55 D4** 9 25S 39 50 E
Mberengwa, Zimbabwe **55 G2** 20 29S 29 57 E
Mberengwa, Mt., Zimbabwe **55 G2** 20 37S 29 55 E
Mbesuma, Zambia **55 E3** 10 0S 32 2 E
Mbeya, Tanzania **55 D3** 8 54S 33 29 E
Mbeya □, Tanzania **54 D3** 8 15S 33 30 E
Mbinga, Tanzania **55 E4** 10 50S 35 0 E
Mbini □, Eq. Guin. **52 D2** 1 30N 10 0 E
Mbour, Senegal **50 F2** 14 22N 16 54W
Mbuji-Mayi, Dem. Rep. of the Congo **54 D1** 6 9S 23 40 E
Mbulu, Tanzania **54 C4** 3 45S 35 30 E
Mburucuyá, Argentina **94 B4** 28 1S 58 14W
Mchinja, Tanzania **55 D4** 9 44S 39 45 E
Mchinji, Malawi **55 E3** 13 47S 32 58 E
Mdantsane, S. Africa **53 L5** 32 56S 27 46 E
Mead, L., U.S.A. **85 J12** 36 1N 114 44W
Meade, U.S.A. **81 G4** 37 17N 100 20W
Meadow Lake, Canada **73 C7** 54 10N 108 26W
Meadow Lake Prov. Park, Canada **73 C7** 54 27N 109 0W
Meadow Valley Wash →, U.S.A. **85 J12** 36 40N 114 34W
Meadville, U.S.A. **78 E4** 41 39N 80 9W
Meaford, Canada **78 B4** 44 36N 80 35W
Mealy Mts., Canada **71 B8** 53 10N 58 0W
Meander River, Canada **72 B5** 59 2N 117 42W
Meares, C., U.S.A. **82 D2** 45 37N 124 0W
Mearim →, Brazil **93 D10** 3 4S 44 35W
Meath □, Ireland **13 C5** 53 40N 6 57W
Meath Park, Canada **73 C7** 53 27N 105 22W
Meaux, France **18 B5** 48 58N 2 50 E
Mebechi-Gawa →, Japan **30 D10** 40 31N 141 31 E
Mecanhelas, Mozam. **55 F4** 15 12S 35 54 E
Mecca = Makkah, Si. Arabia **46 C2** 21 30N 39 54 E
Mecca, U.S.A. **85 M10** 33 34N 116 5W
Mechanicsburg, U.S.A. **78 F8** 40 13N 77 1W
Mechanicville, U.S.A. **79 D11** 42 54N 73 41W
Mechelen, Belgium **15 C4** 51 2N 4 29 E
Mecheria, Algeria **50 B5** 33 35N 0 18W
Mecklenburg, Germany **16 B6** 53 33N 11 40 E
Mecklenburger Bucht, Germany **16 A6** 54 20N 11 40 E
Meconta, Mozam. **55 E4** 14 59S 39 50 E
Medan, Indonesia **36 D1** 3 40N 98 38 E
Medanosa, Pta., Argentina **96 F3** 48 8S 66 0W
Médéa, Algeria **50 A6** 36 12N 2 50 E
Medellín, Colombia **92 B3** 6 15N 75 35W
Medelpad, Sweden **9 E17** 62 33N 16 30 E
Medemblik, Neths. **15 B5** 52 46N 5 8 E
Medford, Mass., U.S.A. **79 D13** 42 25N 71 7W
Medford, Oreg., U.S.A. **82 E2** 42 19N 122 52W
Medford, Wis., U.S.A. **80 C9** 45 9N 90 20W
Medgidia, Romania **17 F15** 44 15N 28 19 E
Media Agua, Argentina **94 C2** 31 58S 68 25W
Media Luna, Argentina **94 C2** 34 45S 66 44W
Medianeira, Brazil **95 B5** 25 17S 54 5W
Mediaş, Romania **17 E13** 46 9N 24 22 E
Medicine Bow, U.S.A. **82 F10** 41 54N 106 12W
Medicine Bow Pk., U.S.A. **82 F10** 41 21N 106 19W
Medicine Bow Ra., U.S.A. **82 F10** 41 10N 106 25W
Medicine Hat, Canada **73 D6** 50 0N 110 45W
Medicine Lake, U.S.A. **80 A2** 48 30N 104 30W
Medicine Lodge, U.S.A. **81 G5** 37 17N 98 35W
Medina = Al Madīnah, Si. Arabia **46 C2** 24 35N 39 52 E
Medina, N. Dak., U.S.A. **80 B5** 46 54N 99 18W
Medina, N.Y., U.S.A. **78 C6** 43 13N 78 23W
Medina, Ohio, U.S.A. **78 E3** 41 8N 81 52W
Medina →, U.S.A. **81 L5** 29 16N 98 29W
Medina del Campo, Spain **19 B3** 41 18N 4 55W
Medina L., U.S.A. **81 L5** 29 32N 98 56W
Medina Sidonia, Spain **19 D3** 36 28N 5 57W
Medinipur, India **43 H12** 22 25N 87 21 E
Mediterranean Sea, Europe **6 H7** 35 0N 15 0 E
Médoc, France **18 D3** 45 10N 0 50W
Medveditsa →, Russia **25 E7** 49 35N 42 41 E
Medvezhi, Ostrava, Russia **27 B17** 71 0N 161 0 E
Medvezhyegorsk, Russia **24 B5** 63 0N 34 25 E
Medway →, U.K. **11 F8** 51 27N 0 46 E
Medway Towns □, U.K. **11 F8** 51 25N 0 32 E
Meekatharra, Australia **61 E2** 26 32S 118 29 E
Meeker, U.S.A. **82 F10** 40 2N 107 55W
Meelpaeg Res., Canada **71 C8** 48 15N 56 33W
Meerut, India **42 E7** 29 1N 77 42 E
Meeteetse, U.S.A. **82 D9** 44 9N 108 52W
Mega, Ethiopia **46 G2** 3 57N 38 19 E
Mégara, Greece **21 F10** 37 58N 23 22 E
Megasini, India **43 J12** 21 38N 86 21 E
Meghalaya □, India **41 G17** 25 50N 91 0 E
Mégiscane, L., Canada **70 C4** 48 35N 75 55W
Meharry, Mt., Australia **60 D2** 22 59S 118 35 E
Mehlville, U.S.A. **80 F9** 38 30N 90 19W
Mehndawal, India **43 F10** 26 58N 83 5 E

Mehr Jān, Iran 45 C7 33 50N 55 6 E
Mehrābād, Iran 44 B5 36 53N 47 55 E
Mehrān, Iran 44 C5 33 7N 46 10 E
Mehrīz, Iran 45 D7 31 35N 54 28 E
Mei Xian, China 34 G4 34 18N 107 55 E
Meiktila, Burma 41 J19 20 53N 95 54 E
Meissen, Germany 16 C7 51 9N 13 29 E
Meizhou, China 33 D6 24 16N 116 6 E
Meja, India 43 G10 25 9N 82 7 E
Mejillones, Chile 94 A1 23 10S 70 30W
Mekele, Ethiopia 46 E2 13 33N 39 30 E
Mekhtar, Pakistan 40 D6 30 30N 69 15 E
Meknès, Morocco 50 B4 33 57N 5 33W
Mekong →, Asia 39 H6 9 30N 106 15 E
Mekongga, Indonesia 37 E6 3 39S 121 15 E
Mekvari = Kür →, Azerbaijan 25 G8 39 29N 49 15 E
Melagiri Hills, India 40 N10 12 20N 77 30 E
Melaka, Malaysia 39 L4 2 15N 102 15 E
Melalap, Malaysia 36 C5 5 10N 116 5 E
Mélambes, Greece 23 D6 35 8N 24 40 E
Melanesia, Pac. Oc. 64 H7 4 0S 155 0 E
Melbourne, Australia 63 F4 37 50S 145 0 E
Melbourne, U.S.A. 77 L5 28 5N 80 37W
Melchor Múzquiz, Mexico 86 B4 27 50N 101 30W
Melchor Ocampo, Mexico 86 C4 24 52N 101 40W
Mélèzes →, Canada 69 C12 57 30N 71 0W
Mélèzes →, Qué., Canada 70 A5 57 40N 69 29W
Melfort, Canada 73 C8 52 50N 104 37W
Melfort, Zimbabwe 55 F3 18 0S 31 25 E
Melhus, Norway 8 E14 63 17N 10 18 E
Melilla, N. Afr. 19 E4 35 21N 2 57W
Melipilla, Chile 94 C1 33 42S 71 15W
Mélissa, Ákra, Greece 23 D6 35 6N 24 33 E
Melita, Canada 73 D8 49 15N 101 0W
Melitopol, Ukraine 25 E6 46 50N 35 22 E
Melk, Austria 16 D8 48 13N 15 20 E
Mellansel, Sweden 8 E18 63 25N 18 17 E
Mellen, U.S.A. 80 B9 46 20N 90 40W
Mellerud, Sweden 9 G15 58 41N 12 28 E
Mellette, U.S.A. 80 C5 45 9N 98 30W
Mellieha, Malta 23 D1 35 57N 14 21 E
Melo, Uruguay 95 C5 32 20S 54 10W
Melolo, Indonesia 37 F6 9 53S 120 40 E
Melouprey, Cambodia 38 F5 13 48N 105 16 E
Melrose, Australia 63 E4 32 42S 146 57 E
Melrose, U.K. 12 F6 55 36N 2 43W
Melrose, Minn., U.S.A. 80 C7 45 40N 94 49W
Melrose, N. Mex., U.S.A. 81 H3 34 26N 103 38W
Melstone, U.S.A. 82 C10 46 36N 107 52W
Melton Mowbray, U.K. 10 E7 52 47N 0 54W
Melun, France 18 B5 48 32N 2 39 E
Melville, Canada 73 C8 50 55N 102 50W
Melville, C., Australia 62 A3 14 11S 144 30 E
Melville, L., Canada 71 B8 53 30N 60 0W
Melville B., Australia 62 A2 12 0S 136 45 E
Melville I., Australia 60 B5 11 30S 131 0 E
Melville I., Canada 4 B2 75 30N 112 0W
Melville Pen., Canada 69 B11 68 0N 84 0W
Memba, Mozam. 55 E5 14 11S 40 30 E
Memboro, Indonesia 37 F5 9 30S 119 30 E
Memel = Klaìpeda, Lithuania 9 J19 55 43N 21 10 E
Memel, S. Africa 57 D4 27 38S 29 36 E
Memmingen, Germany 16 E6 47 58N 10 10 E
Mempawah, Indonesia 36 D3 0 30N 109 5 E
Memphis, Mich., U.S.A. 78 D2 42 54N 82 46W
Memphis, Tenn., U.S.A. 81 H10 35 8N 90 3W
Memphis, Tex., U.S.A. 81 H4 34 44N 100 33W
Memphremagog, L., U.S.A. 79 B12 45 0N 72 12W
Mena, U.S.A. 81 H7 34 35N 94 15W
Menai Strait, U.K. 10 D3 53 11N 4 13W
Ménaka, Mali 50 E6 15 59N 2 18 E
Menam = Chao Phraya →, Thailand 38 F3 13 32N 100 36 E
Menarandra →, Madag. 57 D7 25 17S 44 30 E
Menard, U.S.A. 81 K5 30 55N 99 47W
Mendawai →, Indonesia 36 E4 3 30S 113 0 E
Mende, France 18 D5 44 31N 3 30 E
Mendez, Mexico 87 B5 25 7N 98 34W
Mendhar, India 43 C6 33 35N 74 10 E
Mendip Hills, U.K. 11 F5 51 17N 2 40W
Mendocino, U.S.A. 82 G2 39 19N 123 48W
Mendocino, C., U.S.A. 82 F1 40 26N 124 25W
Mendooran, Australia 63 E4 31 50S 149 6 E
Mendota, Calif., U.S.A. 84 J6 36 45N 120 23W
Mendota, Ill., U.S.A. 80 E10 41 33N 89 7W
Mendoza, Argentina 94 C2 32 50S 68 52W
Mendoza □, Argentina 94 C2 33 0S 69 0W
Mene Grande, Venezuela 92 B4 9 49N 70 56W
Menemen, Turkey 21 E12 38 34N 27 3 E
Menen, Belgium 15 D3 50 47N 3 7 E
Menggala, Indonesia 36 E3 4 30S 105 15 E
Mengjin, China 34 G7 34 55N 112 45 E
Mengyin, China 35 G9 35 40N 117 58 E
Mengzi, China 32 D5 23 20N 103 22 E
Menihek, Canada 71 B6 54 28N 56 36W
Menihek L., Canada 71 B6 54 0N 67 0W
Menin = Menen, Belgium 15 D3 50 47N 3 7 E
Menindee, Australia 63 E3 32 20S 142 25 E
Menindee L., Australia 63 E3 32 20S 142 25 E
Meningie, Australia 63 F2 35 50S 139 18 E
Menlo Park, U.S.A. 84 H4 37 27N 122 12W
Menominee, U.S.A. 76 C2 45 6N 87 37W
Menominee →, U.S.A. 76 C2 45 6N 87 36W
Menomonie, U.S.A. 80 C9 44 53N 91 55W
Menongue, Angola 53 G3 14 48S 17 52 E
Menorca, Spain 22 B11 40 0N 4 0 E
Mentakab, Malaysia 39 L4 3 29N 102 21 E
Mentawai, Kepulauan, Indonesia 36 E1 2 0S 99 0 E
Menton, France 18 E7 43 50N 7 29 E
Mentor, U.S.A. 78 E3 41 40N 81 21W
Menzelinsk, Russia 24 C9 55 47N 53 11 E
Menzies, Australia 61 E3 29 40S 121 2 E
Me'ona, Israel 47 B4 33 1N 35 15 E
Meoqui, Mexico 86 B3 28 17N 105 29W
Mepaco, Mozam. 55 F3 15 57S 30 48 E
Meppel, Neths. 15 B6 52 42N 6 12 E
Merabéllou, Kólpos, Greece 23 D7 35 10N 25 50 E
Merak, Indonesia 37 F12 6 10N 106 26 E
Meramangye, L., Australia 61 E5 28 25S 132 13 E
Meran = Merano, Italy 20 A4 46 40N 11 9 E
Merano, Italy 20 A4 46 40N 11 9 E
Merauke, Indonesia 37 F10 8 29S 140 24 E
Merbein, Australia 63 E3 34 10S 142 2 E
Merca, Somali Rep. 46 G3 1 48N 44 50 E
Merced, U.S.A. 84 H6 37 18N 120 29W
Merced →, U.S.A. 84 H6 37 21N 120 59W
Merced Pk., U.S.A. 84 H7 37 36N 119 24W
Mercedes, Buenos Aires, Argentina 94 C4 34 40S 59 30W
Mercedes, Corrientes, Argentina 94 B4 29 10S 58 5W
Mercedes, San Luis, Argentina 94 C2 33 40S 65 21W
Mercedes, Uruguay 94 C4 33 12S 58 0W
Mercedes, U.S.A. 81 M6 26 9N 97 55W
Merceditas, Chile 94 B1 28 20S 70 35W
Mercer, N.Z. 59 G5 37 16S 175 5 E
Mercer, U.S.A. 78 E4 41 14N 80 15W
Mercer Island, U.S.A. 84 C4 47 35N 122 15W
Mercury, U.S.A. 85 J11 36 40N 115 58W
Mercy C., Canada 69 B13 65 0N 63 30W
Mere, U.K. 11 F5 51 6N 2 16W
Meredith, C., Falk. Is. 96 G4 52 15S 60 40W
Meredith, L., U.S.A. 81 H4 35 43N 101 33W
Mergui, Burma 38 F2 12 26N 98 34 E
Mergui Arch. = Myeik Kyunzu, Burma 39 G1 11 30N 97 30 E
Mérida, Mexico 87 C7 20 58N 89 37W
Mérida, Spain 19 C2 38 55N 6 25W
Mérida, Venezuela 92 B4 8 24N 71 8W
Mérida, Cord. de, Venezuela 90 C3 9 0N 71 0W
Meriden, U.K. 11 E6 52 26N 1 38W
Meriden, U.S.A. 79 E12 41 32N 72 48W
Meridian, Calif., U.S.A. 84 F5 39 9N 121 55W
Meridian, Idaho, U.S.A. 82 E5 43 37N 116 24W
Meridian, Miss., U.S.A. 77 J1 32 22N 88 42W
Merimbula, Australia 63 F4 36 53S 149 54 E
Merinda, Australia 62 C4 20 2S 148 11 E
Meringur, Australia 63 E3 34 20S 141 19 E
Merir, Pac. Oc. 37 D8 4 10N 132 30 E
Merirumã, Brazil 93 C8 1 15N 54 50W
Merkel, U.S.A. 81 J5 32 28N 100 1W
Mermaid Reef, Australia 60 C2 17 6S 119 36 E
Merredin, Australia 61 F2 31 28S 118 18 E
Merrick, U.K. 12 F4 55 8N 4 28W
Merrickville, Canada 79 B9 44 55N 75 50W
Merrill, Oreg., U.S.A. 82 E3 42 1N 121 36W
Merrill, Wis., U.S.A. 80 C10 45 11N 89 41W
Merrimack →, U.S.A. 79 D14 42 49N 70 49W
Merriman, U.S.A. 80 D4 42 55N 101 42W
Merritt, Canada 72 C4 50 10N 120 45W
Merritt Island, U.S.A. 77 L5 28 21N 80 42W
Merriwa, Australia 63 E5 32 6S 150 22 E
Merry I., Canada 70 A4 55 29N 77 31W
Merryville, U.S.A. 81 K8 30 45N 93 33W
Mersch, Lux. 15 E6 49 44N 6 7 E
Mersea I., U.K. 11 F8 51 47N 0 58 E
Merseburg, Germany 16 C6 51 22N 11 59 E
Mersey →, U.K. 10 D4 53 25N 3 1W
Merseyside □, U.K. 10 D4 53 31N 3 2W
Mersin, Turkey 25 G5 36 51N 34 36 E
Mersing, Malaysia 39 L4 2 25N 103 50 E
Merta, India 42 F6 26 39N 74 4 E
Merta Road, India 42 F5 26 43N 73 55 E
Merthyr Tydfil, U.K. 11 F4 51 45N 3 22W
Merthyr Tydfil □, U.K. 11 F4 51 46N 3 21W
Mértola, Portugal 19 D2 37 40N 7 40W
Mertzon, U.S.A. 81 K4 31 16N 100 49W
Meru, Kenya 54 B4 0 3N 37 40 E
Meru, Tanzania 54 C4 3 15S 36 46 E
Mesa, U.S.A. 83 K8 33 25N 111 50W
Mesa Verde National Park, U.S.A. 83 H9 37 11N 108 29W
Mesanagrós, Greece 23 C9 36 1N 27 49 E
Mesaoria □, Cyprus 23 D12 35 12N 33 14 E
Mesarás, Kólpos, Greece 23 D6 35 6N 24 47 E
Mesgouez, L., Canada 70 B5 51 20N 75 0W
Meshed = Mashhad, Iran 45 B8 36 20N 59 35 E
Meshoppen, U.S.A. 79 E8 41 36N 76 3W
Mesilinka →, Canada 72 B4 56 6N 124 30W
Mesilla, U.S.A. 83 K10 32 16N 106 48W
Mesolóngion, Greece 21 E9 38 21N 21 28 E
Mesopotamia = Al Jazirah, Iraq 44 C5 33 30N 44 0 E
Mesopotamia, U.S.A. 78 E4 41 27N 80 57W
Mesquite, U.S.A. 83 H6 36 47N 114 6W
Messad, Algeria 50 B6 34 8N 3 30 E
Messalo →, Mozam. 55 E4 12 25S 39 15 E
Messina, Italy 20 E6 38 11N 15 34 E
Messina, S. Africa 57 C5 22 20S 30 5 E
Messina, Str. di, Italy 20 F6 38 15N 15 35 E
Messíni, Greece 21 F10 37 4N 22 1 E
Messiniakós Kólpos, Greece 21 F10 36 45N 22 5 E
Messonghi, Greece 23 B3 39 29N 19 56 E
Mesta →, Bulgaria 21 D11 40 54N 24 49 E
Meta →, S. Amer. 92 B5 6 12N 67 28W
Meta Incognita Peninsula, Canada 69 B13 62 40N 68 0W
Metabetchouan, Canada 71 C5 48 26N 71 52W
Metairie, U.S.A. 81 L9 29 58N 90 10W
Metaline Falls, U.S.A. 82 B5 48 52N 117 22W
Metán, Argentina 94 B3 25 30S 65 0W
Metangula, Mozam. 55 E3 12 40S 34 50 E
Metengobalame, Mozam. 55 E3 14 49S 34 30 E
Methven, N.Z. 59 K3 43 38S 171 40 E
Metil, Mozam. 55 F4 16 24S 39 0 E
Metlakatla, U.S.A. 68 C6 55 8N 131 35W
Metropolis, U.S.A. 81 G10 37 9N 88 44W
Mettur Dam, India 40 P10 11 45N 77 45 E
Metu, Ethiopia 46 F2 8 18N 35 35 E
Metz, France 18 B7 49 8N 6 10 E
Meulaboh, Indonesia 36 D1 4 11N 96 3 E
Meureudu, Indonesia 36 C1 5 19N 96 10 E
Meuse →, Europe 18 A6 50 45N 5 41 E
Mexia, U.S.A. 81 K6 31 41N 96 29W
Mexiana, I., Brazil 93 D9 0 0 49 30W
Mexicali, Mexico 85 N11 32 40N 115 30W
Mexican Plateau, Mexico 66 G9 25 0N 104 0W
Mexican Water, U.S.A. 83 H9 36 57N 109 32W
México, Mexico 87 D5 19 20N 99 10W
Mexico, Maine, U.S.A. 79 B14 44 34N 70 33W
Mexico, Mo., U.S.A. 80 F9 39 10N 91 53W
Mexico, N.Y., U.S.A. 79 C8 43 28N 76 18W
México □, Mexico 87 D5 19 20N 99 10W
Mexico ■, Cent. Amer. 86 C4 25 0N 105 0W
Mexico, G. of, Cent. Amer. 87 C7 25 0N 90 0W
Mexico B., U.S.A. 79 C8 43 35N 76 20W
Meydān-e Naftūn, Iran 45 D6 31 56N 49 18 E
Meydani, Ra's-e, Iran 45 E8 25 24N 59 6 E
Meymaneh, Afghan. 40 B4 35 53N 64 38 E
Mezen, Russia 24 A7 65 50N 44 20 E
Mezen →, Russia 24 A7 65 44N 44 22 E
Mézenc, Mt., France 18 D6 44 54N 4 11 E
Mezhdurechenskiy, Russia 26 D7 59 36N 65 56 E
Mezökövesd, Hungary 17 E11 47 49N 20 35 E
Mezőtúr, Hungary 17 E11 47 1N 20 41 E
Mezquital, Mexico 86 C4 23 29N 104 23W
Mgeta, Tanzania 55 D4 8 22S 36 6 E
Mhlaba Hills, Zimbabwe 55 F3 18 30S 30 30 E
Mhow, India 42 H6 22 33N 75 50 E
Miahuatlán, Mexico 87 D5 16 21N 96 36W
Miami, Fla., U.S.A. 77 N5 25 47N 80 11W
Miami, Okla., U.S.A. 81 G7 36 53N 94 53W
Miami, Tex., U.S.A. 81 H4 35 42N 100 38W
Miami Beach, U.S.A. 77 N5 25 47N 80 8W
Mian Xian, China 34 H4 33 10N 106 32 E
Mianchi, China 34 G6 34 48N 111 48 E
Mīāndarreh, Iran 45 C7 35 37N 53 39 E
Mīāndowāb, Iran 44 B5 37 0N 46 5 E
Miandrivazo, Madag. 57 B8 19 31S 45 29 E
Mīāneh, Iran 44 B5 37 30N 47 40 E
Mianwali, Pakistan 42 C4 32 38N 71 28 E
Miarinarivo, Madag. 57 B8 18 57S 46 55 E
Miass, Russia 24 D11 54 59N 60 6 E
Michalovce, Slovak Rep. 17 D11 48 47N 21 58 E
Michigan □, U.S.A. 76 C3 44 0N 85 0W
Michigan, L., U.S.A. 76 D2 44 0N 87 0W
Michigan City, U.S.A. 76 E2 41 43N 86 54W
Michipicoten I., Canada 70 C2 47 40N 85 40W
Michoacan □, Mexico 86 D4 19 0N 102 0W
Michurin, Bulgaria 21 C12 42 9N 27 51 E
Michurinsk, Russia 24 D7 52 58N 40 27 E
Mico, Pta., Nic. 88 D3 12 0N 83 30W
Micronesia, Pac. Oc. 64 G7 11 0N 160 0 E
Micronesia, Federated States of ■, Pac. Oc. 64 G7 9 0N 150 0 E
Midai, Indonesia 39 L6 3 0N 107 47 E
Midale, Canada 73 D8 49 25N 103 20W
Middelburg, Neths. 15 C3 51 30N 3 36 E
Middelburg, Eastern Cape, S. Africa 56 E4 31 30S 25 0 E
Middelburg, Mpumalanga, S. Africa 57 D4 25 49S 29 28 E
Middelwit, S. Africa 56 C4 24 51S 27 3 E
Middle Alkali L., U.S.A. 82 F3 41 27N 120 5W
Middle Bass I., U.S.A. 78 E2 41 41N 82 49W
Middle East, Asia 28 F7 38 0N 40 0 E
Middle Fork Feather →, U.S.A. 84 F5 38 33N 121 30W
Middle I., Australia 61 F3 34 6S 123 11 E
Middle Loup →, U.S.A. 80 E5 41 17N 98 24W
Middle Sackville, Canada 71 D7 44 47N 63 42W
Middleboro, U.S.A. 79 E14 41 54N 70 55W
Middleburg, Fla., U.S.A. 77 K5 30 4N 81 52W
Middleburg, N.Y., U.S.A. 79 D10 42 36N 74 20W
Middleburg, Pa., U.S.A. 78 F7 40 47N 77 3W
Middlebury, U.S.A. 79 B11 44 1N 73 10W
Middlemount, Australia 62 C4 22 50S 148 40 E
Middleport, N.Y., U.S.A. 78 C6 43 13N 78 29W
Middleport, Ohio, U.S.A. 76 F4 39 0N 82 3W
Middlesboro, U.S.A. 77 G4 36 36N 83 43W
Middlesbrough, U.K. 10 C6 54 35N 1 13W
Middlesbrough □, U.K. 10 C6 54 28N 1 13W
Middlesex, Belize 88 C2 17 2N 88 31W
Middlesex, N.J., U.S.A. 79 F10 40 36N 74 30W
Middlesex, N.Y., U.S.A. 78 D7 42 42N 77 16W
Middleton, Australia 62 C3 22 22S 141 32 E
Middleton, Canada 71 D6 44 57N 65 4W
Middleton Cr. →, Australia 62 C3 22 35S 141 51 E
Middletown, U.K. 13 B5 54 17N 6 51W
Middletown, Calif., U.S.A. 84 G4 38 45N 122 37W
Middletown, Conn., U.S.A. 79 E12 41 34N 72 39W
Middletown, N.Y., U.S.A. 79 E10 41 27N 74 25W
Middletown, Ohio, U.S.A. 76 F3 39 31N 84 24W
Middletown, Pa., U.S.A. 79 F8 40 12N 76 44W
Midhurst, U.K. 11 G7 50 59N 0 44W
Midi, Canal du →, France 18 E4 43 45N 1 21 E
Midland, Canada 78 B5 44 45N 79 50W
Midland, Calif., U.S.A. 85 M12 33 52N 114 48W
Midland, Mich., U.S.A. 76 D3 43 37N 84 14W
Midland, Pa., U.S.A. 78 F4 40 39N 80 27W
Midland, Tex., U.S.A. 81 K3 32 0N 102 3W
Midlands □, Zimbabwe 55 F2 19 40S 29 0 E
Midleton, Ireland 13 E3 51 55N 8 10W
Midlothian, U.S.A. 81 J6 32 30N 97 0W
Midlothian □, U.K. 12 F5 55 51N 3 5W
Midongy, Tangorombohitr' i, Madag. 57 C8 23 30S 47 0 E
Midongy Atsimo, Madag. 57 C8 23 35S 47 1 E
Midway Is., Pac. Oc. 64 E10 28 13N 177 22W
Midway Wells, U.S.A. 85 N11 32 41N 115 7W
Midwest, U.S.A. 75 B9 42 0N 90 0W
Midwest, Wyo., U.S.A. 82 E10 43 25N 106 16W
Midwest City, U.S.A. 81 H6 35 27N 97 24W
Midyat, Turkey 44 B4 37 25N 41 23 E
Midžor, Bulgaria 21 C10 43 24N 22 40 E
Mie □, Japan 31 G8 34 30N 136 10 E
Międzychód, Poland 16 B8 52 35N 15 53 E
Międzyrzec Podlaski, Poland 17 C12 51 58N 22 45 E
Mielec, Poland 17 C11 50 15N 21 25 E
Mienga, Angola 56 B2 17 12S 19 48 E
Miercurea-Ciuc, Romania 17 E13 46 21N 25 48 E
Mieres, Spain 19 A3 43 18N 5 48W
Mifflintown, U.S.A. 78 F7 40 34N 77 24W
Mifraz Hefa, Israel 47 C4 32 52N 35 0 E
Miguel Alemán, Presa, Mexico 87 D5 18 15N 96 40W
Mihara, Japan 31 G6 34 24N 133 5 E
Mikese, Tanzania 54 D4 6 48S 37 55 E
Mikhaylovgrad = Montana, Bulgaria 21 C10 43 27N 23 16 E
Mikhaylovka, Russia 25 D7 50 3N 43 5 E
Mikkeli, Finland 9 F22 61 43N 27 15 E
Mikkwa →, Canada 72 B6 58 25N 114 46W
Míkonos, Greece 21 F11 37 30N 25 25 E
Mikumi, Tanzania 54 D4 7 26S 37 0 E
Mikun, Russia 24 B9 62 20N 50 0 E
Milaca, U.S.A. 80 C8 45 45N 93 39W
Milagro, Ecuador 92 D3 2 11S 79 36W
Milan = Milano, Italy 18 D8 45 28N 9 12 E
Milan, Mo., U.S.A. 80 E8 40 12N 93 7W
Milan, Tenn., U.S.A. 77 H1 35 55N 88 46W
Milang, Australia 63 F2 35 24S 138 58 E
Milange, Mozam. 55 F4 16 3S 35 45 E
Milano, Italy 18 D8 45 28N 9 12 E
Milâs, Turkey 21 F12 37 20N 27 50 E
Milatos, Greece 23 D7 35 18N 25 34 E
Milazzo, Italy 20 E6 38 13N 15 15 E
Milbank, U.S.A. 80 C6 45 13N 96 38W
Milbanke Sd., Canada 72 C3 52 15N 128 35W
Milden, Canada 73 C7 51 29N 107 32W
Mildenhall, U.K. 11 E8 52 21N 0 32 E
Mildmay, Canada 78 B3 44 3N 81 7W
Mildura, Australia 63 E3 34 13S 142 9 E
Miles, Australia 63 D5 26 40S 150 9 E
Miles City, U.S.A. 80 B2 46 25N 105 51W
Milestone, Canada 73 D8 49 59N 104 31W
Miletus, Turkey 21 F12 37 30N 27 18 E
Milford, Calif., U.S.A. 84 E6 40 10N 120 22W
Milford, Conn., U.S.A. 79 E11 41 14N 73 3W
Milford, Del., U.S.A. 76 F8 38 55N 75 26W
Milford, Mass., U.S.A. 79 D13 42 8N 71 31W
Milford, N.H., U.S.A. 79 D13 42 50N 71 39W
Milford, Pa., U.S.A. 79 E10 41 19N 74 48W
Milford, Utah, U.S.A. 83 G7 38 24N 113 1W
Milford Haven, U.K. 11 F2 51 42N 5 7W
Milford Sd., N.Z. 59 L1 44 41S 167 47 E
Milḥ, Baḥr al, Iraq 44 C4 32 40N 43 35 E
Milikapiti, Australia 60 B5 11 26S 130 40 E
Miling, Australia 61 F2 30 30S 116 17 E
Milk →, U.S.A. 82 B10 48 4N 106 19W
Milk River, Canada 72 D6 49 10N 112 5W
Mill I., Antarctica 5 C8 66 0S 101 30 E
Mill Valley, U.S.A. 84 H4 37 54N 122 32W
Millau, France 18 D5 44 8N 3 4 E
Millbridge, Canada 78 B7 44 41N 77 36W
Millbrook, Canada 78 B6 44 10N 78 29W
Millbrook, U.S.A. 79 E11 41 47N 73 42W
Mille Lacs, L. des, Canada 70 C1 48 45N 90 35W
Mille Lacs L., U.S.A. 80 B8 46 15N 93 39W
Milledgeville, U.S.A. 77 J4 33 5N 83 14W
Millen, U.S.A. 77 J5 32 48N 81 57W
Miller, U.S.A. 80 C5 44 31N 98 59W
Millersburg, Ohio, U.S.A. 78 F3 40 33N 81 55W
Millersburg, Pa., U.S.A. 78 F8 40 32N 76 58W
Millerton, U.S.A. 79 E11 41 57N 73 31W
Millerton L., U.S.A. 84 J7 37 1N 119 41W
Millheim, U.S.A. 78 F7 40 54N 77 29W
Millicent, Australia 63 F3 37 34S 140 21 E
Millington, U.S.A. 81 H10 35 20N 89 53W
Millinocket, U.S.A. 77 C11 45 39N 68 43W
Millmerran, Australia 63 D5 27 53S 151 16 E
Millom, U.K. 10 C4 54 13N 3 16W
Mills L., Canada 72 A5 61 30N 118 20W
Millsboro, U.S.A. 78 G5 40 0N 80 0W
Milltown Malbay, Ireland 13 D2 52 52N 9 24W
Millville, N.J., U.S.A. 76 F8 39 24N 75 2W
Millville, Pa., U.S.A. 79 E8 41 7N 76 32W
Millwood L., U.S.A. 81 J8 33 42N 93 58W
Milne →, Australia 62 C2 21 10S 137 33 E
Milo, U.S.A. 77 C11 45 15N 68 59W
Mílos, Greece 21 F11 36 44N 24 25 E
Milparinka, Australia 63 D3 29 46S 141 57 E
Milton, N.S., Canada 71 D7 44 4N 64 45W
Milton, Ont., Canada 78 C5 43 31N 79 53W
Milton, N.Z. 59 M2 46 7S 169 59 E
Milton, Calif., U.S.A. 84 G6 38 3N 120 51W
Milton, Fla., U.S.A. 77 K2 30 38N 87 3W
Milton, Pa., U.S.A. 78 F8 41 1N 76 51W
Milton, Vt., U.S.A. 79 B11 44 38N 73 7W
Milton-Freewater, U.S.A. 82 D4 45 56N 118 23W
Milton Keynes, U.K. 11 E7 52 1N 0 44W
Milton Keynes □, U.K. 11 E7 52 1N 0 44W
Milverton, Canada 78 C4 43 34N 80 55W
Milwaukee, U.S.A. 76 D2 43 2N 87 55W
Milwaukee Deep, Atl. Oc. 89 C6 19 50N 68 0W
Milwaukie, U.S.A. 84 E4 45 27N 122 38W
Min Jiang →, Fujian, China 33 D6 26 0N 119 35 E
Min Jiang →, Sichuan, China 32 D5 28 45N 104 40 E
Min Xian, China 34 G3 34 25N 104 5 E
Mina Pirquitas, Argentina 94 A2 22 40S 66 30W
Mīnā Su'ud, Si. Arabia 45 D6 28 45N 48 28 E
Mīnā'al Aḥmadī, Kuwait 45 D6 29 5N 48 10 E
Minago →, Canada 73 C9 54 33N 98 59W
Minaki, Canada 73 D10 49 59N 94 40W
Minamata, Japan 31 H5 32 10N 130 30 E
Minami-Tori-Shima, Pac. Oc. 64 E7 24 20N 153 58 E
Minas, Uruguay 95 C4 34 20S 55 10W
Minas, Sierra de las, Guatemala 88 C2 15 9N 89 31W
Minas Basin, Canada 71 C7 45 20N 64 12W
Minas Gerais □, Brazil 93 G9 18 50S 46 0W
Minatitlán, Mexico 87 D6 17 59N 94 31W
Minbu, Burma 41 J19 20 10N 94 52 E
Minchinabad, Pakistan 42 D5 30 10N 73 34 E
Mindanao, Phil. 37 C7 8 0N 125 0 E
Mindanao Sea = Bohol Sea, Phil. 37 C6 9 0N 124 0 E
Mindanao Trench, Pac. Oc. 37 B7 12 0N 126 0 E
Minden, Canada 78 B6 44 55N 78 43W
Minden, Germany 16 B5 52 17N 8 55 E
Minden, La., U.S.A. 81 J8 32 37N 93 17W
Minden, Nev., U.S.A. 84 G7 38 57N 119 46W
Mindiptana, Indonesia 37 F10 5 55S 140 22 E
Mindoro, Phil. 37 B6 13 0N 121 0 E
Mindoro Str., Phil. 37 B6 12 30N 120 30 E
Mine, Japan 31 G5 34 12N 131 7 E
Minehead, U.K. 11 F4 51 12N 3 29W
Mineola, N.Y., U.S.A. 79 F11 40 45N 73 39W
Mineola, Tex., U.S.A. 81 J7 32 40N 95 29W
Mineral King, U.S.A. 84 J8 36 27N 118 36W
Mineral Wells, U.S.A. 81 J5 32 48N 98 7W
Minersville, U.S.A. 79 F8 40 41N 76 16W
Minerva, U.S.A. 78 F3 40 44N 81 6W
Minetto, U.S.A. 79 C8 43 24N 76 28W
Mingäçevir Su Anbarı, Azerbaijan 25 F8 40 57N 46 50 E
Mingan, Canada 71 B7 50 20N 64 0W
Mingechaurskoye Vdkhr. = Mingäçevir Su Anbarı, Azerbaijan 25 F8 40 57N 46 50 E
Mingela, Australia 62 B4 19 52S 146 38 E
Mingenew, Australia 61 E2 29 12S 115 21 E
Mingera Cr. →, Australia 62 C2 20 38S 137 45 E
Mingin, Burma 41 H19 22 50N 94 30 E
Mingo Junction, U.S.A. 78 F4 40 19N 80 37W
Mingyuegue, China 35 C15 43 2N 128 50 E
Minho = Miño →, Spain 19 A2 41 52N 8 40W
Minho, Portugal 19 B1 41 25N 8 20W
Minidoka, U.S.A. 82 E7 42 45N 113 29W

Minigwal, L., *Australia* **61 E3** 29 31S 123 14 E
Minilya →, *Australia* **61 D1** 23 45S 114 0 E
Minilya Roadhouse, *Australia* **61 D1** 23 55S 114 0 E
Minipi L., *Canada* **71 B7** 52 25N 60 45W
Mink L., *Canada* **72 A5** 61 54N 117 40W
Minna, *Nigeria* **50 G7** 9 37N 6 30 E
Minneapolis, *Kans., U.S.A.* **80 F6** 39 8N 97 42W
Minneapolis, *Minn., U.S.A.* **80 C8** 44 59N 93 16W
Minnedosa, *Canada* **73 C9** 50 14N 99 50W
Minnesota □, *U.S.A.* **80 B8** 46 0N 94 15W
Minnesota →, *U.S.A.* **80 C8** 44 54N 93 9W
Minnewaukan, *U.S.A.* **80 A5** 48 4N 99 15W
Minnipa, *Australia* **63 E2** 32 51S 135 9 E
Minnitaki L., *Canada* **70 C1** 49 57N 92 10W
Mino, *Japan* **31 G8** 35 32N 136 55 E
Miño →, *Spain* **19 A2** 41 52N 8 40W
Minorca = Menorca, *Spain* **22 B11** 40 0N 4 0 E
Minot, *U.S.A.* **80 A4** 48 14N 101 18W
Minqin, *China* **34 E2** 38 38N 103 20 E
Minsk, *Belarus* **17 B14** 53 52N 27 30 E
Mińsk Mazowiecki, *Poland* **17 B11** 52 10N 21 33 E
Mintabie, *Australia* **63 D1** 27 15S 133 7 E
Mintaka Pass, *Pakistan* **43 A6** 37 0N 74 58 E
Minteke Daban = Mintaka Pass, *Pakistan* **43 A6** 37 0N 74 58 E
Minto, *Canada* **71 C6** 46 5N 66 5W
Minto, L., *Canada* **70 A5** 57 13N 75 0W
Minton, *Canada* **73 D8** 49 10N 104 35W
Minturn, *U.S.A.* **82 G10** 39 35N 106 26W
Minusinsk, *Russia* **27 D10** 53 43N 91 20 E
Minutang, *India* **41 E20** 28 15N 96 30 E
Miquelon, *Canada* **70 C4** 49 25N 76 27W
Miquelon, *St- P. & M.* **71 C8** 47 8N 56 22W
Mīr Kūh, *Iran* **45 E8** 26 22N 58 55 E
Mīr Shahdād, *Iran* **45 E8** 26 15N 58 29 E
Mira, *Italy* **20 B5** 45 26N 12 8 E
Mira por vos Cay, *Bahamas* **89 B5** 22 9N 74 30W
Miraj, *India* **40 L9** 16 50N 74 45 E
Miram Shah, *Pakistan* **42 C4** 33 0N 70 2 E
Miramar, *Argentina* **94 D4** 38 15S 57 50W
Miramar, *Mozam.* **57 C6** 23 50S 35 35 E
Miramichi, *Canada* **71 C6** 47 2N 65 28W
Miramichi B., *Canada* **71 C7** 47 15N 65 0W
Miranda, *Brazil* **93 H7** 20 10S 56 15W
Miranda →, *Brazil* **92 G7** 19 25S 57 20W
Miranda de Ebro, *Spain* **19 A4** 42 41N 2 57W
Miranda do Douro, *Portugal* **19 B2** 41 30N 6 16W
Mirandópolis, *Brazil* **95 A5** 21 9S 51 6W
Mirango, *Malawi* **55 E3** 13 32S 34 58 E
Mirassol, *Brazil* **95 A6** 20 46S 49 28W
Mirbāṭ, *Oman* **46 D5** 17 0N 54 45 E
Miri, *Malaysia* **36 D4** 4 23N 113 59 E
Miriam Vale, *Australia* **62 C5** 24 20S 151 33 E
Mirim, L., *S. Amer.* **95 C5** 32 45S 52 50W
Mirnyy, *Russia* **27 C12** 62 33N 113 53 E
Mirokhan, *Pakistan* **42 F3** 27 46N 68 6 E
Mirond L., *Canada* **73 B8** 55 6N 102 47W
Mirpur, *Pakistan* **43 C5** 33 32N 73 56 E
Mirpur Batoro, *Pakistan* **42 G3** 24 44N 68 16 E
Mirpur Bibiwari, *Pakistan* **42 E2** 28 33N 67 44 E
Mirpur Khas, *Pakistan* **42 G3** 25 30N 69 0 E
Mirpur Sakro, *Pakistan* **42 G2** 24 33N 67 41 E
Mirtağ, *Turkey* **44 B4** 38 23N 41 56 E
Miryang, *S. Korea* **35 G15** 35 31N 128 44 E
Mirzapur, *India* **43 G10** 25 10N 82 34 E
Mirzapur-cum-Vindhyachal = Mirzapur, *India* **43 G10** 25 10N 82 34 E
Misantla, *Mexico* **87 D5** 19 56N 96 50W
Misawa, *Japan* **30 D10** 40 41N 141 24 E
Miscou I., *Canada* **71 C7** 47 57N 64 31W
Mish'āb, Ra's al, *Si. Arabia* **45 D6** 28 15N 48 43 E
Mishan, *China* **33 B8** 45 37N 131 48 E
Mishawaka, *U.S.A.* **76 E2** 41 40N 86 11W
Mishima, *Japan* **31 G9** 35 10N 138 52 E
Misión, *Mexico* **85 N10** 32 6N 116 53W
Misiones □, *Argentina* **95 B5** 27 0S 55 0W
Misiones □, *Paraguay* **94 B4** 27 0S 56 0W
Miskah, *Si. Arabia* **44 E4** 24 49N 42 56 E
Miskitos, Cayos, *Nic.* **88 D3** 14 26N 82 50W
Miskolc, *Hungary* **17 D11** 48 7N 20 50 E
Misoke, *Dem. Rep. of the Congo* **54 C2** 0 42S 28 2 E
Misool, *Indonesia* **37 E8** 1 52S 130 10 E
Misrātah, *Libya* **51 B9** 32 24N 15 3 E
Missanabie, *Canada* **70 C3** 48 20N 84 6W
Missinaibi →, *Canada* **70 B3** 50 43N 81 29W
Missinaibi L., *Canada* **70 C3** 48 23N 83 40W
Mission, *Canada* **72 D4** 49 10N 122 15W
Mission, *S. Dak., U.S.A.* **80 D4** 43 18N 100 39W
Mission, *Tex., U.S.A.* **81 M5** 26 13N 98 20W
Mission Beach, *Australia* **62 B4** 17 53S 146 6 E
Mission Viejo, *U.S.A.* **85 M9** 33 36N 117 40W
Missisa L., *Canada* **70 B2** 52 20N 85 7W
Missisicabi →, *Canada* **70 B4** 51 14N 79 31W
Mississagi →, *Canada* **70 C3** 46 15N 83 9W
Mississauga, *Canada* **78 C5** 43 32N 79 35W
Mississippi □, *U.S.A.* **81 J10** 33 0N 90 0W
Mississippi →, *U.S.A.* **81 L10** 29 9N 89 15W
Mississippi L., *Canada* **79 A8** 45 5N 76 10W
Mississippi River Delta, *U.S.A.* **81 L9** 29 10N 89 15W
Mississippi Sd., *U.S.A.* **81 K10** 30 20N 89 0W
Missoula, *U.S.A.* **82 C7** 46 52N 114 1W
Missouri □, *U.S.A.* **80 F8** 38 25N 92 30W
Missouri →, *U.S.A.* **80 F9** 38 49N 90 7W
Missouri City, *U.S.A.* **81 L7** 29 37N 95 32W
Missouri Valley, *U.S.A.* **80 E7** 41 34N 95 53W
Mist, *U.S.A.* **84 E3** 45 59N 123 15W
Mistassibi →, *Canada* **71 B5** 48 53N 72 13W
Mistassini, *Canada* **71 C5** 48 53N 72 12W
Mistassini →, *Canada* **71 C5** 48 42N 72 20W
Mistassini, L., *Canada* **70 B5** 51 0N 73 30W
Mistastin L., *Canada* **71 A7** 55 57N 63 20W
Mistinibi, L., *Canada* **71 A7** 55 56N 64 17W
Misty L., *Canada* **73 B8** 58 53N 101 40W
Misurata = Misrātah, *Libya* **51 B9** 32 24N 15 3 E
Mitchell, *Australia* **63 D4** 26 29S 147 58 E
Mitchell, *Canada* **78 C3** 43 28N 81 12W
Mitchell, *Nebr., U.S.A.* **80 E3** 41 57N 103 49W
Mitchell, *Oreg., U.S.A.* **82 D3** 44 34N 120 9W
Mitchell, *S. Dak., U.S.A.* **80 D6** 43 43N 98 2W
Mitchell →, *Australia* **62 B3** 15 12S 141 35 E
Mitchell, Mt., *U.S.A.* **77 H4** 35 46N 82 16W
Mitchell Ranges, *Australia* **62 A2** 12 49S 135 36 E
Mitchelstown, *Ireland* **13 D3** 52 15N 8 16W
Mitha Tiwana, *Pakistan* **42 C5** 32 13N 72 6 E
Mithi, *Pakistan* **42 G3** 24 44N 69 48 E
Mithrao, *Pakistan* **42 F3** 27 28N 69 40 E
Mitilíni, *Greece* **21 E12** 39 6N 26 35 E
Mito, *Japan* **31 F10** 36 20N 140 30 E
Mitrovica = Kosovska Mitrovica, *Serbia, Yug.* **21 C9** 42 54N 20 52 E
Mitsinjo, *Madag.* **57 B8** 16 1S 45 52 E
Mitsiwa, *Eritrea* **46 D2** 15 35N 39 25 E
Mitsukaidō, *Japan* **31 F9** 36 1N 139 59 E
Mittagong, *Australia* **63 E5** 34 28S 150 29 E
Mitú, *Colombia* **92 C4** 1 15N 70 13W
Mitumba, *Tanzania* **54 D3** 7 8S 31 2 E
Mitumba, Mts., *Dem. Rep. of the Congo* **54 D2** 7 0S 27 30 E
Mitwaba, *Dem. Rep. of the Congo* **55 D2** 8 2S 27 17 E
Mityana, *Uganda* **54 B3** 0 23N 32 2 E
Mixteco →, *Mexico* **87 D5** 18 11N 98 30W
Miyagi □, *Japan* **30 E10** 38 15N 140 45 E
Miyah, W. el →, *Syria* **44 C3** 34 44N 39 57 E
Miyake-Jima, *Japan* **31 G9** 34 5N 139 30 E
Miyako, *Japan* **30 E10** 39 40N 141 59 E
Miyako-Jima, *Japan* **31 M2** 24 45N 125 20 E
Miyako-Rettō, *Japan* **31 M2** 24 24N 125 0 E
Miyakonojō, *Japan* **31 J5** 31 40N 131 5 E
Miyani, *India* **42 J3** 21 50N 69 26 E
Miyanoura-Dake, *Japan* **31 J5** 30 20N 130 31 E
Miyazaki, *Japan* **31 J5** 31 56N 131 30 E
Miyazaki □, *Japan* **31 H5** 32 30N 131 30 E
Miyazu, *Japan* **31 G7** 35 35N 135 10 E
Miyet, Bahr el = Dead Sea, *Asia* **47 D4** 31 30N 35 30 E
Miyoshi, *Japan* **31 G6** 34 48N 132 51 E
Miyun, *China* **34 D9** 40 28N 116 50 E
Miyun Shuiku, *China* **35 D9** 40 30N 117 0 E
Mizdah, *Libya* **51 B8** 31 30N 13 0 E
Mizen Hd., *Cork, Ireland* **13 E2** 51 27N 9 50W
Mizen Hd., *Wick., Ireland* **13 D5** 52 51N 6 4W
Mizhi, *China* **34 F6** 37 47N 110 12 E
Mizoram □, *India* **41 H18** 23 30N 92 40 E
Mizpe Ramon, *Israel* **47 E3** 30 34N 34 49 E
Mizusawa, *Japan* **30 E10** 39 8N 141 8 E
Mjölby, *Sweden* **9 G16** 58 20N 15 10 E
Mjøsa, *Norway* **9 F14** 60 40N 11 0 E
Mkata, *Tanzania* **54 D4** 5 45S 38 20 E
Mkokotoni, *Tanzania* **54 D4** 5 55S 39 15 E
Mkomazi, *Tanzania* **54 C4** 4 40S 38 7 E
Mkomazi →, *S. Africa* **57 E5** 30 12S 30 50 E
Mkulwe, *Tanzania* **55 D3** 8 37S 32 20 E
Mkumbi, Ras, *Tanzania* **54 D4** 7 38S 39 55 E
Mkushi, *Zambia* **55 E2** 14 25S 29 15 E
Mkushi River, *Zambia* **55 E2** 13 32S 29 45 E
Mkuze, *S. Africa* **57 D5** 27 10S 32 0 E
Mladá Boleslav, *Czech Rep.* **16 C8** 50 27N 14 53 E
Mlala Hills, *Tanzania* **54 D3** 6 50S 31 40 E
Mlange = Mulanje, *Malawi* **55 F4** 16 2S 35 33 E
Mlanje, Pic, *Malawi* **53 H7** 15 57S 35 38 E
Mława, *Poland* **17 B11** 53 9N 20 25 E
Mljet, *Croatia* **20 C7** 42 43N 17 30 E
Mmabatho, *S. Africa* **56 D4** 25 49S 25 30 E
Mo i Rana, *Norway* **8 C16** 66 20N 14 7 E
Moa, *Cuba* **89 B4** 20 40N 74 56W
Moa, *Indonesia* **37 F7** 8 0S 128 0 E
Moab, *U.S.A.* **83 G9** 38 35N 109 33W
Moala, *Fiji* **59 D8** 18 36S 179 53 E
Moama, *Australia* **63 F3** 36 7S 144 46 E
Moapa, *U.S.A.* **85 J12** 36 40N 114 37W
Moate, *Ireland* **13 C4** 53 24N 7 44W
Moba, *Dem. Rep. of the Congo* **54 D2** 7 0S 29 48 E
Mobārakābād, *Iran* **45 D7** 28 24N 53 20 E
Mobaye, *C.A.R.* **52 D4** 4 25N 21 5 E
Mobayi, *Dem. Rep. of the Congo* **52 D4** 4 15N 21 8 E
Moberley Lake, *Canada* **72 B4** 55 50N 121 44W
Moberly, *U.S.A.* **80 F8** 39 25N 92 26W
Mobile, *U.S.A.* **77 K1** 30 41N 88 3W
Mobile B., *U.S.A.* **77 K2** 30 30N 88 0W
Mobridge, *U.S.A.* **80 C4** 45 32N 100 26W
Mobutu Sese Seko, L. = Albert L., *Africa* **54 B3** 1 30N 31 0 E
Moc Chau, *Vietnam* **38 B5** 20 50N 104 38 E
Moc Hoa, *Vietnam* **39 G5** 10 46N 105 56 E
Mocabe Kasari, *Dem. Rep. of the Congo* **55 D2** 9 58S 26 12 E
Moçambique, *Mozam.* **55 F5** 15 3S 40 42 E
Moçâmedes = Namibe, *Angola* **53 H2** 15 7S 12 11 E
Mocanaqua, *U.S.A.* **79 E8** 41 9N 76 8W
Mochudi, *Botswana* **56 C4** 24 27S 26 7 E
Mocimboa da Praia, *Mozam.* **55 E5** 11 25S 40 20 E
Moclips, *U.S.A.* **84 C2** 47 14N 124 13W
Mocoa, *Colombia* **92 C3** 1 7N 76 35W
Mococa, *Brazil* **95 A6** 21 28S 47 0W
Mocorito, *Mexico* **86 B3** 25 30N 107 53W
Moctezuma, *Mexico* **86 B3** 29 50N 109 0W
Moctezuma →, *Mexico* **87 C5** 21 59N 98 34W
Mocuba, *Mozam.* **55 F4** 16 54S 36 57 E
Mocúzari, Presa, *Mexico* **86 B3** 27 10N 109 10W
Modane, *France* **18 D7** 45 12N 6 40 E
Modasa, *India* **42 H5** 23 30N 73 21 E
Modder →, *S. Africa* **56 D3** 29 2S 24 37 E
Modderrivier, *S. Africa* **56 D3** 29 2S 24 38 E
Módena, *Italy* **20 B4** 44 40N 10 55 E
Modena, *U.S.A.* **83 H7** 37 48N 113 56W
Modesto, *U.S.A.* **84 H6** 37 39N 121 0W
Módica, *Italy* **20 F6** 36 52N 14 46 E
Moe, *Australia* **63 F4** 38 12S 146 19 E
Moebase, *Mozam.* **55 F4** 17 3S 38 41 E
Moengo, *Surinam* **93 B8** 5 45N 54 20W
Moffat, *U.K.* **12 F5** 55 21N 3 27W
Moga, *India* **42 D6** 30 48N 75 8 E
Mogadishu = Muqdisho, *Somali Rep.* **46 G4** 2 2N 45 25 E
Mogador = Essaouira, *Morocco* **50 B4** 31 32N 9 42W
Mogalakwena →, *S. Africa* **57 C4** 22 38S 28 40 E
Mogami-Gawa →, *Japan* **30 E10** 38 45N 140 0 E
Mogán, *Canary Is.* **22 G4** 27 53N 15 43W
Mogaung, *Burma* **41 G20** 25 20N 97 0 E
Mogi das Cruzes, *Brazil* **95 A6** 23 31S 46 11W
Mogi-Guaçu →, *Brazil* **95 A6** 20 53S 48 10W
Mogi-Mirim, *Brazil* **95 A6** 22 29S 47 0W
Mogilev = Mahilyow, *Belarus* **17 B16** 53 55N 30 18 E
Mogilev-Podolskiy = Mohyliv-Podilskyy, *Ukraine* **17 D14** 48 26N 27 48 E
Mogincual, *Mozam.* **55 F5** 15 35S 40 25 E
Mogocha, *Russia* **27 D12** 53 40N 119 50 E
Mogok, *Burma* **41 H20** 23 0N 96 40 E
Mogollon Rim, *U.S.A.* **83 J8** 34 10N 110 50W
Mogumber, *Australia* **61 F2** 31 2S 116 3 E
Mohács, *Hungary* **17 F10** 45 58N 18 41 E
Mohales Hoek, *Lesotho* **56 E4** 30 7S 27 26 E
Mohall, *U.S.A.* **80 A4** 48 46N 101 31W
Moḥammadābād, *Iran* **45 B8** 37 52N 59 5 E
Mohammedia, *Morocco* **50 B4** 33 44N 7 21W
Mohana →, *India* **43 G11** 24 43N 85 0 E
Mohanlalganj, *India* **43 F9** 26 41N 80 58 E
Mohave, L., *U.S.A.* **85 K12** 35 12N 114 34W
Mohawk →, *U.S.A.* **79 D11** 42 47N 73 41W
Mohenjodaro, *Pakistan* **42 F3** 27 19N 68 7 E
Mohicanville Reservoir, *U.S.A.* **78 F3** 40 45N 82 0W
Mohoro, *Tanzania* **54 D4** 8 6S 39 8 E
Mohyliv-Podilskyy, *Ukraine* **17 D14** 48 26N 27 48 E
Moidart, L., *U.K.* **12 E3** 56 47N 5 52W
Moira →, *Canada* **78 B7** 44 21N 77 24W
Moires, *Greece* **23 D6** 35 4N 24 56 E
Moisaküla, *Estonia* **9 G21** 58 3N 25 12 E
Moisie, *Canada* **71 B6** 50 12N 66 1W
Moisie →, *Canada* **71 B6** 50 14N 66 5W
Mojave, *U.S.A.* **85 K8** 35 3N 118 10W
Mojave Desert, *U.S.A.* **85 L10** 35 0N 116 30W
Mojo, *Bolivia* **94 A2** 21 48S 65 33W
Mojokerto, *Indonesia* **37 G15** 7 28S 112 26 E
Mokai, *N.Z.* **59 H5** 38 32S 175 56 E
Mokambo, *Dem. Rep. of the Congo* **55 E2** 12 25S 28 20 E
Mokameh, *India* **43 G11** 25 24N 85 55 E
Mokelumne →, *U.S.A.* **84 G5** 38 13N 121 28W
Mokelumne Hill, *U.S.A.* **84 G6** 38 18N 120 43W
Mokhós, *Greece* **23 D7** 35 16N 25 27 E
Mokhotlong, *Lesotho* **57 D4** 29 22S 29 2 E
Mokokchung, *India* **41 F19** 26 15N 94 30 E
Mokp'o, *S. Korea* **35 G14** 34 50N 126 25 E
Mokra Gora, *Serbia, Yug.* **21 C9** 42 50N 20 30 E
Mol, *Belgium* **15 C5** 51 11N 5 5 E
Molchanovo, *Russia* **26 D9** 57 40N 83 50 E
Mold, *U.K.* **10 D4** 53 9N 3 8W
Moldavia = Moldova ■, *Europe* **17 E15** 47 0N 28 0 E
Molde, *Norway* **8 E12** 62 45N 7 9 E
Moldova ■, *Europe* **17 E15** 47 0N 28 0 E
Moldoveana, Vf., *Romania* **17 F13** 45 36N 24 45 E
Mole →, *U.K.* **11 F7** 51 24N 0 21W
Mole Creek, *Australia* **62 G4** 41 34S 146 24 E
Molepolole, *Botswana* **56 C4** 24 28S 25 28 E
Molfetta, *Italy* **20 D7** 41 12N 16 36 E
Moline, *U.S.A.* **80 E9** 41 30N 90 31W
Molinos, *Argentina* **94 B2** 25 28S 66 15W
Moliro, *Dem. Rep. of the Congo* **54 D3** 8 12S 30 30 E
Mollendo, *Peru* **92 G4** 17 0S 72 0W
Mollerin, L., *Australia* **61 F2** 30 30S 117 35 E
Molodechno = Maladzyechna, *Belarus* **17 A14** 54 20N 26 50 E
Molokai, *U.S.A.* **74 H16** 21 8N 157 0W
Molong, *Australia* **63 E4** 33 5S 148 54 E
Molopo →, *Africa* **56 D3** 27 30S 20 13 E
Molotov = Perm, *Russia* **24 C10** 58 0N 56 10 E
Molson L., *Canada* **73 C9** 54 22N 96 40W
Molteno, *S. Africa* **56 E4** 31 22S 26 22 E
Molu, *Indonesia* **37 F8** 6 45S 131 40 E
Molucca Sea, *Indonesia* **37 E6** 2 0S 124 0 E
Moluccas = Maluku, *Indonesia* **37 E7** 1 0S 127 0 E
Moma, *Dem. Rep. of the Congo* **54 C1** 1 35S 23 52 E
Moma, *Mozam.* **55 F4** 16 47S 39 4 E
Mombasa, *Kenya* **54 C4** 4 2S 39 43 E
Mombetsu, *Japan* **30 B11** 44 21N 143 22 E
Momchilgrad, *Bulgaria* **21 D11** 41 33N 25 23 E
Momi, *Dem. Rep. of the Congo* **54 C2** 1 42S 27 0 E
Mompós, *Colombia* **92 B4** 9 14N 74 26W
Møn, *Denmark* **9 J15** 54 57N 12 20 E
Mon →, *Burma* **41 J19** 20 25N 94 30 E
Mona, Canal de la, *W. Indies* **89 C6** 18 30N 67 45W
Mona, Isla, *Puerto Rico* **89 C6** 18 5N 67 54W
Mona, Pta., *Costa Rica* **88 E3** 9 37N 82 36W
Monaca, *U.S.A.* **78 F4** 40 41N 80 17W
Monaco ■, *Europe* **18 E7** 43 46N 7 23 E
Monadhliath Mts., *U.K.* **12 D4** 57 10N 4 4W
Monadnock, Mt., *U.S.A.* **79 D12** 42 52N 72 7W
Monaghan, *Ireland* **13 B5** 54 15N 6 57W
Monaghan □, *Ireland* **13 B5** 54 11N 6 56W
Monahans, *U.S.A.* **81 K3** 31 36N 102 54W
Monapo, *Mozam.* **55 E5** 14 56S 40 19 E
Monar, L., *U.K.* **12 D3** 57 26N 5 8W
Monarch Mt., *Canada* **72 C3** 51 55N 125 57W
Monashee Mts., *Canada* **72 C5** 51 0N 118 43W
Monasterevin, *Ireland* **13 C4** 53 8N 7 4W
Monastir = Bitola, *Macedonia* **21 D9** 41 1N 21 20 E
Moncayo, Sierra del, *Spain* **19 B5** 41 48N 1 50W
Monchegorsk, *Russia* **24 A5** 67 54N 32 58 E
Mönchengladbach, *Germany* **16 C4** 51 11N 6 27 E
Monchique, *Portugal* **19 D1** 37 19N 8 38W
Moncks Corner, *U.S.A.* **77 J5** 33 12N 80 1W
Monclova, *Mexico* **86 B4** 26 50N 101 30W
Moncton, *Canada* **71 C7** 46 7N 64 51W
Mondego →, *Portugal* **19 B1** 40 9N 8 52W
Mondeodo, *Indonesia* **37 E6** 3 34S 122 9 E
Mondovì, *Italy* **18 D7** 44 23N 7 49 E
Mondrain I., *Australia* **61 F3** 34 9S 122 14 E
Monessen, *U.S.A.* **78 F5** 40 9N 79 54W
Monett, *U.S.A.* **81 G8** 36 55N 93 55W
Moneymore, *U.K.* **13 B5** 54 41N 6 40W
Monforte de Lemos, *Spain* **19 A2** 42 31N 7 33W
Mong Hsu, *Burma* **41 J21** 21 54N 98 30 E
Mong Kung, *Burma* **41 J20** 21 35N 97 35 E
Mong Nai, *Burma* **41 J20** 20 32N 97 46 E
Mong Pawk, *Burma* **41 H21** 22 4N 99 16 E
Mong Ton, *Burma* **41 J21** 20 17N 98 45 E
Mong Wa, *Burma* **41 J22** 21 26N 100 27 E
Mong Yai, *Burma* **41 H21** 22 21N 98 3 E
Mongalla, *Sudan* **51 G12** 5 8N 31 42 E
Mongers, L., *Australia* **61 E2** 29 25S 117 5 E
Monghyr = Munger, *India* **43 G12** 25 23N 86 30 E
Mongibello = Etna, *Italy* **20 F6** 37 50N 14 55 E
Mongo, *Chad* **51 F9** 12 14N 18 43 E
Mongolia ■, *Asia* **27 E10** 47 0N 103 0 E
Mongu, *Zambia* **53 H4** 15 16S 23 12 E
Mônguà, *Angola* **56 B2** 16 43S 15 20 E
Monifieth, *U.K.* **12 E6** 56 30N 2 48W
Monkey Bay, *Malawi* **55 E4** 14 7S 35 1 E
Monkey Mia, *Australia* **61 E1** 25 48S 113 43 E
Monkey River, *Belize* **87 D7** 16 22N 88 29W
Monkoto, *Dem. Rep. of the Congo* **52 E4** 1 38S 20 35 E
Monkton, *Canada* **78 C3** 43 35N 81 5W
Monmouth, *U.K.* **11 F5** 51 48N 2 42W
Monmouth, *Ill., U.S.A.* **80 E9** 40 55N 90 39W
Monmouth, *Oreg., U.S.A.* **82 D2** 44 51N 123 14W
Monmouthshire □, *U.K.* **11 F5** 51 48N 2 54W
Mono L., *U.S.A.* **84 H7** 38 1N 119 1W
Monolith, *U.S.A.* **85 K8** 35 7N 118 22W
Monólithos, *Greece* **23 C9** 36 7N 27 45 E
Monongahela, *U.S.A.* **78 F5** 40 12N 79 56W
Monópoli, *Italy* **20 D7** 40 57N 17 18 E
Monroe, *Ga., U.S.A.* **77 J4** 33 47N 83 43W
Monroe, *La., U.S.A.* **81 J8** 32 30N 92 7W
Monroe, *Mich., U.S.A.* **76 E4** 41 55N 83 24W
Monroe, *N.C., U.S.A.* **77 H5** 34 59N 80 33W
Monroe, *N.Y., U.S.A.* **79 E10** 41 20N 74 11W
Monroe, *Utah, U.S.A.* **83 G7** 38 38N 112 7W
Monroe, *Wash., U.S.A.* **84 C5** 47 51N 121 58W
Monroe, *Wis., U.S.A.* **80 D10** 42 36N 89 38W
Monroe City, *U.S.A.* **80 F9** 39 39N 91 44W
Monroeton, *U.S.A.* **79 E8** 41 43N 76 29W
Monroeville, *Ala., U.S.A.* **77 K2** 31 31N 87 20W
Monroeville, *Pa., U.S.A.* **78 F5** 40 26N 79 45W
Monrovia, *Liberia* **50 G3** 6 18N 10 47W
Mons, *Belgium* **15 D3** 50 27N 3 58 E
Monse, *Indonesia* **37 E6** 4 0S 123 10 E
Mont-de-Marsan, *France* **18 E3** 43 54N 0 31W
Mont-Joli, *Canada* **71 C6** 48 37N 68 10W
Mont-Laurier, *Canada* **70 C4** 46 35N 75 30W
Mont-Louis, *Canada* **71 C6** 49 15N 65 44W
Mont-St-Michel, Le = Le Mont-St-Michel, *France* **18 B3** 48 40N 1 30W
Mont Tremblant, Parc Recr. du, *Canada* **70 C5** 46 30N 74 30W
Montagu, *S. Africa* **56 E3** 33 45S 20 8 E
Montagu I., *Antarctica* **5 B1** 58 25S 26 20W
Montague, *Canada* **71 C7** 46 10N 62 39W
Montague, I., *Mexico* **86 A2** 31 40N 114 56W
Montague Ra., *Australia* **61 E2** 27 15S 119 30 E
Montague Sd., *Australia* **60 B4** 14 28S 125 20 E
Montalbán, *Spain* **19 B5** 40 50N 0 45W
Montalvo, *U.S.A.* **85 L7** 34 15N 119 12W
Montana, *Bulgaria* **21 C10** 43 27N 23 16 E
Montaña, *Peru* **92 E4** 6 0S 73 0W
Montana □, *U.S.A.* **82 C9** 47 0N 110 0W
Montaña Clara, I., *Canary Is.* **22 E6** 29 17N 13 33W
Montargis, *France* **18 C5** 47 59N 2 43 E
Montauban, *France* **18 D4** 44 2N 1 21 E
Montauk, *U.S.A.* **79 E13** 41 3N 71 57W
Montauk Pt., *U.S.A.* **79 E13** 41 4N 71 52W
Montbéliard, *France* **18 C7** 47 31N 6 48 E
Montceau-les-Mines, *France* **18 C6** 46 40N 4 23 E
Montclair, *U.S.A.* **79 F10** 40 49N 74 13W
Monte Albán, *Mexico* **87 D5** 17 2N 96 45W
Monte Alegre, *Brazil* **93 D8** 2 0S 54 0W
Monte Azul, *Brazil* **93 G10** 15 9S 42 53W
Monte Bello Is., *Australia* **60 D2** 20 30S 115 45 E
Monte-Carlo, *Monaco* **18 E7** 43 46N 7 23 E
Monte Caseros, *Argentina* **94 C4** 30 10S 57 50W
Monte Comán, *Argentina* **94 C2** 34 40S 67 53W
Monte Cristi, *Dom. Rep.* **89 C5** 19 52N 71 39W
Monte Lindo →, *Paraguay* **94 A4** 23 56S 57 12W
Monte Patria, *Chile* **94 C1** 30 42S 70 58W
Monte Quemado, *Argentina* **94 B3** 25 53S 62 41W
Monte Rio, *U.S.A.* **84 G4** 38 28N 123 0W
Monte Santu, C. di, *Italy* **20 D3** 40 5N 9 44 E
Monte Vista, *U.S.A.* **83 H10** 37 35N 106 9W
Monteagudo, *Argentina* **95 B5** 27 14S 54 8W
Montebello, *Canada* **70 C5** 45 40N 74 55W
Montecito, *U.S.A.* **85 L7** 34 26N 119 40W
Montecristo, *Italy* **20 C4** 42 20N 10 19 E
Montego Bay, *Jamaica* **88 C4** 18 30N 78 0W
Montélimar, *France* **18 D6** 44 33N 4 45 E
Montello, *U.S.A.* **80 D10** 43 48N 89 20W
Montemorelos, *Mexico* **87 B5** 25 11N 99 42W
Montenegro, *Brazil* **95 B5** 29 39S 51 29W
Montenegro □, *Yugoslavia* **21 C8** 42 40N 19 20 E
Montepuez, *Mozam.* **55 E4** 13 8S 38 59 E
Montepuez →, *Mozam.* **55 E5** 12 32S 40 27 E
Monterey, *U.S.A.* **84 J5** 36 37N 121 55W
Monterey B., *U.S.A.* **84 J5** 36 45N 122 0W
Montería, *Colombia* **92 B3** 8 46N 75 53W
Monteros, *Argentina* **94 B2** 27 11S 65 30W
Monterrey, *Mexico* **86 B4** 25 40N 100 30W
Montes Claros, *Brazil* **93 G10** 16 30S 43 50W
Montesano, *U.S.A.* **84 D3** 46 59N 123 36W
Montesilvano, *Italy* **20 C6** 42 29N 14 8 E
Montevideo, *Uruguay* **95 C4** 34 50S 56 11W
Montevideo, *U.S.A.* **80 C7** 44 57N 95 43W
Montezuma, *U.S.A.* **80 E8** 41 35N 92 32W
Montgomery = Sahiwal, *Pakistan* **42 D5** 30 45N 73 8 E
Montgomery, *U.K.* **11 E4** 52 34N 3 8W
Montgomery, *Ala., U.S.A.* **77 J2** 32 23N 86 19W
Montgomery, *Pa., U.S.A.* **78 E8** 41 10N 76 53W
Montgomery, *W. Va., U.S.A.* **76 F5** 38 11N 81 19W
Montgomery City, *U.S.A.* **80 F9** 38 59N 91 30W
Monticello, *Ark., U.S.A.* **81 J9** 33 38N 91 47W
Monticello, *Fla., U.S.A.* **77 K4** 30 33N 83 52W
Monticello, *Ind., U.S.A.* **76 E2** 40 45N 86 46W
Monticello, *Iowa, U.S.A.* **80 D9** 42 15N 91 12W
Monticello, *Ky., U.S.A.* **77 G3** 36 50N 84 51W
Monticello, *Minn., U.S.A.* **80 C8** 45 18N 93 48W
Monticello, *Miss., U.S.A.* **81 K9** 31 33N 90 7W
Monticello, *N.Y., U.S.A.* **79 E10** 41 39N 74 42W
Monticello, *Utah, U.S.A.* **83 H9** 37 52N 109 21W
Montijo, *Portugal* **19 C1** 38 41N 8 54W
Montilla, *Spain* **19 D3** 37 36N 4 40W
Montluçon, *France* **18 C5** 46 22N 2 36 E
Montmagny, *Canada* **71 C5** 46 58N 70 34W
Montmartre, *Canada* **73 C8** 50 14N 103 27W
Montmorillon, *France* **18 C4** 46 26N 0 50 E
Monto, *Australia* **62 C5** 24 52S 151 6 E
Montoro, *Spain* **19 C3** 38 1N 4 27W
Montour Falls, *U.S.A.* **78 D8** 42 21N 76 51W

Montoursville, U.S.A. 78 E8 41 15N 76 55W
Montpelier, Idaho, U.S.A. 82 E8 42 19N 111 18W
Montpelier, Vt., U.S.A. 79 B12 44 16N 72 35W
Montpellier, France 18 E5 43 37N 3 52 E
Montréal, Canada 79 A11 45 31N 73 34W
Montreal →, Canada 70 C3 47 14N 84 39W
Montreal L., Canada 73 C7 54 20N 105 45W
Montreal Lake, Canada 73 C7 54 3N 105 46W
Montreux, Switz. 18 C7 46 26N 6 55 E
Montrose, U.K. 12 E6 56 44N 2 27W
Montrose, Colo., U.S.A. 83 G10 38 29N 107 53W
Montrose, Pa., U.S.A. 79 E9 41 50N 75 53W
Monts, Pte. des, Canada 71 C6 49 20N 67 12W
Montserrat ■, W. Indies 89 C7 16 40N 62 10W
Montuiri, Spain 22 B9 39 34N 2 59 E
Monywa, Burma 41 H19 22 7N 95 11 E
Monza, Italy 18 D8 45 35N 9 16 E
Monze, Zambia 55 F2 16 17S 27 29 E
Monze, C., Pakistan 42 G2 24 47N 66 37 E
Monzón, Spain 19 B6 41 52N 0 10 E
Mooers, U.S.A. 79 B11 44 58N 73 35W
Mooi River, S. Africa 57 D4 29 13S 29 50 E
Moonah →, Australia 62 C2 22 3S 138 33 E
Moonda, L., Australia 62 D3 25 52S 140 25 E
Moonie, Australia 63 D5 27 46S 150 20 E
Moonie →, Australia 63 D4 29 19S 148 43 E
Moonta, Australia 63 E2 34 6S 137 32 E
Moora, Australia 61 F2 30 37S 115 58 E
Moorcroft, U.S.A. 80 C2 44 16N 104 57W
Moore →, Australia 61 F2 31 22S 115 30 E
Moore, L., Australia 61 E2 29 50S 117 35 E
Moore Park, Australia 62 C5 24 43S 152 17 E
Moore Reefs, Australia 62 B4 16 0S 149 5 E
Moorefield, U.S.A. 76 F6 39 5N 78 59W
Moores Res., U.S.A. 79 B13 44 45N 71 50W
Moorfoot Hills, U.K. 12 F5 55 44N 3 8W
Moorhead, U.S.A. 80 B6 46 53N 96 45W
Moorpark, U.S.A. 85 L8 34 17N 118 53W
Moorreesburg, S. Africa 56 E2 33 6S 18 38 E
Moose →, Canada 70 B3 51 20N 80 25W
Moose →, U.S.A. 79 C9 43 38N 75 24W
Moose Creek, Canada 79 A10 45 15N 74 58W
Moose Factory, Canada 70 B3 51 16N 80 32W
Moose Jaw, Canada 73 C7 50 24N 105 30W
Moose Jaw →, Canada 73 C7 50 34N 105 18W
Moose Lake, Canada 73 C8 53 43N 100 20W
Moose Lake, U.S.A. 80 B8 46 27N 92 46W
Moose Mountain Prov. Park, Canada 73 D8 49 48N 102 25W
Moosehead L., U.S.A. 77 C11 45 38N 69 40W
Mooselookmeguntic L., U.S.A. 77 C10 44 55N 70 49W
Moosilauke, Mt., U.S.A. 79 B13 44 3N 71 40W
Moosomin, Canada 73 C8 50 9N 101 40W
Moosonee, Canada 70 B3 51 17N 80 39W
Moosup, U.S.A. 79 E13 41 43N 71 53W
Mopeia Velha, Mozam. 55 F4 17 30S 35 40 E
Mopipi, Botswana 56 C3 21 6S 24 55 E
Mopoi, C.A.R. 54 A2 5 6N 26 54 E
Mopti, Mali 50 F5 14 30N 4 0W
Moqor, Afghan. 42 C2 32 50N 67 42 E
Moquegua, Peru 92 G4 17 15S 70 46W
Mora, Sweden 9 F16 61 2N 14 38 E
Mora, Minn., U.S.A. 80 C8 45 53N 93 18W
Mora, N. Mex., U.S.A. 83 J11 35 58N 105 20W
Mora →, U.S.A. 81 H2 35 35N 104 25W
Moradabad, India 43 E8 28 50N 78 50 E
Morafenobe, Madag. 57 B7 17 50S 44 53 E
Moramanga, Madag. 57 B8 18 56S 48 12 E
Moran, Kans., U.S.A. 81 G7 37 55N 95 10W
Moran, Wyo., U.S.A. 82 E8 43 53N 110 37W
Moranbah, Australia 62 C4 22 1S 148 6 E
Morant Cays, Jamaica 88 C4 17 22N 76 0W
Morant Pt., Jamaica 88 C4 17 55N 76 12W
Morar, India 42 F8 26 14N 78 14 E
Morar, L., U.K. 12 E3 56 57N 5 40W
Moratuwa, Sri Lanka 40 R11 6 45N 79 55 E
Morava →, Serbia, Yug. 21 B9 44 36N 21 4 E
Morava →, Slovak Rep. 17 D9 48 10N 16 59 E
Moravia, U.S.A. 79 D8 42 43N 76 25W
Moravian Hts. = Českomoravská Vrchovina, Czech Rep. 16 D8 49 30N 15 40 E
Morawa, Australia 61 E2 29 13S 116 0 E
Morawhanna, Guyana 92 B7 8 30N 59 40W
Moray □, U.K. 12 D5 57 31N 3 18W
Moray Firth, U.K. 12 D5 57 40N 3 52W
Morbi, India 42 H4 22 50N 70 42 E
Morden, Canada 73 D9 49 15N 98 10W
Mordovian Republic = Mordvinia □, Russia 24 D7 54 20N 44 30 E
Mordvinia □, Russia 24 D7 54 20N 44 30 E
Morea, Greece 6 H10 37 45N 22 10 E
Moreau →, U.S.A. 80 C4 45 18N 100 43W
Morecambe, U.K. 10 C5 54 5N 2 52W
Morecambe B., U.K. 10 C5 54 7N 3 0W
Moree, Australia 63 D4 29 28S 149 54 E
Morehead, U.S.A. 76 F4 38 11N 83 26W
Morehead City, U.S.A. 77 H7 34 43N 76 43W
Morel →, India 42 F7 26 13N 76 36 E
Morelia, Mexico 86 D4 19 42N 101 7W
Morella, Australia 62 C3 23 0S 143 52 E
Morella, Spain 19 B5 40 35N 0 5W
Morelos, Mexico 86 B3 26 42N 107 40W
Morelos □, Mexico 87 D5 18 40N 99 10W
Morena, India 42 F8 26 30N 78 4 E
Morena, Sierra, Spain 19 C3 38 20N 4 0W
Moreno Valley, U.S.A. 85 M10 33 56N 117 15W
Moresby I., Canada 72 C2 52 30N 131 40W
Moreton I., Australia 63 D5 27 10S 153 25 E
Morey, Spain 22 B10 39 44N 3 20 E
Morgan, U.S.A. 82 F8 41 2N 111 41W
Morgan City, U.S.A. 81 L9 29 42N 91 12W
Morgan Hill, U.S.A. 84 H5 37 8N 121 39W
Morganfield, U.S.A. 76 G2 37 41N 87 55W
Morganton, U.S.A. 77 H5 35 45N 81 41W
Morgantown, U.S.A. 76 F6 39 38N 79 57W
Morgenzon, S. Africa 57 D4 26 45S 29 36 E
Morghak, Iran 45 D8 29 7N 57 54 E
Morhar →, India 43 G11 25 29N 85 11 E
Moriarty, U.S.A. 83 J10 34 59N 106 3W
Morice L., Canada 72 C3 53 50N 127 40W
Morinville, Canada 72 C6 53 49N 113 41W
Morioka, Japan 30 E10 39 45N 141 8 E
Moris, Mexico 86 B3 28 8N 108 32W
Morlaix, France 18 B2 48 36N 3 52W
Mornington, Australia 63 F4 38 15S 145 5 E
Mornington, I., Chile 96 F1 49 50S 75 30W
Mornington I., Australia 62 B2 16 30S 139 30 E
Moro, Pakistan 42 F2 26 40N 68 0 E
Moro →, Pakistan 42 E2 29 42N 67 22 E
Moro G., Phil. 37 C6 6 30N 123 0 E
Morocco ■, N. Afr. 50 B4 32 0N 5 50W
Morogoro, Tanzania 54 D4 6 50S 37 40 E
Morogoro □, Tanzania 54 D4 8 0S 37 0 E
Moroleón, Mexico 86 C4 20 8N 101 32W
Morombe, Madag. 57 C7 21 45S 43 22 E
Moron, Argentina 94 C4 34 39S 58 37W
Morón, Cuba 88 B4 22 8N 78 39W
Morón de la Frontera, Spain 19 D3 37 6N 5 28W
Morona →, Peru 92 D3 4 40S 77 10W
Morondava, Madag. 57 C7 20 17S 44 17 E
Morongo Valley, U.S.A. 85 L10 34 3N 116 37W
Moroni, Comoros Is. 49 H8 11 40S 43 16 E
Moroni, U.S.A. 82 G8 39 32N 111 35W
Morotai, Indonesia 37 D7 2 10N 128 30 E
Moroto, Uganda 54 B3 2 28N 34 42 E
Moroto Summit, Kenya 54 B3 2 30N 34 43 E
Morpeth, U.K. 10 B6 55 10N 1 41W
Morphou, Cyprus 23 D11 35 12N 32 59 E
Morphou Bay, Cyprus 23 D11 35 15N 32 50 E
Morrilton, U.S.A. 81 H8 35 9N 92 44W
Morrinhos, Brazil 93 G9 17 45S 49 10W
Morrinsville, N.Z. 59 G5 37 40S 175 32 E
Morris, Canada 73 D9 49 25N 97 22W
Morris, Minn., U.S.A. 80 C7 45 35N 95 55W
Morris, N.Y., U.S.A. 79 D9 42 33N 75 15W
Morris, Pa., U.S.A. 78 E7 41 35N 77 17W
Morris, Mt., Australia 61 E5 26 9S 131 4 E
Morrisburg, Canada 79 B9 44 55N 75 7W
Morristown, Ariz., U.S.A. 83 K7 33 51N 112 37W
Morristown, N.J., U.S.A. 79 F10 40 48N 74 29W
Morristown, N.Y., U.S.A. 79 B9 44 35N 75 39W
Morristown, Tenn., U.S.A. 77 G4 36 13N 83 18W
Morrisville, N.Y., U.S.A. 79 D9 42 53N 75 35W
Morrisville, Pa., U.S.A. 79 F10 40 13N 74 47W
Morrisville, Vt., U.S.A. 79 B12 44 34N 72 36W
Morro, Pta., Chile 94 B1 27 6S 71 0W
Morro Bay, U.S.A. 84 K6 35 22N 120 51W
Morro del Jable, Canary Is. 22 F5 28 3N 14 23W
Morro Jable, Pta. de, Canary Is. 22 F5 28 2N 14 20W
Morrosquillo, G. de, Colombia 88 E4 9 35N 75 40W
Morrumbene, Mozam. 57 C6 23 31S 35 16 E
Morshansk, Russia 24 D7 53 28N 41 50 E
Morteros, Argentina 94 C3 30 50S 62 0W
Mortlach, Canada 73 C7 50 27N 106 4W
Mortlake, Australia 63 F3 38 5S 142 50 E
Morton, Tex., U.S.A. 81 J3 33 44N 102 46W
Morton, Wash., U.S.A. 84 D4 46 34N 122 17W
Morundah, Australia 63 E4 34 57S 146 19 E
Moruya, Australia 63 F5 35 58S 150 3 E
Morvan, France 18 C6 47 5N 4 3 E
Morven, Australia 63 D4 26 22S 147 5 E
Morvern, U.K. 12 E3 56 38N 5 44W
Morwell, Australia 63 F4 38 10S 146 22 E
Morzhovets, Ostrov, Russia 24 A7 66 44N 42 35 E
Moscos Is. = Maungmagan Is., Burma 38 F1 14 0N 97 30 E
Moscow = Moskva, Russia 24 C6 55 45N 37 35 E
Moscow, Idaho, U.S.A. 82 C5 46 44N 117 0W
Moscow, Pa., U.S.A. 79 E9 41 20N 75 31W
Mosel →, Europe 18 A7 50 22N 7 36 E
Moselle = Mosel →, Europe 18 A7 50 22N 7 36 E
Moses Lake, U.S.A. 82 C4 47 8N 119 17W
Mosgiel, N.Z. 59 L3 45 53S 170 21 E
Moshi, Tanzania 54 C4 3 22S 37 18 E
Moshupa, Botswana 56 C4 24 46S 25 29 E
Mosjøen, Norway 8 D15 65 51N 13 12 E
Moskenesøya, Norway 8 C15 67 58N 13 0 E
Moskenstraumen, Norway 8 C15 67 47N 12 45 E
Moskva, Russia 24 C6 55 45N 37 35 E
Mosomane, Botswana 56 C4 24 2S 26 19 E
Moson-magyaróvár, Hungary 17 E9 47 52N 17 18 E
Mosquera, Colombia 92 C3 2 35N 78 24W
Mosquero, U.S.A. 81 H3 35 47N 103 58W
Mosquitia, Honduras 88 C3 15 20N 84 10W
Mosquito Coast = Mosquitia, Honduras 88 C3 15 20N 84 10W
Mosquito Creek L., U.S.A. 78 E4 41 18N 80 46W
Mosquito L., Canada 73 A8 62 35N 103 20W
Mosquitos, G. de los, Panama 88 E3 9 15N 81 10W
Moss, Norway 9 G14 59 27N 10 40 E
Moss Vale, Australia 63 E5 34 32S 150 25 E
Mossbank, Canada 73 D7 49 56N 105 56W
Mossburn, N.Z. 59 L2 45 41S 168 15 E
Mosselbaai, S. Africa 56 E3 34 11S 22 8 E
Mossendjo, Congo 52 E2 2 55S 12 42 E
Mossgiel, Australia 63 E3 33 15S 144 5 E
Mossman, Australia 62 B4 16 21S 145 15 E
Mossoró, Brazil 93 E11 5 10S 37 15W
Mossuril, Mozam. 55 E5 14 58S 40 42 E
Most, Czech Rep. 16 C7 50 31N 13 38 E
Mosta, Malta 23 D1 35 54N 14 24 E
Moşţafáābād, Iran 45 C7 33 39N 54 53 E
Mostaganem, Algeria 50 A6 35 54N 0 5 E
Mostar, Bos.-H. 21 C7 43 22N 17 50 E
Mostardas, Brazil 95 C5 31 2S 50 51W
Mostiska = Mostyska, Ukraine 17 D12 49 48N 23 4 E
Mosty = Masty, Belarus 17 B13 53 27N 24 38 E
Mostyska, Ukraine 17 D12 49 48N 23 4 E
Mosul = Al Mawşil, Iraq 44 B4 36 15N 43 5 E
Mosŭlpo, S. Korea 35 H14 33 20N 126 17 E
Motagua →, Guatemala 88 C2 15 44N 88 14W
Motala, Sweden 9 G16 58 32N 15 1 E
Moth, India 43 G8 25 43N 78 57 E
Motherwell, U.K. 12 F5 55 47N 3 58W
Motihari, India 43 F11 26 30N 84 55 E
Motozintla de Mendoza, Mexico 87 D6 15 21N 92 14W
Motril, Spain 19 D4 36 31N 3 37W
Mott, U.S.A. 80 B3 46 23N 102 20W
Motueka, N.Z. 59 J4 41 7S 173 1 E
Motueka →, N.Z. 59 J4 41 5S 173 1 E
Motul, Mexico 87 C7 21 0N 89 20W
Mouchalagane →, Canada 71 B6 50 56N 68 41W
Moúdhros, Greece 21 E11 39 50N 25 18 E
Mouila, Gabon 52 E2 1 50S 11 0 E
Moulamein, Australia 63 F3 35 3S 144 1 E
Moulianá, Greece 23 D7 35 10N 25 59 E
Moulins, France 18 C5 46 35N 3 19 E
Moulmein, Burma 41 L20 16 30N 97 40 E
Moulouya, O. →, Morocco 50 B5 35 5N 2 25W
Moultrie, U.S.A. 77 K4 31 11N 83 47W
Moultrie, L., U.S.A. 77 J5 33 20N 80 5W
Mound City, Mo., U.S.A. 80 E7 40 7N 95 14W
Mound City, S. Dak., U.S.A. 80 C4 45 44N 100 4W
Moundou, Chad 51 G9 8 40N 16 10 E
Moundsville, U.S.A. 78 G4 39 55N 80 44W
Moung, Cambodia 38 F4 12 46N 103 27 E
Mount Airy, U.S.A. 77 G5 36 31N 80 37W
Mount Albert, Canada 78 B5 44 8N 79 19W
Mount Barker, S. Austral., Australia 63 F2 35 5S 138 52 E
Mount Barker, W. Austral., Australia 61 F2 34 38S 117 40 E
Mount Beauty, Australia 63 F4 36 47S 147 10 E
Mount Brydges, Canada 78 D3 42 54N 81 29W
Mount Burr, Australia 63 F3 37 34S 140 26 E
Mount Carmel, Ill., U.S.A. 76 F2 38 25N 87 46W
Mount Carmel, Pa., U.S.A. 79 F8 40 47N 76 24W
Mount Charleston, U.S.A. 85 J11 36 16N 115 37W
Mount Clemens, U.S.A. 78 D2 42 35N 82 53W
Mount Coolon, Australia 62 C4 21 25S 147 25 E
Mount Darwin, Zimbabwe 55 F3 16 47S 31 38 E
Mount Desert I., U.S.A. 77 C11 44 21N 68 20W
Mount Dora, U.S.A. 77 L5 28 48N 81 38W
Mount Edziza Prov. Park, Canada 72 B2 57 30N 130 45W
Mount Fletcher, S. Africa 57 E4 30 40S 28 30 E
Mount Forest, Canada 78 C4 43 59N 80 43W
Mount Gambier, Australia 63 F3 37 50S 140 46 E
Mount Garnet, Australia 62 B4 17 37S 145 6 E
Mount Holly, U.S.A. 79 G10 39 59N 74 47W
Mount Holly Springs, U.S.A. 78 F7 40 7N 77 12W
Mount Hope, N.S.W., Australia 63 E4 32 51S 145 51 E
Mount Hope, S. Austral., Australia 63 E2 34 7S 135 23 E
Mount Isa, Australia 62 C2 20 42S 139 26 E
Mount Jewett, U.S.A. 78 E6 41 44N 78 39W
Mount Kisco, U.S.A. 79 E11 41 12N 73 44W
Mount Laguna, U.S.A. 85 N10 32 52N 116 25W
Mount Larcom, Australia 62 C5 23 48S 150 59 E
Mount Lofty Ra., Australia 63 E2 34 35S 139 5 E
Mount Magnet, Australia 61 E2 28 2S 117 47 E
Mount Maunganui, N.Z. 59 G6 37 40S 176 14 E
Mount Molloy, Australia 62 B4 16 42S 145 20 E
Mount Morgan, Australia 62 C5 23 40S 150 25 E
Mount Morris, U.S.A. 78 D7 42 44N 77 52W
Mount Pearl, Canada 71 C9 47 31N 52 47W
Mount Penn, U.S.A. 79 F9 40 20N 75 54W
Mount Perry, Australia 63 D5 25 13S 151 42 E
Mount Pleasant, Iowa, U.S.A. 80 E9 40 58N 91 33W
Mount Pleasant, Mich., U.S.A. 76 D3 43 36N 84 46W
Mount Pleasant, Pa., U.S.A. 78 F5 40 9N 79 33W
Mount Pleasant, S.C., U.S.A. 77 J6 32 47N 79 52W
Mount Pleasant, Tenn., U.S.A. 77 H2 35 32N 87 12W
Mount Pleasant, Tex., U.S.A. 81 J7 33 9N 94 58W
Mount Pleasant, Utah, U.S.A. 82 G8 39 33N 111 27W
Mount Pocono, U.S.A. 79 E9 41 7N 75 22W
Mount Rainier Nat. Park, U.S.A. 84 D5 46 55N 121 50W
Mount Revelstoke Nat. Park, Canada 72 C5 51 5N 118 30W
Mount Robson Prov. Park, Canada 72 C5 53 0N 119 0W
Mount Shasta, U.S.A. 82 F2 41 19N 122 19W
Mount Signal, U.S.A. 85 N11 32 39N 115 37W
Mount Sterling, Ill., U.S.A. 80 F9 39 59N 90 45W
Mount Sterling, Ky., U.S.A. 76 F4 38 4N 83 56W
Mount Surprise, Australia 62 B3 18 10S 144 17 E
Mount Union, U.S.A. 78 F7 40 23N 77 53W
Mount Upton, U.S.A. 79 D9 42 26N 75 23W
Mount Vernon, Ill., U.S.A. 76 F1 38 19N 88 55W
Mount Vernon, Ind., U.S.A. 80 F10 38 17N 88 57W
Mount Vernon, N.Y., U.S.A. 79 F11 40 55N 73 50W
Mount Vernon, Ohio, U.S.A. 78 F2 40 23N 82 29W
Mount Vernon, Wash., U.S.A. 84 B4 48 25N 122 20W
Mountain Ash, U.K. 11 F4 51 40N 3 23W
Mountain Center, U.S.A. 85 M10 33 42N 116 44W
Mountain City, Nev., U.S.A. 82 F6 41 50N 115 58W
Mountain City, Tenn., U.S.A. 77 G5 36 29N 81 48W
Mountain Dale, U.S.A. 79 E10 41 41N 74 32W
Mountain Grove, U.S.A. 81 G8 37 8N 92 16W
Mountain Home, Ark., U.S.A. 81 G8 36 20N 92 23W
Mountain Home, Idaho, U.S.A. 82 E6 43 8N 115 41W
Mountain Iron, U.S.A. 80 B8 47 32N 92 37W
Mountain Pass, U.S.A. 85 K11 35 29N 115 35W
Mountain View, Ark., U.S.A. 81 H8 35 52N 92 7W
Mountain View, Calif., U.S.A. 84 H4 37 23N 122 5W
Mountain View, Hawaii, U.S.A. 74 J17 19 33N 155 7W
Mountainair, U.S.A. 83 J10 34 31N 106 15W
Mountlake Terrace, U.S.A. 84 C4 47 47N 122 19W
Mountmellick, Ireland 13 C4 53 7N 7 20W
Mountrath, Ireland 13 D4 53 0N 7 28W
Moura, Australia 62 C4 24 35S 149 58 E
Moura, Brazil 92 D6 1 32S 61 38W
Moura, Portugal 19 C2 38 7N 7 30W
Mourdi, Dépression du, Chad 51 E10 18 10N 23 0 E
Mourilyan, Australia 62 B4 17 35S 146 3 E
Mourne →, U.K. 13 B4 54 52N 7 26W
Mourne Mts., U.K. 13 B5 54 10N 6 0W
Mourniaí, Greece 23 D6 35 29N 24 1 E
Mournies = Mourniaí, Greece 23 D6 35 29N 24 1 E
Mouscron, Belgium 15 D3 50 45N 3 12 E
Moussoro, Chad 51 F9 13 41N 16 35 E
Moutohara, N.Z. 59 H6 38 27S 177 32 E
Moutong, Indonesia 37 D6 0 28N 121 13 E
Movas, Mexico 86 B3 28 10N 109 25W
Moville, Ireland 13 A4 55 11N 7 3W
Mowandjum, Australia 60 C3 17 22S 123 40 E
Moy →, Ireland 13 B2 54 8N 9 8W
Moyale, Kenya 54 B4 3 30N 39 0 E
Moyen Atlas, Morocco 50 B4 33 0N 5 0W
Moyne, L. le, Canada 71 A6 56 45N 68 47W
Moyo, Indonesia 36 F5 8 10S 117 40 E
Moyobamba, Peru 92 E3 6 0S 77 0W
Moyyero →, Russia 27 C11 68 44N 103 42 E
Moyynty, Kazakstan 26 E8 47 10N 73 18 E
Mozambique = Moçambique, Mozam. 55 F5 15 3S 40 42 E
Mozambique ■, Africa 55 F4 19 0S 35 0 E
Mozambique Chan., Africa 57 B7 17 30S 42 30 E
Mozdok, Russia 25 F7 43 45N 44 48 E
Mozdūrān, Iran 45 B9 36 9N 60 35 E
Mozhnābād, Iran 45 C9 34 7N 60 6 E
Mozyr = Mazyr, Belarus 17 B15 51 59N 29 15 E
Mpanda, Tanzania 54 D3 6 23S 31 1 E
Mpika, Zambia 55 E3 11 51S 31 25 E
Mpulungu, Zambia 55 D3 8 51S 31 5 E
Mpumalanga, S. Africa 57 D5 29 50S 30 33 E
Mpumalanga □, S. Africa 57 B5 26 0S 30 0 E
Mpwapwa, Tanzania 54 D4 6 23S 36 30 E
Msambansovu, Zimbabwe 55 F3 15 50S 30 3 E
M'sila →, Algeria 50 A6 35 30N 4 29 E
Msoro, Zambia 55 E3 13 35S 31 50 E
Mstislavl = Mstsislaw, Belarus 17 A16 54 0N 31 50 E
Mstsislaw, Belarus 17 A16 54 0N 31 50 E
Mtama, Tanzania 55 E4 10 17S 39 21 E
Mtilikwe →, Zimbabwe 55 G3 21 9S 31 30 E
Mtubatuba, S. Africa 57 D5 28 30S 32 8 E
Mtwara-Mikindani, Tanzania 55 E5 10 20S 40 20 E
Mu Gia, Deo, Vietnam 38 D5 17 40N 105 47 E
Mu Us Shamo, China 34 E5 39 0N 109 0 E
Muang Chiang Rai = Chiang Rai, Thailand 38 C2 19 52N 99 50 E
Muang Khong, Laos 36 B3 14 5N 105 52 E
Muang Khong, Laos 38 E5 14 7N 105 51 E
Muang Lamphun, Thailand 38 C2 18 40N 99 2 E
Muar, Malaysia 39 L4 2 3N 102 34 E
Muarabungo, Indonesia 36 E2 1 28S 102 52 E
Muaraenim, Indonesia 36 E2 3 40S 103 50 E
Muarajuloi, Indonesia 36 E4 0 12S 114 3 E
Muarakaman, Indonesia 36 E5 0 2S 116 45 E
Muaratebo, Indonesia 36 E2 1 30S 102 26 E
Muaratembesi, Indonesia 36 E2 1 42S 103 8 E
Muaratewe, Indonesia 36 E4 0 58S 114 52 E
Mubarakpur, India 43 F10 26 6N 83 18 E
Mubarraz = Al Mubarraz, Si. Arabia 45 E6 25 30N 49 40 E
Mubende, Uganda 54 B3 0 33N 31 22 E
Mubi, Nigeria 51 F8 10 18N 13 16 E
Mubur, Pulau, Indonesia 39 L6 3 20N 106 12 E
Mucajaí →, Brazil 92 C6 2 25N 60 52W
Muchachos, Roque de los, Canary Is. 22 F2 28 44N 17 52W
Muchinga Mts., Zambia 55 E3 11 30S 31 30 E
Muck, U.K. 12 E2 56 50N 6 15W
Muckadilla, Australia 63 D4 26 35S 148 23 E
Mucuri, Brazil 93 G11 18 0S 39 36W
Mucusso, Angola 56 B3 18 1S 21 25 E
Muda, Canary Is. 22 F6 28 34N 13 57W
Mudanjiang, China 35 B15 44 38N 129 30 E
Mudanya, Turkey 21 D13 40 25N 28 50 E
Muddy Cr. →, U.S.A. 83 H8 38 24N 110 42W
Mudgee, Australia 63 E4 32 32S 149 31 E
Mudjatik →, Canada 73 B7 56 1N 107 36W
Muecate, Mozam. 55 E4 14 55S 39 40 E
Mueda, Mozam. 55 E4 11 36S 39 28 E
Mueller Ra., Australia 60 C4 18 18S 126 46 E
Muende, Mozam. 55 E3 14 28S 33 0 E
Muerto, Mar, Mexico 87 D6 16 10N 94 10W
Mufulira, Zambia 55 E2 12 32S 28 15 E
Mufumbiro Range, Africa 54 C2 1 25S 29 30 E
Mughal Sarai, India 43 G10 25 18N 83 7 E
Mughayrā', Si. Arabia 44 D3 29 17N 37 41 E
Mugi, Japan 31 H7 33 40N 134 25 E
Mugila, Mts., Dem. Rep. of the Congo 54 D2 7 0S 28 50 E
Muğla, Turkey 21 F13 37 15N 28 22 E
Mugu, Nepal 43 E10 29 45N 82 30 E
Muhammad, Râs, Egypt 44 E2 27 44N 34 16 E
Muhammad Qol, Sudan 51 D13 20 53N 37 9 E
Muhammadabad, India 43 F10 26 4N 83 25 E
Muhesi →, Tanzania 54 D4 7 0S 35 20 E
Mühlhausen, Germany 16 C6 51 12N 10 27 E
Mühlig Hofmann fjell, Antarctica 5 D3 72 30S 5 0 E
Muhos, Finland 8 D22 64 47N 25 59 E
Muhu, Estonia 9 G20 58 36N 23 11 E
Muhutwe, Tanzania 54 C3 1 35S 31 45 E
Muine Bheag, Ireland 13 D5 52 42N 6 58W
Muir, L., Australia 61 F2 34 30S 116 40 E
Mukacheve, Ukraine 17 D12 48 27N 22 45 E
Mukachevo = Mukacheve, Ukraine 17 D12 48 27N 22 45 E
Mukah, Malaysia 36 D4 2 55N 112 5 E
Mukandwara, India 42 G6 24 49N 75 59 E
Mukdahan, Thailand 38 D5 16 32N 104 43 E
Mukden = Shenyang, China 35 D12 41 48N 123 27 E
Mukerian, India 42 D6 31 57N 75 37 E
Mukhtuya = Lensk, Russia 27 C12 60 48N 114 55 E
Mukinbudin, Australia 61 F2 30 55S 118 5 E
Mukishi, Dem. Rep. of the Congo 55 D1 8 30S 24 44 E
Mukomuko, Indonesia 36 E2 2 30S 101 10 E
Mukomwenze, Dem. Rep. of the Congo 54 D2 6 49S 27 15 E
Muktsar, India 42 D6 30 30N 74 30 E
Mukur = Moqor, Afghan. 42 C2 32 50N 67 42 E
Mukutawa →, Canada 73 C9 53 10N 97 24W
Mukwela, Zambia 55 F2 17 0S 26 40 E
Mula, Spain 19 C5 38 3N 1 33W
Mula →, Pakistan 42 F2 27 57N 67 36 E
Mulange, Dem. Rep. of the Congo 54 C2 3 40S 27 10 E
Mulanje, Malawi 55 F4 16 2S 35 33 E
Mulchén, Chile 94 D1 37 45S 72 20W
Mulde →, Germany 16 C7 51 53N 12 15 E
Mule Creek Junction, U.S.A. 80 D2 43 19N 104 8W
Muleba, Tanzania 54 C3 1 50S 31 37 E
Mulejé, Mexico 86 B2 26 53N 112 1W
Muleshoe, U.S.A. 81 H3 34 13N 102 43W
Mulgrave, Canada 71 C7 45 38N 61 31W
Mulhacén, Spain 19 D4 37 4N 3 20W
Mülheim, Germany 33 C6 51 25N 6 54 E

Mulhouse, France 18 C7 47 40N 7 20 E
Muling, China 35 B16 44 35N 130 10 E
Mull, U.K. 12 E3 56 25N 5 56W
Mull, Sound of, U.K. 12 E3 56 30N 5 50W
Mullaittivu, Sri Lanka 40 Q12 9 15N 80 49 E
Mullen, U.S.A. 80 D4 42 3N 101 1W
Mullens, U.S.A. 76 G5 37 35N 81 23W
Muller, Pegunungan, Indonesia 36 D4 0 30N 113 30 E
Mullet Pen., Ireland 13 B1 54 13N 10 2W
Mullewa, Australia 61 E2 28 29S 115 30 E
Mulligan →, Australia 62 D2 25 0S 139 0 E
Mullingar, Ireland 13 C4 53 31N 7 21W
Mullins, U.S.A. 77 H6 34 12N 79 15W
Mullumbimby, Australia 63 D5 28 30S 153 30 E
Mulobezi, Zambia 55 F2 16 45S 25 7 E
Mulroy B., Ireland 13 A4 55 15N 7 46W
Multan, Pakistan 42 D4 30 15N 71 36 E
Mulumbe, Mts., Dem. Rep. of the Congo 55 D2 8 40S 27 30 E
Mulungushi Dam, Zambia 55 E2 14 48S 28 48 E
Mulvane, U.S.A. 81 G6 37 29N 97 15W
Mumbai, India 40 K8 18 55N 72 50 E
Mumbwa, Zambia 55 F2 15 0S 27 0 E
Mun →, Thailand 38 E5 15 19N 105 30 E
Muna, Indonesia 37 F6 5 0S 122 30 E
Munabao, India 42 G4 25 45N 70 17 E
Munamagi, Estonia 9 H22 57 43N 27 4 E
München, Germany 16 D6 48 8N 11 34 E
Munchen-Gladbach = Mönchengladbach, Germany 16 C4 51 11N 6 27 E
Muncho Lake, Canada 72 B3 59 0N 125 50W
Munch'ŏn, N. Korea 35 E14 39 14N 127 19 E
Muncie, U.S.A. 76 E3 40 12N 85 23W
Muncoonie, L., Australia 62 D2 25 12S 138 40 E
Mundabbera, Australia 63 D5 25 36S 151 18 E
Munday, U.S.A. 81 J5 33 27N 99 38W
Münden, Germany 16 C5 51 25N 9 38 E
Mundiwindi, Australia 60 D3 23 47S 120 9 E
Mundo Novo, Brazil 93 F10 11 50S 40 29W
Mundra, India 42 H3 22 54N 69 48 E
Mundrabilla, Australia 61 F4 31 52S 127 51 E
Mungallala, Australia 63 D4 26 28S 147 34 E
Mungallala Cr. →, Australia 63 D4 28 53S 147 5 E
Mungana, Australia 62 B3 17 8S 144 27 E
Mungaoli, India 42 G8 24 24N 78 7 E
Mungari, Mozam. 55 F3 17 12S 33 30 E
Mungbere, Dem. Rep. of the Congo 54 B2 2 36N 28 28 E
Mungeli, India 43 H9 22 4N 81 41 E
Munger, India 43 G12 25 23N 86 30 E
Munich = München, Germany 16 D6 48 8N 11 34 E
Munising, U.S.A. 76 B2 46 25N 86 40W
Munku-Sardyk, Russia 27 D11 51 45N 100 20 E
Muñoz Gamero, Pen., Chile 96 G2 52 30S 73 5W
Munroe L., Canada 73 B9 59 13N 98 35W
Munsan, S. Korea 35 F14 37 51N 126 48 E
Münster, Germany 16 C4 51 58N 7 37 E
Munster □, Ireland 13 D3 52 18N 8 44W
Muntadgin, Australia 61 F2 31 45S 118 33 E
Muntok, Indonesia 36 E3 2 5S 105 10 E
Munyama, Zambia 55 F2 16 5S 28 31 E
Muong Et, Laos 38 B5 20 49N 104 1 E
Muong Hiem, Laos 38 B4 20 5N 103 22 E
Muong Kau, Laos 38 E5 15 6N 105 47 E
Muong Khao, Laos 38 C4 19 38N 103 32 E
Muong Liep, Laos 38 C3 18 29N 101 40 E
Muong May, Laos 38 E6 14 49N 106 56 E
Muong Nong, Laos 38 D6 16 22N 106 30 E
Muong Oua, Laos 38 C3 18 18N 101 20 E
Muong Phalane, Laos 38 D5 16 39N 105 34 E
Muong Phieng, Laos 38 C3 19 6N 101 32 E
Muong Phine, Laos 38 D6 16 32N 106 2 E
Muong Saiapoun, Laos 38 C3 18 24N 101 31 E
Muong Sen, Vietnam 38 C5 19 24N 104 8 E
Muong Soui, Laos 38 C4 19 33N 102 52 E
Muong Xia, Vietnam 38 B5 20 19N 104 50 E
Muonio, Finland 8 C20 67 57N 23 40 E
Muonionjoki →, Finland 8 C20 67 11N 23 34 E
Muping, China 35 F11 37 22N 121 36 E
Muqdisho, Somali Rep. 46 G4 2 2N 45 25 E
Mur →, Austria 17 E9 46 18N 16 52 E
Murakami, Japan 30 E9 38 14N 139 29 E
Murallón, Cerro, Chile 96 F2 49 48S 73 30W
Muranda, Rwanda 54 C2 1 52S 29 20 E
Murang'a, Kenya 54 C4 0 45S 37 9 E
Murashi, Russia 24 C8 59 30N 49 0 E
Murat →, Turkey 25 G7 38 46N 40 0 E
Muratlı, Turkey 21 D12 41 10N 27 29 E
Murayama, Japan 30 E10 38 30N 140 25 E
Murban, U.A.E. 45 F7 23 50N 53 45 E
Murchison →, Australia 61 E1 27 45S 114 0 E
Murchison, Mt., Antarctica 5 D11 73 0S 168 0 E
Murchison Falls, Uganda 54 B3 2 15N 31 30 E
Murchison Ra., Australia 62 C1 20 0S 134 10 E
Murchison Rapids, Malawi 55 F3 15 55S 34 35 E
Murcia, Spain 19 D5 38 5N 1 10W
Murcia □, Spain 19 D5 37 50N 1 30W
Murdo, U.S.A. 80 D4 43 53N 100 43W
Murdoch Pt., Australia 62 A3 14 37S 144 55 E
Mureş →, Romania 17 E11 46 15N 20 13 E
Mureşul = Mureş →, Romania 17 E11 46 15N 20 13 E
Murfreesboro, N.C., U.S.A. 77 G7 36 27N 77 6W
Murfreesboro, Tenn., U.S.A. 77 H2 35 51N 86 24W
Murgab = Murghob, Tajikistan 26 F8 38 10N 74 2 E
Murgab →, Turkmenistan 45 B9 38 18N 61 12 E
Murgenella, Australia 60 B5 11 34S 132 56 E
Murgha Kibzai, Pakistan 42 D3 30 44N 69 25 E
Murghob, Tajikistan 26 F8 38 10N 74 2 E
Murgon, Australia 63 D5 26 15S 151 54 E
Muri, India 43 H11 23 22N 85 52 E
Muria, Indonesia 37 G14 6 36S 110 53 E
Muriaé, Brazil 95 A7 21 8S 42 23W
Muriel Mine, Zimbabwe 55 F3 17 14S 30 40 E
Müritz, Germany 16 B7 53 25N 12 42 E
Murka, Kenya 54 C4 3 27S 38 0 E
Murliganj, India 43 G12 25 54N 86 59 E
Murmansk, Russia 24 A5 68 57N 33 10 E
Muro, Spain 22 B10 39 44N 3 3 E
Murom, Russia 24 C7 55 35N 42 3 E
Muroran, Japan 30 C10 42 25N 141 0 E
Muroto, Japan 31 H7 33 18N 134 9 E
Muroto-Misaki, Japan 31 H7 33 15N 134 10 E
Murphy, U.S.A. 82 E5 43 13N 116 33W
Murphys, U.S.A. 84 G6 38 8N 120 28W
Murray, Ky., U.S.A. 77 G1 36 37N 88 19W
Murray, Utah, U.S.A. 82 F8 40 40N 111 53W
Murray →, Australia 63 F2 35 20S 139 22 E
Murray, L., U.S.A. 77 H5 34 3N 81 13W
Murray Bridge, Australia 63 F2 35 6S 139 14 E
Murray Harbour, Canada 71 C7 46 0N 62 28W
Murraysburg, S. Africa 56 E3 31 58S 23 47 E
Murree, Pakistan 42 C5 33 56N 73 28 E
Murrieta, U.S.A. 85 M9 33 33N 117 13W
Murrumbidgee →, Australia 63 E3 34 43S 143 12 E
Murrumburrah, Australia 63 E4 34 32S 148 22 E
Murrurundi, Australia 63 E5 31 42S 150 51 E
Murshidabad, India 43 G13 24 11N 88 19 E
Murtle L., Canada 72 C5 52 8N 119 38W
Murtoa, Australia 63 F3 36 35S 142 28 E
Murungu, Tanzania 54 C3 4 12S 31 10 E
Mururoa, Pac. Oc. 65 K14 21 52S 138 55W
Murwara, India 43 H9 23 46N 80 28 E
Murwillumbah, Australia 63 D5 28 18S 153 27 E
Mürzzuschlag, Austria 16 E8 47 36N 15 41 E
Muş, Turkey 25 G7 38 45N 41 30 E
Mûsa, Gebel, Egypt 44 D2 28 33N 33 59 E
Musa Khel, Pakistan 42 D3 30 59N 69 52 E
Mūsá Qal'eh, Afghan. 40 C4 32 20N 64 50 E
Musaffargarh, Pakistan 40 D7 30 10N 71 10 E
Musafirkhana, India 43 F9 26 22N 81 48 E
Musala, Bulgaria 21 C10 42 13N 23 37 E
Musala, Indonesia 36 D1 1 41N 98 28 E
Musan, N. Korea 35 C15 42 12N 129 12 E
Musangu, Dem. Rep. of the Congo 55 E1 10 28S 23 55 E
Musasa, Tanzania 54 C3 3 25S 31 30 E
Musay'īd, Qatar 45 E6 25 0N 51 33 E
Muscat = Masqat, Oman 46 C6 23 37N 58 36 E
Muscat & Oman = Oman ■, Asia 46 C6 23 0N 58 0 E
Muscatine, U.S.A. 80 E9 41 25N 91 3W
Musgrave Harbour, Canada 71 C9 49 27N 53 58W
Musgrave Ranges, Australia 61 E5 26 0S 132 0 E
Mushie, Dem. Rep. of the Congo 52 E3 2 56S 16 55 E
Musi →, Indonesia 36 E2 2 20S 104 56 E
Muskeg →, Canada 72 A4 60 20N 123 20W
Muskegon, U.S.A. 76 D2 43 14N 86 16W
Muskegon →, U.S.A. 76 D2 43 14N 86 21W
Muskegon Heights, U.S.A. 76 D2 43 12N 86 16W
Muskogee, U.S.A. 81 H7 35 45N 95 22W
Muskoka, L., Canada 78 B5 45 0N 79 25W
Muskwa →, Canada 72 B4 58 47N 122 48W
Muslīmiyah, Syria 44 B3 36 19N 37 12 E
Musofu, Zambia 55 E2 13 30S 29 0 E
Musoma, Tanzania 54 C3 1 30S 33 48 E
Musquaro, L., Canada 71 B7 50 38N 61 5W
Musquodoboit Harbour, Canada 71 D7 44 50N 63 9W
Musselburgh, U.K. 12 F5 55 57N 3 2W
Musselshell →, U.S.A. 82 C10 47 21N 107 57W
Mussoorie, India 42 D8 30 27N 78 6 E
Mussuco, Angola 56 B2 17 2S 19 3 E
Mustafakemalpaşa, Turkey 21 D13 40 2N 28 24 E
Mustang, Nepal 43 E10 29 10N 83 55 E
Musters, L., Argentina 96 F3 45 20S 69 25W
Musudan, N. Korea 35 D15 40 50N 129 43 E
Muswellbrook, Australia 63 E5 32 16S 150 56 E
Mût, Egypt 51 C11 25 28N 28 58 E
Mut, Turkey 44 B2 36 40N 33 28 E
Mutanda, Mozam. 57 C5 21 0S 33 34 E
Mutanda, Zambia 55 E2 12 24S 26 13 E
Mutare, Zimbabwe 55 F3 18 58S 32 38 E
Muting, Indonesia 37 F10 7 23S 140 20 E
Mutoray, Russia 27 C11 60 56N 101 0 E
Mutshatsha, Dem. Rep. of the Congo 55 E1 10 35S 24 20 E
Mutsu, Japan 30 D10 41 5N 140 55 E
Mutsu-Wan, Japan 30 D10 41 5N 140 55 E
Muttaburra, Australia 62 C3 22 38S 144 29 E
Mutton I., Ireland 13 D2 52 49N 9 32W
Mutuáli, Mozam. 55 E4 14 55S 37 0 E
Muweilih, Egypt 47 E3 30 42N 34 19 E
Muy Muy, Nic. 88 D2 12 39N 85 36W
Muyinga, Burundi 54 C3 3 14S 30 33 E
Muynak, Uzbekistan 26 E6 43 44N 59 10 E
Muzaffarabad, Pakistan 43 B5 34 25N 73 30 E
Muzaffargarh, Pakistan 42 D4 30 5N 71 14 E
Muzaffarnagar, India 42 E7 29 26N 77 40 E
Muzaffarpur, India 43 F11 26 7N 85 23 E
Muzafirpur, Pakistan 42 D3 30 58N 69 9 E
Muzhi, Russia 24 A11 65 25N 64 40 E
Mvuma, Zimbabwe 55 F3 19 16S 30 30 E
Mvurwi, Zimbabwe 55 F3 17 0S 30 57 E
Mwadui, Tanzania 54 C3 3 26S 33 32 E
Mwambo, Tanzania 55 E5 10 30S 40 22 E
Mwandi, Zambia 55 F1 17 30S 24 51 E
Mwanza, Dem. Rep. of the Congo 54 D2 7 55S 26 43 E
Mwanza, Tanzania 54 C3 2 30S 32 58 E
Mwanza, Zambia 55 F1 16 58S 24 28 E
Mwanza □, Tanzania 54 C3 2 0S 33 0 E
Mwaya, Tanzania 55 D3 9 32S 33 55 E
Mweelrea, Ireland 13 C2 53 39N 9 49W
Mweka, Dem. Rep. of the Congo 52 E4 4 50S 21 34 E
Mwene-Ditu, Dem. Rep. of the Congo 52 F4 6 35S 22 27 E
Mwenezi, Zimbabwe 55 G3 21 15S 30 48 E
Mwenezi →, Mozam. 55 G3 22 40S 31 50 E
Mwenga, Dem. Rep. of the Congo 54 C2 3 1S 28 28 E
Mweru, L., Zambia 55 D2 9 0S 28 40 E
Mweza Range, Zimbabwe 55 G3 21 0S 30 0 E
Mwilambwe, Dem. Rep. of the Congo 54 D2 8 7S 25 5 E
Mwimbi, Tanzania 55 D3 8 38S 31 39 E
Mwinilunga, Zambia 55 E1 11 43S 24 25 E
My Tho, Vietnam 39 G6 10 29N 106 23 E
Myajlar, India 42 F4 26 15N 70 20 E
Myanaung, Burma 41 K19 18 18N 95 22 E
Myanmar = Burma ■, Asia 41 J20 21 0N 96 30 E
Myaungmya, Burma 41 L19 16 30N 94 40 E
Mycenæ, Greece 21 F10 37 39N 22 52 E
Myeik Kyunzu, Burma 39 G1 11 30N 97 30 E
Myers Chuck, U.S.A. 72 B2 55 44N 132 11W
Myerstown, U.S.A. 79 F8 40 22N 76 19W
Myingyan, Burma 41 J19 21 30N 95 20 E
Myitkyina, Burma 41 G20 25 24N 97 26 E
Mykines, Færoe Is. 8 E9 62 7N 7 35W
Mykolayiv, Ukraine 25 E5 46 58N 32 0 E
Mymensingh, Bangla. 41 G17 24 45N 90 24 E
Mynydd Du, U.K. 11 F4 51 52N 3 50W
Mýrdalsjökull, Iceland 8 E4 63 40N 19 6W
Myrtle Beach, U.S.A. 77 J6 33 42N 78 53W
Myrtle Creek, U.S.A. 82 E2 43 1N 123 17W
Myrtle Point, U.S.A. 82 E1 43 4N 124 8W
Myrtou, Cyprus 23 D12 35 18N 33 4 E
Mysia, Turkey 21 E12 39 50N 27 0 E
Mysore = Karnataka □, India 40 N10 13 15N 77 0 E
Mysore, India 40 N10 12 17N 76 41 E
Mystic, U.S.A. 79 E13 41 21N 71 58W
Myszków, Poland 17 C10 50 45N 19 22 E
Mytishchi, Russia 24 C6 55 50N 37 50 E
Mývatn, Iceland 8 D5 65 36N 17 0W
Mzimba, Malawi 55 E3 11 55S 33 39 E
Mzimkulu →, S. Africa 57 E5 30 44S 30 28 E
Mzimvubu →, S. Africa 57 E4 31 38S 29 33 E
Mzuzu, Malawi 55 E3 11 30S 33 55 E

N

Na Hearadh = Harris, U.K. 12 D2 57 50N 6 55W
Na Noi, Thailand 38 C3 18 19N 100 43 E
Na Phao, Laos 38 D5 17 35N 105 44 E
Na San, Vietnam 38 B5 21 12N 104 2 E
Naab →, Germany 16 D6 49 1N 12 2 E
Naantali, Finland 9 F19 60 29N 22 2 E
Naas, Ireland 13 C5 53 12N 6 40W
Nababiep, S. Africa 56 D2 29 36S 17 46 E
Nabadwip = Navadwip, India 43 H13 23 34N 88 20 E
Nabari, Japan 31 G8 34 37N 136 5 E
Nabawa, Australia 61 E1 28 30S 114 48 E
Nabberu, L., Australia 61 E3 25 50S 120 30 E
Naberezhnyye Chelny, Russia 24 C9 55 42N 52 19 E
Nabeul, Tunisia 51 A8 36 30N 10 44 E
Nabha, India 42 D7 30 26N 76 14 E
Nabīd, Iran 45 D8 29 40N 57 38 E
Nabire, Indonesia 37 E9 3 15S 135 26 E
Nabisar, Pakistan 42 G3 25 8N 69 40 E
Nabisipi →, Canada 71 B7 50 14N 62 13W
Nabiswera, Uganda 54 B3 1 27N 32 15 E
Nablus = Nābulus, West Bank 47 C4 32 14N 35 15 E
Naboomspruit, S. Africa 57 C4 24 32S 28 40 E
Nābulus, West Bank 47 C4 32 14N 35 15 E
Nacala, Mozam. 55 E5 14 31S 40 34 E
Nacala-Velha, Mozam. 55 E5 14 32S 40 34 E
Nacaome, Honduras 88 D2 13 31N 87 30W
Nacaroa, Mozam. 55 E4 14 22S 39 56 E
Naches, U.S.A. 82 C3 46 44N 120 42W
Naches →, U.S.A. 84 D6 46 38N 120 31W
Nachicapau, L., Canada 71 A6 56 40N 68 5W
Nachingwea, Tanzania 55 E4 10 23S 38 49 E
Nachna, India 42 F4 27 34N 71 41 E
Nacimiento L., U.S.A. 84 K6 35 46N 120 53W
Naco, Mexico 86 A3 31 20N 109 56W
Nacogdoches, U.S.A. 81 K7 31 36N 94 39W
Nácori Chico, Mexico 86 B3 29 39N 109 1W
Nacozari, Mexico 86 A3 30 24N 109 39W
Nadiad, India 42 H5 22 41N 72 56 E
Nador, Morocco 50 B5 35 14N 2 58W
Nadur, Malta 23 C1 36 2N 14 17 E
Nadūshan, Iran 45 C7 32 2N 53 35 E
Nadvirna, Ukraine 17 D13 48 37N 24 30 E
Nadvoitsy, Russia 24 B5 63 52N 34 14 E
Nadvornaya = Nadvirna, Ukraine 17 D13 48 37N 24 30 E
Nadym, Russia 26 C8 65 35N 72 42 E
Nadym →, Russia 26 C8 66 12N 72 0 E
Nærbø, Norway 9 G11 58 40N 5 39 E
Næstved, Denmark 9 J14 55 13N 11 44 E
Naft-e Safīd, Iran 45 D6 31 40N 49 17 E
Naftshahr, Iran 44 C5 34 0N 45 30 E
Nafud Desert = An Nafūd, Si. Arabia 44 D4 28 15N 41 0 E
Naga, Phil. 37 B6 13 38N 123 15 E
Nagahama, Japan 31 G8 35 23N 136 16 E
Nagai, Japan 30 E10 38 6N 140 2 E
Nagaland □, India 41 G19 26 0N 94 30 E
Nagano, Japan 31 F9 36 40N 138 10 E
Nagano □, Japan 31 F9 36 15N 138 0 E
Nagaoka, Japan 31 F9 37 27N 138 51 E
Nagappattinam, India 40 P11 10 46N 79 51 E
Nagar →, Bangla. 43 G13 24 27N 89 12 E
Nagar Parkar, Pakistan 42 G4 24 28N 70 46 E
Nagasaki, Japan 31 H4 32 47N 129 50 E
Nagasaki □, Japan 31 H4 32 50N 129 40 E
Nagato, Japan 31 G5 34 19N 131 5 E
Nagaur, India 42 F5 27 15N 73 45 E
Nagda, India 42 H6 23 27N 75 25 E
Nagercoil, India 40 Q10 8 12N 77 26 E
Nagina, India 43 E8 29 30N 78 30 E
Nagīneh, Iran 45 C8 34 20N 57 15 E
Nagir, Pakistan 43 A6 36 12N 74 42 E
Nagod, India 43 G9 24 34N 80 36 E
Nagoorin, Australia 62 C5 24 17S 151 15 E
Nagorno-Karabakh, Azerbaijan 25 F8 39 55N 46 45 E
Nagornyy, Russia 27 D13 55 58N 124 57 E
Nagoya, Japan 31 G8 35 10N 136 50 E
Nagpur, India 40 J11 21 8N 79 10 E
Nagua, Dom. Rep. 89 C6 19 23N 69 50W
Nagykanizsa, Hungary 17 E9 46 28N 17 0 E
Nagykőrös, Hungary 17 E10 47 5N 19 48 E
Naha, Japan 31 L3 26 13N 127 42 E
Nahan, India 42 D7 30 33N 77 18 E
Nahanni Butte, Canada 72 A4 61 2N 123 31W
Nahanni Nat. Park, Canada 72 A4 61 15N 125 0W
Nahargarh, Mad. P., India 42 G6 24 10N 75 14 E
Nahargarh, Raj., India 42 G7 24 55N 76 50 E
Nahariyya, Israel 44 C2 33 1N 35 5 E
Nahāvand, Iran 45 C6 34 10N 48 22 E
Naicá, Mexico 86 B3 27 53N 105 31W
Naicam, Canada 73 C8 52 30N 104 30W
Naikoon Prov. Park, Canada 72 C2 53 55N 131 55W
Naimisharanya, India 43 F9 27 21N 80 30 E
Nain, Canada 71 A7 56 34N 61 40W
Nā'īn, Iran 45 C7 32 54N 53 0 E
Naini Tal, India 43 E8 29 30N 79 30 E
Nainpur, India 40 H12 22 30N 80 10 E
Nainwa, India 42 G6 25 46N 75 51 E
Nairn, U.K. 12 D5 57 35N 3 53W
Nairobi, Kenya 54 C4 1 17S 36 48 E
Naissaar, Estonia 9 G21 59 34N 24 29 E
Naivasha, Kenya 54 C4 0 40S 36 30 E
Naivasha, L., Kenya 54 C4 0 48S 36 20 E
Najafābād, Iran 45 C6 32 40N 51 15 E
Najd, Si. Arabia 46 B3 26 30N 42 0 E
Najibabad, India 42 E8 29 40N 78 20 E
Najin, N. Korea 35 C16 42 12N 130 15 E
Najmah, Si. Arabia 45 E6 26 42N 50 6 E
Naju, S. Korea 35 G14 35 3N 126 43 E
Nakadōri-Shima, Japan 31 H4 32 57N 129 4 E
Nakalagba, Dem. Rep. of the Congo 54 B2 2 50N 27 58 E
Nakaminato, Japan 31 F10 36 21N 140 36 E
Nakamura, Japan 31 H6 32 59N 132 56 E
Nakano, Japan 31 F9 36 45N 138 22 E
Nakano-Shima, Japan 31 K4 29 51N 129 52 E
Nakashibetsu, Japan 30 C12 43 33N 144 59 E
Nakfa, Eritrea 46 D2 16 40N 38 32 E
Nakhfar al Buşayyah, Iraq 44 D5 30 0N 46 10 E
Nakhichevan = Naxçıvan, Azerbaijan 25 G8 39 12N 45 15 E
Nakhichevan Republic = Naxçıvan □, Azerbaijan 25 G8 39 25N 45 26 E
Nakhl, Egypt 47 F2 29 55N 33 43 E
Nakhl-e Taqī, Iran 45 E7 27 28N 52 36 E
Nakhodka, Russia 27 E14 42 53N 132 54 E
Nakhon Nayok, Thailand 38 E3 14 12N 101 13 E
Nakhon Pathom, Thailand 38 F3 13 49N 100 3 E
Nakhon Phanom, Thailand 38 D5 17 23N 104 43 E
Nakhon Ratchasima, Thailand 38 E4 14 59N 102 12 E
Nakhon Sawan, Thailand 38 E3 15 35N 100 10 E
Nakhon Si Thammarat, Thailand 39 H3 8 29N 100 0 E
Nakhon Thai, Thailand 38 D3 17 5N 100 44 E
Nakhtarana, India 42 H3 23 20N 69 15 E
Nakina, Canada 70 B2 50 10N 86 40W
Nakodar, India 42 D6 31 8N 75 31 E
Nakskov, Denmark 9 J14 54 50N 11 8 E
Naktong →, S. Korea 35 G15 35 7N 128 57 E
Nakuru, Kenya 54 C4 0 15S 36 4 E
Nakuru, L., Kenya 54 C4 0 23S 36 5 E
Nakusp, Canada 72 C5 50 20N 117 45W
Nal, Pakistan 42 F2 27 40N 66 12 E
Nal →, Pakistan 42 G1 25 20N 65 30 E
Nalchik, Russia 25 F7 43 30N 43 33 E
Nalgonda, India 40 L11 17 6N 79 15 E
Nalhati, India 43 G12 24 17N 87 52 E
Naliya, India 42 H3 23 16N 68 50 E
Nallamalai Hills, India 40 M11 15 30N 78 50 E
Nam Can, Vietnam 39 H5 8 46N 104 59 E
Nam-ch'on, N. Korea 35 E14 38 15N 126 26 E
Nam Co, China 32 C4 30 30N 90 45 E
Nam Du, Hon, Vietnam 39 H5 9 41N 104 21 E
Nam Ngum Dam, Laos 38 C4 18 35N 102 34 E
Nam-Phan = Cochin China, Vietnam 39 G6 10 30N 106 0 E
Nam Phong, Thailand 38 D4 16 42N 102 52 E
Nam Tok, Thailand 38 E2 14 21N 99 4 E
Namacunde, Angola 56 B2 17 18S 15 50 E
Namacurra, Mozam. 57 B6 17 30S 36 50 E
Namak, Daryācheh-ye, Iran 45 C7 34 30N 52 0 E
Namak, Kavir-e, Iran 45 C8 34 30N 57 30 E
Namakzār, Daryācheh-ye, Iran 45 C9 34 0N 60 30 E
Namaland, Namibia 56 C2 26 0S 17 0 E
Namangan, Uzbekistan 26 E8 41 0N 71 40 E
Namapa, Mozam. 55 E4 13 43S 39 50 E
Namaqualand, S. Africa 56 E2 30 0S 17 25 E
Namasagali, Uganda 54 B3 1 2N 33 0 E
Namber, Indonesia 37 E8 1 2S 134 49 E
Nambour, Australia 63 D5 26 32S 152 58 E
Nambucca Heads, Australia 63 E5 30 37S 153 0 E
Namcha Barwa, China 32 D4 29 40N 95 10 E
Namche Bazar, Nepal 43 F12 27 51N 86 47 E
Namchonjŏm = Nam-ch'on, N. Korea 35 E14 38 15N 126 26 E
Namecunda, Mozam. 55 E4 14 54S 37 37 E
Nameponda, Mozam. 55 F4 15 50S 39 50 E
Nametil, Mozam. 55 F4 15 40S 39 21 E
Namew L., Canada 73 C8 54 14N 101 56W
Namgia, India 43 D8 31 48N 78 40 E
Namib Desert = Namibwoestyn, Namibia 56 C2 22 30S 15 0 E
Namibe, Angola 53 H2 15 7S 12 11 E
Namibe □, Angola 56 B1 16 35S 12 30 E
Namibia ■, Africa 56 C2 22 0S 18 9 E
Namibwoestyn, Namibia 56 C2 22 30S 15 0 E
Namlea, Indonesia 37 E7 3 18S 127 5 E
Namoi →, Australia 63 E4 30 12S 149 30 E
Nampa, U.S.A. 82 E5 43 34N 116 34W
Namp'o, N. Korea 35 E13 38 52N 125 10 E
Nampō-Shotō, Japan 31 J10 32 0N 140 0 E
Nampula, Mozam. 55 F4 15 6S 39 15 E
Namrole, Indonesia 37 E7 3 46S 126 46 E
Namse Shankou, China 41 E13 30 0N 82 25 E
Namsen →, Norway 8 D14 64 28N 11 37 E
Namsos, Norway 8 D14 64 29N 11 30 E
Namtsy, Russia 27 C13 62 43N 129 37 E
Namtu, Burma 41 H20 23 5N 97 28 E
Namtumbo, Tanzania 55 E4 10 30S 36 4 E
Namu, Canada 72 C3 51 52N 127 50W
Namur, Belgium 15 D4 50 27N 4 52 E
Namur □, Belgium 15 D4 50 17N 5 0 E
Namutoni, Namibia 56 B2 18 49S 16 55 E
Namwala, Zambia 55 F2 15 44S 26 30 E
Namwŏn, S. Korea 35 G14 35 23N 127 23 E
Nan, Thailand 38 C3 18 48N 100 46 E
Nan →, Thailand 38 E3 15 42N 100 9 E
Nan-ch'ang = Nanchang, China 33 D6 28 42N 115 55 E
Nanaimo, Canada 72 D4 49 10N 124 0W
Nanam, N. Korea 35 D15 41 44N 129 40 E
Nanango, Australia 63 D5 26 40S 152 0 E
Nanao, Japan 31 F8 37 0N 137 0 E
Nanchang, China 33 D6 28 42N 115 55 E
Nanching = Nanjing, China 33 C6 32 2N 118 47 E

Nanchong, China 32 C5 30 43N 106 2 E
Nancy, France 18 B7 48 42N 6 12 E
Nanda Devi, India 43 D8 30 23N 79 59 E
Nanda Kot, India 43 D9 30 17N 80 5 E
Nandan, Japan 31 G7 34 10N 134 42 E
Nanded, India 40 K10 19 10N 77 20 E
Nandewar Ra., Australia 63 E5 30 15S 150 35 E
Nandi, Fiji 59 C7 17 42S 177 20 E
Nandigram, India 43 H12 22 1N 87 58 E
Nandurbar, India 40 J9 21 20N 74 15 E
Nandyal, India 40 M11 15 30N 78 30 E
Nanga-Eboko, Cameroon 52 D2 4 41N 12 22 E
Nanga Parbat, Pakistan 43 B6 35 10N 74 35 E
Nangade, Mozam. 55 E4 11 5S 39 36 E
Nangapinoh, Indonesia 36 E4 0 20S 111 44 E
Nangarhār □, Afghan. 40 B7 34 20N 70 0 E
Nangatayap, Indonesia 36 E4 1 32S 110 34 E
Nangeya Mts., Uganda 54 B3 3 30N 33 30 E
Nangong, China 34 F8 37 23N 115 22 E
Nanhuang, China 35 F11 36 58N 121 48 E
Nanjeko, Zambia 55 F1 15 31S 23 30 E
Nanjing, China 33 C6 32 2N 118 47 E
Nanjirinji, Tanzania 55 D4 9 41S 39 5 E
Nankana Sahib, Pakistan 42 D5 31 27N 73 38 E
Nanking = Nanjing, China 33 C6 32 2N 118 47 E
Nankoku, Japan 31 H6 33 39N 133 44 E
Nanning, China 32 D5 22 48N 108 20 E
Nannup, Australia 61 F2 33 59S 115 48 E
Nanpara, India 43 F9 27 52N 81 33 E
Nanpi, China 34 E9 38 2N 116 45 E
Nanping, China 33 D6 26 38N 118 10 E
Nanripe, Mozam. 55 E4 13 52S 38 52 E
Nansei-Shotō = Ryūkyū-rettō, Japan 31 M3 26 0N 126 0 E
Nansen Sd., Canada 4 A3 81 0N 91 0W
Nanshan I., S. China Sea 36 B5 10 45N 115 49 E
Nansio, Tanzania 54 C3 2 3S 33 4 E
Nantes, France 18 C3 47 12N 1 33W
Nanticoke, U.S.A. 79 E8 41 12N 76 0W
Nanton, Canada 72 C6 50 21N 113 46W
Nantong, China 33 C7 32 1N 120 52 E
Nantucket I., U.S.A. 76 E10 41 16N 70 5W
Nantwich, U.K. 10 D5 53 4N 2 31W
Nanty Glo, U.S.A. 78 F6 40 28N 78 50W
Nanuque, Brazil 93 G10 17 50S 40 21W
Nanusa, Kepulauan, Indonesia 37 D7 4 45N 127 1 E
Nanutarra Roadhouse, Australia 60 D2 22 32S 115 30 E
Nanyang, China 34 H7 33 11N 112 30 E
Nanyuan, China 34 E9 39 44N 116 22 E
Nanyuki, Kenya 54 B4 0 2N 37 4 E
Nao, C. de la, Spain 19 C6 38 44N 0 14 E
Naococane, L., Canada 71 B5 52 50N 70 45W
Napa, U.S.A. 84 G4 38 18N 122 17W
Napa →, U.S.A. 84 G4 38 10N 122 19W
Napanee, Canada 78 B8 44 15N 77 0W
Napanoch, U.S.A. 79 E10 41 44N 74 22W
Nape, Laos 38 C5 18 18N 105 6 E
Nape Pass = Keo Neua, Deo, Vietnam 38 C5 18 23N 105 10 E
Napier, N.Z. 59 H6 39 30S 176 56 E
Napier Broome B., Australia 60 B4 14 2S 126 37 E
Napier Pen., Australia 62 A2 12 4S 135 43 E
Napierville, Canada 79 A11 45 11N 73 25W
Naples = Nápoli, Italy 20 D6 40 50N 14 15 E
Naples, U.S.A. 77 M5 26 8N 81 48W
Napo →, Peru 92 D4 3 20S 72 40W
Napoleon, N. Dak., U.S.A. 80 B5 46 30N 99 46W
Napoleon, Ohio, U.S.A. 76 E3 41 23N 84 8W
Nápoli, Italy 20 D6 40 50N 14 15 E
Napopo, Dem. Rep. of the Congo 54 B2 4 15N 28 0 E
Naqqāsh, Iran 45 C6 35 40N 49 6 E
Nara, Japan 31 G7 34 40N 135 49 E
Nara, Mali 50 E4 15 10N 7 20W
Nara □, Japan 31 G8 34 30N 136 0 E
Nara Canal, Pakistan 42 G3 24 30N 69 20 E
Nara Visa, U.S.A. 81 H3 35 37N 103 6W
Naracoorte, Australia 63 F3 36 58S 140 45 E
Naradhan, Australia 63 E4 33 34S 146 17 E
Naraini, India 43 G9 25 11N 80 29 E
Narasapur, India 41 L12 16 26N 81 40 E
Narathiwat, Thailand 39 J3 6 30N 101 48 E
Narayanganj, Bangla. 41 H17 23 40N 90 33 E
Narayanpet, India 40 L10 16 45N 77 30 E
Narbonne, France 18 E5 43 11N 3 0 E
Nardīn, Iran 45 B7 37 3N 55 59 E
Nardò, Italy 21 D8 40 11N 18 2 E
Narembeen, Australia 61 F2 32 7S 118 24 E
Narendranagar, India 42 D8 30 10N 78 18 E
Nares Str., Arctic 66 A13 80 0N 70 0W
Naretha, Australia 61 F3 31 0S 124 45 E
Narew →, Poland 17 B11 52 26N 20 41 E
Nari →, Pakistan 42 F2 28 0N 67 40 E
Narin, Afghan. 40 A6 36 5N 69 0 E
Narindra, Helodranon' i, Madag. 57 A8 14 55S 47 30 E
Narita, Japan 31 G10 35 47N 140 19 E
Narmada →, India 42 J5 21 38N 72 36 E
Narmland, Sweden 9 F15 60 0N 13 30 E
Narnaul, India 42 E7 28 5N 76 11 E
Narodnaya, Russia 24 A10 65 5N 59 58 E
Narok, Kenya 54 C4 1 55S 35 52 E
Narooma, Australia 63 F5 36 14S 150 4 E
Narowal, Pakistan 42 C6 32 6N 74 52 E
Narrabri, Australia 63 E4 30 19S 149 46 E
Narran →, Australia 63 D4 28 37S 148 12 E
Narrandera, Australia 63 E4 34 42S 146 31 E
Narrogin, Australia 61 F2 32 58S 117 14 E
Narromine, Australia 63 E4 32 12S 148 12 E
Narrow Hills Prov. Park, Canada 73 C8 54 0N 104 37W
Narsimhapur, India 43 H8 22 54N 79 14 E
Narsinghgarh, India 42 H7 23 45N 76 40 E
Naruto, Japan 31 G7 34 11N 134 37 E
Narva, Estonia 24 C4 59 23N 28 12 E
Narva →, Russia 9 G22 59 27N 28 2 E
Narvik, Norway 8 B17 68 28N 17 26 E
Narwana, India 42 E7 29 39N 76 6 E
Naryan-Mar, Russia 24 A9 67 42N 53 12 E
Narym, Russia 26 D9 59 0N 81 30 E
Naryn, Kyrgyzstan 26 E8 41 26N 75 58 E
Nasa, Norway 8 C16 66 29N 15 23 E
Naseby, N.Z. 59 L3 45 1S 170 10 E
Naselle, U.S.A. 84 D3 46 22N 123 49W
Naser, Buheirat en, Egypt 51 D12 23 0N 32 30 E
Nashua, Mont., U.S.A. 82 B10 48 8N 106 22W
Nashua, N.H., U.S.A. 79 D13 42 45N 71 28W
Nashville, Ark., U.S.A. 81 J8 33 57N 93 51W
Nashville, Ga., U.S.A. 77 K4 31 12N 83 15W
Nashville, Tenn., U.S.A. 77 G2 36 10N 86 47W
Nasik, India 40 K8 19 58N 73 50 E
Nasirabad, India 42 F6 26 15N 74 45 E
Nasirabad, Pakistan 42 E3 28 23N 68 24 E
Naskaupi →, Canada 71 B7 53 47N 60 51W
Naşrābād, Iran 45 C6 34 8N 51 26 E
Naşriān-e Pā'īn, Iran 44 C5 32 52N 46 52 E
Nass →, Canada 72 C3 55 0N 129 40W
Nassau, Bahamas 88 A4 25 5N 77 20W
Nassau, U.S.A. 79 D11 42 31N 73 37W
Nassau, B., Chile 96 H3 55 20S 68 0W
Nasser, L. = Naser, Buheirat en, Egypt 51 D12 23 0N 32 30 E
Nasser City = Kôm Ombo, Egypt 51 D12 24 25N 32 52 E
Nässjö, Sweden 9 H16 57 39N 14 42 E
Nastapoka →, Canada 70 A4 56 55N 76 33W
Nastapoka, Is., Canada 70 A4 56 55N 76 50W
Nata, Botswana 56 C4 20 12S 26 12 E
Natal, Brazil 93 E11 5 47S 35 13W
Natal, Indonesia 36 D1 0 35N 99 7 E
Natal □, S. Africa 53 K6 28 30S 30 30 E
Naţanz, Iran 45 C6 33 30N 51 55 E
Natashquan, Canada 71 B7 50 14N 61 46W
Natashquan →, Canada 71 B7 50 7N 61 50W
Natchez, U.S.A. 81 K9 31 34N 91 24W
Natchitoches, U.S.A. 81 K8 31 46N 93 5W
Nathalia, Australia 63 F4 36 1S 145 13 E
Nathdwara, India 42 G5 24 55N 73 50 E
Nati, Pta., Spain 22 A10 40 3N 3 50 E
Natimuk, Australia 63 F3 36 42S 142 0 E
Nation →, Canada 72 B4 55 30N 123 32W
National City, U.S.A. 85 N9 32 41N 117 6W
Natitingou, Benin 50 F6 10 20N 1 26 E
Natividad, I., Mexico 86 B1 27 50N 115 10W
Natkyizin, Burma 38 E1 14 57N 97 59 E
Natron, L., Tanzania 54 C4 2 20S 36 0 E
Natrona Heights, U.S.A. 78 F5 40 37N 79 44W
Natuna Besar, Kepulauan, Indonesia 39 L7 4 0N 108 15 E
Natuna Is. = Natuna Besar, Kepulauan, Indonesia 39 L7 4 0N 108 15 E
Natuna Selatan, Kepulauan, Indonesia 39 L7 2 45N 109 0 E
Natural Bridge, U.S.A. 79 B9 44 5N 75 30W
Naturaliste, C., Australia 62 G4 40 50S 148 15 E
Nau Qala, Afghan. 42 B3 34 5N 68 5 E
Naugatuck, U.S.A. 79 E11 41 30N 73 3W
Naumburg, Germany 16 C6 51 9N 11 47 E
Nā'ūr at Tunayb, Jordan 47 D4 31 48N 35 57 E
Nauru ■, Pac. Oc. 64 H8 1 0S 166 0 E
Naushahra = Nowshera, Pakistan 40 C8 34 0N 72 0 E
Naushahro, Pakistan 42 F3 26 50N 68 7 E
Naushon I., U.S.A. 79 E14 41 29N 70 45W
Nauta, Peru 92 D4 4 31S 73 35W
Nautanwa, India 41 F13 27 20N 83 25 E
Nautla, Mexico 87 C5 20 20N 96 50W
Nava, Mexico 86 B4 28 25N 100 46W
Navadwip, India 43 H13 23 34N 88 20 E
Navahrudak, Belarus 17 B13 53 40N 25 50 E
Navajo Reservoir, U.S.A. 83 H10 36 48N 107 36W
Navalmoral de la Mata, Spain 19 C3 39 52N 5 33W
Navan = An Uaimh, Ireland 13 C5 53 39N 6 41W
Navarino, I., Chile 96 H3 55 0S 67 40W
Navarra □, Spain 19 A5 42 40N 1 40W
Navarre, U.S.A. 78 F3 40 43N 81 31W
Navarro →, U.S.A. 84 F3 39 11N 123 45W
Navasota, U.S.A. 81 K6 30 23N 96 5W
Navassa I., W. Indies 89 C5 18 30N 75 0W
Naver →, U.K. 12 C4 58 32N 4 14W
Navibandar, India 42 J3 21 26N 69 48 E
Navidad, Chile 94 C1 33 57S 71 50W
Naviraí, Brazil 95 A5 23 8S 54 13W
Navlakhi, India 42 H4 22 58N 70 28 E
Năvodari, Romania 17 F15 44 19N 28 36 E
Navoi = Nawoiy, Uzbekistan 26 E7 40 9N 65 22 E
Navojoa, Mexico 86 B3 27 0N 109 30W
Navolato, Mexico 86 C3 24 47N 107 42W
Návpaktos, Greece 21 E9 38 24N 21 50 E
Návplion, Greece 21 F10 37 33N 22 50 E
Navsari, India 40 J8 20 57N 72 59 E
Nawa Kot, Pakistan 42 E4 28 21N 71 24 E
Nawab Khan, Pakistan 42 D3 30 17N 69 12 E
Nawabganj, Ut. P., India 43 F9 26 56N 81 14 E
Nawabganj, Ut. P., India 43 E8 28 32N 79 40 E
Nawabshah, Pakistan 42 F3 26 15N 68 25 E
Nawada, India 43 G11 24 50N 85 33 E
Nawakot, Nepal 43 F11 27 55N 85 10 E
Nawalgarh, India 42 F6 27 50N 75 15 E
Nawanshahr, India 43 C6 32 33N 74 48 E
Nawoiy, Uzbekistan 26 E7 40 9N 65 22 E
Naxçıvan, Azerbaijan 25 G8 39 12N 45 15 E
Naxçıvan □, Azerbaijan 25 G8 39 25N 45 26 E
Náxos, Greece 21 F11 37 8N 25 25 E
Nay, Mui, Vietnam 36 B3 12 55N 109 23 E
Nāy Band, Būshehr, Iran 45 E7 27 20N 52 40 E
Nāy Band, Khorāsān, Iran 45 C8 32 20N 57 34 E
Nayakhan, Russia 27 C16 61 56N 159 0 E
Nayarit □, Mexico 86 C4 22 0N 105 0W
Nayoro, Japan 30 B11 44 21N 142 28 E
Nayyāl, W. →, Si. Arabia 44 D3 28 35N 39 4 E
Nazaré, Brazil 93 F11 13 2S 39 0W
Nazareth = Nazerat, Israel 47 C4 32 42N 35 17 E
Nazareth, U.S.A. 79 F9 40 44N 75 19W
Nazas, Mexico 86 B4 25 10N 104 6W
Nazas →, Mexico 86 B4 25 35N 103 25W
Nazca, Peru 92 F4 14 50S 74 57W
Naze, The, U.K. 11 F9 51 53N 1 18 E
Nazerat, Israel 47 C4 32 42N 35 17 E
Nāzīk, Iran 44 B5 39 1N 45 4 E
Nazilli, Turkey 21 F13 37 55N 28 15 E
Nazir Hat, Bangla. 41 H17 22 35N 91 49 E
Nazko, Canada 72 C4 53 1N 123 37W
Nazko →, Canada 72 C4 53 7N 123 34W
Nazret, Ethiopia 46 F2 8 32N 39 22 E
Nazwá, Oman 46 C6 22 56N 57 32 E
Nchanga, Zambia 55 E2 12 30S 27 49 E
Ncheu, Malawi 55 E3 14 50S 34 47 E
Ndala, Tanzania 54 C3 4 45S 33 15 E
Ndalatando, Angola 52 F2 9 12S 14 48 E
Ndareda, Tanzania 54 C4 4 12S 35 30 E
Ndélé, C.A.R. 52 C4 8 25N 20 36 E
Ndjamena, Chad 51 F8 12 10N 14 59 E
Ndola, Zambia 55 E2 13 0S 28 34 E
Ndoto Mts., Kenya 54 B4 2 0N 37 0 E
Nduguti, Tanzania 54 C3 4 18S 34 41 E
Neagh, Lough, U.K. 13 B5 54 37N 6 25W
Neah Bay, U.S.A. 84 B2 48 22N 124 37W
Neale, L., Australia 60 D5 24 15S 130 0 E
Neápolis, Greece 23 D7 35 15N 25 37 E
Near Is., U.S.A. 68 C1 52 30N 174 0 E
Neath, U.K. 11 F4 51 39N 3 48W
Neath Port Talbot □, U.K. 11 F4 51 42N 3 45W
Nebine Cr. →, Australia 63 D4 29 27S 146 56 E
Nebitdag, Turkmenistan 25 G9 39 30N 54 22 E
Nebo, Australia 62 C4 21 42S 148 42 E
Nebraska □, U.S.A. 80 E5 41 30N 99 30W
Nebraska City, U.S.A. 80 E7 40 41N 95 52W
Nébrodi, Monti, Italy 20 F6 37 54N 14 35 E
Necedah, U.S.A. 80 C9 44 2N 90 4W
Nechako →, Canada 72 C4 53 30N 122 44W
Neches →, U.S.A. 81 L8 29 58N 93 51W
Neckar →, Germany 16 D5 49 27N 8 29 E
Necochea, Argentina 94 D4 38 30S 58 50W
Needles, Canada 72 D5 49 53N 118 7W
Needles, U.S.A. 85 L12 34 51N 114 37W
Needles, The, U.K. 11 G6 50 39N 1 35W
Ñeembucú □, Paraguay 94 B4 27 0S 58 0W
Neemuch = Nimach, India 42 G6 24 30N 74 56 E
Neenah, U.S.A. 76 C1 44 11N 88 28W
Neepawa, Canada 73 C9 50 15N 99 30W
Neftçala, Azerbaijan 25 G8 39 19N 49 12 E
Neftekumsk, Russia 25 F7 44 46N 44 50 E
Nefyn, U.K. 10 E3 52 56N 4 31W
Negapatam = Nagappattinam, India 40 P11 10 46N 79 51 E
Negaunee, U.S.A. 76 B2 46 30N 87 36W
Negele, Ethiopia 46 F2 5 20N 39 36 E
Negev Desert = Hanegev, Israel 47 E4 30 50N 35 0 E
Negombo, Sri Lanka 40 R11 7 12N 79 50 E
Negotin, Serbia, Yug. 21 B10 44 16N 22 37 E
Negra, Pta., Peru 92 E2 6 6S 81 10W
Negrais, C. = Maudin Sun, Burma 41 M19 16 0N 94 30 E
Negril, Jamaica 88 C4 18 22N 78 20W
Negro →, Argentina 96 E4 41 2S 62 47W
Negro →, Brazil 92 D7 3 0S 60 0W
Negro →, Uruguay 95 C4 33 24S 58 22W
Negros, Phil. 37 C6 9 30N 122 40 E
Neguac, Canada 71 C6 47 15N 65 5W
Nehalem →, U.S.A. 84 E3 45 40N 123 56W
Nehāvand, Iran 45 C6 35 56N 49 31 E
Nehbandān, Iran 45 D9 31 35N 60 5 E
Nei Monggol Zizhiqu □, China 34 D7 42 0N 112 0 E
Neijiang, China 32 D5 29 35N 104 55 E
Neillsville, U.S.A. 80 C9 44 34N 90 36W
Neilton, U.S.A. 82 C2 47 25N 123 53W
Neiqiu, China 34 F8 37 15N 114 30 E
Neiva, Colombia 92 C3 2 56N 75 18W
Neixiang, China 34 H6 33 10N 111 52 E
Nejanilini L., Canada 73 B9 59 33N 97 48W
Nejd = Najd, Si. Arabia 46 B3 26 30N 42 0 E
Nekā, Iran 45 B7 36 39N 53 19 E
Nekemte, Ethiopia 46 F2 9 4N 36 30 E
Neksø, Denmark 9 J16 55 4N 15 8 E
Nelia, Australia 62 C3 20 39S 142 12 E
Neligh, U.S.A. 80 D5 42 8N 98 2W
Nelkan, Russia 27 D14 57 40N 136 4 E
Nellore, India 40 M11 14 27N 79 59 E
Nelson, Canada 72 D5 49 30N 117 20W
Nelson, N.Z. 59 J4 41 18S 173 16 E
Nelson, U.K. 10 D5 53 50N 2 13W
Nelson, Ariz., U.S.A. 83 J7 35 31N 113 19W
Nelson, Nev., U.S.A. 85 K12 35 42N 114 50W
Nelson →, Canada 73 C9 54 33N 98 2W
Nelson, C., Australia 63 F3 38 26S 141 32 E
Nelson, Estrecho, Chile 96 G2 51 30S 75 0W
Nelson Bay, Australia 63 E5 32 43S 152 9 E
Nelson Forks, Canada 72 B4 59 30N 124 0W
Nelson House, Canada 73 B9 55 47N 98 51W
Nelson L., Canada 73 B8 55 48N 100 7W
Nelspoort, S. Africa 56 E3 32 7S 23 0 E
Nelspruit, S. Africa 57 D5 25 29S 30 59 E
Néma, Mauritania 50 E4 16 40N 7 15W
Neman, Russia 9 J20 55 2N 22 2 E
Neman →, Lithuania 9 J20 55 25N 21 10 E
Nemeiben L., Canada 73 B7 55 20N 105 20W
Némiscau, Canada 70 B4 51 18N 76 54W
Némiscau, L., Canada 70 B4 51 25N 76 40W
Nemunas = Neman →, Lithuania 9 J20 55 25N 21 10 E
Nemuro, Japan 30 C12 43 20N 145 35 E
Nemuro-Kaikyō, Japan 30 C12 43 30N 145 30 E
Nen Jiang →, China 35 B13 45 28N 124 30 E
Nenagh, Ireland 13 D3 52 52N 8 11W
Nenasi, Malaysia 39 L4 3 9N 103 23 E
Nene →, U.K. 11 E8 52 49N 0 11 E
Nenjiang, China 33 B7 49 10N 125 10 E
Neno, Malawi 55 F3 15 25S 34 40 E
Neodesha, U.S.A. 81 G7 37 25N 95 41W
Neosho, U.S.A. 81 G7 36 52N 94 22W
Neosho →, U.S.A. 81 H7 36 48N 95 18W
Nepal ■, Asia 43 F11 28 0N 84 30 E
Nepalganj, Nepal 43 E9 28 5N 81 40 E
Nepalganj Road, India 43 E9 28 1N 81 41 E
Nephi, U.S.A. 82 G8 39 43N 111 50W
Nephin, Ireland 13 B2 54 1N 9 22W
Neptune, U.S.A. 79 F10 40 13N 74 2W
Nerang, Australia 63 D5 27 58S 153 20 E
Nerchinsk, Russia 27 D12 52 0N 116 39 E
Néret, L., Canada 71 B5 54 45N 70 44W
Neretva →, Croatia 21 C7 43 1N 17 27 E
Neringa, Lithuania 9 J19 55 20N 21 5 E
Neryungri, Russia 27 D13 57 38N 124 28 E
Nescopeck, U.S.A. 79 E8 41 3N 76 12W
Ness, L., U.K. 12 D4 57 15N 4 32W
Ness City, U.S.A. 80 F5 38 27N 99 54W
Nesterov, Poland 17 C12 50 4N 23 58 E
Nesvizh = Nyasvizh, Belarus 17 B14 53 14N 26 38 E
Netanya, Israel 47 C3 32 20N 34 51 E
Netarhat, India 43 H11 23 29N 84 16 E
Nete →, Belgium 15 C4 51 7N 4 14 E
Netherdale, Australia 62 C4 21 10S 148 33 E
Netherlands ■, Europe 15 C5 52 0N 5 30 E
Netherlands Antilles ■, W. Indies 92 A5 12 15N 69 0W
Netrang, India 42 J5 21 39N 73 21 E
Nettilling L., Canada 69 B12 66 30N 71 0W
Netzahualcoyotl, Presa, Mexico 87 D6 17 10N 93 30W
Neubrandenburg, Germany 16 B7 53 33N 13 15 E
Neuchâtel, Switz. 18 C7 47 0N 6 55 E
Neuchâtel, Lac de, Switz. 18 C7 46 53N 6 50 E
Neufchâteau, Belgium 15 E5 49 50N 5 25 E
Neumünster, Germany 16 A5 54 4N 9 58 E
Neunkirchen, Germany 16 D4 49 20N 7 9 E
Neuquén, Argentina 96 D3 38 55S 68 0W
Neuquén □, Argentina 94 D2 38 0S 69 50W
Neuruppin, Germany 16 B7 52 55N 12 48 E
Neuse →, U.S.A. 77 H7 35 6N 76 29W
Neusiedler See, Austria 17 E9 47 50N 16 47 E
Neustrelitz, Germany 16 B7 53 21N 13 4 E
Neva →, Russia 24 C5 59 50N 30 30 E
Nevada, Iowa, U.S.A. 80 D8 42 1N 93 27W
Nevada, Mo., U.S.A. 81 G7 37 51N 94 22W
Nevada □, U.S.A. 82 G5 39 0N 117 0W
Nevada, Sierra, Spain 19 D4 37 3N 3 15W
Nevada, Sierra, U.S.A. 82 G3 39 0N 120 30W
Nevada City, U.S.A. 84 F6 39 16N 121 1W
Nevado, Cerro, Argentina 94 D2 35 30S 68 32W
Nevel, Russia 24 C4 56 0N 29 55 E
Nevers, France 18 C5 47 0N 3 9 E
Nevertire, Australia 63 E4 31 50S 147 44 E
Neville, Canada 73 D7 49 58N 107 39W
Nevinnomyssk, Russia 25 F7 44 40N 42 0 E
Nevis, W. Indies 89 C7 17 0N 62 30W
Nevşehir, Turkey 44 B2 38 33N 34 40 E
Nevyansk, Russia 24 C11 57 30N 60 13 E
New →, U.S.A. 76 F5 38 10N 81 12W
New Aiyansh, Canada 72 B3 55 12N 129 4W
New Albany, Ind., U.S.A. 76 F3 38 18N 85 49W
New Albany, Miss., U.S.A. 81 H10 34 29N 89 0W
New Albany, Pa., U.S.A. 79 E8 41 36N 76 27W
New Amsterdam, Guyana 92 B7 6 15N 57 36W
New Angledool, Australia 63 D4 29 5S 147 55 E
New Baltimore, U.S.A. 78 D2 42 41N 82 44W
New Bedford, U.S.A. 79 E14 41 38N 70 56W
New Berlin, N.Y., U.S.A. 79 D9 42 37N 75 20W
New Berlin, Pa., U.S.A. 78 F8 40 50N 76 57W
New Bern, U.S.A. 77 H7 35 7N 77 3W
New Bethlehem, U.S.A. 78 F5 41 0N 79 20W
New Bloomfield, U.S.A. 78 F7 40 25N 77 11W
New Boston, U.S.A. 81 J7 33 28N 94 25W
New Braunfels, U.S.A. 81 L5 29 42N 98 8W
New Brighton, N.Z. 59 K4 43 29S 172 43 E
New Brighton, U.S.A. 78 F4 40 42N 80 19W
New Britain, Papua N. G. 64 H7 5 50S 150 20 E
New Britain, U.S.A. 79 E12 41 40N 72 47W
New Brunswick, U.S.A. 79 F10 40 30N 74 27W
New Brunswick □, Canada 71 C6 46 50N 66 30W
New Caledonia ■, Pac. Oc. 64 K8 21 0S 165 0 E
New Castile = Castilla-La Mancha □, Spain 19 C4 39 30N 3 30W
New Castle, Ind., U.S.A. 76 F3 39 55N 85 22W
New Castle, Pa., U.S.A. 78 F4 41 0N 80 21W
New City, U.S.A. 79 E11 41 9N 73 59W
New Concord, U.S.A. 78 G3 39 59N 81 54W
New Cumberland, U.S.A. 78 F4 40 30N 80 36W
New Cuyama, U.S.A. 85 L7 34 57N 119 38W
New Delhi, India 42 E7 28 37N 77 13 E
New Denver, Canada 72 D5 50 0N 117 25W
New Don Pedro Reservoir, U.S.A. 84 H6 37 43N 120 24W
New England, U.S.A. 80 B3 46 32N 102 52W
New England Ra., Australia 63 E5 30 20S 151 45 E
New Forest, U.K. 11 G6 50 53N 1 34W
New Galloway, U.K. 12 F4 55 5N 4 9W
New Glasgow, Canada 71 C7 45 35N 62 36W
New Guinea, Oceania 28 K17 4 0S 136 0 E
New Hamburg, Canada 78 C4 43 23N 80 42W
New Hampshire □, U.S.A. 79 C13 44 0N 71 30W
New Hampton, U.S.A. 80 D8 43 3N 92 19W
New Hanover, S. Africa 57 D5 29 22S 30 31 E
New Hartford, U.S.A. 79 C9 43 4N 75 18W
New Haven, Conn., U.S.A. 79 E12 41 18N 72 55W
New Haven, Mich., U.S.A. 78 D2 42 44N 82 48W
New Hazelton, Canada 72 B3 55 20N 127 30W
New Hebrides = Vanuatu ■, Pac. Oc. 64 J8 15 0S 168 0 E
New Holland, U.S.A. 79 F8 40 6N 76 5W
New Iberia, U.S.A. 81 K9 30 1N 91 49W
New Ireland, Papua N. G. 64 H7 3 20S 151 50 E
New Jersey □, U.S.A. 76 E8 40 0N 74 30W
New Kensington, U.S.A. 78 F5 40 34N 79 46W
New Lexington, U.S.A. 76 F4 39 43N 82 13W
New Liskeard, Canada 70 C4 47 31N 79 41W
New London, Conn., U.S.A. 79 E12 41 22N 72 6W
New London, Ohio, U.S.A. 78 E2 41 5N 82 24W
New London, Wis., U.S.A. 80 C10 44 23N 88 45W
New Madrid, U.S.A. 81 G10 36 36N 89 32W
New Martinsville, U.S.A. 76 F5 39 39N 80 52W
New Meadows, U.S.A. 82 D5 44 58N 116 18W
New Melones L., U.S.A. 84 H6 37 57N 120 31W
New Mexico □, U.S.A. 83 J10 34 30N 106 0W
New Milford, Conn., U.S.A. 79 E11 41 35N 73 25W
New Milford, Pa., U.S.A. 79 E9 41 52N 75 44W
New Norcia, Australia 61 F2 30 57S 116 13 E
New Norfolk, Australia 62 G4 42 46S 147 2 E
New Orleans, U.S.A. 81 L9 29 58N 90 4W
New Philadelphia, U.S.A. 78 F3 40 30N 81 27W
New Plymouth, N.Z. 59 H5 39 4S 174 5 E
New Plymouth, U.S.A. 82 E5 43 58N 116 49W
New Port Richey, U.S.A. 77 L4 28 16N 82 43W
New Providence, Bahamas 88 A4 25 25N 78 35W
New Quay, U.K. 11 E3 52 13N 4 21W
New Radnor, U.K. 11 E4 52 15N 3 9W
New Richmond, Canada 71 C6 48 15N 65 45W
New Richmond, U.S.A. 80 C8 45 7N 92 32W
New Roads, U.S.A. 81 K9 30 42N 91 26W
New Rochelle, U.S.A. 79 F11 40 55N 73 47W
New Rockford, U.S.A. 80 B5 47 41N 99 8W
New Romney, U.K. 11 G8 50 59N 0 57 E
New Ross, Ireland 13 D5 52 23N 6 57W
New Salem, U.S.A. 80 B4 46 51N 101 25W
New Scone, U.K. 12 E5 56 25N 3 24W
New Siberian I. = Novaya Sibir, Ostrov, Russia 27 B16 75 10N 150 0 E
New Siberian Is. = Novosibirskiye Ostrova, Russia 27 B15 75 0N 142 0 E

New Smyrna Beach, U.S.A. 77 L5 29 1N 80 56W
New South Wales □, Australia 63 E4 33 0S 146 0 E
New Town, U.S.A. 80 B3 47 59N 102 30W
New Tredegar, U.K. 11 F4 51 44N 3 16W
New Ulm, U.S.A. 80 C7 44 19N 94 28W
New Waterford, Canada 71 C7 46 13N 60 4W
New Westminster, Canada 84 A4 49 13N 122 55W
New York, U.S.A. 79 F11 40 45N 74 0W
New York □, U.S.A. 79 D9 43 0N 75 0W
New York Mts., U.S.A. 83 J6 35 0N 115 20W
New Zealand ■, Oceania 59 J6 40 0S 176 0 E
Newaj →, India 42 G7 24 24N 76 49 E
Newala, Tanzania 55 E4 10 58S 39 18 E
Newark, Del., U.S.A. 76 F8 39 41N 75 46W
Newark, N.J., U.S.A. 79 F10 40 44N 74 10W
Newark, N.Y., U.S.A. 78 C7 43 3N 77 6W
Newark, Ohio, U.S.A. 78 F2 40 3N 82 24W
Newark-on-Trent, U.K. 10 D7 53 5N 0 48W
Newark Valley, U.S.A. 79 D8 42 14N 76 11W
Newberg, U.S.A. 82 D2 45 18N 122 58W
Newberry, Mich., U.S.A. 76 B3 46 21N 85 30W
Newberry, S.C., U.S.A. 77 H5 34 17N 81 37W
Newberry Springs, U.S.A. 85 L10 34 50N 116 41W
Newboro L., Canada 79 B8 44 38N 76 20W
Newbridge = Droichead Nua, Ireland 13 C5 53 11N 6 48W
Newburgh, Canada 78 B8 44 19N 76 52W
Newburgh, U.S.A. 79 E10 41 30N 74 1W
Newbury, U.K. 11 F6 51 24N 1 20W
Newbury, N.H., U.S.A. 79 B12 43 19N 72 3W
Newbury, Vt., U.S.A. 79 B12 44 5N 72 4W
Newburyport, U.S.A. 77 D10 42 49N 70 53W
Newcastle, Australia 63 E5 33 0S 151 46 E
Newcastle, N.B., Canada 71 C6 47 1N 65 38W
Newcastle, Ont., Canada 70 D4 43 55N 78 35W
Newcastle, S. Africa 57 D4 27 45S 29 58 E
Newcastle, U.K. 13 B6 54 13N 5 54W
Newcastle, Calif., U.S.A. 84 G5 38 53N 121 8W
Newcastle, Wyo., U.S.A. 80 D2 43 50N 104 11W
Newcastle Emlyn, U.K. 11 E3 52 2N 4 28W
Newcastle Ra., Australia 60 C5 15 45S 130 15 E
Newcastle-under-Lyme, U.K. 10 D5 53 1N 2 14W
Newcastle-upon-Tyne, U.K. 10 C6 54 58N 1 36W
Newcastle Waters, Australia 62 B1 17 30S 133 28 E
Newcastle West, Ireland 13 D2 52 27N 9 3W
Newcomb, U.S.A. 79 C10 43 58N 74 10W
Newcomerstown, U.S.A. 78 F3 40 16N 81 36W
Newdegate, Australia 61 F2 33 6S 119 0 E
Newell, Australia 62 B4 16 20S 145 16 E
Newell, U.S.A. 80 C3 44 43N 103 25W
Newfane, U.S.A. 78 C6 43 17N 78 43W
Newfield, U.S.A. 79 D8 42 18N 76 33W
Newfound L., U.S.A. 79 C13 43 40N 71 47W
Newfoundland, N. Amer. 66 E14 49 0N 55 0W
Newfoundland, U.S.A. 79 E9 41 18N 75 19W
Newfoundland □, Canada 71 B8 53 0N 58 0W
Newhall, U.S.A. 85 L8 34 23N 118 32W
Newhaven, U.K. 11 G8 50 47N 0 3 E
Newkirk, U.S.A. 81 G6 36 53N 97 3W
Newlyn, U.K. 11 G2 50 6N 5 34W
Newman, Australia 60 D2 23 18S 119 45 E
Newman, U.S.A. 84 H5 37 19N 121 1W
Newmarket, Canada 78 B5 44 3N 79 28W
Newmarket, Ireland 13 D2 52 13N 9 0W
Newmarket, U.K. 11 E8 52 15N 0 25 E
Newmarket, N.H., U.S.A. 79 C14 43 4N 70 56W
Newmarket, N.H., U.S.A. 79 C14 43 5N 70 56W
Newnan, U.S.A. 77 J3 33 23N 84 48W
Newport, Ireland 13 C2 53 53N 9 33W
Newport, I. of W., U.K. 11 G6 50 42N 1 17W
Newport, Newp., U.K. 11 F5 51 35N 3 0W
Newport, Ark., U.S.A. 81 H9 35 37N 91 16W
Newport, Ky., U.S.A. 76 F3 39 5N 84 30W
Newport, N.H., U.S.A. 79 C12 43 22N 72 10W
Newport, N.Y., U.S.A. 79 C9 43 11N 75 1W
Newport, Oreg., U.S.A. 82 D1 44 39N 124 3W
Newport, Pa., U.S.A. 78 F7 40 29N 77 8W
Newport, R.I., U.S.A. 79 E13 41 29N 71 19W
Newport, Tenn., U.S.A. 77 H4 35 58N 83 11W
Newport, Vt., U.S.A. 79 B12 44 56N 72 13W
Newport, Wash., U.S.A. 82 B5 48 11N 117 3W
Newport □, U.K. 11 F4 51 33N 3 1W
Newport Beach, U.S.A. 85 M9 33 37N 117 56W
Newport News, U.S.A. 76 G7 36 59N 76 25W
Newport Pagnell, U.K. 11 E7 52 5N 0 43W
Newquay, U.K. 11 G2 50 25N 5 6W
Newry, U.K. 13 B5 54 11N 6 21W
Newton, Ill., U.S.A. 80 F10 38 59N 88 10W
Newton, Iowa, U.S.A. 80 E8 41 42N 93 3W
Newton, Kans., U.S.A. 81 F6 38 3N 97 21W
Newton, Mass., U.S.A. 79 D13 42 21N 71 12W
Newton, Miss., U.S.A. 81 J10 32 19N 89 10W
Newton, N.C., U.S.A. 77 H5 35 40N 81 13W
Newton, N.J., U.S.A. 79 E10 41 3N 74 45W
Newton, Tex., U.S.A. 81 K8 30 51N 93 46W
Newton Abbot, U.K. 11 G4 50 32N 3 37W
Newton Aycliffe, U.K. 10 C6 54 37N 1 34W
Newton Falls, U.S.A. 78 E4 41 11N 80 59W
Newton Stewart, U.K. 12 G4 54 57N 4 30W
Newtonmore, U.K. 12 D4 57 4N 4 8W
Newtown, U.K. 11 E4 52 31N 3 19W
Newtownabbey, U.K. 13 B6 54 40N 5 56W
Newtownards, U.K. 13 B6 54 36N 5 42W
Newtownbarry = Bunclody, Ireland 13 D5 52 39N 6 40W
Newtownstewart, U.K. 13 B4 54 43N 7 23W
Newville, U.S.A. 78 F7 40 10N 77 24W
Neya, Russia 24 C7 58 21N 43 49 E
Neyrīz, Iran 45 D7 29 15N 54 19 E
Neyshābūr, Iran 45 B8 36 10N 58 50 E
Nezhin = Nizhyn, Ukraine 25 D5 51 5N 31 55 E
Nezperce, U.S.A. 82 C5 46 14N 116 14W
Ngabang, Indonesia 36 D3 0 23N 109 55 E
Ngabordamlu, Tanjung, Indonesia 37 F8 6 56S 134 11 E
N'Gage, Angola 52 F3 7 46S 15 15 E
Ngami Depression, Botswana 56 C3 20 30S 22 46 E
Ngamo, Zimbabwe 55 F2 19 3S 27 32 E
Nganglong Kangri, China 41 C12 33 0N 81 0 E
Ngao, Thailand 38 C2 18 46N 99 59 E
Ngaoundéré, Cameroon 52 C2 7 15N 13 35 E
Ngapara, N.Z. 59 L3 44 57S 170 46 E
Ngara, Tanzania 54 C3 2 29S 30 40 E
Ngawi, Indonesia 37 G14 7 24S 111 26 E
Ngoma, Malawi 55 E3 13 8S 33 45 E
Ngomahura, Zimbabwe 55 G3 20 26S 30 43 E
Ngomba, Tanzania 55 D3 8 20S 32 53 E
Ngoring Hu, China 32 C4 34 55N 97 5 E
Ngorongoro, Tanzania 54 C4 3 11S 35 32 E
Ngozi, Burundi 54 C2 2 54S 29 50 E
Ngudu, Tanzania 54 C3 2 58S 33 25 E
Nguigmi, Niger 51 F8 14 20N 13 20 E
Nguiu, Australia 60 B5 11 46S 130 38 E
Ngukurr, Australia 62 A1 14 44S 134 44 E
Ngulu Atoll, Pac. Oc. 37 C9 8 0N 137 30 E
Ngunga, Tanzania 54 C3 3 37S 33 37 E
Nguru, Nigeria 51 F8 12 56N 10 29 E
Nguru Mts., Tanzania 54 D4 6 0S 37 30 E
Nha Trang, Vietnam 39 F7 12 16N 109 10 E
Nhacoongo, Mozam. 57 C6 24 18S 35 14 E
Nhamaabué, Mozam. 55 F4 17 25S 35 5 E
Nhamundá →, Brazil 93 D7 2 12S 56 41W
Nhangutazi, L., Mozam. 57 C5 24 0S 34 30 E
Nhill, Australia 63 F3 36 18S 141 40 E
Nhulunbuy, Australia 62 A2 12 10S 137 20 E
Nia-nia, Dem. Rep. of the Congo 54 B2 1 30N 27 40 E
Niagara Falls, Canada 78 C5 43 7N 79 5W
Niagara Falls, U.S.A. 78 C6 43 5N 79 4W
Niagara-on-the-Lake, Canada 78 C5 43 15N 79 4W
Niah, Malaysia 36 D4 3 58N 113 46 E
Niamey, Niger 50 F6 13 27N 2 6 E
Niangara, Dem. Rep. of the Congo 54 B2 3 42N 27 50 E
Niantic, U.S.A. 79 E12 41 20N 72 11W
Nias, Indonesia 36 D1 1 0N 97 30 E
Niassa □, Mozam. 55 E4 13 30S 36 0 E
Nibāk, Si. Arabia 45 E7 24 25N 50 50 E
Nicaragua ■, Cent. Amer. 88 D2 11 40N 85 30W
Nicaragua, L. de, Nic. 88 D2 12 0N 85 30W
Nicastro, Italy 20 E7 38 59N 16 19 E
Nice, France 18 E7 43 42N 7 14 E
Niceville, U.S.A. 77 K2 30 31N 86 30W
Nichicun, L., Canada 71 B5 53 5N 71 0W
Nichinan, Japan 31 J5 31 38N 131 23 E
Nicholás, Canal, W. Indies 88 B3 23 30N 80 5W
Nicholasville, U.S.A. 76 G3 37 53N 84 34W
Nichols, U.S.A. 79 D8 42 1N 76 22W
Nicholson, Australia 60 C4 18 2S 128 54 E
Nicholson, U.S.A. 79 E9 41 37N 75 47W
Nicholson →, Australia 62 B2 17 31S 139 36 E
Nicholson L., Canada 73 A8 62 40N 102 40W
Nicholson Ra., Australia 61 E2 27 15S 116 45 E
Nicholville, U.S.A. 79 B10 44 41N 74 39W
Nicobar Is., Ind. Oc. 28 J13 9 0N 93 0 E
Nicola, Canada 72 C4 50 12N 120 40W
Nicolls Town, Bahamas 88 A4 25 8N 78 0W
Nicosia, Cyprus 23 D12 35 10N 33 25 E
Nicoya, Costa Rica 88 D2 10 9N 85 27W
Nicoya, G. de, Costa Rica 88 E3 10 0N 85 0W
Nicoya, Pen. de, Costa Rica 88 E2 9 45N 85 40W
Nidd →, U.K. 10 D6 53 59N 1 23W
Niedersachsen □, Germany 16 B5 52 50N 9 0 E
Niekerkshoop, S. Africa 56 D3 29 19S 22 51 E
Niemba, Dem. Rep. of the Congo 54 D2 5 58S 28 24 E
Niemen = Neman →, Lithuania 9 J20 55 25N 21 10 E
Nienburg, Germany 16 B5 52 39N 9 13 E
Nieu Bethesda, S. Africa 56 E3 31 51S 24 34 E
Nieuw Amsterdam, Surinam 93 B7 5 53N 55 5W
Nieuw Nickerie, Surinam 93 B7 6 0N 56 59W
Nieuwoudtville, S. Africa 56 E2 31 23S 19 7 E
Nieuwpoort, Belgium 15 C2 51 8N 2 45 E
Nieves, Pico de las, Canary Is. 22 G4 27 57N 15 35W
Niğde, Turkey 25 G5 37 58N 34 40 E
Nigel, S. Africa 57 D4 26 27S 28 25 E
Niger ■, W. Afr. 50 E7 17 30N 10 0 E
Niger →, W. Afr. 50 G7 5 33N 6 33 E
Nigeria ■, W. Afr. 50 G7 8 30N 8 0 E
Nighasin, India 43 E9 28 14N 80 52 E
Nightcaps, N.Z. 59 L2 45 57S 168 2 E
Nii-Jima, Japan 31 G9 34 20N 139 15 E
Niigata, Japan 30 F9 37 58N 139 0 E
Niigata □, Japan 31 F9 37 15N 138 45 E
Niihama, Japan 31 H6 33 55N 133 16 E
Niihau, U.S.A. 74 H14 21 54N 160 9W
Niimi, Japan 31 G6 34 59N 133 28 E
Niitsu, Japan 30 F9 37 48N 139 7 E
Nijil, Jordan 47 E4 30 32N 35 33 E
Nijkerk, Neths. 15 B5 52 13N 5 30 E
Nijmegen, Neths. 15 C5 51 50N 5 52 E
Nijverdal, Neths. 15 B6 52 22N 6 28 E
Nīk Pey, Iran 45 B6 36 50N 48 10 E
Nikiniki, Indonesia 37 F6 9 49S 124 30 E
Nikkō, Japan 31 F9 36 45N 139 35 E
Nikolayev = Mykolayiv, Ukraine 25 E5 46 58N 32 0 E
Nikolayevsk, Russia 25 E8 50 0N 45 35 E
Nikolayevsk-na-Amur, Russia 27 D15 53 8N 140 44 E
Nikolskoye, Russia 27 D17 55 12N 166 0 E
Nikopol, Ukraine 25 E5 47 35N 34 25 E
Nīkshahr, Iran 45 E9 26 15N 60 10 E
Nikšić, Montenegro, Yug. 21 C8 42 50N 18 57 E
Nîl, Nahr en →, Africa 51 B12 30 10N 31 6 E
Nîl el Abyad →, Sudan 51 E12 15 38N 32 31 E
Nîl el Azraq →, Sudan 51 E12 15 38N 32 31 E
Nila, Indonesia 37 F7 6 44S 129 31 E
Niland, U.S.A. 85 M11 33 14N 115 31W
Nile = Nîl, Nahr en →, Africa 51 B12 30 10N 31 6 E
Niles, Mich., U.S.A. 76 E2 41 50N 86 15W
Niles, Ohio, U.S.A. 78 E4 41 11N 80 46W
Nim Ka Thana, India 42 F6 27 44N 75 48 E
Nimach, India 42 G6 24 30N 74 56 E
Nimbahera, India 42 G6 24 37N 74 45 E
Nîmes, France 18 E6 43 50N 4 23 E
Nimfaíon, Ákra = Pínnes, Ákra, Greece 21 D11 40 5N 24 20 E
Nimmitabel, Australia 63 F4 36 29S 149 15 E
Nīnawá, Iraq 44 B4 36 25N 43 10 E
Nindigully, Australia 63 D4 28 21S 148 50 E
Nineveh = Nīnawá, Iraq 44 B4 36 25N 43 10 E
Ning Xian, China 34 G4 35 30N 107 58 E
Ning'an, China 35 B15 44 22N 129 20 E
Ningbo, China 33 D7 29 51N 121 28 E
Ningcheng, China 35 D10 41 32N 119 53 E
Ningjin, China 34 F8 37 35N 114 57 E
Ningjing Shan, China 32 D4 30 0N 98 20 E
Ningling, China 34 G8 34 25N 115 22 E
Ningpo = Ningbo, China 33 D7 29 51N 121 28 E
Ningqiang, China 34 H4 32 47N 106 15 E
Ningshan, China 34 H5 33 21N 108 21 E
Ningsia Hui A.R. = Ningxia Huizu Zizhiqu □, China 34 F4 38 0N 106 0 E
Ningwu, China 34 E7 39 0N 112 18 E
Ningxia Huizu Zizhiqu □, China 34 F4 38 0N 106 0 E
Ningyang, China 34 G9 35 47N 116 45 E
Ninh Giang, Vietnam 38 B6 20 44N 106 24 E
Ninh Hoa, Vietnam 38 F7 12 30N 109 7 E
Ninh Ma, Vietnam 38 F7 12 48N 109 21 E
Ninove, Belgium 15 D4 50 51N 4 2 E
Nioaque, Brazil 95 A4 21 5S 55 50W
Niobrara, U.S.A. 80 D6 42 45N 98 2W
Niobrara →, U.S.A. 80 D6 42 46N 98 3W
Nioro du Sahel, Mali 50 E4 15 15N 9 30W
Niort, France 18 C3 46 19N 0 29W
Nipawin, Canada 73 C8 53 20N 104 0W
Nipigon, Canada 70 C2 49 0N 88 17W
Nipigon, L., Canada 70 C2 49 50N 88 30W
Nipishish L., Canada 71 B7 54 12N 60 45W
Nipissing, L., Canada 70 C4 46 20N 80 0W
Nipomo, U.S.A. 85 K6 35 3N 120 29W
Nipton, U.S.A. 85 K11 35 28N 115 16W
Niquelândia, Brazil 93 F9 14 33S 48 23W
Nīr, Iran 44 B5 38 2N 47 59 E
Nirasaki, Japan 31 G9 35 42N 138 27 E
Nirmal, India 40 K11 19 3N 78 20 E
Nirmali, India 43 F12 26 20N 86 35 E
Niš, Serbia, Yug. 21 C9 43 19N 21 58 E
Nişāb, Si. Arabia 44 D5 29 11N 44 43 E
Nişāb, Yemen 46 E4 14 25N 46 29 E
Nishinomiya, Japan 31 G7 34 45N 135 20 E
Nishin'omote, Japan 31 J5 30 43N 130 59 E
Nishiwaki, Japan 31 G7 34 59N 134 58 E
Niskibi →, Canada 70 A2 56 29N 88 9W
Nisqually →, U.S.A. 84 C4 47 6N 122 42W
Nissáki, Greece 23 A3 39 43N 19 52 E
Nissum Bredning, Denmark 9 H13 56 40N 8 20 E
Nistru = Dnister →, Europe 17 E16 46 18N 30 17 E
Nisutlin →, Canada 72 A2 60 14N 132 34W
Nitchequon, Canada 71 B5 53 10N 70 58W
Niterói, Brazil 95 A7 22 52S 43 0W
Nith →, Canada 78 C4 43 12N 80 23W
Nith →, U.K. 12 F5 55 14N 3 33W
Nitra, Slovak Rep. 17 D10 48 19N 18 4 E
Nitra →, Slovak Rep. 17 E10 47 46N 18 10 E
Niuafo'ou, Tonga 59 B11 15 30S 175 58W
Niue, Cook Is. 65 J11 19 2S 169 54W
Niut, Indonesia 36 D4 0 55N 110 6 E
Niuzhuang, China 35 D12 40 58N 122 28 E
Nivala, Finland 8 E21 63 56N 24 57 E
Nivelles, Belgium 15 D4 50 35N 4 20 E
Nivernais, France 18 C5 47 15N 3 30 E
Niwas, India 43 H9 23 3N 80 26 E
Nixon, U.S.A. 81 L6 29 16N 97 46W
Nizamabad, India 40 K11 18 45N 78 7 E
Nizamghat, India 41 E19 28 20N 95 45 E
Nizhne Kolymsk, Russia 27 C17 68 34N 160 55 E
Nizhnekamsk, Russia 24 C9 55 38N 51 49 E
Nizhneudinsk, Russia 27 D10 54 54N 99 3 E
Nizhnevartovsk, Russia 26 C8 60 56N 76 38 E
Nizhniy Novgorod, Russia 24 C7 56 20N 44 0 E
Nizhniy Tagil, Russia 24 C10 57 55N 59 57 E
Nizhyn, Ukraine 25 D5 51 5N 31 55 E
Nizip, Turkey 44 B3 37 5N 37 50 E
Nízké Tatry, Slovak Rep. 17 D10 48 55N 19 30 E
Njakwa, Malawi 55 E3 11 1S 33 56 E
Njanji, Zambia 55 E3 14 25S 31 46 E
Njinjo, Tanzania 55 D4 8 48S 38 54 E
Njombe, Tanzania 55 D3 9 20S 34 50 E
Njombe →, Tanzania 54 D4 6 56S 35 6 E
Nkana, Zambia 55 E2 12 50S 28 8 E
Nkayi, Zimbabwe 55 F2 19 41S 29 20 E
Nkhotakota, Malawi 55 E3 12 56S 34 15 E
Nkongsamba, Cameroon 52 D1 4 55N 9 55 E
Nkurenkuru, Namibia 56 B2 17 42S 18 32 E
Nmai →, Burma 41 G20 25 30N 97 25 E
Noakhali = Maijdi, Bangla. 41 H17 22 48N 91 10 E
Nobel, Canada 78 A4 45 25N 80 6W
Nobeoka, Japan 31 H5 32 36N 131 41 E
Noblesville, U.S.A. 76 E3 40 3N 86 1W
Nocera Inferiore, Italy 20 D6 40 44N 14 38 E
Nocona, U.S.A. 81 J6 33 47N 97 44W
Noda, Japan 31 G9 35 56N 139 52 E
Nogales, Mexico 86 A2 31 20N 110 56W
Nogales, U.S.A. 83 L8 31 20N 110 56W
Nōgata, Japan 31 H5 33 48N 130 44 E
Noggerup, Australia 61 F2 33 32S 116 5 E
Noginsk, Russia 27 C10 64 30N 90 50 E
Nogoa →, Australia 62 C4 23 40S 147 55 E
Nogoyá, Argentina 94 C4 32 24S 59 48W
Nohar, India 42 E6 29 11N 74 49 E
Nohta, India 43 H8 23 40N 79 34 E
Noire, Mts., France 18 B2 48 7N 3 28W
Noirmoutier, Î. de, France 18 C2 46 58N 2 10W
Nojane, Botswana 56 C3 23 15S 20 14 E
Nojima-Zaki, Japan 31 G9 34 54N 139 53 E
Nok Kundi, Pakistan 40 E3 28 50N 62 45 E
Nokaneng, Botswana 56 B3 19 40S 22 17 E
Nokia, Finland 9 F20 61 30N 23 30 E
Nokomis, Canada 73 C8 51 35N 105 0W
Nokomis L., Canada 73 B8 57 0N 103 0W
Nola, C.A.R. 52 D3 3 35N 16 4 E
Noma Omuramba →, Namibia 56 B3 18 52S 20 53 E
Nombre de Dios, Panama 88 E4 9 34N 79 28W
Nome, U.S.A. 68 B3 64 30N 165 25W
Nomo-Zaki, Japan 31 H4 32 35N 129 44 E
Nonacho L., Canada 73 A7 61 42N 109 40W
Nonda, Australia 62 C3 20 40S 142 28 E
Nong Chang, Thailand 38 E2 15 23N 99 51 E
Nong Het, Laos 38 C4 19 29N 103 59 E
Nong Khai, Thailand 38 D4 17 50N 102 46 E
Nong'an, China 35 B13 44 25N 125 5 E
Nongoma, S. Africa 57 D5 27 58S 31 35 E
Nonoava, Mexico 86 B3 27 28N 106 44W
Nonoava →, Mexico 86 B3 27 29N 106 45W
Nonthaburi, Thailand 38 F3 13 51N 100 34 E
Noonamah, Australia 60 B5 12 40S 131 4 E
Noord Brabant □, Neths. 15 C5 51 40N 5 0 E
Noord Holland □, Neths. 15 B4 52 30N 4 45 E
Noordbeveland, Neths. 15 C3 51 35N 3 50 E
Noordoostpolder, Neths. 15 B5 52 45N 5 45 E
Noordwijk, Neths. 15 B4 52 14N 4 26 E
Nootka I., Canada 72 D3 49 32N 126 42W
Nopiming Prov. Park, Canada 73 C9 50 30N 95 37W
Noralee, Canada 72 C3 53 59N 126 26W
Noranda = Rouyn-Noranda, Canada 70 C4 48 20N 79 0W
Norco, U.S.A. 85 M9 33 56N 117 33W
Nord-Kivu □, Dem. Rep. of the Congo 54 C2 1 0S 29 0 E
Nord-Ostsee-Kanal, Germany 16 A5 54 12N 9 32 E
Nordaustlandet, Svalbard 4 B9 79 14N 23 0 E
Nordegg, Canada 72 C5 52 29N 116 5W
Norderney, Germany 16 B4 53 42N 7 9 E
Norderstedt, Germany 16 B5 53 42N 10 1 E
Nordfjord, Norway 9 F11 61 55N 5 30 E
Nordfriesische Inseln, Germany 16 A5 54 40N 8 20 E
Nordhausen, Germany 16 C6 51 30N 10 47 E
Norðoyar, Færoe Is. 8 E9 62 17N 6 35W
Nordkapp, Norway 8 A21 71 10N 25 50 E
Nordkapp, Svalbard 4 A9 80 31N 20 0 E
Nordkinn = Kinnarodden, Norway 6 A11 71 8N 27 40 E
Nordkinn-halvøya, Norway 8 A22 70 55N 27 40 E
Nordrhein-Westfalen □, Germany 16 C4 51 45N 7 30 E
Nordvik, Russia 27 B12 74 2N 111 32 E
Nore →, Ireland 13 D4 52 25N 6 58W
Norfolk, Nebr., U.S.A. 80 D6 42 2N 97 25W
Norfolk, Va., U.S.A. 76 G7 36 51N 76 17W
Norfolk □, U.K. 11 E8 52 39N 0 54 E
Norfolk I., Pac. Oc. 64 K8 28 58S 168 3 E
Norfork L., U.S.A. 81 G8 36 15N 92 14W
Norilsk, Russia 27 C9 69 20N 88 6 E
Norma, Mt., Australia 62 C3 20 55S 140 42 E
Normal, U.S.A. 80 E10 40 31N 88 59W
Norman, U.S.A. 81 H6 35 13N 97 26W
Norman →, Australia 62 B3 19 18S 141 51 E
Norman Wells, Canada 68 B7 65 17N 126 51W
Normanby →, Australia 62 A3 14 23S 144 10 E
Normandie, France 18 B4 48 45N 0 10 E
Normandin, Canada 70 C5 48 49N 72 31W
Normandy = Normandie, France 18 B4 48 45N 0 10 E
Normanhurst, Mt., Australia 61 E3 25 4S 122 30 E
Normanton, Australia 62 B3 17 40S 141 10 E
Normétal, Canada 70 C4 49 0N 79 22W
Norquay, Canada 73 C8 51 53N 102 5W
Norquinco, Argentina 96 E2 41 51S 70 55W
Norrbotten □, Sweden 8 C19 66 30N 22 30 E
Norris Point, Canada 71 C8 49 31N 57 53W
Norristown, U.S.A. 79 F9 40 7N 75 21W
Norrköping, Sweden 9 G17 58 37N 16 11 E
Norrland, Sweden 9 E16 62 15N 15 45 E
Norrtälje, Sweden 9 G18 59 46N 18 42 E
Norseman, Australia 61 F3 32 8S 121 43 E
Norsk, Russia 27 D14 52 30N 130 5 E
Norte, Pta. del, Canary Is. 22 G2 27 51N 17 57W
Norte, Serra do, Brazil 92 11 20S 59 0W
North, C., Canada 71 C7 47 2N 60 20W
North Adams, U.S.A. 79 D11 42 42N 73 7W
North Arm, Canada 72 A5 62 0N 114 30W
North Augusta, U.S.A. 77 J5 33 30N 81 59W
North Ayrshire □, U.K. 12 F4 55 45N 4 44W
North Bass I., U.S.A. 78 E2 41 43N 82 49W
North Battleford, Canada 73 C7 52 50N 108 17W
North Bay, Canada 70 C4 46 20N 79 30W
North Belcher Is., Canada 70 A4 56 50N 79 50W
North Bend, Oreg., U.S.A. 82 E1 43 24N 124 14W
North Bend, Pa., U.S.A. 78 E7 41 20N 77 42W
North Bend, Wash., U.S.A. 84 C5 47 30N 121 47W
North Bennington, U.S.A. 79 D11 42 56N 73 15W
North Berwick, U.K. 12 E6 56 4N 2 42W
North Berwick, U.S.A. 79 C14 43 18N 70 44W
North C., Canada 71 C7 47 5N 64 0W
North C., N.Z. 59 F4 34 23S 173 4 E
North Canadian →, U.S.A. 81 H7 35 16N 95 31W
North Canton, U.S.A. 78 F3 40 53N 81 24W
North Cape = Nordkapp, Norway 8 A21 71 10N 25 50 E
North Cape = Nordkapp, Svalbard 4 A9 80 31N 20 0 E
North Caribou L., Canada 70 B1 52 50N 90 40W
North Carolina □, U.S.A. 77 H6 35 30N 80 0W
North Cascades National Park, U.S.A. 82 B3 48 45N 121 10W
North Channel, Canada 70 C3 46 0N 83 0W
North Channel, U.K. 12 F3 55 13N 5 52W
North Charleston, U.S.A. 77 J6 32 53N 79 58W
North Chicago, U.S.A. 76 D2 42 19N 87 51W
North Creek, U.S.A. 79 C11 43 41N 73 59W
North Dakota □, U.S.A. 80 B5 47 30N 100 15W
North Downs, U.K. 11 F8 51 19N 0 21 E
North East, U.S.A. 78 D5 42 13N 79 50W
North East Frontier Agency = Arunachal Pradesh □, India 41 F19 28 0N 95 0 E
North East Lincolnshire □, U.K. 10 D7 53 34N 0 2W
North Eastern □, Kenya 54 B5 1 30N 40 0 E
North Esk →, U.K. 12 E6 56 46N 2 24W
North European Plain, Europe 6 E10 55 0N 25 0 E
North Foreland, U.K. 11 F9 51 22N 1 28 E
North Fork, U.S.A. 84 H7 37 14N 119 21W
North Fork American →, U.S.A. 84 G5 38 57N 120 59W
North Fork Feather →, U.S.A. 84 F5 38 33N 121 30W
North Fork Grand →, U.S.A. 80 C3 45 47N 102 16W
North Fork Red →, U.S.A. 81 H5 34 24N 99 14W
North Frisian Is. = Nordfriesische Inseln, Germany 16 A5 54 40N 8 20 E
North Gower, Canada 79 A9 45 8N 75 43W
North Hd., Australia 61 F1 30 14S 114 59 E
North Henik L., Canada 73 A9 61 45N 97 40W
North Highlands, U.S.A. 84 G5 38 40N 121 23W
North Horr, Kenya 54 B4 3 20N 37 8 E
North I., Kenya 54 B4 4 5N 36 5 E
North I., N.Z. 59 H5 38 0S 175 0 E
North Kingsville, U.S.A. 78 E4 41 54N 80 42W
North Knife →, Canada 73 B10 58 53N 94 45W

North Koel →, *India* ..... **43 G10** 24 45N 83 50 E
North Korea ■, *Asia* ...... **35 E14** 40 0N 127 0 E
North Lakhimpur, *India* ... **41 F19** 27 14N 94 7 E
North Lanarkshire □, *U.K.* . **12 F5** 55 52N 3 56W
North Las Vegas, *U.S.A.* ... **85 J11** 36 12N 115 7W
North Lincolnshire □, *U.K.* . **10 D7** 53 36N 0 30W
North Little Rock, *U.S.A.* .. **81 H8** 34 45N 92 16W
North Loup →, *U.S.A.* ... **80 E5** 41 17N 98 24W
North Magnetic Pole, *Canada* **4 B2** 77 58N 102 8W
North Minch, *U.K.* **12 C3** 58 5N 5 55W
North Moose L., *Canada* .. **73 C8** 54 11N 100 6W
North Myrtle Beach, *U.S.A.* **77 J6** 33 48N 78 42W
North Nahanni →, *Canada* **72 A4** 62 15N 123 20W
North Olmsted, *U.S.A.* **78 E3** 41 25N 81 56W
North Ossetia □, *Russia* ... **25 F7** 43 30N 44 30 E
North Pagai, I. = Pagai Utara, Pulau, *Indonesia* . **36 E2** 2 35S 100 0 E
North Palisade, *U.S.A.* **84 H8** 37 6N 118 31W
North Platte, *U.S.A.* **80 E4** 41 8N 100 46W
North Platte →, *U.S.A.* ... **80 E4** 41 7N 100 42W
North Pole, *Arctic* .... **4 A** 90 0N 0 0 E
North Portal, *Canada* **73 D8** 49 0N 102 33W
North Powder, *U.S.A.* **82 D5** 45 2N 117 55W
North Pt., *U.S.A.* **78 A1** 45 2N 83 16W
North Rhine Westphalia = Nordrhein-Westfalen □, *Germany* .... **16 C4** 51 45N 7 30 E
North River, *Canada* **71 B8** 53 49N 57 6W
North Ronaldsay, *U.K.* **12 B6** 59 22N 2 26W
North Saskatchewan →, *Canada* **73 C7** 53 15N 105 5W
North Sea, *Europe* .... **6 D6** 56 0N 4 0 E
North Seal →, *Canada* ... **73 B9** 58 50N 98 7W
North Somerset □, *U.K.* ... **11 F5** 51 24N 2 45W
North Sporades = Vóriai Sporádhes, *Greece* ..... **21 E10** 39 15N 23 30 E
North Sydney, *Canada* **71 C7** 46 12N 60 15W
North Syracuse, *U.S.A.* ... **79 C8** 43 8N 76 7W
North Taranaki Bight, *N.Z.* . **59 H5** 38 50S 174 15 E
North Thompson →, *Canada* **72 C4** 50 40N 120 20W
North Tonawanda, *U.S.A.* . **78 C6** 43 2N 78 53W
North Troy, *U.S.A.* **79 B12** 45 0N 72 24W
North Truchas Pk., *U.S.A.* . **83 J11** 36 0N 105 30W
North Twin I., *Canada* **70 B4** 53 20N 80 0W
North Tyne →, *U.K.* **10 B5** 55 0N 2 8W
North Uist, *U.K.* **12 D1** 57 40N 7 15W
North Vancouver, *Canada* . **72 D4** 49 19N 123 4W
North Vernon, *U.S.A.* **76 F3** 39 0N 85 38W
North Wabasca L., *Canada* **72 B6** 56 0N 113 55W
North Walsham, *U.K.* ..... **10 E9** 52 50N 1 22 E
North-West □, *S. Africa* ... **56 D4** 27 0S 25 0 E
North West C., *Australia* .. **60 D1** 21 45S 114 9 E
North West Christmas I. Ridge, *Pac. Oc.* **65 G11** 6 30N 165 0W
North West Frontier □, *Pakistan* .... **42 C4** 34 0N 72 0 E
North West Highlands, *U.K.* **12 D4** 57 33N 4 58W
North West River, *Canada* . **71 B7** 53 30N 60 10W
North Western □, *Zambia* . **55 E2** 13 30S 25 30 E
North Wildwood, *U.S.A.* ... **76 F8** 39 0N 74 48W
North York Moors, *U.K.* ... **10 C7** 54 23N 0 53W
North Yorkshire □, *U.K.* ... **10 C6** 54 15N 1 25W
Northallerton, *U.K.* **10 C6** 54 20N 1 26W
Northam, *Australia* .... **61 F2** 31 35S 116 42 E
Northam, *S. Africa* .... **56 C4** 24 56S 27 18 E
Northampton, *Australia* ... **61 E1** 28 27S 114 33 E
Northampton, *U.K.* **11 E7** 52 15N 0 53W
Northampton, *Mass., U.S.A.* **79 D12** 42 19N 72 38W
Northampton, *Pa., U.S.A.* .. **79 F9** 40 41N 75 30W
Northamptonshire □, *U.K.* . **11 E7** 52 16N 0 55W
Northbridge, *U.S.A.* **79 D13** 42 9N 71 39W
Northcliffe, *Australia* ...... **61 F2** 34 39S 116 7 E
Northeast Providence Chan., *W. Indies* **88 A4** 26 0N 76 0W
Northern □, *Malawi* ...... **55 E3** 11 0S 34 0 E
Northern □, *Uganda* ...... **54 B3** 3 5N 32 30 E
Northern □, *Zambia* ...... **55 E3** 10 30S 31 0 E
Northern Cape □, *S. Africa* **56 D3** 30 0S 20 0 E
Northern Circars, *India* .... **41 L13** 17 30N 82 30 E
Northern Indian L., *Canada* **73 B9** 57 20N 97 20W
Northern Ireland □, *U.K.* .. **13 B5** 54 45N 7 0W
Northern Light L., *Canada* . **70 C1** 48 15N 90 39W
Northern Marianas ■, *Pac. Oc.* .... **64 F6** 17 0N 145 0 E
Northern Territory □, *Australia* .... **60 D5** 20 0S 133 0 E
Northern Transvaal □, *S. Africa* .... **57 C4** 24 0S 29 0 E
Northfield, *Minn., U.S.A.* .. **80 C8** 44 27N 93 9W
Northfield, *Vt., U.S.A.* **79 B12** 44 9N 72 40W
Northland □, *N.Z.* .... **59 F4** 35 30S 173 30 E
Northome, *U.S.A.* **80 B7** 47 52N 94 17W
Northport, *Ala., U.S.A.* **77 J2** 33 14N 87 35W
Northport, *Wash., U.S.A.* .. **82 B5** 48 55N 117 48W
Northumberland □, *U.K.* .. **10 B6** 55 12N 2 0W
Northumberland, C., *Australia* .... **63 F3** 38 5S 140 40 E
Northumberland Is., *Australia* .... **62 C4** 21 30S 149 50 E
Northumberland Str., *Canada* **71 C7** 46 20N 64 0W
Northville, *U.S.A.* **79 C10** 43 13N 74 11W
Northwest Providence Channel, *W. Indies* **88 A4** 26 0N 78 0W
Northwest Territories □, *Canada* **68 B9** 67 0N 110 0W
Northwood, *Iowa, U.S.A.* .. **80 D8** 43 27N 93 13W
Northwood, *N. Dak., U.S.A.* **80 B6** 47 44N 97 34W
Norton, *U.S.A.* **80 F5** 39 50N 99 53W
Norton, *Zimbabwe* .... **55 F3** 17 52S 30 40 E
Norton Sd., *U.S.A.* **68 B3** 63 50N 164 0W
Norwalk, *Calif., U.S.A.* **85 M8** 33 54N 118 5W
Norwalk, *Conn., U.S.A.* ... **79 E11** 41 7N 73 22W
Norwalk, *Iowa, U.S.A.* **80 E8** 41 29N 93 41W
Norwalk, *Ohio, U.S.A.* **78 E2** 41 15N 82 37W
Norway, *Maine, U.S.A.* **77 C10** 44 13N 70 32W
Norway, *Mich., U.S.A.* **76 C2** 45 47N 87 55W
Norway ■, *Europe* .... **8 E14** 63 0N 11 0 E
Norway House, *Canada* ... **73 C9** 53 59N 97 50W
Norwegian Sea, *Atl. Oc.* ... **4 C8** 66 0N 1 0 E
Norwich, *Canada* **78 D4** 42 59N 80 36W
Norwich, *U.K.* .... **11 E9** 52 38N 1 18 E
Norwich, *Conn., U.S.A.* ... **79 E12** 41 31N 72 5W
Norwich, *N.Y., U.S.A.* **79 D9** 42 32N 75 32W
Norwood, *Canada* **78 B7** 44 23N 77 59W
Norwood, *U.S.A.* **79 B10** 44 45N 75 0W
Noshiro, *Japan* .... **30 D10** 40 12N 140 0 E
Noşratābād, *Iran* .... **45 D8** 29 55N 60 0 E
Noss Hd., *U.K.* **12 C5** 58 28N 3 3W
Nossob →, *S. Africa* ..... **56 D3** 26 55S 20 45 E
Nosy Barren, *Madag.* ...... **53 H8** 18 25S 43 40 E
Nosy Be, *Madag.* .... **53 G9** 13 25S 48 15 E
Nosy Boraha, *Madag.* ..... **57 B8** 16 50S 49 55 E
Nosy Varika, *Madag.* ..... **57 C8** 20 35S 48 32 E
Noteć →, *Poland* .... **16 B8** 52 44N 15 26 E
Notikewin →, *Canada* ... **72 B5** 57 2N 117 38W
Notodden, *Norway* .... **9 G13** 59 35N 9 17 E
Notre Dame B., *Canada* ... **71 C8** 49 45N 55 30W
Notre Dame de Koartac = Quaqtaq, *Canada* **69 B13** 60 55N 69 40W
Notre-Dame-des-Bois, *Canada* **79 A13** 45 24N 71 4W
Notre Dame d'Ivugivic = Ivujivik, *Canada* **69 B12** 62 24N 77 55W
Notre-Dame-du-Nord, *Canada* **70 C4** 47 36N 79 30W
Nottawasaga B., *Canada* .. **78 B4** 44 35N 80 15W
Nottaway →, *Canada* **70 B4** 51 22N 78 55W
Nottingham, *U.K.* **10 E6** 52 58N 1 10W
Nottingham, City of □, *U.K.* **10 E6** 52 58N 1 10W
Nottingham I., *Canada* **69 B12** 63 20N 77 55W
Nottinghamshire □, *U.K.* .. **10 D6** 53 10N 1 3W
Nottoway →, *U.S.A.* **76 G7** 36 33N 76 55W
Notwane →, *Botswana* ... **56 C4** 23 35S 26 58 E
Nouâdhibou, *Mauritania* ... **50 D2** 20 54N 17 0W
Nouâdhibou, Ras, *Mauritania* **50 D2** 20 50N 17 0W
Nouakchott, *Mauritania* ... **50 E2** 18 9N 15 58W
Nouméa, *N. Cal.* .... **64 K8** 22 17S 166 30 E
Noupoort, *S. Africa* .... **56 E3** 31 10S 24 57 E
Nouveau Comptoir = Wemindji, *Canada* **70 B4** 53 0N 78 49W
Nouvelle-Calédonie = New Caledonia ■, *Pac. Oc.* ... **64 K8** 21 0S 165 0 E
Nova Casa Nova, *Brazil* ... **93 E10** 9 25S 41 5W
Nova Esperança, *Brazil* **95 A5** 23 8S 52 24W
Nova Friburgo, *Brazil* **95 A7** 22 16S 42 30W
Nova Gaia = Cambundi-Catembo, *Angola* .... **52 G3** 10 10S 17 35 E
Nova Iguaçu, *Brazil* **95 A7** 22 45S 43 28W
Nova Iorque, *Brazil* **93 E10** 7 0S 44 5W
Nova Lima, *Brazil* **95 A7** 19 59S 43 51W
Nova Lisboa = Huambo, *Angola* .... **53 G3** 12 42S 15 54 E
Nova Lusitânia, *Mozam.* .... **55 F3** 19 50S 34 34 E
Nova Mambone, *Mozam.* ... **57 C6** 21 0S 35 3 E
Nova Scotia □, *Canada* **71 C7** 45 10N 63 0W
Nova Sofala, *Mozam.* ...... **57 C5** 20 7S 34 42 E
Nova Venécia, *Brazil* **93 G10** 18 45S 40 24W
Nova Zagora, *Bulgaria* .... **21 C11** 42 32N 26 1 E
Novar, *Canada* **78 A5** 45 27N 79 15W
Novara, *Italy* .... **18 D8** 45 28N 8 38 E
Novato, *U.S.A.* **84 G4** 38 6N 122 35W
Novaya Ladoga, *Russia* .... **24 B5** 60 7N 32 16 E
Novaya Lyalya, *Russia* .... **24 C11** 59 4N 60 45 E
Novaya Sibir, Ostrov, *Russia* **27 B16** 75 10N 150 0 E
Novaya Zemlya, *Russia* .... **26 B6** 75 0N 56 0 E
Nové Zámky, *Slovak Rep.* . **17 D10** 48 2N 18 8 E
Novgorod, *Russia* .... **24 C5** 58 30N 31 25 E
Novgorod-Severskiy = Novhorod-Siverskyy, *Ukraine* .... **24 D5** 52 2N 33 10 E
Novhorod-Siverskyy, *Ukraine* .... **24 D5** 52 2N 33 10 E
Novi Lígure, *Italy* .... **18 D8** 44 46N 8 47 E
Novi Pazar, *Serbia, Yug.* ... **21 C9** 43 12N 20 28 E
Novi Sad, *Serbia, Yug.* .... **21 B8** 45 18N 19 52 E
Nôvo Hamburgo, *Brazil* **95 B5** 29 37S 51 7W
Novo Mesto, *Slovenia* ..... **20 B6** 45 47N 15 12 E
Novo Remanso, *Brazil* **93 E10** 9 41S 42 4W
Novoataysk, *Russia* .... **26 D9** 53 30N 84 0 E
Novocherkassk, *Russia* .... **25 E7** 47 27N 40 15 E
Novogrudok = Navahrudak, *Belarus* .... **17 B13** 53 40N 25 50 E
Novohrad-Volynskyy, *Ukraine* .... **17 C14** 50 34N 27 35 E
Novokachalinsk, *Russia* ... **30 B6** 45 5N 132 0 E
Novokazalinsk = Zhangaqazaly, *Kazakstan* **26 E7** 45 48N 62 6 E
Novokuybyshevsk, *Russia* . **24 D8** 53 7N 49 58 E
Novokuznetsk, *Russia* ..... **26 D9** 53 45N 87 10 E
Novomoskovsk, *Russia* .... **24 D6** 54 5N 38 15 E
Novorossiysk, *Russia* ..... **25 F6** 44 43N 37 46 E
Novorybnoye, *Russia* ..... **27 B11** 72 50N 105 50 E
Novoselytsya, *Ukraine* .... **17 D14** 48 14N 26 15 E
Novoshakhtinsk, *Russia* ... **25 E6** 47 46N 39 58 E
Novosibirsk, *Russia* .... **26 D9** 55 0N 83 5 E
Novosibirskiye Ostrova, *Russia* .... **27 B15** 75 0N 142 0 E
Novotroitsk, *Russia* .... **24 D10** 51 10N 58 15 E
Novouzensk, *Russia* ...... **25 D8** 50 32N 48 17 E
Novovolynsk, *Ukraine* ..... **17 C13** 50 45N 24 4 E
Novska, *Croatia* .... **20 B7** 45 19N 17 0 E
Novvy Urengoy, *Russia* .... **26 C8** 65 48N 76 52 E
Novyy Bor, *Russia* .... **24 A9** 66 43N 52 19 E
Novyy Port, *Russia* .... **26 C8** 67 40N 72 30 E
Now Shahr, *Iran* .... **45 B6** 36 40N 51 30 E
Nowa Sól, *Poland* .... **16 C8** 51 48N 15 44 E
Nowata, *U.S.A.* **81 G7** 36 42N 95 38W
Nowbarān, *Iran* .... **45 C6** 35 8N 49 42 E
Nowghāb, *Iran* .... **45 C8** 33 53N 59 4 E
Nowgong, *Assam, India* .... **41 F18** 26 20N 92 50 E
Nowgong, *Mad. P., India* ... **43 G8** 25 4N 79 27 E
Nowra-Bomaderry, *Australia* **63 E5** 34 53S 150 35 E
Nowshera, *Pakistan* .... **40 C8** 34 0N 72 0 E
Nowy Sącz, *Poland* .... **17 D11** 49 40N 20 41 E
Nowy Targ, *Poland* .... **17 D11** 49 29N 20 2 E
Nowy Tomyśl, *Poland* ..... **16 B9** 52 19N 16 10 E
Noxen, *U.S.A.* **79 E8** 41 25N 76 4W
Noxon, *U.S.A.* **82 C6** 48 0N 115 43W
Noyabr'sk, *Russia* .... **26 C8** 64 34N 76 21 E
Noyon, *France* .... **18 B5** 49 34N 2 59 E
Noyon, *Mongolia* .... **34 C2** 43 2N 102 4 E
Nsanje, *Malawi* .... **55 F4** 16 55S 35 12 E
Nsomba, *Zambia* .... **55 E2** 10 45S 29 51 E
Nu Jiang →, *China* .... **32 D4** 29 58N 97 25 E
Nu Shan, *China* .... **32 D4** 26 0N 99 20 E
Nubia, *Africa* .... **48 D7** 21 0N 32 0 E
Nubian Desert = Nûbîya, Es Sahrâ en, *Sudan* .... **51 D12** 21 30N 33 30 E
Nûbîya, Es Sahrâ en, *Sudan* **51 D12** 21 30N 33 30 E
Nuboai, *Indonesia* .... **37 E9** 2 10S 136 30 E
Nubra →, *India* .... **43 B7** 34 35N 77 35 E
Nueces →, *U.S.A.* **81 M6** 27 51N 97 30W
Nueltin L., *Canada* **73 A9** 60 30N 99 30W
Nueva Asunción □, *Paraguay* **94 A3** 21 0S 61 0W
Nueva Gerona, *Cuba* **88 B3** 21 53N 82 49W
Nueva Palmira, *Uruguay* .. **94 C4** 33 52S 58 20W
Nueva Rosita, *Mexico* **86 B4** 28 0N 101 11W
Nueva San Salvador, *El Salv.* **88 D2** 13 40N 89 18W
Nuéve de Julio, *Argentina* . **94 D3** 35 30S 61 0W
Nuevitas, *Cuba* **88 B4** 21 30N 77 20W
Nuevo, G., *Argentina* **96 E4** 43 0S 64 30W
Nuevo Casas Grandes, *Mexico* **86 A3** 30 22N 108 0W
Nuevo Guerrero, *Mexico* .. **87 B5** 26 34N 99 15W
Nuevo Laredo, *Mexico* **87 B5** 27 30N 99 30W
Nuevo León □, *Mexico* **86 C5** 25 0N 100 0W
Nuevo Rocafuerte, *Ecuador* **92 D3** 0 55S 75 27W
Nugget Pt., *N.Z.* .... **59 M2** 46 27S 169 50 E
Nuhaka, *N.Z.* .... **59 H6** 39 3S 177 45 E
Nukey Bluff, *Australia* ..... **63 E2** 32 26S 135 29 E
Nukhuyb, *Iraq* .... **44 C4** 32 4N 42 3 E
Nuku'alofa, *Tonga* **59 E12** 21 10S 174 0W
Nukus, *Uzbekistan* .... **26 E6** 42 27N 59 41 E
Nullagine, *Australia* ...... **60 D3** 21 53S 120 7 E
Nullagine →, *Australia* ... **60 D3** 21 20S 120 20 E
Nullarbor, *Australia* ...... **61 F5** 31 28S 130 55 E
Nullarbor Plain, *Australia* .. **61 F4** 31 10S 129 0 E
Numalla, L., *Australia* .... **63 D3** 28 43S 144 20 E
Numan, *Nigeria* .... **51 G8** 9 29N 12 3 E
Numata, *Japan* .... **31 F9** 36 45N 139 4 E
Numazu, *Japan* .... **31 G9** 35 7N 138 51 E
Numbulwar, *Australia* .... **62 A2** 14 15S 135 45 E
Numfoor, *Indonesia* ...... **37 E8** 1 0S 134 50 E
Numurkah, *Australia* ..... **63 F4** 36 5S 145 26 E
Nunaksaluk I., *Canada* **71 A7** 55 49N 60 20W
Nunavut □, *Canada* **69 B11** 66 0N 85 0W
Nunda, *U.S.A.* **78 D7** 42 35N 77 56W
Nungarin, *Australia* ...... **61 F2** 31 12S 118 6 E
Nungo, *Mozam.* .... **55 E4** 13 23S 37 43 E
Nungwe, *Tanzania* .... **54 C3** 2 48S 32 2 E
Nunivak I., *U.S.A.* **68 C3** 60 10N 166 30W
Nunkun, *India* .... **43 C7** 33 57N 76 2 E
Núoro, *Italy* .... **20 D3** 40 20N 9 20 E
Nūrābād, *Iran* .... **45 E8** 27 47N 57 12 E
Nuremberg = Nürnberg, *Germany* .... **16 D6** 49 27N 11 3 E
Nuri, *Mexico* **86 B3** 28 2N 109 22W
Nuriootpa, *Australia* ...... **63 E2** 34 27S 139 0 E
Nurmes, *Finland* .... **8 E23** 63 33N 29 10 E
Nürnberg, *Germany* ...... **16 D6** 49 27N 11 3 E
Nurpur, *Pakistan* .... **42 D4** 31 53N 71 54 E
Nurran, L. = Terewah, L., *Australia* .... **63 D4** 29 52S 147 35 E
Nurrari Lakes, *Australia* ... **61 E5** 29 1S 130 5 E
Nusa Barung, *Indonesia* ... **37 H15** 8 30S 113 30 E
Nusa Kambangan, *Indonesia* **37 G13** 7 40S 108 10 E
Nusa Tenggara Barat □, *Indonesia* .... **36 F5** 8 50S 117 30 E
Nusa Tenggara Timur □, *Indonesia* .... **37 F6** 9 30S 122 0 E
Nusaybin, *Turkey* .... **25 G7** 37 3N 41 10 E
Nushki, *Pakistan* .... **42 E2** 29 35N 66 0 E
Nuuk, *Greenland* **69 B14** 64 10N 51 35W
Nuwakot, *Nepal* .... **43 E10** 28 10N 83 55 E
Nuweiba', *Egypt* .... **44 D2** 28 59N 34 39 E
Nuweveldberge, *S. Africa* . **56 E3** 32 10S 21 45 E
Nuyts, C., *Australia* ...... **61 F5** 32 2S 132 21 E
Nuyts, Pt., *Australia* ...... **61 G2** 35 4S 116 38 E
Nuyts Arch., *Australia* .... **63 E1** 32 35S 133 20 E
Nxau-Nxau, *Botswana* .... **56 B3** 18 57S 21 4 E
Nyabing, *Australia* .... **61 F2** 33 33S 118 9 E
Nyack, *U.S.A.* **79 E11** 41 5N 73 55W
Nyagan, *Russia* .... **26 C7** 62 30N 65 38 E
Nyahanga, *Tanzania* ...... **54 C3** 2 20S 33 37 E
Nyahua, *Tanzania* .... **54 D3** 5 25S 33 23 E
Nyahururu, *Kenya* .... **54 B4** 0 2N 36 27 E
Nyainqentanglha Shan, *China* .... **32 D4** 30 0N 90 0 E
Nyakanazi, *Tanzania* ..... **54 C3** 3 2S 31 10 E
Nyâlâ, *Sudan* .... **51 F10** 12 2N 24 58 E
Nyamandhlovu, *Zimbabwe* **55 F2** 19 55S 28 16 E
Nyambiti, *Tanzania* .... **54 C3** 2 48S 33 27 E
Nyamwaga, *Tanzania* ..... **54 C3** 1 27S 34 33 E
Nyandekwa, *Tanzania* ..... **54 C3** 3 57S 32 32 E
Nyandoma, *Russia* .... **24 B7** 61 40N 40 12 E
Nyangana, *Namibia* ...... **56 B3** 18 0S 20 40 E
Nyanguge, *Tanzania* ...... **54 C3** 2 30S 33 12 E
Nyanza, *Rwanda* .... **54 C2** 2 20S 29 42 E
Nyanza □, *Kenya* .... **54 C3** 0 10S 34 15 E
Nyanza-Lac, *Burundi* ..... **54 C2** 4 21S 29 36 E
Nyasa, L., *Africa* .... **55 E3** 12 30S 34 30 E
Nyasvizh, *Belarus* .... **17 B14** 53 14N 26 38 E
Nyazepetrovsk, *Russia* ... **24 C10** 56 3N 59 36 E
Nyazura, *Zimbabwe* ...... **55 F3** 18 40S 32 16 E
Nyazwidzi →, *Zimbabwe* . **55 G3** 20 0S 31 17 E
Nybro, *Sweden* .... **9 H16** 56 44N 15 55 E
Nyda, *Russia* .... **26 C8** 66 40N 72 58 E
Nyeri, *Kenya* .... **54 C4** 0 23S 36 56 E
Nyíregyháza, *Hungary* .... **17 E11** 47 58N 21 47 E
Nykøbing, *Storstrøm, Denmark* .... **9 J14** 54 56N 11 52 E
Nykøbing, *Vestsjælland, Denmark* .... **9 J14** 55 55N 11 40 E
Nykøbing, *Viborg, Denmark* **9 H13** 56 48N 8 51 E
Nyköping, *Sweden* .... **9 G17** 58 45N 17 1 E
Nylstroom, *S. Africa* ...... **57 C4** 24 42S 28 22 E
Nymagee, *Australia* ...... **63 E4** 32 7S 146 20 E
Nynäshamn, *Sweden* ..... **9 G17** 58 54N 17 57 E
Nyngan, *Australia* .... **63 E4** 31 30S 147 8 E
Nyoma Rap, *India* .... **43 C8** 33 10N 78 40 E
Nyoman = Neman →, *Lithuania* .... **9 J20** 55 25N 21 10 E
Nysa, *Poland* .... **17 C9** 50 30N 17 22 E
Nysa →, *Europe* .... **16 B8** 52 4N 14 46 E
Nyssa, *U.S.A.* **82 E5** 43 53N 117 0W
Nyunzu, *Dem. Rep. of the Congo* . **54 D2** 5 57S 27 58 E
Nyurba, *Russia* .... **27 C12** 63 17N 118 28 E
Nzega, *Tanzania* .... **54 C3** 4 10S 33 12 E
N'zérékoré, *Guinea* **50 G4** 7 49N 8 48W
Nzeto, *Angola* .... **52 F2** 7 10S 12 52 E
Nzilo, Chutes de, *Dem. Rep. of the Congo* . **55 E2** 10 18S 25 27 E
Nzubuka, *Tanzania* .... **54 C3** 4 45S 32 50 E

O

Ō-Shima, *Japan* .... **31 G9** 34 44N 139 24 E
Oa, Mull of, *U.K.* **12 F2** 55 35N 6 20W
Oacoma, *U.S.A.* **80 D5** 43 48N 99 24W
Oahe, L., *U.S.A.* **80 C4** 44 27N 100 24W
Oahe Dam, *U.S.A.* **80 C4** 44 27N 100 24W
Oahu, *U.S.A.* **74 H16** 21 28N 157 58W
Oak Harbor, *U.S.A.* **84 B4** 48 18N 122 39W
Oak Hill, *U.S.A.* **76 G5** 37 59N 81 9W
Oak Ridge, *U.S.A.* **77 G3** 36 1N 84 16W
Oak View, *U.S.A.* **85 L7** 34 24N 119 18W
Oakan-Dake, *Japan* .... **30 C12** 43 27N 144 10 E
Oakdale, *Calif., U.S.A.* **84 H6** 37 46N 120 51W
Oakdale, *La., U.S.A.* **81 K8** 30 49N 92 40W
Oakes, *U.S.A.* **80 B5** 46 8N 98 6W
Oakesdale, *U.S.A.* **82 C5** 47 8N 117 15W
Oakey, *Australia* .... **63 D5** 27 25S 151 43 E
Oakfield, *U.S.A.* **78 C6** 43 4N 78 16W
Oakham, *U.K.* **11 E7** 52 40N 0 43W
Oakhurst, *U.S.A.* **84 H7** 37 19N 119 40W
Oakland, *U.S.A.* **84 H4** 37 49N 122 16W
Oakley, *Idaho, U.S.A.* **82 E7** 42 15N 113 53W
Oakley, *Kans., U.S.A.* **80 F4** 39 8N 100 51W
Oakover →, *Australia* .... **60 D3** 21 0S 120 40 E
Oakridge, *U.S.A.* **82 E2** 43 45N 122 28W
Oakville, *Canada* **78 C5** 43 27N 79 41W
Oakville, *U.S.A.* **84 D3** 46 51N 123 14W
Oamaru, *N.Z.* .... **59 L3** 45 5S 170 59 E
Oasis, *Calif., U.S.A.* **85 M10** 33 28N 116 6W
Oasis, *Nev., U.S.A.* **84 H9** 37 29N 117 55W
Oates Land, *Antarctica* .... **5 C11** 69 0S 160 0 E
Oatlands, *Australia* .... **62 G4** 42 17S 147 21 E
Oatman, *U.S.A.* **85 K12** 35 1N 114 19W
Oaxaca, *Mexico* **87 D5** 17 2N 96 40W
Oaxaca □, *Mexico* **87 D5** 17 0N 97 0W
Ob →, *Russia* .... **26 C7** 66 45N 69 30 E
Oba, *Canada* **70 C3** 49 4N 84 7W
Obama, *Japan* .... **31 G7** 35 30N 135 45 E
Oban, *U.K.* **12 E3** 56 25N 5 29W
Obbia, *Somali Rep.* .... **46 F4** 5 25N 48 30 E
Obera, *Argentina* **95 B4** 27 21S 55 2W
Oberhausen, *Germany* ..... **16 C4** 51 28N 6 51 E
Oberlin, *Kans., U.S.A.* **80 F4** 39 49N 100 32W
Oberlin, *La., U.S.A.* **81 K8** 30 37N 92 46W
Oberlin, *Ohio, U.S.A.* **78 E2** 41 18N 82 13W
Oberon, *Australia* .... **63 E4** 33 45S 149 52 E
Obi, Kepulauan, *Indonesia* . **37 E7** 1 23S 127 45 E
Obi Is. = Obi, Kepulauan, *Indonesia* .... **37 E7** 1 23S 127 45 E
Óbidos, *Brazil* **93 D7** 1 50S 55 30W
Obihiro, *Japan* .... **30 C11** 42 56N 143 12 E
Obilatu, *Indonesia* .... **37 E7** 1 25S 127 20 E
Obluchye, *Russia* .... **27 E14** 49 1N 131 4 E
Obo, *C.A.R.* .... **54 A2** 5 20N 26 32 E
Oboa, Mt., *Uganda* .... **54 B3** 1 45N 34 45 E
Oboyan, *Russia* .... **26 D4** 51 15N 36 21 E
Obozerskaya = Obozerskiy, *Russia* .... **24 B7** 63 34N 40 21 E
Obozerskiy, *Russia* .... **24 B7** 63 34N 40 21 E
Observatory Inlet, *Canada* . **72 B3** 55 10N 129 54W
Obshchi Syrt, *Russia* ..... **6 E16** 52 0N 53 0 E
Obskaya Guba, *Russia* .... **26 C8** 69 0N 73 0 E
Obuasi, *Ghana* **50 G5** 6 17N 1 40W
Ocala, *U.S.A.* **77 L4** 29 11N 82 8W
Ocampo, *Mexico* **86 B3** 28 9N 108 24W
Ocampo, *Tamaulipas, Mexico* **87 C5** 22 50N 99 20W
Ocaña, *Spain* **19 C4** 39 55N 3 30W
Oconomowoc, *U.S.A.* **80 D10** 43 7N 88 30W
Occidental, Cordillera, *Colombia* **92 C3** 5 0N 76 0W
Ocean City, *Md., U.S.A.* **76 F8** 38 20N 75 5W
Ocean City, *N.J., U.S.A.* ... **76 F8** 39 17N 74 35W
Ocean City, *Wash., U.S.A.* . **84 C2** 47 4N 124 10W
Ocean Falls, *Canada* **72 C3** 52 18N 127 48W
Ocean I. = Banaba, *Kiribati* **64 H8** 0 45S 169 50 E
Ocean Park, *U.S.A.* **84 D2** 46 30N 124 3W
Oceano, *U.S.A.* **85 K6** 35 6N 120 37W
Oceanport, *U.S.A.* **79 F10** 40 19N 74 3W
Oceanside, *U.S.A.* **85 M9** 33 12N 117 23W
Ochil Hills, *U.K.* **12 E5** 56 14N 3 40W
Ocilla, *U.S.A.* **77 K4** 31 36N 83 15W
Ocmulgee →, *U.S.A.* **77 K4** 31 58N 82 33W
Ocniţa, *Moldova* .... **17 D14** 48 25N 27 30 E
Oconee →, *U.S.A.* **77 K4** 31 58N 82 33W
Oconto, *U.S.A.* **76 C2** 44 53N 87 52W
Oconto Falls, *U.S.A.* **76 C1** 44 52N 88 9W
Ocosingo, *Mexico* **87 D6** 17 10N 92 15W
Ocotal, *Nic.* **88 D2** 13 41N 86 31W
Ocotlán, *Mexico* **86 C4** 20 21N 102 42W
Ocotlán de Morelos, *Mexico* **87 D5** 16 48N 96 40W
Ōda, *Japan* .... **31 G6** 35 11N 132 30 E
Ódáðahraun, *Iceland* **8 D5** 65 5N 17 0W
Odate, *Japan* .... **30 D10** 40 16N 140 34 E
Odawara, *Japan* .... **31 G9** 35 20N 139 6 E
Odda, *Norway* .... **9 F12** 60 3N 6 35 E
Odei →, *Canada* **73 B9** 56 6N 96 54W
Ödemiş, *Turkey* .... **21 E13** 38 15N 28 0 E
Odendaalsrus, *S. Africa* ... **56 D4** 27 48S 26 45 E
Odense, *Denmark* .... **9 J14** 55 22N 10 23 E
Oder →, *Europe* .... **16 B8** 53 33N 14 38 E
Odesa, *Ukraine* .... **25 E5** 46 30N 30 45 E
Odessa = Odesa, *Ukraine* . **25 E5** 46 30N 30 45 E
Odessa, *Canada* **79 B8** 44 17N 76 43W
Odessa, *Tex., U.S.A.* **81 K3** 31 52N 102 23W
Odessa, *Wash., U.S.A.* **82 C4** 47 20N 118 41W
Odiakwe, *Botswana* ...... **56 C4** 20 12S 25 17 E
Odienné, *Ivory C.* **50 G4** 9 30N 7 34W
Odintsovo, *Russia* .... **24 C6** 55 39N 37 15 E
O'Donnell, *U.S.A.* **81 J4** 32 58N 101 50W
Odorheiu Secuiesc, *Romania* .... **17 E13** 46 21N 25 21 E
Odra = Oder →, *Europe* . **16 B8** 53 33N 14 38 E
Odzi, *Zimbabwe* .... **57 B5** 19 0S 32 20 E
Oeiras, *Brazil* **93 E10** 7 0S 42 8W
Oelrichs, *U.S.A.* **80 D3** 43 11N 103 14W
Oelwein, *U.S.A.* **80 D9** 42 41N 91 55W
Oenpelli, *Australia* .... **60 B5** 12 20S 133 4 E
Ofanto →, *Italy* .... **20 D7** 41 22N 16 13 E
Offa, *Nigeria* .... **50 G6** 8 13N 4 42 E
Offaly □, *Ireland* **13 C4** 53 15N 7 30W
Offenbach, *Germany* ...... **16 C5** 50 6N 8 44 E
Offenburg, *Germany* ...... **16 D4** 48 28N 7 56 E

Ofotfjorden, Norway 8 B17 68 27N 17 0 E
Ōfunato, Japan 30 E10 39 4N 141 43 E
Oga, Japan 30 E9 39 55N 139 50 E
Oga-Hantō, Japan 30 E9 39 58N 139 47 E
Ogaden, Ethiopia 46 F3 7 30N 45 30 E
Ōgaki, Japan 31 G8 35 21N 136 37 E
Ogallala, U.S.A. 80 E4 41 8N 101 43W
Ogasawara Gunto, Pac. Oc. 28 G18 27 0N 142 0 E
Ogbomosho, Nigeria 50 G6 8 1N 4 11 E
Ogden, U.S.A. 82 F7 41 13N 111 58W
Ogdensburg, U.S.A. 79 B9 44 42N 75 30W
Ogeechee →, U.S.A. 77 K5 31 50N 81 3W
Ogilby, U.S.A. 85 N12 32 49N 114 50W
Oglio →, Italy 20 B4 45 2N 10 39 E
Ogmore, Australia 62 C4 22 37S 149 35 E
Ogoki, Canada 70 B2 51 38N 85 58W
Ogoki →, Canada 70 B2 51 38N 85 57W
Ogoki L., Canada 70 B2 50 50N 87 10W
Ogoki Res., Canada 70 B2 50 45N 88 15W
Ogooué →, Gabon 52 E1 1 0S 9 0 E
Ogowe = Ogooué →, Gabon 52 E1 1 0S 9 0 E
Ogre, Latvia 9 H21 56 49N 24 36 E
Ogurchinskiy, Ostrov, Turkmenistan 45 B7 38 55N 53 2 E
Ohai, N.Z. 59 L2 45 55S 168 0 E
Ohakune, N.Z. 59 H5 39 24S 175 24 E
Ohata, Japan 30 D10 41 24N 141 10 E
Ohau, L., N.Z. 59 L2 44 15S 169 53 E
Ohio □, U.S.A. 78 F2 40 15N 82 45W
Ohio →, U.S.A. 76 G1 36 59N 89 8W
Ohře →, Czech Rep. 16 C8 50 30N 14 10 E
Ohrid, Macedonia 21 D9 41 8N 20 52 E
Ohridsko Jezero, Macedonia 21 D9 41 8N 20 52 E
Ohrigstad, S. Africa 57 C5 24 39S 30 36 E
Oiapoque, Brazil 93 3 50N 51 50W
Oikou, China 35 E9 38 35N 117 42 E
Oil City, U.S.A. 78 E5 41 26N 79 42W
Oil Springs, Canada 78 D2 42 47N 82 7W
Oildale, U.S.A. 85 K7 35 25N 119 1W
Oise →, France 18 B5 49 0N 2 4 E
Ōita, Japan 31 H5 33 14N 131 36 E
Ōita □, Japan 31 H5 33 15N 131 30 E
Oiticica, Brazil 93 E10 5 3S 41 5W
Ojacaliente, Mexico 86 C4 22 34N 102 15W
Ojai, U.S.A. 85 L7 34 27N 119 15W
Ojinaga, Mexico 86 B4 29 34N 104 25W
Ojiya, Japan 31 F9 37 18N 138 48 E
Ojos del Salado, Cerro, Argentina 94 B2 27 0S 68 40W
Oka →, Russia 24 C7 56 20N 43 59 E
Okaba, Indonesia 37 F9 8 6S 139 42 E
Okahandja, Namibia 56 C2 22 0S 16 59 E
Okahukura, N.Z. 59 H5 38 48S 175 14 E
Okanagan L., Canada 72 D5 50 0N 119 30W
Okanogan, U.S.A. 82 B4 48 22N 119 35W
Okanogan →, U.S.A. 82 B4 48 6N 119 44W
Okaputa, Namibia 56 C2 20 5S 17 0 E
Okara, Pakistan 42 D5 30 50N 73 31 E
Okarito, N.Z. 59 K3 43 15S 170 9 E
Okaukuejo, Namibia 56 B2 19 10S 16 0 E
Okavango Swamps, Botswana 56 B3 18 45S 22 45 E
Okaya, Japan 31 F9 36 5N 138 10 E
Okayama, Japan 31 G6 34 40N 133 54 E
Okayama □, Japan 31 G6 35 0N 133 50 E
Okazaki, Japan 31 G8 34 57N 137 10 E
Okeechobee, U.S.A. 77 M5 27 15N 80 50W
Okeechobee, L., U.S.A. 77 M5 27 0N 80 50W
Okefenokee Swamp, U.S.A. 77 K4 30 40N 82 20W
Okehampton, U.K. 11 G4 50 44N 4 0W
Okha, India 42 H3 22 27N 69 4 E
Okha, Russia 27 D15 53 40N 143 0 E
Okhotsk, Russia 27 D15 59 20N 143 10 E
Okhotsk, Sea of, Asia 27 D15 55 0N 145 0 E
Okhotskiy Perevoz, Russia 27 C14 61 52N 135 35 E
Okhtyrka, Ukraine 25 D5 50 25N 35 0 E
Oki-Shotō, Japan 31 F6 36 5N 133 15 E
Okiep, S. Africa 56 D2 29 39S 17 53 E
Okinawa □, Japan 31 L4 26 40N 128 0 E
Okinawa-Guntō, Japan 31 L4 26 40N 128 0 E
Okinawa-Jima, Japan 31 L4 26 32N 128 0 E
Okino-erabu-Shima, Japan 31 L4 27 21N 128 33 E
Oklahoma □, U.S.A. 81 H6 35 20N 97 30W
Oklahoma City, U.S.A. 81 H6 35 30N 97 30W
Okmulgee, U.S.A. 81 H7 35 37N 95 58W
Oknitsa = Ocniţa, Moldova 17 D14 48 25N 27 30 E
Okolo, Uganda 54 B3 2 37N 31 8 E
Okolona, U.S.A. 81 J10 34 0N 88 45W
Okotoks, Canada 72 C6 50 43N 113 58W
Oksibil, Indonesia 37 E10 4 59S 140 35 E
Oksovskiy, Russia 24 B6 62 33N 39 57 E
Oktabrsk = Oktyabrsk, Kazakstan 25 E10 49 28N 57 25 E
Oktyabrsk, Kazakstan 25 E10 49 28N 57 25 E
Oktyabrskiy = Aktsyabrski, Belarus 17 B15 52 38N 28 53 E
Oktyabrskiy, Russia 24 D9 54 28N 53 28 E
Oktyabrskoy Revolyutsii, Ostrov, Russia 27 B10 79 30N 97 0 E
Okuru, N.Z. 59 K2 43 55S 168 55 E
Okushiri-Tō, Japan 30 C9 42 15N 139 30 E
Okwa →, Botswana 56 C3 22 30S 23 0 E
Ola, U.S.A. 81 H8 35 2N 93 13W
Ólafsfjörður, Iceland 8 C4 66 4N 18 39W
Ólafsvík, Iceland 8 D2 64 53N 23 43W
Olancha, U.S.A. 85 J8 36 17N 118 1W
Olancha Pk., U.S.A. 85 J8 36 15N 118 7W
Olanchito, Honduras 88 C2 15 30N 86 30W
Öland, Sweden 9 H17 56 45N 16 38 E
Olary, Australia 63 E3 32 18S 140 19 E
Olascoaga, Argentina 94 D3 35 15S 60 39W
Olathe, U.S.A. 80 F7 38 53N 94 49W
Olavarría, Argentina 94 D3 36 55S 60 20W
Oława, Poland 17 C9 50 57N 17 20 E
Ólbia, Italy 20 D3 40 55N 9 31 E
Olcott, U.S.A. 78 C6 43 20N 78 42W
Old Bahama Chan. = Bahama, Canal Viejo de, W. Indies 88 B4 22 10N 77 30W
Old Baldy Pk. = San Antonio, Mt., U.S.A. 85 L9 34 17N 117 38W
Old Castile = Castilla y Leon □, Spain 19 B3 42 0N 5 0W
Old Crow, Canada 68 B6 67 30N 139 55W
Old Dale, U.S.A. 85 L11 34 8N 115 47W
Old Forge, N.Y., U.S.A. 79 C10 43 43N 74 58W
Old Forge, Pa., U.S.A. 79 E9 41 22N 75 45W
Old Perlican, Canada 71 C9 48 5N 53 1W
Old Shinyanga, Tanzania 54 C3 3 33S 33 27 E
Old Speck Mt., U.S.A. 79 B14 44 34N 70 57W
Old Town, U.S.A. 77 C11 44 56N 68 39W
Old Washington, U.S.A. 78 F3 40 2N 81 27W
Old Wives L., Canada 73 C7 50 5N 106 0W
Oldbury, U.K. 11 F5 51 38N 2 33W
Oldcastle, Ireland 13 C4 53 46N 7 10W
Oldeani, Tanzania 54 C4 3 22S 35 35 E
Oldenburg, Germany 16 B5 53 9N 8 13 E
Oldenzaal, Neths. 15 B6 52 19N 6 53 E
Oldham, U.K. 10 D5 53 33N 2 7W
Oldman →, Canada 72 D6 49 57N 111 42W
Oldmeldrum, U.K. 12 D6 57 20N 2 19W
Olds, Canada 72 C6 51 50N 114 10W
Oldziyt, Mongolia 34 B5 44 40N 109 1 E
Olean, U.S.A. 78 D6 42 5N 78 26W
Olekma →, Russia 27 C13 60 22N 120 42 E
Olekminsk, Russia 27 C13 60 25N 120 30 E
Oleksandriya, Ukraine 17 C14 50 37N 26 19 E
Olema, U.S.A. 84 G4 38 3N 122 47W
Olenegorsk, Russia 24 A5 68 9N 33 18 E
Olenek, Russia 27 C12 68 28N 112 18 E
Olenek →, Russia 27 B13 73 0N 120 10 E
Oléron, Î. d', France 18 D3 45 55N 1 15W
Oleśnica, Poland 17 C9 51 13N 17 22 E
Olevsk, Ukraine 17 C14 51 12N 27 39 E
Olga, Russia 27 E14 43 50N 135 14 E
Olga, L., Canada 70 C4 49 47N 77 15W
Olga, Mt., Australia 61 E5 25 20S 130 50 E
Olhão, Portugal 19 D2 37 3N 7 48W
Olifants →, Africa 57 C5 23 57S 31 58 E
Olifantshoek, S. Africa 56 D3 27 57S 22 42 E
Ólimbos, Óros, Greece 21 D10 40 6N 22 23 E
Olímpia, Brazil 95 A6 20 44S 48 54W
Olinda, Brazil 93 E12 8 1S 34 51W
Oliva, Argentina 94 C3 32 0S 63 38W
Olivehurst, U.S.A. 84 F5 39 6N 121 34W
Olivenza, Spain 19 C2 38 41N 7 9W
Oliver, Canada 72 D5 49 13N 119 37W
Oliver L., Canada 73 B8 56 56N 103 22W
Ollagüe, Chile 94 A2 21 15S 68 10W
Olney, Ill., U.S.A. 76 F1 38 44N 88 5W
Olney, Tex., U.S.A. 81 J5 33 22N 98 45W
Olomane →, Canada 71 B7 50 14N 60 37W
Olomouc, Czech Rep. 17 D9 49 38N 17 12 E
Olonets, Russia 24 B5 61 0N 32 54 E
Olongapo, Phil. 37 B6 14 50N 120 18 E
Olot, Spain 19 A7 42 11N 2 30 E
Olovyannaya, Russia 27 D12 50 58N 115 35 E
Oloy →, Russia 27 C16 66 29N 159 29 E
Olsztyn, Poland 17 B11 53 48N 20 29 E
Olt →, Romania 17 G13 43 43N 24 51 E
Olteniţa, Romania 17 F14 44 7N 26 42 E
Olton, U.S.A. 81 H3 34 11N 102 8W
Olymbos, Cyprus 23 D12 35 21N 33 45 E
Olympia, Greece 21 F9 37 39N 21 39 E
Olympia, U.S.A. 84 D4 47 3N 122 53W
Olympic Dam, Australia 63 E2 30 30S 136 55 E
Olympic Mts., U.S.A. 84 C3 47 55N 123 45W
Olympic Nat. Park, U.S.A. 84 C3 47 48N 123 30W
Olympus, Cyprus 23 E11 34 56N 32 52 E
Olympus, Mt. = Ólimbos, Óros, Greece 21 D10 40 6N 22 23 E
Olympus, Mt. = Uludağ, Turkey 21 D13 40 4N 29 13 E
Olympus, Mt., U.S.A. 84 C3 47 48N 123 43W
Olyphant, U.S.A. 79 E9 41 27N 75 36W
Om →, Russia 26 D8 54 59N 73 22 E
Om Koi, Thailand 38 D2 17 48N 98 22 E
Ōma, Japan 30 D10 41 45N 141 5 E
Ōmachi, Japan 31 F8 36 30N 137 50 E
Omae-Zaki, Japan 31 G9 34 36N 138 14 E
Ōmagari, Japan 30 E10 39 27N 140 29 E
Omagh, U.K. 13 B4 54 36N 7 19W
Omagh □, U.K. 13 B4 54 35N 7 15W
Omaha, U.S.A. 80 E7 41 17N 95 58W
Omak, U.S.A. 82 B4 48 25N 119 31W
Omalos, Greece 23 D5 35 19N 23 55 E
Oman ■, Asia 46 C6 23 0N 58 0 E
Oman, G. of, Asia 45 E8 24 30N 58 30 E
Omaruru, Namibia 56 C2 21 26S 16 0 E
Omaruru →, Namibia 56 C1 22 7S 14 15 E
Omate, Peru 92 G4 16 45S 71 0W
Ombai, Selat, Indonesia 37 F6 8 30S 124 50 E
Omboué, Gabon 52 E1 1 35S 9 15 E
Ombrone →, Italy 20 C4 42 42N 11 5 E
Omdurmân, Sudan 51 E12 15 40N 32 28 E
Omemee, Canada 78 B6 44 18N 78 33W
Omeo, Australia 63 F4 37 6S 147 36 E
Omeonga, Dem. Rep. of the Congo 54 C1 3 40S 24 22 E
Ometepe, I. de, Nic. 88 D2 11 32N 85 35W
Ometepec, Mexico 87 D5 16 39N 98 23W
Ominato, Japan 30 D10 41 17N 141 10 E
Omineca →, Canada 72 B4 56 3N 124 16W
Omitara, Namibia 56 C2 22 16S 18 2 E
Ōmiya, Japan 31 G9 35 54N 139 38 E
Ommen, Neths. 15 B6 52 31N 6 26 E
Ömnögovĭ □, Mongolia 34 C3 43 15N 104 0 E
Omo →, Ethiopia 46 F2 6 25N 36 10 E
Omodhos, Cyprus 23 E11 34 51N 32 48 E
Omolon →, Russia 27 C16 68 42N 158 36 E
Omono-Gawa →, Japan 30 E10 39 46N 140 3 E
Omsk, Russia 26 D8 55 0N 73 12 E
Omsukchan, Russia 27 C16 62 32N 155 48 E
Ōmu, Japan 30 B11 44 34N 142 58 E
Omul, Vf., Romania 17 F13 45 27N 25 29 E
Ōmura, Japan 31 H4 32 56N 129 57 E
Omuramba Omatako →, Namibia 53 H4 17 45S 20 25 E
Ōmuta, Japan 31 H5 33 5N 130 26 E
Onaga, U.S.A. 80 F6 39 29N 96 10W
Onalaska, U.S.A. 80 D9 43 53N 91 14W
Onancock, U.S.A. 76 G8 37 43N 75 45W
Onang, Indonesia 37 E5 3 2S 118 49 E
Onaping L., Canada 70 C3 47 3N 81 30W
Onavas, Mexico 86 B3 28 28N 109 30W
Onawa, U.S.A. 80 D6 42 2N 96 6W
Oncócua, Angola 56 B1 16 30S 13 25 E
Onda, Spain 19 C5 39 55N 0 17W
Ondaejin, N. Korea 35 D15 41 34N 129 40 E
Ondangua, Namibia 56 B2 17 57S 16 4 E
Ondjiva, Angola 56 B2 16 48S 15 50 E
Öndörshil, Mongolia 34 B5 45 13N 108 5 E
Öndverðarnes, Iceland 8 D1 64 52N 24 0W
One Tree, Australia 63 E3 34 11S 144 43 E
Onega, Russia 24 B6 64 0N 38 10 E
Onega →, Russia 24 B6 63 58N 38 2 E
Onega, G. of = Onezhskaya Guba, Russia 24 B6 64 24N 36 38 E
Onega, L. = Onezhskoye Ozero, Russia 24 B6 61 44N 35 22 E
Onehunga, N.Z. 59 G5 36 55S 174 48 E
Oneida, U.S.A. 79 C9 43 6N 75 39W
Oneida L., U.S.A. 79 C9 43 12N 75 54W
O'Neill, U.S.A. 80 D5 42 27N 98 39W
Onekotan, Ostrov, Russia 27 E16 49 25N 154 45 E
Onema, Dem. Rep. of the Congo 54 C1 4 35S 24 30 E
Oneonta, U.S.A. 79 D9 42 27N 75 4W
Oneşti, Romania 17 E14 46 15N 26 45 E
Onezhskaya Guba, Russia 24 B6 64 24N 36 38 E
Onezhskoye Ozero, Russia 24 B6 61 44N 35 22 E
Ongarue, N.Z. 59 H5 38 42S 175 19 E
Ongerup, Australia 61 F2 33 58S 118 28 E
Ongjin, N. Korea 35 F13 37 56N 125 21 E
Ongkharak, Thailand 38 E3 14 8N 101 1 E
Ongniud Qi, China 35 C10 43 0N 118 38 E
Ongoka, Dem. Rep. of the Congo 54 C2 1 20S 26 0 E
Ongole, India 40 M12 15 33N 80 2 E
Ongon = Havirga, Mongolia 34 B7 45 41N 113 5 E
Onida, U.S.A. 80 C4 44 42N 100 4W
Onilahy →, Madag. 57 C7 23 34S 43 45 E
Onitsha, Nigeria 50 G7 6 6N 6 42 E
Onoda, Japan 31 G5 34 2N 131 25 E
Onpyŏng-ni, S. Korea 35 H14 33 25N 126 55 E
Onslow, Australia 60 D2 21 40S 115 12 E
Onslow B., U.S.A. 77 H7 34 20N 77 15W
Ontake-San, Japan 31 G8 35 53N 137 29 E
Ontario, Calif., U.S.A. 85 L9 34 4N 117 39W
Ontario, Oreg., U.S.A. 82 D5 44 2N 116 58W
Ontario □, Canada 70 B2 48 0N 83 0W
Ontario, L., N. Amer. 75 B11 43 20N 78 0W
Ontonagon, U.S.A. 80 B10 46 52N 89 19W
Onyx, U.S.A. 85 K8 35 41N 118 14W
Oodnadatta, Australia 63 D2 27 33S 135 30 E
Ooldea, Australia 61 F5 30 27S 131 50 E
Oombulgurri, Australia 60 C4 15 15S 127 45 E
Oorindi, Australia 62 C3 20 40S 141 1 E
Oost-Vlaanderen □, Belgium 15 C3 51 5N 3 50 E
Oostende, Belgium 15 C2 51 15N 2 54 E
Oosterhout, Neths. 15 C4 51 39N 4 47 E
Oosterschelde →, Neths. 15 C4 51 33N 4 0 E
Oosterwolde, Neths. 15 B6 53 0N 6 17 E
Ootacamund = Udagamandalam, India 40 P10 11 30N 76 44 E
Ootsa L., Canada 72 C3 53 50N 126 2W
Opala, Dem. Rep. of the Congo 54 C1 0 40S 24 20 E
Opanake, Sri Lanka 40 R12 6 35N 80 40 E
Opasatika, Canada 70 C3 49 30N 82 50W
Opasquia Prov. Park, Canada 70 B1 53 33N 93 5W
Opava, Czech Rep. 17 D9 49 57N 17 58 E
Opelika, U.S.A. 77 J3 32 39N 85 23W
Opelousas, U.S.A. 81 K8 30 32N 92 5W
Opémisca, L., Canada 70 C5 49 56N 74 52W
Opheim, U.S.A. 82 B10 48 51N 106 24W
Ophthalmia Ra., Australia 60 D2 23 15S 119 30 E
Opinaca →, Canada 70 B4 52 15N 78 2W
Opinaca, Rés., Canada 70 B4 52 39N 76 20W
Opinnagau →, Canada 70 B3 54 12N 82 25W
Opiscoteo, L., Canada 71 B6 53 10N 68 10W
Opole, Poland 17 C9 50 42N 17 58 E
Oporto = Porto, Portugal 19 B1 41 8N 8 40W
Opotiki, N.Z. 59 H6 38 1S 177 19 E
Opp, U.S.A. 77 K2 31 17N 86 16W
Oppdal, Norway 9 E13 62 35N 9 41 E
Opportunity, U.S.A. 82 C5 47 39N 117 15W
Opua, N.Z. 59 F5 35 19S 174 9 E
Opunake, N.Z. 59 H4 39 26S 173 52 E
Ora, Cyprus 23 E12 34 51N 33 12 E
Oracle, U.S.A. 83 K8 32 37N 110 46W
Oradea, Romania 17 E11 47 2N 21 58 E
Öræfajökull, Iceland 8 D5 64 2N 16 39W
Orai, India 43 G8 25 58N 79 30 E
Oral = Zhayyq →, Kazakstan 25 E9 47 0N 51 48 E
Oral, Kazakstan 25 D9 51 20N 51 20 E
Oran, Algeria 50 A5 35 45N 0 39W
Orange, Australia 63 E4 33 15S 149 7 E
Orange, France 18 D6 44 8N 4 47 E
Orange, Calif., U.S.A. 85 M9 33 47N 117 51W
Orange, Mass., U.S.A. 79 D12 42 35N 72 19W
Orange, Tex., U.S.A. 81 K8 30 6N 93 44W
Orange, Va., U.S.A. 76 F6 38 15N 78 7W
Orange →, S. Africa 56 D2 28 41S 16 28 E
Orange, C., Brazil 93 C8 4 20N 51 30W
Orange Cove, U.S.A. 84 J7 36 38N 119 19W
Orange Free State = Free State □, S. Africa 56 D4 28 30S 27 0 E
Orange Grove, U.S.A. 81 M6 27 58N 97 56W
Orange Walk, Belize 87 D7 18 6N 88 33W
Orangeburg, U.S.A. 77 J5 33 30N 80 52W
Orangeville, Canada 78 C4 43 55N 80 5W
Oranienburg, Germany 16 B7 52 45N 13 14 E
Oranje = Orange →, S. Africa 56 D2 28 41S 16 28 E
Oranje Vrystaat = Free State □, S. Africa 56 D4 28 30S 27 0 E
Oranjemund, Namibia 56 D2 28 38S 16 29 E
Oranjerivier, S. Africa 56 D3 29 40S 24 12 E
Orapa, Botswana 53 J5 21 15S 25 30 E
Oras, Phil. 37 B7 12 9N 125 28 E
Oraşul Stalin = Braşov, Romania 17 F13 45 38N 25 35 E
Orbetello, Italy 20 C4 42 27N 11 13 E
Orbisonia, U.S.A. 78 F7 40 15N 77 54W
Orbost, Australia 63 F4 37 40S 148 29 E
Orcas I., U.S.A. 84 B4 48 42N 122 56W
Orchard City, U.S.A. 83 G10 38 50N 107 58W
Orchila, I., Venezuela 89 D6 11 48N 66 10W
Orcutt, U.S.A. 85 L6 34 52N 120 27W
Ord, U.S.A. 80 E5 41 36N 98 56W
Ord →, Australia 60 C4 15 33S 128 15 E
Ord, Mt., Australia 60 C4 17 20S 125 34 E
Orderville, U.S.A. 83 H7 37 17N 112 38W
Ordos = Mu Us Shamo, China 34 E5 39 0N 109 0 E
Ordu, Turkey 25 F6 40 55N 37 53 E
Ordway, U.S.A. 80 F3 38 13N 103 46W
Ordzhonikidze = Vladikavkaz, Russia 25 F7 43 0N 44 35 E
Ore, Dem. Rep. of the Congo 54 B2 3 17N 29 30 E
Ore Mts. = Erzgebirge, Germany 16 C7 50 27N 12 55 E
Örebro, Sweden 9 G16 59 20N 15 18 E
Oregon, U.S.A. 80 D10 42 1N 89 20W
Oregon □, U.S.A. 82 E3 44 0N 121 0W
Oregon City, U.S.A. 84 E4 45 21N 122 36W
Orekhovo-Zuyevo, Russia 24 C6 55 50N 38 55 E
Orel, Russia 24 D6 52 57N 36 3 E
Orem, U.S.A. 74 B4 40 19N 111 42W
Ören, Turkey 21 F12 37 3N 27 57 E
Orenburg, Russia 24 D10 51 45N 55 6 E
Orense = Ourense, Spain 19 A2 42 19N 7 55W
Orepuki, N.Z. 59 M1 46 19S 167 46 E
Orestiás, Greece 21 D12 41 30N 26 33 E
Orestos Pereyra, Mexico 86 B3 26 31N 105 40W
Orford Ness, U.K. 11 E9 52 5N 1 35 E
Organos, Pta. de los, Canary Is. 22 F2 28 12N 17 17W
Orgaz, Spain 19 C4 39 39N 3 53W
Orgeyev = Orhei, Moldova 17 E15 47 24N 28 50 E
Orhaneli, Turkey 21 E13 39 54N 28 59 E
Orhangazi, Turkey 21 D13 40 29N 29 18 E
Orhei, Moldova 17 E15 47 24N 28 50 E
Orhon Gol →, Mongolia 32 A5 50 21N 106 0 E
Oriental, Cordillera, Colombia 92 B4 6 0N 73 0W
Orientale □, Dem. Rep. of the Congo 54 B2 2 20N 26 0 E
Oriente, Argentina 94 D3 38 44S 60 37W
Orihuela, Spain 19 C5 38 7N 0 55W
Orillia, Canada 78 B5 44 40N 79 24W
Orinoco →, Venezuela 92 B6 9 15N 61 30W
Orion, Canada 73 D6 49 27N 110 49W
Oriskany, U.S.A. 79 C9 43 10N 75 20W
Orissa □, India 41 K14 20 0N 84 0 E
Orissaare, Estonia 9 G20 58 34N 23 5 E
Oristano, Italy 20 E3 39 54N 8 36 E
Oristano, G. di, Italy 20 E3 39 50N 8 29 E
Orizaba, Mexico 87 D5 18 51N 97 6W
Orkanger, Norway 8 E13 63 18N 9 52 E
Orkla →, Norway 8 E13 63 18N 9 51 E
Orkney, S. Africa 56 D4 26 58S 26 40 E
Orkney □, U.K. 12 B5 59 2N 3 13W
Orkney Is., U.K. 12 B6 59 0N 3 0W
Orland, U.S.A. 84 F4 39 45N 122 12W
Orlando, U.S.A. 77 L5 28 33N 81 23W
Orléanais, France 18 C5 48 0N 2 0 E
Orléans, France 18 C4 47 54N 1 52 E
Orleans, U.S.A. 79 B12 44 49N 72 12W
Orléans, I. d', Canada 71 C5 46 54N 70 58W
Ormara, Pakistan 40 G4 25 16N 64 33 E
Ormoc, Phil. 37 B6 11 0N 124 37 E
Ormond, N.Z. 59 H6 38 33S 177 56 E
Ormond Beach, U.S.A. 77 L5 29 17N 81 3W
Ormskirk, U.K. 10 D5 53 35N 2 54W
Ormstown, Canada 79 A11 45 8N 74 0W
Örnsköldsvik, Sweden 8 E18 63 17N 18 40 E
Oro, N. Korea 35 D14 40 1N 127 27 E
Oro →, Mexico 86 B3 25 35N 105 2W
Oro Grande, U.S.A. 85 L9 34 36N 117 20W
Oro Valley, U.S.A. 83 K8 32 26N 110 58W
Orocué, Colombia 92 C4 4 48N 71 20W
Orofino, U.S.A. 82 C5 46 29N 116 15W
Orol Dengizi = Aral Sea, Asia 26 E7 44 30N 60 0 E
Oromocto, Canada 71 C6 45 54N 66 29W
Orono, Canada 78 C6 43 59N 78 37W
Orono, U.S.A. 77 C11 44 53N 68 40W
Oronsay, U.K. 12 E2 56 1N 6 15W
Oroqen Zizhiqi, China 33 A7 50 34N 123 43 E
Oroquieta, Phil. 37 C6 8 32N 123 44 E
Orosháza, Hungary 17 E11 46 32N 20 42 E
Orotukan, Russia 27 C16 62 16N 151 42 E
Oroville, Calif., U.S.A. 84 F5 39 31N 121 33W
Oroville, Wash., U.S.A. 82 B4 48 56N 119 26W
Oroville, L., U.S.A. 84 F5 39 33N 121 29W
Orroroo, Australia 63 E2 32 43S 138 38 E
Orrville, U.S.A. 78 F3 40 50N 81 46W
Orsha, Belarus 24 D5 54 30N 30 25 E
Orsk, Russia 26 D6 51 12N 58 34 E
Orşova, Romania 17 F12 44 41N 22 25 E
Ortaca, Turkey 21 F13 36 49N 28 45 E
Ortegal, C., Spain 19 A2 43 43N 7 52W
Orthez, France 18 E3 43 29N 0 48W
Ortigueira, Spain 19 A2 43 40N 7 50W
Orting, U.S.A. 84 C4 47 6N 122 12W
Ortles, Italy 18 C9 46 31N 10 33 E
Ortón →, Bolivia 92 F5 10 50S 67 0W
Ortonville, U.S.A. 80 C6 45 19N 96 27W
Orūmīyeh, Iran 44 B5 37 40N 45 0 E
Orūmīyeh, Daryācheh-ye, Iran 44 B5 37 50N 45 30 E
Oruro, Bolivia 92 G5 18 0S 67 9W
Orust, Sweden 9 G14 58 10N 11 40 E
Oruzgān □, Afghan. 40 C5 33 30N 66 0 E
Orvieto, Italy 20 C5 42 43N 12 7 E
Orwell, N.Y., U.S.A. 79 C9 43 35N 75 50W
Orwell, Ohio, U.S.A. 78 E4 41 32N 80 52W
Orwell →, U.K. 11 F9 51 59N 1 18 E
Orwigsburg, U.S.A. 79 F8 40 38N 76 6W
Oryakhovo, Bulgaria 21 C10 43 40N 23 57 E
Osa, Russia 24 C10 57 17N 55 26 E
Osa, Pen. de, Costa Rica 88 E3 8 0N 84 0W
Osage, U.S.A. 80 D8 43 17N 92 49W
Osage →, U.S.A. 80 F9 38 35N 91 57W
Osage City, U.S.A. 80 F7 38 38N 95 50W
Ōsaka, Japan 31 G7 34 40N 135 30 E
Osan, S. Korea 35 F14 37 11N 127 4 E
Osawatomie, U.S.A. 80 F7 38 31N 94 57W
Osborne, U.S.A. 80 F5 39 26N 98 42W
Osceola, Ark., U.S.A. 81 H10 35 42N 89 58W
Osceola, Iowa, U.S.A. 80 E8 41 2N 93 46W
Oscoda, U.S.A. 78 B1 44 26N 83 20W
Ösel = Saaremaa, Estonia 9 G20 58 30N 22 30 E
Osgoode, Canada 79 A9 45 8N 75 36W
Osh, Kyrgyzstan 26 E8 40 37N 72 49 E
Oshakati, Namibia 53 H3 17 45S 15 40 E
Oshawa, Canada 78 C6 43 50N 78 50W
Oshkosh, Nebr., U.S.A. 80 E3 41 24N 102 21W
Oshkosh, Wis., U.S.A. 80 C10 44 1N 88 33W

Oshmyany = Ashmyany, *Belarus* **9 J21** 54 26N 25 52 E
Oshnovīyeh, *Iran* **44 B5** 37 2N 45 6 E
Oshogbo, *Nigeria* **50 G6** 7 48N 4 37 E
Oshtorīnān, *Iran* **45 C6** 34 1N 48 38 E
Oshwe, *Dem. Rep. of the Congo* **52 E3** 3 25S 19 28 E
Osijek, *Croatia* **21 B8** 45 34N 18 41 E
Osipenko = Berdyansk, *Ukraine* **25 E6** 46 45N 36 50 E
Osipovichi = Asipovichy, *Belarus* **17 B15** 53 19N 28 33 E
Osiyan, *India* **42 F5** 26 43N 72 55 E
Osizweni, *S. Africa* **57 D5** 27 49S 30 7 E
Oskaloosa, *U.S.A.* **80 E8** 41 18N 92 39W
Oskarshamn, *Sweden* **9 H17** 57 15N 16 27 E
Oskélanéo, *Canada* **70 C4** 48 5N 75 15W
Öskemen, *Kazakstan* **26 E9** 50 0N 82 36 E
Oslo, *Norway* **9 G14** 59 55N 10 45 E
Oslofjorden, *Norway* **9 G14** 59 20N 10 35 E
Osmanabad, *India* **40 K10** 18 5N 76 10 E
Osmaniye, *Turkey* **25 G6** 37 5N 36 10 E
Osnabrück, *Germany* **16 B5** 52 17N 8 3 E
Osorio, *Brazil* **95 B5** 29 53S 50 17W
Osorno, *Chile* **96 E2** 40 25S 73 0W
Osoyoos, *Canada* **72 D5** 49 0N 119 30W
Osøyro, *Norway* **9 F11** 60 9N 5 30 E
Ospika →, *Canada* **72 B4** 56 20N 124 0W
Osprey Reef, *Australia* **62 A4** 13 52S 146 36 E
Oss, *Neths.* **15 C5** 51 46N 5 32 E
Ossa, Mt., *Australia* **62 G4** 41 52S 146 3 E
Óssa, Óros, *Greece* **21 E10** 39 47N 22 42 E
Ossabaw I., *U.S.A.* **77 K5** 31 50N 81 5W
Ossining, *U.S.A.* **79 E11** 41 10N 73 55W
Ossipee, *U.S.A.* **79 C13** 43 41N 71 7W
Ossokmanuan L., *Canada* **71 B7** 53 25N 65 0W
Ossora, *Russia* **27 D17** 59 20N 163 13 E
Ostend = Oostende, *Belgium* **15 C2** 51 15N 2 54 E
Oster, *Ukraine* **17 C16** 50 57N 30 53 E
Osterburg, *U.S.A.* **78 F6** 40 16N 78 31W
Österdalälven, *Sweden* **9 F16** 61 30N 13 45 E
Østerdalen, *Norway* **9 F14** 61 40N 10 50 E
Östersund, *Sweden* **8 E16** 63 10N 14 38 E
Ostfriesische Inseln, *Germany* **16 B4** 53 42N 7 0 E
Ostrava, *Czech Rep.* **17 D10** 49 51N 18 18 E
Ostróda, *Poland* **17 B10** 53 42N 19 58 E
Ostroh, *Ukraine* **17 C14** 50 20N 26 30 E
Ostrołęka, *Poland* **17 B11** 53 4N 21 32 E
Ostrów Mazowiecka, *Poland* **17 B11** 52 50N 21 51 E
Ostrów Wielkopolski, *Poland* **17 C9** 51 36N 17 44 E
Ostrowiec-Świętokrzyski, *Poland* **17 C11** 50 55N 21 22 E
Ostuni, *Italy* **21 D7** 40 44N 17 35 E
Ōsumi-Kaikyō, *Japan* **31 J5** 30 55N 131 0 E
Ōsumi-Shotō, *Japan* **31 J5** 30 30N 130 0 E
Osuna, *Spain* **19 D3** 37 14N 5 8W
Oswegatchie →, *U.S.A.* **79 B9** 44 42N 75 30W
Oswego, *U.S.A.* **79 C8** 43 27N 76 31W
Oswego →, *U.S.A.* **79 C8** 43 27N 76 30W
Oswestry, *U.K.* **10 E4** 52 52N 3 3W
Oświęcim, *Poland* **17 C10** 50 2N 19 11 E
Otago □, *N.Z.* **59 L2** 45 15S 170 0 E
Otago Harbour, *N.Z.* **59 L3** 45 47S 170 42 E
Ōtake, *Japan* **31 G6** 34 12N 132 13 E
Otaki, *N.Z.* **59 J5** 40 45S 175 10 E
Otaru, *Japan* **30 C10** 43 10N 141 0 E
Otaru-Wan = Ishikari-Wan, *Japan* **30 C10** 43 25N 141 1 E
Otavalo, *Ecuador* **92 C3** 0 13N 78 20W
Otavi, *Namibia* **56 B2** 19 40S 17 24 E
Otchinjau, *Angola* **56 B1** 16 30S 13 56 E
Otelnuk L., *Canada* **71 A6** 56 9N 68 12W
Othello, *U.S.A.* **82 C4** 46 50N 119 10W
Otira Gorge, *N.Z.* **59 K3** 42 53S 171 33 E
Otjiwarongo, *Namibia* **56 C2** 20 30S 16 33 E
Otoineppu, *Japan* **30 B11** 44 44N 142 16 E
Otorohanga, *N.Z.* **59 H5** 38 12S 175 14 E
Otoskwin →, *Canada* **70 B2** 52 13N 88 6W
Otra →, *Norway* **9 G13** 58 9N 8 1 E
Otranto, *Italy* **21 D8** 40 9N 18 28 E
Otranto, C. d', *Italy* **21 D8** 40 7N 18 30 E
Otranto, Str. of, *Italy* **21 D8** 40 15N 18 40 E
Otse, *S. Africa* **56 D4** 25 2S 25 45 E
Ōtsu, *Japan* **31 G7** 35 0N 135 50 E
Ōtsuki, *Japan* **31 G9** 35 36N 138 57 E
Ottawa = Outaouais →, *Canada* **70 C5** 45 27N 74 8W
Ottawa, *Canada* **79 A9** 45 27N 75 42W
Ottawa, *Ill., U.S.A.* **80 E10** 41 21N 88 51W
Ottawa, *Kans., U.S.A.* **80 F7** 38 37N 95 16W
Ottawa Is., *Canada* **69 C11** 59 35N 80 10W
Otter Cr. →, *U.S.A.* **79 B11** 44 13N 73 17W
Otter L., *Canada* **73 B8** 55 35N 104 39W
Otterville, *Canada* **78 D4** 42 55N 80 36W
Ottery St. Mary, *U.K.* **11 G4** 50 44N 3 17W
Otto Beit Bridge, *Zimbabwe* **55 F2** 15 59S 28 56 E
Ottosdal, *S. Africa* **56 D4** 26 46S 25 59 E
Ottumwa, *U.S.A.* **80 E8** 41 1N 92 25W
Oturkpo, *Nigeria* **50 G7** 7 16N 8 8 E
Otway, B., *Chile* **96 G2** 53 30S 74 0W
Otway, C., *Australia* **63 F3** 38 52S 143 30 E
Otwock, *Poland* **17 B11** 52 5N 21 20 E
Ou →, *Laos* **38 B4** 20 4N 102 13 E
Ou-Sammyaku, *Japan* **30 E10** 39 20N 140 35 E
Ouachita →, *U.S.A.* **81 K9** 31 38N 91 49W
Ouachita, L., *U.S.A.* **81 H8** 34 34N 93 12W
Ouachita Mts., *U.S.A.* **81 H7** 34 40N 94 25W
Ouagadougou, *Burkina Faso* **50 F5** 12 25N 1 30W
Ouahran = Oran, *Algeria* **50 A5** 35 45N 0 39W
Ouallene, *Algeria* **50 D6** 24 41N 1 11 E
Ouargla, *Algeria* **50 B7** 31 59N 5 16 E
Ouarzazate, *Morocco* **50 B4** 30 55N 6 50W
Oubangi →, *Dem. Rep. of the Congo* **52 E3** 0 30S 17 50 E
Ouddorp, *Neths.* **15 C3** 51 50N 3 57 E
Oude Rijn →, *Neths.* **15 B4** 52 12N 4 24 E
Oudenaarde, *Belgium* **15 D3** 50 50N 3 37 E
Oudtshoorn, *S. Africa* **56 E3** 33 35S 22 14 E
Ouessant, Î. d', *France* **18 B1** 48 28N 5 6W
Ouesso, *Congo* **52 D3** 1 37N 16 5 E
Ouest, Pte. de l', *Canada* **71 C7** 49 52N 64 40W
Ouezzane, *Morocco* **50 B4** 34 51N 5 35W
Oughterard, *Ireland* **13 C2** 53 26N 9 18W
Oujda, *Morocco* **50 B5** 34 41N 1 55W
Oulainen, *Finland* **8 D21** 64 17N 24 47 E
Oulu, *Finland* **8 D21** 65 1N 25 29 E
Oulujärvi, *Finland* **8 D22** 64 25N 27 15 E
Oulujoki →, *Finland* **8 D21** 65 1N 25 30 E
Oum Chalouba, *Chad* **51 E10** 15 48N 20 46 E
Oum Hadjer, *Chad* **51 F9** 13 18N 19 41 E
Ounasjoki →, *Finland* **8 C21** 66 31N 25 40 E
Ounguati, *Namibia* **56 C2** 22 0S 15 46 E
Ounianga Sérir, *Chad* **51 E10** 18 54N 20 51 E
Our →, *Lux.* **15 E6** 49 55N 6 5 E
Ouray, *U.S.A.* **83 G10** 38 1N 107 40W
Ourense, *Spain* **19 A2** 42 19N 7 55W
Ouricuri, *Brazil* **93 E10** 7 53S 40 5W
Ourinhos, *Brazil* **95 A6** 23 0S 49 54W
Ouro Fino, *Brazil* **95 A6** 22 16S 46 25W
Ouro Prêto, *Brazil* **95 A7** 20 20S 43 30W
Ourthe →, *Belgium* **15 D5** 50 29N 5 35 E
Ouse →, *E. Susx., U.K.* **11 G8** 50 47N 0 4 E
Ouse →, *N. Yorks., U.K.* **10 D7** 53 44N 0 55W
Outaouais →, *Canada* **70 C5** 45 27N 74 8W
Outardes →, *Canada* **71 C6** 49 24N 69 30W
Outer Hebrides, *U.K.* **12 D1** 57 30N 7 40W
Outjo, *Namibia* **56 C2** 20 5S 16 7 E
Outlook, *Canada* **73 C7** 51 30N 107 0W
Outokumpu, *Finland* **8 E23** 62 43N 29 1 E
Ouyen, *Australia* **63 F3** 35 1S 142 22 E
Ovalau, *Fiji* **59 C8** 17 40S 178 48 E
Ovalle, *Chile* **94 C1** 30 33S 71 18W
Ovamboland, *Namibia* **56 B2** 18 30S 16 0 E
Overflakkee, *Neths.* **15 C4** 51 44N 4 10 E
Overijssel □, *Neths.* **15 B6** 52 25N 6 35 E
Overland Park, *U.S.A.* **80 F7** 38 55N 94 50W
Overton, *U.S.A.* **85 J12** 36 33N 114 27W
Övertorneå, *Sweden* **8 C20** 66 23N 23 38 E
Ovid, *U.S.A.* **79 D8** 42 41N 76 49W
Oviedo, *Spain* **19 A3** 43 25N 5 50W
Oviši, *Latvia* **9 H19** 57 33N 21 44 E
Ovoot, *Mongolia* **34 B7** 45 21N 113 45 E
Övör Hangay □, *Mongolia* **34 B2** 45 0N 102 30 E
Øvre Årdal, *Norway* **9 F12** 61 19N 7 48 E
Ovruch, *Ukraine* **17 C15** 51 25N 28 45 E
Owaka, *N.Z.* **59 M2** 46 27S 169 40 E
Owambo = Ovamboland, *Namibia* **56 B2** 18 30S 16 0 E
Owando, *Congo* **52 E3** 0 29S 15 55 E
Owasco L., *U.S.A.* **79 D8** 42 50N 76 31W
Owase, *Japan* **31 G8** 34 7N 136 12 E
Owatonna, *U.S.A.* **80 C8** 44 5N 93 14W
Owbeh, *Afghan.* **40 B3** 34 28N 63 10 E
Owego, *U.S.A.* **79 D8** 42 6N 76 16W
Owen Falls Dam, *Uganda* **54 B3** 0 30N 33 5 E
Owen Sound, *Canada* **78 B4** 44 35N 80 55W
Owens →, *U.S.A.* **84 J9** 36 32N 117 59W
Owens L., *U.S.A.* **85 J9** 36 26N 117 57W
Owensboro, *U.S.A.* **76 G2** 37 46N 87 7W
Owl →, *Canada* **73 B10** 57 51N 92 44W
Owo, *Nigeria* **50 G7** 7 10N 5 39 E
Owosso, *U.S.A.* **76 D3** 43 0N 84 10W
Owyhee, *U.S.A.* **82 F5** 41 57N 116 6W
Owyhee →, *U.S.A.* **82 E5** 43 49N 117 2W
Owyhee, L., *U.S.A.* **82 E5** 43 38N 117 14W
Ox Mts. = Slieve Gamph, *Ireland* **13 B3** 54 6N 9 0W
Öxarfjörður, *Iceland* **8 C5** 66 15N 16 45W
Oxbow, *Canada* **73 D8** 49 14N 102 10W
Oxelösund, *Sweden* **9 G17** 58 43N 17 5 E
Oxford, *N.Z.* **59 K4** 43 18S 172 11 E
Oxford, *U.K.* **11 F6** 51 46N 1 15W
Oxford, *Mass., U.S.A.* **79 D13** 42 7N 71 52W
Oxford, *Miss., U.S.A.* **81 H10** 34 22N 89 31W
Oxford, *N.C., U.S.A.* **77 G6** 36 19N 78 35W
Oxford, *N.Y., U.S.A.* **79 D9** 42 27N 75 36W
Oxford, *Ohio, U.S.A.* **76 F3** 39 31N 84 45W
Oxford L., *Canada* **73 C9** 54 51N 95 37W
Oxfordshire □, *U.K.* **11 F6** 51 48N 1 16W
Oxnard, *U.S.A.* **85 L7** 34 12N 119 11W
Oxus = Amudarya →, *Uzbekistan* **26 E6** 43 58N 59 34 E
Oya, *Malaysia* **36 D4** 2 55N 111 55 E
Oyama, *Japan* **31 F9** 36 18N 139 48 E
Oyem, *Gabon* **52 D2** 1 34N 11 31 E
Oyen, *Canada* **73 C6** 51 22N 110 28W
Oykel →, *U.K.* **12 D4** 57 56N 4 26W
Oymyakon, *Russia* **27 C15** 63 25N 142 44 E
Oyo, *Nigeria* **50 G6** 7 46N 3 56 E
Oyster Bay, *U.S.A.* **79 F11** 40 52N 73 32W
Ōyūbari, *Japan* **30 C11** 43 1N 142 5 E
Ozamiz, *Phil.* **37 C6** 8 15N 123 50 E
Ozark, *Ala., U.S.A.* **77 K3** 31 28N 85 39W
Ozark, *Ark., U.S.A.* **81 H8** 35 29N 93 50W
Ozark, *Mo., U.S.A.* **81 G8** 37 1N 93 12W
Ozark Plateau, *U.S.A.* **81 G9** 37 20N 91 40W
Ozarks, L. of the, *U.S.A.* **80 F8** 38 12N 92 38W
Ózd, *Hungary* **17 D11** 48 14N 20 15 E
Ozette L., *U.S.A.* **84 B2** 48 6N 124 38W
Ozona, *U.S.A.* **81 K4** 30 43N 101 12W
Ozuluama, *Mexico* **87 C5** 21 40N 97 50W

P

Pa-an, *Burma* **41 L20** 16 51N 97 40 E
Pa Mong Dam, *Thailand* **38 D4** 18 0N 102 22 E
Pa Sak →, *Thailand* **36 B2** 15 30N 101 0 E
Paamiut = Frederikshåb, *Greenland* **4 C5** 62 0N 49 43W
Paarl, *S. Africa* **56 E2** 33 45S 18 56 E
Paauilo, *U.S.A.* **74 H17** 20 2N 155 22W
Pab Hills, *Pakistan* **42 F2** 26 30N 66 45 E
Pabbay, *U.K.* **12 D1** 57 46N 7 14W
Pabianice, *Poland* **17 C10** 51 40N 19 20 E
Pabna, *Bangla.* **41 G16** 24 1N 89 18 E
Pabo, *Uganda* **54 B3** 3 1N 32 10 E
Pacaja →, *Brazil* **93 D8** 1 56S 50 50W
Pacaraima, Sa., *S. Amer.* **92 C6** 4 0N 62 30W
Pacasmayo, *Peru* **92 E3** 7 20S 79 35W
Pachhar, *India* **42 G7** 24 40N 77 42 E
Pachitea →, *Peru* **92 E4** 8 46S 74 33W
Pachmarhi, *India* **43 H8** 22 28N 78 26 E
Pachpadra, *India* **40 G8** 25 58N 72 10 E
Pachuca, *Mexico* **87 C5** 20 10N 98 40W
Pacific, *Canada* **72 C3** 54 48N 128 28W
Pacific-Antarctic Ridge, *Pac. Oc.* **65 M16** 43 0S 115 0W
Pacific Grove, *U.S.A.* **84 J5** 36 38N 121 56W
Pacific Ocean, *Pac. Oc.* **65 G14** 10 0N 140 0W
Pacific Rim Nat. Park, *Canada* **84 B2** 48 40N 124 45W
Pacifica, *U.S.A.* **84 H4** 37 36N 122 30W
Pacitan, *Indonesia* **37 H14** 8 12S 111 7 E
Packwood, *U.S.A.* **84 D5** 46 36N 121 40W
Padaido, Kepulauan, *Indonesia* **37 E9** 1 5S 138 0 E
Padang, *Indonesia* **36 E2** 1 0S 100 20 E
Padang Endau, *Malaysia* **39 L4** 2 40N 103 38 E
Padangpanjang, *Indonesia* **36 E2** 0 40S 100 20 E
Padangsidempuan, *Indonesia* **36 D1** 1 30N 99 15 E
Paddle Prairie, *Canada* **72 B5** 57 57N 117 29W
Paddockwood, *Canada* **73 C7** 53 30N 105 30W
Paderborn, *Germany* **16 C5** 51 42N 8 45 E
Padma, *India* **43 G11** 24 12N 85 22 E
Pádova, *Italy* **20 B4** 45 25N 11 53 E
Padra, *India* **42 H5** 22 15N 73 7 E
Padrauna, *India* **43 F10** 26 54N 83 59 E
Padre I., *U.S.A.* **81 M6** 27 10N 97 25W
Padstow, *U.K.* **11 G3** 50 33N 4 58W
Padua = Pádova, *Italy* **20 B4** 45 25N 11 53 E
Paducah, *Ky., U.S.A.* **76 G1** 37 5N 88 37W
Paducah, *Tex., U.S.A.* **81 H4** 34 1N 100 18W
Paengnyŏng-do, *S. Korea* **35 F13** 37 57N 124 40 E
Paeroa, *N.Z.* **59 G5** 37 23S 175 41 E
Pafúri, *Mozam.* **57 C5** 22 28S 31 17 E
Pag, *Croatia* **16 F8** 44 25N 15 3 E
Pagadian, *Phil.* **37 C6** 7 55N 123 30 E
Pagai Selatan, Pulau, *Indonesia* **36 E2** 3 0S 100 15 E
Pagai Utara, Pulau, *Indonesia* **36 E2** 2 35S 100 0 E
Pagalu = Annobón, *Atl. Oc.* **49 G4** 1 25S 5 36 E
Pagara, *India* **43 G9** 24 22N 80 1 E
Pagastikós Kólpos, *Greece* **21 E10** 39 15N 23 0 E
Pagatan, *Indonesia* **36 E5** 3 33S 115 59 E
Page, *U.S.A.* **83 H8** 36 57N 111 27W
Pago Pago, *Amer. Samoa* **59 B13** 14 16S 170 43W
Pagosa Springs, *U.S.A.* **83 H10** 37 16N 107 1W
Pagwa River, *Canada* **70 B2** 50 2N 85 14W
Pahala, *U.S.A.* **74 J17** 19 12N 155 29W
Pahang →, *Malaysia* **39 L4** 3 30N 103 9 E
Pahiatua, *N.Z.* **59 J5** 40 27S 175 50 E
Pahokee, *U.S.A.* **77 M5** 26 50N 80 40W
Pahrump, *U.S.A.* **85 J11** 36 12N 115 59W
Pahute Mesa, *U.S.A.* **84 H10** 37 20N 116 45W
Pai, *Thailand* **38 C2** 19 19N 98 27 E
Paia, *U.S.A.* **74 H16** 20 54N 156 22W
Paicines, *U.S.A.* **84 J5** 36 44N 121 17W
Paide, *Estonia* **9 G21** 58 57N 25 31 E
Paignton, *U.K.* **11 G4** 50 26N 3 35W
Päijänne, *Finland* **9 F21** 61 30N 25 30 E
Pailani, *India* **43 G9** 25 45N 80 26 E
Pailin, *Cambodia* **38 F4** 12 46N 102 36 E
Painan, *Indonesia* **36 E2** 1 21S 100 34 E
Painesville, *U.S.A.* **78 E3** 41 43N 81 15W
Paint Hills = Wemindji, *Canada* **70 B4** 53 0N 78 49W
Paint L., *Canada* **73 B9** 55 28N 97 57W
Painted Desert, *U.S.A.* **83 J8** 36 0N 111 0W
Paintsville, *U.S.A.* **76 G4** 37 49N 82 48W
País Vasco □, *Spain* **19 A4** 42 50N 2 45W
Paisley, *Canada* **78 B3** 44 18N 81 16W
Paisley, *U.K.* **12 F4** 55 50N 4 25W
Paisley, *U.S.A.* **82 E3** 42 42N 120 32W
Paita, *Peru* **92 E2** 5 11S 81 9W
Pajares, Puerto de, *Spain* **19 A3** 42 58N 5 46W
Pak Lay, *Laos* **38 C3** 18 15N 101 27 E
Pak Phanang, *Thailand* **39 H3** 8 21N 100 12 E
Pak Sane, *Laos* **38 C4** 18 22N 103 39 E
Pak Song, *Laos* **38 E6** 15 11N 106 14 E
Pakaur, *India* **43 G12** 24 38N 87 51 E
Pakenham, *Canada* **79 A8** 45 18N 76 18W
Pákhnes, *Greece* **23 D6** 35 16N 24 4 E
Pakistan ■, *Asia* **42 E4** 30 0N 70 0 E
Pakkading, *Laos* **38 C4** 18 19N 103 59 E
Pakokku, *Burma* **41 J19** 21 20N 95 0 E
Pakowki L., *Canada* **73 D6** 49 20N 111 0W
Pakpattan, *Pakistan* **42 D5** 30 25N 73 27 E
Paktīā □, *Afghan.* **40 C6** 33 0N 69 15 E
Pakwach, *Uganda* **54 B3** 2 28N 31 27 E
Pakxe, *Laos* **38 E5** 15 5N 105 52 E
Pal Lahara, *India* **43 J11** 21 27N 85 11 E
Pala, *Chad* **51 G9** 9 25N 15 5 E
Pala, *Dem. Rep. of the Congo* **54 D2** 6 45S 29 30 E
Pala, *U.S.A.* **85 M9** 33 22N 117 5W
Palabek, *Uganda* **54 B3** 3 22N 32 33 E
Palacios, *U.S.A.* **81 L6** 28 42N 96 13W
Palagruža, *Croatia* **20 C7** 42 24N 16 15 E
Palaiókastron, *Greece* **23 D8** 35 12N 26 15 E
Palaiokhóra, *Greece* **23 D5** 35 16N 23 39 E
Palam, *India* **40 K10** 19 0N 77 0 E
Palampur, *India* **42 C7** 32 10N 76 30 E
Palana, *Australia* **62 F4** 39 45S 147 55 E
Palana, *Russia* **27 D16** 59 10N 159 59 E
Palanan, *Phil.* **37 A6** 17 8N 122 29 E
Palanan Pt., *Phil.* **37 A6** 17 17N 122 30 E
Palandri, *Pakistan* **43 C5** 33 42N 73 40 E
Palanga, *Lithuania* **9 J19** 55 58N 21 3 E
Palangkaraya, *Indonesia* **36 E4** 2 16S 113 56 E
Palani Hills, *India* **40 P10** 10 14N 77 33 E
Palanpur, *India* **42 G5** 24 10N 72 25 E
Palapye, *Botswana* **56 C4** 22 30S 27 7 E
Palas, *Pakistan* **43 B5** 35 4N 73 14 E
Palashi, *India* **43 H13** 23 47N 88 15 E
Palasponga, *India* **43 J11** 21 47N 85 34 E
Palatka, *Russia* **27 C16** 60 6N 150 54 E
Palatka, *U.S.A.* **77 L5** 29 39N 81 38W
Palau ■, *Pac. Oc.* **28 J17** 7 30N 134 30 E
Palauk, *Burma* **38 F2** 13 10N 98 40 E
Palawan, *Phil.* **36 C5** 9 30N 118 30 E
Palayankottai, *India* **40 Q10** 8 45N 77 45 E
Paldiski, *Estonia* **9 G21** 59 23N 24 9 E
Paleleh, *Indonesia* **37 D6** 1 10N 121 50 E
Palembang, *Indonesia* **36 E2** 3 0S 104 50 E
Palencia, *Spain* **19 A3** 42 1N 4 34W
Palenque, *Mexico* **87 D6** 17 31N 91 58W
Paleokastrítsa, *Greece* **23 A3** 39 40N 19 41 E
Paleometokho, *Cyprus* **23 D12** 35 7N 33 11 E
Palermo, *Italy* **20 E5** 38 7N 13 22 E
Palermo, *U.S.A.* **82 G3** 39 26N 121 33W
Palestina, *Chile* **96 A3** 23 50S 69 47W
Palestine, *Asia* **47 D4** 32 0N 35 0 E
Palestine, *U.S.A.* **81 K7** 31 46N 95 38W
Paletwa, *Burma* **41 J18** 21 10N 92 50 E
Palghat, *India* **40 P10** 10 46N 76 42 E
Palgrave, Mt., *Australia* **60 D2** 23 22S 115 58 E
Pali, *India* **42 G5** 25 50N 73 20 E
Palikir, *Micronesia* **64 G7** 6 55N 158 9 E
Palioúrion, Ákra, *Greece* **21 E10** 39 57N 23 45 E
Palisades Reservoir, *U.S.A.* **82 E8** 43 20N 111 12W
Paliseul, *Belgium* **15 E5** 49 54N 5 8 E
Palitana, *India* **42 J4** 21 32N 71 49 E
Palizada, *Mexico* **87 D6** 18 18N 92 8W
Palk Bay, *Asia* **40 Q11** 9 30N 79 15 E
Palk Strait, *Asia* **40 Q11** 10 0N 79 45 E
Palkānah, *Iraq* **44 C5** 35 49N 44 26 E
Palkot, *India* **43 H11** 22 53N 84 39 E
Palla Road = Dinokwe, *Botswana* **56 C4** 23 29S 26 37 E
Pallanza = Verbánia, *Italy* **18 D8** 45 56N 8 33 E
Pallarenda, *Australia* **62 B4** 19 12S 146 46 E
Pallinup →, *Australia* **61 F2** 34 27S 118 50 E
Pallisa, *Uganda* **54 B3** 1 12N 33 43 E
Pallu, *India* **42 E6** 28 59N 74 14 E
Palm Bay, *U.S.A.* **77 L5** 28 2N 80 35W
Palm Beach, *U.S.A.* **77 M6** 26 43N 80 2W
Palm Coast, *U.S.A.* **77 L5** 29 32N 81 10W
Palm Desert, *U.S.A.* **85 M10** 33 43N 116 22W
Palm Is., *Australia* **62 B4** 18 40S 146 35 E
Palm Springs, *U.S.A.* **85 M10** 33 50N 116 33W
Palma, *Mozam.* **55 E5** 10 46S 40 29 E
Palma, B. de, *Spain* **22 B9** 39 30N 2 39 E
Palma de Mallorca, *Spain* **22 B9** 39 35N 2 39 E
Palma Soriano, *Cuba* **88 B4** 20 15N 76 0W
Palmares, *Brazil* **93 E11** 8 41S 35 28W
Palmas, *Brazil* **95 B5** 26 29S 52 0W
Palmas, C., *Liberia* **50 H4** 4 27N 7 46W
Pálmas, G. di, *Italy* **20 E3** 39 0N 8 30 E
Palmdale, *U.S.A.* **85 L8** 34 35N 118 7W
Palmeira das Missões, *Brazil* **95 B5** 27 55S 53 17W
Palmeira dos Índios, *Brazil* **93 E11** 9 25S 36 37W
Palmer, *U.S.A.* **68 B5** 61 36N 149 7W
Palmer →, *Australia* **62 B3** 16 0S 142 26 E
Palmer Arch., *Antarctica* **5 C17** 64 15S 65 0W
Palmer Lake, *U.S.A.* **80 F2** 39 7N 104 55W
Palmer Land, *Antarctica* **5 D18** 73 0S 63 0W
Palmerston, *Canada* **78 C4** 43 50N 80 51W
Palmerston, *N.Z.* **59 L3** 45 29S 170 43 E
Palmerston North, *N.Z.* **59 J5** 40 21S 175 39 E
Palmerton, *U.S.A.* **79 F9** 40 48N 75 37W
Palmetto, *U.S.A.* **77 M4** 27 31N 82 34W
Palmi, *Italy* **20 E6** 38 21N 15 51 E
Palmira, *Argentina* **94 C2** 32 59S 68 34W
Palmira, *Colombia* **92 C3** 3 32N 76 16W
Palmyra = Tudmur, *Syria* **44 C3** 34 36N 38 15 E
Palmyra, *Mo., U.S.A.* **80 F9** 39 48N 91 32W
Palmyra, *N.J., U.S.A.* **79 F9** 40 1N 75 1W
Palmyra, *N.Y., U.S.A.* **78 C7** 43 5N 77 18W
Palmyra, *Pa., U.S.A.* **79 F8** 40 18N 76 36W
Palmyra Is., *Pac. Oc.* **65 G11** 5 52N 162 5W
Palo Alto, *U.S.A.* **84 H4** 37 27N 122 10W
Palo Verde, *U.S.A.* **85 M12** 33 26N 114 44W
Palopo, *Indonesia* **37 E6** 3 0S 120 16 E
Palos, C. de, *Spain* **19 D5** 37 38N 0 40W
Palos Verdes, *U.S.A.* **85 M8** 33 48N 118 23W
Palos Verdes, Pt., *U.S.A.* **85 M8** 33 43N 118 26W
Palu, *Indonesia* **37 E5** 1 0S 119 52 E
Palu, *Turkey* **25 G7** 38 45N 40 0 E
Palwal, *India* **42 E7** 28 8N 77 19 E
Pamanukan, *Indonesia* **37 G12** 6 16S 107 49 E
Pamiers, *France* **18 E4** 43 7N 1 39 E
Pamir, *Tajikistan* **26 F8** 37 40N 73 0 E
Pamlico →, *U.S.A.* **77 H7** 35 20N 76 28W
Pamlico Sd., *U.S.A.* **77 H8** 35 20N 76 0W
Pampa, *U.S.A.* **81 H4** 35 32N 100 58W
Pampa de las Salinas, *Argentina* **94 C2** 32 1S 66 58W
Pampanua, *Indonesia* **37 E6** 4 16S 120 8 E
Pampas, *Argentina* **94 D3** 35 0S 63 0W
Pampas, *Peru* **92 F4** 12 20S 74 50W
Pamplona, *Colombia* **92 B4** 7 23N 72 39W
Pamplona, *Spain* **19 A5** 42 48N 1 38W
Pampoenpoort, *S. Africa* **56 E3** 31 3S 22 40 E
Pana, *U.S.A.* **80 F10** 39 23N 89 5W
Panaca, *U.S.A.* **83 H6** 37 47N 114 23W
Panaitan, *Indonesia* **37 G11** 6 36S 105 12 E
Panaji, *India* **40 M8** 15 25N 73 50 E
Panamá, *Panama* **88 E4** 9 0N 79 25W
Panama ■, *Cent. Amer.* **88 E4** 8 48N 79 55W
Panamá, G. de, *Panama* **88 E4** 8 4N 79 20W
Panama Canal, *Panama* **88 E4** 9 10N 79 37W
Panama City, *U.S.A.* **77 K3** 30 10N 85 40W
Panamint Range, *U.S.A.* **85 J9** 36 20N 117 20W
Panamint Springs, *U.S.A.* **85 J9** 36 20N 117 28W
Panão, *Peru* **92 E3** 9 55S 75 55W
Panare, *Thailand* **39 J3** 6 51N 101 30 E
Panay, *Phil.* **37 B6** 11 10N 122 30 E
Panay, G., *Phil.* **37 B6** 11 0N 122 30 E
Pančevo, *Serbia, Yug.* **21 B9** 44 52N 20 41 E
Pandan, *Phil.* **37 B6** 11 45N 122 10 E
Pandegelang, *Indonesia* **37 G12** 6 25S 106 5 E
Pandhana, *India* **42 J7** 21 42N 76 13 E
Pandharpur, *India* **40 L9** 17 41N 75 20 E
Pando, *Uruguay* **95 C4** 34 44S 56 0W
Pando, L. = Hope, L., *Australia* **63 D2** 28 24S 139 18 E
Pandokrátor, *Greece* **23 A3** 39 45N 19 50 E
Pandora, *Costa Rica* **88 E3** 9 43N 83 3W
Panevėžys, *Lithuania* **9 J21** 55 42N 24 25 E
Panfilov, *Kazakstan* **26 E9** 44 10N 80 0 E
Pang-Long, *Burma* **41 H21** 23 11N 98 45 E
Pang-Yang, *Burma* **41 H21** 22 7N 98 48 E
Panga, *Dem. Rep. of the Congo* **54 B2** 1 52N 26 18 E
Pangalanes, Canal des, *Madag.* **57 C8** 22 48S 47 50 E
Pangani, *Tanzania* **54 D4** 5 25S 38 58 E
Pangani →, *Tanzania* **54 D4** 5 26S 38 58 E
Pangfou = Bengbu, *China* **35 H9** 32 58N 117 20 E
Pangil, *Dem. Rep. of the Congo* **54 C2** 3 10S 26 35 E
Pangkah, Tanjung, *Indonesia* **37 G15** 6 51S 112 33 E
Pangkajene, *Indonesia* **37 E5** 4 46S 119 34 E
Pangkalanbrandan, *Indonesia* **36 D1** 4 1N 98 20 E
Pangkalanbuun, *Indonesia* **36 E4** 2 41S 111 37 E

Pangkalpinang, Indonesia . 36 E3 2 0S 106 0 E
Pangnirtung, Canada . 69 B13 66 8N 65 54W
Pangong Tso, India . 42 B8 34 40N 78 40 E
Panguitch, U.S.A. . 83 H7 37 50N 112 26W
Pangutaran Group, Phil. . 37 C6 6 18N 120 34 E
Panhandle, U.S.A. . 81 H4 35 21N 101 23W
Pani Mines, India . 42 H5 22 29N 73 50 E
Pania-Mutombo,
Dem. Rep. of the Congo . 54 D1 5 11S 23 51 E
Panikota I., India . 42 J4 20 46N 71 21 E
Panipat, India . 42 E7 29 25N 77 2 E
Panjal Range, India . 42 C7 32 30N 76 50 E
Panjang, Hon, Vietnam . 39 H4 9 20N 103 28 E
Panjgur, Pakistan . 40 F4 27 0N 64 5 E
Panjim = Panaji, India . 40 M8 15 25N 73 50 E
Panjin, China . 35 D12 41 3N 122 2 E
Panjinad Barrage, Pakistan 40 E7 29 22N 71 15 E
Panjnad →, Pakistan . 42 E4 28 57N 70 30 E
Panjwai, Afghan. . 42 D1 31 26N 65 27 E
Panmunjŏm, N. Korea . 35 F14 37 59N 126 38 E
Panna, India . 43 G9 24 40N 80 15 E
Panna Hills, India . 43 G9 24 40N 81 15 E
Pannawonica, Australia . 60 D2 21 39S 116 19 E
Pano Akil, Pakistan . 42 F3 27 51N 69 7 E
Pano Lefkara, Cyprus . 23 E12 34 53N 33 20 E
Pano Panayia, Cyprus . 23 E11 34 55N 32 38 E
Panorama, Brazil . 95 A5 21 21S 51 51W
Pánormon, Greece . 23 D6 35 25N 24 41 E
Pansemal, India . 42 J6 21 39N 74 42 E
Panshan = Panjin, China . 35 D12 41 3N 122 2 E
Panshi, China . 35 C14 42 58N 126 5 E
Pantanal, Brazil . 92 H7 17 30S 57 40W
Pantar, Indonesia . 37 F6 8 28S 124 10 E
Pante Macassar, Indonesia 37 F6 9 30S 123 58 E
Pantelleria, Italy . 20 F4 36 50N 11 57 E
Pánuco, Mexico . 87 C5 22 0N 98 15W
Paola, Malta . 23 D2 35 52N 14 30 E
Paola, U.S.A. . 80 F7 38 35N 94 53W
Paonia, U.S.A. . 83 G10 38 52N 107 36W
Paoting = Baoding, China . 34 E8 38 50N 115 28 E
Paot'ou = Baotou, China . 34 D6 40 32N 110 2 E
Paoua, C.A.R. . 52 C3 7 9N 16 20 E
Pápa, Hungary . 17 E9 47 22N 17 30 E
Papa Stour, U.K. . 12 A7 60 20N 1 42W
Papa Westray, U.K. . 12 B6 59 20N 2 55W
Papagayo →, Mexico . 87 D5 16 36N 99 43W
Papagayo, G. de, Costa Rica 88 D2 10 30N 85 50W
Papakura, N.Z. . 59 G5 37 4S 174 59 E
Papantla, Mexico . 87 C5 20 30N 97 30W
Papar, Malaysia . 36 C5 5 45N 116 0 E
Papeete, Tahiti . 65 J13 17 32S 149 34W
Paphos, Cyprus . 23 E11 34 46N 32 25 E
Papigochic →, Mexico . 86 B3 29 9N 109 40W
Paposo, Chile . 94 B1 25 0S 70 30W
Papoutsa, Cyprus . 23 E12 34 54N 33 4 E
Papua New Guinea ■,
Oceania . 64 H6 8 0S 145 0 E
Papudo, Chile . 94 C1 32 29S 71 27W
Papun, Burma . 41 K20 18 2N 97 30 E
Papunya, Australia . 60 D5 23 15S 131 54 E
Pará = Belém, Brazil . 93 D9 1 20S 48 30W
Pará □, Brazil . 93 D8 3 20S 52 0W
Paraburdoo, Australia . 60 D2 23 14S 117 32 E
Paracatu, Brazil . 93 G9 17 10S 46 50W
Paracel Is., S. China Sea . 36 A4 15 50N 112 0 E
Parachilna, Australia . 63 E2 31 10S 138 21 E
Parachinar, Pakistan . 42 C4 33 55N 70 5 E
Paradhísi, Greece . 23 C10 36 18N 28 7 E
Paradip, India . 41 J15 20 15N 86 35 E
Paradise, Calif., U.S.A. . 84 F5 39 46N 121 37W
Paradise, Nev., U.S.A. . 85 J11 36 9N 115 10W
Paradise →, Canada . 71 B8 53 27N 57 19W
Paradise Hill, Canada . 73 C7 53 32N 109 28W
Paradise River, Canada . 71 B8 53 27N 57 17W
Paradise Valley, U.S.A. . 82 F5 41 30N 117 32W
Parado, Indonesia . 37 F5 8 42S 118 30 E
Paragould, U.S.A. . 81 G9 36 3N 90 29W
Paragua →, Venezuela . 92 B6 6 55N 62 55W
Paraguaçu →, Brazil . 93 F11 12 45S 38 54W
Paraguaçu Paulista, Brazil . 95 A5 22 22S 50 35W
Paraguaná, Pen. de,
Venezuela . 92 A5 12 0N 70 0W
Paraguarí, Paraguay . 94 B4 25 36S 57 0W
Paraguarí □, Paraguay . 94 B4 26 0S 57 10W
Paraguay ■, S. Amer. . 94 A4 23 0S 57 0W
Paraguay →, Paraguay . 94 B4 27 18S 58 38W
Paraíba = João Pessoa,
Brazil . 93 E12 7 10S 34 52W
Paraíba □, Brazil . 93 E11 7 0S 36 0W
Paraíba do Sul →, Brazil . 95 A7 21 37S 41 3W
Parainen, Finland . 9 F20 60 18N 22 18 E
Paraiso, Mexico . 87 D6 18 24N 93 14W
Parak, Iran . 45 E7 27 38N 52 25 E
Parakou, Benin . 50 G6 9 25N 2 40 E
Paralimni, Cyprus . 23 D12 35 2N 33 58 E
Paramaribo, Surinam . 93 B7 5 50N 55 10W
Paramushir, Ostrov, Russia 27 D16 50 24N 156 0 E
Paran →, Israel . 47 E4 30 20N 35 10 E
Paraná, Argentina . 94 C3 31 45S 60 30W
Paranã, Brazil . 93 F9 12 30S 47 48W
Paraná □, Brazil . 95 A5 24 30S 51 0W
Paraná →, Argentina . 94 C4 33 43S 59 15W
Paranaguá, Brazil . 95 B6 25 30S 48 30W
Paranaíba, Brazil . 93 G8 19 40S 51 11W
Paranaíba →, Brazil . 93 H8 20 6S 51 4W
Paranapanema →, Brazil . 95 A5 22 40S 53 9W
Paranapiacaba, Serra do,
Brazil . 95 A6 24 31S 48 35W
Paranavai, Brazil . 95 A5 23 4S 52 56W
Parang, Jolo, Phil. . 37 C6 5 55N 120 54 E
Parang, Mindanao, Phil. . 37 C6 7 23N 124 16 E
Parângul Mare, Vf., Romania 17 F12 45 20N 23 37 E
Parbati →, India . 42 F6 26 54N 77 53 E
Parbati →, India . 42 G7 25 50N 76 30 E
Parbhani, India . 40 K10 19 8N 76 52 E
Parchim, Germany . 16 B6 53 26N 11 52 E
Pardes Hanna-Karkur, Israel 47 C3 32 28N 34 57 E
Pardo →, Bahia, Brazil . 93 G11 15 40S 39 0W
Pardo →, Mato Grosso,
Brazil . 95 A5 21 46S 52 9W
Pardubice, Czech Rep. . 16 C8 50 3N 15 45 E
Pare, Indonesia . 37 G15 7 43S 112 12 E
Pare Mts., Tanzania . 54 C4 4 0S 37 45 E
Parecis, Serra dos, Brazil . 92 F7 13 0S 60 0W
Paren, Russia . 27 C17 62 30N 163 15 E
Parent, Canada . 70 C5 47 55N 74 35W
Parent, L., Canada . 70 C4 48 31N 77 1W
Parepare, Indonesia . 37 E5 4 0S 119 40 E
Párga, Greece . 21 E9 39 15N 20 29 E
Pargo, Pta. do, Madeira . 22 D2 32 49N 17 17W
Pariaguán, Venezuela . 92 B6 8 51N 64 34W
Paricutín, Cerro, Mexico . 86 D4 19 28N 102 15W
Parigi, Indonesia . 37 E6 0 50S 120 5 E
Parika, Guyana . 92 B7 6 50N 58 20W
Parima, Serra, Brazil . 92 C6 2 30N 64 0W
Parinari, Peru . 92 D4 4 35S 74 25W
Pariñas, Pta., S. Amer. . 90 D2 4 30S 82 0W
Parintins, Brazil . 93 D7 2 40S 56 50W
Pariparit Kyun, Burma . 41 M18 14 55N 93 45 E
Paris, Canada . 78 C4 43 12N 80 25W
Paris, France . 18 B5 48 50N 2 20 E
Paris, Idaho, U.S.A. . 82 E8 42 14N 111 24W
Paris, Ky., U.S.A. . 76 F3 38 13N 84 15W
Paris, Tenn., U.S.A. . 77 G1 36 18N 88 19W
Paris, Tex., U.S.A. . 81 J7 33 40N 95 33W
Parish, U.S.A. . 79 C8 43 25N 76 8W
Parishville, U.S.A. . 79 B10 44 38N 74 49W
Park, U.S.A. . 84 B4 48 45N 122 18W
Park City, U.S.A. . 81 G6 37 48N 97 20W
Park Falls, U.S.A. . 80 C9 45 56N 90 27W
Park Head, Canada . 78 B3 44 36N 81 9W
Park Hills, U.S.A. . 81 G9 37 53N 90 28W
Park Range, U.S.A. . 82 G10 40 0N 106 30W
Park Rapids, U.S.A. . 80 B7 46 55N 95 4W
Park River, U.S.A. . 80 A6 48 24N 97 45W
Park Rynie, S. Africa . 57 E5 30 25S 30 45 E
Parkā Bandar, Iran . 45 E8 25 55N 59 35 E
Parkano, Finland . 9 E20 62 1N 23 0 E
Parker, Ariz., U.S.A. . 85 L12 34 9N 114 17W
Parker, Pa., U.S.A. . 78 E5 41 5N 79 41W
Parker Dam, U.S.A. . 85 L12 34 18N 114 8W
Parkersburg, U.S.A. . 76 F5 39 16N 81 34W
Parkes, Australia . 63 E4 33 9S 148 11 E
Parkfield, U.S.A. . 84 K6 35 54N 120 26W
Parkhill, Canada . 78 C3 43 15N 81 38W
Parkland, U.S.A. . 84 C4 47 9N 122 26W
Parkston, U.S.A. . 80 D6 43 24N 97 59W
Parksville, Canada . 72 D4 49 20N 124 21W
Parla, Spain . 19 B4 40 14N 3 46W
Parma, Italy . 18 D9 44 48N 10 20 E
Parma, Idaho, U.S.A. . 82 E5 43 47N 116 57W
Parma, Ohio, U.S.A. . 78 E3 41 23N 81 43W
Parnaguá, Brazil . 93 F10 10 10S 44 38W
Parnaíba, Brazil . 93 D10 2 54S 41 47W
Parnaíba →, Brazil . 93 D10 3 0S 41 50W
Parnassós, Greece . 21 E10 38 35N 22 30 E
Pärnu, Estonia . 9 G21 58 28N 24 33 E
Paroo →, Australia . 63 E3 31 28S 143 32 E
Páros, Greece . 21 F11 37 5N 25 12 E
Parowan, U.S.A. . 83 H7 37 51N 112 50W
Parral, Chile . 94 D1 36 10S 71 52W
Parras, Mexico . 86 B4 25 30N 102 20W
Parrett →, U.K. . 11 F4 51 12N 3 1W
Parris I., U.S.A. . 77 J5 32 20N 80 41W
Parrsboro, Canada . 71 C7 45 30N 64 25W
Parry I., Canada . 78 A4 45 18N 80 10W
Parry Is., Canada . 4 B2 77 0N 110 0W
Parry Sound, Canada . 78 A5 45 20N 80 0W
Parsnip →, Canada . 72 B4 55 10N 123 2W
Parsons, U.S.A. . 81 G7 37 20N 95 16W
Parsons Ra., Australia . 62 A2 13 30S 135 15 E
Partinico, Italy . 20 E5 38 3N 13 7 E
Partridge I., Canada . 70 A2 55 59N 87 37W
Paru →, Brazil . 93 D8 1 33S 52 38W
Parvān □, Afghan. . 40 B6 35 0N 69 0 E
Parvatipuram, India . 41 K13 18 50N 83 25 E
Parvatsar, India . 42 F6 26 52N 74 49 E
Parys, S. Africa . 56 D4 26 52S 27 29 E
Pas, Pta. des, Spain . 22 C7 38 46N 1 26 E
Pasadena, Canada . 71 C8 49 1N 57 36W
Pasadena, Calif., U.S.A. . 85 L8 34 9N 118 9W
Pasadena, Tex., U.S.A. . 81 L7 29 43N 95 13W
Pasaje →, Argentina . 94 B3 25 39S 63 56W
Pascagoula, U.S.A. . 81 K10 30 21N 88 33W
Pascagoula →, U.S.A. . 81 K10 30 23N 88 37W
Paşcani, Romania . 17 E14 47 14N 26 45 E
Pasco, U.S.A. . 82 C4 46 14N 119 6W
Pasco, Cerro de, Peru . 92 F3 10 45S 76 10W
Pasco I., Australia . 60 D2 20 57S 115 20 E
Pascoag, U.S.A. . 79 E13 41 57N 71 42W
Pascua, I. de, Pac. Oc. . 65 K17 27 0S 109 0W
Pasfield L., Canada . 73 B7 58 24N 105 20W
Pashiwari, Pakistan . 43 B6 34 40N 75 10 E
Pashmakli = Smolyan,
Bulgaria . 21 D11 41 36N 24 38 E
Pasir Mas, Malaysia . 39 J4 6 2N 102 8 E
Pasir Putih, Malaysia . 39 K4 5 50N 102 24 E
Pasirian, Indonesia . 37 H15 8 13S 113 8 E
Pasirkuning, Indonesia . 36 E2 0 30S 104 33 E
Paskūh, Iran . 45 E9 27 34N 61 39 E
Pasley, C., Australia . 61 F3 33 52S 123 35 E
Pašman, Croatia . 16 G8 43 58N 15 20 E
Pasni, Pakistan . 40 G3 25 15N 63 27 E
Paso Cantinela, Mexico . 85 N11 32 33N 115 47W
Paso de Indios, Argentina . 96 E3 43 55S 69 0W
Paso de los Libres,
Argentina . 94 B4 29 44S 57 10W
Paso de los Toros, Uruguay 94 C4 32 45S 56 30W
Paso Robles, U.S.A. . 83 J3 35 38N 120 41W
Paspébiac, Canada . 71 C6 48 3N 65 17W
Pasrur, Pakistan . 42 C6 32 16N 74 43 E
Passage West, Ireland . 13 E3 51 52N 8 21W
Passaic, U.S.A. . 79 F10 40 51N 74 7W
Passau, Germany . 16 D7 48 34N 13 28 E
Passero, C., Italy . 20 F6 36 41N 15 10 E
Passo Fundo, Brazil . 95 B5 28 10S 52 20W
Passos, Brazil . 93 H9 20 45S 46 37W
Pastavy, Belarus . 9 J22 55 4N 26 50 E
Pastaza →, Peru . 92 D3 4 50S 76 52W
Pasto, Colombia . 92 C3 1 13N 77 17W
Pasuruan, Indonesia . 37 G15 7 40S 112 44 E
Patagonia, Argentina . 96 F3 45 0S 69 0W
Patagonia, U.S.A. . 83 L8 31 33N 110 45W
Patambar, Iran . 45 D9 29 45N 60 17 E
Patan, India . 40 H8 23 54N 72 14 E
Patan, Maharashtra, India . 42 H5 23 54N 72 14 E
Patan, Nepal . 41 F14 27 40N 85 20 E
Patani, Indonesia . 37 D7 0 20N 128 50 E
Pataudi, India . 42 E7 28 18N 76 48 E
Patchewollock, Australia . 63 F3 35 22S 142 12 E
Patchogue, U.S.A. . 79 F11 40 46N 73 1W
Patea, N.Z. . 59 H5 39 45S 174 30 E
Patensie, S. Africa . 56 E3 33 46S 24 49 E
Paternò, Italy . 20 F6 37 34N 14 54 E
Pateros, U.S.A. . 82 B4 48 3N 119 54W
Paterson, U.S.A. . 79 F10 40 55N 74 11W
Paterson Ra., Australia . 60 D3 21 45S 122 10 E
Pathankot, India . 42 C6 32 18N 75 45 E
Pathfinder Reservoir, U.S.A. 82 E10 42 28N 106 51W
Pathiu, Thailand . 39 G2 10 42N 99 19 E
Pathum Thani, Thailand . 38 E3 14 1N 100 32 E
Pati, Indonesia . 37 G14 6 45S 111 1 E
Patía →, Colombia . 92 C3 2 13N 78 40W
Patiala, India . 42 D7 30 23N 76 26 E
Patiala, India . 43 F8 27 43N 79 1 E
Patkai Bum, India . 41 F19 27 0N 95 30 E
Pátmos, Greece . 21 F12 37 21N 26 36 E
Patna, India . 43 G11 25 35N 85 12 E
Pato Branco, Brazil . 95 B5 26 13S 52 40W
Patonga, Uganda . 54 B3 2 45N 33 15 E
Patos, Brazil . 93 E11 6 55S 37 16W
Patos, L. dos, Brazil . 95 C5 31 20S 51 0W
Patos, Río de los →,
Argentina . 94 C2 31 18S 69 25W
Patos de Minas, Brazil . 93 G9 18 35S 46 32W
Patquía, Argentina . 94 C2 30 2S 66 55W
Pátrai, Greece . 21 E9 38 14N 21 47 E
Pátraikós Kólpos, Greece . 21 E9 38 17N 21 30 E
Patras = Pátrai, Greece . 21 E9 38 14N 21 47 E
Patrocínio, Brazil . 93 G9 18 57S 47 0W
Patta, Kenya . 54 C5 2 10S 41 0 E
Pattani, Thailand . 39 J3 6 48N 101 15 E
Pattaya, Thailand . 36 B2 12 52N 100 55 E
Patten, U.S.A. . 77 C11 46 0N 68 38W
Patterson, Calif., U.S.A. . 84 H5 37 28N 121 8W
Patterson, La., U.S.A. . 81 L9 29 42N 91 18W
Patterson, Mt., U.S.A. . 84 G7 38 29N 119 20W
Patti, Punjab, India . 42 D6 31 17N 74 54 E
Patti, Ut. P., India . 43 G10 25 55N 82 12 E
Pattoki, Pakistan . 42 D5 31 5N 73 52 E
Patton, U.S.A. . 78 F6 40 38N 78 39W
Patuakhali, Bangla. . 41 H17 22 20N 90 25 E
Patuanak, Canada . 73 B7 55 55N 107 43W
Patuca →, Honduras . 88 C3 15 50N 84 18W
Patuca, Punta, Honduras . 88 C3 15 49N 84 14W
Pátzcuaro, Mexico . 86 D4 19 30N 101 40W
Pau, France . 18 E3 43 19N 0 25W
Pauk, Burma . 41 J19 21 27N 94 30 E
Paul I., Canada . 71 A7 56 30N 61 20W
Paul Smiths, U.S.A. . 79 B10 44 26N 74 15W
Paulatuk, Canada . 68 B7 69 25N 124 0W
Paulis = Isiro,
Dem. Rep. of the Congo . 54 B2 2 53N 27 40 E
Paulistana, Brazil . 93 E10 8 9S 41 9W
Paulo Afonso, Brazil . 93 E11 9 21S 38 15W
Paulpietersburg, S. Africa . 57 D5 27 23S 30 50 E
Pauls Valley, U.S.A. . 81 H6 34 44N 97 13W
Pauma Valley, U.S.A. . 85 M10 33 16N 116 58W
Pauri, India . 43 D8 30 9N 78 47 E
Pāveh, Iran . 44 C5 35 3N 46 22 E
Pavia, Italy . 18 D8 45 7N 9 8 E
Pavilion, U.S.A. . 78 D6 42 52N 78 1W
Pāvilosta, Latvia . 9 H19 56 53N 21 14 E
Pavlodar, Kazakstan . 26 D8 52 33N 77 0 E
Pavlograd = Pavlohrad,
Ukraine . 25 E6 48 30N 35 52 E
Pavlohrad, Ukraine . 25 E6 48 30N 35 52 E
Pavlovo, Russia . 24 C7 55 58N 43 5 E
Pavlovsk, Russia . 25 D7 50 26N 40 5 E
Pavlovskaya, Russia . 25 E6 46 17N 39 47 E
Pawayan, India . 43 E9 28 4N 80 6 E
Pawhuska, U.S.A. . 81 G6 36 40N 96 20W
Pawling, U.S.A. . 79 E11 41 34N 73 36W
Pawnee, U.S.A. . 81 G6 36 20N 96 48W
Pawnee City, U.S.A. . 80 E6 40 7N 96 9W
Pawtucket, U.S.A. . 79 E13 41 53N 71 23W
Paximádhia, Greece . 23 E6 35 0N 24 35 E
Paxoí, Greece . 21 E9 39 14N 20 12 E
Paxton, Ill., U.S.A. . 76 E1 40 27N 88 6W
Paxton, Nebr., U.S.A. . 80 E4 41 7N 101 21W
Payakumbuh, Indonesia . 36 E2 0 20S 100 35 E
Payette, U.S.A. . 82 D5 44 5N 116 56W
Payne Bay = Kangirsuk,
Canada . 69 C13 60 0N 70 0W
Payne L., Canada . 69 C12 59 30N 74 30W
Paynes Find, Australia . 61 E2 29 15S 117 42 E
Paynesville, U.S.A. . 80 C7 45 23N 94 43W
Paysandú, Uruguay . 94 C4 32 19S 58 8W
Payson, Ariz., U.S.A. . 83 J8 34 14N 111 20W
Payson, Utah, U.S.A. . 74 B4 40 3N 111 44W
Paz →, Guatemala . 88 D1 13 44N 90 10W
Paz, B. la, Mexico . 86 C2 24 15N 110 25W
Pāzanān, Iran . 45 D6 30 35N 49 59 E
Pazardzhik, Bulgaria . 21 C11 42 12N 24 20 E
Pe Ell, U.S.A. . 84 D3 46 34N 123 18W
Peabody, U.S.A. . 79 D14 42 31N 70 56W
Peace →, Canada . 72 B6 59 0N 111 25W
Peace Point, Canada . 72 B6 59 7N 112 27W
Peace River, Canada . 72 B5 56 15N 117 18W
Peach Springs, U.S.A. . 83 J7 35 32N 113 25W
Peachland, Canada . 72 D5 49 47N 119 45W
Peachtree City, U.S.A. . 77 J3 33 25N 84 35W
Peak, The = Kinder Scout,
U.K. . 10 D6 53 24N 1 52W
Peak District, U.K. . 10 D6 53 10N 1 50W
Peak Hill, N.S.W., Australia 63 E4 32 47S 148 11 E
Peak Hill, W. Austral.,
Australia . 61 E2 25 35S 118 43 E
Peak Ra., Australia . 62 C4 22 50S 148 20 E
Peake Cr. →, Australia . 63 D2 28 2S 136 7 E
Peale, Mt., U.S.A. . 83 G9 38 26N 109 14W
Pearblossom, U.S.A. . 85 L9 34 30N 117 55W
Pearl →, U.S.A. . 81 K10 30 11N 89 32W
Pearl City, U.S.A. . 74 H16 21 24N 157 59W
Pearl Harbor, U.S.A. . 74 H16 21 21N 157 57W
Pearl River, U.S.A. . 79 E10 41 4N 74 2W
Pearsall, U.S.A. . 81 L5 28 54N 99 6W
Peary Land, Greenland . 4 A6 82 40N 33 0W
Pease →, U.S.A. . 81 H5 34 12N 99 2W
Peawanuck, Canada . 69 C11 55 15N 85 12W
Pebane, Mozam. . 55 F4 17 10S 38 8 E
Pebas, Peru . 92 D4 3 10S 71 46W
Pebble Beach, U.S.A. . 84 J5 36 34N 121 57W
Peć, Yugoslavia . 21 C9 42 40N 20 17 E
Pechenga, Russia . 24 A5 69 29N 31 4 E
Pechenizhyn, Ukraine . 17 D13 48 30N 24 48 E
Pechiguera, Pta., Canary Is. 22 F6 28 51N 13 53W
Pechora, Russia . 24 A10 65 10N 57 11 E
Pechora →, Russia . 24 A9 68 13N 54 15 E
Pechorskaya Guba, Russia . 24 A9 68 40N 54 0 E
Pečory, Russia . 9 H22 57 48N 27 40 E
Pecos, U.S.A. . 81 K3 31 26N 103 30W
Pecos →, U.S.A. . 81 L3 29 42N 101 22W
Pécs, Hungary . 17 E10 46 5N 18 15 E
Pedder, L., Australia . 62 G4 42 55S 146 10 E
Peddie, S. Africa . 57 E4 33 14S 27 7 E
Pédernales, Dom. Rep. . 89 C5 18 2N 71 44W
Pedieos →, Cyprus . 23 D12 35 10N 33 54 E
Pedirka, Australia . 63 D2 26 40S 135 14 E
Pedra Azul, Brazil . 93 G10 16 2S 41 17W
Pedreiras, Brazil . 93 D10 4 32S 44 40W
Pedro Afonso, Brazil . 93 E9 9 0S 48 10W
Pedro Cays, Jamaica . 88 C4 17 5N 77 48W
Pedro de Valdivia, Chile . 94 A2 22 55S 69 38W
Pedro Juan Caballero,
Paraguay . 95 A4 22 30S 55 40W
Pee Dee →, U.S.A. . 77 J6 33 22N 79 16W
Peebinga, Australia . 63 E3 34 52S 140 57 E
Peebles, U.K. . 12 F5 55 40N 3 11W
Peekskill, U.S.A. . 79 E11 41 17N 73 55W
Peel, U.K. . 10 C3 54 13N 4 40W
Peel →, Australia . 63 E5 30 50S 150 29 E
Peel →, Canada . 68 B6 67 0N 135 0W
Peel Sound, Canada . 68 A10 73 0N 96 0W
Peera Peera Poolanna L.,
Australia . 63 D2 26 30S 138 0 E
Peerless Lake, Canada . 72 B6 56 37N 114 40W
Peers, Canada . 72 C5 53 40N 116 0W
Pegasus Bay, N.Z. . 59 K4 43 20S 173 10 E
Pegu, Burma . 41 L20 17 20N 96 29 E
Pegu Yoma, Burma . 41 K20 19 0N 96 0 E
Pehuajó, Argentina . 94 D3 35 45S 62 0W
Pei Xian = Pizhou, China . 34 G9 34 44N 116 55 E
Peine, Chile . 94 A2 23 45S 68 8W
Peine, Germany . 16 B6 52 19N 10 14 E
Peip'ing = Beijing, China . 34 E9 39 55N 116 20 E
Peipus, L. = Chudskoye,
Ozero, Russia . 9 G22 58 13N 27 30 E
Peixe, Brazil . 93 F9 12 0S 48 40W
Peixe →, Brazil . 93 H8 21 31S 51 58W
Pekalongan, Indonesia . 37 G13 6 53S 109 40 E
Pekan, Malaysia . 39 L4 3 30N 103 25 E
Pekanbaru, Indonesia . 36 D2 0 30N 101 15 E
Pekin, U.S.A. . 80 E10 40 35N 89 40W
Peking = Beijing, China . 34 E9 39 55N 116 20 E
Pelabuhan Kelang, Malaysia 39 L3 3 0N 101 23 E
Pelabuhan Ratu, Teluk,
Indonesia . 37 G12 7 5S 106 30 E
Pelabuhanratu, Indonesia . 37 G12 7 0S 106 32 E
Pelagie, Is., Italy . 20 G5 35 39N 12 33 E
Pelaihari, Indonesia . 36 E4 3 55S 114 45 E
Peleaga, Vf., Romania . 17 F12 45 22N 22 55 E
Pelée, Mt., Martinique . 89 D7 14 48N 61 10W
Pelee, Pt., Canada . 70 D3 41 54N 82 31W
Pelee I., Canada . 78 E2 41 47N 82 40W
Pelekech, Kenya . 54 B4 3 52N 35 8 E
Peleng, Indonesia . 37 E6 1 20S 123 30 E
Pelican, U.S.A. . 72 B1 57 58N 136 14W
Pelican L., Canada . 73 C8 52 28N 100 20W
Pelican Narrows, Canada . 73 B8 55 10N 102 56W
Pelješac, Croatia . 20 C7 42 55N 17 25 E
Pelkosenniemi, Finland . 8 C22 67 6N 27 28 E
Pella, S. Africa . 56 D2 29 1S 19 6 E
Pella, U.S.A. . 80 E8 41 25N 92 55W
Pello, Finland . 8 C21 66 47N 23 59 E
Pelly →, Canada . 68 B6 62 47N 137 19W
Pelly Bay, Canada . 69 B11 68 38N 89 50W
Peloponnese =
Pelopónnisos □, Greece . 21 F10 37 10N 22 0 E
Pelopónnisos □, Greece . 21 F10 37 10N 22 0 E
Pelorus Sd., N.Z. . 59 J4 40 59S 173 59 E
Pelotas, Brazil . 95 C5 31 42S 52 23W
Pelotas →, Brazil . 95 B5 27 28S 51 55W
Pelvoux, Massif du, France 18 D7 44 52N 6 20 E
Pemalang, Indonesia . 37 G13 6 53S 109 23 E
Pemanggil, Pulau, Malaysia 39 L5 2 37N 104 21 E
Pematangsiantar, Indonesia 36 D1 2 57N 99 5 E
Pemba, Mozam. . 55 E5 12 58S 40 30 E
Pemba, Zambia . 55 F2 16 30S 27 28 E
Pemba Channel, Tanzania . 54 D4 5 0S 39 37 E
Pemba I., Tanzania . 54 D4 5 0S 39 45 E
Pemberton, Australia . 61 F2 34 30S 116 0 E
Pemberton, Canada . 72 C4 50 25N 122 50W
Pembina, U.S.A. . 80 A6 48 58N 97 15W
Pembroke, Canada . 70 C4 45 50N 77 7W
Pembroke, U.K. . 11 F3 51 41N 4 55W
Pembrokeshire □, U.K. . 11 F3 51 52N 4 56W
Pen-y-Ghent, U.K. . 10 C5 54 10N 2 14W
Penang = Pinang, Malaysia 39 K3 5 25N 100 15 E
Penápolis, Brazil . 95 A6 21 30S 50 0W
Peñarroya-Pueblonuevo,
Spain . 19 C3 38 19N 5 16W
Penarth, U.K. . 11 F4 51 26N 3 11W
Peñas, C. de, Spain . 19 A3 43 42N 5 52W
Penas, G. de, Chile . 96 F2 47 0S 75 0W
Peñas del Chache,
Canary Is. . 22 E6 29 6N 13 33W
Pench'i = Benxi, China . 35 D12 41 20N 123 48 E
Pend Oreille →, U.S.A. . 82 B5 49 4N 117 37W
Pend Oreille, L., U.S.A. . 82 C5 48 10N 116 21W
Pendembu, S. Leone . 50 G3 9 7N 11 14W
Pender B., Australia . 60 C3 16 45S 122 42 E
Pendleton, U.S.A. . 82 D4 45 40N 118 47W
Pendra, India . 43 H9 22 46N 81 57 E
Penedo, Brazil . 93 F11 10 15S 36 36W
Penetanguishene, Canada . 78 B5 44 50N 79 55W
Penfield, U.S.A. . 78 E6 41 13N 78 35W
Pengalengan, Indonesia . 37 G12 7 9S 107 30 E
Penge, Kasai-Or.,
Dem. Rep. of the Congo . 54 D1 5 30S 24 33 E
Penge, Sud-Kivu,
Dem. Rep. of the Congo . 54 C2 4 27S 28 25 E
Penglai, China . 35 F11 37 48N 120 42 E
Penguin, Australia . 62 G4 41 8S 146 6 E
Penhalonga, Zimbabwe . 55 F3 18 52S 32 40 E
Peniche, Portugal . 19 C1 39 19N 9 22W
Penicuik, U.K. . 12 F5 55 50N 3 13W
Penida, Indonesia . 36 F5 8 45S 115 30 E
Peninsular Malaysia □,
Malaysia . 39 L4 4 0N 102 0 E
Penitente, Serra do, Brazil . 93 E9 8 45S 46 20W
Penkridge, U.K. . 10 E5 52 44N 2 6W
Penmarch, Pte. de, France . 18 C1 47 48N 4 22W
Penn Hills, U.S.A. . 78 F5 40 28N 79 52W

Penn Yan, *U.S.A.* **78 D7** 42 40N 77 3W
Pennant, *Canada* **73 C7** 50 32N 108 14W
Penner →, *India* **40 M12** 14 35N 80 10 E
Pennines, *U.K.* **10 C5** 54 45N 2 27W
Pennington, *U.S.A.* **84 F5** 39 15N 121 47W
Pennsburg, *U.S.A.* **79 F9** 40 23N 75 29W
Pennsylvania □, *U.S.A.* **76 E7** 40 45N 77 30W
Penny, *Canada* **72 C4** 53 51N 121 20W
Penobscot →, *U.S.A.* **77 C11** 44 30N 68 48W
Penobscot B., *U.S.A.* **77 C11** 44 35N 68 50W
Penola, *Australia* **63 F3** 37 25S 140 48 E
Penong, *Australia* **61 F5** 31 56S 133 1 E
Penonomé, *Panama* **88 E3** 8 31N 80 21W
Penrith, *Australia* **63 E5** 33 43S 150 38 E
Penrith, *U.K.* **10 C5** 54 40N 2 45W
Penryn, *U.K.* **11 G2** 50 9N 5 7W
Pensacola, *U.S.A.* **77 K2** 30 25N 87 13W
Pensacola Mts., *Antarctica* **5 E1** 84 0S 40 0W
Pense, *Canada* **73 C8** 50 25N 104 59W
Penshurst, *Australia* **63 F3** 37 49S 142 20 E
Penticton, *Canada* **72 D5** 49 30N 119 38W
Pentland, *Australia* **62 C4** 20 32S 145 25 E
Pentland Firth, *U.K.* **12 C5** 58 43N 3 10W
Pentland Hills, *U.K.* **12 F5** 55 48N 3 25W
Penza, *Russia* **24 D8** 53 15N 45 5 E
Penzance, *U.K.* **11 G2** 50 7N 5 33W
Penzhino, *Russia* **27 C17** 63 30N 167 55 E
Penzhinskaya Guba, *Russia* **27 C17** 61 30N 163 0 E
Peoria, *Ariz., U.S.A.* **83 K7** 33 35N 112 14W
Peoria, *Ill., U.S.A.* **80 E10** 40 42N 89 36W
Pepacton Reservoir, *U.S.A.* **79 D10** 42 5N 74 58W
Pera Hd., *Australia* **62 A3** 12 55S 141 37 E
Perabumulih, *Indonesia* **36 E2** 3 27S 104 15 E
Perak →, *Malaysia* **39 K3** 4 0N 100 50 E
Pérama, *Kérkira, Greece* **23 A3** 39 34N 19 54 E
Pérama, *Kríti, Greece* **23 D6** 35 20N 24 40 E
Peräpohjola, *Finland* **8 C22** 66 16N 26 10 E
Percé, *Canada* **71 C7** 48 31N 64 13W
Perche, Collines du, *France* **18 B4** 48 30N 0 40 E
Percival Lakes, *Australia* **60 D4** 21 25S 125 0 E
Percy Is., *Australia* **62 C5** 21 39S 150 16 E
Perdido, Mte., *Spain* **19 A6** 42 40N 0 5 E
Perdu, Mt. = Perdido, Mte., *Spain* **19 A6** 42 40N 0 5 E
Pereira, *Colombia* **92 C3** 4 49N 75 43W
Perenjori, *Australia* **61 E2** 29 26S 116 16 E
Pereyaslav-Khmelnytskyy, *Ukraine* **25 D5** 50 3N 31 28 E
Pérez, I., *Mexico* **87 C7** 22 24N 89 42W
Pergamino, *Argentina* **94 C3** 33 52S 60 30W
Pergau →, *Malaysia* **39 K3** 5 23N 102 2 E
Perham, *U.S.A.* **80 B7** 46 36N 95 34W
Perhentian, Kepulauan, *Malaysia* **36 C2** 5 54N 102 42 E
Péribonca →, *Canada* **71 C5** 48 45N 72 5W
Péribonca, L., *Canada* **71 B5** 50 1N 71 10W
Perico, *Argentina* **94 A2** 24 20S 65 5W
Pericos, *Mexico* **86 B3** 25 3N 107 42W
Périgueux, *France* **18 D4** 45 10N 0 42 E
Perijá, Sierra de, *Colombia* **92 B4** 9 30N 73 3W
Peristerona →, *Cyprus* **23 D12** 35 8N 33 5 E
Perito Moreno, *Argentina* **96 F2** 46 36S 70 56W
Perkasie, *U.S.A.* **79 F9** 40 22N 75 18W
Perlas, Arch. de las, *Panama* **88 E4** 8 41N 79 7W
Perlas, Punta de, *Nic.* **88 D3** 12 30N 83 30W
Perm, *Russia* **24 C10** 58 0N 56 10 E
Pernambuco = Recife, *Brazil* **93 E12** 8 0S 35 0W
Pernambuco □, *Brazil* **93 E11** 8 0S 37 0W
Pernatty Lagoon, *Australia* **63 E2** 31 30S 137 12 E
Pernik, *Bulgaria* **21 C10** 42 35N 23 2 E
Peron Is., *Australia* **60 B5** 13 9S 130 4 E
Peron Pen., *Australia* **61 E1** 26 0S 113 10 E
Perow, *Canada* **72 C3** 54 35N 126 10W
Perpendicular Pt., *Australia* **63 E5** 31 37S 152 52 E
Perpignan, *France* **18 E5** 42 42N 2 53 E
Perris, *U.S.A.* **85 M9** 33 47N 117 14W
Perry, *Fla., U.S.A.* **77 K4** 30 7N 83 35W
Perry, *Ga., U.S.A.* **77 J4** 32 28N 83 44W
Perry, *Iowa, U.S.A.* **80 E7** 41 51N 94 6W
Perry, *Okla., U.S.A.* **81 G6** 36 17N 97 14W
Perryton, *U.S.A.* **81 G4** 36 24N 100 48W
Perryville, *U.S.A.* **81 G10** 37 43N 89 52W
Persepolis, *Iran* **45 D7** 29 55N 52 50 E
Pershotravensk, *Ukraine* **17 C14** 50 13N 27 40 E
Persia = Iran ■, *Asia* **45 C7** 33 0N 53 0 E
Persian Gulf = Gulf, The, *Asia* **45 E6** 27 0N 50 0 E
Perth, *Australia* **61 F2** 31 57S 115 52 E
Perth, *Canada* **79 B8** 44 55N 76 15W
Perth, *U.K.* **12 E5** 56 24N 3 26W
Perth & Kinross □, *U.K.* **12 E5** 56 45N 3 55W
Perth Amboy, *U.S.A.* **79 F10** 40 31N 74 16W
Perth-Andover, *Canada* **71 C6** 46 44N 67 42W
Peru, *Ind., U.S.A.* **76 E2** 40 45N 86 4W
Peru, *N.Y., U.S.A.* **79 B11** 44 35N 73 32W
Peru ■, *S. Amer.* **92 D4** 4 0S 75 0W
Peru-Chile Trench, *Pac. Oc.* **92 G3** 20 0S 72 0W
Perúgia, *Italy* **20 C5** 43 7N 12 23 E
Pervomaysk, *Ukraine* **25 E5** 48 10N 30 46 E
Pervouralsk, *Russia* **24 C10** 56 59N 59 59 E
Pésaro, *Italy* **20 C5** 43 54N 12 55 E
Pescara, *Italy* **20 C6** 42 28N 14 13 E
Peshawar, *Pakistan* **42 B4** 34 2N 71 37 E
Peshkopi, *Albania* **21 D9** 41 41N 20 25 E
Peshtigo, *U.S.A.* **76 C2** 45 4N 87 46W
Pesqueira, *Brazil* **93 E11** 8 20S 36 42W
Petah Tiqwa, *Israel* **47 C3** 32 6N 34 53 E
Petaling Jaya, *Malaysia* **39 L3** 3 4N 101 42 E
Petaloudhes, *Greece* **23 C10** 36 18N 28 5 E
Petaluma, *U.S.A.* **84 G4** 38 14N 122 39W
Pétange, *Lux.* **15 E5** 49 33N 5 55 E
Petaro, *Pakistan* **42 G3** 25 31N 68 18 E
Petatlán, *Mexico* **86 D4** 17 31N 101 16W
Petauke, *Zambia* **55 E3** 14 14S 31 20 E
Petawawa, *Canada* **70 C4** 45 54N 77 17W
Petén Itzá, L., *Guatemala* **88 C2** 16 58N 89 50W
Peter I.s Øy, *Antarctica* **5 C16** 69 0S 91 0W
Peter Pond L., *Canada* **73 B7** 55 55N 108 44W
Peterbell, *Canada* **70 C3** 48 36N 83 21W
Peterborough, *Australia* **63 E2** 32 58S 138 51 E
Peterborough, *Canada* **78 B6** 44 20N 78 20W
Peterborough, *U.K.* **11 E7** 52 35N 0 15W
Peterborough, *U.S.A.* **79 D13** 42 53N 71 57W
Peterborough □, *U.K.* **11 E7** 52 35N 0 15W
Peterculter, *U.K.* **12 D6** 57 6N 2 16W
Peterhead, *U.K.* **12 D7** 57 31N 1 48W
Peterlee, *U.K.* **10 C6** 54 47N 1 20W
Petermann Bjerg, *Greenland* **66 B17** 73 7N 28 25W
Petermann Ranges, *Australia* **60 E5** 26 0S 130 30 E
Petersburg, *Alaska, U.S.A.* **68 C6** 56 48N 132 58W
Petersburg, *Pa., U.S.A.* **78 F6** 40 34N 78 3W
Petersburg, *Va., U.S.A.* **76 G7** 37 14N 77 24W
Petersburg, *W. Va., U.S.A.* **76 F6** 39 1N 79 5W
Petersfield, *U.K.* **11 F7** 51 1N 0 56W
Petit Goâve, *Haiti* **89 C5** 18 27N 72 51W
Petit Jardin, *Canada* **71 C8** 48 28N 59 14W
Petit Lac Manicouagan, *Canada* **71 B6** 51 25N 67 40W
Petit-Mécatina →, *Canada* **71 B8** 50 40N 59 30W
Petit-Mécatina, I. du, *Canada* **71 B8** 50 30N 59 25W
Petitcodiac, *Canada* **71 C6** 45 57N 65 11W
Petite Baleine →, *Canada* **70 A4** 56 0N 76 45W
Petite Saguenay, *Canada* **71 C5** 48 15N 70 4W
Petitot →, *Canada* **72 A4** 60 14N 123 29W
Petitsikapau L., *Canada* **71 B6** 54 37N 66 25W
Petlad, *India* **42 H5** 22 30N 72 45 E
Peto, *Mexico* **87 C7** 20 10N 88 53W
Petone, *N.Z.* **59 J5** 41 13S 174 53 E
Petorca, *Chile* **94 C1** 32 15S 70 56W
Petoskey, *U.S.A.* **76 C3** 45 22N 84 57W
Petra, *Jordan* **47 E4** 30 20N 35 22 E
Petra, *Spain* **22 B10** 39 37N 3 6 E
Petra, Ostrova, *Russia* **4 B13** 76 15N 118 30 E
Petra Velikogo, Zaliv, *Russia* **30 C6** 42 40N 132 0 E
Petrich, *Bulgaria* **21 D10** 41 24N 23 13 E
Petrified Forest National Park, *U.S.A.* **83 J9** 35 0N 109 30W
Petrikov = Pyetrikaw, *Belarus* **17 B15** 52 11N 28 29 E
Petrograd = Sankt-Peterburg, *Russia* **24 C5** 59 55N 30 20 E
Petrolândia, *Brazil* **93 E11** 9 5S 38 20W
Petrolia, *Canada* **78 D2** 42 54N 82 9W
Petrolina, *Brazil* **93 E10** 9 24S 40 30W
Petropavl, *Kazakstan* **26 D7** 54 53N 69 13 E
Petropavlovsk = Petropavl, *Kazakstan* **26 D7** 54 53N 69 13 E
Petropavlovsk-Kamchatskiy, *Russia* **27 D16** 53 3N 158 43 E
Petrópolis, *Brazil* **95 A7** 22 33S 43 9W
Petroşani, *Romania* **17 F12** 45 28N 23 20 E
Petrovaradin, *Serbia, Yug.* **21 B8** 45 16N 19 55 E
Petrovsk, *Russia* **24 D8** 52 22N 45 19 E
Petrovsk-Zabaykalskiy, *Russia* **27 D11** 51 20N 108 55 E
Petrozavodsk, *Russia* **24 B5** 61 41N 34 20 E
Petrus Steyn, *S. Africa* **57 D4** 27 38S 28 8 E
Petrusburg, *S. Africa* **56 D4** 29 4S 25 26 E
Peumo, *Chile* **94 C1** 34 21S 71 12W
Peureulak, *Indonesia* **36 D1** 4 48N 97 45 E
Pevek, *Russia* **27 C18** 69 41N 171 19 E
Pforzheim, *Germany* **16 D5** 48 52N 8 41 E
Phagwara, *India* **40 D9** 31 10N 75 40 E
Phaistós, *Greece* **23 D6** 35 2N 24 50 E
Phala, *Botswana* **56 C4** 23 45S 26 50 E
Phalera = Phulera, *India* **42 F6** 26 52N 75 16 E
Phalodi, *India* **42 F5** 27 12N 72 24 E
Phan, *Thailand* **38 C2** 19 28N 99 43 E
Phan Rang, *Vietnam* **39 G7** 11 34N 109 0 E
Phan Ri = Hoa Da, *Vietnam* **39 G7** 11 16N 108 40 E
Phan Thiet, *Vietnam* **39 G7** 11 1N 108 9 E
Phanat Nikhom, *Thailand* **38 F3** 13 27N 101 11 E
Phangan, Ko, *Thailand* **39 H3** 9 45N 100 0 E
Phangnga, *Thailand* **39 H2** 8 28N 98 30 E
Phanh Bho Ho Chi Minh, *Vietnam* **39 G6** 10 58N 106 40 E
Phanom Sarakham, *Thailand* **38 F3** 13 45N 101 21 E
Phaphund, *India* **43 F8** 26 36N 79 28 E
Pharenda, *India* **43 F10** 27 5N 83 17 E
Pharr, *U.S.A.* **81 M5** 26 12N 98 11W
Phatthalung, *Thailand* **39 J3** 7 39N 100 6 E
Phayao, *Thailand* **38 C2** 19 11N 99 55 E
Phelps, *U.S.A.* **78 D7** 42 58N 77 3W
Phelps L., *Canada* **73 B8** 59 15N 103 15W
Phenix City, *U.S.A.* **77 J3** 32 28N 85 0W
Phet Buri, *Thailand* **38 F2** 13 1N 99 55 E
Phetchabun, *Thailand* **38 D3** 16 25N 101 8 E
Phetchabun, Thiu Khao, *Thailand* **38 E3** 16 0N 101 20 E
Phetchaburi = Phet Buri, *Thailand* **38 F2** 13 1N 99 55 E
Phi Phi, Ko, *Thailand* **39 J2** 7 45N 98 46 E
Phiafay, *Laos* **38 E6** 14 48N 106 0 E
Phibun Mangsahan, *Thailand* **38 E5** 15 14N 105 14 E
Phichai, *Thailand* **38 D3** 17 22N 100 10 E
Phichit, *Thailand* **38 D3** 16 26N 100 22 E
Philadelphia, *Miss., U.S.A.* **81 J10** 32 46N 89 7W
Philadelphia, *N.Y., U.S.A.* **79 B9** 44 9N 75 43W
Philadelphia, *Pa., U.S.A.* **79 G9** 39 57N 75 10W
Philip, *U.S.A.* **80 C4** 44 2N 101 40W
Philippeville, *Belgium* **15 D4** 50 12N 4 33 E
Philippi, *U.S.A.* **76 F5** 39 9N 80 3W
Philippi L., *Australia* **62 C2** 24 20S 138 55 E
Philippines ■, *Asia* **37 B6** 12 0N 123 0 E
Philippolis, *S. Africa* **56 E4** 30 15S 25 16 E
Philippopolis = Plovdiv, *Bulgaria* **21 C11** 42 8N 24 44 E
Philipsburg, *Canada* **79 A11** 45 2N 73 5W
Philipsburg, *Mont., U.S.A.* **82 C7** 46 20N 113 18W
Philipsburg, *Pa., U.S.A.* **78 F6** 40 54N 78 13W
Philipstown = Daingean, *Ireland* **13 C4** 53 18N 7 17W
Philipstown, *S. Africa* **56 E3** 30 28S 24 30 E
Phillip I., *Australia* **63 F4** 38 30S 145 12 E
Phillips, *U.S.A.* **80 C9** 45 42N 90 24W
Phillipsburg, *Kans., U.S.A.* **80 F5** 39 45N 99 19W
Phillipsburg, *N.J., U.S.A.* **79 F9** 40 42N 75 12W
Philmont, *U.S.A.* **79 D11** 42 15N 73 39W
Philomath, *U.S.A.* **82 D2** 44 32N 123 22W
Phimai, *Thailand* **38 E4** 15 13N 102 30 E
Phitsanulok, *Thailand* **38 D3** 16 50N 100 12 E
Phnom Dangrek, *Thailand* **36 B2** 14 20N 104 0 E
Phnom Penh, *Cambodia* **39 G5** 11 33N 104 55 E
Phnum Penh = Phnom Penh, *Cambodia* **39 G5** 11 33N 104 55 E
Phoenicia, *U.S.A.* **79 D10** 42 5N 74 14W
Phoenix, *Ariz., U.S.A.* **83 K7** 33 27N 112 4W
Phoenix, *N.Y., U.S.A.* **79 C8** 43 14N 76 18W
Phoenix Is., *Kiribati* **64 H10** 3 30S 172 0W
Phoenixville, *U.S.A.* **79 F9** 40 8N 75 31W
Phon, *Thailand* **38 E4** 15 49N 102 36 E
Phon Tiou, *Laos* **38 D5** 17 53N 104 37 E
Phong →, *Thailand* **38 D4** 16 23N 102 56 E
Phong Tho, *Vietnam* **38 A4** 22 32N 103 21 E
Phonhong, *Laos* **38 C4** 18 30N 102 25 E
Phonum, *Thailand* **39 H2** 8 49N 98 48 E
Phosphate Hill, *Australia* **62 C2** 21 53S 139 58 E
Photharam, *Thailand* **38 F2** 13 41N 99 51 E
Phra Nakhon Si Ayutthaya, *Thailand* **38 E3** 14 25N 100 30 E
Phra Thong, Ko, *Thailand* **39 H2** 9 5N 98 17 E
Phrae, *Thailand* **38 C3** 18 7N 100 9 E
Phrom Phiram, *Thailand* **38 D3** 17 2N 100 12 E
Phu Dien, *Vietnam* **38 C5** 18 58N 105 31 E
Phu Loi, *Laos* **38 B4** 20 14N 103 14 E
Phu Quoc, Dao, *Vietnam* **39 G4** 10 20N 104 0 E
Phuket, *Thailand* **39 J2** 7 52N 98 22 E
Phuket, Ko, *Thailand* **39 J2** 8 0N 98 22 E
Phul, *India* **42 D6** 30 19N 75 14 E
Phulad, *India* **42 G5** 25 38N 73 49 E
Phulchari, *Bangla.* **43 G13** 25 11N 89 37 E
Phulera, *India* **42 F6** 26 52N 75 16 E
Phulpur, *India* **43 G10** 25 31N 82 49 E
Phun Phin, *Thailand* **39 H2** 9 7N 99 12 E
Piacenza, *Italy* **18 D8** 45 1N 9 40 E
Pian Cr. →, *Australia* **63 E4** 30 2S 148 12 E
Pianosa, *Italy* **20 C4** 42 35N 10 5 E
Piapot, *Canada* **73 D7** 49 59N 109 8W
Piatra Neamţ, *Romania* **17 E14** 46 56N 26 21 E
Piauí □, *Brazil* **93 E10** 7 0S 43 0W
Piaui →, *Brazil* **93 E10** 6 38S 42 42W
Piave →, *Italy* **20 B5** 45 32N 12 44 E
Pibor Post, *Sudan* **51 G12** 6 47N 33 3 E
Picardie, *France* **18 B5** 49 50N 3 0 E
Picardy = Picardie, *France* **18 B5** 49 50N 3 0 E
Picayune, *U.S.A.* **81 K10** 30 32N 89 41W
Pichhor, *India* **43 G8** 25 58N 78 20 E
Pichilemu, *Chile* **94 C1** 34 22S 72 0W
Pichor, *India* **42 G8** 25 11N 78 11 E
Pickerel L., *Canada* **70 C1** 48 40N 91 25W
Pickering, *U.K.* **10 C7** 54 15N 0 46W
Pickering, Vale of, *U.K.* **10 C7** 54 14N 0 45W
Pickle Lake, *Canada* **70 B1** 51 30N 90 12W
Pickwick L., *U.S.A.* **77 H1** 35 4N 88 15W
Pico Truncado, *Argentina* **96 F3** 46 40S 68 0W
Picos, *Brazil* **93 E10** 7 5S 41 28W
Picton, *Australia* **63 E5** 34 12S 150 34 E
Picton, *Canada* **78 B7** 44 1N 77 9W
Picton, *N.Z.* **59 J5** 41 18S 174 3 E
Pictou, *Canada* **71 C7** 45 41N 62 42W
Picture Butte, *Canada* **72 D6** 49 55N 112 45W
Picún Leufú, *Argentina* **96 D3** 39 30S 69 5W
Pidurutalagala, *Sri Lanka* **40 R12** 7 10N 80 50 E
Piedmont = Piemonte □, *Italy* **18 D7** 45 0N 8 0 E
Piedmont, *Ala., U.S.A.* **77 J3** 33 55N 85 37W
Piedmont, *S.C., U.S.A.* **75 D10** 34 0N 81 30W
Piedras Negras, *Mexico* **86 B4** 28 42N 100 31W
Pieksämäki, *Finland* **9 E22** 62 18N 27 10 E
Piemonte □, *Italy* **18 D7** 45 0N 8 0 E
Piercefield, *U.S.A.* **79 B10** 44 13N 74 35W
Pierceland, *Canada* **73 C7** 54 20N 109 46W
Pierpont, *U.S.A.* **78 E4** 41 45N 80 34W
Pierre, *U.S.A.* **80 C4** 44 22N 100 21W
Piet Retief, *S. Africa* **57 D5** 27 1S 30 50 E
Pietarsaari, *Finland* **8 E20** 63 40N 22 43 E
Pietermaritzburg, *S. Africa* **57 D5** 29 35S 30 25 E
Pietersburg, *S. Africa* **57 C4** 23 54S 29 25 E
Pietrosul, Vf., *Maramureş, Romania* **17 E13** 47 35N 24 43 E
Pietrosul, Vf., *Suceava, Romania* **17 E13** 47 12N 25 18 E
Pigeon L., *Canada* **78 B6** 44 27N 78 30W
Piggott, *U.S.A.* **81 G9** 36 23N 90 11W
Pigüe, *Argentina* **94 D3** 37 36S 62 25W
Pihani, *India* **43 F9** 27 36N 80 15 E
Pihlajavesi, *Finland* **9 F23** 61 45N 28 45 E
Pijijiapan, *Mexico* **87 D6** 15 42N 93 14W
Pikangikum Berens, *Canada* **73 C10** 51 49N 94 0W
Pikes Peak, *U.S.A.* **80 F2** 38 50N 105 3W
Piketberg, *S. Africa* **56 E2** 32 55S 18 40 E
Pikeville, *U.S.A.* **76 G4** 37 29N 82 31W
Pikou, *China* **35 E12** 39 18N 122 22 E
Pikwitonei, *Canada* **73 B9** 55 35N 97 9W
Piła, *Poland* **17 B9** 53 10N 16 48 E
Pilani, *India* **42 E6** 28 22N 75 33 E
Pilar, *Paraguay* **94 B4** 26 50S 58 20W
Pilaya →, *Bolivia* **92 H6** 20 55S 64 4W
Pilbara, *Australia* **60 D2** 23 35S 117 25 E
Pilcomayo →, *Paraguay* **94 B4** 25 21S 57 42W
Pilibhit, *India* **43 E8** 28 40N 79 50 E
Pilica →, *Poland* **17 C11** 51 52N 21 17 E
Pilkhawa, *India* **42 E7** 28 43N 77 42 E
Pilliga, *Australia* **63 E4** 30 21S 148 54 E
Pílos, *Greece* **21 F9** 36 55N 21 42 E
Pilot Mound, *Canada* **73 D9** 49 15N 98 54W
Pilot Point, *U.S.A.* **81 J6** 33 24N 96 58W
Pilot Rock, *U.S.A.* **82 D4** 45 29N 118 50W
Pilsen = Plzeň, *Czech Rep.* **16 D7** 49 45N 13 22 E
Pima, *U.S.A.* **83 K9** 32 54N 109 50W
Pimba, *Australia* **63 E2** 31 18S 136 46 E
Pimenta Bueno, *Brazil* **92 F6** 11 35S 61 10W
Pimentel, *Peru* **92 E3** 6 45S 79 55W
Pinang, *Malaysia* **39 K3** 5 25N 100 15 E
Pinar, C. des, *Spain* **22 B10** 39 53N 3 12 E
Pinar del Río, *Cuba* **88 B3** 22 26N 83 40W
Pınarhisar, *Turkey* **21 D12** 41 37N 27 30 E
Pinatubo, *Phil.* **37 A6** 15 8N 120 21 E
Pincher Creek, *Canada* **72 D6** 49 30N 113 57W
Pinchi L., *Canada* **72 C4** 54 38N 124 30W
Pinckneyville, *U.S.A.* **80 F10** 38 5N 89 23W
Pińczów, *Poland* **17 C11** 50 32N 20 32 E
Pindar, *Australia* **61 E2** 28 30S 115 47 E
Pindi Gheb, *Pakistan* **42 C5** 33 14N 72 21 E
Pindos Óros, *Greece* **21 E9** 40 0N 21 0 E
Pindus Mts. = Pindos Óros, *Greece* **21 E9** 40 0N 21 0 E
Pine →, *B.C., Canada* **72 B4** 56 8N 120 43W
Pine →, *Sask., Canada* **73 B7** 58 50N 105 38W
Pine, C., *Canada* **71 C9** 46 37N 53 32W
Pine Bluff, *U.S.A.* **81 H9** 34 13N 92 1W
Pine Bluffs, *U.S.A.* **80 E2** 41 11N 104 4W
Pine City, *U.S.A.* **80 C8** 45 50N 92 59W
Pine Cr. →, *U.S.A.* **78 E7** 41 10N 77 16W
Pine Creek, *Australia* **60 B5** 13 50S 131 50 E
Pine Falls, *Canada* **73 C9** 50 34N 96 11W
Pine Flat Res., *U.S.A.* **84 J7** 36 50N 119 20W
Pine Grove, *U.S.A.* **79 F8** 40 33N 76 23W
Pine Pass, *Canada* **72 B4** 55 25N 122 42W
Pine Point, *Canada* **72 A6** 60 50N 114 28W
Pine Ridge, *U.S.A.* **80 D3** 43 2N 102 33W
Pine River, *Canada* **73 C8** 51 45N 100 30W
Pine River, *U.S.A.* **80 B7** 46 43N 94 24W
Pine Valley, *U.S.A.* **85 N10** 32 50N 116 32W
Pinecrest, *U.S.A.* **84 G6** 38 12N 120 1W
Pinedale, *Calif., U.S.A.* **84 J7** 36 50N 119 48W
Pinedale, *Wyo., U.S.A.* **82 E9** 42 52N 109 52W
Pinega →, *Russia* **24 B8** 64 30N 44 19 E
Pinehill, *Australia* **62 C4** 23 38S 146 57 E
Pinehouse L., *Canada* **73 B7** 55 32N 106 35W
Pineimuta →, *Canada* **70 B1** 52 8N 88 33W
Pinerolo, *Italy* **18 D7** 44 53N 7 21 E
Pinetop, *U.S.A.* **83 J9** 34 8N 109 56W
Pinetown, *S. Africa* **57 D5** 29 48S 30 54 E
Pineville, *U.S.A.* **81 K8** 31 19N 92 26W
Ping →, *Thailand* **38 E3** 15 42N 100 9 E
Pingaring, *Australia* **61 F2** 32 40S 118 32 E
Pingding, *China* **34 F7** 37 47N 113 38 E
Pingdingshan, *China* **34 H7** 33 43N 113 27 E
Pingdong, *Taiwan* **33 D7** 22 39N 120 30 E
Pingdu, *China* **35 F10** 36 42N 119 59 E
Pingelly, *Australia* **61 F2** 32 32S 117 5 E
Pingliang, *China* **34 G4** 35 35N 106 31 E
Pinglu, *China* **34 E7** 39 31N 112 30 E
Pingluo, *China* **34 E4** 38 52N 106 30 E
Pingquan, *China* **35 D10** 41 1N 118 37 E
Pingrup, *Australia* **61 F2** 33 32S 118 29 E
P'ingtung, *Taiwan* **33 D7** 22 38N 120 30 E
Pingwu, *China* **34 H3** 32 25N 104 30 E
Pingxiang, *China* **32 D5** 22 6N 106 46 E
Pingyao, *China* **34 F7** 37 12N 112 10 E
Pingyi, *China* **35 G9** 35 30N 117 35 E
Pingyin, *China* **34 F9** 36 20N 116 25 E
Pingyuan, *China* **34 F9** 37 10N 116 22 E
Pinhal, *Brazil* **95 A6** 22 10S 46 46W
Pinheiro, *Brazil* **93 D9** 2 31S 45 5W
Pinheiro Machado, *Brazil* **95 C5** 31 34S 53 23W
Pinhel, *Portugal* **19 B2** 40 50N 7 1W
Pini, *Indonesia* **36 D1** 0 10N 98 40 E
Piniós →, *Greece* **21 E10** 39 55N 22 41 E
Pinjarra, *Australia* **61 F2** 32 37S 115 52 E
Pink Mountain, *Canada* **72 B4** 57 3N 122 52W
Pinnacles, *U.S.A.* **84 J5** 36 33N 121 19W
Pinnaroo, *Australia* **63 F3** 35 17S 140 53 E
Pinnes, Ákra, *Greece* **21 D11** 40 5N 24 20 E
Pinon Hills, *U.S.A.* **85 L9** 34 26N 117 39W
Pinos, *Mexico* **86 C4** 22 20N 101 40W
Pinos, Mt., *U.S.A.* **85 L7** 34 49N 119 8W
Pinos Pt., *U.S.A.* **83 H3** 36 38N 121 57W
Pinotepa Nacional, *Mexico* **87 D5** 16 19N 98 3W
Pinrang, *Indonesia* **37 E5** 3 46S 119 41 E
Pins, Pte. aux, *Canada* **78 D3** 42 15N 81 51W
Pinsk, *Belarus* **17 B14** 52 10N 26 1 E
Pintados, *Chile* **92 H5** 20 35S 69 40W
Pinyug, *Russia* **24 B8** 60 5N 48 0 E
Pioche, *U.S.A.* **83 H6** 37 56N 114 27W
Piombino, *Italy* **20 C4** 42 55N 10 32 E
Pioner, Ostrov, *Russia* **27 B10** 79 50N 92 0 E
Piorini, L., *Brazil* **92 D6** 3 15S 62 35W
Piotrków Trybunalski, *Poland* **17 C10** 51 23N 19 43 E
Pīp, *Iran* **45 E9** 26 45N 60 10 E
Pipar, *India* **42 F5** 26 25N 73 31 E
Pipar Road, *India* **42 F5** 26 27N 73 27 E
Piparia, *Mad. P., India* **42 H8** 22 45N 78 23 E
Piparia, *Mad. P., India* **42 J7** 21 49N 77 37 E
Pipestone, *U.S.A.* **80 D6** 44 0N 96 19W
Pipestone →, *Canada* **70 B2** 52 53N 89 23W
Pipestone Cr. →, *Canada* **73 D8** 49 38N 100 15W
Piplan, *Pakistan* **42 C4** 32 17N 71 21 E
Piploda, *India* **42 H6** 23 37N 74 56 E
Pipmuacan, Rés., *Canada* **71 C5** 49 45N 70 30W
Pippingarra, *Australia* **60 D2** 20 27S 118 42 E
Piqua, *U.S.A.* **76 E3** 40 9N 84 15W
Piquiri →, *Brazil* **95 A5** 24 3S 54 14W
Pīr Sohrāb, *Iran* **45 E9** 25 44N 60 54 E
Piracicaba, *Brazil* **95 A6** 22 45S 47 40W
Piracuruca, *Brazil* **93 D10** 3 50S 41 50W
Piræus = Piraiévs, *Greece* **21 F10** 37 57N 23 42 E
Piraiévs, *Greece* **21 F10** 37 57N 23 42 E
Pirajuí, *Brazil* **95 A6** 21 59S 49 29W
Piram I., *India* **42 J5** 21 36N 72 21 E
Piranè, *Argentina* **94 B4** 25 42S 59 6W
Pirapora, *Brazil* **93 G10** 17 20S 44 56W
Pirawa, *India* **42 G7** 24 10N 76 2 E
Pirgos, *Greece* **21 F9** 37 40N 21 27 E
Piribebuy, *Paraguay* **94 B4** 25 26S 57 2W
Pirimapun, *Indonesia* **37 F9** 6 45S 138 0 E
Pirin Planina, *Bulgaria* **21 D10** 41 40N 23 30 E
Pírineos = Pyrénées, *Europe* **18 E4** 42 45N 0 18 E
Piripiri, *Brazil* **93 D10** 4 15S 41 46W
Pirmasens, *Germany* **16 D4** 49 12N 7 36 E
Pirot, *Serbia, Yug.* **21 C10** 43 9N 22 33 E
Piru, *Indonesia* **37 E7** 3 4S 128 12 E
Piru, *U.S.A.* **85 L8** 34 25N 118 48W
Pisa, *Italy* **20 C4** 43 43N 10 23 E
Pisagua, *Chile* **92 G4** 19 40S 70 15W
Pisco, *Peru* **92 F3** 13 50S 76 12W
Písek, *Czech Rep.* **16 D8** 49 19N 14 10 E
Pishan, *China* **32 C2** 37 30N 78 33 E
Pīshīn, *Iran* **45 E9** 26 6N 61 47 E
Pishin, *Pakistan* **42 D2** 30 35N 67 0 E
Pishin Lora →, *Pakistan* **42 E1** 29 9N 64 5 E
Pising, *Indonesia* **37 F6** 5 8S 121 53 E
Pismo Beach, *U.S.A.* **85 K6** 35 9N 120 38W
Pissis, Cerro, *Argentina* **94 B2** 27 45S 68 48W
Pissouri, *Cyprus* **23 E11** 34 40N 32 42 E
Pistóia, *Italy* **20 C4** 43 55N 10 54 E
Pistol B., *Canada* **73 A10** 62 25N 92 37W
Pisuerga →, *Spain* **19 B3** 41 33N 4 52W
Pit →, *U.S.A.* **82 F2** 40 47N 122 6W
Pitarpunga, L., *Australia* **63 E3** 34 24S 143 30 E
Pitcairn I., *Pac. Oc.* **65 K14** 25 5S 130 5W
Pite älv →, *Sweden* **8 D19** 65 20N 21 25 E
Piteå, *Sweden* **8 D19** 65 20N 21 25 E
Piteşti, *Romania* **17 F13** 44 52N 24 54 E
Pithapuram, *India* **41 L13** 17 10N 82 15 E
Pithara, *Australia* **61 F2** 30 20S 116 35 E
Pithoragarh, *India* **43 E9** 29 35N 80 13 E
Pithoro, *Pakistan* **42 G3** 25 31N 69 23 E
Pitlochry, *U.K.* **12 E5** 56 42N 3 44W

Pitsilia □, Cyprus 23 E12 34 55N 33 0 E
Pitt I., Canada 72 C3 53 30N 129 50W
Pittsburg, Calif., U.S.A. 84 G5 38 2N 121 53W
Pittsburg, Kans., U.S.A. 81 G7 37 25N 94 42W
Pittsburg, Tex., U.S.A. 81 J7 33 0N 94 59W
Pittsburgh, U.S.A. 78 F5 40 26N 80 1W
Pittsfield, Ill., U.S.A. 80 F9 39 36N 90 49W
Pittsfield, Maine, U.S.A. 77 C11 44 47N 69 23W
Pittsfield, Mass., U.S.A. 79 D11 42 27N 73 15W
Pittsfield, N.H., U.S.A. 79 C13 43 18N 71 20W
Pittston, U.S.A. 79 E9 41 19N 75 47W
Pittsworth, Australia 63 D5 27 41S 151 37 E
Pituri →, Australia 62 C2 22 35S 138 30 E
Piura, Peru 92 E2 5 15S 80 38W
Pixley, U.S.A. 84 K7 35 58N 119 18W
Pizhou, China 34 G9 34 44N 116 55 E
Placentia, Canada 71 C9 47 20N 54 0W
Placentia B., Canada 71 C9 47 0N 54 40W
Placerville, U.S.A. 84 G6 38 44N 120 48W
Placetas, Cuba 88 B4 22 15N 79 44W
Plainfield, N.J., U.S.A. 79 F10 40 37N 74 25W
Plainfield, Ohio, U.S.A. 78 F3 40 13N 81 43W
Plainfield, Vt., U.S.A. 79 B12 44 17N 72 26W
Plains, Mont., U.S.A. 82 C6 47 28N 114 53W
Plains, Tex., U.S.A. 81 J3 33 11N 102 50W
Plainview, Nebr., U.S.A. 80 D6 42 21N 97 47W
Plainview, Tex., U.S.A. 81 H4 34 11N 101 43W
Plainwell, U.S.A. 76 D3 42 27N 85 38W
Plaistow, U.S.A. 79 D13 42 50N 71 6W
Pláka, Ákra, Greece 23 D8 35 11N 26 19 E
Plana Cays, Bahamas 89 B5 22 38N 73 30W
Planada, U.S.A. 84 H6 37 16N 120 19W
Plano, U.S.A. 81 J6 33 1N 96 42W
Plant City, U.S.A. 77 M4 28 1N 82 7W
Plaquemine, U.S.A. 81 K9 30 17N 91 14W
Plasencia, Spain 19 B2 40 3N 6 8W
Plaster City, U.S.A. 85 N11 32 47N 115 51W
Plaster Rock, Canada 71 C6 46 53N 67 22W
Plastun, Russia 30 B8 44 45N 136 19 E
Plata, Río de la, S. Amer. 94 C4 34 45S 57 30W
Plátani →, Italy 20 F5 37 23N 13 16 E
Plátanos, Greece 23 D5 35 28N 23 33 E
Platte, U.S.A. 80 D5 43 23N 98 51W
Platte →, Mo., U.S.A. 75 C8 39 16N 94 50W
Platte →, Nebr., U.S.A. 80 E7 41 4N 95 53W
Platteville, U.S.A. 80 D9 42 44N 90 29W
Plattsburgh, U.S.A. 79 B11 44 42N 73 28W
Plattsmouth, U.S.A. 80 E7 41 1N 95 53W
Plauen, Germany 16 C7 50 30N 12 8 E
Plavinas, Latvia 9 H21 56 35N 25 46 E
Playa Blanca, Canary Is. 22 F6 28 55N 13 37W
Playa Blanca Sur, Canary Is. 22 F6 28 51N 13 50W
Playa de las Americas, Canary Is. 22 F3 28 5N 16 43W
Playa de Mogán, Canary Is. 22 G4 27 48N 15 47W
Playa del Inglés, Canary Is. 22 G4 27 45N 15 33W
Playa Esmerelda, Canary Is. 22 F5 28 8N 14 16W
Playgreen L., Canada 73 C9 54 0N 98 15W
Pleasant Bay, Canada 71 C7 46 51N 60 48W
Pleasant Hill, U.S.A. 84 H4 37 57N 122 4W
Pleasant Mount, U.S.A. 79 E9 41 44N 75 26W
Pleasanton, Calif., U.S.A. 84 H5 37 39N 121 52W
Pleasanton, Tex., U.S.A. 81 L5 28 58N 98 29W
Pleasantville, N.J., U.S.A. 76 F8 39 24N 74 32W
Pleasantville, Pa., U.S.A. 78 E5 41 35N 79 34W
Plei Ku, Vietnam 38 F7 13 57N 108 0 E
Plenty →, Australia 62 C2 23 25S 136 31 E
Plenty, B. of, N.Z. 59 G6 37 45S 177 0 E
Plentywood, U.S.A. 80 A2 48 47N 104 34W
Plesetsk, Russia 24 B7 62 43N 40 20 E
Plessisville, Canada 71 C5 46 14N 71 47W
Plétipi, L., Canada 71 B5 51 44N 70 6W
Pleven, Bulgaria 21 C11 43 26N 24 37 E
Plevlja, Montenegro, Yug. 21 C8 43 21N 19 21 E
Plevna, Canada 78 B8 44 58N 76 59W
Płock, Poland 17 B10 52 32N 19 40 E
Plöckenstein, Germany 16 D7 48 46N 13 51 E
Ploieşti, Romania 17 F14 44 57N 26 5 E
Plonge, Lac la, Canada 73 B7 55 8N 107 20W
Plovdiv, Bulgaria 21 C11 42 8N 24 44 E
Plum, U.S.A. 78 F5 40 29N 79 47W
Plum I., U.S.A. 79 E12 41 11N 72 12W
Plumas, U.S.A. 84 F7 39 45N 120 4W
Plummer, U.S.A. 82 C5 47 20N 116 53W
Plumtree, Zimbabwe 55 G2 20 27S 27 55 E
Plungė, Lithuania 9 J19 55 53N 21 59 E
Plymouth, U.K. 11 G3 50 22N 4 10W
Plymouth, Calif., U.S.A. 84 G6 38 29N 120 51W
Plymouth, Ind., U.S.A. 76 E2 41 21N 86 19W
Plymouth, Mass., U.S.A. 79 E14 41 57N 70 40W
Plymouth, N.C., U.S.A. 77 H7 35 52N 76 43W
Plymouth, N.H., U.S.A. 79 C13 43 46N 71 41W
Plymouth, Pa., U.S.A. 79 E9 41 14N 75 57W
Plymouth, Wis., U.S.A. 76 D2 43 45N 87 59W
Plynlimon = Pumlumon Fawr, U.K. 11 E4 52 28N 3 46W
Plzeň, Czech Rep. 16 D7 49 45N 13 22 E
Po →, Italy 20 B5 44 57N 12 4 E
Po Hai = Bo Hai, China 35 E10 39 0N 119 0 E
Pobeda, Russia 27 C15 65 12N 146 12 E
Pobedy, Pik, Kyrgyzstan 26 E8 42 0N 79 58 E
Pocahontas, Ark., U.S.A. 81 G9 36 16N 90 58W
Pocahontas, Iowa, U.S.A. 80 D7 42 44N 94 40W
Pocatello, U.S.A. 82 E7 42 52N 112 27W
Pochutla, Mexico 87 D5 15 50N 96 31W
Pocito Casas, Mexico 86 B2 28 32N 111 6W
Pocomoke City, U.S.A. 76 F8 38 5N 75 34W
Poços de Caldas, Brazil 95 A6 21 50S 46 33W
Podgorica, Montenegro, Yug. 21 C8 42 30N 19 19 E
Podilska Vysochyna, Ukraine 17 D14 49 0N 28 0 E
Podolsk, Russia 24 C6 55 25N 37 30 E
Podporozhye, Russia 24 B5 60 55N 34 2 E
Pofadder, S. Africa 56 D2 29 10S 19 22 E
Pogranitšnyi, Russia 30 B5 44 25N 131 24 E
Poh, Indonesia 37 E6 0 46S 122 51 E
P'ohang, S. Korea 35 F15 36 1N 129 23 E
Pohjanmaa, Finland 8 E20 62 58N 22 50 E
Pohnpei, Micronesia 64 G7 6 55N 158 10 E
Pohri, India 42 G6 25 32N 77 22 E
Poinsett, C., Antarctica 5 C8 65 42S 113 18 E
Point Arena, U.S.A. 84 G3 38 55N 123 41W
Point Baker, U.S.A. 72 B2 56 21N 133 37W
Point Edward, Canada 70 D3 43 0N 82 30W
Point Hope, U.S.A. 68 B3 68 21N 166 47W
Point L., Canada 68 B8 65 15N 113 4W
Point Pedro, Sri Lanka 40 Q12 9 50N 80 15 E
Point Pleasant, N.J., U.S.A. 79 F10 40 5N 74 4W
Point Pleasant, W. Va., U.S.A. 76 F4 38 51N 82 8W
Pointe-à-Pitre, Guadeloupe 89 C7 16 10N 61 30W
Pointe-Claire, Canada 79 A11 45 26N 73 50W
Pointe-Gatineau, Canada 79 A9 45 28N 75 42W
Pointe-Noire, Congo 52 E2 4 48S 11 53 E
Poisonbush Ra., Australia 60 D3 22 30S 121 30 E
Poissonnier Pt., Australia 60 C2 19 57S 119 10 E
Poitiers, France 18 C4 46 35N 0 20 E
Poitou, France 18 C3 46 40N 0 10W
Pojoaque, U.S.A. 83 J11 35 54N 106 1W
Pokaran, India 40 F7 27 0N 71 50 E
Pokataroo, Australia 63 D4 29 30S 148 36 E
Pokhara, Nepal 43 E10 28 14N 83 58 E
Poko, Dem. Rep. of the Congo 54 B2 3 7N 26 52 E
Pokrovsk = Engels, Russia 25 D8 51 28N 46 6 E
Pokrovsk, Russia 27 C13 61 29N 129 0 E
Pola = Pula, Croatia 16 F7 44 54N 13 57 E
Polacca, U.S.A. 83 J8 35 50N 110 23W
Polan, Iran 45 E9 25 30N 61 10 E
Poland ■, Europe 17 C10 52 0N 20 0 E
Polar Bear Prov. Park, Canada 70 A2 55 0N 83 45W
Polatsk, Belarus 24 C4 55 30N 28 50 E
Polcura, Chile 94 D1 37 17S 71 43W
Polessk, Russia 9 J19 54 50N 21 8 E
Polesye = Pripet Marshes, Europe 17 B15 52 10N 28 10 E
Polevskoy, Russia 24 C11 56 26N 60 11 E
Pŏlgyo-ri, S. Korea 35 G14 34 51N 127 21 E
Police, Poland 16 B8 53 33N 14 33 E
Polillo Is., Phil. 37 B6 14 56N 122 0 E
Polis, Cyprus 23 D11 35 2N 32 26 E
Políyiros, Greece 21 D10 40 23N 23 25 E
Polk, U.S.A. 78 E5 41 22N 79 56W
Pollachi, India 40 P10 10 35N 77 0 E
Pollença, Spain 22 B10 39 54N 3 1 E
Pollença, B. de, Spain 22 B10 39 53N 3 8 E
Polnovat, Russia 26 C7 63 50N 65 54 E
Polonne, Ukraine 17 C14 50 6N 27 30 E
Polonnoye = Polonne, Ukraine 17 C14 50 6N 27 30 E
Polson, U.S.A. 82 C6 47 41N 114 9W
Poltava, Ukraine 25 E5 49 35N 34 35 E
Põltsamaa, Estonia 9 G21 58 41N 25 58 E
Polunochnoye, Russia 26 C7 60 52N 60 25 E
Põlva, Estonia 9 G22 58 3N 27 3 E
Polyarny, Russia 24 A5 69 8N 33 20 E
Polynesia, Pac. Oc. 65 J11 10 0S 162 0W
Polynésie française = French Polynesia ■, Pac. Oc. 65 K13 20 0S 145 0W
Pomaro, Mexico 86 D4 18 20N 103 18W
Pombal, Portugal 19 C1 39 55N 8 40W
Pómbia, Greece 23 E6 35 0N 24 51 E
Pomeroy, Ohio, U.S.A. 76 F4 39 2N 82 2W
Pomeroy, Wash., U.S.A. 82 C5 46 28N 117 36W
Pomézia, Italy 20 D5 41 40N 12 30 E
Pomona, Australia 63 D5 26 22S 152 52 E
Pomona, U.S.A. 85 L9 34 4N 117 45W
Pomorskie, Pojezierze, Poland 17 B9 53 40N 16 37 E
Pomos, Cyprus 23 D11 35 9N 32 33 E
Pomos, C., Cyprus 23 D11 35 10N 32 33 E
Pompano Beach, U.S.A. 77 M5 26 14N 80 8W
Pompeys Pillar, U.S.A. 82 D10 45 59N 107 57W
Pompton Lakes, U.S.A. 79 F10 41 0N 74 17W
Ponape = Pohnpei, Micronesia 64 G7 6 55N 158 10 E
Ponask L., Canada 70 B1 54 0N 92 41W
Ponca, U.S.A. 80 D6 42 34N 96 43W
Ponca City, U.S.A. 81 G6 36 42N 97 5W
Ponce, Puerto Rico 89 C6 18 1N 66 37W
Ponchatoula, U.S.A. 81 K9 30 26N 90 26W
Poncheville, L., Canada 70 B4 50 10N 76 55W
Pond, U.S.A. 85 K7 35 43N 119 20W
Pond Inlet, Canada 69 A12 72 40N 77 0W
Pondicherry, India 40 P11 11 59N 79 50 E
Ponds, I. of, Canada 71 B8 53 27N 55 52W
Ponferrada, Spain 19 A2 42 32N 6 35W
Ponnani, India 40 P9 10 45N 75 59 E
Ponnyadaung, Burma 41 J19 22 0N 94 10 E
Ponoka, Canada 72 C6 52 42N 113 40W
Ponorogo, Indonesia 37 G14 7 52S 111 27 E
Ponoy, Russia 24 A7 67 0N 41 13 E
Ponoy →, Russia 24 A7 66 59N 41 17 E
Ponta do Sol, Madeira 22 D2 32 42N 17 7W
Ponta Grossa, Brazil 95 B5 25 7S 50 10W
Ponta Pora, Brazil 95 A4 22 20S 55 35W
Pontarlier, France 18 C7 46 54N 6 20 E
Pontchartrain L., U.S.A. 81 K10 30 5N 90 5W
Ponte do Pungué, Mozam. 55 F3 19 30S 34 33 E
Ponte Nova, Brazil 95 A7 20 25S 42 54W
Ponteix, Canada 73 D7 49 46N 107 29W
Pontevedra, Spain 19 A1 42 26N 8 40W
Pontiac, Ill., U.S.A. 80 E10 40 53N 88 38W
Pontiac, Mich., U.S.A. 76 D4 42 38N 83 18W
Pontian Kecil, Malaysia 39 M4 1 29N 103 23 E
Pontianak, Indonesia 36 E3 0 3S 109 15 E
Pontine Is. = Ponziane, Ísole, Italy 20 D5 40 55N 12 57 E
Pontine Mts. = Kuzey Anadolu Dağları, Turkey 25 F6 41 30N 35 0 E
Pontivy, France 18 B2 48 5N 2 58W
Pontoise, France 18 B5 49 3N 2 5 E
Ponton →, Canada 72 B5 58 27N 116 11W
Pontypool, Canada 78 B6 44 6N 78 38W
Pontypool, U.K. 11 F4 51 42N 3 2W
Ponziane, Ísole, Italy 20 D5 40 55N 12 57 E
Poochera, Australia 63 E1 32 43S 134 51 E
Poole, U.K. 11 G6 50 43N 1 59W
Poole □, U.K. 11 G6 50 43N 1 59W
Poona = Pune, India 40 K8 18 29N 73 57 E
Pooncarie, Australia 63 E3 33 22S 142 31 E
Poopelloe L., Australia 63 E3 31 40S 144 0 E
Poopó, L. de, Bolivia 92 G5 18 30S 67 35W
Popayán, Colombia 92 C3 2 27N 76 36W
Poperinge, Belgium 15 D2 50 51N 2 42 E
Popilta L., Australia 63 E3 33 10S 141 42 E
Popio L., Australia 63 E3 33 10S 141 52 E
Poplar, U.S.A. 80 A2 48 7N 105 12W
Poplar →, Canada 73 C9 53 0N 97 19W
Poplar Bluff, U.S.A. 81 G9 36 46N 90 24W
Poplarville, U.S.A. 81 K10 30 51N 89 32W
Popocatépetl, Volcán, Mexico 87 D5 19 2N 98 38W
Popokabaka, Dem. Rep. of the Congo 52 F3 5 41S 16 40 E
Poprad, Slovak Rep. 17 D11 49 3N 20 18 E
Porali →, Pakistan 42 G2 25 58N 66 26 E
Porbandar, India 40 J6 21 44N 69 43 E
Porcher I., Canada 72 C2 53 50N 130 30W
Porcupine →, Canada 73 B8 59 11N 104 46W
Porcupine →, U.S.A. 68 B5 66 34N 145 19W
Pordenone, Italy 20 B5 45 57N 12 39 E
Pori, Finland 9 F19 61 29N 21 48 E
Porlamar, Venezuela 92 A6 10 57N 63 51W
Poronaysk, Russia 27 E15 49 13N 143 0 E
Poroshiri-Dake, Japan 30 C11 42 41N 142 52 E
Poroto Mts., Tanzania 55 D3 9 0S 33 30 E
Porpoise B., Antarctica 5 C9 66 0S 127 0 E
Porreres, Spain 22 B10 39 31N 3 2 E
Porsangen, Norway 8 A21 70 40N 25 40 E
Porsgrunn, Norway 9 G13 59 10N 9 40 E
Port Alberni, Canada 72 D4 49 14N 124 50W
Port Alfred, S. Africa 56 E4 33 36S 26 55 E
Port Alice, Canada 72 C3 50 20N 127 25W
Port Allegany, U.S.A. 78 E6 41 48N 78 17W
Port Allen, U.S.A. 81 K9 30 27N 91 12W
Port Alma, Australia 62 C5 23 38S 150 53 E
Port Angeles, U.S.A. 84 B3 48 7N 123 27W
Port Antonio, Jamaica 88 C4 18 10N 76 30W
Port Aransas, U.S.A. 81 M6 27 50N 97 4W
Port Arthur = Lüshun, China 35 E11 38 45N 121 15 E
Port Arthur, Australia 62 G4 43 7S 147 50 E
Port Arthur, U.S.A. 81 L8 29 54N 93 56W
Port au Choix, Canada 71 B8 50 43N 57 22W
Port au Port B., Canada 71 C8 48 40N 58 50W
Port-au-Prince, Haiti 89 C5 18 40N 72 20W
Port Augusta, Australia 63 E2 32 30S 137 50 E
Port Austin, U.S.A. 78 B2 44 3N 83 1W
Port Bell, Uganda 54 B3 0 18N 32 35 E
Port Bergé Vaovao, Madag. 57 B8 15 33S 47 40 E
Port Blandford, Canada 71 C9 48 20N 54 10W
Port Bradshaw, Australia 62 A2 12 30S 137 20 E
Port Broughton, Australia 63 E2 33 37S 137 56 E
Port Burwell, Canada 78 D4 42 40N 80 48W
Port Campbell, Australia 63 F3 38 37S 143 1 E
Port Canning, India 43 H13 22 23N 88 40 E
Port-Cartier, Canada 71 B6 50 2N 66 50W
Port Chalmers, N.Z. 59 L3 45 49S 170 30 E
Port Charlotte, U.S.A. 77 M4 26 59N 82 6W
Port Chester, U.S.A. 79 F11 41 0N 73 40W
Port Clements, Canada 72 C2 53 40N 132 10W
Port Clinton, U.S.A. 76 E4 41 31N 82 56W
Port Colborne, Canada 78 D5 42 50N 79 10W
Port Coquitlam, Canada 72 D4 49 15N 122 45W
Port Credit, Canada 78 C5 43 33N 79 35W
Port Curtis, Australia 62 C5 23 57S 151 20 E
Port d'Alcúdia, Spain 22 B10 39 50N 3 7 E
Port Dalhousie, Canada 78 C5 43 13N 79 16W
Port Darwin, Australia 60 B5 12 24S 130 45 E
Port Darwin, Falk. Is. 96 G5 51 50S 59 0W
Port Davey, Australia 62 G4 43 16S 145 55 E
Port-de-Paix, Haiti 89 C5 19 50N 72 50W
Port de Pollença, Spain 22 B10 39 54N 3 4 E
Port de Sóller, Spain 22 B9 39 48N 2 42 E
Port Dickson, Malaysia 39 L3 2 30N 101 49 E
Port Douglas, Australia 62 B4 16 30S 145 30 E
Port Dover, Canada 78 D4 42 47N 80 12W
Port Edward, Canada 72 C2 54 12N 130 10W
Port Elgin, Canada 78 B3 44 25N 81 25W
Port Elizabeth, S. Africa 56 E4 33 58S 25 40 E
Port Ellen, U.K. 12 F2 55 38N 6 11W
Port Erin, U.K. 10 C3 54 5N 4 45W
Port Essington, Australia 60 B5 11 15S 132 10 E
Port Etienne = Nouâdhibou, Mauritania 50 D2 20 54N 17 0W
Port Ewen, U.S.A. 79 E11 41 54N 73 59W
Port Fairy, Australia 63 F3 38 22S 142 12 E
Port Gamble, U.S.A. 84 C4 47 51N 122 35W
Port-Gentil, Gabon 52 E1 0 40S 8 50 E
Port Germein, Australia 63 E2 33 1S 138 1 E
Port Gibson, U.S.A. 81 K9 31 58N 90 59W
Port Glasgow, U.K. 12 F4 55 56N 4 41W
Port Harcourt, Nigeria 50 H7 4 40N 7 10 E
Port Hardy, Canada 72 C3 50 41N 127 30W
Port Harrison = Inukjuak, Canada 69 C12 58 25N 78 15W
Port Hawkesbury, Canada 71 C7 45 36N 61 22W
Port Hedland, Australia 60 D2 20 25S 118 35 E
Port Henry, U.S.A. 79 B11 44 3N 73 28W
Port Hood, Canada 71 C7 46 0N 61 32W
Port Hope, Canada 78 C6 43 56N 78 20W
Port Hope, U.S.A. 78 C2 43 57N 82 43W
Port Hope Simpson, Canada 71 B8 52 33N 56 18W
Port Hueneme, U.S.A. 85 L7 34 7N 119 12W
Port Huron, U.S.A. 78 D2 42 58N 82 26W
Port Jefferson, U.S.A. 79 F11 40 57N 73 3W
Port Jervis, U.S.A. 79 E10 41 22N 74 41W
Port Kelang = Pelabuhan Kelang, Malaysia 39 L3 3 0N 101 23 E
Port Kenny, Australia 63 E1 33 10S 134 41 E
Port Lairge = Waterford, Ireland 13 D4 52 15N 7 8W
Port Laoise, Ireland 13 C4 53 2N 7 18W
Port Lavaca, U.S.A. 81 L6 28 37N 96 38W
Port Leyden, U.S.A. 79 C9 43 35N 75 21W
Port Lincoln, Australia 63 E2 34 42S 135 52 E
Port Loko, S. Leone 50 G3 8 48N 12 46W
Port Louis, Mauritius 49 H9 20 10S 57 30 E
Port Lyautey = Kenitra, Morocco 50 B4 34 15N 6 40W
Port MacDonnell, Australia 63 F3 38 5S 140 48 E
Port McNeill, Canada 72 C3 50 35N 127 6W
Port Macquarie, Australia 63 E5 31 25S 152 25 E
Port Maria, Jamaica 88 C4 18 25N 76 55W
Port Matilda, U.S.A. 78 F6 40 48N 78 3W
Port Mellon, Canada 72 D4 49 32N 123 31W
Port-Menier, Canada 71 C7 49 51N 64 15W
Port Moody, Canada 84 A4 49 17N 122 51W
Port Morant, Jamaica 88 C4 17 54N 76 19W
Port Moresby, Papua N. G. 64 H6 9 24S 147 8 E
Port Musgrave, Australia 62 A3 11 55S 141 50 E
Port Neches, U.S.A. 81 L8 30 0N 93 59W
Port Nolloth, S. Africa 56 D2 29 17S 16 52 E
Port Nouveau-Québec = Kangiqsualujjuaq, Canada 69 C13 58 30N 65 59W
Port of Spain, Trin. & Tob. 89 D7 10 40N 61 31W
Port Orange, U.S.A. 77 L5 29 9N 80 59W
Port Orchard, U.S.A. 84 C4 47 32N 122 38W
Port Orford, U.S.A. 82 E1 42 45N 124 30W
Port Pegasus, N.Z. 59 M1 47 12S 167 41 E
Port Perry, Canada 78 B6 44 6N 78 56W
Port Phillip B., Australia 63 F3 38 10S 144 50 E
Port Pirie, Australia 63 E2 33 10S 138 1 E
Port Radium = Echo Bay, Canada 68 B8 66 5N 117 55W
Port Renfrew, Canada 72 D4 48 30N 124 20W
Port Roper, Australia 62 A2 14 45S 135 25 E
Port Rowan, Canada 78 D4 42 40N 80 30W
Port Safaga = Bûr Safâga, Egypt 44 E2 26 43N 33 57 E
Port Said = Bûr Sa'îd, Egypt 51 B12 31 16N 32 18 E
Port St. Joe, U.S.A. 77 L3 29 49N 85 18W
Port St. Johns, S. Africa 57 E4 31 38S 29 33 E
Port St. Lucie, U.S.A. 77 M5 27 20N 80 20W
Port Sanilac, U.S.A. 78 C2 43 26N 82 33W
Port Severn, Canada 78 B5 44 48N 79 43W
Port Shepstone, S. Africa 57 E5 30 44S 30 28 E
Port Simpson, Canada 72 C2 54 30N 130 20W
Port Stanley = Stanley, Falk. Is. 96 G5 51 40S 59 51W
Port Stanley, Canada 78 D3 42 40N 81 10W
Port Sudan = Bûr Sûdân, Sudan 51 E13 19 32N 37 9 E
Port Sulphur, U.S.A. 81 L10 29 29N 89 42W
Port Talbot, U.K. 11 F4 51 35N 3 47W
Port Townsend, U.S.A. 84 B4 48 7N 122 45W
Port-Vendres, France 18 E5 42 32N 3 8 E
Port Vila, Vanuatu 64 J8 17 45S 168 18 E
Port Vladimir, Russia 24 A5 69 25N 33 6 E
Port Wakefield, Australia 63 E2 34 12S 138 10 E
Port Washington, U.S.A. 76 D2 43 23N 87 53W
Port Weld = Kuala Sepetang, Malaysia 39 K3 4 49N 100 28 E
Porta Orientalis, Romania 17 F12 45 6N 22 18 E
Portadown, U.K. 13 B5 54 25N 6 27W
Portaferry, U.K. 13 B6 54 23N 5 33W
Portage, Pa., U.S.A. 78 F6 40 23N 78 41W
Portage, Wis., U.S.A. 80 D10 43 33N 89 28W
Portage La Prairie, Canada 73 D9 49 58N 98 18W
Portageville, U.S.A. 81 G10 36 26N 89 42W
Portalegre, Portugal 19 C2 39 19N 7 25W
Portales, U.S.A. 81 H3 34 11N 103 20W
Portarlington, Ireland 13 C4 53 9N 7 14W
Portbou, Spain 19 A7 42 25N 3 9 E
Porter L., N.W.T., Canada 73 A7 61 41N 108 5W
Porter L., Sask., Canada 73 B7 56 20N 107 20W
Porterville, S. Africa 56 E2 33 0S 19 0 E
Porterville, U.S.A. 84 J8 36 4N 119 1W
Porthcawl, U.K. 11 F4 51 29N 3 42W
Porthill, U.S.A. 82 B5 48 59N 116 30W
Porthmadog, U.K. 10 E3 52 55N 4 8W
Portile de Fier, Europe 17 F12 44 44N 22 30 E
Portimão, Portugal 19 D1 37 8N 8 32W
Portishead, U.K. 11 F5 51 29N 2 46W
Portknockie, U.K. 12 D6 57 42N 2 51W
Portland, N.S.W., Australia 63 E5 33 20S 150 0 E
Portland, Vic., Australia 63 F3 38 20S 141 35 E
Portland, Canada 79 B8 44 42N 76 12W
Portland, Conn., U.S.A. 79 E12 41 34N 72 38W
Portland, Maine, U.S.A. 69 D12 43 39N 70 16W
Portland, Mich., U.S.A. 76 D3 42 52N 84 54W
Portland, Oreg., U.S.A. 84 E4 45 32N 122 37W
Portland, Pa., U.S.A. 79 F9 40 55N 75 6W
Portland, Tex., U.S.A. 81 M6 27 53N 97 20W
Portland, I. of, U.K. 11 G5 50 33N 2 26W
Portland B., Australia 63 F3 38 15S 141 45 E
Portland Bill, U.K. 11 G5 50 31N 2 28W
Portland Canal, U.S.A. 72 B2 55 56N 130 0W
Portmadoc = Porthmadog, U.K. 10 E3 52 55N 4 8W
Porto, Portugal 19 B1 41 8N 8 40W
Pôrto Alegre, Brazil 95 C5 30 5S 51 10W
Porto Amboim = Gunza, Angola 52 G2 10 50S 13 50 E
Porto Cristo, Spain 22 B10 39 33N 3 20 E
Pôrto de Móz, Brazil 93 D8 1 41S 52 13W
Porto Empédocle, Italy 20 F5 37 17N 13 32 E
Pôrto Esperança, Brazil 92 G7 19 37S 57 29W
Pôrto Franco, Brazil 93 E9 6 20S 47 24W
Porto Mendes, Brazil 95 A5 24 30S 54 15W
Porto Moniz, Madeira 22 D2 32 52N 17 11W
Pôrto Murtinho, Brazil 92 H7 21 45S 57 55W
Pôrto Nacional, Brazil 93 F9 10 40S 48 30W
Porto-Novo, Benin 50 G6 6 23N 2 42 E
Porto Petro, Spain 22 B10 39 22N 3 13 E
Porto Santo, Madeira 50 B2 33 45N 16 25W
Pôrto São José, Brazil 95 A5 22 43S 53 10W
Pôrto Seguro, Brazil 93 G11 16 26S 39 5W
Porto Tórres, Italy 20 D3 40 50N 8 24 E
Pôrto União, Brazil 95 B5 26 10S 51 10W
Pôrto Válter, Brazil 92 E4 8 15S 72 40W
Porto-Vecchio, France 18 F8 41 35N 9 16 E
Pôrto Velho, Brazil 92 E6 8 46S 63 54W
Portobelo, Panama 88 E4 9 35N 79 42W
Portoferráio, Italy 20 C4 42 48N 10 20 E
Portola, U.S.A. 84 F6 39 49N 120 28W
Portoscuso, Italy 20 E3 39 12N 8 24 E
Portoviejo, Ecuador 92 D2 1 7S 80 28W
Portpatrick, U.K. 12 G3 54 51N 5 7W
Portree, U.K. 12 D2 57 25N 6 12W
Portrush, U.K. 13 A5 55 12N 6 40W
Portsmouth, Domin. 89 C7 15 34N 61 27W
Portsmouth, U.K. 11 G6 50 48N 1 6W
Portsmouth, N.H., U.S.A. 77 D10 43 5N 70 45W
Portsmouth, Ohio, U.S.A. 76 F4 38 44N 82 57W
Portsmouth, R.I., U.S.A. 79 E13 41 36N 71 15W
Portsmouth, Va., U.S.A. 76 G7 36 50N 76 18W
Portsmouth □, U.K. 11 G6 50 48N 1 6W
Portsoy, U.K. 12 D6 57 41N 2 41W
Portstewart, U.K. 13 A5 55 11N 6 43W
Porttipahtan tekojärvi, Finland 8 B22 68 5N 26 40 E
Portugal ■, Europe 19 C1 40 0N 8 0W
Portumna, Ireland 13 C3 53 6N 8 14W
Portville, U.S.A. 78 D6 42 3N 78 20W
Porvenir, Chile 96 G2 53 10S 70 16W
Porvoo, Finland 9 F21 60 24N 25 40 E
Posadas, Argentina 95 B4 27 30S 55 50W
Poshan = Boshan, China 35 F9 36 28N 117 49 E
Posht-e-Badam, Iran 45 C7 33 2N 55 23 E
Poso, Indonesia 37 E6 1 20S 120 55 E
Posong, S. Korea 35 G14 34 46N 127 5 E

Posse, *Brazil* **93 F9** 14 4S 46 18W
Possession I., *Antarctica* **5 D11** 72 4S 172 0 E
Possum Kingdom L., *U.S.A.* **81 J5** 32 52N 98 26W
Post, *U.S.A.* **81 J4** 33 12N 101 23W
Post Falls, *U.S.A.* **82 C5** 47 43N 116 57W
Postavy = Pastavy, *Belarus* **9 J22** 55 4N 26 50 E
Poste-de-la-Baleine = Kuujjuarapik, *Canada* **70 A4** 55 20N 77 35W
Postmasburg, *S. Africa* **56 D3** 28 18S 23 5 E
Postojna, *Slovenia* **16 F8** 45 46N 14 12 E
Poston, *U.S.A.* **85 M12** 34 0N 114 24W
Postville, *Canada* **71 B8** 54 54N 59 47W
Potchefstroom, *S. Africa* **56 D4** 26 41S 27 7 E
Poteau, *U.S.A.* **81 H7** 35 3N 94 37W
Poteet, *U.S.A.* **81 L5** 29 2N 98 35W
Potenza, *Italy* **20 D6** 40 38N 15 48 E
Poteriteri, L., *N.Z.* **59 M1** 46 5S 167 10 E
Potgietersrus, *S. Africa* **57 C4** 24 10S 28 55 E
Poti, *Georgia* **25 F7** 42 10N 41 38 E
Potiskum, *Nigeria* **51 F8** 11 39N 11 2 E
Potomac →, *U.S.A.* **76 G7** 38 0N 76 23W
Potosí, *Bolivia* **92 G5** 19 38S 65 50W
Potosi Mt., *U.S.A.* **85 K11** 35 57N 115 29W
Pototan, *Phil.* **37 B6** 10 54N 122 38 E
Potrerillos, *Chile* **94 B2** 26 30S 69 30W
Potsdam, *Germany* **16 B7** 52 25N 13 4 E
Potsdam, *U.S.A.* **79 B10** 44 40N 74 59W
Pottersville, *U.S.A.* **79 C11** 43 43N 73 50W
Pottstown, *U.S.A.* **79 F9** 40 15N 75 39W
Pottsville, *U.S.A.* **79 F8** 40 41N 76 12W
Pottuvil, *Sri Lanka* **40 R12** 6 55N 81 50 E
Pouce Coupé, *Canada* **72 B4** 55 40N 120 10W
Poughkeepsie, *U.S.A.* **79 E11** 41 42N 73 56W
Poulaphouca Res., *Ireland* **13 C5** 53 8N 6 30W
Poulsbo, *U.S.A.* **84 C4** 47 44N 122 39W
Poultney, *U.S.A.* **79 C11** 43 31N 73 14W
Poulton-le-Fylde, *U.K.* **10 D5** 53 51N 2 58W
Pouso Alegre, *Brazil* **95 A6** 22 14S 45 57W
Pouthisat, *Cambodia* **38 F4** 12 34N 103 50 E
Považská Bystrica, *Slovak Rep.* **17 D10** 49 8N 18 27 E
Povenets, *Russia* **24 B5** 62 50N 34 50 E
Poverty B., *N.Z.* **59 H7** 38 43S 178 2 E
Póvoa de Varzim, *Portugal* **19 B1** 41 25N 8 46W
Povungnituk = Puvirnituq, *Canada* **69 B12** 60 2N 77 10W
Powassan, *Canada* **70 C4** 46 5N 79 25W
Poway, *U.S.A.* **85 N9** 32 58N 117 2W
Powder →, *U.S.A.* **80 B2** 46 45N 105 26W
Powder River, *U.S.A.* **82 E10** 43 2N 106 59W
Powell, *U.S.A.* **82 D9** 44 45N 108 46W
Powell, L., *U.S.A.* **83 H8** 36 57N 111 29W
Powell River, *Canada* **72 D4** 49 50N 124 35W
Powers, *U.S.A.* **76 C2** 45 41N 87 32W
Powys □, *U.K.* **11 E4** 52 20N 3 20W
Poyang Hu, *China* **33 D6** 29 5N 116 20 E
Poyarkovo, *Russia* **27 E13** 49 36N 128 41 E
Poza Rica, *Mexico* **87 C5** 20 33N 97 27W
Požarevac, *Serbia, Yug.* **21 B9** 44 35N 21 18 E
Poznań, *Poland* **17 B9** 52 25N 16 55 E
Pozo, *U.S.A.* **85 K6** 35 20N 120 24W
Pozo Almonte, *Chile* **92 H5** 20 10S 69 50W
Pozo Colorado, *Paraguay* **94 A4** 23 30S 58 45W
Pozoblanco, *Spain* **19 C3** 38 23N 4 51W
Pozzuoli, *Italy* **20 D6** 40 49N 14 7 E
Prachin Buri, *Thailand* **38 F3** 14 0N 101 25 E
Prachuap Khiri Khan, *Thailand* **39 G2** 11 49N 99 48 E
Prado, *Brazil* **93 G11** 17 20S 39 13W
Prague = Praha, *Czech Rep.* **16 C8** 50 5N 14 22 E
Praha, *Czech Rep.* **16 C8** 50 5N 14 22 E
Praia, *C. Verde Is.* **49 E1** 14 55N 23 30W
Prainha, *Amazonas, Brazil* **92 E6** 7 10S 60 30W
Prainha, *Pará, Brazil* **93 D8** 1 45S 53 30W
Prairie, *Australia* **62 C3** 20 50S 144 35 E
Prairie City, *U.S.A.* **82 D4** 44 28N 118 43W
Prairie Dog Town Fork →, *U.S.A.* **81 H5** 34 30N 99 23W
Prairie du Chien, *U.S.A.* **80 D9** 43 3N 91 9W
Prairies, L. of the, *Canada* **73 C8** 51 16N 101 32W
Pran Buri, *Thailand* **38 F2** 12 23N 99 55 E
Prapat, *Indonesia* **36 D1** 2 41N 98 58 E
Prasonísi, Ákra, *Greece* **23 D9** 35 42N 27 46 E
Prata, *Brazil* **93 G9** 19 25S 48 54W
Pratabpur, *India* **43 H10** 23 28N 83 15 E
Pratapgarh, *Raj., India* **42 G6** 24 2N 74 40 E
Pratapgarh, *Ut. P., India* **43 G9** 25 56N 81 59 E
Prato, *Italy* **20 C4** 43 53N 11 6 E
Pratt, *U.S.A.* **81 G5** 37 39N 98 44W
Prattville, *U.S.A.* **77 J2** 32 28N 86 29W
Pravia, *Spain* **19 A2** 43 30N 6 12W
Praya, *Indonesia* **36 F5** 8 39S 116 17 E
Precordillera, *Argentina* **94 C2** 30 0S 69 1W
Preeceville, *Canada* **73 C8** 51 57N 102 40W
Preiļi, *Latvia* **9 H22** 56 18N 26 43 E
Premont, *U.S.A.* **81 M5** 27 22N 98 7W
Prentice, *U.S.A.* **80 C9** 45 33N 90 17W
Preobrazheniye, *Russia* **30 C6** 42 54N 133 54 E
Preparis North Channel, *Ind. Oc.* **41 M18** 15 12N 93 40 E
Preparis South Channel, *Ind. Oc.* **41 M18** 14 36N 93 40 E
Přerov, *Czech Rep.* **17 D9** 49 28N 17 27 E
Prescott, *Canada* **79 B9** 44 45N 75 30W
Prescott, *Ariz., U.S.A.* **83 J7** 34 33N 112 28W
Prescott, *Ark., U.S.A.* **81 J8** 33 48N 93 23W
Prescott Valley, *U.S.A.* **83 J7** 34 40N 112 18W
Preservation Inlet, *N.Z.* **59 M1** 46 8S 166 35 E
Presho, *U.S.A.* **80 D4** 43 54N 100 3W
Presidencia de la Plaza, *Argentina* **94 B4** 27 0S 59 50W
Presidencia Roque Saenz Peña, *Argentina* **94 B3** 26 45S 60 30W
Presidente Epitácio, *Brazil* **93 H8** 21 56S 52 6W
Presidente Hayes □, *Paraguay* **94 A4** 24 0S 59 0W
Presidente Prudente, *Brazil* **95 A5** 22 5S 51 25W
Presidio, *Mexico* **86 B4** 29 29N 104 23W
Presidio, *U.S.A.* **81 L2** 29 34N 104 22W
Prešov, *Slovak Rep.* **17 D11** 49 0N 21 15 E
Prespa, L. = Prespansko Jezero, *Macedonia* **21 D9** 40 55N 21 0 E
Prespansko Jezero, *Macedonia* **21 D9** 40 55N 21 0 E
Presque I., *U.S.A.* **78 D4** 42 9N 80 6W
Presque Isle, *U.S.A.* **77 B12** 46 41N 68 1W
Prestatyn, *U.K.* **10 D4** 53 20N 3 24W
Presteigne, *U.K.* **11 E5** 52 17N 3 0W
Preston, *Canada* **78 C4** 43 23N 80 21W
Preston, *U.K.* **10 D5** 53 46N 2 42W
Preston, *Idaho, U.S.A.* **82 E8** 42 6N 111 53W
Preston, *Minn., U.S.A.* **80 D8** 43 40N 92 5W
Preston, C., *Australia* **60 D2** 20 51S 116 12 E
Prestonburg, *U.S.A.* **76 G4** 37 39N 82 46W
Prestwick, *U.K.* **12 F4** 55 29N 4 37W
Pretoria, *S. Africa* **57 D4** 25 44S 28 12 E
Préveza, *Greece* **21 E9** 38 57N 20 47 E
Prey Veng, *Cambodia* **39 G5** 11 35N 105 29 E
Pribilof Is., *U.S.A.* **68 C2** 57 0N 170 0W
Příbram, *Czech Rep.* **16 D8** 49 41N 14 2 E
Price, *U.S.A.* **82 G8** 39 36N 110 49W
Price I., *Canada* **72 C3** 52 23N 128 41W
Prichard, *U.S.A.* **77 K1** 30 44N 88 5W
Priekule, *Latvia* **9 H19** 56 26N 21 35 E
Prienai, *Lithuania* **9 J20** 54 38N 23 57 E
Prieska, *S. Africa* **56 D3** 29 40S 22 42 E
Priest L., *U.S.A.* **82 B5** 48 35N 116 52W
Priest River, *U.S.A.* **82 B5** 48 10N 116 54W
Priest Valley, *U.S.A.* **84 J6** 36 10N 120 39W
Prievidza, *Slovak Rep.* **17 D10** 48 46N 18 36 E
Prikaspiyskaya Nizmennost = Caspian Depression, *Eurasia* **25 E8** 47 0N 48 0 E
Prilep, *Macedonia* **21 D9** 41 21N 21 32 E
Priluki = Pryluky, *Ukraine* **25 D5** 50 30N 32 24 E
Prime Seal I., *Australia* **62 G4** 40 3S 147 43 E
Primrose L., *Canada* **73 C7** 54 55N 109 45W
Prince Albert, *Canada* **73 C7** 53 15N 105 50W
Prince Albert, *S. Africa* **56 E3** 33 12S 22 2 E
Prince Albert Mts., *Antarctica* **5 D11** 76 0S 161 30 E
Prince Albert Nat. Park, *Canada* **73 C7** 54 0N 106 25W
Prince Albert Pen., *Canada* **68 A8** 72 30N 116 0W
Prince Albert Sd., *Canada* **68 A8** 70 25N 115 0W
Prince Alfred, C., *Canada* **4 B1** 74 20N 124 40W
Prince Charles I., *Canada* **69 B12** 67 47N 76 12W
Prince Charles Mts., *Antarctica* **5 D6** 72 0S 67 0 E
Prince Edward I. □, *Canada* **71 C7** 46 20N 63 20W
Prince Edward Is., *Ind. Oc.* **3 G11** 46 35S 38 0 E
Prince Edward Pt., *Canada* **78 C8** 43 56N 76 52W
Prince George, *Canada* **72 C4** 53 55N 122 50W
Prince of Wales, C., *U.S.A.* **66 C3** 65 36N 168 5W
Prince of Wales I., *Australia* **62 A3** 10 40S 142 10 E
Prince of Wales I., *Canada* **68 A10** 73 0N 99 0W
Prince of Wales I., *U.S.A.* **66 C6** 55 47N 132 50W
Prince Patrick I., *Canada* **4 B2** 77 0N 120 0W
Prince Regent Inlet, *Canada* **4 B3** 73 0N 90 0W
Prince Rupert, *Canada* **72 C2** 54 20N 130 20W
Princess Charlotte B., *Australia* **62 A3** 14 25S 144 0 E
Princess May Ranges, *Australia* **60 C4** 15 30S 125 30 E
Princess Royal I., *Canada* **72 C3** 53 0N 128 40W
Princeton, *Canada* **72 D4** 49 27N 120 30W
Princeton, *Calif., U.S.A.* **84 F4** 39 24N 122 1W
Princeton, *Ill., U.S.A.* **80 E10** 41 23N 89 28W
Princeton, *Ind., U.S.A.* **76 F2** 38 21N 87 34W
Princeton, *Ky., U.S.A.* **76 G2** 37 7N 87 53W
Princeton, *Mo., U.S.A.* **80 E8** 40 24N 93 35W
Princeton, *N.J., U.S.A.* **79 F10** 40 21N 74 39W
Princeton, *W. Va., U.S.A.* **76 G5** 37 22N 81 6W
Principe, I. de, *Atl. Oc.* **48 F4** 1 37N 7 27 E
Principe da Beira, *Brazil* **92 F6** 12 20S 64 30W
Prineville, *U.S.A.* **82 D3** 44 18N 120 51W
Prins Harald Kyst, *Antarctica* **5 D4** 70 0S 35 1 E
Prinsesse Astrid Kyst, *Antarctica* **5 D3** 70 45S 12 30 E
Prinsesse Ragnhild Kyst, *Antarctica* **5 D4** 70 15S 27 30 E
Prinzapolca, *Nic.* **88 D3** 13 20N 83 35W
Priozersk, *Russia* **24 B5** 61 2N 30 7 E
Pripet = Prypyat →, *Europe* **17 C16** 51 20N 30 15 E
Pripet Marshes, *Europe* **17 B15** 52 10N 28 10 E
Pripyat Marshes = Pripet Marshes, *Europe* **17 B15** 52 10N 28 10 E
Pripyats = Prypyat →, *Europe* **17 C16** 51 20N 30 15 E
Priština, *Yugoslavia* **21 C9** 42 40N 21 13 E
Privas, *France* **18 D6** 44 45N 4 37 E
Privolzhskaya Vozvyshennost, *Russia* **25 D8** 51 0N 46 0 E
Prizren, *Yugoslavia* **21 C9** 42 13N 20 45 E
Probolinggo, *Indonesia* **37 G15** 7 46S 113 13 E
Proctor, *U.S.A.* **79 C11** 43 40N 73 2W
Proddatur, *India* **40 M11** 14 45N 78 30 E
Prodhromos, *Cyprus* **23 E11** 34 57N 32 50 E
Profítis Ilías, *Greece* **23 C9** 36 17N 27 56 E
Profondeville, *Belgium* **15 D4** 50 23N 4 52 E
Progreso, *Mexico* **87 C7** 21 20N 89 40W
Progreso, *Yucatán, Mexico* **86 B4** 21 17N 89 40W
Prokopyevsk, *Russia* **26 D9** 54 0N 86 45 E
Prokuplje, *Serbia, Yug.* **21 C9** 43 16N 21 36 E
Prome = Pyè, *Burma* **41 K19** 18 49N 95 13 E
Prophet →, *Canada* **72 B4** 58 48N 122 40W
Prophet River, *Canada* **72 B4** 58 6N 122 43W
Propriá, *Brazil* **93 F11** 10 13S 36 51W
Proserpine, *Australia* **62 C4** 20 21S 148 36 E
Prosna →, *Poland* **17 B9** 52 6N 17 44 E
Prospect, *U.S.A.* **79 C9** 43 18N 75 9W
Prosser, *U.S.A.* **82 C4** 46 12N 119 46W
Prostějov, *Czech Rep.* **17 D9** 49 30N 17 2 E
Proston, *Australia* **63 D5** 26 8S 151 32 E
Provence, *France* **18 E6** 43 40N 5 46 E
Providence, *Ky., U.S.A.* **76 G2** 37 24N 87 46W
Providence, *R.I., U.S.A.* **79 E13** 41 49N 71 24W
Providence Bay, *Canada* **70 C3** 45 41N 82 15W
Providence Mts., *U.S.A.* **85 K11** 35 10N 115 15W
Providencia, I. de, *Colombia* **88 D3** 13 25N 81 26W
Provideniya, *Russia* **27 C19** 64 23N 173 18W
Provins, *France* **18 B5** 48 33N 3 15 E
Provo, *U.S.A.* **82 F8** 40 14N 111 39W
Provost, *Canada* **73 C6** 52 25N 110 20W
Prudhoe Bay, *U.S.A.* **68 A5** 70 18N 148 22W
Prudhoe I., *Australia* **62 C4** 21 19S 149 41 E
Prud'homme, *Canada* **73 C7** 52 20N 105 54W
Pruszków, *Poland* **17 B11** 52 9N 20 49 E
Prut →, *Romania* **17 F15** 45 28N 28 10 E
Pruzhany, *Belarus* **17 B13** 52 33N 24 28 E
Prydz B., *Antarctica* **5 C6** 69 0S 74 0 E
Pryluky, *Ukraine* **25 D5** 50 30N 32 24 E
Pryor, *U.S.A.* **81 G7** 36 19N 95 19W
Prypyat →, *Europe* **17 C16** 51 20N 30 15 E
Przemyśl, *Poland* **17 D12** 49 50N 22 45 E
Przhevalsk, *Kyrgyzstan* **26 E8** 42 30N 78 20 E
Psará, *Greece* **21 E11** 38 37N 25 38 E
Psíra, *Greece* **23 D7** 35 12N 25 52 E
Pskov, *Russia* **24 C4** 57 50N 28 25 E
Pskovskoye, Ozero, *Russia* **9 H22** 58 0N 27 58 E
Ptich = Ptsich →, *Belarus* **17 B15** 52 9N 28 52 E
Ptolemaís, *Greece* **21 D9** 40 30N 21 43 E
Ptsich →, *Belarus* **17 B15** 52 9N 28 52 E
Pu Xian, *China* **34 F6** 36 24N 111 6 E
Pua, *Thailand* **38 C3** 19 11N 100 55 E
Puán, *Argentina* **94 D3** 37 30S 62 45W
Puan, *S. Korea* **35 G14** 35 44N 126 44 E
Pucallpa, *Peru* **92 E4** 8 25S 74 30W
Pudasjärvi, *Finland* **8 D22** 65 23N 26 53 E
Pudozh, *Russia* **24 B6** 61 48N 36 32 E
Pudukkottai, *India* **40 P11** 10 28N 78 47 E
Puebla, *Mexico* **87 D5** 19 3N 98 12W
Puebla □, *Mexico* **87 D5** 18 30N 98 0W
Pueblo, *U.S.A.* **80 F2** 38 16N 104 37W
Pueblo Hundido, *Chile* **94 B1** 26 20S 70 5W
Puelches, *Argentina* **94 D2** 38 5S 65 51W
Puelén, *Argentina* **94 D2** 37 32S 67 38W
Puente Alto, *Chile* **94 C1** 33 32S 70 35W
Puente-Genil, *Spain* **19 D3** 37 22N 4 47W
Puerco →, *U.S.A.* **83 J10** 34 22N 107 50W
Puerto, *Canary Is.* **22 F2** 28 5N 17 20W
Puerto Aisén, *Chile* **96 F2** 45 27S 73 0W
Puerto Ángel, *Mexico* **87 D5** 15 40N 96 29W
Puerto Arista, *Mexico* **87 D6** 15 56N 93 48W
Puerto Armuelles, *Panama* **88 E3** 8 20N 82 51W
Puerto Ayacucho, *Venezuela* **92 B5** 5 40N 67 35W
Puerto Barrios, *Guatemala* **88 C2** 15 40N 88 32W
Puerto Bermejo, *Argentina* **94 B4** 26 55S 58 34W
Puerto Bermúdez, *Peru* **92 F4** 10 20S 74 58W
Puerto Bolívar, *Ecuador* **92 D3** 3 19S 79 55W
Puerto Cabello, *Venezuela* **92 A5** 10 28N 68 1W
Puerto Cabezas, *Nic.* **88 D3** 14 0N 83 30W
Puerto Cabo Gracias á Dios, *Nic.* **88 D3** 15 0N 83 10W
Puerto Carreño, *Colombia* **92 B5** 6 12N 67 22W
Puerto Castilla, *Honduras* **88 C2** 16 0N 86 0W
Puerto Chicama, *Peru* **92 E3** 7 45S 79 20W
Puerto Coig, *Argentina* **96 G3** 50 54S 69 15W
Puerto Cortés, *Costa Rica* **88 E3** 8 55N 84 0W
Puerto Cortés, *Honduras* **88 C2** 15 51N 88 0W
Puerto Cumarebo, *Venezuela* **92 A5** 11 29N 69 30W
Puerto de Alcudia = Port d'Alcúdia, *Spain* **22 B10** 39 50N 3 7 E
Puerto de Andraitx, *Spain* **22 B9** 39 32N 2 23 E
Puerto de Cabrera, *Spain* **22 B9** 39 8N 2 56 E
Puerto de Gran Tarajal, *Canary Is.* **22 F5** 28 13N 14 1W
Puerto de la Cruz, *Canary Is.* **22 F3** 28 24N 16 32W
Puerto de Pozo Negro, *Canary Is.* **22 F6** 28 19N 13 55W
Puerto de Sóller = Port de Sóller, *Spain* **22 B9** 39 48N 2 42 E
Puerto del Carmen, *Canary Is.* **22 F6** 28 55N 13 38W
Puerto del Rosario, *Canary Is.* **22 F6** 28 30N 13 52W
Puerto Deseado, *Argentina* **96 F3** 47 55S 66 0W
Puerto Escondido, *Mexico* **87 D5** 15 50N 97 3W
Puerto Heath, *Bolivia* **92 F5** 12 34S 68 39W
Puerto Inírida, *Colombia* **92 C5** 3 53N 67 52W
Puerto Juárez, *Mexico* **87 C7** 21 11N 86 49W
Puerto La Cruz, *Venezuela* **92 A6** 10 13N 64 38W
Puerto Leguízamo, *Colombia* **92 D4** 0 12S 74 46W
Puerto Limón, *Colombia* **92 C4** 3 23N 73 30W
Puerto Lobos, *Argentina* **96 E3** 42 0S 65 3W
Puerto Madryn, *Argentina* **96 E3** 42 48S 65 4W
Puerto Maldonado, *Peru* **92 F5** 12 30S 69 10W
Puerto Manotí, *Cuba* **88 B4** 21 22N 76 50W
Puerto Montt, *Chile* **96 E2** 41 28S 73 0W
Puerto Morazán, *Nic.* **88 D2** 12 51N 87 11W
Puerto Morelos, *Mexico* **87 C7** 20 49N 86 52W
Puerto Natales, *Chile* **96 G2** 51 45S 72 15W
Puerto Padre, *Cuba* **88 B4** 21 13N 76 35W
Puerto Páez, *Venezuela* **92 B5** 6 13N 67 28W
Puerto Peñasco, *Mexico* **86 A2** 31 20N 113 33W
Puerto Pinasco, *Paraguay* **94 A4** 22 36S 57 50W
Puerto Plata, *Dom. Rep.* **89 C5** 19 48N 70 45W
Puerto Pollensa = Port de Pollença, *Spain* **22 B10** 39 54N 3 4 E
Puerto Princesa, *Phil.* **37 C5** 9 46N 118 45 E
Puerto Quepos, *Costa Rica* **88 E3** 9 29N 84 6W
Puerto Rico, *Canary Is.* **22 G4** 27 47N 15 42W
Puerto Rico ■, *W. Indies* **89 C6** 18 15N 66 45W
Puerto Rico Trench, *Atl. Oc.* **89 C6** 19 50N 66 0W
Puerto San Julián, *Argentina* **96 F3** 49 18S 67 43W
Puerto Sastre, *Paraguay* **94 A4** 22 2S 57 55W
Puerto Suárez, *Bolivia* **92 G7** 18 58S 57 52W
Puerto Vallarta, *Mexico* **86 C3** 20 36N 105 15W
Puerto Wilches, *Colombia* **92 B4** 7 21N 73 54W
Puertollano, *Spain* **19 C3** 38 43N 4 7W
Pueyrredón, L., *Argentina* **96 F2** 47 20S 72 0W
Puffin I., *Ireland* **13 E1** 51 50N 10 24W
Pugachev, *Russia* **24 D8** 52 0N 48 49 E
Pugal, *India* **42 E5** 28 30N 72 48 E
Puge, *Tanzania* **54 C3** 4 45S 33 11 E
Puget Sound, *U.S.A.* **82 C2** 47 50N 122 30W
Pugŏdong, *N. Korea* **35 C16** 42 5N 130 0 E
Pugu, *Tanzania* **54 D4** 6 55S 39 4 E
Pūgūnzī, *Iran* **45 E8** 25 49N 59 10 E
Puig Major, *Spain* **22 B9** 39 48N 2 47 E
Puigcerdà, *Spain* **19 A6** 42 24N 1 50 E
Puigpunyent, *Spain* **22 B9** 39 38N 2 32 E
Pujon-chŏsuji, *N. Korea* **35 D14** 40 35N 127 35 E
Pukaki L., *N.Z.* **59 L3** 44 4S 170 1 E
Pukapuka, *Cook Is.* **65 J11** 10 53S 165 49W
Pukaskwa Nat. Park, *Canada* **70 C2** 48 20N 86 0W
Pukatawagan, *Canada* **73 B8** 55 45N 101 20W
Pukchin, *N. Korea* **35 D13** 40 12N 125 45 E
Pukch'ŏng, *N. Korea* **35 D15** 40 14N 128 10 E
Pukekohe, *N.Z.* **59 G5** 37 12S 174 55 E
Pukhrayan, *India* **43 F8** 26 14N 79 51 E
Pula, *Croatia* **16 F7** 44 54N 13 57 E
Pulacayo, *Bolivia* **92 H5** 20 25S 66 41W
Pulandian, *China* **35 E11** 39 25N 121 58 E
Pularumpi, *Australia* **60 B5** 11 24S 130 26 E
Pulaski, *N.Y., U.S.A.* **79 C8** 43 34N 76 8W
Pulaski, *Tenn., U.S.A.* **77 H2** 35 12N 87 2W
Pulaski, *Va., U.S.A.* **76 G5** 37 3N 80 47W
Pulau →, *Indonesia* **37 F9** 5 50S 138 15 E
Puławy, *Poland* **17 C11** 51 23N 21 59 E
Pulga, *U.S.A.* **84 F5** 39 48N 121 29W
Pulicat L., *India* **40 N12** 13 40N 80 15 E
Pullman, *U.S.A.* **82 C5** 46 44N 117 10W
Pulo-Anna, *Pac. Oc.* **37 D8** 4 30N 132 5 E
Pulog, *Phil.* **37 A6** 16 40N 120 50 E
Pułtusk, *Poland* **17 B11** 52 43N 21 6 E
Pumlumon Fawr, *U.K.* **11 E4** 52 28N 3 46W
Puná, I., *Ecuador* **92 D2** 2 55S 80 5W
Punakha, *Bhutan* **41 F16** 27 42N 89 52 E
Punasar, *India* **42 F5** 27 6N 73 6 E
Punata, *Bolivia* **92 G5** 17 32S 65 50W
Punch, *India* **43 C6** 33 48N 74 4 E
Punch →, *Pakistan* **42 C5** 33 12N 73 40 E
Pune, *India* **40 K8** 18 29N 73 57 E
P'ungsan, *N. Korea* **35 D15** 40 50N 128 9 E
Pungue, Ponte de, *Mozam.* **55 F3** 19 0S 34 0 E
Punjab □, *India* **42 D7** 31 0N 76 0 E
Punjab □, *Pakistan* **42 E6** 32 0N 74 30 E
Puno, *Peru* **92 G4** 15 55S 70 3W
Punpun →, *India* **43 G11** 25 31N 85 18 E
Punta Alta, *Argentina* **96 D4** 38 53S 62 4W
Punta Arenas, *Chile* **96 G2** 53 10S 71 0W
Punta de Díaz, *Chile* **94 B1** 28 0S 70 45W
Punta Gorda, *Belize* **87 D7** 16 10N 88 45W
Punta Gorda, *U.S.A.* **77 M5** 26 56N 82 3W
Punta Prieta, *Mexico* **86 B2** 28 58N 114 17W
Punta Prima, *Spain* **22 B11** 39 48N 4 16 E
Puntarenas, *Costa Rica* **88 E3** 10 0N 84 50W
Punto Fijo, *Venezuela* **92 A4** 11 50N 70 13W
Punxsatawney, *U.S.A.* **78 F6** 40 57N 78 59W
Puquio, *Peru* **92 F4** 14 45S 74 10W
Pur →, *Russia* **26 C8** 67 31N 77 55 E
Purace, Vol., *Colombia* **92 C3** 2 21N 76 23W
Puralia = Puruliya, *India* **43 H12** 23 17N 86 24 E
Puranpur, *India* **43 E9** 28 31N 80 9 E
Purbeck, Isle of, *U.K.* **11 G6** 50 39N 1 59W
Purcell, *U.S.A.* **81 H6** 35 1N 97 22W
Purcell Mts., *Canada* **72 D5** 49 55N 116 15W
Puri, *India* **41 K14** 19 50N 85 58 E
Purmerend, *Neths.* **15 B4** 52 32N 4 58 E
Purnia, *India* **43 G12** 25 45N 87 31 E
Pursat = Pouthisat, *Cambodia* **38 F4** 12 34N 103 50 E
Purukcahu, *Indonesia* **36 E4** 0 35S 114 35 E
Puruliya, *India* **43 H12** 23 17N 86 24 E
Purus →, *Brazil* **92 D6** 3 42S 61 28W
Purvis, *U.S.A.* **81 K10** 31 9N 89 25W
Purwa, *India* **43 F9** 26 28N 80 47 E
Purwakarta, *Indonesia* **37 G12** 6 35S 107 29 E
Purwodadi, *Indonesia* **37 G14** 7 7S 110 55 E
Purwokerto, *Indonesia* **37 G13** 7 25S 109 14 E
Puryŏng, *N. Korea* **35 C15** 42 5N 129 43 E
Pusa, *India* **43 G11** 25 59N 85 41 E
Pusan, *S. Korea* **35 G15** 35 5N 129 0 E
Pushkino, *Russia* **25 D8** 51 16N 47 0 E
Putahow L., *Canada* **73 B8** 59 54N 100 40W
Putao, *Burma* **41 F20** 27 28N 97 30 E
Putaruru, *N.Z.* **59 H5** 38 2S 175 50 E
Puthein Myit →, *Burma* **41 M19** 15 56N 94 18 E
Putignano, *Italy* **20 D7** 40 51N 17 7 E
Puting, Tanjung, *Indonesia* **36 E4** 3 31S 111 46 E
Putnam, *U.S.A.* **79 E13** 41 55N 71 55W
Putorana, Gory, *Russia* **27 C10** 69 0N 95 0 E
Puttalam, *Sri Lanka* **40 Q11** 8 1N 79 55 E
Puttgarden, *Germany* **16 A6** 54 30N 11 10 E
Putumayo →, *S. Amer.* **92 D5** 3 7S 67 58W
Putussibau, *Indonesia* **36 D4** 0 50N 112 56 E
Puvirnituq, *Canada* **69 B12** 60 2N 77 10W
Puy-de-Dôme, *France* **18 D5** 45 46N 2 57 E
Puyallup, *U.S.A.* **84 C4** 47 12N 122 18W
Puyang, *China* **34 G8** 35 40N 115 1 E
Pūzeh Rīg, *Iran* **45 E8** 27 20N 58 40 E
Pwani □, *Tanzania* **54 D4** 7 0S 39 0 E
Pweto, *Dem. Rep. of the Congo* **55 D2** 8 25S 28 51 E
Pwllheli, *U.K.* **10 E3** 52 53N 4 25W
Pya-ozero, *Russia* **24 A5** 66 5N 30 58 E
Pyapon, *Burma* **41 L19** 16 20N 95 40 E
Pyasina →, *Russia* **27 B9** 73 30N 87 0 E
Pyatigorsk, *Russia* **25 F7** 44 2N 43 6 E
Pyè, *Burma* **41 K19** 18 49N 95 13 E
Pyetrikaw, *Belarus* **17 B15** 52 11N 28 29 E
Pyhäjoki, *Finland* **8 D21** 64 28N 24 14 E
Pyinmana, *Burma* **41 K20** 19 45N 96 12 E
Pyla, C., *Cyprus* **23 E12** 34 56N 33 51 E
Pymatuning Reservoir, *U.S.A.* **78 E4** 41 30N 80 28W
Pyŏktong, *N. Korea* **35 D13** 40 50N 125 50 E
Pyŏnggang, *N. Korea* **35 E14** 38 24N 127 17 E
P'yŏngt'aek, *S. Korea* **35 F14** 37 1N 127 4 E
P'yŏngyang, *N. Korea* **35 E13** 39 0N 125 30 E
Pyote, *U.S.A.* **81 K3** 31 32N 103 8W
Pyramid L., *U.S.A.* **82 G4** 40 1N 119 35W
Pyramid Pk., *U.S.A.* **85 J10** 36 25N 116 37W
Pyrénées, *Europe* **18 E4** 42 45N 0 18 E
Pyu, *Burma* **41 K20** 18 30N 96 28 E

Q

Qaanaaq = Thule, *Greenland* **4 B4** 77 40N 69 0W
Qachasnek, *S. Africa* **57 E4** 30 6S 28 42 E
Qa'el Jafr, *Jordan* **47 E5** 30 20N 36 25 E
Qa'emābād, *Iran* **45 D9** 31 44N 60 2 E
Qā'emshahr, *Iran* **45 B7** 36 30N 52 53 E
Qagan Nur, *China* **34 C8** 43 30N 114 55 E
Qahar Youyi Zhongqi, *China* **34 D7** 41 12N 112 40 E
Qahremānshahr = Bākhtarān, *Iran* **44 C5** 34 23N 47 0 E
Qaidam Pendi, *China* **32 C4** 37 0N 95 0 E
Qajarīyeh, *Iran* **45 D6** 31 1N 48 22 E
Qala, Ras il, *Malta* **23 C1** 36 1N 14 20 E
Qala-i-Jadid = Spīn Búldak, *Afghan.* **42 D2** 31 1N 66 25 E
Qala Viala, *Pakistan* **42 D2** 30 49N 67 17 E
Qala Yangi, *Afghan.* **42 B2** 34 20N 66 30 E

Qal'at al Akhḑar, Si. Arabia 44 E3 28 0N 37 10 E
Qal'at Dīzah, Iraq 44 B5 36 11N 45 7 E
Qal'at Şaliḩ, Iraq 44 D5 31 31N 47 16 E
Qal'at Sukkar, Iraq 44 D5 31 51N 46 5 E
Qal'eh Shaharak, Afghan. 40 B4 34 10N 64 20 E
Qamdo, China 32 C4 31 15N 97 6 E
Qamruddin Karez, Pakistan 42 D3 31 45N 68 20 E
Qandahār, Afghan. 40 D4 31 32N 65 30 E
Qandahār □, Afghan. 40 D4 31 0N 65 0 E
Qapān, Iran 45 B7 37 40N 55 47 E
Qapshaghay, Kazakstan 26 E8 43 51N 77 14 E
Qaqortoq = Julianehåb, Greenland 4 C5 60 43N 46 0W
Qara Qash →, India 43 B8 35 0N 78 30 E
Qarabutaq, Kazakstan 26 E7 49 59N 60 14 E
Qaraghandy, Kazakstan 26 E8 49 50N 73 10 E
Qārah, Si. Arabia 44 D4 29 55N 40 3 E
Qarataū, Kazakstan 26 E8 43 10N 70 28 E
Qareh →, Iran 44 B5 39 25N 47 22 E
Qareh Tekān, Iran 45 B6 36 38N 49 29 E
Qarqan He →, China 32 C3 39 30N 88 30 E
Qarqaraly, Kazakstan 26 E8 49 26N 75 30 E
Qarshi, Uzbekistan 26 F7 38 53N 65 48 E
Qartabā, Lebanon 47 A4 34 4N 35 50 E
Qaryat al Gharab, Iraq 44 D5 31 27N 44 48 E
Qaryat al 'Ulyā, Si. Arabia 44 E5 27 33N 47 42 E
Qasr 'Amra, Jordan 44 D3 31 48N 36 35 E
Qaşr-e Qand, Iran 45 E9 26 15N 60 45 E
Qasr Farâfra, Egypt 51 C11 27 0N 28 1 E
Qatanā, Syria 47 B5 33 26N 36 4 E
Qatar ■, Asia 45 E6 25 30N 51 15 E
Qatlīsh, Iran 45 B8 37 50N 57 19 E
Qattâra, Munkhafed el, Egypt 51 C11 29 30N 27 30 E
Qattâra Depression = Qattâra, Munkhafed el, Egypt 51 C11 29 30N 27 30 E
Qawām al Ḩamzah, Iraq 44 D5 31 43N 44 58 E
Qāyen, Iran 45 C8 33 40N 59 10 E
Qazaqstan = Kazakstan ■, Asia 26 E8 50 0N 70 0 E
Qazimämmäd, Azerbaijan 45 A6 40 3N 49 0 E
Qazvin, Iran 45 B6 36 15N 50 0 E
Qena, Egypt 51 C12 26 10N 32 43 E
Qeqertarsuaq = Disko, Greenland 4 C5 69 45N 53 30W
Qeqertarsuaq = Godhavn, Greenland 4 C5 69 15N 53 38W
Qeshlāq, Iran 44 C5 34 55N 46 28 E
Qeshm, Iran 45 E8 26 55N 56 10 E
Qeys, Iran 45 E7 26 32N 53 58 E
Qezel Owzen →, Iran 45 B6 36 45N 49 22 E
Qezi'ot, Israel 47 E3 30 52N 34 26 E
Qi Xian, China 34 G8 34 40N 114 48 E
Qian Gorlos, China 35 B13 45 5N 124 42 E
Qian Xian, China 34 G5 34 31N 108 15 E
Qianyang, China 34 G4 34 40N 107 8 E
Qibā', Si. Arabia 44 E5 27 24N 44 20 E
Qikiqtarjuaq, Canada 69 B13 67 33N 63 0W
Qila Safed, Pakistan 40 E2 29 0N 61 30 E
Qila Saifullāh, Pakistan 42 D3 30 45N 68 17 E
Qilian Shan, China 32 C4 38 30N 96 0 E
Qin He →, China 34 G7 35 1N 113 22 E
Qin Ling = Qinling Shandi, China 34 H5 33 50N 108 10 E
Qin'an, China 34 G3 34 48N 105 40 E
Qing Xian, China 34 E9 38 35N 116 45 E
Qingcheng, China 35 F9 37 15N 117 40 E
Qingdao, China 35 F11 36 5N 120 20 E
Qingfeng, China 34 G8 35 52N 115 8 E
Qinghai □, China 32 C4 36 0N 98 0 E
Qinghai Hu, China 32 C5 36 40N 100 10 E
Qinghecheng, China 35 D13 41 28N 124 15 E
Qinghemen, China 35 D11 41 48N 121 25 E
Qingjian, China 34 F6 37 8N 110 8 E
Qingjiang = Huaiyin, China 35 H10 33 30N 119 2 E
Qingshui, China 34 G4 34 48N 106 8 E
Qingshuihe, China 34 E6 39 55N 111 35 E
Qingtongxia Shuiku, China 34 F3 37 50N 105 58 E
Qingxu, China 34 F7 37 34N 112 22 E
Qingyang, China 34 F4 36 2N 107 55 E
Qingyuan, China 35 C13 42 10N 124 55 E
Qingyun, China 35 F9 37 45N 117 20 E
Qinhuangdao, China 35 E10 39 56N 119 30 E
Qinling Shandi, China 34 H5 33 50N 108 10 E
Qinshui, China 34 G7 35 40N 112 8 E
Qinyang = Jiyuan, China 34 G7 35 7N 112 57 E
Qinyuan, China 34 F7 36 29N 112 20 E
Qinzhou, China 32 D5 21 58N 108 38 E
Qionghai, China 38 C8 19 15N 110 26 E
Qiongzhou Haixia, China 38 B8 20 10N 110 15 E
Qiqihar, China 27 E13 47 26N 124 0 E
Qiraīya, W. →, Egypt 47 E3 30 27N 34 0 E
Qiryat Ata, Israel 47 C4 32 47N 35 6 E
Qiryat Gat, Israel 47 D3 31 32N 34 46 E
Qiryat Mal'akhi, Israel 47 D3 31 44N 34 44 E
Qiryat Shemona, Israel 47 B4 33 13N 35 35 E
Qiryat Yam, Israel 47 C4 32 51N 35 4 E
Qishan, China 34 G4 34 25N 107 38 E
Qitai, China 32 B3 44 2N 89 35 E
Qixia, China 35 F11 37 17N 120 52 E
Qızılağac Körfäzi, Azerbaijan 45 B6 39 9N 49 0 E
Qojūr, Iran 44 B5 36 12N 47 55 E
Qom, Iran 45 C6 34 40N 51 0 E
Qomolangma Feng = Everest, Mt., Nepal 43 E12 28 5N 86 58 E
Qomsheh, Iran 45 D6 32 0N 51 55 E
Qostanay, Kazakstan 26 D7 53 10N 63 35 E
Quabbin Reservoir, U.S.A. 79 D12 42 20N 72 20W
Quairading, Australia 61 F2 32 0S 117 21 E
Quakertown, U.S.A. 79 F9 40 26N 75 21W
Qualicum Beach, Canada 72 D4 49 22N 124 26W
Quambatook, Australia 63 F3 35 49S 143 34 E
Quambone, Australia 63 E4 30 57S 147 53 E
Quamby, Australia 62 C3 20 22S 140 17 E
Quan Long = Ca Mau, Vietnam 39 H5 9 7N 105 8 E
Quanah, U.S.A. 81 H5 34 18N 99 44W
Quang Ngai, Vietnam 38 E7 15 13N 108 58 E
Quang Tri, Vietnam 38 D6 16 45N 107 13 E
Quantock Hills, U.K. 11 F4 51 8N 3 10W
Quanzhou, China 33 D6 24 55N 118 34 E
Qu'Appelle, Canada 73 C8 50 33N 103 53W
Quaqtaq, Canada 69 B13 60 55N 69 40W
Quaraí, Brazil 94 C4 30 15S 56 20W
Quartu Sant'Élena, Italy 20 E3 39 15N 9 10 E
Quartzsite, U.S.A. 85 M12 33 40N 114 13W
Quatsino Sd., Canada 72 C3 50 25N 127 58W
Quba, Azerbaijan 25 F8 41 21N 48 32 E
Qūchān, Iran 45 B8 37 10N 58 27 E
Queanbeyan, Australia 63 F4 35 17S 149 14 E
Québec, Canada 71 C5 46 52N 71 13W
Québec □, Canada 71 C6 48 0N 74 0W
Queen Alexandra Ra., Antarctica 5 E11 85 0S 170 0 E
Queen Charlotte City, Canada 72 C2 53 15N 132 2W
Queen Charlotte Is., Canada 72 C2 53 20N 132 10W
Queen Charlotte Sd., Canada 72 C3 51 0N 128 0W
Queen Charlotte Strait, Canada 72 C3 50 45N 127 10W
Queen Elizabeth Is., Canada 66 B10 76 0N 95 0W
Queen Elizabeth Nat. Park, Uganda 54 C3 0 0 30 0 E
Queen Mary Land, Antarctica 5 D7 70 0S 95 0 E
Queen Maud G., Canada 68 B9 68 15N 102 30W
Queen Maud Land, Antarctica 5 D3 72 30S 12 0 E
Queen Maud Mts., Antarctica 5 E13 86 0S 160 0W
Queens Chan., Australia 60 C4 15 0S 129 30 E
Queenscliff, Australia 63 F3 38 16S 144 39 E
Queensland □, Australia 62 C3 22 0S 142 0 E
Queenstown, Australia 62 G4 42 4S 145 35 E
Queenstown, N.Z. 59 L2 45 1S 168 40 E
Queenstown, S. Africa 56 E4 31 52S 26 52 E
Queets, U.S.A. 84 C2 47 32N 124 20W
Queguay Grande →, Uruguay 94 C4 32 9S 58 9W
Queimadas, Brazil 93 F11 11 0S 39 38W
Quelimane, Mozam. 55 F4 17 53S 36 58 E
Quellón, Chile 96 E2 43 7S 73 37W
Quelpart = Cheju do, S. Korea 35 H14 33 29N 126 34 E
Quemado, N. Mex., U.S.A. 83 J9 34 20N 108 30W
Quemado, Tex., U.S.A. 81 L4 28 58N 100 35W
Quemú-Quemú, Argentina 94 D3 36 3S 63 36W
Quequén, Argentina 94 D4 38 30S 58 30W
Querétaro, Mexico 86 C4 20 36N 100 23W
Querétaro □, Mexico 86 C5 20 30N 100 0W
Queshan, China 34 H8 32 55N 114 2 E
Quesnel, Canada 72 C4 53 0N 122 30W
Quesnel →, Canada 72 C4 52 58N 122 29W
Quesnel L., Canada 72 C4 52 30N 121 20W
Questa, U.S.A. 83 H11 36 42N 105 36W
Quetico Prov. Park, Canada 70 C1 48 30N 91 45W
Quetta, Pakistan 42 D2 30 15N 66 55 E
Quezaltenango, Guatemala 88 D1 14 50N 91 30W
Quezon City, Phil. 37 B6 14 38N 121 0 E
Qufār, Si. Arabia 44 E4 27 26N 41 37 E
Qui Nhon, Vietnam 38 F7 13 40N 109 13 E
Quibaxe, Angola 52 F2 8 24S 14 27 E
Quibdo, Colombia 92 B3 5 42N 76 40W
Quiberon, France 18 C2 47 29N 3 9W
Quiet L., Canada 72 A2 61 5N 133 5W
Quiindy, Paraguay 94 B4 25 58S 57 14W
Quila, Mexico 86 C3 24 23N 107 13W
Quilán, C., Chile 96 E2 43 15S 74 30W
Quilcene, U.S.A. 84 C4 47 49N 122 53W
Quilimarí, Chile 94 C1 32 5S 71 30W
Quilino, Argentina 94 C3 30 14S 64 29W
Quill Lakes, Canada 73 C8 51 55N 104 13W
Quillabamba, Peru 92 F4 12 50S 72 50W
Quillagua, Chile 94 A2 21 40S 69 40W
Quillaicillo, Chile 94 C1 31 17S 71 40W
Quillota, Chile 94 C1 32 54S 71 16W
Quilmes, Argentina 94 C4 34 43S 58 15W
Quilon, India 40 Q10 8 50N 76 38 E
Quilpie, Australia 63 D3 26 35S 144 11 E
Quilpué, Chile 94 C1 33 5S 71 33W
Quilua, Mozam. 55 F4 16 17S 39 54 E
Quimilí, Argentina 94 B3 27 40S 62 30W
Quimper, France 18 B1 48 0N 4 9W
Quimperlé, France 18 C2 47 53N 3 33W
Quinault →, U.S.A. 84 C2 47 21N 124 18W
Quincy, Calif., U.S.A. 84 F6 39 56N 120 57W
Quincy, Fla., U.S.A. 77 K3 30 35N 84 34W
Quincy, Ill., U.S.A. 80 F9 39 56N 91 23W
Quincy, Mass., U.S.A. 79 D14 42 15N 71 0W
Quincy, Wash., U.S.A. 82 C4 47 22N 119 56W
Quines, Argentina 94 C2 32 13S 65 48W
Quinga, Mozam. 55 F5 15 49S 40 15 E
Quinns Rocks, Australia 61 F2 31 40S 115 42 E
Quintana Roo □, Mexico 87 D7 19 0N 88 0W
Quintanar de la Orden, Spain 19 C4 39 36N 3 5W
Quintero, Chile 94 C1 32 45S 71 30W
Quirihue, Chile 94 D1 36 15S 72 35W
Quirindi, Australia 63 E5 31 28S 150 40 E
Quirinópolis, Brazil 93 G8 18 32S 50 30W
Quissanga, Mozam. 55 E5 12 24S 40 28 E
Quitilipi, Argentina 94 B3 26 50S 60 13W
Quitman, U.S.A. 77 K4 30 47N 83 34W
Quito, Ecuador 92 D3 0 15S 78 35W
Quixadá, Brazil 93 D11 4 55S 39 0W
Quixaxe, Mozam. 55 F5 15 17S 40 4 E
Qul'ân, Jazâ'ir, Egypt 44 E2 24 22N 35 31 E
Qumbu, S. Africa 57 E4 31 10S 28 48 E
Quneitra, Syria 47 B4 33 7N 35 48 E
Qŭnghirot, Uzbekistan 26 E6 43 6N 58 54 E
Quoin I., Australia 60 B4 14 54S 129 32 E
Quoin Pt., S. Africa 56 E2 34 46S 19 37 E
Quorn, Australia 63 E2 32 25S 138 5 E
Qŭqon, Uzbekistan 26 E8 40 30N 70 57 E
Qurnat as Sawdā', Lebanon 47 A5 34 18N 36 6 E
Quşaybā', Si. Arabia 44 E4 26 53N 43 35 E
Qusaybah, Iraq 44 C4 34 24N 40 59 E
Quseir, Egypt 44 E2 26 7N 34 16 E
Qūshchī, Iran 44 B5 37 59N 45 3 E
Quthing, Lesotho 57 E4 30 25S 27 36 E
Qūţīābād, Iran 45 C6 35 47N 48 30 E
Quwo, China 34 G6 35 38N 111 25 E
Quyang, China 34 E8 38 35N 114 40 E
Quynh Nhai, Vietnam 38 B4 21 49N 103 33 E
Quyon, Canada 79 A8 45 31N 76 14W
Quzhou, China 33 D6 28 57N 118 54 E
Quzi, China 34 F4 36 20N 107 20 E
Qyzylorda, Kazakstan 26 E7 44 48N 65 28 E

R

Ra, Ko, Thailand 39 H2 9 13N 98 16 E
Raahe, Finland 8 D21 64 40N 24 28 E
Raalte, Neths. 15 B6 52 23N 6 16 E
Raasay, U.K. 12 D2 57 25N 6 4W
Raasay, Sd. of, U.K. 12 D2 57 30N 6 8W
Raba, Indonesia 37 F5 8 36S 118 55 E
Rába →, Hungary 17 E9 47 38N 17 38 E
Rabai, Kenya 54 C4 3 50S 39 31 E
Rabat, Malta 23 D1 35 53N 14 25 E
Rabat, Morocco 50 B4 34 2N 6 48W
Rabaul, Papua N. G. 64 H7 4 24S 152 18 E
Rābigh, Si. Arabia 46 C2 22 50N 39 5 E
Râbniţa, Moldova 17 E15 47 45N 29 0 E
Rābor, Iran 45 D8 29 17N 56 55 E
Race, C., Canada 71 C9 46 40N 53 5W
Rach Gia, Vietnam 39 G5 10 5N 105 5 E
Rachid, Mauritania 50 E3 18 48N 11 41W
Racibórz, Poland 17 C10 50 7N 18 18 E
Racine, U.S.A. 76 D2 42 41N 87 51W
Rackerby, U.S.A. 84 F5 39 26N 121 22W
Radama, Nosy, Madag. 57 A8 14 0S 47 47 E
Radama, Saikanosy, Madag. 57 A8 14 16S 47 53 E
Rădăuţi, Romania 17 E13 47 50N 25 59 E
Radcliff, U.S.A. 76 G3 37 51N 85 57W
Radekhiv, Ukraine 17 C13 50 25N 24 32 E
Radekhov = Radekhiv, Ukraine 17 C13 50 25N 24 32 E
Radford, U.S.A. 76 G5 37 8N 80 34W
Radhanpur, India 42 H4 23 50N 71 38 E
Radhwa, Jabal, Si. Arabia 44 E3 24 34N 38 18 E
Radisson, Canada 70 B4 53 47N 77 37W
Radisson, Sask., Canada 73 C7 52 30N 107 20W
Radium Hot Springs, Canada 72 C5 50 35N 116 2W
Radnor Forest, U.K. 11 E4 52 17N 3 10W
Radom, Poland 17 C11 51 23N 21 12 E
Radomsko, Poland 17 C10 51 5N 19 28 E
Radomyshl, Ukraine 17 C15 50 30N 29 12 E
Radstock, C., Australia 63 E1 33 12S 134 20 E
Radviliškis, Lithuania 9 J20 55 49N 23 33 E
Radville, Canada 73 D8 49 30N 104 15W
Rae, Canada 72 A5 62 50N 116 3W
Rae Bareli, India 43 F9 26 18N 81 20 E
Rae Isthmus, Canada 69 B11 66 40N 87 30W
Raeren, Belgium 15 D6 50 41N 6 7 E
Raeside, L., Australia 61 E3 29 20S 122 0 E
Raetihi, N.Z. 59 H5 39 25S 175 17 E
Rafaela, Argentina 94 C3 31 10S 61 30W
Rafah, Gaza Strip 47 D3 31 18N 34 14 E
Rafai, C.A.R. 54 B1 4 59N 23 58 E
Rafḩā, Si. Arabia 44 D4 29 35N 43 35 E
Rafsanjān, Iran 45 D8 30 30N 56 5 E
Raft Pt., Australia 60 C3 16 4S 124 26 E
Raga, Sudan 51 G11 8 28N 25 41 E
Ragachow, Belarus 17 B16 53 8N 30 5 E
Ragama, Sri Lanka 40 R11 7 0N 79 50 E
Ragged, Mt., Australia 61 F3 33 27S 123 25 E
Raghunathpalli, India 43 H11 22 14N 84 48 E
Raghunathpur, India 43 H12 23 33N 86 40 E
Raglan, N.Z. 59 G5 37 55S 174 55 E
Ragusa, Italy 20 F6 36 55N 14 44 E
Raha, Indonesia 37 E6 4 55S 123 0 E
Rahaeng = Tak, Thailand 38 D2 16 52N 99 8 E
Rahatgarh, India 43 H8 23 47N 78 22 E
Raḩīmah, Si. Arabia 45 E6 26 42N 50 4 E
Rahimyar Khan, Pakistan 42 E4 28 30N 70 25 E
Rāhjerd, Iran 45 C6 34 22N 50 22 E
Rahon, India 42 D7 31 3N 76 7 E
Raichur, India 40 L10 16 10N 77 20 E
Raiganj, India 43 G13 25 37N 88 10 E
Raigarh, India 41 J13 21 56N 83 25 E
Raijua, Indonesia 37 F6 10 37S 121 36 E
Raikot, India 42 D6 30 41N 75 42 E
Railton, Australia 62 G4 41 25S 146 28 E
Rainbow Lake, Canada 72 B5 58 30N 119 23W
Rainier, U.S.A. 84 D4 46 53N 122 41W
Rainier, Mt., U.S.A. 84 D5 46 52N 121 46W
Rainy L., Canada 73 D10 48 42N 93 10W
Rainy River, Canada 73 D10 48 43N 94 29W
Raippaluoto, Finland 8 E19 63 13N 21 14 E
Raipur, India 41 J12 21 17N 81 45 E
Raisen, India 42 H8 23 20N 77 48 E
Raisio, Finland 9 F20 60 28N 22 11 E
Raj Nandgaon, India 41 J12 21 5N 81 5 E
Raj Nilgiri, India 43 J12 21 28N 86 46 E
Raja, Ujung, Indonesia 36 D1 3 40N 96 25 E
Raja Ampat, Kepulauan, Indonesia 37 E8 0 30S 130 0 E
Rajahmundry, India 41 L12 17 1N 81 48 E
Rajang →, Malaysia 36 D4 2 30N 112 0 E
Rajanpur, Pakistan 42 E4 29 6N 70 19 E
Rajapalaiyam, India 40 Q10 9 25N 77 35 E
Rajasthan □, India 42 F5 26 45N 73 30 E
Rajasthan Canal, India 42 F5 28 0N 72 0 E
Rajauri, India 43 C6 33 25N 74 21 E
Rajgarh, Mad. P., India 42 G7 24 2N 76 45 E
Rajgarh, Raj., India 42 F7 27 14N 76 38 E
Rajgarh, Raj., India 42 E6 28 40N 75 25 E
Rajgir, India 43 G11 25 2N 85 25 E
Rajkot, India 42 H4 22 15N 70 56 E
Rajmahal Hills, India 43 G12 24 30N 87 30 E
Rajpipla, India 40 J8 21 50N 73 30 E
Rajpur, India 42 H6 22 18N 74 21 E
Rajpura, India 42 D7 30 25N 76 32 E
Rajshahi, Bangla. 41 G16 24 22N 88 39 E
Rajshahi □, Bangla. 43 G13 25 0N 89 0 E
Rajula, India 42 J4 21 3N 71 26 E
Rakaia, N.Z. 59 K4 43 45S 172 1 E
Rakaia →, N.Z. 59 K4 43 36S 172 15 E
Rakan, Ra's, Qatar 45 E6 26 10N 51 20 E
Rakaposhi, Pakistan 43 A6 36 10N 74 25 E
Rakata, Pulau, Indonesia 36 F3 6 10S 105 20 E
Rakhiv, Ukraine 17 D13 48 3N 24 12 E
Rakhni, Pakistan 42 D3 30 4N 69 56 E
Rakhni →, Pakistan 42 E3 29 31N 69 36 E
Rakitnoye, Russia 30 B7 45 36N 134 17 E
Rakops, Botswana 56 C3 21 1S 24 28 E
Rakvere, Estonia 9 G22 59 20N 26 25 E
Raleigh, U.S.A. 77 H6 35 47N 78 39W
Raleigh B., U.S.A. 75 D11 34 50N 76 15W
Ralls, U.S.A. 81 J4 33 41N 101 24W
Ralston, U.S.A. 78 E8 41 30N 76 57W
Ram →, Canada 72 A4 62 1N 123 41W
Rām Allāh, West Bank 47 D4 31 55N 35 10 E
Ram Hd., Australia 63 F4 37 47S 149 30 E
Rama, Nic. 88 D3 12 9N 84 15W
Ramakona, India 43 J8 21 43N 78 50 E
Raman, Thailand 39 J3 6 29N 101 18 E
Ramanathapuram, India 40 Q11 9 25N 78 55 E
Ramanetaka, B. de, Madag. 57 A8 14 13S 47 52 E
Ramanujganj, India 43 H10 23 48N 83 42 E
Ramat Gan, Israel 47 C3 32 4N 34 48 E
Ramatlhabama, S. Africa 56 D4 25 37S 25 33 E
Ramban, India 43 C6 33 14N 75 12 E
Rambipuji, Indonesia 37 H15 8 12S 113 37 E
Ramechhap, Nepal 43 F12 27 25N 86 10 E
Ramganga →, India 43 F8 27 5N 79 58 E
Ramgarh, Bihar, India 43 H11 23 40N 85 35 E
Ramgarh, Raj., India 42 F6 27 16N 75 14 E
Ramgarh, Raj., India 42 F4 27 30N 70 36 E
Rāmhormoz, Iran 45 D6 31 15N 49 35 E
Ramīān, Iran 45 B7 37 3N 55 16 E
Ramingining, Australia 62 A2 12 19S 135 3 E
Ramla, Israel 47 D3 31 55N 34 52 E
Ramnad = Ramanathapuram, India 40 Q11 9 25N 78 55 E
Ramnagar, India 43 E8 29 24N 79 7 E
Ramnagar, Jammu & Kashmir, India 43 C6 32 47N 75 18 E
Râmnicu Sărat, Romania 17 F14 45 26N 27 3 E
Râmnicu Vâlcea, Romania 17 F13 45 9N 24 21 E
Ramona, U.S.A. 85 M10 33 2N 116 52W
Ramore, Canada 70 C3 48 30N 80 25W
Ramotswa, Botswana 56 C4 24 50S 25 52 E
Rampur, H.P., India 42 D7 31 26N 77 43 E
Rampur, Mad. P., India 42 H5 23 25N 73 53 E
Rampur, Ut. P., India 43 E8 28 50N 79 5 E
Rampur Hat, India 43 G12 24 10N 87 50 E
Rampura, India 42 G6 24 30N 75 27 E
Ramrama Tola, India 43 J8 21 52N 79 55 E
Ramree I. = Ramree Kyun, Burma 41 K19 19 0N 94 0 E
Ramree Kyun, Burma 41 K19 19 0N 94 0 E
Rāmsar, Iran 45 B6 36 53N 50 41 E
Ramsey, U.K. 10 C3 54 20N 4 22W
Ramsey, U.S.A. 79 E10 41 4N 74 9W
Ramsey L., Canada 70 C3 47 13N 82 15W
Ramsgate, U.K. 11 F9 51 20N 1 25 E
Ramtek, India 40 J11 21 20N 79 15 E
Rana Pratap Sagar Dam, India 42 G6 24 58N 75 38 E
Ranaghat, India 43 H13 23 15N 88 35 E
Ranahu, Pakistan 42 G3 25 55N 69 45 E
Ranau, Malaysia 36 C5 6 2N 116 40 E
Rancagua, Chile 94 C1 34 10S 70 50W
Rancheria →, Canada 72 A3 60 13N 129 7W
Ranchester, U.S.A. 82 D10 44 54N 107 10W
Ranchi, India 43 H11 23 19N 85 27 E
Rancho Cucamonga, U.S.A. 85 L9 34 10N 117 30W
Randalstown, U.K. 13 B5 54 45N 6 19W
Randers, Denmark 9 H14 56 29N 10 1 E
Randfontein, S. Africa 57 D4 26 8S 27 45 E
Randle, U.S.A. 84 D5 46 32N 121 57W
Randolph, Mass., U.S.A. 79 D13 42 10N 71 2W
Randolph, N.Y., U.S.A. 78 D6 42 10N 78 59W
Randolph, Utah, U.S.A. 82 F8 41 40N 111 11W
Randolph, Vt., U.S.A. 79 C12 43 55N 72 40W
Randsburg, U.S.A. 85 K9 35 22N 117 39W
Råne älv →, Sweden 8 D20 65 50N 22 20 E
Rangae, Thailand 39 J3 6 19N 101 44 E
Rangaunu B., N.Z. 59 F4 34 51S 173 15 E
Rangeley, U.S.A. 79 B14 44 58N 70 39W
Rangeley L., U.S.A. 79 B14 44 55N 70 43W
Rangely, U.S.A. 82 F9 40 5N 108 48W
Ranger, U.S.A. 81 J5 32 28N 98 41W
Rangia, India 41 F17 26 28N 91 38 E
Rangiora, N.Z. 59 K4 43 19S 172 36 E
Rangitaiki →, N.Z. 59 G6 37 54S 176 49 E
Rangitata →, N.Z. 59 K3 43 45S 171 15 E
Rangkasbitung, Indonesia 37 G12 6 21S 106 15 E
Rangon →, Burma 41 L20 16 28N 96 40 E
Rangoon, Burma 41 L20 16 45N 96 20 E
Rangpur, Bangla. 41 G16 25 42N 89 22 E
Rangsit, Thailand 38 F3 13 59N 100 37 E
Ranibennur, India 40 M9 14 35N 75 30 E
Raniganj, Ut. P., India 43 F9 27 3N 82 13 E
Raniganj, W. Bengal, India 41 H15 23 40N 87 5 E
Ranikhet, India 43 E8 29 39N 79 25 E
Raniwara, India 40 G8 24 50N 72 10 E
Rāniyah, Iraq 44 B5 36 15N 44 53 E
Ranka, India 43 H10 23 59N 83 47 E
Ranken →, Australia 62 C2 20 31S 137 36 E
Rankin, U.S.A. 81 K4 31 13N 101 56W
Rankin Inlet, Canada 68 B10 62 30N 93 0W
Rankins Springs, Australia 63 E4 33 49S 146 14 E
Rannoch, L., U.K. 12 E4 56 41N 4 20W
Rannoch Moor, U.K. 12 E4 56 38N 4 48W
Ranobe, Helodranon' i, Madag. 57 C7 23 3S 43 33 E
Ranohira, Madag. 57 C8 22 29S 45 24 E
Ranomafana, Toamasina, Madag. 57 B8 18 57S 48 50 E
Ranomafana, Toliara, Madag. 57 C8 24 34S 47 0 E
Ranong, Thailand 39 H2 9 56N 98 40 E
Rānsa, Iran 45 C6 33 39N 48 18 E
Ransiki, Indonesia 37 E8 1 30S 134 10 E
Rantauprapat, Indonesia 36 D1 2 15N 99 50 E
Rantemario, Indonesia 37 E5 3 15S 119 57 E
Rantoul, U.S.A. 76 E1 40 19N 88 9W
Raoyang, China 34 E8 38 15N 115 45 E
Rapa, Pac. Oc. 65 K13 27 35S 144 20W
Rapallo, Italy 18 D8 44 21N 9 14 E
Rapar, India 42 H4 23 34N 70 38 E
Rāpch, Iran 45 E8 25 40N 59 15 E
Raper, C., Canada 69 B13 69 44N 67 6W
Rapid City, U.S.A. 80 D3 44 5N 103 14W
Rapid River, U.S.A. 76 C2 45 55N 86 58W
Rapla, Estonia 9 G21 59 1N 24 52 E
Rapti →, India 43 F10 26 18N 83 41 E
Raquette →, U.S.A. 79 B10 45 0N 74 42W
Raquette Lake, U.S.A. 79 C10 43 49N 74 40W
Rarotonga, Cook Is. 65 K12 21 30S 160 0W
Ra's al 'Ayn, Syria 44 B4 36 45N 40 12 E
Ra's al Khaymah, U.A.E. 45 E8 25 50N 55 59 E
Ra's an Naqb, Jordan 47 F4 30 0N 35 29 E
Ras Dashen, Ethiopia 46 E2 13 8N 38 26 E
Râs Timirist, Mauritania 50 E2 19 21N 16 30W

Rasca, Pta. de la, *Canary Is.* **22 G3** 27 59N 16 41W
Raseiniai, *Lithuania* **9 J20** 55 25N 23 5 E
Rashmi, *India* **42 G6** 25 4N 74 22 E
Rasht, *Iran* **45 B6** 37 20N 49 40 E
Rasi Salai, *Thailand* **38 E5** 15 20N 104 9 E
Rason L., *Australia* **61 E3** 28 45S 124 25 E
Rasra, *India* **43 G10** 25 50N 83 50 E
Rasul, *Pakistan* **42 C5** 32 42N 73 34 E
Rat Buri, *Thailand* **38 F2** 13 30N 99 54 E
Rat Islands, *U.S.A.* **68 C1** 52 0N 178 0 E
Rat L., *Canada* **73 B9** 56 10N 99 40W
Ratangarh, *India* **42 E6** 28 5N 74 35 E
Raṭāwī, *Iraq* **44 D5** 30 38N 47 13 E
Ratcatchers L., *Australia* **63 E3** 32 38S 143 10 E
Rath, *India* **43 G8** 25 36N 79 37 E
Rath Luirc, *Ireland* **13 D3** 52 21N 8 40W
Rathdrum, *Ireland* **13 D5** 52 56N 6 14W
Rathenow, *Germany* **16 B7** 52 37N 12 19 E
Rathkeale, *Ireland* **13 D3** 52 32N 8 56W
Rathlin I., *U.K.* **13 A5** 55 18N 6 14W
Rathmelton, *Ireland* **13 A4** 55 2N 7 38W
Ratibor = Racibórz, *Poland* **17 C10** 50 7N 18 18 E
Ratlam, *India* **42 H6** 23 20N 75 0 E
Ratnagiri, *India* **40 L8** 16 57N 73 18 E
Ratodero, *Pakistan* **42 F3** 27 48N 68 18 E
Raton, *U.S.A.* **81 G2** 36 54N 104 24W
Rattaphum, *Thailand* **39 J3** 7 8N 100 16 E
Rattray Hd., *U.K.* **12 D7** 57 38N 1 50W
Ratz, Mt., *Canada* **72 B2** 57 23N 132 12W
Raub, *Malaysia* **39 L3** 3 47N 101 52 E
Rauch, *Argentina* **94 D4** 36 45S 59 5W
Raudales de Malpaso, *Mexico* **87 D6** 17 30N 23 30W
Raufarhöfn, *Iceland* **8 C6** 66 27N 15 57W
Raufoss, *Norway* **9 F14** 60 44N 10 37 E
Raukumara Ra., *N.Z.* **59 H6** 38 5S 177 55 E
Rauma, *Finland* **9 F19** 61 10N 21 30 E
Raurkela, *India* **43 H11** 22 14N 84 50 E
Rausu-Dake, *Japan* **30 B12** 44 4N 145 7 E
Rava-Ruska, *Poland* **17 C12** 50 15N 23 42 E
Rava Russkaya = Rava-Ruska, *Poland* **17 C12** 50 15N 23 42 E
Ravalli, *U.S.A.* **82 C6** 47 17N 114 11W
Ravānsar, *Iran* **44 C5** 34 43N 46 40 E
Rāvar, *Iran* **45 D8** 31 20N 56 51 E
Ravena, *U.S.A.* **79 D11** 42 28N 73 49W
Ravenna, *Italy* **20 B5** 44 25N 12 12 E
Ravenna, *Nebr., U.S.A.* **80 E5** 41 1N 98 55W
Ravenna, *Ohio, U.S.A.* **78 E3** 41 9N 81 15W
Ravensburg, *Germany* **16 E5** 47 46N 9 36 E
Ravenshoe, *Australia* **62 B4** 17 37S 145 29 E
Ravensthorpe, *Australia* **61 F3** 33 35S 120 2 E
Ravenswood, *Australia* **62 C4** 20 6S 146 54 E
Ravenswood, *U.S.A.* **76 F5** 38 57N 81 46W
Ravi →, *Pakistan* **42 D4** 30 35N 71 49 E
Rawalpindi, *Pakistan* **42 C5** 33 38N 73 8 E
Rawāndūz, *Iraq* **44 B5** 36 40N 44 30 E
Rawang, *Malaysia* **39 L3** 3 20N 101 35 E
Rawene, *N.Z.* **59 F4** 35 25S 173 32 E
Rawlinna, *Australia* **61 F4** 30 58S 125 28 E
Rawlins, *U.S.A.* **82 F10** 41 47N 107 14W
Rawlinson Ra., *Australia* **61 D4** 24 40S 128 30 E
Rawson, *Argentina* **96 E3** 43 15S 65 5W
Raxaul, *India* **43 F11** 26 59N 84 51 E
Ray, *U.S.A.* **80 A3** 48 21N 103 10W
Ray, C., *Canada* **71 C8** 47 33N 59 15W
Rayadurg, *India* **40 M10** 14 40N 76 50 E
Rayagada, *India* **41 K13** 19 15N 83 20 E
Raychikhinsk, *Russia* **27 E13** 49 46N 129 25 E
Rāyen, *Iran* **45 D8** 29 34N 57 26 E
Rayleigh, *U.K.* **11 F8** 51 36N 0 37 E
Raymond, *Canada* **72 D6** 49 30N 112 35W
Raymond, *Calif., U.S.A.* **84 H7** 37 13N 119 54W
Raymond, *N.H., U.S.A.* **79 C13** 43 2N 71 11W
Raymond, *Wash., U.S.A.* **84 D3** 46 41N 123 44W
Raymond Terrace, *Australia* **63 E5** 32 45S 151 44 E
Raymondville, *U.S.A.* **81 M6** 26 29N 97 47W
Raymore, *Canada* **73 C8** 51 25N 104 31W
Rayna, *India* **43 H12** 23 5N 87 54 E
Rayón, *Mexico* **86 B2** 29 43N 110 35W
Rayong, *Thailand* **38 F3** 12 40N 101 20 E
Rayville, *U.S.A.* **81 J9** 32 29N 91 46W
Raz, Pte. du, *France* **18 C1** 48 2N 4 47W
Razan, *Iran* **45 C6** 35 23N 49 2 E
Razdel'naya = Rozdilna, *Ukraine* **17 E16** 46 50N 30 2 E
Razdolnoye, *Russia* **30 C5** 43 30N 131 52 E
Razeh, *Iran* **45 C6** 32 47N 48 9 E
Razgrad, *Bulgaria* **21 C12** 43 33N 26 34 E
Razim, Lacul, *Romania* **17 F15** 44 50N 29 0 E
Razmak, *Pakistan* **42 C3** 32 45N 69 50 E
Ré, Î. de, *France* **18 C3** 46 12N 1 30W
Reading, *U.K.* **11 F7** 51 27N 0 58W
Reading, *U.S.A.* **79 F9** 40 20N 75 56W
Reading □, *U.K.* **11 F7** 51 27N 0 58W
Realicó, *Argentina* **94 D3** 35 0S 64 15W
Ream, *Cambodia* **39 G4** 10 34N 103 39 E
Reata, *Mexico* **86 B4** 26 8N 101 5W
Reay Forest, *U.K.* **12 C4** 58 22N 4 55W
Rebi, *Indonesia* **37 F8** 6 23S 134 7 E
Rebiana, *Libya* **51 D10** 24 12N 22 10 E
Rebun-Tō, *Japan* **30 B10** 45 23N 141 2 E
Recherche, Arch. of the, *Australia* **61 F3** 34 15S 122 50 E
Rechna Doab, *Pakistan* **42 D5** 31 35N 73 30 E
Rechytsa, *Belarus* **17 B16** 52 21N 30 24 E
Recife, *Brazil* **93 E12** 8 0S 35 0W
Recklinghausen, *Germany* **15 C7** 51 37N 7 12 E
Reconquista, *Argentina* **94 B4** 29 10S 59 45W
Recreo, *Argentina* **94 B2** 29 25S 65 10W
Red →, *La., U.S.A.* **81 K9** 31 1N 91 45W
Red →, *N. Dak., U.S.A.* **68 C10** 49 0N 97 15W
Red Bank, *U.S.A.* **79 F10** 40 21N 74 5W
Red Bay, *Canada* **71 B8** 51 44N 56 25W
Red Bluff, *U.S.A.* **82 F2** 40 11N 122 15W
Red Bluff L., *U.S.A.* **81 K3** 31 54N 103 55W
Red Cliffs, *Australia* **63 E3** 34 19S 142 11 E
Red Cloud, *U.S.A.* **80 E5** 40 5N 98 32W
Red Creek, *U.S.A.* **79 C8** 43 14N 76 45W
Red Deer, *Canada* **72 C6** 52 20N 113 50W
Red Deer →, *Alta., Canada* **73 C7** 50 58N 110 0W
Red Deer →, *Man., Canada* **73 C8** 52 53N 101 1W
Red Deer L., *Canada* **73 C8** 52 55N 101 20W
Red Hook, *U.S.A.* **79 E11** 41 55N 73 53W
Red Indian L., *Canada* **71 C8** 48 35N 57 0W
Red L., *Canada* **73 C10** 51 3N 93 49W
Red Lake, *Canada* **73 C10** 51 3N 93 49W
Red Lake Falls, *U.S.A.* **80 B6** 47 53N 96 16W
Red Lake Road, *Canada* **73 C10** 49 59N 93 25W
Red Lodge, *U.S.A.* **82 D9** 45 11N 109 15W
Red Mountain, *U.S.A.* **85 K9** 35 37N 117 38W
Red Oak, *U.S.A.* **80 E7** 41 1N 95 14W
Red Rock, *Canada* **70 C2** 48 55N 88 15W
Red Rock, L., *U.S.A.* **80 E8** 41 22N 92 59W
Red Rocks Pt., *Australia* **61 F4** 32 13S 127 32 E
Red Sea, *Asia* **46 C2** 25 0N 36 0 E
Red Slate Mt., *U.S.A.* **84 H8** 37 31N 118 52W
Red Sucker L., *Canada* **70 B1** 54 9N 93 40W
Red Tower Pass = Turnu Roşu, P., *Romania* **17 F13** 45 33N 24 17 E
Red Wing, *U.S.A.* **80 C8** 44 34N 92 31W
Redang, *Malaysia* **36 C2** 5 49N 103 2 E
Redange, *Lux.* **15 E5** 49 46N 5 52 E
Redcar, *U.K.* **10 C6** 54 37N 1 4W
Redcar & Cleveland □, *U.K.* **10 C7** 54 29N 1 0W
Redcliff, *Canada* **73 C6** 50 10N 110 50W
Redcliffe, *Australia* **63 D5** 27 12S 153 0 E
Redcliffe, Mt., *Australia* **61 E3** 28 30S 121 30 E
Reddersburg, *S. Africa* **56 D4** 29 41S 26 10 E
Redding, *U.S.A.* **82 F2** 40 35N 122 24W
Redditch, *U.K.* **11 E6** 52 18N 1 55W
Redfield, *U.S.A.* **80 C5** 44 53N 98 31W
Redford, *U.S.A.* **79 B11** 44 38N 73 48W
Redlands, *U.S.A.* **85 M9** 34 4N 117 11W
Redmond, *Oreg., U.S.A.* **82 D3** 44 17N 121 11W
Redmond, *Wash., U.S.A.* **84 C4** 47 41N 122 7W
Redon, *France* **18 C2** 47 40N 2 6W
Redonda, *Antigua* **89 C7** 16 58N 62 19W
Redondela, *Spain* **19 A1** 42 15N 8 38W
Redondo Beach, *U.S.A.* **85 M8** 33 50N 118 23W
Redruth, *U.K.* **11 G2** 50 14N 5 14W
Redvers, *Canada* **73 D8** 49 35N 101 40W
Redwater, *Canada* **72 C6** 53 55N 113 6W
Redwood, *U.S.A.* **79 B9** 44 18N 75 48W
Redwood City, *U.S.A.* **84 H4** 37 30N 122 15W
Redwood Falls, *U.S.A.* **80 C7** 44 32N 95 7W
Redwood National Park, *U.S.A.* **82 F1** 41 40N 124 5W
Ree, L., *Ireland* **13 C3** 53 35N 8 0W
Reed, L., *Canada* **73 C8** 54 38N 100 30W
Reed City, *U.S.A.* **76 D3** 43 53N 85 31W
Reedley, *U.S.A.* **84 J7** 36 36N 119 27W
Reedsburg, *U.S.A.* **80 D9** 43 32N 90 0W
Reedsport, *U.S.A.* **82 E1** 43 42N 124 6W
Reedsville, *U.S.A.* **78 F7** 40 39N 77 35W
Reefton, *N.Z.* **59 K3** 42 6S 171 51 E
Reese →, *U.S.A.* **82 F5** 40 48N 117 4W
Refugio, *U.S.A.* **81 L6** 28 18N 97 17W
Regensburg, *Germany* **16 D7** 49 1N 12 6 E
Réggio di Calábria, *Italy* **20 E6** 38 6N 15 39 E
Réggio nell'Emilia, *Italy* **20 B4** 44 43N 10 36 E
Reghin, *Romania* **17 E13** 46 46N 24 42 E
Regina, *Canada* **73 C8** 50 27N 104 35W
Regina Beach, *Canada* **73 C8** 50 47N 105 0W
Registro, *Brazil* **95 A6** 24 29S 47 49W
Rehar →, *India* **43 H10** 23 55N 82 40 E
Rehli, *India* **43 H8** 23 38N 79 5 E
Rehoboth, *Namibia* **56 C2** 23 15S 17 4 E
Rehovot, *Israel* **47 D3** 31 54N 34 48 E
Reichenbach, *Germany* **16 C7** 50 37N 12 17 E
Reid, *Australia* **61 F4** 30 49S 128 26 E
Reidsville, *U.S.A.* **77 G6** 36 21N 79 40W
Reigate, *U.K.* **11 F7** 51 14N 0 12W
Reims, *France* **18 B6** 49 15N 4 1 E
Reina Adelaida, Arch., *Chile* **96 G2** 52 20S 74 0W
Reindeer →, *Canada* **73 B8** 55 36N 103 11W
Reindeer I., *Canada* **73 C9** 52 30N 98 0W
Reindeer L., *Canada* **73 B8** 57 15N 102 15W
Reinga, C., *N.Z.* **59 F4** 34 25S 172 43 E
Reinosa, *Spain* **19 A3** 43 2N 4 15W
Reitz, *S. Africa* **57 D4** 27 48S 28 29 E
Reivilo, *S. Africa* **56 D3** 27 36S 24 8 E
Reliance, *Canada* **73 A7** 63 0N 109 20W
Remarkable, Mt., *Australia* **63 E2** 32 48S 138 10 E
Rembang, *Indonesia* **37 G14** 6 42S 111 21 E
Remedios, *Panama* **88 E3** 8 15N 81 50W
Remeshk, *Iran* **45 E8** 26 55N 58 50 E
Remich, *Lux.* **15 E6** 49 32N 6 22 E
Remscheid, *Germany* **15 C7** 51 11N 7 12 E
Ren Xian, *China* **34 F8** 37 8N 114 40 E
Rendsburg, *Germany* **16 A5** 54 17N 9 39 E
Renfrew, *Canada* **79 A8** 45 30N 76 40W
Renfrewshire □, *U.K.* **12 F4** 55 49N 4 38W
Rengat, *Indonesia* **36 E2** 0 30S 102 45 E
Rengo, *Chile* **94 C1** 34 24S 70 50W
Reni, *Ukraine* **17 F15** 45 28N 28 15 E
Renmark, *Australia* **63 E3** 34 11S 140 43 E
Rennell Sd., *Canada* **72 C2** 53 23N 132 35W
Renner Springs, *Australia* **62 B1** 18 20S 133 47 E
Rennes, *France* **18 B3** 48 7N 1 41W
Rennie L., *Canada* **73 A7** 61 32N 105 35W
Reno, *U.S.A.* **84 F7** 39 31N 119 48W
Reno →, *Italy* **20 B5** 44 38N 12 16 E
Renovo, *U.S.A.* **78 E7** 41 20N 77 45W
Renqiu, *China* **34 E9** 38 43N 116 5 E
Rensselaer, *Ind., U.S.A.* **76 E2** 40 57N 87 9W
Rensselaer, *N.Y., U.S.A.* **79 D11** 42 38N 73 45W
Rentería, *Spain* **19 A5** 43 19N 1 54W
Renton, *U.S.A.* **84 C4** 47 29N 122 12W
Reotipur, *India* **43 G10** 25 33N 83 45 E
Republic, *Mo., U.S.A.* **81 G8** 37 7N 93 29W
Republic, *Wash., U.S.A.* **82 B4** 48 39N 118 44W
Republican →, *U.S.A.* **80 F6** 39 4N 96 48W
Repulse Bay, *Canada* **69 B11** 66 30N 86 30W
Requena, *Peru* **92 E4** 5 5S 73 52W
Requena, *Spain* **19 C5** 39 30N 1 4W
Reşadiye = Datça, *Turkey* **21 F12** 36 46N 27 40 E
Reserve, *U.S.A.* **83 K9** 33 43N 108 45W
Resht = Rasht, *Iran* **45 B6** 37 20N 49 40 E
Resistencia, *Argentina* **94 B4** 27 30S 59 0W
Reşiţa, *Romania* **17 F11** 45 18N 21 53 E
Resolution I., *Canada* **69 B13** 61 30N 65 0W
Resolution I., *N.Z.* **59 L1** 45 40S 166 40 E
Ressano Garcia, *Mozam.* **57 D5** 25 25S 32 0 E
Reston, *Canada* **73 D8** 49 33N 101 6W
Retalhuleu, *Guatemala* **88 D1** 14 33N 91 46W
Retenue, L. de, *Dem. Rep. of the Congo* **55 E2** 11 0S 27 0 E
Retford, *U.K.* **10 D7** 53 19N 0 56W
Réthimnon, *Greece* **23 D6** 35 18N 24 30 E
Réthimnon □, *Greece* **23 D6** 35 23N 24 28 E
Reti, *Pakistan* **42 E3** 28 5N 69 48 E
Réunion ■, *Ind. Oc.* **49 J9** 21 0S 56 0 E
Reus, *Spain* **19 B6** 41 10N 1 5 E
Reutlingen, *Germany* **16 D5** 48 29N 9 12 E
Reval = Tallinn, *Estonia* **9 G21** 59 22N 24 48 E
Revda, *Russia* **24 C10** 56 48N 59 57 E
Revelganj, *India* **43 G11** 25 50N 84 40 E
Revelstoke, *Canada* **72 C5** 51 0N 118 10W
Reventazón, *Peru* **92 E2** 6 10S 80 58W
Revillagigedo, Is. de, *Pac. Oc.* **86 D2** 18 40N 112 0W
Revuè →, *Mozam.* **55 F3** 19 50S 34 0 E
Rewa, *India* **43 G9** 24 33N 81 25 E
Rewari, *India* **42 E7** 28 15N 76 40 E
Rexburg, *U.S.A.* **82 E8** 43 49N 111 47W
Rey, *Iran* **45 C6** 35 35N 51 25 E
Rey, I. del, *Panama* **88 E4** 8 20N 78 30W
Rey Malabo, *Eq. Guin.* **52 D1** 3 45N 8 50 E
Reyðarfjörður, *Iceland* **8 D6** 65 2N 14 13W
Reyes, Pt., *U.S.A.* **84 H3** 38 0N 123 0W
Reykjahlið, *Iceland* **8 D5** 65 40N 16 55W
Reykjanes, *Iceland* **8 E2** 63 48N 22 40W
Reykjavík, *Iceland* **8 D3** 64 10N 21 57W
Reynolds Ra., *Australia* **60 D5** 22 30S 133 0 E
Reynoldsville, *U.S.A.* **78 E6** 41 5N 78 58W
Reynosa, *Mexico* **87 B5** 26 5N 98 18W
Rēzekne, *Latvia* **9 H22** 56 30N 27 17 E
Rezvān, *Iran* **45 E8** 27 34N 56 6 E
Rhayader, *U.K.* **11 E4** 52 18N 3 29W
Rhein →, *Europe* **15 C6** 51 52N 6 2 E
Rhein-Main-Donau-Kanal, *Germany* **16 D6** 49 15N 11 15 E
Rheine, *Germany* **16 B4** 52 17N 7 26 E
Rheinland-Pfalz □, *Germany* **16 C4** 50 0N 7 0 E
Rhin = Rhein →, *Europe* **15 C6** 51 52N 6 2 E
Rhine = Rhein →, *Europe* **15 C6** 51 52N 6 2 E
Rhinebeck, *U.S.A.* **79 E11** 41 56N 73 55W
Rhineland-Palatinate = Rheinland-Pfalz □, *Germany* **16 C4** 50 0N 7 0 E
Rhinelander, *U.S.A.* **80 C10** 45 38N 89 25W
Rhinns Pt., *U.K.* **12 F2** 55 40N 6 29W
Rhino Camp, *Uganda* **54 B3** 3 0N 31 22 E
Rhir, Cap, *Morocco* **50 B4** 30 38N 9 54W
Rhode Island □, *U.S.A.* **79 E13** 41 40N 71 30W
Rhodes = Ródhos, *Greece* **23 C10** 36 15N 28 10 E
Rhodesia = Zimbabwe ■, *Africa* **55 F3** 19 0S 30 0 E
Rhodope Mts. = Rhodopi Planina, *Bulgaria* **21 D11** 41 40N 24 20 E
Rhodopi Planina, *Bulgaria* **21 D11** 41 40N 24 20 E
Rhön = Rhön, *Germany* **16 C5** 50 24N 9 58 E
Rhön, *Germany* **16 C5** 50 24N 9 58 E
Rhondda, *U.K.* **11 F4** 51 39N 3 31W
Rhondda Cynon Taff □, *U.K.* **11 F4** 51 42N 3 27W
Rhône →, *France* **18 E6** 43 28N 4 42 E
Rhum, *U.K.* **12 E2** 57 0N 6 20W
Rhyl, *U.K.* **10 D4** 53 20N 3 29W
Riachão, *Brazil* **93 E9** 7 20S 46 37W
Riasi, *India* **43 C6** 33 10N 74 50 E
Riau □, *Indonesia* **36 E2** 0 0 102 35 E
Riau, Kepulauan, *Indonesia* **36 D2** 0 30N 104 20 E
Riau Arch. = Riau, Kepulauan, *Indonesia* **36 D2** 0 30N 104 20 E
Ribadeo, *Spain* **19 A2** 43 35N 7 5W
Ribas do Rio Pardo, *Brazil* **93 H8** 20 27S 53 46W
Ribble →, *U.K.* **10 D5** 53 52N 2 25W
Ribe, *Denmark* **9 J13** 55 19N 8 44 E
Ribeira Brava, *Madeira* **22 D2** 32 41N 17 4W
Ribeirão Prêto, *Brazil* **95 A6** 21 10S 47 50W
Riberalta, *Bolivia* **92 F5** 11 0S 66 0W
Riccarton, *N.Z.* **59 K4** 43 32S 172 37 E
Rice, *U.S.A.* **85 L12** 34 5N 114 51W
Rice L., *Canada* **78 B6** 44 12N 78 10W
Rice Lake, *U.S.A.* **80 C9** 45 30N 91 44W
Rich, C., *Canada* **78 B4** 44 43N 80 38W
Richards Bay, *S. Africa* **57 D5** 28 48S 32 6 E
Richardson →, *Canada* **73 B6** 58 25N 111 14W
Richardson Lakes, *U.S.A.* **76 C10** 44 46N 70 58W
Richardson Springs, *U.S.A.* **84 F5** 39 51N 121 46W
Riche, C., *Australia* **61 F2** 34 36S 118 47 E
Richey, *U.S.A.* **80 B2** 47 39N 105 4W
Richfield, *U.S.A.* **83 G8** 38 46N 112 5W
Richfield Springs, *U.S.A.* **79 D10** 42 51N 74 59W
Richford, *U.S.A.* **79 B12** 45 0N 72 40W
Richibucto, *Canada* **71 C7** 46 42N 64 54W
Richland, *Ga., U.S.A.* **77 J3** 32 5N 84 40W
Richland, *Wash., U.S.A.* **82 C4** 46 17N 119 18W
Richland Center, *U.S.A.* **80 D9** 43 21N 90 23W
Richlands, *U.S.A.* **76 G5** 37 6N 81 48W
Richmond, *Australia* **62 C3** 20 43S 143 8 E
Richmond, *N.Z.* **59 J4** 41 20S 173 12 E
Richmond, *U.K.* **10 C6** 54 25N 1 43W
Richmond, *Calif., U.S.A.* **84 H4** 37 56N 122 21W
Richmond, *Ind., U.S.A.* **76 F3** 39 50N 84 53W
Richmond, *Ky., U.S.A.* **76 G3** 37 45N 84 18W
Richmond, *Mich., U.S.A.* **78 D2** 42 49N 82 45W
Richmond, *Mo., U.S.A.* **80 F8** 39 17N 93 58W
Richmond, *Tex., U.S.A.* **81 L7** 29 35N 95 46W
Richmond, *Utah, U.S.A.* **82 F8** 41 56N 111 48W
Richmond, *Va., U.S.A.* **76 G7** 37 33N 77 27W
Richmond, *Vt., U.S.A.* **79 B12** 44 24N 72 59W
Richmond Hill, *Canada* **78 C5** 43 52N 79 27W
Richmond Ra., *Australia* **63 D5** 29 0S 152 45 E
Richwood, *U.S.A.* **76 F5** 38 14N 80 32W
Ridder = Leninogorsk, *Kazakstan* **26 D9** 50 20N 83 30 E
Riddlesburg, *U.S.A.* **78 F6** 40 9N 78 15W
Ridgecrest, *U.S.A.* **85 K9** 35 38N 117 40W
Ridgefield, *Conn., U.S.A.* **79 E11** 41 17N 73 30W
Ridgefield, *Wash., U.S.A.* **84 E4** 45 49N 122 45W
Ridgeland, *U.S.A.* **77 J5** 32 29N 80 59W
Ridgetown, *Canada* **78 D3** 42 26N 81 52W
Ridgewood, *U.S.A.* **79 F10** 40 59N 74 7W
Ridgway, *U.S.A.* **78 E6** 41 25N 78 44W
Riding Mountain Nat. Park, *Canada* **73 C9** 50 50N 100 0W
Ridley, Mt., *Australia* **61 F3** 33 12S 122 7 E
Ried, *Austria* **16 D7** 48 14N 13 30 E
Riesa, *Germany* **16 C7** 51 17N 13 17 E
Riet →, *S. Africa* **56 D3** 29 0S 23 54 E
Rieti, *Italy* **20 C5** 42 24N 12 51 E
Riffe L., *U.S.A.* **84 D4** 46 32N 122 26W
Rifle, *U.S.A.* **82 G10** 39 32N 107 47W
Rift Valley □, *Kenya* **54 B4** 0 20N 36 0 E
Rīga, *Latvia* **9 H21** 56 53N 24 8 E
Riga, G. of, *Latvia* **9 H20** 57 40N 23 45 E
Rīgān, *Iran* **45 D8** 28 37N 58 58 E
Rīgas Jūras Līcis = Riga, G. of, *Latvia* **9 H20** 57 40N 23 45 E
Rigaud, *Canada* **79 A10** 45 29N 74 18W
Rigby, *U.S.A.* **82 E8** 43 40N 111 55W
Rīgestān □, *Afghan.* **40 D4** 30 15N 65 0 E
Riggins, *U.S.A.* **82 D5** 45 25N 116 19W
Rigolet, *Canada* **71 B8** 54 10N 58 23W
Rihand Dam, *India* **43 G10** 24 9N 83 2 E
Riihimäki, *Finland* **9 F21** 60 45N 24 48 E
Riiser-Larsen-halvøya, *Antarctica* **5 C4** 68 0S 35 0 E
Rijeka, *Croatia* **16 F8** 45 20N 14 21 E
Rijssen, *Neths.* **15 B6** 52 19N 6 31 E
Rikuzentakada, *Japan* **30 E10** 39 0N 141 40 E
Riley, *U.S.A.* **82 E4** 43 32N 119 28W
Rimah, Wadi ar →, *Si. Arabia* **44 E4** 26 5N 41 30 E
Rimbey, *Canada* **72 C6** 52 35N 114 15W
Rimersburg, *U.S.A.* **78 E5** 41 3N 79 30W
Rímini, *Italy* **20 B5** 44 3N 12 33 E
Rimouski, *Canada* **71 C6** 48 27N 68 30W
Rimrock, *U.S.A.* **84 D5** 46 38N 121 10W
Rinca, *Indonesia* **37 F5** 8 45S 119 35 E
Rincón de Romos, *Mexico* **86 C4** 22 14N 102 18W
Rinconada, *Argentina* **94 A2** 22 26S 66 10W
Rind →, *India* **43 G9** 25 53N 80 33 E
Ringas, *India* **42 F6** 27 21N 75 34 E
Ringkøbing, *Denmark* **9 H13** 56 5N 8 15 E
Ringvassøy, *Norway* **8 B18** 69 56N 19 15 E
Ringwood, *U.S.A.* **79 E10** 41 7N 74 15W
Rinjani, *Indonesia* **36 F5** 8 24S 116 28 E
Rio Branco, *Brazil* **92 E5** 9 58S 67 49W
Río Branco, *Uruguay* **95 C5** 32 40S 53 40W
Río Bravo del Norte →, *Mexico* **87 B5** 25 57N 97 9W
Rio Brilhante, *Brazil* **95 A5** 21 48S 54 33W
Rio Claro, *Brazil* **95 A6** 22 19S 47 35W
Rio Claro, *Trin. & Tob.* **89 D7** 10 20N 61 25W
Río Colorado, *Argentina* **96 D4** 39 0S 64 0W
Río Cuarto, *Argentina* **94 C3** 33 10S 64 25W
Rio das Pedras, *Mozam.* **57 C6** 23 8S 35 28 E
Rio de Janeiro, *Brazil* **95 A7** 23 0S 43 12W
Rio de Janeiro □, *Brazil* **95 A7** 22 50S 43 0W
Rio do Sul, *Brazil* **95 B6** 27 13S 49 37W
Río Gallegos, *Argentina* **96 G3** 51 35S 69 15W
Rio Grande = Grande, Rio →, *U.S.A.* **81 N6** 25 58N 97 9W
Río Grande, *Argentina* **96 G3** 53 50S 67 45W
Rio Grande, *Brazil* **95 C5** 32 0S 52 20W
Río Grande, *Mexico* **86 C4** 23 50N 103 2W
Río Grande, *Nic.* **88 D3** 12 54N 83 33W
Rio Grande City, *U.S.A.* **81 M5** 26 23N 98 49W
Río Grande de Santiago →, *Mexico* **86 C3** 21 36N 105 26W
Rio Grande del Norte →, *N. Amer.* **75 E7** 26 0N 97 0W
Rio Grande do Norte □, *Brazil* **93 E11** 5 40S 36 0W
Rio Grande do Sul □, *Brazil* **95 C5** 30 0S 53 0W
Río Hato, *Panama* **88 E3** 8 22N 80 10W
Río Lagartos, *Mexico* **87 C7** 21 36N 88 10W
Rio Largo, *Brazil* **93 E11** 9 28S 35 50W
Río Mulatos, *Bolivia* **92 G5** 19 40S 66 50W
Río Muni = Mbini □, *Eq. Guin.* **52 D2** 1 30N 10 0 E
Rio Negro, *Brazil* **95 B6** 26 0S 49 55W
Rio Pardo, *Brazil* **95 C5** 30 0S 52 30W
Rio Rancho, *U.S.A.* **83 J10** 35 14N 106 38W
Río Segundo, *Argentina* **94 C3** 31 40S 63 59W
Río Tercero, *Argentina* **94 C3** 32 15S 64 8W
Rio Verde, *Brazil* **93 G8** 17 50S 51 0W
Río Verde, *Mexico* **87 C5** 21 56N 99 59W
Rio Vista, *U.S.A.* **84 G5** 38 10N 121 42W
Riobamba, *Ecuador* **92 D3** 1 50S 78 45W
Ríohacha, *Colombia* **92 A4** 11 33N 72 55W
Riosucio, *Colombia* **92 B3** 7 27N 77 7W
Riou L., *Canada* **73 B7** 59 7N 106 25W
Ripley, *Canada* **78 B3** 44 4N 81 35W
Ripley, *Calif., U.S.A.* **85 M12** 33 32N 114 39W
Ripley, *N.Y., U.S.A.* **78 D5** 42 16N 79 43W
Ripley, *Tenn., U.S.A.* **81 H10** 35 45N 89 32W
Ripley, *W. Va., U.S.A.* **76 F5** 38 49N 81 43W
Ripon, *U.K.* **10 C6** 54 9N 1 31W
Ripon, *Calif., U.S.A.* **84 H5** 37 44N 121 7W
Ripon, *Wis., U.S.A.* **76 D1** 43 51N 88 50W
Rishā', W. ar →, *Si. Arabia* **44 E5** 25 33N 44 5 E
Rishiri-Tō, *Japan* **30 B10** 45 11N 141 15 E
Rishon le Ziyyon, *Israel* **47 D3** 31 58N 34 48 E
Rison, *U.S.A.* **81 J8** 33 58N 92 11W
Risør, *Norway* **9 G13** 58 43N 9 13 E
Rita Blanca Cr. →, *U.S.A.* **81 H3** 35 40N 102 29W
Ritter, Mt., *U.S.A.* **84 H7** 37 41N 119 12W
Rittman, *U.S.A.* **78 F3** 40 58N 81 47W
Ritzville, *U.S.A.* **82 C4** 47 8N 118 23W
Riva del Garda, *Italy* **20 B4** 45 53N 10 50 E
Rivadavia, *Buenos Aires, Argentina* **94 D3** 35 29S 62 59W
Rivadavia, *Mendoza, Argentina* **94 C2** 33 13S 68 30W
Rivadavia, *Salta, Argentina* **94 A3** 24 5S 62 54W
Rivadavia, *Chile* **94 B1** 29 57S 70 35W
Rivas, *Nic.* **88 D2** 11 30N 85 50W
River Cess, *Liberia* **50 G4** 5 30N 9 32W
River Jordan, *Canada* **84 B2** 48 26N 124 3W
Rivera, *Argentina* **94 D3** 37 12S 63 14W
Rivera, *Uruguay* **95 C4** 31 0S 55 50W
Riverbank, *U.S.A.* **84 H6** 37 44N 120 56W
Riverdale, *U.S.A.* **84 J7** 36 26N 119 52W
Riverhead, *U.S.A.* **79 F12** 40 55N 72 40W
Riverhurst, *Canada* **73 C7** 50 55N 106 50W
Rivers, *Canada* **73 C8** 50 2N 100 14W
Rivers Inlet, *Canada* **72 C3** 51 42N 127 15W
Riversdale, *S. Africa* **56 E3** 34 7S 21 15 E
Riverside, *U.S.A.* **85 M9** 33 59N 117 22W
Riverton, *Australia* **63 E2** 34 10S 138 46 E
Riverton, *Canada* **73 C9** 51 1N 97 0W
Riverton, *N.Z.* **59 M2** 46 21S 168 0 E
Riverton, *U.S.A.* **82 E9** 43 2N 108 23W
Riverton Heights, *U.S.A.* **84 C4** 47 28N 122 17W
Riviera, *U.S.A.* **85 K12** 35 4N 114 35W
Riviera di Levante, *Italy* **18 D8** 44 15N 9 30 E
Riviera di Ponente, *Italy* **18 D8** 44 10N 8 0 E
Rivière-au-Renard, *Canada* **71 C7** 48 59N 64 23W
Rivière-du-Loup, *Canada* **71 C6** 47 50N 69 30W
Rivière-Pentecôte, *Canada* **71 C6** 49 57N 67 1W

Rivière-Pilote, *Martinique* .. **89 D7** 14 26N 60 53W
Rivière St. Paul, *Canada* ... **71 B8** 51 28N 57 45W
Rivne, *Ukraine* .... **17 C14** 50 40N 26 10 E
Rívoli, *Italy* .... **18 D7** 45 3N 7 31 E
Rivoli B., *Australia* .... **63 F3** 37 32S 140 3 E
Riyadh = Ar Riyāḑ,
Si. Arabia .... **46 C4** 24 41N 46 42 E
Rize, *Turkey* .... **25 F7** 41 0N 40 30 E
Rizhao, *China* .... **35 G10** 35 25N 119 30 E
Rizokarpaso, *Cyprus* ...... **23 D13** 35 36N 34 23 E
Rizzuto, C., *Italy* .... **20 E7** 38 53N 17 5 E
Rjukan, *Norway* .... **9 G13** 59 54N 8 33 E
Road Town, *Virgin Is.* **89 C7** 18 27N 64 37W
Roan Plateau, *U.S.A.* **82 G9** 39 20N 109 20W
Roanne, *France* .... **18 C6** 46 3N 4 4 E
Roanoke, *Ala., U.S.A.* **77 J3** 33 9N 85 22W
Roanoke, *Va., U.S.A.* **76 G6** 37 16N 79 56W
Roanoke →, *U.S.A.* **77 H7** 35 57N 76 42W
Roanoke I., *U.S.A.* **77 H8** 35 55N 75 40W
Roanoke Rapids, *U.S.A.* ... **77 G7** 36 28N 77 40W
Roatán, *Honduras* **88 C2** 16 18N 86 35W
Robāt Sang, *Iran* .... **45 C8** 35 35N 59 10 E
Robbins I., *Australia* ...... **62 G4** 40 42S 145 0 E
Robe, *Australia* .... **63 F2** 37 11S 139 45 E
Robe →, *Australia* .... **60 D2** 21 42S 116 15 E
Robert Lee, *U.S.A.* **81 K4** 31 54N 100 29W
Robertsdale, *U.S.A.* **78 F6** 40 11N 78 6W
Robertsganj, *India* .... **43 G10** 24 44N 83 4 E
Robertson, *S. Africa* ...... **56 E2** 33 46S 19 50 E
Robertson I., *Antarctica* **5 C18** 65 15S 59 30W
Robertson Ra., *Australia* .. **60 D3** 23 15S 121 0 E
Robertstown, *Australia* .... **63 E2** 33 58S 139 5 E
Roberval, *Canada* **71 C5** 48 32N 72 15W
Robeson Chan., *Greenland* .. **4 A4** 82 0N 61 30W
Robesonia, *U.S.A.* **79 F8** 40 21N 76 8W
Robinson, *U.S.A.* **76 F2** 39 0N 87 44W
Robinson →, *Australia* ... **62 B2** 16 3S 137 16 E
Robinson Ra., *Australia* ... **61 E2** 25 40S 119 0 E
Robinvale, *Australia* ...... **63 E3** 34 40S 142 45 E
Roblin, *Canada* **73 C8** 51 14N 101 21W
Roboré, *Bolivia* **92 G7** 18 10S 59 45W
Robson, *Canada* **72 D5** 49 20N 117 41W
Robson, Mt., *Canada* **72 C5** 53 10N 119 10W
Robstown, *U.S.A.* **81 M6** 27 47N 97 40W
Roca, C. da, *Portugal* **19 C1** 38 40N 9 31W
Roca Partida, I., *Mexico* ... **86 D2** 19 1N 112 2W
Rocas, I., *Brazil* **93 D12** 4 0S 34 1W
Rocha, *Uruguay* **95 C5** 34 30S 54 25W
Rochdale, *U.K.* **10 D5** 53 38N 2 9W
Rochefort, *Belgium* .... **15 D5** 50 9N 5 12 E
Rochefort, *France* **18 D3** 45 56N 0 57W
Rochelle, *U.S.A.* **80 E10** 41 56N 89 4W
Rocher River, *Canada* **72 A6** 61 23N 112 44W
Rochester, *U.K.* .... **11 F8** 51 23N 0 31 E
Rochester, *Ind., U.S.A.* **76 E2** 41 4N 86 13W
Rochester, *Minn., U.S.A.* ... **80 C8** 44 1N 92 28W
Rochester, *N.H., U.S.A.* ... **79 C14** 43 18N 70 59W
Rochester, *N.Y., U.S.A.* **78 C7** 43 10N 77 37W
Rock →, *Canada* **72 A3** 60 7N 127 7W
Rock Creek, *U.S.A.* **78 E4** 41 40N 80 52W
Rock Falls, *U.S.A.* **80 E10** 41 47N 89 41W
Rock Hill, *U.S.A.* **77 H5** 34 56N 81 1W
Rock Island, *U.S.A.* **80 E9** 41 30N 90 34W
Rock Rapids, *U.S.A.* **80 D6** 43 26N 96 10W
Rock Sound, *Bahamas* **88 B4** 24 54N 76 12W
Rock Springs, *Mont., U.S.A.* **82 C10** 46 49N 106 15W
Rock Springs, *Wyo., U.S.A.* **82 F9** 41 35N 109 14W
Rock Valley, *U.S.A.* **80 D6** 43 12N 96 18W
Rockall, *Atl. Oc.* **6 D3** 57 37N 13 42W
Rockdale, *Tex., U.S.A.* **81 K6** 30 39N 97 0W
Rockdale, *Wash., U.S.A.* ... **84 C5** 47 22N 121 28W
Rockefeller Plateau,
Antarctica **5 E14** 80 0S 140 0W
Rockford, *U.S.A.* **80 D10** 42 16N 89 6W
Rockglen, *Canada* **73 D7** 49 11N 105 57W
Rockhampton, *Australia* ... **62 C5** 23 22S 150 32 E
Rockingham, *Australia* .... **61 F2** 32 15S 115 38 E
Rockingham, *U.S.A.* **77 H6** 34 57N 79 46W
Rockingham B., *Australia* .. **62 B4** 18 5S 146 10 E
Rocklake, *U.S.A.* **80 A5** 48 47N 99 15W
Rockland, *Canada* **79 A9** 45 33N 75 17W
Rockland, *Idaho, U.S.A.* ... **82 E7** 42 34N 112 53W
Rockland, *Maine, U.S.A.* ... **77 C11** 44 6N 69 7W
Rockland, *Mich., U.S.A.* **80 B10** 46 44N 89 11W
Rocklin, *U.S.A.* **84 G5** 38 48N 121 14W
Rockport, *Mass., U.S.A.* ... **79 D14** 42 39N 70 37W
Rockport, *Mo., U.S.A.* **80 E7** 40 25N 95 31W
Rockport, *Tex., U.S.A.* **81 L6** 28 2N 97 3W
Rocksprings, *U.S.A.* **81 K4** 30 1N 100 13W
Rockville, *Conn., U.S.A.* ... **79 E12** 41 52N 72 28W
Rockville, *Md., U.S.A.* **76 F7** 39 5N 77 9W
Rockwall, *U.S.A.* **81 J6** 32 56N 96 28W
Rockwell City, *U.S.A.* **80 D7** 42 24N 94 38W
Rockwood, *Canada* **78 C4** 43 37N 80 8W
Rockwood, *Maine, U.S.A.* .. **77 C11** 45 41N 69 45W
Rockwood, *Tenn., U.S.A.* .. **77 H3** 35 52N 84 41W
Rocky Ford, *U.S.A.* **80 F3** 38 3N 103 43W
Rocky Gully, *Australia* .... **61 F2** 34 30S 116 57 E
Rocky Harbour, *Canada* ... **71 C8** 49 36N 57 55W
Rocky Island L., *Canada* ... **70 C3** 46 55N 83 0W
Rocky Lane, *Canada* **72 B5** 58 31N 116 22W
Rocky Mount, *U.S.A.* **77 H7** 35 57N 77 48W
Rocky Mountain House,
Canada **72 C6** 52 22N 114 55W
Rocky Mountain National
Park, *U.S.A.* **82 F11** 40 25N 105 45W
Rocky Mts., *N. Amer.* **74 C5** 49 0N 115 0W
Rod, *Pakistan* .... **40 E3** 28 10N 63 5 E
Rødbyhavn, *Denmark* ..... **9 J14** 54 39N 11 22 E
Roddickton, *Canada* **71 B8** 50 51N 56 8W
Rodez, *France* .... **18 D5** 44 21N 2 33 E
Rodhopoú, *Greece* .... **23 D5** 35 34N 23 45 E
Ródhos, *Greece* .... **23 C10** 36 15N 28 10 E
Rodney, *Canada* **78 D3** 42 34N 81 41W
Rodney, C., *N.Z.* .... **59 G5** 36 17S 174 50 E
Rodriguez, *Ind. Oc.* .... **3 E13** 19 45S 63 20 E
Roe →, *U.K.* **13 A5** 55 6N 6 59W
Roebling, *U.S.A.* **79 F10** 40 7N 74 47W
Roebourne, *Australia* ..... **60 D2** 20 44S 117 9 E
Roebuck B., *Australia* ..... **60 C3** 18 5S 122 20 E
Roermond, *Neths.* .... **15 C6** 51 12N 6 0 E
Roes Welcome Sd., *Canada* **69 B11** 65 0N 87 0W
Roeselare, *Belgium* .... **15 D3** 50 57N 3 7 E
Rogachev = Ragachow,
Belarus .... **17 B16** 53 8N 30 5 E
Rogagua, L., *Bolivia* **92 F5** 13 43S 66 50W
Rogatyn, *Ukraine* .... **17 D13** 49 24N 24 36 E
Rogdhia, *Greece* .... **23 D7** 35 22N 25 1 E
Rogers, *U.S.A.* **81 G7** 36 20N 94 7W
Rogers City, *U.S.A.* **76 C4** 45 25N 83 49W
Rogersville, *Canada* **71 C6** 46 44N 65 26W
Roggan →, *Canada* **70 B4** 54 24N 79 25W
Roggan L., *Canada* **70 B4** 54 8N 77 50W
Roggeveldberge, *S. Africa* . **56 E3** 32 10S 20 10 E
Rogoaguado, L., *Bolivia* ... **92 F5** 13 0S 65 30W
Rogue →, *U.S.A.* **82 E1** 42 26N 124 26W
Róhda, *Greece* .... **23 A3** 39 48N 19 46 E
Rohnert Park, *U.S.A.* **84 G4** 38 16N 122 40W
Rohri, *Pakistan* .... **42 F3** 27 45N 68 51 E
Rohri Canal, *Pakistan* ..... **42 F3** 26 15N 68 27 E
Rohtak, *India* .... **42 E7** 28 55N 76 43 E
Roi Et, *Thailand* .... **38 D4** 16 4N 103 40 E
Roja, *Latvia* .... **9 H20** 57 29N 22 43 E
Rojas, *Argentina* **94 C3** 34 10S 60 45W
Rojo, C., *Mexico* **87 C5** 21 33N 97 20W
Rokan →, *Indonesia* ..... **36 D2** 2 0N 100 50 E
Rokiškis, *Lithuania* .... **9 J21** 55 55N 25 35 E
Rolândia, *Brazil* **95 A5** 23 18S 51 23W
Rolla, *U.S.A.* **81 G9** 37 57N 91 46W
Rolleston, *Australia* ...... **62 C4** 24 28S 148 35 E
Rollingstone, *Australia* .... **62 B4** 19 2S 146 24 E
Roma, *Australia* .... **63 D4** 26 32S 148 49 E
Roma, *Italy* .... **20 D5** 41 54N 12 29 E
Roma, *Sweden* .... **9 H18** 57 32N 18 26 E
Roma, *U.S.A.* **81 M5** 26 25N 99 1W
Romain C., *U.S.A.* **77 J6** 33 0N 79 22W
Romaine, *Canada* **71 B7** 50 13N 60 40W
Romaine →, *Canada* **71 B7** 50 18N 63 47W
Roman, *Romania* .... **17 E14** 46 57N 26 55 E
Romang, *Indonesia* .... **37 F7** 7 30S 127 20 E
Romani, *Egypt* .... **47 E1** 30 59N 32 38 E
Romania ■, *Europe* .... **17 F12** 46 0N 25 0 E
Romano, Cayo, *Cuba* **88 B4** 22 0N 77 30W
Romanovka =
Basarabeasca, *Moldova* . **17 E15** 46 21N 28 58 E
Romans-sur-Isère, *France* . **18 D6** 45 3N 5 3 E
Romblon, *Phil.* .... **37 B6** 12 33N 122 17 E
Rome = Roma, *Italy* ...... **20 D5** 41 54N 12 29 E
Rome, *Ga., U.S.A.* **77 H3** 34 15N 85 10W
Rome, *N.Y., U.S.A.* **79 C9** 43 13N 75 27W
Rome, *Pa., U.S.A.* **79 E8** 41 51N 76 21W
Romney, *U.S.A.* **76 F6** 39 21N 78 45W
Romney Marsh, *U.K.* ...... **11 F8** 51 2N 0 54 E
Rømø, *Denmark* .... **9 J13** 55 10N 8 30 E
Romorantin-Lanthenay,
France .... **18 C4** 47 21N 1 45 E
Romsdalen, *Norway* ...... **9 E12** 62 25N 7 52 E
Romsey, *U.K.* **11 G6** 51 0N 1 29W
Ron, *Vietnam* .... **38 D6** 17 53N 106 27 E
Rona, *U.K.* **12 D3** 57 34N 5 59W
Ronan, *U.S.A.* **82 C6** 47 32N 114 6W
Roncador, Cayos, *Caribbean* **88 D3** 13 32N 80 4W
Roncador, Serra do, *Brazil* . **93 F8** 12 30S 52 30W
Ronda, *Spain* **19 D3** 36 46N 5 12W
Rondane, *Norway* .... **9 F13** 61 57N 9 50 E
Rondônia □, *Brazil* **92 F6** 11 0S 63 0W
Rondonópolis, *Brazil* **93 G8** 16 28S 54 38W
Rong, Koh, *Cambodia* .... **39 G4** 10 45N 103 15 E
Ronge, L. la, *Canada* **73 B7** 55 6N 105 17W
Rønne, *Denmark* .... **9 J16** 55 6N 14 43 E
Ronne Ice Shelf, *Antarctica* **5 D18** 78 0S 60 0W
Ronsard, C., *Australia* .... **61 D1** 24 46S 113 10 E
Ronse, *Belgium* .... **15 D3** 50 45N 3 35 E
Roodepoort, *S. Africa* ..... **57 D4** 26 11S 27 54 E
Roof Butte, *U.S.A.* **83 H9** 36 28N 109 5W
Roorkee, *India* .... **42 E7** 29 52N 77 59 E
Roosendaal, *Neths.* .... **15 C4** 51 32N 4 29 E
Roosevelt, *U.S.A.* **82 F8** 40 18N 109 59W
Roosevelt →, *Brazil* **92 E6** 7 35S 60 20W
Roosevelt, Mt., *Canada* ... **72 B3** 58 26N 125 20W
Roosevelt I., *Antarctica* ... **5 D12** 79 30S 162 0W
Roper →, *Australia* ...... **62 A2** 14 43S 135 27 E
Roper Bar, *Australia* ...... **62 A1** 14 44S 134 44 E
Roque Pérez, *Argentina* ... **94 D4** 35 25S 59 24W
Roquetas de Mar, *Spain* ... **19 D4** 36 46N 2 36W
Roraima □, *Brazil* **92 C6** 2 0N 61 30W
Roraima, Mt., *Venezuela* .. **92 B6** 5 10N 60 40W
Røros, *Norway* .... **9 E14** 62 35N 11 23 E
Rosa, *Zambia* .... **55 D3** 9 33S 31 15 E
Rosa, L., *Bahamas* **89 B5** 21 0N 73 30W
Rosa, Monte, *Europe* ..... **18 D7** 45 57N 7 53 E
Rosalia, *U.S.A.* **82 C5** 47 14N 117 22W
Rosamond, *U.S.A.* **85 L8** 34 52N 118 10W
Rosario, *Argentina* **94 C3** 33 0S 60 40W
Rosário, *Brazil* **93 D10** 3 0S 44 15W
Rosario, *Baja Calif., Mexico* **86 B1** 30 0N 115 50W
Rosario, *Sinaloa, Mexico* .. **86 C3** 23 0N 105 52W
Rosario, *Paraguay* **94 A4** 24 30S 57 35W
Rosario de la Frontera,
Argentina **94 B3** 25 50S 65 0W
Rosario de Lerma, *Argentina* **94 A2** 24 59S 65 35W
Rosario del Tala, *Argentina* **94 C4** 32 20S 59 10W
Rosário do Sul, *Brazil* **95 C5** 30 15S 54 55W
Rosarito, *Mexico* **85 N9** 32 18N 117 4W
Roscoe, *U.S.A.* **79 E10** 41 56N 74 55W
Roscommon, *Ireland* **13 C3** 53 38N 8 11W
Roscommon □, *Ireland* ... **13 C3** 53 49N 8 23W
Roscrea, *Ireland* **13 D4** 52 57N 7 49W
Rose →, *Australia* .... **62 A2** 14 16S 135 45 E
Rose Blanche, *Canada* **71 C8** 47 38N 58 45W
Rose Pt., *Canada* **72 C2** 54 11N 131 39W
Rose Valley, *Canada* **73 C8** 52 19N 103 49W
Roseau, *Domin.* **89 C7** 15 20N 61 24W
Roseau, *U.S.A.* **80 A7** 48 51N 95 46W
Rosebery, *Australia* ...... **62 G4** 41 46S 145 33 E
Rosebud, *S. Dak., U.S.A.* .. **80 D4** 43 14N 100 51W
Rosebud, *Tex., U.S.A.* **81 K6** 31 4N 96 59W
Roseburg, *U.S.A.* **82 E2** 43 13N 123 20W
Rosedale, *U.S.A.* **81 J9** 33 51N 91 2W
Roseland, *U.S.A.* **84 G4** 38 25N 122 43W
Rosemary, *Canada* **72 C6** 50 46N 112 5W
Rosenberg, *U.S.A.* **81 L7** 29 34N 95 49W
Rosenheim, *Germany* ..... **16 E7** 47 51N 12 7 E
Roses, G. de, *Spain* ...... **19 A7** 42 10N 3 15 E
Rosetown, *Canada* **73 C7** 51 35N 107 59W
Roseville, *Calif., U.S.A.* ... **84 G5** 38 45N 121 17W
Roseville, *Mich., U.S.A.* ... **78 D2** 42 30N 82 56W
Rosewood, *Australia* ...... **63 D5** 27 38S 152 36 E
Roshkhvār, *Iran* .... **45 C8** 34 58N 59 37 E
Rosignano Marittimo, *Italy* **20 C4** 43 24N 10 28 E
Rosignol, *Guyana* **92 B7** 6 15N 57 30W
Roşiori-de-Vede, *Romania* . **17 F13** 44 7N 24 59 E
Roskilde, *Denmark* .... **9 J15** 55 38N 12 3 E
Roslavl, *Russia* .... **24 D5** 53 57N 32 55 E
Rosmead, *S. Africa* .... **56 E4** 31 29S 25 8 E
Ross, *Australia* .... **62 G4** 42 2S 147 30 E
Ross, *N.Z.* .... **59 K3** 42 53S 170 49 E
Ross I., *Antarctica* .... **5 D11** 77 30S 168 0 E
Ross Ice Shelf, *Antarctica* . **5 E12** 80 0S 180 0 E
Ross L., *U.S.A.* **82 B3** 48 44N 121 4W
Ross-on-Wye, *U.K.* **11 F5** 51 54N 2 34W
Ross River, *Australia* ..... **62 C1** 23 44S 134 30 E
Ross River, *Canada* **72 A2** 62 30N 131 30W
Ross Sea, *Antarctica* ..... **5 D11** 74 0S 178 0 E
Rossall Pt., *U.K.* **10 D4** 53 55N 3 3W
Rossan Pt., *Ireland* **13 B3** 54 42N 8 47W
Rossano, *Italy* .... **20 E7** 39 36N 16 39 E
Rossburn, *Canada* **73 C8** 50 40N 100 49W
Rosseau, *Canada* **78 A5** 45 16N 79 39W
Rosseau L., *Canada* **78 A5** 45 10N 79 35W
Rosses, The, *Ireland* **13 A3** 55 2N 8 20W
Rossignol, L., *Canada* **70 B5** 52 43N 73 40W
Rossignol Res., *Canada* ... **71 D6** 44 12N 65 10W
Rossland, *Canada* **72 D5** 49 6N 117 50W
Rosslare, *Ireland* **13 D5** 52 17N 6 24W
Rosso, *Mauritania* **50 E2** 16 40N 15 45W
Rossosh, *Russia* .... **25 D6** 50 15N 39 28 E
Røssvatnet, *Norway* ...... **8 D16** 65 45N 14 5 E
Røst, *Norway* .... **8 C15** 67 32N 12 0 E
Rosthern, *Canada* **73 C7** 52 40N 106 20W
Rostock, *Germany* .... **16 A7** 54 5N 12 8 E
Rostov, *Don, Russia* ...... **25 E6** 47 15N 39 45 E
Rostov, *Yaroslavl, Russia* .. **24 C6** 57 14N 39 25 E
Roswell, *Ga., U.S.A.* **77 H3** 34 2N 84 22W
Roswell, *N. Mex., U.S.A.* .. **81 J2** 33 24N 104 32W
Rotan, *U.S.A.* **81 J4** 32 51N 100 28W
Rother →, *U.K.* .... **11 G8** 50 59N 0 45 E
Rotherham, *U.K.* **10 D6** 53 26N 1 20W
Rothes, *U.K.* **12 D5** 57 32N 3 13W
Rothesay, *Canada* **71 C6** 45 23N 66 0W
Rothesay, *U.K.* **12 F3** 55 50N 5 3W
Roti, *Indonesia* .... **37 F6** 10 50S 123 0 E
Roto, *Australia* .... **63 E4** 33 0S 145 30 E
Rotondo Mte., *France* ..... **18 E8** 42 14N 9 8 E
Rotoroa, L., *N.Z.* .... **59 J4** 41 55S 172 39 E
Rotorua, *N.Z.* .... **59 H6** 38 9S 176 16 E
Rotorua, L., *N.Z.* .... **59 H6** 38 5S 176 18 E
Rotterdam, *Neths.* .... **15 C4** 51 55N 4 30 E
Rotterdam, *U.S.A.* **79 D10** 42 48N 74 1W
Rottnest I., *Australia* ..... **61 F2** 32 0S 115 27 E
Rottumeroog, *Neths.* ..... **15 A6** 53 33N 6 34 E
Rottweil, *Germany* .... **16 D5** 48 9N 8 37 E
Rotuma, *Fiji* .... **64 J9** 12 25S 177 5 E
Roubaix, *France* .... **18 A5** 50 40N 3 10 E
Rouen, *France* .... **18 B4** 49 27N 1 4 E
Rouleau, *Canada* **73 C8** 50 10N 104 56W
Round Mountain, *U.S.A.* .. **82 G5** 38 43N 117 4W
Round Mt., *Australia* ..... **63 E5** 30 26S 152 16 E
Round Rock, *U.S.A.* **81 K6** 30 31N 97 41W
Roundup, *U.S.A.* **82 C9** 46 27N 108 33W
Rousay, *U.K.* **12 B5** 59 10N 3 2W
Rouses Point, *U.S.A.* **79 B11** 44 59N 73 22W
Rouseville, *U.S.A.* **78 E5** 41 28N 79 42W
Roussillon, *France* .... **18 E5** 42 30N 2 35 E
Rouxville, *S. Africa* .... **56 E4** 30 25S 26 50 E
Rouyn-Noranda, *Canada* .. **70 C4** 48 20N 79 0W
Rovaniemi, *Finland* .... **8 C21** 66 29N 25 41 E
Rovereto, *Italy* .... **20 B4** 45 53N 11 3 E
Rovigo, *Italy* .... **20 B4** 45 4N 11 47 E
Rovinj, *Croatia* .... **16 F7** 45 5N 13 40 E
Rovno = Rivne, *Ukraine* ... **17 C14** 50 40N 26 10 E
Rovuma = Ruvuma →,
Tanzania .... **55 E5** 10 29S 40 28 E
Row'ān, *Iran* .... **45 C6** 35 8N 48 51 E
Rowena, *Australia* .... **63 D4** 29 48S 148 55 E
Rowley Shoals, *Australia* .. **60 C2** 17 30S 119 0 E
Roxas, *Phil.* .... **37 B6** 11 36N 122 49 E
Roxboro, *U.S.A.* **77 G6** 36 24N 78 59W
Roxburgh, *N.Z.* .... **59 L2** 45 33S 169 19 E
Roxbury, *U.S.A.* **78 F7** 40 6N 77 39W
Roy, *Mont., U.S.A.* **82 C9** 47 20N 108 58W
Roy, *N. Mex., U.S.A.* **81 H2** 35 57N 104 12W
Roy, *Utah, U.S.A.* **82 F7** 41 10N 112 2W
Royal Canal, *Ireland* **13 C4** 53 30N 7 13W
Royal Leamington Spa, *U.K.* **11 E6** 52 18N 1 31W
Royal Tunbridge Wells, *U.K.* **11 F8** 51 7N 0 16 E
Royan, *France* **18 D3** 45 37N 1 2W
Royston, *U.K.* .... **11 E7** 52 3N 0 0 E
Rozdilna, *Ukraine* .... **17 E16** 46 50N 30 2 E
Rozhyshche, *Ukraine* ..... **17 C13** 50 54N 25 15 E
Rtishchevo, *Russia* .... **24 C7** 52 18N 43 46 E
Ruacaná, *Angola* .... **56 B1** 17 20S 14 12 E
Ruahine Ra., *N.Z.* .... **59 H6** 39 55S 176 2 E
Ruapehu, *N.Z.* .... **59 H5** 39 17S 175 35 E
Ruapuke I., *N.Z.* .... **59 M2** 46 46S 168 31 E
Ruâq, W. →, *Egypt* ...... **47 F2** 30 0N 33 49 E
Rub' al Khālī, *Si. Arabia* ... **46 D4** 18 0N 48 0 E
Rubeho Mts., *Tanzania* .... **54 D4** 6 50S 36 25 E
Rubh a' Mhail, *U.K.* **12 F2** 55 56N 6 8W
Rubha Hunish, *U.K.* **12 D2** 57 42N 6 20W
Rubha Robhanais = Lewis,
Butt of, *U.K.* **12 C2** 58 31N 6 16W
Rubicon →, *U.S.A.* **84 G5** 38 53N 121 4W
Rubio, *Venezuela* **92 B4** 7 43N 72 22W
Rubtsovsk, *Russia* .... **26 D9** 51 30N 81 10 E
Ruby L., *U.S.A.* **82 F6** 40 10N 115 28W
Ruby Mts., *U.S.A.* **82 F6** 40 30N 115 20W
Rubyvale, *Australia* .... **62 C4** 23 25S 147 42 E
Rūd Sar, *Iran* .... **45 B6** 37 8N 50 18 E
Rudall, *Australia* .... **63 E2** 33 43S 136 17 E
Rudall →, *Australia* ...... **60 D3** 22 34S 122 13 E
Rudewa, *Tanzania* .... **55 E3** 10 7S 34 40 E
Rudnyy, *Kazakstan* .... **26 D7** 52 57N 63 7 E
Rudolfa, Ostrov, *Russia* ... **26 A6** 81 45N 58 30 E
Rudyard, *U.S.A.* **76 B3** 46 14N 84 36W
Rufiji →, *Tanzania* .... **54 D4** 7 50S 39 15 E
Rufino, *Argentina* **94 C3** 34 20S 62 50W
Rufunsa, *Zambia* .... **55 F2** 15 4S 29 34 E
Rugby, *U.K.* **11 E6** 52 23N 1 16W
Rugby, *U.S.A.* **80 A5** 48 22N 100 0W
Rügen, *Germany* .... **16 A7** 54 22N 13 24 E
Ruhengeri, *Rwanda* ...... **54 C2** 1 30S 29 36 E
Ruhnu, *Estonia* .... **9 H20** 57 48N 23 15 E
Ruhr →, *Germany* .... **16 C4** 51 27N 6 43 E
Ruhuhu →, *Tanzania* ..... **55 E3** 10 31S 34 34 E
Ruidoso, *U.S.A.* **83 K11** 33 20N 105 41W
Ruivo, Pico, *Madeira* **22 D3** 32 45N 16 56W
Rujm Tal'at al Jamā'ah,
Jordan .... **47 E4** 30 24N 35 30 E
Ruk, *Pakistan* .... **42 F3** 27 50N 68 42 E
Rukhla, *Pakistan* .... **42 C4** 32 27N 71 57 E
Ruki →,
Dem. Rep. of the Congo . **52 E3** 0 5N 18 17 E
Rukwa □, *Tanzania* ...... **54 D3** 7 0S 31 30 E
Rukwa, L., *Tanzania* ..... **54 D3** 8 0S 32 20 E
Rulhieres, C., *Australia* .... **60 B4** 13 56S 127 22 E
Rum = Rhum, *U.K.* **12 E2** 57 0N 6 20W
Rum Cay, *Bahamas* **89 B5** 23 40N 74 58W
Rum Jungle, *Australia* .... **60 B5** 13 0S 130 59 E
Rumāḩ, *Si. Arabia* .... **44 E5** 25 29N 47 10 E
Rumania = Romania ■,
Europe .... **17 F12** 46 0N 25 0 E
Rumaylah, *Iraq* .... **44 D5** 30 47N 47 37 E
Rumbêk, *Sudan* .... **51 G11** 6 54N 29 37 E
Rumford, *U.S.A.* **77 C10** 44 33N 70 33W
Rumia, *Poland* .... **17 A10** 54 37N 18 25 E
Rumoi, *Japan* .... **30 C10** 43 56N 141 39 E
Rumonge, *Burundi* .... **54 C2** 3 59S 29 26 E
Rumson, *U.S.A.* **79 F11** 40 23N 74 0W
Rumuruti, *Kenya* .... **54 B4** 0 17N 36 32 E
Runan, *China* .... **34 H8** 33 0N 114 30 E
Runanga, *N.Z.* .... **59 K3** 42 25S 171 15 E
Runaway, C., *N.Z.* .... **59 G6** 37 32S 177 59 E
Runcorn, *U.K.* **10 D5** 53 21N 2 44W
Rundu, *Namibia* .... **53 H3** 17 52S 19 43 E
Rungwa, *Tanzania* .... **54 D3** 6 55S 33 32 E
Rungwa →, *Tanzania* ..... **54 D3** 7 36S 31 50 E
Rungwe, *Tanzania* .... **55 D3** 9 11S 33 32 E
Rungwe, Mt., *Tanzania* .... **52 F6** 9 8S 33 40 E
Runton Ra., *Australia* ..... **60 D3** 23 31S 123 6 E
Ruoqiang, *China* .... **32 C3** 38 55N 88 10 E
Rupa, *India* .... **41 F18** 27 15N 92 21 E
Rupar, *India* .... **42 D7** 31 2N 76 38 E
Rupat, *Indonesia* .... **36 D2** 1 45N 101 40 E
Rupen →, *India* .... **42 H4** 23 28N 71 31 E
Rupert, *U.S.A.* **82 E7** 42 37N 113 41W
Rupert →, *Canada* **70 B4** 51 29N 78 45W
Rupert B., *Canada* **70 B4** 51 35N 79 0W
Rupert House =
Waskaganish, *Canada* ... **70 B4** 51 30N 78 40W
Rupsa, *India* .... **43 J12** 21 37N 87 1 E
Rurrenabaque, *Bolivia* **92 F5** 14 30S 67 32W
Rusambo, *Zimbabwe* ..... **55 F3** 16 30S 32 4 E
Rusape, *Zimbabwe* .... **55 F3** 18 35S 32 8 E
Ruschuk = Ruse, *Bulgaria* . **21 C12** 43 48N 25 59 E
Ruse, *Bulgaria* .... **21 C12** 43 48N 25 59 E
Rush, *Ireland* **13 C5** 53 31N 6 6W
Rushan, *China* .... **35 F11** 36 56N 121 30 E
Rushden, *U.K.* **11 E7** 52 18N 0 35W
Rushmore, Mt., *U.S.A.* **80 D3** 43 53N 103 28W
Rushville, *Ill., U.S.A.* **80 E9** 40 7N 90 34W
Rushville, *Ind., U.S.A.* **76 F3** 39 37N 85 27W
Rushville, *Nebr., U.S.A.* ... **80 D3** 42 43N 102 28W
Russas, *Brazil* **93 D11** 4 55S 37 50W
Russell, *Canada* **73 C8** 50 50N 101 20W
Russell, *Kans., U.S.A.* **80 F5** 38 54N 98 52W
Russell, *N.Y., U.S.A.* **79 B9** 44 27N 75 9W
Russell, *Pa., U.S.A.* **78 E5** 41 56N 79 8W
Russell L., *Man., Canada* .. **73 B8** 56 15N 101 30W
Russell L., *N.W.T., Canada* . **72 A5** 63 5N 115 44W
Russellkonda, *India* ...... **41 K14** 19 57N 84 42 E
Russellville, *Ala., U.S.A.* ... **77 H2** 34 30N 87 44W
Russellville, *Ark., U.S.A.* ... **81 H8** 35 17N 93 8W
Russellville, *Ky., U.S.A.* ... **77 G2** 36 51N 86 53W
Russia ■, *Eurasia* .... **27 C11** 62 0N 105 0 E
Russian →, *U.S.A.* **84 G3** 38 27N 123 8W
Russkoye Ustie, *Russia* ... **4 B15** 71 0N 149 0 E
Rustam, *Pakistan* .... **42 B5** 34 25N 72 13 E
Rustam Shahr, *Pakistan* ... **42 F2** 26 58N 66 6 E
Rustavi, *Georgia* .... **25 F8** 41 30N 45 0 E
Rustenburg, *S. Africa* ..... **56 D4** 25 41S 27 14 E
Ruston, *U.S.A.* **81 J8** 32 32N 92 38W
Rutana, *Burundi* .... **54 C3** 3 55S 30 0 E
Ruteng, *Indonesia* .... **37 F6** 8 35S 120 30 E
Ruth, *U.S.A.* **78 C2** 43 42N 82 45W
Rutherford, *U.S.A.* **84 G4** 38 26N 122 24W
Rutland, *U.S.A.* **79 C12** 43 37N 72 58W
Rutland □, *U.K.* **11 E7** 52 38N 0 40W
Rutland Water, *U.K.* **11 E7** 52 39N 0 38W
Rutledge →, *Canada* **73 A6** 61 4N 112 0W
Rutledge L., *Canada* **73 A6** 61 33N 110 47W
Rutshuru,
Dem. Rep. of the Congo . **54 C2** 1 13S 29 25 E
Ruvu, *Tanzania* .... **54 D4** 6 49S 38 43 E
Ruvu →, *Tanzania* .... **54 D4** 6 23S 38 52 E
Ruvuma □, *Tanzania* ..... **55 E4** 10 20S 36 0 E
Ruvuma →, *Tanzania* ..... **55 E5** 10 29S 40 28 E
Ruwais, *U.A.E.* .... **45 E7** 24 5N 52 50 E
Ruwenzori, *Africa* .... **54 B2** 0 30N 29 55 E
Ruyigi, *Burundi* .... **54 C3** 3 29S 30 15 E
Ružomberok, *Slovak Rep.* . **17 D10** 49 3N 19 17 E
Rwanda ■, *Africa* .... **54 C3** 2 0S 30 0 E
Ryan, L., *U.K.* **12 G3** 55 0N 5 2W
Ryazan, *Russia* .... **24 D6** 54 40N 39 40 E
Ryazhsk, *Russia* .... **24 D7** 53 45N 40 3 E
Rybache = Rybachye,
Kazakstan .... **26 E9** 46 40N 81 20 E
Rybachiy Poluostrov, *Russia* **24 A5** 69 43N 32 0 E
Rybachye = Ysyk-Köl,
Kyrgyzstan .... **28 E11** 42 26N 76 12 E
Rybachye, *Kazakstan* ..... **26 E9** 46 40N 81 20 E
Rybinsk, *Russia* .... **24 C6** 58 5N 38 50 E
Rybinskoye Vdkhr., *Russia* . **24 C6** 58 30N 38 25 E
Rybnitsa = Râbniţa,
Moldova .... **17 E15** 47 45N 29 0 E
Rycroft, *Canada* **72 B5** 55 45N 118 40W
Ryde, *U.K.* **11 G6** 50 43N 1 9W
Ryderwood, *U.S.A.* **84 D3** 46 23N 123 3W
Rye, *U.K.* .... **11 G8** 50 57N 0 45 E
Rye →, *U.K.* **10 C7** 54 11N 0 44W
Rye Bay, *U.K.* .... **11 G8** 50 52N 0 49 E
Rye Patch Reservoir, *U.S.A.* **82 F4** 40 28N 118 19W
Ryegate, *U.S.A.* **82 C9** 46 18N 109 15W
Ryley, *Canada* **72 C6** 53 17N 112 26W
Rylstone, *Australia* .... **63 E4** 32 46S 149 58 E
Ryōtsu, *Japan* .... **30 E9** 38 5N 138 26 E
Rypin, *Poland* .... **17 B10** 53 3N 19 25 E
Ryūgasaki, *Japan* .... **31 G10** 35 54N 140 11 E
Ryūkyū Is. = Ryūkyū-rettō,
Japan .... **31 M3** 26 0N 126 0 E
Ryūkyū-rettō, *Japan* ..... **31 M3** 26 0N 126 0 E
Rzeszów, *Poland* .... **17 C11** 50 5N 21 58 E
Rzhev, *Russia* .... **24 C5** 56 20N 34 20 E

S

Sa, *Thailand* 38 C3 18 34N 100 45 E
Sa Canal, *Spain* 22 C7 38 51N 1 23 E
Sa Conillera, *Spain* 22 C7 38 59N 1 13 E
Sa Dec, *Vietnam* 39 G5 10 20N 105 46 E
Sa Dragonera, *Spain* 22 B9 39 35N 2 19 E
Sa Mesquida, *Spain* 22 B11 39 55N 4 16 E
Sa Savina, *Spain* 22 C7 38 44N 1 25 E
Sa'ādatābād, *Fārs, Iran* 45 D7 30 10N 53 5 E
Sa'ādatābād, *Hormozgān, Iran* 45 D7 28 3N 55 53 E
Sa'ādatābād, *Kermān, Iran* 45 D7 29 40N 55 51 E
Saale →, *Germany* 16 C6 51 56N 11 54 E
Saalfeld, *Germany* 16 C6 50 38N 11 21 E
Saar →, *Europe* 18 B7 49 41N 6 32 E
Saarbrücken, *Germany* 16 D4 49 14N 6 59 E
Saaremaa, *Estonia* 9 G20 58 30N 22 30 E
Saarijärvi, *Finland* 9 E21 62 43N 25 16 E
Saariselkä, *Finland* 8 B23 68 16N 28 15 E
Sab 'Ābar, *Syria* 44 C3 33 46N 37 41 E
Saba, *W. Indies* 89 C7 17 42N 63 26W
Šabac, *Serbia, Yug.* 21 B8 44 48N 19 42 E
Sabadell, *Spain* 19 B7 41 28N 2 7 E
Sabah □, *Malaysia* 36 C5 6 0N 117 0 E
Sabak Bernam, *Malaysia* 39 L3 3 46N 100 58 E
Sabalān, Kūhhā-ye, *Iran* 44 B5 38 15N 47 45 E
Sabalana, Kepulauan, *Indonesia* 37 F5 6 45S 118 50 E
Sábana de la Mar, *Dom. Rep.* 89 C6 19 7N 69 24W
Sábanalarga, *Colombia* 92 A4 10 38N 74 55W
Sabang, *Indonesia* 36 C1 5 50N 95 15 E
Sabará, *Brazil* 93 G10 19 55S 43 46W
Sabarmati →, *India* 42 H5 22 18N 72 22 E
Sabattis, *U.S.A.* 79 B10 44 6N 74 40W
Saberania, *Indonesia* 37 E9 2 5S 138 18 E
Sabhah, *Libya* 51 C8 27 9N 14 29 E
Sabi →, *India* 42 E7 28 29N 76 44 E
Sabie, *S. Africa* 57 D5 25 10S 30 48 E
Sabinal, *Mexico* 86 A3 30 58N 107 25W
Sabinal, *U.S.A.* 81 L5 29 19N 99 28W
Sabinas, *Mexico* 86 B4 27 50N 101 10W
Sabinas →, *Mexico* 86 B4 27 37N 100 42W
Sabinas Hidalgo, *Mexico* 86 B4 26 33N 100 10W
Sabine →, *U.S.A.* 81 L8 29 59N 93 47W
Sabine L., *U.S.A.* 81 L8 29 53N 93 51W
Sabine Pass, *U.S.A.* 81 L8 29 44N 93 54W
Sabinsville, *U.S.A.* 78 E7 41 52N 77 31W
Sabkhet el Bardawîl, *Egypt* 47 D2 31 10N 33 15 E
Sablayan, *Phil.* 37 B6 12 50N 120 50 E
Sable, *Canada* 71 A6 55 30N 68 21W
Sable, C., *Canada* 71 D6 43 29N 65 38W
Sable, C., *U.S.A.* 75 E10 25 9N 81 8W
Sable I., *Canada* 71 D8 44 0N 60 0W
Sabrina Coast, *Antarctica* 5 C9 68 0S 120 0 E
Sabulubbek, *Indonesia* 36 E1 1 36S 98 40 E
Sabzevār, *Iran* 45 B8 36 15N 57 40 E
Sabzvārān, *Iran* 45 D8 28 45N 57 50 E
Sac City, *U.S.A.* 80 D7 42 25N 95 0W
Săcele, *Romania* 17 F13 45 37N 25 41 E
Sachigo →, *Canada* 70 A2 55 6N 88 58W
Sachigo, L., *Canada* 70 B1 53 50N 92 12W
Sachsen □, *Germany* 16 C7 50 55N 13 10 E
Sachsen-Anhalt □, *Germany* 16 C7 52 0N 12 0 E
Sackets Harbor, *U.S.A.* 79 C8 43 57N 76 7W
Sackville, *Canada* 71 C7 45 54N 64 22W
Saco, *Maine, U.S.A.* 77 D10 43 30N 70 27W
Saco, *Mont., U.S.A.* 82 B10 48 28N 107 21W
Sacramento, *U.S.A.* 84 G5 38 35N 121 29W
Sacramento →, *U.S.A.* 84 G5 38 3N 121 56W
Sacramento Mts., *U.S.A.* 83 K11 32 30N 105 30W
Sacramento Valley, *U.S.A.* 84 G5 39 30N 122 0W
Sada-Misaki, *Japan* 31 H6 33 20N 132 1 E
Sadabad, *India* 42 F8 27 27N 78 3 E
Sadani, *Tanzania* 54 D4 5 58S 38 35 E
Sadao, *Thailand* 39 J3 6 38N 100 26 E
Sadd el Aali, *Egypt* 51 D12 23 54N 32 54 E
Saddle Mt., *U.S.A.* 84 E3 45 58N 123 41W
Sadimi, *Dem. Rep. of the Congo* 55 D1 9 25S 23 32 E
Sado, *Japan* 30 F9 38 0N 138 25 E
Sadon, *Burma* 41 G20 25 28N 97 55 E
Sadra, *India* 42 H5 23 21N 72 43 E
Sadri, *India* 42 G5 25 11N 73 26 E
Sæby, *Denmark* 9 H14 57 21N 10 30 E
Saegertown, *U.S.A.* 78 E4 41 43N 80 9W
Şafājah, *Si. Arabia* 44 E3 26 25N 39 0 E
Säffle, *Sweden* 9 G15 59 8N 12 55 E
Safford, *U.S.A.* 83 K9 32 50N 109 43W
Saffron Walden, *U.K.* 11 E8 52 1N 0 16 E
Safi, *Morocco* 50 B4 32 18N 9 20W
Şafīābād, *Iran* 45 B8 36 45N 57 58 E
Safīd Dasht, *Iran* 45 C6 33 27N 48 11 E
Safīd Kūh, *Afghan.* 40 B3 34 45N 63 0 E
Safīd Rūd →, *Iran* 45 B6 37 23N 50 11 E
Safipur, *India* 43 F9 26 44N 80 21 E
Safwān, *Iraq* 44 D5 30 7N 47 43 E
Sag Harbor, *U.S.A.* 79 F12 41 0N 72 18W
Saga, *Japan* 31 H5 33 15N 130 16 E
Saga □, *Japan* 31 H5 33 15N 130 20 E
Sagae, *Japan* 30 E10 38 22N 140 17 E
Sagamore, *U.S.A.* 78 F5 40 46N 79 14W
Sagar, *India* 40 M9 14 14N 75 6 E
Sagar, *Mad. P., India* 43 H8 23 50N 78 44 E
Sagara, L., *Tanzania* 54 D3 5 20S 31 0 E
Saginaw, *U.S.A.* 76 D4 43 26N 83 56W
Saginaw →, *U.S.A.* 76 D4 43 39N 83 51W
Saginaw B., *U.S.A.* 76 D4 43 50N 83 40W
Saglouc = Salluit, *Canada* 69 B12 62 14N 75 38W
Sagŏ-ri, *S. Korea* 35 G14 35 25N 126 49 E
Sagua la Grande, *Cuba* 88 B3 22 50N 80 10W
Saguache, *U.S.A.* 83 G10 38 5N 106 8W
Saguaro Nat. Park, *U.S.A.* 83 K8 32 12N 110 38W
Saguenay →, *Canada* 71 C5 48 22N 71 0W
Sagunt, *Spain* 19 C5 39 42N 0 18W
Sagunto = Sagunt, *Spain* 19 C5 39 42N 0 18W
Sagwara, *India* 42 H6 23 41N 74 1 E
Sahagún, *Spain* 19 A3 42 18N 5 2W
Saḩam al Jawlān, *Syria* 47 C4 32 45N 35 55 E
Sahand, Kūh-e, *Iran* 44 B5 37 44N 46 27 E
Sahara, *Africa* 50 D6 23 0N 5 0 E
Saharan Atlas = Saharien, Atlas, *Algeria* 50 B6 33 30N 1 0 E
Saharanpur, *India* 42 E7 29 58N 77 33 E
Saharien, Atlas, *Algeria* 50 B6 33 30N 1 0 E
Saharsa, *India* 43 G12 25 53N 86 36 E
Sahasinaka, *Madag.* 57 C8 21 49S 47 49 E
Sahaswan, *India* 43 E8 28 5N 78 45 E
Sahel, *Africa* 50 E5 16 0N 5 0 E
Sahibganj, *India* 43 G12 25 12N 87 40 E
Sāḩilīyah, *Iraq* 44 C4 33 43N 42 42 E
Sahiwal, *Pakistan* 42 D5 30 45N 73 8 E
Şaḩneh, *Iran* 44 C5 34 29N 47 41 E
Sahuaripa, *Mexico* 86 B3 29 0N 109 13W
Sahuarita, *U.S.A.* 83 L8 31 57N 110 58W
Sahuayo, *Mexico* 86 C4 20 4N 102 43W
Sai →, *India* 43 G10 25 39N 82 47 E
Sai Buri, *Thailand* 39 J3 6 43N 101 45 E
Sa'id Bundas, *Sudan* 51 G10 8 24N 24 48 E
Sa'īdābād, *Kermān, Iran* 45 D7 29 30N 55 45 E
Sa'īdābād, *Semnān, Iran* 45 B7 36 8N 54 11 E
Sa'īdīyeh, *Iran* 45 B6 36 20N 48 55 E
Saidpur, *Bangla.* 41 G16 25 48N 89 0 E
Saidpur, *India* 43 G10 25 33N 83 11 E
Saidu, *Pakistan* 43 B5 34 43N 72 24 E
Saigon = Phanh Bho Ho Chi Minh, *Vietnam* 39 G6 10 58N 106 40 E
Saijō, *Japan* 31 H6 33 55N 133 11 E
Saikhoa Ghat, *India* 41 F19 27 50N 95 40 E
Saiki, *Japan* 31 H5 32 58N 131 51 E
Sailana, *India* 42 H6 23 28N 74 55 E
Sailolof, *Indonesia* 37 E8 1 7S 130 46 E
Saimaa, *Finland* 9 F23 61 15N 28 15 E
Şa'in Dezh, *Iran* 44 B5 36 40N 46 25 E
St. Abb's Head, *U.K.* 12 F6 55 55N 2 8W
St. Alban's, *Canada* 71 C8 47 51N 55 50W
St. Albans, *U.K.* 11 F7 51 45N 0 19W
St. Albans, *Vt., U.S.A.* 79 B11 44 49N 73 5W
St. Albans, *W. Va., U.S.A.* 76 F5 38 23N 81 50W
St. Alban's Head, *U.K.* 11 G5 50 34N 2 4W
St. Albert, *Canada* 72 C6 53 37N 113 32W
St. Andrew's, *Canada* 71 C8 47 45N 59 15W
St. Andrews, *U.K.* 12 E6 56 20N 2 47W
St-Anicet, *Canada* 79 A10 45 8N 74 22W
St. Ann B., *Canada* 71 C7 46 22N 60 25W
St. Ann's Bay, *Jamaica* 88 C4 18 26N 77 15W
St. Anthony, *Canada* 71 B8 51 22N 55 35W
St. Anthony, *U.S.A.* 82 E8 43 58N 111 41W
St. Antoine, *Canada* 71 C7 46 22N 64 45W
St. Arnaud, *Australia* 63 F3 36 40S 143 16 E
St-Augustin →, *Canada* 71 B8 51 16N 58 40W
St-Augustin-Saguenay, *Canada* 71 B8 51 13N 58 38W
St. Augustine, *U.S.A.* 77 L5 29 54N 81 19W
St. Austell, *U.K.* 11 G3 50 20N 4 47W
St. Barbe, *Canada* 71 B8 51 12N 56 46W
St-Barthélemy, *W. Indies* 89 C7 17 50N 62 50W
St. Bees Hd., *U.K.* 10 C4 54 31N 3 38W
St. Bride's, *Canada* 71 C9 46 56N 54 10W
St. Brides B., *U.K.* 11 F2 51 49N 5 9W
St-Brieuc, *France* 18 B2 48 30N 2 46W
St. Catharines, *Canada* 78 C5 43 10N 79 15W
St. Catherines I., *U.S.A.* 77 K5 31 40N 81 10W
St. Catherine's Pt., *U.K.* 11 G6 50 34N 1 18W
St-Chamond, *France* 18 D6 45 28N 4 31 E
St. Charles, *Ill., U.S.A.* 76 E1 41 54N 88 19W
St. Charles, *Mo., U.S.A.* 80 F9 38 47N 90 29W
St. Charles, *Va., U.S.A.* 76 F7 36 48N 83 4W
St. Christopher-Nevis = St. Kitts & Nevis ■, *W. Indies* 89 C7 17 20N 62 40W
St. Clair, *Mich., U.S.A.* 78 D2 42 50N 82 30W
St. Clair, *Pa., U.S.A.* 79 F8 40 43N 76 12W
St. Clair →, *U.S.A.* 78 D2 42 38N 82 31W
St. Clair, L., *Canada* 70 D3 42 30N 82 45W
St. Clair, L., *U.S.A.* 78 D2 42 27N 82 39W
St. Clairsville, *U.S.A.* 78 F4 40 5N 80 54W
St. Claude, *Canada* 73 D9 49 40N 98 20W
St-Clet, *Canada* 79 A10 45 21N 74 13W
St. Cloud, *Fla., U.S.A.* 77 L5 28 15N 81 17W
St. Cloud, *Minn., U.S.A.* 80 C7 45 34N 94 10W
St. Cricq, C., *Australia* 61 E1 25 17S 113 6 E
St. Croix, *Virgin Is.* 89 C7 17 45N 64 45W
St. Croix →, *U.S.A.* 80 C8 44 45N 92 48W
St. Croix Falls, *U.S.A.* 80 C8 45 24N 92 38W
St. David's, *Canada* 71 C8 48 12N 58 52W
St. David's, *U.K.* 11 F2 51 53N 5 16W
St. David's Head, *U.K.* 11 F2 51 54N 5 19W
St-Denis, *France* 18 B5 48 56N 2 22 E
St-Dizier, *France* 18 B6 48 38N 4 56 E
St. Elias, Mt., *U.S.A.* 68 B5 60 18N 140 56W
St. Elias Mts., *Canada* 72 A1 60 33N 139 28W
St. Elias Mts., *U.S.A.* 68 C6 60 0N 138 0W
St-Étienne, *France* 18 D6 45 27N 4 22 E
St. Eugène, *Canada* 79 A10 45 30N 74 28W
St. Eustatius, *W. Indies* 89 C7 17 20N 63 0W
St-Félicien, *Canada* 70 C5 48 40N 72 25W
St-Flour, *France* 18 D5 45 2N 3 6 E
St. Francis, *U.S.A.* 80 F4 39 47N 101 48W
St. Francis →, *U.S.A.* 81 H9 34 38N 90 36W
St. Francis, C., *S. Africa* 56 E3 34 14S 24 49 E
St. Francisville, *U.S.A.* 81 K9 30 47N 91 23W
St-François, L., *Canada* 79 A10 45 10N 74 22W
St-Gabriel, *Canada* 70 C5 46 17N 73 24W
St. Gallen = Sankt Gallen, *Switz.* 18 C8 47 26N 9 22 E
St-Gaudens, *France* 18 E4 43 6N 0 44 E
St. George, *Australia* 63 D4 28 1S 148 30 E
St. George, *Canada* 71 C6 45 11N 66 50W
St. George, *S.C., U.S.A.* 77 J5 33 11N 80 35W
St. George, *Utah, U.S.A.* 83 H7 37 6N 113 35W
St. George, C., *Canada* 71 C8 48 30N 59 16W
St. George, C., *U.S.A.* 77 L3 29 40N 85 5W
St. George Ra., *Australia* 60 C4 18 40S 125 0 E
St. George's, *Canada* 71 C8 48 26N 58 31W
St-Georges, *Canada* 71 C5 46 8N 70 40W
St. George's, *Grenada* 89 D7 12 5N 61 43W
St. George's B., *Canada* 71 C8 48 24N 58 53W
St. Georges Basin, *N.S.W., Australia* 63 F5 35 7S 150 36 E
St. Georges Basin, *W. Austral., Australia* 60 C4 15 23S 125 2 E
St. George's Channel, *Europe* 13 E6 52 0N 6 0W
St. Georges Hd., *Australia* 63 F5 35 12S 150 42 E
St. Gotthard P. = San Gottardo, P. del, *Switz.* 18 C8 46 33N 8 33 E
St. Helena, *U.S.A.* 82 G2 38 30N 122 28W
St. Helena ■, *Atl. Oc.* 49 H3 15 55S 5 44W
St. Helena, Mt., *U.S.A.* 84 G4 38 40N 122 36W
St. Helena B., *S. Africa* 56 E2 32 40S 18 10 E
St. Helens, *Australia* 62 G4 41 20S 148 15 E
St. Helens, *U.K.* 10 D5 53 27N 2 44W
St. Helens, *U.S.A.* 84 E4 45 52N 122 48W
St. Helens, Mt., *U.S.A.* 84 D4 46 12N 122 12W
St. Helier, *U.K.* 11 H5 49 10N 2 7W
St-Hubert, *Belgium* 15 D5 50 2N 5 23 E
St-Hyacinthe, *Canada* 70 C5 45 40N 72 58W
St. Ignace, *U.S.A.* 76 C3 45 52N 84 44W
St. Ignace I., *Canada* 70 C2 48 45N 88 0W
St. Ignatius, *U.S.A.* 82 C6 47 19N 114 6W
St. Ives, *U.K.* 11 G2 50 12N 5 30W
St. James, *U.S.A.* 80 D7 43 59N 94 38W
St-Jean →, *Canada* 71 B7 50 17N 64 20W
St-Jean, L., *Canada* 71 C5 48 40N 72 0W
St-Jean-Port-Joli, *Canada* 71 C5 47 15N 70 13W
St-Jean-sur-Richelieu, *Canada* 79 A11 45 20N 73 20W
St-Jérôme, *Canada* 70 C5 45 47N 74 0W
St. John, *Canada* 71 C6 45 20N 66 8W
St. John, *U.S.A.* 81 G5 38 0N 98 46W
St. John →, *U.S.A.* 77 C12 45 12N 66 5W
St. John, C., *Canada* 71 C8 50 0N 55 32W
St. John's, *Antigua* 89 C7 17 6N 61 51W
St. John's, *Canada* 71 C9 47 35N 52 40W
St. Johns, *Ariz., U.S.A.* 83 J9 34 30N 109 22W
St. Johns, *Mich., U.S.A.* 76 D3 43 0N 84 33W
St. Johns →, *U.S.A.* 77 K5 30 24N 81 24W
St. John's Pt., *Ireland* 13 B3 54 34N 8 27W
St. Johnsbury, *U.S.A.* 79 B12 44 25N 72 1W
St. Johnsville, *U.S.A.* 79 D10 43 0N 74 43W
St. Joseph, *La., U.S.A.* 81 K9 31 55N 91 14W
St. Joseph, *Mich., U.S.A.* 75 B9 42 6N 86 29W
St. Joseph, *Mo., U.S.A.* 80 F7 39 46N 94 50W
St. Joseph →, *U.S.A.* 76 D2 42 7N 86 29W
St. Joseph, I., *Canada* 70 C3 46 12N 83 58W
St. Joseph, L., *Canada* 70 B1 51 10N 90 35W
St-Jovite, *Canada* 70 C5 46 8N 74 38W
St. Kilda, *N.Z.* 59 L3 45 53S 170 31 E
St. Kitts & Nevis ■, *W. Indies* 89 C7 17 20N 62 40W
St. Laurent, *Canada* 73 C9 50 25N 97 58W
St. Lawrence, *Australia* 62 C4 22 16S 149 31 E
St. Lawrence, *Canada* 71 C8 46 54N 55 23W
St. Lawrence →, *Canada* 71 C6 49 30N 66 0W
St. Lawrence, Gulf of, *Canada* 71 C7 48 25N 62 0W
St. Lawrence I., *U.S.A.* 68 B3 63 30N 170 30W
St. Leonard, *Canada* 71 C6 47 12N 67 58W
St. Lewis →, *Canada* 71 B8 52 26N 56 11W
St-Lô, *France* 18 B3 49 7N 1 5W
St. Louis, *Senegal* 50 E2 16 8N 16 27W
St. Louis, *U.S.A.* 80 F9 38 37N 90 12W
St. Louis →, *U.S.A.* 80 B8 47 15N 92 45W
St. Lucia ■, *W. Indies* 89 D7 14 0N 60 50W
St. Lucia, L., *S. Africa* 57 D5 28 5S 32 30 E
St. Lucia Channel, *W. Indies* 89 D7 14 15N 61 0W
St. Maarten, *W. Indies* 89 C7 18 0N 63 5W
St. Magnus B., *U.K.* 12 A7 60 25N 1 35W
St-Malo, *France* 18 B2 48 39N 2 1W
St-Marc, *Haiti* 89 C5 19 10N 72 41W
St. Maries, *U.S.A.* 82 C5 47 19N 116 35W
St-Martin, *W. Indies* 89 C7 18 0N 63 0W
St. Martin, L., *Canada* 73 C9 51 40N 98 30W
St. Mary Pk., *Australia* 63 E2 31 32S 138 34 E
St. Marys, *Australia* 62 G4 41 35S 148 11 E
St. Marys, *Canada* 78 C3 43 20N 81 10W
St. Mary's, *Corn., U.K.* 11 H1 49 55N 6 18W
St. Mary's, *Orkney, U.K.* 12 C6 58 54N 2 54W
St. Marys, *Ga., U.S.A.* 77 K5 30 44N 81 33W
St. Marys, *Pa., U.S.A.* 78 E6 41 26N 78 34W
St. Mary's, C., *Canada* 71 C9 46 50N 54 12W
St. Mary's B., *Canada* 71 C9 46 50N 53 50W
St. Marys Bay, *Canada* 71 D6 44 25N 66 10W
St-Mathieu, Pte., *France* 18 B1 48 20N 4 45W
St. Matthew I., *U.S.A.* 68 B2 60 24N 172 42W
St. Matthews, I. = Zadetkyi Kyun, *Burma* 39 H2 10 0N 98 25 E
St-Maurice →, *Canada* 70 C5 46 21N 72 31W
St-Nazaire, *France* 18 C2 47 17N 2 12W
St. Neots, *U.K.* 11 E7 52 14N 0 15W
St-Niklaas, *Belgium* 15 C4 51 10N 4 8 E
St-Omer, *France* 18 A5 50 45N 2 15 E
St-Pamphile, *Canada* 71 C6 46 58N 69 48W
St. Pascal, *Canada* 71 C6 47 32N 69 48W
St. Paul, *Canada* 72 C6 54 0N 111 17W
St. Paul, *Minn., U.S.A.* 80 C8 44 57N 93 6W
St. Paul, *Nebr., U.S.A.* 80 E5 41 13N 98 27W
St-Paul →, *Canada* 71 B8 51 27N 57 42W
St. Paul, I., *Ind. Oc.* 3 F13 38 55S 77 34 E
St. Paul I., *Canada* 71 C7 47 12N 60 9W
St. Peter, *U.S.A.* 80 C8 44 20N 93 57W
St. Peter Port, *U.K.* 11 H5 49 26N 2 33W
St. Peters, *N.S., Canada* 71 C7 45 40N 60 53W
St. Peters, *P.E.I., Canada* 71 C7 46 25N 62 35W
St. Petersburg = Sankt-Peterburg, *Russia* 24 C5 59 55N 30 20 E
St. Petersburg, *U.S.A.* 77 M4 27 46N 82 39W
St-Pie, *Canada* 79 A12 45 30N 72 54W
St-Pierre, *St- P. & M.* 71 C8 46 46N 56 12W
St-Pierre, L., *Canada* 70 C5 46 12N 72 52W
St-Pierre et Miquelon □, *St- P. & M.* 71 C8 46 55N 56 10W
St. Quentin, *Canada* 71 C6 47 30N 67 23W
St-Quentin, *France* 18 B5 49 50N 3 16 E
St. Regis, *U.S.A.* 82 C6 47 18N 115 6W
St. Sebastien, Tanjon' i, *Madag.* 57 A8 12 26S 48 44 E
St-Siméon, *Canada* 71 C6 47 51N 69 54W
St. Simons I., *U.S.A.* 77 K5 31 12N 81 15W
St. Simons Island, *U.S.A.* 77 K5 31 9N 81 22W
St. Stephen, *Canada* 71 C6 45 16N 67 17W
St. Thomas, *Canada* 78 D3 42 45N 81 10W
St. Thomas I., *Virgin Is.* 89 C7 18 20N 64 55W
St-Tite, *Canada* 70 C5 46 45N 72 34W
St-Tropez, *France* 18 E7 43 17N 6 38 E
St. Troud = St. Truiden, *Belgium* 15 D5 50 48N 5 10 E
St. Truiden, *Belgium* 15 D5 50 48N 5 10 E
St. Vincent, G., *Australia* 63 F2 35 0S 138 0 E
St. Vincent & the Grenadines ■, *W. Indies* 89 D7 13 0N 61 10W
St. Vincent Passage, *W. Indies* 89 D7 13 30N 61 0W
St-Vith, *Belgium* 15 D6 50 17N 6 9 E
St. Walburg, *Canada* 73 C7 53 39N 109 12W
Ste-Agathe-des-Monts, *Canada* 70 C5 46 3N 74 17W
Ste-Anne, L., *Canada* 71 B6 50 0N 67 42W
Ste-Anne-des-Monts, *Canada* 71 C6 49 8N 66 30W
Ste. Genevieve, *U.S.A.* 80 G9 37 59N 90 2W
Ste-Marguerite →, *Canada* 71 B6 50 9N 66 36W
Ste-Marie, *Martinique* 89 D7 14 48N 61 1W
Ste-Marie de la Madeleine, *Canada* 71 C5 46 26N 71 0W
Ste-Rose, *Guadeloupe* 89 C7 16 20N 61 45W
Ste. Rose du Lac, *Canada* 73 C9 51 4N 99 30W
Saintes, *France* 18 D3 45 45N 0 37W
Saintes, I. des, *Guadeloupe* 89 C7 15 50N 61 35W
Saintfield, *U.K.* 13 B6 54 28N 5 49W
Sainthiya, *India* 43 H12 23 57N 87 40 E
Saintonge, *France* 18 D3 45 40N 0 50W
Saipan, *Pac. Oc.* 64 F6 15 12N 145 45 E
Sairang, *India* 41 H18 23 50N 92 45 E
Sairecábur, Cerro, *Bolivia* 94 A2 22 43S 67 54W
Saitama □, *Japan* 31 F9 36 25N 139 30 E
Saiyid, *Pakistan* 42 C5 33 7N 73 2 E
Sajama, *Bolivia* 92 G5 18 7S 69 0W
Sajószentpéter, *Hungary* 17 D11 48 12N 20 44 E
Sajum, *India* 43 C8 33 20N 79 0 E
Sak →, *S. Africa* 56 E3 30 52S 20 25 E
Sakai, *Japan* 31 G7 34 30N 135 30 E
Sakaide, *Japan* 31 G6 34 15N 133 50 E
Sakaiminato, *Japan* 31 G6 35 38N 133 11 E
Sakākah, *Si. Arabia* 44 D4 30 0N 40 8 E
Sakakawea, L., *U.S.A.* 80 B4 47 30N 101 25W
Sakami →, *Canada* 70 B4 53 40N 76 40W
Sakami, L., *Canada* 70 B4 53 15N 77 0W
Sakania, *Dem. Rep. of the Congo* 55 E2 12 43S 28 30 E
Sakarya, *Turkey* 25 F5 40 48N 30 25 E
Sakashima-Guntō, *Japan* 31 M2 24 46N 124 0 E
Sakata, *Japan* 30 E9 38 55N 139 50 E
Sakchu, *N. Korea* 35 D13 40 23N 125 2 E
Sakeny →, *Madag.* 57 C8 20 0S 45 25 E
Sakha □, *Russia* 27 C14 66 0N 130 0 E
Sakhalin, *Russia* 27 D15 51 0N 143 0 E
Sakhalinskiy Zaliv, *Russia* 27 D15 54 0N 141 0 E
Šakiai, *Lithuania* 9 J20 54 59N 23 2 E
Sakon Nakhon, *Thailand* 38 D5 17 10N 104 9 E
Sakrand, *Pakistan* 42 F3 26 10N 68 15 E
Sakri, *India* 43 F12 26 13N 86 5 E
Sakrivier, *S. Africa* 56 E3 30 54S 20 28 E
Sakti, *India* 43 H10 22 2N 82 58 E
Sakuma, *Japan* 31 G8 35 3N 137 49 E
Sakurai, *Japan* 31 G7 34 30N 135 51 E
Sala, *Sweden* 9 G17 59 58N 16 35 E
Sala Consilina, *Italy* 20 D6 40 23N 15 36 E
Sala-y-Gómez, *Pac. Oc.* 65 K17 26 28S 105 28W
Salaberry-de-Valleyfield, *Canada* 79 A10 45 15N 74 8W
Saladas, *Argentina* 94 B4 28 15S 58 40W
Saladillo, *Argentina* 94 D4 35 40S 59 55W
Salado →, *Buenos Aires, Argentina* 94 D4 35 44S 57 22W
Salado →, *La Pampa, Argentina* 96 D3 37 30S 67 0W
Salado →, *Santa Fe, Argentina* 94 C3 31 40S 60 41W
Salado →, *Mexico* 81 M5 26 52N 99 19W
Salaga, *Ghana* 50 G5 8 31N 0 31W
Sālah, *Syria* 47 C5 32 40N 36 45 E
Sálakhos, *Greece* 23 C9 36 17N 27 57 E
Salālah, *Oman* 46 D5 16 56N 53 59 E
Salamanca, *Chile* 94 C1 31 46S 70 59W
Salamanca, *Spain* 19 B3 40 58N 5 39W
Salamanca, *U.S.A.* 78 D6 42 10N 78 43W
Salāmatābād, *Iran* 44 C5 35 39N 47 50 E
Salamis, *Cyprus* 23 D12 35 11N 33 54 E
Salamís, *Greece* 21 F10 37 56N 23 30 E
Salar de Atacama, *Chile* 94 A2 23 30S 68 25W
Salar de Uyuni, *Bolivia* 92 H5 20 30S 67 45W
Salatiga, *Indonesia* 37 G14 7 19S 110 30 E
Salavat, *Russia* 24 D10 53 21N 55 55 E
Salaverry, *Peru* 92 E3 8 15S 79 0W
Salawati, *Indonesia* 37 E8 1 7S 130 52 E
Salaya, *India* 42 H3 22 19N 69 35 E
Salayar, *Indonesia* 37 F6 6 7S 120 30 E
Salcombe, *U.K.* 11 G4 50 14N 3 47W
Saldanha, *S. Africa* 56 E2 33 0S 17 58 E
Saldanha B., *S. Africa* 56 E2 33 6S 18 0 E
Saldus, *Latvia* 9 H20 56 38N 22 30 E
Sale, *Australia* 63 F4 38 6S 147 6 E
Salé, *Morocco* 50 B4 34 3N 6 48W
Sale, *U.K.* 10 D5 53 26N 2 19W
Salekhard, *Russia* 26 C7 66 30N 66 35 E
Salem, *India* 40 P11 11 40N 78 11 E
Salem, *Ill., U.S.A.* 76 F1 38 38N 88 57W
Salem, *Ind., U.S.A.* 76 F2 38 36N 86 6W
Salem, *Mass., U.S.A.* 79 D14 42 31N 70 53W
Salem, *Mo., U.S.A.* 81 G9 37 39N 91 32W
Salem, *N.H., U.S.A.* 79 D13 42 45N 71 12W
Salem, *N.J., U.S.A.* 76 F8 39 34N 75 28W
Salem, *N.Y., U.S.A.* 79 C11 43 10N 73 20W
Salem, *Ohio, U.S.A.* 78 F4 40 54N 80 52W
Salem, *Oreg., U.S.A.* 82 D2 44 56N 123 2W
Salem, *S. Dak., U.S.A.* 80 D6 43 44N 97 23W
Salem, *Va., U.S.A.* 76 G5 37 18N 80 3W
Salerno, *Italy* 20 D6 40 41N 14 47 E
Salford, *U.K.* 10 D5 53 30N 2 18W
Salgótarján, *Hungary* 17 D10 48 5N 19 47 E
Salgueiro, *Brazil* 93 E11 8 4S 39 6W
Salibabu, *Indonesia* 37 D7 3 51N 126 40 E
Salida, *U.S.A.* 74 C5 38 32N 106 0W
Salihli, *Turkey* 21 E13 38 28N 28 8 E
Salihorsk, *Belarus* 17 B14 52 51N 27 27 E
Salima, *Malawi* 53 G6 13 47S 34 28 E
Salina, *Italy* 20 E6 38 34N 14 50 E
Salina, *Kans., U.S.A.* 80 F6 38 50N 97 37W
Salina, *Utah, U.S.A.* 83 G8 38 58N 111 51W
Salina Cruz, *Mexico* 87 D5 16 10N 95 10W
Salinas, *Brazil* 93 G10 16 10S 42 10W
Salinas, *Chile* 94 A2 23 31S 69 29W
Salinas, *Ecuador* 92 D2 2 10S 80 58W
Salinas, *U.S.A.* 84 J5 36 40N 121 39W
Salinas →, *Guatemala* 87 D6 16 28N 90 31W
Salinas →, *U.S.A.* 84 J5 36 45N 121 48W
Salinas, B. de, *Nic.* 88 D2 11 4N 85 45W
Salinas, Pampa de las, *Argentina* 94 C2 31 58S 66 42W
Salinas Ambargasta, *Argentina* 94 B3 29 0S 65 0W

Salinas de Hidalgo, *Mexico* **86 C4** 22 30N 101 40W
Salinas Grandes, *Argentina* **94 C3** 30 0S 65 0W
Saline →, *Ark., U.S.A.* **81 J8** 33 10N 92 8W
Saline →, *Kans., U.S.A.* **80 F6** 38 52N 97 30W
Salines, *Spain* **22 B10** 39 21N 3 3 E
Salines, C. de ses, *Spain* **22 B10** 39 16N 3 4 E
Salinópolis, *Brazil* **93 D9** 0 40S 47 20W
Salisbury = Harare, *Zimbabwe* **55 F3** 17 43S 31 2 E
Salisbury, *U.K.* **11 F6** 51 4N 1 47W
Salisbury, *Md., U.S.A.* **76 F8** 38 22N 75 36W
Salisbury, *N.C., U.S.A.* **77 H5** 35 40N 80 29W
Salisbury I., *Canada* **69 B12** 63 30N 77 0W
Salisbury Plain, *U.K.* **11 F6** 51 14N 1 55W
Şalkhad, *Syria* **47 C5** 32 29N 36 43 E
Salla, *Finland* **8 C23** 66 50N 28 49 E
Salliq, *Canada* **69 B11** 64 8N 83 10W
Sallisaw, *U.S.A.* **81 H7** 35 28N 94 47W
Salluit, *Canada* **69 B12** 62 14N 75 38W
Salmās, *Iran* **44 B5** 38 11N 44 47 E
Salmo, *Canada* **72 D5** 49 10N 117 20W
Salmon, *U.S.A.* **82 D7** 45 11N 113 54W
Salmon →, *Canada* **72 C4** 54 3N 122 40W
Salmon →, *U.S.A.* **82 D5** 45 51N 116 47W
Salmon Arm, *Canada* **72 C5** 50 40N 119 15W
Salmon Gums, *Australia* **61 F3** 32 59S 121 38 E
Salmon River Mts., *U.S.A.* **82 D6** 45 0N 114 30W
Salo, *Finland* **9 F20** 60 22N 23 10 E
Salome, *U.S.A.* **85 M13** 33 47N 113 37W
Salon, *India* **43 F9** 26 2N 81 27 E
Salon-de-Provence, *France* **18 E6** 43 39N 5 6 E
Salonica = Thessaloníki, *Greece* **21 D10** 40 38N 22 58 E
Salonta, *Romania* **17 E11** 46 49N 21 42 E
Salpausselkä, *Finland* **9 F22** 61 0N 27 0 E
Salsacate, *Argentina* **94 C2** 31 20S 65 5W
Salsk, *Russia* **25 E7** 46 28N 41 30 E
Salso →, *Italy* **20 F5** 37 6N 13 57 E
Salt →, *Canada* **72 B6** 60 0N 112 25W
Salt →, *U.S.A.* **83 K7** 33 23N 112 19W
Salt Fork Arkansas →, *U.S.A.* **75 C7** 36 36N 97 3W
Salt Lake City, *U.S.A.* **82 F8** 40 45N 111 53W
Salt Range, *Pakistan* **42 C5** 32 30N 72 25 E
Salta, *Argentina* **94 A2** 24 57S 65 25W
Salta □, *Argentina* **94 A2** 24 48S 65 30W
Saltash, *U.K.* **11 G3** 50 24N 4 14W
Saltburn by the Sea, *U.K.* **10 C7** 54 35N 0 58W
Saltcoats, *U.K.* **12 F4** 55 38N 4 47W
Saltee Is., *Ireland* **13 D5** 52 7N 6 37W
Saltfjellet, *Norway* **8 C16** 66 40N 15 15 E
Saltfjorden, *Norway* **8 C16** 67 15N 14 10 E
Saltillo, *Mexico* **86 B4** 25 25N 101 0W
Salto, *Argentina* **94 C3** 34 20S 60 15W
Salto, *Uruguay* **94 C4** 31 27S 57 50W
Salto →, *Italy* **20 C5** 42 26N 12 25 E
Salto del Guaíra, *Paraguay* **95 A5** 24 3S 54 17W
Salton City, *U.S.A.* **85 M11** 33 29N 115 51W
Salton Sea, *U.S.A.* **85 M11** 33 15N 115 45W
Saltsburg, *U.S.A.* **78 F5** 40 29N 79 27W
Saluda →, *U.S.A.* **77 J5** 34 1N 81 4W
Salûm, *Egypt* **51 B11** 31 31N 25 7 E
Salur, *India* **41 K13** 18 27N 83 18 E
Salvador, *Brazil* **93 F11** 13 0S 38 30W
Salvador, *Canada* **73 C7** 52 10N 109 32W
Salvador, L., *U.S.A.* **81 L9** 29 43N 90 15W
Salween →, *Burma* **41 L20** 16 31N 97 37 E
Salyan, *Azerbaijan* **25 G8** 39 33N 48 59 E
Salzach →, *Austria* **16 D7** 48 12N 12 56 E
Salzburg, *Austria* **16 E7** 47 48N 13 2 E
Salzgitter, *Germany* **16 B6** 52 9N 10 19 E
Salzwedel, *Germany* **16 B6** 52 52N 11 10 E
Sam, *India* **42 F4** 26 50N 70 31 E
Sam Ngao, *Thailand* **38 D2** 17 18N 99 0 E
Sam Rayburn Reservoir, *U.S.A.* **81 K7** 31 4N 94 5W
Sam Son, *Vietnam* **38 C5** 19 44N 105 54 E
Sam Teu, *Laos* **38 C5** 19 59N 104 38 E
Sama de Langreo = Langreo, *Spain* **19 A3** 43 18N 5 40W
Samagaltay, *Russia* **27 D10** 50 36N 95 3 E
Samales Group, *Phil.* **37 C6** 6 0N 122 0 E
Samana, *India* **42 D7** 30 10N 76 13 E
Samaná □, *Dom. Rep.* **89 C6** 19 15N 69 27W
Samana Cay, *Bahamas* **89 B5** 23 3N 73 45W
Samanga, *Tanzania* **55 D4** 8 20S 39 13 E
Samangwa, *Dem. Rep. of the Congo* **54 C1** 4 23S 24 10 E
Samani, *Japan* **30 C11** 42 7N 142 56 E
Samar, *Phil.* **37 B7** 12 0N 125 0 E
Samara, *Russia* **24 D9** 53 8N 50 6 E
Samaria = Shōmrōn, *West Bank* **47 C4** 32 15N 35 13 E
Samariá, *Greece* **23 D5** 35 17N 23 58 E
Samarinda, *Indonesia* **36 E5** 0 30S 117 9 E
Samarkand = Samarqand, *Uzbekistan* **26 F7** 39 40N 66 55 E
Samarqand, *Uzbekistan* **26 F7** 39 40N 66 55 E
Sāmarrā, *Iraq* **44 C4** 34 12N 43 52 E
Samastipur, *India* **43 G11** 25 50N 85 50 E
Samba, *Dem. Rep. of the Congo* **54 C2** 4 38S 26 22 E
Samba, *India* **43 C6** 32 32N 75 10 E
Sambalpur, *India* **41 J14** 21 28N 84 4 E
Sambar, Tanjung, *Indonesia* **36 E4** 2 59S 110 19 E
Sambas, *Indonesia* **36 D3** 1 20N 109 20 E
Sambava, *Madag.* **57 A9** 14 16S 50 10 E
Sambawizi, *Zimbabwe* **55 F2** 18 24S 26 13 E
Sambhal, *India* **43 E8** 28 35N 78 37 E
Sambhar, *India* **42 F6** 26 52N 75 6 E
Sambhar L., *India* **42 F6** 26 55N 75 12 E
Sambiase, *Italy* **20 E7** 38 58N 16 17 E
Sambir, *Ukraine* **17 D12** 49 30N 23 10 E
Sambor, *Cambodia* **38 F6** 12 46N 106 0 E
Samborombón, B., *Argentina* **94 D4** 36 5S 57 20W
Samch'ŏk, *S. Korea* **35 F15** 37 30N 129 10 E
Samch'onp'o, *S. Korea* **35 G15** 35 0N 128 6 E
Same, *Tanzania* **54 C4** 4 2S 37 38 E
Samfya, *Zambia* **55 E2** 11 22S 29 31 E
Samnah, *Si. Arabia* **44 E3** 25 10N 37 15 E
Samo Alto, *Chile* **94 C1** 30 22S 71 0W
Samokov, *Bulgaria* **21 C10** 42 18N 23 35 E
Sámos, *Greece* **21 F12** 37 45N 26 50 E
Samothráki = Mathráki, *Greece* **23 A3** 39 48N 19 31 E
Samothráki, *Greece* **21 D11** 40 28N 25 28 E
Sampacho, *Argentina* **94 C3** 33 20S 64 50W
Sampang, *Indonesia* **37 G15** 7 11S 113 13 E
Sampit, *Indonesia* **36 E4** 2 34S 113 0 E
Sampit, Teluk, *Indonesia* **36 E4** 3 5S 113 3 E
Samrong, *Cambodia* **38 E4** 14 15N 103 30 E
Samrong, *Thailand* **38 E3** 15 10N 100 40 E
Samsø, *Denmark* **9 J14** 55 50N 10 35 E
Samsun, *Turkey* **25 F6** 41 15N 36 22 E
Samui, Ko, *Thailand* **39 H3** 9 30N 100 0 E
Samusole, *Dem. Rep. of the Congo* **55 E1** 10 2S 24 0 E
Samut Prakan, *Thailand* **38 F3** 13 32N 100 40 E
Samut Songkhram →, *Thailand* **36 B1** 13 24N 100 1 E
Samwari, *Pakistan* **42 E2** 28 30N 66 46 E
San, *Mali* **50 F5** 13 15N 4 57W
San →, *Cambodia* **38 F5** 13 32N 105 57 E
San →, *Poland* **17 C11** 50 45N 21 51 E
San Agustin, C., *Phil.* **37 C7** 6 20N 126 13 E
San Agustín de Valle Fértil, *Argentina* **94 C2** 30 35S 67 30W
San Ambrosio, *Pac. Oc.* **90 F3** 26 28S 79 53W
San Andreas, *U.S.A.* **84 G6** 38 12N 120 41W
San Andrés, I. de, *Caribbean* **88 D3** 12 42N 81 46W
San Andres Mts., *U.S.A.* **83 K10** 33 0N 106 30W
San Andrés Tuxtla, *Mexico* **87 D5** 18 30N 95 20W
San Angelo, *U.S.A.* **81 K4** 31 28N 100 26W
San Anselmo, *U.S.A.* **84 H4** 37 59N 122 34W
San Antonio, *Belize* **87 D7** 16 15N 89 2W
San Antonio, *Chile* **94 C1** 33 40S 71 40W
San Antonio, *N. Mex., U.S.A.* **83 K10** 33 55N 106 52W
San Antonio, *Tex., U.S.A.* **81 L5** 29 25N 98 30W
San Antonio →, *U.S.A.* **81 L6** 28 30N 96 54W
San Antonio, C., *Argentina* **94 D4** 36 15S 56 40W
San Antonio, C., *Cuba* **88 B3** 21 50N 84 57W
San Antonio, Mt., *U.S.A.* **85 L9** 34 17N 117 38W
San Antonio de los Baños, *Cuba* **88 B3** 22 54N 82 31W
San Antonio de los Cobres, *Argentina* **94 A2** 24 10S 66 17W
San Antonio Oeste, *Argentina* **96 E4** 40 40S 65 0W
San Ardo, *U.S.A.* **84 J6** 36 1N 120 54W
San Augustín, *Canary Is.* **22 G4** 27 47N 15 32W
San Augustine, *U.S.A.* **81 K7** 31 30N 94 7W
San Bartolomé, *Canary Is.* **22 F6** 28 59N 13 37W
San Bartolomé de Tirajana, *Canary Is.* **22 G4** 27 54N 15 34W
San Benedetto del Tronto, *Italy* **20 C5** 42 57N 13 53 E
San Benedicto, I., *Mexico* **86 D2** 19 18N 110 49W
San Benito, *U.S.A.* **81 M6** 26 8N 97 38W
San Benito →, *U.S.A.* **84 J5** 36 53N 121 34W
San Benito Mt., *U.S.A.* **84 J6** 36 22N 120 37W
San Bernardino, *U.S.A.* **85 L9** 34 7N 117 19W
San Bernardino Mts., *U.S.A.* **85 L10** 34 10N 116 45W
San Bernardino Str., *Phil.* **37 B7** 13 0N 125 0 E
San Bernardo, *Chile* **94 C1** 33 40S 70 50W
San Bernardo, I. de, *Colombia* **92 B3** 9 45N 75 50W
San Blas, *Mexico* **86 B3** 26 4N 108 46W
San Blas, Arch. de, *Panama* **88 E4** 9 50N 78 31W
San Blas, C., *U.S.A.* **77 L3** 29 40N 85 21W
San Borja, *Bolivia* **92 F5** 14 50S 66 52W
San Buenaventura, *Mexico* **86 B4** 27 5N 101 32W
San Carlos = Sant Carles, *Spain* **22 B8** 39 3N 1 34 E
San Carlos, *Argentina* **94 C2** 33 50S 69 0W
San Carlos, *Chile* **94 D1** 36 10S 72 0W
San Carlos, *Mexico* **86 B4** 29 0N 100 54W
San Carlos, *Mexico* **86 C2** 24 47N 112 6W
San Carlos, *Nic.* **88 D3** 11 12N 84 50W
San Carlos, *Phil.* **37 B6** 10 29N 123 25 E
San Carlos, *Uruguay* **95 C5** 34 46S 54 58W
San Carlos, *U.S.A.* **83 K8** 33 21N 110 27W
San Carlos, *Venezuela* **92 B5** 9 40N 68 36W
San Carlos de Bariloche, *Argentina* **96 E2** 41 10S 71 25W
San Carlos de Bolívar, *Argentina* **96 D4** 36 15S 61 6W
San Carlos del Zulia, *Venezuela* **92 B4** 9 1N 71 55W
San Carlos L., *U.S.A.* **83 K8** 33 11N 110 32W
San Clemente, *Chile* **94 D1** 35 30S 71 29W
San Clemente, *U.S.A.* **85 M9** 33 26N 117 37W
San Clemente I., *U.S.A.* **85 N8** 32 53N 118 29W
San Cristóbal = Es Migjorn Gran, *Spain* **22 B11** 39 57N 4 3 E
San Cristóbal, *Argentina* **94 C3** 30 20S 61 10W
San Cristóbal, *Dom. Rep.* **89 C5** 18 25N 70 6W
San Cristóbal, *Venezuela* **92 B4** 7 46N 72 14W
San Cristóbal de la Casas, *Mexico* **87 D6** 16 50N 92 33W
San Diego, *Calif., U.S.A.* **85 N9** 32 43N 117 9W
San Diego, *Tex., U.S.A.* **81 M5** 27 46N 98 14W
San Diego, C., *Argentina* **96 G3** 54 40S 65 10W
San Diego de la Unión, *Mexico* **86 C4** 21 28N 100 52W
San Dimitri, Ras, *Malta* **23 C1** 36 4N 14 11 E
San Estanislao, *Paraguay* **94 A4** 24 39S 56 26W
San Felipe, *Chile* **94 C1** 32 43S 70 42W
San Felipe, *Mexico* **86 A2** 31 0N 114 52W
San Felipe, *Venezuela* **92 A5** 10 20N 68 44W
San Felipe →, *U.S.A.* **85 M11** 33 12N 115 49W
San Felix, *Chile* **94 B1** 28 56S 70 28W
San Félix, *Pac. Oc.* **90 F2** 26 23S 80 0W
San Fernando = Sant Ferran, *Spain* **22 C7** 38 42N 1 28 E
San Fernando, *Chile* **94 C1** 34 30S 71 0W
San Fernando, *Mexico* **86 B1** 29 55N 115 10W
San Fernando, *Tamaulipas, Mexico* **87 C5** 24 51N 98 10W
San Fernando, *La Union, Phil.* **37 A6** 16 40N 120 23 E
San Fernando, *Pampanga, Phil.* **37 A6** 15 5N 120 37 E
San Fernando, *Spain* **19 D2** 36 28N 6 17W
San Fernando, *Trin. & Tob.* **89 D7** 10 20N 61 30W
San Fernando, *U.S.A.* **85 L8** 34 17N 118 26W
San Fernando de Apure, *Venezuela* **92 B5** 7 54N 67 15W
San Fernando de Atabapo, *Venezuela* **92 C5** 4 3N 67 42W
San Francisco, *Argentina* **94 C3** 31 30S 62 5W
San Francisco, *U.S.A.* **84 H4** 37 47N 122 25W
San Francisco →, *U.S.A.* **83 K9** 32 59N 109 22W
San Francisco, Paso de, *S. Amer.* **94 B2** 27 0S 68 0W
San Francisco de Macorís, *Dom. Rep.* **89 C5** 19 19N 70 15W
San Francisco del Monte de Oro, *Argentina* **94 C2** 32 36S 66 8W
San Francisco del Oro, *Mexico* **86 B3** 26 52N 105 50W
San Francisco Javier = Sant Francesc de Formentera, *Spain* **22 C7** 38 42N 1 26 E
San Francisco Solano, Pta., *Colombia* **90 C3** 6 18N 77 29W
San Gabriel, *Chile* **94 C1** 33 47S 70 15W
San Gabriel Mts., *U.S.A.* **85 L9** 34 20N 118 0W
San Gorgonio Mt., *U.S.A.* **85 L10** 34 7N 116 51W
San Gottardo, P. del, *Switz.* **18 C8** 46 33N 8 33 E
San Gregorio, *Uruguay* **95 C4** 32 37S 55 40W
San Gregorio, *U.S.A.* **84 H4** 37 20N 122 23W
San Ignacio, *Belize* **87 D7** 17 10N 89 0W
San Ignacio, *Bolivia* **92 G6** 16 20S 60 55W
San Ignacio, *Mexico* **86 B2** 27 27N 113 0W
San Ignacio, *Paraguay* **88 C2** 26 52S 57 3W
San Ignacio, L., *Mexico* **86 B2** 26 50N 113 11W
San Ildefonso, C., *Phil.* **37 A6** 16 0N 122 1 E
San Isidro, *Argentina* **94 C4** 34 29S 58 31W
San Jacinto, *U.S.A.* **85 M10** 33 47N 116 57W
San Jaime = Sant Jaume, *Spain* **22 B11** 39 54N 4 4 E
San Javier, *Misiones, Argentina* **95 B4** 27 55S 55 5W
San Javier, *Santa Fe, Argentina* **94 C4** 30 40S 59 55W
San Javier, *Bolivia* **92 G6** 16 18S 62 30W
San Javier, *Chile* **94 D1** 35 40S 71 45W
San Jeronimo Taviche, *Mexico* **87 D5** 16 38N 96 32W
San Joaquin, *U.S.A.* **84 J6** 36 36N 120 11W
San Joaquin →, *U.S.A.* **84 G5** 38 4N 121 51W
San Joaquin Valley, *U.S.A.* **84 J6** 37 20N 121 0W
San Jon, *U.S.A.* **81 H3** 35 6N 103 20W
San Jordi = Sant Jordi, *Spain* **22 B9** 39 33N 2 46 E
San Jorge, *Argentina* **94 C3** 31 54S 61 50W
San Jorge, *Spain* **22 C7** 38 54N 1 24 E
San Jorge, B. de, *Mexico* **86 A2** 31 20N 113 20W
San Jorge, G., *Argentina* **96 F3** 46 0S 66 0W
San Jorge, G. of, *Argentina* **90 H4** 46 0S 66 0W
San José = San Josep, *Spain* **22 C7** 38 55N 1 18 E
San José, *Costa Rica* **88 E3** 9 55N 84 2W
San José, *Guatemala* **88 D1** 14 0N 90 50W
San José, *Mexico* **86 C2** 25 0N 110 50W
San Jose, *Luzon, Phil.* **37 A6** 15 45N 120 55 E
San Jose, *Mind. Or., Phil.* **37 B6** 12 27N 121 4 E
San Jose, *U.S.A.* **84 H5** 37 20N 121 53W
San Jose →, *U.S.A.* **83 J10** 34 25N 106 45W
San Jose de Buenavista, *Phil.* **37 B6** 10 45N 121 56 E
San José de Chiquitos, *Bolivia* **92 G6** 17 53S 60 50W
San José de Feliciano, *Argentina* **94 C4** 30 26S 58 46W
San José de Jáchal, *Argentina* **94 C2** 30 15S 68 46W
San José de Mayo, *Uruguay* **94 C4** 34 27S 56 40W
San José del Cabo, *Mexico* **86 C3** 23 0N 109 40W
San José del Guaviare, *Colombia* **92 C4** 2 35N 72 38W
San Josep, *Spain* **22 C7** 38 55N 1 18 E
San Juan, *Argentina* **94 C2** 31 30S 68 30W
San Juan, *Mexico* **86 C4** 21 20N 102 50W
San Juan, *Puerto Rico* **89 C6** 18 28N 66 7W
San Juan □, *Argentina* **94 C2** 31 9S 69 0W
San Juan □, *Dom. Rep.* **89 C5** 18 45N 71 25W
San Juan →, *Argentina* **94 C2** 32 20S 67 25W
San Juan →, *Nic.* **88 D3** 10 56N 83 42W
San Juan →, *U.S.A.* **83 H8** 37 16N 110 26W
San Juan Bautista = Sant Joan Baptista, *Spain* **22 B8** 39 5N 1 31 E
San Juan Bautista, *Paraguay* **94 B4** 26 37S 57 6W
San Juan Bautista, *U.S.A.* **84 J5** 36 51N 121 32W
San Juan Bautista Valle Nacional, *Mexico* **87 D5** 17 47N 96 19W
San Juan Capistrano, *U.S.A.* **85 M9** 33 30N 117 40W
San Juan Cr. →, *U.S.A.* **84 J5** 35 40N 120 22W
San Juan de Guadalupe, *Mexico* **86 C4** 24 38N 102 44W
San Juan de la Costa, *Mexico* **86 C2** 24 23N 110 45W
San Juan de los Morros, *Venezuela* **92 B5** 9 55N 67 21W
San Juan del Norte, *Nic.* **88 D3** 10 58N 83 40W
San Juan del Norte, B. de, *Nic.* **88 D3** 11 0N 83 40W
San Juan del Río, *Mexico* **87 C5** 20 25N 100 0W
San Juan del Sur, *Nic.* **88 D2** 11 20N 85 51W
San Juan I., *U.S.A.* **84 B3** 48 32N 123 5W
San Juan Mts., *U.S.A.* **83 H10** 37 30N 107 0W
San Justo, *Argentina* **94 C3** 30 47S 60 30W
San Kamphaeng, *Thailand* **38 C2** 18 45N 99 8 E
San Lázaro, C., *Mexico* **86 C2** 24 50N 112 18W
San Lázaro, Sa., *Mexico* **86 C3** 23 25N 110 0W
San Leandro, *U.S.A.* **84 H4** 37 44N 122 9W
San Lorenzo = Sant Llorenç des Cardassar, *Spain* **22 B10** 39 37N 3 17 E
San Lorenzo, *Argentina* **94 C3** 32 45S 60 45W
San Lorenzo, *Ecuador* **92 C3** 1 15N 78 50W
San Lorenzo, *Paraguay* **94 B4** 25 20S 57 32W
San Lorenzo →, *Mexico* **86 C3** 24 15N 107 24W
San Lorenzo, I., *Mexico* **86 B2** 28 35N 112 50W
San Lorenzo, Mte., *Argentina* **96 F2** 47 40S 72 20W
San Lucas, *Bolivia* **92 H5** 20 5S 65 7W
San Lucas, *Baja Calif. S., Mexico* **86 C3** 22 53N 109 54W
San Lucas, *Baja Calif. S., Mexico* **86 B2** 27 10N 112 14W
San Lucas, *U.S.A.* **84 J5** 36 8N 121 1W
San Lucas, C., *Mexico* **86 C3** 22 50N 110 0W
San Luis, *Argentina* **94 C2** 33 20S 66 20W
San Luis, *Cuba* **88 B3** 22 17N 83 46W
San Luis, *Guatemala* **88 C2** 16 14N 89 27W
San Luis, *Ariz., U.S.A.* **83 K6** 32 29N 114 47W
San Luis, *Colo., U.S.A.* **83 H11** 37 12N 105 25W
San Luis □, *Argentina* **94 C2** 34 0S 66 0W
San Luis, I., *Mexico* **86 B2** 29 58N 114 26W
San Luis, Sierra de, *Argentina* **94 C2** 32 30S 66 10W
San Luis de la Paz, *Mexico* **86 C4** 21 19N 100 32W
San Luis Obispo, *U.S.A.* **85 K6** 35 17N 120 40W
San Luis Potosí, *Mexico* **86 C4** 22 9N 100 59W
San Luis Potosí □, *Mexico* **86 C4** 22 10N 101 0W
San Luis Reservoir, *U.S.A.* **84 H5** 37 4N 121 5W
San Luis Río Colorado, *Mexico* **86 A2** 32 29N 114 58W
San Manuel, *U.S.A.* **83 K8** 32 36N 110 38W
San Marcos, *Guatemala* **88 D1** 14 59N 91 52W
San Marcos, *Mexico* **86 B2** 27 13N 112 6W
San Marcos, *Calif., U.S.A.* **85 M9** 33 9N 117 10W
San Marcos, *Tex., U.S.A.* **81 L6** 29 53N 97 56W
San Marino, *San Marino* **16 G7** 43 55N 12 30 E
San Marino ■, *Europe* **20 C5** 43 56N 12 25 E
San Martín, *Argentina* **94 C2** 33 5S 68 28W
San Martín →, *Bolivia* **92 F6** 13 8S 63 43W
San Martín, L., *Argentina* **96 F2** 48 50S 72 50W
San Martín de los Andes, *Argentina* **96 E2** 40 10S 71 20W
San Mateo = Sant Mateu, *Spain* **22 B7** 39 3N 1 23 E
San Mateo, *U.S.A.* **84 H4** 37 34N 122 19W
San Matías, *Bolivia* **92 G7** 16 25S 58 20W
San Matías, G., *Argentina* **96 E4** 41 30S 64 0W
San Miguel = Sant Miquel, *Spain* **22 B7** 39 3N 1 26 E
San Miguel, *El Salv.* **88 D2** 13 30N 88 12W
San Miguel, *Panama* **88 E4** 8 27N 78 55W
San Miguel, *U.S.A.* **84 K6** 35 45N 120 42W
San Miguel →, *Bolivia* **92 F6** 13 52S 63 56W
San Miguel de Tucumán, *Argentina* **94 B2** 26 50S 65 20W
San Miguel del Monte, *Argentina* **94 D4** 35 23S 58 50W
San Miguel I., *U.S.A.* **85 L6** 34 2N 120 23W
San Nicolás, *Canary Is.* **22 G4** 27 58N 15 47W
San Nicolás de los Arroyas, *Argentina* **94 C3** 33 25S 60 10W
San Nicolas I., *U.S.A.* **85 M7** 33 15N 119 30W
San Onofre, *U.S.A.* **85 M9** 33 22N 117 34W
San Pablo, *Bolivia* **94 A2** 21 43S 66 38W
San Pablo, *U.S.A.* **84 H4** 37 58N 122 21W
San Pedro, *Argentina* **94 C4** 33 40S 59 40W
San Pedro, *Buenos Aires, Argentina* **95 B5** 26 30S 54 10W
San Pedro, *Chile* **94 C1** 33 54S 71 28W
San Pedro, *Ivory C.* **50 H4** 4 50N 6 33W
San Pedro, *Mexico* **86 C2** 23 55N 110 17W
San Pedro □, *Paraguay* **94 A4** 24 0S 57 0W
San Pedro →, *Chihuahua, Mexico* **86 B3** 28 20N 106 10W
San Pedro →, *Nayarit, Mexico* **86 C3** 21 45N 105 30W
San Pedro →, *U.S.A.* **83 K8** 32 59N 110 47W
San Pedro, Pta., *Chile* **94 B1** 25 30S 70 38W
San Pedro Channel, *U.S.A.* **85 M8** 33 30N 118 25W
San Pedro de Atacama, *Chile* **94 A2** 22 55S 68 15W
San Pedro de Jujuy, *Argentina* **94 A3** 24 12S 64 55W
San Pedro de las Colonias, *Mexico* **86 B4** 25 50N 102 59W
San Pedro de Macorís, *Dom. Rep.* **89 C6** 18 30N 69 18W
San Pedro del Norte, *Nic.* **88 D3** 13 4N 84 33W
San Pedro del Paraná, *Paraguay* **94 B4** 26 43S 56 13W
San Pedro Mártir, Sierra, *Mexico* **86 A1** 31 0N 115 30W
San Pedro Mixtepec, *Mexico* **87 D5** 16 2N 97 7W
San Pedro Ocampo = Melchor Ocampo, *Mexico* **86 C4** 24 52N 101 40W
San Pedro Sula, *Honduras* **88 C2** 15 30N 88 0W
San Pietro, *Italy* **20 E3** 39 8N 8 17 E
San Quintín, *Mexico* **86 A1** 30 29N 115 57W
San Rafael, *Argentina* **94 C2** 34 40S 68 21W
San Rafael, *Calif., U.S.A.* **84 H4** 37 58N 122 32W
San Rafael, *N. Mex., U.S.A.* **83 J10** 35 7N 107 53W
San Rafael Mt., *U.S.A.* **85 L7** 34 41N 119 52W
San Rafael Mts., *U.S.A.* **85 L7** 34 40N 119 50W
San Ramón de la Nueva Orán, *Argentina* **94 A3** 23 10S 64 20W
San Remo, *Italy* **18 E7** 43 49N 7 46 E
San Roque, *Argentina* **94 B4** 28 25S 58 45W
San Roque, *Spain* **19 D3** 36 17N 5 21W
San Rosendo, *Chile* **94 D1** 37 16S 72 43W
San Saba, *U.S.A.* **81 K5** 31 12N 98 43W
San Salvador, *El Salv.* **88 D2** 13 40N 89 10W
San Salvador, *Spain* **22 B10** 39 27N 3 11 E
San Salvador de Jujuy, *Argentina* **94 A3** 24 10S 64 48W
San Salvador I., *Bahamas* **89 B5** 24 0N 74 40W
San Sebastián = Donostia-San Sebastián, *Spain* **19 A5** 43 17N 1 58W
San Sebastián, *Argentina* **96 G3** 53 10S 68 30W
San Sebastian de la Gomera, *Canary Is.* **22 F2** 28 5N 17 7W
San Serra = Son Serra, *Spain* **22 B10** 39 43N 3 13 E
San Severo, *Italy* **20 D6** 41 41N 15 23 E
San Simeon, *U.S.A.* **84 K5** 35 39N 121 11W
San Simon, *U.S.A.* **83 K9** 32 16N 109 14W
San Telmo = Sant Telm, *Spain* **22 B9** 39 35N 2 21 E
San Telmo, *Mexico* **86 A1** 30 58N 116 6W
San Tiburcio, *Mexico* **86 C4** 24 8N 101 32W
San Valentin, Mte., *Chile* **96 F2** 46 30S 73 30W
San Vicente de la Barquera, *Spain* **19 A3** 43 23N 4 29W
San Vito, *Costa Rica* **88 E3** 8 50N 82 58W
Sana', *Yemen* **46 D3** 15 27N 44 12 E
Sana →, *Bos.-H.* **16 F9** 45 3N 16 23 E
Sanaga →, *Cameroon* **52 D1** 3 35N 9 38 E
Sanaloa, Presa, *Mexico* **86 C3** 24 50N 107 20W
Sanana, *Indonesia* **37 E7** 2 4S 125 58 E
Sanand, *India* **42 H5** 22 59N 72 25 E
Sanandaj, *Iran* **44 C5** 35 18N 47 1 E
Sanandita, *Bolivia* **94 A3** 21 40S 63 45W
Sanawad, *India* **42 H7** 22 11N 76 5 E
Sancellas = Sencelles, *Spain* **22 B9** 39 39N 2 54 E
Sanchahe, *China* **35 B14** 44 50N 126 2 E

Sánchez, Dom. Rep. 89 C6 19 15N 69 36W
Sanchor, India 42 G4 24 45N 71 55 E
Sancti Spíritus, Cuba 88 B4 21 52N 79 33W
Sancy, Puy de, France 18 D5 45 32N 2 50 E
Sand ~►, S. Africa 57 C5 22 25S 30 5 E
Sand Hills, U.S.A. 80 D4 42 10N 101 30W
Sand Springs, U.S.A. 81 G6 36 9N 96 7W
Sanda, Japan 31 G7 34 53N 135 14 E
Sandakan, Malaysia 36 C5 5 53N 118 4 E
Sandan = Sambor, Cambodia 38 F6 12 46N 106 0 E
Sandanski, Bulgaria 21 D10 41 35N 23 16 E
Sanday, U.K. 12 B6 59 16N 2 31W
Sandefjord, Norway 9 G14 59 10N 10 15 E
Sanders, U.S.A. 83 J9 35 13N 109 20W
Sanderson, U.S.A. 81 K3 30 9N 102 24W
Sandersville, U.S.A. 77 J4 32 59N 82 48W
Sandfire Roadhouse, Australia 60 C3 19 45S 121 15 E
Sandfly L., Canada 73 B7 55 43N 106 6W
Sandía, Peru 92 F5 14 10S 69 30W
Sandila, India 43 F9 27 5N 80 31 E
Sandnes, Norway 9 G11 58 50N 5 45 E
Sandnessjøen, Norway 8 C15 66 2N 12 38 E
Sandoa, Dem. Rep. of the Congo 52 F4 9 41S 23 0 E
Sandomierz, Poland 17 C11 50 40N 21 43 E
Sandover ~►, Australia 62 C2 21 43S 136 32 E
Sandoway, Burma 41 K19 18 20N 94 30 E
Sandoy, Færoe Is. 8 F9 61 52N 6 46W
Sandpoint, U.S.A. 82 B5 48 17N 116 33W
Sandray, U.K. 12 E1 56 53N 7 31W
Sandringham, U.K. 10 E8 52 51N 0 31 E
Sandstone, Australia 61 E2 27 59S 119 16 E
Sandusky, Mich., U.S.A. 78 C2 43 25N 82 50W
Sandusky, Ohio, U.S.A. 78 E2 41 27N 82 42W
Sandviken, Sweden 9 F17 60 38N 16 46 E
Sandwich, C., Australia 62 B4 18 14S 146 18 E
Sandwich B., Canada 71 B8 53 40N 57 15W
Sandwich B., Namibia 56 C1 23 25S 14 20 E
Sandwip Chan., Bangla. 41 H17 22 35N 91 35 E
Sandy, Oreg., U.S.A. 84 E4 45 24N 122 16W
Sandy, Pa., U.S.A. 78 E6 41 6N 78 46W
Sandy, Utah, U.S.A. 82 F8 40 35N 111 50W
Sandy Bay, Canada 73 B8 55 31N 102 19W
Sandy Bight, Australia 61 F3 33 50S 123 20 E
Sandy C., Queens., Australia 62 C5 24 42S 153 15 E
Sandy C., Tas., Australia 62 G3 41 25S 144 45 E
Sandy Cay, Bahamas 89 B4 23 13N 75 18W
Sandy Cr. ~►, U.S.A. 82 F9 41 51N 109 47W
Sandy L., Canada 70 B1 53 2N 93 0W
Sandy Lake, Canada 70 B1 53 0N 93 15W
Sandy Valley, U.S.A. 85 K11 35 49N 115 36W
Sanford, Fla., U.S.A. 77 L5 28 48N 81 16W
Sanford, Maine, U.S.A. 77 D10 43 27N 70 47W
Sanford, N.C., U.S.A. 77 H6 35 29N 79 10W
Sanford ~►, Australia 61 E2 27 22S 115 53 E
Sanford, Mt., U.S.A. 68 B5 62 13N 144 8W
Sang-i-Masha, Afghan. 42 C2 33 8N 67 27 E
Sanga, Mozam. 55 E4 12 22S 35 21 E
Sanga ~►, Congo 52 E3 1 5S 17 0 E
Sangamner, India 40 K9 19 37N 74 15 E
Sangar, Afghan. 42 C1 32 56N 65 30 E
Sangar, Russia 27 C13 64 2N 127 31 E
Sangar Sarai, Afghan. 42 B4 34 27N 70 35 E
Sangarh ~►, Pakistan 42 D4 30 43N 70 44 E
Sangay, Ecuador 92 D3 2 0S 78 20W
Sange, Dem. Rep. of the Congo 54 D2 6 58S 28 21 E
Sangeang, Indonesia 37 F5 8 12S 119 6 E
Sanger, U.S.A. 84 J7 36 42N 119 33W
Sangerhausen, Germany 16 C6 51 28N 11 18 E
Sanggan He ~►, China 34 E9 38 12N 117 15 E
Sanggau, Indonesia 36 D4 0 5N 110 30 E
Sanghar, Pakistan 42 F3 26 2N 68 57 E
Sangihe, Kepulauan, Indonesia 37 D7 3 0N 126 0 E
Sangihe, Pulau, Indonesia 37 D7 3 45N 125 30 E
Sangju, S. Korea 35 F15 36 25N 128 10 E
Sangkapura, Indonesia 36 F4 5 52S 112 40 E
Sangkhla, Thailand 38 E2 14 57N 98 28 E
Sangkulirang, Indonesia 36 D5 0 59N 117 58 E
Sangla, Pakistan 42 D5 31 43N 73 23 E
Sangli, India 40 L9 16 55N 74 33 E
Sangmélima, Cameroon 52 D2 2 57N 12 1 E
Sangod, India 42 G7 24 55N 76 17 E
Sangre de Cristo Mts., U.S.A. 81 G2 37 30N 105 20W
Sangrur, India 42 D6 30 14N 75 50 E
Sangudo, Canada 72 C6 53 50N 114 54W
Sangue ~►, Brazil 92 F7 11 1S 58 39W
Sanibel, U.S.A. 77 M4 26 26N 82 1W
Sanirajak, Canada 69 B11 68 46N 81 12W
Sanjawi, Pakistan 42 D3 30 17N 68 21 E
Sanje, Uganda 54 C3 0 49S 31 30 E
Sanjo, Japan 30 F9 37 37N 138 57 E
Sankh ~►, India 43 H11 22 15N 84 48 E
Sankt Gallen, Switz. 18 C8 47 26N 9 22 E
Sankt Moritz, Switz. 18 C8 46 30N 9 50 E
Sankt-Peterburg, Russia 24 C5 59 55N 30 20 E
Sankt Pölten, Austria 16 D8 48 12N 15 38 E
Sankuru ~►, Dem. Rep. of the Congo 52 E4 4 17S 20 25 E
Sanliurfa, Turkey 25 G6 37 12N 38 50 E
Sanlúcar de Barrameda, Spain 19 D2 36 46N 6 21W
Sanmenxia, China 34 G6 34 47N 111 12 E
Sanming, China 33 D6 26 15N 117 40 E
Sannaspos, S. Africa 56 D4 29 6S 26 34 E
Sannicandro Gargánico, Italy 20 D6 41 50N 15 34 E
Sânnicolau Mare, Romania 17 E11 46 5N 20 39 E
Sannieshof, S. Africa 56 D4 26 30S 25 47 E
Sannīn, J., Lebanon 47 B4 33 57N 35 52 E
Sanniquellie, Liberia 50 G4 7 19N 8 38W
Sanok, Poland 17 D12 49 35N 22 10 E
Sanquhar, U.K. 12 F5 55 22N 3 54W
Sant Antoni Abat, Spain 22 C7 38 59N 1 19 E
Sant Carles, Spain 22 B8 39 3N 1 34 E
Sant Feliu de Guíxols, Spain 19 B7 41 45N 3 1 E
Sant Ferran, Spain 22 C7 38 42N 1 28 E
Sant Francesc de Formentera, Spain 22 C7 38 42N 1 26 E
Sant Jaume, Spain 22 B11 39 54N 4 4 E
Sant Joan Baptista, Spain 22 B8 39 5N 1 31 E
Sant Jordi, Spain 22 B9 39 33N 2 46 E
Sant Jordi, G. de, Spain 19 B6 40 53N 1 2 E
Sant Llorenç des Cardassar, Spain 22 B10 39 37N 3 17 E
Sant Mateu, Spain 22 B7 39 3N 1 23 E
Sant Miquel, Spain 22 B7 39 3N 1 26 E
Sant Telm, Spain 22 B9 39 35N 2 21 E
Santa Agnés, Spain 22 B7 39 3N 1 21 E
Santa Ana, Bolivia 92 F5 13 50S 65 40W
Santa Ana, El Salv. 88 D2 14 0N 89 31W
Santa Ana, Mexico 86 A2 30 31N 111 8W
Santa Ana, U.S.A. 85 M9 33 46N 117 52W
Sant' Antíoco, Italy 20 E3 39 4N 8 27 E
Santa Barbara, Chile 94 D1 37 40S 72 1W
Santa Barbara, Honduras 88 D2 14 53N 88 14W
Santa Bárbara, Mexico 86 B3 26 48N 105 50W
Santa Barbara, U.S.A. 85 L7 34 25N 119 42W
Santa Barbara Channel, U.S.A. 85 L7 34 15N 120 0W
Santa Barbara I., U.S.A. 85 M7 33 29N 119 2W
Santa Catalina, Gulf of, U.S.A. 85 N9 33 10N 117 50W
Santa Catalina, I., Mexico 86 B2 25 40N 110 50W
Santa Catalina I., U.S.A. 85 M8 33 23N 118 25W
Santa Catarina □, Brazil 95 B6 27 25S 48 30W
Santa Catarina, I. de, Brazil 95 B6 27 30S 48 40W
Santa Cecília, Brazil 95 B5 26 56S 50 18W
Santa Clara, Cuba 88 B4 22 20N 80 0W
Santa Clara, Calif., U.S.A. 84 H5 37 21N 121 57W
Santa Clara, Utah, U.S.A. 83 H7 37 8N 113 39W
Santa Clara, El Golfo de, Mexico 86 A2 31 42N 114 30W
Santa Clara de Olimar, Uruguay 95 C5 32 50S 54 54W
Santa Clarita, U.S.A. 85 L8 34 24N 118 30W
Santa Clotilde, Peru 92 D4 2 33S 73 45W
Santa Coloma de Gramenet, Spain 19 B7 41 27N 2 13 E
Santa Cruz, Argentina 96 G3 50 0S 68 32W
Santa Cruz, Bolivia 92 G6 17 43S 63 10W
Santa Cruz, Chile 94 C1 34 38S 71 27W
Santa Cruz, Costa Rica 88 D2 10 15N 85 35W
Santa Cruz, Madeira 22 D3 32 42N 16 46W
Santa Cruz, Phil. 37 B6 14 20N 121 24 E
Santa Cruz, U.S.A. 84 J4 36 58N 122 1W
Santa Cruz ~►, Argentina 96 G3 50 10S 68 20W
Santa Cruz de la Palma, Canary Is. 22 F2 28 41N 17 46W
Santa Cruz de Tenerife, Canary Is. 22 F3 28 28N 16 15W
Santa Cruz del Norte, Cuba 88 B3 23 9N 81 55W
Santa Cruz del Sur, Cuba 88 B4 20 44N 78 0W
Santa Cruz do Rio Pardo, Brazil 95 A6 22 54S 49 37W
Santa Cruz do Sul, Brazil 95 B5 29 42S 52 25W
Santa Cruz I., U.S.A. 85 M7 34 1N 119 43W
Santa Cruz Is., Solomon Is. 64 J8 10 30S 166 0 E
Santa Domingo, Cay, Bahamas 88 B4 21 25N 75 15W
Santa Elena, Argentina 94 C4 30 58S 59 47W
Santa Elena, C., Costa Rica 88 D2 10 54N 85 56W
Santa Eulàlia des Riu, Spain 22 C8 38 59N 1 32 E
Santa Fe, Argentina 94 C3 31 35S 60 41W
Santa Fe, U.S.A. 83 J11 35 41N 105 57W
Santa Fé □, Argentina 94 C3 31 50S 60 55W
Santa Fé do Sul, Brazil 93 H8 20 13S 50 56W
Santa Filomena, Brazil 93 E9 9 6S 45 50W
Santa Gertrudis, Spain 22 C7 39 0N 1 26 E
Santa Inês, Brazil 93 F11 13 17S 39 48W
Santa Inés, I., Chile 96 G2 54 0S 73 0W
Santa Isabel = Rey Malabo, Eq. Guin. 52 D1 3 45N 8 50 E
Santa Isabel, Argentina 94 D2 36 10S 66 54W
Santa Isabel do Morro, Brazil 93 F8 11 34S 50 40W
Santa Lucía, Corrientes, Argentina 94 B4 28 58S 59 5W
Santa Lucía, San Juan, Argentina 94 C2 31 30S 68 30W
Santa Lucía, Uruguay 94 C4 34 27S 56 24W
Santa Lucia Range, U.S.A. 84 K5 36 0N 121 20W
Santa Magdalena, I., Mexico 86 C2 24 40N 112 15W
Santa Margarita, Argentina 94 D3 38 28S 61 35W
Santa Margarita, Spain 22 B10 39 42N 3 6 E
Santa Margarita, U.S.A. 84 K6 35 23N 120 37W
Santa Margarita ~►, U.S.A. 85 M9 33 13N 117 23W
Santa Margarita, I., Mexico 86 C2 24 30N 111 50W
Santa María, Argentina 94 B2 26 40S 66 0W
Santa Maria, Brazil 95 B5 29 40S 53 48W
Santa Maria, U.S.A. 85 L6 34 57N 120 26W
Santa María ~►, Mexico 86 A3 31 0N 107 14W
Santa María, B. de, Mexico 86 B3 25 10N 108 40W
Santa Maria da Vitória, Brazil 93 F10 13 24S 44 12W
Santa Maria del Camí, Spain 22 B9 39 38N 2 47 E
Santa Maria di Léuca, C., Italy 21 E8 39 47N 18 22 E
Santa Marta, Colombia 92 A4 11 15N 74 13W
Santa Marta, Sierra Nevada de, Colombia 92 A4 10 55N 73 50W
Santa Marta Grande, C., Brazil 95 B6 28 43S 48 50W
Santa Maura = Levkás, Greece 21 E9 38 40N 20 43 E
Santa Monica, U.S.A. 85 M8 34 1N 118 29W
Santa Paula, U.S.A. 85 L7 34 21N 119 4W
Santa Ponsa, Spain 22 B9 39 30N 2 28 E
Santa Rita, U.S.A. 83 K10 32 48N 108 4W
Santa Rosa, La Pampa, Argentina 94 D3 36 40S 64 17W
Santa Rosa, San Luis, Argentina 94 C2 32 21S 65 10W
Santa Rosa, Brazil 95 B5 27 52S 54 29W
Santa Rosa, Calif., U.S.A. 84 G4 38 26N 122 43W
Santa Rosa, N. Mex., U.S.A. 81 H2 34 57N 104 41W
Santa Rosa de Copán, Honduras 88 D2 14 47N 88 46W
Santa Rosa de Río Primero, Argentina 94 C3 31 8S 63 20W
Santa Rosa del Sara, Bolivia 92 G6 17 7S 63 35W
Santa Rosa I., U.S.A. 85 M6 33 58N 120 6W
Santa Rosa Range, U.S.A. 82 F5 41 45N 117 40W
Santa Rosalía, Mexico 86 B2 27 20N 112 20W
Santa Sylvina, Argentina 94 B3 27 50S 61 10W
Santa Tecla = Nueva San Salvador, El Salv. 88 D2 13 40N 89 18W
Santa Teresa, Argentina 94 C3 33 25S 60 47W
Santa Teresa, Australia 62 C1 24 8S 134 22 E
Santa Teresa, Mexico 87 B5 25 17N 97 51W
Santa Vitória do Palmar, Brazil 95 C5 33 32S 53 25W
Santa Ynez, U.S.A. 85 L6 34 37N 120 5W
Santa Ynez ~►, U.S.A. 85 L6 35 41N 120 36W
Santa Ynez Mts., U.S.A. 85 L6 34 30N 120 0W
Santa Ysabel, U.S.A. 85 M10 33 7N 116 40W
Santai, China 32 C5 31 5N 104 58 E
Santana, Madeira 22 D3 32 48N 16 52W
Santana, Coxilha de, Brazil 95 C4 30 50S 55 35W
Santana do Livramento, Brazil 95 C4 30 55S 55 30W
Santander, Spain 19 A4 43 27N 3 51W
Santander Jiménez, Mexico 87 C5 24 11N 98 29W
Santanyí, Spain 22 B10 39 20N 3 5 E
Santaquin, U.S.A. 82 G8 39 59N 111 47W
Santarém, Brazil 93 D8 2 25S 54 42W
Santarém, Portugal 19 C1 39 12N 8 42W
Santaren Channel, W. Indies 88 B4 24 0N 79 30W
Santee, U.S.A. 85 N10 32 50N 116 58W
Santee ~►, U.S.A. 77 J6 33 7N 79 17W
Santiago, Brazil 95 B5 29 11S 54 52W
Santiago, Chile 94 C1 33 24S 70 40W
Santiago, Panama 88 E3 8 0N 81 0W
Santiago □, Chile 94 C1 33 30S 70 50W
Santiago ~►, Mexico 66 G9 25 11N 105 26W
Santiago ~►, Peru 92 D3 4 27S 77 38W
Santiago de Compostela, Spain 19 A1 42 52N 8 37W
Santiago de Cuba, Cuba 88 C4 20 0N 75 49W
Santiago de los Cabelleros, Dom. Rep. 89 C5 19 30N 70 40W
Santiago del Estero, Argentina 94 B3 27 50S 64 15W
Santiago del Estero □, Argentina 94 B3 27 40S 63 15W
Santiago del Teide, Canary Is. 22 F3 28 17N 16 48W
Santiago Ixcuintla, Mexico 86 C3 21 50N 105 11W
Santiago Papasquiaro, Mexico 86 C3 25 0N 105 20W
Santiaguillo, L. de, Mexico 86 C4 24 50N 104 50W
Santo Amaro, Brazil 93 F11 12 30S 38 43W
Santo Anastácio, Brazil 95 A5 21 58S 51 39W
Santo André, Brazil 95 A6 23 39S 46 29W
Santo Ângelo, Brazil 95 B5 28 15S 54 15W
Santo Antônio do Içá, Brazil 92 D5 3 5S 67 57W
Santo Antônio do Leverger, Brazil 93 G7 15 52S 56 5W
Santo Domingo, Dom. Rep. 89 C6 18 30N 69 59W
Santo Domingo, Baja Calif., Mexico 86 A1 30 43N 116 2W
Santo Domingo, Baja Calif. S., Mexico 86 B2 25 32N 112 2W
Santo Domingo, Nic. 88 D3 12 14N 84 59W
Santo Domingo de los Colorados, Ecuador 92 D3 0 15S 79 9W
Santo Domingo Pueblo, U.S.A. 83 J10 35 31N 106 22W
Santo Tomás, Mexico 86 A1 31 33N 116 24W
Santo Tomás, Peru 92 F4 14 26S 72 8W
Santo Tomé, Argentina 95 B4 28 40S 56 5W
Santo Tomé de Guayana = Ciudad Guayana, Venezuela 92 B6 8 0N 62 30W
Santoña, Spain 19 A4 43 29N 3 27W
Santoríni = Thíra, Greece 21 F11 36 23N 25 27 E
Santos, Brazil 95 A6 24 0S 46 20W
Santos Dumont, Brazil 95 A7 22 55S 43 10W
Sanwer, India 42 H6 22 59N 75 50 E
Sanyuan, China 34 G5 34 35N 108 58 E
São Bernardo do Campo, Brazil 95 A6 23 45S 46 34W
São Borja, Brazil 95 B4 28 39S 56 0W
São Carlos, Brazil 95 A6 22 0S 47 50W
São Cristóvão, Brazil 93 F11 11 1S 37 15W
São Domingos, Brazil 93 F9 13 25S 46 19W
São Francisco, Brazil 93 G10 16 0S 44 50W
São Francisco ~►, Brazil 93 F11 10 30S 36 24W
São Francisco do Sul, Brazil 95 B6 26 15S 48 36W
São Gabriel, Brazil 95 C5 30 20S 54 20W
São Gonçalo, Brazil 95 A7 22 48S 43 5W
Sao Hill, Tanzania 55 D4 8 20S 35 12 E
São João da Boa Vista, Brazil 95 A6 22 0S 46 52W
São João da Madeira, Portugal 19 B1 40 54N 8 30W
São João del Rei, Brazil 95 A7 21 8S 44 15W
São João do Araguaia, Brazil 93 E9 5 23S 48 46W
São João do Piauí, Brazil 93 E10 8 21S 42 15W
São Joaquim, Brazil 95 B6 28 18S 49 56W
São Jorge, Pta. de, Madeira 22 D3 32 50N 16 53W
São José, Brazil 95 B5 27 38S 48 39W
São José do Norte, Brazil 95 C5 32 1S 52 3W
São José do Rio Prêto, Brazil 95 A6 20 50S 49 20W
São José dos Campos, Brazil 95 A6 23 7S 45 52W
São Leopoldo, Brazil 95 B5 29 50S 51 10W
São Lourenço, Brazil 95 A6 22 7S 45 3W
São Lourenço ~►, Brazil 93 G7 17 53S 57 27W
São Lourenço, Pta. de, Madeira 22 D3 32 44N 16 39W
São Lourenço do Sul, Brazil 95 C5 31 22S 51 58W
São Luís, Brazil 93 D10 2 39S 44 15W
São Luís Gonzaga, Brazil 95 B5 28 25S 55 0W
São Marcos ~►, Brazil 93 G9 18 15S 47 37W
São Marcos, B. de, Brazil 93 D10 2 0S 44 0W
São Mateus, Brazil 93 G11 18 44S 39 50W
São Mateus do Sul, Brazil 95 B5 25 52S 50 23W
São Miguel do Oeste, Brazil 95 B5 26 45S 53 34W
São Paulo, Brazil 95 A6 23 32S 46 37W
São Paulo □, Brazil 95 A6 22 0S 49 0W
São Paulo, I., Atl. Oc. 2 D8 0 50N 31 40W
São Paulo de Olivença, Brazil 92 D5 3 27S 68 48W
São Roque, Madeira 22 D3 32 46N 16 48W
São Roque, C. de, Brazil 93 E11 5 30S 35 16W
São Sebastião, I. de, Brazil 95 A6 23 50S 45 18W
São Sebastião do Paraíso, Brazil 95 A6 20 54S 46 59W
São Tomé, Atl. Oc. 48 F4 0 10N 6 39 E
São Tomé, C. de, Brazil 95 A7 22 0S 40 59W
São Tomé & Principe ■, Africa 49 F4 0 12N 6 39 E
São Vicente, Brazil 95 A6 23 57S 46 23W
São Vicente, Madeira 22 D2 32 48N 17 3W
São Vicente, C. de, Portugal 19 D1 37 0N 9 0W
Saona, I., Dom. Rep. 89 C6 18 10N 68 40W
Saône ~►, France 18 D6 45 44N 4 50 E
Saonek, Indonesia 37 E8 0 22S 130 55 E
Saparua, Indonesia 37 E7 3 33S 128 40 E
Sapele, Nigeria 50 G7 5 50N 5 40 E
Sapelo I., U.S.A. 77 K5 31 25N 81 12W
Saposoa, Peru 92 E3 6 55S 76 45W
Sapphire, Australia 62 C4 23 28S 147 43 E
Sappho, U.S.A. 84 B2 48 4N 124 16W
Sapporo, Japan 30 C10 43 0N 141 21 E
Sapulpa, U.S.A. 81 H6 35 59N 96 5W
Saqqez, Iran 44 B5 36 15N 46 20 E
Sar Dasht, Iran 45 C6 32 32N 48 52 E
Sar Gachīneh, Iran 45 D6 30 31N 51 31 E
Sar Planina, Macedonia 21 C9 42 0N 21 0 E
Sara Buri = Saraburi, Thailand 38 E3 14 30N 100 55 E
Sarāb, Iran 44 B5 37 55N 47 40 E
Sarabadi, Iraq 44 C5 33 1N 44 48 E
Saraburi, Thailand 38 E3 14 30N 100 55 E
Sarada ~►, India 41 F12 27 21N 81 23 E
Saradiya, India 42 J4 21 34N 70 2 E
Saragossa = Zaragoza, Spain 19 B5 41 39N 0 53W
Saraguro, Ecuador 92 D3 3 35S 79 16W
Sarai Naurang, Pakistan 42 C4 32 50N 70 47 E
Saraikela, India 43 H11 22 42N 85 56 E
Sarajevo, Bos.-H. 21 C8 43 52N 18 26 E
Sarakhs, Turkmenistan 45 B9 36 32N 61 13 E
Saran, Gunung, Indonesia 36 E4 0 30S 111 25 E
Saranac L., U.S.A. 79 B10 44 20N 74 10W
Saranac Lake, U.S.A. 79 B10 44 20N 74 8W
Saranda, Tanzania 54 D3 5 45S 34 59 E
Sarandí del Yi, Uruguay 95 C4 33 18S 55 38W
Sarandí Grande, Uruguay 94 C4 33 44S 56 20W
Sarangani B., Phil. 37 C7 6 0N 125 13 E
Sarangani Is., Phil. 37 C7 5 25N 125 25 E
Sarangarh, India 41 J13 21 30N 83 5 E
Saransk, Russia 24 D8 54 10N 45 10 E
Sarapul, Russia 24 C9 56 28N 53 48 E
Sarasota, U.S.A. 77 M4 27 20N 82 32W
Saratoga, Calif., U.S.A. 84 H4 37 16N 122 2W
Saratoga, Wyo., U.S.A. 82 F10 41 27N 106 49W
Saratoga Springs, U.S.A. 79 C11 43 5N 73 47W
Saratok, Malaysia 36 D4 1 55N 111 17 E
Saratov, Russia 25 D8 51 30N 46 2 E
Saravane, Laos 38 E6 15 43N 106 25 E
Sarawak □, Malaysia 36 D4 2 0N 113 0 E
Saray, Turkey 21 D12 41 26N 27 55 E
Sarayköy, Turkey 21 F13 37 55N 28 54 E
Sarbāz, Iran 45 E9 26 38N 61 19 E
Sarbīsheh, Iran 45 C8 32 30N 59 40 E
Sarda = Sarada ~►, India 41 F12 27 21N 81 23 E
Sardarshahr, India 42 E6 28 30N 74 29 E
Sardegna □, Italy 20 D3 40 0N 9 0 E
Sardhana, India 42 E7 29 9N 77 39 E
Sardina, Pta., Canary Is. 22 F4 28 9N 15 44W
Sardinia = Sardegna □, Italy 20 D3 40 0N 9 0 E
Sardis, Turkey 21 E12 38 28N 28 2 E
Sārdūīyeh = Dar Mazār, Iran 45 D8 29 14N 57 20 E
S'Arenal, Spain 22 B9 39 30N 2 45 E
Sargasso Sea, Atl. Oc. 66 G13 27 0N 72 0W
Sargodha, Pakistan 42 C5 32 10N 72 40 E
Sarh, Chad 51 G9 9 5N 18 23 E
Sārī, Iran 45 B7 36 30N 53 4 E
Saria, India 43 J10 21 38N 83 22 E
Sariab, Pakistan 42 D2 30 6N 66 59 E
Sarıgöl, Turkey 21 E13 38 14N 28 41 E
Sarikei, Malaysia 36 D4 2 8N 111 30 E
Sarila, India 43 G8 25 46N 79 41 E
Sarina, Australia 62 C4 21 22S 149 13 E
Sarita, U.S.A. 81 M6 27 13N 97 47W
Sariwŏn, N. Korea 35 E13 38 31N 125 46 E
Sarju ~►, India 43 F9 27 21N 81 23 E
Sark, U.K. 11 H5 49 25N 2 22W
Sarkari Tala, India 42 F4 27 39N 70 52 E
Şarköy, Turkey 21 D12 40 36N 27 6 E
Sarlat-la-Canéda, France 18 D4 44 54N 1 13 E
Sarmi, Indonesia 37 E9 1 49S 138 44 E
Sarmiento, Argentina 96 F3 45 35S 69 5W
Särna, Sweden 9 F15 61 41N 13 8 E
Sarnia, Canada 78 D2 42 58N 82 23W
Sarolangun, Indonesia 36 E2 2 19S 102 42 E
Saronikós Kólpos, Greece 21 F10 37 45N 23 45 E
Saros Körfezi, Turkey 21 D12 40 30N 26 15 E
Sarpsborg, Norway 9 G14 59 16N 11 7 E
Sarre = Saar ~►, Europe 18 B7 49 41N 6 32 E
Sarreguemines, France 18 B7 49 5N 7 4 E
Sarthe ~►, France 18 C3 47 33N 0 31W
Saruna ~►, Pakistan 42 F2 26 31N 67 7 E
Sarvar, India 42 F6 26 4N 75 0 E
Sarvestān, Iran 45 D7 29 20N 53 10 E
Sary-Tash, Kyrgyzstan 26 F8 39 44N 73 15 E
Saryshagan, Kazakstan 26 E8 46 12N 73 38 E
Sasan Gir, India 42 J4 21 10N 70 36 E
Sasaram, India 43 G11 24 57N 84 5 E
Sasebo, Japan 31 H4 33 10N 129 43 E
Saser, India 43 B7 34 50N 77 50 E
Saskatchewan □, Canada 73 C7 54 40N 106 0W
Saskatchewan ~►, Canada 73 C8 53 37N 100 40W
Saskatoon, Canada 73 C7 52 10N 106 38W
Saskylakh, Russia 27 B12 71 55N 114 1 E
Sasolburg, S. Africa 57 D4 26 46S 27 49 E
Sasovo, Russia 24 D7 54 25N 41 55 E
Sassandra, Ivory C. 50 H4 4 55N 6 8W
Sassandra ~►, Ivory C. 50 H4 4 58N 6 5W
Sássari, Italy 20 D3 40 43N 8 34 E
Sassnitz, Germany 16 A7 54 29N 13 39 E
Sassuolo, Italy 20 B4 44 33N 10 47 E
Sasumua Dam, Kenya 54 C4 0 45S 36 40 E
Sasyk, Ozero, Ukraine 17 F15 45 45N 29 20 E
Sata-Misaki, Japan 31 J5 31 0N 130 40 E
Satadougou, Mali 50 F3 12 25N 11 25W
Satakunta, Finland 9 F20 61 45N 23 0 E
Satara, India 40 L8 17 44N 73 58 E
Satbarwa, India 43 H11 23 55N 84 16 E
Satevó, Mexico 86 B3 27 57N 106 7W
Satilla ~►, U.S.A. 77 K5 30 59N 81 29W
Satka, Russia 24 C10 55 3N 59 1 E
Satmala Hills, India 40 J9 20 15N 74 40 E
Satna, India 43 G9 24 35N 80 50 E
Sátoraljaújhely, Hungary 17 D11 48 25N 21 41 E

Satpura Ra., *India* 40 J10 21 25N 76 10 E
Satsuna-Shotō, *Japan* 31 K5 30 0N 130 0 E
Sattahip, *Thailand* 38 F3 12 41N 100 54 E
Satu Mare, *Romania* 17 E12 47 46N 22 55 E
Satui, *Indonesia* 36 E5 3 50S 115 27 E
Satun, *Thailand* 39 J3 6 43N 100 2 E
Saturnina →, *Brazil* 92 F7 12 15S 58 10W
Sauce, *Argentina* 94 C4 30 5S 58 46W
Sauceda, *Mexico* 86 B4 25 55N 101 18W
Saucillo, *Mexico* 86 B3 28 1N 105 17W
Sauda, *Norway* 9 G12 59 40N 6 20 E
Sauðarkrókur, *Iceland* 8 D4 65 45N 19 40W
Saudi Arabia ■, *Asia* 46 B3 26 0N 44 0 E
Sauerland, *Germany* 16 C4 51 12N 7 59 E
Saugeen →, *Canada* 78 B3 44 30N 81 22W
Saugerties, *U.S.A.* 79 D11 42 5N 73 57W
Saugus, *U.S.A.* 85 L8 34 25N 118 32W
Sauk Centre, *U.S.A.* 80 C7 45 44N 94 57W
Sauk Rapids, *U.S.A.* 80 C7 45 35N 94 10W
Sault Ste. Marie, *Canada* 70 C3 46 30N 84 20W
Sault Ste. Marie, *U.S.A.* 69 D11 46 30N 84 21W
Saumlaki, *Indonesia* 37 F8 7 55S 131 20 E
Saumur, *France* 18 C3 47 15N 0 5W
Saunders C., *N.Z.* 59 L3 45 53S 170 45 E
Saunders I., *Antarctica* 5 B1 57 48S 26 28W
Saunders Point, *Australia* 61 E4 27 52S 125 38 E
Saurimo, *Angola* 52 F4 9 40S 20 12 E
Sausalito, *U.S.A.* 84 H4 37 51N 122 29W
Savá, *Honduras* 88 C2 15 32N 86 15W
Sava →, *Serbia, Yug.* 21 B9 44 50N 20 26 E
Savage, *U.S.A.* 80 B2 47 27N 104 21W
Savage I. = Niue, *Cook Is.* 65 J11 19 2S 169 54W
Savage River, *Australia* 62 G4 41 31S 145 14 E
Savai'i, *W. Samoa* 59 A12 13 28S 172 24W
Savalou, *Benin* 50 G6 7 57N 1 58 E
Savane, *Mozam.* 55 F4 19 37S 35 8 E
Savanna, *U.S.A.* 80 D9 42 5N 90 8W
Savanna-la-Mar, *Jamaica* 88 C4 18 10N 78 10W
Savannah, *Ga., U.S.A.* 77 J5 32 5N 81 6W
Savannah, *Mo., U.S.A.* 80 F7 39 56N 94 50W
Savannah, *Tenn., U.S.A.* 77 H1 35 14N 88 15W
Savannah →, *U.S.A.* 77 J5 32 2N 80 53W
Savannakhet, *Laos* 38 D5 16 30N 104 49 E
Savant L., *Canada* 70 B1 50 16N 90 44W
Savant Lake, *Canada* 70 B1 50 14N 90 40W
Savanur, *India* 40 M9 14 59N 75 21 E
Save →, *Mozam.* 57 C5 21 16S 34 0 E
Sāveh, *Iran* 45 C6 35 2N 50 20 E
Savelugu, *Ghana* 50 G5 9 38N 0 54W
Savo, *Finland* 8 E22 62 45N 27 30 E
Savoie □, *France* 18 D7 45 26N 6 25 E
Savona, *Italy* 18 D8 44 17N 8 30 E
Savona, *U.S.A.* 78 D7 42 17N 77 13W
Savonlinna, *Finland* 24 B4 61 52N 28 53 E
Savoy = Savoie □, *France* 18 D7 45 26N 6 25 E
Savur, *Turkey* 44 B4 37 34N 40 53 E
Sawahlunto, *Indonesia* 36 E2 0 40S 100 52 E
Sawai, *Indonesia* 37 E7 3 0S 129 5 E
Sawai Madhopur, *India* 42 G7 26 0N 76 25 E
Sawang Daen Din, *Thailand* 38 D4 17 28N 103 28 E
Sawankhalok, *Thailand* 38 D2 17 19N 99 50 E
Sawara, *Japan* 31 G10 35 55N 140 30 E
Sawatch Range, *U.S.A.* 83 G10 38 30N 106 30W
Sawel Mt., *U.K.* 13 B4 54 50N 7 2W
Sawi, *Thailand* 39 G2 10 14N 99 5 E
Sawmills, *Zimbabwe* 55 F2 19 30S 28 2 E
Sawtooth Range, *U.S.A.* 82 E6 44 3N 114 58W
Sawu, *Indonesia* 37 F6 10 35S 121 50 E
Sawu Sea, *Indonesia* 37 F6 9 30S 121 50 E
Saxby →, *Australia* 62 B3 18 25S 140 53 E
Saxmundham, *U.K.* 11 E9 52 13N 1 30 E
Saxony = Sachsen □, *Germany* 16 C7 50 55N 13 10 E
Saxony, Lower = Niedersachsen □, *Germany* 16 B5 52 50N 9 0 E
Saxton, *U.S.A.* 78 F6 40 13N 78 15W
Sayabec, *Canada* 71 C6 48 35N 67 41W
Sayaboury, *Laos* 38 C3 19 15N 101 45 E
Sayán, *Peru* 92 F3 11 8S 77 12W
Sayan, Vostochnyy, *Russia* 27 D10 54 0N 96 0 E
Sayan, Zapadnyy, *Russia* 27 D10 52 30N 94 0 E
Saydā, *Lebanon* 47 B4 33 35N 35 25 E
Sayhandulaan = Oldziyt, *Mongolia* 34 B5 44 40N 109 1 E
Sayhūt, *Yemen* 46 D5 15 12N 51 10 E
Saynshand, *Mongolia* 34 B6 44 55N 110 11 E
Sayre, *Okla., U.S.A.* 81 H5 35 18N 99 38W
Sayre, *Pa., U.S.A.* 79 E8 41 59N 76 32W
Sayreville, *U.S.A.* 79 F10 40 28N 74 22W
Sayula, *Mexico* 86 D4 19 50N 103 40W
Sayward, *Canada* 72 C3 50 21N 125 55W
Sazanit, *Albania* 21 D8 40 30N 19 20 E
Sázava →, *Czech Rep.* 16 D8 49 53N 14 24 E
Sazin, *Pakistan* 43 B5 35 35N 73 30 E
Scafell Pike, *U.K.* 10 C4 54 27N 3 14W
Scalloway, *U.K.* 12 A7 60 9N 1 17W
Scalpay, *U.K.* 12 D3 57 18N 6 0W
Scandia, *Canada* 72 C6 50 20N 112 0W
Scandicci, *Italy* 20 C4 43 45N 11 11 E
Scandinavia, *Europe* 6 C8 64 0N 12 0 E
Scapa Flow, *U.K.* 12 C5 58 53N 3 3W
Scappoose, *U.S.A.* 84 E4 45 45N 122 53W
Scarba, *U.K.* 12 E3 56 11N 5 43W
Scarborough, *Trin. & Tob.* 89 D7 11 11N 60 42W
Scarborough, *U.K.* 10 C7 54 17N 0 24W
Scariff I., *Ireland* 13 E1 51 44N 10 15W
Scarp, *U.K.* 12 C1 58 1N 7 8W
Scebeli, Wabi →, *Somali Rep.* 46 G3 2 0N 44 0 E
Schaffhausen, *Switz.* 18 C8 47 42N 8 39 E
Schagen, *Neths.* 15 B4 52 49N 4 48 E
Schaghticoke, *U.S.A.* 79 D11 42 54N 73 35W
Schefferville, *Canada* 71 B6 54 48N 66 50W
Schelde →, *Belgium* 15 C4 51 15N 4 16 E
Schell Creek Ra., *U.S.A.* 82 G6 39 15N 114 30W
Schellsburg, *U.S.A.* 78 F6 40 3N 78 39W
Schenectady, *U.S.A.* 79 D11 42 49N 73 57W
Schenevus, *U.S.A.* 79 D10 42 33N 74 50W
Schiedam, *Neths.* 15 C4 51 55N 4 25 E
Schiermonnikoog, *Neths.* 15 A6 53 30N 6 15 E
Schio, *Italy* 20 B4 45 43N 11 21 E
Schleswig, *Germany* 16 A5 54 31N 9 34 E
Schleswig-Holstein □, *Germany* 16 A5 54 30N 9 30 E
Schoharie, *U.S.A.* 79 D10 42 40N 74 19W
Schoharie →, *U.S.A.* 79 D10 42 57N 74 18W
Scholls, *U.S.A.* 84 E4 45 24N 122 56W
Schouten I., *Australia* 62 G4 42 20S 148 20 E
Schouten Is. = Supiori, *Indonesia* 37 E9 1 0S 136 0 E
Schouwen, *Neths.* 15 C3 51 43N 3 45 E
Schreiber, *Canada* 70 C2 48 45N 87 20W
Schroon Lake, *U.S.A.* 79 C11 43 50N 73 46W
Schuler, *Canada* 73 C6 50 20N 110 6W
Schumacher, *Canada* 70 C3 48 30N 81 16W
Schurz, *U.S.A.* 82 G4 38 57N 118 49W
Schuyler, *U.S.A.* 80 E6 41 27N 97 4W
Schuylerville, *U.S.A.* 79 C11 43 6N 73 35W
Schuylkill →, *U.S.A.* 79 G9 39 53N 75 12W
Schuylkill Haven, *U.S.A.* 79 F8 40 37N 76 11W
Schwäbische Alb, *Germany* 16 D5 48 20N 9 30 E
Schwaner, Pegunungan, *Indonesia* 36 E4 1 0S 112 30 E
Schwarzwald, *Germany* 16 D5 48 30N 8 20 E
Schwedt, *Germany* 16 B8 53 3N 14 16 E
Schweinfurt, *Germany* 16 C6 50 3N 10 14 E
Schweizer-Reneke, *S. Africa* 56 D4 27 11S 25 18 E
Schwenningen = Villingen-Schwenningen, *Germany* 16 D5 48 3N 8 26 E
Schwerin, *Germany* 16 B6 53 36N 11 22 E
Schwyz, *Switz.* 18 C8 47 2N 8 39 E
Sciacca, *Italy* 20 F5 37 31N 13 3 E
Scilla, *Italy* 20 E6 38 15N 15 43 E
Scilly, Isles of, *U.K.* 11 H1 49 56N 6 22W
Scioto →, *U.S.A.* 76 F4 38 44N 83 1W
Scituate, *U.S.A.* 79 D14 42 12N 70 44W
Scobey, *U.S.A.* 80 A2 48 47N 105 25W
Scone, *Australia* 63 E5 32 5S 150 52 E
Scoresbysund, *Greenland* 4 B6 70 20N 23 0W
Scotia, *Calif., U.S.A.* 82 F1 40 29N 124 6W
Scotia, *N.Y., U.S.A.* 79 D11 42 50N 73 58W
Scotia Sea, *Antarctica* 5 B18 56 5S 56 0W
Scotland, *Canada* 78 C4 43 1N 80 22W
Scotland □, *U.K.* 12 E5 57 0N 4 0W
Scott, C., *Australia* 60 B4 13 30S 129 49 E
Scott City, *U.S.A.* 80 F4 38 29N 100 54W
Scott Glacier, *Antarctica* 5 C8 66 15S 100 5 E
Scott I., *Antarctica* 5 C11 67 0S 179 0 E
Scott Is., *Canada* 72 C3 50 48N 128 40W
Scott L., *Canada* 73 B7 59 55N 106 18W
Scott Reef, *Australia* 60 B3 14 0S 121 50 E
Scottburgh, *S. Africa* 57 E5 30 15S 30 47 E
Scottdale, *U.S.A.* 78 F5 40 6N 79 35W
Scottish Borders □, *U.K.* 12 F6 55 35N 2 50W
Scottsbluff, *U.S.A.* 80 E3 41 52N 103 40W
Scottsboro, *U.S.A.* 77 H3 34 40N 86 2W
Scottsburg, *U.S.A.* 76 F3 38 41N 85 47W
Scottsdale, *Australia* 62 G4 41 9S 147 31 E
Scottsdale, *U.S.A.* 83 K7 33 29N 111 56W
Scottsville, *Ky., U.S.A.* 77 G2 36 45N 86 11W
Scottsville, *N.Y., U.S.A.* 78 C7 43 2N 77 47W
Scottville, *U.S.A.* 76 D2 43 58N 86 17W
Scranton, *U.S.A.* 79 E9 41 25N 75 40W
Scugog, L., *Canada* 78 B6 44 10N 78 55W
Scunthorpe, *U.K.* 10 D7 53 36N 0 39W
Seabrook, L., *Australia* 61 F2 30 55S 119 40 E
Seaford, *U.K.* 11 G8 50 47N 0 7 E
Seaford, *U.S.A.* 76 F8 38 39N 75 37W
Seaforth, *Australia* 62 C4 20 55S 148 57 E
Seaforth, *Canada* 78 C3 43 35N 81 25W
Seaforth, L., *U.K.* 12 D2 57 52N 6 36W
Seagraves, *U.S.A.* 81 J3 32 57N 102 34W
Seaham, *U.K.* 10 C6 54 50N 1 20W
Seal →, *Canada* 73 B10 59 4N 94 48W
Seal L., *Canada* 71 B7 54 20N 61 30W
Sealy, *U.S.A.* 81 L6 29 47N 96 9W
Searchlight, *U.S.A.* 85 K12 35 28N 114 55W
Searcy, *U.S.A.* 81 H9 35 15N 91 44W
Searles L., *U.S.A.* 85 K9 35 44N 117 21W
Seascale, *U.K.* 10 C4 54 24N 3 29W
Seaside, *Calif., U.S.A.* 84 J5 36 37N 121 50W
Seaside, *Oreg., U.S.A.* 84 E3 46 0N 123 56W
Seaspray, *Australia* 63 F4 38 25S 147 15 E
Seattle, *U.S.A.* 84 C4 47 36N 122 20W
Seaview Ra., *Australia* 62 B4 18 40S 145 45 E
Sebago L., *U.S.A.* 79 C14 43 52N 70 34W
Sebago Lake, *U.S.A.* 79 C14 43 51N 70 34W
Sebastián Vizcaíno, B., *Mexico* 86 B2 28 0N 114 30W
Sebastopol = Sevastopol, *Ukraine* 25 F5 44 35N 33 30 E
Sebastopol, *U.S.A.* 84 G4 38 24N 122 49W
Sebewaing, *U.S.A.* 76 D4 43 44N 83 27W
Sebha = Sabhah, *Libya* 51 C8 27 9N 14 29 E
Şebinkarahisar, *Turkey* 25 F6 40 22N 38 28 E
Sebring, *Fla., U.S.A.* 77 M5 27 30N 81 27W
Sebring, *Ohio, U.S.A.* 78 F3 40 55N 81 2W
Sebringville, *Canada* 78 C3 43 24N 81 4W
Sebta = Ceuta, *N. Afr.* 19 E3 35 52N 5 18W
Sebuku, *Indonesia* 36 E5 3 30S 116 25 E
Sebuku, Teluk, *Malaysia* 36 D5 4 0N 118 10 E
Sechelt, *Canada* 72 D4 49 25N 123 42W
Sechura, Desierto de, *Peru* 92 E2 6 0S 80 30W
Secretary I., *N.Z.* 59 L1 45 15S 166 56 E
Secunderabad, *India* 40 L11 17 28N 78 30 E
Security-Widefield, *U.S.A.* 80 F2 38 45N 104 45W
Sedalia, *U.S.A.* 80 F8 38 42N 93 14W
Sedan, *France* 18 B6 49 43N 4 57 E
Sedan, *U.S.A.* 81 G6 37 8N 96 11W
Seddon, *N.Z.* 59 J5 41 40S 174 7 E
Seddonville, *N.Z.* 59 J4 41 33S 172 1 E
Sedé Boqér, *Israel* 47 E3 30 52N 34 47 E
Sedeh, *Fārs, Iran* 45 D7 30 45N 52 11 E
Sedeh, *Khorāsān, Iran* 45 C8 33 20N 59 14 E
Sederot, *Israel* 47 D3 31 32N 34 37 E
Sédhiou, *Senegal* 50 F2 12 44N 15 30W
Sedley, *Canada* 73 C8 50 10N 104 0W
Sedona, *U.S.A.* 83 J8 34 52N 111 46W
Sedova, Pik, *Russia* 26 B6 73 29N 54 58 E
Sedro Woolley, *U.S.A.* 84 B4 48 30N 122 14W
Seeheim, *Namibia* 56 D2 26 50S 17 45 E
Seekoei →, *S. Africa* 56 E4 30 18S 25 1 E
Seeley's Bay, *Canada* 79 B8 44 29N 76 14W
Seferihisar, *Turkey* 21 E12 38 10N 26 50 E
Seg-ozero, *Russia* 24 B5 63 20N 33 46 E
Segamat, *Malaysia* 39 L4 2 30N 102 50 E
Segesta, *Italy* 20 F5 37 56N 12 50 E
Seget, *Indonesia* 37 E8 1 24S 130 58 E
Segezha, *Russia* 24 B5 63 44N 34 19 E
Ségou, *Mali* 50 F4 13 30N 6 16W
Segovia = Coco →, *Cent. Amer.* 88 D3 15 0N 83 8W
Segovia, *Spain* 19 B3 40 57N 4 10W
Segre →, *Spain* 19 B6 41 40N 0 43 E
Séguéla, *Ivory C.* 50 G4 7 55N 6 40W
Seguin, *U.S.A.* 81 L6 29 34N 97 58W
Segundo →, *Argentina* 94 C3 30 53S 62 44W
Segura →, *Spain* 19 C5 38 3N 0 44W
Seh Konj, Kūh-e, *Iran* 45 D8 30 6N 57 30 E
Seh Qal'eh, *Iran* 45 C8 33 40N 58 24 E
Sehitwa, *Botswana* 56 C3 20 30S 22 30 E
Sehore, *India* 42 H7 23 10N 77 5 E
Sehwan, *Pakistan* 42 F2 26 28N 67 53 E
Seil, *U.K.* 12 E3 56 18N 5 38W
Seiland, *Norway* 8 A20 70 25N 23 15 E
Seiling, *U.S.A.* 81 G5 36 9N 98 56W
Seinäjoki, *Finland* 9 E20 62 40N 22 51 E
Seine →, *France* 18 B4 49 26N 0 26 E
Sekayu, *Indonesia* 36 E2 2 51S 103 51 E
Seke, *Tanzania* 54 C3 3 20S 33 31 E
Sekenke, *Tanzania* 54 C3 4 18S 34 11 E
Sekondi-Takoradi, *Ghana* 50 H5 4 58N 1 45W
Sekuma, *Botswana* 56 C3 24 36S 23 50 E
Selah, *U.S.A.* 82 C3 46 39N 120 32W
Selama, *Malaysia* 39 K3 5 12N 100 42 E
Selaru, *Indonesia* 37 F8 8 9S 131 0 E
Selby, *U.K.* 10 D6 53 47N 1 5W
Selby, *U.S.A.* 80 C4 45 31N 100 2W
Selçuk, *Turkey* 21 F12 37 56N 27 22 E
Selden, *U.S.A.* 80 F4 39 33N 100 34W
Sele →, *Italy* 20 D6 40 29N 14 56 E
Selebi-Pikwe, *Botswana* 57 C4 21 58S 27 48 E
Selemdzha →, *Russia* 27 D13 51 42N 128 53 E
Selenga = Selenge Mörön →, *Asia* 32 A5 52 16N 106 16 E
Selenge Mörön →, *Asia* 32 A5 52 16N 106 16 E
Seletan, Tanjung, *Indonesia* 36 E4 4 10S 114 40 E
Sélibabi, *Mauritania* 50 E3 15 10N 12 15W
Seligman, *U.S.A.* 83 J7 35 20N 112 53W
Selîma, El Wâhât el, *Sudan* 51 D11 21 22N 29 19 E
Selinda Spillway, *Botswana* 56 B3 18 35S 23 10 E
Selinsgrove, *U.S.A.* 78 F8 40 48N 76 52W
Selkirk, *Canada* 73 C9 50 10N 96 55W
Selkirk, *U.K.* 12 F6 55 33N 2 50W
Selkirk I., *Canada* 73 C9 53 20N 99 6W
Selkirk Mts., *Canada* 68 C8 51 15N 117 40W
Selliá, *Greece* 23 D6 35 12N 24 23 E
Sells, *U.S.A.* 83 L8 31 55N 111 53W
Selma, *Ala., U.S.A.* 77 J2 32 25N 87 1W
Selma, *Calif., U.S.A.* 84 J7 36 34N 119 37W
Selma, *N.C., U.S.A.* 77 H6 35 32N 78 17W
Selmer, *U.S.A.* 77 H1 35 10N 88 36W
Selowandoma Falls, *Zimbabwe* 55 G3 21 15S 31 50 E
Selpele, *Indonesia* 37 E8 0 1S 130 5 E
Selsey Bill, *U.K.* 11 G7 50 43N 0 47W
Seltso, *Russia* 24 D5 53 22N 34 4 E
Selu, *Indonesia* 37 F8 7 32S 130 55 E
Selva, *Argentina* 94 B3 29 50S 62 0W
Selvas, *Brazil* 92 E5 6 30S 67 0W
Selwyn L., *Canada* 73 B8 60 0N 104 30W
Selwyn Mts., *Canada* 68 B6 63 0N 130 0W
Selwyn Ra., *Australia* 62 C3 21 10S 140 0 E
Semani →, *Albania* 21 D8 40 47N 19 30 E
Semarang, *Indonesia* 37 G14 7 0S 110 26 E
Sembabule, *Uganda* 54 C3 0 4S 31 25 E
Semeru, *Indonesia* 37 H15 8 4S 112 55 E
Semey, *Kazakstan* 26 D9 50 30N 80 10 E
Seminoe Reservoir, *U.S.A.* 82 F10 42 9N 106 55W
Seminole, *Okla., U.S.A.* 81 H6 35 14N 96 41W
Seminole, *Tex., U.S.A.* 81 J3 32 43N 102 39W
Seminole Draw →, *U.S.A.* 81 J3 32 27N 102 20W
Semipalatinsk = Semey, *Kazakstan* 26 D9 50 30N 80 10 E
Semirara Is., *Phil.* 37 B6 12 0N 121 20 E
Semitau, *Indonesia* 36 D4 0 29N 111 57 E
Semiyarka, *Kazakstan* 26 D8 50 55N 78 23 E
Semiyarskoye = Semiyarka, *Kazakstan* 26 D8 50 55N 78 23 E
Semmering P., *Austria* 16 E8 47 41N 15 45 E
Semnān, *Iran* 45 C7 35 40N 53 23 E
Semnān □, *Iran* 45 C7 36 0N 54 0 E
Semporna, *Malaysia* 37 D5 4 30N 118 33 E
Semuda, *Indonesia* 36 E4 2 51S 112 58 E
Sen →, *Cambodia* 36 B3 13 45N 105 12 E
Senā, *Iran* 45 D6 28 27N 51 36 E
Sena, *Mozam.* 55 F4 17 25S 35 0 E
Sena Madureira, *Brazil* 92 E5 9 5S 68 45W
Senador Pompeu, *Brazil* 93 E11 5 40S 39 20W
Senanga, *Zambia* 56 B3 16 2S 23 14 E
Senatobia, *U.S.A.* 81 H10 34 37N 89 58W
Sencelles, *Spain* 22 B9 39 39N 2 54 E
Sendai, *Kagoshima, Japan* 31 J5 31 50N 130 20 E
Sendai, *Miyagi, Japan* 30 E10 38 15N 140 53 E
Sendai-Wan, *Japan* 30 E10 38 15N 141 0 E
Sendhwa, *India* 42 J6 21 41N 75 6 E
Seneca, *U.S.A.* 77 H4 34 41N 82 57W
Seneca Falls, *U.S.A.* 79 D8 42 55N 76 48W
Seneca L., *U.S.A.* 78 D8 42 40N 76 54W
Senecaville L., *U.S.A.* 78 G3 39 55N 81 25W
Senegal ■, *W. Afr.* 50 F3 14 30N 14 30W
Senegal →, *W. Afr.* 50 E2 15 48N 16 32W
Senegambia, *Africa* 48 E2 12 45N 12 0W
Senekal, *S. Africa* 57 D4 28 20S 27 36 E
Senga Hill, *Zambia* 55 D3 9 19S 31 11 E
Senge Khambab = Indus →, *Pakistan* 42 G2 24 20N 67 47 E
Sengua →, *Zimbabwe* 55 F2 17 7S 28 5 E
Senhor-do-Bonfim, *Brazil* 93 F10 10 30S 40 10W
Senigállia, *Italy* 20 C5 43 43N 13 13 E
Senj, *Croatia* 16 F8 45 0N 14 58 E
Senja, *Norway* 8 B17 69 25N 17 30 E
Senkaku-Shotō, *Japan* 31 L1 25 45N 124 0 E
Senlis, *France* 18 B5 49 13N 2 35 E
Senmonorom, *Cambodia* 38 F6 12 27N 107 12 E
Senneterre, *Canada* 70 C4 48 25N 77 15W
Seno, *Laos* 38 D5 16 35N 104 50 E
Sens, *France* 18 B5 48 11N 3 15 E
Senta, *Serbia, Yug.* 21 B9 45 55N 20 3 E
Sentani, *Indonesia* 37 E10 2 36S 140 37 E
Sentery, *Dem. Rep. of the Congo* 54 D2 5 17S 25 42 E
Sentinel, *U.S.A.* 83 K7 32 52N 113 13W
Seo de Urgel = La Seu d'Urgell, *Spain* 19 A6 42 22N 1 23 E
Seohara, *India* 43 E8 29 15N 78 33 E
Seonath →, *India* 43 J10 21 44N 82 28 E
Seondha, *India* 43 F8 26 9N 78 48 E
Seoni, *India* 43 H8 22 5N 79 30 E
Seoni Malwa, *India* 42 H8 22 27N 77 28 E
Seoul = Sŏul, *S. Korea* 35 F14 37 31N 126 58 E
Sepīdān, *Iran* 45 D7 30 20N 52 5 E
Sepo-ri, *N. Korea* 35 E14 38 57N 127 25 E
Sepone, *Laos* 38 D6 16 45N 106 13 E
Sept-Îles, *Canada* 71 B6 50 13N 66 22W
Sequim, *U.S.A.* 84 B3 48 5N 123 6W
Sequoia National Park, *U.S.A.* 84 J8 36 30N 118 30W
Seraing, *Belgium* 15 D5 50 35N 5 32 E
Seraja, *Indonesia* 39 L7 2 41N 108 35 E
Serakhis →, *Cyprus* 23 D11 35 13N 32 55 E
Seram, *Indonesia* 37 E7 3 10S 129 0 E
Seram Sea, *Indonesia* 37 E7 2 30S 128 30 E
Serang, *Indonesia* 37 G12 6 8S 106 10 E
Serasan, *Indonesia* 39 L7 2 29N 109 4 E
Serbia □, *Yugoslavia* 21 C9 43 30N 21 0 E
Serdobsk, *Russia* 24 D7 52 28N 44 10 E
Seremban, *Malaysia* 39 L3 2 43N 101 53 E
Serengeti Plain, *Tanzania* 54 C4 2 40S 35 0 E
Serenje, *Zambia* 55 E3 13 14S 30 15 E
Sereth = Siret →, *Romania* 17 F14 45 24N 28 1 E
Sergino, *Russia* 26 C7 62 25N 65 12 E
Sergipe □, *Brazil* 93 F11 10 30S 37 30W
Sergiyev Posad, *Russia* 24 C6 56 20N 38 10 E
Seria, *Brunei* 36 D4 4 37N 114 23 E
Serian, *Malaysia* 36 D4 1 10N 110 31 E
Seribu, Kepulauan, *Indonesia* 36 F3 5 36S 106 33 E
Sérifos, *Greece* 21 F11 37 9N 24 30 E
Sérigny →, *Canada* 71 A6 56 47N 66 0W
Seringapatam Reef, *Australia* 60 B3 13 38S 122 5 E
Sermata, *Indonesia* 37 F7 8 15S 128 50 E
Serov, *Russia* 24 C11 59 29N 60 35 E
Serowe, *Botswana* 56 C4 22 25S 26 43 E
Serpentine Lakes, *Australia* 61 E4 28 30S 129 10 E
Serpukhov, *Russia* 24 D6 54 55N 37 28 E
Serra do Navio, *Brazil* 93 C8 0 59N 52 3W
Sérrai, *Greece* 21 D10 41 5N 23 31 E
Serrezuela, *Argentina* 94 C2 30 40S 65 20W
Serrinha, *Brazil* 93 F11 11 39S 39 0W
Sertanópolis, *Brazil* 95 A5 23 4S 51 2W
Serua, *Indonesia* 37 F8 6 18S 130 1 E
Serui, *Indonesia* 37 E9 1 53S 136 10 E
Serule, *Botswana* 56 C4 21 57S 27 20 E
Sese Is., *Uganda* 54 C3 0 20S 32 20 E
Sesepe, *Indonesia* 37 E7 1 30S 127 59 E
Sesfontein, *Namibia* 56 B1 19 7S 13 39 E
Sesheke, *Zambia* 56 B3 17 29S 24 13 E
S'Espalmador, *Spain* 22 C7 38 47N 1 26 E
S'Espardell, *Spain* 22 C7 38 48N 1 29 E
S'Estanyol, *Spain* 22 B9 39 22N 2 54 E
Setana, *Japan* 30 C9 42 26N 139 51 E
Sète, *France* 18 E5 43 25N 3 42 E
Sete Lagôas, *Brazil* 93 G10 19 27S 44 16W
Sétif, *Algeria* 50 A7 36 9N 5 26 E
Seto, *Japan* 31 G8 35 14N 137 6 E
Setonaikai, *Japan* 31 G6 34 20N 133 30 E
Settat, *Morocco* 50 B4 33 0N 7 40W
Setting L., *Canada* 73 C9 55 0N 98 38W
Settle, *U.K.* 10 C5 54 5N 2 16W
Settlement Pt., *Bahamas* 77 M6 26 40N 79 0W
Setúbal, *Portugal* 19 C1 38 30N 8 58W
Setúbal, B. de, *Portugal* 19 C1 38 40N 8 56W
Seul, Lac, *Canada* 68 C10 50 20N 92 30W
Sevan, Ozero = Sevana Lich, *Armenia* 25 F8 40 30N 45 20 E
Sevana Lich, *Armenia* 25 F8 40 30N 45 20 E
Sevastopol, *Ukraine* 25 F5 44 35N 33 30 E
Seven Sisters, *Canada* 72 C3 54 56N 128 10W
Severn →, *Canada* 70 A2 56 2N 87 36W
Severn →, *U.K.* 11 F5 51 35N 2 40W
Severn L., *Canada* 70 B1 53 54N 90 48W
Severnaya Zemlya, *Russia* 27 B11 79 0N 100 0 E
Severnyye Uvaly, *Russia* 24 C8 60 0N 50 0 E
Severo-Kurilsk, *Russia* 27 D16 50 40N 156 8 E
Severo-Yeniseyskiy, *Russia* 27 C10 60 22N 93 1 E
Severodvinsk, *Russia* 24 B6 64 27N 39 58 E
Severomorsk, *Russia* 24 A5 69 5N 33 27 E
Severouralsk, *Russia* 24 B10 60 9N 59 57 E
Sevier, *U.S.A.* 83 G7 38 39N 112 11W
Sevier →, *U.S.A.* 83 G7 39 4N 113 6W
Sevier Desert, *U.S.A.* 82 G7 39 40N 112 45W
Sevier L., *U.S.A.* 82 G7 38 54N 113 9W
Sevilla, *Spain* 19 D2 37 23N 5 58W
Seville = Sevilla, *Spain* 19 D2 37 23N 5 58W
Sevlievo, *Bulgaria* 21 C11 43 2N 25 6 E
Sewani, *India* 42 E6 28 58N 75 39 E
Seward, *Alaska, U.S.A.* 68 B5 60 7N 149 27W
Seward, *Nebr., U.S.A.* 80 E6 40 55N 97 6W
Seward, *Pa., U.S.A.* 78 F5 40 25N 79 1W
Seward Peninsula, *U.S.A.* 68 B3 65 30N 166 0W
Sewell, *Chile* 94 C1 34 10S 70 23W
Sewer, *Indonesia* 37 F8 5 53S 134 40 E
Sewickley, *U.S.A.* 78 F4 40 32N 80 12W
Sexsmith, *Canada* 72 B5 55 21N 118 47W
Seychelles ■, *Ind. Oc.* 29 K9 5 0S 56 0 E
Seyðisfjörður, *Iceland* 8 D6 65 16N 13 57W
Seydişehir, *Turkey* 25 G5 37 25N 31 51 E
Seydvān, *Iran* 44 B5 38 34N 45 2 E
Seyhan →, *Turkey* 44 B2 36 43N 34 53 E
Seym →, *Ukraine* 25 D5 51 27N 32 34 E
Seymour, *Australia* 63 F4 37 0S 145 10 E
Seymour, *S. Africa* 57 E4 32 33S 26 46 E
Seymour, *Conn., U.S.A.* 79 E11 41 24N 73 4W
Seymour, *Ind., U.S.A.* 76 F3 38 58N 85 53W
Seymour, *Tex., U.S.A.* 81 J5 33 35N 99 16W
Sfântu Gheorghe, *Romania* 17 F13 45 52N 25 48 E
Sfax, *Tunisia* 51 B8 34 49N 10 48 E
Shaanxi □, *China* 34 G5 35 0N 109 0 E
Shaba = Katanga □, *Dem. Rep. of the Congo* 54 D2 8 0S 25 0 E
Shabogamo L., *Canada* 71 B6 53 15N 66 30W
Shabunda, *Dem. Rep. of the Congo* 54 C2 2 40S 27 16 E
Shache, *China* 32 C2 38 20N 77 10 E
Shackleton Ice Shelf, *Antarctica* 5 C8 66 0S 100 0 E
Shackleton Inlet, *Antarctica* 5 E11 83 0S 160 0 E
Shādegān, *Iran* 45 D6 30 40N 48 38 E
Shadi, *India* 43 C7 33 24N 77 14 E
Shadrinsk, *Russia* 26 D7 56 5N 63 32 E
Shadyside, *U.S.A.* 78 G4 39 58N 80 45W

Shafter, U.S.A. **85 K7** 35 30N 119 16W
Shaftesbury, U.K. **11 F5** 51 0N 2 11W
Shagram, Pakistan **43 A5** 36 24N 72 20 E
Shah Alizai, Pakistan **42 E2** 29 25N 66 33 E
Shah Bunder, Pakistan **42 G2** 24 13N 67 56 E
Shahabad, Punjab, India **42 D7** 30 10N 76 55 E
Shahabad, Raj., India **42 G7** 25 15N 77 11 E
Shahabad, Ut. P., India **43 F8** 27 36N 79 56 E
Shahadpur, Pakistan **42 G3** 25 55N 68 35 E
Shahba, Syria **47 C5** 32 52N 36 38 E
Shahdād, Iran **45 D8** 30 30N 57 40 E
Shahdād, Namakzār-e, Iran **45 D8** 30 20N 58 20 E
Shahdadkot, Pakistan **42 F2** 27 50N 67 55 E
Shahdol, India **43 H9** 23 19N 81 26 E
Shahe, China **34 F8** 37 0N 114 32 E
Shahganj, India **43 F10** 26 3N 82 44 E
Shahgarh, India **40 F6** 27 15N 69 50 E
Shahjahanpur, India **43 F8** 27 54N 79 57 E
Shahpur, India **42 H7** 22 12N 77 58 E
Shahpur, Baluchistan, Pakistan **42 E3** 28 46N 68 27 E
Shahpur, Punjab, Pakistan **42 C5** 32 17N 72 26 E
Shahpur Chakar, Pakistan **42 F3** 26 9N 68 39 E
Shahpura, Mad. P., India **43 H9** 23 10N 80 45 E
Shahpura, Raj., India **42 G6** 25 38N 74 56 E
Shahr-e Bābak, Iran **45 D7** 30 7N 55 9 E
Shahr-e Kord, Iran **45 C6** 32 15N 50 55 E
Shāhrakht, Iran **45 C9** 33 38N 60 16 E
Shahrig, Pakistan **42 D2** 30 15N 67 40 E
Shahukou, China **34 D7** 40 20N 112 18 E
Shaikhabad, Afghan. **42 B3** 34 2N 68 45 E
Shajapur, India **42 H7** 23 27N 76 21 E
Shakargarh, Pakistan **42 C6** 32 17N 75 10 E
Shakawe, Botswana **56 B3** 18 28S 21 49 E
Shaker Heights, U.S.A. **78 E3** 41 29N 81 32W
Shakhty, Russia **25 E7** 47 40N 40 16 E
Shakhunya, Russia **24 C8** 57 40N 46 46 E
Shaki, Nigeria **50 G6** 8 41N 3 21 E
Shallow Lake, Canada **78 B3** 44 36N 81 5W
Shalqar, Kazakstan **26 E6** 47 48N 59 39 E
Shaluli Shan, China **32 C4** 30 40N 99 55 E
Shām, Iran **45 E8** 26 39N 57 21 E
Shām, Bādiyat ash, Asia **44 C3** 32 0N 40 0 E
Shamâl Kordofân □, Sudan **48 E6** 15 0N 30 0 E
Shamattawa, Canada **70 A1** 55 51N 92 5W
Shamattawa →, Canada **70 A2** 55 1N 85 23W
Shamīl, Iran **45 E8** 27 30N 56 55 E
Shāmkūh, Iran **45 C8** 35 47N 57 50 E
Shamli, India **42 E7** 29 32N 77 18 E
Shammar, Jabal, Si. Arabia **44 E4** 27 40N 41 0 E
Shamo = Gobi, Asia **34 C6** 44 0N 110 0 E
Shamo, L., Ethiopia **46 F2** 5 45N 37 30 E
Shamokin, U.S.A. **79 F8** 40 47N 76 34W
Shamrock, U.S.A. **81 H4** 35 13N 100 15W
Shamva, Zimbabwe **55 F3** 17 20S 31 32 E
Shan □, Burma **41 J21** 21 30N 98 30 E
Shan Xian, China **34 G9** 34 50N 116 5 E
Shanchengzhen, China **35 C13** 42 20N 125 20 E
Shāndak, Iran **45 D9** 28 28N 60 27 E
Shandon, U.S.A. **84 K6** 35 39N 120 23W
Shandong □, China **35 G10** 36 0N 118 0 E
Shandong Bandao, China **35 F11** 37 0N 121 0 E
Shang Xian = Shangzhou, China **34 H5** 33 50N 109 58 E
Shanga, Nigeria **50 F6** 11 12N 4 33 E
Shangalowe, Dem. Rep. of the Congo **55 E2** 10 50S 26 30 E
Shangani →, Zimbabwe **55 F2** 18 41S 27 10 E
Shangbancheng, China **35 D10** 40 50N 118 1 E
Shangdu, China **34 D7** 41 30N 113 30 E
Shanghai, China **33 C7** 31 15N 121 26 E
Shanghe, China **35 F9** 37 20N 117 10 E
Shangnan, China **34 H6** 33 32N 110 50 E
Shangqiu, China **34 G8** 34 26N 115 36 E
Shangrao, China **33 D6** 28 25N 117 59 E
Shangshui, China **34 H8** 33 42N 114 35 E
Shangzhi, China **35 B14** 45 22N 127 56 E
Shangzhou, China **34 H5** 33 50N 109 58 E
Shanhetun, China **35 B14** 44 33N 127 15 E
Shannon, N.Z. **59 J5** 40 33S 175 25 E
Shannon →, Ireland **13 D2** 52 35N 9 30W
Shannon, Mouth of the, Ireland **13 D2** 52 30N 9 55W
Shannon Airport, Ireland **13 D3** 52 42N 8 57W
Shansi = Shanxi □, China **34 F7** 37 0N 112 0 E
Shantar, Ostrov Bolshoy, Russia **27 D14** 55 9N 137 40 E
Shantipur, India **43 H13** 23 17N 88 25 E
Shantou, China **33 D6** 23 18N 116 40 E
Shantung = Shandong □, China **35 G10** 36 0N 118 0 E
Shanxi □, China **34 F7** 37 0N 112 0 E
Shanyang, China **34 H5** 33 31N 109 55 E
Shanyin, China **34 E7** 39 25N 112 56 E
Shaoguan, China **33 D6** 24 48N 113 35 E
Shaoxing, China **33 D7** 30 0N 120 35 E
Shaoyang, China **33 D6** 27 14N 111 25 E
Shap, U.K. **10 C5** 54 32N 2 40W
Shapinsay, U.K. **12 B6** 59 3N 2 51W
Shaqra', Si. Arabia **44 E5** 25 15N 45 16 E
Shaqrā', Yemen **46 E4** 13 22N 45 44 E
Sharafkhāneh, Iran **44 B5** 38 11N 45 29 E
Sharbot Lake, Canada **79 B8** 44 46N 76 41W
Shari, Japan **30 C12** 43 55N 144 40 E
Sharjah = Ash Shāriqah, U.A.E. **45 E7** 25 23N 55 26 E
Shark B., Australia **61 E1** 25 30S 113 32 E
Sharon, Mass., U.S.A. **79 D13** 42 7N 71 11W
Sharon, Pa., U.S.A. **78 E4** 41 14N 80 31W
Sharon Springs, Kans., U.S.A. **80 F4** 38 54N 101 45W
Sharon Springs, N.Y., U.S.A. **79 D10** 42 48N 74 37W
Sharp Pt., Australia **62 A3** 10 58S 142 43 E
Sharpe L., Canada **70 B1** 54 24N 93 40W
Sharpsville, U.S.A. **78 E4** 41 15N 80 29W
Sharya, Russia **24 C8** 58 22N 45 20 E
Shashemene, Ethiopia **46 F2** 7 13N 38 33 E
Shashi, Botswana **57 C4** 21 15S 27 27 E
Shashi, China **33 C6** 30 25N 112 14 E
Shashi →, Africa **55 G2** 21 14S 29 20 E
Shasta, Mt., U.S.A. **82 F2** 41 25N 122 12W
Shasta L., U.S.A. **82 F2** 40 43N 122 25W
Shatt al'Arab →, Iraq **45 D6** 29 57N 48 34 E
Shaunavon, Canada **73 D7** 49 35N 108 25W
Shaver L., U.S.A. **84 H7** 37 9N 119 18W
Shaw →, Australia **60 D2** 20 21S 119 17 E
Shaw I., Australia **62 C4** 20 30S 149 2 E
Shawanaga, Canada **78 A4** 45 31N 80 17W
Shawangunk Mts., U.S.A. **79 E10** 41 35N 74 30W
Shawano, U.S.A. **76 C1** 44 47N 88 36W
Shawinigan, Canada **70 C5** 46 35N 72 50W
Shawnee, U.S.A. **81 H6** 35 20N 96 55W
Shay Gap, Australia **60 D3** 20 30S 120 10 E
Shaybārā, Si. Arabia **44 E3** 25 26N 36 47 E
Shaykh, J. ash, Lebanon **47 B4** 33 25N 35 50 E
Shaykh Miskīn, Syria **47 C5** 32 49N 36 9 E
Shaykh Sa'īd, Iraq **44 C5** 32 34N 46 17 E
Shcherbakov = Rybinsk, Russia **24 C6** 58 5N 38 50 E
Shchuchinsk, Kazakstan **26 D8** 52 56N 70 12 E
She Xian, China **34 F7** 36 30N 113 40 E
Shebele = Scebeli, Wabi →, Somali Rep. **46 G3** 2 0N 44 0 E
Sheboygan, U.S.A. **76 D2** 43 46N 87 45W
Shediac, Canada **71 C7** 46 14N 64 32W
Sheelin, L., Ireland **13 C4** 53 48N 7 20W
Sheep Haven, Ireland **13 A4** 55 11N 7 52W
Sheerness, U.K. **11 F8** 51 26N 0 47 E
Sheet Harbour, Canada **71 D7** 44 56N 62 31W
Sheffield, U.K. **10 D6** 53 23N 1 28W
Sheffield, Ala., U.S.A. **77 H2** 34 46N 87 41W
Sheffield, Mass., U.S.A. **79 D11** 42 5N 73 21W
Sheffield, Pa., U.S.A. **78 E5** 41 42N 79 3W
Sheikhpura, India **43 G11** 25 9N 85 53 E
Shekhupura, Pakistan **42 D5** 31 42N 73 58 E
Shelburne, N.S., Canada **71 D6** 43 47N 65 20W
Shelburne, Ont., Canada **78 B4** 44 4N 80 15W
Shelburne, Vt., U.S.A. **79 B11** 44 22N 73 13W
Shelburne, Vt., U.S.A. **79 B11** 44 23N 73 14W
Shelburne B., Australia **62 A3** 11 50S 142 50 E
Shelburne Falls, U.S.A. **79 D12** 42 36N 72 45W
Shelby, Mich., U.S.A. **76 D2** 43 37N 86 22W
Shelby, Miss., U.S.A. **81 J9** 33 57N 90 46W
Shelby, Mont., U.S.A. **82 B8** 48 30N 111 51W
Shelby, N.C., U.S.A. **77 H5** 35 17N 81 32W
Shelby, Ohio, U.S.A. **78 F2** 40 53N 82 40W
Shelbyville, Ill., U.S.A. **80 F10** 39 24N 88 48W
Shelbyville, Ind., U.S.A. **76 F3** 39 31N 85 47W
Shelbyville, Ky., U.S.A. **76 F3** 38 13N 85 14W
Shelbyville, Tenn., U.S.A. **77 H2** 35 29N 86 28W
Sheldon, U.S.A. **80 D7** 43 11N 95 51W
Sheldrake, Canada **71 B7** 50 20N 64 51W
Shelikhova, Zaliv, Russia **27 D16** 59 30N 157 0 E
Shell Lakes, Australia **61 E4** 29 20S 127 30 E
Shellbrook, Canada **73 C7** 53 13N 106 24W
Shellharbour, Australia **63 E5** 34 31S 150 51 E
Shelter I, U.S.A. **79 E12** 41 5N 72 21W
Shelton, Conn., U.S.A. **79 E11** 41 19N 73 5W
Shelton, Wash., U.S.A. **84 C3** 47 13N 123 6W
Shen Xian, China **34 F8** 36 15N 115 40 E
Shenandoah, Iowa, U.S.A. **80 E7** 40 46N 95 22W
Shenandoah, Pa., U.S.A. **79 F8** 40 49N 76 12W
Shenandoah, Va., U.S.A. **76 F6** 38 29N 78 37W
Shenandoah →, U.S.A. **76 F7** 39 19N 77 44W
Shenandoah National Park, U.S.A. **76 F6** 38 35N 78 22W
Shenchi, China **34 E7** 39 8N 112 10 E
Shendam, Nigeria **50 G7** 8 49N 9 30 E
Shendī, Sudan **51 E12** 16 46N 33 22 E
Shengfang, China **34 E9** 39 3N 116 42 E
Shenjingzi, China **35 B13** 44 40N 124 30 E
Shenmu, China **34 E6** 38 50N 110 29 E
Shenqiu, China **34 H8** 33 25N 115 5 E
Shenqiucheng, China **34 H8** 33 24N 115 2 E
Shensi = Shaanxi □, China **34 G5** 35 0N 109 0 E
Shenyang, China **35 D12** 41 48N 123 27 E
Sheo, India **42 F4** 26 11N 71 15 E
Sheopur Kalan, India **40 G10** 25 40N 76 40 E
Shepetivka, Ukraine **17 C14** 50 10N 27 10 E
Shepetovka = Shepetivka, Ukraine **17 C14** 50 10N 27 10 E
Shepparton, Australia **63 F4** 36 23S 145 26 E
Sheppey, I. of, U.K. **11 F8** 51 25N 0 48 E
Shepton Mallet, U.K. **11 F5** 51 11N 2 33W
Sheqi, China **34 H7** 33 12N 112 57 E
Sher Qila, Pakistan **43 A6** 36 7N 74 2 E
Sherborne, U.K. **11 G5** 50 57N 2 31W
Sherbro I., S. Leone **50 G3** 7 30N 12 40W
Sherbrooke, Canada **71 C7** 45 8N 61 59W
Sherbrooke, Qué., Canada **79 A13** 45 28N 71 57W
Sherburne, U.S.A. **79 D9** 42 41N 75 30W
Shergarh, India **42 F5** 26 20N 72 18 E
Sherghati, India **43 G11** 24 34N 84 47 E
Sheridan, Ark., U.S.A. **81 H8** 34 19N 92 24W
Sheridan, Wyo., U.S.A. **82 D10** 44 48N 106 58W
Sheringham, U.K. **10 E9** 52 56N 1 13 E
Sherkin I., Ireland **13 E2** 51 28N 9 26W
Sherkot, India **43 E8** 29 22N 78 35 E
Sherman, U.S.A. **81 J6** 33 40N 96 35W
Sherpur, India **43 G10** 25 34N 83 47 E
Sherridon, Canada **73 B8** 55 8N 101 5W
Sherwood Forest, U.K. **10 D6** 53 6N 1 7W
Sherwood Park, Canada **72 C6** 53 31N 113 19W
Sheslay →, Canada **72 B2** 58 48N 132 5W
Shethanei L., Canada **73 B9** 58 48N 97 50W
Shetland □, U.K. **12 A7** 60 30N 1 30W
Shetland Is., U.K. **12 A7** 60 30N 1 30W
Shetrunji →, India **42 J5** 21 19N 72 7 E
Sheyenne →, U.S.A. **80 B6** 47 2N 96 50W
Shibām, Yemen **46 D4** 16 0N 48 36 E
Shibata, Japan **30 F9** 37 57N 139 20 E
Shibecha, Japan **30 C12** 43 17N 144 36 E
Shibetsu, Japan **30 B11** 44 10N 142 23 E
Shibogama L., Canada **70 B2** 53 35N 88 15W
Shibushi, Japan **31 J5** 31 25N 131 8 E
Shickshinny, U.S.A. **79 E8** 41 9N 76 9W
Shickshock Mts. = Chic-Chocs, Mts., Canada **71 C6** 48 55N 66 0W
Shidao, China **35 F12** 36 50N 122 25 E
Shido, Japan **31 G7** 34 19N 134 10 E
Shiel, L., U.K. **12 E3** 56 48N 5 34W
Shield, C., Australia **62 A2** 13 20S 136 20 E
Shiga □, Japan **31 G8** 35 20N 136 0 E
Shiguaigou, China **34 D6** 40 52N 110 15 E
Shihchiachuangi = Shijiazhuang, China **34 E8** 38 2N 114 28 E
Shijiazhuang, China **34 E8** 38 2N 114 28 E
Shikarpur, India **42 E8** 28 17N 78 7 E
Shikarpur, Pakistan **42 F3** 27 57N 68 39 E
Shikohabad, India **43 F8** 27 6N 78 36 E
Shikoku □, Japan **31 H6** 33 30N 133 30 E
Shikoku-Sanchi, Japan **31 H6** 33 30N 133 30 E
Shiliguri, India **41 F16** 26 45N 88 25 E
Shilka, Russia **27 D12** 52 0N 115 55 E
Shilka →, Russia **27 D13** 53 20N 121 26 E
Shillelagh, Ireland **13 D5** 52 45N 6 32W
Shillington, U.S.A. **79 F9** 40 18N 75 58W
Shillong, India **41 G17** 25 35N 91 53 E
Shilo, West Bank **47 C4** 32 4N 35 18 E
Shilou, China **34 F6** 37 0N 110 48 E
Shimabara, Japan **31 H5** 32 48N 130 20 E
Shimada, Japan **31 G9** 34 49N 138 10 E
Shimane □, Japan **31 G6** 35 0N 132 30 E
Shimanovsk, Russia **27 D13** 52 15N 127 30 E
Shimizu, Japan **31 G9** 35 0N 138 30 E
Shimodate, Japan **31 F9** 36 20N 139 55 E
Shimoga, India **40 N9** 13 57N 75 32 E
Shimoni, Kenya **54 C4** 4 38S 39 20 E
Shimonoseki, Japan **31 H5** 33 58N 130 55 E
Shimpuru Rapids, Angola **56 B2** 17 45S 19 55 E
Shin, L., U.K. **12 C4** 58 5N 4 30W
Shinano-Gawa →, Japan **31 F9** 36 50N 138 30 E
Shināş, Oman **45 E8** 24 46N 56 28 E
Shīndand, Afghan. **40 C3** 33 12N 62 8 E
Shinglehouse, U.S.A. **78 E6** 41 58N 78 12W
Shingū, Japan **31 H7** 33 40N 135 55 E
Shinjō, Japan **30 E10** 38 46N 140 18 E
Shinshār, Syria **47 A5** 34 36N 36 43 E
Shinyanga, Tanzania **54 C3** 3 45S 33 27 E
Shinyanga □, Tanzania **54 C3** 3 50S 34 0 E
Shio-no-Misaki, Japan **31 H7** 33 25N 135 45 E
Shiogama, Japan **30 E10** 38 19N 141 1 E
Shiojiri, Japan **31 F8** 36 6N 137 58 E
Shipchenski Prokhod, Bulgaria **21 C11** 42 45N 25 15 E
Shiping, China **32 D5** 23 45N 102 23 E
Shipki La, India **40 D11** 31 45N 78 40 E
Shippegan, Canada **71 C7** 47 45N 64 45W
Shippensburg, U.S.A. **78 F7** 40 3N 77 31W
Shippenville, U.S.A. **78 E5** 41 15N 79 28W
Shiprock, U.S.A. **83 H9** 36 47N 108 41W
Shiqma, N. →, Israel **47 D3** 31 37N 34 30 E
Shiquan, China **34 H5** 33 5N 108 15 E
Shiquan He = Indus →, Pakistan **42 G2** 24 20N 67 47 E
Shīr Kūh, Iran **45 D7** 31 39N 54 3 E
Shiragami-Misaki, Japan **30 D10** 41 24N 140 12 E
Shirakawa, Fukushima, Japan **31 F10** 37 7N 140 13 E
Shirakawa, Gifu, Japan **31 F8** 36 17N 136 56 E
Shirane-San, Gumma, Japan **31 F9** 36 48N 139 22 E
Shirane-San, Yamanashi, Japan **31 G9** 35 42N 138 9 E
Shiraoi, Japan **30 C10** 42 33N 141 21 E
Shīrāz, Iran **45 D7** 29 42N 52 30 E
Shire →, Africa **55 F4** 17 42S 35 19 E
Shiretoko-Misaki, Japan **30 B12** 44 21N 145 20 E
Shirinab →, Pakistan **42 D2** 30 15N 66 28 E
Shiriya-Zaki, Japan **30 D10** 41 25N 141 30 E
Shiroishi, Japan **30 F10** 38 0N 140 37 E
Shīrvān, Iran **45 B8** 37 30N 57 50 E
Shirwa, L. = Chilwa, L., Malawi **55 F4** 15 15S 35 40 E
Shivpuri, India **42 G7** 25 26N 77 42 E
Shixian, China **35 C15** 43 5N 129 50 E
Shizuishan, China **34 E4** 39 15N 106 50 E
Shizuoka, Japan **31 G9** 34 57N 138 24 E
Shizuoka □, Japan **31 G9** 35 15N 138 40 E
Shklov = Shklow, Belarus **17 A16** 54 16N 30 15 E
Shklow, Belarus **17 A16** 54 16N 30 15 E
Shkoder = Shkodra, Albania **21 C8** 42 4N 19 32 E
Shkodra, Albania **21 C8** 42 4N 19 32 E
Shkumbini →, Albania **21 D8** 41 2N 19 31 E
Shmidta, Ostrov, Russia **27 A10** 81 0N 91 0 E
Shō-Gawa →, Japan **31 F8** 36 47N 137 4 E
Shoal L., Canada **73 D9** 49 33N 95 1W
Shoal Lake, Canada **73 C8** 50 30N 100 35W
Shōdo-Shima, Japan **31 G7** 34 30N 134 15 E
Sholapur = Solapur, India **40 L9** 17 43N 75 56 E
Shologontsy, Russia **27 C12** 66 13N 114 0 E
Shōmrōn, West Bank **47 C4** 32 15N 35 13 E
Shoreham by Sea, U.K. **11 G7** 50 50N 0 16W
Shori →, Pakistan **42 E3** 28 29N 69 44 E
Shorkot Road, Pakistan **42 D5** 30 47N 72 15 E
Shoshone, Calif., U.S.A. **85 K10** 35 58N 116 16W
Shoshone, Idaho, U.S.A. **82 E6** 42 56N 114 25W
Shoshone L., U.S.A. **82 D8** 44 22N 110 43W
Shoshone Mts., U.S.A. **82 G5** 39 20N 117 25W
Shoshong, Botswana **56 C4** 22 56S 26 31 E
Shoshoni, U.S.A. **82 E9** 43 14N 108 7W
Shouguang, China **35 F10** 37 52N 118 45 E
Shouyang, China **34 F7** 37 54N 113 8 E
Show Low, U.S.A. **83 J9** 34 15N 110 2W
Shreveport, U.S.A. **81 J8** 32 31N 93 45W
Shrewsbury, U.K. **11 E5** 52 43N 2 45W
Shri Mohangarh, India **42 F4** 27 17N 71 18 E
Shrirampur, India **43 H13** 22 44N 88 21 E
Shropshire □, U.K. **11 E5** 52 36N 2 45W
Shu, Kazakstan **26 E8** 43 36N 73 42 E
Shu →, Kazakstan **28 E10** 45 0N 67 44 E
Shuangcheng, China **35 B14** 45 20N 126 15 E
Shuanggou, China **35 G9** 34 2N 117 30 E
Shuangliao, China **35 C12** 43 29N 123 30 E
Shuangshanzi, China **35 D10** 40 20N 119 8 E
Shuangyang, China **35 C13** 43 28N 125 40 E
Shuangyashan, China **33 B8** 46 28N 131 5 E
Shuguri Falls, Tanzania **55 D4** 8 33S 37 22 E
Shuiye, China **34 F8** 36 7N 114 8 E
Shujalpur, India **42 H7** 23 18N 76 46 E
Shukpa Kunzang, India **43 B8** 34 22N 78 22 E
Shulan, China **35 B14** 44 28N 127 0 E
Shule, China **32 C2** 39 25N 76 3 E
Shumagin Is., U.S.A. **68 C4** 55 7N 160 30W
Shumen, Bulgaria **21 C12** 43 18N 26 55 E
Shumikha, Russia **26 D7** 55 10N 63 15 E
Shuo Xian = Shuozhou, China **34 E7** 39 20N 112 33 E
Shuozhou, China **34 E7** 39 20N 112 33 E
Shūr →, Fārs, Iran **45 D7** 28 30N 55 0 E
Shūr →, Kermān, Iran **45 D8** 30 52N 57 37 E
Shūr →, Yazd, Iran **45 D7** 31 45N 55 15 E
Shūr Āb, Iran **45 C6** 34 23N 51 11 E
Shūr Gaz, Iran **45 D8** 29 10N 59 20 E
Shūrāb, Iran **45 C8** 33 43N 56 29 E
Shūrjestān, Iran **45 D7** 31 24N 52 25 E
Shurugwi, Zimbabwe **55 F3** 19 40S 30 0 E
Shūsf, Iran **45 D9** 31 50N 60 5 E
Shūshtar, Iran **45 D6** 32 0N 48 50 E
Shuswap L., Canada **72 C5** 50 55N 119 3W
Shuyang, China **35 G10** 34 10N 118 42 E
Shūzū, Iran **45 D7** 29 52N 54 30 E
Shwebo, Burma **41 H19** 22 30N 95 45 E
Shwegu, Burma **41 G20** 24 15N 96 26 E
Shweli →, Burma **41 H20** 23 45N 96 45 E
Shymkent, Kazakstan **26 E7** 42 18N 69 36 E
Shyok, India **43 B8** 34 13N 78 12 E
Shyok →, Pakistan **43 B6** 35 13N 75 53 E
Si Chon, Thailand **39 H2** 9 0N 99 54 E
Si Kiang = Xi Jiang →, China **33 D6** 22 5N 113 20 E
Si-ngan = Xi'an, China **34 G5** 34 15N 109 0 E
Si Prachan, Thailand **38 E3** 14 37N 100 9 E
Si Racha, Thailand **38 F3** 13 10N 100 48 E
Si Xian, China **35 H9** 33 30N 117 50 E
Siahaf →, Pakistan **42 E3** 29 3N 68 57 E
Siahan Range, Pakistan **40 F4** 27 30N 64 40 E
Siaksriindrapura, Indonesia **36 D2** 0 51N 102 0 E
Sialkot, Pakistan **42 C6** 32 32N 74 30 E
Siam = Thailand ■, Asia **38 E4** 16 0N 102 0 E
Sian = Xi'an, China **34 G5** 34 15N 109 0 E
Siantan, Indonesia **36 D3** 3 10N 106 15 E
Sīāreh, Iran **45 D9** 28 5N 60 14 E
Siargao, Phil. **37 C7** 9 52N 126 3 E
Siari, Pakistan **43 B7** 34 55N 76 40 E
Siasi, Phil. **37 C6** 5 34N 120 50 E
Siau, Indonesia **37 D7** 2 50N 125 25 E
Šiauliai, Lithuania **9 J20** 55 56N 23 15 E
Sibâi, Gebel el, Egypt **44 E2** 25 45N 34 10 E
Sibay, Russia **24 D10** 52 42N 58 39 E
Sibayi, L., S. Africa **57 D5** 27 20S 32 45 E
Šibenik, Croatia **20 C6** 43 48N 15 54 E
Siberia, Russia **4 D13** 60 0N 100 0 E
Siberut, Indonesia **36 E1** 1 30S 99 0 E
Sibi, Pakistan **42 E2** 29 30N 67 54 E
Sibil = Oksibil, Indonesia **37 E10** 4 59S 140 35 E
Sibiti, Congo **52 E2** 3 38S 13 19 E
Sibiu, Romania **17 F13** 45 45N 24 9 E
Sibley, U.S.A. **80 D7** 43 24N 95 45W
Sibolga, Indonesia **36 D1** 1 42N 98 45 E
Sibsagar, India **41 F19** 27 0N 94 36 E
Sibu, Malaysia **36 D4** 2 18N 111 49 E
Sibuco, Phil. **37 C6** 7 20N 122 10 E
Sibuguey B., Phil. **37 C6** 7 50N 122 45 E
Sibut, C.A.R. **52 C3** 5 46N 19 10 E
Sibutu, Phil. **37 D5** 4 45N 119 30 E
Sibutu Passage, E. Indies **37 D6** 4 50N 120 0 E
Sibuyan, Phil. **37 B6** 12 25N 122 40 E
Sibuyan Sea, Phil. **37 B6** 12 30N 122 20 E
Sicamous, Canada **72 C5** 50 49N 119 0W
Siccus →, Australia **63 E2** 31 26S 139 30 E
Sichuan □, China **32 C5** 31 0N 104 0 E
Sicilia, Italy **20 F6** 37 30N 14 30 E
Sicily = Sicilia, Italy **20 F6** 37 30N 14 30 E
Sicuani, Peru **92 F4** 14 21S 71 10W
Sidári, Greece **23 A3** 39 47N 19 41 E
Siddhapur, India **42 H5** 23 56N 72 25 E
Siddipet, India **40 K11** 18 5N 78 51 E
Sidhauli, India **43 F9** 27 17N 80 50 E
Sidheros, Ákra, Greece **23 D8** 35 19N 26 19 E
Sidhi, India **43 G9** 24 25N 81 53 E
Sidi-bel-Abbès, Algeria **50 A5** 35 13N 0 39W
Sidlaw Hills, U.K. **12 E5** 56 32N 3 2W
Sidley, Mt., Antarctica **5 D14** 77 2S 126 2W
Sidmouth, U.K. **11 G4** 50 40N 3 15W
Sidmouth, C., Australia **62 A3** 13 25S 143 36 E
Sidney, Canada **72 D4** 48 39N 123 24W
Sidney, Mont., U.S.A. **80 B2** 47 43N 104 9W
Sidney, N.Y., U.S.A. **79 D9** 42 19N 75 24W
Sidney, Nebr., U.S.A. **80 E3** 41 8N 102 59W
Sidney, Ohio, U.S.A. **76 E3** 40 17N 84 9W
Sidney Lanier L., U.S.A. **77 H4** 34 10N 84 4W
Sidoarjo, Indonesia **37 G15** 7 27S 112 43 E
Sidon = Saydā, Lebanon **47 B4** 33 35N 35 25 E
Sidra, G. of = Surt, Khalīj, Libya **51 B9** 31 40N 18 30 E
Siedlce, Poland **17 B12** 52 10N 22 20 E
Sieg →, Germany **16 C4** 50 46N 7 6 E
Siegen, Germany **16 C5** 50 51N 8 0 E
Siem Pang, Cambodia **38 E6** 14 7N 106 23 E
Siem Reap = Siemreab, Cambodia **38 F4** 13 20N 103 52 E
Siemreab, Cambodia **38 F4** 13 20N 103 52 E
Siena, Italy **20 C4** 43 19N 11 21 E
Sieradz, Poland **17 C10** 51 37N 18 41 E
Sierra Blanca, U.S.A. **83 L11** 31 11N 105 22W
Sierra Blanca Peak, U.S.A. **83 K11** 33 23N 105 49W
Sierra City, U.S.A. **84 F6** 39 34N 120 38W
Sierra Colorada, Argentina **96 E3** 40 35S 67 50W
Sierra Gorda, Chile **94 A2** 22 50S 69 15W
Sierra Leone ■, W. Afr. **50 G3** 9 0N 12 0W
Sierra Madre, Mexico **87 D6** 16 0N 93 0W
Sierra Mojada, Mexico **86 B4** 27 19N 103 42W
Sierra Nevada, U.S.A. **84 H8** 37 30N 119 0W
Sierra Vista, U.S.A. **83 L8** 31 33N 110 18W
Sierraville, U.S.A. **84 F6** 39 36N 120 22W
Sífnos, Greece **21 F11** 37 0N 24 45 E
Sifton, Canada **73 C8** 51 21N 100 8W
Sifton Pass, Canada **72 B3** 57 52N 126 15W
Sighetu-Marmaţiei, Romania **17 E12** 47 57N 23 52 E
Sighişoara, Romania **17 E13** 46 12N 24 50 E
Sigli, Indonesia **36 C1** 5 25N 96 0 E
Siglufjörður, Iceland **8 C4** 66 12N 18 55W
Signal, U.S.A. **85 L13** 34 30N 113 38W
Signal Pk., U.S.A. **85 M12** 33 20N 114 2W
Sigsig, Ecuador **92 D3** 3 0S 78 50W
Sigüenza, Spain **19 B4** 41 3N 2 40W
Siguiri, Guinea **50 F4** 11 31N 9 10W
Sigulda, Latvia **9 H21** 57 10N 24 55 E
Sihanoukville = Kampong Saom, Cambodia **39 G4** 10 38N 103 30 E
Sihora, India **43 H9** 23 29N 80 6 E
Siikajoki →, Finland **8 D21** 64 50N 24 43 E
Siilinjärvi, Finland **8 E22** 63 4N 27 39 E
Sijarira Ra., Zimbabwe **55 F2** 17 36S 27 45 E
Sika, India **42 H3** 22 26N 69 47 E
Sikao, Thailand **39 J2** 7 34N 99 21 E
Sikar, India **42 F6** 27 33N 75 10 E
Sikasso, Mali **50 F4** 11 18N 5 35W
Sikeston, U.S.A. **81 G10** 36 53N 89 35W
Sikhote Alin, Khrebet, Russia **27 E14** 45 0N 136 0 E
Sikhote Alin Ra. = Sikhote Alin, Khrebet, Russia **27 E14** 45 0N 136 0 E

Síkinos, *Greece* 21 F11 36 40N 25 8 E
Sikkani Chief →, *Canada* 72 B4 57 47N 122 15W
Sikkim □, *India* 41 F16 27 50N 88 30 E
Sikotu-Ko, *Japan* 30 C10 42 45N 141 25 E
Sil →, *Spain* 19 A2 42 27N 7 43W
Silacayoapan, *Mexico* 87 D5 17 30N 98 9W
Silawad, *India* 42 J6 21 54N 74 54 E
Silchar, *India* 41 G18 24 49N 92 48 E
Siler City, *U.S.A.* 77 H6 35 44N 79 28W
Silesia = Śląsk, *Poland* 16 C9 51 0N 16 30 E
Silgarhi Doti, *Nepal* 43 E9 29 15N 81 0 E
Silghat, *India* 41 F18 26 35N 93 0 E
Silifke, *Turkey* 25 G5 36 22N 33 58 E
Siliguri = Shiliguri, *India* 41 F16 26 45N 88 25 E
Siling Co, *China* 32 C3 31 50N 89 20 E
Silistra, *Bulgaria* 21 B12 44 6N 27 19 E
Silivri, *Turkey* 21 D13 41 4N 28 14 E
Siljan, *Sweden* 9 F16 60 55N 14 45 E
Silkeborg, *Denmark* 9 H13 56 10N 9 32 E
Silkwood, *Australia* 62 B4 17 45S 146 2 E
Sillajhuay, Cordillera, *Chile* 92 G5 19 46S 68 40W
Sillamäe, *Estonia* 9 G22 59 24N 27 45 E
Silloth, *U.K.* 10 C4 54 52N 3 23W
Siloam Springs, *U.S.A.* 81 G7 36 11N 94 32W
Silsbee, *U.S.A.* 81 K7 30 21N 94 11W
Šilutė, *Lithuania* 9 J19 55 21N 21 33 E
Silva Porto = Kuito, *Angola* 53 G3 12 22S 16 55 E
Silvani, *India* 43 H8 23 18N 78 25 E
Silver City, *U.S.A.* 83 K9 32 46N 108 17W
Silver Cr. →, *U.S.A.* 82 E4 43 16N 119 13W
Silver Creek, *U.S.A.* 78 D5 42 33N 79 10W
Silver L., *U.S.A.* 84 G6 38 39N 120 6W
Silver Lake, *Calif., U.S.A.* 85 K10 35 21N 116 7W
Silver Lake, *Oreg., U.S.A.* 82 E3 43 8N 121 3W
Silver Streams, *S. Africa* 56 D3 28 20S 23 33 E
Silverton, *Colo., U.S.A.* 83 H10 37 49N 107 40W
Silverton, *Tex., U.S.A.* 81 H4 34 28N 101 19W
Silvies →, *U.S.A.* 82 E4 43 34N 119 2W
Simaltala, *India* 43 G12 24 43N 86 33 E
Simanggang = Bandar Sri Aman, *Malaysia* 36 D4 1 15N 111 32 E
Simard, L., *Canada* 70 C4 47 40N 78 40W
Simav, *Turkey* 21 E13 39 4N 28 58 E
Simba, *Tanzania* 54 C4 2 10S 37 36 E
Simbirsk, *Russia* 24 D8 54 20N 48 25 E
Simbo, *Tanzania* 54 C2 4 51S 29 41 E
Simcoe, *Canada* 78 D4 42 50N 80 20W
Simcoe, L., *Canada* 78 B5 44 25N 79 20W
Simdega, *India* 43 H11 22 37N 84 31 E
Simeria, *Romania* 17 F12 45 51N 23 1 E
Simeulue, *Indonesia* 36 D1 2 45N 95 45 E
Simferopol, *Ukraine* 25 F5 44 55N 34 3 E
Sími, *Greece* 21 F12 36 35N 27 50 E
Simi Valley, *U.S.A.* 85 L8 34 16N 118 47W
Simikot, *Nepal* 43 E9 30 0N 81 50 E
Simla, *India* 42 D7 31 2N 77 9 E
Simmie, *Canada* 73 D7 49 56N 108 6W
Simmler, *U.S.A.* 85 K7 35 21N 119 59W
Simojoki →, *Finland* 8 D21 65 35N 25 1 E
Simojovel, *Mexico* 87 D6 17 12N 92 38W
Simonette →, *Canada* 72 B5 55 9N 118 15W
Simonstown, *S. Africa* 56 E2 34 14S 18 26 E
Simplonpass, *Switz.* 18 C8 46 15N 8 3 E
Simpson Desert, *Australia* 62 D2 25 0S 137 0 E
Simpson Pen., *Canada* 69 B11 68 34N 88 45W
Simpungdong, *N. Korea* 35 D15 40 56N 129 29 E
Simrishamn, *Sweden* 9 J16 55 33N 14 22 E
Simsbury, *U.S.A.* 79 E12 41 53N 72 48W
Simushir, Ostrov, *Russia* 27 E16 46 50N 152 30 E
Sin Cowe I., *S. China Sea* 36 C4 9 53N 114 19 E
Sinabang, *Indonesia* 36 D1 2 30N 96 24 E
Sinadogo, *Somali Rep.* 46 F4 5 50N 47 0 E
Sinai = Es Sînâ', *Egypt* 47 F3 29 0N 34 0 E
Sinai, Mt. = Mûsa, Gebel, *Egypt* 44 D2 28 33N 33 59 E
Sinai Peninsula, *Egypt* 47 F3 29 30N 34 0 E
Sinaloa □, *Mexico* 86 C3 25 0N 107 30W
Sinaloa de Leyva, *Mexico* 86 B3 25 50N 108 20W
Sinarádhes, *Greece* 23 A3 39 34N 19 51 E
Sincelejo, *Colombia* 92 B3 9 18N 75 24W
Sinch'ang, *N. Korea* 35 D15 40 7N 128 28 E
Sinchang-ni, *N. Korea* 35 E14 39 24N 126 8 E
Sinclair, *U.S.A.* 82 F10 41 47N 107 7W
Sinclair Mills, *Canada* 72 C4 54 5N 121 40W
Sinclair's B., *U.K.* 12 C5 58 31N 3 5W
Sinclairville, *U.S.A.* 78 D5 42 16N 79 16W
Sincorá, Serra do, *Brazil* 93 F10 13 30S 41 0W
Sind, *Pakistan* 42 G3 26 0N 68 30 E
Sind □, *Pakistan* 42 G3 26 0N 69 0 E
Sind →, *India* 43 F8 26 26N 79 13 E
Sind →, *Jammu & Kashmir, India* 43 B6 34 18N 74 45 E
Sind Sagar Doab, *Pakistan* 42 D4 32 0N 71 30 E
Sindangan, *Phil.* 37 C6 8 10N 123 5 E
Sindangbarang, *Indonesia* 37 G12 7 27S 107 1 E
Sinde, *Zambia* 55 F2 17 28S 25 51 E
Sindri, *India* 43 H12 23 45N 86 42 E
Sines, *Portugal* 19 D1 37 56N 8 51W
Sines, C. de, *Portugal* 19 D1 37 58N 8 53W
Sineu, *Spain* 22 B10 39 38N 3 1 E
Sing Buri, *Thailand* 38 E3 14 53N 100 25 E
Singa, *Sudan* 51 F12 13 10N 33 57 E
Singapore ■, *Asia* 39 M4 1 17N 103 51 E
Singapore, Straits of, *Asia* 39 M5 1 15N 104 0 E
Singaraja, *Indonesia* 36 F5 8 6S 115 10 E
Singida, *Tanzania* 54 C3 4 49S 34 48 E
Singida □, *Tanzania* 54 D3 6 0S 34 30 E
Singitikós Kólpos, *Greece* 21 D11 40 6N 24 0 E
Singkaling Hkamti, *Burma* 41 G19 26 0N 95 39 E
Singkang, *Indonesia* 37 E6 4 8S 120 1 E
Singkawang, *Indonesia* 36 D3 1 0N 108 57 E
Singkep, *Indonesia* 36 E2 0 30S 104 25 E
Singleton, *Australia* 63 E5 32 33S 151 0 E
Singleton, Mt., *N. Terr., Australia* 60 D5 22 0S 130 46 E
Singleton, Mt., *W. Austral., Australia* 61 E2 29 27S 117 15 E
Singoli, *India* 42 G6 25 0N 75 22 E
Singora = Songkhla, *Thailand* 39 J3 7 13N 100 37 E
Singosan, *N. Korea* 35 E14 38 52N 127 25 E
Sinhung, *N. Korea* 35 D14 40 11N 127 34 E
Sînî □, *Egypt* 47 F3 30 0N 34 0 E
Sinjai, *Indonesia* 37 F6 5 7S 120 20 E
Sinjār, *Iraq* 44 B4 36 19N 41 52 E
Sinkat, *Sudan* 51 E13 18 55N 36 49 E
Sinkiang Uighur = Xinjiang Uygur Zizhiqu □, *China* 32 C3 42 0N 86 0 E
Sinmak, *N. Korea* 35 E14 38 25N 126 14 E
Sinnamary, *Fr. Guiana* 93 B8 5 25N 53 0W
Sinni →, *Italy* 20 D7 40 8N 16 41 E
Sinop, *Turkey* 25 F6 42 1N 35 11 E
Sinor, *India* 42 J5 21 55N 73 20 E
Sinp'o, *N. Korea* 35 E15 40 0N 128 13 E
Sinsk, *Russia* 27 C13 61 8N 126 48 E
Sintang, *Indonesia* 36 D4 0 5N 111 35 E
Sinton, *U.S.A.* 81 L6 28 2N 97 31W
Sintra, *Portugal* 19 C1 38 47N 9 25W
Sinŭiju, *N. Korea* 35 D13 40 5N 124 24 E
Siocon, *Phil.* 37 C6 7 40N 122 10 E
Siófok, *Hungary* 17 E10 46 54N 18 3 E
Sioma, *Zambia* 56 B3 16 25S 23 28 E
Sion, *Switz.* 18 C7 46 14N 7 20 E
Sion Mills, *U.K.* 13 B4 54 48N 7 29W
Sioux City, *U.S.A.* 80 D6 42 30N 96 24W
Sioux Falls, *U.S.A.* 80 D6 43 33N 96 44W
Sioux Lookout, *Canada* 70 B1 50 10N 91 50W
Sioux Narrows, *Canada* 73 D10 49 25N 94 10W
Siping, *China* 35 C13 43 8N 124 21 E
Sipiwesk L., *Canada* 73 B9 55 5N 97 35W
Sipra →, *India* 42 H6 23 55N 75 28 E
Sipura, *Indonesia* 36 E1 2 18S 99 40 E
Siquia →, *Nic.* 88 D3 12 10N 84 20W
Siquijor, *Phil.* 37 C6 9 12N 123 35 E
Siquirres, *Costa Rica* 88 D3 10 6N 83 30W
Şîr Banī Yās, *U.A.E.* 45 E7 24 19N 52 37 E
Sir Edward Pellew Group, *Australia* 62 B2 15 40S 137 10 E
Sir Graham Moore Is., *Australia* 60 B4 13 53S 126 34 E
Sir James MacBrien, Mt., *Canada* 68 B7 62 8N 127 40W
Sira →, *Norway* 9 G12 58 23N 6 34 E
Siracusa, *Italy* 20 F6 37 4N 15 17 E
Sirajganj, *Bangla.* 43 G13 24 25N 89 47 E
Sirathu, *India* 43 G9 25 39N 81 19 E
Sīrdān, *Iran* 45 B6 36 39N 49 12 E
Sirdaryo = Syrdarya →, *Kazakstan* 26 E7 46 3N 61 0 E
Siren, *U.S.A.* 80 C8 45 47N 92 24W
Sirer, *Spain* 22 C7 38 56N 1 22 E
Siret →, *Romania* 17 F14 45 24N 28 1 E
Sirghāyā, *Syria* 47 B5 33 51N 36 8 E
Sirmaur, *India* 43 G9 24 51N 81 23 E
Sirohi, *India* 42 G5 24 52N 72 53 E
Sironj, *India* 42 G7 24 5N 77 39 E
Síros, *Greece* 21 F11 37 28N 24 57 E
Sirretta Pk., *U.S.A.* 85 K8 35 56N 118 19W
Sirrī, *Iran* 45 E7 25 55N 54 32 E
Sirsa, *India* 42 E6 29 33N 75 4 E
Sirsa →, *India* 43 F8 26 51N 79 4 E
Sisak, *Croatia* 16 F9 45 30N 16 21 E
Sisaket, *Thailand* 38 E5 15 8N 104 23 E
Sishen, *S. Africa* 56 D3 27 47S 22 59 E
Sishui, *Henan, China* 34 G7 34 48N 113 15 E
Sishui, *Shandong, China* 35 G9 35 42N 117 18 E
Sisipuk L., *Canada* 73 B8 55 45N 101 50W
Sisophon, *Cambodia* 38 F4 13 38N 102 59 E
Sisseton, *U.S.A.* 80 C6 45 40N 97 3W
Sīstān, *Asia* 45 D9 30 50N 61 0 E
Sīstān, Daryācheh-ye, *Iran* 40 D2 31 0N 61 0 E
Sīstān va Balūchestān □, *Iran* 45 E9 27 0N 62 0 E
Sisters, *U.S.A.* 82 D3 44 18N 121 33W
Siswa Bazar, *India* 43 F10 27 9N 83 46 E
Sitamarhi, *India* 43 F11 26 37N 85 30 E
Sitapur, *India* 43 F9 27 38N 80 45 E
Siteki, *Swaziland* 57 D5 26 32S 31 58 E
Sitges, *Spain* 19 B6 41 17N 1 47 E
Sitía, *Greece* 23 D8 35 13N 26 6 E
Sitka, *U.S.A.* 72 B1 57 3N 135 20W
Sitoti, *Botswana* 56 C3 23 15S 23 40 E
Sittang Myit →, *Burma* 41 L20 17 20N 96 45 E
Sittard, *Neths.* 15 C5 51 0N 5 52 E
Sittingbourne, *U.K.* 11 F8 51 21N 0 45 E
Sittwe, *Burma* 41 J18 20 18N 92 45 E
Situbondo, *Indonesia* 37 G16 7 42S 114 0 E
Siuna, *Nic.* 88 D3 13 37N 84 45W
Siuri, *India* 43 H12 23 50N 87 34 E
Sīvand, *Iran* 45 D7 30 5N 52 55 E
Sivas, *Turkey* 25 G6 39 43N 36 58 E
Siverek, *Turkey* 44 B3 37 50N 39 19 E
Sivomaskinskiy, *Russia* 24 A11 66 40N 62 35 E
Sivrihisar, *Turkey* 25 G5 39 30N 31 35 E
Sîwa, *Egypt* 51 C11 29 11N 25 31 E
Siwa Oasis, *Egypt* 48 D6 29 10N 25 30 E
Siwalik Range, *Nepal* 43 F10 28 0N 83 0 E
Siwan, *India* 43 F11 26 13N 84 21 E
Siwana, *India* 42 G5 25 38N 72 25 E
Sixmilebridge, *Ireland* 13 D3 52 44N 8 46W
Sixth Cataract, *Sudan* 51 E12 16 20N 32 42 E
Siziwang Qi, *China* 34 D6 41 25N 111 40 E
Sjælland, *Denmark* 9 J14 55 30N 11 30 E
Sjumen = Shumen, *Bulgaria* 21 C12 43 18N 26 55 E
Skadarsko Jezero, *Montenegro, Yug.* 21 C8 42 10N 19 20 E
Skaftafell, *Iceland* 8 D5 64 1N 17 0W
Skagafjörður, *Iceland* 8 D4 65 54N 19 35W
Skagastølstindane, *Norway* 9 F12 61 28N 7 52 E
Skagaströnd, *Iceland* 8 D3 65 50N 20 19W
Skagen, *Denmark* 9 H14 57 43N 10 35 E
Skagerrak, *Denmark* 9 H13 57 30N 9 0 E
Skagit →, *U.S.A.* 84 B4 48 23N 122 22W
Skagway, *U.S.A.* 68 C6 59 28N 135 19W
Skala-Podilska, *Ukraine* 17 D14 48 50N 26 15 E
Skala Podolskaya = Skala-Podilska, *Ukraine* 17 D14 48 50N 26 15 E
Skalat, *Ukraine* 17 D13 49 23N 25 55 E
Skåne, *Sweden* 9 J15 55 59N 13 30 E
Skaneateles, *U.S.A.* 79 D8 42 57N 76 26W
Skaneateles L., *U.S.A.* 79 D8 42 51N 76 22W
Skara, *Sweden* 9 G15 58 25N 13 30 E
Skardu, *Pakistan* 43 B6 35 20N 75 44 E
Skarżysko-Kamienna, *Poland* 17 C11 51 7N 20 52 E
Skeena →, *Canada* 72 C2 54 9N 130 5W
Skeena Mts., *Canada* 72 B3 56 40N 128 30W
Skegness, *U.K.* 10 D8 53 9N 0 20 E
Skeldon, *Guyana* 92 B7 5 55N 57 20W
Skellefte älv →, *Sweden* 8 D19 64 45N 21 10 E
Skellefteå, *Sweden* 8 D19 64 45N 20 50 E
Skelleftehamn, *Sweden* 8 D19 64 40N 21 9 E
Skerries, The, *U.K.* 10 D3 53 25N 4 36W
Ski, *Norway* 9 G14 59 43N 10 52 E
Skíathos, *Greece* 21 E10 39 12N 23 30 E
Skibbereen, *Ireland* 13 E2 51 33N 9 16W
Skiddaw, *U.K.* 10 C4 54 39N 3 9W
Skidegate, *Canada* 72 C2 53 15N 132 1W
Skien, *Norway* 9 G13 59 12N 9 35 E
Skierniewice, *Poland* 17 C11 51 58N 20 10 E
Skikda, *Algeria* 50 A7 36 50N 6 58 E
Skilloura, *Cyprus* 23 D12 35 14N 33 10 E
Skipton, *U.K.* 10 D5 53 58N 2 3W
Skirmish Pt., *Australia* 62 A1 11 59S 134 17 E
Skíros, *Greece* 21 E11 38 55N 24 34 E
Skive, *Denmark* 9 H13 56 33N 9 2 E
Skjálfandafljót →, *Iceland* 8 D5 65 59N 17 25W
Skjálfandi, *Iceland* 8 C5 66 5N 17 30W
Skoghall, *Sweden* 9 G15 59 20N 13 30 E
Skole, *Ukraine* 17 D12 49 3N 23 30 E
Skópelos, *Greece* 21 E10 39 9N 23 47 E
Skopí, *Greece* 23 D8 35 11N 26 2 E
Skopje, *Macedonia* 21 C9 42 1N 21 26 E
Skövde, *Sweden* 9 G15 58 24N 13 50 E
Skovorodino, *Russia* 27 D13 54 0N 124 0 E
Skowhegan, *U.S.A.* 77 C11 44 46N 69 43W
Skull, *Ireland* 13 E2 51 32N 9 34W
Skunk →, *U.S.A.* 80 E9 40 42N 91 7W
Skuodas, *Lithuania* 9 H19 56 16N 21 33 E
Skvyra, *Ukraine* 17 D15 49 44N 29 40 E
Skye, *U.K.* 12 D2 57 15N 6 10W
Skykomish, *U.S.A.* 82 C3 47 42N 121 22W
Skyros = Skíros, *Greece* 21 E11 38 55N 24 34 E
Slættaratindur, *Færoe Is.* 8 E9 62 18N 7 1W
Slagelse, *Denmark* 9 J14 55 23N 11 19 E
Slamet, *Indonesia* 37 G13 7 16S 109 8 E
Slaney →, *Ireland* 13 D5 52 26N 6 33W
Śląsk, *Poland* 16 C9 51 0N 16 30 E
Slate Is., *Canada* 70 C2 48 40N 87 0W
Slatina, *Romania* 17 F13 44 28N 24 22 E
Slatington, *U.S.A.* 79 F9 40 45N 75 37W
Slaton, *U.S.A.* 81 J4 33 26N 101 39W
Slave →, *Canada* 72 A6 61 18N 113 39W
Slave Coast, *W. Afr.* 50 G6 6 0N 2 30 E
Slave Lake, *Canada* 72 B6 55 17N 114 43W
Slave Pt., *Canada* 72 A5 61 11N 115 56W
Slavgorod, *Russia* 26 D8 53 1N 78 37 E
Slavonski Brod, *Croatia* 21 B8 45 11N 18 1 E
Slavuta, *Ukraine* 17 C14 50 15N 27 2 E
Slavyanka, *Russia* 30 C5 42 53N 131 21 E
Slavyansk = Slovyansk, *Ukraine* 25 E6 48 55N 37 36 E
Slawharad, *Belarus* 17 B16 53 27N 31 0 E
Sleaford, *U.K.* 10 D7 53 0N 0 24W
Sleaford B., *Australia* 63 E2 34 55S 135 45 E
Sleat, Sd. of, *U.K.* 12 D3 57 5N 5 47W
Sleeper Is., *Canada* 69 C11 58 30N 81 0W
Sleepy Eye, *U.S.A.* 80 C7 44 18N 94 43W
Slemon L., *Canada* 72 A5 63 13N 116 4W
Slide Mt., *U.S.A.* 79 E10 42 0N 74 25W
Slidell, *U.S.A.* 81 K10 30 17N 89 47W
Sliema, *Malta* 23 D2 35 54N 14 30 E
Slieve Aughty, *Ireland* 13 C3 53 4N 8 30W
Slieve Bloom, *Ireland* 13 C4 53 4N 7 40W
Slieve Donard, *U.K.* 13 B6 54 11N 5 55W
Slieve Gamph, *Ireland* 13 B3 54 6N 9 0W
Slieve Gullion, *U.K.* 13 B5 54 7N 6 26W
Slieve Mish, *Ireland* 13 D2 52 12N 9 50W
Slievenamon, *Ireland* 13 D4 52 25N 7 34W
Sligeach = Sligo, *Ireland* 13 B3 54 16N 8 28W
Sligo, *Ireland* 13 B3 54 16N 8 28W
Sligo, *U.S.A.* 78 E5 41 6N 79 29W
Sligo □, *Ireland* 13 B3 54 8N 8 42W
Sligo B., *Ireland* 13 B3 54 18N 8 40W
Slippery Rock, *U.S.A.* 78 E4 41 3N 80 3W
Slite, *Sweden* 9 H18 57 42N 18 48 E
Sliven, *Bulgaria* 21 C12 42 42N 26 19 E
Sloan, *U.S.A.* 85 K11 35 57N 115 13W
Sloansville, *U.S.A.* 79 D10 42 45N 74 22W
Slobodskoy, *Russia* 24 C9 58 40N 50 6 E
Slobozia, *Romania* 17 F14 44 34N 27 23 E
Slocan, *Canada* 72 D5 49 48N 117 28W
Slonim, *Belarus* 17 B13 53 4N 25 19 E
Slough, *U.K.* 11 F7 51 30N 0 36W
Slough □, *U.K.* 11 F7 51 30N 0 36W
Sloughhouse, *U.S.A.* 84 G5 38 26N 121 12W
Slovak Rep. ■, *Europe* 17 D10 48 30N 20 0 E
Slovakia = Slovak Rep. ■, *Europe* 17 D10 48 30N 20 0 E
Slovakian Ore Mts. = Slovenské Rudohorie, *Slovak Rep.* 17 D10 48 45N 20 0 E
Slovenia ■, *Europe* 16 F8 45 58N 14 30 E
Slovenija = Slovenia ■, *Europe* 16 F8 45 58N 14 30 E
Slovenské Rudohorie, *Slovak Rep.* 17 D10 48 45N 20 0 E
Slovyansk, *Ukraine* 25 E6 48 55N 37 36 E
Sluch →, *Ukraine* 17 C14 51 37N 26 38 E
Sluis, *Neths.* 15 C3 51 18N 3 23 E
Słupsk, *Poland* 17 A9 54 30N 17 3 E
Slurry, *S. Africa* 56 D4 25 49S 25 42 E
Slutsk, *Belarus* 17 B14 53 2N 27 31 E
Slyne Hd., *Ireland* 13 C1 53 25N 10 10W
Slyudyanka, *Russia* 27 D11 51 40N 103 40 E
Småland, *Sweden* 9 H16 57 15N 15 25 E
Smalltree L., *Canada* 73 A8 61 0N 105 0W
Smallwood Res., *Canada* 71 B7 54 0N 64 0W
Smara, *Morocco* 50 B4 32 9N 8 16W
Smarhon, *Belarus* 17 A14 54 20N 26 24 E
Smartt Syndicate Dam, *S. Africa* 56 E3 30 45S 23 10 E
Smartville, *U.S.A.* 84 F5 39 13N 121 18W
Smeaton, *Canada* 73 C8 53 30N 104 49W
Smederevo, *Serbia, Yug.* 21 B9 44 40N 20 57 E
Smerwick Harbour, *Ireland* 13 D1 52 12N 10 23W
Smethport, *U.S.A.* 78 E6 41 49N 78 27W
Smidovich, *Russia* 27 E14 48 36N 133 49 E
Smith, *Canada* 72 B6 55 10N 114 0W
Smith Center, *U.S.A.* 80 F5 39 47N 98 47W
Smith Sund, *Greenland* 4 B4 78 30N 74 0W
Smithburne →, *Australia* 62 B3 17 3S 140 57 E
Smithers, *Canada* 72 C3 54 45N 127 10W
Smithfield, *S. Africa* 57 E4 30 9S 26 30 E
Smithfield, *N.C., U.S.A.* 77 H6 35 31N 78 21W
Smithfield, *Utah, U.S.A.* 82 F8 41 50N 111 50W
Smiths Falls, *Canada* 79 B9 44 55N 76 0W
Smithton, *Australia* 62 G4 40 53S 145 6 E
Smithville, *Canada* 78 C5 43 6N 79 33W
Smithville, *U.S.A.* 81 K6 30 1N 97 10W
Smoky →, *Canada* 72 B5 56 10N 117 21W
Smoky Bay, *Australia* 63 E1 32 22S 134 13 E
Smoky Hill →, *U.S.A.* 80 F6 39 4N 96 48W
Smoky Hills, *U.S.A.* 80 F5 39 15N 99 30W
Smoky Lake, *Canada* 72 C6 54 10N 112 30W
Smøla, *Norway* 8 E13 63 23N 8 3 E
Smolensk, *Russia* 24 D5 54 45N 32 5 E
Smolikas, Óros, *Greece* 21 D9 40 9N 20 58 E
Smolyan, *Bulgaria* 21 D11 41 36N 24 38 E
Smooth Rock Falls, *Canada* 70 C3 49 17N 81 37W
Smoothstone L., *Canada* 73 C7 54 40N 106 50W
Smorgon = Smarhon, *Belarus* 17 A14 54 20N 26 24 E
Smyrna = İzmir, *Turkey* 21 E12 38 25N 27 8 E
Smyrna, *U.S.A.* 76 F8 39 18N 75 36W
Snæfell, *Iceland* 8 D6 64 48N 15 34W
Snaefell, *U.K.* 10 C3 54 16N 4 27W
Snæfellsjökull, *Iceland* 8 D2 64 49N 23 46W
Snake →, *U.S.A.* 82 C4 46 12N 119 2W
Snake I., *Australia* 63 F4 38 47S 146 33 E
Snake Range, *U.S.A.* 82 G6 39 0N 114 20W
Snake River Plain, *U.S.A.* 82 E7 42 50N 114 0W
Snåsavatnet, *Norway* 8 D14 64 12N 12 0 E
Sneek, *Neths.* 15 A5 53 2N 5 40 E
Sneeuberge, *S. Africa* 56 E3 31 46S 24 20 E
Snelling, *U.S.A.* 84 H6 37 31N 120 26W
Sněžka, *Europe* 16 C8 50 41N 15 50 E
Snizort, L., *U.K.* 12 D2 57 33N 6 28W
Snøhetta, *Norway* 9 E13 62 19N 9 16 E
Snohomish, *U.S.A.* 84 C4 47 55N 122 6W
Snoul, *Cambodia* 39 F6 12 4N 106 26 E
Snow Hill, *U.S.A.* 76 F8 38 11N 75 24W
Snow Lake, *Canada* 73 C8 54 52N 100 3W
Snow Mt., *Calif., U.S.A.* 84 F4 39 23N 122 45W
Snow Mt., *Maine, U.S.A.* 79 A14 45 18N 70 48W
Snow Shoe, *U.S.A.* 78 E7 41 2N 77 57W
Snowbird L., *Canada* 73 A8 60 45N 103 0W
Snowdon, *U.K.* 10 D3 53 4N 4 5W
Snowdrift →, *Canada* 73 A6 62 24N 110 44W
Snowflake, *U.S.A.* 83 J8 34 30N 110 5W
Snowshoe Pk., *U.S.A.* 82 B6 48 13N 115 41W
Snowtown, *Australia* 63 E2 33 46S 138 14 E
Snowville, *U.S.A.* 82 F7 41 58N 112 43W
Snowy →, *Australia* 63 F4 37 46S 148 30 E
Snowy Mt., *U.S.A.* 79 C10 43 42N 74 23W
Snowy Mts., *Australia* 63 F4 36 30S 148 20 E
Snug Corner, *Bahamas* 89 B5 22 33N 73 52W
Snyatyn, *Ukraine* 17 D13 48 27N 25 38 E
Snyder, *Okla., U.S.A.* 81 H5 34 40N 98 57W
Snyder, *Tex., U.S.A.* 81 J4 32 44N 100 55W
Soahanina, *Madag.* 57 B7 18 42S 44 13 E
Soalala, *Madag.* 57 B8 16 6S 45 20 E
Soan →, *Pakistan* 42 C4 33 1N 71 44 E
Soanierana-Ivongo, *Madag.* 57 B8 16 55S 49 35 E
Sobat, Nahr →, *Sudan* 51 G12 9 22N 31 33 E
Sobhapur, *India* 42 H8 22 47N 78 17 E
Sobradinho, Reprêsa de, *Brazil* 93 E10 9 30S 42 0 E
Sobral, *Brazil* 93 D10 3 50S 40 20W
Soc Trang, *Vietnam* 39 H5 9 37N 105 50 E
Socastee, *U.S.A.* 77 J6 33 41N 79 1W
Soch'e = Shache, *China* 32 C2 38 20N 77 10 E
Sochi, *Russia* 25 F6 43 35N 39 40 E
Société, Is. de la, *Pac. Oc.* 65 J12 17 0S 151 0W
Society Is. = Société, Is. de la, *Pac. Oc.* 65 J12 17 0S 151 0W
Socompa, Portezuelo de, *Chile* 94 A2 24 27S 68 18W
Socorro, *N. Mex., U.S.A.* 83 J10 34 4N 106 54W
Socorro, *Tex., U.S.A.* 83 L10 31 39N 106 18W
Socorro, I., *Mexico* 86 D2 18 45N 110 58W
Socotra, *Ind. Oc.* 46 E5 12 30N 54 0 E
Soda L., *U.S.A.* 83 J5 35 10N 116 4W
Soda Plains, *India* 43 B8 35 30N 79 0 E
Soda Springs, *U.S.A.* 82 E8 42 39N 111 36W
Sodankylä, *Finland* 8 C22 67 29N 26 40 E
Soddy-Daisy, *U.S.A.* 77 H3 35 17N 85 10W
Söderhamn, *Sweden* 9 F17 61 18N 17 10 E
Söderköping, *Sweden* 9 G17 58 31N 16 20 E
Södermanland, *Sweden* 9 G17 58 56N 16 55 E
Södertälje, *Sweden* 9 G17 59 12N 17 39 E
Sodiri, *Sudan* 51 F11 14 27N 29 0 E
Sodus, *U.S.A.* 78 C7 43 14N 77 4W
Soekmekaar, *S. Africa* 57 C4 23 30S 29 55 E
Soest, *Neths.* 15 B5 52 9N 5 19 E
Sofia = Sofiya, *Bulgaria* 21 C10 42 45N 23 20 E
Sofia →, *Madag.* 57 B8 15 27S 47 23 E
Sofiya, *Bulgaria* 21 C10 42 45N 23 20 E
Sōfu-Gan, *Japan* 31 K10 29 49N 140 21 E
Sogamoso, *Colombia* 92 B4 5 43N 72 56W
Sogār, *Iran* 45 E8 25 53N 58 6 E
Sogndalsfjøra, *Norway* 9 F12 61 14N 7 5 E
Søgne, *Norway* 9 G12 58 5N 7 48 E
Sognefjorden, *Norway* 9 F11 61 10N 5 50 E
Sŏgwipo, *S. Korea* 35 H14 33 13N 126 34 E
Soh, *Iran* 45 C6 33 26N 51 27 E
Sohâg, *Egypt* 51 C12 26 33N 31 43 E
Sohagpur, *India* 42 H8 22 42N 78 12 E
Sŏhori, *N. Korea* 35 D15 40 7N 128 23 E
Soignies, *Belgium* 15 D4 50 35N 4 5 E
Soissons, *France* 18 B5 49 25N 3 19 E
Sōja, *Japan* 31 G6 34 40N 133 45 E
Sojat, *India* 42 G5 25 55N 73 45 E
Sokal, *Ukraine* 17 C13 50 31N 24 15 E
Söke, *Turkey* 21 F12 37 48N 27 28 E
Sokelo, *Dem. Rep. of the Congo* 55 D1 9 55S 24 36 E
Sokhumi, *Georgia* 25 F7 43 0N 41 0 E
Sokodé, *Togo* 50 G6 9 0N 1 11 E
Sokol, *Russia* 24 C7 59 30N 40 5 E
Sokółka, *Poland* 17 B12 53 25N 23 30 E
Sokołów Podlaski, *Poland* 17 B12 52 25N 22 15 E
Sokoto, *Nigeria* 50 F7 13 2N 5 16 E
Sol Iletsk, *Russia* 24 D10 51 10N 55 0 E
Solai, *Kenya* 54 B4 0 2N 36 12 E
Solan, *India* 42 D7 30 55N 77 7 E
Solano, *Phil.* 37 A6 16 31N 121 15 E
Solapur, *India* 40 L9 17 43N 75 56 E
Soldotna, *U.S.A.* 68 B4 60 29N 151 3W
Soléa □, *Cyprus* 23 D12 35 5N 33 4 E
Soledad, *Colombia* 92 A4 10 55N 74 46W
Soledad, *U.S.A.* 84 J5 36 26N 121 20W
Soledad, *Venezuela* 92 B6 8 10N 63 34W
Solent, The, *U.K.* 11 G6 50 45N 1 25W
Solfonn, *Norway* 9 F12 60 2N 6 57 E

Solhan, Turkey 44 B4 38 57N 41 3 E
Soligalich, Russia 24 C7 59 5N 42 10 E
Soligorsk = Salihorsk, Belarus 17 B14 52 51N 27 27 E
Solihull, U.K. 11 E6 52 26N 1 47W
Solikamsk, Russia 24 C10 59 38N 56 50 E
Solila, Madag. 57 C8 21 25S 46 37 E
Solimões = Amazonas →, S. Amer. 93 D9 0 5S 50 0W
Solingen, Germany 16 C4 51 10N 7 5 E
Sollefteå, Sweden 8 E17 63 12N 17 20 E
Sóller, Spain 22 B9 39 46N 2 43 E
Solo →, Indonesia 37 G15 6 47S 112 22 E
Sologne, France 18 C4 47 40N 1 45 E
Solok, Indonesia 36 E2 0 45S 100 40 E
Sololá, Guatemala 88 D1 14 49N 91 10W
Solomon, N. Fork →, U.S.A. 80 F5 39 29N 98 26W
Solomon, S. Fork →, U.S.A. 80 F5 39 25N 99 12W
Solomon Is. ■, Pac. Oc. 64 H7 6 0S 155 0 E
Solon, China 33 B7 46 32N 121 10 E
Solon Springs, U.S.A. 80 B9 46 22N 91 49W
Solor, Indonesia 37 F6 8 27S 123 0 E
Solothurn, Switz. 18 C7 47 13N 7 32 E
Šolta, Croatia 20 C7 43 24N 16 15 E
Solṭānābād, Khorāsān, Iran 45 C8 34 13N 59 58 E
Solṭānābād, Khorāsān, Iran 45 B8 36 29N 58 5 E
Solunska Glava, Macedonia 21 D9 41 44N 21 31 E
Solvang, U.S.A. 85 L6 34 36N 120 8W
Solvay, U.S.A. 79 C8 43 3N 76 13W
Sölvesborg, Sweden 9 H16 56 5N 14 35 E
Solvychegodsk, Russia 24 B8 61 21N 46 56 E
Solway Firth, U.K. 10 C4 54 49N 3 35W
Solwezi, Zambia 55 E2 12 11S 26 21 E
Sōma, Japan 30 F10 37 40N 140 50 E
Soma, Turkey 21 E12 39 10N 27 35 E
Somali Pen., Africa 48 F8 7 0N 46 0 E
Somali Rep. ■, Africa 46 F4 7 0N 47 0 E
Somalia = Somali Rep. ■, Africa 46 F4 7 0N 47 0 E
Sombor, Serbia, Yug. 21 B8 45 46N 19 9 E
Sombra, Canada 78 D2 42 43N 82 29W
Sombrerete, Mexico 86 C4 23 40N 103 40W
Sombrero, Anguilla 89 C7 18 37N 63 30W
Somdari, India 42 G5 25 47N 72 38 E
Somers, U.S.A. 82 B6 48 5N 114 13W
Somerset, Ky., U.S.A. 76 G3 37 5N 84 36W
Somerset, Mass., U.S.A. 79 E13 41 47N 71 8W
Somerset, Pa., U.S.A. 78 F5 40 1N 79 5W
Somerset □, U.K. 11 F5 51 9N 3 0W
Somerset East, S. Africa 56 E4 32 42S 25 35 E
Somerset I., Canada 68 A10 73 30N 93 0W
Somerset West, S. Africa 56 E2 34 8S 18 50 E
Somersworth, U.S.A. 79 C14 43 16N 70 52W
Somerton, U.S.A. 83 K6 32 36N 114 43W
Somerville, U.S.A. 79 F10 40 35N 74 38W
Someș →, Romania 17 D12 47 49N 22 43 E
Somme →, France 18 A4 50 11N 1 38 E
Somnath, India 42 J4 20 53N 70 22 E
Somosierra, Puerto de, Spain 19 B4 41 4N 3 35W
Somoto, Nic. 88 D2 13 28N 86 37W
Somport, Puerto de, Spain 18 E3 42 48N 0 31W
Son →, India 43 G11 25 42N 84 52 E
Son Ha, Vietnam 38 E7 15 3N 108 34 E
Son Hoa, Vietnam 38 F7 13 2N 108 58 E
Son Serra, Spain 22 B10 39 43N 3 13 E
Soná, Panama 88 E3 8 0N 81 20W
Sonamarg, India 43 B6 34 18N 75 21 E
Sonamukhi, India 43 H12 23 18N 87 27 E
Sonar →, India 43 G8 24 24N 79 56 E
Sŏnch'ŏn, N. Korea 35 E13 39 48N 124 55 E
Sondags →, S. Africa 56 E4 33 44S 25 51 E
Sondar, India 43 C6 33 28N 75 56 E
Sønderborg, Denmark 9 J13 54 55N 9 49 E
Sóndrio, Italy 18 C8 46 10N 9 52 E
Sone, Mozam. 55 F3 17 23S 34 55 E
Sonepur, India 41 J13 20 55N 83 50 E
Song, Thailand 38 C3 18 28N 100 11 E
Song Cau, Vietnam 38 F7 13 27N 109 18 E
Song Xian, China 34 G7 34 12N 112 8 E
Songch'ŏn, N. Korea 35 E14 39 12N 126 15 E
Songea, Tanzania 55 E4 10 40S 35 40 E
Songhua Hu, China 35 C14 43 35N 126 50 E
Songhua Jiang →, China 33 B8 47 45N 132 30 E
Songjin, N. Korea 35 D15 40 40N 129 10 E
Songjŏng-ni, S. Korea 35 G14 35 8N 126 47 E
Songkhla, Thailand 39 J3 7 13N 100 37 E
Songnim, N. Korea 35 E13 38 45N 125 39 E
Songo, Angola 52 F2 7 22S 14 51 E
Songo, Mozam. 53 H6 15 34S 32 38 E
Songo, Sudan 51 G10 9 47N 24 21 E
Songpan, China 32 C5 32 40N 103 30 E
Songwe, Dem. Rep. of the Congo 54 C2 3 20S 26 16 E
Songwe →, Africa 55 D3 9 44S 33 58 E
Sonhat, India 43 H10 23 29N 82 31 E
Sonid Youqi, China 34 C7 42 45N 112 48 E
Sonipat, India 42 E7 29 0N 77 5 E
Sonkach, India 42 H7 22 59N 76 21 E
Sonmiani, Pakistan 42 G2 25 25N 66 40 E
Sonmiani B., Pakistan 42 G2 25 15N 66 30 E
Sono →, Brazil 93 E9 9 58S 48 11W
Sonoma, U.S.A. 84 G4 38 18N 122 28W
Sonora, Calif., U.S.A. 84 H6 37 59N 120 23W
Sonora, Tex., U.S.A. 81 K4 30 34N 100 39W
Sonora □, Mexico 86 B2 29 0N 111 0W
Sonora →, Mexico 86 B2 28 50N 111 33W
Sonora Desert, U.S.A. 85 L12 33 40N 114 15W
Sonoyta, Mexico 86 A2 31 51N 112 50W
Sŏnsan, S. Korea 35 F15 36 14N 128 17 E
Sonsonate, El Salv. 88 D2 13 43N 89 44W
Sonsorol Is., Pac. Oc. 37 C8 5 30N 132 15 E
Soochow = Suzhou, China 33 C7 31 19N 120 38 E
Sooke, Canada 84 B3 48 13N 123 43W
Sop Prap, Thailand 38 D2 17 53N 99 20 E
Sopi, Indonesia 37 D7 2 34N 128 28 E
Sopot, Poland 17 A10 54 27N 18 31 E
Sopron, Hungary 17 E9 47 45N 16 32 E
Sopur, India 43 B6 34 18N 74 27 E
Sør-Rondane, Antarctica 5 D4 72 0S 25 0 E
Sorah, Pakistan 42 F3 27 13N 68 56 E
Soraon, India 43 G9 25 37N 81 51 E
Sorel, Canada 70 C5 46 0N 73 10W
Sórgono, Italy 20 D3 40 1N 9 6 E
Soria, Spain 19 B4 41 43N 2 32W
Soriano, Uruguay 94 C4 33 24S 58 19W
Sorkh, Kuh-e, Iran 45 C8 35 40N 58 30 E
Soroca, Moldova 17 D15 48 8N 28 12 E
Sorocaba, Brazil 95 A6 23 31S 47 27W
Sorochinsk, Russia 24 D9 52 26N 53 10 E
Soroki = Soroca, Moldova 17 D15 48 8N 28 12 E
Sorol Atoll, Pac. Oc. 37 C10 7 45N 140 45 E
Sorong, Indonesia 37 E8 0 55S 131 15 E
Soroní, Greece 23 C10 36 21N 28 1 E
Soroti, Uganda 54 B3 1 43N 33 35 E
Sørøya, Norway 8 A20 70 40N 22 30 E
Sørøysundet, Norway 8 A20 70 25N 23 0 E
Sorrell, Australia 62 G4 42 47S 147 34 E
Sorsele, Sweden 8 D17 65 31N 17 30 E
Sorsogon, Phil. 37 B6 13 0N 124 0 E
Sortavala, Russia 24 B5 61 42N 30 41 E
Sortland, Norway 8 B16 68 42N 15 25 E
Sŏsan, S. Korea 35 F14 36 47N 126 27 E
Soscumica, L., Canada 70 B4 50 15N 77 27W
Sosnogorsk, Russia 24 B9 63 37N 53 51 E
Sosnowiec, Poland 17 C10 50 20N 19 10 E
Sŏsura, N. Korea 35 C16 42 16N 130 36 E
Sot →, India 43 F8 27 27N 79 37 E
Sotkamo, Finland 8 D23 64 8N 28 23 E
Soto la Marina →, Mexico 87 C5 23 40N 97 40W
Sotuta, Mexico 87 C7 20 29N 89 43W
Souanké, Congo 52 D2 2 10N 14 3 E
Souderton, U.S.A. 79 F9 40 19N 75 19W
Soúdha, Greece 23 D6 35 29N 24 4 E
Soúdhas, Kólpos, Greece 23 D6 35 25N 24 10 E
Soufrière, St. Lucia 89 D7 13 51N 61 3W
Soukhouma, Laos 38 E5 14 38N 105 48 E
Sŏul, S. Korea 35 F14 37 31N 126 58 E
Sound, The, U.K. 11 G3 50 20N 4 10W
Sources, Mt. aux, Lesotho 57 D4 28 45S 28 50 E
Soure, Brazil 93 D9 0 35S 48 30W
Souris, Man., Canada 73 D8 49 40N 100 20W
Souris, P.E.I., Canada 71 C7 46 21N 62 15W
Souris →, Canada 80 A5 49 40N 99 34W
Sousa, Brazil 93 E11 6 45S 38 10W
Sousse, Tunisia 51 A8 35 50N 10 38 E
South Africa ■, Africa 56 E3 32 0S 23 0 E
South America 90 E5 10 0S 60 0W
South Atlantic Ocean 90 H7 20 0S 10 0W
South Aulatsivik I., Canada 71 A7 56 45N 61 30W
South Australia □, Australia 63 E2 32 0S 139 0 E
South Ayrshire □, U.K. 12 F4 55 18N 4 41W
South Baldy, U.S.A. 83 J10 33 59N 107 11W
South Bass I., U.S.A. 78 E2 41 39N 82 49W
South Bend, Ind., U.S.A. 76 E2 41 41N 86 15W
South Bend, Wash., U.S.A. 84 D3 46 40N 123 48W
South Boston, U.S.A. 77 G6 36 42N 78 54W
South Branch, Canada 71 C8 47 55N 59 2W
South Brook, Canada 71 C8 49 26N 56 5W
South Carolina □, U.S.A. 77 J5 34 0N 81 0W
South Charleston, U.S.A. 76 F5 38 22N 81 44W
South China Sea, Asia 36 C4 10 0N 113 0 E
South Dakota □, U.S.A. 80 C5 44 15N 100 0W
South Deerfield, U.S.A. 79 D12 42 29N 72 37W
South Downs, U.K. 11 G7 50 52N 0 25W
South East C., Australia 62 G4 43 40S 146 50 E
South East Is., Australia 61 F3 34 17S 123 30 E
South Esk →, U.K. 12 E6 56 43N 2 31W
South Foreland, U.K. 11 F9 51 8N 1 24 E
South Fork American →, U.S.A. 84 G5 38 45N 121 5W
South Fork Feather →, U.S.A. 84 F5 39 17N 121 36W
South Fork Grand →, U.S.A. 80 C3 45 43N 102 17W
South Fork Republican →, U.S.A. 80 E4 40 3N 101 31W
South Georgia, Antarctica 96 G9 54 30S 37 0W
South Gloucestershire □, U.K. 11 F5 51 32N 2 28W
South Hadley, U.S.A. 79 D12 42 16N 72 35W
South Haven, U.S.A. 76 D2 42 24N 86 16W
South Henik, L., Canada 73 A9 61 30N 97 30W
South Honshu Ridge, Pac. Oc. 64 E6 23 0N 143 0 E
South Horr, Kenya 54 B4 2 12N 36 56 E
South I., Kenya 54 B4 2 35N 36 35 E
South I., N.Z. 59 L3 44 0S 170 0 E
South Indian Lake, Canada 73 B9 56 47N 98 56W
South Invercargill, N.Z. 59 M2 46 26S 168 23 E
South Knife →, Canada 73 B10 58 55N 94 37W
South Koel →, India 43 H11 22 32N 85 14 E
South Korea ■, Asia 35 G15 36 0N 128 0 E
South Lake Tahoe, U.S.A. 84 G6 38 57N 119 59W
South Lanarkshire □, U.K. 12 F5 55 37N 3 53W
South Loup →, U.S.A. 80 E5 41 4N 98 39W
South Magnetic Pole, Antarctica 5 C9 64 8S 138 8 E
South Milwaukee, U.S.A. 76 D2 42 55N 87 52W
South Molton, U.K. 11 F4 51 1N 3 51W
South Moose L., Canada 73 C8 53 46N 100 8W
South Nahanni →, Canada 72 A4 61 3N 123 21W
South Nation →, Canada 79 A9 45 34N 75 6W
South Natuna Is. = Natuna Selatan, Kepulauan, Indonesia 39 L7 2 45N 109 0 E
South Negril Pt., Jamaica 88 C4 18 14N 78 30W
South Orkney Is., Antarctica 5 C18 63 0S 45 0W
South Ossetia □, Georgia 25 F7 42 21N 44 2 E
South Pagai, I. = Pagai Selatan, Pulau, Indonesia 36 E2 3 0S 100 15 E
South Paris, U.S.A. 79 B14 44 14N 70 31W
South Pass, U.S.A. 74 B5 42 20N 108 58W
South Pittsburg, U.S.A. 77 H3 35 1N 85 42W
South Platte →, U.S.A. 80 E4 41 7N 100 42W
South Pole, Antarctica 5 E 90 0S 0 0 E
South Porcupine, Canada 70 C3 48 30N 81 12W
South Portland, U.S.A. 77 D10 43 38N 70 15W
South Pt., U.S.A. 78 B1 44 52N 83 19W
South River, Canada 70 C4 45 52N 79 23W
South River, U.S.A. 79 F10 40 27N 74 23W
South Ronaldsay, U.K. 12 C6 58 48N 2 58W
South Sandwich Is., Antarctica 5 B1 57 0S 27 0W
South Saskatchewan →, Canada 73 C7 53 15N 105 5W
South Seal →, Canada 73 B9 58 48N 98 8W
South Shetland Is., Antarctica 5 C18 62 0S 59 0W
South Shields, U.K. 10 C6 55 0N 1 25W
South Sioux City, U.S.A. 80 D6 42 28N 96 24W
South Taranaki Bight, N.Z. 59 H5 39 40S 174 5 E
South Thompson →, Canada 72 C4 50 40N 120 20W
South Twin I., Canada 70 B4 53 7N 79 52W
South Tyne →, U.K. 10 C5 54 59N 2 8W
South Uist, U.K. 12 D1 57 20N 7 15W
South West Africa = Namibia ■, Africa 56 C2 22 0S 18 9 E
South West C., Australia 62 G4 43 34S 146 3 E
South West Rocks, Australia 63 E5 30 52S 153 3 E
South Williamsport, U.S.A. 78 E8 41 13N 77 0W
South Yorkshire □, U.K. 10 D6 53 27N 1 36W
Southampton, Canada 78 B3 44 30N 81 25W
Southampton, U.K. 11 G6 50 54N 1 23W
Southampton, U.S.A. 79 F12 40 53N 72 23W
Southampton □, U.K. 11 G6 50 54N 1 23W
Southampton I., Canada 69 B11 64 30N 84 0W
Southaven, U.S.A. 81 H9 34 59N 90 2W
Southbank, Canada 72 C3 54 2N 125 46W
Southbridge, N.Z. 59 K4 43 48S 172 16 E
Southbridge, U.S.A. 79 D12 42 5N 72 2W
Southend, Canada 73 B8 56 19N 103 22W
Southend-on-Sea, U.K. 11 F8 51 32N 0 44 E
Southend-on-Sea □, U.K. 11 F8 51 32N 0 44 E
Southern □, Malawi 55 F4 15 0S 35 0 E
Southern □, Uganda 54 C3 0 15S 31 30 E
Southern □, Zambia 55 F2 16 20S 26 20 E
Southern Alps, N.Z. 59 K3 43 41S 170 11 E
Southern Cross, Australia 61 F2 31 12S 119 15 E
Southern Indian L., Canada 73 B9 57 10N 98 30W
Southern Ocean, Antarctica 5 C6 62 0S 60 0 E
Southern Pines, U.S.A. 77 H6 35 11N 79 24W
Southern Uplands, U.K. 12 F5 55 28N 3 52W
Southington, U.S.A. 79 E12 41 36N 72 53W
Southold, U.S.A. 79 E12 41 4N 72 26W
Southport, Australia 63 D5 27 58S 153 25 E
Southport, U.K. 10 D4 53 39N 3 0W
Southport, Fla., U.S.A. 77 K3 30 17N 85 38W
Southport, N.Y., U.S.A. 78 D8 42 3N 76 49W
Southwest C., N.Z. 59 M1 47 17S 167 28 E
Southwold, U.K. 11 E9 52 20N 1 41 E
Soutpansberg, S. Africa 57 C4 23 0S 29 30 E
Sovetsk, Kaliningd., Russia 9 J19 55 6N 21 50 E
Sovetsk, Kirov, Russia 24 C8 57 38N 48 53 E
Sovetskaya Gavan = Vanino, Russia 27 E15 48 50N 140 5 E
Soweto, S. Africa 57 D4 26 14S 27 54 E
Sōya-Kaikyō = La Perouse Str., Asia 30 B11 45 40N 142 0 E
Sōya-Misaki, Japan 30 B10 45 30N 141 55 E
Sozh →, Belarus 17 B16 51 57N 30 48 E
Spa, Belgium 15 D5 50 29N 5 53 E
Spain ■, Europe 19 B4 39 0N 4 0W
Spalding, Australia 63 E2 33 30S 138 37 E
Spalding, U.K. 10 E7 52 48N 0 9W
Spangler, U.S.A. 78 F6 40 39N 78 48W
Spanish, Canada 70 C3 46 12N 82 20W
Spanish Fork, U.S.A. 82 F8 40 7N 111 39W
Spanish Town, Jamaica 88 C4 18 0N 76 57W
Sparks, U.S.A. 84 F7 39 32N 119 45W
Sparta = Spárti, Greece 21 F10 37 5N 22 25 E
Sparta, Mich., U.S.A. 76 D3 43 10N 85 42W
Sparta, N.J., U.S.A. 79 E10 41 2N 74 38W
Sparta, Wis., U.S.A. 80 D9 43 56N 90 49W
Spartanburg, U.S.A. 77 H5 34 56N 81 57W
Spartansburg, U.S.A. 78 E5 41 49N 79 41W
Spárti, Greece 21 F10 37 5N 22 25 E
Spartivento, C., Calabria, Italy 20 F7 37 55N 16 4 E
Spartivento, C., Sard., Italy 20 E3 38 53N 8 50 E
Sparwood, Canada 72 D6 49 44N 114 53W
Spassk Dalniy, Russia 27 E14 44 40N 132 48 E
Spátha, Ákra, Greece 23 D5 35 42N 23 43 E
Spatsizi →, Canada 72 B3 57 42N 128 7W
Spatsizi Plateau Wilderness Park, Canada 72 B3 57 40N 128 0W
Spean →, U.K. 12 E4 56 55N 4 59W
Spearfish, U.S.A. 80 C3 44 30N 103 52W
Spearman, U.S.A. 81 G4 36 12N 101 12W
Speculator, U.S.A. 79 C10 43 30N 74 25W
Speightstown, Barbados 89 D8 13 15N 59 39W
Speke Gulf, Tanzania 54 C3 2 20S 32 50 E
Spencer, Idaho, U.S.A. 82 D7 44 22N 112 11W
Spencer, Iowa, U.S.A. 80 D7 43 9N 95 9W
Spencer, N.Y., U.S.A. 79 D8 42 13N 76 30W
Spencer, Nebr., U.S.A. 80 D5 42 53N 98 42W
Spencer, C., Australia 63 F2 35 20S 136 53 E
Spencer B., Namibia 56 D1 25 30S 14 47 E
Spencer G., Australia 63 E2 34 0S 137 20 E
Spencerville, Canada 79 B9 44 51N 75 33W
Spences Bridge, Canada 72 C4 50 25N 121 20W
Spennymoor, U.K. 10 C6 54 42N 1 36W
Spenser Mts., N.Z. 59 K4 42 15S 172 45 E
Sperrin Mts., U.K. 13 B5 54 50N 7 0W
Spey →, U.K. 12 D5 57 40N 3 6W
Speyer, Germany 16 D5 49 29N 8 25 E
Spezand, Pakistan 42 E2 29 59N 67 0 E
Spili, Greece 23 D6 35 13N 24 31 E
Spīn Būldak, Afghan. 42 D2 31 1N 66 25 E
Spinalónga, Greece 23 D7 35 18N 25 44 E
Spirit Lake, U.S.A. 84 D4 46 15N 122 9W
Spirit River, Canada 72 B5 55 45N 118 50W
Spiritwood, Canada 73 C7 53 24N 107 33W
Spithead, U.K. 11 G6 50 45N 1 10W
Spitzbergen = Svalbard, Arctic 4 B8 78 0N 17 0 E
Spjelkavik, Norway 9 E12 62 28N 6 22 E
Split, Croatia 20 C7 43 31N 16 26 E
Split L., Canada 73 B9 56 8N 96 15W
Split Lake, Canada 73 B9 56 8N 96 15W
Spofford, U.S.A. 81 L4 29 10N 100 25W
Spokane, U.S.A. 82 C5 47 40N 117 24W
Spoleto, Italy 20 C5 42 44N 12 44 E
Spooner, U.S.A. 80 C9 45 50N 91 53W
Sporyy Navolok, Mys, Russia 26 B7 75 50N 68 40 E
Sprague, U.S.A. 82 C5 47 18N 117 59W
Spratly I., S. China Sea 36 C4 8 38N 111 55 E
Spratly Is., S. China Sea 36 C4 8 20N 112 0 E
Spray, U.S.A. 82 D4 44 50N 119 48W
Spree →, Germany 16 B7 52 32N 13 13 E
Sprengisandur, Iceland 8 D5 64 52N 18 7W
Spring City, U.S.A. 79 F9 40 11N 75 33W
Spring Creek, U.S.A. 82 F6 40 45N 115 38W
Spring Garden, U.S.A. 84 F6 39 52N 120 47W
Spring Hill, U.S.A. 77 L4 28 27N 82 41W
Spring Mts., U.S.A. 83 H6 36 0N 115 45W
Spring Valley, U.S.A. 85 N10 32 45N 117 5W
Springbok, S. Africa 56 D2 29 42S 17 54 E
Springboro, U.S.A. 78 E4 41 48N 80 22W
Springdale, Canada 71 C8 49 30N 56 6W
Springdale, U.S.A. 81 G7 36 11N 94 8W
Springer, U.S.A. 81 G2 36 22N 104 36W
Springerville, U.S.A. 83 J9 34 8N 109 17W
Springfield, Canada 78 D4 42 50N 80 56W
Springfield, N.Z. 59 K3 43 19S 171 56 E
Springfield, Colo., U.S.A. 81 G3 37 24N 102 37W
Springfield, Ill., U.S.A. 80 F10 39 48N 89 39W
Springfield, Mass., U.S.A. 79 D12 42 6N 72 35W
Springfield, Mo., U.S.A. 81 G8 37 13N 93 17W
Springfield, Ohio, U.S.A. 76 F4 39 55N 83 49W
Springfield, Oreg., U.S.A. 82 D2 44 3N 123 1W
Springfield, Tenn., U.S.A. 77 G2 36 31N 86 53W
Springfield, Vt., U.S.A. 79 C12 43 18N 72 29W
Springfontein, S. Africa 56 E4 30 15S 25 40 E
Springhill, Canada 71 C7 45 40N 64 4W
Springhill, U.S.A. 81 J8 33 0N 93 28W
Springhouse, Canada 72 C4 51 56N 122 7W
Springs, S. Africa 57 D4 26 13S 28 25 E
Springsure, Australia 62 C4 24 8S 148 6 E
Springvale, U.S.A. 79 C14 43 28N 70 48W
Springville, Calif., U.S.A. 84 J8 36 8N 118 49W
Springville, N.Y., U.S.A. 78 D6 42 31N 78 40W
Springville, Utah, U.S.A. 82 F8 40 10N 111 37W
Springwater, U.S.A. 78 D7 42 38N 77 35W
Spruce-Creek, U.S.A. 78 F6 40 36N 78 9W
Spruce Mt., U.S.A. 79 B12 44 12N 72 19W
Spur, U.S.A. 81 J4 33 28N 100 52W
Spurn Hd., U.K. 10 D8 53 35N 0 8 E
Spuzzum, Canada 72 D4 49 37N 121 23W
Squam L., U.S.A. 79 C13 43 45N 71 32W
Squamish, Canada 72 D4 49 45N 123 10W
Square Islands, Canada 71 B8 52 47N 55 47W
Squires, Mt., Australia 61 E4 26 14S 127 28 E
Srbija = Serbia □, Yugoslavia 21 C9 43 30N 21 0 E
Sre Ambel, Cambodia 39 G4 11 8N 103 46 E
Sre Khtum, Cambodia 39 F6 12 10N 106 52 E
Sre Umbell = Sre Ambel, Cambodia 39 G4 11 8N 103 46 E
Srebrenica, Bos.-H. 21 B8 44 6N 19 18 E
Sredinny Ra. = Sredinnyy Khrebet, Russia 27 D17 57 0N 160 0 E
Sredinnyy Khrebet, Russia 27 D17 57 0N 160 0 E
Srednekolymsk, Russia 27 C16 67 27N 153 40 E
Śrem, Poland 17 B9 52 6N 17 2 E
Sremska Mitrovica, Serbia, Yug. 21 B8 44 59N 19 38 E
Srepok →, Cambodia 38 F6 13 33N 106 16 E
Sretensk, Russia 27 D12 52 10N 117 40 E
Sri Lanka ■, Asia 40 R12 7 30N 80 50 E
Srikakulam, India 41 K13 18 14N 83 58 E
Srinagar, India 43 B6 34 5N 74 50 E
Staaten →, Australia 62 B3 16 24S 141 17 E
Stade, Germany 16 B5 53 35N 9 29 E
Stadskanaal, Neths. 15 A6 53 4N 6 55 E
Staffa, U.K. 12 E2 56 27N 6 21W
Stafford, U.K. 10 E5 52 49N 2 7W
Stafford, U.S.A. 81 G5 37 58N 98 36W
Stafford Springs, U.S.A. 79 E12 41 57N 72 18W
Staffordshire □, U.K. 10 E5 52 53N 2 10W
Staines, U.K. 11 F7 51 26N 0 29W
Stakhanov, Ukraine 25 E6 48 35N 38 40 E
Stalingrad = Volgograd, Russia 25 E7 48 40N 44 25 E
Staliniri = Tskhinvali, Georgia 25 F7 42 14N 44 1 E
Stalino = Donetsk, Ukraine 25 E6 48 0N 37 45 E
Stalinogorsk = Novomoskovsk, Russia 24 D6 54 5N 38 15 E
Stalis, Greece 23 D7 35 17N 25 25 E
Stalowa Wola, Poland 17 C12 50 34N 22 3 E
Stalybridge, U.K. 10 D5 53 28N 2 3W
Stamford, Australia 62 C3 21 15S 143 46 E
Stamford, U.K. 11 E7 52 39N 0 29W
Stamford, Conn., U.S.A. 79 E11 41 3N 73 32W
Stamford, N.Y., U.S.A. 79 D10 42 25N 74 38W
Stamford, Tex., U.S.A. 81 J5 32 57N 99 48W
Stamps, U.S.A. 81 J8 33 22N 93 30W
Standerton, S. Africa 57 D4 26 55S 29 7 E
Standish, U.S.A. 76 D4 43 59N 83 57W
Stanford, U.S.A. 82 C8 47 9N 110 13W
Stanger, S. Africa 57 D5 29 27S 31 14 E
Stanislaus →, U.S.A. 84 H5 37 40N 121 14W
Stanislav = Ivano-Frankivsk, Ukraine 17 D13 48 40N 24 40 E
Stanke Dimitrov, Bulgaria 21 C10 42 17N 23 9 E
Stanley, Australia 62 G4 40 46S 145 19 E
Stanley, Canada 73 B8 55 24N 104 22W
Stanley, Falk. Is. 96 G5 51 40S 59 51W
Stanley, U.K. 10 C6 54 53N 1 41W
Stanley, Idaho, U.S.A. 82 D6 44 13N 114 56W
Stanley, N. Dak., U.S.A. 80 A3 48 19N 102 23W
Stanley, N.Y., U.S.A. 78 D7 42 48N 77 6W
Stanovoy Khrebet, Russia 27 D14 55 0N 130 0 E
Stanovoy Ra. = Stanovoy Khrebet, Russia 27 D14 55 0N 130 0 E
Stansmore Ra., Australia 60 D4 21 23S 128 33 E
Stanthorpe, Australia 63 D5 28 36S 151 59 E
Stanton, U.S.A. 81 J4 32 8N 101 48W
Stanwood, U.S.A. 84 B4 48 15N 122 23W
Staples, U.S.A. 80 B7 46 21N 94 48W
Star City, Canada 73 C8 52 50N 104 20W
Star Lake, U.S.A. 79 B9 44 10N 75 2W
Stara Planina, Bulgaria 21 C10 43 15N 23 0 E
Stara Zagora, Bulgaria 21 C11 42 26N 25 39 E
Starachowice, Poland 17 C11 51 3N 21 2 E
Staraya Russa, Russia 24 C5 57 58N 31 23 E
Starbuck I., Kiribati 65 H12 5 37S 155 55W
Stargard Szczeciński, Poland 16 B8 53 20N 15 0 E
Staritsa, Russia 24 C5 56 33N 34 55 E
Starke, U.S.A. 77 L4 29 57N 82 7W
Starogard Gdański, Poland 17 B10 53 59N 18 30 E
Starokonstantinov = Starokonstyantyniv, Ukraine 17 D14 49 48N 27 10 E
Starokonstyantyniv, Ukraine 17 D14 49 48N 27 10 E
Start Pt., U.K. 11 G4 50 13N 3 39W
Staryy Chartoriysk, Ukraine 17 C13 51 15N 25 54 E
State College, U.S.A. 78 F7 40 48N 77 52W
Stateline, U.S.A. 84 G7 38 57N 119 56W

Staten, I. = Estados, I. de Los, *Argentina* **96 G4** 54 40S 64 30W
Staten I., *U.S.A.* **79 F10** 40 35N 74 9W
Statesboro, *U.S.A.* **77 J5** 32 27N 81 47W
Statesville, *U.S.A.* **77 H5** 35 47N 80 53W
Stauffer, *U.S.A.* **85 L7** 34 45N 119 3W
Staunton, *Ill., U.S.A.* **80 F10** 39 1N 89 47W
Staunton, *Va., U.S.A.* **76 F6** 38 9N 79 4W
Stavanger, *Norway* **9 G11** 58 57N 5 40 E
Staveley, *N.Z.* **59 K3** 43 40S 171 32 E
Stavelot, *Belgium* **15 D5** 50 23N 5 55 E
Stavern, *Norway* **9 G14** 59 0N 10 1 E
Stavoren, *Neths.* **15 B5** 52 53N 5 22 E
Stavropol, *Russia* **25 E7** 45 5N 42 0 E
Stavros, *Cyprus* **23 D11** 35 1N 32 38 E
Stavrós, *Greece* **23 D6** 35 12N 24 45 E
Stavros, Ákra, *Greece* **23 D6** 35 26N 24 58 E
Stawell, *Australia* **63 F3** 37 5S 142 47 E
Stawell →, *Australia* **62 C3** 20 20S 142 55 E
Stayner, *Canada* **78 B4** 44 25N 80 5W
Stayton, *U.S.A.* **82 D2** 44 48N 122 48W
Steamboat Springs, *U.S.A.* **82 F10** 40 29N 106 50W
Steele, *U.S.A.* **80 B5** 46 51N 99 55W
Steelton, *U.S.A.* **78 F8** 40 14N 76 50W
Steen River, *Canada* **72 B5** 59 40N 117 12W
Steenkool = Bintuni, *Indonesia* **37 E8** 2 7S 133 32 E
Steens Mt., *U.S.A.* **82 E4** 42 35N 118 40W
Steenwijk, *Neths.* **15 B6** 52 47N 6 7 E
Steep Pt., *Australia* **61 E1** 26 8S 113 8 E
Steep Rock, *Canada* **73 C9** 51 30N 98 48W
Stefanie L. = Chew Bahir, *Ethiopia* **46 G2** 4 40N 36 50 E
Stefansson Bay, *Antarctica* **5 C5** 67 20S 59 8 E
Steiermark □, *Austria* **16 E8** 47 26N 15 0 E
Steilacoom, *U.S.A.* **84 C4** 47 10N 122 36W
Steinbach, *Canada* **73 D9** 49 32N 96 40W
Steinkjer, *Norway* **8 D14** 64 1N 11 31 E
Steinkopf, *S. Africa* **56 D2** 29 18S 17 43 E
Stellarton, *Canada* **71 C7** 45 32N 62 30W
Stellenbosch, *S. Africa* **56 E2** 33 58S 18 50 E
Stendal, *Germany* **16 B6** 52 36N 11 53 E
Steornabhaigh = Stornoway, *U.K.* **12 C2** 58 13N 6 23W
Stepanakert = Xankändi, *Azerbaijan* **25 G8** 39 52N 46 49 E
Stephens Creek, *Australia* **63 E3** 31 50S 141 30 E
Stephens I., *Canada* **72 C2** 54 10N 130 45W
Stephens L., *Canada* **73 B9** 56 32N 95 0W
Stephenville, *Canada* **71 C8** 48 31N 58 35W
Stephenville, *U.S.A.* **81 J5** 32 13N 98 12W
Stepnoi = Elista, *Russia* **25 E7** 46 16N 44 14 E
Steppe, *Asia* **28 D9** 50 0N 50 0 E
Sterkstroom, *S. Africa* **56 E4** 31 32S 26 32 E
Sterling, *Colo., U.S.A.* **80 E3** 40 37N 103 13W
Sterling, *Ill., U.S.A.* **80 E10** 41 48N 89 42W
Sterling, *Kans., U.S.A.* **80 F5** 38 13N 98 12W
Sterling City, *U.S.A.* **81 K4** 31 51N 101 0W
Sterling Heights, *U.S.A.* **76 D4** 42 35N 83 0W
Sterling Run, *U.S.A.* **78 E6** 41 25N 78 12W
Sterlitamak, *Russia* **24 D10** 53 40N 56 0 E
Stérnes, *Greece* **23 D6** 35 30N 24 9 E
Stettin = Szczecin, *Poland* **16 B8** 53 27N 14 27 E
Stettiner Haff, *Germany* **16 B8** 53 47N 14 15 E
Stettler, *Canada* **72 C6** 52 19N 112 40W
Steubenville, *U.S.A.* **78 F4** 40 22N 80 37W
Stevenage, *U.K.* **11 F7** 51 55N 0 13W
Stevens Point, *U.S.A.* **80 C10** 44 31N 89 34W
Stevenson, *U.S.A.* **84 E5** 45 42N 121 53W
Stevenson L., *Canada* **73 C9** 53 55N 96 0W
Stevensville, *U.S.A.* **82 C6** 46 30N 114 5W
Stewart, *B.C., Canada* **72 B3** 55 56N 129 57W
Stewart, *N.W.T., Canada* **68 B6** 63 19N 139 26W
Stewart, *U.S.A.* **84 F7** 39 5N 119 46W
Stewart, C., *Australia* **62 A1** 11 57S 134 56 E
Stewart, I., *Chile* **96 G2** 54 50S 71 15W
Stewart I., *N.Z.* **59 M1** 46 58S 167 54 E
Stewarts Point, *U.S.A.* **84 G3** 38 39N 123 24W
Stewartville, *U.S.A.* **80 D8** 43 51N 92 29W
Stewiacke, *Canada* **71 C7** 45 9N 63 22W
Steynsburg, *S. Africa* **56 E4** 31 15S 25 49 E
Steyr, *Austria* **16 D8** 48 3N 14 25 E
Steytlerville, *S. Africa* **56 E3** 33 17S 24 19 E
Stigler, *U.S.A.* **81 H7** 35 15N 95 8W
Stikine →, *Canada* **72 B2** 56 40N 132 30W
Stilfontein, *S. Africa* **56 D4** 26 51S 26 50 E
Stillwater, *N.Z.* **59 K3** 42 27S 171 20 E
Stillwater, *Minn., U.S.A.* **80 C8** 45 3N 92 49W
Stillwater, *N.Y., U.S.A.* **79 D11** 42 55N 73 41W
Stillwater, *Okla., U.S.A.* **81 G6** 36 7N 97 4W
Stillwater Range, *U.S.A.* **82 G4** 39 50N 118 5W
Stillwater Reservoir, *U.S.A.* **79 C9** 43 54N 75 3W
Stilwell, *U.S.A.* **81 H7** 35 49N 94 38W
Štip, *Macedonia* **21 D10** 41 42N 22 10 E
Stirling, *Canada* **78 B7** 44 18N 77 33W
Stirling, *U.K.* **12 E5** 56 8N 3 57W
Stirling □, *U.K.* **12 E4** 56 12N 4 18W
Stirling Ra., *Australia* **61 F2** 34 23S 118 0 E
Stittsville, *Canada* **79 A9** 45 15N 75 55W
Stjernøya, *Norway* **8 A20** 70 20N 22 40 E
Stjørdalshalsen, *Norway* **8 E14** 63 29N 10 51 E
Stockerau, *Austria* **16 D9** 48 24N 16 12 E
Stockholm, *Sweden* **9 G18** 59 20N 18 3 E
Stockport, *U.K.* **10 D5** 53 25N 2 9W
Stocksbridge, *U.K.* **10 D6** 53 29N 1 35W
Stockton, *Calif., U.S.A.* **84 H5** 37 58N 121 17W
Stockton, *Kans., U.S.A.* **80 F5** 39 26N 99 16W
Stockton, *Mo., U.S.A.* **81 G8** 37 42N 93 48W
Stockton-on-Tees, *U.K.* **10 C6** 54 35N 1 19W
Stockton-on-Tees □, *U.K.* **10 C6** 54 35N 1 19W
Stockton Plateau, *U.S.A.* **81 K3** 30 30N 102 30W
Stoeng Treng, *Cambodia* **38 F5** 13 31N 105 58 E
Stoer, Pt. of, *U.K.* **12 C3** 58 16N 5 23W
Stoke-on-Trent, *U.K.* **10 D5** 53 1N 2 11W
Stoke-on-Trent □, *U.K.* **10 D5** 53 1N 2 11W
Stokes Pt., *Australia* **62 G3** 40 10S 143 56 E
Stokes Ra., *Australia* **60 C5** 15 50S 130 50 E
Stokksnes, *Iceland* **8 D6** 64 14N 14 58W
Stokmarknes, *Norway* **8 B16** 68 34N 14 54 E
Stolac, *Bos.-H.* **21 C7** 43 5N 17 59 E
Stolbovoy, Ostrov, *Russia* **27 D17** 74 44N 135 14 E
Stolbtsy = Stowbtsy, *Belarus* **17 B14** 53 30N 26 43 E
Stolin, *Belarus* **17 C14** 51 53N 26 50 E
Stomíon, *Greece* **23 D5** 35 21N 23 32 E
Stone, *U.K.* **10 E5** 52 55N 2 9W
Stoneboro, *U.S.A.* **78 E4** 41 20N 80 7W
Stonehaven, *U.K.* **12 E6** 56 59N 2 12W
Stonehenge, *Australia* **62 C3** 24 22S 143 17 E
Stonehenge, *U.K.* **11 F6** 51 9N 1 45W
Stonewall, *Canada* **73 C9** 50 10N 97 19W
Stony L., *Man., Canada* **73 B9** 58 51N 98 40W
Stony L., *Ont., Canada* **78 B6** 44 30N 78 5W
Stony Point, *U.S.A.* **79 E11** 41 14N 73 59W
Stony Pt., *U.S.A.* **79 C8** 43 50N 76 18W
Stony Rapids, *Canada* **73 B7** 59 16N 105 50W
Stony Tunguska = Tunguska, Podkamennaya →, *Russia* **27 C10** 61 50N 90 13 E
Stonyford, *U.S.A.* **84 F4** 39 23N 122 33W
Stora Lulevatten, *Sweden* **8 C18** 67 10N 19 30 E
Storavan, *Sweden* **8 D18** 65 45N 18 10 E
Stord, *Norway* **9 G11** 59 52N 5 23 E
Store Bælt, *Denmark* **9 J14** 55 20N 11 0 E
Storm B., *Australia* **62 G4** 43 10S 147 30 E
Storm Lake, *U.S.A.* **80 D7** 42 39N 95 13W
Stormberge, *S. Africa* **56 E4** 31 16S 26 17 E
Stormsrivier, *S. Africa* **56 E3** 33 59S 23 52 E
Stornoway, *U.K.* **12 C2** 58 13N 6 23W
Storozhinets = Storozhynets, *Ukraine* **17 D13** 48 14N 25 45 E
Storozhynets, *Ukraine* **17 D13** 48 14N 25 45 E
Storrs, *U.S.A.* **79 E12** 41 49N 72 15W
Storsjön, *Sweden* **8 E16** 63 9N 14 30 E
Storuman, *Sweden* **8 D17** 65 5N 17 10 E
Storuman, sjö, *Sweden* **8 D17** 65 13N 16 50 E
Stouffville, *Canada* **78 C5** 43 58N 79 15W
Stoughton, *Canada* **73 D8** 49 40N 103 0W
Stour →, *Dorset, U.K.* **11 G6** 50 43N 1 47W
Stour →, *Kent, U.K.* **11 F9** 51 18N 1 22 E
Stour →, *Suffolk, U.K.* **11 F9** 51 57N 1 4 E
Stourbridge, *U.K.* **11 E5** 52 28N 2 8W
Stout L., *Canada* **73 C10** 52 0N 94 40W
Stove Pipe Wells Village, *U.S.A.* **85 J9** 36 35N 117 11W
Stow, *U.S.A.* **78 E3** 41 10N 81 27W
Stowbtsy, *Belarus* **17 B14** 53 30N 26 43 E
Stowmarket, *U.K.* **11 E9** 52 12N 1 0 E
Strabane, *U.K.* **13 B4** 54 50N 7 27W
Strahan, *Australia* **62 G4** 42 9S 145 20 E
Stralsund, *Germany* **16 A7** 54 18N 13 4 E
Strand, *S. Africa* **56 E2** 34 9S 18 48 E
Stranda, *Møre og Romsdal, Norway* **9 E12** 62 19N 6 58 E
Stranda, *Nord-Trøndelag, Norway* **8 E14** 63 33N 10 14 E
Strangford L., *U.K.* **13 B6** 54 30N 5 37W
Stranraer, *U.K.* **12 G3** 54 54N 5 1W
Strasbourg, *Canada* **73 C8** 51 4N 104 55W
Strasbourg, *France* **18 B7** 48 35N 7 42 E
Stratford, *Canada* **78 C4** 43 23N 81 0W
Stratford, *N.Z.* **59 H5** 39 20S 174 19 E
Stratford, *Calif., U.S.A.* **84 J7** 36 11N 119 49W
Stratford, *Conn., U.S.A.* **79 E11** 41 12N 73 8W
Stratford, *Tex., U.S.A.* **81 G3** 36 20N 102 4W
Stratford-upon-Avon, *U.K.* **11 E6** 52 12N 1 42W
Strath Spey, *U.K.* **12 D5** 57 9N 3 49W
Strathalbyn, *Australia* **63 F2** 35 13S 138 53 E
Strathaven, *U.K.* **12 F4** 55 40N 4 5W
Strathcona Prov. Park, *Canada* **72 D3** 49 38N 125 40W
Strathmore, *Canada* **72 C6** 51 5N 113 18W
Strathmore, *U.K.* **12 E5** 56 37N 3 7W
Strathmore, *U.S.A.* **84 J7** 36 9N 119 4W
Strathnaver, *Canada* **72 C4** 53 20N 122 33W
Strathpeffer, *U.K.* **12 D4** 57 35N 4 32W
Strathroy, *Canada* **78 D3** 42 58N 81 38W
Strathy Pt., *U.K.* **12 C4** 58 36N 4 1W
Strattanville, *U.S.A.* **78 E5** 41 12N 79 19W
Stratton, *U.S.A.* **79 A14** 45 8N 70 26W
Stratton Mt., *U.S.A.* **79 C12** 43 4N 72 55W
Straubing, *Germany* **16 D7** 48 52N 12 34 E
Straumnes, *Iceland* **8 C2** 66 26N 23 8W
Strawberry →, *U.S.A.* **82 F8** 40 10N 110 24W
Streaky B., *Australia* **63 E1** 32 48S 134 13 E
Streaky Bay, *Australia* **63 E1** 32 51S 134 18 E
Streator, *U.S.A.* **80 E10** 41 8N 88 50W
Streetsboro, *U.S.A.* **78 E3** 41 14N 81 21W
Streetsville, *Canada* **78 C5** 43 35N 79 42W
Strelka, *Russia* **27 D10** 58 5N 93 3 E
Streng →, *Cambodia* **38 F4** 13 12N 103 37 E
Streymoy, *Færoe Is.* **8 E9** 62 8N 7 5W
Strezhevoy, *Russia* **26 C8** 60 42N 77 34 E
Strimón →, *Greece* **21 D10** 40 46N 23 51 E
Strimonikós Kólpos, *Greece* **21 D11** 40 33N 24 0 E
Stroma, *U.K.* **12 C5** 58 41N 3 7W
Strómboli, *Italy* **20 E6** 38 47N 15 13 E
Stromeferry, *U.K.* **12 D3** 57 21N 5 33W
Stromness, *U.K.* **12 C5** 58 58N 3 17W
Stromsburg, *U.S.A.* **80 E6** 41 7N 97 36W
Strömstad, *Sweden* **9 G14** 58 56N 11 10 E
Strömsund, *Sweden* **8 E16** 63 51N 15 33 E
Strongsville, *U.S.A.* **78 E3** 41 19N 81 50W
Stronsay, *U.K.* **12 B6** 59 7N 2 35W
Stroud, *U.K.* **11 F5** 51 45N 2 13W
Stroud Road, *Australia* **63 E5** 32 18S 151 57 E
Stroudsburg, *U.S.A.* **79 F9** 40 59N 75 12W
Stroumbi, *Cyprus* **23 E11** 34 53N 32 29 E
Struer, *Denmark* **9 H13** 56 30N 8 35 E
Strumica, *Macedonia* **21 D10** 41 28N 22 41 E
Struthers, *Canada* **70 C2** 48 41N 85 51W
Struthers, *U.S.A.* **78 E4** 41 4N 80 39W
Stryker, *U.S.A.* **82 B6** 48 41N 114 46W
Stryy, *Ukraine* **17 D12** 49 16N 23 48 E
Strzelecki Cr. →, *Australia* **63 D2** 29 37S 139 59 E
Stuart, *Fla., U.S.A.* **77 M5** 27 12N 80 15W
Stuart, *Nebr., U.S.A.* **80 D5** 42 36N 99 8W
Stuart →, *Canada* **72 C4** 54 0N 123 35W
Stuart Bluff Ra., *Australia* **60 D5** 22 50S 131 52 E
Stuart L., *Canada* **72 C4** 54 30N 124 30W
Stuart Ra., *Australia* **63 D1** 29 10S 134 56 E
Stull, L., *Canada* **70 B1** 54 24N 92 0W
Stung Treng = Stoeng Treng, *Cambodia* **38 F5** 13 31N 105 58 E
Stupart →, *Canada* **70 A1** 56 0N 93 25W
Sturgeon B., *Canada* **73 C9** 52 0N 97 50W
Sturgeon Bay, *U.S.A.* **76 C2** 44 50N 87 23W
Sturgeon Falls, *Canada* **70 C4** 46 25N 79 57W
Sturgeon L., *Alta., Canada* **72 B5** 55 6N 117 32W
Sturgeon L., *Ont., Canada* **70 C1** 50 0N 90 45W
Sturgeon L., *Ont., Canada* **78 B6** 44 28N 78 43W
Sturgis, *Canada* **73 C8** 51 56N 102 36W
Sturgis, *Mich., U.S.A.* **76 E3** 41 48N 85 25W
Sturgis, *S. Dak., U.S.A.* **80 C3** 44 25N 103 31W
Sturt Cr. →, *Australia* **60 C4** 19 8S 127 50 E
Stutterheim, *S. Africa* **56 E4** 32 33S 27 28 E
Stuttgart, *Germany* **16 D5** 48 48N 9 11 E
Stuttgart, *U.S.A.* **81 H9** 34 30N 91 33W
Stuyvesant, *U.S.A.* **79 D11** 42 23N 73 45W
Stykkishólmur, *Iceland* **8 D2** 65 2N 22 40W
Styria = Steiermark □, *Austria* **16 E8** 47 26N 15 0 E
Su Xian = Suzhou, *China* **34 H9** 33 41N 116 59 E
Suakin, *Sudan* **51 E13** 19 8N 37 20 E
Suan, *N. Korea* **35 E14** 38 42N 126 22 E
Suaqui, *Mexico* **86 B3** 29 12N 109 41W
Suar, *India* **43 E8** 29 2N 79 3 E
Subang, *Indonesia* **37 G12** 6 34S 107 45 E
Subansiri →, *India* **41 F18** 26 48N 93 50 E
Subarnarekha →, *India* **43 H12** 22 34N 87 24 E
Subayhah, *Si. Arabia* **44 D3** 30 2N 38 50 E
Subi, *Indonesia* **39 L7** 2 58N 108 50 E
Subotica, *Serbia, Yug.* **21 A8** 46 6N 19 39 E
Suceava, *Romania* **17 E14** 47 38N 26 16 E
Suchan, *Russia* **30 C6** 43 8N 133 9 E
Suchitoto, *El Salv.* **88 D2** 13 56N 89 0W
Suchou = Suzhou, *China* **33 C7** 31 19N 120 38 E
Süchow = Xuzhou, *China* **35 G9** 34 18N 117 10 E
Suck →, *Ireland* **13 C3** 53 17N 8 3W
Sucre, *Bolivia* **92 G5** 19 0S 65 15W
Sucuriú →, *Brazil* **93 H8** 20 47S 51 38W
Sud, Pte. du, *Canada* **71 C7** 49 3N 62 14W
Sud-Kivu □, *Dem. Rep. of the Congo* **54 C2** 3 30S 28 0 E
Sud-Ouest, Pte. du, *Canada* **71 C7** 49 23N 63 36W
Sudan, *U.S.A.* **81 H3** 34 4N 102 32W
Sudan ■, *Africa* **51 E11** 15 0N 30 0 E
Sudbury, *Canada* **70 C3** 46 30N 81 0W
Sudbury, *U.K.* **11 E8** 52 2N 0 45 E
Sûdd, *Sudan* **51 G12** 8 20N 30 0 E
Sudeten Mts. = Sudety, *Europe* **17 C9** 50 20N 16 45 E
Sudety, *Europe* **17 C9** 50 20N 16 45 E
Suðuroy, *Færoe Is.* **8 F9** 61 32N 6 50W
Sudi, *Tanzania* **55 E4** 10 11S 39 57 E
Sudirman, Pegunungan, *Indonesia* **37 E9** 4 30S 137 0 E
Sueca, *Spain* **19 C5** 39 12N 0 21W
Suemez I., *U.S.A.* **72 B2** 55 15N 133 20W
Suez = El Suweis, *Egypt* **51 C12** 29 58N 32 31 E
Suez, G. of = Suweis, Khalîg el, *Egypt* **51 C12** 28 40N 33 0 E
Suez Canal = Suweis, Qanâ es, *Egypt* **51 B12** 31 0N 32 20 E
Suffield, *Canada* **72 C6** 50 12N 111 10W
Suffolk, *U.S.A.* **76 G7** 36 44N 76 35W
Suffolk □, *U.K.* **11 E9** 52 16N 1 0 E
Sugargrove, *U.S.A.* **78 E5** 41 59N 79 21W
Sugarive →, *India* **43 F12** 26 16N 86 24 E
Sugluk = Salluit, *Canada* **69 B12** 62 14N 75 38W
Şuḩār, *Oman* **45 E8** 24 20N 56 40 E
Sühbaatar □, *Mongolia* **34 B8** 45 30N 114 0 E
Suhl, *Germany* **16 C6** 50 36N 10 42 E
Sui, *Pakistan* **42 E3** 28 37N 69 19 E
Sui Xian, *China* **34 G8** 34 25N 115 2 E
Suide, *China* **34 F6** 37 30N 110 12 E
Suifenhe, *China* **35 B16** 44 25N 131 10 E
Suihua, *China* **33 B7** 46 32N 126 55 E
Suining, *China* **35 H9** 33 56N 117 58 E
Suiping, *China* **34 H7** 33 10N 113 59 E
Suir →, *Ireland* **13 D4** 52 16N 7 9W
Suisun City, *U.S.A.* **84 G4** 38 15N 122 2W
Suiyang, *China* **35 B16** 44 30N 130 56 E
Suizhong, *China* **35 D11** 40 21N 120 20 E
Sujangarh, *India* **42 F6** 27 42N 74 31 E
Sukabumi, *Indonesia* **37 G12** 6 56S 106 50 E
Sukadana, *Indonesia* **36 E4** 1 10S 110 0 E
Sukagawa, *Japan* **31 F10** 37 17N 140 23 E
Sukaraja, *Indonesia* **36 E4** 2 28S 110 25 E
Sukarnapura = Jayapura, *Indonesia* **37 E10** 2 28S 140 38 E
Sukch'ŏn, *N. Korea* **35 E13** 39 22N 125 35 E
Sukhona →, *Russia* **24 C6** 61 15N 46 39 E
Sukhothai, *Thailand* **38 D2** 17 1N 99 49 E
Sukhumi = Sokhumi, *Georgia* **25 F7** 43 0N 41 0 E
Sukkur, *Pakistan* **42 F3** 27 42N 68 54 E
Sukkur Barrage, *Pakistan* **42 F3** 27 40N 68 50 E
Sukri →, *India* **42 G4** 25 4N 71 43 E
Sukumo, *Japan* **31 H6** 32 56N 132 44 E
Sukunka →, *Canada* **72 B4** 55 45N 121 15W
Sula, Kepulauan, *Indonesia* **37 E7** 1 45S 125 0 E
Sulaco →, *Honduras* **88 C2** 15 2N 87 44W
Sulaiman Range, *Pakistan* **42 D3** 30 30N 69 50 E
Sülär, *Iran* **45 D6** 31 53N 51 54 E
Sulawesi □, *Indonesia* **37 E6** 2 0S 120 0 E
Sulawesi Sea = Celebes Sea, *Indonesia* **37 D6** 3 0N 123 0 E
Sulawesi Selatan □, *Indonesia* **37 E6** 2 30S 120 0 E
Sulawesi Utara □, *Indonesia* **37 D6** 1 0N 122 30 E
Sulima, *S. Leone* **50 G3** 6 58N 11 32W
Sulina, *Romania* **17 F15** 45 10N 29 40 E
Sulitjelma, *Norway* **8 C17** 67 9N 16 3 E
Sullana, *Peru* **92 D2** 4 52S 80 39W
Sullivan, *Ill., U.S.A.* **80 F10** 39 36N 88 37W
Sullivan, *Ind., U.S.A.* **76 F2** 39 6N 87 24W
Sullivan, *Mo., U.S.A.* **80 F9** 38 13N 91 10W
Sullivan Bay, *Canada* **72 C3** 50 55N 126 50W
Sullivan I. = Lambi Kyun, *Burma* **39 G2** 10 50N 98 20 E
Sulphur, *La., U.S.A.* **81 K8** 30 14N 93 23W
Sulphur, *Okla., U.S.A.* **81 H6** 34 31N 96 58W
Sulphur Pt., *Canada* **72 A6** 60 56N 114 48W
Sulphur Springs, *U.S.A.* **81 J7** 33 8N 95 36W
Sultan, *Canada* **70 C3** 47 36N 82 47W
Sultan, *U.S.A.* **84 C5** 47 52N 121 49W
Sultanpur, *India* **43 F10** 26 18N 82 4 E
Sultanpur, *Mad. P., India* **42 H8** 23 9N 77 56 E
Sultanpur, *Punjab, India* **42 D6** 31 13N 75 11 E
Sulu Arch., *Phil.* **37 C6** 6 0N 121 0 E
Sulu Sea, *E. Indies* **37 C6** 8 0N 120 0 E
Suluq, *Libya* **51 B10** 31 44N 20 14 E
Sulzberger Ice Shelf, *Antarctica* **5 D10** 78 0S 150 0 E
Sumalata, *Indonesia* **37 D6** 1 0N 122 31 E
Sumampa, *Argentina* **94 B3** 29 25S 63 29W
Sumatera □, *Indonesia* **36 D2** 0 40N 100 20 E
Sumatera Barat □, *Indonesia* **36 E2** 1 0S 101 0 E
Sumatera Utara □, *Indonesia* **36 D1** 2 30N 98 0 E
Sumatra = Sumatera □, *Indonesia* **36 D2** 0 40N 100 20 E
Sumba, *Indonesia* **37 F5** 9 45S 119 35 E
Sumba, Selat, *Indonesia* **37 F5** 9 0S 118 40 E
Sumbawa, *Indonesia* **36 F5** 8 26S 117 30 E
Sumbawa Besar, *Indonesia* **36 F5** 8 30S 117 26 E
Sumbawanga □, *Tanzania* **52 F6** 8 0S 31 30 E
Sumbe, *Angola* **52 G2** 11 10S 13 48 E
Sumburgh Hd., *U.K.* **12 B7** 59 52N 1 17W
Sumdeo, *India* **43 D8** 31 26N 78 44 E
Sumdo, *India* **43 B8** 35 6N 78 41 E
Sumedang, *Indonesia* **37 G12** 6 52S 107 55 E
Šumen = Shumen, *Bulgaria* **21 C12** 43 18N 26 55 E
Sumenep, *Indonesia* **37 G15** 7 1S 113 52 E
Sumgait = Sumqayıt, *Azerbaijan* **25 F8** 40 34N 49 38 E
Summer L., *U.S.A.* **82 E3** 42 50N 120 45W
Summerland, *Canada* **72 D5** 49 32N 119 41W
Summerside, *Canada* **71 C7** 46 24N 63 47W
Summersville, *U.S.A.* **76 F5** 38 17N 80 51W
Summerville, *Ga., U.S.A.* **77 H3** 34 29N 85 21W
Summerville, *S.C., U.S.A.* **77 J5** 33 1N 80 11W
Summit Lake, *Canada* **72 C4** 54 20N 122 40W
Summit Peak, *U.S.A.* **83 H10** 37 21N 106 42W
Sumner, *Iowa, U.S.A.* **80 D8** 42 51N 92 6W
Sumner, *Wash., U.S.A.* **84 C4** 47 12N 122 14W
Sumoto, *Japan* **31 G7** 34 21N 134 54 E
Šumperk, *Czech Rep.* **17 D9** 49 59N 16 59 E
Sumqayıt, *Azerbaijan* **25 F8** 40 34N 49 38 E
Sumter, *U.S.A.* **77 J5** 33 55N 80 21W
Sumy, *Ukraine* **25 D5** 50 57N 34 50 E
Sun City, *Ariz., U.S.A.* **83 K7** 33 36N 112 17W
Sun City, *Calif., U.S.A.* **85 M9** 33 42N 117 11W
Sun City Center, *U.S.A.* **77 M4** 27 43N 82 18W
Sun Lakes, *U.S.A.* **83 K8** 33 10N 111 52W
Sun Valley, *U.S.A.* **82 E6** 43 42N 114 21W
Sunagawa, *Japan* **30 C10** 43 29N 141 55 E
Sunan, *N. Korea* **35 E13** 39 15N 125 40 E
Sunart, L., *U.K.* **12 E3** 56 42N 5 43W
Sunburst, *U.S.A.* **82 B8** 48 53N 111 55W
Sunbury, *Australia* **63 F3** 37 35S 144 44 E
Sunbury, *U.S.A.* **79 F8** 40 52N 76 48W
Sunchales, *Argentina* **94 C3** 30 58S 61 35W
Suncho Corral, *Argentina* **94 B3** 27 55S 63 27W
Sunch'ŏn, *S. Korea* **35 G14** 34 52N 127 31 E
Suncook, *U.S.A.* **79 C13** 43 8N 71 27W
Sunda, Selat, *Indonesia* **36 F3** 6 20S 105 30 E
Sunda Is., *Indonesia* **28 K14** 5 0S 105 0 E
Sunda Str. = Sunda, Selat, *Indonesia* **36 F3** 6 20S 105 30 E
Sundance, *Canada* **73 B10** 56 32N 94 4W
Sundance, *U.S.A.* **80 C2** 44 24N 104 23W
Sundar Nagar, *India* **42 D7** 31 32N 76 53 E
Sundarbans, The, *Asia* **41 J16** 22 0N 89 0 E
Sundargarh, *India* **41 H14** 22 4N 84 5 E
Sundays = Sondags →, *S. Africa* **56 E4** 33 44S 25 51 E
Sunderland, *Canada* **78 B5** 44 16N 79 4W
Sunderland, *U.K.* **10 C6** 54 55N 1 23W
Sundre, *Canada* **72 C6** 51 49N 114 38W
Sundsvall, *Sweden* **9 E17** 62 23N 17 17 E
Sung Hei, *Vietnam* **39 G6** 10 20N 106 2 E
Sungai Kolok, *Thailand* **39 J3** 6 2N 101 58 E
Sungai Lembing, *Malaysia* **39 L4** 3 55N 103 3 E
Sungai Petani, *Malaysia* **39 K3** 5 37N 100 30 E
Sungaigerong, *Indonesia* **36 E2** 2 59S 104 52 E
Sungailiat, *Indonesia* **36 E3** 1 51S 106 8 E
Sungaipenuh, *Indonesia* **36 E2** 2 1S 101 20 E
Sungari = Songhua Jiang →, *China* **33 B8** 47 45N 132 30 E
Songhua Chiang = Songhua Jiang →, *China* **33 B8** 47 45N 132 30 E
Sunland Park, *U.S.A.* **83 L10** 31 50N 106 40W
Sunndalsøra, *Norway* **9 E13** 62 40N 8 33 E
Sunnyside, *U.S.A.* **82 C3** 46 20N 120 0W
Sunnyvale, *U.S.A.* **84 H4** 37 23N 122 2W
Suntar, *Russia* **27 C12** 62 15N 117 30 E
Suomenselkä, *Finland* **8 E21** 62 52N 24 0 E
Suomussalmi, *Finland* **8 D23** 64 54N 29 10 E
Suoyarvi, *Russia* **24 B5** 62 3N 32 20 E
Supai, *U.S.A.* **83 H7** 36 15N 112 41W
Supaul, *India* **43 F12** 26 10N 86 40 E
Superior, *Ariz., U.S.A.* **83 K8** 33 18N 111 6W
Superior, *Mont., U.S.A.* **82 C6** 47 12N 114 53W
Superior, *Nebr., U.S.A.* **80 E5** 40 1N 98 4W
Superior, *Wis., U.S.A.* **80 B8** 46 44N 92 6W
Superior, L., *N. Amer.* **70 C2** 47 0N 87 0W
Suphan Buri, *Thailand* **38 E3** 14 14N 100 10 E
Suphan Dağı, *Turkey* **44 B4** 38 54N 42 48 E
Supiori, *Indonesia* **37 E9** 1 0S 136 0 E
Supung Shuiku, *China* **35 D13** 40 35N 124 50 E
Sûq Suwayq, *Si. Arabia* **44 E3** 24 23N 38 27 E
Suqian, *China* **35 H10** 33 54N 118 8 E
Sūr, *Lebanon* **47 B4** 33 19N 35 16 E
Sūr, *Oman* **46 C6** 22 34N 59 32 E
Sur, Pt., *U.S.A.* **84 J5** 36 18N 121 54W
Sura →, *Russia* **24 C8** 56 6N 46 0 E
Surab, *Pakistan* **42 E2** 28 25N 66 15 E
Surabaja = Surabaya, *Indonesia* **37 G15** 7 17S 112 45 E
Surabaya, *Indonesia* **37 G15** 7 17S 112 45 E
Surakarta, *Indonesia* **37 G14** 7 35S 110 48 E
Surat, *Australia* **63 D4** 27 10S 149 6 E
Surat, *India* **40 J8** 21 12N 72 55 E
Surat Thani, *Thailand* **39 H2** 9 6N 99 20 E
Suratgarh, *India* **42 E5** 29 18N 73 55 E
Surendranagar, *India* **42 H4** 22 45N 71 40 E
Surf, *U.S.A.* **85 L6** 34 41N 120 36W
Surgut, *Russia* **26 C8** 61 14N 73 20 E
Suriapet, *India* **40 L11** 17 10N 79 40 E
Surigao, *Phil.* **37 C7** 9 47N 125 29 E
Surin, *Thailand* **38 E4** 14 50N 103 34 E
Surin Nua, Ko, *Thailand* **39 H1** 9 30N 97 55 E
Surinam ■, *S. Amer.* **93 C7** 4 0N 56 0W
Suriname = Surinam ■, *S. Amer.* **93 C7** 4 0N 56 0W
Suriname →, *Surinam* **93 B7** 5 50N 55 15W
Sūrmaq, *Iran* **45 D7** 31 3N 52 48 E
Surrey □, *U.K.* **11 F7** 51 15N 0 31W
Sursand, *India* **43 F11** 26 39N 85 43 E
Sursar →, *India* **43 F12** 26 14N 87 3 E

Surt, Libya 51 B9 31 11N 16 39 E
Surt, Khalīj, Libya 51 B9 31 40N 18 30 E
Surtanahu, Pakistan 42 F4 26 22N 70 0 E
Surtsey, Iceland 8 E3 63 20N 20 30W
Suruga-Wan, Japan 31 G9 34 45N 138 30 E
Susaki, Japan 31 H6 33 22N 133 17 E
Sūsangerd, Iran 45 D6 31 35N 48 6 E
Susanville, U.S.A. 82 F3 40 25N 120 39W
Susner, India 42 H7 23 57N 76 5 E
Susquehanna, U.S.A. 79 E9 41 57N 75 36W
Susquehanna —►, U.S.A. 79 G8 39 33N 76 5W
Susques, Argentina 94 A2 23 35S 66 25W
Sussex, Canada 71 C6 45 45N 65 37W
Sussex, U.S.A. 79 E10 41 13N 74 37W
Sussex, E. □, U.K. 11 G8 51 0N 0 20 E
Sussex, W. □, U.K. 11 G7 51 0N 0 30W
Sustut —►, Canada 72 B3 56 20N 127 30W
Susuman, Russia 27 C15 62 47N 148 10 E
Susunu, Indonesia 37 E8 3 20S 133 25 E
Susurluk, Turkey 21 E13 39 54N 28 8 E
Sutherland, S. Africa 56 E3 32 24S 20 40 E
Sutherland, U.S.A. 80 E4 41 10N 101 8W
Sutherland Falls, N.Z. 59 L1 44 48S 167 46 E
Sutherlin, U.S.A. 82 E2 43 23N 123 19W
Suthri, India 42 H3 23 3N 68 55 E
Sutlej —►, Pakistan 42 E4 29 23N 71 3 E
Sutter, U.S.A. 84 F5 39 10N 121 45W
Sutter Creek, U.S.A. 84 G6 38 24N 120 48W
Sutton, Canada 79 A12 45 6N 72 37W
Sutton, Nebr., U.S.A. 80 E6 40 36N 97 52W
Sutton, W. Va., U.S.A. 76 F5 38 40N 80 43W
Sutton —►, Canada 70 A3 55 15N 83 45W
Sutton Coldfield, U.K. 11 E6 52 35N 1 49W
Sutton in Ashfield, U.K. 10 D6 53 8N 1 16W
Sutton L., Canada 70 B3 54 15N 84 42W
Suttor —►, Australia 62 C4 21 36S 147 2 E
Suttsu, Japan 30 C10 42 48N 140 14 E
Suva, Fiji 59 D8 18 6S 178 30 E
Suva Planina, Serbia, Yug. 21 C10 43 10N 22 5 E
Suvorov Is. = Suwarrow Is., Cook Is. 65 J11 15 0S 163 0W
Suwałki, Poland 17 A12 54 8N 22 59 E
Suwannaphum, Thailand 38 E4 15 33N 103 47 E
Suwannee —►, U.S.A. 77 L4 29 17N 83 10W
Suwanose-Jima, Japan 31 K4 29 38N 129 43 E
Suwarrow Is., Cook Is. 65 J11 15 0S 163 0W
Suwayq aş Şuqban, Iraq 44 D5 31 32N 46 7 E
Suweis, Khalîg el, Egypt 51 C12 28 40N 33 0 E
Suweis, Qanâ es, Egypt 51 B12 31 0N 32 20 E
Suwŏn, S. Korea 35 F14 37 17N 127 1 E
Suzdal, Russia 24 C7 56 29N 40 26 E
Suzhou, Anhui, China 34 H9 33 41N 116 59 E
Suzhou, Jiangsu, China 33 C7 31 19N 120 38 E
Suzu, Japan 31 F8 37 25N 137 17 E
Suzu-Misaki, Japan 31 F8 37 31N 137 21 E
Suzuka, Japan 31 G8 34 55N 136 36 E
Svalbard, Arctic 4 B8 78 0N 17 0 E
Svappavaara, Sweden 8 C19 67 40N 21 3 E
Svartisen, Norway 8 C15 66 40N 13 50 E
Svay Chek, Cambodia 38 F4 13 48N 102 58 E
Svay Rieng, Cambodia 39 G5 11 9N 105 45 E
Svealand □, Sweden 9 G16 60 20N 15 0 E
Sveg, Sweden 9 E16 62 2N 14 21 E
Svendborg, Denmark 9 J14 55 4N 10 35 E
Sverdlovsk = Yekaterinburg, Russia 26 D7 56 50N 60 30 E
Sverdrup Is., Canada 4 B3 79 0N 97 0W
Svetlaya, Russia 30 A9 46 33N 138 18 E
Svetlogorsk = Svyetlahorsk, Belarus 17 B15 52 38N 29 46 E
Svir —►, Russia 24 B5 60 30N 32 48 E
Svishtov, Bulgaria 21 C11 43 36N 25 23 E
Svislach, Belarus 17 B13 53 3N 24 2 E
Svobodnyy, Russia 27 D13 51 20N 128 0 E
Svolvær, Norway 8 B16 68 15N 14 34 E
Svyetlahorsk, Belarus 17 B15 52 38N 29 46 E
Swabian Alps = Schwäbische Alb, Germany 16 D5 48 20N 9 30 E
Swainsboro, U.S.A. 77 J4 32 36N 82 20W
Swakopmund, Namibia 56 C1 22 37S 14 30 E
Swale —►, U.K. 10 C6 54 5N 1 20W
Swan —►, Australia 61 F2 32 3S 115 45 E
Swan —►, Canada 73 C8 52 30N 100 45W
Swan Hill, Australia 63 F3 35 20S 143 33 E
Swan Hills, Canada 72 C5 54 43N 115 24W
Swan Is., W. Indies 88 C3 17 22N 83 57W
Swan L., Canada 73 C8 52 30N 100 40W
Swan Peak, U.S.A. 82 C7 47 43N 113 38W
Swan Ra., U.S.A. 82 C7 48 0N 113 45W
Swan Reach, Australia 63 E2 34 35S 139 37 E
Swan River, Canada 73 C8 52 10N 101 16W
Swanage, U.K. 11 G6 50 36N 1 58W
Swansea, Australia 62 G4 42 8S 148 4 E
Swansea, Canada 78 C5 43 38N 79 28W
Swansea, U.K. 11 F4 51 37N 3 57W
Swansea □, U.K. 11 F3 51 38N 4 3W
Swar —►, Pakistan 43 B5 34 40N 72 5 E
Swartberge, S. Africa 56 E3 33 20S 22 0 E
Swartmodder, S. Africa 56 D3 28 1S 20 32 E
Swartruggens, S. Africa 56 D4 25 39S 26 42 E
Swastika, Canada 70 C3 48 7N 80 6W
Swatow = Shantou, China 33 D6 23 18N 116 40 E
Swaziland ■, Africa 57 D5 26 30S 31 30 E
Sweden ■, Europe 9 G16 57 0N 15 0 E
Sweet Home, U.S.A. 82 D2 44 24N 122 44W
Sweetgrass, U.S.A. 82 B8 48 59N 111 58W
Sweetwater, Nev., U.S.A. 84 G7 38 27N 119 9W
Sweetwater, Tenn., U.S.A. 77 H3 35 36N 84 28W
Sweetwater, Tex., U.S.A. 81 J4 32 28N 100 25W
Sweetwater —►, U.S.A. 82 E10 42 31N 107 2W
Swellendam, S. Africa 56 E3 34 1S 20 26 E
Świdnica, Poland 17 C9 50 50N 16 30 E
Świdnik, Poland 17 C12 51 13N 22 39 E
Świebodzin, Poland 16 B8 52 15N 15 31 E
Świecie, Poland 17 B10 53 25N 18 30 E
Swift Current, Canada 73 C7 50 20N 107 45W
Swiftcurrent —►, Canada 73 C7 50 38N 107 44W
Swilly, L., Ireland 13 A4 55 12N 7 33W
Swindon, U.K. 11 F6 51 34N 1 46W
Swindon □, U.K. 11 F6 51 34N 1 46W
Swinemünde = Świnoujście, Poland 16 B8 53 54N 14 16 E
Swinford, Ireland 13 C3 53 57N 8 58W
Świnoujście, Poland 16 B8 53 54N 14 16 E
Switzerland ■, Europe 18 C8 46 30N 8 0 E
Swords, Ireland 13 C5 53 28N 6 13W
Swoyerville, U.S.A. 79 E9 41 18N 75 53W
Sydenham —►, Canada 78 D2 42 33N 82 25W
Sydney, Australia 63 E5 33 53S 151 10 E
Sydney, Canada 71 C7 46 7N 60 7W
Sydney L., Canada 73 C10 50 41N 94 25W
Sydney Mines, Canada 71 C7 46 18N 60 15W
Sydprøven, Greenland 4 C5 60 30N 45 35W
Sydra, G. of = Surt, Khalīj, Libya 51 B9 31 40N 18 30 E
Sykesville, U.S.A. 78 E6 41 3N 78 50W
Syktyvkar, Russia 24 B9 61 45N 50 40 E
Sylacauga, U.S.A. 77 J2 33 10N 86 15W
Sylarna, Sweden 8 E15 63 2N 12 13 E
Sylhet, Bangla. 41 G17 24 54N 91 52 E
Sylt, Germany 16 A5 54 54N 8 22 E
Sylvan Beach, U.S.A. 79 C9 43 12N 75 44W
Sylvan Lake, Canada 72 C6 52 20N 114 3W
Sylvania, U.S.A. 77 J5 32 45N 81 38W
Sylvester, U.S.A. 77 K4 31 32N 83 50W
Sym, Russia 26 C9 60 20N 88 18 E
Symón, Mexico 86 C4 24 42N 102 35W
Synnott Ra., Australia 60 C4 16 30S 125 20 E
Syracuse, Kans., U.S.A. 81 G4 37 59N 101 45W
Syracuse, N.Y., U.S.A. 79 C8 43 3N 76 9W
Syracuse, Nebr., U.S.A. 80 E6 40 39N 96 11W
Syrdarya —►, Kazakstan 26 E7 46 3N 61 0 E
Syria ■, Asia 44 C3 35 0N 38 0 E
Syrian Desert = Shām, Bādiyat ash, Asia 44 C3 32 0N 40 0 E
Syzran, Russia 24 D8 53 12N 48 30 E
Szczecin, Poland 16 B8 53 27N 14 27 E
Szczecinek, Poland 17 B9 53 43N 16 41 E
Szczeciński, Zalew = Stettiner Haff, Germany 16 B8 53 47N 14 15 E
Szczytno, Poland 17 B11 53 33N 21 0 E
Szechwan = Sichuan □, China 32 C5 31 0N 104 0 E
Szeged, Hungary 17 E11 46 16N 20 10 E
Székesfehérvár, Hungary 17 E10 47 15N 18 25 E
Szekszárd, Hungary 17 E10 46 22N 18 42 E
Szentes, Hungary 17 E11 46 39N 20 21 E
Szolnok, Hungary 17 E11 47 10N 20 15 E
Szombathely, Hungary 17 E9 47 14N 16 38 E

T

Ta Khli Khok, Thailand 38 E3 15 18N 100 20 E
Ta Lai, Vietnam 39 G6 11 24N 107 23 E
Tabacal, Argentina 94 A3 23 15S 64 15W
Tabaco, Phil. 37 B6 13 22N 123 44 E
Ţābah, Si. Arabia 44 E4 26 55N 42 38 E
Ţabas, Khorāsān, Iran 45 C9 32 48N 60 12 E
Ţabas, Khorāsān, Iran 45 C8 33 35N 56 55 E
Tabasará, Serranía de, Panama 88 E3 8 35N 81 40W
Tabasco □, Mexico 87 D6 17 45N 93 30W
Tabāsīn, Iran 45 D8 31 12N 57 54 E
Tabatinga, Serra da, Brazil 93 F10 10 30S 44 0W
Taber, Canada 72 D6 49 47N 112 8W
Taberg, U.S.A. 79 C9 43 18N 75 37W
Tablas, Phil. 37 B6 12 25N 122 2 E
Table B. = Tafelbaai, S. Africa 56 E2 33 35S 18 25 E
Table B., Canada 71 B8 53 40N 56 25W
Table Mt., S. Africa 56 E2 34 0S 18 22 E
Table Rock L., U.S.A. 81 G8 36 36N 93 19W
Tabletop, Mt., Australia 62 C4 23 24S 147 11 E
Tábor, Czech Rep. 16 D8 49 25N 14 39 E
Tabora, Tanzania 54 D3 5 2S 32 50 E
Tabora □, Tanzania 54 D3 5 0S 33 0 E
Tabou, Ivory C. 50 H4 4 30N 7 20W
Tabrīz, Iran 44 B5 38 7N 46 20 E
Tabuaeran, Pac. Oc. 65 G12 3 51N 159 22W
Tabūk, Si. Arabia 44 D3 28 23N 36 36 E
Tacámbaro de Codallos, Mexico 86 D4 19 14N 101 28W
Tacheng, China 32 B3 46 40N 82 58 E
Tach'ing Shan = Daqing Shan, China 34 D6 40 40N 111 0 E
Tacloban, Phil. 37 B6 11 15N 124 58 E
Tacna, Peru 92 G4 18 0S 70 20W
Tacoma, U.S.A. 84 C4 47 14N 122 26W
Tacuarembó, Uruguay 95 C4 31 45S 56 0W
Tademaït, Plateau du, Algeria 50 C6 28 30N 2 30 E
Tadjoura, Djibouti 46 E3 11 50N 42 55 E
Tadmor, N.Z. 59 J4 41 27S 172 45 E
Tadoule, L., Canada 73 B9 58 36N 98 20W
Tadoussac, Canada 71 C6 48 11N 69 42W
Tadzhikistan = Tajikistan ■, Asia 26 F8 38 30N 70 0 E
Taechŏn-ni, S. Korea 35 F14 36 21N 126 36 E
Taegu, S. Korea 35 G15 35 50N 128 37 E
Taegwan, N. Korea 35 D13 40 13N 125 12 E
Taejŏn, S. Korea 35 F14 36 20N 127 28 E
Tafalla, Spain 19 A5 42 30N 1 41W
Tafelbaai, S. Africa 56 E2 33 35S 18 25 E
Tafermaar, Indonesia 37 F8 6 47S 134 10 E
Tafí Viejo, Argentina 94 B2 26 43S 65 17W
Tafīhān, Iran 45 D7 29 25N 52 39 E
Tafresh, Iran 45 C6 34 45N 49 57 E
Taft, Iran 45 D7 31 45N 54 14 E
Taft, Phil. 37 B7 11 57N 125 30 E
Taft, U.S.A. 85 K7 35 8N 119 28W
Taftān, Kūh-e, Iran 45 D9 28 40N 61 0 E
Taga Dzong, Bhutan 41 F16 27 5N 89 55 E
Taganrog, Russia 25 E6 47 12N 38 50 E
Tagbilaran, Phil. 37 C6 9 39N 123 51 E
Tagish, Canada 72 A2 60 19N 134 16W
Tagish L., Canada 72 A2 60 10N 134 20W
Tagliamento —►, Italy 20 B5 45 38N 13 6 E
Tagomago, Spain 22 B8 39 2N 1 39 E
Taguatinga, Brazil 93 F10 12 16S 42 26W
Tagum, Phil. 37 C7 7 33N 125 53 E
Tagus = Tejo —►, Europe 19 C1 38 40N 9 24W
Tahakopa, N.Z. 59 M2 46 30S 169 23 E
Tahan, Gunong, Malaysia 39 K4 4 34N 102 17 E
Tahat, Algeria 50 D7 23 18N 5 33 E
Tāherī, Iran 45 E7 27 43N 52 20 E
Tahiti, Pac. Oc. 65 J13 17 37S 149 27W
Tahlequah, U.S.A. 81 H7 35 55N 94 58W
Tahoe, L., U.S.A. 84 G6 39 6N 120 2W
Tahoe City, U.S.A. 84 F6 39 10N 120 9W
Tahoka, U.S.A. 81 J4 33 10N 101 48W
Taholah, U.S.A. 84 C2 47 21N 124 17W
Tahoua, Niger 50 F7 14 57N 5 16 E
Tahrūd, Iran 45 D8 29 26N 57 49 E
Tahsis, Canada 72 D3 49 55N 126 40W
Tahta, Egypt 51 C12 26 44N 31 32 E
Tahulandang, Indonesia 37 D7 2 27N 125 23 E
Tahuna, Indonesia 37 D7 3 38N 125 30 E
Tai Shan, China 35 F9 36 25N 117 20 E
Tai'an, China 35 F9 36 12N 117 8 E
Taibei = T'aipei, Taiwan 33 D7 25 2N 121 30 E
Taibique, Canary Is. 22 G2 27 42N 17 58W
Taibus Qi, China 34 D8 41 54N 115 22 E
T'aichung, Taiwan 33 D7 24 9N 120 37 E
Taieri —►, N.Z. 59 M3 46 3S 170 12 E
Taigu, China 34 F7 37 28N 112 30 E
Taihang Shan, China 34 G7 36 0N 113 30 E
Taihape, N.Z. 59 H5 39 41S 175 48 E
Taihe, China 34 H8 33 20N 115 42 E
Taikang, China 34 G8 34 5N 114 50 E
Tailem Bend, Australia 63 F2 35 12S 139 29 E
Taimyr Peninsula = Taymyr, Poluostrov, Russia 27 B11 75 0N 100 0 E
Tain, U.K. 12 D4 57 49N 4 4W
T'ainan, Taiwan 33 D7 23 0N 120 10 E
Tainaron, Ákra, Greece 21 F10 36 22N 22 27 E
T'aipei, Taiwan 33 D7 25 2N 121 30 E
Taiping, Malaysia 39 K3 4 51N 100 44 E
Taipingzhen, China 34 H6 33 35N 111 42 E
Tairbeart = Tarbert, U.K. 12 D2 57 54N 6 49W
Taita Hills, Kenya 54 C4 3 25S 38 15 E
Taitao, Pen. de, Chile 96 F2 46 30S 75 0W
T'aitung, Taiwan 33 D7 22 43N 121 4 E
Taivalkoski, Finland 8 D23 65 33N 28 12 E
Taiwan ■, Asia 33 D7 23 30N 121 0 E
Taïyetos Óros, Greece 21 F10 37 0N 22 23 E
Taiyiba, Israel 47 C4 32 36N 35 27 E
Taiyuan, China 34 F7 37 52N 112 33 E
Taizhong = T'aichung, Taiwan 33 D7 24 9N 120 37 E
Ta'izz, Yemen 46 E3 13 35N 44 2 E
Tājābād, Iran 45 D7 30 2N 54 24 E
Tajikistan ■, Asia 26 F8 38 30N 70 0 E
Tajima, Japan 31 F9 37 12N 139 46 E
Tajo = Tejo —►, Europe 19 C1 38 40N 9 24W
Tajrīsh, Iran 45 C6 35 48N 51 25 E
Tak, Thailand 38 D2 16 52N 99 8 E
Takāb, Iran 44 B5 36 24N 47 7 E
Takachiho, Japan 31 H5 32 42N 131 18 E
Takada, Japan 31 F9 37 7N 138 15 E
Takahagi, Japan 31 F10 36 43N 140 45 E
Takaka, N.Z. 59 J4 40 51S 172 50 E
Takamatsu, Japan 31 G7 34 20N 134 5 E
Takaoka, Japan 31 F8 36 47N 137 0 E
Takapuna, N.Z. 59 G5 36 47S 174 47 E
Takasaki, Japan 31 F9 36 20N 139 0 E
Takatsuki, Japan 31 G7 34 51N 135 37 E
Takaungu, Kenya 54 C4 3 38S 39 52 E
Takayama, Japan 31 F8 36 18N 137 11 E
Take-Shima, Japan 31 J5 30 49N 130 26 E
Takefu, Japan 31 G8 35 50N 136 10 E
Takengon, Indonesia 36 D1 4 45N 96 50 E
Takeo, Japan 31 H5 33 12N 130 1 E
Tākestān, Iran 45 C6 36 0N 49 40 E
Taketa, Japan 31 H5 32 58N 131 24 E
Takev, Cambodia 39 G5 10 59N 104 47 E
Takh, India 43 C7 33 6N 77 32 E
Takht-Sulaiman, Pakistan 42 D3 31 40N 69 58 E
Takikawa, Japan 30 C10 43 33N 141 54 E
Takla L., Canada 72 B3 55 15N 125 45W
Takla Landing, Canada 72 B3 55 30N 125 50W
Takla Makan = Taklamakan Shamo, China 32 C3 38 0N 83 0 E
Taklamakan Shamo, China 32 C3 38 0N 83 0 E
Taku —►, Canada 72 B2 58 30N 133 50W
Tal Halāl, Iran 45 D7 28 54N 55 1 E
Tala, Uruguay 95 C4 34 21S 55 46W
Talagang, Pakistan 42 C5 32 55N 72 25 E
Talagante, Chile 94 C1 33 40S 70 50W
Talamanca, Cordillera de, Cent. Amer. 88 E3 9 20N 83 20W
Talara, Peru 92 D2 4 38S 81 18W
Talas, Kyrgyzstan 26 E8 42 30N 72 13 E
Talâta, Egypt 47 E1 30 36N 32 20 E
Talaud, Kepulauan, Indonesia 37 D7 4 30N 127 10 E
Talaud Is. = Talaud, Kepulauan, Indonesia 37 D7 4 30N 127 10 E
Talavera de la Reina, Spain 19 C3 39 55N 4 46W
Talayan, Phil. 37 C6 6 52N 124 24 E
Talbandh, India 43 H12 22 3N 86 20 E
Talbot, C., Australia 60 B4 13 48S 126 43 E
Talbragar —►, Australia 63 E4 32 12S 148 37 E
Talca, Chile 94 D1 35 28S 71 40W
Talcahuano, Chile 94 D1 36 40S 73 10W
Talcher, India 41 J14 21 0N 85 18 E
Taldy Kurgan = Taldyqorghan, Kazakstan 26 E8 45 10N 78 45 E
Taldyqorghan, Kazakstan 26 E8 45 10N 78 45 E
Tālesh, Iran 45 B6 37 58N 48 58 E
Tālesh, Kūhhā-ye, Iran 45 B6 37 42N 48 55 E
Tali Post, Sudan 51 G12 5 55N 30 44 E
Taliabu, Indonesia 37 E6 1 50S 125 0 E
Talibon, Phil. 37 B6 10 9N 124 20 E
Talibong, Ko, Thailand 39 J2 7 15N 99 23 E
Talihina, U.S.A. 81 H7 34 45N 95 3W
Taliwang, Indonesia 36 F5 8 50S 116 55 E
Tall 'Afar, Iraq 44 B4 36 22N 42 27 E
Tall Kalakh, Syria 47 A5 34 41N 36 15 E
Talladega, U.S.A. 77 J2 33 26N 86 6W
Tallahassee, U.S.A. 77 K3 30 27N 84 17W
Tallangatta, Australia 63 F4 36 15S 147 19 E
Tallering Pk., Australia 61 E2 28 6S 115 37 E
Talli, Pakistan 42 E3 29 32N 68 8 E
Tallinn, Estonia 9 G21 59 22N 24 48 E
Tallmadge, U.S.A. 78 E3 41 6N 81 27W
Tallulah, U.S.A. 81 J9 32 25N 91 11W
Taloyoak, Canada 68 B10 69 32N 93 32W
Talpa de Allende, Mexico 86 C4 20 23N 104 51W
Talsi, Latvia 9 H20 57 10N 22 30 E
Taltal, Chile 94 B1 25 23S 70 33W
Taltson —►, Canada 72 A6 61 24N 112 46W
Talwood, Australia 63 D4 28 29S 149 29 E
Talyawalka —►, Australia 63 E3 32 28S 142 22 E
Tam Chau, Vietnam 39 G5 10 48N 105 12 E
Tam Ky, Vietnam 38 E7 15 34N 108 29 E
Tam Quan, Vietnam 38 E7 14 35N 109 3 E
Tama, U.S.A. 80 E8 41 58N 92 35W
Tamale, Ghana 50 G5 9 22N 0 50W
Tamano, Japan 31 G6 34 29N 133 59 E
Tamanrasset, Algeria 50 D7 22 50N 5 30 E
Tamaqua, U.S.A. 79 F9 40 48N 75 58W
Tamar —►, U.K. 11 G3 50 27N 4 15W
Tamarinda, Spain 22 B10 39 55N 3 49 E
Tamashima, Japan 31 G6 34 32N 133 40 E
Tamaulipas □, Mexico 87 C5 24 0N 99 0W
Tamaulipas, Sierra de, Mexico 87 C5 23 30N 98 20W
Tamazula, Mexico 86 C3 24 55N 106 58W
Tamazunchale, Mexico 87 C5 21 16N 98 47W
Tambacounda, Senegal 50 F3 13 45N 13 40W
Tambelan, Kepulauan, Indonesia 36 D3 1 0N 107 30 E
Tambellup, Australia 61 F2 34 4S 117 37 E
Tambo, Australia 62 C4 24 54S 146 14 E
Tambo de Mora, Peru 92 F3 13 30S 76 8W
Tambohorano, Madag. 57 B7 17 30S 43 58 E
Tambora, Indonesia 36 F5 8 12S 118 5 E
Tambov, Russia 24 D7 52 45N 41 28 E
Tambuku, Indonesia 37 G15 7 8S 113 40 E
Tâmega —►, Portugal 19 B1 41 5N 8 21W
Tamenglong, India 41 G18 25 0N 93 35 E
Tamiahua, L. de, Mexico 87 C5 21 30N 97 30W
Tamil Nadu □, India 40 P10 11 0N 77 0 E
Tamluk, India 43 H12 22 18N 87 58 E
Tammerfors = Tampere, Finland 9 F20 61 30N 23 50 E
Tammisaari, Finland 9 F20 60 0N 23 26 E
Tamo Abu, Pegunungan, Malaysia 36 D5 3 10N 115 5 E
Tampa, U.S.A. 77 M4 27 57N 82 27W
Tampa B., U.S.A. 77 M4 27 50N 82 30W
Tampere, Finland 9 F20 61 30N 23 50 E
Tampico, Mexico 87 C5 22 20N 97 50W
Tampin, Malaysia 39 L4 2 28N 102 13 E
Tamu, Burma 41 G19 24 13N 94 12 E
Tamworth, Australia 63 E5 31 7S 150 58 E
Tamworth, Canada 78 B8 44 29N 77 0W
Tamworth, U.K. 11 E6 52 39N 1 41W
Tamyang, S. Korea 35 G14 35 19N 126 59 E
Tan An, Vietnam 39 G6 10 32N 106 25 E
Tan-Tan, Morocco 50 C3 28 29N 11 1W
Tana —►, Kenya 54 C5 2 32S 40 31 E
Tana —►, Norway 8 A23 70 30N 28 14 E
Tana, L., Ethiopia 46 E2 13 5N 37 30 E
Tana River, Kenya 54 C4 2 0S 39 30 E
Tanabe, Japan 31 H7 33 44N 135 22 E
Tanafjorden, Norway 8 A23 70 45N 28 25 E
Tanaga, Pta., Canary Is. 22 G1 27 42N 18 10W
Tanahbala, Indonesia 36 E1 0 30S 98 30 E
Tanahgrogot, Indonesia 36 E5 1 55S 116 15 E
Tanahjampea, Indonesia 37 F6 7 10S 120 35 E
Tanahmasa, Indonesia 36 E1 0 12S 98 39 E
Tanahmerah, Indonesia 37 F10 6 5S 140 16 E
Tanakpur, India 43 E9 29 5N 80 7 E
Tanakura, Japan 31 F10 37 10N 140 20 E
Tanami, Australia 60 C4 19 59S 129 43 E
Tanami Desert, Australia 60 C5 18 50S 132 0 E
Tanana —►, U.S.A. 68 B4 65 10N 151 58W
Tananarive = Antananarivo, Madag. 57 B8 18 55S 47 31 E
Tánaro —►, Italy 18 D8 44 55N 8 40 E
Tancheng, China 35 G10 34 25N 118 20 E
Tanch'ŏn, N. Korea 35 D15 40 27N 128 54 E
Tanda, Ut. P., India 43 F10 26 33N 82 35 E
Tanda, Ut. P., India 43 E8 28 57N 78 56 E
Tandag, Phil. 37 C7 9 4N 126 9 E
Tandaia, Tanzania 55 D3 9 25S 34 15 E
Tandaué, Angola 56 B2 16 58S 18 5 E
Tandil, Argentina 94 D4 37 15S 59 6W
Tandil, Sa. del, Argentina 94 D4 37 30S 59 0W
Tandlianwala, Pakistan 42 D5 31 3N 73 9 E
Tando Adam, Pakistan 42 G3 25 45N 68 40 E
Tando Allahyar, Pakistan 42 G3 25 28N 68 43 E
Tando Bago, Pakistan 42 G3 24 47N 68 58 E
Tando Mohommed Khan, Pakistan 42 G3 25 8N 68 32 E
Tandou L., Australia 63 E3 32 40S 142 5 E
Tandragee, U.K. 13 B5 54 21N 6 24W
Tane-ga-Shima, Japan 31 J5 30 30N 131 0 E
Taneatua, N.Z. 59 H6 38 4S 177 1 E
Tanen Tong Dan, Burma 38 D2 16 30N 98 30 E
Tanezrouft, Algeria 50 D6 23 9N 0 11 E
Tang, Koh, Cambodia 39 G4 10 16N 103 7 E
Tang, Ra's-e, Iran 45 E8 25 21N 59 52 E
Tang Krasang, Cambodia 38 F5 12 34N 105 3 E
Tanga, Tanzania 54 D4 5 5S 39 2 E
Tanga □, Tanzania 54 D4 5 20S 38 0 E
Tanganyika, L., Africa 54 D3 6 40S 30 0 E
Tanger = Tangier, Morocco 50 A4 35 50N 5 49W
Tangerang, Indonesia 37 G12 6 11S 106 37 E
Tanggu, China 35 E9 39 2N 117 40 E
Tanggula Shan, China 32 C4 32 40N 92 10 E
Tanghe, China 34 H7 32 47N 112 50 E
Tangier, Morocco 50 A4 35 50N 5 49W
Tangorin, Australia 62 C3 21 47S 144 12 E
Tangshan, China 35 E10 39 38N 118 10 E
Tangtou, China 35 G10 35 28N 118 30 E
Tanimbar, Kepulauan, Indonesia 37 F8 7 30S 131 30 E
Tanimbar Is. = Tanimbar, Kepulauan, Indonesia 37 F8 7 30S 131 30 E
Taninthari = Tenasserim □, Burma 38 F2 14 0N 98 30 E
Tanjay, Phil. 37 C6 9 30N 123 5 E
Tanjong Malim, Malaysia 39 L3 3 42N 101 31 E
Tanjore = Thanjavur, India 40 P11 10 48N 79 12 E
Tanjung, Indonesia 36 E5 2 10S 115 25 E
Tanjungbalai, Indonesia 36 D1 2 55N 99 44 E
Tanjungbatu, Indonesia 36 D5 2 23N 118 3 E
Tanjungkarang Telukbetung, Indonesia 36 F3 5 20S 105 10 E
Tanjungpandan, Indonesia 36 E3 2 43S 107 38 E
Tanjungpinang, Indonesia 36 D2 1 5N 104 30 E
Tanjungredeb, Indonesia 36 D5 2 9N 117 29 E
Tanjungselor, Indonesia 36 D5 2 55N 117 25 E
Tank, Pakistan 42 C4 32 14N 70 25 E
Tankhala, India 42 J5 21 58N 73 47 E
Tannersville, U.S.A. 79 E9 41 3N 75 18W
Tannu-Ola, Russia 27 D10 51 0N 94 0 E
Tannum Sands, Australia 62 C5 23 57S 151 22 E

Tanout, *Niger* **50 F7** 14 50N 8 55 E
Tanta, *Egypt* **51 B12** 30 45N 30 57 E
Tantoyuca, *Mexico* **87 C5** 21 21N 98 10W
Tantung = Dandong, *China* **35 D13** 40 10N 124 20 E
Tanunda, *Australia* **63 E2** 34 30S 139 0 E
Tanzania ■, *Africa* **54 D3** 6 0S 34 0 E
Tanzilla →, *Canada* **72 B2** 58 8N 130 43W
Tao, Ko, *Thailand* **39 G2** 10 5N 99 52 E
Tao'an = Taonan, *China* **35 B12** 45 22N 122 40 E
Tao'er He →, *China* **35 B13** 45 45N 124 5 E
Taolanaro, *Madag.* **57 D8** 25 2S 47 0 E
Taole, *China* **34 E4** 38 48N 106 40 E
Taonan, *China* **35 B12** 45 22N 122 40 E
Taos, *U.S.A.* **83 H11** 36 24N 105 35W
Taoudenni, *Mali* **50 D5** 22 40N 3 55W
Tapa, *Estonia* **9 G21** 59 15N 25 50 E
Tapa Shan = Daba Shan, *China* **33 C5** 32 0N 109 0 E
Tapachula, *Mexico* **87 E6** 14 54N 92 17W
Tapah, *Malaysia* **39 K3** 4 12N 101 15 E
Tapajós →, *Brazil* **93 D8** 2 24S 54 41W
Tapaktuan, *Indonesia* **36 D1** 3 15N 97 10 E
Tapanahoni →, *Surinam* **93 C8** 4 20N 54 25W
Tapanui, *N.Z.* **59 L2** 45 56S 169 18 E
Tapauá →, *Brazil* **92 E6** 5 40S 64 21W
Tapes, *Brazil* **95 C5** 30 40S 51 23W
Tapeta, *Liberia* **50 G4** 6 29N 8 52W
Taphan Hin, *Thailand* **38 D3** 16 13N 100 26 E
Tapirapecó, Serra, *Venezuela* **92 C6** 1 10N 65 0W
Tapuaenuku, Mt., *N.Z.* **59 K4** 42 0S 173 39 E
Tapul Group, *Phil.* **37 C6** 5 35N 120 50 E
Tapurucuará, *Brazil* **92 D5** 0 24S 65 2W
Ţaqţaq, *Iraq* **44 C5** 35 53N 44 35 E
Taquara, *Brazil* **95 B5** 29 36S 50 46W
Taquari →, *Brazil* **92 G7** 19 15S 57 17W
Tara, *Australia* **63 D5** 27 17S 150 31 E
Tara, *Canada* **78 B3** 44 28N 81 9W
Tara, *Russia* **26 D8** 56 55N 74 24 E
Tara, *Zambia* **55 F2** 16 58S 26 45 E
Tara →, *Montenegro, Yug.* **21 C8** 43 21N 18 51 E
Tarabagatay, Khrebet, *Kazakstan* **26 E9** 48 0N 83 0 E
Tarābulus, *Lebanon* **47 A4** 34 31N 35 50 E
Tarābulus, *Libya* **51 B8** 32 49N 13 7 E
Taradehi, *India* **43 H8** 23 18N 79 21 E
Tarajalejo, *Canary Is.* **22 F5** 28 12N 14 7W
Tarakan, *Indonesia* **36 D5** 3 20N 117 35 E
Tarakit, Mt., *Kenya* **54 B4** 2 2N 35 10 E
Tarama-Jima, *Japan* **31 M2** 24 39N 124 42 E
Taran, Mys, *Russia* **9 J18** 54 56N 19 59 E
Taranagar, *India* **42 E6** 28 43N 74 50 E
Taranaki □, *N.Z.* **59 H5** 39 25S 174 30 E
Tarancón, *Spain* **19 B4** 40 1N 3 0W
Taranga Hill, *India* **40 H8** 24 0N 72 40 E
Taransay, *U.K.* **12 D1** 57 54N 7 0W
Táranto, *Italy* **20 D7** 40 28N 17 14 E
Táranto, G. di, *Italy* **20 D7** 40 8N 17 20 E
Tarapacá, *Colombia* **92 D5** 2 56S 69 46W
Tarapacá □, *Chile* **94 A2** 20 45S 69 30W
Tarapoto, *Peru* **92 E3** 6 30S 76 20W
Tararua Ra., *N.Z.* **59 J5** 40 45S 175 25 E
Tarashcha, *Ukraine* **17 D16** 49 30N 30 31 E
Tarauacá, *Brazil* **92 E4** 8 6S 70 48W
Tarauacá →, *Brazil* **92 E5** 6 42S 69 48W
Tarawa, *Kiribati* **64 G9** 1 30N 173 0 E
Tarawera, *N.Z.* **59 H6** 39 2S 176 36 E
Tarawera L., *N.Z.* **59 H6** 38 13S 176 27 E
Tarazona, *Spain* **19 B5** 41 55N 1 43W
Tarbat Ness, *U.K.* **12 D5** 57 52N 3 47W
Tarbela Dam, *Pakistan* **42 B5** 34 8N 72 52 E
Tarbert, *Arg. & Bute, U.K.* **12 F3** 55 52N 5 25W
Tarbert, *W. Isles, U.K.* **12 D2** 57 54N 6 49W
Tarbes, *France* **18 E4** 43 15N 0 3 E
Tarboro, *U.S.A.* **77 H7** 35 54N 77 32W
Tarcoola, *Australia* **63 E1** 30 44S 134 36 E
Tarcoon, *Australia* **63 E4** 30 15S 146 43 E
Taree, *Australia* **63 E5** 31 50S 152 30 E
Tarfaya, *Morocco* **50 C3** 27 55N 12 55W
Târgovişte, *Romania* **17 F13** 44 55N 25 27 E
Târgu-Jiu, *Romania* **17 F12** 45 5N 23 19 E
Târgu Mureş, *Romania* **17 E13** 46 31N 24 38 E
Ţarif, *U.A.E.* **45 E7** 24 3N 53 46 E
Tarifa, *Spain* **19 D3** 36 1N 5 36W
Tarija, *Bolivia* **94 A3** 21 30S 64 40W
Tarija □, *Bolivia* **94 A3** 21 30S 63 30W
Tariku →, *Indonesia* **37 E9** 2 55S 138 26 E
Tarim Basin = Tarim Pendi, *China* **32 B3** 40 0N 84 0 E
Tarim He →, *China* **32 C3** 39 30N 88 30 E
Tarim Pendi, *China* **32 B3** 40 0N 84 0 E
Taritatu →, *Indonesia* **37 E9** 2 54S 138 27 E
Tarka →, *S. Africa* **56 E4** 32 10S 26 0 E
Tarkastad, *S. Africa* **56 E4** 32 0S 26 16 E
Tarkhankut, Mys, *Ukraine* **25 E5** 45 25N 32 30 E
Tarko Sale, *Russia* **26 C8** 64 55N 77 50 E
Tarkwa, *Ghana* **50 G5** 5 20N 2 0W
Tarlac, *Phil.* **37 A6** 15 29N 120 35 E
Tarma, *Peru* **92 F3** 11 25S 75 45W
Tarn →, *France* **18 E4** 44 5N 1 6 E
Târnăveni, *Romania* **17 E13** 46 19N 24 13 E
Tarnobrzeg, *Poland* **17 C11** 50 35N 21 41 E
Tarnów, *Poland* **17 C11** 50 3N 21 0 E
Tarnowskie Góry, *Poland* **17 C10** 50 27N 18 54 E
Ţārom, *Iran* **45 D7** 28 11N 55 46 E
Taroom, *Australia* **63 D4** 25 36S 149 48 E
Taroudannt, *Morocco* **50 B4** 30 30N 8 52W
Tarpon Springs, *U.S.A.* **77 L4** 28 9N 82 45W
Tarragona, *Spain* **19 B6** 41 5N 1 17 E
Tarraleah, *Australia* **62 G4** 42 17S 146 26 E
Tarrasa = Terrassa, *Spain* **19 B7** 41 34N 2 1 E
Tarrytown, *U.S.A.* **79 E11** 41 4N 73 52W
Tarshiha = Me'ona, *Israel* **47 B4** 33 1N 35 15 E
Tarso Emissi, *Chad* **51 D9** 21 27N 18 36 E
Tarsus, *Turkey* **25 G5** 36 58N 34 55 E
Tartagal, *Argentina* **94 A3** 22 30S 63 50W
Tartu, *Estonia* **9 G22** 58 20N 26 44 E
Ţarţūs, *Syria* **44 C2** 34 55N 35 55 E
Tarumizu, *Japan* **31 J5** 31 29N 130 42 E
Tarutao, Ko, *Thailand* **39 J2** 6 33N 99 40 E
Tarutung, *Indonesia* **36 D1** 2 0N 98 54 E
Taseko →, *Canada* **72 C4** 52 8N 123 45W
Tash-Kömür, *Kyrgyzstan* **26 E8** 41 40N 72 10 E
Tash-Kumyr = Tash-Kömür, *Kyrgyzstan* **26 E8** 41 40N 72 10 E
Tashauz = Dashhowuz, *Turkmenistan* **26 E6** 41 49N 59 58 E
Tashi Chho Dzong = Thimphu, *Bhutan* **41 F16** 27 31N 89 45 E
Ţashk, Daryācheh-ye, *Iran* **45 D7** 29 45N 53 35 E
Tashkent = Toshkent, *Uzbekistan* **26 E7** 41 20N 69 10 E
Tashtagol, *Russia* **26 D9** 52 47N 87 53 E
Tasikmalaya, *Indonesia* **37 G13** 7 18S 108 12 E
Tåsjön, *Sweden* **8 D16** 64 15N 15 40 E
Taskan, *Russia* **27 C16** 62 59N 150 20 E
Tasman B., *N.Z.* **59 J4** 40 59S 173 25 E
Tasman Mts., *N.Z.* **59 J4** 41 3S 172 25 E
Tasman Pen., *Australia* **62 G4** 43 10S 148 0 E
Tasman Sea, *Pac. Oc.* **64 L8** 36 0S 160 0 E
Tasmania □, *Australia* **62 G4** 42 0S 146 30 E
Tassili n'Ajjer, *Algeria* **50 C7** 25 47N 8 1 E
Tatabánya, *Hungary* **17 E10** 47 32N 18 25 E
Tatahouine, *Tunisia* **51 B8** 32 56N 10 27 E
Tatar Republic = Tatarstan □, *Russia* **24 C9** 55 30N 51 30 E
Tatarbunary, *Ukraine* **17 F15** 45 50N 29 39 E
Tatarsk, *Russia* **26 D8** 55 14N 76 0 E
Tatarstan □, *Russia* **24 C9** 55 30N 51 30 E
Tateyama, *Japan* **31 G9** 35 0N 139 50 E
Tathlina L., *Canada* **72 A5** 60 33N 117 39W
Tathra, *Australia* **63 F4** 36 44S 149 59 E
Tati →, *India* **40 J8** 21 8N 72 41 E
Tatinnai L., *Canada* **73 A9** 60 55N 97 40W
Tatla L., *Canada* **72 C4** 52 0N 124 20W
Tatnam, C., *Canada* **73 B10** 57 16N 91 0W
Tatra = Tatry, *Slovak Rep.* **17 D11** 49 20N 20 0 E
Tatry, *Slovak Rep.* **17 D11** 49 20N 20 0 E
Tatshenshini →, *Canada* **72 B1** 59 28N 137 45W
Tatsuno, *Japan* **31 G7** 34 52N 134 33 E
Tatta, *Pakistan* **42 G2** 24 42N 67 55 E
Tatuī, *Brazil* **95 A6** 23 25S 47 53W
Tatum, *U.S.A.* **81 J3** 33 16N 103 19W
Tat'ung = Datong, *China* **34 D7** 40 6N 113 18 E
Tatvan, *Turkey* **25 G7** 38 31N 42 15 E
Taubaté, *Brazil* **95 A6** 23 0S 45 36W
Tauern, *Austria* **16 E7** 47 15N 12 40 E
Taumarunui, *N.Z.* **59 H5** 38 53S 175 15 E
Taumaturgo, *Brazil* **92 E4** 8 54S 72 51W
Taung, *S. Africa* **56 D3** 27 33S 24 47 E
Taungdwingyi, *Burma* **41 J19** 20 1N 95 40 E
Taunggyi, *Burma* **41 J20** 20 50N 97 0 E
Taungup, *Burma* **41 K19** 18 51N 94 14 E
Taungup Pass, *Burma* **41 K19** 18 40N 94 45 E
Taungup Taunggya, *Burma* **41 K18** 18 20N 93 40 E
Taunsa, *Pakistan* **42 D4** 30 42N 70 39 E
Taunsa Barrage, *Pakistan* **42 D4** 30 42N 70 50 E
Taunton, *U.K.* **11 F4** 51 1N 3 5W
Taunton, *U.S.A.* **79 E13** 41 54N 71 6W
Taunus, *Germany* **16 C5** 50 13N 8 34 E
Taupo, *N.Z.* **59 H6** 38 41S 176 7 E
Taupo, L., *N.Z.* **59 H5** 38 46S 175 55 E
Taurage, *Lithuania* **9 J20** 55 14N 22 16 E
Tauranga, *N.Z.* **59 G6** 37 42S 176 11 E
Tauranga Harb., *N.Z.* **59 G6** 37 30S 176 5 E
Taureau, Rés., *Canada* **70 C5** 46 46N 73 50W
Taurianova, *Italy* **20 E7** 38 21N 16 1 E
Taurus Mts. = Toros Dağları, *Turkey* **25 G5** 37 0N 32 30 E
Tavda, *Russia* **26 D7** 58 7N 65 8 E
Tavda →, *Russia* **26 D7** 57 47N 67 18 E
Taveta, *Tanzania* **54 C4** 3 23S 37 37 E
Taveuni, *Fiji* **59 C9** 16 51S 179 58W
Tavira, *Portugal* **19 D2** 37 8N 7 40W
Tavistock, *Canada* **78 C4** 43 19N 80 50W
Tavistock, *U.K.* **11 G3** 50 33N 4 9W
Tavoy = Dawei, *Burma* **38 E2** 14 2N 98 12 E
Taw →, *U.K.* **11 F3** 51 4N 4 4W
Tawa →, *India* **42 H8** 22 48N 77 48 E
Tawas City, *U.S.A.* **76 C4** 44 16N 83 31W
Tawau, *Malaysia* **36 D5** 4 20N 117 55 E
Tawitawi, *Phil.* **37 C6** 5 10N 120 0 E
Taxco de Alarcón, *Mexico* **87 D5** 18 33N 99 36W
Taxila, *Pakistan* **42 C5** 33 42N 72 52 E
Tay →, *U.K.* **12 E5** 56 37N 3 38W
Tay, Firth of, *U.K.* **12 E5** 56 25N 3 8W
Tay, L., *Australia* **61 F3** 32 55S 120 48 E
Tay, L., *U.K.* **12 E4** 56 32N 4 8W
Tay Ninh, *Vietnam* **39 G6** 11 20N 106 5 E
Tayabamba, *Peru* **92 E3** 8 15S 77 16W
Taylakova, *Russia* **26 D8** 59 13N 74 0 E
Taylakovy = Taylakova, *Russia* **26 D8** 59 13N 74 0 E
Taylor, *Canada* **72 B4** 56 13N 120 40W
Taylor, *Nebr., U.S.A.* **80 E5** 41 46N 99 23W
Taylor, *Pa., U.S.A.* **79 E9** 41 23N 75 43W
Taylor, *Tex., U.S.A.* **81 K6** 30 34N 97 25W
Taylor, Mt., *U.S.A.* **83 J10** 35 14N 107 37W
Taylorville, *U.S.A.* **80 F10** 39 33N 89 18W
Taymā, *Si. Arabia* **44 E3** 27 35N 38 45 E
Taymyr, Oz., *Russia* **27 B11** 74 20N 102 0 E
Taymyr, Poluostrov, *Russia* **27 B11** 75 0N 100 0 E
Tayport, *U.K.* **12 E6** 56 27N 2 52W
Tayshet, *Russia* **27 D10** 55 58N 98 1 E
Taytay, *Phil.* **37 B5** 10 45N 119 30 E
Taz →, *Russia* **26 C8** 67 32N 78 40 E
Taza, *Morocco* **50 B5** 34 16N 4 6W
Tāzah Khurmātū, *Iraq* **44 C5** 35 18N 44 20 E
Tazawa-Ko, *Japan* **30 E10** 39 43N 140 40 E
Tazin, *Canada* **73 B7** 59 48N 109 55W
Tazin L., *Canada* **73 B7** 59 44N 108 42W
Tazovskiy, *Russia* **26 C8** 67 30N 78 44 E
Tbilisi, *Georgia* **25 F7** 41 43N 44 50 E
Tchad = Chad ■, *Africa* **51 F8** 15 0N 17 15 E
Tchad, L., *Chad* **51 F8** 13 30N 14 30 E
Tch'eng-tou = Chengdu, *China* **32 C5** 30 38N 104 2 E
Tchentlo L., *Canada* **72 B4** 55 15N 125 0W
Tchibanga, *Gabon* **52 E2** 2 45S 11 0 E
Tch'ong-k'ing = Chongqing, *China* **32 D5** 29 35N 106 25 E
Tczew, *Poland* **17 A10** 54 8N 18 50 E
Te Anau, L., *N.Z.* **59 L1** 45 15S 167 45 E
Te Aroha, *N.Z.* **59 G5** 37 32S 175 44 E
Te Awamutu, *N.Z.* **59 H5** 38 1S 175 20 E
Te Kuiti, *N.Z.* **59 H5** 38 20S 175 11 E
Te Puke, *N.Z.* **59 G6** 37 46S 176 22 E
Te Waewae B., *N.Z.* **59 M1** 46 13S 167 33 E
Teague, *U.S.A.* **81 K6** 31 38N 96 17W
Teapa, *Mexico* **87 D6** 18 35N 92 56W
Tebakang, *Malaysia* **36 D4** 1 6N 110 30 E
Tébessa, *Algeria* **50 A7** 35 22N 8 8 E
Tebicuary →, *Paraguay* **94 B4** 26 36S 58 16W
Tebingtinggi, *Indonesia* **36 D1** 3 20N 99 9 E
Tebintingii, *Indonesia* **36 E2** 1 0N 102 45 E
Tecate, *Mexico* **85 N10** 32 34N 116 38W
Tecka, *Argentina* **96 E2** 43 29S 70 48W
Tecomán, *Mexico* **86 D4** 18 55N 103 53W
Tecopa, *U.S.A.* **85 K10** 35 51N 116 13W
Tecoripa, *Mexico* **86 B3** 28 37N 109 57W
Tecuala, *Mexico* **86 C3** 22 23N 105 27W
Tecuci, *Romania* **17 F14** 45 51N 27 27 E
Tecumseh, *Canada* **78 D2** 42 19N 82 54W
Tecumseh, *Mich., U.S.A.* **76 D4** 42 0N 83 57W
Tecumseh, *Okla., U.S.A.* **81 H6** 35 15N 96 56W
Tedzhen = Tejen, *Turkmenistan* **26 F7** 37 23N 60 31 E
Tees →, *U.K.* **10 C6** 54 37N 1 10W
Tees B., *U.K.* **10 C6** 54 40N 1 9W
Teeswater, *Canada* **78 C3** 43 59N 81 17W
Tefé, *Brazil* **92 D6** 3 25S 64 50W
Tegal, *Indonesia* **37 G13** 6 52S 109 8 E
Tegid, L. = Bala, L., *U.K.* **10 E4** 52 53N 3 37W
Tegucigalpa, *Honduras* **88 D2** 14 5N 87 14W
Tehachapi, *U.S.A.* **85 K8** 35 8N 118 27W
Tehachapi Mts., *U.S.A.* **85 L8** 35 0N 118 30W
Tehoru, *Indonesia* **37 E7** 3 19S 129 37 E
Tehrān, *Iran* **45 C6** 35 44N 51 30 E
Tehri, *India* **43 D8** 30 23N 78 29 E
Tehuacán, *Mexico* **87 D5** 18 30N 97 30W
Tehuantepec, *Mexico* **87 D5** 16 21N 95 13W
Tehuantepec, G. de, *Mexico* **87 D5** 15 50N 95 12W
Tehuantepec, Istmo de, *Mexico* **87 D6** 17 0N 94 30W
Teide, *Canary Is.* **22 F3** 28 15N 16 38W
Teifi →, *U.K.* **11 E3** 52 5N 4 41W
Teign →, *U.K.* **11 G4** 50 32N 3 32W
Teignmouth, *U.K.* **11 G4** 50 33N 3 31W
Tejam, *India* **43 E9** 29 57N 80 11 E
Tejen, *Turkmenistan* **26 F7** 37 23N 60 31 E
Tejen →, *Turkmenistan* **45 B9** 37 24N 60 38 E
Tejo →, *Europe* **19 C1** 38 40N 9 24W
Tejon Pass, *U.S.A.* **85 L8** 34 49N 118 53W
Tekamah, *U.S.A.* **80 E6** 41 47N 96 13W
Tekapo, L., *N.Z.* **59 K3** 43 53S 170 33 E
Tekax, *Mexico* **87 C7** 20 11N 89 18W
Tekeli, *Kazakstan* **26 E8** 44 50N 79 0 E
Tekirdağ, *Turkey* **21 D12** 40 58N 27 30 E
Tekkali, *India* **41 K14** 18 37N 84 15 E
Tekoa, *U.S.A.* **82 C5** 47 14N 117 4W
Tel Aviv-Yafo, *Israel* **47 C3** 32 4N 34 48 E
Tel Lakhish, *Israel* **47 D3** 31 34N 34 51 E
Tel Megiddo, *Israel* **47 C4** 32 35N 35 11 E
Tela, *Honduras* **88 C2** 15 40N 87 28W
Telanaipura = Jambi, *Indonesia* **36 E2** 1 38S 103 30 E
Telavi, *Georgia* **25 F8** 42 0N 45 30 E
Telde, *Canary Is.* **22 G4** 27 59N 15 25W
Telegraph Creek, *Canada* **72 B2** 58 0N 131 10W
Telekhany = Tsyelyakhany, *Belarus* **17 B13** 52 30N 25 46 E
Telemark, *Norway* **9 G12** 59 15N 7 40 E
Telén, *Argentina* **94 D2** 36 15S 65 31W
Teleng, *Iran* **45 E9** 25 47N 61 3 E
Teles Pires →, *Brazil* **92 E7** 7 21S 58 3W
Telescope Pk., *U.S.A.* **85 J9** 36 10N 117 5W
Telfer Mine, *Australia* **60 C3** 21 40S 122 12 E
Telford, *U.K.* **11 E5** 52 40N 2 27W
Telford and Wrekin □, *U.K.* **10 E5** 52 45N 2 27W
Telkwa, *Canada* **72 C3** 54 41N 127 5W
Tell City, *U.S.A.* **76 G2** 37 57N 86 46W
Tellicherry, *India* **40 P9** 11 45N 75 30 E
Telluride, *U.S.A.* **83 H10** 37 56N 107 49W
Teloloapán, *Mexico* **87 D5** 18 21N 99 51W
Telpos Iz, *Russia* **24 B10** 63 16N 59 13 E
Telsen, *Argentina* **96 E3** 42 30S 66 50W
Telšiai, *Lithuania* **9 H20** 55 59N 22 14 E
Teluk Anson = Teluk Intan, *Malaysia* **39 K3** 4 3N 101 0 E
Teluk Betung = Tanjungkarang Telukbetung, *Indonesia* **36 F3** 5 20S 105 10 E
Teluk Intan, *Malaysia* **39 K3** 4 3N 101 0 E
Telukbutun, *Indonesia* **39 K7** 4 13N 108 12 E
Telukdalem, *Indonesia* **36 D1** 0 33N 97 50 E
Tema, *Ghana* **50 G5** 5 41N 0 0 E
Temax, *Mexico* **87 C7** 21 10N 88 50W
Temba, *S. Africa* **57 D4** 25 20S 28 17 E
Tembagapura, *Indonesia* **37 E9** 4 20S 137 0 E
Tembe, *Dem. Rep. of the Congo* **54 C2** 0 16S 28 14 E
Temblor Range, *U.S.A.* **85 K7** 35 20N 119 50W
Teme →, *U.K.* **11 E5** 52 11N 2 13W
Temecula, *U.S.A.* **85 M9** 33 30N 117 9W
Temerloh, *Malaysia* **36 D2** 3 27N 102 25 E
Teminabuan, *Indonesia* **37 E8** 1 26S 132 1 E
Temir, *Kazakstan* **25 E10** 49 1N 57 14 E
Temirtau, *Kazakstan* **26 D8** 50 5N 72 56 E
Temirtau, *Russia* **26 D9** 53 10N 87 30 E
Témiscamie →, *Canada* **71 B5** 50 59N 73 5W
Témiscaming, *Canada* **70 C4** 46 44N 79 5W
Témiscamingue, L., *Canada* **70 C4** 47 10N 79 25W
Temosachic, *Mexico* **86 B3** 28 58N 107 50W
Tempe, *U.S.A.* **83 K8** 33 25N 111 56W
Tempiute, *U.S.A.* **84 H11** 37 39N 115 38W
Temple, *U.S.A.* **81 K6** 31 6N 97 21W
Temple B., *Australia* **62 A3** 12 15S 143 3 E
Templemore, *Ireland* **13 D4** 52 47N 7 51W
Templeton, *U.S.A.* **84 K6** 35 33N 120 42W
Templeton →, *Australia* **62 C2** 21 0S 138 40 E
Tempoal, *Mexico* **87 C5** 21 31N 98 23W
Temuco, *Chile* **96 D2** 38 45S 72 40W
Temuka, *N.Z.* **59 L3** 44 14S 171 17 E
Tenabo, *Mexico* **87 C6** 20 2N 90 12W
Tenaha, *U.S.A.* **81 K7** 31 57N 94 15W
Tenakee Springs, *U.S.A.* **72 B1** 57 47N 135 13W
Tenali, *India* **40 L12** 16 15N 80 35 E
Tenancingo, *Mexico* **87 D5** 19 0N 99 33W
Tenango, *Mexico* **87 D5** 19 7N 99 33W
Tenasserim, *Burma* **39 F2** 12 6N 99 3 E
Tenasserim □, *Burma* **38 F2** 14 0N 98 30 E
Tenby, *U.K.* **11 F3** 51 40N 4 42W
Tenda, Colle di, *France* **18 D7** 44 7N 7 36 E
Tendaho, *Ethiopia* **46 E3** 11 48N 40 54 E
Tendukhera, *India* **43 H8** 23 24N 79 33 E
Ténéré, *Niger* **50 E7** 19 0N 10 30 E
Tenerife, *Canary Is.* **22 F3** 28 15N 16 35W
Tenerife, Pico, *Canary Is.* **22 G1** 27 43N 18 1W
Teng Xian, *China* **35 G9** 35 5N 117 10 E
Tengah □, *Indonesia* **37 E6** 2 0S 122 0 E
Tengah, Kepulauan, *Indonesia* **36 F5** 7 5S 118 15 E
Tengchong, *China* **32 D4** 25 0N 98 28 E
Tengchowfu = Penglai, *China* **35 F11** 37 48N 120 42 E
Tenggara □, *Indonesia* **37 E6** 3 0S 122 0 E
Tenggarong, *Indonesia* **36 E5** 0 24S 116 58 E
Tenggol, Pulau, *Malaysia* **39 K4** 4 48N 103 41 E
Tengiz, Ozero, *Kazakstan* **26 D7** 50 30N 69 0 E
Tenino, *U.S.A.* **84 D4** 46 51N 122 51W
Tenkasi, *India* **40 Q10** 8 55N 77 20 E
Tenke, *Katanga, Dem. Rep. of the Congo* **55 E2** 11 22S 26 40 E
Tenke, *Katanga, Dem. Rep. of the Congo* **55 E2** 10 32S 26 7 E
Tennant Creek, *Australia* **62 B1** 19 30S 134 15 E
Tennessee □, *U.S.A.* **77 H2** 36 0N 86 30W
Tennessee →, *U.S.A.* **76 G1** 37 4N 88 34W
Teno, Pta. de, *Canary Is.* **22 F3** 28 21N 16 55W
Tenom, *Malaysia* **36 C5** 5 4N 115 57 E
Tenosique, *Mexico* **87 D6** 17 30N 91 24W
Tenryū-Gawa →, *Japan* **31 G8** 35 39N 137 48 E
Tenterden, *U.K.* **11 F8** 51 4N 0 42 E
Tenterfield, *Australia* **63 D5** 29 0S 152 0 E
Teófilo Otoni, *Brazil* **93 G10** 17 50S 41 30W
Tepa, *Indonesia* **37 F7** 7 52S 129 31 E
Tepalcatepec →, *Mexico* **86 D4** 18 35N 101 59W
Tepehuanes, *Mexico* **86 B3** 25 21N 105 44W
Tepetongo, *Mexico* **86 C4** 22 28N 103 9W
Tepic, *Mexico* **86 C4** 21 30N 104 54W
Teplice, *Czech Rep.* **16 C7** 50 40N 13 48 E
Tepoca, C., *Mexico* **86 A2** 30 20N 112 25W
Tequila, *Mexico* **86 C4** 20 54N 103 47W
Ter →, *Spain* **19 A7** 42 2N 3 12 E
Ter Apel, *Neths.* **15 B7** 52 53N 7 5 E
Teraina, *Kiribati* **65 G11** 4 43N 160 25W
Téramo, *Italy* **20 C5** 42 39N 13 42 E
Terang, *Australia* **63 F3** 38 15S 142 55 E
Tercero →, *Argentina* **94 C3** 32 58S 61 47W
Terebovlya, *Ukraine* **17 D13** 49 18N 25 44 E
Terek →, *Russia* **25 F8** 44 0N 47 30 E
Teresina, *Brazil* **93 E10** 5 9S 42 45W
Terewah, L., *Australia* **63 D4** 29 52S 147 35 E
Teridgerie Cr. →, *Australia* **63 E4** 30 25S 148 50 E
Termez = Termiz, *Uzbekistan* **26 F7** 37 15N 67 15 E
Términi Imerese, *Italy* **20 F5** 37 59N 13 42 E
Términos, L. de, *Mexico* **87 D6** 18 35N 91 30W
Termiz, *Uzbekistan* **26 F7** 37 15N 67 15 E
Térmoli, *Italy* **20 C6** 42 0N 15 0 E
Ternate, *Indonesia* **37 D7** 0 45N 127 25 E
Terneuzen, *Neths.* **15 C3** 51 20N 3 50 E
Terney, *Russia* **27 E14** 45 3N 136 37 E
Terni, *Italy* **20 C5** 42 34N 12 37 E
Ternopil, *Ukraine* **17 D13** 49 30N 25 40 E
Ternopol = Ternopil, *Ukraine* **17 D13** 49 30N 25 40 E
Terowie, *Australia* **63 E2** 33 8S 138 55 E
Terra Bella, *U.S.A.* **85 K7** 35 58N 119 3W
Terra Nova Nat. Park, *Canada* **71 C9** 48 33N 53 55W
Terrace, *Canada* **72 C3** 54 30N 128 35W
Terrace Bay, *Canada* **70 C2** 48 47N 87 5W
Terracina, *Italy* **20 D5** 41 17N 13 15 E
Terralba, *Italy* **20 E3** 39 43N 8 39 E
Terranova = Ólbia, *Italy* **20 D3** 40 55N 9 31 E
Terrassa, *Spain* **19 B7** 41 34N 2 1 E
Terre Haute, *U.S.A.* **76 F2** 39 28N 87 25W
Terrebonne B., *U.S.A.* **81 L9** 29 5N 90 35W
Terrell, *U.S.A.* **81 J6** 32 44N 96 17W
Terrenceville, *Canada* **71 C9** 47 40N 54 44W
Terry, *U.S.A.* **80 B2** 46 47N 105 19W
Terryville, *U.S.A.* **79 E11** 41 41N 73 3W
Terschelling, *Neths.* **15 A5** 53 25N 5 20 E
Teruel, *Spain* **19 B5** 40 22N 1 8W
Tervola, *Finland* **8 C21** 66 6N 24 49 E
Teryaweyna L., *Australia* **63 E3** 32 18S 143 22 E
Teshio, *Japan* **30 B10** 44 53N 141 44 E
Teshio-Gawa →, *Japan* **30 B10** 44 53N 141 45 E
Tesiyn Gol →, *Mongolia* **32 A4** 50 40N 93 20 E
Teslin, *Canada* **72 A2** 60 10N 132 43W
Teslin →, *Canada* **72 A2** 61 34N 134 35W
Teslin L., *Canada* **72 A2** 60 15N 132 57W
Tessalit, *Mali* **50 D6** 20 12N 1 0 E
Test →, *U.K.* **11 G6** 50 56N 1 29W
Testigos, Is. Las, *Venezuela* **89 D7** 11 23N 63 7W
Tetachuck L., *Canada* **72 C3** 53 18N 125 55W
Tetas, Pta., *Chile* **94 A1** 23 31S 70 38W
Tete, *Mozam.* **55 F3** 16 13S 33 33 E
Tete □, *Mozam.* **55 F3** 15 15S 32 40 E
Teterev →, *Ukraine* **17 C16** 51 1N 30 5 E
Teteven, *Bulgaria* **21 C11** 42 58N 24 17 E
Tethul →, *Canada* **72 A6** 60 35N 112 12W
Tetiyev, *Ukraine* **17 D15** 49 22N 29 38 E
Teton →, *U.S.A.* **82 C8** 47 56N 110 31W
Tétouan, *Morocco* **50 A4** 35 35N 5 21W
Tetovo, *Macedonia* **21 C9** 42 1N 20 59 E
Teuco →, *Argentina* **94 B3** 25 35S 60 11W
Teulon, *Canada* **73 C9** 50 23N 97 16W
Teun, *Indonesia* **37 F7** 6 59S 129 8 E
Teutoburger Wald, *Germany* **16 B5** 52 5N 8 22 E
Tevere →, *Italy* **20 D5** 41 44N 12 14 E
Teverya, *Israel* **47 C4** 32 47N 35 32 E
Teviot →, *U.K.* **12 F6** 55 29N 2 38W
Tewantin, *Australia* **63 D5** 26 27S 153 3 E
Tewkesbury, *U.K.* **11 F5** 51 59N 2 9W
Texada I., *Canada* **72 D4** 49 40N 124 25W
Texarkana, *Ark., U.S.A.* **81 J8** 33 26N 94 2W
Texarkana, *Tex., U.S.A.* **81 J7** 33 26N 94 3W
Texas, *Australia* **63 D5** 28 49S 151 9 E
Texas □, *U.S.A.* **81 K5** 31 40N 98 30W
Texas City, *U.S.A.* **81 L7** 29 24N 94 54W
Texel, *Neths.* **15 A4** 53 5N 4 50 E
Texline, *U.S.A.* **81 G3** 36 23N 103 2W
Texoma, L., *U.S.A.* **81 J6** 33 50N 96 34W
Tezin, *Afghan.* **42 B3** 34 24N 69 30 E
Teziutlán, *Mexico* **87 D5** 19 50N 97 22W
Tezpur, *India* **41 F18** 26 40N 92 45 E
Tezzeron L., *Canada* **72 C4** 54 43N 124 30W
Tha-anne →, *Canada* **73 A10** 60 31N 94 37W
Tha Deua, *Laos* **38 D4** 17 57N 102 53 E
Tha Deua, *Laos* **38 C3** 19 26N 101 50 E
Tha Pla, *Thailand* **38 D3** 17 48N 100 32 E
Tha Rua, *Thailand* **38 E3** 14 34N 100 44 E
Tha Sala, *Thailand* **39 H2** 8 40N 99 56 E

Tha Song Yang, *Thailand* **38 D1** 17 34N 97 55 E
Thaba Putsoa, *Lesotho* **57 D4** 29 45S 28 0 E
Thabana Ntlenyana, *Lesotho* **57 D4** 29 30S 29 16 E
Thabazimbi, *S. Africa* **57 C4** 24 40S 27 21 E
Thādiq, *Si. Arabia* **44 E5** 25 18N 45 52 E
Thai Muang, *Thailand* **39 H2** 8 24N 98 16 E
Thailand ■, *Asia* **38 E4** 16 0N 102 0 E
Thailand, G. of, *Asia* **39 G3** 11 30N 101 0 E
Thakhek, *Laos* **38 D5** 17 25N 104 45 E
Thal, *Pakistan* **42 C4** 33 28N 70 33 E
Thal Desert, *Pakistan* **42 D4** 31 10N 71 30 E
Thala La, *Burma* **41 E20** 28 25N 97 23 E
Thalabarivat, *Cambodia* **38 F5** 13 33N 105 57 E
Thallon, *Australia* **63 D4** 28 39S 148 49 E
Thames, *N.Z.* **59 G5** 37 7S 175 34 E
Thames →, *Canada* **78 D2** 42 20N 82 25W
Thames →, *U.K.* **11 F8** 51 29N 0 34 E
Thames →, *U.S.A.* **79 E12** 41 18N 72 5W
Thames Estuary, *U.K.* **11 F8** 51 29N 0 52 E
Thamesford, *Canada* **78 C4** 43 4N 81 0W
Thamesville, *Canada* **78 D3** 42 33N 81 59W
Than, *India* **42 H4** 22 34N 71 11 E
Than Uyen, *Vietnam* **38 B4** 22 0N 103 54 E
Thana Gazi, *India* **42 F7** 27 25N 76 19 E
Thandla, *India* **42 H6** 23 0N 74 34 E
Thane, *India* **40 K8** 19 12N 72 59 E
Thanesar, *India* **42 D7** 30 1N 76 52 E
Thanet, I. of, *U.K.* **11 F9** 51 21N 1 20 E
Thangool, *Australia* **62 C5** 24 38S 150 42 E
Thanh Hoa, *Vietnam* **38 C5** 19 48N 105 46 E
Thanh Hung, *Vietnam* **39 H5** 9 55N 105 43 E
Thanh Pho Ho Chi Minh = Phanh Bho Ho Chi Minh, *Vietnam* **39 G6** 10 58N 106 40 E
Thanh Thuy, *Vietnam* **38 A5** 22 55N 104 51 E
Thanjavur, *India* **40 P11** 10 48N 79 12 E
Thano Bula Khan, *Pakistan* **42 G2** 25 22N 67 50 E
Thaolinta L., *Canada* **73 A9** 61 30N 96 25W
Thap Sakae, *Thailand* **39 G2** 11 30N 99 37 E
Thap Than, *Thailand* **38 E2** 15 27N 99 54 E
Thar Desert, *India* **42 F5** 28 0N 72 0 E
Tharad, *India* **42 G4** 24 30N 71 44 E
Thargomindah, *Australia* **63 D3** 27 58S 143 46 E
Tharrawaddy, *Burma* **41 L19** 17 38N 95 48 E
Tharthār, Mileh, *Iraq* **44 C4** 34 0N 43 15 E
Tharthār, W. ath →, *Iraq* **44 C4** 33 59N 43 12 E
Thásos, *Greece* **21 D11** 40 40N 24 40 E
Thatcher, *Ariz., U.S.A.* **83 K9** 32 51N 109 46W
Thatcher, *Colo., U.S.A.* **81 G2** 37 33N 104 7W
Thaton, *Burma* **41 L20** 16 55N 97 22 E
Thaungdut, *Burma* **41 G19** 24 30N 94 40 E
Thayer, *U.S.A.* **81 G9** 36 31N 91 33W
Thayetmyo, *Burma* **41 K19** 19 20N 95 10 E
Thazi, *Burma* **41 J20** 21 0N 96 5 E
The Alberga →, *Australia* **63 D2** 27 6S 135 33 E
The Bight, *Bahamas* **89 B4** 24 19N 75 24W
The Coorong, *Australia* **63 F2** 35 50S 139 20 E
The Dalles, *U.S.A.* **82 D3** 45 36N 121 10W
The English Company's Is., *Australia* **62 A2** 11 50S 136 32 E
The Frome →, *Australia* **63 D2** 29 8S 137 54 E
The Great Divide = Great Dividing Ra., *Australia* **62 C4** 23 0S 146 0 E
The Hague = 's-Gravenhage, *Neths.* **15 B4** 52 7N 4 17 E
The Hamilton →, *Australia* **63 D2** 26 40S 135 19 E
The Macumba →, *Australia* **63 D2** 27 52S 137 12 E
The Neales →, *Australia* **63 D2** 28 8S 136 47 E
The Officer →, *Australia* **61 E5** 27 46S 132 30 E
The Pas, *Canada* **73 C8** 53 45N 101 15W
The Range, *Zimbabwe* **55 F3** 19 2S 31 2 E
The Rock, *Australia* **63 F4** 35 15S 147 2 E
The Salt L., *Australia* **63 E3** 30 6S 142 8 E
The Sandheads, *India* **43 J13** 21 10N 88 20 E
The Stevenson →, *Australia* **63 D2** 27 6S 135 33 E
The Warburton →, *Australia* **63 D2** 28 4S 137 28 E
The Woodlands, *U.S.A.* **81 K7** 30 9N 95 27W
Thebes = Thívai, *Greece* **21 E10** 38 19N 23 19 E
Thebes, *Egypt* **51 C12** 25 40N 32 35 E
Thedford, *Canada* **78 C3** 43 9N 81 51W
Thedford, *U.S.A.* **80 E4** 41 59N 100 35W
Theebine, *Australia* **63 D5** 25 57S 152 34 E
Thekulthili L., *Canada* **73 A7** 61 3N 110 0W
Thelon →, *Canada* **73 A8** 62 35N 104 3W
Theodore, *Australia* **62 C5** 24 55S 150 3 E
Theodore, *Canada* **73 C8** 51 26N 102 55W
Theodore, *U.S.A.* **77 K1** 30 33N 88 10W
Theodore Roosevelt National Memorial Park, *U.S.A.* **80 B3** 47 0N 103 25W
Theodore Roosevelt Res., *U.S.A.* **83 K8** 33 46N 111 0W
Thepha, *Thailand* **39 J3** 6 52N 100 58 E
Theresa, *U.S.A.* **79 B9** 44 13N 75 48W
Thermaïkós Kólpos, *Greece* **21 D10** 40 15N 22 45 E
Thermopolis, *U.S.A.* **82 E9** 43 39N 108 13W
Thermopylae P., *Greece* **21 E10** 38 48N 22 35 E
Thessalon, *Canada* **70 C3** 46 20N 83 30W
Thessaloníki, *Greece* **21 D10** 40 38N 22 58 E
Thessaloniki, Gulf of = Thermaïkós Kólpos, *Greece* **21 D10** 40 15N 22 45 E
Thetford, *U.K.* **11 E8** 52 25N 0 45 E
Thetford Mines, *Canada* **71 C5** 46 8N 71 18W
Theun →, *Laos* **38 C5** 18 19N 104 0 E
Theunissen, *S. Africa* **56 D4** 28 26S 26 43 E
Thevenard, *Australia* **63 E1** 32 9S 133 38 E
Thibodaux, *U.S.A.* **81 L9** 29 48N 90 49W
Thicket Portage, *Canada* **73 B9** 55 19N 97 42W
Thief River Falls, *U.S.A.* **80 A6** 48 7N 96 10W
Thiel Mts., *Antarctica* **5 E16** 85 15S 91 0W
Thiers, *France* **18 D5** 45 52N 3 33 E
Thiès, *Senegal* **50 F2** 14 50N 16 51W
Thika, *Kenya* **54 C4** 1 1S 37 5 E
Thikombia, *Fiji* **59 B9** 15 44S 179 55W
Thimphu, *Bhutan* **41 F16** 27 31N 89 45 E
þingvallavatn, *Iceland* **8 D3** 64 11N 21 9W
Thionville, *France* **18 B7** 49 20N 6 10 E
Thíra, *Greece* **21 F11** 36 23N 25 27 E
Third Cataract, *Sudan* **51 E12** 19 49N 30 19 E
Thirsk, *U.K.* **10 C6** 54 14N 1 19W
Thisted, *Denmark* **9 H13** 56 58N 8 40 E
Thistle I., *Australia* **63 F2** 35 0S 136 8 E
Thívai, *Greece* **21 E10** 38 19N 23 19 E
þjórsá →, *Iceland* **8 E3** 63 47N 20 48W
Thlewiaza →, *Man., Canada* **73 B8** 59 43N 100 5W
Thlewiaza →, *N.W.T., Canada* **73 A10** 60 29N 94 40W
Thmar Puok, *Cambodia* **38 F4** 13 57N 103 4 E
Tho Vinh, *Vietnam* **38 C5** 19 16N 105 42 E
Thoa →, *Canada* **73 A7** 60 31N 109 47W
Thoen, *Thailand* **38 D2** 17 43N 99 12 E
Thoeng, *Thailand* **38 C3** 19 41N 100 12 E
Thohoyandou, *S. Africa* **53 J6** 22 58S 30 29 E
Tholdi, *Pakistan* **43 B7** 35 5N 76 6 E
Thomas, *U.S.A.* **81 H5** 35 45N 98 45W
Thomas, L., *Australia* **63 D2** 26 4S 137 58 E
Thomaston, *U.S.A.* **77 J3** 32 53N 84 20W
Thomasville, *Ala., U.S.A.* **77 K2** 31 55N 87 44W
Thomasville, *Ga., U.S.A.* **77 K4** 30 50N 83 59W
Thomasville, *N.C., U.S.A.* **77 H5** 35 53N 80 5W
Thompson, *Canada* **73 B9** 55 45N 97 52W
Thompson, *U.S.A.* **79 E9** 41 52N 75 31W
Thompson →, *Canada* **72 C4** 50 15N 121 24W
Thompson →, *U.S.A.* **80 F8** 39 46N 93 37W
Thompson Falls, *U.S.A.* **82 C6** 47 36N 115 21W
Thompson Pk., *U.S.A.* **82 F2** 41 0N 123 0W
Thompson Springs, *U.S.A.* **83 G9** 38 58N 109 43W
Thompsontown, *U.S.A.* **78 F7** 40 33N 77 14W
Thomson, *U.S.A.* **77 J4** 33 28N 82 30W
Thomson →, *Australia* **62 C3** 25 11S 142 53 E
Thomson's Falls = Nyahururu, *Kenya* **54 B4** 0 2N 36 27 E
þórisvatn, *Iceland* **8 D4** 64 20N 18 55W
Thornaby on Tees, *U.K.* **10 C6** 54 33N 1 18W
Thornbury, *Canada* **78 B4** 44 34N 80 26W
Thorne, *U.K.* **10 D7** 53 37N 0 57W
Thornhill, *Canada* **72 C3** 54 31N 128 32W
Thorold, *Canada* **78 C5** 43 7N 79 12W
þórshöfn, *Iceland* **8 C6** 66 12N 15 20W
Thouin, C., *Australia* **60 D2** 20 20S 118 10 E
Thousand Oaks, *U.S.A.* **85 L8** 34 10N 118 50W
Thrace, *Turkey* **21 D12** 41 0N 27 0 E
Three Forks, *U.S.A.* **82 D8** 45 54N 111 33W
Three Hills, *Canada* **72 C6** 51 43N 113 15W
Three Hummock I., *Australia* **62 G3** 40 25S 144 55 E
Three Points, C., *Ghana* **50 H5** 4 42N 2 6W
Three Rivers, *Calif., U.S.A.* **84 J8** 36 26N 118 54W
Three Rivers, *Tex., U.S.A.* **81 L5** 28 28N 98 11W
Three Sisters, *U.S.A.* **82 D3** 44 4N 121 51W
Three Springs, *Australia* **61 E2** 29 32S 115 45 E
Throssell, L., *Australia* **61 E3** 27 33S 124 10 E
Throssell Ra., *Australia* **60 D3** 22 3S 121 43 E
Thuan Hoa, *Vietnam* **39 H5** 8 58N 105 30 E
Thubun Lakes, *Canada* **73 A6** 61 30N 112 0W
Thuin, *Belgium* **15 D4** 50 20N 4 17 E
Thule, *Greenland* **4 B4** 77 40N 69 0W
Thun, *Switz.* **18 C7** 46 45N 7 38 E
Thunder B., *U.S.A.* **78 B1** 45 0N 83 20W
Thunder Bay, *Canada* **70 C2** 48 20N 89 15W
Thung Song, *Thailand* **39 H2** 8 10N 99 40 E
Thunkar, *Bhutan* **41 F17** 27 55N 91 0 E
Thuong Tra, *Vietnam* **38 D6** 16 2N 107 42 E
Thüringer Wald, *Germany* **16 C6** 50 35N 11 0 E
Thurles, *Ireland* **13 D4** 52 41N 7 49W
Thurrock □, *U.K.* **11 F8** 51 31N 0 23 E
Thursday I., *Australia* **62 A3** 10 30S 142 3 E
Thurso, *Canada* **70 C4** 45 36N 75 15W
Thurso, *U.K.* **12 C5** 58 36N 3 32W
Thurso →, *U.K.* **12 C5** 58 36N 3 32W
Thurston I., *Antarctica* **5 D16** 72 0S 100 0W
Thutade L., *Canada* **72 B3** 57 0N 126 55W
Thyolo, *Malawi* **55 F4** 16 7S 35 5 E
Thysville = Mbanza Ngungu, *Dem. Rep. of the Congo* **52 F2** 5 12S 14 53 E
Ti Tree, *Australia* **62 C1** 22 5S 133 22 E
Tian Shan, *Asia* **32 B3** 42 0N 76 0 E
Tianjin, *China* **35 E9** 39 8N 117 10 E
Tianshui, *China* **34 G3** 34 32N 105 40 E
Tianzhen, *China* **34 D8** 40 24N 114 5 E
Tianzhuangtai, *China* **35 D12** 40 43N 122 5 E
Tiaret, *Algeria* **50 A6** 35 20N 1 21 E
Tibagi, *Brazil* **95 A5** 24 30S 50 24W
Tibagi →, *Brazil* **95 A5** 22 47S 51 1W
Tiber = Tevere →, *Italy* **20 D5** 41 44N 12 14 E
Tiberias = Teverya, *Israel* **47 C4** 32 47N 35 32 E
Tiberias, L. = Yam Kinneret, *Israel* **47 C4** 32 45N 35 35 E
Tibesti, *Chad* **51 D9** 21 0N 17 30 E
Tibet = Xizang Zizhiqu □, *China* **32 C3** 32 0N 88 0 E
Tibet, Plateau of, *Asia* **28 F12** 32 0N 86 0 E
Tibnī, *Syria* **44 C3** 35 36N 39 50 E
Tibooburra, *Australia* **63 D3** 29 26S 142 1 E
Tiburón, I., *Mexico* **86 B2** 29 0N 112 30W
Ticino →, *Italy* **18 D8** 45 9N 9 14 E
Ticonderoga, *U.S.A.* **79 C11** 43 51N 73 26W
Ticul, *Mexico* **87 C7** 20 20N 89 31W
Tidaholm, *Sweden* **9 G15** 58 12N 13 58 E
Tiddim, *Burma* **41 H18** 23 28N 93 45 E
Tidioute, *U.S.A.* **78 E5** 41 41N 79 24W
Tidjikja, *Mauritania* **50 E3** 18 29N 11 35W
Tidore, *Indonesia* **37 D7** 0 40N 127 25 E
Tiel, *Neths.* **15 C5** 51 53N 5 26 E
Tieling, *China* **35 C12** 42 20N 123 55 E
Tielt, *Belgium* **15 C3** 51 0N 3 20 E
Tien Shan = Tian Shan, *Asia* **32 B3** 42 0N 76 0 E
Tien-tsin = Tianjin, *China* **35 E9** 39 8N 117 10 E
Tien Yen, *Vietnam* **38 B6** 21 20N 107 24 E
T'ienching = Tianjin, *China* **35 E9** 39 8N 117 10 E
Tienen, *Belgium* **15 D4** 50 48N 4 57 E
Tientsin = Tianjin, *China* **35 E9** 39 8N 117 10 E
Tieri, *Australia* **62 C4** 23 2S 148 21 E
Tierra Amarilla, *Chile* **94 B1** 27 28S 70 18W
Tierra Amarilla, *U.S.A.* **83 H10** 36 42N 106 33W
Tierra Colorada, *Mexico* **87 D5** 17 10N 99 35W
Tierra de Campos, *Spain* **19 A3** 42 10N 4 50W
Tierra del Fuego, I. Gr. de, *Argentina* **96 G3** 54 0S 69 0W
Tiétar →, *Spain* **19 C3** 39 50N 6 1W
Tietê →, *Brazil* **95 A5** 20 40S 51 35W
Tiffin, *U.S.A.* **76 E4** 41 7N 83 11W
Tiflis = Tbilisi, *Georgia* **25 F7** 41 43N 44 50 E
Tifton, *U.S.A.* **77 K4** 31 27N 83 31W
Tifu, *Indonesia* **37 E7** 3 39S 126 24 E
Tighina, *Moldova* **17 E15** 46 50N 29 30 E
Tigil, *Russia* **27 D16** 57 49N 158 40 E
Tignish, *Canada* **71 C7** 46 58N 64 2W
Tigre →, *Peru* **92 D4** 4 30S 74 10W
Tigre →, *Venezuela* **92 B6** 9 20N 62 30W
Tigris = Dijlah, Nahr →, *Asia* **44 D5** 31 0N 47 25 E
Tigyaing, *Burma* **41 H20** 23 45N 96 10 E
Tījara, *India* **42 F7** 27 56N 76 31 E
Tijuana, *Mexico* **85 N9** 32 30N 117 10W
Tikal, *Guatemala* **88 C2** 17 13N 89 24W
Tikamgarh, *India* **43 G8** 24 44N 78 50 E
Tikhoretsk, *Russia* **25 E7** 45 56N 40 5 E
Tikhvin, *Russia* **24 C5** 59 35N 33 30 E
Tikrīt, *Iraq* **44 C4** 34 35N 43 37 E
Tiksi, *Russia* **27 B13** 71 40N 128 45 E
Tilamuta, *Indonesia* **37 D6** 0 32N 122 23 E
Tilburg, *Neths.* **15 C5** 51 31N 5 6 E
Tilbury, *Canada* **78 D2** 42 17N 82 23W
Tilbury, *U.K.* **11 F8** 51 27N 0 22 E
Tilcara, *Argentina* **94 A2** 23 36S 65 23W
Tilden, *U.S.A.* **80 D6** 42 3N 97 50W
Tilhar, *India* **43 F8** 28 0N 79 45 E
Tilichiki, *Russia* **27 C17** 60 27N 166 5 E
Tílissos, *Greece* **23 D7** 35 20N 25 1 E
Till →, *U.K.* **10 B5** 55 41N 2 13W
Tillamook, *U.S.A.* **82 D2** 45 27N 123 51W
Tillsonburg, *Canada* **78 D4** 42 53N 80 44W
Tillyeria □, *Cyprus* **23 D11** 35 6N 32 40 E
Tílos, *Greece* **21 F12** 36 27N 27 27 E
Tilpa, *Australia* **63 E3** 30 57S 144 24 E
Tilsit = Sovetsk, *Russia* **9 J19** 55 6N 21 50 E
Tilt →, *U.K.* **12 E5** 56 46N 3 51W
Tilton, *U.S.A.* **79 C13** 43 27N 71 36W
Tiltonsville, *U.S.A.* **78 F4** 40 10N 80 41W
Timagami, L., *Canada* **70 C3** 47 0N 80 10W
Timanskiy Kryazh, *Russia* **24 A9** 65 58N 50 5 E
Timaru, *N.Z.* **59 L3** 44 23S 171 14 E
Timau, *Kenya* **54 B4** 0 4N 37 15 E
Timbákion, *Greece* **23 D6** 35 4N 24 45 E
Timber Creek, *Australia* **60 C5** 15 40S 130 29 E
Timber Lake, *U.S.A.* **80 C4** 45 26N 101 5W
Timber Mt., *U.S.A.* **84 H10** 37 6N 116 28W
Timbuktu = Tombouctou, *Mali* **50 E5** 16 50N 3 0W
Timi, *Cyprus* **23 E11** 34 44N 32 31 E
Timimoun, *Algeria* **50 C6** 29 14N 0 16 E
Timişoara, *Romania* **17 F11** 45 43N 21 15 E
Timmins, *Canada* **70 C3** 48 28N 81 25W
Timok →, *Serbia, Yug.* **21 B10** 44 10N 22 40 E
Timor, *Indonesia* **37 F7** 9 0S 125 0 E
Timor Sea, *Ind. Oc.* **60 B4** 12 0S 127 0 E
Timor Timur □, *Indonesia* **37 F7** 9 0S 125 0 E
Tin Can Bay, *Australia* **63 D5** 25 56S 153 0 E
Tin Mt., *U.S.A.* **84 J9** 36 50N 117 10W
Tinaca Pt., *Phil.* **37 C7** 5 30N 125 25 E
Tinajo, *Canary Is.* **22 E6** 29 4N 13 42W
Tindal, *Australia* **60 B5** 14 31S 132 22 E
Tindouf, *Algeria* **50 C4** 27 42N 8 10W
Tinggi, Pulau, *Malaysia* **39 L5** 2 18N 104 7 E
Tingo Maria, *Peru* **92 E3** 9 10S 75 54W
Tingrela, *Ivory C.* **50 F4** 10 27N 6 25W
Tinh Bien, *Vietnam* **39 G5** 10 36N 104 57 E
Tinnevelly = Tirunelveli, *India* **40 Q10** 8 45N 77 45 E
Tinogasta, *Argentina* **94 B2** 28 5S 67 32W
Tínos, *Greece* **21 F11** 37 33N 25 8 E
Tinpahar, *India* **43 G12** 24 59N 87 44 E
Tintina, *Argentina* **94 B3** 27 2S 62 45W
Tintinara, *Australia* **63 F3** 35 48S 140 2 E
Tioga, *N. Dak., U.S.A.* **80 A3** 48 23N 102 56W
Tioga, *Pa., U.S.A.* **78 E7** 41 55N 77 8W
Tioman, Pulau, *Malaysia* **39 L5** 2 50N 104 10 E
Tionesta, *U.S.A.* **78 E5** 41 30N 79 28W
Tipongpani, *India* **41 F19** 27 20N 95 55 E
Tipperary, *Ireland* **13 D3** 52 28N 8 10W
Tipperary □, *Ireland* **13 D4** 52 37N 7 55W
Tipton, *Calif., U.S.A.* **84 J7** 36 4N 119 19W
Tipton, *Iowa, U.S.A.* **80 E9** 41 46N 91 8W
Tipton Mt., *U.S.A.* **85 K12** 35 32N 114 12W
Tiptonville, *U.S.A.* **81 G10** 36 23N 89 29W
Tīrān, *Iran* **45 C6** 32 45N 51 8 E
Tirana, *Albania* **21 D8** 41 18N 19 49 E
Tiranë = Tirana, *Albania* **21 D8** 41 18N 19 49 E
Tiraspol, *Moldova* **17 E15** 46 55N 29 35 E
Tire, *Turkey* **21 E12** 38 5N 27 45 E
Tirebolu, *Turkey* **25 F6** 40 58N 38 45 E
Tiree, *U.K.* **12 E2** 56 31N 6 55W
Tiree, Passage of, *U.K.* **12 E2** 56 30N 6 30W
Tîrgovişte = Târgovişte, *Romania* **17 F13** 44 55N 25 27 E
Tîrgu-Jiu = Târgu-Jiu, *Romania* **17 F12** 45 5N 23 19 E
Tîrgu Mureş = Târgu Mureş, *Romania* **17 E13** 46 31N 24 38 E
Tirich Mir, *Pakistan* **40 A7** 36 15N 71 55 E
Tírnavos, *Greece* **21 E10** 39 45N 22 18 E
Tirodi, *India* **40 J11** 21 40N 79 44 E
Tirol □, *Austria* **16 E6** 47 3N 10 43 E
Tirso →, *Italy* **20 E3** 39 53N 8 32 E
Tiruchchirappalli, *India* **40 P11** 10 45N 78 45 E
Tirunelveli, *India* **40 Q10** 8 45N 77 45 E
Tirupati, *India* **40 N11** 13 39N 79 25 E
Tiruppur, *India* **40 P10** 11 5N 77 22 E
Tiruvannamalai, *India* **40 N11** 12 15N 79 5 E
Tisa, *India* **42 C7** 32 50N 76 9 E
Tisa →, *Serbia, Yug.* **21 B9** 45 15N 20 17 E
Tisdale, *Canada* **73 C8** 52 50N 104 0W
Tishomingo, *U.S.A.* **81 H6** 34 14N 96 41W
Tisza = Tisa →, *Serbia, Yug.* **21 B9** 45 15N 20 17 E
Tit-Ary, *Russia* **27 B13** 71 55N 127 2 E
Tithwal, *Pakistan* **43 B5** 34 21N 73 50 E
Titicaca, L., *S. Amer.* **92 G5** 15 30S 69 30W
Titograd = Podgorica, *Montenegro, Yug.* **21 C8** 42 30N 19 19 E
Titule, *Dem. Rep. of the Congo* **54 B2** 3 15N 25 31 E
Titusville, *Fla., U.S.A.* **77 L5** 28 37N 80 49W
Titusville, *Pa., U.S.A.* **78 E5** 41 38N 79 41W
Tivaouane, *Senegal* **50 F2** 14 56N 16 45W
Tiverton, *U.K.* **11 G4** 50 54N 3 29W
Tívoli, *Italy* **20 D5** 41 58N 12 45 E
Tizi-Ouzou, *Algeria* **50 A6** 36 42N 4 3 E
Tizimín, *Mexico* **87 C7** 21 0N 88 1W
Tjeggelvas, *Sweden* **8 C17** 66 37N 17 45 E
Tjirebon = Cirebon, *Indonesia* **37 G13** 6 45S 108 32 E
Tjörn, *Sweden* **9 G14** 58 0N 11 35 E
Tlacotalpan, *Mexico* **87 D5** 18 37N 95 40W
Tlahualilo, *Mexico* **86 B4** 26 20N 103 30W
Tlaquepaque, *Mexico* **86 C4** 20 39N 103 19W
Tlaxcala, *Mexico* **87 D5** 19 20N 98 14W
Tlaxcala □, *Mexico* **87 D5** 19 30N 98 20W
Tlaxiaco, *Mexico* **87 D5** 17 18N 97 40W
Tlemcen, *Algeria* **50 B5** 34 52N 1 21W
To Bong, *Vietnam* **38 F7** 12 45N 109 16 E
Toad →, *Canada* **72 B4** 59 25N 124 57W
Toad River, *Canada* **72 B3** 58 51N 125 14W
Toamasina, *Madag.* **57 B8** 18 10S 49 25 E
Toamasina □, *Madag.* **57 B8** 18 0S 49 0 E
Toay, *Argentina* **94 D3** 36 43S 64 38W
Toba, *Japan* **31 G8** 34 30N 136 51 E
Toba, Danau, *Indonesia* **36 D1** 2 30N 97 30 E
Toba Kakar, *Pakistan* **42 D3** 31 30N 69 0 E
Toba Tek Singh, *Pakistan* **42 D5** 30 55N 72 25 E
Tobago, *W. Indies* **89 D7** 11 10N 60 30W
Tobelo, *Indonesia* **37 D7** 1 45N 127 56 E
Tobermory, *Canada* **78 A3** 45 12N 81 40W
Tobermory, *U.K.* **12 E2** 56 38N 6 5W
Tobi, *Pac. Oc.* **37 D8** 2 40N 131 10 E
Tobin, *U.S.A.* **84 F5** 39 55N 121 19W
Tobin, L., *Australia* **60 D4** 21 45S 125 49 E
Tobin L., *Canada* **73 C8** 53 35N 103 30W
Toboali, *Indonesia* **36 E3** 3 0S 106 25 E
Tobol →, *Russia* **26 D7** 58 10N 68 12 E
Toboli, *Indonesia* **37 E6** 0 38S 120 5 E
Tobolsk, *Russia* **26 D7** 58 15N 68 10 E
Tobruk = Tubruq, *Libya* **51 B10** 32 7N 23 55 E
Tobyhanna, *U.S.A.* **79 E9** 41 11N 75 25W
Tobyl = Tobol →, *Russia* **26 D7** 58 10N 68 12 E
Tocantinópolis, *Brazil* **93 E9** 6 20S 47 25W
Tocantins □, *Brazil* **93 F9** 10 0S 48 0W
Tocantins →, *Brazil* **93 D9** 1 45S 49 10W
Toccoa, *U.S.A.* **77 H4** 34 35N 83 19W
Tochi →, *Pakistan* **42 C4** 32 49N 70 41 E
Tochigi, *Japan* **31 F9** 36 25N 139 45 E
Tochigi □, *Japan* **31 F9** 36 45N 139 45 E
Toconao, *Chile* **94 A2** 23 11S 68 1W
Tocopilla, *Chile* **94 A1** 22 5S 70 10W
Tocumwal, *Australia* **63 F4** 35 51S 145 31 E
Tocuyo →, *Venezuela* **92 A5** 11 3N 68 23W
Todd →, *Australia* **62 C2** 24 52S 135 48 E
Todeli, *Indonesia* **37 E6** 1 38S 124 34 E
Todenyang, *Kenya* **54 B4** 4 35N 35 56 E
Todgarh, *India* **42 G5** 25 42N 73 58 E
Todos os Santos, B. de, *Brazil* **93 F11** 12 48S 38 38W
Todos Santos, *Mexico* **86 C2** 23 27N 110 13W
Toe Hd., *U.K.* **12 D1** 57 50N 7 8W
Tofield, *Canada* **72 C6** 53 25N 112 40W
Tofino, *Canada* **72 D3** 49 11N 125 55W
Tofua, *Tonga* **59 D11** 19 45S 175 5W
Tōgane, *Japan* **31 G10** 35 33N 140 22 E
Togian, Kepulauan, *Indonesia* **37 E6** 0 20S 121 50 E
Togliatti, *Russia* **24 D8** 53 32N 49 24 E
Togo ■, *W. Afr.* **50 G6** 8 30N 1 35 E
Togtoh, *China* **34 D6** 40 15N 111 10 E
Tōhoku □, *Japan* **30 E10** 39 50N 141 45 E
Töhöm, *Mongolia* **34 B5** 44 27N 108 2 E
Toinya, *Sudan* **51 G11** 6 17N 29 46 E
Toiyabe Range, *U.S.A.* **82 G5** 39 30N 117 0W
Tojikiston = Tajikistan ■, *Asia* **26 F8** 38 30N 70 0 E
Tojo, *Indonesia* **37 E6** 1 20S 121 15 E
Tōjō, *Japan* **31 G6** 34 53N 133 16 E
Tok, *U.S.A.* **68 B5** 63 20N 142 59W
Tok-do, *Japan* **31 F5** 37 15N 131 52 E
Tokachi-Dake, *Japan* **30 C11** 43 17N 142 5 E
Tokachi-Gawa →, *Japan* **30 C11** 42 44N 143 42 E
Tokala, *Indonesia* **37 E6** 1 30S 121 40 E
Tōkamachi, *Japan* **31 F9** 37 8N 138 43 E
Tokanui, *N.Z.* **59 M2** 46 34S 168 56 E
Tokara-Rettō, *Japan* **31 K4** 29 37N 129 43 E
Tokarahi, *N.Z.* **59 L3** 44 56S 170 39 E
Tokashiki-Shima, *Japan* **31 L3** 26 11N 127 21 E
Tokat □, *Turkey* **25 F6** 40 15N 36 30 E
Tŏkch'ŏn, *N. Korea* **35 E14** 39 45N 126 18 E
Tokeland, *U.S.A.* **84 D3** 46 42N 123 59W
Tokelau Is., *Pac. Oc.* **64 H10** 9 0S 171 45W
Tokmak, *Kyrgyzstan* **26 E8** 42 49N 75 15 E
Toko Ra., *Australia* **62 C2** 23 5S 138 20 E
Tokoro-Gawa →, *Japan* **30 B12** 44 7N 144 5 E
Tokuno-Shima, *Japan* **31 L4** 27 56N 128 55 E
Tokushima, *Japan* **31 G7** 34 4N 134 34 E
Tokushima □, *Japan* **31 H7** 33 55N 134 0 E
Tokuyama, *Japan* **31 G5** 34 3N 131 50 E
Tōkyō, *Japan* **31 G9** 35 45N 139 45 E
Tolaga Bay, *N.Z.* **59 H7** 38 21S 178 20 E
Tolbukhin = Dobrich, *Bulgaria* **21 C12** 43 37N 27 49 E
Toledo, *Brazil* **95 A5** 24 44S 53 45W
Toledo, *Spain* **19 C3** 39 50N 4 2W
Toledo, *Ohio, U.S.A.* **76 E4** 41 39N 83 33W
Toledo, *Oreg., U.S.A.* **82 D2** 44 37N 123 56W
Toledo, *Wash., U.S.A.* **82 C2** 46 26N 122 51W
Toledo, Montes de, *Spain* **19 C3** 39 33N 4 20W
Toledo Bend Reservoir, *U.S.A.* **81 K8** 31 11N 93 34W
Tolga, *Australia* **62 B4** 17 15S 145 29 E
Toliara, *Madag.* **57 C7** 23 21S 43 40 E
Toliara □, *Madag.* **57 C8** 21 0S 45 0 E
Tolima, *Colombia* **92 C3** 4 40N 75 19W
Tolitoli, *Indonesia* **37 D6** 1 5N 120 50 E
Tollhouse, *U.S.A.* **84 H7** 37 1N 119 24W
Tolo, Teluk, *Indonesia* **37 E6** 2 20S 122 10 E
Toluca, *Mexico* **87 D5** 19 20N 99 40W
Tom Burke, *S. Africa* **57 C4** 23 5S 28 0 E
Tom Price, *Australia* **60 D2** 22 40S 117 48 E
Tomah, *U.S.A.* **80 D9** 43 59N 90 30W
Tomahawk, *U.S.A.* **80 C10** 45 28N 89 44W
Tomakomai, *Japan* **30 C10** 42 38N 141 36 E
Tomales, *U.S.A.* **84 G4** 38 15N 122 53W
Tomales B., *U.S.A.* **84 G3** 38 15N 123 58W
Tomar, *Portugal* **19 C1** 39 36N 8 25W
Tomaszów Mazowiecki, *Poland* **17 C10** 51 30N 20 2 E
Tomatlán, *Mexico* **86 D3** 19 56N 105 15W
Tombador, Serra do, *Brazil* **92 F7** 12 0S 58 0W
Tombigbee →, *U.S.A.* **77 K2** 31 8N 87 57W
Tombouctou, *Mali* **50 E5** 16 50N 3 0W
Tombstone, *U.S.A.* **83 L8** 31 43N 110 4W
Tombua, *Angola* **56 B1** 15 55S 11 55 E

Tomé, Chile 94 D1 36 36S 72 57W
Tomelloso, Spain 19 C4 39 10N 3 2W
Tomini, Indonesia 37 D6 0 30N 120 30 E
Tomini, Teluk, Indonesia 37 E6 0 10S 122 0 E
Tomintoul, U.K. 12 D5 57 15N 3 23W
Tomkinson Ranges, Australia 61 E4 26 11S 129 5 E
Tommot, Russia 27 D13 59 4N 126 20 E
Tomnop Ta Suos, Cambodia 39 G5 11 20N 104 15 E
Tomo →, Colombia 92 B5 5 20N 67 48W
Toms Place, U.S.A. 84 H8 37 34N 118 41W
Toms River, U.S.A. 79 G10 39 58N 74 12W
Tomsk, Russia 26 D9 56 30N 85 5 E
Tonalá, Mexico 87 D6 16 8N 93 41W
Tonantins, Brazil 92 D5 2 45S 67 45W
Tonasket, U.S.A. 82 B4 48 42N 119 26W
Tonawanda, U.S.A. 78 D6 43 1N 78 53W
Tonbridge, U.K. 11 F8 51 11N 0 17 E
Tondano, Indonesia 37 D6 1 35N 124 54 E
Tone →, Australia 61 F2 34 25S 116 25 E
Tone-Gawa →, Japan 31 F9 35 44N 140 51 E
Tonekābon, Iran 45 B6 36 45N 51 12 E
Tong Xian, China 34 E9 39 55N 116 35 E
Tonga ■, Pac. Oc. 59 D11 19 50S 174 30W
Tonga Trench, Pac. Oc. 64 J10 18 0S 173 0W
Tongaat, S. Africa 57 D5 29 33S 31 9 E
Tongareva, Cook Is. 65 H12 9 0S 158 0W
Tongatapu, Tonga 59 E12 21 10S 174 0W
Tongchŏn-ni, N. Korea 35 E14 39 50N 127 25 E
Tongchuan, China 34 G5 35 6N 109 3 E
Tongeren, Belgium 15 D5 50 47N 5 28 E
Tongguan, China 34 G6 34 40N 110 25 E
Tonghua, China 35 D13 41 42N 125 58 E
Tongjosŏn Man, N. Korea 35 E15 39 30N 128 0 E
Tongking, G. of, Asia 32 E5 20 0N 108 0 E
Tongliao, China 35 C12 43 38N 122 18 E
Tongling, China 33 C6 30 55N 117 48 E
Tongnae, S. Korea 35 G15 35 12N 129 5 E
Tongobory, Madag. 57 C7 23 32S 44 20 E
Tongoy, Chile 94 C1 30 16S 71 31W
Tongres = Tongeren, Belgium 15 D5 50 47N 5 28 E
Tongsa Dzong, Bhutan 41 F17 27 31N 90 31 E
Tongue, U.K. 12 C4 58 29N 4 25W
Tongue →, U.S.A. 80 B2 46 25N 105 52W
Tongwei, China 34 G3 35 0N 105 5 E
Tongxin, China 34 F3 36 59N 105 58 E
Tongyang, N. Korea 35 E14 39 9N 126 53 E
Tongyu, China 35 B12 44 45N 123 4 E
Tonj, Sudan 51 G11 7 20N 28 44 E
Tonk, India 42 F6 26 6N 75 54 E
Tonkawa, U.S.A. 81 G6 36 41N 97 18W
Tonkin = Bac Phan, Vietnam 38 B5 22 0N 105 0 E
Tonle Sap, Cambodia 38 F5 13 0N 104 0 E
Tono, Japan 30 E10 39 19N 141 32 E
Tonopah, U.S.A. 83 G5 38 4N 117 14W
Tonosí, Panama 88 E3 7 20N 80 20W
Tons →, Haryana, India 42 D7 30 30N 77 39 E
Tons →, Ut. P., India 43 F10 26 1N 83 33 E
Tønsberg, Norway 9 G14 59 19N 10 25 E
Toobanna, Australia 62 B4 18 42S 146 9 E
Toodyay, Australia 61 F2 31 34S 116 28 E
Tooele, U.S.A. 82 F7 40 32N 112 18W
Toompine, Australia 63 D3 27 15S 144 19 E
Toora, Australia 63 F4 38 39S 146 23 E
Toora-Khem, Russia 27 D10 52 28N 96 17 E
Toowoomba, Australia 63 D5 27 32S 151 56 E
Top-ozero, Russia 24 A5 65 35N 32 0 E
Top Springs, Australia 60 C5 16 37S 131 51 E
Topaz, U.S.A. 84 G7 38 41N 119 30W
Topeka, U.S.A. 80 F7 39 3N 95 40W
Topley, Canada 72 C3 54 49N 126 18W
Topocalma, Pta., Chile 94 C1 34 10S 72 2W
Topock, U.S.A. 85 L12 34 46N 114 29W
Topol'čany, Slovak Rep. 17 D10 48 35N 18 12 E
Topolobampo, Mexico 86 B3 25 40N 109 4W
Toppenish, U.S.A. 82 C3 46 23N 120 19W
Toraka Vestale, Madag. 57 B7 16 20S 43 58 E
Torata, Peru 92 G4 17 23S 70 1W
Torbalı, Turkey 21 E12 38 10N 27 21 E
Torbat-e Heydārīyeh, Iran 45 C8 35 15N 59 12 E
Torbat-e Jām, Iran 45 C9 35 16N 60 35 E
Torbay, Canada 71 C9 47 40N 52 42W
Torbay □, U.K. 11 G4 50 26N 3 31W
Tordesillas, Spain 19 B3 41 30N 5 0W
Torfaen □, U.K. 11 F4 51 43N 3 3W
Torgau, Germany 16 C7 51 34N 13 0 E
Torhout, Belgium 15 C3 51 5N 3 7 E
Tori-Shima, Japan 31 J10 30 29N 140 19 E
Torin, Mexico 86 B2 27 33N 110 15W
Torino, Italy 18 D7 45 3N 7 40 E
Torit, Sudan 51 H12 4 27N 32 31 E
Torkamān, Iran 44 B5 37 35N 47 23 E
Tormes →, Spain 19 B2 41 18N 6 29W
Tornado Mt., Canada 72 D6 49 55N 114 40W
Torne älv →, Sweden 8 D21 65 50N 24 12 E
Torneå = Tornio, Finland 8 D21 65 50N 24 12 E
Torneträsk, Sweden 8 B18 68 24N 19 15 E
Tornio, Finland 8 D21 65 50N 24 12 E
Tornionjoki →, Finland 8 D21 65 50N 24 12 E
Tornquist, Argentina 94 D3 38 8S 62 15W
Toro, Spain 22 B11 39 59N 4 8 E
Toro, Cerro del, Chile 94 B2 29 10S 69 50W
Toro Pk., U.S.A. 85 M10 33 34N 116 24W
Toroníios Kólpos, Greece 21 D10 40 5N 23 30 E
Toronto, Canada 78 C5 43 39N 79 20W
Toronto, U.S.A. 78 F4 40 28N 80 36W
Toropets, Russia 24 C5 56 30N 31 40 E
Tororo, Uganda 54 B3 0 45N 34 12 E
Toros Dağları, Turkey 25 G5 37 0N 32 30 E
Torpa, India 43 H11 22 57N 85 6 E
Torquay, Australia 63 F3 38 20S 144 19 E
Torquay, U.K. 11 G4 50 27N 3 32W
Torrance, U.S.A. 85 M8 33 50N 118 19W
Torre de Moncorvo, Portugal 19 B2 41 12N 7 8W
Torre del Greco, Italy 20 D6 40 47N 14 22 E
Torrejón de Ardoz, Spain 19 B4 40 27N 3 29W
Torrelavega, Spain 19 A3 43 20N 4 5W
Torremolinos, Spain 19 D3 36 38N 4 30W
Torrens, L., Australia 63 E2 31 0S 137 50 E
Torrens Cr. →, Australia 62 C4 22 23S 145 9 E
Torrens Creek, Australia 62 C4 20 48S 145 3 E
Torrent, Spain 19 C5 39 27N 0 28W
Torreón, Mexico 86 B4 25 33N 103 26W
Torres, Brazil 95 B5 29 21S 49 44W
Torres, Mexico 86 B2 28 46N 110 47W
Torres Strait, Australia 64 H6 9 50S 142 20 E
Torres Vedras, Portugal 19 C1 39 5N 9 15W
Torrevieja, Spain 19 D5 37 59N 0 42W
Torrey, U.S.A. 83 G8 38 18N 111 25W
Torridge →, U.K. 11 G3 51 0N 4 13W
Torridon, L., U.K. 12 D3 57 35N 5 50W
Torrington, Conn., U.S.A. 79 E11 41 48N 73 7W
Torrington, Wyo., U.S.A. 80 D2 42 4N 104 11W
Tórshavn, Færoe Is. 8 E9 62 5N 6 56W
Tortola, Virgin Is. 89 C7 18 19N 64 45W
Tortosa, Spain 19 B6 40 49N 0 31 E
Tortosa, C., Spain 19 B6 40 41N 0 52 E
Tortue, I. de la, Haiti 89 B5 20 5N 72 57W
Ţorūd, Iran 45 C7 35 25N 55 5 E
Toruń, Poland 17 B10 53 2N 18 39 E
Tory I., Ireland 13 A3 55 16N 8 14W
Tosa, Japan 31 H6 33 24N 133 23 E
Tosa-Shimizu, Japan 31 H6 32 52N 132 58 E
Tosa-Wan, Japan 31 H6 33 15N 133 30 E
Toscana □, Italy 20 C4 43 25N 11 0 E
Toshkent, Uzbekistan 26 E7 41 20N 69 10 E
Tostado, Argentina 94 B3 29 15S 61 50W
Tostón, Pta. de, Canary Is. 22 F5 28 42N 14 2W
Tosu, Japan 31 H5 33 22N 130 31 E
Toteng, Botswana 56 C3 20 22S 22 58 E
Totma, Russia 24 C7 60 0N 42 40 E
Totnes, U.K. 11 G4 50 26N 3 42W
Totness, Surinam 93 B7 5 53N 56 19W
Totonicapán, Guatemala 88 D1 14 58N 91 12W
Totten Glacier, Antarctica 5 C8 66 45S 116 10 E
Tottenham, Australia 63 E4 32 14S 147 21 E
Tottenham, Canada 78 B5 44 1N 79 49W
Tottori, Japan 31 G7 35 30N 134 15 E
Tottori □, Japan 31 G7 35 30N 134 12 E
Toubkal, Djebel, Morocco 50 B4 31 0N 8 0W
Tougan, Burkina Faso 50 F5 13 11N 2 58W
Touggourt, Algeria 50 B7 33 6N 6 4 E
Toul, France 18 B6 48 40N 5 53 E
Toulon, France 18 E6 43 10N 5 55 E
Toulouse, France 18 E4 43 37N 1 27 E
Toummo, Niger 51 D8 22 45N 14 8 E
Toungoo, Burma 41 K20 19 0N 96 30 E
Touraine, France 18 C4 47 20N 0 30 E
Tourane = Da Nang, Vietnam 38 D7 16 4N 108 13 E
Tourcoing, France 18 A5 50 42N 3 10 E
Touriñán, C., Spain 19 A1 43 3N 9 18W
Tournai, Belgium 15 D3 50 35N 3 25 E
Tournon-sur-Rhône, France 18 D6 45 4N 4 50 E
Tours, France 18 C4 47 22N 0 40 E
Tousidé, Pic, Chad 51 D9 21 1N 16 29 E
Toussora, Mt., C.A.R. 52 C4 9 7N 23 14 E
Touwsrivier, S. Africa 56 E3 33 20S 20 2 E
Towada, Japan 30 D10 40 37N 141 13 E
Towada-Ko, Japan 30 D10 40 28N 140 55 E
Towanda, U.S.A. 79 E8 41 46N 76 27W
Towang, India 41 F17 27 37N 91 50 E
Tower, U.S.A. 80 B8 47 48N 92 17W
Towerhill Cr. →, Australia 62 C3 22 28S 144 35 E
Towner, U.S.A. 80 A4 48 21N 100 25W
Townsend, U.S.A. 82 C8 46 19N 111 31W
Townshend I., Australia 62 C5 22 10S 150 31 E
Townsville, Australia 62 B4 19 15S 146 45 E
Towson, U.S.A. 76 F7 39 24N 76 36W
Towuti, Danau, Indonesia 37 E6 2 45S 121 32 E
Toya-Ko, Japan 30 C10 42 35N 140 51 E
Toyama, Japan 31 F8 36 40N 137 15 E
Toyama □, Japan 31 F8 36 45N 137 30 E
Toyama-Wan, Japan 31 F8 37 0N 137 30 E
Toyohashi, Japan 31 G8 34 45N 137 25 E
Toyokawa, Japan 31 G8 34 48N 137 27 E
Toyonaka, Japan 31 G7 34 50N 135 28 E
Toyooka, Japan 31 G7 35 35N 134 48 E
Toyota, Japan 31 G8 35 3N 137 7 E
Tozeur, Tunisia 50 B7 33 56N 8 8 E
Trá Li = Tralee, Ireland 13 D2 52 16N 9 42W
Tra On, Vietnam 39 H5 9 58N 105 55 E
Trabzon, Turkey 25 F6 41 0N 39 45 E
Tracadie, Canada 71 C7 47 30N 64 55W
Tracy, Calif., U.S.A. 84 H5 37 44N 121 26W
Tracy, Minn., U.S.A. 80 C7 44 14N 95 37W
Trafalgar, C., Spain 19 D2 36 10N 6 2W
Trail, Canada 72 D5 49 5N 117 40W
Trainor L., Canada 72 A4 60 24N 120 17W
Trákhonas, Cyprus 23 D12 35 12N 33 21 E
Tralee, Ireland 13 D2 52 16N 9 42W
Tralee B., Ireland 13 D2 52 17N 9 55W
Tramore, Ireland 13 D4 52 10N 7 10W
Tramore B., Ireland 13 D4 52 9N 7 10W
Tran Ninh, Cao Nguyen, Laos 38 C4 19 30N 103 10 E
Tranås, Sweden 9 G16 58 3N 14 59 E
Trancas, Argentina 94 B2 26 11S 65 20W
Trang, Thailand 39 J2 7 33N 99 38 E
Trangahy, Madag. 57 B7 19 7S 44 31 E
Trangan, Indonesia 37 F8 6 40S 134 20 E
Trangie, Australia 63 E4 32 4S 148 0 E
Trani, Italy 20 D7 41 17N 16 25 E
Tranoroa, Madag. 57 C8 24 42S 45 4 E
Tranqueras, Uruguay 95 C4 31 13S 55 45W
Transantarctic Mts., Antarctica 5 E12 85 0S 170 0W
Transilvania, Romania 17 E12 46 30N 24 0 E
Transilvanian Alps = Carpaţii Meridionali, Romania 17 F13 45 30N 25 0 E
Transvaal □, S. Africa 53 K5 25 0S 29 0 E
Transylvania = Transilvania, Romania 17 E12 46 30N 24 0 E
Trápani, Italy 20 E5 38 1N 12 29 E
Trapper Pk., U.S.A. 82 D6 45 54N 114 18W
Traralgon, Australia 63 F4 38 12S 146 34 E
Trasimeno, L., Italy 20 C5 43 8N 12 6 E
Trat, Thailand 39 F4 12 14N 102 33 E
Tratani →, Pakistan 42 E3 29 19N 68 20 E
Traun, Austria 16 D8 48 14N 14 15 E
Travellers L., Australia 63 E3 33 20S 142 0 E
Travemünde, Germany 16 B6 53 57N 10 52 E
Travers, Mt., N.Z. 59 K4 42 1S 172 45 E
Traverse City, U.S.A. 76 C3 44 46N 85 38W
Travis, L., U.S.A. 81 K5 30 24N 97 55W
Travnik, Bos.-H. 21 B7 44 17N 17 39 E
Trébbia →, Italy 18 D8 45 4N 9 41 E
Třebíč, Czech Rep. 16 D8 49 14N 15 55 E
Trebinje, Bos.-H. 21 C8 42 44N 18 22 E
Trebonne, Australia 62 B4 18 37S 146 5 E
Tregaron, U.K. 11 E4 52 14N 3 56W
Tregrosse Is., Australia 62 B5 17 41S 150 43 E
Treherne, Canada 73 D9 49 38N 98 42W
Treinta y Tres, Uruguay 95 C5 33 16S 54 17W
Trelew, Argentina 96 E3 43 10S 65 20W
Trelleborg, Sweden 9 J15 55 20N 13 10 E
Tremadog Bay, U.K. 10 E3 52 51N 4 18W
Tremonton, U.S.A. 82 F7 41 43N 112 10W
Tremp, Spain 19 A6 42 10N 0 52 E
Trenche →, Canada 70 C5 47 46N 72 53W
Trenčín, Slovak Rep. 17 D10 48 52N 18 4 E
Trenggalek, Indonesia 37 H14 8 3S 111 43 E
Trenque Lauquen, Argentina 94 D3 36 5S 62 45W
Trent →, Canada 78 B7 44 6N 77 34W
Trent →, U.K. 10 D7 53 41N 0 42W
Trento, Italy 20 A4 46 4N 11 8 E
Trenton, Canada 78 B7 44 10N 77 34W
Trenton, Mo., U.S.A. 80 E8 40 5N 93 37W
Trenton, N.J., U.S.A. 79 F10 40 14N 74 46W
Trenton, Nebr., U.S.A. 80 E4 40 11N 101 1W
Trepassey, Canada 71 C9 46 43N 53 25W
Tres Arroyos, Argentina 94 D3 38 26S 60 20W
Três Corações, Brazil 95 A6 21 44S 45 15W
Três Lagoas, Brazil 93 H8 20 50S 51 43W
Tres Lomas, Argentina 94 D3 36 27S 62 51W
Tres Marías, Islas, Mexico 86 C3 21 25N 106 28W
Tres Montes, C., Chile 96 F1 46 50S 75 30W
Tres Pinos, U.S.A. 84 J5 36 48N 121 19W
Três Pontas, Brazil 95 A6 21 23S 45 29W
Tres Puentes, Chile 94 B1 27 50S 70 15W
Tres Puntas, C., Argentina 96 F3 47 0S 66 0W
Três Rios, Brazil 95 A7 22 6S 43 15W
Tres Valles, Mexico 87 D5 18 15N 96 8W
Tresco, U.K. 11 H1 49 57N 6 20W
Treviso, Italy 20 B5 45 40N 12 15 E
Triabunna, Australia 62 G4 42 30S 147 55 E
Triánda, Greece 23 C10 36 25N 28 10 E
Tribulation, C., Australia 62 B4 16 5S 145 29 E
Tribune, U.S.A. 80 F4 38 28N 101 45W
Trichinopoly = Tiruchchirappalli, India 40 P11 10 45N 78 45 E
Trichur, India 40 P10 10 30N 76 18 E
Trida, Australia 63 E4 33 1S 145 1 E
Trier, Germany 16 D4 49 45N 6 38 E
Trieste, Italy 20 B5 45 40N 13 46 E
Triglav, Slovenia 16 E7 46 21N 13 50 E
Tríkkala, Greece 21 E9 39 34N 21 47 E
Trikomo, Cyprus 23 D12 35 17N 33 52 E
Trikora, Puncak, Indonesia 37 E9 4 15S 138 45 E
Trim, Ireland 13 C5 53 33N 6 48W
Trincomalee, Sri Lanka 40 Q12 8 38N 81 15 E
Trindade, Brazil 93 G9 16 40S 49 30W
Trindade, I., Atl. Oc. 2 F8 20 20S 29 50W
Trinidad, Bolivia 92 F6 14 46S 64 50W
Trinidad, Cuba 88 B4 21 48N 80 0W
Trinidad, Uruguay 94 C4 33 30S 56 50W
Trinidad, U.S.A. 81 G2 37 10N 104 31W
Trinidad, W. Indies 89 D7 10 30N 61 15W
Trinidad →, Mexico 87 D5 17 49N 95 9W
Trinidad & Tobago ■, W. Indies 89 D7 10 30N 61 20W
Trinity, Canada 71 C9 48 59N 53 55W
Trinity, U.S.A. 81 K7 30 57N 95 22W
Trinity →, Calif., U.S.A. 82 F2 41 11N 123 42W
Trinity →, Tex., U.S.A. 81 L7 29 45N 94 43W
Trinity B., Canada 71 C9 48 20N 53 10W
Trinity Is., U.S.A. 68 C4 56 33N 154 25W
Trinity Range, U.S.A. 82 F4 40 15N 118 45W
Trinkitat, Sudan 51 E13 18 45N 37 51 E
Trinway, U.S.A. 78 F2 40 9N 82 1W
Tripoli = Tarābulus, Lebanon 47 A4 34 31N 35 50 E
Tripoli = Tarābulus, Libya 51 B8 32 49N 13 7 E
Trípolis, Greece 21 F10 37 31N 22 25 E
Tripolitania, Libya 48 C5 31 0N 12 0 E
Tripolitania, N. Afr. 51 B8 31 0N 13 0 E
Tripura □, India 41 H18 24 0N 92 0 E
Tripylos, Cyprus 23 E11 34 59N 32 41 E
Tristan da Cunha, Atl. Oc. 49 K2 37 6S 12 20W
Trisul, India 43 D8 30 19N 79 47 E
Trivandrum, India 40 Q10 8 41N 77 0 E
Trnava, Slovak Rep. 17 D9 48 23N 17 35 E
Trochu, Canada 72 C6 51 50N 113 13W
Trodely I., Canada 70 B4 52 15N 79 26W
Troglav, Croatia 20 C7 43 56N 16 36 E
Troilus, L., Canada 70 B5 50 50N 74 35W
Trois-Pistoles, Canada 71 C6 48 5N 69 10W
Trois-Rivières, Canada 70 C5 46 25N 72 34W
Troitsk, Russia 26 D7 54 10N 61 35 E
Troitsko Pechorsk, Russia 24 B10 62 40N 56 10 E
Trölladyngja, Iceland 8 D5 64 54N 17 16W
Trollhättan, Sweden 9 G15 58 17N 12 20 E
Trollheimen, Norway 8 E13 62 46N 9 1 E
Trombetas →, Brazil 93 D7 1 55S 55 35W
Tromsø, Norway 8 B18 69 40N 18 56 E
Trona, U.S.A. 85 K9 35 46N 117 23W
Tronador, Mte., Argentina 96 E2 41 10S 71 50W
Trøndelag, Norway 8 D14 64 17N 11 50 E
Trondheim, Norway 8 E14 63 36N 10 25 E
Trondheimsfjorden, Norway 8 E14 63 35N 10 30 E
Troodos, Cyprus 23 E11 34 55N 32 52 E
Troon, U.K. 12 F4 55 33N 4 39W
Tropic, U.S.A. 83 H7 37 37N 112 5W
Trostan, U.K. 13 A5 55 3N 6 10W
Trout →, Canada 72 A5 61 19N 119 51W
Trout L., N.W.T., Canada 72 A4 60 40N 121 14W
Trout L., Ont., Canada 73 C10 51 20N 93 15W
Trout Lake, Canada 72 B6 56 30N 114 32W
Trout Lake, U.S.A. 84 E5 46 0N 121 32W
Trout River, Canada 71 C8 49 29N 58 8W
Trout Run, U.S.A. 78 E7 41 23N 77 3W
Trouville-sur-Mer, France 18 B4 49 21N 0 5 E
Trowbridge, U.K. 11 F5 51 18N 2 12W
Troy, Turkey 21 E12 39 57N 26 12 E
Troy, Ala., U.S.A. 77 K3 31 48N 85 58W
Troy, Kans., U.S.A. 80 F7 39 47N 95 5W
Troy, Mo., U.S.A. 80 F9 38 59N 90 59W
Troy, Mont., U.S.A. 82 B6 48 28N 115 53W
Troy, N.Y., U.S.A. 79 D11 42 44N 73 41W
Troy, Ohio, U.S.A. 76 E3 40 2N 84 12W
Troy, Pa., U.S.A. 79 E8 41 47N 76 47W
Troyes, France 18 B6 48 19N 4 3 E
Truchas Peak, U.S.A. 81 H2 35 58N 105 39W
Trucial States = United Arab Emirates ■, Asia 45 F7 23 50N 54 0 E
Truckee, U.S.A. 84 F6 39 20N 120 11W
Trudovoye, Russia 30 C6 43 17N 132 5 E
Trujillo, Honduras 88 C2 16 0N 86 0W
Trujillo, Peru 92 E3 8 6S 79 0W
Trujillo, Spain 19 C3 39 28N 5 55W
Trujillo, U.S.A. 81 H2 35 32N 104 42W
Trujillo, Venezuela 92 B4 9 22N 70 38W
Truk, Micronesia 64 G7 7 25N 151 46 E
Trumann, U.S.A. 81 H9 35 41N 90 31W
Trumansburg, U.S.A. 79 D8 42 33N 76 40W
Trumbull, Mt., U.S.A. 83 H7 36 25N 113 8W
Trundle, Australia 63 E4 32 53S 147 35 E
Trung-Phan = Annam, Vietnam 38 E7 16 0N 108 0 E
Truro, Canada 71 C7 45 21N 63 14W
Truro, U.K. 11 G2 50 16N 5 4W
Truskavets, Ukraine 17 D12 49 17N 23 30 E
Trutch, Canada 72 B4 57 44N 122 57W
Truth or Consequences, U.S.A. 83 K10 33 8N 107 15W
Trutnov, Czech Rep. 16 C8 50 37N 15 54 E
Truxton, U.S.A. 79 D8 42 45N 76 2W
Tryonville, U.S.A. 78 E5 41 42N 79 48W
Tsaratanana, Madag. 57 B8 16 47S 47 39 E
Tsaratanana, Mt. de, Madag. 57 A8 14 0S 49 0 E
Tsarevo = Michurin, Bulgaria 21 C12 42 9N 27 51 E
Tsau, Botswana 56 C3 20 8S 22 22 E
Tselinograd = Astana, Kazakstan 26 D8 51 10N 71 30 E
Tsetserleg, Mongolia 32 B5 47 36N 101 32 E
Tshabong, Botswana 56 D3 26 2S 22 29 E
Tshane, Botswana 56 C3 24 5S 21 54 E
Tshela, Dem. Rep. of the Congo 52 E2 4 57S 13 4 E
Tshesebe, Botswana 57 C4 21 51S 27 32 E
Tshibeke, Dem. Rep. of the Congo 54 C2 2 40S 28 35 E
Tshibinda, Dem. Rep. of the Congo 54 C2 2 23S 28 43 E
Tshikapa, Dem. Rep. of the Congo 52 F4 6 28S 20 48 E
Tshilenge, Dem. Rep. of the Congo 54 D1 6 17S 23 48 E
Tshinsenda, Dem. Rep. of the Congo 55 E2 12 20S 28 0 E
Tshofa, Dem. Rep. of the Congo 54 D2 5 13S 25 16 E
Tshwane, Botswana 56 C3 22 24S 22 1 E
Tsigara, Botswana 56 C4 20 22S 25 54 E
Tsihombe, Madag. 57 D8 25 10S 45 41 E
Tsiigehtchic, Canada 68 B6 67 15N 134 0W
Tsimlyansk Res. = Tsimlyanskoye Vdkhr., Russia 25 E7 48 0N 43 0 E
Tsimlyanskoye Vdkhr., Russia 25 E7 48 0N 43 0 E
Tsinan = Jinan, China 34 F9 36 38N 117 1 E
Tsineng, S. Africa 56 D3 27 5S 23 5 E
Tsinghai = Qinghai □, China 32 C4 36 0N 98 0 E
Tsingtao = Qingdao, China 35 F11 36 5N 120 20 E
Tsinjomitondraka, Madag. 57 B8 15 40S 47 8 E
Tsiroanomandidy, Madag. 57 B8 18 46S 46 2 E
Tsivory, Madag. 57 C8 24 4S 46 5 E
Tskhinvali, Georgia 25 F7 42 14N 44 1 E
Tsna →, Russia 24 D7 54 55N 41 58 E
Tso Moriri, L., India 43 C8 32 50N 78 20 E
Tsodilo Hill, Botswana 56 B3 18 49S 21 43 E
Tsogttsetsiy = Baruunsuu, Mongolia 34 C3 43 43N 105 35 E
Tsolo, S. Africa 57 E4 31 18S 28 37 E
Tsomo, S. Africa 57 E4 32 0S 27 42 E
Tsu, Japan 31 G8 34 45N 136 25 E
Tsu L., Canada 72 A6 60 40N 111 52W
Tsuchiura, Japan 31 F10 36 5N 140 15 E
Tsugaru-Kaikyō, Japan 30 D10 41 35N 141 0 E
Tsumeb, Namibia 56 B2 19 9S 17 44 E
Tsumis, Namibia 56 C2 23 39S 17 29 E
Tsuruga, Japan 31 G8 35 45N 136 2 E
Tsurugi-San, Japan 31 H7 33 51N 134 6 E
Tsuruoka, Japan 30 E9 38 44N 139 50 E
Tsushima, Gifu, Japan 31 G8 35 10N 136 43 E
Tsushima, Nagasaki, Japan 31 G4 34 20N 129 20 E
Tsuyama, Japan 31 G7 35 3N 134 0 E
Tsyelyakhany, Belarus 17 B13 52 30N 25 46 E
Tual, Indonesia 37 F8 5 38S 132 44 E
Tuam, Ireland 13 C3 53 31N 8 51W
Tuamotu Arch. = Tuamotu Is., Pac. Oc. 65 J13 17 0S 144 0W
Tuamotu Is., Pac. Oc. 65 J13 17 0S 144 0W
Tuamotu Ridge, Pac. Oc. 65 K14 20 0S 138 0W
Tuao, Phil. 37 A6 17 55N 121 22 E
Tuapse, Russia 25 F6 44 5N 39 10 E
Tuatapere, N.Z. 59 M1 46 8S 167 41 E
Tuba City, U.S.A. 83 H8 36 8N 111 14W
Tuban, Indonesia 37 G15 6 54S 112 3 E
Tubarão, Brazil 95 B6 28 30S 49 0W
Tūbās, West Bank 47 C4 32 20N 35 22 E
Tübingen, Germany 16 D5 48 31N 9 4 E
Tubruq, Libya 51 B10 32 7N 23 55 E
Tubuai Is., Pac. Oc. 65 K13 25 0S 150 0W
Tuc Trung, Vietnam 39 G6 11 1N 107 12 E
Tucacas, Venezuela 92 A5 10 48N 68 19W
Tuchodi →, Canada 72 B4 58 17N 123 42W
Tuckanarra, Australia 61 E2 27 7S 118 5 E
Tucson, U.S.A. 83 K8 32 13N 110 58W
Tucumán □, Argentina 94 B2 26 48S 66 2W
Tucumcari, U.S.A. 81 H3 35 10N 103 44W
Tucupita, Venezuela 92 B6 9 2N 62 3W
Tucuruí, Brazil 93 D9 3 42S 49 44W
Tucuruí, Reprêsa de, Brazil 93 D9 4 0S 49 30W
Tudela, Spain 19 A5 42 4N 1 39W
Tudmur, Syria 44 C3 34 36N 38 15 E
Tudor, L., Canada 71 A6 55 50N 65 25W
Tugela →, S. Africa 57 D5 29 14S 31 30 E
Tuguegarao, Phil. 37 A6 17 35N 121 42 E
Tugur, Russia 27 D14 53 44N 136 45 E
Tui, Spain 19 A1 42 3N 8 39W
Tuineje, Canary Is. 22 F5 28 19N 14 3W
Tukangbesi, Kepulauan, Indonesia 37 F6 6 0S 124 0 E
Tukarak I., Canada 70 A4 56 15N 78 45W
Tukayyid, Iraq 44 D5 29 47N 45 36 E
Tuktoyaktuk, Canada 68 B6 69 27N 133 2W
Tukums, Latvia 9 H20 56 58N 23 10 E

Tukuyu, Tanzania 55 D3 9 17S 33 35 E
Tula, Hidalgo, Mexico 87 C5 20 5N 99 20W
Tula, Tamaulipas, Mexico 87 C5 23 0N 99 40W
Tula, Russia 24 D6 54 13N 37 38 E
Tulancingo, Mexico 87 C5 20 5N 99 22W
Tulare, U.S.A. 84 J7 36 13N 119 21W
Tulare Lake Bed, U.S.A. 84 K7 36 0N 119 48W
Tularosa, U.S.A. 83 K10 33 5N 106 1W
Tulbagh, S. Africa 56 E2 33 16S 19 6 E
Tulcán, Ecuador 92 C3 0 48N 77 43W
Tulcea, Romania 17 F15 45 13N 28 46 E
Tulchyn, Ukraine 17 D15 48 41N 28 49 E
Tūleh, Iran 45 C7 34 35N 52 33 E
Tulemalu L., Canada 73 A9 62 58N 99 25W
Tuli, Zimbabwe 55 G2 21 58S 29 13 E
Tulia, U.S.A. 81 H4 34 32N 101 46W
Tulita, Canada 68 B7 64 57N 125 30W
Ţulkarm, West Bank 47 C4 32 19N 35 2 E
Tulla, Ireland 13 D3 52 53N 8 46W
Tullahoma, U.S.A. 77 H2 35 22N 86 13W
Tullamore, Australia 63 E4 32 39S 147 36 E
Tullamore, Ireland 13 C4 53 16N 7 31W
Tulle, France 18 D4 45 16N 1 46 E
Tullow, Ireland 13 D5 52 49N 6 45W
Tully, Australia 62 B4 17 56S 145 55 E
Tully, U.S.A. 79 D8 42 48N 76 7W
Tulsa, U.S.A. 81 G7 36 10N 95 55W
Tulsequah, Canada 72 B2 58 39N 133 35W
Tulua, Colombia 92 C3 4 6N 76 11W
Tulun, Russia 27 D11 54 32N 100 35 E
Tulungagung, Indonesia 37 H14 8 5S 111 54 E
Tuma →, Nic. 88 D3 13 6N 84 35W
Tumaco, Colombia 92 C3 1 50N 78 45W
Tumatumari, Guyana 92 B7 5 20N 58 55W
Tumba, Sweden 9 G17 59 12N 17 48 E
Tumba, L., Dem. Rep. of the Congo 52 E3 0 50S 18 0 E
Tumbarumba, Australia 63 F4 35 44S 148 0 E
Tumbaya, Argentina 94 A2 23 50S 65 26W
Tumbes, Peru 92 D2 3 37S 80 27W
Tumbwe, Dem. Rep. of the Congo 55 E2 11 25S 27 15 E
Tumby Bay, Australia 63 E2 34 21S 136 8 E
Tumd Youqi, China 34 D6 40 30N 110 30 E
Tumen, China 35 C15 43 0N 129 50 E
Tumen Jiang →, China 35 C16 42 20N 130 35 E
Tumeremo, Venezuela 92 B6 7 18N 61 30W
Tumkur, India 40 N10 13 18N 77 6 E
Tump, Pakistan 40 F3 26 7N 62 16 E
Tumpat, Malaysia 39 J4 6 11N 102 10 E
Tumu, Ghana 50 F5 10 56N 1 56W
Tumucumaque, Serra, Brazil 93 C8 2 0N 55 0W
Tumut, Australia 63 F4 35 16S 148 13 E
Tumwater, U.S.A. 84 C4 47 1N 122 54W
Tuna, India 42 H4 22 59N 70 5 E
Tunas de Zaza, Cuba 88 B4 21 39N 79 34W
Tunbridge Wells = Royal Tunbridge Wells, U.K. 11 F8 51 7N 0 16 E
Tuncurry-Forster, Australia 63 E5 32 17S 152 29 E
Tundla, India 42 F8 27 12N 78 17 E
Tunduru, Tanzania 55 E4 11 8S 37 25 E
Tundzha →, Bulgaria 21 C11 41 40N 26 35 E
Tunga Pass, India 41 E19 29 0N 94 14 E
Tungabhadra →, India 40 M11 15 57N 78 15 E
Tungla, Nic. 88 D3 13 24N 84 21W
Tungsten, Canada 72 A3 61 57N 128 16W
Tunguska, Nizhnyaya →, Russia 27 C9 65 48N 88 4 E
Tunguska, Podkamennaya →, Russia 27 C10 61 50N 90 13 E
Tunica, U.S.A. 81 H9 34 41N 90 23W
Tunis, Tunisia 51 A8 36 50N 10 11 E
Tunisia ■, Africa 51 A7 33 30N 9 10 E
Tunja, Colombia 92 B4 5 33N 73 25W
Tunkhannock, U.S.A. 79 E9 41 32N 75 57W
Tunliu, China 34 F7 36 13N 112 52 E
Tunnsjøen, Norway 8 D15 64 45N 13 25 E
Tunungayualok I., Canada 71 A7 56 0N 61 0W
Tunuyán, Argentina 94 C2 33 35S 69 0W
Tunuyán →, Argentina 94 C2 33 33S 67 30W
Tuolumne, U.S.A. 84 H6 37 58N 120 15W
Tuolumne →, U.S.A. 84 H5 37 36N 121 13W
Tūp Āghāj, Iran 44 B5 36 3N 47 50 E
Tupā, Brazil 95 A5 21 57S 50 28W
Tupelo, U.S.A. 77 H1 34 16N 88 43W
Tupinambaranas, Brazil 92 D7 3 0S 58 0W
Tupiza, Bolivia 94 A2 21 30S 65 40W
Tupman, U.S.A. 85 K7 35 18N 119 21W
Tupper, Canada 72 B4 55 32N 120 1W
Tupper Lake, U.S.A. 79 B10 44 14N 74 28W
Tupungato, Cerro, S. Amer. 94 C2 33 15S 69 50W
Tuquan, China 35 B11 45 18N 121 38 E
Túquerres, Colombia 92 C3 1 5N 77 37W
Tura, Russia 27 C11 64 20N 100 17 E
Turabah, Si. Arabia 46 C3 28 20N 43 15 E
Tūrān, Iran 45 C8 35 39N 56 42 E
Turan, Russia 27 D10 51 55N 95 0 E
Ţurayf, Si. Arabia 44 D3 31 41N 38 39 E
Turda, Romania 17 E12 46 34N 23 47 E
Turek, Poland 17 B10 52 3N 18 30 E
Turen, Venezuela 92 B5 9 17N 69 6W
Turfan = Turpan, China 32 B3 43 58N 89 10 E
Turfan Depression = Turpan Hami, China 28 E12 42 40N 89 25 E
Turgeon →, Canada 70 C4 50 0N 78 56W
Tŭrgovishte, Bulgaria 21 C12 43 17N 26 38 E
Turgutlu, Turkey 21 E12 38 30N 27 43 E
Turia →, Spain 19 C5 39 27N 0 19W
Turiaçu, Brazil 93 D9 1 40S 45 19W
Turiaçu →, Brazil 93 D9 1 36S 45 19W
Turin = Torino, Italy 18 D7 45 3N 7 40 E
Turkana, L., Africa 54 B4 3 30N 36 5 E
Turkestan = Türkistan, Kazakstan 26 E7 43 17N 68 16 E
Turkey ■, Eurasia 25 G6 39 0N 36 0 E
Turkey Creek, Australia 60 C4 17 2S 128 12 E
Türkistan, Kazakstan 26 E7 43 17N 68 16 E
Türkmenbashi, Turkmenistan 25 G9 40 5N 53 5 E
Turkmenistan ■, Asia 26 F6 39 0N 59 0 E
Turks & Caicos Is. ■, W. Indies 89 B5 21 20N 71 20W
Turks Island Passage, W. Indies 89 B5 21 30N 71 30W
Turku, Finland 9 F20 60 30N 22 19 E
Turkwel →, Kenya 54 B4 3 6N 36 6 E
Turlock, U.S.A. 84 H6 37 30N 120 51W
Turnagain →, Canada 72 B3 59 12N 127 35W
Turnagain, C., N.Z. 59 J6 40 28S 176 38 E
Turneffe Is., Belize 87 D7 17 20N 87 50W
Turner, U.S.A. 82 B9 48 51N 108 24W
Turner Pt., Australia 62 A1 11 47S 133 32 E
Turner Valley, Canada 72 C6 50 40N 114 17W
Turners Falls, U.S.A. 79 D12 42 36N 72 33W
Turnhout, Belgium 15 C4 51 19N 4 57 E
Turnor L., Canada 73 B7 56 35N 108 35W
Tŭrnovo = Veliko Tŭrnovo, Bulgaria 21 C11 43 5N 25 41 E
Turnu Măgurele, Romania 17 G13 43 46N 24 56 E
Turnu Roşu, P., Romania 17 F13 45 33N 24 17 E
Turpan, China 32 B3 43 58N 89 10 E
Turpan Hami, China 28 E12 42 40N 89 25 E
Turriff, U.K. 12 D6 57 32N 2 27W
Tursāq, Iraq 44 C5 33 27N 45 47 E
Turtle Head I., Australia 62 A3 10 56S 142 37 E
Turtle L., Canada 73 C7 53 36N 108 38W
Turtle Lake, U.S.A. 80 B4 47 31N 100 53W
Turtleford, Canada 73 C7 53 23N 108 57W
Turukhansk, Russia 27 C9 65 21N 88 5 E
Tuscaloosa, U.S.A. 77 J2 33 12N 87 34W
Tuscany = Toscana □, Italy 20 C4 43 25N 11 0 E
Tuscarawas →, U.S.A. 78 F3 40 24N 81 25W
Tuscarora Mt., U.S.A. 78 F7 40 55N 77 55W
Tuscola, Ill., U.S.A. 76 F1 39 48N 88 17W
Tuscola, Tex., U.S.A. 81 J5 32 12N 99 48W
Tuscumbia, U.S.A. 77 H2 34 44N 87 42W
Tuskegee, U.S.A. 77 J3 32 25N 85 42W
Tustin, U.S.A. 85 M9 33 44N 117 49W
Tuticorin, India 40 Q11 8 50N 78 12 E
Tutóia, Brazil 93 D10 2 45S 42 20W
Tutong, Brunei 36 D4 4 47N 114 40 E
Tutrakan, Bulgaria 21 B12 44 2N 26 40 E
Tuttle Creek L., U.S.A. 80 F6 39 22N 96 40W
Tuttlingen, Germany 16 E5 47 58N 8 48 E
Tutuala, Indonesia 37 F7 8 25S 127 15 E
Tutuila, Amer. Samoa 59 B13 14 19S 170 50W
Tutume, Botswana 53 J5 20 30S 27 5 E
Tututepec, Mexico 87 D5 16 9N 97 38W
Tuva □, Russia 27 D10 51 30N 95 0 E
Tuvalu ■, Pac. Oc. 64 H9 8 0S 178 0 E
Tuxpan, Mexico 87 C5 20 58N 97 23W
Tuxtla Gutiérrez, Mexico 87 D6 16 50N 93 10W
Tuy = Tui, Spain 19 A1 42 3N 8 39W
Tuy An, Vietnam 38 F7 13 17N 109 16 E
Tuy Duc, Vietnam 39 F6 12 15N 107 27 E
Tuy Hoa, Vietnam 38 F7 13 5N 109 10 E
Tuy Phong, Vietnam 39 G7 11 14N 108 43 E
Tuya L., Canada 72 B2 59 7N 130 35W
Tuyen Hoa, Vietnam 38 D6 17 50N 106 10 E
Tūysarkān, Iran 45 C6 34 33N 48 27 E
Tuz Gölü, Turkey 25 G5 38 42N 33 18 E
Ţūz Khurmātū, Iraq 44 C5 34 56N 44 38 E
Tuzla, Bos.-H. 21 B8 44 34N 18 41 E
Tver, Russia 24 C6 56 55N 35 55 E
Twain, U.S.A. 84 E5 40 1N 121 3W
Twain Harte, U.S.A. 84 G6 38 2N 120 14W
Tweed, Canada 78 B7 44 29N 77 19W
Tweed →, U.K. 12 F6 55 45N 2 0W
Tweed Heads, Australia 63 D5 28 10S 153 31 E
Tweedsmuir Prov. Park, Canada 72 C3 53 0N 126 20W
Twentynine Palms, U.S.A. 85 L10 34 8N 116 3W
Twillingate, Canada 71 C9 49 42N 54 45W
Twin Bridges, U.S.A. 82 D7 45 33N 112 20W
Twin Falls, Canada 71 B7 53 30N 64 32W
Twin Falls, U.S.A. 82 E6 42 34N 114 28W
Twin Valley, U.S.A. 80 B6 47 16N 96 16W
Twinsburg, U.S.A. 78 E3 41 18N 81 26W
Twitchell Reservoir, U.S.A. 85 L6 34 59N 120 19W
Two Harbors, U.S.A. 80 B9 47 2N 91 40W
Two Hills, Canada 72 C6 53 43N 111 52W
Two Rivers, U.S.A. 76 C2 44 9N 87 34W
Two Rocks, Australia 61 F2 31 30S 115 35 E
Twofold B., Australia 63 F4 37 8S 149 59 E
Tyachiv, Ukraine 17 D12 48 1N 23 35 E
Tychy, Poland 17 C10 50 9N 18 59 E
Tyler, U.S.A. 75 D7 32 18N 95 17W
Tyler, Minn., U.S.A. 80 C6 44 18N 96 8W
Tyler, Tex., U.S.A. 81 J7 32 21N 95 18W
Tynda, Russia 27 D13 55 10N 124 43 E
Tyndall, U.S.A. 80 D6 43 0N 97 50W
Tyne →, U.K. 10 C6 54 59N 1 32W
Tyne & Wear □, U.K. 10 B6 55 6N 1 17W
Tynemouth, U.K. 10 B6 55 1N 1 26W
Tyre = Sūr, Lebanon 47 B4 33 19N 35 16 E
Tyrifjorden, Norway 9 F14 60 2N 10 8 E
Tyrol = Tirol □, Austria 16 E6 47 3N 10 43 E
Tyrone, U.S.A. 78 F6 40 40N 78 14W
Tyrone □, U.K. 13 B4 54 38N 7 11W
Tyrrell →, Australia 63 F3 35 26S 142 51 E
Tyrrell, L., Australia 63 F3 35 20S 142 50 E
Tyrrell L., Canada 73 A7 63 7N 105 27W
Tyrrhenian Sea, Medit. S. 20 E5 40 0N 12 30 E
Tysfjorden, Norway 8 B17 68 7N 16 25 E
Tyulgan, Russia 24 D10 52 22N 56 12 E
Tyumen, Russia 26 D7 57 11N 65 29 E
Tywi →, U.K. 11 F3 51 48N 4 21W
Tywyn, U.K. 11 E3 52 35N 4 5W
Tzaneen, S. Africa 57 C5 23 47S 30 9 E
Tzermiádhes, Greece 23 D7 35 12N 25 29 E
Tzukong = Zigong, China 32 D5 29 15N 104 48 E

U

U Taphao, Thailand 38 F3 12 35N 101 0 E
U.S.A. = United States of America ■, N. Amer. 74 C7 37 0N 96 0W
Uatumã →, Brazil 92 D7 2 26S 57 37W
Uaupés, Brazil 92 D5 0 8S 67 5W
Uaupés →, Brazil 92 C5 0 2N 67 16W
Uaxactún, Guatemala 88 C2 17 25N 89 29W
Ubá, Brazil 95 A7 21 8S 43 0W
Ubaitaba, Brazil 93 F11 14 18S 39 20W
Ubangi = Oubangi →, Dem. Rep. of the Congo 52 E3 0 30S 17 50 E
Ubauro, Pakistan 42 E3 28 15N 69 45 E
Ubayyiḑ, W. al →, Iraq 44 C4 32 34N 43 48 E
Ube, Japan 31 H5 33 56N 131 15 E
Úbeda, Spain 19 C4 38 3N 3 23W
Uberaba, Brazil 93 G9 19 50S 47 55W
Uberlândia, Brazil 93 G9 19 0S 48 20W
Ubolratna Res., Thailand 38 D4 16 45N 102 30 E
Ubombo, S. Africa 57 D5 27 31S 32 4 E
Ubon Ratchathani, Thailand 38 E5 15 15N 104 50 E
Ubondo, Dem. Rep. of the Congo 54 C2 0 55S 25 42 E
Ubort →, Belarus 17 B15 52 6N 28 30 E
Ubundu, Dem. Rep. of the Congo 54 C2 0 22S 25 30 E
Ucayali →, Peru 92 D4 4 30S 73 30W
Uchiura-Wan, Japan 30 C10 42 25N 140 40 E
Uchquduq, Uzbekistan 26 E7 41 50N 62 50 E
Uchur →, Russia 27 D14 58 48N 130 35 E
Ucluelet, Canada 72 D3 48 57N 125 32W
Uda →, Russia 27 D14 54 42N 135 14 E
Udagamandalam, India 40 P10 11 30N 76 44 E
Udainagar, India 42 H7 22 33N 76 13 E
Udaipur, India 42 G5 24 36N 73 44 E
Udaipur Garhi, Nepal 43 F12 27 0N 86 35 E
Udala, India 43 J12 21 35N 86 34 E
Uddevalla, Sweden 9 G14 58 21N 11 55 E
Uddjaur, Sweden 8 D17 65 56N 17 49 E
Uden, Neths. 15 C5 51 40N 5 37 E
Udgir, India 40 K10 18 25N 77 5 E
Udhampur, India 43 C6 33 0N 75 5 E
Údine, Italy 20 A5 46 3N 13 14 E
Udmurtia □, Russia 24 C9 57 30N 52 30 E
Udon Thani, Thailand 38 D4 17 29N 102 46 E
Udupi, India 40 N9 13 25N 74 42 E
Udzungwa Range, Tanzania 55 D4 9 30S 35 10 E
Ueda, Japan 31 F9 36 24N 138 16 E
Uedineniya, Os., Russia 4 B12 78 0N 85 0 E
Uele →, Dem. Rep. of the Congo 52 D4 3 45N 24 45 E
Uelen, Russia 27 C19 66 10N 170 0W
Uelzen, Germany 16 B6 52 57N 10 32 E
Ufa, Russia 24 D10 54 45N 55 55 E
Ufa →, Russia 24 D10 54 40N 56 0 E
Ugab →, Namibia 56 C1 20 55S 13 30 E
Ugalla →, Tanzania 54 D3 5 8S 30 42 E
Uganda ■, Africa 54 B3 2 0N 32 0 E
Ugie, S. Africa 57 E4 31 10S 28 13 E
Uglegorsk, Russia 27 E15 49 5N 142 2 E
Ugljan, Croatia 16 F8 44 12N 15 10 E
Uhrichsville, U.S.A. 78 F3 40 24N 81 21W
Uibhist a Deas = South Uist, U.K. 12 D1 57 20N 7 15W
Uibhist a Tuath = North Uist, U.K. 12 D1 57 40N 7 15W
Uig, U.K. 12 D2 57 35N 6 21W
Uíge, Angola 52 F2 7 30S 14 40 E
Uijŏngbu, S. Korea 35 F14 37 48N 127 0 E
Ŭiju, N. Korea 35 D13 40 15N 124 35 E
Uinta Mts., U.S.A. 82 F8 40 45N 110 30W
Uitenhage, S. Africa 56 E4 33 40S 25 28 E
Uithuizen, Neths. 15 A6 53 24N 6 41 E
Ujh →, India 42 C6 32 10N 75 18 E
Ujhani, India 43 F8 28 0N 79 6 E
Uji-guntō, Japan 31 J4 31 15N 129 25 E
Ujjain, India 42 H6 23 9N 75 43 E
Ujung Pandang, Indonesia 37 F5 5 10S 119 20 E
Uka, Russia 27 D17 57 50N 162 0 E
Ukara I., Tanzania 54 C3 1 50S 33 0 E
Uke-Shima, Japan 31 K4 28 2N 129 14 E
Ukerewe I., Tanzania 54 C3 2 0S 33 0 E
Ukhrul, India 41 G19 25 10N 94 25 E
Ukhta, Russia 24 B9 63 34N 53 41 E
Ukiah, U.S.A. 84 F3 39 9N 123 13W
Ukki Fort, India 43 C7 33 28N 76 54 E
Ukmerge, Lithuania 9 J21 55 15N 24 45 E
Ukraine ■, Europe 25 E5 49 0N 32 0 E
Uku, Angola 53 G2 11 24S 14 22 E
Ukwi, Botswana 56 C3 23 29S 20 30 E
Ulaan-Uul, Mongolia 34 B6 44 13N 111 10 E
Ulaanbaatar, Mongolia 27 E11 47 55N 106 53 E
Ulaangom, Mongolia 32 A4 50 5N 92 10 E
Ulaanjirem, Mongolia 34 B3 45 5N 105 30 E
Ulamba, Dem. Rep. of the Congo 55 D1 9 3S 23 38 E
Ulan Bator = Ulaanbaatar, Mongolia 27 E11 47 55N 106 53 E
Ulan Ude, Russia 27 D11 51 45N 107 40 E
Ulaya, Morogoro, Tanzania 54 D4 7 3S 36 55 E
Ulaya, Tabora, Tanzania 54 C3 4 25S 33 30 E
Ulcinj, Montenegro, Yug. 21 D8 41 58N 19 10 E
Ulco, S. Africa 56 D3 28 21S 24 15 E
Ulefoss, Norway 9 G13 59 17N 9 16 E
Ulhasnagar, India 40 K8 19 15N 73 10 E
Uliastay, Mongolia 32 B4 47 56N 97 28 E
Ulithi Atoll, Pac. Oc. 37 B9 10 0N 139 30 E
Ulladulla, Australia 63 F5 35 21S 150 29 E
Ullapool, U.K. 12 D3 57 54N 5 9W
Ullswater, U.K. 10 C5 54 34N 2 52W
Ullŭng-do, S. Korea 31 F5 37 30N 130 30 E
Ulm, Germany 16 D5 48 23N 9 58 E
Ulmarra, Australia 63 D5 29 37S 153 4 E
Ulongué, Mozam. 55 E3 14 37S 34 19 E
Ulricehamn, Sweden 9 H15 57 46N 13 26 E
Ulsan, S. Korea 35 G15 35 20N 129 15 E
Ulsta, U.K. 12 A7 60 30N 1 9W
Ulster □, U.K. 13 B5 54 35N 6 30W
Ulubat Gölü, Turkey 21 D13 40 9N 28 35 E
Uludağ, Turkey 21 D13 40 4N 29 13 E
Uluguru Mts., Tanzania 54 D4 7 15S 37 40 E
Ulungur He →, China 32 B3 47 1N 87 24 E
Uluru = Ayers Rock, Australia 61 E5 25 23S 131 5 E
Uluru Nat. Park, Australia 61 E5 25 15S 131 20 E
Ulutau, Kazakstan 26 E7 48 39N 67 1 E
Ulva, U.K. 12 E2 56 29N 6 13W
Ulverston, U.K. 10 C4 54 13N 3 5W
Ulverstone, Australia 62 G4 41 11S 146 11 E
Ulya, Russia 27 D15 59 10N 142 0 E
Ulyanovsk = Simbirsk, Russia 24 D8 54 20N 48 25 E
Ulyasutay = Uliastay, Mongolia 32 B4 47 56N 97 28 E
Ulysses, U.S.A. 81 G4 37 35N 101 22W
Umala, Bolivia 92 G5 17 25S 68 5W
Uman, Ukraine 17 D16 48 40N 30 12 E
Umaria, India 41 H12 23 35N 80 50 E
Umarkot, Pakistan 40 G6 25 15N 69 40 E
Umarpada, India 42 J5 21 27N 73 30 E
Umatilla, U.S.A. 82 D4 45 55N 119 21W
Umba, Russia 24 A5 66 42N 34 11 E
Umbagog L., U.S.A. 79 B13 44 46N 71 3W
Umbakumba, Australia 62 A2 13 47S 136 50 E
Umbrella Mts., N.Z. 59 L2 45 35S 169 5 E
Ume älv →, Sweden 8 E19 63 45N 20 20 E
Umeå, Sweden 8 E19 63 45N 20 20 E
Umera, Indonesia 37 E7 0 12S 129 37 E
Umfuli →, Zimbabwe 55 F2 17 30S 29 23 E
Umgusa, Zimbabwe 55 F2 19 29S 27 52 E
Umkomaas, S. Africa 57 E5 30 13S 30 48 E
Umlazi, S. Africa 53 L6 29 59S 30 54 E
Umm ad Daraj, J., Jordan 47 C4 32 18N 35 48 E
Umm al Qaywayn, U.A.E. 45 E7 25 30N 55 35 E
Umm al Qittayn, Jordan 47 C5 32 18N 36 40 E
Umm Bāb, Qatar 45 E6 25 12N 50 48 E
Umm el Fahm, Israel 47 C4 32 31N 35 9 E
Umm Keddada, Sudan 51 F11 13 36N 26 42 E
Umm Lajj, Si. Arabia 44 E3 25 0N 37 23 E
Umm Ruwaba, Sudan 51 F12 12 50N 31 20 E
Umnak I., U.S.A. 68 C3 53 15N 168 20W
Umniati →, Zimbabwe 55 F2 16 49S 28 45 E
Umpqua →, U.S.A. 82 E1 43 40N 124 12W
Umreth, India 42 H5 22 41N 73 4 E
Umtata, S. Africa 57 E4 31 36S 28 49 E
Umuarama, Brazil 95 A5 23 45S 53 20W
Umvukwe Ra., Zimbabwe 55 F3 16 45S 30 45 E
Umzimvubu = Port St. Johns, S. Africa 57 E4 31 38S 29 33 E
Umzingwane →, Zimbabwe 55 G2 22 12S 29 56 E
Umzinto, S. Africa 57 E5 30 15S 30 45 E
Una, India 42 J4 20 46N 71 8 E
Una →, Bos.-H. 16 F9 45 0N 16 20 E
Unadilla, U.S.A. 79 D9 42 20N 75 19W
Unalakleet, U.S.A. 68 B3 63 52N 160 47W
Unalaska, U.S.A. 68 C3 53 53N 166 32W
Unalaska I., U.S.A. 68 C3 53 35N 166 50W
'Unayzah, Si. Arabia 44 E4 26 6N 43 58 E
'Unāzah, J., Asia 44 C3 32 12N 39 18 E
Uncía, Bolivia 92 G5 18 25S 66 40W
Uncompahgre Peak, U.S.A. 83 G10 38 4N 107 28W
Uncompahgre Plateau, U.S.A. 83 G9 38 20N 108 15W
Underbool, Australia 63 F3 35 10S 141 51 E
Ungarie, Australia 63 E4 33 38S 146 56 E
Ungarra, Australia 63 E2 34 12S 136 2 E
Ungava, Pén. d', Canada 69 C12 60 0N 74 0W
Ungava B., Canada 69 C13 59 30N 67 30W
Ungeny = Ungheni, Moldova 17 E14 47 11N 27 51 E
Unggi, N. Korea 35 C16 42 16N 130 28 E
Ungheni, Moldova 17 E14 47 11N 27 51 E
União da Vitória, Brazil 95 B5 26 13S 51 5W
Unimak I., U.S.A. 68 C3 54 45N 164 0W
Union, Miss., U.S.A. 81 J10 32 34N 89 7W
Union, Mo., U.S.A. 80 F9 38 27N 91 0W
Union, S.C., U.S.A. 77 H5 34 43N 81 37W
Union City, Calif., U.S.A. 84 H4 37 36N 122 1W
Union City, N.J., U.S.A. 79 F10 40 45N 74 2W
Union City, Pa., U.S.A. 78 E5 41 54N 79 51W
Union City, Tenn., U.S.A. 81 G10 36 26N 89 3W
Union Gap, U.S.A. 82 C3 46 33N 120 28W
Union Springs, U.S.A. 77 J3 32 9N 85 43W
Uniondale, S. Africa 56 E3 33 39S 23 7 E
Uniontown, U.S.A. 76 F6 39 54N 79 44W
Unionville, U.S.A. 80 E8 40 29N 93 1W
United Arab Emirates ■, Asia 45 F7 23 50N 54 0 E
United Kingdom ■, Europe 7 E5 53 0N 2 0W
United States of America ■, N. Amer. 74 C7 37 0N 96 0W
Unity, Canada 73 C7 52 30N 109 5W
University Park, U.S.A. 83 K10 32 17N 106 45W
Unjha, India 42 H5 23 46N 72 24 E
Unnao, India 43 F9 26 35N 80 30 E
Unst, U.K. 12 A8 60 44N 0 53W
Unuk →, Canada 72 B2 56 5N 131 3W
Uozu, Japan 31 F8 36 48N 137 24 E
Upata, Venezuela 92 B6 8 1N 62 24W
Upemba, L., Dem. Rep. of the Congo 55 D2 8 30S 26 20 E
Upernavik, Greenland 4 B5 72 49N 56 20W
Upington, S. Africa 56 D3 28 25S 21 15 E
Upleta, India 42 J4 21 46N 70 16 E
Upolu, W. Samoa 59 A13 13 58S 172 0W
Upper Alkali L., U.S.A. 82 F3 41 47N 120 8W
Upper Arrow L., Canada 72 C5 50 30N 117 50W
Upper Foster L., Canada 73 B7 56 47N 105 20W
Upper Hutt, N.Z. 59 J5 41 8S 175 5 E
Upper Klamath L., U.S.A. 82 E3 42 25N 121 55W
Upper Lake, U.S.A. 84 F4 39 10N 122 54W
Upper Musquodoboit, Canada 71 C7 45 10N 62 58W
Upper Red L., U.S.A. 80 A7 48 8N 94 45W
Upper Sandusky, U.S.A. 76 E4 40 50N 83 17W
Upper Volta = Burkina Faso ■, Africa 50 F5 12 0N 1 0W
Uppland, Sweden 9 F17 59 59N 17 48 E
Uppsala, Sweden 9 G17 59 53N 17 38 E
Upshi, India 43 C7 33 48N 77 52 E
Upstart, C., Australia 62 B4 19 41S 147 45 E
Upton, U.S.A. 80 C2 44 6N 104 38W
Ur, Iraq 44 D5 30 55N 46 25 E
Urad Qianqi, China 34 D5 40 40N 108 30 E
Urakawa, Japan 30 C11 42 9N 142 47 E
Ural = Zhayyq →, Kazakstan 25 E9 47 0N 51 48 E
Ural, Australia 63 E4 33 21S 146 12 E
Ural Mts. = Uralskie Gory, Eurasia 24 C10 60 0N 59 0 E
Uralla, Australia 63 E5 30 37S 151 29 E
Uralsk = Oral, Kazakstan 25 D9 51 20N 51 20 E
Uralskie Gory, Eurasia 24 C10 60 0N 59 0 E
Urambo, Tanzania 54 D3 5 4S 32 0 E
Urana, Australia 63 F4 35 15S 146 21 E
Urandangi, Australia 62 C2 21 32S 138 14 E
Uranium City, Canada 73 B7 59 34N 108 37W
Uraricoera →, Brazil 92 C6 3 2N 60 30W
Urawa, Japan 31 G9 35 50N 139 40 E
Uray, Russia 26 C7 60 5N 65 15 E
'Uray'irah, Si. Arabia 45 E6 25 57N 48 53 E
Urbana, Ill., U.S.A. 76 E1 40 7N 88 12W
Urbana, Ohio, U.S.A. 76 E4 40 7N 83 45W
Urbino, Italy 20 C5 43 43N 12 38 E
Urbión, Picos de, Spain 19 A4 42 1N 2 52W
Urcos, Peru 92 F4 13 40S 71 38W

Urdinarrain, *Argentina* 94 C4 32 37S 58 52W
Urdzhar, *Kazakstan* 26 E9 47 5N 81 38 E
Ure →, *U.K.* 10 C6 54 5N 1 20W
Ures, *Mexico* 86 B2 29 30N 110 30W
Urfa = Sanliurfa, *Turkey* 25 G6 37 12N 38 50 E
Urganch, *Uzbekistan* 26 E7 41 40N 60 41 E
Urgench = Urganch, *Uzbekistan* 26 E7 41 40N 60 41 E
Ürgüp, *Turkey* 44 B2 38 38N 34 56 E
Uri, *India* 43 B6 34 8N 74 2 E
Uribia, *Colombia* 92 A4 11 43N 72 16W
Uriondo, *Bolivia* 94 A3 21 41S 64 41W
Urique, *Mexico* 86 B3 27 13N 107 55W
Urique →, *Mexico* 86 B3 26 29N 107 58W
Urk, *Neths.* 15 B5 52 39N 5 36 E
Urla, *Turkey* 21 E12 38 20N 26 47 E
Urmia = Orūmīyeh, *Iran* 44 B5 37 40N 45 0 E
Urmia, L. = Orūmīyeh, Daryācheh-ye, *Iran* 44 B5 37 50N 45 30 E
Uroševac, *Yugoslavia* 21 C9 42 23N 21 10 E
Uruaçu, *Brazil* 93 F9 14 30S 49 10W
Uruapan, *Mexico* 86 D4 19 30N 102 0W
Urubamba →, *Peru* 92 F4 10 43S 73 48W
Uruçara, *Brazil* 92 D7 2 20S 57 50W
Uruçuí, *Brazil* 93 E10 7 20S 44 28W
Uruguai →, *Brazil* 95 B5 26 0S 53 30W
Uruguaiana, *Brazil* 94 B4 29 50S 57 0W
Uruguay ■, *S. Amer.* 94 C4 32 30S 56 30W
Uruguay →, *S. Amer.* 94 C4 34 12S 58 18W
Urumchi = Ürümqi, *China* 26 E9 43 45N 87 45 E
Ürümqi, *China* 26 E9 43 45N 87 45 E
Urup, Ostrov, *Russia* 27 E16 46 0N 151 0 E
Usa →, *Russia* 24 A10 66 16N 59 49 E
Uşak, *Turkey* 25 G4 38 43N 29 28 E
Usakos, *Namibia* 56 C2 21 54S 15 31 E
Usedom, *Germany* 16 B8 53 55N 14 2 E
Useless Loop, *Australia* 61 E1 26 8S 113 23 E
Ush-Tobe, *Kazakstan* 26 E8 45 16N 78 0 E
Ushakova, Ostrov, *Russia* 4 A12 82 0N 80 0 E
Ushant = Ouessant, Î. d', *France* 18 B1 48 28N 5 6W
Ushashi, *Tanzania* 54 C3 1 59S 33 57 E
Ushibuka, *Japan* 31 H5 32 11N 130 1 E
Ushuaia, *Argentina* 96 G3 54 50S 68 23W
Ushumun, *Russia* 27 D13 52 47N 126 32 E
Usk, *Canada* 72 C3 54 38N 128 26W
Usk →, *U.K.* 11 F5 51 33N 2 58W
Uska, *India* 43 F10 27 12N 83 7 E
Usman, *Russia* 24 D6 52 5N 39 48 E
Usoke, *Tanzania* 54 D3 5 8S 32 24 E
Usolye Sibirskoye, *Russia* 27 D11 52 48N 103 40 E
Uspallata, P. de, *Argentina* 94 C2 32 37S 69 22W
Uspenskiy, *Kazakstan* 26 E8 48 41N 72 43 E
Ussuri →, *Asia* 30 A7 48 27N 135 0 E
Ussuriysk, *Russia* 27 E14 43 48N 131 59 E
Ussurka, *Russia* 30 B6 45 12N 133 31 E
Ust-Aldan = Batamay, *Russia* 27 C13 63 30N 129 15 E
Ust Amginskoye = Khandyga, *Russia* 27 C14 62 42N 135 35 E
Ust-Bolsheretsk, *Russia* 27 D16 52 50N 156 15 E
Ust Chaun, *Russia* 27 C18 68 47N 170 30 E
Ust Ilimpeya = Yukta, *Russia* 27 C11 63 26N 105 42 E
Ust-Ilimsk, *Russia* 27 D11 58 3N 102 39 E
Ust Ishim, *Russia* 26 D8 57 45N 71 10 E
Ust-Kamchatsk, *Russia* 27 D17 56 10N 162 28 E
Ust-Kamenogorsk = Öskemen, *Kazakstan* 26 E9 50 0N 82 36 E
Ust Khayryuzovo, *Russia* 27 D16 57 15N 156 45 E
Ust-Kut, *Russia* 27 D11 56 50N 105 42 E
Ust Kuyga, *Russia* 27 B14 70 1N 135 43 E
Ust Maya, *Russia* 27 C14 60 30N 134 28 E
Ust-Mil, *Russia* 27 D14 59 40N 133 11 E
Ust-Nera, *Russia* 27 C15 64 35N 143 15 E
Ust-Nyukzha, *Russia* 27 D13 56 34N 121 37 E
Ust Olenek, *Russia* 27 B12 73 0N 120 5 E
Ust-Omchug, *Russia* 27 C15 61 9N 149 38 E
Ust Port, *Russia* 26 C9 69 40N 84 26 E
Ust Tsilma, *Russia* 24 A9 65 28N 52 11 E
Ust Urt = Ustyurt Plateau, *Asia* 26 E6 44 0N 55 0 E
Ust Usa, *Russia* 24 A10 66 2N 56 57 E
Ust Vorkuta, *Russia* 24 A11 67 24N 64 0 E
Ústí nad Labem, *Czech Rep.* 16 C8 50 41N 14 3 E
Ústica, *Italy* 20 E5 38 42N 13 11 E
Ustinov = Izhevsk, *Russia* 24 C9 56 51N 53 14 E
Ustyurt Plateau, *Asia* 26 E6 44 0N 55 0 E
Usu, *China* 32 B3 44 27N 84 40 E
Usuki, *Japan* 31 H5 33 8N 131 49 E
Usulután, *El Salv.* 88 D2 13 25N 88 28W
Usumacinta →, *Mexico* 87 D6 17 0N 91 0W
Usumbura = Bujumbura, *Burundi* 54 C2 3 16S 29 18 E
Usure, *Tanzania* 54 C3 4 40S 34 22 E
Uta, *Indonesia* 37 E9 4 33S 136 0 E
Utah □, *U.S.A.* 82 G8 39 20N 111 30W
Utah L., *U.S.A.* 82 F8 40 10N 111 58W
Utarni, *India* 42 F4 26 5N 71 58 E
Utatlan, *Guatemala* 88 C1 15 2N 91 11W
Ute Creek →, *U.S.A.* 81 H3 35 21N 103 50W
Utena, *Lithuania* 9 J21 55 27N 25 40 E
Utete, *Tanzania* 54 D4 8 0S 38 45 E
Uthai Thani, *Thailand* 38 E3 15 22N 100 3 E
Uthal, *Pakistan* 42 G2 25 44N 66 40 E
Utiariti, *Brazil* 92 F7 13 0S 58 10W
Utica, *N.Y., U.S.A.* 79 C9 43 6N 75 14W
Utica, *Ohio, U.S.A.* 78 F2 40 14N 82 27W
Utikuma L., *Canada* 72 B5 55 50N 115 30W
Utopia, *Australia* 62 C1 22 14S 134 33 E
Utraula, *India* 43 F10 27 19N 82 25 E
Utrecht, *Neths.* 15 B5 52 5N 5 8 E
Utrecht, *S. Africa* 57 D5 27 38S 30 20 E
Utrecht □, *Neths.* 15 B5 52 6N 5 7 E
Utrera, *Spain* 19 D3 37 12N 5 48W
Utsjoki, *Finland* 8 B22 69 51N 26 59 E
Utsunomiya, *Japan* 31 F9 36 30N 139 50 E
Uttar Pradesh □, *India* 43 F9 27 0N 80 0 E
Uttaradit, *Thailand* 38 D3 17 36N 100 5 E
Uttoxeter, *U.K.* 10 E6 52 54N 1 52W
Uummannarsuaq = Farvel, Kap, *Greenland* 4 D5 59 48N 43 55W
Uusikaarlepyy, *Finland* 8 E20 63 32N 22 31 E
Uusikaupunki, *Finland* 9 F19 60 47N 21 25 E
Uva, *Russia* 24 C9 56 59N 52 13 E
Uvalde, *U.S.A.* 81 L5 29 13N 99 47W
Uvat, *Russia* 26 D7 59 5N 68 50 E
Uvinza, *Tanzania* 54 D3 5 5S 30 24 E
Uvira, *Dem. Rep. of the Congo* 54 C2 3 22S 29 3 E
Uvs Nuur, *Mongolia* 32 A4 50 20N 92 30 E
'Uwairidh, Harrat al, *Si. Arabia* 44 E3 26 50N 38 0 E
Uwajima, *Japan* 31 H6 33 10N 132 35 E
Uweinat, Jebel, *Sudan* 51 D10 21 54N 24 58 E
Uxbridge, *Canada* 78 B5 44 6N 79 7W
Uxin Qi, *China* 34 E5 38 50N 109 5 E
Uxmal, *Mexico* 87 C7 20 22N 89 46W
Üydzin, *Mongolia* 34 B4 44 9N 107 0 E
Uyo, *Nigeria* 50 G7 5 1N 7 53 E
Uyûn Mûsa, *Egypt* 47 F1 29 53N 32 40 E
Uyuni, *Bolivia* 92 H5 20 28S 66 47W
Uzbekistan ■, *Asia* 26 E7 41 30N 65 0 E
Uzen, *Kazakstan* 25 F9 43 29N 52 54 E
Uzen, Mal →, *Kazakstan* 25 E8 49 4N 49 44 E
Uzerche, *France* 18 D4 45 25N 1 34 E
Uzh →, *Ukraine* 17 C16 51 15N 30 12 E
Uzhgorod = Uzhhorod, *Ukraine* 17 D12 48 36N 22 18 E
Uzhhorod, *Ukraine* 17 D12 48 36N 22 18 E
Užice, *Serbia, Yug.* 21 C8 43 55N 19 50 E
Uzunköprü, *Turkey* 21 D12 41 16N 26 43 E

V

Vaal →, *S. Africa* 56 D3 29 4S 23 38 E
Vaal Dam, *S. Africa* 57 D4 27 0S 28 14 E
Vaalwater, *S. Africa* 57 C4 24 15S 28 8 E
Vaasa, *Finland* 8 E19 63 6N 21 38 E
Vác, *Hungary* 17 E10 47 49N 19 10 E
Vacaria, *Brazil* 95 B5 28 31S 50 52W
Vacaville, *U.S.A.* 84 G5 38 21N 121 59W
Vach = Vakh →, *Russia* 26 C8 60 45N 76 45 E
Vache, Î. à, *Haiti* 89 C5 18 2N 73 35W
Vadnagar, *India* 42 H5 23 47N 72 40 E
Vadodara, *India* 42 H5 22 20N 73 10 E
Vadsø, *Norway* 8 A23 70 3N 29 50 E
Vaduz, *Liech.* 18 C8 47 8N 9 31 E
Værøy, *Norway* 8 C15 67 40N 12 40 E
Vágar, *Færoe Is.* 8 E9 62 5N 7 15W
Vågsfjorden, *Norway* 8 B17 68 50N 16 50 E
Váh →, *Slovak Rep.* 17 D9 47 43N 18 7 E
Vahsel B., *Antarctica* 5 D1 75 0S 35 0W
Váï, *Greece* 23 D8 35 15N 26 18 E
Vaigach, *Russia* 26 B6 70 10N 59 0 E
Vail, *U.S.A.* 74 C5 39 40N 106 20W
Vaisali →, *India* 43 F8 26 28N 78 53 E
Vakh →, *Russia* 26 C8 60 45N 76 45 E
Val-d'Or, *Canada* 70 C4 48 7N 77 47W
Val Marie, *Canada* 73 D7 49 15N 107 45W
Valahia, *Romania* 17 F13 44 35N 25 0 E
Valandovo, *Macedonia* 21 D10 41 19N 22 34 E
Valcheta, *Argentina* 96 E3 40 40S 66 8W
Valdayskaya Vozvyshennost, *Russia* 24 C5 57 0N 33 30 E
Valdepeñas, *Spain* 19 C4 38 43N 3 25W
Valdés, Pen., *Argentina* 96 E4 42 30S 63 45W
Valdez, *U.S.A.* 68 B5 61 7N 146 16W
Valdivia, *Chile* 96 D2 39 50S 73 14W
Valdosta, *U.S.A.* 77 K4 30 50N 83 17W
Valdres, *Norway* 9 F13 61 5N 9 5 E
Vale, *U.S.A.* 82 E5 43 59N 117 15W
Vale of Glamorgan □, *U.K.* 11 F4 51 28N 3 25W
Valemount, *Canada* 72 C5 52 50N 119 15W
Valença, *Brazil* 93 F11 13 20S 39 5W
Valença do Piauí, *Brazil* 93 E10 6 20S 41 45W
Valence, *France* 18 D6 44 57N 4 54 E
Valencia, *Spain* 19 C5 39 27N 0 23W
Valencia, *U.S.A.* 83 J10 34 48N 106 43W
Valencia, *Venezuela* 92 A5 10 11N 68 0W
Valencia □, *Spain* 19 C5 39 20N 0 40W
Valencia, G. de, *Spain* 19 C6 39 30N 0 20 E
Valencia de Alcántara, *Spain* 19 C2 39 25N 7 14W
Valencia I., *Ireland* 13 E1 51 54N 10 22W
Valenciennes, *France* 18 A5 50 20N 3 34 E
Valentim, Sa. do, *Brazil* 93 E10 6 0S 43 30W
Valentin, *Russia* 30 C7 43 8N 134 17 E
Valentine, *Nebr., U.S.A.* 74 B6 42 52N 100 33W
Valentine, *Tex., U.S.A.* 81 K2 30 35N 104 30W
Valera, *Venezuela* 92 B4 9 19N 70 37W
Valga, *Estonia* 9 H22 57 47N 26 2 E
Valier, *U.S.A.* 82 B7 48 18N 112 16W
Valjevo, *Serbia, Yug.* 21 B8 44 18N 19 53 E
Valka, *Latvia* 9 H21 57 42N 25 57 E
Valkeakoski, *Finland* 9 F20 61 16N 24 2 E
Valkenswaard, *Neths.* 15 C5 51 21N 5 29 E
Vall de Uxó = La Vall d'Uixó, *Spain* 19 C5 39 49N 0 15W
Valladolid, *Mexico* 87 C7 20 40N 88 11W
Valladolid, *Spain* 19 B3 41 38N 4 43W
Valldemossa, *Spain* 22 B9 39 43N 2 37 E
Valle de la Pascua, *Venezuela* 92 B5 9 13N 66 0W
Valle de las Palmas, *Mexico* 85 N10 32 20N 116 43W
Valle de Santiago, *Mexico* 86 C4 20 25N 101 15W
Valle de Suchil, *Mexico* 86 C4 23 38N 103 55W
Valle de Zaragoza, *Mexico* 86 B3 27 28N 105 49W
Valle Fértil, Sierra del, *Argentina* 94 C2 30 20S 68 0W
Valle Hermoso, *Mexico* 87 B5 25 35N 97 40W
Valledupar, *Colombia* 92 A4 10 29N 73 15W
Vallehermoso, *Canary Is.* 22 F2 28 10N 17 15W
Vallejo, *U.S.A.* 84 G4 38 7N 122 14W
Vallenar, *Chile* 94 B1 28 30S 70 50W
Valletta, *Malta* 23 D2 35 54N 14 31 E
Valley Center, *U.S.A.* 85 M9 33 13N 117 2W
Valley City, *U.S.A.* 80 B6 46 55N 98 0W
Valley Falls, *Oreg., U.S.A.* 82 E3 42 29N 120 17W
Valley Falls, *R.I., U.S.A.* 79 E13 41 54N 71 24W
Valley Springs, *U.S.A.* 84 G6 38 12N 120 50W
Valley View, *U.S.A.* 79 F8 40 39N 76 33W
Valley Wells, *U.S.A.* 85 K11 35 27N 115 46W
Valleyview, *Canada* 72 B5 55 5N 117 17W
Vallimanca, Arroyo, *Argentina* 94 D4 35 40S 59 10W
Valls, *Spain* 19 B6 41 18N 1 15 E
Valmiera, *Latvia* 9 H21 57 37N 25 29 E
Valognes, *France* 18 B3 49 30N 1 28W
Valona = Vlóra, *Albania* 21 D8 40 32N 19 28 E
Valozhyn, *Belarus* 17 A14 54 3N 26 30 E
Valparaíso, *Chile* 94 C1 33 2S 71 40W
Valparaíso, *Mexico* 86 C4 22 50N 103 32W
Valparaiso, *U.S.A.* 76 E2 41 28N 87 4W
Valparaíso □, *Chile* 94 C1 33 2S 71 40W
Vals →, *S. Africa* 56 D4 27 23S 26 30 E
Vals, Tanjung, *Indonesia* 37 F9 8 26S 137 25 E
Valsad, *India* 40 J8 20 40N 72 58 E
Valverde, *Canary Is.* 22 G2 27 48N 17 55W
Valverde del Camino, *Spain* 19 D2 37 35N 6 47W
Vammala, *Finland* 9 F20 61 20N 22 54 E
Vámos, *Greece* 23 D6 35 24N 24 13 E
Van, *Turkey* 25 G7 38 30N 43 20 E
Van, L. = Van Gölü, *Turkey* 25 G7 38 30N 43 0 E
Van Alstyne, *U.S.A.* 81 J6 33 25N 96 35W
Van Blommestein Meer, *Surinam* 93 C7 4 45N 55 5W
Van Buren, *Canada* 71 C6 47 10N 67 55W
Van Buren, *Ark., U.S.A.* 81 H7 35 26N 94 21W
Van Buren, *Maine, U.S.A.* 77 B11 47 10N 67 58W
Van Buren, *Mo., U.S.A.* 81 G9 37 0N 91 1W
Van Canh, *Vietnam* 38 F7 13 37N 109 0 E
Van Diemen, C., *N. Terr., Australia* 60 B5 11 9S 130 24 E
Van Diemen, C., *Queens., Australia* 62 B2 16 30S 139 46 E
Van Diemen G., *Australia* 60 B5 11 45S 132 0 E
Van Gölü, *Turkey* 25 G7 38 30N 43 0 E
Van Horn, *U.S.A.* 81 K2 31 3N 104 50W
Van Ninh, *Vietnam* 38 F7 12 42N 109 14 E
Van Rees, Pegunungan, *Indonesia* 37 E9 2 35S 138 15 E
Van Wert, *U.S.A.* 76 E3 40 52N 84 35W
Vanadzor, *Armenia* 25 F7 40 48N 44 30 E
Vanavara, *Russia* 27 C11 60 22N 102 16 E
Vancouver, *Canada* 72 D4 49 15N 123 10W
Vancouver, *U.S.A.* 84 E4 45 38N 122 40W
Vancouver, C., *Australia* 61 G2 35 2S 118 11 E
Vancouver I., *Canada* 72 D3 49 50N 126 0W
Vandalia, *Ill., U.S.A.* 80 F10 38 58N 89 6W
Vandalia, *Mo., U.S.A.* 80 F9 39 19N 91 29W
Vandenburg, *U.S.A.* 85 L6 34 35N 120 33W
Vanderbijlpark, *S. Africa* 57 D4 26 42S 27 54 E
Vandergrift, *U.S.A.* 78 F5 40 36N 79 34W
Vanderhoof, *Canada* 72 C4 54 0N 124 0W
Vanderkloof Dam, *S. Africa* 56 E3 30 4S 24 40 E
Vanderlin I., *Australia* 62 B2 15 44S 137 2 E
Vänern, *Sweden* 9 G15 58 47N 13 30 E
Vänersborg, *Sweden* 9 G15 58 26N 12 19 E
Vang Vieng, *Laos* 38 C4 18 58N 102 32 E
Vanga, *Kenya* 54 C4 4 35S 39 12 E
Vangaindrano, *Madag.* 57 C8 23 21S 47 36 E
Vanguard, *Canada* 73 D7 49 55N 107 20W
Vanino, *Russia* 27 E15 48 50N 140 5 E
Vanna, *Norway* 8 A18 70 6N 19 50 E
Vännäs, *Sweden* 8 E18 63 58N 19 48 E
Vannes, *France* 18 C2 47 40N 2 47W
Vanrhynsdorp, *S. Africa* 56 E2 31 36S 18 44 E
Vansbro, *Sweden* 9 F16 60 32N 14 15 E
Vansittart B., *Australia* 60 B4 14 3S 126 17 E
Vantaa, *Finland* 9 F21 60 18N 24 58 E
Vanua Levu, *Fiji* 59 C8 16 33S 179 15 E
Vanua Mbalavu, *Fiji* 59 C9 17 40S 178 57W
Vanuatu ■, *Pac. Oc.* 64 J8 15 0S 168 0 E
Vanwyksvlei, *S. Africa* 56 E3 30 18S 21 49 E
Vanzylsrus, *S. Africa* 56 D3 26 52S 22 4 E
Vapnyarka, *Ukraine* 17 D15 48 32N 28 45 E
Varanasi, *India* 43 G10 25 22N 83 0 E
Varanger-halvøya, *Norway* 8 A23 70 25N 29 30 E
Varangerfjorden, *Norway* 8 A23 70 3N 29 25 E
Varaždin, *Croatia* 16 E9 46 20N 16 20 E
Varberg, *Sweden* 9 H15 57 6N 12 20 E
Vardar = Axiós →, *Greece* 21 D10 40 57N 22 35 E
Varde, *Denmark* 9 J13 55 38N 8 29 E
Vardø, *Norway* 8 A24 70 23N 31 5 E
Varella, Mui, *Vietnam* 38 F7 12 54N 109 26 E
Varena, *Lithuania* 9 J21 54 12N 24 30 E
Varese, *Italy* 18 D8 45 48N 8 50 E
Varginha, *Brazil* 95 A6 21 33S 45 25W
Varillas, *Chile* 94 A1 24 0S 70 10W
Varkaus, *Finland* 9 E22 62 19N 27 50 E
Varna, *Bulgaria* 21 C12 43 13N 27 56 E
Värnamo, *Sweden* 9 H16 57 10N 14 3 E
Vars, *Canada* 79 A9 45 21N 75 21W
Varysburg, *U.S.A.* 78 D6 42 46N 78 19W
Varzaneh, *Iran* 45 C7 32 25N 52 40 E
Vasa Barris →, *Brazil* 93 F11 11 10S 37 10W
Vascongadas = País Vasco □, *Spain* 19 A4 42 50N 2 45W
Vasht = Khāsh, *Iran* 40 E2 28 15N 61 15 E
Vasilevichi, *Belarus* 17 B15 52 15N 29 50 E
Vasilkov = Vasylkiv, *Ukraine* 17 C16 50 7N 30 15 E
Vaslui, *Romania* 17 E14 46 38N 27 42 E
Vassar, *Canada* 73 D9 49 10N 95 55W
Vassar, *U.S.A.* 76 D4 43 22N 83 35W
Västerås, *Sweden* 9 G17 59 37N 16 38 E
Västerbotten, *Sweden* 8 D18 64 36N 20 4 E
Västerdalälven →, *Sweden* 9 F16 60 30N 14 7 E
Västervik, *Sweden* 9 H17 57 43N 16 33 E
Västmanland, *Sweden* 9 G16 59 45N 16 20 E
Vasto, *Italy* 20 C6 42 8N 14 40 E
Vasylkiv, *Ukraine* 17 C16 50 7N 30 15 E
Vatersay, *U.K.* 12 E1 56 55N 7 32W
Vatican City ■, *Europe* 20 D5 41 54N 12 27 E
Vatili, *Cyprus* 23 D12 35 6N 33 40 E
Vatnajökull, *Iceland* 8 D5 64 30N 16 48W
Vatoa, *Fiji* 59 D9 19 50S 178 13W
Vatólakkos, *Greece* 23 D5 35 27N 23 53 E
Vatoloha, *Madag.* 57 B8 17 52S 47 48 E
Vatomandry, *Madag.* 57 B8 19 20S 48 59 E
Vatra-Dornei, *Romania* 17 E13 47 22N 25 22 E
Vatrak →, *India* 42 H5 23 9N 73 2 E
Vättern, *Sweden* 9 G16 58 25N 14 30 E
Vaughn, *Mont., U.S.A.* 82 C8 47 33N 111 33W
Vaughn, *N. Mex., U.S.A.* 83 J11 34 36N 105 13W
Vaujours L., *Canada* 70 A5 55 27N 74 15W
Vaupés = Uaupés →, *Brazil* 92 C5 0 2N 67 16W
Vaupes □, *Colombia* 92 C4 1 0N 71 0W
Vauxhall, *Canada* 72 C6 50 5N 112 9W
Vav, *India* 42 G4 24 22N 71 31 E
Vava'u, *Tonga* 59 D12 18 36S 174 0W
Vawkavysk, *Belarus* 17 B13 53 9N 24 30 E
Växjö, *Sweden* 9 H16 56 52N 14 50 E
Vaygach, Ostrov, *Russia* 26 C7 70 0N 60 0 E
Váyia, Ákra, *Greece* 23 C10 36 15N 28 11 E
Vechte →, *Neths.* 15 B6 52 34N 6 6 E
Vedea →, *Romania* 17 G13 43 42N 25 41 E
Vedia, *Argentina* 94 C3 34 30S 61 31W
Veendam, *Neths.* 15 A6 53 5N 6 52 E
Veenendaal, *Neths.* 15 B5 52 2N 5 34 E
Vefsna →, *Norway* 8 D15 65 48N 13 10 E
Vega, *Norway* 8 D14 65 40N 11 55 E
Vega, *U.S.A.* 81 H3 35 15N 102 26W
Vegreville, *Canada* 72 C6 53 30N 112 5W
Vejer de la Frontera, *Spain* 19 D3 36 15N 5 59W
Vejle, *Denmark* 9 J13 55 43N 9 30 E
Velas, C., *Costa Rica* 88 D2 10 21N 85 52W
Velasco, Sierra de, *Argentina* 94 B2 29 20S 67 10W
Velddrif, *S. Africa* 56 E2 32 42S 18 11 E
Velebit Planina, *Croatia* 16 F8 44 50N 15 20 E
Veles, *Macedonia* 21 D9 41 46N 21 47 E
Vélez-Málaga, *Spain* 19 D3 36 48N 4 5W
Vélez Rubio, *Spain* 19 D4 37 41N 2 5W
Velhas →, *Brazil* 93 G10 17 13S 44 49W
Velika Kapela, *Croatia* 16 F8 45 10N 15 5 E
Velikaya →, *Russia* 24 C4 57 48N 28 10 E
Velikaya Kema, *Russia* 30 B8 45 30N 137 12 E
Veliki Ustyug, *Russia* 24 B8 60 47N 46 20 E
Velikiye Luki, *Russia* 24 C5 56 25N 30 32 E
Veliko Tŭrnovo, *Bulgaria* 21 C11 43 5N 25 41 E
Velikonda Range, *India* 40 M11 14 45N 79 10 E
Velletri, *Italy* 20 D5 41 41N 12 47 E
Vellore, *India* 40 N11 12 57N 79 10 E
Velsk, *Russia* 24 B7 61 10N 42 5 E
Velva, *U.S.A.* 80 A4 48 4N 100 56W
Venado Tuerto, *Argentina* 94 C3 33 50S 62 0W
Vendée □, *France* 18 C3 46 50N 1 35W
Vendôme, *France* 18 C4 47 47N 1 3 E
Venézia, *Italy* 20 B5 45 27N 12 21 E
Venézia, G. di, *Italy* 20 B5 45 15N 13 0 E
Venezuela ■, *S. Amer.* 92 B5 8 0N 66 0W
Venezuela, G. de, *Venezuela* 92 A4 11 30N 71 0W
Vengurla, *India* 40 M8 15 53N 73 45 E
Venice = Venézia, *Italy* 20 B5 45 27N 12 21 E
Venice, *U.S.A.* 77 M4 27 6N 82 27W
Venkatapuram, *India* 41 K12 18 20N 80 30 E
Venlo, *Neths.* 15 C6 51 22N 6 11 E
Vennesla, *Norway* 9 G12 58 15N 7 59 E
Venray, *Neths.* 15 C6 51 31N 6 0 E
Ventana, Punta de la, *Mexico* 86 C3 24 4N 109 48W
Ventana, Sa. de la, *Argentina* 94 D3 38 0S 62 30W
Ventersburg, *S. Africa* 56 D4 28 7S 27 9 E
Venterstad, *S. Africa* 56 E4 30 47S 25 48 E
Ventnor, *U.K.* 11 G6 50 36N 1 12W
Ventotène, *Italy* 20 D5 40 47N 13 25 E
Ventoux, Mt., *France* 18 D6 44 10N 5 17 E
Ventspils, *Latvia* 9 H19 57 25N 21 32 E
Ventuarí →, *Venezuela* 92 C5 3 58N 67 2W
Ventucopa, *U.S.A.* 85 L7 34 50N 119 29W
Ventura, *U.S.A.* 85 L7 34 17N 119 18W
Venus B., *Australia* 63 F4 38 40S 145 42 E
Vera, *Argentina* 94 B3 29 30S 60 20W
Vera, *Spain* 19 D5 37 15N 1 51W
Veracruz, *Mexico* 87 D5 19 10N 96 10W
Veracruz □, *Mexico* 87 D5 19 0N 96 15W
Veraval, *India* 42 J4 20 53N 70 27 E
Verbánia, *Italy* 18 D8 45 56N 8 33 E
Vercelli, *Italy* 18 D8 45 19N 8 25 E
Verdalsøra, *Norway* 8 E14 63 48N 11 30 E
Verde →, *Argentina* 96 E3 41 56S 65 5W
Verde →, *Goiás, Brazil* 93 G8 18 1S 50 14W
Verde →, *Mato Grosso do Sul, Brazil* 93 H8 21 25S 52 20W
Verde →, *Chihuahua, Mexico* 86 B3 26 29N 107 58W
Verde →, *Oaxaca, Mexico* 87 D5 15 59N 97 50W
Verde →, *Veracruz, Mexico* 86 C4 21 10N 102 50W
Verde →, *Paraguay* 94 A4 23 9S 57 37W
Verde →, *U.S.A.* 74 D4 33 33N 111 40W
Verde, Cay, *Bahamas* 88 B4 23 0N 75 5W
Verden, *Germany* 16 B5 52 55N 9 14 E
Verdi, *U.S.A.* 84 F7 39 31N 119 59W
Verdun, *France* 18 B6 49 9N 5 24 E
Vereeniging, *S. Africa* 57 D4 26 38S 27 57 E
Verga, C., *Guinea* 50 F3 10 30N 14 10W
Vergara, *Uruguay* 95 C5 32 56S 53 57W
Vergemont Cr. →, *Australia* 62 C3 24 16S 143 16 E
Vergennes, *U.S.A.* 79 B11 44 10N 73 15W
Verin, *Spain* 19 B2 41 57N 7 27W
Verkhnevilyuysk, *Russia* 27 C13 63 27N 120 18 E
Verkhniy Baskunchak, *Russia* 25 E8 48 14N 46 44 E
Verkhoyansk, *Russia* 27 C14 67 35N 133 25 E
Verkhoyansk Ra. = Verkhoyanskiy Khrebet, *Russia* 27 C13 66 0N 129 0 E
Verkhoyanskiy Khrebet, *Russia* 27 C13 66 0N 129 0 E
Vermilion, *Canada* 73 C6 53 20N 110 50W
Vermilion, *U.S.A.* 78 E2 41 25N 82 22W
Vermilion →, *Alta., Canada* 73 C6 53 22N 110 51W
Vermilion →, *Qué., Canada* 70 C5 47 38N 72 56W
Vermilion, B., *U.S.A.* 81 L9 29 45N 91 55W
Vermilion Bay, *Canada* 73 D10 49 51N 93 34W
Vermilion L., *U.S.A.* 80 B8 47 53N 92 26W
Vermillion, *U.S.A.* 80 D6 42 47N 96 56W
Vermont □, *U.S.A.* 79 C12 44 0N 73 0W
Vernal, *U.S.A.* 82 F9 40 27N 109 32W
Vernalis, *U.S.A.* 84 H5 37 36N 121 17W
Verner, *Canada* 70 C3 46 25N 80 8W
Verneukpan, *S. Africa* 56 E3 30 0S 21 0 E
Vernon, *Canada* 72 C5 50 20N 119 15W
Vernon, *U.S.A.* 81 H5 34 9N 99 17W
Vernonia, *U.S.A.* 84 E3 45 52N 123 11W
Vero Beach, *U.S.A.* 77 M5 27 38N 80 24W
Véroia, *Greece* 21 D10 40 34N 22 12 E
Verona, *Canada* 79 B8 44 29N 76 42W
Verona, *Italy* 20 B4 45 27N 10 59 E
Verona, *U.S.A.* 80 D10 42 59N 89 32W
Versailles, *France* 18 B5 48 48N 2 8 E
Vert, C., *Senegal* 50 F2 14 45N 17 30W
Verulam, *S. Africa* 57 D5 29 38S 31 2 E
Verviers, *Belgium* 15 D5 50 37N 5 52 E
Veselovskoye Vdkhr., *Russia* 25 E7 46 58N 41 25 E
Vesoul, *France* 18 C7 47 40N 6 11 E
Vesterålen, *Norway* 8 B16 68 45N 15 0 E

Vestfjorden, *Norway* 8 C15 67 55N 14 0 E
Vestmannaeyjar, *Iceland* 8 E3 63 27N 20 15W
Vestspitsbergen, *Svalbard* 4 B8 78 40N 17 0 E
Vestvågøy, *Norway* 8 B15 68 18N 13 50 E
Vesuvio, *Italy* 20 D6 40 49N 14 26 E
Vesuvius, Mt. = Vesuvio, *Italy* 20 D6 40 49N 14 26 E
Veszprém, *Hungary* 17 E9 47 8N 17 57 E
Vetlanda, *Sweden* 9 H16 57 24N 15 3 E
Vetlugu →, *Russia* 24 C8 56 36N 46 4 E
Vettore, Mte., *Italy* 20 C5 42 49N 13 16 E
Veurne, *Belgium* 15 C2 51 5N 2 40 E
Veys, *Iran* 45 D6 31 30N 49 0 E
Vezhen, *Bulgaria* 21 C11 42 50N 24 20 E
Vi Thanh, *Vietnam* 39 H5 9 42N 105 26 E
Viacha, *Bolivia* 92 G5 16 39S 68 18W
Viamão, *Brazil* 95 C5 30 5S 51 0W
Viana, *Brazil* 93 D10 3 13S 44 55W
Viana do Alentejo, *Portugal* 19 C2 38 17N 7 59W
Viana do Castelo, *Portugal* 19 B1 41 42N 8 50W
Vianden, *Lux.* 15 E6 49 56N 6 12 E
Vianópolis, *Brazil* 93 G9 16 40S 48 35W
Viaréggio, *Italy* 20 C4 43 52N 10 14 E
Vibo Valéntia, *Italy* 20 E7 38 40N 16 6 E
Viborg, *Denmark* 9 H13 56 27N 9 23 E
Vic, *Spain* 19 B7 41 58N 2 19 E
Vicenza, *Italy* 20 B4 45 33N 11 33 E
Vich = Vic, *Spain* 19 B7 41 58N 2 19 E
Vichada →, *Colombia* 92 C5 4 55N 67 50W
Vichy, *France* 18 C5 46 9N 3 26 E
Vicksburg, *Ariz., U.S.A.* 85 M13 33 45N 113 45W
Vicksburg, *Miss., U.S.A.* 81 J9 32 21N 90 53W
Victor, *India* 42 J4 21 0N 71 30 E
Victor, *U.S.A.* 78 D7 42 58N 77 24W
Victor Harbor, *Australia* 63 F2 35 30S 138 37 E
Victoria = Labuan, *Malaysia* 36 C5 5 20N 115 14 E
Victoria, *Argentina* 94 C3 32 40S 60 10W
Victoria, *Canada* 72 D4 48 30N 123 25W
Victoria, *Chile* 96 D2 38 13S 72 20W
Victoria, *Malta* 23 C1 36 2N 14 14 E
Victoria, *Kans., U.S.A.* 80 F5 38 52N 99 9W
Victoria, *Tex., U.S.A.* 81 L6 28 48N 97 0W
Victoria □, *Australia* 63 F3 37 0S 144 0 E
Victoria →, *Australia* 60 C4 15 10S 129 40 E
Victoria, Grand L., *Canada* 70 C4 47 31N 77 30W
Victoria, L., *Africa* 54 C3 1 0S 33 0 E
Victoria, L., *Australia* 63 E3 33 57S 141 15 E
Victoria Beach, *Canada* 73 C9 50 40N 96 35W
Victoria de Durango = Durango, *Mexico* 86 C4 24 3N 104 39W
Victoria de las Tunas, *Cuba* 88 B4 20 58N 76 59W
Victoria Falls, *Zimbabwe* 55 F2 17 58S 25 52 E
Victoria Harbour, *Canada* 78 B5 44 45N 79 45W
Victoria I., *Canada* 68 A8 71 0N 111 0W
Victoria L., *Canada* 71 C8 48 20N 57 27W
Victoria Ld., *Antarctica* 5 D11 75 0S 160 0 E
Victoria Nile →, *Uganda* 54 B3 2 14N 31 26 E
Victoria River, *Australia* 60 C5 16 25S 131 0 E
Victoria Str., *Canada* 68 B9 69 30N 100 0W
Victoria Taungdeik, *Burma* 41 J18 21 15N 93 55 E
Victoria West, *S. Africa* 56 E3 31 25S 23 4 E
Victoriaville, *Canada* 71 C5 46 4N 71 56W
Victorica, *Argentina* 94 D2 36 20S 65 30W
Victorville, *U.S.A.* 85 L9 34 32N 117 18W
Vicuña, *Chile* 94 C1 30 0S 70 50W
Vicuña Mackenna, *Argentina* 94 C3 33 53S 64 25W
Vidal, *U.S.A.* 85 L12 34 7N 114 31W
Vidal Junction, *U.S.A.* 85 L12 34 11N 114 34W
Vidalia, *U.S.A.* 77 J4 32 13N 82 25W
Vídho, *Greece* 23 A3 39 38N 19 55 E
Vidin, *Bulgaria* 21 C10 43 59N 22 50 E
Vidisha, *India* 42 H7 23 28N 77 53 E
Vidzy, *Belarus* 9 J22 55 23N 26 37 E
Viedma, *Argentina* 96 E4 40 50S 63 0W
Viedma, L., *Argentina* 96 F2 49 30S 72 30W
Vielsalm, *Belgium* 15 D5 50 17N 5 54 E
Vienna = Wien, *Austria* 16 D9 48 12N 16 22 E
Vienna, *Ill., U.S.A.* 81 G10 37 25N 88 54W
Vienna, *Mo., U.S.A.* 80 F9 38 11N 91 57W
Vienne, *France* 18 D6 45 31N 4 53 E
Vienne →, *France* 18 C4 47 13N 0 5 E
Vientiane, *Laos* 38 D4 17 58N 102 36 E
Vientos, Paso de los, *Caribbean* 89 C5 20 0N 74 0W
Vierzon, *France* 18 C5 47 13N 2 5 E
Vietnam ■, *Asia* 38 C6 19 0N 106 0 E
Vigan, *Phil.* 37 A6 17 35N 120 28 E
Vigévano, *Italy* 18 D8 45 19N 8 51 E
Vigia, *Brazil* 93 D9 0 50S 48 5W
Vigía Chico, *Mexico* 87 D7 19 46N 87 35W
Víglas, Ákra, *Greece* 23 D9 35 54N 27 51 E
Vigo, *Spain* 19 A1 42 12N 8 41W
Vihowa, *Pakistan* 42 D4 31 8N 70 30 E
Vihowa →, *Pakistan* 42 D4 31 8N 70 41 E
Vijayawada, *India* 41 L12 16 31N 80 39 E
Vík, *Iceland* 8 E4 63 25N 19 1W
Vikeke, *Indonesia* 37 F7 8 52S 126 23 E
Viking, *Canada* 72 C6 53 7N 111 50W
Vikna, *Norway* 8 D14 64 55N 10 58 E
Vila da Maganja, *Mozam.* 55 F4 17 18S 37 30 E
Vila de João Belo = Xai-Xai, *Mozam.* 57 D5 25 6S 33 31 E
Vila do Bispo, *Portugal* 19 D1 37 5N 8 53W
Vila do Chibuto, *Mozam.* 57 C5 24 40S 33 33 E
Vila Franca de Xira, *Portugal* 19 C1 38 57N 8 59W
Vila Gamito, *Mozam.* 55 E3 14 12S 33 0 E
Vila Gomes da Costa, *Mozam.* 57 C5 24 20S 33 37 E
Vila Machado, *Mozam.* 55 F3 19 15S 34 14 E
Vila Mouzinho, *Mozam.* 55 E3 14 48S 34 25 E
Vila Nova de Gaia, *Portugal* 19 B1 41 8N 8 37W
Vila Real, *Portugal* 19 B2 41 17N 7 48W
Vila-real de los Infantes, *Spain* 19 C5 39 55N 0 3W
Vila Real de Santo António, *Portugal* 19 D2 37 10N 7 28W
Vila Vasco da Gama, *Mozam.* 55 E3 14 54S 32 14 E
Vila Velha, *Brazil* 95 A7 20 20S 40 17W
Vilagarcía de Arousa, *Spain* 19 A1 42 34N 8 46W
Vilaine →, *France* 18 C2 47 30N 2 27W
Vilanandro, Tanjona, *Madag.* 57 B7 16 11S 44 27 E
Vilanculos, *Mozam.* 57 C6 22 1S 35 17 E
Vilanova i la Geltrú, *Spain* 19 B6 41 13N 1 40 E
Vileyka, *Belarus* 17 A14 54 30N 26 53 E
Vilhelmina, *Sweden* 8 D17 64 35N 16 39 E
Vilhena, *Brazil* 92 F6 12 40S 60 5W
Viliga, *Russia* 27 C16 61 36N 156 56 E
Viliya →, *Lithuania* 9 J21 55 8N 24 16 E
Viljandi, *Estonia* 9 G21 58 28N 25 30 E
Vilkitskogo, Proliv, *Russia* 27 B11 78 0N 103 0 E
Vilkovo = Vylkove, *Ukraine* 17 F15 45 28N 29 32 E
Villa Abecia, *Bolivia* 94 A2 21 0S 68 18W
Villa Ahumada, *Mexico* 86 A3 30 38N 106 30W
Villa Ana, *Argentina* 94 B4 28 28S 59 40W
Villa Ángela, *Argentina* 94 B3 27 34S 60 45W
Villa Bella, *Bolivia* 92 F5 10 25S 65 22W
Villa Bens = Tarfaya, *Morocco* 50 C3 27 55N 12 55W
Villa Cañás, *Argentina* 94 C3 34 0S 61 35W
Villa Cisneros = Dakhla, *W. Sahara* 50 D2 23 50N 15 53W
Villa Colón, *Argentina* 94 C2 31 38S 68 20W
Villa Constitución, *Argentina* 94 C3 33 15S 60 20W
Villa de María, *Argentina* 94 B3 29 55S 63 43W
Villa Dolores, *Argentina* 94 C2 31 58S 65 15W
Villa Frontera, *Mexico* 86 B4 26 56N 101 27W
Villa Guillermina, *Argentina* 94 B4 28 15S 59 29W
Villa Hayes, *Paraguay* 94 B4 25 5S 57 20W
Villa Iris, *Argentina* 94 D3 38 12S 63 12W
Villa Juárez, *Mexico* 86 B4 27 37N 100 44W
Villa María, *Argentina* 94 C3 32 20S 63 10W
Villa Mazán, *Argentina* 94 B2 28 40S 66 30W
Villa Montes, *Bolivia* 94 A3 21 10S 63 30W
Villa Ocampo, *Argentina* 94 B4 28 30S 59 20W
Villa Ocampo, *Mexico* 86 B3 26 29N 105 30W
Villa Ojo de Agua, *Argentina* 94 B3 29 30S 63 44W
Villa San José, *Argentina* 94 C4 32 12S 58 15W
Villa San Martín, *Argentina* 94 B3 28 15S 64 9W
Villa Unión, *Mexico* 86 C3 23 12N 106 14W
Villacarlos, *Spain* 22 B11 39 53N 4 17 E
Villacarrillo, *Spain* 19 C4 38 7N 3 3W
Villach, *Austria* 16 E7 46 37N 13 51 E
Villafranca de los Caballeros, *Spain* 22 B10 39 34N 3 25 E
Villagrán, *Mexico* 87 C5 24 29N 99 29W
Villaguay, *Argentina* 94 C4 32 0S 59 0W
Villahermosa, *Mexico* 87 D6 17 59N 92 55W
Villajoyosa, *Spain* 19 C5 38 30N 0 12W
Villalba, *Spain* 19 A2 43 26N 7 40W
Villanueva, *U.S.A.* 81 H2 35 16N 105 22W
Villanueva de la Serena, *Spain* 19 C3 38 59N 5 50W
Villanueva y Geltrú = Vilanova i la Geltrú, *Spain* 19 B6 41 13N 1 40 E
Villarreal = Vila-real de los Infantes, *Spain* 19 C5 39 55N 0 3W
Villarrica, *Chile* 96 D2 39 15S 72 15W
Villarrica, *Paraguay* 94 B4 25 40S 56 30W
Villarrobledo, *Spain* 19 C4 39 18N 2 36W
Villavicencio, *Argentina* 94 C2 32 28S 69 0W
Villavicencio, *Colombia* 92 C4 4 9N 73 37W
Villaviciosa, *Spain* 19 A3 43 32N 5 27W
Villazón, *Bolivia* 94 A2 22 0S 65 35W
Ville-Marie, *Canada* 70 C4 47 20N 79 30W
Ville Platte, *U.S.A.* 81 K8 30 41N 92 17W
Villena, *Spain* 19 C5 38 39N 0 52W
Villeneuve-d'Ascq, *France* 18 A5 50 38N 3 9 E
Villeneuve-sur-Lot, *France* 18 D4 44 24N 0 42 E
Villiers, *S. Africa* 57 D4 27 2S 28 36 E
Villingen-Schwenningen, *Germany* 16 D5 48 3N 8 26 E
Vilna, *Canada* 72 C6 54 7N 111 55W
Vilnius, *Lithuania* 9 J21 54 38N 25 19 E
Vilvoorde, *Belgium* 15 D4 50 56N 4 26 E
Vilyuy →, *Russia* 27 C13 64 24N 126 26 E
Vilyuysk, *Russia* 27 C13 63 40N 121 35 E
Viña del Mar, *Chile* 94 C1 33 0S 71 30W
Vinarós, *Spain* 19 B6 40 30N 0 27 E
Vincennes, *U.S.A.* 76 F2 38 41N 87 32W
Vincent, *U.S.A.* 85 L8 34 33N 118 11W
Vinchina, *Argentina* 94 B2 28 45S 68 15W
Vindelälven →, *Sweden* 8 E18 63 55N 19 50 E
Vindeln, *Sweden* 8 D18 64 12N 19 43 E
Vindhya Ra., *India* 42 H7 22 50N 77 0 E
Vineland, *U.S.A.* 76 F8 39 29N 75 2W
Vinh, *Vietnam* 38 C5 18 45N 105 38 E
Vinh Linh, *Vietnam* 38 D6 17 4N 107 2 E
Vinh Long, *Vietnam* 39 G5 10 16N 105 57 E
Vinita, *U.S.A.* 81 G7 36 39N 95 9W
Vinkovci, *Croatia* 21 B8 45 19N 18 48 E
Vinnitsa = Vinnytsya, *Ukraine* 17 D15 49 15N 28 30 E
Vinnytsya, *Ukraine* 17 D15 49 15N 28 30 E
Vinton, *Calif., U.S.A.* 84 F6 39 48N 120 10W
Vinton, *Iowa, U.S.A.* 80 D8 42 10N 92 1W
Vinton, *La., U.S.A.* 81 K8 30 11N 93 35W
Virac, *Phil.* 37 B6 13 30N 124 20 E
Virachei, *Cambodia* 38 F6 13 59N 106 49 E
Virago Sd., *Canada* 72 C2 54 0N 132 30W
Viramgam, *India* 42 H5 23 5N 72 0 E
Virananşehir, *Turkey* 44 B3 37 13N 39 45 E
Virawah, *Pakistan* 42 G4 24 31N 70 46 E
Virden, *Canada* 73 D8 49 50N 100 56W
Vire, *France* 18 B3 48 50N 0 53W
Vírgenes, C., *Argentina* 96 G3 52 19S 68 21W
Virgin →, *U.S.A.* 83 H6 36 28N 114 21W
Virgin Gorda, *Virgin Is.* 89 C7 18 30N 64 26W
Virgin Is. (British) ■, *W. Indies* 89 C7 18 30N 64 30W
Virgin Is. (U.S.) ■, *W. Indies* 89 C7 18 20N 65 0W
Virginia, *S. Africa* 56 D4 28 8S 26 55 E
Virginia, *U.S.A.* 80 B8 47 31N 92 32W
Virginia □, *U.S.A.* 76 G7 37 30N 78 45W
Virginia Beach, *U.S.A.* 76 G8 36 51N 75 59W
Virginia City, *Mont., U.S.A.* 82 D8 45 18N 111 56W
Virginia City, *Nev., U.S.A.* 84 F7 39 19N 119 39W
Virginia Falls, *Canada* 72 A3 61 38N 125 42W
Virginiatown, *Canada* 70 C4 48 9N 79 36W
Viroqua, *U.S.A.* 80 D9 43 34N 90 53W
Virovitica, *Croatia* 20 B7 45 51N 17 21 E
Virpur, *India* 42 J4 21 51N 70 42 E
Virton, *Belgium* 15 E5 49 35N 5 32 E
Virudunagar, *India* 40 Q10 9 30N 77 58 E
Vis, *Croatia* 20 C7 43 4N 16 10 E
Visalia, *U.S.A.* 84 J7 36 20N 119 18W
Visayan Sea, *Phil.* 37 B6 11 30N 123 30 E
Visby, *Sweden* 9 H18 57 37N 18 18 E
Viscount Melville Sd., *Canada* 4 B2 74 10N 108 0W
Visé, *Belgium* 15 D5 50 44N 5 41 E
Višegrad, *Bos.-H.* 21 C8 43 47N 19 17 E
Viseu, *Brazil* 93 D9 1 10S 46 5W
Viseu, *Portugal* 19 B2 40 40N 7 55W
Vishakhapatnam, *India* 41 L13 17 45N 83 20 E
Visnagar, *India* 42 H5 23 45N 72 32 E
Viso, Mte., *Italy* 18 D7 44 38N 7 5 E
Visokoi I., *Antarctica* 5 B1 56 43S 27 15W
Vista, *U.S.A.* 85 M9 33 12N 117 14W
Vistula = Wisła →, *Poland* 17 A10 54 22N 18 55 E
Vitebsk = Vitsyebsk, *Belarus* 24 C5 55 10N 30 15 E
Viterbo, *Italy* 20 C5 42 25N 12 6 E
Viti Levu, *Fiji* 59 C7 17 30S 177 30 E
Vitigudino, *Spain* 19 B2 41 1N 6 26W
Vitim, *Russia* 27 D12 59 28N 112 35 E
Vitim →, *Russia* 27 D12 59 26N 112 34 E
Vitória, *Brazil* 93 H10 20 20S 40 22W
Vitória da Conquista, *Brazil* 93 F10 14 51S 40 51W
Vitória de São Antão, *Brazil* 93 E11 8 10S 35 20W
Vitoria-Gasteiz, *Spain* 19 A4 42 50N 2 41W
Vitsyebsk, *Belarus* 24 C5 55 10N 30 15 E
Vittória, *Italy* 20 F6 36 57N 14 32 E
Vittório Véneto, *Italy* 20 B5 45 59N 12 18 E
Viveiro, *Spain* 19 A2 43 39N 7 38W
Vivian, *U.S.A.* 81 J8 32 53N 93 59W
Vizcaíno, Desierto de, *Mexico* 86 B2 27 40N 113 50W
Vizcaíno, Sierra, *Mexico* 86 B2 27 30N 114 0W
Vize, *Turkey* 21 D12 41 34N 27 45 E
Vizianagaram, *India* 41 K13 18 6N 83 30 E
Vjosa →, *Albania* 21 D8 40 37N 19 24 E
Vlaardingen, *Neths.* 15 C4 51 55N 4 21 E
Vladikavkaz, *Russia* 25 F7 43 0N 44 35 E
Vladimir, *Russia* 24 C7 56 15N 40 30 E
Vladimir Volynskiy = Volodymyr-Volynskyy, *Ukraine* 17 C13 50 50N 24 18 E
Vladivostok, *Russia* 27 E14 43 10N 131 53 E
Vlieland, *Neths.* 15 A4 53 16N 4 55 E
Vlissingen, *Neths.* 15 C3 51 26N 3 34 E
Vlóra, *Albania* 21 D8 40 32N 19 28 E
Vltava →, *Czech Rep.* 16 D8 50 21N 14 30 E
Vo Dat, *Vietnam* 39 G6 11 9N 107 31 E
Voe, *U.K.* 12 A7 60 21N 1 16W
Vogelkop = Doberai, Jazirah, *Indonesia* 37 E8 1 25S 133 0 E
Vogelsberg, *Germany* 16 C5 50 31N 9 12 E
Voghera, *Italy* 18 D8 44 59N 9 1 E
Vohibinany, *Madag.* 57 B8 18 49S 49 4 E
Vohimarina = Iharana, *Madag.* 57 A9 13 25S 50 0 E
Vohimena, Tanjon' i, *Madag.* 57 D8 25 36S 45 8 E
Vohipeno, *Madag.* 57 C8 22 22S 47 51 E
Voi, *Kenya* 54 C4 3 25S 38 32 E
Voiron, *France* 18 D6 45 22N 5 35 E
Voisey B., *Canada* 71 A7 56 15N 61 50W
Vojmsjön, *Sweden* 8 D17 64 55N 16 40 E
Vojvodina □, *Serbia, Yug.* 21 B9 45 20N 20 0 E
Volborg, *U.S.A.* 80 C2 45 51N 105 41W
Volcano Is. = Kazan-Rettō, *Pac. Oc.* 64 E6 25 0N 141 0 E
Volda, *Norway* 9 E12 62 9N 6 5 E
Volga →, *Russia* 25 E8 46 0N 48 30 E
Volga Hts. = Privolzhskaya Vozvyshennost, *Russia* 25 D8 51 0N 46 0 E
Volgodonsk, *Russia* 25 E7 47 33N 42 5 E
Volgograd, *Russia* 25 E7 48 40N 44 25 E
Volgogradskoye Vdkhr., *Russia* 25 E8 50 0N 45 20 E
Volkhov →, *Russia* 24 B5 60 8N 32 20 E
Volkovysk = Vawkavysk, *Belarus* 17 B13 53 9N 24 30 E
Volksrust, *S. Africa* 57 D4 27 24S 29 53 E
Volochanka, *Russia* 27 B10 71 0N 94 28 E
Volodymyr-Volynskyy, *Ukraine* 17 C13 50 50N 24 18 E
Vologda, *Russia* 24 C6 59 10N 39 45 E
Vólos, *Greece* 21 E10 39 24N 22 59 E
Volovets, *Ukraine* 17 D12 48 43N 23 11 E
Volozhin = Valozhyn, *Belarus* 17 A14 54 3N 26 30 E
Volsk, *Russia* 24 D8 52 5N 47 22 E
Volta →, *Ghana* 48 F4 5 46N 0 41 E
Volta, L., *Ghana* 50 G6 7 30N 0 0 E
Volta Redonda, *Brazil* 95 A7 22 31S 44 5W
Voltaire, C., *Australia* 60 B4 14 16S 125 35 E
Volterra, *Italy* 20 C4 43 24N 10 51 E
Volturno →, *Italy* 20 D5 41 1N 13 55 E
Volzhskiy, *Russia* 25 E7 48 56N 44 46 E
Vondrozo, *Madag.* 57 C8 22 49S 47 20 E
Vopnafjörður, *Iceland* 8 D6 65 45N 14 50W
Vóriai Sporádhes, *Greece* 21 E10 39 15N 23 30 E
Vorkuta, *Russia* 24 A11 67 48N 64 20 E
Vormsi, *Estonia* 9 G20 59 1N 23 13 E
Voronezh, *Russia* 25 D6 51 40N 39 10 E
Voroshilovgrad = Luhansk, *Ukraine* 25 E6 48 38N 39 15 E
Voroshilovsk = Alchevsk, *Ukraine* 25 E6 48 30N 38 45 E
Võrts Järv, *Estonia* 9 G22 58 16N 26 3 E
Vöru, *Estonia* 9 H22 57 48N 26 54 E
Vosges, *France* 18 B7 48 20N 7 10 E
Voss, *Norway* 9 F12 60 38N 6 26 E
Vostok I., *Kiribati* 65 J12 10 5S 152 23W
Votkinsk, *Russia* 24 C9 57 0N 53 55 E
Votkinskoye Vdkhr., *Russia* 24 C10 57 22N 55 12 E
Votsuri-Shima, *Japan* 31 M1 25 45N 123 29 E
Vouga →, *Portugal* 19 B1 40 41N 8 40W
Voúxa, Ákra, *Greece* 23 D5 35 37N 23 32 E
Vozhe, Ozero, *Russia* 24 B6 60 45N 39 0 E
Voznesensk, *Ukraine* 25 E5 47 35N 31 21 E
Voznesenye, *Russia* 24 B6 61 0N 35 28 E
Vrangelya, Ostrov, *Russia* 27 B19 71 0N 180 0 E
Vranje, *Serbia, Yug.* 21 C9 42 34N 21 54 E
Vratsa, *Bulgaria* 21 C10 43 15N 23 30 E
Vrbas →, *Bos.-H.* 20 B7 45 8N 17 29 E
Vrede, *S. Africa* 57 D4 27 24S 29 6 E
Vredefort, *S. Africa* 56 D4 27 0S 27 22 E
Vredenburg, *S. Africa* 56 E2 32 56S 18 0 E
Vredendal, *S. Africa* 56 E2 31 41S 18 35 E
Vrindavan, *India* 42 F7 27 37N 77 40 E
Vríses, *Greece* 23 D6 35 23N 24 13 E
Vršac, *Serbia, Yug.* 21 B9 45 8N 21 20 E
Vryburg, *S. Africa* 56 D3 26 55S 24 45 E
Vryheid, *S. Africa* 57 D5 27 45S 30 47 E
Vu Liet, *Vietnam* 38 C5 18 43N 105 23 E
Vukovar, *Croatia* 21 B8 45 21N 18 59 E
Vulcan, *Canada* 72 C6 50 25N 113 15W
Vulcan, *Romania* 17 F12 45 23N 23 17 E
Vulcaneşti, *Moldova* 17 F15 45 41N 28 18 E
Vulcano, *Italy* 20 E6 38 24N 14 58 E
Vulkaneshty = Vulcaneşti, *Moldova* 17 F15 45 41N 28 18 E
Vunduzi →, *Mozam.* 55 F3 18 56S 34 1 E
Vung Tau, *Vietnam* 39 G6 10 21N 107 4 E
Vyatka = Kirov, *Russia* 24 C8 58 35N 49 40 E
Vyatka →, *Russia* 24 C9 55 37N 51 28 E
Vyatskiye Polyany, *Russia* 24 C9 56 14N 51 5 E
Vyazemskiy, *Russia* 27 E14 47 32N 134 45 E
Vyazma, *Russia* 24 C5 55 10N 34 15 E
Vyborg, *Russia* 24 B4 60 43N 28 47 E
Vychegda →, *Russia* 24 B8 61 18N 46 36 E
Vychodné Beskydy, *Europe* 17 D11 49 20N 22 0 E
Vyg-ozero, *Russia* 24 B5 63 47N 34 29 E
Vylkove, *Ukraine* 17 F15 45 28N 29 32 E
Vynohradiv, *Ukraine* 17 D12 48 9N 23 2 E
Vyrnwy, L., *U.K.* 10 E4 52 48N 3 31W
Vyshniy Volochek, *Russia* 24 C5 57 30N 34 30 E
Vyškov, *Czech Rep.* 17 D9 49 17N 17 0 E
Vytegra, *Russia* 24 B6 61 0N 36 27 E

W

W.A.C. Bennett Dam, *Canada* 72 B4 56 2N 122 6W
Waal →, *Neths.* 15 C5 51 37N 5 0 E
Waalwijk, *Neths.* 15 C5 51 42N 5 4 E
Wabana, *Canada* 71 C9 47 40N 53 0W
Wabasca →, *Canada* 72 B5 58 22N 115 20W
Wabasca-Desmarais, *Canada* 72 B6 55 57N 113 56W
Wabash, *U.S.A.* 76 E3 40 48N 85 49W
Wabash →, *U.S.A.* 76 G1 37 48N 88 2W
Wabigoon L., *Canada* 73 D10 49 44N 92 44W
Wabowden, *Canada* 73 C9 54 55N 98 38W
Wabuk Pt., *Canada* 70 A2 55 20N 85 5W
Wabush, *Canada* 71 B6 52 55N 66 52W
Waco, *U.S.A.* 81 K6 31 33N 97 9W
Waconichi, L., *Canada* 70 B5 50 8N 74 0W
Wad Hamid, *Sudan* 51 E12 16 30N 32 45 E
Wâd Medanî, *Sudan* 51 F12 14 28N 33 30 E
Wad Thana, *Pakistan* 42 F2 27 22N 66 23 E
Wadai, *Africa* 48 E5 12 0N 19 0 E
Wadayama, *Japan* 31 G7 35 19N 134 52 E
Waddeneilanden, *Neths.* 15 A5 53 20N 5 10 E
Waddenzee, *Neths.* 15 A5 53 6N 5 10 E
Waddington, *U.S.A.* 79 B9 44 52N 75 12W
Waddington, Mt., *Canada* 72 C3 51 23N 125 15W
Waddy Pt., *Australia* 63 C5 24 58S 153 21 E
Wadebridge, *U.K.* 11 G3 50 31N 4 51W
Wadena, *Canada* 73 C8 51 57N 103 47W
Wadena, *U.S.A.* 80 B7 46 26N 95 8W
Wadeye, *Australia* 60 B4 14 28S 129 52 E
Wadhams, *Canada* 72 C3 51 30N 127 30W
Wādī as Sīr, *Jordan* 47 D4 31 56N 35 49 E
Wadi Halfa, *Sudan* 51 D12 21 53N 31 19 E
Wadsworth, *Nev., U.S.A.* 82 G4 39 38N 119 17W
Wadsworth, *Ohio, U.S.A.* 78 E3 41 2N 81 44W
Waegwan, *S. Korea* 35 G15 35 59N 128 23 E
Wafangdian, *China* 35 E11 39 38N 121 58 E
Wafrah, *Si. Arabia* 44 D5 28 33N 47 56 E
Wageningen, *Neths.* 15 C5 51 58N 5 40 E
Wager B., *Canada* 69 B11 65 26N 88 40W
Wagga Wagga, *Australia* 63 F4 35 7S 147 24 E
Waghete, *Indonesia* 37 E9 4 10S 135 50 E
Wagin, *Australia* 61 F2 33 17S 117 25 E
Wagner, *U.S.A.* 80 D5 43 5N 98 18W
Wagon Mound, *U.S.A.* 81 G2 36 1N 104 42W
Wagoner, *U.S.A.* 81 H7 35 58N 95 22W
Wah, *Pakistan* 42 C5 33 45N 72 40 E
Wahai, *Indonesia* 37 E7 2 48S 129 35 E
Wahiawa, *U.S.A.* 74 H15 21 30N 158 2W
Wâḩid, *Egypt* 47 E1 30 48N 32 21 E
Wahnai, *Afghan.* 42 C1 32 40N 65 50 E
Wahoo, *U.S.A.* 80 E6 41 13N 96 37W
Wahpeton, *U.S.A.* 80 B6 46 16N 96 36W
Wai, Koh, *Cambodia* 39 H4 9 55N 102 55 E
Waiau →, *N.Z.* 59 K4 42 47S 173 22 E
Waibeem, *Indonesia* 37 E8 0 30S 132 59 E
Waigeo, *Indonesia* 37 E8 0 20S 130 40 E
Waihi, *N.Z.* 59 G5 37 23S 175 52 E
Waihou →, *N.Z.* 59 G5 37 15S 175 40 E
Waika, *Dem. Rep. of the Congo* 54 C2 2 22S 25 42 E
Waikabubak, *Indonesia* 37 F5 9 45S 119 25 E
Waikari, *N.Z.* 59 K4 42 58S 172 41 E
Waikato →, *N.Z.* 59 G5 37 23S 174 43 E
Waikerie, *Australia* 63 E3 34 9S 140 0 E
Waikokopu, *N.Z.* 59 H6 39 3S 177 52 E
Waikouaiti, *N.Z.* 59 L3 45 36S 170 41 E
Wailuku, *U.S.A.* 74 H16 20 53N 156 30W
Waimakariri →, *N.Z.* 59 K4 43 24S 172 42 E
Waimate, *N.Z.* 59 L3 44 45S 171 3 E
Wainganga →, *India* 40 K11 18 50N 79 55 E
Waingapu, *Indonesia* 37 F6 9 35S 120 11 E
Waini →, *Guyana* 92 B7 8 20N 59 50W
Wainwright, *Canada* 73 C6 52 50N 110 50W
Waiouru, *N.Z.* 59 H5 39 28S 175 41 E
Waipara, *N.Z.* 59 K4 43 3S 172 46 E
Waipawa, *N.Z.* 59 H6 39 56S 176 38 E
Waipiro, *N.Z.* 59 H7 38 2S 178 22 E
Waipu, *N.Z.* 59 F5 35 59S 174 29 E
Waipukurau, *N.Z.* 59 J6 40 1S 176 33 E
Wairakei, *N.Z.* 59 H6 38 37S 176 6 E
Wairarapa, L., *N.Z.* 59 J5 41 14S 175 15 E
Wairoa, *N.Z.* 59 H6 39 3S 177 25 E
Waitaki →, *N.Z.* 59 L3 44 56S 171 7 E
Waitara, *N.Z.* 59 H5 38 59S 174 15 E
Waitsburg, *U.S.A.* 82 C5 46 16N 118 9W
Waiuku, *N.Z.* 59 G5 37 15S 174 45 E
Wajima, *Japan* 31 F8 37 30N 137 0 E
Wajir, *Kenya* 54 B5 1 42N 40 5 E
Wakasa, *Japan* 31 G7 35 20N 134 24 E
Wakasa-Wan, *Japan* 31 G7 35 40N 135 30 E
Wakatipu, L., *N.Z.* 59 L2 45 5S 168 33 E
Wakaw, *Canada* 73 C7 52 39N 105 44W
Wakayama, *Japan* 31 G7 34 15N 135 15 E
Wakayama □, *Japan* 31 H7 33 50N 135 30 E
Wake Forest, *U.S.A.* 77 H6 35 59N 78 30W

Wake I., Pac. Oc. 64 F8 19 18N 166 36 E
WaKeeney, U.S.A. 80 F5 39 1N 99 53W
Wakefield, N.Z. 59 J4 41 24S 173 5 E
Wakefield, U.K. 10 D6 53 41N 1 29W
Wakefield, Mass., U.S.A. 79 D13 42 30N 71 4W
Wakefield, Mich., U.S.A. 80 B10 46 29N 89 56W
Wakema, Burma 41 L19 16 30N 95 11 E
Wakkanai, Japan 30 B10 45 28N 141 35 E
Wakkerstroom, S. Africa 57 D5 27 24S 30 10 E
Wakool, Australia 63 F3 35 28S 144 23 E
Wakool →, Australia 63 F3 35 5S 143 33 E
Wakre, Indonesia 37 E8 0 19S 131 5 E
Wakuach, L., Canada 71 A6 55 34N 67 32W
Walamba, Zambia 55 E2 13 30S 28 42 E
Wałbrzych, Poland 16 C9 50 45N 16 18 E
Walbury Hill, U.K. 11 F6 51 21N 1 28W
Walcha, Australia 63 E5 30 55S 151 31 E
Walcheren, Neths. 15 C3 51 30N 3 35 E
Walcott, U.S.A. 82 F10 41 46N 106 51W
Wałcz, Poland 16 B9 53 17N 16 27 E
Waldburg Ra., Australia 61 D2 24 40S 117 35 E
Walden, Colo., U.S.A. 82 F10 40 44N 106 17W
Walden, N.Y., U.S.A. 79 E10 41 34N 74 11W
Waldport, U.S.A. 82 D1 44 26N 124 4W
Waldron, U.S.A. 81 H7 34 54N 94 5W
Walebing, Australia 61 F2 30 41S 116 13 E
Wales □, U.K. 11 E3 52 19N 4 43W
Walgett, Australia 63 E4 30 0S 148 5 E
Walgreen Coast, Antarctica 5 D15 75 15S 105 0W
Walker, U.S.A. 80 B7 47 6N 94 35W
Walker, L., Canada 71 B6 50 20N 67 11W
Walker L., Canada 73 C9 54 42N 95 57W
Walker L., U.S.A. 82 G4 38 42N 118 43W
Walkerston, Australia 62 C4 21 11S 149 8 E
Walkerton, Canada 78 B3 44 10N 81 10W
Wall, U.S.A. 80 D3 44 0N 102 8W
Walla Walla, U.S.A. 82 C4 46 4N 118 20W
Wallace, Idaho, U.S.A. 82 C6 47 28N 115 56W
Wallace, N.C., U.S.A. 77 H7 34 44N 77 59W
Wallaceburg, Canada 78 D2 42 34N 82 23W
Wallachia = Valahia, Romania 17 F13 44 35N 25 0 E
Wallal, Australia 63 D4 26 32S 146 7 E
Wallam Cr. →, Australia 63 D4 28 40S 147 20 E
Wallambin, L., Australia 61 F2 30 57S 117 35 E
Wallan, Australia 63 F3 37 26S 144 59 E
Wallangarra, Australia 63 D5 28 56S 151 58 E
Wallaroo, Australia 63 E2 33 56S 137 39 E
Wallenpaupack, L., U.S.A. 79 E9 41 25N 75 15W
Wallingford, U.S.A. 79 E12 41 27N 72 50W
Wallis & Futuna, Is., Pac. Oc. 64 J10 13 18S 176 10W
Wallowa, U.S.A. 82 D5 45 34N 117 32W
Wallowa Mts., U.S.A. 82 D5 45 20N 117 30W
Walls, U.K. 12 A7 60 14N 1 33W
Wallula, U.S.A. 82 C4 46 5N 118 54W
Wallumbilla, Australia 63 D4 26 33S 149 9 E
Walmsley, L., Canada 73 A7 63 25N 108 36W
Walney, I. of, U.K. 10 C4 54 6N 3 15W
Walnut Creek, U.S.A. 84 H4 37 54N 122 4W
Walnut Ridge, U.S.A. 81 G9 36 4N 90 57W
Walpole, Australia 61 F2 34 58S 116 44 E
Walpole, U.S.A. 79 D13 42 9N 71 15W
Walsall, U.K. 11 E6 52 35N 1 58W
Walsenburg, U.S.A. 81 G2 37 38N 104 47W
Walsh, U.S.A. 81 G3 37 23N 102 17W
Walsh →, Australia 62 B3 16 31S 143 42 E
Walterboro, U.S.A. 77 J5 32 55N 80 40W
Walters, U.S.A. 81 H5 34 22N 98 19W
Waltham, U.S.A. 79 D13 42 23N 71 14W
Waltman, U.S.A. 82 E10 43 4N 107 12W
Walton, U.S.A. 79 D9 42 10N 75 8W
Walton-on-the-Naze, U.K. 11 F9 51 51N 1 17 E
Walvis Bay, Namibia 56 C1 23 0S 14 28 E
Walvisbaai = Walvis Bay, Namibia 56 C1 23 0S 14 28 E
Wamba, Dem. Rep. of the Congo 54 B2 2 10N 27 57 E
Wamba, Kenya 54 B4 0 58N 37 19 E
Wamego, U.S.A. 80 F6 39 12N 96 18W
Wamena, Indonesia 37 E9 4 4S 138 57 E
Wamsutter, U.S.A. 82 F9 41 40N 107 58W
Wamulan, Indonesia 37 E7 3 27S 126 7 E
Wan Xian, China 34 E8 38 47N 115 7 E
Wana, Pakistan 42 C3 32 20N 69 32 E
Wanaaring, Australia 63 D3 29 38S 144 9 E
Wanaka, N.Z. 59 L2 44 42S 169 9 E
Wanaka L., N.Z. 59 L2 44 33S 169 7 E
Wanapitei L., Canada 70 C3 46 45N 80 40W
Wandel Sea = McKinley Sea, Arctic 4 A7 82 0N 0 0 E
Wanderer, Zimbabwe 55 F3 19 36S 30 1 E
Wandhari, Pakistan 42 F2 27 42N 66 48 E
Wandoan, Australia 63 D4 26 5S 149 55 E
Wanfu, China 35 D12 40 8N 122 38 E
Wang →, Thailand 38 D2 17 8N 99 2 E
Wang Noi, Thailand 38 E3 14 13N 100 44 E
Wang Saphung, Thailand 38 D3 17 18N 101 46 E
Wang Thong, Thailand 38 D3 16 50N 100 26 E
Wanga, Dem. Rep. of the Congo 54 B2 2 58N 29 12 E
Wangal, Indonesia 37 F8 6 8S 134 9 E
Wanganella, Australia 63 F3 35 6S 144 49 E
Wanganui, N.Z. 59 H5 39 56S 175 3 E
Wangaratta, Australia 63 F4 36 21S 146 19 E
Wangary, Australia 63 E2 34 35S 135 29 E
Wangdu, China 34 E8 38 40N 115 7 E
Wangerooge, Germany 16 B4 53 47N 7 54 E
Wangi, Kenya 54 C5 1 58S 40 58 E
Wangiwangi, Indonesia 37 F6 5 22S 123 37 E
Wangqing, China 35 C15 43 12N 129 42 E
Wankaner, India 42 H4 22 35N 71 0 E
Wanless, Canada 73 C8 54 11N 101 21W
Wanning, Taiwan 38 C8 23 15N 121 17 E
Wanon Niwat, Thailand 38 D4 17 38N 103 46 E
Wanquan, China 34 D8 40 50N 114 40 E
Wanrong, China 34 G6 35 25N 110 50 E
Wantage, U.K. 11 F6 51 35N 1 25W
Wanxian, China 33 C5 30 42N 108 20 E
Wapakoneta, U.S.A. 76 E3 40 34N 84 12W
Wapato, U.S.A. 82 C3 46 27N 120 25W
Wapawekka L., Canada 73 C8 54 55N 104 40W
Wapikopa L., Canada 70 B2 52 56N 87 53W
Wapiti →, Canada 72 B5 55 5N 118 18W
Wappingers Falls, U.S.A. 79 E11 41 36N 73 55W
Wapsipinicon →, U.S.A. 80 E9 41 44N 90 19W
Warangal, India 40 L11 17 58N 79 35 E
Waraseoni, India 43 J9 21 45N 80 2 E
Waratah, Australia 62 G4 41 30S 145 30 E
Waratah B., Australia 63 F4 38 54S 146 5 E
Warburton, Vic., Australia 63 F4 37 47S 145 42 E
Warburton, W. Austral., Australia 61 E4 26 8S 126 35 E
Warburton Ra., Australia 61 E4 25 55S 126 28 E
Ward, N.Z. 59 J5 41 49S 174 11 E
Ward →, Australia 63 D4 26 28S 146 6 E
Ward Mt., U.S.A. 84 H8 37 12N 118 54W
Warden, S. Africa 57 D4 27 50S 29 0 E
Wardha, India 40 J11 20 45N 78 39 E
Wardha →, India 40 K11 19 57N 79 11 E
Ware, Canada 72 B3 57 26N 125 41W
Ware, U.S.A. 79 D12 42 16N 72 14W
Waregem, Belgium 15 D3 50 53N 3 27 E
Wareham, U.S.A. 79 E14 41 46N 70 43W
Waremme, Belgium 15 D5 50 43N 5 15 E
Warialda, Australia 63 D5 29 29S 150 33 E
Wariap, Indonesia 37 E8 1 30S 134 5 E
Warin Chamrap, Thailand 38 E5 15 12N 104 53 E
Warkopi, Indonesia 37 E8 1 12S 134 9 E
Warm Springs, U.S.A. 83 G5 38 10N 116 20W
Warman, Canada 73 C7 52 19N 106 30W
Warmbad, Namibia 56 D2 28 25S 18 42 E
Warmbad, S. Africa 57 C4 24 51S 28 19 E
Warminster, U.K. 11 F5 51 12N 2 10W
Warminster, U.S.A. 79 F9 40 12N 75 6W
Warner Mts., U.S.A. 82 F3 41 40N 120 15W
Warner Robins, U.S.A. 77 J4 32 37N 83 36W
Waroona, Australia 61 F2 32 50S 115 58 E
Warracknabeal, Australia 63 F3 36 9S 142 26 E
Warragul, Australia 63 F4 38 10S 145 58 E
Warrego →, Australia 63 E4 30 24S 145 21 E
Warrego Ra., Australia 62 C4 24 58S 146 0 E
Warren, Australia 63 E4 31 42S 147 51 E
Warren, Ark., U.S.A. 81 J8 33 37N 92 4W
Warren, Mich., U.S.A. 76 D4 42 30N 83 0W
Warren, Minn., U.S.A. 80 A6 48 12N 96 46W
Warren, Ohio, U.S.A. 78 E4 41 14N 80 49W
Warren, Pa., U.S.A. 78 E5 41 51N 79 9W
Warrenpoint, U.K. 13 B5 54 6N 6 15W
Warrensburg, Mo., U.S.A. 80 F8 38 46N 93 44W
Warrensburg, N.Y., U.S.A. 79 C11 43 29N 73 46W
Warrenton, S. Africa 56 D3 28 9S 24 47 E
Warrenton, U.S.A. 84 D3 46 10N 123 56W
Warri, Nigeria 50 G7 5 30N 5 41 E
Warrina, Australia 63 D2 28 12S 135 50 E
Warrington, U.K. 10 D5 53 24N 2 35W
Warrington, U.S.A. 77 K2 30 23N 87 17W
Warrington □, U.K. 10 D5 53 24N 2 35W
Warrnambool, Australia 63 F3 38 25S 142 30 E
Warroad, U.S.A. 80 A7 48 54N 95 19W
Warruwi, Australia 62 A1 11 36S 133 20 E
Warsa, Indonesia 37 E9 0 47S 135 55 E
Warsak Dam, Pakistan 42 B4 34 11N 71 19 E
Warsaw = Warszawa, Poland 17 B11 52 13N 21 0 E
Warsaw, Ind., U.S.A. 76 E3 41 14N 85 51W
Warsaw, N.Y., U.S.A. 78 D6 42 45N 78 8W
Warsaw, Ohio, U.S.A. 78 F3 40 20N 82 0W
Warszawa, Poland 17 B11 52 13N 21 0 E
Warta →, Poland 16 B8 52 35N 14 39 E
Warthe = Warta →, Poland 16 B8 52 35N 14 39 E
Waru, Indonesia 37 E8 3 30S 130 36 E
Warwick, Australia 63 D5 28 10S 152 1 E
Warwick, U.K. 11 E6 52 18N 1 35W
Warwick, N.Y., U.S.A. 79 E10 41 16N 74 22W
Warwick, R.I., U.S.A. 79 E13 41 42N 71 28W
Warwickshire □, U.K. 11 E6 52 14N 1 38W
Wasaga Beach, Canada 78 B4 44 31N 80 1W
Wasagaming, Canada 73 C9 50 39N 99 58W
Wasatch Ra., U.S.A. 82 F8 40 30N 111 15W
Wasbank, S. Africa 57 D5 28 15S 30 9 E
Wasco, Calif., U.S.A. 85 K7 35 36N 119 20W
Wasco, Oreg., U.S.A. 82 D3 45 36N 120 42W
Waseca, U.S.A. 80 C8 44 5N 93 30W
Wasekamio L., Canada 73 B7 56 45N 108 45W
Wash, The, U.K. 10 E8 52 58N 0 20 E
Washago, Canada 78 B5 44 45N 79 20W
Washburn, N. Dak., U.S.A. 80 B4 47 17N 101 2W
Washburn, Wis., U.S.A. 80 B9 46 40N 90 54W
Washim, India 40 J10 20 3N 77 0 E
Washington, U.K. 10 C6 54 55N 1 30W
Washington, D.C., U.S.A. 76 F7 38 54N 77 2W
Washington, Ga., U.S.A. 77 J4 33 44N 82 44W
Washington, Ind., U.S.A. 76 F2 38 40N 87 10W
Washington, Iowa, U.S.A. 80 E9 41 18N 91 42W
Washington, Mo., U.S.A. 80 F9 38 33N 91 1W
Washington, N.C., U.S.A. 77 H7 35 33N 77 3W
Washington, N.J., U.S.A. 79 F10 40 46N 74 59W
Washington, Pa., U.S.A. 78 F4 40 10N 80 15W
Washington, Utah, U.S.A. 83 H7 37 8N 113 31W
Washington □, U.S.A. 82 C3 47 30N 120 30W
Washington, Mt., U.S.A. 79 B13 44 16N 71 18W
Washington Court House, U.S.A. 76 F4 39 32N 83 26W
Washington I., U.S.A. 76 C2 45 23N 86 54W
Washougal, U.S.A. 84 E4 45 35N 122 21W
Wasian, Indonesia 37 E8 1 47S 133 19 E
Wasilla, U.S.A. 68 B5 61 35N 149 26W
Wasior, Indonesia 37 E8 2 43S 134 30 E
Waskaganish, Canada 70 B4 51 30N 78 40W
Waskaiowaka, L., Canada 73 B9 56 33N 96 23W
Waskesiu Lake, Canada 73 C7 53 55N 106 5W
Wasserkuppe, Germany 16 C5 50 29N 9 55 E
Waswanipi, Canada 70 C4 49 40N 76 29W
Waswanipi, L., Canada 70 C4 49 35N 76 40W
Watampone, Indonesia 37 E6 4 29S 120 25 E
Water Park Pt., Australia 62 C5 22 56S 150 47 E
Water Valley, U.S.A. 81 H10 34 10N 89 38W
Waterberge, S. Africa 57 C4 24 10S 28 0 E
Waterbury, Conn., U.S.A. 79 E11 41 33N 73 3W
Waterbury, Vt., U.S.A. 79 B12 44 20N 72 46W
Waterbury L., Canada 73 B8 58 10N 104 22W
Waterdown, Canada 78 C5 43 20N 79 53W
Waterford, Canada 78 D4 42 56N 80 17W
Waterford, Ireland 13 D4 52 15N 7 8W
Waterford, Calif., U.S.A. 84 H6 37 38N 120 46W
Waterford, Pa., U.S.A. 78 E5 41 57N 79 59W
Waterford □, Ireland 13 D4 52 10N 7 40W
Waterford Harbour, Ireland 13 D5 52 8N 6 58W
Waterhen L., Canada 73 C9 52 10N 99 40W
Waterloo, Belgium 15 D4 50 43N 4 25 E
Waterloo, Ont., Canada 78 C4 43 30N 80 32W
Waterloo, Qué., Canada 79 A12 45 22N 72 32W
Waterloo, Ill., U.S.A. 80 F9 38 20N 90 9W
Waterloo, Iowa, U.S.A. 80 D8 42 30N 92 21W
Waterloo, N.Y., U.S.A. 78 D8 42 54N 76 52W
Watersmeet, U.S.A. 80 B10 46 16N 89 11W
Waterton Nat. Park, U.S.A. 82 B7 48 45N 115 0W
Watertown, Conn., U.S.A. 79 E11 41 36N 73 7W
Watertown, N.Y., U.S.A. 79 C9 43 59N 75 55W
Watertown, S. Dak., U.S.A. 80 C6 44 54N 97 7W
Watertown, Wis., U.S.A. 80 D10 43 12N 88 43W
Waterval-Boven, S. Africa 57 D5 25 40S 30 18 E
Waterville, Canada 79 A13 45 16N 71 54W
Waterville, Maine, U.S.A. 77 C11 44 33N 69 38W
Waterville, N.Y., U.S.A. 79 D9 42 56N 75 23W
Waterville, Pa., U.S.A. 78 E7 41 19N 77 21W
Waterville, Wash., U.S.A. 82 C3 47 39N 120 4W
Watervliet, U.S.A. 79 D11 42 44N 73 42W
Wates, Indonesia 37 G14 7 51S 110 10 E
Watford, Canada 78 D3 42 57N 81 53W
Watford, U.K. 11 F7 51 40N 0 24W
Watford City, U.S.A. 80 B3 47 48N 103 17W
Wathaman →, Canada 73 B8 57 16N 102 59W
Wathaman L., Canada 73 B8 56 58N 103 44W
Watheroo, Australia 61 F2 30 15S 116 0 E
Wating, China 34 G4 35 40N 106 38 E
Watkins Glen, U.S.A. 78 D8 42 23N 76 52W
Watling I. = San Salvador I., Bahamas 89 B5 24 0N 74 40W
Watonga, U.S.A. 81 H5 35 51N 98 25W
Watrous, Canada 73 C7 51 40N 105 25W
Watrous, U.S.A. 81 H2 35 48N 104 59W
Watsa, Dem. Rep. of the Congo 54 B2 3 4N 29 30 E
Watseka, U.S.A. 76 E2 40 47N 87 44W
Watson, Australia 61 F5 30 29S 131 31 E
Watson, Canada 73 C8 52 10N 104 30W
Watson Lake, Canada 72 A3 60 6N 128 49W
Watsontown, U.S.A. 78 E8 41 5N 76 52W
Watsonville, U.S.A. 84 J5 36 55N 121 45W
Wattiwarriganna Cr. →, Australia 63 D2 28 57S 136 10 E
Watuata = Batuata, Indonesia 37 F6 6 12S 122 42 E
Watubela, Kepulauan, Indonesia 37 E8 4 28S 131 35 E
Watubela Is. = Watubela, Kepulauan, Indonesia 37 E8 4 28S 131 35 E
Wau, Sudan 49 F6 7 45N 28 1 E
Waubamik, Canada 78 A4 45 27N 80 1W
Waubay, U.S.A. 80 C6 45 20N 97 18W
Wauchope, N.S.W., Australia 63 E5 31 28S 152 45 E
Wauchope, N. Terr., Australia 62 C1 20 36S 134 15 E
Waukarlycarly, L., Australia 60 D3 21 18S 121 56 E
Waukegan, U.S.A. 75 B9 42 22N 87 50W
Waukesha, U.S.A. 76 D1 43 1N 88 14W
Waukon, U.S.A. 80 D9 43 16N 91 29W
Waupaca, U.S.A. 80 C10 44 21N 89 5W
Waupun, U.S.A. 80 D10 43 38N 88 44W
Waurika, U.S.A. 81 H6 34 10N 98 0W
Wausau, U.S.A. 80 C10 44 58N 89 38W
Wautoma, U.S.A. 80 C10 44 4N 89 18W
Wauwatosa, U.S.A. 76 D2 43 3N 88 0W
Waveney →, U.K. 11 E9 52 35N 1 39 E
Waverley, N.Z. 59 H5 39 46S 174 37 E
Waverly, Iowa, U.S.A. 80 D8 42 44N 92 29W
Waverly, N.Y., U.S.A. 79 E8 42 1N 76 32W
Wavre, Belgium 15 D4 50 43N 4 38 E
Wâw, Sudan 51 G11 7 45N 28 1 E
Wāw al Kabīr, Libya 51 C9 25 20N 16 43 E
Wawa, Canada 70 C3 47 59N 84 47W
Wawanesa, Canada 73 D9 49 36N 99 40W
Wawona, U.S.A. 84 H7 37 32N 119 39W
Waxahachie, U.S.A. 81 J6 32 24N 96 51W
Way, L., Australia 61 E3 26 45S 120 16 E
Waycross, U.S.A. 77 K4 31 13N 82 21W
Wayland, U.S.A. 78 D7 42 34N 77 35W
Wayne, Nebr., U.S.A. 80 D6 42 14N 97 1W
Wayne, W. Va., U.S.A. 76 F4 38 13N 82 27W
Waynesboro, Ga., U.S.A. 77 J4 33 6N 82 1W
Waynesboro, Miss., U.S.A. 77 K1 31 40N 88 39W
Waynesboro, Pa., U.S.A. 76 F7 39 45N 77 35W
Waynesboro, Va., U.S.A. 76 F6 38 4N 78 53W
Waynesburg, U.S.A. 76 F5 39 54N 80 11W
Waynesville, U.S.A. 77 H4 35 28N 82 58W
Waynoka, U.S.A. 81 G5 36 35N 98 53W
Wazirabad, Pakistan 42 C6 32 30N 74 8 E
We, Indonesia 36 C1 5 51N 95 18 E
Weald, The, U.K. 11 F8 51 4N 0 20 E
Wear →, U.K. 10 C6 54 55N 1 23W
Weatherford, Okla., U.S.A. 81 H5 35 32N 98 43W
Weatherford, Tex., U.S.A. 81 J6 32 46N 97 48W
Weaverville, U.S.A. 82 F2 40 44N 122 56W
Webb City, U.S.A. 81 G7 37 9N 94 28W
Webequie, Canada 70 B2 52 59N 87 21W
Webster, Mass., U.S.A. 79 D13 42 3N 71 53W
Webster, N.Y., U.S.A. 78 C7 43 13N 77 26W
Webster, S. Dak., U.S.A. 80 C6 45 20N 97 31W
Webster City, U.S.A. 80 D8 42 28N 93 49W
Webster Springs, U.S.A. 76 F5 38 29N 80 25W
Weda, Indonesia 37 D7 0 21N 127 50 E
Weda, Teluk, Indonesia 37 D7 0 30N 127 50 E
Weddell I., Falk. Is. 96 G4 51 50S 61 0W
Weddell Sea, Antarctica 5 D1 72 30S 40 0W
Wedderburn, Australia 63 F3 36 26S 143 33 E
Wedgeport, Canada 71 D6 43 44N 65 59W
Wedza, Zimbabwe 55 F3 18 40S 31 33 E
Wee Waa, Australia 63 E4 30 11S 149 26 E
Weed, U.S.A. 82 F2 41 25N 122 23W
Weed Heights, U.S.A. 84 G7 38 59N 119 13W
Weedsport, U.S.A. 79 C8 43 3N 76 35W
Weedville, U.S.A. 78 E6 41 17N 78 30W
Weenen, S. Africa 57 D5 28 48S 30 7 E
Weert, Neths. 15 C5 51 15N 5 43 E
Wei He →, Hebei, China 34 F8 36 10N 115 45 E
Wei He →, Shaanxi, China 34 G6 34 38N 110 15 E
Weichang, China 35 D9 41 58N 117 49 E
Weichuan, China 34 G7 34 20N 113 59 E
Weiden, Germany 16 D7 49 41N 12 10 E
Weifang, China 35 F10 36 44N 119 7 E
Weihai, China 35 F12 37 30N 122 6 E
Weimar, Germany 16 C6 50 58N 11 19 E
Weinan, China 34 G5 34 31N 109 29 E
Weipa, Australia 62 A3 12 40S 141 50 E
Weir →, Australia 63 D4 28 20S 149 50 E
Weir →, Canada 73 B10 56 54N 93 21W
Weir River, Canada 73 B10 56 49N 94 6W
Weirton, U.S.A. 78 F4 40 24N 80 35W
Weiser, U.S.A. 82 D5 44 10N 117 0W
Weishan, China 35 G9 34 47N 117 5 E
Weiyuan, China 34 G3 35 7N 104 10 E
Wejherowo, Poland 17 A10 54 35N 18 12 E
Wekusko L., Canada 73 C9 54 40N 99 50W
Welch, U.S.A. 76 G5 37 26N 81 35W
Welkom, S. Africa 56 D4 28 0S 26 46 E
Welland, Canada 78 D5 43 0N 79 15W
Welland →, U.K. 11 E7 52 51N 0 5W
Wellesley Is., Australia 62 B2 16 42S 139 30 E
Wellingborough, U.K. 11 E7 52 19N 0 41W
Wellington, Australia 63 E4 32 35S 148 59 E
Wellington, Canada 78 C7 43 57N 77 20W
Wellington, N.Z. 59 J5 41 19S 174 46 E
Wellington, S. Africa 56 E2 33 38S 19 1 E
Wellington, Somst., U.K. 11 G4 50 58N 3 13W
Wellington, Telford & Wrekin, U.K. 11 E5 52 42N 2 30W
Wellington, Colo., U.S.A. 80 E2 40 42N 105 0W
Wellington, Kans., U.S.A. 81 G6 37 16N 97 24W
Wellington, Nev., U.S.A. 84 G7 38 45N 119 23W
Wellington, Ohio, U.S.A. 78 E2 41 10N 82 13W
Wellington, Tex., U.S.A. 81 H4 34 51N 100 13W
Wellington, I., Chile 96 F2 49 30S 75 0W
Wellington, L., Australia 63 F4 38 6S 147 20 E
Wells, U.K. 11 F5 51 13N 2 39W
Wells, Maine, U.S.A. 79 C14 43 20N 70 35W
Wells, N.Y., U.S.A. 79 C10 43 24N 74 17W
Wells, Nev., U.S.A. 82 F6 41 7N 114 58W
Wells, L., Australia 61 E3 26 44S 123 15 E
Wells, Mt., Australia 60 C4 17 25S 127 8 E
Wells Gray Prov. Park, Canada 72 C4 52 30N 120 15W
Wells-next-the-Sea, U.K. 10 E8 52 57N 0 51 E
Wells River, U.S.A. 79 B12 44 9N 72 4W
Wellsboro, U.S.A. 78 E7 41 45N 77 18W
Wellsburg, U.S.A. 78 F4 40 16N 80 37W
Wellsville, N.Y., U.S.A. 78 D7 42 7N 77 57W
Wellsville, Ohio, U.S.A. 78 F4 40 36N 80 39W
Wellsville, Utah, U.S.A. 82 F8 41 38N 111 56W
Wellton, U.S.A. 83 K6 32 40N 114 8W
Wels, Austria 16 D8 48 9N 14 1 E
Welshpool, U.K. 11 E4 52 39N 3 8W
Welwyn Garden City, U.K. 11 F7 51 48N 0 12W
Wem, U.K. 10 E5 52 52N 2 44W
Wembere →, Tanzania 54 C3 4 10S 34 15 E
Wemindji, Canada 70 B4 53 0N 78 49W
Wen Xian, China 34 G7 34 55N 113 5 E
Wenatchee, U.S.A. 82 C3 47 25N 120 19W
Wenchang, China 38 C8 19 38N 110 42 E
Wenchi, Ghana 50 G5 7 46N 2 8W
Wenchow = Wenzhou, China 33 D7 28 0N 120 38 E
Wenden, U.S.A. 85 M13 33 49N 113 33W
Wendeng, China 35 F12 37 15N 122 5 E
Wendesi, Indonesia 37 E8 2 30S 134 17 E
Wendover, U.S.A. 82 F6 40 44N 114 2W
Wenlock →, Australia 62 A3 12 2S 141 55 E
Wenshan, China 32 D5 23 20N 104 18 E
Wenshang, China 34 G9 35 45N 116 30 E
Wenshui, China 34 F7 37 26N 112 1 E
Wensleydale, U.K. 10 C6 54 17N 2 0W
Wensu, China 32 B3 41 15N 80 10 E
Wensum →, U.K. 10 E8 52 40N 1 15 E
Wentworth, Australia 63 E3 34 2S 141 54 E
Wentzel L., Canada 72 B6 59 2N 114 28W
Wenut, Indonesia 37 E8 3 11S 133 19 E
Wenxi, China 34 G6 35 20N 111 10 E
Wenxian, China 34 H3 32 43N 104 36 E
Wenzhou, China 33 D7 28 0N 120 38 E
Weott, U.S.A. 82 F2 40 20N 123 55W
Wepener, S. Africa 56 D4 29 42S 27 3 E
Werda, Botswana 56 D3 25 24S 23 15 E
Weri, Indonesia 37 E8 3 10S 132 38 E
Werra →, Germany 16 C5 51 24N 9 39 E
Werrimull, Australia 63 E3 34 25S 141 38 E
Werris Creek, Australia 63 E5 31 18S 150 38 E
Weser →, Germany 16 B5 53 36N 8 28 E
Wesiri, Indonesia 37 F7 7 30S 126 30 E
Weslemkoon L., Canada 78 A7 45 2N 77 25W
Wesleyville, Canada 71 C9 49 8N 53 36W
Wesleyville, U.S.A. 78 D4 42 9N 80 0W
Wessel, C., Australia 62 A2 10 59S 136 46 E
Wessel Is., Australia 62 A2 11 10S 136 45 E
Wessington Springs, U.S.A. 80 C5 44 5N 98 34W
West, U.S.A. 81 K6 31 48N 97 6W
West →, U.S.A. 79 D12 42 52N 72 33W
West Baines →, Australia 60 C4 15 38S 129 59 E
West Bank □, Asia 47 C4 32 6N 35 13 E
West Bend, U.S.A. 76 D1 43 25N 88 11W
West Bengal □, India 43 H13 23 0N 88 0 E
West Berkshire □, U.K. 11 F6 51 25N 1 17W
West Beskids = Západné Beskydy, Europe 17 D10 49 30N 19 0 E
West Branch, U.S.A. 76 C3 44 17N 84 14W
West Branch Susquehanna →, U.S.A. 79 F8 40 53N 76 48W
West Bromwich, U.K. 11 E6 52 32N 1 59W
West Burra, U.K. 12 A7 60 5N 1 21W
West Canada Cr. →, U.S.A. 79 C10 43 1N 74 58W
West Cape Howe, Australia 61 G2 35 8S 117 36 E
West Chazy, U.S.A. 79 B11 44 49N 73 28W
West Chester, U.S.A. 79 G9 39 58N 75 36W
West Columbia, U.S.A. 81 L7 29 9N 95 39W
West Covina, U.S.A. 85 L9 34 4N 117 54W
West Des Moines, U.S.A. 80 E8 41 35N 93 43W
West Dunbartonshire □, U.K. 12 F4 55 59N 4 30W
West End, Bahamas 88 A4 26 41N 78 58W
West Falkland, Falk. Is. 96 G5 51 40S 60 0W
West Fargo, U.S.A. 80 B6 46 52N 96 54W
West Farmington, U.S.A. 78 E4 41 23N 80 58W
West Fjord = Vestfjorden, Norway 8 C15 67 55N 14 0 E
West Fork Trinity →, U.S.A. 81 J6 32 48N 96 54W
West Frankfort, U.S.A. 80 G10 37 54N 88 55W
West Hartford, U.S.A. 79 E12 41 45N 72 44W
West Haven, U.S.A. 79 E12 41 17N 72 57W
West Hazleton, U.S.A. 79 F9 40 58N 76 0W
West Helena, U.S.A. 81 H9 34 33N 90 38W
West Hurley, U.S.A. 79 E10 41 59N 74 7W
West Ice Shelf, Antarctica 5 C7 67 0S 85 0 E

West Indies, *Cent. Amer.* . . **89 D7** 15 0N 65 0W
West Jordan, *U.S.A.* **82 F8** 40 36N 111 56W
West Lorne, *Canada* **78 D3** 42 36N 81 36W
West Lothian □, *U.K.* **12 F5** 55 54N 3 36W
West Lunga →, *Zambia* . . **55 E1** 13 6S 24 39 E
West Memphis, *U.S.A.* **81 H9** 35 9N 90 11W
West Midlands □, *U.K.* **11 E6** 52 26N 2 0W
West Mifflin, *U.S.A.* **78 F5** 40 22N 79 52W
West Milton, *U.S.A.* **78 E8** 41 1N 76 50W
West Monroe, *U.S.A.* **81 J8** 32 31N 92 9W
West Newton, *U.S.A.* **78 F5** 40 14N 79 46W
West Nicholson, *Zimbabwe* **55 G2** 21 2S 29 20 E
West Palm Beach, *U.S.A.* . . **77 M5** 26 43N 80 3W
West Plains, *U.S.A.* **81 G9** 36 44N 91 51W
West Point, *N.Y., U.S.A.* . . . **79 E11** 41 24N 73 58W
West Point, *Nebr., U.S.A.* . . **80 E6** 41 51N 96 43W
West Point, *Va., U.S.A.* **76 G7** 37 32N 76 48W
West Pt. = Ouest, Pte. de l',
Canada **71 C7** 49 52N 64 40W
West Pt., *Australia* . . . . **63 F2** 35 1S 135 56 E
West Road →, *Canada* . . . **72 C4** 53 18N 122 53W
West Rutland, *U.S.A.* **75 B12** 43 38N 73 5W
West Schelde =
Westerschelde →, *Neths.* **15 C3** 51 25N 3 25 E
West Seneca, *U.S.A.* **78 D6** 42 51N 78 48W
West Siberian Plain, *Russia* **28 C11** 62 0N 75 0 E
West Sussex □, *U.K.* **11 G7** 50 55N 0 30W
West-Terschelling, *Neths.* . . **15 A5** 53 22N 5 13 E
West Valley City, *U.S.A.* . . . **82 F8** 40 42N 111 57W
West Virginia □, *U.S.A.* . . . **76 F5** 38 45N 80 30W
West-Vlaanderen □,
Belgium . . . . **15 D2** 51 0N 3 0 E
West Walker →, *U.S.A.* . . **84 G7** 38 54N 119 9W
West Wyalong, *Australia* . . **63 E4** 33 56S 147 10 E
West Yellowstone, *U.S.A.* . **82 D8** 44 40N 111 6W
West Yorkshire □, *U.K.* . . . **10 D6** 53 45N 1 40W
Westall Pt., *Australia* . . . . . **63 E1** 32 55S 134 4 E
Westbrook, *U.S.A.* **77 D10** 43 41N 70 22W
Westbury, *Australia* . . . . . . **62 G4** 41 30S 146 51 E
Westby, *U.S.A.* **80 A2** 48 52N 104 3W
Westend, *U.S.A.* **85 K9** 35 42N 117 24W
Westerland, *Germany* . . . . . **9 J13** 54 54N 8 17 E
Westerly, *U.S.A.* **79 E13** 41 22N 71 50W
Western □, *Kenya* . . . . **54 B3** 0 30N 34 30 E
Western □, *Uganda* . . . . . . **54 B3** 1 45N 31 30 E
Western □, *Zambia* . . . . . . **55 F1** 15 15S 24 30 E
Western Australia □,
Australia . . . . **61 E2** 25 0S 118 0 E
Western Cape □, *S. Africa* . **56 E3** 34 0S 20 0 E
Western Dvina =
Daugava →, *Latvia* . . . . **9 H21** 57 4N 24 3 E
Western Ghats, *India* . . . . . **40 N9** 14 0N 75 0 E
Western Isles □, *U.K.* **12 D1** 57 30N 7 10W
Western Sahara ■, *Africa* . **50 D3** 25 0N 13 0W
Western Samoa ■, *Pac. Oc.* **59 B13** 14 0S 172 0W
Westernport, *U.S.A.* **76 F6** 39 29N 79 3W
Westerschelde →, *Neths.* . **15 C3** 51 25N 3 25 E
Westerwald, *Germany* . . . . **16 C4** 50 38N 7 56 E
Westfield, *Mass., U.S.A.* . . . **79 D12** 42 7N 72 45W
Westfield, *N.Y., U.S.A.* **78 D5** 42 20N 79 35W
Westfield, *Pa., U.S.A.* **78 E7** 41 55N 77 32W
Westhill, *U.K.* **12 D6** 57 9N 2 19W
Westhope, *U.S.A.* **80 A4** 48 55N 101 1W
Westland Bight, *N.Z.* . . . . . **59 K3** 42 55S 170 5 E
Westlock, *Canada* **72 C6** 54 9N 113 55W
Westmar, *Australia* . . . . . . **63 D4** 27 55S 149 44 E
Westmeath □, *Ireland* **13 C4** 53 33N 7 34W
Westminster, *U.S.A.* **76 F7** 39 34N 76 59W
Westmont, *U.S.A.* **78 F6** 40 19N 78 58W
Westmorland, *U.S.A.* **85 M11** 33 2N 115 37W
Weston, *Oreg., U.S.A.* **82 D4** 45 49N 118 26W
Weston, *W. Va., U.S.A.* **76 F5** 39 2N 80 28W
Weston I., *Canada* **70 B4** 52 33N 79 36W
Weston-super-Mare, *U.K.* . . **11 F5** 51 21N 2 58W
Westover, *U.S.A.* **78 F6** 40 45N 78 40W
Westport, *Canada* **79 B8** 44 40N 76 25W
Westport, *Ireland* **13 C2** 53 48N 9 31W
Westport, *N.Z.* . . . . **59 J3** 41 46S 171 37 E
Westport, *N.Y., U.S.A.* **79 B11** 44 11N 73 26W
Westport, *Oreg., U.S.A.* **84 D3** 46 8N 123 23W
Westport, *Wash., U.S.A.* . . . **84 D2** 46 53N 124 6W
Westray, *Canada* **73 C8** 53 36N 101 24W
Westray, *U.K.* **12 B5** 59 18N 3 0W
Westree, *Canada* **70 C3** 47 26N 81 34W
Westville, *U.S.A.* **84 F6** 39 8N 120 42W
Westwood, *U.S.A.* **82 F3** 40 18N 121 0W
Wetar, *Indonesia* . . . . **37 F7** 7 30S 126 30 E
Wetaskiwin, *Canada* **72 C6** 52 55N 113 24W
Wete, *Tanzania* . . . . **52 F7** 5 4S 39 43 E
Wetherby, *U.K.* **10 D6** 53 56N 1 23W
Wethersfield, *U.S.A.* **79 E12** 41 42N 72 40W
Wetteren, *Belgium* . . . . **15 D3** 51 0N 3 53 E
Wetzlar, *Germany* . . . . **16 C5** 50 32N 8 31 E
Wewoka, *U.S.A.* **81 H6** 35 9N 96 30W
Wexford, *Ireland* **13 D5** 52 20N 6 28W
Wexford □, *Ireland* **13 D5** 52 20N 6 25W
Wexford Harbour, *Ireland* . **13 D5** 52 20N 6 25W
Weyburn, *Canada* **73 D8** 49 40N 103 50W
Weymouth, *Canada* **71 D6** 44 30N 66 1W
Weymouth, *U.K.* **11 G5** 50 37N 2 28W
Weymouth, *U.S.A.* **79 D14** 42 13N 70 58W
Weymouth, C., *Australia* . . **62 A3** 12 37S 143 27 E
Wha Ti, *Canada* **68 B8** 63 8N 117 16W
Whakatane, *N.Z.* . . . . **59 G6** 37 57S 177 1 E
Whale →, *Canada* **71 A6** 58 15N 67 40W
Whale Cove, *Canada* **73 A10** 62 11N 92 36W
Whales, B. of, *Antarctica* . . **5 D12** 78 0S 165 0W
Whalsay, *U.K.* **12 A8** 60 22N 0 59W
Whangamomona, *N.Z.* . . . . **59 H5** 39 8S 174 44 E
Whangarei, *N.Z.* . . . . **59 F5** 35 43S 174 21 E
Whangarei Harb., *N.Z.* . . . . **59 F5** 35 45S 174 28 E
Wharfe →, *U.K.* **10 D6** 53 51N 1 9W
Wharfedale, *U.K.* **10 C5** 54 6N 2 1W
Wharton, *N.J., U.S.A.* **79 F10** 40 54N 74 35W
Wharton, *Pa., U.S.A.* **78 E6** 41 31N 78 1W
Wharton, *Tex., U.S.A.* **81 L6** 29 19N 96 6W
Wheatland, *Calif., U.S.A.* . . **84 F5** 39 1N 121 25W
Wheatland, *Wyo., U.S.A.* . . . **80 D2** 42 3N 104 58W
Wheatley, *Ont., Canada* . . . **78 D2** 42 6N 82 27W
Wheatley, *Ont., Canada* . . . **78 D2** 42 6N 82 27W
Wheaton, *Md., U.S.A.* **76 F7** 39 3N 77 3W
Wheaton, *Minn., U.S.A.* **80 C6** 45 48N 96 30W
Wheelbarrow Pk., *U.S.A.* . . **84 H10** 37 26N 116 5W
Wheeler, *Oreg., U.S.A.* **82 D2** 45 41N 123 53W
Wheeler, *Tex., U.S.A.* **81 H4** 35 27N 100 16W
Wheeler →, *Canada* **71 A6** 57 2N 67 13W
Wheeler L., *U.S.A.* **77 H2** 34 48N 87 23W
Wheeler Pk., *N. Mex., U.S.A.* **83 H11** 36 34N 105 25W
Wheeler Pk., *Nev., U.S.A.* . . **83 G6** 38 57N 114 15W
Wheeler Ridge, *U.S.A.* **85 L8** 35 0N 118 57W
Wheeling, *U.S.A.* **78 F4** 40 4N 80 43W
Whernside, *U.K.* **10 C5** 54 14N 2 24W
Whiskey Jack L., *Canada* . . **73 B8** 58 23N 101 55W
Whistleduck Cr. →,
Australia . . . . **62 C2** 20 15S 135 18 E
Whistler, *Canada* **72 C4** 50 7N 122 58W
Whitby, *Canada* **78 C6** 43 52N 78 56W
Whitby, *U.K.* **10 C7** 54 29N 0 37W
White →, *Ark., U.S.A.* **81 J9** 33 57N 91 5W
White →, *Ind., U.S.A.* **76 F2** 38 25N 87 45W
White →, *S. Dak., U.S.A.* . **80 D5** 43 42N 99 27W
White →, *Tex., U.S.A.* **81 J4** 33 14N 100 56W
White →, *Utah, U.S.A.* . . . **82 F9** 40 4N 109 41W
White →, *Vt., U.S.A.* **79 C12** 43 37N 72 20W
White →, *Wash., U.S.A.* . . **84 C4** 47 12N 122 15W
White, L., *Australia* . . . . **60 D4** 21 9S 128 56 E
White B., *Canada* **71 C8** 50 0N 56 35W
White Bird, *U.S.A.* **82 D5** 45 46N 116 18W
White Butte, *U.S.A.* **80 B3** 46 23N 103 18W
White City, *U.S.A.* **82 E2** 42 26N 122 51W
White Cliffs, *Australia* . . . . . **63 E3** 30 50S 143 10 E
White Hall, *U.S.A.* **80 F9** 39 26N 90 24W
White Haven, *U.S.A.* **79 E9** 41 4N 75 47W
White Horse, Vale of, *U.K.* . **11 F6** 51 37N 1 30W
White I., *N.Z.* . . . . **59 G6** 37 30S 177 13 E
White L., *Canada* **79 A8** 45 18N 76 31W
White L., *U.S.A.* **81 L8** 29 44N 92 30W
White Mountain Peak,
U.S.A. **83 G4** 37 38N 118 15W
White Mts., *Calif., U.S.A.* . . **84 H8** 37 30N 118 15W
White Mts., *N.H., U.S.A.* . . . **75 B12** 44 15N 71 15W
White Mts., *N.H., U.S.A.* . . . **76 C10** 44 10N 71 20W
White Nile = Nîl el
Abyad →, *Sudan* . . . . . . **51 E12** 15 38N 32 31 E
White Otter L., *Canada* **70 C1** 49 5N 91 55W
White Pass, *U.S.A.* **84 D5** 46 38N 121 24W
White Plains, *U.S.A.* **79 E11** 41 2N 73 46W
White River, *Canada* **70 C2** 48 35N 85 20W
White River, *S. Africa* . . . . . **57 D5** 25 20S 31 0 E
White River, *U.S.A.* **80 D4** 43 34N 100 45W
White Rock, *Canada* **84 A4** 49 2N 122 48W
White Russia = Belarus ■,
Europe . . . . **17 B14** 53 30N 27 0 E
White Sea = Beloye More,
Russia . . . . **24 A6** 66 30N 38 0 E
White Sulphur Springs,
Mont., U.S.A. **82 C8** 46 33N 110 54W
White Sulphur Springs,
W. Va., U.S.A. **76 G5** 37 48N 80 18W
White Swan, *U.S.A.* **84 D6** 46 23N 120 44W
Whitecliffs, *N.Z.* . . . . **59 K3** 43 26S 171 55 E
Whitecourt, *Canada* **72 C5** 54 10N 115 45W
Whiteface Mt., *U.S.A.* **79 B11** 44 22N 73 54W
Whitefield, *U.S.A.* **79 B13** 44 23N 71 37W
Whitefish, *U.S.A.* **82 B6** 48 25N 114 20W
Whitefish L., *Canada* **73 A7** 62 41N 106 48W
Whitefish Point, *U.S.A.* **76 B3** 46 45N 84 59W
Whitegull, L., *Canada* **71 A7** 55 27N 64 17W
Whitehall, *Mich., U.S.A.* . . . **76 D2** 43 24N 86 21W
Whitehall, *Mont., U.S.A.* . . . **82 D7** 45 52N 112 6W
Whitehall, *N.Y., U.S.A.* **79 C11** 43 33N 73 24W
Whitehall, *Wis., U.S.A.* **80 C9** 44 22N 91 19W
Whitehaven, *U.K.* **10 C4** 54 33N 3 35W
Whitehorse, *Canada* **72 A1** 60 43N 135 3W
Whitemark, *Australia* . . . . . **62 G4** 40 7S 148 3 E
Whiteriver, *U.S.A.* **83 K9** 33 50N 109 58W
Whitesand →, *Canada* . . . **72 A5** 60 9N 115 45W
Whitesboro, *N.Y., U.S.A.* . . . **79 C9** 43 7N 75 18W
Whitesboro, *Tex., U.S.A.* . . . **81 J6** 33 39N 96 54W
Whiteshell Prov. Park,
Canada **73 D9** 50 0N 95 40W
Whitesville, *U.S.A.* **78 D7** 42 2N 77 46W
Whiteville, *U.S.A.* **77 H6** 34 20N 78 42W
Whitewater, *U.S.A.* **76 D1** 42 50N 88 44W
Whitewater Baldy, *U.S.A.* . . **83 K9** 33 20N 108 39W
Whitewater L., *Canada* **70 B2** 50 50N 89 10W
Whitewood, *Australia* . . . . . . **62 C3** 21 28S 143 30 E
Whitewood, *Canada* **73 C8** 50 20N 102 20W
Whithorn, *U.K.* **12 G4** 54 44N 4 26W
Whitianga, *N.Z.* . . . . **59 G5** 36 47S 175 41 E
Whitman, *U.S.A.* **79 D14** 42 5N 70 56W
Whitney, *Canada* **78 A6** 45 31N 78 14W
Whitney, Mt., *U.S.A.* **84 J8** 36 35N 118 18W
Whitney Point, *U.S.A.* **79 D9** 42 20N 75 58W
Whitstable, *U.K.* . . . . **11 F9** 51 21N 1 3 E
Whitsunday I., *Australia* . . . **62 C4** 20 15S 149 4 E
Whittier, *U.S.A.* **85 M8** 33 58N 118 3W
Whittlesea, *Australia* . . . . . . **63 F4** 37 27S 145 9 E
Wholdaia L., *Canada* **73 A8** 60 43N 104 20W
Whyalla, *Australia* . . . . **63 E2** 33 2S 137 30 E
Wiarton, *Canada* **78 B3** 44 40N 81 10W
Wiay, *U.K.* **12 D1** 57 24N 7 13W
Wibaux, *U.S.A.* **80 B2** 46 59N 104 11W
Wichian Buri, *Thailand* . . . . **38 E3** 15 39N 101 7 E
Wichita, *U.S.A.* **81 G6** 37 42N 97 20W
Wichita Falls, *U.S.A.* **81 J5** 33 54N 98 30W
Wick, *U.K.* **12 C5** 58 26N 3 5W
Wicked Pt., *Canada* **78 C7** 43 52N 77 15W
Wickenburg, *U.S.A.* **83 K7** 33 58N 112 44W
Wickepin, *Australia* . . . . **61 F2** 32 50S 117 30 E
Wickham, *Australia* . . . . **60 D2** 20 42S 117 11 E
Wickham, C., *Australia* . . . . **62 F3** 39 35S 143 57 E
Wickliffe, *U.S.A.* **78 E3** 41 36N 81 28W
Wicklow, *Ireland* **13 D5** 52 59N 6 3W
Wicklow □, *Ireland* **13 D5** 52 57N 6 25W
Wicklow Hd., *Ireland* **13 D6** 52 58N 6 0W
Wicklow Mts., *Ireland* **13 C5** 52 58N 6 26W
Widgeegoara Cr. →,
Australia . . . . **63 D4** 28 51S 146 34 E
Widgiemooltha, *Australia* . . **61 F3** 31 30S 121 34 E
Widnes, *U.K.* **10 D5** 53 23N 2 45W
Wieluń, *Poland* . . . . **17 C10** 51 15N 18 34 E
Wien, *Austria* . . . . **16 D9** 48 12N 16 22 E
Wiener Neustadt, *Austria* . . **16 E9** 47 49N 16 16 E
Wiesbaden, *Germany* . . . . . . **16 C5** 50 4N 8 14 E
Wigan, *U.K.* **10 D5** 53 33N 2 38W
Wiggins, *Colo., U.S.A.* **80 E2** 40 14N 104 4W
Wiggins, *Miss., U.S.A.* **81 K10** 30 51N 89 8W
Wight, I. of □, *U.K.* **11 G6** 50 40N 1 20W
Wigston, *U.K.* **11 E6** 52 35N 1 6W
Wigton, *U.K.* **10 C4** 54 50N 3 10W
Wigtown, *U.K.* **12 G4** 54 53N 4 27W
Wigtown B., *U.K.* **12 G4** 54 46N 4 15W
Wilber, *U.S.A.* **80 E6** 40 29N 96 58W
Wilberforce, *Canada* **78 A6** 45 2N 78 13W
Wilberforce, C., *Australia* . . **62 A2** 11 54S 136 35 E
Wilburton, *U.S.A.* **81 H7** 34 55N 95 19W
Wilcannia, *Australia* . . . . **63 E3** 31 30S 143 26 E
Wilcox, *U.S.A.* **78 E6** 41 35N 78 41W
Wildrose, *U.S.A.* **85 J9** 36 14N 117 11W
Wildspitze, *Austria* . . . . **16 E6** 46 53N 10 53 E
Wilge →, *S. Africa* . . . . . . **57 D4** 27 3S 28 20 E
Wilhelm II Coast, *Antarctica* **5 C7** 68 0S 90 0 E
Wilhelmshaven, *Germany* . . **16 B5** 53 31N 8 7 E
Wilhelmstal, *Namibia* . . . . . **56 C2** 21 58S 16 21 E
Wilkes-Barre, *U.S.A.* **79 E9** 41 15N 75 53W
Wilkie, *Canada* **73 C7** 52 27N 108 42W
Wilkinsburg, *U.S.A.* **78 F5** 40 26N 79 53W
Wilkinson Lakes, *Australia* . **61 E5** 29 40S 132 39 E
Willandra Creek →,
Australia . . . . **63 E4** 33 22S 145 52 E
Willapa B., *U.S.A.* **82 C2** 46 40N 124 0W
Willapa Hills, *U.S.A.* **84 D3** 46 35N 123 25W
Willard, *N.Y., U.S.A.* **78 D8** 42 40N 76 50W
Willard, *Ohio, U.S.A.* **78 E2** 41 3N 82 44W
Willcox, *U.S.A.* **83 K9** 32 15N 109 50W
Willemstad, *Neth. Ant.* **89 D6** 12 5N 69 0W
Willet, *U.S.A.* **79 D9** 42 28N 75 55W
William →, *Canada* **73 B7** 59 8N 109 19W
William 'Bill' Dannely Res.,
U.S.A. **77 J2** 32 10N 87 10W
William Creek, *Australia* . . . **63 D2** 28 58S 136 22 E
Williams, *Australia* . . . . **61 F2** 33 2S 116 52 E
Williams, *Ariz., U.S.A.* **83 J7** 35 15N 112 11W
Williams, *Calif., U.S.A.* **84 F4** 39 9N 122 9W
Williams Harbour, *Canada* . **71 B8** 52 33N 55 47W
Williams Lake, *Canada* **72 C4** 52 10N 122 10W
Williamsburg, *Ky., U.S.A.* . . **77 G3** 36 44N 84 10W
Williamsburg, *Pa., U.S.A.* . . **78 F6** 40 28N 78 12W
Williamsburg, *Va., U.S.A.* . . **76 G7** 37 17N 76 44W
Williamson, *N.Y., U.S.A.* . . . **78 C7** 43 14N 77 11W
Williamson, *W. Va., U.S.A.* . **76 G4** 37 41N 82 17W
Williamsport, *U.S.A.* **78 E7** 41 15N 77 0W
Williamston, *U.S.A.* **77 H7** 35 51N 77 4W
Williamstown, *Australia* . . . **63 F3** 37 51S 144 52 E
Williamstown, *Ky., U.S.A.* . . **76 F3** 38 38N 84 34W
Williamstown, *Mass., U.S.A.* **79 D11** 42 41N 73 12W
Williamstown, *N.Y., U.S.A.* . **79 C9** 43 26N 75 53W
Willimantic, *U.S.A.* **79 E12** 41 43N 72 13W
Willingboro, *U.S.A.* **76 E8** 40 3N 74 54W
Willis Group, *Australia* . . . . **62 B5** 16 18S 150 0 E
Williston, *S. Africa* . . . . **56 E3** 31 20S 20 53 E
Williston, *Fla., U.S.A.* **77 L4** 29 23N 82 27W
Williston, *N. Dak., U.S.A.* . . **80 A3** 48 9N 103 37W
Williston L., *Canada* **72 B4** 56 0N 124 0W
Willits, *U.S.A.* **82 G2** 39 25N 123 21W
Willmar, *U.S.A.* **80 C7** 45 7N 95 3W
Willoughby, *U.S.A.* **78 E3** 41 39N 81 24W
Willow Bunch, *Canada* **73 D7** 49 20N 105 35W
Willow L., *Canada* **72 A5** 62 10N 119 8W
Willow Wall, The, *China* . . . **35 C12** 42 10N 122 0 E
Willowick, *U.S.A.* **78 E3** 41 38N 81 28W
Willowlake →, *Canada* . . . **72 A4** 62 42N 123 8W
Willowmore, *S. Africa* . . . . . **56 E3** 33 15S 23 30 E
Willows, *U.S.A.* **84 F4** 39 31N 122 12W
Willowvale = Gatyana,
S. Africa . . . . **57 E4** 32 16S 28 31 E
Wills, L., *Australia* . . . . **60 D4** 21 25S 128 51 E
Wills Cr. →, *Australia* . . . **62 C3** 22 43S 140 2 E
Willsboro, *U.S.A.* **79 B11** 44 21N 73 24W
Willunga, *Australia* . . . . **63 F2** 35 15S 138 30 E
Wilmette, *U.S.A.* **76 D2** 42 5N 87 42W
Wilmington, *Australia* . . . . . **63 E2** 32 39S 138 7 E
Wilmington, *Del., U.S.A.* . . . **76 F8** 39 45N 75 33W
Wilmington, *N.C., U.S.A.* . . . **77 H7** 34 14N 77 55W
Wilmington, *Ohio, U.S.A.* . . . **76 F4** 39 27N 83 50W
Wilmington, *Vt., U.S.A.* **79 D12** 42 52N 72 52W
Wilmslow, *U.K.* **10 D5** 53 19N 2 13W
Wilpena →, *Australia* . . . . **63 E2** 31 25S 139 29 E
Wilsall, *U.S.A.* **82 D8** 45 59N 110 38W
Wilson, *N.C., U.S.A.* **77 H7** 35 44N 77 55W
Wilson, *N.Y., U.S.A.* **78 C6** 43 19N 78 50W
Wilson, *Pa., U.S.A.* **79 F9** 40 41N 75 15W
Wilson →, *Australia* . . . . . **60 C4** 16 48S 128 16 E
Wilson Bluff, *Australia* . . . . **61 F4** 31 41S 129 0 E
Wilson Inlet, *Australia* . . . . **61 G2** 35 0S 117 22 E
Wilsons Promontory,
Australia . . . . **63 F4** 38 55S 146 25 E
Wilton, *U.S.A.* **80 B4** 47 10N 100 47W
Wilton →, *Australia* . . . . . **62 A1** 14 45S 134 33 E
Wiltshire □, *U.K.* **11 F6** 51 18N 1 53W
Wiltz, *Lux.* . . . . **15 E5** 49 57N 5 55 E
Wiluna, *Australia* . . . . **61 E3** 26 36S 120 14 E
Wimborne Minster, *U.K.* . . . **11 G6** 50 48N 1 59W
Wimmera →, *Australia* . . . **63 F3** 36 8S 141 56 E
Winam G., *Kenya* . . . . **54 C3** 0 20S 34 15 E
Winburg, *S. Africa* . . . . **56 D4** 28 30S 27 2 E
Winchendon, *U.S.A.* **79 D12** 42 41N 72 3W
Winchester, *U.K.* **11 F6** 51 4N 1 18W
Winchester, *Conn., U.S.A.* . . **79 E11** 41 53N 73 9W
Winchester, *Idaho, U.S.A.* . . **82 C5** 46 14N 116 38W
Winchester, *Ind., U.S.A.* . . . **76 E3** 40 10N 84 59W
Winchester, *Ky., U.S.A.* **76 G3** 38 0N 84 11W
Winchester, *N.H., U.S.A.* . . . **79 D12** 42 46N 72 23W
Winchester, *Nev., U.S.A.* . . . **85 J11** 36 6N 115 10W
Winchester, *Tenn., U.S.A.* . . **77 H2** 35 11N 86 7W
Winchester, *Va., U.S.A.* **76 F6** 39 11N 78 10W
Wind →, *U.S.A.* **82 E9** 43 12N 108 12W
Wind River Range, *U.S.A.* . . **82 E9** 43 0N 109 30W
Windau = Ventspils, *Latvia* **9 H19** 57 25N 21 32 E
Windber, *U.S.A.* **78 F6** 40 14N 78 50W
Winder, *U.S.A.* **77 J4** 34 0N 83 45W
Windermere, *Cumb., U.K.* . . **10 C5** 54 23N 2 55W
Windermere, *Cumb., U.K.* . . **10 C5** 54 22N 2 56W
Windhoek, *Namibia* . . . . **56 C2** 22 35S 17 4 E
Windom, *U.S.A.* **80 D7** 43 52N 95 7W
Windorah, *Australia* . . . . **62 D3** 25 24S 142 36 E
Window Rock, *U.S.A.* **83 J9** 35 41N 109 3W
Windrush →, *U.K.* **11 F6** 51 43N 1 24W
Windsor, *Australia* . . . . **63 E5** 33 37S 150 50 E
Windsor, *N.S., Canada* **71 D7** 44 59N 64 5W
Windsor, *Ont., Canada* **78 D2** 42 18N 83 0W
Windsor, *U.K.* **11 F7** 51 29N 0 36W
Windsor, *Colo., U.S.A.* **80 E2** 40 29N 104 54W
Windsor, *Conn., U.S.A.* **79 E12** 41 50N 72 39W
Windsor, *Mo., U.S.A.* **80 F8** 38 32N 93 31W
Windsor, *N.Y., U.S.A.* **79 D9** 42 5N 75 37W
Windsor, *Vt., U.S.A.* **79 C12** 43 29N 72 24W
Windsor & Maidenhead □,
U.K. **11 F7** 51 29N 0 40W
Windsorton, *S. Africa* . . . . . **56 D3** 28 16S 24 44 E
Windward Is., *W. Indies* . . . **89 D7** 13 0N 61 0W
Windward Passage =
Vientos, Paso de los,
Caribbean **89 C5** 20 0N 74 0W
Winefred L., *Canada* **73 B6** 55 30N 110 30W
Winfield, *U.S.A.* **81 G6** 37 15N 96 59W
Wingate Mts., *Australia* . . . . **60 B5** 14 25S 130 40 E
Wingham, *Australia* . . . . **63 E5** 31 48S 152 22 E
Wingham, *Canada* **78 C3** 43 55N 81 20W
Winisk, *Canada* **70 A2** 55 20N 85 15W
Winisk →, *Canada* **70 A2** 55 17N 85 5W
Winisk L., *Canada* **70 B2** 52 55N 87 22W
Wink, *U.S.A.* **81 K3** 31 45N 103 9W
Winkler, *Canada* **73 D9** 49 10N 97 56W
Winlock, *U.S.A.* **84 D4** 46 30N 122 56W
Winnebago, L., *U.S.A.* **76 D1** 44 0N 88 26W
Winnecke Cr. →, *Australia* **60 C5** 18 35S 131 34 E
Winnemucca, *U.S.A.* **82 F5** 40 58N 117 44W
Winnemucca L., *U.S.A.* **82 F4** 40 7N 119 21W
Winnett, *U.S.A.* **82 C9** 47 0N 108 21W
Winnfield, *U.S.A.* **81 K8** 31 56N 92 38W
Winnibigoshish, L., *U.S.A.* . **80 B7** 47 27N 94 13W
Winnipeg, *Canada* **73 D9** 49 54N 97 9W
Winnipeg →, *Canada* **73 C9** 50 38N 96 19W
Winnipeg, L., *Canada* **73 C9** 52 0N 97 0W
Winnipeg Beach, *Canada* . . **73 C9** 50 30N 96 58W
Winnipegosis, *Canada* **73 C9** 51 39N 99 55W
Winnipegosis L., *Canada* . . **73 C9** 52 30N 100 0W
Winnipesaukee, L., *U.S.A.* . . **79 C13** 43 38N 71 21W
Winnisquam L., *U.S.A.* **79 C13** 43 33N 71 31W
Winnsboro, *La., U.S.A.* **81 J9** 32 10N 91 43W
Winnsboro, *S.C., U.S.A.* **77 H5** 34 23N 81 5W
Winnsboro, *Tex., U.S.A.* **81 J7** 32 58N 95 17W
Winokapau, L., *Canada* **71 B7** 53 15N 62 50W
Winona, *Minn., U.S.A.* **80 C9** 44 3N 91 39W
Winona, *Miss., U.S.A.* **81 J10** 33 29N 89 44W
Winooski, *U.S.A.* **79 B11** 44 29N 73 11W
Winooski →, *U.S.A.* **79 B11** 44 32N 73 17W
Winschoten, *Neths.* . . . . **15 A7** 53 9N 7 3 E
Winsford, *U.K.* **10 D5** 53 12N 2 31W
Winslow, *Ariz., U.S.A.* **83 J8** 35 2N 110 42W
Winslow, *Wash., U.S.A.* **84 C4** 47 38N 122 31W
Winsted, *U.S.A.* **79 E11** 41 55N 73 4W
Winston-Salem, *U.S.A.* **77 G5** 36 6N 80 15W
Winter Garden, *U.S.A.* **77 L5** 28 34N 81 35W
Winter Haven, *U.S.A.* **77 M5** 28 1N 81 44W
Winter Park, *U.S.A.* **77 L5** 28 36N 81 20W
Winterhaven, *U.S.A.* **85 N12** 32 47N 114 39W
Winters, *U.S.A.* **84 G5** 38 32N 121 58W
Wintersville, *U.S.A.* **78 F4** 40 23N 80 42W
Winterswijk, *Neths.* . . . . **15 C6** 51 58N 6 43 E
Winterthur, *Switz.* . . . . **18 C8** 47 30N 8 44 E
Winthrop, *U.S.A.* **82 B3** 48 28N 120 10W
Winton, *Australia* . . . . **62 C3** 22 24S 143 3 E
Winton, *N.Z.* . . . . **59 M2** 46 8S 168 20 E
Wirrulla, *Australia* . . . . **63 E1** 32 24S 134 31 E
Wisbech, *U.K.* . . . . **11 E8** 52 41N 0 9 E
Wisconsin □, *U.S.A.* **80 C10** 44 45N 89 30W
Wisconsin →, *U.S.A.* **80 D9** 43 0N 91 15W
Wisconsin Rapids, *U.S.A.* . . **80 C10** 44 23N 89 49W
Wisdom, *U.S.A.* **82 D7** 45 37N 113 27W
Wishaw, *U.K.* **12 F5** 55 46N 3 54W
Wishek, *U.S.A.* **80 B5** 46 16N 99 33W
Wisła →, *Poland* . . . . **17 A10** 54 22N 18 55 E
Wismar, *Germany* . . . . **16 B6** 53 54N 11 29 E
Wisner, *U.S.A.* **80 E6** 41 59N 96 55W
Witbank, *S. Africa* . . . . **57 D4** 25 51S 29 14 E
Witdraai, *S. Africa* . . . . **56 D3** 26 58S 20 48 E
Witham, *U.K.* . . . . **11 F8** 51 48N 0 40 E
Witham →, *U.K.* . . . . **10 E7** 52 59N 0 2 E
Withernsea, *U.K.* . . . . **10 D8** 53 44N 0 1 E
Witney, *U.K.* **11 F6** 51 48N 1 28W
Witnossob →, *Namibia* . . . **56 D3** 26 55S 20 37 E
Wittenberge, *Germany* . . . . . **16 B6** 53 0N 11 45 E
Wittenoom, *Australia* . . . . . . **60 D2** 22 15S 118 20 E
Wkra →, *Poland* . . . . **17 B11** 52 27N 20 44 E
Wlingi, *Indonesia* . . . . **37 H15** 8 5S 112 25 E
Włocławek, *Poland* . . . . **17 B10** 52 40N 19 3 E
Włodawa, *Poland* . . . . **17 C12** 51 33N 23 31 E
Woburn, *U.S.A.* **79 D13** 42 29N 71 9W
Wodian, *China* . . . . **34 H7** 32 50N 112 35 E
Wokam, *Indonesia* . . . . **37 F8** 5 45S 134 28 E
Woking, *U.K.* **11 F7** 51 19N 0 34W
Wokingham □, *U.K.* **11 F7** 51 25N 0 51W
Wolf →, *Canada* **72 A2** 60 17N 132 33W
Wolf Creek, *U.S.A.* **82 C7** 47 0N 112 4W
Wolf L., *Canada* **72 A2** 60 24N 131 40W
Wolf Point, *U.S.A.* **80 A2** 48 5N 105 39W
Wolfe I., *Canada* **79 B8** 44 7N 76 20W
Wolfeboro, *U.S.A.* **79 C13** 43 35N 71 13W
Wolfsberg, *Austria* . . . . **16 E8** 46 50N 14 52 E
Wolfsburg, *Germany* . . . . **16 B6** 52 25N 10 48 E
Wolin, *Poland* . . . . **16 B8** 53 50N 14 37 E
Wollaston, Is., *Chile* **96 H3** 55 40S 67 30W
Wollaston L., *Canada* **73 B8** 58 7N 103 10W
Wollaston Lake, *Canada* **73 B8** 58 3N 103 33W
Wollaston Pen., *Canada* **68 B8** 69 30N 115 0W
Wollongong, *Australia* . . . . . **63 E5** 34 25S 150 54 E
Wolmaransstad, *S. Africa* . . **56 D4** 27 12S 25 59 E
Wolseley, *S. Africa* . . . . **56 E2** 33 26S 19 7 E
Wolsey, *U.S.A.* **80 C5** 44 24N 98 28W
Wolstenholme, C., *Canada* . **66 C12** 62 35N 77 30W
Wolvega, *Neths.* . . . . **15 B6** 52 52N 6 0 E
Wolverhampton, *U.K.* **11 E5** 52 35N 2 7W
Wondai, *Australia* . . . . **63 D5** 26 20S 151 49 E
Wongalarroo L., *Australia* . . **63 E3** 31 32S 144 0 E
Wongan Hills, *Australia* . . . . **61 F2** 30 51S 116 37 E
Wŏnju, *S. Korea* . . . . **35 F14** 37 22N 127 58 E
Wonosari, *Indonesia* . . . . **37 G14** 7 58S 110 36 E
Wonosobo, *Indonesia* . . . . . . **37 G13** 7 22S 109 54 E
Wonowon, *Canada* **72 B4** 56 44N 121 48W
Wŏnsan, *N. Korea* . . . . **35 E14** 39 11N 127 27 E
Wonthaggi, *Australia* . . . . . . **63 F4** 38 37S 145 37 E
Wood Buffalo Nat. Park,
Canada **72 B6** 59 0N 113 41W
Wood Is., *Australia* . . . . **60 C3** 16 24S 123 19 E
Wood L., *Canada* **73 B8** 55 17N 103 17W
Woodah I., *Australia* . . . . **62 A2** 13 27S 136 10 E
Woodbourne, *U.S.A.* **79 E10** 41 46N 74 36W
Woodbridge, *Canada* **78 C5** 43 47N 79 36W
Woodbridge, *U.K.* . . . . **11 E9** 52 6N 1 20 E
Woodburn, *U.S.A.* **82 D2** 45 9N 122 51W
Woodenbong, *Australia* . . . . **63 D5** 28 24S 152 39 E

Woodend, *Australia* **63 F3** 37 20S 144 33 E
Woodford, *Australia* **63 D5** 26 58S 152 47 E
Woodfords, *U.S.A.* **84 G7** 38 47N 119 50W
Woodlake, *U.S.A.* **84 J7** 36 25N 119 6W
Woodland, *Calif., U.S.A.* **84 G5** 38 41N 121 46W
Woodland, *Maine, U.S.A.* **77 C12** 45 9N 67 25W
Woodland, *Pa., U.S.A.* **78 F6** 40 59N 78 21W
Woodland, *Wash., U.S.A.* **84 E4** 45 54N 122 45W
Woodland Caribou Prov. Park, *Canada* **73 C10** 51 0N 94 45W
Woodridge, *Canada* **73 D9** 49 20N 96 9W
Woodroffe, Mt., *Australia* **61 E5** 26 20S 131 45 E
Woods, L., *Australia* **62 B1** 17 50S 133 30 E
Woods, L. of the, *Canada* **73 D10** 49 15N 94 45W
Woodside, *Australia* **63 F4** 38 31S 146 52 E
Woodstock, *Australia* **62 B4** 19 35S 146 50 E
Woodstock, *N.B., Canada* **71 C6** 46 11N 67 37W
Woodstock, *Ont., Canada* **78 C4** 43 10N 80 45W
Woodstock, *U.K.* **11 F6** 51 51N 1 20W
Woodstock, *Ill., U.S.A.* **80 D10** 42 19N 88 27W
Woodstock, *Vt., U.S.A.* **79 C12** 43 37N 72 31W
Woodsville, *U.S.A.* **79 B13** 44 9N 72 2W
Woodville, *N.Z.* **59 J5** 40 20S 175 53 E
Woodville, *Miss., U.S.A.* **81 K9** 31 6N 91 18W
Woodville, *Tex., U.S.A.* **81 K7** 30 47N 94 25W
Woodward, *U.S.A.* **81 G5** 36 26N 99 24W
Woody, *U.S.A.* **85 K8** 35 42N 118 50W
Woody →, *Canada* **73 C8** 52 31N 100 51W
Woolamai, C., *Australia* **63 F4** 38 30S 145 23 E
Wooler, *U.K.* **10 B5** 55 33N 2 1W
Woolgoolga, *Australia* **63 E5** 30 6S 153 11 E
Woomera, *Australia* **63 E2** 31 5S 136 50 E
Woonsocket, *R.I., U.S.A.* **79 E13** 42 0N 71 31W
Woonsocket, *S. Dak., U.S.A.* **80 C5** 44 3N 98 17W
Wooramel →, *Australia* **61 E1** 25 47S 114 10 E
Wooramel Roadhouse, *Australia* **61 E1** 25 45S 114 17 E
Wooster, *U.S.A.* **78 F3** 40 48N 81 56W
Worcester, *S. Africa* **56 E2** 33 39S 19 27 E
Worcester, *U.K.* **11 E5** 52 11N 2 12W
Worcester, *Mass., U.S.A.* **79 D13** 42 16N 71 48W
Worcester, *N.Y., U.S.A.* **79 D10** 42 36N 74 45W
Worcestershire □, *U.K.* **11 E5** 52 13N 2 10W
Workington, *U.K.* **10 C4** 54 39N 3 33W
Worksop, *U.K.* **10 D6** 53 18N 1 7W
Workum, *Neths.* **15 B5** 52 59N 5 26 E
Worland, *U.S.A.* **82 D10** 44 1N 107 57W
Worms, *Germany* **16 D5** 49 37N 8 21 E
Worsley, *Canada* **72 B5** 56 31N 119 8W
Wortham, *U.S.A.* **81 K6** 31 47N 96 28W
Worthing, *U.K.* **11 G7** 50 49N 0 21W
Worthington, *Minn., U.S.A.* **80 D7** 43 37N 95 36W
Worthington, *Pa., U.S.A.* **78 F5** 40 50N 79 38W
Wosi, *Indonesia* **37 E7** 0 15S 128 0 E
Wou-han = Wuhan, *China* **33 C6** 30 31N 114 18 E
Wousi = Wuxi, *China* **33 C7** 31 33N 120 18 E
Wowoni, *Indonesia* **37 E6** 4 5S 123 5 E
Wrangel I. = Vrangelya, Ostrov, *Russia* **27 B19** 71 0N 180 0 E
Wrangell, *U.S.A.* **72 B2** 56 28N 132 23W
Wrangell Mts., *U.S.A.* **68 B5** 61 30N 142 0W
Wrath, C., *U.K.* **12 C3** 58 38N 5 1W
Wray, *U.S.A.* **80 E3** 40 5N 102 13W
Wrekin, The, *U.K.* **11 E5** 52 41N 2 32W
Wrens, *U.S.A.* **77 J4** 33 12N 82 23W
Wrexham, *U.K.* **10 D4** 53 3N 3 0W
Wrexham □, *U.K.* **10 D5** 53 1N 2 58W
Wright, *U.S.A.* **80 D2** 43 47N 105 30W
Wright Pt., *Canada* **78 C3** 43 48N 81 44W
Wrightson Mt., *U.S.A.* **83 L8** 31 42N 110 51W
Wrightwood, *U.S.A.* **85 L9** 34 21N 117 38W
Wrigley, *Canada* **68 B7** 63 16N 123 37W
Wrocław, *Poland* **17 C9** 51 5N 17 5 E
Września, *Poland* **17 B9** 52 21N 17 36 E
Wu Jiang →, *China* **32 D5** 29 40N 107 20 E
Wu'an, *China* **34 F8** 36 40N 114 15 E
Wubin, *Australia* **61 F2** 30 6S 116 37 E
Wubu, *China* **34 F6** 37 28N 110 42 E
Wuchang, *China* **35 B14** 44 55N 127 5 E
Wucheng, *China* **34 F9** 37 12N 116 20 E
Wuchuan, *China* **34 D6** 41 5N 111 28 E
Wudi, *China* **35 F9** 37 40N 117 35 E
Wuding He →, *China* **34 F6** 37 2N 110 23 E
Wudinna, *Australia* **63 E2** 33 0S 135 22 E
Wudu, *China* **34 H3** 33 22N 104 54 E
Wuhan, *China* **33 C6** 30 31N 114 18 E
Wuhe, *China* **35 H9** 33 10N 117 50 E
Wuhsi = Wuxi, *China* **33 C7** 31 33N 120 18 E
Wuhu, *China* **33 C6** 31 22N 118 21 E
Wukari, *Nigeria* **50 G7** 7 51N 9 42 E
Wulajie, *China* **35 B14** 44 6N 126 33 E
Wulanbulang, *China* **34 D6** 41 5N 110 55 E
Wular L., *India* **43 B6** 34 20N 74 30 E
Wulian, *China* **35 G10** 35 40N 119 12 E
Wuliaru, *Indonesia* **37 F8** 7 27S 131 0 E
Wuluk'omushih Ling, *China* **32 C3** 36 25N 87 25 E
Wulumuchi = Ürümqi, *China* **26 E9** 43 45N 87 45 E
Wundowie, *Australia* **61 F2** 31 47S 116 23 E
Wunnummin L., *Canada* **70 B2** 52 55N 89 10W
Wuntho, *Burma* **41 H19** 23 55N 95 45 E
Wuppertal, *Germany* **16 C4** 51 16N 7 12 E
Wuppertal, *S. Africa* **56 E2** 32 13S 19 12 E
Wuqing, *China* **35 E9** 39 23N 117 4 E
Wurtsboro, *U.S.A.* **79 E10** 41 35N 74 29W
Würzburg, *Germany* **16 D5** 49 46N 9 55 E
Wushan, *China* **34 G3** 34 43N 104 53 E
Wusuli Jiang = Ussuri →, *Asia* **30 A7** 48 27N 135 0 E
Wutai, *China* **34 E7** 38 40N 113 12 E
Wuting = Huimin, *China* **35 F9** 37 27N 117 28 E
Wutonghaolai, *China* **35 C11** 42 50N 120 5 E
Wutongqiao, *China* **32 D5** 29 22N 103 50 E
Wuwei, *China* **32 C5** 37 57N 102 34 E
Wuxi, *China* **33 C7** 31 33N 120 18 E
Wuxiang, *China* **34 F7** 36 49N 112 50 E
Wuyang, *China* **34 H7** 33 25N 113 35 E
Wuyi, *China* **34 F8** 37 46N 115 56 E
Wuyi Shan, *China* **33 D6** 27 0N 117 0 E
Wuyuan, *China* **34 D5** 41 2N 108 20 E
Wuzhai, *China* **34 E6** 38 54N 111 48 E
Wuzhi Shan, *China* **38 C7** 18 45N 109 45 E
Wuzhong, *China* **34 E4** 38 2N 106 12 E
Wuzhou, *China* **33 D6** 23 30N 111 18 E
Wyaaba Cr. →, *Australia* **62 B3** 16 27S 141 35 E
Wyalkatchem, *Australia* **61 F2** 31 8S 117 22 E
Wyalusing, *U.S.A.* **79 E8** 41 40N 76 16W
Wyandotte, *U.S.A.* **76 D4** 42 12N 83 9W
Wyandra, *Australia* **63 D4** 27 12S 145 56 E
Wyangala Res., *Australia* **63 E4** 33 54S 149 0 E
Wyara, L., *Australia* **63 D3** 28 42S 144 14 E
Wycheproof, *Australia* **63 F3** 36 5S 143 17 E
Wye →, *U.K.* **11 F5** 51 38N 2 40W
Wyemandoo, *Australia* **61 E2** 28 28S 118 29 E
Wymondham, *U.K.* **11 E9** 52 35N 1 7 E
Wymore, *U.S.A.* **80 E6** 40 7N 96 40W
Wyndham, *Australia* **60 C4** 15 33S 128 3 E
Wyndham, *N.Z.* **59 M2** 46 20S 168 51 E
Wynne, *U.S.A.* **81 H9** 35 14N 90 47W
Wynyard, *Australia* **62 G4** 41 5S 145 44 E
Wynyard, *Canada* **73 C8** 51 45N 104 10W
Wyola L., *Australia* **61 E5** 29 8S 130 17 E
Wyoming, *Canada* **78 D2** 42 57N 82 7W
Wyoming □, *U.S.A.* **82 E10** 43 0N 107 30W
Wyomissing, *U.S.A.* **79 F9** 40 20N 75 59W
Wyong, *Australia* **63 E5** 33 14S 151 24 E
Wytheville, *U.S.A.* **76 G5** 36 57N 81 5W

X

Xaçmaz, *Azerbaijan* **25 F8** 41 31N 48 42 E
Xai-Xai, *Mozam.* **57 D5** 25 6S 33 31 E
Xainza, *China* **32 C3** 30 58N 88 35 E
Xangongo, *Angola* **56 B2** 16 45S 15 5 E
Xankändi, *Azerbaijan* **25 G8** 39 52N 46 49 E
Xánthi, *Greece* **21 D11** 41 10N 24 58 E
Xanxerê, *Brazil* **95 B5** 26 53S 52 23W
Xapuri, *Brazil* **92 F5** 10 35S 68 35W
Xar Moron He →, *China* **35 C11** 43 25N 120 35 E
Xátiva, *Spain* **19 C5** 38 59N 0 32W
Xau, L., *Botswana* **56 C3** 21 15S 24 44 E
Xavantina, *Brazil* **95 A5** 21 15S 52 48W
Xenia, *U.S.A.* **76 F4** 39 41N 83 56W
Xeropotamos →, *Cyprus* **23 E11** 34 42N 32 33 E
Xhora, *S. Africa* **57 E4** 31 55S 28 38 E
Xhumo, *Botswana* **56 C3** 21 7S 24 35 E
Xi Jiang →, *China* **33 D6** 22 5N 113 20 E
Xi Xian, *China* **34 F6** 36 41N 110 58 E
Xia Xian, *China* **34 G6** 35 8N 111 12 E
Xiachengzi, *China* **35 B16** 44 40N 130 18 E
Xiaguan, *China* **32 D5** 25 32N 100 16 E
Xiajin, *China* **34 F9** 36 56N 116 0 E
Xiamen, *China* **33 D6** 24 25N 118 4 E
Xi'an, *China* **34 G5** 34 15N 109 0 E
Xian Xian, *China* **34 E9** 38 12N 116 6 E
Xiang Jiang →, *China* **33 D6** 28 55N 112 50 E
Xiangcheng, *Henan, China* **34 H8** 33 29N 114 52 E
Xiangcheng, *Henan, China* **34 H7** 33 50N 113 27 E
Xiangfan, *China* **33 C6** 32 2N 112 8 E
Xianggang = Hong Kong □, *China* **33 D6** 22 11N 114 14 E
Xianghuang Qi, *China* **34 C7** 42 2N 113 50 E
Xiangning, *China* **34 G6** 35 58N 110 50 E
Xiangquan, *China* **34 F7** 36 30N 113 1 E
Xiangquan He = Sutlej →, *Pakistan* **42 E4** 29 23N 71 3 E
Xiangshui, *China* **35 G10** 34 12N 119 33 E
Xiangtan, *China* **33 D6** 27 51N 112 54 E
Xianyang, *China* **34 G5** 34 20N 108 40 E
Xiao Hinggan Ling, *China* **33 B7** 49 0N 127 0 E
Xiao Xian, *China* **34 G9** 34 15N 116 55 E
Xiaoyi, *China* **34 F6** 37 8N 111 48 E
Xiawa, *China* **35 C11** 42 35N 120 38 E
Xiayi, *China* **34 G9** 34 15N 116 10 E
Xichang, *China* **32 D5** 27 51N 102 19 E
Xichuan, *China* **34 H6** 33 0N 111 30 E
Xieng Khouang, *Laos* **38 C4** 19 17N 103 25 E
Xifei He →, *China* **34 H9** 32 45N 116 40 E
Xifeng, *Gansu, China* **34 G4** 35 40N 107 40 E
Xifeng, *Liaoning, China* **35 C13** 42 42N 124 45 E
Xifengzhen = Xifeng, *China* **34 G4** 35 40N 107 40 E
Xigazê, *China* **32 D3** 29 5N 88 45 E
Xihe, *China* **34 G3** 34 2N 105 20 E
Xihua, *China* **34 H8** 33 45N 114 30 E
Xiliao He →, *China* **35 C12** 43 32N 123 35 E
Xin Xian = Xinzhou, *China* **34 E7** 38 22N 112 46 E
Xinavane, *Mozam.* **57 D5** 25 2S 32 47 E
Xinbin, *China* **35 D13** 41 40N 125 2 E
Xing Xian, *China* **34 E6** 38 27N 111 7 E
Xing'an, *China* **33 D6** 25 38N 110 40 E
Xingcheng, *China* **35 D11** 40 40N 120 45 E
Xinghe, *China* **34 D7** 40 55N 113 55 E
Xinghua, *China* **35 H10** 32 58N 119 48 E
Xinglong, *China* **35 D9** 40 25N 117 30 E
Xingping, *China* **34 G5** 34 20N 108 28 E
Xingtai, *China* **34 F8** 37 3N 114 32 E
Xingu →, *Brazil* **93 D8** 1 30S 51 53W
Xingyang, *China* **34 G7** 34 45N 112 52 E
Xinhe, *China* **34 F8** 37 30N 115 15 E
Xining, *China* **32 C5** 36 34N 101 40 E
Xinjiang, *China* **34 G6** 35 34N 111 11 E
Xinjiang Uygur Zizhiqu □, *China* **32 C3** 42 0N 86 0 E
Xinjin = Pulandian, *China* **35 E11** 39 25N 121 58 E
Xinkai He →, *China* **35 C12** 43 32N 123 35 E
Xinle, *China* **34 E8** 38 25N 114 40 E
Xinlitun, *China* **35 D12** 42 0N 122 8 E
Xinmin, *China* **35 D12** 41 59N 122 50 E
Xintai, *China* **35 G9** 35 55N 117 45 E
Xinxiang, *China* **34 G7** 35 18N 113 50 E
Xinzhan, *China* **35 C14** 43 50N 127 18 E
Xinzheng, *China* **34 G7** 34 20N 113 45 E
Xinzhou, *China* **34 E7** 38 22N 112 46 E
Xiong Xian, *China* **34 E9** 38 59N 116 8 E
Xiongyuecheng, *China* **35 D12** 40 12N 122 5 E
Xiping, *Henan, China* **34 H8** 33 22N 114 5 E
Xiping, *Henan, China* **34 H6** 33 25N 111 8 E
Xique-Xique, *Brazil* **93 F10** 10 50S 42 40W
Xisha Qundao = Paracel Is., *S. China Sea* **36 A4** 15 50N 112 0 E
Xiuyan, *China* **35 D12** 40 18N 123 11 E
Xixabangma Feng, *China* **41 E14** 28 20N 85 40 E
Xixia, *China* **34 H6** 33 25N 111 29 E
Xixiang, *China* **34 H4** 33 0N 107 44 E
Xiyang, *China* **34 F7** 37 38N 113 38 E
Xizang Zizhiqu □, *China* **32 C3** 32 0N 88 0 E
Xlendi, *Malta* **23 C1** 36 1N 14 12 E
Xuan Loc, *Vietnam* **39 G6** 10 56N 107 14 E
Xuanhua, *China* **34 D8** 40 40N 115 2 E
Xuchang, *China* **34 G7** 34 2N 113 48 E
Xun Xian, *China* **34 G8** 35 42N 114 33 E
Xunyang, *China* **34 H5** 32 48N 109 22 E
Xunyi, *China* **34 G5** 35 8N 108 20 E
Xúquer →, *Spain* **19 C5** 39 5N 0 10W
Xushui, *China* **34 E8** 39 2N 115 40 E
Xuyen Moc, *Vietnam* **39 G6** 10 34N 107 25 E
Xuzhou, *China* **35 G9** 34 18N 117 10 E
Xylophagou, *Cyprus* **23 E12** 34 54N 33 51 E

Y

Ya Xian, *China* **38 C7** 18 14N 109 29 E
Yaamba, *Australia* **62 C5** 23 8S 150 22 E
Yaapeet, *Australia* **63 F3** 35 45S 142 3 E
Yablonovy Ra. = Yablonovyy Khrebet, *Russia* **27 D12** 53 0N 114 0 E
Yablonovyy Khrebet, *Russia* **27 D12** 53 0N 114 0 E
Yabrai Shan, *China* **34 E2** 39 40N 103 0 E
Yabrūd, *Syria* **47 B5** 33 58N 36 39 E
Yacheng, *China* **33 E5** 18 22N 109 6 E
Yacuiba, *Bolivia* **94 A3** 22 0S 63 43W
Yacuma →, *Bolivia* **92 F5** 13 38S 65 23W
Yadgir, *India* **40 L10** 16 45N 77 5 E
Yadkin →, *U.S.A.* **77 H5** 35 29N 80 9W
Yaeyama-Rettō, *Japan* **31 M1** 24 30N 123 40 E
Yagodnoye, *Russia* **27 C15** 62 33N 149 40 E
Yahila, *Dem. Rep. of the Congo* **54 B1** 0 13N 24 28 E
Yahk, *Canada* **72 D5** 49 6N 116 10W
Yahuma, *Dem. Rep. of the Congo* **52 D4** 1 0N 23 10 E
Yaita, *Japan* **31 F9** 36 48N 139 56 E
Yaiza, *Canary Is.* **22 F6** 28 57N 13 46W
Yakima, *U.S.A.* **82 C3** 46 36N 120 31W
Yakima →, *U.S.A.* **82 C3** 47 0N 120 30W
Yakobi I., *U.S.A.* **72 B1** 58 0N 136 30W
Yakovlevka, *Russia* **30 B6** 44 26N 133 28 E
Yaku-Shima, *Japan* **31 J5** 30 20N 130 30 E
Yakumo, *Japan* **30 C10** 42 15N 140 16 E
Yakutat, *U.S.A.* **68 C6** 59 33N 139 44W
Yakutia = Sakha □, *Russia* **27 C14** 66 0N 130 0 E
Yakutsk, *Russia* **27 C13** 62 5N 129 50 E
Yala, *Thailand* **39 J3** 6 33N 101 18 E
Yale, *U.S.A.* **78 C2** 43 8N 82 48W
Yalgoo, *Australia* **61 E2** 28 16S 116 39 E
Yalinga, *C.A.R.* **52 C4** 6 33N 23 10 E
Yalkubul, Punta, *Mexico* **87 C7** 21 32N 88 37W
Yalleroi, *Australia* **62 C4** 24 3S 145 42 E
Yalobusha →, *U.S.A.* **81 J9** 33 33N 90 10W
Yalong Jiang →, *China* **32 D5** 26 40N 101 55 E
Yalova, *Turkey* **21 D13** 40 41N 29 15 E
Yalta, *Ukraine* **25 F5** 44 30N 34 10 E
Yalu Jiang →, *China* **35 E13** 40 0N 124 22 E
Yam Ha Melah = Dead Sea, *Asia* **47 D4** 31 30N 35 30 E
Yam Kinneret, *Israel* **47 C4** 32 45N 35 35 E
Yamada, *Japan* **31 H5** 33 33N 130 49 E
Yamagata, *Japan* **30 E10** 38 15N 140 15 E
Yamagata □, *Japan* **30 E10** 38 30N 140 0 E
Yamaguchi, *Japan* **31 G5** 34 10N 131 32 E
Yamaguchi □, *Japan* **31 G5** 34 20N 131 40 E
Yamal, Poluostrov, *Russia* **26 B8** 71 0N 70 0 E
Yamal Pen. = Yamal, Poluostrov, *Russia* **26 B8** 71 0N 70 0 E
Yamanashi □, *Japan* **31 G9** 35 40N 138 40 E
Yamantau, Gora, *Russia* **24 D10** 54 15N 58 6 E
Yamba, *Australia* **63 D5** 29 26S 153 23 E
Yambarran Ra., *Australia* **60 C5** 15 10S 130 25 E
Yâmbiô, *Sudan* **51 H11** 4 35N 28 16 E
Yambol, *Bulgaria* **21 C12** 42 30N 26 30 E
Yamdena, *Indonesia* **37 F8** 7 45S 131 20 E
Yame, *Japan* **31 H5** 33 13N 130 35 E
Yamethin, *Burma* **41 J20** 20 29N 96 18 E
Yamma-Yamma, L., *Australia* **63 D3** 26 16S 141 20 E
Yamoussoukro, *Ivory C.* **50 G4** 6 49N 5 17W
Yampa →, *U.S.A.* **82 F9** 40 32N 108 59W
Yampi Sd., *Australia* **60 C3** 16 8S 123 38 E
Yampil, *Moldova* **17 D15** 48 15N 28 15 E
Yampol = Yampil, *Moldova* **17 D15** 48 15N 28 15 E
Yamuna →, *India* **43 G9** 25 30N 81 53 E
Yamunanagar, *India* **42 D7** 30 7N 77 17 E
Yamzho Yumco, *China* **32 D4** 28 48N 90 35 E
Yana →, *Russia* **27 B14** 71 30N 136 0 E
Yanagawa, *Japan* **31 H5** 33 10N 130 24 E
Yanai, *Japan* **31 H6** 33 58N 132 7 E
Yan'an, *China* **34 F5** 36 35N 109 26 E
Yanaul, *Russia* **24 C10** 56 25N 55 0 E
Yanbu 'al Baḥr, *Si. Arabia* **46 C2** 24 0N 38 5 E
Yanchang, *China* **34 F6** 36 43N 110 1 E
Yancheng, *Henan, China* **34 H8** 33 35N 114 0 E
Yancheng, *Jiangsu, China* **35 H11** 33 23N 120 8 E
Yanchep Beach, *Australia* **61 F2** 31 33S 115 37 E
Yanchi, *China* **34 F4** 37 48N 107 20 E
Yanchuan, *China* **34 F6** 36 51N 110 10 E
Yanco, *Australia* **63 E4** 34 38S 146 27 E
Yanco Cr. →, *Australia* **63 F4** 35 14S 145 35 E
Yandoon, *Burma* **41 L19** 17 0N 95 40 E
Yang Xian, *China* **34 H4** 33 15N 107 30 E
Yangambi, *Dem. Rep. of the Congo* **54 B1** 0 47N 24 20 E
Yangcheng, *China* **34 G7** 35 28N 112 22 E
Yangch'ü = Taiyuan, *China* **34 F7** 37 52N 112 33 E
Yanggao, *China* **34 D7** 40 21N 113 55 E
Yanggu, *China* **34 F8** 36 8N 115 43 E
Yangliuqing, *China* **35 E9** 39 2N 117 5 E
Yangon = Rangoon, *Burma* **41 L20** 16 45N 96 20 E
Yangpingguan, *China* **34 H4** 32 58N 106 5 E
Yangquan, *China* **34 F7** 37 58N 113 31 E
Yangtse = Chang Jiang →, *China* **33 C7** 31 48N 121 10 E
Yangtze Kiang = Chang Jiang →, *China* **33 C7** 31 48N 121 10 E
Yangyang, *S. Korea* **35 E15** 38 4N 128 38 E
Yangyuan, *China* **34 D8** 40 1N 114 10 E
Yangzhou, *China* **33 C6** 32 21N 119 26 E
Yanji, *China* **35 C15** 42 59N 129 30 E
Yankton, *U.S.A.* **80 D6** 42 53N 97 23W
Yanonge, *Dem. Rep. of the Congo* **54 B1** 0 35N 24 38 E
Yanqi, *China* **32 B3** 42 5N 86 35 E
Yanqing, *China* **34 D8** 40 30N 115 58 E
Yanshan, *China* **35 E9** 38 4N 117 22 E
Yanshou, *China* **35 B15** 45 28N 128 22 E
Yantabulla, *Australia* **63 D4** 29 21S 145 0 E
Yantai, *China* **35 F11** 37 34N 121 22 E
Yanzhou, *China* **34 G9** 35 35N 116 49 E
Yao Xian, *China* **34 G5** 34 55N 108 59 E
Yao Yai, Ko, *Thailand* **39 J2** 8 0N 98 35 E
Yaoundé, *Cameroon* **52 D2** 3 50N 11 35 E
Yaowan, *China* **35 G10** 34 15N 118 3 E
Yap I., *Pac. Oc.* **64 G5** 9 30N 138 10 E
Yapen, *Indonesia* **37 E9** 1 50S 136 0 E
Yapen, Selat, *Indonesia* **37 E9** 1 20S 136 10 E
Yapero, *Indonesia* **37 E9** 4 59S 137 11 E
Yappar →, *Australia* **62 B3** 18 22S 141 16 E
Yaqui →, *Mexico* **86 B2** 27 37N 110 39W
Yar-Sale, *Russia* **26 C8** 66 50N 70 50 E
Yaraka, *Australia* **62 C3** 24 53S 144 3 E
Yaransk, *Russia* **24 C8** 57 22N 47 49 E
Yare →, *U.K.* **11 E9** 52 35N 1 38 E
Yaremcha, *Ukraine* **17 D13** 48 27N 24 33 E
Yarensk, *Russia* **24 B8** 62 11N 49 15 E
Yari →, *Colombia* **92 D4** 0 20S 72 20W
Yarkand = Shache, *China* **32 C2** 38 20N 77 10 E
Yarker, *Canada* **79 B8** 44 23N 76 46W
Yarkhun →, *Pakistan* **43 A5** 36 17N 72 30 E
Yarmouth, *Canada* **71 D6** 43 50N 66 7W
Yarmūk →, *Syria* **47 C4** 32 42N 35 40 E
Yaroslavl, *Russia* **24 C6** 57 35N 39 55 E
Yarqa, W. →, *Egypt* **47 F2** 30 0N 33 49 E
Yarra Yarra Lakes, *Australia* **61 E2** 29 40S 115 45 E
Yarram, *Australia* **63 F4** 38 29S 146 39 E
Yarraman, *Australia* **63 D5** 26 50S 152 0 E
Yarras, *Australia* **63 E5** 31 25S 152 20 E
Yartsevo, *Russia* **27 C10** 60 20N 90 0 E
Yarumal, *Colombia* **92 B3** 6 58N 75 24W
Yasawa Group, *Fiji* **59 C7** 17 0S 177 23 E
Yaselda, *Belarus* **17 B14** 52 7N 26 28 E
Yasin, *Pakistan* **43 A5** 36 24N 73 23 E
Yasinski, L., *Canada* **70 B4** 53 16N 77 35W
Yasinya, *Ukraine* **17 D13** 48 16N 24 21 E
Yasothon, *Thailand* **38 E5** 15 50N 104 10 E
Yass, *Australia* **63 E4** 34 49S 148 54 E
Yatağan, *Turkey* **21 F13** 37 20N 28 10 E
Yates Center, *U.S.A.* **81 G7** 37 53N 95 44W
Yathkyed L., *Canada* **73 A9** 62 40N 98 0W
Yatsushiro, *Japan* **31 H5** 32 30N 130 40 E
Yatta Plateau, *Kenya* **54 C4** 2 0S 38 0 E
Yavari →, *Peru* **92 D4** 4 21S 70 2W
Yávaros, *Mexico* **86 B3** 26 42N 109 31W
Yavatmal, *India* **40 J11** 20 20N 78 15 E
Yavne, *Israel* **47 D3** 31 52N 34 45 E
Yavoriv, *Ukraine* **17 D12** 49 55N 23 20 E
Yavorov = Yavoriv, *Ukraine* **17 D12** 49 55N 23 20 E
Yawatahama, *Japan* **31 H6** 33 27N 132 24 E
Yazd, *Iran* **45 D7** 31 55N 54 27 E
Yazd □, *Iran* **45 D7** 32 0N 55 0 E
Yazd-e Khvāst, *Iran* **45 D7** 31 31N 52 7 E
Yazman, *Pakistan* **42 E4** 29 8N 71 45 E
Yazoo →, *U.S.A.* **81 J9** 32 22N 90 54W
Yazoo City, *U.S.A.* **81 J9** 32 51N 90 25W
Yding Skovhøj, *Denmark* **9 J13** 55 59N 9 46 E
Ye Xian = Laizhou, *China* **35 F10** 37 8N 119 57 E
Ye Xian, *China* **34 H7** 33 35N 113 25 E
Yebyu, *Burma* **38 E2** 14 15N 98 13 E
Yechŏn, *S. Korea* **35 F15** 36 39N 128 27 E
Yecla, *Spain* **19 C5** 38 35N 1 5W
Yécora, *Mexico* **86 B3** 28 20N 108 58W
Yedintsy = Edineţ, *Moldova* **17 D14** 48 9N 27 18 E
Yegros, *Paraguay* **94 B4** 26 20S 56 25W
Yehuda, Midbar, *Israel* **47 D4** 31 35N 35 15 E
Yei, *Sudan* **51 H12** 4 9N 30 40 E
Yekaterinburg, *Russia* **26 D7** 56 50N 60 30 E
Yekaterinodar = Krasnodar, *Russia* **25 E6** 45 5N 39 0 E
Yelarbon, *Australia* **63 D5** 28 33S 150 38 E
Yelets, *Russia* **24 D6** 52 40N 38 30 E
Yelizavetgrad = Kirovohrad, *Ukraine* **25 E5** 48 35N 32 20 E
Yell, *U.K.* **12 A7** 60 35N 1 5W
Yell Sd., *U.K.* **12 A7** 60 33N 1 15W
Yellow Sea, *China* **35 G12** 35 0N 123 0 E
Yellowhead Pass, *Canada* **72 C5** 52 53N 118 25W
Yellowknife, *Canada* **72 A6** 62 27N 114 29W
Yellowknife →, *Canada* **72 A6** 62 31N 114 19W
Yellowstone →, *U.S.A.* **80 B3** 47 59N 103 59W
Yellowstone L., *U.S.A.* **82 D8** 44 27N 110 22W
Yellowstone National Park, *U.S.A.* **82 D9** 44 40N 110 30W
Yelsk, *Belarus* **17 C15** 51 50N 29 10 E
Yemen ■, *Asia* **46 E3** 15 0N 44 0 E
Yenangyaung, *Burma* **41 J19** 20 30N 95 0 E
Yenbo = Yanbu 'al Baḥr, *Si. Arabia* **46 C2** 24 0N 38 5 E
Yenda, *Australia* **63 E4** 34 13S 146 14 E
Yenice, *Turkey* **21 E12** 39 55N 27 17 E
Yenisey →, *Russia* **26 B9** 71 50N 82 40 E
Yeniseysk, *Russia* **27 D10** 58 27N 92 13 E
Yeniseyskiy Zaliv, *Russia* **26 B9** 72 20N 81 0 E
Yennádhi, *Greece* **23 C9** 36 2N 27 56 E
Yenyuka, *Russia* **27 D13** 57 57N 121 15 E
Yeo →, *U.K.* **11 G5** 51 2N 2 49W
Yeo, L., *Australia* **61 E3** 28 0S 124 30 E
Yeo I., *Canada* **78 A3** 45 24N 81 48W
Yeola, *India* **40 J9** 20 2N 74 30 E
Yeoryioúpolis, *Greece* **23 D6** 35 20N 24 15 E
Yeovil, *U.K.* **11 G5** 50 57N 2 38W
Yeppoon, *Australia* **62 C5** 23 5S 150 47 E
Yerbent, *Turkmenistan* **26 F6** 39 30N 58 50 E
Yerbogachen, *Russia* **27 C11** 61 16N 108 0 E
Yerevan, *Armenia* **25 F7** 40 10N 44 31 E
Yerington, *U.S.A.* **82 G4** 38 59N 119 10W
Yermak, *Kazakstan* **26 D8** 52 2N 76 55 E
Yermo, *U.S.A.* **85 L10** 34 54N 116 50W
Yerólakkos, *Cyprus* **23 D12** 35 11N 33 15 E
Yeropol, *Russia* **27 C17** 65 15N 168 40 E
Yeropótamos →, *Greece* **23 D6** 35 3N 24 50 E
Yeroskipos, *Cyprus* **23 E11** 34 46N 32 28 E
Yershov, *Russia* **25 D8** 51 23N 48 27 E
Yerushalayim = Jerusalem, *Israel* **47 D4** 31 47N 35 10 E
Yes Tor, *U.K.* **11 G4** 50 41N 4 0W
Yesan, *S. Korea* **35 F14** 36 41N 126 51 E
Yeso, *U.S.A.* **81 H2** 34 26N 104 37W
Yessey, *Russia* **27 C11** 68 29N 102 10 E
Yetman, *Australia* **63 D5** 28 56S 150 48 E
Yeu, Î. d', *France* **18 C2** 46 42N 2 20W
Yevpatoriya, *Ukraine* **25 E5** 45 15N 33 20 E
Yeysk, *Russia* **25 E6** 46 40N 38 12 E

Yezd = Yazd, *Iran* **45 D7** 31 55N 54 27 E
Yhati, *Paraguay* **94 B4** 25 45S 56 35W
Yhú, *Paraguay* **95 B4** 25 0S 56 0W
Yi →, *Uruguay* **94 C4** 33 7S 57 8W
Yi 'Allaq, G., *Egypt* **47 E2** 30 22N 33 32 E
Yi He →, *China* **35 G10** 34 10N 118 8 E
Yi Xian, *Hebei, China* **34 E8** 39 20N 115 30 E
Yi Xian, *Liaoning, China* **35 D11** 41 30N 121 22 E
Yialiás →, *Cyprus* **23 D12** 35 9N 33 44 E
Yialousa, *Cyprus* **23 D13** 35 32N 34 10 E
Yianisádhes, *Greece* **23 D8** 35 20N 26 10 E
Yiannitsa, *Greece* **21 D10** 40 46N 22 24 E
Yibin, *China* **32 D5** 28 45N 104 32 E
Yichang, *China* **33 C6** 30 40N 111 20 E
Yicheng, *China* **34 G6** 35 42N 111 40 E
Yichuan, *China* **34 F6** 36 2N 110 10 E
Yichun, *China* **33 B7** 47 44N 128 52 E
Yidu, *China* **35 F10** 36 43N 118 28 E
Yijun, *China* **34 G5** 35 28N 109 8 E
Yıldız Dağları, *Turkey* **21 D12** 41 48N 27 36 E
Yilehuli Shan, *China* **33 A7** 51 20N 124 20 E
Yimianpo, *China* **35 B15** 45 7N 128 2 E
Yinchuan, *China* **34 E4** 38 30N 106 15 E
Yindarlgooda, L., *Australia* **61 F3** 30 40S 121 52 E
Ying He →, *China* **34 H9** 32 30N 116 30 E
Ying Xian, *China* **34 E7** 39 32N 113 10 E
Yingkou, *China* **35 D12** 40 37N 122 18 E
Yining, *China* **26 E9** 43 58N 81 10 E
Yinmabin, *Burma* **41 H19** 22 10N 94 55 E
Yiofiros →, *Greece* **23 D7** 35 20N 25 6 E
Yirga Alem, *Ethiopia* **46 F2** 6 48N 38 22 E
Yirrkala, *Australia* **62 A2** 12 14S 136 56 E
Yishan, *China* **32 D5** 24 28N 108 38 E
Yishui, *China* **35 G10** 35 47N 118 30 E
Yíthion, *Greece* **21 F10** 36 46N 22 34 E
Yitiaoshan, *China* **34 F3** 37 5N 104 2 E
Yitong, *China* **35 C13** 43 13N 125 20 E
Yiyang, *Henan, China* **34 G7** 34 27N 112 10 E
Yiyang, *Hunan, China* **33 D6** 28 35N 112 18 E
Yli-Kitka, *Finland* **8 C23** 66 8N 28 30 E
Ylitornio, *Finland* **8 C20** 66 19N 23 39 E
Ylivieska, *Finland* **8 D21** 64 4N 24 28 E
Yoakum, *U.S.A.* **81 L6** 29 17N 97 9W
Yog Pt., *Phil.* **37 B6** 14 6N 124 12 E
Yogyakarta, *Indonesia* **37 G14** 7 49S 110 22 E
Yoho Nat. Park, *Canada* **72 C5** 51 25N 116 30W
Yojoa, L. de, *Honduras* **88 D2** 14 53N 88 0W
Yŏju, *S. Korea* **35 F14** 37 20N 127 35 E
Yokadouma, *Cameroon* **52 D2** 3 26N 14 55 E
Yokkaichi, *Japan* **31 G8** 34 55N 136 38 E
Yoko, *Cameroon* **52 C2** 5 32N 12 20 E
Yokohama, *Japan* **31 G9** 35 27N 139 28 E
Yokosuka, *Japan* **31 G9** 35 20N 139 40 E
Yokote, *Japan* **30 E10** 39 20N 140 30 E
Yola, *Nigeria* **51 G8** 9 10N 12 29 E
Yolaina, Cordillera de, *Nic.* **88 D3** 11 30N 84 0W
Yoloten, *Turkmenistan* **45 B9** 37 18N 62 21 E
Yom →, *Thailand* **36 A2** 15 35N 100 1 E
Yonago, *Japan* **31 G6** 35 25N 133 19 E
Yonaguni-Jima, *Japan* **31 M1** 24 27N 123 0 E
Yŏnan, *N. Korea* **35 F14** 37 55N 126 11 E
Yonezawa, *Japan* **30 F10** 37 57N 140 4 E
Yong Peng, *Malaysia* **39 M4** 2 0N 103 3 E
Yong Sata, *Thailand* **39 J2** 7 8N 99 41 E
Yongamp'o, *N. Korea* **35 E13** 39 56N 124 23 E
Yongcheng, *China* **34 H9** 33 55N 116 20 E
Yŏngch'ŏn, *S. Korea* **35 G15** 35 58N 128 56 E
Yongdeng, *China* **34 F2** 36 38N 103 25 E
Yŏngdŏk, *S. Korea* **35 F15** 36 24N 129 22 E
Yŏngdŭngpo, *S. Korea* **35 F14** 37 31N 126 54 E
Yonghe, *China* **34 F6** 36 46N 110 38 E
Yŏnghŭng, *N. Korea* **35 E14** 39 31N 127 18 E
Yongji, *China* **34 G6** 34 52N 110 28 E
Yŏngju, *S. Korea* **35 F15** 36 50N 128 40 E
Yongnian, *China* **34 F8** 36 47N 114 29 E
Yongning, *China* **34 E4** 38 15N 106 14 E
Yongqing, *China* **34 E9** 39 25N 116 28 E
Yŏngwŏl, *S. Korea* **35 F15** 37 11N 128 28 E
Yonibana, *S. Leone* **50 G3** 8 30N 12 19W
Yonkers, *U.S.A.* **79 F11** 40 56N 73 54W
Yonne →, *France* **18 B5** 48 23N 2 58 E
York, *Australia* **61 F2** 31 52S 116 47 E
York, *U.K.* **10 D6** 53 58N 1 6W
York, *Nebr., U.S.A.* **80 E6** 40 52N 97 36W
York, *Pa., U.S.A.* **76 F7** 39 58N 76 44W
York, C., *Australia* **62 A3** 10 42S 142 31 E
York, City of □, *U.K.* **10 D6** 53 58N 1 6W
York, Kap, *Greenland* **4 B4** 75 55N 66 25W
York, Vale of, *U.K.* **10 C6** 54 15N 1 25W
York Haven, *U.S.A.* **78 F8** 40 7N 76 46W
York Sd., *Australia* **60 C4** 15 0S 125 5 E
Yorke Pen., *Australia* **63 E2** 34 50S 137 40 E
Yorketown, *Australia* **63 F2** 35 0S 137 33 E
Yorkshire Wolds, *U.K.* **10 C7** 54 8N 0 31W
Yorkton, *Canada* **73 C8** 51 11N 102 28W
Yorkville, *U.S.A.* **84 G3** 38 52N 123 13W
Yoro, *Honduras* **88 C2** 15 9N 87 7W
Yoron-Jima, *Japan* **31 L4** 27 2N 128 26 E
Yos Sudarso, Pulau = Dolak, Pulau, *Indonesia* **37 F9** 8 0S 138 30 E
Yosemite National Park, *U.S.A.* **84 H7** 37 45N 119 40W
Yosemite Village, *U.S.A.* **84 H7** 37 45N 119 35W
Yoshkar Ola, *Russia* **24 C8** 56 38N 47 55 E
Yŏsu, *S. Korea* **35 G14** 34 47N 127 45 E
Yotvata, *Israel* **47 F4** 29 55N 35 2 E
Youbou, *Canada* **84 B2** 48 53N 124 13W
Youghal, *Ireland* **13 E4** 51 56N 7 52W
Youghal B., *Ireland* **13 E4** 51 55N 7 49W
Young, *Australia* **63 E4** 34 19S 148 18 E
Young, *Canada* **73 C7** 51 47N 105 45W
Young, *Uruguay* **94 C4** 32 44S 57 36W
Younghusband, L., *Australia* **63 E2** 30 50S 136 5 E
Younghusband Pen., *Australia* **63 F2** 36 0S 139 25 E
Youngstown, *Canada* **73 C6** 51 35N 111 10W
Youngstown, *N.Y., U.S.A.* **78 C5** 43 15N 79 3W
Youngstown, *Ohio, U.S.A.* **78 E4** 41 6N 80 39W
Youngsville, *U.S.A.* **78 E5** 41 51N 79 19W
Youngwood, *U.S.A.* **78 F5** 40 14N 79 34W
Youyu, *China* **34 D7** 40 10N 112 20 E
Yozgat, *Turkey* **25 G5** 39 51N 34 47 E
Ypané →, *Paraguay* **94 A4** 23 29S 57 19W
Ypres = Ieper, *Belgium* **15 D2** 50 51N 2 53 E
Yreka, *U.S.A.* **82 F2** 41 44N 122 38W
Ystad, *Sweden* **9 J15** 55 26N 13 50 E
Ysyk-Köl, *Kyrgyzstan* **28 E11** 42 26N 76 12 E
Ysyk-Köl, Ozero, *Kyrgyzstan* **26 E8** 42 25N 77 15 E
Ythan →, *U.K.* **12 D7** 57 19N 1 59W
Ytyk Kyuyel, *Russia* **27 C14** 62 30N 133 45 E
Yu Jiang →, *China* **33 D6** 23 22N 110 3 E
Yu Xian = Yuzhou, *China* **34 G7** 34 10N 113 28 E
Yu Xian, *Hebei, China* **34 E8** 39 50N 114 35 E
Yu Xian, *Shanxi, China* **34 E7** 38 5N 113 20 E
Yuan Jiang →, *China* **33 D6** 28 55N 111 50 E
Yuanqu, *China* **34 G6** 35 18N 111 40 E
Yuanyang, *China* **34 G7** 35 3N 113 58 E
Yuba →, *U.S.A.* **84 F5** 39 8N 121 36W
Yuba City, *U.S.A.* **84 F5** 39 8N 121 37W
Yūbari, *Japan* **30 C10** 43 4N 141 59 E
Yūbetsu, *Japan* **30 B11** 44 13N 143 50 E
Yucatán □, *Mexico* **87 C7** 21 30N 86 30W
Yucatán, Canal de, *Caribbean* **88 B2** 22 0N 86 30W
Yucatán, Península de, *Mexico* **66 H11** 19 30N 89 0W
Yucatán Basin, *Cent. Amer.* **66 H11** 19 0N 86 0W
Yucatan Str. = Yucatán, Canal de, *Caribbean* **88 B2** 22 0N 86 30W
Yucca, *U.S.A.* **85 L12** 34 52N 114 9W
Yucca Valley, *U.S.A.* **85 L10** 34 8N 116 27W
Yucheng, *China* **34 F9** 36 55N 116 32 E
Yuci, *China* **34 F7** 37 42N 112 46 E
Yuendumu, *Australia* **60 D5** 22 16S 131 49 E
Yugoslavia ■, *Europe* **21 B9** 43 20N 20 0 E
Yukon →, *U.S.A.* **68 B3** 62 32N 163 54W
Yukon Territory □, *Canada* **68 B6** 63 0N 135 0W
Yukta, *Russia* **27 C11** 63 26N 105 42 E
Yukuhashi, *Japan* **31 H5** 33 44N 130 59 E
Yulara, *Australia* **61 E5** 25 10S 130 55 E
Yule →, *Australia* **60 D2** 20 41S 118 17 E
Yuleba, *Australia* **63 D4** 26 37S 149 24 E
Yulin, *Shaanxi, China* **34 E5** 38 20N 109 30 E
Yulin, *Shensi, China* **38 C7** 38 15N 109 30 E
Yuma, *Ariz., U.S.A.* **85 N12** 32 43N 114 37W
Yuma, *Colo., U.S.A.* **80 E3** 40 8N 102 43W
Yuma, B. de, *Dom. Rep.* **89 C6** 18 20N 68 35W
Yumbe, *Uganda* **54 B3** 3 28N 31 15 E
Yumbi, *Dem. Rep. of the Congo* **54 C2** 1 12S 26 15 E
Yumen, *China* **32 C4** 39 50N 97 30 E
Yun Ho →, *China* **35 E9** 39 10N 117 10 E
Yuna, *Australia* **61 E2** 28 20S 115 0 E
Yuncheng, *Henan, China* **34 G8** 35 36N 115 57 E
Yuncheng, *Shanxi, China* **34 G6** 35 2N 111 0 E
Yungas, *Bolivia* **92 G5** 17 0S 66 0W
Yungay, *Chile* **94 D1** 37 10S 72 5W
Yunnan □, *China* **32 D5** 25 0N 102 0 E
Yunta, *Australia* **63 E2** 32 34S 139 36 E
Yunxi, *China* **34 H6** 33 0N 110 22 E
Yupyongdong, *N. Korea* **35 D15** 41 49N 128 53 E
Yurga, *Russia* **26 D9** 55 42N 84 51 E
Yurimaguas, *Peru* **92 E3** 5 55S 76 7W
Yuryung Kaya, *Russia* **27 B12** 72 48N 113 23 E
Yuscarán, *Honduras* **88 D2** 13 58N 86 45W
Yushe, *China* **34 F7** 37 4N 112 58 E
Yushu, *Jilin, China* **35 B14** 44 43N 126 38 E
Yushu, *Qinghai, China* **32 C4** 33 5N 96 55 E
Yutai, *China* **34 G9** 35 0N 116 45 E
Yutian, *China* **35 E9** 39 53N 117 45 E
Yuxarı Qarabağ = Nagorno-Karabakh, *Azerbaijan* **25 F8** 39 55N 46 45 E
Yuxi, *China* **32 D5** 24 30N 102 35 E
Yuzawa, *Japan* **30 E10** 39 10N 140 30 E
Yuzhno-Sakhalinsk, *Russia* **27 E15** 46 58N 142 45 E
Yuzhou, *China* **34 G7** 34 10N 113 28 E
Yvetot, *France* **18 B4** 49 37N 0 44 E

Z

Zaanstad, *Neths.* **15 B4** 52 27N 4 50 E
Zāb al Kabīr →, *Iraq* **44 C4** 36 1N 43 24 E
Zāb aş Şagīr →, *Iraq* **44 C4** 35 17N 43 29 E
Zabaykalsk, *Russia* **27 E12** 49 40N 117 25 E
Zābol, *Iran* **45 D9** 31 0N 61 32 E
Zābolī, *Iran* **45 E9** 27 10N 61 35 E
Zabrze, *Poland* **17 C10** 50 18N 18 50 E
Zacapa, *Guatemala* **88 D2** 14 59N 89 31W
Zacapu, *Mexico* **86 D4** 19 50N 101 43W
Zacatecas, *Mexico* **86 C4** 22 49N 102 34W
Zacatecas □, *Mexico* **86 C4** 23 30N 103 0W
Zacatecoluca, *El Salv.* **88 D2** 13 29N 88 51W
Zachary, *U.S.A.* **81 K9** 30 39N 91 9W
Zacoalco, *Mexico* **86 C4** 20 14N 103 33W
Zacualtipán, *Mexico* **87 C5** 20 39N 98 36W
Zadar, *Croatia* **16 F8** 44 8N 15 14 E
Zadetkyi Kyun, *Burma* **39 H2** 10 0N 98 25 E
Zafarqand, *Iran* **45 C7** 33 11N 52 29 E
Zafra, *Spain* **19 C2** 38 26N 6 30W
Żagań, *Poland* **16 C8** 51 39N 15 22 E
Zagaoua, *Chad* **51 E10** 15 30N 22 24 E
Zagazig, *Egypt* **51 B12** 30 40N 31 30 E
Zāgheh, *Iran* **45 C6** 33 30N 48 42 E
Zagorsk = Sergiyev Posad, *Russia* **24 C6** 56 20N 38 10 E
Zagreb, *Croatia* **16 F9** 45 50N 15 58 E
Zāgros, Kūhhā-ye, *Iran* **45 C6** 33 45N 48 5 E
Zagros Mts. = Zāgros, Kūhhā-ye, *Iran* **45 C6** 33 45N 48 5 E
Zāhedān, *Fārs, Iran* **45 D7** 28 46N 53 52 E
Zāhedān, *Sīstān va Balūchestān, Iran* **45 D9** 29 30N 60 50 E
Zahlah, *Lebanon* **47 B4** 33 52N 35 50 E
Zaïre = Congo →, *Africa* **52 F2** 6 4S 12 24 E
Zaječar, *Serbia, Yug.* **21 C10** 43 53N 22 18 E
Zakamensk, *Russia* **27 D11** 50 23N 103 17 E
Zakhodnaya Dzvina = Daugava →, *Latvia* **9 H21** 57 4N 24 3 E
Zākhū, *Iraq* **44 B4** 37 10N 42 50 E
Zákinthos, *Greece* **21 F9** 37 47N 20 57 E
Zakopane, *Poland* **17 D10** 49 18N 19 57 E
Zákros, *Greece* **23 D8** 35 6N 26 10 E
Zalaegerszeg, *Hungary* **17 E9** 46 53N 16 47 E
Zalău, *Romania* **17 E12** 47 12N 23 3 E
Zaleshchiki = Zalishchyky, *Ukraine* **17 D13** 48 45N 25 45 E
Zalew Wiślany, *Poland* **17 A10** 54 20N 19 50 E
Zalingei, *Sudan* **51 F10** 12 51N 23 29 E
Zalishchyky, *Ukraine* **17 D13** 48 45N 25 45 E
Zama L., *Canada* **72 B5** 58 45N 119 5W
Zambeke, *Dem. Rep. of the Congo* **54 B2** 2 8N 25 17 E
Zambeze →, *Africa* **55 F4** 18 35S 36 20 E
Zambezi = Zambeze →, *Africa* **55 F4** 18 35S 36 20 E
Zambezi, *Zambia* **53 G4** 13 30S 23 15 E
Zambezia □, *Mozam.* **55 F4** 16 15S 37 30 E
Zambia ■, *Africa* **55 F2** 15 0S 28 0 E
Zamboanga, *Phil.* **37 C6** 6 59N 122 3 E
Zamora, *Mexico* **86 D4** 20 0N 102 21W
Zamora, *Spain* **19 B3** 41 30N 5 45W
Zamość, *Poland* **17 C12** 50 43N 23 15 E
Zandvoort, *Neths.* **15 B4** 52 22N 4 32 E
Zanesville, *U.S.A.* **78 G2** 39 56N 82 1W
Zangābād, *Iran* **44 B5** 38 26N 46 44 E
Zangue →, *Mozam.* **55 F4** 17 50S 35 21 E
Zanjān, *Iran* **45 B6** 36 40N 48 35 E
Zanjān □, *Iran* **45 B6** 37 20N 49 30 E
Zanjān →, *Iran* **45 B6** 37 8N 47 47 E
Zante = Zákinthos, *Greece* **21 F9** 37 47N 20 57 E
Zanthus, *Australia* **61 F3** 31 2S 123 34 E
Zanzibar, *Tanzania* **54 D4** 6 12S 39 12 E
Zaouiet El-Kala = Bordj Omar Driss, *Algeria* **50 C7** 28 10N 6 40 E
Zaouiet Reggane, *Algeria* **50 C6** 26 32N 0 3 E
Zaozhuang, *China* **35 G9** 34 50N 117 35 E
Zap Suyu = Zāb al Kabīr →, *Iraq* **44 C4** 36 1N 43 24 E
Zapadnaya Dvina = Daugava →, *Latvia* **9 H21** 57 4N 24 3 E
Západné Beskydy, *Europe* **17 D10** 49 30N 19 0 E
Zapala, *Argentina* **96 D2** 39 0S 70 5W
Zapaleri, Cerro, *Bolivia* **94 A2** 22 49S 67 11W
Zapata, *U.S.A.* **81 M5** 26 55N 99 16W
Zapolyarnyy, *Russia* **24 A5** 69 26N 30 51 E
Zaporizhzhya, *Ukraine* **25 E6** 47 50N 35 10 E
Zaporozhye = Zaporizhzhya, *Ukraine* **25 E6** 47 50N 35 10 E
Zara, *Turkey* **44 B3** 39 58N 37 43 E
Zaragoza, *Coahuila, Mexico* **86 B4** 28 30N 101 0W
Zaragoza, *Nuevo León, Mexico* **87 C5** 24 0N 99 46W
Zaragoza, *Spain* **19 B5** 41 39N 0 53W
Zarand, *Kermān, Iran* **45 D8** 30 46N 56 34 E
Zarand, *Markazī, Iran* **45 C6** 35 18N 50 25 E
Zaranj, *Afghan.* **40 D2** 30 55N 61 55 E
Zarasai, *Lithuania* **9 J22** 55 40N 26 20 E
Zarate, *Argentina* **94 C4** 34 7S 59 0W
Zard, Kūh-e, *Iran* **45 C6** 32 22N 50 4 E
Zāreh, *Iran* **45 C6** 35 7N 49 9 E
Zaria, *Nigeria* **50 F7** 11 0N 7 40 E
Zarneh, *Iran* **44 C5** 33 55N 46 10 E
Zarós, *Greece* **23 D6** 35 8N 24 54 E
Zarqā', Nahr az →, *Jordan* **47 C4** 32 10N 35 37 E
Zarrīn, *Iran* **45 C7** 32 46N 54 37 E
Zaruma, *Ecuador* **92 D3** 3 40S 79 38W
Żary, *Poland* **16 C8** 51 37N 15 10 E
Zarzis, *Tunisia* **51 B8** 33 31N 11 2 E
Zaskar →, *India* **43 B7** 34 13N 77 20 E
Zaskar Mts., *India* **43 C7** 33 15N 77 30 E
Zastron, *S. Africa* **56 E4** 30 18S 27 7 E
Zavāreh, *Iran* **45 C7** 33 29N 52 28 E
Zavitinsk, *Russia* **27 D13** 50 10N 129 20 E
Zavodovski, I., *Antarctica* **5 B1** 56 0S 27 45W
Zawiercie, *Poland* **17 C10** 50 30N 19 24 E
Zāwiyat al Bayḑā = Al Bayḑā, *Libya* **51 B10** 32 50N 21 44 E
Zāyā, *Iraq* **44 C5** 33 33N 44 13 E
Zāyandeh →, *Iran* **45 C7** 32 35N 52 0 E
Zaysan, *Kazakstan* **26 E9** 47 28N 84 52 E
Zaysan, Oz., *Kazakstan* **26 E9** 48 0N 83 0 E
Zayü, *China* **32 D4** 28 48N 97 27 E
Zbarazh, *Ukraine* **17 D13** 49 43N 25 44 E
Zdolbuniv, *Ukraine* **17 C14** 50 30N 26 15 E
Zduńska Wola, *Poland* **17 C10** 51 37N 18 59 E
Zeballos, *Canada* **72 D3** 49 59N 126 50W
Zebediela, *S. Africa* **57 C4** 24 20S 29 17 E
Zeebrugge, *Belgium* **15 C3** 51 19N 3 12 E
Zeehan, *Australia* **62 G4** 41 52S 145 25 E
Zeeland □, *Neths.* **15 C3** 51 30N 3 50 E
Zeerust, *S. Africa* **56 D4** 25 31S 26 4 E
Ẓefat, *Israel* **47 C4** 32 58N 35 29 E
Zeil, Mt., *Australia* **60 D5** 23 30S 132 23 E
Zeila, *Somali Rep.* **46 E3** 11 21N 43 30 E
Zeist, *Neths.* **15 B5** 52 5N 5 15 E
Zeitz, *Germany* **16 C7** 51 2N 12 7 E
Zelenograd, *Russia* **24 C6** 56 1N 37 12 E
Zelenogradsk, *Russia* **9 J19** 54 53N 20 29 E
Zelienople, *U.S.A.* **78 F4** 40 48N 80 8W
Zémio, *C.A.R.* **54 A2** 5 2N 25 5 E
Zemun, *Serbia, Yug.* **21 B9** 44 51N 20 25 E
Zenica, *Bos.-H.* **21 B7** 44 10N 17 57 E
Žepče, *Bos.-H.* **21 B8** 44 28N 18 2 E
Zevenaar, *Neths.* **15 C6** 51 56N 6 5 E
Zeya, *Russia* **27 D13** 53 48N 127 14 E
Zeya →, *Russia* **27 D13** 51 42N 128 53 E
Zêzere →, *Portugal* **19 C1** 39 28N 8 20W
Zghartā, *Lebanon* **47 A4** 34 21N 35 53 E
Zgorzelec, *Poland* **16 C8** 51 10N 15 0 E
Zhabinka, *Belarus* **17 B13** 52 13N 24 2 E
Zhailma, *Kazakstan* **26 D7** 51 37N 61 33 E
Zhambyl, *Kazakstan* **26 E8** 42 54N 71 22 E
Zhangaqazaly, *Kazakstan* **26 E7** 45 48N 62 6 E
Zhangbei, *China* **34 D8** 41 10N 114 45 E
Zhangguangcai Ling, *China* **35 B15** 45 0N 129 0 E
Zhangjiakou, *China* **34 D8** 40 48N 114 55 E
Zhangwu, *China* **35 C12** 42 43N 123 52 E
Zhangye, *China* **32 C5** 38 50N 100 23 E
Zhangzhou, *China* **33 D6** 24 30N 117 35 E
Zhanhua, *China* **35 F10** 37 40N 118 8 E
Zhanjiang, *China* **33 D6** 21 15N 110 20 E
Zhannetty, Ostrov, *Russia* **27 B16** 76 43N 158 0 E
Zhanyi, *China* **32 D5** 25 38N 103 48 E
Zhanyu, *China* **35 B12** 44 30N 122 30 E
Zhao Xian, *China* **34 F8** 37 43N 114 45 E
Zhaocheng, *China* **34 F6** 36 22N 111 38 E
Zhaotong, *China* **32 D5** 27 20N 103 44 E
Zhaoyuan, *Heilongjiang, China* **35 B13** 45 27N 125 0 E
Zhaoyuan, *Shandong, China* **35 F11** 37 20N 120 23 E
Zhashkiv, *Ukraine* **17 D16** 49 15N 30 5 E
Zhashui, *China* **34 H5** 33 40N 109 8 E
Zhayyq →, *Kazakstan* **25 E9** 47 0N 51 48 E
Zhdanov = Mariupol, *Ukraine* **25 E6** 47 5N 37 31 E
Zhecheng, *China* **34 G8** 34 7N 115 20 E
Zhejiang □, *China* **33 D7** 29 0N 120 0 E
Zheleznodorozhnyy, *Russia* **24 B9** 62 35N 50 55 E
Zheleznogorsk-Ilimskiy, *Russia* **27 D11** 56 34N 104 8 E
Zhen'an, *China* **34 H5** 33 27N 109 9 E
Zhengding, *China* **34 E8** 38 8N 114 32 E
Zhengzhou, *China* **34 G7** 34 45N 113 34 E
Zhenlai, *China* **35 B12** 45 50N 123 5 E
Zhenping, *China* **34 H7** 33 10N 112 16 E
Zhenyuan, *China* **34 G4** 35 35N 107 30 E
Zhetiqara, *Kazakstan* **26 D7** 52 11N 61 12 E
Zhezqazghan, *Kazakstan* **26 E7** 47 44N 67 40 E
Zhidan, *China* **34 F5** 36 48N 108 48 E
Zhigansk, *Russia* **27 C13** 66 48N 123 27 E
Zhilinda, *Russia* **27 C12** 70 0N 114 20 E
Zhitomir = Zhytomyr, *Ukraine* **17 C15** 50 20N 28 40 E
Zhlobin, *Belarus* **17 B16** 52 55N 30 0 E
Zhmerinka = Zhmerynka, *Ukraine* **17 D15** 49 2N 28 2 E
Zhmerynka, *Ukraine* **17 D15** 49 2N 28 2 E
Zhob, *Pakistan* **42 D3** 31 20N 69 31 E
Zhob →, *Pakistan* **42 C3** 32 4N 69 50 E
Zhodino = Zhodzina, *Belarus* **17 A15** 54 5N 28 17 E
Zhodzina, *Belarus* **17 A15** 54 5N 28 17 E
Zhokhova, Ostrov, *Russia* **27 B16** 76 4N 152 40 E
Zhongdian, *China* **32 D4** 27 48N 99 42 E
Zhongning, *China* **34 F3** 37 29N 105 40 E
Zhongtiao Shan, *China* **34 G6** 35 0N 111 10 E
Zhongwei, *China* **34 F3** 37 30N 105 12 E
Zhongyang, *China* **34 F6** 37 20N 111 11 E
Zhoucun, *China* **35 F9** 36 47N 117 48 E
Zhouzhi, *China* **34 G5** 34 10N 108 12 E
Zhuanghe, *China* **35 E12** 39 40N 123 0 E
Zhucheng, *China* **35 G10** 36 0N 119 27 E
Zhugqu, *China* **34 H3** 33 40N 104 30 E
Zhumadian, *China* **34 H8** 32 59N 114 2 E
Zhuo Xian = Zhuozhou, *China* **34 E8** 39 28N 115 58 E
Zhuolu, *China* **34 D8** 40 20N 115 12 E
Zhuozhou, *China* **34 E8** 39 28N 115 58 E
Zhuozi, *China* **34 D7** 41 0N 112 25 E
Zhytomyr, *Ukraine* **17 C15** 50 20N 28 40 E
Zīārān, *Iran* **45 B6** 36 7N 50 32 E
Ziarat, *Pakistan* **42 D2** 30 25N 67 49 E
Zibo, *China* **35 F10** 36 47N 118 3 E
Zichang, *China* **34 F5** 37 18N 109 40 E
Zielona Góra, *Poland* **16 C8** 51 57N 15 31 E
Zierikzee, *Neths.* **15 C3** 51 40N 3 55 E
Zigey, *Chad* **51 F9** 14 43N 15 50 E
Zigong, *China* **32 D5** 29 15N 104 48 E
Ziguinchor, *Senegal* **50 F2** 12 35N 16 20W
Zihuatanejo, *Mexico* **86 D4** 17 38N 101 33W
Žilina, *Slovak Rep.* **17 D10** 49 12N 18 42 E
Zillah, *Libya* **51 C9** 28 30N 17 33 E
Zima, *Russia* **27 D11** 54 0N 102 5 E
Zimapán, *Mexico* **87 C5** 20 54N 99 20W
Zimba, *Zambia* **55 F2** 17 20S 26 11 E
Zimbabwe, *Zimbabwe* **55 G3** 20 16S 30 54 E
Zimbabwe ■, *Africa* **55 F3** 19 0S 30 0 E
Zimnicea, *Romania* **17 G13** 43 40N 25 22 E
Zinder, *Niger* **50 F7** 13 48N 9 0 E
Zinga, *Tanzania* **55 D4** 9 16S 38 49 E
Zion National Park, *U.S.A.* **83 H7** 37 15N 113 5W
Ziros, *Greece* **23 D8** 35 5N 26 8 E
Zitácuaro, *Mexico* **86 D4** 19 28N 100 21W
Zitundo, *Mozam.* **57 D5** 26 48S 32 47 E
Ziway, L., *Ethiopia* **46 F2** 8 0N 38 50 E
Ziyang, *China* **34 H5** 32 32N 108 31 E
Zlatograd, *Bulgaria* **21 D11** 41 22N 25 7 E
Zlatoust, *Russia* **24 C10** 55 10N 59 40 E
Zlín, *Czech Rep.* **17 D9** 49 14N 17 40 E
Zmeinogorsk, *Kazakstan* **26 D9** 51 10N 82 13 E
Znojmo, *Czech Rep.* **16 D9** 48 50N 16 2 E
Zobeyrī, *Iran* **44 C5** 34 10N 46 40 E
Zobia, *Dem. Rep. of the Congo* **54 B2** 3 0N 25 59 E
Zoetermeer, *Neths.* **15 B4** 52 3N 4 30 E
Zolochev = Zolochiv, *Ukraine* **17 D13** 49 45N 24 51 E
Zolochiv, *Ukraine* **17 D13** 49 45N 24 51 E
Zomba, *Malawi* **55 F4** 15 22S 35 19 E
Zongo, *Dem. Rep. of the Congo* **52 D3** 4 20N 18 35 E
Zonguldak, *Turkey* **25 F5** 41 28N 31 50 E
Zonqor Pt., *Malta* **23 D2** 35 51N 14 34 E
Zorritos, *Peru* **92 D2** 3 43S 80 40W
Zou Xiang, *China* **34 G9** 35 30N 116 58 E
Zouar, *Chad* **51 D9** 20 30N 16 32 E
Zouérate = Zouîrât, *Mauritania* **50 D3** 22 44N 12 21W
Zouîrât, *Mauritania* **50 D3** 22 44N 12 21W
Zoutkamp, *Neths.* **15 A6** 53 20N 6 18 E
Zrenjanin, *Serbia, Yug.* **21 B9** 45 22N 20 23 E
Ẓufār, *Oman* **46 D5** 17 40N 54 0 E
Zug, *Switz.* **18 C8** 47 10N 8 31 E
Zugspitze, *Germany* **16 E6** 47 25N 10 59 E
Zuid-Holland □, *Neths.* **15 C4** 52 0N 4 35 E
Zuidbeveland, *Neths.* **15 C3** 51 30N 3 50 E
Zuidhorn, *Neths.* **15 A6** 53 15N 6 23 E
Zula, *Eritrea* **46 D2** 15 17N 39 40 E
Zumbo, *Mozam.* **55 F3** 15 35S 30 26 E
Zumpango, *Mexico* **87 D5** 19 48N 99 6W
Zunhua, *China* **35 D9** 40 18N 117 58 E
Zuni, *U.S.A.* **83 J9** 35 4N 108 51W
Zunyi, *China* **32 D5** 27 42N 106 53 E
Zuoquan, *China* **34 F7** 37 5N 113 22 E
Zurbātīyah, *Iraq* **44 C5** 33 9N 46 3 E
Zürich, *Switz.* **18 C8** 47 22N 8 32 E
Zutphen, *Neths.* **15 B6** 52 9N 6 12 E
Zuwārah, *Libya* **51 B8** 32 58N 12 1 E
Zūzan, *Iran* **45 C8** 34 22N 59 53 E
Zverinogolovskoye, *Russia* **26 D7** 54 26N 64 50 E
Zvishavane, *Zimbabwe* **55 G3** 20 17S 30 2 E
Zvolen, *Slovak Rep.* **17 D10** 48 33N 19 10 E
Zwelitsha, *S. Africa* **53 L5** 32 55S 27 22 E
Zwettl, *Austria* **16 D8** 48 35N 15 9 E
Zwickau, *Germany* **16 C7** 50 44N 12 30 E
Zwolle, *Neths.* **15 B6** 52 31N 6 6 E
Zwolle, *U.S.A.* **81 K8** 31 38N 93 39W
Żyrardów, *Poland* **17 B11** 52 3N 20 28 E
Zyryan, *Kazakstan* **26 E9** 49 43N 84 20 E
Zyryanka, *Russia* **27 C16** 65 45N 150 51 E
Zyryanovsk = Zyryan, *Kazakstan* **26 E9** 49 43N 84 20 E
Żywiec, *Poland* **17 D10** 49 42N 19 10 E
Zyyi, *Cyprus* **23 E12** 34 43N 33 20 E

World: Regions in the News

YUGOSLAVIA
Population 10,500,000
(Serb 62.6%, Albanian 16.5%, Montenegrin 5%, Hungarian 3.3%, Muslim 3.2%)
Serbia Population: 5,799,800
(Serb 87.7%, excluding the provinces of Kosovo and Vojvodina)
Kosovo Population: 2,084,4000
(Albanian 81.6%, Serb 9.9%)
Vojvodena Population: 1,980,800
(Serb 56.8%, Hungarian 16.9%)
Montenegro Population: 635,000
(Montenegrin 61.9%, Muslim 14.6%, Albanian 7%)

CROATIA
Population: 4,672,000
(Croat 78.1%, Serb 12.2%)

SLOVENIA
Population: 1,972,000
(Slovene 88%, Croat 3%, Serb 2%)

MACEDONIA (F. Y. R. O. M.)
Population: 2,009,000
(Macedonian 64%, Albanian 21.7%, Turkish 5%, Romanian 3%, Serb 2%)

BOSNIA-HERZEGOVINA
Population: 3,366,000
(Muslim 49%, Serb 31.2%, Croat 17.2%)

AUSTRIA
HUNGARY
SLOVENIA
Ljubljana
Maribor
Zagreb
CROATIA
Rijeka
Osijek
Vukovar
Vojvodina
Novi Sad
Subotica
ROMANIA
Timişoara
Beograd (Belgrade)
Banja Luka
Bihać
BOSNIA-HERZEGOVINA
Tuzla
Zenica
Sarajevo
Mostar
Split
Dubrovnik
ADRIATIC SEA
YUGOSLAVIA
SERBIA
Smederevo
Kraljevo
Niš
MONTENEGRO
Podgorica
Priština
Kosovo
Skopje
MACEDONIA
Bitola
Tirana
ALBANIA
BULGARIA
GREECE
ITALY
Drava
Sava
Danube
Tisa
Morava
0 100 200 km
International boundaries
Republic boundaries
Province boundaries
Capital cities
Dayton Peace Agreement Boundary
Muslim–Croat Federation
Bosnian Serb Republic

FORMER YUGOSLAVIA AND KOSOVO

The former Yugoslavia, a federation of six republics, split apart in 1991–2. Fearing Serb domination, Croatia, Slovenia, Macedonia and Bosnia-Herzegovina declared themselves independent. This left two states, Serbia and Montenegro, to continue as Yugoslavia. The presence in Croatia and Bosnia-Herzegovina of Orthodox Christian Serbs, Roman Catholic Croats, and Muslims led to civil war and 'ethnic cleansing'. In 1995, the war ended when the Dayton Peace Accord affirmed Bosnia-Herzegovina as a single state partitioned into a Muslim-Croat Federation and a Serbian Republic.

But the status of Kosovo, a former autonomous Yugoslav region, remained unresolved. Kosovo's autonomy had been abolished in 1989 and the Albanian-speaking, Muslim Kosovars were forced to accept direct Serbian rule. After 1995, support grew for the rebel Kosovo Liberation Army. The Serbs hit back and thousands of Kosovars were forced to flee their homes. In March 1999, NATO launched an aerial offensive against Serbia in an attempt to halt the 'ethnic cleansing'. A Serb military withdrawal from Kosovo was finally agreed in June.

SERBIA
Prokuplje
Toplica
Novi Pazar
Kopaonik
Leskovac
YUGOSLAVIA
Berane
MONTENEGRO
Mokra Gora
Kosovska Mitrovica
Podujevo
Vučitrn
Sitnica
Peć
Priština
Vranje
Kosovo
Gnjilane
Đakovica
Orahovac
Uroševac
Beli Drim
Suva Reka
ALBANIA
Prizren
Crna Gora
Kukës
Tetovo
Skopje
Šar Planina
MACEDONIA
KOSOVO
0 20 40 km
Capital city
Other towns
International boundaries

TURKEY
Mosul
Irbil
As Sulaymānīyah
SYRIA
Kirkuk
Bākhtaran
Euphrates
Tigris
Ba'qūbah
IRAN
IRAQ
Ar Ramādī
Al 'Azamiyah
Baghdad
Karbalā
Al Ḩillah
Mesopotamia
An Najaf
Al 'Amārah
An Nāşirīyah
Basra
SAUDI ARABIA
Kuwait City
KUWAIT
NO-FLY ZONE
0 100 200 km
Capital cities
Cities
Kurdish region
No-fly zone

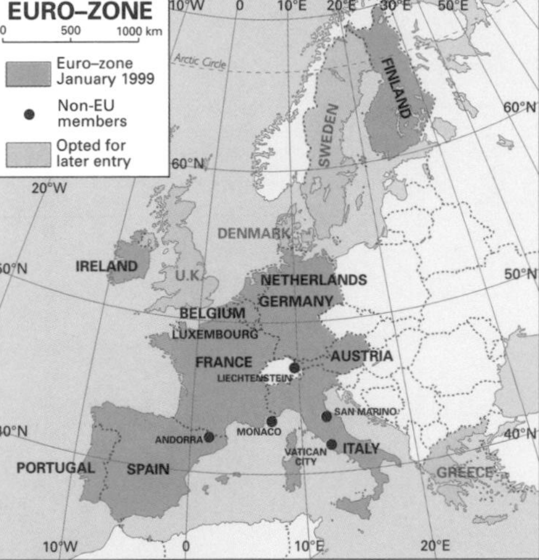
EURO–ZONE
0 500 1000 km
Euro–zone January 1999
Non-EU members
Opted for later entry
Arctic Circle
FINLAND
SWEDEN
DENMARK
IRELAND
U.K.
NETHERLANDS
GERMANY
BELGIUM
LUXEMBOURG
FRANCE
LIECHTENSTEIN
AUSTRIA
SAN MARINO
ANDORRA
MONACO
VATICAN CITY
ITALY
PORTUGAL
SPAIN
GREECE

THE EURO

The euro (€) is the single currency which will eventually replace the national currencies of the countries of the European Economic and Monetary Union (EMU). Euro notes and coins will come into circulation in January 2000. The euro will be used alongside national currencies until July 2002 when it will become the sole legal tender in the EMU countries.

1 euro (€) = US$ 1.66* = £ 0.66*
*market rate 24.05.99

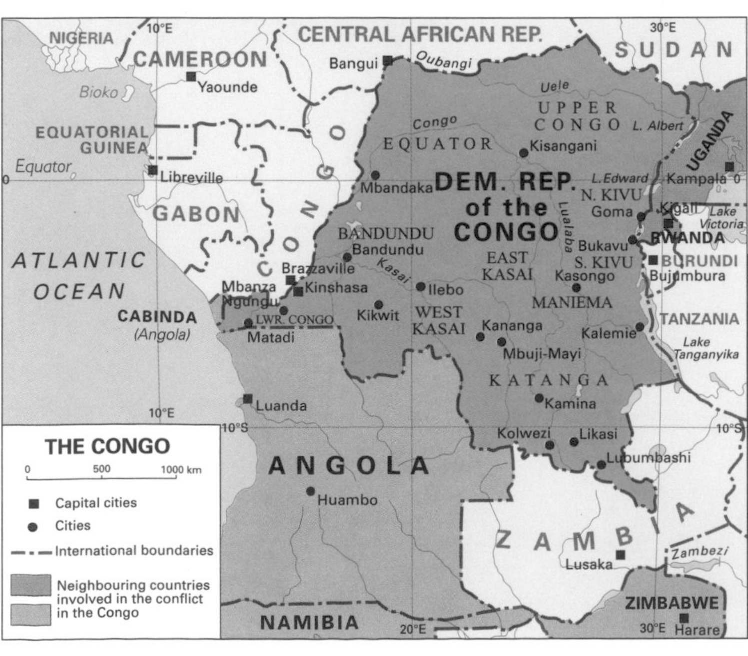
NIGERIA
CENTRAL AFRICAN REP.
SUDAN
CAMEROON
Bangui
Ubangi
Yaounde
Bioko
Uele
UPPER CONGO
L. Albert
EQUATORIAL GUINEA
Equator
EQUATOR
Kisangani
UGANDA
Libreville
Mbandaka
DEM. REP. of the CONGO
L. Edward
Kampala
N. KIVU
GABON
CONGO
Goma
Kigali
RWANDA
Lake Victoria
BANDUNDU
Bandundu
Bukavu
S. KIVU
BURUNDI
Bujumbura
ATLANTIC OCEAN
Brazzaville
Kinshasa
Kasai
Ilebo
EAST KASAI
Kasongo
MANIEMA
Lualaba
CABINDA (Angola)
Kikwit
WEST KASAI
Kananga
Kalemie
TANZANIA
Matadi
Mbuji-Mayi
Lake Tanganyika
KATANGA
Luanda
Kamina
Kolwezi
Likasi
Lubumbashi
ANGOLA
Huambo
ZAMBIA
Lusaka
Zambezi
ZIMBABWE
Harare
NAMIBIA
THE CONGO
0 500 1000 km
Capital cities
Cities
International boundaries
Neighbouring countries involved in the conflict
in the Congo

CONGO

The Congo gained independence from Belgium in 1960 and was renamed Zaïre in 1971. Ethnic rivalries caused instability until 1965, when the country became a one-party state, ruled by President Mobuto. The government allowed the formation of political parties in 1990, but elections were repeatedly postponed. In 1996, fighting broke out in eastern Zaïre, as the Tutsi-Hutu conflict in Burundi and Rwanda spilled over. The rebel leader Laurent Kabila took power in 1997, ousting Mobutu and renaming the country. A rebellion against Kabila broke out in 1998. Rwanda and Uganda supported the rebels, while Angola, Chad, Namibia and Zimbabwe sent troops to assist Kabila.

THE NEAR EAST
0 25 50 km
1949 Armistice Line
1974 Cease-fire Line
Main Jewish settlements in the West Bank and Gaza Strip
Main Palestinian Arab towns in the West Bank and Gaza Strip
Capital cities
Saydā
Beqaa Valley
LEBANON
Litani
Şūr (Tyre)
Qiryat Shemona
SYRIA
Golan Heights
Nahariyya
Zefat
Akko
Yam Kinneret
Hefa
Terverya
Nazerat
MEDITERRANEAN SEA
ISRAEL
Irbid
Hadera
Janīn
West Bank
Tūbās
Netanya
Tūlkarm
Shavel Shomron
Elon More
Kedumim
Nabulus
Qalqīlya
Emanuel
Karne Shomron
Kfar Tapuah
Tel Aviv-Yafo
Elkana
Ariel
Shiloh
As Salt
Rehovot
Al Birah
Rām Allāh
Beit El
El Arīhā (Jericho)
'Ammān
Ashdod
Beit Horon
Maale Adumim
Jerusalem
Ashqelon
Bayt Lahm (Bethlehem)
Efrata
Tkoa
Dead Sea
Halhul
Al Khalīl (Hebron)
Qiryat Arba
Gaza
Gaza Strip
Khān Yūnis
Be'er Sheva
EGYPT
JORDAN

ISRAEL
Population: 5,644,000 (inc. East Jerusalem and Jewish settlers in the areas under Israeli administration. Jewish 82%, Arab Muslim 13.8%, Arab Christian 2.5%, Druze 1.7%)

West Bank
Population: 1,122,900 (Palestinian Arabs 97% [of whom Arab Muslim 85%, Jewish 7%, Christian 8%])

Gaza Strip
Population: 748,400 (Arab 98%)

JORDAN
Population: 4,435,000 (Arab 99% [of whom about 50% are Palestinian Arab])

LEBANON
Population: 3,506,000 (Arab 93% [of whom 83% are Lebanese Arab and 10% Palestinian Arab])

KEY TO WORLD MAP PAGES

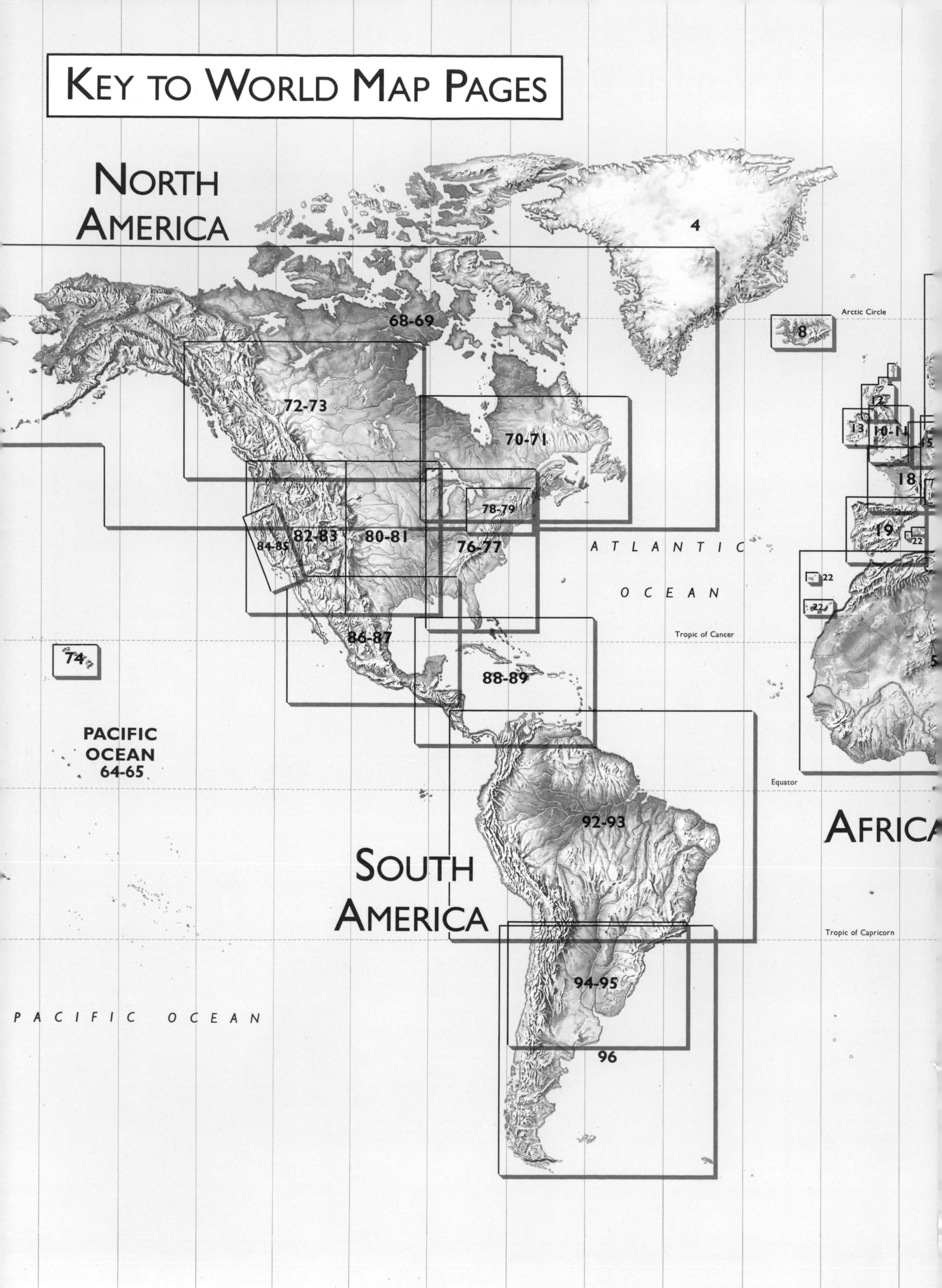

NORTH AMERICA
4
68-69
72-73
70-71
78-79
82-83
80-81
84-85
76-77
86-87
88-89
74
8
Arctic Circle
12
13
10-11
18
19
22
22
22
ATLANTIC
OCEAN
Tropic of Cancer
PACIFIC OCEAN 64-65
Equator
92-93
AFRICA
SOUTH AMERICA
Tropic of Capricorn
94-95
96
PACIFIC OCEAN

Personal Financial Planning Theory and Practice

Michael A. Dalton, Ph.D., JD, CPA, CLU, ChFC, CFP®
James F. Dalton, MBA, MS, CPA/PFS, CFA, CFP®
Randal R. Cangelosi, JD, MBA
Randall S. Guttery, Ph.D., CLU, ChFC
Scott A. Wasserman, CPA/PFS, CLU, ChFC, CASL, RFC, CFP®

KAPLANFinancial™

143 Mallard Street, Suite E
St. Rose, Louisiana 70087
(504) 464-9772 • (504) 461-9860 Fax
www.kaplanfinancial.com

To submit comments or suggestions, please send an email to errata@kaplan.com.

PERSONAL FINANCIAL PLANNING THEORY AND PRACTICE

Published by DF Institute, Inc.

Printed in the United States of America.

ISBN: 1-4195-4049-1

PPN: 4303-2601

05	06	10	9	8	7	6	5	4	3	2	1
J	F	M	A	M	J	J	A	S	O	N	**D**

Other texts in Kaplan Financial's Personal Financial Planning Series include:

ISBN 1-931629-10-2 Understanding Your Financial Calculator
ISBN 1-931629-07-2 Personal Financial Planning Cases and Applications

For additional information on Kaplan Financial's live instructional reviews for the CFP® Certification Examination and related study materials, please email fpsupport@kaplan.com or visit our website at www.kaplanfinancial.com.

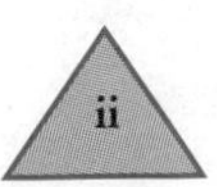

ORIGINAL AUTHORS

MICHAEL A. DALTON, PH.D., JD, CPA, CLU, CHFC, CFP®

- ▲ Former Chair of the Board of Dalton Publications, L.L.C.
- ▲ Former Senior Vice President, Education at BISYS Group
- ▲ Personal financial planning instructor at Georgetown University's Executive Certificate in Financial Planning Program
- ▲ Provider of litigation support for NASD securities arbitration and serves as expert in securities litigation
- ▲ Associate professor of Accounting and Taxation at Loyola University in New Orleans, Louisiana
- ▲ Ph.D. in Accounting from Georgia State University
- ▲ Juris Doctorate from Louisiana State University in Baton Rouge, Louisiana
- ▲ MBA and BBA in Management and Accounting from Georgia State University
- ▲ Former board member of the CFP Board's Board of Examiners, Board of Standards, and Board of Governors
- ▲ Former member (and chair) of the CFP Board's Board of Examiners
- ▲ Member of the Financial Planning Association
- ▲ Member of the *Journal of Financial Planning* Editorial Advisory Board
- ▲ Member of the *Journal of Financial Planning* Editorial Review Board
- ▲ Member of the LSU Law School Board of Trustees (2000 - Present)
- ▲ Author of *Dalton Review for the CFP® Certification Examination: Volume I – Outlines and Study Guides, Volume II – Problems and Solutions, Volume III - Case Exam Book, Mock Exams A-1* and *A-2* (1st – 8th Editions)
- ▲ Author of *Estate Planning for Financial Planners* (1st - 3rd Editions)
- ▲ Author of *Retirement Planning and Employee Benefits for Financial Planners* (1st - 3rd Editions)
- ▲ Co-author of *Dalton CFA® Study Notes Volumes I* and *II* (1st - 2nd Editions)
- ▲ Co-author of *Personal Financial Planning: Theory and Practice* (1st - 3rd Editions)
- ▲ Co-author of *Personal Financial Planning: Cases and Applications* (1st - 4th Editions)
- ▲ Co-author of *Cost Accounting: Traditions and Innovations* published by West Publishing Company
- ▲ Co-author of the *ABCs of Managing Your Money* published by National Endowment for Financial Education

JAMES F. DALTON, MBA, MS, CPA/PFS, CFA, CFP®

- ▲ Senior Vice President of Kaplan Financial
- ▲ Former Senior Manager of an international accounting firm, concentrating in Personal Financial Planning, investment planning, and litigation services
- ▲ MBA from Loyola University New Orleans
- ▲ Masters of Accounting in Taxation from the University of New Orleans
- ▲ BS in accounting from Florida State University in Tallahassee, Florida
- ▲ Member of the CFP Board of Standards July 1996, Comprehensive CFP® Exam Pass Score Committee
- ▲ Member of the AICPA and the Louisiana Society of CPAs
- ▲ Member of the Financial Planning Association
- ▲ Member of the *Journal of Financial Planning* Editorial Review Board
- ▲ Member of the New Orleans Estate Planning Council
- ▲ Author of *Kaplan Financial's Personal Financial Planning Series – Understanding Your Financial Calculator*
- ▲ Author of Kaplan Financial's Understanding Your Financial Calculator for the CFA® Exam
- ▲ Co-author of *BISYS CFA® Study Notes Volumes I and II*
- ▲ Co-author of *Kaplan Financial's Personal Financial Planning Series – Cases and Applications*
- ▲ Co-author of *Kaplan Financial Review for the CFP® Certification Examination: Volume I – Outlines and Study Guides, Volume II – Problems and Solutions, Volume III - Case Exam Book, Mock Exams A-1 and A-2, Financial Planning Flashcards*

CONTRIBUTING AUTHORS

RANDAL R. CANGELOSI, JD, MBA

- ▲ Practicing litigator throughout Louisiana, in commercial law and litigation, wills and trust litigation, environmental law and litigation, medical malpractice defense, and insurance law and litigation
- ▲ Has successfully defended numerous corporations, businesses and doctors in jury and judge tried cases throughout Louisiana
- ▲ J.D. from Loyola University New Orleans
- ▲ Master of Business from Loyola University New Orleans
- ▲ BS in Finance from Louisiana State University
- ▲ Member of the American & Federal Bar Associations
- ▲ Member of the New Orleans and Baton Rouge Bar Associations
- ▲ Former Chairman of New Orleans Bar Association, Community Service Committee and Food and Clothing Drives
- ▲ Co-author of *Professional Ethics for Financial Planners*

RANDALL S. GUTTERY, PH.D., CLU, CHFC

- ▲ CFP Program Director at the University of North Texas for 10 years
- ▲ Associate Professor of Finance and Real Estate at the University of North Texas
- ▲ Ph.D. in Finance at the University of Connecticut
- ▲ Master of Finance from Louisiana State University
- ▲ BBA in Finance and Risk Management from the University of Texas
- ▲ Holds a Louisiana real estate brokers license
- ▲ Published several academic articles and professional journals
- ▲ Published a Real Estate Principles text for Prentice-Hall
- ▲ Research has been featured in several print media

SCOTT A. WASSERMAN, CPA/PFS, CLU, CHFC, CASL, RFC, CFP®

- ▲ Director in the Tax Technology practice of an international accounting firm, specializing in financial planning software solutions.
- ▲ BBA from the University of Texas in Austin, Texas
- ▲ Member of American Institute of Certified Public Accountants
- ▲ Member of the Texas Society of Certified Public Accountants
- ▲ Member of the Financial Planning Association
- ▲ Former Board member of the Financial Planning Association of Dallas-Ft. Worth
- ▲ Instructor of various financial planning courses, including Life Insurance Law, Health Insurance Financing, Understanding the Older Client, and Estate Planning Applications
- ▲ Financial planning speaker for large employee groups and insurance agents, covering areas including investments, income taxes, estate planning, and retirement planning
- ▲ Co-author of *Kaplan Financial's Financial Planning Flashcards*
- ▲ Instructor of Tax, Retirement, and Estates for the Kaplan Financial Review for the CFP® Certification Examination
- ▲ Contributing author of *Kaplan Financial Review for the CFP® Certification Examination: Volume I – Outlines and Study Guides* and *Kaplan Financial Review for the CFP® Certification Examination: Volume II – Problems and Solutions*
- ▲ Technical reviewer of *Kaplan Financial Review for the CFP® Certification Examination: Volume III – Case Exam Book* and *Kaplan Financial Review for the CFP® Certification Examination: Mock Exams*

CONTRIBUTORS TO CURRENT EDITION

KATHY L. BERLIN

- Content Developer and Technical Editor for Kaplan Financial
- Successfully passed November 2004 CFP® Certification Examination
- Certified Public Accountant (Inactive)
- BA from Loyola University of New Orleans, Louisiana
- Former CFO a of large nonprofit organization

CINDY R. HART, CLU, CHFC, CFP®

- Director of Product Development, Advanced Designations for Kaplan Financial
- BS in Business Administration from Louisiana State University in Baton Rouge, Louisiana
- Member of the Financial Planning Association
- Former Director of Marketing Development for an international insurance and financial services company

LISA T. KELEHER, MS, CFA

- Content Developer and Technical Editor for Kaplan Financial
- Successfully passed November 2003 CFP® Certification Examination
- MS from Tulane University in New Orleans, Louisiana
- BA from University of San Diego
- Member of the CFA Institute
- Former financial analyst for real estate developer and property management companies

BOBBY M. KOSH, AAMS, CFP®

- Content Developer and Technical Editor for Kaplan Financial
- BS in International Trade & Finance/Economics from Louisiana State University in Baton Rouge, Louisiana
- Former client account manager for an international mutual fund and brokerage company

MARGUERITE F. MERRITT, M.ED.

- Senior Copy Editor for Kaplan Financial
- M.Ed. from the University of New Orleans in New Orleans, Louisiana
- BS from the University of New Orleans in New Orleans, Louisiana
- Former communications specialist for an international utility company

CLAUDIA C. SCHMITT

- Administrative Assistant and Page Layout Specialist for Kaplan Financial
- Former Administrative Assistant at Tulane Medical School and Children's Hospital in New Orleans, LA

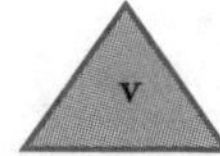

PREFACE

Personal Financial Planning – Theory and Practice was written in response to numerous pleas from instructors and students requesting a fundamental financial planning textbook. Through this text, the authors hope to convey their knowledge of financial planning and reflect their enthusiasm for the subject.

This text is written for graduate and undergraduate students who are interested in acquiring an in-depth understanding of personal financial planning from a professional planning viewpoint. The text is also intended to serve as a reference for practicing professional financial planners.

CONTENT AND THEMES

The Financial Planner's Pyramid of Knowledge is depicted throughout this text. The base of the pyramid identifies the core knowledge that every financial planner should possess. Chapters 8 – 17 detail this foundation of knowledge upon which a successful financial planning profession can be built. The second layer of the pyramid, presented in Chapters 6 and 7, focuses on the basic financial planning tools a financial planner must be familiar with and capable of implementing. The third and fourth layers of the pyramid, presented in Chapters 1 – 5, describe the basic financial planning skills every professional financial planner must possess. Finally, the pyramid's pinnacle explores the financial planning profession and the ethical responsibilities faced by a professional financial planner. Chapters 18 and 19 cover these topics.

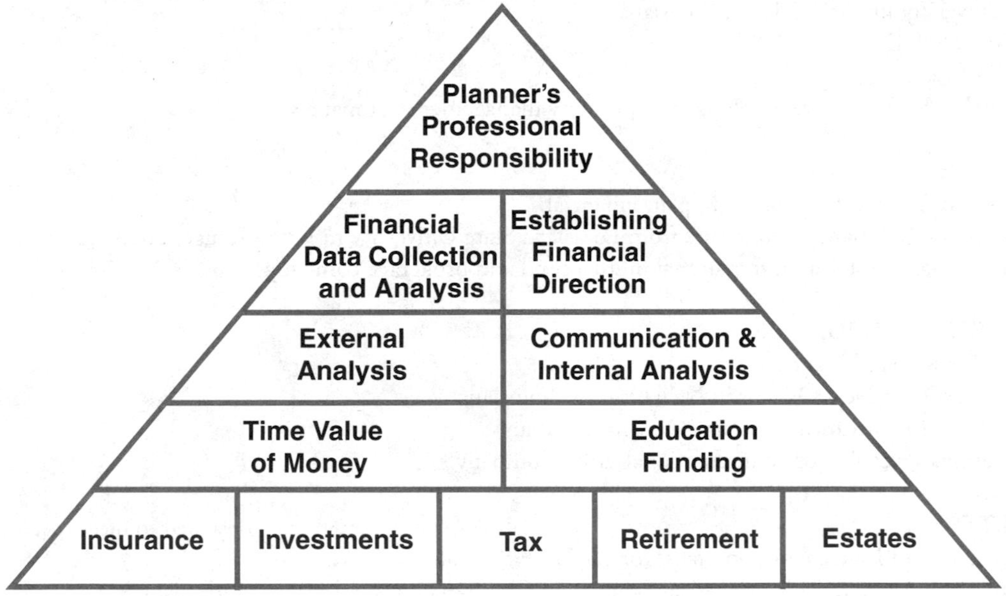
Planner's Professional Responsibility
Financial Data Collection and Analysis
Establishing Financial Direction
External Analysis
Communication & Internal Analysis
Time Value of Money
Education Funding
Insurance
Investments
Tax
Retirement
Estates

Throughout the text, two themes are identified. The first theme of the text is that personal financial planning is about attaining financial goals and managing financial risks. There are perhaps as many goals as there are clients. Generally, the majority of clients are looking to achieve one or more of the following goals: to attain financial security for themselves, to accumulate assets to fund their children's education, to save a specific lump sum to cover future expenditures, or to prepare their assets for transfer to heirs. There are many risks threatening the attainment of these goals, including disability, ill health and untimely death. This text will identify these risks and present ways to manage them.

The second theme emphasized throughout the text is that the professional practice of personal financial planning emphasizes data collection and analysis. For the professional financial planner, this requires knowledge of external environmental influences and skill at data collection, interviewing and administering questionnaires. Analytical skills are invaluable when applying time-value-of-money concepts, and when preparing and analyzing personal financial statements. Excellent communication skills, including displaying empathy and using verbal and nonverbal pacing, are essential when dealing with clients. Finally, helping clients set reasonable goals that are objectively measurable in time and form, and using good follow-up and evaluation skills, are most valuable to the professional financial planner.

SPECIAL FEATURES

A variety of tools and presentation methods are used throughout this text to assist in the learning process. Some of the features presented in this text that are designed to enhance the readers' understanding and learning process include:

Section Break Features

- **The Financial Planner's Pyramid of Knowledge** – The financial planning pyramid is shown on every section break to focus the student's attention to the section topic. We have shaded the corresponding area on the pyramid to identify the broad knowledge topic discussed in the section. The pyramid's intricacies are discussed more fully in Chapter 1.
- **Knowledge Level "In Brief"** – The knowledge level "In Brief" section allows us to be more specific on the topics covered in the section. The topics are listed by difficulty, with the easier topics in the top box, medium topics in the middle, and more difficult topics in the bottom box. This was done to help the student be aware of and prepared for the difficulty of the topics. It also allowed us to give a brief "keyword" overview of the section.
- **Goal and Risk Identification** – Common goals and risks are identified on the section break to focus the reader's attention on the ever-present conflict between goal attainment and risk avoidance.
- **Data Collection and Analysis Requirements** – Data collection and data analysis requirements are identified to help the reader become adept at identifying relevant information.

Chapter Features

- **Professional Focus** – Responses to questions posed to practicing professionals are presented throughout the text to provide real-life application scenarios.
- **"Where On The Web"** – Each chapter has a "Where On The Web" section that provides the reader with useful website domains.
- **Bolded Keywords** – Keywords appear in **boldfaced type** throughout the text to assist in the identification of important concepts and terminology. Keyword definitions appear in the margin for quick access to important concepts.
- **Examples** – Examples are used frequently to illustrate the concepts being discussed.
- **Exhibits** – The written text is enhanced and simplified by using exhibits where appropriate.

4TH EDITION CHANGES

- In response to editorial comments from instructors and students, sections have been added on the following topics: bankruptcy laws, tort law, financial institutions, FDIC insurance, and negotiable instruments.
- The Insurance section has been expanded to discuss insurance as a risk management tool designed to meet specific insurance needs. The risk management process is covered more extensively. Universal life and long-term care insurance are detailed. Additional examples have been added to clarify insurance topics.
- The Investment section is now comprised of an introductory chapter and three supplements. "Introduction to Investment Planning" provides a survey of investment theory and terms. The supplements that follow offer more detailed information on investment concepts and the characteristics of equity, fixed-income, and mutual fund securities.
- The Tax section has been updated for law changes through 2005. Material moved to a tax supplement includes information on tax planning, the IRS audit selection and screening process, family limited partnerships, and taxation and legal liabilities of partnerships, corporations and S corporations.
- Retirement statistics have been updated. Information regarding qualified plans has been detailed, and a discussion of hybrid plans has been added.
- The Estates section has been combined into one introductory chapter and several exhibits have been moved to an Appendix in the section.

ACKNOWLEDGEMENTS & SPECIAL THANKS

We are most appreciative of the tremendous support and encouragement we have received throughout this project. We are extremely grateful to the instructors and program directors of CFP Board-Registered programs who provided valuable comments concerning past editions. We are fortunate to have dedicated, careful readers at several institutions who were willing to share their needs, expectations, and time with us. We also owe a debt of gratitude to all the reviewers and students who have read and commented on many drafts of *Personal Financial Planning – Theory and Practice*.

This book would not have been possible without the extraordinary dedication, skill, and knowledge of those people who helped with previous editions: Joe Bellows, Cassie Bradley, Amy Breaux, Phyllis Brierre, Allison Dalton, Donna Dalton, Jan Dupont, C.J. Guenzel, Jacob Guidry, Ann Lopez, Marguerite Merritt, Rob Sabrio and Kristi Tafalla. To each of these individuals we extend our deepest gratitude and appreciation.

We owe a special thanks to David Bergmann, Peter Blackwell, Robert Borek, Jr., Cassie Bradley, Connie Brezik, James Coleman, Joe Devanny, Edwin Duett, David Durr, Jill Peetluk Feinstein, John Gisolfi, Robert Glovsky, E. Vance Grange, Charlotte Hartmann-Hansen, A. Perry Hubbs II, Robert Kirby, Stan Roesler, John Rossi, Bradley Van Vechten, and Evan Wardner for their contribution to the "Professional Focus" feature of the text. We greatly appreciate their willingness to offer their valuable time and professional observations.

The 4th edition is the result of thoughtful and thorough comments from many people. We feel it is only fitting to mention a few special people who went above and beyond. We would like to thank Peter Blackwell, Joe Gillice, and Robert Redmond who reviewed the text and offered many valuable comments. Finally, we would like to thank the National Association of Securities Dealers who allowed us to use their Registered Investment Advisor materials.

We have received so much help from so many people, it is possible that we have inadvertently overlooked thanking someone. If so, it is our shortcoming, and we apologize in advance. Please let us know if you are that someone, and we will make it right in our next printing.

PROFESSIONAL FOCUS

DAVID R. BERGMANN, CLU, CHFC, EA, CFP®

David is a two-time past President and Chairman of the Los Angeles Society of the Institute of Certified Financial Planners. He served five years on the National Board of Directors of the Institute and has been a seven-time mentor in the Financial Planning Association's Residency Program. Starting in 2006 David will be a FPA Residency Dean. David has twice been named to the Mutual Fund Magazine's Top 100 Financial Advisors list. He has been quoted in numerous national publications including the Wall Street Journal and Money Magazine and has served on the editorial review board of The Journal of Financial Planning since the publication's inception. David teaches financial analysis and federal income taxation at UCLA Extension in the Personal Financial Planning Certification Program. He oversees UCLA's internship program as well. David has twenty years of experience as a CFP® practitioner.

PETER BLACKWELL, MBA, CFP®

Peter has served as the Academic Coordinator and Program Director of the CFP Board-Approved Education Program at University of Central Florida since 1997 after serving in the same capacity for four years at Rollins College in Winter Park, FL. Peter has authored teaching materials and exam questions and cases, in addition to the supplemental teaching materials used in the UCF Financial Planning Certificate Program. Prior to becoming a full-time educator, Peter was a full-time CFP® practitioner and co-owner of Aegis Financial Advisors, Inc., a Registered Investment Advisor. Peter is an instructor for the Kaplan Financial Review for the CFP Certification Examination and many of Kaplan Financial's corporate classes.

ROBERT W. BOREK, JR., CLU, CHFC, CFP®

Robert is currently managing an independent financial consulting firm in Honolulu, Hawaii. He is also a member of the Financial Planning Association, the Honolulu Rotary, the Hawaii Chamber of Commerce and the Hawaii Committee for Employer Support of the Guard and Reserve.

CASSIE BRADLEY, PH.D., CFP®

Cassie is an Assistant Professor at Mercer University in Atlanta, GA and also is President of Market Results, a business advisory and educational services firm. Previously, she was also a Senior Tax Manager with Federal Express Corporation. She is a member of the American Accounting Association and the American Taxation Association. Cassie is also a co-author to the *Kaplan Financial Review for the CFP® Certification Examination: Volume I—Outlines and Study Guides* and a contributing author to the *Kaplan Financial Review for the CFP® Certification Examination: Volume II—Problems and Solutions.*

CONNIE BREZIK, CPA/PFS

Connie is President of Asset Strategies, Inc., where she is an investment advisor and financial planner. She manages the Casper, Wyoming, and Scottsdale, Arizona offices of ASI. Connie previously worked with a large national accounting and consulting firm. She is a frequent speaker and authors a monthly column on financial planning and investment topics. *Worth* named Connie as one of the top advisors in the country for three years. In 2001 and 2002, *Accounting Today* included Connie in the list of top people to know in financial planning. Connie is on the board of the Association of CPA Financial Planners and has served on various committees for the PFP Division of the AICPA. She is a member of the Wyoming and Arizona Societies of CPAs, the Financial Planning Association (FPA), the National Association of Personal Financial Advisors (NAPFA), the Arizona Valley Estate Planners and the All-Star Financial Group (ASFG). Connie is a founding shareholder of National Advisors Trust.

JAMES COLEMAN, PH.D. CPA, CFP®

James is an Assistant Professor at Mercer University Atlanta, Georgia. He previously held several management positions in the Finance, Investor Relations and Public Relations departments at Federal Express Corporation. James is also an instructor for the BISYS Review for the CFP® Certification Examination where he teaches investments, insurance, and fundamentals of financial planning.

JOE DEVANNEY, MA, CLU, PFP

Joe is the President of Insurance/Investment Corporation of Mission Hills, California, which specializes in providing consultation services in insurance and investments. He also teaches several courses in Insurance and Financial Planning at the UCLA Extension Program. Joe just received the continuing education field's equivalent of a lifetime achievement award, also known as the University of Continuing Education Association's Award for Excellence in Teaching.

EDWIN DUETT, PH.D.

Edwin is professor of finance at Mississippi State University and is the Peter K. Lutken Chair of Insurance at the university. He is a member of American Risk and Insurance, the Financial Management Association, the Southern Finance Association and the Financial Planning Association. Edwin also serves on the editorial board of *The Journal of Economics and Finance* and on the review board of *Financial Decisions.*

DAVID DURR, PH.D., CFA, CFP®

David holds the Endowed Chair in Investment Management at Murray State University, Murray, Kentucky. He is associate professor of finance at Murray State University where he teaches classes in investments and portfolio management. David is a member of the Financial Planning Association and the American Finance Association. He has published articles in *Advances in Investment Analysis and Portfolio Management, Review of Quantitative Finance and Accounting,* and *Advances in Taxation.* David is also an instructor for the BISYS Review for the CFP® Certification Examination where he teaches investments, insurance, and fundamentals of financial planning.

JILL PEETLUK FEINSTEIN, CFP®

Jill is a Long Island financial planner in private practice. She has taught in the CFP Board-Registered program at the C.W. Post Campus of Long Island University. She has also been a consultant to Chase Bank, training their employees to better educate the public on financial alternatives. As a respected financial planner and educator, Jill was invited to serve on the Item Writing Committee of the CFP Board of Standards and Practices and has also served on the Board of the Long Island Society of the Financial Planning Association.

JOHN A. GISOLFI, MS, RFC, CFP®

John is an Adjunct professor of Personal Financial Planning at Moravian College in Bethlehem, Pennsylvania and an independent contractor serving as Director of Plan Design at Integrated Asset Management. He has conducted advanced educational conferences at both Muhlenberg College and Lehigh University on strategies for money management as well as other presentations on Modern Portfolio Theory. He holds NASD Series 7 and 63 general securities licenses, a Series 65 Investment Advisor license, and a Series 24 Securities Principal license.

ROBERT J. GLOVSKY, JD, LLM, CLU, CHFC, CFP®

Bob is the President of Mintz Levin Financial Advisors, LLC, providing customized financial planning and investment advisory services to individuals and families. He is also the Director of Boston University's Program for Financial Planners and served as Chair of the CFP Board of Examiners. Bob has lectured and taught extensively throughout the country on financial planning topics. *Worth* magazine selected him as one of the "Best Financial Advisors in the Country" for each of the past six years. Bob is renowned for his financial expertise, and currently hosts the "The Bob Glovsky Show" airing five days a week on Boston business radio.

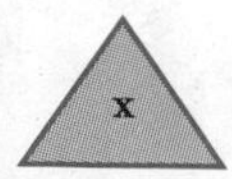

E. VANCE GRANGE, PH.D. CPA, CFP®

Vance is Director of Tax and Personal Financial Planning Programs in the College of Business at Utah State University. He is also the President of Beacon Financial Planning LLC. Vance is a member of the American Institute of Certified Public Accountants and of the Financial Planning Association where he serves on the board of directors of its Utah Chapter. He is also an academic affiliate of the National Association of Personal Financial Advisors. Vance served as a member and chair of the CFP Board's Board of Examiners and has served on the CFP Board of Governors. He is currently involved with others in research to determine factors associated with success on the CFP® Certification Examination and is assisting the Academy of Financial Services and CFP Board in their efforts to develop a model curriculum in personal financial planning.

CHARLOTTE HARTMANN-HANSEN, MS, CLU, CHFC, LUTCF

Charlotte is president of Hartmann-Hansen Financial Services as a financial services consultant/insurance advisor since 1978. She is a Registered Representative and Investment Advisor Representative with Woodbury Financial Services, Inc. and an adjunct professor with Moravian College's Division of Continuing and Graduate Studies CFP Board-approved certificate program where she teaches and serves on their advisory board. She is active in her community providing programs and seminars for communities, professional associations (as a board member and president), non-profit groups, businesses, Chambers of Commerce and both locally and regionally for Rotary International.

A. PERRY HUBBS II, MBA, CFP®

Perry is a CFP® practitioner with expertise in asset allocation and pension planning. He is the President of Arden & Associates, a full service financial planning company. He is Program Head for the Financial Planners Certification Program with the Division of Professional & Workforce Development at the University of South Florida where he teaches investments, retirement planning and employee benefits at the Master's level. He is the past president of the Tampa Bay Society of the Institute of Certified Financial Planners where he was Board Member for ten years.

ROBERT KIRBY, JD, CFP®

Robert is an attorney in private law practice in Winter Park, Florida, specializing in estate planning, probate litigation, and trust administration. He is also an educator, having been an Assistant Professor of Financial Planning at Florida Institute of Technology since 1997 and an adjunct instructor in trusts and estates at the University of Central Florida since 1995. Robert is a member of the State Bars of both Florida and Texas.

STAN ROESLER, MBA, CFP®

Stan is the Principal of PDP Financial Planning Group in Vernon, Connecticut, and the Program Coordinator for the CFP Board-Registered Program at Manchester Community College in Manchester, Connecticut. He is registered with the Connecticut Department of Banking as an Investment Adviser.

JOHN D. ROSSI, III, MBA, CPA/PFS, CMA, CFM, CVA, CFP®

John is a full-time member of the Accounting Faculty at Moravian College in Bethlehem, PA. He is also the Director of Personal Financial Planning Education and Administration and Moravian College's CFP Board-Registered program. John is a frequent presenter of workshops and continuing professional education programs on technical, tax, valuation, and business management issues. John is also president of JR3 Management Services, P.C. providing accounting, tax and consulting services, including business valuation, financial planning, financial reporting, and taxation. John also writes on tax and accounting issues as a contributing columnist for the *Eastern Pennsylvania Business Journal.*

BRADLEY VAN VECHTEN, CLU, CHFC, CIMA, CFP®

Brad is a veteran financial planner, investment manager analyst, and a Registered Investment Advisor. He holds NASD Series 7 and 63 general securities licenses, a Series 65 Investment Advisor license, and a Series 24 General Securities Principal license. He also holds State of California Life Insurance and Annuity licenses, and Long Term Care license. Bradley is also an active member of The Financial Planning Association and The Investment Management Consultants Association.

EVAN S. WARDNER, MBA, CFP®

Evan is the Program Director of the CFP Board-Registered Program at Medaille College in Buffalo, New York. A former president of the Western New York Chapter of the Financial Planning Association, he remains active in the local chapter leadership. In addition to his work in education, Evan is a private practitioner advising individual and business clients across New York State.

BASIC FINANCIAL PLANNING SKILLS 1

Chapter 1: Introduction To Personal Financial Planning 3

Personal Financial Planning Defined 4
Benefits of Personal Financial Planning 4
Financial Success is a Relative Concept 5
Resource Allocation in Financial Planning 6
Why do People Hire Professional Financial Planners? 7
The Financial Planner's Pyramid of Knowledge 7
Basic Financial Planning Skills 8
Basic Financial Planning Tools 9
Core Topics 9
The Financial Planning Profession 11
Discussion Questions 12

Chapter 2: External Environmental Analysis 13

The External Environment 14
Analyzing the External Environment 17
Why Study the External Environment? 18
The Economic and Legal Environments 18
Importance of the Economic Environment 19
The General Economy 20
Business Cycles 24
Inflation 27
Monetary and Fiscal Policy 31
The Nature of Interest Rates 32
Expansion and Recession 33
Forecasting the Economy – Index of Leading Economic Indicators 33
Importance of the Legal Environment 35
Torts 35
Property Ownership 37
Consumer Protection 37
Worker Protection (Employer/Employee Relations) 41
Financial Institutions 42
FDIC Insurance 44
Negotiable Instruments 47
Investor Protection (The Securities Acts of 1933 and 1934) 48
Forms of Business Organizations 49
Importance of the Social Environment 49
Importance of the Technological Environment 50
Importance of the Political Environment 51
Importance of the Taxation Environment 51
Discussion Questions 54
Exercises 54
Problems 55

Chapter 3: Communication and Internal Environmental Analysis 57

Communication Skills 58
Be Respectful of Your Client 58
Communicate with Your Client 59
Professional Liability 62
Educate Your Client 63
Understand the Client's Thinking Phase 64
Internal Analysis 67
Life Cycle Positioning 67
Attitudes and Beliefs 72
Special Needs 73
Financial Position 76
Client's Perception of Their Financial Situation 77
Discussion Questions 79
Exercises 79
Problems 80
Appendix 3-A: Client Data Questionnaire 81

Chapter 4: Personal Financial Statements (Preparation and Analysis) 91

Introduction 92
Decision-Making Uses of Financial Statements and Financial Statement Analysis 92
Rules Regarding Financial Statements 93
Preparation of Financial Statements 93
The Balance Sheet 93
Balance Sheet Terms and Presentation Order 94
Categories and Classifications of Assets 95
Categories and Classifications of Liabilities 96
Valuation of Assets and Liabilities 97
The Nelson Family Balance Sheet 97
Valuation of Assets and Liabilities—The Nelsons 100
Information Sources 100
Identification of Ownership of Assets and Liabilities 103
Footnotes to the Balance Sheet 103
The Income and Expense Statement 103
Income and Expense Statement Terms and Order of Their Presentation 104
Information Sources 104
Compromise in Information Reporting 107
The Relationship of the Balance Sheet to the Income and Expense Statement 107
The Statement of Cash Flows 107
Other Classification Issues 109
Adjustments to Cash Flows from Operations 109
Rationales for Cash Flow Categories 111
The Statement of Changes in Net Worth 111
Nelson Example Recap 114

Financial Analysis of Personal Financial Statements 115
Ratio Analysis 115
Vertical Analysis 125
Growth Analysis 128
Limitations of Financial Statement Analysis 128
Sensitivity Analysis 129
Risk Analysis 129
Budgeting 129
Description 129
Steps 129
Nelson Budgeting Plan 130
Saving and Consumption Habits 133
Debt Management 133
Personal Use—Assets and Liabilities 133
Home Mortgages 134
Discussion Questions 139
Exercises 139
Problems 142

Chapter 5: Establishing Financial Direction 145
The Process 146
Step One – Develop the Mission 149
Step Two – Identify Relevant Environmental Information 150
Step Three – Establish Financial Goals – 151
Step Four – Develop Financial Objectives 154
Step Five – SWOT Analysis 157
Step Six – Formulate Feasible Strategy Alternatives 159
Step Seven – Select the Most Appropriate Strategy 162
Step Eight – Strategy Implementation and Monitoring 165
Discussion Questions 167
Exercises 167
Problems 167
Chapter 5 Supplement169
Calculations for Retirement Needs and Key West Home for the Nelsons 169

BASIC FINANCIAL PLANNING TOOLS 173

Chapter 6: Time Value of Money 175
Understanding Time Value of Money 176
Future Value and The Power of Compound Interest 177
Basic Tools for Time Value of Money (TVM) Analysis 179
Timelines 179
TVM Tables 179
Financial Calculators 180
Computer Software 181
Accumulation Schedules 181
Future Value of an Ordinary Annuity (FVOA) 182
FVOA Timeline 182
FVOA Using Mathematics 182
FVOA Using TVM Tables 183
FVOA Using a Financial Calculator 183
FVOA Using an Accumulation Schedule 184
Future Value of an Annuity Due (FVAD) 184
FVAD Timeline 185
FVAD Using Mathematics 185
FVAD Using TVM Tables 186
FVAD Using a Financial Calculator 186
FVAD Using an Accumulation Schedule 187
Comparison of Ordinary Annuity and Annuity Due Calculations 187
Present Value of a dollar (PV) 188
PV Timeline 189
PV Using Mathematics 189
PV Using TVM Tables 189
PV Using a Financial Calculator 190
PV Using an Accumulation Schedule 190
Present Value of an Ordinary Annuity (PVOA) 191
PVOA Timeline 191
PVOA Using Mathematics 192
PVOA Using TVM Tables 193
PVOA Using a Financial Calculator 194
PVOA Using an Accumulation Schedule 194
Present Value of an Annuity Due (PVAD) 194
PVAD Timeline 195
PVAD Using Mathematics 195
PVAD Using TVM Tables 196
PVAD Using a Financial Calculator 196
PVAD Using an Accumulation Schedule 197
Other TVM Concepts 197
Uneven Cash Flows 197
Combining Sum Certains with Annuities 199
Net Present Value Analysis 201
Internal Rate of Return (IRR) 202
Yield to Maturity 203
Solving for Term Given the Other Variables 205
Selecting the Rate of Interest for Accumulating or Discounting 205
Serial Payments 207
Perpetuties 209
Other TVM Tools 209
Amortization Tables 209
The Rule of 72 212
Discussion Questions 215
Exercises 215
Problems 217

Chapter 7: Education Funding 219
Introduction 220
Issues and Goals 221
Information Gathering 222

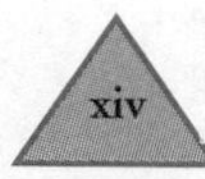

Determining Financial Need 224
Financial Aid Programs 226
Federal Pell Grants 226
Direct and FFEL Stafford Loans 227
PLUS Loans 229
Consolidation Loans 229
Campus-Based Student Financial Aid 230
State Governmental Aid 231
Other Financial Aid Sources 231
Tax Advantages From Educational Expenses and Tax Issues 232
Qualified Tuition Plans 233
Prepaid Tuition Plans 233
Savings Plans 234
Coverdell Education Savings Accounts 236
Traditional IRA 237
Roth IRA 237
The HOPE Scholarship Credit 238
The Lifetime Learning Credit 238
Series EE Bonds 239
Uniform Gift to Minor's Act 239
Uniform Transfer to Minor's Act 239
Interest on Educational Loans 240
Employer's Educational Assistance Program 240
Deduction for Qualified Higher Education Expenses 241
Equity Lines of Credit 241
Highlights of Benefits for Higher Education 241
Educational Funding/Savings Regimen Example 243
Investment Strategies to Accomplish Education Goals 246
Discussion Questions 249
Exercises 249
Problems 251

INSURANCE PLANNING 253

Chapter 8: An Introduction to Insurance and Risk Management 255
Introduction 256
Understanding Risk 256
Risk Classification 256
Pure versus Speculative Risk 256
Dynamic versus Static Risk 257
Subjective versus Objective Risk 257
Particular versus Fundamental Risk 257
Financial versus Nonfinancial Risk 257
Probability of Loss 258
Law of Large Numbers 258
Responses to Pure Risk 259
Risk Avoidance 259
Risk Reduction 259
Risk Retention or Assumption 260
Risk Transfer 260
Insurance as a Risk Management Tool 260
Transfer Of Losses 261
Sharing Losses with Others 261
Causes of Insured Losses 262
Perils 262
Hazards 262
Adverse Selection 263
Insurable Losses 264
Insurance versus Gambling 264
Requisites for an Insurable Risk 264
The Law of Insurance Contracts 265
Elements of a Valid Contract 266
Legal Principles of the Insurance Contract 267
Legal Form 270
Distinguishing Characteristics of Insurance Contracts 270
The Law of Agency 271
Agents and Brokers 271
Agency Relationships 272
Important Features of Insurance Contracts 273
Exclusions 273
Riders and Endorsements 273
Valuation of Insured Losses 273
Coinsurance 275
Individual Loss Exposures and Insurance Coverages 276
Perils that Can Reduce and/or Eliminate the Ability to Earn Income 276
Perils that Can Destroy or Deplete Existing Assets 277
Selecting an Insurance Company 278
Rating Agencies 278
NAIC Criteria 279
Characteristics of Insurance Companies 280
Types of Ownership 280
Insurance Underwriting 281
Reinsurance 281
Federal and State Regulation 281
The Risk Management Process 282
Determining the Objectives of the Risk Management Program 282
Identifying the Risk Exposure 282
Evaluating the Identified Risks 283
Determining and Selecting the Best Risk-Management Alternative 283
Implementing a Risk-Management Plan Based on the Selected Alternatives 284
Periodically Evaluating and Reviewing the Risk Management Program 284
Discussion Questions 286
Exercises 286

Chapter 9: Managing Life, Health and Disability Risks 289

Introduction 291
Identifying Risks Associated with Premature Death 291
Inadequate Financial Resources 291
Estate Preservation 292
Measuring Needs related to premature death 293
Human Life Value Approach 294
Financial Needs Approach 295
Capital Retention Approach 298
Individual Life Insurance Policies 300
Term Insurance 300
Whole Life Insurance 303
Universal Life Insurance 310
Group Life Insurance 314
Group Term Insurance 315
Group Whole Life Insurance 315
Group Universal Life Insurance 315
Policy Replacement 316
Life Insurance Policy Provisions 317
Life Insurance Settlement Options 320
Annuity Contracts 321
Types of Annuities 322
Timing of Annuity Payments 322
Taxation of Life Insurance and Annuities 324
Life Insurance 324
Viatical Agreements 326
Annuities 327
Individual Health Insurance 327
Purpose 327
Cost Concerns 328
Eligibility 328
Medical Expense Insurance 328
Major Medical Insurance 329
Long-Term Care Insurance 330
Health and Disability Insurance Policy Provisions 338
Group Health Insurance 339
Eligibility 339
Characteristics 340
Portability of Group Plans 346
Discussion Questions 347
Exercises 347
Problems 349
CASE 351

Chapter 10: Personal Property and Liability Insurance 355

Introduction 356
Personal Property and Liability Insurance 356
Homeowners (HO) Insurance: Basic Coverage 357
Section I Coverage 358
Summary of Section II Coverage 362
Homeowners (HO) Insurance: Basic Forms 365
HO-2: Broad Form 366
HO-3: Special Form 366
HO-4: Contents Broad Form (for tenants) 366
HO-5: Comprehensive Form 366
HO-6: Unit Owners Form (for condominium owners) 366
HO-8: Modified Form 367
Homeowners (HO) Insurance: Additional Coverages 367
Homeowners (HO) Insurance: Endorsements 368
Replacement Cost for Personal Property 368
Inflation Protection 368
Earthquake Endorsement 368
Water Backup Coverage 369
Building Law & Ordinance Coverage 369
Personal Injury 369
Open Perils 369
Homeowners Insurance Contractual Conditions 369
Section I Conditions 369
Section II Conditions 372
Sections I and II Conditions 372
Automobile Insurance 375
Personal Auto Policy (PAP) Coverages 375
Policy Overview 375
Part A: Liability Coverage 376
Part B: Medical Payments 380
Part C: Uninsured Motorists 381
Part D: Coverage for Damage to Your Auto 382
Part E: Duties after an Accident or Loss 384
Part F: General Provisions 384
Legal Liability 384
Personal Liability Umbrella Policy 385
Purpose 385
Characteristics 385
Exclusions 386
Business and Professional Use of Property and Liability Insurance 386
The Commercial Package Policy (CPP) 386
Inland Marine Policies 386
The Business Owner's Policy (BOP) 386
Business Liability Insurance 387
Workers Compensation 387
Business Auto 387
Business Liability Umbrella 387
Malpractice Insurance 387
Errors and Omissions 387
Product Liability 388
Discussion Questions 390
Exercises 390
Problems 391
Cases 393
The Bannisters 393
The Nelsons 395

Chapter 11: Social Security and Other Social Insurance 399

Overview of the U.S. Social Security System 400
The History of Social Security Benefits 401
Social Security Taxes and Contributions 402
The Social Security Trust Funds and Their Relative Solvency 403
Social Security Benefits – Eligibility and Calculations 405
Covered Workers and Insured Status 405
Social Security Beneficiaries 406
Social Security Retirement Benefits – A Closer Look 407
The Social Security Statement 407
The Retirement Benefit Calculation 408
Taxation of Social Security Benefits 415
Other Social Security Benefits 416
Disability Benefits and Disability Insured 416
Family Benefits 416
Survivors Benefits 417
The Maximum Family Benefit 418
Other Medicare Health Plan Choices 421
Applying for Medicare Benefits and Coverage 422
Supplemental Security Income Benefits 423
Filing for Social Security Claims 423
Social Security Changes for 2005 424
Other Issues 425
Effect of Marriage or Divorce on Benefits 425
Change of Name 425
Leaving the United States 425
Discussion Questions 427
Exercises 427
Problems 428
Appendix 11.1: Social Security Statement 430
Appendix 11.2: Form 7004 434

INVESTMENT, INCOME TAX, BUSINESS, RETIREMENT AND ESTATE PLANNING 436

Chapter 12: Introduction to Investment Concepts 439

Introduction to Investing 440
Establishing Financial Goals 440
Typical Financial Planning Goals 440
Common Investment Goals 441
Budgeting 442
Methods of Increasing Savings 443
Investment Risks 444
Systematic Risks 445
Unsystematic Risks 447
Risk and Return 448
Liquidity and Marketability 449
Investment Choices 449
Lending Investments 449
Ownership Investments in Business (Common and Preferred Stock) 450
Ownership Investments in Real Estate 451
Derivatives 452
Direct vs. Indirect Investing 454
Historical Performance 454
Measures of Risk 455
Beta 455
Standard Deviation 455
Semivariance 455
Measures of Return 456
Holding Period Return 456
Arithmetic Mean 456
Geometric Mean 457
Internal Rate of Return 458
Real Rate of Return 459
Modern Portfolio Theory 459
Software Inputs 461
Software Outputs 465
Investment Strategies and Theories 468
Efficient Market Hypothesis 468
Active vs. Passive Investing 469
Indexing 469
Timing the Market 470
Discussion Questions 472
Exercises 472
Problems 473

Chapter 12 Supplement A: Fixed-Income Securities 475

Basic Concepts of Lending Securities 476
Valuation of Fixed-Income Securities 476
Basic Calculation Example 477
Calculation Inputs 478
Measures of Return 479
Current Yield 479
Yield to Maturity 480
Yield to Maturity for a Zero-Coupon Bond 481
Yield to Call (YTC) 482
Comparing Corporate Returns and Municipals Returns 482
Types of Fixed-Income Securities 484
The Money Market 484
Treasury Notes and Bonds 486
United States Savings Bonds 488
Federal Agency Securities 491
Municipal Bonds 491
Corporate Bonds 492

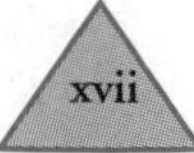

Convertible Bonds 493
Mortgage-Backed Securities and Collateralized Mortgage Obligations 494
Rating Agencies 496
Risks of Fixed-Income Securities 498
Interest-Rate Risk 498
Default (or Credit) Risk 500
Reinvestment-Rate Risk 500
Call Risk 501
Exchange-Rate Risk 501
Liquidity Risk 501
Volatility of Fixed-Income Securities 502
Coupon Rate 502
Maturity 502
Term Structure of Interest Rates 503
Yield Curves 503
Yield Curve Theories 504
Duration & Immunization 506
Calculating Duration 506
Duration as a Measure of a Bond's Volatility 508
Estimating the Change in the Price of a Bond Based on Changes in Interest Rates 509
Using Duration to Immunize Bond Portfolios 510
Traditional Methods of Immunizing Bond Portfolios 512

Chapter 12 Supplement B: Equity Securities 515

Introduction 516
Basic Concepts of Ownership-Type Investments 516
What Ownership Means 516
Types of Equity Securities 519
Common Stock 519
Preferred Stock 522
Foreign Securities 523
Risks of Equity Securities 525
Systematic Risks 525
Unsystematic Risks 527
Equity Markets and Benchmarks 528
Primary Market 528
Secondary Market 529
Third and Fourth Markets 529
Market Indexes and Averages 530
Benchmarks 533
Measures of Return 534
Holding Period Return 534
Arithmetic Mean 534
Geometric Mean 535
Time-Weighted and Dollar-Weighted Returns 536
Dividend Yield 539
Purchasing Equity Securities 539
Long Positions 539
Short Positions 539
Margin Accounts 540
Types of Orders 542
Methods of Analysis 544
Technical Analysis 544
Fundamental Analysis 545
Valuation Models 546
Valuing Preferred Stock 546
Dividend Discount Model 546
Price to Earnings (P/E) Ratio 547
Valuing the Company versus Valuing the Stock 548
Capital Asset Pricing Model 549

Chapter 12 Supplement C: Mutual Funds 553

Introduction to Mutual Funds 554
Types of Investment Companies 555
Unit Investment Trusts 556
Exchange Traded Funds (ETFs) 556
Closed-End Investment Companies 557
Open-End Investment Companies (Mutual Funds) 560
Mutual Fund Fees 562
Loads or Sales Charges 562
Other Mutual Fund Fees 562
Mutual Fund Classification 563
Load versus No-Load Funds 563
Classes of Load Fund Shares 563
How Do Fund Expenses Impact Performance? 564
Expense Ratios for Different Types of Funds 565
Advantages of Mutual Funds 565
Low Initial Investment 565
Diversification 566
Ease of Access 566
Professional Management 566
Tax Efficiency of Management Fees 567
Liquidity 567
Transaction Cost Efficiency 567
Variety of Mutual Funds 567
Services 567
Disadvantages of Mutual Funds 568
Performance 568
Fees, Loads, and Expenses 569
The Abundance of Choices 569
Liquidity 569
Execution 569
Classification System for Mutual Funds 569
Built-In Gains 570
Types and Objectives of Mutual Funds 570
Money Market Mutual Funds 572
Fixed-Income Mutual Funds 573
Equity Mutual Funds 575
Hybrid or Balanced Funds 575
Asset Allocation Using Mutual Funds 576

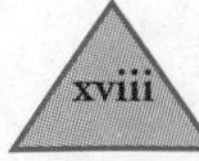

How Do Professional Investment Advisers Select Mutual Funds? 578
Examine the Prospectus 578
Modern Portfolio Theory (MPT) Statistics and Performance Measures 584
R2 (Coefficient of Determination) 584
Beta 584
Measures of Performance 585
Issues To Look For When Managing Portfolios Of Mutual Funds 587
Changing Asset Size 587
Style Shift 588
Manager Changes 588
Capital Gain Exposure 588

Chapter 13: Individual Income Tax and Tax Planning 591

Income Tax Planning 592
History 592
Objectives of the Federal Income Tax Law 592
Individual Income Tax Rates 593
Ordinary Rates 593
Capital Gain Rates 594
Determining Income Tax Liability 598
Total Income and Gross Income 598
Adjusted Gross Income (AGI) 599
Itemized Deductions and the Standard Deduction 599
Personal and Dependency Exemptions 601
Taxable Income and Tax Rates 602
Tax Credits 602
IRS Guidance 603
Penalties and Interest 604
Payroll Taxes 605
FICA Taxes for Employers and Employees 606
Self-Employment Tax 606
Federal Unemployment Tax Act 608
Tax-Advantaged Investments 608
Investment in Tax-Exempt Securities 609
Tax Shelters 609
Acceleration of Deductions 610
Deferral of Tax Gains 610
Exemption Opportunities 611
In Conclusion 612
Discussion Questions 614
Exercises 614
Problems 617
Case Scenario 619
Appendix 13.1: 2005 Tax Rates and Brackets 623
Appendix 13.2: Form W-2 624

Chapter 14: Business Entities 625

Business Entities 626
Sole Proprietorship 626
Management Operation and Decision Making of a Proprietorship 627
Legal Liability of a Proprietorship 627
Taxation of a Proprietorship 627
Partnership 628
Management Operation and Decision Making of a Partnership 629
Legal Liability of a Partnership 629
Taxation of a Partnership 630
Limited Liability Partnership 631
Management Operation and Decision Making of a Limited Liability Partnership 631
Legal Liability of a Limited Liability Partnership 631
Taxation of Limited Liability Partnerships 632
Corporation 632
Management Operation and Decision Making of a Corporation 632
Legal Liability of a Corporation 633
Taxation of a Corporation 633
S Corporation 635
Management Operation and Decision Making of an S Corporation 636
Legal Liability of an S Corporation 636
Taxation of an S Corporation 636
Limited Liability Company 637
Management Operation and Decision Making of a Limited Liability Company 638
Legal Liability of a Limited Liability Company 639
Taxation of a Limited Liability Company 639
Selecting the Proper Business Legal Form 640
Simplicity of Formation and Operation 641
Ownership Restrictions 641
Limited Liability 642
Management Operations 642
Tax Characteristics 643
Discussion Questions 645
Exercises 645
Problems 647
Appendix 14.1: Schedule C of Form 1040 649
Appendix 14.2: Schedule SE (2004) 650
Appendix 14.3: Form 1065—Schedule K-1 651
Appendix 14.4: Corporation schedule K-1 652
Appendix 14.5: Form 8832 653

Chapter 14: Tax Planning Supplement 655

Data Collection and Risk Analysis 656
Client Questionnaire 656
Prior Income Tax Returns 656
Information Forms 657
Tax Avoidance vs. Tax Evasion 658

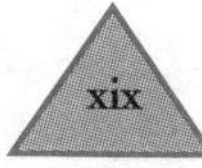

Audit Process 658
Selection and Screening Process 659
Types of Audits 660
Outcomes of Audits 660
Business Entities 662
Partnership 662
Taxation of a Partnership 662
Family Limited Partnership 663
Management Operation and Decision Making of a Family Limited Partnership 664
Legal Liability of a Family Limited Partnership 664
Taxation of a Family Limited Partnership 664
Corporation 664
Legal Liability of a Corporation 664
Taxation of a Corporation 665
S Corporation 665
Taxation of an S Corporation 665

Chapter 15: Introduction to Retirement Planning 667

Introduction 668
Basic Factors Affecting Retirement Planning 668
Remaining Work Life Expectancy (RWLE) 668
Retirement Life Expectancy (RLE) 669
The WLE and the RLE Relationship 670
Savings Concepts 671
Savings Amount 671
Savings Rate 672
Timing of Savings 672
Investment Decisions 673
Inflation 674
Defining The Retirement Goal (needs) 675
Planning for Retirement—Pretax or After Tax 676
Wage Replacement Ratio (WRR) 676
Calculating the Wage Replacement Ratio 677
The Sources Of Retirement Income 680
Social Security 680
Private Pension and Company-Sponsored Retirement Plans 681
Personal Savings 681
Qualitative Factors in Retirement – Advising Clients 682
Summary Of Factors Affecting Retirement Planning 683
Risks to Financial Independence 684
Capital Needs Analysis 685
Basic Planning – Annuity Method 685
Accurate Assumptions are Essential 687
Advanced Planning – Capital Preservation Model (CP) 688
Advanced Planning – Purchasing Power Preservation Model (PPP) 689
Discussion Questions 692
Exercises 692
Problems 694

Chapter 16: Basic Retirement Plans 695

Retirement Plans 696
Qualified Retirement Plans 696
Characteristics of Qualified Retirement Plans 697
Disadvantages of Qualified Retirement Plans 701
Benefits of Tax Deferral 705
Types of Qualified Retirement Plans 707
Pension Plans 707
Profit-Sharing Plans 708
Defined-Benefit, Defined-Contribution, and Target/Age-Weighted (Hybrid) Plans 710
Target/Age-Weighted Plan. 712
Contributory Versus Noncontributory Plans 713
Corporate Versus Keogh Plans 713
Other Tax-Advantaged Plans 715
Individual Retirement Account (IRA) or IRA Annuity 715
Simplified Employee Pensions (SEP) 717
SIMPLE (IRA) Plans 717
403(b) Plans 718
Distributions from Qualified and Other Tax-Advantaged Plans 719
Nonqualified Plans 720
Deferred-Compensation Plans 721
Section 457 Plans 721
Split-Dollar Life Insurance 722
Employee Stock Option Plan 722
The Financial PLanner's Role In Retirement Planning 723
Discussion Questions 725
Exercises 725
Problems 727

Chapter 17: Introduction to Estate Planning 729

Basics Of Estate Planning 730
Estate Planning Reform 730
Estate Planning Defined 730
The Objectives of Estate Planning 730
The Estate Planning Team 731
The Estate Planning Process 732
Collecting Client Information and Defining Transfer Objectives 732
Basic Documents Included In An Estate Plan 733
Wills 733
Power of Attorney 735
Durable Power of Attorney for Health Care or Property 735
Living Wills and Advanced Medical Directives 736
A Side Instruction Letter or Personal Instruction Letter 736
The Probate Process Defined 736
Property Passing Through Probate 737
Property Passing Outside of the Probate Process 739
Advantages of the Probate Process 739
Disadvantages of the Probate Process 739
Ownership And Transfer of Property 739
Probate and Property Interests (Title and Ownership) 740

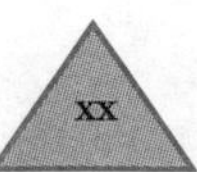

Less Than Complete Ownership Interests 741
Methods of Transfer 742
Consequences of Property Transfers 742
Introduction To Trusts 743
Grantor Trusts 746
Reducing the Gross Estate 747
The Use of Life Insurance in Estate Planning 748
Common Estate Planning Mistakes 749
Invalid, Out-of-Date, or Poorly Drafted Wills 749
Simple Wills ("Sweetheart" or "I Love You" Wills) 749
Improperly Arranged or Inadequate Life Insurance 749
Possible Adverse Consequences of Jointly Held Property 750
Estate Liquidity Problems 750
Wrong Executor/Trustee/Manager 750
The Unified Gift and Estate Transfer Tax System 752
The Federal Gift Tax System 754
Purpose and Definition 754
Annual Exclusion 755
Applicable Credit Amount 758
Qualified Transfers 758
Gifts to Spouses 759
Payments for Support 759
Reporting and Paying Taxes 759
The Federal Estate Tax System 762
Purpose and Definition 762
Reporting and Paying Taxes 763
The Gross Estate 763
Deductions From the Gross Estate 764
The Charitable Deduction 765
Definition 765
Types of Charitable Bequests 765
The Marital Deduction 766
Definition 766
Qualifications for the Marital Deduction 766
Direct Bequests to a Spouse 767
Qualified Terminable Interest Property Trust (QTIP) 767
Power of Appointment Trust 768
Optimizing the Marital Deduction 768
The Bypass Trust (Credit Equivalency) 768
The Mechanics of the Bypass Trust (Credit Equivalency) 769
Use of Disclaimers 771
Alien Surviving Spouses 771
Generation-Skipping Transfer Tax (GSTT) 772
The Role of the Financial Planner in Estate Planning 772
Concluding Comments on the Unification Scheme of Gifts and Estates 773
Discussion Questions 776
Exercises 776
Problems 781
Case Scenario 782
Personal Background and Information 782
General Goals (not prioritized) 783
Insurance Information 783
Investment Information 783
Income Tax Information 784
Education Information 784
Gifts, Estates, Trusts, and Will Information 784
Relevant External Environmental Information 784
Appendix 17.3: Power of Attorney 790
Appendix 17.4: medical power of attorney 792

THE FINANCIAL PLANNING PROFESSION 797

Chapter 18: The Practice of Financial Planning 799

Introduction 800
The Financial Planning Profession 800
Financial Planning Institutions 801
Financial Planning Professionals 803
Compensation Methods 805
Compliance Issues 806
Developing a Professional Practice 808
Building a Practice 808
Maintaining Clients 809
Education and Continuing Education 810
Technology 810
Discussion Questions 811

Chapter 19: Ethical Responsibilities 813

Ethics, Law, and Codes of Ethics 814
CFP Board and the Code of Ethics 815
Note on Civil Liability 816
Principle 1: Integrity 817
Rules that Relate to the Principle of Integrity 817
Principle 2: Objectivity 820
Rules that Relate to the Principle of Objectivity 820
Principle 3: Competence 821
Rules that Relate to the Principle of Competence 822
Principle 4: Fairness 822
Rules that Relate to the Principle of Fairness 824
Principle 5: Confidentiality 827
Rules that Relate to the Principle of Confidentiality 827
Principle 6: Professionalism 829
Rules that Relate to the Principle of Professionalism 830
Principle 7: Diligence 833
Rules that Relate to the Principle of Diligence 833
Disciplinary Rules And Procedures 834
Notes on Burdens of Proof 834
Grounds for and Forms of Discipline 835
Report, Findings of Fact, and Recommendation 837
Conviction of a Crime or Professional Suspension 838

Settlement Procedure 838
Required Action after Revocation or Suspension 838
The Practice Standards 839
The 100 Series 839
The 200 Series 839
The 300 Series 840
The 400 Series 840
The 500 Series 841
The 600 Series 841
The Importance of Ethics 842
Discussion Questions 843

APPENDICES 845

Appendix A
Comprehensive Case 847
Appendix B-1
Present Value of a Dollar 853
Appendix B-1
Present Value of a Dollar (continued) 854
Appendix B-2
Future Value of a Dollar 855
Appendix B-2
Future Value of a Dollar (continued) 856
Appendix B-3
Present Value of an Ordinary Annuity 857
Appendix B-3
Present Value of an Ordinary Annuity (continued) 858
Appendix B-4
Future Value of an Ordinary Annuity 859
Appendix B-4
Future Value of an Ordinary Annuity (continued) 860
Appendix B-5
Present Value of an Annuity Due 861
Appendix B-5
Present Value of an Annuity Due (continued) 862
Appendix B-6
Future Value of an Annuity Due 863
Appendix B-6
Future Value of an Annuity Due (Continued) 864
Appendix C
Regulatory Requirements 865
Regulatory Requirements—Federal Securities Regulation 865
Introduction 865
The Securities Act of 1933 865
The Securities Exchange Act of 1934 (SEA) 866
NASD 867
The Investment Advisors Act of 1940 867
Registration 869
Reform of Previous Acts 870
Investment Company Act of 1940 871
Appendix D
Topic List for the CFP® Certification Examination 873

GLOSSARY 875

INDEX 903

Basic Financial Planning Skills

in BRIEF

- Personal financial planning
- The Financial Planner's Pyramid of Knowledge
- The external environment
- Communication skills of the financial planner
- Internal analysis
- Life cycle positioning

↓

- Financial statement preparation
- Ratio analysis and comparison to benchmarks
- Trend analysis
- Sensitivity and risk analysis

↓

- Financial mission
- Financial goals
- Financial objectives
- Alternative strategies
- Strategy selection and financial direction

SECTION I

Basic Financial Planning Skills

CHAPTER 1 Introduction to Personal Financial Planning
CHAPTER 2 External Environmental Analysis
CHAPTER 3 Communication and Internal Environmental Analysis
CHAPTER 4 Financial Data Collection and Analysis
CHAPTER 5 Establishing Financial Direction

Risks

- Inadequate data collection
- Incorrect data analysis
- Miscommunication to client
- Poor strategy
- No client buy-in

Data Collection

- Economic information
- Legal information
- Personal information
- Financial information
- Tax returns
- Mission
- Goals
- Objectives
- Strategic alternatives

Goals

- Establish appropriate mission statement
- Establish goals
- Establish objectives

Data Analysis

- Economic analysis
- Personal financial analysis
- Savings analysis
- Investment analysis
- Risk tolerance of client
- Strategic alternatives

CHAPTER 1

Introduction To Personal Financial Planning

LEARNING OBJECTIVES:

After learning the material in this chapter, you will be able to:

1. Define personal financial planning.
2. Discuss the benefits of personal financial planning.
3. Explain how the financial planning process promotes efficient allocation of a client's resources.
4. Explain how financial success is a relative concept.
5. Identify why people hire professional financial planners.
6. Describe the Financial Planner's Pyramid of Knowledge and explain the importance of each component.

PERSONAL FINANCIAL PLANNING DEFINED

personal financial planning - the process, both artistic and scientific, of formulating, implementing and monitoring multifunctional decisions that enable an individual or family to achieve financial goals

Comprehensive **personal financial planning** is the process, both artistic and scientific, of formulating, implementing and monitoring multifunctional decisions that enable an individual or family to achieve financial goals. Personal financial planning involves the management of personal financial risks through cost benefit analysis. It capitalizes on personal and financial strengths while managing financial risks and weaknesses. Financial planning professionals and those studying financial planning should understand and appreciate the comprehensive nature of a competently prepared personal financial plan and what it is intended to accomplish for the person who implements it effectively.

BENEFITS OF PERSONAL FINANCIAL PLANNING

A financial plan integrates a financial mission, goals and objectives into one cohesive plan that allocates financial resources consistently. Individuals and families with no formal financial plan actually have an *informal* financial plan. This informal financial plan is their historical pattern of financial decisions and financial behavior which, when woven together, establishes their informal plan. For example, consistent late debt repayments suggest a pattern (plan), and such a pattern eventually leads to financial consequences. Conversely, consistent long-term savings and investment without any formal plan creates a pattern (plan) that also leads to financial consequences. The historical pattern of personal or family financial behavior is as difficult to change as any other personal habit. Thus, the professional financial planner is not only a strategist and planner, but may also serve as counselor and financial therapist.

benefits of personal financial planning -
- goals identified are more likely to be achieved
- helps to clearly identify risk exposures
- is proactive rather than reactive
- creates a framework for feedback, evaluation and control
- establishes measurable goals and expectations
- develops an improved awareness of financial choices
- provides an opportunity for an increased commitment to financial goals

Clients can derive many **benefits from the process of personal financial planning.** Perhaps the most important benefit is that goals identified and planned for are more likely to be achieved. The planning process helps to clearly identify risks that can undermine goals. Once identified, these risks can be managed with a variety of techniques. The financial planning process is one of learning, growing and choosing wisely. The process is proactive rather than reactive, thus giving clients more control over their financial destiny. By using a more logical, systematic and rational approach to decision-making, clients make better strategic choices about using resources. The process also creates a framework for feedback, evaluation and control. It establishes measurable goals and expectations that can be compared to actual results.

During the financial planning process, the client develops an improved awareness of financial choices and of how internal and external environments affect those choices. The process also provides the client an opportunity to increase commitment to selected goals. When clients and their families understand what they want to achieve, why they want to achieve it, and how and when it can be achieved, they often take ownership of their financial plan and become more committed to it.

A comprehensive personal financial plan helps to establish rationality and reality and purge the client of "pie in the sky" ideas and wishful thinking. For example, it is common for persons to want to retire early and maintain their preretirement lifestyle while currently spending more than 100 percent of their personal disposable income with no plan to save or invest. A comprehensive personal financial plan will quickly demonstrate the irrationality of such an approach and assist the client in identifying changes necessary to achieve a more realistic plan.

The financial planning process brings financial order and discipline. It instills confidence that goals can be achieved and identifies the behavioral changes necessary to accomplish those goals. It provides a forum for rationalizing the need for change and helps to view change as an opportunity rather than a threat.

Financially successful individuals—not necessarily those who are wealthy, but, rather, those who meet their financial goals—tend to do more financial planning to prepare themselves for the inevitable fluctuations in their internal and external environments. They tend to make more informed financial decisions. They also tend to better anticipate both the short-run and long-run consequences of their decisions. Conversely, individuals who are not as financially successful, tend to underestimate the value of planning and may attribute their lack of financial success to uncontrollable factors such as a poor economy, foreign competition, government interference, or just bad luck.

There are no absolutes in financial planning any more than there are absolutes about anything in the future. Financial planning will not guarantee desired results. The ultimate outcome of a plan may vary from its prediction for a variety of reasons. The probability is, however, that the more we plan, the better we get at planning and the less risky our plan will be.

FINANCIAL SUCCESS IS A RELATIVE CONCEPT

Financial success means different things to different people. The fisherman who lives in a poor village in a developing country and who has a slightly larger boat than most of the other local fishermen may feel financially successful. Conversely, the millionaire whose friends are all billionaires, may feel less financially successful. In a way, financial success is a comparison with the client's own benchmarks or standards. Thus, from the client's perspective, financial success is both a relative concept and a subjective one. The professional financial planner needs to keep in mind that, to a particular client, financial success is a relative concept, the description of which may be subjectively determined by the client.

financial success - for most individuals, financial success means accomplishing one's financial goals

While **subjectivity** tends to dominate the client's thinking about financial success, **objectivity** should dominate the planner's thinking about financial planning. Accomplishing specific goals is objectively determined if objectively defined. Risks that exist in the external environment are objective and real to the professional planner. The client may have a subjective perception of the same risks. For example, the risk of untimely death can be measured actuarially, regardless of the subjective perception of the client. Another example of objectivity is recognizing the risk of permanent disability for a particular job. Consider the example of the NFL running back. The National Football League knows (and teams know, too) that the average playing life expectancy for a professional running back is approximately four years. Some players, through poor performance, are cut from the roster, and others may suffer a disabling injury on the playing field. The number of running backs who are disabled each year is a predictable percentage, league-wide. Regardless of how the players subjectively feel about their chances of suffering a disabling injury, it is mathematically objective that a certain percentage of running backs will be injured and will be unable to play in any given year. With full knowledge of this objective risk and its catastrophic financial consequences, a professional financial planner should strongly advise his running back client to purchase long-term disability insurance that pays benefits if the player is injured while playing professional football. Most professional planners would agree with that

subjectivity - relating to the client's perception of reality

objectivity - relating to facts without distortion by personal feelings or prejudices

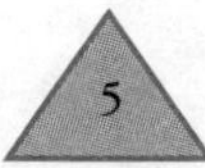

advice even though the policy premiums will be extremely high. (The premiums are high because the insurers also understand the objective risks, and they set premiums that will cover losses and make a profit.)

RESOURCE ALLOCATION IN FINANCIAL PLANNING

personal utility curves - economic curves that describe the satisfaction that an individual receives from a selected item and/or additional units of that item

opportunity cost - the highest valued alternative not chosen

Financial planning is about making financial choices and allocating scarce resources. People make choices because scarcity exists. At any moment in time, all people want the highest level of overall satisfaction from their choices. People are aware from an early age that there are alternative financial choices to be made, such as whether to consume today or to defer consumption until later. The internal psychological analysis that people perform when they decide among choices is a subjective evaluation and application of their own **personal utility curves** to the alternatives identified and presented to them. Personal utility curves are subjectively based and reflect our knowledge, values, and beliefs and, therefore, may be quite different for each person. Some individuals place a high value on spending time alone while some value spending time with others in social settings. If a client believes there is no tomorrow, he may as well consume today. If, however, he believes in a long "tomorrow" during which he plans not to work (some call it retirement), he may be willing to forego consumption today, deferring those unconsumed resources for the future.

When making choices, we are faced with alternatives. Each alternative poses risks and consequences. Doing nothing is always one alternative. The highest-valued alternative not chosen is called the **opportunity cost**. Opportunity cost represents what is forgone by choosing another alternative. For example, if a client chooses to spend $2,500 on a vacation cruise as an alternative to saving for the future, the opportunity cost is the value of the $2,500 in the client's investment portfolio at a future point in time. Five years after taking the cruise, the client has fond memories and beautiful photos of the trip. Alternatively, had he skipped the cruise and invested the money in a well-structured investment portfolio for those five years, he might have doubled his investment to $5,000.

When choosing among alternatives, people have to put those alternatives into some framework for comparison. When making comparisons, human nature tends to discount anything in the future in favor of immediate gratification. In the cruise example above, the client decided to spend the $2,500 now to take the cruise, even if the client objectively knew that the money would double in five years if invested wisely. For this client, the current subjective satisfaction expected from taking the cruise is worth more today than the increased future value of the investment portfolio.

Once a financial planner presents a client with a framework of objective alternatives that identifies the opportunity cost associated with each alternative, the client can make a more informed, more rational choice among alternatives. In this way, the financial planning process promotes efficient allocation of a client's resources and avoids commitment of resources to more costly, less rational choices.

WHY DO PEOPLE HIRE PROFESSIONAL FINANCIAL PLANNERS?

Many people seek the advice of professionals, such as doctors, lawyers, and accountants, on a regular basis. Generally, professionals have a more comprehensive knowledge of their subject field than does the public. In some cases, it is simply a matter of opportunity cost. It is a lot less expensive in total satisfaction and cost to retain an "expert" than to invest the time to learn to "do it ourselves." We may lack the day-to-day cognitive references, financial benchmarks, and comparisons needed to know when a plan is competent or attainable. Even though people may have a limited knowledge of a certain subject, they may lack the confidence to make important decisions based on that limited knowledge. Essentially, people seek out and retain professional financial planners for the same reasons. People hire professional financial planners because they believe that doing so is more effective and efficient than attempting to create and implement a financial plan on their own.

The public has a reasonable expectation that a professional financial planner is knowledgeable and competent in the financial planning field. The planner should have an understanding of objective risks in the environment, such as the risks of untimely death, health problems, disability, property loss, and negligence suits and awards. The public can reasonably expect that a professional financial planner will have knowledge of life expectancies and, thus, an understanding of the average expected length of years of retirement. Planners should know that in general it takes 60-80 percent of preretirement income to maintain the preretirement lifestyle in retirement. Planners should know that for low-income workers, Social Security provides a good wage replacement, but for highly paid workers it may only replace 10-20 percent of preretirement income. Professional planners should know the risk of inflation and its historical patterns. Planners should also know the historical investment returns for various classes of assets, and which asset allocation schemes have produced the best overall investment returns for selected risk levels. Building the professional financial planner's knowledge and skill base, understanding the financial planning process, and recognizing the environment in which financial planning exists, is what this text is about.

THE FINANCIAL PLANNER'S PYRAMID OF KNOWLEDGE

The Financial Planner's Pyramid of Knowledge, as depicted in Exhibit 1.1, is presented throughout this text. The Pyramid identifies both the skills and the basic tools that the financial planner must possess, as well as the core topics of which the planner must be knowledgeable. Just as the strength of any structure depends on a solid foundation, the success of any professional financial planner relies on a well-built foundation of knowledge, competency, and skill. The base of the Financial Planner's Pyramid of Knowledge identifies the core knowledge and skill sets that every financial planner should possess. Collectively, these competencies make up the financial planner's toolkit—a foundation on which a successful profession in financial planning can be built. Out of necessity in this text, these skills, tools, and knowledge are presented serially and compartmentally. It is important to note, however, that they are not performed sequentially or independently. Rather, they are performed simultaneously throughout the many aspects of the financial planning process.

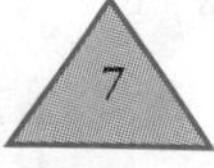

EXHIBIT 1.1: FINANCIAL PLANNER'S PYRAMID OF KNOWLEDGE

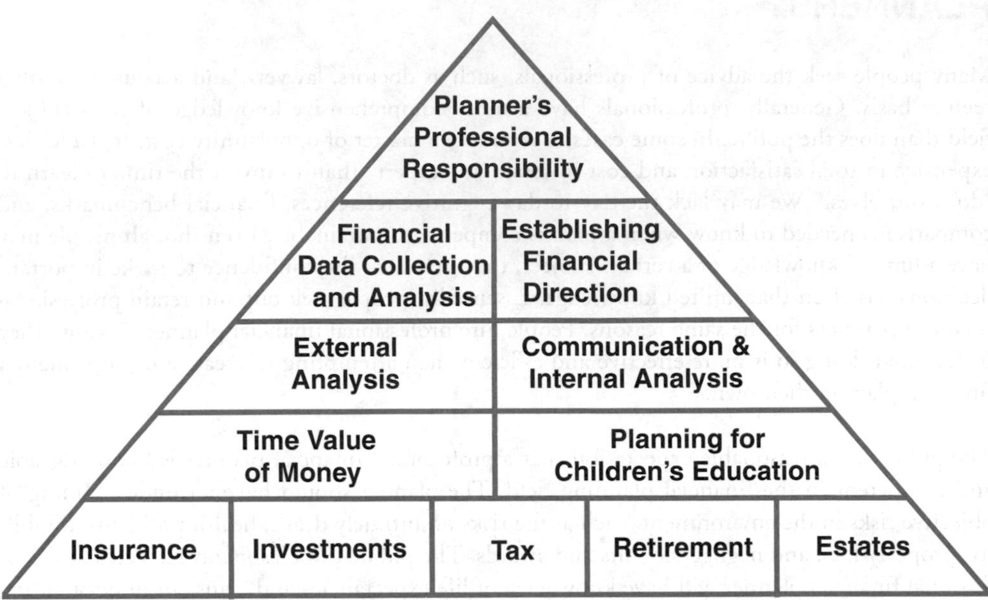
Planner's Professional Responsibility
Financial Data Collection and Analysis
Establishing Financial Direction
External Analysis
Communication & Internal Analysis
Time Value of Money
Planning for Children's Education
Insurance
Investments
Tax
Retirement
Estates

Throughout the text, we also focus on two themes. The first theme of the text is that personal financial planning is about attaining financial goals and managing financial risks. There are perhaps as many goals as there are clients. Generally, the majority of clients are looking to achieve one or more of the following goals: to attain financial security for themselves, to create an accumulation of assets to fund their children's education, to save a specific lump sum to cover future expenditures, or to prepare their assets for transfer to heirs. There are many risks threatening the attainment of these goals, including disability, ill health, or untimely death. The text will identify these risks and suggest ways for managing these risks.

The second theme emphasized throughout the text is that the professional practice of personal financial planning emphasizes data collection and analysis. For the professional financial planner, this requires a good education in the external environmental influences and good data collection skills for interviewing and administering questionnaires. Analytical skills are invaluable when applying time value of money concepts, and when preparing and analyzing personal financial statements. Excellent communication skills, including displaying empathy and using verbal and nonverbal pacing, are essential when gathering information and communicating with clients. Finally, helping clients set reasonable goals that are objectively measurable in time and form, and using good follow-up and evaluation skills are most valuable to the professional financial planner.

Basic Financial Planning Skills

financial phases - accumulation, conservation/protection, and distribution/gifting

The first section of the text explains that the practice of personal financial planning requires the financial planner to master good communication, data collection, and analysis skills. These skills are necessary when applying financial planning tools and when working with clients. The planner must be aware that individuals generally progress through **financial phases** during their lives. These phases include the asset accumulation phase, the conservation/protection phase, and the distribution/gifting phase. These phases are not mutually exclusive. A client may function in two or three phases simultaneously. If a professional planner can identify which phase or phases a client is in, the planner will have better insight into the client's financial behavior and a better understanding of the client's approach to goals and risks.

This section also identifies the process of establishing financial direction. Establishing a **financial mission** begins the process. Once the mission is identified and embraced, the planner must consider relevant internal and external environmental information. The planner should use objective analysis and rational judgment to guide the client to effective decision-making. The client's **financial goals** and **financial objectives** are then identified and prioritized so that feasible alternative strategies can be created. After examining the alternatives, the planner aids the client in selecting the optimal alternative strategy. The last step in the process is where the plan is implemented and monitored; but by no means is the process finished. The responsible financial planner will then provide regular feedback to the client on the plan's performance.

financial mission - a broad and enduring statement that identifies the client's purpose for wanting a financial plan

financial goals - high-level statements of financial desires that may be for the short run or the long run

financial objectives - statements of financial desire that contain time and measurement attributes making them more specific than financial goals

Basic Financial Planning Tools

The second section of the text identifies two basic financial planning tools; **time value of money** and planning for children's education.

time value of money - the concept that money received today is worth more than the same amount of money received sometime in the future

In Chapter 6, we discuss time value of money (TVM) concepts, one of the most useful and important concepts in finance and personal financial planning. The chapter includes in-depth discussions on TVM concepts, terms, and tools such as present value, future value, amortization tables, net present value (NPV) and internal rate of return (IRR), yield to maturity, debt management, and the inflation rate.

Chapter 7 covers developing a plan for funding children's education. A primary financial goal of most parents is to provide an education for their children. Education funding is a common area of concern for those seeking financial planning advice because paying for higher education is one of the largest financial burdens a family will face. In our discussion, we identify the various issues that parents should consider when setting goals for financing their children's education, examine the types of financial aid information that can be gathered from a college's financial aid office, and explain the importance of the EFC (Expected Family Contribution) formula in student financial aid application. We describe the major student financial assistance programs available, and explain how time value of money concepts are used to help calculate the cost of their child's education.

Core Topics

Chapters 8 through 11 are dedicated to insurance planning. Chapter 8 discusses the legal foundation of insurance and the transference or sharing of risks using insurance contracts. Chapter 9 identifies the risks associated with premature death, catastrophic illness, disability, and the need for long-term care. Chapter 10 identifies the risks to property and liability exposures. Chapter 11 covers Social Security and other types of social insurance.

Chapters 12 through 17 provide an introduction to investments, income tax, retirement, and estate needs. Chapter 12 and its Supplements A, B, and C, offer a discussion on investment

Where on the Web

Association for Financial Counseling and Planning Education *www.afcpe.org*
Barron's Online *www.barrons.com*
Bloomberg *www.bloomberg.com*
Certified Financial Planner Board of Standards *www.cfp-board.org*
Financial Planning Association *www.fpanet.org*
Forbes Magazine *www.forbes.com*
Fortune Magazine *www.fortune.com*
Kiplinger *www.kiplinger.com*
Money Magazine *money.cnn.com*
National Association of Personal Financial Advisors *www.napfa.org*
Smart Money Magazine *www.smartmoney.com*
Society of Financial Service Professionals *www.financialpro.org/welcome.cfm*
TIAA-CREF *www.tiaa-cref.org/index.html*
Wall Street Journal *www.wsj.com*
Worth Magazine *www.worth.com*

planning. Chapter 12 introduces investment goals common to most investors, the risks that threaten those goals, and discusses modern portfolio theory and investment strategies. Supplement 12A discusses investing in lending securities, such as bonds. Supplement 12B covers equity securities, namely common and preferred stock. Supplement 12C discusses mutual funds as an investment opportunity.

Chapters 13 and 14 cover individual income tax and tax planning and the formation and taxation of business entities. Chapter 13 includes discussions on the objectives of the Federal Income Tax Law, the three different tax rate structures under which income can be taxed, how to perform the calculation to determine a client's income tax liability, the types of IRS rulings issued as guidance to taxpayers, payroll taxes, the various civil penalties imposed on tax law violators, and the various tax-advantaged investment options available to taxpayers. Chapter 14 identifies the several different types of business entities that a business owner may choose as a legal form of business and characterizes each type of business entity with regard to formation requirements, operation, ownership restrictions, tax treatment, legal liability risk, and management operations. The chapter goes on to discuss the basic factors that a business owner should consider when selecting a legal form of business and explains how each type of business entity differs with regard to simplicity of formation and operation, ownership restrictions, limited liability, management operations, and tax characteristics.

Chapters 15 and 16 examine retirement planning. Chapter 15 identifies and explains the major factors that affect retirement planning. Chapter 16 provides an introduction to private retirement plans, including qualified retirement plans, other tax-advantaged retirement plans, and nonqualified plans.

Chapter 17 presents the goals of efficient and effective wealth transfer, during life or at death, and the risks that are associated with such transfers. It introduces estate planning, describes the estate planning process, discusses the objectives of and the benefits derived from planning an estate, lists the types of client information necessary to begin and complete the estate planning process, and describes the probate process and lists its advantages and disadvantages. Chapter 17 also explains why a unified gift and estate tax system exists, identifies the basic strategies for transferring wealth through gifting, explains the purpose of the federal estate tax, defines the marital deduction and how it affects estate planning, and discusses the various estate tax reduction techniques available.

THE FINANCIAL PLANNING PROFESSION

Chapter 18 describes the financial planning profession today. It describes and differentiates financial institutions from individual financial professionals. The chapter outlines the methods of compensation and closes with ideas about developing and maintaining a practice. Chapter 19 covers the ethical responsibilities of a financial planner, provides a legal framework for malpractice and civil liability, and details the CFP Board's Standards of Professional Conduct, which covers its code of ethics and professional responsibility, disciplinary rules and procedures, and practice standards for CFP® certificants.

DISCUSSION QUESTIONS

1. What is personal financial planning?
2. What does it mean to say that financial success is a "relative" concept?
3. How does the financial planning process promote efficient allocation of a client's resources?
4. Why do people hire professional financial planners?
5. What does the Financial Planner's Pyramid of Knowledge identify?
6. What benefits can a client derive from the process of personal financial planning?
7. What concepts must the professional financial planner balance in order to create a successful financial plan?
8. Through what activities is the personal financial planner expected to guide the client?

CHAPTER 2

External Environmental Analysis

LEARNING OBJECTIVES:

After learning the material in this chapter, you will be able to:

1. Differentiate between the external and internal environments in which financial planning occurs.
2. Discuss how external environmental factors link to the different areas of financial planning.
3. Give examples of how external environmental factors might affect clients from different economic levels.
4. Give reasons why external environmental analysis is important.
5. Explain how economic factors, such as interest rates, taxes, and inflation, affect areas of financial planning.
6. Define the several phases and important extreme points that make up a business cycle and describe their effect on the economy.
7. Calculate the rate of inflation.
8. Define the consumer price index, the gross domestic product deflator, and the producer price index.
9. Explain how changes in monetary and fiscal policy affect the economy.
10. Discuss the different types of financial institutions and negotiable instruments.
11. Explain how FDIC coverage works.
12. Identify federal consumer protection/bankruptcy laws and give a brief description of each.
13. List federal programs that offer protection for workers on the jobsite.
14. Give examples of how other external environmental factors—social, technological, political, and taxation—affect a client's personal financial plan.

THE EXTERNAL ENVIRONMENT

The success of a client's financial planning is affected by both internal and external environmental factors. Internal environmental forces, which will be examined fully in subsequent chapters, include a client's current and projected financial situation, tolerance for risk, discipline regarding savings and investments, consumption patterns, and financial goals. Exhibit 2.1 shows how the internal environment fits within the external environment.

EXHIBIT 2.1: INTERNAL AND EXTERNAL ENVIRONMENTS

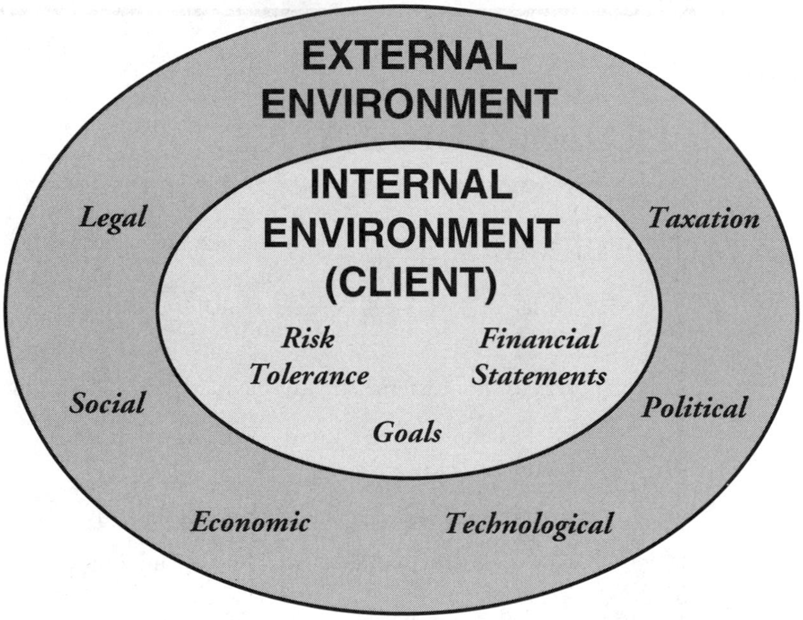

EXTERNAL ENVIRONMENT
Legal
Taxation
INTERNAL ENVIRONMENT (CLIENT)
Risk Tolerance
Financial Statements
Goals
Social
Political
Economic
Technological

external environment - the whole complex of external factors that influence the financial planning process, including economic, legal, social, technological, political, and taxation factors

The **external environment** is made up of a variety of factors, or "sub" environments, that are broad in scope but have at least some influence on the financial planning process. The external environment includes economic, legal, social, technological, political, and taxation factors. An abbreviated list of factors for each of the external environmental influences is presented in Exhibit 2.2.

EXHIBIT 2.2: ABBREVIATED LIST OF EXTERNAL FACTORS*

Economic Factors	Legal Factors
Gross Domestic Product (GDP)	*Antitrust Acts*
Inflation (Consumer Price Index)	*Consumer Protection Acts*
Interest Rates	*Bankruptcy Acts*
Trade Payments	*Securities Acts (1933-1934)*
Consumer Income/Debt/Spending	*Forms of Business Organization*
Unemployment	*Employer/Employee Relations*
Population Age	*Workers Compensation*
Index of Leading Economic Indicators	*Continuation of Benefits (COBRA)*
	Social Security

Social Factors	Technological Factors
Age of Population – Life Expectancy	*Current State of Technology*
Customs and Beliefs	*Creation of New Technology*
Attitudes and Motivations	*Human and Business Solutions*
Status Symbols/Social Institutions	*Advances in Service & Engineering*

Political Factors	Taxation Factors
Form of Government	*Income Taxes (Federal and State)*
Political Ideology/Stability	*Property Taxes*
Foreign Trade Policy	*Transfer Taxes (Gift and Estate)*
Degree of Government Protectionism	*Payroll Taxes*
	Sales Taxes

*There are many other factors than those listed; however, a full discussion of all factors is beyond the scope of this text.

This chapter describes the external environment in which financial planning occurs. The external environment is characterized by opportunities and threats. For the financial planner, the purpose of studying the external environment is to scan for those opportunities and threats that may relate to particular clients and their financial goals. The financial planner may forecast external trends (or use experts to forecast trends) to help clients achieve goals and avoid external risks.

As stated previously, external environmental factors include economic, legal, social, technological, political, and taxation forces. Everyone is influenced by these forces to differing degrees as shown by the links in Exhibit 2.3 and the selected examples in Exhibit 2.4. Exhibit 2.3 summarizes how the basic external environmental factors link to financial planning.

EXHIBIT 2.3: GENERAL LINKAGES OF EXTERNAL ENVIRONMENT TO FINANCIAL PLANNING

External Environment	Fundamentals of Financial Planning	Insurance Planning	Investments Planning	Income Taxation Planning	Retirement Planning	Estate Planning and Taxation
Economic Environment	✘		✘		✘	
Legal Environment	✘	✘	✘			✘
Social Environment	✘	✘			✘	
Technological Environment	✘		✘	✘		
Political Environment	✘	✘	✘	✘	✘	✘
Taxation Environment		✘	✘	✘	✘	✘

Note: The ✘ indicates predominant linkages, but other linkages may exist.

Because some clients are more affected by certain environmental factors than others (as illustrated in Exhibit 2.4), it is the professional planner's responsibility to decide the influences relevant to a particular client at a particular time.

EXHIBIT 2.4: EXTERNAL ENVIRONMENTAL IMPACT ON FINANCIAL PLANNING (SELECTED EXAMPLES)

Client's Economic Level	EXTERNAL ENVIRONMENTAL FORCES					
	Economic	Legal	Social	Political	Taxation	Technological
High Income Clients	• Gross Domestic Product • Interest rates	• Antitrust • Form of business organization	• Status symbols • Life expectancy	• Political • Ideology/ stability	• Income and transfer taxes • Property taxes	• Investments • Internet
Middle Income Clients	• Inflation • Interest rates	• Form of business organization • Employer/ employee relationships • Consumer protection • COBRA • Social Security	• Customs/ Beliefs • Life expectancy	• Foreign Trade Policy	• Property taxes • Income taxes • Payroll taxes	• Investments • Jobs • Electronic tax filing • Internet
Low Income Clients	• Unemployment • Inflation	• Workers compensation • Consumer protection • COBRA • Social Security	• Social institutions • Life expectancy • Customs/ beliefs	• Government protectionism	• Sales taxes • Payroll taxes	• Electronic tax filing • Internet

ANALYZING THE EXTERNAL ENVIRONMENT

External environmental analysis is the process of identifying and monitoring the environment in which a client lives and the opportunities and threats that are present. External environmental analysis is important for a variety of reasons.

- ▲ External trends and particular events play a significant role in effecting change in the world and in the behavior of individuals.
- ▲ Changes in external forces impact beliefs, economics, unemployment, inflation, and a society's well-being.
- ▲ The external environment shapes the way people live, work, spend, save, and think.

Professional financial planners need to have an understanding of these forces and should develop a methodology for staying abreast of the changes occurring in the external environment.

In performing external environmental analysis, the financial planner must determine the relevance of one or more external environmental factors for each client. The relevance of such factors may be dependent on the client's age, goals, net worth, or income. Consider the following examples:

EXAMPLE Mr. Jones is 70 years old, married, has five adult children, seven grandchildren, and has a net worth of ten million dollars. One of his goals is to leave as much money as he can to his heirs. Since the tax environment incorporates gift taxes, estate taxes, generation-skipping transfer taxes, and in some cases, state inheritance taxes, the tax environment is highly relevant to Mr. Jones's personal financial planning.

EXAMPLE Mr. Smith, age 36, is married, has three young children, and has debts in excess of his assets. He was injured on the job and may never return to work. While the tax environment may have some relevance to Mr. Smith, it is going to be a minor influence relative to Mr. Jones. The legal environment, which addresses consumer protection, bankruptcy, workmans' compensation, Medicaid, COBRA, Social Security disability benefits, and civil lawsuits, may be of utmost importance to Mr. Smith.

Why Study the External Environment?

Regular observation and monitoring of the external environment is essential to providing high quality financial planning services to clients. Financial planners may study the external environment formally or informally. Formal study will usually include university-level courses in economics, taxation, political science, sociology, and the legal environment. The external environment may also be studied informally using a variety of sources, such as general economic and business periodicals, books, academic and professional journals, newspapers, government statistical studies, and by obtaining environmental briefings from various information providers. Financial planners also take continuing professional education courses to stay abreast of the ever-changing external environment.

The Economic and Legal Environments

The external environment—particularly the economic and legal environment—exerts far-reaching, yet often subtle influence on accomplishing financial goals and reducing risks. For example, consider an economic environment characterized by low interest rates, modest growth, and low inflation. Such an environment is ideal for businesses to prosper and for investors to achieve excellent investment returns with relatively moderate levels of risk. Alternatively, economic periods of high interest rates and growing inflation are not as suitable for businesses, investors, or retirees who, living on fixed incomes, are losing purchasing power. The legal environment, especially consumer protection, is important because it establishes the legal rules by which consumers must abide and creates the legal rights to which consumers are entitled.

IMPORTANCE OF THE ECONOMIC ENVIRONMENT

Of all the external environments, the economic environment has the most direct influence on personal financial planning. It is the rationing system among resources, scarcity, and outputs. The economic environment includes many factors, such as gross domestic product, inflation rates, interest rates, trade payments, consumer income/debt/spending, unemployment, population age, and the index of leading economic indicators. Many of these factors, namely, interest rates, inflation, unemployment, and gross domestic product, play a key role in real investment returns and, therefore, in the accomplishment of financial goals.

Professional financial planners must understand the current economic environment to better forecast the economic future. By identifying the opportunities and risks that lie ahead, planners can help clients adapt to that future. The planner needs an understanding of the current economy's general condition, the current interest rate environment, the current rate of inflation, and recent changes in monetary and fiscal policy. It is essential that the planner have the ability to anticipate each element's behavior and its potential effect on a client's financial plan. Exhibit 2.5 illustrates several selected economic factors and their relationship to various areas of financial planning.

EXHIBIT 2.5: THE ECONOMIC ENVIRONMENT AND FINANCIAL PLANNING

Selected Economic Factors	Financial Planning Areas Affected	How They Are Affected
Interest rates	Investment returns	Inversely
	Purchasing power and, therefore, the costs of goods and services in the future including education, retirement funding, and health care	Inversely
Taxes	Redistribution of income through government	Directly
	Production of goods	Inversely
	Distribution of wealth	Directly
Inflation	The cost of goods, services, money, and unemployment	Directly
Unemployment	Wage rates and other costs/expansion/contraction/consumption	Inversely
Monetary and fiscal policy	Economic expansion/contraction/expectations	Directly

Remember, these economic factors are not mutually exclusive, but, rather, are interrelated. As Exhibit 2.5 illustrates, one economic factor may influence several areas of financial planning in different ways. It is important for professional financial planners to "read" the external economic environment accurately, so that they can adjust their clients' financial plans accordingly.

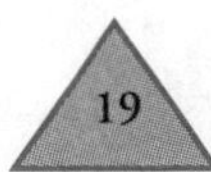

The General Economy

The economy is a resource-allocation market system that achieves its objectives through a pricing mechanism. Prices are essentially determined in the marketplace at the point where supply and demand reach equilibrium. If supply or demand is affected, prices will change.

In the News...
Consider that when the pope lifted the ban on eating meat on Friday for Catholics in 1966, the average price per pound of fish dropped 12.5%. However, with the current awareness of health issues, the price of fish has risen faster than general inflation. Thus, if demand is affected, prices will also be affected. (Frederick W. Bell "The Pope and the Price of Fish," American Economic Review 58 (December 1968): 1346-1350)

Demand

demand - the quantity of a particular good that people are willing to buy. Demand is heavily dependent on price.

demand curve - the graphic depiction that illustrates the relationship between a particular good's price and the quantity demanded

The **demand** for a particular good is that quantity which people are willing to buy. Demand is heavily dependent on price. The **demand curve** (Exhibit 2.6) illustrates the general relationship between a particular good's price and the quantity demanded.

EXHIBIT 2.6: THE DEMAND CURVE

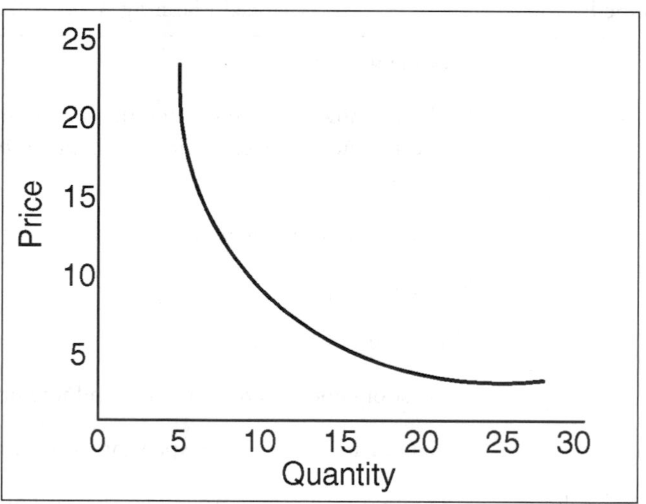
Price
25
20
15
10
5
0
5
10
15
20
25
30
Quantity

substitution effect - the phenomenon in which consumers substitute less expensive goods for similar, expensive goods. This is one of two reasons why the demand curve slopes downward.

Downward sloping demand indicates that if the price increases, the quantity demanded will fall. Conversely, when the price falls, quantity demanded increases. There are two reasons demand declines when the price increases. The first reason is consumers are ingenious about substituting other, less expensive goods when the price for a particular good rises. This phenomenon is called the **substitution effect**. The second reason demand declines is that consumers curb consumption when prices rise. For example, assume Exhibit 2.6 shows the demand curve for Ben's consumption of ice cream. Then, if the price of ice cream is $5 per pint, Ben will consume 15 pints of ice cream. However, if the price of ice cream increases to $8 per pint, Ben will only consume 10 pints of ice cream. Ben could substitute cupcakes for ice cream or simply reduce his overall con-

sumption of desserts. These movements along the demand curve in response to a change in price are called **changes in quantity demanded.**

changes in quantity demanded - the movements along the demand curve in response to a change in price

When the entire curve shifts to the right or the left, we say that there is a **change in demand.** When the curve shifts, quantity demanded at each price level changes. The average income or standard of living is a key determinant of demand. As incomes increase, individuals demand and purchase more goods at each price level. The size of the market and the price and availability of related, substitute goods also influence the demand for a particular good.

change in demand - this occurs when the entire curve shifts to the right or left

Event	Effect on Demand Curve
Increase in the price of the good	Downward movement along the demand curve
Increase in average income	Upward (right) shift of demand curve
Increase in population	Upward shift of demand curve
Increase in the price of related goods	Upward shift of demand curve
Increase in the price of complement goods	Downward (left) shift of demand curve
Increase in taste preference	Upward shift of demand curve
Increases in price and economic expectations	Upward shift of demand curve

The opposite effects of these events (i.e. a decrease in average income) will result in an opposite effect on the demand curve (downward shift in the demand curve). Any changes or influences other than the price of a good, cause a shift in the demand curve. Price changes simply cause movement along the demand curve.

Supply

The **supply** of a particular good is that quantity which businesses are willing to produce and sell. The **supply curve** (Exhibit 2.7) depicts the general relationship between the market price of a particular good and the quantity supplied.

supply - the quantity of a particular good which businesses are willing to produce or sell

supply curve - the graphic depiction that shows the relationship between the market price of a particular good and the quantity supplied

EXHIBIT 2.7: THE SUPPLY CURVE

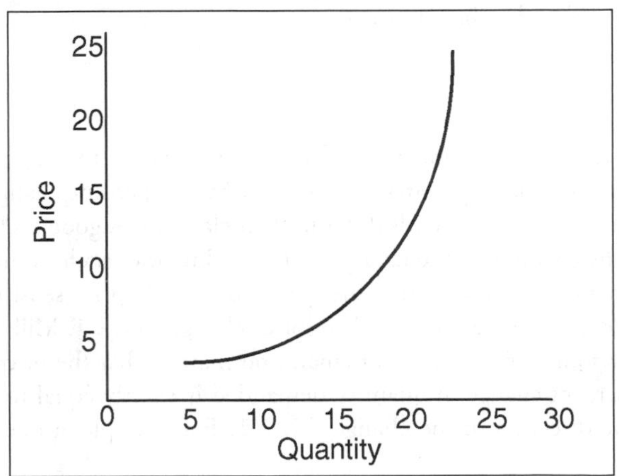

Price
25
20
15
10
5
0
5
10
15
20
25
30
Quantity

The factors that affect supply include the price of the good, technological advances, input prices, prices of related goods, and special influences like price expectations.

Substitutes and Complements

Often in markets, goods are related to each other. If good A and good B are related, then a price change for good A will affect the quantity demanded of good A and of good B. Whether this relationship is positively or negatively correlated depends on whether the goods are substitutes or complements. Substitutes are products that serve similar purposes. They are related such that an increase in the price of one will cause an increase in demand for the other. For example, if the price of chicken suddenly rose sharply, the demand for pork would probably increase, even though the price of pork was initially unchanged. Consumers would eat more pork and reduce their consumption of the now expensive chicken. Conversely, complements are products that are usually consumed jointly. They are related such that an increase in the price of one will cause a decrease in demand for the other. For example, when the price of jelly goes up, the supermarket can expect the demand for peanut butter to decrease slightly because the two products are complements.

Event	Effect on Supply Curve
Increase in the price of the good	Upward movement along the supply curve
Increase in technology	Rightward shift (increase) of supply curve
Increase in input prices	Leftward shift (decrease) of supply curve
Increase in the price of related goods	Rightward shift of supply curve

Diminishing Marginal Utility

The law of diminishing marginal utility states that as the rate of consumption increases, the marginal utility derived from consuming additional units of a good will decline. Marginal utility is the additional utility received from the consumption of an additional unit of a good. For example, if Richard's favorite food was steak, he might eat steak often. However, if Richard ate steak for "n" consecutive days for dinner, the enjoyment, or utility, that he received from the dinner would be higher the first day than on the last.

Price Elasticity

price elasticity - the quantity demanded of a good in response to changes in that good's price. A good is elastic when its quantity demanded responds greatly to price changes (luxuries). A good is inelastic when its quantity demanded responds little to price changes

Price elasticity is the quantity demanded of a good in response to changes in that good's price. The percent change in quantity demanded divided by the percent change in price is a relative measure of price elasticity (PE). Goods differ in their elasticity. A good is elastic when its quantity demanded responds greatly to price changes, PE > 1. Luxuries such as movie tickets and liquor could be considered elastic because they are, generally, highly price sensitive. A good is inelastic when its quantity demanded responds little to price changes, PE < 1. Milk and electricity, considered necessities by some, will remain in demand no matter what the price. Unit elastic demand exists when the percent change in quantity demanded is exactly equal to the percent change in price, ignoring the direction of the change, PE = 1. For example, a one percent drop in price causes a one percent increase in the amount sold. Exhibit 2.8 illustrates the relative elasticity of gasoline consumption to price for the period 1973-2002.

EXHIBIT 2.8: GASOLINE PRICES AND CONSUMPTION (U.S.)

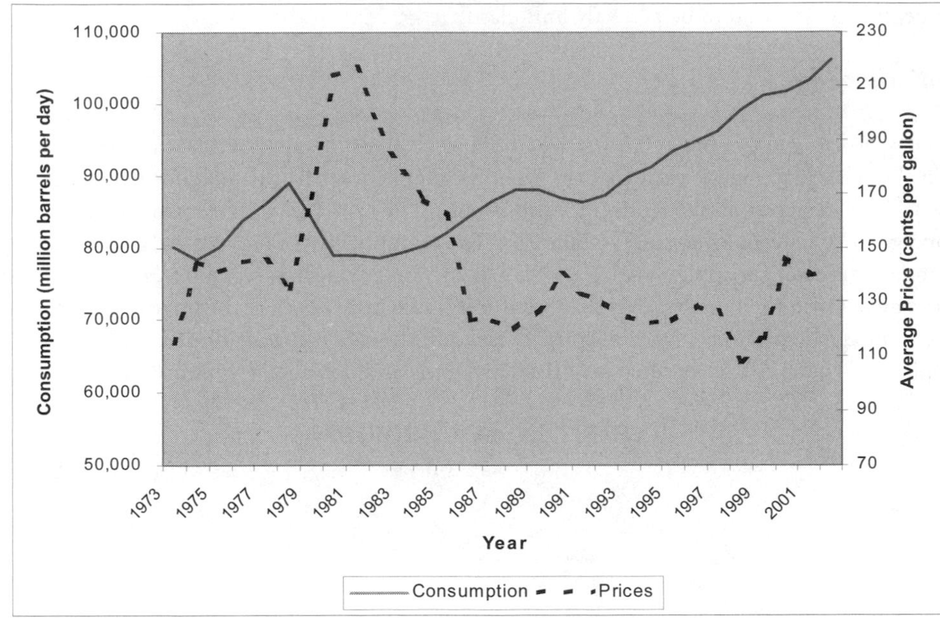

Consumption (million barrels per day)
110,000
100,000
90,000
80,000
70,000
60,000
50,000
230
210
190
170
150
130
110
90
70
Average Price (cents per gallon)
1973
1975
1977
1979
1981
1983
1985
1987
1989
1991
1993
1995
1997
1999
2001
Year
Consumption
Prices

We can calculate the price elasticity (PE) of gasoline over the 1973 – 2002 time period.

EXAMPLE

$$\frac{\text{\% Change in Quantity Demanded}}{\text{\% Change in Price}} = \frac{\left(\frac{105{,}000 - 80{,}000}{80{,}000}\right)}{\frac{(140 - 120)}{120}} = \frac{31.25\%}{16.67\%} = 1.875$$

Since PE > 1, we say that the demand for gasoline is elastic.

Price elasticity can also have an affect on a company's total revenues. When the demand for a good is price inelastic, a price decrease reduces total revenues. When the demand is price elastic, a price decrease increases total revenue. In the case of unit-elastic demand, a price decrease lends to no change in total revenue.

EXAMPLE

Consider a gas company that derives its revenues from the price of gasoline (an inelastic good). The company typically sells 1 million gallons per day at $5.50 per gallon. this translates into sales of $5.5 million per day. If the price of gasoline increases to $6 a gallon, then revenues would increase to $6 million per day, giving the company an extra $500,000 of revenue.

With inelastic goods, the demand curve becomes vertical because the price has no effect on the quantity demanded. It may, however, shift right or left depending on various factors.

EXAMPLE

To explain unit-elastic demand and its effects on company revenues, consider a grocer selling apples for $1 a pound. He typically sells 500 pounds a week for a gross revenue of $500. One week, he decided to raise the price of apples to $2 per pound and only ended up selling 250 pounds and maintaining a gross revenue of $500. Since the change in price had no effect on total revenue, this good is said to be perfectly unit-elastic.

Equilibrium

equilibrium - the state of the market where quantity demanded equals quantity supplied

In a competitive market, prices are free to adjust to changes in supply and consumer demand. When the price of a good is such that the quantity supplied equals the quantity demanded, the market for that good is said to be in **equilibrium**. The conditions of a competitive market encourage price movement toward equilibrium. For example, if more apples are grown than are demanded, the price for apples will fall which will encourage consumers to buy. Similarly, if consumers are demanding more bananas than producers are supplying, then the price of bananas will rise, discouraging consumers from buying. Theses adjustments continue until the market prices of apples and bananas achieve equal quantities of supply and demand – equilibrium.

EXHIBIT 2.9: EQUILIBRIUM

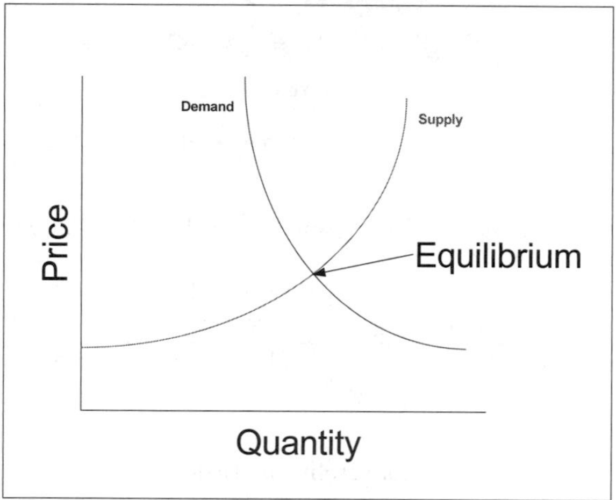
Demand
Supply
Price
Equilibrium
Quantity

BUSINESS CYCLES

business cycles - swings in total national output, income, and employment marked by widespread expansion or contraction in many sectors of the economy

Business cycles are swings in total national output, income, and employment marked by widespread expansion or contraction in many sectors of the economy. These cycles generally occur because of shifts in aggregate demand. The financial planner should be familiar with the impact of business cycles on the economy, as different investments will perform differently during various phases of a business cycle. For example, cyclical industries such as the automobile or housing industry generally perform well during an economic boom and poorly during a bust.

The business cycle (as depicted in Exhibit 2.10) consists of two general phases, expansion and contraction; and two points, peak and trough. Each phase of the business cycle passes into the next phase and is characterized by different economic conditions.

The expansion phase ends and moves into the contraction phase at the upper turning point, or peak. Similarly, the contraction phase gives way to expansion at the lower turning point, or trough. The emphasis here is not so much on high or low business activity as on the dynamic aspects of the rise and fall of business activity.

EXHIBIT 2.10: A HYPOTHETICAL BUSINESS CYCLE

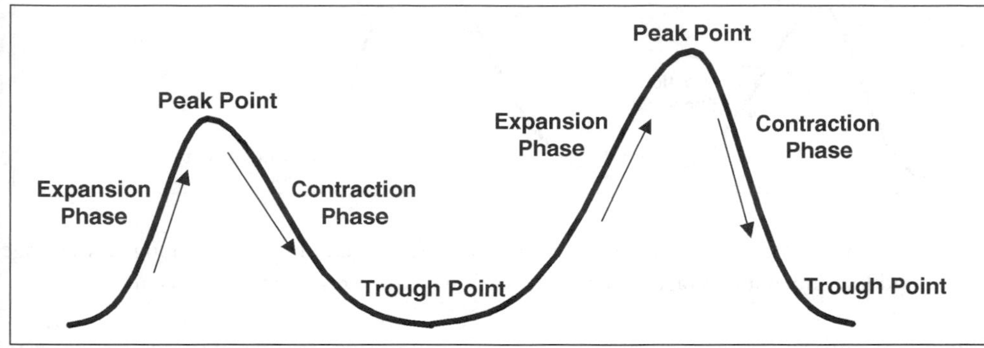
Peak Point
Peak Point
Expansion Phase
Contraction Phase
Expansion Phase
Contraction Phase
Trough Point
Trough Point

Note: The actual business cycle is not as symmetrical as drawn here. The pattern is more irregular and unpredictable. See Exhibit 2.12 for an illustration of the changes in the actual business cycle.

expansion phase - one of the two general business cycle phases characterized by a rise in business sales, growth of the Gross Domestic Product, and a decline in unemployment

peak - the point in the business cycle that appears at the end of the expansion phase when most businesses are operating at full capacity and Gross Domestic Product is increasing rapidly

Business Cycle Components and Their Effect on the Economy

The **expansion phase** leads to the peak point. During the expansion phase, business sales rise, Gross Domestic Product (GDP) grows, and unemployment declines. (GDP is the value of all goods and services produced in the country.)

The **peak** point appears at the end of the expansion phase when most businesses are operating at full capacity and GDP is increasing rapidly. The peak is the point at which GDP is at its highest and exceeds the long-run average GDP. Usually employment levels also peak at this point. (See Exhibit 2.11 for a depiction of the relationship between long-run GDP and the business cycle.)

contraction phase - one of the two general business cycle phases characterized by a fall in business sales, decreased growth of the Gross Domestic Product, and increased unemployment

The **contraction phase** leads to the trough point. During the contraction phase, business sales fall, GDP growth falls, and unemployment increases.

The **trough** point appears at the end of the contraction phase where businesses are generally operating at their lowest capacity levels. The trough point is characterized by GDP growth being at its lowest. Unemployment is rapidly increasing and finally peaks when sales fall rapidly.

trough - the point in the business cycle that appears at the end of the contraction phase when most businesses are operating at their lowest capacity levels and the Gross Domestic Product is at its lowest

Recession is a decline in real GDP for two or more successive quarters characterized by:

- Declining consumer purchases
- Expanding business inventories
- Decreasing capital investment
- Decreasing demand for labor
- High unemployment
- Falling commodity prices
- Decreasing business profits
- Falling interest rates due to reduced demand for money

recession - a decline in real Gross Domestic Product for two or more successive quarters

depression - a persistent recession that brings a severe decline in economic activity

capital formation - production of buildings, machinery, tools, and other equipment that will assist in the ability of economic participants to produce in the future

durable goods - products that are not consumed or quickly disposed of, and can be used for several years such as automobiles, furniture, and computers

consumption movements - economic variables that fluctuate during the business cycle; describe changes in consumer purchases

Depression is a persistent recession that brings a severe decline in economic activity.

EXHIBIT 2.11: THE BUSINESS CYCLE & GDP

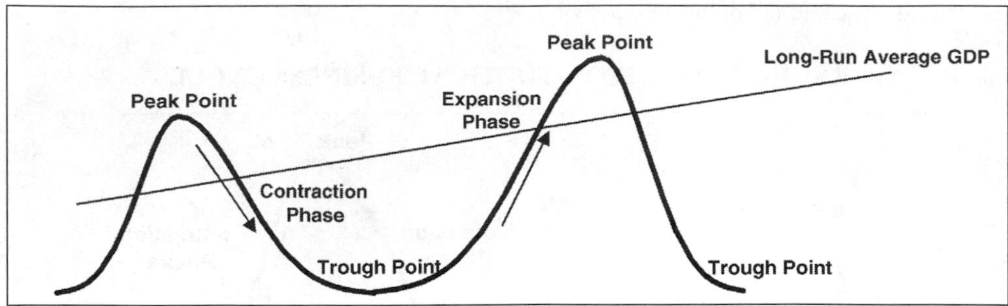
Peak Point
Long-Run Average GDP
Peak Point
Expansion Phase
Contraction Phase
Trough Point
Trough Point

Exhibit 2.11 illustrates that in spite of the expansion/contraction cycle, the long-run average GDP trend line shows an average historical expansion of the economy of +3 percent.

While there are many economic variables that fluctuate during the business cycle, certain economic variables always show greater fluctuation than others. **Capital formation** rises and falls significantly with expansion and contraction, usually leading the trend. **Durable goods,** also a trend leader, is subject to violently erratic patterns of demand. It is the economy's durable, or capital, goods sector that by far shows the greatest cyclical fluctuation. There is good reason to believe that the movement of durable goods represents key causes in the direction of expansion or contraction. **Consumption movements,** which lags behind trends, seems to be the effect of the business cycle phase rather than its cause.

Business Cycle Theories

Two opposing types of theories attempt to explain the fluctuations in the business cycle—external theories and internal theories. External theories find the root of the business cycle in the fluctuations of something outside the economic system such as wars, revolutions, political events, rates of population growth and migration, discoveries of new resources, scientific and technological discoveries, and innovation. Internal theories look for mechanisms within the economic system that give rise to self-generating business cycles. Thus, every expansion breeds recession and contraction. Every contraction, in turn, breeds revival and expansion in a quasi-regular, repeating, never-ending chain. Each peak and valley, however, is higher than the last and leads to growth in the economy over the long term despite the business cycle.

Actual Business Cycle

The actual business cycle for the United States as depicted below has averaged growth of approximately 3.0 percent per year. Growth, as measured by gross domestic product, will exceed the average in some years while in other years growth will be less than the average. Exhibit 2.12 illustrates the actual change in the business cycle as a percentage.

EXHIBIT 2.12: ACTUAL BUSINESS CYCLE ANNUAL CHANGE IN GROSS DOMESTIC PRODUCT

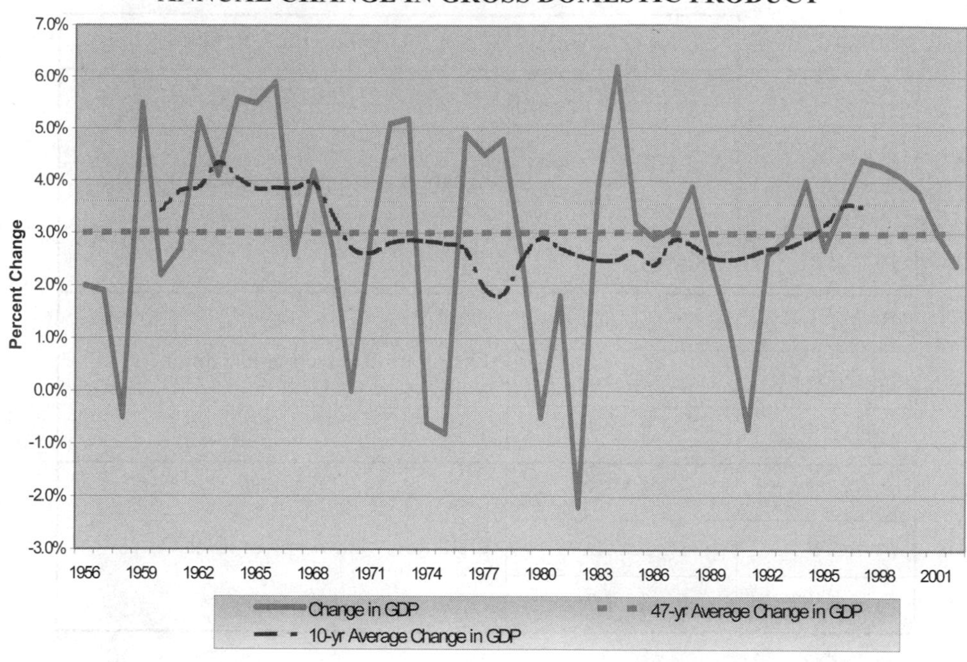
7.0%
6.0%
5.0%
4.0%
3.0%
2.0%
1.0%
0.0%
-1.0%
-2.0%
-3.0%
Percent Change
1956
1959
1962
1965
1968
1971
1974
1977
1980
1983
1986
1989
1992
1995
1998
2001
Change in GDP
47-yr Average Change in GDP
10-yr Average Change in GDP

INFLATION

Inflation is another important element affecting the economic environment. Inflation is an increase in the price level of goods and services. Inflation increases the cost of buying a home, durable goods, and consumption goods. For retirees on fixed incomes, substantial increases in inflation can dramatically affect their financial plan. Likewise, for wage earners, the rate of inflation may sometimes be greater than the individual's wage increases, resulting in a real loss of purchasing power. Professional financial planners need to understand how the rate of inflation is calculated, how it affects the economy, and how it is measured.

The opposite of inflation is **deflation**, which occurs when the general level of prices is falling. **Disinflation** is the term used to denote a decline in the rate of inflation. **Moderate inflation** is characterized by slowly rising prices. **Galloping inflation** occurs when money loses its value very quickly and real interest rates can be negative 50 or 100 percent per year. During a period of galloping inflation, people hold only the bare minimum of cash needed for daily transactions. Financial markets are in turmoil or disappear, and funds are generally allocated by rationing rather than by interest rates. People hoard goods, buy houses, and never lend money at the low nominal interest rate. Remember though, that during periods of inflation, all prices and wages do not increase at the same rate.

inflation - an increase in the price level of goods and services

deflation - the opposite of inflation, it occurs when the general level of prices is falling

disinflation - the term used to denote a decline in the rate of inflation

moderate inflation - inflation characterized by slowly rising prices

galloping inflation - inflation that occurs when money loses its value very quickly and when real interest rates can be minus 50 or 100 percent per year

EXAMPLE

	Price of Goods	Economic Climate
Period 1	*$1.00*	**Inflation** - rising price level
Period 2	*$1.50*	
Period 3	*$2.10*	
Period 4	*$2.75*	
Period 5	*$2.80*	**Disinflation** - decline in rate of inflation
Period 6	*$2.82*	
Period 7	*$2.85*	
Period 8	*$2.55*	**Deflation** - falling price level
Period 9	*$2.40*	
Period 10	*$2.10*	

Calculating Inflation

Inflation denotes a rise in the general level of prices. The rate of inflation is the rate of change in the general price level and is calculated as follows:

Rate of inflation (year t):

$$\frac{\text{Price level (year t)} - \text{Price level (year t–1)}}{\text{Price level (year t–1)}} \times 100$$

EXAMPLE Last year Rachel paid $20,000 for her college tuition. This year Rachel will pay $21,000 for tuition, with the increase being solely attributable to inflation. Calculate the inflation rate for Rachel's education expense.

Answer:

The inflation rate attributable to Rachel's increase in tuition is 5%. It is calculated as follows.

$$\frac{21{,}000 - 20{,}000}{20{,}000} \times 100 = 5\%$$

Effects of Inflation

Unexpected inflation causes a redistribution of income and wealth among different classes of people in our economy. Changes are created in the relative prices and outputs of different goods, or sometimes in output and employment for the economy as a whole. The major redistributive impact of inflation occurs through its effect on the real value of people's wealth. In general, unanticipated inflation redistributes wealth from creditors to debtors. Said another way, unanticipated or unforeseen inflation helps those who have previously borrowed money and hurts those who have loaned money. An unanticipated decline in inflation has the opposite effect. If, however, inflation is anticipated, prices adjust as expected and there is little redistribution of wealth.

real interest rate adjustment - the rate of interest expressed in dollars of constant value (adjusted for inflation) and equal to the nominal interest rate less the rate of inflation

Inflation affects the real economy in two specific areas: total output and economic efficiency. The relationship between prices and output is not necessarily direct. Inflation may be associated with a higher or a lower level of output and employment. Generally, the higher the inflation rate, the greater the changes in relative prices of goods. Distortions occur when price changes accelerate relative to changes in costs and demand.

price index - a weighted average of the prices of numerous goods and services, (for example, the consumer price index, the gross national product deflator, and the producer price index)

If inflation persists for a long time, markets begin to adapt, and an allowance for inflation is built into the market interest rate. This is known as the **real interest rate adjustment**. This phenomenon is consistent with anticipated price increases.

Measures of Inflation

A **price index** is a weighted average of the prices of numerous goods and services. The most well known price indexes are the consumer price index (CPI), the gross domestic product (GDP) deflator, the gross national product (GNP) deflator, and the producer price index (PPI).

The **Consumer Price Index (CPI)** measures the cost of a "market basket" of 364 items of consumer goods and services, including prices of food, clothing, housing, property taxes, fuels, transportation, medical care, college tuition, and other commodities purchased for day-to-day living. The CPI is constructed by weighting each price according to the economic importance of the commodity in question. Each item is assigned a fixed weight proportional to its relative importance in consumer expenditure budgets as determined by a survey of expenditures covering 1982 through 1984.

Consumer Price Index (CPI) - a price index that measures the cost of a "market basket" of consumer goods and services purchased for day-to-day living

The **Gross Domestic Product (GDP)** is the market value of final goods and services produced within a country over a specific time period, usually a year. The GDP deflator is the ratio of nominal GDP to real GDP and gives an overall measure of prices in the economy. Real GDP only measures increases or decreases in production output. Nominal GDP is affected by changes in prices as well as increases and decreases in production. The GDP deflator is a broader price index than the CPI. In addition to consumer goods, the GDP deflator includes prices for capital goods and other goods and services purchased by businesses and government.

Gross Domestic Product (GDP) - the value of all goods and services produced in the country; GDP is the broadest measure of the general state of the economy

Exhibit 2.13 presents data for both the CPI and GDP deflator. Even though the two indexes are based on different market baskets of goods with different base years, the two measures of the annual rate of inflation are quite similar. The differences between these two measures of inflation have been small, usually only a few tenths of a percentage point per year. The closeness of the two rates is not a surprise because consumer spending makes up about two-thirds of GDP.

EXHIBIT 2.13: CONSUMER PRICE INDEX AND GDP DEFLATOR PERCENT CHANGE

1980-2002

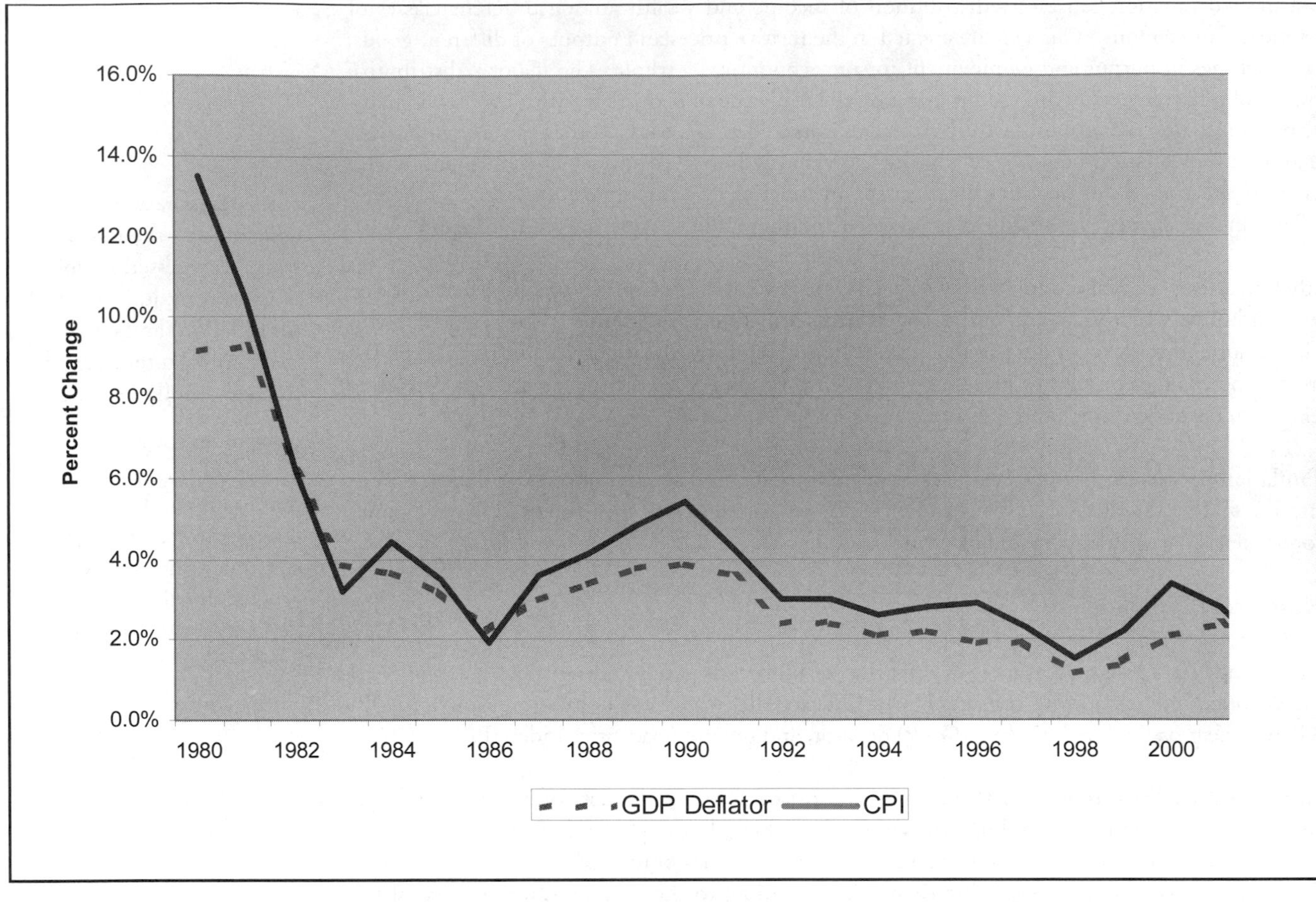
16.0%
14.0%
12.0%
10.0%
8.0%
6.0%
4.0%
2.0%
0.0%
Percent Change
1980
1982
1984
1986
1988
1990
1992
1994
1996
1998
2000
GDP Deflator
CPI

Price indexes are not problem free. The cost of living, as estimated by the CPI, is considered over-estimated in the situation where consumers substitute relatively inexpensive goods for relatively expensive goods. The CPI does not accurately capture changes in the quality of goods. Although the CPI is modified from time to time, the CPI is not corrected for quality improvements in goods and services.

The GNP deflator is the ratio of nominal gross national product to real gross national product. The difference between Gross Domestic Product (GDP) and Gross National Product (GNP) is subtle. GDP measures goods and services produced within the country, regardless of the citizenship of the owners. For example, automobiles produced at a Honda plant in Ohio would be included in the United States' GDP. GNP, on the other hand, measures goods and services produced by citizens of the country regardless of where they are produced. For example, wages paid to an American working for Honda in Tokyo would be included in GNP, but not in GDP.

Producer Price Index (PPI) - the oldest continuous statistical series published by the Labor Department that measures the level of prices at the wholesale or producer stage

The **Producer Price Index (PPI)** is the oldest continuous statistical series published by the Labor Department. It measures the level of prices at the wholesale or producer stage. It is based on approximately 3,400 commodity prices including prices of foods, manufactured products, and mining products.

For professional planners, the CPI is a good proxy for overall consumer price changes. However, due to the general nature of the market basket of goods described above, it is likely that many clients' inflation experience will be different from the general CPI. Consider the fact that many people have fixed-rate mortgages rather than rent, thus the cost of the housing payment (principal and interest) associated with the mortgage payment is unaffected by inflation. The property taxes and insurance costs on the above home, however, are subject to inflation, as are any maintenance or repair costs. Also consider that some households will need to factor in the effect of inflation on their savings plans for their children's education, while other households are relatively unaffected by the costs of higher education. The planner with clients on a fixed income can review a line-item budget to determine which costs are subject to inflation and adjust their overall financial plan accordingly. Having listed some of the more dominant ways individuals are affected by inflation, it should be realized that every individual is affected in a consequential way by inflation because they pay for groceries, clothing, automobiles, fuel, and medical care.

MONETARY AND FISCAL POLICY

Monetary policy and fiscal policy exert far-reaching influence on the economic environment. Competent financial planners must identify those changes in monetary and fiscal policy that will be the most beneficial and most detrimental to their client's financial goals and objectives. Once identified, the planner should forecast the likelihood of the important policy changes and adjust the financial plan accordingly.

Monetary Policy

The **Federal Reserve** (Fed) is charged with three primary responsibilities. The first is to maintain sustainable long-term economic growth. The second is to maintain price levels that are supported by that economic growth. The third is to maintain full employment. The Fed goes about its mission primarily using the tools of monetary policy. The Fed controls the supply of money, which enables it to significantly impact short-term interest rates. The Fed will follow a "loose," or *easy*, monetary policy when it wants to increase the money supply, and thus, expand the level of income and employment. In times of inflation and when it wants to constrict the supply of money, the Fed will follow a *tight* monetary policy.

Federal Reserve - the banking and financial system developed under the Federal Reserve Act of 1913 that makes the basic policy decisions that regulate the country's money and banking

Easy monetary policy

When the Fed wants to stimulate the money supply, it lowers the cost of short-term loans to commercial banks. The supply of money increases, resulting in the circulation of more money. This leads to more funds available for banks to lend and, ultimately, to a decline in short-term interest rates.

Tight monetary policy

When the Fed wants to tighten the money supply, it raises the price of short-term borrowing for commercial banks. The supply of money is restricted, resulting in less money available for banks to lend. This leads to an increase in short-term interest rates.

reserve requirement - for a member bank of the Federal Reserve, it is the percent of deposit liabilities that must be held in reserve. As the reserve requirement is increased, less money is available to be loaned, resulting in a restriction of the money supply.

Federal Reserve discount rate - the rate at which Federal Reserve member banks can borrow funds to meet reserve requirements. The Fed will lower the discount rate when it wants to increase the money supply.

open market operations - the process by which the Federal Reserve purchases and sells government securities in the open

fiscal policy - taxation, expenditures, and debt management of the federal government

deficit spending - occurs when governmental expenditures exceed the government's tax collections

The Fed has several methods for controlling the money supply, including raising the reserve requirements, raising the Federal Reserve discount rates, and using open market operations.

The **reserve requirement** for a member bank of the Federal Reserve is the percent of deposit liabilities that must be held in reserve. As this requirement is increased, less money is available to be loaned to customers resulting in a restriction of the money supply. Conversely, as reserve requirements are decreased, more money is made available for loans.

The **Federal Reserve discount rate** is the rate at which member banks can borrow funds from the Federal Reserve to meet reserve requirements. When the Fed raises the discount rate, it increases short-term borrowing costs and discourages member banks from borrowing funds. This results in the money supply contracting. The Fed will lower the discount rate when it wants to increase the money supply. Banks are able to borrow funds at lower rates and lend more money, which increases the money supply.

Note: The Federal Reserve discount rate is the borrowing rate from the Federal Reserve. The federal funds rate is the overnight lending rate between member banks.

Open market operations is the process by which the Federal Reserve purchases and sells government securities in the open market. The Fed buys government securities to cause more money to circulate, resulting in lower interest rates, increased lending, and growth of the money supply. The Fed sells government securities to restrict the money supply. As investors purchase government securities, more money leaves circulation, which increases interest rates and decreases lending.

Fiscal Policy

Taxation, expenditures, and debt management of the federal government is called **fiscal policy**. Economic growth, price stability, and full employment are other goals that may be pursued by changes in fiscal policy.

Changes in taxation affect corporate earnings, disposable earnings, and the overall economy. As tax rates increase, corporations' after-tax income declines, which reduces their ability to pay dividends. This may cause the price for equities to decrease. Tax rate increases also reduce an individuals' disposable income and limit the amount of money entering the economy. The demand for tax-free investments is also influenced by changes in taxation levels. As increases in proportional tax rates occur, the attractiveness of tax-free instruments also increases, reducing yields.

Deficit spending occurs when governmental expenditures exceed tax collections of the government. By selling debt securities to the public to finance deficits, Treasury Securities compete with other issuers of debt securities. This demand drives the value of debt down due to the increased supply of debt, causing the yields on debt instruments to rise to meet competition.

THE NATURE OF INTEREST RATES

The economic environment is greatly influenced by interest rates. Decreases in interest rates are often followed by periods of economic expansion, while increases are generally followed by economic contractions. Investment returns and purchasing power are just two of the areas that are affected by the rise and fall of interest rates. Simply stated, the interest rate is the price of money. The discount rate is the interest rate charged by the Fed on a loan that it makes to a member bank. The nominal interest rate is the stated interest rate. The return on investments in terms of real goods and services is a real interest rate measure. The return in terms of dollars is an absolute measure. The real interest rate measures the quantity of goods we receive tomorrow for goods forgone today. The real interest rate is obtained by correcting nominal or dollar interest rates for the rate of inflation.

EXPANSION AND RECESSION

As discussed earlier, the economy is in a constant state of flux. Some economic factors tend to expand the economy and some tend to contract the economy. In the following section, we discuss the factors that contribute to the economy's rise and fall.

Periods of economic expansion are characterized by high employment, high resource demand, and output in excess of the historical gross domestic product average of 3 percent. As the economy expands, real wages rise, as do real interest rates. Higher interest rates decrease capital expenditures, and higher resource costs increase overall costs and reduce aggregate demand ultimately ending the expansionary period. The economy experienced such periods of expansion during the 1960s, and in 1973, 1978, 1983, and from 1992 to 1998.

Periods of recession are characterized by high unemployment, low resource demand, falling real wages, and decreasing real interest rates. The economy eventually pulls itself out of recession as prices for money and resources fall. The economy saw periods of recession in 1970, 1974, 1975, 1979, 1982, 1990, 1991, 2000, 2001, and 2002.

Recall Exhibit 2.10 (the drawing of the Business Cycle) with its peaks and troughs. The peaks are simply the top of the expansion, and the troughs, the bottom of the recession. Each is characterized by high and low real interest rates and changes in nonfarm hourly payroll. Real interest rates are at their highest at the peak and at their lowest at the trough. The rate of change in nonfarm hourly labor costs is at its highest at peaks and at its lowest in troughs.

A reasonable question to ask at this point is whether the economy is self-correcting. It appears to be so, although slowly. This slowness is evidenced by a recession's prolonged high unemployment and below-capacity utilization. As a result of the belief that the economy is too slow to self-correct, there is widespread support for monetary and fiscal policy stimulation during periods of recession, and, alternatively, for monetary and fiscal restriction during periods of excessive economic expansion. Thus, monetary and fiscal policy tools are used to guide the economy to stability and long-run prosperity. The degree of policy discretion remains controversial. There are economists who believe in less discretion and more constant growth models, including the management of money supply, inflation, unemployment, and budget deficits. Then, there are economists who believe in greater discretion and aggressive monetary and fiscal management.

FORECASTING THE ECONOMY – INDEX OF LEADING ECONOMIC INDICATORS

Can anyone successfully predict the future economy? Some say that monitoring the Gross Domestic Product is useful in forecasting the economy. Others look to the Index of Leading

Economic Indicators (the Index). Monitoring both GDP and the Index may be the best approach to forecasting the economy.

Gross Domestic Product (GDP) is the value of all goods and services produced in the country. It is the broadest measure of the general state of the economy. The historical growth rate is about 3 percent. Growth of GDP less than 2 percent is considered low and signals a possible recession. Growth in excess of 4 percent is robust and suggests the possibility of expansion. Monitoring GDP growth is useful in forecasting the peaks and troughs in the economy.

Another indication of future economic activity of which financial planners should be keenly aware is the Index of Leading Economic Indicators. This Index is a composite index of 10 variables. It has had a reasonable track record in predicting recessions, and has accurately predicted every recession since 1950, but has also predicted five that did not happen. When the Index declines for three months in a row, it signals a slowdown in economic growth. The Index only predicts the direction of economic activity and not the magnitude. The ten components listed below make up the Index.

Components of the Index of Leading Economic Indicators:

1. Length of average work week in hours, manufacturing
2. Initial weekly claims for unemployment
3. New orders placed with manufacturers for consumer goods
4. Percent of companies receiving slower deliveries from supplier
5. Contracts and orders for new plant and equipment
6. Permits for new housing starts
7. Interest rate spread, 10-year Treasury bond less federal funds rate
8. S&P 500 Index
9. Money supply (M2)
10. Index of consumer expectations

In addition to leading economic indicators, there are lagging economic indicators. These economic statistics fall or rise three to twelve months after the general economy. The lagging index gives a good picture of where the economy has been. The seven components of the lagging index for the United States are:

1. Average duration of unemployment
2. Inventories to sales ratio, manufacturing and trade
3. Labor cost per unit of output, manufacturing
4. Average prime rate
5. Commercial and industrial loans
6. Consumer installment credit to personal income ratio
7. Consumer price index for services

Although the word "recession" for some investors may have a less-than-positive connotation in periods of declining economic growth, interest rates generally fall, making the purchases of fixed instruments prior to the decline in interest rates an attractive investment opportunity. Likewise, generally the best time to buy stocks and hold them through economic recovery may be when the economy is at its worst.

IMPORTANCE OF THE LEGAL ENVIRONMENT

The legal environment is another component of the external environment that may have far-reaching influence on the accomplishment of financial goals and risk exposure. The rules of property ownership; consumer rights and protections; worker rights and protections; investor rights and protections; and the rules regarding formation of a business are established within this environment. With a high level of competence and knowledge of the legal environment, the personal financial planner can guide clients toward their financial goals while avoiding legal risks and protecting the clients' rights.

TORTS

Tort (private wrongs) is an infringement on the rights of another. The wrongdoer is a tortfeasor and creates a right in the damaged party to bring a civil action. Intentional torts—battery (harmful touching), assault (threat causing apprehension), libel (written falsehood), slander (oral falsehood), false imprisonment (unlawfully holding against will), trespass to land, invasion of privacy, and intentional infliction of emotional distress—are not covered by liability insurance. Unintentional torts (negligence) are acts or failures to act in a reasonably prudent manner thereby causing harm to another. Elements of unintentional torts include duty, breach of duty, causation and actual loss. Did the person exercise the proper degree of care to carry out his or her duty, and if not, was that the cause of the actual loss suffered by the other party? If so, the person performing the act may be liable for negligence.

Persons who may be liable (other than normal adults) include minors, mental incompetents and employees. Children and minors may be liable depending on their mental capacity. Their parents or guardians may be **vicariously liable** for the acts of such persons. Mental incompetents may, nonetheless, be required to exercise some duty of care. If that level of care is not exercised, such incompetents may be liable. Employers may be vicariously liable for the acts of employees.

vicarious liability - one person may become legally liable for the torts of another (e.g., parent/child, employer/employee acting in the scope of employment)

Standards of care

Negligence is defined as the failure to act in a way that a reasonably prudent person would have acted under the circumstances—in short, negligence is imprudent behavior. Types of liability created from negligent behavior include:

- ▲ Strict (absolute) liability - The two terms are used interchangeably. It is a liability without regard to negligence or fault. It applies to damage resulting from some extraordinarily dangerous activity or other statutorily defined activity (e.g., product liability, hazardous materials, blasting operations). Negligence does not have to be proved; however, defenses may be allowed to refute or lessen liability. Workers are indemnified for employment-connected injuries regardless of who was at fault (e.g., workers compensation). Negligence does not have to be proved on the part of the employer nor are defenses permitted by the employer to refute or lessen liability.
- ▲ Negligence per se - The act itself constitutes negligence, thereby relieving the burden to prove negligence (e.g., drunk driving).

Burden of proof is initially borne by the injured party. Standard of proof in most civil cases is the preponderance of the evidence (more than 50%). Other concepts to consider include *res ipsa loquitur* ("the act speaks for itself"). *Res ipsa loquitur* is a doctrine of the law of negligence that is concerned with the circumstances and the types of accidents, which afford reasonable evidence if a specific explanation of negligence is not available. For example, if a plane crashed, there is negligence. It does not have to be proven. The mere fact that a plane crashed implies negligence. Planes just don't fall out of the sky.

Damages

A tort can result in two forms of injury - bodily injury and property damage. Bodily injury may lead to medical expense, loss of income, pain and suffering, mental anguish and loss of consortium. The damages for bodily injury can be:

- Special damages to compensate for measurable losses.
- General damages to compensate for intangible losses (pain and suffering).
- Punitive damages - amounts assessed against the negligent party as punishment.

Property damage is usually measured by the actual monetary loss.

The collateral source rule holds that damages assessed against a negligent party should not be reduced simply because the injured party has other sources of recovery available such as insurance or employee benefits (health or disability insurance).

Vicarious liability

One person may become legally liable for the torts of another (e.g., parent/child, employer/employee acting in the scope of employment).

Defenses to negligence

There are various defenses available to alleged negligent parties that can relieve them of legal liability in spite of negligent behavior.

Assumption of the risk - The injured party fully understood and recognized the dangers that were involved in an activity and voluntarily chose to proceed. This defense is not available in all states.

Negligence on the part of the injured party - This can be either contributory negligence, where there is evidence that the injured party did not look out for his own safety, or comparative negligence, where the amount of damage is adjusted to reflect the injured party's proportion of contribution to the cause of the injury (same with multiple defendants). Contributory negligence theories usually cause the entire action to fail, thus effecting a harsh result. Many states allow recovery for that portion of damage not caused by the injured party (comparative negligence). The "last clear chance" rule may apply. This rule states that a claimant who is endangered by his own negligence may recover if the defendant had a "last clear chance" to avoid the accident and failed to do so.

Property Ownership

Property ownership rules are generally determined by individual states and will be discussed in Chapter 17 dealing with estate planning.

Consumer Protection

There are arguments for and against consumer protection legislation. In general, the arguments favoring such legislation suggest a necessity to equalize economic power (that is, to protect the so-called "weak" individual from the so-called "powerful" corporation). A second reason given to support such legislation is to protect honest businesses from competition with unscrupulous businesses. The arguments against consumer protection laws question the increased costs of such protection and the inability to measure its effectiveness (no amount of laws will ever overcome consumer ignorance).

Consumer protection laws are passed at both the state and federal levels. Federal laws preempt state laws where the state law provides less protection than the federal law. However, states do have the right to grant their citizens additional protection in excess of federal laws.

Consumer protection laws accomplish their goals by affecting contractual obligations. Without the right to enforce contracts, there would certainly be less private enterprise. Thus, certain consumer protection laws allow for the recission of illegal contracts and provide for monetary damages or injunctive relief for the injured party.

Federal Trade Commission (FTC) - the federal organization created in 1914 to keep competition free and fair and to protect U. S. consumers

Federal consumer protection began with the creation of the **Federal Trade Commission** (FTC) in 1914. Its charge was to keep competition free and fair and to protect consumers. The FTC promotes competition through the enforcement of antitrust laws. It also assures consumer protection by trade practice regulation prohibiting "unfair or deceptive acts or practices in commerce."

The FTC also prohibits the unfair and deceptive advertising of prices and practices, such as "bait-and-switch" promotions. Credit and packaging also fall under FTC regulation. Federal credit regulations are a response to the magnitude of credit transactions. The laws include the regulation of credit extension and discrimination, and the collection and dissemination of credit report information. Laws also regulate consumer warranties and debt collection practices. What follows is a brief description of several FTC laws that have a direct effect on consumers.

Where on the Web

Board of Governors of the Federal Reserve System *www.federalreserve.gov*
Bureau of Economic Analysis *www.bea.gov*
Bureau of Labor Statistics *www.bls.gov*
CPI Home Page *www.bls.gov/cpi*
Department of Commerce *www.commerce.gov*
Economic Policy Institute *www.epinet.org*
Economy at a Glance *stats.bls.gov/eag/eag.us.htm*
Federal Interagency Council on Statistical Policy *www.fedstats.gov*
LawLinks (Information on Bankruptcy) *www.lawlinks.com*
National Council on Economic Education *www.ncee.net*
National Foundation for Credit Counseling *www.nfcc.org*
National Institute for Consumer Education *www.nice.emich.edu*
PPI Home Page *www.bls.gov/ppi*
U.S. Census Bureau *www.census.gov*
U.S. Department of Treasury (Bureau of Public Debt) *www.publicdebt.treas.gov*

EXHIBIT 2.14: THE FTC AND FEDERAL CONSUMER PROTECTION LAWS

LAW	PURPOSE
Fair Packaging and Labeling Act	To prohibit deceptive labeling and require disclosure
Equal Credit Opportunity Act	To prohibit discrimination in granting credit
Fair Credit Reporting Act	To regulate the consumer credit reporting industry
Fair Credit Billing Act	To regulate consumer credit billing practices
Truth in Lending Act	To require disclosure of terms
Magnuson-Moss Warranty Act	To regulate consumer product warranty
Fair Debt Collection Act	To prevent abusive or deceptive debt collection practices
Federal Bankruptcy Laws	To adjust consumer debt and allow for a “fresh-start”
Consumer Protection at State Level	To protect against unfair business practices
Antitrust Legislation	To prevent monopolistic price practices
Federal Trade Commission Act	To prohibit unfair and deceptive acts of commerce

The *Equal Credit Opportunity Act of 1975* was designed to prohibit discrimination in credit extension. The law prohibits those to whom it applies from discouraging a consumer from seeking credit based on sex, race, religion, marital status, national origin, or because of the receipt of welfare payments.

The *Fair Credit Reporting Act* applies to anyone preparing or using a credit report in connection with extending credit, selling insurance, or hiring or terminating an employee. The purpose of the law is to prevent unjust injury to an individual because of inaccurate or arbitrary information in a credit report. It is also designed to prevent undue invasion of privacy in the collection and dissemination of a person's credit record or information. The law provides consumers with the right to require the reporting agency to reveal the information given in a credit report and the right to correct incorrect information or explain the consumer's version regarding disputed facts. The act is designed to cover credit-reporting agencies, not individual businesses. A consumer has 60 days to make a written request as to the nature of information received, upon which an adverse credit decision was made. If challenged, the credit agency must investigate and respond to the consumer within 30 days of such challenge.

The *Fair Credit Billing Act* (FCBA) provides a mechanism for consumers to correct credit card billing errors. The consumer must provide a written billing complaint to a creditor within 60 days of receiving the alleged erroneous bill. The creditor must acknowledge the complaint within 30 days and explain the alleged error in writing or correct the error within two billing periods not to exceed 90 days.

The *Truth in Lending Act* imposes a duty on those persons regularly extending credit to private individuals to inform those individuals fully as to the cost of the credit, including financial charges and the annual percentage rate of interest (APR). The purpose of the law is to promote informed decisions about the cost and use of credit.

The *Magnuson-Moss Warranty Act* covers express consumer warranties. The terms of the warranty must be simple and in readily understandable language, and if the price of the product is greater than $10, the warranty must be labeled as "full" or "limited."

The *Fair Debt Collections Practice Act* (FDCPA) applies to agencies and individuals whose primary business is the collection of debts for others. The law regulates collectors by prohibiting the collector from physically threatening the debtor or from using obscene language. The collector cannot falsely represent himself as an attorney or threaten the debtor with arrest or garnishment unless the collector can and intends to do so. The collector must disclose that he is a collector and must limit telephone calls to after 8:00 a.m. and before 9:00 p.m. The collector cannot telephone repeatedly with the intent to annoy the debtor. The collector cannot place collect calls to the debtor or use any unfair or unconscionable means to collect the debt.

Consumers and businesses receive further protection from creditors through the *federal bankruptcy laws.* **Bankruptcy** proceedings are held in a separate federal bankruptcy court with the filing of a voluntary (debtor) or involuntary (creditor-forced) petition. When a debtor is determined by the court to be unable to pay creditors, the court will provide or order relief in either liquidation (also known as "Chapter 7") or adjusted debts ("Chapter 13"). Businesses and the self-employed may also enter bankruptcy under reorganization ("Chapter 11"). Debtor rehabilitation is the main objective of the bankruptcy proceeding allowing the consumer or business entity a "fresh start."

bankruptcy - the financial condition when a debtor is determined by the court to be unable to pay creditors

With Chapter 7 bankruptcy, individuals are required to relinquish their assets in order to satisfy the claims of creditors. An individual is permitted, however, to retain certain assets. These assets include interest in personal household goods; clothing, books, animals, etc., up to $400 for any single item but not exceeding $8,000; interest in jewelry up to $1,000; equity in a home and burial plot not exceeding $15,000; interest in one motor vehicle up to $2,000; other property worth up to $800 plus up to $7,500 of the unused part of the $15,000 exemption for equity in a home and/or burial plot; item used in trade or business up to $1,500; interests in life insurance policies; professionally prescribed health aids; federal and state benefits such as Social Security, veteran's disability, and unemployment benefits; alimony; child support; pensions; annuities and rights to receive certain personal injury and other awards. Once Chapter 7 bankruptcy is completed, most debts are discharged completely and the debtor is no longer responsible for their repayment; however, there are certain nondischargeable debts. These nondischargeable debts include back taxes (going back three years); those debts based upon fraud, embezzlement, misappropriation, or defalcation against the debtor acting in a fiduciary capacity; alimony; child support; intentional tort claims; property or money obtained by the debtor under fraudulent or false pretenses; student loans (unless paying the loan will impose an undue hardship on the debtor or the debtor 's dependents); unscheduled claims (those not listed while filing for bankruptcy); claims from prior bankruptcy action in which the debtor was denied a discharge; consumer debts of more than $500 for luxury goods or services owed a single creditor within 40 days of relief; cash advances aggregating more than $1,000 as extensions of open-end consumer credit obtained by the debtor within 20 days of the order relief; and judgments or consent decrees awarded against the debtor for liability incurred as a result of the debtor's operation of a motor vehicle while intoxicated.

Chapter 13 bankruptcy tends to be more favorable for creditors because they receive at least some portion of what is owed to them. Chapter 7 bankruptcy does not guarantee that creditors will receive anything. In order to quality for Chapter 13, the individual must be a wage earner or have regular income. Also, the debtor's non contingent, liquidated, unsecured debts amount to less than $100,000 and secured debts amount to less than $350,000. Payments to creditors are reduced in accordance to an establish plan. The debtor is not required to relinquish assets in order to discharge debts.

Certain states have moved to protect citizens from unfair and deceptive acts and practices by enacting legislation that closes gaps in federal law or provides additional *protection for consumers under the state law.* An example of such state consumer protection is state-ordered "lemon laws" dealing with defective new automobiles. Such legislation creates public and/or private remedies for undesirable activities (illegal activities under the law). Public remedies include injunction, restitution, fines, and revocation of licenses. Private remedies include loss recovery, punitive damages, injunctions, recission, and redhibition.

antitrust legislation - laws passed to protect consumers from monopolistic price practices and to protect investors by promoting fair competition

monopoly - a single seller of a well-defined product with no valid substitutes

oligopoly - small number of rival seller firms; incentive to collude; high

The purpose of **antitrust legislation** is to protect consumers from monopolistic price practices and to protect investors by promoting fair competition. A **monopoly** is a single seller of a well-defined product with no valid substitute. Usually monopolies exist in industries with high barriers to entry, meaning it is cost prohibitive for new producers to enter the market. Since there is no competition, monopolies can control the market price of their products by adjusting output. Multiple sellers of goods can also engage in monopolistic practices when there is a small number of producers with a high incentive to collude. Such groups are called oligopolies. The Organization of Petroleum Exporting Countries (OPEC) is an example of an **oligopoly**. Some of the most important antitrust legislation include the Sherman Act and the Clayton Act.

The Sherman Act states, "Every contract, combination...or conspiracy in restraint of trade is illegal." It also states, "Every person who shall monopolize or attempt to monopolize shall be guilty of a misdemeanor."

The Clayton Act contains several sections that regulate monopolization, pricing practices, and competition. The following four sections are of particular interest to financial planners.

Section 2 prohibits sellers from discriminating in price between similarly situated buyers of goods (not services) where the effect of such discrimination may be to substantially lessen competition or create a monopoly (Robinson-Patman Act). The objective is to prevent large firms from using predatory pricing practices to drive out small competitors. *Section 3* states that persons engaged in commerce shall not contract, lease, or sell where the effect of such contract, lease, or sale may be to substantially lessen competition or tend to create a monopoly. This legislation deals with tying contracts, exclusive dealing, and requirements contracts. *Section 7* states that corporate mergers are illegal if they tend to create a monopoly in any line of business. *Section 8* prohibits persons from being directors of competing corporations. Once again, the legislation is intended to prohibit a lessening of competition.

The Federal Trade Commission Act protects consumers through trade practice regulation. It prohibits unfair methods of competition in or affecting commerce or deceptive acts or practices in commerce. The Federal Trade Commission enforces the Clayton Act provisions on price discrimination, tying and exclusive contracts, mergers and acquisitions, and interlocking directories. The FTC Act is broader in scope than the Sherman Act or the Clayton Act and may be used to curtail activities that prevent fair competition but do not rise to the level regulated in the Sherman or Clayton Acts.

Worker Protection (Employer/Employee Relations)

Worker protection is another facet of the legal environment. There are two fundamental areas of worker protection: job safety and financial security. The reasons for such protections are the same as for consumer protection, except that they apply specifically to employees.

The Occupational Safety and Health Act (OSHA) ensures safe and healthy working conditions for employees. The Secretary of Labor issues federal standards for safe employment environments to safeguard employees' health.

Workers' Compensation Acts are enacted both at the federal and state level and impose a form of strict liability on employers for accidental injuries occurring in the workplace. The legislation essentially removes the right of the injured employee to sue the employer for acts of ordinary negligence and replaces that right with the right to collect benefits—solely funded by employers—from an administrative agency. Workers' compensation protects against financial losses due to accidental injury, death, or disease resulting from employment. Generally, workmans' compensation is the exclusive remedy to employment accidents. However, courts are now carving out exceptions to the so-called "exclusive remedy rule" recognizing that workers compensation laws may not adequately compensate those injured workers with the greatest injuries and for situations that exceed normal negligence on the employer's part.

Other federal programs that offer protection for workers are discussed below.

Unemployment compensation is a federal and state financial security program that provides for temporary payments to workers who, through no fault of their own, become unemployed. Unemployment benefits are funded with a tax on employers based on an extensive rating system.

Social Security is a federal financial security program for providing some replacement income lost due to retirement, disability, and survivorship. Additionally, Social Security provides a death benefit and Medicare benefits, all of which are more thoroughly discussed in Chapter 11.

The *Employee Retirement Income Security Act (ERISA)* was passed to protect the financial security of employees by protecting employee rights in qualified retirement plans. Chapter 16 discusses ERISA and qualified retirement plans.

The *Consolidated Omnibus Budget Reconciliation Act of 1986 (COBRA)* requires that employees and certain dependents of employees be allowed to continue their group health insurance coverage following a qualifying loss of coverage. Chapter 9 contains a discussion of COBRA.

FINANCIAL INSTITUTIONS

Commercial Banks

Commercial banks are chartered under federal and state regulations. They offer numerous consumer services such as checking, savings, loans, safe-deposit boxes, investment services, financial counseling, and automatic payment of bills. Approximately 8,000 commercial banks exist nationwide with over 70,000 branch offices. Each account in a federally chartered bank is insured against loss up to $100,000 in principal and interest per account by the Bank Insurance Fund (BIF) of the Federal Deposit Insurance Corporation (FDIC), an agency of the federal government, subject to an aggregate limit of $100,000 for each person's accounts at that bank titled similarly (see discussion later).

Savings and Loan Associations

The purpose of Savings and Loan Associations (S&Ls), also known as thrift institutions, is to accept savings and provide home loans. They can also make installment loans for consumer products (e.g., automobiles and appliances). S&Ls are not permitted to provide demand deposits (such as checking accounts with a commercial bank); however, they can offer interest-bearing NOW accounts, which are similar to demand deposit accounts. The FDIC insures accounts in all federally chartered S&Ls up to $100,000 in principal and interest per account through its Savings Association Insurance Fund (SAIF) as well as some state-chartered institutions.

S&Ls are either mutual or corporate. The mutual savings and loans, which are more common, have the depositors as the actual owners of the association (shareowners). Corporate savings and loans operate as corporations and issue common and preferred stock to denote ownership.

Mutual savings banks

A mutual savings bank (MSB) is quite similar to a savings and loan association (S&L). Historically, they accepted deposits in order to make housing loans, but they primarily compete for consumer loans and offer interest-bearing negotiable order of withdrawal (NOW) accounts. Technically, the depositors of savings are the owners of the institution. MSBs are state chartered and have either FDIC's BIF insurance or a state-approved insurance program up to $100,000 per account. They are not, however, permitted in all states. Most are located in the Northeast.

Credit unions

Credit unions are not-for-profit cooperative ventures that are largely run by volunteers. They are developed to pool the deposits of members. These funds are used to invest or lend to members/ owners. Members are usually joined by a common bond such as work, union, or fraternal association, and regulations make it possible for people to remain members of a credit union after the common bond has been severed. Credit unions with federal charters have their accounts insured up to $100,000 through the National Credit Union Share Insurance Fund (NCUSIF), administered by the National Credit Union Administration (NCUA), that provides the same safety as deposits insured by the FDIC. Credit unions accept deposits and make loans for consumer products. They also make home loans. Employment-related credit unions typically make use of payroll deductions for deposits and loan repayments, often offer free term life insurance up to certain limits, and usually offer free credit life insurance.

Money Market Mutual Funds

A mutual fund is an investment company that raises money by selling shares to the public and investing the money in a diversified portfolio of securities. The investments are professionally managed with securities purchased and sold at the discretion of the fund manager. Many mutual fund companies have created money market mutual funds (MMMF) that serve as money market accounts. The accounts can be used for purposes of cash management.

A MMMF is a mutual fund that pools the cash of many investors and specializes in earning a relatively safe and high return by buying securities that have short-term maturities (always less than one year). The average maturity for the portfolio cannot exceed 120 days. This reduces price swings so that the money funds maintain a constant share value. Securities are bought and sold almost daily in money markets that result in payment of the highest daily rates available to small investors. Money deposited in mutual funds is not insured by the federal government; however, MMMFs are considered extremely safe due to the high quality of the securities. Accounts in money market mutual funds provide a convenient and safe place to keep money while awaiting alternative investment opportunities.

Stock Brokerage Firms

A stock brokerage firm is a licensed financial institution that specializes in selling and buying investment securities. Such firms usually receive a commission for the advice and assistance they provide. Commissions are based on the buy/sell orders they execute. Stock brokerage firms usually offer money market fund accounts where clients may place money while waiting to make investments in stocks and bonds. Money held in a money market mutual fund at a stock brokerage firm is not insured against loss by any government agency; however, most brokerage firms purchase private insurance against such losses.

Financial Services Companies

Financial services companies are national or regional corporations that offer a number of financial services to consumers, including traditional checking, savings, lending, credit card accounts, and MMMFs as well as advice on investments, insurance, real estate, and general financial planning. Financial services companies are also referred to as nonbank banks because they provide limited traditional banking services, either accepting deposits or making commercial loans, but not both.

FDIC Insurance

Any person or entity can have FDIC insurance on a deposit. A depositor does not have to be a United States citizen, or even a resident of the United States. The FDIC insures deposits in some, but not all, banks and savings associations. Federal deposit insurance protects deposits that are payable in the United States. The FDIC does not insure the following items.

- Deposits that are only payable overseas.
- Securities, mutual funds, and similar types of investments.
- Creditors (other than depositors) and shareholders of a failed bank or savings association.
- Treasury securities (bills, notes, and bonds) purchased by an insured depository institution on a customer's behalf.

All types of deposits received by a qualifying financial institution in its usual course of business are insured. For example, savings deposits, checking deposits, deposits in NOW accounts, Christmas Club accounts, and time deposits (including certificates of deposit, or CDs), are all FDIC insured deposits. The FDIC also insures the following.

- Cashiers' checks, money orders, officers' checks, and outstanding drafts.
- Certified checks, letters of credit, and travelers' checks for which an insured depository institution is primarily liable are also insured, when issued in exchange for money or its equivalent, or for a charge against a deposit account.

Deposits in different qualified institutions are insured separately. If an institution has one or more branches, however, the main office and all branch offices are considered to be one institution. Thus, deposits at the main office and at branch offices of the same institution are added together when calculating deposit insurance coverage. Financial institutions owned by the same holding company but separately chartered are separately insured. The FDIC presumes that funds are owned as shown on the "deposit account records" of the insured depository institution. The basic FDIC insured amount of a depositor is $100,000. Accrued interest is included when calculating insurance coverage. Deposits maintained in different categories of legal ownership are separately insured. Accordingly, a depositor can have more than $100,000 insurance coverage in a single institution if the funds are owned and deposited in different ownership categories. The most common categories of ownership are single (or individual) ownership, joint ownership, and testamentary accounts. Separate insurance is also available for funds held for retirement and business purposes. Federal deposit insurance is not determined on a per-account basis. A depositor cannot increase FDIC insurance by dividing funds owned in the same ownership category among different accounts within the same institutions. The type of account (whether checking, savings, certificate of deposit, outstanding official checks, or other form of deposit) has no bearing on the amount of insurance coverage.

Single ownership accounts.

A single (or individual) ownership account is an account owned by one person. Single ownership accounts include accounts in the owner's name, accounts established for the benefit of the owner by agents, nominees, guardians, custodians, or conservators, and accounts established by a business that is a sole proprietorship. All single ownership accounts established by, or for the benefit of, the same person are added together and the total is insured up to a maximum of $100,000. If an individual owns and deposits funds in his or her own name but then gives another person the right to withdraw funds from the account, the account will generally be insured as a joint ownership account.

Depositor	Type of Deposit	Amount Deposited
A	Savings Account	$25,000
A	CD	100,000
A	NOW Account	25,000
A's Restaurant (A Sole Proprietorship)	Checking	25,000
Total Deposited		$175,000
Maximum Amount of Insurance Available		(100,000)
Uninsured Amount		$75,000

The Uniform Gifts to Minors Act is a state law that allows an adult to make an irrevocable gift to a minor. Funds given to a minor under the Uniform Gifts to Minors Act are held in the name of a custodian for the minor's benefit. The funds are added to any other single ownership accounts of the minor, and the total is insured up to a maximum of $100,000.

Joint accounts

A joint account is an account owned by two or more individuals. They are insured separately from single ownership account if each of the following conditions are met:

- All co-owners must be natural persons. This means that legal entities such as corporations or partnerships are not eligible for joint account deposit insurance coverage.
- Each of the co-owners must have a right of withdrawal on the same basis as the other co-owners. For example, if one co-owner can withdraw funds on his or her signature alone, but the other co-owner can withdraw funds only on the signature of both co-owners, then this requirement has not been satisfied; the co-owners do not have equal withdrawal rights. Likewise, if a co-owner's right to withdraw funds is limited to a specified dollar amount, the funds in the account will be allocated between the co-owners according to their withdrawal rights and insured as single ownership funds. So, for example, if $100,000 is deposited in the names of A and B, but A has the right to withdraw only up to $5,000 from the account, $5,000 is allocated to A and the remainder is allocated to B. The funds, as allocated, are then added to any other single ownership funds of A or B, respectively.

- Each of the co-owners must have personally signed a deposit account signature card. The execution of an account signature card is not required for certificates of deposit, deposit obligations evidenced by a negotiable instrument, or accounts maintained by an agent, nominee, guardian, custodian, or conservator, but the deposit must in fact be jointly owned.

The interests of each individual in all joint accounts he or she owns at the same FDIC-insured depository institution are added together and insured up to $100,000 maximum. Each person's interest (or share) in a joint account is deemed equal unless otherwise stated on the deposit account records.

Account	Owners	Balance
#1	A and B	$100,000
#2	B and A	25,000
#3	A, B, and C	75,000
#4	D and A	80,000

A deposit account held in two or more names that does not qualify for joint account deposit insurance coverage is treated as being owned by each named owner as an individual, corporation, partnership, or unincorporated association, as the case may be, according to each co-owner's actual ownership interest. As such, each owner's interest is added to any other single ownership accounts or, in the case of a corporation, partnership, or unincorporated association, to other accounts of such entity, and the total is insured up to $100,000.

Business accounts

Funds deposited by a corporation, partnership, or unincorporated association, are FDIC insured up to a maximum of $100,000. Funds deposited by a corporation, partnership, or unincorporated association, are insured separately from the personal accounts of the stockholders, partners, or members. To qualify for this coverage, the entity must be engaged in an independent activity. "Independent activity" means that the entity is operated primarily for some purpose other than to increase deposit insurance. Funds owned by a business that is a sole proprietorship are treated as the individually owned funds of the person who is the sole proprietor. Consequently, funds deposited in the name of the sole proprietorship are added to any other single ownership accounts of the sole proprietor and the total is insured to a maximum of $100,000.

Retirement accounts

Retirement accounts established at FDIC-insured institutions also qualify for FDIC insurance. The total amount insured across all retirement accounts held at a single institution is limited to $100,000. This is provided that they are in bank investments and not securities and are not securities secured from the bank's investment arm.

NEGOTIABLE INSTRUMENTS

Negotiable instruments serve two important functions; they serve as an extension of credit, and also as substitute for money. In order for an instrument to be negotiable, it must have all of the following requirements on the face of the instrument:

- In writing.
- Signed by maker or drawer.
- Contain an unconditional promise or order to pay.
- State a fixed amount in money.
- Payable on demand or at a definite time.
- Payable to order or to bearer, unless it is a check.

Commercial paper is a typical form of negotiable instrument, and there are several different types.

The first type is known as a draft, and it has three parties in which one person or entity (drawer) orders another (drawee) to pay a third party (payee) a sum of money.

August 29, 2006

On August 29, 2005, pay to the order of Allison $1,000 plus 6% annual interest from August 29, 2006.

To: Acme Publications, Inc.

(signed) **Donna Jones**

A check is a special type of draft that is payable on demand, and the drawee must be a bank. The check writer is the drawer.

A promissory note is another type of commercial paper that is a two-party instrument. With a promissory note, Party A (the maker) promises to pay a specified sum of money to Party B (the payee). The note may be payable on demand or at a definite time. The following example is a promissory note in which Jean Smith is the maker and Kristin Fourroux is the payee.

August 29, 2005

I promise to pay to the order of Kristin Fourroux $1,000 plus 6% annual interest on August 29, 2006.

To: Acme Publications, Inc.

(signed) **Jean Smith**

A certificate of deposit is an acknowledgment by a financial institution of receipt of money and a promise to repay it. It is actually a special type of promissory note in which the maker is the financial institution.

Investor Protection (The Securities Acts of 1933 and 1934)

The *Securities Acts of 1933 and 1934* were passed to protect investors and to regulate those providing investment services. It is important that all professional financial analysts be familiar with the Securities Acts and the related Acts that followed them.

The Securities Act of 1933 is primarily concerned with new issues of securities or issues in the primary market. It requires that all relevant information on new issues be fully disclosed, that new securities be registered with the Securities and Exchange Commission (SEC), that audited financial statements be filed with the registration statements, and forbids fraud and deception. When sold, all securities must be accompanied by a prospectus. Small issues (under $1,500,000) and private issues are not required to comply with the Securities Act of 1933 requirements of full disclosure.

While the Securities Act of 1933 was limited to new issues, the 1934 Securities Exchange Act (SEA) extended the regulation to securities sold in the secondary markets. The Act provided the following provisions:

- ▲ Establishment of the SEC - The SEC's primary function is to regulate the securities markets.
- ▲ Disclosure requirements for Secondary Marke - Annual reports and other financial reports are required to be filed with the SEC prior to listing on the organized exchanges. These reports include the annual 10K Report, which must be audited, and the quarterly 10Q Report, which is not required to be audited.
- ▲ Registration of organized exchanges - All organized exchanges must register with the SEC and provide copies of their rules and bylaws.
- ▲ Credit regulation - Congress gave the Federal Reserve Board the power to set margin requirements for credit purchases of securities. Securities dealers' indebtedness was also limited to 20 times their owners' equity capital by this act.
- ▲ Proxy solicitation - Specific rules governing solicitation of proxies were established.
- ▲ Exemptions - Securities of federal, state, and local governments, securities that are not traded across state lines, and any other securities specified by the SEC are exempt from registering with the SEC. This includes Treasury bonds and municipal bonds.
- ▲ Insider activities - A public report, called an insider report, must be filed with the SEC in every month that a change in the holding of a firm's securities occurs for an officer, director, or 10% or more of the shareholders. The 1934 SEA forbids insiders profiting from securities held less than 6 months and requires these profits be returned to the organization. In addition, short sales are not permitted by individuals considered to be insiders.
- ▲ Price manipulation - The SEA of 1934 forbids price manipulation schemes such as wash sales, pools, circulation of manipulative information, and false and misleading statements about securities.

For a complete discussion on Regulatory Requirements, see Appendix C.

FORMS OF BUSINESS ORGANIZATIONS

Each state's legal environment establishes the forms of business organizations that may be created within that state. This chapter introduces the legal forms of business. A more detailed discussion of business organizations is covered in Chapter 14—Business Entities.

There are seven legal forms of organization that a business can use: sole proprietorship, general partnership, limited partnership, limited liability partnership, limited liability company, corporation, and S corporation. A sole proprietorship is a business owned by an individual who is personally liable for the obligations of the business. A general partnership is an association of two or more persons, who jointly control and carry on a business as co-owners for making a profit. The partners are personally liable for the obligations of the business. A limited partnership is an organization in which at least one partner is a general partner and at least one other is a limited partner with limited management participation and limited liability. A limited liability partnership (LLP) is usually a professional partnership (CPAs, attorneys) wherein the partners have limited liability to the extent of investment except where personally liable through malpractice. This form protects the individual assets of the partners who do not commit malpractice. A limited liability company (LLC) is an entity where the owners, or members, have limited liability for debts and claims of the business even while participating in management. The governing document is called an operating agreement. Some states prohibit single member LLCs. A corporation is a separate legal entity that is created by state law and operates under a common name through its elected management. Owners (shareholders) have limited liability. An S corporation is a domestic corporation with 100 shareholders or less, comprised of individuals (excluding nonresident aliens), estates, certain trusts, and exempt organizations and having no more than one class of stock.

There are several other forms of business organizations:

- A joint venture is an association formed to carry out a single transaction or a series of similar transactions that, for tax purposes, is treated the same as a partnership (although no partnership tax return is filed).
- A syndicate or investment group contains a number of persons who pool their resources in order to finance a business venture.
- A business trust involves a number of people who turn over management and legal title of property to one or more trustees who then distribute the profits to the participants (the beneficiaries of the trust).
- A cooperative is an association (may be incorporated) organized in order to provide an economic service to its members (or shareholders).

IMPORTANCE OF THE SOCIAL ENVIRONMENT

A society's culture affects the way a society lives and what it values. Culture changes slowly, but it does change. How does a changing social environment affect a client's financial plan? Financial planners must accurately assess the social environment and forecast the threats and opportunities that change will bring. Some of the characteristics of a changing social environment include:

- Advancing population age.

- ▲ Increasing life expectancy.
- ▲ Changing customs, norms, values, folkways, and morals.
- ▲ Shifts in attitudes and motivations.
- ▲ Dedication to or alienation from traditional religious beliefs.
- ▲ Evolving global languages.
- ▲ Acceptance or rejection of traditional status symbols and social institutions.

One likely forecast for the U.S. is the flow of new cultures from around the globe into the workforce. These modern-day settlers bring new customs and cultures to be assimilated into this country. How they interpret the so-called "American Dream" may well determine the country's future social environment.

Statistics show that the U.S. population is aging. At some point in the future, retirees will outnumber active workers. The larger number of retirees will put additional pressure on the finances of the Social Security system. There will be new investment opportunities as our country is faced with the challenges of an aging population with increased life expectancies, geographic mobility, and financial freedom.

IMPORTANCE OF THE TECHNOLOGICAL ENVIRONMENT

Perhaps the most rapidly changing environment is that of technology. Technological advancement has affected our workplace, our homes, and our investment planning. Think back to when there was no Internet, no electronic income tax filing. It will not be long before the majority of tax filers file income tax returns electronically. Already, the Internet, through large institutions, provides basic financial planning to anyone with access to a computer. Such assistance may include income tax preparation; credit assessment and counseling; mortgage qualification; education planning; preparation of basic personal financial statements; determination of investment selection for 401(k) plan contributions; and retirement planning. Why do these institutions provide these services, especially free of charge? The answer is to get more assets under management. Assets under management equals fee revenues. Such technology has displaced some financial planners who were providing the same service for persons in the same market niche. Astute financial planners learn to recognize how the technological environment can best serve them and their clients. Success comes from keeping a constant vigil on the characteristics that make up the technological environment:

- ▲ Current state of technology.
- ▲ Information processing and communication.
- ▲ Production equipment and processes.
- ▲ Medical advances.
- ▲ Creation of new technology.
- ▲ New patents, trademarks, copyrights.
- ▲ Human and business solutions.
- ▲ Biotechnology.
- ▲ Gene identification and cloning.
- ▲ Advances in service and engineering.

IMPORTANCE OF THE POLITICAL ENVIRONMENT

The political environment is especially important to risk analysis in investments. Political stability means less investment risk. To evaluate the political environment of any country, the financial planner should assess the country's:

- Form of government.
- Political ideology/stability.
- Social unrest.
- Relative strength of opposing political groups and views.
- Foreign trade policy.
- Degree of government protectionism regarding foreign goods.

This analysis becomes increasingly important as the world moves to a global economy and investors try to diversify investment portfolios using worldwide investments.

IMPORTANCE OF THE TAXATION ENVIRONMENT

Taxation, in its myriad forms, leaves the taxpayer with less disposable income. In that sense, all taxes, including income taxes, estate transfer taxes, payroll taxes, property taxes, and sales taxes, have a dampening effect on consumer spending and consumption.

Many of the taxes we pay are the result of complex tax laws about which the average taxpayer has little knowledge or understanding. Enter the income tax expert, the transfer tax expert, and even the property tax expert—each offering a specialized knowledge and distinctive expertise.

Some of the taxes we pay are the result of economic choice, some from a lack of understanding of the alternatives. This is especially true in the area of transfer taxes (estate and gift taxes). If people were more keenly aware of the way to avoid transfer taxes, many would. Because of the potential burden of transfer taxes (up to 47% in 2005, 46% in 2006, 45% in 2007), there is a great opportunity to avoid these transfer taxes through competent tax planning.

The changing nature of taxes and tax legislation has the potential to broadly affect large segments of the financial planning community. Consider that in 2001 Congress passed a bill to eliminate death or transfer taxes (effective in 2010). Even though transfer taxes affect only 5 percent of the U.S. population (roughly 13,750,000 out of 275,000,000), those affected are the country's wealthiest. Many of these persons spend substantial amounts to avoid or mitigate the costs of transfer taxes. They spend this money with estate planners, lawyers, CPAs, and insurance professionals because it is cheaper to pay these professionals than to pay the tax. If the transfer tax were eliminated, many of the transaction costs associated with avoiding the transfer tax would also be eliminated. What would happen to the estate-planning bar? What would happen to the insurance professional that sells only multimillion-dollar second-to-die whole life policies? What would happen to the CPA who practices primarily or exclusively in the estate planning area? Perhaps many of the services, products, and devices used to avoid the transfer taxes would disappear.

The tax environment itself is constantly changing. It is common for Congress to write new tax laws as frequently as annually. If a professional financial planner is to assist clients in minimizing their legal taxes, thus giving them more disposable income for consumption, savings, and investments, the planner must have a basic education in taxation and must develop ways to remain current in the field.

PROFESSIONAL FOCUS

CERTIFI
FINA
PLANN
Robert

When analyzing the External Environment for a client, which economic indicators do you find most effective and why?

Interest rates, consumer spending, unemployment, manufacturer's new orders, building permits, the money supply and the CPI fluctuate endlessly. Clients are afraid they may not be able to meet future financial obligations and desires. Since the beginning of recorded history, consultants have used a variety of means to attempt to predict the future. In our profession, we use economic indicators, theories about business cycles, and wave theories in an attempt to take the uncertainty out of the future. A planner should be prepared to discuss the nature of economic indicators and The Conference Board's Index of Leading Economic Indicators. However, planners should emphasize these are indicators, not accurate predictors of future economic behavior.

What method do you use to forecast inflation and how does inflation affect your clients' financial plans?

Our nation's best economists have trouble turning the predictions of The Conference Board and the contents of The Beige Book into accurate predictions of inflation. How can a planner be expected to predict inflation, select the most appropriate investments, persuade his client to buy them, monitor performance and make appropriate changes each time a new inflation-related statistic is released? We know that interest rates, inflation, employment, consumer confidence and other indicators are going to change. What we don't know is the direction or rate of change. We don't know tomorrow's breaking news story. We don't know the effect on individual portfolio positions. On the other hand, we know what assets our clients own. We know our clients' earning capacity. We know our clients' financial dreams. Rather than trying to predict the economy, we should prepare our clients for uncertainty. Use the predictive tools of our profession to describe probable economic futures to our clients. Then, design portfolios that have adequate amounts of cash and fixed income to give clients the staying power they need to weather downturns in the market: adequate amounts of equities to preserve purchasing power in times of inflation.

For clients that are not knowledgeable of their external environment, do you, as their financial planner, feel it your responsibility to educate them? If so, how much should they know and what steps do you use to educate them?

When clients question individual investment performance, gently draw them back and refocus their attention on their goals and objectives. Remind them the future holds risk and uncertainty. Show them how you have arrayed their assets to help increase the possibility of achieving their goals. With help, they may be able to write a check for what they want, when they want it.

Do your clients understand the impact of inflation on their overall financial planning goals? Explain.

A major concern for planners and clients is anticipating how the external environment will affect client finances. Clients understand the impact of inflation. They know from experience that most items cost more than they did a few years ago. They are confident that goods and services will cost more in the future.

ROBERT W. BOREK, JR., CLU, CHFC, CFP®

DISCUSSION QUESTIONS

1. How do the external and internal environments in which financial planning occurs differ?
2. How does each external environmental factor link to the different areas of financial planning?
3. What are some examples of how each external environmental factor might affect clients from different economic levels?
4. Why is external environmental analysis so important?
5. How is the external environment analyzed?
6. Why is the economic environment so important to financial planning?
7. What is price elasticity?
8. What is unit elastic demand?
9. What is marginal utility?
10. What is diminishing marginal utility?
11. How do interest rates, taxes, and inflation affect areas of financial planning?
12. What are the components of the business cycle and how do they affect the economy?
13. What is the formula for the rate of inflation?
14. What are the Consumer Price Index, the Gross Domestic Product deflator, and the Producer Price Index?
15. What is monetary policy?
16. What is fiscal policy?
17. What are the Federal Reserve's three economic goals?
18. What is the index of leading economic indicators?
19. For what is the index of leading economic indicators used?
20. How good is the index of leading economic indicators as a predictor?
21. What are five of the components of the index of leading economic indicators?
22. What is negligence?
23. What are considered "nondischargable debts" in Chapter 7 bankruptcy?
24. List some examples of federal consumer protection laws.
25. What are some examples of federal programs that offer protection for workers on the job-site?
26. Identify two federal securities acts that protect investors.
27. How do the external environmental factors—social, technological, political, and taxation—affect a client's financial plan?

EXERCISES

1. Define the laws of supply and demand.
2. What does it mean if the demand for a product is inelastic?
3. What action might the Federal Reserve take if it wanted to lower interest rates?
4. What is the price adjustment process in a competitive market and how does it shift?
5. What happens in the marketplace when the supply curve decreases, or shifts to the left?
6. Describe what has occurred when the price of a particular product decreases and consumers buy more of that product.
7. Consumer demand for sugar at 80 cents per pound results in 1,000 pounds sold. A drop in sugar price to 50 cents per pound results in 1,250 pounds sold. Is the demand for sugar inelastic, elastic, or unit elastic? (Ignore negative signs for PE calculations.)

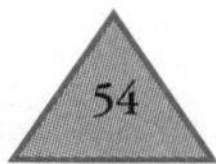

8. If a substitute good is readily available for a product, is the product demand likely to be elastic or inelastic?
9. Give an example illustrating the law of downward-sloping demand.
10. An increase in the price of product A causes a decrease in the demand for product B. What is the relationship between the two products?
11. Describe reasons for a change in consumer demand.
12. Which of the following might cause an increase in supply?
    - ▲ A decrease in productivity.
    - ▲ Fewer sellers in the marketplace.
    - ▲ More efficient technology.
    - ▲ A decrease in government subsidies.
13. Identify several determinants of demand elasticity.
14. If the quantity supplied does not change significantly with a change in price, is the type of supply elastic or inelastic?
15. Define inflation.
16. How would someone living on a fixed income be affected by inflation?
17. When the economy is slowing and unemployment is increasing, what phase of the business cycle are we in?
18. Which of the following economic activities represent examples of monetary policy?
    - ▲ The federal funds rate is increased.
    - ▲ The Federal Reserve lowers bank reserve requirements.
    - ▲ The Federal Open Market Committee sells securities.
19. What action taken by the Fed will lead to increased money supply?
20. Identify the phases and points of a typical business cycle.
21. In a typical business cycle, which phases exhibit periods of increasing employment and increasing output?

PROBLEMS

1. Identify whether each of the following involves a shift in the demand curve or a change in the quantity demanded:
    - ▲ Fish prices fall after the Pope allows Catholics to eat meat on Friday.
    - ▲ Auto sales decrease due to increased unemployment.
    - ▲ Gasoline consumption increases as some gasoline taxes are lowered.
    - ▲ After a drought hits Louisiana, crawfish sales decrease.
2. If the cost of one year of college education on January 1 of 2004, 2005, and 2006 are $15,000, $16,000, and $17,500, respectively, what was the rate of education inflation for 2004 and 2005? What was the annualized education inflation rate from 2004 to year 2006?

3. Homer, age 38, is married with three children. He has the following liquid assets on deposits with his bank, which is an FDIC insured institutions.

Account	Ownership	Balance
CD	Homer	150,000
Savings	Homer with wife	50,000
IRA	Homer	75,000
Checking Account	Homer	90,000

How much is currently insured by the FDIC?

CHAPTER 3

Communication and Internal Environmental Analysis

LEARNING OBJECTIVES:

After learning the material in this chapter, you will be able to:

1. Explain how a financial planner can successfully communicate respect, trust, and empathy to a client.
2. List several techniques that reduce the risk of misinterpretation and misunderstanding when communicating with a client.
3. Identify professional liability risks affecting the financial planner.
4. List the four phases of thinking through which a client often progresses in the financial planning process.
5. Describe the Auditory Learning Style, the Visual Learning Style, and the Kinetic, or Tactile, Learning Style by discussing how a client with each style prefers to learn.
6. Identify the five categories that make up a client's internal environment.
7. List the factors that make up Life Cycle Positioning.
8. Name the Life Cycle Phases through which most financial planning clients eventually pass.
9. Explain how a client's tolerance for risk; savings and consumption habits; views about employment, retirement, and leisure time; and attitudes on government (especially taxation) affect the setting of their financial goals.
10. Identify "special needs" that may influence the successful development of a client's financial plan.
11. Identify the financial statements and other information needed to develop an accurate assessment of a client's financial position.
12. Explain how a client's subjective perception of his or her financial position affects the objective reality of the financial position provided by a financial planner.

COMMUNICATION SKILLS

The importance of a good working relationship between the personal financial planner and the client cannot be overemphasized. The relationship requires excellent interpersonal skills, proficient communication skills, and the ability to educate. As indicated in the Planner's Pyramid of Knowledge, these skills are essential to achieving a successful financial plan. Specifically, they are required to efficiently gather accurate information from the client and to educate the client throughout the financial planning process. With a good working relationship, the client is more willing to share information and less resistant to accepting a planner's advice. A good relationship is one in which all persons involved are treated with respect, trust, and empathy.

EXHIBIT 3.1: FINANCIAL PLANNER'S PYRAMID OF KNOWLEDGE

Planner's Professional Responsibility				
Financial Data Collection and Analysis	Establishing Financial Direction			
External Analysis	Communication & Internal Analysis			
Time Value of Money	Planning for Children's Education			
Insurance	Investments	Tax	Retirement	Estates

BE RESPECTFUL OF YOUR CLIENT

Respect can be conveyed in several ways. One obvious way is the manner in which the client is addressed. When first meeting a client, use a courteous title such as Mr., Ms., Dr., etc. If later, the client indicates a preference to be called by a first name or some other nickname, that desire should be met. Listening to clients, not talking over them, and showing value for their time also portray respect. Always return phone calls when you say you will. Be on time for appointments. Let the client know how long a meeting is expected to last. If you are exceeding the time, ask if the meeting should continue or be rescheduled for another time. These issues may seem elementary, but being mindful of them will assist in developing a professional relationship with your client.

Trust must be developed between the planner and the client. Trust has to be earned, but the process is expedited by showing evidence that others deem you trustworthy. Provide prospective clients with letters of reference from previous clients, especially those that cite specific examples of how they benefited from your skills. Care must be taken to maintain confidentiality. The client needs to know that any information they share with you will remain strictly confidential. Therefore, if specific examples are provided, make sure the client knows that permission was received prior to any disclosure.

Respect is shown by being empathetic and viewing the client as an individual. Empathy is the identification with and understanding of another's situations, feelings, and motives. Remember, financial success is a relative concept. The client defines success subjectively. The client's definition is based on personal situations, feelings, and motives. The financial planner needs to understand the client's perspective and show regard for those views and values.

Communicate with Your Client

A good relationship cannot be developed with the client without first mastering communication skills. Communications between the financial planner and client are difficult because of subjectivity, paradigms, and unspoken words that lead to misinterpretation and misunderstanding.

For example, suppose the client states a desire to take at least one nice vacation each year. The keen financial planner might ask for the vacation destination. Suppose that destination is the Caribbean. The planner may now believe that enough information has been gathered to include this objective into the financial plan. However, enough information has probably not been gathered. It might be assumed the client intends to vacation for one week, because that is the norm in the United States. However, the client may be planning a month-long vacation. Additionally, it is not known how the client plans to travel. Are they going to fly? If so, do they plan to fly first class or coach? In what type of accommodations do they plan to stay? As you can see, by attributing the standards of the financial planner or by assuming the client's standards, the goal of taking one nice vacation a year is easily misinterpreted. This misinterpretation may lead to inappropriate financial planning.

Use Communication Techniques

Fortunately, there are several communication techniques that can greatly reduce the chance of misinterpretation and misunderstanding. Below are a few of the techniques that the financial planner should use when speaking with a client.

Keep the client informed. Tell the client what will happen, what is happening as it happens, and what has happened when it is completed. Although you may be very experienced in the financial planning process, the client is not. Consider the client's perspective. If they do not know what to expect, they will probably be apprehensive. If they are not informed of the significance of particular questions, they may be resistant to answer them or may only provide partial information.

Clarify statements and remove ambiguity. Avoid general statements by using clarification techniques such as restating, paraphrasing, and summarizing. Apply the ideas of "Is" and "Is Not." For example, in describing the purpose of property insurance, you may state that property insurance is intended to help minimize loss in the event of a disaster. It is not intended to eliminate loss in the event of a disaster.

Seek information to understand the client's situation and goals. Use open-ended questions to draw out relevant information. Do not make assumptions. Question everything. Question the answers to the questions. When the client can no longer generate an answer, all the information the client has may be known. However, that does not mean the planner has all the information necessary. It may be necessary to obtain information from other sources.

Be specific. When communicating with the client, identify the "What, Where, When, Responsible Party, and Extent" to describe a task or a result. Avoid the use of slang and colloquialisms. Articulate goals in terms of time, place, and form. A financial plan is useless if it cannot be accurately and precisely communicated to the client.

The Engagement Letter

engagement letter - a tool of communication between client and financial planner that sets down in writing information about any agreements or understandings obtained at client/planner meetings including the plan of action for developing a financial plan, the expected outcome of the engagement, and the method of compensation

An **engagement letter** is a useful tool in communicating with your client. An engagement letter is written near the beginning of the client/planner relationship, usually following the first meeting. The letter should summarize and memorialize the previous meetings and conversations with the client. The letter should also contain information about any agreements or understandings that were obtained during previous meetings, including the plan of action for developing a financial plan, the expected outcome of the engagement, and the method and amounts of compensation. Exhibit 3.2 illustrates a sample engagement letter.

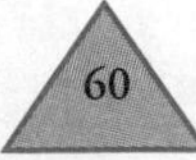

EXHIBIT 3.2: SAMPLE ENGAGEMENT LETTER

(Date)

(Name of Client)
(Address of Client)

Dear (Name of Client):

Thank you for meeting with me on *(date)*. Per our discussions, I understand your goals are as follows:
1. *(list goal)*
2. *(list goal)*
3. *(list goal)*

This letter sets forth our understanding of the terms and objectives of our engagement to provide personal financial planning services to you. The scope and nature of the services to be provided are as follows:

1. **Review and Evaluation**
   We will review and analyze all information furnished to us including:
   (list items)

2. **Written Plan**
   Based on our review and analysis, we will prepare a written analysis of your:
   (list items)

   We will also prepare, in writing, specific initial recommendations to address your concerns and issues, including goals, objectives, and risks with respect to:
   (list items)

   Our recommendations will include strategies based on our analysis of your circumstances. Where appropriate, we will include financial illustrations and financial projections to enhance your understanding of the potential outcomes of the alternatives.

   We will meet with you to discuss our analysis and will provide you with a preliminary draft copy of our recommended strategies. You will be given an opportunity to concur with the preliminary recommendations or suggest modifications. Following agreement on your personal financial goals and the strategies to be used to achieve them, we will provide you with a finalized version of the plan.

3. **Fees**
   Our fee for these services is based on our standard hourly rates and the number of hours required. We expect our fees to be no less than $_______________ but not to exceed $_______________. We will bill you beginning with our next regular billing cycle. The final payment will be adjusted to reflect actual time expended, not to exceed the maximum total amount quoted for the year, and will be due upon completion of the engagement.

4. **Implementation**
   We will assist you in implementing the strategies that have been agreed upon. Accordingly, we will be available on an ongoing basis, by telephone or in person, to answer questions, to assist you or your other advisors to take necessary actions, and to make recommendations regarding these matters. We will bill you for these additional services based on time expended at our standard hourly rate.

5. **Limitation on Scope of Services**

   These services are not intended to include:
   (list items)

We will bill separately for any such additional services provided, based on time expended at our standard hourly rates.

If this letter correctly sets forth your understanding of the terms and objectives of the engagement, please so indicate by signing in the space provided below.

Respectfully yours,

(Name of Planner)
(Name of Firm)

The above letter sets forth my understanding of the terms and objectives of the engagement to provide personal financial planning services.

Signed: ____ Date: ______________________________

PROFESSIONAL LIABILITY

As members of a profession, financial planners are expected to comply with standards of ethics and to perform their services in accordance with accepted principles and standards. Financial planners who fail to carry out such duties may be civilly liable to their clients, for whom they have agreed to provide services, and to third parties, who may have relied upon statements prepared by the financial planner. Civil and criminal liability may also be imposed upon financial planners through statutes, such as the federal securities law.

Common Law Liability to Clients

Common law liability - liability based on breach of contract, tort, or fraud

Common law liability to which a financial planner may be subject is based upon breach of contract, tort of negligence, or fraud. The failure to perform one's contractual duties is a breach of contract for which one is liable to the party to whom the performance was to be rendered. Thus, if a financial planner has agreed to perform certain services for a client and fails to honestly, properly, and completely carry out those contractual duties, the financial planner will be civilly liable. In most cases, if there has been a breach of contract by a financial planner, courts will award compensatory damages as a remedy to the client.

A financial planner has a duty to exercise the same standard of care that a reasonably prudent and skillful financial planner in the community would exercise under similar circumstances. A violation of generally accepted principles and standards is sufficient evidence of negligence but not necessary for an action to be deemed negligent. A financial planner may comply with accepted principles and standards and still be negligent for failure to act with reasonable care. The financial planner, however, is not liable for errors in judgment if made according to accepted practices and with reasonable care, or if the client's own negligence or intentional acts contributed significantly to the client's loss.

In an action based upon fraud, the client must establish that the financial planner made a false representation of a material fact. The misrepresentation by the financial planner must have been made with the knowledge that it was false (actual fraud) or with reckless disregard for its truth or falsity (constructive fraud). For the fact to be deemed material, the financial planner must have intentionally made the misrepresentation to induce the client to act or discourage the client from acting, and the client must have been injured as a result of his reasonable reliance on the misrepresentation. Damages for common law liability will be equal to the actual or anticipated losses incurred by the client as a result of the breach of contract, negligent act, or fraud and may include the cost of securing services of another financial planner.

Common Law Liability to Third Parties

Third parties are not clients of the financial planner but are persons who had knowledge of documents prepared by the financial planner. Traditionally, in common law, a financial planner does not owe contractual duties to third parties unless they are direct parties to or third party beneficiaries of a contract for the services of the financial planner. The financial planner may, however, be subject to tort liability which is based upon negligence in failing to exercise ordinary, reasonable care. If a third party is injured because he relied upon documents prepared by a financial planner who failed to act with reasonable care, the financial planner will be liable and compensatory damages will be awarded.

Statutory Liability

The financial planner is subject to criminal liability imposed by the Securities Act of 1933, the Securities Exchange Act of 1934, the Investment Advisers Act of 1940 (discussed in Chapter 19), and other federal statutes and state criminal codes. The **Securities Act of 1933** provided rules and regulations related to new issues of investment securities such as initial public offerings. Before the issuer can offer the securities to the public, a registration statement that includes financial statements of the firm must be filed with the Securities and Exchange Commission (SEC).

Securities Act of 1933 - federal law that provides rules and regulations related to new issues of investment securities

The **Securities Exchange Act of 1934** provided rules and regulations related to the purchase and sale of investment securities in the market after the initial offering by the firm. Under this act financial planners are liable for false or misleading statements of material facts that are made in applications, reports, documents, and registration statements prepared by the financial planner and filed with the SEC. Liability is also imposed on financial planners who have access to material non-public information and trade in the securities without making a disclosure. It is unlawful to use any manipulative or deceptive device in connection with the sale or purchase of securities including attempts to defraud, making untrue statements of material facts, and omitting true statements of material facts. The financial planner will be liable to a person who was injured because he purchased or sold securities as a result of such misrepresentation. For more information with regards to the regulatory requirements, see Appendix C.

Securities Exchange Act of 1934 - federal law that provides rules and regulations related to the purchase and sale of investment securities in the secondary market

EDUCATE YOUR CLIENT

A significant role of a personal financial planner is that of educator. The client may need to be taught the meaning of common financial planning terminology, such as the time value of money and opportunity costs. The professional financial planner should be an expert in the use of time value of money to be able to assist clients in putting financial choices into a logical, systematic, and quantifiable framework. For most clients, the most understandable time reference is today. The planner may project that the client will need one million dollars at age 62 to quit working (achieve financial independence) and continue to maintain the same preretirement lifestyle. If the client is currently 35 years old, the million dollars and the 27 years until the client will need the money may have little relevance. The planner can create relevance and understanding, however, by calculating the need in today's dollars. In this example, the million dollars is equal to $100,000 in invested assets or, alternatively, if the client has no investments, $731.25 will need to be saved each month. (This calculation was determined by assuming 324 months of saving $731.25 at an earnings rate of 9 percent per year to accumulate the million dollars at age 62.) The reality of the $100,000 or the $731.25 each month is much more meaningful to the client than the distant million dollars. People have a much better understanding of today's realities and values than of those in the future.

learning styles (auditory, visual, kinetic or tactile) - the conditions under which people learn best—clients whose preferred learning style is auditory learn best by hearing information; clients who prefer a visual learning style learn best by reading and viewing; those who prefer a kinetic, or tactile, style learn best through manipulation and testing information

Clients may need education during the development of goals and objectives or the selection and implementation of the financial strategy. Undoubtedly, clients will need to be educated on many aspects of the financial planning process throughout the relationship. Therefore, it is beneficial for the planner to understand how individuals learn. Learning is made easier, and is more effective, when people are taught in a manner conducive to their learning style. People who learn best by listening prefer the auditory learning style. Those who prefer to learn by seeing are "visual" learners. Kinetic, or tactile, learners learn best by "doing." Most likely, clients will not know their preferred **learning style**. Exhibit 3.3 may help you gain a better understanding of a client's learning style.

EXHIBIT 3.3: DETERMINING LEARNING STYLES

If your client...	Their learning style is most likely ...	They should be educated by...
Talks about situations; expresses emotions verbally; enjoys listening, but cannot wait to talk; tends to move lips or sub-vocalize when reading.	Auditory	Providing verbal instruction and repeating yourself often.
Seems to enjoy watching demonstrations; has intense concentration and ability to visually imagine information; writes things down and takes detailed notes; doodles and looks around studying the environment; often becomes impatient when extensive listening is involved.	Visual	Providing them with written information, especially with charts, graphs, and pictures. They learn best by studying alone.
Fidgets when reading; is easily distracted when not able to move; expresses emotions physically by jumping and gesturing; does not listen well and tries things out by touching, feeling, and manipulating; needs frequent breaks during meetings.	Kinetic or Tactile	Providing them with exercises or assignments to perform. They learn best by manipulating and testing information.

UNDERSTAND THE CLIENT'S THINKING PHASE

The financial planner should be aware that the financial planning process can be both comforting and confusing to a client: comforting because action is being taken to accomplish goals; confusing because this is usually when the client realizes the magnitude of the planning choices and decisions required. It is the responsibility of the planner to assist the client throughout this process and provide education and reassurance when necessary. Exhibit 3.4 depicts the common phases of thinking through which a client often progresses while establishing a financial plan. The objective is for the client to achieve the high cognitive thinking phase. The financial planner should be knowledgeable about these common phases of thinking and assist the client in progressing through them while establishing financial direction. The planner should help the client transition from the outer edge of the circle to the inner circle in Exhibit 3.4.

EXHIBIT 3.4: COMMON THINKING PHASES

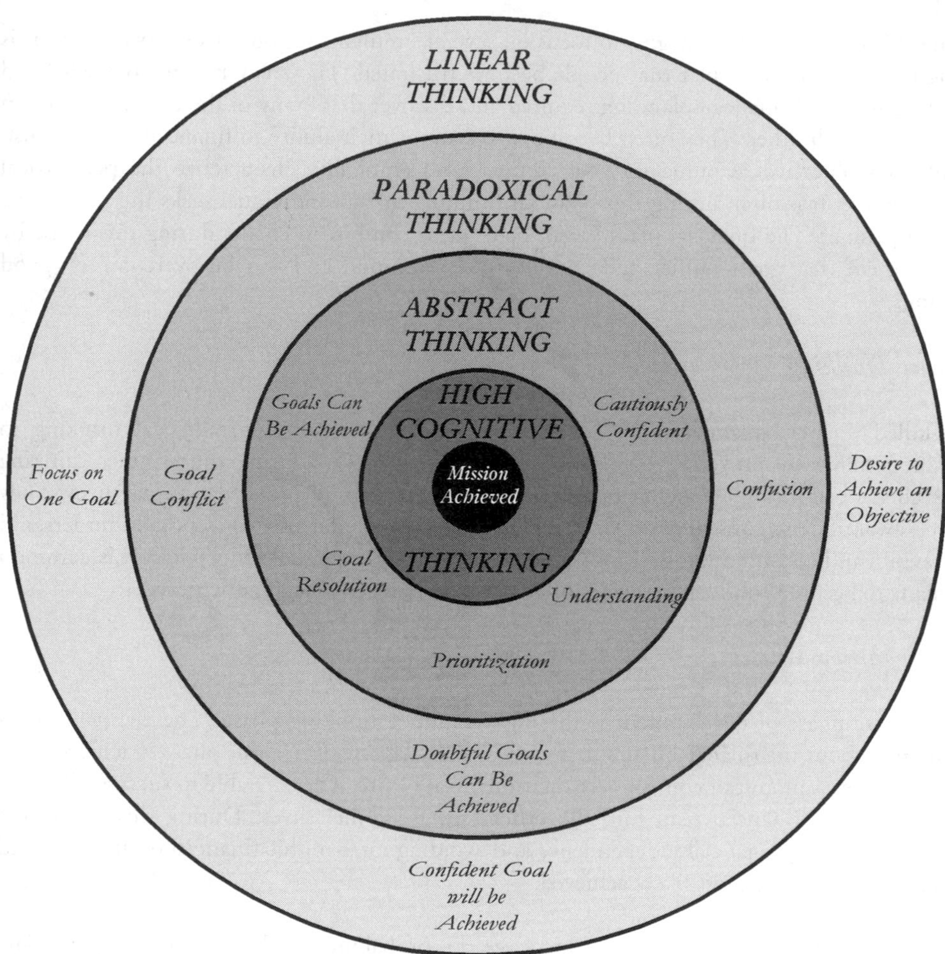

LINEAR THINKING
PARADOXICAL THINKING
ABSTRACT THINKING
HIGH COGNITIVE THINKING
Mission Achieved
Goals Can Be Achieved
Cautiously Confident
Focus on One Goal
Goal Conflict
Confusion
Desire to Achieve an Objective
Goal Resolution
Understanding
Prioritization
Doubtful Goals Can Be Achieved
Confident Goal will be Achieved

Linear Thinking

Generally, individuals who are just beginning to plan financially are in the outer phase of thinking, referred to as linear thinking. Focusing on accomplishing a particular goal or objective describes the concept of linear thinking. During this phase, an individual's financial plan is compartmentalized and simplistic. The primary interest is in achieving one or two narrow objectives. Confidence that objectives can and will be achieved is high. However, once the individual begins to face the reality that saving for one objective means forgoing funds in another area because funds are limited, confidence in the ability to achieve overall goals is often questioned and the person may give up. During this phase, the client may increase savings and/or set up a special savings account to save for something only to find that those funds must be used for day-to-day or unexpected expenses. Due to the frequent failure to achieve all goals, clients frequently give up the idea of developing a financial plan. However, if success is achieved in the linear phase, the client's thinking usually changes from linear to paradoxical.

Paradoxical Thinking

During this phase, the client begins to focus on several simultaneous objectives. As a result, it is during this phase in particular that people become frustrated. They may become overwhelmed with the amount of financial planning required and discover that many of their objectives are in conflict with each other. They often become uncertain of their ability to financially accomplish any of their objectives. Confusion, goal conflict, and ambiguity characterize the paradoxical thinking phase. It is often during this phase of thinking that an individual seeks the advice of a financial planner. The financial planner can be of great comfort to clients during this phase by assuring them that goal conflict and confusion are common and can be overcome by good planning.

Abstract Thinking

The skilled financial planner can assist a client in advancing from paradoxical thinking to abstract thinking by providing education and encouragement. During the abstract thinking phase, clients begin to integrate elements of the financial plan into their day-to-day lives. They become aware of the consequences of their financial actions and can conceptually understand how savings and consumption decisions impact their financial plan. At this point, it is common for clients to become confident that identified goals and objectives can be achieved.

High Cognitive Thinking

The ultimate phase of development is the high cognitive thinking phase. The client becomes enlightened about the financial issues that exist in everyday life. Once this phase is achieved, clients have a great amount of control over their financial future. They are able to successfully integrate their entire financial plan into the other aspects of their lives. During this phase, the mission of achieving financial independence and avoiding catastrophic financial occurrences and financial dependence is most likely achieved.

The personal financial planner greatly increases the probability of developing an appropriate financial strategy and having it properly implemented if a good relationship with the client is established, communication skills are practiced, the client's preferred learning style is identified, and the financial planner understands the client's current phase of thinking.

INTERNAL ANALYSIS

The internal environment defines the way people live, work, spend, save, and think. Internal data about the client is needed to understand the environment in which the individual exists and the strengths and weaknesses that are present. Once a good working relationship is developed with the client, and communication lines are open, it is easy to collect most of the internal data that is needed. The key is to know what information to collect and how to collect it efficiently and accurately. Internal data can be divided into five general categories, which include the client's:

- Life cycle position.
- Attitudes and beliefs.
- Special needs.
- Financial position.
- Perception of their financial situation.

LIFE CYCLE POSITIONING

Life cycle positioning information is needed because it plays a significant role in affecting the goals and behaviors of individuals. It also suggests which financial risks currently exist. In order to identify the client's life cycle position, the planner needs to have information about the client's:

life cycle positioning - using information about a client's age, marital status, dependents, income level, and net worth to help determine goals and risks

- Age.
- Marital status.
- Dependents.
- Income level.
- Net worth.

Age

Age is one of the most important and revealing factors in financial planning. Generally, young people give little thought or consideration to retirement goals or wealth-transfer goals. As people age, they become aware that adequate retirement income requires funding. At some time, they begin to seriously plan for this financial goal. In the recent past, it was common for persons to become conscious about their "retirement reality" as late as age 50. Today, clients are beginning to become aware of this issue at a much younger age. Perhaps this phenomenon is due to the increased amount of readily available information on the cost of retirement and the necessity to plan early.

Marital Status

The second factor that affects goal determination is marital status. The desire to provide for one's dependents creates a host of goals to achieve and risks to avoid. It is common for married couples to combine their future economic resources to jointly purchase assets, such as a house, by jointly committing to indebtedness. The purchase of a personal residence through indebtedness, which can only be afforded by combining both incomes, creates an interdependency of one spouse on the other. In the event one spouse were to suffer unemployment, untimely death, disability, or some other catastrophic event, the commitment to the repayment of the debt may not be met.

Dependents

A third factor affecting the creation of goals is the existence of dependents. Dependents may be children, grandchildren, or elderly parents. Parents commonly have goals of providing education for their children. Education can be an expensive goal that requires substantial expenditures made over a finite period. For example, the annual cost of a college education at some private universities in the U.S. is currently $30,000. If we assume two children and four years in college, the current total cost of such an education would be $240,000. Whatever the cost, it is probably a substantial amount on a relative basis, for most 40-year-old clients to take on. Even public university education is high - currently about $25,000 for each student for four years. Not all persons feel obligated to provide their children with a college education. However, many parents do, and many more wish they were able to do so.

Grandchildren may also be considered dependents. A person may have grandchildren as early as in their 30s but more commonly in their 50s or older. The significance of grandchildren as a factor is not that they are actual dependents, but rather that grandchildren may signal the initial phase of wealth transfer. Grandparents may find themselves with more assets and income than they feel necessary to sustain their lifestyle. They may then begin to provide financially for their grandchildren.

Other examples of dependencies that affect goals are caring for an aging parent or providing special care to a handicapped child or sibling. It is important for the planner to realize that married persons with children are not the only ones with dependents. Single, childless persons may have financial dependents by taking on the obligations of aging parents or other loved ones.

Income and Net Worth

Income and net worth are the last two factors concerning life cycle positioning. Substantial income suggests an opportunity to achieve financial goals as long as the goals are realistic relative to the income. Lower income presents greater challenges in achieving financial security and financial independence. Persons with a low income and low net worth generally have a more difficult time overcoming financial setbacks. Whereas, a person with substantial net worth is generally less likely to suffer catastrophic consequences as a result of a single financial setback. Substantial net worth also implies a need for increased management of assets and planning. Generally, the greater the income or net worth the greater the interest in tax deferral or avoidance.

Life Cycle Phases and Characteristics

life cycle phase - an interval in a client's life cycle that tends to give a planner insight into the client's financial objectives and concerns—the Asset Accumulation phase, the Conservation/Protection phase, the Distribution/Gifting phase

As people progress through their lives, there is a tendency to move subtly but surely among financial objectives due to changes in personal financial circumstances. We have identified and labeled these **life cycle phases** and characteristics as the Asset Accumulation Phase, the Conservation/Protection Phase, and the Distribution/Gifting Phase. While not all people move through these phases at the same rate, a sufficient percent of people do, so that financial planners can gain valuable insight into their client's objectives and concerns by identifying which phase or phases their client is in at a particular point in time. Exhibit 3.5 illustrates the life cycle phases and the typical characteristics of each phase.

EXHIBIT 3.5: LIFE CYCLE PHASES AND CHARACTERISTICS

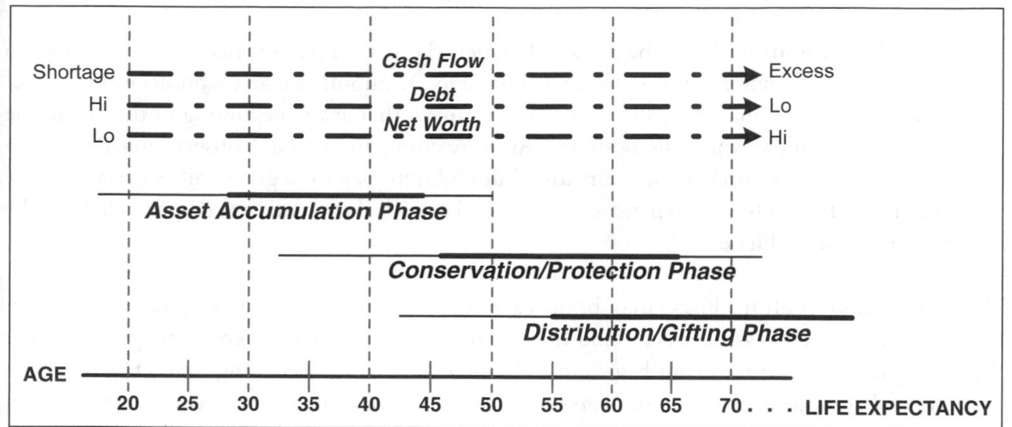
Shortage
Hi
Lo
Cash Flow
Debt
Net Worth
Excess
Lo
Hi
Asset Accumulation Phase
Conservation/Protection Phase
Distribution/Gifting Phase
AGE
20 25 30 35 40 45 50 55 60 65 70. . . LIFE EXPECTANCY

Asset Accumulation

The **Asset Accumulation Phase** usually begins somewhere between the ages of 20 and 25 and lasts until about age 50. The beginning of the phase is characterized by limited excess cash flow for investing, a relatively high degree of debt, and a low net worth. At the beginning of the phase, there is generally a low appreciation for the risks that exist. As the person moves through the Asset Accumulation Phase, cash for investments generally increases, there is less use of debt as a percent of total assets, and there is an increase in net worth.

Asset Accumulation Phase - life cycle phase through which clients pass. Usually begins somewhere between the ages of 20 and 25 and lasts until about age 50, characterized by limited excess funds for investing, high degree of debt, and low net worth

Conservation/Protection

The **Conservation/Protection Phase** begins when one has acquired some assets, usually in late 30s or 40s, and may last throughout the work life expectancy. It is characterized by an increase in cash flow, assets, and net worth with some decrease in the proportional use of debt. People generally become more risk averse as they acquire more assets. From an investments viewpoint, they are more concerned about losing what they have acquired than acquiring more. They become aware and concerned with many of the risks they ignored at the beginning of the Asset Accumulation Phase, including an increased awareness of life's risks (untimely death, unemployment, disability, etc.). This is not to say that they have completely left the Asset Accumulation Phase. At least at the beginning, they are simultaneously in both phases (trying to accumulate, while trying not to lose what they have).

Conservation/Protection Phase - life cycle phase through which clients pass characterized by an increase in cash flow, assets, and net worth with some decrease in the proportional use of debt

Making payments for children's education and saving for retirement frequently characterize the Conservation/Protection Phase. This phase is where the real struggle between current-consumption needs and deferred-consumption necessities is waged. It is also during this period that the client is most financially confused because of the conflicting goals and perceived risks. During this phase one of the greatest opportunities exists for the professional financial planner to assist the client.

Distribution/Gifting

Distribution/Gifting Phase - life cycle phase through which clients pass characterized by excess relative cash flows, low debt, and high relative net worth

The **Distribution/Gifting Phase** begins subtly when the person realizes that they can afford to spend on things they never believed possible. The Asset Accumulation and Conservation/Protection Phases make this phase possible. It is quite common that at the beginning of this phase the person is also simultaneously in both the Asset Accumulation and Conservation/Protection Phases. When parents purchase new cars for adult children, pay for a grandchild's private school tuition, or take themselves on expensive vacations relative to their tradition, they are likely in the Distribution/Gifting Phase.

The Distribution/Gifting Phase may begin as early as the late 40s and continue until death. Excess relative cash flows, low debt, and high relative net worth characterize this phase. At the beginning of the phase the client begins to feel financial pressures declining, starts to believe life is short and should be enjoyed, and cares less about material things. Now clients start asking, Where did yesterday go? It is also during this period that life's risks are put into perspective. Frequently, during this phase life insurance is dropped, deductibles are raised, and the client achieves more financial balance and confidence.

It is common for people to be in two or more life cycle phases simultaneously, although not necessarily to the same degree. By determining where the client is in terms of these phases, we can gain some insight as to the person's financial goals, concerns, and behaviors, which will help to better serve the client. Throughout the text, we will refer to whether the client, in a specific application, is predominately in the Asset Accumulation, Conservation/Protection, or Distribution/Gifting Phase or some combination. We do so to put the client's goals and risks into perspective and to gain insight into appropriate financial planning solutions.

Once life cycle positioning is completed, the experienced financial planner can develop a generic financial plan to meet clients' needs who are in similar life cycle phases. Exhibit 3.6 illustrates some generalized life cycle positions and the likely goals and risks associated with each. Remember, however, these are only generalizations. Although enough information has been obtained to provide a framework with which to begin developing a client's financial plan, much more information is required before an accurate financial plan can be developed for a particular individual.

EXHIBIT 3.6: SELECTED LIFE CYCLE POSITIONS AND RELATED GOALS/RISKS

Life Cycle Position	Phase	Common Goals	Risks					
			L	H	D	LTC	P	LB
25- to 35-year-old single (S/25-35) modest income/net worth	AAP	Savings; investment; wealth accumulation; personal residence; debt management	✘	✔	✔	✘	✔	✔
25- to 35-year-old married with small dependent children (MWC/25-35); moderate income/net worth	AAP	Educational funding; savings; investment; wealth accumulation; personal residence; debt management	✔	✔	✔	✘	✔	✔
40- to 50-year-old with dependent children	AAP, CPP	Retirement planning; educational funding; savings; investment; wealth accumulation; debt management	✔	✔	✔	✘	✔	✔
62- to 68-year-old retired with adult children and grandchildren	CPP, DGP	Estate planning	✘	✔	✘	?	?	✔

Key:
L = Life
H = Health
D = Disability
LTC = Long-Term Care
P = Property
LB = Liability

✔ = The risk is likely
✘ = The risk is not likely
? = The risk is possible

AAP = Asset Accumulation Phase
CPP = Conservation/Protection Phase
DGP = Distribution/Gifting Phase

Client Data Collection Questionnaire - a survey used by financial planners to gather internal data from clients, such as their tolerance for risk and their personal perception of their financial situation, as well as tax-related data, Social Security numbers, information relating to their dependents, and so on

Life cycle positioning is one of the easiest types of internal data to collect. The client is usually comfortable providing this information because it is not too personal and the client probably expects to be asked such questions. This information may be gathered during a face-to-face meeting, a telephone meeting, or by using a **Client Data Collection Questionnaire** similar to the one in the Appendix at the end of the chapter.

Attitudes and Beliefs

The second type of internal data identifies the client's attitudes and beliefs. Attitudes and beliefs are important because they play a significant role in affecting the goals and behaviors of individuals. Information that should be gathered includes the client's:

- Risk tolerance levels.
- Savings and consumption habits.
- Views about employment, retirement, and leisure time.
- Attitude regarding government, especially taxation.

Risk Tolerance Levels

risk tolerance - the level of risk exposure with which an individual is comfortable

Knowledge of **risk tolerance** levels is needed to assist the financial planner in determining the types of investments and the style of risk management best suited for the client. The style of risk management refers to the degree to which insurance is sought for mitigation of small to moderate losses. Risk management involves balancing lower premiums and self-reliance for small losses with higher premiums and less loss exposure. Stated risk tolerance levels may be misinterpreted because they are subjective. The statement, "I am not very risk tolerant," may mean different things to different clients. Therefore, additional questioning is needed to ensure understanding. Implementing the communication techniques discussed earlier can assist the planner. The Client Data Collection Questionnaire can also help in gathering information about the client's risk tolerance level. The concept of risk management will be emphasized throughout the text with special emphasis in the chapters on insurance and investments.

Savings and Consumption Habits

Information about a client's savings and consumption habits assists the planner in developing a successful strategic financial plan for the client. If the client does not have a history of saving money consistently, it would be wise to develop a strategy in which money is directed into savings prior to the client receiving a check from the employer. Similarly, if the client has a history of making impulsive large-dollar purchases, it would be wise to encourage investments in assets with early withdrawal penalties or those where withdrawal is difficult. Withdrawal penalties or delays discourage clients from making such impulse purchases. Historical behavior is the best indicator of future behavior. A good way to collect information about the client's savings and consumption habits is to ask the client detailed questions and to review income and expenses for previous years.

Views on Employment, Retirement, Leisure Time

A client's view on employment, retirement, and leisure time is useful information to a financial planner because it provides information about likely behavior. If a person is discontented with his

Where on the Web

American Savings Education Council *www.asec.org*
Bankruptcy Action *www.bankruptcyaction.com*
Better Business Bureau *www.bbb.org*
Consolidated Credit Counseling Services, Inc. *www.debtfree.org*
Consumer Action *www.consumeraction.org*
Consumer Federation of America *www.consumerfed.org*
The Foundation for Taxpayer & Consumer Rights *www.consumerwatchdog.org*
Consumer Information Center *www.pueblo.gsa.gov*
Federal Trade Commission *www.ftc.gov*
National Consumers League *www.natlconsumersleague.org*
National Institute of Consumer Education *www.nice.emich.edu*
NCL's National Fraud Information Center *www.fraud.org*

job or places a high value on leisure time, he may be more likely to take spontaneous vacations. The financial planner may want to incorporate these likely-but-unplanned expenditures into the financial strategy. Suppose a client is 55 years old, married with no dependent children, and is unsatisfied with his employment situation. Although this client may intend to work until the age of 62, the financial planner should be aware that this client might decide to retire earlier than planned, if financially able. The skilled financial planner will develop a strategy that includes contingency plans for various possibilities. Information about a client's views is best gathered through question and answer sessions with the client.

Attitude Toward Government

The last type of information about a client's attitudes and beliefs is their attitude toward government fiscal responsibility and taxation. If a client believes that government expenditures are wise and useful to the public, that client would probably be less resistant to taxation than a client who believes that government essentially wastes whatever money it receives. These attitudes toward tax and government translate into financial planning issues in numerous ways. Some clients ignore the role taxes play in financial planning. Other clients are tax conscious and simply view the tax environment as one in which they live and must take into consideration. Still other clients are so focused on tax minimization, that they spend extraordinary time and resources on the tax minimization objective, sometimes to the detriment of other goals.

Special Needs

The third type of internal data to be gathered concerns the client's special needs. Special needs may include planning for divorce, remarriage, aging parents, disabled children, terminal illness, nontraditional families, career changes, and unemployment.

Divorce

The financial planner can assist divorcing couples in determining an equitable division of marital assets and planning for the financial changes that accompany the separation of a household.

Sources of income and expenses may change dramatically making a review of the client's budget necessary. Other areas for review include:

- Legally changing client's name, changing beneficiaries of retirement plans, and evaluation of retirement funds
- Amending wills, setting-up trusts for the benefit of children
- Requiring life insurance from former spouse for benefit of client or children and changing beneficiaries
- Maintaining or acquiring health insurance for client or children
- Evaluating need for disability or long-term care insurance
- Requiring funding from former spouse for college education of children and assessing educational funding requirements

Remarriage

Many of the areas discussed in divorce planning are relevant in financial planning for remarriage. Besides continuation of insurance for the client and children and reviewing beneficiary designations, the financial planner should make clients aware of income that will be unavailable after remarriage and discuss integration of families for estate planning and education funding. Frequently divorce decrees retire alimony payments when the receiver remarries, and Social Security benefits available to the client based on the ex-spouse's earnings generally disappear. Child support, payment of insurance premiums, retirement benefits, and other sources of income from the former spouse may diminish or be eliminated. Finding replacement sources of income or helping the client adjust to a different standard of living is an important role of the financial planner.

When remarriage combines families, the financial planner will have an even larger role. Estate planning and education funding must be performed with knowledge and understanding of the new couple's relationship with children from each other's previous marriage. Questions such as who should inherit the house to how much college tuition will the couple fund should be asked. The financial planner can offer an objective view on the fairness of property gifting and education funding from the perspective of children and stepchildren.

Aging Parents

With the increase in life expectancy, adults may be caring for their aging parents and grandparents for ten or twenty years. The financial planner can reduce stress for the client faced with prolonged care of an elderly family member by helping them discuss living wills, powers of attorney, and long-term care options with their parents and by helping the client prepare financially for medical and living expenses. Some of the tax advantages that may apply include deductibility of medical expenses paid by the client for a dependent parent and the dependent-care tax credit. Using a loan against life insurance and a reverse mortgage, where the homeowner "sells" the equity in the home, to pay expenses are options that can be discussed with the aging family member. In planning for the care of a client's parents, financial planners will be challenged to act objectively and with sensitivity.

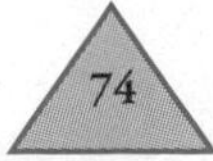

Disabled Dependents

Approximately fifteen percent of Americans have a child or spouse with a disability. Often, the client with special needs dependents will be the primary caregiver. The financial planner can assist the client in planning for continuous care for the life of the child or spouse. Wills may need to be modified to provide a custodian for the dependent. Trusts can be created to secure assets for care after the death of the client. For disabled children, second-to-die life insurance, which pays out after both parents have died, may be appropriate.

Terminal Illness

Families of a loved one with a terminal illness may come to the financial planner in a state of shock or denial. The financial planner can benefit the terminally ill client and family by retaining a level of detachment and being proactive in addressing financial issues. At the same time the financial planner must be considerate and empathetic of family members' feelings. Some financial planning topics to address are:

- Estimation of medical or assisted living expenses for physician, pharmacy, hospital, home health, and hospice care
- Budgeting for medical expenses, loss of income from inability to work or desire not to work, and last wishes such as a special trip
- Coverage provided under health and disability insurance, COBRA options, and government benefits such as Medicare, Medicaid, and Social Security
- Using life insurance benefits through a policy's accelerated benefits clause or through a viatical settlement (the sale of life insurance to a third party)
- Review of investment portfolio goals and time horizons
- Availability of benefits from retirement plans
- Powers of attorney, wills, living wills, and beneficiaries

Nontraditional Families

Unmarried heterosexual couples, same-sex couples, and other nontraditional families can benefit greatly from the services of a financial planner. Certain rights and advantages available to married persons are not available to unmarried adults sharing a residence and common goals. For example, unmarried couples do not qualify for married-filing-jointly income tax status, the unlimited marital deduction for estate taxes, survivorship benefits from Social Security, the ability to direct medical treatment for each other, and legal transfer of assets at death without a will or proper titling of property. It is common for employer-provided retirement benefits and health insurance to be available only to the employee, a spouse, or relative. Besides addressing these disadvantages, the financial planner can help nontraditional families take advantage of their tax status. Since they are not married, both members receive the single standard deduction and may qualify for head of household status, which would reduce their tax liability. Mortgage interest paid on a first and second home is tax deductible. For married couples, this means they can deduct interest on two homes. For unmarried couples, they can each deduct interest on two homes.

Career Change and Unemployment

Career changes and unemployment present similar challenges to the client and his or her family. The family budget will need revising. Income will be reduced and expenses may increase for the purchase of new business clothes, education or training, and resume preparation and for job hunting. Severance packages and unemployment benefits will help replace lost income for a short period of time. Health, life and disability insurance may be eliminated or premiums may increase. Retirement plans and investment portfolios should be reviewed. The financial planner can assist the client in making these adjustments.

FINANCIAL POSITION

The fourth type of internal data needed is the client's current financial position. This information is so important Chapter 4 has been dedicated to it. We will simply introduce the topic here. The gathering of information on financial position is the most time consuming for two reasons. First, the client often does not readily know the answers to the questions. Therefore, some information may need to be collected from third parties, such as stockbrokers, accountants, employers, and lawyers. Secondly, the financial planner may need to prepare the client's personal financial statements. Financial statements include the balance sheet, the income statement, and the statement of changes in net worth.

Information that needs to be collected to develop these financial statements includes:

- ▲ Assets
  - Cash, checking accounts, savings accounts
  - Mutual funds, ownership of business, Treasury bonds
  - Personal residence, jewelry, art collection, automobile
- ▲ Liabilities
  - Credit card debt, rent due on apartment
  - Auto loan, home mortgage
- ▲ Income
  - Salaries, bonuses
  - Interest income, employer contributions to retirement plan
- ▲ Expenses
  - Rent or mortgage payments, utilities, groceries
  - Insurance premiums, interest payments on credit cards, taxes
  - Deposits to savings accounts and retirement plans, donations to charity

In addition to developing financial statements, the financial planner must collect information about the client's insurance policies and coverage, investments, retirement, and other employee benefits. The client's historical tax returns are useful, as is information about any wills, trusts, or other estate planning documents. The planner should be aware of any powers of attorney the client may possess or may have given to others. How to obtain each of these items and how to judge their relevance will be discussed fully in the following chapter.

CLIENT'S PERCEPTION OF THEIR FINANCIAL SITUATION

The fifth and final type of internal data is the client's subjective evaluation of their own financial situation. This is how the client thinks they are doing. The client's perception is useful because it assesses the client's knowledge of his or her own financial situation. It gives the financial planner an opportunity to assess the client's subjective perception compared to the objective reality of the situation. The gap between perception and reality directly influences the amount of client education necessary. The greater the gap between the subjective perception of the client and economic reality, the greater the education needed. This information may be gathered by using the Client Data Collection Questionnaire in the Appendix at the end of the chapter.

It is common for the client's internal data to change over time. Therefore, it is essential to regularly revisit the data. If a good client/planner relationship has been developed, the client will notify the financial planner when a major life change occurs. The financial planner, however, should not rely on the client for notification. A competent financial planner will contact the client with sufficient frequency (usually quarterly) to learn how the financial plan is working and to ask if any significant changes have occurred. Contacting clients by phone, e-mail, or in writing should be done in addition to regularly scheduled face-to-face meetings.

PROFESSIONAL FOCUS

Do you find that your clients are educated about the financial planning process?
Generally, I find that most prospective clients are not well-informed regarding the nature of the financial planning process. Initially, they tend to think of "financial planning" rather narrowly, i.e. dealing only with the one or two issues that initially moved them to action, such as college funding, or proper allocation of their 401(k) plan investments.

During our initial meeting, I introduce the notion that financial planning is a systematic, comprehensive process, noting that "square one" is establishing and defining the client-planner relationship. Fortunately, CFP Board has some excellent resources in this regard ("*What You Should Know About Financial Planning,*" which contains "*Common Mistakes Consumers Make When Approaching Financial Planning*"), which I share with prospective clients.

The general public's limited awareness regarding the nature of the financial planning process may be due, at least in part, to the popular financial media, which tends to emphasize single-issue or episodic "financial planning," like, "The Hottest New Fund," "3 Ways to Bet on Internet Stocks," and "10 Ways to Cut Your Taxes Now."

What techniques do you use to determine your clients' attitudes and beliefs with regard to risk tolerance levels, savings, consumption, employment, retirement, and the government?
I have learned that, to a considerable extent, my role is to be a good, active listener. Over time, once an environment of trust, confidentiality, and confidence has been established, clients will reveal what you need to know to prepare a financial plan that is responsive to their needs. Your role as a financial planner is to properly evaluate and interpret *all* of the evidence and data, financial and otherwise, so that your recommendations are suitable and appropriate for your clients.

Other techniques include using one or more of the excellent risk profile questionnaires that are readily available from broker-dealers and mutual funds. In this regard, it is important to compare the client's risk tolerance as expressed by the risk profile instrument with the *actual* risk tolerance indicated by the client's investment portfolio. Some clients tend to overstate their risk tolerance. For example, the risk profile assessment tool may indicate a rather high risk tolerance, which is belied by a portfolio dominated by bonds, bond funds, CDs, and money market funds, or preferred stocks.

Another effective discovery technique is to carefully review the cash flow statement prepared by your clients. Preparing a personal cash flow statement for the first time can be an epiphany for your clients, as they are confronted by their priorities and attitudes toward consumption vs. investment. The cash flow statement is a road map detailing the clients' economic behavior that you can use to point out in an appropriate way the consequence and impact of various resource allocation options and alternatives that are available.

Do you find that your clients have an unrealistic perception of their financial position?
Initially, they may have a sense that they need to have a trained professional "take a look at what we've done," in order to determine if their present financial position is sufficient to achieve their goals, such as early retirement or college funding. The financial position of your client may be the result of a somewhat *ad hoc*, reactive approach to personal finance matters over many years.

If, through the financial planning process, it becomes apparent that their perception is unrealistic, i.e. retiring at age 54, or sending the three children to competitive private colleges, then the task becomes one of working with the client to reframe their goals and examine alternative strategies.

STAN ROESLER, MBA, CFP®

DISCUSSION QUESTIONS

1. How does a financial planner successfully communicate respect, trust, and empathy to a client?
2. Which techniques can be used to reduce the risk of misinterpretation and misunderstanding when communicating with a client?
3. What is the purpose of an engagement letter?
4. To what common law liabilities is the financial planner exposed?
5. How do the Securities Act of 1933 and the Securities Exchange Act of 1934 affect financial planners?
6. What four thinking phases does a client progress through during the financial planning process? What can the financial planner do to assist the client in progressing through the common thinking phases? In which phase is it most common for a client to seek the assistance of a financial planner? In which phase is the financial mission most likely to be achieved?
7. What is the Auditory Learning Style, the Visual Learning Style, and the Kinetic, or Tactile, Learning Style, and how does a client with each style prefer to learn?
8. What five categories make up a client's internal environment?
9. Which factors make up Life Cycle Positioning?
10. What are the Life Cycle Phases through which financial planning clients usually pass?
11. How does a client's tolerance for risk; savings and consumption habits; views about employment, retirement, and leisure time; and attitudes on government (especially taxation) affect the setting of their financial goals?
12. What are the "special needs" that may influence the successful development of a client's financial plan?
13. Which financial statements are needed to develop an accurate assessment of a client's financial position? What other information is important?
14. How does a client's subjective perception of his or her financial position affect the objective reality of the financial position provided by a financial planner?

EXERCISES

1. Upon your first meeting, how should you address your client?
2. What are some techniques that can be used to clarify statements when speaking with a client?
3. Nancy is a financial planner. Her client, Mr. Martin, is 60 years old and retired. His Social Security and pension plan benefits barely cover his living expenses. His two assets are his personal residence and a brokerage account of $600,000 invested in conservative mutual funds. Nancy advises Mr. Martin to sell all of his mutual fund shares and invest the proceeds in commercial real estate. If Mr. Martin follows Nancy's advice and subsequently loses $300,000, will Nancy be liable for fraud?
4. If you noticed that your client was taking notes and occasionally doodling while you spoke with them, what would you assume their learning style to be, and how would you go about educating them regarding financial planning information?
5. If your client is 30 years old, has no children and has a moderate income and net worth, what risks is he or she most likely seeking to avoid?
6. If your clients are 73 years old, retired and have adult children and grandchildren and a high net worth, which life cycle phase are they most likely in?

7. What might be the common goals of a client who is 24 years old and single with a modest income?
8. If your client is interested in saving for retirement, but has a history of using savings planned for the long-term on current purchases such as vacations, vehicles, etc., what type of savings plan would you recommend?

PROBLEMS

1. Write an engagement letter to conduct comprehensive personal financial planning for the Nelsons.
2. Identify the lifecycle position and related risks most likely to affect the achievement of the Nelsons' general goals.

NELSON FAMILY CASE SCENARIO

The Nelsons recently visited you, their financial planner. After initial discussions and completion of a client data questionnaire similar to the one presented in Appendix 3-A, you have gathered the following information. (The Nelson family will be used throughout the text for various examples and explanations.)

DAVID AND DANA NELSON

As of 1/1/2006

PERSONAL BACKGROUND AND INFORMATION

David Nelson (Age 37) is a bank vice president. He has been employed there for twelve years and has an annual salary of $70,000. Dana Nelson (Age 37) is a full-time housewife. David and Dana have been married for eight years. They have two children, John (Age 6) and Gabrielle (Age 3), and are expecting their third child in two weeks. They have always lived in this community and expect to remain in their current residence indefinitely.

GENERAL GOALS (not prioritized)

Save for college education.

Reduce debt.

Save for retirement.

Estate planning.

Invest wisely.

APPENDIX 3-A: CLIENT DATA QUESTIONNAIRE

Client Name____________________

Date____________________

PERSONAL INFORMATION

Your Full Name ____________________ Social Security No. ____________________

U.S. Citizen? ❒ Yes ❒ No Date and Place of Birth ____________________

Employer ____________________ Position ____________________

Work Phone ____________________ Years with current employer ____________________

Married ________ Single ________ Divorced ________

Spouse's Full Name (if married) ____________________ Social Security No. ____________________

U.S. Citizen? ❒ Yes ❒ No Date and Place of Birth ____________________

Employer ____________________ Position ____________________

Work Phone ____________________ Years with current employer ____________________

Home Address ____________________

Home Phone ____________________ Home Fax ____________________

E-mail address ____________________

Previous Marriages

Have you been previously married? ❒ Yes ❒ No Has your spouse been previously married? ❒ Yes ❒ No

Children

Name(s)	Date(s)of Birth	Social Security Number(s)	Tax Dependent
			❒ Yes ❒ No
			❒ Yes ❒ No
			❒ Yes ❒ No
			❒ Yes ❒ No

Grandchildren

Name(s)	Date(s)of Birth	Social Security Number(s)	Tax Dependent
			❒ Yes ❒ No
			❒ Yes ❒ No

Other Income Tax/Financial Dependents

Does anyone other than your children depend on you or your spouse for financial support? ❒ Yes ❒ No

If so, provide names, ages, and relationships: ____________________

____

____

Health Issues

Do you or any members of your family have serious health problems? ❒ Yes ❒ No

Describe: ____________________

Professional Advisers (include names, addresses, phone numbers, fax numbers, and e-mail addresses)

Attorney ____________________

Accountant (CPA) ____________________

Insurance Agent ____________________

Banker ____________________

Investment Adviser ____________________

Page 1 Initial _____ Date _____

APPENDIX 3-A: CLIENT DATA QUESTIONNAIRE (CONT.)

FINANCIAL PLANNING GOALS AND OBJECTIVES

Financial Objectives (Please select and indicate degree of importance)	Degree of Importance (1-high/5-low)				
	1	**2**	**3**	**4**	**5**
Retire and maintain preretirement lifestyle					
Retire early - Indicate age ____________					
Protection from risks to person/property/liability					
Provide education for children/grandchildren					
Major purchases (car, boat, second home)					
Establish an emergency fund					
Save more					
Invest for safety					
Invest for growth					
Invest for income					
Transfer of wealth					
Minimize income taxes					
Minimize transfer taxes (estates and gifts)					
Other:					

Page 2 Initial _____ Date _____

APPENDIX 3-A: CLIENT DATA QUESTIONNAIRE (CONT.)

ASSETS

Cash Accounts (indicate current ($) dollar balance for each account)

Type of Account	Your Name	Spouse's Name	Joint w/ Spouse	Other
Cash on hand				
Checking accounts				
Savings accounts				
CDs				
Money market funds				
Treasury securities				
U.S. Savings Bonds				
Total				

Brokerage Accounts (Stocks)

Name of Security	No. of Shares	Market Value

Mutual Funds (Stocks)

Name of Institution (Fund Name)	No. of Shares	Market Value

Mutual Funds (Bonds)

Name of Institution (Fund Name)	No. of Shares	Market Value

Bonds Owned

Name of Institution	Maturity Face Value	Market Value

Page 3 Initial _____ Date _____

APPENDIX 3-A: CLIENT DATA QUESTIONNAIRE (CONT.)

Stock Options and/or Stock Purchase Plans

Do you or your spouse participate in a company stock option plan or stock purchase plan? ❒ Yes ❒ No

Receivables (owed to you and/or your spouse)

Type	Description	Interest Rate	Amount	Maturity Date
Notes Receivable				
Other Receivables				

Retirement Accounts (indicate vested values)

Type	Description	Fair Market Value You	Fair Market Value Your Spouse
IRA – Regular			
IRA – Roth			
401(k) or 403(b) plan			
Keogh plan			
Pension plan			
Profit-sharing plan			
Employee stock bonus plan			
Employee stock ownership plan			
SEP			
SIMPLE			

Real Estate (Personal Use)

Address	Type*	State Located	Original Cost	Fair Market Value	Current Mortgage Amount

* PR = Personal Residence VH = Vacation Home

Real Estate (Held for Investment)

Address	Type*	State Located	Original Cost	Fair Market Value	Current Mortgage Amount

* R = Rental O = Other

Page 4 Initial _____ Date _____

APPENDIX 3-A: CLIENT DATA QUESTIONNAIRE (CONT.)

***Closely Held Business Interest** (attach financial statement if available)*

Description	Type of Entity*	Date Acquired	Percentage Owned	Est. Fair Market Value

* P = Proprietorship PTR = Partnership S = S corporation C = C corporation LLC = Limited Liability Company

Any Other Investments

Description	Date Acquired	Est. Fair Market Value

Personal Use Property

Type	Estimated Fair Market Value
Furniture & household goods	
Jewelry & furs	
Automobiles	
Boats, aircraft	
Recreational vehicles	
Art & antiques	
Other collectibles (stamps, baseball cards)	
Other items of significant value	

Page 5 Initial _____ Date _____

APPENDIX 3-A: CLIENT DATA QUESTIONNAIRE (CONT.)

LIABILITIES

	Amount Owed		Monthly Payments	
	You	Spouse	You	Spouse
Bank Loans				
Student Loans				
Insurance Policy Loans				
Personal Loans				
Taxes Payable				
Installment Debt (Automobile)				
Credit Cards				
Other Unpaid Bills				
Alimony/Child Support Obligations				
Charitable Pledges				
Other (__________________)				
Other (__________________)				
Other (__________________)				

Page 6 Initial _____ Date _____

APPENDIX 3-A: CLIENT DATA QUESTIONNAIRE (CONT.)

INCOME SOURCES

	You	Spouse	Joint
Employment Income			
Gross Salary			
Bonuses			
Commissions			
Other (Describe____________________)			
Investment Income			
Taxable Interest			
Nontaxable Interest			
Dividends			
Net Rental Income			
Business Income			
Annuities			
Social Security Benefits			
Pension/Retirement Plan			
Other (Describe____________________)			
Miscellaneous Income (Expected)			
Inheritances			
Alimony			
Child Support			
Other (Describe____________________)			

Page 7 Initial _____ Date _____

APPENDIX 3-A: CLIENT DATA QUESTIONNAIRE (CONT.)

INSURANCE

Life Insurance (Bring in policies)

Type	Policy Owner	Face Amount	Cash Value	Beneficiary	Premium Paid by Employer/ You
Term – You					
Term - Your Spouse					
Permanent – You					
Permanent - Your Spouse					
Other - You (____________)					
Other - Your Spouse (______)					

General Insurance (Check the ones you have and bring in the policies and premium statements)

Type	
Dental	
Health	
Short-term disability	
Long-term disability	
Automobile (Property and Liability)	
Homeowners/Renters	
Specified Personal Property	
Personal Umbrella Liability	
Other (________________________)	
Other (________________________)	

Page 8 Initial _____ Date _____

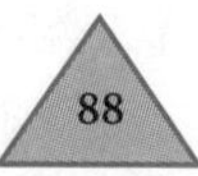

APPENDIX 3-A: CLIENT DATA QUESTIONNAIRE (CONT.)

RETIREMENT PLANNING AND ESTATE PLANNING

At what age do you and your spouse plan to retire? ____________ You

____________ Spouse

Describe your plans for retirement. Include a description of your retirement lifestyle.

____

____

____

____

____

____

____

	You		Your Spouse	
	Yes	**No**	**Yes**	**No**
Do you have a recent will?	❐	❐	❐	❐
Are you planning to make any changes to the will?	❐	❐	❐	❐
Do you have a medical directive?	❐	❐	❐	❐
Have you given a Power of Attorney for healthcare and property?	❐	❐	❐	❐

Page 9 Initial _____ Date _____

CHAPTER 4

Personal Financial Statements (Preparation and Analysis)

LEARNING OBJECTIVES:

After learning the material in this chapter, you will be able to:

1. Explain the need for financial statements.
2. Explain the need for financial statement preparation.
3. Identify and describe each financial statement, its content, and its objective.
4. Be able to prepare financial statements.
5. Identify the tools of financial statement analysis.
6. Calculate ratios.
7. Perform financial statement analysis.
8. Identify the ratios used to determine debt utilization, liquidity, and asset performance.
9. Discuss the limitations of financial statement analysis.
10. Define fair market value.
11. Define liquidity.
12. List the steps necessary to create a budget.
13. Discuss the importance of debt management and differentiate between the types of home mortgages.

INTRODUCTION

Personal financial statements serve as a fundamental planning tool for the financial planner by providing important financial information and by giving the planner an opportunity to analyze such information so as to assist the client in financial decision making. Financial statements are intended to provide information about financial resources available to the client, how these resources were acquired, and what the client has accomplished financially using these resources. Financial statements represent the scoring mechanism for recording and evaluating an individual's financial performance. Information obtained from financial statements can be used to analyze the financial well-being of the client and determine what factors influence the client's earnings and cash flows. Personal financial statements are different from business financial statements primarily in the valuation of assets. Business financial statements use historical values and personal financial statements use current fair market values.

Personal financial statements include the balance sheet, the income and expense statement, and the statement of changes in net worth. This chapter will include a discussion of each financial statement, how it is prepared, and from where the data is obtained. The chapter provides examples illustrating the different financial statements based on the Nelson family introduced in the previous chapter. Information from the Nelsons is also used to demonstrate a thorough treatment of financial statement analysis, including ratio analysis, vertical analysis, and growth analysis.

DECISION-MAKING USES OF FINANCIAL STATEMENTS AND FINANCIAL STATEMENT ANALYSIS

Personal financial statements provide planners, clients, and lenders the necessary information to make adequate financial decisions. Clients prepare personal budgets to assist in understanding their spending patterns, to gain more control over their financial affairs, and to improve the likelihood of reaching their financial goals. As we will see in this chapter, financial statements are used by clients to benchmark goal achievement, by planners to help clients decide financial direction, and by creditors and lenders to make decisions to extend, continue, or call indebtedness. Exhibit 4.1 presents financial actions using the different financial information that can be gathered, the most likely user of the information, and the types of decisions that can be made from the gathering and analysis of the financial information.

EXHIBIT 4.1: FINANCIAL INFORMATION COLLECTION AND ANALYSIS

FINANCIAL ACTIONS	LIKELY USER	TYPE OF DECISION
Preparing personal budgets	Client/Planner	Basic planning
Evaluating spending patterns	Client/Planner	Efficiency/effectiveness
Determining the financial solvency of the client	Client/Planner/Lender	Debt management
Determining if financial goals are being achieved	Client/Planner	Redirect or steady course
Determining if the client is making adequate progress toward retirement	Client/Planner	Capital needs analysis
Evaluating the relative risk and performance of the investment portfolio	Client/Planner	Asset allocation
Evaluating the client's use and cost of debt	Client/Planner/Lender	Refinance
Determining the adequacy of income replacement insurance	Client/Planner	Insurance/estate planning
Determining the adequacy of liquidity for estate planning	Client/Planner	Liquidity at death
Evaluating net worth	Client/Planner/Lender	Lending
Financial statements required for loans	Lender	Lending

RULES REGARDING FINANCIAL STATEMENTS

The **Financial Accounting Standards Board** (FASB) is a nongovernmental board that sets the standards for financial statements and generally accepted accounting principles (also known as GAAP). While these principles (GAAP) generally apply to businesses, they are also useful in the development of personal financial statements. The objectives in following such accounting conventions include consistency and comparability in the preparation and presentation of financial statements. Therefore, objective rather than subjective judgments of value should generally be used in presentation and decision-making.

Financial Accounting Standards Board (FASB) - a nongovernmental board that sets the standards for financial statements and generally accepted accounting principles (GAAP)

PREPARATION OF FINANCIAL STATEMENTS

It is rare that a client is able to provide the financial planner with a complete set of competent personal financial statements. The client many times does not have the necessary documentation or a clear understanding of his or her own current financial position. With that in mind, the planner can either personally prepare the client's financial statements or have someone else prepare them, usually the client's CPA. Personally preparing and analyzing a client's financial statements provides the planner with a wealth of information and insight about the client. Because financial statement preparation and analysis are fundamental to financial planning, all competent financial planners should have a basic understanding of the terminology, evaluation and valuation methods, and the current and relevant accounting and reporting principles to develop such financial statements.

THE BALANCE SHEET

The **balance sheet** is a listing of assets, liabilities, and net worth that depicts resources and tells how those resources were obtained or financed. The statement is a financial "snapshot" of the client at a moment in time (the date of the statement). Historically, the balance sheet was the

balance sheet - a listing of assets, liabilities, and net worth

primary financial statement given to and relied upon by third parties, especially lenders. It was originally designed to meet the needs of creditors who wanted information about assets, collateral, and a person's ability (net worth) to repay debts. Now, lenders generally require copies of all personal financial statements, not just the balance sheet.

Balance Sheet Terms and Presentation Order

assets - property owned completely or partially by the client

liquidity - the ability to buy or sell an asset quickly and at known price

current assets - assets expected to be converted to cash within one year

liability - money owed by the client

net worth - the amount of wealth or equity the client has in owned assets

An **asset** is property owned completely or partially by the client. Some examples of assets are cash, investments, personal residences, and automobiles. The classification of the list of assets on the balance sheet is generally based on liquidity. **Liquidity** is the ability to buy or sell an asset quickly and at a known price. Assets expected to be converted to cash within one year are **current assets.** Therefore, cash and cash equivalents are presented first, followed by assets held as investments, and, finally, assets held for personal use.

A **liability** is money owed by the client. Some examples of liabilities are bank loans, student loans, automobile loans, credit card debt, home mortgages, and taxes owed. On the liability side, liabilities that will or should be paid within one year are presented as current liabilities in their expected order of payoff. Liabilities extending beyond a year are presented as long-term liabilities.

Net worth is the amount of wealth or equity the client has in owned assets. It is the amount of money that would remain after selling all owned assets at their estimated fair market values and paying off all liabilities. The client's net worth is therefore calculated by taking the difference between total assets and total liabilities.

Traditionally, assets are listed on the left side of the balance sheet and liabilities on the right side. The net worth is shown below liabilities on the right side. Depending on the client and the purpose of the balance sheet, the categories may be subdivided into more detail. Regardless of the categorization of assets and liabilities, the statement must always balance. The basic balance sheet formula is Assets – Liabilities = Net Worth. Exhibit 4.2 shows the basic balance sheet format.

EXHIBIT 4.14: BALANCE SHEET FORMAT

ABBREVIATED BALANCE SHEET			
Cash and cash equivalents	$ xxx	Current liabilities	$ xxx
Investment assets	xxx	Long-term liabilities	xxx
Personal-use assets	xxx	Total liabilities	$ xxx
		Net worth	xxx
Total assets	$ xxx	Total liabilities and net worth	$ xxx

Categories and Classifications of Assets

Cash and Cash Equivalents

Cash and cash equivalents include cash on hand, checking accounts, savings accounts, certificates of deposit, cash value in life insurance policies (if intended for current use as cash and cash equivalents; otherwise, classify permanent insurance policies as investments), money market accounts, income tax refunds due, and accounts receivable that are expected to be collected quickly. These are assets easily converted to cash for regular or emergency expenses and assets that are expected to convert to cash within one year.

Investment Assets

Investment assets include stocks, bonds, mutual funds, real estate, collectibles (i.e., stamps and art) held for investment, cash value in life insurance policies (if not intended for use as cash and cash equivalents), and interests in closely held corporations or businesses. Generally, investment assets are held for growth or income. Assets may also be distinguished in the balance sheet as tax advantaged or not tax advantaged. This distinction is useful for tax and distribution purposes.

Personal-Use Assets

Personal-use assets include the personal residence, personal property (furniture, clothing, etc.) jewelry, automobiles, other vehicles, and recreational boats. These assets are generally long lived and are not expected to be liquidated in the short term but rather are to be used to maintain the client's quality of life. Exhibit 4.3 lists some commonly held assets.

EXHIBIT 4.15: COMMONLY HELD ASSETS

CASH & CASH EQUIVALENTS	INVESTMENTS	PERSONAL-USE ASSETS
▲ Cash on-hand	▲ Stocks and bonds	▲ Primary residence
▲ Checking accounts	▲ Certificates of Deposit (> 1 yr)	▲ Vacation home
▲ Savings accounts	▲ Mutual funds	▲ Automobiles
▲ Money market accounts	▲ Real estate	▲ Recreational equipment
▲ Certificates of Deposit (≤1 yr)	▲ Business ownership	▲ Household items
	▲ Cash value of life insurance (generally)	▲ Jewelry
	▲ Cash value of pensions	
	▲ Retirement accounts	
	▲ Collectibles	
	▲ Annuities	
	▲ Other investment vehicles	

Categories and Classifications of Liabilities

Current Liabilities

current liability - debt owed by the client that is expected to be paid off within the year (current ≤ 12 months

Current liabilities include any short-term credit card debt and unpaid bills. These bills represent money the client currently owes. Unpaid credit card balances, taxes payable, bank loans, and other debts that will or should be paid off within one year are also considered current liabilities.

Long-Term Liabilities

long-term liability - debt extending beyond one year (long-term > 12 months)

Long-term liabilities are those debts that will not be paid off within one year, usually debts of larger assets. Generally, loans such as mortgages, automobile loans, long-term notes payable, and student loans are considered long-term liabilities. Where the debt is long term, the current portion due is listed under current liabilities.

Exhibit 4.4 gives several examples of common personal liabilities.

EXHIBIT 4.14: COMMON PERSONAL LIABILITIES

CURRENT LIABILITIES	LONG-TERM LIABILITIES
▲ Current portion of mortgages due	▲ Primary residence mortgage
▲ Utility bills due	▲ Vacation home mortgage
▲ Credit card balances due	▲ Other mortgages
▲ Insurance premiums due	▲ Automobile loans
▲ Taxes due	▲ Home improvement loans
▲ Medical bills due	▲ Student loans
▲ Repair bills due	▲ Other loans

Valuation of Assets and Liabilities

For personal financial statements, assets and liabilities on the balance sheet are stated at the current fair market value. Presenting assets and liabilities at fair market value is not an easy task. There are problems with the precise determination of fair market value for many of the assets listed. Liabilities are more straight forward in terms of valuation.

fair market value - the price at which an exchange will take place between a willing buyer and a willing seller both informed and neither under duress to exchange

Fair market value is defined as the price at which an exchange will take place between a willing buyer and a willing seller, both reasonably informed and neither under duress to exchange. Fair market value for certain assets like cash, cash equivalents, some investment account balances, and most liabilities is readily available from institutional statements and/or by contacting the institution holding the asset. For those assets, such a determination should be made. However, for certain other assets, the determination of fair market value is difficult and may require an appraisal by an expert or an estimate by the client. In some cases, the cost of an appraisal is not warranted because the information gained by appraisal is not worth the cost expended. For example, a small change in the value of a personal residence from year to year may not be relevant to the financial statements, especially where the client has no intent to dispose of the personal residence. The same is true for the valuation of closely held business interests where there is no intent to dispose of such business interests.

The Nelson Family Balance Sheet

Exhibit 4.5 is the Nelsons' beginning financial statement for the year 2005. Exhibit 4.6 is an ending balance sheet for 12/31/05. Notice the changes in net worth, assets, and liabilities. Even though these changes are readily apparent by comparing the numbers, there is no explanation as to what transactions caused those changes. This is one of the weaknesses of the balance sheet.

For example, in Exhibits 4.5 and 4.6, ABC stock increased from $12,500 to $14,050. Did the Nelsons buy more stock? Did the value of the stock increase? Do the Nelsons still hold the same number of shares? The two balance sheets really do not reveal the answer to these questions. A comparison only reveals an increase in the Nelsons' total assets from $423,072 to $459,197 and an increase in their net worth from $207,626 to $241,823—an increase of $34,197. Is the increase good or bad? Obviously, an increase (for an asset) is better than a decrease, but what was the cause? Once again, the two balance sheets do not reveal the answer. In order to answer these questions, other financial statements need to be prepared for the Nelson family, namely, the revenue and expense statement, the cash flow statement, and the statement of changes in net worth. Once all of the financial statements are prepared, they can be analyzed to gain a better understanding of the underlying financial transactions that occurred during the year. All the financial statements for the Nelsons will be presented and analyzed in this chapter. As you will see, the balance sheet does not tell the whole financial story.

EXHIBIT 4.15: NELSONS' BEGINNING BALANCE SHEET

Dana and David Nelson
Balance Sheet
01/01/05

Assets			Liabilities and Net Worth		
Cash/Cash Equivalents			**Current Liabilities**		
JT	Checking Account	$1,425	JT	Credit Cards	$4,000
JT	Savings Account	$950	JT	Mortgage on Principal Residence	$1,234
			H	Boat Loan	$1,493
	Total Cash/Cash Equiv.	$2,375		**Total Current Liabilities**	$6,727
Invested Assets			**Long-Term Liabilities**		
W	ABC Stock	$12,500	JT	Mortgage on Principal Residence	$196,654
JT	Educational Fund	$14,000	H	Boat Loan	$12,065
H	401(k)	$32,197			
	Total Invested Assets	$58,697		**Total Long-Term Liabilities**	$208,719
Personal-Use Assets			**Total Liabilities**		**$215,446**
JT	Principal Residence	$245,000			
JT	Automobile	$18,000			
H	Boat A	$25,000	**Net Worth**		**$207,626**
W	Jewelry	$13,000			
JT	Furniture/Household	$61,000			
	Total Personal-Use Assets	$362,000			
Total Assets		**$423,072**	**Total Liabilities and Net Worth**		**$423,072**

Notes to Financial Statements:

- Assets are stated at fair market value.
- The ABC stock was inherited from Dana's aunt on November 15, 2001. Her aunt originally paid $20,000 for it on October 31, 2001. The fair market value at the aunt's death was $12,000.
- Liabilities are stated at principal only.
- H = Husband; W = Wife; JT = Joint Tenancy

EXHIBIT 4.16: NELSONS' ENDING BALANCE SHEET

Dana and David Nelson
Balance Sheet
12/31/05

Assets			Liabilities and Net Worth		
Cash/Cash Equivalents			**Current Liabilities**		
JT	Checking Account	$1,518	JT	Credit Cards	$3,655
JT	Savings Account	$950	JT	Mortgage on Principal Residence	$1,370
	Total Cash/Cash Equiv.	$2,468	H	Boat Loan	$1,048
				Total Current Liabilities	$6,073
Invested Assets			**Long-Term Liabilities**		
W	ABC Stock	$14,050	JT	Mortgage on Principal Residence	$195,284
JT	Educational Fund	$15,560	H	Boat Loan	$16,017
H	401(k)	$38,619		**Total Long-Term Liabilities**	$211,301
H	XYZ Stock	$10,000			
	Total Invested Assets	$78,229			
Personal-Use Assets			**Total Liabilities**		**$217,374**
JT	Principal Residence	$250,000			
JT	Automobile	$15,000			
H	Jet Ski	$10,000	**Net Worth**		**$241,823**
H	Boat B	$30,000			
W	Jewelry	$13,500			
JT	Furniture/Household	$60,000			
	Total Personal-Use Assets	$378,500			
Total Assets		**$459,197**	**Total Liabilities and Net Worth**		**$459,197**

Notes to Financial Statements:

- Assets are stated at fair market value.
- The ABC stock was inherited from Dana's aunt on November 15, 2001. Her aunt originally paid $20,000 for it on October 31, 2001. The fair market value at the aunt's death was $12,000.
- Liabilities are stated at principal only.
- H = Husband; W = Wife; JT = Joint Tenancy

VALUATION OF ASSETS AND LIABILITIES - THE NELSONS

Reviewing the 1/1/05 and the 12/31/05 balance sheets for the Nelsons, notice that the value of their personal residence has increased by $5,000 ($245,000 - $250,000). If we assume that there were no improvements to the residence, and that we did not have a real estate appraisal, where did the $250,000 number come from? Probably, the planner and client estimated inflation at 2 percent and rounded the increase in value to $5,000, assuming that real estate generally appreciates at the same rate as inflation. What are the relative merits of such estimation for valuation? If you have no plans to sell an asset, but you need a valuation and no ready valuation is available, estimation is a reasonable idea. Anyone familiar with financial statements knows that if they plan to rely on financial statements, then it is incumbent upon them to verify the valuations of important assets and liabilities. In reality, no individual is going to have an appraisal on an annual basis for their personal residence, furnishings, automobile, or other personal-use assets. Therefore, the reader of personal financial statements should be skeptical of the valuations given for personal-use assets.

There is always some imprecision in valuing certain assets and liabilities. The extent to which such imprecision is acceptable to the user depends on the particular use of the financial statements. It is frequently appropriate to have the client estimate a value, particularly for a personal residence. Usually clients know what property has been selling for in their neighborhood and have no intent to dispose of the property. Likewise, it is reasonable to have the client estimate the value of an interest in a closely held business, especially when there is no current intent to dispose of such business interest. Precise valuation may be necessary when the financial statements are used to obtain a loan from a third party, and that third party cannot or will not accept estimates. For example, if the client is refinancing a home, the mortgage lender will require an appraisal.

INFORMATION SOURCES

The financial planner needs to thoroughly review the client's various assets and liabilities in order to prepare the financial statements. The planner will need to access many different documents to determine valuation, payment schedules, and applicable interest concerns. The detail desired of the financial planning engagement will determine the thoroughness of the planner's assessment of these documents. Exhibit 4.7 lists important sources of financial information and the types of information that may be obtained from the sources for the preparation of the balance sheet.

EXHIBIT 4.17: SOURCES AND TYPES OF INFORMATION FOR BALANCE SHEET

SOURCE OF INFORMATION	TYPES OF INFORMATION THAT CAN BE OBTAINED FROM SOURCE
Bank statements	Bank balances and possible loan creation or repayments
Investment account statements	Investment account balance and types
Life insurance statements	Cash value of life insurance and any indebtedness
Real estate purchase agreement	Purchase price of real estate
Mortgage notes	Indebtedness of real estate and terms of indebtedness
Auto purchase agreements	Purchase price of automobile
Auto notes	Terms of indebtedness for automobile
Employer benefit statements	Vested and nonvested account balance/options/contributions by employee and employer to retirement plan
Credit card statements	Purchase price of use assets, balances of credit card indebtedness, payments, interest rates, late charges
Appraisals	Value of the asset appraised
Installment notes	Value of installment notes or liability and terms
Client	All documents and estimates of value regarding assets and liabilities

In the case of the assets and liabilities other than personal-use assets, there are a wide variety of sources and documents to assist the financial planner in the preparation of the balance sheet.

Exhibit 4.8 presents each account on the balance sheet and where the best source of information is to determine the correct balance sheet amount. In addition, alternative sources are presented where the cost/benefit of finding precise data does not warrant collection from the best source.

EXHIBIT 4.18: BALANCE SHEET INFORMATION BY ACCOUNT TYPE

ACCOUNTS AND ACCOUNT BALANCES	BEST SOURCE OF BALANCE SHEET INFORMATION FOR VALUATION	ALTERNATIVE SOURCE
ASSETS		
Cash and Cash Equivalents		
Checking account	Bank statements of client	Client/planner estimate
Savings account	Bank statements of client	
Certificates of Deposit	Bank statements of client	
Investment Assets		
Stocks	Brokerage or investment statements	Client/planner estimate
Bonds	Brokerage or investment statements	
Mutual funds	Account statements	
401(k) account	Account statements	
403(b) account	Account statements	
IRA/SEP	Account statements	
Personal-Use Assets		
Personal residence	Appraisal if warranted	Client/planner estimate
Personal furniture & fixtures	Appraisal if warranted	
Investment real estate	Appraisal if warranted	
Closely Held Business Interests	Appraisal if warranted	Client/planner estimate
Automobiles	Blue book, Bank, Credit Union	Client/planner estimate
LIABILITIES		
Current Liabilities		
Credit card debt	Credit card statements	Client estimate
Bank loans	Lender	Client estimate
Long-Term Liabilities		
Mortgage loans	Amortization table/Lender/Annual statements	Client/planner estimate
Auto Loans	Coupon/Lender	Client/planner estimate

Identification of Ownership of Assets and Liabilities

It is useful to indicate the type of property ownership and the titling of assets and liabilities on the balance sheet when preparing financial statements for married persons. Identifying ownership is especially helpful for estate planning and where one individual has separately owned property not subject to the claims of the other spouse's creditors.

Common abbreviations for property ownership and titling on personal balance sheets are:

H	=	separate property of husband
W	=	separate property of wife
JT	=	property held jointly with survivorship rights by H and W (husband and wife)
CP	=	community property of H and W (husband and wife)

Footnotes to the Balance Sheet

Generally, footnotes are used to provide additional information or to clarify the item footnoted on the financial statements. Examples of common footnotes to the balance sheet include:

- Assets are stated at fair market value.
- Property title listings.
- Existing contingent liabilities (guarantors/co-signed obligations).
- Additional notes regarding property that may be needed at a later date (i.e., basis of gifted property, date of asset acquisition).

THE INCOME AND EXPENSE STATEMENT

The **income and expense statement** presents a summary of the client's income and expenses during an interval of time, usually one year. The income and expense statement may focus on realized transactions, and if so, is helpful when comparing to budgeted financial goals. The income and expense statement may also be prepared pro forma (in advance) and, therefore, can be used for budgeting and/or projections. The basic income and expense statement equation is:

income and expense statement - summary of the client's income and expenses during an interval of time, usually one year

Income – Expenses = **Discretionary Cash Flow.**

The bottom line on a personal income and expense statement shows the amount of discretionary cash flow available to the client. As defined in the equation, discretionary cash flow represents the excess of cash flows to the individual from income, less expenses and committed savings. Such discretionary cash flow may be used for consumption, reduction of debt, additional savings, or for cash gifts, or the purchase of gifts. If such discretionary cash flows are used to reduce debt or are added to savings, balance sheet ratios are improved.

discretionary cash flow - money available after all expenses are accounted for

Income and Expense Statement Terms and Order of Their Presentation

Income

income - all monies received from employment, investments and other sources

Income includes all monies received, usually on a cash basis, from employment, investments, and other sources.

- Employment income includes wages, salaries, bonuses, and commissions.
- Investment income includes interest and dividends from savings and investment accounts, proceeds from the sale of assets, income from annuities, and any other investment-related activities.
- Other income sources may include Social Security benefits, child support, alimony, gifts, scholarships, tax refunds, pension income, and any other income that is received on a regular basis.

Savings

savings - deferred consumption

Savings reduces income available for expenses. Savings is deferred consumption and will be treated as an increase to assets on the balance sheet.

Expenses

expenses - recurring obligations

fixed expenses - expenses that remain constant over a period of time and over which the client has little control

variable expenses - expenses that fluctuate from time to time over which the client has some control

discretionary expenses - luxuries or expenses over which the client has complete control

Expenses are recurring obligations paid, or monthly expenses paid. The three main categories of expenses are fixed, variable, and discretionary.

Fixed expenses are expenses that remain constant over a period of time and over which the client has little control. Examples of fixed expenses include rent or mortgage payments, insurance premiums, tuition, and loan payments.

Variable expenses are expenses that fluctuate in amount from time to time, over which the client has some control. Examples of variable expenses include food, utilities, and transportation costs.

Discretionary expenses are luxuries or expenses over which the client has complete control. Examples of discretionary expenses are vacations, entertainment expenses, and gifts.

Information Sources

The financial planner will need to thoroughly review the client's various income sources and personal expenditures in order to create the income and expense statement. Exhibit 4.9 lists some of the more common sources of financial information that may be used in the collection of data for the preparation of the income and expense statement.

EXHIBIT 4.14: PERSONAL INCOME & EXPENDITURE SOURCES

Income Sources	Information Source
Salary	Form W-2/tax return
Interest (taxable)	Form 1099/tax return
Dividends	Form 1099

Expenditures (Savings and Expenses)	Information Source
Savings	Bank statements/401(k) statements/1099s
Food	Budget/check register/receipts/credit card statement
Clothing	Budget/check register/receipts/credit card statement
Child care	Budget/check register/receipts/credit card statement
Entertainment	Budget/check register/receipts/credit card statement
Utilities	Actual bills/check register/receipts
Auto maintenance	Budget/check register/receipts/credit card statement
Church	Checks and receipts
401(k) loan repayments	Participant statement
Credit card interest	Statements
Mortgage payment	Mortgage statement
Automobile/Boat loan	Loan agreement/check register
Insurance premiums	Invoice/policy/check register
Tuition and education expenses	Invoice/check stubs
Federal income tax (W/H)	Form W-2/tax return
State (and City) income tax	Form W-2/tax return
FICA	Form W-2/tax return
Property tax for real estate	Mortgage statement/check register

Exhibit 4.10 is the Nelsons' statement of income and expenses showing their income, savings, expenses, and discretionary cash flow for the year 2005.

EXHIBIT 4.15: STATEMENT OF INCOME AND EXPENSES

Dana and David Nelson Statement of Income and Expenses For the year 2005		
INCOME		
Salary - David		$70,000
Investment Income		
Interest Income	$900	
Dividend Income	$150	$1,050
Total Inflow		**$71,050**
Savings		
Reinvestment (Interest/Dividends)	$1,050	
401(k) Deferrals	$3,803	
Educational Fund	$1,000	
Total Savings		**$5,853**
Available for Expenses		**$65,197**
EXPENSES		
Ordinary Living Expenses		
Food	$6,000	
Clothing	$3,600	
Child Care	$600	
Entertainment	$1,814	
Utilities	$3,600	
Auto Maintenance	$2,000	
Church	$3,500	
Total Ordinary Living Expenses		**$21,114**
Debt Payments		
Credit Card Payments Principal	$345	
Credit Card Payments Interest	$615	
Mortgage Payment Principal	$1,234	
Mortgage Payment Interest	$20,720	
Boat Loan Principal	$1,493	
Boat Loan Interest	$1,547	
Total Debt Payments		**$25,954**
Insurance Premiums		
Automobile Insurance Premiums	$900	
Disability Insurance Premiums	$761	
Homeowners Insurance Premiums	$950	
Total Insurance Premiums		**$2,611**
Tuition and Education Expenses		**$1,000**
Taxes		
Federal Income Tax (W/H)	$7,500	
State (and City) Income Tax	$820	
FICA	$5,355	
Property Tax (Principal Residence)	$1,000	
Total Taxes		**$14,675**
Total Expenses		**$65,354**
Discretionary Cash Flow (negative)		**($157)**

Compromise in Information Reporting

The income and expense statement is a compromise in information reporting. For an individual, the income and expense statement is almost a full cash flow statement. The exceptions, those transactions that are not considered income or expenses, but are cash flows, are generally not included in the income and expense statement. As an example, while conventional corporate accounting would only include the interest portion from any repayment of debt as an expense, it is common for personal financial statements to include both the principal and the interest in debt repayment as an expense or cash flow of the period (e.g., mortgage payments, credit card payments, bank loan repayments).

The astute planner will notice that an income and expense statement for an individual is not truly an accrual income and expense statement nor is it a full cash flow statement. Because the income statement for individuals is frequently prepared pro forma (in advance) and used as a budget, it is a presentation of recurring inflows and outflows presented in a conventional manner, and is, therefore, a compromise. If it were a full cash flow statement, it would have to consider the acquisition and disposition of all assets for and by cash.

The income statement generally does not consider the sale or purchase of assets during the period. The income statement also does not consider employer matches to qualified retirement accounts. As we will soon see, other financial statements must be prepared to present the complete financial picture of the client.

The Relationship of the Balance Sheet to the Income and Expense Statement

The balance sheet represents the financial picture of the individual at a moment in time setting forth assets, liabilities, and net worth. The income and expense statement presents recurring revenues, savings, expenses, and discretionary cash flow over a period of time. The income statement provides a partial picture of what has happened between two balance sheet dates. As discussed previously, neither statement by itself, nor when taken together, presents the entire financial picture of the individual. This deficiency creates the need for other financial statements, such as the statement of cash flows and the statement of changes in net worth, to help further clarify the complete financial picture of the client. The purpose of the statement of cash flows is to bridge the gap between the beginning and the ending cash balance and the intervening income and expense statement.

THE STATEMENT OF CASH FLOWS

The **statement of cash flows** assists in the reconciliation of the income statement to changes between two balance sheets. For a given period, the statement of cash flows shows the inflows and outflows and the net changes in cash between two balance sheets and identifies the changes in some of the accounts from one balance sheet to the next.

statement of cash flows - summary of the client's changes to the cash account

There are numerous financial transactions involving cash flows that occur between balance sheet dates that do not show up as either a revenue (income) or expense and, therefore, are not accounted for on the income and expense statement. Such transactions include where two balance sheet accounts are affected without affecting an income or expense account.

EXAMPLE

Examples of transactions that affect cash flows but are generally not included on the personal income and expense statement include:

- Purchasing or selling a personal-use asset for cash (automobile).
- Taking out a loan.
- Purchasing or selling an investment.
- Receiving a gift or inheritance in cash.
- Giving a gift of cash.

CLASSIFICATIONS

The statement of cash flows supplements the information from the income and expense statement and balance sheets to help explain the changes in account balances that have occurred between the beginning and ending balance sheets. The classification of individual items is what provides information content. The statement of cash flows has three sections: cash flows from operations, cash flows from financing activities, and cash flows from investing activities. The sum of all cash flows for the three sections is equal to the net change in cash as presented on the beginning and ending balance sheets.

Cash Flows from Operations

cash flows from operations - net cash generated or used due to normal work and living

Cash flows from operations measure the amount of net cash generated or used by the individual due to normal work and normal living. For short periods, deficits may occur but, generally, net positive discretionary cash flows are essential to produce long-term growth. Discretionary funds can then be used for (1) investments, (2) to replace use assets such as automobiles, or (3) to pay debt. Because it is a common practice to include savings, recurring investments, and recurring debt principal repayments in the income and expense statement there is a need to adjust those items out of operating cash flow and reclassify them appropriately as cash flows to investment and financing activities, respectively. This section (cash flow from operations) lists the discretionary cash flow from normal household operations on the income and expense statements and changes in the balances of current assets and liabilities (excluding cash).

Cash Flows from Investing Activities

cash flows from investing - cash receipts or expenditures for the sale or purchase of assets

Cash flows from investing are the cash outflows used to acquire assets and cash inflows from the sale of assets (investments and personal-use assets) during the period. These cash flows are necessary to maintain a lifestyle and to save for future goals (i.e. education or retirement). The cash flows from investing activities section details the acquisition and disposition of invested assets and personal-use assets. Cash that is invested through savings is reclassified from operating cash flows to cash outflows from investing.

Cash Flows from Financing Activities

Cash flows from financing include cash inflows from the issuance of additional debt (notes payable) and cash outflows for the repayment of debt (principal) during the period. This section details the cash obtained from financing sources and the cash used to repay those sources. Increases in cash flows are created by actions increasing long-term indebtedness where cash is received at the inception of the transaction (i.e. obtaining a loan). Decreases in cash flows result from repayments of debt. For personal financial statements, it is useful to list the repayment of principal for indebtedness related to mortgages or automobiles even though they are initially accounted for in the income and expense statement. We can accomplish this with an adjustment to the operating cash flows from the income and expense statement as shown in Exhibit 4.11, the Nelsons' statement of cash flows.

cash flows from financing - cash inflows from the issuance of additional debt and cash outflows for the repayment of debt

OTHER CLASSIFICATION ISSUES

Several classification issues exist regarding the cash flow statement for individuals that generally do not exist for businesses. Perhaps the most common item of savings not reflected in the income and expense statement is an employer match contribution to a retirement plan. Inheritances received in cash and cash outflows of nonrecurring gifts are also among the most common for individuals but uncommon for businesses. The question is where to classify such transactions on the statement of cash flows. We have chosen, for convenience and convention, to record employer contributions under investing cash flows, and inheritances received and gifts given under investment activities. For example, an inheritance received in cash is a source of investment cash flow, and the corresponding use occurs when the cash is placed in an investment account. Conversely, gifts of property made by a donor are essentially a reduction of investments to the donor.

ADJUSTMENTS TO CASH FLOWS FROM OPERATIONS

There are a number of adjustments that need to be made to the operating cash flows of an individual to provide a clear financial picture of the client. These adjustments remove savings and debt repayments from the income statement and more properly reclassify these as cash flows to investments or to financing activities. The cash flows on the income statement used for savings are reclassified as cash flows to investing. The cash flows from principal debt repayments (included in income and expense statement), including mortgage, bank loan, auto loan, credit card and student loan payments, are reclassified as cash flows to financing activities.

EXHIBIT 4.16: STATEMENT OF CASH FLOWS

Dana and David Nelson Statement of Cash Flows For the Year Ending 12/31/05		
Cash from/for Operations (Income Statement)		
Discretionary Cash Flow from Income Statement		($157)
Adjustments to operating cash flows		
Increase of Investments from Savings		
Interest/Dividends	$1,050	
Educational Fund	$1,000	
401(k)	$3,803	$5,853
Decrease in Liabilities from Principal Repayments		
Mortgage on Principal Residence	$1,234	
Boat Loan	$1,493	
Credit Card Debt	$345	$3,072
Total Cash from Operations		**$8,768**
Cash from/(for) Investment Activities		
Jet ski		($10,000)
Increases of Investments from Savings		
ABC Stock	($1,050)	
Educational Fund	($1,000)	
401(k)	($3,803)	($5,853)
Inheritance		$10,250
Boat B		($5,000)
Total Cash from Investments		**($10,603)**
Cash from/(for) Financing Activities		
Decreases in Liabilities from Principal Repayments		
Mortgage on Principal Residence	($1,234)	
Boat Loan	($1,493)	
Credit Card Debt	($345)	($3,072)
Boat Loan		$5,000
Total Cash from Finance		**$1,928**
Net Increase (Decrease) in Cash Flows		$93
Ending Cash and Cash Equivalents		$2,468
Beginning Cash and Cash Equivalents		($2,375)
Net Increase (Decrease) in Cash Flows		$93

RATIONALES FOR CASH FLOW CATEGORIES

The rationale for the adoption of the three categories (cash flows from operations, cash flows from investing activities, and cash flows from financing activities) on the cash flow statement is that such classification assists the reader in learning where cash comes from and where it is being used. The income and expense statement does not include borrowings, repayments, investment changes, and other items that are not routine and recurring, but still need to be accounted for. The different ways in which cash flows may be grouped can be argued and may be somewhat arbitrary; however, the statement of cash flows, when presented with two balance sheets (beginning and end), and the intervening income and expense statement, provide a wealth of financial information about the client.

THE STATEMENT OF CHANGES IN NET WORTH

Throughout the preparation of the three previously mentioned financial statements, we have tried to provide financial information useful to the client and the planner. We now need to be able to explain the changes in net worth between two balance sheets. So far, using the income statement and the statement of cash flows, we are able to explain all of the balance sheet account changes that were affected by cash. Unfortunately, there are changes in net worth that do not affect cash flows. Therefore, even when these three financial statements (balance sheet, income statement, and cash flow statement) are taken together, they cannot fully account for all the changes between the beginning and ending balance sheets. Thus, there is a need for a fourth and final statement to summarize noncash flow changes in net worth that would not have been recorded on either the income or the cash flow statement. This fourth financial statement is called the **statement of changes in net worth**. To the extent that we have not been able to ascertain all of the exact changes in the net worth, this statement will allow us to do so. Examples of transactions or changes in account balances that would not be included in the income statement are listed below:

statement of changes in net worth - summary of changes from one balance sheet to the next

- ▲ Changes in value for assets due to either appreciation or depreciation.
- ▲ If an asset other than cash is exchanged for some other assets (real estate for real estate).
- ▲ If assets other than cash are received by gift or inheritance (property).
- ▲ If assets other than cash are given to charities or noncharitable donees (automobiles, buildings, or investments).

EXAMPLE

Below are some sample transactions and how the transactions affect Net Worth:

- ▲ The client buys $5,000 of furniture on credit. The effect: Assets (furniture) increase by $5,000 and Liabilities (debt) increase by $5,000; no change in Net Worth.
- ▲ The client's IRA appreciates by $10,000 this year. The effect: Assets (IRA) increase by $10,000 and Liabilities remain the same, so Net Worth increases by $10,000.
- ▲ The clients buy a house for $200,000 by paying a 5% down payment and financing the balance. The effect: Assets decrease by $10,000 (cash) and increase by $200,000 (house) and Liabilities increase by the $190,000 (mortgage). There is then no change in Net Worth.

Exhibit 4.12 depicts the statement of changes in net worth for the Nelson family. The Nelsons' net worth statement ties together the overall change in their net worth. It reflects each noncash item that was altered during the year. Transactions that were not previously reported on any of the other statements include:

- An inheritance of $10,000 in XYZ stock from David's grandmother.
- Appreciation in value of the jewelry, residence, ABC stock, Educational Fund, and 401(k).
- Employer contribution to David's 401(k) plan ($2,100).
- Gift of a table to Dana's mother ($1,000 value).

EXHIBIT 4.17: STATEMENT OF CHANGES IN NET WORTH

Dana and David Nelson **Statement of Changes in Net Worth** **For the Year Ending** **12/31/05**	
Additions to Net Worth	
Add (Non Cash Flow Adjustments to Net Worth)	
Increases in Assets:	
Inheritance	
XYZ Stock	$10,000
Appreciation of Assets	
Jewelry	$500
Residence	$5,000
Adjustment from Even Exchange	
Boat B	$30,000
Purchase	
Jet Ski	$10,000
Appreciation of Investments	
ABC Stock	$500
Educational fund	$560
401(k)	$519
Increase of Investment Contributions	
ABC Stock	$1,050
Educational Fund	$1,000
401(k)-employee contribution	$3,803
401(k)-employer contribution	$2,100
Decrease in Liabilities (Debt Repayments):	
Mortgage on Principal Residence	$1,234
Boat Loan	$1,493
Credit Card Debt	$345
Total	**$68,104**
Reductions in Net Worth	
Less (Non Cash Flow Adjustments to Net Worth)	
Decrease in Assets:	
Depreciation of Assets	
Auto	($3,000)
Gifts	
Table to Mother	($1,000)
Adjustment from Even Exchange	
Boat A	($25,000)
Increase in liabilities	
Addition to Boat Loan	($5,000)
Total	**($34,000)**
Net - Non Cash Flow change in Net Worth	**$34,104**
Beginning Net Worth (Beginning Balance Sheet)	$207,626
Plus Changes from Cash Flow Statement	$93
Plus Change from Statement of Changes in Net Worth	$34,104
Ending Net Worth (Ending Balance Sheet)	**$241,823**

Where on the Web

Consolidated Credit Counseling Services, Inc. *www.consolidatedcredit.org*

Credit Union National Association *www.cuna.org*

Equifax *www.equifax.com*

Federal Citizen Information Center *www.pueblo.gsa.gov*

Myvesta.org *www.dca.org or www.myvesta.org*

Sallie Mae *www.salliemae.com*

NELSON EXAMPLE RECAP

Recall that the initial balance sheet and the ending balance sheet are not equal. Based on this observation, we know that there were circumstances in which the overall financial status of the Nelsons changed during the year. Exhibit 4.13 illustrates a spreadsheet reconciliation of the changes for the Nelsons from one balance sheet date to the next.

EXHIBIT 4.14: SPREADSHEET RECONCILIATION OF CHANGES IN NET WORTH

Asset	1/1/2005 Balance Sheet	Income (Cash Flow) Statement	Net Worth	12/31/2005 Balance Sheet
Checking Account	$1,425	$93		$1,518
Savings Account	$950			$950
ABC Stock	$12,500		$1,550	$14,050
Educational Fund	$14,000		$1,560	$15,560
401(k)	$32,197		$6,422	$38,619
XYZ Stock	$0		$10,000	$10,000
Principal Residnece	$245,000		$5,000	$250,000
Automobile	$18,000		($3,000)	$15,000
Jet Ski	$0		$10,000	$10,000
Boat A	$25,000		($25,000)	$0
Boat B	$0		($30,000)	$30,000
Jewerly	$13,000		$500	$13,500
Furniture/Househould	$61,000		($1,000)	$60,000
Credit Cards	($4,000)		$345	($3,655)
Mortagage on Residence*	($197,888)		$1,234	($196,654)
Boat Loan*	($13,558)		($3,507)	($17,065)
Net Worth	$207,626	$93	$34,104	$241,823

**Includes current and long-term liabilities*

FINANCIAL ANALYSIS OF PERSONAL FINANCIAL STATEMENTS

Once the balance sheet, income and expense statement, and statement of changes in net worth have been properly prepared, financial statement analysis can be performed to gain insight into the financial strengths and weaknesses of the client. The financial planner may look upon this activity as a form of diagnosing the financial health of the client. It should be stressed that financial analysis, while somewhat comprehensive, is only one tool of the competent financial planner. Financial analysis by its very nature is limited to the past and, therefore, is not necessarily predictive of the future. Even with its inherent limitations, however, financial statement analysis is a useful and powerful tool to gain insight into the financial well-being of the client.

We begin with a traditional approach to analyzing the four financial statements, and then broaden our analysis to improve our insights. Our traditional approach utilizes ratio, vertical, and growth analysis.

Financial statement analysis (in general) and ratio analysis (in particular) can assist us in answering the following questions about a client:

- Can the client financially withstand a sudden negative financial disruption to income (such as unemployment or loss of a significant asset)?
- Can the client meet short-term obligations?
- Does the client manage debt well?
- Does the client have an appropriate balance among various classes of expenditures relative to income?
- Is the client's income growing at an appropriate rate?
- Is the client's savings and savings rate appropriate for the given income and income growth?
- Is the client making a satisfactory total return on investments and savings?
- Is the client's net worth growing at an appropriate rate?
- Is the client making satisfactory progress toward funding retirement?

RATIO ANALYSIS

There are many financial ratios one might use to gain insight into the client's financial well-being. The ratios that we have selected are only suggestive. Other financial planners may have ratios that they use which we have neglected. Furthermore, some decisions require exhaustive **ratio analysis** while other decisions are quite simple and may require only the calculation of a few simple ratios. Thus, there is no one set of ratios that needs to be used all of the time, nor is there a particular ratio that is always calculated. The ratios are used to clarify and to improve the understanding of the data and are used in comparison to established benchmarks, such as those established in the mortgage lending industry, to make judgments as to their appropriateness for a particular client. We would expect, for example, that at higher income levels, there are greater amounts of savings and larger net worths. Therefore, we must be careful to use relevant benchmarks to which we compare the financial ratios of each individual.

ratio analysis - the relationship or relative value of two characteristics used to analyze an individual's financial health and to conduct comparison and trend analysis

Financial statement analysis is both art and science. While anyone can mathematically calculate ratios, the ability to understand the implications of those ratios and to motivate the client to take actions to affect those ratios where appropriate, is truly an art. The art will only come with practice and experience.

Ratio analysis is intended to provide additional perspective on the financial statements. The selection of each numerator and denominator to calculate a particular ratio must be done with care. Not every ratio is relevant for every client. The objective of ratio analysis is twofold: to gain additional insight into the financial situation and behavior of the client, and to generate questions for the client to answer to further gain such insight.

The ratios selected for discussion in this chapter are ones that the authors have found to be particularly useful. The key to ratio analysis is, does the ratio answer the question asked, and then, is there some standard or benchmark to determine whether the result is appropriate for this particular client. Ratio analysis uses both the balance sheet and income and expense statement.

Liquidity Ratios

Liquidity ratios measure the ability of the client to meet short-term financial obligations. They compare current financial obligations such as current liabilities or financial requirements to current assets or cash flows available to meet those financial obligations. These liquidity ratios include the emergency fund ratio and the current ratio.

The Emergency Fund Ratio

The emergency fund ratio assists the planner in determining the ability of the client to withstand a sudden negative financial disruption to income. Such a financial disruption could occur as a result of a layoff, untimely death, disability, or some other event that causes the cash flows to cease or be reduced. It is calculated by comparing the amount of liquid assets to the monthly expenses of the client. The emergency fund ratio should generally be three to six months of non-discretionary cash flows to accommodate unemployment, losses of significant assets, or other unexpected major expenditures.

Reviewing Exhibit 4.6, the 12/31/2005 balance sheet, the Nelsons had $2,468 in liquid assets. In reviewing the income and expense statement, they have monthly expenses totaling $5,446 ($65,354 ÷12). A closer review of the monthly expenditures reveals that there are certain expenses that could be reduced if necessary. Assume that the following costs could be eliminated:

Child Care[1]	$600
Entertainment	1,814
Federal Taxes[2]	7,500
State and City Taxes[2]	820
FICA[2]	5,355
Eliminated Expenses	$16,089

[1] Dana is a full-time housewife. In an emergency, child care costs could be eliminated.

[2] If David lost his source of income, the Nelsons would not pay taxes.

Thus, the real nondiscretionary monthly expenses are $4,105 [($65,354 - $16,089) ÷ 12]. (Note that in consultation with the client, the church contribution of $3,500 was not considered discretionary.) The emergency fund ratio is calculated by dividing the current assets (numerator) by the nondiscretionary monthly expenses (denominator) to provide the resultant.

$$\text{Emergency Fund Ratio (EFR)} = \frac{\text{Current Assets}}{\text{Monthly Nondiscretionary Expenses}} = \text{Target of 3 to 6 Months}$$

$$\text{Nelsons' EFR} \quad \frac{\$2{,}468}{\$4{,}105} = 0.60 \text{ months}$$

The emergency fund ratio of 0.60 months is substantially below the target goal of three to six months, suggesting a substantial risk to the overall financial plan. You may observe that the Nelsons could liquidate some of their investments or borrow from their 401(k) plan in the event of an emergency. While both observations are correct, generally, it is disruptive to a long-term investment plan to have such forced liquidations. Therefore, we would place building the emergency fund as one of our current objectives with a quantitative target of initially 3 months, and over a longer time of 6 months.

While it is generally desirable for the client to maintain a 3-6 month EFR using only current assets in the numerator, each client's situation is unique. Some clients may be at little risk of losing income to cover basic living expenses and may desire higher rates of return than can be achieved with checking and savings accounts. In such a case, substitutions for current assets may be made in the EFR calculation. For example, the client may be willing, and able, to sell marketable securities or obtain a low-interest line of credit.

The Current Ratio

The current ratio examines the relationship between current assets and current liabilities. The current ratio indicates the ability to meet short-term obligations. The ratio is calculated by dividing current assets (numerator) by current liabilities (denominator).

$$\text{Current Ratio (CR)} = \frac{\text{Current Assets}}{\text{Current Liabilities}} = \text{Target of 1.0 to 2.0}$$

In reviewing the 12/31/2006 balance sheet of the Nelsons, we find current assets of $2,468 and current liabilities of $6,073.

$$\text{Nelsons' CR} \quad \frac{\$2{,}468}{\$6{,}073} = 0.41$$

The current ratio of 0.41 is low relative to the target of 1.0 to 2.0. It suggests insufficient current assets, or too many current liabilities, or some combination of both. Therefore, we would suggest increasing the current ratio to 1.0 over a reasonable period of time. By increasing the emergency fund ratio, the Nelsons may also increase the current ratio.

Debt Ratios and Debt Analysis

Debt ratios indicate how well the person manages debt. Debt is not inherently good or bad. All debt carries some cost, at a minimum, interest costs. Quality debt is debt that is low in cost and has a term structure that does not exceed the economic life of the asset that created the debt. When a person consistently repays debt as agreed, such repayment creates a history of good credit ratings, the borrower gains confidence in handling debt, and lenders gain confidence in extending credit to such a borrower. Excessive debt or expensive debt is a warning sign that default risk is a serious threat. It is impossible to determine exactly how much debt a person should have, but various ratios give signals as to the person's ability to handle debt and whether or not the person may be overextended. The initial debt ratios include total debt to net worth, long-term debt to net worth, debt to total assets, and long-term debt to total assets. These debt ratios are compared from one year to the next in order to identify trends, rather than having a particular target, as with liquidity ratios.

Total Debt to Net Worth

$$\text{Total Debt to Net Worth} = \frac{\text{Total Debt}}{\text{Net Worth}}$$

The ratio indicates the portion of a person's assets derived from debt compared to net worth. Generally, we would expect the debt to net worth ratio to decline over a person's lifetime.

Reviewing the two balance sheets for the Nelsons (1/1/2006 and 12/31/2006), we find the total debt to net worth ratio to be:

$$1/1/2005 \quad \frac{\$215{,}446}{\$207{,}626} = 1.04$$

$$12/31/2005 \quad \frac{\$217{,}374}{\$241{,}823} = 0.90$$

The total debt ratio has improved this year, as a lower proportion of debt indicates less financial risk.

Long-Term Debt to Net Worth

The long-term debt ratio removes short-term debt from the numerator to get a look at the long-term capital structure. The ratio is calculated as follows:

$$\text{Long-Term Debt to Net Worth} = \frac{\text{Long-Term Debt}}{\text{Net Worth}}$$

Net worth should be increasing and long-term debt should be declining over time. Therefore, we expect a decreasing ratio when comparing from one year to the next.

Again, after reviewing the two balance sheets for the Nelsons, we find long-term debt to net worth to be:

$$1/1/2005 \quad \frac{\$208{,}719}{\$207{,}626} = 1.01$$

$$12/31/2005 \quad \frac{\$211{,}301}{\$241{,}823} = 0.87$$

Note that the long-term debt to net worth ratios are very close to the total debt to net worth ratios, which suggests that most of the Nelsons' debt is long term. An examination of the long-term debt of the Nelsons reveals that the primary debt is the mortgage on the principal residence, which (as opposed to credit card debt) is generally considered high quality debt.

Total Debt to Total Assets

The ratio of total debt to total assets indicates the proportion of assets furnished by creditors as a percentage of total assets.

$$\text{Total Debt to Total Assets} = \frac{\text{Total Debt}}{\text{Total Assets}}$$

Reviewing the Nelsons' two balance sheets, we find total debt to total assets to be:

$$1/1/2005 \quad \frac{\$215{,}446}{\$423{,}072} = 0.51$$

$$12/31/2005 \quad \frac{\$217{,}374}{\$459{,}197} = 0.47$$

Once again, the resultant ratio has modestly improved over the last year.

Long-Term Debt to Total Assets

The long-term debt to total assets ratio is a numerator refinement on the previous ratio to focus on long-term debt as a proportion of total assets.

$$\text{Long-Term Debt to Total Assets} = \frac{\text{Long-Term Debt}}{\text{Total Assets}}$$

Once again, we use the two balance sheets for the Nelsons to determine the long-term debt to total assets:

$$1/1/2005 \quad \frac{\$208{,}719}{\$423{,}072} = 0.49$$

$$12/31/2005 \quad \frac{\$211{,}301}{\$459{,}197} = 0.46$$

The ratio has modestly declined. For the Nelsons, this decline does not add very much insight due to the debt mix. However, for a client with different debt mixes, this ratio could be very revealing.

Analysis of Debt

The proper use of debt is to match the economic benefit period of the asset purchased with the repayment period of the debt such that the economic benefit period equals or exceeds the repayment period. We expect that there is a life cycle of indebtedness beginning at the asset accumulation phase, peaking sometime in the conservation/preservation phase, and declining rapidly during or before the gifting phase. Debt is useful for asset accumulation, but it has a cost. Once it is established that the person can manage debt well, lenders are willing to extend more debt up to the point where default risk is increased. At some point, persons who have acquired assets using debt wish to be out of debt to devote the repayment resources to other goals, such as, saving for retirement.

Certain types of debt are often thought of as reasonable, such as student loans, mortgages, and auto loans. The underlying assets of education, housing, and transportation create long-lived economic benefits and are expensive. These assets are commonly purchased with some debt financing. Exhibit 4.14 presents the types of debts, the benefits created by those debts, the expected economic benefits period of the asset purchased, and the common repayment period. Many items may be purchased with credit cards; however, credit card debt is considered the worst kind of debt due to its high costs. Many people use credit cards to purchase consumable goods and then find themselves repaying the debt long after the period of consumption. There are some positive ways to use credit cards, such as paying off the balance monthly without increasing debt.

EXHIBIT 4.14: TYPES OF DEBT: ECONOMIC BENEFIT AND REPAYMENT PERIODS

TYPE OF DEBT	TYPE OF BENEFIT CREATED	EXPECTED BENEFIT PERIOD*	COMMON REPAYMENT PERIOD
Student loans	Education	Lifetime	10 years
Mortgage or principal residence	Shelter	40 years	15-30 years
Auto loans	Transportation	3-10 years	3-5 years
Bank loans	Various	Various	Various
Credit cards	Various[1]	Various	30 days to 1 year[2] or more

*Assumes asset held for entire economic life.

[1] Various, but usually, consumption.

[2] If credit cards are paid at the minimum payment, the interest may be high (18-21 percent), and the debt will last a very long time.

Monthly Housing Costs to Monthly Gross Income

Mortgage lenders are sophisticated lenders. They have benchmarks for loans secured with real estate used as a personal residence. The first such benchmark is:

$$\frac{\text{Monthly Housing Costs (P+Int+T+Ins)}}{\text{Monthly Gross Income}} \leq 28\ \%\ \text{Monthly Gross Income}$$

Where:

P	=	Principal
Int	=	Interest
T	=	Taxes (Real Estate)
Ins	=	Insurance

Housing costs include the monthly principal and interest to repay the loan, real estate taxes, and homeowners insurance. This sum is divided by monthly gross income (income before taxes and other deductions). Generally, to issue a mortgage loan at prevailing market interest rates, lenders require this ratio to be less than or equal to 28 percent.

housing costs - principal and interest to pay the mortgage loan, real estate taxes and homeowners insurance

For the Nelsons:

$$\frac{(\$20{,}720 + \$1{,}234 + \$1{,}000 + \$950) \div 12}{\$71{,}050 \div 12} = \$1{,}992 \div \$5{,}921 = 33.6\%$$

This ratio, which for the Nelsons significantly exceeds the benchmark of 28 percent, suggests that the Nelsons have taken on housing debt in excess of what is reasonable for their income.

Monthly Housing Costs and Other Debt Repayments to Monthly Gross Income

The second ratio that lenders use is adjusts the previous numerator to reflect all monthly debt repayments. This ratio should be less than or equal to 36 percent.

$$\frac{\text{Housing Costs (from above) + Other Monthly Debt Pmts.}}{\text{Monthly Gross Income}} \leq 36\%\ \text{Monthly Gross Income}$$

This ratio of housing costs and all other monthly debt repayments must be less than or equal to 36 percent. A mortgage applicant must generally meet both the requirements of the 28 percent benchmark and the 36 percent benchmark to qualify for a mortgage loan at the best interest rates.

For the Nelsons:

$$\frac{\text{Housing Costs + Credit Cards + Boat Loan}}{\text{Monthly Gross Income}} \leq 36\%\ \text{Monthly Gross Income}$$

$$\frac{\$1{,}992 + (\$960 \div 12) + (\$3{,}040 \div 12)}{\$5{,}921} = \$2{,}325.33 \div \$5{,}921 = 39.3\%$$

The Nelsons have also exceeded the second benchmark. This should serve as a warning sign that the Nelsons have too much debt for their current income level. The second housing ratio is not grossly deficient (over the target). If the Nelsons paid off the credit cards and boat with invested assets, the second ratio would be within the established benchmark.

Because these ratios are so widely used by mortgage lenders for both initial mortgage indebtedness and for mortgage refinance, they are useful benchmark ratios to calculate for any client to determine if the client is at risk of having too much debt. The ratios indicate that monthly housing nondiscretionary costs should not exceed 28 percent of monthly gross income, and that all monthly debt repayments should not exceed 36 percent of monthly gross income. The second ratio suggests that if the full initial 28 percent of gross income is used for housing, there is only 8 percent of gross income left for auto loans, furniture loans, student loans, and monthly credit card repayments. Many clients tend to stretch beyond their means when buying a home and should be cautioned by the planner. These ratios can bring a sense of reality to a client regarding the debt picture and indebtedness decisions.

Performance Ratios - Savings

Performance ratios are designed to assess the financial flexibility of the client, as well as to assess the client's progress toward financial goal achievement. These ratios are the savings ratio and discretionary cash flow plus savings to gross income ratio.

The Savings Ratio

The savings ratio indicates the amount that is actually being saved as a percent of gross income.

$$\frac{\text{Annual Savings (Personal and Employer Related)}}{\text{Annual Gross Income}} = \text{Annual Rate of Savings} = \text{Target of 10\%}$$

The long-run savings rate for a client is the level of savings that has been achieved on a consistent basis and is reasonably likely to persist. The long-run combined savings rate should be about 10 percent of gross income if the client begins saving by age 30 expecting to retire at the age of 62. If savings begin later, retirement must be delayed or the savings rate must be increased. For example, beginning to save at age 40 and retiring at 65 would require a 15 percent savings rate. For these savings rates to be effective, there is also an earnings rate assumption of real market returns on a growth investment portfolio. Unfortunately, many clients do not save enough to create adequate retirement capital. Some clients also do not invest wisely and, therefore, do not achieve growth investment portfolio returns.

In reviewing the Nelsons' income and expense statement, Exhibit 4.10, we have determined their savings rate to be:

$$\frac{\$5{,}853 + \$2{,}100}{\$71{,}050} = 11.2\%$$

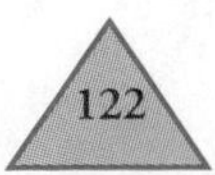

The Nelsons have a good combined savings rate of 11.2 percent, which includes the 3 percent match from David's employer.

Discretionary Cash Flows Plus Savings to Gross Income

This ratio indicates the amount that could be saved as opposed to what is saved. The ratio is calculated using net discretionary cash flow from the statement of income and expense and adding scheduled savings. This sum is then divided by total gross income.

$$\frac{\text{DCF + Savings}}{\text{Annual Gross Income}} \geq \text{10\% Target}$$

Reviewing the Nelsons' statement of income and expenses, we determine that the ratio is:

$$\frac{(\$157) + \$5{,}853 + \$2{,}100}{\$71{,}050} = 11\%$$

While this ratio is unrevealing for the Nelsons, it may be useful for other clients where the savings rate is lower or where there are significant discretionary cash flows.

Performance Ratios - Investments

Investment performance ratios are designed to assist the reader in understanding the returns on investments. They include income on investments, rate of return on investments, and investment assets to gross income.

Income on Investments

The income on investments is calculated by dividing the investment returns by the average invested assets.

$$\frac{\text{Income from Investment Returns}}{\text{Average Invested Assets}} = \text{Target depends on the client's situation}$$

Using the income and expense statement and the balance sheet for the Nelsons, we calculate their income on investments to be:

$$\frac{\$900 + \$150}{(\$58{,}697 + \$78{,}229) \div 2} = \frac{\$1{,}050}{\$68{,}463} = 0.015$$

The ratio of 0.015 indicates a low level of income from investments. A review of the rate of return on all investments, however, including any unrealized appreciation in investment assets, will provide additional information that may be useful regarding investment performance.

Rate of Return on Investments (ROI)

This ratio provides us with a return on investments that we can compare to a previously established benchmark or to an appropriate investment index. The numerator is the change in investment assets from one year to the next (Ending Investments (EI) – Beginning Investments (BI)) less any savings or gifts/inheritances received that went into investments. The denominator is the average invested assets. ROI is calculated as:

$$\frac{\text{EI} - \text{BI} - \text{Savings} - \text{Gifts Received}}{\text{Average Invested Assets}} = \text{Target of 9 - 12\%}$$

$$\frac{\text{BI} + \text{EI}}{2} = \text{Average Invested Assets}$$

Again, using the Nelsons' income and expense statement and balance sheet, the ROI is calculated to be:

$$\frac{\$78{,}229 - \$58{,}697 - \$7{,}953 - \$10{,}000}{(\$58{,}697 + \$78{,}229) \div 2} = \frac{\$1{,}579}{\$68{,}463} = 0.023$$

The rate of return on investments for the Nelsons for the year 2005 was 2.3 percent. While at first glance, that may seem a poor rate of return, it will need to be compared with portfolios with similar asset allocations to determine exactly how the performance compared to a relevant benchmark. Obviously, it is a poor rate of return against the general benchmark of 9-12 percent needed annually to provide a sufficient capital base for retirement. It may, however, only represent one "down" year among many "up" years that exceeded the target.

Investment Assets to Gross Income

Calculating investment assets as a percent of gross income provides a peek into the capital-needed-at-retirement issue. A simple example will help us. Assume that a person about to retire has investment assets devoted to retirement of $1,000,000; has gross income of $100,000; can invest at a rate of return of 10 percent with no inflation. The investment asset to income ratio is 10 ($1,000,000 ÷ $100,000), and the client can produce that income in perpetuity. We expect investment assets to be equal to or greater than 10 times preretirement income at normal retirement age. This ratio calculated over time helps us to benchmark the progress toward retirement. The ratio should be about 3–4, 10 years prior to retirement, and about 1, 20 years before retirement.

$$\frac{\text{Investment Assets}}{\text{Gross Income}} = \text{Target depends on the client's situation and age}$$

Using the Nelsons' income and expense statement and balance sheet, the ratio is calculated as:

$$\frac{\$78{,}229}{\$71{,}050} = 1.10$$

This investment ratio is excellent for the Nelsons at their age if all the investment assets were held for retirement. Even when the education fund is deducted from the invested assets, the ratio equals 0.88, which is good progress toward retirement for their age.

Exhibit 4.15 gives a summary of the ratio analysis for the Nelson family.

EXHIBIT 4.14: SUMMARY OF RATIO ANALYSIS
(TARGETS AND NELSONS')
YEAR END 12/31/05

				Target	Nelsons'
Liquidity Ratios					
Emergency Fund Ratio	=	Current Assets / Monthly Nondiscretionary Expenses	=	3–6	0.60
Current Ratio	=	Current Assets / Current Liabilities	=	1–2	0.41
Debt Ratios					
Total Debt to Net Worth	=	Total Debt / Net Worth	=	*	0.90
Long-Term Debt to Net Worth	=	Long-Term Debt / Net Worth	=	*	0.87
Total Debt to Total Assets	=	Total Debt / Total Assets	=	*	0.47
Long-Term Debt to Total Assets	=	Long-Term Debt / Total Assets	=	*	0.46
Monthly Housing Costs to Monthly Gross Income	=	Monthly Housing Costs / Monthly Gross Income	=	≤ 28%	33.6%
Monthly Housing Costs and Other Debt Repayments to Monthly Gross Income	=	Housing Costs and Debt Repayments / Monthly Gross Income	=	≤ 36%	39.3%
Savings Ratios					
Savings Ratio	=	Personal Saving & Employer Contribution / Annual Gross Income	=	≤ 10%	11.2%
Discretionary Cash Flow plus Savings to Annual Gross Income	=	Discretionary Cash Flow + Savings / Annual Gross Income	=	> 10%	11%
Performance Ratios					
Income on Investments	=	Dividends and Interest / Average Investments	=	*	1.5%
Return on Investments	=	EI – BI – Savings – Gifts / Average Investments	=	9–12%	2.3%
Investment Assets to Annual Gross Income	=	Investment Assets / Annual Gross Income	=	*	1.10

*Target depends on the individual's age or investment objectives.

VERTICAL ANALYSIS

Vertical Analysis and Common Size Analysis

Vertical analysis of financial statements presents each statement in percentage terms. Usually, the balance sheet is presented with each item as a percentage of total assets while the income statement is prepared with each item as a percentage of total income. Percentage items allow us to compare items over time when we have multiple-year financial statements for the same client.

The comparison of one statement on a percentage basis is called common size analysis because the percentages calculated ignore absolute dollars and provide information regarding stability or instability of each account in percentage terms. Exhibit 4.16 presents the two balance sheets in a vertical analysis format and Exhibit 4.17 presents the Nelsons' income statement using vertical analysis.

EXHIBIT 4.15: BALANCE SHEET - VERTICAL ANALYSIS

Dana and David Nelson
Balance Sheet-Vertical Analysis
2005

		01/01/05	12/31/05	Difference
Assets				
Cash/Cash Equivalents				
JT	Checking Account	0.34%	0.33%	-0.01%
JT	Savings Account	0.22%	0.21%	-0.02%
	Total Cash/Cash Equiv.	0.56%	0.54%	-0.02%
Invested Assets				
W	ABC Stock	2.95%	3.06%	0.11%
JT	Educational Fund	3.31%	3.39%	0.08%
JT	401(k)	7.61%	8.41%	0.80%
H	XYZ Stock	0.00%	2.18%	2.18%
	Total Invested Assets	13.87%	17.04%	3.17%
Personal-Use Assets				
JT	Principal Residence	57.91%	54.44%	-3.47%
JT	Automobile	4.25%	3.27%	-0.98%
H	Jet Ski	0.00%	2.18%	2.18%
H	Boat A	5.91%	0.00%	-5.91%
H	Boat B	0.00%	6.53%	6.53%
W	Jewelry	3.07%	2.94%	-0.13%
JT	Furniture/Household	14.42%	13.07%	-1.35%
	Total Personal-Use Assets	85.56%	82.42%	-3.14%
Total Assets		**100.00%**	**100.00%**	**0.00%**
Liabilities and Net Worth				
Current Liabilities				
JT	Credit Cards	0.95%	0.80%	-0.15%
JT	Mortgage on Principal Residence	0.29%	0.30%	0.01%
H	Boat Loan	0.35%	0.23%	-0.12%
	Total Current Liabilities	1.59%	1.33%	-0.26%
Long-Term Liabilities				
JT	Mortgage on Principal Residence	46.48%	42.53%	-3.95%
H	Boat Loan	2.85%	3.49%	0.64%
	Total Long-Term Liabilities	49.33%	46.02%	-3.31%
Total Liabilities		**50.92%**	47.35%	-3.58%
Net Worth		**49.08%**	**52.65%**	3.57%
Total Liabilities and Net Worth		**100.00%**	**100.00%**	**0.00%**

EXHIBIT 4.16: STATEMENT OF INCOME AND EXPENSES

Dana and David Nelson Statement of Income and Expenses For the year 2005		
INCOME		
Salary - David		98.52%
Investment Income		
Interest Income	1.27%	
Dividend Income	0.21%	1.48%
Total Inflow		100.00%
Savings		
Reinvestment (Interest/dividends)	1.48%	
401(k) Deferrals	5.35%	
Educational Fund	1.41%	
Total Savings		8.24%
Available for Expenses		91.76%
EXPENSES		
Ordinary Living Expenses		
Food	8.44%	
Clothing	5.07%	
Child Care	0.84%	
Entertainment	2.55%	
Utilities	5.07%	
Auto Maintenance	2.81%	
Church	4.93%	
Total Ordinary Living Expenses		29.72%
Debt Payments		
Credit Card Payments Principal	0.48%	
Credit Card Payments Interest	0.87%	
Mortgage Payment Principal	1.74%	
Mortgage Payment Interest	29.16%	
Boat Loan Principal	2.10%	
Boat Loan Interest	2.18%	
Total Debt Payments		36.53%
Insurance Premiums		
Automobile Insurance Premiums	1.27%	
Disability Insurance Premiums	1.07%	
Homeowners Insurance Premiums	1.34%	
Total Insurance Premiums		3.67%
Tuition and Education Expenses		1.41%
Taxes		
Federal Income Tax (W/H)	10.56%	
State (and City) Income Tax	1.15%	
FICA	7.54%	
Property Tax (Principal Residence)	1.41%	
Total Taxes		20.65%
Total Expenses		91.98%
Discretionary Cash Flow (negative)		-0.22%

Growth Analysis

The purpose of growth analysis is to calculate the growth rate of certain financial variables over time using time value of money tools. We expect that increases in gross income will exceed increases in the consumer price index (CPI) by more than 1 percent. Exhibit 4.18 lists the financial variables for which growth rates should be calculated. The second column of Exhibit 4.17 presents the growth rates that are appropriate for the particular financial variable.

EXHIBIT 4.14: FINANCIAL VARIABLES AND GROWTH RATES

Variable		Growth Rate
Inflation	-	Should equal CPI
Gross Income	-	Should exceed CPI
Savings Increase	-	Should exceed CPI
Savings Rate	-	Should remain constant or increase
Discretionary Cash Flows (DCF)	-	Should grow somewhat
DCF + Savings	-	Should grow somewhat
Net Worth	-	Should exceed CPI
Investment Assets	-	Should grow exponentially due to combining returns and savings contributions

Limitations of Financial Statement Analysis

Inflation

Because inflation exists, comparing multiple reporting periods will require adjusting certain numbers either to current dollars (inflated dollars) or to some base percentage or index. Inflation reduces the comparability of multiperiod financial statements and ratios even when adjusted for such inflation. It is especially important to adjust growth rates for income and savings to real dollars. It is also useful to adjust nominal investment returns for inflation to determine real economic returns.

Use of Estimates

Whenever estimates of values are used, even if provided by expert appraisers, there is some risk that the estimated value is different from the actual fair market value. Such risks should be evaluated considering the purpose of the financial statement analysis. For example, net worth may very well be dependent on the estimated value of personal-use assets (which are very difficult to value). Since net worth is used as a denominator for several ratios, an error in the denominator will affect the result of any ratio using that denominator.

Benchmarks

For corporations and industries there are published financial statements and, therefore, clear benchmarks with which to compare ratios for companies in the same industry. Unfortunately, there are few published personal financial statements and, therefore, fewer clearly established benchmarks for individuals. Recall the housing mortgage ratios where benchmarks exist at 28 percent and 36 percent of gross pay.

Sensitivity Analysis

Some ratios are more important than others. For example, the long-term savings rate and emergency fund ratio are critical, while the current ratio is less so. The relative size of the numerator and denominator may cause some ratios to be more sensitive to changes. Sensitivity analysis allows us to manipulate the numerators and denominators by small increments to determine the impact on the ratio.

Risk Analysis

Risk analysis examines the uncertainty of cash flows to the individual. Uncertainty regarding the asset side of the balance sheet is called business or investment risk. Specifically, earnings may vary due to fluctuations in the value of investments and personal-use assets. Financial risk is the risk on the liability side of the balance sheet. Indebtedness is accompanied with fixed interest and principal repayments. There is always some risk as to whether debt repayments can be made. The debt/net worth ratio and other debt ratios help to measure the financial risk of the individual.

BUDGETING

Description

Planners and clients should remember that good budgeting is a learned phenomenon, and, as such, there is a learning curve (the more you do it, the better you get at it). Budgeting requires planning for the expected, the recurring and supposedly unexpected (every month it's something). **Budgeting** is a process of projecting, monitoring, adjusting and controlling future income and expenditures. It may be used to determine the Wage Replacement Ratio for capital needs analysis for retirement where the client is sufficiently close to retirement to be able to estimate the retirement budget.

budgeting - a process of projecting, monitoring, adjusting, and controlling future income and

Steps

1. Start with a year of bank statements, checks and check stubs. Create a spreadsheet of all expenditures by month by category. If needed, retrieve a year's copies of credit card expenditure information to assist in determining the amounts and categories of expenditures.
2. Once the dollar amounts are determined per category per month, calculate these as a percentage of gross income. Analyze each category looking for consistent percentage expenditures to develop a predictive model for that particular expenditure.
3. Identify which costs are sensitive to general inflation and are fixed. Examples include,
    - ▲ Ordinary living expenses (food, clothing, utilities, etc.).
    - ▲ Home mortgage payments (interest).
    - ▲ Credit card payments (interests).
    - ▲ Other interest based payments (i.e., boat payments).
4. Forecast next year's income on a monthly basis.

5. Determine how much expenditures will amount to and in which months the expenditure will occur. Often insurance bills are paid annually or semiannually. If they arrive at the wrong time, they can play havoc with cash flows.
6. Project the budget for the next 12 months.
7. Compare actual expenditures for the month to expected expenditures. Adjust the next 11 months accordingly.
8. Continue to analyze, picking out specific expenditure categories that you can control. Utilities are an example of a cost that can be managed. Long distance telephone bills may be reduced by changing carriers.

NELSON BUDGETING PLAN

We are now going to look at how a budgeting plan would help the Nelson's achieve their financial goals. First, we will look at the statement of income and expenses in order to gauge what costs they are incurring against their income. Fortunately, the statement presented for the Nelson's is already projected for the next year. However in most situations, the planner will have to forecast next year's income and expenses using current financial statements and client discussions.

EXHIBIT 4.14: STATEMENT OF INCOME AND EXPENSES

Dana and David Nelson Statement of Income and Expenses For the year 2005		
INCOME		
Salary - David		$70,000
Investment Income		
Interest Income	$900	
Dividend Income	$150	$1,050
Total Inflow		**$71,050**
Savings		
Reinvestment (Interest/Dividends)	$1,050	
401(k) Deferrals	$3,803	
Educational Fund	$1,000	
Total Savings		**$5,853**
Available for Expenses		**$65,197**
EXPENSES		
Ordinary Living Expenses		
Food	$6,000	
Clothing	$3,600	
Child Care	$600	
Entertainment	$1,814	
Utilities	$3,600	
Auto Maintenance	$2,000	
Church	$3,500	
Total Ordinary Living Expenses		**$21,114**
Debt Payments		
Credit Card Payments Principal	$345	
Credit Card Payments Interest	$615	
Mortgage Payment Principal	$1,234	
Mortgage Payment Interest	$20,720	
Boat Loan Principal	$1,493	
Boat Loan Interest	$1,547	
Total Debt Payments		**$25,954**
Insurance Premiums		
Automobile Insurance Premiums	$900	
Disability Insurance Premiums	$761	
Homeowners Insurance Premiums	$950	
Total Insurance Premiums		**$2,611**
Tuition and Education Expenses		**$1,000**
Taxes		
Federal Income Tax (W/H)	$7,500	
State (and City) Income Tax	$820	
FICA	$5,355	
Property Tax (Principal Residence)	$1,000	
Total Taxes		**$14,675**
Total Expenses		**$65,354**
Discretionary Cash Flow (negative)		**($157)**

The next step is to focus on the expenses and what percentage of available income they represent. It is also beneficial to break down the amounts further into monthly projections. This way the figures seem more manageable.

EXHIBIT 4.14: MONTHLY PROJECTIONS

Available for Expenses (monthly)	$5,433.08	Percentage of available Income
EXPENSES (monthly)		
Ordinary Living Expenses		
Food	$500	9.2%
Clothing	$300	5.5%
Child Care	$ 50	.9%
Entertainment	$151.16	2.8%
Utilities	$300	5.5%
Auto Maintenance	$167.67	3.1%
Church	$291.67	5.4%
Total Ordinary Living Expenses	**$1,759.50**	**32.4%**
Debt Payments		
Credit Card Payments Principal	$28.75	.5%
Credit Card Payments Interest	$51.25	.9%
Mortgage Payment Princip al	$102.83	1.9%
Mortgage Payment Interest	$1,726.66	31.8%
Boat Loan Principal	$124.42	2.3%
Boat Loan Interest	$128.92	2.4%
Total Debt Payments	**$2,162.83**	**39.8%**
Insurance Premiums		
Automobile Insurance Premiums	$75	1.4%
Disability Insurance Premiums	$63.42	1.2%
Homeowners Insurance Premiums	$79.16	1.5%
Total Insurance Premiums	**$217.58**	**4.0%**
Tuition and Education Expenses	$83.33	1.5%

We can now see what expense percentages are higher than others, and thus ones that need greater control. This is where the planner and client begin to discuss the control of costs and establish a budget. With the Nelson's ordinary living expenses, we see that a large percentage is devoted to food, clothing and utilities. These are expenses that can be controlled and managed in order to decrease overall expenditures. The planner would also discuss with the Nelson's what other living expenses could possibly also be managed.

Debt payments and insurance premiums are also areas where proper management can control costs. There are several techniques in order to decrease premium payments for insurance. For example, increasing deductibles, and managing appropriate risks and coverage can have dramatic effects on the costs of premiums. Savings with insurance costs and ordinary living expenses can be used in several ways. They can be utilized towards savings, investments, emergency funds, self-insurance, education funding, etc. or they may also be used to pay down large amounts of debt. A large portion of the Nelson's expenditures goes toward debt payments. They could use the savings to pay off their credit card debt, or make additional principal payments on their boat or home. Mortgage payments have certain tax advantages associated with them, so depending on the situation, the planner would most likely pay off the other debt payments first.

Once the Nelson's have agreed upon a certain cost controls, the planner can then establish a monthly budget projected for next year. The budget should then be strictly adhered to and reviewed each month in order to make sure the goals of the budget are being met. Adjustments and restructuring can be done for those costs that are proving difficult to manage.

SAVING AND CONSUMPTION HABITS

Information about a client's saving and consumption habits assists the planner in developing a successful strategic financial plan for the client. If the client does not have a history of saving money consistently, it is wise to develop a strategy in which money is directed into savings prior to the client receiving a check from their employer. Similarly, if the client has a history of making large dollar purchases impulsively, it would be wise to encourage investments in assets with early withdrawal penalties and/or those where withdrawal is difficult. Withdrawal penalties or delays may discourage the client from making such impulse purchases. Historical behavior is the best indicator of future behavior. Therefore, a good way to collect information about the client's saving and consumption habits is by asking the client about their previous saving and consumption habits.

DEBT MANAGEMENT

PERSONAL USE - ASSETS AND LIABILITIES

Debt is appropriate when matched properly with the economic life of the asset and the ability to repay.

EXAMPLE

For example, the purchase of an automobile that is expected to be used for three years (36 months) has a maximum realistic economic life of five years (60 months). Ideally it would be financed over 36 months but certainly no longer than 60 months.

There are a number of risks to consider when taking on debt. The risks include:

- ▲ A shorter than expected economic life.
- ▲ Increasing cash outflows for repairs as the asset ages.
- ▲ The changing of the initial utility curves of the purchaser during the holding period unexpectedly reducing the overall utility of the asset.

Debt repayment cash flows should be matched to the economic life of the asset. Generally, the cash flows considered are not just the principal and interest to retire the debt. Also included are the cash flows associated with the increase in repairs and maintenance due to asset aging (both real and personal property) as well as the prospect of higher executory costs (insurance and taxes).

The cost of the replacement asset will have to either be borne entirely by future cash flows, or the current asset value will help to offset replacement costs. One question is whether the cost of the new asset is increasing in price faster than the old asset. Another question is whether the value of the old asset (exchange value to another buyer) is diminishing faster than the debt is being extinguished. If so, the purchasers of such an asset may find that they are in a negative equity position. This is the primary reason that lenders insist on down payments and generally establish a repayment schedule to ensure that the borrower will always be in a positive equity position. Such a position will reduce the likelihood that the borrower will abandon the property.

HOME MORTGAGES

Types:

- 30-year fixed mortgage.
- 15-year fixed mortgage.
- Variable mortgage.
- Balloon mortgage.

Fixed-Rate Mortgages

Fixed-rate mortgages offer a level interest rate for the term of the loan and a fixed payment amortization schedule. An amortization schedule outlines the portion of each payment allocated to interest and the portion allocated to principal reduction. The payments are selected such that at the end of the term (30 years or 15 years), the principal is completely repaid.

EXAMPLE

If John purchases his home using a 15-year fixed-rate mortgage of $120,000 with a 6.5 percent interest rate, John will pay 6.5 percent interest on the outstanding balance every month. His monthly payment will be $1,045.33 for the 15-year term of the loan. For the first month, John owes 6.5 percent ÷ 12 = 0.5417 percent on $120,000, which equals $650. The remaining $395.33 will go towards repayment of the loan. After this payment, John owes $120,000 – $395.33 = $119,604.67. The $119,604.67 will be the new balance on which the 6.5 percent interest is calculated. Thus, for each subsequent payment the portion allocated to interest is reduced and the portion allocated to principal repayment is increased.

Variable-Rate Mortgages or Adjustable-Rate Mortgages (ARMs)

With a variable-rate loan, or adjustable-rate mortgage (ARM), the borrower is charged interest based on a benchmark such as the 90-day Treasury bill rate. The interest rate will change monthly based on changes in the benchmark rate. Variable-rate loans typically have amortization schedules with fixed payments. The payment is determined by selecting an interest rate and computing the payment necessary to retire a fixed-rate mortgage with that interest rate. Since the actual interest rate varies, the portion of the mortgage payment allocated to principal repayment will not always be greater than the previous month's allocation as it is under a fixed mortgage. If the actual interest rate is much higher than the rate used to calculate the mortgage payment, there will still be principal outstanding at the end of the term. In that case, the borrower will be required to repay the remaining balance in a lump sum. On the other hand, if the actual interest rate is much lower than the rate used to calculate the mortgage payment, the loan will be repaid before the end of the term.

EXAMPLE

John has a 2/6 ARM. His 30-year mortgage interest rate is currently 4%. This means that John's interest rate cannot increase more than 2% per year or 6% over the life of the loan. His maximum interest rate is 10%.

Many variable-rate mortgages limit the amount by which the interest rate can change on a monthly and yearly basis. For example, an ARM may state that the interest rate can only adjust by 0.5 percent each month and no more than 2.0 percent per year. Another common feature of adjustable-rate mortgages is conversion from a fixed rate after a period of time, usually five to seven years. Most ARMs used for personal residences begin as fixed-rate mortgages and then convert to adjustable rate. The borrower pays a fixed rate of interest, usually lower than that for a comparable fixed-rate mortgage, for five to seven years, and then the interest rate adjusts monthly based on the predetermined benchmark.

Balloon Mortgages

Besides the fixed-rate and variable-rate mortgages, a prospective homeowner may acquire a balloon mortgage. Balloon mortgages can have fixed interest rates or adjustable interest rates, but the term will be less than the period required to amortize the loan.

EXAMPLE

Shelly obtains a seven-year balloon mortgage of $80,000 with a fixed interest rate of 5.75 percent. The lender determines Shelly's payments based on a 30-year amortization, which results in a fixed monthly payment of $466.86. Shelly will pay $466.86 per month for seven years. At the end of the seventh year, the outstanding balance on Shelly's loan is $71,386.82. Since the term of the loan is seven years, Shelly will be required to pay off the remaining balance in a lump sum. Instead of paying cash, Shelly would probably refinance, replacing her original $80,000 loan with one for $71,386.82.

Several issues must be addressed in the selection of mortgages. They include the length of time expected to stay in the house, cash flow capacity and tolerance for risk. A determination should be made of spread between yields after a quantitative analysis comparison of fixed-to-fixed rates and fixed-to-variable rates.

If the time expected to be in the house is short, the more likely that an adjustable rate mortgage (ARM) is the mortgage of choice. This is simply because most ARMs have a 2 – 3% lower interest rate than a 30-year fixed-rate mortgage and have 2/6 caps (2% maximum interest rate increase per year, 6% life of loan). The downside risk to an ARM is the prospect of the interest rate increasing periodically causing the payment to increase proportionally. An advantage of an ARM is that, due to the low initial interest rate, the principal and interest (P&I) payments are low relative to a 30-year fixed-rate mortgage. It is easier to qualify for a mortgage using the traditional lender hurdle rates of 28%/36%.

EXAMPLE When comparing a 15-year to a 30-year fixed rate mortgage, the interest rates will usually be about 0.5% different assuming the same down payment. The cash flows will differ depending on the interest rate and the size of the mortgage.

	Sales Price	Down Payment	Paid Closing Costs	Mortgage Amount	Term Months	Interest Rate	P & I Payment
Fixed 30 Year	$180,000	$36,000	$5,760	$144,000	360	5.5%	$818
Fixed 15 Year	$180,000	$36,000	$5,760	$144,000	180	5.0%	$1,139
ARM 30 Year	$180,000	$36,000	$5,760	$144,000	360	3.0%	$607

While the ARM has the current lowest payment, the risk is that at some point in the life of the ARM the interest rate will be 9.0%, assuming a 2%/6% cap, at which time the monthly P&I payment would be $1,158.66 over a 30-year period. It should be pointed out that in this particular example, loan qualifying would be easier using the ARM because the initial payment is lower (assuming $200 per month taxes and $75 per month insurance):

- 30-year fixed rate - Total monthly housing costs = $818 + $200 + $75 = $1,093; monthly gross income needed to qualify for loan = $1,093 ÷ 0.28 = $3,903.57.
- 15-year fixed rate - Total monthly housing costs = $1,139 + $200 + $75 = $1,414; monthly gross income needed to qualify for loan = $1,414 ÷ 0.28 = $5,050.
- ARM - Total monthly housing costs = $607 + $200 + $75 = $882; monthly gross income needed to qualify for loan = $882 ÷ 0.28 = $3,150.

If a client has a low tolerance for fluctuating payments, a fixed mortgage should be selected. Assuming a higher risk tolerance, the planner will have to consider the length of expected ownership (shorter term will mitigate risk) and the opportunity cost of alternative investments. The client may consider an ARM. It is generally not appropriate to select an ARM (using the first year teaser rate) simply to qualify for a loan and hope that cash flows will be sufficient to pay for any interest increases.

EXAMPLE The savings due to mortgage selection is a result of (1) the 15-year mortgage causing earlier retirement of the principal indebtedness and (2) the slightly lower interest rate. Many 30-year loans are selected simply as a necessity to meet lender qualification requirements. If no prepayment penalties exist, most of the savings can be achieved by paying a 30-year loan according to a 15-year amortization schedule.

	Number of Payments	Monthly Payment	Total Payment	Loan Principal	Interest Paid
30-Year Fixed	360	$818	$294,341.80	$144,000	$150,341.80
15-Year Fixed	180	$1,139	$204,973.71	$144,000	$60,973.71
Savings			$89,368.09	$0	$89,368.09

The total interest paid is determined by multiplying the amount of the payment by the number of payments and then subtracting the principal borrowed.

PROFESSIONAL FOCUS

How do you gather client information?

We send out questionnaires that ask for cash flow information, asset listings, and biographical information. We ask the clients to complete them in detail and bring them to our initial meeting. These questionnaires also inquire about financial objectives and require the client to think about their risk tolerance level. Finally, we ask the client to bring all estate documents, tax returns, insurance policies, and investments statements with them to the initial meeting. Whenever possible, we use these original source materials.

Which sources of information are the most helpful?

The original source material seems to be the most helpful since we know it to be accurate. Additionally, spending just a couple of hours with the client in the initial face-to-face meeting is very valuable. This is where we define, refine, and quantify their goals and risk tolerance. Of all the sources of information we use, original source material and face-to-face meetings yield the most value.

Do you have tips on how to get all of the client information from your clients?

Having clients supply original source material is easiest for them. It motivates the client, with very little effort, to provide us with accurate data. All clients have account statements, copies of wills, tax returns, and so on. Oftentimes, though, with cash flow information, clients are less detail oriented. Sometimes we have to apply some "tricks" by backing into their spending. By looking at income the client takes home and what is left at the end of the year, we can then do a calculation that gets us close to what they *actually* spent. Unfortunately, it does not tell us *where* the money was spent.

Do you prepare balance sheets, income statements, statements of cash flow, and/or changes in net worth for your clients?

We do prepare balance sheets, in particular, for our clients. We find balance sheets to be most useful, especially the investable assets balance sheet. This enables us to advise the client around issues such as asset allocation and investment repositioning. We do not prepare cash flow statements. Since most of our clients are high net worth individuals, cash flow is not an issue. We do provide changes in net worth on a quarter-by-quarter basis for all of our clients while we are monitoring their investments. We show them performance rates of return as well as comparative indices and change of value. Again, this is an investment valuation change, not an overall net worth change.

ROBERT GLOVSKY, JD, LLM, CLU, ChFC, CFP®

DISCUSSION QUESTIONS

1. What is the relationship between GAAP/FASB and personal financial statements?
2. Describe some of the uses of personal financial statements.
3. What is the purpose of the balance sheet?
4. What items are included on the balance sheet?
5. Discuss the presentation of the balance sheet (i.e., how items are listed and why).
6. What is the purpose of the income statement?
7. What items are included on the income statement?
8. Discuss the presentation of the income statement (i.e., how items are listed and why).
9. What is the purpose of the statement of changes in net worth?
10. What items are included on the statement of net worth?
11. Discuss the presentation of the statement of net worth (i.e., how items are listed and why).
12. What are the differences between long-term and current assets/liabilities?
13. Why are financial ratios important to financial planning?
14. What is the importance of keeping accurate and up-to-date financial statements?
15. What is fair market value?
16. What is liquidity?
17. Why do we prepare four financial statements?
18. Discuss the importance of vertical analysis.
19. What are some of the limitations of personal financial statements?
20. What is the purpose of budgeting?
21. List the different types of home mortgages and their characteristics.

EXERCISES

1. What is the balancing equation for the balance sheet?
2. What do current assets and current liabilities have in common?
3. Your client purchased a new living room set for $6,500 last month. Which financial statement(s) would this purchase affect and how?
4. How would each of the following items affect net worth?
   a. Repayment of a loan using funds from a savings account.
   b. Purchase of an automobile that is 75 percent financed with a 25 percent down payment.
   c. The S&P 500 increases, and the client has an S&P Indexed Mutual Fund.
   d. Interest rates increase, and the client has a substantial bond portfolio.
5. Lauren and Herb have the following assets and liabilities:

Liquid assets	$6,750
Investment assets	$16,250
House	$125,000
Current liabilities	$3,100
Long-term liabilities	$86,000

Compute the total assets, total liabilities, and net worth.

6. Compute the current ratio based on the facts given in the previous question.
7. After reviewing Kenny and Jane's financial statements, the following information wa determined:

Liquid assets	$3,976
Investment assets	$10,738
Annual nondiscretionary expenses	$13,913
Current liabilities	$9,247

Compute this couple's emergency fund ratio. Does it fall within the target goal?
8. After reviewing Matt and Jennifer's Annual Statement of Income and Expenses, the fol lowing information was determined:

Mortgage principal	$5,467
Mortgage interest	$21,500
Property tax	$2,000
Homeowners insurance premium	$1,800

The couple has monthly gross income of $9,500. Has this couple taken on debt in exces of what is reasonable for their income, according to benchmarks set by mortgage lenders?
9. In addition to the information given above, Matt and Jennifer had other annual debt pay ments of $11,600. Compute the monthly housing costs and other debt repayments t monthly gross income ratio. Do Matt and Jennifer qualify for a mortgage loan?
10. Mariska and Bryant Hahn have the following assets and liabilities:

Checking account	$2,000
House	$125,000
Savings account	$3,000
CDs	$5,000
Automobile	$13,500
Stocks	$10,000
Utilities	$500
Mortgage	$80,000
Auto loan	$5,000
Credit card bills	$1,500

Determine their net worth.

11. Use the following items to determine total assets, total liabilities, net worth, total income (cash inflows), and total expenses (cash outflows):

Net monthly salary	$2,280
Rent	$750
Savings account balance	$2,000
Auto loan payment	$416
Money market investments account balance	$4,800
Clothing expense	$150
Value of home computer	$1,200
Groceries expense	$220
Entertainment expense	$130
Value of autos	$10,800
Student loan payment	$212
Utilities expense	$510
Laundry expense	$46
Insurance premium	$368
Balance of student loan	$8,625

Note: Income and expense items are monthly.

12. The Coopers have a net worth of $250,000 before any of the following transactions:
    - ▲ Paid off credit cards of $9,000 using a savings account.
    - ▲ Transferred $5,000 from checking to their IRAs.
    - ▲ Purchased $2,500 of furniture with credit.

    What is the net worth of the Coopers after these transactions?
13. What are the advantages of performing vertical analysis on financial statements?
14. Explain how inflation limits financial statement analysis.
15. Bart has a history of making large dollar purchases impulsively. As Bart's planner what could you do to help remedy this situation?

PROBLEMS

1. Given the following information develop a beginning-of-the-year balance sheet.

Beginning Date	1/1/2006
End Date	12/31/2006
Client Name	Frank and Lois Fox
Year	2006

	Beginning Balance	Ending Balance	Income/Expenses Amount (Yearly)
401(k)			$750
401(k) - Frank	$0	$1,500	
403(b)			$990
403(b) - Lois	$0	$990	
Auto Loan	$15,432	$10,436	
Auto Loan Interest			$381
Auto Loan Principal			$4,996
Auto Maintenance			$600
Automobile - Frank	$20,000	$18,000	
Automobile - Lois	$5,750	$5,175	
Automobile Insurance Premiums			$2,124
Checking	$10,000	$15,570	
Child Support			$2,400
Clothing			$3,600
Credit Card	$10,870	$10,418	
Credit Card Payments Interest			$1,707
Credit Card Payments Principal			$453
Entertainment			$4,200
Federal Income Tax (W/H)			$7,018
FICA			$4,431
Food			$4,800
Furniture/Household	$36,000	$34,000	
Go-cart	$0	$1,200	
Homeowners Insurance Premiums			$534
Jewelry	$6,000	$6,100	
Maid/child care			$4,800
Mortgage on Residence	$72,960	$72,164	
Mortgage Payment Interest			$5,808
Mortgage Payment Principal			$796
Personal Residence	$85,000	$89,250	
Property Tax (Principal Residence)			$850
Reinvestment in Savings Account/Trust			$5,675
Salary - Frank			$25,000
Salary - Lois			$33,000
Savings	$13,500	$14,175	
Savings Account/Trust Fund Interest			$5,675
Trust Fund	$100,000	$105,000	
Tuition and Education Expenses			$2,893
Utilities			$2,100

Additional Transactions:
Gift of bedroom set worth $2,000 to Frank's little sister
401(k) match = 3% of income
Bought a go-cart for son for $1,200
Inheritance of $5,000 from Lois's father

2. Use the data in Problem 1 to create an income statement.
3. Use the data in Problem 1 to create a statement of net worth.
4. Use the data in Problem 1 to create an end-of-the-year balance sheet.
5. Use the results from the above problems to compute the following ratios for year end:
   a. Emergency Fund
   b. Current Ratio
   c. Total Debt to Net Worth
   d. Long-Term Debt to Net Worth
   e. Total Debt to Total Assets
   f. Long-Term Debt To Total Assets
   g. Monthly Housing Costs To Monthly Gross Income
   h. Monthly Housing Costs And Other Debt Repayments To Monthly Gross Income
   i. Savings Ratio
   j. Discretionary Cash Flow Plus Savings To Annual Gross Income
   k. Income On Investments
   l. Return On Investments
   m. Investment Assets To Annual Gross Income
6. Discuss the financial position of the Foxes based on the ratios you calculated in the previous problem.
7. Prepare a vertical analysis of the ending balance sheet and the income and expense statement for the Foxes.
8. Lisa recently bought a house for $150,000 using a fixed 30-year home loan with a 5% interest rate. She used 20% if the amount towards the down payment and paid the $5,000 in closing costs out of pocket. How much mortgage interest can Lisa expect to pay the course of this loan?

CHAPTER 5

Establishing Financial Direction

LEARNING OBJECTIVES:

After learning the material in this chapter, you will be able to:

1. Identify the 8 steps for establishing financial direction.
2. Assist clients in identifying an appropriate financial mission.
3. Identify external and internal environmental information that is relevant for a particular client.
4. Assist clients in identifying financial goals and objectives.
5. Analyze a client's internal strengths and weaknesses.
6. Analyze external environmental opportunities and threats as they apply to a client.
7. Formulate appropriate financial strategies.
8. Assist clients in analyzing and selecting the financial strategy that best meets their needs and desires.
9. Assist clients in implementing and monitoring their financial plan.

THE PROCESS

Once the financial planner has an understanding of the external environment and has gathered the client's internal and financial data, the process of establishing financial direction may begin. As depicted in Exhibit 5.1, this process has eight steps:

EXHIBIT 5.1: STEPS FOR ESTABLISHING FINANCIAL DIRECTION

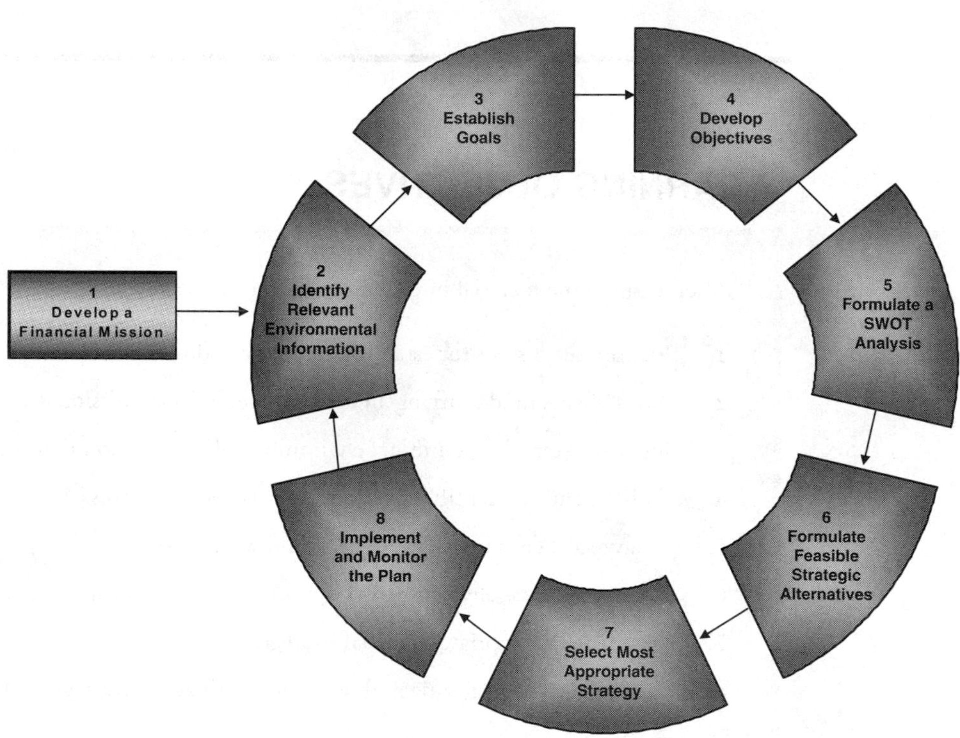
1
Develop a
Financial Mission
2
Identify
Relevant
Environmental
Information
3
Establish
Goals
4
Develop
Objectives
5
Formulate a
SWOT
Analysis
6
Formulate
Feasible
Strategic
Alternatives
7
Select Most
Appropriate
Strategy
8
Implement
and Monitor
the Plan

Step 1 - Develop a Financial Mission.
Step 2 - Identify Relevant Environmental Information.
Step 3 - Establish Goals.
Step 4 - Develop Objectives.
Step 5 - Formulate a SWOT Analysis.
Step 6 - Formulate Feasible Strategic Alternatives.
Step 7 - Select the Most Appropriate Strategy.
Step 8 - Implement and Monitor the Plan.

The eight steps of establishing financial direction are completed in sequential order because each step is dependent upon the previous step. The elimination of any step may result in the loss of direction and possibly result in an inappropriate financial strategy. Furthermore, the financial planner must periodically monitor the external and internal environments so that changes in the environment may be responded to appropriately. Monitoring is a continuous and ongoing process that does not end once the plan has been implemented. Modifications to the plan must be made as changes in situations and circumstances require.

To establish financial direction in a manner that is concise and systematic, we recommend the use of a Client/Planner Worksheet for Establishing Financial Direction as illustrated in Exhibit 5.2. The application of this worksheet will be demonstrated throughout this chapter. Notice that the worksheet has a header for the client's name and date, a footer for the planner's name, a section for the financial mission, a section for financial goals and objectives, and a section where each goal/objective is identified and classified as a need or want, with the want objectives ranked from 1 (nice to have) to 5 (of great importance).

The process of interviewing the client and gathering necessary paperwork could take several weeks. Financial planners may find it helpful to ask the client to bring bank statements, pay check stubs, investment account statements, and insurance policies to the first meeting. A completed client questionnaire may also be requested before the meeting. Having these support documents will speed the analysis phase and allow the planner to ask pointed questions at the first appointment.

EXHIBIT 5.2: CLIENT/PLANNER WORKSHEET - BLANK FORM

Client/Planner Worksheet for Establishing Financial Direction

Client Name____ **Date**________________________

FINANCIAL MISSION

1. Educate the client as to what a financial mission is and the importance of it being broad and enduring.
2. Working with your client, develop a financial mission that your client is willing to embrace.

____

____

Financial Goals & Objectives

1. Discuss and explain common financial goals with client.
2. Identify goals the client is interested in achieving.
3. Write client objective under appropriate goal classification.
4. Ensure all "need" objectives have been identified and documented.
5. Classify each objective as a want or a need; remember to remain objective.
6. For each "want" objective, the client must assign a weight between 1 and 5 (1 = objective would be nice to have, 5 = objective is of great importance).

Goal:		
Objectives:	**Need**	**Want**
	•	• ____
	•	• ____
	•	• ____

Goal		
Objectives:	**Need**	**Want**
	•	• ____
	•	• ____
	•	• ____

Goal:		
Objectives:	**Need**	**Want**
	•	• ____
	•	• ____
	•	• ____

Goal:		
Objectives:	**Need**	**Want**
	•	• ____
	•	• ____
	•	• ____

Planner's Name ____

STEP ONE – DEVELOP THE MISSION

The first step in establishing financial direction is the development of a **financial mission**. A financial mission is a broad and enduring statement that identifies the client's long-term purpose for wanting a financial plan. Since the mission statement is broad and enduring, it should not change throughout the planning process. The purpose of a financial mission is twofold. First, it ensures a common understanding between the client and the planner as to why the financial plan is being created and implemented. Second, it provides a basis for the creation of feasible alternative goals, objectives, and strategies, and for selecting among strategic alternatives. Throughout the text, we have assumed that the financial mission for most clients is to achieve financial independence and to avoid catastrophic financial occurrences that could result in financial dependence.

financial mission - a broad and enduring statement that identifies the client's long-term purpose for wanting a financial plan

Occasionally, clients may believe that their mission is to buy a house, a boat, or some other personal property. This type of thinking is common while in the **linear-thinking** phase. This misunderstanding is usually due to shortsightedness and a lack of financial planning knowledge. Through sufficient education, the planner can assist the client in understanding the difference between a goal, an objective, and a mission. It is the responsibility of the financial planner to ensure that the client either embraces this mission or develops and embraces another, more suitable mission. To embrace a mission, the client must have a clear understanding of it and must want to achieve it.

linear-thinking - the initial phase of a client's thinking process when setting financial direction in which a client focuses on accomplishing one particular goal or narrow objective using a very compartmentalized, simplistic, self-designed financial plan

Appropriate financial planning requires a holistic approach. All aspects of a client's past, present, and projected financial situation need to be evaluated. It is inappropriate to only focus on one or two aspects of a client's situation since all aspects are interrelated and interdependent. That is why developing an appropriate financial mission is so important. The financial planner can use the Client/Planner Worksheet for Establishing Financial Direction to begin formalizing the financial planning process when working with the client.

Exhibit 5.3 identifies how the Nelsons, the couple introduced at the end of Chapter 3, might complete the Financial Mission section of the Client/Planner Worksheet for Establishing Financial Direction. When completing the Financial Mission section, the first step is for the financial planner to communicate with and educate the client so that a realistic, enduring, and broad financial mission is developed. Once the client has embraced the mission, it should be documented on the worksheet. Throughout this chapter, we will assume the Nelsons have embraced the mission, "To achieve financial independence and to avoid catastrophic financial occurrences resulting in financial dependence."

EXHIBIT 5.3: CLIENT/PLANNER WORKSHEET - FINANCIAL MISSION

Client/Planner Worksheet for Establishing Financial Direction

Client Name *David and Dana Nelson* Date *February 16, 2006*

FINANCIAL MISSION

1. Educate the client as to what a financial mission is and the importance of it being broad and enduring.
2. Working with your client, develop a financial mission that your client is willing to embrace.

To achieve financial independence and to avoid catastrophic financial occurrences that may result in financial dependence

STEP TWO – IDENTIFY RELEVANT ENVIRONMENTAL INFORMATION

Once the mission is established and embraced, the financial planner should identify the relevant external and internal environmental information that applies to the client. During this step, the planner should apply the skills and information discussed in Chapter 2 – The External Environment, to identify external environmental information that is current and relevant to the client. The planner must also be able to identify the relevant information that has been collected about the client. Lessons learned in Chapter 3 – Communication and Internal Environmental Analysis should also be applied during this step. It is important to keep the mission in mind to determine whether information is relevant or not. Only relevant information should be listed in order to keep the amount of information collected manageable. During this step, we will only gather and list the facts. Analysis will be conducted and conclusions will be drawn later while developing the SWOT Analysis, during step 5.

The following external and internal environmental information has been gathered and determined to be relevant to the Nelsons.

Relevant External Environmental Information

- ▲ Mortgage rates are 6.0 percent for 30 years and 5.5 percent for 15 years, fixed.
- ▲ Gross Domestic Product is expected to grow at less than 3 percent.
- ▲ Inflation is expected to be 2.6 percent.
- ▲ Expected return on investment is 10.4 percent for common stocks, 12.1 percent for small company stocks, and 1.1 percent for U.S. Treasury bills.
- ▲ College education costs are $15,000 per year ($15,000 for 5 years equals $75,000).

Relevant Internal Environmental Information

- David has been employed at the bank for twelve years and has a salary of $70,000 and a gross income of $71,050.
- The Nelsons are in the Asset Accumulation Phase.
- Relevant financial ratios, identified in Chapter 4, are as follows:
  - Current assets to monthly nondiscretionary expenses ratio is 0.60.
  - Housing costs to gross income ratio is 33.6 percent.
  - All debt payments to gross income ratio is 39.3 percent.
  - Annual savings to annual gross income ratio is 11.2 percent.
  - Investment asset ratio is 1.09 for the previous year.
- The family is insured under David's company indemnity plan. There is a $200 family deductible with 80/20 major medical coverage and $500,000 lifetime limit for each family member.
- David has a term life insurance policy provided by his employer with a face amount of $25,000.
- David has a private disability insurance policy covering accidental disability for "own occupation" with a 30-day elimination period. The benefit is $2,700 per month until age 65, and it has an annual premium of $761.
- The Nelsons have a homeowners insurance (HO3) policy with dwelling extension and replacement cost on contents. The deductible is $250 with an annual premium of $950.
- David currently contributes 5.43 percent of his salary into the company's 401(k) plan. The company contributes dollar-for-dollar up to 3 percent. David's maximum contribution is 16 percent.
- David and Dana are just within the 15 percent marginal federal income tax bracket.

STEP THREE – ESTABLISH FINANCIAL GOALS

The next step toward establishing financial direction is the establishment of **financial goals**. Goals are high-level statements of desires that may be for either the short run or the long run. Short-run goals are those that will occur within five years. Long-run goals are those that will occur sometime beyond five years. Identifying goals requires the client to consider all aspects of a financial plan. If all goals are identified and prioritized, the client is less likely to overlook some goals while focusing on others. Performing this process of defining and prioritizing goals, however, often results in the client entering the second common phase of thinking—**paradoxical thinking**. Remember that advancing to the paradoxical thinking level is where the client may begin to become discouraged or frustrated with the process due to a new awareness of the extent of financial planning required to achieve multiple and often conflicting goals. During this phase, the planner should keep explanations simple and should discuss goals in present dollar value terms since future value terms are more difficult for the client to understand.

financial goals - high-level statements of financial desire that may be for the short run or the long run

paradoxical thinking - the second phase of a client's thinking process when setting financial direction in which a client tries to focus on several simultaneous objectives, causing confusion, goal conflict, and ambiguity. The paradoxical thinking phase is where a client often seeks the advice of a financial planner.

Generally, financial goals can be divided into 5 categories. Each category will be discussed fully in subsequent chapters.

- Insurance Planning – The goal is to mitigate the risks of catastrophic losses to persons, property, and liability by maintaining appropriate insurance coverage while paying efficient premiums.

- ▲ Retirement Planning –The goal is to adequately provide inflation-protected retirement income at an appropriate age for full life expectancy, conservatively estimated.
- ▲ Estate Planning – The goal is to have a proper estate plan consistent with transfer goals.
- ▲ Tax Planning – The goal is to arrange income tax affairs to mitigate income tax liability and take advantage of incentives in the income tax law as appropriate.
- ▲ Investment Planning – The goal is to save and invest so to accumulate capital for retirement, wealth transfer, and other expenditure objectives such as the purchase of personal property, education funding, lump-sum payments, and emergencies.

The financial planner can again use the Client/Planner Worksheet for Establishing Financial Direction to assist in establishing financial goals. As the Nelson's financial planner, you should work with and educate them so that they become familiar with the common financial goals. Next, you should assist them in identifying the goals they are interested in achieving. Once the Nelsons understand the importance and interdependence of all common financial goals, the goals should be documented in the Financial Goals section of the worksheet. Exhibit 5.4 identifies the goals that are relevant to the Nelsons.

EXHIBIT 5.4: ESTABLISHING FINANCIAL DIRECTION - FINANCIAL GOALS

Client/Planner Worksheet for Establishing Financial Direction

Client Name *David and Dana Nelson* **Date** *February 16, 2006*

FINANCIAL MISSION

1. Educate the client as to what a financial mission is and the importance of it being broad and enduring.
2. Working with your client, develop a financial mission that your client is willing to embrace.

To achieve financial independence and to avoid catastrophic financial occurrences that may result in financial dependence

Financial Goals & Objectives

1. Discuss and explain common financial goals with client.
2. Identify goals the client is interested in achieving.

Goal: *Mitigate risk of catastrophic losses by maintaining appropriate insurance coverage while paying efficient premiums.*		
Objectives:	**Need**	**Want**
	❒	❒ ____

Goal: *Provide inflation-protected retirement income, assuming a life expectancy of 92 years of age.*		
Objectives:	**Need**	**Want**
	❒	❒ ____

Goal: *Develop an appropriate estate plan consistent with transfer goals.*		
Objectives:	**Need**	**Want**
	❒	❒ ____

Goal: *Arrange income tax affairs to minimize income tax liability and take advantage of tax law incentives.*		
Objectives:	**Need**	**Want**
	❒	❒ ____

Goal: *Accumulate capital, through saving and investing, for the purchase of personal property, education, and emergencies.*		
Objectives:	**Need**	**Want**
	❒	❒ ____

Where on the Web

Association for Financial Consulting and Planning Education *www.afcpe.org*
Bloomberg *www.bloomberg.com*
Bureau of Economic Analysis (U.S. Department of Commerce) *www.bea.gov*
Bureau of Labor Statistics (U.S. Department of Labor) *www.bls.gov*
CPI Home Page (U.S.) *www.bls.gov/cpi*
Economy at a Glance (U.S.) *stats.bls.gov/eag/eag.us.htm*
Forbes Magazine *www.forbes.com*
Fortune Magazine *www.fortune.com*
National Association of Personal Financial Advisors *www.napfa.org*
Service Corps of Retired Executives *www.score.org*
Society of Financial Service Professionals *www.financialpro.org*
U.S. Small Business Association *www.sba.gov*

STEP FOUR – DEVELOP FINANCIAL OBJECTIVES

financial objectives - statements of financial desire that contain time and measurement attributes, making them more specific than financial goals

The fourth step in establishing financial direction is the development of **financial objectives**. Objectives are more specific than goals. Several objectives may be developed for each goal category and should include time and measurement attributes when appropriate.

Usually, clients are immersed in paradoxical thinking during this step. The client has the propensity to become confused and frustrated due to the conflicting issue of unlimited wants and limited resources. The planner can greatly assist the client by presenting information in a clear, concise, systematic, and objective manner.

Once objectives have been identified for each goal category, each objective must then be classified as either a "want" or "need." Generally, the client is more focused on identifying the "want" objectives. Therefore, the planner is responsible for ensuring that all of the "need" objectives are identified. The planner should keep the mission and relevant environmental factors in mind when assisting the client in the development of financial objectives.

Distinguishing between a "want" and "need" can be difficult for clients because subjectivity and strong desires become an issue. This potential difficulty can be eliminated by asking both of the following questions of each objective:

- Is this objective necessary to accomplish the financial mission?
- Does the law require that this objective be implemented?

If the answer to <u>either</u> of these questions is yes, the objective is a "need." If the answer to <u>both</u> of these questions is no, the objective is a "want."

For example, under the goal of Protection Against Risk, the objectives of property insurance on an old car and auto liability coverage may have been identified. If we ask the questions above in reference to auto property insurance, we find that in this case auto property insurance is a "want" objective. Implementation of this objective is not necessary to accomplish the mission of achieving financial independence and to avoid catastrophic financial occurrences nor does law require it since it is an older car and is paid for in full. Asking the same questions with respect to liability insurance, however, we may find that liability insurance is a "need" objective because the state law requires all licensed automobile owners to carry liability insurance.

Objectives classified as "wants" are further analyzed by having the client attach weights to them. Assigning weights to objectives allows the planner and the client to objectively evaluate a subjective desire. A weight is a number between "1" and "5" assigned by the client to each "want" objective to express the importance or desirability of that objective relative to the others. A "5" should be assigned to a "want" objective of great importance—something the client has a strong desire to achieve. A "1" should be assigned to a "want" objective that the client would like to have but could do without, if the objective was not achieved. The weight assignment will be used during strategy selection to assist in determining which "want" objectives will be implemented. It is probable that not all of the "want" objectives will be achieved; however, all of the "need" objectives must be implemented in order to achieve the financial mission and/or comply with the law. Therefore, objectives classified as "needs" do not require weight assignment.

As the Nelsons' financial planner you should continue using the Client/Planner Worksheet for Establishing Financial Direction to document and formalize the Nelsons' desired objectives. The first step is to identify all of the objectives that are relevant to the Nelsons. Next, each objective must be classified as either a "want" or a "need" objective. To assist in the classification of each objective, you should determine whether the objective is necessary to accomplish the mission, and whether the implementation of the objective is required by law. The final step is to assist the Nelsons in establishing a weight for all of the "want" objectives. The weight indicates how important implementing that objective is to the Nelsons. Exhibit 5.5 identifies a partial list of objectives that are important to the Nelsons. Throughout this chapter, we will only address a partial list of objectives in order to keep the amount of material manageable.

EXHIBIT 5.5: CLIENT/PLANNER WORKSHEET - FINANCIAL OBJECTIVES

Client/Planner Worksheet for Establishing Financial Direction

Client Name David and Dana Nelson **Date** February 16, 2006

FINANCIAL MISSION

1. Educate the client as to what a financial mission is and the importance of it being broad and enduring.
2. Working with your client, develop a financial mission that your client is willing to embrace.

To achieve financial independence and to avoid catastrophic financial occurrences that may result in financial dependence.

Financial Goals & Objectives

1. Discuss and explain common financial goals with client.
2. Identify goals the client is interested in achieving.
3. Write client objective under appropriate goal classification.
4. Ensure all "need" objectives have been identified and documented.
5. Classify each objective as a "want" or a "need." Remember to remain objective.
6. For each "want" objective, the client must assign a weight between 1 and 5. (1 = objective would be nice to have, 5 = objective is of great importance).

Goal: *Mitigate risk of catastrophic losses by maintaining appropriate insurance coverage while paying efficient premiums.*		
Objectives:	**Need**	**Want**
Within 6 months, modify Life Insurance to include $500,000 term, 20-year.	✔	❒ ___
Within 6 months, modify Disability Insurance to include disability by sickness.	✔	❒ ___
Within 6 months, modify Health Insurance to include major medical with $10,000 deductible due to lifetime limit.	✔	❒ ___

Goal: *Provide inflation-protected retirement income, assuming a life expectancy of 92 years of age.*		
Objectives:	**Need**	**Want**
Retire at age 67 with an 80% wage replacement, thereby, maintaining lifestyle.	✔	❒ ___
Retire at age 62 with an 80% wage replacement, thereby, maintaining lifestyle.	❒	✔ 5

Goal: *Develop an appropriate estate plan consistent with transfer goals.*		
Objectives:	**Need**	**Want**
Develop a will for David, within three months.	✔	❒ ___
Develop a will for Dana, within three months.	✔	❒ ___

Goal: *Arrange income tax affairs so that income tax liability is minimized and to take advantage of tax law incentives.*		
Objectives:	**Need**	**Want**
Reduce tax payments to the minimum amount allowable by law.	❒	✔ 5
Within 2 months, modify contributions into 401(k) plan to ensure adequate retirement income and to reduce income tax liability.	✔	❒ ___

Goal: *Accumulate capital, through saving and investing, for the purchase of personal property, education, and emergencies.*		
Objectives:	**Need**	**Want**
Purchase a $200,000 home in Key West within 5 years.	❒	✔ 4
Save for college tuition so that money is available when John, Gabrielle, and new baby begin college.	❒	✔ 3
Purchase a new car in two years, twelve years, and at retirement.	❒	✔ 2
Eliminate credit card debt within six years	❒	✔ 3

STEP FIVE – SWOT ANALYSIS

A **SWOT analysis** is a useful tool to assist the planner in converting several bits of relevant information into an understandable format. It helps the planner understand how the internal and external environments impact the client's situation—a critical element to developing feasible and responsive strategies. The acronym, SWOT, stands for Strengths, Weaknesses, Opportunities, and Threats. A SWOT analysis is developed by analyzing the relevant environmental factors that were identified in Step 2 of the process, then listing the client's internal strengths and weaknesses and the external environment's opportunities and threats. Once the strengths, weaknesses, opportunities, and threats are identified, the planner systematically analyzes the SWOT list to assist in the generation of feasible alternative strategies.

SWOT analysis - an analysis that helps the financial planner understand how internal and external environmental factors impact the client's financial situation. The acronym, SWOT, stands for Strengths, Weaknesses, Opportunities, and Threats.

When identifying the strengths, the planner should consider the internal and financial data collected from the client. Client strengths, such as appropriate consumption and savings behaviors and positive attitudes and beliefs with regard to financial planning and financial stability should also be considered. The planner should indicate whether the timing of the plan is appropriate to the client's goals and objectives and if the client's subjective perception of his financial situation is similar to the planner's objective appraisal of the client's financial situation. The planner should consider areas in which the client has adequate insurance coverage for life, health, disability, long-term care, property, and liability. Finally, the financial ratios that meet or exceed recommended levels should be listed.

When identifying weaknesses, the planner should again consider the internal and financial data collected from the client. Client weaknesses, such as poor savings behaviors and unwise consumption habits, a poor attitude toward financial planning, special needs, and financial instability should be identified. The planner should indicate whether the timing of the plan is inappropriate for the client and if the client's subjective perception of their financial situation is dissimilar to the objective financial situation. The planner should consider areas in which the client has inadequate insurance coverage for life, health, disability, long-term care, property, and liability. Lastly, the financial ratios that do not meet recommended levels should be listed.

When identifying external environmental opportunities, the planner should consider monetary trends, favorable interest rates and inflation levels, technological breakthroughs, governmental controls, social attitudes towards businesses, and the emergence of new industries. The planner should also list favorable trends and forecasts that may positively impact the client's financial plan.

When identifying external environmental threats, the planner should consider unfavorable interest rates and inflation forecasts, technological breakthroughs, governmental controls, public distrust of businesses, and emergence of new industries. The planner should also list unfavorable trends and forecasts that may negatively impact the client's financial plan.

Using the Nelsons as an example, the following SWOT may be developed.

STRENGTHS	▲ David has a job in a stable industry that provides the family with sufficient income. ▲ Their net worth is reasonable for their age. ▲ Their investment assets-to-income ratio exceeds the target ratio for their age.
WEAKNESSES	▲ Insufficient annual savings to drive goals. ▲ Inadequate life and disability insurance. ▲ Inappropriate investment risk. ▲ Too much debt. ▲ Unrealistic goals for current savings and investments. ▲ Deficient health insurance policy. ▲ No estate planning. ▲ Poor housing-cost-to-income ratio.
OPPORTUNITIES	▲ Mortgage rates are favorable for refinancing. ▲ Expected return on investments for stocks is high. ▲ Expected inflation rate is low. ▲ Current interest rates are low. ▲ Leading Economic Index signals expansion.
THREATS	▲ The current cost of college (room and board, tuition) is $15,000 per year per child. ▲ Economy is slow and unemployment is high, so investments may not provide expected returns.

STEP SIX – FORMULATE FEASIBLE STRATEGY ALTERNATIVES

EXHIBIT 5.6: STRATEGY FORMULATION

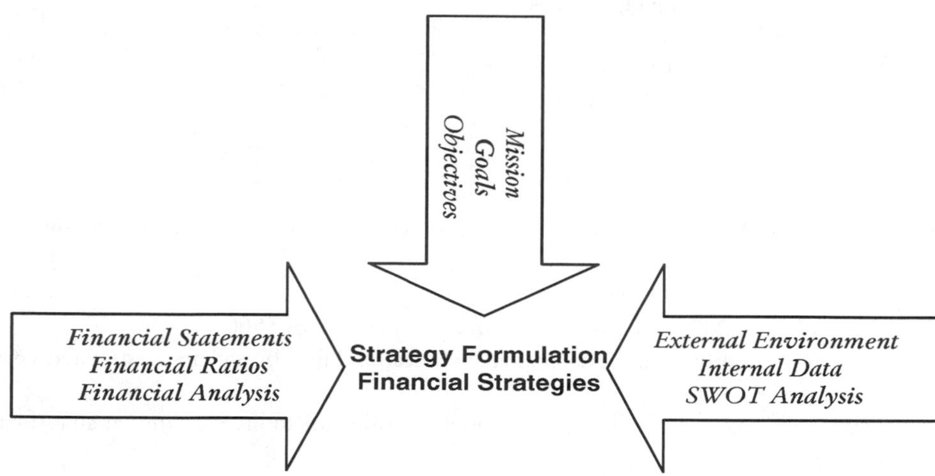
Mission
Goals
Objectives
Financial Statements
Financial Ratios
Financial Analysis
Strategy Formulation
Financial Strategies
External Environment
Internal Data
SWOT Analysis

As depicted in Exhibit 5.6, several financial, environmental and internal client aspects must be considered and analyzed before feasible strategies can be formulated for the client.

- ▲ The client's financial situation must be analyzed using financial data collection techniques (Chapter 4).
- ▲ The external environment and its effect on the client must be considered (Chapter 2).
- ▲ The client's internal data and life cycle positioning must be understood (Chapter 3).
- ▲ The client's mission, goals, and objectives must also remain central to the development of strategies.

When formulating feasible strategies, we recommend that you begin by developing an abbreviated Income Statement to identify the client's current cash flow situation. Then, identify the costs associated with implementing the "need" objectives and add the required cash outflows necessary to meet the need requirements to the existing cash flow. This will provide an estimate of the cash flow required to implement a plan that will accomplish the "need" objectives. Do not be concerned that the addition of these costs may cause the discretionary cash flow to be negative. If a negative discretionary cash flow exists, it may help bring the client into financial reality.

Using the Nelsons as an example and the initial income statement information gathered in Chapter 4, we can estimate the costs for implementing the "need" objectives.

EXHIBIT 5.7: ABBREVIATED INCOME STATEMENT OF CURRENT CASH FLOWS

Income	$ 71,050
Savings	(5,853)
Ordinary Living Expenses	(21,114)
Other Payments	(25,954)
Insurance Payments	(2,611)
Tuition and Education	(1,000)
Total Taxes	(14,675)
Discretionary Total Cash Flow (Deficit)	$ (157)

The estimated costs for implementing the "need" objectives for the Nelsons are as follows.

Acquire appropriate amount of insurance

- Life – add $500,000 term, 20-year, for an estimated cost of $500.
- Disability – modify coverage so that it includes disability by sickness, estimated cost of $1,400.
- Health – add major medical with $10,000 deductible due to lifetime limit at an estimated cost of $1,000.

Retire and maintain lifestyle

- David should save 10 percent of his salary based on his age. Since his company matches 3 percent, David should save at least 7 percent in his 401(k) plan. David is currently saving 5.43 percent (3,803/70,000). Therefore, he intends to increase his 401(k) savings by $1,099 (1.57 percent).
- By increasing his 401(k) savings, however, David will reduce his tax payments by $165 ($1,099 @ 15 percent = $164.85 rounded to nearest dollar). Therefore, the change in cash flow is an increased outflow of $934 ($1,099 – $165).

Reduce debt

- The Nelsons should increase their payments toward their credit card debt; however, no estimated amounts will be identified at this time. This objective will be addressed when selecting a strategy with the client.

Prepare appropriate wills

- David and Dana should *each* have an appropriate will created. The estimated cost of having a will drawn up is $500 each, for a total of $1,000.

The Nelsons currently have a cash flow deficit of $157; however, the implementation of all "need" objectives would increase the deficit by $4,834 ($2,900 for insurance, $934 for 401(k) savings, $1,000 for wills) for a total deficit of $4,991 ($4,834 + $157).

EXHIBIT 5.8: DISCRETIONARY CASH FLOWS AFTER IMPLEMENTATION OF "NEED" OBJECTIVES

Discretionary Cash Flow	$ (157)
Life Insurance	(500)
Disability Insurance	(1,400)
Health Insurance	(1,000)
Additional 401(k) contribution	(1,099)
Reduction of tax due to 401(k) savings	165
Will	(1,000)
Discretionary cash flow after implementation of "need" objectives	$ (4,991)

Often, as in the case of the Nelsons, the analysis of the abbreviated Income Statement and the addition of costs associated with "need" objectives indicates that there is a shortage of cash. Therefore, either more cash inflow, less cash outflow, or a combination of the two, is required. There are common sources of available cash flows to increase inflows or reduce outflows including:

- Cutting discretionary expenses such as entertainment, vacations, utilities, charitable contributions, etc.
- Refinancing mortgages to reduce payment or decrease the debt term.
- Raising insurance deductibles to reduce premiums.
- Making use of tax-advantaged savings.
- Obtaining additional income from employment.

After determining the cash flow situation, including the implementation of "need" objectives, the next step is to develop strategies that create a positive discretionary cash flow while at the same time resolving weaknesses that were identified in the SWOT analysis and accomplishing, at a minimum, the "need" objectives. Therefore, the planner should consider each of the common methods to increase cash inflow or reduce cash outflow, the opportunities identified in the SWOT analysis, and each of the objectives previously identified by the client and the planner.

While developing alternative strategies, the planner must determine how each strategy might affect cash flow and the client's objectives. Remember, all "need" objectives should be resolved first, and then the "want" objectives should be considered. These alternative strategies will be presented to the client and, with the assistance of the planner, the client will ultimately choose which strategy to implement.

Revisiting the SWOT analysis and taking advantage of the available external opportunities indicate that the Nelsons should refinance their home. Refinancing their home mortgage at 6 percent will reduce their annual mortgage payment by $7,716.52 (($1,829.48 – $1,186.44) × 12). (Assume 30-year loan at 6%. N=360, I=0.50 (6/12), PV=197,887.67 (prepaid closing costs), PMT=1,186.44.) While analyzing the financial statements and tax returns, it was also discovered that the Nelson's income taxes are currently over-withheld annually by $4,412. This type of discovery is common, and an adjustment to increase receivables will be made on a future balance sheet. The combination of refinancing the home and properly adjusting their income tax withholdings will increase the Nelson's cash flow by $12,128.52.

If we now compare the total cash flow deficit of $4,991 to the newly found cash inflows of $12,128.52, we find that the Nelsons now have a positive net cash flow of $7,137.52. Some of this positive cash flow should be used to reduce credit card debt. The remainder of the cash flow may be used to achieve some of the "want" objectives, to create an emergency fund, or increase savings and investments.

Recall that the two "want" objectives that were most important to the Nelsons (each with a 5 ranking) were to minimize payment of income taxes and to retire at age 62. The next most important objective, with a 4 ranking, was to purchase a home in Key West, Florida.

The objective of minimizing the payment of income taxes was resolved while focusing on the "need" objectives. In order for David to retire at age 62 he will either need exceptional investment returns or an increase in periodic savings for retirement by $1,649 annually. Purchasing a $200,000 home in Key West will require annual savings of $6,684 for 5 years to create a 20 percent down payment, then monthly mortgage payments of $1,197.55 ($14,371 annually). (See supplement on pages 149-151 for detailed calculations.)

Since we have already taken advantage of refinancing and tax savings, we must now consider cutting discretionary expenses, raising deductibles on insurance, or obtaining additional income. Raising deductibles is usually the next option that is considered since it has little impact on the client's daily life or overall financial plan. Clients seem to be more resistant to cutting discretionary expenses or obtaining additional income since those options can have a significant impact on the client's daily life.

STEP SEVEN – SELECT THE MOST APPROPRIATE STRATEGY

Strategy selection is a collaborative effort between planner and client. The planner ensures that the client understands all of the aspects of the alternative strategies and educates the client on how to analyze the selection in a systematic and quantitative manner. The client, however, makes the final decision and is responsible for implementing the plan. Therefore, the client's involvement and commitment to the process and the strategy is essential to the successful implementation of the plan.

abstract thinking - the third phase of a client's thinking process in establishing financial direction, where a client becomes aware of the consequences of financial actions and understands how day-to-day savings and consumption decisions impact a financial plan

Strategy selection is made simpler when analyzed in a quantitative manner. It also helps the client move on to the **abstract thinking** level. Using the Strategy Selection Worksheet, as shown in Exhibit 5.9, can assist in this analysis. During the evaluation of each alternative, the planner should discuss with the client actions that must be taken, what must occur to implement the strategy, and how the strategy might change the client's current consumption and savings behavior, existing savings rate, time horizon, and asset allocation.

While considering the above-mentioned issues, the client should answer the following questions with the planner's assistance:

1. How easy will it be to implement this strategy?
2. How committed am I to implementing this strategy considering the required sacrifices?

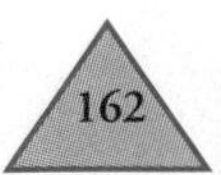

The client should respond to each of these questions using a weighting scale of 1 to 5. For the first question, a 5 would indicate the strategy is *very easy* to implement. For the second, a 5 would indicate the client is *very committed* to implementing the strategy. The answer weightings of each question are multiplied to result in a ranking for that strategy. The strategies with the highest rankings are the ones most likely to be successful.

The ranking of the "want" objectives include one additional measure. The weight of the objective that was identified on the Client/Planner Worksheet for Establishing Financial Direction should be considered when obtaining the ranking for that strategy. Again, the strategies with the highest rankings are most likely to be successful and, therefore, should be seriously considered. Exhibit 5.9 indicates how the Nelsons may have completed the Strategy Selection Worksheet.

EXHIBIT 5.9: STRATEGY SELECTION WORKSHEET

Strategy Selection Worksheet

Client Name David and Dana Nelson **Date** February 16, 2006

a) List strategy options.
b) For each strategy option, indicate the objective(s) that is resolved.
c) Discuss, with the client, the impact of implementing the objective.
d) For each strategy option, the client should answer the following questions by ranking the answers 1 to 5.
   - ✓ How easy will it be to implement this strategy? (A 5 ranking indicates very easy to implement.)
   - ✓ How committed am I to implementing this strategy? (A 5 ranking indicates very committed.)
e) For "want" objectives, consider the original importance ranking that was identified when completing the **Client/Planner Worksheet**.

Strategy (Discuss how each strategy impacts relevant objectives)	**Benefits of Implementing Strategy**	**Behavior Change Required**	**Ease of Implementation**	**Commitment Level**	**Ranking**
Refinance Home	*Increases annual cash flow by $7,717*	*None*	*5*	*5*	*25*
Adjust tax withholdings	*Increases annual cash flow by $4,412*	*None*	*5*	*5*	*25*
Increase Savings to 401(k)	*Takes advantage of tax-free savings*	*None since other strategies will increase current cash flow*	*5*	*5*	*25*
Raise Insurance Deductibles	*Increases cash flow by $200*	*Acceptance of additional risk*	*5*	*3*	*15*
Cut discretionary expenses	*Increases annual cash flow by maximum of $2,414*	*Do not use paid babysitters, eliminate entertainment expenses, etc.*	*1*	*2*	*2*
Dana acquires part-time job	*Increases annual cash flow*	*Put Gabby in daycare*	*2*	*1*	*2*
David acquires a second job	*Increases annual cash flow*	*Spend less time with family*	*2*	*1*	*2*

After completing the Strategy Selection Worksheet, the Nelsons have decided to refinance their home, adjust their tax withholdings, and increase their contribution to the 401(k) plan. This increase in cash flow will allow them to meet all of their "need" objectives. They have also decided to reduce their credit card debt using the surplus cash flow and to begin putting money toward an emergency fund. The Nelsons now realize that purchasing a vacation home in Key West is not reasonable at this time and have decided to revisit this objective in five years. David also realizes that retiring at age 62 may not be possible; however, he has made a promise to himself to increase his 401(k) savings each time he gets a raise until he reaches the maximum allowable contribution.

David and Dana do not want to raise their insurance deductibles because they enjoy the peace of mind of having low insurance deductibles. They do not want to acquire an additional job because spending time with family is very important to both of them.

STEP EIGHT – STRATEGY IMPLEMENTATION AND MONITORING

Successful strategy implementation is primarily dependent upon the client. The client must implement the plan and make it work. The financial planner can improve the probability of successful implementation by ensuring that the client has a detailed understanding of the current strategy, can measure progress toward the attainment of objectives, and, through periodic monitoring, can adjust the plan as necessary. The planner can be reasonably assured that the client has a detailed understanding of the plan if the client actively participates in the development of the goals and objectives and in the selection of the best implementation strategy.

Establishing targets and measures aids in monitoring the client's progress toward attaining objectives. A minimum of one target and one measure should be established for each objective. Both the planner and the client should monitor targets and achievement. Therefore, the planner should present the client with the established targets and measures for each objective and show how they apply to each.

Periodic monitoring of the plan is critical. Internal and external circumstances change, and plans do not always work as expected. Clients get married, have children, and may eventually divorce. Some remarry and begin second families. Economic forces change and technology advances. For a host of reasons, quarterly monitoring is recommended, along with annual face-to-face meetings with the client. Therefore, just as situations are expected to change over time, so is it necessary to modify the financial plan.

PROFESSIONAL FOCUS

Do you use the client/planner worksheet (i.e. a fact finder) to determine the goals and objectives of your clients?

I believe client/planner worksheets are an invaluable tool for data collection. These fact finders offer clients a structured format for assembling essential planning documents such as wills and trusts, or even a foundation for developing a rudimentary balance sheet and income statement. This preliminary data assembly most often enables our initial interview to be more productive. Probing questions attempt to highlight any potential obstacles, both financial and emotional, that may prevent a client from achieving their stated goals and objectives. These worksheets, however, can never fully replace the value of a one-on-one interview. Such interactions often produce candid conversation on delicate planning subjects. It is important to note that the human element of emotion is often lost among the sterile context of checklists, pen, and paper.

Do you find clients are aware of their financial goals and objectives or do they require more assistance from you in this area?

I find that many clients have used a fragmented approach to their own financial affairs. Most are a piecemeal assembly of mis-matched documents, haphazard investment positions, and well-intentioned yet ineffectual attempts at risk management. In short, their "comprehensive financial strategies" lack clarity of purpose and are more a result of default than design. Most lack coordination and efficiency. My role as a professional adviser is to aid clients in both identifying and prioritizing their goals and objectives. We then map out a strategy designed to achieve those goals and commit it to writing. This declaration represents an explicit linkage between a client's long-term objectives and the need to execute those actions necessary to achieve the stated goals.

How do you approach clients who have unrealistic goals?

Each of us has a finite dimension to both our capital and our time. These constraints may undermine our ability to achieve all of our stated goals and objectives. At least on some level, all clients are faced with making a choice between immediate capital consumption and long-term savings accumulations. Their decision is based, in large part, on the clients' perception for future investment performance. Sometimes overly optimistic expectations expose clients to a risk of failure. Our role is to temper this exuberance and refocus on the long-term historic normalcy of market performance. Clients must be directed to review their statements of goals and objectives in light of their limited capital resources and realistic expectations for future investment performance. They are faced with the following choices:

- ▲ Save more aggressively today at the expense of instant gratification.
- ▲ Begin investing more aggressively with the potential, but not the guarantee, of achieving greater investment performance.
- ▲ Reduce their expectations of retirement age.

When have you had the best success with clients following the financial plan you created for them?

The greatest success I have experienced as a professional planner rests squarely on my ability to help clients effectively organize their financial lives. By providing an inter-disciplinary perspective I am able to integrate structural efficiencies in both plan design and implementation. Whether it's estate or retirement planning, charitable inclinations, investment, tax or risk management, finding creative solutions to solve clients' unique problems affords a very fulfilling and rewarding career as a financial planner.

JOHN GISOLFI, MS, RFC, CFP®

DISCUSSION QUESTIONS

1. What are the eight steps in establishing financial direction?
2. What is the definition of a financial mission?
3. What are the most common financial goals?
4. How do financial goals and financial objectives differ?
5. Why must a financial planner keep abreast of the external environment?
6. How does client subjectivity affect the establishment of financial objectives?
7. What is the difference between "need" and "want" objectives?
8. What questions can be asked of financial objectives to determine if the objective is a "need" or a "want" objective?
9. What does the acronym SWOT stand for?
10. How can a SWOT analysis be useful to a financial planner?
11. What must be considered when formulating strategy alternatives?
12. What are common methods to increase cash inflow or reduce cash outflow?
13. What should be considered when selecting strategies to implement?
14. How can the planner improve the probability of successful implementation of strategies?
15. How often should a financial plan be monitored?

EXERCISES

1. Suppose Wilma and Fred contacted you, a financial planner, to assist them in saving for a car, their children's education, and a boat. Which thinking phase are they probably demonstrating?
2. What would you do if a client came to you insisting that his financial mission was to buy a 1965 Mustang?
3. If you were working with a client to distinguish between a "want" and a "need" objective and the client wanted to categorize buying a vacation home as a "need," what would you do?
4. What would you say or do to assist a client in understanding the difference between a goal and an objective?
5. What should a planner and a client take into consideration when determining strategies to implement?

PROBLEMS

1. Assume that you had a client with multiple objectives requiring monthly cash flows of $400, $250, $150, $750, and $325, respectively. Also assume that the client's current discretionary cash flow per month is $380.
   a. What technique would you use to bring the client into economic reality?
   b. How would you distinguish between "need" objectives and "want" objectives?
   c. Where might you look for additional available cash flows to meet this client's objectives?

2. Suppose a couple hired you as their financial planner. Upon brief investigation you collect the following information. The couple has been married for 5 years. They have no children. They take expensive vacations several times a year. They both have good jobs and both save the maximum allowed in their 401(k) plans. The mortgage on the house is at a 10.3 percent rate. The current mortgage rate is 8.15 percent. Their credit card balance has been about $1,500, which they never pay in full, and they have a monthly discretionary cash flow deficit of $98. What would be your recommendations to increase their monthly discretionary cash flow?

CHAPTER 5 SUPPLEMENT

CALCULATIONS FOR RETIREMENT NEEDS AND KEY WEST HOME FOR THE NELSONS

Retirement Needs Analysis Using Capital Needs Analysis and the Annuity Method

Step 1. Determine gross dollar needs.

We assume the Nelsons wish to maintain their current lifestyle at retirement. At retirement, the Nelsons will have eliminated Social Security taxes (FICA), 401(k) contributions, child care expenses, and disability insurance premiums.

Current Salary	$70,000
FICA	– 5,355
401(k) Savings	– 4,900
Child Care	– 600
Disability Insurance	– 2,161
	$56,984 yearly retirement needs in today's dollars

Step 2. Determine net dollar needs.

We estimate David's Social Security benefits at $7,400 per year in today's dollars.

Gross Retirement Needs	$56,984
Social Security Benefits	– 7,400
	$49,584 net retirement needs per year

Step 3. Calculate inflated preretirement dollar needs.

N	=	25 (62 – 37)
I	=	2.6 (inflation estimate)
PV	=	$49,584
PMT	=	0
FV	=	$94,194.51 first year needs for retirement

Step 4. Calculate capital needs at retirement.

N	=	30 (92 – 62) Expect to live to age 92
I	=	6.24 [(1.09/1.026 – 1) × 100] (Return on investments of 9%)
FV	=	0
PMT	=	$94,194.51
PV	=	$1,263,943.93 Total capital needed at retirement

Step 5. Calculate yearly deposits to savings.

N	=	25 (62 – 37)
I	=	9 (Estimated return on investment)
FV	=	$1,263,943.93
PV	=	– $61,619 (Balance sheet: 401(k) + stocks at end of 2006)
PMT	=	$8,649.24 needs to be saved each year to achieve goal

Required savings	$8,649.24
Current savings	– 7,000.00 (includes employer contribution)
	$1,649.24 additional savings required

Key West house purchase

N	=	5
I	=	9 (Estimated return on investment)
PV	=	0
FV	=	$40,000 (20% × $200,000)
PMT	=	$6,683.70 required savings

Key West mortgage payment

N	=	360 (30 × 12)
I	=	0.667 (8 / 12) (Assumes 8% interest on 30-year mortgages in 5-years.)
PV	=	$163,200 ($200,000 – $40,000 down payment + 2% closing costs)
FV	=	0
PMT	=	$1,197.55 monthly payment

Basic Financial Planning Tools

in BRIEF

- The power of compound interest
- Basic tools for time value of money
- Future value of an ordinary annuity
- Future value of an annuity due
- Present value of a dollar
- Present value of an ordinary annuity
- Present value of an annuity due
- Financial aid programs
- Tax advantages related to education

↓

- Uneven cash flows
- Internal rate of return and net present value
- Yield to maturity
- Solving for terms or yield
- Serial payments

↓

- Discount rate selection
- Amortization tables
- Rule of 72
- Education funding
- Investments for education

SECTION II

Basic Financial Planning Tools

CHAPTER 6 Time Value of Money
CHAPTER 7 Planning for Children's Education

Risks

- Misunderstanding the impact of inflation
- Failure to understand compounding

Data Collection

- Financial aid programs
- Financial aid information of client
- Current cost of education
- Inflation rate
- Expected earnings rate
- Tax-advantaged education programs

Goals

- Understanding the importance of time value of money to financial planning
- Adequate resources for education of children

Data Analysis

- Projected cost of education
- Education funding choices
- Educational funding analysis
- Investment selections

CHAPTER 6

Time Value of Money

LEARNING OBJECTIVES:

After learning the material in this chapter, you will be able to:

1. Define the time value of money (TVM) concept and explain why it is such an important financial planning concept.
2. Define the terms present value and future value and illustrate their roles in the calculation of compound interest.
3. Calculate the future value and the present value of a dollar.
4. List and explain the tools used in TVM analysis.
5. Calculate the present and future values of an ordinary annuity and an annuity due.
6. Explain the differences between an ordinary annuity and an annuity due.
7. Reconcile the difference between an ordinary annuity and an annuity due.
8. Prepare an amortization table for debt repayment.
9. Explain the Rule of 72 and its uses.
10. Apply the Rule of 72.
11. Understand how unequal cash flows and serial payments affect the future value of an investment.
12. Compare and contrast the concepts of net present value (NPV) and internal rate of return (IRR).
13. Define yield to maturity and explain how it is used to determine a bond's earnings.
14. Explain how "Solving for Term Given the Other Variables" is useful in debt management.
15. Understand how the inflation rate affects the real rate of return of an investment.
16. Define perpetuities and explain how they affect financial planning.

UNDERSTANDING TIME VALUE OF MONEY

TVM (Time Value of Money) - the concept that money received today is worth more than the same amount of money received sometime in the future

Time Value of Money (TVM) is one of the most useful and important concepts in finance and personal financial planning. Essentially, the concept of TVM is that money received today is worth more than the same amount of money received sometime in the future. A dollar received today is worth more than a dollar received one year from today because the dollar received today can be invested and will be worth more in one year. Alternatively, a dollar to be received a year from now is worth less than a dollar today. Comparisons of dollars received and paid at the same point in time are necessary to solve many financial planning problems and to make sound financial decisions. Thus, TVM calculations are fundamental to financial planning. The TVM calculation is one tool that allows financial planners to properly plan a client's goals and objectives.

present value - what a sum of money to be received in a future year is worth in today's dollars based on a specific discount rate

future value - the future amount to which a sum of money today will increase based on a defined interest rate and a period of time

There are two time periods and two values in TVM analysis: the future and future value, and the present and present value. Future value is the future dollar amount to which a sum certain today will increase compounded at a defined interest rate over a period of time. Present value is the current dollar value of a future sum discounted at a defined interest rate over a period of time. Future value is calculated using a process called compounding. Present value is calculated using a process called discounting. Suppose, for example, that a dollar was invested in a bank savings account paying 5 percent annual interest. At the end of the year, the dollar would have grown to $1.05. The initial dollar would be referred to as the **present value**. The 5 percent represents the interest rate. The term is for one year. The $1.05 equals the **future value**. The interest earned (in this case $0.05) is compensation for delaying consumption for one year into the future. We will discuss compounding and discounting later in the chapter.

The initial mathematical relationship between the present value and the future value is expressed as:

$$FV = PV(1+i)^n$$

Where:	PV	=	Present Value
	i	=	Interest Rate
	FV	=	Future Value
	n	=	Number of Periods

Conversely, $PV = \dfrac{FV}{(1+i)^n}$

and thus, $FV = PV(1+i)^n$

In the above example:

$$
\begin{aligned}
FV &= PV(1+i) \\
&= (\$1)(1 + 0.05) \\
&= \$1.05 \text{ (where 5 percent is the annual interest rate on savings)}
\end{aligned}
$$

There are numerous important questions in financial planning that can be answered using TVM concepts.

- If I have a certain dollar amount today, how much will it be worth at some time in the future if it is invested at a certain rate of earnings (interest)?
- If I invested a certain dollar amount on a regular interval basis and at a constant earnings rate, how much would I accumulate at some future date?
- If I wanted to save for the college education of my children, how much would I need to save starting today on a regular interval basis to pay for that education?
- If I wanted to pay off my house mortgage early, how many dollars would I need to add to each monthly payment?
- What is the present value of my expected Social Security retirement benefits?
- How much investment capital will I need to retire at a particular age and still maintain my preretirement lifestyle?

All of these questions and many other financial planning questions can be answered by applying TVM concepts.

FUTURE VALUE AND THE POWER OF COMPOUND INTEREST

Understanding **compound interest** is essential to understanding the future value of money. Basically, compound interest is interest earned on interest. If you take the interest that you earn on an investment and reinvest it, you then earn interest on both the principal and the reinvested interest. Therefore, the interest you earn grows, or compounds. Mathematically, the growth is exponential (a power function) as opposed to a linear function. An investment earns compound interest anytime the investment is held beyond one period, where interest is applied to both contributions and earnings, and where the earnings are reinvested in the investment.

compound interest - interest earned on interest

If the entire \$1.05 in the above example remained in the investment for a second year in the same bank earning 5 percent annually, the future value at the end of the second year would be \$1.1025.

$$FV = PV\,(1 + i)$$

$$FV = \$1.05(1 + 0.05)$$

$$FV = \$1.1025$$

The earnings in the second year, \$0.0525, reflect the interest on the original dollar (\$0.05) and the interest on the 5 cents earned in the first year (\$0.0025).

The mathematical expression for compounding interest at a constant rate is:

$$FV = PV\,(1 + i)^n, \text{ where}$$

n represents the number of periods (term) the investment is to be held. Notice that *i* must be expressed in the same terms as *n* (yearly, semiannually, quarterly, monthly, etc). If *i* is expressed as an annual interest or earnings rate then *n* must also be expressed annually.

To illustrate this compounding phenomena, assume that $2,000 is invested by a 25-year-old in an individual retirement account (IRA) and left for 5 years earning 12 percent compounded annually. What would be the future value of the investment at the end of 5 years when our investor is age 30?

$$FV = PV\,(1 + i)^n$$

$$FV = (\$2{,}000)(1.12)^5$$

'V = ($2,000)(1.7623) [The exact mathematical factor calculated using an HP 12C]

$$FV = \$3{,}524.68$$

Future value calculations of this type can be performed a variety of different ways using the tools available for TVM calculations. Generally the illustrated examples in this chapter have been calculated using an HP 12C calculator. Where multiple steps were required to solve a problem, we did not round the intermediate steps. If you are attempting to calculate the problems in the chapter and are using table factors, a different calculator, or if you round intermediate steps, then you may receive an answer slightly different from that calculated in the chapter. Where we used table factors you will notice some rounding error. Where we used mathematical exponentials you will also notice differences from calculator or table results. For example, if the problem above had been calculated with rounded interest, then the answer would be $3,524.60 (rounding error of

BASIC TOOLS FOR TIME VALUE OF MONEY (TVM) ANALYSIS

cash flow timeline - TVM analysis tool that graphically depicts cash inflows (cash received) and cash outflows (cash deposited or invested) over a certain period of time (the term)

In addition to mathematical equations, there are a number of other tools that the financial planner can use to understand TVM problems, to assist the client in answering TVM questions, and to present such quantitative information to clients. Among these tools are **cash flow timelines**, TVM tables, financial calculators, cash flow computer software, and accumulation schedules. We will illustrate the various tools of TVM by calculating the future value for the previous example ($2,000 invested for 5 years earning 12 percent compounded annually).

TIMELINES

Timelines are a useful tool to visualize cash flows—both inflows and outflows. Below is a timeline based on the previous example. Notice that the $2,000 invested in time period "0" is listed with a parenthesis indicating that it is an outflow. Respectively, the future value of $3,524.68 is presented as an inflow at time period "5."

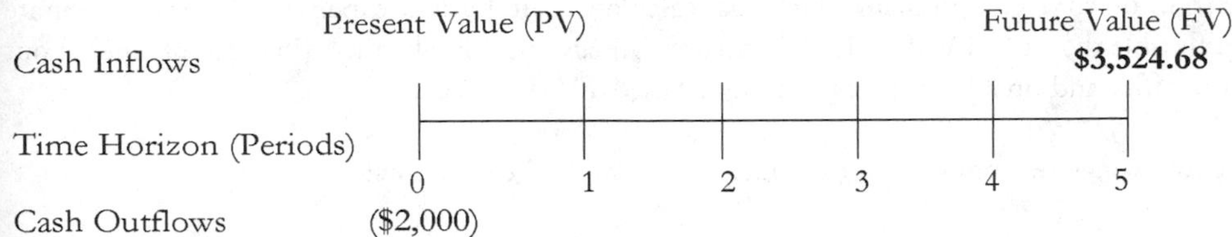
Present Value (PV)
Future Value (FV)
Cash Inflows
$3,524.68
Time Horizon (Periods)
0
1
2
3
4
5
Cash Outflows
($2,000)

The more complex the TVM problem, the more useful a timeline can be in illustrating the positions of the cash flows.

TVM TABLES

TVM tables represent the various values for combinations of *i* and *n*. These tables can be found in the Appendix (B-1 through B-6). The Future Value of a Dollar table is necessary to calculate the answer to our problem. The amounts given in the table represent the value of a dollar deposited today (received in the future) and compounded at a defined rate (i) for a defined period (*n*). The interest factor in Table 1 for 12 percent and for 5 years is 1.7623 (rounded). This number is the equivalent of $(1.12)^5$ or (1.12)(1.12)(1.12)(1.12)(1.12) = 1.7623. Thus, when using TVM tables, the future value formula is also represented as FV = PV × (Table 1 factor at 12 percent for 5 years). In our example: $2,000 × 1.7623 = $3,524.60.

Table 1: Future Value Factor of a Dollar

(Excerpt from Appendix B-2)

Period	2%	4%	6%	8%	10%	12%
1	1.0200	1.0400	1.0600	1.0800	1.1000	1.1200
2	1.0404	1.0816	1.1236	1.1664	1.2100	1.2544
3	1.0612	1.1249	1.1910	1.2597	1.3310	1.4049
4	1.0824	1.1699	1.2625	1.3605	1.4641	1.5735
5	1.1041	1.2167	1.3382	1.4693	1.6105	1.7623

Notice that the tables have been rounded off to four decimals for presentation convenience. The rounding in the tables will cause a slight error in calculation. The amount of the error in the above example is $0.08; $3,524.60 (1.7623 x $2,000) vs. $3,524.68 (1.762341683 x $2,000).

FINANCIAL CALCULATORS

There are a wide variety of useful hand-held financial calculators that will accurately calculate the solution to TVM problems. Financial calculators are fairly inexpensive and more accurate and flexible than the TVM tables. Calculators are also useful when the financial planner is out of the office and unable to access computer-based TVM software.

The following are among the most widely used financial calculators:

- Hewlett Packard: HP 17BII.
- Hewlett Packard: HP 12C.
- Hewlett Packard: HP 10BII.
- Texas Instruments: TI BAII Plus.
- Sharp: EL – 733A.

Each of these has its own mathematical algorithm for solving TVM problems, and to master each calculator requires some practice. It is strongly recommended, regardless of which calculator you select, that you review your calculator's user manual and become familiar with the various keys. Familiarity with the following keys is essential:

[PV] = stores/calculates the present value
[FV] = stores/calculates the future value
[PMT] = stores/calculates the amount of each payment
[n] = stores/calculates the total number of payments or time periods
[i] = stores/calculates the interest or discount rate

It is also helpful to use an application-based calculator text such as "*Understanding Your Financial Calculator.*" In calculating the TVM problems throughout this chapter and this text, we have used the HP 12C.

We will illustrate the keystrokes (for the HP 12C) used to solve the previous future value problem.

Keystroke	Display
2,000[CHS][PV]	–2,000.0000
5[n]	5.0000
12[i]	12.0000
0[PMT]	0.0000
[FV]	3,524.6834

COMPUTER SOFTWARE

Essentially, computer software uses the same or similar mathematical algorithms as the hand-held calculators. In fact, TVM software testers usually use a hand-held calculator to assure the computer algorithm's accuracy. TVM software and application software using TVM concepts are widely available to aid both individuals and practitioners. A discussion of the available TVM software is beyond the scope of this text.

ACCUMULATION SCHEDULES

Knowing the future value of a deposit made today is useful for investment planning for expenditures. It is also useful to know both the amount of earnings and the balance of an investment account on a yearly or periodic basis. To determine the investment earnings and investment accumulation on a periodic basis, prepare a basic accumulation schedule similar to Exhibit 6.1.

EXHIBIT 6.1: ACCUMULATION SCHEDULE

Year (Col 1)	Beginning Balance (Col 2)	Interest (Col 3)	Ending Balance (Col 2) + (Col 3) = (Col 4)
1	$2,000.00	$ 240.00	$ 2,240.00
2	$2,240.00	$ 268.80	$ 2,508.80
3	$2,508.80	$ 301.06	$ 2,809.86
4	$2,809.86	$ 337.18	$ 3,147.04
5	$3,147.04	$ 377.64	$ 3,524.68
Totals	$2,000.00 Total Deposits	$1,524.68 Total Interest	$3,524.68 Final Balance

Column 1 is the year in question, Column 2 is the account balance at the beginning of each year, Column 3 is the interest earned during the year (Column 2 × 12 percent), and Column 4 is the balance at the year-end for each year (Column 2 + Column 3). The Total row shows the original amount deposited, $2,000; interest earned over the 5 years, $1,524.68, and the final balance, $3,524.68. As we will demonstrate, this type of schedule can be expanded or modified to illustrate the extinguishments of debt and is also useful for a variety of other illustrative purposes.

While useful for learning, professional financial planners do not generally rely on TVM tables and accumulation schedules. Rather, they rely on hand-held financial calculators or computer software.

FUTURE VALUE OF AN ORDINARY ANNUITY (FVOA)

Thus far we have calculated the future value of a single deposit made at the beginning of a period. Now consider, instead of a single deposit, that a series of deposits are made into an account. Instead of our previous example of the $2,000 deposited once in the IRA, our investor deposits $2,000 each year in the IRA and does so for 5 years earning an annual rate of return of 12 percent. The series of deposits of equal size is known as an annuity when deposited over a finite number of equal interval time periods. However, it will make a difference whether the deposits are made at the end of each period (known as an ordinary annuity) or deposited at the beginning of every period (known as an annuity due). The ordinary annuity is quite common in investments and in debt repayment. It is sometimes referred to as a payment made in arrears. An annuity due calculation is commonly used in educational funding and for retirement planning. We will discuss the annuity due concept in the following section.

future value of an ordinary annuity - the future amount to which a series of deposits of equal size will amount to when deposited over a finite number of equal interval time periods, based on a defined interest rate, and the deposits are made at the <u>end</u> of each time period

To demonstrate the calculation of the **future value of an ordinary annuity**, assume Davin deposits $2,000 per year at year-end for 5 years into an IRA earning 12 percent annually. For purposes of our illustration, we will present the problem in the context of the basic TVM tools: timelines, mathematics, TVM tables, a hand-held financial calculator, and an accumulation schedule.

FVOA TIMELINE

The ordinary annuity timeline below depicts a pattern of deposits at the end of each period (1–5).

Cash Inflows (Accumulation)

Time Horizon (Periods)

Cash Outflows (Deposits)

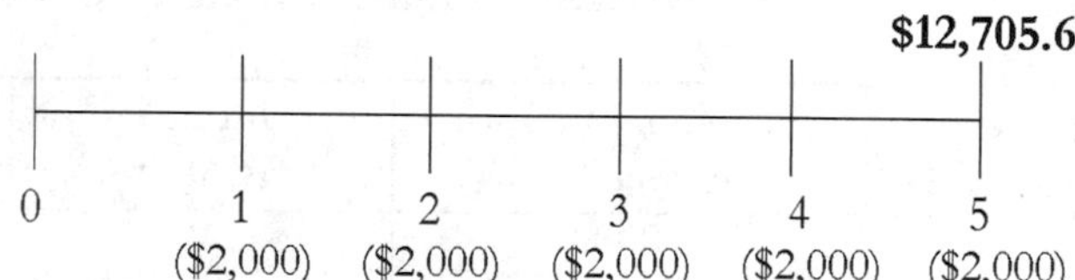

$12,705.69
0
1
2
3
4
5
($2,000)
($2,000)
($2,000)
($2,000)
($2,000)

As shown on the timeline, the future value of the accumulation is equal to $12,705.69 and is shown as an inflow. The deposits of $2,000 are shown as outflows at each year-end.

FVOA USING MATHEMATICS

The mathematical calculation for the ordinary annuity is presented below.

$$FVOA = \$2{,}000(1.12)^0 + \$2{,}000(1.12)^1 + \$2{,}000(1.12)^2 + \$2{,}000(1.12)^3 + \$2{,}000(1.12)^4 = \$12{,}705.69$$

Notice that the future value of an ordinary annuity (FVOA) is calculated by multiplying each deposit of $2,000 by one plus the interest rate of 12 percent raised to the power associated with the term (e.g., the fifth deposit is raised by the zero power because it is made at the end of Year

5 and, therefore, earns no interest). These totals are then summed to determine the future value of the annuity.

Exhibit 6.2 below presents a tabular accumulation using the table factors for each deposit from the last (Deposit 5) to the first (Deposit 1). Notice that the summation of the factor column is equal to 6.3528 and the total future dollar equals $12,705.60.

EXHIBIT 6.2: FUTURE VALUE OF AN ORDINARY ANNUITY CALCULATION

Deposit Number	Amount		Factor	′	Deposit	=	Amount
5	$\$2{,}000\ (1.12)^0$	=	1.0000	×	$2,000	=	$2,000.00
4	$\$2{,}000\ (1.12)^1$	=	1.1200	×	$2,000	=	$2,240.00
3	$\$2{,}000\ (1.12)^2$	=	1.2544	×	$2,000	=	$2,508.80
2	$\$2{,}000\ (1.12)^3$	=	1.4049	×	$2,000	=	$2,809.80
1	$\$2{,}000\ (1.12)^4$	=	1.5735	×	$2,000	=	$3,147.00
Total			6.3528				$12,705.60

($0.09 rounding error due to using table factors) Note: An amount raised to a zero power is equal to 1(1.12^0=1.00).

FVOA Using TVM Tables

We can also calculate the future value of an ordinary annuity using the TVM table for Future Value of an Ordinary Annuity (Appendix B-4). An excerpt of this table, identified as Table 2, is depicted below. The TVM factor for an ordinary annuity of 5 periods at 12% is 6.3528, the same as the interest-compounding factor calculated above. The future value is then calculated as $12,705.60 [($2,000 × 6.3528) = $12,705.60], a difference of $0.09 from the mathematical calculation but the same as the calculation using the table factors in Exhibit 6.2.

Table 2: Future Value Factor of an Ordinary Annuity
(Excerpt from Appendix B-4)

Period	2%	4%	6%	8%	10%	12%
1	1.0000	1.0000	1.0000	1.0000	1.0000	1.0000
2	2.0200	2.0400	2.0600	2.0800	2.1000	2.1200
3	3.0604	3.1216	3.1836	3.2464	3.3100	3.3744
4	4.1216	4.2465	4.3746	4.5061	4.6410	4.7793
5	5.2040	5.4163	5.6371	5.8666	6.1051	6.3528

FVOA Using a Financial Calculator

Your financial calculator will have a feature (generally a [BEGIN] or [END] key) that will allow you to switch between an ordinary annuity (use END) and an annuity due (use BEGIN).

Calculate the future value of the ordinary annuity using the following keystrokes (using the HP 12C):

Keystroke	Display
5[n]	5.0000
12[i]	12.0000
2,000[CHS][PMT]	–2,000.0000
0[PV]	0.0000
[FV]	12,705.6947

FVOA Using an Accumulation Schedule

Exhibit 6.3 is the accumulation schedule, which shows the beginning balance, deposits, interest earned, and ending balance for each year. It also shows the total deposited, total interest earned, and the final accumulation balance of $12,705.70.

EXHIBIT 6.3: ORDINARY ANNUITY ACCUMULATION SCHEDULE

Year	Beginning Balance	Interest	Deposits	Ending Balance
1	$0.00	$0.00	$2,000.00	$2,000.00
2	$2,000.00	$240.00	$2,000.00	$4,240.00
3	$4,240.00	$508.80	$2,000.00	$6,748.80
4	$6,748.80	$809.86	$2,000.00	$9,558.66
5	$9,558.66	$1,147.04	$2,000.00	$12,705.70
Total		$2,705.70	$10,000.00	$12,705.70

($0.01 error due to rounding)

The timeline depicted above and the accumulation schedule in Exhibit 6.3 are different methods of presenting the information related to this particular problem. The timeline is best used by the planner to initially understand the position of the cash flows, while the accumulation schedule is probably the most useful exhibit to present to a client.

FUTURE VALUE OF AN ANNUITY DUE (FVAD)

The application for an annuity due is exactly the same as the ordinary annuity, except that the first deposit or payment for the annuity due is made immediately. This is opposite to the ordinary annuity pattern, where the first payment is made at the end of the first term. The annuity due pattern of payments is quite common for educational funding where the educational institution demands tuition payments be made in advance rather than in arrears. Other common uses of the annuity due concept are for rents and for retirement income, which are both commonly paid in advance.

Using the previous example, we once again present the problem in the context of the basic TVM tools: timelines, mathematics, TVM tables, the financial calculator, and an accumulation schedule.

FVAD TIMELINE

Using the previous example, notice that the pattern of annuity due deposits shifts one period to the left from the ordinary annuity. The difference is essentially Deposit 5 of the ordinary annuity versus Deposit 1 of the annuity due. (Deposits 1, 2, 3, and 4 of the ordinary annuity correspond exactly with deposits 2, 3, 4 and 5 of the annuity due.) Notice that the annuity due timeline illustrates a pattern of deposits made at the beginning of each period instead of at the end of each period.

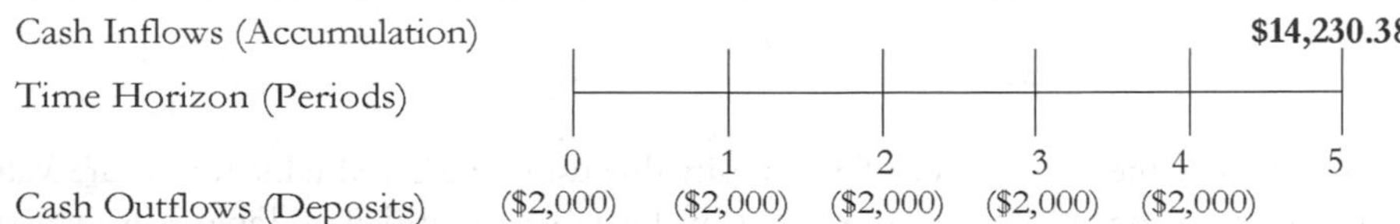
Cash Inflows (Accumulation)
$14,230.38
Time Horizon (Periods)
0
1
2
3
4
5
Cash Outflows (Deposits)
($2,000)
($2,000)
($2,000)
($2,000)
($2,000)

As shown in the timeline, the future value of the accumulation is equal to $14,230.38 and is shown as an inflow. The $2,000 deposits are shown as outflows at the beginning of each year.

We therefore have interest accumulating on all five deposits. Previously the fifth deposit was made at the end of Year 5. That deposit did not accumulate any interest. Now that we have shifted the deposit pattern to that of an annuity due, the last deposit is made at the beginning of Year 5 and, therefore, earns one full year of interest. For this reason, the **future value of an annuity due** will always be greater by one period's interest than the same deposits made for an ordinary annuity of the same term and interest rate. Using the above example, you should note that $12,705.70 x (1.12) = $14,230.38.

future value of an annuity due - the future value to which a series of deposits of equal size will amount when deposited over a definite number of equal interval time periods, based on a defined interest rate, and the deposits are made at the beginning of each time period

FVAD USING MATHEMATICS

The mathematical calculation for the annuity due is presented below.

$$FVAD = \$2{,}000(1.12)^1 + \$2{,}000(1.12)^2 + \$2{,}000(1.12)^3 + \$2{,}000(1.12)^4 + \$2{,}000(1.12)^5 = \$14{,}230.38$$

Notice that the future value of an annuity due (FVAD) is calculated by raising each deposit of $2,000 by the interest rate of 12 percent and at the power associated with the term (e.g. the fifth deposit is raised by the power of one because the deposit is made at the beginning of Year 5 and receives one year of interest).

Exhibit 6.4 below presents a tabular accumulation using the table factors for each deposit from the last (Deposit 5) to the first (Deposit 1). Notice that the summation of the factor column is equal to 7.1151 (FVOA factor of 6.3528 × 1.12) and the total future dollars equals $14,230.20 (off $0.18 due to roundings in table factors).

EXHIBIT 6.4: FUTURE VALUE OF AN ANNUITY DUE CALCULATION

Deposit Number	Amount		Factor	´	Deposit	=	Amount
5	$2,000 (1.12)^1$	=	1.1200	×	$2,000	=	$2,240.00
4	$2,000 (1.12)^2$	=	1.2544	×	$2,000	=	$2,508.80
3	$2,000 (1.12)^3$	=	1.4049	×	$2,000	=	$2,809.80
2	$2,000 (1.12)^4$	=	1.5735	×	$2,000	=	$3,147.00
1	$2,000 (1.12)^5$	=	1.7623	×	$2,000	=	$3,524.60
Total			7.1151				$14,230.20

FVAD Using TVM Tables

We can also calculate the future value of an annuity due using the TVM table for Future Value of an Annuity Due (Appendix B-6). An excerpt of this table, identified as Table 3, is depicted below. The TVM factor for an annuity due of 5 periods at 12% is 7.1152, a difference of 0.0001 from the interest-compounding factor calculated above. The future value is then calculated as $14,230.40 [($2,000 × 7.1152) = $14,230.40] ($0.02 error due to table rounding and $0.20 greater than table factors that were summed to be $14,230.20).

Table 3: Future Value Factor of an Annuity Due
(Excerpt from Appendix B-6)

Period	2%	4%	6%	8%	10%	12%
1	1.0200	1.0400	1.0600	1.0800	1.1000	1.1200
2	2.0604	2.1216	2.1836	2.2464	2.3100	2.3744
3	3.1216	3.2465	3.3746	3.5061	3.6410	3.7793
4	4.2040	4.4163	4.6371	4.8666	5.1051	5.3528
5	5.3081	5.6330	5.9753	6.3359	6.7156	7.1152

FVAD Using a Financial Calculator

We can solve the problem using the HP 12C. Notice that the calculator should be set to the "Begin" mode to indicate an annuity due calculation.

Keystroke	Display
[g][BEG]	0.0000_{BEGIN}
5[n]	5.0000
12[i]	12.0000
2,000[CHS] [PMT]	–2,000.0000
0[PV]	0.0000
[FV]	14,230.3781

FVAD Using an Accumulation Schedule

Exhibit 6.5 is the accumulation schedule, which shows the beginning balance, deposits, interest earned, and ending balance for each year. It also shows the total deposited, total interest earned, and the final accumulation balance of **$14,230.38** (notice the same as the timeline and mathematics).

EXHIBIT 6.5: ANNUITY DUE ACCUMULATION SCHEDULE

Year	Beginning Balance	Deposit	Beginning Balance After Deposit	Interest	Year Ending Balance
1	$0.00	$2,000.00	$2,000.00	$240.00	$2,240.00
2	$2,240.00	$2,000.00	$4,240.00	$508.80	$4,748.80
3	$4,748.80	$2,000.00	$6,748.80	$809.86	$7,558.66
4	$7,558.66	$2,000.00	$9,558.66	$1,147.04	$10,705.69
5	$10,705.69	$2,000.00	$12,705.69	$1,524.68	$14,230.38
Total		$10,000.00		$4,230.38	$14,230.38

(Accurate to the penny)

Comparison of Ordinary Annuity and Annuity Due Calculations

The annuity due has an accumulation account balance at the end of Year 5 of $14,230.38 while the ordinary annuity had an account balance of $12,705.69. The difference of $1,524.69 is equal to the total interest earned in the fifth year ($12,705.69 × 0.12 = $1,524.68). Another way to reconcile this difference is to calculate the interest on the first deposit for the annuity due and subtract the interest on the fifth deposit for the ordinary annuity.

We can prove that the difference between the annuity due and the ordinary annuity is simply the difference between the interest earned on the first deposit using the annuity due and the last deposit using the ordinary annuity. This concept is depicted in the timeline below.

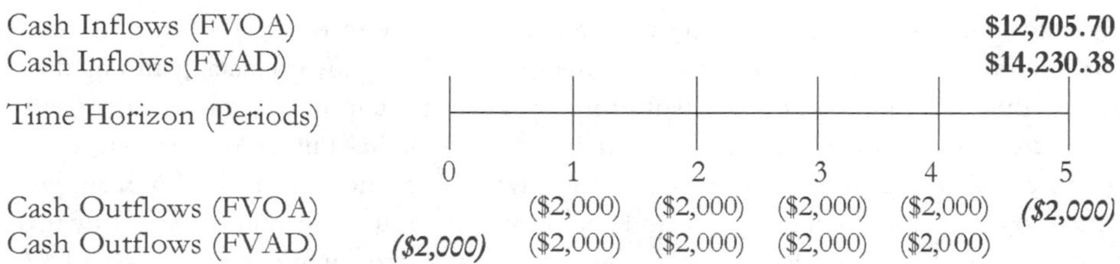
Cash Inflows (FVOA)
Cash Inflows (FVAD)
$12,705.70
$14,230.38
Time Horizon (Periods)
0
1
2
3
4
5
Cash Outflows (FVOA)
($2,000) ($2,000) ($2,000) ($2,000) ($2,000)
Cash Outflows (FVAD)
($2,000) ($2,000) ($2,000) ($2,000) ($2,000)

Notice that the deposits made at the end of years 1, 2, 3, and 4 are identical. We know that the future value of $2,000 deposited at the end of Year 5 for the ordinary annuity is equal to $2,000 [($2,000) × $(1.12)^0$]. The future value of Deposit 1 for the annuity due is equal to $3,524.68 [($2,000) × $(1.12)^5$].

FVAD (1)	$3,524.68
FVOA (5)	$2,000.00
Difference	$1,524.68

Proof of the reconciliation of total accumulation under the annuity due versus the ordinary annuity is depicted below:

FVAD	$14,230.38	
FVOA	$12,705.69	
Difference	$1,524.69	($0.01 rounding error)

We could also reconcile the two accounts using the TVM table by subtracting the ordinary annuity factor by the annuity due factor and then multiplying the result by $2,000, as demonstrated below.

Annuity Due Factor	7.1152	
Ordinary Annuity Factor	(6.3528)	
	0.7624	
Multiplied By	$2,000.00	
Equals	$1,524.80	($0.12 rounding error)

There is a slight rounding error in the total of $0.12 due to rounding the factors in the TVM tables. All factors are rounded to the fourth decimal, which may result in a slight discrepancy.

PRESENT VALUE OF A DOLLAR (PV)

This calculation is used to determine what a sum of money to be received in a future year is worth in today's dollars based on a specific discount rate. For many financial planning decisions, such as education funding or retirement funding, it is important to determine the present value of a future amount rather than the future value of a present amount. In this section, we explain how to calculate the present value of a future investment amount. To illustrate, suppose you wanted to have $20,000 in five years, and could earn an annual return of 8 percent by investing in a certificate of deposit. How much do you need to invest today to meet your goal of $20,000 in 5 years?

We return to our basic tools and present the timeline, mathematical approach, the TVM factor tables, the financial calculator, and the accumulation schedule to calculate the present value of a future sum certain of $20,000 in 5 years.

PV Timeline

Notice that the $20,000 is located as an inflow at Year 5. We must determine the present value dollar amount at Year 0.

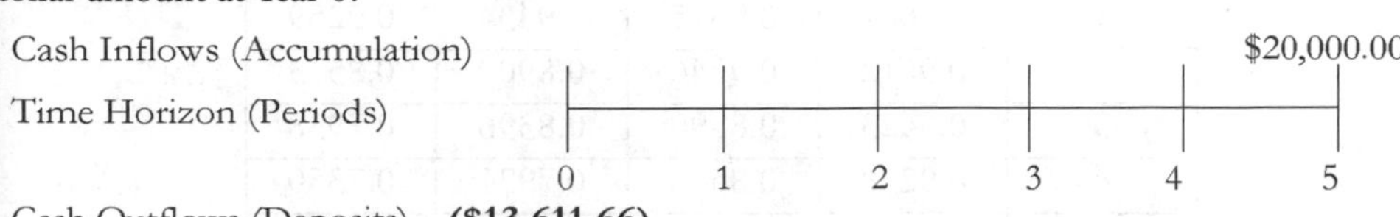
Cash Inflows (Accumulation)
$20,000.00
Time Horizon (Periods)
0
1
2
3
4
5
Cash Outflows (Deposits)
($13,611.66)

As shown in the timeline, the present value of $20,000 five years from now is $13,611.66. In other words, $13,611.66 is the amount that should be deposited today earning 8 percent interest compounded annually to equal $20,000 in five years.

PV Using Mathematics

Mathematically, the solution to this type of problem can be derived from the original future value equation as presented below.

$$PV(1+i)^n = FV$$

$$PV = \left[\frac{FV}{(1+i)^n}\right]$$

$$PV = \left[\frac{\$20,000}{(1+0.08)^5}\right]$$

$$PV = \left[\frac{\$20,000}{1.469328}\right]$$

$$PV = \$13,611.66$$

Where: PV = Present Value
i = interest rate for each term
n = Term
FV = Future Value of $20,000

Again, the amount to deposit today to have $20,000 five years from today, assuming an annual earnings rate of 8 percent, is $13,611.66.

PV Using TVM Tables

We can also calculate the present value using the TVM table for Present Value of a Dollar (Appendix B-1). An excerpt of this table, identified as Table 4, is depicted below. The TVM factor for the present value of a dollar of 5 periods at 8% is 0.6806. Therefore, the present value is calculated by multiplying the $20,000 future value times the TVM table factor of 0.6806 for a present value of $13,612 (rounded) [($20,000 × 0.6806) = $13,612.00].

Table 4: Present Value Factor of a Dollar
(Excerpt from Appendix B-1)

Period	2%	4%	6%	8%
1	0.9804	0.9615	0.9434	0.9259
2	0.9612	0.9246	0.8900	0.8573
3	0.9423	0.8890	0.8396	0.7938
4	0.9238	0.8548	0.7921	0.7350
5	0.9057	0.8219	0.7473	**0.6806**

Another method of calculating the TVM factor for the present value of a dollar is to take the factor in the denominator from the previous equation (1.469328) and divide it into 1. The result is 0.6806, the same factor in Table 4 at a term of 5 years and at 8% interest.

PV Using a Financial Calculator

Keystroke	Display
20,000 [FV]	20,000.0000
8[i]	8.0000
5[n]	5.0000
0[PMT]	0.0000
[PV]	– 13,611.6639

PV Using an Accumulation Schedule

Exhibit 6.6 is the accumulation schedule to prove the results and to present a complete picture of the account accumulation for a client. In Exhibit 6.6, we have the original balance of $13,611.66, the interest for the year, the ending balance for each year, the totals for interest earned of $6,385.93, and the correct final balance of $20,000 (corrected for $0.01 rounding error).

EXHIBIT 6.6: ACCUMULATION SCHEDULE OF INVESTMENT

Year	Beginning Balance	Interest Earned	Ending Balance
1	$13,611.66	$1,088.93	$14,700.59
2	$14,700.59	$1,176.05	$15,876.64
3	$15,876.64	$1,270.13	$17,146.77
4	$17,146.77	$1,371.74	$18,518.51
5	$18,518.51	$1,481.48	$19,999.99
Total		$6,388.33	$19,999.99

You can use the accumulation schedule to determine the present value, if you start with the Ending Balance and use the equality:

Ending Balance = Beginning Balance x (1 + interest rate)

Or

Beginning Balance = Ending Balance ÷ (1 + interest rate)

EXHIBIT 6.7: ACCUMULATION SCHEDULE IN REVERSE

Year	Ending Balance	Interest Earned	Beginning Balance
5	$20,000.00	$1,481.48	$18,518.52
4	$18,518.52	$1,371.74	$17,146.78
3	$17,146.78	$1,270.13	$15,876.65
2	$15,876.65	$1,176.05	$14,700.60
1	$14,700.60	$1,088.93	$13,611.67
Total		$6,388.33	$13,611.67

PRESENT VALUE OF AN ORDINARY ANNUITY (PVOA)

It is common for persons or businesses to receive a series of equal payments for a finite period from debt repayment, from a life insurance settlement, from an annuity, or as a pension payment. The question usually asked is, what is the present value of such a series of payments? Remember that the ordinary annuity assumed that each payment is made at the end of each period (arrears). As an example, consider that you are to receive $25,000 per year for the next 5 years with each payment made at year-end. Also assume that your earnings rate is 8 percent. What is the present value in dollars of that income stream? Once again, we can apply the basic tools of TVM to solve this problem.

PVOA TIMELINE

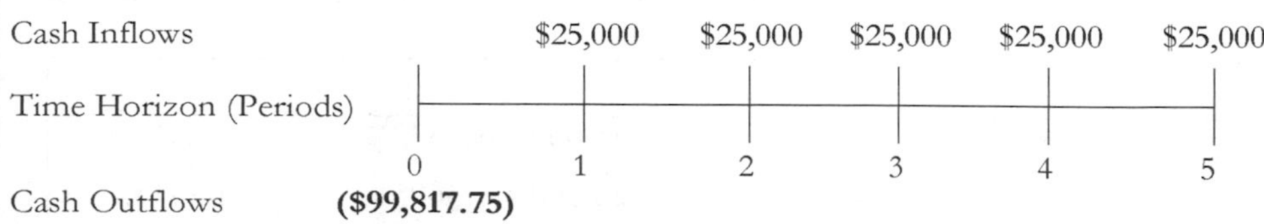
Cash Inflows
$25,000
$25,000
$25,000
$25,000
$25,000
Time Horizon (Periods)
0
1
2
3
4
5
Cash Outflows
($99,817.75)

The timeline suggests that we need to calculate the present value of $25,000 to be received annually for 5 years with each payment occurring at the end of the year and assuming an 8 percent earnings rate. As the timeline depicts, the PV equals $99,817.75.

PVOA Using Mathematics

We solve this problem using a mathematical formula:

$$PVOA = PMT\left[\frac{1-\frac{1}{(1+i)^n}}{i}\right]$$

where: PVOA = Present value of an ordinary annuity
i = Interest rate for each term
n = Term
PMT = Periodic payment

$$PVOA = \$25{,}000\left[\frac{1-\frac{1}{(1+0.08)^5}}{0.08}\right]$$

$$PVOA = \$25{,}000\left[\frac{1-\frac{1}{1.4693}}{0.08}\right]$$

$$PVOA = \$25{,}000\left[\frac{1-0.6806}{0.08}\right]$$

$$PVOA = \$25{,}000\,[3.99275]$$

$PVOA = \$99{,}817.75$ (answer will be slightly different depending on the rounding technique used throughout the problem)

Exhibit 6.8 presents the present value calculation in tabular form for each payment and for the payments in total. Notice that the present value of five annual payments of $25,000 is approximately $99,817.76 ($0.01 rounding error) when discounted at 8 percent.

EXHIBIT 6.8: PRESENT VALUES OF AN ORDINARY ANNUITY CALCULATION

Year	Payment				
5	$25,000 ÷ (1+0.08)^5	=	$25,000 ÷ 1.4693	=	$17,014.58
4	$25,000 ÷ (1+0.08)^4	=	$25,000 ÷ 1.3605	=	$18,375.75
3	$25,000 ÷ (1+0.08)^3	=	$25,000 ÷ 1.2597	=	$19,845.81
2	$25,000 ÷ (1+0.08)^2	=	$25,000 ÷ 1.1664	=	$21,433.47
1	$25,000 ÷ (1+0.08)^1	=	$25,000 ÷ 1.0800	=	$23,148.15
Total					$99,817.76

PVOA Using TVM Tables

We can also calculate the **present value of an ordinary annuity** using the TVM table for Present Value of an Ordinary Annuity (Appendix B-3). An excerpt of this table, identified as Table 5, is depicted below. The TVM factor for present value of an ordinary annuity of 5 periods at 8% is 3.9927. Therefore, the present value is calculated by multiplying the $25,000 payment times the TVM table factor of 3.9927 for a present value of $99,817.50 (rounded).

present value of an ordinary annuity - the value today of a series of equal payments made at the end of each period for a finite number of periods

($25,000 x 3.9927) = $99,817.50

Table 5: Present Value Factor of an Ordinary Annuity

(Excerpt from Appendix B-3)

Period	2%	4%	6%	8%
1	0.9804	0.9615	0.9434	0.9259
2	1.9416	1.8861	1.8334	1.7833
3	2.8839	2.7751	2.6730	2.5771
4	3.8077	3.6299	3.4651	3.3121
5	4.7135	4.4518	4.2124	3.9927

Another method of calculating the TVM factor for the present value of an ordinary annuity is to take the sum of the factors for the present value of a dollar (Table 4) for each of the five years at the 8% interest rate. The total of the five individual factors will approximately equal the present value of an ordinary annuity factor (Table 5) as shown below.

Year	PV Factor (from Table 4)	
1	0.9259	
2	0.8573	
3	0.7938	
4	0.7350	
5	0.6806	
	3.9926	(off due to rounding)

Thus, the present value of an ordinary annuity table is constructed by taking the summation of the present value of an amount for the appropriate term at the appropriate interest rate.

PVOA Using a Financial Calculator

Keystroke	Display
5[n]	5.0000
8[i]	8.0000
25,000[PMT]	25,000.0000
0[FV]	0.0000
[PV]	–99,817.7509

PVOA Using an Accumulation Schedule

An accumulation schedule (Exhibit 6.9) can be presented to the client to help explain how the account balance will change based on an initial deposit of $99,817.75 and an earnings rate of 8 percent.

EXHIBIT 6.9: ACCUMULATION SCHEDULE OF INVESTMENT

Year	Beginning Balance	Interest Earned	Year End Withdrawals	Ending Balance
1	$99,817.75	7,985.42	$25,000.00	$82,803.17
2	82,803.17	6,624.25	25,000.00	64,427.42
3	64,427.42	5,154.19	25,000.00	44,581.62
4	44,581.62	3,566.53	25,000.00	23,148.15
5	23,148.15	1,851.85	25,000.00	0.00

Notice that we placed the withdrawal column to the right of the interest column to indicate that the interest was earned on the entire beginning balance for each year and the withdrawals were made at year end each year. Also, the final withdrawal of $25,000 at the end of Year 5 depletes the account, proving once again that the original present value calculation was correct.

PRESENT VALUE OF AN ANNUITY DUE (PVAD)

present value of an annuity due - the value today of a series of equal payments made at the beginning of each period for a finite number of periods

The difference between the **present value of an annuity due** and the present value of an ordinary annuity is that the annuity due's payments are made at the beginning of each period rather than at the end, as for an ordinary annuity. This makes the present value of an annuity due always larger than the present value of an ordinary annuity with the same payments over the same time period. The annuity due calculation is quite common in financial planning and is most often used for educational funding and for retirement capital needs analysis. Using the previous problem, and assuming that this is an educational funding problem where the parent is to pay $25,000 each year for 5 years with payments occurring at the beginning of each year and the earnings rate is 8 percent, we can calculate the present value using the basic TVM tools. (For simplicity, we have assumed an inflation rate of zero.)

PVAD Timeline

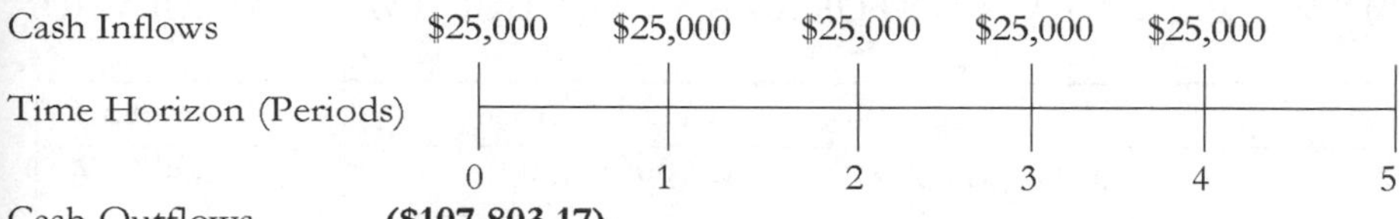
Cash Inflows
$25,000
$25,000
$25,000
$25,000
$25,000
Time Horizon (Periods)
0
1
2
3
4
5
Cash Outflows
($107,803.17)

The timeline suggests that while $107,803.17 is deposited today, $25,000 is immediately withdrawn.

PVAD Using Mathematics

The present value of an annuity due is illustrated below.

$$PVAD = PMT\left[\frac{1-\frac{1}{(1+i)^{n-1}}}{i}+1\right]$$

where: PVAD = Present value of annuity due
PMT = Cash flow payment ($25,000)
i = Interest rate (discount rate)
n = Term (n - 1 = 4)

$$PVAD = PMT\left[\frac{1-\frac{1}{(1+0.08)^{5-1}}}{0.08}+1\right]$$

$$PVAD = \$25,\ 000\left[\frac{1-\frac{1}{1.3605}}{0.08}+1\right]$$

$$PVAD = \$25,\ 000\left[\frac{1-0.7350}{0.08}+1\right]$$

$$PVAD = \$25,\ 000\left[\frac{0.2650}{0.08}+1\right]$$

$$PVAD = \$25,\ 000 \times 4.3121$$

$$PVAD = \$107{,}803.17$$

The mathematical calculation of $25,000 paid as an annuity due for five payments earning 8 percent is equal to a present value of $107,803.18 ($0.01 rounding error).

Exhibit 6.10 below presents the calculation by year in tabular form.

EXHIBIT 6.10: PRESENT VALUES FOR AN ANNUITY DUE (PVAD) CALCULATION

Year	PMTs	=	PMTs ÷ Factors	=	PV Amount
5	25,000 ÷ $(1+.08)^4$	=	25,000 ÷ 1.3605	=	$18,375.75
4	25,000 ÷ $(1+.08)^3$	=	25,000 ÷ 1.2597	=	$19,845.81
3	25,000 ÷ $(1+.08)^2$	=	25,000 ÷ 1.1664	=	$21,433.47
2	25,000 ÷ $(1+.08)^1$	=	25,000 ÷ 1.0800	=	$23,148.15
1	25,000 ÷ $(1+.08)^0$	=	25,000 ÷ 1.0000	=	$25,000.00
Total					$107,803.18

PVAD Using TVM Tables

We can also calculate the present value of an annuity due using the TVM tables for Present Value of an Annuity Due (Appendix B-5). An excerpt of this table, identified as Table 6, is depicted below. The TVM factor for present value of an annuity due of 5 periods at 8% is 4.3121. Therefore, the present value is calculated by multiplying the $25,000 payment times the TVM table factor of 4.3121 for a present value of $107,802.50 (rounded) [($25,000 × 4.3121) = $107,802.50].

Table 6: Present Value Factor of an Annuity Due
(Excerpt from Appendix B-5)

Period	2%	4%	6%	8%
1	1.0000	1.0000	1.0000	1.0000
2	1.9804	1.9615	1.9434	1.9259
3	2.9416	2.8861	2.8334	2.7833
4	3.8839	3.7751	3.6730	3.5771
5	4.8077	4.6299	4.4651	4.3121

PVAD Using a Financial Calculator

Keystroke	Display
[g][BEG]	0.0000 BEGIN
5[n]	5.0000
8[i]	8.0000
25,000[PMT]	25,000.0000
0[FV]	0.0000
[PV]	-107,803.1710

VAD USING AN ACCUMULATION SCHEDULE

n accumulation schedule (Exhibit 6.11) can be presented to the client by illustrating the initial eposit of $107,803.17, the annual withdrawals of $25,000 to pay the college at the beginning each year, the interest rate earned each year, and the year-end account balance. The interest is id on the beginning balance less $25,000 each year.

EXHIBIT 6.11: ACCUMULATION SCHEDULE OF INVESTMENT

Year	Beginning Balance	Withdrawals	Interest Earned	Ending Balance
1	$107,803.17	$25,000.00	$6,624.25	$89,427.42
2	89,427.42	25,000.00	5,154.19	69,581.61
3	69,581.61	25,000.00	3,566.53	48,148.14
4	48,148.14	25,000.00	1,851.85	24,999.99
5	24,999.99	24,999.99	0.00	0.00

uneven cash flows - investment returns or deposits that are not single interval deposits nor equal payments

OTHER TVM CONCEPTS

ow that we have a better understanding of the concepts and basic mathematics and mechanics f TVM, it is time to discuss some of the common TVM applications. Included in these pplications are **uneven cash flows**, combining sum certains with annuities, **net present value** NPV), **internal rate of return** (IRR), yield to maturity (YTM), solving for term, selecting the iterest rate, serial payments, perpetuities, educational funding, and capital needs analysis for tirement. In the next section of this chapter, we are going to present the basics of most of these VM concepts. YTM will be covered more extensively in Chapter 12 Supplement A (Fixed-icome Securities). We will defer coverage of education funding until Chapter 7 (Education unding) and capital needs analysis until Chapter 15 (Introduction to Retirement Planning).

net present value (NPV) - the difference between the initial cash outflow (investment) and the present value of discounted cash inflows, i.e., NPV = PV of CF - Cost of Investment

internal rate of return (IRR) - the discount rate that causes cash inflows to equal cash outflows, thus allowing comparison of rates of return on alternative investments

UNEVEN CASH FLOWS

ivestment returns or deposits are not always single interval deposits or equal payments. For xample, assume that a person deposits $400, $500, $600, and $700 into an investment ccount at the end of each of four years, respectively. How much would the investment be orth if the earnings rate was a constant 8 percent annually? For this situation, without a nancial calculator or computer, this future value problem must be solved separately for each ear since the cash flows are uneven. Once again, the cash flows can be presented in a timeline.

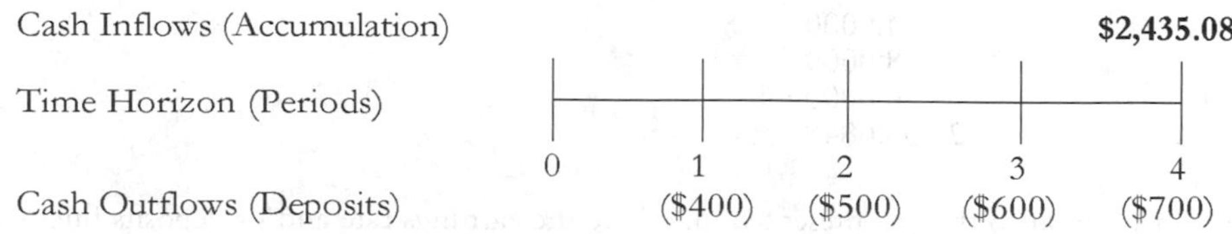

Cash Inflows (Accumulation)
$2,435.08
Time Horizon (Periods)
0
1
2
3
4
Cash Outflows (Deposits)
($400)
($500)
($600)
($700)

Mathematically, the future value of each cash flow can be determined using the equation $FV = PV(1+i)^n$ as follows:

$\$400(1.08)^3 + \$500(1.08)^2 + \$600(1.08)^1 + \$700(1.08)^0$

$\$503.88 + \$583.20 + \$648.00 + \$700.00 = \$2,435.08$

This problem can also be solved using an accumulation schedule as illustrated in Exhibit 6.12.

EXHIBIT 6.12: SCHEDULE OF INVESTMENT ACCUMULATION

Year	Beginning Balance	8% Interest Earned	Year End Deposit	Ending Balance
1	$0.00	$0.00	$400.00	$400.00
2	$400.00	$32.00	$500.00	$932.00
3	$932.00	$74.56	$600.00	$1,606.56
4	$1,606.56	$128.52	$700.00	$2,435.08
Total		$235.08	$2,200.00	$2,435.08

Using a financial calculator (HP12C), we can easily calculate the problem by using the uneven cash flow keys. The first step in the calculation determines the present value of the uneven deposits. The second step calculates the future value. The keystrokes for the uneven cash flow problem are below:

Step 1:

Keystroke	Display
0[g][CF_o]	0.0000
400 [CHS][g][CF_j]	–400.0000
500 [CHS][g][CF_j]	–500.0000
600 [CHS][g][CF_j]	–600.0000
700 [CHS][g][CF_j]	–700.0000
8[i]	8.0000
f[NPV]	–1,789.8600

Step 2:

Keystroke	Display	
[PV]	–1,789.8600	(this step inputs the NPV from Step 1 as the PV for Step 2)
4[n]	4.0000	
8[i]	8.0000	
0[PMT]	0.0000	
[FV]	2,435.0848	

For problems similar to the one presented, or where the earnings rate and/or deposits fluctuate in either rate or amount, using a financial calculator or computer is more efficient than manual methods.

COMBINING SUM CERTAINS WITH ANNUITIES

For some investments, bonds for example, the investment returns are received in the form of both an annuity and a sum certain. Assume that an investor purchased a 3-year $1,000 corporate bond paying $30 interest twice a year (semiannually) and then paying $1,000 (the maturity value) back to the holder at the end of the 3-year period. If the holder expected an 8 percent annual return, what amount should be paid for the bond at the beginning of the 3-year period? Assume that the interest is paid as an ordinary annuity (arrears).

This problem is no different than combining two different problems, one the present value of an ordinary annuity and the second the present value of a future amount. To solve the problem, complete the following steps:

Step 1 – Draw a cash flow timeline
Step 2 – Determine the PV of the ordinary annuity
Step 3 – Determine the PV of the sum certain (maturity value)
Step 4 – Add the results of Steps 2 and 3

<u>Step 1</u> – Draw a timeline

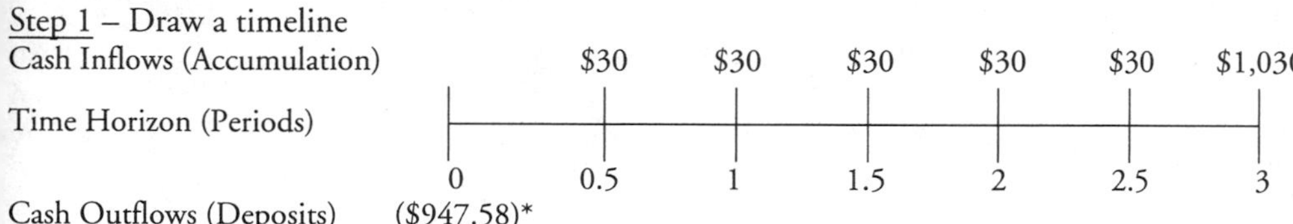
Cash Inflows (Accumulation)
$30
$30
$30
$30
$30
$1,030
Time Horizon (Periods)
0
0.5
1
1.5
2
2.5
3
Cash Outflows (Deposits)
($947.58)*

*presently unknown

Step 2 – Determine the PV of the Annuity

PVOA $30 for 6 periods at 4 percent (double the periods and halve the rate for semiannual interest)

$$PVOA = PMT\left[\frac{1-\frac{1}{(1+i)^n}}{i}\right]$$

$$PVOA = \$30\left[\frac{1-\frac{1}{(1+0.04)^6}}{0.04}\right]$$

$$PVOA = \$30\left[\frac{1-\frac{1}{1.2653}}{0.04}\right]$$

$$PVOA = \$30\left[\frac{0.2097}{0.04}\right]$$

$$PVOA = \$30 \times 5.2421$$

$$PVOA = \$157.26$$

Step 3 – Determine the PV of the Sum Certain

PV of $1,000 at 4 percent for 6 periods

$PV = \$1,000 \div (1+0.04)^6$

$PV = \$1,000 \div 1.2653$

$PV = \$790.31$

Step 4 – Add the results of Steps 2 and 3

$157.26	Present Value of Annuity Interest (ordinary)
790.31	Present Value of Final Payment
$947.57	PV of Bond (rounded)

Many investments take the form of a series of equal cash flows and then one lump sum payment (stocks with dividends, bonds). By drawing a cash flow timeline it is easier to visualize how a problem may be divided into single payments and annuities. Alternatively, the problem is easily solved using a financial calculator. The keystrokes for such a solution are :

Keystroke	Display
6[n]	6.0000
4[i]	4.0000
30[PMT]	30.0000
1000[FV]	1000.0000
[PV]	–947.5786

Obviously, the calculator reduces the amount of work necessary to solve this type of problem. We have now taken a sum certain problem and combined it with an annuity.

NET PRESENT VALUE ANALYSIS

Net present value analysis (NPV) is a commonly used TVM technique employed by businesses and investors to evaluate the cash flows associated with capital projects and capital expenditures. The concept is common to capital budgeting. NPV analysis helps to answer the question of whether one should select one capital investment over another capital investment. The result of the analysis is in terms of dollars. The method discounts the future cash flows at an appropriate discount rate and allows the present value of inflows to be compared to the present value of outflows. This technique is important to financial planners in assisting clients in making decisions as to which investment projects the client should consider undertaking.

The model itself is deterministic, that is, it assumes information is known about the future (cash flows, life, etc.). The NPV model assumes that all reinvestments of cash flows received are made at the weighted average cost of the capital of the firm or the required rate of return of the investor.

NPV equals the difference between the initial cash outflow (investment) and the present value of discounted cash inflows. For example, if the present value of a series of cash flows is $200 and the initial outflow is $150, then the NPV equals $50. Businesses generally look for investments with a positive NPV.

EXAMPLE

Assume you are a financial planner debating whether to purchase a copy machine. You currently pay 12 cents a copy for reproducing materials and expect to make 3,000 copies per month. The copier you are considering costs $5,000 and is expected to last 5 years with a $1,000 salvage value. Your cost for reproducing on the new copier would be 7 cents per copy. Assuming a 12 percent discount rate, what is the net present value of the copier?

To solve this problem, first convert the relevant data to monthly figures. If you purchase a copy machine, each copy would save you $0.05 ($0.12 – $0.07 = $0.05). If you made 3,000 copies per month, you would save $150 per month ($0.05 × 3,000 = $150). We must then calculate

the present value of the cash flow discounted at 12 percent (1 percent monthly). The keystroke for this calculation (using the HP 12C) are below:

Keystroke	Display
150 [PMT]	150.000
1,000 [FV]	1,000.0000
60 [n]	60.0000
1 [i]	1.0000
[PV]	–7,293.7054

The present value of the copier is $7,293.71. It is displayed as a negative number on the calculator, indicating that the stream of cash inflows is worth an initial cash outflow (purchase) of $7,293.71. Subtracting the actual cost of $5,000 indicates the net present value of the copier is $2,293.71. Therefore, the positive NPV indicates that you should purchase the copy machine. The purchase essentially will save you $2,293.71 in today's dollars.

Internal Rate of Return (IRR)

The internal rate of return (IRR) is the discount rate that equates the discounted cash inflows and outflows of a specific investment or project. IRR calculations allow the financial planner to compare rates of return on alternative investments of unequal size and investment amounts. The NPV model and the IRR model make different assumptions about the reinvestment rate of cash flows received during the period of investment. Recall that NPV assumes the reinvestment rate to be the weighted average cost of capital or the required return. The IRR calculation assumes the reinvestment rate equals the IRR. NPV is considered a superior model to IRR, when comparing investment projects of unequal lives because assuming reinvestment at the required return is more reasonable than at the IRR.

The formula below describes the basic present value model used for discounting cash flows.

$$PV = \frac{Cf_1}{(1+k)^1} + \frac{Cf_2}{(1+k)^2} + \cdots + \frac{Cf_n}{(1+k)^n}$$

PV	=	The value of the security or asset today.
Cf_n	=	The cash flow for a particular period, *n*.
k	=	The discount rate or IRR.
n	=	The number of cash flows to be evaluated.

The formula states that the PV of a series of cash flows is equal to each cash flow divided by one plus the discount rate raised to a power equal to the period in which the cash flow occurs.

The internal rate of return is the exact discount rate (labeled as "k" in the above formula) that makes the discounted future cash inflows equal to the initial cash outflow, or investment. One of the underlying assumptions in the above equation is that the cash flows that are received during the investment period will be reinvested at the investment's internal rate of return.

EXAMPLE

Meg owns 1 share of Herring, Inc. stock. She purchased this share of stock three years ago for $50. The current market value of the stock is $40 per share. Since buying the stock, the following dividends have been paid:

Dividend year 1 (end) $4.80 per share
Dividend year 2 (end) $5.90 per share
Dividend year 3 (end) $7.25 per share

What is the IRR that Meg has earned on her investment? Because the IRR is the rate of discount that equalizes the cash inflows and outflows, using a financial calculator is the easiest method. The financial calculator keystrokes (HP 12C) are below.

Keystroke	Display
50 [CHS][g][CF_o]	–50.0000
4.8 [g][CF_j]	4.8000
5.9 [g][CF_j]	5.9000
7.25 [ENTER]	7.2500
40 [+][g][CF_j]	47.2500
[f][IRR]	5.5695

We can check our result of 5.5695%:

Period	Cash Flow (CF)	Divisor (×)	Factor (1/×)	Present Value (CF × Factor)
1	4.80	$1 \div (1.055695)^1$	0.9472	4.5468
2	5.90	$1 \div (1.055695)^2$	0.8973	5.2939
3	47.25	$1 \div (1.055695)^3$	0.8499	40.1593
				50.0000

YIELD TO MATURITY

Yield to maturity (YTM) is the calculation of the rate of return that will make the discounted cash flows of a bond equal to the current price of that bond. It is the application of the IRR model to bond investments. YTM is generally calculated based on semiannual coupon payments (even with zero-coupon bonds). Financial planners need to understand YTM to begin understanding bonds and other debt investments.

There are three adjustments that have to be made in order to calculate YTM for a bond that makes semiannual coupon payments:

- *n* – The number of periods is determined by multiplying the number of years by two so as to reflect two coupon payments per year. For example, the *n* for a 10-year bond would be 20 to reflect 20 coupon payments.

- PMT – The coupon rate is stated as a percent of the face value of the bond. (Face value = $1,000.) Therefore, a 10 percent coupon bond will pay a total of $100 each year ($50 twice per year). The adjustment is to divide the $100 by two to reflect the two payments of $50 during the year.
- YTM – The YTM that will be calculated will be a semiannual YTM rate. Therefore, it is necessary to multiply the calculated YTM by two to determine the annual YTM.

EXAMPLE Ann is considering the purchase of a 5-year, $1,000 bond that is selling for $1,162.22. What is the YTM for this bond if it has a 12 percent coupon, paid semiannually? The yield to maturity is 8 percent annually or 4 percent per semiannual interest payment. The proof of this calculation is illustrated below.

Period	Cash Flow (CF)	Divisor (×)	Factor (1/×)	Present Value (CF × Factor)
1	60.0000	$1 \div (1.04)^1$	0.9615	57.6923
2	60.0000	$1 \div (1.04)^2$	0.9246	55.4734
3	60.0000	$1 \div (1.04)^3$	0.8890	53.3398
4	60.0000	$1 \div (1.04)^4$	0.8548	51.2883
5	60.0000	$1 \div (1.04)^5$	0.8219	49.3156
6	60.0000	$1 \div (1.04)^6$	0.7903	47.4189
7	60.0000	$1 \div (1.04)^7$	0.7599	45.5951
8	60.0000	$1 \div (1.04)^8$	0.7307	43.8414
9	60.0000	$1 \div (1.04)^9$	0.7026	42.1552
10	1,060.0000	$1 \div (1.04)^{10}$	0.6756	716.0980
				1,162.2179

To calculate the yield to maturity using a financial calculator:

Keystroke	Display	
10[n]	10.0000	Semiannual payment
1162.22[CHS][PV]	–1,162.2200	The current cost of the bond
60[PMT]	60	The semiannual interest payment for a 12% annual coupon
1000 [FV]	1,000	Maturity value of the bond
[i]	4.0000	(Yield to maturity – YTM)(multiply by 2 = 8 percent)

SOLVING FOR TERM GIVEN THE OTHER VARIABLES

This kind of analysis answers the question of how long (in days, months, quarters, or years) to save or pay to accomplish some goal, if you save or pay at a given rate. This type of analysis is particularly useful in debt management, such as determining the:

- Term to pay off student loans.
- Term to pay off a mortgage.
- Term to save for college education.
- Term to save for a special purchase (car, home, vacation).

EXAMPLE

Margaret bought a house using a mortgage loan of $240,000 issued for 15 years at 6.25 percent per year on May 1, 2005. Her first payment was June 1, 2005. On January 1st of 2006, she has made 7 payments of $2,057.81 and has 173 payments remaining and a remaining mortgage balance of $234,256.20. Margaret wants to know how many more months she will have to pay if she increases her monthly payment by $500 to $2,557.81. Using a financial calculator (HP 12C), we calculate the term using the following keystrokes:

Keystroke	Display	
234,256.20[PV]	234,256.2000	Current balance
0 [FV]	0.0000	Future value
2,557.81 [CHS][PMT]	–2,557.8100	New payment
6.25 ÷ 12 = 0.5208[i]	0.5208333	Monthly interest rate
[n]	125.0000	Number of payments remaining

Margaret is thus able to reduce her remaining payments from 173 to 125 by increasing her monthly payment by $500 to $2,557.81. Her last payment (payment 125) will be $1,982.12.

When solving for [n] on the HP 12C, only integers (whole numbers) are displayed as a solution. This calculator cannot solve for non-integers (numbers with decimals). Therefore, your initial answer may be incorrect and will not match answers of other calculators. To calculate the correct term, you will have to substitute numbers for the term until you get the correct future value or present value. If the future value or present value does not match, you must adjust the term up or down and recalculate. This process must be done until the term you substitute equals the future value or present value. The place to begin is with the term initially calculated.

opportunity cost - when faced with investment alternatives, it is the highest-valued alternative not chosen—it represents what is forgone by choosing another alternative. When discounting a future sum or series of payments back to present value, it is the composite rate of return on the client's assets with similar risk to the assets being examined.

SELECTING THE RATE OF INTEREST FOR ACCUMULATING OR DISCOUNTING

When utilizing TVM analysis, the planner is frequently faced with the issue of which interest rate or earnings rate to use. The choices include the expected rate of earnings for a particular investment, the client's **opportunity cost**, the riskless rate, the consumer price index (CPI) for some future expenditures, the specific inflation rate for particular services (educational and medical), or the **real rate of return,** which accommodates both the nominal earnings rate and some measure of inflation.

real rate of return - the combination of the nominal earnings rate reduced mathematically by the inflation rate

Generally, when projecting the future value of an investment, either a lump-sum investment or one made with annuity contributions, the appropriate compounding rate will be the expected rate of return for that particular investment. When discounting a future sum or series of payments back to present value, however, either the client's opportunity cost or the riskless rate of return will be used. The client's opportunity cost is usually the composite rate of return on the client's assets with similar risk to the assets being examined. The riskless rate is the Treasury rate for the selected period or term.

Consumer Price Index **(CPI)** - a price index that measures the cost of a "market basket" of consumer goods and services purchased for day-to-day living

When calculating the amount of dollars that retirement will cost in the future, it is common to use the general **Consumer Price Index**, while in the case of college education, the recent and projected rate of inflation for college education should be used.

It is also useful to use an inflation-adjusted earnings rate for problems like retirement capital needs or education funding. The reason for using such a rate is that the costs in the future are generally increasing at one rate (the inflation rate) and the investments are growing at a different rate (the earnings rate). Thus, the way to make the increasing cash outflows equal is to treat them as real dollars of purchasing power and use an inflation-adjusted discount rate that takes into consideration the earnings rate and inflation rate. For example, if inflation is 5 percent, a product costing $1,000 today will cost $1,050 one year from now, but will only be $1,000 of real purchasing power one year from now in today's dollars. The combination of the nominal earnings rate reduced mathematically by the inflation rate is known as the real rate of return.

The loss of purchasing power is one of the risks that investors must overcome to achieve their financial goals. Real economic returns reflect the earnings from an investment that are above the inflation rate. Simply subtracting the rate of inflation from the nominal earnings rate, however, will not yield the real economic rate of return. Real economic returns must be calculated by using the following formula.

$$\left[\frac{1+R_n}{1+i}-1\right]\times 100$$

where R_n = nominal rate of return

i = inflation rate

Assume that $1,000 is invested at the beginning of the year and earns 10 percent, resulting in a balance at the end of the year of $1,100. Also assume that over the same period inflation has been 4 percent. Thus, $1,040 at the end of the year is equal to the initial investment of $1,000 at the beginning of the year, in terms of real dollars or purchasing power. The real return is equal to the difference between the earnings ($100) and the increase as a result of inflation ($40), which is $60, divided by the initial investment adjusted for inflation ($1,040). This result equals a real rate of return of 5.77 percent.

- Conceptually, the return of 5.77 percent makes sense, in that the absolute return was 10 percent and the inflation was 4 percent, with the difference being 6 percent.

$$\left[\frac{1 + 0.10}{1 + 0.04} - 1\right] \times 100 = 5.7692$$

- The nominal earnings for this investment are \$100. The real earnings are \$57.69 in today's dollars (\$60.00 ÷ 1.04 = \$57.69).

SERIAL PAYMENTS

A **serial payment** is a payment that increases at a constant rate (usually inflation) on an annual (ordinary) basis. There are situations when investors are more comfortable increasing payments or deposits on an annual basis because the investor is expecting increases in salary or wages with which to make those increasing payments. Examples include investment deposits, life insurance premiums, educational needs, and retirement needs, or for any lump-sum future expenditure.

serial payment - a payment that increases at a constant rate (usually, the rate of inflation) on an annual (ordinary) basis

Serial payments differ from fixed annuity payments (both ordinary annuities and annuities due) because the payments themselves are increasing at a constant rate. The result is that the initial serial payment will be less than a fixed annuity but the last deposit or payment will be greater than the fixed annuity payment.

EXAMPLE

Consider that Kathy wants to start her own business in 3 years, and she needs to accumulate \$100,000 (in today's dollars) to do so. Kathy expects inflation to be 4 percent, and she expects to earn 8 percent on her investments. What serial payment should Kathy make each year to attain her goal?

The serial payment is calculated by adjusting the earnings rate for inflation to determine the real economic rate of return (nominal rate 8 percent, adjusted for inflation, 4 percent). This adjustment is accomplished using the following formula:

$$\left[\frac{1 + R_n}{1 + i} - 1\right] \times 100$$

where R_n = nominal rate of return

i = inflation rate

$$\left[\frac{1 + 0.08}{1 + 0.04} - 1\right] \times 100 = 3.8462$$

Therefore, the real rate of return used for the calculation is 3.8462.

The next step is to calculate the amount of an ordinary annuity payment for 3 years that would result in a $100,000 future value. This amount equals the payment needed today if made at the beginning of each year. If the payments, as in this case, are made at year end, the initial payment of $32,083.16 must be inflated by 4 percent.

FV	=	PMT ($1.038462^2 + 1.038462^1 + 1.038462^0$)
$100,000	=	PMT (1.0784 + 1.0385 +1)
PMT	=	$100,000 ÷ 3.1168
PMT	=	$32,083.16 (if payments are made at the beginning of the year)
PMT	=	$32,083.16 × 1.04 (inflation) or $33,366.49 (if made at year end)

The second and third payments must be increased by 4 percent to reflect inflation. The $100,000 payment today grows with inflation to $112,486.40 ($100,000 × $(1.04)^3$) by the end of year 3, which is when Kathy needs it. The Schedule of Investment below proves the increasing payments are correct.

EXHIBIT 6.13: ACCUMULATION SCHEDULE OF INVESTMENT

Year	Beginning Balance Needed	Deposit (Payments)	8% Interest Earned	Accumulation Ending Balance
1	$100,000.00	$33,366.87	$0.00	$33,366.87
2	$104,000.00	$34,701.55	$2,669.35	$70,737.77
3	$108,160.00	$36,089.61	$5,659.02	$112,486.40
End of Year 3	**$112,486.40**	**$104,158.03**	**$8,328.37**	$112,486.40

Note: She could have saved $34,649.58 per year. An annuity of this amount would have provided her with the same future value of $112,486.40. This payment is calculated as follows:

FV	=	$112,486.40
N	=	3
i	=	8
PMT	=	$34,649.58

Notice that the payment of $34,649.58 is greater than the first serial payment, but less than the last one.

PERPETUTIES

A perpetuity is a payment cash flow stream that remains constant indefinitely. An example of a common perpetuity is preferred stock, which generally pays a set dividend each year. To determine the value of this type of payment stream, simply divide the payment (PMT) by the discount rate (i).

$$PV = \frac{PMT}{i}$$

EXAMPLE

Assume Smith Corporation always pays a $4.00 preferred stock dividend and the client's required rate of return is 10 percent. The value of the preferred stock equals $40 as illustrated below:

$$PV = \frac{PMT}{i}$$

$$PV = \frac{\$4.00}{0.10}$$

$$PV = \$40$$

OTHER TVM TOOLS

Timelines, mathematics, TVM tables, accumulation schedules, financial calculators, and computer software are basic tools of time value of money. There are other TVM tools, including amortization tables and the Rule of 72. An understanding of each of these tools will assist the financial planner in solving other complex TVM problems.

AMORTIZATION TABLES

An **amortization table** is an extension of the accumulation schedules illustrated earlier in the chapter. Amortization tables are primarily used to illustrate the amortization, or extinguishment, of debt. Initially we create a table with the beginning balance of debt, a level payment, the portion of the payment that is interest, the portion of the payment that is used to reduce the principal indebtedness, and the ending balance of the indebtedness for each year.

amortization table - TVM tool used primarily to illustrate the amortization, or extinguishments of debt. The table presents the number of years of indebtedness, the beginning balance, level payments, interest amount, principal reduction, and ending balance of indebtedness.

Where on the Web

American Savings Education Council *www.asec.org*
Investor Desktop, Financial and Insurance Calculators *www.quickcalcs.com*
Kiplinger Online (calculator) *www.kiplinger.com*
Money Magazine *www.money.cnn.com*
Mortgage Calculator *www.mcalculator.com*
NASD *www.nasd.com*
USA Today (calculator) *www.usatoday.com/money/perfi/calculators/calculator.htm*
U.S. News *www.usnews.com*

EXHIBIT 6.14: AMORTIZATION TABLE (BLANK)

Month (Col. 1)	Beginning Balance (Col. 2)	Payment (Col. 3)	6.25% Interest (Col. 4) = 6.25% / 12 x (Col. 2)	Principal Reduction (Col. 5) = (3)–(4)	Ending Mortgage Balance (Col. 6) = (2)–(5)
–	–	–	–	–	–
–	–	–	–	–	–

The beginning balance of the indebtedness less the principal amount of reduction will equal the ending balance of the indebtedness. The remainder of the payment was interest as determined in the interest amount column. The common usage for amortization tables is for mortgages, but as a tool it can be used to illustrate any indebtedness repayment schedule.

EXAMPLE Consider that Josh takes out a $240,000 mortgage with the first payment to be made in January and repaid over 15 years on a monthly basis at 6.25% annual interest.

EXHIBIT 6.15: MORTGAGE AMORTIZATION TABLE

Month (Col. 1)	Beginning Balance (Col. 2)	Payment (Col. 3)	6.25% Interest (Col. 4) = 6.25% / 12 × (Col. 2)	Principal Reduction (Col. 5) = (3)–(4)	Ending Mortgage Balance (Col. 6) = (2)–(5)
Yr 1 - Jan	$240,000.00	$2,057.81	$1,250.00	$807.81	$239,192.19
Yr 1 - Feb	$239,192.19	$2,057.81	$1,245.79	$812.02	$238,380.17
Yr 1 - Mar	$238,380.17	$2,057.81	$1,241.56	$816.25	$237,563.92
...	...	...	...	...	...
Yr 1 - Dec	$230,878.98	$2,057.81	$1,202.49	$855.32	$230,023.66
Total Yr 1		**$24,693.72**	**$14,717.44**	**$9,976.34**	

PV	=	\$240,000	Mortgage amount
n	=	180 months	Term in months
i	=	6.25 ÷ 12	Interest per month
PMT	=	-\$2,057.8166	Payment of an ordinary annuity
FV_{12}	=	\$230,023.66	Balance of mortgage after 12 payments

Notice that Column 2 of Exhibit 6.15 is the beginning balance of indebtedness of \$240,000. Josh then makes 12 monthly payments of \$2,057.81 (total \$24,693.72) during Year 1 of which \$14,717.44 is interest and the remainder \$9,976.34 is used to reduce the mortgage balance so that at the end of Year 1, Josh owes \$230,023.66 on the mortgage (Column 6).

The amortization table can be extended for the full 15 years and is useful to illustrate exactly when the balance of the mortgage will reach any certain amount, the amount of interest for a given period, and the amount of principal reduction during a given period. The table may be presented for only one year as above, or may be presented yearly or monthly for the entire indebtedness period. In the event the mortgage begins sometime other than January, the table can be modified so that the mortgage interest expense for each calendar year can be shown for use in estimating the mortgage interest income tax deduction for federal income tax.

Qualified residence interest expense is deductible for those taxpayers who itemize their expenses on their federal income tax return. The mortgage company sends the interest payer a Form 1098 (Mortgage Interest Statement) providing the payer with the amount of interest paid for the prior year. This amount may also be obtained from the amortization table, assuming payments are made as agreed. For example, Josh should have received a Form 1098 for the first year of \$14,717.44 interest paid. The amortization table is a useful tool to estimate the interest deduction for future years and can be used to assist the planner in estimating future income tax liability and other income tax planning.

EXHIBIT 6.16: FORM 1098 (MORTGAGE INTEREST STATEMENT)

8181 ☐ VOID ☐ CORRECTED

RECIPIENT'S/LENDER'S name, address, and telephone number		OMB No. 1545-0901 2005 Form 1098	**Mortgage Interest Statement**
RECIPIENT'S Federal identification no.	PAYER'S social security number	1 Mortgage interest received from payer(s)/borrower(s) \$	**Copy A For Internal Revenue Service Center**
PAYER'S/BORROWER'S name		2 Points paid on purchase of principal residence \$	**File with Form 1096.**
Street address (including apt. no.)		3 Refund of overpaid interest \$	For Privacy Act and Paperwork Reduction Act Notice, see the **2005 General Instructions for Forms 1099, 1098, 5498, and W-2G.**
City, state, and ZIP code		4	
Account number (see instructions)			

Form **1098** Cat. No. 14402K Department of the Treasury - Internal Revenue Service

THE RULE OF 72

Frequently, professionals want to approximate rates of earnings or the time needed to achieve a certain financial goal where the earnings rate or the time, but not both, is known. The professional may only need an estimate rather than a mathematically precise answer and/or does not have access to the appropriate tool to perform precise calculations.

Rule of 72 - a method of approximation that estimates the time that it takes to double the value of an investment where the earnings (interest) rate is known (by dividing 72 by the interest rate). Alternatively, it can also estimate the earnings (interest) rate necessary to double an investment value if the time is known (by dividing 72 by the period of investment).

The **Rule of 72** is such a method of approximation. Initially used by accountants, it is now used by financial planners to estimate the time that it takes to double the value of an investment where the earnings rate is known. Alternatively, the Rule of 72 will estimate the earnings rate necessary to double an investment value if the time is known. The Rule of 72 states that if you know a rate of return, you can determine the period of time that it takes to double the value of the investment by dividing 72 by the interest rate. For example, if the annual interest rate is 6 percent, then 72 ÷ 6 = 12. Therefore, if a dollar is invested at 6 percent for 12 years, it should be equal to $2 at the end of the 12-year term. Conversely, if the term is known to be 12 years and you need an amount to double during that term, you can divide 72 by 12 to determine the interest rate necessary [72 ÷ 12 = 6]. Therefore, you would need an interest rate of 6 percent in order to double your investment in 12 years.

Mathematically, the rule is described by the formula below

$$PV = \left[\frac{FV}{(1+i)^n}\right]$$

$$1 = \left[\frac{2}{(1+i)^n}\right]$$

If you know *i*, you can determine *n* by dividing 72 by 100*i*. Conversely, if you know *n*, you can determine 100*i* by dividing 72 by *n*.

EXHIBIT 6.17: RULE OF 72 EXAMPLE

Interest Rate	Period to Double (n)
4%	18.0
6%	12.0
8%	9.0
9%	8.0
10%	7.2

Consider the following question: Approximately how long does it take to double an investment that is earning 9 percent annually? Using Exhibit 6.17, we know that a 9 percent interest rate will take 8 years to double according to the Rule of 72 [72 ÷ 9 = 8 years].

While an extremely helpful tool as an approximator and as a control on the reasonableness of an answer determined by a calculator or computer, the Rule of 72 has a small error in it, especially at extremely low or high rates or terms. Consider, for example, how long it would take to double $1 if the rate of interest were 72 percent annually. According to the Rule of 72, 72 ÷ 72 = 1, indicating to us that we should double our money in one year, but we know that the value at the end of one year is $1.72 not $2. Many financial planners are using the Rule of 72 without consideration of the error factor. Exhibit 6.18 is a table of the error percentage rate for the Rule of 72 at various interest rates.

EXHIBIT 6.18: ERROR RATE USING THE RULE OF 72

Interest Rate	Error %
1	2.4
2	2.0
3	1.6
4	1.3
5	1.0
6	0.6
7	0.3
8	0.05
9	<0.4>
10	<0.6>
11	<0.9>
12	<1.3>
13	<1.4>
14	<1.8>
15	<2.1>
18	<3.1>
24	<4.7>
40	<7.6>
50	<8.5>
72*	<14.0>

**The error rate for a given interest rate equal to or greater than 72 percent will always be 14 percent.*

The error rate is calculated above using the actual value of $2 as the numerator and the actual calculated amount as the denominator to get the error percentage. The < > signs indicate that the actual value is less than the Rule of 72 estimated by the calculated percentage. The values that are not bracketed are greater than the Rule of 72 estimated by the calculated percentage indicated. For example, at 1 percent, the actual value of $1 at 1 percent for 72 periods is $2.047 or 2.4 percent above $2.

As you can see from Exhibit 6.18, the error rate as a percent of the future value can range from +2.4 percent to –14 percent. Therefore, while the Rule of 72 is a good approximation, especially at interest rates between 6 percent and 10 percent, it loses some of its precision when outside the 6 percent to 10 percent interest rate range.

PROFESSIONAL FOCUS

How do you convince your younger clients to take advantage of the power of compound interest for retirement planning or saving for children's education?

I explain that $2,000 invested annually for 40 years at 12% equals $1,534,000. They are usually impressed that the invested amount is $80,000 and the earning growth is $1,454,000. I usually recommend they maximize any pretax savings at their companies to take advantage of any employer match. Having maximized those savings, the Roth IRA is ideal for young persons with currently low income tax rates. I also explain to the 25-to-35-year-old clients that they can retire comfortably at age 55 if they will annually save 10-13% of their gross income and invest in a broadly diversified portfolio of common stocks.

How frequently do you use TVM concepts and in what ways? Do you often make use of the perpetuities model?

I use TVM concepts almost every day. Among my other activities I teach investments. Understanding investments requires a thorough understanding of TVM concepts. In making investments in fixed-income securities, TVM concepts are essential to determine the price of a bond, yield to maturity, and yield to call. I also use TVM concepts for valuing common stock investments using the concepts of fundamental analysis.

When calculating TVM problems, do you usually use a nominal rate or the real rate, and where do you get them?

When calculating the solution to an education funding situation, or when planning for retirement, I use a rate of return for discounting based on the asset allocation chosen and the expected historical return for such an allocation. The inflation rate that I use is usually the current CPI for retirement plus 1 percent for conservatism. For education funding I use a tuition inflation rate, which is a little higher and more representative of the recent experience of tuition increases. I would only use nominal rates of return without inflation for relatively short-term investment horizons.

Are serial payments really applicable to financial planning?

Yes. In fact, serial payments are very appropriate to financial planning. Since the serial payment is to be increased by inflation each year, it is generally consistent with a client's ability to pay and save more over time.

DAVID DURR, PH.D., CFA, CFP®

DISCUSSION QUESTIONS

1. What is the Time Value of Money (TVM) concept and why is it so important in financial planning?
2. What are the important questions in financial planning that can be answered using TVM concepts?
3. What is meant by present value and future value and how are these two concepts used in the calculation of compound interest?
4. What are the basic tools used in TVM analysis?
5. How are TVM tables computed?
6. What is the difference between the future value of an ordinary annuity (FVOA) and the present value of an ordinary annuity (PVOA)?
7. What is the difference between the future value of an annuity due (FVAD) and the present value of an annuity due (PVAD)?
8. When would you use an ordinary annuity or an annuity due in financial planning?
9. What are the formulas for calculating the present and future values of an ordinary annuity and an annuity due?
10. What are some TVM concepts other than annuities?
11. How do unequal cash flows affect the future value of an investment?
12. How do net present value (NPV) and internal rate of return (IRR) differ in financial planning calculations?
13. What is the yield to maturity (YTM) and how is it used to determine a bond's earnings?
14. How is the concept of "Solving for Term Given the Other Variables" useful in debt management?
15. What alternative rate choices exist when selecting the rate of interest for accumulating or discounting?
16. How is the real return of an investment affected by the inflation rate?
17. How do serial payments affect the future value of an investment?
18. What are perpetuities and how do they affect financial planning?
19. How can amortization tables and the Rule of 72 assist in solving present TVM problems?

EXERCISES

1. Calculate the present value of $10,000 to be received in exactly 10 years, assuming an annual interest rate of 9 percent.
2. Calculate the future value of $10,000 invested for 10 years, assuming an annual interest rate of 9 percent.
3. Calculate the present value of an ordinary annuity of $5,000 received annually for 10 years, assuming a discount rate of 9 percent.
4. Calculate the present value of an annuity of $5,000 received annually that begins today and continues for 10 years, assuming a discount rate of 9 percent.
5. Calculate the future value of an ordinary annuity of $5,000 received for 10 years, assuming an earnings rate of 9 percent.
6. Calculate the future value of an annual annuity of $5,000 beginning today and continuing for 10 years, assuming an earnings rate of 9 percent.
7. Mike borrows $240,000 at 8 percent for a mortgage for 15 years. Prepare an annual amortization table assuming the first payment is due January 30, 2006 exactly 30 days after the loan.

8. Joan invested $5,000 in an interest-bearing promissory note earning an 8 percent annual rate of interest compounded monthly. How much will the note be worth at the end of 5 years, assuming all interest is reinvested at the 8 percent rate?
9. Callie expects to receive $50,000 in 2 years. Her opportunity cost is 10 percent compounded monthly. What is the sum worth to Callie today?
10. Lola purchased a zero-coupon bond 9 years ago for $600. If the bond matures today and the face value is $1,000, what is the average annual compound rate of return (calculated semiannually) that Lola realized on her investment?
11. Today Evan put all of his cash into an account earning an annual interest rate of 10 percent. Assuming he makes no withdrawals or additions into this account, approximately how many years must Evan wait to double his money? Use the Rule of 72 to determine the answer.
12. Anthony has been investing $1,500 at the end of each year for the past 12 years. How much has accumulated assuming he has earned 8 percent compounded annually on his investment?
13. Dennis has been dollar cost averaging in a mutual fund by investing $1,000 at the beginning of every quarter for the past 5 years. He has been earning an average annual compound return of 11 percent compounded quarterly on this investment. How much is the fund worth today?
14. Casey, injured in an automobile accident, won a judgment that provides him $2,500 at the end of each 6-month period over the next 3 years. If the escrow account that holds Casey's settlement award earns an average annual rate of 10 percent compounded semiannually, how much was the defendant initially required to pay Casey to compensate him for his injuries?
15. Stacey wants to withdraw $3,000 at the beginning of each year for the next 5 years. She expects to earn 8 percent compounded annually on her investment. What lump sum should Stacey deposit today?
16. Gary wants to purchase a beach condo in 7 years for $100,000. What periodic payment should he invest at the beginning of each quarter to attain the goal if he can earn 11 percent annual interest, compounded quarterly on investments?
17. Ann purchased a car for $25,000. She is financing the auto at a 10 percent annual interest rate, compounded monthly for 4 years. What payment is required at the end of each month to finance Ann's car?
18. Josh purchased a house for $215,000 with a down payment of 20 percent. If he finances the balance at 10 percent over 30 years, how much will his monthly payment be?
19. Chase purchased a house for $300,000. He put 20 percent down and financed the remaining amount over 30 years at 8 percent. How much interest will be paid over the life of the loan assuming he pays the loan as agreed? (Round to the nearest dollar.)

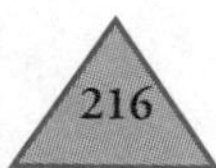

PROBLEMS

1. Lucy wants to give her son $80,000 on his wedding day in 4 years. How much should she invest today at an annual interest rate of 9.5 percent compounded annually to have $80,000 in 4 years? Alternatively, how much would she need to invest today if she could have her interest compounded monthly? Explain which interest option would be most beneficial to Lucy.
2. Rachel, who just turned 18, deposits a $15,000 gift into an interest-bearing account earning a 7.5 percent annual rate of interest. How much will she have in the account when she retires at age 60 assuming all interest is reinvested at the 7.5 percent rate? If Rachel decided she only needed $300,000 at retirement, could she retire at 59? Explain.
3. Kerri won the lottery today. She has two options. She can receive $30,000 at the end of each year for the next 15 years or take a lump-sum distribution of $200,000. Her opportunity cost is 12 percent compounded annually. Based on present values which option should she choose?
4. Darrin wants to donate $8,000 to his church at the beginning of each year for the next 20 years. What lump sum should Darrin deposit today if he expects to earn 11 percent compounded annually on his investment? Alternatively, how much should he deposit if he wants to have $50,000 left at the end of the 20 years?
5. James deposited $800 at the end of the last 16 years to purchase his granddaughter, Kali, a car. James earned 8 percent interest compounded annually on his investment. If the car Kali chooses costs $22,999, would she have enough money in the account to purchase the vehicle? What would be the deficit or surplus?
6. Brenda has been investing $150 at the beginning of each month for the past 20 years. How much has she accumulated assuming she has earned an 11 percent annual return compounded monthly on her investment? If instead of earning 11 percent, Brenda was only able to earn 10 percent (compounded monthly), how much would her payments need to be to have the same accumulated amount?
7. Kenneth took out a loan today to purchase a boat for $160,000. He will repay the loan over a 30-year period at 9 percent interest (with payments occurring monthly). What will be his remaining principal balance at the end of the first year?
8. Cody estimates his opportunity cost on investments at 9 percent compounded annually. Which one of the following is the best investment opportunity?
   - ▲ To receive $100,000 today.
   - ▲ To receive $400,000 at the end of 15 years.
   - ▲ To receive $1,500 at the end of each month for 10 years compounded monthly.
   - ▲ To receive $75,000 in 5 years and $100,000 5 years later.
   - ▲ To receive $75,000 in 5 years and $175,000 10 years later.
9. Patricia and Scott Johnson are ready to retire. They want to receive the equivalent of $30,000 in today's dollars at the beginning of each year for the next 20 years. They assume inflation will average 4 percent over the long run, and they can earn an 8 percent compound annual after-tax return on investments. What lump sum do Patricia and Scott need to invest today to attain their goal?
10. Margaret wants to retire in 9 years. She needs an additional $200,000 in today's dollars in 10 years to have sufficient funds to finance this objective. She assumes inflation will average 5.0 percent over the long run, and she can earn a 4.0 percent compound annual after-tax return on investments. What serial payment should Margaret invest at the end of the first year to attain her objective?

11. Determine the future value of a periodic deposit of $5,000 made at the beginning of each year for 5 years to a mutual fund expected to earn 11 percent compounded quarterly during the projection period.
12. Kristi wants to buy a house in 10 years. She estimates she will need $200,000 at that time. She currently has ten zero-coupon bonds with a market value of $4,600 that she will use as part of the required amount. The zero-coupon bonds have a total face value of $10,000 and will mature in 10 years. The bond has a semiannual effective interest rate of 4.323 percent. In addition to the bond, she wants to save a monthly amount to reach her goal. What is Kristi's required monthly payment made at the beginning of each month in order to accumulate the $200,000, including the zero-coupon bond, at an assumed interest rate of 11 percent?

CHAPTER 7

Education Funding

LEARNING OBJECTIVES:

After learning the material in this chapter, you will be able to:

1. Discuss the various issues that parents should consider when setting goals for financing their children's education.
2. List the types of financial aid information that can be gathered from a college's financial aid office.
3. Explain the importance of the EFC (Expected Family Contribution) formula in student financial aid application.
4. Describe the major student financial assistance programs available through the U.S. Department of Education.
5. Describe the campus-based student financial aid programs available to college students.
6. Describe the several financial aid programs available to college students.
7. List the benefits of Qualified Tuition Plans (QTPs).
8. Describe the various income-tax saving financial aid vehicles.
9. Understand how time value of money concepts are used to help calculate the cost of a child's education.

INTRODUCTION

One of the most common financial planning goals of parents is to provide an education for their children. Education funding is a common area of concern for those seeking financial planning advice because paying for higher education is one of the largest financial burdens a family will face. Even clients with high-income levels must take into account paying for their children's tuition and school-related expenses. Recently, educational costs have dramatically outpaced inflation. Over the past ten years, tuition at colleges and universities throughout the country increased at an average annual rate of 6 percent. The Consumer Price Index (CPI) over the past ten years averaged 2 percent. Also, recent trends show an increase in the number of years students remain in college and increased requirements for postgraduate education. Along with the expense of a home and taxes, providing for a child's education is one of the largest expenses for families, and one of the most important decisions.

EXHIBIT 7.1: ANNUAL TUITION INCREASE TO CPI (1996–2005)

8.0%
7.0%
6.0%
5.0%
4.0%
3.0%
2.0%
1.0%
0.0%

1996 1997 1998 1999 2000 2001 2002 2003 2004 2005

☐ Education Inflation ■ CPI Inflation

Source: Trends in College Pricing 2005. Copyright 2005 by College Entrance Examination Board. www.collegeboard.com

Exhibit 7.1 above illustrates that, on average, tuition costs have increased at a rate 3 percent to 4 percent greater than inflation. It is important for a financial planner to determine these types of economic factors when developing clients plans to fund their children's education.

This chapter discusses how to develop a plan for funding a child's education by addressing the issues that must be raised, the information that must be gathered, and the goals that should be set, taking the family's circumstances into account. Once the goals have been set, the implementation of the plan will depend on the sources of funding available, which may include a savings campaign, financial aid, and various payment options. Once the plan is designed and the strategies have been identified, action must be taken to implement and monitor the plan.

ISSUES AND GOALS

In order to formulate a plan that best meets the needs of the particular family, goals must be identified and agreed upon, so that appropriate provisions can be made to achieve those goals. The key is to set feasible, realistic goals.

When formulating a plan for the education of a child, one of the most significant considerations is how much time exists before the child enters college. There are many options available for parents of very young children who are years away from entering college. Those parents with children nearing college age or currently entering college do not have as many options and savings methods. It cannot be stressed enough that, as with most areas of planning, time is crucial in planning for a child's education. Time allows consistent and persistent contributions toward savings vehicles, allowing them to grow and, hopefully, meet or surpass the cost of tuition. Meanwhile, inflation will continue to drive tuition costs higher over the time horizon. It will clearly be less stressful and easier to manage tuition costs, however, with the benefit of ten, fifteen or more years of saving versus evaluating options, one's ability to pay, and formulating a plan during the student's junior or senior year in high school. In addition to concerns about college tuition, families should set goals as to whether they want to fund private elementary and secondary school education for their children. A family should also decide if they desire to provide some or all funding for graduate or professional school education.

One way for parents to ultimately defray the cost of education is paying for only a portion of the child's college expenses, while leaving some of the expenses to be paid by the child. Some view this method as a way of building character for the child and of "educating" the child in accepting responsibility, without forcing the child to assume all financial responsibility for college-related expenses that may burden the child with overwhelming loans and debt when beginning a career. Again, decisions such as these will depend on the preferences and desires of the parents.

During the goal-setting process, some individuals struggle with the notion of sending their children to public elementary and/or secondary school while investing resources during this time to a college education fund. This decision is often based on the quality of the public education available to the child. The parents should also consider that, while private elementary and/or secondary education will require more funds, there may be a "return" on that investment through the child obtaining a more advanced education and perhaps acceptance to prestigious colleges that may provide less stringent financial aid requirements or scholarships. Of course, these are issues that a financial planner should discuss with the parents so that they can make an informed decision based upon their own circumstances. Although there are many important issues and financial decisions to be made regarding elementary and secondary education, the majority of this chapter will deal with preparation and planning for a child's college expenses.

Parents should be reminded that families are in a better position to fund college expenses over a long time period because their income will likely increase in future years. This will motivate some parents to begin a savings regimen that does not meet all financial requirements right away, but can be increased as the years progress, and provide an incentive to increase savings as college years grow nearer.

INFORMATION GATHERING

During the goal-setting process, financial planners must forecast anticipated tuition and related expenses. This forecasting can be accomplished by first determining current tuition and related expenses for the schools in the area and for the schools that the parents believe would be appropriate for the child. This information can be found by calling the school's administrative office. Additionally, there are numerous college guides in bookstores and local libraries that provide tuition and room and board expenses at colleges and universities throughout the country. Such information is available on the Internet by using the search query "college tuition and financial aid," or by accessing *www.collegeboard.com* and its publications, including Trends in College Pricing or Trends in Student Aid.

Once these expenses are obtained, the financial planner must adjust these expenses to account for inflation until the child enters college. The planner must assume a tuition inflation rate, probably between 5 and 8 percent per year for college and related expenses, and then calculate the anticipated expenses for each year the child will attend college.

EXAMPLE

Assumptions:

- Child's current age — 10 yrs.
- Anticipated college age — 18–22 yrs.
- Current tuition and room and board — $13,000/year
- Tuition inflation rate — 6 percent

Estimated costs (future value or actual cost) of tuition and room and board:

- Freshman Year — $20,720 [$13,000 × $(1.06)^8$]
- Sophomore Year — $21,963 [$13,000 × $(1.06)^9$]
- Junior Year — $23,281 [$13,000 × $(1.06)^{10}$]
- Senior Year — $24,678 [$13,000 × $(1.06)^{11}$]

Once these expenses have been identified and adjusted for inflation, one can determine the estimated 4-year cost of a college education. As will be discussed later in this chapter, depending on how much money will be available when the child enters college, a formula can be used to determine how much money must be invested now, over time, to meet the amount of savings necessary for college (i.e., the Expected Family Contribution). Other expenses that should be considered are books and school supplies, transportation, travel expenses, entertainment and the like, as shown in Exhibit 7.2.

Because college is such a major investment, families should carefully evaluate potential schools. Some of the information families should obtain includes a copy of the documents describing the school's accreditation and licensing, current school tuition, and on-campus room and board. Also, families should ask about the school's loan default rate. The default rate is the percentage of students who attend the school, obtain federal student loans, and ultimately fail to repay the loan. This information is important because schools with high default rates may not be eligible to obtain federal aid for certain federal financial assistance programs. This may also indicate a pattern of poorly matched students with the school.

EXHIBIT 7.2: COLLEGE EXPENSES CHECKLIST

These are the college expenses that most families should keep in mind when planning for payment of a child's education:

- Tuition and tuition-related expenses.
- Books, school supplies, and equipment (calculator, computer).
- Lodging.
- Meals.
- Transportation.
- Entertainment (school sporting events) and leisure (health club).
- Travel expenses.
- Tutoring (if necessary).
- Extra-curricular (fraternity/sorority dues).
- Clothing and attire.
- Other considerations particular to the student or family.

If a school advertises its job placement rates, it must also publish the most recent employment statistics, graduation statistics, and any other information that would justify its representations. Another relevant item of information is the school's refund policy. If a student enrolls but never attends classes, the student should be refunded the majority of his or her money. If a student begins attending classes but leaves prior to completing his or her coursework, the student may be able to receive a partial refund. Many state universities and certain private colleges allow for prepayment of tuition at current prices for enrollment in the future, up to even ten years prior to the child's enrollment. The individual schools can provide information on these programs and the inherent risks in participating in them. Prepaid tuition plans are discussed later in this chapter.

A prospective student can obtain the following financial aid availability information from a school:

- Availability of financial assistance, including information on all federal, state, local, private, and institutional financial aid programs.
- Procedures and deadlines for submitting financial aid program applications.
- The school's process for determining a financial aid applicant's eligibility.
- The school's method for determining a student's financial need.
- The school's method for determining each type and amount of assistance in a student's financial aid package.
- How and when the student will receive financial aid.
- The school's method for determining whether the student is making satisfactory academic progress, and the consequences if the student is not (whether the student continues to receive federal financial aid depends, in part, on whether the student makes satisfactory academic progress).
- If the student is awarded a job through the Federal Work-Study program, what type of job is involved, the amount of hours the student must work, the duties of the student in that job, the rate of pay, and how and when the student will be paid.
- The availability and counseling procedures of the school's financial aid office.

The client may also wish to ask the school for a copy of its "equity-in-athletics" report. Any coeducational school where a student can receive federal financial aid that has an interschool athletic program must prepare an equity-in-athletics report giving financial and statistical information for men's and women's sports. This information is designed to advise students of a school's commitment to providing equitable athletic opportunities for its men and women students.

The client should also be encouraged to consult with high school counselors, local employers, and the state higher education agency. These are invaluable sources of information for those exploring options of higher education.

DETERMINING FINANCIAL NEED

As mentioned earlier, most financial aid packages depend heavily on the financial need of the student. It is, therefore, important to evaluate whether a client may have the requisite financial need when estimating costs of tuition and availability of funds for college.

FAFSA - an application form that must be submitted by a college student to become eligible for federal financial aid

The financial aid process is initiated by filling out financial aid forms available from high schools, the United States Department of Education, or from the college the student will attend. This financial aid application form is called a **FAFSA**," which stands for "**Free Application for Federal Student Aid**." A FAFSA must be submitted by the student applicant to become eligible for federal financial aid. The student can obtain and complete a FAFSA application in one of the following ways:

- ▲ Complete and mail a paper FAFSA, which can be obtained from the student's high school, potential college to attend, or college where attending.
- ▲ Have the student's school submit the completed FAFSA electronically.
- ▲ Use "FAFSA on the Web" (*www.fafsa.ed.gov*) through the Internet.

Colleges usually appoint an agency to conduct an analysis of the financial need of the student and the student's family. The completed information on the FAFSA is sent to colleges requested by the applicant. The college may also have the applicant complete other forms to enable the college to conduct its own needs analysis of the student. Once the student is accepted to a college, the college may inform the student at that time of any available financial aid.

EFC - (Expected Family Contribution) a formula that indicates how much of a student's family's resources ought to be available to assist in paying for the student's college education. Some of the factors used in this calculation include taxable and nontaxable income, assets, retirement funds, and benefits, such as unemployment and Social Security

When applying for student financial assistance, the information reported by the applicant is used in a formula established by Congress. The formula is called the **Expected Family Contribution** or "**EFC**" for a child's education. The EFC indicates how much of a student's family's resources ought to be available to assist in paying for the student's education. Some of the factors used in this calculation include taxable and nontaxable income, assets, retirement funds, and benefits, such as unemployment and Social Security.

Although low-income families are more likely to qualify for financial aid than higher-income families, higher-income families should not be discouraged from applying for aid because the EFC formula also takes into account various factors including the number of children in private school or college, the size of the family, the amount of years until the parents' retirement, and large financial burdens, such as medical bills. The EFC calculation is used to determine eligibility for financial aid programs, except for unsubsidized student loans and PLUS loans, which are provided regardless of financial need. If the EFC is below a certain amount, the student may be eligible for financial aid, such as a Federal Pell Grant, assuming other eligibility requirements are met. Such eligibility requirements include the cost of attendance at the school (tuition, room and board, and related expenses), full-time, half-time or part-time status, and academic standing.

There is no maximum EFC because the EFC is used in a calculation depending on where the student attends school and the cost of attendance at that school. Here is how it works. When the student consults with his or her school's financial aid administrator, the financial aid administrator will calculate the student's financial need by subtracting the student's EFC from the cost of attendance at the school. The remaining figure equals the student's *financial need.* The formula is as follows:

Tuition/Cost of Attendance	$ Amount
– Expected Family Contribution (EFC)	– $ Amount
Financial Need	$ Amount

As is evident from the above calculation, a student may have financial need at one school but not another, because financial need turns on the cost of attendance, whereas the student's EFC remains constant for the year regardless of which school the student attends. Financial aid administrators, however, in their discretion, can adjust the cost of attendance or adjust data in calculating a student's EFC if circumstances so require. For more information on the EFC calculation, the *EFC Formula Book* describes how a student's EFC is calculated and can be obtained through the Federal Student Aid Information Center, 1-800-433-3243, or on the Internet at *http://studentaid.ed.gov.*

It is at this point that most individuals ask how can they reduce their EFC. In other words, how can a family reduce the amount of money that it is expected to contribute to a child's education in order to receive more financial assistance? There are various methods that a family can use to reduce EFC. First, however, one must determine the dependency status of the student.

The income and assets of the student's family will only be counted if the student is considered dependent on the parents. If the student applying for financial aid is independent, then only the student's income and assets will be considered. The reasoning behind this rule is that a student who has access to parental support should not be able to reap the benefits of student financial aid programs to the exclusion of those needy, independent students who do not have access to parental support. A student is considered independent if he or she meets <u>any one</u> of the following criteria:

- ▲ Over the age of 23.
- ▲ Married.
- ▲ Is working on a master's or doctorate degree.
- ▲ Has legal dependents other than a spouse.
- ▲ Is an orphan or ward of the court, or was a ward of the court until age 18.
- ▲ Is a veteran of the U.S. Armed Forces.

Another common method for reducing a family's EFC is creating a trust for the child and diminishing the family's estate through gifts. This may create problems, however, because the child's own assets will be considered in the child's financial needs analysis. A family may also reduce its

EFC by providing all information surrounding the factors that tend to diminish their EFC, such as high medical bills and more than one child in the family attends college. Finally, the school's financial aid advisor may be able to adjust a family's EFC if the circumstances so require. Here, the burden is on the family or student to communicate information to the financial aid advisor that may reduce their EFC.

FINANCIAL AID PROGRAMS

The United States Department of Education has the following major student financial assistance programs:

- Federal Pell Grant.
- Stafford Loan.
- PLUS Loan.
- Consolidation Loan.
- Federal Supplemental Educational Opportunity Grant (FSEOG).
- Federal Work-Study and Federal Perkins Loans.

These federal programs are the largest sources of student aid in the United States. According to the U.S. Department of Education, available student aid topped $122 billion in 2004.

EXHIBIT 7.3: FEDERAL AID AWARDED

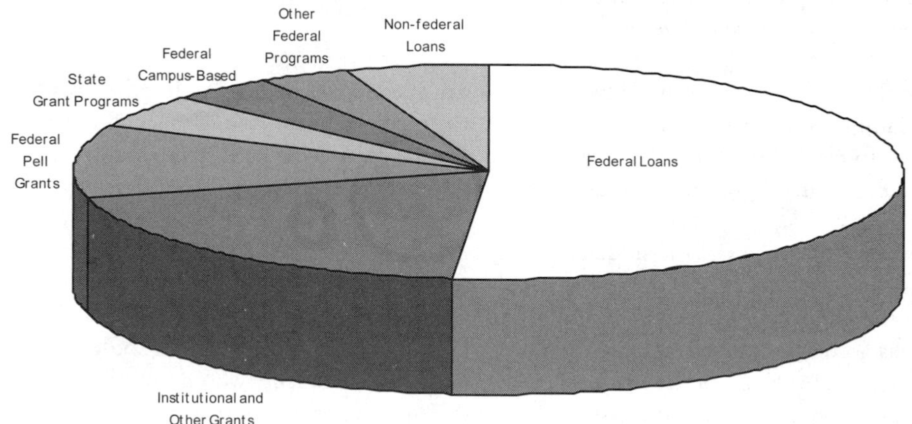
Other Federal Programs
Non-federal Loans
Federal Campus-Based
State Grant Programs
Federal Pell Grants
Federal Loans
Institutional and Other Grants

Reproduced with permission from the College Board. Copyright 2004 by College Entrance Examination Board. All Rights Reserved.

Pell Grant - a grant from the federal government awarded to undergraduate students who have not earned bachelors or professional degrees. The EFC calculation, which is based on one's financial need, is used to determine a student's eligibility for a Pell Grant and how much is awarded to a student.

The subsections below identify and describe these federal programs, as well as some state, and other programs.

FEDERAL PELL GRANTS

A Federal **Pell Grant** is not a loan. It is a grant from the federal government that does not require repayment. The EFC calculation, which is based on one's financial need, is used to determine a student's eligibility for a Pell Grant and how much is awarded to a student. Pell

Grants are awarded to undergraduate students who have not earned bachelors or professional degrees. Graduate, professional, and postgraduate students are not awarded Pell Grants. Maximum awards for Pell Grants were $4,050 per student for the 2004-2005 school year. The application deadline for the 2004-2005 award period is June 30, 2005. Each year's awards depend on program funding for that year. A student can receive only one Pell Grant award per year. A student can still receive a Pell Grant if enrolled part time, but will not receive as much as he or she would have received if enrolled full time.

Direct and FFEL Stafford Loans

The **Stafford Loan** is the primary type of financial aid provided by the United States Department of Education. There are two types of Stafford Loans, those being Direct Stafford Loans ("Direct Loans") and Federal Family Education Stafford Loans, or "FFEL Loans." The major differences between Direct and FFEL Stafford Loans are the sources of the loan funds and the available repayment plans. Under the **Direct Stafford Loan** system, funds are provided directly to the borrower by the United States government, whereas funds for **FFEL Stafford Loans** are loaned to the student through a lender (such as a bank or other approved financial institution) that participates in the FFEL program.

Stafford Loans are either subsidized or unsubsidized. A subsidized loan means that there is no interest charged on the loan until repayment of the loan begins, which is typically six months after one of the following occurs:

- Graduation.
- Leaving school.
- Dropping below half-time status.

Half-time status is considered half of the minimum hours to be considered full time. For instance, if a school on a semester basis has a 12-hour minimum requirement each semester for a student to be considered full time, the student is considered half time if he or she is enrolled in at least 6 credit hours each semester. The only federal student aid programs that require at least half-time enrollment are the Stafford Direct and FFEL Loan programs. Half-time enrollment is not a requirement in the other financial aid programs, including the Federal Pell Grant, FSEOG, Federal Work Study, and Federal Perkins Loan programs.

The application process differs for each Stafford Loan program. If the school participates in the Direct Stafford Loan program, the Free Application for Federal Student Aid ("FAFSA") serves as the Stafford Loan application. If the school participates in the FFEL Stafford Loan program, the student completes a separate application in addition to the FAFSA.

A subsidized loan is based on the financial need of the student as determined by the EFC formula. An unsubsidized Stafford Loan is a loan in which the borrower is charged interest on the principal from the moment of disbursement until the loan is paid off. Those who receive unsubsidized loans have the option of allowing the interest to be capitalized (which means that the interest accumulates and is added to the principal during the life of the loan until principal reduction payments are required), or the option of paying the interest as it accrues. The process of capitalization costs more over the long-term because the interest that accumulates is added to the principal balance, and subsequent interest is charged on the entire outstanding balance.

Stafford Loan - the primary type of financial aid provided by the United States Department of Education. There are two types of Stafford Loans: Direct Stafford Loans ("Direct Loans") and Federal Family Education Stafford Loans, or "FFEL Loans".

Direct Stafford Loan - federal financial aid funds provided by the U.S. Dept. of Education directly to the student

FFEL Stafford Loans - are loaned to the student through a lender (such as a bank or other approved financial institution) that participates in the FFEL program

However, some students or their families may not be in a financial position to pay the interest while the student is in school, and the capitalization method provides them with the option of postponing payment. All Stafford Loans have below-market interest rates that cannot exceed 8.25 percent.

When Stafford Loans are disbursed to a student, approximately 4 percent of the loan is deducted to help defray the cost of the loan and help pay for the administrative costs of the Stafford Loan program. Thus, when determining the amount of funds through Stafford Loans required for a school term, the student must remember that the disbursement for a $7,000 Stafford Loan, for example, will only be $6,720 [$7,000 × 4 percent = $280; $7,000 – $280 = $6,720] or [$7,000 × 96 percent = $6,720]. In other words, the actual disbursement to the student will be roughly 4 percent less than the face amount of the loan, which the student must pay back.

Repayment of Stafford Loans begins after a grace period of six months following graduation, leaving school, or dropping below half-time enrollment. The subsidized Stafford Loan is attractive because no interest is charged and no principal payment is required during the six-month grace period. Essentially, the student has received a free loan during school and for six months thereafter under the subsidized loan program. Once the grace period is over, however, the subsidized loan begins to accrue interest, and principal and interest reduction payments must begin. Although interest is charged during the grace period on an unsubsidized Stafford Loan, no repayment of principal or interest is required during the grace period. By not paying the interest on an unsubsidized loan during the grace period, the interest accrues and continues to be capitalized.

Students may obtain a "deferment" of the loan, which is a temporary postponement of payments on the loan. If the student has a subsidized loan, interest will not be charged during the period of deferment. For unsubsidized loans, the interest is capitalized during deferment unless the student chooses to pay the interest as it accrues during deferment. A deferment is allowed only after proving "special circumstances" to the agency, sender, or holder of the loan. The circumstances that may give rise to a deferment of repayment on a Stafford Loan include the following:

- At least half-time enrollment at a post-secondary school.
- Enrollment in an approved fellowship program.
- Enrollment in an approved rehabilitation training program for the disabled.
- Economic hardship (for up to 3 years).
- Former student's inability to attain full-time employment (for up to 3 years).

Forbearance is a period of time when repayment of a loan is temporarily postponed upon request of a borrower and authorization by the lender. While forbearance also postpones repayment, subsidized loans accrue interest during the period of forbearance. Direct Stafford Loans can be repaid under several payment plans. Each payment plan has a different term ranging from 10 to 32 years. FFEL Stafford Loans can also be repaid under several payment plans, but cannot exceed a 10-year term.

Under certain conditions Stafford loans may be canceled or recipients may receive repayment assistance. One of the following conditions must be met for the loan to be canceled:

- ▲ Death of the student or borrower (i.e. parent of student).
- ▲ The borrower becomes totally and permanently disabled.
- ▲ The student is a full-time teacher for five consecutive years in a designated elementary or secondary school serving students from low-income families.
- ▲ The loan is discharged in bankruptcy.
- ▲ The student's school closes before the student completes the program.
- ▲ The school falsely certifies the loan.

Repayment assistance may be available to students who serve in the military or become registered nurses and serve in eligible facilities in areas experiencing a nursing shortage.

PLUS Loans

PLUS Loans (Parent Loans for Undergraduate Students) are loans that are available through the Direct Loan and FFEL programs. PLUS Loans allow parents with good credit histories to borrow funds for a child's educational expenses. The child must be a dependent student in at least half-time enrollment and be enrolled in an eligible program at an eligible school. The parents complete a PLUS Loan application and Promissory Note with the school's financial aid office. As long as the parents do not have an adverse credit history, they may be entitled to receive a loan equal to the cost of attendance less any other available financial aid.

PLUS Loans (Parent Loans for Undergraduate Students) - loans available through the Direct Loan and FFEL programs that allow parents with good credit histories to borrow funds for a child's educational expenses

For instance, if the cost of attendance is $7,500 and the student has $5,000 in other financial aid, then the parents could borrow up to, but no more than, $2,500. The interest rate on a PLUS Loan is variable, but will never exceed 9 percent. Interest accrues on the loan from the moment of disbursement until the loan is paid off. As with Stafford Loans, a fee of roughly 4 percent is deducted from the funds disbursed to help defray the cost of the loan to the government. At least two disbursements of funds are made because no installment may exceed half of the loan amount.

Normally, parents must begin repaying PLUS Loans within 60 days after the final loan disbursement for the current academic year. Parents must commence repayment of both principal and interest while the student is in school. The same rules that apply to deferment or forbearance of Stafford Loans apply to PLUS Loans as well. However, because PLUS Loans are not subsidized, interest will continue to accrue and will thus be capitalized during the period of deferment or forbearance. PLUS Loans must be repaid within 10 years.

Consolidation Loans

A **Consolidation Loan** provides borrowers with a vehicle to consolidate various types of federal student loans that have separate repayment schedules into one loan. The Consolidation Loan program benefits student and parent borrowers by extending the term of repayment, requiring only one payment per month, and in some cases providing a lower interest rate than on one or more of the loans. The loan interest rate is capped at 8.25 percent. The school's financial aid adviser can explain the many combinations of Consolidation Loan options.

Consolidation Loan - a loan that provides borrowers with a way to consolidate various types of federal student loans that have separate repayment schedules into one loan

Campus-Based Student Financial Aid

There are three "campus-based" programs that are administered directly by the financial aid office at participating schools. The three programs are:

- The Federal Supplemental Education Opportunity Grant (FSEOG) Program.
- The Federal Work-Study Program.
- The Federal Perkins Loan Program.

Each program extends aid based on financial need of the student and the availability of funds at the school.

FSEOG (Federal Supplemental Education Opportunity Grant) - campus-based student financial aid grant awarded to undergraduate students with low EFCs that gives priority to students who receive federal Pell Grants

The Federal Supplemental Education Opportunity Grant Program

A **FSEOG** is a grant, an outright gift, which need not be repaid. The FSEOG is awarded to undergraduate students with low EFCs who have not obtained a bachelor's or professional degree and gives priority to students who receive Federal Pell Grants. The difference between a Federal Pell Grant and an FSEOG is that the United States Department of Education guarantees that each eligible school will receive sufficient funds to pay Federal Pell Grants to all eligible students, whereas an FSEOG is paid to eligible students if funds are available. Once all available FSEOG funds are used at the school, remaining eligible students will not receive an FSEOG grant. The FSEOG is in the range of $100 to $4,000 per academic year. The amount paid depends on the level of need, the time of application, and the school's funding level.

Federal Work-Study Program - campus-based student financial aid program that enables undergraduate and graduate students to earn money for education expenses through jobs that pay at least current minimum wages but do not exceed the award received through the program

The Federal Work-Study Program

Federal Work-Study Programs enable undergraduate and graduate students with financial need to earn money for education expenses through jobs that pay at least current minimum wages. Some jobs may pay higher hourly rates depending on the work done and skill required. The amount earned through the Federal Work-Study program cannot exceed the award received through the program. Federal Work-Study jobs are both on campus and off campus depending on the employer participating in the program.

The Federal Perkins Loan Program

Federal Perkins Loan - campus-based, low-interest student loan that is provided to undergraduate and graduate students that have exceptional financial need, that is, very low EFCs

A **Federal Perkins Loan** is a loan that is provided to undergraduate and graduate students that have exceptional financial need (i.e., very low EFCs). Although the loan is made with government funds, the school is the lender. The student must repay the loan, but the benefit of the Perkins Loan is that it is a low 5 percent interest loan. Unlike Stafford and PLUS Loans, there is no 4 percent charge or fee for a Perkins Loan. After graduation, leaving school, or dropping below half-time status, there is a nine-month grace period for repayment of a Perkins Loan. The Perkins Loan must be repaid within 10 years from the start of repayment. In addition to the same rules as Stafford and PLUS Loans for deferment, forbearance, repayment assistance, and cancellation, the Perkins Loan can also be canceled under the following conditions:

- The student is a full-time employee of a public or nonprofit agency that provides services to high-risk children and their families.
- The student is a full-time qualified professional provider of early intervention services for the disabled.
- The student is a full-time nurse, medical technician, law enforcement officer, or teacher in a field designated as a teacher shortage area.
- The student is serving in the Armed Forces in areas of hostilities or imminent danger.
- The student is a full-time staff member in the education component of a Head Start Program.
- The student is a Vista or Peace Corps volunteer.

These cancellation conditions are subject to certain tests and can be explained by the school's financial aid adviser.

For more information about federal education programs and financial aid applications, visit the United States Department of Education's website at *www.ed.gov.*

State Governmental Aid

Most states have programs that are very similar to the federal student financial aid programs discussed above. The state programs rely heavily on the financial need of the student as well as the student's superior academic performance. States also require that the student be a resident of the state and attend a college or university in that state. Information on a given state's financial aid programs can be obtained from the school to be attended or that state's Department of Education.

Other Financial Aid Sources

Aid Directly From The Institution

Each school has its own method of providing aid through loans, scholarships, discounts, and campus jobs. The school's financial aid advisor should adequately explain to the student the school's available options and programs. Some schools will allow a student to pay tuition on a monthly installment plan, which may provide more flexibility to the student and parents. Other schools may offer discounts or scholarships for superior athletic or academic performance either prior to or after enrollment. The school has an incentive to entice superior athletes and academic students in order to increase their level of top students and to better compete with other schools, which in turn enhances the school's image.

Aid from Armed Forces

The U.S. Armed Forces have numerous programs and scholarships that may pay for tuition, fees, and books for those who enlist or enroll in the military. The student may also receive monthly payments for other expenses. Information regarding the many programs available through the U.S. Armed Forces can be obtained from the college attended or from the Administrative Office of the desired branch of military. On the Internet, try any of the following websites for Armed Forces aid:

- *www.armyrotc.com*
- *www.goarmy.com/benefits/education.jsp*
- *www.gibill.va.gov*
- *www.usmc.mil*
- *www.af.mil*
- *www.uscg.mil*

Other Grants, Scholarships, and Fellowships

There are many forms of scholarships that are awarded by groups that are separate and apart from the school and state, or federal government. For instance, there are numerous civic organizations, like the American Legion, the Knights of Columbus, and the Boy Scouts of America, that award scholarships based on need, merit, and/or the student's or parents' affiliation with that civic organization. Of course, there are various types of scholarships available to students who have high grades and high standardized (entrance) test scores, including National Merit Scholarships. Also, scholarships can be provided through a particular church or religious organization. Although finding out about these scholarships will take some effort, it may prove to be time well spent.

In addition to scholarships, which typically do not include funds for living expenses, many organizations offer grants and fellowships. Grants and fellowships are similar to scholarships in that the funds awarded do not require repayment. Grants, however, are need-based awards, and fellowships are generally awarded to graduate students based on academic merit and include living expenses as well as funds for tuition and fees.

TAX ADVANTAGES FROM EDUCATIONAL EXPENSES AND TAX ISSUES

Although much time has been spent in this chapter discussing the costs of education and the rise in educational expenses, there is some tax relief available. There are various vehicles available that allow the family or taxpayer who bear the brunt of education expenses to realize tax savings and benefits.

QUALIFIED TUITION PLANS

One increasingly popular vehicle used to prepare for college tuition and related costs are **"qualified Tuition Plans," or QTPs**. In 1996, Congress enacted Section 529 of the Internal Revenue Code (IRC) through the Small Business Job Protection Act of 1996. Section 529 was modified by the Taxpayer Relief Act of 1997. The Taxpayer Relief Act of 1997 also created Roth IRAs and the Coverdell Education Savings Account(s) (or Coverdell ESA). Section 529 provides tax-exempt status to QTPs created, sponsored, and maintained by individual states. QTPs are also commonly referred to as "529 Plans" after IRC Section 529. The Internal Revenue Code permits the states to enact and tailor their own QTPs within the parameters established by Section 529. All fifty states have 529 Plans/QTPs, and tax laws have made it possible for institutions of higher education to establish their own 529 Plans. In addition to state sponsored plans and plans associated with a specific college or university, the Tuition Plan Consortium, a nonprofit consortium of independent colleges and universities, offers a national prepaid tuition plan for private institutions.

QTPs - (Qualified Tuition Plans) also known as 529 plans, QTPs allow individuals to either participate in prepaid tuition plans in which tuition credits are purchased for a designated beneficiary for payment or waiver of higher education expenses, or participate in savings plans in which contributions of money are made to an account to eventually pay for higher education expenses of a designated beneficiary

The Benefits of QTPs

The benefits of QTPs are:

- Tax-deferred growth.
- Distributions from qualified tuition programs are excludible from gross income.
- The contributor can remove assets from his or her taxable estate.
- QTPs generally charge low commissions and have low management fees.
- Many states provide state tax deductions and/or tax exemptions for at least a portion of contributions.
- The contributor/owner has full control of the asset and can change the beneficiary.

Although each state's QTP legislation varies and has different features, all basically provide for at least one of two types of plans, Prepaid Tuition Plans and Savings Plans. QTPs allow individuals to either participate in Prepaid Tuition Plans whereby tuition credits are purchased for a designated beneficiary for payment or waiver of higher education expenses, or participate in Savings Plans whereby contributions of money are made to an account to eventually pay for higher education expenses of a designated beneficiary.

PREPAID TUITION PLANS

Prepaid Tuition Plans are plans where prepayment of tuition is allowed at current prices for enrollment in the future. In other words, the parent can "lock in" future tuition at current rates. Participating in a school's prepayment program presupposes that the child will ultimately attend that school for college. The parents also assume the risk that the child will not meet the school's academic and admission requirements. Starting a tuition prepayment plan years in advance further prevents the student from choosing his or her own college. Other risks include the possibility that the student may be the recipient of a scholarship to that or another college. More particularly, the college chosen for tuition prepayment, although a well-respected and accredited school, could have a less than desirable curriculum in the student's major or particular area of interest. The client should weigh these risks with the benefits obtained at the particular school through tuition prepayment. Unused prepaid tuition benefits can be transferred to another family member held for possible future use. Refund and transfer options are available, but it is

Prepaid Tuition Plans - plans where prepayment of college tuition is allowed at current prices for enrollment in the future; in other words, a parent can "lock in" future tuition at current rates

recommended that the family fully investigate the terms and conditions of the specific prepaid tuition plan so that the family will understand the consequences if the student attends a different college, fails to meet academic qualifications, or does not attend college at all. Various prepaid tuition plans treat these and other events differently.

SAVINGS PLANS

Savings Plan - a type of QTP similar to Coverdell Education Savings Accounts (Coverdell ESAs) where the owner of the account, (the parent or grandparent of the student) contributes cash to the account so that the contributions can grow tax deferred and, hopefully, realize a higher return on the investment than could be achieved outside of the plan

Savings Plans are similar to Coverdell Education Savings Accounts (Coverdell ESAs), but have different attributes, rules, and tax ramifications, as will be seen below. In a Savings Plan, the owner of the account, the parent or grandparent, contributes money to the account so that the contributions can grow tax deferred and, hopefully, realize a higher return on the investment than could be achieved outside of the plan. Section 529 requires that all contributions to the program be made exclusively in cash.

QTPs are attractive to states because they can provide incentives to residents and nonresidents (depending on the state's individual plan) to invest in higher education and into that state's educational system. These plans are inexpensive for states to run, as many states provide turn-key contracts to financial services firms or investment companies to professionally manage the statewide plan. For instance, Merrill Lynch manages all QTPs for Maine, Fidelity Investments manages all QTPs for New Hampshire, and Salomon Smith Barney manages QTPs for Colorado.

It is generally recognized that Savings Plans have distinct advantages over Prepaid Tuition Plans. First, payment to a state's Savings Plan does not prohibit the owner/contributor from withdrawing money and paying for tuition at an out-of-state school. Savings Plans allow the owner/contributor to invest his or her money into a pool and experience growth on the return on the investment. Prepaid Tuition Plans allow the owner/contributor to "lock in" on current tuition rates for college in later years, which is only attractive if the rising rate of tuition exceeds the client's after-tax rate of return. One perceived disadvantage of Savings Plans is that the owner/contributor does not have the right to choose how contributions are invested. However, a plan can permit the contributor/owner to select among different investment strategies (i.e. conservative) designed exclusively for the program when the initial contribution is made to establish the account. Managers of Savings Plans generally decrease the percentage of investment in growth/equity funds as the beneficiary gets older and closer to college, while the percentage of investment into bonds and money market funds increases as the beneficiary ages. However, the income tax and estate tax advantages of QTPs and the risks inherent in Prepaid Tuition Plans, as discussed earlier, generally make Savings Plans more advantageous for those who take time to plan their tax and saving strategies.

One of the most alluring attributes of QTPs is that the owner/contributor controls the account, makes the withdrawals to pay for expenses, and can change beneficiaries. Do not confuse control of the account with control of the specific investments. A plan can permit the contributor to select among different investment strategies designed exclusively for the program when the initial contribution is made to establish the account. The Internal Revenue Code (IRC) states that neither the contributor nor the beneficiary can direct the investment. However, the account owner can change the investment strategy selection one time per year. The owner/contributor, not the student/beneficiary, controls the withdrawal and payment of expenses. In contrast, the Uniform Gift to Minors Act, for instance (discussed later in this chapter), provides no safeguard to the contributor if the student decides not to attend college and uses the funds to go sailing to Australia!

The Mechanics of QTPs

The mechanics of QTPs are simple. The owner/contributor withdraws funds from the account to pay for "qualified higher education expenses." Under Section 529, qualified higher education expenses are defined as tuition, fees, books, supplies, and equipment required for attendance or enrollment at an eligible educational institution, as well as certain room and board expenses for students who attend an eligible educational institution at least half time. An eligible educational institution is an accredited postsecondary educational institution that offers credit toward a Bachelor's degree, an Associate's degree, a graduate-level or professional degree, or another recognized postsecondary credential. The institution must be eligible to participate in Department of Education student aid programs.

Withdrawals used to pay for qualified higher education expenses are free from federal income tax. If, however, a portion or all of the withdrawal is spent on anything other than qualified higher education expenses, the owner/contributor will be taxed at his or her own tax rate on the earnings portion of the withdrawal and will be subject to a 10 percent penalty. A penalty is not imposed if the beneficiary dies or becomes disabled or if the beneficiary receives a scholarship.

A qualified program must provide adequate safeguards to prevent contributions in excess of those necessary to provide for the qualified higher education expenses of the beneficiary. Some states utilize the highest tuition in the state as a limit on contributions. Many states with college savings plans have maximum contribution limits of more than $200,000, although some states limit contributions to no more than $3,000 per year.

Taxes and the QTP

As previously discussed, a student's financial aid eligibility depends on the student's and family's financial condition. The existence of a QTP may affect the formula calculation for a student depending on the type of plan involved. For instance, a Savings Plan is deemed an asset of the parent who is the owner/contributor of the account.

Contributions to QTPs are deemed to qualify for the annual $11,000 gift tax exclusion. A five-year averaging election for purposes of the gift tax annual exclusion may be applied to the transfer. If one's contributions exceed $11,000, the contributor is permitted to spread out one contribution over a five-year period. For example, if John (father-contributor) contributes $35,000 to a QTP account for Matthew (beneficiary-child) in one year, then John can elect to spread this contribution over five years, that is, $7,000 per year, and avoid a gift tax (less than the $11,000 annual exclusion). The QTP thus permits the owner/contributor to shift his or her taxable estate to the beneficiary without taxation.

Any distribution or in-kind benefit that is transferred within 60 days under a QTP to the credit of a new designated beneficiary who is a family member of the old designated beneficiary shall not be treated as a distribution, and thus is beyond income taxation and penalty. A change in the designated beneficiary of an interest in a QTP shall not be treated as a distribution if the new beneficiary is a family member of the old beneficiary. Unless the transfer occurs between spouses, the transfer is a taxable gift from the old beneficiary to the new beneficiary regardless of whether the new beneficiary is a member of the family. In addition, the transfer will be subject to the generation-skipping transfer tax if the new beneficiary is assigned to a generation that is two or more levels lower than the generation assignment of the old beneficiary.

Except to the extent provided in the regulations, a tuition program maintained by a private institution is not treated as qualified unless it has received a ruling or determination from the IRS that the program satisfies applicable requirements. This exclusion from gross income for qualified education expenses is extended to distributions from qualified tuition programs established and maintained by an entity other than a State for distributions made in taxable years after December 31, 2003. The tax-exempt status of these non-state sponsored distributions will end on December 31, 2010.

QTPs are extremely useful tools that provide significant tax savings, allow for substantial investments for a child's education, and provide a tool for avoidance of gift and estate taxes if used correctly. When comparing the tax savings alone from a QTP Savings Plan versus a taxable account, the tax benefits can prove to be substantial. If a family contributes $300 per month to a taxable account earning 10 percent annually for 16 years, the accumulated value of the account would be approximately $100,000 if the assumed federal and state tax rates total 34 percent. However, if that same $300 monthly contribution is made for 16 years into a QTP earning 10 percent annually the account would be worth approximately $140,000. The difference is a tax savings of approximately $40,000.

Coverdell Education Savings Account (Coverdell ESAs) - an investment account established with cash contributions are that grow tax free within the account. Money withdrawn from the account remains free from tax or penalty if the funds are used for higher educational expenses. If not, the earnings are subject to income tax and a 10 percent penalty.

COVERDELL EDUCATION SAVINGS ACCOUNTS

Coverdell Education Savings Accounts (Coverdell ESAs), formerly known as Educational IRAs, were also authorized by the Taxpayer Relief Act of 1997. Coverdell ESAs are designed to offer tax benefits to those individuals who wish to save money for a child/grandchild's qualified education expenses. A Coverdell is an investment account established with cash that is not tax deductible. The contributions are made for the benefit of children who are under 18 years of age. The contributions are allowed to grow tax free within the account. Money withdrawn from the account is free from tax or penalty if the funds are used for qualified educational expenses. If the funds are used for anything other than qualified education expenses, the earnings are subject to income tax and a 10 percent penalty.

Coverdell ESA permit up to $2,000 in annual contributions, whereas QTPs allow large contributions. However, if the individual family plans to contribute only $2,000 or less annually to the student/beneficiary's college fund, then Coverdell ESAs might be more attractive because they offer the same tax benefits as 529 plans and the owner/contributor has the power to direct the specific investments. A person contributing funds to a Coverdell ESA may also contribute funds to a QTP in the same year for the same beneficiary.

A Coverdell can be established for any child under the age of 18 by a parent, grandparent, other family members or friends, or even by the child, as long as the contributor who establishes the account does not have $220,000 ($110,000 for singles) or more of modified family annual gross income (phaseout is $190,000 to $220,000 for married filing jointly and $95,000 to $110,000 for single filers). If, however, money from the Coverdell is not used for qualified education expenses by the designated beneficiary by the time the beneficiary turns 30 years of age, then that eneficiary may not use the money without tax and penalties. However, if the beneficiary reaches 0 years, the Coverdell may be rolled over into a Coverdell for a family member of the original eneficiary.

No contributions can be made to the account once the beneficiary turns 18 years of age. Distributions or withdrawals from Coverdell ESAs are comprised of principal and earnings. The principal portion is always excluded from taxation, whereas earnings are excluded if used to pay for qualified educational expenses. Although contributors may establish more than one account in a given child's name, the aggregate maximum annual contribution is $2,000. Withdrawals are tax free whether the student is enrolled full-time, half-time, or less than half-time as long as the withdrawals do not exceed the child's qualified educational expenses.

The definition of qualified education expenses (beyond under graduate or graduate level courses) that may be paid tax free from a Coverdell ESA include qualified elementary and secondary school expenses. These expenses include: (1) tuition, fees, academic tutoring, special need services, books, supplies, and other equipment incurred in connection with the enrollment or attendance of the beneficiary at a public, private, or religious school providing elementary or secondary education (kindergarten through grade 12) as determined under state law, (2) room and board, uniforms, transportation, and supplementary items or services (including extended day programs) required or provided by such a school in connection with such enrollment or attendance of the beneficiary, and (3) the purchase of any computer technology or equipment or Internet access and related services, if such technology, equipment, or services are to be used by the beneficiary and the beneficiary's family during any of the years the beneficiary is in school.

TRADITIONAL IRA

Generally speaking, if a taxpayer withdraws funds from his or her traditional IRA prior to age 59½, the taxpayer is required to pay a 10 percent early withdrawal penalty on all or part of the amount withdrawn. However, the 10 percent penalty does not apply if a taxpayer withdraws funds from a traditional IRA to pay for qualified higher educational expenses for the taxpayer, the taxpayer's spouse or the child or grandchild of the taxpayer or taxpayer's spouse. Unlike a Coverdell, the taxpayer will owe federal income tax on the amount withdrawn.

ROTH IRA

The **Roth IRA** was also created by the Taxpayer Relief Act of 1997. The Roth IRA does not provide tax deductions for contributions. However, contributions grow tax free within the IRA. Contributions are limited to $4,000 for years 2005 through 2007; and $5,000 in 2008 and thereafter. Contributions can be made as late as the due date of the individual's tax return for the previous tax year. Contributions to a Roth IRA can be made for years beyond age 70½, whereas traditional IRAs prevent contributions after attainment of age 70½. Contributions to Roth IRAs are phased out for joint filers with adjusted gross income between $150,000 and $160,000, and for single taxpayers with adjusted gross income between $95,000 and $110,000.

Roth IRA - an IRA created by the Taxpayer Relief Act of 1997. Contributions to a Roth IRA are nondeductible; qualified distributions are excluded from an individuals taxable income. Distributions used for qualified educational expenses can also avoid the 10 percent penalty.

A distribution from a Roth IRA is not includible in the owner's gross income if it is a "qualified distribution," or to the extent that it is a return of the owner's contributions to the Roth IRA. Qualified distributions are distributions that occur after a five-year holding period and on account of one of the following four reasons:

- ▲ Death.
- ▲ Disability.
- ▲ Attainment of age 59½.
- ▲ First-time house purchase (limit of $10,000).

If a distribution is not a qualified distribution and it exceeds contribution (and conversions) t Roth IRAs, then the distribution will be subject to income tax and may be subject to the 10 per cent penalty. However, these excess distributions can avoid the 10 percent penalty if the proceed are used for qualified higher education costs. Qualified higher educational expenses are tuition fees, and room and board. The taxpayer is always able to withdraw amounts up to their total con tribution without income tax or penalty.

In short, Roth IRAs may be an even more attractive vehicle for education savings than Coverdel ESAs because the age of the student is irrelevant (versus the 30-year-old limit) and because con tribution limits are higher. In addition, funds in a Roth IRA not used for education can be used for retirement.

THE HOPE SCHOLARSHIP CREDIT

HOPE scholarship credit - a tax credit available for qualified tuition and enrollment fees incurred and paid in the first two years of post-secondary education for the taxpayer, spouse, or dependent

The **HOPE scholarship credit** is another by-product of the Taxpayer Relief Act of 1997. This tax credit is available for qualified tuition and enrollment fees incurred and paid in the first two years of post-secondary education for the taxpayer, spouse, or dependent. The HOPE credit is comprised of 100 percent of the first $1,000 of qualified expenses paid in the tax year, plus 50 percent of the next $1,000. The maximum credit allowed in a given year is $1,500 per student. A student must be enrolled no less than half time to be eligible. The HOPE credit is subject to a phaseout based on the taxpayer's adjusted gross income as follows:

AGI PHASEOUT FOR HOPE AND LIFETIME LEARNING CREDITS

	2005	2006 (Projected)
Married filing jointly	$87,000 – $107,000	$89,000 – $107,000
All other taxpayers	$43,000 – $ 53,000	$44,000 – $ 54,000

NOTE: AGI, for purposes of this chart, includes AGI and foreign earned income exclusions and United States possessions and Puerto Rico income exclusions.

THE LIFETIME LEARNING CREDIT

Lifetime learning credit - a tax credit available to pay for tuition and enrollment fees for undergraduate or graduate degree programs

The **Lifetime learning credit** is another by-product of the Taxpayer Relief Act of 1997. This tax credit is available for tuition and enrollment fees for undergraduate or graduate degree programs or courses that help students acquire or improve job skills. The Lifetime learning credit provides annual reimbursement for college tuition and fees per family in the amount of $2,000 per year. The taxpayer must spend $10,000 annually on qualified expenses in order to qualify for the full credit. This credit is based on a 20 percent factor of the qualified expenses.

The Lifetime learning credit can be claimed for an unlimited number of years. If two or more children in the same household incur qualified expenses in the same year, the parents may claim

Lifetime learning credit or HOPE scholarship credit for both children, or a Lifetime learning ·edit for one child and a HOPE scholarship credit for the other. However, only one credit is lowed per child per year. Also note that the maximum credit of $2,000 applies to the family, ot per student as with the HOPE scholarship credit. Like the HOPE scholarship credit, the ifetime learning credit is subject to the phaseout based on the taxpayer's adjusted gross income ; shown on the chart in the previous section.

axpayers may claim a HOPE credit or lifetime learning credit for a taxable year and exclude om gross income amounts distributed from a Coverdell ESA or qualified tuition program on ehalf of the same student as long as the distribution is not used for the same expenses for which credit was claimed.

ERIES EE BONDS

nother vehicle that may be used to save for college is **Series EE United States Savings Bonds "EE bonds")**. EE bonds are useful tools for college tuition. Face values of EE bonds start as low ; $50 and max out at $10,000. EE bonds are purchased at one-half of their face value. They an have varying interest rates, but must be purchased after 1989 to be a qualified education ivings bond. Bonds purchased after 5/05 will earn fixed rate of interest, and rates for these sues will be adjusted each May 1 and November 1, with each new rate effective for all bonds sued through the following six months. Interest accrues in an amount equal to the increase in edemption value as indicated in the table of redemption values shown on the bond.

Series EE United States Savings Bonds ("EE bonds") - if used to pay for qualified higher education expenses at an eligible institution or state tuition plan, EE bonds bestow significant tax savings; that is, no federal income tax on the interest

 used to pay for qualified higher education expenses at an eligible institution or state tuition lan, EE bonds bestow significant tax savings, that is, no federal income tax is payable on the iterest. To attain tax-free status, EE bonds must be purchased in the name of one or both parnts of the student/child. The parent(s) are considered the owners of the bond, and must be at east 24 years old before the first day of the month of the issue date of the bond. Also, the owners iust redeem the bonds in the same year that the student/child's qualified higher education xpenses are paid. It is worth noting that the newly issued Series I bonds have the same tax benets as EE bonds for purposes of qualified higher education costs.

JNIFORM GIFT TO MINOR'S ACT

he **Uniform Gift to Minor's Act** (UGMA) allows parents to put cash and securities in a custoial account for a child. UGMA accounts give the child full ownership of the assets at the age of iajority (age 18 or 21, depending on the state). If the child is under 14 years of age, all income ver $1,600 for 2005 earned by the assets is taxed at the income tax rate of the parents. If the hild is 14 years or older, the income earned by the assets is taxed at the tax rate of the child. Notably, this is considered an asset of the child and is considered in determining financial aid. Therefore, the account can significantly reduce a student's eligibility for need-based financial id.

Uniform Gift to Minor's Act (UGMA) - allows parents to put cash and securities in a custodial account for a child

Uniform Transfer to Minor's Act (UTMA) - allows parents to put cash, securities, and real property in a custodial account for a child

JNIFORM TRANSFER TO MINOR'S ACT

he **Uniform Transfer to Minor's Act** (UTMA) is similar to the Uniform Gift to Minor's Act. It rovides for the transfer of assets to a custodial account for the benefit of a minor. The taxation reatment of the income earned on the assets is the same as for UGMA, and an UTMA account

Where on the Web

American Savings Education Council *www.asec.org*

College Savings Plans Network (the official website for State 529 Plans/QTPs; affiliated with the National Association of State Treasuries; provides links on the internet to individual State plans) *www.collegesavings.org*

Education Commission of the States *www.ecs.org*

Federal Student Aid - Information for Financial Aid Professionals *http://ifap.ed.gov*

Information on Armed Forces programs and scholarships *www.armyrotc.com, www.goarmy.com/benefits/education.jsp, www.gibill.va.gov, www.usmc.mil, www.af.mil,* www.uscg.mil

The College Board (a not-for-profit education association that created and controls the SAT and PSAT/ NMSQT Examinations) *www.collegeboard.com*

The National Association for College Admission Counseling *www.nacac.com*

The National Association of Student Financial Aid Administrators *www.nasfaa.org*

The Smart Student Guide to Financial Aid (discusses financial aid eligibility and calculations; student loan analysis; scholarship availability) *www.finaid.org*

US Department of Education - College is Possible (A resource guide for parents, students, and education professionals) *www.collegeispossible.org*

is considered an asset of the child for financial aid purposes. There are differences between the two acts. UTMA is more flexible than UGMA. Parents may transfer real property as well as cash and securities to an UTMA account.

Interest on Educational Loans

Up to $2,500 of interest paid on student loans for undergraduate and graduate education may be deducted as an adjustment to the taxpayer's AGI. The loaned funds must have been spent on tuition and enrollment fees, books, supplies, equipment, room and board, transportation, or other necessary expenses. There is now a phaseout of this deduction for taxpayers filing jointly with an AGI from $105,000 to $135,000 and for single filers with an AGI from $50,000 to $65,000.

Employer's Educational Assistance Program - under this program, an employer can pay for an employee's undergraduate tuition, enrollment fees, books, supplies, and equipment while these employer benefits are excluded from the employee's income up to $5,250

Employer's Educational Assistance Program

Under the **Employer's Educational Assistance Program**, an employer can pay for an employee's tuition (both graduate and undergraduate), enrollment fees, books, supplies, and equipment while these employer benefits are excluded from the employee's income up to $5,250. However, the employer or employee cannot also claim an educational credit.

DEDUCTION FOR QUALIFIED HIGHER EDUCATION EXPENSES

For tax years 2002 through 2005, an above-the-line deduction is permitted for qualified higher education expenses paid by the taxpayer during a taxable year. After 2005, this deduction will no longer be available. Qualified higher education expenses are defined in the same manner as for purposes of the HOPE credit.

In 2005, taxpayers with adjusted gross income that does not exceed $65,000 ($130,000 in the case of married taxpayers filing joint returns) are entitled to a maximum deduction of $4,000, and taxpayers with adjusted gross income that does not exceed $80,000 ($160,000 in the case of married taxpayers filing joint returns) are entitled to a maximum deduction of $2,000. Taxpayers with adjusted gross income above these thresholds are not entitled to a deduction.

Taxpayers are not eligible to claim the deduction and a HOPE or lifetime learning credit in the same year with respect to the same student. A taxpayer may not claim a deduction for amounts taken into account in determining the amount excludable due to a distribution (i.e., the earnings and the contribution portion of a distribution) from a Coverdell or the amount of interest excludable with respect to education savings bonds.

EQUITY LINES OF CREDIT

A home equity loan or line of credit is yet another vehicle that can be used to fund college-related expenses. Because home equity loans are secured by a house, the interest rate on a home equity loan may be lower than rates for an unsecured student loan. Many state schools do not consider the value of the home when determining eligibility for financial aid, but numerous private colleges take equity in the home into account. If equity in the home is considered in the financial aid equation, a home equity loan could decrease home equity and possibly improve one's eligibility for financial aid. Further, the interest on home equity loans is normally deductible from the taxpayer's AGI. As a general rule, using home equity loans and lines of credit to pay for higher education expenses should be a last resort, or at least done after researching all other options, rates and conditions for alternative funding. Borrowing too much against the home could result in foreclosure or other difficult situations.

HIGHLIGHTS OF BENEFITS FOR HIGHER EDUCATION

The following exhibit provides the highlights of the various vehicles covered in this section.

EXHIBIT 7.4: HIGHLIGHTS OF TAX BENEFITS FOR HIGHER EDUCATION FOR 2005

	HOPE Credit	Lifetime Learning Credit	Coverdell Education Savings Account[1]	Traditional and Roth IRAs[1]	Student Loan Interest	Qualified Tuition Programs (Section 529 Plans)	Education Savings Bond Program[1]	Employer's Educational Assistance Program[1]	Qualified Higher Education Expenses[3]
What is your benefit?	Credits can reduce the amount of tax you must pay		Earnings are not taxed	No 10% additional tax on early withdrawal	You can deduct the interest	Earnings are not taxed	Interest is not taxed	Employer benefits are not taxed	Deduction of expenses "for AGI"
What is the annual limit?	Up to $1,500 per student	Up to $2,000 per family	$2,000 contribution per beneficiary	Amount of qualifying expenses	$2,500	None	Amount of qualifying expenses	$5,250	2005 $4,000
What expenses qualify besides tuition and required enrollment fees?	None		Books Supplies Equipment Room & board if at least a half-time student Payments to qualified tuition program	Books Supplies Equipment Room & board if at least a half-time student	Books Supplies Equipment Room & board Trans-portation Other necessary expenses	Books Supplies Equipment Room & board if at least a half-time student	Payments to Coverdell ESAs Payments to qualified tuition program	Books Supplies Equipment	None
What education qualifies?	1st 2 years of under-graduate	All undergraduate and graduate[2]							
What are some of the other conditions that apply?	Can be claimed only for 2 years Must be enrolled at least half-time in a degree program		Can also contribute to qualified tuition programs in the same year Cannot contribute after 18th birthday of beneficiary. Must withdraw assets at age 30		No longer a 60 month limit Must have been at least half-time student in a degree program	Distribution is excluded from gross income Hope and Lifetime Learning Credit are permitted in the same year but not for the same expenses	Applies only to qualified series EE bonds issued after 1989 or series I bonds		Cannot claim Hope or Lifetime Learning Credit in same year for the same student
In what income range do benefits phase out?	2005 $43,000 - $53,000 $87,000 - $107,000 for joint returns		$95,000 – $110,000; $190,000 – $220,000 for joint returns	No phaseout[4]	$50,000 - $65,000 $105,000 - $135,000 for joint returns	No phaseout	2005 $61,200 – $76,200 $91,850 – $121,850	No phaseout	2005 Single $65,000 – $80,000 MFJ $130,000 – $160,000

[1] Any nontaxable withdrawal is limited to the amount that does not exceed qualifying educational expenses.

[2] For Coverdell ESAs, qualified elementary and secondary school expenses are also permitted.

[3] For years 2004 – 2005 AGI less than $65,000 ($130,000 married) can take a maximum deduction of $4,000 and taxpayers with AGI between $65,000 and $80,000 ($130,000 and $160,000 married) can take a deduction of $2,000. This deduction expires for years after 2005.

[4] Phaseouts exist at the time of contribution. They are not relevant for withdrawals.

EDUCATIONAL FUNDING/SAVINGS REGIMEN EXAMPLE

Now that all sources of educational funding have been discussed and the investment vehicles and tax benefits identified, the most pressing issue is how much does the parent or family need to save now in order to pay for the child's college education. Calculating the cost of a child's college education through a savings plan is always a helpful exercise.

There are numerous ways to calculate the required funding necessary to pay for a child's college education. In the following example, John plans to pay for the college education of his daughter, Claire. As a general rule, John should establish a savings schedule for Claire's college fund. This savings schedule can be created using time value of money concepts discussed in Chapter 6.

The type of information needed to conduct this analysis includes the age of the child, the age the child will attend college, the parents' after-tax annual earnings rate, the current cost of tuition, related costs and books, and the tuition inflation rate. John is willing to fund Claire's room and board either out of his own pocket when those expenses are incurred or by Claire working to pay them. John nonetheless is comfortable with assuming the risk of paying or funding room and board as the expense is incurred.

Claire is one day old, and John anticipates that Claire will be 18 years old when she begins college. John expects to earn an after-tax annual rate of return over the 18-year period of 11 percent. The current cost of tuition, tuition-related expenses, and books and equipment at Claire's projected category of schools is $25,000 per year. The rate of increase of tuition and tuition-related expenses is assumed to be 6 percent. The CPI inflation rate for this 18-year period is assumed to be 4 percent, which is less than the rate of increase of tuition. Therefore, to be conservative, the higher rate of 6 percent for tuition increases will be used instead of the CPI inflation rate. Other assumptions and necessary data for this exercise are:

- John's annual investment, or "savings payments," will begin at the end of each year from now until the day Claire starts college (expected to be in 18 years).
- John will stop making savings payments once Claire starts college, so that he can pay for Claire's monthly room and board expenses.
- Scholarship money and financial aid will not be considered in these calculations.
- John will postpone his decision as to whether he will place any burden of education-related expenses on Claire while she is in school until a later date (i.e., work or loans).
- John desires to fund all college education expenses without having to borrow any funds.

This problem can be viewed in terms of a timeline (below) from year zero until year 21.

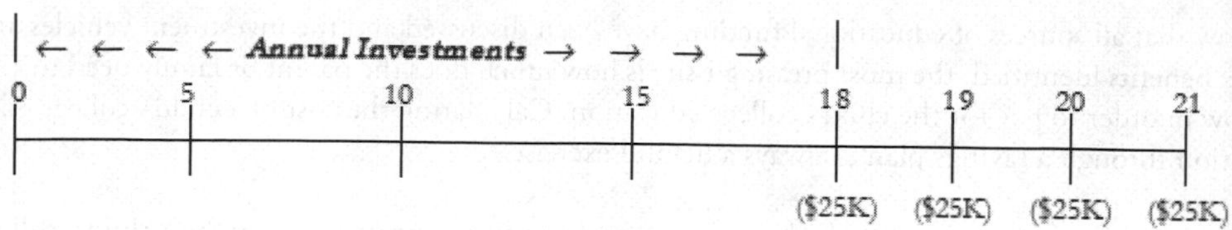
← ← ← ← Annual Investments → → → →
0
5
10
15
18
19
20
21
($25K)
($25K)
($25K)
($25K)

Using what is referred to as the "uneven cash flow" method, there are two series of cash flows that are important, the first being the cash flows invested annually into the account by John over an 18-year span and the second being the four annual payments out of the account starting at the beginning of year 18 and continuing through year 21 for Claire's college education.

STEP 1: Determine the Cost of College Tuition for the 4-Year Period, in Today's Dollars

The first step in this calculation is to determine the present value of the four consecutive annual payments of tuition in years 18 through 21 as of period zero, which is of present day. Using a financial calculator, enter a cash flow of zero for 18 years, and a cash flow of $25,000 for the next four years. Then, discount these cash flows to the present day by an adjusted, assumed earnings rate of 4.7170 percent. The earnings rate of 11 percent is adjusted for the annual increase in tuition of 6 percent as follows:

$$\left(\frac{1+\text{assumed earnings rate}}{1+\text{assumed tuition increase rate}}-1\right)\text{x}\,100=\text{adjusted assumed annual rate}$$

FORMULA CALCULATION pertaining to John and Claire's circumstances:

John's annual earnings rate $1 + 0.11 = 1.11$

John's assumed tuition inflation rate $1 + 0.06 = 1.06$

$[(1.11 \div 1.06) - 1] \times 100 = 4.7170$ percent

Earnings per year are thus assumed in the calculation to be 4.7170 percent. The net present value of the 4 cash flows of $25,000 (today's dollars) at the beginning of years 18 through 21 equals $40,760.80.

This calculation is broken down step by step on the following chart, using an HP-12C calculator:

Keystroke	Display
[f][CLX]	0.0000
0[g][CFj]	0.0000
17[g][Nj]	17.0000
25000[g][CFj]	25,000.0000
4[g][Nj]	4.0000
1.11[enter]	1.1100
1.06[÷]	1.0472
1[–]	0.0472
100[×]	4.7170
[i]	4.7170
[f][NPV]	40,760.8045

Note: For more information on how to utilize a financial calculator or how to calculate a savings schedule for education funding, see Understanding Your Financial Calculator, published by BISYS Education, a Kaplan Financial Company.

STEP 2: Determine the Annual Payments Needed to Fund College Tuition Costs

The next step is to determine the annual payments from year zero through the end of year 17 that are needed to fund the outgoing cash flows for tuition at the beginning of years 18 through 21. Using a financial calculator, the required annual investment or payment is $5,292.50. This calculation is broken down step by step on the following chart, using an HP-12C Calculator:

Keystroke	Display
40,760.80 [PV]	40,760.8000
18 [n]	18.0000
11 [i]	11.0000
0 [FV]	0.0000
[PMT]	5,292.4993

Therefore, John must save $5,292.50 per year beginning one year from now, the start of year zero, and continuing until the end of year 17 (a total of 18 payments) so that when Claire attends college at the start of year 18, John can pay for her college education.

INVESTMENT STRATEGIES TO ACCOMPLISH EDUCATION GOALS

It is important to bear in mind that the investment strategies employed by the family should rely heavily on the amount of time that exists until the child will be enrolled in school. In other words, the time horizon is probably the most important factor (besides risk tolerance) to consider in deciding what securities to invest in, how much to invest, and when to invest. The more time that exists before the child enrolls in school inevitably provides the parents or family with more options and more time for accumulation of principal and growth for a savings regimen.

Using the education funding example above, if John wants to completely pay for his one-day-old daughter, Claire's, college tuition, he has a time horizon of 18 years to invest enough money to fund 4 years of tuition. The funds invested by John will have numerous years to grow and accumulate, and John's risk tolerance for investments will be higher than those parents who start to save for their children's college expenses years after they are born. John could invest in more growth- and equity-oriented funds with higher potential rates of return between 10 and 14 percent.

Let's compare John's situation to that of Tad, a parent with a 10-year-old son named Ken. Tad will have only 8 years to save and invest money to pay for 4 years of college for Ken. Tad does not have the luxury of time. Further, Tad cannot tolerate as much risk as John because there is less time to recover from a bear market. Therefore, Tad would probably invest substantially more conservatively than John.

As discussed earlier in this chapter, QTPs follow this investment principle. QTPs generally require a decrease in risk levels of investments the closer the child gets to the targeted year to begin college. This method is referred to as "Age-banding." Various QTP managers will generally comply with the sequence illustrated in the exhibit below.

EXHIBIT 7.5: AGE-BANDING EXAMPLE

Student's Age	Stocks	Bonds	Money Market/Cash
0–13	70–100 percent	0–30 percent	0
14–17	25–40 percent	35–50 percent	10–40 percent
18–	0–10 percent	20–30 percent	60–80 percent

Depending upon the specifics of a state's QTP legislation, which varies from one state to another, managers of QTPs must comply with this decrease (or a similar decrease) in the percentage of investment in growth and equity funds because, as the child ages, the risk of losing principal and earnings is too great considering that the prospect of attending college hangs in the balance.

Finally, after the analysis is complete and a savings plan has been developed and begun, the contributor must monitor and reassess the plan on a consistent, periodic basis (at least annually). This review process is necessary because the parents' financial situation may change or the goals may be changed. If a family experiences a significant increase in income or finances, an increase in the savings amount may be in order to alleviate the risks of the assumptions made in the

analysis, or to broaden the potential colleges and universities the child may consider. If a family experiences a decrease in income or finances, it may be more realistic to lower the expectations or assumptions in the analysis or determine if the family would qualify for financial aid or assistance, such as a Pell Grant.

Other assumptions may also change over time. For instance, in our earlier example, John's daughter, Claire, may prove to be an extraordinary student or athlete, and the increased likelihood of her receiving a scholarship could be factored into John's plan.

In conclusion, the education funding savings plan should be developed and implemented as early as possible to take advantage of time-horizon principles. Once the plan is in place, the plan should be monitored and updated because numerous assumptions and unknowns enter into the analysis. The amount necessary to fund college must be identified, but the family can attempt to minimize the contributions it must make through identifying the issues addressed above, setting goals, gathering the necessary information regarding financial aid, school loans, scholarships and other assistance, maximizing tax benefits, choosing the best investment vehicles for themselves, and making choices that are best suited to the family's needs, expectations, and desires.

PROFESSIONAL FOCUS

What do you advise clients regarding §529 Plans?

The contributions to these plans are not deductible, but earnings grow tax free so the withdrawals for payment of qualified educational expenses are tax free. For conservative clients with a low risk tolerance, I might advise a Prepaid Plan. The downside of the Prepaid Plan is the lack of investment flexibility since plan administrators direct asset investment. Another disadvantage is that the Prepaid Plan is considered to be the student's asset which can directly reduce available financial aid. On the other hand, the Savings Plan has the advantage of more investment options with some states offering up to 30 different mutual fund investments. In addition, the §529 Savings Plan asset is considered to be property of the account owner (usually the parent). Since only 5.6% of the parent's assets are considered in financial aid formulas compared to 35% of the child's assets, the Savings Plan has a less negative impact on financial aid. I advise my clients of all of the risks and benefits and try to help them choose the best answer based on their needs. There are currently over 85 separate state plans. I suggest clients browse www.collegesavings.org, www.savingforcollege.com, and Business Week's Guide to College Savings Plans, all which are excellent sources of information on the various state offerings. Attributes that a client needs to examine include fund expenses (some are quite high), a variety of good investments (some offer both static and aged-adjusted portfolios) and, if investing in their own state plan, whether special incentives are offered for residents. More sophisticated clients will be able to enroll directly in a state plan and avoid costly broker fees. Finally, as with all asset acquisition, clients need to consider their investment goals and the risk tolerance. Remember, however, to max out your retirement accounts first....you can borrow for college tuition but not for retirement expenses!

How do you feel about putting assets in the name of the child for education?

The advantages of putting assets in the name of the child or in a custodial account are the absence of income limitations, absence of contribution limitations and the flexibility in distributions. However, a number of issues apply to this situation. First, assets held in a child's name count more heavily against a family's qualification for college financial aid than assets held in the parents' names. Secondly, there is always the issue of control of the assets since UGMA/UTMA assets are irrevocable gifts to the child and custodianship terminates when the minor reaches majority which is established under state law (generally 18 or 21). As the child ages, it is not uncommon for the child's goals to be different from the parents'. I always explain to clients who are new parents that while younger children may be compliant and easy to control, these characteristics generally disappear as the children grow older. In addition, the kiddie tax will apply to unearned income of a child under the age of fourteen. Of course, the kiddie tax can be avoided simply by investing in non-dividend stocks and holding the portfolio until after the child turns 14.

What do you think of the Coverdell education savings account?

Coverdell plans have only about $3 billion in assets, compared to $55 million in §529 plans. Tax legislation has increased the contribution amount to $2,000 per beneficiary making the Coverdell account a much more useful vehicle for educational funding. AGI limitations are still imposed but at much higher levels beginning at $190,000 for joint return filers). The new law now also allows contributions to both a Coverdell account and to a qualified tuition program. A Coverdell account provides more flexibility than a qualified tuition plan by allowing distributions for elementary or secondary school costs and the transfer feature is valuable to the client who has multiple children, some who may get scholarships or loans, and others who may decide not to go to college. It can also be a helpful way for grandparents to assist the family by making a Coverdell contribution annually for each grandchild, as the amount would pass to the grandchild tax free. In comparison to the prepaid state tuition plan, the Coverdell education savings account offers greater control and choice of fund investments, but much lower contribution limits than §529 plans; however the 5-year gift election that is available for §529 plans is not available for the Coverdell accounts. That said, the Coverdell Education Savings Account can be useful as an adjunct or alternative to a §529 plan.

CASSIE BRADLEY, PH.D., CFP®

DISCUSSION QUESTIONS

1. What are the issues and goals of education funding?
2. What education funding information should students and parents gather?
3. How is financial need determined?
4. What is a Federal Pell Grant?
5. What is Direct and FFEL Stafford Loans?
6. What is the difference between a subsidized student loan and an unsubsidized student loan?
7. What are PLUS Loans?
8. What is a Consolidation Loan?
9. What campus-based student financial aid is available?
10. What are the tax advantages and issues with respect to educational expenses?
11. What are the benefits of Qualified Tuition Plans and how are they taxed?
12. What are prepaid tuition plans and how do they work?
13. How do contributions to QTPs affect gift taxes?
14. What is a Coverdell Education Savings Account?
15. How can a Roth IRA be used for education funding?
16. What is the maximum credit allowed with the HOPE scholarship credit?
17. What are the eligibility requirements to take a Lifetime learning credit?
18. What are Series EE bonds?
19. What is the Uniform Gift to Minor's Act?
20. What is the Employer's Educational Assistance Program?

EXERCISES

1. Compare and contrast grants, scholarships, and fellowships.
2. Compare and contrast Direct and FFEL Stafford loans.
3. Shawna, age 18, recently graduated from high school with a 3.6 GPA. Shawna currently lives at home and works part-time as an office assistant. She has been accepted to Texas State University. Her parents cannot afford to assist her. She wants to obtain a college education, but is having trouble affording tuition and other college expenses. What financial aid programs would you recommend to Shawna, and why?
4. Karen, age 20, is in her second year at the University of California. She will not be able to hold down a part-time job and complete her bachelor's degree program in four years. She will receive approximately $30,000 from a trust fund left to her by her grandmother on her 22nd birthday. What federal aid programs are available to Karen? Would you recommend that Karen borrow against the trust fund in order to support herself during the next two years? Why or why not?
5. Gordon and Rhonda want to start saving now for their two-year-old daughter's college education. Tuition and fees at a four-year public university is currently $3,500 per year, and tuition has increased approximately 7 percent each year. How much should Gordon and Rhonda expect to pay for college when their daughter turns 18 years old?
6. Christian and Emily have two children, Bethany, age 5, and Taylor, age 7. Christian's parents would like to pay for Bethany and Taylor's college education. They are considering gifting the money to Bethany and Taylor by setting up savings accounts for them. Would you recommend this approach? Why or why not? If not, who should the grandparents pass the money to and why?

7. Brandon and Myra are married and have an adjusted gross income of $55,000. They have two children, Beth, age 18, and Brett, age 20. Both Beth and Brett are full-time students attending the local university. Are Brandon and Myra eligible to take advantage of any educational tax credits? If so, which ones, and what is the maximum credit they are allowed?
8. Leslie is in her third year of college and has received subsidized Stafford loans to help her pay for college. She does not have to borrow any more money before she receives her degree. She wants to start paying off her student loans now. Given the choices for repaying student loans, what would you recommend to Leslie?
9. Brad was recently awarded some financial aid through his university. Although the aid he was awarded helps, he still needs more financial aid than the school offered. What would you recommend to Brad to help him pay for college?
10. Tyra plans to attend the local university next year. Her parents make too much money to qualify for federal aid programs, but Tyra still needs help. What financial aid, if any, is available for Tyra?
11. Julie's parents would like to assist her with the cost of college tuition. Tuition and fees are estimated at $13,000 per school year. Julie's parents apply and qualify for a PLUS loan. How much can they borrow?
12. John and Sue, both age 30, have a child born today. They plan to save the maximum amount in their respective IRAs until their child goes to college in 18 years. Would you recommend a Roth IRA or a Coverdell ESA? Explain why.
13. David intends to open a QTP Savings Plan for his daughter, but wants to know if he can direct the specific investments himself. Can David direct where and how much of the contributions are invested? Can David direct how much of the funds are used to purchase stock or bonds? Explain.
14. In the prior exercise, David was interested in placing a percentage of the funds in the QTP Savings Plan into stocks and a percentage into bonds. What is this principle called? Also, provide an example as to how it is used.
15. Robby plans to attend college but cannot afford tuition. He decides to apply for federal financial aid. Generally, how will Robby's financial aid eligibility be calculated?
16. Bob established a QTP Savings Plan for his son Ricky at age 5. When Ricky turned 18 years old, Ricky decided not to attend college and began working as a bartender in the Bahamas. Can Ricky withdraw funds from the QTP account, which has a value of $100,000? What can Bob do (if anything) with the account?
17. Claire established a QTP Savings Plan for Matt, her son. While Matt was attending college Matt asked Claire for money to spend on a ski boat. Claire agreed, withdrew $10,000 from the QTP account, and purchased the boat for Matt in Matt's name. Will this $10,000 withdrawal and payment be taxed, and if so, whose tax rate will be used? Would it be important to know what portion of the $10,000 represents contributions and what portion represents earnings? Explain.
18. Let's take the prior exercise (exercise 17) one step further. Would there be any penalty assessed on the $10,000 withdrawal? Would it be important to know what portion of the $10,000 is contributed and what portion is earnings?
19. What if in the prior exercise (exercise 17), Matt had received a full scholarship for his remaining years in college, the semester before Claire gave him $10,000 for the boat?

PROBLEMS

1. Rena and Hunter Alesio have two children, ages 5 and 7. The Alesios want to start saving for their children's education. Each child will spend 6 years at college and will begin at age 18. College currently costs $20,000 per year and is expected to increase at 6 percent per year. Assuming the Alesios can earn an annual compound return of 12 percent and inflation is 4 percent, how much must the Alesios deposit at the end of each year to pay for their children's educational requirements until the youngest is out of school? Assume that educational expenses are withdrawn at the beginning of each year and that the last deposit will be made at the beginning of the last year of the youngest child.
2. Chelsea was recently divorced and has two children. The divorce decree requires that she pay 1/3 of the college tuition cost for her children. Tuition cost is currently $15,000 per year and has been increasing at 7 percent per year. Her son and daughter are 12 and 16, respectively, and will attend college for four years beginning at age 18. Assume that her after-tax rate of return will be 9 percent and that general inflation has been 4 percent. How much should she save each month, beginning today for the next five years to finance both children's education?
3. Ken and Amy Charvet have two children, ages 4 and 6. The Charvets want to start saving for their children's education. Each child will spend 5 years in college and will begin at age 18. College currently costs $30,000 per year and is expected to increase at 7 percent per year. Assuming the Charvets can earn an annual compound investment return of 12 percent and inflation is 4 percent, how much must the Charvets deposit at the end of each year to pay for their children's educational requirements until the youngest goes to school? Assume that educational expenses are withdrawn at the beginning of each year and that the last deposit will be made at the beginning of the first year of the youngest child.
4. Barry and Virginia have a five-year-old son, Daniel. They have plans for Daniel to attend a four-year private university at age 18. Currently, tuition at the local private university is $15,000 per year and is expected to increase at 7 percent per year. Assuming Barry and Virginia can earn an annual compound return of 10 percent and inflation is 4 percent, how much do Barry and Virginia need to start saving per year, starting today to be able to pay for Daniel's college education? Assume their last payment is made at the beginning of Daniel's first year in college.

Insurance Planning

in BRIEF

- Risk
- Perils and hazards
- Adverse selection
- Insurable losses
- Law of insurance contracts
- Insurance policy features
- Selecting an insurance company
- Risk management process

- Measuring needs related to premature death
- Characteristics of life, health and disability policies
- Annuities
- Long -term care insurance

- Automobile insurance
- Homeowners insurance
- Liability insurance
- Property insurance
- Business insurance

- Social Security insurance and benefits
- Taxation of Social Security benefits
- Medicare benefits

SECTION III

Insurance Planning

CHAPTER 8 Introduction to Insurance and Risk Management
CHAPTER 9 Managing Life, Health, and Disability Risks
CHAPTER 10 Personal Property and Liability Insurance
CHAPTER 11 Social Security and Other Social Insurance

Risks

- Untimely death
- Disability
- Unemployment
- Medical illness
- Long-term health care
- Damage to property
- Tort liability

Data Collection

- Life insurance policies
- Disability policies
- Employer benefit summaries
- Health plan policies
- Long-term care policies
- Automobile policies
- Homeowners policies, riders, etc.
- Personal liability umbrella policies
- Business policies

Goals

- Appropriate insurance coverage and reasonable premiums for the risks identified to person, property and/or liabilities of the client.

Data Analysis

- Life insurance policy analysis
- Health insurance policy analysis
- Disability insurance policy analysis
- Homeowners policy analysis
- Automobile insurance analysis
- Liability insurance analysis
- Business insurance analysis

CHAPTER 8

An Introduction to Insurance and Risk Management

LEARNING OBJECTIVES:

After learning the material in this chapter, you will be able to:

1. Define risk, the different types of risk and understand how each risk impacts the personal financial planning process.
2. Understand the insurable loss exposures faced by the typical individual client.
3. Understand the responses to pure risk and how they can be incorporated into a risk management plan.
4. Define insurance and understand how it is used as a risk management tool.
5. Distinguish between a peril and a hazard and understand how each relates to the need for insurance.
6. Define adverse selection and explain its impact on the insurance process.
7. Summarize the requisites for an insurable risk and understand what distinguishes insurance from gambling.
8. Explain the elements of a valid contract and identify the distinguishing features of insurance contracts.
9. Understand the reason for, and the effect of, various contractual features in insurance contracts.
10. Know the types of authority of agents to act on behalf of an insurance company.
11. Understand the methods of valuation for insured losses.
12. Know the insurance company rating agencies and how they evaluate the financial conditions of insurers.
13. Define risk management and explain the steps in the risk management process.

INTRODUCTION

Proper insurance coverage, both private and social, is essential to a client's financial plan. Most people do not have the right amount of insurance coverage and, therefore, are either overinsured or underinsured. Financial planners must have a basic understanding of risk and insurance in order to properly assist their clients in assessing their insurance needs and evaluating their current insurance coverage. For most clients, basic insurance needs can be covered with life insurance, health insurance, disability insurance, homeowners or renters insurance, long-term care, automobile insurance, and personal liability insurance. This section of the text is designed as an introduction to these areas of insurance. Chapter 8 discusses risk, the legal foundation of insurance and the transference of risks using insurance contracts. Chapter 9 identifies the risks to the person, namely premature death, catastrophic illness, disability, and the need for long-term care. Chapter 10 identifies the risks to property and liability exposures. Chapter 11 covers the types and availability of social insurance.

UNDERSTANDING RISK

risk - the chance of loss, possibility of loss, uncertainty, or a variation of actual from expected results

Risk can be defined as the chance of loss, possibility of loss, uncertainty, or a variation of actual from expected results. The insured who owns a home knows that in most years he will not suffer a house fire. But the possibility of fire does exist, and its consequences could be financially devastating. Thus, the insured transfers the risk of fire to an insurance company and pays the insurer a premium to accept such risk.

There has to be some chance that a loss will occur for risk to exist. The person who does not own a boat has no need for boat owners insurance because there is no risk to be transferred. The person who owns a boat, however, must be concerned with the financial consequences of the boat being stolen, damaged by fire, or involved in an accident. While the boat owner hopes that none of these losses occurs, there is the chance that they might, so the risk must be managed in an appropriate manner.

RISK CLASSIFICATION

PURE VERSUS SPECULATIVE RISK

pure risk - a risk in which the results are either a loss or no loss

speculative risk - a risk where profit, loss or no loss may occur

A **pure risk** is one in which the results are either loss or no loss. An example of a pure risk is death. While death is a certainty, there is still risk in determining when each person will die. A **speculative risk**, on the other hand, is one where profit, loss, or no loss may occur. Entrepreneurs regularly encounter speculative risk when they begin a new business or sell a new product. Speculative risks are generally undertaken voluntarily and are not insurable.

Consider the risks associated with the purchase of a home. A speculative risk is the potential fluctuation in the value of the house after it is purchased. The market value of the home could remain the same as the original purchase price, increase, or even decline. There are also a variety of pure risks associated with home ownership, such as the risk of a fire, flood, or theft of property. If a fire occurs, the insured will suffer a loss; otherwise, there is no change in the condition of the house. To summarize, a pure risk has two possible outcomes—loss or no loss, while a speculative risk has three. Only pure risks are commercially insurable.

Dynamic versus Static Risk

Risks that can be classified in terms of whether they are affected by society or the economy are called **dynamic risks.** For example, changes in technology can make a company's product obsolete, leading to great financial loss. Dynamic losses are difficult to predict; therefore, insurance companies are not inclined to assume this type of risk.

Static risks, on the other hand, involve losses that would occur even though there were no changes in society or the economy. The death of a family's breadwinner is an example of such a loss. Static losses tend to occur with regularity over time, and are therefore generally predictable. For this reason, insurance companies are more willing to accept these types of risks.

dynamic risk – a risk that results from changes in society or the economy (i.e., inflation)

static risk – a risk dependent on factors other than a change in economy (e.g., natural disaster - earthquake/ flood)

Subjective versus Objective Risk

Subjective risk is a particular person's perception of risk, and varies greatly among individuals. Consider two people, each having slept only two hours in the last two days, who need to drive home from work late at night. The first person drinks coffee habitually and considers an hour drive no problem, thus, reflecting a low level of subjective risk. The second person does not drink coffee and knows he is very tired. He either does not drive home at all or drives very carefully because he knows he has fallen asleep behind the wheel before under similar circumstances. The second person's perception is an example of high subjective risk. A perception of low subjective risk often results in less prudent conduct, whereas a perception of high subjective risk may result in more prudent conduct.

Objective risk is a concrete concept and does not depend on a particular person's perception. It is the relative variation of an actual loss from an expected loss. Suppose an auto insurer has 1,000 new cars insured each year. On average, 100 cars, or 10 percent, file collision claims each year. If in the first year 110 cars file claims, and the next year only 90 filed claims, there is a 10-car variation each year, equaling a 10 percent objective risk. Objective risk varies inversely with the number of exposures involved. As the number of exposures increases, the insurance company can predict more accurately its future loss experience based on the law of large numbers (to be discussed later in the chapter).

subjective risk - a particular person's perception of risk, varying greatly among individuals

objective risk - the relative variation of an actual loss from an expected loss

particular risk – personal risk that involves a possible loss for an individual or a small group

Particular versus Fundamental Risk

Risks can also be classified in terms of how large of a population they affect. **Particular risks** are personal and involve a possible loss for individuals or small groups of individuals, rather than a large segment of the population. Theft of a family's personal property is an example of particular risk. **Fundamental risks**, on the other hand, is impersonal and involves a possible loss for a large group. For example, the possibility of rising waters during a hurricane is a fundamental risk.

fundamental risk – an impersonal risk that involves a possible loss for a large group

Financial versus Nonfinancial Risk

Whether or not a risk involves financial loss is another means of classification. **Financial risks** involve monetary losses. The possibility that a family may be faced with a significant loss of income in the event of its breadwinner's disability is an example of a financial risk. There may also be **nonfinancial risk** associated with a breadwinner's disability, such as pain and suffering on the part of the breadwinner. Generally, insurance is intended for financial losses, although some

financial risk – a risk that involves a monetary loss

nonfinancial risk – a risk that involves a non-monetary loss liability policies will compensate for nonfinancial losses that arise out of legal liability. For example, pain and suffering caused by the insured is given a monetary value and covered by a liability policy.

PROBABILITY OF LOSS

For an insurer to estimate how many losses will occur in a given year, its actuary must know the chance of loss for members of the insurance pool. The chance of loss is more commonly referred to as the probability of loss and is a measure of the long-run frequency with which an event occurs.

EXAMPLE

For example, if 700 out of 100,000 homes suffer a fire each year, then the probability of a fire can be calculated as 700 divided by 100,000 or 0.007. For each individual member of the pool, the probability of loss is a moot point. Whether the probability is 7 in 1,000 or 7 in 100, the insured's concern is that it will be his home that burns, and that such a loss will be financially devastating. Probability analysis is useful information for the insurer, however, because it allows the insurer to determine the number of insureds who will suffer losses and to estimate the aggregate claims. The expected total cost of claims can then be evenly distributed among the members of the pool.

Notice that probability is the *long-run* chance. This implies that numerous events must occur before probability can be calculated with reasonable accuracy. To illustrate, consider how one might determine the probability of a tossed coin landing with the head side up. The probability is 0.5 (or a 50 percent chance), but suppose one did not know this. To discover the probability of tossing a head, assume the coin is tossed ten times. With many iterations of the same test, some might obtain five out of 10 heads, but others will not. When seven heads turn up, one may erroneously conclude that the probability is 0.7 (7 out of 10). To calculate a true probability, one should toss the coin several thousand times, recording each of the results. Perhaps there were 5,021 heads, resulting in a better estimate of the true probability (5,021 ÷ 10,000 = 0.5021) than tossing the coin just ten times.

How does probability relate to objective risk? Objective risk is the chance that predictions about losses will be wrong. Those predictions are based on probability. The more reliable the probability figures are, the more accurate the predictions will be and, thus, the lower the objective risk.

LAW OF LARGE NUMBERS

law of large numbers - the chance that probable results will accurately reflect true results increases as the number of exposures increases

Probability figures must be determined over time. The previous coin toss example illustrates that the more times one repeats an experiment, the more likely it is that the true probability will reveal itself. So, the larger the number of exposure units, the more likely it is that the predictions will be accurate. A related conclusion is that the **law of large numbers** helps reduce objective risk, which depends on the variation in, or uncertainty of, possible outcomes.

EXAMPLE

As an illustration, consider the risk faced by an insurer that has 1,000 insureds in a life insurance pool, versus that of an insurer with 100,000 insureds. If the probability of death is 5 in 1,000, or .005, the insurer with the smaller pool estimates that 5 people in the pool will die this year. The larger insurer estimates that 500 people will die. Suppose five additional people in each pool die, above and beyond what each insurer predicted. For the smaller insurer, these extra deaths result in a 100 percent increase in claims beyond what was originally predicted. For the larger insurer, however, the five additional deaths result in an increase of only 1 percent. Because there are more observations in the larger pool, the variation in possible outcomes declines, which reduces the insurer's objective risk.

RESPONSES TO PURE RISK

Individuals and businesses may respond to pure risk exposures in one or more ways:

- Risk avoidance.
- Risk reduction.
- Risk retention or assumption.
- Risk transfer.

RISK AVOIDANCE

risk avoidance - the avoidance of any chance of loss

Risk avoidance is simply the avoidance of any chance of loss. If the probability of loss becomes zero, there is no risk of future losses. How does one eliminate the possibility of dying in an airplane crash? Avoid air travel!

EXAMPLE

Avoidance works for some loss exposures, but it is impossible to avoid all possible loss exposures. For example, the person who wishes to avoid dying in a plane crash can certainly avoid flying, but then how does he get from one distant place to another? Perhaps using a car, but many people would also prefer to avoid dying in an automobile accident. So, those persons would have to walk. In today's society, it is not feasible for many persons to avoid driving or flying.

If one risk is avoided, another risk likely will replace it. Certain risks can be avoided, however, when their potential frequency and severity are too high to justify *not* avoiding them. As an example, some doctors have left private practice because of the fear of medical malpractice suits. They find other ways to earn a living (teaching or research, for example), thus, avoiding the risk of a malpractice suit completely.

RISK REDUCTION

Risk reduction consists of activities that reduce the frequency or severity of losses. A person who cannot avoid driving faces the risk of an auto accident, but has several risk reduction devices at her disposal. Taking a defensive driving class and practicing defensive driving techniques are means of preventing accidents. In the same way, wearing a seatbelt minimizes injuries sustained in an automobile accident.

Risk reduction measures are undertaken only when they are cost feasible. To minimize the severity of injuries sustained in a car accident, one might decide to purchase the safest automobile on the market; however, if that automobile costs $50,000, it may be cost prohibitive.

risk reduction – activities that reduce the frequency or severity of losses

Certain risk reduction features that reduce the severity of losses, such as seat belts, may give some drivers a false sense of security. Those drivers might increase undesirable behavior, such as speeding, which may increase the frequency of losses, thus mitigating the risk reduction advantage.

Risk Retention or Assumption

risk assumption - bearing all or part of the financial burden in the event of a loss

When a person or firm is exposed to risk and decides to bear all or part of the financial burden if a loss occurs, this is known as risk retention, or **risk assumption**. It may occur in one of two forms, active or passive. Active risk retention means that one is fully aware of the chance for loss and consciously plans to retain all or part of the risk. The person who has a $100,000 home may choose to retain the first $500 of any loss through a deductible clause, whereas the person with a $1,500 automobile may choose to retain the whole risk of property damage by not carrying comprehensive and collision because the severity of loss is low.

Passive risk retention is being unaware of a risk and, thus, taking no steps to manage it. When another method is not actively chosen, retention is selected by default.

Risk Transfer

risk transfer - shifting the probability of loss to another party, such as an insurance company

Risk transfer involves shifting the probability of loss to another party, such as an insurance company. The purchase of insurance is a way to transfer a pure risk. Three other techniques for handling the transfer of risk include contracts, hedging, and incorporation. Contractual agreements may often include guarantees at the time of sale, often known as warranties. Hedging is a means of trying to match profit on one transaction to the expected loss of another. In stock market transactions, a speculator can hedge unfavorable price fluctuations by buying and selling futures contracts. Incorporation results in limited liability for business owners. In situations where a business is operated as a sole proprietorship or a partnership, liability is unlimited for the owners; however, if a business is incorporated, stockholder liability is limited and the risk of insufficient funds or assets to meet the demands of business expenses rests with the corporation or is shifted to creditors.

INSURANCE AS A RISK MANAGEMENT TOOL

Individuals and businesses can obtain protection against certain risks of financial loss though the use of insurance. While there are many ways to suffer a financial loss, this type of risk management tool is designed specifically to deal with the financial consequences of pure risks. As you will recall, pure risk involves situations in which there is only the possibility of loss or no loss. Unlike speculative risk, there is no chance of gain. The possibility of loss when owning property is an example of pure risk. A homeowner is confronted with the possibility that something may damage his home. The potential consequences are loss or no loss.

Insurance is the pooling of unexpected losses by the transfer of risks to insurers who agree to indemnify insureds for such losses, to provide other pecuniary benefits on their occurrence, or to render services connected with the risk. Insurance provides that the insurer will pay for unexpected losses and, thus, provide financial security to the insured. Insurance is a valuable tool for protecting the individual against fortuitous accidental losses because it allows for the transfer of losses and for the sharing of losses with others.

insurance - the pooling of unexpected losses by the transfer of risks to insurers who agree to indemnify insureds for such losses, to provide other pecuniary benefits on their occurrence, or to render services connected with the risk

Transfer Of Losses

Insurance transfers the risk of loss to the insurer—a financial intermediary that specializes in assuming risk. The insured pays the insurer a premium to agree that if certain events (losses) occur, money will be provided to the insured to pay for the consequences of those losses. In exchange, the insurer provides the insured with a legally binding contract—the insurance policy—that spells out, among other things, covered losses, how those losses will be valued, and what duties are owed by each party to the contract. Almost any risk can be transferred for the right price. Of course, the greater the chance that a loss will occur, the higher the price of the insurance premium and the lower the likelihood that an insurance company will agree to insure.

Sharing Losses with Others

Cooperation and sharing are essential to the insurance process. Insureds facing similar risks of loss are pooled together. The insurer mathematically predicts the expected losses for the entire pool, and then divides the cost of those losses among each insured, then adds a charge for the insurer's operating expenses and profit margin.

Each insured person contributes a fair share of money to the pool. Those who possess a greater amount of risk contribute more to the pool, and vice versa. Actuarial science allows insurance companies to estimate losses and, thus, to estimate premiums for each person in a pool.

EXAMPLE

For example, assume First Mutual Insurance Company has a life insurance pool of 1,000 thirty-year-old males. Each insured joined the pool because he was concerned about dying during the year and wanted to leave money behind to provide for his financial obligations. Human life expectancy is quite predictable, so the actuary can determine with considerable certainty how many of those in this particular pool will die during the year. Suppose the actuary determines that two of the 1,000 men in the pool will die this year. If each man in the pool purchased $100,000 of life insurance coverage, this means that the actuary expects the insurer to pay $200,000 for the year in claims. If the $200,000 in claims (losses) is divided among the 1,000 people in the pool, each person's share is $200. The insurer will add a charge for expenses and profit, perhaps $50 per insured. Thus, the cost of insurance (premium) for each person in the pool for that year will be $250.

Each insured in the pool voluntarily pays $250 for the security of knowing that if he is one of the two insureds to die, his beneficiary will receive $100,000. At the same time, each insured hopes that he does not die, and that his $250 will be paid as someone else's death claim under the life insurance policy.

Notice that in the second year, there are only 998 insureds left in the pool if two died the preceding year. Suppose the actuary determines that, once again, only two people in the pool will die. For the $100,000 death benefit to be paid on each claim, the insurer must again collect a total of $200,000. When this amount is spread over 998 insureds, each is responsible for $200.40. When the insurer's expenses (again, assume they are $50) are added, the total premium charged is $250.40. This premium is slightly higher than for the previous year. Note that it would be even higher had the actuary determined that three or more people in the pool would likely die the following year.

Because death rates increase as people get older, life insurance premiums rise at an increasing rate. This occurs because the number of people dropping out of the pool increases each year due to death and to lapsing policies. Thus, there are fewer persons remaining in the pool to share the expense of future death claims.

CAUSES OF INSURED LOSSES

PERILS

peril - the proximate, or actual, cause of a loss

open-perils policy - a policy in which all perils or causes of loss are covered, unless they are specifically listed under the exclusions section

named-perils policy - a policy which provides protection against losses caused only by the perils specifically listed in the policy

Too often the concept of risk, or the chance of loss, is confused with the terms "peril" and "hazard." A **peril** is the proximate or actual cause of a loss. Some common perils are fire, windstorm, tornado, earthquake, burglary, and collision.

Insurance policies may be written in either an open-perils or named-perils format. Historically, open-perils policies were called "all-risks" policies, because they covered all risks of loss (perils) not specifically excluded. The name "all-risks" proved to be somewhat misleading to typical consumers, implying that "all" things were covered. So, the industry has moved toward the use of the term "open-perils" to describe this type of coverage agreement. An **open-perils policy** is one in which all perils or causes of loss are covered, unless they are specifically listed under the exclusions section. A **named-perils policy** provides protection against losses caused only by the perils specifically listed in the policy. Because there is always a chance of loss being caused by an unknown peril, an open-perils policy is preferable to a named-perils policy. Consequently, the open-perils policy premium is higher because it provides broader coverage.

HAZARDS

hazard - a condition that creates or increases the likelihood of a loss occurring

physical hazard - a tangible condition or circumstance that increases the probability of a peril occurring and/or the severity of damages that result from a peril

A **hazard** is a condition that creates or increases the likelihood of a loss occurring. The three main types of hazard are:

- Physical hazard.
- Moral hazard.
- Morale hazard.

Physical Hazard

A **physical hazard** is a tangible condition or circumstance that increases the probability of a peril occurring and/or the severity of damages that result from a peril. Common examples of physical hazard include poor lighting, icy roads, storing gasoline in a household garage, and defective wiring.

Moral Hazard

Moral hazard is a character flaw or level of dishonesty an individual possesses that causes or increases the chance for loss. In property insurance claims, a good example of a moral hazard is arson. Fraud in auto and health claims also occurs frequently. Dishonest insureds justify their claims by thinking, "the insurer has plenty of money, and some of it is mine, so I'm entitled to it." Unfortunately, these types of losses result in premium increases for all insureds. When an insured submits an inflated or intentionally caused claim, he is "stealing" from himself and from his fellow insureds.

moral hazard - a character flaw or level of dishonesty an individual possesses that causes or increases the chance for loss

Morale Hazard

Morale hazard is indifference to a loss based on the existence of insurance. Many people think that because they have insurance there is no need to be concerned about protecting their property. As a direct result, the chance of loss is increased. An individual may contend that because he is insured, there is no reason to lock his home or lock his car. This should not be confused with moral hazard, which, for example, would be burning one's own house down or purposely rear-ending another motor vehicle to collect insurance.

morale hazard - indifference to a loss based on the existence of insurance

Adverse Selection

Adverse selection is the tendency of higher-than-average risks (i.e., people who need insurance the most) to purchase or renew insurance policies. Calculating insurance premiums depends on the existence of a balance of both favorable and unfavorable risks in the pool. When higher-than-average loss levels occur among insureds, meaning a greater proportion of bad versus good risks, there may exist a problem of adverse selection.

adverse selection - the tendency of higher-than-average risks (people who need insurance the most) to purchase or renew insurance policies

For instance, if someone with no insurance needs surgery, lives in a flood-prone area, or has recently acquired a life-threatening disease, that person is more likely to seek insurance. Adverse selection makes insurance less affordable for all insureds. It is reasonable to conclude that if all people were to purchase insurance only when they knew that they would incur a financial loss, then insurance would not exist. The premiums insurers collect would be depleted before all the claims could be accounted for, thus, causing insurance companies to go out of business.

The problem of adverse selection is primarily managed through effective underwriting, which is the process of selecting and classifying insureds according to their respective risk levels. Each level of risk can be thought of as a pool, and the insureds within that pool must all be similar in terms of expected losses, so that they can be charged a premium representative of their risk levels. While a person with a terminal illness may wish to purchase life insurance (a clear example of adverse selection), the underwriting process should detect the condition and result in the underwriter's rejection of the application for insurance. Insurers also manage adverse selection after the fact by raising premiums, by nonrenewal, and, in the case of life insurance, by applying surrender charges to policies terminated.

INSURABLE LOSSES

INSURANCE VERSUS GAMBLING

Many people view insurance and gambling as similar activities. A commonly asked question is "Isn't insurance a gamble because the insurance company and the insured are betting if and when an unfortunate event will occur?" While it is true that in insurance there are monetary transactions that take place on the basis of chance, insurance and gambling differ in terms of their respective purposes.

Insurance allows the insured to transfer a risk to the insurer, whereas gambling creates a risk where none previously existed. In gambling, the risk of loss is created when the transaction itself occurs. For example, when a card player bets $100 on a hand against the dealer, he has immediately created a speculative risk (risk of gain or loss) for himself. Insurance takes the consequences of a pure risk (loss, no loss), and makes them manageable for the insured.

REQUISITES FOR AN INSURABLE RISK

There are several conditions that must exist before a pure risk is considered to be an insurable risk. These conditions are:

- A large number of homogeneous (similar) exposure units must exist.
- Insured losses must be accidental from the insured's standpoint.
- Insured losses must be measurable and determinable.
- Loss must not pose a catastrophic risk for the insurer.

A Large Number of Homogeneous (Similar) Exposure Units Must Exist

The insurance process depends on the establishment of fair and accurate premiums for insureds. If accurate estimates of the probability of an occurrence are to be made, a large number of cases need to be considered. The law of large numbers states that in order to predict the average frequency and severity of a loss with accuracy, a sufficient number of homogeneous exposure units needs to be present within each class.

It is important to note the distinction between homogeneous and heterogeneous groups at this point. If dissimilar exposure units are placed in the same group to be observed, predictions on their loss experience will likely be inaccurate. Imagine a pool of homeowners that consists of people from California, Texas, Montana, and Maine. Because the natural disaster perils that each state faces are somewhat different, the resulting expected loss predictions would be imprecise. It makes more sense to estimate losses for homeowners in California as a group, and to make separate loss estimates for persons living in the other states. The exposure units must be homogeneous, or similar in nature, to obtain an accurate measure of the underlying probability for the loss experience of an insured group.

Insured Losses Must be Accidental from the Insured's Standpoint

Losses need to be unintentional and unexpected from the insured's perspective in order to be insurable. If it were not for this requirement, moral hazards would be created and encouraged; and if intentional losses were paid, premiums would skyrocket. As a direct result, fewer people would purchase insurance. This in turn would change the ability of companies to predict probabilities based on a large number of homogeneous units.

Insured Losses Must be Measurable and Determinable

In order to prevent fraud, insurance companies' policies state whether a loss is covered and how much will be paid for that loss. A loss must be both measurable and determinable as to reason, time, location, and price before accurate loss predictions can be made. Difficult risks to predict include flood, earthquake, and nuclear contamination. Losses that are difficult to measure and determine include sentimental value of property (such as the value of a family pet) and cash losses. Although proving that a house or car existed and what each was worth is straightforward, proving how much cash one had on hand at the time a wallet is stolen is not. Thus, insurers typically provide very limited coverage for losses of cash, while they readily pay for fire damage to houses and for theft of automobiles.

Losses Must Not Pose a Catastrophic Risk for the Insurer

Logically, an insurer cannot provide coverage against some loss that could cause it to become financially insolvent. Dangerous risks for an insurer include those that are not accurately predictable and those that can cause damage to a significant portion of the insurer's pool.

Recall that insurable losses must be predictable and measurable. Otherwise, the insurer likely cannot accurately estimate the appropriate premium for the coverage. A war is an example of a risk that is simply not predictable. There is no statistical trend that can be used to determine future losses. For this reason, insurers virtually never provide coverage against war-related losses.

Another source of catastrophic risk for an insurer is any peril that could cause loss to a significant portion of the insureds in the pool. Hurricane risk is a good example of this type of loss. Imagine the loss exposure faced by an insurer that sells property coverages only in the state of Florida. With the hurricane risk faced by a large portion of that state, one such storm could damage a significant portion of the insureds' property. Compare this situation with an insurer that sells coverage in all fifty states, and does only a small portion of its business in Florida. A hurricane in Florida would not be as financially devastating in such a case.

THE LAW OF INSURANCE CONTRACTS

A contract is valid only if the legal system enforces its terms and conditions. Our legal system has established certain principles upon which insurance contracts are based, and by which insurance contracts are interpreted when claims or disputes arise. The following sections address these various principles, but first is a discussion of what constitutes a legally binding contract.

ELEMENTS OF A VALID CONTRACT

The elements of a valid contract are:

- Offer and acceptance.
- Legal competency of all parties.
- Legal consideration.
- Lawful purpose.

Offer and Acceptance

A valid contract exists only if it is based on mutual assent, or a "meeting of the minds" of th contracting parties. Mutual assent consists of a valid offer made by one party and an acceptanc of that offer by the other party. In most cases, an offer is made by the prospective insured to a insurer via its agent by filling out and signing an application that is accompanied by the initia premium. Next, the insurance company must decide whether to accept, counter-offer, or rejec the offer. In order for a contract to become effective, acceptance of the offer by the insurer or b the agent acting on behalf of the company is necessary.

Legal Competency of All Parties to the Contract

The law requires that both the offeror and offeree be legally competent. The vast majority o persons are considered legally competent, so it is easier to explain which persons are legall incompetent. These may include insane persons, intoxicated persons, and minors. Those unde 18 are subject to special state provisions in order to provide a basis for competency.

While it is not *specifically* illegal to enter into a contract with someone who is incompetent i the eyes of the law, it is dangerous to do so. This is because the contract is generally voidable a the option of the incompetent party once he becomes competent, or once someone responsibl for the incompetent party discovers the existence of the contract.

EXAMPLE

Suppose Joe, 16, buys a life insurance policy and pays premiums on it until he is 18 years old. I upon turning 18 Joe becomes legally competent, it is generally possible for him to void th contract on the grounds that he was not competent when he first entered into it. By voiding th contract, Joe is stating that he never wanted to be a part of it and is entitled to a refund of al premiums paid. Yet, had Joe died during the two years the policy was in force, the insurer woul have been legally required to pay the death claim. So, from the insurer's standpoint, entering int a contract with anyone who is not legally competent is ill advised.

Legal Consideration

Each party to a contract must provide something of value, known as "consideration." Paymen (or the promise of payment) of a first premium is generally consideration on the part of th insured. The insurer's consideration is its promise to pay losses covered by the policy and uphol the terms of the policy.

Lawful Purpose

In a court of law, a contract deemed to have an illegal purpose, or a purpose that is against the benefit of public interest in general, is invalid. Any insurance contract that promotes actions contrary to public interest is unenforceable. For example, an insurer will not pay the beneficiary of a life insurance policy if the beneficiary murders the insured. To do so would encourage murder, which is illegal and against public policy. Recall that moral hazards are character flaws in persons who may intentionally create losses. They are willing to commit illegal acts to profit from insurance. If insurance policies did not eliminate coverage for these illegal activities, they would encourage crime and, thus, be against public policy.

LEGAL PRINCIPLES OF THE INSURANCE CONTRACT

In light of the previous discussion on what constitutes a legally enforceable contract, the three legal principles of insurance contracts follow.

The Principle of Indemnity

Insurance is a contract of indemnity, which means that a person is entitled to compensation only to the extent that a financial loss has been suffered. Insurance exists only to indemnify a person's losses, not to place him or her in a better financial position than before the loss occurred. If an insured could make money from the perils covered by insurance policies, she would have an incentive to make sure those perils occurred.

In some cases, an insured will exaggerate an insurance claim. This is a violation of the **principle of indemnity**. If the insured suffers a theft of a leather jacket purchased at a discount store for $100, yet tells the insurance company the jacket was a designer item that cost $1,000, and the insurer pays the claim without question, the insured has actually made a profit from insurance. Making a profit from insurance is clearly a violation of the principle of indemnity, and also an inducement to moral hazard.

principle of indemnity - states that a person is entitled to compensation only to the extent that financial loss has been suffered

People fail to realize that the more money an insurance company pays for losses, the higher will be the premiums charged to everyone in the pool. Thus, even when insureds are able to violate the principle of indemnity without being caught, they are only taking money from themselves and others in their pool.

subrogation clause - states that the insured cannot indemnify herself from both the insurance company and a negligent third party for the same claim

One means by which insurers enforce the principle of indemnity is by including a subrogation clause in property and liability policies. The **subrogation clause** states that the insured cannot indemnify herself from both the insurance company and a negligent third party for the same claim. If the insured collects against the policy, she then relinquishes the right to collect damages from the negligent party.

principle of insurable interest - to have an insurable interest, an insured must be subject to emotional or financial hardship resulting from damage, loss, or destruction

The Principle of Insurable Interest

An insured must be subject to emotional or financial hardship resulting from damage, loss, or destruction in order to have an insurable interest. The **principle of insurable interest** as a legal principle is clearly congruent with the principle of indemnity. For example, if Susan is allowed to insure a building she does not own and has no financial interest in, she has every incentive to destroy the building. Similarly, if she were allowed to insure the life of someone with whom she had no financial or emotional attachment, she would have an incentive to, at least, use insurance as a gambling device, and, at worst, kill the insured.

In property and liability insurance, an insurable interest must be present both at the time of policy inception and at the time of loss. In the case of life insurance, however, an insurable interest is necessary only when the policy is issued. These rules exist in part because life insurance is a long-term investment, whereas property and liability contracts are short-term contracts usually renewed at six-month or one-year intervals. To require a property owner to give up insurance on property he no longer owns does not impose a financial burden on him. On the other hand, the policyowner who insures her spouse for 20 years and then gets divorced might suffer a severe financial penalty and loss of investment if the policy were automatically terminated due to the loss of insurable interest.

The Principle of Utmost Good Faith

principle of utmost good faith - also known as the principle of fair dealing, the principle of utmost good faith requires that the insured and the insurer both be forthcoming with all relevant facts about the insured risk and the coverage provided for that risk

Also known as the principle of fair dealing, the **principle of utmost good faith** requires that both the insured and the insurer be forthcoming with all relevant facts about the insured risk and the coverage provided for that risk. Recall that to have a binding contract, there must be both a valid offer and a valid acceptance, which together constitute mutual assent. Unless all pertinent facts are revealed by the insured in the application process, the insurer does not have a valid offer on which to base its acceptance. The same is true of any counteroffer the insurer might make to the insured before binding coverage.

Throughout the life of the insurance policy, it is presumed that both parties will tell each other the truth about all matters relevant to the contract. If this standard of honesty is not upheld, then the insured could legally commit insurance fraud (thus violating the principle of indemnity). Similarly, the insurer could refuse to pay claims for which the insured is legally entitled to receive compensation. The insurer is expected to comply with all terms of the contract and all provisions of the insurance law in the state(s) where it operates. The legal system recognizes three different areas of enforcement that apply to the insured:

- Warranty.
- Representation.
- Concealment.

Warranty

A warranty is merely a promise made by the insured to the insurer that is part of the insurance contract and, as such, must be adhered to. The promise can be that something is true when coverage is applied for (also called an affirmative warranty), or it can be a promise that the insured will or will not do something during the life of the policy (promissory warranty). Historically, any violation of warranty was grounds for contract avoidance; however, most U.S. jurisdictions have determined that statements made on an application for insurance coverage are not affirmative warranties, but are instead representations. The legal effects of representations are covered below.

The effect of a breach of a promissory warranty is much clearer and more severe. For example, consider a homeowner who promises to purchase and maintain a security system for his home as part of the insurance contract. He decides that he needs to save money, so he disconnects his security service. If he is burglarized three months later, the insurer likely will not have to pay the claim because a breach of warranty is grounds for voiding a policy.

Representation

Representations are statements made by the insured to the insurer in the application process. Material (relevant) misrepresentations give the insurer the right to void the policy once they are discovered. Why? Once again, mutual assent is a necessary element to any contract. If the insured lies to the insurer in the application (offer) process, then the insurer has not received a valid offer, so mutual assent is never reached.

representation - statement made by the insured to the insurer in the application process

The misrepresentation must be *material* before the insurer may void the policy and ultimately deny payment of a claim. The test of materiality is a simple one—if the insurer had known the truth, would it have affected the insurer's underwriting decision to such an extent that the policy would not have been issued? For example, if Carmen states on her application for life insurance that she does not smoke when in fact she does, it definitely would have affected the insurer's underwriting decision. While coverage might have still been sold to Carmen, she would have been placed into a different underwriting class and, thus, charged a higher premium.

Now, suppose on Carmen's life insurance application the insurer asked if she had ever been seen by a doctor for any medical condition over the past five years (which is a very vague question), and she said "no." In reality, she had been seen once a year for an annual check-up and was treated for the flu two years ago. If the insurer discovered the misrepresentation and wanted to void the policy, it would have to prove that knowing she had annual check-ups plus one case of the flu would have changed its underwriting decision. In reality, this type of routine medical treatment probably would not affect the underwriting decision, so the insurer would be barred from voiding the policy.

Concealment

Concealment occurs when the insured is silent about a fact that is material to the risk. If an insured does not reveal material information that he knows and that he is not specifically asked about, then he has concealed that information. Contrast the notion of concealment with that of misrepresentation. A misrepresentation is an untruthful answer to a question, whereas concealment is not revealing a fact that is of importance to the insurer.

concealment - occurs when the insured is silent about a fact that is material to the risk

In practice, most insurers do not void coverage on the grounds of concealment because it is very difficult to prove. U.S. law requires the insurer to prove the concealed information was important to the underwriting process, and that the insured knew that it was important but intentionally kept it a secret. This is a very difficult standard of proof because the typical consumer has no way of knowing precisely what is relevant to an underwriter's decision.

Legal Form

Although not required to be written, the form and content of insurance contracts are generall governed by state law. Each contract must be filed and approved by a state regulatory agenc before the insurance policy may be sold in a particular state.

Distinguishing Characteristics of Insurance Contracts

Insurance is a contract of adhesion. It is also aleatory, unilateral, and conditional.

Adhesion (A "take it or leave it" contract)

adhesion - a characteristic of insurance which means that insurance is "a take it or leave it" contract. The insured must accept (or adhere to) the contract as written, without any bargaining over its terms and conditions.

In most cases, two parties form a contract through the bargaining process. In insuranc however, this is not the case because insurance is a contract of **adhesion**. Adhesion means th insured must accept the contract as written, without any bargaining over its terms an conditions. Most insurance companies today use standardized policy forms that may not b modified by the insurer to meet individual needs, and in the vast majority of cases the insure cannot bargain over the specific terms and conditions contained in the contract.

If the drafter of the contract, (in this case, the insurer) leaves the contract ambiguous in any wa such ambiguities will be interpreted in favor of the person who was not allowed to bargain ove the terms of the contract (in this case, the insured). This legal doctrine imposes a stringen burden on the insurer to use very precise wording in its contractual products. The test o ambiguity is, "How would a reasonable layperson (not an insurance expert) interpret thi contract?" If a court determines that a contractual provision is ambiguous to the average person it will require the insurer to interpret the provision in a manner that is most favorable to th insured.

Aleatory (Money exchange may be unequal)

aleatory - a characteristic of insurance meaning that monetary values exchanged by each party in an insurance agreement are unequal

Monetary values exchanged by each party in an insurance agreement are unequal. This is know as the **aleatory** feature of insurance contracts. While the insured pays a small premium, th insurer might ultimately pay a large dollar amount as the result of a claim. There have bee cases, for example, where the insured died within a few days of the life insurance policy' issuance. Perhaps one $80 premium payment was made, yet the insurer had to pay a $250,00 death claim.

Unilateral (Only one promise, made by insurer)

Insurance policies are unilateral contracts because only one party, the insurer, agrees to a legally enforceable promise to provide the coverages shown in the policy and to abide by all terms and conditions of the policy. On the other hand, the insured is not legally obligated to uphold his agreement to pay premiums. Although the insured must continue to pay premiums if he wants to keep his insurance protection, the insurer cannot legally force him to remain in the contract and to continue paying premiums.

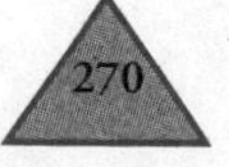

Conditional (Conditioned on paying the premium)

Every contract lists provisions or conditions that outline the duties of each party involved. An insurance policy is conditional in that the insurer is obligated only to compensate the insured if certain conditions are met. Due to this characteristic, it is the duty of every insured to carefully read and understand the conditions listed in a policy before it is signed.

THE LAW OF AGENCY

AGENTS AND BROKERS

It is important for financial planners to understand the relationship between insurers, insureds, agents, and brokers. Often clients will not be aware of potential conflicts of interest inherent in certain agent-insurer or broker-insurer relationships. The financial planner has a responsibility to make his clients aware of such relationships and inform them of the various methods of obtaining recommended insurance coverage.

An **agent** is a legal representative of the insurer and has authority to enter into agreements on its behalf. Agents are used by insurance companies as a marketing and sales tool. Types of agencies include general agencies, branch agencies, independent agencies, and surplus-line agencies. In contrast, **brokers** are legal representatives of the insured and can offer products from many insurers. Many are also licensed agents, which facilitates issuance of policies.

agent - legal representative of the insurer that has authority to enter into agreements on its behalf

broker - legal representative of the insured who can offer products from many insurers

A **general agent** is an independent businessperson who represents only one insurer for a designated territory. The agent is responsible for hiring, training, and paying other agents to work under his supervision. The general agent is compensated by commissions received from the insurance company for sales produced by his agency, and the insurer may provide some financing for office expenses.

general agent - an independent businessperson who represents only one insurer for a designated territory

Insurance companies may also market their products via a branch office. The manager in charge of the office is an agent similar to a general agent with respect to duties and compensation, but the manager is an employee of the insurer instead of an independent contractor. The difference between the general agent and the branch manager would not be apparent to the public, and their relationship with insureds is identical.

Independent agents are insurance agents that represent multiple unrelated insurers. Conflicts of interest can easily arise in the independent agency system since commissions are based on the product line offered and which insurer writes the policy. Agents have an incentive to sell products that offer high commissions and are under pressure to maintain a certain level of product sales offered by the insurance companies they represent. These characteristics of independent agencies may prevent the consumer from obtaining the best policy for his needs.

independent agent - an agent that represents multiple insurers

Sometimes the policy requested by a consumer would require an admitted (in-state) insurer to be exposed to too great a risk. In this situation, **surplus-line agents** will be employed. These agents have the authority to place business with unadmitted (out-of-state) insurers when necessary insurance is not available within the state.

surplus-line agent - an agent that has the authority to engage in business with out-of-state insurers in order to meet unavailable in-state consumer needs

AGENCY RELATIONSHIPS

Because brokers are representatives of the insured and not of the insurer, the insurance companies are not bound by statements made by the broker to the insured. Disagreements will not involve the insurer. Instead, the broker and the insured will be the parties involved if legal controversy arises.

Agents, on the other hand, are designated by the insurance companies as legal representatives. Thus, the insurer, known as the principal in the relationship, is generally responsible for statements made by the agent to the insured. Agency relationships legally cannot be presumed without basis, which could include the agent possessing a rate book, business cards, or blank application forms. The authority of an agent is derived from three sources: express authority, implied authority, and apparent authority.

express authority - the actual authority that a insurance company gives its representatives

Express authority is the actual authority that an insurance company gives its representatives (agents). It involves powers that are explicitly given or denied to the agent by the insurer in writing. Usually these are stated in the agency agreement between the agent and the insurer. Typical powers are the ability to solicit applicants for insurance products. Limits on the amount of insurance the agent can offer may be included in the agreement as a restriction on his authority. The insurance company is responsible for the acts of its agents per the express authority.

implied authority - the authority that the public reasonably perceives the agent to possess, even without express authority

Implied authority is the authority that the public reasonably perceives the agent to possess, even without express authority. It gives the agent the power to perform any incidental act required in fulfilling obligations of the agency agreement. For example, the agent may have express authority to deliver policies to the insured. Accepting the first premium due under the policy would be an implied power of the agent. Under implied authority, an insurer is liable for the acts of its agents even if the agent knowingly misleads the insured.

apparent authority - the insured is led to believe that the agent has authority, either express or implied, where no such authority actually exists

Apparent authority is when the insured is led to believe that the agent has authority, either express or implied, where no such authority actually exists. The insurer may be liable for misstatements by the agent even if it is unaware of such acts. For example, if an agent tells a client that the premium for insurance can be paid 10 days late then the insurer is required to provide coverage during those 10 days even if the stated policy of the insurance company is different.

EXAMPLE

An insurer may be liable for unauthorized actions of its agents if the company was aware of the actions, but did nothing to stop them. Apparent authority is based on this principle of estoppel. For example, an agent who has an insurer's logo on his stationery and on the sign in front of his office has the apparent authority to represent that insurer to the public. Should the insurer withdraw the agent's authority to represent it, but not make certain that the company's logo is removed from the stationery and the sign, the insurer could still be bound by the agent's actions on its behalf.

IMPORTANT FEATURES OF INSURANCE CONTRACTS

EXCLUSIONS

Exclusions are a necessary part of every insurance contract, because not every peril or property can be covered in every policy. Moreover, some items are simply uninsurable because they do not meet the requisites of an insurable risk.

The exclusions in an insurance contract outline what specifically will not be covered. The doctrine of concurrent causation makes it necessary for even named-perils policies to include numerous exclusions. Concurrent causation exists when a loss can be attributed to more than one peril. The law states that if at least one of the contributing perils is covered, then the insurer must pay the entire loss. So, even though a named-perils policy might agree to cover fire, the insurer may not wish to cover fires that result from an earthquake. If the insurer does not specifically state that fires caused by earthquake are excluded from coverage, then when an earthquake occurs, and even a small fire results, the entire loss will have to be paid.

Insurers may exclude coverage for perils (such as war and flood), losses (the cost of a private hospital room when a semiprivate room will do), or specific items of property (valuable papers and money are typically excluded from homeowners coverage).

RIDERS AND ENDORSEMENTS

Riders and **endorsements** are two terms used interchangeably by the insurance industry. They are written additions to an insurance contract that modify its original provisions. They make it possible to customize an insurance contract to fit an individual's needs. These attachments to the contract may extend coverage, change premiums, or make corrections to the policy that take precedence over any conflicting terms in the preprinted policy form.

riders/endorsements - written additions to an insurance contract that modify its original provisions

VALUATION OF INSURED LOSSES

Insurance policies must not only specify what is covered and what is excluded, they must also explain how losses will be paid. Without valuation provisions in the policy, the insured and the insurer could have numerous disputes over how much a particular claim is worth.

Most insurance policies value losses in one of three ways:

- Replacement cost.
- Actual cash value.
- Agreed-upon value.

Replacement Cost

Replacement cost is the current cost of replacing property with new materials of like kind and quality. If, for example, a house were damaged by fire, the damaged carpet would be replaced with new carpet, even though the old carpet was somewhat worn and soiled. Replacement cost is

Where on the Web

A.M. Best Company *www.ambest.com*
Fitch Ratings Insurance Group *www.fitchratings.com*
Independent Insurance Agents and Brokers of America *www.independentagent.com*
Insurance Information Institute *www.iii.org*
Insurance Marketplace Standards Association (IMSA) *www.imsaethics.org*
Investor Desktop *www.quickcalcs.com*
Life and Health Insurance Foundation for Education *www.life-line.org*
Moody's Investor Service *www.moodys.com*
National Association of Insurance Commissioners *www.naic.org*
Property and Casualty Information *www.propertyandcasualty.com*
Standard & Poors *www.standardpoors.com*
Quicken InsureMarket *www.quicken.com/insurance*
Weiss Ratings *www.weissratings.com*

often found by comparing what was once owned with what is currently on the market. Many homeowners policies have replacement cost provisions.

Actual Cash Value (ACV)

actual cash value - one of three ways in which losses are valued in most insurance policies. Actual cash value (ACV) is calculated as replacement cost minus functional depreciation.

Actual cash value is equal to replacement cost minus functional depreciation. For example, if the functional life of a roof is 20 years, and it is destroyed after five years, the roof is assumed to be 25 percent depreciated at the time of the loss. The insurer would thus pay 75 percent of the roof's replacement cost if the policy valued losses on an ACV basis.

From the standpoint of a homeowner, ACV coverage can impose a serious financial burden if a severe loss occurs on older property. Replacement cost coverage is therefore suggested, even though it is more expensive. Virtually all automobile policies use ACV, rather than replacement cost, because automobiles depreciate so rapidly. The cost of providing replacement cost coverage on autos would be too high for most consumers to purchase it.

Agreed-upon Value

Due to the difficulty of valuing certain losses, amounts paid for a loss are agreed upon by the insurer and the insured at the time a policy is issued. In writing a contract of this type, there is no violation of the principle of indemnity because the insurer will generally agree to a value that is reflective of the property's fair market value. Fine arts are often insured under the valued policy principle, as are antiques. Life insurance is a valued policy because it is impossible to determine the precise value of a person's life objectively, and there is no such thing as the replacement cost of a person.

Deductibles and Copayments

A **deductible** is a stated amount of money the insured is required to pay on a loss before the insurer will make any payments under the policy conditions. Deductibles help to eliminate small claims, reduce premiums, and decrease morale hazard. Deductibles are used mainly in property, health, and automobile insurance contracts. They are not used in life insurance contracts, however, because death is a complete loss (there is never a partial claim under a life insurance policy). Disability policies use an elimination period, which essentially provides a deductible.

deductible - a stated amount of money the insured is required to pay on a loss before the insurer will make any payments under the policy conditions

Copayments are in addition to deductibles and are commonly used in health insurance policies. **Copayments** are loss-sharing arrangements in which the insured pays a percentage of the loss in excess of the deductible. One example of a copayment is when a person must pay the first $500 of medical expenses each year, and then 20 percent of all expenses over that amount. The insurer pays 80 percent of covered medical expenses that exceed the $500 deductible.

copayments - a loss-sharing arrangement in which the insured pays a percentage of the loss in excess of the deductible

COINSURANCE

Coinsurance defines the percentage of financial responsibility that the insured and the insurer must uphold in order to achieve equity in rating. Coinsurance exists primarily in property insurance and encourages all insureds to cover their property to at least a stated percentage of the property's value, or else suffer a financial penalty. Because the vast majority of property losses are partial, without coinsurance clauses many insureds would attempt to save money on insurance by purchasing less insurance than the full value of their property. While underinsuring is not an illegal practice, it presents a problem for the underwriter and actuary who base expected loss estimates, and thus premiums, on the full value of the properties in the pool.

coinsurance - the percentage of financial responsibility that the insured and the insurer must uphold in order to achieve equity in rating

The amount paid on a property insurance claim with a coinsurance clause is determined by comparing several values. If the insured purchases coverage that meets or exceeds the coinsurance requirement (usually 80 percent of replacement value for homeowners insurance), then payment on a claim for a loss will be the lesser of the face value of the policy, replacement cost, or actual expenditures. However, if the insured purchases coverage that is less than the coinsurance requirement (say, 60 percent of the replacement value), then payment on a claim for a loss will be the greater of the actual cash value (ACV) or the result of the following formula subject to the face value of the policy:

$$\frac{\text{Amount of Coverage Purchased}}{\text{Coinsurance}} \times \text{Replacement Cost}$$

EXAMPLE For example, Martin owns a home with a replacement value of $300,000 and a depreciate actual value equal to 50 percent of the replacement value. He purchases $200,000 of insuranc with a coinsurance requirement of 80 percent. If Martin experiences a $100,000 loss, th insurance company will pay the greater of:

Actual Cash Value = 50% × $100,000 = **$50,000**

or

$$\frac{\text{Amt Purchased}}{\text{Coinsurance}} \times \text{Replacement Cost} = \frac{\$200{,}000}{80\% \times \$300{,}000} \times \$100{,}000 = \mathbf{\$83{,}333}$$

Since the coinsurance formula results in the greater value, Martin will receive $83,333 for hi $100,000 loss.

Coinsurance is also a term used in medical insurance indemnity policies. In these policies coinsurance refers to the percentages paid by the insurer and the insured for claims after th deductible has been met and before the stop-loss limit is reached. For example, in a plan wit 80/20 coinsurance, a $500 deductible, and a $1,000 stop-loss limit, the insured would pay 10 percent of costs until the $500 deductible was reached. After the first $500 in claims, the insure would pay 20 percent of costs until claims reached $5,500 ($1,000 stop-loss / 20% + $50 deductible) and then 0 percent. The insurance company would be responsible for 100 percent o all further claims during that policy period.

INDIVIDUAL LOSS EXPOSURES AND INSURANCE COVERAGES

PERILS THAT CAN REDUCE AND/OR ELIMINATE THE ABILITY TO EARN INCOME

There are three main types of pure risk that can interrupt one's earned income stream: dying to soon, living too long, and disability.

Dying Too Soon

The risk of a person dying before reaching full life expectancy is known as premature death. In most cases, the person who dies prematurely has a number of financial obligations, including a family to support, a mortgage to pay, and children to send through college. To prevent a great economic struggle for surviving dependents, proper financial and estate planning using life insurance will provide for those dependents in the event of the premature death of a breadwinner.

Living Too Long

While it may sound ridiculous to say that someone lived "too long," there is the risk of outliving one's financial resources (called superannuation). Medical and technological advances have led to substantial increases in human life expectancy. Currently, the average person retiring at age 65 is expected to live another 20 years. Approximately fifty percent of all retirees will live beyond the normal life expectancy of 20 years. How does one make certain that savings and other assets will last until death? Various financial planning products make it possible to assure that one does not outlive one's assets.

Disability

An unexpected accident or illness may result not only in high medical costs, but also in the inability to work and earn income. The cost of medical treatment continues to rise at a rate that exceeds general inflation. The cost of providing a lifetime of medical care, while simultaneously being unable to earn an income, can be astronomical. Long-term disability insurance can be used to mitigate this risk.

PERILS THAT CAN DESTROY OR DEPLETE EXISTING ASSETS

With the income earned in one's lifetime, various assets such as cash, real estate, and automobiles are acquired. Even if the individual's ability to earn an income is never hindered, financial loss could result if existing assets are destroyed or lost by theft. There are two main exposures that exist in this category: damage to property and legal liability for injuries inflicted upon others.

Damage to Property

A host of perils threaten the individual's property, including natural disasters, crimes, and careless accidents. The financial consequences of these perils and their resulting damage can be severe.

Damage to property can result in one of two types of financial losses: direct and indirect. A direct loss is an immediate result of an insured peril. The cost of repairing fire damage to one's house is a direct loss. An indirect loss occurs as a result of a direct property loss. The types of expenses that are incurred as indirect losses are numerous. If a section of the fire-damaged house mentioned above is being rented out, the lost rent due to the property being uninhabitable is an example of an indirect loss. Because the fire damage leaves the house untenable, the family also has to pay for the cost of hotel accommodations until the house can be repaired, which is another indirect loss resulting from the fire damage. If the hotel does not accept pets, the family will have to pay a kennel or other boarding facility to keep the pets until the home is repaired. All of these expenses add up quickly and can easily exceed the cost of the direct property loss.

Legal Liability for Injuries Inflicted upon Others

Under the U.S. legal system, one is held legally liable if he causes bodily injury or property damage to another. Personal savings and other assets can be seized to pay for this liability.

Liability risk is especially dangerous from a financial standpoint because there is no upper limit on the amount of loss one can suffer. Consider the physician who treats 20 to 40 patients each day. If one of those patients is injured as a result of the doctor's malpractice, she might be willing to accept a small settlement of $10,000 for her pain and suffering, whereas another patient suffering the exact same injury might demand $10 million. Assuming a court of law finds the doctor guilty of malpractice, the injured patient might very well be awarded $10 million (or even more). In addition to the damages claimed by the injured party, the insured also suffers another loss—the cost of settling and/or defending lawsuits. With professional legal fees starting at abou $150 per hour, a person found to be free of causing an injury could have enormous legal bills.

SELECTING AN INSURANCE COMPANY

Several rating agencies specialize in the financial assessments of insurers. Due to recent financia crises encountered by some insurers, the evaluations of these companies have become more an more important to consumers. The ratings of these agencies reflect their opinions of th insurance companies' financial condition and their ability to meet their obligations to thei policyowners.

The financial stability of an insurance company is essential for all types of insurance. Thes ratings may be of greater significance to life insurance policyowners, however, due to the long term nature of the life insurance contract. Policyowners need to be concerned with financia stability for obvious investment reasons, and, as a professional, the financial planner should b diligent when recommending insurance products.

RATING AGENCIES

Presently there are five private rating agencies that evaluate the financial condition of insurers anc make their ratings available to the public. The factors of the insurance companies examined vary among the rating companies and include recent performance. financial statements, leverage and management stability. External factors, such as competition, diversification and market presence may also be considered. Each organization provides a description of its analysis and defines its rating scores (see Exhibit 8.1).

A.M. Best Co. has been providing ratings for insurance companies since 1899. Specializing in insurance companies, it is the largest and longest-established company devoted to issuing in-depth reports and financial-strength ratings.

Fitch Ratings provides credit opinions for over 800 insurance companies. Fitch acquired Duff & Phelps Credit Rating Co. in 2000.

Moody's Investors Service is a source for credit ratings, research and the risk analysis of thousands of companies, including insurers. Generally, Moody's analyzes the financial condition of a company at its request, therefore using internal and external information. It also rates some companies with only information available to the public.

Standard & Poor's provides two types of ratings. Claims-paying ability ratings are issued by request of a company. There is a cost to the requesting company for this service. Qualified solvency ratings are issued using public information only and are free of charge.

Weiss Ratings publishes "safety ratings." Weiss analyzes companies using public information only and is the only company that does not charge companies for its ratings.

When purchasing insurance products, the consumer ideally will use a company that has received a top-tier rating from the majority of the agencies. For safety's sake, any company that has received a low-tier rating from any of the agencies should be avoided.

EXHIBIT 8.1: INSURER RATING AGENCIES' TOP AND BOTTOM-TIER FINANCIAL RATINGS

	A.M. Best's	Fitch	Moody's	Standard & Poor	Weiss
Highest Ratings	A++ (superior) A/A– (excellent)	AAA (highest) AA+/AA/ AA– (very high)	Aaa (exceptional) Aa1/Aa2 (excellent)	AAA (superior) AA+/AA/AA– (excellent)	A+/A/A– (excellent) B+/B/B– (good)
Lowest Ratings	C/C– (weak) D (poor)	B+/B/B- CCC+/ CCC/CCC–	B1/B2/B3 (poor) Caa	B+/B/B- (vulnerable) CC+/CCC/CCC– (extremely vulnerable)	F (failed) U (unrated)

NAIC Criteria

The National Association of Insurance Commissioners was created by state insurance regulators in 1871 to coordinate regulation of multistate insurance companies. It continues to provide support to state insurance commissioners in their role as consumer advocates in the insurance industry. NAIC produces a watchlist of insurance companies with financial ratios that indicate regulatory action may be required. A company will land on the watchlist if at least 4 of the following ratios fall outside the usual range.

- Net Change in Capital and Surplus
- Gross Change in Capital and Surplus
- Net Gain to Total Income
- Net Investment Income to Interest Required
- Admitted to Nonadmitted Assets
- Total Real Estate and Mortgage Loans to Cash and Invested Assets
- Investments in Affiliates to Capital and Surplus
- Net Commissions and Expense Allowances on Reinsurance and Changes in Surplus for Reinsurance to Capital and Surplus
- Change in Premium
- Change in Product Mix
- Change in Asset Mix
- Change in Reserving Ratio

NAIC also created the Risk-Based Capital (RBC) Model Act that adjusts the insurer's capital bas according to the amount and types of risk to which it is exposed. States that adopted this ac require insurance companies to file annual reports detailing the following risks:

- Risk associated with assets of the insurer
- Risk associated with adverse experience of the insurer related to liabilities and obligations
- Interest rate risk associated with the insurer's business
- Other relevant business risks as outlined in the RBC instructions

If the risk-based capital ratios fall to low levels, the state commissioners office will put th company under regulatory control and will attempt rehabilitation or declare the insuranc company insolvent.

Besides insurance ratings and NAIC ratios, consumers should also consider the following wher deciding on an insurance provider.

- Asset size and age of the company
- Track record
- Financial operating ratios
- Lapse ratio – percentage of policies that are terminated each year
- Average policy size
- Product lines offered
- Average investment returns
- Treatment of loans against policies
- Form of ownership
- Membership in the Insurance Marketplace Standards Association (IMSA), a voluntary trade association of life insurance providers that commit to ethical market conduct

CHARACTERISTICS OF INSURANCE COMPANIES

TYPES OF OWNERSHIP

Capital Stock Insurance Company

capital stock insurance company - operated for profit, owned by stockholders

This type of insurance company is operated for profit and is owned by stockholders. Stockholders purchase shares in the insurance company. The capital received provides funding for operating expenses until premiums and investment earnings are sufficient. Stockholders receive a return on their investment through dividends and capital appreciation of the shares of the company. The Board of Directors, who are elected by the shareholders, declare dividends at their discretion.

Mutual Insurance Company

mutual insurance company - owned by policyholders; distributes profit in the form of dividends

Mutual insurance company is owned by the policyholders. Usually it is formed by a group of individuals with the goal of providing insurance to members. Most mutual insurance companies

operate in the same manner as capital stock insurance companies and distribute profits in the form of dividends to policyholders.

Insurance Underwriting

As discussed earlier, one difficulty with loss prediction for the insurance company is adverse selection. Insurance companies, therefore, employ underwriters. Underwriters classify insureds in a such a way as to adequately protect the insurance company from adverse selection. Actuaries develop rates that can be translated into insurance premiums based on particular risk characteristics. It is the job of the underwriter to decide which risk characteristics describe the individual or group applying for coverage. After determining relevant risk exposures, the underwriter will designate the prospect as insurable or uninsurable according to company guidelines. If the potential insured is deemed insurable, the underwriter will determine the appropriate premium to charge based on the actuarial tables and level of risk associated with the insured.

Reinsurance

Reinsurance is insurance for insurance companies. It provides sharing of risk across two or more insurance providers. With reinsurance, a company can reduce its exposure to risk of catastrophic loss which could cause it to become insolvent. One method of reinsurance is excess-loss. Under this method the reinsurer is liable for losses that exceed a specified limit. Thus, the original insurer is protected from large claims. The reinsurer will receive premiums from many policies, but will likely have only a few claims. Many firms that self-insure for employer-provided health insurance reinsure using the excess-loss method.

Example

For example, Company A is willing to expose itself to $500,000 of risk (its "retention limit"). Reinsurer B accepts the risk in excess of Company A's $500,000 retention limit. For acceptance of the excess risk, Reinsurer B receives a premium from Company A.

Federal and State Regulation

Historically, the insurance industry has been regulated by state governments. Since 1941, the federal government has had authority under interstate commerce and antitrust laws to regulate insurance companies, but most legislative and administrative actions involving insurance are still performed at the state level. In 1945 with the passage of the McCarran-Ferguson Act, regulation of insurance companies was explicitly given to the states. If a state has inadequate resources, however, the federal government may step in.

Each state has an insurance commissioner who is either appointed by the governor or is elected. The commissioner oversees the execution of state and federal laws related to the insurance industry. Among the commissioner's duties are licensing insurance agents and companies, approving proposed rate changes, investigating consumer complaints, reviewing insurance forms, and regularly auditing insurance companies to ensure solvency.

THE RISK MANAGEMENT PROCESS

Risk management is a systematic process for identifying, evaluating, and managing pure risk exposures faced by a firm or individual. The six steps in the risk management process are:

- Determining the objectives of the risk management program.
- Identifying the risks to which the company is exposed.
- Evaluating the identified risks as to the probability of outcome and potential loss.
- Determining alternatives for managing risks and selecting the most appropriate alternative for each risk.
- Implementing a risk-management plan based on the selected alternatives.
- Periodically evaluating and reviewing the risk management program.

DETERMINING THE OBJECTIVES OF THE RISK MANAGEMENT PROGRAM

The first step in the risk management process is determining the goals of the risk management program. Unfortunately, this step in the process is one of the most ignored. As a result, many parts of a client's risk management program conflict and are disjointed This is often due to vague risk management objectives. Risk management objectives can range from obtaining the most cost-effective protection against risk, to stabilizing operations or continuing income after a loss.

IDENTIFYING THE RISK EXPOSURE

The next step is to identify all possible pure risk exposures of the client. Though it is difficult to generalize risks that companies face due to differences in structure and conditions, potential exposures mirror those described for individuals. Businesses, of course, are concerned with damage to existing assets and any perils that might interrupt their ability to generate income. As most businesses generate income through the efforts of their personnel, risk managers are also concerned with the recruitment, selection, hiring, training, health, and welfare of personnel.

In order for a corporate risk manager to identify the risks that his company faces, he must delve into the operations of the firm. Some common methods of research are physical inspection, risk analysis questionnaires, flow process charts, review of financial statements and reports on past losses.

For the individual consumer, identifying risks is a somewhat simpler process. Analyzing and valuing the properties owned or leased, recognizing activities that could result in injuries to others, and determining how to protect one's ability to generate an income are all reasonably straightforward activities.

Evaluating the Identified Risks

The next logical step in the risk management process is to evaluate the potential frequency and severity of losses. **Loss frequency** is the expected number of losses that will occur within a given period of time. **Loss severity** refers to the potential size or damage of a loss. By identifying loss frequency and severity, a risk manager can prioritize the urgency of dealing with each specific risk.

loss frequency - the expected number of losses that will occur within a given period of time

loss severity - potential size or damage of a loss

Recall that probability is useful when applied to large numbers. Relying solely on probability-based predictions for an individual, however, is not recommended. Of greater concern to the individual is the potential severity of the losses that occur. The person who owns a $200,000 home has a maximum possible severity of loss on that asset equal to $200,000. This would be, for the vast majority of consumers, a high severity loss. On the other hand, the person who owns a car worth $1,500 has a fairly low severity loss potential. To a particular person the $1,500 loss might be severe, however, and could even adversely affect income generation if they could no longer drive to work.

Determining and Selecting the Best Risk-Management Alternative

Insurance is not necessary, nor is it even available, for each and every risk of loss an individual faces. Choosing the appropriate risk management tool depends largely on the potential severity and frequency of the loss exposures faced. Where more than one tool is deemed appropriate, the costs and benefits of each should be examined to determine which is most economical and beneficial.

As discussed earlier, there are generally four ways to manage a risk – avoid it, reduce it, retain it, or transfer it. How does one know the best risk management technique for a particular risk? Exhibit 8.2, based on the frequency and severity of expected losses, can be used as a general guideline for selecting an appropriate tool.

EXHIBIT 8.2: RISK MANAGEMENT GUIDELINES

	HIGH FREQUENCY	LOW FREQUENCY
HIGH SEVERITY	Avoidance	Insurance
LOW SEVERITY	Retention/Reduction	Retention

EXAMPLE

The first type of loss exposure is a combination of high severity and high frequency. This is perhaps the most serious type of exposure and is often handled by avoidance. Assume John applies for the position of chauffeur for Divine Limousine Company. He has previously been arrested for miscellaneous misdemeanors and convicted twice for driving while intoxicated. He is clearly an unsafe driver and hiring him as an employee creates potential liability for Divine. It makes sense for Divine Limousine to avoid this exposure by not hiring John.

Exposures that are low in frequency yet high in potential severity are best handled by insurance. The high severity losses can leave a person in a dire financial position, yet the low frequency makes sharing the cost of losses with others economically feasible. Examples of high severity/low frequency loss exposures include fire damage to a house and losses due to automobile collisions.

The remaining types of losses are both low severity in nature. Transferring low severity losses to an insurer is not economically feasible because the insurer will have substantial expenses associated with processing numerous small claims. The risk of low severity losses is generally retained. When low severity losses occur with high frequency, their aggregate impact can have financially devastating effects. So, it is suggested that high frequency, low severity losses not just be retained, but also controlled in an effort to reduce frequency. For an individual, low severity losses include dings on cars, road-damaged tires, minor injuries and illnesses, and small kitchen grease fires in the home.

IMPLEMENTING A RISK-MANAGEMENT PLAN BASED ON THE SELECTED ALTERNATIVES

The risk-management plan must reflect the chosen response to risk. If risk-reduction is the appropriate response to a given risk, then the proper risk-reduction program must be designed and implemented. If a decision is made to retain a risk, the individual or company must determine whether a reserve fund will be used. If the response to a given risk is to transfer the risk through insurance, an assessment and selection of an insurer are usually followed by negotiations and purchase of the appropriate insurance products.

PERIODICALLY EVALUATING AND REVIEWING THE RISK MANAGEMENT PROGRAM

The purpose for periodic evaluation and review is twofold. First, the risk management process does not take place independent of external influences. Things change over time and risk exposure can change as well. The risk management technique that was most suitable last year may not be the most prudent this year, and adjustments will have to be made. Second, errors in judgment may occur, and periodic review allows the risk manager to discover such errors and revise the risk management plan as necessary.

PROFESSIONAL FOCUS

Do you feel that many of your clients underestimate their need for insurance?

Clients often misjudge their need for insurance to manage their various risk exposures. In some cases they underestimate the insurance need, while in other cases they overestimate. There is a tendency to focus on protection of ownership interests in real and tangible property, while underestimating the need to insure liability exposures. An uncovered loss of a piece of property such as an automobile or home can have a major financial impact, but the liability exposure related to the ownership and operation of that automobile or home can be much more significant. An uncovered adverse lawsuit decision can have a devastating effect on a client's financial prospect and lifestyle. One big liability claim can literally wipe out years of financial planning and wealth accumulation.

What have you found to be the best way to evaluate an individual's insurance risks?

There is no substitute for good, old-fashioned, "roll-up-your-sleeves" work to accomplish a comprehensive evaluation of a client's risk exposures. This is one area where the "know your customer" rule is of critical importance. An in-depth investigation of a client's lifestyle will often uncover exposures that had never occurred to the client. A careful inspection of the client's insurance policies is certainly a necessary element of a comprehensive review of his risk management program, but this step should arguably be delayed until after the initial fact-finding interview. Focusing on in-force policies from the start can skew the perspective of the planner, possibly causing neglect of exposures that are not covered by a policy.

How do you approach situations where you have found a misrepresentation or concealment in the insurance contract by the client?

When misrepresentation, concealment, or other fraudulent activity may exist, it is important to clearly explain the potential ramifications of such acts, without being unduly judgmental or accusatory. Clients can thereby make informed decisions to rectify situations that could void essential coverage. Certainly, in cases where the planner is also acting as the agent or broker providing the coverage, a higher standard of diligence is required.

Do you believe that your clients read their insurance policy and are fully aware of the specifics of the contract?

The vast majority either does not read the policy at all, or does not read it carefully enough to understand the coverage provided under the contract. In fact, a reading of the contracts alone may not provide a precise understanding of coverage, as many words and phrases used in insurance contracts have specific meanings which do not mirror common, everyday language. For a complete understanding, a client should read his policy and then confirm his understanding with his planner or insurance professional. Frankly, many financial planners have insufficient knowledge of the various insurance forms and coverage and, therefore, should defer the provision of specific advice to a competent insurance professional.

In general, are clients more eager to purchase insurance to cover their risks or to self-insure?

Generally clients will purchase insurance or self-insure based on common practice. For example, many people will carry property coverage on a low-value automobile just because they have always done so. Yet, at the same time, they will choose to self-insure an expensive recreational vehicle because they have traditionally gone without insurance, even though this might be the more substantial exposure. This relates to the question of estimation of the need for insurance: This same client may be carrying a low (e.g., $100 or $250) deductible on the low-value automobile, while tacitly "choosing" to self-insure the theoretically unlimited liability exposure of the recreational vehicle. The planner serves a vital role in making clients aware of these sorts of inconsistencies and gaps in the client's risk management program.

EVAN WARDNER, MBA, CFP®

DISCUSSION QUESTIONS

1. What is risk?
2. What are the different types of risk and how does each impact the personal financial planning process?
3. What is the difference between subjective and objective risk?
4. Name the common responses to risk. Of these responses, for which is insurance an appropriate risk management tool?
5. How does a peril differ from a hazard, and how does each relate to the need for insurance?
6. What is adverse selection and how does it affect the insurance mechanism?
7. What are the requisites for an insurable risk and what distinguishes insurance from gambling?
8. What are the elements of a valid contract? What distinguishing features do insurance contracts have?
9. What is the reason for, and the effect of, various contractual features in insurance contracts?
10. What is the principle of indemnity?
11. What is the principle of insurable interest?
12. What is adhesion?
13. Distinguish between an agent and a broker.
14. Differentiate between a general agent, an independent agent and a surplus-line agent.
15. The authority of an agent can be derived from what sources? Describe each source of authority.
16. What are the insurable-loss exposures faced by the typical individual consumer?
17. What are the various insurance company rating agencies? Describe each.
18. What are the steps in the risk management process?
19. What does frequency of loss and severity of loss have to do with risk management?

EXERCISES

1. Briefly explain the difference between pure and speculative risk. Give an example.
2. Name three perils that could cause a loss around your home or apartment. What are the hazards that may increase the probability of such perils?
3. Explain the difference between moral hazard and morale hazard. Give two examples of each.
4. Differentiate between gambling and insurance.
5. How would you reduce or manage the risk of adverse selection in a group dental insurance program?
6. John has an insurance policy for $150,000 on a building located at 175 Pine Street. The policy expires December 31, 2005. John sold the property to Bill on October 31, 2005, for $150,000. That very night, the building burned to the ground. Can John collect on the policy? If so, how much? If not, what legal characteristics would prevent him from collecting? Will John get any money from the insurer?

7. Which of the following people have an insurable interest in Mike's life?
   - ▲ Angel, Mike's 25-year-old daughter
   - ▲ James, Mike's 30-year-old son
   - ▲ Cassie, Mike's former wife and mother of Angel
   - ▲ John, Mike's former business partner
   - ▲ Donna, Mike's daughter-in-law
   - ▲ Scott, Mike's current business partner
   - ▲ Rita, Mike's new girlfriend

8. Leon is the risk manager for ABC, Inc. He has evaluated the following risks in terms of frequency and severity and asks your opinion as to which risk management tool to use.

		Probability/ Frequency	Severity per Occurrence
A	Fire destroys plant	0.0001	$10,000,000
B	Loss of property through employee theft	0.1	$1,000
C	On-the-job employee disability	0.01	$1,500,000
D	Loss due to misplaced inventory (computer)	0.1	$2,000
E	Loss due to failure to reduce energy bill (lights off, air conditioner off on weekends)	0.02	$400
F	Air conditioning unit goes out (compressor)	0.01	$2,000

CHAPTER 9

Managing Life, Health and Disability Risks

LEARNING OBJECTIVES:

After learning the material in this chapter, you will be able to:

1. Identify the risks associated with premature death.
2. Measure the needs related to premature death.
3. List and define the various types of term life insurance.
4. List and define the various types of whole life insurance.
5. List and define the various types of universal life insurance.
6. Distinguish between term, whole life and universal life insurance, and explain the advantages and disadvantages of each.
7. List and describe the major types of employer-provided health and disability coverages.
8. Describe the important policy provisions and major contractual features of individual health and disability coverages.
9. Explain the differences between annuities and life insurance contracts.
10. List and define the various types of annuities.
11. Describe the tax treatment of life insurance and annuities.
12. Describe the important policy provisions and contractual features of life and annuity contracts.
13. Explain the need for health insurance.
14. List and describe the major types of individual health coverage.
15. Be familiar with important policy provisions and major contractual features of individual health coverage.
16. Determine how much the insured must pay out of pocket and how much the insured will collect from the insurer, given information about particular health coverage.
17. Understand the purpose of disability income insurance, and be able to define and discuss the various definitions of disability.

- more -

18. Describe the major types of disability coverage.
19. Describe the important policy provisions and contractual features of disability income insurance.
20. Describe the tax treatment of health and disability coverages.
21. Distinguish between indemnity plans and managed care plans.
22. Explain how group health coverage may be continued or transferred when employment terminates.
23. Describe the important policy provisions and contractual features of long-term care insurance.

INTRODUCTION

Life, health, and disability risks include premature death, catastrophic illness, the inability to work, and the need for long-term care. While these risks are generally low in frequency, they are potentially catastrophic in severity. Thus, the financial planner must assist the client in mitigating the impact of such risks by selecting and implementing appropriate insurance coverage. This chapter examines each of the above catastrophic risks and describes insurance products, particularly life insurance and health insurance, that can mitigate those risks.

Life insurance is a fundamental element in a comprehensive financial plan for most clients, particularly those with dependents. The financial planner should be familiar with each type of life insurance in order to identify and meet client needs.

Health insurance is crucial for each member of the family, since an uninsured illness can disrupt income security and reduce personal wealth. The financial planner must be familiar with not only major medical insurance, but also disability and long-term care insurance.

IDENTIFYING RISKS ASSOCIATED WITH PREMATURE DEATH

While it may be impossible to predict the timing of a person's death, it is possible to protect the survivors from the financial distress that they can suffer from the loss of an income provider. The purchase of life insurance is one of the most effective methods of protecting against the financial consequences of untimely death. Financial planners recognize two fundamental needs for the monies generated by a life insurance policy: replacing income and preserving assets.

INADEQUATE FINANCIAL RESOURCES

Life insurance policy proceeds can replace the income lost when a breadwinner dies. There are several different needs that can be addressed using life insurance proceeds.

Providing Income for the Readjustment Period

The loss of a breadwinner may have a significant financial impact on surviving dependent family members, at least in the short run. Family income will diminish, and the risk that family members may experience a lower standard of living is great. Ultimately, the family may adjust its standard of living to fit its new income level, or other members of the family may be able to work to replace the lost income of the deceased. However, after a family suffers the loss of a loved one, it usually encounters an unsettling and emotionally stressful readjustment period. It will take time for the surviving spouse or other dependents to reconcile grief and resume their lives. In many cases, a surviving spouse may have to be educated and trained to enter the workforce for the first time. Life insurance made payable directly to the family members or heirs of one's estate can provide for the family's financial support during such a period of readjustment.

Providing Financial Support to Dependents

When a breadwinner has dependents, the concern for their financial well-being exists. The mother who is the sole support of two children concerns herself with how their financial needs will be met if she dies prematurely. A life insurance policy guarantees that when the insured dies, a certain amount of money will be available to support those dependents.

When considering how much money is needed for this particular life insurance need, two important points need to be considered. First, who actually qualifies as a "dependent"? For tax purposes, most people are able to claim only persons who are children as their dependents. However, many other people may be financially dependent upon the insured. Perhaps the insured's parents, who are older and on a fixed income, rely on the insured for a certain amount of support. There may be a spouse who either does not work outside the home or does not earn enough income to survive without the insured's wages. Responsible financial planning considers the needs of all dependents, not just underage children.

Second, how much financial support should be given to various dependents? Should dependent children be supported until they are 18 years old, or should they be supported until they complete college? What standard of living does the insured wish to guarantee for survivors? These questions must be answered before the insured can accurately determine life insurance needs.

Earmarking Funds for Specific Goals

In addition to the fundamental notion of providing survivors with income, insureds may also wish to provide survivors with funds to achieve a specific goal. Such goals might include prepaying a mortgage so the surviving spouse no longer has to make a mortgage payment, or paying for college tuition for each child.

ESTATE PRESERVATION

People work throughout their lives to accumulate wealth in the form of various assets. A common fear of most consumers is that after they die, those assets will be lost. The following types of posthumous expenses that are imposed on dependents make it clear why this is a reasonable fear.

Medical Expenses Prior to Death

Even when death is sudden and swift, final medical expenses are typically incurred. In more extreme situations, one can incur exorbitant medical bills fighting to live, yet still not prevail in the fight. In many cases, a loss of life occurs after months or even years of treatment and hospital stays. Unless adequate health insurance exists to cover the bulk of such expenses, the survivors must worry about paying those final medical expenses. Even when health insurance has been purchased, many policies have a lifetime maximum benefit of $1 million or $2 million. A serious illness could easily exhaust those coverage limits, leaving many unpaid medical bills.

Disposal and Ceremonial Expenses

Each person has specific preferences about how their body should be handled after death. Some people prefer cremation, while others prefer burial. Still, there are others who wish to be placed in a mausoleum and even those who wish to have their bodies donated to medical science. Some of these procedures can be very expensive. The final ceremonies or services held for a person, whether they include a simple memorial service or an elaborate funeral, must also be paid. The amount of money that should be available to survivors to pay for these types of expenses will vary depending upon personal preferences, but one thing to remember is that they often are much more expensive than one might imagine. Adequate life insurance proceeds prevent survivors from having to liquidate other assets to pay disposal and ceremonial expenses.

Probate Expenses

After death, a person's estate may go through the probate court for final settlement of all financial matters. The probate process provides for the distribution of the deceased's assets that are under the will and for payment of debts. Life insurance proceeds may be used to expedite the prompt settlement of a person's probate estate, including the payment of court costs, taxes, and outstanding debts.

Taxes. During the probate process, federal and state estate taxes, accrued property taxes, and federal and state income taxes for the current year, as well as any back taxes due, will be collected by the appropriate agencies. If cash is not available to survivors to pay such taxes, then assets may have to be liquidated to satisfy the debts. Life insurance can provide the liquidity to satisfy the tax liabilities.

Debt Retirement. Most people die with outstanding debts, including credit card charges, accrued taxes, unpaid bills, student loans, automobile loans, and other miscellaneous consumer loans. An executor fund may be set up to retire some or all of a person's debts after death in order to avoid saddling survivors with such obligations.

MEASURING NEEDS RELATED TO PREMATURE DEATH

Generally, there are three methods used to evaluate needs related to premature death:

- The Human Life Value Approach.
- The Financial Needs Approach.
- The Capital Retention Approach

human life value approach - uses an individual's income-earning ability as the basis for risk measurement

HUMAN LIFE VALUE APPROACH

The **human life value approach** uses an individual's income-earning ability as the basis for risk measurement. This approach projects the income of the individual throughout his or her remaining work-life expectancy, including raises. Then, utilizing a discount rate (usually the risk-free rate of return and adjusted for inflation), the present value (human life value) is determined. Note that cash flows may be adjusted downward for what the individual would have personally consumed or paid in taxes on the income. The net amount is known as the FSE (Family's Share of Earnings).

Alex, who is married and the father of 4, is 45 and expects to work to age 65. He earns $70,000 per year and expects annual salary increases of 5%. Alex expects inflation to be 4.2% over his working life, and the discount rate is 5%. His personal consumption is equal to 10% of after-tax earnings, and the combined federal and state marginal tax bracket is 20%.

Step 1 Calculate the Family's Share of Earnings (FSE)

Annual Earnings = $70,000   Annual Taxes = $70,000 × .20 = $14,000

Personal Consumption	=	(After-Tax Income × Consumption %age)
	=	($70,000 – 14,000) × .10)]
	=	($56,000 × .10)
	=	$5,600

FSE	=	$70,000 – (14,000 + 5,600)
	=	Annual Earnings – (Annual Taxes + Annual Personal Consumption)
	=	$70,000 – 19,600
	=	**$50,400**

Step 2 Calculate Work Life Expectancy (WLE)

WLE	=	Expected Age of Retirement – Current Age
	=	65 – 45
	=	20 years

Step 3 Determine Human Life Value

FV	=	0
PMT	=	$50,400
I	=	.7678% [[(1.05/1.042)–1] × 100]
N	=	20

Human Life Value = $938,270

Financial Needs Approach

The **financial needs approach** to determining the adequate amount of life insurance evaluates the income replacement and lump sum needs of an individual's survivors in the event of untimely death. The effects of inflation on these needs over the years must also be recognized A family that loses a breadwinner is likely to have common needs. Funds are often necessary for the needs listed below.

financial needs approach - evaluates the income replacement needs of one's survivors in the event of untimely death

Lump-sum (cash) needs	Income (cash flow) needs
Final expenses and debts	Readjustment period
Mortgage liquidation or payment fund	Dependency period
Education expenses	Spousal life income (pre- & post-retirement)
Emergency expenses	

Final Expenses and Debts

A fund for final expenses and debts, commonly known as a **cleanup fund**, is needed by the survivors immediately. These expenses include out-of-pocket medical expenses prior to death, funeral costs, and other unplanned expenditures. Estate administration expenses, federal estate taxes, state death taxes, inheritance taxes, and income taxes must also be funded from a source outside the estate if there are illiquid assets in the estate to cover these costs

cleanup fund - fund needed immediately by survivors to cover final expenses and debts of decedent

Mortgage Liquidation or Payment Fund

The family may choose to set aside funds to pay off a mortgage. If there is no mortgage prepayment penalty, this can be an effective way to reduce the cash flow needed by the surviving family members. A fund may also be established from which monthly mortgage payments may be made (it may be advantageous for the surviving spouse to have an annual interest deduction for tax purposes).

Education Expenses

If an education funding plan is not already in place, funds may be set aside for private school at a secondary level, as well as for college and post-college education. If the survivors choose not to set aside funds, and there will be educational expenses in the future, these expenses should be factored into the life income needed by the family.

Emergency Expenses

The purpose of this fund is to provide survivors with a reserve for unforeseen expenses that may arise as the family makes a transition to life without the deceased.

Readjustment Period Income Needs

readjustment period - lasts for one to two years following the death of a breadwinner

Typically, the **readjustment period** lasts for one to two years following the death of a breadwinner. During this period, the family should receive approximately the same amount of income it received while the deceased was alive. Families will usually have certain nonrecurring expenses as they adjust to a new lifestyle. For a family that will experience a decline in its standard of living, this period allows the family to achieve the necessary readjustment.

Dependency Period Income Needs

dependency period - period in which others (the deceased's spouse, children and, in some cases, parents) would have been dependent on the deceased had he or she

The **dependency period** is one in which others (the deceased's spouse, children, and, in some cases, parents) would have been dependent on the deceased had he or she survived. In most cases, the income needs are largest during this period. The length of the dependency period is determined by the number of dependents, their ages and the deceased's contribution to the family's total income.

If both spouses earned an income prior to death, a smaller percentage of total family income must be replaced upon one of the spouse's deaths. If, however, the sole breadwinner of the family has died, the ability (or desire) of the surviving spouse to secure employment must be considered.

In most cases, the children of the deceased will be entitled to Social Security benefits (see Chapter 11, *Social Security Benefits*). The benefits received by the spouse, as caretaker of the children and on behalf of the children, will decrease the income needs of the family during the dependency period. Additionally, if parents were dependents of the deceased, any Social Security benefits received by them due to the death of their child may also decrease the income needs during this period.

Spousal Life Income Needs

At some point, the children are no longer dependent on the surviving spouse and begin lives of their own. The surviving spouse, however, may still need to replace a part of the wage earner's income, especially if the spouse does not work outside the home Spouses that reenter the workforce after years at home may find it difficult to find employment that would maintain their standards of living. Therefore, it is advisable to plan for a life income for the spouse.

blackout period - the time when Social Security benefits to the spouse are discontinued (usually when a child reaches age 16), to the time when the spouse begins to receive Social Security benefits at age 60 or later

Generally, there are two income periods to consider: 1) the blackout period, and 2) the period in which the spouse receives Social Security benefits. The **blackout period** refers to the time when Social Security benefits to the spouse are discontinued (usually when a child reaches age 16), to the time when the spouse begins to receive Social Security benefits at age 60 or later. During the blackout period, income must be provided by employment, insurance, investments, or some other source. Once Social Security benefits resume, the amount of supplemental income needed can be reduced.

EXAMPLE

Assume Frank is a consultant who earns $72,000 annually. His spouse, Julie, is a homemaker, and they have one child, Betty. There is life insurance on Frank's life in the amount of $200,000. Frank and Julie have set the following goals.

Income needed - readjustment period (1 yr.)	$ 72,000/yr.
Income needed - dependency period	48,000/yr.
Income needed - "empty nest" period	36,000/yr.
Estate expenses and debts	15,000
Education fund needed (in today's dollars)	180,000
Emergency fund	15,000
Investment assets (cash/cash equivalents)	100,000
Julie's life expectancy	Age 85
Discount rate	4%

Given the above information and a discount rate of 4%, how much life insurance should be purchased on Frank's life?

. Calculate the family's income (cash flow) needs for each period:

	Readjustment (1 year)	Child's Age (4 – 16)	Child's Age (17 – 18)	Blackout Period (age 46 – 60)	Retirement (25 yrs.)
Annual Income Needed	$72,000	$48,000	$48,000	$36,000	$36,000
OASDI (Soc. Sec.)	– 26,400	– 26,400	– 10,800	0	– 18,000
Net Annual Income Needed (PMT)	45,600	21,600	37,200	36,000	18,000
$i = \left(\frac{1.06}{1.03} - 1\right) 100 =$	2.9126	2.9126	2.9126	2.9126	2.9126
Years Needed	1	11	2	15	25
PV of Net Annual Income Needed (use begin mode)	$45,600	$206,677	$73,347	$445,092	$325,730
PV of Total Annual Income Needed: **$1,096,446**					

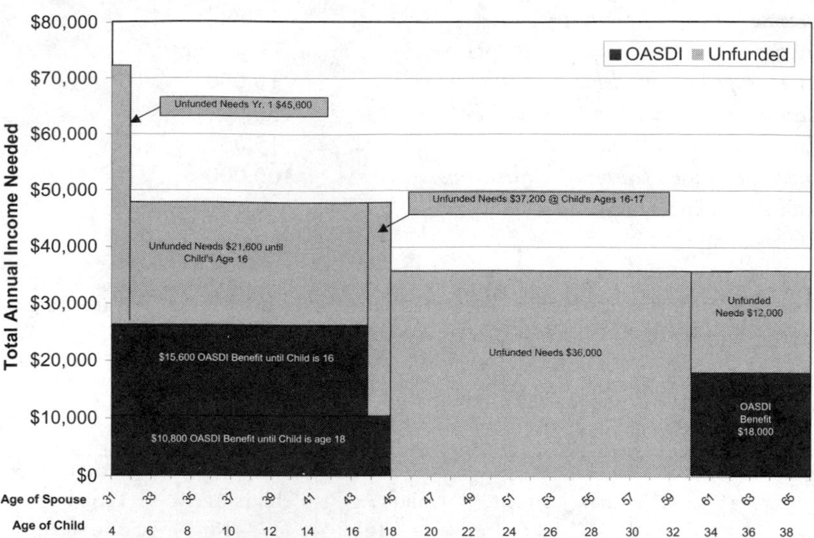

$80,000
$70,000
$60,000
$50,000
$40,000
$30,000
$20,000
$10,000
$0
Total Annual Income Needed
OASDI Unfunded
Unfunded Needs Yr. 1 $45,800
Unfunded Needs $37,200 @ Child's Ages 16-17
Unfunded Needs $21,600 until Child's Age 16
$15,600 OASDI Benefit until Child is 16
$10,800 OASDI Benefit until Child is age 18
Unfunded Needs $36,000
Unfunded Needs $12,000
OASDI Benefit $18,000
Age of Spouse
Age of Child
4 6 8 10 12 14 16 18 20 22 24 26 28 30 32 34 36 38

2. Calculate the family's lump sum funding needs:

Estate expenses and debts	$ 15,000
Education fund needed (in today's dollars)	180,000
Emergency fund	15,000
Total lump sum funding needs	**$ 210,000**

3. Calculate the life insurance death benefit needed:

Total Need	$1,306,446	($1,096,446 + $210,000)
Less Life Insurance Already in Place	– 200,000	
Less Liquid Assets	– 100,000	
Net Death Benefit Need	**$1,006,446**	

CAPITAL RETENTION APPROACH

capital retention approach - provides a death benefit amount that is sufficient to provide investment income that will cover the projected needs of the family

Unlike the financial needs approach, the **capital retention approach** provides a death benefit amount that is sufficient, along with the family's other assets, to provide investment income that will cover the projected needs of the family. The family's needs are met from the earnings of the assets, not the assets themselves. Therefore, the income-producing assets are later available for distribution to the children or other heirs.

The Capital Retention Approach involves three steps:

1. *Prepare a personal balance sheet.* List all assets and liabilities. Since this is a projected balance sheet at death, assets should include any life insurance from other sources, such as existing personal policies, coverage through employers, or death benefits available through retirement plans.

2. *Calculate the capital available for income.* Subtract liabilities, cash needs and non-income producing capital from total assets.
3. *Determine the amount of additional capital required.* Compare the family's income objectives with other sources of income available, such as Social Security.

EXAMPLE

Nicholas wants to provide his family with $50,000 of annual income in the event of his death. He wants to provide his children with an inheritance upon the death of his spouse, Kelly. He also wants to establish an emergency fund of $15,000 and an education fund of $60,000 for his children should he die. Additionally, Nicholas would like to pay off his mortgage at his death. He assumes that, over the years, any principal used to provide income will earn a return on investment (ROI) of 6%, and that final expenses upon his death will be $15,000. Assume that the family will receive $20,000 of income from other sources each year after Nicholas' death.

1. Prepare Nicholas and Kelly's balance sheet.

Assets		Liabilities	
House	$300,000	Mortgage	$220,000
Automobiles	30,000	Auto loans	20,000
Personal property	25,000	Credit card debt	10,000
Investments	20,000		
Life Insurance	200,000	Total	$250,000
Total	$575,000		

2. Calculate the capital available for income.

Total assets		$ 575,000
Less:		
Mortgage	$ 220,000	
Other liabilities	30,000	
Emergency fund	15,000	
Education fund	60,000	
Final expenses	15,000	
Non-income producing capital (Equity in home, autos, personal property)	135,000	
Total deductions		– 475,000
Capital available for income (CAI)		$ 100,000

3. Determine the amount of additional capital required

Annual income objective for the family	$ 60,000
Less:	
Capital currently available for income (CAI x ROI = $100,000 x .06)	– 6,000
Annual income from other sources	– 20,000
Annual income shortfall	$ 34,000
Total additional capital required (Shortfall/ROI - $34,000/.06)	**$ 566,667**

Unlike the Financial Needs Approach, the Capital Retention Approach has the advantages c simplicity and preservation of capital. In addition, this approach provides protection fror inflation, or can be used to hedge against rising costs. A key disadvantage, however, is the large amount of life insurance needed so that assets can be conserved for heirs.

INDIVIDUAL LIFE INSURANCE POLICIES

Life insurance is an economic means by which an individual's risk of premature death is poole among a large group of insureds. Unlike other forms of insurance, the event insured under a lif insurance policy – death – will eventually occur. The insurable risk covered under a lif insurance policy is not *whether* the individual is going to die, but *when.* This risk increases a time goes on, and actuaries can use mortality experience to calculate the number of death within an insured pool with a considerable degree of accuracy.

Consumers have a wide array of life insurance choices. Policies vary based upon the term o coverage, the flexibility of the premium or death benefit, whether the policy has cash value and if so, whether the interest rate is fixed or variable. Additionally, riders and other options, such a waiver of premium or accidental death benefit, may be added to a policy.

Life insurance policies are commonly categorized in the following manner:

- Term insurance.
- Whole life.
- Universal life.

TERM INSURANCE

term insurance - provides life insurance protection for a given period

Term insurance is commonly known as "pure insurance" because it provides nothing more thar insurance protection for a given period or term. Generally, this type of insurance is purchasec for a stated period of time and a death benefit is paid only if the insured dies during this period Term insurance has no cash value, although some long-term policies build up a small reserve tc cover future mortality costs and expenses. This reserve, however, is used up by the end of the policy term.

renewable - policyowner may continue a term policy for an additional period without evidence of insurability at a premium based on the insured's current age

convertible - a term policy that may be exchanged for a cash value life insurance policy without evidence of insurability

Most term insurance policies are **renewable**, which gives the policyowner the right to continue coverage for an additional period without evidence of insurability at a premium based on the insured's current age. The period of renewal is usually the same length as the original term period. The majority of term insurance policies are also **convertible**, which means that the term policy may be exchanged for a cash value life insurance policy without evidence of insurability Together, the renewability and convertibility features protect the policyowner against the loss of insurability.

Types of Term Insurance Policies

There are several forms of term insurance available on the market today. Generally, these policies vary by premium and death benefit design.

Annual renewable term (ART). Also known as yearly renewal term (YRT), this policy is issued for one year, and the policyowner can renew for subsequent periods to a stated age without evidence of insurability. Premiums increase each year as the insured ages.

A key advantage of yearly renewable term is that no evidence of insurability is required at the time of renewal. One disadvantage, however, is that premiums are reevaluated at the end of each annual term and will increase as the death rate increases. Because the rate of death rises at an increasing rate with age, the premiums for this type of policy may become prohibitively expensive as the insured ages. Although initially less expensive than a level premium whole life policy, ART premiums will far exceed the level premium as the insured ages. Exhibit 9.1 illustrates the premium comparison of an ART policy with a level premium policy. Notice the exponential nature of the annual renewable term premium reflecting the increased probability of mortality as people age.

annual renewable term (ART) - term insurance issued for one year; renewable for subsequent periods to a stated age without evidence of insurability

EXHIBIT 9.1: ANNUAL RENEWABLE TERM PREMIUM AND PREMIUM FOR ORDINARY LIFE

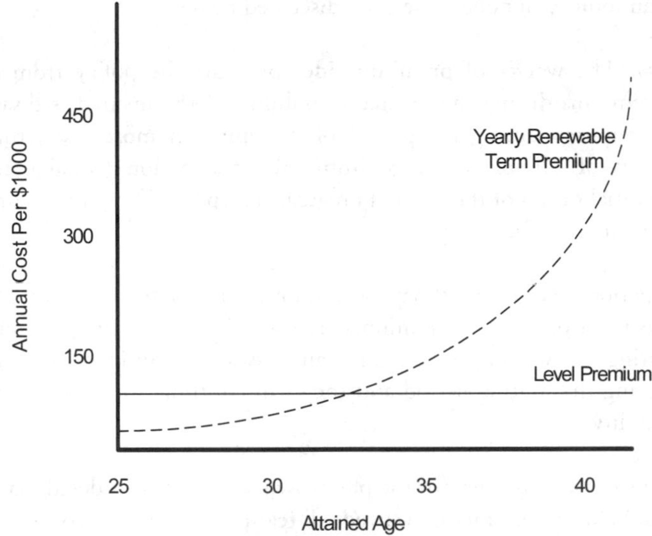
Annual Cost Per $1000
450
300
150
Yearly Renewable
Term Premium
Level Premium
25
30
35
40
Attained Age

Level term. **Level term** insurance has a level death benefit and a fixed premium for a stated period. Common term periods for this type of policy are 5, 10, 15, 20 and 30 years. In most cases, premiums for the early years of the term are higher than those for a yearly renewable term policy. This "overpayment" in early years funds the coverage for later ages when premiums for an ART policy would have been exceedingly expensive and unaffordable.

level term - a policy with a level death benefit and a fixed premium for a stated period

Term to Age 65 or 70. This policy provides protection until the insured reaches age 65 or 70, at which time coverage ceases. Often, this policy may be converted to a cash value policy, but the policyowner must covert the policy before a particular age, often age 60.

term to age 65 or 70 - a policy that provides protection until the insured reaches age 65 or 70, at which time coverage ceases

Decreasing term. **Decreasing term** insurance has a level premium with a decreasing death benefit. In some policies, premiums discontinue a few years before the coverage ends. Decreasing term policies are most commonly used to provide a death benefit to pay off a mortgage in the event a

decreasing term - term insurance that has a level premium with a decreasing death benefit

breadwinner dies. Since mortgage balances decrease over time, a decreasing term policy is most appropriate to meet this need.

reentry term - the insurer may renew coverage at a lower premium rate if the insured provides satisfactory evidence of insurability

Reentry term. **Reentry term** is a policy under which the company may renew coverage at a lower premium rate than would otherwise apply, provided that at the time of renewal, the insured furnishes evidence of insurability (e.g., medical exam, etc.) satisfactory to the company. The ability to apply for lower rates may or may not be guaranteed in the contract. Rate schedules are provided in the policy, and there is a "guaranteed maximum" rate that the policyowner must pay if the insured no longer qualifies for the preferred rates. These policies reward insureds that remain in good health, while maintaining the insurance coverage of those who no longer qualify as "preferred risks."

Term Policy Riders

rider - provides additional coverage for something specifically not covered within the primary policy

A **rider** provides additional coverage for something specifically not covered within the primary policy. The rider is added to the primary policy and the policyholder pays an extra amount to cover the rider. Common term policy riders are discussed below.

waiver of premium rider - if the insured is disabled, premium payments are not required during the period of disability

Waiver of Premium. The **waiver of premium rider** prevents the policy from lapsing due to nonpayment of premiums during the insured's disability. If the insured is disabled, premium payments are not required during the period of disability. In most cases, total disability is required. Definitions of "disability" range from own occupation ("unable to perform the material and substantial duties of the insured's regular occupation") to any occupation ("unable to engage in any paying work").

accidental death benefit rider - pays the beneficiary an additional death benefit if the insured dies accidentally

Standard waiting periods vary from 90 days to 6 months; in other words, for a 90-day waiting period, ninety days must pass before premiums are waived. The policyowner must continue to pay premiums during the waiting period. In many cases, the company will then return the premiums paid during the waiting period and they will continue to waive the premiums until the end of the disability.

accelerated death benefit rider - allows the policyowner to receive a portion of the policy's death benefit during the insured's lifetime if the insured is inflicted with a terminal illness

Note that premiums waived on behalf of the policyowner are not considered loans and, as such, need not be repaid. While premiums are waived, all features and benefits of the policy continue just as if the insured were paying the premiums.

Accidental Death Benefit. The **accidental death benefit rider** pays the beneficiary an additional death benefit if the insured dies accidentally, as defined in the rider. The definition of "accident" usually requires that death occur within 90 days of a purely unexpected event, and not be related to any medical condition of the insured. An accidental death benefit is termed "double indemnity" when twice the face amount is paid for an accidental death.

return of premium rider - returns the premium paid for a policy (less any administrative charges, fees, or rider premiums) back to the policyowner at the end of the insurance term

Accelerated Death Benefit. The **accelerated death benefit rider** allows the policyowner to receive a portion of the policy's death benefit during the insured's lifetime in the event the insured is inflicted with a terminal illness and has a limited life expectancy. This rider is also known as a living benefits rider, and is often provided without additional cost.

Return of Premium. The **return of premium rider** returns the premium paid for a policy (less any administrative charges, fees, or rider premiums) back to the policyowner at the end of the insurance term. In the event the insured dies before the end of the insurance term, the beneficiary will receive the death benefit and the amount of premiums paid up to death

Spouse/Child Insurance. The **spouse insurance** and **child insurance riders** provide life insurance coverage on the lives of the insured's spouse or children, respectively. One child rider usually covers all children of the insured.

spouse insurance and **child insurance riders** - provide life insurance coverage on the lives of the insured's spouse or children

Advantages

Affordability. Term life, because it is temporary pure death protection, tends to be very affordable in the early years of the policy. Premium rates on term insurance policies are less expensive than rates for cash value policies for two reasons: 1) the death benefit is payable during a specified term only and, 2) there is no savings element (cash value) for this type of policy.

Maximum Coverage per Premium Dollar. Since term insurance provides pure death protection for a specified term only, it is less expensive than a cash value policy that provides coverage for life. Term insurance premiums cover mortality, administrative expenses, and a profit margin. Because part of the premium is not allocated for cash value accumulation, as in cash value policies, it is less expensive dollar-for-dollar of death benefit

Meets Temporary Need for Coverage. Insurance protection under term insurance is temporary. Since the insurer provides coverage for a specified period only, term insurance is ideal for temporary needs, such as the payoff of a mortgage in the event of a breadwinner's death.

Ensures Insurability. A person with a current need for a larger amount of coverage and limited funds with which to purchase it can purchase a lower-cost term policy. Later, the term policy can be converted to a cash value, permanent policy at the same death benefit level, even if the insured develops a medical condition that renders him uninsurable.

Limitations

Cost Prohibitive at Older Ages. Perhaps the most notable limitation of term insurance is the increasing premiums on the basis of age. This makes term insurance impractical for many older people. Term insurance should never be viewed as a form of lifetime protection because it generally may not be renewed after age 65 or 70.

No Savings Feature. A term insurance policy does not possess a tax-deferred cash value buildup or savings feature as does an ordinary (whole) life policy (see below). Its primary function is to provide pure death protection. If one's goal is to accumulate wealth for retirement or education funding through an insurance policy, term life is inappropriate.

WHOLE LIFE INSURANCE

Whole life insurance pays a death benefit during the lifetime of the insured as long as the premiums are paid according to the policy contract. This type of insurance generates a cash value that can be made available to the policyowner during the insured's lifetime.

whole life insurance - pays a death benefit during the lifetime of the insured as long as the premiums are paid according to the policy contract

Whole life policies offer permanent protection for the insured's "whole life" at a relatively moderate premium because mortality costs and other expenses are spread over the full policy period (usually to age 100). All whole life policies involve the prepayment of future mortality costs. This is one reason that whole life policies have cash value. Cash value also represents the investment feature of a whole life policy.

Cash Value Buildup

Unlike term insurance, which exists solely for the purpose of providing death protection, whole life policies may be purchased for protection against the risk of death for their low-risk investment component. (Note, however, that there is no FDIC-type insurance for the cash value build-up.) Cash values in traditional whole life policies increase at a steady rate, equaling the policy face amount at age 100.

Traditional whole life insurance policies pay a low rate of interest on the cash value accumulation. This low rate of return is unattractive to many consumers, so traditional whole life should not be purchased solely for investment purposes. However, permanent insurance can be used as part of an overall investment and risk management plan. The insurance protection can serve as a risk management component, and the cash value may provide a low-risk investment vehicle.

Exhibit 9.2 illustrates the savings element of permanent life insurance. Notice that the original per thousand premium of $13.50 is substantially greater than the $1.95 per thousand mortality cost at the inception of the policy.

EXHIBIT 9.2: THE SAVINGS ELEMENT OF A LEVEL-PREMIUM, WHOLE LIFE INSURANCE POLICY

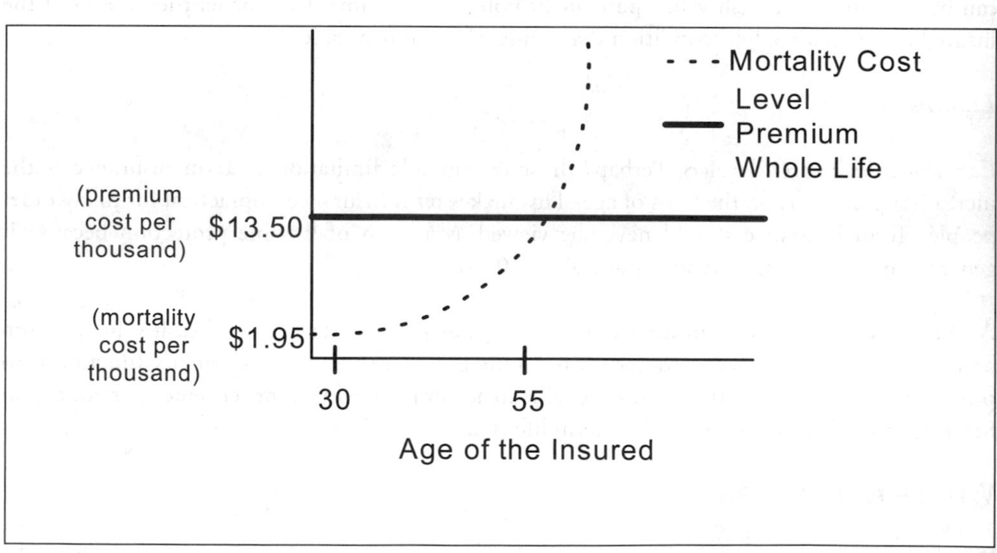

- - - Mortality Cost
Level Premium Whole Life
(premium cost per thousand)
$13.50
(mortality cost per thousand)
$1.95
30
55
Age of the Insured

Characteristics

Level Premium. Unlike term life in which premiums increase with age, whole life policies are generally based on a level premium throughout the duration of the payment period. Whole life policies build early cash values by prepaying premiums in the first several years and investing the excess to pay premiums in the later years of the policies. The excess premiums in the early years are kept in a **legal reserve**, which is a fund that is accumulated and maintained by the insurer to meet future obligations, such as administrative expenses and mortality charges.

legal reserve - a fund that is accumulated and maintained by the insurer to meet future obligations, such as administrative expenses and mortality charges

Mortality Charge. All whole life policies include a **mortality charge**, which is the amount of money the insurance company charges (usually monthly) for providing the death benefit. Few people die at younger ages, so the mortality charge is fairly low. As the insureds age, however, mortality increases and so do mortality charges.

mortality charge - the amount of money the insurance company charges (usually monthly) for providing a death benefit

Administrative Costs and Insurer Profit. As with all types of insurance, whole life premiums cover not only mortality charges, but administrative expenses and a profit margin.

Cash Value. Cash value, a savings element, is usually accumulated by payment of a periodic dividend or interest payments made towards the policy after it has been in force for a certain length of time. The policy may be surrendered for its cash value (surrender charges may apply) or it may be borrowed under a loan provision.

Types of Whole Life Policies

Ordinary Life. (Straight Life). In this continuous-premium policy, premiums are paid regularly until either the date of death or age 100. The insured may choose from various premium modes - annually, semiannually, quarterly, monthly, etc. The continuous premium policy provides the maximum permanent death protection for the lowest possible premium, but consumers should be aware that those premiums must be paid continuously, even past retirement, until death. If the insured is alive at age 100, the face amount is paid to the policyowner at that time.

ordinary (straight) life - a continuous-premium whole life policy in which premiums are paid regularly until either the date of death or age 100

Limited-Payment. Under a **limited-payment policy**, the insurance is permanent and the insured has lifetime protection. Premiums, however, are payable for only a limited number of years, after which the policy becomes paid up for its stated face amount. A **paid-up policy** is one for which no future premium payments are due, but the policy remains in effect. Because the years in which premiums are paid are fewer than those of an ordinary life policy, limited-payment premiums are higher.

limited-payment policy - permanent insurance for which premiums are payable for a limited number of years, after which the policy becomes paid up for its stated face amount

paid-up policy - a policy for which no future premium payments are due, and the policy remains in effect

Life insurance benefits under a paid-up, limited-payment policy are contractually guaranteed once premiums cease. This differs from a vanishing premium policy, however, for which no such guarantee exists, although the values are *expected* to sustain the policy throughout the insured's lifetime. If dividend projections for a vanishing premium policy fall short of actual dividend payments, premiums that have been discontinued may "unvanish", and policyowners may find themselves paying additional premiums to keep the policy in force.

The premiums for limited-payment policies may be fixed for any number of years (e.g., 10 years) or to a stated age. The name of the policy reflects the premium period; for example, if a premium payment is required for 10 years, the policy is usually known as a 10-payment whole life policy. The greater the number of premium payments, the closer the policy form is to an ordinary life policy.

Individuals who anticipate a limited number of high-income years during which they can best afford life insurance premium payments often choose limited-payment policies. Limited-payment policies are not suited for individuals with a restricted amount of financial resources and a need for a high death benefit.

modified whole life - premiums are lower for the first few years after policy issue, typically three to five years, and increase thereafter

Modified Life. Under a **modified whole life policy**, premiums are lower for the first few years after policy issue (typically three to five years) and increase thereafter. Modified life is merely traditional whole life insurance with a unique premium payment arrangement offered to the policyowner who has a lower current cash flow, but expects to have the funds needed for a higher premium in later years.

Single Premium. The single premium whole life policy is the ultimate example of a limited-payment policy. A single lump-sum payment is made at policy issue and no future premiums are due. This type of policy may be suited for a policyowner with a cash windfall and a death benefit need.

Although single-premium whole life policies build immediate cash value, they are usually classified as a modified endowment contract (MEC) and, as such, may be subject to taxation and penalties on loans or withdrawals. Refer to the section in this chapter titled "Modified Endowment Contracts" for additional information.

current assumption whole life - uses new-money interest rates and current mortality assumptions to determine cash values

Current Assumption (Interest-Sensitive). **Current assumption whole life** (CAWL) uses new-money interest rates and current mortality assumptions to determine cash values. In essence, the insurer shares its investment experience and profits with the policyowner. Interest rates fluctuate with the experience of the insurer, but have a stated guaranteed minimum. Mortality costs vary as well, with maximum mortality charges stated in the policy.

variable life - a fixed-premium whole life policy in which the death benefit and cash values fluctuate based on the investment of a separate account maintained by

Variable Life. **Variable life,** a type of whole life insurance, is a fixed-premium policy in which the death benefit and cash values fluctuate based on the investment of a separate account maintained by the insurer. The policyowner directs the investment of the policy's cash values and bears the investment risk.

With a variable life policy, cash values are not guaranteed and rise or fall based on the performance of the portfolio in which the net premiums (premiums less expenses and mortality charges) have been invested. The policyowner has the option to invest in a variety of investments, such as stock funds, bond funds, balanced funds, or money market funds. If the investment experience is weak, the death benefit amount may be reduced, but will never fall below the original face amount.

joint life - covers two or more lives under one policy at a cost lower than premiums for multiple separate policies

Since securities are used as variable life investment options, the policy must be approved by the Securities and Exchange Commission (SEC). Agents and brokers who sell variable life products must be licensed to sell both life insurance and securities.

first-to-die policy - pays the face amount to the beneficiaries upon the first death of two or more insureds

Joint Life. **Joint life insurance** covers two or more lives under one policy at a cost lower than premiums for multiple separate policies. A **first-to-die policy** pays the face amount to the

beneficiaries upon the first death of two or more insureds. Spouses may use this type of policy to provide for mortgage payments or educational funding. A **last-to-die policy**, also known as a survivorship policy, makes a death benefit payment upon the last death of multiple insureds. This is an effective estate planning tool when the unlimited marital deduction is used and estate taxes are due at the death of the surviving spouse. Premiums for this type of policy are usually based on the characteristics of the covered individual with the longest life expectancy.

last-to-die policy - makes a death benefit payment upon the last death of multiple insureds

Dividend Options

If a whole life policy pays dividends, it is considered a **participating** policy. (Policies that do not pay dividends are considered **non-participating**.) For the most part, dividends represent a refund of a portion of the gross premium if the insurer has favorable interest, expense, and mortality experience. Dividends are not guaranteed because they are based upon these variables. Owners of participating whole life policies are entitled to receive policy dividends declared by the insurer. Below are the several options under which dividends may be taken.

participating - a policy that pays dividends

non-participating - a policy that does not pay dividends

Cash. Under the cash option, you will receive a check on your policy anniversary equal to the full amount of the declared dividend. In most cases, cash dividends are payable only after the policy has been in force for a certain period of time as designated in the policy.

Paid-Up Additions. If the policyowner chooses the paid-up additions option, dividends are used to purchase additional paid-up life insurance coverage, which increases the policy's total death benefit and cash value. The additional amount is what a single premium equal to the dividends would purchase for the same whole life plan. No evidence of insurability is required.

Dividends to Accumulate at Interest. When the dividends to accumulate at interest option is chosen, dividends are left on deposit with the insurance company and interest is earned on the dividends. The amount accumulated is added to the death benefit if the insured dies, or to the cash value if the policy is surrendered. Interest earned is taxable.

Dividends to Reduce Premium. With the dividends to reduce premium option, dividends will be applied toward the payment of your premium. The policyowner pays the difference between the total premium and the annual dividend.

One-Year Term Insurance (5th Dividend Option). Under the one-year term insurance option, dividends are used to purchase one-year term insurance. In many cases, the face amount of the term insurance policy is the death benefit amount that an annual premium equal to the dividend amount will purchase as annually renewable term. Alternately, the dividends can be used to purchase a one-year term policy equal to the cash value of the original policy. Any remaining dividends are used to purchase increments of paid-up life insurance or are accumulated at interest.

Nonforfeiture Options

Nonforfeiture options are benefits available from a whole life insurance policy if it is discontinued during the insured's lifetime. Under this provision the insured, by lapsing or surrendering the policy, does not forfeit the cash value accumulation, but instead chooses how policy cash values are used The most common nonforfeiture options are discussed below.

Cash Surrender Value. The cash surrender value option allows the policyowner who discontinues premium payments to surrender the policy and receive the policy's cash surrender value (cash value less any surrender charges). Policyowners who surrender policies may incur an income tax liability on part of the cash value accumulation. This option is appropriate for a policyowner who no longer has a need for the original life insurance protection.

Reduced Paid-Up Insurance. With the reduced paid-up insurance option, the net cash value of the original life insurance policy is used as a net single premium to purchase a lesser amount of fully paid-up insurance. The insurance purchased under this option is the same type of policy as the policy being discontinued. The face amount of the new policy is dependent upon the cash value of the original policy, age of the insured, and policy expenses. This option is suitable for the policyowner who wants to maintain some level of permanent death protection, but wants no future premium outlay.

Extended Term Insurance. The extended term insurance option uses the net cash surrender value of the original policy as a net single premium to purchase a paid-up term insurance policy. The term policy face amount is equal to the original face amount (less any outstanding policy loans) for a specified (usually shorter) period of time. The length of the term protection is dependent upon the insured's age at the time the option is exercised. The net single premium will also be determined by the company's current premium rates. This option is most appropriate for someone who wants to preserve death protection equal to the original policy's net face value for a limited time.

Whole Life Riders

spouse and children riders - allows the policyowner to purchase term insurance on the spouse and/or children of the insured

term insurance rider - offers additional, affordable term life insurance on the

living benefits rider - gives the policyowner access to a portion of the policy's eligible death benefit if the insured is diagnosed with a terminal illness with a life expectancy of 12 months or less

Waiver of Premium. A waiver of premium rider assures that valuable insurance coverage is not lost when the policyholder is unable to pay premiums due to a disability. With this rider, the insurance company waives all premiums should the insured become totally disabled.

Accidental Death Benefit. The accidental death benefit rider pays the beneficiary an additional death benefit if the insured dies accidentally, as defined in the rider. The definition of "accident" usually requires that death occur within 90 days of a purely unexpected event, and not be related to any medical condition of the insured. An accidental death benefit is termed "double indemnity" when twice the face amount is paid for an accidental death.

Spouse and Children's Insurance. With the **spouse and children riders**, the policyowner may purchase term insurance on the spouse and/or children of the insured.

Term Insurance. A **term insurance rider** offers additional, affordable term life insurance on the insured. Premiums are usually guaranteed for a specified number of years; thereafter, premiums may increase annually. Often, this rider can be converted into permanent insurance on an attained age basis.

Living Benefits. The **living benefits rider**, also known as an accelerated death benefit rider, gives the policyowner access to a portion of the policy's eligible death benefit should the insured be iagnosed with a terminal illness with a life expectancy of 12 months or less. (Some states have stablished other life expectancy periods once terminal illness is diagnosed.)

)ption to Purchase Paid-Up Additions. The **option to purchase paid-up additions** is an conomical way to increase the death benefit protection and build additional cash value. 'remiums for this rider are used to purchase additional, paid-up whole life insurance in ddition to the original whole life death benefit.

Jnemployment Rider. The **unemployment rider** allows the policy to stay in force during the nsured's unemployment. Commonly, policy premiums will be waived for up to one year rovided the primary insured meets certain prior employment requirements.

option to purchase paid-up additions - increases the whole life death benefit protection; builds additional cash value

unemployment rider - policy premiums will be waived for a specified period during the insured's unemployment provided the insured meets certain prior employment requirements

Advantages

Fixed premiums. In traditional policies, whole life premiums remain unchanged even if the nsured's health deteriorates. This is a major advantage over term insurance policies.

Tax-deferred accumulation. The policyowner pays no current income on the cash value growth of a whole life policy. Compared to other taxable investments, a whole life policy may yield higher after-tax values in later years.

Lifetime coverage. Whole life policies provide death benefit protection over the insured's lifetime as long as premiums are paid as stipulated in the policy.

Limitations

Inflexible premiums. Policyowners cannot modify whole life premiums in the event their financial situations change. Therefore, much-needed death benefits may lapse if policyowners become ill, unemployed, or find themselves in unfavorable financial circumstances. In some cases, riders can protect the policyowner from these adverse situations.

Inadequate coverage. Due to higher premiums, additional whole life protection may be difficult for a policyowner to afford, thus resulting in an individual being underinsured.

Gradual cash value growth. Cash values can be insignificant in the early years of a whole life policy, but steadily increase over the duration of the policy. Compared to other tax-deferred investments, such as IRAs or 401(k)s, the internal rate of return of a whole life policy may be inferior.

Surrender charges. Most insurers heavily penalize the policyowner for not continuing the whole life policy, especially during the first few years of the policy. This penalty is administered through surrender charges, which are deducted from the cash value. As the insurer's major expenses associated with the policy issuance are incurred up front (e.g., underwriting costs and agents' commissions), the insurer imposes surrender charges so that it can recoup some of these costs should the policy lapse.

Universal Life Insurance

Overview

universal life insurance - gives policyowners the ability to adjust the premiums, death benefit, and cash values up or down to meet their individual needs (within certain limits)

Universal life insurance (UL), which originated as a variation of whole life insurance, give policyowners the ability to adjust the premiums, death benefit, and cash value up or down t meet their individual needs (within certain limits). In this type of policy, premiums are based o interest rates in excess of the policy's guaranteed interest rate. Therefore, some of the investmen risk is shifted to the policyowner. For universal life policies, the policyowner has no ability t direct the investment of the policy's cash value.

Exhibit 9.3 illustrates the basic structure of a universal life policy. The flow is as follows: Th policyowner pays at least a minimum premium into the policy. This is often referred to as th "target" premium, which is often required for the first few policy years.

From the initial premium, mortality charges based on the insured's age and the policy's ne amount at risk, along with the cost of any optional riders, is deducted. Administrative expense are then subtracted. This cash value is credited with interest, most often at new-money rates resulting in the end-of-period cash (accumulated) value. This cash value, less any surrende charges yields the policy's cash surrender value. This value is available to the policyowner in th event of a surrender.

EXHIBIT 9.3: STRUCTURE OF A UNIVERSAL LIFE POLICY

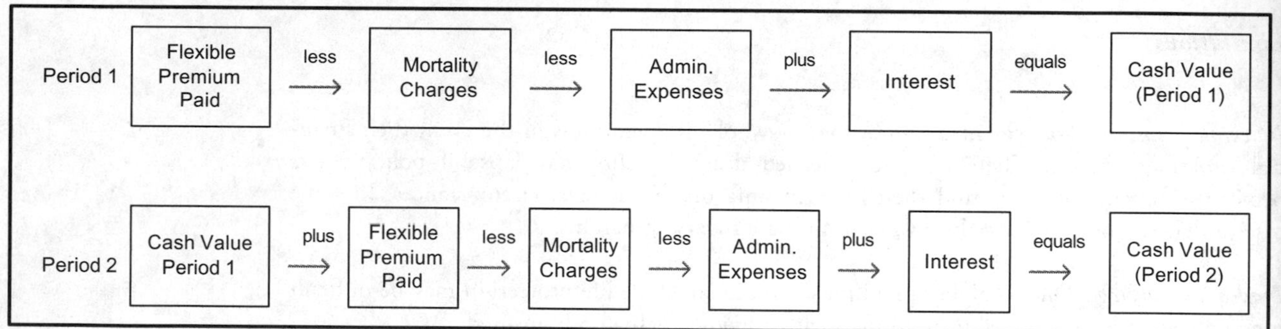
Period 1
Flexible Premium Paid
less
Mortality Charges
less
Admin. Expenses
plus
Interest
equals
Cash Value (Period 1)
Period 2
Cash Value Period 1
plus
Flexible Premium Paid
less
Mortality Charges
less
Admin. Expenses
plus
Interest
equals
Cash Value (Period 2)

Death Benefit Options

Universal life offers two death benefits options: Option A and Option B.

Option A (Option 1). Option A pays a level death benefit. The net amount of risk (NAR) for a universal life policy is the difference between the cash value and the death benefit. Therefore, for an Option A policy, the NAR decreases as the cash value increases, as Exhibit 9.4 shows.

EXHIBIT 9.4: DEATH BENEFIT OPTIONS

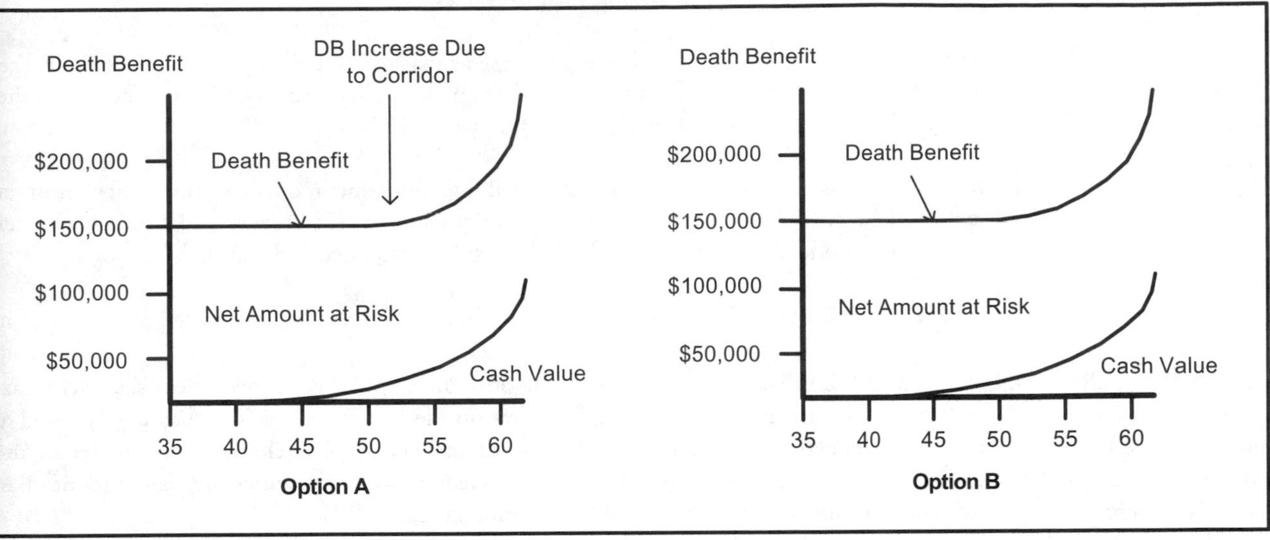

Death Benefit
DB Increase Due to Corridor
$200,000
Death Benefit
$150,000
$100,000
Net Amount at Risk
$50,000
Cash Value
35
40
45
50
55
60
Option A
Death Benefit
$200,000
Death Benefit
$150,000
$100,000
Net Amount at Risk
$50,000
Cash Value
35
40
45
50
55
60
Option B

In some cases, an Option A death benefit will begin to increase in the later years. This is due to the fact that tax law imposes a "corridor" of NAR if the cash value becomes too large (as defined by law) relative to the death benefit. Thus, the death benefit will begin to increase to maintain the required corridor (see Exhibit 9.4 above).

Option B (Option 2). Option B provides an increasing death benefit, which is the net amount at risk plus the cash value. Therefore, the NAR under this option remains level throughout the policy.

Premium Payments

Universal life policyowners can choose the amount of premium they pay into their policies, subject to insurer minimums and maximums. This premium flexibility can be a disadvantage in some cases where insufficient premiums cause the policy to lapse. For this reason, insurers require a target, or planned, premium for a given number of years, after which the policyowner can determine the premiums paid into the policy. As long as there is cash value in the policy to cover mortality charges and administrative expenses, additional premium is not required.

Variable Universal Life

variable universal life insurance (VUL) - combines the investment direction of variable life, and the premium, death benefit, and cash value flexibility of universal life

A **variable universal life policy** (VUL) combines the investment direction of variable life, and the premium, death benefit and cash value flexibility of universal life. Its features include increasing or decreasing death benefits, and flexible premium payments that mirror the universal life policy options.

As with variable life, the policyowner directs the investment of the policy's cash values and bears the investment risk; the cash value is maintained in one or more separate accounts. These cash values reflect the policyowner's pro rata share of assets held in the separate account and are subject to fluctuation just like variable life cash values.

The basic structure of a VUL policy is the same as that of a UL policy, with mortality charge and administrative expenses being deducted from the policy's cash value and the cash value being credited with interest. (See Exhibit 9.3 on page 310.)

Since securities are used as variable universal life investment options, the policy must be approved by the Securities and Exchange Commission (SEC). Agents and brokers who sell variable life products must be licensed to sell both life insurance and securities.

Modified Endowment Contracts

modified endowment contract (MEC) - a policy that fails the "7-pay" test; distributions receive LIFO tax treatment and are subject to a 10% penalty if under age 59 ½ (taxed under annuity rules)

IRC Sect. 7702A discourages the use of a life insurance policy as an investment that yields tax-advantaged income by imposing a "7-pay" test on life insurance policies. A policy is tested at issue and when the policy undergoes a material change, which includes certain increases and decrease in the anticipated benefits of a policy. Frequently, a material change is the result of an increase in death benefit due to flexible premium payments.

A policy is considered a MEC if it takes in too much premium during the first seven policy years, or in the seven years after a material change. A net level premium is established for the policy, and if, at any point during the seven-year period, the sum of premiums paid exceed the sum of the net level premium needed for a paid-up policy at the end of the period, it is a MEC.

MECs are treated differently than policies that pass the "7-pay" test. Loans and most withdrawals are subject to LIFO (last-in, first-out) treatment. In other words, taxable policy gains are distributed first (and, as such, taxed) and, once gain is loaned or withdrawn, subsequent distributions are considered a return of basis. Additionally, a 10% penalty is assessed to any taxable amount, unless the policyowner has reached age 59½.

Riders and Optional Benefits

Waiver of Premium. The waiver of premium (or, waiver of monthly deductions) **rider** waives mortality and expense charges if the insured becomes totally and permanently disabled before a stated age, usually age 65. The policy continues as if the policyowner were paying an amount equal to these charges. Policies have a waiting period, often for six months, before the waiver of monthly deductions commences. Once the waiting period is satisfied, all monthly deductions are waived as long as total and permanent disability continues. Deductions made during the waiting period are often reimbursed as well.

Accidental Death Benefit. The accidental death benefit rider pays the beneficiary an additional death benefit if the insured dies accidentally, as defined in the rider. The definition of "accident" usually requires that death occur within 90 days of a purely unexpected event, and not be related to any medical condition of the insured. An accidental death benefit is termed "double indemnity" when twice the face amount is paid for an accidental death.

Other Insured. The **other insured rider** offers level term insurance coverage on the insured, the insured's spouse, children, or business partners. In general, coverage is convertible to permanent insurance up until specified ages.

other insured rider- offers level term insurance coverage on the insured, the insured's spouse, children or business partners

Living Benefits. The living benefits rider, also known as an accelerated death benefit rider, gives the policyowner access to a portion of the policy's eligible death benefit if the insured is diagnosed with a terminal illness and has a life expectancy of 12 months or less. (Some states have established other life expectancy periods once terminal illness is diagnosed.)

Advantages

Premium flexibility. The ability to adjust the amount of premium payments is beneficial when financial circumstances change.

Ability to change death benefit amount. Universal life offers cost-effective increases in death benefit without the need to purchase a separate policy. The death benefit can also be decreased if the full current death benefit is no longer needed by the policyowner.

Current assumptions. Because interest rates and mortality are based on current experience , the accumulated values of a universal life policy are often higher than those of a whole life policy. Additionally, the cost for a universal life policy may be lower than that of a whole life policy.

Limitations

Premium flexibility. This can also be a disadvantage. Policyowners may decide not to make premium payments at certain times, thus resulting in a significant decrease in accumulated values or lapse of the policy. Owners of universal life policies must be self-disciplined enough to make the premium payments needed to yield the desired accumulated values and keep the policy in force.

Fewer guarantees. The accumulated values of a universal life policy can drop to zero if sufficient premiums are not paid. Often, even the target premium for some policies will not carry the policy into later years. The premium required to keep the policy in force may actually be higher than whole life premiums in some years.

On the other hand, whole life policies are guaranteed to have a specified cash value and death benefit at a given time as long as premiums are paid While universal life policies can guarantee a minimum accumulated cash value and death benefit, the premium necessary for this guarantee may not be much less than a whole life policy.

EXHIBIT 9.5: FEATURE COMPARISON OF COMMON LIFE INSURANCE POLICIES

	Term Life	Whole (Ordinary) Life	Universal Life	Variable Life	Variable Universal Life
Premium Amount	Fixed or Variable	Fixed	Variable, subject to a required minimum	Fixed	Variable, subject to a required minimum
Death Benefits	Fixed	Fixed	May increase above initial face amount, depending on cash value accumulation	Has a guaranteed minimum, but can increase if investment experience on cash value is good	Has a guaranteed minimum, but can increase if investment experience on cash value is good
Policyowner's Control Over Cash Value Investments	None	None	None	Complete	Complete
Rate of Return on Cash Value Investment	None	Fixed rate	Minimum guaranteed rate, but may be higher depending on interest rates	No minimum guarantee, but positive investment experience can yield very high returns	No minimum guarantee, but positive investment experience can yield very high returns
Use	Large need, limited resources	Want guarantees	Flexibility without investment responsibility	Flexibility with investment responsibility, fixed premiums	Flexibility with investment responsibility, variable premiums

GROUP LIFE INSURANCE

Group life insurance covers a large group of insureds under a single master contract. The employer holds the master contract and is responsible for making premium payments to the insurer. The employer can fund premium payments in whole or in part and, in many cases, the employee pays no portion of the premium at all. Where employees are expected to pay some or all of the cost of the life insurance, the employer generally collects the employee contributions through payroll deductions.

Group insurance is typically less expensive than individual insurance because of the savings the insurer realizes in terms of lower administrative expenses and underwriting costs. Individual underwriting is not required of group insurance participants, so no evidence of insurability is required and no medical examinations are necessary. The employer may set up its requirements for eligibility. Eligibility requirements for a typical plan might include that participating employees be full-time workers and satisfy a minimum probationary period.

Group Term Insurance

Group term insurance is the most common form of group insurance selected by employers. Group term offers the same benefits as an individual term insurance policy. Group term premiums, like those of individual term policies, increase with age. When an employer provides group term insurance, there are no tax consequences to the employee if the death benefit under the policy does not exceed $50,000. The imputed cost of coverage in excess of $50,000 must be included in income using the IFS Premium Table, and is subject to Social Security and Medicare taxes (IRC §79). The actual premiums paid by the employer for group term insurance are tax-deductible to the employer as a business expense.

The amount of coverage provided by an employer through a group term plan must be determined by some formula that precludes adverse selection on the part of employees. Most employers provide employees with either a flat amount of coverage, such as $25,000, or coverage equal to a multiple of the employee's annual salary is provided. In some cases employees are then allowed to purchase additional amounts of coverage in pre-specified multiple amounts. The insurer may require proof of insurability for these optional higher coverage amounts.

A covered employee typically has the right to convert a group term policy, upon termination from the company, to a regular cash value policy at a rate based on his attained age. The insurer usually grants a 31-day **grace period** after an employee withdraws from the group in which basic death benefits remain in effect. The conversion privilege is advantageous to the insured because no evidence of insurability is required upon conversion.

grace period - period during which a group term policy may be converted, upon termination from a company, to a cash value policy at a rate based upon the insured's attained age

Group Whole Life Insurance

Group whole life insurance allows the insured to obtain death benefit coverage, as well as accumulate a level of savings through the policy's cash value. Group whole life insurance is not a frequently chosen employee benefit because it does not have the tax advantages that group term life insurance offers. Generally, the employee must report the premiums paid by the employer for a group whole life policy as taxable income.

Group Universal Life Insurance

Some employers are now offering group universal life plans. Often, these policies serve as optional supplements to the more traditional group term plans. In most cases, employees pay the entire cost of the coverage; the premiums are paid through payroll deductions, so there are some administrative cost savings for the insurer. These savings are then passed on to employees in the form of lower premiums. Most plans allow the employee to purchase coverage up to a specified maximum face value without providing evidence of insurability.

POLICY REPLACEMENT

The decision to replace one policy with another should be made cautiously. The methodology for such a decision includes fact gathering, calculations, and benchmark comparisons. One such comparison uses the Belth price of protection model:

$$CPT = \frac{(P + CV_0)(1 + i) - (CV_1 + D)}{(DB - CV_1)(0.001)}$$

CPT = Cost per thousand

P = Annual premium

CV_0 = Cash value at beginning of year

i = Net after-tax earning rate

CV_1 = Cash value at year end

D = Current dividend

DB = Death benefit

Belth Benchmark Table

Age	Benchmark Price of Insurance per $1,000
< 30	1.50
30 – 34	2.00
35 – 39	3.00
40 – 44	4.00
45 – 49	6.50
50 – 54	10.00
55 – 60	15.00
60 – 64	25.00
65 – 69	35.00
70 – 74	50.00
75 – 79	80.00
80 – 84	125.00

(Joseph M. Belth, author)

To use this model, the insured should calculate the cost per thousand (CPT) for his or her current insurance and compare the result to the appropriate Belth benchmark per thousand. If the CPT is more than twice the benchmark price, the insured should consider replacement.

EXAMPLE

For example, Joan is 62 years old and has a whole life policy with the following features:

- Annual premium = $800.00
- Cash value on January 1, 2003 = $400,000
- Cash value on December 31, 2003 = $405,000
- After-tax earning rate = 4.2%
- Current dividend = $600.00
- Death benefit = $750,000

$$CPT = \frac{(P + CV_0)(1 + i) - (CV_1 + D)}{(DB - CV_1)(0.001)}$$

$$CPT = \frac{(800 + 400,000)(1 + 0.042) - (405,000 + 600)}{(750,000 - 405,000)(0.001)}$$

$$CPT = 34.88$$

The Belth benchmark for a 62-year-old individual is 25.00. Since the CPT for Joan's current insurance is less than 50 (2 × 25.00), she should retain her current policy.

LIFE INSURANCE POLICY PROVISIONS

Grace Period

Life insurance policies allow for a grace period (typically 31 days) after the premium due date in which the policyowner may pay the overdue premium. During this grace period, the policy remains in force. If the policyowner pays the premium during the grace period, the policy is continued. In some cases, interest may be charged on the overdue premium. If the insured dies within the grace period, the insurer deducts it (and, in some cases, pro rata premium) from the death benefit payable to the beneficiary.

Incontestability

The **incontestability clause** in a life insurance policy prevents the insurer from canceling the policy after it has been in force for two years (one year for some companies) in the event the life insurer discovers material misrepresentation or concealment.

incontestability clause - prevents the insurer from canceling the policy after it has been in force for two years (one year for some companies) in the event the life insurer discovers material misrepresentation or concealment

entire contract clause - maintains that the life insurance policy and the policyowner's application comprises the complete life insurance contract

Entire Contract Clause

The entire contract clause maintains that the life insurance policy and the policyowner's application comprise the complete life insurance contract. As a result, any statements made on the application are part of the contract and, if these statements are false, can be used as basis to void or alter the contract.

misstatement of age or gender provision - if a misstatement is made, the insurer can adjust the face amount to what the premium would have purchased had the age or gender been correctly stated

Misstatement of Age or Gender

The **misstatement of age or gender provision** provides that if a misstatement of age is discovered after the policy is issued, the life insurance company can adjust the face amount of the policy to an amount that the premium would have purchased had the insured's age or gender been correctly stated.

EXAMPLE

Suppose Abby is age 45, but looks much younger. She incorrectly states her age as 35 on a life insurance application for a $100,000 policy. She is charged a $100 monthly premium for her policy. The insurer, however, would have charged Abby $200 per month had it known she were 45. If she dies and the insurer discovers the misstatement of age, it will recalculate her death benefit based on the premium amount she *should* have paid. Because she paid only half as much as she should have ($100 instead of $200), the insurer will pay only half the death benefit, or $50,000.

Assignment

An assignment is an agreement under which the policyowner (the assignor) transfers some or all of his ownership rights in a policy to another party (the assignee). Generally there are two types of assignments, absolute and collateral.

absolute assignment - all life insurance policy ownership rights are transferred to a designated assignee

Absolute assignment. An **absolute assignment** is an assignment of a life insurance policy under which the policyowner transfers all policy ownership rights to a designated assignee.

collateral assignment - a life insurance policy is transferred to a creditor as security for a loan or debt

Collateral assignment. A **collateral assignment** is the assignment of a life insurance policy to a creditor as security for a loan or debt. The creditor is entitled to receive the proceeds or cash values of the policy only to the extent of its interest. The assignment terminates when the debt is paid.

suicide clause - asserts that, if the insured commits suicide within a specified period of time, the policy will be voided and premiums will be refunded to the beneficiary

Suicide

To mitigate against the risk that a person will purchase a life insurance policy in contemplation of suicide, life insurance policies include a **suicide clause.** This clause asserts that, if the insured commits suicide within a specified period of time, the policy will be voided and premiums will be refunded to the beneficiary. Most suicide clauses have a specified time limit of one or two years.

reinstatement clause - outlines the conditions under which a lapsed policy may be reinstated

Reinstatement

A life insurance policy will lapse if the premium payments made by the insured are not paid as stated in the policy. The **reinstatement clause** in a policy outlines the conditions under which a

lapsed policy may be reinstated. In most cases, evidence of insurability is not needed if the reinstatement takes place within 31 days of the grace period. Thereafter, the policy may be reinstated during the reinstatement period (typically up to five years) with submission of unpaid premiums plus interest and satisfactory evidence of insurability.

Policy Loan Provision

A **policy loan provision** allows the policyowner to borrow (with interest) against the cash surrender value of a permanent insurance policy. Any loans and interest payments outstanding at the time of the insured's death will be deducted from the death proceeds.

policy loan provision - allows the policyowner to borrow (with interest) against the cash surrender value of a permanent insurance policy

Some whole life policies include a provision for an **automatic premium loan** (APL), which directs the insurance company to pay an overdue premium by making an interest-bearing loan against the policy's cash value. The policyowner must specifically request this provision either on the initial coverage application or in writing at a later date. As with the policy loan provision, any outstanding loans and interest payments at the insured's death will be withheld from the death benefit paid to the beneficiary.

automatic premium loan (APL) - directs the insurance company to pay an overdue premium by making an interest-bearing loan against the policy's cash value

Beneficiary Designations

The proceeds of a life insurance policy are distributed upon death to a beneficiary selected by the policyowner. A life insurance beneficiary can be an individual, a group of individuals, the insured's estate, or an entity (non-natural person).

Revocable and irrevocable beneficiaries. A **revocable beneficiary** can be changed by the policyowner at any time. An **irrevocable beneficiary** cannot be changed without the beneficiary's consent. An irrevocable beneficiary must give his or her consent before the policyowner can change beneficiaries. This type of beneficiary designation is often used in divorce settlements to guarantee one parent with a death benefit in the event the other parent dies.

revocable beneficiary - can be changed by the policyowner at any time

irrevocable beneficiary - cannot be changed without the beneficiary's consent

Primary and contingent beneficiaries. The **primary beneficiary** of a life insurance policy is the party designated by the policyowner to receive death benefits. A **contingent beneficiary** is an individual, group, or entity designated to receive the policy proceeds if the primary beneficiary should die before the insured dies. Contingent beneficiaries can be secondary (receives benefits if primary beneficiary is deceased at the insured's death), or tertiary (receives a benefit when both the primary and secondary beneficiaries predecease the insured).

primary beneficiary - the party designated by the policyowner to receive death benefits

contingent beneficiary - an individual, group or entity designated to receive the policy proceeds if the primary beneficiary should die before the insured dies

If the primary beneficiary is deceased, and any contingent beneficiaries are deceased or non-existent, the death benefit proceeds will be paid to the insured or policyowner's estate. In this event, the proceeds will be included in the probate estate and, therefore, subject to costs and delays.

Survivorship clause. The **survivorship clause** in a life insurance policy requires that a beneficiary must survive the insured by a specified period (usually 30 or 60 days) in order to receive the death benefit proceeds. Otherwise, the policy proceeds will be paid as though the beneficiary had predeceased the insured. This clause, also known as a common disaster clause, is inserted as part of the policy by the policyowner.

survivorship clause - requires that a beneficiary must survive the insured by a specified period (usually 30 to 60 days) in order to receive the death benefit proceeds

Aviation Exclusion

Though no longer a common exclusion in policies issued today, the aviation exclusion denies coverage for those who die in noncommercial flights, such as private pilots, their passengers and military pilots. The death benefit is not paid; however, premiums are usually returned to the beneficiary.

War Exclusion

war exclusion - allows the insurer to deny the death claim if the insured's death is related to war or military service

The **war exclusion** allows the insurer to deny the death claim if the insured's death is related to war or military service. In lieu of paying the death benefit, premiums are usually returned to the beneficiary with interest.

Simultaneous Death Provisions

A situation may arise in which the insured and the beneficiary both die within a short time of each other in an accident and it is not readily determinable who died first. Patterned after the Uniform Simultaneous Death Act, which has been adopted by most states, the simultaneous death provision establishes that the proceeds of the life insurance policy will be distributed as though the insured survived the beneficiary. If more than one beneficiary has been named on the policy, the next in the line of succession shall receive the proceeds. If no other beneficiaries are designated, the proceeds will be paid to the insured or policyowner's estate.

LIFE INSURANCE SETTLEMENT OPTIONS

settlement options - allow the policyowner or beneficiary to choose either cash or one of several alternatives to how the death benefit will be paid

Most life insurance policies provide alternatives to a beneficiary receiving a lump sum check at the death of an insured. **Settlement options** allow the policyowner or beneficiary to choose either cash or one of these alternatives. These alternatives may protect a beneficiary who is unable to manage a large lump sum of cash. Below are settlement options offered by insurers.

Interest Only

interest-only option - the insurance company retains the death benefit and pays the primary beneficiary interest on that sum

Under the **interest-only option**, the insurance company retains the death benefit and pays the primary beneficiary interest on that sum. In some cases, the primary beneficiary may be given the right to withdraw some or all of the proceeds in a lump sum. The policyowner or primary beneficiary may name a contingent beneficiary to receive the balance of the proceeds at the primary beneficiary's death.

Fixed Amount

fixed-amount option - specifies that a designated amount of income will be provided to the beneficiary on a regular basis until the proceeds and accumulated interest are depleted

The **fixed-amount option** specifies that a designated amount of income will be provided to the beneficiary on a regular basis until the proceeds and accumulated interest are depleted. If the beneficiary dies with a balance of unpaid proceeds and accumulated interest, this balance is paid to a contingent beneficiary or included in the deceased beneficiary's estate.

Fixed Period

If the **fixed-period option** is chosen, the beneficiary will receive the maximum periodic payments that the death benefit proceeds will purchase for a specified time period. If the beneficiary dies within the payment period, the balance is paid to a contingent beneficiary or included in the estate of the deceased beneficiary.

fixed-period option - the beneficiary will receive the maximum periodic payments that the death benefit proceeds will purchase for a specified time period

Life Income

A **life income option** allows the beneficiary to periodically receive a specified monthly payment for his or her lifetime. The amount of the proceeds and the life expectancy of the beneficiary at the time of the insured's death are used to determine the amount of life income payable.

life income option - allows the beneficiary to periodically receive a specified monthly payment for his or her lifetime

Life Income with Period Certain

The **life income with period certain option** provides an income to the beneficiary for his or her lifetime, or a specified period, if greater. The balance of the payments will be made to a contingent beneficiary if the primary beneficiary dies during the certain period. For example, a life income with 20 years certain option will provide a specified amount for at least twenty years (either to the primary beneficiary, if living, or to a contingent beneficiary, if the primary dies) or longer if the primary beneficiary outlives the 20-year period.

life income with period certain option - provides an income to the beneficiary for his or her lifetime, or a specified period, if greater

Life Income with Refund

Under the **life income with refund option**, the life insurance company agrees that, if the primary beneficiary dies before the total amount paid under the option equals the proceeds of the policy, the life insurance company will pay the difference to a contingent beneficiary.

life income with refund option - the life insurance company agrees that, if the primary beneficiary dies before the total amount paid under the option equals the proceeds of the policy, the company will pay the difference to a contingent beneficiary

Joint and Last Survivor Income

The **joint and last survivor income option** provides joint beneficiaries a stated amount of income during their lives, and a continuation of the original or reduced amount for the remaining beneficiary's life. A certain period may also be stipulated as part of this option.

joint and last survivor income option - provides joint beneficiaries a stated amount of income during their lives, and a continuation of the original or reduced amount for the remaining beneficiary's life

ANNUITY CONTRACTS

An annuity is a contract designed to provide payments to the holder at specified intervals, usually for a fixed period, for the annuitant's life or for the lives of two or more joint annuitants. Sold by insurance companies, annuities are commonly used to fund retirement benefits. Similar to life insurance benefits, annuity payments are based on the pooling of the risk and life expectancy of a group.

Types of Annuities

Immediate vs. Deferred

immediate annuity - one in which the first annuity payment is due one payment interval from its purchase date

The insured has the option of having annuity payments made monthly, quarterly, semiannually or annually. In addition, the insured may also specify whether he would like the annuity payments to be immediate or deferred. An **immediate annuity** is one in which the first annuity payment is due one payment interval from its purchase date. Immediate annuities are purchased with a single lump-sum premium.

deferred annuity - provides income at some date in the future

A **deferred annuity** provides income at some date in the future. The most popular form of a deferred annuity is a retirement annuity in which monetary value accumulates for a number of years and is paid in installments when the insured reaches retirement. Deferred annuities are purchased with either a single premium or periodic level premiums.

Flexible Premium vs. Single Premium

flexible premium annuity - allows the insured the option to vary premium deposits

A **flexible premium annuity** allows the insured the option to vary premium deposits. The amount of retirement income will relate directly to the accumulated sum in the annuity when it becomes due. Under a flexible premium plan, the insured spreads payments out over a designated period of time by making periodic premium payments.

single premium annuity - an annuity purchased with a single lump sum

An annuity purchased with a single lump sum is known as a **single premium annuity**. Proceeds from life insurance policies can be used to purchase single premium annuities at special rates under life income settlement options.

Fixed vs. Variable

fixed annuity - the insurer agrees to credit a specified interest rate over a stated period of time

With a **fixed annuity**, the insurer agrees to credit a specified interest rate over a stated period of time. As a result, the insurance company can guarantee a certain annuity payment amount at annuitization. A fixed annuity provides more security of principal than a variable annuity, but has limited upside potential.

variable annuity - does not guarantee specific payments; however, it has a potential for greater returns

Variable annuities do not guarantee specific annuity payments; however, they have a potential for greater returns. In a variable annuity, the annuity owner invests in one or more "subaccounts," which can own stocks or bonds or a combination of stocks and bonds. Therefore, interest rates credited to the annuity are based on the performance on the stocks or bonds in which the annuity values are invested. The owner of a variable annuity accepts more short-term volatility because the value of the annuity fluctuates with the stock and bond markets. This is simply a trade-off of risk and return.

Timing of Annuity Payments

Straight Life Annuity

straight life annuity - provides a lifetime income to the annuitant regardless of how long he or she lives

Often referred to as a pure life annuity, a **straight life annuity** provides a lifetime income to the annuitant regardless of how long he or she lives. After the annuitant dies, no further annuity

Where on the Web

A.M. Best Company *www.ambest.com*
American Council of Life Insurers *www.acli.org*
Centers For Medicare and Medicaid Services *www.cms.hhs.gov*
Fitch Ratings *www.fitchibca.com*
Health Insurance Association of America *www.hiaa.org*
Insure.com (S & P and Fitch ratings) *http://info.insure.com/ratings/*
Life-Line (website of the Life and Health Insurance Foundation) *www.life-line.org*
Long-Term Care Education *www.longtermcareeducation.com*
Medicare *www.medicare.gov*
Moody's Investors Service *www.moodys.com*
National Hospice and Palliative Care Organization *www.nhpco.org*
Standard & Poor's Index Services *www.spglobal.com*
TIAA-CREF Life Insurance Information *www.tiaa-cref.org*
U.S. Government's Agency for Healthcare Research and Quality *www.ahcpr.gov/consumer*
Weiss Ratings Inc. *www.weissratings.com*

payments are made by the insurer. For a given purchase price, the highest amount of lifetime income per dollar spent is earned through the pure life annuity.

For a straight life annuity, there is no guaranteed minimum number of payments the insurer must make, and the dependents of the annuitant receive nothing from the contract once the annuitant has died. Therefore, the pure life annuity is ideal for the person who needs maximum income spread out over his or her lifetime and has no living dependents to whom he wishes to leave assets.

Life Annuity with a Period Certain

A life annuity with a period certain guarantees that the annuitant either receives a minimum number of payments or will have lifetime income, whichever is greater. Two common guarantee options are the ten-year period certain and the twenty-year period certain. If the annuitant dies before the guarantee period expires, a named beneficiary receives the remaining guaranteed payments. If the annuitant outlives the guarantee period, payments continue until the annuitant's death.

Installment Refund Annuity

The **installment refund annuity** is similar to the one described previously, except the insurer promises to continue periodic payments after the annuitant has died until the sum of all annuity payments equals the purchase price of the annuity or, with the cash refund option, the balance is paid in cash to a beneficiary at the annuitant's death.

installment refund annuity - the insurer promises to continue periodic payments after the annuitant has died until the sum of all annuity payments equals the purchase price of the annuity or, with the cash refund option, the balance is paid in cash to a beneficiary at the annuitant's death

Joint and Survivor Annuity

A **joint and survivor annuity** is based on the lives of two or more annuitants, most often husband and wife. Annuity payments are made until the last annuitant dies. A joint and 100% survivor annuity pays the full monthly payment to both parties and continues the same payment to the survivor. Some persons, however, choose a joint and survivor annuity that pays the survivor only a portion of the payment that was paid on both lives. For example, a joint and 75% survivor annuity would pay the survivor 75% of the payment received during both annuitant's lifetimes. Joint and last survivor is the most popular form of the multilife (2+ annuitants) annuity today.

joint and survivor annuity - based on the lives of two or more annuitants, most often husband and wife

TAXATION OF LIFE INSURANCE AND ANNUITIES

LIFE INSURANCE

Favorable Tax Treatment

There are several ways in which life insurance contracts receive favorable tax treatment. First, proceeds paid to beneficiaries are generally excludable from taxable income. Second, dividends earned on the cash surrender value are not taxable to the owner of the policy until withdrawn. In other words, the funds accumulate tax-free. If the insured dies without surrendering the policy or withdrawing the cash value, the cash value accumulated will never be subject to income tax. Third, excluding modified endowment contracts, loans against life insurance policies are tax-free. Fourth, under Section 1035 of the Internal Revenue Code, exchanges of one life insurance policy for another or for an annuity will not result in any recognition of gain. The owner's cost basis for the original life insurance policy will transfer to the new life insurance policy or annuity.

Taxation of Benefits Received During Life

Dividends. Generally, dividends distributed are not taxable, but instead are considered a return of a portion of premium payments that reduce the policyowner's basis. If dividends distributed exceed premiums, however, the excess amount of dividends are taxed to the owner as ordinary income.

Withdrawals. Withdrawals from a life insurance policy receive FIFO (first-in, first-out) treatment. In other words, withdrawals of principal are tax-free until the accumulated premiums (less any prior withdrawals or loans) have been paid out [IRC §72(e)].

Withdrawals, or policy loans, of living benefits within the first fifteen years of a life insurance policy are subject to LIFO (last-in, first-out) treatment if the withdrawals result in a reduction of death benefits. Under LIFO treatment, withdrawals will be considered distributions of dividends or interest, which are taxable as ordinary income, until the cash value equals accumulated premiums. Subsequent distributions will be considered return of principal, which is not taxable. In this case, withdrawals made after the first fifteen years of the policy will receive FIFO treatment.

Modified endowment contracts (MECs) will be subject to LIFO treatment for the life of the policy and a 10% penalty on taxable gains withdrawn before age 59½. See "Modified Endowment Contracts" section on page 284.

Surrenders. When the owner of a policy surrenders a life insurance contract, the insurer is no longer obligated to pay the death benefit to the beneficiary. The policyowner will receive the cash value of the policy by one of three methods – lump-sum payment, interest payments, or installment payments. Under the **lump-sum payment method**, the total cash value of the life insurance policy is paid to the policyowner. A lump-sum payment of the cash value above the owner's cost basis is taxable to the owner as ordinary income. The owner's cost basis is equal to accumulated premiums paid less any withdrawals, dividends paid, or outstanding loans considered to be a return of premium.

lump-sum payment method - the total cash value of the life insurance policy is paid to the policyowner

Upon cash surrender of the policy, the owner may choose to leave the cash value proceeds with the insurer and receive only interest payments on the cash value. This is known as the **interest payment method.** In this case, the interest is taxable as ordinary income when received or credited to the payee.

interest payment method - upon cash surrender of the policy, the owner may choose to leave the cash value proceeds with the insurer and receive only interest payments on the cash value

Under the **installment payment method**, the policyowner receives the cash value and accrued interest over a period of time, usually in fixed amounts. This payment method is similar to an annuity and each payment will include a return of basis and interest.

installment payment method - the policyowner receives the cash value and accrued interest over a period of time, usually in fixed amounts

For example, Nicholas selected the installment payment option on a policy with a cash value of $150,000. He will receive $1,000 per month for the remainder of his life, which according to life expectancy tables will be 20 more years.

Total expected payments = $1,000 × 12 × 20 = $240,000

Nicholas' tax basis = $150,000

The exclusion ratio = $150,000 / $240,000 = 0.625

Thus, 62.5% or $625 of each payment is excludable from gross income.

If the beneficiary who chose the installment method for receipt of death benefits survives beyond his or her life expectancy, the annuity payments will retain the original exclusion ratio for income tax purposes. If the beneficiary dies before the projected life expectancy, no basis can be recovered and annuity payments will end.

Transfer of Policy. If an existing policy is transferred for valuable consideration (transfer for value), the insurance proceeds are includible in the gross income of the transferee to the extent the proceeds exceed the basis. Thus, the usual income tax exclusion for life insurance proceeds is lost. There are five instances when the transfer of a policy will not result in inclusion of proceeds in the income of the transferee. They are:

- A transfer to the insured
- A transfer to a business partner of the insured
- A transfer to a partnership of which the insured is a partner

- A transfer to a corporation of which the insured is an officer or shareholder
- A transfer that results in the transferee's basis being determined by reference to the transferor's basis, such as a gift

Premiums. Generally, premium payments for individual life insurance policies are not tax deductible. Life insurance premiums that are considered alimony, however, are tax deductible to the payor and taxable as income to the beneficiary. Group life insurance premiums are usually tax deductible when paid by the employer. If a corporation pays the premium on a policy covering an employee and the corporation is not a beneficiary, the premium is considered compensation and is deductible by the employer and includable in the employee's income.

Taxation of Benefits Received after Death

The beneficiary of a life insurance policy generally has the same options for payment as the policyowner does when surrendering a contract. However, the taxation of proceeds may be different. Lump-sum death benefit proceeds received as a result of the insured's death are excludable from gross income and are therefore tax-exempt for income tax purposes. Under the interest-only payment option, the insurer pays interest earned on the death benefit to the beneficiary. Since these distributions are 100 percent interest and 0 percent death benefits, they are fully includable in the gross income of the beneficiary. Installment payments will generally be made in the form of an annuity and each payment will include a return of basis and interest. The return of basis component is equal to the ratio of the face value of the policy to the total amount of expected payments to be received.

For example, Benjamin selected the installment payment option on a policy with a face value of $300,000. He will receive $1,750 per month for the remainder of his life, which according to life expectancy tables will be 25 more years.

Total expected payments = $1,750 × 12 × 25 = $525,000

Benjamin's tax basis = $300,000

The exclusion ratio = $300,000 / $525,000 = 0.5714

Thus, 57.14%, or $1,000, of each payment is excludable from gross income.

VIATICAL AGREEMENTS

viatical agreement - the owner of a policy covering a terminally ill insured sells a life insurance policy to a third party or receives accelerated death benefits from the insurer without the proceeds being subject to income tax

Terminal illness. When the insured of a life insurance policy owns a policy and becomes terminally ill (defined as having a life expectancy of 24 months or less) he or she may sell the policy to a third party or receive accelerated death benefits from the insurer without the proceeds being subject to income tax. These types of settlements are known as **viatical agreements**. The third party purchaser will receive the death benefit of the policy upon the death of the insured and will incur income tax liability for proceeds that exceed the purchase price and any subsequent premiums paid.

Chronic illness. Another type of viatical agreement with the same tax advantages for the insured is the sale of a life insurance policy when the proceeds are used to pay for long-term care for the insured. In this case, the insured must be chronically ill or suffer from substantial cognitive impairment, or be unable to perform at least 2 of 6 activities of daily living (ADLs). ADLs are discussed in the long-term care section of this chapter.

ANNUITIES

Each payment from a fixed annuity is considered a partially tax-free return of basis and partially taxable income using an exclusion ratio. In general, the numerator for the exclusion ratio is the investment in the annuity. The denominator is the total expected return from the annuity. Unlike annuities resulting from life insurance settlements, any annuity payments from purchased annuities that occur beyond the original life expectancy are fully taxable as ordinary income to the annuitant. If the annuitant dies before full recovery of basis, the unrecovered basis may be deducted on the decedents' final IRS 1040 Form.

Part of each fixed annuity payment an annuitant receives is considered to be a return of principal, which is not taxed. The remaining portion of the payment is taxable because it consists of interest earnings. The exclusion ratio determines the taxable and nontaxable portions of each payment. The exclusion ratio formula is:

$$\frac{\text{Investment in the Contract}}{\text{Expected Return}}$$

The exclusion ratio is no longer used once the principal in the contract has been received. In other words, when the entire amount of principal has been exhausted, the entire annuity payment will then be taxable.

INDIVIDUAL HEALTH INSURANCE

Prudent financial planning includes preparation for the financial impact of a serious injury or illness. Not only may medical bills be incurred, but there might also be a loss of income if the ill or injured person is unable to continue working. Various forms of health insurance can compensate for these losses.

Persons not covered under a social insurance program, such as Medicare or Medicaid, or who do not have some form of privately funded health insurance, should consider purchasing at least some minimum level of medical expense coverage. The probability of needing medical attention during one's life is very high. However, the severity of the illness and the ultimate cost of treatment are unknown. While treating the flu is generally affordable for most people, obtaining a heart or liver transplant is not.

PURPOSE

Individual health insurance coverages allow the individual to customize his or her own insurance package. Provided the insured has no health problems that limit insurability, health insurers typically allow insureds to choose from a wide array of coverages to meet individual needs. There exists a direct relationship between the amount of coverage desired and the price of the premium. Naturally, the more coverages one chooses, the higher the premium.

Cost Concerns

Most people who have health insurance coverages today obtain them through either a group plan or a social insurance program. Individual health coverages are not as popular as group coverages, because the insured must pay the full cost of the coverage with *after-tax* dollars and individual health coverages are typically not as generous as those offered through group plans.

Eligibility

To obtain individual health insurance coverage, proof of insurability must be provided to the insurer. The completion of a fairly lengthy application is required and the insured must usually submit to some form of medical examination. The underwriter may also wish to see copies of previous medical records before making a coverage decision. Proof of insurability is not required for group plans.

Medical Expense Insurance

Basic Medical Insurance Coverages

There are three coverages an insured can purchase to cover a variety of medical expenses: hospital expense insurance, surgical expense insurance, and physician's expense insurance.

hospital expense insurance - provides payment for expenses incurred by the insured while in the hospital

Hospital Expense Insurance. **Hospital expense insurance** provides payment for expenses incurred by the insured while in the hospital. Coverage under hospital expense insurance includes a daily hospital benefit and a miscellaneous expense benefit. The daily hospital benefit pays a specified amount for room and board charges incurred during each day the insured is hospitalized. This benefit may be paid on a reimbursement basis, subject to a maximum daily limit, or it may be a flat amount per day. These plans also have a maximum number of days covered, such as 90 or 180.

A lump-sum benefit may be paid if the patient incurs miscellaneous expenses for items such as X-rays, medications, surgical supplies, and use of the operating room. The miscellaneous expense benefit will, of course, be subject to a maximum dollar amount.

Caution must be exercised in purchasing this type of coverage because many expensive procedures are now performed outside of a hospital. Also, physician and surgeon's fees are billed separately from hospital services, so hospital expense coverage does not provide for payment of those fees. Purchasing only hospital expense coverage is not sufficient to meet the needs of most individuals.

surgical expense insurance - may be added to a hospital expense insurance policy to provide payment of surgeon's fees, even when procedures are not performed in a hospital

Surgical Expense Insurance. **Surgical expense insurance** may be added to a hospital expense insurance policy to provide for the payment of the surgeon's fees, even when surgery is not performed in a hospital. Insurers typically base maximum benefits payable on a generic list of surgical procedures and their estimated costs, but some other benefit determination formula may be used.

Physician's Expense Insurance. **Physician's expense insurance** pays for fees charged by physicians who provide the insured with nonsurgical care. Treatment can be administered in the doctor's office, the patient's home, or the hospital. Again, maximum coverage limits will be specified.

physician's expense insurance - pays for fees charged by physicians that provide nonsurgical care

Limitations

Basic medical coverages set rigid limits on the amount payable for any one event. The maximum benefit provided for a single illness or injury may not be enough to pay the actual expenses incurred. While having these coverages is better than having no coverage at all, insureds must be aware that benefit levels are restricted.

MAJOR MEDICAL INSURANCE

Characteristics

Major medical insurance is designed to provide broad coverage of all reasonable and necessary expenses associated with an illness or injury, whether incurred at a doctor's office, a hospital, or the insured's home. Some major medical policies are "stand-alone" coverages that pay for a wide range of medical services. Others are written in conjunction with a basic medical plan to provide coverage in excess of that provided by the basic coverages. Many consumers are attracted to major medical insurance because it generally covers a wide range of expenses including hospitalization charges, physician and surgeon's fees, physical therapy, prescription drugs, wheelchairs and other medical supplies. High limits of coverage are usually provided, such as a $1 million lifetime maximum.

major medical insurance - health insurance that provides broad coverage of all reasonable and necessary expenses associated with an illness or injury, whether incurred at a doctor's office, a hospital, or the insured's home

Major medical policies have few exclusions. Routine eye exams and dental care typically are not covered, nor are self-inflicted injuries, injuries sustained in war, and elective cosmetic procedures.

Most major medical policies have a deductible of $500 or less. The deductible may apply per illness, per person per year, or per family per year. After the deductible has been met, the insurer typically pays some percentage of all remaining expenses that are usual and customary. Coinsurance is the division of expenses between the insured and the insurer in health insurance, with a common amount being 80 percent/20 percent. This clause requires the insurer to pay 80 percent of medical bills above the deductible and the insured to pay the remaining 20 percent.

After a deductible is met, the insured usually has a maximum time in which to incur expenses associated with one illness or injury. The period of time major medical benefits will be paid after the deductible is fulfilled is referred to as the benefit period. When the benefit period expires, the insured must then satisfy another deductible to be eligible for benefits again.

Limitations

In addition to a lifetime maximum benefit limit, many policies contain internal coverage limits, such as a maximum allowable daily charge for hospitalization, or perhaps a $25,000 lifetime maximum on mental health benefits. While these limits may satisfy the needs of most insureds, some may find them too restrictive.

Another problem with major medical insurance is the insurer's agreement to pay only 80 percent (or whatever the designated coinsurance percentage is) of *usual and customary* medical expenses. If the insurer determines that a particular surgical procedure should cost $10,000, it will pay only $8,000 of that amount, even if the surgeon's charges are $13,000 or $14,000.

Finally, unless the policy provides for some maximum out-of-pocket limit on the insured's portion of the coinsurance, a serious illness can still be financially devastating to the insured. Considering that all treatment associated with a heart transplant can easily cost $1 million, it is easy to see that most insureds could not afford their 20 percent (or even 10 percent) of that amount.

EXAMPLE

Assume that Brenda has a major medical insurance policy with a $500 annual aggregate deductible, a 90 percent/10 percent cost-sharing provision, and a $2,000 out-of-pocket cap (also referred to as a "stop loss provision.") If Brenda has surgery that costs $8,000, her plan will require her to pay $500, and then 10 percent of the remaining $7,500 in expenses, or $750. So, Brenda's total out-of-pocket expense for the surgery will be $1,250. If later the same year she has another illness that results in $10,000 of covered medical expenses, she will have to pay $750 (not $1,000) because once she has spent $2,000 of her own money during the year, the insurer will pay 100 percent of all remaining covered expenses.

long-term care insurance - provides coverage for nursing home stays and other types of routine care that are not covered by health insurance. Levels of coverage are skilled nursing care, intermediate nursing care, custodial care, home health care, and adult day care.

LONG-TERM CARE INSURANCE

An elderly person might be able to live alone, but may need assistance once each day with dressing and bathing. Medical expense policies (including Medicare coverage provided through the federal government) do not cover these types of expenses, nor do they pay for stays in extended care facilities such as nursing homes. **Long-term care insurance** provides coverage for nursing home stays and other types of routine care that are not covered by health insurance.

skilled nursing care - daily nursing care and rehabilitation services ordered and monitored by a physician

The premiums charged for long-term care coverage depend on the extent of benefits provided. There are seven types of coverage: skilled nursing care, intermediate nursing care, home health care, custodial care, assisted living, adult day care, and hospice care.

Types of Coverage

intermediate nursing care - occasional nursing and rehabilitative care ordered and monitored by a physician

Skilled nursing care is the highest level of medical care and is provided by traditional nursing homes. Daily nursing care is provided, along with rehabilitation services, and the patient's care is ordered and monitored by a physician. **Intermediate nursing care** is similar to skilled nursing care, except care is provided occasionally rather than on a daily basis. Again, a physician must order this type of treatment.

home health care - part-time skilled nursing care and rehabilitative therapy provided at the patient's home

Home health care allows the patient to remain at home and receive part-time skilled nursing care, rehabilitative therapy, and other necessary assistance. Depending upon the level of treatment needed, these services may be provided by a skilled professional or nonmedical personnel.

Custodial care provides assistance with regular tasks of daily life, such as eating, dressing, bathing, and taking medications. These services can normally be provided by nonmedical personnel and do not have to be ordered or supervised by a physician.

custodial care - assistance provided for tasks of daily life, such as eating, dressing, bathing, and taking medications

Assisted living facilities generally provide apartment-style housing, support services, and basic healthcare for individuals who need help with tasks of daily living. Some assisted living facilities are connected with skilled nursing facilities and allow patients to transfer back and forth as required by their health status.

assisted living - apartment-style housing combined with support services and basic health care

Adult day care is provided for persons who need assistance and supervision during the day, but whose spouse or other family members must work. The purpose of adult day care is quite similar to that of infant and child day care—to allow family members living with a person who cannot take care of herself to maintain their careers.

adult day care - basic assistance and supervision provided outside the home usually during the primary caregiver's working hours

Hospice care is care for the terminally ill and can take place at the patient's home, in a hospice care center, hospital, or nursing facility. Unlike most healthcare services, hospice care does not seek to cure the patient of an ailment. Instead, the goals of hospice care are pain management, emotional and spiritual support, and offering treatment that provides the patient with dignity and comfort.

hospice care - care that provides dignity and comfort to terminally ill patients and their

The need for long-term care insurance is often overlooked in the financial planning process. When an individual requires long-term care that health insurance will not pay for, assets may be quickly depleted paying for such care. In extreme cases, some people ultimately liquidate all assets so they can qualify for long-term care benefits through the Medicaid (welfare) insurance program. As many long-term care facilities are not Medicaid providers, the insured's choice of care facilities may be severely restricted under these impoverished circumstances.

Benefits

Long-term care insurance is a recent innovation prompted by the increasing costs of healthcare associated with the extension of life provided by today's technology. The two benefit approaches used are the defined period approach and the pool of money approach. The **defined-period approach** is the more popular method and provides coverage for a defined period following an elimination period of up to 180 days. Benefits may be provided for a specified period of time or until death. Under the **pool of money concept**, the insured is covered up to a specific dollar amount regardless of the time period.

defined-period approach - long-term care coverage provided for a specified period of time following an elimination period

Most long-term care policies provide skilled nursing, intermediate nursing, and custodial care. Some policies will also cover home health care, assisted living, adult day care, and hospice care. Medicare provides limited coverage for skilled nursing, intermediate nursing, home health, and hospice care. Most of the features of health insurance policies are also found in long-term care insurance policies, including deductibles and waivers of premium. When determining the appropriateness and desirable characteristics of long-term care insurance, financial planners should consider the benefits available under Medicare and the client's assets and family health history.

pool of money concept - long-term care coverage that provides coverage up to a specific dollar amount, regardless of time period

A new class of long-term care insurance policies called tax-qualified long-term care insurance was established with the passage of the Health Insurance Portability and Accountability Act of

1996 (HIPAA). Policies that meet standards set forth in this act state on their cover and in marketing materials that the policy is intended to be a qualified plan. The word "intend" or "intended" is used because the federal government does not have a mechanism for certifying that policies are qualified. However, a policy that clearly does not meet the standards cannot state that it is intended to be a qualified plan.

A tax-qualified long-term care policy (TQ) is any insurance contract that provides only coverage of qualified long-term care services and meets the following additional requirements:

- the contract must be guaranteed renewable;
- the contract must not provide for a cash surrender value or other money that can be paid, assigned, borrowed, or pledged;
- refunds under the contract (other than refunds paid upon the death of the insured or complete surrender or cancellation of the contract) and dividends may only be used to reduce future premiums or to increase future benefits;
- the contract must meet certain consumer protection standards (See Exhibit 9.6); and
- the contract must coordinate benefits with Medicare (unless Medicare is a secondary payor) or the contract is an indemnity or per diem contract.

qualified long-term care services - as defined by HIPAA, necessary diagnostic, preventative, therapeutic, caring, treating, rehabilitative services, and maintenance or personal care services required by a chronically ill or cognitively impaired person and provided by a plan prescribed by a licensed health care practitioner

chronically ill individual - a person who has an illness or injury resulting in the inability to perform, without substantial assistance, at least two of the six activities of daily living for

EXHIBIT 9.6: CONSUMER PROTECTION

In order to qualify for favorable tax treatment under HIPAA, an LTC policy must have certain consumer protection features. These protections include the following:

- All contracts must be guaranteed renewable.
- Preexisting conditions can be excluded up to a maximum of six months after issue (If a new contract replaces another contract, the new contract must recognize the previous contract's satisfaction of the insured's six-month preexisting condition.)
- Contracts cannot require prior hospitalization before paying nursing home benefits or require prior institutionalization before paying home care benefits.
- Contracts cannot exclude any specific illnesses (such as Alzheimer's disease).
- Contracts must provide protection against unintentional lapses because of a physical or cognitive impairment.
- Companies cannot utilize post-claims underwriting.
- Contracts providing home care benefit cannot restrict allowable care to only skilled care, and must provide coverage for a meaningful length of time.
- Contracts must offer inflation protection.
- Companies must offer a nonforfeiture option.

Qualified long-term care services include necessary diagnostic, preventative, therapeutic, caring, treating, rehabilitative services, as well as maintenance or personal care services that are required by a **chronically ill individual** and are provided in accordance with a plan of care prescribed by a licensed health care practitioner.

A chronically ill individual is any individual certified within the previous 12 months by a licensed health practitioner as (1) being unable to perform at least two **activities of daily living (ADLs)** for a period expected to last at least 90 days owing to a loss of functional capacity; (2) requiring substantial supervision to protect the person from threats to health and safety because of severe cognitive impairment; or (3) having a similar level of disability as designated by some future regulation.

activities of daily living (ADLs) - eating, bathing, dressing, transferring from bed to chair, using a toilet, and continence

Under the ADL trigger, the policy must take into account at least five of the following ADLs in determining whether an individual is chronically ill: eating, toileting, transferring, bathing, dressing, and continence.

Plans that do not meet these requirements are considered nontax-qualified long-term care insurance (NTQ). These plans are identified by one or more of the following characteristics:

- physical impairment does not need to be expected to last at least 90 days;
- physical impairment requirement can be met with just one ADL impairment;
- physical impairment requirement can be met with an impairment with two or more of any ADLs;
- fewer than five ADLs can be assessed in determining whether an individual is chronically ill;
- physical impairment requirement can be met with an impairment of instrumental activities of daily living (IADLs) only;
- the physical impairment requirement can be met without reference to the need for "substantial" assistance;
- the insured can qualify for benefits:
  - because of a medical necessity;
  - without a severe cognitive impairment; and
  - without a plan of care submitted to the insurance company;
- benefits reimburse for actual charges but do not coordinate with Medicare;
- plan pays benefits for services received from unskilled providers or family members*;
- plan pays benefits for services not related to caring for the insured;
- plan pays for capital improvements to a home; or
- plan includes a cash payment return of premium at lapse that pays in excess of the premiums paid for the policy.

*A tax-qualified long-term care insurance plan (TQ) can also pay benefits for unskilled providers or family members and does not have to coordinate benefits with Medicare if the benefits are paid without regard to actual cost. These types of plans are normally referred to as indemnity plans. Plans that are concerned with actual cost are referred to as reimbursement plans.

HIPAA allows favorable tax treatment for premiums paid to and benefits received from qualified plans. Premiums paid by the individual are deductible as medical expenses for itemized deduction purposes depending on the individual's age. Exhibit 9.7 outlines the maximum annual premium allowed to be deducted for income tax purposes. If an employer pays for long-term care insurance, the premiums are tax-deductible to the employer and are not taxable income to the employee. Long-term care benefits cannot be included in a cafeteria plan or a flexible spending account on a tax-advantaged basis. In other words, if the premiums are deducted from the employee's pay, they must be deducted on an after-tax basis. Regardless of who makes the premium payments, benefits received from qualified plans are excluded from income.

EXHIBIT 9.7: MAXIMUM ALLOWABLE FEDERAL INCOME TAX DEDUCTION FOR LONG-TERM CARE PREMIUMS (2005)

Age of Insured	Maximum Deduction
≤40	$270
41 – 50	$510
51 – 60	$1,020
61 – 70	$2,720
> 70	$3,400

DISABILITY INCOME INSURANCE

Purpose

disability income insurance - a type of insurance that provides a regular income while the insured is unable to work because of illness or injury

Disability income insurance provides replacement income while the insured is unable to work because of illness or injury. Premiums for this coverage are a function of the insured's health, occupation, gender, age, and the level of income benefits provided by the policy. Most insureds purchase either a flat dollar amount of coverage, such as $2,000 per month, or coverage that replaces some portion of predisability earnings (such as 60 to 80 percent).

morbidity - relates to the probability of becoming disabled

To qualify for disability income, one must become totally disabled while the policy is in force and remain so until the elimination (exclusion) period has ended. Once these qualifications are met, monthly indemnity will be made payable at the end of each month of disability. Premiums for disability insurance are based partially on morbidity rates for the benefit term. The **morbidity** rate is the probability of a person becoming disabled.

Definitions of Disability

A key feature of disability income insurance is that it specifies what constitutes a "disability" for the purposes of receiving policy benefits. Unless the insured person's condition complies with the disability definition in the policy, the insurer does not pay income benefits. Different types of disability definitions exist. The most common ones are "any occupation," "own occupation," and a combination of the two.

"any occupation" - definition of disability in which an insured is considered totally disabled if duties of *any* occupation cannot be performed

Any Occupation. A person insured under the "**any occupation**" clause is considered totally disabled if he or she cannot perform the duties of *any* occupation. The courts have interpreted this clause to mean any occupation for which the insured is suited by education, experience, and training. Thus, a disabled brain surgeon can draw benefits from the policy even if he is still able o work at a fast food restaurant. But, if the surgeon is able to teach, lecture, or do research elated to his field of expertise, then the insurer would likely not consider him disabled.

Own Occupation. The "**own occupation**" definition is much more liberal than the any occupation definition. It states that the insured must be able to perform each and every duty of his *own* occupation, or he is considered disabled. This means that a surgeon who cannot perform surgery due to a broken hand is considered totally disabled even if he moves to a hospital administration position. Because he cannot perform all of the duties of his chosen profession, he is considered totally disabled.

"own occupation" - definition of disability in which an insured is considered totally disabled if he cannot perform each and every duty of his *own* occupation

Split Definition. Many disability income insurance policies today include a combination of the any and own occupation clauses. Typically, the own occupation definition of disability will apply only during the first one-to-five years after an illness or injury. After that, the any occupation definition applies.

Disability insurance may cover injuries only or injuries and illness. Coverage for injury and illness is preferred but will result in a higher premium. Injury is defined in the policy as either accidental bodily injury or bodily injury by accidental means. **Accidental bodily injury** requires only that the injury incurred be accidental. **Bodily injury by accidental means** requires accidental injury by accidental means. Thus, if Gerry's coworker intentionally drops a computer monitor on Gerry's foot, Gerry's disability insurance would provide coverage if it provides for accidental bodily injuries. Gerry would not be covered, however, if his policy defined injury as bodily injury by accidental means, since the coworker intentionally dropped the monitor. The definition of illness usually precludes preexisting conditions and may require a probationary period.

accidental bodily injury - only the injury incurred is accidental

bodily injury by accidental means - requires accidental injury by accidental means

It is important to realize that Social Security may also provide disability benefits to a disabled person; however, the Social Security definition of disability is much more restrictive than most definitions used in private disability income insurance. The Social Security program requires the disabled person to wait five months before receiving benefits. The disabled person also must prove that he cannot engage in *any* gainful employment, and that the disability is expected to last at least twelve months or end in death.

Characteristics

Benefit period. Disability insurance distinguishes between short-term and long-term coverage. **Short-term disability** provides coverage for up to two years. Many employers offer group short-term disability insurance that provides employees with a percentage of their salary while disabled. **Long-term disability** provides coverage until normal retirement age, until death, or for a specified term greater than two years. Some employers offer group long-term disability insurance with premiums generally paid for by the employee. Employer-sponsored plans are usually not portable and terminate when the employee leaves the firm unless the reason for leaving employment is directly related to the disability.

short-term disability - provides coverage for up to two years

long-term disability - provides coverage for specified term greater than two years, until specified age, or until death

elimination period - the amount of time that must pass before benefits are paid

partial disability - the insured cannot perform all of the substantial and material duties of the job, or is prevented from working at least 80% of his normal work schedule

cost of living rider - increases benefits being received by the policyowner each year; based on an index, such as the CPI

Elimination Period. To reduce unnecessary small claims and moral hazards, an **elimination period** of one month to one year from the date of disability is included in a disability income policy. During this waiting period, disability income benefits are not being paid. Shorter elimination periods require higher premium payments since the probability that the insurer will make disability income payments to the policyowner is greater.

Partial Disability. Many policies include coverage for **partial disability**, defined as a disability that prevents the insured from performing all of the substantial and material duties of the job or prevents the insured from working at least 80% of the insured's normal work schedule. The partial disability provision provides payments that are less than those paid for total disability but these benefits usually last for only a short time (such as six months). By covering partial disability in this manner, the insurer gives the insured some incentive to return to work sooner than he or she otherwise might.

Waiver of Premium. The waiver of premium rider removes the requirement that the policyowner make premium payments after the insured has been disabled for 90 days, or the elimination period, if shorter. In many cases, premiums paid during the 90 days are refunded. When the insured recovers from the disability, premiums normally resume, although some companies will waive premiums for 90 days following recovery. However, as long as the insured remains disabled, premiums are waived. Some policies will refund premiums if they are paid during this period.

Cost of Living Rider. The **cost of living rider** preserves the purchasing power of the insured's disability income benefits. It takes effect only if a monthly benefit is being paid for disability.

Disability insurance claims often result in benefit payments that last for a number of years. This rider protects benefits from the effects of inflation. A cost of living adjustment is made each year benefits are paid to the insured. Adjustments are computed by using the same rate of change as, say, the Consumer Price Index. The rate of change is limited to a specific rate of inflation, usually between 5 percent and 10 percent compounded annually with a maximum cumulative rate. This is an expensive rider that may increase premiums by 25 to 40 percent.

Future Increase Option. The future increase option protects future earnings by allowing the policyowner to increase the potential monthly benefit as the insured gets older and earns more, regardless of any health changes. This rider guarantees insurability for a certain period of time (normally to age 55) for additional premium. Note that this option affects the benefit coverage; in other words the potential benefit paid in the event a disability occurs is increased.

Automatic Increase Rider. The automatic increase rider raises the total monthly benefit coverage each year for a specified number of years, and no increase thereafter (a common increase is 5% per year for five years). Premiums increase as the monthly coverage increases. This rider is often used to have the monthly benefit coverage keep pace with inflation. Thus, the policyowner receives a benefit that reflects rises in inflation should the insured become disabled.

Taxation of Benefits

ndividual disability income insurance premiums are generally not tax deductible by the nsured. As a result, benefit payments received during a period of disability are not subject to ncome taxation. If before-tax dollars fund the premium, benefits will be subject to income taxation.

Integration of Benefits

A disability income policy may "integrate" with Social Security disability coverage. A policy that ntegrates with Social Security will reduce payable benefits by the amount of Social Security the disabled person is eligible to receive. This type of coverage is less expensive than a similar policy that does not integrate with Social Security, because the insurer expects to pay out lower benefits if the insured is disabled for a lengthy period of time.

The insured may have a $2,000 monthly disability benefit provided by the policy, but if she is also eligible for a $1,200 monthly Social Security disability benefit, the individual policy might pay only $800 per month. When shopping for an individual disability income policy, the insured should be aware that some policies contain such integration provisions.

Termination of Benefits

Benefit payments cease at either the end of the benefit period or the date one is no longer disabled, whichever occurs first.

Residual Benefits

residual benefits provision - policyowner receives a percentage of the disability benefit based on the percentage of income loss due to sickness or injury

Under the **residual benefits provision**, the policyowner receives a percentage of the disability benefit based on the percentage of income loss due to sickness or injury. The benefit payable is equal to a proportionate amount of the monthly benefit.

EXAMPLE

For example, assume Dr. Peyton earns $10,000 per month as a practicing physician. He becomes disabled, and returns to work as a consultant earning $6,000 per month – a drop in income of 40%. Dr. Peyton had a disability income policy with residual benefits and a monthly benefit of $5,000. Under the residual benefit provision of the policy he would receive $2,000 per month (40% of the $5,000 monthly benefit).

EXHIBIT 9.8: LONG-TERM DISABILITY INSURANCE CHECKLIST

Characteristic	Desirable Coverage
Amount of Benefit	60% to 70% of gross pay
Benefit Term	Work life expectancy
Covered Conditions	Injury and illness
Elimination Period	Based on client's liquid assets and emergency fund
Definition of Disability	Own occupation or split definition
Integration	To reduce premiums, integration with Social Security or workers compensation may be desirable

Health and Disability Insurance Policy Provisions

pre-existing condition - a medical condition that required treatment during a specified period of time prior to the insured's effective date of coverage

pre-existing conditions clause - excludes coverage for pre-existing conditions for possibly as long as 12 months after the effective date of coverage

Pre-existing Conditions

A **pre-existing condition** is a medical condition that required treatment during a specified period of time (e.g., 6 months) prior to the insured's effective date of coverage under a health insurance plan. In some policies, the definition of pre-existing condition includes medical conditions known to the insured, even though no medical care was provided for the condition during the specified period. A **preexisting conditions clause** excludes coverage for pre-existing conditions for possibly as long as 12 months after the effective date of coverage. This clause helps insurance companies control adverse selection.

Grace Period

A grace period is a period of time (usually 31 days) beyond the premium due date during which an insurance premium payment may be made without cancellation of the coverage. During the grace period, the policy remains in force.

Reinstatement

Included in every health insurance policy is a procedure for policy reinstatement, should coverage lapse due to nonpayment of premium. A reinstatement clause specifies a time limit within which the insured may reinstate the policy, and indicates whether proof of insurability is required. Reinstated policies usually have pre-existing clauses that exclude coverage for illnesses incurred during a given time period.

incontestable clause - the insurer may not contest the validity of the contract after it has been in force for a certain period of time

Incontestable Clause

The **incontestable clause** of a health insurance policy is an optional clause that may be used in noncancelable or guaranteed renewable health insurance contracts. This clause provides that the insurer may not contest the validity of the contract after it has been in force for a certain period (typically two years).

Guaranteed Renewable

If a health or disability insurance policy is **guaranteed renewable**, the insurance company is required to renew a policy for a specified amount of time (e.g., to age 65) regardless of changes to the health of the insured. Under this agreement, premiums must be paid when due. The renewal of the policy is at the sole discretion of the insured. The insurance company, however, reserves the right to increase premiums as deemed necessary, as long as the premium increase is for an entire class of policyowners.

guaranteed renewable - the insurer is required to renew the policy for a specified amount of time regardless of changes to the insured's health (premiums may be increased)

Noncancellable

A health or disability insurance policy that is **noncancellable** provides the greatest amount of security for the insured. The insurance company guarantees the renewal of the policy for a given period or to a stated age. Additionally, the insurer may not make changes to the policy, including increases in premiums.

noncancellable - insurer guarantees the renewal of the policy for a given period or to a stated age without an increase in

Conditionally Renewable

A policy that is **conditionally renewable** cannot be canceled by the insurance company during the policy term (usually one year), but it may refuse to renew the contract for another term if certain conditions exist as stipulated in the policy.

conditionally renewable - cannot be canceled by the insurer during the policy term, but insurer may refuse to renew the contract for another term if certain conditions exist

Renewable at Insurer's Option

Under a policy that is **renewable at the insurer's option**, the insurance company may not cancel the policy during its term (usually one year), but it may decline to renew the policy for a subsequent term at its discretion. This offers very little security to the insured.

renewable at the insurer's option - the insurer may not cancel the policy during its term, but the insurer may decline to renew the policy for a subsequent term at its

GROUP HEALTH INSURANCE

The vast majority of all medical expense insurance coverage sold today is in the form of a group policy. By pooling together a large number of employees, the administrative costs of providing coverage are lowered and adverse selection is usually reduced. As a result, more features and benefits are usually provided through a group health insurance plan.

ELIGIBILITY

To be eligible for group health care coverage, one must be a member of a group that has come together for some purpose other than to purchase insurance. Some examples of eligible groups are debtor-creditor groups, labor union groups, multiple-employer trusts, trade and professional associations, and any single employer group. Most eligible groups require that their participants:

- Be a full-time employee (or a qualifying member) of the group.
- Satisfy a probationary period.
- Be actively at work the day coverage begins.

CHARACTERISTICS

Group underwriting procedures are different from those for individual health coverages. Instead of looking at each insured on an individual basis, the underwriter looks at the overall composition of the insured group. All employees in the group are automatically eligible for coverage under a group contract.

The employer holds the master contract and employees are given individual coverage certificates. The employer generally pays most, or all, of the premium, which further prevents adverse selection. The employer is responsible for enrolling new employees and collecting any premiums due from employees. The insurer thus saves a great deal on administrative expenses and those savings are passed on to the employer or employees in the form of lower premiums.

Basic and Major Medical

Group basic medical insurance provides coverage for hospital, surgical, and physician's expenses that are similar to those discussed previously under Individual Health Coverages. Basic medical plans have low maximum limits on coverage and are often used in conjunction with major medical plans.

group supplemental plans - often attached to basic medical expense coverages, these policies allow the employer to use more than one provider for coverage, offer first-dollar coverage, or use different contribution rates for basic and supplemental coverages

Group major medical expense coverage is also very similar to individual major medical coverage. The two main types of group major medical plans are supplemental and comprehensive. **Group supplemental plans**, often attached to basic medical expense coverages, allow the employer to use more than one provider for coverage, offer first-dollar coverage, or use different contribution rates for basic and supplemental coverages.

comprehensive major medical - stand-alone coverage that provides for a broad range of medical services and has high limits of coverage

Comprehensive major medical is a stand-alone coverage that provides for a broad range of medical services and has high limits of coverage. Deductibles are usually low and employees pay some percentage of all medical expenses above the deductible, subject to some maximum out-of-pocket dollar limit. As with individual plans, these group major medical plans cover all necessary medical expenses unless they are specifically excluded in the contract. Recently, coverages under these plans have expanded to pay for items such as extended care facilities, home health care centers, hospice care, ambulatory care, birthing centers, diagnostic x-ray and laboratory services, radiation therapy, supplemental accident benefits, prescription drugs, and vision care.

EXAMPLE

Assume that Alexander's employer offers him comprehensive group major medical coverage. The policy has a $250 per person annual deductible and after that pay 80 percent of all covered charges. The policy might further limit Alexander's out-of-pocket expenses to $1,000 per year (including the deductible). After Alexander has spent $1,000 of his own money, the insurer will then pay 100 percent of covered medical expenses up to the maximum benefit stated in the contract, frequently $1,000,000 or more.

If Alexander is involved in a boating accident and incurs $1,250 of medical expenses, he must pay the first $250 of these covered expenses. Then, the insurer will pay 80 percent of the remaining $1,000, or $800, and Jerry will pay $200. If two months later, Alexander suffers another injury, he does not have to pay the $250 deductible again because he has a "per person per year" deductible. He only has to pay 20 percent of his medical expenses. Once he has paid $1,000 out of his pocket for the entire year (including the deductible), his insurer will begin paying 100 percent of all covered expenses.

Dental and Vision

Many medical health insurance plans do not provide coverage for dental or optical care. However, most companies today offer supplemental plans for vision and dental coverage. Preventive care is usually encouraged under these plans, so routine check-ups are often covered. They are thus quite popular with employees, even when the employees must pay 100 percent of the cost of coverage. These are the types of coverage where the risk of adverse selection is so high that benefits are quite limited and premiums frequently adjusted.

Disability Income

Group disability income insurance is structured in much the same fashion as individual disability income coverage. Under a group disability income plan, however, payments are based on the disability being either long term or short term. Generally, short-term disability payments are made from either the first day of injury resulting from an accident or the eighth day of disability resulting from sickness. Benefits are payable on a weekly basis for up to 13, 26, or 52 weeks. Long-term disability coverage will pay when short-term benefits expire or when the insured has satisfied the required long-term elimination period. Long-term disability benefits under a group plan are usually paid until the disability ends or until the insured reaches age 65, whichever occurs first. It is always advisable, however, to check the term of benefits, since they may not be as long as the employee's remaining work life expectancy.

Managed Care

The goal of managed care techniques is to reduce the overall costs of providing health coverage, while simultaneously ensuring the quality of medical services delivered. Much variation exists among managed care plans, but most plans will, at a minimum, arrange for the delivery of medical and health services, review the quality and appropriateness of services rendered, and reimburse the providers who deliver services to plan participants.

The consumer must join a plan and agree to its contractual terms. The consumer is then able to obtain health care with a small copayment or other deductible. The managed care plan assembles a network of doctors and other health care providers who agree to provide services to plan participants. The health care providers are under contract with the plan and must agree to abide by the plan's terms and conditions, plus agree to accept whatever compensation the plan allows without penalizing the patient.

When the need for care arises, the consumer will access the plan through a primary care physician who either provides treatment or refers the patient to a medical specialist. Each doctor collects the required copayment from the patient and then bills the managed care plan for other charges allowed by the plan.

EXAMPLE

Assume that Blue Hope Managed Care Plan provides coverage to Betty. Betty goes to her primary care physician (PCP) and asks him to look at a cyst on her arm. The PCP determines that the cyst is severe enough to use the services of a surgeon, so he refers Betty to one of the plan's surgeons. When the surgeon removes the cyst, she charges Betty the plan's required co-pay of $20. Her usual fee for that type of surgery is $1,000, so she bills Blue Hope for the remaining $980. If Blue Hope allows the surgeon only $500 for the procedure (it will pay $480, because Betty has already paid $20), the surgeon may not then go back to Betty and ask her to pay the remaining $500.

It is important to clarify the major differences between a managed care plan and an indemnity plan. The major medical coverages discussed previously are examples of indemnity plans. An indemnity plan agrees to pay a certain percentage of covered medical expenses the insured person incurs, while a managed care plan agrees to provide needed medical services. There is no contractual arrangement between the major medical insurer and the doctor (or other service provider). A managed care plan, however, contracts with doctors and hospitals and other health care providers *and* it contracts with persons who wish to receive health care services.

Health Maintenance Organization (HMO) - organized system of health care that provides comprehensive health services to its members for a fixed prepaid fee

HMOs. As a direct result of the HMO Act of 1973, **Health Maintenance Organizations (HMOs)** have flourished in the United States. All HMOs share common goals of comprehensive care, delivery of services, and cost control. An HMO assumes the responsibility and risk of providing a broad range of services to its members, including preventive medical services such as check-ups and mammograms, in exchange for a fixed monthly or annual enrollment fee. HMOs usually allow their members very little choice of service providers. The patient must generally use a contract provider or no benefits are paid. A $10 to $20 copayment must usually be paid by the insured for each office visit.

Primary care doctors are either salaried employees of the HMO, or they are in private practice and receive a monthly fee ("capitation payment") for each patient they agree to treat, whether the patient receives care or not. Specialists may also be salaried employees or they may be in private practice and receive fees for only the services they provide.

Preferred Provider Organization (PPO) - a contractual arrangement between the insured, the insurer, and the health care provider that allows the insurer to receive discounted rates from service providers

PPOs. A **Preferred Provider Organization (PPO)** is merely a contractual arrangement between the insured, the insurer, and the health care provider that allows the insurer to receive discounted rates from service providers. PPOs are structured in much the same way as HMOs with two main exceptions: members are allowed to use non-PPO providers, although they will be required to pay higher deductibles and coinsurance than required when they use PPO doctors, and primary care doctors (as well as specialists) are paid on a fee-for-service basis rather than as employees under the usual HMO.

PPOs offer insureds a greater choice of health care providers than most HMOs. Many find the HMO concept objectionable because benefits are not provided if the covered person uses a doctor outside of the HMO's network of providers (in other than an emergency). Although the insured pays more out of her pocket by going outside the network of preferred providers offered by a PPO, medical benefits are still payable.

Advantages and Disadvantages. Managed health care companies are highly competitive and often improve services or reduce costs to gain market share. Most managed health care plans are service-oriented and focus on assisting the patient to receive the most appropriate care for the money. To maintain quality of care, managed care plans provide coordination and continuity in the process of delivering care that is deemed medically necessary.

The primary disadvantage of managed care is reduced choice for the patient. While many managed care plans allow the insured to go outside the network of preferred providers, the vast majority of plans do not allow physicians to perform certain procedures without prior approval from the plan. This in turn reduces the patient's options for care. Furthermore, some managed care organizations put "gag clauses" in their contracts with providers. These clauses require the provider to remain silent about treatment options for the patient if the managed care plan excludes coverage for those procedures, such as experimental bone marrow transplants. Much criticism focuses on the fact that nonmedical personnel are controlling the medical options offered to patients by their doctors.

Coordination of Benefits

Due to the rising number of dual-income families across America today, measures have been taken by insurers to prevent insureds from making a profit by receiving benefits twice for the same ailment. One such measure is known as the **coordination of benefits (COB) clause**. The goal of this measure is to avoid duplicate payments for a single service. COB is used in all group health insurance plans to prevent the insured who is covered by both her own employer's plan and her spouse's plan from receiving more than 100 percent of the actual cost of health care received.

coordination of benefits clause - prevents an insured from receiving greater than 100% of the cost of health care received when covered by multiple policies

Termination of Benefits

Upon permanent termination of employment with a company, one may still maintain group health insurance benefits for 31 days. This opportunity is extended to the former employee so that he or she will have adequate time to replace the group insurance with individual insurance. If new employment provides health insurance for the terminated employee, the previous employer's coverage automatically expires even if the 31-day period has not ended.

Consolidated Omnibus Budget Reconciliation Act (COBRA)

Employees and dependents previously covered under a group health insurance may have that group coverage extended under a federal law known as the ***Consolidated Omnibus Budget Reconciliation Act (COBRA).*** COBRA requires certain employers to provide the previously covered persons (including dependents and spouses) with the same coverage he or she received prior to unemployment or other event affecting health care coverage. The benefit recipient must pay the full cost of the coverage, however, which may be prohibitively expensive if the recipient is unemployed. The employer is also allowed to charge up to 2 percent of the premium to cover administrative expenses, but under no circumstances may the employee be charged more than 102 percent of the total cost of the plan during the period of coverage.

Consolidated Omnibus Budget Reconciliation Act (COBRA) - requires certain employers to provide previously covered persons with the same coverage received prior to discontinuation of coverage

To continue health insurance coverage through COBRA, the group coverage must terminate because of a qualifying event, including:

- Voluntary or involuntary termination of the employee (except for gross misconduct).

PROFESSIONAL FOCUS

How much insurance does an individual need?

The justification for the purchase of life insurance is based on the need of the insured to provide financial support for dependents in the event of premature death by the insured. The basic definition of a premature death is if the insured has unfulfilled financial obligations. We typically look at this from the standpoint of the head of the family, but most individuals will have financial obligations, even after their death.

Do you use the needs approach or the human value approach, why or why not?

In many ways, the needs approach is easier for the insured to comprehend and agree with the amount of life insurance needed as opposed to the human value approach or capital retention approach. This is typically the case if the insured is using life insurance to manage the unfulfilled obligations and not using life insurance as a type of estate protection. The needs approach is very straightforward. You start by estimating the funds needed for estate clearance and include needs such as income for dependents, income for a surviving spouse, college education funds for dependents, and others. The amount in the estate clearance should be enough to cover possible unpaid medical bills, funeral costs, taxes, and legal fees. Most people can easily come up with the amount needed in the absence of a breadwinner. If using the needs approach, the insured definitely needs to review the amount of life insurance needed and carried on a regular basis. Obviously at different times in an insured's life, the need for life insurance varies with financial responsibilities.

How do you help clients choose between term and permanent life insurance?

If income is limited and the need is temporary, term life insurance is definitely the way to go. If you are not only trying to deal with the possibility of premature death, but also want to include retirement planning or saving for a specific need, various whole-life policies can help. Insurance agents prefer to sell the more expensive cash-value policies, which generate higher commissions than term. Their justification is that the insured will not buy term and invest the difference in cost, but buy term and spend the difference. They are probably correct in most cases. However, approximately 12 percent of consumers that buy the higher cost cash-value policies allow them to lapse within the first year and an estimated 40 percent drop these policies during the first 10 years.

Who should receive the death benefit?

The insured must carefully consider the designation of a beneficiary. In most families, spouses name the remaining spouse as primary beneficiary and the children as contingent beneficiaries. If both spouses die and the children are minors, most states will not allow the proceeds to go directly to the minor. There are variations in different states. Payments can be delayed as a guardian for the minor children is selected. An easy solution is to name a guardian in the couple's wills.

EDWIN H. DUETT, PH.D.

- Death of the covered employee.
- Reduction of employee's hours from full-time to part-time.
- Divorce or legal separation of covered employee from spouse.
- Employee becomes eligible for Medicare.
- A dependent child is no longer eligible for coverage under the employee's plan, as would be the case when the child left school, reached a certain age, or married.

COBRA applies only to employees who offer a group health plan and have at least 20 employees. Affected employers must offer coverage for a specified period of time, dependent on the type of qualifying event.

- Termination or part-time status: 18 months *
- Death of covered employee: 36 months
- Divorce or legal separation: 36 months
- Medicare eligibility: 36 months

*Up to 29 months if employee meets Social Security definition of disabled, or up to 36 months if the beneficiary experiences, during a period of COBRA coverage, a second COBRA qualifying event.

Coverage for Elderly Employees

Employees who are 65 and older, and who are also eligible for Medicare benefits, must still be covered by the employer's group health coverage. The group plan is the primary payor of benefits and Medicare is the secondary payor.

Coverage for Retirees

Historically, many companies continued group health insurance coverage on their retired employees, although Medicare was the primary payor of benefits and the group plan served to fill coverage gaps in the Medicare program. The employer would pay some or all of the premiums on the retiree's coverage. In 1993, however, the Federal Accounting Standards Board (FASB) began requiring employers to recognize (on the balance sheet) the present value of the cost of providing retiree coverage *during the employee's active working years.* This ruling had a very negative effect on the earnings of most employers; so many employers have stopped offering paid benefits to retirees.

Another problem employers face in offering paid health benefits to retirees is the tendency of U.S. courts to prohibit a reduction in benefits after retirement. If an employer offers a retiree benefits, it may have to continue those benefits as long as the retiree desires them. This is a rather lengthy commitment for the employer that could prove financially burdensome during periods of reduced sales or profits.

Taxation of Group Health Benefits

Currently, employer-provided medical expense coverages are not taxable as income to the employee and the premiums paid by the employer are tax deductible as a business expense.

Employer-paid premiums for disability income coverage are not taxed as current income to the employee, but if a disability occurs, the benefits paid by the plan are taxable as income to the employee. If the employee pays the entire cost of disability income coverage, the premiums are not tax deductible for the employee. However, any disability benefits received from an employee-paid policy are not subject to income tax. If the employer and employee share the cost of disability income coverage, then disability benefits that are attributable to employer contributions are taxable as income to the employee.

Portability of Group Plans

In 1997, President Clinton signed into law the *Health Insurance Portability and Accountability Act (HIPAA).* This law eliminates the previously detrimental effects of changing jobs and starting a new health plan with a new pre-existing exclusions clause.

Example

For example, suppose Sherri worked at ABC Industries for 10 years and was covered under their group health plan. She then took a job at XYZ Consolidated. Prior to the passage of HIPAA, Sherri would have to satisfy a new pre-existing conditions exclusion period (usually at least 6 months and sometimes as long as 18 or 24 months) before benefits would be payable under XYZ's health plan. Thus, if Sherri had some type of serious medical condition, she would probably be unable to change jobs.

HIPAA guarantees that persons who change jobs do not suffer such penalties. HIPAA requires that employers give departing employees a certificate of creditable coverage to take to their next employer. This certificate shows how many months the employee was covered by the employer's group plan. When the employee enrolls in a new group plan, both of the following rules apply:

- Pre-existing conditions can be excluded for a maximum of 12 months.
- The 12-month pre-existing conditions exclusion under the new plan must be reduced for every month of coverage the employee had under a previous plan.

A pre-existing condition is defined as any medical condition that was treated or diagnosed within six months prior to enrolling in the new group plan.

Example

In the previous example HIPAA would thus require that XYZ ignore the pre-existing conditions exclusion in Sherri's case, since she already has creditable coverage of 10 years in a previous employer's plan. Had Sherri only worked for ABC for 8 months and been a participant in the ABC plan for 7 months, XYZ would have to give him 7 months of credit on its pre-existing conditions exclusion. So, Sherri's illness would be excluded, but only for five months.

DISCUSSION QUESTIONS

1. What are some of the risks associated with premature death? How can life insurance reduce (or eliminate) these risks?
2. What are the three recognized methods of measuring the needs related to premature death?
3. What is used as the basis for risk measurement under the human value life approach to identifying life insurance needs?
4. What are component needs that make up the financial needs approach to the amount of life insurance needed?
5. How do term, whole life, and universal life insurance differ? What are the advantages and disadvantages of each?
6. Identify and discuss the various types of term life insurance.
7. Identify and discuss the various types of whole life insurance.
8. Identify and discuss the death benefit options offered for a universal life policy.
9. What differentiates variable life insurance from variable universal life insurance?
10. At what threshold is an employee taxed on group term life insurance provided by an employer?
11. How do annuities differ from life insurance contracts?
12. What are the various types of annuities?
13. What are the tax implications of life insurance and annuities?
14. What are the various contractual provisions and options that pertain to life and annuity contracts?
15. What are the major types of individual health coverage?
16. What are the important policy provisions and major contractual features of individual health coverage?
17. What are the major types of employer-provided group health coverages?
18. What are the important policy provisions and major contractual features of group health coverage?
19. What is the purpose of disability income insurance? What are some of the various definitions of disability?
20. What are the major types of disability coverage?
21. What are the important policy provisions and major contractual features of disability income insurance?
22. What is the tax treatment of health and disability coverages?
23. How do indemnity plans and managed care plans differ?
24. How can group health coverage be continued or transferred when employment terminates?

EXERCISES

1. Comment on each of the following statements concerning the methods of providing life insurance protection:
   - ▲ An insurance company can use three approaches to provide life insurance protection: term insurance, which is temporary; whole life insurance, which is permanent protection that builds up a reserve or savings component; and universal life, which is protection that accrues cash value at interest rates higher than the guaranteed interest rate.

- Term insurance is a form of life insurance in which the death proceeds are payable in the event of the insured's death during a specified period and nothing is paid if the insured survives to the end of that period.
- The net premium for term insurance is determined by the mortality rate for the attained age of the individual involved.
- Because death rates rise at an increasing rate as ages increase, the net premium for term insurance also rises at an increasing rate.
- Because many individuals need insurance that can be continued until death, at whatever age it might occur, whole life and universal life insurance were developed.
- Universal life insurance offers the policyowner more flexibility than traditional whole life policies.

2. Identify circumstances for which the following types of life insurance would be most appropriate:
   - term insurance
   - whole life insurance
   - variable life insurance
   - universal life insurance
   - variable universal life insurance
3. Compare the primary functions of life insurance and annuities.
4. Discuss the following types of annuities:
   - immediate vs. deferred
   - flexible premium vs. single premium
   - fixed vs. variable
5. Identify and describe the features of a major medical plan.
6. Identify and describe the features of a long-term disability insurance policy.
7. Comment on the need for long-term care insurance.
8. Frank, age 45, who is married to Julie, makes $120,000 per year. He has 2 children, ages 9 and 10. He pays income taxes of $26,000 per year and FICA taxes of $5,000 per year. Frank consumes $20,000 per year of the family's expenses. He expects raises of 4 percent annually, and plans to retire at age 65. The return on low-risk investments is 5 percent, and inflation is 3 percent. Calculate the amount of life insurance needed using the human life approach.
9. Describe the distinguishing features of whole life, universal life, variable life, and variable universal life in terms of premium amount, death benefit, the policyowner's control over investment, and the expected rate of return from the cash value invested.
10. Calculate the amount of money a medical insurance policy will pay if:
    - The surgeon's charge is $12,500
    - There is a 80/20 coinsurance clause
    - The deductible is $500
    - The usual and customary charge for this surgery is $10,000

11. Briefly explain the purpose of an elimination period in a long-term disability policy.

12. Differentiate between an HMO and a PPO.

13. What are the qualifying events that allow for COBRA benefits? What is the maximum benefit period for each qualifying event?

PROBLEMS

Problem 1

Julian Grant, age 27, has two children, ages 4 and 3, from his first marriage. He is now married to Marie. The children live with their mother, Alice. Julian and Marie each make $26,000 per year and have recently bought a house for $100,000, using a mortgage of $95,000. They have the following life, health, and disability coverage:

Life Insurance:

	Policy A	Policy B	Policy C
Insured	Julian	Julian	Marie
Face Amount	$250,000	$78,000	$20,000
Type	Whole Life	Group Term	Group Term
Cash Value	$2,000	$0	$0
Annual Premium	$2,100	$156	$50
Who pays premium	Trustee	Employer	Employer
Beneficiary	Trustee[1]	Alice	Julian
Policyowner	Trust	Julian	Marie
Settlement options clause selected	None	None	None

[1] Children are beneficiaries of the trust required by divorce decree.

Health Insurance:

Julian and Marie are covered under Julian's employer plan, which is an indemnity plan with a $200 deductible per person per year, an 80/20 major medical coinsurance clause with a family annual stop loss of $1,500, and lifetime benefit maximum of $500,000.

Long Term Disability Insurance:

Julian is covered by an "own occupation" policy with premiums paid by his employer. The benefits equal 60 percent of his gross pay after a 180-day elimination period. The policy covers both sickness and accidents. The term of benefits is five full years (60 months). Marie is not covered by disability insurance.

1. Assume that Julian dies. Who would receive the proceeds of the insurance policies?
2. Does Julian have adequate life insurance?
3. Is Julian's health and disability coverage adequate? If not, why not?

4. Should Marie have disability insurance? Why or why not?
5. Are any of the premiums or benefits received from the life, health, or disability insurance taxable to the Grants?

Problem 2

Sanchez Richard graduated from State University with a Bachelor of Science degree in accounting. He has been employed at Knoth & Cartez, a small local accounting firm (50 employees) for almost 7 years. He makes $31,000 per year. Sanchez has been married to Marianne for 6 years. She graduated from Private University with a Bachelor of Science degree in elementary education. She is employed as a fourth grade teacher at Riverside Preparatory private school. She makes $22,000 per year. Sanchez and Marianne have three children: Carlos, age four; and twin girls, Maria and Anna, ages two.

The Richards have the following insurance:

Health Insurance:

Health insurance is provided for the entire family by Knoth & Cartez. The Richards are covered by an HMO. Doctor's visits are $10 per visit, while prescriptions are $5 for generic brands and $10 for other brands. There is no copayment for hospitalization in semiprivate accommodations. Private rooms are provided when medically necessary. For emergency treatment, a $50 copayment is required.

Life Insurance:

Sanchez has a $50,000 group term life insurance policy through Knoth & Cartez. Marianne has a $20,000 group term policy through Riverside Preparatory School. The owners of the policies are Sanchez and Marianne, respectively, with each other as the respective beneficiary.

Disability Insurance:

Sanchez has disability insurance through the accounting firm. Short term disability benefits begin for any absence due to accident or illness over 6 days and will continue for up to 6 months at 80 percent of his salary. Long term disability benefits are available if disability continues over 6 months. If Sanchez is unable to perform the duties of his own current position, the benefits provide him with 60 percent of his gross salary while disabled until recovery, death, retirement, or age 65 (whichever occurs first). All disability premiums are paid by Knoth & Cartez.

Marianne currently has no disability insurance.

1. What happens to the Richards' health insurance if Sanchez is terminated from his job? What are the alternatives?
2. Does Sanchez have adequate life insurance?
3. How much life insurance does Sanchez need?
4. Do either of the group term policies cause taxable income to the Richards?
5. Should Marianne have disability insurance?

CASE

Use the information provided to answer the following questions regarding the Nelson family.

NELSON FAMILY CASE SCENARIO

DAVID AND DANA NELSON

As of 1/1/2006

PERSONAL BACKGROUND AND INFORMATION

David Nelson (age 37) is a bank vice president. He has been employed there for twelve years and has an annual salary of $70,000. Dana Nelson (age 37) is a full-time housewife. David and Dana have been married for eight years. They have two children, John (age 6) and Gabrielle (age 3), and are expecting their third child in two weeks. They have always lived in this community and expect to remain indefinitely in their current residence.

INSURANCE INFORMATION

Health Insurance: The entire family is insured under David's company plan (an indemnity plan). There is a $200 family deductible, and it provides 80/20 major medical coverage. The plan has a $500,000 lifetime limit for each family member. David's employer pays the entire health insurance premium.

Life Insurance: David has a term life insurance policy with a face amount of $25,000 provided by his employer. The policy beneficiary is Dana.

Disability Insurance: David has a private disability insurance policy covering accidental disability for "own occupation" with a 30-day elimination period. In the event that David is disabled as provided under the policy, the benefit is $2,700 per month until age 65. The annual premium is $761 and is paid by David.

RELEVANT EXTERNAL ENVIRONMENTAL INFORMATION

- Mortgage rates are 6.0 percent for 30 years and 5.5 percent for 15 years, fixed.
- Gross Domestic Product is expected to grow at less than 3 percent.
- Inflation is expected to be 2.6 percent.
- Expected return on investment is 10.4 percent for common stocks, 12.1 percent for small company stocks, and 1.1 percent for U.S. Treasury bills.
- College education costs are $15,000 per year.

Dana and David Nelson
Balance Sheet
12/31/05

	Assets			Liabilities and Net Worth	
	Cash/Cash Equivalents			**Current Liabilities**	
JT	Checking Account	$1,518	JT	Credit Cards	$3,655
JT	Savings Account	$950	JT	Mortgage on Principal Residence	$1,370
	Total Cash/Cash Eq.	$2,468	H	Boat Loan	$1,048
				Total Current Liabilities	$6,073
	Invested Assets			**Long-term Liabilities**	
W	ABC Stock	$14,050	JT	Mortgage on Principal Residence	$195,284
JT	Educational Fund	$15,560	H	Boat Loan	$16,017
JT	401(k)	$38,619		**Total Long-term Liabilities**	$211,301
H	XYZ Stock	$10,000			
	Total Invested Assets	$78,229		**Total Liabilities**	**$217,374**
	Personal Use Assets			**Net Worth**	**$241,823**
JT	Principal Residence	$250,000			
JT	Automobile	$15,000			
H	Jet Ski	$10,000			
H	Boat B	$30,000			
W	Jewelry	$13,500			
JT	Furniture/Household	$60,000			
	Total Personal Use Assets	$378,500			
Total Assets		**$459,197**		**Total Liabilities and Net Worth**	**$459,197**

Notes to Financial Statements:

- Assets are stated at fair market value.
- The ABC stock was inherited from Dana's aunt on November 15, 2001. Her aunt originally paid $20,000 for it on October 31, 2001. The fair market value at the aunt's death was $12,000.
- Liabilities are stated at principal only.
- H = Husband; W = Wife; JT = Joint Tenancy

1. The Nelsons are evaluating their life insurance coverage. David would like to have enough insurance to provide the family with 60 percent of his current salary. ABC stock and XYZ stock have average annual returns of 9 percent. The educational fund is invested 100 percent in U.S. Treasuries. David's 401(k) plan is invested 50 percent in a diversified common stock fund and 50 percent in a small company stock fund. Using the capital retention approach, an interest rate of 8 percent, and ignoring Social Security benefits, how much additional life insurance do the Nelsons need?
2. Evaluate the Nelsons' disability insurance coverage.
3. Assume that the Nelsons incurred the following medical expenses in 2006:
   - Dana's visits to her obstetrician = $450
   - Hospital and physician charges for delivery of third child = $10,600
   - Visits to pediatrician = $1,500
   - Regular dental cleanings performed by the hygienist = $300
   - David's visit to the emergency room and subsequent surgery = $7,500
   - Follow-up visits to David's doctor = $430
   - Vision check and purchase of prescription glasses = $385

   What was the total cost to the Nelsons for the above services?

CHAPTER 10

Personal Property and Liability Insurance

LEARNING OBJECTIVES:

After learning the material in this chapter, you will be able to:

1. Identify the need for homeowners, auto, and umbrella insurance coverages.
2. List and define the basic coverages provided by a homeowners policy.
3. Be aware of the various homeowners forms that are available.
4. Understand and explain the various contractual options and provisions in homeowners insurance.
5. List and define the basic coverages provided by a personal automobile insurance policy.
6. Understand and explain the various contractual options and provisions in personal automobile insurance.
7. Identify the need for a personal umbrella policy and explain the umbrella's distinguishing characteristics.
8. Identify the coverages available to businesses and business owners.

INTRODUCTION

A home is, in most cases, the largest investment a family will make. Although the frequency of perils causing financial loss to the home is small, the severity of loss is potentially large. Therefore, it is important that this valuable asset be protected against damage and destruction. The professional financial planner should be knowledgeable about these property risks, as well as the liability risks associated with a client's property. While property insurance protects the assets the client already owns, liability insurance protects the client against financial loss from legal action. Therefore, coverage for both property and liability risks is an essential part of a client's financial plan.

Automobiles are also major assets that individuals own. The automobile policy is a means to mitigate the risk of loss to the automobile and those involved in an automobile accident. For a client, automobile insurance may be among the most expensive aspects of owning a car. Another type of insurance, a personal liability umbrella policy, provides coverage in excess of the liability coverage provided in the homeowners and automobile policies.

Various types of insurance coverage, such as the commercial package policy, the business owner's policy, and professional insurance, provide protection for business owners and self-employed professionals.

This chapter introduces each of these types of insurance to help the planner adequately evaluate his client's property and liability needs and recommend appropriate coverage.

PERSONAL PROPERTY AND LIABILITY INSURANCE

A home and automobiles can represent a substantial portion of a person's assets. Thus, insurance on each is a significant concern in financial planning.

The United States' legal system makes individuals responsible for bodily injuries and property damage they cause to others. When one is legally liable for injuries to another, the law requires that payment be made for those injuries. Where money is not available to make the necessary restitution, other assets may be seized, thus jeopardizing an individual's standard of living. Liability insurance provides the insured with financial protection against lawsuits and other claims for damages that result from the insured's actions.

In this chapter, the three policies used most commonly to protect against personal property and liability risks are discussed: homeowners insurance, automobile insurance, and personal umbrella liability insurance. Homeowners and automobile insurance are package policies that provide both property and liability coverage in one contract. The personal umbrella policy provides a layer of personal liability protection above the coverage provided under the homeowners and automobile policies, in the unfortunate event that those policies do not provide adequate compensation to injured parties.

Each of the following discussions is based on the standard policy forms issued by the Insurance Services Office (ISO). Since insurance is regulated at the state level, each state may require certain modifications to the standard ISO form. Thus, the ensuing discussions are general in nature. Absolute statements cannot be made about a particular policy without reading the policy thoroughly.

Homeowners (HO) Insurance: Basic Coverage

Homeowners insurance is a package insurance policy that provides both property and liability coverage for the insured dwelling, other structures, personal property, and loss of use. Each homeowners insurance form consists of two sections: Section I provides property coverage, and Section II provides liability coverage.

Levels of Coverage

A **peril**, as indicated in a homeowners insurance policy, is a cause of financial loss. The level of coverage afforded by a homeowners insurance policy is determined by the perils it covers.

Named-perils coverage. **Named-perils coverage** is coverage that provides protection from perils that are specifically listed in the policy. **Broad coverage** includes eighteen named perils.

homeowners insurance - a package insurance policy that provides both property and liability coverage for the insured dwelling, other structures, personal property, and loss of use

peril - a cause of financial loss

named-perils coverage - coverage that provides protection from perils that are specifically listed in the policy

broad coverage - includes eighteen named perils

EXHIBIT 10.1: LIST OF BROAD NAMED PERILS

1. Fire
2. Lightning
3. Windstorm
4. Hail
5. Riot or civil commotion
6. Aircraft
7. Vehicles
8. Smoke
9. Vandalism or malicious mischief
10. Explosion
11. Theft
12. Volcanic eruption
13. Falling objects.
14. Weight of ice, snow, sleet.
15. Accidental discharge or overflow of water or steam.
16. Sudden and accidental tearing apart, cracking, burning, or bulging of a steam, hot water, air conditioning, or automatic fire protective sprinkler system, or from within a household appliance.
17. Freezing of a plumbing, heating, air conditioning, or automatic fire sprinkler system, or of a household appliance.
18. Sudden and accidental damage from artificially generated electrical current.

open-perils coverage - coverage designed to protect against all perils except those specifically excluded from coverage

Open-perils coverage. **Open-perils coverage** is designed to protect against all perils except those specifically excluded from coverage. This increased coverage results in a higher premium for the insured.

Perils Generally Excluded

Perils that are excluded from most homeowners policies are:

Movement of the ground. Property damage arising from earth movement is excluded. This includes damage from an earthquake, volcanic eruption, or landslide.

Ordinance or law. A loss due to an ordinance or law that regulates the construction, repair, or demolition of a building or structure is excluded.

Damage from water. Property damage from the following are specifically excluded from coverage under the homeowners policy:

- Floods, surface water, waves, tidal water, and overflow or spray of a body of water.
- Water below the surface of the ground that exerts pressure on or seeps through a building, sidewalk, driveway, foundation, swimming pool, or other structure.
- Water backing through sewers or drains.

Coverage for naturally occurring floods is available through the National Flood Insurance Program offered by the federal government. Coverage for sewer backup is available in some areas as an endorsement to the HO policy.

War or nuclear hazard. Property damage from war or nuclear hazard, including radiation, or radioactive contamination is excluded. If a radiation leak from a nuclear power plant near an insured's home contaminates his or her property, there is no coverage for the loss.

Power failure. Losses due to power failure caused by an uninsured peril, such as a freezer thawing out and its contents spoiling because of local power plant malfunctions, are not covered. If, however, a covered peril such as fire or lightning on the premises causes the power failure, then the resulting damage is covered.

Intentional act. If a loss is discovered to be an intentional act on the part of any insured, it is not covered. For example, one cannot intentionally burn his house down and recover insurance benefits.

Neglect. If an insured fails to use all reasonable and necessary means to save and preserve his property during or after the loss, or when the property is endangered by an insured peril, the loss is not covered.

SECTION I COVERAGE

Section I protects property and belongings. This section helps the policyowner repair, rebuild or completely replace a house, furniture and belongings in the event of a casualty. Section I provides fives types of coverage as listed below. Each coverage type is covered in a separate part of Section I.

- ▲ Section A - Dwelling
- ▲ Section B - Other structures
- ▲ Section C - Personal property
- ▲ Section D - Loss of use
- ▲ Additional coverage - Debris removal, damage to trees, credit card loss, etc.

Coverage A: Dwelling

Section A provides coverage for repair or replacement of damage to a **dwelling**, a residential structure covered under a homeowners policy. This section also covers attached structures and building materials on the premises. The homeowner typically buys an amount of coverage equal to the replacement cost of the dwelling, and in some cases, will be required to carry even more if the property is mortgaged. A mortgage lender usually demands an amount of coverage on the dwelling at least equal to the total amount of the mortgage.

dwelling - residential structure covered under a homeowners policy

Covered losses to the dwelling and other structures are paid on the basis of replacement cost with no deduction for depreciation. **Replacement cost** is the amount necessary to purchase, repair, or replace the dwelling with materials of the same or similar quality at current prices. The insured must carry insurance of at least 80 percent of the replacement cost (coinsurance) at the time of the loss or the insured will receive the larger of the following:

replacement cost - the amount necessary to purchase, repair, or replace the dwelling with materials of the same or similar quality at current prices

- ▲ Actual cash value of the part of the dwelling that is damaged
- ▲ [(Insurance Carried) ÷ (Coinsurance % × Replacement Value)] × Amount of Loss

EXAMPLE

For example, assume Joanne owns a home with a replacement value of \$280,000 and a depreciated actual value equal to 50 percent of the replacement value. She purchases \$200,000 of insurance with a coinsurance requirement of 80 percent. If Joanne experiences a \$100,000 loss, the insurance company will pay the greater of:

$$\text{Actual Cash Value} = 50\% \times \$100{,}000 = \$50{,}000$$

or

$$\frac{\text{Insurance Purchased}}{\text{Coinsurance}} \times \text{Amount of Loss} = \frac{\$200{,}000}{80\% \times \$280{,}000} \times \$100{,}000 = \$89{,}286 \text{ less any deductible}$$

Since the coinsurance formula results in the greater value, Joanne will receive \$89,286, less any applicable deductible.

Certain properties attached to the dwelling or considered an integral part of the dwelling are covered only on an actual cash value basis. These properties include awnings, household appliances, outdoor antennas, outdoor appliances, and non-building structures.

Coverage B: Other Structures

other structures - structure not attached to a dwelling, such as detached garages, small greenhousees, storage buildings, and gazebos

Coverage B provides coverage for small, detached structures on the dwelling property. These **other structures** include detached garages, small greenhouses, storage buildings, and gazebos. The limit of insurance in Coverage B is typically 10 percent of the Coverage A (dwelling) limit. Like the dwelling coverage, this coverage also pays on a replacement cost basis.

Note that detached structures used for business purposes are not covered under Section B of a personal homeowners policy. Additionally, Section B does not apply to any structure rented to someone who is not a tenant of the dwelling, unless the structure is used solely as a private garage.

Coverage C: Personal Property

Under Coverage C, personal property refers to the belongings possessed by the policyowner, as well as the personal property of any resident family members. This property includes furniture, clothing, electronics, and other personally owned possessions, regardless of where the property is located at the time of loss. The limit of insurance for Coverage C is typically 50 percent of the Coverage A (dwelling) limit.

actual cash value - the depreciated value of personal property (replacement cost minus depreciation)

Note that the standard HO form provides only actual cash value (ACV) coverage on personal property. **Actual cash value** is the depreciated value of personal property. An optional endorsement is available to increase coverage up to the replacement cost, and this option is recommended for most homeowners. Since the contents of a home depreciate rapidly, a homeowner could suffer a serious financial loss if replacement cost coverage were not provided.

Consider the price of a gentleman's suit. The typical suit starts at $300. Assume that a short time later the suits depreciate to a value of $150 each and the homeowner loses five suits due to fire. Under the ACV option, the insurer will only pay what the suits are worth at the time of loss, in this case a total of $750. If the homeowner has an optional replacement endorsement, the insurance company will pay the replacement cost of the suits.

Certain kinds of personal property have maximum dollar limits on the amount that will be paid for any loss. A typical HO policy contains the following limits of liability:

- $ 200 – cash and currency, bank notes, bullion, coin collections, and medals.
- $ 500 – loss of business use property not on premises.
- $1,500 – securities, manuscripts, stamp collections, valuable papers, and airline tickets.
- $1,500 – theft of jewelry, watches, gems, precious metals, and real furs.
- $1,500 – watercraft (including motor and trailer), trailers (not boat affiliated) and equipment.
- $1,500 – loss of electronic apparatus.
- $2,500 – theft of firearms.
- $2,500 – theft of silverware, goldware, pewterware, and similar property.
- $2,500 – loss of business use property on premises.

Types of property having considerable value, such as jewelry, furs, or stamp collections may be protected by additional amounts of insurance beyond the special limits listed above. These items may be covered under a **scheduled personal property endorsement**. This endorsement provides open-peril coverage under the same terms as if separate contracts were purchased for each type of property. Types of property that may be covered under this type of endorsement include jewelry, musical instruments, silverware, fine art, cameras, furs, coin collections, and stamp collections. In most cases, the amount for which an item is insured is considered the value of the item if a loss is incurred.

scheduled personal property endorsement - provides open-peril coverage under the same terms as if separate contracts were purchased for each type of property; the amount for which an item is insured is considered the value of the item if a loss is

Certain items of personal property are excluded from coverage because they are either uninsurable or outside the "normal" range of properties owned by the typical homeowner. Because there is an unusual risk exposure for these types of property, the homeowner must request special coverage outside of their homeowners coverage. The following types of personal property are specifically excluded from coverage under a homeowners policy:

- Animals, birds, and fish.
- Articles separately described and specifically insured.
- Motorized land vehicles used off premises.
- Property of roomers or boarders not related to the insured.
- Aircraft and parts.
- Furnishings on property rented out to others.
- Property held as samples, held for sale, or sold but not delivered.
- Business data, credit cards, and funds transfer cards.
- Business property held away from the residence premises.

Coverage D: Loss of Use

loss of use - coverage that provides reimbursement to an insured homeowner for additional living expenses or loss of fair rental value

Loss of use coverage may provide reimbursement to an insured homeowner for additional living expenses or loss of fair rental value.

Additional living expenses. Loss of use coverage provides repayment of any extra living expenses incurred due to having to live elsewhere while the home is being restored following a Coverage A loss. **Additional living expenses** are defined as the difference between the cost of living in temporary arrangements and the normal costs that would have been incurred had there been no loss. Typically, coverage is limited to a maximum of 20 percent of the Coverage A (dwelling) limit.

additional living expenses - the difference between the cost of living in temporary arrangements and the normal costs that would have been incurred had there been no loss

Assume that Scott cannot live in his house for several weeks due to severe damage, which is covered by his homeowners policy. He incurs hotel charges of $4,000, pays $1,500 for meals, and has $150 in laundry costs while living away from home. Had there been no loss, his expenses for his home, meals and laundry would have been $3,250. Loss of use protection would provides $2,400 in additional living expenses to compensate him for the extra costs (hotel accommodations and meals, etc.) associated with being temporarily displaced from his home while it is being repaired. [($4,000 + $1,500 + $150) – $3,250 = $2,400]

loss of fair rental value - the gross rental value less charges and expenses that do not continue during the period in which the property is uninhabitable

Loss of fair rental value. Under Coverage D, an insured lessor may recover the loss of fair rental value on property held for rental purposes. Benefits for **loss of fair rental value** are paid on the basis of the gross rental value less charges and expenses that do not continue during the period in which the property is uninhabitable. In this case, coverage is usually limited to a maximum o 20 percent of the Coverage A (dwelling) limit.

Suppose Janice owns a house in which she rents a section to a university student for $300 pe month. The house is deemed uninhabitable for two months after a fire. Each month she ha maintenance expenses for this section of the house totaling $50, which she does not incu during the repair of the house. Janice can recover $500 [($300 – $50) × 2] for the loss of ren during the restoration of the house.

If a civil authority prevents an insured from using his or her premises due to damage by a covered peril to a neighborhood, loss of use coverage typically will be provided for up to two weeks. This is a unique feature of the HO form, considering that the insured need not directly experience any damage to his or her property to collect for loss of use. Consider the various forest fire episodes in California. If a civil authority orders a homeowner to vacate the premises due to the spread of fire in the area, loss of use coverage can provide reimbursement of additional living expenses incurred due to the evacuation.

Preferred Provisions

Exhibit 10.2 summarizes the preferred provisions of homeowners insurance.

EXHIBIT 10.2: HOMEOWNERS CHECKLIST

Part A – Dwelling	• Replacement cost • Open perils
Part B – Other Structures	• Replacement cost • Open perils
Part C – Personal Property	• Replacement cost* • Open perils* • Scheduled items
Part D – Loss of Use	• Additional living expenses • Loss of fair rental value
Riders	• Extra coverage for valuable personal property • Aircraft • Watercraft • Furnishings on property rented out to others • Business property • Earthquake insurance • Sewer backup coverage
*An endorsement is required for HO-3 policies.	

occurrence - an accident, including exposure to conditions, which results in bodily injury or property damage during the policy period

SUMMARY OF SECTION II COVERAGE

Coverage E: Personal Liability

Coverage E protects the insured homeowner and all resident family members against liability for bodily injury and property damage for which they are legally responsible. The standard limit of liability is $100,000 per occurrence, although this limit may be increased. An **occurrence** is an accident, including exposure to conditions, which results in bodily injury or property

damage during the policy period. For example, covered occurrences may include a guest to an insured's home falling on a patch of ice on his walkway or a dog biting a mail carrier in an insured's yard.

As part of the coverage, the insurer pays all defense and settlement costs associated with a claim for damages made by an injured party. Personal liability coverage does not, however, cover the homeowner for liability arising from the operation of a business in his or her home.

Coverage F: Medical Payments to Others

This coverage pays necessary medical expenses of others that result from bodily injury. The bodily injuries must arise out of the insured's activities, premises, or animal(s). Medical expenses must be incurred within three years of the accident, and it is important to note that this coverage will *not* pay for medical expenses incurred by the insured or any regular resident of the household, except a residence employee (such as a maid or butler).

On the surface, this coverage may seem to duplicate the coverage provided in Coverage E; however, there is an important difference between the two. Coverage F is a "no-fault" coverage that will automatically pay for bodily injuries, while Coverage E pays for both bodily injuries and property damage *for which the insured is legally liable.* Generally, Coverage F will pay up to $1,000 per person per occurrence. For example, if five people become ill from the food at Marie's dinner party, each person may receive up to $1,000 to cover necessary medical expenses that result.

EXAMPLE

Suppose Lisa hosts a party at her house and invites Dennis. While dancing on the coffee table, Dennis slips, falls, and is injured. Lisa rushes Dennis to the hospital. Coverage F will pay for his medical expenses incurred by the incident, even though his injuries are his own fault, because they occurred on Lisa's premises. If, on the following day, Dennis files a lawsuit against Lisa, asking her for $1 million for pain and suffering damages, her homeowners policy will defend her, but if a court determines that Dennis' injuries were his own fault, it may deny payment to him under a theory that Lisa is not legally liable.

Medical Payment Exclusions to Coverage E and Coverage F

Neither Coverage E nor Coverage F will pay for injuries or damages:

- That are *expected or intended* by the insured.
- Resulting from the *insured's business or professional activities.*
- Resulting from *the rental of premises* (however, coverage will be provided when 1) part of an insured location is rented either on an occasional basis, or when part of an insured location is rented out solely as a residence to no more than two roomers or boarders, and 2) part of an insured location is rented out as an office, school, studio, or private garage).
- Arising out of premises the insured owns, rents, or leases to others *that have not been declared an insured location.*
- Arising out of the *ownership or use of watercraft, motorized vehicles, and aircraft* (however, certain vehicles and watercraft are covered for liability):
    - Trailers that are not connected to a motorized land conveyance.

- A vehicle designed primarily for use off public roads that the insured does not own or that the insured does own but that is on an insured location.
- Motorized golf carts while being used on a golf course.
- Vehicles not subject to motor vehicle registration that include lawnmowers, motorized wheelchairs, and vehicles in dead storage on the insured location.
- Nonmotorized watercraft (canoes and rowboats, for example).
- Low-powered boats the insured owns or rents, and small (under 26 feet long) sailboats.
- Model and hobby aircraft that are not designed to carry people or cargo.
- Note that the exclusions of watercraft liability are very detailed. Any time the insured plans to purchase, rent, or use a watercraft, the HO policy should be consulted to determine whether or not coverage exists.

- Caused by *war or nuclear weapons* of any kind.
- Caused by the *transmission of a communicable disease.*
- Arising out of *sexual molestation, corporal punishment, or physical or mental abuse.*
- Resulting from *the use, sale, manufacture, delivery, transfer, or possession of a controlled substance* (other than legally-obtained prescription drugs).
- Note that liability for injuries to a residence employee (e.g., a maid or butler) is generally covered. This type of liability coverage is provided to protect the homeowner who needs to hire domestic help, but who is not required to purchase workers compensation coverage for such employees.

Exclusions to Coverage E Only

Certain exclusions pertain only to Coverage E of the policy. They are:

- Damage to *property of any insured* (should be covered under Section I).
- Damage to *premises the insured is renting* or has control of, unless caused by fire, smoke or explosion.
- *Contractual liability*; (however, two types of contractual liability are covered). First, where the insured has entered into a contract that directly relates to the ownership, maintenance, or use of an insured location, coverage is provided. Second, where the liability of others is assumed by the insured in a contract prior to an occurrence, coverage is provided.
- Liability for *loss assessments charged against the insured* as a member of an association or organization of property owners (e.g., a condominium association charges individual unit owners for damage to community property).
- Liability for injuries to employees that falls under a *workers compensation or other disability law.*
- Liability for *bodily injury or property damage for which the insured is also covered by a nuclear energy liability policy.*

Exclusions to Coverage F Only

Coverage F will not provide coverage for bodily injuries:

- Sustained by the *insured* or any *family member.*
- Sustained by *a regular resident* of an insured location.

- Sustained by a *residence employee* of the insured that occur outside of the scope of employment.
- Sustained by anyone eligible to receive benefits for their injuries under a *workers compensation or similar disability law.*
- Resulting from *nuclear reaction radiation*, etc., regardless of how caused.

EXHIBIT 10.3: SUMMARY OF LIABILITY EXCLUSIONS APPLICABLE TO COVERAGE E & F

EXCLUSION	COVERAGE E: PERSONAL LIABILITY	COVERAGE F: MEDICAL PAYMENTS
Intentional Injury	✔	✔
Business & Professional Activities	✔	✔
Rental of Property	✔	✔
Professional Liability	✔	✔
Uninsured Premises	✔	✔
Motor Vehicles	✔	✔
Watercraft	✔	✔
Aircraft	✔	✔
War	✔	✔
Communicable Disease	✔	✔
Sexual Molestation or Abuse	✔	✔
Nuclear Exclusion	✔	✔
Workers Compensation	✔	✔
Controlled Substance	✔	✔
Contractual Liability	✔	–
Property owned by or in custody of Insured	✔	–
Residence Employee Away from Premises	–	✔
Persons Residing on Premises	–	✔

HOMEOWNERS (HO) INSURANCE: BASIC FORMS

The basic homeowners (HO) insurance forms available are:

- HO-2: Broad Form (named perils).
- HO-3: Special Form (open perils).
- HO-4: Contents Broad Form (for tenants).
- HO-5: Comprehensive Form (open perils, Parts A, B, C, D).
- HO-6: Unit Owners Form (for condominium owners).
- HO-8: Modified Form.

HO-2: Broad Form

The HO-2 policy offers broader protection that covers you for loss from the perils specificall named in the policy.

HO-3: Special Form

This is the most popular and widely purchased of the basic homeowners policies, accounting fo nearly 80 percent of all homeowners policies sold today. Under an HO-3 policy, real property i covered on an open-perils (or "all risks") basis, unless the peril is specifically excluded by th policy. Personal property is covered on named-perils basis.

"Open-perils" means that unless a peril is specifically excluded in the policy, it will be covered HO-3 policies cover all of the perils listed in an HO-2 policy and any other peril not excluded The value of the HO-3 is that it will cover certain unusual losses not specifically named as peril in the HO-2. For example, suppose the insured homeowner with HO-2 policy has his hous trampled by a herd of cattle. As none of the named perils addresses this particular situation, th loss would not be covered. However, had the house been insured under an HO-3 policy, th damage would have been covered since HO-3 policies generally have no such exclusions.

HO-4: Contents Broad Form (for tenants)

HO-4 is designed for tenants who do not own their dwelling. In such cases, the tenant has need only for personal liability coverage, plus coverage for contents and loss of use. The HO-4 policy does not protect the actual building or dwelling (Coverage A or Coverage B), which should be covered by the landlord's policy.

The Contents Broad Form provides protection against losses caused by the eighteen perils listed in an HO-2 policy The minimum amount of coverage sold under the HO-4 is $4,000 o personal property coverage (Coverage C). Coverage D (Loss of Use) limit is commonly equal tc 20 percent of the Coverage C limit.

HO-5: Comprehensive Form

The HO-5 is similar to HO-3 except that Coverage C (personal property) for an HO-5 policy is written on an open-perils basis. HO-5 had been withdrawn from use in 1984, but was reintroduced by the ISO (Insurance Services Offices) in 2000. In the interim, an HO-15 endorsement was added to an HO-3 policy to provide coverage similar to that of an HO-5 policy.

HO-6: Unit Owners Form (for condominium owners)

The insurance needs of condominium owners differ from those of single-family residence owners because the condo property's common areas (e.g., elevators, hallways, lobbies, laundry rooms, etc.) are covered by insurance policies owned by the condo association. An HO-6 policy provides coverage for the condo owner's personal belongings and any structural part of the building which he owns. In most cases, the minimum amount of insurance that must be

urchased for Coverage C (personal property) under HO-6 is $6,000. Loss of use coverage is mited to 40 percent of Coverage C. HO-6 policies do provide liability protection.

HO-8: Modified Form

The HO-8 policy provides coverage for those that live in an older home whose replacement cost xceeds its market value. This policy uses a functional replacement cost provision for loss. Under the functional replacement cost, the insurance company agrees to pay the amount necessary to repair damage, but the coverage cannot be more than the materials and labor that make the dwelling functionally equivalent to its original style. The HO-8 policy covers basic perils only. Liability and medical payments coverage are also part of this policy.

EXHIBIT 10.4: SUMMARY OF PERILS COVERED UNDER VARIOUS BASIC FORMS OF HOMEOWNERS INSURANCE

	HO-2	HO-3	HO-4	HO-5	HO-6	HO-8
Coverage A Dwelling	Broad	Open	N/A	Open	Broad	Basic
Coverage B Other Structures	Broad	Open	N/A	Open	N/A	Basic
Coverage C Personal Property	Broad	Broad	Broad	Open	Broad	Basic
Coverage D Loss of Use	Broad	Open/ Broad	Broad	Open	Broad	Basic

* HO-1 Coverage is no longer offered in most states. This basic coverage is included in other forms.

HOMEOWNERS (HO) INSURANCE: ADDITIONAL COVERAGES

Additional coverage is available under homeowners insurance policies. Most of these may be included in an HO-3 policy without additional cost, and not all additional coverage features are available on all policies.

- All-risk coverage for property while it is being moved from one place to another and for an additional thirty days thereafter.
- Removal of debris from covered property damaged by an insured peril
- A fire department service charge up to $500 for loss by an insured peril; however, a fire department call for rescuing a cat from a tree or people in a home being threatened by a flood is not covered
- The cost of reasonable repairs to protect the property from further damage after a covered loss occurs
- Damage to trees, shrubs, plants, and lawns from all covered perils except for wind (limited to five percent of the dwelling coverage, but not more than $1,000 for any one tree or plant)

- Up to $1,000 per loss for assessments against an insured by a group of property owners arising from loss or damage to property jointly owned by all of the members collectively (e.g., condominium owners)
- Costs resulting from damage to property arising from the collapse of a building caused by an insured peril in addition to several circumstances per the insurance contract
- Damage caused by breakage of glass or safety glazing material that is part of the building, storm doors, or storm windows
- Up to $2,500 for damage to landlord's furnishings in an apartment on the insured's dwelling premises
- Up to $1,000 for loss due to unauthorized use of credit cards, fund transfer cards, forgery of checks, acceptance of counterfeit money, and any incurred court costs or attorney fees may be available.
- Theft coverage for property of students while away at school
- Damage caused by the accidental discharge of water from a waterbed

HOMEOWNERS (HO) INSURANCE: ENDORSEMENTS

Several endorsements are available for homeowners policies at an additional cost. Available endorsements include those listed below.

REPLACEMENT COST FOR PERSONAL PROPERTY

All of the forms previously discussed provide personal property coverage on the basis of actual cash value (ACV) of the personal property. With this endorsement, covered losses are paid on the basis of what it costs to replace the property without a deduction for depreciation.

INFLATION PROTECTION

An inflation protection endorsement provides for an annual pro-rata increase in the limits of liability under Coverages A, B, C, and D. The insured specifies the percentage increase, for example 6%, when he purchases the endorsement.

Assume the homeowner chooses an inflation protection endorsement with an annual pro-rata increase of 6 percent. The homeowner's house, originally insured for $200,000 would have coverage of $206,000 at the end of six months.

Since it is uncommon for a home to increase in value at precisely the same rate of inflation, note that an inflation protection endorsement is not a comprehensive form of protection against inflation and should not be a substitute for regular and careful review of adequate insurance coverage.

EARTHQUAKE ENDORSEMENT

An earthquake endorsement can be added to Section I of a homeowners policy to provide coverage for earthquakes, landslides, and earth movement. A minimum deductible of $250 applies to any one loss, and there is an up to 10 percent deductible of the total amount of applicable insurance that applies to the loss.

Water Backup Coverage

This endorsement to Section I of a homeowners policy provides coverage for loss to property as a result of water that backs up through a sewer or drain. It also covers an overflow from a sump, even if the overflow is the result of a mechanical failure of the sump.

Building Law & Ordinance Coverage

Coverage under this endorsement arises from a homeowner's legal responsibility to abide by building laws, ordinances, and codes. If a homeowner is legally required to demolish a partially destroyed house, or if the building codes require more costly construction methods or materials in the replacement or restoration of a structure, this endorsement provides coverage on the basis of the extra costs.

Personal Injury

Section II of the standard HO policy protects the insured only against liability for bodily injury and property damage. An insured may be liable for personal injury or damage to someone's reputation as well. The HO policies can be endorsed to provide limited personal injury protection to the insured. This endorsement adds coverage for the following *unintentional* offenses (remember that if the loss is intentionally caused, the policy will not provide coverage):

- False arrest, detention or imprisonment, or malicious prosecution.
- Libel, slander, defamation of character, or violation of the right of privacy.
- Invasion of right of private occupation, wrongful eviction, or wrongful entry.

Open Perils

An endorsement may be purchased to change coverage to open perils for non-HO-5 policies.

HOMEOWNERS INSURANCE CONTRACTUAL CONDITIONS

Section I Conditions

Loss Settlement

This condition specifies how certain property items will be valued (whether on an ACV basis or a replacement cost basis, etc.). The coinsurance provision of the policy is also contained in this clause.

Duties after a Loss

If there is a loss to an insured's property, the insured is required to fulfill a number of obligations before the loss can be settled. Immediately following the loss the insured must:

1. Give notice immediately to the insurance company or agent.

2. Protect the property from any further damage.
3. Prepare an inventory of loss to the building and personal property.
4. File written proof of the loss with the insurance company, given the company's tim constraints. The insurer must provide a state-approved form for the proof of loss.

Appraisal

This clause gives the insured the right to dispute the amount of settlement offered by th insurer. If the insured and the insurer disagree on the amount of loss, either party may deman an appraisal by a competent appraiser. Both the insurer and the insured hire their ow appraisers. If the two appraisers cannot reach an agreement on the loss amount, an "umpire mediates their differences. Each party pays for its own appraiser, and both the insured and th insurer equally share the expense of hiring the umpire.

Settlement at Insurer's Option

The insurer retains the right to repair or replace any part of damaged property with simila property, as long as it notifies the insured of this right within 30 days after receiving th insured's sworn proof of loss.

Mortgage Clause

Because many homes are mortgaged, the insurer includes this clause to protect the mortgagee' (lender's) interest in the insured home. This clause gives the mortgagee important rights. The mortgagee has the right to receive payment for valid claims on the property to the extent of its interest, even if the insurer has denied the insured's claim (which would happen in the case of misrepresentation by the insured or an intentionally caused loss). The mortgagee also has the right to receive notice of policy cancellation or non-renewal at least 10 days before the coverage on the property ends.

This clause also imposes certain obligations on the mortgagee. The mortgagee is responsible for notifying the insurer if there is a change in ownership or occupancy of the mortgaged property. The mortgagee must also pay any homeowner premiums that are due but that the insured has neglected to pay, and file proof of loss statements if the insured fails to do so.

Abandonment of Property

The insurance company does not have to accept property abandoned by an insured. A homeowner who suffers fire damage, for example, might try to force the insurer to take control of the house and be responsible for cleanup and repairs, and even mortgage payments.

Recovered Property

When the insured or the insurer recovers property for which the insurer has already paid a claim (as might be the case following a theft), each must notify the other party of the recovery. The insured then has the option either to return the recovered property to the insurer or to keep the ecovered property. If the insured keeps the property, the loss payment must be adjusted ccordingly.

Loss to a Pair or a Set

When there has been a loss to a pair or a set (such as a partial loss of a set of china, or the theft of only one earring), the insurer may either repair or replace the damaged or lost items, or pay he difference between the value of the property as a set (before the loss) and the value after the oss.

Other Insurance

When a loss covered under this policy is also covered by another policy, the insured cannot collect from each policy in full. To do so would place him in a better position after the loss than he was before the loss, thus violating the principle of indemnity. The Other Insurance clause states that when more than one policy covers a loss, the insurer will only pay a proportion of the loss based on the limits of coverage provided by each policy.

Suppose Debbie has two homeowners policies. One provides a limit of $50,000; the other provides a limit of $100,000. Debbie's house is worth only $100,000; and after a fire destroys it, she will collect a proportion of the loss from each insurer. Because the first insurer provides 1/3 of all coverage provided ($50,000 / $150,000), it will pay 1/3 of the loss, or $33,333. The second insurer will pay 2/3 of the loss, or $66,667.

Suit against the Insurance Company

This clause gives the insured the right to sue the insurer *only after* he has complied with all the policy provisions It also requires that the suit be brought within one year of the date of the loss.

Loss Payment

The insurer has 60 days after an agreement is reached regarding the amount of loss to provide payment to the insured.

No Benefit to Bailee

A **bailee** is a party that holds the property of another. If the insured has left property with a bailee, such as a moving company or dry cleaner, the insurer will not pay for loss or damaged property on behalf of the bailee. This clause does not say that claims by the insured will not be paid; it merely states that the coverage will not protect or benefit the bailee. If, for example, a fire on the premises of a dry cleaner destroyed the insured's personal property, the insurer would pay the insured's claim; however, it would then subrogate against, or seek restitution from, the dry cleaner.

bailee - a party that holds the property of another

Volcanic Eruption Period

All volcanic eruptions occurring within a 72-hour period are considered one occurrence. Because volcanoes tend to erupt gradually over a period of days, this clause protects the insured from having to pay a new deductible for each eruption.

SECTION II CONDITIONS

Limit of Liability

The insurer will not pay more than the policy's coverage limit for each occurrence, regardless of the number of suits or claims filed against the insured for any one event.

Duties after a Loss

The insured is expected to give notice of any accident or occurrence to the insurer or its agent. The insured must also promptly forward to the insurer all summons and demand letters. The insured must cooperate and assist the insurer in the investigation and settlement of any claims. Finally, the insured must not voluntarily make payments for anything other than first aid at the time a bodily injury is sustained.

Duties of an Injured Person - Coverage F

An injured person or a representative must give the insurer written proof of a claim as soon as practical after a loss, and give the insurer permission to obtain medical records of the injured person. The injured person must also submit to a physical exam by the insurer's doctor, if instructed to do so by the insurer.

Payment of Claim - Coverage F

This clause states that paying any claim under Coverage F is in no way an admission of liability by the insurer or the insured.

Bankruptcy of Insurance Company

The bankruptcy or insolvency of any insurer does not terminate coverage or relieve the insurer of its obligations under the policy.

SECTIONS I AND II CONDITIONS

Concealment or Fraud

Dishonesty either before or after a loss may void the policy. Examples of dishonesty that will void the policy include intentionally concealing or misrepresenting material facts, and intentionally causing losses to occur.

Cancellation and Nonrenewal

State laws regarding insurer's right of cancellation and nonrenewal vary, so it is important to examine the specific policy to understand the law. Generally, however, the insured may cancel the policy at any time by notifying the insurer, while the insurer may cancel the policy only for certain reasons: nonpayment of premium, material misrepresentation of fact, or a substantial change in the risk. In most cases, the insurer must only provide a 10-day notice of cancellation when it is canceling a newly-issued policy, or when it is canceling for nonpayment of premium. Other cancellations and nonrenewals usually require a 30-day notice. Cancellations generally result in a pro-rata refund of unused premium.

Assignment

For a homeowners policy, the insured may not assign rights under the policy without the insurer's written consent.

Subrogation

The insurer may require the insured to assign rights of recovery for payments made by the insurer. This allows the insurer to take over the insured's subrogation rights against negligent third parties. The insurer does not, however, subrogate for claims made under Coverage F of the policy.

EXHIBIT 10.5: SUMMARY OF HOMEOWNERS INSURANCE POLICIES

	HO-2 (Broad Form)	HO-3 (Special Form)	HO-8 (For Older Homes)	HO-4 (Renter's Contents Broad Form)	HO-6 (For Condominium Owners)
Perils covered	Perils 1 – 18	All perils except those specifically excluded from buildings; perils 1-18 on personal property.	Perils 1 - 12	Perils 1 - 18	Perils 1 - 18
Section 1: Property coverages/limits					
House and any other attachments	Amount based on replacement cost, minimum $15,000	Amount based on replacement cost, minimum $20,000	Amount based on actual cash value of the home Minimum $15,000	10% of personal property insurance on additions and alterations to the apartment	$1,000 on owner's additions and alterations to the unit
Detached buildings	10 % of insurance on the home	10% of insurance on the home	10% of insurance on the home	Not covered	Included in Dwelling Coverage
Trees, shrubs, plants, etc.	5% of insurance on the home, $500 maximum per item	5% of insurance on the home, $500 maximum per item	5% of insurance on the home, $250 maximum per item	10% of personal property insurance, $500 maximum per item	10% of personal property insurance, $500 maximum per item
Personal Property (Contents)	50% of insurance on the home	50% of insurance on the home Covers same as Broad Form	50% of insurance on the home	Chosen by the tenant to reflect the value of the items, minimum $6,000	Chosen by home owner to reflect the value of the items, minimum $6,000
Loss of use and/or add'l living expense	20% of insurance on the home	20% of insurance on the home	10% of insurance on the home	20% of personal property insurance	40% of personal property insurance
Credit card, forgery, counterfeit money	$500	$500	$500	$500	$500
Section 2: Liability					
Comprehensive personal liability	$100,000	$100,000	$100,000	$100,000	$100,000
Damage to property of others	$250 - $500	$250 - $500	$250 - $500	$250 - $500	$250 - $500
Medical payments	$1,000	$1,000	$1,000	$1,000	$1,000
Special limits of liability*	*Special limits apply on a per-occurrence basis (e.g. per fire or theft): money, coins, bank notes, precious metals (gold, silver, etc.) - $200; securities, deeds, stocks, bonds, tickets, stamp - $1,500; watercraft and trailers, including furnishings, equipment, and outboard motors trailers other than for watercraft - $1,500; trailers other than for watercraft, $1,500; jewelry, watches, furs, $1,500; silverware, goldware, etc. - $2,500; guns - $2,500.				

AUTOMOBILE INSURANCE

Automobile insurance is required in every state, although to varying degrees. Mandatory automobile insurance laws expressly require the purchase of liability insurance before owning or operating a motor vehicle. Some states require the purchase of "no-fault" coverage that pays for bodily injuries on a first-party basis. Each state implicitly requires automobile insurance by compelling motorists to be "financially responsible" for a minimum amount of bodily injury and property damage.

In addition to these statutory requirements, many people purchase automobile insurance because their automobiles are financed, and the lender requires the borrower to carry coverage for direct physical damage on the auto. Finally, many people purchase increased amounts of automobile insurance because they recognize that the financial burden associated with an automobile accident could be devastating. One at-fault accident could result in thousands of dollars of damage, and the insured would be responsible for those damages. In addition, with most new cars costing into the multiple tens of thousands, the damage to the insured's vehicle could be very costly to repair.

The owner and operator of an automobile should be concerned about the following losses:

- ▲ Damage to or loss of the insured's vehicle
- ▲ Injury to the insured or family members
- ▲ Legal liability for injuries and damages to other persons

PERSONAL AUTO POLICY (PAP) COVERAGES

The **personal automobile policy** (PAP) is an insurance package policy that can provide protection against the three major losses listed above. A PAP may be used to provide physical damage insurance, medical payments, liability coverage, and uninsured motorist protection. It may also provide no-fault benefits in states that require this type of protection. **No-fault insurance** is used in states that require drivers to carry insurance for their own protection. It also places limits on the insured's ability to sue other drivers for damages. Under this type of insurance, a driver's insurance company pays for his damages (up to policy limits), and the other driver's insurance company pays for his damages, regardless of who was at fault for the accident. Most insurers use the ISO (Insurance Standards Office) Program; however, various state laws may result in different policy provisions and coverage. It is always important that each policy be read carefully.

personal automobile policy (PAP) - provides physical damage insurance, medical payments, liability coverage, and uninsured motorist protection

no-fault insurance - used in states that require drivers to carry insurance for their own protection; places limits on the insured's ability to sue other drivers for damages

Policy Overview

Eligible Vehicles

The PAP may be used to insure four-wheel passenger automobiles, pickup trucks, and vans that are owned by individuals or leased for at least six months. The vehicle must be owned by an individual or by a husband and wife who are residents of the same household. Pickups and vans must have a gross vehicle weight of less than 10,000 pounds and not be used primarily for business purposes (other than farming, ranching, or the installation, maintenance, or repair of equipment or furnishings). The policy may be used to insure one vehicle or all the vehicles owned in a household (usually subject to a maximum of four vehicles on one policy). It is generally less expensive to insure all the vehicles in one household on the same policy than to insure each vehicle with a separate policy.

The PAP may be used to insure vehicles that are used for pleasure and recreation (e.g., motorcycles, recreational vehicles, or golf carts). An endorsement is used to provide coverage when it is used for these types of vehicles.

Policy Design

Throughout the personal automobile policy, "you" and "your" refer to the named insured and spouse. "We," "us," and "our" refer to the insurance company. Policy language is usually simplified as much as possible while maintaining the required legal form.

The PAP is arranged into six parts listed as follows:

- Part A—Liability Coverage.
- Part B—Medical Payments Coverage.
- Part C—Uninsured Motorists Coverage.
- Part D—Coverage for Damage to Your Auto.
- Part E—Duties After an Accident or Loss.
- Part F—General Provisions.

Parts A through D are four separate types of coverage that may be included in a PAP. Each part has its own insuring agreement, insured persons covered, and exclusions. Each type of coverage is effective by declaration in the policy and payment of the premium for the coverage.

PART A: LIABILITY COVERAGE

In the PAP's Liability Coverage section, the insurance company agrees to pay damages due to an accident, up to the policy limit, for which the insured is legally responsible. The insurer retains the right to defend or settle any claim or suit, and settlement and defense costs are paid in addition to the policy limits.

Covered Persons and Autos

Definition of "Insured". An "insured" is defined in Part A as:

- You or any family member for the ownership, maintenance, or use of any auto or trailer (this includes the use of borrowed autos, and even rental cars).
- Any person using "your covered auto" with permission or belief of right to use.
- Any organization that is responsible for the conduct of someone driving "your covered auto" (such as an employer or charitable organization).
- Any organization that is responsible for your conduct or the conduct of a family member, while you are driving a non-owned automobile (such as an employer that might be responsible for your actions when you are using a coworker's car for business purposes).

Primarily, coverage is provided for the insured or spouse residing in the same household (referred to as "you" in the policy), or any family member for the use of any auto or trailer. "Family member" refers to a person related to the named insured by blood, marriage, adoption, or a foster child residing with the insured. The insured and family members are covered when operating any auto, which includes both the covered auto and rented or borrowed vehicles.

Individuals other than the named insured and family members are covered while using the covered auto. The person using the vehicle, however, must have a reasonable belief that he or she has the right to do so.

Coverage under a PAP extends to an individual or organization held vicariously liable for damage or injury. Vicarious liability exists when one party is liable for the negligent actions of another, even though the first party was not directly responsible for the injury. The following parties would be covered under a PAP:

- Those that are vicariously liable for the operation of the insured automobile. Assume Erin is the insured under a PAP policy, which covers her 1979 Mustang. She uses this automobile to run an errand for her employer, Austen. While running the errand, Erin collides with Billy's vehicle and injures him. Billy not only brings suit against Erin for damages, he also sues Austen as Erin's employer. Under the PAP, Austen is covered in addition to Erin because, as Erin's employer, Austen is vicariously liable for the injuries she causes.

EXAMPLE

- Those held vicariously liable for the operation of a non-owned vehicle by the named insured or family member. Assume Lara is insured under a PAP policy. Lara borrows Lee's 2006 Hummer to call on a client of John, her employer. Lara rear-ends Peggy's vehicle as she returns to the office. Peggy is injured and files suit against both Lara and John as Lara's employer. Lara's PAP policy will provide coverage for John's vicarious liability. However, it will not cover Lee should she be sued as owner of the Hummer. Lee would, however, be covered under her own PAP.

EXAMPLE

"Covered Auto" Defined. "Your covered auto" is defined as any of the following:

- Any vehicle shown in the policy declarations.
- Any new vehicle *in addition to* those shown in the declarations, but only for a specified period (policies vary, most often for a 14 or 30 day period) or until the new vehicle is reported to the insurer. The insurer will charge a premium from the date the vehicle was acquired. The new vehicle will have the broadest coverage provided on any declared vehicle for the specified period.
- Any new vehicle *that replaces* a vehicle shown in the declarations. The new vehicle will have the same coverage as the vehicle it replaced. The insured must report the new vehicle within 30 days *only if* coverage for damage to your auto is desired.
- Any trailer the insured owns.
- Any auto or trailer that the insured does not own, but that is used as a temporary substitute while a covered vehicle is unavailable due to loss, breakdown, repair, service, or destruction.

Exclusions

PAP liability coverage is quite broad in nature. However, it excludes coverage for the following persons and situations.

- *Vehicle used by auto dealer.* No coverage is provided for any auto dealer or other person in the automobile business that is driving your car. A person in the automobile business should have coverage under his own policy.
- *Bodily injury to an employee*—No coverage is provided for injuries to an employee, such injuries are most often covered by workers compensation benefits. One exception is that the insured will be covered for liability for injuries to a domestic employee.
- *Insured's owned property*—Liability insurance is designed to pay for damages caused by the insured to third parties. By definition, liability insurance does not pay for damages to the insured's owned property. Therefore, in an auto accident, damages to the insured's car and its contents are not paid by the liability coverage – Part A. Damage to the car would be covered by the PAP's Part D – *Damage to Your Auto*, and damage to contents of the vehicle may be covered by homeowners coverage.
- *Property in the insured's care, custody, and control*—Along the same lines as the previous exclusion, this one prohibits the insured from recovering under his or her own liability insurance for items that are not true liability losses. When property such as a rental car is damaged in an automobile accident, the PAP treats it as if it were the insured's owned auto. The insured may not use the liability coverage to pay for damages to the rental car.
- *Intentional acts*—Any person who intentionally causes an auto accident is not covered for liability by the policy.
- *Public livery*—Coverage is not provided for any person or vehicle while transporting people or property for a fee. A share-the-expense car pool is not considered a for-fee activity and is, thus, covered.
- *Commercial vehicles used in business*—This exclusion eliminates coverage for business use of automobiles, but then gives back coverage for business use of any private passenger auto, or any owned pickup or van, or any temporary or substitute pickup or van. The intent is to limit business coverage on autos to either private passenger autos or owned pickups and vans.
- *Using auto without permission*—No coverage is provided for any person who uses an automobile without having a reasonable belief that he or she has permission to do so.
- *Regular use of nonowned or nondeclared auto*—When the insured has the regular use of an automobile that is not shown on the declarations page, either because the employer provides a company car or because the insured owns a nondeclared vehicle, coverage is not provided. If the insured has a company vehicle, the employer should provide coverage or the insured should declare the vehicle as a nonowned vehicle and purchase coverage for it. Recall that the named insured is covered while using "any" auto. If this exclusion were not in the policy, the insured could own ten vehicles, buy coverage on only one, but have coverage on all ten. This exclusion makes it clear that the insurer will only cover those owned vehicles that have been declared and for which a premium has been paid.
- *Autos with less than four wheels*—Motorcycles and recreational vehicles having fewer than four wheels must be specifically insured under a different policy. No coverage is provided for these types of vehicles, regardless of whether they are owned or borrowed.

Coverage Limits

The limits of coverage for Part A are shown on the declarations page, and in most cases represent three separate liability coverage limits—two for bodily injury, and one for property damage. These "**split limits**" are often written as follows: 50/100/25, and are expressed in thousands. All limits are on a per occurrence basis. The first number represents a *per person* bodily injury limit. A per person limit of $50,000 indicates that any one injured person may not receive more than $50,000 for bodily injuries. The second number represents a *per occurrence* bodily injury limit for *all* bodily injuries. If this limit were $100,000, the insurer would pay up to $100,000 for all the bodily injuries sustained in one accident, regardless of the number of persons injured. The third number represents the property damage limit It specifies the most the insurer will pay for all property damage caused by one accident.

split limits - lists the *per person* bodily injury limit, the *per occurrence* bodily injury limit for *all* bodily injuries, and the property damage limit

EXAMPLE

Assume that Paul carried 50/100/25 coverage and had a major accident that is deemed to be his fault. The following claims were filed by injured parties in the other vehicle: Eddie sustains $75,000 in bodily injuries, Chris sustains $22,000 in bodily injuries, and Bill sustains $53,000 in bodily injuries. Paul, the driver, also incurs $17,000 in automobile repair and rental car costs. Dyann, a nearby homeowner on whose lawn the two cars ultimately landed, sustained $9,000 in lawn and shrubbery damage. Assume that all claims are settled in the order they are mentioned above.

First, address the bodily injury claims. Eddie is allowed to collect only $50,000, because that is the per person limit. Note that Eddie likely will sue for the $25,000 deficiency. Chris may collect the full $22,000. Bill will collect only $28,000 because at that point, the $100,000 per occurrence limit has been reached. Claims are paid in the order that they are settled, not on a pro rata basis, so it is important that claimants begin the settlement process as soon as possible.

Next, consider the property damage claims. The policy provides a total of $25,000 of coverage, yet there is a total of $26,000 in property damage claims. Thus, the insurer will pay all of Paul's damages, and Dyann will receive only $8,000.

Increased Limits in Another State

As mentioned previously, all states require some minimum level of financial responsibility or automobile liability insurance. When the insured in one state drives to another state and has an accident, the insured must generally have sufficient limits to meet the requirements of the state in which the accident occurred.

EXAMPLE

A driver from Arizona who has only the minimum required limits of 15/30/10 who drives to Texas, where the minimum limits are 20/40/15, would be expected to have those coverage limits if an accident occurred in Texas. The PAP automatically provides the increased limits required by state law. Therefore, the Arizona driver's policy would pay up to 20/40/15 if an accident occurred while in Texas.

It is important to note that this policy provision never reduces the limits of liability the insured has purchased. If a Texas driver having the 20/40/15 coverage limits drives to Arizona, her policy will pay up to those limits for any accident. The policy will not reduce the amount of coverage provided to 15/30/10.

Loss Sharing with Other Coverage

When more than one auto policy covers a loss, the general rule is that insurance on the automobile is primary, while insurance on the driver is excess.

EXAMPLE

If Harry borrows Anna's car and has an accident while driving it, Anna's PAP coverage will pay first. When Anna's limits of coverage have been exhausted, then Harry's policy will pay on an excess basis. If more than one policy is primary (for example, if an automobile is declared and covered by two separate policies), then the primary policies share losses on a proportionate basis (similar to homeowners insurance).

PART B: MEDICAL PAYMENTS

medical payments - a no-fault, first-party insurance coverage designed to pay for bodily injuries sustained in an auto accident

Medical payments are optional no-fault, first-party coverage designed to pay for bodily injuries sustained in an auto accident. Expenses must be incurred within three years of the auto accident. Limits of insurance are provided on a per person, per occurrence basis. A typical limit of coverage is $5,000 per person per occurrence. This means that if four covered persons are injured in an auto accident, each may collect up to $5,000 for reasonable and necessary medical and funeral expenses.

Who is Covered?

An insured in this coverage is defined as any of the following:

- You or any family member while occupying a motor vehicle.
- You or any family member as a pedestrian when struck by a motor vehicle.
- Any other person while occupying "your covered auto."

Exclusions

Medical payment coverages exclude the following:

- *Public livery*—No coverage is provided while the vehicle is used to carry persons or property for a fee.
- *Auto used as a residence*—Although trailers are included as covered autos, this exclusion prevents someone from having medical payments coverage on a house trailer. This type of nonstandard risk must be specifically insured.
- *Injury while working*—Any benefits that are payable under workers compensation or other disability benefit laws preclude coverage under this policy.
- *Using auto without permission*—No coverage is provided for any person who uses an automobile without having a reasonable belief that he or she has permission to do so.
- *Regular use of nonowned or nondeclared auto*—When the insured has the regular use of an automobile that is not shown on the declarations page, either because the employer

provides a company car or because the insured owns a nondeclared vehicle, coverage is not provided.

- *Autos with less than four wheels*—Motorcycles and recreational vehicles having fewer than four wheels must be specifically insured under a different policy. No coverage is provided for these types of vehicles, regardless of whether they are owned or borrowed.
- *Auto used in insured's business*—The same exclusion that was discussed in Part A applies here. Coverage is provided for private passenger autos used in business and for owned pickups and vans used in business.
- *War and nuclear hazard injuries*—Consistent with other policies, this coverage does not apply to any injuries sustained because of acts of war or because of nuclear contamination or radioactive hazards.
- *Racing*—No coverage is provided when the vehicle is located inside a racing facility or when the vehicle is practicing for, preparing for, or competing in any type of racing or speed contest.

Part C: Uninsured Motorists

Purpose

Because so many drivers do not obey financial responsibility and compulsory automobile insurance laws, the PAP offers insureds the option of purchasing uninsured motorist coverage that acts as the liability insurance for an uninsured or underinsured motorist.

What is Covered?

Part C will pay for bodily injuries and, in many states, property damages that are sustained by an insured because of an uninsured or underinsured motorist. In other words this coverage will pay what the uninsured, at-fault motorist's liability insurance *should* have paid, had it been in place.

Who is Covered?

An insured for this coverage is defined as follows:

- You or any family member.
- Any other person occupying "your covered auto."
- Any person who might also be entitled to damages (such as a spouse or child) for the injuries sustained by a person described above.

Definitions of an Uninsured/Underinsured Auto

An **uninsured or underinsured motorist** is defined as one who has no liability coverage, one who has limits of liability coverage less than those required by the insured's home state law, one who is an unidentified hit-and-run driver, or one who has liability insurance, but whose insurer cannot or will not pay the claim. For the insured to collect from this coverage, the uninsured or underinsured driver *must be at fault* in the accident.

uninsured/underinsured motorist - motorist without liability coverage or whose insurer cannot or will not pay the claim, hit-and-run driver, or motorist with insufficient liability coverage according to state law

Where on the Web

Federal Emergency Management Agency *www.fema.gov*

Independent Insurance Agents and Brokers of America *www.independentagent.com*

Insurance Information Institute *www.iii.org*

The Insurance Guide *www.insure.com*

Instant Insurance Quotes *www.insure.com/index.html*

Quicken Insurance Quotes *www.quicken.com/insurance*

Exclusions and Limitations

Many of the exclusions contained in Part B are repeated in this coverage:

- Public livery.
- Regular use of nonowned auto.
- Injury while working.
- Regular use of nondeclared auto.
- Using auto without permission.
- Auto used in insured's business.

In addition, the insurer will not pay for any bodily injuries when the insured or legal representatives settle a bodily injury claim without the insurer's consent. Furthermore, this coverage will not pay for punitive damages.

PART D: COVERAGE FOR DAMAGE TO YOUR AUTO

Coverage D provides direct damage coverage on "your covered auto," plus any "nonowned auto." "A nonowned" auto is any private passenger auto, pickup, van, or trailer not owned by or furnished for the use of a family member that is in your (or a family member's) custody. This would include a borrowed car, a rental car, and a temporary substitute auto.

Two Coverages Available

Part D provides the insured with two different direct damage coverages: collision and comprehensive. The insured may purchase one, both, or none of these coverages. Automobile lenders will generally require the insured to carry both coverages.

Collision coverage protects the insured against upset and collision damages, such as those sustained in an accident involving other vehicles or those sustained when an auto runs, for example, off the road and into a lake.

collision - auto insurance coverage that protects the insured against upset and collision damages, such as those sustained in an accident involving other vehicles or those sustained when an auto runs off the road and into a lake

Comprehensive coverage protects the insured against the following perils: missiles or falling objects, fire, theft, explosion, earthquake, windstorm, hail, water or flood, malicious mischief or vandalism, riot or civil commotion, contact with bird or animal, and breakage of glass. These perils are typically viewed as accidental and out of the insured's control. Thus, the premium for this coverage is lower than that for collision coverage.

comprehensive - auto insurance coverage that protects the insured's auto against perils out of the insured's control, such as missiles or falling objects, fire, theft, earthquake, hail, flood, and vandalism

Dispute Resolution (Appraisal Clause)

If the insured and the insurer do not agree on the amount of a loss, the insured may demand an appraisal process similar to that provided for in the homeowners policy.

Loss Payment

The insurer retains the sole option either to pay for repairs or to declare the vehicle a "total loss" and pay the actual cash value of the vehicle, less any deductible. The collision coverage deductible is typically twice as high as the other-than-collision (comprehensive) deductible. In most cases, insureds should carry a minimum $250 other-than-collision deductible and $500 collision deductible. Higher (and lower) deductibles are available, however. Higher deductibles generally reduce premiums.

Loss Sharing with Other Policies

EXAMPLE

When more than one auto policy covers a loss, insurance on the automobile is primary, while insurance on the driver is excess. Therefore, if Joe borrows Fred's car and has an accident while driving it, Fred's collision damage coverage will pay first. Joe's policy will pay on an excess basis, but will not pay more than the loss, and will still require Joe to pay his own deductible.

If more than one policy is primary (for example, if an automobile is declared and covered by two separate policies), then the primary policies share losses on a proportionate basis (similar to homeowners insurance).

Exclusions

Many of the exclusions described in other coverages apply here:

- Public livery.
- Custom furnishings on a pickup or van.
- Using auto without permission.
- Radar detectors.
- Racing.
- Most electronic equipment (except permanently installed sound reproducing equipment).
- War.
- Nuclear damages.

As with most direct property coverages, the PAP excludes coverage for normal wear and tear, and ordinary maintenance losses such as road damage to tires. Loss caused by destruction or confiscation by governmental authorities is also excluded, as could occur if the insured vehicle were involved in a crime. Losses to nonowned autos are not covered when the auto is used or maintained by anyone in the automobile business.

Finally, no coverage is provided for a rental vehicle if the insured has purchased a loss damage waiver from the rental car company. Loss damage waivers relieve the insured of liability for damage to the rented vehicle, so the insurer will not provide coverage.

Part E: Duties after an Accident or Loss

After a loss, the insured should notify the insurer, file proof of loss, and cooperate with the insurer in the investigation and settlement of any claim. In addition, the insured must file a police report to have theft coverage for a stolen vehicle, or to have uninsured motorist coverage for a hit-and-run incident.

Part F: General Provisions

There are several general provisions and conditions of the auto policy that are similar to those contained in the HO policies. One, however, deserves special attention: the PAP coverage territory.

The PAP provides coverage *only in* the United States, its territories and possessions, Puerto Rico, and Canada. When the insured travels to Mexico (where auto accidents are automatically criminal offenses), or to any other country outside the coverage territory, PAP is not effective. If the insured intends to drive in such a locale, the appropriate local coverages must be arranged.

LEGAL LIABILITY

intentional interference - intentional act committed against another that causes injury

slander - verbal statement that causes harm to another

libel - written statement that causes harm to

strict and absolute liability - liability resulting from law; strict liability allows for defense, absolute liability does not

Clients may be exposed to three types of risk – torts (civil wrongs), breach of contract, and crimes (public wrongs). Liability insurance will cover certain classes of torts, but not breaches of contract or criminal offenses. If a court decides that an individual is liable for a civil wrong that causes injury to another, the individual will be required to make restitution usually in the form of monetary compensation.

There are three general types of torts related to liability – intentional interference, strict and absolute liability, and negligence. **Intentional interference** is an intentional act committed against another that causes injury. Many of the actions that fall under intentional interference are also criminal acts and would not be covered under liability insurance. Slander and libel, however, are usually covered under personal liability insurance policies. **Slander** is defamation or harm caused by a verbal statement, and **libel** is defamation caused by a written statement.

Under **strict and absolute liability**, one party is held legally liable regardless of who is responsible for the injury. Workers compensation laws are examples of absolute liability. Under workers compensation laws the employer is liable for any injury to an employee while he is engaged in business activities. Even if the employee causes injury to himself, the employer will

be liable unless the employer can prove the injury was due to intoxication or failure to follow orders. If workers compensation laws provided for absolute liability, the employer would be liable even if the employee was intoxicated. Under strict liability, responsible parties have few options for defense, but under absolute liability, the responsible party has no options for defense.

If an individual causes harm to another by failing to act with appropriate care, she will be subject to liability due to **negligence**. In determining whether an individual has acted with appropriate care, the courts use the "prudent man" standard. The standard is met if a reasonable person confronted with the same circumstances would have performed the same acts. **Direct negligence** refers to acts or omissions directly attributable to an individual. An individual may also be liable for **vicarious acts**, which are negligent acts performed by someone else but for which the individual is held at least partially responsible. For example, in many states bartenders are vicariously liable for the negligent acts of intoxicated patrons. Liability insurance generally covers both types of negligence.

negligence - tort caused by acting without reasonable care

direct negligence - involves acts or omissions directly attributable to an individual

vicarious acts - negligent acts performed by someone else but for which the individual is held at least partially responsible

PERSONAL LIABILITY UMBRELLA POLICY

Purpose

The **personal umbrella policy** (PUP) is designed to provide a catastrophic layer of liability coverage on top of the individual's homeowners and automobile insurance policies. A standard amount of coverage is $1 million, although higher limits may be purchased. The need for the PUP is largely dictated by the insured's personal wealth. The more the insured stands to lose, the more likely it is that a PUP is a suitable purchase.

personal umbrella policy - coverage designed to provide a catastrophic layer of liability coverage on top of the individual's homeowners and automobile insurance policies

Characteristics

Most PUP insurers will require the insured to maintain certain underlying limits of coverage through an HO and a PAP; and, if the insured also has other liability exposures to insure, such as watercraft liability, minimum limits of coverage will be required for those policies as well.

In most cases, the PUP provides the insured with a large amount of coverage at an affordable price. The coverage provided is generally quite broad, and may even provide coverages in addition to those provided by the underlying policies. For example, the PUP might provide personal injury coverage (for defamation of character, false arrest, etc.) even though the underlying HO policy does not. Where these additional coverages are provided, the insured is usually required to pay a **self-insured retention** (SIR) for each loss. This SIR is similar to a deductible.

self-insured retention - a payment similar to a deductible that an insured is usually required to pay for each loss under a personal umbrella policy

Where both the umbrella and an underlying policy cover a loss, the umbrella does not pay any claims until the underlying coverage has exhausted its limits. From there, the umbrella picks up with no SIR imposed on the insured.

EXAMPLE

If Bob has an HO policy with a Coverage E (Personal Liability) limit of $200,000, and a $1 million PUP, and is held liable for bodily injuries totaling $700,000, his HO policy will pay the first $200,000 of the claims, then the PUP will pay the remaining $500,000.

Exclusions

PUP forms are nonstandard, so it is difficult to generalize about what exclusions will be included in each policy. Certain exclusions almost universally found in PUPs include: damage to the insured's property; injuries sustained by the insured or a family member; injuries that were intentionally inflicted or caused by the insured; injuries to another party that should be paid under a workers compensation law; and business and professional liability incidents.

BUSINESS AND PROFESSIONAL USE OF PROPERTY AND LIABILITY INSURANCE

Some of the policies used by businesses to cover property and liability include the commercial package policy, inland marine policies, the business owners policy, business liability insurance, workers compensation, business automobile, business liability umbrella policies, professional insurance, and errors and omissions.

The Insurance Services Office (ISO) has developed a commercial insurance program including a package policy (two or more coverages).

The Commercial Package Policy (CPP)

commercial package policy (CPP) - property and liability coverage combined into a single policy

The **commercial package policy (CPP)** is both a property and a liability coverage combined into a single policy. The advantages of such a policy include lower premiums and fewer gaps in overall coverage. Workers compensation coverage and surety coverages are not part of a CPP. A CPP policy format includes: (1) a declarations page, (2) a policy conditions page, and (3) two or more coverage parts or forms (property, general liability, crime, boiler and machinery, inland marine, commercial auto, farm). Each part or form of the CPP will specify covered property, additional coverages, extension of coverages, other provisions, deductibles, coinsurance, valuation provisions, optional coverages, and a cause-of-loss form. Coverages for causes of loss are basic, broad, special, or earthquake form. These forms are similar to the parallel homeowners forms. Business interruption insurance may be added. Also, a builders-risk-coverage form can be added to the CPP for buildings under construction.

Inland Marine Policies

Inland marine policies cover domestic goods in transit, property held by bailees, mobile equipment and property, property of certain dealers, and means of transportation and communication. They may also be used to increase coverage limits on nonmovables, such as furs and jewelry.

The Business Owner's Policy (BOP)

The business owner's policy is specifically designed for the needs of small-to-medium-size businesses and covers buildings and business personal property (two forms: basic and special). Basic covers listed perils, as distinguished from special, which covers all perils not excluded. The policy has a standard $250 deductible and covers business liability for bodily injury and property damage.

Business Liability Insurance

General liability is the legal liability arising out of business activities not related to autos, motorized vehicles, aircraft, and employee (workers compensation) injuries. Liability issues, not including the exceptions mentioned, are covered by commercial general liability policies (CGL). CGL can be written either as a stand-alone policy or as a part of a commercial package policy (CPP). The usual coverage, Coverage A, is for bodily injury, property damage, and legal defense, but it has significant exclusions. Coverage B is for personal and advertising injury liability, and part C covers medical payments.

Workers Compensation

Most businesses are required to carry insurance providing the following coverages: workers compensation insurance, employer liability insurance, and other state insurance. Part One, workers compensation insurance, covers benefits provided by the insurer (state). Part Two covers lawsuits by employees injured in the course of employment, but not covered by state workers compensation law. Part Three provides coverage for other listed states (for business trips, etc.).

Business Auto

Businesses also use commercial automobile insurance policies covering both physical damage to property and liability insurance.

Business Liability Umbrella

Businesses may make use of commercial liability umbrella policies for excess coverage on liability beyond the coverage provided by the firm's basic liability policy.

Malpractice Insurance

Most people understand malpractice insurance as liability insurance for health service providers, especially physicians and surgeons. Malpractice insurance, however, is available for all professional service providers and generally covers intentional as well as unintentional negligent acts committed by the insured. A typical policy will have a maximum per incident limit and an aggregate limit. The insurer is usually allowed to settle claims out of court without obtaining consent from the insured.

Errors and Omissions

Errors and omissions coverage provides protection against loss from negligent acts, errors, and omissions by the insured. Many professionals (real estate agents, insurance agents, accountants, stockbrokers, attorneys, engineers) need errors and omissions coverage for negligent acts, omissions, or failure to act within their own profession that may cause legal liability. Policies usually have large deductibles ($1,000).

error and omissions insurance coverage - provides protection against loss from negligent acts, errors, and omissions by the

A special type of errors and omissions coverage, called Directors and Officers Errors and Omissions insurance, is available for business executives. Directors and officers insurance provides protection against liability due to mismanagement. Policies usually have high deductibles and require that the insured be financially responsible for a percentage of any claims.

Product Liability

Businesses that manufacture products are subject to liability with respect to those products. Acts that can expose a company to product liability include:

- Manufacturing a harmful product
- Selling a defective product
- Packaging the product inappropriately
- Providing insufficient directions or warnings for use

EXHIBIT 10.6: SUMMARY OF INSURANCE FOR BUSINESSES AND PROFESSIONALS

	BUSINESSES	PROFESSIONALS
Property Insurance - Buildings	CPP	CPP
Property Insurance - Personalty	CPP	CPP
General Liability Insurance	As needed	As needed
Inland Marine Coverage	If transporting goods	If transporting goods
Business Interruption Coverage	As needed	As needed
Builders' Risk Insurance	If construction	If construction
Workers' Compensation	If employees	If employees
Commercial Auto Insurance	If autos	If autos
Commercial Umbrella Policy	Excess liability coverage	Excess liability coverage
Malpractice	N/A	Yes
Errors and Omissions	N/A	Yes
Product Liability	If manufacturer	N/A

PROFESSIONAL FOCUS

Do your clients really understand the difference between a listed-peril homeowners policy HO2 and an open-peril policy? Do your clients understand the difference between an actual cash value policy and a replacement value policy on contents? Explain.

Unfortunately, many clients have very little understanding of even basic homeowners insurance policies. We regularly recommend open-perils policies as opposed to listed-perils policies. We also recommend endorsing the homeowners policies for open perils on contents and for replacement value on contents. Most clients who have actual cash value coverage on contents do not realize that in the event of a loss they may not receive a sufficient settlement to provide them with adequate funds to replace the lost items.

What information collection procedures do you use to determine if a client has an item that they mistakenly believe is insured, when in fact it is not?

We regularly use questionnaires to determine if property has been acquired (such as boats, motorcycles, airplanes, second homes, and rental property) that may not be sufficiently insured from both a property loss point of view and from a liability perspective. We try to help clients understand that boats, motorcycles, and airplanes need their own separate policies from any personal automobile policy. We also see clients who erroneously think that rental property or vacation homes with mixed use are sufficiently covered for renter liability exposure under their homeowners policy. We also like to list all serious liability exposures with the excess liability provider of the personal liability policy. We also recommend that they periodically review their actual property with the agent involved, especially if they acquire any significantly valuable art work, antiques, electronics or jewelry, since these items have low coverage limits in the typical homeowners policy.

How do you determine what advice to give to clients about how much personal liability umbrella coverage to purchase? Do you review quantitative studies or consider the net worth? Do you find resistance from insurers in issuing large personal umbrella policies, such as 5 and 10 million?

We generally look for one to three million dollars in personal liability umbrella excess coverage. We are less concerned with the size of the client's net worth than the risk exposures and their loss potential to the client. We find great resistance in purchasing umbrella excess liability coverage in the five to ten million dollar range due to the severity of the underwriting and the possible need for reinsurance at that level. We find that one million is adequate for most clients and three million is appropriate for our high net worth clients.

JAMES COLEMAN, PH.D., CPA, CFP®

DISCUSSION QUESTIONS

1. Describe the need for homeowners, auto, and umbrella insurance coverages.
2. List and define the basic coverages provided by a homeowners policy.
3. List the available homeowners forms.
4. Explain the various contractual options and provisions in homeowners insurance.
5. List and define the basic coverages provided by a personal automobile insurance policy (PAP).
6. Explain the various contractual options and provisions in personal automobile insurance.
7. Explain the distinguishing characteristics of a personal umbrella policy.
8. For what type of coverage does Section 1 of a homeowners policy provide?
9. For what type of coverage does Section 2 of a homeowners policy provide?
10. Are intentional acts usually covered by insurance?

EXERCISES

1. What are the three types of property and liability loss exposures facing families and business?
2. What is a named-perils policy?
3. Why is it that property insurance policies only pay for the policyowner's insurable interest in a loss?
4. How do property insurance polices determine how losses will be valued?
5. List some examples of types of property with limited coverage under a typical homeowners policy.
6. List two major exclusions in almost all homeowners insurance policies that cover real property.
7. List the 18 perils that constitute broad coverage.
8. If Joe is injured in an automobile wreck, will his own auto policy pay for his medical injuries?
9. Differentiate between the HO-2 and HO-3 form of homeowners insurance.
10. Jan rents an apartment and has $40,000 contents coverage. If she is unable to occupy her apartment due to a negligent fire, for how many months could she rent a $700 apartment if her damaged apartment rented for $600 per month?
11. Patrice lives in Nebraska where she carries the state-mandated minimum liability insurance on her car (10/25/10) through her personal automobile policy (PAP). She is driving through Texas and has a wreck. Texas requires minimum liability insurance of 25/50/20. She injures Sherri in an amount equal to $30,000 and Sherri's vehicle in an amount of $15,000. How much will Sherri collect from Patrice's PAP?
12. Pat and Matt are fraternity brothers who frequently drive each other's cars. Their automobiles are insured as follows:

Insured	Insurance Company	Amount
Pat	XYZ Co.	25/50/10
Matt	All Auto	100/300/25

Pat is negligent while driving Matt's car and has an accident and the bodily injury loss to the other party involved in the accident is $30,000. Which insurer will pay and how much will be paid?

PROBLEMS

1. Jimmy and Mary Sue North are married, age 28 and 27, respectively, and have net worth of $100,000. They both work, Jimmy has a 1980 Chevy truck, and Mary Sue has a 1994 Toyota Corolla. They also own a 1964 Indian motorcycle. They rent an apartment and have the following automobile and renter's insurance policies:

Renters Insurance:

- ▲ The Norths have an HO-4 renter's policy without endorsements.
- ▲ Content Coverage – $25,000; Liability – $100,000.

Automobile Insurance:

- ▲ Both Car and Truck

Type	PAP
Bodily Injury	$25,000/$50,000
Property Damage	$10,000
Medical Payments	$5,000 per person
Physical Damage	Actual Cash Value
Uninsured Motorist	$25,000/$50,000
Comprehensive Deductible	$200
Collision Deductible	$500
Premium (annual)	$3,300

- ▲ What risk exposures are not covered by the HO-4 policy?
- ▲ Comment on the efficiency and effectiveness of the PAP.
- ▲ Is the motorcycle covered under the PAP?
- ▲ Do they have adequate liability coverage? If not, what would you suggest?

2. The Nicholsons recently purchased a fabulous stereo system (FMV $10,000). They asked and received permission to alter their apartment to build speakers into every room. The agreement with the landlord requires them to leave the speakers if they move, as they are permanently installed and affixed to the property. The replacement value of the installed speakers is $4,500, and the noninstalled components are valued at $5,500. The cost of the entire system was $10,000. The Nicholsons have an HO-4 policy with $25,000 content coverage and $100,000 of liability coverage.
   - ▲ If the Nicholsons were burglarized and had their movable stereo system components stolen, would the burglary be covered under the HO-4 policy, and, if so, for what value?
   - ▲ If there was a fire in the Nicholsons' apartment building and their in-wall speaker system was destroyed, would they be covered under the HO-4 policy, and if so, to what extent?
   - ▲ If a fire forces them to move out of their apartment for a month and rent elsewhere at a higher cost, would the HO-4 policy provide any coverage?

3. Ken and Mary Claire Powell are married, both age 40. They own their own home, with the land valued at $80,000 and the dwelling valued at $150,000. They have a total net worth of $550,000. They have the following property/liability insurance coverages:

Homeowners Insurance:
The Powells currently have an HO-3 policy with a replacement value endorsement on contents. The policy is an open-perils coverage. The deductible is $250 and the premium is $533.60 per year.

The building coverage is $100,000, contents $50,000, and liability $100,000.

Automobile Insurance:

The Powells have full coverage on both cars, including:

$100,000 bodily injury for one person
$300,000 bodily injury for all persons
$50,000 property damage
$100,000 uninsured motorist

Deductibles are:

$500 comprehensive
$1,000 collision

This insurance includes medical payments, car rentals, and towing.

The cost of the auto insurance is $2,123.50 per year because of the number of speeding tickets Mary Claire has received.

- ▲ The Powells suffer a burglary and lose personal property items for which they paid $20,000 and that have a replacement value of $27,000. How much will the insurance company pay?
- ▲ If a fire destroys 2/3 of their house and the loss is $100,000, how much will the insurance company pay?
- ▲ Do the Powells have adequate liability coverage?
- ▲ What would you recommend regarding liability coverage?
- ▲ While Mary Claire's car was parked in a parking lot next to a playground, a young student missed a ball being thrown and it dented the hood of Mary Claire's car. The damage was estimated to cost $1,840 to repair. How much will the insurer pay?

CASES

THE BANNISTERS

Derek Bannister, age 26, is employed at a computer store as a salesperson and trainer. He has been employed with this company for 5 years. He earns $30,000 per year. His wife, Olga Bannister, age 26, is a German citizen and is employed as a floral designer for a local florist. She earns $28,000 per year. Derek and Olga have been married for 2 years and have 1 child, Prissy, age 1.

Insurance Information:

Life Insurance	
Insured	Derek
Owner	Derek
Beneficiary	Olga
Face Amount	$50,000
Cash Value	0
Type of Policy	Term
Settlement Options	Lump Sum
Premium	Employer provided
Health Insurance	
Premium	Employer provided for Derek; Olga and Prissy are dependents under Derek's policy
Coverage	Major medical with a $500,000 lifetime limit on a 80/20 basis. Maternity coverage also has 80/20 coinsurance Dental coverage is not provided
Deductible	$250 per person (3 person maximum)
Family out-of-pocket limit	$2,500
Disability Insurance	
Neither Derek nor Olga has disability insurance.	
Automobile Insurance	
Premium	$1,000 total annual premium for both vehicles
Bodily Injury and Property Damage	$10,000/$25,000/$5,000 for each vehicle
Comprehensive	$250 deductible
Collision	$500 deductible
Renter's Insurance	
Type	HO-4
Contents Coverage	$35,000
Premium	$600 annually
Deductible	$250
Liability	$100,000
Medical Payments	$1,000 per person

HOMEOWNERS O4 POLICY DECLARATION PAGE

Policy Number: **H04-123-ZA-996**
Policy Period: **12:01 a.m. Central Time at the residence premises**
From: **January 1, 2005** To: **December 31, 2005**

Name insured and mailing address:
Derek and Olga Bannister
123 Raleigh Way, Apartment 8
Anytown, State 00001

The residence premises covered by this policy is located at the above address unless otherwise indicated.
Same as above.

Coverage is provided where a premium or limit of liability is shown for the coverage.

SECTION I COVERAGES	Limit of Liability	Premium
A. Dwelling	N/A	N/A
B. Other Structures	N/A	N/A
C. Personal property	$35,000	$475
D. Loss of use	N/A	N/A
SECTION II COVERAGES		
A. Personal liability: each occurrence	$100,000	$100
B. Medical payments to others: each occurrence	$1,000	$ 25
Total premium for endorsements listed below		
	Policy Total	$600

Forms and endorsements made part of this policy:

Number	Edition Date	Title	Premium

Not applicable.

DEDUCTIBLE - Section I: **$250**
In case of a loss under Section I, we cover only that part of the loss over the deductible stated.
Section II: Other insured locations: **Not applicable.**

[Mortgagee/Lienholder (Name and address)]
Not applicable.

Countersignature of agent/date Signature/title - company officer

While on a vacation in Colorado, the Bannisters had several unfortunate incidents.

- A deer collided with their car causing $800 worth of damage.
- Derek rented a motorcycle. While riding the motorcycle, his wallet was stolen, but Derek thought he had lost the wallet on the mountain during a fall, so he did not report the loss to the credit card company until he returned home.
- Derek, not experienced driving in the mountains, drove the motorcycle into another motorcycle on the road causing damage to both motorcycles and to Derek. The driver of the other motorcycle, Oscar Applebaum, suffered a broken arm.
- Upon returning home, the Bannisters discovered that their apartment building had been destroyed by fire.

1. How much will the insurance company pay to have the front of the car repaired from the collision with the deer?
2. The fire that destroyed the apartment building also destroyed all of their personal property. While the depreciated or actual cash value of all their property is $8,000, it would cost the Bannisters about $37,000 to replace all of their lost items. How much will the insurance company pay for this loss?
3. Derek's collision with the motorcycle caused $2,000 of damage to the motorcycle owned by Mr. Oscar Applebaum. Will the HO-4 liability policy cover this loss?
4. Mr. Applebaum, the motorcycle owner, suffered $350 in emergency medical expense to reset his broken arm caused by the incident. Will the HO-4 cover this loss?
5. In the motorcycle accident, Derek suffered medical expenses of $1,850. Is Derek covered by the HO-4 for this loss?
6. What deficiencies do you think are in the Bannisters' overall insurance program?

THE NELSONS

David Nelson (age 37) is a bank vice president. He has been employed there for twelve years and has an annual salary of $70,000. Dana Nelson (age 37) is a full-time housewife. David and Dana have been married for eight years. They have two children, John (age 6) and Gabrielle (age 3), and are expecting their third child in two weeks. They have always lived in this community and expect to remain indefinitely in their current residence.

Insurance Information:

- Health Insurance: The entire family is insured under David's company plan (an indemnity plan). There is a $200 family deductible, and it provides 80/20 major medical coverage. The plan has a $500,000 lifetime limit for each family member. David's employer pays the entire health insurance premium.
- Homeowners Insurance: The Nelsons have an HO-3 policy with replacement cost on contents. There is a $250 deductible. The annual premium is $950.
- Automobile Insurance: The Nelsons have automobile liability and bodily injury coverage of $100,000/$300,000/$100,000. They have both comprehensive coverage and collision. The deductibles are $250 (comprehensive) and $500 (collision), respectively. The annual premium is $900.

Dana and David Nelson
Balance Sheet
12/31/05

Assets			Liabilities and Net Worth		
Cash/Cash Equivalents			**Current Liabilities**		
JT	Checking Account	$1,518	JT	Credit Cards	$3,655
JT	Savings Account	$950	JT	Mortgage on Principal Residence	$1,370
	Total Cash/Cash Eq.	$2,468	H	Boat Loan	$1,048
				Total Current Liabilities	$6,073
Invested Assets			**Long-term Liabilities**		
W	ABC Stock	$14,050	JT	Mortgage on Principal Residence	$195,284
JT	Educational Fund	$15,560	H	Boat Loan	$16,017
JT	401(k)	$38,619		**Total Long-term Liabilities**	$211,301
H	XYZ Stock	$10,000			
	Total Invested Assets	$78,229		**Total Liabilities**	$217,374
Personal Use Assets				**Net Worth**	**$241,823**
JT	Principal Residence	$250,000			
JT	Automobile	$15,000			
H	Jet Ski	$10,000			
H	Boat B	$30,000			
W	Jewelry	$13,500			
JT	Furniture/Household	$60,000			
Total Personal Use Assets		$378,500			
Total Assets		**$459,197**		**Total Liabilities and Net Worth**	**$459,197**

Notes to Financial Statements:

- Assets are stated at fair market value.
- The ABC stock was inherited from Dana's aunt on November 15, 2001. Her aunt originally paid $20,000 for it on October 31, 2001. The fair market value at the aunt's death was $12,000.
- Liabilities are stated at principal only.
- H = Husband; W = Wife; JT = Joint Tenancy

1. Evaluate the Nelson's personal property and liability insurance coverage.
2. What business and professional insurance may be relevant to the Nelsons?
3. The Nelson's homeowners insurance provides dwelling coverage for $180,000 with an 80 percent coinsurance clause. On December 31, 2005, a stampeding herd of cattle ran through their house causing $100,000 of damage to the home and $40,000 of damage to furniture and other personal property. How much of the $140,000 of damage will be paid for by their insurance? Assume a replacement value for the home of $240,000.
4. On a trip to the supermarket, a deer ran into the Nelson's car. The damage to the car was $3,000, and Dana, the driver, required $1,200 of medical care. How much will this accident cost Dana and David?

CHAPTER 11

Social Security and Other Social Insurance

LEARNING OBJECTIVES:

After learning the material in this chapter, you will be able to:

1. Identify the six major categories of benefits administered by the Social Security Administration.
2. Understand how the Social Security program works.
3. Explain the structure of the Social Security system of trust funds.
4. List the eligibility requirements that must be satisfied for a person to qualify as a Social Security beneficiary.
5. Describe how the Social Security eligibility system works.
6. Calculate a worker's average indexed monthly earnings (AIME) and primary insurance amount (PIA).
7. Discuss how "bend points" affect a worker's Social Security benefit.
8. Understand how early and late retirement options affect a worker's Social Security benefit.
9. List the ways that a worker's Social Security benefit might be reduced.
10. Explain how modified adjusted gross income affects the taxation of Social Security benefits.
11. Understand how Medicare is structured and the benefits it offers.

OVERVIEW OF THE U.S. SOCIAL SECURITY SYSTEM

Social Security benefits were never intended to provide total financial support upon retirement. Social Security was created to supplement one's pension, savings, investments and assets. Typically, individuals who retire need seventy to eighty percent of their preretirement income to maintain the same preretirement standard of living.

Through Social Security, low wage earners receive benefits of roughly sixty percent of preretirement income. However, average wage earners receive only forty-two percent of their preretirement income from Social Security benefits, while high wage earners receive only twenty-six percent of their preretirement income.

EXHIBIT 11.1: SOCIAL SECURITY BENEFITS AS A PERCENTAGE OF PRERETIREMENT INCOME

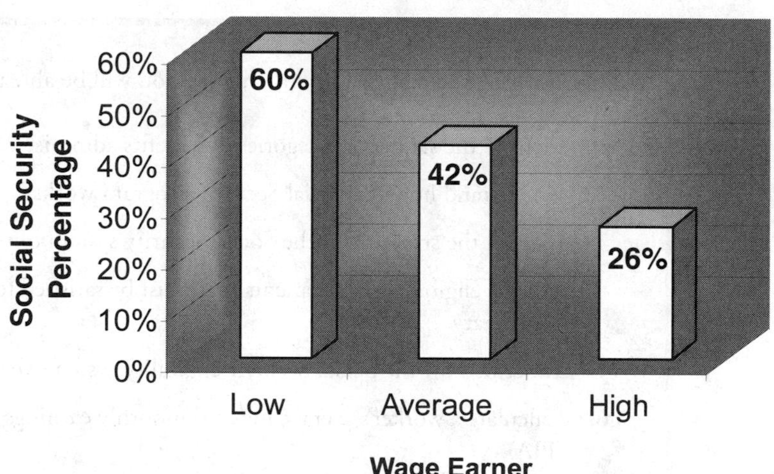
60%
50%
40%
30%
20%
10%
0%
Social Security Percentage
60%
42%
26%
Low
Average
High
Wage Earner

From a financial planning standpoint it is important to understand Social Security and the various benefits that are available. This chapter provides a basic overview of the Social Security system and its benefits. There are six major categories of benefits administered by the Social Security Administration: (1) Retirement Benefits, (2) Disability Benefits, (3) Family Benefits, (4) Survivors' Benefits, (5) Medicare, and (6) Supplemental Security Income (SSI) Benefits. SSI benefits are not funded by Social Security taxes, but are funded by the general Treasury.

retirement benefit - the most familiar Social Security benefit, full retirement benefits are payable at full retirement age with reduced benefits as early as age 62, to anyone who has obtained at least a minimum amount of Social Security credits

The **retirement benefit** is the benefit of which most people are aware. Full retirement benefits are payable at "full retirement age," with reduced benefits as early as age 62, to anyone who has obtained at least a minimum amount of Social Security credits. Based on a change in Social Security law in 1983, the age when full retirement benefits are paid began to rise from age 65 in the year 2000 and increases to age 67 by the year 2027. Those workers who delay retirement beyond the full retirement age will receive a special increase in their retirement benefits when they ultimately retire.

The **disability benefit** is payable at any age to workers who have sufficient credits under the Social Security system. Recipients must have a severe physical or mental impairment that is expected to prevent them from performing "substantial" work for at least a year or result in death. Earnings of $830 or more monthly is considered substantial. The disability insurance program has built-in incentives to smooth the transition back to the workforce including continuation of benefits and health care coverage.

The **family benefit** is provided to certain family members of workers eligible for retirement or disability benefits. Such family members include spouses age 62 or older, spouses under age 62 but caring for a child under age 16, unmarried children under 18, unmarried children under age 19 and full-time students in secondary schools, and unmarried children of any age who were disabled before age 22. **Survivors benefits** apply to certain members of the worker's family if the worker earned sufficient Social Security credits. Family members entitled to survivors benefits include those listed for family benefits, and may also include the worker's parents if the worker was their primary means of support. A special one-time payment of $255 may be made to the spouse or minor children upon the death of a Social Security covered worker.

The next benefit, **Medicare**, provides hospital and medical insurance. Those who have attained the full retirement age or those who receive disability benefits for at least 2 years automatically qualify for Medicare. Others must file an application to become qualified.

Finally, **Supplemental Security Income** (**SSI**) (funded by general tax revenues and not by Social Security taxes) is another benefit of monthly payments to those disabled or at full retirement age who have a low income and few assets. Generally, those who receive SSI also qualify for Medicaid, food stamps and other assistance.

THE HISTORY OF SOCIAL SECURITY BENEFITS

Ever-changing social and economic conditions have dictated the social welfare structure of the United States. During its infancy, the country's economy was predominantly agricultural. As late as 1870, over half of the nation's adult workers were farmers. The country then began to transform. With the advent of the Industrial Revolution, the country began to specialize. One of the consequences of this industrialization and specialization was more dependence on wages and income to maintain and provide for the family.

Federal, state and local governmental bodies throughout the country recognized the inherent risks in an industrialized and ever-specializing economy. It was perceived that such risks could best be handled through an approach dominated by a philosophy of social insurance. Social insurance is the act of contributing financing over time to social programs to provide protection as a matter of right to everyone without regard to need. Social insurance has its roots in workers' compensation laws dating back to as early as 1908. Various social and other retirement programs developed gradually and were implemented in piecemeal fashion. The federal government began programs to provide benefits to those who served in the Armed Forces.

disability benefit - Social Security benefit available to recipients who have a severe physical or mental impairment that is expected to prevent them from performing "substantial" work for at least a year or result in death, and who have the sufficient amount of Social Security credits

family benefit - Social Security benefit available to certain family members of workers eligible for retirement or disability benefits

survivors benefit - Social Security benefit available to surviving family members of a deceased, eligible worker

Medicare - a federal health insurance plan for those who have attained full retirement age or have been disabled whether retired or still working

SSI (Supplemental Security Income) - program administered by the Social Security Administration and funded by the general Treasury that is available to those at full retirement age or disabled who have a low income and few assets

The Depression of the 1930s necessitated action by the federal government. State and local governmental entities could not shoulder the immense needs of so many Americans. The federal government extended loans and grants to the states to provide relief and created special programs. By 1935, however, President Franklin D. Roosevelt proposed that Congress enact economic security legislation, resulting in the passage of the Social Security Act signed into law August 14, 1935.

The Social Security Act established two national social insurance programs: old-age benefits and unemployment benefits. The old-age benefits were intended for retired workers employed in industry and commerce, while unemployment benefits were for breadwinners faced with limited employment opportunities. Congress added benefits to dependents of retired and deceased workers in 1939.

COLA - cost-of-living adjustments provided for Social Security benefits

By 1950, the Social Security program was expanded to cover a number of jobs that had previously been excluded. The range of the program was further broadened by the inclusion, in 1956, of disability insurance for severely disabled workers aged 50 or older and for adult disabled children of deceased or retired workers. The requirement of attaining age 50 was removed in 1960, and disability benefits were available to widows and widowers by 1967. Annual cost-of-living adjustments ("**COLA**") based on the Consumer Price Index were implemented through legislation in 1972, as was the delayed retirement credit that increased benefits for workers for those retiring after the full retirement age.

Medicaid - provides medical assistance for persons with low incomes and resources

The Medicare program was established through the 1965 amendments to the Social Security Act. The program provided for medical coverage for those aged 65 or older, regardless of income. Legislation passed in 1965 also created **Medicaid**, which provides medical assistance for persons with low incomes and resources. Medicare and Medicaid have been subject to numerous legislative changes since 1965. In 1972, the state-administered assistance programs for the aged, blind, and disabled were replaced by the essentially federally administered SSI program.

The 1983 amendments made coverage compulsory for federal civilian employees and for employees of nonprofit organizations, and state and local governments were prohibited from opting out of the system. Gradual increases in the age of eligibility for full retirement benefits from age 65 to age 67 were implemented to begin with persons attaining the age 62 in the year 2000 and ending in 2027. Benefits also became subject to income tax for those with higher income.

SOCIAL SECURITY TAXES AND CONTRIBUTIONS

Although the Social Security retirement benefits program is thought by many to be one of the most complicated and confusing programs created, the basic concept is quite simple. The basic theory is that employees, employers, and self-employed individuals pay Social Security taxes, that is, FICA taxes, during their working years. These payments are pooled in special trust funds. Contributing workers become "covered" workers, meaning that they will fall under the Social Security umbrella of benefits, after contributing for approximately 10 years, and will receive retirement benefits based on those contributions.

ICA stands for the **Federal Insurance Contributions Act**, the law allowing Social Security axes, including Medicare, to be deducted from paychecks. These deductions are called Social ecurity taxes, which are used to pay for Social Security benefits. A portion of these FICA taxes ays part of the Medicare coverage. Separate and apart from Social Security taxes, general tax evenues are used to finance Supplemental Security Income, commonly referred to as "SSI." SI is a program administered by the Social Security Administration that pays benefits to ersons who have limited income and assets.

FICA (Federal Insurance Contributions Act) - the law allowing Social Security taxes, including Medicare, to be deducted from paychecks

mployers and employees pay the taxes for Social Security and Medicare. For the year 2005, an mployer and employee each pay 6.2 percent of the employee's gross salary up to a limit of 90,000 for **OASDI (Old Age and Survivor Disability Insurance)**. The salary limit rises nnually based on annual increases in average wages. Self-employed workers pay 12.4 percent 6.2 percent × 2) of their taxable income up to the same salary limit. The Medicare portion of he Social Security tax is 1.45 percent for employers and employees each and is 2.9 percent for elf-employed workers. For example, if an employee earns a salary of $100,000 in 2005, the first 90,000 of the employee's salary will receive a tax of 7.65 (6.2 + 1.45) percent, while the emaining $10,000 will be subject to a tax of only 1.45 percent. The employer pays the same mount as the employee.

OASDI - Old Age and Survivor Disability Insurance, commonly referred to as Social Security

THE SOCIAL SECURITY TRUST FUNDS AND THEIR RELATIVE SOLVENCY

The United States Social Security system operates on a "pay-as-you-go" basis. Social Security axes are collected and divided among several trust funds. The federal Old-Age and Survivors nsurance ("OASI") Trust Fund pays retirement and survivors' benefits. The OASI Trust Fund eceives 5.30 percent of the FICA tax. The federal Disability Insurance ("DI") Trust Fund pays enefits to workers with disabilities and their families. The DI Trust Fund receives 0.90 percent of the FICA tax. OASI and DI are the two trust funds used for payment of Social Security enefits.

The two Medicare trust funds are the federal Hospital Insurance ("HI") Trust Fund, that pays for services covered under the hospital insurance provisions of Medicare (Part A), and the federal Supplementary Medical Insurance ("SMI") Trust Fund that pays for services covered under the medical insurance provisions of Medicare, known as Part B. The SMI Trust Fund is partially funded by the general fund of the Treasury, with the remainder funding coming from monthly premiums paid by the individuals enrolled in Part B.

EXHIBIT 11.2: SOURCES OF FUNDING TO SOCIAL SECURITY TRUST FUNDS

Fund	Source
OASI Trust Fund	5.30 percent (limited to the maximum taxable earnings)
DI Trust Fund	0.90 percent (limited to the maximum taxable earnings)
HI Trust Fund	1.45 percent (all earnings are taxed)(In 1993, the Omnibus Budget Reconciliation Act of 1993 abolished the ceiling on taxable earnings for Medicare)
SMI Trust Fund	-0- (no FICA taxes used; funded by general federal tax revenues and monthly premiums paid by enrollees)

On average, for every Social Security tax dollar, 68 cents goes to retirement and survivo benefits, 19 cents goes to Medicare benefits, 12 cents goes to disability benefits, and 1 cent goe to administrative costs.

Tax revenues are deposited into the trust funds daily. Social Security benefits are paid from thes funds. Money that is not needed to pay benefits is invested daily in Unites States governmen bonds. This method of investing leftover funds into U.S. government bonds is called th "partial reserve" method of funding, which has been utilized since 1983. For example, in 2004 the Social Security Trust Funds earned over $89 billion in interest, representing an effectiv annual interest rate of roughly 5.7 percent. The goal is to receive more revenue than that whicl is paid out so as to accumulate large reserve funds to aid in paying benefits to the increasin number of retired workers. The increase in retired workers represents a society that is livin longer due to medical improvements, better health information, and less stressful lifestyles. Th number of retired workers will continue to rise within the next ten years because of the bab boom generation (born from 1946 to 1964) that will begin retirement around 2010.

The trust funds are governed by The Board of Trustees of the Social Security and Medicare Trust Funds. Members of the Board of Trustees are the Secretary of the Treasury, Secretary of Labor, Secretary of Health and Human Services, the Commissioner of Social Security, and two public trustees with 4-year terms. By law, the trust funds can only be used to pay Social Security benefits and pay for administrative costs of the program. However, recent legislation has been adopted to help control future HI program costs and to extend the retirement age to receive retirement benefits. These and other measures may help extend the useful life of the trust funds. A recent report from the Board of Trustees released in April 2005 estimated that in 2041, the OASI and DI Trust Funds would become exhausted, while the HI Trust Fund will be able to pay benefits for only 15 more years. It must be recognized that the Social Security system and benefits as they exist today are likely to change.

Based on the Board of Trustees 2005 Summary Annual Report, by the end of 2004 approximately 39.7 million individuals were receiving OASI benefits, 7.9 million individuals were receiving DI benefits and over 41 million individuals were covered by Medicare. The operations of the trust funds for the year 2004 are summarized in Exhibit 11.3:

EXHIBIT 11.3: TRUST FUNDS OPERATIONS, 2004 (DOLLARS IN BILLIONS)

Trust Fund	OASI	DI	HI	SMI
Assets (end of 2003)	$1,355.3	$175.4	$256.0	$24.0
Income for 2004	$566.3	$91.4	$183.9	$133.8
Expenses for 2004	$421.0	$80.6	$170.6	$138.3
Net change in assets	$145.3	$10.8	$13.3	-$4.5
Assets (end of 2004)	$1,500.6	$186.2	$269.3	$19.4

Source: *2005 Annual Report by the Board of Trustees*

SOCIAL SECURITY BENEFITS – ELIGIBILITY AND CALCULATIONS

COVERED WORKERS AND INSURED STATUS

To qualify for retirement benefits, a worker must be "fully insured," which means that a worker has earned a certain number of quarters of coverage under the Social Security system. Since 1978, quarters of coverage have been determined based on annual earnings. In other words, earning a designated amount of money, regardless of when it was earned during the year, will credit the worker with a quarter of coverage for that year. In 2004, the designated amount for a quarter of coverage was $900, while it is $920 for 2005. Thus, workers who earned at least $3,600 are credited with 4 quarters of coverage for 2004, and workers who earned at least $3,680 are credited with 4 quarters of coverage for 2005. No worker may earn more than 4 quarters in one year, regardless of earnings. The following is a list of the designated amounts for a quarter of coverage dating back to 1980:

EXHIBIT 11.4: DESIGNATED AMOUNTS FOR A QUARTER OF SOCIAL SECURITY COVERAGE

Year	Amount Needed to Receive a Credit for One Quarter	Year	Amount Needed to Receive a Credit for One Quarter
1980	$290	1993	$590
1981	$310	1994	$620
1982	$340	1995	$630
1983	$370	1996	$640
1984	$390	1997	$670
1985	$410	1998	$700
1986	$440	1999	$740
1987	$460	2000	$780
1988	$470	2001	$830
1989	$500	2002	$870
1990	$520	2003	$890
1991	$540	2004	$900
1992	$570	2005	$920

For most persons, 40 quarters of coverage (10 years of work in employment covered by Social Security) or 1 quarter of coverage per year past beginning at age 21 will fully insure a worker for life. Fully insured workers are entitled to the benefits under the Social Security system, although some benefits, like survivor's benefits, are available to "currently" (although not necessarily fully) insured individuals. "Currently" insured workers are those individuals that have at least 6 quarters of coverage out of the previous 13 quarters.

SOCIAL SECURITY BENEFICIARIES

As we discussed, Social Security benefits are paid upon retirement, disability, or death, if the eligibility requirements are satisfied. The worker's spouse and children may also be eligible to receive benefits when the worker satisfies eligibility requirements. Generally, monthly Social Security benefits can be paid to:

- A disabled insured worker under age 65.
- A retired insured worker at age 62.
- The spouse of a retired or disabled worker entitled to benefits who:
  - is at least 62 years old, or
  - is caring for a child under age 16 or disabled.
- The divorced spouse of a retired or disabled worker entitled to benefits if age 62 and married to the worker for at least 10 years and not remarried by age 60.
- The divorced spouse of a fully insured worker who has not yet filed a claim for benefits if both are at least age 62, were married for at least 10 years, and have been finally divorced for at least 2 continuous years.
- The dependent, unmarried child of a retired or disabled worker entitled to benefits, or of a deceased insured worker if the child is:
  - under age 18, or
  - under age 19 and a full-time elementary or secondary school student; or
  - age 18 or over but under a disability that began before age 22.
- The surviving spouse (including a surviving divorced spouse) of a deceased insured worker if the widow(er) is age 60.
- The disabled surviving spouse (including a surviving divorced spouse in some cases) of a deceased insured worker if the widow(er) is age 50.
- The surviving spouse (including a surviving divorced spouse) of a deceased insured worker, regardless of age, if caring for an entitled child of the deceased who is either under age 16 or disabled before age 22.
- The dependent parents of a deceased insured worker at age 62.

In addition to monthly survivors benefits, a lump-sum death payment of $255 is payable upon the death of an insured worker. The PIA is the retirement benefit that the worker would receive if he or she retires at full retirement age.

SOCIAL SECURITY RETIREMENT BENEFITS – A CLOSER LOOK

The most commonly known Social Security benefit is the Retirement Benefit. Until 2000, full retirement age, the age where full retirement benefits are available to the retiree, was 65 years. The age at which full benefits are paid began to rise in the year 2000. Exhibit 11.5 shows the phaseout, which raises full retirement age with full benefits to age 67:

EXHIBIT 11.5: AGE FULL RETIREMENT BENEFITS BEGIN

Full Retirement Age With Full Benefits	Year Born
65 years	Before 1938
65 years, 2 months	1938
65 years, 4 months	1939
65 years, 6 months	1940
65 years, 8 months	1941
65 years, 10 months	1942
66 years	1943–1954
66 years, 2 months	1955
66 years, 4 months	1956
66 years, 6 months	1957
66 years, 8 months	1958
66 years, 10 months	1959
67 years	1960–present

People who delay retirement beyond full retirement age receive an increase in their benefit when they do retire. People who take early retirement, currently as early as age 62, receive an actuarially reduced monthly benefit equal to a reduction of 5/9ths of one percent for each month of early retirement. (Early and late retirement options are discussed later in this chapter.)

When engaging in financial planning for an individual, it may be appropriate to compute the individual's expected Social Security retirement benefit or ask the client to request a Social Security statement and consider the benefit in that individual's retirement plan. Some financial planners, however, choose not to consider the estimated retirement benefit in order to be conservative in developing a financial plan. Others justify exclusion of Social Security retirement benefits from financial planning based on fear of drastic changes to the Social Security system through legislative action or through economically driven forces.

Social Security Statement, Form SSA-7005 - a written report mailed by the Social Security Administration to all workers age 25 and over who are not yet receiving Social Security benefits that provides an estimate of the worker's eventual Social Security benefits and instructions on how to qualify for those benefits

THE SOCIAL SECURITY STATEMENT

As of October 1999, the Social Security Administration began automatically mailing a **Social Security Statement—Form SSA-7005**, to all workers age 25 and over who are not yet receiving Social Security benefits. The Social Security Statement should prove to be a valuable tool in the process of personal financial planning for the worker and his or her family. The statement, formerly known as the Social Security Personal Earnings and Benefits Estimate Statement ("PEBES") is a written report that provides an estimate of the worker's eventual Social Security benefits and instructions on how to qualify for those benefits.

The new Social Security Statement includes the worker's lifetime earnings history as it has been reported to the Social Security Administration, an estimate of the amount of Social Security taxes (FICA) and Medicare taxes (FICA-Med) that the worker and employer (if applicable) have paid, and forecasts the ultimate benefits to be paid to the worker and family through retirement, disability and/or survivorship.

The mail out campaign is designed to keep the worker informed as to his or her earnings history and to ensure the accuracy and completeness of the Social Security Administration's records. If any earnings are incorrect or incomplete, the worker can notify the Social Security Administration of the problem well in advance of the time of the worker's retirement age. The statement also serves as a quick and reliable reference to the worker for use in financial planning and forecasting, whether done by the individual worker or by a financial planner. The statement will be mailed to the individual worker roughly three months prior to his or her birthday and will continue to be mailed at or near that time every year until the worker begins to receive Social Security benefits. An example of the Social Security Statement is provided at the end of this chapter (Chapter Appendix 11.1).

Workers can also request a Social Security Statement at any time from the Social Security Administration. A statement can be requested by the worker from the Social Security Administration by filling out and mailing a Request for a Social Security Statement, SSA Form 7004 (Chapter Appendix 11.2), or by requesting it online at *www.ssa.gov.* Applicants can also obtain the request form by calling Social Security at 1-800-772-1213 and asking for the Form SSA-7004. The Social Security Administration will also answer questions and set up appointments with local Social Security offices through the toll-free number. Even with an estimate, financial planners may still want to explain to their clients exactly how the clients' benefit is determined.

The Retirement Benefit Calculation

AIME (average indexed monthly earnings) - amount that adjusts, or indexes, a worker's actual earnings to current dollars

PIA (primary insurance amount) - amount on which a worker's retirement benefit is based, the PIA determines the amount the applicant will receive at his or her full retirement age, based on the year in which the retiree turns 62. The PIA is indexed to the Consumer Price Index (CPI) annually.

Determining a worker's retirement benefit requires specific, detailed information pertaining to age, earnings history and the worker's retirement date. Social Security benefits are based on earnings averaged over most of a worker's lifetime. Actual earnings are first adjusted or "indexed" to current dollars to account for changes in average wages since the year the earnings were received. Then, the Social Security Administration calculates **average indexed monthly earnings ("AIME")** during the 35 years in which the applicant earned the most. The Social Security Administration applies a formula to these earnings and arrives at a basic benefit, which is referred to as the **primary insurance amount** or **PIA**. The Social Security retirement benefit is based on the worker's PIA. The PIA determines the amount the applicant will receive at his or her full retirement age, but the amount of the benefit depends on the year in which the retiree turns age 62. The PIA is indexed to the consumer price index (CPI) annually.

Figuring the Worker's Average Indexed Monthly Earnings (AIME)

To determine a worker's AIME, the worker's annual earnings from age 22 to 62 must be converted into current dollars by multiplying the worker's total annual earnings for each year by an indexing factor. The indexing factor is the result of dividing the national average wage for the year in which the worker attains age <u>60</u> by the national average wage for the actual year being indexed. For instance, for a worker age 63 in 2001, the indexing factor for the year 1970 is determined by dividing the national average wage for 1998 (when the worker attained age 60), which was $28,861.44, by the national average wage for 1970 (the year being indexed), which was $6,186.23, yielding a factor of 4.66543. Exhibit 11.6 provides national average wages from 1953 to 2003.

EXHIBIT 11.6: NATIONAL AVERAGE WAGE INDEXING SERIES, 1953-2003

Year	Amount	Year	Amount	Year	Amount
1953	3,139.44	1970	6,186.24	1987	18,426.51
1954	3,155.64	1971	6,497.08	1988	19,334.04
1955	3,301.44	1972	7,133.80	1989	20,099.55
1956	3,532.36	1973	7,580.16	1990	21,027.98
1957	3,641.72	1974	8,030.76	1991	21,811.60
1958	3,673.80	1975	8,630.92	1992	22,935.42
1959	3,855.80	1976	9,226.48	1993	23,132.67
1960	4,007.12	1977	9,779.44	1994	23,753.53
1961	4,086.76	1978	10,556.03	1995	24,705.66
1962	4,291.40	1979	11,479.46	1996	25,913.90
1963	4,396.64	1980	12,513.46	1997	27,426.00
1964	4,576.32	1981	13,773.10	1998	28,861.44
1965	4,658.72	1982	14,531.34	1999	30,469.84
1966	4,938.36	1983	15,239.24	2000	32,154.82
1967	5,213.44	1984	16,135.07	2001	32,921.92
1968	5,571.16	1985	16,822.51	2002	33,252.09
1969	5,893.76	1986	17,321.82	2003	34,064.95

Source: Social Security Administration (www.ssa.gov)

Next, each year's annual earnings must be multiplied by its indexing factor to arrive at the indexed earnings for the years from age 22 to 60. Note that the indexing factor will always equal one for the years in which the worker is 60 or older. After all annual earnings are indexed or converted to current dollar amounts, the highest 35 years of indexed earnings are added together for a total. The sum of the highest 35 years is then divided by 420 (which represents 35 years multiplied by 12 months per year). This yields the average amount of monthly earnings for all indexed years, hence the name average indexed monthly earnings, or AIME. Once the worker's AIME is determined, the next step in determining the worker's retirement benefit is to calculate the primary insurance amount, or PIA, for the worker.

Figuring the Worker's Primary Insurance Amount (PIA)

Generally, the PIA is the actual Social Security retirement benefit for the retiree who retires at full retirement age. For those who retire early or late and for family or surviving beneficiaries, the PIA is not the actual amount of the benefit, but the PIA is used to determine their actual benefit.

The PIA is a figure derived from the worker's AIME. The PIA is calculated by applying a "benefit formula" to AIME. This benefit formula changes from year to year and depends on the worker's first year of eligibility, that is, when the worker turns 62, becomes disabled or dies.

bend points - the three separate percentages of portions of the AIME that are summed to arrive at the PIA

The PIA is the sum of three separate percentages of portions of the AIME. These portions are also known as "**bend points.**" For the year 2005, these portions are the first $627 of AIME, the amount of AIME between $627 and $3,779, and the AIME over $3,779. The bend points for 2004 are thus $627 and $3,779. For individuals who first become eligible for retirement benefits or disability insurance benefits in 2005 or who die in 2005 before becoming eligible for benefits, their PIA will be the sum of:

90 percent of the first $627 of their AIME, *plus*
32 percent of their AIME over $627 up to $3,779, *plus*
15 percent of their AIME that exceeds $3,779.

The sum of these three calculations is rounded down to the next lower multiple of $0.10 (if it is not already a multiple of $0.10). For calculations in subsequent years, it is useful to know how to determine a given year's bend points. Exhibit 11.7 shows the established bend points from 1979 through 2005.

EXHIBIT 11.7: BEND POINT TABLE

	Dollar Amounts (bend points) in PIA Formula	
Year	First	Second
1979	$180	$1,085
1980	194	1,171
1981	211	1,274
1982	230	1,388
1983	254	1,528
1984	267	1,612
1985	280	1,691
1986	297	1,790
1987	310	1,866
1988	319	1,922
1989	339	2,044
1990	356	2,145
1991	370	2,230
1992	387	2,333
1993	401	2,420
1994	422	2,545
1995	426	2,567
1996	437	2,635
1997	455	2,741
1998	477	2,875
1999	505	3,043
2000	531	3,202
2001	561	3,381
2002	592	3,567
2003	606	3,653
2004	612	3,689
2005	627	3,779

Source: Social Security Administration (www.ssa.gov)

In order to determine future years' bend points, the 1979 bend points are converted into dollars for that year. The bend points for 2001 were determined by multiplying the 1979 bend points ($180 and $1,085) by the ratio between the national average wage for 1999, which was $30,469.84, and the national average wage for 1977, which was $9,779.44, rounded to the nearest dollar. $30,469.84 divided by $9,779.44 is 3.1157040. When multiplying the 1979 bend points of $180 and $1,085 by 3.1157040, the rounded results are $561 and $3,381, the bend points for 2001. For subsequent years, the 1979 bend points should be indexed by multiplying them by the ratio for the national average wage for the year the worker attains age 60 over the national average wage for 1977.

These figures for the PIA rise each year based on a cost-of-living adjustment (COLA) that is applied to reflect changes in the cost of living. Recent COLAs, which are based on inflation, are shown in Exhibit 11.8.

EXHIBIT 11.8: COST OF LIVING ADJUSTMENT (COLA) PER YEAR

COLA	YEAR
4.7%	1990
5.4%	1991
3.7%	1992
3.0%	1993
2.6%	1994
2.8%	1995
2.6%	1996
2.9%	1997
2.1%	1998
1.3%	1999
2.5%	2000
3.5%	2001
2.6%	2002
1.4%	2003
2.1%	2004
2.7%	2005

Annual COLA increases are determined by October of each year and go into effect in time so that they first appear on monthly benefit checks received in January. In 2005, the maximum monthly retirement benefit for retirees at full retirement age is $1,939, compared to $1,825 in 2004.

Early and Late Retirement Options

Workers entitled to retirement benefits can currently take early retirement benefits as early as age 62. The worker will receive a reduced benefit because he or she will receive more monthly benefit payments than if the worker had waited and retired at full retirement age. The reduction to one's monthly benefit for early retirement is permanent. Conversely, a delayed or postponed retirement will permanently increase the monthly retirement benefit for a worker.

For each month of early retirement, a worker will receive a reduction in his or her monthly retirement benefit of 0.555 percent, or 1/180, for each month of early retirement taken up to the first 36 months. For subsequent months of early retirement, the permanent reduction percentage is 0.416 percent, or 1/240, per month.

EXAMPLE Korie, a fully insured worker born in 1940, took retirement benefits at age 64 years and 7 months in 2004. Korie will receive her retirement benefit, less 11/180ths, because Korie retired 11 months before her full retirement age. If Korie's monthly retirement benefit at full retirement age (FRA) of 65 years and 6 months was $1,000, she would receive $938 per month instead, for the remainder of her life, subject to COLA adjustments.

Although the full retirement age will increase to age 67, workers will still have the option of taking early retirement at age 62. However, the reduction percentage that is applied to the monthly retirement benefit will increase until 2027. Before 2000, those who retired at age 62 received 80 percent of their retirement benefit, but the increase in full retirement age has increased the number of months from 62 until full retirement age. For instance, in the year 2009, covered workers who retire at age 62 will receive 75 percent of their monthly retirement benefit, that is, 25 percent less than his or her full retirement benefit. By 2027, a covered worker retiring at age 62 (full retirement age would be 67) will receive only 70 percent of his or her monthly retirement benefit. Exhibit 11.9, which was compiled by the Social Security Administration, shows the phase-in of the Social Security full retirement age and accompanying reductions for early retirement at age 62.

EXHIBIT 11.9: SOCIAL SECURITY FULL RETIREMENT AND REDUCTIONS* BY AGE

Year of Birth	Full Retirement Age	Age 62 Reduction Months	Monthly Percent Reduction	Total Percent Reduction
1937 or earlier	65	36	.555	20.00
1938	65 & 2 months	38	.548	20.83
1939	65 & 4 months	40	.541	21.67
1940	65 & 6 months	42	.535	22.50
1941	65 & 8 months	44	.530	23.33
1942	65 & 10 months	46	.525	24.17
1943-1954	66	48	.520	25.00
1955	66 & 2 months	50	.516	25.84
1956	66 & 4 months	52	.512	26.66
1957	66 & 6 months	54	.509	27.50
1958	66 & 8 months	56	.505	28.33
1959	66 & 10 months	58	.502	29.17
1960 and later	67	60	.500	30.00

**Percentage monthly and total reductions are approximate due to rounding. The actual reductions are .555 or 5/9 of 1 percent per month for the first 36 months and .416 or 5/12 of 1 percent for subsequent months.*

Source: Social Security Administration (www.ssa.gov)

No matter what your full retirement age is, you may start receiving benefits as early as age 62. You can also retire at any time between age 62 and full retirement age; however, if you start at one of these early ages, your benefits are reduced a fraction of a percent for each month before your full retirement age.

EXAMPLE

Let's assume that Josephine, a worker born in 1939, decided to retire on her 62nd birthday. Assume that her full retirement benefit would have been $1,429.20 at age 65 and 4 months, her full retirement age. If she retires at age 62, what will her monthly retirement benefit be?

The answer is $1,119. Josephine is retiring 40 months early. The monthly retirement benefit reduction percentage is 1/180 for the first 36 months (1/180 × 36 = 20 percent) and 1/240 for the 4 subsequent months of early retirement (1/240 × 4 = 1.6668 percent), yielding a total permanent reduction to Josephine's monthly retirement benefit of 21.6667 percent. 21.6667 percent × $1,429.20 = $309.66. $1,429.20 – $309.66 = $1,119.50 (rounded off).

EXAMPLE

What if Josephine retires at age 64 and 6 months? What will her permanent monthly retirement benefit be? (subject to COLA increases)

The answer is $1,349. 1/180 × 10 = 5.5556 percent. 5.5556 percent × $1,429.20 = $79.40. $1,429.20 – $79.40 = $1,349.80 (rounded off).

For those covered individuals who postpone retirement, that is, take late retirement, or when benefits are lost due to the earnings limitation, the monthly retirement benefit and the benefit paid to the surviving spouse will increase each year (until age 70) as follows:

EXHIBIT 11.10: PERCENTAGE INCREASES FOR DELAYED RETIREMENT

Increase for Year Born	Annual Percentage Each Year of Late Retirement	After Age
1917-1924	3.0%	65
1925-1926	3.5%	65
1927-1928	4.0%	65
1929-1930	4.5%	65
1931-1932	5.0%	65
1933-1934	5.5%	65
1935-1936	6.0%	65
1937	6.5%	65
1938	6.5%	65 and 2 months
1939	7.0%	65 and 4 months
1940	7.0%	65 and 6 months
1941	7.5%	65 and 8 months
1942	7.5%	65 and 10 months
1943	8.0%	66

Those taking delayed retirement receive a permanent increase to their monthly retirement benefit.

Although the calculations explained above can provide estimates of what benefits a retiring worker may receive, a financial planner should have the client obtain his or her entire earnings history up to the moment of retirement from the Social Security Administration to get the most accurate benefit estimate.

Reduction of Social Security Benefits

retirement earnings limitations test - one of the ways in which Social Security benefits are reduced based on earnings

Besides early retirement, there are two other manners in which beneficiaries can have their benefits reduced. The first method is through reduction of benefits based on earnings, referred to as the **retirement earnings limitations test**. The other method is through taxation of Social Security benefits. Both of these measures reduce one's net benefits.

A person can continue to work even though he or she is considered "retired" under Social Security. The earnings received by the beneficiary cannot exceed certain limitations without triggering a reduction in Social Security benefits. Beneficiaries can earn up to the limitation and receive all of their benefits, but if those earnings exceed the designated limit for the calendar year, then some or all benefits will be withheld. The law provided for earnings limitations of $12,000 for those under the full retirement age for 2005. The Social Security Administration deducted $1 in benefits for each $2 earned by those beneficiaries above $12,000. In the year that the retiree reaches full retirement age, $1 in benefits will be deducted for each $3 earned above the given year's limit, but only for earnings before the month the retiree reaches full retirement age. For 2005, the limit for earnings in the year the retiree reaches full retirement age was $31,800. The earnings limitation increases every year as median earnings nationwide increase.

In the event that a beneficiary's earnings exceed the limitation, that beneficiary's benefits will be reduced depending on his or her age. The beneficiary must file an annual report of his or her earnings to the Social Security Administration by April 15 of the year following the year worked and must provide the exact earnings for that year and an estimate for the current year. The filing of a federal tax return with the IRS does not satisfy the filing requirement with the Social Security Administration. Also, the wages count toward the earnings limitation when they are earned, not when paid, whereas income for the self-employed normally counts when paid, not earned. If other family members receive benefits based on the beneficiary's Social Security record, then the total family benefits may be affected by the beneficiary's earnings that exceed the earnings limitation. In such a case, the Social Security Administration will withhold not only the worker's benefits, but will withhold those benefits payable to family members as well.

EXAMPLE

Matthew is 64 years old and, despite being retired from his occupation as an attorney, earned $20,000 in 2005 while working as a golf instructor at a local golf course. Matthew's monthly retirement benefit from Social Security is normally $1,200, which totals $14,400 for the entire year. Because Matthew exceeded the retirement earnings limitation, how much money will be deducted from Matthew's retirement benefit for 2005?

Matthew's total earnings in 2005	$20,000
Earnings Limitation	(12,000)
Remainder Excess	$8,000
One-half deduction	÷ 2
	$ 4,000

The Social Security Administration will thus deduct $4,000 from Matthew's benefits for the year. Matthew will receive $10,400 in retirement benefits ($14,400 annual retirement benefit less $4,000 reduction). Matthew's total income for 2005 would be $30,400, instead of $34,400.

Another commonly asked question is what income counts toward the retirement earnings limitation. Generally, only wages and net self-employment income count, whereas income from savings, investments, and insurance does not. The following is a nonexclusive list of sources of income that DO NOT count toward the earnings limitation:

- Pension or retirement pay.
- 401(k) and IRA withdrawals.
- Dividends and interest from investments.
- Capital gains.
- Rental income.
- Workers' compensation benefits.
- Unemployment benefits.
- Court-awarded judgments, less components of award that include lost wages.
- Contest winnings.

TAXATION OF SOCIAL SECURITY BENEFITS

Separate and apart from the earnings limitation scenario, some beneficiaries may be required to pay taxes on their Social Security benefits. For persons with substantial income in addition to Social Security benefits, up to 85 percent of their annual benefits may be subject to federal income tax. The Social Security Administration is concerned with beneficiaries' **modified adjusted gross income**. On the 1040 federal tax return, modified adjusted gross income is the sum of adjusted gross income, nontaxable interest, and foreign-earned income.

modified adjusted gross income - on the 1040 federal tax return, modified adjusted gross income is the sum of adjusted gross income, nontaxable interest, and foreign-earned income

Generally, up to 50 percent of Social Security benefits are subject to federal income taxes for beneficiaries who file a federal tax return as an "individual" and have a modified adjusted gross income between $25,000 and $34,000. For those with a modified adjusted gross income over $34,000, up to 85 percent of their Social Security benefits will be subject to federal income taxation. For those beneficiaries that file a joint federal tax return and have a modified adjusted gross income with their spouse between $32,000 and $44,000, up to 50 percent of their Social Security benefits will be subject to federal income taxes. Finally, if beneficiaries filing a joint tax return have a modified adjusted-gross income that exceeds $44,000, up to 85 percent of their Social Security benefits will be subject to federal income taxation.

In sum, for persons with substantial income in addition to their Social Security benefits, up to 85 percent of their annual benefits may be subject to federal income tax. The amount of benefits subject to federal income tax for taxpayers with modified adjusted gross income under $34,000 ($44,000 if married-filing-jointly) is the smaller of:

- One-half of their benefits.
- One-half of the amount by which their adjusted gross income, plus tax-exempt interest, plus foreign-earned income, plus one-half of their Social Security exceeds:
  - ❐ $25,000 if single.
  - ❐ $25,000 if married and not filing a joint return and did not live with a spouse at any time during the year.
  - ❐ $32,000 if married and filing a joint return.
  - ❐ $0 if married and not filing a joint return and did live with a spouse at any time during the year.

OTHER SOCIAL SECURITY BENEFITS

DISABILITY BENEFITS AND DISABILITY INSURED

Benefits are payable at any age to people who have enough Social Security credits and who hav a severe physical or mental impairment that is expected to prevent them from doin "substantial" work for a year or more or who have a condition that is expected to result in death Workers are insured for disability if they are fully insured and, except for persons who are blin or disabled before age 31, have a total of at least 20 quarters of coverage during the 40-quarte period ending with the quarter in which the worker became disabled. Workers who are disable before age 31 must have total quarters of coverage equal to half the calendar quarters whic have elapsed since the worker reached age 21, ending in the quarter in which the worker becam disabled. However, a minimum of 6 quarters is required.

Currently, earnings of $830 or more per month are considered substantial. The disabilit program includes incentives to smooth the transition back into the workforce, includin continuation of benefits and health care coverage. Disability under the Social Security system i defined as an inability to engage in substantial gainful activity by reason of a physical or ment impairment expected to last at least 12 months or to result in death. The impairment must be o such severity that the applicant is not only unable to do his or her previous work but cannot considering age, education, and work experience, engage in any other kind of substantial gainfu work that exists in the national economy.

FAMILY BENEFITS

If an individual is eligible for retirement or disability benefits, other members of the individual' family might receive benefits as well. Family members who may receive benefits include th following:

- A spouse caring for a child under age 16, or caring for a child who was disabled befor age 22.
- A child, if the child is unmarried and under age 18, under age 19 but still in secondar school, or age 18 or older but disabled before age 22.

For those workers who are entitled to retirement or disability benefits, an ex-spouse could als be eligible for benefits on the worker's record.

A child's benefit stops the month before the child reaches 18, unless the child is unmarried and i either disabled or is a full-time elementary or secondary school student. Approximately fiv months before the child's 18th birthday, the person receiving the child's benefits will get a form explaining how benefits can continue. A child whose benefits stop at 18 can have them starte again if the child becomes disabled before reaching 22 or becomes a full-time elementary o secondary school student before reaching 19. If the child continues to receive benefits after ag 18 due to a disability, the child also may qualify for SSI disability benefits. When a student's 19t birthday occurs during a school term, benefits can be continued up to two months to allow completion of the school term.

SURVIVORS BENEFITS

If a worker earned enough Social Security credits during his or her lifetime, certain members of the worker's family may be eligible for benefits when the worker dies. The family members of the deceased worker who may be entitled to survivors' benefits include:

- A widow or widower age 60, age 50 if disabled, or any age if caring for a child under age 16 or a disabled child.
- A child of the deceased worker, if the child is unmarried and under age 18, under age 19 but still in school, or age 18 or older but disabled.
- Parents of the deceased worker, if the deceased worker was their primary means of support, and dependent parent(s) is/are age 62 or older.

A special one-time payment of $255 may be made to a deceased worker's spouse or minor children upon death. If a spouse was living with the beneficiary at the time of death, the spouse will receive a one-time payment of $255. The payment may be made to a spouse who was not living with the beneficiary at the time of death or an ex-spouse if the spouse or ex-spouse was receiving Social Security benefits based on the deceased's earnings record. If there is no surviving spouse, a child (or children) who is eligible for benefits on the deceased's work record in the month of death may claim the payment.

EXHIBIT 11.11: SUMMARY OF SOCIAL SECURITY OASDI BENEFITS

Assuming Full Retirement Age of the worker

	Retirement	Survivorship		Disabilit y
	Fully Insured (2)	Fully Insured (2)	Currently Insured (3)	(4)
Participant	100%	Deceased	Deceased	100%
Child Under 18 (6)	50%	75%	75%	50%
Spouse with child under 16 (7)	50%	75%	75%	50%
Spouse - Age 65 (1)	50%	100%	0%	50%
Spouse - Age 62 (1)	40%	83%	0%	40%
Spouse - Age 60 (1)	N/A	71.5%	0%	N/A
Dependent Parent (age 62)	0%	75/82.5 (5)	0%	0%

(1) Includes divorced spouse if married at least 10 years (unless they have remarried). Survivorship benefits are also available to divorced spouse if remarried after age 60.
(2) Fully insured is 40 quarters of coverage or 1 quarter for each year after age 21 but before age 62.
(3) Currently insured is at least six quarters of coverage in the last 13 quarters.
(4) Disability insured is based on age as follows:
- Before age 24 - Must have 6 quarters of coverage in the last 12 quarters.
- Age 24 through 30 - Must be covered for half of the available quarters after age 21.
- Age 31 or older - Must be fully insured and have 20 quarters of coverage in the last 40 quarters.

(5) Parent benefit is 82.5% for one parent, and 75% for each parent if two parents.
(6) Child under age 19 and a full-time student in secondary school or of any age and disabled before age 22 also qualifies.
(7) Spouse with child disabled before age 22 also qualifies.

THE MAXIMUM FAMILY BENEFIT

maximum family benefit - the limit on the amount of monthly Social Security benefits that may be paid to a family

When a person dies, his or her survivors receive a percentage of the worker's Social Security benefits ranging from 75 percent to 100 percent each. There is a limit on the amount of monthly Social Security benefits that may be paid to a family. This limit is called the **maximum family benefit**, which is determined through a formula based on the worker's PIA. While the limit varies, it is equal to roughly 150 percent to 180 percent of the deceased worker's PIA. If the sum of the family members' benefits exceeds the limit, the family members' benefits are proportionately reduced. For old-age and survivor family benefits, the formula computes the sum of four separate percentages of portions of the worker's PIA. For 2005, these portions are the first $801 of PIA, the amount between $801 and $1,156, the amount between $1,156 and $1,508, and the amount over $1,508. These are the bend points for the maximum family benefit formula for the year 2005, with the following percentage calculations:

> 150 percent of the first $801 of the worker's PIA, *plus*
> 272 percent of the worker's PIA over $801 through $1,156, *plus*
> 134 percent of the worker's PIA over $1,156 through $1,508, *plus*
> 175 percent of the worker's PIA over $1,508.

This number is rounded to the next lower $0.10.

MEDICARE BENEFITS

Medicare is a federal health insurance plan for people who are 65 and over, whether retired or still working. People who are disabled or have permanent kidney failure can get Medicare at any age. The Health Care Financing Administration, part of the United States Department of Health and Human Services, administers Medicare. Medicare is the nation's largest health insurance program, covering over 41.7 million individuals. There are two parts to Medicare: Hospital Insurance (Part A) and Medical Insurance (Part B).

Generally, individuals who are age 65 and over qualify for Medicare. Also, individuals who have received Social Security disability benefits for at least two years automatically qualify for Medicare. All other individuals must file an application for Medicare.

Part A, Hospital Insurance, is paid for by a portion of the Social Security tax. Part A helps pay for necessary medical care and services furnished by Medicare-certified hospitals, inpatient hospital care, skilled nursing care, home health care, hospice care and other services. The number of days that Medicare covers care in hospitals and skilled nursing facilities is measured in what is termed **benefit periods**. A benefit period begins on the first day a patient receives services as a patient in a hospital or skilled nursing facility and ends after 60 consecutive days of no further skilled care. There is no limit to the number of benefit periods a beneficiary may have.

benefit periods - the number of days that Medicare covers care in hospitals and skilled nursing facilities

Benefit periods are identified because deductibles, coinsurance and premiums relate to a benefit period instead of a calendar year. For instance, for coverage under Medicare under Part A, a deductible of $912 applies per benefit period. For the 61st through the 90th day of each benefit period, the insured individual must pay $228 a day in the form of coinsurance. Any days over 90 in a benefit period are considered lifetime reserve days. There are 60 lifetime reserve days available with coinsurance of $456 per day. Lifetime reserve days do not renew with each benefit period. It is important, therefore, to determine the number of days used in each benefit period.

EXHIBIT 11.12: MEDICARE DEDUCTIBLE, COINSURANCE AND PREMIUM AMOUNTS FOR 2005

Hospital Insurance (Part A)

- **Deductible** - $912 per Benefit Period
- **Coinsurance**
  - $228 a day for the 61st through the 90th day, per Benefit Period;
  - $456 a day for the 91st through the 150th day for each lifetime reserve day (total of 60 lifetime reserve days – nonrenewable).
- **Skilled Nursing Facility coinsurance** - $114 a day for the 21st through the 100th day per Benefit Period;
- **Hospital Insurance Premium** - $375 per month (Note: This premium is paid only by individuals who are not otherwise eligible for premium-free hospital insurance and have less than 30 quarters of Medicare covered employment.)
- **Reduced Hospital Insurance Premium** - $206 (Note: For individuals having 30 to 39 quarters of coverage.)

Medical Insurance (Part B)

- **Deductible** - $110 per year
- **Monthly Premium** - $78.20

Source: Social Security Administration (www.ssa.gov)

Medicare Part A helps pay for up to 90 days of inpatient hospital care during each benefit period. Covered services for inpatient hospital care include: semiprivate room and meal, operating and recovery room cost, intensive care, drugs, laboratory tests, x-rays, general nursing services, and any other necessary medical services and supplies. Convenience items such as television and telephones provided by hospitals in private rooms (unless medically necessary) are generally not covered. Medicare does not pay for custodial services for daily living activities such as eating, bathing, and getting dressed. Medicare does, however, pay for skilled nursing facility care for rehabilitation, such as recovery time after a hospital discharge. Part A may help pay for up to 100 days in a participating skilled nursing facility in each benefit period. Medicare pays all approved charges for the first 20 days relating to skilled nursing facility care, and the patient pays a coinsurance amount for days 21 through 100. Medicare may also pay the full, approved cost of covered home health care services, which includes part-time or intermittent skilled nursing services prescribed by a physician for treatment or rehabilitation of homebound patients. Normally, the only cost to the insured for home health care is a 20 percent coinsurance charge for medical equipment, like wheelchairs and walkers.

Medicare Part B pays for 80 percent of approved charges for most covered services. Unless an individual declines Part B medical insurance protection, the premium will automatically be deducted from their Social Security benefits. The 2005 premium amount is $78.20 a month. The deductible for Part B is $110 per year. The insured is responsible for paying a $110 deductible per calendar year and the remaining 20 percent of the Medicare-approved charge. Medicare Part B usually does not cover charges for routine physical examinations or services unrelated to treatment of injury or illness. Dental care, dentures, cosmetic surgery, hearing aids and eye examinations are not covered by Part B. Prescription drugs are also excluded from coverage; however a prescription drug discount card is available to individuals enrolled in Part A or B and not enrolled in Medicaid. This card gives the bearer access to negotiated prescription discounts.

Various plans under Medicare are available to insureds. The original Medicare Plan is the means by which most individuals get their Medicare Part A and Part B benefits. This is the traditional payment-per-service arrangement where the individual insured may go to any doctor, specialist, or hospital that accepts Medicare, and Medicare pays its share after services are rendered. Medicare carriers and fiscal intermediaries are private insurance organizations that handle claims under the original Medicare Plan. Carriers handle Part B claims, while fiscal intermediaries handle Part A plans. The Social Security Administration does not handle claims or Medicare payments.

Medicare Advantage - a managed care plan that uses a network of doctors, hospitals and health care providers approved by Medicare

An individual may opt instead to enroll in a Medicare managed care plan, called **Medicare Advantage**. These plans are offered by private Medicare-approved companies and are networks of doctors, hospitals, and other health care providers that agree to give care in return for a set monthly payment from Medicare. Individuals are eligible to enroll in Medicare Advantage if they are enrolled in Medicare Parts A and B, pay the Part B premium, do not have end-stage renal disease, and live in the plan's service area.

medical savings account (MSA) - used to pay the out-of-pocket medical expenses of an insured enrolled in a high-deductible insurance

Another option is a high-deductible insurance plan and a **Medical Savings Account** (MSA). Funds from the MSA can be used to pay the out-of-pocket medical expenses of an insured enrolled in a high-deductible insurance plan. Medicare will pay the premium and will also make contributions to the MSA. These contributions are equal to the amount Medicare would pay to a Medicare Advantage plan in the individual's area less the premium for the high-deductible insurance plan.

Many private insurance companies sell Medicare supplemental insurance policies, Medigap, and Medicare SELECT. These supplemental policies help bridge the coverage gaps in the original Medicare Plan. These supplemental policies also help pay Medicare's coinsurance amounts and deductibles, as well as other out-of-pocket expenses for health care.

When a worker is first enrolled in Part B at age 65, there is a six-month open enrollment period in Medigap. During the time of open enrollment, the health status of the applicant cannot be used as a reason to refuse a Medigap policy or to charge more than other open enrollment applicants. The insurer may require a six-month waiting period for coverage of pre-existing conditions. If, however, the open enrollment period has expired, the applicant may be denied a policy based on health status or may be charged higher rates.

Other Medicare Health Plan Choices

Medicare offers alternative methods of obtaining Medicare benefits through other health plan choices. Choices that vary by area include coordinated-care or Medicare managed care plans, such as Health Maintenance Organizations (HMOs), HMOs with a point of service option, Provider Sponsored Organizations (PSOs), and Preferred Provider Organizations (PPOs). These plans involve specific groups of doctors, hospitals and other providers who provide care to the insured as a member of the plan, like many employer-sponsored plans throughout the country. Medicare managed care plans not only provide the same services that are covered by Part A and Part B, but most Medicare managed plans offer a variety of additional benefits like preventative care, prescription drugs, dental care, eyeglasses and other items not covered by the original Medicare Plan. The cost of these extra benefits varies among the plans.

Where on the Web

Centers for Medicare and Medicaid Services *www.cms.hhs.gov*
HealthMetrix Research, Inc. *www.hmos4seniors.com*
Medicare Rights Center *www.medicarerights.org*
National Organization of Social Security Claimants' Representatives *www.nosscr.org*
Social Security Administration *www.ssa.gov*
Social Security Disability *www.ssa.gov/disability*
Social Security Forms *www.ssa.gov/online/forms.html*
Social Security Medicare *www.ssa.gov/mediinfo.htm*
Social Security Privatization and Reform *www.socialsecurity.org*
U.S. Government Website for Medicare *www.medicare.gov*

Other Medicare health plan choices beyond the original Medicare Plan and Medicare managed care plans include: Private Fee for Service Plans, Medicare Medical Savings Account Plans (MSAs), or religious fraternal benefits plans. These plans provide all services covered by both Part A and Part B, as well as a variety of additional benefits. MSAs are funded through a lump-sum payment from traditional Medicare to obtain a high deductible insurance policy. Any remaining balance can be used by the beneficiary for payment of medical expenses not covered by traditional Medicare or for other use. This amount could be subject to taxation if not used for medically related purposes. For information about these various health plan choices, the official Internet site of Medicare at *www.medicare.gov* is very helpful and provides many links to other informative sources.

Applying for Medicare Benefits and Coverage

If a worker applies for retirement or survivors' benefits before his or her 65th birthday, there is no need to file a separate application for Medicare. The worker will receive information in the mail before he or she turns 65, explaining what needs to be done. Coverage starts automatically at age 65, even without receiving a Medicare card in the mail.

Those who are not receiving Social Security benefits must file an application for Medicare benefits. Spouses can qualify for Medicare Part A at age 65 based on the other spouse's work record if the other spouse is eligible for monthly Social Security benefits or if the other spouse is receiving Social Security disability benefits. Applications should be submitted three months before the applicant's 65th birthday. If the worker does not enroll and delays taking Part B for one year, that worker's monthly premiums for Part B will increase. For each 12 months the worker could have used Part B, but does not take it, the monthly premium increases by 10 percent. If the worker decides to delay opting into Part B because of the worker's current group health plan coverage (if applicable), the worker may be able to avoid the increased monthly premium by applying for Part B (i) while participating in the group coverage or (ii) within eight months after the employment ends or group health coverage ends, whichever occurs first.

Even if an individual continues to work after turning 65, he or she should sign up for Part A of Medicare. Part A may help defray some costs not otherwise covered by group health plans. Applying for Part B may or may not be advantageous if the worker has health insurance through an employer. The worker would be required to pay the monthly Part B premium, yet the Part B benefits may be of limited value because the employer plan is the primary source of payment of medical bills.

For those who receive Medicare and have low income and few resources, states may pay Medicare premiums, and, in some cases, other out-of-pocket Medicare expenses such as deductibles and coinsurance. The state decides if individuals qualify. For more general information about Medicare, the Social Security Administration's leaflet *Medicare Savings for Qualified Beneficiaries* (HCFA Publication No. 02184) is helpful, as are the websites *www.ssa.gov* and *www.medicare.gov.*

SUPPLEMENTAL SECURITY INCOME BENEFITS

SSI makes monthly payments to individuals with low incomes and few assets. In order to obtain SSI benefits, an individual must be age 65, disabled, or blind. The definition of disability is satisfied when the individual is unable to engage in any substantial gainful activity due to a physical or mental problem expected to last at least a year or expected to result in death. Children as well as adults qualify for SSI disability payments. As its name implies, Supplemental Security Income supplements the beneficiary's income up to various levels, depending on where the beneficiary lives. If an otherwise eligible SSI applicant lives in another's household and receives support from that person, the federal SSI benefit is reduced by one-third.

The federal government pays a basic rate. In 2005 the basic monthly SSI check is $579 per month for one person and $869 per month for married couples. Some states supply additional funds to qualified individuals. To ascertain the SSI benefit rates in a certain state, the financial planner or client can contact a local Social Security office in that state, or visit the Social Security Administration's website. Generally, individuals who receive SSI benefits also qualify for Medicaid, food stamps, and other assistance.

FILING FOR SOCIAL SECURITY CLAIMS

The Social Security Administration reports that many people fail to file claims with the Social Security Administration or fail to do so in a timely fashion. Individuals should file for Social Security or SSI disability benefits as soon they become too disabled to work or for survivors benefits when a family breadwinner dies. Social Security benefits do not start automatically. Social Security will not begin payment of benefits until the beneficiary files an application. When filling for benefits, applicants must submit documents that show eligibility, such as a birth certificate for each family member applying for benefits, a marriage certificate if a spouse is applying, and the most recent W-2 forms or tax returns.

To file for benefits, obtain information, or to speak to a Social Security representative, individuals must call the Social Security Administration's toll-free number, 800-772-1213, or visit the Social Security Administration's website. The toll-free number can be used to schedule an appointment at a local Social Security office. The Social Security Administration treats all calls confidentially. Periodically, a second Social Security representative will monitor incoming and outgoing telephone calls to ensure accurate and courteous service.

SOCIAL SECURITY CHANGES FOR 2005

Each year the Social Security Commissioner issues a Fact Sheet summarizing the changes in Social Security. The following is the Commissioner's Fact Sheet for 2005.

EXHIBIT 11.14: SOCIAL SECURITY CHANGES FOR 2005

Cost-of-Living Adjustment (COLA):
Based on the increase in the Consumer Price Index (CPI-W) from the third quarter of 2003 through the third quarter of 2004, Social Security beneficiaries and Supplemental Security Income (SSI) recipients received a 2.7 percent COLA for 2005. Other important 2005 Social Security information is as follows:

Tax Rate:	**2004**	**2005**
Employee	7.65%	7.65%
Self-Employed	15.30%	15.30%

NOTE: The 7.65% tax rate is the combined rate for Social Security and Medicare. The Social Security portion (OASDI) is 6.20% on earnings up to the applicable maximum taxable amount (see below). The Medicare portion (HI) is 1.45% on all earnings.

Maximum Earnings Taxable:	**2004**	**2005**
Social Security (OASDI only)	$87,900	$90,000
Medicare (HI only)	No Limit	No Limit
Quarter of Coverage:	$900	$920

Retirement Earnings Test Exempt Amounts:
As of January 2000, the Retirement Earnings Test has been eliminated for individuals age 65-69. It remains in effect for those ages 62 through 64. A modified test applies for the year an individual reaches age 65. (The Senior Citizens' Freedom To Work Act of 2000, signed into law by President Clinton on April 7, 2000.)

2004
Year individual reaches full retirement age - $31,080/yr. ($2,590/mo.)
--Applies only to earnings for months prior to attaining age 65. One dollar in benefits will be withheld for every $3 in earnings above the limit. There is no limit on earnings beginning the month an individual attains age 65.
Under full retirement age - $11,640/yr. ($970/mo.)
--One dollar in benefits will be withheld for every $2 in earnings above the limit.

2005
Year individual reaches full retirement age - $31,800/yr. ($2,650/mo.)
--Applies only to earnings for months prior to attaining age 65. One dollar in benefits will be withheld for every $3 in earnings above the limit. There is no limit on earnings beginning the month an individual attains age 65.
Under full retirement age - $12,000/yr. ($1,000/mo.)
--One dollar in benefits will be withheld for every $2 in earnings above the limit.

SSI Federal Payment Standard:	**2004**	**2005**
Individual	$564/mo.	$579/mo.
Couple	$846/mo.	$869/mo.
SSI Resources Limits:		
Individual	$2,000	$2,000
Couple	$3,000	$3,000
Estimated Average Monthly Social Security Benefits Payable in January 2004:		
	Before 2.7% COLA	**After 2.7% COLA**
All Retired Workers	$930	$955
Aged Couple, Both Receiving Benefits	$1,532	$1,574
Widowed Mother and Two Children	$1,927	$1,979
Aged Widow(er) Alone	$896	$920
Disabled Worker, Spouse and One or More Children	$1,458	$1,497
All Disabled Workers	$871	$895

OTHER ISSUES

EFFECT OF MARRIAGE OR DIVORCE ON BENEFITS

Marriage or divorce may affect one's Social Security benefits, depending on the kind of benefits received. If a worker receives retirement benefits based on his or her own earnings record, the worker's retirement benefits will continue whether married or divorced. If an individual receives benefits based on his or her spouse's record, the individual's benefits will cease upon divorce unless the individual is age 62 or older and was married at least 10 years. Widows and widowers, whether divorced or not, will continue to receive survivors' benefits upon remarriage if the widow or widower is age 60 or older. Disabled widows and widowers, whether divorced or not, will continue to receive survivors' benefits upon remarriage if the disabled widow or widower is age 50 or older.

For all other forms of Social Security benefits, benefits will cease upon remarriage, except in special circumstances. When a person marries, it is presumed that at least one person in the marriage can provide adequate support. Likewise, Social Security benefits may recommence based on the previous spouse's benefits if the marriage ends.

CHANGE OF NAME

If an individual changes his or her name due to marriage, divorce or a court order, that individual must notify the Social Security Administration of the name change so the Social Security Administration will be able to show the new name in their records and properly credit that individual for earnings. This will ensure that the individual's work history will be accurately recorded and maintained.

LEAVING THE UNITED STATES

Beneficiaries who are United States citizens may travel or live in most foreign countries without affecting their eligibility for Social Security benefits. However, there are a few countries where Social Security checks cannot be sent. These countries currently include Cuba, Cambodia, North Korea, Vietnam, and the republics that were formerly in the U.S.S.R. (except Armenia, Estonia, Latvia, Lithuania, and Russia).

Beneficiaries should inform the Social Security Administration of their plans to go outside the United States for a trip that lasts 30 days or more. By providing the name of the country or countries to be visited and the expected departure and return dates, the Social Security Administration will send special reporting instructions to the beneficiaries and arrange for delivery of checks while abroad.

PROFESSIONAL FOCUS

Do you find clients are aware of the limitations of Social Security (i.e. that it may run out, that it may not provide enough income to higher income workers)?

Yes, my clients are concerned that Social Security benefits may run out. These clients generally fall into two categories: (1) Those in 50+ age bracket who are really concerned because they have included Social Security benefits as a major component of their retirement plan and (2) those clients in the 30-50 age bracket who are of the strong opinion that the Social Security benefits may no longer exist by the time they reach retirement age. As a planner what I try to do with the first group is get them to voluntarily spend a little less and save small amounts in a growth portfolio to offset the risk that Social Security benefits will be reduced or eliminated. For the second group we plan without Social Security benefits. We are fairly certain that for the older members of this group there will be some benefits which we plan to invest in growth securities because we never counted on them anyway. My expectation is that while Social Security benefits will change, the legislated changes are unlikely to adversely affect those persons who are 50 and are registered to vote.

Do you find clients are aware of the benefits they should receive from Social Security? Are they surprised by the amount (i.e. they find it lower than they expected)?

Until recently, clients were totally unaware how much they would receive in Social Security benefits from retirement. They still have little knowledge when we are speaking of early (before normal age) retirement and families who receive survivor or disability benefits. The ability to file the SSA 7004 and receive the SSA 7005 has helped both planners and clients to estimate realistic Social Security benefits. Social Security for a covered worker with a nonworking, same age spouse may replace from 20 percent to 57 percent of pre-retirement income. Social Security retirement benefits, in spite of the issues regarding soundness of the system, continue to represent a major source of retirement income for many, especially the lower and middle class.

What steps do you take to ensure your client is aware of the need to file for Social Security benefits?

We create retirement projections and plans as early as the client allows us. We regularly monitor and review our retirement projections as we meet with clients quarterly and annually. We begin serious discussions of Social Security benefits and other retirement sources of income around age 55. We also discuss early retirement and the resulting reduction in Social Security benefits. For some of our very early retirees (age 55), we use Social Security as a predictable boost in cash inflows that will enter the picture at age 62. If such a client has sufficient assets and income to maintain their preretirement lifestyle for the 7 or so years, Social Security benefits give them a boost in lifestyle at age 62. We regularly review all income, assets, and investment performance on a quarterly or annual basis for each client regardless of age. We do, however, pay particular attention to our seniors.

Do you believe Medicare is an adequate source of health insurance for the aged. If not, what types of products do you recommend to supplement Medicare.

We find that Medicare is not an adequate source of health insurance for seniors except for those in very good health. We review supplemental plan (A-J), Medigap plans, and we explore the need for Long-Term Care Insurance policies that have become much more affordable and now provide better benefits for less cost. As always the purchase of long-term care policies requires a cost/risk/benefits analysis.

We are increasingly alarmed with the number of HMOs that are dropping Medicare enrollees. We expect that Congress will have to address this issue by either raising the fees paid to providers or the HMO Medicare enrollees will have to turn back to regular indemnity Medicare plans.

JOE DEVANNEY, MA, CLU, PFP

DISCUSSION QUESTIONS

1. For purposes of Social Security and disability benefits, what is the meaning of "substantial" work?
2. When was Social Security legislation passed?
3. When was Social Security cost of living adjusted?
4. How are Social Security benefits financed?
5. Is there a maximum payroll amount to which Social Security taxes apply?
6. In order to qualify for OASDI disability benefits, what definition of disability must be met?
7. Describe the major benefits under the Social Security program.
8. Identify and describe the benefits available to those covered under OASDI.
9. How would a person who is entitled to Social Security benefits become ineligible for benefits?
10. What are the coverages that comprise the Medicare program?
11. Define and explain the meaning of fully insured, currently insured, and disability insured under the OASDI program.
12. What are the requirements to be "fully insured" under OASDI?
13. What Social Security benefits are available to the dependents of a deceased worker who was only currently insured?
14. What Social Security benefits would a "fully insured" worker have that a "currently insured" worker would not have?
15. What requirements must a person satisfy to collect Social Security (OASDI) disability income benefits?
16. How is Social Security funded?
17. To qualify for Social Security OASDI benefits, how many credits does one need? How is a credit determined?
18. What percentage of income does Social Security typically replace?
19. How is OASDI insured status determined, and why is it important?
20. How are monthly payments under OASDI determined?
21. What is normal retirement age in year 2005 for OASDI benefits?
22. For a recipient of Social Security benefits, is there a risk of loss from purchasing power declines?
23. What are the four benefits payable under the OASDI program?
24. If a taxpayer's income exceeds a specified base amount, as much as 50% or 85% of Social Security retirement benefits must be included in gross income. What would be the taxable amount of Social Security benefits at the 50% level?

EXERCISES

1. Michael was divorced after 15 years of marriage. He has 2 dependent children ages 4 and 6 who are cared for by their mother. He was currently, but not fully, insured under Social Security at the time of his death. What are the benefits that his survivors are entitled to under Social Security?

2. In 2005, James earned $4,000 from employment subject to Social Security between January 1 and March 31. He was then unemployed for the remainder of the year. How many quarters of coverage did he earn for Social Security for 2005?
3. Charles, age 38, has just died. He has been credited with the last 30 consecutive quarters of Social Security coverage since he left school. He did not work before leaving school. Which of the following persons are eligible to receive Social Security survivor benefits as a result of Charles' death?
   - Bill, Charles' 16-year-old son.
   - Dawn, Charles' 18-year-old daughter.
   - Margaret, Charles' 38-year-old widow.
   - Betty, Charles' 60-year-old dependent mother.
4. Under Social Security (OASDI), what benefits are available to the survivors of a deceased who was currently insured only ?
5. Which of the following persons are eligible to receive immediate survivor income benefits based on a deceased worker's Primary Insurance Amount (PIA), under OASDI (Social Security)?
   - A surviving spouse caring for an under-16-year-old child.
   - Unmarried children under age 18 who are dependents.
   - Unmarried disabled children who became disabled before age 22.
   - Any surviving divorced spouse over 50, with no children who was married to decedent for over 10 years and who is disabled.
6. How is a worker's insured status determined under Social Security?
7. Philip began his professional corporation single practitioner CPA firm 38 years ago at age 27. He worked profitably as a sole practitioner for the full 38 years and is now age 63 and 2 months. He retired December 31, 2004. On January 1st of 2005 he sold his practice for $400,000 to be received in 4 equal annual annuity due payments to be made on January 1st of each of the next four years beginning January 1st, 2005. Is Philip eligible for Social Security retirement benefits during this year? Why or why not?

PROBLEMS

1. Larry was married at the following ages and to the following wives. Larry is now 62 and married to Dawn.

	Wife	Current Age	Larry's Age at Marriage	Current Marital Status	Length of Marriage
1	Alice	62	20	Single	10 years, 1 month
2	Betty	63	31	Single	10 years, 1 month
3	Claire	64	42	Single	9 years
4	Dawn	65	53	Married	9 years

   Who, among the wives, may be eligible to receive Social Security retirement benefits based upon Larry's earnings if Larry is retired or not retired?

2. Rob earned $62,000 last year. Calculate his FICA contribution for the year. How much did his employer pay toward FICA?

3. Last year Michelle, filing single, received $10,400 in Social Security benefits. For the entire year, she had adjusted gross income of $28,000. How much, if any, of her Social Security benefit is taxable?
4. Mike is 66 years old. He has a full-time job working as a masseur. This year (2006) he anticipates earning $22,000 from his job. How much, in dollars, will Mike's Social Security benefits be reduced?
5. A married couple with adjusted gross income of $38,000, no tax-exempt interest, and $11,000 of Social Security benefits who file jointly must include how much of their Social Security benefits in gross income?

CHAPTER APPENDIX 11.1: SOCIAL SECURITY STATEMENT

Prevent identity theft—protect your Social Security number

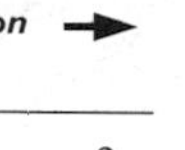

Your Social Security Statement

Prepared especially for Wanda Worker

March 31, 2005

See inside for your personal information 

WANDA WORKER
456 ANYWHERE AVENUE
MAINTOWN, USA 11111-1111

What's inside...

▼ Your Estimated Benefits 2
▼ Your Earnings Record 3
▼ Some Facts About Social Security 4
▼ If You Need More Information 4
▼ To Request This Statement In Spanish 4
(Para Solicitar Una Declaración en Español)

What Social Security Means to You

This *Social Security Statement* will help you understand what Social Security means to you and your family. This *Statement* can help you better plan for your financial future. It gives you estimates of your Social Security benefits under current law. Each year, we will send you an updated *Statement* including your latest reported earnings.

Be sure to read this *Statement* carefully. If you think there may be a mistake, please let us know. That's important because your benefits will be based on our record of your lifetime earnings. We recommend you keep a copy of this *Statement* with your financial records.

Social Security is for people of all ages...
It can help you whether you're young or old, male or female, single or with a family. It's there for you when you retire, but it's more than a retirement program. Social Security also can provide benefits if you become disabled and help support your family when you die.

Work to build a secure future...
Social Security is the largest source of income for most elderly Americans today. It is very important to remember that Social Security was never intended to be your only source of income when you retire. Social Security can't do it all. You also will need other savings, investments, pensions or retirement accounts to make sure you have enough money to live comfortably when you retire.

About Social Security's future...
Social Security is a compact between generations. For more than 60 years, America has kept the promise of security for its workers and their families. But now, the Social Security system is facing serious future financial problems, and action is needed soon to make sure that the system is sound when today's younger workers are ready for retirement.

Today there are almost 36 million Americans age 65 or older. Their Social Security retirement benefits are funded by today's workers and their employers who jointly pay Social Security taxes—just as the money they paid into Social Security was used to pay benefits to those who retired before them. Unless action is taken soon to strengthen Social Security, in just 12 years we will begin paying more in benefits than we collect in taxes. Without changes, by 2041 the Social Security Trust Fund will be exhausted.* By then, the number of Americans 65 or older is expected to have doubled. There won't be enough younger people working to pay all of the benefits owed to those who are retiring. At that point, there will be enough money to pay only about 74 cents for each dollar of scheduled benefits. We will need to resolve these issues soon to make sure Social Security continues to provide a foundation of protection for future generations as it has done in the past.

Social Security on the Net...
Visit ***www.socialsecurity.gov*** on the Internet to learn more about Social Security. You can read our publications, use the *Social Security Benefit Calculators* to calculate future benefits, apply for retirement, spouse's or disability benefits, or subscribe to *eNews* for up-to-date information about Social Security.

Jo Anne B. Barnhart
Commissioner

*These estimates of the future financial status of the Social Security program were produced by the actuaries at the Social Security Administration based on the intermediate assumptions from the Social Security Trustees' Annual Report to the Congress.

Your Estimated Benefits

To qualify for benefits, you earn "credits" through your work—up to four each year. This year, for example, you earn one credit for each $920 of wages or self-employment income. When you've earned $3,680, you've earned your four credits for the year. Most people need 40 credits, earned over their working lifetime, to receive retirement benefits. For disability and survivors benefits, young people need fewer credits to be eligible.

We checked your records to see whether you have earned enough credits to qualify for benefits. If you haven't earned enough yet to qualify for any type of benefit, we can't give you a benefit estimate now. If you continue to work, we'll give you an estimate when you do qualify.

What we assumed—If you have enough work credits, we estimated your benefit amounts using your average earnings over your working lifetime. For 2005 and later (up to retirement age), we assumed you'll continue to work and make about the same as you did in 2003 or 2004. We also included credits we assumed you earned last year and this year.

We can't provide your actual benefit amount until you apply for benefits. **And that amount may differ from the estimates stated below because:**

(1) Your earnings may increase or decrease in the future.

(2) Your estimated benefits are based on current law. **The law governing benefit amounts may change.***

(3) Your benefit amount may be affected by **military service, railroad employment or pensions earned through work on which you did not pay Social Security tax. Visit *www.socialsecurity.gov/mystatement* to see whether your Social Security benefit amount will be affected.**

Generally, estimates for older workers are more accurate than those for younger workers because they're based on a longer earnings history with fewer uncertainties such as earnings fluctuations and future law changes.

These estimates are in today's dollars. After you start receiving benefits, they will be adjusted for cost-of-living increases.

▼ *Retirement You have earned enough credits to qualify for benefits. At your current earnings rate, if you stop working and start receiving benefits...

At age 62, your payment would be about .... $ 903 a month

If you continue working until...

your full retirement age (67 years), your payment would be about .... $ 1,309 a month

age 70, your payment would be about .... $ 1,633 a month

▼ *Disability You have earned enough credits to qualify for benefits. If you became disabled right now,

Your payment would be about .... $ 1,197 a month

▼ *Family If you get retirement or disability benefits, your spouse and children also may qualify for benefits.

▼ *Survivors You have earned enough credits for your family to receive survivors benefits. If you die this year, certain members of your family **may** qualify for the following benefits.

Your child .... $ 933 a month

Your spouse who is caring for your child .... $ 933 a month

Your spouse, if benefits start at full retirement age .... $ 1,245 a month

Total family benefits cannot be more than .... $ 2,287 a month

Your spouse or minor child may be eligible for a special one-time death benefit of $255.

▼ Medicare You have enough credits to qualify for Medicare at age 65. Even if you do not retire at age 65, be sure to contact Social Security three months before your 65th birthday to enroll in Medicare.

***Your estimated benefits are based on current law. Congress has made changes to the law in the past and can do so at any time. The law governing benefit amounts may change because, by 2041, the payroll taxes collected will be enough to pay only about 74 percent of scheduled benefits.**

We based your benefit estimates on these facts:

Your date of birth .... May 5, 1964

Your estimated taxable earnings per year after 2004 .... $35,897

Your Social Security number (only the last four digits are shown to help prevent identity theft) XXX-XX-1234

2

Help Us Keep Your Earnings Record Accurate

You, your employer and Social Security share responsibility for the accuracy of your earnings record. Since you began working, we recorded your reported earnings under your name and Social Security number. We have updated your record each time your employer (or you, if you're self-employed) reported your earnings.

Remember, it's your earnings, not the amount of taxes you paid or the number of credits you've earned, that determine your benefit amount. When we figure that amount, we base it on your average earnings over your lifetime. If our records are wrong, you may not receive all the benefits to which you're entitled.

▼**Review this chart carefully** using your own records to make sure our information is correct and that we've recorded each year you worked. You are the only person who can look at the earnings chart and know whether it is complete and correct.

Some or all of your earnings from **last year** may not be shown on your *Statement*. It could be that we still were processing last year's earnings reports when your *Statement* was prepared. Your complete earnings for last year will be shown on next year's *Statement*. **Note:** If you worked for more than one employer during any year, or if you had both earnings and self-employment income, we combined your earnings for the year.

▼**There's a limit on the amount of earnings on which you pay Social Security taxes each year.** The limit increases yearly. Earnings above the limit will not appear on your earnings chart as Social Security earnings. (For Medicare taxes, the maximum earnings amount began rising in 1991. Since 1994, **all** of your earnings are taxed for Medicare.)

▼**Call us right away** at **1-800-772-1213** (7 a.m.–7 p.m. your local time) if any earnings for years **before last year** are shown incorrectly. If possible, have your W-2 or tax return for those years available. (If you live outside the U.S., follow the directions at the bottom of page 4.)

Your Earnings Record at a Glance

Years You Worked	Your Taxed Social Security Earnings	Your Taxed Medicare Earnings
1980	505	505
1981	1,226	1,226
1982	2,087	2,087
1983	3,418	3,418
1984	4,710	4,710
1985	5,809	5,809
1986	7,112	7,112
1987	9,293	9,293
1988	11,403	11,403
1989	13,262	13,262
1990	15,122	15,122
1991	16,876	16,876
1992	18,780	18,780
1993	19,847	19,847
1994	21,113	21,113
1995	22,633	22,633
1996	24,355	24,355
1997	26,330	26,330
1998	28,222	28,222
1999	30,373	30,373
2000	32,510	32,510
2001	33,833	33,833
2002	34,646	34,646
2003	35,897	35,897
2004	Not yet recorded	

Did you know... Social Security is more than just a retirement program? It's here to help you when you need it most.

You and your family may be eligible for valuable benefits:

▼When you die, your family may be eligible to receive survivors benefits.

▼Social Security may help you if you become disabled—even at a young age.

▼It is possible for a young person who has worked and paid Social Security taxes in as few as two years to become eligible for disability benefits.

Social Security credits you earn move with you from job to job throughout your career.

Total Social Security and Medicare taxes paid over your working career through the last year reported on the chart above:

Estimated taxes paid for Social Security:		Estimated taxes paid for Medicare:	
You paid:	$25,757	You paid:	$6,056
Your employers paid:	$25,757	Your employers paid:	$6,056

Note: You currently pay 6.2 percent of your salary, up to $90,000, in Social Security taxes and 1.45 percent in Medicare taxes on your entire salary. Your employer also pays 6.2 percent in Social Security taxes and 1.45 percent in Medicare taxes for you. If you are self-employed, you pay the combined employee and employer amount of 12.4 percent in Social Security taxes and 2.9 percent in Medicare taxes on your net earnings.

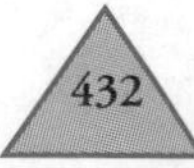

Some Facts About Social Security

About Social Security and Medicare...
Social Security pays retirement, disability, family and survivors benefits. Medicare, a separate program run by the Centers for Medicare and Medicaid Services, helps pay for inpatient hospital care, nursing care, doctors' fees, and other medical services and supplies to people age 65 and older, or to people who have been receiving Social Security disability benefits for two years or more. Your Social Security covered earnings qualify you for both programs. For more information about Medicare, visit ***www.medicare.gov*** or call **1-800-633-4227** (TTY **1-877-486-2048** if you are deaf or hard of hearing).

Here are some facts about Social Security's benefits:

▼**Retirement**—If you were born before 1938, your full retirement age is 65. Because of a 1983 change in the law, the full retirement age will increase gradually to 67 for people born in 1960 and later.

Some people retire before their full retirement age. You can retire as early as age 62 and take your benefits at a reduced rate. If you continue working after your full retirement age, you can receive higher benefits because of additional earnings and special credits for delayed retirement.

▼**Disability**—If you become disabled before full retirement age, you can receive disability benefits after six months if you have:

— enough credits from earnings (depending on your age, you must have earned six to 20 of your credits in the three to 10 years before you became disabled); and

— a physical or mental impairment that is expected to prevent you from doing "substantial" work for a year or more *or* result in death.

▼**Family**—If you're eligible for disability or retirement benefits, your current or divorced spouse, minor children or adult children disabled before age 22 also may receive benefits. Each may qualify for up to about 50 percent of your benefit amount. The total amount depends on how many family members qualify.

▼**Survivors**—When you die, certain members of your family may be eligible for benefits:

— your spouse age 60 or older (50 or older if disabled, or any age if caring for your children younger than age 16); and

— your children if unmarried and younger than age 18, still in school and younger than 19 years old, or adult children disabled before age 22.

If you are divorced, your ex-spouse could be eligible for a widow's or widower's benefit on your record when you die.

Receive benefits and still work...
You can continue to work and still get retirement or survivors benefits. If you're younger than your full retirement age, there are limits on how much you can earn without affecting your benefit amount. The limits change each year. When you apply for benefits, we'll tell you what the limits are at that time and whether work would affect your monthly benefits. When you reach full retirement age, the earnings limits no longer apply.

Before you decide to retire...
Think about your benefits for the long term. Everyone's situation is different. For example, be sure to consider the advantages and disadvantages of early retirement. If you choose to receive benefits before you reach full retirement age, your benefits will be permanently reduced. However, you'll receive benefits for a longer period of time.

To help you decide when is the best time for you to retire, we offer a free booklet, *Social Security — Retirement Benefits* (Publication No. 05-10035), that provides specific information about retirement. You can calculate future retirement benefits on our website at ***www.socialsecurity.gov*** by using the *Social Security Benefit Calculators.* There are other free publications that you may find helpful, including:

▼*Understanding The Benefits* (No. 05-10024) — a general explanation of all Social Security benefits;

▼*How Your Retirement Benefit Is Figured* (No. 05-10070) — an explanation of how you can calculate your benefit;

▼*The Windfall Elimination Provision* (No. 05-10045) — how it affects your retirement or disability benefits;

▼*Government Pension Offset* (No. 05-10007) — explanation of a law that affects spouse's or widow(er)'s benefits; and

▼*Identity Theft And Your Social Security Number* (No. 05-10064) — what to do if you're a victim of identity theft.

We also have other leaflets and fact sheets with information about specific topics such as military service, self-employment or foreign employment. You can request Social Security publications at ***www.socialsecurity.gov*** or by calling us at **1–800–772–1213**.

If you need more information—Visit ***www.socialsecurity.gov/mystatement*** on the Internet, contact any Social Security office, call **1–800–772–1213** or write to Social Security Administration, Office of Earnings Operations, P.O. Box 33026, Baltimore, MD 21290-3026. If you are deaf or hard of hearing, call TTY **1–800–325–0778**. If you have questions about your personal information, you must provide your complete Social Security number. If your address is incorrect on this *Statement*, ask the Internal Revenue Service to send you a Form 8822. We do not keep your address if you are not receiving Social Security benefits.

Para solicitar una *Declaración* en español, llame al 1-800-772-1213.

CHAPTER APPENDIX 11.2: FORM 7004

Form Approved
OMB No. 0960-0466

SP

Request for Social Security Statement

☐ Please check this box if you want to get your statement in Spanish instead of English.

Please print or type your answers. When you have completed the form, fold it and mail it to us. (If you prefer to send your request using the Internet, contact us at *www.ssa.gov*)

1. Name shown on your Social Security card:

   First Name ______ Middle Initial ______

   Last Name Only ______

2. Your Social Security number as shown on your card:

   ☐☐☐ - ☐☐ - ☐☐☐☐

3. Your date of birth (Mo.-Day-Yr.)

   ☐☐ - ☐☐ - ☐☐☐☐

4. Other Social Security numbers you have used:

   ☐☐☐ - ☐☐ - ☐☐☐☐

   ☐☐☐ - ☐☐ - ☐☐☐☐

5. Your Sex: ☐ Male ☐ Female

For items 6 and 8 show only earnings covered by Social Security. Do NOT include wages from State, local or Federal Government employment that are NOT covered for Social Security or that are covered ONLY by Medicare.

6. Show your actual earnings (wages and/or net self-employment income) for last year and your estimated earnings for this year.

   A. Last year's actual earnings: *(Dollars Only)*

   $☐☐☐,☐☐☐.0 0

   B. This year's estimated earnings: *(Dollars Only)*

   $☐☐☐,☐☐☐.0 0

7. Show the age at which you plan to stop working.

   ☐☐ *(Show only one age)*

8. Below, show the average yearly amount (not your total future lifetime earnings) that you think you will earn between now and when you plan to stop working. Include performance or scheduled pay increases or bonuses, but not cost-of-living increases.

   If you expect to earn significantly more or less in the future due to promotions, job changes, part-time work, or an absence from the work force, enter the amount that most closely reflects your future average yearly earnings.

   If you don't expect any significant changes, show the same amount you are earning now (the amount in 6B).

   Future average yearly earnings: *(Dollars Only)*

   $☐☐☐,☐☐☐.0 0

9. Do you want us to send the statement:
   - To you? Enter your name and mailing address.
   - To someone else (your accountant, pension plan, etc.)? Enter your name with "c/o" and the name and address of that person or organization.

   "C/O" or Street Address (Include Apt. No., P.O. Box, Rural Route)

   Street Address

   Street Address (If Foreign Address, enter City, Province, Postal Code)

   U.S. City, State, Zip code (If Foreign Address, enter Name of Country

NOTICE:
I am asking for information about my own Social Security record or the record of a person I am authorized to represent. I understand that if I deliberately request information under false pretenses, I may be guilty of a Federal crime and could be fined and/or imprisoned. I authorize you to use a contractor to send the Social Security Statement to the person and address in item 9.

▶

Please sign your name (Do Not Print)

Date (Area Code) Daytime Telephone No.

Form **SSA-7004-SM** (6-2002) EF (08-2002)
Destroy prior editions

Investment, Income Tax, Business, Retirement and Estate Planning

in
BRIEF

- Risk and return of asset classes
- Types of investment vehicles

- The Internal Revenue Service and Administration
- Income tax liability, audits, interest, and penalties
- Selecting the proper business form

- Retirement income needs analysis
- Qualified and other tax-advantaged retirement savings plans
- Nonqualified retirement plans and deferred compensation

- Estate planning goals and documents
- Probate process
- Gift and estate taxation
- Use of trusts

nvestment, Income Tax, Business, Retirement and Estate Planning

SECTION IV

CHAPTER 12 Introduction to Investment Concepts
CHAPTER 13 Individual Income Tax and Tax Planning
CHAPTER 14 Business Entities
CHAPTER 15 Introduction to Retirement Planning
CHAPTER 16 Basic Retirement Plans
CHAPTER 17 Introduction to Estate Planning

Risks

- Unrealized financial planning goals
- Investment losses
- Systematic and unsystematic risk
- Excessive tax liability (income, estate, gift)
- Excessive general liability exposure
- Outliving one's assets
- Failure to provide for survivors
- Inefficient distribution of estate assets
- Failure to meet assisted living and end-of-life care needs

Data Collection

- Business entity characteristics
- Financial statements
- Family health history
- Projected inflation rate
- Investment history
- Risk tolerance
- Tax returns and information forms
- Current investment and asset allocation
- Life insurance policies and property titles
- Retirement plan and deferred compensation information
- Estate planning documents and trust information

Goals

- Minimize tax liability
- Match business goals with entity formation
- Ensure inflation-protected retirement income
- Efficient transfer of assets

Data Analysis

- Liquidity needs
- Investment portfolio risks and returns benchmark comparison
- Tax efficiency of investments
- Tax-saving strategies
- Retirement needs analysis
- Adequacy of life insurance and other wealth transfer techniques

CHAPTER 12

Introduction to Investment Concepts

LEARNING OBJECTIVES:

After learning the material in this chapter, you will be able to:

1. List the investment goals common to most investors and how to achieve them.
2. Differentiate between systematic risk and unsystematic risk, giving examples of each.
3. Define lending investments and ownership investments and discuss the differences between them.
4. Explain the difference between direct investing and indirect investing.
5. Describe the two common measures of risk—beta and standard deviation.
6. Discuss several measures of return—holding period return, arithmetic mean, geometric mean, internal rate of return, and real rate of return.
7. Define the "efficient frontier" and explain its role in modern portfolio theory.
8. Describe the "Efficient Market Hypothesis" and compare it to investment strategies and theories.

INTRODUCTION TO INVESTING

As this text's opening chapters point out, the professional financial planner's purpose is to assist clients in achieving their financial goals and objectives, while helping them reduce certain personal and financial risks. Investment planning and portfolio evaluation are key elements in achieving many financial planning goals, such as saving for retirement, saving for children's education, and the accumulation and preservation of wealth. This chapter will provide the financial planner with the background and reference information necessary to develop a solid foundation of investment planning—an essential ingredient in the financial planning process.

Investing is based on the concept that forgoing immediate consumption provides for greater future consumption. Investing provides an opportunity for discretionary funds to grow and to accumulate over time to facilitate future consumption. Therefore, the first step in investing is to save instead of consume. This current sacrifice implies an expectation that funds saved today will provide for greater expenditures in the future.

Without the ability to invest and grow through savings, interest income, dividend payments, rental income, and capital appreciation, investors would find it very difficult to achieve their financial goals. However, financial growth is only one element to consider in achieving financial goals. Taxes, inflation, and other investment risks stand in the way. The starting point in the investment planning process is to establish financial goals.

ESTABLISHING FINANCIAL GOALS

Goals establish the financial target. Strategies establish the path to reach the target. The more specific and measurable the goals are, the more useful they become. In general, goals should be **SMART**.

- Specific
- Measurable
- Attainable
- Realistic
- Timely

The time horizon for goals can be short, intermediate, or long term. Short-term goals are those accomplished within two years, such as saving for small purchases or for a down payment for an automobile. We think of intermediate goals as those that can be accomplished within two to ten years, such as funding for a child's college education or saving for a down payment on a home. Long-term goals are those that generally take over ten years to accomplish, such as saving for retirement. A discussion of the different approaches to investing for goals with different time horizons appears later in this chapter.

TYPICAL FINANCIAL PLANNING GOALS

Although clients may have financial planning goals that are unique to them, most individuals share a certain number of goals with other people. These typical goals include saving for the purchase of a home, funding children's education, and planning for retirement.

Purchasing a home is likely one of the largest financial commitments your client will make. Most people begin the process by saving for a few years to accumulate a down payment. If the price of an average home is $100,000, many people attempt to make a down payment of approximately $20,000, or 20 percent. The average time it takes for someone to save for a down payment is generally between two and five years. This short time period leaves little room for growth and even less opportunity to tolerate a significant amount of risk. Therefore, the appropriate types of securities for this investment situation are relatively conservative.

One typical goal for most parents is funding their children's college tuition. The cost of higher education can be as low as a few thousand dollars to over thirty thousand dollars annually. In some cases, parents will pay the entire cost of education from their current budget. However, with tuition costs increasing at an inflation rate of approximately five to seven percent per year, it is becoming increasingly difficult to pay for college education. As a result, many parents are beginning to plan and save for college as soon as their child is born, giving themselves an investment time horizon of approximately eighteen years. Other parents with young children may not have the resources to begin planning for college until the child is beginning high school. In their case, the time horizon for saving and investing is closer to four or five years. Clearly, the 18-year horizon allows a longer compounding period of growth and a greater amount of risk tolerance than does the shorter time horizon.

Even individuals and couples without children, or those whose children choose not to attend college, still need to plan for retirement. Today's Social Security system will not provide enough income for most individuals to maintain their lifestyle during retirement. Today, the burden of funding one's retirement income falls mainly upon the individual. As people become more knowledgeable about financial planning, they are beginning to save for retirement earlier. Someone who is 25 years old has forty years to save for retirement, assuming retirement begins at age 65. Others will not begin to save until much later, but will still have a long-term investment time horizon since the average person will spend ten to twenty years in retirement.

In each of these cases, accomplishing the specific financial planning goal requires that the individual save and invest funds for a certain period. However, since the time horizon of each goal is different, the ability to tolerate fluctuation in the value of the invested assets is also different. Obviously, there is more tolerance for fluctuation when planning for retirement than when saving for a down payment on a home. Although each of these financial planning goals may be different and have a different time horizon, in most cases, investors will have basic, common investment goals.

Common Investment Goals

In addition to the financial planning goals mentioned above, it is probably fair to say that all investors, both individuals and institutions, are concerned about the more fundamental investment goals of capital accumulation, capital preservation, maximizing returns, and minimizing risk. While these goals seem, and are, contradictory in nature, they are fundamental elements that must be addressed by every investor.

Capital Accumulation

Accumulation of capital is the reason for investment. Without a need to accumulate capital, there would be no reason to invest.

Preservation of Capital

Preservation of capital is one of the most basic investment objectives. Investors are generally willing to take some degree of risk with the idea that they will be increasing their wealth. Capital preservation provides inflation protection for accumulated wealth with minimal risk.

Maximizing Returns

Maximizing returns is another goal for which investors strive. However, since risk and return are related, it is unlikely that one can maximize returns, and simultaneously preserve capital and reduce risk.

Minimizing Risk

Minimizing risk is the fourth basic objective of most investors. Investors are often willing to accept risk, but complain in the event of the first downturn in the market value of their investments. Therefore, the planner must be able to assist the investor in balancing these four somewhat contradictory goals and help the investor achieve his or her specific goals.

BUDGETING

Unless a client is already financially secure, a key element in achieving his financial goals will be the ability to save money from the current budget. Those who cannot live within their current budget will be hard pressed to achieve their financial goals. Many people spend more money than they earn. Often their credit cards have large balances and worse, they are paying interest rates as high as 21 percent. Purchases with short-term credit, such as with credit cards, should generally be limited to an amount that can be easily paid off each month.

The purpose of budgeting is to manage the amount of income and expenses on a monthly basis. Income for most people is reasonably fixed in the short term. That is, most people have a salary with which they can anticipate a certain fixed amount of income each month. Expenses may vary widely throughout the year. For example, some items are paid monthly, such as utilities, mortgage payments, and phone bills, while other items are paid semiannually, such as automobile insurance. In addition, certain expenses are necessities, such as mortgage payments, groceries, and utilities, while other expenses are discretionary, such as dining out or purchasing new clothes. Having determined which expenses are necessary every month and which expenses are discretionary, one can then begin to find ways to reduce expenses and increase savings. For those who live on a relatively fixed salary, the only way to increase savings is to ultimately reduce expenditures.

Methods of Increasing Savings

Reducing expenditures, especially discretionary expenditures, is an excellent way to increase savings for investment. One way to accomplish this is a savings method called "pay yourself first." Paying yourself first means that the first bill paid every pay period is what the investor owes to his or her savings. With savings set aside, the investor must then live within the reduced budget. This method of savings is very effective for those people without much savings discipline because it can be accomplished automatically. For instance, mutual funds accounts can be set up to automatically draft a certain amount of savings from the primary checking account every month or each pay period. Paying yourself first assures saving on a regular basis and promotes living within budget.

Exhibit 12.1 below illustrates the calculation by the Bureau of Economic Analysis for personal savings as a percentage of disposable personal income for the years 1929 – 2004. Notice the dramatic decrease in the savings rate over the last decade.

EXHIBIT 12.1: NATIONAL SAVINGS RATE

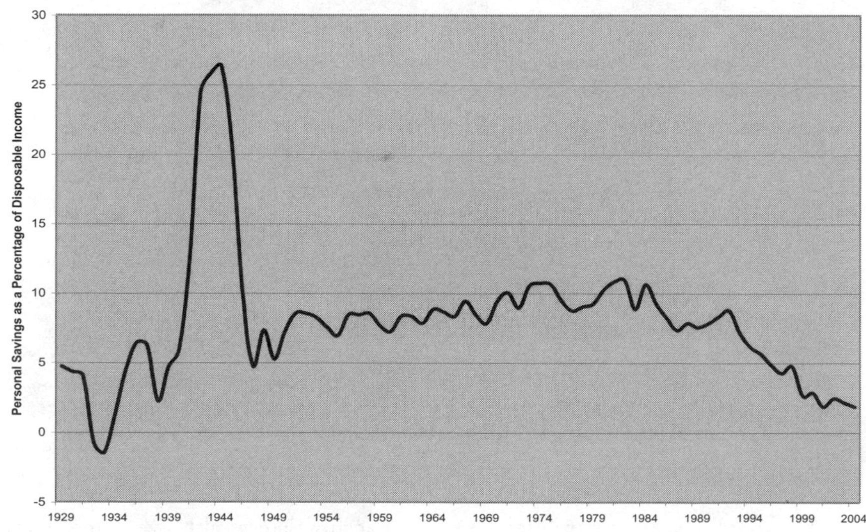
Personal Savings as a Percentage of Disposable Income
30
25
20
15
10
5
0
-5
1929 1934 1939 1944 1949 1954 1959 1964 1969 1974 1979 1984 1989 1994 1999 2004

Another method to increase savings over time is to allocate a portion of future raises to savings. As increases in salary occur, increases in savings should also occur. If an investor was able to live on $4,000 last month and received a ten percent raise, the investor should be able to live on less than $4,400 next month and can allocate up to $400 of the raise to savings.

Elective savings programs, such as 401(k) plans (cash or deferred arrangements) are another excellent method of increasing savings and net worth. These plans not only facilitate automatic savings in the form of payroll deduction, they also increase the current budget by saving on a pre-tax basis instead of on an after-tax basis. Most of the time, salary deferrals are accompanied by employer-matching contributions. These employer contributions are like "free money," and individuals should take full advantage of these contributions. A 401(k) plan can facilitate both the "paying yourself first" and the "allocating raises" methods of increasing savings.

Dividend reinvestment plans (DRIPs) allow individuals to accumulate wealth over time by reinvesting dividends back into their equity holdings. DRIPs have traditionally been programs established by corporations to allow their shareholders to purchase additional shares without the need of a broker and to automatically reinvest dividend payments. These programs can provide cost efficient investing for the average investor.

EXAMPLE

Probably the most important step in achieving financial goals is to begin today. Time is a great asset in achieving financial planning objectives. In the area of investing, time is crucial to success. For example, a 25-year-old saving $2,000 per year for ten years will accumulate more by age 65 than a 35-year-old saving $2,000 for 30 years. Although the younger investor invested only one-third of the amount of the older investor, the younger investor has more assets at age 65. How can this be? The simple answer is time. The 25-year-old investor had the advantage of time. Exhibit 12.2 demonstrates this concept at three earnings rates.

EXHIBIT 12.2: TIME/SAVINGS EXAMPLE (ACCUMULATION AT AGE 65)

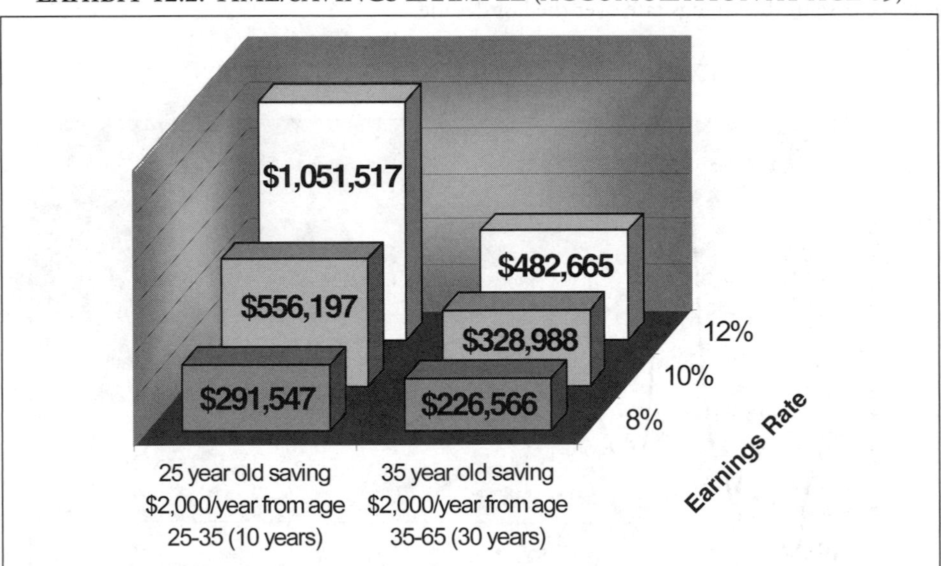
$1,051,517
$556,197
$291,547
$482,665
$328,988
$226,566
12%
10%
8%
Earnings Rate
25 year old saving $2,000/year from age 25-35 (10 years)
35 year old saving $2,000/year from age 35-65 (30 years)

Each of these methods can be an effective way to accumulate wealth over time. However, all investors are subject to factors outside their control that may negatively affect the accomplishment of their financial goals. These factors, known as investment risks, are discussed next.

INVESTMENT RISKS

Individuals, corporations, and institutions all invest to grow wealth. The investor's returns, however, are indeterminable at the inception of the investment due to uncertainty. This uncertainty is risk, and it can mean different things to different investors. Risk can be thought of as the uncertainty of future outcomes, or risk might be defined as the probability of an adverse result. In either case, investors expect higher returns when they accept higher levels of uncertainty or risk. This concept is fundamental to the topic of investments.

Investors must choose to accept a certain level of risk. Some investors think that they can completely avoid all risk; however, certain risks influence all securities, such as the risk of inflation and fluctuations in interest rates. Even the most conservative investors, who invest in the least risky fixed-income securities, are subject to purchasing power risk (inflation) and interest rate risk (changes in interest rates). Other types of risk may only affect a single security, industry, or country. Based on these differences, there are two broad categories of risk: systematic risks and unsystematic risks. Exhibit 12.3 summarizes the types of risks under each category.

EXHIBIT 12.3: SYSTEMATIC AND UNSYSTEMATIC RISKS

SYSTEMATIC RISKS	UNSYSTEMATIC RISKS
• Purchasing Power Risk	• Business Risk
• Reinvestment Rate Risk	• Financial Risk
• Interest Rate Risk	• Default Risk
• Market Risk	• Country Risk
• Foreign Currency Risk	• Regulation Risk

SYSTEMATIC RISKS

Systematic risks are those risks impacted by broad macroeconomic factors that influence all securities. These risks include market risk, interest rate risk, purchasing power risk, foreign currency risk, and reinvestment risk. Diversification cannot eliminate all systematic risk because at least one of these factors affects every security.

systematic risks - investment risks impacted by broad macroeconomic factors that influence all securities

Purchasing Power Risk

The risk that inflation will erode the real value of the investor's assets is **purchasing power risk.** As the price of goods increases, the purchasing power of assets decreases. The objective of investment planning is to generate returns in excess of inflation so that the real value of assets does not erode. Unexpected inflation is the main cause of purchasing power risk. Bonds held to maturity are likely to suffer from purchasing power risk because maturity value and coupon payments remain constant regardless of price changes.

purchasing power risk - a systematic risk where inflation will erode the real value of the investor's assets

Reinvestment Risk

Reinvestment risk is the risk that earnings (cash flows) distributed from current investments cannot be reinvested at a rate of return equal to the expected yield of the current investments. For example, if a bond is purchased today to yield 8 percent and the market interest rate subsequently declines, interest payments from the bond cannot be reinvested at 8 percent; thus, the overall yield to maturity will decline. Zero-coupon bonds, bonds that do not make regular periodic interest payments, are not subject to reinvestment rate risk during the term of the bond because payments are not made to the investor until maturity.

reinvestment risk - a systematic risk where earnings (cash flows) distributed from current investments cannot be reinvested at a rate of return equal to the expected yield of the current investments

Interest Rate Risk

interest rate risk - a systematic risk where changes in interest rates will affect the value of securities

market risk - a systematic risk where securities tend to move with the market

foreign currency risk - a systematic risk due to the potential change in the relationship between the value of the dollar (or investor's currency) and the value of the foreign currency during the period of investment; also known as exchange rate risk

The risk that changes in interest rates will affect the value of securities is known as **interest rate risk**. There exists an inverse relationship between the value of fixed investments and changes in interest rates—as interest rates increase, the value of bonds declines. Rising interest rates generally have a negative effect on stocks as well. Reasons for this negative pressure include the increased discount rate utilized for valuation of cash flows, increased borrowing costs for corporations (thus, an expectancy of lower earnings), and increased yields on alternative investments, such as bonds.

Market Risk

The tendency for securities to move with the market is **market risk**. When the market is rising, stocks have a tendency to increase in value. Conversely, most stocks tend to fall with declines in the market. Often, a move in the market is prefaced by some change in the economic environment. (About 85 percent of stocks are positively correlated to some degree with the market).

Foreign Currency Risk (or Exchange Rate Risk)

Foreign currency risk is the risk that a change in the relationship between the value of the dollar (or investor's currency) and the value of the foreign currency will occur during the period the investment is held. The risk affects investments in foreign stocks and bonds as well as domestic corporations who export products or import factors of production.

EXAMPLE

John invests $1,000,000 in the Orval Corporation based in Mexico. If the conversion rate for pesos to dollars is ten to one, John would have to invest 10 million pesos in Orval Corporation. Orval Corporation does extremely well, and John is able to sell his interest for 15 million pesos. If John attempts to convert the pesos into dollars when the exchange rate has changed to 12 to 1, he will receive $1,250,000 (15,000,000 ÷ 12).

This gain is comprised of a 50 percent (5,000,000 pesos) gain on the investment and a loss of 16.67 percent ([10 pesos / $ ÷ 12 pesos / $] – 1) or $250,000 from the change in the currency rate. The net result is a 25 percent gain on the original investment; however, it is only half of the gain generated from the appreciation of Orval Corporation.

EXAMPLE

Assume the same facts as in the previous example except that the exchange rate is now 8 to 1 instead of 12 to 1. In this case, John liquidates his interest in Orval Corporation and converts the pesos to $1,875,000. This $875,000 gain consists of $500,000 from the appreciation of Orval Corporation and $375,000 from the devaluation of the dollar relative to the peso.

In the first example, John's gain decreases by 50 percent, and in the second example, John's gain increases by 75 percent. Money managers often attempt to avoid such drastic changes in gains and losses by hedging against currency fluctuations. Forward or futures contracts are often used as hedging devices against currency risk.

UNSYSTEMATIC RISKS

Unsystematic risks are those risks that are unique to a single security, company, industry, or country. These risks include default risk, business risk, financial risk, and country risk. Unlike systematic risk, these risks can be eliminated through diversification. Several studies have found that unsystematic risk declines significantly with a portfolio consisting of as few as ten randomly chosen stocks. As more stocks are added to a portfolio, the less impact the losses of one company in the portfolio will have on the total performance of the portfolio of securities. This concept is illustrated in the example below.

unsystematic risks - types of investment risks unique to a single company, industry, or country that can be eliminated by portfolio diversification

EXHIBIT 12.4: TOTAL PORTFOLIO RISK

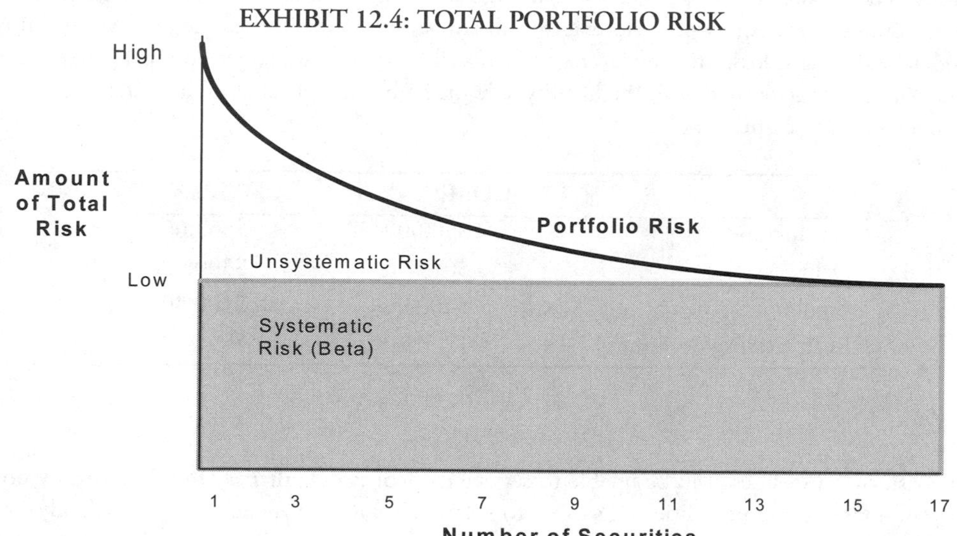
High
Amount of Total Risk
Portfolio Risk
Unsystematic Risk
Low
Systematic Risk (Beta)
1
3
5
7
9
11
13
15
17
Number of Securities

The figure above illustrates the concept of diversification. As more securities are added to the portfolio, the overall risk of the portfolio declines. There are several other points of interest. First, unsystematic risk can be reduced and effectively eliminated. This is not the case for systematic risk. Systematic risk cannot be eliminated because it represents the risk to all securities. Systematic risk is generally measured by beta, whereas total risk is measured by standard deviation. For portfolios that have significantly reduced unsystematic risk, beta is a good measure of total risk. However, when unsystematic risk is not reduced, beta does a poor job of estimating total risk.

Business Risk

Business risk, or the level of risk of the specific business, includes the speculative nature of the business, the management of the business, the philosophy of the business, and so on. Different types of businesses will have different levels of risk. For instance, searching for gold would generally be riskier than operating a grocery store. However, each has unique risks associated with that type of business. Business risk can also be thought of as the uncertainty of operating income. Utility companies have relatively stable and predictable income streams and, therefore, have lower business risk. Since cyclical companies, such as auto manufacturers, have unsteady or fluctuating operating income levels, they have higher business risk. Business risk relates to the activities of the company.

business risk - an unsystematic risk based on predictability of operating income for a specific business; dependent upon management and industry characteristics

financial risk - an unsystematic risk based on the inclusion of debt in the capital structure of a firm which affects the return on equity (ROE) for a company

Financial Risk

Financial risk is based on the capital structure of a firm. Firms with debt in their capital structures have financial risk. Financial risk is the additional risk that shareholders bear because of the decision to finance some of the firm's assets with debt. The use of debt magnifies the return on equity (ROE) and makes gains and losses more volatile.

EXAMPLE

For example, a firm that is financed with 75 percent debt (25 percent equity) will have an ROE four times larger than a similar firm with the same net income and financed 100 percent with equity. This financial leverage occurs because the return is based on a smaller amount of equity. In this example, the equity of the leveraged company is one-fourth that of the nonleveraged firm, so that returns and losses for the leveraged firm will be four times larger on a percentage basis. Financial risk is associated with the liability side of the balance sheet since it relates to the debt ratio a company maintains.

	COMPANY A	COMPANY B
Net Income	$50,000	$50,000
Debt	$0	$300,000
Equity	$400,000	$100,000
ROE (Return on Equity)	12.5%	50%

Default Risk

default risk - an unsystematic risk where a business will be unable to service its debt

The risk that a business will be unable to service its debt is **default risk**. Bonds issued by both corporations and municipalities are subject to default risk. Rating agencies, such as Moody's and Standard & Poor's, rate bonds issued by corporations and municipalities from the highest grade to default. Obligations of the U.S. Government (Treasuries and Ginnie Maes) are considered free from default risk. In addition, equity investments are not subject to default risk.

Country (or Regulation) Risk

country (or regulation) risk - an unsystematic risk where changes in a country's laws or political situation will have an adverse effect on an investment

International investments are subject to **country risk**, which is the unique risk associated with each country. These risks include political and economic risks. The United States is generally thought to have the lowest country risk, since its political and economic systems are the most stable. An investor is able to minimize country risk by investing in several countries instead of just a few.

RISK AND RETURN

There is a direct relationship between risk and expected return. As the level of risk increases, the expected return increases. Meanwhile, as the level of risk declines, the expected return declines. Thus, to receive higher returns, an investor must accept the trade-off of greater risk and typically more volatile returns. As mentioned previously, this concept of risk and return is essential to the theories within investments and is important when planning for the financial well-being of clients.

Liquidity and Marketability

Liquidity is the ability to sell an investment quickly and at a competitive price, with no loss of principal and little price concession. Liquidity is a risk that investors must face. If the security markets do not have sufficient liquidity to absorb a trade, then the trader may find that a price concession is necessary to execute the trade. **Marketability** refers to the ability of an investor to find a ready market where the investor may sell his or her investment. There is a subtle difference between liquidity and marketability. For instance, real estate is marketable but may not be liquid. Treasury bills are both liquid and marketable. Liquidity and marketability should be thought of as a spectrum with cash being the most liquid and the most marketable.

liquidity - the ability to sell an investment quickly and at a competitive price, with no loss of principal and little price concession

marketability - the ability of an investor to find a ready market where the investor may sell his or her investment

INVESTMENT CHOICES

The level of risk and the specific risks an investor must face greatly influence the investor's choice of investments. Investors today have a wide variety of investment options, ranging from interest-bearing checking accounts to sophisticated derivatives. Although investments can be extremely complicated and risky, as in the case of derivatives, investments generally fall within one of two categories: lending investments or ownership investments.

Lending Investments

Savings accounts and bonds are both examples of lending investments. When cash is deposited into a savings account, it is as if the owner has loaned money to the bank. The bank, which will lend money to others in the form of a mortgage or some other loan, will in return pay the owner interest, which is the payment for the use of the money. Interest can be paid based on a fixed rate, or it can vary based on some agreed upon variable-rate benchmark, such as the 91-day Treasury bill rate.

Bonds are more structured investments than savings accounts. For example, bonds have specific maturity dates, specified face values, and defined interest (coupon) payments. While a savings account is, in effect, an indefinite loan, bonds have a specific maturity date. This date is the time at which the borrower (bond issuer) must repay the loan. The maturity of a bond can range from a few months, as with a 91-day Treasury bill, to thirty years or more.

Bonds generally have a standard, or par, value (face value) of $1,000. Therefore, to invest $10,000, a purchase of ten bonds trading at par would be made. Bond issuers compensate the lender (bondholder) by making specified interest payments. These interest payments, generally paid semiannually (twice per year), are based on a rate of interest called the coupon rate. For example, a bond with a stated coupon rate of 10 percent will pay interest of $50 ($1,000 × 10 percent × ½) twice each year for a total of $100 per year. These coupon payments, which are really the payment by the lender for the use of the money, continue over the life of the bond. Therefore, a thirty-year bond will generally make sixty coupon payments. At the time the bond matures, the investor will also receive the par (face) value of the bond (generally $1,000). This payment is the repayment of the original loan proceeds.

Bonds provide investors with a certain level of security since they generally make regular, specified payments to the bondholders. Many investors, especially retired individuals, rely on these coupon payments as a source of income. Although bonds provide some certainty, there are risks inherent in investing in bonds. Two of the more important risks are default risk and interest rate risk.

Default Risk

Because bonds are essentially loans to an organization or corporation, bond investors must be concerned with the ability of the organization to repay the proceeds of the loan. The risk that an institution or government will fail to repay its loan is called credit risk or default risk. Default risk is an unsystematic risk that can be either diversified or eliminated. Diversifying default risk is accomplished by investing in several bond issues instead of a single issue. This strategy reduces the potential exposure to any one of the borrowers (issuers). Default risk can be eliminated by purchasing bonds that are direct obligations of the United States government. U.S. Treasuries are default risk-free and are, therefore, a good choice for those investors concerned about default risk. However, the basic principle of risk and return still holds: as default risk is reduced for a bond, so is the related return. Investors will require higher investment returns from investments that have higher default risk.

Interest Rate Risk

Even if credit risk were eliminated, as in the case of U.S. Treasuries, bonds are still impacted in several ways by fluctuations in interest rates. Changes in interest rates influence both the current market price of the bond, and the value of the reinvested coupon payments. As interest rates increase, the current value and price of outstanding bonds should decline. This decline results because bonds, which are a series of cash flows, must be reevaluated or repriced in accordance with the new market rate of interest.

If an increase in interest rates results in a decline in the value of a bond, how would the reinvested coupon payments be impacted? If an investor was reinvesting the cash flow from the coupon payments that were received from the bond, then these coupon payments could be reinvested to earn higher rates of return. Thus, when interest rates increase, there is a decline in the value of a bond, but an increase in the value of the reinvested cash flows from the coupon payments.

Ownership Investments in Business (Common and Preferred Stock)

Ownership investments take the form of common or preferred stock. Common stockholders accept the risks inherent in owning a company. While bondholders have a right to be repaid funds that were loaned, common stockholders have invested in the potential future profitability of the business. If the company is successful, then the value of the common stock will increase. If the company is unsuccessful, then the value of the common stock will decline. Investors in common stock are rewarded for accepting risk in two ways. The first is through appreciation in the value of the stock. The second is from earnings that are paid to the shareholders in the form of dividends. A dividend is a payment made by the corporation to the shareholders as their share of the profits of the corporation.

There is more risk for common stockholders than for bondholders since, in the event of bankruptcy, bondholders are paid before stockholders. Investors require higher returns for common stock to compensate them for the increased risks associated with owning equity securities. In addition, equities tend to have more price volatility than bonds.

Preferred stock has characteristics of both bonds and common stock. Like bonds, preferred stock generally pays a fixed payment, called a preferred stock dividend, which is determined as a percentage of the par value of the preferred stock. Preferred stock is valued similarly to bonds and is subject to many of the same risks as bonds. Many preferred stocks have mandatory redemption dates that occur thirty years or more after issuance; however, bonds typically mature within thirty years. Some preferred stocks have no redemption features, similar to common stocks, and continue for the life of the company unless retired.

Ownership Investments in Real Estate

Real estate is another type of ownership asset. Real estate is clearly a valuable asset to investors. In fact, a personal residence is often the largest asset owned by an individual. Stocks, bonds, money market securities, and derivatives are all intangible financial assets while real estate is a tangible asset. Real estate differs from financial assets due to the following attributes:

- Each parcel of land or real estate is unique in its location and composition.
- Real estate is immovable.
- Real estate is virtually indestructible.
- There is a limited supply of real estate.

An investor can make an investment in a variety of real estate, including residential real estate, commercial real estate, partnerships and limited partnerships, developed land, undeveloped land, and real estate investment trusts (REITs). Most real estate investments have the following advantages:

Cash Flow

Generally, real estate investments generate a generous amount of cash flow through rents. Some real estate investments, however, like undeveloped land, may not have this advantage.

Depreciation Deductions

Many real estate investments have deductions for depreciation that can offset taxable income from the investment and from other sources. In many cases, real estate investments can generate positive cash flow without having taxable income. In some cases, taxable losses are generated along with positive cash flow. These taxable losses are due to the deductibility of depreciation. However, the Tax Reform Act of 1986 limited this advantage with the creation of the passive activity loss rules.

Low Correlation to Other Asset Classes

As will be discussed in the portfolio theory section, it is often advantageous to add asset classes that have a low correlation to equities and fixed-income securities to portfolios to reduce the overall risk of the portfolio. Real estate has a low correlation of returns to common stock, preferred stock, and bonds.

Derivatives

Investors have become increasingly aware of the concept of derivatives in recent years. Much of this awareness is due to the devastating financial results that derivatives have had on certain organizations. These disastrous outcomes have generally been due to mismanagement of derivatives within the organizations. When derivatives are used properly, however, they can provide investors with an investment tool that can create many benefits, including the reduction of risk.

derivatives - securities whose value is based on the value of some other security or proxy

Derivatives are securities whose value is based on the value of some other security or proxy. For example, an IBM option contract will derive its value from the value of IBM stock. Changes in the value of IBM stock will cause the associated option contract to also change in value. This text's discussion of derivatives will be limited to options contracts and futures contracts.

Options Contracts

options - derivatives that give the holder or buyer the right to do something

Options are derivatives that give the holder or buyer the right to do something. **Call options** give the holder the right to purchase the underlying asset, generally stock, at a specified price within a specified period.

EXAMPLE

call options - a derivative that gives the holder the right to purchase the underlying asset, generally stock, at a specified price within a specified period of time

For example, assume Brooke wants to purchase ABC Company stock, which is currently trading at $50 per share. She expects the company to greatly increase in value over the next couple of months. However, she does not have enough cash to purchase the security today, but will have the funds in three months when she receives her partnership distribution. Brooke could purchase a call option on ABC stock that would give her the right to purchase the stock in three months for $50 per share.

put option - a derivative that gives the holder the right to sell the underlying asset, generally stock, at a specified price within a specified period

Put options give the holder the right to sell the underlying asset, generally stock, at a specified price within a specified period. Options can either be purchased or sold (also referred to as written). Therefore, there are four unique positions that an investor could take with an option: to purchase a call option, to sell (write) a call option, to purchase a put option, or to sell (write) a put option. However, investors will often combine multiple options positions or combine an option position with a stock position to create different risk-return characteristics.

exercise price - the price at which an underlying stock will either be sold (put) or purchased (call) by the holder of an option

premium - the cost of an option contract

The **exercise price** of an option contract is the price at which the underlying stock will either be sold (put) or purchased (call) by the holder of the option. The **premium** for any option is simply the cost of the option contract. The premium is generally impacted by the following factors: price of the underlying security, the exercise price of the underlying security, the time until the option expires, the volatility of the underlying security, and the risk-free rate.

What are the reasons that an investor might enter into an option contract? As with most derivatives, options can be used for specific purposes or simply as a leveraged investment. Investors who believe that the underlying security is going to appreciate may purchase call options. Investors will generally sell (write) call options when they believe that the underlying security is going to either remain flat or decline in value. Often, when an investor is holding a long position in a stock that

as appreciated rapidly within a short period, the investor will sell (write) a call option to generte the premium for additional income. As long as the stock does not continue to appreciate, the nvestor will have enhanced his return by the amount of the call option premium.

ut options are generally purchased to establish a floor or protect against a decline in the value of long position in a stock. For example, an investor might own Microsoft and be concerned that he stock is overvalued. In such a case, the investor might purchase a put option at a level slightly elow the current market price. In the event that the stock decreased in value, the investor could ell the stock at the put exercise price. In other words, the put provides downside protection ecause it establishes the minimum price at which the investor will be able to sell the Microsoft tock.

ut options can be sold (written) by an investor to generate an option premium for a stock that he investor believes will increase in price and that he may own or wish to own. If the investor is orrect and the stock does increase, then the investor will receive the option premium as income. n the event that the stock should go down and someone "puts" the stock to the investor (forces he investor to purchase the stock), the investor probably would still believe that the stock was a ood purchase and a good stock to own.

utures Contracts

Jnlike options, which give the holder a *right* to purchase or sell a specific security, a **futures contract** is an agreement to do something in the future. Generally, purchasing (selling) a futures ontract obligates the buyer (seller) to take delivery (make delivery) of a specific commodity at a pecific time in the future. Since a futures contract is an agreement to make or take delivery in he future, the investor will be required to put up a good faith deposit until the agreement is fulilled, known as an initial margin.

futures contract - an agreement to do something in the future—generally, purchasing/selling a futures contract obligates the buyer to take delivery/make delivery of a specific commodity at a specific time in the future

)ver time, the futures contract, which is required to be marked-to-market on a daily basis, will enerate gains and losses. Each of these daily gains and losses will either add to or reduce the inial margin. If the initial amount put up is reduced to a level below the maintenance margin, the nvestor will be required to restore the initial margin. Both the initial margin percentage and the naintenance margin amount are set at the inception of the contract.

peculators and hedgers use futures contracts for different reasons. Speculators use futures conracts as a leveraged investment. Government studies have suggested that approximately 90 perent of individual investors who speculate in futures lose money. The majority of these investors nvest in futures contracts only once. Unlike speculators, hedgers use futures contracts to reduce r offset certain risks.

or example, farmers who sell commodities, such as cotton, are concerned about decreasing comnodity prices. To offset this risk, farmers can sell futures contracts to ensure that the cotton prouced sells at a specific price. This type of hedge, referred to as a short hedge, protects against ecreasing prices.

)ther investors who hedge using futures contracts include manufacturers who use commodities s raw material. For example, if a furniture manufacturer was concerned about rising lumber rices, the manufacturer might purchase lumber futures contracts to lock in the price at which to buy lumber in the future. This type of hedge, referred to as a long hedge, protects against rising prices. The following table summarizes the two types of hedge positions.

Hedger	Cash Position	Hedge Needed	Action
Grower	Long	Short	Sell futures contracts
Manufacturer	Short	Long	Buy futures contracts

In general, derivatives provide investors with a variety of speculative and hedging strategies that would not be available using traditional investment alternatives and allows for a more complete market.

DIRECT VS. INDIRECT INVESTING

direct investing - a process of investing where investors purchase actual securities

indirect investing - a process of investing where investors invest in companies that invest directly

Investing in bonds or stocks can be accomplished by purchasing the actual securities or by investing in companies that purchase actual securities. **Direct investing** occurs when investors purchase actual securities. For example, an investor who purchased an IBM corporate bond or the common stock of Microsoft would be investing directly. Direct investing can be accomplished by investing through a brokerage account or some other source, such as a Dividend Reinvestment Plan (DRIP).

Indirect investing is a process of investing in securities like mutual funds, that invest directly. Mutual funds are companies that invest in stocks, bonds, and other securities.

Over the last 20 years, indirect investing has gained in popularity. In fact, there are currently more investment companies (mutual funds) than there are listed securities. Investment companies or mutual funds provide a variety of benefits to shareholders, including ease of access, diversification, professional management, and investor services.

HISTORICAL PERFORMANCE

All assets do not have the same historical investment returns. Exhibit 12.5 provides the historical investment returns, inflation-adjusted returns, and the standard deviation of various asset classes.

EXHIBIT 12.5: AVERAGE HISTORICAL RETURNS, INFLATION-ADJUSTED RETURNS, AND STANDARD DEVIATION OF ASSET CLASSES (1932 - 2001)

ASSET CLASS	HISTORICAL RETURNS	INFLATION-ADJUSTED RETURNS	STANDARD DEVIATION
Small Capitalization Stocks	13	10	30
Large Capitalization Stocks	11	8	20
Fixed-Income Securities	6	3	8
Consumer Price Index (CPI)	3	N/A	4

Exhibit 12.5 illustrates how risk and return are closely related. Small capitalization stocks have had the highest returns among the asset classes, but have also been the most volatile. After

adjusting for inflation, returns on fixed-income securities have been extremely low. Once the effects of taxation are considered, these returns are further reduced. Therefore, it is important to include equity investments in portfolios to provide for real after-tax growth, instead of relying solely on fixed-income securities.

MEASURES OF RISK

We defined risk earlier in the chapter as the probability of an adverse outcome. In the field of investments and financial planning, risk is generally measured in terms of volatility. Clients are very concerned about fluctuations in their portfolio. As was the case in the years 2000 through 2002, the markets can be extremely volatile. These market moves cause investors' portfolios to significantly change in value without significant changes in the economy. As previously discussed, the two common measures of risk, from the standpoint of volatility, are beta and standard deviation. Semivariance is a third measure of risk that is gaining popularity.

BETA

Beta is a commonly used measure of risk derived from regression analysis. It is a measure of systematic risk and provides an indication of the volatility of a portfolio compared to the market. The market is defined as having a beta of 1.0. Portfolios with a beta greater than 1.0 are more volatile than the market, while portfolios with a beta less than 1.0 are less volatile than the market. A portfolio with a beta of 1.5 is considered to be 50 percent more volatile than the market. Similarly, a portfolio with a beta of 0.7 is considered to be 30 percent less volatile than the market.

beta - a commonly used measure of systematic risk that is derived from regression analysis

Since beta measures systematic risk, it is a good measure of risk for fully diversified portfolios. Diversified portfolios have minimal unsystematic risk, which means that beta is capturing the majority of the risk of the portfolio. However, when the diversification of the portfolio is low and the portfolio has a substantial amount of unsystematic risk, then beta does not capture all of the volatility within the portfolio. Beta is more appropriate for portfolios and mutual funds that are well-diversified and, therefore, highly correlated to the market.

STANDARD DEVIATION

Unlike beta, **standard deviation** measures total volatility of the portfolio and total risk (that is systematic and unsystematic risk) of the portfolio. Standard deviation is a statistical measure of how far actual returns deviate from the mean return. Although there have been many articles on the limitations of standard deviation, it remains one of the most prominent and vital measures of risk used by investment practitioners.

standard deviation - measures a portfolio's total volatility and its total risk (that is, systematic and unsystematic risk)

SEMIVARIANCE

Semivariance is another statistical measure of risk. However, it differs from standard deviation in that semivariance only considers the downside risk of an investment. Specifically, semivariance measures the variability of returns that fall below the average or expected return.

Critics of standard deviation state that investors do not complain, nor are concerned, about volatility above the average return. Rather, investors are only concerned about volatility below the average return. Therefore, a portfolio manager with a large standard deviation may be punished for having superior positive returns. Semivariance attempts to correct for this perceived flaw by only considering returns and volatility below the expected or average return.

MEASURES OF RETURN

There are a variety of measures of return, including holding period return, arithmetic mean, geometric mean, internal rate of return, and real rate of return. Each of these calculations of return has certain advantages and disadvantages. Each measure of return is discussed below:

HOLDING PERIOD RETURN

holding period return - measures the total return an investor receives over a specific time period

The **holding period return** (HPR) measures the total return an investor receives from an investment over a specific time period. It is written as:

$$HPR = \frac{\text{Ending Value of Investment} - \text{Beginning Value of Investment} \ +/- \text{Cash flows}}{\text{Beginning Value of Investment}}$$

EXAMPLE

Assume Glen purchases a stock for \$50 per share and sells it for \$75 and the stock paid dividend of \$10, then the holding period return equals 70 percent as follows:

$$HPR = \frac{\$75 - \$50 + \$10}{\$50} = 70\%$$

Is a 70 percent return a good return? At first, you might think that a 70 percent return is great However, we have no idea how long the investment was held. Therefore, there is no way to compare a HPR to other alternative investments, such as the risk-free rate of return. Because the HPR does not address the time value of money, it is not commonly used as a return measure.

ARITHMETIC MEAN

arithmetic mean- a measure of investment return that is the result of averaging periodic returns

The **arithmetic mean** is a measure of investment return that is the result of averaging periodic returns.

EXAMPLE

Assume a client had the following returns for years 2002 through 2005:

YEAR	RETURN
2002	12%
2003	3%
2004	10%
2005	15%

The arithmetic mean equals 10 percent, calculated as follows:

$$AM = \frac{12\% + 3\% + 10\% + 15\%}{4} = 10\%$$

geometric mean - is a method of calculating the internal rate of return based on periodic rates of return

GEOMETRIC MEAN

The **geometric mean** is a method of calculating the internal rate of return based on periodic rates of return.

EXAMPLE

Assume a client had the following returns for years 2002 through 2005 (same example as above):

YEAR	RETURN
2002	12%
2003	3%
2004	10%
2005	15%

The geometric mean equals 9.91 percent, calculated as follows:

Assume a deposit of $100 at the beginning of 2002.

PV = -100
FV = 100(1+.12)(1+.03)(1+.10)(1+.15) = 145.93
n = 4

Solve for I = 9.91%

Using the same example has resulted in a different outcome for the arithmetic mean and the geometric mean. This difference is a result of the geometric mean taking into consideration the compounding of the investment returns over time, whereas the arithmetic mean does not.

In this case, the geometric mean is less than the arithmetic mean. Will this always be the case? No, but the geometric mean will always be less than or equal to the arithmetic mean. They will be equal only when the periodic returns are identical, such as 10 percent for every year. The difference between the two measures will increase as the volatility in returns increases. The following example illustrates this increase.

EXAMPLE

John invests $100 at the beginning of the year. At the end of the year, his investment is worth $200. At the end of the following year, the investment is worth $100. The returns for the two years are as follows:

YEAR	BEGINNING OF THE YEAR	END OF THE YEAR	RATE OF RETURN
1	$100	$200	100%
2	$200	$100	(50%)

The arithmetic mean equals 25 percent, calculated as follows:

$$AM = \frac{100\% + (50\%)}{2} = 25\%$$

The geometric mean equals 0.00 percent, calculated as follows:

PV = –100
FV = 100
n = 2
i = 0%

Obviously, there is a big difference between a 25 percent return and a 0 percent return. In addition, it should be clear that if you began with $100 and ended up with $100 that your return is zero. Therefore, the arithmetic mean is not as practical for evaluating investment returns as the geometric mean. The difference is even greater when returns are more volatile.

internal rate of return - a measure of return that equates discounted future cash flows to the present value of an asset

INTERNAL RATE OF RETURN

The **internal rate of return** (IRR) is one of the most common measures of return. It equates discounted future cash flows to the present value of an asset. Consider the basic present value model:

$$PV = \frac{CF_1}{(1+k)^1} + \frac{CF_2}{(1+k)^2} + \ldots + \frac{CF_n}{(1+k)^n}, \text{ where}$$

PV = Present value of future cash flows

CF_n = Cash flows for period n

n = Number of cash flows in the analysis

k = Internal rate of return

An important assumption of this model is that any cash flows that occur before the end of the investment will be reinvested at the IRR. If these cash flows are not reinvested at the IRR, then the actual return received by the investor will be different than expected.

EXAMPLE

A bond that is selling for par ($1,000) and has an annual coupon rate of 10 percent (coupon payments of $100) will have an IRR of 10 percent. If the annual coupon payments of $100 are reinvested at a rate of return of 10 percent, then the actual return received by the investor will be 10 percent. However, if the coupon payments are invested at a rate of return less (or greater) than 10 percent, then the actual return the investor receives will be less (or greater) than 10 percent. This is an example of reinvestment risk.

REAL RATE OF RETURN

As discussed earlier in the chapter, inflation erodes returns and the purchasing power of assets. Therefore, it is important to understand both nominal returns as well as real returns. The **nominal return** is the stated return from the investment. The **real rate of return** is the nominal return adjusted for inflation.

nominal return - the stated return from an investment

real rate of return - the nominal return adjusted for inflation

The formula for the real return as we saw in the chapter on education funding is as follows:

$$\text{Real return} = \frac{(1 + R_n)}{(1 + I)} - 1, \text{ where}$$

R_n = Nominal rate of return

I = Rate of inflation

MODERN PORTFOLIO THEORY

Just about everyone is familiar with the saying, "Don't put all your eggs in one basket." The interpretation of this saying is that it is safer to spread your risk around than to concentrate it in one area. The same concept applies to investing. Investors diversify risk by investing in more than one security or more than one asset class. Through diversification, investors are able to reduce the risk to their investment portfolios.

The reason diversification works is that unsystematic risks to which a security is subject, can be minimized by adding additional securities to the portfolio. Similarly, adding additional asset classes to a portfolio can minimize or reduce the unique risks to which an asset class is subject.

Modern portfolio theory (MPT) is the concept that describes this diversification process among asset classes. Harry Markowitz, considered the father of modern portfolio theory, was responsible for the development of MPT and received the Nobel Prize in economics in 1990 for his work.

Modern Portfolio Theory (MPT) - theory created by Harry Markowitz that describes portfolio diversification gained by combining securities with varying characteristics

Markowitz found that by combining different asset classes and varying the weightings of each asset class, he could create portfolios that had higher returns with less portfolio volatility (risk). Markowitz uses standard deviation as a measure of risk. The portfolios that had the highest expected return for the given level of risk he called "efficient portfolios." By combining these efficient portfolios, he created the **efficient frontier**. The following figure is a graphical representation of the efficient frontier.

efficient frontier - consists of investment portfolios with the highest expected return for a given level of risk

EXHIBIT 12.6: THE EFFICIENT FRONTIER

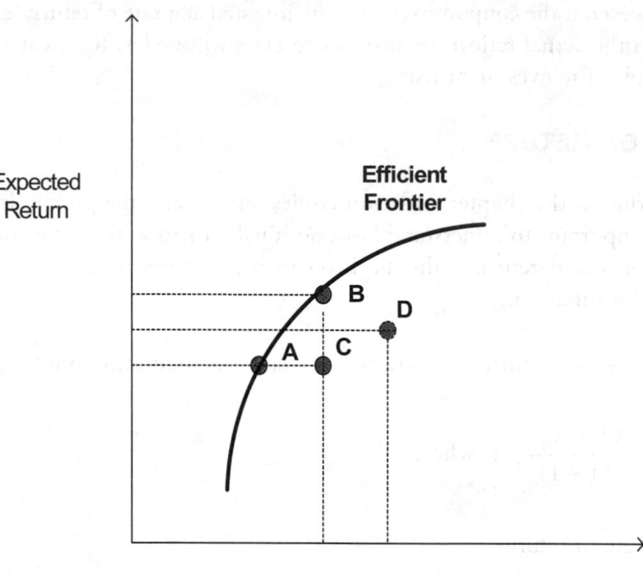
Expected Return
Efficient Frontier
B
D
A
C
Risk

The efficient frontier consists of portfolios with the highest expected return for a given level of risk. Notice in Exhibit 12.6 above that portfolios A and B are efficient portfolios. Portfolios C and D are not. Portfolio A is more efficient than Portfolio C because it has the same expected return with less risk. Portfolio B is more efficient than Portfolio C because it has a much higher expected return for the same level of risk. Portfolio B is also more efficient than Portfolio D because B has a higher expected return and less risk. Markowitz came up with the following three rules for choosing efficient portfolios:

Markowitz's Three Rules:

1. Same return, choose lower risk.
2. Same risk, choose higher return.
3. Choose higher return with lower

- For any two portfolios with the same expected return, choose the one with the lower risk.
- For any two portfolios with the same risk, choose the one with the higher expected return.
- Choose any portfolio that has a higher expected return and lower risk.

Portfolios, such as Portfolios C and D above, are considered inefficient, since they have not maximized the return for a given level of risk. Portfolios do not exist above the efficient frontier since the efficient frontier consists of the most efficient portfolios (portfolios of assets with the <u>highest</u> expected return for a given level of risk).

Markowitz developed a model to estimate the efficient frontier by using security standard deviations, correlation coefficients, and expected returns in calculating the standard deviation of a multi-asset portfolio and the expected return of a portfolio.

These calculations are the foundation for most of the asset allocation (mean-variance optimization) software packages used by financial planners. The purpose of these software packages is to build an investment portfolio capable of accomplishing the goals of the client, while matching he level of risk in the portfolio to the investor's tolerance for risk. Most financial planners who provide investment counseling use some type of mean-variance optimization software to determine an optimum portfolio or asset allocation based on a client's goals, risk tolerance, time horizon, tax situation, and economic forecasts.

The goal in using these software packages is to build an efficient portfolio for the client. Remember that an efficient portfolio is one that has the highest level of return (in practice, the return should be an after-tax return) for the given level of risk.

SOFTWARE INPUTS

These software packages generally make use of the following inputs:

ECONOMIC VARIABLES	CLIENT VARIABLES
Asset classes	Risk tolerance
Expected returns for each asset class	Time horizon of goals
Standard deviation of each asset class	Tax bracket
Correlation coefficient of each asset class to every other asset class	

Asset Classes

The asset classes to be included in the analysis are an important starting point for the economic variables. Since there are numerous asset classes to consider, and practitioners often have limited access to some of them, the asset classes to be considered must be designated for the analysis. Exhibit 12.7 is a sample of some of the asset classes that might be included in an analysis.

EXHIBIT 12.7: ASSET CLASSES

Large-cap value	Small/mid-cap core	U.S. Treasury fixed-income
Large-cap core	Small/mid-cap value	U.S. Corporate fixed-income
Large-cap growth	International equity	U.S. Municipal fixed-income
Small/mid-cap growth	Emerging market equity	International fixed-income

Another common reason to limit asset class inclusion is the investment restrictions on certain types of asset pools, such as government funds, retirement plans, and trust assets. Often, these pools are not permitted to invest in certain asset classes, or they may have limitations on the amount of certain securities that are included in the portfolio. As a result, it may be appropriate to exclude these asset classes from the analysis.

Expected Returns

The expected return for each asset class must be included in the analysis to determine which combination of investments produces the highest level of return for the appropriate level of risk for the client. Expected returns can be based on historical data or can be an estimate of what future returns will be. As with most of these variables, different methods of calculating the variable result in a different input. It is the financial planner's responsibility to determine t most appropriate method for determining these variables.

Standard Deviation

The standard deviation for each asset class must be included in the analysis to help determi which combinations of investments produce low portfolio risk. Standard deviation is a measu of dispersion around a mean and is really a method of quantifying the volatility of investment As with expected return, standard deviation is forecasted based on expectations or calculat based on historical data.

Correlation Coefficient

correlation coefficient - a statistical measure of the direction and strength of the relationship between two sets of data. Correlation coefficients close to +1.0 are strongly positively correlated and those close to –1.0 are strongly negatively correlated.

The **correlation coefficient**, generally denoted with the symbol "R," is a statistical measure ge erated from a regression analysis that provides insight into the relationship between two secu ties, two portfolios, or two indexes. The correlation coefficient indicates the direction of t relationship between the two indexes or securities and the strength between the two items. T correlation coefficient ranges between +1.0 and –1.0. At +1.0, there is perfect positive correl tion between the two items. In other words, the two items will move together over time. At 1.0, there is perfect negative correlation between the two items. The two items will move opposite directions over time. At a correlation of zero, there is no relationship between the tw items and they will move independent of each other. Exhibit 12.8 depicts these relationships.

The correlation coefficient is key to the concept of asset allocation. When the correlation coeff cient between two asset classes is less than 1.0, then combining the asset classes will reduce t overall risk of the investment portfolio. The lower the correlation, the lower the standard devi tion of the combined portfolio and, therefore, the lower the risk.

EXHIBIT 12.8: CORRELATION COEFFICIENTS

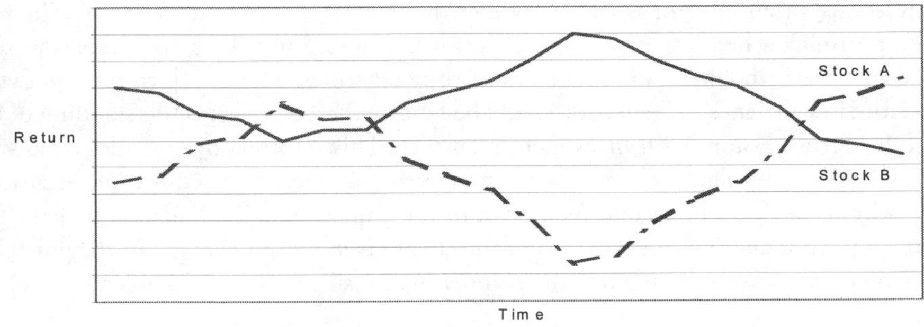
Figure 1: r = -1.0
Stock A
Return
Stock B
Time

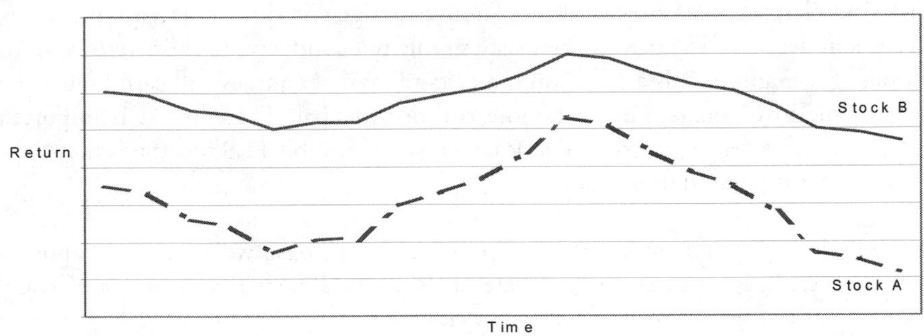
Figure 2: r = 1.0
Stock B
Return
Stock A
Time

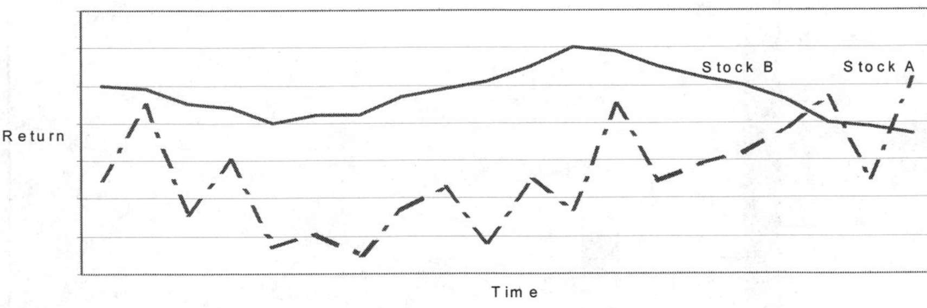
Figure 3: r = 0.0
Stock B
Stock A
Return
Time

Coefficient of Determination

The **coefficient of determination** (R^2) is calculated by squaring the correlation coefficient. The coefficient of determination describes the percentage of variability of returns of an asset that can be explained by changes in the returns of another asset. For example, assume that the correlation coefficient between portfolio X and the S & P 500 Index is 0.95. The coefficient of determination would be $(0.95)^2 = 0.9025$. This means that approximately 90% of the variability of portfolio X is explained by changes in the Index. The remaining 10% of the movement of portfolio X is caused by other variables. If we consider the S & P Index as a measure of the market, then the 10% would be considered unsystematic risk.

coefficient of determination (R^2) - percentage of variability in the dependent variable that is explained by variability in the independent variable

Risk Tolerance

risk tolerance - an estimate of the level of risk an investor is willing to accept in his or her portfolio

The **risk tolerance** of an investor is an estimate of the level of risk that he or she is willing to accept in a portfolio. There are clearly those investors who are unwilling to accept any risk while there are others who invest in only the most risky securities. There are two common ways a planner estimates a client's tolerance for risk. The first method is a clear understanding of the client and the client's history with investment securities. This information provides a basis for determining how comfortable a client is with investments in equities, fixed-income securities and other risky securities. The second method is to use a questionnaire designed to elicit feelings about risky assets and the comfort level of the client given certain changes in the portfolio. These two methods combined can guide the planner in assessing a client's risk tolerance.

Time Horizon

Along with risk tolerance, the time horizon of an investor's goal is vital in determining an appropriate investment decision. Some investments are simply not conducive to short-term investment time horizons. For example, it is a common understanding that equities will earn higher returns than fixed-income investments, but have more risk of principal. Therefore, it is important to expect to invest in equities for a period of at least ten years. Exhibit 12.9 illustrates that the volatility of asset classes is reduced over time.

Very often people saving money for a down payment on a house will ask about appropriate investment vehicles. In most cases, the purchase of a house will be within a couple of years and thus, eliminate most of the long-term investment choices.

EXHIBIT 12.9: TIME DIVERSIFICATION

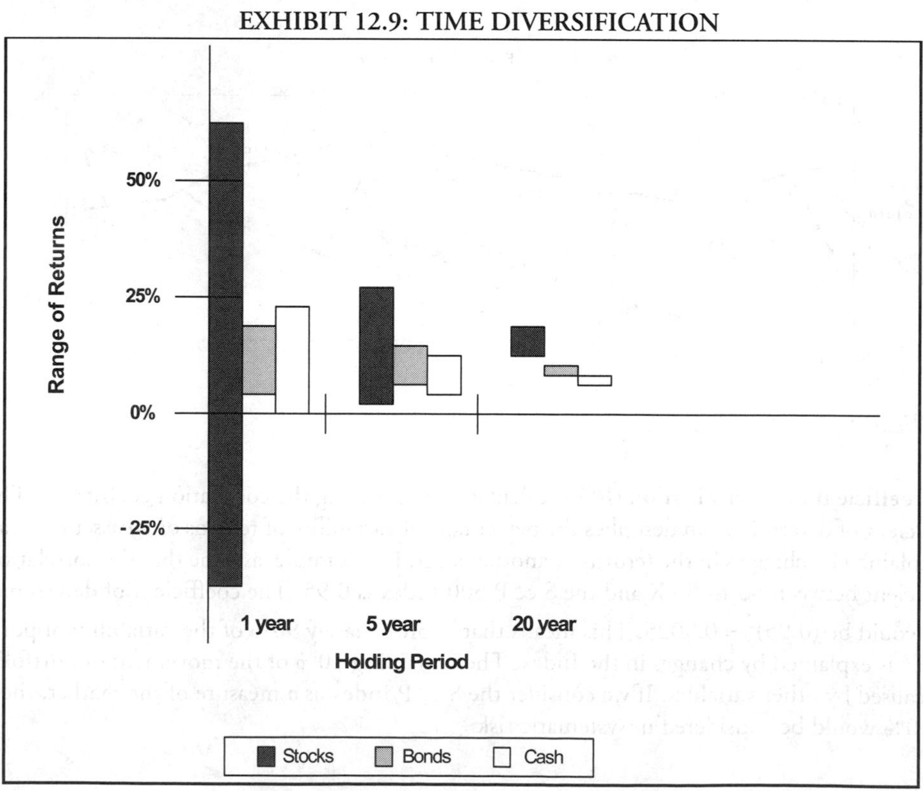
50%
25%
0%
- 25%
Range of Returns
1 year
5 year
20 year
Holding Period
Stocks
Bonds
Cash

Investor Tax Bracket

Tax issues are another important consideration in the investment planning process. The most apparent issue impacted by an investor's tax bracket is whether to invest in taxable or tax-free municipal fixed-income securities. For high net worth investors, municipal bonds generally provide a higher after-tax return, while for taxpayers in lower tax brackets, taxable bonds will generally provide higher after-tax returns. However, assets in qualified plans or other tax-deferred accounts should generally not be invested in municipal bonds, since returns for these securities are traditionally lower than the returns for taxable fixed-income securities.

The tax bracket of the investor also affects the type and style of equity investments. For investors in higher tax brackets, equities that do not pay dividends are preferred for tax purposes since they do not generate current taxable income. In the same regard, high turnover investment styles are not as conducive to tax efficiency as lower turnover styles. In other words, when portfolio managers buy and sell at high turnover rates during the year, it can often generate more taxable income with short-term rather than long-term capital gains. A strategy that emphasizes more of a buy-and-hold strategy will reduce the recognition of current taxable income and minimize transaction costs.

SOFTWARE OUTPUTS

Mean-variance optimization software packages provide advisers with a useful tool in assisting clients with the achievement of their investment goals and other financial planning goals. Among the outputs to these types of packages are asset allocations, expected returns (both before tax and after tax), expected standard deviation of the portfolio, and projections on the future value of the portfolio.

Asset Allocation

The primary purpose of a mean-variance optimization model is to determine an efficient allocation for an investor's portfolio based on the goals of the client and tolerance for risk. An **asset allocation** provides an investor with a guide as to how much of the portfolio should be invested in each asset class. Exhibit 12.10 illustrates three possible asset allocations: one for a conservative investor, one for a moderate investor, and one for an aggressive investor.

asset allocation - the distribution of investments in a portfolio by asset class

Expected Return

Investors are clearly interested in the return they can anticipate from their portfolios. In many cases, a financial planner can calculate the rate of return necessary to achieve some financial planning goal. Generally, these software packages provide for both pretax and after-tax rates of return.

Expected Volatility (Standard Deviation)

Investors are certainly wary about large fluctuations in the value of their invested assets. Therefore, understanding the expected volatility of their portfolio is an important factor to consider when choosing a final asset allocation.

Where on the Web

Chicago Board of Trade *www.cbot.com*

Commodity Futures Trading Commission *www.cftc.gov*

CNBC *http://moneycentral.msn.com/investor/home.asp*

Investor Guide *www.investorguide.com*

National Futures Association *www.nfa.futures.org*

North American Securities Administrators Association *www.nasaa.org*

Securities and Exchange Commission - Investor Education and Assistance *www.sec.gov/investor/students.shtml*

The Investor's Clearinghouse *www.investoreducation.org*

Projected Portfolio Values

Based on the expected returns and the expected volatility, these packages can project the future value of an investor's portfolio. This process is useful in estimating whether or not a goal will be within reach, or if the goal needs to be revised. This projection should be updated at least annually to determine whether the client is on track to meet his objectives. If the portfolio is not doing as well as anticipated, the investor should evaluate why and make any necessary changes.

EXHIBIT 12.10: SAMPLE ASSET ALLOCATIONS

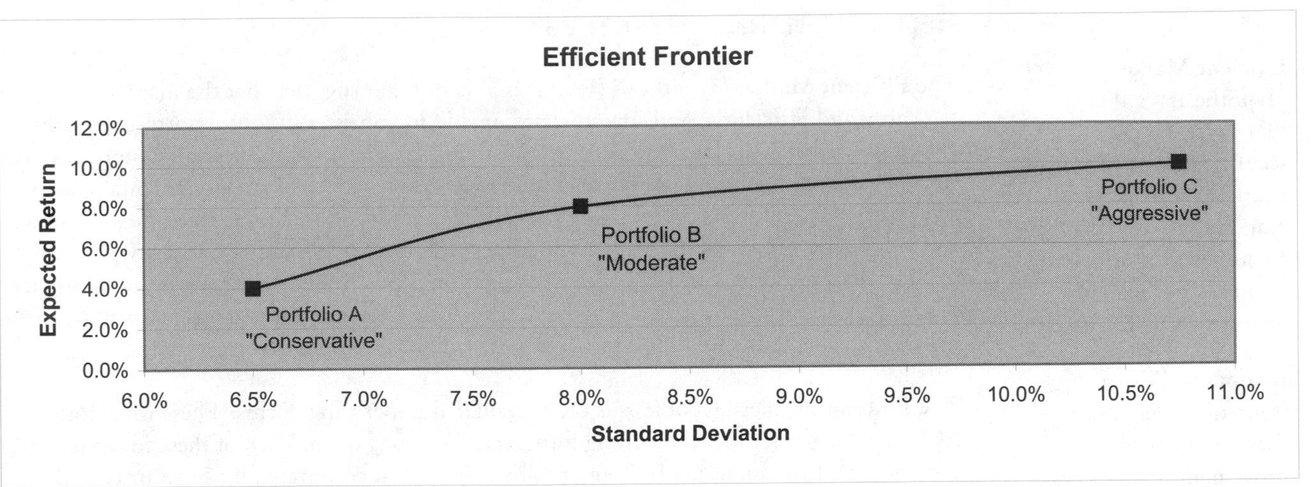
Efficient Frontier
Expected Return
12.0%
10.0%
8.0%
6.0%
4.0%
2.0%
0.0%
Portfolio A
"Conservative"
Portfolio B
"Moderate"
Portfolio C
"Aggressive"
6.0%
6.5%
7.0%
7.5%
8.0%
8.5%
9.0%
9.5%
10.0%
10.5%
11.0%
Standard Deviation

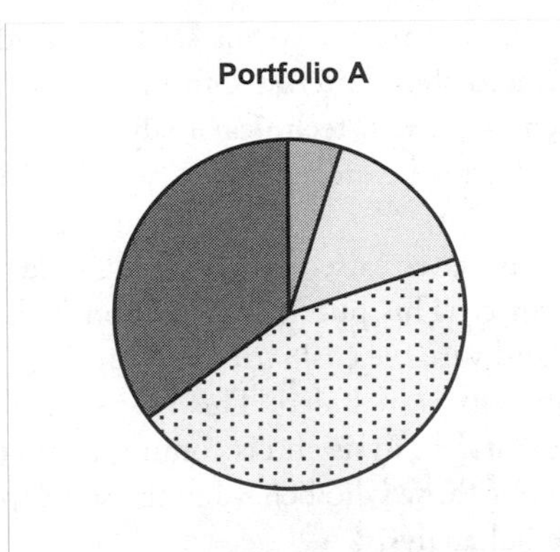
Portfolio A

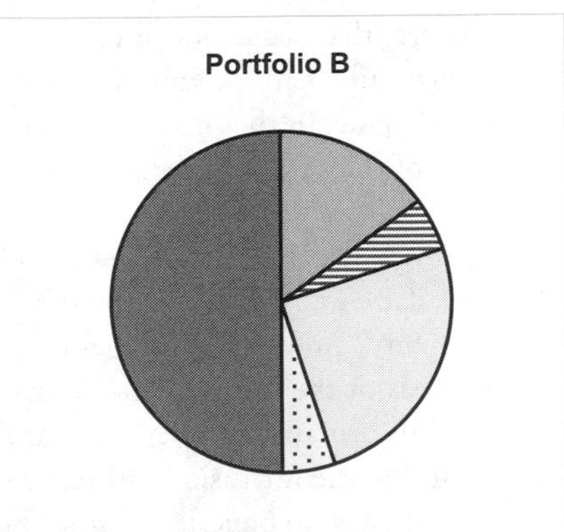
Portfolio B

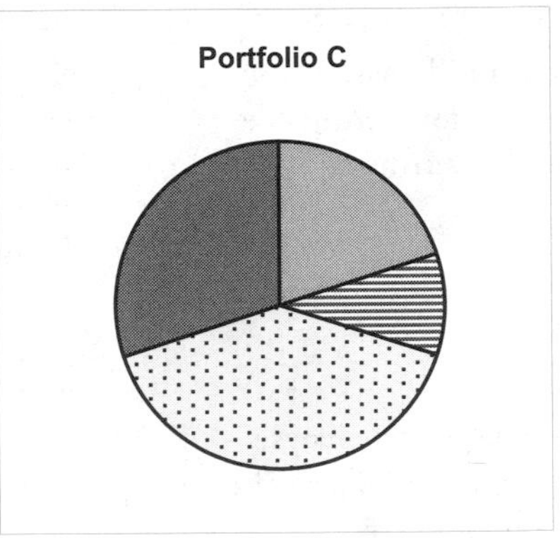
Portfolio C

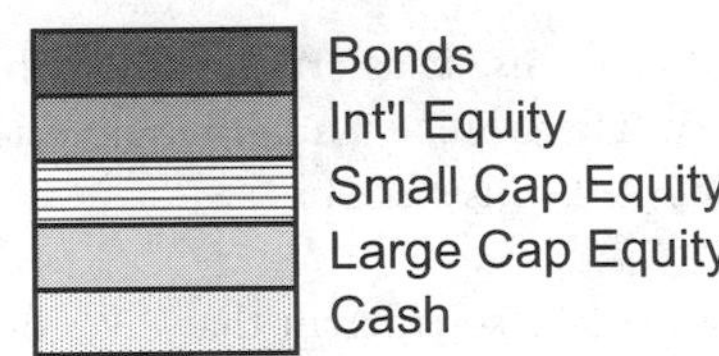
Bonds
Int'l Equity
Small Cap Equity
Large Cap Equity
Cash

INVESTMENT STRATEGIES AND THEORIES

EFFICIENT MARKET HYPOTHESIS

Efficient Market Hypothesis - a theory that suggests that securities are priced fairly and efficiently by the market, and investors are unable to consistently outperform the market on a risk-adjusted basis

random walk - an unpredictable pattern that describes the movement of security prices over time.

The **Efficient Market Hypothesis** (EMH) is a theory that suggests that the market prices securities fairly and efficiently, and investors are unable to consistently outperform the market on a risk-adjusted basis. In fact, the EMH states that securities prices reflect all historical information. Therefore, analyzing historical information using technical or fundamental analysis will not provide an advantage in investing. The only information that will affect the price of a security will be new, unknown information. As new information affecting a security is released, the price of the security will increase if the information is positive and decrease if the information is negative. Since new information is by its very nature unknown, it is random, or unpredictable. Thus, security prices should follow a **random walk**, or an unpredictable pattern.

The Efficient Market Hypothesis is often evaluated under three forms. These three forms of the EMH are the weak form, semistrong form, and the strong form. Each of these forms differs as to the level of information that is thought to be efficiently incorporated into a security's price.

technical analysis - the search for identifiable and recurring stock price patterns

The weak form asserts that securities prices reflect information related to the security's trading data, including price information, volume information, and short-interest information. Under this form, analyzing trends in the price of securities, such as done in **technical analysis**, is irrelevant since the price of the security should already fully reflect this information.

fundamental analysis - the analysis of a stock's value using basic, publicly available data such as the stock's earnings, sales, risk, and

The semistrong form asserts that securities prices not only reflect a security's trading data, but also all publicly available information related to the security. This public information includes analysis of the company's products, management, fixed and variable cost structure, earnings and cash flow, and analysis of the industry in which the company is included. This type of analysis of publicly available information is referred to as **fundamental analysis** and is commonly used in attempts of determining the intrinsic value of a security. For those who believe in the semistrong form of the EMH, there is no benefit to using fundamental analysis.

The strong form goes even farther than the other forms. It asserts that all public and private information is included in the price of a security. Therefore, even corporate inside information will not allow investors to outperform the market on a consistent basis.

Is the Efficient Market Hypothesis correct? Are markets so efficient that investors are unable to consistently outperform on a risk-adjusted basis? These questions have been plaguing the investment community for decades without a definitive answer. For our purposes, it is fair to say many of the aspects of the EMH are correct. Stock prices will generally move because of new information. It is difficult for investors to outperform the market on a consistent basis, as evidenced by the thousands of mutual funds that do not outperform the market each year (especially after adjusting for transaction costs and expenses).

anomalies - occurrences in the stock market that are not supported by the concept of the Efficient Market Hypothesis

However, there are certainly counterarguments to the validity of the EMH. The most obvious of these includes **anomalies**. Anomalies are occurrences in the stock market that are not supported by the concept of an efficient market. For example, if a method of trading results in superior returns, then the trading method implies that the market is not perfectly efficient.

There are numerous anomalies that have been studied at great length. Some of these anomalies end up supporting the EMH based on the extended research, while others are still unexplained in accordance with the EMH.

The October 1987 crash of the stock market is an example that the markets may not be as efficient as explained in the EMH. According to the research, there was no change in expectations that could account for the 23 percent decline in the market. This type of volatility is not based on new information received by the market. Therefore, there are arguments that may imply that the EMH is not entirely correct.

Finally, it is fair to say that the markets are efficient, without defining the level of efficiency, and that it is certainly difficult for professional portfolio managers to outperform the market. In addition, certain markets are more efficient than other markets. For example, the U.S. large-cap equity market is more efficient than the international emerging equity market. The U.S. large-cap market has fewer barriers to entry and the financial statements of large publicly traded U.S. companies are publicly available and commonly reviewed by analysts. The degree to which you believe in the efficiency of the market will impact your choice as to active or passive management of investment portfolios.

Active vs. Passive Investing

Active and passive investment strategies are commonly used approaches to investing. Active management is an attempt to outperform the returns that are available to those investors using a passive approach. It is through the process of finding undervalued or mispriced securities that active managers attempt to earn these higher returns. Active management generally requires more research and support than passive strategies. Therefore, the expenses associated with active management are generally higher than for passively managed approaches.

A passive approach to investment management does not attempt to find undervalued securities. Instead, this approach assumes, as does the Efficient Market Hypothesis, that investors will be unable to consistently outperform the market over the long term. As a result, managers will not employ active strategies and will generally hold a well-diversified portfolio, often based on an asset allocation strategy. Over time, the portfolio may have to be rebalanced, due to different rates of return for different asset classes within the portfolio. However, a passive approach will have lower costs, both transaction fees and management fees. One method of passive investing is the use of index funds.

Indexing

An obvious and natural question that investors ask about their investment performance is, "How did my portfolio perform compared to the market?" The market is generally represented by an index, or benchmark, such as the Standard & Poor's 500 Index. These indexes provide investors with a benchmark for the performance of different segments of the market.

Indexing is the concept of investing in the same securities and in the same proportions represented by an index. For instance, an investor might purchase the same securities that make up the S&P 500 Index. However, purchasing 500 stocks and purchasing them in the correct proportions requires a substantial investment. Therefore, investors will often invest in index mutual

funds. These funds provide an inexpensive method for investors to receive the performance of an index without the hassle of having to mimic the structure of the index.

Indexing has proved to be an effective investment strategy. Historical return results indicate that the majority of active managers do not produce returns in excess of returns earned by indexes or index mutual funds.

TIMING THE MARKET

Market-timing is a strategy whereby investors attempt to be fully invested in periods of upward movements in the market and to be out of the market when it is declining. This type of strategy can be applied to equities, fixed-income securities, or portfolios. Knowing when to buy and when to sell is the inherent difficulty with this type of strategy. Although there are a vast number of methods to time the market, many of which can be found on the Internet, the majority of academic studies indicate that it is not possible to outperform the market by attempting to time its rise and fall. According to The Hulbert Financial Digest, a publication that rates market-timing newsletters, only 25 out of 201 market-timing newsletters in 1999 were able to beat the Wilshire 5000 index. Exhibit 12.11 illustrates the ineffectiveness of market-timing newsletters over 1-year, 5-year, 10-year, and 15-year periods.

EXHIBIT 12.11: MARKET-TIMING NEWSLETTERS THAT BEAT THE WILSHIRE 500

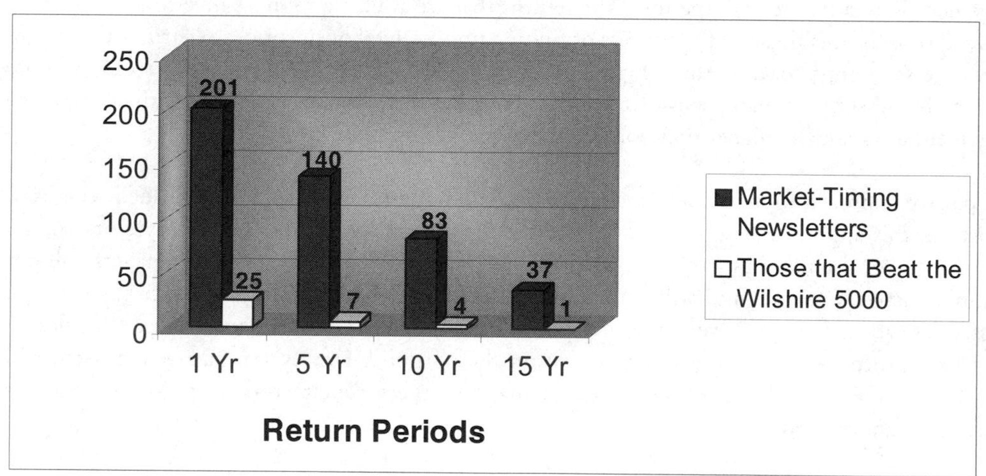
250
200
150
100
50
0
201
25
140
7
83
4
37
1
1 Yr
5 Yr
10 Yr
15 Yr
Return Periods
Market-Timing Newsletters
Those that Beat the Wilshire 5000

PROFESSIONAL

FOCUS

How difficult is it to come up with goals and objectives for clients, and what do you do to minimize the difficulty?

The job of setting goals and objectives becomes easier when a client is willing to inventory their assets including financial, personal, business and family and then review their obligations, needs, desires, and goals for the long and short term. All prospects are offered the opportunity to meet with me for a one to two hour consultation to determine what our expectations are before deciding to work together. If they attend the initial meeting with a prepared financial profile, I know the chances are that this is a serious prospect and we can move ahead. I frequently refer prospects to other professionals (accountants, attorneys, estate, tax, and eldercare specialists) before we proceed with planning and prioritizing their objectives.

When a potential client is willing to explore what their current situation is, and to plan for specific things they expect for themselves and their families, I feel they are ready for the services of a financial adviser. They may require a "reality check" to recognize that they are "playing the lottery" and it is not the soundest way of building a secure financial foundation.

Under what circumstances do you have your best success convincing your clients to follow the investment plan that you set up?

There are various programs and processes I draw from to lead the clients through the planning process. They include protection of their life, property and financial assets, savings approaches, wealth creation and preservation, distribution techniques, tax saving strategies (current and future), employee benefits, retirement and estate planning and senior planning issues. In the first visit I follow a track using a visual system that helps put the present and future needs into perspective. Keeping a positive attitude and looking ahead to what can be accomplished, not emphasizing what should have been done, gives clients reasonable expectations. Working closely with clients to prioritize their goals and objectives and decide when they want to accomplish them, I find they are enthusiastic and motivated to take the actions we have outlined together. It is also reassuring to see I have good client retention, some with my firm over 25 years.

How do you convey the concepts and benefits of asset allocation to your clients?

The risk/financial profiles that many insurance and investment companies offer financial planners make it very easy to educate clients in marketplace idiosyncrasies and prepare them for the asset mixes that match their risk tolerance and expectations. The "dream" of high returns with no risk comes into focus as we review historical performance of securities and funds in different blends, leading clients to face more realistic planning. For the majority of my clients I tend to lean more toward passive rather than active managed securities and funds. The concepts presented are adapted to the people needs and wants, and depend on whether they are strong enough to ignore the noise and "investment pornography" generated in the media and elsewhere. I use "Modern Portfolio Theory" materials showing diversified portfolios, asset class investing for the long term and construction of portfolios which takes some of the mystery out of investing. I share samples of client portfolios (used with client approval and/or free of client identifying information) which demonstrate the success of "staying the course" portfolios over at least five or six years showing the historical performance of the diversified asset allocations going back over 30 years.

Charlotte Hartmann-Hansen, CLU, ChFC, LUTCF, CSA, is a Registered Representative and Investment Adviser Representative affiliated with Woodbury Financial Services, Inc., member NASD, SPIC and Registered Investment Advisor 500 Bielenberg Drive, Woodbury, MN 55125, 800-800-2000. The viewpoint presented is that of Charlotte Hartmann-Hansen and not necessarily that of Woodbury Financial Services, Inc.

Charlotte Hartmann-Hansen, MS, CLU, ChFC, LUTCF

DISCUSSION QUESTIONS

1. How does investment planning fit into the overall framework of financial planning?
2. What investment goals are common to most investors and how are these goals achieved?
3. What are two methods of increasing savings for an investor?
4. How do systematic risk and unsystematic risk differ?
5. What are lending investments and ownership investments, and how to they differ?
6. What are the benefits of owning real estate in an investment portfolio?
7. What are the two types of derivatives discussed in the chapter?
8. What are the differences in the obligations and rights with regard to option contracts and futures contracts?
9. What is the difference between direct investing and indirect investing?
10. How does the historical performance, in terms of returns and standard deviation, differ among small capitalization stocks, large capitalization stocks, and fixed-income securities?
11. How do the two common measures of risk—beta and standard deviation—differ?
12. What are the differences between the arithmetic mean and the geometric mean?
13. How are the nominal rate of return and real rate of return different?
14. What is the efficient frontier, and what is its role in modern portfolio theory?
15. What type of information is conveyed by the correlation coefficient?
16. What is the Efficient Market Hypothesis (EMH)?
17. What makes timing the market such a difficult process?
18. What are anomalies, and how do they provide a counterargument to the validity of the EMH?
19. What is indexing, and how is it used?
20. What is the difference between active and passive portfolio management?

EXERCISES

1. List five systematic risks and explain each.
2. List four unsystematic risks and explain each.
3. Michael invests $10,000 in Bonsai Inc., which is based in Japan. The conversion rate at the time of the investment is 100 yen to 1 dollar. Michael sells his interest six months later for 1,750,000 yen. However, the exchange rate now is 125 yen to 1 dollar. What is Michael's return on the investment (before yen to dollars), return due to exchange rate risk, and net result on the original investment?
4. Compare and contrast common and preferred stock.
5. Hewkard stock has recently had a market correction. If Bill likes the long-term potential of the stock, what option positions might he choose and why?
6. Harry bought XYZ Company fifteen years ago. The stock has greatly appreciated recently and Harry is concerned about a correction. List two alternatives that he could implement to minimize losses in the event of a correction.
7. Kyle purchases one lot (100 shares) of Superstock for $6,500. One year later, he sells the lot when the stock is trading for $79 per share. Superstock does not pay dividends. What is Kyle's holding period return?
8. Eric had the following returns on his portfolio from 2001 through 2005: 10 percent, 8 percent, 13 percent, 15 percent, 11 percent. What is the arithmetic mean for Eric's portfolio?

1. Tyler had the following returns on his high-risk portfolio over a five-year period: 35 percent, –10 percent, 25 percent, 65 percent, –5 percent. What is the geometric mean for Tyler's portfolio?
2. Sandra expects to earn an after-tax rate of return over a long period of time of 10 percent. If inflation is expected to continue at 3 percent, what is Sandra's real rate of return?
3. The Efficient Market Hypothesis is often evaluated under three forms. List and explain how each of these forms differs as to the level of information that is efficiently incorporated into a security's price.
4. If portfolio A has a coefficient of determination, when compared to the S & P 500 Index, of 0.64, then what portion of the risk of the portfolio is considered unsystematic risk?
5. If Portfolio B has a correlation with the market of 0.70, then what portion of the risk of the portfolio can be eliminated through diversification?

PROBLEMS

1. Use the chart to answer the following questions:

YEAR	RETURN
1	10%
2	–5%
3	18%
4	6%
5	1%

- Calculate the arithmetic mean for the five-year period.
- Calculate the geometric mean for the five-year period.

2. Janet has a portfolio that has a correlation with the market of 0.8 and a standard deviation of 20 percent. Determine how much unsystematic risk is within Janet's portfolio.
3. What is the implication of the historical performance of various asset classes on the investment choices made by investors in different stages of the life cycle?

CHAPTER 12 SUPPLEMENT A

Fixed-Income Securities

This supplement provides additional information on fixed-income securities. Topics covered include:

- Valuation
- Return Measures
- Types of Fixed-Income Securities
- Risks
- Term Structure of Interest Rates
- Duration and Immunization

fixed-income securities - securities with specified payment dates and amounts, primarily bonds

lending securities - securities where an investor of bonds lends funds to the issuer in exchange for a promise of a stream of periodic interest payments and a repayment of the loaned principal at the maturity

coupon payments - interest payments paid to the bondholder on a semiannual basis and based on a percentage of the face value, or par value, of the bond

maturity - the period of time through which the issuer has control over the bond proceeds and the period of time it must continue to pay coupon payments

BASIC CONCEPTS OF LENDING SECURITIES

As described in this chapter, **fixed-income securities**, including bonds, are known as **lending securities** or instruments. An investor of bonds lends funds to the issuer in exchange for a promise of a stream of periodic interest payments and a repayment of the loaned principal at the maturity of the bond. Generally, these interest payments are called coupon payments and are often paid on a semiannual basis, or twice per year. **Coupon payments** are based on a percentage of the face value, or par value, of the bond, which is typically $1,000. For example, a bond that contains a 10 percent coupon will pay $100 per year (generally, $50 twice per year) for the life of the bond. Coupon payments can vary widely and can be as low as zero in the case of zero-coupon bonds.

Bonds provide investors with an excellent alternative to other types of securities and can be used for the purpose of diversifying portfolios or providing income to individuals who are in need of a stream of cash flows. Although bonds generally have lower returns than equity investments, they are generally less risky than equities and provide higher returns than bank certificates of deposit, savings accounts, and other lending alternatives.

There are a variety of issuers of bonds including domestic and foreign governments and domestic and foreign companies; however, the U.S. federal government, its agencies, municipalities, and domestic corporations issue the majority of the fixed-income securities. The bonds of each of the issuers may be issued in public or private markets and generally have different characteristics. Each of the differences in the characteristics of bonds will impact the perceived value of the bond, and as a result, impact the required returns.

One of the key features of a bond is the length of its term, or **maturity**. The maturity of the bond indicates the period of time through which the issuer has control over the bond proceeds and the period of time it must continue to pay coupon payments. The maturity of a bond also impacts the yield that is received by the investor. Generally, the yield that is received by the investor will be higher for longer maturity bonds. However, as we will see later, this depends on the shape of the yield curve. The maturity also impacts the volatility of the bond and can impact other types of risk associated with the bond.

Although most bonds are issued with maturities ranging from one to thirty years, bonds are sometimes issued with maturities as long as 100 years. In addition, some issuers will include features in the bond agreement that allows the issuer to call the bond from the holder. A call feature allows the issuer to redeem the bond issue prior to its scheduled maturity, which may be beneficial to the issuer if interest rates have declined. In such a case, the bond issuer may call the bonds from the holder and issue new bonds at a lower coupon rate, thereby reducing the cost of its debt. Call features will be discussed later in this section.

VALUATION OF FIXED-INCOME SECURITIES

As with most financial securities, the value of a bond is equal to the present value of the expected future cash flows. Conceptually, the cash flows of a bond are generally straightforward: fixed- coupon payments on a periodic basis and a return of principal at maturity. To determine the present value of a bond, these expected cash flows are discounted at an appropriate discount rate, which depends on the market yields being offered on comparable fixed-income securities. The value of a bond is determined in the same manner as the value of an annuity using the time value of money concepts.

BASIC CALCULATION EXAMPLE

EXAMPLE

Assume a three-year bond (face value of $1,000) is issued by XYZ Company that pays an 8 percent coupon semiannually ($40 twice each year). What is the value of the bond if comparable bonds are yielding 10 percent?

$$P_0 = \frac{Cf_1}{(1+k)^1} + \frac{Cf_2}{(1+k)^2} + \frac{Cf_3}{(1+k)^3} + \frac{Cf_4}{(1+k)^4} + \frac{Cf_5}{(1+k)^5} + \frac{Cf_6}{(1+k)^6}$$

$$P_0 = \frac{40}{(1.05)^1} + \frac{40}{(1.05)^2} + \frac{40}{(1.05)^3} + \frac{40}{(1.05)^4} + \frac{40}{(1.05)^5} + \frac{1{,}040}{(1.05)^6}$$

$$P_0 = 38.10 + 36.28 + 34.55 + 32.91 + 31.34 + 776.06$$

$$P_0 = \$949.24 \text{ (The bond should sell for \$949.24)}$$

Each cash flow is discounted by first raising the sum of 1 plus the periodic discount rate to the power in which the cash flow occurs and then dividing the cash flow by this amount. For example, the present value of the first cash flow is equal to $40 divided by (1 plus 0.05) resulting in a discounted value of $38.10. We used 5 percent since it is half of the 10 percent yield to reflect the semiannual payments.

The method for valuing a bond is summarized in the following formula:

$$PV = \sum_{t=1}^{2n} \frac{C/2}{(1+i/2)^t} + \frac{P_P}{(1+i/2)^{2n}}, \text{ where}$$

- PV = Present value of the future cash flows (price of the bond)
- n = Number of years to maturity
- C = Annual coupon interest payment
- i = Current yield to maturity for the bond
- P_p = Par value of the bond

The value of a bond can also be calculated using a financial calculator. Using the example above, a bond's value would be calculated using the following method:

Present Value of a Bond			
n	=	6 (3 years × 2)	Term
i	=	5 (10 ÷ 2)	Discount Rate or YTM
PMT_{OA}	=	\$40 (\$80 ÷ 2)	Semiannual coupon
FV	=	\$1,000	Maturity Value
PV	=	(\$949.24)	Present Value

Calculation Inputs

In the above examples, all of the inputs to the calculation were provided. However, in practice, this is not always the case. Therefore, the following section discusses two of the most important inputs, including the cash flows from the security and the appropriate discount rate to use in the valuation.

Cash Flows

As we said before, the cash flows for the bond will consist of periodic coupon payments and the par value, or maturity value, of the bond. The coupon payments can be made over any period, but are more often paid on a semiannual or annual basis. Although the examples above illustrate the first coupon payment occurring exactly six months from the valuation point, in practice, this is not always the case. If the first coupon payment does not occur exactly six months from the valuation point, then it will occur earlier and will require an adjustment to be made to the calculation to account for this short period. The par value, or maturity value, of the bond will generally be the face value of \$1,000. However, if the bond contains a call feature, then the term of the bond to be used for purposes of valuation will likely change, as will the expected maturity value of the bond.

asset-backed securities - securities issued against some type of asset-linked debts bundled together, such as credit card receivables or mortgages

Asset-backed securities, such as mortgage-backed securities and collateralized mortgage obligations, contain more uncertainty with regard to their cash flows. First, coupon payments and repayment of principal are based on payments made by the mortgagors who often have the right to prepay principal. Prepayments cause the schedule of cash flows to change, which adjusts the value of the bond. The second issue related to asset-backed securities concerns the potential for defaults. Clearly, in a large pool of mortgages, it is likely that some of the mortgages will result in default. In such a case, the cash flows are impacted, causing the value of the bond to change. Each of these issues can be incorporated into the projection of the expected cash flows and, therefore, incorporated into the valuation of the asset-backed securities. Mortgage-backed securities and collateralized mortgage obligations will be discussed in more detail later in this chapter.

Discount Rate

The other important factor in determining the value of the bond is the discount rate, or the rate at which the cash flows are discounted. The yield that an investor expects to earn from a bond is

determined by evaluating yields being offered in the market on similar instruments. Similar instruments are those that have the same maturity and credit quality. The yield that is used in the valuation of a fixed-income security is generally stated in the form of an annual rate of return. This annual return is simply divided by two to adjust for semiannual payments. In the above example, the annual yield of 10 percent was divided by 2 resulting in a periodic rate of 5 percent.

Zero-Coupon Bonds

A **zero-coupon bond** is a bond that does not pay periodic coupon or interest payments; therefore, these bonds always sell at a discount from (less than) par. As a result, the only cash flow that occurs and that needs to be considered in the valuation of a zero-coupon bond is the maturity value or principal value. Although coupon payments are not actually paid, the number of periods that are used when valuing zeros is the same as if the coupon payments were being paid. In other words, the number of periods will equal the number of years until maturity of the bond multiplied by two. Therefore, the valuation methodology of a zero-coupon bond will be consistent with and comparable to the valuation methodology of a bond that makes coupon payments.

zero-coupon bond - a bond that does not pay periodic coupon or interest payments

MEASURES OF RETURN

One of the important issues relating to bonds is the determination of various measures of return. Investors of fixed-income securities will be rewarded with interest or coupon payments, capital appreciation (or loss), and the reinvestment of coupon payments. Each of the following types of return takes into consideration some or all of these factors.

CURRENT YIELD

The **current yield** of a bond is an indication of the income or cash flow an investor will receive based on the coupon payment and the current price. The current yield measure is calculated by dividing the annual coupon payment by the current price of the security. The formula for calculating the current yield is:

current yield - a bond's annual coupon divided by the current market price

$$\text{Current yield} = \frac{\text{Annual coupon payment in dollars}}{\text{Current market price}}$$

EXAMPLE

For example, a ten-year bond that has a 10 percent coupon and is currently selling for $850 will have a current yield of 11.76 percent calculated as follows:

$$\text{Current yield} = \frac{\$1{,}000 \times 10\%}{\$850}$$

$$\text{Current yield} = \frac{\$100}{\$850}$$

$$\text{Current yield} = 11.76\%$$

This type of measure is useful for determining the income or cash flow that can be earned on the purchase of a bond. For example, a person living on a fixed-income might choose to invest in fixed-income securities if the yield is sufficiently high enough to cover living and other expenses. Notice that the calculation does not consider appreciation of the bond or reinvestment of the coupon payments. Therefore, it is not as complete a measure as other measures, such as yield to maturity.

YIELD TO MATURITY

yield to maturity (YTM) - the compounded rate of return on a bond purchased at the current market price and held to maturity

In the previous section, we illustrated the method for determining the price of a bond, which is based on the cash flows from the bond and the discount rate. The discount rate that is used in the calculation is generally the **yield to maturity** (YTM) and is determined by solving for the earnings rate that equates the current market price of the bond to the discounted cash flows from the bond. In calculating the yield to maturity, you would solve for the "k" that equates the present value of the bond to the discounted cash flows from the bond.

$$P_o = \frac{Cf_1}{(1+k)^1} + \frac{Cf_2}{(1+k)^2} + \frac{Cf_3}{(1+k)^3} + \frac{Cf_4}{(1+k)^4} + \frac{Cf_5}{(1+k)^5} + ... + \frac{Cfn}{(1+k)^n}$$

Where

P = Present value

Cf_n = Cash flow for period *n*

k = Yield to maturity

EXAMPLE

Calculating yield to maturity using the above formula is a long and arduous process. Instead, we generally use a financial calculator to calculate the yield to maturity using the present value of the bond, term of the bond, coupon payments of the bond, and the par value of the bond. For example, a 30-year bond that pays a coupon of 9 percent semiannually and is selling for $1,249.45 has a yield to maturity of 7 percent, calculated as follows:

Present Value of a Bond			
PV	=	($1,249.45)	Current Bond Price
n	=	60 (30 years x 2)	Semiannual periods
PMT_{OA}	=	$45 ($90 ÷ 2)	Semiannual cash flow
FV	=	$1,000	Maturity value
i	=	3.5 × 2 = 7%	Yield to maturity

If you were to check the answer, you would find that the present value equals $1,249.45 by using 7 percent as the annualized discount rate. The present value is reflected as a negative number to illustrate that the purchase of the bond requires a cash outflow being paid from the investor, whereas the coupon payments and the future value are positive to reflect the payments made to the investor.

The calculation of the yield to maturity is based on certain important assumptions. It assumes that the investor will hold the bond until it matures and the calculation accounts for the timing of the cash flows. This calculation also assumes that any cash flows that occur during the life of the bond will be reinvested at the calculated yield to maturity rate of return. This is an important limitation of the model. If the reinvestment rate differs from the yield to maturity, then the actual yield received on the bond will be different from the expected yield calculated at inception. Specifically, if the reinvestment rate is less than the yield to maturity, then the actual yield earned on the bond will be less than the calculated yield to maturity. If the reinvestment rate is greater than the yield to maturity, then the actual yield earned on the bond will be greater than the calculated yield to maturity.

As stated above, the calculation assumes that the bond is held until it matures. If the investor sells the bond prior to maturity and the bond is sold at either a premium or discount, then the actual yield will differ from the calculated yield to maturity, because of the capital gain or loss. A premium occurs when the bond sells for a price in excess of par, while a discount occurs when the price of a bond is less than par. Note the following relationships between the price of a bond, the coupon rate, the current yield and the yield to maturity:

Bond Selling At:			Relationship:		
Par	Coupon Rate	=	Current Yield	=	Yield to Maturity
Discount	Coupon Rate	<	Current Yield	<	Yield to Maturity
Premium	Coupon Rate	>	Current Yield	>	Yield to Maturity

YIELD TO MATURITY FOR A ZERO-COUPON BOND

Calculating the yield to maturity for a zero-coupon bond can be done using the same method described above. The only difference is that the periodic payments are equal to zero. Since there are no coupon payments to consider, however, you can use a simplified method to calculate the YTM. The formula for this simplified method is as follows:

$$\text{Yield to Maturity} = (\text{FV Factor})^{\frac{1}{n}} - 1\text{, where}$$

$$\text{FV Factor} = \frac{\text{Maturity value of bond}}{\text{Purchase price of a bond}}$$

For example, the yield to maturity for a twenty-year, zero-coupon bond that is selling for $156.26 equals 9.5 percent, calculated as follows:

$$\text{FV Factor} = \frac{\$1{,}000}{\$156.26} = 6.3996$$

$$\text{Yield to Maturity} = \left[(6.3996)^{\frac{1}{40}} - 1\right] \times 2 = 0.0950 = 9.5\%$$

Two adjustments must be made to account for semiannual compounding. First, 40 payments or periods are used instead of 20. Second, the YTM that results from the equation must be multiplied by 2 to reflect an annual rate instead of a semiannual rate. Solving the same example using the time-value-of-money keys on a financial calculator results in the same answer, as illustrated below:

Present Value of a Bond			
PV	=	($156.26)	Current price
n	=	40 (20 years × 2)	Semiannual periods
PMT_{OA}	=	$0	Coupon payment
FV	=	$1,000	Maturity value
i	=	4.75 × 2 = 9.5%	Yield to maturity

YIELD TO CALL (YTC)

yield to call (YTC) - the expected return on a bond from the purchase date to the date that the bond may be called

Yield to call (YTC) is the rate of return that equates the present value of the bond (purchase price) to the expected cash flows, adjusted for the call feature. Calculating yield to call is performed using the same methodology as calculating yield to maturity, with two adjustments. A bond containing a call feature generally allows the issuer the right to call the bond prior to the standard maturity, but usually at a premium above par value. Therefore, in the calculation of yield to call, the number of periods will need to be adjusted to reflect the shorter term of the bond resulting from the call feature, and the future value must be adjusted to reflect the premium paid by the issuer.

For example, assume a 30-year bond ($1,000) that pays a coupon of 9 percent semiannually is selling for $1,249.45, has a yield to maturity of 7 percent, and has a call provision. If the call provision provides that the bond may be called in 5 years at 104 (meaning 104 percent of the par value), then the yield to call equals 4.15 percent, calculated as follows:

Present Value of a Bond			
PV	=	($1,249.45)	Present value
n	=	10 (5 years × 2)	Semiannual periods
PMT_{OA}	=	$45 ($90 ÷ 2)	Semiannual coupon payments
FV	=	$1,040 (104% × $1,000)	Par value plus premium
i	=	2.076 × 2 = 4.152%	Yield to call

taxable bond market - one of two markets that make up the United States bond market, and that consists of U.S. Treasury bonds, U.S. government agency bonds, and corporate bonds

Note that the yield to call is different from the yield to maturity. It is important for investors who are considering the purchase of a callable bond to calculate both the YTM and the YTC in case the issuer decides to call the bond. The lesser of the YTM or YTC is the more conservative estimate of the actual yield.

COMPARING CORPORATE RETURNS AND MUNICIPALS RETURNS

The taxable bond market and the tax-exempt bond market make up the United States bond market. The **taxable bond market** consists of U.S. Treasury bonds, U.S. government agency bonds, and corporate bonds. The **tax-exempt bond market** consists of bonds issued by municipalities, which includes states, counties, cities, and parishes. The exemption from federal income tax is why municipal bonds are referred to as tax exempt. Interest from bonds issued by these municipalities is exempt from federal income tax, and in some cases, exempt from state income tax. Interest from U.S. Treasury securities is subject to federal income tax, but is not subject to state income tax. Corporate bond interest and interest derived from U.S. agency bonds are subject to federal and state income tax. Since the various types of bonds have different tax treatment, it is essential to compare yields for different bonds on a consistent basis. This comparison can be performed on an after-tax basis or a pretax basis.

tax-exempt bond market - one of the two markets that make up the United States bond market, and that consists of municipal bonds

An investor can convert a municipal bond yield to an equivalent taxable yield using the following formula:

$$\text{Pretax yield} = \frac{\text{Tax-exempt yield}}{1 - \text{marginal tax rate}}$$

EXAMPLE

For example, Tom, who is in the 35 percent tax bracket, is considering the purchase of a Big State municipal bond that is offering a 5 percent yield, while comparable credit-worthy corporate bonds are offering a yield of 7.5 percent. To determine which bond is preferred, based on yield, Tom could determine the pretax yield for the municipal bond, as illustrated:

$$\text{Pretax yield} = \frac{0.05}{1 - 0.35} = 0.077 = 7.7\%$$

Since the pretax equivalent yield equals 7.7 percent, the municipal bond yield of 5 percent is preferable to the corporate bond yield of 7.5 percent. The comparison can also be made on an after-tax basis by multiplying the taxable yield of the corporate bond by the difference between 1 and the marginal tax rate, as follows:

$$\text{After-tax yield} = 0.075 \times (1 - 0.35) = 0.049 = 4.9\%$$

Since the 5 percent tax-free municipal yield is greater than the 4.9 percent after-tax corporate bond yield, the municipal bond appears to be the better choice, based on yield. A third method of comparison is to determine the equilibrium tax rate. This rate is the marginal tax rate at which the yields of the taxable bonds are equal to the yields of the municipal bonds. Using the example above, the equilibrium tax rate equals 33 percent:

$$\text{Pretax yield} = \frac{\text{Tax-exempt yield}}{1 - \text{marginal tax rate}}$$

$$(1 - \text{marginal tax rate}) = \frac{\text{Tax-exempt yield}}{\text{Pretax yield}}$$

$$(1 - \text{marginal tax rate}) = \frac{0.050}{0.075}$$

$$(1 - \text{marginal tax rate}) = 0.6667$$

$$\text{marginal tax rate} = 0.3333$$

Since the equilibrium tax rate is 33 percent, investors in a marginal tax bracket that exceeds 33 percent, such as Tom, will want to invest in municipal bonds, while those investors in a tax bracket below 33 percent will be better off with taxable bonds.

For tax-exempt entities, there is almost never a reason to purchase a municipal bond over a taxable bond because pretax yields on taxable instruments are generally higher than yields for tax-exempt securities of similar risk. Similarly, municipal bonds should not be used in tax-deferred accounts, such as IRAs and 401(k) plans. The yields on municipals will usually be lower than yields on taxable bonds.

money market - consists of debt securities that have the following characteristics: short-term maturity, low credit risk, and high liquidity

secondary market - the market where investors can freely buy and sell securities with other investors

primary market - the market where new issues of securities are first offered to the public

TYPES OF FIXED-INCOME SECURITIES

The Money Market

The **money market** consists of debt securities that have the following characteristics: short-term maturity, low credit risk, and high liquidity. These securities include Treasury bills, commercial paper, certificates of deposit, banker's acceptances, and repurchase agreements.

Treasury Bills

The U.S. Treasury issues 4-week, 13-week, and 26-week bills in denominations of $1,000. The Treasury auctions these bills on a weekly basis. In addition to being purchased directly from the Treasury, these securities can be purchased and sold in the **secondary market**. The secondary market allows investors to freely buy and sell securities with other investors. The **primary market** is the place where securities are first offered to the public.

EXHIBIT 12A.1: RECENT TREASURY BILL AUCTION RESULTS

Term	Issue Date	Maturity Date	Discount Rate %	Investment Rate %	Price Per $100	CUSIP
28-DAY	08-25-2005	09-22-2005	3.275	3.329	99.745	912795VS7
92-DAY	08-25-2005	11-25-2005	3.460	3.539	99.116	912795WB3
182-DAY	08-25-2005	02-23-2006	3.690	3.812	99.134	912795WQ0
28-DAY	08-25-2005	09-15-2005	3.260	3.314	99.746	912795VR9
91-DAY	08-18-2005	11-17-2005	3.470	3.549	99.123	912795WA5
182-DAY	08-18-2005	02-16-2006	3.705	3.828	98.127	912795WP2
28-DAY	08-11-2005	09-08-2005	3.330	3.385	99.741	912795VQ1

Note: The CUSIP number is a unique number identifying each security.

Source: http://www.publicdebt.treas.gov/servlet/OFBills

Treasury bills are issued at a discount or percentage of face value. For example, the 28-day bills (first line in the table above) issued on 8-25-2005 were issued at a price of $99.745 per $100. An investor would have paid $997.45 for a $1,000 bill. The bill will mature at its face value of $1,000, providing the investor with income of $2.55.

EXAMPLE

The discount rate, price, and investment yield are determined in each auction. Bidding is in terms of the discount rate, which is calculated

$$\text{Discount Rate} = \frac{\text{Par} - \text{Price}}{\text{Par}} \times \frac{360}{\text{Days to Maturity}}$$

Par is simply the face value of the bill or the principal paid at maturity. The discount rate gives a yield based on the face value of the security and uses a 360-day year. The investment rate gives a rate used for comparison with other securities by basing the yield on a 365-day year and the purchase price. The calculation for the investment rate is

$$\text{Investment Rate} = \frac{\text{Par} - \text{Price}}{\text{Price}} \times \frac{365}{\text{Days to Maturity}}$$

Competitive and noncompetitive bids are awarded at the highest rate of bids accepted in the auction. The single-price auction technique became effective for all sales of Treasury marketable securities beginning on November 2, 1998.

Commercial Paper

Commercial paper consists of a private sector company's issue of short-term, unsecured promissory notes. This type of debt is issued in denominations of $100,000 or more and serves as a substitute for short-term bank financing. Maturities for commercial paper are 270 days or less (costly SEC registration procedures are required for securities issued with maturities over 270 days) and are often backed by lines of credit from banks. In comparison to Treasury bills, these instruments have a slightly higher default risk and are slightly less liquid. Therefore, commercial paper has slightly higher yields than T-bills of similar term structures.

Certificates of Deposit

Negotiable certificates of deposit (also known as Jumbo CDs) are deposits of $100,000 or more placed with commercial banks at a specific stated rate of interest. These short-term securities can be bought and sold in the open market. These instruments usually yield slightly higher returns than T-bills because they have more default risk and less marketability. CDs with smaller denominations (as low as $500) are sold by some banks; however, these smaller CDs are not negotiable certificates of deposit and, thus, are not traded on the open market.

Banker's Acceptances

Bankers' acceptances are securities that act as a line of credit issued from a bank. Usually, the bank acts as an intermediary between a U.S. company and a foreign company. Companies that are too small to issue commercial paper will use banker's acceptances to fund short-term debt needs. These securities usually have slightly higher interest rates than commercial pape reflecting greater default risk and less liquidity.

Repurchase Agreements

Securities dealers use repurchase agreements (known as "repos") to finance large inventories c marketable securities from one to a few days. The issuer or seller both sells and agrees t repurchase the underlying security at a specific price and specific date. The repurchase price i higher than the selling price, creating the required return to compensate the holde participating in the repurchase agreement.

TREASURY NOTES AND BONDS

Treasury Notes and Bonds

U.S. Treasury notes and bonds have virtually the same characteristics with the exception c maturity. U.S. Treasury notes are issued with maturities of at least one year, but not exceeding te years. U.S. Treasury bonds are sold with maturities greater than 10 years. The minimur purchase amount for both types of securities is $1,000 with additional amounts purchased i $1,000 increments. Treasury notes and bonds are coupon securities that pay interest on semiannual basis. Like Treasury bills, pricing for notes and bonds is done through the auctio process.

Inflation Indexed Treasury Notes and Bonds

In 1997, the Treasury began issuing notes and bonds that are indexed with the consumer pric index. These securities have the same basic characteristics as noninflation-adjusted Treasur notes and bonds, except for the inflation-adjustment feature.

The interest rate paid on these securities is determined through the auction process, just as th other Treasury obligations; however, the principal value of the bond is adjusted for changes i the consumer price index. Thus, the semiannual interest payments received by the investor ar determined by multiplying the inflation-adjusted principal value by one-half of the state coupon payment.

One of the primary risks to which fixed-income securities are subject is change in interest rates both from devaluation in principal and from loss of purchasing power. The indexed Treasurie provide protection from both of these risks making them an attractive security for thos investors concerned about rising inflation and devaluation due to loss of purchasing power.

STRIPS - acronym for Separate Trading of Registered Interest and Principal of Securities—a program that permits investors to hold and trade the individual interest and principal components of eligible Treasury notes and bonds as separate securities

Like the nonindexed Treasury notes and bonds, indexed Treasury securities are eligible for th STRIPS program discussed below.

Treasury STRIPS

The Treasury STRIPS program was introduced in February 1985. **STRIPS** is the acronym fo Separate Trading of Registered Interest and Principal of Securities. The STRIPS progran permits investors to hold and trade the individual interest and principal components of eligibl

Treasury notes and bonds as separate securities. The Treasury does not issue or sell STRIPS directly to investors. STRIPS can be purchased and held only through financial institutions and government securities brokers and dealers who are the parties that separate the original security into its component parts.

When a Treasury fixed-principal or inflation-indexed note or bond is stripped, each interest payment and the principal payment becomes a separate zero-coupon security. Each component has its own identifying number and can be held or traded separately. For example, a Treasury note with 10 years remaining to maturity consists of a single principal payment at maturity and 20 interest payments, one every six months for 10 years. When this note is converted to STRIPS form, each of the 20 interest (coupon) payments and the principal payment become a separate (zero-coupon) security. STRIPS are also called zero-coupon securities because the only time an investor receives a payment during the life of a STRIP is when it matures.

How is a Treasury Security stripped?

A financial institution, government securities broker, or government securities dealer can convert an eligible Treasury security into interest and principal components through the commercial book-entry system. Generally, an eligible security can be stripped at any time from its issue date until its call or maturity date.

Securities are assigned a standard identification code known as a CUSIP number. CUSIP is the acronym for Committee on Uniform Security Identification Procedures. Just as a fully constituted security has a unique CUSIP number, each STRIPS component has a unique CUSIP number. All interest STRIPS that are payable on the same day, even when stripped from different securities, have the same generic CUSIP number. The principal STRIPS from each note or bond, however, have a unique CUSIP number.

For example, if several fixed-principal notes and bonds that pay interest on May 15 and November 15 are stripped, the interest STRIPS that are payable on the same day (for example, May 15, 2005) have the same CUSIP number. The principal STRIPS of each fixed-principal note and bond have a unique CUSIP number, however, and principal STRIPS with different CUSIP numbers that pay on the same day are not interchangeable (or "fungible").

In the case of inflation-indexed notes and bonds, the semiannual interest STRIPS that are payable on the same day (for example, April 15, 2005) have the same CUSIP number. The principal STRIPS also have a unique CUSIP number. The CUSIP numbers for STRIPS from inflation-indexed securities are different from those for STRIPS from fixed-principal securities.

Source: http://www.publicdebt.treas.gov/of/ofstrips.htm

Generally, an investor must report as income, for federal income tax purposes, the interest earned on STRIPS in the year in which it is earned. Inflation adjustments to principal on inflation-indexed securities must also be reported in the year earned. Income must be reported even though it is not received until maturity or the STRIPS are sold. Every investor in STRIPS receives a report each year displaying the amount of STRIPS interest income from the financial institution, government securities broker, or government securities dealer that maintains the account in which the STRIPS are held. This statement is known as IRS Form 1099-OID, the acronym for original issue discount. The income-reporting requirement has meant that STRIPS are attractive investments for tax-deferred accounts, such as individual retirement accounts and 401(k) plans, and for nontaxable accounts, which include pension funds.

UNITED STATES SAVINGS BONDS

Series EE Savings Bonds

The Series E bond was designed to encourage more people to save money. It was sold in denominations of $25, $100, $500, and up to $10,000. Series E bonds were sold at a discount and paid no annual interest, similar to zero-coupon bonds. The Treasury issued the new Series EE savings bond beginning July 1, 1980 in order to replace the older Series E bond. The rate of interest earned on Series EE savings bonds is a fixed rate determined by the Department of the Treasury and is based on the yield for the 10-year Treasury note. A new earnings rate is announced each May and November.

Series EE bonds are accrual bonds, whose price on original issue is half of the face amount (This discounting only applies to paper issues. Electronic sales of Series EE Savings bonds are issued at face value.) Series EE bonds are issued in face amounts of $50, $75, $100, $200, $500, $1,000, $5,000, and $10,000. Series EE bonds issued on or after June 1, 2003, reach original maturity at 20 years after the date of issue and reach final maturity at 30 years after the date of issue. Bonds cease to earn interest at final maturity. Bonds may be redeemed at anytime subject to the following restrictions and penalties. Bonds must be held for at least 12 months. If a bond that is less than 5 years old is redeemed, the penalty is forfeiture of the last three months of interest.

One of the attractions of Series EE bonds is the special tax treatment of the income attributable to these securities. Interest earned from bonds that are issued at a discount, such as zero-coupon bonds and STRIPS, is required to be reported as taxable income on an annual basis even though cash may not be received during the year. Because of the special tax treatment afforded Series EE bonds, however, the interest accrued on these securities is generally not taxed on an annual basis, but rather is taxed upon redemption. However, taxpayers are permitted to make an election to include for tax purposes the income from these securities on an annual basis. This elected tax treatment can be beneficial under certain circumstances, such as for a child with income under the standard deduction. In such a case, basis can be established without incurring tax.

Another tax benefit of Series EE bonds is that the interest earned on these securities can be completely excluded from taxable income if the proceeds from the bonds are used for qualified higher education costs of the taxpayer, spouse, or dependents. These costs include books, tuition, and fees for these family members.

Series HH Savings Bonds

Unlike Series EE bonds that are sold for cash, Series HH savings bonds could only be acquired through an exchange of Series E or EE bonds or with redemption proceeds of another H bond (and savings notes issued prior to 1970). Series HH bonds were issued at 100 percent of the face amount in denominations of $500, $1,000, $5,000, and $10,000 until September 1, 2004, when they were discontinued. Series HH bonds pay interest semiannually at a fixed rate set on the date of issuance and adjusted on the 10th anniversary. The interest payments are required to be included in income for federal income tax purposes.

Series HH bonds have an original maturity period of 10 years and have been granted one 10-year extension of maturity with interest, bringing their final maturity to 20 years. Like EE bonds, HH bonds are issued only in registered physical form and are not transferable. In other words, EE and HH bonds are not marketable securities.

Like Treasury securities, neither EE nor HH bonds are subject to state or local income tax. The tax treatment of these savings bonds can be quite beneficial in those states and cities with an income tax.

Series I Savings Bonds

The Treasury began selling Series I savings bonds on September 1, 1998 in an attempt to offer individuals a way to accrue income and to protect the purchasing power of their investment. Series I bonds are issued at 100 percent of the face amount in denominations of $50, $75, $100, $200, $500, $1,000, $5,000, and $10,000. The bonds have an interest-paying life of 30 years after the date of issue and cease to increase in value on that date. Like EE and HH bonds, Series I bonds are not transferable or marketable.

The Series I bond earnings rate is a combination of two separate rates: a fixed rate of return and a semiannual inflation rate. Each May and November, the Treasury announces a fixed rate of return that applies to all Series I bonds issued during the six-month period beginning with the effective date of the announcement, May 1 or November 1. The fixed rate for any given Series I bond remains the same for the life of the bond.

In addition, every May and November, the Treasury announces a semiannual inflation rate based on changes in the Consumer Price Index for all Urban consumers (CPI-U). The semiannual inflation rate announced in May is a measure of inflation from the previous October through March; the rate announced in November is a measure of inflation from the previous April through September. The CPI-U is published monthly by the Department of Labor's Bureau of through Labor Statistics. The semiannual inflation rate is then combined with the fixed rate of the Series I bond to determine the bond's earnings rate for the next six months.

Eight Americans are honored on the Series I Bonds, representing the diversity that built this country. Portraits of the following prominent Americans appear on the eight Series I Bond denominations:

- **$50 - Helen Keller** - Noted author and advocate for people with disabilities; responsible for Braille becoming the standard for printed communications with the blind.
- **$75 - Dr. Hector P. Garcia** - Physician; leading advocate for Mexican-American veterans' rights; activist in Latino civil rights movement and founder of the American G.I. Forum.
- **$100 - Dr. Martin Luther King, Jr.** - Prominent civil rights leader; minister; Nobel Peace Prize recipient.
- **$200 - Chief Joseph** - a Native American leader who resisted the U.S. government's attempts to force the Nez Perce onto a reservation.
- **$500 - General George C. Marshall** - U.S. Army Chief of Staff during World War II; Secretary of State; Secretary of Defense; Nobel Peace Prize recipient.
- **$1,000 - Albert Einstein** - Physicist; author of the Theory of Relativity; Nobel Prize recipient for Physics.
- **$5,000 - Marian Anderson** - World-renowned vocalist (contralto); first African-American to sing with the Metropolitan Opera.
- **$10,000 - Spark Matsunaga** - U.S. Senator and Congressman; World War II hero; obtained redress for survivors of World War II internment camps.

Source: U.S. Treasury at www.publicdebt.treas.gov/sav/sbiwho.htm

Series I bonds are U.S. Treasury securities backed by the U.S. Government. Series I bonds even protect investors from the effects of deflation. In the rare event that the CPI-U is negative during a period of deflation and the decline in the CPI-U is greater than the fixed rate, the redemption value of the Series I bonds remains the same until the earnings rate becomes greater than zero.

Like EE bonds, Series I bonds receive special income tax treatment. The interest from Series I bonds is not subject to state and local income tax. Interest is accrued for Series I bonds and is not taxable until redeemed. In addition, the interest can be completely excluded from taxable income if the proceeds are used for qualified higher education expenses of the taxpayer, spouse or dependents.

Series I bonds can be redeemed anytime twelve months after the issue date to get the original investment plus the earnings, however, Series I bonds are meant to be longer-term investments. So, if a Series I bond is redeemed within the first five years, there is a 3-month earnings penalty. For example, if a Series I bond is redeemed after 18-months, only 15 months of earnings will be awarded. The following exhibit illustrates the primary differences between the three types of savings bonds.

EXHIBIT 12A.2: SUMMARY OF U.S. SAVINGS BONDS

	Series EE	Series HH	Series I
Denominations	$50, $75, $100, $200, $500, $1,000, $5,000, $10,000	$500, $1,000, $5,000, $10,000	$50, $75, $100, $200, $500, $1,000, $5,000, $10,000
Purchased	With cash	By exchanging E or EE bonds	With cash
Issued at	50% of face value	100% face value	100% face value
Maturity	30 years	20 years	30 years
Interest Rate	Fixed rate based on 10-year Treasury	1.5% fixed rate	Combination of fixed and variable rates
Interest	Accrues	Paid semiannually	Accrues
Taxation of Interest	Deferred	Taxable annually	Deferred
Interest Can be Completely Excluded for Qualified Higher Education Costs	Yes	No	Yes

EDERAL AGENCY SECURITIES

Governmental agencies, such as the Federal Home Loan Bank and the Federal National Mortgage Association, issue public debt as a means of raising funds for operations of the espective agency. Although not issued by the Treasury, **federal agency securities** are extremely afe and have minimal credit risk as a group. These securities have slightly higher yields than Treasuries due to the minimal increase in credit risk.

federal agency securities - public debt issued by agencies of the U.S. government as a means of raising funds for operations of the respective agency

MUNICIPAL BONDS

Municipalities include states, counties, parishes, cities, and towns. These governmental agencies ssue debt instruments, referred to as **municipal bonds**. The unique characteristic of municipal bonds is their income tax treatment. The interest from municipal bonds is not subject to federal ncome tax, and in some cases, not subject to state income tax. Although the yields on nunicipals are generally lower than that of Treasuries, their special tax treatment makes them he choice for higher income investors because of their higher after-tax yields. Two common ypes of municipal bonds are general obligation bonds and revenue bonds.

municipal bonds - debt instruments issued by municipalities (states, counties, parishes, cities, towns) as general obligation bonds or revenue bonds

General obligation bonds are backed by the full faith and credit of the government issuing the lebt and are repaid through taxes collected by the government body. These bonds are backed by he taxing authority of the municipality and, therefore, have minimal default risk.

Revenue bonds are issued by governmental bodies in order to raise funds to finance specific evenue producing projects. Examples of revenue bonds include airport revenue bonds, college and university revenue bonds, hospital revenue bonds, sewer revenue bonds, toll road revenue bonds, and water revenue bonds. These bonds are not backed by the full faith and credit of the ssuing body. Instead, the interest and principal are repaid from revenue generated from the project that was financed with the bond proceeds. Because the revenue generated from the project may differ from what is expected, these bonds are more risky than general obligation bonds and, thus, require higher yields for similar maturities.

There are other differences between municipal bonds besides sources of repayment. Fc example, municipal bonds may be either term bonds or serial bonds. The principal for terı bonds is repaid in full upon maturity, whereas, serial bonds require that the municipality retire certain amount of the bond issue each year.

Another important characteristic of municipal bonds is whether they are classified as priva activity issues. Interest from municipal bonds that are considered private activity bonds taxable for alternative minimum tax purposes. Investors with large amounts of private activi bonds could be required to pay alternative minimum tax. Generally, a private activity bond part of a state or local government bond issue for which the proceeds are to be used for a priva business use, such as a sports stadium.

Although relatively safe, municipal bonds are often insured by third party insurance compani to further reduce credit risk. Three of the more common insurance companies that insu municipal bonds include: Ambac Financial Group (American Municipal Bond Assuranc Corporation), MBIA Insurance Corporation (a subsidiary of MBIA, Inc., formally known a Municipal Bond Insurance Association and Municipal Bond Investors Assurance), an Financial Guaranty Insurance Company (FGIC). Since insured municipal bonds have lowe risk, they will have lower returns.

CORPORATE BONDS

Corporations raise funds by issuing both equity and debt obligations. A discussion on equit obligations appears in Supplement B. Debt obligations provide corporations with a method o raising needed capital funds without diluting the ownership of the entity; however, excessiv amounts of debt can cause strain on the financial health of the company by using preciou resources for debt service. In general, debt increases the leverage of a company and specifically, i impacts the return on equity. Excessive use of debt can cause increased fluctuations in the shar price of the common stock.

The corporate bond market is very broad and is typically classified by the type of issuer. The fiv broad categories of corporate bonds are banks and finance companies, industrials, publi utilities, transportations, and international. Each of these categories can be further subdivided For example, transportation can be divided into airlines, railroads, and trucking. Thes subcategory classifications can assist investors in analyzing and comparing various debt issues.

bond indenture agreement - the legal document that sets forth the repayment schedules, restrictions, and promises between the issuer of a corporate bond and the borrower

The **bond indenture agreement** is the legal document that sets forth the repayment schedules restrictions, and promises between the issuer and the borrower. Some of the information tha may be found in the indenture agreement includes call provisions, sinking fund provisions collateral provisions, and conversion options.

Call Provisions

call provision - right to redeem the bond issue prior to maturity

A **call provision** provides the issuer of the debt instrument the right to redeem the bond issu prior to maturity. Generally, a call provision will require the issuer to pay a premium if the bonc issue is redeemed prior to maturity. When interest rates decline, call provisions allow the issue to redeem the outstanding debt and reissue it at a lower interest rate. By refinancing the debt

companies can save significant amounts of interest payments that would have been paid to the creditors.

From the investor's point of view, the worst time for a company to redeem a bond issue is when interest rates have declined. Such a redemption requires investors to reinvest the proceeds in an interest rate environment that is unfavorable to the investor. Since the potential for a call provision is disadvantageous, investors require that bonds with call provisions have higher yields than bonds without call provisions. Call provisions also create risk because they introduce uncertainty with regard to the stream of cash flows from the bond.

Sinking Fund Provisions

Sinking funds may be established and funded by the bond issuer each year and may accumulate to pay off debt upon maturity. These funds are usually held by a trustee to ensure the repayment of the borrowed principal.

sinking funds - funds usually held by trustee to ensure repayment of borrowed principal

Collateral Provisions

Bonds may be unsecured or secured. If a bond is secured then it has a claim on specific assets of the issuing company in the event of liquidation. A **mortgage bond** is secured by real property. Generally, a mortgage bond will have a lien on the specified property, but could have a lien on all assets of the firm. Mortgage bonds may be open-ended, limited open-ended, or closed-ended, which indicates the degree to which additional debt may be issued against the same property.

mortgage bond - bond secured by real property

Collateral trust bonds are usually secured by stocks and bonds of other companies held in trust. For companies that have insufficient real property, providing a lien on securities held by the company is a method of providing security to its creditors. The investments that are pledged act as collateral for the loan.

collateral trust bonds - bonds secured by securities issued by other companies

Companies are willing to provide security for bond issues to reduce and minimize interest payments and expense. The market interest rate required for secured bonds will be less than that of unsecured bonds.

Unsecured bonds are called **debentures**. Investors who hold debentures do not have a claim to specific assets of the corporation. Instead, debenture holders are general creditors of the issuing corporation and will be paid in liquidation only after secured creditors have been repaid. Subordinated debentures have an even lower claim on assets than general creditors, such as debenture holders.

debentures - unsecured corporate bonds whose holders have no claim to specific assets of the issuing corporation

CONVERTIBLE BONDS

Corporate bonds may contain provisions permitting the conversion of the fixed-income security into equity securities. **Convertible bonds** are hybrid securities that permit the holder to acquire shares of common stock from the issuing company by exchanging the currently held debt security under a specific formula. Similar to an option contract, the holder's ability to convert the current security into common stock is a right that the holder has, not an obligation. The conversion decision hinges on the value of the stock upon conversion. If the value of the stock

convertible bonds - hybrid securities that permit the holder to acquire shares of common stock from the issuing company by exchanging the currently held debt security for a specific number of common stock shares

after conversion were less than the value of the bond, then the investor would be wise to hold on to the fixed-income security.

Convertible securities allow the issuer to reduce the cost of interest for a bond issue by paying a lower yield. The lower yield is a result of the buyer purchasing not only a steady stream of cash flows, but also an option to convert the bond to common stock.

Convertible securities provide investors with several advantages over nonconvertible securities. They provide the holder with a steady stream of income and the ability to participate in the growth of the underlying company. Convertible bonds have a relatively low correlation with bonds and only a moderate correlation to stocks, thus providing the opportunity to diversify a portfolio. Convertible securities are senior securities in terms of liquidation when compared to common stock and are generally very marketable.

Mortgage-Backed Securities and Collateralized Mortgage Obligations

Although relatively new, the market for mortgage-backed securities has seen tremendous growth since its inception in the 1970s. Mortgage-backed securities are ownership claims on a pool of mortgages. The originating mortgage lender will sell loans to investors in the secondary market. These investors pool mortgages together and sell interests in the pool to other investors. This process of transforming nonpublicly traded securities into marketable assets is known as **securitization.**

securitization - the process of transforming nonnegotiable securities into negotiable securities

mortgage-backed securities (MBSs) - ownership claims on a pool of mortgages

Mortgage-Backed Securities

Mortgage-backed securities (MBSs) are often referred to as "pass-through" securities because the monthly mortgage payments are passed along to the holders of the MBSs, less a small servicing fee. These monthly mortgage payments consist of scheduled interest and principal payments, as well as unscheduled principal prepayments. These unscheduled principal prepayments result from borrowers making additional principal payments on their loans or from paying off loans, such as in the case of refinancing.

Because MBSs are backed by mortgages, many of which are backed by the government and all of which are secured by real property, they have little credit risk. However, MBSs are subject to other risks. Just like other fixed-income obligations, these securities are subject to the fluctuation in interest rates. As interest rates increase, the value of the MBS decreases, and as interest rates decrease, the value of the MBS increases.

Since MBSs pass through payments on a monthly basis, the investor must reinvest these cash flows in some other investment. This reinvestment rate risk impacts MBSs in the same manner as other fixed-income securities that have cash flows occurring during the life of the security.

prepayment risk - the risk that homeowners will pay off their loans before the scheduled loan maturity date

Unlike other fixed-income obligations, MBSs are subject to **prepayment risk**, which is the risk that homeowners will pay off their loans before the scheduled loan maturity date. Since the value of these securities is based on the schedule of cash flows, any mortgage prepayments will impact the return an investor receives on a mortgage-backed security. In addition to creating uncertainty as to the timing of the cash flows, these prepayments create a situation in which the

investor must reinvest the additional principal payments perhaps at a lower interest rate, furthering the reinvestment risk.

EXHIBIT 12A.3: HISTORICAL LANDMARKS OF THE SECONDARY MORTGAGE MARKET

1934	Congress established FHA under the National Housing Act of 1934.
1938	Congress established Fannie Mae to serve as refinance facility for FHA-insured mortgages.
1944	VA given authority to guarantee mortgages for U.S. veterans under the Servicemen's Readjustment Act of 1944.
1968	Fannie Mae rechartered as a private corporation. Ginnie Mae established by the Housing and Urban Development Act as a government corporation to serve as a secondary mortgage market institution for FHA/VA/RHS loans.
1970	Under the Emergency Home Finance Act, the Federal Home Loan Mortgage Corporation (Freddie Mac) was chartered as a government-sponsored private corporation to purchase conventional mortgages.
1970	Ginnie Mae issued the first mortgage-backed security (MBS).
1983	The first collateralized mortgage obligation (CMO) was issued using Ginnie Mae MBS pools as collateral, spawning market innovations in multiple-class securities. It was issued by an investment bank called Lehman Brothers Kuhn Loeb.
1986	The Tax Reform Act of 1986 propelled CMOs by creating REMICs, a vehicle that minimizes tax liability for multiple-class MBSs.
1988	The Basle Agreement was issued by the Basle Committee on Banking Supervision, establishing risk-based capital guidelines. It affected the treatment of mortgage products on institution's balance sheets.

Source: GNMA

The majority of the mortgage-backed securities have been issued by three government agencies. These include the Federal National Mortgage Association (FNMA or "Fannie Mae"), the Government National Mortgage Association (GNMA or "Ginnie Mae"), and the Federal Home Loan Mortgage Corporation (FHLMC or "Freddie Mac"). In 1938, the federal government established Fannie Mae to expand the flow of mortgage money by creating a secondary market. Fannie Mae became a private-shareholder company in 1968 and was listed on the New York and Pacific stock exchanges two years later. Ginnie Mae was created in 1968 and remains a government agency within the Department of Housing and Urban Development (HUD). Freddie Mac is a stockholder-owned corporation chartered by Congress in 1970 to create a continuous flow of funds to mortgage lenders in support of home ownership and rental housing. Freddie Mac became a private corporation in 1989. With the exception of minor differences, the pass-through securities of each of the three organizations are virtually the same.

collateralized mortgage obligations (CMOs) - mortgage-backed securities that are divided into principal repayment tranches

Collateralized Mortgage Obligations (CMOs)

Due to the popularity of the mortgage-backed securities, private investment firms have created their own pass-through securities, which are referred to as **collateralized mortgage obligations**

(CMOs). Collateralized mortgage obligations are similar to MBSs in that they are backed by mortgages. They differ from MBSs, however, in that the cash flows associated with a pool of mortgages are divided into repayment periods called tranches. In the traditional MBS, each investor will receive a pro-rata share of principal and interest each month. In effect, the note is being paid off every month.

The principal repayment method is different for collateralized mortgage obligations than for MBSs. As described above, tranches, or repayment periods, are established which dictate when an investor will receive principal repayments. Each of the tranches will receive regular interest payments with the investors of the first tranche receiving all principal payments until they are completely repaid their principal. Once the obligations of the first tranche are satisfied, all principal payments are made to the second tranche, and so on until all of the tranches are repaid. The holders of the CMOs of the first tranche have less interest rate risk than the holders of the CMOs for the last tranche since the maturity is longer for the securities of the last tranche.

Rating Agencies

Rating agencies are responsible for assisting investors in evaluating the default risk of fixed-income securities. Bond rating agencies analyze the financial information of thousands of companies attempting to determine a credit rating for the various debt issues in the market. The two largest and most popular rating agencies are Standard & Poor's and Moody's. Their credit rating system is listed in Exhibit 12A.4.

EXHIBIT 12A.4: STANDARD CREDIT RATING SYSTEM

Bonds	Standard & Poor's	Moody's
Investment Grade:		
▲ High Grade	AAA – AA	Aaa – Aa
▲ Medium Grade	A – BBB	A – Baa
Noninvestment Grade:		
▲ Speculative	BB – B	Ba – B
▲ Default	CCC – D	Caa – C
Overall Range	AAA – D	Aaa – C

Investment grade bonds have a high probability of timely payment of both interest and repayment of principal, while noninvestment grade bonds are those where a significant risk exists to interest or principal payments. The definition of each rating follows:

EXHIBIT 12A.5: DEFINITION OF CREDIT RATINGS

AAA/Aaa	The highest rating and indicates very high ability to service debt.
AA/Aa	Only slightly lower than AAA/Aaa, this rating indicates a very high rating but not as much protection as AAA/Aaa.
A/A	These companies are strong and possess favorable characteristics, but may not be able to sustain adverse economic conditions.
BBB/Baa	These issuers currently have the capacity to service debt, but do not possess the financial strength to withstand weakened economic conditions.
BBBa	This rating and the ratings below are considered junk bonds. There is little protection for payment of principal and interest.
B/B	There is little assurance that principal and interest will be paid for these bonds.
CCC/Caa	These issues are in default or may soon be in default.
CC/Ca	Very poor quality issue that is likely in default or extremely close to default.
C/C	No interest is being paid on these bonds. This is Moody's lowest rating, indicating that the company may be in bankruptcy soon.
D	These bonds are in default and interest and principal payments are in arrears.

Besides Standard & Poor's and Moody's, there are two other large rating agencies: Duff and Phelps and Fitch. In general, the rating agencies will generally provide the same rating for a specific debt issue. In some cases, there may be a slight difference between the ratings of a specific issue by the different agencies. If there is a difference in a bond rating between rating agencies, this difference is referred to as a split rating.

The first four ratings are considered investment grade bonds. Anything below BBB or Baa is considered junk bonds.

Where on the Web

Bloomberg.com *www.bloomberg.com*

Bureau of the Public Debt *www.publicdebt.treas.gov*

The Bond Market Association *www.bondmarkets.com*

CNN Money *http://money.cnn.com*

Electronic Municipal Statistics *www.emuni.com*

Ginnie Mae (GNMA) *www.ginniemae.com*

Marketwatch from Dow Jones *www.marketwatch.com*

Moody's Investors Service *www.moodys.com*

MSN Money *http://moneycentral.msn.com/investor*

Standard & Poor's *www2.standardpoors.com*

Treasury Direct (U.S. Savings Bonds) *www.savingsbonds.gov*

RISKS OF FIXED-INCOME SECURITIES

Fixed-income securities can provide substantial returns to investors; however, there are a variety of risks that investors of fixed-income securities are subject to, including interest-rate risk, default risk, reinvestment-rate risk, purchasing-power risk, call risk, exchange-rate risk, and liquidity risk. These risks are discussed below.

SYSTEMATIC RISKS	UNSYSTEMATIC RISKS
▲ Interest-Rate Risk	▲ Default (Credit) Risk
▲ Reinvestment-Rate Risk	▲ Call Risk
▲ Purchasing-Power Risk	▲ Liquidity Risk
▲ Exchange-Rate Risk	

INTEREST-RATE RISK

Interest-rate risk is the risk that fluctuations in interest rates will adversely impact the value of a security. This risk is generally the greatest risk for an investor of bonds. There is an inverse relationship between changes in interest rates and bond prices. As interest rates fall, bond prices increase. Conversely, as interest rates increase, the value of bonds declines.

EXAMPLE

A 10-year $1,000 bond (that pays interest semiannually) yields 10 percent and sells at par or 100 percent of face value ($1,000). If prevailing interest rates increase to 12 percent, buyers will pay less than par value for the bond so that the yield equals 12 percent (that is, the prevailing market interest rate). Because of the increase in market interest rates, investors will only be willing to pay $885.30 (a $114.70 discount) for the bond, which sold for $1,000 when the prevailing interest rates were 10 percent. Thus, this bond will sell for a discount due to the coupon rate of the bond being less than the prevailing rate of interest for bonds of similar risk and maturity.

Prior to Interest Rate Changes 10%			After Interest Rates Change to 12%			After Interest Rates Change to 8%		
(Bond Sells at Par)			(Bond Sells at a Discount)			(Bond Sells at a Premium)		
n	=	20 (10 × 2)	n	=	20 (10 × 2)	n	=	20 (10 × 2)
i	=	5 (10 ÷ 2)	i	=	6 (12 ÷ 2)	i	=	4 (8 ÷ 2)
PMT_{OA}	=	$50 (100 ÷ 2)	PMT_{OA}	=	$50 (100 ÷ 2)	PMT_{OA}	=	$50 (100 ÷ 2)
FV	=	$1,000	FV	=	$1,000	FV	=	$1,000
PV	=	($1,000)	PV	=	($885.30)	PV	=	($1,135.90)

Similarly, as interest rates decline, bond prices will increase. Considering the bond above, if prevailing interest rates drop from 10 percent to 8 percent, then the price of the bond will increase to $1,135.90 (a $135.90 premium). The inverse relationship between interest rates and bond prices is not a linear relationship. Instead, as the following chart indicates, the relationship between bond prices and interest rates is curvilinear:

EXHIBIT 12A.6: RELATIONSHIP BETWEEN PRICE AND YTM

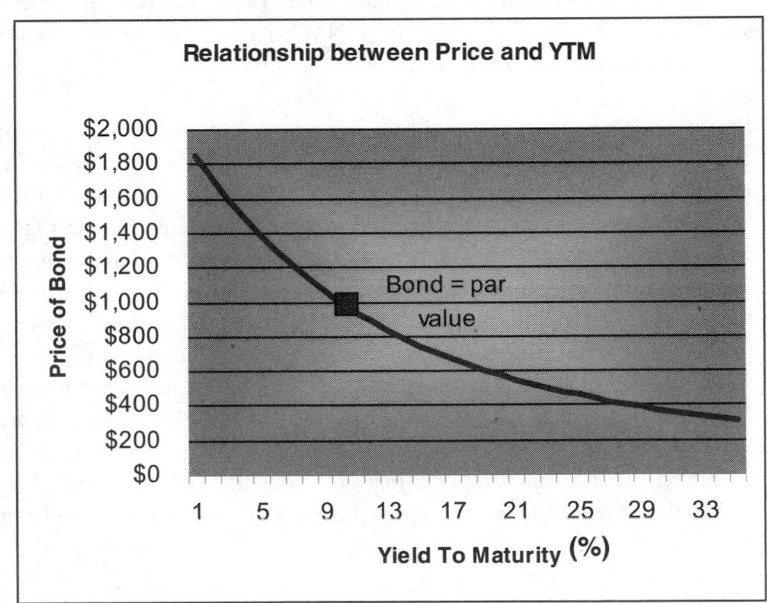
Relationship between Price and YTM
$2,000
$1,800
$1,600
$1,400
$1,200
$1,000
$800
$600
$400
$200
$0
Price of Bond
Bond = par value
1
5
9
13
17
21
25
29
33
Yield To Maturity (%)

Notice that as the yield to maturity increases, the bond price decreases.

It is important to understand that a decline in the value of a bond, which is attributable to an increase in interest rates, is of little relevance to an investor holding the bond to maturity. In such a case, the decline in value of the bond is simply a reflection of the change in market interest rates. The investor will still receive the scheduled coupon payments and will still receive the par value (usually $1,000) upon maturity. For an investor who sells prior to maturity, an increase in interest rates means that the investor will incur a capital loss. Interest rate risk impacts bonds, bond portfolios, and bond mutual funds.

Default (or Credit) Risk

As discussed earlier, investing in a fixed-income obligation is a process of lending money. The bond issuer is effectively borrowing money from the investor in return for a promise to make periodic interest (coupon) payments and to repay the principal at the maturity of the bond. However, since bonds are often issued with maturities exceeding ten, twenty, and thirty years, there is a risk that the financial well-being of the bond issuer will change over this long period of time. In some cases, the financial health of a company will be in such turmoil that the company cannot uphold its promise to repay the borrowed proceeds. The risk that this might occur is referred to as credit risk or default risk. Rating agencies, such as Moody's, Standard & Poor's, and Duff & Phelps, provide investors with analysis of the financial stability of companies and their ability to service their debt.

Fortunately, default risk is an unsystematic risk that can be eliminated (or at least minimized) through choice of investment and through diversification. Investors who are overly concerned about default risk can eliminate it by investing exclusively in U.S. Treasury fixed-income securities. These securities are considered default-risk-free since they are backed by the full faith and credit of the United States government. In addition to Treasuries, fixed-income securities of the Government National Mortgage Association (GNMAs) are also backed by the full faith and credit of the U.S. government and considered default-risk-free.

Municipal bonds provide a sufficient level of protection against default risk, especially ones that are insured; however, there still remains some level of default risk, even with these insured municipal bonds. To minimize default risk with municipals, corporates, and other fixed-income obligations, it is very important to diversify fixed-income portfolios. Purchasing a variety of fixed-income obligations minimizes the impact that any single security has on the overall bond portfolio. This is the basic concept of diversification.

Another issue of default risk is the impact that a change in a company's financial well-being will have on the value of a bond issue. When a company's financial health diminishes, it increases the likelihood, or probability, of default. Because of this increased likelihood of default, as small as it may be, the market value of the bond will decline relative to other bonds with similar characteristics. Therefore, it is not simply a matter of default, but also how changes in the general financial health of the bond issuer impact the price of a fixed-income security.

Reinvestment-Rate Risk

Simply put, reinvestment rate risk is the risk that cash flows received during the holding period of an investment will not be able to be invested at a rate that is at least as great as the expected internal rate of return of the original investment. As we discussed in calculating the yield to maturity for a bond, there is an implicit assumption that cash flows are reinvested at the YTM rate. If cash flows are reinvested at a rate that is less than the YTM rate, then the actual earnings will be less than the YTM rate calculated at inception. Likewise, if the cash flows are reinvested at a rate that is greater than the YTM rate, then the actual earnings will be greater than the YTM rate calculated at inception.

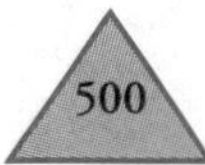

EXAMPLE

A 10-year $1,000 bond making coupon payments (semiannually) of 10 percent ($50 twice per ear) and selling for par or 100 percent of face value ($1,000) must have a YTM of 10 percent. The YTM is calculated assuming the $50 coupon payments will be reinvested to earn 10 percent. What happens if the coupon payments are invested in a savings account earning 5 percent? If the coupon payments are invested to earn 5 percent for the 10 years, the final future alue (the amount of money at the maturity of the bond) will be $2,277.23. The future value onsists of the reinvested coupon payments and the return of principal. Using a present value of $1,000 (the current value of the bond) and a future value of $2,277 will result in an actual yield of 8.4 percent instead of the expected yield of 10 percent.

Calculation of YTM Prior to Interest Rate Changes		Calculation of FV of Coupon Payments Earning 5%		Calculation of Actual Yield after Adjusting for Coupons Earning 5%	
n	= 20 (10 × 2)	PMT$_{OA}$	= $50 (100 ÷ 2)	PV	= ($1,000)
PMT$_{OA}$	= $50 (100 ÷ 2)	i	= 2.5 (5 ÷ 2)	n	= 20 (10 × 2)
FV	= $1,000	n	= 20 (10 × 2)	PMT$_{OA}$	= 0
PV	= ($1,000)	PV	= 0	FV	= $2,277.23 ($1,000 + $1,277.23)
i	= 5% × 2 = 10%	FV	= ($1,277.23)	i	= 4.2% × 2 = 8.4%

Because it is a systematic risk, purchasing power risk cannot be eliminated. Purchasing power risk is the risk that inflation will erode the purchasing power of investor's assets. Bondholders can especially be impacted by purchasing power risk. For example, if an investor owns a bond with a coupon of 5 percent when inflation is 6 percent, then he is losing purchasing power at a rate of 1 percent per year. As discussed above, there are certain inflation-adjusted bonds, such as the ones issued by the U.S. Treasury, that can minimize the adverse impact of inflation.

CALL RISK

For bonds that have a call feature, there is a risk that the bond will be called from the investor. Bond issuers will generally call a bond when interest rates decline, which means that the investor will have to reinvest the proceeds in an environment of lower interest rates. One of the characteristics that appeals to bondholders is the scheduled and known cash flows of a bond. Call features increase the uncertainty of the cash flows of a bond.

EXCHANGE-RATE RISK

Bonds issued by foreign governments or foreign companies are subject to the fluctuations in currency rates. Investors may benefit from or be harmed by currency rate changes. In addition to currency risk, foreign bonds are subject to other risks such as political risk and country risk.

LIQUIDITY RISK

The primary measure of liquidity is the spread between the bid price and the ask price for a fixed-income security. The level of risk is directly related to the spread. The larger the spread, the greater the liquidity risk. Typically, the greater the volume of transactions in a bond market, the smaller the spread will be for the security. For example, because the Treasury market is ver large, spreads are very small.

VOLATILITY OF FIXED-INCOME SECURITIES

As we have discussed, bond prices fluctuate with changes in interest rates. The value of differen bonds, however, will vary by different amounts. The two key factors that influence volatility ar coupon rate and maturity.

COUPON RATE

The volatility in price for a bond is inversely related to the bond's coupon payment whe interest rates change. Bonds with higher coupon rates are more stable with regards to interes rate changes than bonds with lower coupon rates. A zero-coupon bond will generally be mor volatile in value than a bond with a 10 percent coupon.

MATURITY

Bonds with longer terms are subject to more volatility in an environment of changing interes rates than bonds with shorter terms. A 30-year Treasury bond will be more volatile than a 5-yea Treasury note when interest rates change. This is illustrated in the following example:

EXAMPLE

Bond A is a 5-year bond with a 10 percent coupon rate. Bond B is a 30-year bond also with a 1(percent coupon rate. Since Bond B has a longer maturity, it will experience more volatility whe interest rates change.

EXHIBIT 12A.7: IMPACT OF MATURITY ON BOND VOLATILITY

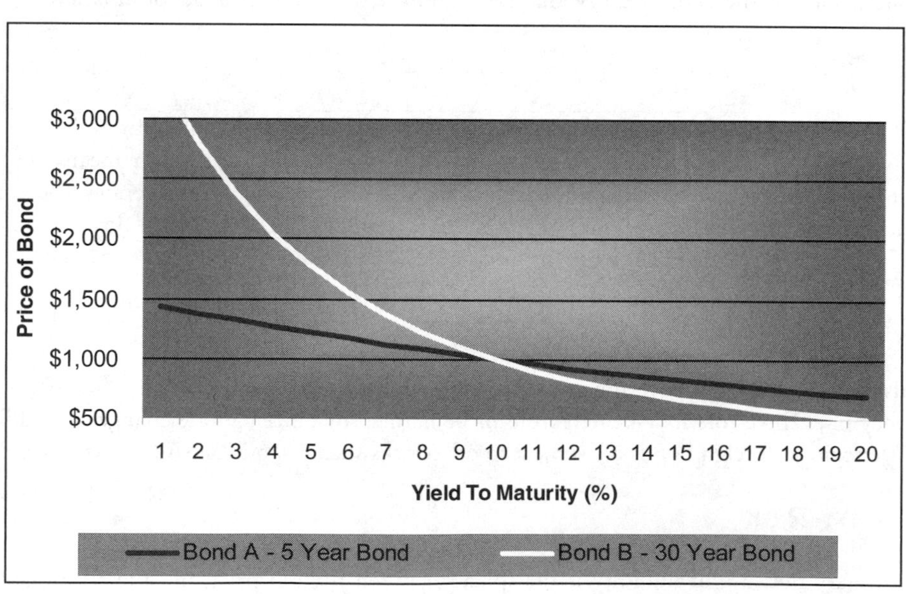

$3,000
$2,500
$2,000
$1,500
$1,000
$500
Price of Bond
1 2 3 4 5 6 7 8 9 10 11 12 13 14 15 16 17 18 19 20
Yield To Maturity (%)
Bond A - 5 Year Bond
Bond B - 30 Year Bond

Notice that Bond B's slope is steeper than Bond A's. At a YTM of 10 percent, the price of the bonds is equal at $1,000. When interest rates decrease, the price of Bond B increases more than Bond A. When interest rates increase, the price of Bond B decreases more than Bond A.

TERM STRUCTURE OF INTEREST RATES

YIELD CURVES

Traditionally, interest rates for bonds have been reflected in graphical representations called **yield curves**. These yield curves reflect current market interest rates for various bond maturities. The most popular of these yield curves is the Treasury yield curve, which depicts current yields for Treasury securities. The yield curve is generally upward sloping indicating that yields on longer-term bonds are higher than yields on shorter-term bonds. However, there have been times when the structure of interest rates has caused the yield curve to be shaped differently. The yield curve is generally described as upward sloping (normal), flat, or downward sloping (inverted) as shown in Exhibit 12A.8.

yield curves - graphical representations that reflect current market interest rates for various bond maturities

EXHIBIT 12A.8: YIELD CURVES

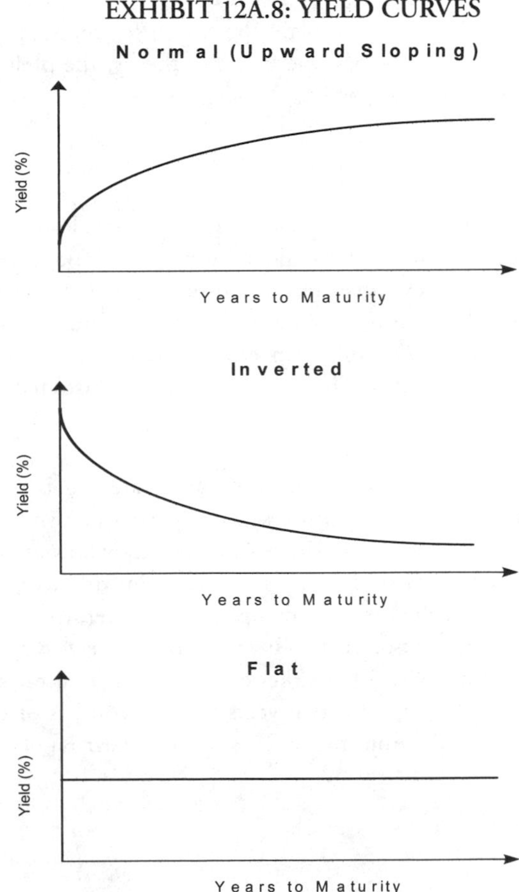

Normal (Upward Sloping)
Yield (%)
Years to Maturity
Inverted
Yield (%)
Years to Maturity
Flat
Yield (%)
Years to Maturity

The Treasury yield curve is often used as a benchmark for other fixed-income securities. The Treasury yield curve is an effective benchmark for pricing bonds and determining yields of bonds in other sectors since it is not impacted by credit risk or liquidity risk. Treasuries are backed by the full faith and credit of the U.S. government and are, therefore, not subject to credit risk. The Treasury market is extremely liquid, since it is the largest and most actively traded bond market.

The traditional method for valuing or pricing non-Treasury bonds has been to use the yield on the Treasury yield curve for the appropriate maturity, plus a premium for additional risk.

An alternative way to consider the valuation of bonds is to consider them as a series of individual cash flows with each cash flow being viewed as an independent zero-coupon bond. For example, a ten-year, 10 percent coupon Treasury note could be viewed as 20 separate and distinct zero-coupon bonds. These individual cash flows can then be valued based on market yields for zero-coupon Treasuries with similar maturities.

YIELD CURVE THEORIES

There are several theories that attempt to explain the reason for the shape of the yield curve. These include the pure expectations theory, the liquidity theory, the preferred habitat theory, and the market segmentation theory.

The Pure Expectations Theory

pure expectations theory - yield curve theory that asserts that long-term interest rates are based on expectations about future short-term interest rates

The **pure expectations theory** asserts that longer-term rates are based on expected future short-term rates. In other words, forward rates should indicate the market's perception of which direction rates will be moving. For example, an upward sloping yield curve would indicate that future short-term rates would be increasing; a flat yield curve indicates that future short-term rates will remain constant; and a downward, or inverted, yield curve represents the expectation that short-term rates will be declining. This concept can be illustrated with the following example.

EXAMPLE

Assume that the 1-year rate equals 6 percent and the 2-year rate equals 8 percent. Under this assumption, an investor who was willing to invest for a period of two years could receive a return of 8 percent for each of the two years, whereas the investor who was only willing to invest one year would receive 6 percent. There is a 2-percentage-point difference in the returns that the 2-year investor will receive in the first year compared to the return for the 1-year investor. Under the expectations theory, the reason that an investor could receive 8 percent over two years and only 6 percent for one year is that the market expects short-term rates to increase in one year. In other words, the 8 percent rate for two years actually consists of the 1-year rate of 6 percent and the 1-year rate one year from today. This future 1-year rate turns out to be 10.04 percent, as follows:

Future Value of 2-Year Bond	= 1.08 × 1.08	= 1.1664	The investor should have 16.64% more than the initial investment at the end of 2 years.
Future 1-Year Rate	= 1.1664 ÷ 1.06	= 1.1004 – 1.00 = 10.04%	Since the 1-year rate equals 6%, the future 1-year rate must equal 10.04%.
Proof	= 1.06 × 1.1004	= 1.1664	A rate of 6% for the first year plus a rate of 10.04% for the second year is equal to a 2-year rate of 8%.

One shortcoming of this theory is that it does not reflect the inherent increased risk or uncertainty in longer-term bonds. There is clearly more uncertainty with a 2-year bond than with a 1-year bond. In the above example, the theory explains that the 2-year return of 8 percent results from a 6 percent return the first year and a 10.04 percent return the second year. Based on this theory, it seems reasonable that an investor with a 1-year time horizon would purchase the 2-year bond to earn 8 percent for the first year and then sell it at the end of one year. However, there is no guarantee that the bond could be sold at a specific price at the end of one year, which introduces the element of risk into the decision. As a result, an investor with a 1-year time horizon might choose the 1-year bond instead of the 2-year bond, even though the return for the 1-year bond is lower. Therefore, it seems as though the forward rate, in our example 10.04 percent, may consist of a risk premium as well as expectations of higher future rates.

The Liquidity Preference Theory

According to the **liquidity preference theory**, investors prefer certainty and expect to be compensated for uncertainty. This theory incorporates a liquidity premium into the expectations theory model. Under this theory, investors require premiums for the increased exposure to interest rate risk inherent in long-term bonds. Yield curves will generally be upward sloping, reflecting higher premiums for longer-term bonds.

liquidity preference theory - yield curve theory that asserts that long-term bonds have greater yields to compensate investors for increased interest-rate

The Preferred Habitat Theory

The **preferred habitat theory** is similar to the market segmentation theory (described later) and states that institutions (generally financial institutions) prefer to match the maturity of their assets to that of their liabilities. In other words, institutions generally try to match the maturity or duration of their assets and liabilities. Under this theory, institutions are incentivized to shift their maturities or duration if the premiums for the switch are significant enough. Therefore, it is possible to have any shape yield curve under this theory.

preferred habitat theory - yield curve theory that asserts that financial institutions prefer to match asset maturities to liability maturities

Market Segmentation Theory

market segmentation theory - yield curve theory that asserts that yields are determined by the laws of supply and demand for specific bond maturities

According to the **market segmentation theory**, interest rates for varying maturities are determined by supply and demand. Institutions may have liabilities that are short term, intermediate term, or long term and will generally want to match the maturity of their assets with the maturity of their liabilities. As a result, there are certain types of institutions that lend and borrow at the different categories of maturities. This results in a separate market for short-term borrowings, intermediate-term borrowings, and long-term borrowings. Each market has its own balance between supply and demand. Therefore, based on the supply and demand in each maturity market, the yield curve can be any shape.

DURATION & IMMUNIZATION

duration - a concept developed by Fred Macaulay in 1938 that provides a time-weighted measure of a security's cash flows in terms of payback

The concept of **duration**, developed by Frederick Macaulay in 1938, provides a time-weighted measure of a security's cash flows in terms of payback. There are three important uses for duration:

1. Measuring of a bond's volatility;
2. Estimating the change in the price of a bond based on changes in interest rates; and
3. Immunizing a bond or bond portfolio against interest-rate risk.

CALCULATING DURATION

The formula for the Macaulay duration is:

$$D = \frac{\sum_{t=1}^{n} \frac{t\,Cf_t}{(1+k)^t}}{\sum_{t=1}^{n} \frac{Cf_t}{(1+k)^t}}$$

where: n = Number of periods until maturity

Cf_t = Cash flow that occurs in period t

k = Yield to maturity

t = Time period

The denominator is the market price of the bond, defined as the present value of future cash flows. The numerator is the sum of each discounted cash flow adjusted for the period in which it occurs.

EXAMPLE

For example, the duration for a 10-year bond that pays a 10 percent coupon annually and is yielding 10 percent can be calculated as follows:

(A) Period	(B) Cash Flow	(C) PV Factor *	(D) PV @ 10%	(E) PV x Period
1	$100.00	0.9091	$90.91	$90.91
2	$100.00	0.8264	$82.64	$165.29
3	$100.00	0.7513	$75.13	$225.39
4	$100.00	0.6830	$68.30	$273.21
5	$100.00	0.6209	$62.09	$310.46
6	$100.00	0.5645	$56.45	$338.68
7	$100.00	0.5132	$51.32	$359.21
8	$100.00	0.4665	$46.65	$373.21
9	$100.00	0.4241	$42.41	$381.69
10	$1,100.00	0.3855	$424.10	$4,240.98
			$1,000.00	$6,759.02

(F) Duration $= \frac{\$6,759.02}{\$1,000.00}$ = 6.76 years

* The PV factor is $1 \div (1.10)^t$, where t = period.

The calculation of duration requires five broad steps. The first step is to list the periods relevant to the bond (**A**). In the above example, there are ten periods associated with the bond. The second step is to list the cash flow for each period (**B**). The cash flows will consist of coupon payments and/or principal payments. The third step is to calculate the present value of each of the cash flows. This can be done by multiplying column **B** by column **C**. Column **C** lists the present value factors used to discount a future cash flow back *n* periods. The fourth step is to multiply column **A** by column **D**. For example, in the third period, 3 is multiplied by $75.13, which equals $225.39. The final step is to divide the sum of column **E** by the sum of column **D**. The result of this fifth step is the duration in years (**F**).

Duration can be calculated on a periodic basis to accurately account for semiannual coupon payments by listing each semiannual period and cash flow. This adjustment will result in an answer in terms of period, which can be converted into years simply by dividing by two (for semiannual payments).

The previous multiple-step method can also be solved using the closed-end formula:

$$\text{Dur} = \frac{1+k}{k} - \frac{(1+k)+T(C-k)}{C\left[(1+k)^{T}-1\right]+k}, \text{ where}$$

k = Yield to maturity, as a decimal

T = Time until maturity, in periods

C = Coupon rate, as a decimal

The calculation of this formula can be illustrated using the above example:

$$\text{Dur} = \frac{1+0.10}{0.10} - \frac{(1+0.10)+10(0.10-0.10)}{0.10[(1+0.10)^{10}-1]+0.10}$$

$$\text{Dur} = 11 - \frac{1.10}{0.25937}$$

$$\text{Dur} = 11 - 4.24$$

$$\text{Dur} = 6.76 \text{ years}$$

Duration as a Measure of a Bond's Volatility

Duration provides investors with a method of easily comparing a bond's volatility to the volatility of other bonds. Very simply, bonds with higher durations are more volatile when interest rates change than bonds with lower durations. Therefore, the volatility of bonds increases as the duration increases. The main factors that impact a bond's duration are coupon rate and maturity.

Coupon Rate

There is an inverse relationship between a bond's coupon rate and its duration. The duration of a bond cannot exceed the maturity of a bond. Generally, the duration of a bond is less than its term to maturity. A bond's duration will only equal its maturity if the bond is a zero-coupon bond.

When the coupon rate is increased, the investor is receiving cash flows faster, decreasing the time the investor must wait to be paid back the initial investment. A quicker payback means a shorter duration.

Maturity

There is a direct relationship between a bond's maturity and its duration. Bonds with greater maturities have longer durations. However, the increase in duration is at a diminishing rate. The following figure illustrates this point. It is a graph of the duration for a bond with a 10 percent coupon and a 10 percent YTM, calculated for maturities ranging between 1 year and 30 years.

EXHIBIT 12A.1: DURATION AT VARIOUS MATURITIES FOR A 10% COUPON BOND WITH YTM OF 10%

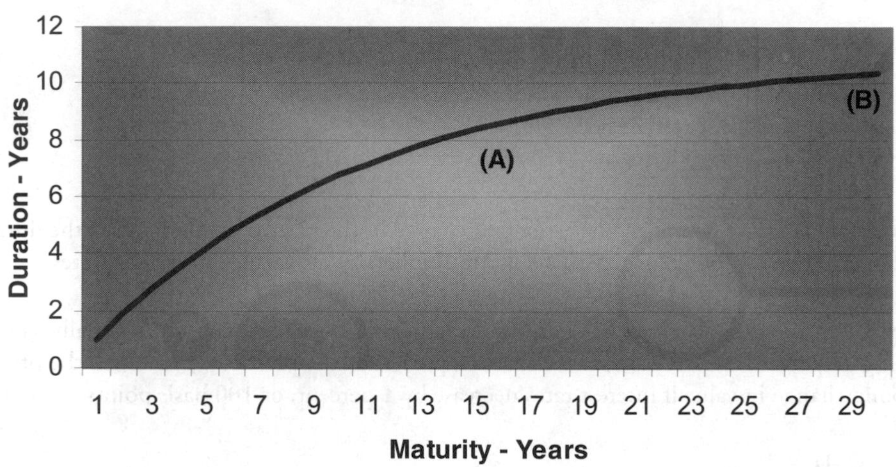

Duration - Years
0
2
4
6
8
10
12
(A)
(B)
1 3 5 7 9 11 13 15 17 19 21 23 25 27 29
Maturity - Years

As illustrated in Exhibit 12A.9, duration is directly impacted by maturity, however, at a decreasing rate. In this example, the duration for a maturity of 15 years is approximately 8.4 years (**A**), while the duration for a maturity of 30 years is only 10.4 years (**B**). Although the actual maturity doubled, the duration of the bond increased by only 2 years. It should also be noted that the coupon rate will impact the degree to which the duration changes.

Yield to Maturity

Like the coupon rate of a bond, the market rate of interest, or current yield to maturity, is inversely related to duration. As the level of interest rates increases, the durations of bonds decrease, and if interest rates decrease, durations will increase. A reduction in market rates of interest results in a lower reinvestment rate for coupon payments, which extends the payback period for the bond.

ESTIMATING THE CHANGE IN THE PRICE OF A BOND BASED ON CHANGES IN INTEREST RATES

Another important application of duration is its use in determining the price change in a bond or bond portfolio based on changes in interest rates. As interest rates change, bond prices are impacted. What is important to a fixed-income investor is the exposure to interest-rate risk. What is the percent change in the bond or bond portfolio given a specific change in interest rates? The answer to this question can be determined by understanding the relationship between a bond's price and its duration. As we discussed, coupon, maturity, and YTM all impact duration. These same factors also determine the price of a bond. Therefore, duration can assist us in determining the estimated change in the price of a bond based on changes in interest rates. The following formula provides an estimate of the percentage change in the price of a bond based on the duration and the change in market interest rates:

$$\frac{\Delta P}{P} = \frac{-D}{1 + YTM} \times \Delta YTM \text{ , where}$$

$\Delta P/P$ = Percentage change in the price of a bond

D = Duration of the bond

YTM = Yield to maturity for the bond

ΔYTM = Change in YTM as a decimal

As the formula above describes, the estimated change in the price of a bond equals the duratio of a bond divided by one plus the YTM and multiplied by the change in interest rates.

EXAMPLE

For example, the duration for a 10-year bond that pays a 10 percent coupon, annually, and is yielding 10 percent is 6.76 years, as we saw in a previous example. How much will the price of the bond change in value if interest rates decrease by 1 percent, or 100 basis points, to 9 percent?

$$\frac{\Delta P}{P} = \frac{-D}{1 + YTM} \times \Delta YTM$$

$$\frac{\Delta P}{P} = \frac{-6.76}{1 + 0.10} \times (0.09 - 0.10)$$

$$\frac{\Delta P}{P} = -6.1455 \times -0.01$$

$$\frac{\Delta P}{P} = 0.06145 = 6.145\%$$

Based on the above formula, the price of the bond should increase by approximately 6.1 percent. This estimation of the price change of a bond is very useful in analyzing the exposur that a bond portfolio has to interest-rate risk. Based on this estimate, we would expect the nev price of the bond to be $1,061.45 ($1,000 x 1.06145). This estimate can be verified b calculating the price of the bond using time value of money concepts.

FV	=	$1,000
n	=	10
i	=	9%
PMT	=	$100
PV	=	($1,064.18)

Based on this calculation, our estimate is off by $2.73 or 0.25 percent. The estimation model i very effective for small changes in interest rates; and in the market, we rarely find large change in interest rates.

Using Duration to Immunize Bond Portfolios

As we have emphasized, interest-rate risk is one of the major concerns of fixed-income investors as well as managers of fixed-income portfolios. As interest rates increase, the price of bonds wil decline. However, there is an offsetting position that must be considered. When interest rate increase, the reinvested coupon payments can be invested at higher rates, offsetting the declin in the value of the bond. This offsetting of price and reinvested coupon payments is illustrated in the following table:

Interest Rates Move	Value of Bond (Inverse to interest rates)	Value of Reinvested Coupon Payments (Move is direct to interest rates)
↑	↓	↑
↓	↑	↓

As you can see, when interest rates increase, the value of bonds decline, but the value of reinvested coupon payments increase. Similarly, as interest rates decline, bond prices increase and the value of reinvested coupon payments decreases. This offsetting is the basis for immunizing a bond or bond portfolio against interest rate risk.

Immunization is the concept of minimizing the impact of changes in interest rates on the value of investments. The goal of immunization is to protect the bond portfolio from interest-rate fluctuations and reinvestment-rate risk. The purpose of immunization is to provide a stable compound rate of return that equals the calculated YTM at the purchase of the bond, despite interest-rate fluctuations. The portfolio is considered immunized if the realized rate of return is at least as great as the computed YTM calculated at inception. Another way to think of immunization is that a bond portfolio is immunized when the actual future value is at least as great as had been expected at inception.

immunization - the concept of minimizing the impact of changes in interest rates on the value of investments

A bond portfolio is initially immunized at the point of duration. Therefore, if an investor were to match the duration of a bond portfolio to the time horizon of his goal, then his portfolio is initially immunized. This can be easily accomplished with a zero-coupon bond. An investor who had a cash need in ten years could simply purchase a ten-year, zero-coupon bond and hold it to maturity. This will eliminate all reinvestment-rate and interest-rate risk. However, purchasing zero-coupon bonds with the desired maturities is not always feasible. Although not as ideal as zeros, ordinary coupon bonds can effectively immunize a portfolio. Consider the following example.

EXAMPLE

Assumptions:

- Coupon rate of 8 percent, paid annually.
- Term of bond is 10 years.
- The yield on the bond equals 10 percent.
- The duration of the bond is approximately 7 years.
- Time horizon of client's cash needs is 7 years.

IMMUNIZATION EXAMPLE

	Assuming Interest Rates Remain at:	Interest Rates Change to the Following:			
	10%	8%	9%	11%	12%
Coupon Payment Reinvested					
PMT	$ 80.00	$ 80.00	$ 80.00	$ 80.00	$ 80.00
i	10.00%	8.00%	9.00%	11.00%	12.00%
n	7.000	7.000	7.000	7.000	7.000
FV@7years	$758.97	$ 713.82	$ 736.03	$ 782.66	$ 807.12
Proceeds of Bond Sales @ Year 7					
FV	$ 1,000.00	$ 1,000.00	$ 1,000.00	$ 1,000.00	$ 1,000.00
PMT	$ 80.00	$ 80.00	$ 80.00	$ 80.00	$ 80.00
i	10.00%	8.00%	9.00%	11.00%	12.00%
n	3.000	3.000	3.000	3.000	3.000
PV@7years	$950.26	$1,000.00	$ 974.69	$ 926.69	$ 903.93
Reinvested Coupon Pmts.	$758.97	$ 713.82	$ 736.03	$ 782.66	$ 807.12
Bond Sale Proceeds	$950.26	$1,000.00	$ 974.69	$ 926.69	$ 903.93
Total@7years	$1,709.24	$1,713.82	$1,710.72	$1,709.35	$1,711.05

The example above illustrates the concept of immunization. The investor should have $1,709.24 at the end of seven years, assuming yields remain steady at 10 percent. The $1,709.24 consists of the reinvested coupon payments ($758.97) plus the sales proceeds of the bond ($950.26) at year seven. Thus, $1,709.24 is the future value at the point of duration that we are expecting assuming no change in interest rates. This bond will be considered immunized if the future value at other rates of return is at least as great as $1,709.24. As the chart illustrates, although the interest rate changes from 10 percent, the future value at the point of duration (7 years) for these other points is at least as great as the future value if the interest rates had remained at 10 percent. Therefore, an investor who had a cash need in seven years could use this bond as a method of minimizing the exposure to interest-rate risk.

It should be noted that matching the duration to the investor's cash need immunizes the portfolio against initial changes in interest rates. As time passes, however, the bond portfolio will need to be rebalanced so that the duration and remaining time continue to match. Rebalancing should be done once or twice per year. If rebalancing is performed more frequently than twice per year, then the transaction costs will minimize any benefit derived through rebalancing.

Traditional Methods of Immunizing Bond Portfolios

Traditional strategies for immunizing bond portfolios from interest-rate risk include the ladder strategy, the barbell strategy, and the bullet strategy.

The Ladder Strategy

The **ladder strategy** is accomplished by establishing a portfolio of bonds with staggered maturities. For example, ten $20,000 bonds could be purchased with maturities ranging from one to ten years for a total portfolio of $200,000. The shorter maturity bonds would be less subject to price fluctuation than the longer term bonds, and they would combine to provide the desired duration. This approach provides two advantages. First, since there is a combination of long-term and short-term bonds in the portfolio, the laddered portfolio will provide higher yields than a portfolio consisting entirely of short-term bonds. Second, because one bond matures each year, cash is regularly available to the investor.

ladder strategy - portfolio immunization strategy that uses a portfolio of bonds with staggered maturities

The Barbell Strategy

Under the **barbell strategy**, one-half of the portfolio is invested in short-term bonds, while the other half of the portfolio is invested in long-term bonds. Again, the combined portfolio has the desired duration. For example, a $200,000 fixed-income portfolio might be invested as $100,000 in 5-year bonds and $100,000 in 15-year bonds.

barbell strategy - portfolio immunization strategy that uses a portfolio of short-term and long-term

The Bullet Strategy

When investors purchase a series of bonds with similar maturities, focused around a single point in time, it is considered a **bullet strategy**. Like the previous two strategies, the portfolio is created to achieve the desired duration.

bullet strategy - portfolio immunization strategy that uses a portfolio of bonds with similar

PROFESSIONAL FOCUS

When do you prefer to use individual fixed-income securities over mutual funds?

Fixed-income investments can reduce the volatility of the overall portfolio, increase diversification to reduce risk, and provide steady cash flow. It is important to determine the needs and concerns of the client.

Individual fixed-income securities can be used when clients want to remove interest rate risk. Generally we are buying highly rated securities with the intent to hold them to maturity.

Individual securities provide a known source of cash flow as interest is paid and investments mature. We often will ladder the maturity date of these securities to generate a steady stream of cash flow over a number of years. This works well for clients that also need growth in their portfolio, but are risk averse. Once you can show them they will have a steady source of cash flow for living expenses, they are more comfortable having the remainder of the portfolio invested in equities for long-term growth.

Bond mutual funds can be used to reduce the volatility of the overall portfolio and to capture a diversified mix of bonds. For example, we may want to include a combination of taxable and tax-free, short-term and intermediate term, and domestic and international securities in a portfolio. Bond funds are easier to manage than individual securities and fund managers may have access to securities you will not.

How do you make decisions with regard to allocating among short-, medium- and long-term fixed-income securities?

We use fixed-income securities to reduce volatility and/or produce cash flow while using stocks or stock funds to produce growth. If a client is willing to take higher risks, we will invest in stocks for long-term growth.

Research has shown that the risk of owning fixed-income securities can increase after 5 years while the returns do not. Bond values will fluctuate with changes in interest rates, however, shorter-term bonds have less interest rate risk than longer-term bonds. Therefore, we generally invest in short- to intermediate-term securities.

Short-term bond funds are also used as a holding place for cash when interest rates are low and individual CDs and bonds are not a good option.

When do you use individual fixed-income securities for your client's portfolio and why?

Municipal bond and or bond funds can be used for clients in high federal and state income tax brackets. Depending on the state, inventories of highly rated municipals may be low at times and the use of a bond fund or bond manager may be appropriate.

Municipals should not be purchased in tax-deferred accounts, as the yields are lower for municipals than taxable bonds. The after-tax yield of securities will need to be compared when deciding which is better for a client.

CONNIE BREZIK, CPA/PFS

CHAPTER 12 SUPPLEMENT B

Equity Securities

This supplement provides additional information on equity securities. Topics covered include:

- General characteristics of equities
- Types of common stock
- Preferred stock
- Foreign securities
- Risks associated with equities
- Equity markets
- Benchmarks
- Market indexes and averages
- Measures of equity returns
- Market positions
- Margin accounts
- Market orders
- Methods of analysis
- Equity valuation models

INTRODUCTION

Equity securities play a vital role in the investment strategies of many investors. Historically, thei returns have been significantly better than the returns for many other asset classes. These hig returns are a key aspect in the attractiveness of equity investments . This section explains th basic concepts of equity-type investments, the risks of equity investments, how equity securitie are traded, and how equity securities are valued.

BASIC CONCEPTS OF OWNERSHIP-TYPE INVESTMENTS

WHAT OWNERSHIP MEANS

dividends - distributions of cash or additional shares of stock paid to the shareholders of a corporation

In Chapter 12, we discussed the two general types of securities—lending securities and owner ship securities. Lending securities, which are investments with interest payments made to th investor (lender) for the use of the loaned funds, were discussed in the previous supplemen (Chapter 12 Supplement A). By ownership securities, we mean securities that represent som form of ownership interest in a corporation. Corporations are artificial, legal entities whose cre ation and operation are controlled by state statutes. To become a corporation, a business mus incorporate within a state. As part of the incorporation process and as one method of raisin additional capital, a corporation issues shares of common stock. Holders of these shares have cer tain rights and benefits, including the right to receive dividends, the right to vote on corporat issues, the right to limited liability, and finally, the right to ultimate distribution of assets in th event of liquidation.

date of declaration - date on which a corporation's board of directors declares a dividend payment creating an obligation on the company to make a dividend payment to shareholders

Numerous risks are inherent in owning common stock. The primary reason that investors ar willing to accept these risks is that equities have earned significantly higher returns than othe types of investments over long periods. These returns consist of two primary sources – dividend and capital appreciation.

date of record - the date at which an owner of the common stock of a corporation is entitled to receive the dividend payment

Dividends

Companies have positive net income when their earnings are greater than their expenses. A com pany has two choices with regard to the excess earnings. This additional cash can be reinveste into the business in the form of new or existing projects, or it can be paid to the shareholders o the corporation. These payments to shareholders are referred to as cash dividends.

ex-dividend date - the date on which the market reflects the dividend payment

From a theoretical standpoint, the company should reinvest the additional income if it is able t earn returns that are higher than shareholders could earn on their own. If this is not the case then companies should pay the additional cash to the shareholders in the form of **dividends**.

date of payment - the date that the dividend will actually be paid

Four dates are important when discussing payment of a dividend. These dates include the **dat of declaration**, the **date of record**, the **ex-dividend date**, and the **date of payment**. The board o directors declares a dividend payment, which creates an obligation for the company to make dividend payment to shareholders. The date of record represents the date on which an owner o the common stock is entitled to receive the dividend payment. If a shareholder owns the stoc as of the date of record, he is entitled to receive the dividend.

The ex-dividend date is the date at which the market reflects the dividend payment. If a stock is currently valued at $100 and the company declares a $5 dividend, then the stock should decline in value by $5 to $95 on the ex-dividend date. From an economic standpoint, the shareholder is in the same position after the ex-dividend date as before. Prior to the dividend, the shareholders owned a stock worth $100. After the dividend payment, the shareholders own a stock worth $95 and have $5 in cash.

EXAMPLE

Finally, the date of payment is simply the date on which the dividend will actually be paid. Remember that the dividend will be paid to those who owned shares as of the date of record. Therefore, someone who sells his or her shares after the date of record, but before the date of payment, will receive the dividend payment.

Capital Appreciation

A company must choose how to use the income it generates. Even if the company is highly profitable, it may choose to retain the earnings and invest in additional projects. In such a case, the owner or investor receives his return in the form of appreciation of the stock, which is referred to as **capital appreciation**. Amgen is a good example of a company that does not pay dividends, but has generated significant stock appreciation (Exhibit 12B.1).

capital appreciation - when a company chooses to retain the earnings and invest in additional projects, the investor receives his return in the form of appreciation of the stock

EXHIBIT 12B.1: AMGEN'S STOCK PRICE 1984-2005

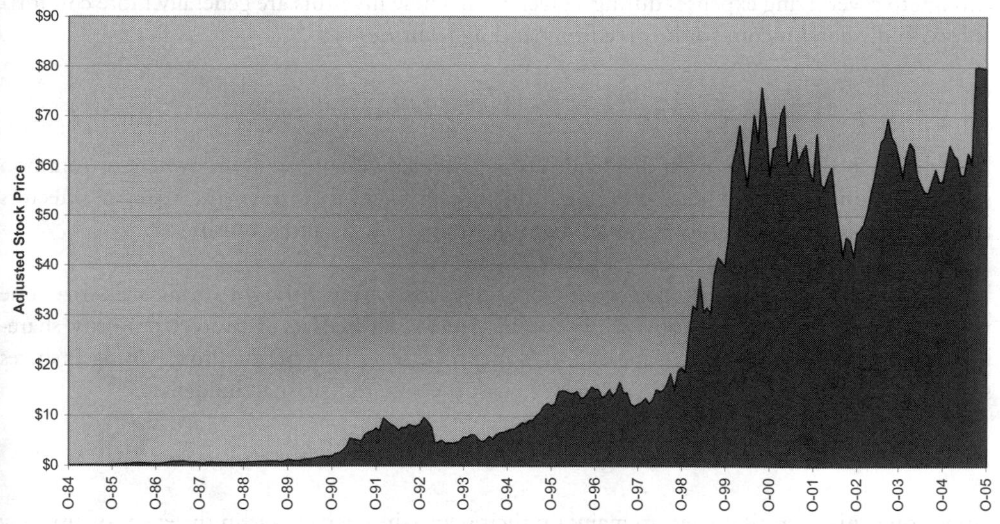

Adjusted Stock Price
$90
$80
$70
$60
$50
$40
$30
$20
$10
$0
O-84
O-85
O-86
O-87
O-88
O-89
O-90
O-91
O-92
O-93
O-94
O-95
O-96
O-97
O-98
O-99
O-00
O-01
O-02
O-03
O-04
O-05

Exhibit 12B.1 shows that investors who purchased Amgen stock during the 1980's have received huge gains from the appreciation of the stock. The company was able to earn returns higher than most investors could have earned through other investments.

Dividends or Capital Appreciation: Which is better?

There are two primary differences between dividend income and capital appreciation that need to be considered before answering the question, "Which is better?" These two differences include the tax treatment and the perceived risk between the two types of income.

Since 2003, most dividends are taxed as capital gains in the year in which the dividend payment is received. The tax rates for long-term capital gains range from 5 percent to 15 percent. Appreciation in the price of a stock is also taxed as a capital gain but is taxed only when the stock has been sold. Therefore, from a tax standpoint, capital gains may be preferred over dividend income due to the delay in taxation.

If capital gain income is preferred over dividend income from a tax standpoint, then why do individual investors often prefer dividend income? To answer this question, we have to understand the nature of dividend income versus income from the sale of appreciated stock.

Generally, a company's dividend policy will remain relatively constant over a period of time. In other words, if a company paid a $2.00 dividend last year, then it is reasonable to expect the company to pay $2.00 or a little more this year and next year. Companies do not generally change their dividend payments drastically from one year to the next, thus allowing investors to have confidence in the amount of dividend income they will receive from their investment.

Price appreciation is much less reliable than dividend income, meaning there is more risk associated with gain from the sale of stock than with dividend income. Therefore, investors with long-time horizons prefer capital appreciation, because they are more able to control the recognition and taxation of the income and because with higher risk generally comes higher returns. Investors who need current income cannot afford the risk of whether a stock will appreciate enough to cover living expenses during a given year. These investors are generally more comfortable with dividend income or income from lending securities.

Voting

straight voting - one vote per share of common stock

cumulative voting - number of votes per share equal to number of seats on the board of directors

proxy voting - authorizing an agent to cast the vote for the

preemptive right - allows shareholder to maintain ownership percentage by requiring new issues of stock to be offered first to current shareholders

In addition to the returns from dividend income and capital appreciation, owners of common stock have voting rights. These voting rights include the right to vote for the board of directors and the right to vote on corporate issues, such as certain mergers and acquisitions.

Voting can take the form of straight voting or cumulative voting. **Straight voting** authorizes one vote per share of common stock, while **cumulative voting** is used to protect minority shareholder interests. In addition, voting can be done in person or by proxy. **Proxy voting** involves sending a written authorization to an agent to cast the vote for the shareholder.

Maintaining Ownership Percentage

Some companies permit owners to maintain their ownership percentage in the event of any new offering of their stock. For example, an investor who owned 10 percent of a company might be given the opportunity to purchase 10 percent of any new stock offering. This right allows him to maintain his ownership percentage. This type of right is known as a **preemptive right**.

Liability

Because corporations are separate legal entities, they are generally responsible for all debts and claims arising from all sources. As a result, shareholders are protected from personal liability.

TYPES OF EQUITY SECURITIES

COMMON STOCK

Common stock represents an ownership interest in a firm. If the company succeeds, then the investor will receive high returns from his investment. However, if the company does not perform well, then the value of the stock will decline. Since there are thousands of companies, a classification system has developed to categorize equity securities. One classification system is based on the type of stock. This classification system includes defensive stocks, cyclical stocks, blue chip stocks, growth stocks, income stocks, interest-sensitive stocks, value stocks, and new economy stocks.

common stock - ownership interest in a company

Defensive Stocks

Stocks that are relatively unaffected by general fluctuations in the economy are considered **defensive stocks.** These companies tend to have steady (although slow) growth, become popular during economic recessions, and lose popularity during economic booms. Many of these companies provide products that are necessary for everyday life. Thus, the demand for the products will not be adversely affected by changing economic cycles. Since the demand for these products does not change, the demand for these products is considered inelastic. Defensive stocks are usually found in the following industries:

defensive stocks - stock of companies that are relatively unaffected by general fluctuations in the economy

- Utilities.
- Soft drinks.
- Groceries.
- Candy.
- Drug/Pharmaceuticals.
- Tobacco.

Another way to think of defensive stocks is that they have low systematic risk, since they are not greatly affected by changes in the economy and the market. Therefore, these securities will typically have low betas relative to the overall market.

Cyclical Stocks

Cyclical stocks tend to prosper in expanding economies and tend to do poorly during down business cycles. When the economy is growing, demand strengthens, and these companies are able to make large profits. When the economy is in a downturn, these companies are hurt by declines in demand and are less profitable. In recessions, they begin cost cutting measures to improve the bottom line (earnings) and as a result, these companies end up in a healthy financial position for the next economic upturn. The companies regarded as cyclicals usually have large investments in plant and equipment and, therefore, high fixed costs. These stocks come from industries that include the following:

cyclical stocks - stock of companies that tend to prosper in expanding economies and do poorly during down business cycles

- Automobiles.
- Cement.
- Paper.

- Airlines.
- Railroads.
- Machinery.
- Steel.

Because these stocks typically perform well when the economy is booming and perform poorly when the economy is in recession, cyclical stocks are highly correlated with the overall stock market. In addition, these stocks will typically have higher betas than the overall market.

Blue Chip Stocks

blue chip stocks - stock issued by older, well-established companies that maintain the ability to pay dividends both in years the company has income and in years the company has losses

Stocks issued by highly regarded investment quality companies are called **blue chip stocks**. These companies tend to be older, well-established companies that maintain the ability to pay dividends both in years the company has income and in years the company has losses. These companies are generally leaders in their respective industries. They tend to offer investors quality investments with both steady dividend streams and relatively consistent growth. Examples of blue chip stocks include:

- General Electric.
- General Motors.
- ExxonMobil.
- Wal-Mart.
- IBM.

Although blue chip companies are by definition high-quality, sound financial companies, are they good investments? The answer to this question depends on a variety of issues related to the company. However, it is certainly the case that some good companies may be poor investments. This distinction occurs because the price for quality companies may be so high that it makes the investment a poor decision.

Growth Stocks

growth stocks - stock issued by companies whose sales, earnings, and market share are growing at higher rates than average or the general

Growth stocks are stocks issued by companies that have sales, earnings, and market share growing at higher rates than average or the general economy. Many blue chip stocks can also be classified as growth stocks. Because these companies are growing and expanding, they do not typically pay large dividends. Most of the earnings generated from these companies are reinvested in the company to support future growth. An example of this type of stock is Amgen, which has never paid a dividend, but whose stock has appreciated substantially over the last twenty years. These companies are expected to grow and appreciate more rapidly than ordinary companies.

Price appreciation is appealing to investors because it remains untaxed until the appreciation is recognized (that is, there is no taxable gain until the stock is sold and the gain is recognized for tax purposes). This growth acts as an income tax deferral and allows for higher compounding returns. Since investors trying to accumulate wealth do not usually need current income, these stocks match their financial needs better than other investments due to smaller dividends and tax deferred appreciation.

Long-term (held for a year and a day) capital gains currently receive favorable tax treatment. These gains are ordinarily taxed at a maximum rate of 15 percent (some long-term capital gains are taxed at an intermediate rate of 28 percent, such as collectibles), whereas ordinary income can be taxed at marginal rates of 35 percent. This large difference in tax rates causes investors to adjust their asset allocations to maximize after-tax returns at their level of risk tolerance.

In addition to growth stocks, there are emerging growth stocks for smaller and younger growth companies. These companies have survived the early years and are just beginning to grow and expand. Emerging growth stocks have great potential for investment, but are also subject to tremendous risk.

Income Stocks

As discussed earlier, dividends are one of the two ways investors benefit from investing in common stock. Some stocks are attractive because they make large divided payments relative to other firms in the economy. Often these companies are in the maturity phase of the industry life cycle and payout the majority of their earnings in the form of dividends. These companies will generally appreciate moderately, but will continue to be profitable and grow over time. Utilities are a good example of an **income stock.**

income stock - stock issued by companies in the maturity phase of the industry life cycle and that payout the majority of their earnings in the form of dividends

Interest-Sensitive Stocks

Because the performance of some companies is largely affected by changes in interest rates, their stock is considered **interest-sensitive stock**. For example, the housing industry is more productive and has more demand when interest rates are low since it is cheaper for consumers to purchase homes. When interest rates increase, the cost of purchasing homes goes up, causing the demand for new homes to decline. These trends also affect lumber, plumbing, furnishing, and household equipment companies. Rising interest rates cause the cost of debt to increase; therefore, companies that have large amounts of debt will have increasing interest expense. These companies, like consumers, have the opportunity to refinance their debt during low interest rate periods.

interest-sensitive stock - stock issued by companies whose performance is largely affected by changes in interest rates

Some companies that are heavily affected by interest rates are:

- ▲ Insurance companies.
- ▲ Savings and loans.
- ▲ Commercial banks.
- ▲ Telephone companies.
- ▲ Utility companies.

Value Stocks

Stocks trading at prices that are low given their historical earnings and current asset value are referred to as **value stocks**. These securities tend to have low price-to-earnings ratios and tend to be out of favor in the market. Value managers attempt to find these high quality companies that are temporarily undervalued by the market in hopes that the market will recognize their true value, and the stock's price will increase.

value stocks - stock trading at prices that are low given the stock's historical earnings and current asset value

New Economy Stocks

new economy stocks - stock of companies within the technology industry that are expected to benefit greatly from the popularity and mainstreaming of the internet

During the early part of the year 2000, the term "**new economy stocks**" became popular. This new term was used to describe the stocks within the technology industry that were expected to benefit greatly from the popularity and mainstreaming of the internet. These companies included companies selling products to consumers directly over the internet, such as Amazon, E-Bay, Yahoo, and numerous others. In addition, companies providing access to the internet, such as cable companies and telephone companies, were benefiting from the new economy. Providers of hardware, such as Cisco Systems, were seeing tremendous growth and prosperity due to the demand for internet systems.

preferred stock - a type of stock that has characteristics of both fixed-income investments and of common stock in that dividend payments must be paid each year prior to paying a dividend to the common shareholders

Within a short period, these companies and many more had benefited from the Internet. The media hype on Internet and technology stocks led many to believe that we had entered into a new era and that traditional methods of valuation were somehow outdated and not in touch with the new economy. During the latter part of 2000 and in 2001, the euphoria of the Internet and technology stocks dissipated and the markets took a nosedive, losing more than 60 percent of their market capitalization. Investors found that despite the hype, traditional valuation models do hold.

Equities can be classified in other ways. For example, equities might be segregated into sectors of the economy (healthcare, energy, technology) or classified by size (large-cap, mid-cap, small-cap).

cumulative preferred stock - preferred stock that requires receipt of previously unpaid preferred dividends before common shareholders receive dividend payments

PREFERRED STOCK

Preferred stock has characteristics of both fixed-income investments and of common stock. Shareholders of preferred stock generally receive dividends each year equal to a stated percentage of the par value of the stock if the corporation declares them. For instance, a $100 par, 5.5 percent issue of preferred stock pays a dividend of $5.50 each year for each share owned. The corporation must satisfy these dividend payments each year before paying a dividend to the common shareholders. If the corporation is required to pay any unpaid preferred dividends from prior years before paying a dividend to the common stockholders, the preferred stock is referred to as **cumulative**.

participating preferred stock - preferred stock that receives dividend based on the performance of the firm in addition to the specified preferred dividend

Preferred stock may also be participating, meaning that preferred shareholders share in the profits of the corporation. With **participating preferred**, the preferred shareholders generally receive dividend payments. Then, holders of common stock will receive dividends equal to the amount paid to the preferred shareholders. Additional funds for dividends will then be allocated between the participating preferred and common shareholders according to stock agreements.

convertible preferred stock - preferred stock that includes the right to convert preferred stock into a specific number of common shares at the option of the stockholder

Preferred stock has a preferential right over common shareholders to the assets of the corporation equal to the par value of the stock. This right must be satisfied before the common shareholders receive any assets upon liquidation. However, secured and unsecured creditors will be compensated before preferred shareholders receive any assets of the corporation.

Convertible preferred stock has a conversion right that allows holders to redeem or trade in the preferred stock for a specified number of common shares. Convertible preferred stock provides the safety of a fixed-income security with the growth potential of a stock.

Foreign Securities

Although the United States is the largest financial market in the world, as measured by market capitalization, it only represents approximately 50 to 55 percent of the world financial market capitalization. This means that approximately half of the world's market capitalization is created by companies outside the United States. Thus, **foreign securities** may provide significant benefits to United States investors.

foreign securities - securities issued by non-U.S. firms

First, securities outside the U.S. have substantial return potential. Many of the countries outside the U.S. are less developed and, therefore, provide opportunities for significant growth. Second, foreign markets are generally not as efficient as the U.S. market and, therefore, provide opportunities to find undervalued securities. Third, foreign securities provide benefits of diversification. The returns and movements in the equity markets of most foreign countries are not highly correlated with that of the U.S. market. Therefore, adding foreign asset classes to a portfolio may increase the efficiency of the portfolio.

Foreign securities are generally classified as being from developed countries or emerging markets. Developed countries include countries such as the Canada, Japan, England, and France. Emerging markets include those countries with significant growth potential, but that are currently underdeveloped. Examples of emerging markets include Argentina, Brazil, Chile, Taiwan, and Venezuela. The returns from emerging market countries are generally less correlated to the returns of the U.S. market than that of developed countries. However, the returns of emerging markets can be extremely volatile.

There are currently several methods for U.S. investors to invest in foreign securities. These include purchasing American Depositary Receipts, investing in international or foreign mutual funds, investing in international or foreign closed-end funds, purchasing foreign shares on foreign stock exchanges, and purchasing international iShares.

American Depositary Receipts (ADRs)

American Depositary Receipts (ADRs) are one of the easiest methods of acquiring individual foreign securities. They are certificates issued by U.S. banks representing ownership in shares of stock of a foreign company that are held on deposit in a bank in the firm's home country. ADRs are denominated in U.S. dollars and pay dividends in U.S. dollars. Although they are denominated in U.S. currency, they do not protect holders from exchange rate risk. Changes in currency rates between the firm's currency and the U.S. dollar will be reflected by a change in the value of the ADR.

American Depositary Receipts (ADRs) - certificates issued by U.S. banks representing ownership in shares of stock of a foreign company that are held on deposit in a bank in the firm's home country

ADRs are considered "cross listed" since the foreign shares are listed on the U.S. stock exchange as well as the foreign exchange. One of the benefits of ADRs is that the foreign company must satisfy the requirements of U.S. exchanges including compliance with U.S. GAAP (Generally Accepted Accounting Principles) and certain disclosure and reporting requirements.

foreign mutual funds - securities that provide investors with the easiest method of investing in foreign markets in the context of a diversified portfolio

Foreign Mutual Funds

Today, numerous mutual funds have the objective of investing internationally. These **foreign mutual funds** provide investors with the easiest method of investing in foreign markets in the context of a diversified portfolio. These foreign funds have a variety of objectives, ranging from regions of the world to size of the market. International funds generally invest in securities throughout the world, while foreign funds strictly invest outside the U.S.

Foreign Closed-end Funds

foreign closed-end funds - closed-end funds that invest in foreign firms

Foreign closed-end funds provide the same basic benefits as foreign mutual funds. However, because closed-end funds trade on exchanges, they do not have the cash inflow and outflow that mutual funds frequently experience. This fixed capitalization allows managers of closed-end funds to invest in less liquid securities without fear that investors will wish to liquidate their positions, forcing the manager to liquidate the illiquid securities in the portfolio.

Purchasing Foreign Shares on Foreign Stock Exchanges

Direct purchasing of foreign securities on foreign exchanges is more difficult than indirect purchasing. However, with the advance of technology, the process has become simpler. Establishing a brokerage account in a foreign country or using a foreign branch of a U.S. broker can accomplish the purchase of foreign shares on foreign exchanges. The foreign transactions require completion in the local currency. Monitoring direct foreign investments is certainly more difficult than monitoring a mutual fund.

International iShares

iShares - passively managed international index funds

In 1996, Barclays Global Investors introduced World Equity Benchmark Shares (commonly referred to as WEBS) as an alternative method of investing in foreign markets. WEBS, now **iShares**, are investment companies that are designed and structured to mimic the Morgan Stanley Capital International (MSCI) stock market indexes for individual foreign countries, foreign regions and foreign firms by market capitalization. Effectively, WEBS are passively managed index funds that invest in foreign firms.

International iShares are designed after Standard & Poor's Depositary Receipts (SPDRs), which track the S&P 500 index. They are similar to open-end investment companies (mutual funds) in that they are open-ended and the shares trade at or near net asset value (NAV). However, like closed-end funds, iShares trade in the secondary market.

Although relatively new, there are already iShares for forty-seven various international indexes. These represent indexes in Europe, Asia, Africa, North and South America, as well as regional and global indexes.

International iShares, along with the other methods of foreign investing, provide investors with numerous advantages over investing strictly in domestic equities. When foreign investment is combined with domestic investment, these advantages include higher potential returns, lower levels of risk, and portfolios that are more efficient.

RISKS OF EQUITY SECURITIES

As with all securities and investments, there are certain inherent risks (both systematic and unsystematic) associated with equity investments that must be considered. The most important systematic risks that we will discuss are market risk, interest rate risk, and exchange rate risk. The key unsystematic risks that we will discuss are business risk, financial risk, and country risk.

SYSTEMATIC RISKS

Systematic risks are those that affect all securities. In other words, these risks cannot be diversified away. Systematic risks include market risk, interest rate risk, and exchange rate risk.

systematic risk - investment risk impacted by broad macroeconomic factors that influence all securities

Market Risk

Market risk represents the tendency for changes in the market to influence the prices of equities. When the market is on the rise, most stocks increase in value. Conversely, stocks tend to fall with declines in the market. Often, a move in the market is prefaced by some change in the broad economic environment.

market risk - a systematic risk describing the tendency of stocks to move with the market

The equity market is quite volatile and its value can change significantly over short periods of time. No direct cause may be attributable to this volatility. When the change occurs, especially on the downside, equities tend to decline in value. The volatility of the U.S. equity market, as represented by the S&P 500 index, is illustrated . in Exhibit 12B.2 below.

EXHIBIT 12B.2: S&P 500 INDEX

January 2000 to January 2005

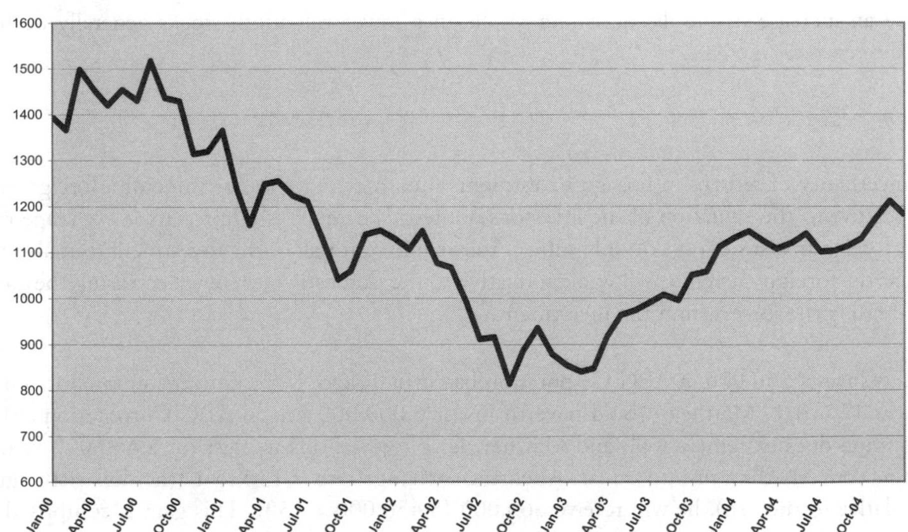
1600
1500
1400
1300
1200
1100
1000
900
800
700
600
Jan-00
Apr-00
Jul-00
Oct-00
Jan-01
Apr-01
Jul-01
Oct-01
Jan-02
Apr-02
Jul-02
Oct-02
Jan-03
Apr-03
Jul-03
Oct-03
Jan-04
Apr-04
Jul-04
Oct-04

Notice that when the market changes direction, it does so rapidly and the changes are often significant. These ups and downs in the market cause the value of investor's portfolios to change dramatically within short periods of time.

Interest Rate Risk

interest rate risk - a systematic risk where changes in interest rates will affect the value of securities

Interest rate risk is one of the major risks affecting fixed-income securities and bond portfolios. Equity securities also are impacted by changes in interest rates. When interest rates increase there is negative pressure on the value of common stocks, and when interest rates decrease stocks tend to increase in value. There are three primary reasons for this relationship: increased borrowing costs, attractiveness of alternative investments, and the valuation of securities.

Increased Borrowing Costs

Most companies use debt as a means of financing capital expansion and acquisition of assets. The cost of debt is interest payments. When interest rates increase, the cost of future borrowing increases. This increased borrowing cost can cause earnings to decline. When earnings decrease the value of the company is reduced. Therefore, changes in interest rates have a direct impact on the cost of borrowing and, thus, on the earnings of a firm.

Attractiveness of Alternative Investments

When interest rates increase, so do the corresponding yields on fixed-income securities. As yields increase, bonds become more attractive. Investors become unwilling to assume the additional risk inherent in equities when the spread between the expected return on bonds and stocks is small (the value of equities). Therefore, as investors decrease investments in equities so that they can take advantage of the fixed-income yields, there is downward pressure on the equity market causing it to decline.

The Value of Equities

exchange rate risk - a systematic risk associated with a change in the relationship between the value of the dollar (or investor's currency) and the value of the foreign currency during the period of investment; also known as foreign currency risk

The value of a security today is the sum of the discounted future cash flows expected from the investment. As interest rates increase, the discount rate used to value a security must also increase. Because an increase in the discount rate results in a lower valuation, stocks generally decline when interest rates increase.

Exchange Rate Risk

The uncertainty of returns in foreign investments due to changes in the value of a foreign currency relative to the valuation of the investor's domestic currency is referred to as **exchange rate risk**. A foreign investment is not only subject to the inherent risk of the investment, but also the risk that the foreign currency will weaken relative to the domestic currency, decreasing the gains (or increasing the losses) from the investment.

EXAMPLE

Matthew invests $50,000 in ABC Corporation based in Tokyo. If the conversion rate for yen to dollars is 120 to 1, Matthew would have to invest 6,000,000 yen in ABC Corporation. ABC Corporation does extremely well, and Matthew is able to sell his interest for 8,450,000 yen. If Matthew converts the yen into dollars when the exchange rate is 130 to 1 (the dollar strengthened relative to the yen), he will receive $65,000 (8,450,000 ÷ 130). This gain is comprised of 40.8 percent (2,450,000 yen) gain on the investment and a loss of 7.7 percent (120 ÷ 130 – 1) or $3,846 from the change in the currency rate. The net result is a 30 percent gain on the original investment.

Assume the same facts as in the previous example except that the exchange rate is now 110 to 1 instead of 130 to 1. In this case, Matthew liquidates his interest in ABC Corporation and converts the yen to $76,820 (8,450,000 ÷ 110). This $26,820 gain is attributable to the appreciation of ABC Corporation and the devaluation of the dollar relative to the yen.

International equity managers attempt to avoid such drastic results from the change in currency rates by hedging against currency fluctuations. Forward or futures contracts may be used as hedging devices against currency risk. However, academic studies have shown that over long periods of time, hedged and unhedged portfolios will perform similarly.

UNSYSTEMATIC RISKS

Unsystematic risks are those risks that are unique to individual securities, industries, or countries. These risks include business risk, financial risk, and country risk.

unsystematic risks - types of investment risks unique to a single company, industry, or country that can be eliminated by portfolio diversification

Business Risk

Business risk is the riskiness of a specific business, which includes the speculative nature of the business, the management of the business, and the philosophy of the business. Different types of businesses will have different levels of risk. For instance, we generally consider technology securities more risky than defensive stocks. However, both will have an unique risk associated with their specific type of business.

business risk - an unsystematic risk based on predictability of operating income for a specific business; dependent upon management and industry characteristics

Business risk can also be thought of as the uncertainty of operating income. Utility companies have relatively stable and steady operating income streams and, therefore, have lower business risk. Because they have unsteady or fluctuating operating income levels, cyclical companies (such as auto manufacturers) have higher business risk. .

Financial Risk

The method by which a firm acquires its assets is directly related to **financial risk** or financial leverage. Companies have two choices with regard to their capital structure: firms may use debt through the issuance of bonds or they may issue equity securities. When a company chooses debt to finance the purchase of additional assets, it increases the financial risk of the firm. This increased leverage is the same as for individuals when they use margin to purchase securities.

financial risk - an unsystematic risk based on the capital structure of a firm that affects the return on equity (ROE) for a company

EXAMPLE

Consider two firms that each earn $50,000 of net income. Both firms are in the same business, and each has $400,000 of assets. Company A has not issued debt and has financed all of its assets with equity. Company B has issued $300,000 of debt and $100,000 of equity.

	Company A	Company B
Net Income	$50,000	$50,000
Debt	$0	$300,000
Equity	$400,000	$100,000
ROE (Return on Equity)	12.5%	50%

Notice that while each company's earnings and assets are the same, the return on equity is quit[e] different. This difference results from the different capital structures of the firms. Because Company B has chosen to use debt as a method of financing, it has increased the leverage of the firm. Company B's returns are likely to be more volatile over time than Company A's returns. Financial risk is directly related to the capital structure of the firm and, therefore, to the liability side of the balance sheet.

country risk - an unsystematic risk where changes in a country's laws or political situation will have an adverse effect on an investment

Country Risk

International investments are subject to **country risk**, which is the unique risk within each country. These risks include political and economic risks. The United States is generally thought to have the lowest country risk, since its political and economic systems are the most stable.

or country. Therefore, these risks can be diversified away, unlike systematic risks.

primary market - the market where new issues of securities are first offered to the public

initial public offering - first offering of equity securities to the general public

EQUITY MARKETS AND BENCHMARKS

PRIMARY MARKET

The **primary market** is the place where securities are initially offered to the public. These security offerings are in the form of **initial public offerings**, commonly referred to as IPOs. IPOs allow businesses and entrepreneurs access to the capital markets. Business owners may issue additional shares to the public to raise capital for the expansion and growth of their business. While an IPO will dilute the ownership of the existing shareholders, it can provide the capital and resources to dramatically expand the business.

underwriting - the process by which investment bankers purchase an issue of securities from a firm and resell it to the public

Underwriting

To issue shares to the public, companies enlist the assistance of investment bankers to underwrite the stock issue. In the process of **underwriting** an IPO, the investment banker may assume some of the risk associated with selling the securities to the public. For example, an investment banker might agree to purchase an issue for $12 per share and then resell the issue to the public for $13 per share. This $1 profit is referred to as an underwriter's spread. In addition, underwriters often help the issuing firm determine its financial needs and the best investment vehicle to achieve the needed funds. Underwriting can take one of four forms. These include firm commitment, stand-by underwriting, best efforts, and private placement.

firm commitment - equity underwriting in which the underwriter purchases the entire issue at a specific price from the firm and resells it on the open market

Firm Commitment

With a **firm commitment**, the underwriter purchases the entire issue of securities at a specific price then attempts to sell it at a higher price. This arrangement shifts all risk to the underwriter. If the issue cannot be resold at a price above the purchase price, the underwriter will lose money on the transaction. Often, a syndicate of underwriters will be setup to spread the potential risk.

Stand-By Underwriting

When the underwriter purchases the remaining securities at a predetermined price after an initial offering (usually to existing shareholders/owners), the form of underwriting is called **stand-by underwriting.**

stand-by underwriting - equity underwriting in which the underwriter purchases any securities remaining after an initial offering

Best-Efforts

Under a **best-efforts agreement**, the underwriter sells as much of the issue as possible, and the remainder is returned to the issuing company. No risk is shifted to the underwriter. This arrangement occurs when the issuing company is confident that the issue will be sold or the underwriter is concerned about the financial stability of the company.

best-efforts agreement - equity underwriting in which the firm agrees to repurchase any securities remaining after the initial offering is made by the underwriter

Private Placement

The main attraction of a **private placement** is the lack of registration requirements associated with an IPO. It is, therefore, less expensive and less time consuming. Generally, the issue can be placed quickly and at a low cost. Underwriters help find investors and receive a finder's fee or commission ranging from 0.25 percent to 1.5 percent. Bonds have been the most common privately placed issues. A private placement cannot be sold to more than 35 unaccredited investors. An unaccredited investor is one who does not fit into one of the following categories:

- Net worth of more than $1,000,000, or
- Gross income in excess of $200,000 for each of the past two years, with the anticipation of the same level of income.

private placement - equity underwriting in which the underwriter assists in identifying private purchasers of an issue

In addition to reduced cost, private placements avoid the registration requirements of the SEC and the public access to information that occurs when conforming to SEC requirements. Although private placements are limited to 35 unaccredited investors, there is no limit to the number of accredited investors.

SECONDARY MARKET

The **secondary market** is where investors buy and sell securities that have been issued previously in the primary markets. The secondary market provides liquidity to the capital markets and allows for the free trade of public securities.

secondary market - the market where investors can buy and sell securities with other investors

The secondary markets consist of exchanges, such as the New York Stock Exchange and the American Stock Exchange, and Over the Counter (OTC) Trading. These exchanges house the buying and selling of securities that are listed on the particular exchange. This buying and selling represents the primary function of the secondary market.

third market - over-the-counter trading of equity shares that are listed on an exchange

THIRD AND FOURTH MARKETS

The **third market** consists of over-the-counter trading of equity shares that are listed on an exchange. This market is especially important when the exchange is not trading a security and outside the normal operating hours of the exchange.

fourth market - comprised of institutional traders that trade without the help of brokers

The **fourth market** is comprised of traders who trade without the help of brokers. They trade directly with other interested parties. These traders make use of communication systems such as

Instinet to find other interested parties. Most of these traders are institutional type investors who are interested in trading large volumes of securities.

EXHIBIT 12B.3: THIRD AND FOURTH MARKETS

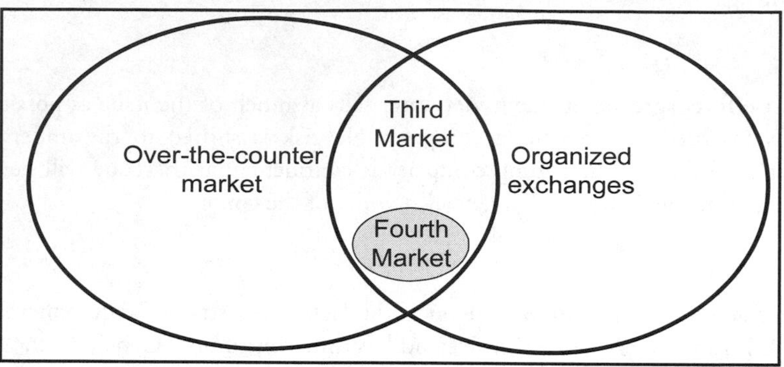
Third Market
Over-the-counter market
Organized exchanges
Fourth Market

MARKET INDEXES AND AVERAGES

The purpose of a market index or average is to provide information to investors and advisors concerning the overall movement and performance of the securities markets. Since most securities are positively correlated with their respective index, the securities tend to increase when their index is increasing and decrease when their index is decreasing.

Dow Jones Industrial Average

Dow Jones Industrial Average (DJIA) - a financial index that is a price-weighted average of thirty leading industrial stocks used to measure the status of the equity market

The **Dow Jones Industrial Average** (**DJIA**) is probably the best-known financial index in the United States. It is a price-weighted average of thirty leading industrial stocks used to measure the status of the equity market. The thirty stocks currently included in the DJIA are identified in Exhibit 12B.4.

EXHIBIT 12B.4: DJIA STOCKS
(As of April 2004)

Alcoa	General Electric	Merck
Altria (formerly Philip Morris)	General Motors	Microsoft
American Express	Hewlett-Packard	Minnesota Mining & Mfr. (3M)
American International Group, Inc. (AIG)	Home Depot	Pfizer
Boeing	Honeywell	Proctor & Gamble
Caterpillar	IBM	SBC Communications
Citigroup	Intel	United Technologies
Coca Cola	J P Morgan Chase	Verizon Communications
Du Pont	Johnson & Johnson	Wal-Mart
ExxonMobil	McDonalds	Walt Disney

The DJIA consists of stocks that are considered blue-chip stocks. Although these companies are often leaders in their industry, the composition of the average does change over time.

Standard & Poor's 500 Index

The **Standard & Poor's Index (S&P 500)** traditionally has been the measure of the U.S. large capitalization market used by academics and financial professionals. It consists of 500 U.S. equities chosen for market size, liquidity, and industry group representation. These 500 stocks are represented by the industries described in Exhibit 12B.5.

Standard & Poor's Index (S&P 500) - a financial index of 500 U.S. equities chosen for market size, liquidity, and industry group representation

EXHIBIT 12B.5: S&P 500 INDUSTRY GROUP REPRESENTATION
(As of October 3, 2005)

Industry	# of Companies	# of Companies As % of 500
Consumer Discretionary	89	17.8%
Financials	84	16.8%
Information Technology	78	15.6%
Health Care	56	11.2%
Industrials	53	10.6%
Consumer Staples	37	7.4%
Utilities	33	6.6%
Materials	32	6.4%
Energy	29	5.8%
Telecommunications Services	9	1.8%

The S&P 500 index is a market-value-weighted index. This means that a company's **market capitalization** (outstanding shares times the current stock price) is represented in the index. Market- value indexes typically provide a better measure of the market than averages, such as the DJIA (however, the DJIA is highly correlated to the S&P 500 index). The 500 securities that make up the index have a market value of over $10 trillion.

market capitalization - the product of the number of outstanding common stock shares and current stock price

In addition to the S&P 500 index, Standard & Poor's maintains numerous other U.S. indexes, including:

- S&P Mid-Cap 400 Index
- S&P Small-Cap 600 Index
- S&P SuperComposite 1500
- S&P 100 Index
- S&P/BARRA Growth and Value Indexes

Each of these indexes provides a different view of the U.S. market.

Nasdaq

The **Nasdaq** system began in 1971 and was the first electronic trading system. The Nasdaq is one of the fastest growing indexes in the world. Many of today's leading technology and internet-related companies are listed on the Nasdaq. Exhibit 12B.6 describes the history of this stock market.

Nasdaq - the first electronic trading system made up of leading technology and internet-related companies

EXHIBIT 12B.6: HISTORY OF THE NASDAQ STOCK MARKET

1961	In an effort to improve overall regulation of the securities industry, Congress asks the U.S. Securities and Exchange Commission (SEC) to conduct a special study of all securities markets.
1963	The SEC releases the completed study, in which it characterizes the over-the-counter (OTC) securities market as fragmented and obscure. The SEC proposes a solution–automation–and charges The National Association of Securities Dealers, Inc. (NASD) with its implementation.
1968	Construction begins on the automated over-the-counter securities system–then known as the National Association of Securities Dealers Automated Quotation–or "Nasdaq"–System.
1971	Nasdaq® celebrates its first official trading day on February 8th–the first day of operation for the completed Nasdaq automated system, which displays median quotes for more than 2,500 over-the-counter securities.
1975	Nasdaq establishes new listing standards–which it requires all listed companies to meet–effectively separating Nasdaq-listed securities from other OTC securities.
1980	Nasdaq begins to display inside quotations–the market's best bid and offer prices–on-screen. As a result, both displayed and published spreads decline on more than 85 percent of Nasdaq stocks.
1982	The top Nasdaq companies split off to form the Nasdaq National Market®, which requires higher listing standards. The Nasdaq National Market also offers real-time trade reporting, which provides investors with broader access to market information.
1984	Nasdaq introduces the Small Order Execution System (SOES℠). Designed to automatically execute small orders against the best quotations, SOES enhances Nasdaq's trading capacity and efficiency.
1986	The Federal Reserve Board grants Nasdaq National Market stocks marginability, meaning that customers can purchase these securities on credit extended by a broker/dealer.
1990	Nasdaq formally changes its name to "The Nasdaq Stock Market." Creation of the OTC Bulletin Board℠ (OTCBB) gives investors information on and access to securities not listed on Nasdaq.
1991	Nasdaq National Market securities attain virtual parity with the NYSE and AMEX on blue-sky laws–applicable state laws concerning the registration and sale of new securities. (*Note: The National Securities Market Improvement Act of 1996 mandated that all states must exempt Nasdaq National Market securities from state blue-sky regulations*).
1992	Nasdaq International℠ Service begins operation, allowing Nasdaq National Market securities to be traded during early morning hours, when the London financial markets are open. Real-time trade reporting is initiated for The Nasdaq SmallCap Market℠.
1994	A landmark year: The Nasdaq Stock Market surpasses the New York Stock Exchange in annual share volume.
1997	The SEC approves Nasdaq's request to begin quoting in 1/16ths of a dollar for stocks trading above $10. Nasdaq implements new order handling rules. In combination with Nasdaq's move to quoting in 1/16ths, these rules produce better prices and an average spread reduction of 40%.
1998	Merger between the NASD and the AMEX creates The Nasdaq-Amex Market Group.
1999	Nasdaq becomes the top stock market in the world based on dollar volume. Nasdaq Europe and Nasdaq Canada are born. Partnership with Stock Exchange of Hong Kong is finalized.
2001	Nasdaq meets ISO 9001 quality standards. Decimal pricing for all equity securities is enacted.

Nasdaq Highlights: 2004

- As of 12/31/04 NASDAQ's market value was 3.7 trillion.
- Total share volume was 445 billion shares and the average daily share volume was 1.8 billion shares.
- 65% of all U.S. IPO's were offered through NASDAQ.

Source: www.nasdaq.com

Russell Indexes

The Frank Russell Company maintains 24 U.S. stock indexes, as well as foreign indexes in Australia, Canada, Japan, and the United Kingdom. All of the **Russell Indexes** are market capitalization weighted, and 22 of the U.S. indexes are subsets of the Russell 3000 Index, which represents the 98 percent of investable U.S. equities. The Russell 2000 Index is a well-known index that is used to benchmark small capitalization companies. The Russell 1000 Index represents the thousand largest companies in the Russell 3000 Index. Russell also maintains numerous value and growth indexes that allow for comparisons with various portfolio manager styles.

Russell Indexes - a collection of financial indexes made up of 24 U.S. stock indexes, as well as foreign indexes in Australia, Canada, Japan, and the United Kingdom, maintained by the Frank Russell Company

Wilshire 5000 Index

The **Wilshire 5000 Index** is another well-known index that is used as a measure of the U.S. broad market. It consists of over 5,000 U.S. based companies and is often used as a measure of the overall market within the United States.

Wilshire 5000 Index - a financial index consisting of over 5,000 U.S.-based companies that is often used as a measure of the overall market within the U.S.

EAFE Index

In 1969, the Europe, Australia, and Far East (**EAFE) index** was created as a measure of the international securities markets. It provides an indication of how a portfolio consisting of companies outside the United States might perform over time. It is probably the most well-known measure of international markets.

EAFE Index - the Europe, Australia, and Far East (EAFE) index created as a measure of the international securities markets

BENCHMARKS

The indexes discussed above can be used for comparison with a portfolio's results to evaluate the manager's performance. Although many investors use comparisons with other managers as a measure of performance, benchmarks should have certain characteristics. The characteristics of a good benchmark include the following:

- ▲ Unambiguous. The composition and weighting of the components of the benchmark must be clearly delineated.
- ▲ Investable. The option to invest in the benchmark is available.
- ▲ Measurable. It should be possible to calculate the benchmark's return on a relatively frequent basis.
- ▲ Appropriate. The benchmark must be consistent with the manager's investment philosophy and style.
- ▲ Reflective of current investment opinions. The manager has current investment knowledge of the securities that make up the benchmark.
- ▲ Specified in advance. The benchmark should be constructed before the beginning of the evaluation period.

These six properties improve the usefulness of a benchmark as an investment management tool and allow for a better measure of a portfolio manager's performance.

MEASURES OF RETURN

The primary purpose of investing is to earn a positive return. Investors seek out investments that are consistent with their risk and return preferences in an attempt to achieve financial goals. Therefore, it is important to understand and be able to calculate the returns from equity securities. There are several methods of calculating returns from equity securities, each with their advantages and disadvantages. We will examine holding period return, arithmetic mean, geometric mean, time-weighted return, dollar-weighted return, and dividend yield.

HOLDING PERIOD RETURN

holding period return - measures the total return an investor receives over a specific time period

The **holding period return** is a basic measure of an investment's rate of return over a specific time period. It is sometimes referred to as the single period rate of return. The holding period return measures the change in value of an investment over the holding period and is calculated as follows:

$$HPR = \frac{Ending\ Value\ of\ Investment - Beginning\ Value\ of\ Investment +/- Cash\ Flows}{Beginning\ Value\ of\ Investment}$$

EXAMPLE

Morgan buys one share of ABC stock for $25 and sells it for $35. During the holding period, the stock pays total dividends of $5. The holding period return for this investment is calculated as follows:

$$HPR = \frac{\$35 - \$25 + \$5}{\$25} = 0.60 \text{ or } 60\%$$

Therefore, the holding period return for Morgan is 60 percent. However, knowing this return does not indicate how well the investment performed because there is no indication of the time over which the investment was held. If the investment was held for a week, the 60 percent return is very good. However, if the investment was held for ten years, it may not be very good. The holding period return is often used as a measure of return for a single period, such as a year or a month.

ARITHMETIC MEAN

arithmetic mean - also called the arithmetic average rate of return; a measure of investment return that is the result of averaging period returns

Investors often evaluate holding period returns of an investment for a certain length of time. One easy method of evaluating these periodic returns is to determine the **arithmetic mean**. The arithmetic mean is calculated by dividing the sum of the returns for each period by the total number of periods (n) being evaluated. The formula is written as follows:

$$AM = \frac{\sum_{t=1}^{n} HPR_t}{n}$$

EXAMPLE

Assume ABC stock earned the following returns over the last five years:

Year	Return
1	10%
2	5%
3	20%
4	0%
5	–12%

The arithmetic return is calculated as follows:

$$AM = \frac{10\% + 5\% + 20\% + 0\% + -12\%}{5} = 4.6\%$$

Therefore, ABC stock has earned an average return over the five-year period of 4.6 percent per year.

GEOMETRIC MEAN

geometric mean - also known as geometric average return; a method of calculating the internal rate of return based on periodic rates of return

Although the arithmetic mean is an extremely common measure, the **geometric mean** is considered a better and truer measure of the return from a security over time. The geometric mean is calculated using the following formula:

$$GM = \sqrt[n]{(1+R_1)(1+R_2)\cdots(1+R_n)} - 1$$, where

R_n = Return for period n

n = Number of periods in the analysis

EXAMPLE

Using the historical data for ABC stock from above, the GM is calculated as follows:

$$GM = \sqrt[5]{(1+.10)(1+.05)(1+.20)(1+0)(1+-.12)} - 1$$

$$GM = \sqrt[5]{1.21968} - 1$$

$$GM = 4.05\%$$

Notice that the return for the geometric mean is less than the arithmetic mean. The geometric mean will always be less than the arithmetic mean, except when the returns for each period are the same. The difference between the arithmetic mean and the geometric mean will be exaggerated as the volatility of returns increases. The calculation of the geometric mean is one method of calculating the time-weighted rate of return.

Another way to calculate the geometric mean is to use the present value keys of a financial calculator. Assume that $100 is invested into an account that earns 10 percent the first year, 5 percent the second year, 20 percent the third year, zero in the fourth year, and loses 12 percent in the fifth year. How much is in the account at the end of the fifth year? The answer is $121.97, which can be calculated by multiplying the $100 times the sum of one plus each year's return (just as we did in the GM calculation). Once the future value is determined, it is simple to determine the GM.

Keystroke	Display
100 [CHS][PV]	–100.0000
5[n]	5.0000
121.97[FV]	121.9700
[i]	4.0520

Therefore, over the five-year period, the investment earned an annualized return of 4.05 percent per year.

time-weighted returns - a method of determining an internal rate of return by evaluating the performance of portfolio managers without the influence of additional investor deposits or withdrawals to or from the portfolio

TIME-WEIGHTED AND DOLLAR-WEIGHTED RETURNS

Although time-weighted returns and dollar-weighted returns are both methods of determining an internal rate of return, they have very different purposes. **Time-weighted returns** are used to evaluate the performance of portfolio managers separate from the influence of additional investor deposits or withdrawals. **Dollar-weighted returns** are used to determine the rate of return an individual investor earned based on the investor's particular cash flows into and out of the portfolio. The following example illustrates the difference between dollar-weighted returns and time-weighted returns.

dollar-weighted returns - a method of determining the internal rate of return that an individual investor earned based on the investor's particular cash flow into and out of the portfolio

Assume we are comparing two portfolios, A and B. Over a four-year period, they each earn exactly the same return per period. However, each portfolio has a different set of investor deposits and withdrawals.

PORTFOLIO A				
Period	Investor Deposits or Withdrawals	Beginning of Period Value	End of Period Value	Periodic Rate of Return
0	1000	1000	1200	20.00%
1	(400)	800	700	–12.50%
2	300	1000	1400	40.00%
3	(200)	1200	1000	–16.67%
4	(1000)	–	–	–
DWR =	8.2311%		TWR =	5.2044%

PORTFOLIO B				
Period	Investor Deposits or Withdrawals	Beginning of Period Value	End of Period Value	Periodic Rate of Return
0	1000	1000	1200	20.00%
1	400	1600	1400	–12.50%
2	(400)	1000	1400	40.00%
3	400	1800	1500	–16.67%
4	(1500)	–	–	–
DWR =	2.0245%		TWR =	5.2044%

Using the uneven cash flow keys of a financial calculator, we have calculated the dollar-weighted return (DWR) for Portfolio A to be 8.23 percent, while the DWR for Portfolio B equals 2.02 percent. Is it reasonable to use a methodology that results in drastically different returns when each portfolio produced the same periodic rates of return? The answer depends on our goal. To evaluate the overall return for the portfolio, we want to use DWR. This provides the investor with his or her actual return. For portfolio managers, we generally do not use DWR. This is because managers do not control the timing of additional investments into the portfolio or the timing of withdrawals from the portfolio. A more accurate measure of the portfolio manager's ability is the time-weighted return.

Time-Weighted Return

The time-weighted return is used to compare returns achieved by portfolio managers without the influence of investor deposits and withdrawals. The above example shows what can happen when dollar-weighted returns are used to evaluate portfolio manager performance. The investor-specific cash flows of Portfolio A helped its overall performance while the investor-specific cash flows of Portfolio B hurt its performance.

To compare the managers of the two portfolios, we can use the geometric mean calculation to determine the time-weighted return:

$$TWR = \sqrt[4]{(1+.20)(1+-.1250)(1+.40)(1+-.1667)} - 1$$

$$TWR = \sqrt[4]{1.225} - 1$$

$$TWR = 5.2044\%$$

Since each portfolio had the same periodic returns over the four periods, their time-weighted returns both equal 5.20 percent.

Dollar-Weighted Return

Although we illustrated how the dollar-weighted return can erroneously influence our decision about the performance of a portfolio manager, the dollar-weighted return has its use. The dollar-weighted return is appropriate for determining a client's return over time when the client is either investing additional money into the account or removing money from the account. For example, assume the above charts actually represent different clients with their unique cash flows.

Although each client had the same periodic returns, their overall dollar-weighted returns would be quite different and quite relevant to each client.

The dollar-weighted return is calculated using the cash flows for each period. The above DWRs are calculated as follows:

Portfolio A

Keystroke	Display
[f][CLX]	0.0000
1000[CHS]	–1,000
[g] [CF_o]	–1,000.0000
400[g][CF_j]	400.0000
300[CHS]	–300
[g][CF_j]	–300.0000
200[g][CF_j]	200.0000
1000[g][CF_j]	1,000.0000
[f][IRR]	8.2311

Portfolio B

Keystroke	Display
[f][CLX]	0.0000
1000[CHS]	–1,000
[g] [CF_o]	–1,000.0000
400[CHS]	–400
[g][CF_j]	–400.0000
400 [g][CF_j]	400.0000
400[CHS]	–400
[g][CF_j]	–400.0000
1500[g][CF_j]	1,500.0000
[f][IRR]	2.0245

The primary reason that the DWR for each client is so different is that in the case of client A, the cash inflows were in periods of positive performance and the cash outflows were in periods of negative performance. For client B, just the opposite is true. Cash inflows were in periods of negative performance, while cash outflows were in periods of positive performance.

DIVIDEND YIELD

We defined income stocks as those with high dividend payments compared to other stocks. The measure used to compare the dividend payments from one company to another is called the **dividend yield** and is calculated as follows:

dividend yield - the measure of a security's annual dividend payment as a percent of the current market price

$$DY = \frac{\text{Annual Dividend per Share}}{\text{Market Price of the Stock}}$$

EXAMPLE

If XYZ Company is paying a dividend of $4 per share and the current market price of the stock is $50, then the dividend yield of XYZ equals 8 percent ($4 ÷ $50).

The dividend yield measure is useful for selecting stocks for inclusion in a portfolio of an investor who needs the income derived from the portfolio. Stocks that have high dividend yields are included, while those that have low dividend yields are excluded.

PURCHASING EQUITY SECURITIES

LONG POSITIONS

The most prevalent type of position investors take is referred to as a long position. A **long position** is the purchase of a stock in hopes that it will appreciate over time. If a stock is purchased for $45 and is sold for $100, then the stock has increased, resulting in a gain of $55.

long position - the purchase of a stock in hopes that it will appreciate over time

SHORT POSITIONS

Investors may also benefit in the market when they find securities that are overvalued. A short sale allows the investor to benefit from the decline in the value of the security. A short sale is selling shares that are not owned by the investor. This transaction is accomplished by borrowing shares of stock from a broker. Once the shares are sold in the market, the investor is credited with the proceeds. However, the investor must, at some point, replace the borrowed shares. This is known as covering the **short position** and is accomplished by purchasing the shares in the market and replacing the shares that were borrowed.

short position - a type of position investors take by selling borrowed shares in hopes that the stock price will decline over time

The short seller will be profitable if the shares can be purchased at a price less than the price at which the shares were sold. If the stock appreciates after the shares are sold short, then the investor will lose money.

Three technical issues must be discussed regarding short selling. First, a short sale must occur on an uptick or zero plus tick. A zero plus tick is a zero tick which has been proceeded by a plus tick or uptick. The uptick rule requires that the security trade up in price before the short sale can be executed.

EXAMPLE

If ABC stock trades at the following prices: $45.00, $44.50, $44.50, $41.00, $41.50, $41.50, $42.00, then a short sale could not occur until the stock price moved from $41.00 to $41.50. The price of $41.50 represents the first uptick in the series. The second trade at $41.50 represents a zero tick or zero plus tick.

The second issue concerning short sales is that of dividend payments that occur before closing the short position. A short sale involves borrowing stock and selling it in the market. At the time of a short sale, two investors believe that they own the stock and are entitled to receive any dividend payment that is declared and paid. However, the company declaring the dividend will only recognize one owner (the third party who purchased the shares in the market) and will only make one dividend payment. Therefore, it is the responsibility of the short seller to make up the other dividend payment to the party from whom the stock was originally borrowed. From an economic standpoint, paying this dividend is irrelevant since the price of the security should decline by the same amount as the dividend payment.

The third issue is that short sellers are required to have a margin account and post margin as if the investor was acquiring stock. If the stock increases, then the short seller may be required to restore his margin. This issue is discussed below from the standpoint of an investor acquiring stock.

cash accounts - a type of brokerage account that requires that all securities purchased by the investor be paid for in full without any indebtedness

margin accounts - a type of brokerage account that allows the investor to borrow funds from the broker to purchase additional securities without adding cash to the account

MARGIN ACCOUNTS

When an investor opens a brokerage account, it is either a cash account or a margin account. **Cash accounts** require that all securities purchased by the investor be paid for in full without any indebtedness. If a cash account is fully invested in securities, then the only way to purchase additional securities is to add cash to the account or sell some of the current securities to generate cash. In contrast, **margin accounts** allow the investor to borrow funds from the broker to purchase additional securities without adding cash to the account. Margin accounts give investors flexibility and the ability to leverage the account.

Margin accounts require that the account owner pay for a certain percentage of the cost of an investment. The margin percentage that must be established for the purchase of a security is referred to as the initial margin. The Federal Reserve sets the minimum initial margin percentage, currently 50 percent. Therefore, the initial purchase of a security requires the investor to put up at least 50 percent of the initial purchase.

In addition to the amount that must be initially put up by the investor, the investor must maintain an equity position in the account that equals or exceeds the maintenance margin. The maintenance margin is typically 35 percent, which means that the equity in the account must equal or exceed 35 percent. If the equity in the account drops below the maintenance margin, then the account holder receives a margin call from the broker. A margin call is a request for funds to restore the account equity to the maintenance margin.

Determining the Price for a Margin Call

The account equity is defined as the market value of the securities in the account less the outstanding debt. The equity percentage equals the account equity divided by the market value of the securities. The price at which a margin call is received occurs when the equity percentage drops below the maintenance margin. We can solve for the price (or account value) when a margin call will be received by setting the equity percentage equal to the maintenance margin, as follows:

$$\frac{\text{Account Value} - \text{Debt}}{\text{Account Value}} = \text{Maintenance Margin}$$

$$\text{Account Value} - \text{Debt} = \text{Maintenance Margin} \times \text{Account Value}$$

$$\text{Account Value} - (\text{Maintenance Margin} \times \text{Account Value}) = \text{Debt}$$

$$\text{Account Value} \times (1 - \text{Maintenance Margin}) = \text{Debt}$$

$$\text{Account Value} = \frac{\text{Debt}}{1 - \text{Maintenance Margin}}$$

EXAMPLE

Hardy purchases one share of Solvent Company for $104. Hardy uses a margin account with a 50 percent initial margin for the purchase and is concerned about receiving a margin call. If the maintenance margin equals 35 percent, then Hardy will receive a margin call if the stock falls below $80, as illustrated below:

$$\text{Account Value} = \frac{\text{Debt}}{1 - \text{Maintenance Margin}}$$

$$\text{Account Value} = \frac{\$52}{1 - 0.35} = \$80$$

Determining How Much to Put Up to Restore the Account Equity

If the stock or account drops below the price at which there is a margin call, then the account owner must deposit sufficient funds to restore the account equity to the maintenance margin. This amount can be determined by asking two questions. How much equity does the broker require? And, how much equity does the investor currently have?

Using the above example, assume that the stock drops in value to $70. In such a case, Hardy would be required to put up $6.50 per share ($24.50 – $18.00).

Required Equity	
Current Value of Stock	$70.00
Equity %	35%
Required Equity	$24.50

Current Equity Position	
Current Value of Stock	$70.00
Loan Amount	(52.00)
Equity	$18.00

The investor must maintain an equity position of 35 percent, which is the given maintenance margin. Because the price of the stock is currently $70, Hardy must have $24.50 ($70 × 35%) of equity in his account. To determine Hardy's current equity position, subtract the outstanding debt from the value of the stock. Since his current equity position equals $18, and he must have $24.50 of equity, Hardy must fund the account with the difference of $6.50.

TYPES OF ORDERS

When purchasing equity investments it is important to understand the different types of orders that can be used to acquire shares of common stock. The four standard types of orders include market orders, limit orders, stop loss orders, and stop limit orders. All orders are considered day orders unless otherwise specified. If an order is not filled within the trading day, it will expire. Orders can be good for a specific length of time, or they can be "good-til-canceled." Time limits are often used with limit and stop orders because they are not as likely to be filled during the day, as are market orders.

Market Order

market orders - type of securities order that requires the trade be made at the best current market price

The majority of orders are **market orders**. In fact, 75 percent to 80 percent of all orders have traditionally been market orders, and these orders have the highest priority. A market order is an order to buy or sell a security at the best current market price. These orders must be filled prior to other types of orders being considered. While these are the fastest orders, they do not have limits or a specific price and, therefore, are subject to the fluctuations and time lines of the market.

It is possible that an investor puts in a market order to buy when the stock is trading at $22 per share, and his order is filled at $23. This might occur because there are more buy orders than sell orders, which causes the market price to increase.

Limit Order

limit order - type of securities order that requires the trade be made at a specified price or better

The objective of a **limit order** is to acquire or sell a security at a specific price; one that is better than the market at the time the order is placed. The price acts as a ceiling for purchases and as a floor for sales, and the order will be held until filled or canceled. Limit orders are maintained in chronological order. Higher priced purchase limit orders take priority over lower priced purchase limit orders. Even if the price for the stock is below (or above) the limit order, there is no guarantee that it will be filled.

EXAMPLE

David, a shrewd investor, has analyzed all the relevant financial information and has determined that the Ashbey Corporation is worth $45 per share. While the stock is trading between $48 and $50, he places a limit order at $45. This will assure that if the order is filled to purchase shares of Ashbey Corporation, David's price will be no higher than $45. If Ashbey continues to trade above $45, David's order will not be filled.

Stop Loss Order

stop loss orders - a type of securities order that becomes a market order when the security's price reaches a specific level

Stop loss orders are used to protect investors from large losses. If the market price reaches a certain point, the stop order will turn into a market order. For instance, an investor who is long in a security might place a stop order at 10 points below the current market price to protect the appreciation of the stock against serious declines in market price. Likewise, these orders can be used to limit losses in connection with short sales.

Steve purchased Roland, Inc. for $29 per share. It is now trading at $73 per share. He has an unrealized gain of $44. If Steve is concerned about the price of the stock declining, he can place a stop order at $70. If the stock price drops to $70, a market order is placed immediately. However, it may be filled at $69 or $68. The stop order protects his profit position.

EXAMPLE

Stop Limit Order

Stop limit orders are similar to stop loss orders except they turn into limit orders when triggered. The stop order price and the limit order price are both specified. Stop limit orders are the least used type of order.

stop limit orders - a type of securities order that becomes a limit order when the security's price reaches a specific level

If Dina owns 5,000 shares of Prez's Pretzels, which is sell for $35 per share, and she is concerned about the price dropping, she may want to place a stop limit order. If she places the order "sell 5,000 shares at $32 stop, $30 limit," and the price drops to $32, the broker will attempt to sell the stock for $32 but will not sell below the $30 limit order.

EXAMPLE

Online Trading

With access to the Internet increasing, online trading of securities is increasingly popular. **Online trading** is a method of buying and selling securities over the internet without the use of a broker. While Schwab was the first brokerage house to allow account holders to trade over the internet, most brokerage houses now have the ability to accept trades over the internet. Trading over the internet has become so popular that there are brokerage houses that tailor themselves to online traders.

online trading - a method of buying and selling securities over the internet without the use of a broker

Exhibit 12B.7 is a sample of TD Waterhouse's webBroker that allows customers to buy and sell securities over the internet. The form allows for trades of stocks, options, mutual funds, and bonds. The form also allows for market orders, limit orders, and stop loss orders.

In addition to enhancing the trading of securities over the internet, these online brokers allow customers to research securities directly from their personal computers. Although trading over the internet is relatively new, it seems to be a trend that will continue for some time.

EXHIBIT 14.9: SAMPLE OF TD WATERHOUSE'S WEBBROKER

TD WATERHOUSE webBroker

Help | Customer Service | Log Off

Welcome | Trading | Account | Quotes | Research | Tools | IPO Center | webBanking

Order Status | Stocks | Options | Mutual Funds | Extended Hours | Bonds

Stocks

Account: XXXXXXXX

webBroker Trading Limitations

Bottom of Form

Order to:	Select Action	
Number of Shares:	☐ All or none	Trading in volatile markets
Symbol:		
Order Type:	Select an Order Type	*Please note that "stop-limit" orders cannot be placed via TD Waterhouse webBroker. Please contact an Account Officer to place a "stop-limit" order.*
Limit or Stop Price:		
Time Limit:	Good for the Day	
Account Type:	Please Select Account	
Telephone #:	Ext.	

METHODS OF ANALYSIS

There are two primary methods of analyzing equity securities. These methods are technical analysis and fundamental analysis. Each method is discussed below.

TECHNICAL ANALYSIS

technical analysis - the search for identifiable and recurring stock price patterns

Technical analysis is an attempt to determine the demand side of the supply/demand equation for a particular stock or set of stocks. This methodology is based on the belief that studying the history of security trades will help predict movements in the future. Technical analysts, or chartists, referring to the reliance on charts, believe that the history of the stock price will tell the whole story of the security and that there is no need to be concerned with earnings, financial leverage, product mix, and management philosophy. Recall that technical analysis is in direct contradiction to the efficient market hypothesis which, at all levels, states that the current price already reflects all historical price data. Technical analysts believe there are basic economic assumptions that support the theories of technical analysis. These assumptions include the following:

- The interaction between supply and demand is the foundation for the value of all goods and services.

- Both rational and irrational factors control supply and demand. The market weighs each of these factors.
- The market and individual securities tend to move in similar trends that endure for substantial lengths of time.
- Variations in the relationship between supply and demand can change prevailing trends.
- Shifts or variations in supply and demand can be detected in the movement of the market.

Technical analysts use a variety of techniques to predict the trend of the market, such as moving averages, relative strength analysis, contrary opinion rules, and breadth of the market indicators. One of the most significant stock price and volume techniques is called the Dow theory.

The Dow theory was developed initially by Charles H. Dow and later expanded by William Hamilton. It is the basis for many of the theories of technical analysis. The Dow theory suggests three types of price movements. Primary moves are the first type of movement and represent large trends that last anywhere from one to four years. These moves are considered bull or bear markets for up or down moves, respectively. The second type of movement is called an intermediate move that is a temporary change in movement called a technical correction. The time frame for these corrections is generally less than two months. The final type of movement is referred to as a ripple that occurs during both primary and secondary movements and represents a small change in comparison to the first two movements. It is believed that all three of these movements are occurring at the same time.

The Dow Theory uses the Dow Jones Industrial Average (DJIA) and the Dow Jones Transportation Average (DJTA) as indicators of the market. This theory is based on the concept that measures of stock prices, such as averages and indexes, should move coincidentally. Thus, if the DJIA is moving upwards, the DJTA should also be increasing. Support from both market indicators would suggest a strong bull market. Likewise, if both averages are declining, there is considerable support for a strong bear market. When the averages are moving in opposite directions, then the future direction of stock prices is unclear.

Fundamental Analysis

Fundamental analysis is the process of determining the true value of a security. This true value is referred to as the intrinsic value and it is generally thought of as the present value of the future cash flows (oftentimes the dividend stream of an equity security). Through fundamental analysis, investors attempt to determine what the company is worth. Once the value is determined, it is compared to the market value of the security. If the market value of the security is less than the intrinsic value, then the investor will purchase the security. If the market value of the security is greater than the intrinsic value, then the investor should sell shares currently held or delay purchase of shares.

fundamental analysis - the analysis of a stock's value using basic, publicly available data such as the stock's earnings, sales, risk, and industry analysis

The process of determining the value of a security encompasses many aspects. The fundamental analyst incorporates broad macroeconomic trends, industry analysis, and company analysis into an estimate of the value of a security. The analysis of broad economic trends includes analyzing growth of the economy, analyzing monetary and fiscal policy, interest rates, unemployment, consumer spending, and inflation. Analysts look at industry data to determine market competitiveness, strengths and weaknesses, and other factors that impact on the value of a security within the context of its industry. At the company level, fundamental analysts use financial statement analysis, valuation models, and ratio analysis to assist in determining a company's worth. Once forecasts about future cash flows are developed, a fundamental analyst uses the valuation models to determine the value of the company.

VALUATION MODELS

One of the components of selecting a stock in which to invest is determining its value. The value of a common stock is equal to the present value of its future cash flows. We use the same model to value all securities, whether bonds, preferred stock, or common stock. However, each case has unique issues for which we must account.

The basic model for valuing any security or project is as follows:

$$PV = \frac{Cf_1}{(1+k)^1} + \frac{Cf_2}{(1+k)^2} + \cdots + \frac{Cf_n}{(1+k)^n} \quad \text{or} \quad PV = \sum_{t=1}^{n} \frac{Cf_t}{(1+k)^t}$$

In this model, Cf_n represents the cash flow for period *n,* and *k* represents the internal rate of return or the required rate of return. The series of cash flows are discounted at an appropriate discount rate to determine the value of the security.

VALUING PREFERRED STOCK

Because preferred stock generally pays a fixed dividend and often has no maturity, it is considered a perpetuity. In other words, the dividend continues indefinitely. Therefore, we can use a simplified version of the above model to determine the value of preferred stock. The model used to value preferred stock is as follows:

$$V = \frac{D}{k}$$

The value of preferred stock equals the dividend (*D*) divided by the required rate of return of the investor (*k*). For example, if a preferred stock is paying a dividend of $6 and the investor's required rate of return equals 12 percent, then the value of the preferred stock should equal $50:

$$V = \frac{\$6}{0.12} = \$50$$

If the current market price of the security was greater than $50, then the investor should not purchase the preferred stock as an investment. However, if the stock were trading at a price of $50 or less, then the purchase of the security would be a wise decision.

DIVIDEND DISCOUNT MODEL

Common stock dividends do not typically remain steady over time. Generally, the dividend from common stock grows over time. Assuming a constant rate of growth for the dividend, we can expand the above model to accommodate the growth component of the dividend stream. The following formula is used to value common stock with a constant growing dividend:

$$V_0 = \frac{D_1}{k - g}$$

The value of common stock equals the dividend one period from today (D_1) divided by the difference between the investor's required rate of return (k) and the growth of the dividend (g).

EXAMPLE

A common stock is paying a dividend that is currently \$6 and is growing at a constant rate of 6 percent per year. If the investor's required rate of return equals 12 percent, then the value of the common stock equals \$106:

$$V = \frac{\$6(1.06)}{0.12 - 0.06} = \$106$$

D_1 must be determined by multiplying the current dividend (D_0) by one plus the growth rate (1+ g). The model is based on a constant growing dividend and on the required return of the investor. Notice that the model will not work if the growth rate (g) equals or exceeds the required rate of return of the investor (k).

Both the preferred stock and the common stock are currently paying a dividend of \$6 per share. However, the value of the common stock is \$56 more than the value of the preferred stock. The reason for this difference is the growth of future dividends. Therefore, the growth of future dividends can be valued at \$56.

PRICE TO EARNINGS (P/E) RATIO

The price to earnings (P/E) ratio is a measure of how much the market is willing to pay for each dollar of earnings of a company. The **P/E ratio** is determined by dividing the current market price of the security by the earnings per share (EPS) for the company:

P/E ratio - a measure of how much the market is willing to pay for each dollar of earnings of a company; the price per earnings ratio

$$\text{Price to Earnings Ratio} = \frac{\text{Market Price per Share}}{\text{Earnings per Share}}$$

EXAMPLE

If XYZ stock is trading at \$50 per share and it has earnings per share of \$4, then its P/E ratio equals 12.5.

The P/E ratio can be viewed differently by using the constant growth dividend model as the price and dividing both sides of the equation by earnings (E). This is illustrated below:

$$V = P = \frac{D_1}{k - g}$$

$$P/\ E = \frac{D_1/\ E}{k - g}$$

Based on this model, the P/E ratio is dependent on three components. The first component is referred to as the payout ratio (D_1/E). The payout ratio represents the portion of earnings that a company pays to the shareholders in the form of dividend payments. The second component is the required return for the security, and the third is the growth of the dividend payment.

The P/E ratio may be used to compare companies within an industry. Better quality companies generally have higher P/E ratios than lower quality companies. Investors are willing to pay more for each dollar of earnings from a high quality company.

VALUING THE COMPANY VERSUS VALUING THE STOCK

Up to this point, we have confined our valuation methodology to those stocks that pay dividends. With preferred stock, we use the valuation of a perpetuity to determine its price. Similarly, we valued common stock with a constant growing dividend. What about those companies that do not generally pay dividends, such as Amgen? Since these companies do not pay dividends, our valuation models do not seem to work. Our focus, however, simply needs to shift from the valuation of the stock to the valuation of the company. Instead of looking at the cash flows from the security, we need to address the cash flows that are generated by the company.

By using the models developed for finding the present value of a stream of cash flows, the value of the company can be obtained. The inputs in the model are the relevant cash flows and the discount rate.

free cash flow to equity - term that describes the available cash after meeting all of the firm's operating and financial needs; used to calculate the value a company

The term **"free cash flow to equity"** describes the available cash after meeting all of the firms operating and financial needs. It is generally calculated as follows:

	Revenue
–	Operating expenses
=	**Earnings before interest, taxes and depreciation** (EBITDA)
–	Depreciation
–	Amortization
=	**Earnings before interest and taxes** (EBIT)
–	Interest
–	Taxes
=	Net Income
+	Depreciation
+	Amortization
=	*Cash flow from operations*
–	Preferred dividends
–	Capital expenditures
–	Working capital needs
–	Principal repayments (loan)
+	Proceeds from new debt issues
=	*Free cash flow to equity*

Once the cash flow is forecasted, then it can be used to value the company. The discount rate that is used can be derived from reviewing comparable companies in the market or by using models such as the Capital Asset Pricing Model, which is discussed below.

Once the value of the company is established, then the value of the stock can be derived from the company's valuation. However, valuing the share price of the stock is not as simple as dividing the value of the company by the outstanding shares of common stock. The value of the company reflects an inherent control premium. This premium reflects the ability to change the board of directors, change the dividend policy, and influence the business opportunities that are undertaken. The concept of the control premium can be seen in the market anytime a company acquires another company. The acquiring company is willing to pay more than the current market price of the stock because it is acquiring control. Therefore, the value of a share of stock as listed on an exchange has been discounted from the proportionate value of the company because the stock represents a minority interest.

CAPITAL ASSET PRICING MODEL

The **Capital Asset Pricing Model** (CAPM) is an asset pricing model that developed from the Markowitz efficient frontier (discussed in Chapter 12) and the introduction of a risk-free asset. As you recall from the discussion of Markowitz, any portfolio that lies on the efficient frontier is considered an efficient portfolio, and, thus, it has the highest level of return for the given level of risk. However, by introducing a risk-free asset (R_f), a new set of portfolios can be created that is more efficient than the Markowitz efficient frontier. Exhibit 12B.8 illustrates this concept.

Capital Asset Pricing Model (CAPM) - an asset pricing model that developed from the Markowitz efficient frontier and the introduction of a risk-free asset

EXHIBIT 12B.8: CAPITAL MARKET LINE

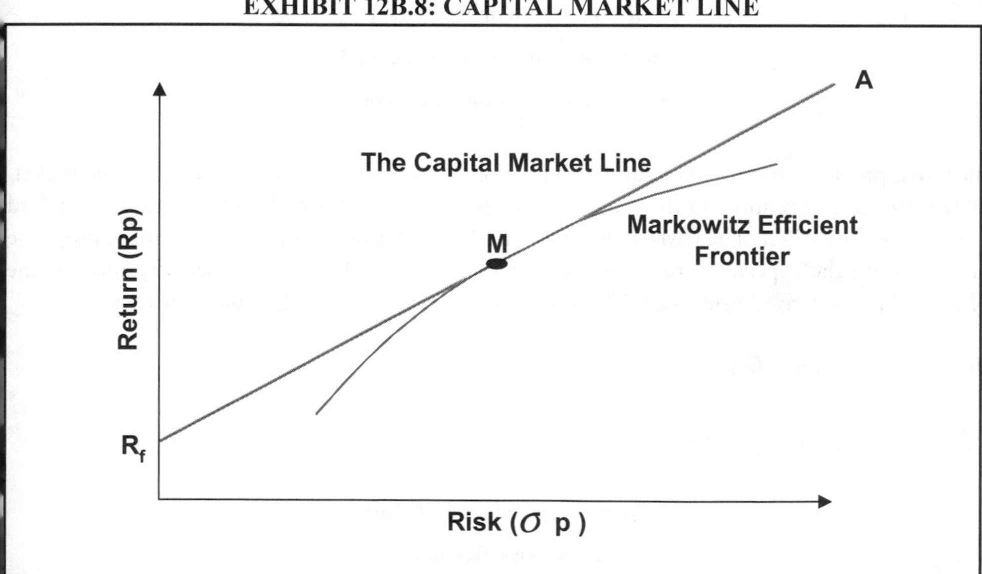
A
The Capital Market Line
Markowitz Efficient Frontier
M
Return (Rp)
Rf
Risk (σ p)

The capital market line (CML) is the new efficient frontier. However, instead of providing a maximum return, as did the efficient frontier of Markowitz, the CML provides an expected return based on the level of risk. The equation for the CML is written as follows:

Where on the Web

American Association of Individual Investors *www.aaii.com*
American Stock Exchange *www.amex.com*
Barron's Online *www.barrons.com*
Bloomberg.com *www.bloomberg.com*
CNBC *http://moneycentral.msn.com*
CNN Money *www.money.cnn.com*
Dow Jones Industrial Average *www.djindexes.com*
Kiplinger *www.kiplinger.com*
Nasdaq *www.nasdaq.com*
New York Stock Exchange *www.nyse.com*
TD Waterhouse *www.tdwaterhouse.com*
U.S. Securities and Exchange Commission *www.sec.gov*Yahoo Finance *finance.yahoo.com*

$E(R_p) = R_f + \left(\frac{[R_m - R_f]}{\sigma_m}\right) \times \sigma_p$, where

$E(R_p)$ = Expected return of the portfolio
R_f = Risk-free rate
R_m = Return on the market
σ_m = Standard deviation of the market
σ_p = Standard deviation of the portfolio

The CML provides an expected return for a portfolio based on the expected return of the market, the risk-free rate of return and the standard deviation of the portfolio in relation to the standard deviation of the market. The CML is generally used with efficient portfolios. It is not appropriate for estimating the expected return for individual securities. However, the security market line (SML), which is derived from the CML, does allow us to evaluate individual securities.

The SML is written as follows:

$E(R_i) = R_f + B_i(R_m - R_f)$, where

$E(R_i)$ = Expected return for asset *i*
R_f = Risk-free rate
R_m = Return on the market
B_i = Beta of asset *i*

The security market line determines the expected return for a security (i) based on its beta and the expectations about the market and the risk-free rate.

EXAMPLE

If the beta of ABC Company is 1.2 and the market return is expected to be 13 percent with a risk-free return of 3 percent, then the expected return of ABC is 15 percent, as follows:

$$E(R_i) = R_f + B_i(R_m - R_f)$$
$$E(R_i) = 0.03 + 1.2(0.13 - 0.03) = 0.15 \text{ or } 15\%$$

Therefore, based on the level of systematic risk of ABC Company, it should earn a return of 15 percent. The SML helps identify how the characteristics of a portfolio will be impacted when a security is added to the portfolio.

PROFESSIONAL FOCUS

Do you prefer using individual equity securities or mutual funds in your clients' portfolios and why?

It depends on many factors, such as how much money we are talking about investing, whether there are existing positions in an account that have tax consequences if you reposition them, and what percentage of the account is fixed income.

If we were talking about investing $25,000, my inclination would be to invest all of the money in a diversified portfolio of mutual funds. Why? Because we do not have enough money to take a meaningful position in individual equities.

If we were talking about investing $100,000 in cash, my response might be to invest a small portion in individual equities or fixed income to spice up the mix, but the majority in a diversified portfolio of actively managed mutual funds. Depending on my client's age, risk tolerance, investment experience, etc., his recommended asset allocation may require some exposure to foreign equities, small and mid-cap domestic equities, REITS, and so on. I would certainly be inclined to invest in mutual funds in the areas that require special research, or that are highly volatile, such as small-cap and international. I rely heavily on the use of Shape Ratio and Alpha as a measure of fund manager effectiveness.

If we were to invest $500,000 or more, I would be inclined to place portions, (subject to asset allocation) with various private money managers who specialize within asset categories. My experience has been that they are accountable for style drift, and they can be sensitive to issues such as capital gain exposure. Transparency of the portfolio is very appealing to my clients and me.

Do you believe that the equity markets are efficient or that active management can indeed add value?

In spite of evidence that only a limited number of mutual fund managers consistently beat the indices they are measured against, there is no question in my mind that actively managed portfolios add value. The concern I have with index funds is that investors are of the mistaken impression that they are getting a diversified portfolio of stocks, when because of capitalization weighting, they are not. When the top 25 (5 percent) companies of the 500 that comprise the S&P Index represent 40 percent of the entire value of the index, the client is exposed to a far greater degree of risk than they may be aware. Index funds tend to look great when the market is up, but when the market is down, I believe that a manager who has the ability to get out of a troubled holding in a hurry is of great value.

What is the process that you use to select individual equities for clients' portfolios?

When I propose a stock for consideration to my clients, it is generally a large, well-known company, that may look attractive for valuation reasons. They are always long-term holds. I find that it helps clients stay "enrolled" in the process if they can look up their individual equity positions or discuss them with friends. The problem with mutual funds is that they are a passive item to most investors, as they don't know what the holdings are within the fund at any given time.

BRADLEY VAN VECHTEN, CFP®

CHAPTER 12 SUPPLEMENT C

Mutual Funds

This supplement provides additional information on mutual funds. Topics covered include:

- Types of investment companies
  - ▲ Unit investment trusts
  - ▲ Exchange-traded funds
  - ▲ Closed-end investment companies
  - ▲ Mutual funds
- Mutual fund fees
- Mutual fund classification
- Mutual fund expenses and their impact on performance
- Mutual fund expense ratios
- Advantages of mutual funds
- Disadvantages of mutual funds
- Types and objectives of mutual funds
- Mutual fund selection
- Modern Portfolio Theory
- Performance measures
- Portfolio management

INTRODUCTION TO MUTUAL FUNDS

mutual funds - open-end investment companies that sell shares of stock to the public and use the proceeds to invest in a portfolio of securities on behalf of their shareholders

Mutual funds are investment vehicles that provide individual investors and institutional investors with easy access to capital markets. They are a type of investment company that sells shares of stock to the public and uses the proceeds to invest in a portfolio of securities on behalf of its shareholders. The many benefits to investing in mutual funds will be discussed in this section.

Over the past few decades, mutual funds have become the predominant method for small investors to gain access to equity and fixed-income investments. The growing popularity of mutual funds is evidenced by the increasing number of mutual funds available to investors as well as the amount of assets invested in mutual funds. In the U. S. there are now more than eight thousand mutual funds, meaning that there are more mutual funds than there are listed equity securities.

EXHIBIT 12C.1: MUTUAL FUND ASSETS (TRILLIONS OF DOLLARS)

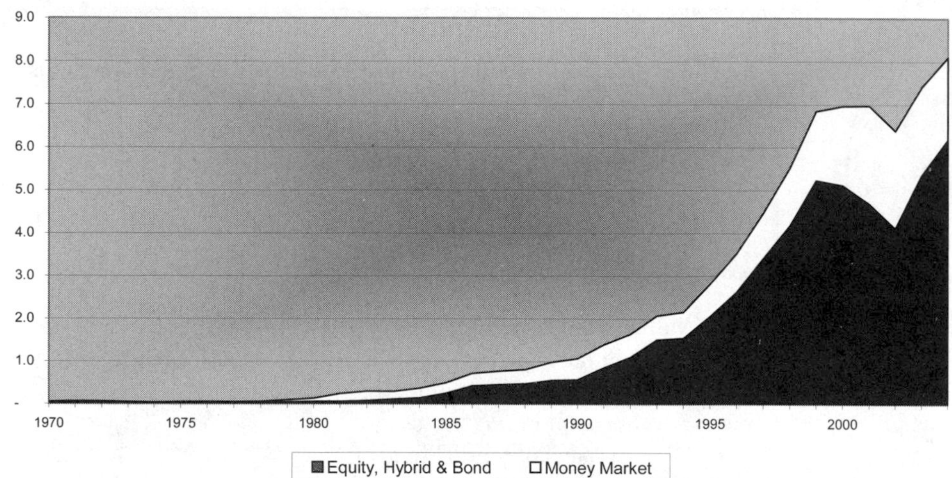
9.0
8.0
7.0
6.0
5.0
4.0
3.0
2.0
1.0
-
1970
1975
1980
1985
1990
1995
2000
Equity, Hybrid & Bond
Money Market

Source: 2005 Mutual Fund Fact Book, Investment Company Institute, Washington, DC

As illustrated in Exhibit 12C.1, assets invested in mutual funds have increased to $8.11 trillion by year-end 2004. This increase in mutual fund assets has grown at a tremendous rate and is attributable to several important changes that have occurred in recent decades.

The work place environment has changed significantly in the last twenty to thirty years. Gone are the days when employees would stay with a company for their entire career. In the past, employers and employees had a great deal of mutual loyalty and, as a result, companies generally provided significant retirement benefits to employees. These benefits, along with Social Security, traditionally provided sufficient income during retirement to maintain preretirement life styles. Today, such mutual loyalty is rare. Employees change employers frequently, and employers are quick to terminate employees in an attempt to become more competitive. Employers today are also reducing the retirement benefits that were once provided. Instead of employer-funded retirement plans, companies are establishing an increasing number of 401(k) plans, which allow individuals to save for retirement on a pretax basis. These changes have caused individuals to become self-reliant in an attempt to sufficiently save for their own retirement. In most cases, these retirement plan savings are invested in mutual funds.

In addition to changes occurring in the work place, the public is becoming more aware of the need for financial planning and the potential investment returns that are available in the securities markets. The public, being more educated about investments, is more willing to accept the additional risk of equities and fixed-income securities. Mutual funds are allowing these individuals easy access to investment securities and markets.

Another cause for increased savings in 401(k) plans and increased self-reliance is the public awareness of increasing life expectancies. At the time Social Security was created, the remaining life expectancy for someone entitled to receive full retirement benefits was at most fifteen years. Today, the remaining life expectancy for someone retiring at 65 may be twenty to thirty years. The increased time spent in retirement increases the amount of money needed for retirement and increases the amount that must be saved prior to retirement.

Mutual funds are considered an indirect method of investing and are an alternative to investing directly in equities and other securities. Mutual funds provide numerous benefits to investors, many of which are unavailable from other methods of investing. Investors need to be cautious, however, when investing in mutual funds because of certain disadvantages and complexities that are presented later in this section.

TYPES OF INVESTMENT COMPANIES

Mutual funds are actually a subcategory of what is referred to as regulated investment companies. **Investment companies** are financial services companies that sell shares of stock to the public and use the proceeds to invest in a portfolio of securities. Although each investor or shareholder may have a relatively small investment in total, the funds of all shareholders pooled together allow the investment company to create a widely diversified portfolio with certain economies of scale.

investment companies - financial services companies that sell shares of stock to the public and use the proceeds to invest in a portfolio of securities

Investment companies are generally nontaxable entities. These companies do not pay federal or state income tax. Instead, investment companies act as flow-through entities or conduits whereby interest income, dividends, and capital gains all flow through from the investment company to the shareholders and are reported on the investor's individual tax return. The income that flows through retains its character as to ordinary income or capital gain and is allocated to each shareholder based on the number of shares owned. The tax treatment of investment companies is similar in concept to the tax treatment of partnerships and S-corporations.

To qualify for nontaxable treatment, investment companies, under Internal Revenue Code Section 851, must meet the following criteria:

- The investment company must earn at least 90 percent of its income from interest, dividends, and capital gains derived from investing in stocks, bonds, currencies, or other securities.
- At least 90 percent of the investment company's taxable income must be distributed to its shareholders.
- For 50 percent of the portfolio, an investment in securities of any one issuer is limited to an amount not greater than 5 percent of the total assets of the fund, and no more than 10 percent of the outstanding voting securities of such issuer.
- No more than 25 percent of the value of a fund's total assets can be invested in the securities of one issuer.

In addition to meeting specific requirements of the Internal Revenue Code, investment companies are also regulated by the Securities Exchange Commission (SEC) under the Investment Company Act of 1940. Investment companies are also regulated under the Securities Act of 1933, the Securities Exchange Act of 1934, and the Investment Advisors Act of 1940. For more information on these Acts, see Appendix C at the end of the text.

As indicated above, mutual funds are only one type of investment company. The four types of investment companies are unit investment trusts, exchange-traded funds, closed-end funds, and open-end investment companies (mutual funds).

Unit Investment Trusts

unit investment trust (UIT) - a registered investment company that is passively managed and may invest in stocks, bonds, or other securities

A **unit investment trust** (UIT) is a registered investment company that is passively managed and may invest in stocks, bonds or other securities. Investors generally purchase units, which are sold at net asset value plus a commission, with the idea that they will hold the units until they mature. As income is earned and securities mature, investors will receive both income (interest and/or dividends) and principal from the trust.

In the case of UITs that invest in stocks, the trust will have a defined maturity date at which time the investor will have the option of rolling over the proceeds, receiving a pro-rata distribution of the UIT's underlying securities, or receiving cash from the investment.

UITs are known as unmanaged, or passively managed, funds because professional managers initially select securities to be included in the portfolio, and those securities are generally held until they mature. For example, a UIT investing in municipal bond securities may have a portfolio of municipal bonds with staggered maturities. These bonds will generally be held until they mature. As coupon payments are received from the bond issuer, they are passed along to the unit holders. When a bond matures, the face value will be passed through to the unit holders. Although the holdings of UITs are monitored, the securities within the fund generally remain the same throughout the life of the fund.

The traditional UIT invested in fixed-income securities. Today, however, there are a variety of UITs available to meet the objectives and risk tolerances of investors. UITs invest in a wide array of securities, including municipal bonds, corporate bonds, U.S. government bonds, international bonds, and mortgage-backed securities.

The intent of most investors is to hold these UITs until maturity. However, for investors who wish to divest themselves of the units, trusts are required to redeem units at net asset value.

Exchange Traded Funds (ETFs)

exchange traded funds (ETFs) - a type of investment company whose investment objective is to achieve the same return as a particular market index

Exchange traded funds (ETFs) are portfolios or baskets of stocks that are traded on an exchange (offerings are generally traded on the American Stock Exchange). ETFs are index-based equity instruments that represent ownership in either a fund or a unit investment trust and give investors the opportunity to buy and sell shares of an entire stock portfolio as a single security. Common examples include QQQQ (Nasdaq-100) and SPDRs (Standard & Poor's Depositary Receipts, tracking the S&P 500 index, or sectors of the index).

Unlike mutual funds, ETFs can be purchased and sold throughout the day. In addition, they can be bought on margin and can be sold short (and are not subject to the uptick rule). These ETFs typically have lower annual expenses compared to mutual funds. However, since ETFs are traded on exchanges, it is possible that in a market correction, investors may be unable to sell their shares. Recall that mutual funds must redeem investors' shares upon request.

ETFs are passively managed. They generally track a specific index, sector, or region. Although ETFs are traded on exchanges, investors may be able to buy or redeem shares from the fund family, generally in 50,000 share blocks. However, redemptions generally require the delivery of the underlying shares of stock. Generally, investors will buy and sell ETFs in the secondary market by using a broker. The price of ETF shares is certainly based on the value of the underlying securities; however, it may not be equal to NAV due to supply and demand for the shares. Although the price of ETF shares may trade at a discount or premium, the difference should be minimal. If the shares were selling at a discount, then a large financial institution could purchase a large quantity (in blocks of 50,000 shares) of ETF shares and then redeem the shares for the underlying securities. These securities could then be sold in the market for a profit. Arbitrageurs can employ a similar strategy in the event that shares are trading at a premium. Generally, however, the gap from NAV is small to nonexistent in free markets where arbitrageurs can operate.

Generally, the annual expense ratio for ETF shares is lower than for the majority of index mutual funds. For example, the annual expense ratio is 11 basis points (0.11%) for SPDRs, while Vanguard's 500 Index Fund charges 18 basis points (0.18%). However, ETF shares that are purchased using a broker will require a commission to be paid. Depending on the commission and the size of the investment, one alternative may be better than the other. ETFs have low turnover and, therefore, lower taxable distributions than most mutual funds. When there is a substantial amount of selling of mutual fund shares, the manager is forced to sell some of the underlying securities to generate enough cash for redemptions. This does not occur in an ETF. Shares are either sold or redeemed in-kind.

Most mutual funds have cash that is not invested, which is a result of new contributions into the fund or cash that is maintained for redemptions. ETFs do not have this cash management problem and may have better performance than similar mutual funds.

HOLDRs (Holding Company Depositary Receipts) have many of the same characteristics as ETFs except that HOLDRs are depositary receipts that represent an investor's ownership in the common stock or ADRs (American depositary receipts) of specified companies in a particular industry, sector, or group. The following table compares various types of ETFs, the index they track, and the annual expenses associated with each exchange traded fund.

CLOSED-END INVESTMENT COMPANIES

A **closed-end fund** is a type of investment company whose shares trade in the same manner that publicly traded stocks trade in the secondary market. Shares of closed-end funds are listed on a stock exchange or trade in the over-the-counter market. Because shares trade in the same manner as other stocks, their prices are subject to the fluctuations in the supply and demand for the shares in the market. Although it is relatively easy to determine the value of securities held within the fund, the share price for the fund will rarely be directly equal to the value of the

closed-end fund - a type of investment company whose shares trade in the same manner that publicly traded stocks trade in the secondary market

EXHIBIT 12C.2: EXCHANGE TRADED FUNDS (ETFs)

Exchange Traded Funds	Index	Annual Expenses
DIAMONDS	DJIA	18 bp
HOLDRs (Holding Company Depositary Receipts) Merrill Lynch	Various sectors	$8 per 100 shares
Ishares	Various sectors and regions	9 to 75 bp
SPDRs (Standard & Poor's Depositary Receipts)	S&P 500	11 bp
Midcap SPDRs	S&P 400	25 bp
NASDAQ-100 Index Tracking Stock (QQQQ)	Nasdaq-100	20 bp
Select Sector SPDRs	Sectors of S&P 500	27 bp
streetTRACKS	Various Dow Jones and MS indexes	20-50 bp

bp = basis points

underlying securities. Since the shares for closed-end funds are subject to supply and demand the shares will generally sell at a premium or discount relative to the net asset value of the fund.

After the initial public offering, a closed-end fund will generally not issue additional shares in the market. Unlike an open-end fund, a closed-end fund's capitalization is considered to be fixed since it does not generally add assets to the fund after initial capitalization.

Since the pool of assets to be invested for a closed-end fund is fixed and shares are not redeemed, the manager of a closed-end fund has a great deal of flexibility in managing the assets within the fund. He does not have to worry about or plan for cash redemptions like a mutual fund (open-end investment company). This one characteristic of closed-end funds allows the manager to invest in less liquid securities that may have higher expected returns than more liquid securities.

Closed-end funds invest in a wide array of securities, including municipal bonds, corporate bonds, U.S. government bonds, international bonds, mortgage-backed securities, convertible securities, domestic equities, and foreign equities. A particularly interesting closed-end fund is what is known as an equity dual-purpose fund. This type of fund invests primarily in securities of U.S. companies but has two classes of shares. The first class of shares consists of income shares that receive all dividend income, but no capital appreciation. The second class of shares consists of capital shares that receive all capital appreciation, but no dividend income. An investor interested in income only, such as a retiree, might purchase the first class of shares. This class of shares would provide a steady stream of income. Alternatively, an investor who had a long-term time horizon and did not have any need for current income would most likely be interested in long-term growth securities. The second class of shares would provide this long-term growth with little or no current income tax cost.

Although closed-end investment companies have been around since before the economic depression of the 1930s, the growth of these funds has paled in comparison to the growth of open-end investment companies (mutual funds).

EXHIBIT 12C.3: GROWTH OF CLOSED-END FUNDS VS. OPEN-END FUNDS

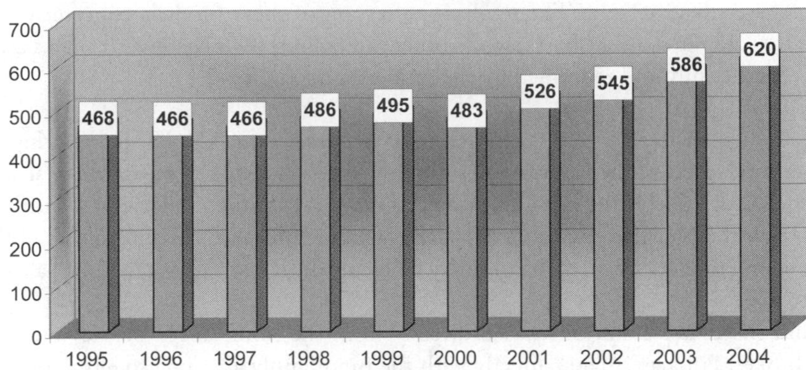
Closed-end Funds
700
600
500
400
300
200
100
0
468
466
466
486
495
483
526
545
586
620
1995
1996
1997
1998
1999
2000
2001
2002
2003
2004

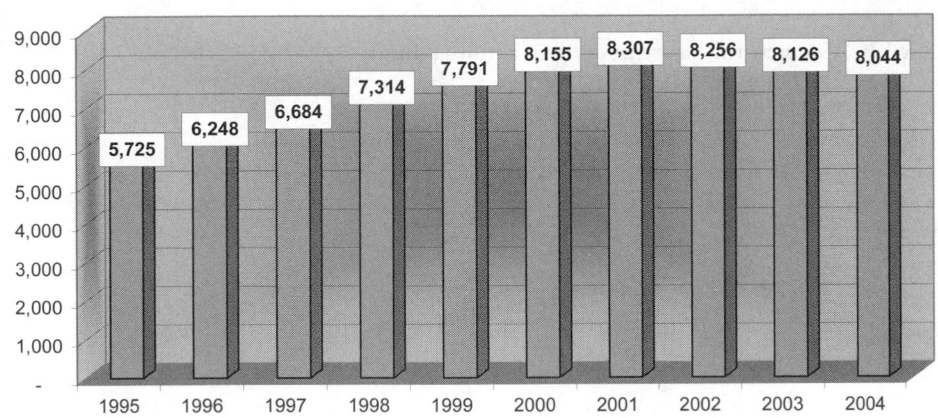
Open-end Funds
9,000
8,000
7,000
6,000
5,000
4,000
3,000
2,000
1,000
-
5,725
6,248
6,684
7,314
7,791
8,155
8,307
8,256
8,126
8,044
1995
1996
1997
1998
1999
2000
2001
2002
2003
2004

Source: Investment Company Institute, Washington, D.C.

One likely reason that closed-end funds have not been as popular as open-end funds is that the fees that can be generated by the fund managers and operators are not as high as those with open-ended funds. Good performance in an open-end fund attracts significant increases in fund assets resulting in a larger base of assets upon which to charge the management fee. A closed-end fund that has great performance may have shares selling at a premium, but additional funds are generally not forthcoming. Therefore, it is easier to increase the management fees through an open-end mutual fund than a closed-end fund.

Another reason that closed-end funds may not have been as popular as open-end funds is the requirement of a broker to buy or sell shares for a closed-end fund. With an open-end fund, an investor must simply call the fund to request the shares be redeemed. The process of purchasing mutual fund shares directly from a fund family is easier than setting up a brokerage account and purchasing closed-end fund shares. In addition, open-end funds are easier for investors to comprehend since their share price is solely based on the price of the underlying securities. Remember, closed-end fund shares may sell at a premium or discount to net asset value.

open-end investment company - an investment company whose capitalization constantly changes as new shares are sold and outstanding shares are redeemed

net asset value (NAV) - the price at which shares of an open-end investment company are sold. The NAV of a fund is determined by subtracting total liabilities from total assets of the fund and dividing the difference by the outstanding shares.

Open-End Investment Companies (Mutual Funds)

Open-end investment companies are referred to as open-end because they are not limited in the number of shares that are sold. The total capitalization of these funds is constantly changing. Some investors are purchasing shares, while others are selling their shares. All shares are sold by the mutual fund family and redeemed by the mutual fund family.

The price at which shares are sold is referred to as **net asset value** (NAV). Subtracting total liabilities from total assets of the fund and dividing the difference by the outstanding shares determines the net asset value of the fund. Each day, as the prices of the underlying securities change in value, so will the NAV for the fund. All shares will be purchased for and sold at NAV. However, commissions and other sales charges may be charged against the purchase or sale of shares.

Mutual fund shares are either purchased directly from the fund family or they are purchased through a broker. Purchases made directly with the fund family are done so either by mail, telephone, Internet, or by visiting office locations. Shares purchased through a broker or other financial services person will generally be charged a commission or a sales charge. These fees serve to compensate the broker as an investment adviser.

Exhibit 12C.4 depicts the basic structure of a mutual fund.

EXHIBIT 12C.4: MUTUAL FUND STRUCTURE

Shareholders

Board of directors
Oversees the fund's activities, including approval of the contract with the management company and certain other service providers.

Mutual fund

Investment adviser
Manages the fund's portfolio according to the objectives and policies described in the fund's prospectus.

Principal underwriter
Sells fund shares, either directly to the public or through other firms.

Custodian
Holds the fund assets, maintaining them separately to protect shareholder interests.

Independent public accountant
Certifies the fund's financial statements.

Transfer agent
Executes transactions—such as orders to buy and sell fund shares—on behalf of fund shareholders, maintains records of those transactions and other shareholder account activity, and sends account information—such as fund statements and transaction confirmations—to shareholders.

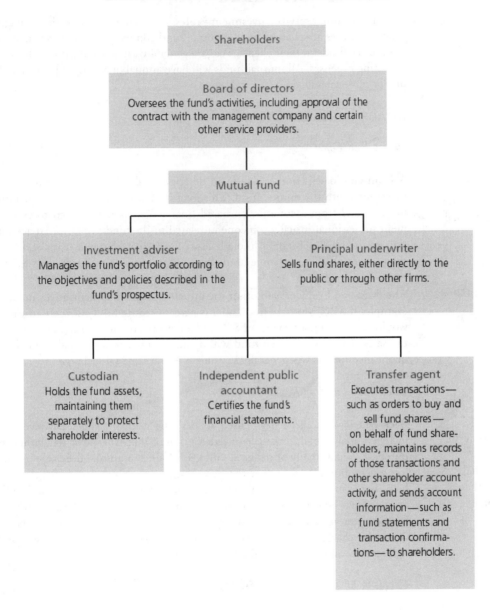

Source: 2003 Mutual Fund Fact Book, Investment Company Institute, Washington, D.C.

MUTUAL FUND FEES

Just like any other service, investment professionals charge fees for the management of an investor's assets. Fees are charged by the mutual fund company and by investment professionals who sell mutual funds to their clients. Fees are generally categorized into loads or sales charges and operating expenses. All mutual funds will have annual operating expenses, and many also have one or more sales charges.

LOADS OR SALES CHARGES

Front-End Load

front-end load - a sales charge based on the initial investment into a mutual fund

A **front-end load** is simply a term to describe a sales charge based on the value of the initial investment into the mutual fund. This load is incurred when an investor purchases shares of a mutual fund from a commission-based financial adviser. It is used to compensate the investment professional (usually someone unrelated to the fund itself) for advice related to the selection of the mutual funds. Although most funds that charge a front-end load will charge less than 6 percent, there are some funds that impose sales charges as high as 8.5 percent.

EXAMPLE

The front-end load works to offset the initial, or any subsequent, investment into the fund. For example, if ABC Mutual Fund had a 6 percent front-end load, then an investment of $1,000 would result in a sales charge of $60 and a net investment into the mutual fund of $940. Once the sales charge is paid, the fund will operate similar to a no-load fund. However, any subsequent investments will generally be subject to the same sales charge.

Back-End Load or Redemption Fee

back-end load - a sales charge incurred upon the ultimate sale or redemption of mutual fund shares rather than at the time of purchase

Back-end load is also a term used to describe a sales charge. However, the sales charge is incurred upon the ultimate sale or redemption of mutual fund shares rather than at the time of purchase. Today, many of the back-end loads found in mutual funds are in the form of a declining redemption fee, such that the percentage sales charge declines each year that the fund is held. For example, a fund might charge a five percent declining redemption fee. In such a case, an investor would pay 5 percent of the amount invested into the fund for redemption within the first year, 4 percent within the second year, and so on. After five years, no redemption fee would be charged in such a case. A back-end load is typically assessed on the lesser of the redemption value or the initial investment value.

OTHER MUTUAL FUND FEES

12b-1 Fees

12b-1 fee - a fee that pays for the services of brokers who sell mutual funds and who maintain the client relationship

Under the Investment Company Act of 1940, Section 12b-1, fees are permitted to pay for marketing and distribution expenses directly from a fund's asset base. The so-called **12b-1 fee** charged by the mutual fund company is used to pay for the services of brokers who sell the mutual funds and who maintain the client relationships. This fee is often paid in the form of trailing commissions, where commissions are paid to the broker over a period of years. The trailing commissions are based on the size of the investment in the mutual fund. Brokers will eceive larger commissions for larger investments. As the investment in the mutual fund grows over time, so does the trailing commission that the broker receives.

The maximum 12b-1 fee that can be charged is 75 basis points per year. However, another 25 basis points can be charged as a "service fee," which effectively raises the annual potential 12b-1 charge to 100 basis points or 1 percent of assets per year.

Management Fees

The **management fee** is the fee that is charged by the investment adviser for the management of the fund assets. This fee is generally the single largest expense of a mutual fund and is included in the expense ratio.

management fee - a fee charged by an investment adviser for the management of a mutual fund's assets

Expense Ratio

The **expense ratio** is disclosed by all mutual funds in the fund prospectus and is an indication of the annual fund expenses and is stated as a percentage of total assets. Included in this figure are the management fees, the 12b-1 fees, and other operating expenses related to running and operating the fund (e.g., rent, computer). The expense ratio does not include sales charges.

expense ratio - disclosed by all mutual funds in their fund prospectuses as an indication of the annual fund expenses, stated as a percentage of total assets

It is important for an investor to realize that reducing the expense ratio by one percent is essentially the same as increasing the rate of return by 1 percent. Therefore, managing the expenses paid for the management of mutual fund assets is an important element of the investment planning process.

MUTUAL FUND CLASSIFICATION

There are no-load funds and load funds. No-load funds are sold directly by the fund to the investor and do not charge front or back-end loads as described below. An investment of $100 goes directly into the fund at the NAV. Load funds are discussed below.

Load versus No-Load Funds

Mutual funds that charge either a front-end load or a back-end load are considered **load funds**. As stated above, sales charges are used to compensate the brokers or sales force for the fund. In addition, funds without a front-end load or a back-end load that have a 12b-1 fee that exceeds 25 basis points (0.25 percent or 0.0025) are also considered load funds. Only if the 12b-1 fee is 25 basis points or less can the fund be called a no-load fund. Generally, **no-load funds** are purchased directly through the mutual fund family without the assistance of a broker. These funds do not charge annual sales charges, but will have operating expenses, as do other mutual funds.

load funds - mutual funds that charge either a front-end load or back-end load

no-load funds - mutual funds purchased directly through the mutual fund family without the assistance of a broker

Classes of Load Fund Shares

Many of the fund families that offer load funds have different classes of shares that contain different sets of loads and expenses. Although there are no legal requirements as to the classification of shares of a load fund, most of the industry follows a similar classification system. Shares are generally classified into three classes, known as class A shares, class B shares, and class C shares:

- *Class A shares* – These shares usually charge a front-end load with a smaller 12b-1 fee.
- *Class B shares* – These shares usually charge a deferred redemption fee plus the maximum 1 percent 12b-1 fee. In addition, many of the class B shares will have a conversion feature that automatically converts the class B shares to class A shares after a period of years. The advantage of the conversion feature is that the investor will save expenses because the 12b-1 fee is lower for class A shares than for class B shares.
- *Class C shares* – These shares will often have a level deferred sales charge (often 1 percent) plus the maximum 1 percent 12b-1 fee. However, these shares do not convert to class A shares.

Many fund families have additional classes of shares that have a variety of meanings. As a result investors should carefully review the prospectus of each fund to determine the actual fees that are being charged to shareholders for each class of shares for a particular fund.

HOW DO FUND EXPENSES IMPACT PERFORMANCE?

High quality funds may have high or low expense ratios. However, as a general rule, the higher the expenses of the mutual fund, the more the fund manager will have to overcome to achieve strong return performance. Consider the following example:

EXAMPLE Assume an investment of $10,000 into two funds, each with an annual return of 10 percent, before expenses. Fund A has an expense ratio of 1 percent while Fund B has an expense ratio of 1.6 percent. The investment in the Fund B will grow to $112,429 after 30 years. The investment in Fund A will grow to $132,677 after 30 years. The $20,248 (18 percent) difference is attributable to the higher expenses of Fund B.

EXHIBIT 12C.5: GROWTH OF $10,000 AFTER EXPENSES

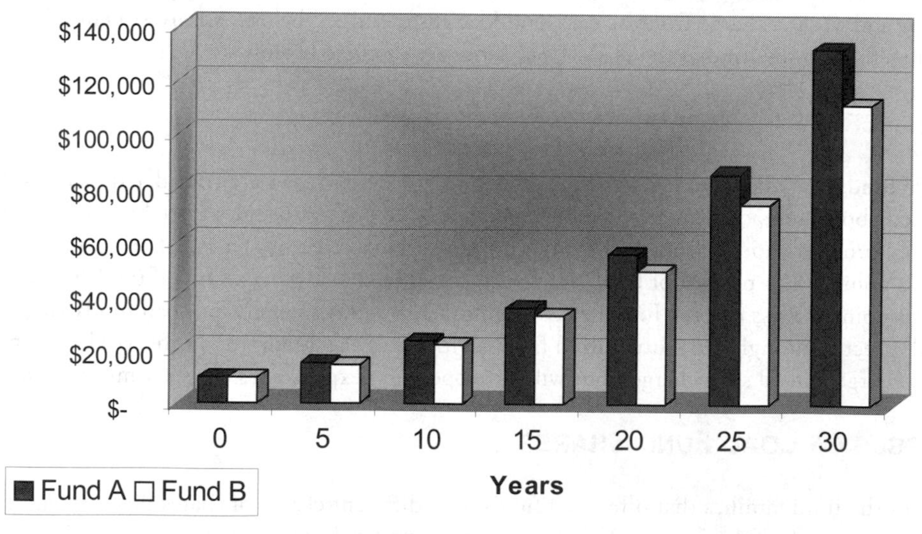

$140,000
$120,000
$100,000
$80,000
$60,000
$40,000
$20,000
$-
0
5
10
15
20
25
30
Years
Fund A
Fund B

As illustrated by Exhibit 12C.5, mutual fund expenses can make a significant difference in an investor's wealth over a period of years. It is important to realize the impact of expenses on overall performance of a potential mutual fund. However, it is also important to realize that the returns reported by the various mutual funds are net of annual fees. This makes it easier for investors to compare returns of one fund with those of another.

EXPENSE RATIOS FOR DIFFERENT TYPES OF FUNDS

What expense ratio is appropriate for a mutual fund? The answer to this question depends on the objectives of the mutual fund. For example, actively managed funds (those that frequently buy and sell securities) require more research and support than passively managed index funds. Therefore, most actively managed funds will have higher expense ratios than passively managed funds. Similarly, it is more costly to manage international equities than domestic equities because there are many more companies internationally than within the United States. In addition, the availability of accounting and financial information outside the U.S. is not as sufficient as within, thus making research more difficult and more costly. Therefore, it is quite common for international equity funds to have higher expense ratios relative to domestic equity funds.

ADVANTAGES OF MUTUAL FUNDS

Mutual funds provide many benefits to investors including easy access to a diversified portfolio with professional management, as well as other benefits that are not found in typical securities, such as low initial investment amounts, easy access, tax efficiency, liquidity, transaction cost efficiency, and services.

LOW INITIAL INVESTMENT

The majority of mutual funds have very low minimum investment requirements, allowing smaller investors access to many choices of mutual funds. In fact, approximately 61 percent of mutual funds have minimums of $1,000 or under, and 82 percent have minimums of $5,000 or under (see Exhibit 12C.6). These low minimum investment requirements allow individuals, who would otherwise be precluded from such investments, access to the equity and fixed-income markets.

EXHIBIT 12C.6: MUTUAL FUND MINIMUM INVESTMENT REQUIREMENTS, 2002

*Percent distribution of funds by minimum investment requirement**

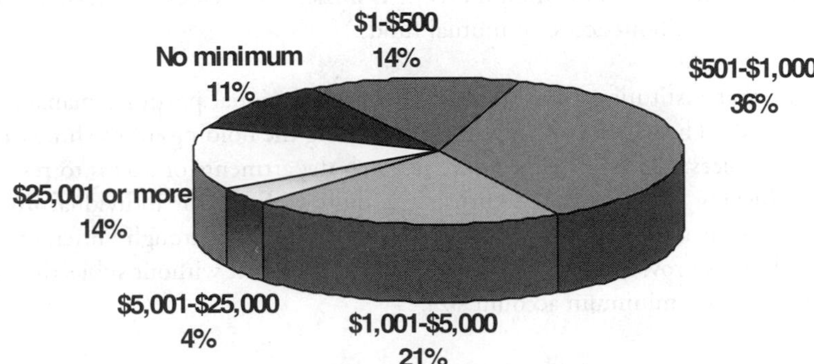
$1-$500
14%
No minimum
11%
$501-$1,000
36%
$25,001 or more
14%
$5,001-$25,000
4%
$1,001-$5,000
21%

**Many mutual funds offer lower investment minimums for Individual Retirement Accounts and automatic investment plans.*
Source: 2003 Mutual Fund Fact Book, Investment Company Institute, Washington, DC.

DIVERSIFICATION

Mutual funds provide an easy way to diversify a portfolio at a low cost. Some mutual funds have as many as 2,000 different securities in a single portfolio. Most mutual funds have 100 to 1,000 different securities in one portfolio. Such broad diversification, coupled with a minimum investment requirement, achieves diversification at a very low cost. Minimum initial investments for mutual funds are usually less than $5,000 allowing investors to achieve broad diversification without requiring them to invest large sums of money into individual stocks and bonds. There is really no other way to achieve the same level of diversification with such a small investment.

Trying to achieve the same level of diversification that a mutual fund can offer would require a substantially greater investment than the usual minimum fund requirement. In addition, the transaction costs in acquiring a diversified portfolio would be high. For example, buying 40 equity securities in round lots (100 shares) at an average price of $25 per share would require an investment of $100,000. This investment is far more than an initial investment in most mutual funds. In addition, the transaction cost of purchasing 40 issues could range from $500 to $1,600.

EASE OF ACCESS

Investors can purchase mutual funds easily. Mutual funds can be purchased directly from the mutual fund family or through a broker, bank, or other financial institution. To invest in a mutual fund directly through the fund family, an investor must call the fund family for an account application and prospectus, complete the application, and return the application to the fund family with a check for the amount of the initial investment. Investing in a mutual fund through a broker is as easy as calling the broker and requesting the purchase of the mutual fund. Usually, a brokerage account must be established before the purchase of the mutual fund can be made.

PROFESSIONAL MANAGEMENT

Individuals and institutions that manage money usually charge a fee in the form of a percent of the assets managed. For example, a manager might charge 1 percent of assets annually to manage a portfolio. For an account with a value of $1 million, the fee at 1 percent of assets equals $10,000 annually. However, most professional money managers have minimum account size requirements. These minimum account sizes can be $1 million, $5 million, $50 million, or more for institutional managers. Institutional managers only manage very large pools of assets. Since most managers have specific account minimums, it is difficult to achieve professional management for small investors without access to mutual funds.

The same benefits that institutional investors find with professional portfolio managers can be found in mutual funds. The manager is constantly evaluating the holdings of the funds and alternative investment choices. Managers either have research departments or access to research that assists them in achieving above average returns. It is quite difficult for individual investors to match the performance of professional managers over time and through different markets. Therefore, mutual funds provide access to professional management without subjecting investors to the same restrictions on minimum account size.

TAX EFFICIENCY OF MANAGEMENT FEES

Mutual funds have a tax benefit compared to separately managed accounts. Separately managed accounts are pools of assets that are separately managed by an investment adviser. These funds are not commingled with assets of other investors, as in the case of a mutual fund. Advisers managing separately managed accounts typically charge a management fee based on a percent of assets under management.

The fee that is charged for the management of investments is deductible for income tax purposes as an itemized deduction. If an investor pays $20,000 for an investment adviser to manage his assets, then the investor can deduct the $20,000 as an itemized deduction. However, since the fee can only be deducted as an itemized deduction, it is a deduction after adjusted gross income (AGI) and may be limited by the 2 percent floor or the phaseout of itemized deductions.

Management fees for mutual funds are deducted from the returns of the fund and, therefore, are not reported for tax purposes by the investor. The returns that investors receive from mutual funds are after the charge for the management of the assets. Since the returns are after the management fee, AGI is automatically reduced, which lowers the threshold for various other tax limits. Therefore, mutual funds provide a tax benefit that is not available to separately managed accounts.

LIQUIDITY

Investors of mutual funds are always able to redeem their shares because mutual funds are required to redeem shares when requested by investors. These shares will be redeemed at net asset value, which is the price of the mutual fund shares based on the underlying assets.

TRANSACTION COST EFFICIENCY

Since mutual funds generally have hundreds of millions, and some have billions, of dollars under management, they have economies of scale with regard to transaction costs. Many of their investment trades can be executed for pennies per share, or less. These transaction costs are significantly less on a per share and dollar basis than most individuals could achieve on their own. However, with the increased online securities trading over the Internet, investor's direct transaction costs are also being reduced. In fact, shares of common stock can be traded at less than $0.01 per share with online trading.

VARIETY OF MUTUAL FUNDS

With more than 8,000 mutual funds, an investor has a plethora of choices of how to invest in mutual funds. There are mutual funds that can meet almost any investor's objectives, whether a growth fund, sector fund, or a **"green" fund**.

green fund - a fund that invests in environmentally friendly companies

SERVICES

Mutual funds provide investors with a variety of services that they would not have with an individual portfolio of securities. Basic services such as reporting may include monthly or quarterly statements that provide the investor with a variety of information about their investments. This information generally includes number of shares owned, net asset value of shares, and value of

the mutual fund investment. In addition, statements will often provide information on the investor's rate of return that has been earned and an investor's tax basis in the fund.

Other services that are extremely helpful in accomplishing certain goals include automatic investing (purchasing) into the fund, often called dollar-cost averaging. Investors can set up a mutual fund account such that an automatic electronic transfer of a certain dollar amount from the investor's checking or savings account is invested into the fund on a certain day each month. This allows an investor to automatically invest on a periodic basis, similar to payroll reduction with a 401(k) plan.

Similar to automatic investing is automatic withdrawals or sales. Individuals who need a certain sum of money every month can set up a directive to the mutual fund so that it automatically sells a certain number of shares to provide for this need. The proceeds from the sale are then transferred into the investor's checking or savings account.

Other services that are common to mutual funds include automatic reinvestment of dividends and capital gain distributions, check writing privileges, maintaining the shareholder adjusted taxable basis, and telephone and wire redemptions. All of these services provide convenience and flexibility to investors that would not be provided by a single individual portfolio.

DISADVANTAGES OF MUTUAL FUNDS

Although mutual funds provide tremendous advantages to investors, there are certain disadvantages that investors should be aware of including poor performance and unreasonable expenses of some mutual funds.

PERFORMANCE

Many, if not most, mutual funds do not outperform their appropriate investment benchmarks. For example, consider large-cap equity funds reported by Morningstar (period ended September 30, 1999). The average large-cap equity fund underperformed the S&P 500 index for both the ten and fifteen-year periods by more than 300 basis points (3 percent). For the three- and five-year periods, the average large-cap equity fund underperformed the S&P 500 index by more than 600 basis points (6 percent). Such performance should give the investor sufficient notice to be cautious when selecting a particular mutual fund. Exhibit 12C.7 illustrates this same point (for the period ended September 30, 1999).

EXHIBIT 12C.7: HOW MUTUAL FUNDS COMPARE TO THE S&P 500 INDEX

	3 Years	5 Years	10 Years	15 Years
Annualized S&P 500 Index return for period	25%	25%	17%	18%
Approx. number of equity funds reporting for each period	4,324	2,677	941	486
Approx. number of equity funds outperforming index	278	119	98	45
Percentage of funds outperforming the S&P 500 index	6.4%	4.4%	10.4%	9.3%

Only a small percentage of mutual funds outperform the appropriate index over time. One explanation for this underperformance is that mutual funds have expenses that must be incurred for the operation of the fund. Performance for indexes does not include expenses or transaction costs. Although many of the funds underperform, they provide good returns when compared to returns achieved by unsophisticated investors.

Fees, Loads, and Expenses

Investors should be conscious of fees, loads, and expenses of mutual funds. While all funds will have operating and management expenses, some funds have sales charges (loads) that can be as high as 8.5 percent. The higher the fund costs, the more difficult it will be to outperform the appropriate benchmark.

The Abundance of Choices

With more than 8,000 funds available, it may be difficult for an investor to choose only one, or a few, mutual funds. There are now more mutual funds than listed equities. Mutual fund selection will be discussed later in this chapter.

Liquidity

While liquidity is one of the primary advantages of mutual funds, it can also be a disadvantage. To accommodate cash flowing into and out of the fund on a regular basis, fund managers must maintain a certain amount of cash on hand at all times. This cash reserve may cause funds to not be fully invested, thus leading to lower returns than otherwise possible were the fund fully invested at all times.

Execution

Recall that one of the advantages of mutual funds is that they trade in large volumes, resulting in low transaction costs. However, since the volume of trades made by mutual funds is high, there is some risk that such buying and selling may cause the market price of securities to increase or decrease. This potential effect of flooding the market can result in purchasing shares at a higher price than expected and selling shares at a lower price than expected. The effect of flooding may result in lower returns on mutual fund assets than otherwise could have been achieved.

Classification System for Mutual Funds

A mutual fund classification system can assist investors in choosing funds that are consistent with their goals and objectives. Using an objective-based classification system, an investor can compare mutual funds under consideration with the other funds within the classification category. Once a comparison is made, the investor can make a more informed choice about which funds are suitable for that particular investor. Mutual fund investors should be aware, however, that funds have a tendency to be misclassified. One reason for such misclassification is that there is not a specific classification system that defines each category. Although the SEC regulates investment companies, it does not provide a system for differentiating between types of mutual funds. Since there are mutual funds that are misclassified, it is more difficult for investors to select appropriate funds relative to their objectives.

Built-In Gains

Mutual funds will generally have appreciated securities within their portfolio. This appreciation is considered a built-in gain inside the mutual fund. Selling these appreciated securities by the mutual fund causes income to be recognized for income tax purposes by the fund and then passed through to the investor. Taxable investors who purchase shares of mutual funds having these built-in gains subject themselves to potential taxable income without any associated economic gain. The built-in gain on mutual funds can range widely and depends on past performance of the fund. Investors should be cautious when purchasing mutual funds with large amounts of unrealized appreciation.

Overall, the dramatic growth of mutual funds has provided a great service to the small investor. This growth has allowed more and more individuals to have access to professional money managers, in both 401(k) plans and taxable investment accounts. When calculating mutual fund investments, however, investors must be careful to consider the risks that are inherent in investing in the underlying securities and in selecting a particular mutual fund.

TYPES AND OBJECTIVES OF MUTUAL FUNDS

While the classification system for mutual funds is not completely standardized or precise, there are certainly specific types and objectives of mutual funds that can be discussed. Mutual funds can be categorized into equity funds, bond funds, balanced (hybrid) funds, or money market funds. As Exhibit 12C.8 shows, by the end of 2004, there were 4,550 equity funds, 2,041 bond funds, 510 hybrid funds, and 943 money market funds.

EXHIBIT 12C.8: NUMBER OF MUTUAL FUNDS (2004)

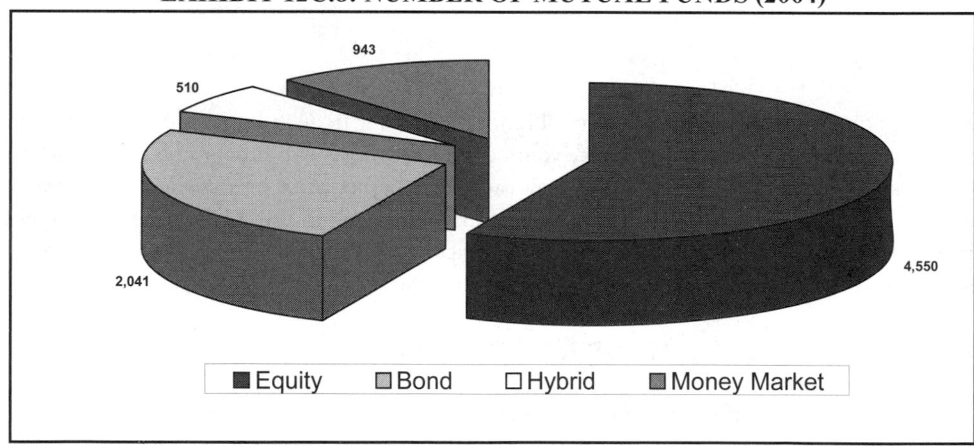
943
510
2,041
4,550
Equity
Bond
Hybrid
Money Market

EXHIBIT 12C.9: TYPES OF MUTUAL FUNDS

Equity Funds

- **Aggressive growth funds** invest primarily in common stock of small, growth companies with potential for capital appreciation.
- **Emerging market equity funds** invest primarily in equity securities of companies based in less-developed regions of the world.
- **Global equity funds** invest primarily in worldwide equity securities, including those of U.S. companies.
- **Growth and income funds** attempt to combine long-term capital growth with steady income dividends. These funds pursue this goal by investing primarily in common stocks of established companies with the potential for both growth and good dividends.
- **Growth funds** invest primarily in common stocks of well-established companies with the potential for capital appreciation. These funds' primary aim is to increase the value of their investments (capital gain) rather than generate a flow of dividends.
- **Income equity funds** seek income by investing primarily in equity securities of companies with good dividends. Capital appreciation is not an objective.
- **International equity funds** invest at least two-thirds of their portfolios in equity securities of companies located outside the United States.
- **Regional equity funds** invest in equity securities of companies based in specific world regions, such as Europe, Latin America, the Pacific Region or individual countries.
- **Sector equity funds** seek capital appreciation by investing in companies in related fields or specific industries, such as financial services, health care, natural resources, technology or utilities.

Bond Funds

- **Corporate bond general funds** seek a high level of income by investing two-thirds or more of their portfolios in corporate bonds and have no explicit restrictions on average maturity.
- **Corporate bond intermediate-term funds** seek a high level of income with two-thirds or more of their portfolios invested at all times in corporate bonds. Their average maturity is five to ten years.
- **Corporate bond short-term funds** seek a high level of current income with two-thirds or more of their portfolios invested at all times in corporate bonds. Their average maturity is one to five years.
- **Global bond general funds** invest in worldwide debt securities and have no stated average maturity or an average maturity of more than five years. Up to 25 percent of their portfolios' securities (not including cash) may be invested in companies located in the United States.
- **Global bond short-term funds** invest in worldwide debt securities and have an average maturity of one to five years. Up to 25 percent of their portfolios' securities (not including cash) may be invested in companies located in the United States.
- **Government bond general funds** invest at least two-thirds of their portfolios in U.S. government securities and have no stated average maturity.
- **Government bond intermediate-term funds** invest at least two-thirds of their portfolios in U.S. government securities and have an average maturity of five to 10 years.
- **Government bond short-term funds** invest at least two-thirds of their portfolios in U.S. government securities and have an average maturity of one to five years.
- **High yield funds** seek a high level of current income by investing at least two-thirds of their portfolios in lower-rated corporate bonds (Baa or lower by Moody's and BBB or lower by Standard and Poor's rating services).
- **Mortgage-backed funds** invest at least two-thirds of their portfolios in pooled mortgage-backed securities.
- **National municipal bond general funds** invest predominantly in municipal bonds and have an average maturity of more than five years or no stated average maturity. The funds' bonds are usually exempt from federal income tax but may be taxed under state and local laws.
- **National municipal bond short-term funds** invest predominantly in municipal bonds and have an average maturity of one to five years. The funds' bonds are usually exempt from federal income tax but may be taxed under state and local laws.
- **Other world bond funds** invest at least two-thirds of their portfolios in a combination of foreign government and corporate debt. Some funds in this category invest primarily in debt securities of emerging markets.
- **State municipal bond general funds** invest primarily in municipal bonds of a single state and have an average maturity of more than five years or no stated average maturity. The funds' bonds are exempt from federal and state income taxes for residents of that state.
- **State municipal bond short-term funds** invest predominantly in municipal bonds of a single state and have an average maturity of one to five years. The funds' bonds are exempt from federal and state income taxes for residents of that state.
- **Strategic income funds** invest in a combination of domestic fixed-income securities to provide high current income.

Hybrid Funds

- **Asset allocation funds** seek high total return by investing in a mix of equities, fixed-income securities and money market instruments. Unlike Flexible Portfolio funds (defined below), these funds are required to strictly maintain a precise weighting in asset classes.
- **Balanced funds** invest in a specific mix of equity securities and bonds with the three-part objective of conserving principal, providing income and achieving long-term growth of both principal and income.
- **Flexible portfolio funds** seek high total return by investing in common stock, bonds and other debt securities, and money market securities. Portfolios may hold up to 100 percent of any one of these types of securities and may easily change, depending on market conditions.
- **Income mixed funds** seek a high level of current income by investing in a variety of income-producing securities, including equities and fixed-income securities. Capital appreciation is not a primary objective.

Money Market Funds

- **National tax-exempt money market funds** seek income not taxed by the federal government by investing in municipal securities with relatively short maturities.
- **State tax-exempt money market funds** invest predominantly in short-term municipal obligations of a single state, which are exempt from federal and state income taxes for residents of that state.
- **Taxable money market government funds** invest principally in short-term U.S. Treasury obligations and other short-term financial instruments issued or guaranteed by the U.S. government, its agencies or instrumentalities.
- **Taxable money market nongovernment funds** invest in a variety of money market instruments, including certificates of deposit of large banks, commercial paper and banker's acceptances.

Source: Investment Company Institute: "A Guide to Mutual Funds"

MONEY MARKET MUTUAL FUNDS

money market mutual funds - a mutual fund that invests in money market instruments, such as Treasury bills and negotiable CDs

Although not created until 1974, **money market mutual funds** had tremendous growth in the late '70s and early '80s due to the extremely high short-term interest rates during that period. Money market mutual funds provided investors with an easy method of investing in short-term fixed-income securities during this period of high interest rates without buying the actual securities. Although short-term interest rates have decreased significantly since the early '80s, money market mutual funds still provide investors an easy and effective method of investing in money market instruments and provide a good alternative to the returns that can be earned on bank certificates of deposit and bank savings accounts.

Money market mutual funds provide investors the opportunity to earn competitive money market returns with the added benefits of ease of access and liquidity. Investors that have a portion of their portfolio invested in cash, or those who create cash by selling other long-term securities can use money market mutual funds as an appropriate, competitive money market investment or as a temporary holding place for cash. In addition, investors can choose to invest in either taxable or tax-exempt money market mutual funds, depending on the investor's tax situation. Many high net worth clients use tax-exempt funds due to their income tax bracket, while qualified retirement assets (tax-advantaged funds, such as funds in a 401(k) plan or IRA) should always use taxable funds because the rate of return for taxable funds is higher than the rate of return for municipal funds.

Money market instruments include securities such as Treasury bills, commercial paper, negotiable certificates of deposit, repurchase agreements, and short-term municipal debt. Taxable money market mutual funds will often invest in a variety of these short-term securities or they may only invest in Treasury bills. Tax-exempt funds will generally invest exclusively in short-term municipal debt resulting in earnings that are exempt from federal tax and may be fully or partially excluded from state and local income tax. As mentioned above, these tax-exempt funds are popular with taxpayers in the higher marginal tax brackets.

The majority of money market mutual funds have securities with maturities of less than two months. The Securities Exchange Commission regulations prohibit the average maturity of money market mutual funds from exceeding 90 days.

With such short maturities, these funds have minimal interest rate risk, and because of the quality and diversity of the investments, these funds have little or no credit risk. Although these funds have minimal interest rate risk and credit risk, they are subject to reinvestment risk and purchasing power risk.

Money market mutual funds have net asset values of one dollar. Interest for these funds is earned and credited on a daily basis. Most of these funds allow investors check-writing privileges as long as a minimum balance is maintained. This check-writing feature allows competitive short-term returns with the flexibility of a checking account.

Unlike some fixed-income and equity mutual funds, money market mutual funds do not charge front-end loads or redemption fees. However, a fee is charged for the management of the assets within the fund.

Fixed-Income Mutual Funds

Fixed-income, or bond, mutual funds invest primarily in fixed-income securities ranging in maturity from several months to thirty years or longer. Just like money market mutual funds, bond funds invest in numerous bond issues to diversify the investment portfolio from default risk. Fixed-income funds provide investors with current income making them ideal for inclusion in portfolios of retired investors who need continuing income generated by their investments for retirement expenditures. In addition, bond funds are appropriate for other investors wishing to allocate a certain portion of their portfolio to fixed-income securities.

fixed-income (or bond) mutual funds - a mutual fund that invests in fixed-income securities ranging in maturity of several months to thirty years or longer. Bond funds invest in numerous bond issues to diversify the investment portfolio from default risk.

The risks that investors accept when making investments in bond funds are the same risks that any investor faces with fixed-income securities. Since the mutual fund portfolio is well diversified, there is minimum default risk with bond mutual funds. As with other fixed-income securities, purchasing power risk is a relevant factor to consider when investing in bond mutual funds. However, the most significant risk associated with bond mutual funds is interest rate risk. Recall that interest rate risk is the risk that fluctuations in interest rates will have a negative impact on the value of investments. Just as the value of an individual bond will decline when interest rates increase, so will the value of a bond mutual fund. Conversely, as interest rates decrease, the value of bond mutual funds will increase. During the '80s and '90s, we witnessed a continual decline in interest rates making bond mutual funds' performance excellent (Exhibit 12C.10).

EXHIBIT 12C.10: CONSTANT MATURITY RATES OF U.S. TREASURY SECURITIES

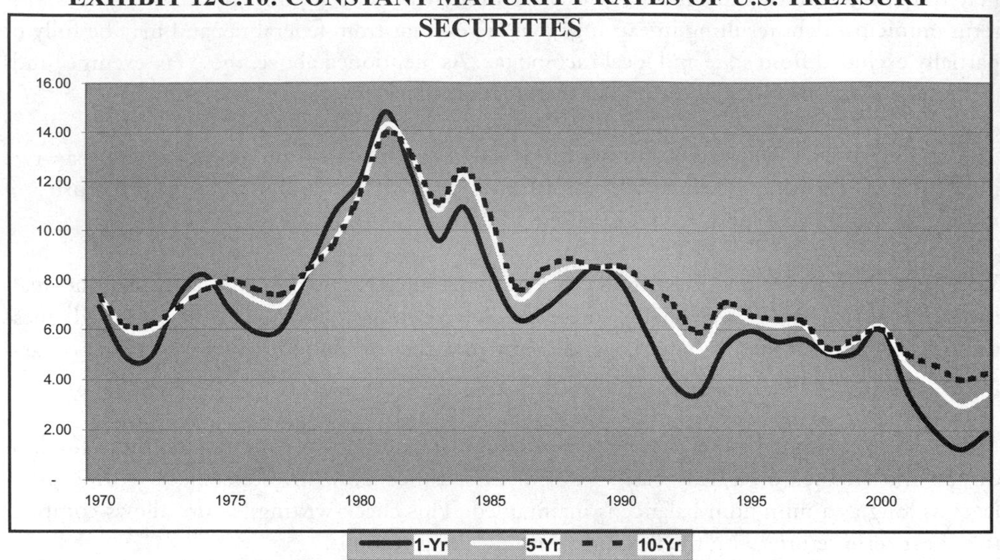
16.00
14.00
12.00
10.00
8.00
6.00
4.00
2.00
-
1970
1975
1980
1985
1990
1995
2000
1-Yr
5-Yr
10-Yr

Source: Federal Reserve Board

The overall net worth of an individual with bond mutual funds in his investment portfolio will decline when interest rates increase. However, is the income he receives on a monthly basis impacted? The answer to the question is a difficult one. If the bond fund portfolio remains the same (no trading of the underlying securities), then theoretically, the income should also remain constant, since the interest coupon payments from the bonds within the portfolio will remain the same. As time elapses, however, other issues become relevant. If the fund manager were to purchase new bonds in the market with the proceeds from principal repayments, bond maturities, or bond sales, then the proceeds would be invested at a higher yield, producing more income, thereby reflecting the increase in interest rates. Therefore, as interest rates increase, the net asset value of the bond mutual fund may decline, but the yield on the fund should begin to increase to reflect higher interest rates (and the lower NAV). If the investor were not living off the monthly income distributions, but rather, was reinvesting them back into the bond fund, then the reinvested dividends would be purchasing shares of the fund at a lower NAV, resulting in a higher number of shares. When interest rates decline, the value of the bond fund will increase, offsetting previous losses by the investor. Thus, bond mutual funds are very similar to other fixed-income securities with regard to interest rate risk.

Bond mutual funds may have a variety of fees, costs, and expenses, including management fees, sales charges (both front-end and deferred), and 12b-1 fees. As is indicated in Exhibit 12C.9: Types of Mutual Funds, there are a variety of objectives for bond funds. With regard to the management fee, some of the objectives will require higher management fees than others. For example, a fund that matches the Lehman Brothers index will require less cost and time than a fund that is actively managed because no research is required to determine which securities to select. Most bond funds have an expense ratio of 1 percent or under, with higher expenses for actively managed and international bond funds.

Equity Mutual Funds

Equity mutual funds invest primarily in equity securities and have a variety of objectives (as we saw in Exhibit 12C.9: Types of Mutual Funds). These funds have become tremendously popular over the last few decades and in fact, have the highest percentage of the total assets invested in mutual funds (Exhibit 12C.11: How Mutual Fund Assets are Invested).

equity mutual funds - a mutual fund that invests primarily in equity securities, such as preferred stock and

EXHIBIT 12C.11: HOW MUTUAL FUND ASSETS ARE INVESTED (2004)

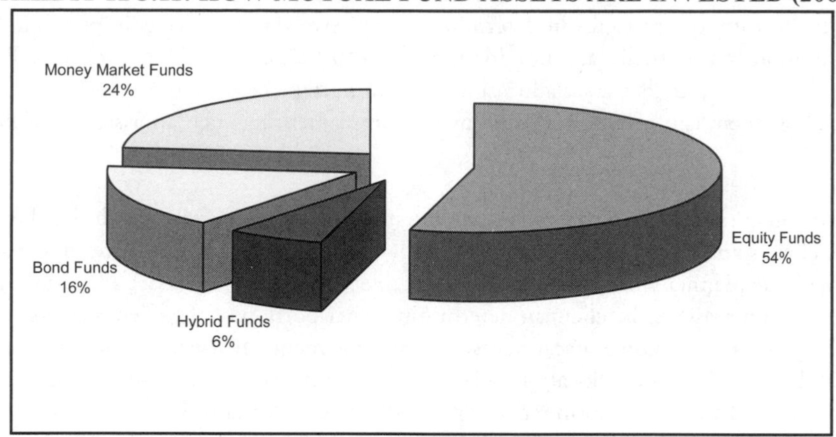
Money Market Funds
24%
Equity Funds
54%
Bond Funds
16%
Hybrid Funds
6%

Source: 2005 Mutual Fund Fact Book, Investment Company Institute, Washington, DC.

As we previously discussed, equities have had significantly higher returns than have fixed-income securities, and equity mutual funds provide investors easy access to common stock securities in an efficient method. The public's increased awareness of higher returns is a major contributing factor to the popularity of equity mutual funds. Another contributing factor is the increase in the number of 401(k) plans that employers are establishing. With the increase in 401(k) plans, there is an increase in assets invested in mutual funds, and especially equity funds.

Just as bond mutual funds have a variety of risks, so do equity mutual funds. One of the most important risks that an equity mutual fund investor must consider is market risk. Recall that market risk is the risk that movements in the market will have a detrimental effect on the value of an investment. There is a strong tendency for equities and equity mutual funds to fluctuate in the same direction and at a similar rate as the entire market. If the market has a sudden decline, it is likely that most equity funds also will decline in value.

For those investors who invest similar amounts on a monthly basis into an equity mutual fund, temporary declines in the market and equity funds provide the opportunity to invest at lower prices. Equity funds are, however, generally more volatile than bond funds, but historically have earned higher returns over a long-term horizon.

Hybrid or Balanced Funds

hybrid (or balanced) mutual funds - a mutual fund that invests in a combination of cash, fixed-income securities, and equity securities

Hybrid mutual funds are those mutual funds that cannot be categorized into any of the three types of fund classifications discussed above (money market, bond, or equity). These funds generally have an objective of investing in a balanced fashion, such that a portion of the portfolio is invested in cash, fixed-income securities, and equity securities.

Investors can build appropriate asset allocated portfolios by investing in a combination of selected money market funds, bond funds, and equity funds. Alternatively, investors can simply select a hybrid fund, such as an asset allocation fund, that meets their asset allocation objective and use it as their only or primary investment vehicle.

ASSET ALLOCATION USING MUTUAL FUNDS

Research (by Brinson, Hood, Beebower, 1986 and Vanguard, 2003) has shown that asset allocation is the most important factor in determining long-term variation (risk) in portfolio returns. Asset allocation may actually account for more than 90 percent of such variation. Based on these studies, it is clear that asset allocation is an important facet of the investment planning process. How, then, can mutual funds be used in implementing such an asset allocation strategy?

Early in the investment planning process, an investment planner, together with the client, identifies the client's goals and objectives, as well as the client's risk tolerance. Once these have been determined, the planner will often help the client select an appropriate asset allocation. In other words, the planner assists the client in determining what portion of the client's assets should be invested in cash, fixed-income investments, equity investments, real estate, international investments, and so on. The asset allocation decision usually involves a narrowing process where the allocation to fixed-income investments is separated into municipal (tax free) versus taxable, and an appropriate average duration is chosen. Similarly, the equity portion of the portfolio will be subdivided into core, value, and growth investment styles and then separated into large, mid, and small capitalization equities. International investments are generally separated into large capitalization or emerging markets and could be divided into different regions or countries around the world.

EXAMPLE

James and Stacey, who are age 40 and 37, respectively, would like to develop an investment plan for their retirement. Assume that after evaluating the timing of their goal and through discussions with them, their financial planner classifies them as moderately aggressive investors. Also, assume that an appropriate asset allocation for them is a portfolio that is 80 percent equity (60 percent domestic equities and 20 percent foreign equities) and 20 percent fixed-income investments, with no allocation to cash or money markets. The allocation might be further divided as shown in the following table:

Equities		Fixed Income	
Large-cap value	10%	Taxable fixed income	8%
Large-cap core	20%	Municipal fixed income	8%
Large-cap growth	10%	Foreign fixed income	4%
Mid-cap growth	10%		
Small-cap growth	10%		
Large-cap foreign	20%		
Total equity allocation	80%	Total fixed-income allocation	20%

The above asset allocation provides James and Stacey with an investment portfolio that is heavily weighted toward equity investments. This equity allocation is divided between domestic and foreign and between large, mid, and small capitalization securities. The fixed-income allocation is also divided between domestic and foreign, as well as taxable and municipal.

Once the asset allocation decision has been made, mutual funds can be used as the vehicle to implement the investment plan. It is important to select mutual funds that are consistent with the concepts and underlying assumptions of the asset allocation process. Specifically, an asset allocation for a client's portfolio is derived through a **mean-variance optimization model**. This type of model is used to determine the highest level of return (based on combinations of asset classes and different weightings of asset classes) for a specified level of risk. This level of risk is generally the client's risk level or risk tolerance. A mean-variance optimization model generally uses all of the following inputs for each asset class represented in the model:

mean-variance optimization model - used to determine the highest level of return (based on combinations of asset classes and different weightings of asset classes) for a specified level of risk tolerance

- Historical return or expected return for each asset class.
- Standard deviation of each asset class (historical or expected).
- Correlation coefficients (historical or expected) for each asset class compared to all other asset classes.

Most of the time, these inputs for the asset classes are derived from indexes that represent the asset class. For example, the large cap equity asset class is usually represented by the S&P 500 index. Small cap equities are often represented by the Russell 2000 index, and fixed-income securities may be represented by one of the Lehman Brothers indexes.

Since the assumptions that are used in the model are derived from indexes, funds to be used for implementation should have characteristics consistent with the index they are representing. This means that if there is an allocation to the large-cap, growth-asset class, then the fund that is chosen to represent this asset class should have consistent risk and return characteristics with that index. This does not mean, however, that index funds are the only choice for implementing an asset allocation strategy. It simply means that the funds that are chosen should be highly correlated with the index that is being represented.

As with all facets of financial planning, the investment planning process is not complete at implementation. The portfolio selections and allocations must be monitored on a continual basis to ensure that the quality of the investments has not changed and that the allocations and risk tolerances of the client have not significantly changed. This monitoring process generally includes quarterly, semiannual, or annual performance measurement reports and meetings with the client.

An investment performance report should include sufficient information to determine whether the investment portfolio has performed as intended and what, if any, changes should be made to the investment portfolio. The report should indicate the return for the overall portfolio, as well as the return for each asset class. These returns should be reported for the recent quarter, as well as the past year, 3-year, and 5-year periods (if available). Each of these returns should be compared to an appropriate benchmark to determine the performance of the fund or investment.

In addition to return information, performance reports should provide the investor with information about the risk characteristics of the overall portfolio. This includes measures for standard deviation and possibly beta.

HOW DO PROFESSIONAL INVESTMENT ADVISERS SELECT MUTUAL FUNDS?

With the thousands of mutual funds available to investors, how does an investor or a professional adviser select a mutual fund for inclusion in a portfolio? In other words, what distinguishes a good mutual fund from a not-so-good mutual fund? The first step is to identify the goals of the investor. Once the goals and objectives of the investor have been established, the next step is to find funds that meet those objectives. In general, a good fund is one that meets the client's objectives and has a good risk-adjusted historical performance.

Professionals use databases of mutual fund information, such as Morningstar or Wiesenberger, to help narrow the thousands of mutual funds down to a few that meet the objectives of the investor. These databases contain a substantial amount of information about each mutual fund and allow advisers to search through voluminous information quickly to select appropriate funds for clients. Much of this information comes from the mutual fund prospectus; the remainder comes from the database company's analysis of the funds. Information that can be found in the prospectus includes the mutual fund objective, the investment policy and strategy, the fund manager's background and tenure with the fund, the fund's historical performance, the portfolio turnover for the fund, the fees and expenses, how to purchase and sell shares, the minimal initial investments, and the investor services available from the fund.

EXAMINE THE PROSPECTUS

Mutual Fund Objective

The goals for a mutual fund are broadly defined in the prospectus objective. Generally, the objective indicates two things: the type of securities that the fund invests in, and whether the fund is trying to achieve income, capital appreciation, or some combination of both. If the fund invests in fixed-income securities, the prospectus objective will often specify the type of fixed-income securities and the duration or maturity of those securities (that is, whether the securities are short-term, intermediate, or long-term). Fixed-income securities can be domestic corporates, Treasuries, municipals, municipals confined to a single state, high yield, or international. If the fund invests in equity securities, the predominant capitalization will often be indicated, as well as the investment style. Equities are generally classified as large-cap, mid-cap, or small-cap, and the investment style will either be growth, value, or a blend (core) strategy.

It is important to know the fund's objective in order to match the appropriate investments to the goals of the investor (or for inclusion in an asset allocation strategy). Younger, more aggressive investors will often want equities with substantial growth potential and minimal income. When returns consist of capital appreciation instead of income, the investor's after-tax returns will generally be higher. The reason for the higher returns is twofold. First, long-term capital gains are taxed at lower rates than ordinary income, such as interest payments. Second, capital appreciation is only taxed when the capital gain is recognized (security is sold).

Although it is important to match the stated objectives of the fund to the needs of the investor, in many cases, the fund does not invest exactly as stated in its objective. This inconsistency may occur because of manager turnover, changes in market condition or other reasons. However, in building a portfolio of mutual funds, or including a mutual fund in a portfolio, one of the primary concerns of the investment adviser should be the consistency of the fund to its stated objectives. This type of information is generally not found in the fund prospectus, but can be found in the databases of information discussed above.

Investment Policy and Strategy

The investment strategy more clearly defines the investment approach of the mutual fund. For example, most funds will provide limits on the portion of the fund that is invested in securities listed in the "objectives" section. Ranges will often be provided for the portion of the portfolio that will normally be invested in cash, fixed-income securities, and equities. In addition, whether the company invests in foreign securities and to what extent is often found in this section. This type of information is especially important for pools of investable assets that have restrictions on the types of securities that can be included in the portfolio, and restrictions on the amount or percentage of certain securities that are included in a mutual fund.

Manager Tenure

The fund manager is listed in the fund prospectus with a description of his or her background and tenure with the fund. If you are selecting a fund based on "good" historical performance, it is important that the manager responsible for the "good" performance is still in charge of the fund. Some funds operate using a team approach, which makes it more difficult for shareholders and potential investors to monitor changes in the management structure.

Historical Performance

Funds generally provide total annual return information for the most recent 1-year, 5-year, and 10-year periods, as available. Total returns from the inception of the fund are also provided for most funds. In many cases, the fund will provide index performance for the given time periods so that a comparison can be made between the fund's performance and an appropriate benchmark. These comparisons are easy to make when the information is included in some type of database.

Portfolio Turnover

The fund will generally have a specific investment style that leads to low, medium, or high portfolio turnover. Higher turnover involves buying and selling securities more often throughout the year resulting in higher transaction costs. Higher turnover can result in more short-term capital gains and can accelerate other taxable income. Such short-term capital gains that flow through from mutual funds are generally taxed as ordinary income, instead of the lower, long-term capital gains tax rate. Funds that have higher turnover will often cause the recognition of more frequent taxable gains through the selling of securities. Since the recognition of capital gains by the mutual fund requires shareholders to report these gains as income for federal income tax purposes, higher turnover funds accelerate the tax payments of the investor.

Where on the Web

American Association of Individual Investors *www.aaii.com*
American Stock Exchange (AMEX) *www.amex.com*
Bloomberg *www.bloomberg.com*
Closed-End Fund Association *www.closed-endfunds.com*
CNBC *www.moneycentral.msn.com*
CNN Money *www.money.cnn.com*
Investment Company Institute *www.ici.org*
Kiplinger *www.kiplinger.com*
Morningstar *www.morningstar.com*
Mutual Fund Investor's Center *www.mfea.com*
Unit Investment Trust Net *www.uitnet.com*

Since combined federal and state tax rates can range from 10 percent to over 40 percent, it is clear that taxes are the highest expense attributable to an investment. For example, management fees average about 1 percent, significantly lower than the tax rates just mentioned. Therefore, it is extremely important to manage the taxation of mutual funds and be aware of the fund's portfolio turnover. This being said, turnover is of minimal concern for tax-deferred accounts, such as pension plans, 401(k) plans, and IRAs since the gains are not taxed until distributed by such plan, usually at or during retirement.

Fees and Expenses

The costs to which an investor is subject are described in the Fees and Expenses section of the prospectus, including loads, management fees, other operating costs, and 12b-1 fees. There will often be an example of the fees a shareholder will pay over a period of years based on certain rate of return assumptions.

Buying and Selling Shares

The prospectus explains how potential investors can purchase shares and how shareholders can sell or redeem shares. Often, investors can redeem shares by mail, phone, fax, or via the Internet.

Minimum Initial Investment

All mutual funds have minimum initial investments. As described earlier in the section, most of these minimums are low. When selecting mutual funds, it is important to establish what the minimum investment is, so as to exclude funds that are not economically feasible due to the minimum requirement. In most cases, this information is found in the prospectus and on the mutual fund account application.

Investor Services

Mutual funds provide a variety of services to shareholders, including automatic investments, automatic redemptions, telephone representatives to answer questions, reports to shareholders, and so on. All of this information will be found within the prospectus.

Although all of the above information can be helpful in determining whether or not a fund is appropriate for an investor, the above is certainly not an exhaustive list of what a professional should review before recommending a fund. In addition to the above information, funds should be evaluated based on risk-adjusted returns, load-adjusted returns, tax-adjusted returns, relative performance compared with similar funds, capital gain exposure, risk characteristics, sector weightings, price earnings ratios, etc. These additional characteristics of mutual funds are not generally found in fund prospectuses, but can be found in the Morningstar database. In addition to the above, most planners consider modern portfolio theory statistics when choosing funds for a portfolio.

EXHIBIT 12C.12: SAMPLE MORNINGSTAR ANALYSIS

Data through July 31, 2003

Legg Mason Value Prim

Ticker	Load	NAV	Yield	Total Assets	Mstar Category
LMVTX	12b-1 only	$50.43	0.0%	$11,396 mil	Large Blend

Manager Strategy

Manager Bill Miller looks at value relative to a firm's growth potential, not just on an absolute basis. This fund reflects that expansive view: Stakes in pricey technology stocks rub elbows with a comparatively large weighting in bargain-priced financials and beaten-down turnaround plays. Miller will also let favored names run, so top positions can soak up a large percentage of assets.

Portfolio Manager(s)

William H. Miller III. Since 04-82. BA'72 Washington & Lee U. Other funds currently managed: Legg Mason Value FI, Masters' Select Value, Masters' Select Equity.

Historical Profile

Return: High
Risk: High
Rating: ★★★★ Above Avg

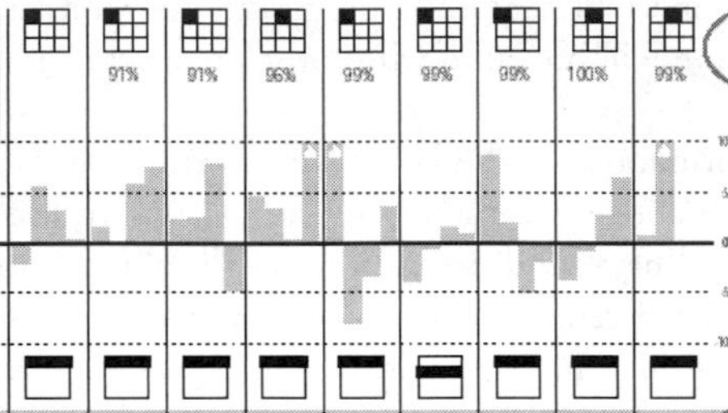

Investment Style
Equity
Stock %

	1995	1996	1997	1998	1999	2000	2001	2002	07-03
Stock %		91%	91%	96%	99%	99%	99%	100%	99%

▼ Manager Change
▽ Partial Manager Change

Fund Performance vs. Category Average.
Quarterly Fund Return +/- Category Average
— Category Baseline

Performance Quartile (within Category)

History

1992	1993	1994	1995	1996	1997	1998	1999	2000	2001	2002	07-03	History
17.32	18.87	19.04	25.19	32.99	42.74	61.58	75.27	55.44	50.06	40.59	50.43	NAV
11.44	11.26	1.39	40.76	38.43	37.05	48.04	26.71	-7.14	-9.29	-18.92	24.24	Total Return %
—	—	—	—	—	—	—	—	—	—	—	10.52	+/-S&P 500
—	—	—	—	—	—	—	—	—	—	—	9.66	+/-Russ 1000
1.02	1.04	0.27	0.93	0.66	0.11	0.00	0.00	0.00	0.00	0.00	—	Income Return %
10.42	10.22	1.12	39.83	37.77	36.94	48.04	26.71	-7.14	-9.29	-18.92	24.24	Capital Return %
21	43	21	2	2	3	1	19	49	20	17	1	Total Rtn % Rank Cat
0.16	0.18	0.05	0.17	0.16	0.04	0.00	0.00	0.00	0.00	0.00	0.00	Income $
0.00	0.20	0.04	1.24	1.53	2.32	1.41	2.46	14.47	0.26	0.00	0.00	Capital Gains $
1.90	1.86	1.82	1.81	1.82	1.77	1.73	1.69	1.68	1.69	1.68	1.72	Expense Ratio %
1.70	1.10	0.50	0.50	0.80	0.40	-0.10	-0.40	-0.60	-0.50	-0.50	-0.40	Income Ratio %
39	22	26	20	20	11	13	19	20	27	24	25	Turnover Rate %
842	914	933	1,340	1,976	3,683	8,079	12,540	10,597	9,788	7,218	9,047	Net Assets $mil

Performance 07-31-03

	1st Qtr	2nd Qtr	3rd Qtr	4th Qtr	Total
1999	18.69	-0.58	-9.70	18.91	26.71
2000	-0.01	-3.31	1.78	-5.63	-7.14
2001	-3.08	7.33	-20.01	9.02	-9.29
2002	-3.66	-13.73	-13.96	13.38	-18.92
2003	-2.91	25.48	—	—	—

Trailing	Total Return%	+/- S&P 500	+/- Russ 1000	%Rank Cat	Growth of $10,000
3 Mo	14.17	5.68	4.94	3	11,417
6 Mo	24.61	7.84	7.19	2	12,461
1 Yr	30.99	20.36	19.80	1	13,099
3 Yr Avg	-4.22	—	—	8	8,787
5 Yr Avg	4.77	5.82	5.39	3	12,624
10 Yr Avg	16.70	6.43	6.51	1	46,850
15 Yr Avg	14.25	2.68	2.65	3	73,764

Tax Analysis	Tax-Adj Rtn%	%Rank Cat	Tax-Cost Rat	%Rank Cat
3 Yr Avg	-5.07	7	0.89	39
5 Yr Avg	3.65	4	1.07	43
10 Yr Avg	15.42	1	1.10	24

Potential Capital Gain Exposure: 15% of assets

Rating and Risk

Time Period	Load-Adj Return %	Morningstar Rtn vs Cat	Morningstar Risk vs Cat	Morningstar Risk-Adj Rating
1 Yr	30.99			
3 Yr	-4.22	High	High	★★★★
5 Yr	14.25	High	High	★★★★
10 Yr	16.70	High	High	★★★★★
Incept	16.82			

Other Measures	Standard Index S&P 500	Best Fit Index S&P 500
Alpha	10.4	10.4
Beta	1.20	1.20
R-Squared	88	88
Standard Deviation	23.69	
Mean	-4.22	
Sharpe Ratio	-0.31	

Portfolio Analysis 06-30-03

Share change since 03-03 Total Stocks:32	Sector	PE	YTD Ret%	% Assets
⊖ Amazon.com	Consumer	—	142.72	7.64
⊖ Nextel Communications	Telecom	6.5	56.36	7.18
Tyco International	Ind Mtrls	—	16.64	5.83
⊕ UnitedHealth Group	Health	22.6	16.68	5.72
☼ InterActiveCorp	—	—	—	5.36
⊖ Washington Mutual	Financial	9.6	15.31	4.18
⊖ Waste Management	Business	18.5	13.44	3.48
⊖ J.P. Morgan Chase & Co.	Financial	34.7	45.83	3.46
⊕ Qwest Comms Intl	Telecom	—	-14.60	3.32
⊖ MGIC Invest	Financial	9.4	33.75	3.28
McKesson HBOC	Health	19.0	24.66	3.23
Eastman Kodak	Goods	10.8	-18.46	3.21
Citigroup	Financial	16.5	24.27	3.09
⊕ AES	Utilities	—	108.28	2.94
⊕ AOL Time Warner	Media	—	20.15	2.91
⊖ Bank One	Financial	13.9	8.65	2.89
Home Depot	Consumer	19.6	36.18	2.78
⊖ Albertson's	Consumer	9.1	-4.51	2.76
⊖ Kroger	Consumer	10.9	22.65	2.48
Fannie Mae	Financial	12.1	0.30	2.44

Current Investment Style

Value Blend Growth / Large Mid Small (style box: Large Blend)

Market Cap %	
Giant	18.0
Large	61.3
Mid	20.7
Small	0.0
Micro	0.0
Avg $mil:	20,293

Value Measures		Rel S&P 500
Price/Earnings	15.28	0.87
Price/Book	1.08	0.40
Price/Sales	0.78	0.57
Price/Cash Flow	5.31	0.78
Dividend Yield %	1.01	0.59

Growth Measures	%	Rel S&P 500
Long-Term Erngs	13.51	1.20
Book Value	11.74	1.79
Sales	6.24	2.51
Cash Flow	4.59	0.71
Historical Erngs	6.84	3.10

Profitability	%	Rel S&P 500
Return on Equity	17.90	1.16
Return on Assets	5.65	0.77
Net Margin	5.64	0.57

Sector Weightings	% of Stocks	Rel S&P 500	3 Year High	3 Year Low
Info	21.01	0.92		
Software	1.85	0.39	2	0
Hardware	2.31	0.22	12	2
Media	5.59	1.36	9	5
Telecom	11.26	3.15	11	5
Service	65.62	1.35		
Health	15.13	1.07	15	12
Consumer	17.50	1.92	18	15
Business	7.87	1.93	10	7
Financial	25.12	1.19	40	25
Mfg	13.31	0.47		
Goods	3.44	0.38	5	3
Ind Mtrls	6.73	0.60	7	0
Energy	0.00	0.00	0	0
Utilities	3.14	1.20	3	0

Composition

Cash	1.4
Stocks	98.6
Bonds	0.0
Other	0.0
Foreign (% of Stock)	10.5

Morningstar's Take by Christopher Traulsen 06-09-03

Maybe Bill Miller wasn't quite so wrong, after all.

Miller has caught his share of grief over the years from those who argue that his definition of value doesn't jibe with normative approaches such as simple multiple analysis. Picks such as Amazon.com and Nextel seem to be the sort of thing that alarmed people the most.

But if you want to beat the market--and Miller has done so with unmatched consistency--you can't just do what everyone else does. You need to find opportunities that others have missed and have enough confidence in your analysis to follow through and commit meaningful capital to your picks.

Miller and his staff excel at this. While everyone else was wringing their hands about a potential cash crunch at Amazon, Miller was buying the stock by the shovelful. More recently, he has bought shares of Intuit, the financial-software firm whose shares sold off sharply after it guided estimates down. Miller notes that the firm has a great balance sheet, is growing earnings and revenues rapidly, and is attractively priced.

After three years of losses, albeit market- and peer-beating losses, the fund is up 21.8% for the year to date through June 6. That's 8.6 percentage points ahead of the S&P 500 and in the top 1% of all large-blend funds (and large-value funds) for the period. Among the fund's biggest winners? Amazon.com and Nextel.

Such a brief period isn't very meaningful, but Miller's long-term results here are also sparkling. A glance at the portfolio also shows that it has substantially lower valuations and higher growth rates than the S&P 500--an attractive combination. Investors here need to accept the risks of Miller's style--the portfolio is compact; some of his tech and telecom picks get buffeted by the momentum crowd; and sometimes he's just plain wrong. But for long-term investors who can accept those risks, the fund's potential rewards and skilled management make it a great core holding.

Address:	100 Light St. P.O. Box 1476 Baltimore, MD 21203-1476 800-577-8589	Minimum Purchase:	$1000	Add: $100	IRA: $1000
		Min Auto Inv Plan:	$1000	Add: $50	
		Sales Fees:	0.70%B, 0.25%S		
Web Address:	www.leggmason.com	Management Fee:	1.00% mx./0.65% mn.		
Inception:	04-16-82	Actual Fees:	Mgt:0.66%	Dist:0.95%	
Advisor:	Legg Mason Funds Management	Expense Projections:	3Yr:$530	5Yr:$913	10Yr:$1987
Subadvisor:	None	Income Distrib:	Quarterly		
NTF Plans:	TD Waterhouse Ins NT	Total Cost (relative to category):	—		

EQ

MORNINGSTAR® Mutual Funds

Continuation of Exhibit 12C.12

Manager Strategy: *Describes the objective of the fund.*

Performance: *Provides historical performance over several time periods. Compares performance to several indexes, and provides information on the tax efficiency of the fund.*

Morningstar's Take: *Analyst's review – provides analysis of fund, including information obtained through interviews with the fund's manager.*

Rating and Risk: *The Morningstar ranking of the fund's risk and return relative to other funds with the same broad investment style. Also, the Morningstar Risk-Adjusted Ranking ranging from 1 to 5 stars.*

Other Measures: *Provides modern portfolio theory statistics for the fund, including alpha, beta, R^2, standard deviation, and the Sharpe ratio.*

Investment Style: *Shows the historical trend of the fund's investment style. Makes it easy to identify fundamental changes in the fund's approach.*

History: *Provides information on income and capital gain distributions, as well as the turnover of the fund, and NAV.*

Portfolio Analysis: *Details the top holdings within the fund, including sector, P/E ratio, Year-To-Date (YTD) return percentage, and percentage of the fund.*

Current Investment Style: *A detailed explanation of Morningstar's investment style box is given in the following exhibit.*

EXHIBIT 12C.13: MORNINGSTAR'S INVESTMENT STYLE BOXES

Equity Style Box:

Risk	Value	Blend	Growth	Median Market Capitalization
Low	*Large-Cap Value*	*Large-Cap Blend*	*Large-Cap Growth*	Large
Moderate	*Mid-Cap Value*	*Mid-Cap Blend*	*Mid-Cap Growth*	Medium
High	*Small-Cap Value*	*Small-Cap Blend*	*Small-Cap Growth*	Small

The equity style box contains nine possible combinations, ranging from large-cap value to small-cap growth.

Source: Morningstar Mutual Funds, 2000. Morningstar, Inc., Chicago, IL

Fixed-Income Style Box:

Risk	Short	Interm	Long	Quality
Low	*Short-Term High Quality*	*Interm-Term High Quality*	*Long-Term High Quality*	High
Moderate	*Short-Term Medium Quality*	*Interm-Term Medium Quality*	*Long-Term Medium Quality*	Medium
High	*Short-Term Low Quality*	*Interm-Term Low Quality*	*Long-Term Low Quality*	Low

The fixed-income style box contains nine possible combinations, ranging from short maturity, high quality for the safest funds to long maturity, low quality for the riskiest.

MODERN PORTFOLIO THEORY (MPT) STATISTICS AND PERFORMANCE MEASURES

As described in Chapter 12, the concepts of modern portfolio theory have been widely accepted among financial practitioners. These MPT statistics provide insight into the fund's risk-return characteristics. Some of the more common statistics that are considered include the coefficient of determination, beta, Jensen's alpha, Sharpe ratio, and Treynor ratio.

R^2 (COEFFICIENT OF DETERMINATION)

(R^2) coefficient of determination - a modern portfolio theory statistic that indicates the percent change in a portfolio or mutual fund that can be explained by changes in the market (generally defined by an index)

The **coefficient of determination**, which is generally referred to as $\mathbf{R^2}$, is found by squaring the correlation coefficient. The correlation coefficient, generally denoted with the symbol "R", is a statistical measure generated from a regression analysis that provides insight into the relationship between two securities or two indexes. The correlation coefficient indicates the direction of the relationship between the two indexes or securities and the strength of the relationship between the two items.

R^2 is an indication of the percentage change in a dependent variable that can be explained by changes in an independent variable. In the context of portfolios, it is an indication of percent change in a portfolio or mutual fund that can be explained by changes in the market (generally defined by an index). R^2 ranges from 0 to 100. When R^2 equals 100 (such as with an index fund), it indicates that 100 percent of the change in the portfolio or mutual fund is attributable to changes in the market. When R^2 equals 50, it indicates that 50 percent of the change in the portfolio or mutual fund is attributable to changes in the market.

Since R^2 provides insight into the changes in a portfolio that are attributable to a market or index, it actually provides insight into the percentage of systematic risk included in the portfolio. For example, a mutual fund that has an R^2 of 85 indicates that 85 percent of the change in the portfolio results from changes in the market. The remaining 15 percent (100 percent - 85 percent) of the change in the portfolio is from some other source. This other source, since it is not systematic risk, must be unsystematic risk. Therefore, 15 percent of the change in the portfolio must be attributable to business risk, financial risk or a combination of unsystematic risks.

When using an asset allocation strategy, it is important to select funds that are highly correlated to the asset classes included in the portfolio. Funds or portfolios that have a high R^2 are funds that are highly correlated to the market.

BETA

beta - a commonly used measure of systematic risk that provides an indication of the volatility of a portfolio compared to the market

Beta is a commonly used measure of risk that is also derived from regression analysis. It is a measure of systematic risk and provides an indication of the volatility of a portfolio compared to the market. The market is defined as having a beta of 1.0. Portfolio betas greater than 1.0 are more volatile than the market, while portfolios with betas less than 1.0 are said to be less volatile than the market. A portfolio with a beta of 1.5 is considered to be 50 percent more volatile than the market. Similarly, a portfolio with a beta of 0.7 is considered to be 30 percent less volatile than the market.

Since beta measures systematic risk, it is a good measure of risk if the portfolio is sufficiently diversified. Diversified portfolios have minimal unsystematic risk, which means that beta is capturing the majority of the risk of the portfolio. However, when the R^2 of the portfolio is low, then the portfolio has a substantial amount of unsystematic risk and beta does not capture all of the relevant risk. Therefore, beta is more appropriate for portfolios and mutual funds that are highly correlated to the market and sufficiently diversified.

MEASURES OF PERFORMANCE

Three performance measures commonly used with mutual funds include Jensen's Alpha, Sharpe ratio, and Treynor ratio. As with all investments, investors are concerned about both returns and risk. These performance measures provide a method of quantifying the risk-adjusted performance of investments, including mutual funds.

Jensen's Alpha

Jensen's Alpha is an absolute measure of performance. It indicates how the actual performance of the investment compares with the expected performance. The expected performance is calculated using the Capital Asset Pricing Model (discussed in Chapter 12 Supplement B), which uses beta as its measure of risk.

Jensen's Alpha - an absolute measure of performance - it indicates how the actual performance of an investment compares with the expected performance

The formula for alpha is often written as follows:

$$\alpha = R_p - [R_f + \beta(R_m - R_f)], \text{ where}$$

α = Alpha

R_p = Actual return of the portfolio

R_f = Risk-free rate of return

β = Beta of the portfolio

R_m = Expected return of the market

EXAMPLE

Notice that alpha is equal to the difference between the actual return (R_p) and the expected return, which is found by using the Capital Asset Pricing Model (security market line): $R_f + \beta(R_m - R_f)$. A higher alpha indicates that the actual return of the investment is better than what was expected, based on the level of risk of the investment. For instance, if the actual return of a portfolio is 25 percent and the expected return was 20 percent, then the alpha equals 5 percent. In other words, the portfolio performed five percentage points better than expected on a risk-adjusted basis. Similarly, a negative alpha implies that the return of the investment was less than expected based on the level of risk. An alpha of zero means that the investment performed as expected.

It is worth mentioning that since alpha uses beta as its measure of risk, it is important to understand the limitations of beta. As we said, beta is less reliable when R^2 is low. Therefore, if beta is unreliable, then the output, alpha, is also unreliable.

Sharpe Ratio

Sharpe ratio - a measure of risk-adjusted portfolio performance that uses standard deviation as the risk measure

The **Sharpe ratio** is also a measure of risk-adjusted performance. However, like the Treynor model, it is a relative measure of performance, meaning that the ratio by itself has little or no meaning. The ratio is only meaningful when compared to alternative investments. The formula for the Sharpe ratio is written as follows:

$$S_p = \frac{R_p - R_f}{\sigma_p}, \text{ where}$$

S_p = Sharpe ratio

R_p = Actual return of the portfolio

R_f = Risk-free rate of return

σ_p = Standard deviation of the portfolio

EXAMPLE

The Sharpe ratio is calculated by dividing the incremental return that the portfolio has generated above the risk-free rate of return by the standard deviation of the portfolio. For example, if ABC growth mutual fund returned 12 percent, while the risk-free rate was 3 percent and the standard deviation was 20 percent, then the Sharpe ratio would equal 0.45. Again, the ratio of 0.45 has no meaning in and of itself; however, when compared to alternative investments, it becomes meaningful. For instance, the Sharpe ratios for the following mutual funds are provided:

Fund Name	Sharpe Ratio
High Growth Mutual Fund	1.20
S&P 500 Index Mutual Fund	0.95
ABC Growth Mutual Fund	0.45
XYZ Growth Mutual Fund	0.30

In the above table, it now seems clear that on a risk-adjusted basis, XYZ Growth Mutual Fund (0.30 Sharpe Ratio) and ABC Growth Mutual Fund (0.45 Sharpe Ratio) are mediocre performing funds. Two better alternatives appear to be the High Growth Mutual Fund (1.20 Sharpe Ratio) and the S&P 500 Index Mutual Fund (.95 Sharpe Ratio).

Since the Sharpe ratio uses standard deviation as the measure of risk, it incorporates total risk (both systematic and unsystematic risk) into the calculation. Therefore, Sharpe ratio does not have the same limitations as alpha with regards to R^2.

Treynor Ratio

The **Treynor ratio** is a similar relative performance measure to the Sharpe ratio except for its measure of risk. Treynor uses beta as its measure of risk. Therefore, the same issues with regard to the use of beta in the calculation of alpha also apply to the calculation of the Treynor ratio. The formula for the Treynor ratio is generally depicted as:

Treynor ratio - a measure of risk adjusted portfolio performance that uses beta as the risk measure

$$T_p = \frac{R_p - R_f}{\beta_p}, \text{ where}$$

T_p = Treynor ratio

R_p = Actual return of the portfolio

R_f = Risk-free rate of return

β_p = Beta of the portfolio

The Treynor ratio also evaluates the incremental return above the risk-free rate of return. Alternative investments should be ranked in order from the highest to the lowest ratio. The investment with the highest Treynor ratio is the one that has the highest risk-adjusted return.

If all of the performance measures provide a quantification of the risk-adjusted return of investments, should the rankings, from highest to lowest, for each of the three measures be the same? The answer to this question is that "it depends." Specifically, it depends on the value of R^2. If R^2 is high, then the three performance measures will provide similar rankings. However, if R^2 is not high, then the three performance measures may not provide similar rankings. This inconsistency occurs because of the use of beta instead of standard deviation as the measure of risk in two of the performance measures.

ISSUES TO LOOK FOR WHEN MANAGING PORTFOLIOS OF MUTUAL FUNDS

Once an investment strategy, including one that involves mutual funds, has been implemented, the portfolio must be monitored. Certain aspects of mutual funds should be monitored to be certain that the fund is performing as anticipated. These characteristics include changing asset size, style shift, manager changes, and capital gain exposure.

CHANGING ASSET SIZE

When mutual funds have good performance for several years in a row, new assets flow to these funds making them bigger. This changing asset size can result in a change in the basic dynamics of the fund. This is especially true for funds that invest in small-cap and mid-cap asset classes. There are only a limited number of small and mid-sized companies to invest in and, as we discussed above, mutual funds have restrictions on the amount that can be invested in any one particular company. Therefore, when a small-cap mutual fund dramatically increases its asset base, the fund may no longer be able to invest the additional assets as efficiently or effectively as it had in the past. If this occurs, returns suffer and assets may begin to leave the fund. To prevent this problem, some funds will close temporarily to new investors, thus limiting the asset base of the fund to protect the dynamics of the fund. Therefore, it is important to monitor the asset size of small-cap and mid-cap equity funds to be sure they are not growing too fast.

STYLE SHIFT

As part of the asset allocation process, the large-cap equity allocation is often segregated into value, growth, and core styles. The purpose of this segregation is to have one growth fund, one value fund, and one core fund, for example. What happens, though, if the value fund begins using more of a growth style? All of a sudden, the diversified portfolio is now more heavily weighted toward growth. It may be that the portfolio is performing well at this time, but it is also likely that when the growth style goes out of favor the portfolio may decline significantly. Therefore, it is important that the fund's style remains consistent with the fund's stated objective.

MANAGER CHANGES

The reason managers of mutual funds are well compensated is that they are the ones making the buy-and-sell decisions, which causes the fund to have good or poor performance. Since the manager is responsible for the performance of the fund, it is important to watch for changes in the management structure of the fund. In most cases one person manages the fund, while in other cases a team manages the fund. A change in investment management means that there is increased risk that the fund will not be managed as before and, therefore, historical returns may be less significant in predicting future returns.

CAPITAL GAIN EXPOSURE

All equity funds have some amount of unrecognized built-in capital gains within the portfolio. This results from the unrealized appreciation of securities within the portfolio. This capital gain exposure is important to monitor for a fund in an existing portfolio, but is critical to consider when initially evaluating whether to purchase a particular fund.

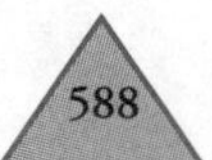

PROFESSIONAL FOCUS

When you are using Mutual Funds as the investment vehicle for a client's portfolio how many funds do you generally use?

A client's financial situation will dictate the number of funds I utilize in a portfolio. The number of funds is determined by the amount of assets to be invested and the best way to achieve a diversified asset allocation. This allocation will usually include investments in large cap growth and value, small cap growth and value, mid-cap growth and value, international securities, domestic fixed-income, and cash.

The amount of assets we have to invest will drive fund selection. If possible, I will recommend funds in each of these asset classes, but sometimes there are not enough dollars to go around. In that case, I will select funds that incorporate more than one investment class, such as global funds or balanced funds.

What are the key investment issues that you consider when selecting among fixed-income mutual funds?

When selecting fixed-income mutual funds, I first determine whether a taxable or tax-exempt fund is appropriate. Once the universe has been narrowed down to taxable or tax-exempt fund, I evaluate the average credit quality of the fund. Whether I select a fund with investment grade or noninvestment grade issues is determined by the risk tolerance and goals of my client.

Evaluating the average duration is very important in minimizing interest rate risk. I match the average duration of the funds I choose to my client's time horizon, and I try to incorporate a range of durations into the portfolio.

What are the key investment issues that you consider when selecting among equity mutual funds?

My goal in the selection of equity funds is to include five funds, at a minimum: a small cap growth fund, a small cap value fund, a large cap growth fund, a large cap value fund and an international equity fund. If the client has enough assets, I will also include a mid-cap growth fund and a mid-cap value fund. Therefore, the manager's investment style will be my first consideration. The weighting in each of these classes will be determined by the client's risk tolerance and time horizon. The more aggressive we can be, the heavier the weighting in small cap and foreign stocks.

I usually choose funds with at least a five-year track record, 10 years is preferable, although there are some exceptions to that. Once I have narrowed the universe of equity funds based on asset class and track record, I then evaluate the critical risk measures of like funds. I will compare the standard deviation, beta, Sharpe ratio and alpha on each of the funds I am considering in order to select the fund that, historically, has had the best risk-adjusted returns over the long haul. Although this is no guarantee of future performance, it's a starting point.

When building a portfolio based on asset allocation how important is the correlation coefficient (r) in your selection of funds?

When I am building a portfolio based on asset allocation, my investment class selection is driven by correlation. I want to incorporate assets in the portfolio that have little correlation, no correlation or negative correlation with one another in order to achieve maximum diversification and minimize risk.

For your taxable clients how important is your funds turnover rate?

Consideration of the turnover rate is important in fund selection but not a driving force. High turnover rates will increase fund expenses, which will cut into return. In addition, the net return will be reduced after taxes are paid on the distributions generated by turnover. In this regard, I am cognizant of historic after-tax returns for funds with high turnover rates. If a fund has managed to consistently perform well on a risk-adjusted basis in spite of its high turnover rate, I will consider it for the portfolio. The best solution to this dilemma is to put a high turnover fund in a nontaxable account where taxable distributions are irrelevant.

JILL PEETLUK FEINSTEIN, CFP®

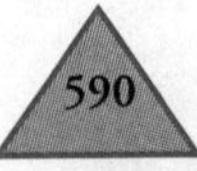

CHAPTER 13

Individual Income Tax and Tax Planning

LEARNING OBJECTIVES:

After learning the material in this chapter, you will be able to:

1. List the objectives of the Federal Income Tax Law, and give examples of each.
2. Name three different tax rate structures under which income can be taxed, and discuss how those rate structures differ.
3. Perform the calculation to determine a client's income tax liability.
4. Describe the types of IRS rulings issued as guidance to taxpayers.
5. List the various civil penalties imposed on taxpayers who violate the tax law.
6. Identify the various payroll taxes imposed on individuals through the Federal Insurance Contributions Act (FICA) and the Federal Unemployment Tax Act (FUTA).
7. Discuss the various tax-advantaged investment options available to taxpayers.

INCOME TAX PLANNING

One of the most important areas of financial planning is income tax planning. Income taxes have an impact on almost every business and investment decision as well as many personal decisions. The objective of tax planning is to pay the lowest tax legally permissible consistent with overall financial planning objectives. The financial planner must not only consider the tax ramifications of a proposed action or transaction; they must also develop an appropriate tax planning strategy consistent with the client's goals and objectives.

Effective tax planning has been complicated over the years by the constant changes to the tax law. The federal income tax system in the United States is among the most complex tax systems in the world. In the 1980s and 1990s changes were made frequently to the Internal Revenue Code in an attempt to raise revenues for the federal government.

HISTORY

Under the United States Constitution, any direct tax imposed by Congress was required to be apportioned among the individual states based on that state's relative population. In 1913, the Sixteenth Amendment to the U.S. Constitution was ratified, which allowed Congress to levy taxes on all income without apportionment among the states.

The Sixteenth Amendment states:

"The Congress shall have the power to lay and collect taxes on incomes, from whatever source derived, without apportionment among the several states, and without regard to any census or enumeration."

After 1913, Congress exercised its taxing authority with the passage of several revenue acts, adding to the complexity of the income tax system. In an attempt to resolve confusion, Congress combined the separate sources of the tax law in 1939. This legislation, named the Internal Revenue Code of 1939, systematically arranged all previous legislation and provided the basis for a standardized income tax law.

The 1939 Code was revised in 1954 and again in 1986. The governing federal income tax law today is the Internal Revenue Code of 1986 (the Code), as amended.

OBJECTIVES OF THE FEDERAL INCOME TAX LAW

There are several objectives of the federal income tax law. These objectives can be classified as revenue raising, economic, and/or social in nature.

The revenue-raising objective is the most important of these objectives. The primary goal of taxation is to provide the resources necessary to fund governmental expenditures. Individual income taxes provide more than 50 percent of the annual revenues of the federal government.

EXHIBIT 13.1: INTERNAL REVENUE COLLECTIONS BY PRINCIPAL SOURCES (2004)

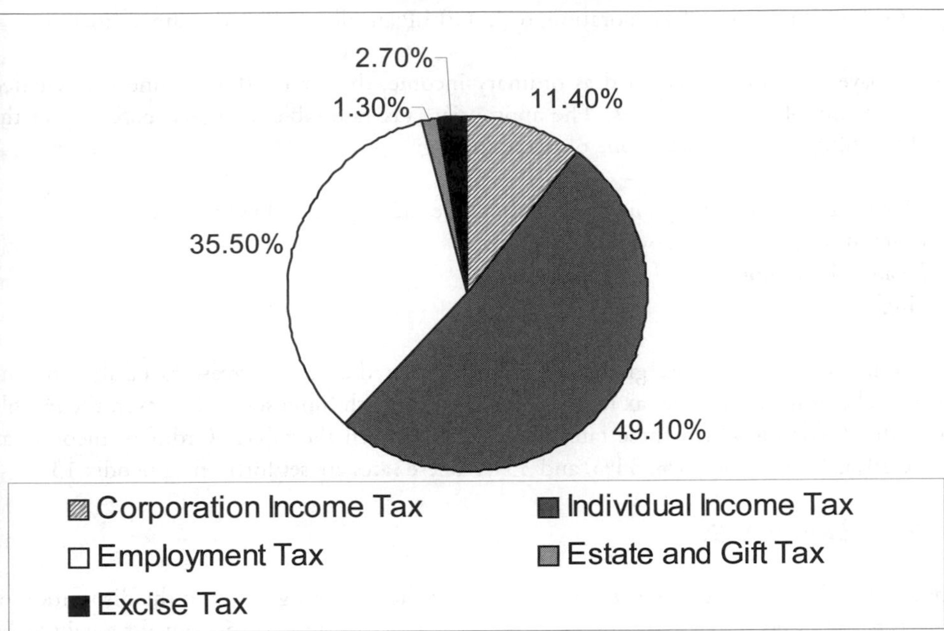
2.70%
1.30%
11.40%
35.50%
49.10%
Corporation Income Tax
Individual Income Tax
Employment Tax
Estate and Gift Tax
Excise Tax

Internal Revenue Collections by Type of Tax (2004)

The federal income tax system is also used as a means to address certain economic goals. Taxation is a major tool used by the government to achieve the goals of economic growth and full employment. During periods of recession, taxes can be lowered, thereby increasing the disposable income in the hands of taxpayers. This allows individuals to spend more money, thus increasing demand, resulting in economic growth.

Social objectives are also accomplished through effective income tax legislation. The Internal Revenue Code (the Code) contains many economic incentives designed to encourage certain social behavior. For example, contributions to charitable organizations are socially desirable. Therefore, to encourage such contributions, the Code permits limited deductions for contributions of money or property to qualified charitable organizations. In addition, the Code provides various tax benefits for homeowners and those saving for retirement.

INDIVIDUAL INCOME TAX RATES

Tax rates are applied to an individual's taxable income to determine the amount of tax due. Currently, income can be taxed under three different rate structures: ordinary tax rates, capital gain tax rates, and alternative minimum tax (AMT) rates.

ORDINARY RATES

Once taxable income has been calculated, the income must be separately classified as ordinary or capital, since different tax rates may apply to capital gains.

ordinary income - any income that arises from services, or from property that is not classified as a capital asset

head of household - the filing status that identifies a taxpayer as an unmarried individual who maintains a household for another and satisfies certain conditions set forth in the Internal Revenue Code

capital asset - broadly speaking, all assets are capital except those specifically excluded by the Internal Revenue Code. Excluded assets include property held for resale in the normal course of business (inventory), trade accounts and notes receivable, and depreciable property and real estate used in a trade or business.

Ordinary income includes any income that arises from services, or from property that is not classified as a capital asset. Salaries, interest, dividends, rents, and income earned from a sole proprietorship, partnership, S corporation, or LLC/LLP are all considered ordinary income.

If the taxpayer's income is classified as ordinary income, the tax on this income is calculated based upon one of four rate tables. The appropriate tax rate table is chosen based upon the individual's filing status, which is one of the following:

- ▲ Married individuals filing joint returns (includes qualifying widow/widower).
- ▲ Married individuals filing separate returns.
- ▲ **Head of household**.
- ▲ Single.

The income tax rate tables are graduated, meaning that the rates increase as taxable income increases. The ordinary income tax rates are the same for each filing status; however, the taxable income thresholds for which these rates apply vary between the tables. Ordinary income tax rates are 10%, 15%, 25%, 28%, 33%, and 35%. These rates are set forth in Appendix 13.1.

Capital Gain Rates

Taxpayers may be eligible to use lower tax rates when they incur a gain upon the disposition of certain types of assets, known as capital assets. Several factors must be present for a gain to be afforded preferential treatment. In general, the asset must be:

- ▲ A capital asset.
- ▲ Sold or exchanged.
- ▲ Held for a long-term period.

Capital Asset

The Internal Revenue Code defines a **capital asset** by listing the types of assets that are not considered capital. All other assets disposed of are presumably capital assets. The following types of assets are not considered capital assets:

- ▲ Inventory or property held for sale to customers in the ordinary course of the taxpayer's trade or business.
- ▲ Accounts or notes receivable arising in the ordinary course of a trade or business.
- ▲ Depreciable real or personal property used in a trade or business.
- ▲ Copyrights or creative works held by the creator.
- ▲ A United States government publication held by a taxpayer who received it other than by purchase.

Therefore, property held for personal use is a capital asset, as is property used for the production of income. Examples of capital assets include securities held for investment, a personal residence, and a personal automobile.

Sale or Exchange

Gains or losses from the disposition of property will not qualify as a capital gain or loss unless the property is disposed of by a sale or exchange. A sale is a transfer of property for an amount of money or money equivalent that is fixed or determinable. An exchange is a transfer of property for property other than money.

It is generally not difficult to determine whether a sale or exchange has occurred. However, the Internal Revenue Code has provided for several situations in which capital gain treatment is afforded even though a sale or exchange has not occurred. For example, capital loss treatment is allowed for a security that becomes worthless during the year, even though no sale or exchange has occurred.

Long-Term Holding Period

Once it has been determined that the asset is a capital asset that has been sold or exchanged, the taxpayer may qualify for lower capital gain tax rates if the property is held long term. In general, a capital asset is held long term if the taxpayer owned the asset for more than one year (that is, a year and one day). The date the asset is disposed of is part of the holding period. For example, if property is acquired on March 3, 2005, the property would need to be sold on or after March 4, 2006, to be considered long term.

long-term capital gain - a gain from a sale or exchange of a capital asset that has been held for more than one year

Tax Treatment of Long-Term Capital Gains

If the taxpayer recognizes a **long-term capital gain**, the gain may be taxed at a lower rate than the individual's ordinary income tax rate. In general, long-term capital gains are taxed at a rate of 15 percent unless the individual is in the 10 percent or 15 percent ordinary income tax bracket, in which case the capital gain is taxed at a rate of 5 percent. The 5 percent rate is scheduled to drop to 0 percent for tax years beginning in 2008.

If the asset is a collectible, such as a work of art, or if the asset is small business stock (as defined in Section 1202), the maximum capital gain rate is 28 percent. In addition, capital gains on sales of depreciable real estate are taxed at a rate of 25 percent, to the extent of any unrecaptured straight-line depreciation on the property. The following table summarizes the different capital gain rates:

EXHIBIT 13.2: CAPITAL GAIN RATES (2005)

Type of Capital Asset	Minimum Holding Period	Maximum Rate
Collectibles (antiques, etc.)or section 1202 stock	Greater than 1 year	28%
Depreciable real estate	Greater than 1 year	25%
Other capital assets (taxpayer is not in 10% or 15% ordinary income tax bracket)	Greater than 1 year	15%
Other capital assets (taxpayer is in 10% or 15% ordinary income tax bracket)	Greater than 1 year	–5%

Tax Treatment of Short-Term Capital Gains

short-term capital gain - a gain from a sale or exchange of a capital asset that has been held for one year or less

A **short-term capital gain** receives no special treatment, and is taxed as ordinary income.

Tax Treatment of Dividends

For taxpayers in the 25 percent and above ordinary income tax rate bracket, dividends received from domestic and most foreign corporations are taxed at 15 percent. For taxpayers in the lower tax brackets, such dividends are taxed at 5 percent.

Tax Treatment of Capital Losses

capital loss - a loss from the sale or exchange of a capital asset

An individual taxpayer may deduct **capital losses** only to the extent of capital gains plus the lesser of $3,000 or the net capital loss. The net capital loss is the excess of capital losses for the year over capital gains for the year.

EXAMPLE

For example, if an individual has a short-term capital loss of $200 and a long-term capital loss of $3,700, the taxpayer is permitted a deduction from ordinary income of $3,000. The remaining loss of $900 ($200 + $3,700 – $3,000) can be carried forward to later years indefinitely until it is absorbed. The short-term loss is utilized first, so the carryover is $900 of long-term capital loss.

Alternative Minimum Tax Rates

The Alternative Minimum Tax (AMT) is a separate tax system that parallels the regular tax system. The AMT system was designed to ensure individuals with large deductions and other tax benefits pay at least a minimum amount of tax.

The AMT calculation begins with the individual's taxable income, which is adjusted to arrive at alternative minimum taxable income (AMTI). AMT tax rates are then applied to AMTI, resulting in the tentative minimum tax. If the tentative minimum tax exceeds the individual's regular tax liability, the excess amount is the alternative minimum tax. The AMT calculation is summarized in the table below.

EXHIBIT 13.3: ALTERNATIVE MINIMUM TAX CALCULATION

	Taxable Income
+	Positive AMT adjustments
–	Negative AMT adjustments
=	**Taxable income after AMT adjustments**
+	Tax preferences (always positive)
=	**Alternative Minimum Taxable Income (AMTI)**
–	AMT exemption
=	**Minimum tax base**
×	AMT rate
=	**Tentative AMT**
–	Regular income tax on taxable income
=	**AMT**

A taxpayer may incur an AMT liability if he or she has one or more of the following items of deduction or income, which are added back to the taxpayer's taxable income to determine AMTI:

- State and local income taxes.
- Real property taxes.
- Accelerated depreciation.
- Interest income on certain private activity bonds.
- Exercise of incentive stock options.
- Gain on sale of small business stock (as defined in Section 1202).

For 2005, the AMT exemption is $58,000 for married filing jointly, $40,250 for single filers, and $29,000 for married filing separately. The tentative minimum tax is applied at a rate of 26 percent of AMTI up to $175,000. AMTI exceeding $175,000 is taxed at a 28 percent rate.

DETERMINING INCOME TAX LIABILITY

Of all the sources providing revenues to the federal government, the individual income tax is the largest. Computing an individual's income tax liability can be very complicated. The tax liability itself is a product of the taxpayer's taxable income, which is summarized in the following formula:

EXHIBIT 13.4: TAXABLE INCOME

Total Income (From Whatever Source Derived)	$xx,xxx
Less: Exclusions From Gross Income	(x,xxx)
Gross Income	$xx,xxx
Less: Deductions for Adjusted Gross Income	(x,xxx)
Adjusted Gross Income (AGI)	$xx,xxx
Less: The Larger of:	
Standard Deduction or Itemized Deductions	(x,xxx)
Less: Personal and Dependency Exemptions	(x,xxx)
Taxable Income	$xx,xxx

TOTAL INCOME AND GROSS INCOME

The tax computation begins with the determination of the taxpayer's total income, from whatever source derived. In general, all income is taxable unless Congress has specifically exempted the income from taxation. In tax terminology, income exempt from tax and not included in a taxpayer's **gross income** is referred to as an "**exclusion**."

gross income - income subject to the federal income tax. Gross income does not include income for which the IRC permits exclusion treatment.

exclusion - income exempt from tax and not included in a taxpayer's gross income

In determining gross income, the taxpayer may exclude many different types of income received. A list of the more common types of income that may be excluded appears below:

- 401(k) salary deferrals.
- 403(b) salary deferrals.
- Accident insurance proceeds.
- Bequests received.
- Child support payments received.
- Certain employee fringe benefits.
- Gifts received.
- Group term life insurance premiums (limited).
- Inheritances.
- Interest received from municipal bonds.
- Life insurance proceeds received.
- Meals and lodging (furnished for the convenience of the employer on the employer's premises).
- Scholarship grants (for tuition and books of a degree candidate).
- Workers' compensation.

The amount of income remaining after removing the exclusions is termed the taxpayer's gross income. Gross income is generally the starting point for the federal individual income tax return (Form 1040).

EXAMPLE

During 2005, Joe received salary of $60,000, dividends of $2,000, tax-exempt interest of $500, and a gift of $20,000 from his parents. Joe has total income for 2005 of $82,500, since total income is based on income from all sources. However, Joe's gross income reported on his tax return is $62,000, the sum of the $60,000 salary and the $2,000 taxable dividend income. The remaining $500 of tax-exempt interest income and $20,000 gift is excluded from gross income.

ADJUSTED GROSS INCOME (AGI)

The gross income can further be reduced by allowed deductions. Deductions that reduce gross income directly are referred to as "deductions *for* AGI" or **"above-the-line" deductions**. The "line" referred to in this phrase is **Adjusted Gross Income**, commonly referred to as AGI.

"above-the-line" deductions - an above-the-line deduction (also known as a deduction *for* AGI) is one that reduces gross income directly

AGI is a very important concept for individual income taxation. It represents the basis for computing percentage limitations on certain itemized deductions such as the charitable, medical, and miscellaneous itemized deductions. AGI also serves as a benchmark for percentage limitations of total itemized deductions, personal and dependency exemptions, and passive rental real estate losses.

adjusted gross income - a determination peculiar to individual taxpayers that represents gross income less business expenses, expenses attributable to the production of rent or royalty income, the allowed capital loss deduction, and certain personal expenses (deductions for AGI)

In determining adjusted gross income, the taxpayer may reduce gross income by the following:

- ▲ Ordinary and necessary expenses incurred in a trade or business.
- ▲ Net capital losses (limited).
- ▲ One-half of self-employment tax paid.
- ▲ Alimony paid to an ex-spouse.
- ▲ Certain payments to a Keogh, SIMPLE or SEP retirement plan.
- ▲ Contributions to a traditional IRA (limited).
- ▲ Qualifying moving expenses.
- ▲ Forfeited interest penalty for premature withdrawal of time deposits.
- ▲ Self-employed health insurance premiums and qualified long-term care premiums.
- ▲ Interest paid on qualifying education loans (limited).
- ▲ Qualified higher education expenses.
- ▲ Educator expenses up to $250.

Deductions for AGI are more favorable than itemized deductions because they are generally subject to fewer limits than itemized deductions, and they do not require the taxpayer to itemize to receive a benefit from the deduction. They also reduce AGI, which reduces calculated hurdles for itemized deductions, and can reduce phased-out items.

ITEMIZED DEDUCTIONS AND THE STANDARD DEDUCTION

Several deductions are allowed to reduce adjusted gross income. These deductions are often referred to as "deductions *from* AGI" or **"below-the-line" deductions**.

"below-the-line" deductions - (also known as a deduction from AGI) is one that is subtracted *from* AGI in arriving at taxable income

basic standard deduction - the amount allowed all taxpayers who do not itemize their deductions

The **basic standard deduction** is the amount allowed all taxpayers who do not itemize their deductions. It represents the government's estimate of tax-deductible expenses a taxpayer might have. The allowed standard deduction is based on the tax year and the taxpayer's filing status. The allowed basic standard deduction for 2005 is summarized in the table below:

EXHIBIT 13.5: 2005 ALLOWED BASIC STANDARD DEDUCTION

Filing Status	Basic Standard Deduction 2005
Single	$5,000
Married, Filing Jointly	$10,000
Qualifying Widow(er)	$10,000
Head of Household	$7,300
Married, Filing Separately	$5,000

itemized deductions - deductions that are in excess of the standard deduction and are used in lieu of the standard deduction

Taxpayers who have deductible expenses in excess of the standard deduction may choose to itemize and deduct these itemized expenses instead of taking the standard deduction. These expenses, referred to as **itemized deductions**, are generally expenses that are personal in nature. In addition, some of the itemized deductions have separate AGI limitations that may reduce their deductibility.

EXAMPLE

For example, medical expenses are only deductible to the extent they exceed 7.5 percent of the taxpayer's AGI. If an itemizing taxpayer's AGI is $100,000, and he incurs unreimbursed medical expenses during the year of $8,000, only $500 ($8,000 – ($100,000 × 7.5%)) of the medical expenses is deductible.

The following is a brief list of some of the more common itemized deductions. It should be noted that some of the deductions listed below are subject to AGI or income limitations.

- ▲ Medical expenses. *
- ▲ State and local income taxes.
- ▲ Real estate taxes.
- ▲ Personal property taxes.
- ▲ Mortgage interest.
- ▲ Investment interest. *
- ▲ Charitable contributions. *
- ▲ Casualty and theft losses. *
- ▲ Miscellaneous expenses (such as tax return preparation fees, etc.). *

* AGI or Income Limited

EXAMPLE

Mary is a single taxpayer. In the year 2005, she paid mortgage interest of $3,500, real estate taxes of $1,500, state income taxes of $2,000, and incurred medical expenses of $600. Assuming Mary's AGI is $50,000, her itemized deductions would total $7,000 ($3,500 + $1,500 + $2,000). The medical expenses are not deductible as itemized deductions, since they do not exceed 7.5 percent of Mary's AGI. Since Mary is a single taxpayer, her standard deduction would only be $5,000 for 2005, and therefore it would be beneficial for Mary to itemize her deductions. If Mary were married, she and her husband should take the standard deduction of $10,000 for 2005.

Not all individuals are entitled to the standard deduction. No standard deduction is allowed for the following individuals:

- ▲ A married person filing a separate return if his or her spouse itemizes deductions.
- ▲ A nonresident alien.
- ▲ An individual filing a tax return for a period of less than 12 months.

The basic standard deduction is reduced under IRC Section 63(c)(5) for an individual who may be claimed under Section 151 as a dependent of another taxpayer for a taxable year beginning in the calendar year in which the individual's taxable year begins. The basic standard deduction is limited to the greater of $850 (2005) or the sum of $250 and such individual's earned income, limited to a maximum of $5,000 (2005).

In addition to the basic standard deduction, a taxpayer will be entitled to an additional standard deduction if he or she is blind or attains the age of 65 by the end of the tax year.

EXHIBIT 13.6: 2005 ADDITIONAL STANDARD DEDUCTION

Filing Status	Additional Standard Deduction 2005
Single	$1,250
Married, Filing Jointly	$1,000 ea.
Qualifying Widow(er)	$1,000
Head of Household	$1,250
Married, Filing Separately	$1,000 ea.

PERSONAL AND DEPENDENCY EXEMPTIONS

Every taxpayer is entitled to a basic deduction to support himself or herself, the spouse, and any **dependents**. The deduction allowed for the taxpayer is called the personal **exemption**, while the deduction allowed for the spouse and dependents is called the dependency exemption. For 2005, the personal and dependency exemption amount is $3,200. Therefore, a married taxpayer with three dependent children will be entitled to a personal and dependency exemption for 2005 in the amount of $16,000 ($3,200 × 5). The allowed exemption amount is phased out for higher income taxpayers.

dependent - an individual who can be claimed by a taxpayer for an exemption on an income tax return

exemptions - a basic deduction to which a taxpayer is entitled for self support (personal exemption) or for the support of a spouse and/or dependent (dependency exemption)

In order to claim an individual as a dependent, five tests must be met:

Support test – the taxpayer must provide over half the support to the dependent (unless a multiple-support agreement exists).

Relationship test – the dependent must be a relative of the taxpayer, or a member of the taxpayer's household.

Gross income test – the dependent's income must be less than $3,200 for 2005, (unless an exception is met, such as a child of taxpayer who is under age 19 or age 24 if a full-time student).

Joint return test – the dependent cannot file a joint income tax return, except to receive a refund of income tax withheld.

Citizenship test – the dependent must be a citizen or resident of the United States (or a resident of Canada or Mexico).

TAXABLE INCOME AND TAX RATES

Taxable income is calculated by reducing the adjusted gross income by the standard or itemized deduction, and further reducing this amount by the personal and dependency exemptions. Taxable income is the tax base upon which the tax rates are applied to determine the taxpayer's tax liability before credits.

The tax rate schedule is based on the current tax year and the individual's filing status. The 2005 tax rates for all filing statuses are listed in Appendix 13.1.

TAX CREDITS

Once the individual's tax liability is determined, it may further be reduced by any allowable tax credits. Tax credits result in a direct, dollar-for-dollar reduction in tax liability. A credit may be either refundable or nonrefundable. Most credits are nonrefundable, meaning that the credit can reduce an individual's tax liability to zero, but not below zero. Common tax credits include the Foreign Tax Credit, the Child and Dependent Care Credit, the Child Tax Credit, the HOPE Scholarship Credit, and the Lifetime Learning Credit.

IRS GUIDANCE

Due to the complexity of the federal tax law, the IRS often issues guidance as to how it will treat certain transactions for tax purposes. This guidance is often given using letter rulings, determination letters, revenue rulings, revenue procedures, and technical advice memoranda.

A **letter ruling** is essentially a statement by the IRS of the way it will treat a prospective or contemplated transaction for tax purposes. In response to a written request from a taxpayer, the National Office prepares the letter ruling. A ruling is generally honored only with respect to the specific taxpayer to whom the ruling was issued. Other taxpayers cannot assume that the IRS will apply the letter ruling to them, even if they engage in the same transaction set out in the letter ruling. It does, however, provide other taxpayers with an idea of the IRS's application of the law.

A **determination letter** is a written statement issued by a District Director of the IRS. The letter applies the principles and precedents announced by the National Office to a given set of facts. Determination letters are issued only if the issue can be resolved based on clearly established rules. They are typically used when establishing a qualified retirement plan, such as a pension or profit-sharing plan.

The National Office of the IRS issues **revenue rulings**. They provide an official interpretation on how the law should be applied to a specific set of facts. They are typically issued because of many requests for **private letter rulings** with respect to an area of the tax law. Taxpayers may rely on revenue rulings in determining the tax consequences of their transactions; however, taxpayers must determine if their facts closely resemble the facts presented in the ruling.

Revenue procedures are statements reflecting the internal management practices of the IRS that affect the rights and duties of taxpayers.

Technical advice memoranda give advice or guidance in memorandum form and are furnished by the National Office of the IRS. An IRS agent typically requests the memorandum during an audit. The purpose of technical advice is to help IRS personnel close cases and maintain consistent holdings throughout the IRS.

letter ruling - a written statement issued by the National Office of the IRS that gives guidance on the way the IRS will treat a prospective or contemplated transaction for tax purposes

determination letter - a written statement issued by an IRS district director that applies the principles and precedents announced by the National Office to a given set of facts

revenue rulings - official pronouncements of the National Office of the IRS

private letter rulings - statements issued for a fee upon a taxpayer's request that describe how the IRS will treat a proposed transaction for tax purposes

revenue procedures - statements reflecting the internal management practices of the IRS that affect the rights and duties of taxpayers

technical advice memoranda - advice or guidance in memorandum form furnished by the National Office of the IRS to IRS agents who request such advice or guidance during an audit. Technical Advice Memoranda help to close cases and maintain consistent holdings throughout the IRS.

PENALTIES AND INTEREST

Various civil penalties are imposed on taxpayers and tax return preparers who violate the tax law. Included in the civil penalties are failure-to-file penalties, failure-to-pay-tax penalties, accuracy-related penalties, and fraud penalties.

Failure-to-File-Tax-Return Penalty

failure-to-file penalty - a civil penalty imposed on taxpayers and tax return preparers who fail to file tax returns according to the requirements of tax

The **failure-to-file penalty** was enacted to ensure the timely filing of tax returns. Generally, a return is considered filed on the date it is delivered to the IRS.

The penalty is 5 percent of the amount of tax required to be shown on the return for each month or fraction of a month that the failure continues, up to a maximum penalty of 25 percent. The penalty period runs from the due date of the tax return, including extensions, to the date the IRS actually receives the return.

The failure-to-file penalty is reduced by any failure-to-pay penalty.

failure-to-pay-tax penalty - a civil penalty imposed on taxpayers who, without reasonable cause, fail to pay the tax shown on their return

Failure-to-Pay-Tax Penalty

The **failure-to-pay-tax penalty** is imposed on taxpayers who, without reasonable cause, fail to pay the tax shown on a return. The penalty is one-half of one percent of the tax shown for each month or fraction of a month that it is not paid, up to a maximum penalty of 25 percent.

Jim files his tax return 40 days after the due date. He remits a check for $7,000 that represents the balance of the tax due. Jim's failure-to-file and failure-to-pay penalties total $700, calculated as follows:

Failure-to-Pay ($7,000 × .5% × 2 months)		$70
Failure-to-File ($7,000 × 5% × 2 months)	$700	
Less: Failure-to-Pay Penalty	(70)	$630
Total Penalty		$700

Interest is generally payable whenever any tax or civil penalty is not paid when due, even if the taxpayer has been granted an extension of time to pay the tax. Interest on unpaid tax liabilities runs from the last day prescribed by the Code for payment to the date paid.

accuracy-related penalty - a penalty of 20% of the portion of the tax underpayment attributable to negligence, substantial understatement of tax, or substantial valuation misstatement without intent to defraud

Accuracy-Related Penalties

The **accuracy-related penalty** is a penalty of 20 percent of the portion of the tax underpayment attributable to negligence, substantial understatement of tax, or substantial valuation misstatement.

Negligence includes any failure to make a reasonable attempt to comply with the tax laws, exercise reasonable care in return preparation, and keep proper books and records or properly substantiate items. If the IRS has evidence that the taxpayer was negligent, the taxpayer must establish that he or she was not negligent by a preponderance of the evidence.

A substantial understatement of income tax occurs when an individual fails to report on his or her income tax return the appropriate amount of tax that should be imposed, and this understatement exceeds the larger of (a) 10 percent of the correct tax, or (b) $5,000.

Substantial valuation misstatement occurs when a taxpayer undervalues or overvalues property or services, resulting in the understatement of income tax liability. The valuation misstatement is considered substantial if the value claimed on the return is 200 percent or more of the correct value. However, the penalty does not apply unless the understatement of tax liability exceeds $5,000.

EXAMPLE

Scott, who is in the 33% marginal tax rate, contributes artwork to a charitable organization and claims a deduction of $40,000. Assuming the actual fair market value of the art is $18,000, Scott would be subject to the 20 percent accuracy-related penalty since the overstatement of the asset's value was more than 200 percent of the correct value, and the understatement of tax liability is more than $5,000.

The accuracy-related penalty does not apply with respect to any portion of an underpayment if the taxpayer has a reasonable cause for the position taken on the return. The determination of whether a taxpayer acted with reasonable cause and in good faith is made on a case-by-case basis, taking into account all pertinent facts and circumstances.

Fraud Penalties

The fraud penalty is a penalty of 75 percent of the portion of the tax underpayment attributable to the fraud. The IRS must prove that there was an underpayment and that the underpayment was attributable to fraud.

For the **fraud penalty** to apply, there must be a willful attempt to evade tax. The taxpayer must have intended to mislead the IRS or conceal information to prevent the collection of taxes. Civil fraud has not been clearly defined, but courts have inferred fraudulent intent from factors such as understatement of income, failure to file tax returns, and failure to cooperate with tax authorities.

fraud penalty - a penalty levied against a taxpayer by the IRS after it has proven an underpayment of tax by the taxpayer and proven that the underpayment was attributable to a willful attempt to evade tax

The fraud penalty does not apply with respect to any portion of an underpayment if the taxpayer has a reasonable cause for the position taken on the return. In addition, the imposition of the fraud penalty precludes the imposition of the accuracy-related penalty on the same underpayment.

PAYROLL TAXES

The federal government, through the Federal Insurance Contributions Act (FICA), imposes employment taxes on employers, employees, and self-employed individuals. These taxes provide for a federal system of old age, survivors, disability, and hospital insurance.

The Federal Unemployment Tax Act (FUTA) provides for payments of unemployment compensation to workers who have lost their jobs.

FICA Taxes for Employers and Employees

The Federal Insurance Contributions Act (FICA) created several different programs designed to prevent people from becoming poverty stricken. The two most important and well-recognized programs created by FICA are the Old Age, Survivor, and Disability benefits program (OASDI), better known as Social Security, and the Hospital Insurance (HI) program, better known as Medicare. These taxes have different tax rates and only OASDI tax has a wage base limit.

Contributions to these programs are made by salary reductions for employees and by direct payments to the government by employers and self-employed individuals. FICA taxes are imposed on employees at a combined rate of 7.65 percent. This rate represents the total of the 6.2 percent rate for the Social Security (OASDI) portion, and the 1.45 percent rate for the Medicare (HI) portion. These rates are applied to the employee's total wages for the year, up to a maximum of $90,000 for the year 2005 for the Social Security portion of the tax. The employer is required to make a matching contribution for each employee.

EXAMPLE

For example, if Tom earns a salary of $100,000 for ABC Company, he will have $6,844 withheld from his paycheck for FICA taxes, computed as follows:

Social Security portion (6.2% × $90,000)	$5,580.00
Medicare portion (1.45% × $100,000)	$1,450.00
Total FICA taxes	$7,030.00

ABC Company will be required to pay the amount withheld from Tom's paycheck, plus their own equal matching contribution. ABC Company will also receive a deduction for their share of the FICA taxes paid.

self-employment tax - tax paid by self-employed individuals that is based on net earnings, not on the individual's wages. Since the self-employed must bear the burden of both the employer and employee portion of FICA, the self-employment tax rate is 15.3%—double the employee's rate of 7.65%.

Self-Employment Tax

Self-employed individuals must bear the burden of both the employer and employee portion of FICA taxes. Therefore, the **self-employment tax** rate is 15.3 percent, double the employee's rate of 7.65 percent. This tax is calculated on Schedule SE, which is attached to the individual's Form 1040.

Self-employment tax is calculated in the same fashion as FICA tax; however, the tax is based on net earnings from self-employment, not on the individual's wages. The net earnings from self-employment is the gross income from the trade or business, less any allowable deductions. Before applying the income tax rates, net earnings may be reduced by 7.65 percent, which is one-half of the self-employment tax rate.

For example, if Andrea owns her own business, and during the year her income after allowed deductions is $200,000, she would incur $16,516.30 in self-employment tax, calculated as follows:

EXAMPLE

Net earnings from self-employment	$200,000
Less: 7.65% of net earnings	($15,300)
Amount subject to self-employment tax	$184,700

Social Security portion (12.4% × $90,000)	$11,160.00
Medicare portion (2.9% × $184,700)	$5,356.30
Total self-employment taxes	$16,516.30

Andrea will report the self-employment tax on her income tax return and will receive a deduction of $8,258.15, one-half of the self-employment tax. This amount will be deducted in arriving at Adjusted Gross Income (above-the-line deduction).

EXHIBIT 13.7: FORM 1040 - ADJUSTMENTS TO INCOME

Section	Line	Description	Box	Line
Income	7	Wages, salaries, tips, etc. Attach Form(s) W-2		7
	8a	**Taxable** interest. Attach Schedule B if required		8a
Attach Forms W-2 and W-2G here. Also attach Form(s) 1099-R if tax was withheld.	b	**Tax-exempt** interest. **Do not** include on line 8a	8b	
	9a	Ordinary dividends. Attach Schedule B if required		9a
	b	Qualified dividends (see page 23)	9b	
	10	Taxable refunds, credits, or offsets of state and local income taxes (see page 23)		10
	11	Alimony received		11
	12	Business income or (loss). Attach Schedule C or C-EZ		12
	13a	Capital gain or (loss). Attach Schedule D if required. If not required, check here ▶ ☐		13a
	b	If box on 13a is checked, enter post-May 5 capital gain distributions	13b	
If you did not get a W-2, see page 22.	14	Other gains or (losses). Attach Form 4797		14
	15a	IRA distributions 15a — b Taxable amount (see page 25)		15b
	16a	Pensions and annuities 16a — b Taxable amount (see page 25)		16b
Enclose, but do not attach, any payment. Also, please use **Form 1040-V.**	17	Rental real estate, royalties, partnerships, S corporations, trusts, etc. Attach Schedule E		17
	18	Farm income or (loss). Attach Schedule F		18
	19	Unemployment compensation		19
	20a	Social security benefits 20a — b Taxable amount (see page 27)		20b
	21	Other income. List type and amount (see page 27)		21
	22	Add the amounts in the far right column for lines 7 through 21. This is your **total income** ▶		22
Adjusted Gross Income	23	Educator expenses (see page 29)	23	
	24	IRA deduction (see page 29)	24	
	25	Student loan interest deduction (see page 31)	25	
	26	Tuition and fees deduction (see page 32)	26	
	27	Moving expenses. Attach Form 3903	27	
	28	One-half of self-employment tax. Attach Schedule SE	28	
	29	Self-employed health insurance deduction (see page 33)	29	
	30	Self-employed SEP, SIMPLE, and qualified plans	30	
	31	Penalty on early withdrawal of savings	31	
	32a	Alimony paid b Recipient s SSN ▶	32a	
	33	Add lines 23 through 32a		33
	34	Subtract line 33 from line 22. This is your **adjusted gross income** ▶		34

For Disclosure, Privacy Act, and Paperwork Reduction Act Notice, see page 77. Cat. No. 11320B Form **1040** (2003)

Where on the Web

American Bar Association *www.abanet.org*
American Institute of Certified Public Accountants (CPA/PFS) *www.aicpa.org*
Certified Financial Planner Board of Standards *www.cfp.net*
College for Financial Planning *www.fp.edu*
Financial Planning Association *www.fpanet.org*
Internal Revenue Service *www.irs.gov*
National Association of Personal Financial Advisors *www.napfa.org*
National Association of State Boards of Accountancy *www.nasba.org*
National Association of Tax Professionals *www.natptax.com*
RIA (Research Institute of America) *www.riahome.com*
Society of Financial Service Professionals *www.sfsp.com*
The American College *www.amercoll.edu*

FEDERAL UNEMPLOYMENT TAX ACT

The Federal Unemployment Tax Act (FUTA) provides for payments of unemployment compensation to workers who have lost their jobs. Most employers pay both a federal and state unemployment tax. The employee is not responsible for the payment of unemployment tax.

Federal unemployment taxes are imposed on employers who pay wages of $1,500 or more during any calendar quarter during the year or who employ at least one individual on each of 20 days during the current or previous year. The FUTA tax rate is 6.2 percent, and it is applied to the first $7,000 the employer pays each employee as wages during the year. Therefore, the maximum FUTA payment required for a covered employee is $434 ($7,000 × 6.2%).

TAX-ADVANTAGED INVESTMENTS

One goal shared by most financial planners and their clients is the minimization of all current and future taxes. Since taxes are often an individual's highest expenditure each year, effective reduction of taxes is of extreme importance.

Although Congress has significantly reduced the opportunities available to minimize income taxes, there are still a few opportunities available for investors interested in or already involved in tax-advantaged investments. Included in these opportunities are investments in tax-exempt securities, investment in tax shelters and vacation homes, use of tax-advantaged employee benefits, use of acceleration/deferral techniques, and awareness of exemption opportunities.

INVESTMENT IN TAX-EXEMPT SECURITIES

As a rule, interest income is taxable regardless of its source. However, interest income from certain state and local bonds and interest on educational savings bonds is excluded from income for federal income tax purposes.

Interest on obligations of a state, territory, U.S. possession (such as Puerto Rico), or any of their political subdivisions is nontaxable. If an individual has money to invest, he or she may wish to invest in state bonds if income tax reduction is an important goal. It should be noted, however, that state governments typically offer lower interest rates on these bonds than the rate offered on taxable investments. Therefore, to determine if an investment in a tax-exempt security is a wise choice, one can calculate an interest rate that a tax-exempt investment must earn to "break even" with the higher rate offered by a taxable investment. The formula to determine the break-even interest rate is:

$$\text{Taxable Interest Rate} \times (1 - \text{Marginal Tax Rate}) = \text{Tax-Free Rate}$$

EXAMPLE

Joe has a 35 percent marginal income tax rate, and he would like to invest in state of Kentucky bonds. If similar taxable investments yield 10 percent, Joe must earn a rate of return on the state of Kentucky bonds of at least 6.5% (10% × (1 – 35%)) to make this a worthwhile investment.

In addition to state bonds, interest on U.S. savings bonds such as Series EE bonds may be either tax deferred or tax exempt. The interest earned on the bond is tax deferred until the year the bond matures or is redeemed by the individual. The interest income from a Series EE bond is completely tax free if the bond was issued after 1989, and if the accrued interest and principal amount of the bond is used to pay for qualified educational expenses of the taxpayer, spouse, or dependents, subject to AGI limitations.

TAX SHELTERS

Under prior law, an individual could reduce or eliminate his or her tax liability by investing in "tax shelters" that produced losses that could be used to offset other income. These shelters often created paper losses in excess of the amount of capital the investor provided, causing the tax shelter business to grow into a thriving industry.

Typically, tax shelters took the form of limited partnerships, thus allowing losses to flow through to the individual partners. In the first few years of the partnerships' operation, losses were generally high due to low revenues and high expenses, such as interest, taxes, and accelerated depreciation.

The Tax Reform Act of 1986 significantly curtailed the benefits available to investors in tax shelters by the introduction of the passive activity loss limits. Passive activities include all rental operations and all other businesses in which the taxpayer does not materially participate. An individual meets the material participation test only if he or she is involved in the operation of the activity on a regular, continuous, and substantial basis.

Although there are many exceptions, a taxpayer will be considered a material participant if he or she spends more than 500 hours in the activity during the year, or if he or she spends more than

100 hours in the activity and no other individual spends more time on the activity. If the investor is not a material participant, the activity is considered passive. Investors may not use passive activity losses to offset ordinary taxable income, such as salary, interest, and dividends. Passive losses can only be used to offset income from passive investments. If a loss is disallowed (suspended), it can subsequently be utilized when the taxpayer disposes of the activity.

Even though deductions for passive losses are generally disallowed, there are situations in which a taxpayer would benefit by investing in a tax shelter. For example, if the taxpayer has an investment in a passive activity that is generating income, any passive losses could be used to offset the passive income. In addition, a taxpayer may deduct a limited amount of loss against active income when the taxpayer invests in rental real estate.

A taxpayer who actively participates in a rental real estate activity may deduct up to $25,000 of losses annually. A taxpayer is considered an active participant if he or she participates in management decisions such as approving new tenants, and owns at least a 10 percent interest in the activity. The $25,000 allowance is reduced by 50 percent of the excess of the individual's AGI over $100,000, and is therefore completely phased out when the taxpayer's AGI reaches $150,000.

Acceleration of Deductions

In addition to pursuing tax-advantaged investments, the taxpayer may take advantage of opportunities to accelerate income tax deductions or defer income tax gains.

The Internal Revenue Code allows individual taxpayers to claim deductions for various personal, investment, and business expenses. The deduction can generally be claimed in the year in which the expenses are paid; therefore, individuals have some flexibility with respect to the timing of deductions. A taxpayer wishing to reduce or eliminate a potential tax liability can accelerate deductions by prepaying the expense. For example, state income taxes can be paid during the current tax year rather than waiting until the following year when the tax is due. Taxpayers can also make additional contributions to charity before the close of the tax year, resulting in an income tax deduction in the current year.

Deferral of Tax Gains

When a taxpayer disposes of property, any resulting gain is usually reported, or recognized, on the individual's income tax return in the year of disposition. However, there are several situations where a taxpayer can dispose of property and defer recognition of the gain until a later date.

Section 1031 of the IRC allows a taxpayer to exchange certain types of property without recognizing a gain. These "like-kind" exchanges are afforded beneficial tax treatment if the property exchanged is qualifying like-kind property. If property other than like-kind property, commonly called **boot**, is received in the exchange, gain may be recognized.

boot - property (other than like-kind property) that qualifies as a tax gain when received in a property exchange

Like-kind property is generally any property other than the following:

- Personal-use assets, such as a personal automobile.

- ▲ Ordinary assets, including inventory.
- ▲ Stocks, bonds, and other securities.
- ▲ Personal property exchanged for real property.
- ▲ Domestic property exchanged for foreign property.
- ▲ Different-sex livestock.

If a taxpayer is not required to recognize gain from a like-kind exchange, the basis of the property received by the taxpayer must be reduced by the unrecognized (deferred) gain, resulting in recognition of the deferred gain when the acquired property is subsequently sold.

EXAMPLE

Assume Jack received business equipment worth $60,000 in exchange for business equipment with a tax basis to Jack of $35,000. Assuming the equipment qualifies as like-kind property, Jack's realized gain of $25,000 ($60,000 – $35,000) will not be reported on his income tax return. Jack's basis in the equipment received will be $35,000 ($60,000 – $25,000 deferred gain).

Taxpayers do not always dispose of their property intentionally. Occasionally, property is lost due to theft or to a casualty such as a fire or storm. When this occurs, the taxpayer may receive some sort of compensation such as insurance proceeds. The proceeds received may even exceed the taxpayer's basis in the property, resulting in a gain. Absent special provisions, the gain would be fully taxable in the year of the conversion, resulting in a potential financial hardship for the taxpayer.

EXEMPTION OPPORTUNITIES

The IRC has traditionally provided tax breaks for homeowners, including the allowance of deductions for mortgage interest and property taxes. The tax law also provides for the exclusion of some or all of the gain on the sale of a residence. The provision applies to residence sales as frequently as every two years, to gains in amounts up to $250,000 for single taxpayers and $500,000 for married taxpayers.

The exclusion is applicable to the sale of a residence owned by the taxpayer and used as a principal residence for two of the five years preceding the sale. If the taxpayer fails the use and/or ownership test, a partial exclusion may be available if the home is sold due to a change in employment, health, or other unforeseen circumstances. The allowed exclusion is based on a ratio of the number of qualifying months to 24 months.

EXAMPLE

Assume Mary, a single taxpayer, owned and used her home as a principal residence for 18 months. She then sold her home because of a new job in another city, realizing a gain on the sale of $300,000. Mary would be entitled to an exclusion of $187,500 ($250,000 × 18/24), resulting in a reportable capital gain of $112,500 ($300,000 – $187,500).

If a married couple filing jointly does not meet the conditions for claiming the full $500,000 exclusion, the excludible gain will be the sum of the exclusion that each spouse would be entitled to if both were single. For this purpose, each spouse is treated as owning the home for the period that either spouse owned the home.

EXAMPLE

The rules for married couples can be clarified with an example. When Al and Susan were married, Susan moved into the home Al had owned and had been using as his principal residence for over 20 years. They used the home as their principal residence for six months, then sold the home (gain of $600,000) because of a new job. The couple can exclude $312,500 of the gain, since Al will receive the full $250,000 exclusion and Susan will be entitled to a partial exclusion of $62,500 ($250,000 × 6/24).

Another exemption opportunity exists for taxpayers owning vacation homes. If the home is rented to others for 14 days or less during the year, any rental income from the home is excludible from the taxpayer's gross income, no matter how much rent is charged.

IN CONCLUSION

The federal tax system in the United States is among the most complex tax systems in the world. A financial planner must realize the importance of gaining a comprehensive understanding of the tax law, since income taxes are often the largest single expenditure of a client in a given year.

While changes to the law have made income tax avoidance much more difficult over the last few years, many tax planning opportunities still exist. It is the financial planner's duty to a client to be aware of these opportunities to prevent the client from paying more tax than he or she is obligated to pay.

PROFESSIONAL FOCUS

Do your clients use of statutory fringe benefits like day care and athletic facilities as a form of nontaxable compensation?

When the taxpayer learns that they must earn $1.54 in the 35% bracket in order to buy $1 of fringe benefit with after-tax dollars, it piques their interest. The new 100% above-the-line deduction for health and long-term care insurance deductions puts the Schedule C filer on parity with the corporate structure for these deductions. Antidiscrimination rules always weigh in the business owner's decision because he has to cover employees. But that should not stop a business owner from reviewing current law changes regarding benefit plans to see how his specific situation may be benefited by retirement plan tax credits and plan design changes; tax credits from both federal and, in some cases, the state for employee dependent care benefit plans implemented; and numerous other opportunities for some serious tax planning

Has the change in capital gains rate versus ordinary income rates caused you to change your asset allocation towards mutual funds with less turnover of holdings?

Never let the tax tail wag the investment dog! Review investments for their utility in your portfolio then compare and contrast on tax efficiencies. That being said, however, taxes do have a decimating impact on wealth accumulation. Studies have shown that taxes gobble up around 2.5 to 3.3 percentage points of return. Some tax efficient funds have "*significant built-in gains*" that could be realized in a market downturn.

What tips do you give to your clients who are being audited by the IRS?

I remind them that this is why we substantiate and document all of our tax activities. I recommend keeping records three years for personal deductible items; seven years for trade, business, or production of income activities; and all home capital improvement receipts (in case we exceed the exemption threshold or we convert to rental) until three years after the home is sold. When an aggressive tax position is being taken, I always make sure the client understands and agrees to the aggressive tax position and the added potential for examination or audit.

What tips would you give to a new professional who is handling a client's audit for a client?

Be a Boy Scout - BE PREPARED. Bring your documentation and have your arguments prepared with relevant statutory authority or case law cites. Be professional. The auditor or examiner is a professional as you are - give them the same due respect.

How do you encourage your clients to come to you prior to completing a transaction, so tax planning can be done before rather than after the fact?

I have a standing policy with all tax clients: Call me anytime you have a tax or financial question or decision. I make this clear to them each and every time I do their returns. As their tax professional, I can fairly easily answer most questions without research and with a few minutes of conversation. I do not charge for these nonresearch queries so that it might encourage them to keep me in the loop before the fact.

Do you find clients are aware of simple things they can do to save taxes, like hold an asset just a little longer to have a long-term gain rather than a short-term gain?

Clients are becoming more sophisticated and savvy but, as the old adage goes, "having enough knowledge to be dangerous" can be so painfully true in this case. There are wonderful sources of tax information out there, but many times because of exceptions to the rule, the application of phaseouts, or other tax nuances, the information can be useless to the client's specific circumstances. Tax planning requires some number-crunching analysis to be able to articulate to the client quantitative factors and/or results, involving a course of action. Then the client's qualitative factors are overlaid and a decision is made. Encouraging the client to review and discuss the issues with you, including their impact on the client before the matter is transacted, is why we call it "planning." Weaving the management of tax issues into the fabric of the financial plan makes for a stronger cloth.

David R. Bergmann, EA, CLU, ChFC, CFP®

DISCUSSION QUESTIONS

1. What are the objectives of the Federal Income Tax Law?
2. What is the Alternative Minimum Tax?
3. What is a capital asset?
4. What is the formula for determining a client's income tax liability?
5. What are some of the types of government rulings issued as guidance to taxpayers?
6. When taxpayers violate the tax laws, what civil penalties might they expect to incur?
7. What payroll taxes did the Federal Insurance Contributions Act and the Federal Unemployment Tax Act create?
8. What tax-advantaged investment options are available to taxpayers?

EXERCISES

1. Dee made the following payments during 2005:

Interest on credit card accounts	$400
Interest on home mortgage	$7,500
Interest on bank loan (proceeds of loan were used to purchase tax-exempt bonds)	$3,100
Interest on credit union loan (proceeds of loan were used for a family vacation)	$1,600

How much of the above amounts may Dee deduct as an itemized deduction for interest expense on her federal income tax return?

2. Joe, a self-employed individual, earns $100,000 in self-employment income. How much self-employment tax will Joe owe for the year 2005?

3. Kay sold the following investments during the current year:

Property	Date Sold	Date Acquired	Sales Price	Adjusted Basis
ABC stock	2/3/05	1/2/04	$3,300	$1,300
Bond	2/5/05	2/5/04	$1,200	$1,400
Land	4/5/05	5/4/04	$4,300	$3,400

What is the amount of net long-term gain and net short-term gain on the sale of the investments?

4. Cindy sold 300 shares of XYZ stock for $5,200. She had paid $3,000 for the stock. Commissions of $300 on the sale and $180 on the purchase were paid.

What is Cindy's amount realized and her gain realized, respectively, on this sale?

5. Don incurred $28,000 of medical expenses in the current year. His insurance company reimbursed him in the amount of $6,000. Assuming his AGI is $100,000, what is the amount of medical expense deduction Don can claim for the year?
6. The Durrs are a married couple with two school-age children they fully support. Use the following information about their year 2005 finances to answer the following question.

Gross income	$91,350
Deductions for AGI	$6,000
Itemized deductions	$4,800

Assuming the Durrs file a joint income tax return, what is their taxable income for 2005?

7. Assuming the same facts as the previous question, how much income tax will the Durrs owe on their 2003 income tax return (ignoring any credits)?
8. Susan, a single taxpayer, sold her home because she has a new job in another city. On the sale date, she had owned the home and used it as a personal residence for 18 months. What is the maximum gain that Susan can exclude on the sale of the residence?
9. During the current year, Scott had long-term capital losses of $2,000 and short-term capital losses of $1,500. If this is the first year he has experienced capital gains or losses, what amount of these losses may Scott deduct this year?
10. Pablo, a single individual, purchased a new personal residence for $375,000. Pablo sold the property 12 months later for $550,000, so he could take a new job that involved a promotion. How much gain must Pablo recognize?
11. David exchanged an apartment complex that he had owned for 8 years for farmland. The farmland was worth $1,050,000, and David's basis in the apartment complex was $475,000. David received $100,000 cash in the transaction. How much is David's gain realized and gain recognized because of this exchange?
12. Barbara exchanges investment land with an adjusted basis of $70,000 for another parcel of investment land with a fair market value of $50,000 plus $12,000 in cash. What is Barbara's realized and recognized loss on this exchange?
13. Doug and Susan, ages 45 and 40, are married, and file a joint return for 2005. The following pertains to their return for the year:

Adjusted gross income	$31,600
Itemized deductions	$11,000
Personal exemptions	2 (no children)

The standard deduction for married persons filing a joint return is $10,000 (2005). What is their taxable income and tax liability for 2005?

14. Joe is a single taxpayer in the 35 percent tax bracket. During the current year, he sold the following assets:

Investment	Gain
ABC company stock	$4,500
XYZ company stock	$1,000
Baseball card collection	$2,000
Corporate bonds	$6,000
Antiques	$8,000

All of the assets were held longer than one year. How much capital gains tax will Joe have to pay because of the sales?

15. Susan filed her tax return 70 days after the due date. She remitted a check for $8,000 that represented the balance of the tax due. Calculate her failure-to-file and failure-to-pay penalties.
16. Jim is in the 33% marginal income tax rate, and he would like to invest in state of Louisiana bonds. If similar taxable investments yield 12%, how much must Jim earn to make this a worthwhile investment?
17. J.J. actively participates in a rental real estate activity. During the year, he received rental income of $85,000, and incurred rental expenses of $120,000. Assuming his AGI is $120,000, how much of the rental real estate loss can he deduct in the current year?
18. Allison is age 12 and has the following income:

Investment Income	$1,800
Income from a Summer Job	$2,200

Assuming her parents claim Allison as a dependent, what is her taxable income for 2005?

19. John is age 15 and has the following income:

Investment Income	$3,550
Income from a Summer Job	$400

Assuming his parents claim John as a dependent, what is his taxable income and tax due for 2005?

20. Billy sold the following investments during the year:

Description	Holding Period	Gain/(Loss)
ABC Stock	Short-Term	$30,000
XYZ Stock	Long-Term	$45,000
Bonds	Short-Term	($20,000)
Real Estate	Long-Term	($60,000)

What is the net short-term or long-term gain or loss, and how much must Billy include or deduct in the current year?

PROBLEMS

1. David and Sue Dell are married and file a joint return. They have two children, Billy and Suzy, ages 8 and 6, respectively.

   David is a self-employed real estate appraiser, and the results for his business for the current year are as follows (he paid self-employment tax of $4,700):

Gross Receipts	$50,000
Expenses:	
Advertising	$900
Insurance	$1,000
Interest	$500
Dues	$700
Depreciation	$1,200
Office Rent	$12,000
Meals and Entertainment	$800

   Sue, who is employed by a marketing company, earned a salary of $40,000 for the current year. She participates in the company 401(k) plan, and made contributions to the plan of $6,000 for the current year (the company does not provide any matching contributions).

   David and Sue also received the following income during the year:

   Interest:

Second National Bank, Dallas	$1,100
State of Louisiana Municipal Bonds	$500

   Dividends:

ABC Company Cash Dividend	$350
XYZ Company Cash Dividend	$400

   They sold their principal residence after owning and living in the home for five years. The following information relates to the sale of the residence:

Sales Price	$700,000
Original Cost	$150,000

   David and Sue incurred the following expenses during the current year:

Real Estate Taxes	$10,000
Mortgage Interest	$4,500
Sales Taxes	$800

   Assuming David paid $5,000 in alimony to his ex-wife, calculate the Dells' taxable income for the current year.

2. Scott and Laura Davis are married and file a joint income tax return. They have taxable income for the current year of $65,000. In arriving at taxable income, they took the following deductions:

Mortgage Interest	$8,000
Real Estate Taxes	$10,000
State Income Taxes	$8,000
Charitable Deductions	$300
Accelerated Depreciation	$2,000

In addition, Scott and Laura received the following tax-exempt interest:

Municipal Bonds	$600
Private Activity Bonds	$3,000

Laura also exercised incentive stock options during the year. The option entitled her to purchase 500 shares at $50 per share. The stock was worth $110 per share at the time of exercise.

Calculate the Davis' Alternative Minimum Tax liability.

3. Steve and Elaine exchange real estate investments. Steve gives up property with an adjusted basis of $250,000 (FMV $400,000). In return for this property, Steve receives property with a FMV of $300,000 (adjusted basis $200,000) and cash of $100,000.What are Steve and Elaine's realized, recognized, and deferred gains because of the exchange?

4. Anne Love, a CPA employed by CPAsRUs.com, is an unmarried taxpayer. She earned a salary of $100,000 for the current year (2005), and did not participate in the firm's 401(k) plan. Anne also received the following income and incurred the following expenses during the year:

Income:

Interest	$2,000
Dividends	$900

Expenses:

Medical (Unreimbursed)	$1,500
Real Estate Taxes	$7,000
Mortgage Interest	$5,000
Interest on Auto Loan	$2,500

Ignoring any credits, how much lower would Anne's tax liability have been had she made a deductible employee contribution ($12,000) to the 401(k) plan?

CASE SCENARIO

Use the information provided to answer the following questions regarding the Nelson family.

NELSON FAMILY CASE SCENARIO
DAVID AND DANA NELSON
As of 1/1/2006

PERSONAL BACKGROUND AND INFORMATION

David Nelson (age 37) is a bank vice president. He has been employed there for twelve years and has an annual salary of $70,000. Dana Nelson (age 37) is a full-time housewife. David and Dana have been married for eight years. They have two children, John (age 6) and Gabrielle (age 3), and are expecting their third child in two weeks. They have always lived in this community and expect to remain indefinitely in their current residence.

INVESTMENT INFORMATION

The bank offers a 401(k) plan in which David is an active participant. The bank matches contributions dollar for dollar up to 3% of David's salary. David currently contributes 5.43% of his salary. His employer's plan allows for employee contributions of up to 16%. In the 401(k), the Nelsons have the opportunity to invest in a Money Market Fund, a Bond Fund, a Growth and Income Fund, and a Small Cap Stock Fund. The Nelsons consider themselves to have a moderate investment risk tolerance.

INCOME TAX INFORMATION

David and Dana tell you that they are in the 15% federal income tax bracket. They pay $820 annually in state and local income taxes.

Dana and David Nelson Statement of Income and Expenses For the year 2005		
INCOME		
Salary - David		$70,000
Investment Income		
Interest Income	$900	
Dividend Income	$150	$1,050
Total Inflow		**$71,050**
Savings		
Reinvestment (Interest/Dividends)	$1,050	
401(k) Deferrals	$3,803	
Educational Fund	$1,000	
Total Savings		**$5,853**
Available for Expenses		**$65,197**
EXPENSES		
Ordinary Living Expenses		
Food	$6,000	
Clothing	$3,600	
Child Care	$600	
Entertainment	$1,814	
Utilities	$3,600	
Auto Maintenance	$2,000	
Church	$3,500	
Total Ordinary Living Expenses		**$21,114**
Debt Payments		
Credit Card Payments Principal	$345	
Credit Card Payments Interest	$615	
Mortgage Payment Principal	$1,234	
Mortgage Payment Interest	$20,720	
Boat Loan Principal	$1,493	
Boat Loan Interest	$1,547	
Total Debt Payments		**$25,954**
Insurance Premiums		
Automobile Insurance Premiums	$900	
Disability Insurance Premiums	$761	
Homeowners Insurance Premiums	$950	
Total Insurance Premiums		**$2,611**
Tuition and Education Expenses		**$1,000**
Taxes		
Federal Income Tax (W/H)	$7,500	
State (and City) Income Tax	$820	
FICA	$5,355	
Property Tax (Principal Residence)	$1,000	
Total Taxes		**$14,675**
Total Expenses		**$65,354**
Discretionary Cash Flow (negative)		**($157)**

Dana and David Nelson
Balance Sheet
01/01/05

Assets			**Liabilities and Net Worth**		
Cash/Cash Equivalents			**Current Liabilities**		
JT	Checking Account	$1,425	JT	Credit Cards	$4,000
JT	Savings Account	$950	JT	Mortgage on Principal Residence	$1,234
			H	Boat Loan	$1,493
	Total Cash/Cash Equiv.	$2,375		**Total Current Liabilities**	$6,727
Invested Assets			**Long-Term Liabilities**		
W	ABC Stock	$12,500	JT	Mortgage on Principal Residence	$196,654
JT	Educational Fund	$14,000	H	Boat Loan	$12,065
H	401(k)	$32,197			
	Total Invested Assets	$58,697		**Total Long-Term Liabilities**	$208,719
Personal-Use Assets			**Total Liabilities**		**$215,446**
JT	Principal Residence	$245,000			
JT	Automobile	$18,000			
H	Boat A	$25,000	**Net Worth**		**$207,626**
W	Jewelry	$13,000			
JT	Furniture/Household	$61,000			
	Total Personal-Use Assets	$362,000			
Total Assets		**$423,072**	**Total Liabilities and Net Worth**		**$423,072**

Dana and David Nelson
Balance Sheet
12/31/05

	Assets			Liabilities and Net Worth	
	Cash/Cash Equivalents			**Current Liabilities**	
JT	Checking Account	$1,518	JT	Credit Cards	$3,655
JT	Savings Account	$950	JT	Mortgage on Principal Residence	$1,370
	Total Cash/Cash Equiv.	$2,468	H	Boat Loan	$1,048
				Total Current Liabilities	$6,073
	Invested Assets			**Long-Term Liabilities**	
W	ABC Stock	$14,050	JT	Mortgage on Principal Residence	$195,284
JT	Educational Fund	$15,560	H	Boat Loan	$16,017
H	401(k)	$38,619		**Total Long-Term Liabilities**	$211,301
H	XYZ Stock	$10,000			
	Total Invested Assets	$78,229			
	Personal-Use Assets			**Total Liabilities**	**$217,374**
JT	Principal Residence	$250,000			
JT	Automobile	$15,000			
H	Jet Ski	$10,000		**Net Worth**	**$241,823**
H	Boat B	$30,000			
W	Jewelry	$13,500			
JT	Furniture/Household	$60,000			
	Total Personal-Use Assets	$378,500			
	Total Assets	**$459,197**		**Total Liabilities and Net Worth**	**$459,197**

1. Calculate the Nelson's taxable income and tax liability for 2005 (ignoring any credits).
2. Are the Nelsons subject to the alternative minimum tax? If so, what is their AMT for 2005?
3. The Nelsons exchanged their boat (Boat A) plus $5,000 for Boat B on December 31, 2005. David had paid $22,000 for Boat A in 2004. What are the realized gain and recognized gain from this transaction?
4. If David maximized his contributions to his 401(k) plan, what would be the reduction in the Nelson's tax liability?

APPENDIX 13.1: 2005 TAX RATES AND BRACKETS

Single – Schedule X

If taxable income is: Over —	But not over —	The tax is:	Of the amount over —
$0	$7,300	-------------- 10.0%	$0
7,300	29,700	$730.00 + 15%	7,300
29,700	71,950	4,090.00 + 25%	29,700
71,950	150,150	14,652.50 + 28%	71,950
150,150	326,450	36,548.50 + 33%	150,150
326,450	----------	94,727.50 + 35%	326,450

Head of Household – Schedule Z

If taxable income is: Over —	But not over —	The tax is:	Of the amount over —
$0	$10,450	--------------- 10%	$0
10,450	39,800	$1,045.00 + 15%	10,450
39,800	102,800	5,447.50 + 25%	39,800
102,800	166,450	21,197.50 + 28%	102,800
166,450	326,450	39,019.50 + 33%	166,450
326,450	------------	91,819.50 + 35%	326,450

Married Filing Jointly or Qualifying Widow(er) – Schedule Y-1

If taxable income is: Over —	But not over —	The tax is:	Of the amount over —
$0	$14,600	--------------- 10%	$0
14,600	59,400	$1,460.00 + 15%	14,600
59,400	119,950	8,180.00 + 25%	59,400
119,950	182,800	23,317.50 + 28%	119,950
182,800	326,450	40,915.50 + 33%	182,800
326,450	------------	88,320.00 + 35%	326,450

Married Filing Separately – Schedule Y-2

If taxable income is: Over —	But not over —	The tax is:	Of the amount over —
$0	$7,300	--------------- 10%	$0
7,300	29,700	$730.00 + 15%	7,300
29,700	59,975	4,140.00 + 25%	29,700
59,975	91,400	11,658.75 + 28%	59,975
91,400	163,255	20,457.75 + 33%	91,400
163,225	------------	44,160.00 + 35%	163,225

APPENDIX 13.2: FORM W-2

a Control number	22222	Void ☐	For Official Use Only ► OMB No. 1545-0008	
b Employer identification number (EIN)			1 Wages, tips, other compensation	2 Federal income tax withheld
c Employer's name, address, and ZIP code			3 Social security wages	4 Social security tax withheld
			5 Medicare wages and tips	6 Medicare tax withheld
			7 Social security tips	8 Allocated tips
d Employee's social security number			9 Advance EIC payment	10 Dependent care benefits
e Employee's first name and initial	Last name		11 Nonqualified plans	12a See instructions for box 12 Code
			13 Statutory employee ☐ Retirement plan ☐ Third-party sick pay ☐	12b Code
			14 Other	12c Code
				12d Code
f Employee's address and ZIP code				

15 State	Employer's state ID number	16 State wages, tips, etc.	17 State income tax	18 Local wages, tips, etc.	19 Local income tax	20 Locality name

Form **W-2** **Wage and Tax Statement** **2005**

Department of the Treasury—Internal Revenue Service

For Privacy Act and Paperwork Reduction Act Notice, see back of Copy D.

Copy A For Social Security Administration — Send this entire page with Form W-3 to the Social Security Administration; photocopies are **not** acceptable.

Cat. No. 10134D

Do Not Cut, Fold, or Staple Forms on This Page — Do Not Cut, Fold, or Staple Forms on This Page

CHAPTER 14

Business Entities

LEARNING OBJECTIVES:

After learning the material in this chapter, you will be able to:

1. Identify the different types of business entities that a business owner may choose as a legal form of business.
2. Characterize each type of business entity listed below with regard to formation requirements, operation, ownership restrictions, tax treatment, legal liability risk, and management operations:
   - ▲ Sole Proprietorship
   - ▲ Partnership
   - ▲ Limited Liability Partnership
   - ▲ Corporation
   - ▲ S Corporation
   - ▲ Limited Liability Company
3. List the basic factors that a business owner should consider when selecting a legal form of business.
4. Explain how each type of business entity differs with regard to simplicity of formation and operation, ownership restrictions, limited liability, management operations, and tax characteristics.

BUSINESS ENTITIES

One of the major decisions confronting a business owner from a tax and legal perspective concerns selecting the form in which the business will operate. The business owner can choose from several different business forms, each with its own advantages and disadvantages.

Business owners may choose to run their business as a sole proprietorship, a partnership, a limited liability partnership (LLP), a corporation, or a limited liability company (LLC). Each of these business forms has different formation requirements, tax rules, legal liability risk, and type of management.

Once a business entity has been created, the next step is operating the business. The type of entity chosen will help determine which individuals will be responsible for making the day-to-day business decisions.

Another major consideration in the selection of a legal form of business entity is the legal liability of the owners. A major concern of business owners is the preservation and growth of personal assets, especially in today's litigious society. Therefore, it is critical to select a form of business entity that provides the desired asset protection, while allowing the appropriate level of freedom to run the company.

Income tax considerations play a major role in the selection of a business entity. Although many of the entities are taxed in a similar fashion, each entity is subject to a set of rules that provides the business owner with tax consequences that are either advantageous or detrimental. The following sections detail the different tax consequences of the formation and operation of sole proprietorships, partnerships, limited liability partnerships (LLPs), corporations, and limited liability companies (LLCs).

The creator of a new business can choose from several legal business forms. The owner must carefully analyze the available options to determine which type of business entity is most appropriate. As a personal financial planner, it is important to understand the different types of business forms available. The most common forms and their basic characteristics are discussed in this chapter.

SOLE PROPRIETORSHIP

sole proprietorship - a business owned and controlled by one person who is personally liable for all debts and claims against the business

A **sole proprietorship** is a business owned and controlled by one person who is personally liable for all debts and claims against the business. Separate accounting books and records are regularly maintained. However, for tax purposes, the sole proprietorship is not treated as a separate taxable entity. Rather, the income and deductions of the business are reported directly on the individual owner's federal income tax return (specifically, Schedule C of Form 1040).

proprietor - the owner of a sole proprietorship

Advantages of a sole proprietorship include its ease of formation and its simplicity of operation and taxation. **Proprietors** own all business property and need not consult partners or other managers before making business decisions. In addition, this form of business entity may provide some state and federal tax advantages over other entities. For example, if the proprietorship incurs a loss for the year, the loss will be reported on the individual's income tax

return where it may provide an immediate tax break because the loss may be deductible against other taxable income.

Management Operation and Decision Making of a Proprietorship

The proprietor is responsible for the day-to-day operation of the business and is responsible for making all of the business decisions. This allows for great flexibility in the operation of the business. For example, the owner may choose to add a new line of business or discontinue an existing line of business without the approval of others.

Legal Liability of a Proprietorship

The major disadvantage of the sole proprietorship is that the proprietor has unlimited personal liability for the indebtedness of the sole proprietorship. Therefore, any business liabilities may be satisfied from the owner's personal assets, and any personal liabilities may be satisfied from the business assets. The owner may purchase business liability insurance. While this insurance does not exempt the owner from creditor's claims, it provides protection against lawsuits.

Taxation of a Proprietorship

Although separate accounting books and records are maintained for tax purposes, the sole proprietorship is not treated as a separate taxable entity.

Tax Ramifications of Formation of a Proprietorship

The formation of a sole proprietorship is very straightforward. No formal transfer of assets to the business is required to enable a proprietorship to engage in business activities. Also, the owner generally is not required to file documents with local authorities (except, perhaps, for a business license), unless the owner is planning to operate the business under an assumed name. When a sole proprietorship is established, there are no federal income tax ramifications.

Tax Ramifications of Business Operation of a Proprietorship

When the proprietorship generates income and incurs losses, it is not required to file a separate federal income tax return. Instead, the income or loss from the business is reported directly on Schedule C of the proprietor's individual income tax return Form 1040. When reported, the income or loss is combined with the proprietor's other income to determine the taxpayer's adjusted gross income (AGI). The income from the business is taxed at ordinary income tax rates applicable to individual taxpayers and is generally subject to self-employment taxes.

Schedule C of Form 1040 is used to report the name of the proprietor, as well as the name, address, and accounting method of the proprietorship. This form also contains separate sections to report income earned by the business, such as gross receipts, and expenses incurred by the business, such as advertising, supplies, and wages paid. A sole proprietorship generally may deduct ordinary and necessary business expenses as incurred. A self-employed business owner is allowed an above-the-line (above AGI) deduction for 100 percent of health insurance premiums and qualified long-term care premiums paid not to exceed net earnings from self-employment and appropriate contributions to retirement plans.

The net profit or loss from Schedule C is reflected on page 1 of the individual income tax return Form 1040. If Schedule C reflects a net profit for the year, this profit is subject to self-employment tax. Self-employment tax is calculated in the same fashion as FICA tax; however the tax will be based on net earnings from the sole proprietorship instead of wages. Before applying the tax rates, net earnings are reduced by 7.65 percent, which is one-half of the self-employment tax rate.

EXHIBIT 14.1: NET PROFIT/LOSS LINE FROM SCHEDULE C (ON PAGE ONE OF FORM 1040)

Attach Forms W-2 and W-2G here. Also attach Form(s) 1099-R if tax was withheld.	**b**	**Tax-exempt** interest. **Do not** include on line 8a . . . **8b**	
	9	Ordinary dividends. Attach Schedule B if required	**9**
	10	Taxable refunds, credits, or offsets of state and local income taxes (see page 24)	**10**
	11	Alimony received	**11**
	12	Business income or (loss). Attach Schedule C or C-EZ	**12**
	13	Capital gain or (loss). Attach Schedule D if required. If not required, check here ▶ ☐	**13**
	14	Other gains or (losses). Attach Form 4797	**14**
If you did not get a W-2, see page 23.	15a	IRA distributions **15a** / **b** Taxable amount (see page 25)	**15b**
	16a	Pensions and annuities **16a** / **b** Taxable amount (see page 25)	**16b**
	17	Rental real estate, royalties, partnerships, S corporations, trusts, etc. Attach Schedule E	**17**

EXAMPLE

If Stan owns his own proprietorship business, and during the year his business income after allowed deductions is $200,000, he would incur $16,144.30 in self-employment tax, calculated as follows:

Net earnings from Sole Proprietorship	$200,000
Less: 7.65% of Net Earnings	($15,300)
Amount Subject to Self-Employment Tax	$184,700
Social Security Portion (12.4% × $90,000)	$11,160.00
Medicare Portion (2.9% × $184,700)	$5,356.30
Total Self-Employment Taxes	$16,516.30

The self-employment tax is calculated on Schedule SE, which is attached to the proprietor's Form 1040. The proprietor is allowed a deduction for one-half of the self-employment tax paid, or $8,258.15, in the above example. This amount will be deducted in arriving at Adjusted Gross Income (above-the-line deduction).

partnership - an association of two or more entities or individuals that carry on as co-owners of a business for the purpose of making a profit

partner - an individual, corporation, trust, estate, or other partnership that has an ownership interest in a partnership

PARTNERSHIP

A **partnership** is an association of two or more entities or individuals that carry on as co-owners of a business for the purpose of making a profit. Generally, forming a partnership is a simple process, since formality is ordinarily unnecessary. The partnership form of business is very flexible, as there are no limitations on the number of **partners**, and partners can be individuals, corporations, trusts, estates, and even other partnerships. There are two types of partnerships, general and limited. These differ primarily in the nature of the rights and obligations of the partners. General partnerships are owned entirely by general partners. Each partner can act on behalf of the partnership. A limited partnership is a partnership formed under the limited

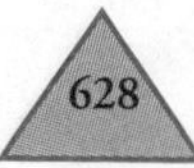

partnership laws of a state. This partnership must have at least one general partner and at least one limited partner.

Management Operation and Decision Making of a Partnership

Ordinarily, when a partnership is formed, a partnership agreement is drafted outlining the identity of the partners, the division of profits and losses, and the duties of each partner in the management of the partnership business.

General Partnership

In a **general partnership**, the general partners participate in the management of the partnership and are directly responsible for the day-to-day operation of the business. With management and ownership consolidated among the same individuals, partners are relatively free to change operating policy. Thus, the partnership can change its operational direction at any time and relatively quickly.

general partnership - a type of business entity owned entirely by general partners, each of whom can act on behalf of the partnership

Limited Partnership

In a **limited partnership**, limited partners are not allowed to participate in the management of the partnership affairs. If the limited partners do participate in management, they will become general partners and lose their limited liability status. It should be noted that even though limited partners are not allowed to participate in management, they generally are entitled to vote on major changes affecting the structure of the partnership, such as a change in the type of investments purchased.

limited partnership - In a limited partnership, limited partners are not allowed to participate in the management of operations, but generally are allowed to vote on major changes affecting the structure of the partnership

Legal Liability of a Partnership

General Partnership

General partnerships are owned entirely by general partners. While the partnership form of business has many advantages, it also has several disadvantages. The most significant disadvantage is the unlimited personal liability of the partners.

A general partner has unlimited liability for the acts of the partnership, the other partners, and obligations made by any partner or the partnership in the performance of partnership duties. If the partnership assets are insufficient to satisfy the liabilities of the partnership, the partnership's creditors can collect against the personal assets of the general partners. The creditors have the right to make any one partner, or several partners, satisfy the entire amount of the partnership's obligations. As a result, one partner may have to make good on the partnership's obligations and then may not be able to recover these amounts from the other partners.

Limited Partnership

A limited partner is liable for partnership indebtedness only to the extent of the capital the partner has contributed or agreed to contribute. In this respect, the limited partner is treated as an investor, liable only for the amount of his or her investment. Although the status of a limited partner generally provides the individual with limited liability, the limited liability status may disappear, and the partner will be liable as a general partner under any of the following circumstances:

- ▲ The surname of the limited partner is included in the partnership name. This does not apply if there is a general partner with the same surname.
- ▲ The limited partner acts as a general partner by participating in the management of the business operations.
- ▲ The limited partner learns that the firm is defectively formed and fails to withdraw from the partnership.

TAXATION OF A PARTNERSHIP

For federal income tax purposes, each general partner's share of partnership trade or business income is considered self-employment income, subject to self-employment taxes. A limited partner, however, is not allowed to participate in the management and control of the business and, therefore, is not subject to self-employment taxes on partnership earnings. A limited partner's income and losses are generally considered passive activities while a general partner's income and losses are ordinary.

flow-through entity - a type of business entity where the results of business operations are reported directly on the owner's income tax return

A partnership is similar to a sole proprietorship in that both entities are **flow-through entities** for federal income tax purposes. In other words, the results of business operations for both entities are reported directly on the owner's income tax return. For federal income tax purposes, partners must take into account their distributive share of partnership taxable income and any additional items the partnership is required to report separately, such as interest and dividend income. Consequently, the partnership is not, as an entity, subject to federal income tax. The partnership items of income and expense are completely taxable to the partners at their own personal income tax rates, but are reported initially on the partnership tax return (Form 1065) and then reported to each partner (Form K-1).

Tax Ramifications of Formation of a Partnership

Partners may form a partnership by contributing cash, property, or services to the partnership in exchange for an ownership interest. When a partner contributes cash or property to the partnership, no gain or loss is recognized and the partner's basis in the partnership is equal to the value of the cash contributed or the adjusted basis of the property contributed. If a partner contributes personal or professional services to the partnership, the partner must recognize ordinary compensation income for the value of the services. The amount of income recognized becomes the partner's basis in his or her partnership interest.

EXAMPLE

Assume Tom contributes the following to the ABC partnership in exchange for a 50 percent general partnership interest in the partnership:

Contribution	Fair Market Value
Cash	$10,000
Land (Tom's basis is $40,000)	$50,000
Services	$5,000

Tom would recognize ordinary income of $5,000, the value of the services he contributed to the partnership. His basis in the partnership interest would be $55,000 ($10,000 + 40,000 + 5,000).

Tax Ramifications of Business Operation of a Partnership

Once the partnership has been created, it is treated for federal income tax purposes as an aggregate of the separate partners, rather than as a separate taxable entity. The partnership itself is not required to pay any income tax, but must file an information return, Form 1065, detailing the items of income and expense that will be reported on the partner's individual income tax return.

Partners must take into account their distributive share of partnership taxable income and any separately stated items in computing their individual taxable incomes. Generally, a partner's interest in the partnership's capital and profits determines the partner's share of income, gain, loss, deduction, or credit. The partners may change the traditional allocation of tax items through the partnership agreement. This "special allocation" of an item or items must have a substantial economic effect to be valid. In many cases, special allocations allow the benefits of deductions to pass to those partners who have a greater use for such deductions.

Each partner's distributive share of items is reported on Form 1065 Schedule K-1, which is furnished by the partnership to both the Internal Revenue Service (IRS) and to each partner. Schedule K-1 details the partner's share of partnership ordinary income, which is the net profit or loss resulting from the partnership's trade or business. If the partner is a general partner, this allocation of ordinary income will be subject not only to ordinary income tax, but also to self-employment tax, similar to the proprietorship.

The Form 1065 Schedule K-1 also reflects various items that must be reported separately from ordinary income. These separately stated items—dividend income, interest income, and capital gains—are afforded special treatment on the partner's individual income tax return.

LIMITED LIABILITY PARTNERSHIP

limited liability partnership (LLP) - a form of business entity similar to a general partnership, except that an LLP provides additional liability protection to the partners

A **limited liability partnership** (LLP) is similar to a general partnership, except an LLP provides additional liability protection to the partners. Only certain professionals are eligible for LLPs.

MANAGEMENT OPERATION AND DECISION MAKING OF A LIMITED LIABILITY PARTNERSHIP

The management of an LLP is the same as that of a general partnership. The partners participate in the management of the partnership and are directly responsible for the day-to-day operation of the business. With management and ownership consolidated among the same individuals, partners are relatively free to change operating policy. Thus, the partnership can change its operational direction at any time and relatively quickly.

LEGAL LIABILITY OF A LIMITED LIABILITY PARTNERSHIP

In an LLP, partners are personally liable for their own acts of wrongdoing, but their personal assets (those outside the partnership entity) are protected from claims arising from the wrongful acts of other partners. This liability protection in many states extends only to tort law, not contract law.

Taxation of Limited Liability Partnerships

For federal income tax purposes, an LLP is treated in the same fashion as a partnership. The LLP is considered a conduit, or flow-through entity, that is not subject to federal income tax. Partners must take into account their distributive share of partnership taxable income and any additional items the partnership is required to report separately.

CORPORATION

C corporation - a business entity created by state law that is separate and distinct from its shareholders/owners

shareholders - the owners of a corporation who elect the corporation's board of directors

A corporation (regular **C corporation**) is an entity created by state law that is separate and distinct from its owners, who are called **shareholders**. A corporation can be closely held if owned by a few shareholders, or publicly held if owned by many shareholders.

The shareholders enjoy limited liability—they can only lose the amount they have invested in the corporation. They do not represent the corporation, but vote for a board of directors, which determines corporate policy and appoints officers. The officers manage the corporation.

For federal income tax purposes, the corporation is treated as a separate taxable entity. The profits of a corporation are taxed to the corporation at special corporate rates. There is a major tax disadvantage of a corporation from an income tax standpoint. When a corporation distributes a dividend to its shareholders, the corporation does not receive an income tax deduction for the dividend payment. The shareholder is required to include the amount of dividend received as ordinary taxable income. As a result, the corporate form of business will result in the double taxation of income—once at the corporate level and once at the shareholder level. The impact of this double taxation is lowered due to the fact that most dividends are taxed at the relatively low long-term capital gains rates.

directors - individuals who, acting as a group known as the board of directors, manage the business affairs of a corporation

board of directors - the governing body of a corporation whose members are elected by shareholders

Management Operation and Decision Making of a Corporation

Corporations have management advantages over other business forms. With a corporation, there is a separation of management from ownership so that the mere ownership of corporate stock does not give the owner the right to participate in management. The management is centralized, with the directors and officers handling management of corporate affairs.

Directors are individuals who, acting as a group known as the board of directors, manage the business affairs of a corporation. The **board of directors** is the governing body of a corporation. Shareholders elect its members. Directors may be shareholders or individuals with no financial interest in the corporation. The directors are responsible for selecting the officers and for the supervision and general control of the corporation.

officers - individuals appointed by a corporation's board of directors to carry out the board's policies and make day-to-day operating decisions

Officers of a corporation are individuals appointed by the board of directors. Like directors, officers may be shareholders or individuals with no financial interest in the corporation. The officers are responsible for carrying out the board's policies and for making day-to-day operating decisions.

The decisions made by the officers and directors are based in part on the corporation's bylaws. Bylaws are the regulations of a corporation that, subject to statutory law and the articles of incorporation, provide the basic rules for the conduct of the corporation's business affairs.

Legal Liability of a Corporation

Because a corporation is an entity created by state law that is separate and distinct from its shareholder/owners, one of the major advantages of the corporate form of ownership is the limited liability they enjoy.

Taxation of a Corporation

A corporation is an entity created under state law that is separate and distinct from its owners. It may be formed only through compliance with state incorporation statutes. For federal income tax purposes, the corporation is treated as a separate taxable entity, not as a flow-through entity.

Tax Ramifications of Formation of a Corporation

When a corporation is formed, cash or property is generally transferred to the corporation in exchange for shares of stock. When cash is transferred to the corporation, the transferor will recognize no gain or loss for federal income tax purposes. He or she will have a basis in the shares received equal to the cash transferred.

In the case of property transfers, no gain or loss will be recognized if the transfer meets the requirements of IRC Section 351. Section 351 provides that gain or loss is not recognized if property is transferred to a corporation in exchange for stock in the corporation, and, if immediately after the transfer, the transferors are in control of the corporation.

Tax Ramifications of Business Operation of a Corporation

A corporation is treated as a separate entity for federal income tax purposes. Computing a corporation's income tax liability can be complicated. The tax liability itself is a product of the corporation's taxable income, which is summarized in the formula shown in Exhibit 14.2:

EXHIBIT 14.2: CORPORATE TAXABLE INCOME FORMULA

Total Income (From Whatever Source Derived)	$xx,xxx
Less: Exclusions From Gross Income	(x,xxx)
Gross Income	$xx,xxx
Less: Deductions	(x,xxx)
Taxable Income	$xx,xxx

Total Income and Gross Income: The tax computation begins with the determination of the corporation's total income, from whatever source derived. In general, all income is taxable unless Congress has specifically exempted the income from taxation. In tax terminology, income exempt from tax and not included in a taxpayer's gross income is referred to as an exclusion. The amount of income remaining after removing the exclusions is the corporation's gross income, which is generally the starting point for the corporate income tax return (Form 1120).

Deductions: Several deductions are allowed to reduce gross income in arriving at corporate taxable income. Fewer restrictions are placed on corporate deductions than are placed on individual deductions since all activities of a corporation are considered business activities. For example, casualty losses incurred are fully deductible by a corporation, but are subject to a $100 floor and a 10 percent of AGI limitation for individuals.

dividends-received deduction (DRD) - a deduction for dividends received by one corporation from another corporation. The amount of the DRD is based on the percentage owned by the corporation receiving the dividend.

Some deductions are allowed only for corporations. For example, corporations are allowed a deduction for dividends received from other corporations. The amount of the **dividends-received deduction** (DRD) is based on the percentage owned by the corporation receiving the dividend. If the dividend-receiving corporation owns less than 20 percent of the dividend-paying corporation, the dividends-received deduction will be 70 percent of the dividend actually received. Exhibit 14.3 summarizes the dividend-received deduction for different ownership levels.

EXHIBIT 14.3: DIVIDEND-RECEIVED DEDUCTION BASED ON CORPORATE OWNERSHIP LEVEL

OWNERSHIP %	DRD
Less than 20%	70%
At least 20% and less than 80%	80%
At least 80% (Affiliated corporations)	100%

EXAMPLE

If ABC Company owns 15 percent of XYZ Company, and XYZ pays a $10,000 dividend during the year to ABC Company, ABC will include the $10,000 of dividend income in its gross income. However, ABC will be entitled to a dividends-received deduction of $7,000 ($10,000 × 70%).

Taxable Income and Tax: The corporate taxable income is calculated by subtracting allowed deductions from the corporation's gross income. The tax on this income is calculated using the rate table shown in Exhibit 14.4.

EXHIBIT 14.4: CORPORATION INCOME TAX RATES

Taxable Income			% on	of the
Over	But Not Over	Pay	Excess	Amount Over
$ 0-	$ 50,000	$ 0	15	$ 0
50,000-	75,000	7,500	25	50,000
75,000-	100,000	13,750	34	75,000
100,000-	335,000	22,250	39	100,000
335,000-	10,000,000	113,900	34	335,000
10,000,000-	15,000,000	3,400,000	35	10,000,000
15,000,000-	18,333,333	5,150,000	38	15,000,000
18,333,333-	....	6,416,667	35	18,333,333

Taxable income of certain personal service corporations is taxed at a flat rate of 35%.

If a corporation incurs a net operating loss for the year, the loss may be carried back two years where it can be used to offset any corporate taxable income. If the loss is not fully utilized by the carryback, it can then be carried forward for up to 20 years.

personal service corporation (PSC) - a C corporation in which substantially all of the activities involve the performance of services in the fields of health, law, engineering, architecture, accounting, actuarial science, or consulting

Personal Service Corporation: A **personal service corporation (PSC)** is defined as a C corporation in which substantially all of the activities involve the performance of services in the fields of health, law, engineering, architecture, accounting, actuarial science, or consulting, and substantially all of the stock is owned by employees. The taxable income of a personal service corporation is taxed at a flat rate of 35 percent, not at the regular corporate income tax rates. This provision was designed to encourage employee-owners of PSCs to take more salary out of the corporation.

Tax Ramifications of Withdrawals or Distributions from a Corporation

double taxation of dividends - the taxation of income at the corporate level and the subsequent taxation of dividend distributions at the individual shareholder's level

One of the major tax disadvantages of the corporate legal form of business entity is the **double taxation of dividends** paid by the corporation to its shareholders. Double taxation refers to the taxation of income at the corporate level and the subsequent taxation of dividend distributions at the individual shareholder's level. There is no deduction from the taxable income of a corporation for dividends distributed to shareholders.

EXAMPLE

For example, if a corporation has taxable income of $1,000 that is taxed at the 34 percent rate, there will only be $660 remaining to distribute to shareholders. If the shareholders are in the 35 percent tax bracket, the $660 dividend received will result in an additional tax of $99 (15 percent capital gains rate), leaving the shareholder with only $561 in cash. This double taxation may be enough incentive to discourage incorporation.

S corporation - a special type of corporation formed under state law like a regular corporation; however, for income tax purposes, is treated similar to a partnership

S CORPORATION

An **S corporation** is a special type of corporation for federal income tax purposes. The corporation is formed like a regular corporation (with limited liability as a separate entity)

under state law; however, it is treated similar to a partnership for income tax purposes. Therefore, all items of corporation income and deduction are passed through to the shareholders and reported on their personal income tax returns. The entity itself files an informational tax return (Form 1120S).

These corporations are called "S corporations" because they must satisfy the requirements of Subchapter S of the Internal Revenue Code to receive this special tax treatment. The essential elements of an S corporation include that the corporation must be a domestic corporation and may not have more than 100 shareholders. In addition, nonresident aliens, C corporations, partnerships, and certain trusts are not allowed to hold stock in an S corporation.

Management Operation and Decision Making of an S Corporation

S corporations are identical to regular corporations in terms of their management characteristics. However, closely held S corporations are often managed in a similar fashion to partnerships.

Legal Liability of an S Corporation

As with regular corporations, one of the major advantages of the S corporation is the limited liability enjoyed by shareholders.

The shareholders' liability for the acts, omissions, debts, and other obligations of the corporation generally is limited to the shareholders' capital contributions. There are several situations, however, in which the S corporation's shareholders will be personally liable for the debts of the corporation:

- A lender to a closely held corporation requires that the primary shareholders guarantee the loan to the corporation. If this is the case, the shareholders are liable to the extent of their guarantees, in addition to their capital contribution.
- A court may ignore the legal fiction of the corporation as an entity (pierce the corporate veil) when the corporation has been used to perpetuate fraud, circumvent law, accomplish an illegal purpose, or otherwise evade law.
- The courts may disregard the corporate form of entity if the corporation is not maintained as a separate entity from its shareholders. This arises occasionally in the case of closely held corporations.

Taxation of an S Corporation

Even though an S corporation is similar to a regular, or "C" corporation in that it is an entity created under state law that is separate and distinct from its owners, the federal income tax treatment of an S corporation is similar to the treatment of a partnership.

In order for a corporation to be taxed according to the rules of Subchapter S, an election must be filed on Form 2553 within 2 months and 15 days after the corporation's taxable year begins. A corporation must meet all of the following requirements at all times for the "S" election to be initially and continually valid:

- ▲ *Maximum of 100 Shareholders:* An S corporation cannot have more than 100 eligible shareholders. Stock owned by a husband and wife is treated as owned by one shareholder.
- ▲ *Eligible Shareholders:* Ownership of S corporation stock is restricted to individuals who are U.S. citizens or residents, estates, certain trusts, and charitable organizations. Nonresident aliens, C corporations, and partnerships are prohibited from holding stock in an S corporation.
- ▲ *Domestic Corporation:* The corporation must be an eligible corporation created under the laws of the United States or of any state.
- ▲ *Eligible Corporation:* Insurance companies, domestic international sales corporation (DISCs), and certain financial institutions are not eligible for S corporation status.
- ▲ *One Class of Stock:* The corporation is allowed only one class of outstanding stock. The shares generally must provide identical rights to all shareholders. However, an S corporation may have two classes of stock if the only difference is that one class has voting rights and the other class does not.

Tax Ramifications of Formation of an S Corporation

An S corporation is formed in the same manner as a C corporation, with the rules of Section 351 (see above) applying to transfers of property to the corporation. Therefore, under qualifying circumstances, property can be transferred to the corporation without gain or loss recognition by the transferors receiving stock.

Conceptually, the computation of a shareholder's basis in S corporation stock is similar to that for partners in a partnership. Both calculations are designed to ensure that there is neither a double taxation of income nor double deduction of expenses.

Tax Ramifications of Business Operation of an S Corporation

Once the S corporation election has been made, the corporation is treated for federal income tax purposes in a similar fashion to a partnership. The S corporation itself is generally not required to pay any income tax, but must file an information return, Form 1120S, detailing the items of income and expense that will be reported on the shareholder's individual income tax return.

Shareholders must take into account their distributive share of corporate taxable income and any separately stated items in computing their taxable incomes. A shareholder's weighted average ownership in the stock of the company determines his or her share of income, gain, loss, deduction, or credit. "Special allocations" are not allowed with S corporations. All items of income must be allocated based on pro-rata ownership.

Each shareholder's distributive share of items is reported on Schedule K-1, which is furnished by the S corporation to both the IRS and the shareholder. The K-1 for an S corporation is similar to that of a partnership, except the K-1 for an S corporation does not include a reconciliation of capital accounts or a line for guaranteed payments.

The S corporation K-1 details the shareholder's share of partnership ordinary income, which is the net profit or loss resulting from the corporation's trade or business. Ordinary income allocated to a shareholder from an S corporation is <u>not</u> subject to self-employment tax. The Schedule K-1 also reflects various items that must be reported separately from ordinary income.

These separately stated items, which include dividend income, interest income, and capital gains, are afforded special treatment on the shareholder's individual income tax return.

LIMITED LIABILITY COMPANY

limited liability company (LLC) - a relatively new and versatile form of business entity created under state law by filing articles of organization—versatile because it can be taxed as a sole proprietorship, partnership, C corporation, or S corporation

members - the owners of a limited liability company (LLC) who can be individuals, partnerships, trusts, corporations, or other

articles of organization - document filed in compliance with state law to create a limited liability company (LLC)

managers - individuals who are responsible for the maintenance, administration, and management of the affairs of a limited liability company

A **limited liability company** (LLC) is a relatively new type of business entity and is one of the most versatile. An LLC is created under state law by filing articles of organization. Its owners, referred to as **members**, can be individuals, partnerships, trusts, corporations, or other LLCs. A limited liability company is an entity that is generally able to provide the limited personal liability of corporations and the flow-through taxation of partnerships or S corporations.

One reason for their versatility is that they can be taxed as a sole proprietorship, partnership, C corporation, or S corporation. Generally, however, LLCs are usually treated as general partnerships for federal income tax purposes. If the LLC is taxed as a partnership or sole proprietorship, then all items of LLC income and expense are reported on the individual member's income tax return. Unlike a general partnership or sole proprietorship, however, members are not personally liable for the obligations of the LLC. This protection from personal liability for members, coupled with the favorable flow-through federal income tax treatment, has made the LLC a popular choice as a business entity.

Management Operation and Decision Making of a Limited Liability Company

When an LLC is formed through the filing of **articles of organization**, the LLC is registered with the state. When drafting the articles of organization, the members of the LLC must determine whether the LLC will be managed directly by all of its members or whether the administration of the LLC will be delegated to one or more managers.

Managers are individuals who are responsible for the maintenance, administration, and management of the affairs of the LLC. In most states, the managers serve a particular term and report to and serve at the discretion of the members. Specific duties of the managers may be detailed in the articles of organization or the operating agreement of the LLC. In some states, the members of an LLC may also serve as the managers.

Legal Liability of a Limited Liability Company

A member of an LLC has no personal liability for the debts or obligations of the LLC. This limited liability applies to both members who participate in management and those who do not. The ability to participate in management and still have limited liability is one of the most attractive features of LLCs. A member that participates in management is similar to a general partner in a partnership, except the member of the LLC has limited liability.

Taxation of a Limited Liability Company

An LLC with two or more owners is generally treated as a partnership for federal income tax purposes, unless it elects to be treated as a corporation. The election to be treated as a corporation is made by checking a box on IRS Form 8832, the Entity Classification Election

form. If the LLC has only one member, it may be treated as a sole proprietorship unless the LLC elects to be taxed as an S corporation in those states that permit one member LLCs . In some states, the LLCs that elect to be treated as a corporation for federal income tax purposes are also permitted to elect small business treatment causing the LLC to be taxed as an S corporation. The election of S corporation treatment for an LLC is accomplished in the same manner as a regular C corporation, by the filing of Form 2553.

A major advantage of an LLC is the limited liability of its members. The protection of owners from personal liability for obligations of the entity, coupled with the flow-through federal income tax treatment, has spurred the enactment of LLC legislation in most states.

Tax Ramifications of Formation of a Limited Liability Company

Generally, limited liability companies are classified as partnerships for federal income tax purposes. As such, the income tax consequences applicable to the formation of an LLC are identical to those applicable to a partnership. When a member contributes cash or property to the LLC, no gain or loss is recognized and the member's basis in the LLC interest is equal to the value of the cash contributed or the basis of the property contributed. If a member instead contributes services to the LLC, the member must recognize ordinary income for the value of the services contributed.

Tax Ramifications of Business Operation of a Limited Liability Company

An LLC with two or more members can be taxed as a partnership or a corporation. If the LLC is classified as a partnership for income tax purposes, the LLC must file an information return, Form 1065, detailing the items of income and expense that will be reported on the member's individual income tax return. The members each receive a Schedule K-1 detailing their allocable amounts of income, loss, deduction, and credit. If the LLC is classified as a corporation, the LLC must file Form1120 and will be responsible for any tax on business income.

If the LLC is comprised of only one member, all results from the business will be reported directly on Schedule C of the member's individual income tax return unless the LLC makes a timely election to be treated as an S corporation. Therefore, the income from the business is taxed at the member's individual income tax rate.

SELECTING THE PROPER BUSINESS LEGAL FORM

The selection of an appropriate business legal form has probably never been as challenging as it is today. Each business entity has its own characteristics that make it more suitable or attractive in a particular situation. The basic factors that should be considered in selecting a business entity include simplicity of formation and operation, ownership restrictions, limited liability, management operations, and tax characteristics. Exhibit 14.5 summarizes some of the more critical legal liability and tax considerations for various business entities.

EXHIBIT 14.5: SUMMARY OF LEGAL LIABILITY & TAX CONSIDERATIONS FOR VARIOUS BUSINESS ENTITIES

	Sole Proprietor	Partnership*	LLP	LLC**	S Corp	Corporation
What type of liability do the owner's have?	Unlimited	General Partnership - Unlimited; Limited Partnership - Limited	Limited	Limited	Limited	Limited
What federal tax form is required to be filed for the organization?	Form 1040, Schedule C	Form 1065	Form 1065	Form 1040, Schedule C or Form 1065 or Form 1120 or Form 1120S	Form 1120S	Form 1120
Under what concept is the organization taxed?	Individual Level	Flow-through	Flow-through	LLCs can be taxed as sole proprietorships, partnerships, C corporations, or S corporations	Flow-through	Entity Level
On what tax form is the owner's compensation reported?	Form 1040, Schedule C	Schedule K-1	Schedule K-1	Form 1040, Schedule C, or Schedule K-1, or Form W-2 and Schedule K-1, or Form W-2	Form W-2 and Schedule K-1	Form W-2 (dividends are reported on Form 1099-div)
What is the nature of the owner's income from the organization?	Self-employment income	Self-employment income for general partners; ordinary income for limited partners	Self-employment income	Self-employment income, or W-2 income and ordinary income, W-2 income	W-2 income and ordinary income	W-2 income and dividend income

Flow-through: all items of income will flow from the entity to the individual partner's/owner's/member's return while retaining the character of the income at the entity level.

* Limited Partners will generally not have self-employment income.

** The LLC will have the same tax characteristics and attributes as the type of entity it has elected to be taxed as.

SIMPLICITY OF FORMATION AND OPERATION

If the main factor in the determination of a business legal form is simplicity of formation, either the sole proprietorship or the general partnership is the business form of choice. No special documents need to be prepared for a sole proprietorship or general partnership to begin activities. However, it is customary for a general partnership to draft a written partnership agreement, and the partnership must file a separate income (informational) tax return each year.

The formation of a limited partnership requires the filing of a certificate of limited partnership with the Secretary of State in the state where the partnership is being organized. Otherwise, the operation of the limited partnership is similar to the general partnership, in that income and losses are allocated to the partners, and the limited partnership is required to file a separate informational tax return each year.

A corporation is often the most expensive form of entity to organize and operate. If the corporate form is selected, the business owners must prepare a certificate of incorporation, articles of incorporation, and bylaws, and must pay filing fees. Corporations must file annual reports with the state and must file annual federal income tax returns and state franchise tax returns. An S corporation also must make an initial election to be treated as an S corporation for tax purposes.

A limited liability company is formed by filing articles of organization with the state in which the entity is to be registered. This process is similar to filing articles of incorporation for a corporation. Limited liability companies are generally classified as partnerships for federal income tax purposes. As such, the income tax consequences applicable to an LLC are almost identical to those applicable to a partnership.

OWNERSHIP RESTRICTIONS

Some business forms place restrictions on the number and types of owners. The ownership structure of the business must be considered before selecting a type of business entity.

C corporations are extremely flexible in the number and types of owners allowed. A regular C corporation can have an unlimited number of shareholders, and the shareholders are not limited to individuals. However, ownership of an S corporation is limited to 100 eligible shareholders. Eligible shareholders are individuals who are U.S. citizens or residents, estates, certain trusts, and charitable organizations. Nonresident aliens, C corporations, and partnerships are prohibited from holding stock in an S corporation.

No limit is placed on the number of members of an LLC. In addition, almost any type of entity may be a member. This flexibility in the number and types of owners makes an LLC more attractive than an S corporation in many situations.

A sole proprietorship can have only one owner. Therefore, this type of business form is unacceptable for joint owners of a business. No limit is placed on the number of partners in a general or limited partnership; however, a limited partnership must have at least one general partner and at least one limited partner.

Where on the Web

BNA Portfolios *www.bna.com/prodcatalog/index.html*
Cornell Law School *www.law.cornell.edu*
Internal Revenue Service *www.irs.gov*
LSU Libraries Federal Agencies Directory *www.lib.lsu.edu/gov/fedgov.html*
National Association of Financial and Estate Planning *www.nafep.com/business_entities*
National Association of Tax Practitioners *www.natptax.com*
Research Institute of America *www.riahome.com*
Small Business Center *www.quicken.com/small_business*
Small Business Taxes & Management *www.smbiz.com*
Tax and Accounting Sites Directory *www.taxsites.com*
United States Small Business Administration *www.sba.gov*

Limited Liability

A major concern of most business owners is the risk of personal liability. As a result, the limited liability company, although relatively new, has become a very popular business form. Members of an LLC have no personal liability for the debts or obligations of the LLC. The ability to participate in management without assuming personal liability for debt is one of the most attractive features of an LLC. Limited liability status also applies to C corporations and S corporations.

A general partner has unlimited liability for the acts of the partnership, the other partners, and obligations made by any partner or the partnership in the performance of partnership duties. If the partnership assets are insufficient to satisfy the liabilities of the partnership, the partnership's creditors can collect against the personal assets of the general partners. Therefore, if legal liability is a major concern for the business, a general partnership is a poor choice of business form.

Management Operations

Another consideration in the selection of a business legal form is the structure and flexibility provided to management.

The management of sole proprietorships and partnerships is straightforward. With a sole proprietorship, the proprietor is responsible for the day-to-day operation of the business and for making all of the business decisions. This allows for great flexibility in the operation of the business. With partnerships, the general partners participate directly in the management of the partnership and are directly responsible for the day-to-day operation of the business. Limited partners are not allowed to participate in management.

Corporations have management advantages and disadvantages over other business forms. One advantage is that there is a separation of management from ownership so that the mere ownership of corporate stock does not give the owner the right to participate in the management.

The management is centralized, with the directors and officers handling management of corporate affairs. A disadvantage, however, is that the decision process may become time consuming and expensive due to the formalities involved.

In the case of an LLC, the members of the LLC must determine initially whether the LLC will be managed directly by all of its members, similar to a partnership, or whether the administration of the LLC will be delegated to one or more managers, similar to a corporation.

TAX CHARACTERISTICS

Startup Losses

A business that expects losses in the first few years of operation will typically opt for a different type of business legal form than that of a business expecting immediate profits. If the business expects losses, a flow-through entity such as a partnership, S corporation, or limited liability corporation, is generally the entity of choice. Losses will flow through to the owners of the entity and can generally be used immediately to offset other income at the individual level.

In contrast, losses incurred by a C corporation can only benefit the corporation. Therefore, several years may pass before the loss can be utilized against corporate profits.

Double Taxation of Dividends

As discussed earlier in this chapter, one of the major tax disadvantages of the corporate form is the double taxation of dividends paid by the corporation to its shareholders. Double taxation refers to the taxation of income at the corporate level and the subsequent taxation of dividend distributions at the individual shareholder's level. There is no deduction from the taxable income of a corporation for dividends distributed to shareholders. This double taxation may be enough incentive to discourage the use of the regular C corporation form.

PROFESSIONAL FOCUS

What criteria do you use to help clients choose their form of business entity?

I generally use three criteria in helping clients choose a business entity. The first and most important is income tax considerations. The choice of business entity can have a significant impact on both federal and state taxes. Generally, for organizations involved in real estate activities or personal services, a partnership can provide creative tax planning opportunities with provisions such as the "Optional Adjustment to Basis" election and flexibility in distribution of flow-through items, such as income/loss, credits, and so on. An S Corporation offers significant tax savings opportunities over a C Corporation for a closely held business by avoiding the "Built-in Gains Tax," "Personal Holding Company Penalty Tax," and additional taxes levied against "Personal Service Corporations."

The second consideration that I evaluate is liability. I often establish a meeting between myself, my client, and my client's attorney to evaluate the liability and related exposure between the various choices of business entities. Generally, where partnerships offer tax advantages, the potential liability exposure can outweigh these benefits. Based upon the attorney's recommendation, clients often choose either a corporation or limited liability company to avoid undesirable personal liability.

The final consideration is the client's personality and business practices. I often explain to clients that if you want to be a "duck" you must "walk and quack like a duck." A client who wants to be a corporation must be willing to play by the rules by clearly separating personal items from business, maintaining corporate minutes, and other legal requirements. Many clients are better suited for the simplicity of a sole proprietorship. If a client forms a corporation and doesn't act like a corporation, related tax problems are bound to appear, and the legal protection of a corporation is often in jeopardy.

Each client is unique and all of the relevant criteria must be adequately considered before making a recommendation. The final decision is and must always be up to the client.

For your S Corporation clients, what recommendations do you make regarding splits between compensation and dividends?

The IRS continues to aggressively challenge S Corporation dividend distributions under the belief, often well founded, that they represent a technique to avoid Social Security taxes. I have been involved in several IRS audits where the agent challenged distributions under the provision of unreasonable compensation. One situation that occurred about ten years ago involved a restaurant client, whose restaurant (a C Corporation) was professionally managed, and the owner worked less than twenty hours per week. The IRS agent challenged the owner's compensation level as excessively high relative to the time spent working. They successfully reclassified part of the compensation as a C Corporation dividend. We then advised the client to become an S Corporation to avoid this problem. In a subsequent audit, (the owner continued to work less than twenty hours per week) the IRS agent challenged the owner's compensation as excessively low. They unsuccessfully attempted to have part of the distribution reclassified as wages subject to Social Security and other payroll taxes. The agent's justification for the change in attitude was very simple, "My job is to support the position which will benefit the government not the taxpayer."

Another issue that must be considered is that distributions reduce the taxpayer's basis in the corporation and can have an effect on the shareholder's ability to deduct losses on the personal income tax return.

JOHN ROSSI III, MBA, CPA/PFS, CMA, CFM, CVA, CFP®

DISCUSSION QUESTIONS

1. What are the different types of business entities that a business owner may choose as a legal form of business?
2. How is a Limited Liability Partnership taxed?
3. What are the differences between General and Limited partnerships?
4. How does each type of business entity differ from other forms of business with regard to the personal liability of owners?
5. What are the tax ramifications of withdrawals or distributions from a C corporation?
6. What type of business entity should owners choose if they expect the business to produce losses the first few years?
7. What is the tax treatment of a Limited Liability Corporation?
8. What type of business entity should an owner choose if simplicity of formation and operation is a major priority?

EXERCISES

1. A bookkeeper performed services for ABC Partnership and, in lieu of her normal fee, accepted a 20 percent unrestricted capital interest in the partnership with a fair market value of $7,500. How much income from this arrangement should the bookkeeper report on her tax return?

2. An S corporation has the following information for its taxable year:

Net income *before* the items below	$60,000
Salary to employee	(18,000)
Rental income	22,000
Rental expenses	(29,000)
Net income	$35,000

John is a 40 percent owner of the S corporation, and he performs services for the business. What is John's self-employment income from the corporation, which is subject to self-employment tax?

3. During the year, Susan purchased 5 shares of an S corporation's 100 shares of common stock outstanding. She held the shares for 146 days during the taxable year. If the S corporation reported taxable income of $200,000, what must Susan include on her personal income tax return?

4. Alpha Company (a C corporation) owns 25 percent of Zeta Company. During the year, Zeta Company paid a $30,000 dividend to Alpha Company. For tax purposes, how will Alpha Company treat the dividend received?

5. Nelson Van Houten received a 70 percent capital interest in a general partnership by contributing the following:

Item Transferred	Nelson's Basis	FMV
Land	$60,000	$100,000
Debt (on Land)	N/A	(50,000)
Inventory	$10,000	$8,000
Services	N/A	$2,500

What is Nelson's basis in the partnership after the contribution?

6. Brooke Industries, Inc. (a C corporation) had the following income and loss items during the year:

Gross Receipts	$200,000
Cost of Goods Sold	(50,000)
Dividend income from ABC Corp (Brooke owns 15% of ABC)	$20,000
Operating Expenses	(40,000)
Net Operating Loss Carryforward	(12,000)

What is Brooke Industries' taxable income and tax due for the year?

7. In its first year of business, Sanifone Corp (a C corporation) had gross income of $160,000 and deductions of $40,000. The company also paid a dividend of $20,000 to its only shareholder, Joe Taylor, who is in the 35 percent individual income tax bracket. What are the tax implications to Sanifone and Joe?

8. Tommy is a general partner in RichTech, a general partnership. Tommy received a K-1 from the partnership, which contained the following items:

Partnership Taxable Income	$200,000
Dividend Income	$2,500
Long-Term Capital Gain (on investments)	$6,000

How much self-employment tax will Tommy have to pay?

9. Discuss the management structure of a C corporation.

10. What are the requirements for an S Corporation?

PROBLEMS

1. Hugh Elliott is a single taxpayer with no children. He is a self-employed real estate appraiser, and the results for his business for the current year are as follows:

Gross Receipts	$150,000
Expenses:	
Advertising	$2,000
Insurance	$1,000
Dues	$1,500
Office Rent	$12,000
Meals and Entertainment	$800

Hugh also received the following income during the year:

Interest	$1,100
Dividends	$1,400

Hugh incurred the following expenses during the current year:

Real Estate Taxes	$9,000
Mortgage Interest	$5,000

Assuming Hugh paid $10,000 in alimony to his ex-wife, calculate his taxable income and self-employment tax for the current year.

2. Pete Johnson is a single taxpayer with no dependents. During the year, he invested $40,000 in an S corporation. He received the following information on the K-1 from the S Corporation:

Net income *before* salary	$60,000
Salary to Pete (S Corporation)	18,000
Interest Income	2,000
Dividend Income	1,000
Long-Term Capital Gain	4,500
Charitable Contributions	2,000

Pete also received a distribution of $5,500 from the S corporation, and earned a salary of $50,000 at his full time job. Calculate Pete's taxable income, as well as his adjusted taxable basis in the S corporation stock at the end of the year.

3. Doug Tanner (a single taxpayer) will be starting a new business in the year 2005. He is not sure whether to operate the business as a C corporation or as a S corporation. Given the following estimates of income and expenses, determine the total tax that would be due under either scenario.

Gross Profit	$150,000
Operating Expenses (excluding salary)	(70,000)
Salary paid to Doug	40,000
Cash distribution to Doug	10,000

APPENDIX 14.1: SCHEDULE C OF FORM 1040

SCHEDULE C (Form 1040)

Department of the Treasury
Internal Revenue Service

Profit or Loss From Business

(Sole Proprietorship)

▶ Partnerships, joint ventures, etc., must file Form 1065 or 1065-B.

▶ Attach to Form 1040 or 1041. ▶ See Instructions for Schedule C (Form 1040).

OMB No. 1545-0074

2004

Attachment Sequence No. **09**

Name of proprietor | **Social security number (SSN)**

A Principal business or profession, including product or service (see page C-2 of the instructions) | **B Enter code from pages C-7, 8, & 9** ▶

C Business name. If no separate business name, leave blank. | **D Employer ID number (EIN), if any**

E Business address (including suite or room no.) ▶
City, town or post office, state, and ZIP code

F Accounting method: (1) ☐ Cash (2) ☐ Accrual (3) ☐ Other (specify) ▶

G Did you "materially participate" in the operation of this business during 2004? If "No," see page C-3 for limit on losses ☐ Yes ☐ No

H If you started or acquired this business during 2004, check here ▶ ☐

Part I Income

1	Gross receipts or sales. **Caution.** If this income was reported to you on Form W-2 and the "Statutory employee" box on that form was checked, see page C-3 and check here ▶ ☐	1	
2	Returns and allowances	2	
3	Subtract line 2 from line 1	3	
4	Cost of goods sold (from line 42 on page 2)	4	
5	**Gross profit.** Subtract line 4 from line 3	5	
6	Other income, including Federal and state gasoline or fuel tax credit or refund (see page C-3)	6	
7	**Gross income.** Add lines 5 and 6 ▶	7	

Part II Expenses. Enter expenses for business use of your home **only** on line 30.

8	Advertising	8		19	Pension and profit-sharing plans	19	
9	Car and truck expenses (see page C-3)	9		20	Rent or lease (see page C-5):		
					a Vehicles, machinery, and equipment	20a	
10	Commissions and fees	10			b Other business property	20b	
11	Contract labor (see page C-4)	11		21	Repairs and maintenance	21	
12	Depletion	12		22	Supplies (not included in Part III)	22	
13	Depreciation and section 179 expense deduction (not included in Part III) (see page C-4)	13		23	Taxes and licenses	23	
				24	Travel, meals, and entertainment:		
					a Travel	24a	
14	Employee benefit programs (other than on line 19)	14			b Meals and entertainment		
15	Insurance (other than health)	15			c Enter nondeductible amount included on line 24b (see page C-5)		
16	Interest:						
a	Mortgage (paid to banks, etc.)	16a			d Subtract line 24c from line 24b	24d	
b	Other	16b		25	Utilities	25	
17	Legal and professional services	17		26	Wages (less employment credits)	26	
18	Office expense	18		27	Other expenses (from line 48 on page 2)	27	

28	**Total expenses** before expenses for business use of home. Add lines 8 through 27 in columns ▶	28	
29	Tentative profit (loss). Subtract line 28 from line 7	29	
30	Expenses for business use of your home. Attach **Form 8829**	30	
31	**Net profit or (loss).** Subtract line 30 from line 29. • If a profit, enter on **Form 1040, line 12,** and **also** on **Schedule SE, line 2** (statutory employees, see page C-6). Estates and trusts, enter on Form 1041, line 3. • If a loss, you **must** go to line 32.	31	
32	If you have a loss, check the box that describes your investment in this activity (see page C-6). • If you checked 32a, enter the loss on **Form 1040, line 12,** and **also** on **Schedule SE, line 2** (statutory employees, see page C-6). Estates and trusts, enter on Form 1041, line 3. • If you checked 32b, you **must** attach **Form 6198.**	32a ☐ All investment is at risk. 32b ☐ Some investment is not at risk.	

For Paperwork Reduction Act Notice, see Form 1040 instructions. Cat. No. 11334P **Schedule C (Form 1040) 2004**

APPENDIX 14.2: SCHEDULE SE (2004)

Schedule SE (Form 1040) 2004 — Attachment Sequence No. **17** — Page **2**

Name of person with **self-employment** income (as shown on Form 1040)	Social security number of person with **self-employment** income ▶	

Section B—Long Schedule SE

Part I Self-Employment Tax

Note. If your only income subject to self-employment tax is **church employee income,** skip lines 1 through 4b. Enter -0- on line 4c and go to line 5a. Income from services you performed as a minister or a member of a religious order **is not** church employee income. See page SE-1.

A If you are a minister, member of a religious order, or Christian Science practitioner **and** you filed Form 4361, but you had $400 or more of **other** net earnings from self-employment, check here and continue with Part I . . . . . . ▶ ☐

1	Net farm profit or (loss) from Schedule F, line 36, and farm partnerships, Schedule K-1 (Form 1065), box 14, code A. **Note.** Skip this line if you use the farm optional method (see page SE-4)		1		
2	Net profit or (loss) from Schedule C, line 31; Schedule C-EZ, line 3; Schedule K-1 (Form 1065), box 14, code A (other than farming); and Schedule K-1 (Form 1065-B), box 9. Ministers and members of religious orders, see page SE-1 for amounts to report on this line. See page SE-2 for other income to report. **Note.** Skip this line if you use the nonfarm optional method (see page SE-4)		2		
3	Combine lines 1 and 2		3		
4a	If line 3 is more than zero, multiply line 3 by 92.35% (.9235). Otherwise, enter amount from line 3		4a		
b	If you elect one or both of the optional methods, enter the total of lines 15 and 17 here . . .		4b		
c	Combine lines 4a and 4b. If less than $400, **stop**; you do not owe self-employment tax. **Exception.** If less than $400 and you had **church employee income,** enter -0- and continue. . . . . . . ▶		4c		
5a	Enter your **church employee income** from Form W-2. See page SE-1 for definition of church employee income	5a			
b	Multiply line 5a by 92.35% (.9235). If less than $100, enter -0-		5b		
6	**Net earnings from self-employment.** Add lines 4c and 5b		6		
7	Maximum amount of combined wages and self-employment earnings subject to social security tax or the 6.2% portion of the 7.65% railroad retirement (tier 1) tax for 2004		7	87,900	00
8a	Total social security wages and tips (total of boxes 3 and 7 on Form(s) W-2) and railroad retirement (tier 1) compensation. If $87,900 or more, skip lines 8b through 10, and go to line 11	8a			
b	Unreported tips subject to social security tax (from Form 4137, line 9)	8b			
c	Add lines 8a and 8b		8c		
9	Subtract line 8c from line 7. If zero or less, enter -0- here and on line 10 and go to line 11 . ▶		9		
10	Multiply the **smaller** of line 6 or line 9 by 12.4% (.124)		10		
11	Multiply line 6 by 2.9% (.029)		11		
12	**Self-employment tax.** Add lines 10 and 11. Enter here and on **Form 1040, line 57**		12		
13	**Deduction for one-half of self-employment tax.** Multiply line 12 by 50% (.5). Enter the result here and on **Form 1040, line 30**	13			

Part II Optional Methods To Figure Net Earnings (see page SE-3)

Farm Optional Method. You may use this method **only** if **(a)** your gross farm income[1] was not more than $2,400 **or (b)** your net farm profits[2] were less than $1,733.

14	Maximum income for optional methods	14	1,600	00
15	Enter the **smaller** of: two-thirds (⅔) of gross farm income[1] (not less than zero) **or** $1,600. Also include this amount on line 4b above	15		

Nonfarm Optional Method. You may use this method **only** if **(a)** your net nonfarm profits[3] were less than $1,733 and also less than 72.189% of your gross nonfarm income[4] **and (b)** you had net earnings from self-employment of at least $400 in 2 of the prior 3 years.

Caution. You may use this method no more than five times.

16	Subtract line 15 from line 14	16		
17	Enter the **smaller** of: two-thirds (⅔) of gross nonfarm income[4] (not less than zero) **or** the amount on line 16. Also include this amount on line 4b above	17		

[1] From Sch. F, line 11, and Sch. K-1 (Form 1065), box 14, code B.

[2] From Sch. F, line 36, and Sch. K-1 (Form 1065), box 14, code A.

[3] From Sch. C, line 31; Sch. C-EZ, line 3; Sch. K-1 (Form 1065), box 14, code A; and Sch. K-1 (Form 1065-B), box 9.

[4] From Sch. C, line 7; Sch. C-EZ, line 1; Sch. K-1 (Form 1065), box 14, code C; and Sch. K-1 (Form 1065-B), box 9.

Schedule SE (Form 1040) 2004

APPENDIX 14.3: FORM 1065—SCHEDULE K-1

6511

☐ Final K-1 ☐ Amended K-1 OMB No. 1545-0099

Schedule K-1 (Form 1065) **2004**

Department of the Treasury
Internal Revenue Service

Tax year beginning ____________, 2004
and ending ____________, 20__

Partner's Share of Income, Deductions, Credits, etc. ► **See back of form and separate instructions.**

Part I Information About the Partnership

A Partnership's employer identification number

B Partnership's name, address, city, state, and ZIP code

C IRS Center where partnership filed return

D ☐ Check if this is a publicly traded partnership (PTP)

E ☐ Tax shelter registration number, if any ____________

F ☐ Check if Form 8271 is attached

Part II Information About the Partner

G Partner's identifying number

H Partner's name, address, city, state, and ZIP code

I ☐ General partner or LLC member-manager ☐ Limited partner or other LLC member

J ☐ Domestic partner ☐ Foreign partner

K What type of entity is this partner? ____________

L Partner's share of profit, loss, and capital:

	Beginning	Ending
Profit	%	%
Loss	%	%
Capital	%	%

M Partner's share of liabilities at year end:

Nonrecourse . . . . $____________
Qualified nonrecourse financing . . $____________
Recourse . . . . $____________

N Partner's capital account analysis:

Beginning capital account . . . . $____________
Capital contributed during the year . $____________
Current year increase (decrease) . . $____________
Withdrawals & distributions . . . $(____________)
Ending capital account . . . . $____________

☐ Tax basis ☐ GAAP ☐ Section 704(b) book
☐ Other (explain)

Part III Partner's Share of Current Year Income, Deductions, Credits, and Other Items

1 Ordinary business income (loss)
2 Net rental real estate income (loss)
3 Other net rental income (loss)
4 Guaranteed payments
5 Interest income
6a Ordinary dividends
6b Qualified dividends
7 Royalties
8 Net short-term capital gain (loss)
9a Net long-term capital gain (loss)
9b Collectibles (28%) gain (loss)
9c Unrecaptured section 1250 gain
10 Net section 1231 gain (loss)
11 Other income (loss)
12 Section 179 deduction
13 Other deductions
14 Self-employment earnings (loss)
15 Credits & credit recapture
16 Foreign transactions
17 Alternative minimum tax (AMT) items
18 Tax-exempt income and nondeductible expenses
19 Distributions
20 Other information

*See attached statement for additional information.

For IRS Use Only

For Privacy Act and Paperwork Reduction Act Notice, see Instructions for Form 1065. Cat. No. 11394R **Schedule K-1 (Form 1065) 2004**

APPENDIX 14.4: CORPORATION SCHEDULE K-1

6711

☐ Final K-1 ☐ Amended K-1 OMB No. 1545-0130

Schedule K-1 (Form 1120S) **2004**
Department of the Treasury
Internal Revenue Service

Tax year beginning ____________, 2004
and ending ____________, 20__

Shareholder's Share of Income, Deductions, Credits, etc. ► See back of form and separate instructions.

Part I Information About the Corporation

A Corporation's employer identification number

B Corporation's name, address, city, state, and ZIP code

C IRS Center where corporation filed return

D ☐ Tax shelter registration number, if any ____________
E ☐ Check if Form 8271 is attached

Part II Information About the Shareholder

F Shareholder's identifying number

G Shareholder's name, address, city, state and ZIP code

H Shareholder's percentage of stock ownership for tax year . . . . ____________ %

For IRS Use Only

Part III Shareholder's Share of Current Year Income, Deductions, Credits, and Other Items

1	Ordinary business income (loss)	13	Credits & credit recapture
2	Net rental real estate income (loss)		
3	Other net rental income (loss)		
4	Interest income		
5a	Ordinary dividends		
5b	Qualified dividends	14	Foreign transactions
6	Royalties		
7	Net short-term capital gain (loss)		
8a	Net long-term capital gain (loss)		
8b	Collectibles (28%) gain (loss)		
8c	Unrecaptured section 1250 gain		
9	Net section 1231 gain (loss)		
10	Other income (loss)	15	Alternative minimum tax (AMT) items
11	Section 179 deduction	16	Items affecting shareholder basis
12	Other deductions		
		17	Other information

* See attached statement for additional information.

For Privacy Act and Paperwork Reduction Act Notice, see Instructions for Form 1120S. Cat. No. 11520D **Schedule K-1 (Form 1120S) 2004**

APPENDIX 14.5: FORM 8832

Form **8832** (Rev. September 2002) Department of the Treasury Internal Revenue Service	**Entity Classification Election**	OMB No. 1545-1516

Type or Print	Name of entity	EIN ▶
	Number, street, and room or suite no. If a P.O. box, see instructions.	
	City or town, state, and ZIP code. If a foreign address, enter city, province or state, postal code and country.	

1 **Type of election** (see instructions):

a ☐ Initial classification by a newly-formed entity.

b ☐ Change in current classification.

2 **Form of entity** (see instructions):

a ☐ A domestic eligible entity electing to be classified as an association taxable as a corporation.

b ☐ A domestic eligible entity electing to be classified as a partnership.

c ☐ A domestic eligible entity with a single owner electing to be disregarded as a separate entity.

d ☐ A foreign eligible entity electing to be classified as an association taxable as a corporation.

e ☐ A foreign eligible entity electing to be classified as a partnership.

f ☐ A foreign eligible entity with a single owner electing to be disregarded as a separate entity.

3 **Disregarded entity information** (see instructions):

a Name of owner ▶ ....

b Identifying number of owner ▶ ....

c Country of organization of entity electing to be disregarded (if foreign) ▶ ....

4 Election is to be effective beginning (month, day, year) (see instructions) . . . . ▶ ___/___/___

5 Name and title of person whom the IRS may call for more information	6 That person s telephone number ( )

Consent Statement and Signature(s) (see instructions)

Under penalties of perjury, I (we) declare that I (we) consent to the election of the above-named entity to be classified as indicated above, and that I (we) have examined this consent statement, and to the best of my (our) knowledge and belief, it is true, correct, and complete. If I am an officer, manager, or member signing for all members of the entity, I further declare that I am authorized to execute this consent statement on their behalf.

Signature(s)	Date	Title

For Paperwork Reduction Act Notice, see page 4. Cat. No. 22598R Form **8832** (Rev. 9-2002)

CHAPTER 14 SUPPLEMENT A

Tax Planning Supplement

After learning the material in this supplement, you will be able to:

- Identify the sources of tax related client information, and explain how each affects tax planning.
- Discuss the difference between tax avoidance and tax evasion.
- Understand the IRS audit selection and screening process.
- Discuss Family Limited Partnerships and how FLPs are used in estate planning.
- Discuss taxation and legal liabilities of partnerships, corporations and S corporations.

DATA COLLECTION AND RISK ANALYSIS

Before a financial planner can provide tax advice or prepare tax estimates for a client, sufficient data must be gathered from the client. The data gathered will help the planner understand a client's economic situation, his or her tolerance for risk, and the role income taxes play in the client's overall financial plan.

Tax data can be gathered from many sources. Three major sources of data include the client questionnaire, prior income tax returns, and information forms sent to the client by various individuals, corporations, and partnerships. Each of these sources of data is discussed below.

CLIENT QUESTIONNAIRE

The client questionnaire is frequently the starting point of comprehensive financial planning engagements. The questionnaire, which is completed by the client, contains information about the client, the client's financial position, and the client's family. The planner can use several elements of the questionnaire to devise a tax projection and develop tax planning strategies. See the Appendix in Chapter 3 for a sample Client Data Collection Questionnaire.

Although questionnaires can be prepared and presented to clients in many ways, several items of information should always be requested from a client in the questionnaire. Many of these items can assist the planner in the tax planning process.

The following is an overview of the tax-related information items that should appear in a client questionnaire:

- Client and spouse name, address, age, and Social Security numbers.
- Family information, including the names of children and parents and their Social Security numbers.
- Detail of investment assets and retirement plans.
- Detail of personal residence and rental property.
- Salaries, bonuses, and other sources of income.
- Detail of expenses and other deductions for budgeting and income tax.

Each of the items listed above may provide the planner with information necessary to provide a comprehensive tax projection. For example, the family information section of the questionnaire may allow the planner to determine if the client's parents can be claimed as dependents by the taxpayer.

PRIOR INCOME TAX RETURNS

Prior income tax returns are generally a major source of information to the planner. The returns should be carefully analyzed to ascertain key client financial information, as well as to determine the client's general tolerance for risk. This can be determined by the investment return sources (for example, money markets, aggressive mutual funds, etc.) When reviewing prior tax returns, the planner should ask the following questions:

- ▲ Do the tax returns indicate the taking of aggressive tax positions?
- ▲ Is the client's tax return risk-taking consistent with other client risk-taking, such as investment risk?
- ▲ How does the client feel regarding a potential IRS audit?
- ▲ What is the client's lifestyle and personality?

The financial planner can also determine whether to accept the individual as a client based on the positions taken on prior tax returns. If the client has taken positions on prior returns that are contrary to tax law, the planner may not want to accept the engagement by such an individual.

INFORMATION FORMS

When a taxpayer provides goods or performs services during the year, the taxpayer will receive compensation in the form of income. This **earned income** (as well as any **unearned income** such as interest or dividends) must be reported on the individual's tax return. The payer of both earned and unearned income usually must provide the recipient with a written statement detailing the amount paid. These written statements, known as **information returns**, provide the taxpayer with a significant portion of the information needed to prepare the federal income tax return.

There are a large number of information returns, each serving a different purpose. The most common are the Form W-2, Form 1098, and the Form 1099 series, and K-1s. These forms are discussed below.

If the taxpayer is an employee, he or she will receive a Form W-2 from the employer no later than January 31 following the tax year. The form discloses the amount of taxable wages and other compensation paid to the employee, as well as income taxes withheld and Social Security (FICA) taxes withheld. In addition, this form details employee contributions to 401(k) plans, distributions received from deferred-compensation plans, taxable fringe benefits, taxable group term life insurance coverage, and state wages and withholding.

If income other than salary is received during the tax year, the taxpayer may receive one or more of the Form 1099 series. The payer of the income is required to furnish the appropriate Form 1099 to the recipient of the income. In addition, the payer must also file the form with the IRS.

- ▲ Form 1099 INT is the form used to report interest income paid to any individual. Reportable interest includes interest on deposits with banks, brokers, or investment companies.
- ▲ Form 1099 DIV is the form used to report dividend income paid to any individual. Reportable dividends include corporate dividends paid to shareholders.
- ▲ Form 1099 G is the form used to report certain government payments made to an individual. For example, a state income tax refund would be reported on this form.
- ▲ Form 1099 R is the form used to report distributions from retirement plans. Retirement plans include pension plans, profit-sharing plans, and IRAs.
- ▲ Form 1099 MISC is the form used to report other income, such as income from rental property, royalties, and self-employment income.
- ▲ Form 1098 is the form used to report payments of mortgage interest by a taxpayer.

earned income - income from personal services as distinguished from income generated by property

unearned income - also referred to as investment income, it includes such income as interest, dividends, capital gains, passive income (rents, royalties), and pension and annuity income

information returns - a written statement provided to the taxpayer after the end of each tax year detailing the amount of income (as well as unearned income such as interest or dividends) earned by the taxpayer. The most common information return is the Form W-2.

The form must also include any points paid by the buyer of a residence.

TAX AVOIDANCE VS. TAX EVASION

tax avoidance - the legal minimization of taxes, which is accomplished by applying knowledge of the IRC and the Treasury regulations to an individual's income tax situation

The goal of most income tax planning is the reduction and minimization of the amount of tax that a person must pay to the government. **Tax avoidance** is the legal minimization of taxes. This avoidance is accomplished by applying knowledge of the Internal Revenue Code and the Treasury regulations to an individual's income tax situation. Every individual has the right to reduce his or her tax burden within the scope of the law.

The taxpayers' legal right to minimize or reduce personal income taxes has been upheld by the courts. In the case of Commissioner vs. Newman, Judge Learned Hand wrote:

"Over and over again courts have said that there is nothing sinister in so arranging one's affairs so as to keep taxes as low as possible. Everybody does so, rich or poor, and all do right, for nobody owes any public duty to pay more than the law demands; taxes are enforced extractions, not voluntary contributions. To demand more in the name of morals is mere cant."

Tax planning and tax avoidance involve only legal actions. Tax planning is the process of arranging one's actions in light of their tax consequences. In many cases, tax planning can be accomplished simply by changing the form of a transaction. For example, if an individual is invested in tax-exempt bonds, the individual is not required to pay tax on the interest income earned by the bonds, and therefore his or her tax liability is less than if he or she invested in taxable bonds.

tax evasion - any of the various fraudulent methods by which a taxpayer may pay less than his or her proper tax liability

While tax avoidance is the term applied to the legal interpretation of the tax laws to minimize tax liabilities, **tax evasion** is the term generally applied to any of the various fraudulent methods by which a taxpayer may pay less than his or her proper tax liability.

For example, if an individual works part-time at home babysitting the neighbors' children, the income received must be reported as income on the individual's income tax return. Since the babysitting income may not be reported to the government by the individual's neighbors, the individual may decide illegally to exclude the income from the tax return.

This example of tax evasion may lead to additional tax liability, as well as interest and penalties, if the tax return is audited. The amount of interest and penalties depends on the amount of understatement. Criminal tax evasion can even lead to fines and an occasional jail sentence.

AUDIT PROCESS

A goal of the IRS is to promote the highest degree of compliance with the Internal Revenue Code. Tax compliance is a voluntary process. Without some sort of audit process, the IRS would have no means by which to ensure compliance with the law. Before conducting an audit, the IRS must use a screening process to determine which taxpayers will be subject to audit, who will perform the audit, and what type of audit will be conducted.

The percentage of returns audited each year varies depending on the IRS's available staff. Returns on which all or most of the income is subject to withholding and where taxpayers did not itemize their deductions are the returns least likely to be audited.

EXHIBIT 14A.1: INDIVIDUAL INCOME TAX RETURNS EXAMINED

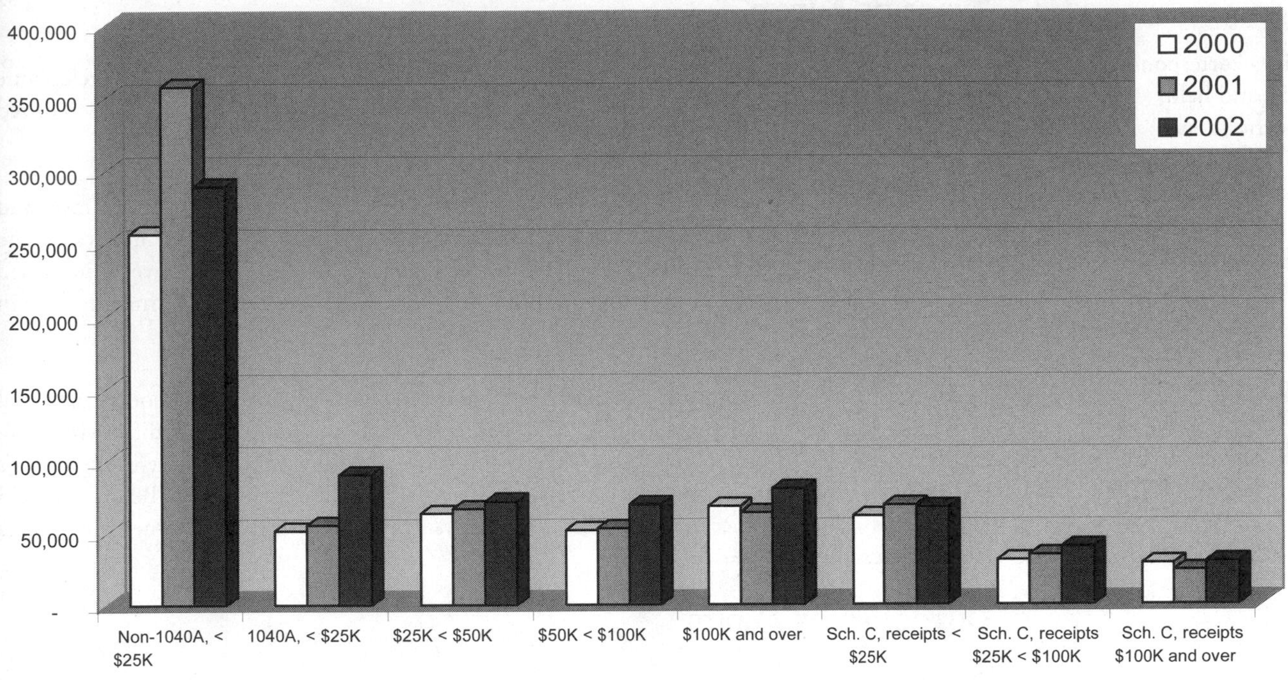

400,000
350,000
300,000
250,000
200,000
150,000
100,000
50,000
-
2000
2001
2002
Non-1040A, < $25K
1040A, < $25K
$25K < $50K
$50K < $100K
$100K and over
Sch. C, receipts < $25K
Sch. C, receipts $25K < $100K
Sch. C, receipts $100K and over

SELECTION AND SCREENING PROCESS

The IRS employs various methods and procedures for identifying and selecting individual returns for examination.

One selection method employed by the IRS is the **Discriminant Index Function System** (DIF). The DIF system is a mathematical technique used to classify tax returns as to their examination potential. Under this system, returns are divided into different audit classes. Weights are then assigned to certain return characteristics in accordance with a formula that varies with each audit class. These weights are added together to arrive at the total DIF score for the return. DIF returns with the highest scores are made available to the examination division of the IRS for manual screening.

Discriminant Index Function System (DIF) - a mathematical technique used to classify tax returns as to their examination potential

Although DIF scores indicate examination potential, tax examiners must manually screen returns to identify issues in need of examination and to eliminate those returns where an audit is not warranted. Either revenue agents or tax auditors, depending on the complexity of the issues involved and the degree of auditing skills required to perform the examination, manually screen individual returns.

If an audit examination is to be conducted, a classification check sheet is prepared and attached to the return. The check sheet lists significant items to be considered and identifies whether a correspondence audit, an office audit, or a field audit will be performed. The determination of which type of audit to conduct is made based on the complexity of the return and which type of audit is most conducive to effective and efficient tax administration.

Types of Audits

audits - correspondence, office, and field inspections and verification of a taxpayer's return or other transactions possessing tax consequences. Correspondence audits are conducted by mail; office audits are conducted in the tax agent's office; field audits are conducted on the business premises of the taxpayer or in the office of the tax practitioner representing the taxpayer.

A **correspondence audit** is conducted almost entirely by written correspondence and telephone contact with the taxpayer. These audits typically involve simple issues, such as itemized deductions, IRA contribution limits, and self-employment tax.

Office audits usually involve issues too complicated to be resolved by mail, such as travel and entertainment expenses, income from rents, and large itemized deductions. In most cases, the audit is conducted at the IRS office located near the taxpayer's home. The taxpayer is informed that his or her tax return is being audited and is usually requested to furnish certain information.

Field audits are conducted for complex individual returns with business or other financial activities. IRS revenue agents handle field audits, as opposed to office audits, which are conducted by less-skilled tax auditors. These audits are typically conducted at the taxpayer's business location or at the location where the taxpayer's books are maintained. Before the field audit begins, the examiner makes a precontact analysis of the return to determine which items should be examined.

Outcomes of Audits

Once the audit is complete, there are four possible outcomes to determinations made by the examiner.

No Change to the Return– the examiner proposes no change in the taxpayer's tax liability.

Taxpayer Agrees with Examiner's Findings – if the taxpayer agrees with the examiner's proposed changes, the taxpayer signs an agreement form and pays any additional taxes and interest owed. The taxpayer may even receive a refund because of the audit.

Taxpayer Does Not Agree with Examiner's Findings – if the taxpayer does not agree with the examiner's proposed changes, the taxpayer has the right to appeal. The IRS will send the taxpayer a "30-day letter" notifying the taxpayer of his or her right to appeal the proposed changes within 30 days. If the taxpayer does not respond within 30 days, the IRS will send a "90-day letter," which is a notice of deficiency.

The notice of deficiency officially informs the taxpayer that the IRS has determined that a tax deficiency exists and details the basis for and the amount of the deficiency. Once an individual has received a "90-day letter," he or she may pay the deficiency, file a Tax Court petition, or take no action.

Taxpayer Partially Agrees with Examiner's Findings – the taxpayer agrees with some, but not all, of the examiner's proposed changes.

If a taxpayer has exhausted all of his or her administrative remedies, he or she may litigate a case in court. The following chart details the court system as it applies to tax litigation.

The litigation begins in a court of original jurisdiction, or trial court. The U.S. Tax Court, U.S. District Court, and U.S. Court of Federal Claims are all trial courts that may hear tax cases.

EXHIBIT 14A.2: INCOME TAX APPEAL PROCEDURE

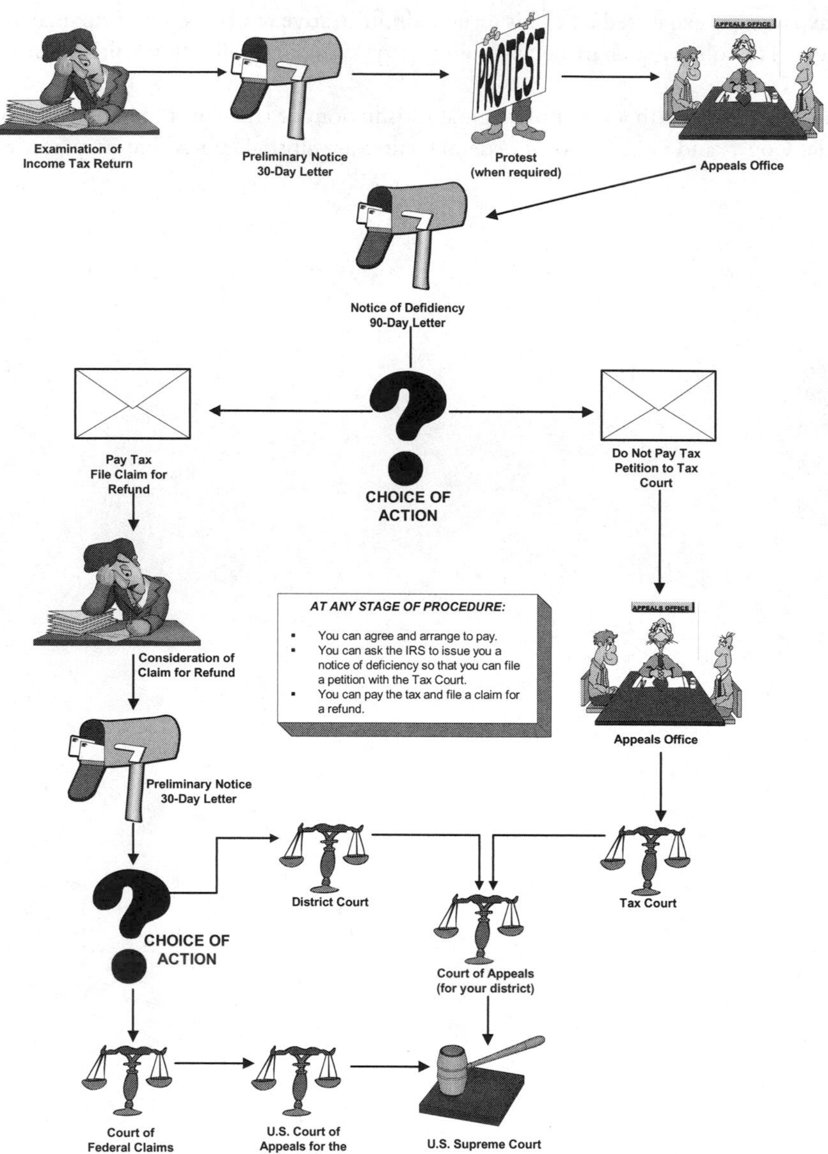

PROTEST
APPEALS OFFICE
Examination of Income Tax Return
Preliminary Notice 30-Day Letter
Protest (when required)
Appeals Office
Notice of Defidiency 90-Day Letter
Pay Tax File Claim for Refund
CHOICE OF ACTION
Do Not Pay Tax Petition to Tax Court
AT ANY STAGE OF PROCEDURE:
You can agree and arrange to pay.
You can ask the IRS to issue you a notice of deficiency so that you can file a petition with the Tax Court.
You can pay the tax and file a claim for a refund.
Consideration of Claim for Refund
Appeals Office
Preliminary Notice 30-Day Letter
District Court
Tax Court
CHOICE OF ACTION
Court of Appeals (for your district)
Court of Federal Claims
U.S. Court of Appeals for the Federal Circuit
U.S. Supreme Court

The U.S. Tax Court tries only tax cases. The taxpayer does not pay the alleged deficiency, but files suit against the IRS Commissioner to stop the collection of tax. The court consists of 19 judges, and a jury trial is not available. The Small Claims Division may try the case if the deficiency is equal to or less than $50,000.

The U.S. District Court tries tax cases, as well as many other types of civil and criminal cases. The taxpayer pays the alleged deficiency and files suit against the U.S. government for a refund.

There are 95 district courts, and a jury trial is available. If the taxpayer has filed for bankruptcy, the Federal Bankruptcy Division may try the case.

The U.S. Court of Federal Claims tries tax cases, as well as other cases against the federal government. The taxpayer pays the alleged deficiency and files suit against the U.S. government for a refund. The court consists of 16 judges, and a jury trial is not available.

The table below summarizes the courts of original jurisdiction.

EXHIBIT 14A.3: COURTS OF ORIGINAL JURISDICTION

	U.S. Tax Court	U.S. District Court	U.S. Claims Court
Number of Courts	1	95	1
Number of Judges	19	1 (per court)	16
Jurisdiction	National	District	National
Subject Matter	Tax Only	Criminal & Civil	Claims Against Govt.
Pay Deficiency?	No	Yes	Yes
Jury Available?	No	Yes	No
Where to Appeal?	US Court of Appeals	US Court of Appeals	US Court of Appeals - Fed Circuit

The appropriate appellate court depends on which trial court hears the case. If the case is tried in the Tax Court or District Court, the appeals are taken to the U.S. Court of Appeals. Appeals from the Claims Court are taken to the U.S. Court of Appeals for the Federal Circuit.

BUSINESS ENTITIES

PARTNERSHIP

TAXATION OF A PARTNERSHIP

Tax Ramifications of Business Operation of a Partnership

The partner's adjusted taxable basis in his or her partnership interest must be adjusted each year to reflect the allocated items of income and expense. Adjusted taxable basis is increased by a partner's distributive share of both taxable and nontaxable partnership income, and is decreased by the partner's share of partnership losses, nondeductible expenses, and distributions.

Continuing with the example above, if the ABC partnership reported earnings of $40,000 for the first year, Tom, a 50 percent partner, would report $20,000 of ordinary income on his federal income tax return even if no cash was actually distributed. His basis in the partnership after the first year would be adjusted to $75,000 ($55,000 original basis + $20,000 of allocated

income). Since Tom is a general partner, the $20,000 distributable share of partnership earnings would also be subject to self-employment tax.

Tax Ramifications of Withdrawals or Distributions from a Partnership

Partners may withdraw cash or property from the partnership to meet their needs or as advance payments of their share of partnership income. Regardless of the reason for the withdrawal, the recipient partner generally recognizes no gain on the distribution. Instead, the withdrawal is treated as a return of capital that reduces the partner's adjusted taxable basis in the partnership. For example, if Tom, the ABC partner, withdrew the $20,000 earned, his adjusted taxable basis would return to $55,000. Once the partner's basis has been reduced to zero, any additional withdrawals taken from the partnership will result in a capital gain to the partner.

FAMILY LIMITED PARTNERSHIP

family limited partnership (FLP) - a limited partnership of family members that is used to generate valuation discounts for estate and gift tax purposes on the transfer of the limited interest in the partnership

A **family limited partnership** (FLP) is an estate planning technique utilizing a limited partnership of family members. The arrangement is generally structured so that a senior family member transfers appreciating, capital intensive property, such as real estate, to a limited partnership in return for a minimal general partnership interest (typically 1 percent) and a significant limited partnership interest (typically 99 percent). Over the senior family member's lifetime, the limited partnership interests are transferred to junior family members by gift or sale.

One of the primary objectives of the family limited partnership arrangement is to generate valuation discounts for estate and gift tax purposes on the transfer of the limited interest in the partnership. The estate and gift tax value of a limited partnership interest in a properly structured family limited partnership typically is determined by applying minority interest and lack of marketability discounts.

- *Minority Interest Discount* - A reduction in value of an asset transferred is often allowed if the asset transferred represents a minority interest in a business. A minority interest is any interest that, in terms of voting, is not a controlling interest. Since minority owners cannot control the business or compel its sale or liquidation, outside buyers would not be willing to pay the same amount for a minority interest as they would for a majority or controlling interest.
- *Lack of Marketability Discount* - A reduction in value of an asset transferred is often allowed if the asset transferred has an inherent lack of marketability. Limited partnership interests in a family limited partnership are more difficult to sell than interests in other assets such as publicly traded stock. Therefore, a discount is often allowed for the lack of marketability.

The family limited partnership has many advantages. One of the major advantages is that the senior family member can retain control of the business, since the senior family member is the only family member with a general partnership interest (limited partners are not allowed to participate in the management of the business). Additional advantages of this technique include creditor protection and the ability to place restrictions on transfers of limited partnership interests by junior family members. Also, it can allow income shifting from higher to lower tax bracket family members.

Management Operation and Decision Making of a Family Limited Partnership

The management of a family limited partnership is the same as that of a limited partnership. The general partner manages the partnership and is directly responsible for the day-to-day operation of the business. Thus, the partnership can change its operational direction at any time and relatively quickly.

Legal Liability of a Family Limited Partnership

The general partner (senior family member) has unlimited liability for the acts of the partnership, the other partners, and obligations made by any partner or the partnership in the performance of partnership duties. The limited partners (junior family members) are treated as investors, liable only for the amount of his or her investment and their respective shares of profits and losses are subject to the passive activity rules.

Taxation of a Family Limited Partnership

The partnership agreement will govern how partnership income is divided among the partners. Generally, both general and limited partners share income and cash flow based on their percentage interest in the partnership. The taxable income of the FLP is reported annually and allocated to each partner on the basis of that partner's percentage interest. The allocation is noted on the Form K-1 issued to each partner. Usually, the general partner annually distributes at least enough cash to pay the income tax liability attributable to each partner. Distributions from the partnership are not taxable to the extent the partner has basis in the partnership interest. Distributions to the extent of basis are return of capital. The partnership itself (unlike a corporation) is not subject to tax, because it passes through all items of income and deduction to the partners.

CORPORATION

Legal Liability of a Corporation

The shareholders' liability for the acts, omissions, debts, and other obligations of the corporation generally is limited to the shareholders' capital contributions. There are several situations, however, in which the shareholders will be held personally liable for the debts of the corporation:

- A lender to a closely held corporation requires that the primary shareholders guarantee the loan to the corporation. If this is the case, the shareholders are liable to the extent of their guarantees, in addition to their capital contribution.
- A court may ignore the legal fiction of the corporation as an entity (pierce the corporate veil) when the corporation has been used to perpetuate fraud, circumvent law, accomplish an illegal purpose, or otherwise evade law.
- The courts may disregard the corporate form of entity if the corporation is not maintained

CHAPTER 15

Introduction to Retirement Planning

LEARNING OBJECTIVES:

After learning the material in this chapter, you will be able to:

1. Define financial security.
2. Identify and understand the major factors that affect retirement planning.
3. Understand the work life expectancy/retirement life expectancy dilemma.
4. Explain the impact that timeliness of savings has on savings accumulation.
5. Discuss the balance that must be achieved between increasing and decreasing retirement income needs.
6. Define the Wage Replacement Ratio (WRR) and explain how it is used to estimate retirement income needs.
7. Differentiate between the top-down approach and the budgeting approach to calculating the Wage Replacement Ratio.
8. Discuss the qualitative factors that affect retirement planning.
9. Differentiate among the three capital needs analysis calculations: the basic, pure annuity model, the capital preservation model (CP), and the purchasing power preservation model (PPP).
10. Determine capital needs for various clients.
11. Make projections to prepare a capital needs analysis presentation.

INTRODUCTION

One of the main goals for many individuals is long-term financial security and independence. This goal is realized when a person is financially secure enough to live at his or her desired comfort level without the need for employment income. Financial security at retirement requires individuals to carefully plan. Unfortunately, the majority of American workers have no idea how much money they will need to fund their retirement. When coupled with changes in Social Security, tax laws, the economy, and the value structure of our society, retirement planning becomes a necessary, but difficult and time-consuming process. Due to the complex nature of retirement planning, financial planners often are enlisted to provide direction and guidance. This chapter discusses the fundamental concepts that financial planners must know to effectively plan for a client's retirement. Chapter 16 discusses the characteristics of actual retirement plans.

BASIC FACTORS AFFECTING RETIREMENT PLANNING

There are several basic factors that affect retirement planning. The following areas must be considered: the remaining work life expectancy (WLE), the retirement life expectancy (RLE), basic savings concepts, the annual income needed (needs), the wage replacement ratio (WRR), the sources of retirement income, inflation, investment returns, and other qualitative factors.

REMAINING WORK LIFE EXPECTANCY (RWLE)

work life expectancy (WLE) - the years that a person spends in the work force, generally 30-40

remaining work life expectancy (RWLE) - work period remaining at a certain point in time prior to retirement

Work life expectancy (WLE) is the period of time a person is in the work force, generally 30-40 years. There has been a substantial decline in the overall work life expectancy (WLE) due to increased education, which causes later entry into the workforce, and early retirement.

Remaining work life expectancy (RWLE) is the work period that remains at a certain point in time before retirement. For example, a 50-year-old client who expects to retire at age 62 has a RWLE of 12 years. Determining the remaining work life expectancy is important for the financial planner because it tells the planner the remaining number of years the client has to save for retirement. In the past normal retirement age was most often 65, because it was the retirement age historically set forth by the Social Security Administration. Today, however, the average retirement age is several years less than 65, with 62 being a common retirement age. People often opt for early retirement because of a heightened awareness of retirement planning, as well as the substantial economic growth that many individuals attained through wise investment decisions. This early retirement trend is illustrated in Exhibit 15.1.

EXHIBIT 15.1: MEDIAN RETIREMENT AGE FROM 1965-2005

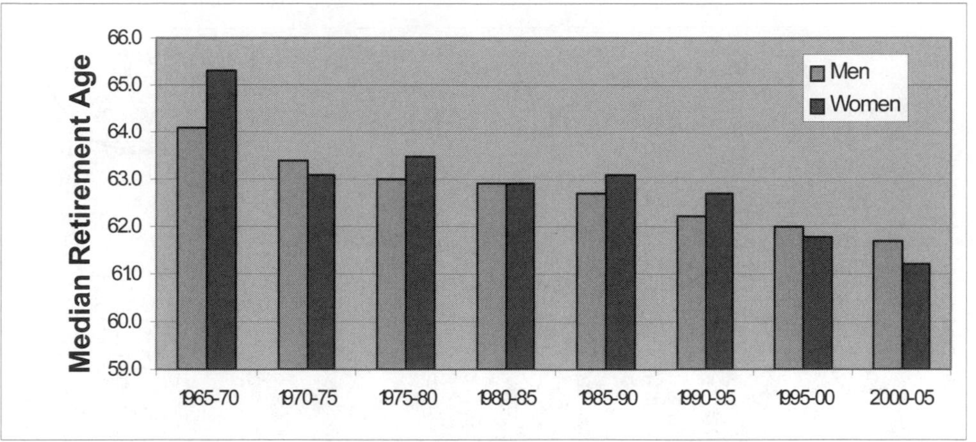

Median Retirement Age
66.0
65.0
64.0
63.0
62.0
61.0
60.0
59.0
Men
Women
1965-70
1970-75
1975-80
1980-85
1985-90
1990-95
1995-00
2000-05

Source: U.S. Bureau of Labor Statistics

As the chart illustrates, both men and women are retiring earlier. Exhibit 15.2 presents a skewed distribution of all retirees' retirement ages. Notice that the area identified as A represents 93 percent of the area of the curve, illustrating that approximately 93 percent of all individuals retire between ages 62 and 65 (inclusive). Exhibit 15.2 is significant to financial planners as it demonstrates that most clients will retire between 62 and 65 years of age.

EXHIBIT 15.2: AVERAGE RETIREMENT AGE (U.S.)

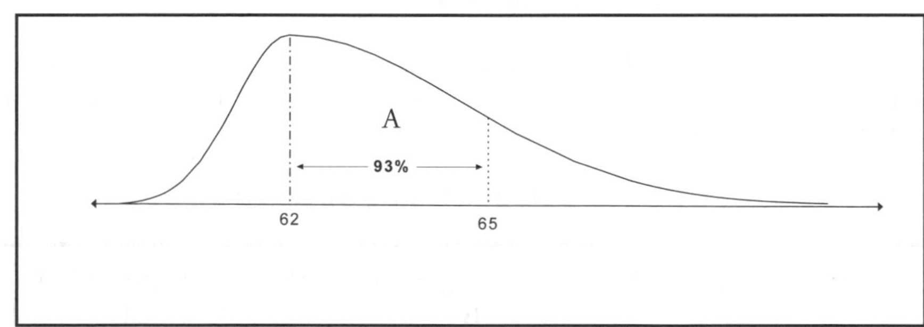

A
93%
62
65

RETIREMENT LIFE EXPECTANCY (RLE)

Retirement life expectancy (RLE) is the time period beginning at retirement and extending until death. While the average RLE for a group of 65-year-olds is approximately 20 years, it is common that clients live beyond this statistical average. In 1900, the average life expectancy for a newborn was 47 years. The average life expectancy has risen to 77.6 years for those born in 2003. This increase in life expectancy, and the corresponding increase in RLE, is a direct result of a decline in the death rate, especially the birth mortality rate. The overall death rate has declined due to medical and technological advances in disease diagnoses, cures, and prevention. With each new medical advancement, life expectancy will, no doubt, increase. Exhibit 15.3 presents the data depicting the increase in life expectancy from 1980 to 2003.

retirement life expectancy (RLE) - that time period beginning at retirement and extending until death; the RLE is the period of retirement that must be funded

EXHIBIT 15.3: LIFE EXPECTANCY AT BIRTH (U.S. 1980 – 2003)

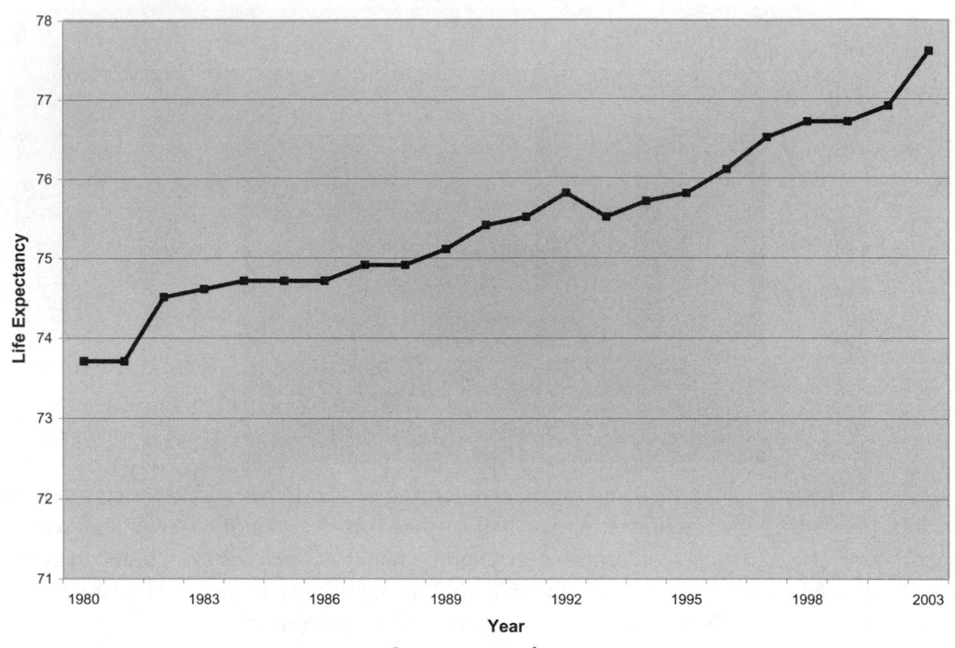
78
77
76
75
74
73
72
71
Life Expectancy
1980
1983
1986
1989
1992
1995
1998
2003
Year

Source: www.cdc.gov

THE WLE AND THE RLE RELATIONSHIP

It is important that the financial planner understand the WLE and the RLE relationship. If either period changes, the other period is affected. Exhibit 15.4 presents the work life expectancy/retirement life expectancy dilemma.

EXHIBIT 15.4: THE WLE/RLE DILEMMA

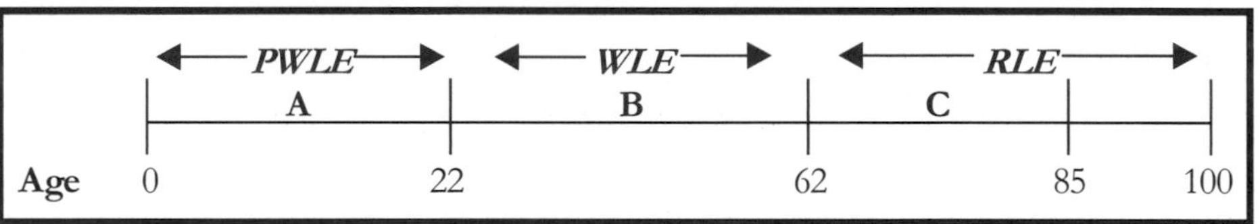
PWLE
WLE
RLE
A
B
C
Age
0
22
62
85
100

Area A represents the prework life expectancy (PWLE) and lasts until the person enters the work force on a full-time basis. Generally, the PWLE ends between ages 18 - 26, with an average age of 22. Area B, the work life expectancy (WLE), represents the period of working years before retirement. This period begins at the end of the PWLE and ends at the beginning of C, the retirement life expectancy (RLE), usually around age 62. The RLE (Area C) generally lasts to age 85, but may continue beyond age 100. With a longer RLE period to finance and a shortened WLE in which to save and accumulate assets, careful planning is needed to meet the funding requirements for a financially secure retirement.

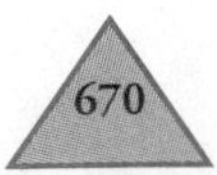

SAVINGS CONCEPTS

The savings amount, the savings rate, the timing of savings, and investment decisions are important concepts in retirement planning. If our society were adequately saving for retirement beginning at an early age, people would be saving about 10 percent of their gross annual income and investing in a broad portfolio of growth investments over their entire work life. They would be ever mindful of investment returns and inflation to ensure sufficient savings. Unfortunately, workers save at a much lower rate than is necessary, are not investment savvy, and are, generally, insensitive to the impact of inflation.

SAVINGS AMOUNT

In general, persons who begin the financial security planning process at an early age (25-30) should save 10-15 percent of their gross annual pay. If individuals do not begin at an early age, then they must save a greater amount of their gross pay to compensate for the missed years of contributions and compounding. Exhibit 15.5 shows how much individuals must save if they choose to wait until later years to begin saving for retirement.

EXHIBIT 15.5: REQUIRED SAVINGS RATE FOR RETIREMENT

Age beginning regular and recurring savings*	Savings (as percent of gross pay) rate required to create appropriate capital*
25–35	10–13%
35–45	15–18%
45–55	20–25%
55-65	30–35%

*Assumes appropriate asset allocation for reasonable-risk investor through accumulation year; also assumes normal raises and an 80 percent wage replacement ratio at Social Security normal retirement age.

Exhibit 15.5 illustrates a major problem with delaying retirement savings. Namely, many individuals find it difficult to begin saving such large amounts even if they are accustomed to saving. Saving requires foregoing current consumption, and most individuals find it difficult to decrease consumption by 20-30 percent, especially when they have been accustomed to maintaining a certain standard of living for long periods of time.

SAVINGS RATE

Exhibit 15.5 identifies a major concern for any planner because the average personal savings rate in the U.S. has plummeted to less than 4 percent in the year 2004. Exhibit 15.6 illustrates this sharp decline.

EXHIBIT 15.6: U.S. PERSONAL SAVINGS RATE (1990-2004)

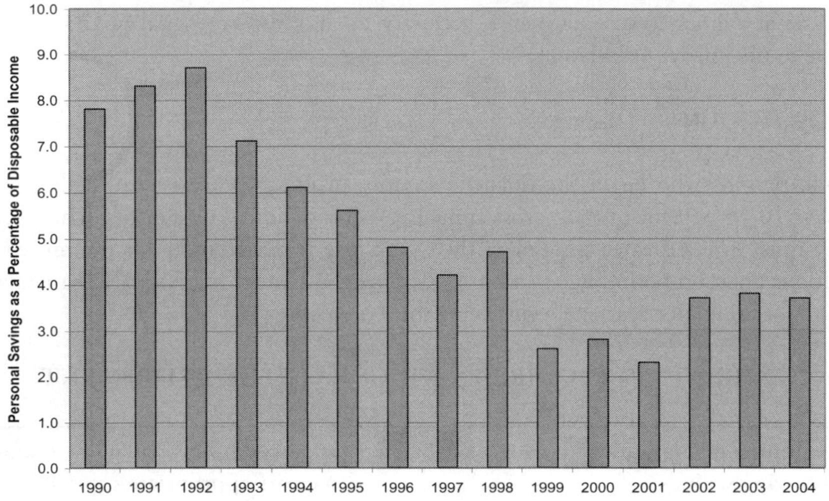

TIMING OF SAVINGS

The earlier a person saves, the greater the number of future compounding periods available before retirement. A greater number of compounding periods leads to a lower required savings rate and a larger accumulation of capital at retirement. When savings is delayed, the power of compounding is lost and individuals must compensate by saving a greater percentage of their disposable income.

EXAMPLE

Ann saves $3,000 a year from age 25-34 inclusively and invests in an account earning 8 percent annually. Ann stops investing at age 34, but does not withdraw the accumulation until age 65. Ann's accumulation at age 65 is $472,300 even though she only deposited $30,000. In contrast, Bob saves $3,000 a year from age 35-65 inclusively and invests in a similar account to Ann, earning 8 percent annually. Even though Bob saved $93,000 more than Ann, he will have accumulated $102,300 less than Ann at age 65. The deposits and balance at age 65 for Ann and Bob are presented in Exhibit 15.7.

EXHIBIT 15.7: TIME/SAVINGS EXAMPLE (ACCUMULATION AT AGE 65)

	Ann	Bob
Total Invested (OA)	$30,000	$93,000
Balance at 65	$472,300	$370,000
Earnings Rate	8%	8%

It may seem strange that while Bob invested more than three times as much as Ann, Ann has 28 percent more than Bob at age 65. This result demonstrates the power of compound earnings over the longer period of 41 years versus 31 years. Exhibit 15.8 shows this phenomenon graphically.

EXHIBIT 15.8: EXAMPLE ACCUMULATION

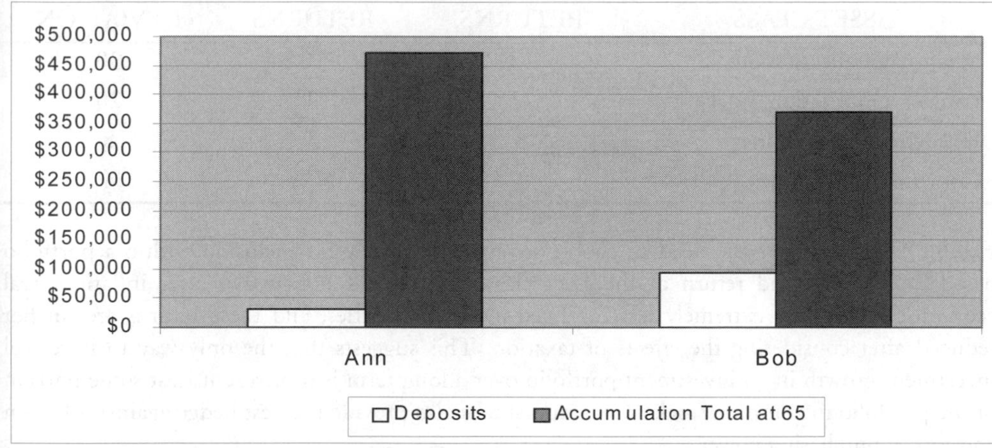
$500,000
$450,000
$400,000
$350,000
$300,000
$250,000
$200,000
$150,000
$100,000
$50,000
$0
Ann
Bob
Deposits
Accumulation Total at 65

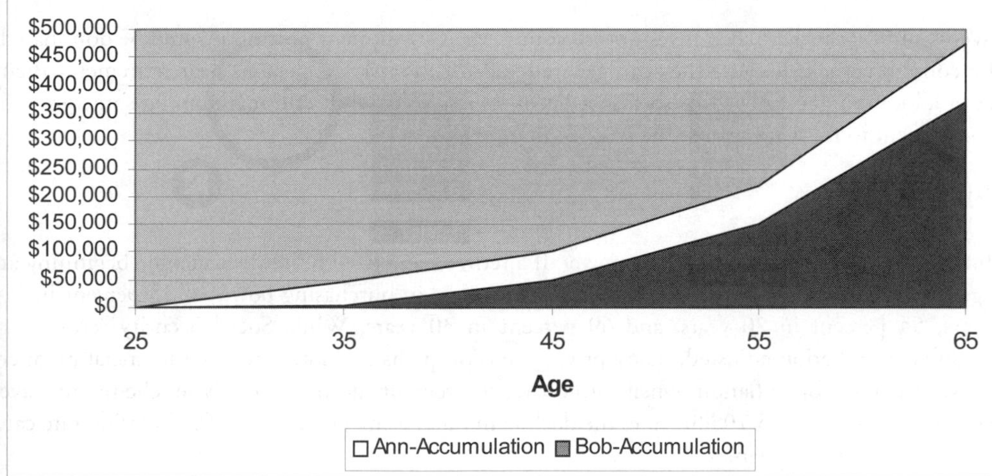
$500,000
$450,000
$400,000
$350,000
$300,000
$250,000
$200,000
$150,000
$100,000
$50,000
$0
25
35
45
55
65
Age
Ann-Accumulation
Bob-Accumulation

INVESTMENT DECISIONS

A fundamental understanding of investment decisions and their consequences is essential to retirement planning. In this chapter, we will briefly identify some of the relationships between investments and retirement planning. More in-depth investment information is provided in Chapter 12 of this book.

All assets do not have the same historical investment returns. When planning for retirement, it is important to have a historical perspective of investment returns for various investment alternatives. Exhibit 15.9 provides a 70 year perspective on historical investment returns, inflation- adjusted returns, and risk as measured by standard deviation.

EXHIBIT 15.9: HISTORICAL RETURNS, INFLATION-ADJUSTED RETURNS, AND STANDARD DEVIATION OF ASSET CLASSES (1932 – 2001)

ASSET CLASS	HISTORICAL RETURNS	INFLATION-ADJUSTED RETURNS	STANDARD DEVIATION
Small-Capitalization Stocks	13	10	30
Large-Capitalization Stocks	11	8	20
Fixed-Income Securities	6	3	8
Consumer Price Index (CPI)	3	N/A	4

Exhibit 15.9 illustrates the need to choose investments wisely for inclusion within a portfolio based on the risk and return of the asset class. You should notice that after inflation, real economic returns are extremely low for fixed-income securities, and these returns are further reduced after considering the effects of taxation. This suggests that the only way to have real investment growth in an investment portfolio over a long term is to invest at least some portion of the portfolio in common stocks. Common stocks also provide the best hedge against inflation and loss of purchasing power.

We would expect that when investors are young, their investment portfolio would be dominated by common stocks because they can generally afford the risk. As persons near retirement, their asset allocation generally shifts so that it becomes less risky while still maintaining some growth component to mitigate against the risk of inflation.

INFLATION

Inflation causes a loss of purchasing power. If a retiree has a fixed retirement income beginning at age 65 and inflation is 4 percent, the retiree has a loss in purchasing power of 33 percent in 10 years, 54 percent in 20 years, and 69 percent in 30 years. While Social Security retirement benefits are inflation adjusted, many private pension plans are not. Thus, the financial planner must account for inflation when projecting retirement needs and advise clients to save accordingly. Exhibit 15.10 illustrates the decline in purchasing power that a 4% inflation rate can cause over a 50-year span.

EXHIBIT 15.10: IMPACT OF INFLATION

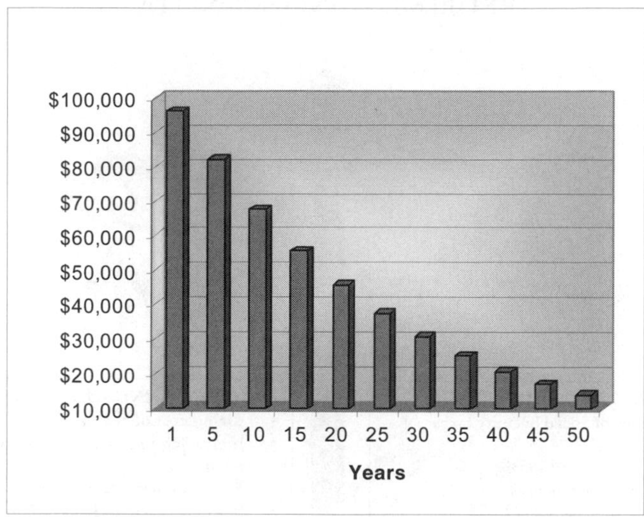
$100,000
$90,000
$80,000
$70,000
$60,000
$50,000
$40,000
$30,000
$20,000
$10,000
1 5 10 15 20 25 30 35 40 45 50
Years

DEFINING THE RETIREMENT GOAL (NEEDS)

How much money and/or income does a person need to be financially independent? Most persons entering retirement intend to maintain the same lifestyle they had prior to retirement. Clients generally do not radically reduce their expenses downward unless it is necessary. When a retirement budget is prepared, it should have similar amounts as the preretirement budget with a few adjustments. Some costs in retirement will decrease, and others will increase. The reduced costs in retirement may include: (1) the elimination of costs associated with employment (certain clothing costs, parking, some meal costs); (2) the elimination of mortgage costs if the mortgage debt is scheduled to be repaid by retirement; (3) the elimination of costs of children (tuition, clothes); (4) the elimination of payroll costs—FICA; and (5) the elimination of savings because the plan will require the use of accumulated savings. For some persons, retirement can bring increased spending on travel and other lifestyle changes. Some retirees are at risk for increases in health care costs. Exhibit 15.11 presents lists of potential decreasing and increasing costs when entering retirement.

EXHIBIT 15.11: BALANCING INCREASING AND DECREASING RETIREMENT INCOME NEEDS

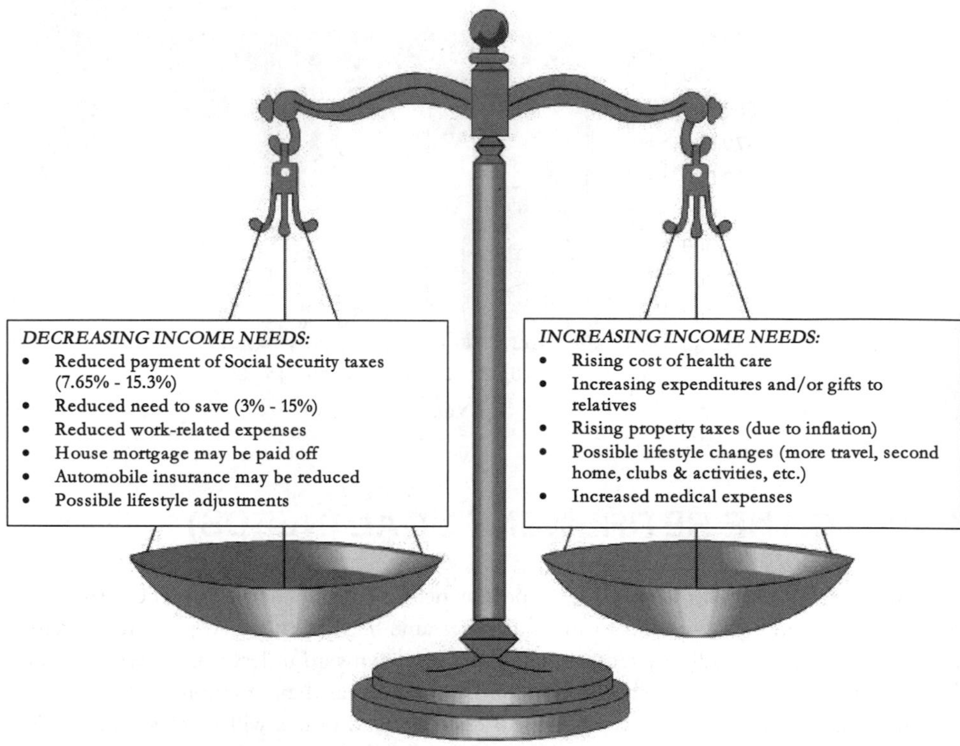
DECREASING INCOME NEEDS:
Reduced payment of Social Security taxes (7.65% - 15.3%)
Reduced need to save (3% - 15%)
Reduced work-related expenses
House mortgage may be paid off
Automobile insurance may be reduced
Possible lifestyle adjustments
INCREASING INCOME NEEDS:
Rising cost of health care
Increasing expenditures and/or gifts to relatives
Rising property taxes (due to inflation)
Possible lifestyle changes (more travel, second home, clubs & activities, etc.)
Increased medical expenses

PLANNING FOR RETIREMENT - PRETAX OR AFTER TAX

It is possible to plan retirement needs either pretax or after tax. Many financial planners calculate needs in pretax dollars believing that pretax is what their clients best understand. The pretax assumption is that clients are more likely to know their gross income than to know their net after-tax cash flow. Therefore, planners create retirement plans pretax, and the clients simply pay whatever income taxes for which they are liable out of their gross retirement income, similar to what clients do during preretirement years. Many CPAs think in terms of after-tax dollars and, therefore, plan for retirement after tax. After-tax planning assumes that income taxes are paid before other retirement needs. Planning can be effective either way as long as the client understands the pretax or after-tax planning choice.

wage replacement ratio (WRR) - an estimate of the percent of income needed at retirement compared to earnings prior to retirement

WAGE REPLACEMENT RATIO (WRR)

The **wage replacement ratio** (WRR) is an estimate of the percent of annual income needed during retirement compared to income earned prior to retirement. The wage replacement ratio or percentage is calculated by dividing the amount of money needed on an annual basis in retirement by the preretirement income. For example, if a client in the last year of work (prior to retirement) makes $100,000, and that client needs $80,000 in the first retirement year to

maintain the same preretirement lifestyle, the wage replacement ratio (WRR) is 80 percent (80,000 ÷ 100,000).

CALCULATING THE WAGE REPLACEMENT RATIO

There are two alternative methods to calculate the wage replacement ratio—the top-down approach and the budgeting approach (or bottom-up approach).

Top-Down Approach

The top-down approach is commonly used with younger clients where expenditure patterns are likely to change dramatically over time. As clients approach retirement age, a more precise wage replacement ratio should be calculated using a budgeting approach. The top-down approach estimates the wage replacement ratio using common sense and percentages.

EXAMPLE

To illustrate, assume a 40-year-old client earns $50,000 a year, pays 7.65 percent of his gross pay in Social Security payroll taxes, and saves 10 percent of his gross income annually. If we assume that any work-related savings resulting from retirement are expected to be completely offset by additional spending adjustments during retirement, and that the client wants to maintain his exact preretirement lifestyle, we would expect that the client would need a wage replacement ratio of 82.35% (100% – 7.65% - 10%).

$50,000	=	100.00%	of salary
(5,000)	=	(10.00%)	current savings
(3,825)	=	(7.65%)	payroll taxes
$41,175	=	82.35%	wage replacement ratio

Notice that the client is currently living on 82.35 percent of his gross pay. The remaining 17.65 percent is paid to FICA taxes and savings. Therefore, the 82.35 percent is a reasonable estimate, or proxy, of the amount necessary, as a percentage of current income, to maintain the preretirement lifestyle.

Budgeting Approach

The second method used to calculate the wage replacement ratio is called the budgeting approach. It is used with older clients because as a person nears retirement, it is possible to examine the actual expenditure patterns of the person. In cooperation with the client, the planner can determine which costs in the current (preretirement) budget will change (plus or minus) in the retirement budget, and thus determine with greater precision than the top-down approach an estimate of actual retirement needs.

EXAMPLE

A and *B* each make $100,000 in preretirement income. *A* has arranged his financial affairs such that he will have no mortgage payment or car payment while in retirement. *B*, on the other hand, expects to continue to have both a mortgage payment and a car payment throughout the majority of his retirement years. Exhibit 15.12 illustrates that while *A* will need a 59.1 percent WRR, *B* will need a 77.1 percent WRR. The difference is due to *B's* $15,000 mortgage payment and $3,000 car payment.

EXHIBIT 15.12: BUDGETING APPROACH TO WAGE REPLACEMENT RATIO

	Client A & B Budget	Client A Retirement Budget	Client B Retirement Budget
Income (Current) Budget	$100,000	$100,000	$100,000
Expenses:	Current	Retirement	Retirement
Income Taxes	$27,650	$20,000	$20,000
Food	4,800	4,800	4,800
Utilities/Phone	2,400	2,400	2,400
Mortgage	15,000	0	15,000
Social Security Taxes	2,500	0	0
Health Insurance	1,000	1,000	1,000
Auto Insurance	1,000	1,000	1,000
Entertainment	5,000	5,000	5,000
Clothing	2,000	1,500	1,500
Auto Maintenance/Operation	1,000	750	750
Auto Payment	3,000	0	3,000
Church	4,800	4,800	4,800
Savings	12,000	0	0
Miscellaneous	17,850	17,850	17,850
Total Expenses	$100,000	$59,100	$77,100
Wage Replacement Percent Needed		59.1%	77.1%

Does a person really need the same wage replacement percentage throughout the entire retirement period? There are clear indications that consumption slows dramatically as people age. The 70-80 percent wage replacement ratio is probably most appropriate from the beginning of retirement regardless of age, until the late 70s. It appears that a person's consumption past the age of 80 declines primarily due to limited mobility. While this may be correct for society at large, certain individuals will incur dramatic medical costs during the latter part of their retirement period. Therefore, while most who study retirement expenditures would suggest a consumption function similar to the one provided in Exhibit 15.13 below, such a model may not apply to a particular individual.

EXHIBIT 15.13: REAL CONSUMPTION BY AGE

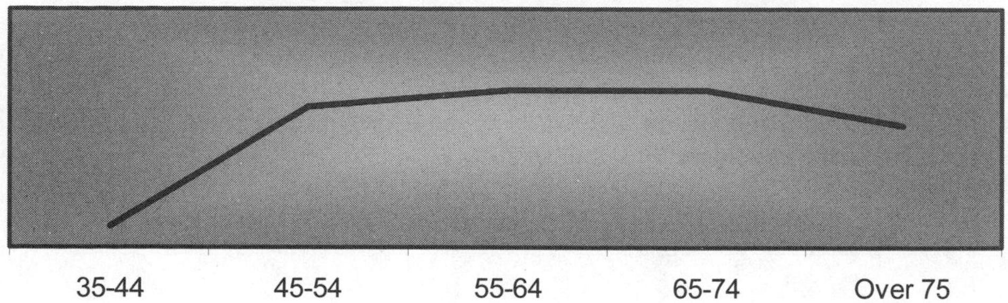
35-44
45-54
55-64
65-74
Over 75

Exhibit 15.14 presents the adjustments from preretirement to retirement in terms of estimated percentages. Notice that many of the adjustments in Exhibit 15.14 will be client-specific.

EXHIBIT 15.14: ADJUSTMENTS FROM PRERETIREMENT TO RETIREMENT

From Preretirement Income to Retirement Income Needs Adjustments to Expenditures	
Adjustments which decrease income needs:	Amount or Percent Saved
▲ No longer pay Social Security taxes	7.65% to 15.3%
▲ No longer need to save	3% to 15%
▲ No longer pay house mortgage	Maybe
▲ No longer pay work-related expenses	*
▲ Auto insurance may be reduced	*
▲ Possible lifestyle adjustments	*
Adjustments which may increase income needs:	
▲ Increasing cost of health care	*
▲ Lifestyle changes	*
▲ Increase in travel	*
▲ Second home	*
▲ Clubs and activities	*
▲ Expenditures on family/gifts/grandchildren	*
▲ Increased property taxes	*

* Amounts must be estimated for each individual

Many expert financial planners conclude that most clients need approximately 70-80 percent of their preretirement current income to retire and maintain their preretirement lifestyle. While many clients would fall into this range, there are also those particularly frugal clients who may need as little as 40 percent of preretirement income, and others who need substantially more than the 80 percent wage replacement ratio (usually due to corporate perks that are discontinued in retirement).

THE SOURCES OF RETIREMENT INCOME

Retirees generally rely on three sources of income for retirement. These sources include: Social Security, private pension plans, and personal savings. All three sources complement each other to provide adequate retirement income. Exhibit 15.15 shows the average amount of income for the average retiree from each of these three sources.

EXHIBIT 15.15: RETIREMENT INCOME SOURCES

Pensions
20%

Social Security
38%

Savings
42%

Source: Social Security Administration, Fast Facts and Figures about Social Security, June 2003

SOCIAL SECURITY

Social Security provides the foundation of retirement earnings. Social Security covers almost all occupational groups (except 25 percent of state and local government employees) with retirement benefits adjusting for inflation. It is considered the safety net of a secure income, but for most income levels it will not be a sufficient source of income replacement during retirement. Social Security retirement benefits provide a wage replacement ratio ranging from less than 20 percent (for high-income earners) to approximately 80 percent (for low-income earners who have a same age, nonworking spouse). As demonstrated in Exhibit 15.16, Social Security is an adequate wage replacement for lower wage earners to maintain their lifestyle, but is clearly inadequate to provide sufficient replacement income for middle-to-upper-wage earners. (Social Security and Social Security benefits are covered in detail in Chapter 11).

EXHIBIT 15.16: SOCIAL SECURITY AS A WAGE REPLACEMENT PERCENTAGE (FOR INDIVIDUALS OF VARIOUS EARNINGS)

Current Earnings	Wage Replacement Ratio Provided by Social Security*	With Same Age, Nonworking Spouse
$13,100	52%	78%
$20,000	41%	62%
$25,000	37%	56%
$28,924	35%	53%
$35,000	33%	49%
$46,663	30%	45%
$72,100	25%	38%
$100,000	21%	31%
$200,000	11%	16%

*Estimated based on single person at normal retirement age in 2005. A same age, nonworking spouse would receive 50 percent of the benefits of the covered worker.

PRIVATE PENSION AND COMPANY-SPONSORED RETIREMENT PLANS

Private pension plans are the second source of retirement income. Private pension plans provided by employers are covered in Chapter 16. As you will see, private pension plans have dramatically changed over the last few years from employer-sponsored and funded plans to employee self-reliance plans, putting more and more emphasis on personal savings as the primary source of retirement income for middle-to-upper-wage workers.

PERSONAL SAVINGS

Personal savings is the third source of retirement income and is the one that is most influenced by the individual. The more personal savings put aside for retirement, the larger the accumulation at retirement and the larger the retirement income for the individual.

Exhibit 15.6 showed the significant decrease in personal savings since 1990. As shown, the savings rate has fallen from 7.9 percent of disposable income in 1990 to 3.7 percent in 2004.

Whenever a retiree has income from invested assets, it can mean a substantially higher overall retirement income. The median income of those retirees with asset income is more than twice as large as the income of retirees with no asset income. As the two pie charts in Exhibit 15.17 illustrate, retirees without asset income are concentrated in the lowest income categories.

EXHIBIT 15.17: RETIREES WITH INCOME FROM PERSONAL ASSETS

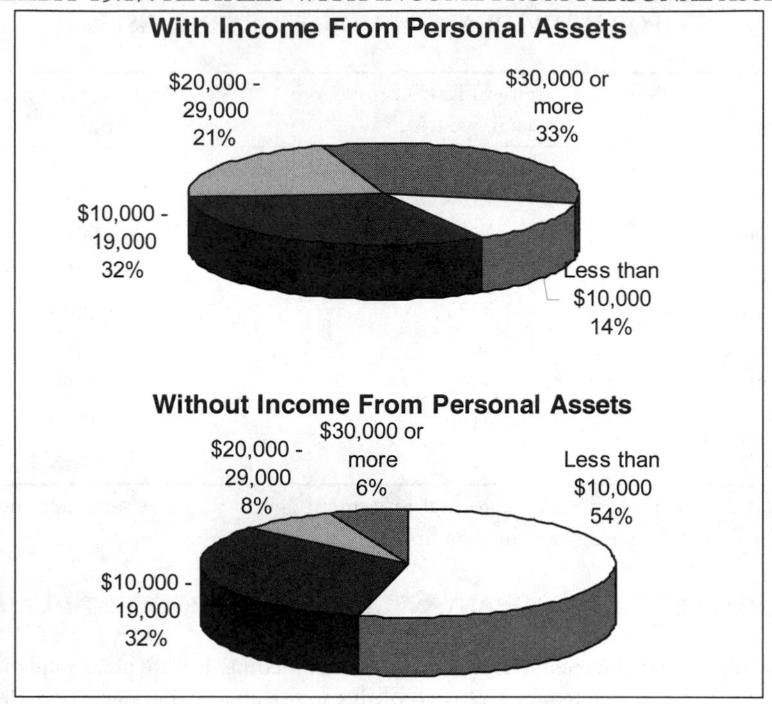

With Income From Personal Assets
$20,000 - 29,000 21%
$30,000 or more 33%
$10,000 - 19,000 32%
Less than $10,000 14%
Without Income From Personal Assets
$30,000 or more 6%
$20,000 - 29,000 8%
Less than $10,000 54%
$10,000 - 19,000 32%

QUALITATIVE FACTORS IN RETIREMENT—ADVISING CLIENTS

Qualitative factors associated with retirement are no less important than the financial or quantitative factors. Qualitative factors include involuntary versus voluntary retirement; emotional and psychological factors, such as loss of esteem and boredom; and the decision to relocate.

The best overall advice financial planners can give their clients is to know themselves and their support system; have a well-planned qualitative side to retirement; and have a system in place to maintain their egos and self-esteem. Many persons in our culture define themselves by what they do. The mere act of going to work may be a ritual or a habit that provides that person with a sense of self worth and with a reason to live. A trusted colleague at the workplace may be a source of support and personal gratification. Voluntary retirement, even when well planned, means change—and change is difficult.

Involuntary retirement, if perceived as undesirable, can be as devastating an impact on an individual as the death of a loved one or a bitter divorce. The client may follow the same psychological pattern of grief—shock, anger, denial, and acceptance. Financial planning professionals need to recognize the emotional state of clients and realize that when someone is emotionally troubled, major decisions, financial or otherwise, are sometimes best delayed. Rather than abruptly making important financial decisions, it may be better to do the minimum financial maneuvering during a grieving period. Such grieving may last for a period of a year or longer. Trying to optimize the financial situation when the client is emotionally unable to determine his or her goals or priorities is probably counterproductive and may add stress to the situation.

A client's decision to change physical locations after retirement (for example, move to another state) should be carefully considered over a long period of planning. Some retirees do not realize that when they move, they will have a completely new environment to adjust to, as well as a substantial loss of their former support system of friends and family. Someone considering moving should conduct a trial transition over a number of years, spending increasingly longer periods at the desired location. This gradual adjustment will help determine if what the retiree believes will actually enhance retirement will, in fact, be true. Persons considering retiring abroad will encounter even more change, thereby necessitating even more detailed planning.

SUMMARY OF FACTORS AFFECTING RETIREMENT PLANNING

Financial planners may encounter clients who subjectively "feel" they are financially secure because they have a good job and/or a good net worth. If a good job is lost through premature death, disability, lay off, job termination, unexpected illness, etc., or if the net worth decreases dramatically, the client's financial security is suddenly lost. Thus, the actual determination of financial security is objective rather than subjective. Therefore, the financial planner is the intermediary between the client's subjective feelings and the overall objective of financial security.

Other factors that complicate the retirement planning process include at least two societal issues. Our society has become more mobile with the traditional family unit deteriorating. Having lost the close connection to family, older persons may not be able to depend on family to provide retirement assistance. Thus, there is a greater need for financial independence for each individual. Additionally, because our society seems to place more value on youth than on age and wisdom in the workplace, retirees have less chance of being hired for part-time employment, which could supplement retirement income.

Many people begin planning for retirement too late in life and save too little to effectively meet retirement capital accumulation needs. Some people do not give retirement funding a thought until they are in their 40s. Even when people do save, many of them make poor investment choices and, therefore, have poor investment returns.

Inflation reduces purchasing power. To recipients of fixed incomes, inflation is like a progressive tax causing declining purchasing power. Exhibit 15.18 lists the factors that frustrate effective retirement planning and the negative impact associated with each factor.

Where on the Web

AARP (formerly American Association of Retired Persons) *www.aarp.org*

American Society on Aging *www.asaging.org*

International Foundation for Retirement Education *www.infre.org*

MSN Money - Retirement, and Wills *www.moneycentral.msn.com/retire/home.asp*

National Council on the Aging *www.ncoa.org*

Senior Law *www.seniorlaw.com*

Social Security Online *www.ssa.gov*

The Retire Early Homepage *www.retireearlyhomepage.com*

The U.S. Administration on Aging *www.aoa.gov*

U.S. Census Bureau *www.census.gov*

EXHIBIT 15.18: FACTORS THAT NEGATIVELY AFFECT RETIREMENT PLANNING AND THEIR IMPACT ON THE PLANNING PROCESS

FACTORS	IMPACT
Reduced WLE	Insufficient savings period
Increased RLE	Increases capital needs
Reduced family reliance	Fewer alternatives in retirement
Reduced ability to work	Fewer alternatives in retirement
Planned too late	Fewer compounding periods
Low savings rate	Unable to meet capital requirements
Inflation	Reduces purchasing power
Poor earnings rate and asset allocation	Unable to meet capital requirements

Long-term financial security does not happen automatically. It requires careful planning, a clear understanding of the quantification of the goal, and identification and management of the risks that are present. Retirement planning requires the collection and projection of data and must be conducted meticulously and conservatively.

RISKS TO FINANCIAL INDEPENDENCE

There are many risks to achieving financial independence. Selected risks are identified in Exhibit 15.19. It is a wise idea to start saving early, save a sufficient amount, invest wisely, and not underestimate retirement needs or the impact of inflation. The risks identified in Part B of Exhibit 15.19 are more thoroughly discussed in the chapters on risk management and insurance.

EXHIBIT 15.19: SUMMARY OF FACTORS AFFECTING RETIREMENT PLANNING

FACTOR	RISK	MITIGATOR
PART A: Risks Discussed in this Chapter		
Work Life Expectancy (WLE)	Shortened due to untimely death, disability, health, unemployment	Life insurance, disability insurance, health insurance, education, training, experience
Retirement Life Expectancy (RLE)	Lengthened	Adequate capital accumulation
Savings rate, amount, and timing	Too low and too late	Save enough; start early
Inflation	Greater than expected	Conservatively estimate inflation and needs
Retirement needs	Underestimated	Use wage replacement estimators
Investment returns	Inadequate to create necessary retirement capital	Knowledge of and investments in broad portfolio of diversified investments and proper asset allocation
Sources of retirement income	Overestimation of Social Security benefits, private pension plans, or personal income (or adverse changes in taxation of such income)	Conservatively estimate and plan for such income Monitor income projections and tax policy
PART B: Risks Discussed in Insurance Chapters		
Qualitative factors including changes in lifestyle, employment, and major assets	Unexpected cost increases due to changes in personal situation; losses due to perils	Plan conservatively to provide for the unexpected; property and liability insurance

CAPITAL NEEDS ANALYSIS

Capital needs analysis is the process of calculating the amount of investment capital needed at retirement to maintain the preretirement lifestyle and mitigate the impact of inflation during the retirement years. There are three methods for analyzing capital needs: the basic annuity method, the capital preservation model, and the purchasing power preservation model.

capital needs analysis - the process of calculating the amount of investment capital needed at retirement to maintain the preretirement lifestyle and mitigate the impact of inflation during the retirement years

Basic Planning – Annuity Method

The following steps are used to determine the capital necessary at the beginning of retirement to fund the retirement period:

Step 1 - Calculate WRR. Determine the wage replacement ratio (WRR) today using one of the two methods identified earlier (top-down or budgeting).
Step 2 – Determine gross dollar needs. Determine the wage replacement amount in today's dollars from Step 1.
Step 3 – Determine net dollar needs. Reduce the result from Step 2 by any expected Social Security benefits in today's dollars or other benefits that are indexed to inflation.
Step 4 – Calculate preretirement dollar needs inflated. Inflate the result from Step 3 to the retirement age at the CPI rate to determine the first annual retirement payment.

Step 5 – Calculate capital needed at retirement age. Calculate the present value at retirement of an annuity due for an annual payment equal to the result from Step 4 over the full retirement life expectancy (estimate life expectancy conservatively at 90-93) and use the inflation-adjusted earnings rate.

Step 6- Determine the amount to save during the work life expectancy. Discount the capital needed at retirement using the savings rate and investment earnings rate, being mindful as to whether the client is expected to save annually or more frequently, and whether the client is expected to save under an annuity due or an ordinary annuity scheme.

EXAMPLE

Mary Jones, age 41, currently makes $80,000. Her wage replacement ratio is determined to be 80 percent. She expects that inflation will average 3 percent for her entire life expectancy. She expects to earn 10 percent on her investments and retire at age 62, living possibly to age 90. She has sent for and received her Social Security benefit statement, which indicated that her Social Security retirement benefit in today's dollars adjusted for early retirement is $12,000 per year.

1. Calculate Mary's capital needed at retirement at age 62.
2. Calculate the amount she must save monthly, at month end, assuming she has no current savings to accumulate the capital needed for retirement at age 62.
3. Calculate the amount she must save monthly, at month end, assuming that she has $50,000 in current retirement savings.
4. Calculate her capital needed at retirement at age 62.

Step 1	80% WRR		
Step 2	($80,000 × 0.80)	=	$64,000 Total needs in today's dollars
Step 3			– 12,000 Less Social Security in today's dollars
			$52,000 Annual amount needed in today's dollars
Step 4	n	=	21 (62 – 41)
	i	=	3 (inflation)
	PV	=	$52,000 (Step 3)
	PMT	=	0
	FV	=	$96,735.32 (Step 4) First year needs for retirement
Step 5	n	=	28 (90 – 62)
	i	=	6.7961 [(1 + earnings rate/1 + inflation rate) – 1] × 100
			[(1.10 ÷ 1.03) – 1] × 100
	FV	=	0
	PMT_{AD}	=	$96,735.32 (from Step 4) this is also an annuity due
	$PV_{AD@62}$	=	$1,278,954.49 (Step 5 – amount needed at age 62)

5. Calculate the amount she must save monthly, at month end, assuming she has no current savings to accumulate the capital needed for retirement at age 62.

$FV_{@62}$	=	\$1,278,954.46 (from Step 5)
n	=	252 (21 years × 12 months)
i	=	0.83333 (10% ÷ 12)
PV	=	0
PMT_{OA}	=	\$1,502.09 (monthly savings necessary)

6. Calculate the amount she must save monthly, at month end, assuming she has \$50,000 in current retirement savings.

$FV_{@62}$	=	\$1,278,954.46
n	=	252
i	=	0.83333
PV	=	– \$50,000
PMT_{OA}	=	\$1,026.70 (monthly savings necessary)

Accurate Assumptions are Essential

Assumptions are made for the wage replacement ratio, the work life expectancy, the retirement life expectancy, inflation, earnings, Social Security and any other benefits. If these assumptions are inaccurate, the projection using those assumptions will be flawed. The wage replacement ratio should be carefully calculated, especially for a client near retirement. Estimating life expectancy usually begins with the IRS tables and is conservatively estimated at 90-93, due to the risk of outliving retirement money. Where family history indicates a particularly long life expectancy, that age could be increased. The estimate of the work life expectancy is critical, as one less year of work means one less year of saving and one less year of retirement funding. Conversely, working one additional year may make an otherwise unworkable retirement plan work quite nicely due to the additional year of savings, the additional year of earnings accumulation, and one less year of consumption.

The assumptions regarding inflation and earnings rates are obviously essential ingredients in capital needs analysis. Historical data is available for inflation; however, inflation is hard to predict. Perhaps the best estimate is the inflation rate for the most recent few years. Earnings rates are dependent on the client's asset allocation and the markets, but can be estimated for a well-diversified portfolio over a long period. It is wise to conservatively estimate inflation (up a little) and conservatively estimate earnings (down a little). Such estimation provides a little conservatism in case one or more of the assumptions are not realized. Social Security benefits and pension benefits that are inflation protected should be carefully determined and documented. The retirement plan and capital needs analysis can be adjusted on an annual basis as information becomes more certain.

As one might expect, small changes in earnings, life expectancy, and needs may have a dramatic impact on the retirement plan. The uncertainty of these assumptions can be accommodated in some of the latest retirement planning software packages that incorporate Monte Carlo analysis

(MCA). MCA uses a random number generator for inputs into a software package that will provide an output with specific probabilities of outcomes. MCA provides insight into the most likely outcome, but with other possible outcomes. Provided with this analysis, the financial planner also gets a best-case scenario and a worst-case scenario with which to make decisions.

Advanced Planning – Capital Preservation Model (CP)

pure annuity concept - the basic capital needs analysis approach that is generally prepared on a pretax basis

capital preservation model (CP) - a capital needs analysis method that assumes that at life expectancy, the client has exactly the same account balance as he did at retirement

The basic capital needs analysis is a **pure annuity concept,** generally prepared on a pretax basis. The annuity concept means that if all of the assumptions happen exactly as expected, the person will die exactly at the assumed life expectancy with a retirement account balance of zero. There is a substantial risk that many clients could outlive their assets using an annuity approach. Therefore, they will actually need more money at retirement. Two models used to mitigate the risk of outliving money are the capital preservation model and the purchasing power preservation model. The **capital preservation model** assumes that at life expectancy, as estimated in the annuity model, the client has exactly the same account balance as he did at retirement. The purchasing power preservation model assumes that the client will have a capital balance of equal purchasing power at life expectancy as he did at retirement. In spite of any conservatism that we may have built into the annuity model with our assumptions, it is always possible that one or more of our assumptions will be unrealized. To mitigate against the risk of the assumptions being overly optimistic, we can make use of a capital preservation model or a purchasing power preservation model rather than a simple annuity model to determine capital needs. These two additional models help to overcome the risks of the pure annuity model (primarily the risk of running out of money).

The capital preservation model maintains the original capital balance needed at retirement for the entire retirement life expectancy. Recall that the amount needed for Mary Jones at age 62 calculated from our previous example was $1,278,954.46. If we discount that amount at the expected earnings rate of 10%, then we can determine the additional amount of capital necessary to leave an estate of $1,278,954.46.

$n = 28$

$i = 10$

$FV_{@90}$ = $1,278,954.46 (amount at life expectancy)

$PV_{@62}$ = $88,686.99

1,367,641.48 = 88,686.99 + 1,278,954.49 (amt. needed for capital preservation model)

Thus, the capital preservation model will require $88,686.99 more at retirement than the pure annuity model, but will reduce the risk of running out of money (superannuation). Such an increase in capital will also require that savings be increased in the Mary Jones example Parts B and C.

EXHIBIT 15.20: COMPARISON OF THE CAPITAL PRESERVATION MODEL WITH THE ANNUITY METHOD (MARY JONES)

	CAPITAL PRESERVATION MODEL		ANNUITY MODEL	
	No Savings	Savings	No Savings	Savings
	B	C	B	C
$FV_{@62}$	$1,367,641.48	$1,367,641.48	$1,278,954.49	$1,278,954.49
n	252	252	252	252
i	0.83333	0.83333	0.8333	0.8333
PV	0	– $50,000	0	– $50,000
PMT_{OA}	$1,606.25	$1,130.86	$1,502.09	$1,026.70

Even though the capital preservation model would increase the savings need of Mary Jones by about $100 per month, it would mitigate against many of the risks in the traditional capital needs annuity approach.

Advanced Planning—Purchasing Power Preservation Model (PPP)

An even more conservative approach to capital needs analysis is the **purchasing power preservation model**. This model essentially maintains the purchasing power of the original capital balance at retirement.

purchasing power preservation model (PPP) - a capital needs analysis method that assumes that the client will have a capital balance of equal purchasing power at life expectancy as he did at retirement

The capital balance of $1,278,954.49 is used as the future value, and then the entire calculation made in the original capital preservation model is repeated. By doing this, the $1,278,954.46 is simultaneously inflated at the rate of inflation and discounted at the earnings rate.

n = 28

i = 6.7961

FV = 1,278,954.49

PMT = $96,735.32 (amount needed the first year of retirement

$PV_{AD@62}$ = $1,481,866.64(capital needed for purchasing power preservation model)

The additional accumulation at retirement using a purchasing power model is $202,912.18 greater than the pure annuity approach.

The answers to B and C in the example would change.

EXHIBIT 15.21: COMPARISON OF THE PURCHASING POWER MODEL WITH THE ANNUITY METHOD (MARY JONES)

	PURCHASING POWER MODEL		ANNUITY MODEL	
	No Savings B	Savings C	No Savings B	Savings C
$FV_{@62}$	$1,481,866.64	$1,481,866.64	$1,278,954.49	$1,278,954.49
n	252	252	252	252
I	0.83333	0.83333	0.8333	0.8333
PV	0	– $50,000	0	– $50,000
PMT_{OA}	$1,740.41	$1,265.02	$1,502.09	$1,026.70

EXHIBIT 15.22: CAPITAL NEEDS ANALYSIS SUMMARY FOR MARY JONES

	ANNUITY MODEL	CAPITAL PRESERVATION MODEL	PURCHASING POWER PRESERVATION MODEL
Capital needed at retirement (A)	$1,278,954.49	$1,367,641.45	$1,481,866.64
Monthly savings with no initial balance (B)	$1,502.09	$1,606.25	$1,740.41
Monthly savings with $50,000 initial balance (C)	$1,026.70	$1,130.86	$1,265.02

There are other methods of mitigating risk in projections, including sensitivity analysis, that are beyond the scope of this text, most of which would be covered in a full semester course on retirement planning.

PROFESSIONAL FOCUS

What percentage do you use to calculate wage replacement ratio?

I normally use 70% to 85% of preretirement income or wages as an estimate of the beginning retirement income needed in today's dollars. The specific percentage depends on a variety of factors. For clients who are near retirement, I often help them prepare a beginning retirement budget rather than using an income or wage replacement ratio.

What are your expectations of (and your clients') of Social Security?

I believe that Social Security retirement benefits will continue for current retirees at substantially the same rates. I believe that benefits for future retirees will be reduced in some way, especially for younger clients. The population demographics will require changes in contributions, benefits or rates of return on reserves for Social Security to remain viable. For most of my clients, I include Social Security benefits in the retirement calculations, but some younger clients ask me to leave them out. I occasionally prepare a plan with and without Social Security benefits at the request of the clients. I will consider actual changes in Social Security benefits in financial plan updates.

Do you help your clients determine their appropriate ages for retirement?

My new clients normally come to me with an idea of when they want to retire. I sometimes need to encourage them to choose a more realistic retirement age by showing them some preliminary calculations. Since reducing the retirement age by one year both reduces the saving/investment period by one year and increases the distribution period by one year, the quantitative impact of a one-year change can be significant. If clients begin planning early, they can usually prepare financially for a retirement or financial independence age that is earlier than normal.

How do you determine life expectancy for retirement planning?

I usually visit briefly with clients about their ancestors' life spans and hereditary diseases, about their own health and lifestyles, and about medical developments. Then I encourage them to plan to live to at least age 90 for financial planning purposes. Depending on our discussion and family circumstances, we often plan for even longer life expectancies.

What qualitative issues do you discuss with your clients prior to retirement to make their transition into retirement smoother?

I often discuss with clients the importance of having interesting things to do during retirement, adjustments to spending more time with each other (for couples), travel plans, health issues, continuing to work on a part-time basis, unexpected consequences of moving at the time of retirement and a variety of other qualitative issues. Since I know my clients rather well, the topics I mention are usually customized for the individual client. Most importantly, I encourage clients to talk to their friends who have retired recently about retirement transitions. My clients who get along well with each other and who have interesting things planned for retirement normally make the transition very well.

E. Vance Grange, Ph.D., CPA, CFP®

DISCUSSION QUESTIONS

1. What is the U.S. savings rate?
2. List the steps necessary to calculate capital needs analysis.
3. What is the difference between capital needs analysis prepared on an annuity basis and capital needs analysis prepared using a capital preservation model? A purchasing power presentation model?
4. What are the three sources of retirement income?
5. What are the two methods for determining the wage replacement ratio?
6. Which method for determining the wage replacement ratio is appropriate for a client who is 50 years old? Why?
7. How is financial security defined?
8. List the financial factors that affect retirement planning.
9. Should retirement planning (capital needs analysis) be prepared on a pretax basis or an after-tax basis? Why?
10. What percent of retirement income is provided by Social Security for the average retiree?
11. Does Social Security favor lower-wage or higher-wage individuals in terms of retirement benefits and wage replacement? How and why?
12. What is the central mission for individuals regarding personal financial planning?
13. When is financial security realized?
14. What is the WLE?
15. What is the RWLE?
16. How has life expectancy changed since 1980?
17. How and why does the timing of savings affect the ultimate amount of accumulation?
18. How does inflation affect retirement planning?
19. What adjustments are normally made to the preretirement budget to arrive at the retirement budget?
20. What is the wage replacement ratio?
21. Does the wage replacement ratio remain constant over the retirement life expectancy?
22. What wage replacement ratio does Social Security provide for a worker with $20,000 income and a same age spouse?
23. What is capital needs analysis?
24. What advanced methods are used to perform capital needs analysis?

EXERCISES

1. Donna, age 45, is self-employed and makes $70,000 today. She is fairly settled in her lifestyle. She currently saves 15 percent of her gross income. Her mortgage payment (P&I) is fixed at $1,166.67 per month. She has scheduled her mortgage payments to cease at retirement. What do you expect Donna's wage replacement ratio to be based on the above information?
2. Kim, age 30, begins saving $2,500 per year at year-end, continues for 8 years, then she quits saving. Joy, age 40, begins saving $2,500 per year at year-end and saves continuously until age 65. Assume that both Kim and Joy earn 12 percent compounded annually. Calculate the total amount of savings and the accumulated balance for Kim and Joy, respectively, at age 65. Explain the difference.

Use the following information for Exercises 3 – 10:

Mike, age 48, currently has $60,000 saved for retirement. He is currently saving $5,000 of his annual income of $50,000 on a monthly basis. His employer matches his savings contributions with $1,500 annually, paid on a monthly basis. Mike projects that inflation will be 3.5 percent and he can earn 9.5 percent before and during retirement. Mike needs a wage replacement ratio of 75 percent of his preretirement income. He plans to retire at age 62 with Social Security benefits of $10,000 in today's dollars. His life expectancy is to age 90.

3. How much will Mike's salary be at age 62 if he receives raises equal to inflation?
4. How much are the Social Security benefits expected to be at age 62?
5. What will be Mike's retirement needs in the 1st year of retirement, excluding Social Security?
6. How much capital will Mike need at age 62 to fund his retirement?
7. How much will Mike have at 62, assuming he continues his current savings and investment program?
8. How much additional monthly savings would be required for Mike to retire at age 62?
9. After reflection, Mike wants to know at what age he can retire, assuming he continues to follow his current savings plan. Make a schedule for years 62, 64, and 66 so Mike can make some choices.
10. You remind Mike that if he waits to age 66 to retire, he will receive $14,344 in Social Security benefits in today's dollars rather than the reduced benefit of $10,000 he was to receive at age 62. Would this additional cash flow suggest that he could retire at age 66, or perhaps earlier?
11. Mary Blue, age 65, is a pensioner who receives a fixed pension of $17,500 for life from her employer's pension plan. Mary also receives $12,000 currently from Social Security. Mary is concerned about how inflation will affect her rent, food, and other expenses. She estimates that inflation will be 3 percent per year for the next 10 years. What loss of purchasing power will she have in today's dollars in 10 years?
12. George Michael, a financial planner, has determined that Dennis Zabloski, his client, needs $2,000,000 at age 66 to retire using an annuity method based on a retirement income of $150,337.75 per year for 24 years to age 90. If the earnings rate was 10 percent and the inflation rate was 3 percent, what additional amount would be needed at age 66 to provide a capital preservation model solution?
13. Referring to Exercise 12, how much would Dennis need at age 66 to fund a purchasing power presentation model?

PROBLEMS

Bill, age 45, wants to retire at age 60. He currently makes $60,000 per year. He has an objective to replace 80 percent of his preretirement income. He wants the retirement income to be inflation adjusted. Bill has an investment portfolio valued at $150,000, which is currently earning 10 percent average annual returns. Bill expects inflation to average 3 percent and based on his family health he predicts he will live to age 90. Bill is currently saving 7 percent of his gross income at each year-end and expects to continue this level savings amount. Bill wants to ignore any Social Security benefits for purposes of planning.

1. What will Bill's annual needs be at age 60?
2. Will the need be for an ordinary annuity or an annuity due?
3. How much total capital will Bill need at age 60?
4. How much will Bill have at age 60?
5. Will Bill have enough?
6. What is the earliest age that Bill could retire utilizing the current savings and investment plan?
7. How much would Bill need to increase his savings on an annual basis to meet his goal of retiring at age 60?
8. Even assuming that Bill increases his savings to an appropriate amount, what are the risks that may affect the success of the plan?
9. How would you modify the capital needs analysis to reduce the risks identified above?

CHAPTER 16

Basic Retirement Plans

LEARNING OBJECTIVES:

After learning the material in this chapter, you will be able to:

1. Describe a qualified retirement plan.
2. Identify and articulate the characteristics of qualified retirement plans.
3. Describe some disadvantages of qualified retirement plans.
4. Define vesting and list two accepted vesting schedules.
5. Identify the reasons for the creation of qualified retirement plans.
6. Calculate and determine the benefits of tax deferral in a qualified retirement plan.
7. Identify the various types of qualified retirement plans.
8. Distinguish between pension and profit-sharing plans.
9. Distinguish between defined-benefit plans and defined-contribution plans.
10. Distinguish between noncontributory and contributory plans.
11. Describe the operations and benefits of a 401(k) plan.
12. Distinguish between Keogh and corporate plans.
13. Identify other tax-advantaged, but nonqualified, retirement plans.
14. Describe IRAs, SEPs, SIMPLEs, and 403(b) plans.
15. Describe distributions from qualified retirement plans and other tax-advantaged retirement plans.
16. Describe and identify nonqualified plans.
17. Clarify why nonqualified plans are useful to employers.

RETIREMENT PLANS

In the previous retirement chapter, we discussed the three general sources of funding used to provide retirement income—Social Security, private retirement plans, and personal savings. It was determined that the retirement benefits from Social Security alone provided a poor wage replacement ratio during retirement except for those beneficiaries who are the lowest wage earners. This chapter provides an introduction to private retirement plans, including qualified retirement plans, other tax-advantaged retirement plans, and nonqualified plans. Exhibit 16.1 illustrates the various types of retirement plans.

EXHIBIT 16.1: RETIREMENT PLANS

QUALIFIED PLANS		OTHER TAX-ADVANTAGED PLANS	NONQUALIFIED PLANS
Pension Plans	Profit-Sharing Plans		
Defined-Benefit Plans	Profit-Sharing Plans	SEPs	Deferred-Compensation Plans
Cash-Balance Plans	Stock Bonus Plans	IRAs (including Roth)	Nonqualified Stock Option Plans
Money-Purchase Pension Plans	ESOPs	403(b) Plans	Incentive Stock Option Plans
Target-Benefit Plans	401(k) Plans	SIMPLE (IRA)	Phantom Stock Plans
	Thrift Plans		Split-Dollar Life Insurance
	SIMPLE 401(k)		457 Plans
	Age-Based, Profit-Sharing Plans		
	New Comparability Plans		

QUALIFIED RETIREMENT PLANS

Qualified retirement plans are sponsored by either a self-employed individual or another employer. The word "qualified" means that the plan meets Internal Revenue Service requirements. To encourage retirement savings, Congress has created or approved various savings schemes that are somewhat tax advantaged. As a result of being qualified, there are tax advantages that accrue to the employer who sponsors the plan and to the employees who participate in the plan.

Exhibit 16.2 summarizes the advantages and disadvantages of qualified plans.

EXHIBIT 16.2: ADVANTAGES AND DISADVANTAGES OF QUALIFIED RETIREMENT PLANS

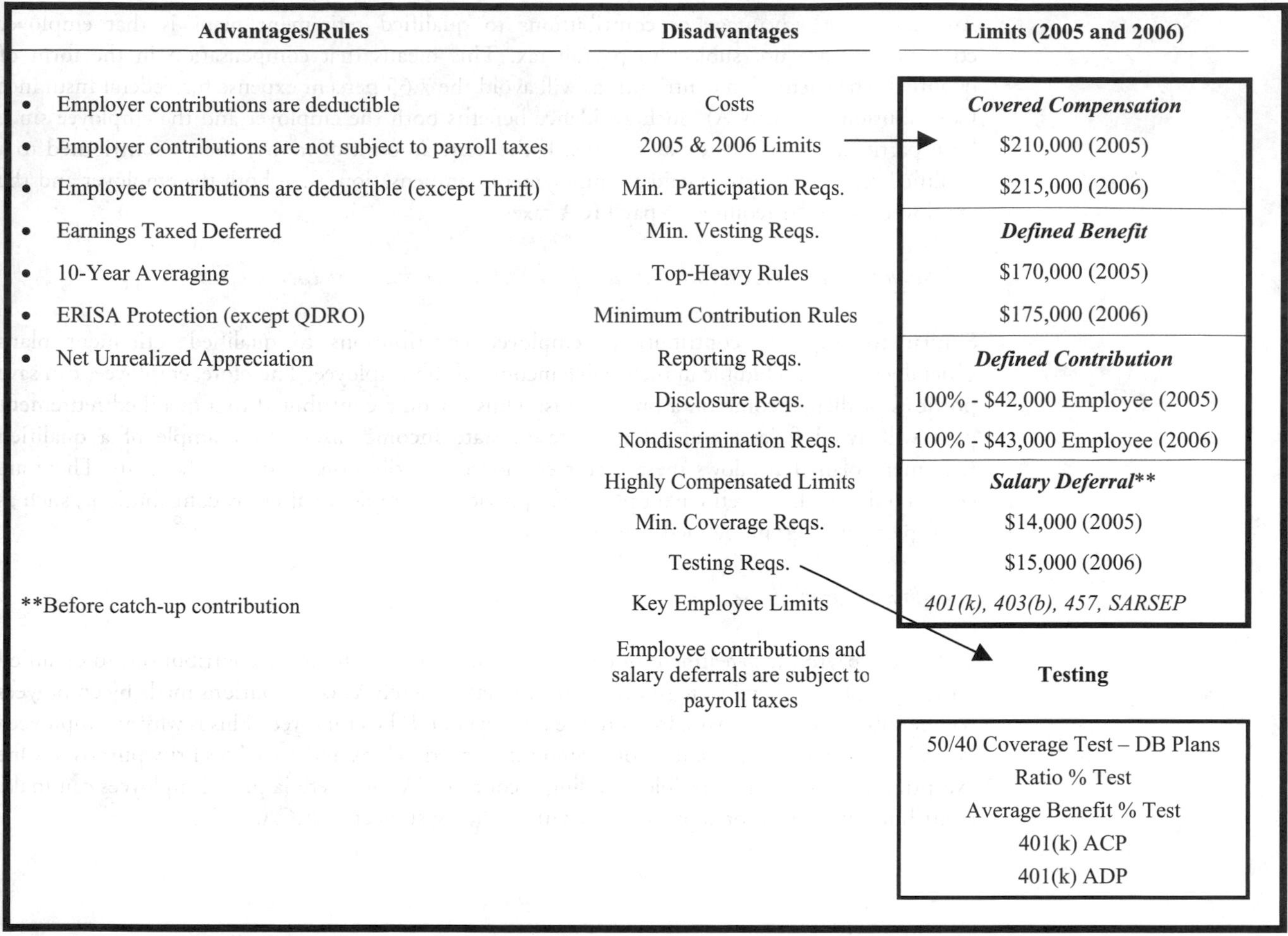

Advantages/Rules	Disadvantages	Limits (2005 and 2006)
• Employer contributions are deductible	Costs	***Covered Compensation***
• Employer contributions are not subject to payroll taxes	2005 & 2006 Limits →	$210,000 (2005)
• Employee contributions are deductible (except Thrift)	Min. Participation Reqs.	$215,000 (2006)
• Earnings Taxed Deferred	Min. Vesting Reqs.	***Defined Benefit***
• 10-Year Averaging	Top-Heavy Rules	$170,000 (2005)
• ERISA Protection (except QDRO)	Minimum Contribution Rules	$175,000 (2006)
• Net Unrealized Appreciation	Reporting Reqs.	***Defined Contribution***
	Disclosure Reqs.	100% - $42,000 Employee (2005)
	Nondiscrimination Reqs.	100% - $43,000 Employee (2006)
	Highly Compensated Limits	***Salary Deferral*****
	Min. Coverage Reqs.	$14,000 (2005)
	Testing Reqs. →	$15,000 (2006)
**Before catch-up contribution	Key Employee Limits	*401(k), 403(b), 457, SARSEP*
	Employee contributions and salary deferrals are subject to payroll taxes	**Testing**
		50/40 Coverage Test – DB Plans Ratio % Test Average Benefit % Test 401(k) ACP 401(k) ADP

Characteristics of Qualified Retirement Plans

Employer Contributions are Not Subject to Federal Income Tax

Unlike most business transactions that result in an income tax deduction for one party and taxable income for another party, contributions made to qualified retirement plans result in a mismatch of income and deductions. Employer contributions to a qualified plan are deductible for income tax purposes for the year in which they were made, but they are not included in current employee taxable income. This favorable tax treatment is a major advantage for both employers and employees. Employers receive a current deduction, while employees receive deferral of income. Because of this favorable tax treatment, however, qualified retirement plans must satisfy numerous testing requirements to ensure that a certain percentage of the nonhighly compensated employees are benefiting from the plan.

Employer Contributions are Not Subject to Payroll Tax

Another major advantage of contributions to qualified retirement plans is that employer contributions are not subject to payroll tax. This means that compensation in the form of qualified retirement plan contributions will avoid the 7.65 percent expense for Federal Insurance Contributions Act (FICA). Such avoidance benefits both the employer and the employee since both parties are required to pay this tax. If the same amount of money that is contributed to a qualified retirement plan is paid as employment compensation, then both the employer and the employee would be required to pay FICA taxes.

Employee Pretax Contributions are Not Subject to Federal Income Tax

Similar to employer contributions, employee contributions to qualified retirement plans generally are not includible in the taxable income of the employee. Therefore, employees can save portions of their income on a pretax basis. Thus, income contributed to a qualified retirement plan will avoid federal and, in most cases, state income taxes. An example of a qualified retirement plan that allows these pretax employee contributions is the 401(k) plan. There are certain older qualified retirement plans that provide for employee after tax contributions, such as thrift plans and certain defined-benefit plans.

Employee Contributions are Subject to Payroll Tax

Unlike the payroll tax treatment of employer contributions, employee contributions to qualified retirement plans generally are subject to payroll tax. Therefore, contributions made by employees will be subject to FICA taxes, for both the employer and the employee. This is why an employee's Form W-2 may have different income amounts for federal tax and Social Security purposes. One exception to this rule is a flexible spending account (FSA) or cafeteria plan. Employees can make contributions to FSAs on a pretax basis without being subject to FICA.

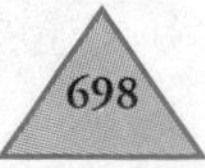

EXHIBIT 16.3: FORM W-2

a Control number	22222	Void ☐	For Official Use Only ▶ OMB No. 1545-0008
b Employer identification number (EIN)	1 Wages, tips, other compensation	2 Federal income tax withheld	
c Employer's name, address, and ZIP code	3 Social security wages	4 Social security tax withheld	
	5 Medicare wages and tips	6 Medicare tax withheld	
	7 Social security tips	8 Allocated tips	
d Employee's social security number	9 Advance EIC payment	10 Dependent care benefits	
e Employee's first name and initial / Last name	11 Nonqualified plans	12a See instructions for box 12 Code	
	13 Statutory employee ☐ Retirement plan ☐ Third-party sick pay ☐	12b Code	
	14 Other	12c Code	
f Employee's address and ZIP code		12d Code	

15 State	Employer's state ID number	16 State wages, tips, etc.	17 State income tax	18 Local wages, tips, etc.	19 Local income tax	20 Locality name

Form **W-2** **Wage and Tax Statement** **2005**

Department of the Treasury—Internal Revenue Service

For Privacy Act and Paperwork Reduction Act Notice, see back of Copy D.

Copy A For Social Security Administration — Send this entire page with Form W-3 to the Social Security Administration; photocopies are **not** acceptable.

Cat. No. 10134D

Do Not Cut, Fold, or Staple Forms on This Page — Do Not Cut, Fold, or Staple Forms on This Page

Tax-Deferred Growth

Assets that are contributed to a qualified retirement plan are held in trust for the benefit of the employees/participants or their beneficiaries. Qualified retirement plan trusts are tax-exempt entities; therefore, the earnings accruing from contributions from both employers and employees grow income-tax-deferred until distributed. The tax-deferred growth of both contributions and earnings is a major benefit that qualified retirement plans provide.

Special Income Tax Averaging

There is a provision for special ten-year-forward income tax averaging on lump-sum distributions made from qualified retirement plans. This provision may reduce the federal income tax liability for taxpayers taking a full and complete distribution from a qualified retirement plan. Only those taxpayers who were born prior to January 1, 1936, however, are eligible for this special rule.

In addition to receiving special income tax averaging, taxpayers born prior to January 1, 1936, may also be eligible to receive capital gains treatment on a portion of their lump-sum distribution. The portion of a distribution that may receive capital gains treatment is that which is attributable to participation in the qualified plan prior to 1974.

Net Unrealized Appreciation

In general, distributions from qualified retirement plans are made in cash and are taxable as ordi income. There is an exception, however, for lump-sum distributions of employer securities (gene stock) that have appreciated while being held in a qualified retirement plan. When such securities distributed (typically in the form of a lump-sum distribution) from a qualified retirement plan, appreciation above the cost basis, called net unrealized appreciation (NUA), is not subject to inc tax upon distribution. In addition, the net unrealized appreciation will be taxed as a capital gain as ordinary income), when the securities are sold. With the large disparity between ordinary inc tax rates (35%) and capital gains tax rates (15%), this exception provides significant benefit taxpayers who receive qualifying distributions of employer securities. It should be noted that special treatment is not available for distributions from Individual Retirement Accounts (IR Therefore, a rollover of otherwise qualifying securities from a qualified retirement plan to an IRA eliminate this potential benefit.

ERISA Protection

Assets held in a qualified retirement plan are protected from creditors by the Employee Retiren Income Security Act (ERISA). ERISA prohibits the alienation of benefits, which means that benefits of the qualified retirement plan may be used only by the participant or by the particip family members. Therefore, even those unfortunate individuals who are forced into bankruptcy l protection for their qualified retirement plan assets.

Timing of Income Tax Deduction

Under the U.S. federal income tax system, when an individual or entity (payer) receives an income deduction for a payment, generally the recipient (payee) must simultaneously recognize the receip taxable income. Such is not the case with qualified retirement and other tax-advantaged retiren plans. Rather, the employer receives a current income tax deduction and the employee is allowe defer the income for current income tax purposes until distribution, usually at age 59½ or older.

Qualified retirement plans were Congressionally created to provide incentives for employer sponsor and promote retirement savings. Congress has known for some time that Social Secu would not provide an adequate wage replacement for many workers. However, whenever Cong creates a plan that provides for income tax relief or tax advantage, there are usually costs, limitati or disadvantages to the successful implementation of such a plan. Some of these disadvantages discussed below.

Small Business Tax Credit

The Economic Growth and Tax Relief Reconciliation Act of 2001 (EGTRRA 2001) provide nonrefundable income tax credit equal to 50 percent of the administrative and retirement-educa expenses paid or incurred after December 31, 2001 for any small business that adopts a qualified, defined-benefit or defined-contribution plan (including a Section 401(k) plan), a SIM plan, or a Simplified Employee Pension (SEP). The credit applies to 50 percent of the first $1,00 administrative and retirement-education expenses for the plan for each of the first three years of plan. The credit is available to an employer that did not employ, in the preceding year, more than employees with compensation in excess of $5,000. To be eligible for the credit, the plan must cover at least one nonhighly compensated employee. In addition, if the credit is for the cost of a payroll deduction IRA arrangement, the arrangement must be made available to all employees of the employer who have worked with the employer for at least three months.

Retirement Plans as Part of a Compensation Package

From the perspective of the employees in the labor market, many qualified retirement plans have essentially become part of their overall compensation package. The employee recognizes the need for retirement savings and accepts an overall compensation package as salary, retirement plan, and other employee fringe benefits, rather than just salary, such that the employee's compensation utility curves are maximized to the greatest extent possible.

This does not suggest that the employee chooses the qualified retirement plan. The employer chooses the type of qualified retirement plan, and it usually becomes part of an overall compensation package offered to current and future employees. The employees then evaluate the complete compensation package, given their personal goals and opportunity costs, to make appropriate employment decisions. Today employees are aware of the benefits of using a qualified retirement plan's taxable income deferral as an alternative to receiving additional current compensation, which would be currently subject to income tax.

In the late 1990s, many employees chose to work for companies that provided minimal salaries, but offered employee stock options. Employees recognized these hi-tech companies as having tremendous growth potential. Employees were willing to sacrifice current income in hopes that their employer's stock would appreciate significantly enough to compensate them for their current sacrifice of higher salaries elsewhere.

Microsoft is a good example of this phenomenon. Base salaries were small, but the right to participate in the ownership of the company was tremendously enticing to potential employees. As it turns out, many of these employees became quite wealthy because of their stock options and other fringe benefits.

DISADVANTAGES OF QUALIFIED RETIREMENT PLANS

Costs to Qualify the Plan

To establish a qualified retirement plan, employers must have a legal document, known as a plan document, drafted by a pension attorney or one pre-approved by the IRS (a prototype plan). The plan document sets forth the rules for administration of the plan, provides for how benefits are earned and allocated to employees, and names which classes of employees will benefit under the plan. Generally, there are attorney costs to having a plan document drafted. A determination letter is generally obtained from the Internal Revenue Service (IRS) to ensure that the plan meets the requirements of Internal Revenue Code (IRC) Section 401(a). The determination letter assures the sponsor of the plan that the plan meets the requirements to be a qualified retirement plan. EGTRRA 2001 allows some small employers to receive determination letters without paying a fee.

It should be noted that many financial institutions have prototype plans available to their clients. Prototype plans are qualified retirement plan documents that have already been approved by the IRS as meeting the requirements of IRC Section 401(a). These prototype plans usually have only a few options for the client to select regarding the plan's operation. These options are selected by the client on what is referred to as an adoption agreement. The remainder of the document is a standard form. Prototype plans are inexpensive to establish and are preapproved by the IRS.

Costs to Fund the Plan

To meet qualification requirements, qualified retirement plans must be funded on a regular basis. Pension plans must be funded at least annually, whereas, contributions to profit-sharing plans must only be substantial and recurring. Qualified plan contributions may be as much as 25 percent of payroll. In years of poor earnings, this benefit can be a substantial drain on a company's cash flow.

Costs of Administering the Plan

Qualified retirement plans require ongoing administration and maintenance. Information compliance tax returns (such as the IRS Form 5500) must be filed with the IRS annually. Allocation of contributions to employees' accounts, or determination of accrued benefits, must also be completed at least annually. Other administrative duties include annual testing to comply with IRS regulations and amending the plan document for tax law changes. Besides performing administrative duties, the plan sponsor must retain and supervise an investment adviser to assure that plan assets are managed for the sole benefit of participants and their beneficiaries. The plan sponsor may outsource each of these tasks to a third party administrator or other provider.

Annual Compensation Limit

The Internal Revenue Code limits the amount of compensation that can be considered for purposes of funding qualified retirement plans. This compensation limit, although indexed, was decreased in the 1993 law change in an attempt to limit the contribution to highly compensated employees and increase the contributions to nonhighly compensated employees. Exhibit 16.4 illustrates the annual compensation limits for the years from 1993 to 2005.

EXHIBIT 16.4: ANNUAL COMPENSATION LIMIT (1993 – 2005)

Year	Compensation Limit	Year	Compensation Limit
1993	$235,850	1999	$160,000
1994	$150,000	2000	$170,000
1995	$150,000	2001	$170,000
1996	$150,000	2002	$200,000
1997	$160,000	2003	$200,000
1998	$160,000	2004	$205,000
		2005	$210,000

When the compensation limit was reduced in 1994 (from $235,850 to $150,000), it caused employers to increase the percentage of contributions to rank-and-file employees so the highly compensated could maintain their contribution amounts from previous years.

For 2005, up to $210,000 of compensation can be considered for purposes of funding a qualified plan. Any income earned above this limit is disregarded. The compensation limit is indexed annually to the CPI in $5,000 increments. When an employer wants to provide benefits on earnings above the annual limit, it is generally done in the form of deferred compensation, which does not have the same tax benefits as qualified plans.

Eligibility Requirements

There are minimal standards that need to be met by an employee in order to be eligible to participate in a qualified retirement plan provided by an employer. Generally, all employees who are at least age 21 and have one year of service (defined as 1,000 hours within a twelve-month period) are considered eligible for the plan. As the number of eligible employees for the plan increases, so does the number that have to benefit under the plan for the plan to remain qualified. Obviously, an increase in the number of employees under the plan increases the cost of the plan. Union employees, who are covered by a separate collective bargaining agreement, are not required to be covered by their employer's qualified retirement plan. The reason for the exception of union employees is that these individuals generally have retirement benefits provided from the union, and employers are generally required to contribute to these union plans.

Coverage of Employees

A qualified retirement plan must benefit a broad range of employees, not just the highly compensated. Although there are exceptions, in general, employers are required to cover 70 percent of the eligible nonhighly compensated employees. For defined-benefit plans only, the employer also must cover 50 employees or 40 percent of those eligible, whichever is less. Coverage under the plan means that the employee is somehow benefiting, either from employer contributions or from the ability to defer employee taxable income in the plan (such as a 401(k) plan). Highly compensated employees are defined as those employees who owned more than 5 percent of the company stock or had income above a certain limit in the previous year ($95,000 in 2005). An election is also available that allows only the top 20 percent of wage earners to be considered highly compensated. Nonhighly compensated employees are those employees who are not classified as highly compensated.

As long as the qualified retirement plan meets the coverage requirement, it is permitted to exclude certain groups of eligible employees from participating in the plan. For example, salaried employees or commissioned employees might be excluded from the plan as a class. These types of class exclusions may reduce the employer's contribution to the plan and reduce the overall cost of the plan. The plan must meet the basic coverage rules, however, and the class exclusions should be considered in the overall context of employee compensation and as a business decision.

Vesting Requirements

vesting - an employee's nonforfeitable right to receive a present or future pension benefit

Vesting is the process by which employees accrue benefits in the form of ownership provided by an employer's contribution. In the context of qualified retirement plans, an employee is vested

when he has ownership rights to the contributions (or benefits) provided by the employer. In general, employees vest over a specific period.

The two standard vesting schedules preapproved by the IRS are referred to as "five-year-cliff" and "three-to-seven-graduated" vesting. The five-year-cliff-vesting schedule requires an employee to complete five years of service. After five years of service (a year of service generally is defined as 1,000 hours within a twelve-month period), the employee is fully or 100 percent vested, meaning that the employee has ownership rights to all previous employer contributions and any contributions made on his behalf in the future. Graduated vesting allows employees to become partially vested over a period of years. In the case of three-to-seven-year graduated vesting, employees accrue ownership rights as follows:

EXHIBIT 16.5: GRADUATED VESTING (STANDARD AND TOP-HEAVY)

VESTING SCHEDULE (5-YEAR CLIFF)		VESTING SCHEDULE (3-7 GRADUATED)	
Years of Service	Portion Vested	Years of Service	Portion Vested
1	0%	1	0%
2	0%	2	0%
3	0%	3	20%
4	0%	4	40%
5	100%	5	60%
		6	80%
		7	100%

Graduated vesting allows those employees who worked for 4 years, for example, to leave the company with some benefit; whereas, under the five-year-cliff vesting schedule, such employees would receive nothing from the contributions made by the employer, nor from the earnings on employer contributions. Contributions and the earnings on contributions made by the employee (such as with a 401(k) plan), however, are always 100 percent vested and remain the property of the employee.

It should be noted that the vesting schedule an employer selects could be more liberal than the prescribed vesting schedules under the Internal Revenue Code. For instance, instead of choosing a five-year-cliff vesting schedule, an employer may elect to have employees' accounts vest over four years at 25 percent each year. However, the employer may not select a vesting schedule that is more restrictive than the five-year-cliff or three-to-seven-year graduated methods.

Employer-matching contributions and top-heavy plans are required to vest at least as quickly as a three-year-cliff or two-to-six-year graduated vesting schedule. (See Exhibit 16.6)

EXHIBIT 16.6: VESTING FOR EMPLOYER MATCHING CONTRIBUTIONS AND TOP-HEAVY PLANS

VESTING SCHEDULE (3-YEAR CLIFF)		VESTING SCHEDULE (2-6 GRADUATED)	
Years of Service	Portion Vested	Years of Service	Portion Vested
1	0%	1	0%
2	0%	2	20%
3	100%	3	40%
4	100%	4	60%
5	100%	5	80%
6	100%	6	100%

Top-Heavy Plans

Under IRC Section 416(g), qualified retirement plans are considered top heavy if more than 60 percent of the benefits are attributable to a group of owners and officers called key employees. If a plan is top heavy, then there are two consequences. First, the standard vesting schedules are required to be shortened (cliff vesting to 3 years and graduated using a two-to-six-year schedule) such that benefits vest quicker for the nonkey employee group. Second, there are certain minimum contributions that must be provided to the nonkey employees based on the benefits accrued or contributions made for the key employees. The top-heavy rules ensure that a qualified retirement plan actually benefits the rank-and-file employees of the company, not just owners and officers.

Disclosure Requirements

The employer is required to provide a summary of the details of the qualified retirement plan to employees, participants, and beneficiaries under pay status. The employer also is required to provide to the plan participants notices of any plan amendments or changes. These documents help to inform the employee of his rights under ERISA and of the rights of the qualified retirement plan.

Annual Testing of Qualified Retirement Plans

As described previously, there are many recurring requirements that must be met to maintain a qualified retirement plan. Therefore, annual testing is necessary to ensure that the plan continues to meet each of these requirements.

BENEFITS OF TAX DEFERRAL

For an employee who participates in a qualified retirement plan, tax deferral is perhaps the biggest benefit. Neither the contributions to the plan nor the earnings on these contributions are currently subject to income tax. The expectation is that in retirement, when distributions begin, the plan participant will be in a lower income tax bracket than during the working years.

EXAMPLE Your client's employer will either (A) pay your client $1,000 that is subject to payroll and income tax, or (B) contribute $1,000 to a qualified retirement plan. Your client would save the net received from (A) and earn 12 percent per year for 40 years. The contribution made to the qualified retirement plan, (B), is made by the employer.

	A Not Tax Advantaged		B Qualified Plan	
Deposit	$1,000.00		$1,000.00	
Less	76.50	Payroll tax	0.00	Payroll tax
Less	280.00	28% assumed income tax rate	0.00	Tax rate
Net Deposited	$ 643.50		$1,000.00	
PV	$ 643.50		$1,000.00	
i	8.64%	(12% × 0.72) (28% tax rate)	12%	
n	40 years		40	
FV	$17,706.75		$93,050.97	
Net of tax	$17,706.75		$66,996.70	(28% tax bracket)

The assumption made in the above example (A) was that the 12 percent earnings were subject to income tax each year, thus the use of the 8.64 earnings rate (1 - tax rate)(ER) = (1 - 0.28)(12) = 8.64. However, even if we assumed a portfolio of nondividend paying stocks that were only subject to capital gains rates of 15 percent at the end of 40 years, the advantage would still be to the qualified retirement plan.

	A Not Tax Advantaged	B Qualified Plan
Deposit	$643.50	$1,000.00
PV	$643.50	$1,000.00
n	40	40
i	12%	12%
FV	$59,878.30	$93,050.97
Tax rate	15% on capital gains ($59,878.30 – $643.50)	28% on ordinary income
Net after tax	$50,349.58 [(FV – basis) × .85]	$66,996.70 (FV × (1 – 0.28))

The difference between *A* and *B* in both examples above is partially due to the payroll tax, which was not applicable to the qualified retirement plan, and partially due to the current income tax on the nontax-advantaged fund (A).

TYPES OF QUALIFIED RETIREMENT PLANS

Qualified retirement plans may be classified as:

- ▲ Pension or profit-sharing plans,
- ▲ Defined-benefit, defined-contribution plans, target/age-weighted (hybrid) plans,
- ▲ Contributory or noncontributory plans, and
- ▲ Corporate or Keogh plans.

Exhibit 16.7 identifies eleven common types of qualified retirement plans.

EXHIBIT 16.7: QUALIFIED RETIREMENT PLANS

TYPES	PENSION PLANS	PROFIT-SHARING PLANS
Defined-Benefit Plans	1. Defined-Benefit Pension Plan 2. Cash-Balance Pension Plan	NONE
Defined-Contribution Plans	1. Target-Benefit Pension Plan 2. Money-Purchase Pension Plan	1. Profit-Sharing Plans 2. 401(k) Plans 3. Thrift Plans 4. Stock Bonus Plans 5. Employee Stock Ownership Plans 6. Age-Based Profit-Sharing Plans 7. New Comparability Plans

PENSION PLANS

The legal requirement or "promise" of a **pension plan** is to regularly pay a fixed sum of money at retirement. Because of this promise, pension plans have certain requirements and characteristics. The first requirement is that pension plans have mandatory funding. This means that, in general, pension plans must be funded on an annual basis, regardless of whether the company has sufficient cash flow. The reason for annual funding is to ensure that sufficient assets will be available to fulfill the promise of a pension during retirement.

pension plan - a qualified plan structured to provide a regularly paid, fixed sum at retirement

The second requirement is that pension plans are not permitted to allow in-service withdrawals. An in-service withdrawal is an employee distribution while the employee is still in the active service of the employer. It is worth noting that loans are not considered in-service withdrawals.

The third requirement is that pension plans are limited to investing no more than 10 percent of the assets in the qualified retirement plan in employer securities. To be consistent with the underlying promise of the pension plan, the investments of the qualified retirement plan should be reasonably diversified to limit the amount of risk undertaken by the portfolio. Investing more than 10 percent in the employer's securities would not be a prudent investment decision and would be inconsistent with the notion of paying pension benefits.

The fourth characteristic of pension plans is the generous limit on contributions. An employer can contribute up to, and in some cases exceed, 25 percent of covered compensation. The term, "covered compensation," describes the portion of payroll that may be considered for qualified retirement plan purposes. These high contribution limits provide ample opportunity for the employer to fulfill the promise of pension benefits.

There are four pension plans as indicated in Exhibit 16.7. These four pension plans differ from each other in complexity and costs. The defined-benefit plan is the most complex and costly, requiring the annual services of an actuary. The money-purchase pension plan is the least complex and least costly. A prototype plan for a money-purchase pension plan is available from almost any financial institution. A target-benefit plan is a special type of money-purchase plan. Each pension plan has particular applications that make it a better choice than the others depending on the employer-sponsor's goals, the number of participants, and the census of participants, including length of service, age, and compensation levels. Cash balance plans are a special type of defined-benefit plan and are beyond the scope of this text.

Small businesses, with the exception of self-employed professional persons, tend to avoid pension plans due to the strict requirement of mandatory funding. Small businesses prefer profit-sharing plans or other tax-advantaged retirement plans that permit more discretion over the funding of contributions.

profit-sharing plan - a qualified defined-contribution plan featuring a flexible (discretionary) employer-contribution provision. Profit-sharing plans are structured to offer employees participation in company profits that they may use for retirement

PROFIT-SHARING PLANS

A **profit-sharing plan** is a qualified defined-contribution plan featuring a flexible (discretionary) employer-contribution provision. The funding discretion is regardless of cash flows or profits. An employer is permitted to fund a profit-sharing plan (including stock bonus plans) in any amount up to 25 percent of covered employee compensation.

stock bonus plan - a defined-contribution profit-sharing plan in which all employer contributions are in the form of employer stock; distributions to participants can be made in the form of employer stock

The legal promise of a profit-sharing plan is to defer taxes rather than provide retirement benefits. There is no particular time requirement for the deferral of taxes. The deferral period could be until retirement, in which case in-service withdrawals would not be permitted. Alternatively, a profit-sharing plan may be designed to allow in-service withdrawals as early as after two years of participation. The plan document (the plan legal description) will dictate what is, or is not, permitted.

Unlike the restriction of pension plans, profit-sharing plans do not have restrictions on the amount of employer securities that can be purchased within the plan. Profit-sharing plans are permitted to invest 100 percent of the qualified retirement plan assets in employer securities. **Stock bonus plans** and employee stock ownership plans (ESOPs) are examples of profit-sharing type plans that often invest entirely in employer securities.

401(k) profit-sharing plan - a defined-contribution profit-sharing plan that gives participants the option of reducing their taxable salary and contributing the salary reduction on a tax-deferred basis to an individual account for retirement purposes

There are seven different profit-sharing plans as shown in Exhibit 16.7. Each one has a particular application depending on costs, complexity, sponsor goals, and the census of employees, including age, length of service and compensation levels.

The one type of profit-sharing plan so common and important that it deserves mentioning is the **401(k) profit-sharing plan**. It is the most popular self-reliant qualified retirement plan. The 401(k) plan permits an employee to save, pretax, up to $14,000 (for the year 2005) or a certain percentage of income per year (indexed to inflation); and in some cases, that savings is matched, or partially matched, by the employer. The limit will increase to $15,000 in 2006. After 2006, the limit will be indexed in increments of $500.

Some matching schemes call for the employee to contribute up to 6 percent of salary with the employer matching $0.50 on the dollar contributed by the employee up to 3 percent per year. The employee may contribute more than the 6 percent if the plan permits, but the employer match usually is maximized at 3 percent. The advantage of this kind of plan to the employer is that the funding is heavily employee dependent and self-reliant. Advantages to the employee are the size of the pretax savings, any employer match, and the prospects for a substantial accumulation over the work life expectancy.

EXAMPLE

Assume Joe G, age 25, participates in a 401(k) plan and his salary is $50,000. Joe annually contributes 6 percent to his 401(k) plan and the contribution is matched with 3 percent from his employer. Joe intends to contribute the same amount each month for the next 40 years. Assume that Joe can earn 10 percent annually, compounded monthly, on his and his employer's contributions and balances. How much will Joe accumulate at age 65 assuming no increase in salary or in the amount of the monthly contribution?

PV	=	0
n	=	480 (40 × 12) months
i	=	0.83333 (10 ÷ 12)
PMT_{OA}	=	\$375.00 [(50,000 × 6%) + (50,000 × 3%)] ÷ 12
$FV_{@65}$	=	\$2,371,529.84

The accumulation is remarkable! Joe and his employer deposited only $180,000 ($375 × 12 × 40), and at age 65, Joe has $2,371,530. The rate of return on earnings was reasonable at 10 percent, but Joe started early and reaped the benefits of a long period of compounding. In actual practice, we would hope and expect that as Joe's salary increased, he would maintain at least a 6 percent savings rate, as opposed to the $375 per month, thus increasing his contributions with each raise. Joe's contribution, as well as the employer match, would increase with each raise in salary, thus increasing the deposits and the accumulation at age 65.

The 401(k) plan has become one of the most popular and widely used qualified retirement plans. It is self-reliant and easily understood by employees. It is popular with employers because it is relatively inexpensive since employees provide most of the funding.

The 2001 tax act (EGTRRA) made a significant change to 401(k) plans for years beginning after December 31, 2005. This change allows 401(k) plans (and 403(b) plans) to include a "qualified plus contribution program" that permits a participant to elect to have all or a portion of the participant's elective deferrals under the plan treated as Roth contributions. As with contributions to Roth IRAs, these participant-elective deferrals would be subject to current taxation (not tax deferred), but would be exempt from taxation when distributed if certain requirements were met. These after-tax contributions can accumulate in the Roth account on a tax-deferred basis. This addition to 401(k) plans may be one of the most beneficial aspects of qualified plans that has been seen in many years.

The elective deferrals are not considered in the contribution limitations of qualified plans. Therefore, employers are allowed to make higher total contributions to qualified plans. Additional contributions may be made to 401(k) plans, 403(b) plans, SARSEPs, SEPs, and 457 plans for employees who are over the age of 50. These catch-up contributions allow employees who are at least age 50 to make the following additional contributions:

Year	50 Plus Years of Age Additional Catch-Up Contributions
2005	$4,000
2006	$5,000
2007	The $5,000 amount is increased in $500 increments based on cost-of-living adjustments

Exhibit 16.8 summarizes the major differences between pension plans and profit-sharing plans.

EXHIBIT 16.8: MAJOR DIFFERENCES BETWEEN PENSION AND PROFIT-SHARING PLANS

PLAN FEATURES	PENSION PLANS	PROFIT-SHARING PLANS
In-Service Withdrawals	Not permitted	Permitted after 2 years
Mandatory Funding	Yes	No
Percentage of Employer Stock Permitted in the Plan	10%	100%
Employer-Contribution Limit	25% of covered compensation (defined-contribution plans)	25%

DEFINED-BENEFIT, DEFINED-CONTRIBUTION, AND TARGET/AGE-WEIGHTED (HYBRID) PLANS

Qualified retirement plans are characterized as either defined-benefit or defined-contribution plans. In a defined-benefit plan, the contributions are actuarially determined to produce a certain future benefit under a formula at retirement. The annual funding for a defined-benefit plan depends on six factors: (1) the life expectancies of the participants, (2) the mortality experience in the employee group, (3) the earnings rate and expected earnings rate on plan assets, (4) the expected wage increases of employees, (5) the expected inflation rate associated with plan costs, and (6) the expected turnover rate of employees. An actuary makes an annual analysis of the above six variables to determine the annual funding. Obviously, defined-benefit plans are both costly and complex. There are only two defined-benefit plans, the traditional **defined-benefit pension plan**, and the cash-balance pension plan. Generally, large corporations use these where the costs of administration, including actuarial costs, can be spread over a large number of employee participants.

defined-benefit plan - a retirement plan that specifies the benefits that each employee receives at retirement. Defined-benefit plans actuarially determine the benefit to be paid at normal retirement age.

Defined-benefit plan assets are invested and managed by the employer or by an outside trustee. Actuaries for the defined-benefit plans determine the benefit to be paid at normal retirement age (frequently age 65). Contributions to defined-benefit plans generally are provided by the employer only. Since the employer is responsible for meeting the benefit obligations, it bears the

Where on the Web

American Society of Pension Actuaries *www.aspa.org*
American Benefits Council *www.appwp.org*
Benefits Link *www.benefitslink.com*
ESOP Association *www.esopassociation.org*
Employee Benefit Research Institute *www.ebri.org*
Employee Benefits Security Administration *www.dol.gov/ebsa*
Internal Revenue Service *www.irs.gov*
International Foundation of Employee Benefit Plans *www.ifebp.org*
National Institute of Pension Administrators *www.nipa.org*
National Tax Sheltered Accounts Association (403(b) and 457 plans) *www.ntsaa.org*
Pension Benefit Guaranty Corporation (PBGC) *www.pbgc.gov*
Profit Sharing/401(k) Council of America *www.psca.org*

investment risk for the funding. If the performance of the fund assets is better than expected, then contributions can be reduced. If investment returns are less than expected, however, the employer is required to make higher contributions than anticipated.

The benefits payable under a defined-benefit plan commonly are paid as a lifetime annuity, although some plans provide a cash-out option at retirement. Since funding requirements are greater the older a person enters into the plan, defined-benefit plans are said to favor older-age entrants and long-term employees.

Since there is some risk that the employer will be unable to sustain the payment of retirement benefits from a defined-benefit plan, sponsors of these plans generally are required to participate in the Pension Benefit Guarantee Corporation (PBGC) termination insurance program. The PBGC is a federal agency that guarantees benefits to participants of defined-benefit plans. It is a type of government insurance company, similar to the FDIC, where plan sponsors make premium payments to the PBGC based on the number of plan participants and based on the level of plan funding. The PBGC does not guarantee the full amount of benefits, but only a set amount as limited by law (currently about $45,000 per year). The PBGC does not guarantee benefits of defined-contribution plans.

Defined-contribution plans specify the annual employer current contribution (as opposed to an ultimate future benefit). The amount of benefit that an employee receives at retirement or termination of employment depends on the account balance. Therefore, the investment risk of a defined-contribution plan is borne by the employee.

defined-contribution plan - a retirement plan that specifies the annual employer current contribution. The amount of benefit received by an employee depends on the account balance at retirement.

There are two defined-contribution pension plans and seven defined-contribution profit-sharing plans. Usually, defined-contribution plan funding is borne solely by the employer (except for the 401(k) and thrift plan), but the assets are maintained in each participant's individual account.

The investment risk is borne by the participants with the investment of the plan assets often being self-directed. Defined-contribution plans favor younger participants who have a longer compounding and accumulation period. Unlike defined-benefit plans, defined-contribution profit-sharing plans have no annual mandatory funding requirement. Thus, accumulations in these accounts are dependent on the contributions made and the earnings performance that may or may not be realized.

Exhibit 16.9 summarizes the characteristics and differences between defined-benefit and defined-contribution plans.

EXHIBIT 16.9: CHARACTERISTICS OF SELECTED RETIREMENT PLAN

	DEFINED BENEFIT	DEFINED CONTRIBUTION
Plan typically benefits older, long-term employees	Yes	No
Requires PBGC insurance	Yes	No
Benefits insured by PBGC	Yes	No
Actuarial costs	Yes	No*
Can encourage early retirement	Yes	No
Can provide benefits based on prior service	Yes	No
Benefit up to $170,000 for 2005	Yes	No
Higher plan costs and complexity	Yes	No
Individual accounts	No	Yes
Contribution is % of compensation	No	Yes
Investment risk	Employer	Employee
Contributions limited to lesser of 100% or $42,000 for 2005	No	Yes
Forfeitures reduce plan costs	Yes	Maybe
Assets in plan	Commingled Funds	Separate Accounts
*except target-benefit plans		

target plan - an age-weighted money-purchase pension plan; a hybrid between a defined-contribution plan and a defined-benefit plan

TARGET/AGE-WEIGHTED PLAN.

A target or other age-weighted plan and formula, for a defined-contribution plan, allows higher contribution levels (as a percentage of compensation) for older plan entrants. Broad types of age-weighted plans include:

The traditional **target plan** is an age-weighted money-purchase pension plan. A traditional target plan is a hybrid between a defined-contribution pension plan and a defined-benefit plan.

age-based profit-sharing plan - a profit-sharing plan with an age-weighted factor in the allocation formula

The **age-based profit-sharing plan** is a profit-sharing plan with an age-weighted factor in the allocation formula. Since the plan allocations are age-weighted, older plan entrants are favored.

The **new comparability plan** represents an attempt to push age weighting to its maximum limit under the cross-testing provisions of the proposed nondiscrimination regulations.

new comparability plan - a defined-contribution plan that maximizes the age-weighted discrepancy permitted under the cross-testing provisions of proposed nondiscrimination

CONTRIBUTORY VERSUS NONCONTRIBUTORY PLANS

Qualified retirement plans may be distinguished as either contributory (employee makes some contribution) or noncontributory (employer pays all). Most pension and profit-sharing plans are noncontributory. The common exceptions are the 401(k) plan and the thrift plan (an after-tax savings plan). The reason that most qualified retirement plans are noncontributory is that both employers and employees view them as a part of an overall compensation package paid for by the employer. Because noncontributory plans are so prevalent, vesting is an important issue. Vesting occurs when the employee has a federal property right in the employer contributions and earnings on those contributions.

CORPORATE VERSUS KEOGH PLANS

Qualified retirement plans are either corporate-sponsored (regular C corporations and S corporations) or Keogh (self-employed, Schedule C, partnerships, LLCs filing as partnerships) plans. Corporations can adopt any of the qualified retirement plans, pension plans, or profit-sharing plans discussed above, as well as other tax-advantaged plans that are not qualified. Self-employed persons can adopt the majority of qualified retirement plans (except stock bonus and ESOP plans) and can adopt other tax-advantaged plans called SEPs and SIMPLEs. These will be covered in the next section of this chapter.

The intent of Congressional legislation regarding self-employed individuals was to put **Keogh plans** in parity with corporate plans. There are two important differences, however, between corporate plans and Keogh plans. The first is the calculation of the maximum contribution allowed by the self-employed person; and the second is the availability of loans from the Keogh plan to these self-employed individuals.

Keogh plan - a qualified plan for unincorporated businesses

Self-Employed Maximum Contribution Calculation

Traditional employees receive a Form W-2 that reflects their earnings for the current year. There is a limit that no more than the lesser of 100 percent of an employee's compensation or $42,000 (year 2005) can be contributed to the defined-contribution plans sponsored by the employer within a given year. Contributions include employer contributions, employee contributions, and **forfeitures**. For example, an employee who had compensation of $100,000 would be limited to $42,000 in contributions for a single year.

forfeitures - employer contributions that are not fully vested and thus revert to the employer in the event that an employee terminates service

Unfortunately for self-employed individuals, their maximum contribution calculation is more complicated. These individuals are limited in their contributions to the lesser of 25 percent of earned income or $42,000 for 2005. Earned income is different than compensation and is defined as self-employment income reduced by ½ self-employment tax (net self-employment income) and reduced by the retirement plan contribution. Reducing the income that can be used as the base for the retirement plan contribution by the retirement plan contribution creates what is known as a circular equation. To resolve this circular equation, the retirement plan contribution percentage is divided by the sum of 1 plus the retirement plan contribution percentage. This factor is then multiplied by the difference between self-employment income and ½ self-employment tax.

EXAMPLE Bob has self-employment income of $105,000 and self-employment tax of $10,000 in 2005, his contribution is limited to a maximum of $20,000, as follows:

KEOGH PLAN CONTRIBUTION CALCULATION			
1.	Self-employment income	$105,000	
2.	Less ½ self-employment tax	$5,000	½ × $10,000
3.	Equals net self-employment income	$100,000	
4.	Less Keogh plan contribution	($20,000)	$100,000 × (0.25/1.25)
5.	Equals Earned Income	$80,000	
6.	Times Keogh contribution percentage	× 25%	
7.	Equals Keogh plan contribution	$20,000	

Notice that the contribution of $20,000 is calculated by multiplying $100,000 by 20 percent, which equals earned income (line 5 above) multiplied by 25 percent. Therefore, it is not necessary to extend the analysis through steps 5 to 7. Determining the contribution is usually calculated by dividing the plan percentage by the sum of 1 plus the plan percentage and multiplying the result by the difference between self-employment earnings and ½ self-employment tax. The following table depicts the percentage that is often used for Keogh calculations depending on the plan contribution percentage limit.

PLAN PERCENTAGE	KEOGH LIMIT
1%	0.9901%
2%	1.9608%
3%	2.9126%
4%	3.8462%
5%	4.7619%
6%	5.6604%
7%	6.5421%
8%	7.4074%
9%	8.2569%
10%	9.0909%
11%	9.9099%
12%	10.7143%
13%	11.5044%

PLAN PERCENTAGE	KEOGH LIMIT
14%	12.2807%
15%	13.0435%
16%	13.7931%
17%	14.5299%
18%	15.2542%
19%	15.9664%
20%	16.6667%
21%	17.3554%
22%	18.0328%
23%	18.6992%
24%	19.3548%
25%	20.0000%

OTHER TAX-ADVANTAGED PLANS

Other than qualified retirement plans, there are individually sponsored and employer-sponsored retirement plans that are tax advantaged, but are not technically qualified. Generally, these plans appeal to individuals or small employers, have lower contribution limits, function about the same as qualified retirement plans as to earnings deferrals and contribution deductions, but are less costly (except for 403(b) plans). They might be thought of as the poor man's substitute for a qualified retirement plan. Exhibit 16.10 lists these plans.

EXHIBIT 16.10: OTHER TAX-ADVANTAGED PLANS

Individual Retirement Account or Annuity (IRA)
▲ Deductible
▲ Nondeductible
▲ Roth IRA
Simplified Employee Plan (SEP)
Savings Incentive Match Plan for Employees (SIMPLE)
403(b) Plans (Tax-Sheltered Annuities)

INDIVIDUAL RETIREMENT ACCOUNT (IRA) OR IRA ANNUITY

In general, the IRA is a tax-deferred investment and savings account that serves as a personal retirement fund for persons with earned income.

An individual worker with earned income who is under age 70½ can contribute to an IRA. Annual IRA contributions are limited to the lesser of $4,000 or earned income for 2005. If a married person has a nonworking spouse, the annual contribution limit is increased to $8,000 for 2005 ($4,000 per individual account).

The contribution limit for IRAs is increased using the following schedule:

2005	$4,000
2006	$4,000
2007	$4,000
2008	$5,000
2009 and later	Increased for inflation in $500 increments

Deductibility rules.

The IRA contribution may be tax deductible, depending on whether the worker is covered by a qualified retirement plan or SEP and depending on the amount of his or her adjusted gross income. For taxpayers who are not active participants in a qualified plan, SEP, SARSEP,

SIMPLE, or 403(b) plan, contributions to a traditional IRA are fully deductible, regardless of the taxpayer's AGI. For taxpayers who are active participants in a qualified plan, SEP, SARSEP, SIMPLE, or 403(b) plan, the deduction for Traditional IRA contributions is limited (or eliminated) when a taxpayer's adjusted income reaches certain levels. These phaseout levels are listed in Exhibit 16.11.

EXHIBIT 16.11: IRA CURRENT PHASEOUT LIMITS

Tax Year	Taxpayer Filing Status	
	Phaseout Range Single	Phaseout Range Married Filing Jointly
2005	$50,000 – 60,000	$70,000 – 80,000
2006	$50,000 – 60,000	$75,000 – 85,000
2007 and after	$50,000 – 60,000	$80,000 – 100,000

An individual will not be considered an "active participant" in an employer-sponsored retirement plan solely because his or her spouse is an active participant. However, when only one spouse is an active participant, the nonparticipant spouse will have his or her deduction phased out at AGI levels between $150,000-$160,000.

Catch-up contributions are available for individuals over 50 years old. Any individual who attains 50 by the end of the taxable year can make the following additional contributions:

2004	$500
2005	$500
2006 and later	$1,000

Thus, a taxpayer age 50 or older in year 2006 could contribute a total of $5,000 to his IRA. This contribution consists of the annual limit plus the catch-up contribution.

The Roth IRA

Roth IRA - an individual retirement account in which contributions are made on an after-tax basis and qualifying distributions are made tax free

The **Roth IRA** is a special type of nondeductible IRA. Like the traditional IRA, the Roth IRA accumulates contributions (nondeductible and after tax) and earnings (tax free). Unlike the traditional IRA, distributions from a Roth IRA generally are tax exempt. Taxpayers can contribute to Roth IRAs after the age of 70½, and are not forced to receive minimum distributions at age 70½, as with traditional IRAs. Only taxpayers with incomes less than those listed below qualify to make a contribution to a Roth IRA.

Taxpayer	Phaseout AGI (modified)
Single	$95,000 – $110,000
Married filing jointly	$150,000 – $160,000
Married filing separately	$0 – $10,000

EXAMPLE

Another big advantage of the Roth IRA is that owners always have the ability to distribute without tax or penalty an amount up to the total contributions to the Roth IRA without being subjected to income tax or penalties. For instance, Bob contributes $3,000 to his Roth IRA each year for five years. The account has grown to $23,000. Bob is able to distribute up to $15,000 (his total contributions) from the Roth IRA without tax or penalties. In a traditional IRA, distributions generally are taxable as ordinary income and distributions prior to age 59½ are generally subject to a 10 percent penalty.

SIMPLIFIED EMPLOYEE PENSIONS (SEP)

simplified employee pension (SEP) - a tax-deferred, noncontributory retirement plan that uses an individual retirement account (IRA) as the receptacle for contributions

A **Simplified Employee Pension** (SEP) is tax-deferred noncontributory retirement plan that is employer sponsored and is similar to a qualified profit-sharing plan with regard to funding requirements and contribution limits. In contrast to qualified profit-sharing plans, SEPs require almost none of the same filing requirements. SEPs use individual retirement accounts (IRAs) to hold the retirement benefits, making the benefits of the employees portable. Individual retirement accounts are established for each eligible employee. The funding is discretionary on the part of the employer up to 25 percent of covered employee compensation to a maximum of $210,000 (as indexed for year 2005) not to exceed $42,000. All contributions to a SEP are immediately and full vested. The advantage of a SEP versus an IRA is the possible amount of funding—$42,000 versus $4,000 for the traditional or Roth IRA. The plan is uncomplicated and low cost compared to qualified retirement plans. Generally, the individual participant has the responsibility and risk for investment returns. SEPs may not be appropriate for small businesses with permanent part-time employees because part-time employees must be covered under the plan. A major advantage of a SEP is that it can be established as late as the due date of the employer's federal income tax return, including extensions. IRAs, on the other hand, must be established by April 15th following the tax year.

SIMPLE (IRA) PLANS

A SIMPLE (IRA) plan (Savings Incentive Match Plan for Employees) is a tax-deferred, employer-sponsored retirement plan that more closely resembles an IRA. Like the SEP, it has minimal filing requirements. The SIMPLE plan allows employees to make elective contributions to an individual retirement account (IRA) up to $10,000 for 2005. The limit increases as follows:

2004	$ 9,000
2005	$10,000
2006 and later	Increased in $500 increments

Catch-up provisions are available for individuals at least 50 years old. Any individual who attains 50 by the end of the taxable year may be eligible to make the following additional contributions:

Year	50 Plus Years of Age Additional Catch-Up Contributions
2004	$1,500
2005	$2,000
2006	$2,500
2007 and later	The $2,500 is indexed for inflation in $500 increments

Unlike most qualified retirement plans, there is no percentage limitation on the deferral amount. In other words, an employee who earned $10,000 (2005) could defer the entire amount. The employer is required to provide one of the following two types of benefits to the employees in the plan: 1) provide a dollar-for-dollar match up to 3 percent of the employee's compensation, or 2) make a 2 percent-of-compensation contribution for each eligible employee without regard to the employee's contribution. The total combined contribution is limited to $24,000 ($10,000 + $2,000 catch-up + match of $12,000) annually. There are no vesting provisions, which means that once contributed, the funds cannot be forfeited or revert back to the employer. The benefits are portable; however, withdrawals made within two years of participation are subject to a 25 percent premature-distribution penalty tax.

The advantage of the SIMPLE over the traditional IRA is the larger amount of contribution allowed. The advantage of the SIMPLE over the SEP is that the SIMPLE plan is funded mostly through employee contributions and there is no percentage limit for contributions to a SIMPLE plan.

To sponsor a SIMPLE plan, the employer must have fewer than 100 employees. SIMPLE plans are essentially governed by the same rules as IRAs. Individual accounts are created, and employees choose the investments from those offered by the plan.

One big disadvantage of a SIMPLE is that no other types of qualified retirement plans are permitted to be simultaneously maintained by the employer. Therefore, if the employer wanted to sponsor a pension or profit-sharing plan, the SIMPLE would have to be terminated.

403(b) Plans

403(b) plan - a retirement plan similar to a 401(k) plan that is available to certain tax-exempt organizations and to public schools

Congress established 403(b) plans to encourage workers in certain tax-exempt organizations to establish retirement savings programs. The name, like that of 401(k) plans, refers to the relevant section of the Internal Revenue Code. A **403(b) plan** is a tax-deferred savings and retirement plan that, while not a qualified plan, provides many of the same benefits and is governed by many of the same rules that govern qualified retirement plans. It is essentially the 401(k) of the not-for-profit industry. Participants contractually reduce their salaries, subject to the same limits as 401(k)s, with their employer for equivalent pretax contributions made either to mutual funds or tax-sheltered annuities. The contributions and earnings grow tax deferred until distribution, and the benefit received is equal to the account balance at the accumulation date (usually retirement). Similar to 401(k) and other defined-contribution plans, the responsibility and risk of investment returns is on the individual participant.

Nonrefundable Credit for Elective Deferrals

For years 2002 through 2006, a special nonrefundable tax credit is available to low-income and moderate-income savers for elective deferrals or contributions made to a 401(k) plan, section 403(b) annuity, eligible deferred-compensation arrangement of a state or local government (a "Section 457 plan"), SIMPLE, SEP, or IRA.

The maximum annual contribution eligible for the credit is $2,000. The credit rates based on AGI are as follows:

Joint Filers	Head of Households	All Other Filers	Credit Rate	Max. Amount of Credit
$0 – $30,000	$0 – $22,500	$0 – $15,000	50 percent	$1,000
$30,000 – $32,500	$22,500 – $24,375	$15,000 – $16,250	20 percent	$400
$32,500 – $50,000	$24,375 – $37,500	$16,250 – $25,000	10 percent	$200
Over $50,000	Over $37,500	Over $25,000	0 percent	$0

The credit is in addition to any deduction or exclusion that would otherwise apply with respect to the contribution. The credit offsets minimum tax liability as well as regular tax liability. The credit is available to individuals who are 18 or over, other than individuals who are full-time students or claimed as a dependent on another taxpayer's return.

The amount of any contribution eligible for the credit is reduced by taxable distributions received by the taxpayer and his or her spouse from any savings arrangement described above or any other qualified retirement plan during the taxable year for which the credit is claimed, the two taxable years prior to the year the credit is claimed, and during the period after the end of the taxable year and prior to the due date for filing the taxpayer's return for the year. In the case of a distribution from a Roth IRA, this rule applies to any such distributions, whether taxable or not.

DISTRIBUTIONS FROM QUALIFIED AND OTHER TAX-ADVANTAGED PLANS

Distributions from qualified retirement plans and other tax-advantaged retirement plans generally have the same federal income tax consequences. In general, distributions made prior to age 59½, death, disability, or retirement are penalized by a premature penalty tax of 10 percent. Annual distributions from qualified retirement plans must begin no later than the year in which the participant attains age 70½, although the first distribution may be delayed until April 1 of the following year. There is an exception if the employee/participant has not yet retired from the sponsor of that plan; in that case, distribution is not required until the year of the participant's retirement. This exception does not apply to other tax-advantaged accounts (IRAs, SEPs, SIMPLEs), nor does it apply to a greater-than-5% owner. Therefore, distributions from other tax-advantaged accounts must begin by age 70½ (or April 1 of the following year).

Distributions from qualified retirement plans and other tax-advantaged plans generally are subject to the following income tax treatment: If the contributions were pretax, then both contributions and earnings are treated as ordinary income equal to the distribution, and thus receive ordinary income tax treatment. If the contributions were after tax (thrift plan and nondeductible IRA), the contributions are treated as a return of capital and the earnings are treated as ordinary income. Each distribution is prorated as to return of taxable basis and ordinary income subject to income tax. This information is summarized in Exhibit 16.12.

EXHIBIT 16.12: TAXATION OF DISTRIBUTIONS

CONTRIBUTIONS	DISTRIBUTION	EARNINGS ON CONTRIBUTIONS
Pretax	Taxable as ordinary income	Ordinary income
After-tax	Nontaxable return of capital	Ordinary income

The two common exceptions to the general income tax treatment of distributions from tax-advantaged retirement accounts are Roth IRA distributions and lump-sum distributions consisting of employer securities. A Roth IRA has nondeductible contributions, but generally provides for tax-exempt distributions and is not subject to the rules on minimum distributions at age 70½.

As previously discussed, distributions that consist of employer securities receive deferred recognition treatment of the net unrealized appreciation in the securities, and the gains are taxable at capital gains rates instead of ordinary income tax rates.

NONQUALIFIED PLANS

nonqualified plan - a retirement plan that can discriminate in favor of executives but which is not eligible for the special tax benefits available for qualified or other tax-advantaged retirement plans

A **nonqualified plan** is any retirement plan, savings plan, or deferred-compensation plan or agreement that does not meet the tax requirements of the Internal Revenue Code. All qualified retirement plans and other tax-advantaged plans are in some way a form of deferred compensation, but with some form of current income tax deduction and/or deferral of taxation on earnings. For the nonqualified plans, no such favorable tax treatment occurs. The employer receives a deduction for contributions only when the participant recognizes the distribution as income for income tax purposes. If the nonqualified plan agreement delays when the participant receives taxable income, then the employer/sponsor's income tax deduction also is delayed.

Employers use nonqualified plans to provide additional financial benefits that are not, or cannot be, provided in qualified retirement plans. Nonqualified plans can reward employees (usually key executives) on a more selective basis than qualified retirement plans that require broad participation, coverage, and nondiscrimination. An example of one benefit that can be provided by a nonqualified plan is a deferred-compensation plan to provide retirement benefits to a key employee in excess of the limits that may be provided under a qualified retirement plan. Recall that the limit for covered compensation that can be considered for purposes of qualified retirement plans is $210,000 for 2005. Employees who earn exactly $210,000 in 2005 have a much higher wage replacement ratio than those who make $1,000,000 under the same qualified retirement plan. Even though the person is earning $1,000,000, their qualified retirement plan acts as if they are making only $210,000 in 2005. The deferred-compensation, nonqualified plan is used to mitigate this perceived wage replacement ratio inequity.

Nonqualified plans do not permit 10-year-forward-averaging income tax treatment, as do qualified retirement plans for individuals born before 1936. Nonqualified plans generally have some risk as to whether the employee/participant will receive the benefits (a substantial risk of forfeiture or a lack of funding is essential for the plan to defer taxation to the employee/participant). If there is no substantial risk of forfeiture and the benefit is funded there is constructive receipt of the funds, and the benefits are currently taxable rather than being deferred. In addition, nonqualified plans are not protected from creditors under ERISA's nonalienation of benefits rules.

There are a number of nonqualified plans that may be used to attract, compensate, and retain key personnel on a discriminatory or selective basis. These include deferred-compensation plans, split-dollar life insurance plans, and employee stock option plans.

Deferred-Compensation Plans

Nonqualified, deferred-compensation agreements are contractual arrangements between the employer and selected employees. **Deferred-compensation plans** take the form of either salary reduction, or more commonly, salary continuation. Either way, compensation is deferred generally until retirement, disability, death, or termination of employment, but usually only at normal retirement age. In effect, no retirement, no benefits.

deferred-compensation plan - a nonqualified plan that is a contractual agreement between the employer and selected employees; takes the form of either salary reduction or salary continuation. Compensation is deferred until retirement, disability, death, or termination of employment, but usually only at normal retirement age.

The employer does not receive any tax deduction unless and until the employee recognizes taxable income. The presumption is that the executive employee may be in a lower income tax bracket in retirement than in the maximum earnings years of employment. Another reason for using nonqualified plans is to delay the receipt of taxable cash flow to the executive until it is actually needed.

Section 457 Plans

A Section 457 plan is a deferred compensation plan of governmental units, governmental agencies, and nonchurch controlled, tax-exempt organizations. The amount deferred annually by an employee under a Section 457 plan cannot exceed the lesser of $14,000 (for 2005) or 100% (for 2005) of the employee's compensation currently includible in gross income. In addition, individuals who have attained age 50 may make additional catch-up contributions. The additional catch-up amount is $4,000 for 2005 and $5,000 for 2006 (indexed after 2006).

The following table summarizes the maximum contributions to a 457 plan:

Year	Maximum Contribution Before Age 50	Maximum Contribution Age 50 or Older
2005	$14,000	$18,000
2006	$15,000	$20,000
2007	Indexed	Indexed

The contribution limit is doubled in the three years prior to an individual's retirement. During this three-year period (before retirement), the catch-up rule does not apply.

Plan distributions cannot be made before one of the following:

a. The calendar year in which the participant attains age 70½.

b. Separation from service.

c. An unforeseeable emergency as defined in regulations.

d. In-service withdrawals are allowed for accounts ≤ $3,500.

Distributions must begin no later than April 1st of the calendar year after the year in which the plan participant attains age 70½.

SPLIT-DOLLAR LIFE INSURANCE

Split-dollar life insurance is an arrangement using permanent life insurance where there is a split between the employer and employee of premiums, ownership, and benefits. There is complete flexibility to arrange such splits any way agreed to by employer and employee. A common split-dollar plan, however, has the employer paying 100 percent of the premium and owning the policy. The employer names itself as beneficiary for an amount equal to the premiums paid to the date of death, and the employee names the beneficiary for the balance of the proceeds. The arrangement is essentially an interest-free loan to the employee. The employer receives no income tax deduction for the payment of the premiums. The employee must recognize taxable income annually to the extent of the true mortality costs using a schedule of mortality costs as determined by the Internal Revenue Service. Ownership and split arrangements can take many different forms and result in various different methods of taxation to the employee. Essentially, the benefit to the employee of split-dollar life insurance is free, permanent insurance to the extent there is value in excess of the true mortality costs.

EMPLOYEE STOCK OPTION PLAN

In employee stock option plans, the employer grants to the employee a right (option) to purchase a fixed number of shares of the employer's stock for a set price (exercise price) during a specified period of time. The purpose of granting such stock options to employees is to align executive compensation to stock performance more closely. These options may be nonqualified stock options (NQSOs) or incentive stock options (ISOs). The NQSO is taxable to the recipient at the

time of exercise to the extent of the difference between the fair market value of the stock and the exercise price as ordinary Form W-2 income. The exercise of ISOs does not create taxable income, as with NQSOs. There is income, however, for alternative minimum tax purposes created upon the exercise of the ISO. When employees exercise numerous ISOs, it may cause them to pay an alternative minimum tax. In addition, the shares that are acquired through the ISO exercise cannot be sold before one year from the date of exercise or two years from the date of grant. If this holding period is satisfied, the gain upon the sale of the ISO shares will be long-term capital gain; otherwise, the income will be ordinary. Therefore, ISOs provide some important advantages to the employees, but also have certain restrictions on the number that can be granted and when the shares can be sold.

THE FINANCIAL PLANNER'S ROLE IN RETIREMENT PLANNING

The financial planner's role in retirement planning is to assist clients in the accomplishment of their retirement goals. Retirement plans have many tax advantages, business benefits, and other advantages. Financial planners must be able to identify the objectives of the client and assist the client in choosing a retirement plan that meets those objectives.

PROFESSIONAL FOCUS

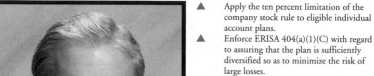

When do you recommend a qualified plan over a nonqualified plan and vice versa?

Prior to proposing a qualified or a nonqualified plan to a client we use a very detailed process for gathering client information. Our concerns are numerous, but we focus in three primary areas of concerns: Does the client have a will? Does the client have an emergency fund? Has the client resolved his risk exposure? After making these determinations we advise and review the tax laws with our clients to determine the need for pretax and tax deferred vehicles, such as retirement plans. We then move our clients on to tax-deferred investments (nonqualified plans; no load annuities) and then to the mainstream of investing.

What characteristics of a qualified plan do you find most appealing?

By far the most interesting of all plans are the profit-sharing/401(k) plans. From a planning standpoint, they allow the planner to offer the business owner a great deal of flexibility. The discretionary aspect of the plans provides the owner the flexibility to deal with the uncertainty of the business environment. Their design permits the business owner the opportunity to take advantage of the plans' intrinsic benefits provided in the tax code.

Do you find that corporate clients are hesitant to fund a retirement plan for employees because they would rather direct all the funds to themselves, or do many of your corporate clients seem concerned about their employees' retirement future?

The majority of our clients have a concern for their employees. The concern is based more on the retention aspect rather than from a retirement point of view. As far as directing all the funds to themselves; if the plan is designed correctly the business owner will benefit. The tax savings alone is easily demonstrated, and when combined with the long-term savings on a pretax and a tax-deferred basis, the benefits become obvious to the business owner.

What are the major issues raising doubts that a 401(k) plan will be able to deliver on its pledge of providing an adequate retirement?

Over the last two decades the increasing use of 401(k) plans has provided employees with a method of savings on a pretax and tax-deferred basis for their retirement. The effect has been to turn these employees into their own money managers. With less than an estimated 20% of the participants having the knowledge to direct their own investment decisions, these plans have lost an enormous amount of their intrinsic value. Participants are now faced with two separate and distinct problems. One is the Social Security crisis. The second is the dramatic decline of their 401(k) plan assets. Participants who planned for their golden years are now facing an austere future. There are steps, however, that can be taken to reduce the catastrophic circumstances of the past several years.

- ▲ Apply the ten percent limitation of the company stock rule to eligible individual account plans.
- ▲ Enforce ERISA 404(a)(1)(C) with regard to assuring that the plan is sufficiently diversified so as to minimize the risk of large losses.
- ▲ Do not chase past performance, but create an investment mix that matches the goals and risk tolerance, and stay the course.
- ▲ Rebalance and adjust the portfolio once a year to maintain its asset allocation.
- ▲ Keep an eye on expenses. This information is available in the fund prospectus.
- ▲ Gain the assistance of an investment adviser to assist participants using asset allocation to develop a portfolio that matches their risk/reward spectrum.

401(k) plans are long-term investment vehicles and should not be looked upon as short-term slush funds. Again, participants should stay the course and not forget that asset allocation is responsible for much of the success that participants will enjoy in the golden years.

How do you recommend individuals receive distributions from 401(k) plans and other tax-deferred distributions?

One of our biggest complaints is that the government has provided retirement incentives for employers to provide to their employees without providing any counseling prior to their retirement. With the risk of employees outliving their money there must be in place alternatives in order to avoid these consequences.

Much of the problem could be resolved by having easier access to annuity-type services to insure that these funds will provide a guarantee payment for life. It is basically up to the government and the insurance companies to step up to the plate and recognize that this problem exists.

A. PERRY HUBBS II, MBA, CFP®

DISCUSSION QUESTIONS

1. What is a qualified retirement plan?
2. What are the advantages of a qualified retirement plan, and what are its disadvantages?
3. What is vesting?
4. What are the two accepted vesting schedules?
5. Why were qualified retirement plans created?
6. What are the benefits of tax deferral in a qualified retirement plan, and how can they be calculated?
7. What are the different types of qualified retirement plans?
8. How do pension plans and profit-sharing plans differ?
9. How do defined-benefit plans and defined-contribution plans differ?
10. How do noncontributory plans and contributory plans differ?
11. What is a 401(k) plan, and how does it operate?
12. How do Keogh plans and corporate plans differ?
13. What are some examples of tax-advantaged, but nonqualified, retirement plans?
14. What are IRAs, SEPs, SIMPLEs, and 403(b) plans?
15. How are distributions from qualified retirement plans and other tax-advantaged retirement plans the same, and how do they differ?
16. What is a nonqualified plan, and what are some examples of this type of plan?
17. Why are nonqualified plans useful to employers?
18. Which qualified retirement plans permit in-service withdrawals?
19. Which qualified retirement plans require immediate vesting of employer contributions?

EXERCISES

1. Shawna, a 73-year-old single taxpayer, retired two years ago and is receiving a pension of $700 per month from her previous employer's qualified pension plan. She recently started a new job with a discount retail outlet that has no pension plan. She will receive $12,000 in compensation from her current job, as well as the $8,400 from her pension. How much can she contribute to a deductible IRA this year (2005)?
2. How much can the following individuals contribute to a deductible IRA in 2005? Assume that none of the persons listed or their spouses participate in an employer-sponsored pension plan.

Person	Marital Status	AGI
Larry	Single	$ 32,000
Mark	Married	$ 87,000
Lee Anne	Single	$ 56,000
Dennis	Married	$120,000

3. Tom and Denise are married and filed a joint income tax return for the tax year 2005. Tom earned a salary of $70,000 that year. Tom and Denise earned interest of $5,000 in 2005 on their joint savings account. Denise is not employed, and the couple had no other income. What amount could Tom and Denise contribute to IRAs for the year 2005 to take advantage of their maximum allowable IRA deduction on their 2005 tax return?

4. Evan and Jody, both age 52, are married and filed a joint income tax return for the year 2005. Their 2005 adjusted gross income was $100,000. The couple had no other income and neither spouse was covered by an employer-sponsored pension plan. What amount could Evan and Jody contribute to IRAs for 2005 to take advantage of their maximum allowable IRA deduction on their 2005 tax return?
5. Darlene and Rick are married and file a joint income tax return. They are both covered by a qualified retirement plan. Their 2005 adjusted gross income was $85,000. The couple had no other income. Assuming the couple is under age 50, what amount could Darlene and Rick contribute to a Roth IRA this year?
6. In January of the current year, Phil Black (age 47) took a premature distribution from a rollover IRA in the amount of $500,000, leaving him a balance in his IRA of $1,000,000. On October 31 of the current year, Phil died with the IRA account balance of $1,200,000. Which penalty or penalties will apply to Phil as a result of these facts?
7. The deductible contribution to a defined-contribution qualified pension plan on behalf of Ann, a self-employed individual whose income from self-employment is $25,000 and whose Social Security taxes are $3,825 is limited to what dollar amount?
8. Refer back to the above exercise concerning Ann, the self-employed person. What is the maximum Ann could contribute to a profit-sharing plan?
9. Robbins, Inc., a regular C corporation, is considering the adoption of a qualified retirement plan. The company has had fluctuating cash flows in the recent past and such fluctuations are expected to continue. The average age of nonowner employees is 24 and the average number of years of service is 3 with the high being 4 and the low 1. Approximately 25 percent of the 12-person labor force turns over each year. The 2 owners receive about two-thirds of the total covered compensation. Which is the most appropriate vesting schedule for Robbins, Inc.?
10. What is the minimum number of employees that must be covered in a defined-benefit plan to conform to ERISA requirements for a company having 100 eligible employees?

PROBLEMS

1. The XYZ Company has 2 employees - John, who earns $300,000 annually and his assistant, Kim, age 26 who has worked for John for 4 years. Kim makes $20,000. XYZ has a contributory pension plan using graduated vesting. Kim's account balance reflects the following:

Contributions		Earnings from Contributions		Kim's Total Balance
Employee	Employer	Employee	Employer	
$1,500	$2,000	$800	$1,200	$5,500

Reviewing the account and assuming that Kim terminated employment when the account balance was as above after 4 years of employment, how much could she take with her, plan permitting?

2. Yarbrough, Inc. has only the following employees, compensation, and other employer characteristics for years 2005 and 2006. Yarbrough, Inc. has an employer-contributing plan with no employee contributions and uses cliff vesting.

	Compensation	Ownership Interest	Years of Service*	Plan Account Balance*
A	$250,000	5%	2	$ 20,000
B	$180,000	8%	10	$300,000
C	$100,000	6%	8	$180,000
D	$ 60,000	1%	3	$ 27,000
E	$ 40,000	0%	2	$ 7,500
				* as of 12/31/06

Please answer all of the following questions:

- ▲ What is the total covered compensation for 2005?
- ▲ What would be the maximum profit-sharing contribution Yarbrough could make in 2005?
- ▲ Which of the employees is highly compensated?
- ▲ Is the plan top heavy?
- ▲ If D and E quit in January 2006, how much do they take with them, plan permitting?

PROBLEMS

1. The XYZ Company [illegible] John, who earns $800,000 annually, and his assistant, Kim, age [illegible] [illegible] for John for 4 years. Kim makes $70,000. XYZ has a [illegible] [illegible] graduated vesting. Kim's account balance reflects the following:

[illegible]	[illegible]	Employee	[illegible]
$1,000	[illegible]	$800	[illegible] $5,000

Reviewing the account, [illegible] Kim's [illegible] employment [illegible] the account balance was as above [illegible] of employment, how much could [illegible] plan participant?

2. Yarbrough, Inc. has only [illegible] following [illegible] and other employer characteristics for years 2005 and 2006. [illegible] plan with [illegible] employee contributions and [illegible]:

[illegible]		[illegible]	[illegible]		
$ 20,000		[illegible]	[illegible]	$200,000	A
$40,000		[illegible]	[illegible]	[illegible]	B
$180,000		[illegible]	[illegible]	$150,000	C
$ 27,000		[illegible]	[illegible]	[illegible]	[illegible]
$ 7,500		[illegible]	[illegible]	[illegible]	[illegible]
Total $[illegible]		[illegible]	[illegible]		

[illegible] the following questions:

a. What [illegible] 2005?
b. What [illegible] 2005?
c. [illegible]
d. Is [illegible]
e. [illegible]

CHAPTER 17

Introduction to Estate Planning

LEARNING OBJECTIVES:

After learning the material in this chapter, you will be able to:

1. Define estate planning and describe the estate planning process.
2. Discuss the objectives of and the benefits derived from planning an estate.
3. Explain the risks of failing to plan for estate transfer.
4. Identify the steps in the estate planning process.
5. List the types of client information necessary to begin and complete the estate planning process.
6. Identify the most common estate transfer objectives.
7. Discuss the types of property ownership interests and how each interest is transferred at death.
8. Identify and describe the basic essential estate planning documents.
9. Describe the probate process and list its advantages and disadvantages.
10. Understand why a unified gift and estate tax system exists.
11. Define the annual exclusion and explain its tax ramifications.
12. Explain the concept of gift splitting.
13. Identify the basic strategies for transferring wealth through the process of making gifts.
14. Define and explain the purpose of the federal estate tax.
15. Describe the gross estate, what assets are included in the gross estate, and the expenses and deductions that reduce the gross estate.
16. Describe how charitable planning impacts estate planning.
17. Define the marital deduction, and explain how it affects estate planning.
18. Define the generation-skipping transfer tax, and explain how it affects estate planning.

BASICS OF ESTATE PLANNING

This chapter presents the goals of efficient and effective wealth transfer, during life or at death, and the risks that are associated with such transfers. When a personal financial planner begins the estate planning process for a client, certain personal and financial data are collected from the client and analyses of that data are performed. Client interest in the estate planning process generally begins at or near the beginning of the distribution/gifting phase of the client's personal lifecycle. However, all clients need to have at least basic documents (e.g., will, durable power of attorney, and advanced medical directives) and provisions in the will for the care of minor children.

ESTATE PLANNING REFORM

The Economic Growth and Tax Relief Reconciliation Act of 2001 (herein referred to as EGTRRA 2001) was signed by President George W. Bush in June of 2001 providing a $1.35 trillion tax cut. While the estate and generation-skipping transfer tax are repealed in 2010, the repeal is phased in over a nine-year period (2001 - 2009). The new law also allows the previous (2001) estate tax rules, rates, and exemptions to come back in effect in 2011. Therefore, it is essential that the financial planner be familiar with the changing laws.

ESTATE PLANNING DEFINED

Estate planning may be broadly defined as the process of accumulation, management, conservation, and transfer of wealth considering legal, tax, and personal objectives. It is financial planning for our inevitable death. The goal of estate planning is the effective and efficient transfer of assets. An effective transfer occurs when the client's assets are transferred to the person or institution intended by the client. An efficient transfer occurs when wealth transfer costs are minimized consistent with the greatest assurance of effectiveness.

THE OBJECTIVES OF ESTATE PLANNING

Common objectives of estate planning include transferring (distributing) property to particular persons or entities consistent with client wishes; minimizing all taxes (income, gift, estate, state inheritance, and generation-skipping taxes); minimizing the transaction costs associated with the transfer (costs of documents, lawyers, and the legal probate process); and providing liquidity to the estate of the decedent at the time of death to pay for costs which commonly arise, such as taxes, funeral expenses, and final medical costs.

EXHIBIT 17.1: ESTATE PLANNING OBJECTIVES

- Fulfill client's property transfer wishes.
- Minimize taxes.
- Minimize costs.
- Provide needed liquidity.

Everyone needs a basic estate plan to provide for health care and property decisions and for transferring their property according to their wishes. An important estate planning objective is to assure that the decedent's property is received by the person, persons, or entities that the client desires.

Risks associated with failing to plan for estate transfer include the transfer of property contrary to the client's wishes; insufficient financial provision for the client's family; and liquidity problems at the time of death. Any of these risks could be catastrophic to the decedent's **heirs** and family. For example, a decedent's assets could be tied up in probate court for an indefinite period of time if that person has no will or has competing and conflicting heirs. Another consideration in estate planning is the excessively high transfer tax rates. The unified gift and estate taxation scheme is a progressive tax scheme and rises to 47 percent (2005) of the taxable estate transferred for estates exceeding $2,000,000. This amount decreases to 45 percent for estates over $1,500,000 in 2009.

heir - one who inherits; beneficiary

EXHIBIT 17.2: RISKS IN FAILING TO PLAN AN ESTATE

- Client's property transfer wishes go unfulfilled.
- Taxes are excessive.
- Transfer costs are excessive.
- Client's family not properly provided for.
- Insufficient liquidity to cover client's debts.

THE ESTATE PLANNING TEAM

The estate planning team consists of the attorney, accountant, life insurance consultant, trust officer, and financial planner. The role of the professional financial planner is to help integrate the work of the estate planning team in developing the overall estate plan.

The estate planning process is complex and somewhat confusing. A CPA is usually involved as a member of the estate planning team because the process requires the identification of assets, the calculation of the related adjusted tax basis, and other tax issues. An insurance specialist, such as a CLU or ChFC, is usually involved to help assure liquidity at death and protection for the client from the risks of untimely death. A licensed attorney is almost always a part of the team, as the process requires drafting numerous legal documents. The financial planner may serve as the team captain and assist in data collection, analysis, and investment decisions. While each member of the planning team may individually be an estate expert, each specialty brings with it a particular and unique perspective, the combination of which is more likely to produce a better result for the client. The financial planner, unless a licensed attorney, should be careful not to engage in any act that could be found to be the unauthorized practice of law.

The Estate Planning Process

There are eight basic steps to the estate planning process:

1. Gather client information, including the client's current financial statements.
2. Establish the client's transfer objectives, including family and charitable objectives.
3. Define any problem areas, such as the disposition of assets, liquidity issues, excessive taxes or costs, and other situational needs, such as disability of an identified heir.
4. Determine the estate liquidity needs now and at five-year intervals for the life expectancy of the transferor, including estate transfer costs.
5. Establish priorities for all client objectives.
6. Develop a comprehensive plan of transfer consistent with all information and objectives.
7. Implement the estate plan.
8. Review the estate plan periodically, and update the plan when necessary (especially for changes in family situations).

Steps 1 and 2 are briefly discussed below. An estate planning course would cover Steps 3 through 8.

Collecting Client Information and Defining Transfer Objectives

The collection of information is essential to gain a complete financial and family picture of the client and to assist the client in identifying financial risks. Information about prospective heirs and legatees needs to be collected to properly arrange for any transfer that the client wants to make.

To begin the estate planning process, the planner should collect:

- Current financial statements.
- Family information (that is, parents, children, ages, health).
- A detailed list of assets and liabilities, including the fair market value, adjusted taxable basis, and expected growth rate for all assets, how title is held, and the date acquired.
- Copies of medical and disability insurance policies.
- Copies of all life insurance policies in force identifying the ownership of each policy, the named insured, and the designated beneficiaries.
- Copies of annuity contracts.
- Copies of wills and trusts.
- Identification of powers of attorney and general powers of appointment.
- Copies of all previously filed income tax and gift tax returns (as available).
- Identification of assets previously gifted.
- Other pertinent information.

Once client and family information is collected, the process of determining the transfer objectives can be completed. Usually the most important objective of the client is to transfer assets as the client wishes. Secondly, the client generally wishes to avoid the shrinkage of the estate resulting from costs associated with the transfer. Exhibit 17.3 provides a list of common transfer objectives.

EXHIBIT 17.3: COMMON TRANSFER OBJECTIVES

- ▲ Minimizing estate and transfer taxes to maximize the assets received by heirs.
- ▲ Avoiding the probate process.
- ▲ Using lifetime transfers – gifts.
- ▲ Meeting liquidity needs at death.
- ▲ Planning for children.
- ▲ Planning for the incapacity of the transferor.
- ▲ Providing for the needs of the surviving spouse of the transferor.
- ▲ Fulfilling charitable intentions of the transferor.

BASIC DOCUMENTS INCLUDED IN AN ESTATE PLAN

The basic documents used in estate planning include wills, living wills or medical directives, durable powers of attorney for health care or property, and side letters.

WILLS

A **will** is a legal document that provides the testator, or will maker, the opportunity to control the distribution of property and avoid the state's intestacy law distribution scheme. In general, a will is valid when the will maker is at least 18 years old or an emancipated minor, and when the will maker is "of sound mind," that is, possessing **testamentary capacity**. The "sound mind" rules are not as rigorous as those rules that are required to form contracts. In other words, a person who may not have the legal capacity to form a contract may have sufficient legal capacity to make a will to transfer his or her assets.

Intestacy

To die "**intestate**" is to die without a valid will. In such a case, the state directs how the decedent's property will be distributed by creating a hypothetical will according to the state's **intestacy laws**. Just as "one size does <u>not</u> fit all," the intestacy laws are not likely to distribute property the way every person would wish, had they written their own will. There are possible adverse consequences of intestacy. In certain states, a spouse's share of the decedent's estate will be equal to a child's. For example, the surviving spouse's share with one child might be one-half, but with nine children it will be one-tenth. Certain states provide that a spouse's share is only a life estate with the true owner being the children. When there are no children, the surviving spouse may be forced to share with the deceased spouse's parents or brothers and sisters. Although each child's needs may be quite different, children may be treated equally, and, therefore, not necessarily equitably. Intestacy may require the appointment of an **administrator** who will usually have to furnish a surety bond, thereby raising the costs of administration. The court, not the decedent, will select any administrator of the estate.

will - a legal document used in estate planning that provides the testator, or will maker, the opportunity to control the distribution of property and avoid the state's intestacy law distribution scheme

testamentary capacity - having the mental capability to make a will to transfer assets; being of sound mind

intestate - to die without a valid will

intestacy laws - state laws that direct how a decedent's property will be distributed when the decedent dies without a will

administrator - in the event a decedent dies intestate (without a valid will), or where an executor cannot be appointed by the probate court, the court appoints an administrator with powers called letters of administration which enable the administrator to carry out duties set

Types of Wills

holographic will - handwritten will dated and signed by the testator

nuncupative/oral will - dying declarations made before sufficient witnesses

statutory will - generally drawn by an attorney, signed in the presence of witnesses, complying with the statutes for wills of the domiciliary state

There are three types of wills: holographic, oral/nuncupative, and statutory.

- **Holographic wills** are handwritten. The material provisions of the will are in the testator's handwriting. The will is dated and signed by the testator and does not need to be witnessed. Holographic wills are valid in most states.
- **Nuncupative (Oral) wills** are dying declarations made before sufficient witnesses. In some states, oral/nuncupative wills may only be able to pass personal property, not real property. The use of oral/nuncupative wills is fairly restricted and is illegal in some states.
- **Statutory (Formal) wills** are generally drawn by an attorney, complying with the statutes for wills of the domiciliary state. They are usually signed in the presence of two witnesses. A person who is a beneficiary under the will usually cannot be a valid witness.

Common Clauses

While all wills are different, there are certain clauses that appear in almost all wills. Common clauses that are generally found in even the simplest will include:

residuary clause - a general provision in a will that provides for the transfer of the balance of any assets not specifically mentioned in the will to someone or to some institution named by the testator

- An introductory clause to identify the testator.
- The establishment of the testator's domicile and residence.
- A declaration that this is the last will and testament of the testator.
- A revocation of all prior wills and codicils by the testator.
- The identification and selection of the executor/executrix and successor executor/executrix by the testator.
- A directive for the payment of debts clause.
- A directive for the payment of taxes clause.
- A disposition of tangible personal property clause.
- A disposition of real estate clause (that is, the residence and other real estate).
- Clauses regarding specific bequests of intangibles and cash.
- A **residuary clause** - the transfer of the balance of any other assets to someone or to some institution. (Note that the failure to have a residuary clause will result in the risk of having intestate assets [that is, assets accumulated after the will was prepared] which pass through probate. Also, taxes will be paid from the residuary unless specifically directed otherwise.)
- An appointment and powers clause, naming fiduciaries, guardians, tutors, trustees, etc.
- A testator's signature clause.
- An attestation clause, or witness clause.
- A self-proving clause.

simultaneous death clause - in the event that both spouses die simultaneously, this clause provides an assumption that one spouse (predetermined) predeceased the other spouse

survivorship clause - provides that the beneficiary must survive the decedent for a specified period in order to receive the inheritance or bequest

Other Clauses

More sophisticated wills often have additional clauses that dictate specific wishes regarding the handling of the estate. Additional clauses may include:

- A **simultaneous death clause** - In the event that both spouses die simultaneously, this clause provides an assumption of which spouse dies first.
- A **survivorship clause** – This clause provides that the beneficiary must survive the decedent for a specified period in order to receive the inheritance or bequest. This clause prevents property from being included in two different estates in rapid succession. In order for

transfers to qualify for the unlimited marital deduction, the survival period included in a survivorship clause for a spouse can be no longer than six months.

- A **disclaimer clause** – A disclaimer clause simply reminds the heir that disclaiming inheritances may be an effective tool in estate planning. A disclaimer allows property to pass from one party to another without gift tax consequences.
- A no-contest clause – This clause discourages heirs from contesting the will by substantially decreasing or eliminating their bequest if they file a formal contest to the will.
- A codicil – This document, which is separate from the will, amends a will (that is, where additional children are born after the original will is made).
- A spendthrift clause – This clause bars transfer of a beneficiary interest to a third party and stipulates that the interest is not subject to claims of the beneficiary's creditors. This clause is usually ineffective in a will.

disclaimer clause - a common clause in a decedent's will that allows property to pass from one party to another without gift tax consequences

POWER OF ATTORNEY

People frequently need another trusted person to make decisions for them regarding property or to make health care decisions for them under certain circumstances. A power of attorney is the legal document that allows the trusted person to act in one's place. It gives the right to one person, the **attorney-in-fact** (the power holder), to act in the place of the other person, the **principal** (power giver). A power of attorney may be very broad or very specific. The broadest power a person can give another is a **general power of attorney or appointment**. Such a power grants to the holder the power to do anything the giver could have done, including the power to make gifts to the holder or pay the holder's creditors. A **special or limited power of attorney or appointment** may be extremely narrow (that is, "I give you the power to pay my bills.") or very broad (that is, "You can do anything I can do, except appoint my assets to yourself, your creditors, your heirs, or their creditors."). All powers are revocable by the giver and all powers cease at the death of giver. A durability feature should be included if the giver intends that the power survive the incapacity or disability of the giver. The principal (the power giver) must be 18 years old and legally competent. A general power of attorney may result in inclusion in the gross estate of the assets over which one has power, if the power holder dies before the principal. In other words, if Jane has general power of attorney over Mary's assets, Mary's assets may be included in Jane's gross estate should she predecease Mary.

attorney-in-fact - the person designated by the principal in a power of attorney to act in place of the principal on the principal's behalf

principal - in a power of attorney document, the person (power giver) who designates another person or persons to act as his attorney-in-fact

general power of attorney/ appointment - gives the appointee the power to do anything the principal could do

special or limited power of attorney/appointment - limits the appointee to specific standards such as Health, Education, Maintenance and Support (HEMS), or nearly as broad as a general power, except no appointments to one's self, creditors, estate or one's estate's creditors

DURABLE POWER OF ATTORNEY FOR HEALTH CARE OR PROPERTY

A specific form of power of attorney is a **durable power of attorney issued either for health care or for property**. These powers are frequently issued to separate persons or, in the case of property, a financial institution. The power of attorney for health care or property eliminates the necessity to petition a local court to appoint a guardian ad litem or conservator to make health care or property decisions for a person who is incapacitated. It provides for continuity in the management of affairs in the event of disability and/or incapacity. The power may be springing or immediately effective (nonspringing). Generally, if the power is springing, the device must indicate that the power springs upon disability or incapacity and is not affected by subsequent disability or incapacity. The power is revocable by the principal. Durable powers of attorney are generally less expensive to set up and administer than a living trust or conservatorship. Durable powers of attorney can be abused, so the principal should give serious consideration to choosing the person to hold such power. The **durable feature** means the power survives incapacity and disability of the principal.

durable power of attorney issued either for health care or for property - a written document enabling the principal to designate another person or persons to act as his or her "attorney-in-fact"

durable feature - the power survives incapacity and disability of the principal

Note: A person possessing a durable power of attorney, in most cases, is not permitted to make gifts to himself or other family members (usually in conjunction with estate planning). If the power to gift to charitable or noncharitable donees is a desirable feature of the power of attorney, it should be separately and explicitly stated.

Living Wills and Advanced Medical Directives

A living will (also known as an advanced medical directive) is not a will at all, but rather the maker's last wishes regarding sustainment of life. It establishes the medical situations and circumstances in which the maker of the document no longer wants life-sustaining treatment. Such a document, though authorized in all states, must generally meet the requirements of a formally drafted state statute. A living will, or advanced medical directive, only covers a narrow range of situations, and usually applies only to terminal patients. Generally, a durable power of attorney issued for health care is insufficient to make decisions regarding the termination of life-sustaining procedures.

A Side Instruction Letter or Personal Instruction Letter

side instruction letter - also known as a personal instruction letter, separate from a will; details the testator's wishes regarding the disposition of tangible possessions (household goods), the disposition of the decedent's body, and funeral arrangements

A **side instruction letter**, or personal instruction letter, details the testator's wishes regarding the disposition of tangible possessions (household goods), the disposition of the decedent's body, and funeral arrangements. Because the side instruction letter exists separately from the will itself, it avoids cluttering the will with small details that may cause conflict among heirs. The letter is given to the executor or executrix. Such a letter may contain information regarding the location of important personal documents, safe deposit boxes, outstanding loans, and other personal and financial information that is invaluable to the executor. While, in most cases, the letter has no legal standing, the executor will generally carry out the wishes of the decedent.

THE PROBATE PROCESS DEFINED

probate process - serves to prove the validity of any will, supervise the orderly distribution of assets to the heirs, and protect creditors by insuring that valid debts of the estate are paid. Probate is also the legal process that performs the function of changing property title from a decedent's name to an heir's name.

The **probate process** serves to prove the validity of any will, supervise the orderly distribution of assets to the heirs, and protect creditors by insuring that valid debts of the estate are paid. In addition, when a person dies, there must be some legal way for the surviving heir to obtain legal title to the property inherited by that heir. Probate is the legal process that performs the function of changing title to those properties that do not change title any other way.

Exhibit 17.4 identifies the primary duties of an executor or administrator in the probate process. In the case of a valid will in which an executor is named, the probate court usually accepts such person and provides the executor with powers called letters testamentary. In the event of intestacy, or where an executor cannot be appointed by the probate court, the court will appoint an administrator (generally, a family member of the decedent). The court provides any appointed administrator with powers called letters of administration. The main differences between an executor and an administrator are that the decedent chooses the executor, the probate court names the administrator, and the administrator (but not the executor) must post a bond.

EXHIBIT 17.4: DUTIES OF EXECUTOR AND/OR ADMINISTRATOR

When the Decedent Dies Testate (with a will)	When the Decedent Dies Intestate (without a will)
The Executor:	The Administrator:
▲ Locates and proves the will.	▲ Petitions court for his or her own appointment.
▲ Locates witnesses to the will.	▲ Receives letters of administration.
▲ Receives letters testamentary from court.	▲ Posts the required bond.

Duties of the Executor or Administrator
▲ Locates and assembles property.
▲ Safeguards, manages, and invests property.
▲ Advertises in legal newspapers that person has died and creditors and other interested parties are on notice.
▲ Locates and communicates with potential beneficiaries.
▲ Pays the expenses of the decedent.
▲ Pays the debts of the decedent.
▲ Files federal and state tax returns, such as Forms 1040, 1041, and 706, and makes tax payments.
▲ Distributes assets to beneficiaries according to the will or the laws of intestacy.

Property Passing Through Probate

Property passing through probate includes property disposed of by a will, such as the fee simple (title), tenancy in common, and all other willed property. The next major section will discuss the different ways to title property. Also included in probate is property owned but not covered by a will, such as intestate property resulting from the failure to provide a residuary clause. Exhibit 17.5 illustrates various assets that pass through and around probate.

EXHIBIT 17.5: ASSETS PASSING THROUGH AND AROUND THE PROBATE PROCESS

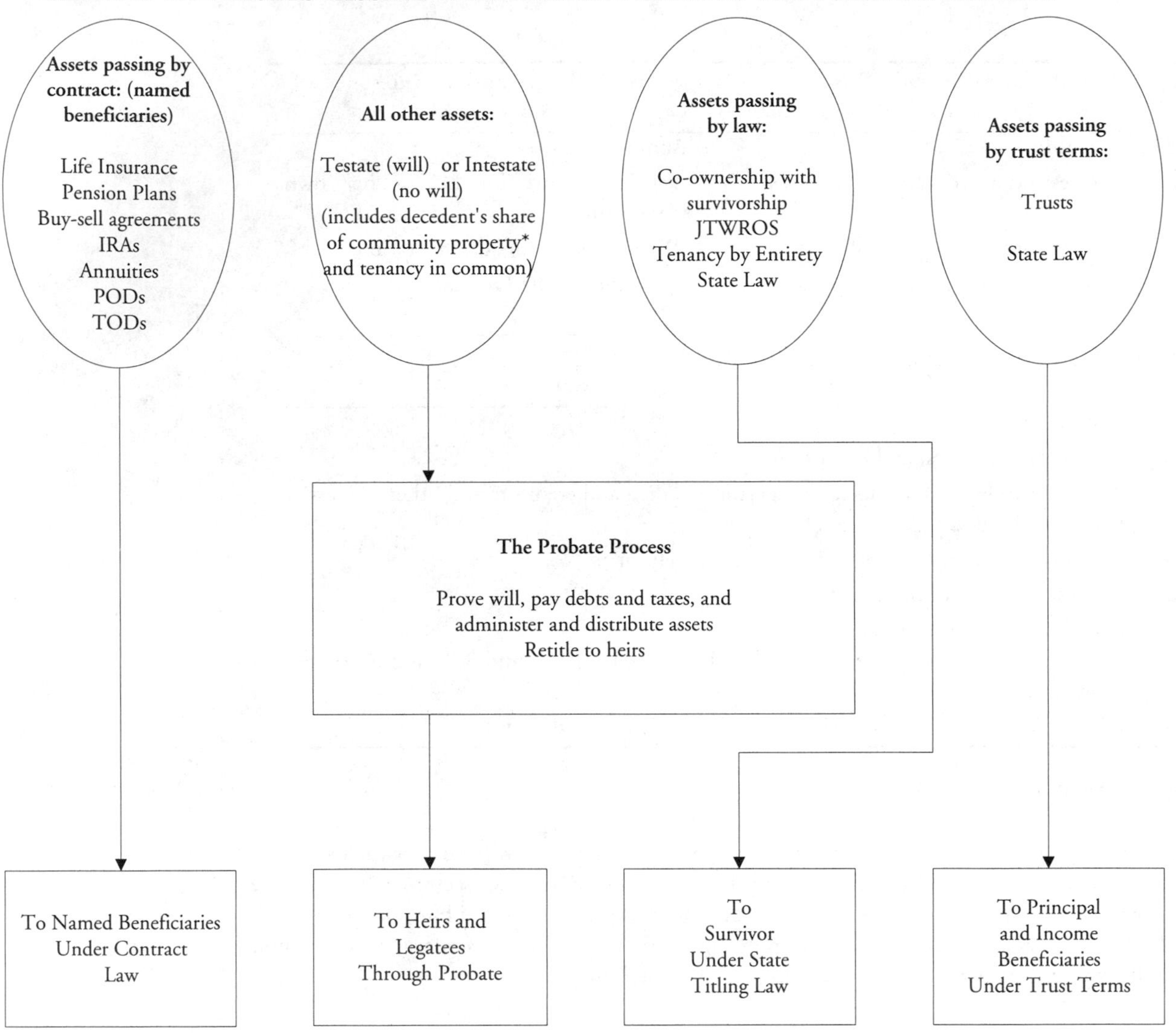
Assets passing by contract: (named beneficiaries)
Life Insurance
Pension Plans
Buy-sell agreements
IRAs
Annuities
PODs
TODs
All other assets:
Testate (will) or Intestate (no will)
(includes decedent's share of community property* and tenancy in common)
Assets passing by law:
Co-ownership with survivorship
JTWROS
Tenancy by Entirety
State Law
Assets passing by trust terms:
Trusts
State Law
The Probate Process
Prove will, pay debts and taxes, and administer and distribute assets
Retitle to heirs
To Named Beneficiaries Under Contract Law
To Heirs and Legatees Through Probate
To Survivor Under State Titling Law
To Principal and Income Beneficiaries Under Trust Terms

**Note that community property states vary on their probate treatment of community property passed to spouses*

PROPERTY PASSING OUTSIDE OF THE PROBATE PROCESS

Property that passes outside of the probate process includes contractual properties and those that are retitled by law. Contractual properties include life insurance proceeds with a named beneficiary, all pension plans and IRAs with named beneficiaries, all annuities with named joint annuitants, and pay-on-death/transfer-on-death accounts. Examples of other types of property that legally pass outside probate include property held by joint tenants with survivorship rights (JTWROS or Tenants by Entirety), and all trust property according to trust terms under state trust laws.

ADVANTAGES OF THE PROBATE PROCESS

The probate process has many advantages. It protects creditors by insuring that the debts of the estate are paid prior to distribution to heirs. It implements the disposition objectives of the testator of the valid will. It provides clean title to heirs or legatees. It increases the chances that all parties in interest have notice of the proceedings and, therefore, a right to be heard. Finally, it provides for an orderly administration of the decedent's assets. The probate process requires the executor or administrator to advertise the upcoming probate for a period of time in legal newspapers to give interested parties notice to enter into the process.

DISADVANTAGES OF THE PROBATE PROCESS

The probate process also has disadvantages. Probate can be both costly and complex. The legal notice requirement, attorney fees, and court costs create some of the costs. Delays are frequently caused by identification of property, valuation, identification of creditors and heirs, court delays, conflicts, and filing of taxes, to name a few. Real property located in a state outside the testator's domicile will require a separate ancillary probate in that state. One of the biggest disadvantages is loss of privacy since probate is open to public scrutiny.

OWNERSHIP AND TRANSFER OF PROPERTY

At any point in time, all property is owned by someone. Property may be described as real (land and buildings), tangible personalty (property that may be touched and is not realty – not affixed to the land, generally moveable), or intangible (stocks, bonds, patents, copyrights). Some property is specifically titled to a named person. Examples include real estate, automobiles (assuming the state has a motor vehicle title law), stocks, bonds, bank accounts, and retirement accounts. Other property may not have a specific title, for example, household goods. The state law in which a person is domiciled, or situs (location) of the property, determines the various types of ownership interests and the ways in which these interests can be transferred from one person to another, either during life or at death. Not all states have every alternative type or form of property interest. The forms have developed over time for the convenience of the citizens of the states that have adopted such forms.

The financial planning professional needs a working knowledge of the various forms of property interest and how each is transferred. Clients will need to be advised as to the initial ownership form depending on the client's objectives and the process the client will have to go through to transfer the property during life or at death.

PROBATE AND PROPERTY INTERESTS (TITLE AND OWNERSHIP)

Property interests take several different legal forms and include fee simple, tenancy in common, joint tenancy, tenancy by the entirety, community property, pay-on-death accounts, and transfer-on-death accounts. In addition, there are property ownerships that are less than complete, including life estates, usufructs, and interests for term.

Fee Simple

fee simple - the complete individual ownership of property with all rights associated with outright ownership, such as the right to use, sell, gift, alienate, or convey

Fee simple is the complete individual ownership of property with all rights associated with outright ownership, such as the right to use, sell, gift, alienate, or convey. When the property passes through the probate process, this type of property ownership interest is known as fee simple absolute.

Tenancy in Common

tenancy in common - two or more persons hold an undivided interest in a whole property

Tenancy in common is where two or more persons hold an undivided interest in the whole property. The percent owned by each party may differ. The property interest is treated as if it were owned outright and the owner's interest can be used, sold, donated, willed, or passed with or without a will. When one of the owners dies, the other owner does not necessarily receive the decedent's interest. The property passes through the probate process for retitling purposes. There is a right of partition, called the right to sever, in the event the owning parties cannot agree.

Joint Tenancy With Right of Survivorship (JTWROS) - Nonspouses

joint tenancy - two or more persons, called equal owners, hold the same fractional interest in a property

Joint tenancy is where two or more persons, called equal owners, hold the same fractional interest in a property. The right of survivorship (JTWROS) is normally implied. Joint tenants have the right to sever their interest in property without the consent of the other joint tenant, thereby destroying the survivorship right. Property held JTWROS at the time of death of a tenant passes to the surviving tenant(s) outside of the probate process according to state law regarding survivorship rights.

Tenancy by the Entirety - (JTWROS) - Between spouses only

tenancy by the entirety - a joint tenancy with right of survivorship (JTWROS) that can only occur between a husband and wife

Tenancy by the entirety is a JTWROS that can only occur between a husband and wife. Generally, neither tenant is able to sever their interest without the consent of the other tenant spouse. At the death of the first tenant, the property is passed to the surviving spouse according to the state law regarding tenancy by the entirety. Because the state law provides for retitling upon presentation of a legal death certificate, there is no need for this property to go through the probate process.

Community Property

community property - a regime where married individuals own an equal undivided interest in all wealth accumulated during marriage

Community property is a regime where married individuals own an equal undivided interest in all wealth accumulated during the marriage. Spouses may also own separate property that was acquired before marriage, inherited, or received by gift. It is possible to create separate property out of a community property by donating a spouse's interest to the other spouse. Community property does not have a survivorship feature, and thus, the decedent's half will generally require the probate process for retitling. If a spouse passes away, one-half of the community property is included in the gross estate of the decedent spouse. There is also a step to fair market value for both halves of the community property at the death of the first spouse. This is in contrast to noncommunity property that receives a step to fair market value only on the decedent spouse's share. Community property may be dissolved by death, divorce, or by agreement between the spouses.

Pay-on-Death (POD), Transfer-on-Death (TOD) Accounts

Pay-on-death bank accounts are fairly new devices. Most states have adopted these devices for bank accounts (PODs) and/or for investment accounts (TODs). Essentially they provide that if the owner of the account has a named beneficiary for such account, that account will legally transfer to the named beneficiary without going through the probate process. Such transfers reduce transfer transaction costs and may improve liquidity for the named heirs, thereby providing estate liquidity. A similar transfer mechanism has existed for a long time with regard to IRAs and other retirement accounts, annuities, and life insurance where a named person is the beneficiary of the accounts or policy. These beneficiary transfer mechanisms are easy and efficient and avoid the probate process, as they have no need to retitle.

Less Than Complete Ownership Interests

There are instances that provide for the creation of, or transfer of, less than the full and complete ownership of property under state law. Three of the most common types of less than full ownership are the life estate, the usufruct, and the interest for term.

Life Estate

A **life estate** is an interest in property that ceases upon the death of the owner of the life interest or estate. A life estate provides a right to income or a right to use, or both. It may be thought of as a right for a life term. Generally at the date of death of the party having the life estate, the property is transferred to the person who has the remainder interest. An example of a life estate is where one person leaves another the use of their beach property for the life of the other.

life estate - an interest in property that ceases upon the death of the owner of the life interest or estate

Usufruct

A **usufruct** is a Louisiana device similar to a life estate. A usufruct provides the holder with the right to use property and/or the right to income from a particular property. At the death of the usufructuary (the person with the usufruct), the property passes to the named owners (remaindermen).

usufruct - a Louisiana legal device similar to a life estate that provides the holder with the right to use, and/or the right to income from, a particular property

Interest for Term

An interest for term is another version of the life estate or usufruct, but instead of a life interest, the interest is for a definite term. An interest for term could involve an income or a use interest, or both. At the end of the interest for term, the property is transferred to the remainderman.

METHODS OF TRANSFER

In general, property ownership can be transferred during life or at death using one of the following three methods: outright, legal, or beneficial. In an outright transfer, the transferee receives both the legal title and beneficial, or economic, ownership. In a legal transfer, the transferee, such as a trust officer, receives only the legal title but not the beneficial or economic ownership. In a beneficial transfer, the transferee receives beneficial or economic ownership, as in a trust, but not the legal title.

Transfers During Life (Inter Vivos)

Property ownership transfers during life include transfer by sale, by gift, and by partial gift or sale. Transfer by sale is a transfer for the full value and full consideration (that is, straight sale or installment sale). Transfer by completed gift is a transfer for less than full fair market value. The concept of a completed gift is where the donor cannot recall, and no longer has, any control over the property that constituted the gift. Transfer by partial gift or sale is when the value received by the transferor is less than the fair market value of the property, the balance of which is treated as a gift referred to as a bargain sale. This type of transaction may be treated as a completed sale for state property law, but will be treated by the IRS as a transfer without full and adequate consideration.

Transfers at Death (Testamentary)

Transfers at death include transfers by will, by laws of intestacy, by other laws such as jointly held property with a survivorship feature (that is, JTWROS, or tenants by the entirety), by contract, and by trust. Transfers at death by contract with a named beneficiary other than the estate of the decedent include insurance policies, IRAs, retirement plan assets such as 401(k) plans, marriage contracts, and annuities. Transfers at death by trust instrument include revocable trusts and irrevocable trusts. All revocable trusts become irrevocable at death.

Transfers at death require retitling of the property from the decedent to the new owner. There are various retitling mechanisms, including state laws, which automatically retitle jointly held property where a survivorship feature exists. There are also legal contracts, which call for immediate retitling, such as life insurance and annuities, retirement accounts, and PODs/TODs with named beneficiaries. Where property is not automatically retitled under one of these other mechanisms, it will go through the probate process either provided by the decedent's will (testate) or following the state laws of intestacy for retitling to the heirs.

CONSEQUENCES OF PROPERTY TRANSFERS

The consequences of transfers of property ownership depend on the method of transfer. If there is a loss of control by the transferor, the transfer is by gift. Gift taxes may be due for *inter vivos* (during life) transfers and are usually paid by the donor/transferor. If the transfer is by sale, there is a loss of the sold asset and the possibility of capital gain taxes; however, the consideration received replaces the asset sold. If the transfer is at death through probate, either testate or intestate, there are the issues of costs, federal and state estate taxes, delays, and publicity.

INTRODUCTION TO TRUSTS

A **trust** is a legal arrangement (usually provided for under state law) in which property is transferred by a grantor to a trustee for the management and conservation of the property for the benefit of the named beneficiaries. The trustee could be either an individual or a financial institution (that is, bank). There are usually three parties to a trust: the grantor, the trustee, and the beneficiary. The grantor, or creator, transfers property to a trustee who takes legal title to those assets for the benefit of all trust beneficiaries. The trustee must adhere to the trust provisions regarding investments, distributions of income and corpus, and eventual termination of the trust. The trust earns income on the trust assets and may distribute such income to those entitled to it, called income beneficiaries. Usually, the grantor has created two types of beneficiaries—the income beneficiary and the remainder beneficiary. The remainder beneficiary receives the trust corpus upon termination of the trust. The income beneficiary and remainder beneficiary may in some cases be the same person, in which case we refer to such a trust as a single beneficiary trust. Exhibit 17.6 illustrates the basic structure of a trust.

trust - a legal arrangement, usually provided for under state law, in which property is transferred by a grantor to a trustee for the management and conservation of the property for the benefit of the named beneficiaries

EXHIBIT 17.6: STRUCTURE OF A TRUST

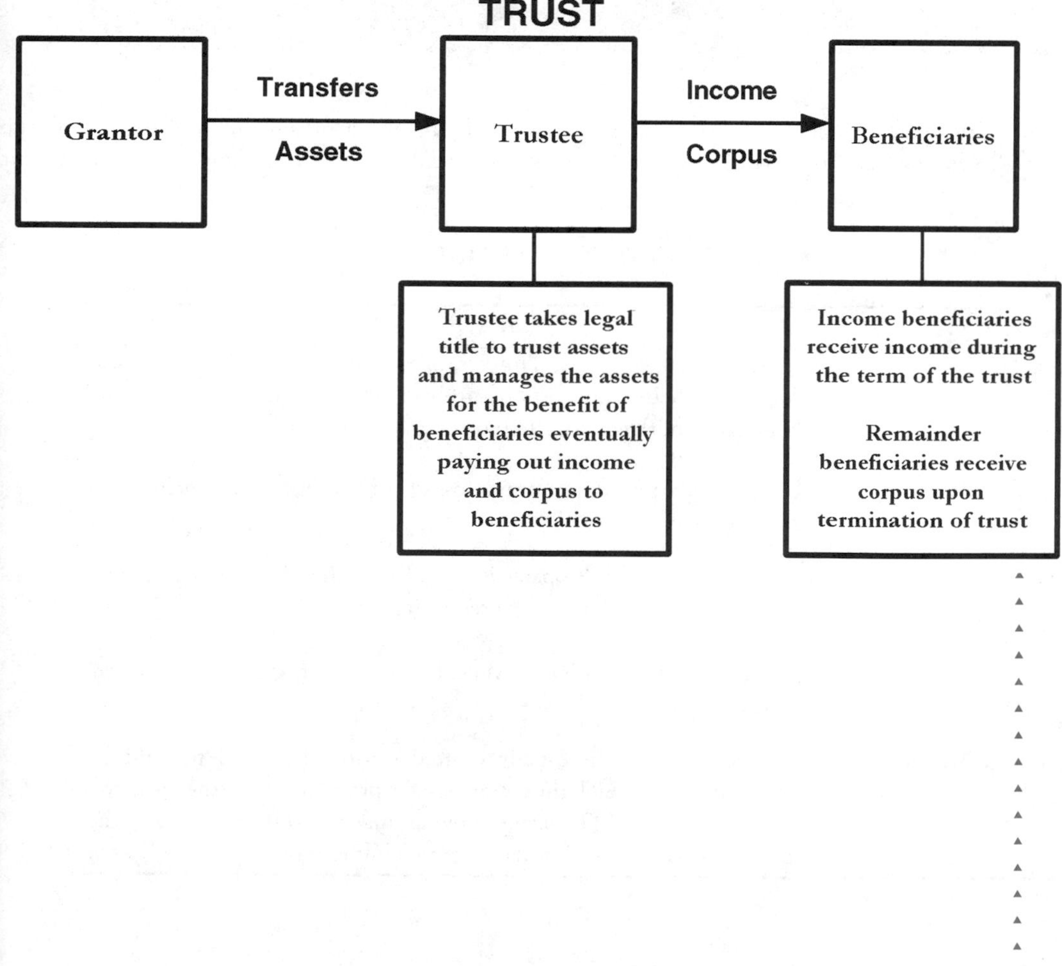
TRUST
Grantor
Transfers
Assets
Trustee
Income
Corpus
Beneficiaries
Trustee takes legal title to trust assets and manages the assets for the benefit of beneficiaries eventually paying out income and corpus to beneficiaries
Income beneficiaries receive income during the term of the trust
Remainder beneficiaries receive corpus upon termination of trust

Where on the Web

American Bar Association *www.abanet.org*

American Bar Assn's Probate and Trust Law Section *www.abanet.org/rppt*

American College of Trust and Estate Counsel *www.actec.org*

Cornell Law School *www.law.cornell.edu*

Estate Planning *www.estateplanninglinks.com*

FindLaw Internet Legal Resources *www.findlaw.com*

Internet Law Library: Trusts and Estates *www.lawguru.com/ilawlib*

National Association of Financial and Estate Planning Website *www.nafep.com*

Nolo Press Self-Help Law Center *www.nolo.com*

U.S. Estate Planning Law (Cornell University) *www.law.cornell.edu*

WebTrust *www.webtrust.com*

Wills of the Famous *www.courttv.com/legaldocs/newsmakers/wills*

Trusts are created for a variety of purposes, including the avoidance of probate, transfer tax reduction, and the management of the trust assets. Exhibit 17.7 lists some types of trusts and their uses.

EXHIBIT 17.7: TYPES AND USES OF TRUSTS

TYPE OF TRUST	USE OF TRUST
Living Trust (Revocable)	Used to manage assets. Protects in emergencies, such as medical. Avoids publicity and costs of probate. Property is included in the gross estate of the grantor (a type of grantor trust).
Irrevocable Trusts (Inter Vivos)	Used to make gifts. Grantor has loss of control. Assets not included in gross estate of grantor.
Testamentary Trusts	Created by the will. Property is included in the gross estate and does not avoid probate. Generally used to manage assets of heirs.
Trust for Minors	Manages assets for minors. May shift income tax burden to lower-bracket taxpayer.
Irrevocable Life Insurance Trust (ILIT)	An irrevocable trust, usually created during life, used to hold an insurance policy, and thus remove the proceeds from the insured's gross estate. The ILIT usually provides income to the spouse and the remainder interest to children or grandchildren.

Whether a trust is selected depends somewhat on the transfer goals of the grantor; the size of the estate; the nature of the relationship with and the financial competence of the spouse; any income needs of the spouse; the nature of the relationship with and financial security and competence of any adult children; any minor children; and any charitable intentions of the grantor. Where there is a split interest in assets (an income interest to one party, and the remainder interest to a different party) a trust is called for to reduce the risk that the income party will utilize all of the assets leaving nothing for the remaindermen. Common split interest trusts include the irrevocable life insurance trust, the credit equivalency trust, and QTIP trust, all of which may call for income to the decedent's spouse and the remainder to children or grandchildren. Trusts are also created to provide income to a noncharitable beneficiary (grantor/grantor spouse) with the remainder to a charity.

Trusts are either revocable or irrevocable and are either created during life (inter vivos) or at death (testamentary or mortis causa). If the trust is revocable, the property will be included in the gross estate of the grantor. A revocable trust will avoid the costs and process of probate, but will not reduce federal estate taxes since the grantor will still have ownership rights. If irrevocable, the property will generally <u>not</u> be included in the gross estate of the grantor. Irrevocable lifetime trusts are used to reduce estate taxes and to avoid probate. One example is the irrevocable life insurance trust (ILIT).

The inter vivos trust is created during the life of the grantor and may be revocable or irrevocable by the grantor. The property in an inter vivos trust avoids the probate process because it does not require the probate process to change title, as it is titled to the trust and not to the decedent. Alternatively, the property used to fund trusts created testamentary (by the will) first goes through the probate process prior to being retitled to the trust.

Although testamentary trusts neither reduce the estate tax nor avoid the costs and process of probate, they are useful in estate planning to protect the interests of minors, incompetents, or spendthrifts. Testamentary trusts are also useful when there is a split interest (income to one person and the remainder to someone else) such that the grantor did not want either party to be dependent on the other party for their interest.

EXHIBIT 17.8: TRUSTS SUMMARY BOX

Established During Life	Probate	Gross Estate	Income Tax	Gift Tax
Revocable	Avoid	Included	To grantor	None at creation
Irrevocable	Avoid	Excluded	To trust or beneficiary	May be subject to
Established by Will				
Testamentary	Does not avoid	Included	To trust or beneficiary	Not applicable

Living Trusts

A living trust is one in which the grantor creates an inter vivos trust that is funded with part or all of the grantor's property. The advantage of a living trust is that the property does not pass through probate at death, but rather transfer at death is accomplished according to the trust provisions and with a minimum of publicity, expense, and delays.

A revocable living trust is revocable during the grantor's life, and becomes irrevocable at the grantor's death. The fair market value of the assets in a revocable trust is included in the gross estate of the grantor. The transferor incurs no gift tax at the time of creation of a revocable trust, because there is no completed gift.

For an irrevocable trust created during life, the grantor places property into a trust that he cannot rescind or amend. Transfers of property to an irrevocable trust constitute completed gifts and any gift tax applies at the time the trust is created and funded. Assuming the grantor of such trust has no retained ownership interest in the irrevocable trust assets during life and at the time of his death, such assets are generally not included in the gross estate of the transferor (grantor), thereby providing both income tax and estate tax benefits to the grantor.

Grantor Trusts

A grantor trust is a trust in which the grantor transfers property into a trust but retains some right of enjoyment of the property, usually an income right. The Internal Revenue Code provides that if a grantor has control over the trust then a completed gift has not been made. The grantor still has ownership of the assets, and the trust is not a separate taxable entity. Consequently, all the income, deductions, and credits of the trust are attributable to the grantor for income tax purposes and possibly estate tax purposes.

Later in this chapter, we identify some other trusts that are useful in certain situations and are used to reduce transfer taxes. These application trusts listed in Exhibit 17.9 include:

EXHIBIT 17.9: APPLICATION TRUSTS AND THEIR USES

APPLICATION TRUSTS	TRUST USES
Credit Equivalency Trust (B Trust - B stands for "bypassing the spouse's estate")	A trust usually created by the will (testamentary) that provides an amount equal to any credit equivalency ($1.5 million for 2004 and 2005) to be placed in trust with the spouse, the usual income beneficiary, and the children or grandchildren, the remaindermen. The principal of the trust is not included in the estate of the surviving spouse.
Power of Appointment Trust (POA)	A power of appointment trust is usually created by will (testamentary) providing all income annually to the spouse and with the spouse having a power to invade the principal. The assets in this trust qualify for the unlimited marital deduction at the death of the first spouse. The assets will be included in the estate of the surviving spouse.
Qualified Terminable Interest Property Trust (QTIP)	A trust created testamentary whereby the executor elects QTIP status. The assets selected for this trust qualify for the unlimited marital deduction. The income beneficiary is always the spouse for all the income, paid at least annually. The remaindermen are chosen by the decedent. The assets remaining at the death of the surviving spouse are included in the estate of the surviving spouse.
Charitable Remainder Trusts (CRTs)	Charitable remainder trusts are irrevocable and may be created during life or testamentary. They are created to provide income to noncharitable beneficiaries (sometimes the grantor and/or spouse) with the remainder interest going to a charity at the end of the trust term.

REDUCING THE GROSS ESTATE

Generally, the smaller the gross estate, the smaller the estate tax liability. Appropriate use of qualified transfers (qualifying transfers directly to medical or educational institutions), gifts under the annual exclusion, and the lifetime use of the exemption equivalency, will all serve to reduce the size of the gross estate at death. Obviously, personal consumption and lifetime transfers to charities will also reduce the gross estate. Removing the proceeds value of life insurance from the gross estate can have a dramatic effect on reducing the size of the gross estate.

There is generally little value in a decedent having an ownership interest in a life insurance policy where the decedent is the insured. The insured has no way to benefit from the proceeds during life and is usually attempting to benefit heirs at the time of the decedent's death. Why not then let heirs (beneficiaries) or an ILIT trust own the insurance policy on the life of the insured? These are the two preferred financial and estate planning methods of owning life insurance. However, like everything else in financial planning, there are no absolutes and, careful consideration should be given as to whom should own any insurance policy for a particular insured.

It is relatively easy to have a zero estate tax liability – either leave the entire taxable estate to a charity or leave the estate in a qualifying way to the decedent's spouse. However, the decedent may not have any charitable intentions and/or may not have a spouse, or not a spouse to whom the decedent wants to leave the balance of the estate.

If a first spouse decedent leaves everything in a qualifying way to the surviving spouse, that will cause the deferral of estate tax until the death of the second spouse, which may (and many times does) occur shortly after the first death. In addition, since qualified transfers to a surviving spouse are added to the surviving spouse's personally owned assets to determine the gross estate of the surviving spouse, such transfers could increase the combined federal estate tax rate and amount of tax for the surviving spouse.

There are a wide variety of estate planning techniques for reducing the estate tax, all of which would be thoroughly covered in an estate planning course, but are beyond the scope of this text. However, consider that only "qualified" transfers to a spouse are deductible. Is it possible to have a spouse benefit from assets without those assets qualifying for the unlimited marital deduction? The answer is yes, and as a result, the first decedent can transfer an amount equal to the lifetime exemption to nonspouse beneficiaries, simultaneously providing the spouse with a life income interest from that same transfer. Because this type of transfer is a so-called split interest (an income interest to the spouse and a remainder interest to someone else) the arrangement calls for a trust to insure that neither party is dependent on the other for their interest.

The Use of Life Insurance in Estate Planning

The federal estate tax return (Form 706) and the tax liability are due within nine months of the decedent's death. Thus, estate liquidity planning is essential and may require the purchase of life insurance since the life insurance proceeds are quickly available from the insurer upon presentation of a proper death certificate to the insurer.

There is usually a need for liquid assets at the time of someone's death. The hospital wants to be paid, the funeral home and cemetery must be paid, and creditors want to be paid. Even the costs associated with getting a death certificate from the coroner must be paid. Often the need for liquidity at death is satisfied with life insurance proceeds because life insurance is one of the quickest sources of liquidity. The beneficiary only needs to send a certified copy of the death certificate to the insurer and the proceeds are generally paid immediately. While insurance is an effective tool to provide liquidity at death, the proceeds of such insurance will be included in the decedent's gross estate if the insured (decedent) has any incidents of ownership in the life insurance policy at death or if the decedent assigned or transferred gratuitously the policy within three years prior to death. Therefore, it is commonly thought wise that life insurance on one's life should be owned by either the beneficiary of such insurance or alternatively owned by an irrevocable life insurance trust. Either of these arrangements will avoid the proceeds of the life insurance policy being included in the insured's (decedent's) gross estate.

COMMON ESTATE PLANNING MISTAKES

INVALID, OUT-OF-DATE, OR POORLY DRAFTED WILLS

Having an invalid, out-of-date, or poorly drafted will can be detrimental to estate planning. There is nothing worse than spending time developing an estate plan only to have it fall apart due to an inadequate will. An invalid will subjects the estate to intestacy laws that may distribute property contrary to the decedent's wishes. The will is often deemed invalid because it does not meet statutory requirements, or because the decedent has moved to another state or domicile and has not reflected the new state's laws in the will. An outdated will often fails to minimize estate taxes because it does not contemplate changes in the tax law. Poorly drafted wills generally lack residuary clauses or other common drafting specificities, which can leave estate issues unresolved.

SIMPLE WILLS ("SWEETHEART" OR "I LOVE YOU" WILLS)

A simple will leaves everything to the decedent's spouse. Leaving everything to a spouse can cause an overqualification of the estate because it fails to take advantage of the credit equivalency for the first spouse who dies. The second spouse to die may pay estate taxes that could have been avoided with a credit equivalency trust or bequest. There is also the risk of a mismanagement of assets. Assets may be put in the hands of a spouse who does not have the education, experience, training, or desire to manage them efficiently and effectively.

IMPROPERLY ARRANGED OR INADEQUATE LIFE INSURANCE

Improperly arranged or inadequate life insurance can defeat successful estate planning. One common way an insurance policy is improperly arranged is when the proceeds are included in the decedent's gross estate. Inclusion will occur when the policy is owned by the decedent, the proceeds are made payable to the estate, or if the decedent has any incidents of ownership. Inclusion will also occur if the insurance was transferred within the last three years of the decedent's life.

A second, common way an insurance policy can be improperly arranged is when the beneficiary is ill equipped (emotionally, in legal capacity, or is a minor) to receive and manage those assets. A trust may provide the needed management of the insurance needs.

Another way an insurance policy can be improperly arranged is when the decedent fails to name a contingent beneficiary. If the original beneficiary predeceases the decedent, then the proceeds may be placed back in the estate where it may be subject to creditor claims, state inheritance laws, federal estate taxes, or all three.

Another improper arrangement of life insurance that should be avoided is the so-called "unholy trinity." The policy is owned by the spouse in the insured's life, and the spouse then names a child the beneficiary. At the death of the insured, the spouse has made a gift to the child.

An insurance policy is generally inadequate when it does not cover the needs of the insured including survivor needs and estate liquidity needs. Survivor needs are generally calculated as the present value of the lost income (net of taxes and the decedent's consumption) over the remaining work life expectancy. An industry rule of thumb is to use 10 times salary to offset inflation. However, either or both of these may be inadequate with regard to providing sufficient estate liquidity where the majority of the other assets in the estate are both large in value and illiquid (real estate or a closely held business).

Possible Adverse Consequences of Jointly Held Property

While having jointly held property with survivorship rights (JTWROS) offers some benefits, it can also pose several problems. One problem that may be encountered is that the decedent will not be able to direct the property to the person or entity to whom he or she wishes because the survivor will have the ultimate opportunity to name the remainderman. Another problem is that some jointly held property might result in a completed gift. The consequence of this may be a federal and state gift tax liability as well as an estate tax liability.

Estate Liquidity Problems

Insufficient cash assets and inadequate planning are two estate liquidity problems that should be avoided. When there are insufficient cash assets and estate planning has been inadequate, the estate may be forced to liquidate assets at a time when they are not fully valued or have not reached their potential value. The result is that assets may have to be sold at less than full value.

Wrong Executor/Trustee/Manager

Having the wrong executor/trustee/manager can cause several problems in the estate plan. When the named executor/trustee is incapable of administering the estate efficiently and effectively, it can make costs increase due to poor estate management. It can also cause potential conflicts of interest when there are proximity problems or family conflicts.

PROFESSIONAL FOCUS

Do many of your clients believe they do not need estate planning, and if so, how do you convince them of its importance?

As an attorney specializing in estate planning, clients are referred to me because they have recognized a need for estate planning. However, this recognition often occurs because some other professional—a financial planner, accountant, stock broker, or insurance agent—has reviewed some aspect of the client's assets and identified one or more estate planning issues that need to be resolved. Absent this threshold contact with another professional, few clients would recognize the complex issues involved in planning for their death or incompetence.

What do you believe are the biggest risks in failing to plan an estate?

▲ The decedent's property may not be distributed to the people or organizations he would have chosen or it may be distributed too soon (e.g., at what age should children receive assets?).

▲ The decedent's estate may be subject to probate. A common scenario involves a married couple who own property together with a right of survivorship and name each other as beneficiaries of life insurance, IRAs, and qualified plan (e.g., 401k) assets. If both spouses are killed in a common accident, all those assets are subject to probate.

▲ The decedent's estate may owe estate taxes. Few people recognize that they own assets of sufficient value to incur estate taxes at their death. While the use of a Credit Equivalency Trust is a relatively simple estate planning technique to achieve estate tax savings for a married couple, without professional assistance the couple would most likely not understand the problem, or comprehend the solution.

▲ Guardianship of minor children. A decedent may nominate in advance a guardian for his minor children. If no guardianship preferences have been expressed by the decedent, the appointed guardian may not be the person the decedent would have chosen.

What advantages and disadvantages do you give your clients for having their assets pass through probate versus through the operation of law, contract or lifetime giving?

The probate process is both costly (7 - 10% of the estate's value) and lengthy (averaging 18 - 24 months). The advantages of probate are primarily to creditors and disappointed heirs who are given the opportunity to litigate their claims against the decedent's estate. One way to avoid probate is to pass property at death by operation of law (e.g., JTWROS). However, this solution raises other problems—adding a joint owner to the title of property can create issues regarding asset protection, income taxes, and gift taxes. Passing property by contract (e.g., a life insurance beneficiary) also is preferable to probate, but a client must plan for the contingency that the beneficiary will predecease him. My preference is to have assets owned by a revocable living trust and/or to have that trust named as primary or contingent beneficiary of property passing by contract. This avoids all of the problems discussed above. Lifetime giving is usually desirable if the donor can afford to give the asset away, but the recipient is denied a "stepped-up" basis in the asset for income tax purposes.

Do you recommend the use of trusts to your clients? If so, which ones?

I strongly favor the use of a revocable living trust in conjunction with a will and with property passing by contract. I often structure such a trust to activate subtrusts upon the occurrence of a certain condition (e.g., death). Depending on the needs of the client, these subtrusts may include a Power of Appointment Trust, Credit Equivalency Trust, Disclaimer Trust, Qualified Terminable Interest Property Trust / QTIP and Qualified Domestic Trust /QDOT. In addition to the above, to meet the needs of high net worth clients, I use Irrevocable Life Insurance Trusts and Charitable Remainder Trusts.

ROBERT KIRBY, JD, CFP®

THE UNIFIED GIFT AND ESTATE TRANSFER TAX SYSTEM

The federal estate tax exists as a method of raising revenue for the federal government. It also functions as a method of social reallocation of wealth. The estate tax system prevents large masses of wealth from being transferred from one generation to subsequent generations. When a taxpayer with a large estate dies, a large portion of the estate will be paid to the federal government in the form of estate tax and thus, will be reallocated to other members of society.

The unified estate and gift transfer tax system exists for the purpose of preventing individuals (donors) from freely transferring property to family members (donees) in an attempt to minimize income and estate tax. Congress, being ever mindful of the resolve and ingenuity with which some taxpayers try to avoid federal taxes, established an excise tax for gifts during life. The excise tax is applied to the transfer of property gratuitously during life. In 1976, Congress unified the gift and estate tax schedules (Exhibit 17.10) to prevent taxpayers from manipulating transfers during life and death.

unified gift and estate transfer tax system - unified tax transfer system created by Congress to ensure that at the time of transfer of property, either during life (gifts) or at death (bequests), the transferor will pay the same tax rate or amount for the transfer, regardless of when the transfer is made

The general theory behind the **unified gift and estate transfer tax system** is that at the time of transfer of property, either during life (gifts) or at death (bequests), the transferor will pay the same tax rate or amount for the transfer, regardless of when the transfer is made. Later in the chapter, we will point out major differences between transfers made during life and those made at death. Observe in Exhibit 17.10 that the unified gift and estate transfer tax rates begin at 18 percent and progress to 47 percent in 2005. The maximum rate is decreasing through 2009 (see Exhibit 17.11). As with many other types of taxes, there are ways to arrange one's financial affairs to reduce or eliminate the transfer tax, thus preserving a greater portion of the estate for heirs.

EXHIBIT 17.10: UNIFIED TAX RATE SCHEDULE FOR GIFTS AND ESTATES FOR 2005

Over $0 but not over $10,000	**18%** of such amount.
Over $10,000 but not over $20,000	$1,800 plus **20%** of the excess of such amount over $10,000
Over $20,000 but not over $40,000	$3,800 plus **22%** of the excess of such amount over $20,000
Over $40,000 but not over $60,000	$8,200 plus **24%** of the excess of such amount over $40,000
Over $60,000 but not over $80,000	$13,000 plus **26%** of the excess of such amount over $60,000
Over $80,000 but not over $100,000	$18,200 plus **28%** of the excess of such amount over $80,000
Over $100,000 but not over $150,000	$23,800 plus **30%** of the excess of such amount over $100,000
Over $150,000 but not over $250,000	$38,800 plus **32%** of the excess of such amount over $150,000
Over $250,000 but not over $500,000	$70,800 plus **34%** of the excess of such amount over $250,000
Over $500,000 but not over $750,000	$155,800 plus **37%** of the excess of such amount over $500,000
Over $750,000 but not over $1,000,000	$248,300 plus **39%** of the excess of such amount over $750,000
Over $1,000,000 but not over $1,250,000	$345,800 plus **41%** of the excess of such amount over $1,000,000
Over $1,250,000 but not over $1,500,000	$448,300 plus **43%** of the excess of such amount over $1,250,000
Over $1,500,000 but not over $2,000,000	$555,800 plus **45%** of the excess of such amount over $1,500,000
Over $2,000,000	$780,800 plus **47%** of the excess of such amount over $2,000,000

The estate and gift tax rates and credit exemption amount for estate tax purposes for 2005 through 2009 are as shown in Exhibit 17.11.

EXHIBIT 17.11: ESTATE AND GIFT TAX RATES AND CREDIT EXEMPTION AMOUNT FOR 2005-2010

Calendar Year	Estate and GST Tax Deathtime Transfer Exemption	Highest Estate and Gift Tax Rates
2005	$1.5 million	47%
2006	$2 million	46%
2007	$2 million	45%
2008	$2 million	45%
2009	$3.5 million	45%
2010	N/A (taxes repealed)	Top individual rate under the bill (gift tax only)

In 2010, the estate and generation-skipping transfer taxes are repealed (EGTRRA 2001). Also beginning in 2010, the top gift tax rate will be the top individual income tax rate as provided under the bill, and except as provided in regulations, a transfer to trust will be treated as a taxable gift, unless the trust is treated as wholly owned by the donor or the donor's spouse under the grantor trust provisions of the Code.

After repeal of the estate and generation-skipping transfer taxes, the present-law rules providing for a fair market value (i.e., stepped-up) basis for property acquired from a decedent are repealed. A modified carryover basis regime generally takes effect, which provides that recipients of property transferred at the decedent's death will receive a basis equal to the lesser of the adjusted basis of the decedent or the fair market value of the property on the date of the decedent's death.

THE FEDERAL GIFT TAX SYSTEM

PURPOSE AND DEFINITION

gift - in estate planning, a direct transfer of property or cash made during life

Recall that one of the estate planning objectives mentioned earlier in this chapter was the effective and efficient transfer of property. What could be more effective or efficient than a direct **gift** from the client during life to a loved one? First, since the client is still living, the transferor can assure the completion of the gift. Second, the direct gift generally has little transaction cost except for perhaps the cost to change the title to the asset (such as in the case of retitling a car in the name of the donee). Third, the client (transferor) is able to see the beneficial effect of his transfer and the joy the gift brings to the donee while also enjoying the pleasure of making the gift. Unfortunately, whenever a gift is made, the client loses control of the asset given and loses income from the asset, which may be needed currently or at some point in the future. The creation of a joint bank account is not a gift until the joint tenant removes the money for his or her own benefit. Also, the client has financially empowered the donee (transferee), which may turn out to be ill-advised. The transferee may not use the property wisely, as the transferor intended, or may no longer behave in a way in which the transferor desired. Even with these noted disadvantages, lifetime gifts remain a cornerstone of estate planning for the reasons stated above, and for reasons discussed below.

If the overall objective of the client is estate reduction, it may be wise to transfer the property belonging to the transferor that has the greatest potential for future appreciation, rather than to transfer cash or property that has already appreciated. A gift of property will be valued for gift tax purposes at the fair market value as of the date of the gift or transfer. Therefore, any future appreciation on the transferred property will be to the transferee (donee) and, thus, out of the transferor's gross estate. Property, which commonly has substantial future appreciation includes, but is not limited to, (1) business interests, (2) real estate, (3) art or other collections, (4) investment securities (stocks and bonds), and (5) other intangible rights (patents, copyrights, royalties). Thus, the selection of property for gifting requires careful financial and estate planning consideration.

Annual Exclusion

annual exclusion - a result of a de minimis rule by Congress to help reduce income tax reporting by eliminating the need for taxpayers to keep an account of, or report, small gifts. All individuals are allowed to gift, tax free, up to $11,000 (for 2005) per donee per year.

All individuals are allowed to gift, tax free, up to $11,000 (for 2005) per donee per year. This **annual exclusion** is a result of a de minimis rule by Congress to help reduce reporting requirements of taxpayers for small gifts. However, to qualify for the annual exclusion, the gift must be of a present interest, which means that the donee can currently benefit from the gift. If the gift is of a future interest, such as a gift of a remainder interest in a trust, then the gift does not qualify for the annual exclusion and must be reported. The $11,000 annual exclusion is indexed to the CPI.

If a person (transferor) is married and joins with his spouse to use both annual exclusions for a particular donee, the exclusion is effectively increased to $22,000 per donee per year. Since the exclusion per donee perishes annually, the spouse donor is essentially using the exclusion right for this particular donee, this particular year, because the nondonor spouse would not have used it. When one donor makes the gift, but the donor's spouse consents and agrees to use their annual exclusion for that donee, then the joint gift is called a **split gift**. A gift tax return (Form 709) is required for all split gifts, and both spouses are required to sign the gift tax return. In addition, if an election to split gifts is made, it applies to all gifts made from both spouses during the year while the spouses were married. Only gifts made while the donors are married qualify for split-gift treatment.

split gift - a joint gift made by spouses which has the effect of doubling the annual exclusion of gifts to the donee. Requires the consent of the spouse and spouse's signature on Form 709.

Not all joint gifts are subject to gift splitting. Gifts of community property, for example, do not require gift splitting, since each spouse is deemed to own one-half of any community property. Therefore, any gift of community property is a joint gift not subject to gift splitting. Gift splitting was enacted as a way to equalize community and noncommunity property states. Since gifts of community property are not considered gift splits, a return is not required unless the gifts constitute taxable gifts. (i.e., exceed $22,000 to an individual recipient).

EXAMPLE

Gift Splitting

Kelly made the following gifts in the current year:

Gift		Donee	Value
Cash		Nephew	$12,000
6-month CD		Niece	8,000
Antique rifle		Friend	20,000
Bonds in trust:	Life estate to:	Father	60,000
	Remainder to:	Niece	18,000
		Total	$118,000

Kelly's total taxable gifts for the current year equal $77,000 as described below:

Donee	FMV	Less Annual Exclusion	Total Taxable Gifts
Nephew	$12,000	$11,000	$1,000
Niece	8,000	8,000	0
Friend	20,000	11,000	9,000
Father	60,000	11,000	49,000
Niece	18,000	--	18,000
Total Gifts	$118,000	$41,000	$77,000

All of Kelly's gifts qualified for the annual exclusion except the gift to her niece consisting of the remainder interest in a trust. Because her niece is unable to currently use the gift, it is not a gift of a present interest, and therefore, does not qualify for the annual exclusion. All of the other gifts qualify since they are of a present interest.

EXAMPLE

Gift-Splitting Comparison

John and Mary made the following gifts during the current year:

	From John	From Mary	Total
To son, Paul	$40,000	$16,000	$56,000
To daughter, Virginia	40,000	6,000	46,000
To granddaughter, Terry	20,000	4,000	24,000
	$100,000	$26,000	$126,000

A comparison of gift splitting and not using gift splitting is provided for John and Mary's taxable gifts below.

If Gift Splitting is Elected (The parties must split all gifts made during year)

	From John	From Mary	Total
To Paul	$28,000	$28,000	$56,000
To Virginia	23,000	23,000	46,000
To Terry	12,000	12,000	24,000
Total Gross Gifts	$63,000	$63,000	$126,000
Less Annual Exclusions			
For Paul	$11,000	$11,000	$22,000
For Virginia	$11,000	$11,000	$22,000
For Terry	$11,000	$11,000	$22,000
Total Exclusions	$33,000	$33,000	$66,000
Equals Current Taxable Gifts	$30,000	$30,000	$60,000

If Gift Splitting is Not Elected

	From John	From Mary	Total
To Paul	$40,000	$16,000	$56,000
To Virginia	40,000	6,000	46,000
To Terry	20,000	4,000	24,000
Total Gross Gifts	$100,000	$26,000	$126,000
Less Annual Exclusions			
For Paul	$11,000	$11,000	$22,000
For Virginia	$11,000	$6,000	$17,000
For Terry	$11,000	$4,000	$15,000
Total Exclusions	$33,000	$21,000	$54,000
Equals Current Taxable Gifts	$67,000	$5,000	$72,000

Electing to split gifts in the above example results in a decrease in the total taxable gifts from $72,000 to $60,000. The $12,000 difference is a result of Mary not making full use of her annual exclusion for gifts to Virginia ($11,000 – $6,000 = $5,000) and gifts to Terry ($11,000 – $4,000 = $7,000).

APPLICABLE CREDIT AMOUNT

In addition to the annual exclusion, there is a lifetime gift and estate tax credit that is used to offset the gift and estate tax on inter vivos and testamentary transfers. This credit allows taxpayers to transfer during life, assets totaling $1,000,000 or $1,500,000 at death (for 2005) without incurring any transfer tax.

EXHIBIT 17.12: APPLICABLE EXCLUSION AMOUNT AND CREDIT AMOUNT 2005)

	2005
Applicable Exclusion Amount	
Gift Tax	$1,000,000
Estate Tax	$1,500,000
Applicable Credit Amount	
Gift Tax	$345,800
Estate Tax	$555,800

The applicable credit amount available at death increases until the estate tax is repealed in 2010. The increase is depicted in Exhibit 17.13.

EXHIBIT 17.13: APPLICABLE CREDIT AMOUNT FOR ESTATE TAX (2005-2010)

Year of Death	Applicable Credit Amount	Applicable Exclusion Amount
2005	$555,800	$1,500,000
2006 – 2008	$780,800	$2,000,000
2009	$1,455,800	$3,500,000
2010	Repealed	Repealed

qualified transfer - a payment made directly to an educational institution for tuition and fees or to a medical provider for medical expenses for the benefit of someone else

QUALIFIED TRANSFERS

Certain transfers, called qualified transfers, are not subject to transfer tax. A **qualified transfer** is a payment made directly to an educational institution for tuition and fees or a payment made directly to a medical provider for medical expenses for the benefit of someone else. These qualified transfers allow taxpayers to effectively transfer wealth to others without being subject to transfer tax. However, to qualify for this treatment, the payments must be paid directly to the specific institution.

EXAMPLE

Jennifer, who is single, gave an outright gift of $60,000 to her friend, Tiffany, who needed the money to pay her medical expenses. Because the gift was made to Tiffany, instead of being paid directly to the medical institution, it cannot be considered a qualified transfer. However, the gift is of a present interest and, therefore, qualifies for the $11,000 annual exclusion. Therefore, Jennifer has made taxable gifts of $49,000 and must file a gift tax return to report the gift. If Jennifer had paid the medical expenses directly to the medical institution for Tiffany, the entire $60,000 received for Tiffany would have escaped gift taxes. In addition, Jennifer would have been able to give Tiffany another $11,000 that would qualify for the annual exclusion.

Because qualified transfers are not subject to gift tax and there is no limitation on the amount of the qualified transfer, it allows family members to provide assistance to other family members without worrying about transfer taxes. In addition, families can make use of the rules to minimize gift tax within the family by allowing, for example, grandparents to pay for college education for their grandchildren instead of making taxable gifts to the parents, who would, in turn, pay for the college expenses.

GIFTS TO SPOUSES

The law allows for unlimited transfers to be made between spouses during life or at death. However, to be eligible for the unlimited **marital deduction**, the donee spouse must be a citizen of the United States. The unlimited marital deduction allows for one spouse to leave their entire estate to the surviving spouse without encumbering it with transfer taxes. Therefore, the surviving spouse will have full use of all property that was held by the deceased spouse.

marital deduction - unlimited amount for transfers to spouse of property during life (gifts) or at death

PAYMENTS FOR SUPPORT

Payments for legal support are transfers to children that are essentially legal support obligations. Payments of support are exempt from the gift tax rules.

payments for legal support - transfers to children that are essentially legal support obligations; exempt from gift tax rules

REPORTING AND PAYING TAXES

Taxable gifts are reported on the federal gift tax return, which is Form 709. The gift tax return is due April 15th, but may be extended until October 15th, as with individual income tax returns. However, the gift tax is not extended as a result of the extension of time to file, and is therefore due on April 15th, similar to individual income tax. The donor is liable for any gift tax due. The gift tax return is also used to report transfers that are subject to generation-skipping transfer tax, which is discussed later in the chapter.

EXHIBIT 17.14: BASIC STRATEGIES FOR TRANSFERRING WEALTH THROUGH GIFTING

Generally, if the objective of the transferor is to reduce the size of the transferor's gross estate, the transferor can use the following lifetime gifting techniques to achieve a lower gross estate at death:
▲ Make optimal use of qualified educational transfers (pay tuition for children and grandchildren from private school through professional education).
▲ Pay medical costs for children, grandchildren, and heirs directly to provider institutions.
▲ Make optimal use of the \$11,000 annual gift exclusion (\$22,000 if the gift is made jointly with the spouse). Example: John is married to Joan and has 3 adult children who all have stable marriages and there are 7 grandchildren. John and Joan can gift \$286,000 per year without incurring any gift tax. (\$22,000 × 13 transferees – 3 children, 3 spouses, 7 grandchildren)
▲ A spouse may make unlimited lifetime gifts to their spouse who is a U.S. citizen.
▲ If the above four strategies are completely exhausted, the transferor can begin using his or her applicable gift exclusion amount (\$1,000,000 for gifts) while still paying no gift tax until the summation of lifetime taxable gifts exceeds the lifetime credit equivalency amount.
▲ Any gift tax paid on gifts prior to three years of death will also reduce the estate of the transferor. This is discussed later in this chapter.

EXHIBIT 17.15: FORM 709

Form **709** — Department of the Treasury, Internal Revenue Service

United States Gift (and Generation-Skipping Transfer) Tax Return

(For gifts made during calendar year 2004)

▶ **See separate instructions.**

OMB No. 1545-0020

2004

Part 1—General Information

1 Donor's first name and middle initial	2 Donor's last name	3 **Donor's social security number**
4 Address (number, street, and apartment number)		5 Legal residence (domicile) (county and state)
6 City, state, and ZIP code		7 Citizenship

		Yes	No
8	If the donor died during the year, check here ▶ ☐ and enter date of death .... , ...		
9	If you received an extension of time to file this Form 709, check here ▶ ☐ and attach the Form 4868, 2688, 2350, or 8892		
10	Enter the total number of donees listed on Schedule A—count each person only once. ▶		
11a	Have you (the donor) previously filed a Form 709 (or 709-A) for any other year? If "No," skip line 11b		
11b	If the answer to line 11a is "Yes," has your address changed since you last filed Form 709 (or 709-A)?		
12	Gifts by husband or wife to third parties.—Do you consent to have the gifts (including generation-skipping transfers) made by you and by your spouse to third parties during the calendar year considered as made one-half by each of you? (See instructions.) (If the answer is "Yes," the following information must be furnished and your spouse must sign the consent shown below. **If the answer is "No," skip lines 13–18 and go to Schedule A.**)		
13	Name of consenting spouse — 14 SSN		
15	Were you married to one another during the entire calendar year? (see instructions)		
16	If 15 is "No," check whether ☐ married ☐ divorced or ☐ widowed/deceased, and give date (see instructions) ▶		
17	Will a gift tax return for this year be filed by your spouse? (If "Yes," mail both returns in the same envelope.)		
18	**Consent of Spouse**—I consent to have the gifts (and generation-skipping transfers) made by me and by my spouse to third parties during the calendar year considered as made one-half by each of us. We are both aware of the joint and several liability for tax created by the execution of this consent.		

Consenting spouse's signature ▶   **Date** ▶

Part 2—Tax Computation

1	Enter the amount from Schedule A, Part 4, line 11	1		
2	Enter the amount from Schedule B, line 3	2		
3	Total taxable gifts (add lines 1 and 2)	3		
4	Tax computed on amount on line 3 (see Table for Computing Tax in separate instructions)	4		
5	Tax computed on amount on line 2 (see Table for Computing Tax in separate instructions)	5		
6	Balance (subtract line 5 from line 4)	6		
7	Maximum unified credit (nonresident aliens, see instructions)	7	345,800	00
8	Enter the unified credit against tax allowable for all prior periods (from Sch. B, line 1, col. C)	8		
9	Balance (subtract line 8 from line 7)	9		
10	Enter 20% (.20) of the amount allowed as a specific exemption for gifts made after September 8, 1976, and before January 1, 1977 (see instructions)	10		
11	Balance (subtract line 10 from line 9)	11		
12	Unified credit (enter the smaller of line 6 or line 11)	12		
13	Credit for foreign gift taxes (see instructions)	13		
14	Total credits (add lines 12 and 13)	14		
15	Balance (subtract line 14 from line 6) (do not enter less than zero)	15		
16	Generation-skipping transfer taxes (from Schedule C, Part 3, col. H, Total)	16		
17	Total tax (add lines 15 and 16)	17		
18	Gift and generation-skipping transfer taxes prepaid with extension of time to file	18		
19	If line 18 is less than line 17, enter **balance due** (see instructions)	19		
20	If line 18 is greater than line 17, enter **amount to be refunded**	20		

Attach check or money order here.

Sign Here

Under penalties of perjury, I declare that I have examined this return, including any accompanying schedules and statements, and to the best of my knowledge and belief, it is true, correct, and complete. Declaration of preparer (other than donor) is based on all information of which preparer has any knowledge.

▶ Signature of donor   Date

Paid Preparer's Use Only

Preparer's signature ▶   Date   Check if self-employed ▶ ☐

Firm's name (or yours if self-employed), address, and ZIP code ▶   Phone no. ▶ ( )

For Disclosure, Privacy Act, and Paperwork Reduction Act Notice, see page 12 of the separate instructions for this form. Cat. No. 16783M Form **709** (2004)

THE FEDERAL ESTATE TAX SYSTEM

PURPOSE AND DEFINITION

federal estate tax - an excise tax on the right to transfer assets by a decedent

The **federal estate tax** is an excise tax on the right to transfer assets by a decedent. In order to properly determine the estate tax liability, the executor must first determine what assets are included in the gross estate. Generally, the gross estate includes all property that the decedent owned at the time of death at the fair market value of the decedent's interest.

The gross estate (Exhibit 17.16, line 1) less the enumerated deductible expenses (lines 2–7) equals the adjusted gross estate (line 8). From the adjusted gross estate (line 8) are two deductions: (1) the value of property left to a qualified charity, and (2) the value of qualified property left to the decedent's spouse. The net result of the adjusted gross estate (line 8) less any marital deduction (line 10) and any charitable deduction (line 9) equals the taxable estate (line 11).

Following the determination of the taxable estate, any taxable gifts (those transfers that did not qualify for the annual exclusion) made after 1976 are added to determine the tentative tax base (line 11 + line 12 = line 13). The tentative tax (line 14) is calculated using the Unified Estate and Gift Tax Schedule as shown in Exhibit 17.10. From the tentative tax are subtracted any credits, such as previous gift tax paid (line 15), the applicable credit amount (line 16) obtained from Exhibit 17.12, to determine the federal estate tax liability (line 17).

EXHIBIT 17.16: THE ESTATE TAX FORMULA

(1)	Gross Estate (GE)		$	Gross Estate
	Less Deductions:			
(2)	Last Medical	$		
(3)	Administrative Costs	$		
(4)	Funeral	$		
(5)	Debts	$		
(6)	State Death Tax Paid	$	$	
(7)	Losses During Estate Administration	$	$	Deductions
(8)	Equals: Adjusted Gross Estate (AGE)		$	Adjusted Gross Estate
(9)	Less: Charitable Deduction	$		
(10)	Less: Marital Deduction	$	$	
(11)	Equals: Taxable Estate (TE)		$	Taxable Estate
(12)	Add: Previous Taxable Gifts (post-1976)		$	Post-1976 Gifts
(13)	Equals: Tentative Tax Base (TTB)		$	Tentative Tax Base
(14)	Tentative Tax (TT) (Exhibit 17.10)		$	Tentative Tax
	Less: Credits			
(15)	Previous Gift Tax Paid	$		
(16)	Applicable Credit Amount (Exhibit 17.12)	$		
(17)	Equals: Federal Estate Tax Liability (FETL)		$	Federal Estate Tax Liability

Reporting and Paying Taxes

Federal estate tax is reported on the federal estate tax return (Form 706). The federal estate tax return is due nine months from the date of death, but may be extended six months. However, an extension of time for filing does not extend the time for paying the estate tax. Therefore, unless permitted by one of the statutory exceptions, estate tax is payable nine months after the date of death.

The Gross Estate

gross estate - all assets included in a decedent's estate including, but not limited to, cash, stocks, bonds, annuities, retirement accounts, notes receivable, personal residences, automobiles, art collections, life insurance proceeds, and income tax refunds due

The financial planner must have a clear understanding of the size of the client's **gross estate** in order to develop a meaningful estate plan. The size and types of assets included in the gross estate will directly determine which planning techniques should be implemented. Exhibit 17.17 illustrates most of the asset types that are included in the gross estate as covered in Section 2033 (the relevant code section) of the Internal Revenue Code:

EXHIBIT 17.17: ASSETS INCLUDED IN THE GROSS ESTATE

Cash
Stocks and bonds
Annuities
Retirement accounts
Notes receivable
Personal residence
Other real estate
Household goods
Automobiles
Business interests
Proceeds of life insurance
Collections (art, wine, jewelry)
Vested future rights
Outstanding loans due decedent from others
Income tax refunds due
Patents/copyrights
Damages owed decedent
Dividends declared and payable
Income in respect of decedent
Decedent's share of property held with others
Other tangible personal property

**List may not be all-inclusive.*

Note that the gross estate includes the decedent's interest in any jointly held property and the proceeds of life insurance on the decedents life where (1) the decedent had any incidents of ownership in the policy at the time of death or (2) where the decedent had assigned (gifted) the insurance to someone else within three years of the decedent's death. The valuation of property included in the gross estate is either the fair market value at the date of death, or if properly elected, the value for the alternate valuation date (six months from the date of death). Because death is presumed to be involuntary, the alternate valuation date is provided so as to give relief to a decedent who just happened to die on a date where the gross estate was valued at a very high value due to the temporary market conditions. Certain requirements must be met in order to elect the alternate valuation date.

DEDUCTIONS FROM THE GROSS ESTATE

adjusted gross estate - gross estate less deductions provided for by law in recognition that the entire value of the gross estate will not be transferred to the heirs due to costs, debts, and certain other deductions

Once the assets are identified and the value of the gross estate is determined, the next step is to determine the allowed deductions to arrive at the **adjusted gross estate** (see Exhibit 17.16). The deductions are provided for by law in recognition that the entire value of the gross estate will not be transferred to the heirs due to costs, debts, and certain other deductions. Rather, a smaller amount than the full gross estate will be transferred to heirs.

The adjusted gross estate is determined by deducting the following:

- Funeral expenses.
- Last medical costs.
- Administration expenses.
- Debts.
- Losses during estate administration.
- State death taxes paid (for years 2005-2009)

Funeral Costs

Reasonable expenditures related to the funeral, such as interment costs, burial plot, grave marker, and transportation of the body to the place of burial, are deductible for estate tax purposes.

Last Medical Costs

Medical costs related to the decedent's last illness are deductible from the gross estate as long as they are not deducted on the decedent's final federal income tax return.

Administrative Expenses

Any expenses related to the administration of the estate are deductible from either the estate tax return (Form 706) or the estate's income tax return (Form 1041). These expenses generally include attorney and accountant fees for preparing the estate tax return, the final Form 1040, and the estate income tax return, and expenses related to the retitling of assets through the probate process. These costs may also include appraisal and valuation fees necessary to determine values of assets included in the gross estate for estate tax purposes.

Debts

All debts of the decedent are deductible from the gross estate. These debts include any amounts the decedent was obligated to pay while alive, plus interest accrued to the date of death. Debts generally include such items as outstanding mortgages, income tax due, credit card balances, and other miscellaneous outstanding debts.

Losses During Estate Administration

Any losses to the estate during the period of administration, including casualty and theft losses, are deductible expenses to the extent they exceed insurance reimbursements.

State Death Taxes

Effective for 2005, the state death credit has been repealed and replaced with a deduction (not a credit) for death taxes actually paid to any state.

THE CHARITABLE DEDUCTION

DEFINITION

Internal Revenue Code 170(c) defines a charitable contribution as a gift made to a qualified organization. To be a **charitable deduction**, a contribution must be made to one of the following organizations:

charitable deduction - a charitable contribution made as a gift to a qualified organization

- A state or possession of the United States or any subdivision thereof.
- A corporation, trust, or community chest, fund, or foundation that is situated in the United States and is organized exclusively for religious, charitable, scientific, literary, or educational purposes, or for the prevention of cruelty to children or animals.
- A veteran's organization.
- A fraternal organization operating under the lodge system.
- A cemetery company.

The IRS publishes a list (Publication 78) of organizations that have applied for and received tax-exempt status under section 501 of the Internal Revenue Code.

charitable remainder trust (CRT) - a split-interest trust. If created during life, the income goes to one or more parties, usually the grantor, or grantor and spouse for life, and upon the income beneficiary's death, the principal (remainder) is transferred to a charity. If the CRT is created testamentary, the usual income beneficiary is the spouse for life.

TYPES OF CHARITABLE BEQUESTS

Direct Charitable Bequests

A direct charitable bequest of any property to a qualifying organization is fully deductible from the gross estate in arriving at the taxable estate.

Charitable Trusts

A **charitable remainder trust (CRT)** is an estate planning vehicle used to reduce the impact of income and estate taxes. A CRT is created by transferring property to a charitable trust. Although the property transferred to the trust may be cash, it generally consists of appreciated property. Because it is a nontaxable entity, the CRT can dispose of property without incurring taxable income upon the disposition. The trust is established so that an income interest, which may be in the form of an annuity or a unitrust payment, is paid to either the donor or a family member of the donor. At the termination of the income interest, which generally occurs at the death of the income beneficiary, the remaining assets in the CRT are transferred to the charity named in the trust document. Because there are two beneficiaries, the income beneficiary or annuitant and the named charity of a CRT, the CRT is considered a split-interest trust.

Charitable remainder trusts can be established during life or at the death of the donor. CRTs that are established during life provide several benefits. First, the donor will receive an income tax deduction equal to the value of the property transferred to the trust less the value of the income stream that is expected to be received by the income beneficiary. Second, the asset that was transferred to the trust is no longer included in the gross estate, thereby reducing the estate tax of the donor. Third, the CRT provides an income stream to the donor or the donor's family member. Finally, if the property transferred to the trust was highly appreciated, the trust is able to dispose of the property without current income taxation. CRTs that are established at death are primarily used to reduce the estate tax and to provide an income stream to one of the donor's heirs. This amounts to social reallocation of wealth by the donor's choice.

charitable lead trust (CLT) - a split-interest trust where a charity is the income beneficiary and there is a noncharitable remainderman

In some cases, the income beneficiary is the charity with the remaining property being passed to one of the donor's heirs. This type of arrangement is called a **charitable lead trust** (**CLT**). A CLT is generally used as a method of transferring property to heirs in the future while paying gift tax at the current valuation of the property. Any appreciation in the value of the property will escape transfer tax.

THE MARITAL DEDUCTION

DEFINITION

A marital deduction occurs when the decedent's estate claims as a deduction from the adjusted gross estate an unlimited qualifying bequest or transfer of property to a surviving spouse. This treatment parallels the unlimited marital deduction for gifts and for gift tax purposes. As discussed previously, the donee spouse must be a U.S. citizen for the transfer to qualify for the unlimited marital deduction.

QUALIFICATIONS FOR THE MARITAL DEDUCTION

terminable interest - an interest that ends upon an event or contingency

To qualify for the marital deduction, the property must be included in the decedent's gross estate and must be passed to the decedent's spouse. The interest in the property must not be one that is a terminable interest. A **terminable interest** is defined as an interest that ends upon an event or contingency. In other words, if the spouse initially gets the interest in the property and then later this interest terminates upon some event (usually death), then the interest passes to someone else, it is a terminable interest. Terminal interests do not qualify for the unlimited marital deduction unless they meet one of the exceptions to the "terminal interest rule."

The following are some exceptions to the terminable interest rule:

- ▲ When the only condition of a bequest is that the survivor spouse lives for a period not exceeding six months, the marital deduction is allowed if the surviving spouse actually lives for the period specified.
- ▲ When there is a right to a life annuity coupled with a power of appointment.
- ▲ When there is a bequest to a spouse of income from a Charitable Remainder Annuity Trust or a Charitable Remainder Unitrust and the spouse is the only noncharitable beneficiary.
- ▲ Certain marital trusts are exceptions to the terminable interest rule (that is, Qualified Terminal Interest Property, or QTIP).

DIRECT BEQUESTS TO A SPOUSE

In a **direct bequest**, the first spouse who dies leaves everything outright to the surviving spouse. The estate of the decedent spouse gets a 100 percent marital deduction equal to the adjusted gross estate. The property will ultimately be consumed by the surviving spouse or will be included in the gross estate of the surviving spouse. The advantages of direct bequests are that they are simple and inexpensive. The surviving spouse gets unfettered control over all of the assets of the decedent. One disadvantage of this approach is that a direct bequest may overqualify the estate since the first spouse to die does not take advantage of the decedent's available applicable credit amount or its equivalency. Overqualification means that the decedent failed to make use of his applicable exclusion opportunity to pass his exemption equivalency amount ($1,500,000 for 2005) to someone other than the spouse and still pay no estate tax. If an estate is overqualified, the total estate tax on the death of the second spouse may be greater than it would have been had they arranged their affairs differently. Another disadvantage is that the first spouse is unable to retain control over the ultimate disposition of the assets.

direct bequest (to a spouse) - the first spouse who dies, leaves everything outright to the surviving spouse

QUALIFIED TERMINABLE INTEREST PROPERTY TRUST (QTIP)

If a direct bequest to a spouse is determined to be inappropriate and the decedent wishes no transfer tax at the first death, the alternatives are a QTIP or a Power of Appointment trust. A **qualified terminable interest property trust**, sometimes called a "C" Trust or a "Q" Trust, allows a terminable interest to be passed to a surviving spouse and the property to still qualify for the unlimited marital deduction. The election is made by the executor on IRS Form 706. There are certain rules associated with QTIPs that must be followed to qualify the transfer for the unlimited marital deduction.

qualified terminable interest property trust (QTIP) - allows a terminable interest to be passed to a surviving spouse and the property to still qualify for the unlimited marital deduction. The election is made by the executor on IRS Form 706.

Any income from the trust must be payable to the surviving spouse at least annually and for life. The trust income cannot be payable to anyone other than the surviving spouse. The trust assets will be included in the gross estate of the surviving spouse at death. The first spouse to die determines the ultimate disposition of the property from the trust (names the remainder beneficiaries) in the trust provisions. This is an especially useful device when the surviving spouse is not the parent of the children of the decedent spouse.

power of appointment trust - allows a terminable interest to be passed to a surviving spouse and the property to still qualify for the marital deduction. Unlike a QTIP Trust, no election is required.

POWER OF APPOINTMENT TRUST

A **Power of Appointment Trust**, sometimes called an "A" Trust, allows a terminable interest to be passed to a surviving spouse and the property to still qualify for the marital deduction. Unlike a QTIP Trust, no election is required. The rules require that income from the trust must be payable to the surviving spouse at least annually for life. Any assets in the trust will be included in the gross estate of the surviving spouse at death. The surviving spouse is given a general power of appointment (the power to appoint the assets to anyone, including herself) over the property during life or at death. The first spouse to die may not control the ultimate disposition of the property because the surviving spouse has a general power of appointment over the trust assets.

OPTIMIZING THE MARITAL DEDUCTION

If the objective of the married decedent is to have a zero-tax-liability estate, he can simply leave all assets in a qualifying way to the surviving spouse. The problem with such a strategy is that it fails to utilize the decedent's right to leave the applicable exclusion amount ($1,500,000 for 2005) to someone other than the spouse. Therefore, all assets, less the applicable exclusion amount ($1,500,000), can be left to the spouse in a qualifying way and still have a zero estate tax liability for the first spouse. Although the $1,500,000 is left to another heir, the decedent spouse may provide that income from the property is to be paid exclusively to the surviving spouse while the spouse is alive. The common method of leaving the applicable exclusion amount where the spouse has a need for the income from such assets is called a bypass trust. In the event a spouse has no need for the income or assets from the credit equivalency amount, such spouse can disclaim, as discussed below. Keep in mind, however, that only citizen spouses can qualify for the unlimited marital deduction. Alien surviving spouses have special rules described later in this section.

THE BYPASS TRUST (CREDIT EQUIVALENCY)

bypass trust - avoids inclusion in, or bypasses, the surviving spouse's gross estate—the assets transfer to a future generation free of estate taxes. The purpose of a bypass trust (known as a "B" trust) is to take advantage of the applicable credit amount.

A **bypass trust** avoids inclusion in, or bypasses, the surviving spouse's gross estate. The assets transfer to a future generation free of estate taxes. The purpose of a bypass trust (known as a "B" trust) is to take advantage of the applicable credit amount. The property does not qualify for the unlimited marital deduction and is therefore taxed in the estate of the first spouse to die. A common scenario is for the first spouse to leave everything to the surviving spouse except for the credit equivalent amount, which goes into a bypass trust. The surviving spouse may be the income beneficiary of the bypass trust and may also be able to invade the trust for health, education, maintenance or support. When the surviving spouse dies, the bypass trust assets are not included in that spouse's gross estate, but rather pass to children or other heirs.

A bypass trust can be used instead of an outright bypass bequest to heirs who are not sufficiently sophisticated or mature enough to handle property. In addition, the bypass trust is used where the surviving spouse needs the income from the trust but wants to avoid inclusion of the assets in the surviving spouse's gross estate. In this case, the choice of the trust over the simple bequest does not save any estate tax dollars, but may give the transferor some peace of mind. Often, highly appreciating assets are placed into the bypass trust. This freezes the value for estate tax purposes for the spouses at the death of the first spouse. A bypass trust may also be called a credit equivalency trust, a credit shelter trust, a family trust, or a "B" Trust.

The Mechanics of the Bypass Trust (Credit Equivalency)

Recall that the property that qualified for the marital deduction reduced the taxable estate of the decedent and that the amount of such transfer is unlimited. Also recall that each individual has a lifetime exemption (Exhibit 17.12) and that such exemption would be lost to the first spouse were he or she to transfer to the surviving spouse all of their property in a qualifying way. A credit equivalency (bypass) trust can be used to avoid these problems. Usually testamentary, a credit equivalency trust is provided for in the will with a provision to fund such trust with an amount of money equal to the current (at the time of death) applicable exclusion amount with the spouse having a lifetime interest in the income and the remaindermen being someone else, usually children. Such a transfer does not qualify for the marital deduction, and therefore those assets will not be included in the gross estate of the surviving spouse when such surviving spouse dies. However, the assets are included in the taxable estate of the grantor, but will not result in any federal estate tax liability as demonstrated in the following example.

EXAMPLE

Sherri and Gary are married with two children. They have community property of $5,000,000. Each spouse has a will bequeathing all property to the surviving spouse.

Calculation of the total estate tax paid, assuming Gary dies first on January 1, 2005.

	Gary	Sherri	
Assets	$2,500,000	$2,500,000	
Inheritance		2,500,000	
Gross Estate	$2,500,000	$5,000,000	
Marital Deductions	(2,500,000)	-0-	
Taxable Estate	-0-	$5,000,000	
Tentative Tax	-0-	2,190,800	
Applicable Credit	-0-	(555,800)	(2005)
Estate Tax	$ -0-	$1,635,000	
Total estate tax paid by family	$1,635,000		

Calculation of the total estate tax paid assuming Gary dies on January 1, 2005, using a maximized credit equivalency trust with the children as beneficiaries.

	Gary	Sherri	
Assets	$2,500,000	$2,500,000	
Inheritance	-0-	1,000,000	
Gross Estate	$2,500,000	$3,500,000	
Marital Deductions	(1,000,000)	-0-	
Taxable Estate	$1,500,000	$3,500,000	
Tentative Tax	$555,800	$1,485,800	
Applicable Credit	(555,800)	(555,800)	(2005)
Estate Tax	$ -0-	$930,000	
Total estate tax paid by family	$930,000		

Conclusion: By using the credit equivalency trust, the family saved $720,000 [$1,635,000 (without shelter) – $930,000 (with shelter) = $705,000 savings] in estate tax. This savings is a result of the couple taking full advantage of the applicable credit amount by placing the applicable exclusion amount of funds at the first death in a credit equivalency trust for the children. Sherri can receive income from the trust for the remainder of her life and have the right to withdraw limited amounts of principal. The credit equivalency trust assets will pass untaxed to the children at Sherri's death.

The applicable exclusion amount of $1,500,000 was not taxed in Example 2. The savings that resulted was equal to the marginal tax bracket (47 percent) times the applicable exclusion amount.

$$\begin{array}{r} \$1,500,000 \\ \times\ 47\% \\ \hline \$\ 705,000 \end{array}$$

Note that the savings amount will vary with the size of the estate and the marginal estate tax rate.

If we assume instead that Gary and Sherri's community property was only worth $2,000,000, then the savings would fall to $225,000, because the size of the estate falls in a lower progressive tax bracket. However, if the community property is worth $10,000,000, then the savings is, again, $705,000 (like the original example $1,500,000 x 47 percent) because the tax rates have caused the savings to stabilize. The conclusion here is that the use of a credit equivalency trust will save estate taxes to varying degrees, with increasing savings as the assets increase, but there will be a stabilizing effect that will occur due to the leveling of the 47 percent tax bracket.

	Net Community Property = $2,000,000		Net Community Property = $10,000,000	
	No Bypass Trust	Bypass Trust	No Bypass Trust	Bypass Trust
Taxable Estate	$ 2,000,000	$ 1,000,000	$10,000,000	$ 8,500,000
Tentative Tax	$ 780,800	$ 345,800	$ 4,540,800	$ 3,835,800
Applicable Credit	(555,800)	(555,800)	(555,800)	(555,800)
Tax Liability	$ 225,000	$ 0	$ 3,985,000	$ 3,280,000
Total Savings	$225,000		$705,000	

Use of Disclaimers

A **disclaimer** allows a spouse or anyone else to disclaim or renounce receiving any part of a bequest. A specific direction to disclaim is not necessary in the will or trust device. If the spouse disclaims property, his or her interest in and control over the property is extinguished. Since disclaimers must be made within nine months of the first spouse's death, the surviving spouse may find it difficult to give up property at a time when he or she may not be feeling emotionally or financially secure. When a person disclaims, they are not making a gift, but rather the person is simply bypassed.

disclaimer - the refusal of the receipt of an estate. The use of disclaimers allows an individual to disclaim or renounce receiving any part of an estate.

Alien Surviving Spouses

Section 2056(d) disallows the unlimited marital deduction if the surviving spouse is not a U.S. citizen. If a noncitizen spouse becomes a citizen before the federal estate tax return is filed (Form 706 within nine months), Section 2056(d) does not apply. For a noncitizen spouse who was a U.S. resident at the time of the decedent's death, the marital deduction is allowed if the property is placed in a **Qualified Domestic Trust (QDOT)** that passes to a noncitizen surviving spouse. The trust document for a QDOT requires at least one trustee to be U.S. citizen or U.S. corporation. The trustee must have a right to withhold estate tax on distribution of assets or income and must meet requirements of the U.S. Treasury. The executor must make an irrevocable election to establish a QDOT. A special annual exclusion is available for non-U.S. sponsors. The U.S. citizen spouse can give $117,000 (in 2005, adjusted for inflation) per year to the non-U.S. citizen spouse.

qualified domestic trust (QDOT) - for a non-citizen spouse who was a U.S. resident at the time of the decedent's death, the marital deduction is allowed if the property is placed in a QDOT that passes to a non-citizen surviving spouse

GENERATION-SKIPPING TRANSFER TAX (GSTT)

generation-skipping transfer tax (GSTT) - a tax that is in addition to the unified gift and estate tax and is designed to tax large transfers that skip a generation (that is, from grandparent to

The **generation-skipping transfer tax** (GSTT) is in addition to the unified gift and estate tax and is designed to tax large transfers that skip a generation (that is, from grandparent to grandchild). The purpose of the tax is to collect potentially lost tax dollars from the skipped generation. But for the generation-skipping tax, one could leave all of one's assets to a grandchild and avoid the unified gift and estate tax on the middle generation. The current unified tax scheme would tax from the first to the second generation and from the second to the third generation. For a transfer made from the first generation directly to the third generation, some unified gift and estate tax is avoided. The generation-skipping transfer tax attempts to make up for that loss of tax.

The GSTT rate is the highest marginal rate for the unified gift and estate tax rates (47 percent in 2005). There are several exceptions to this tax. First, the annual exclusion also applies to a generation-skipping transfer ($11,000 in 2005). Second, there is a lifetime exemption per donor ($1,500,000 in 2005). There is also an exception for transfers to a person of a skipped generation where a parent has predeceased the transferee prior to the transfer. For example, if a parent died, the grandparent may donate or bequest to the grandchild without the grandchild being considered a skip person. In effect, the grandchild steps into the shoes of the deceased parent. Finally, qualified transfers, such as medical costs and tuition are also excluded from GSTT. Gift splitting is available for the annual exclusion exceptions as long as both spouses elect to split gifts. The generation-skipping transfer tax is repealed after 2009.

THE ROLE OF THE FINANCIAL PLANNER IN ESTATE PLANNING

Estate planning is very personal in nature and requires the financial planner to seek out the particulars that characterize each client's individual situation and goals. Financial planners must be able to ascertain the objectives of the client, while forecasting the long-range ramifications of the plan.

Reducing the estate tax is a matter of taking full advantage of various planning opportunities (summarized in Exhibit 17.18). Initially, getting the life insurance out of the gross estate is generally a wise idea. The next step for most clients is to make full use of the qualified transfers to educational and medical institutions. Then, the client should be encouraged to make optimal use of the annual exclusion ($11,000, $22,000 if split) on a yearly basis. At some time, either during life or at death, the client should make effective use of the gift tax applicable exclusion amount ($1,000,000 during life and $1,500,000 at death for 2005) by transferring these assets so as to avoid inclusion in the surviving spouse's gross estate. Then the spouse who has accomplished all of the above can leave the balance of the gross estate to his spouse in a qualifying way and, thus, have an estate tax liability of zero. Charitable contributions during life will reduce his gross estate, and the income on those transferred assets will not be taxed to the transferor. Charitable transfers at death are deductible from the adjusted gross estate and thus, are not taxable.

EXHIBIT 17.18: ESTATE TAX REDUCTION TECHNIQUES

There are several techniques to reduce estate tax:

- Do not overqualify the estate. Use the applicable exclusion amount.
- Do not underqualify the estate. Use an appropriate amount for the marital deduction, generally to reduce estate tax to zero.
- Generally, remove life insurance from the estate of the client.
- Change the ownership of life insurance or use irrevocable life insurance trust (must remove all incidents of ownership).
- Use lifetime gifts. Make use of annual exclusions with gift splitting.
- Use basic trusts.
- Use charitable contributions, transfers, and trusts.

Estate planning calls for a broad range of sophisticated talents. An attorney and CPA may need to be called into the estate team at this point, if not before, to cover the legal and tax aspects.

CONCLUDING COMMENTS ON THE UNIFICATION SCHEME OF GIFTS AND ESTATES

While it may appear that the unification scheme (the unified tax table) for gifts and estates provides equality or parity for transfers during life or at death, there are at least four important distinctions.

First, the annual exclusion of $11,000 per donee per year that is provided for gifts is essentially lost if the transfer does not occur until death. Thus, the annual exclusion is a perishable right, the total value of which declines with each passing year. A married couple with four children and two grandchildren can transfer $132,000 ($22,000 to each descendent) per year total during life to the six donees without any gift tax consequences. If this money is not transferred by gift or consumed by the decedent, it will be included in the gross estate at the decedent's death and may be subject to estate tax.

The second, and perhaps the most important advantage of making lifetime gifts, is that any future appreciation of any asset transferred is not included in the gross estate of the transferor at death. For example, suppose Mr. William Brown gave his son, James, some XYZ.com stock, having a fair market value of $11,000. Mr. Brown (donor) pays no gift tax on the transfer because it is equal to the annual exclusion amount of $11,000. Now assume that James holds the stock for ten years and that at the end of the ten-year period the stock is worth $300,000, and William dies. No part of the value of the stock is included in William Brown's gross estate. If William Brown had retained the stock, he would have had to include the entire $300,000 in his gross estate. Thus, for assets that appreciate, transfers during life are more advantageous than transfers at death in reducing the gross estate.

Third, if any gift tax is paid on gifts made, that gift tax is also not included in the gross estate of the donor unless such gift tax is paid on gifts made within three years of death.

For example, suppose John Hurly gave $10,000 cash under the annual exclusion and a taxable gift of $1,000,000 of stock in XYZ to his son, Patrick, in 1996. He would have paid $153,000 in gift tax. That $153,000 would have been excluded from John's gross estate as long as he died after 1999 (three years after the gift).

Fourth, the transfer of property during life subjects the transferee (donee) to the income tax consequences associated with the property, as opposed to subjecting the transferor (donor) to such income tax consequences. Thus, not only does future appreciation of assets get transferred, so does the future income, and, therefore, the income tax associated with the income earned from the transferred asset.

PROFESSIONAL FOCUS

How do you approach the subject of lifetime gifting for older clients, who have lived through the Depression Era and are unwilling to relinquish assets?

Not only Depression Era clients, but other clients as well are reluctant to give up assets. The question then becomes one of education—would you rather give it to your kids and grandchildren or Uncle Sam? The quantification of estate erosion from estate taxes usually gets their attention. An aggressive gifting program can save hundreds of thousands of dollars in estate taxes and pass the money to their beneficiaries rather than sending it to Washington.

Additionally, gifting has some nontax advantages:

- ▲ The donees show their appreciation while the donors are alive, and
- ▲ The donors can see how the donees manage the gifts, thereby assisting in the decision process of testamentary bequests in cash or in trust.

Do you recommend that clients participate in gifting of the yearly annual exclusion? If so, do you focus on clients of a particular wealth status?

Gifting and use of the annual exclusions can be beneficial to clients of various net worth levels. Those with a taxable estate in excess of the exemption equivalent level should seriously consider gifting to reduce or eliminate estate taxes.

Gifting of assets not needed for the donors' long-term well-being has the additional potential advantages of possibly shifting income to a lower income tax bracket, getting potentially appreciating assets out of one's estate and providing financial assistance for beneficiaries who have current needs.

Care needs to be taken that gifted assets may not be needed by the donor in an era of expanding longevity. Also, clients need to be willing to give up control, something that some clients have difficulty doing.

What techniques do you use to reduce your clients' estate and gift taxes?

One of the exciting aspects of estate planning is that there is no patented or textbook answer. The answer(s) depend on the clients' financial situation, their wishes and their mentalities.

- ▲ Do they have charitable desires? If so, a Charitable Remainder Trust might be advised.
- ▲ Do they wish to pass on a closely held business interest? If so, a Family Limited Partnership might be a possible solution.
- ▲ Is this a second marriage? If so, a QTIP trust could be used to protect the interests of the respective offspring.

Even though a decedent cannot continue to control from the grave, as much postmortem flexibility as possible is desirable. The use of Qualified Disclaimers is a very potent postmortem tool. However, the decedent's will needs to direct where disclaimed property would go to best use this tool. In special cases and selected circumstances, more sophisticated approaches may be warranted, such as Grantor Retained Annuity Trusts, Qualified Personal Residence Trusts and installment sales to Intentionally Defective Trusts.

Estate planning is an area in which proper planning can significantly serve the client, and the recommended solutions can be as varied as the unique client circumstances.

PETER BLACKWELL, MBA, CFP®

DISCUSSION QUESTIONS

1. What is estate planning and what are its objectives?
2. What risks are associated with failing to plan for an estate transfer?
3. Which professionals make up the estate planning team?
4. What steps make up the estate planning process?
5. What client information needs to be gathered to begin a successful estate transfer?
6. What are some common estate transfer objectives?
7. What are the basic documents used in estate planning?
8. What is the probate process, and what are its advantages and disadvantages?
9. Why is having a will important?
10. What are the three types of wills, and how do they differ?
11. What are the characteristics of a valid will?
12. What is a power of attorney?
13. What is a durable power of attorney for health care?
14. What are the definitions of the terms community property, separate property, and tenancy-by-the-entirety?
15. What are the types of property ownership interests, and how are they transferred?
16. What are the duties of the executor/administrator of a will?
17. What is a living trust?
18. What is a grantor trust?
19. How can the gross estate be reduced?
20. What are the common estate planning mistakes?
21. What is the applicable credit amount and how does it affect an individual's federal estate tax liability?
22. How can the annual gift tax exclusion be used as an estate planning tool?
23. What is gift splitting?
24. What are qualified transfers?
25. When is the gift tax return due?
26. What are the advantages and disadvantages of the unlimited marital deduction?
27. What are the steps in calculating the estate tax?
28. What are at least three estate planning techniques available to reduce gift and estate taxes?
29. When is the estate tax return due to be filed with the IRS?
30. What are the applicable credit amounts against federal gift and estate taxes for 2005?
31. On which IRS form do you file funeral expenses?
32. What is a trust, and what are the benefits of creating one?
33. What are different types of trusts that can be created?
34. What is the generation-skipping tax?

EXERCISES

1. Which of the following persons need estate planning?
   - ▲ Steve, who has a wife and one small child, and a net worth of $350,000.
   - ▲ Earl, married with nine children, six grandchildren, and a net worth of $4,000,000.
   - ▲ Ellen, divorced, whose only son is severely mentally challenged.
   - ▲ Mary, who is single, has a net worth of $150,000, and has two cats who she considers as "her children."

2. Place the following estate planning steps in their proper order.
   - ▲ Establish priorities for estate objectives.
   - ▲ Prepare a written plan.
   - ▲ Define problem areas including liquidity, taxes, etc.
   - ▲ Gather client information and establish objectives.
3. List and describe the arrangements that are plausible when dealing with unanticipated incapacity.
4. Describe why each of the following would be considered potential problems of an estate plan.
   - ▲ Ancillary probate.
   - ▲ A will that includes funeral instructions.
   - ▲ A will that attempts to disinherit a spouse and/or minor children.
5. Describe each of the following common provisions in a well-drafted will.
   - ▲ Establishment of the domicile of testator.
   - ▲ An appointment and powers clause.
   - ▲ A survivorship clause.
   - ▲ A residuary clause.
6. Which of the following statements is/are incorrect?
   - ▲ A durable power of attorney for health care is always a direct substitute for a living will.
   - ▲ A living will only covers a narrow range of situations.
   - ▲ A living will must generally meet the requirements of a formally drafted state statute.
   - ▲ Many well-intentioned living wills have failed due to vagueness and/or ambiguities.
7. Marleen has a general power of appointment over her mother's assets. Which of the following is/are true regarding the power?
   - ▲ Marleen can appoint her mother's money to pay for the needs of her mother.
   - ▲ Marleen can appoint money to Marleen's creditors.
   - ▲ Marleen must only appoint money using an ascertainable standard (health, education, maintenance, and support).
   - ▲ If Marleen were to die before her mother, Marleen's gross estate would include her mother's assets although they were not previously appointed to Marleen.
8. Describe each of the following property ownership arrangements.
   - ▲ Tenancy in common.
   - ▲ Joint tenancy with right of survivorship.
   - ▲ Tenancy by the entirety.
   - ▲ Community property.
9. Which of the following statements regarding joint tenancy is/are correct?
   - ▲ Under a joint tenancy, each tenant has an undivided interest in the property.
   - ▲ Joint tenancies may only be established between spouses.
   - ▲ Community property is the same as joint tenancy and has been adopted in many states.
   - ▲ Assuming a spousal joint tenancy, the full value of the property will be included in the gross estate of the first spouse to die without regard to the contribution of each spouse.

10. Generally speaking, which of the following property is included in the probate estate?
    - ▲ Property owned outright in one's own name at the time of death.
    - ▲ An interest in property held as a tenant in common with others.
    - ▲ Life insurance, and other death proceeds, payable to one's estate at death.
    - ▲ The decedent's half of any community property.
11. Describe at least 3 advantages and 3 disadvantages of the probate process.
12. Identify alternatives to probate regarding disposition of property.
13. John and Mary Hurley are both 36 years old with one child, Patrick, age 6. What documents do the Hurleys need for estate planning?
14. Given Mark's assets below, which will go through the probate process if Mark dies?

Life Insurance	Face	$100,000	Beneficiary is Mary
IRA	Balance	$200,000	Beneficiary is Mary
Personal Residence	Value	$280,000	Titled JTWROS with Mary
Automobile	Value	$4,000	Owned by Mark

15. Ann is married to Roy. They have no children. Given that Ann has the following assets, what could she do to reduce her gross estate?

Life Insurance	Face	$1,000,000	Owner is Ann
Cash	Amount	$2,000,000	Owner is Ann

16. During this year, Bob gave $100,000 to his son and $100,000 to his daughter. Bob's wife, Lori, also gave $5,000 to their son. No other gifts were made during the year. Bob and Lori elected to split the gifts on their gift tax returns. What is the amount of taxable gifts made by Bob and Lori?
17. Which of the following situations would not constitute a taxable transfer under the gift tax statutes?
    - ▲ Father creates an irrevocable trust under the terms of which his son is to receive income for life and his grandson the remainder at his son's death.
    - ▲ Father, with personal funds, purchases real property and has title conveyed to himself and his brother as joint tenants with right of survivorship.
    - ▲ Father creates a trust giving income for life to wife and providing that, at her death, the corpus is to be distributed to their daughter. Father reserves the right to revoke the transfer at any time.
18. Stephen created a joint bank account for himself and his friend, Anna. When is there a gift to Anna?
19. During this year, Mr. and Mrs. Buzzetta made joint gifts of the following items to their son:
    - ▲ A bond with an adjusted basis of $12,000 and a fair market value of $40,000.
    - ▲ Stock with an adjusted basis of $22,000 and a fair market value of $33,000.
    - ▲ An auto with an adjusted basis of $12,000 and a fair market value of $14,000.
    - ▲ An interest-free loan of $6,000 for a computer (for the son's personal use) on January 1st, which was paid by their son on December 31st. Assume the applicable federal rate was 8 percent per annum.

    What is the gross amount of gifts includible in Mr. and Mrs. Buzzetta's gift tax returns for this year?

20. Tamara, who is single, gave an outright gift of $50,000 to a friend, Heather, who needed the money to pay her medical expenses. In filing the gift tax return, how much is Tamara entitled to exclude?
21. Which of the following situations constitutes a transfer that comes within the gift tax statutes?
    - ▲ Mark creates a trust under the terms of which his son is to get income for life and his grandson the remainder at his son's death.
    - ▲ Mark purchases real property and has the title conveyed to himself and to his brother as joint tenants.
    - ▲ Mark creates an irrevocable trust giving income for life to his wife and providing that upon her death the corpus is to be distributed to his daughter.
    - ▲ Mark purchases a U.S. Savings Bond made payable to himself and his wife. The wife surrenders the bond for cash to be used for her benefit.
22. Which of the following situations would not constitute a transfer that comes within the gift tax statutes?
    - ▲ Robin creates a trust under the terms of which her daughter is to get income for life and her granddaughter the remainder at the daughter's death.
    - ▲ Robbie purchases real property and has title conveyed to himself and to his brother, Ritchie, as joint tenants.
    - ▲ Randal creates an irrevocable trust giving income for life to his wife and providing that at her death the corpus is to be distributed to his son.
    - ▲ Ray purchases a U.S. Savings Bond made payable to himself and his wife, Raquel. Raquel cashes the bond to be used for her own benefit.
    - ▲ Rose creates a joint bank account for herself and her daughter, Daisy. There have been no withdrawals from the account.
23. Which of the following represent taxable gifts?
    - ▲ The transfer of wealth by a parent to a dependent child that represents legal support.
    - ▲ Payment of a child's tuition to Loyola's Law School by a parent.
    - ▲ Payment of $20,000 from a grandparent to a grandchild for educational purposes.
    - ▲ Payment of $11,000 of medical bills for a friend paid directly to the medical institution.
24. Victor wants to begin a program of lifetime giving to his 3 grandchildren and 5 great-grandchildren. He wants to control the amount of annual gifts to avoid the imposition of federal gift tax, and he does not desire to use any of his or his wife's (Veronica) unified tax credit. Veronica is willing to split each gift over a period of 10 years. What is the total amount of gifts, including gift splitting, that Victor can give over the 10-year period? (Assume the annual exclusion for all years is the same as for 2005.)
25. Rodney and his wife, Lois, have 4 children, each over the age of majority, 2 grandchildren over age 21, and 6 minor grandchildren. Rodney and Lois want to make gifts to their children and grandchildren sufficient to make maximum use of the tax provisions providing for annual exclusions from federal gift tax. Considering that desire only, what is the total amount of gifting that Rodney and Lois can make during the year?

26. Kurt died on July 31st. His assets and their fair market value at the time of his death were:

Cash	$15,000
Personal Residence	$250,000
Life insurance on Kurt's life	$150,000
Series EE bonds	$20,000

Kurt had a balance on his residence mortgage of $15,000. What is the total of Kurt's gross estate?

27. Evelyn died on August 1st this year. What is her gross estate?
    - ▲ In 2000, Evelyn gave cash of $30,000 to her friend. No gift tax was paid on the gift.
    - ▲ Evelyn held property jointly with her brother. Each paid $45,000 of the total purchase price of $90,000. Fair market value of the property at date of death was $200,000.
    - ▲ In 2000, Evelyn purchased a life insurance policy on her own life and gave it as a gift to her sister. Evelyn retained the right to change the beneficiary. Upon Evelyn's death, her sister received $200,000 under the policy.
    - ▲ In 1985, Evelyn gave her son a summer home (fair market value in 1982, $100,000). Evelyn continued to use it until her death pursuant to an understanding with her son. The fair market value at date of death was $190,000.
28. Jane died on May 2nd of the current year, leaving an adjusted gross estate of $1,200,000 at the date of death. Under the terms of the will, $375,000 was bequeathed outright to her husband. The remainder of the estate was left to her mother. No taxable gifts were made during her lifetime. In computing the taxable estate, how much should the executor claim as a marital deduction?
29. Joshua died in 2005 with a taxable estate of $2,000,000. He had made no previous taxable gifts during his lifetime. How much is his federal estate tax?
30. Joseph died in 2005 with a taxable estate of $1,600,000 and had previously given adjusted taxable gifts of $700,000. During his life he used gift tax applicable credits of $64,800. What amount will Joseph subtract on his estate tax return for his applicable credit?
31. Identify at least 3 alternative methods of limiting, reducing, or avoiding federal estate taxes.
32. Which of the following transfers qualify for the unlimited marital deduction?
    - ▲ Outright bequest to resident alien spouse.
    - ▲ Property passing to citizen spouse in QTIP.
    - ▲ Income beneficiary of CRT is a nonresident alien spouse (Trust is not a QDOT).
    - ▲ Outright bequest to resident spouse who, prior to the decedent's death was a noncitizen, but who after the decedent's death and before the estate return was filed became an U.S. citizen.
33. Who among the following would be skip persons for purposes of the GSTT? Matt is the transferor and is 82 years old.
    - ▲ Tim, the grandson of Matt whose mother, Bonnie, is living but whose father, Ben, son of Matt, is deceased.
    - ▲ Mindy is the great-grandchild of Matt. Both Mindy's parents and grandparents are living.
    - ▲ Sharon is the 21-year-old wife of Matt's second son, Alan, age 65.

34. Rosalie, who is single, is diagnosed with a serious disease and expects to be completely incapacitated in three years. Rosalie has two daughters and two grandchildren. She has $500,000 in net worth including her principal residence. Which of the following estate planning tools would you recommend for Rosalie?
    - Set up a durable power of attorney.
    - Immediately gift annual exclusion amounts to children and grandchildren.
    - Set up a revocable living trust.
    - Set up an irrevocable living trust.
    - Set up a QTIP trust.

On April 30th, Dennis transfers property to a trust over which he retains a right to revoke one-fourth of the trust. The trust is to pay Kim 5 percent of the trust assets valued annually for her life with the remainder to be paid to a qualified charity. On August 31st, Dennis dies and the trust becomes irrevocable. Identify the type of trust.

PROBLEMS

1. Kristi and Patrick Moore are 35 years old with two children, Christopher (4 years old) and Andrew (2 years old). The Moore's have simple wills that leave everything to each other. They have asked you to help them update their will. What would you recommend?
2. Tiger Tree is a wealthy golfer who would prefer that his assets not be subject to public scrutiny when he dies. What tools can he use to accomplish his goal?
3. George owns the following property:

    - Boat (fee simple).
    - Condominium on the beach (tenancy in common with his brother and sister).
    - House and two cars with his wife, Ann (tenancy by the entirety).
    - Checking account with his son, Bill (POD).
    - Karate business (JTWROS with his partner, Eric).

    Which items will go through probate? Which property ownership could he sell?

4. Neal is a widower with a taxable estate of $1,400,000. He had made no taxable lifetime gifts. What is his federal estate tax due before the applicable credit if Neal dies in 2005? What is the amount of the applicable credit?
5. Denise and Barry are married and have a taxable estate of $2 million. What is the gross tax on the estate? What is the net tax due? Assume Barry dies in January 2005 and leaves everything to Denise, who dies in November 2005.
6. In 2005, Georgia gave a $10,000 cash gift to her friend, Mary. How much is the taxable gift?
7. For each of the past 10 years, Jessica has given $12,000 to each of her six grandchildren and $25,000 each to her son and daughter. What is the total amount of gifts, and how much gift tax is due? (Assume the annual exclusion for all 10 years is the same as 2005.)

8. Ken and Libby have the following assets:
   - $800,000 house in Ken's name.
   - $1,100,000 investment account in Libby's name.
   - $600,000 in rental property jointly owned with JTWROS.
   - $300,000 beach condo that Libby co-owns with her sister as tenants in common.

   They have two adult children and have made no previous taxable gifts. How much can they transfer to the children free of all transfer tax?

9. Chance is an 85-year-old widower with two sons and a daughter, three grandchildren, and a 27-year old girlfriend. He has an estate currently worth $650,000, including a house worth $300,000. His estate also includes a life insurance policy on his life with a face value of $120,000, and the primary beneficiaries are his children. Chance was recently diagnosed with Alzheimers. The doctors predict a rapid progression and recommend that Chance go into a nursing home soon. He currently has a will that leaves all of his assets equally to his children. He has not taken advantage of any other estate planning techniques. Which of the following would you recommend to Chance while he still has all his mental faculties, and why?
   - Create a living will, a general power of attorney, and a power of attorney for health care.
   - Transfer ownership of his residence to his children so that it will not be counted as a resource when he goes into the nursing home.
   - Create an irrevocable trust containing all of his assets and naming his children as beneficiaries.
   - Create a revocable trust containing all of his assets and naming his children as beneficiaries.
   - Create a QTIP trust naming his girlfriend as the income beneficiary and his children as the remaindermen beneficiaries.

CASE SCENARIO

Use the information provided to answer the following questions regarding the Nelson family.

NELSON FAMILY CASE SCENARIO
DAVID AND DANA NELSON
AS OF 1/1/2006

PERSONAL BACKGROUND AND INFORMATION

David Nelson (age 37) is a bank vice president. He has been employed there for twelve years and has an annual salary of $70,000. Dana Nelson (age 37) is a full-time housewife. David and Dana have been married for eight years. They have two children, John (age 6) and Gabrielle (age 3), and are expecting their third child in two weeks. They have always lived in this community and expect to remain indefinitely in their current residence.

General Goals (Not Prioritized)

- Save for college education.
- Reduce debt.
- Save for retirement.
- Estate planning.
- Invest wisely.

Insurance Information

Health Insurance

The entire family is insured under David's company plan (an indemnity plan). There is a $200 family deductible, and it provides 80/20 major medical coverage. The plan has a $500,000 lifetime limit for each family member. David's employer pays the entire health insurance premium.

Life Insurance

David has a term life insurance policy with a face amount of $25,000 provided by his employer. The policy beneficiary is Dana.

Disability Insurance

David has a private disability insurance policy covering accidental disability for "own occupation" with a 30-day elimination period. In the event that David is disabled as provided under the policy, the benefit is $2,700 per month until age 65. The annual premium is $761 and is paid by David.

Homeowners Insurance

The Nelsons have an HO-3 policy with replacement cost on contents. There is a $250 deductible. The annual premium is $950.

Automobile Insurance

The Nelsons have automobile liability and bodily injury coverage of $100,000/$300,000/ $100,000. They have both comprehensive coverage and collision. The deductibles are $250 (comprehensive) and $500 (collision), respectively. The annual premium is $900.

Investment Information

The bank offers a 401(k) plan in which David is an active participant. The bank matches contributions dollar for dollar up to 3% of David's salary. David currently contributes 5.43% of his salary. His employer's plan allows for employee contributions of up to 16%. In the 401(k), the Nelsons have the opportunity to invest in a Money Market Fund, a Bond Fund, a Growth and Income Fund, and a Small Cap Fund. The Nelsons consider themselves to have a moderate investment risk tolerance.

Income Tax Information

David and Dana tell you that they are in the 15% federal income tax bracket. They pay $820 annually in state and local income taxes.

Education Information

John is 6 years old and currently attending first grade at a private school. Gabrielle is 3 years old. She will attend private school from pre-kindergarten through high school. The current balance of the college fund is $14,000. They expect to contribute $1,000 at the end of each year to this fund.

Gifts, Estates, Trusts, and Will Information

David has made Dana his primary beneficiary on his 401(k) and the children are the contingent beneficiaries. Since most of their assets are owned jointly, David doesn't see the need for a will. Dana also does not have a will.

Relevant External Environmental Information

- Mortgage rates are 6.0 percent for 30 years and 5.5 percent for 15 years, fixed.
- Gross Domestic Product is expected to grow at less than 3 percent.
- Inflation is expected to be 2.6 percent.
- Expected return on investment is 10.4 percent for common stocks, 12.1 percent for small company stocks and 1.1 percent for U.S. Treasury bills.
- College education costs are $15,000 per year.

Dana and David Nelson
Balance Sheet
12/31/05

Assets			Liabilities and Net Worth		
Cash/Cash Equivalents			**Current Liabilities**		
JT	Checking Account	$1,518	JT	Credit Cards	$3,655
JT	Savings Account	$950	JT	Mortgage on Principal Residence	$1,370
	Total Cash/Cash Equiv.	$2,468	H	Boat Loan	$1,048
				Total Current Liabilities	$6,073
Invested Assets			**Long-Term Liabilities**		
W	ABC Stock	$14,050	JT	Mortgage on Principal Residence	$195,284
JT	Educational Fund	$15,560	H	Boat Loan	$16,017
H	401(k)	$38,619		**Total Long-Term Liabilities**	$211,301
H	XYZ Stock	$10,000			
	Total Invested Assets	$78,229			
Personal-Use Assets			**Total Liabilities**		**$217,374**
JT	Principal Residence	$250,000			
JT	Automobile	$15,000			
H	Jet Ski	$10,000	**Net Worth**		**$241,823**
H	Boat B	$30,000			
W	Jewelry	$13,500			
JT	Furniture/Household	$60,000			
	Total Personal-Use Assets	$378,500			
Total Assets		**$459,197**	**Total Liabilities and Net Worth**		**$459,197**

Notes to Financial Statements:

- Assets are stated at fair market value.
- The ABC stock was inherited from Dana's aunt on November 15, 2001. Her aunt originally paid $20,000 for it on October 31, 2001. The fair market value at the aunt's death was $12,000.
- Liabilities are stated at principal only.
- H = Husband; W = Wife; JT = Joint Tenancy

Dana and David Nelson
Statement of Income and Expenses
For the year 2005

INCOME		
Salary - David		$70,000
Investment Income		
Interest Income	$900	
Dividend Income	$150	$1,050
Total Inflow		**$71,050**
Savings		
Reinvestment (Interest/Dividends)	$1,050	
401(k) Deferrals	$3,803	
Educational Fund	$1,000	
Total Savings		**$5,853**
Available for Expenses		**$65,197**
EXPENSES		
Ordinary Living Expenses		
Food	$6,000	
Clothing	$3,600	
Child Care	$600	
Entertainment	$1,814	
Utilities	$3,600	
Auto Maintenance	$2,000	
Church	$3,500	
Total Ordinary Living Expenses		**$21,114**
Debt Payments		
Credit Card Payments Principal	$345	
Credit Card Payments Interest	$615	
Mortgage Payment Principal	$1,234	
Mortgage Payment Interest	$20,720	
Boat Loan Principal	$1,493	
Boat Loan Interest	$1,547	
Total Debt Payments		**$25,954**
Insurance Premiums		
Automobile Insurance Premiums	$900	
Disability Insurance Premiums	$761	
Homeowners Insurance Premiums	$950	
Total Insurance Premiums		**$2,611**
Tuition and Education Expenses		**$1,000**
Taxes		
Federal Income Tax (W/H)	$7,500	
State (and City) Income Tax	$820	
FICA	$5,355	
Property Tax (Principal Residence)	$1,000	
Total Taxes		**$14,675**
Total Expenses		**$65,354**
Discretionary Cash Flow (negative)		**($157)**

1. Given David's current attitudes about the necessity for a will for himself and Dana, what problems has David created should he or Dana die today?
2. What will provisions should David have in his will?
3. What will provisions should Dana have in her will?
4. Assume that David and Dana have implemented recommendations for debt repayment to increase their discretionary cash available and have increased life insurance coverage on David to a total of $450,000. The disability coverage has been changed to add coverage for illness as well as accident. As their financial planner, what other insurance coverages should you recommend to the Nelsons?

CHAPTER APPENDIX 17.1: JFK, JR.'S LAST WILL AND TESTAMENT

THE LAST WILL AND TESTAMENT OF JOHN F. KENNEDY, JR.

John F. Kennedy, Jr. planned to leave the bulk of his holdings to his wife, Caroline Bessette-Kennedy, or their children. But John and Caroline died together in a plane crash in July of 1999 without leaving any issue (children). Therefore, his property will go to the children of his sister, Caroline Kennedy Schlossberg. The bulk of his estate is left to the beneficiaries of a trust he established in 1983. Kennedy also left the scrimshaw set, or carved whale ivory set, once owned by his father to nephew John B.K. Schlossberg. Kennedy's cousin, Timothy P. Shriver was named executor of the will. Kennedy's estate is reportedly worth $100 million.

I, JOHN F. KENNEDY, JR., of New York, New York, make this my last will, hereby revoking all earlier wills and codicils. I do not by this will exercise any power of appointment.

FIRST: I give all my tangible property (as distinguished from money, securities and the like), wherever located, other than my scrimshaw set previously owned by my father, to my wife, Carolyn Bessette-Kennedy, if she is living on the thirtieth day after my death, or if not, by right of representation to my then living issue, or if none, by right of representation to the then living issue of my sister, Caroline Kennedy Schlossberg, or if none, to my said sister, Caroline, if she is then living. If I am survived by issue, I leave this scrimshaw set to said wife, Carolyn, if she is then living, or if not, by right of representation, to my then living issue. If I am not survived by issue, I give said scrimshaw set to my nephew John B.K. Schlossberg, if he is then living, or if not, by right of representation to the then living issue of my said sister, Caroline, or if none, to my said sister Caroline, if she is then living. I hope that whoever receives my tangible personal property will dispose of certain items of it in accordance with my wishes, however made unknown, but I impose no trust, condition or enforceable obligation of any kind in this regard. **SECOND**: I give and devise all my interest in my cooperative apartment located at 20-26 Moore Street, Apartment 9E, in said New York, including all my shares therein and any proprietary leases with respect thereto, to my said wife, Carolyn, if she is living on the thirtieth day after my death.

THIRD: If no issue of mine survive me, I give and devise all my interests in real estate, wherever located, that I own as tenants in common with my said sister, Caroline, or as tenants in common with any of her issue, by right of representation to Caroline's issue who are living on the thirtieth day after my death, or if none, to my said sister Caroline, if she is then living. References in this Article THIRD to "real estate" include shares in cooperative apartments and proprietary leases with respect thereto.

FOURTH: I give and devise the residue of all the property, of whatever kind and wherever located, that I own at my death to the then trustees of the John F. Kennedy Jr. 1983 Trust established October 13, 1983 by me, as Donor, of which John T. Fallon, of Weston, Massachusetts, and I are currently the trustees (the "1983 Trust"), to be added to the principal of the 1983 Trust and administered in accordance with the provisions thereof, as amended by a First Amendment dated April 9, 1987 and by a Second Amendment and Complete Restatement dated earlier this day, and as from time to hereafter further amended whether before or after my death. I have provided in the 1983 Trust for my children and more remote issue and for the method of paying all federal and state taxes in the nature of estate, inheritance, succession and like taxes occasioned by my death.

FIFTH: I appoint my wife, Carolyn Bessette-Kennedy, as guardian of each child of our marriage during minority. No guardian appointed in this will or a codicil need furnish any surety on any official bond.

SIXTH: I name my cousin Anthony Stanislaus Radziwill as my executor; and if for any reason, he fails to qualify or ceases to serve in that capacity, I name my cousin Timothy P. Shriver as my executor in his place. References in this will or a codicil to my "executor" mean the one or more executors (or administrators with this will annexed) for the time being in office. No executor or a codicil need furnish any surety on any official bond. In any proceeding for the allowance of an account of my executor, I request the Court to dispense with the appointment of a guardian ad litem to represent any person or interest. I direct that in any proceeding relating to my estate, service of process upon any person under a disability shall not made when another person not under a disability is a party to the proceeding and has the same interest as the person under the disability.

SEVENTH: In addition to other powers, my executor shall have power from time to time at discretion and without license of court: To retain, and to invest and reinvest in, any kind or amount of property; to vote and exercise other rights of security holders; to make such elections for federal and state estate, gift, income and generation-skipping transfer tax purposes as my executor may deem advisable; to compromise or admit to arbitration any matters in dispute; to borrow money, and to sell, mortgage, pledge, exchange, lease and contract with respect to any real or personal property, all without notice to any beneficiary and in such manner, for such consideration and on such terms as to credit or otherwise as my executor may deem advisable, whether or not the effect thereof extends beyond the period settling my estate; and in distributing my estate, to allot property, whether real or personal, at then current values, in lieu of cash.

Source: Courtroom Television Network, LLC

APPENDIX 17.2: MARILYN MONROE'S LAST WILL AND TESTAMENT

THE WILL OF MARILYN MONROE

The legendary sex symbol, who tragically committed suicide in 1962, left most of her fortune to her friends and family.

I, MARILYN MONROE, do make, publish and declare this to be my Last Will and Testament.

FIRST: I hereby revoke all former Wills and Codicils by me made.

SECOND: I direct my Executor, hereinafter named, to pay all of my just debts, funeral expenses and testamentary charges as soon after my death as can conveniently be done.

THIRD: I direct that all succession, estate or inheritance taxes which may be levied against my estate and/or against any legacies and/or devises hereinafter set forth shall be paid out of my residuary estate.

FOURTH: (a) I give and bequeath to BERNICE MIRACLE, should she survive me, the sum of $10,000.00.

(b) I give and bequeath to MAY REIS, should she survive me, the sum of $10,000.00.

(c) I give and bequeath to NORMAN and HEDDA ROSTEN, or to the survivor of them, or if they should both predecease me, then to their daughter, PATRICIA ROSTEN, the sum of $5,000.00, it being my wish that such sum be used for the education of PATRICIA ROSTEN.

(d) I give and bequeath all of my personal effects and clothing to LEE STRASBERG, or if he should predecease me, then to my Executor hereinafter named, it being my desire that he distribute these, in his sole discretion, among my friends, colleagues and those to whom I am devoted.

FIFTH: I give and bequeath to my Trustee, hereinafter named, the sum of $100,000.00, in Trust, for the following uses and purposes:

(a) To hold, manage, invest and reinvest the said property and to receive and collect the income therefrom.

(b) To pay the net income therefrom, together with such amounts of principal as shall be necessary to provide $5,000.00 per annum, in equal quarterly installments, for the maintenance and support of my mother, GLADYS BAKER, during her lifetime.

(c) To pay the net income therefrom, together with such amounts of principal as shall be necessary to provide $2,500.00 per annum, in equal quarterly installments, for the maintenance and support of MRS. MICHAEL CHEKHOV during her lifetime.

(d) Upon the death of the survivor between my mother, GLADYS BAKER, and MRS. MICHAEL CHEKHOV to pay over the principal remaining in the Trust, together with any accumulated income, to DR. MARIANNE KRIS to be used by her for the furtherance of the work of such psychiatric institutions or groups as she shall elect.

SIXTH: All the rest, residue and remainder of my estate, both real and personal, of whatsoever nature and wheresoever situate, of which I shall die seized or possessed or to which I shall be in any way entitled, or over which I shall possess any power of appointment by Will at the time of my death, including any lapsed legacies, I give, devise and bequeath as follows:

(a) to MAY REIS the sum of $40,000.00 or 25% of the total remainder of my estate, whichever shall be the lesser,

(b) To DR. MARIANNE KRIS 25% of the balance thereof, to be used by her as set forth in ARTICLE FIFTH (d) of this my Last Will and Testament.

(c) To LEE STRASBERG the entire remaining balance.

SEVENTH: I nominate, constitute and appoint AARON R. FROSCH Executor of this my Last Will and Testament. In the event that he should die or fail to qualify, or resign or for any other reason be unable to act, I nominate, constitute and appoint L. ARNOLD WEISSBERGER in his place and stead.

EIGHTH: I nominate, constitute and appoint AARON R. FROSCH Trustee under this my Last Will and Testament. In the event he should die or fail to qualify, or resign or for any other reason be unable to act, I nominate, constitute and appoint L. Arnold Weissberger in his place and stead.

Marilyn Monroe (L.S.)

SIGNED, SEALED, PUBLISHED and DECLARED by MARILYN MONROE, the Testatrix above named, as and for her Last Will and Testament, in our presence and we, at her request and in her presence and in the presence of each other, have hereunto subscribed our names as witnesses this 14th day of January, One Thousand Nine Hundred Sixty-One

Source: Courtroom Television Network, LLC

APPENDIX 17.3: POWER OF ATTORNEY

UNITED STATES OF AMERICA
STATE OF LOUISIANA
PARISH OF JEFFERSON

Be it known, that on this ______day of _________, in the year _________:

1. Before me, the undersigned authority, a Notary Public duly commissioned and qualified in and for the State and Parish set forth above, therein residing, and in the presence of the undersigned competent witnesses, personally came and appeared: ____________________ a person of the full age of majority and domiciled in St. Rose, Louisiana (the "Principal"), who declared that the Principal appoints his children,________(the "Agent," whether one or more, with either authorized to act alone), as the Principal's true and lawful agent and attorney-in-fact, general and special, granting unto the Agent full power and authority for the Principal and in the Principal's name and behalf, and to the Principal's use, to conduct, manage and transact all of the Principal's affairs, business, concerns and matters of whatever nature or kind, without any reservation whatsoever, except as hereinafter specifically set forth and subject to the following effective date. The Power of Attorney shall not become effective unless and until a personal physician of the Principal certifies in writing that the Principal is mentally or physically incapable of administering her affairs. In furtherance of this general grant of authority to the Agent, but not in limitation thereof, the Principal specifically authorizes the Agent to perform all of the following acts and exercise all of the following powers for the Principal and in the Principal's name.
2. To open all letters or correspondence addressed to the Principal and answer them.
3. To open accounts with any bank, brokerage or other entity; to deposit funds (whether represented by cash, checks or otherwise) in any account maintained by or for the Principal with any bank or other entity; to endorse all checks, bills of exchange and other instruments; to withdraw funds from any account maintained by the Principal with any bank or other person; to sign checks, bills or exchange and other instruments; to deposit any obligation with any bank or other entity for collection.
4. To represent the Principal in the Principal's capacity as a creditor or obligee of any person; to collect any funds or things owed the Principal by any person; and to attend any meeting of creditors in which the Principal may be interested and to vote in the Principal's name on all matters that may be submitted to the meeting.
5. To represent the Principal in the Principal's capacity as a stockholder of any corporation, partner in any partnership, beneficiary of any trust or member of any association or entity or as a security holder thereof. This authority shall include (but is not limited to) the authority to execute consent agreements and to attend any meetings of stockholders, partners, members, or beneficiaries or security holders of any corporation, partnership, association, trust or entity and to agree or vote (or execute proxies in favor of others to agree or vote) in the name of the Principal on all questions, including merger, sale, consolidation, any type of reorganization or matters.
6. To borrow any amounts of money for the Principal and in the Principal's name upon such terms and conditions as the Agent may in the Agent's sole discretion deem appropriate.
7. To sell, exchange, donate, transfer, or convey any property, whether immovable (real), movable (personal), tangible or intangible or corporeal or incorporeal, including stocks, bonds, notes, bills or any other security, belonging to the Principal or any interest therein and to receive the price or other consideration thereof.
8. To make gifts or other gratuitous transfers of any property belonging to the Principal either outright or in trust (including the forgiveness of debt), to any of the Principal's descendants or to the agent.
9. To purchase, acquire by exchange or otherwise acquire any property for and in the name of the Principal and to make payment therefore out of the Principal's funds or assets.
10. To create servitudes, building restrictions, other real rights, easements and covenants of any kind that burden, benefit or otherwise affect any property of the Principal.
11. To accept donations.
12. To lease, rent, let or hire (as lessor) any property belonging to the Principal.
13. To lease, rent, hire or let (as lessee) any property.
14. To encumber, mortgage, pledge, pawn or otherwise grant any security interest in any property of the Principal, whether to secure obligations of the Principal or any other person or entity.
15. To grant or convey oil, gas, and other mineral leases, net profits interests, production payments, royalty interests, mineral servitudes and other interests in oil, gas and any other minerals on or under any property of the Principal; to sign division orders and transfer orders; to grant rights-of-way and easements; and otherwise to execute documents incident to the exploration for oil, gas or other minerals on or underlying property of the Principal.

POWER OF ATTORNEY (CONT.)

16. To enter into transactions pursuant to which the Principal is lessee, grantee or vendee under or of any oil, gas or mineral lease, net profits interest, production payment, royalty deed, mineral servitude or any other interest in oil, gas or other minerals.
17. To undertake any obligations for the Principal, to act for the Principal in agreeing to guarantee any obligations of others or agreeing to defend and indemnify any person or entity against any claims, obligations or liabilities.
18. To act for the Principal and be the Principal's substitute in all cases in which the Principal may be appointed the agent or attorney of others.
19. To refer matters to arbitration and to initiate, prosecute, defend and otherwise represent the Principal in any judicial or arbitration proceeding (whether as plaintiff or defendant) and to settle and compromise any claim, dispute or proceeding; to apply for and obtain any attachments, sequestrations, injunctions, and appeals, give the requisite security, and sign the necessary bonds.
20. To represent the Principal in connection with any succession or estate in which the Principal may be or become interested (whether as heir, legatee, creditor, executor, administrator or otherwise), including the execution of any acceptance or renunciation thereof on the Principal's behalf; to apply for the administration thereof, and to demand, obtain and execute all orders and decrees as the Agent may deem proper; to settle, compromise, and liquidate the Principal's interest therein; and to receive and receipt for all property to which Principal may be entitled in respect of successions or estates.
21. To acknowledge any debt of the Principal.
22. To settle and compromise any dispute or matter involving the Principal.
23. To file any United States, State or other tax returns (including but not limited to income tax returns); to apply for extensions of time to file tax returns; and to represent the Principal in connection with any matter or dispute relating to United States, State or other taxes.
24. The Principal further authorizes and empowers the Agent to take any other action concerning the affairs, business or assets of the Principal as fully, completely and effectively and for all intents and purposes with the same validity as though the action had been expressly provided for herein and as though the Principal had taken the action in person.
25. The transactions entered into by the Agent for the Principal shall be on such terms and conditions as to payment and otherwise as the Agent may in the Agent's sole discretion determine.
26. The Agent is authorized to make, sign and execute in the name of the Principal all agreements, contracts, and instruments that may be necessary or convenient in the Agent's sole discretion to carry out transactions entered into by the Agent for the Principal or to enable the Agent fully to exercise the powers granted herein and to include therein any terms, conditions and provisions that the Agent shall deem appropriate and to bind the Principal thereby as fully as though each instrument had been signed by the Principal in person.
27. The agency created by this Power of Attorney shall be "durable" as provided by Louisiana Civil Code article 3027(B) and shall not be deemed revoked by the Principal's disability or incapacity.
28. The Principal agrees to ratify and confirm all actions that the Agent shall take pursuant to this Power of Attorney.
29. References herein to one gender shall be deemed to include the other whenever appropriate.
30. The term "property" means all kinds of property, whether movable, immovable, real, personal, mixed, corporeal, incorporeal, tangible or intangible. The term "entity" includes natural persons, corporations, partnerships, trusts, associations and any other form of legal entity and governmental and political organizations.
31. THUS DONE AND PASSED in multiple originals on the date first above written in the presence of the undersigned competent witnesses, who sign their names with the Principal and me, Notary, after reading of the whole.

WITNESSES:

______________________________ ______________________________

Print Name:______________________ Principal

____

Print Name:______________________

____

Notary Public

APPENDIX 17.4: MEDICAL POWER OF ATTORNEY

MEDICAL POWER OF ATTORNEY

1. BE IT KNOWN, that on this _____ day of __________, in the year Two Thousand:
2. BEFORE ME, the undersigned authority, a Notary Public duly commissioned and qualified in and for the State and Parish set forth above, therein residing, and in the presence of the undersigned competent witnesses, personally came and appeared:
   (The "Principal"), who after being duly sworn, declared that the Principal appoints his children, ___________________ (the "Agent", whether one or more, with either authorized to act alone), as the Principal's true and lawful agent and attorney-in-fact, granting unto the Agent full power and authority regarding the matters set forth below.
3. Durability. This agency is "durable" and shall not be deemed revoked by the Principal's disability or incapacity.

HEALTH CARE

4. The Principal grants unto the Agent full power and authority regarding the following health care matters that the Principal could exercise on the Principal's own behalf, if capable of doing so. The Principal specifically authorizes the Agent to:
   4.1 Medical Records. Have access to any medical information in any form regarding the Principal's physical condition, and to execute such consents as may be necessary to obtain such medical information.
   4.2 Professionals. Retain, compensate and discharge any health care professionals the Agent deems necessary to examine, evaluate or treat the Principal, whether for emergency, elective, recuperative, convalescent or other care.
   4.3 Institutionalization. Admit the Principal to any health care facility recommended by a qualified health care professional, whether for physical or mental care or treatment, and remove the Principal from such institution at any time, even if contrary to medical advice.
   4.4 Treatment. Consent on the Principal's behalf to tests, treatment, medication, surgery, organ transplant or other procedures, and to revoke that consent, even if contrary to medical advice.
   4.5 Chemical Dependency. Consent on the Principal's behalf to a course of treatment for chemical dependency, whether suspected or diagnosed, and to revoke such consent.
   4.6 Pain Relief. Consent on the Principal's behalf to pain relief procedures, even if they are unconventional or experimental, even if they risk addiction, injury or foreshortening the Principal's life.
   4.7 Releases. Release from liability any health care professional or institution that acts on the Principal's behalf in reliance on the Agent.

PERSONAL CARE

5. The Principal grants unto the Agent full power and authority regarding the following personal care matters that the Principal could act on the Principal's own behalf, if capable of doing so. The Principal specifically authorizes the Agent to:
   5.1 Home Care. Provide for the Principal's continued maintenance and support. As nearly as possible, the Principal expressly authorizes the Agent to maintain the Principal's accustomed standard of living. The Agent shall provide the Principal with a suitable place to live by maintaining the Principal in the Principal's family residence or apartment (home), paying principal, interest, taxes, insurance and repairs as necessary. The Agent may retain or discharge domestic servants, attendants, companions, nurses, sitters or other persons who provide care to the Principal and the Principal's home. The Agent may authorize purchases of food, clothing, medical care and customary luxuries on the Principal's behalf.
   5.2 Institutional Care. Arrange and contract for institutional health care (hospital, retirement facility, nursing home, hospice or other) on the Principal's behalf if recommended by the Principal's physician. If reasonably advised that the Principal's return home is unlikely because of the Principal's condition, the Agent may sell, exchange, lease, sublease or dispose of the Principal's home and such of its contents as are no longer useful to the Principal and are not specifically bequeathed in the Principal's will, all on such terms as to price, payment and security as the Agent deems reasonable.
   5.3 Religious Needs. Continue the Principal's affiliation with the Principal's church, keeping the Principal accessible to the Principal's clergy, members and other representatives, continuing and renewing any pledge made by the Principal whether for capital, operations or other purposes, and generally to assist the Principal in maintaining the Principal's church relationships to the extent the Principal's health permits.
   5.4 Companions and Recreation. Hire, discharge, direct and compensate such companions as may be necessary for the Principal's health, recreation, travel, and general well-being.
   5.5 Funeral Arrangements. Arrange and contract for the Principal's funeral including appropriate arrangements and instruction for the Principal's funeral service or memorial service, including purchase of a burial plot or other appropriate disposition of the Principal's body. The Agent shall comply with any known written instructions as the Principal may have or leave.

MEDICAL POWER OF ATTORNEY (CONT.)

5.6 Curator or Guardian. Nominate on the Principal's behalf any person the Agent deems qualified, including the Agent, as the Principal's curator, undercurator, curator ad hoc, guardian, or conservator or any other fiduciary office the Principal has a right to nominate or designate, to waive any bond on the Principal's behalf and to grant to that fiduciary or representative any powers that the Principal might extend on the Principal's own behalf.

REFUSAL OF MEDICAL TREATMENT

6. The Principal declares that the Principal does not wish the Principal's dying to be prolonged artificially through extraordinary or heroic means if the Principal's condition is terminal. Even over the objection of members of the Principal's family, the Principal authorizes the Agent to:

6.1 Withdraw or Withhold Life Support. Sign on behalf of the Principal any documents, waivers or releases necessary to withdraw, withhold or cease any procedure calculated only to prolong the Principal's life, including the use of a respirator, cardiopulmonary resuscitation, surgery, dialysis, blood transfusion, antibiotics, antiarrhythmic and pressor drugs or transplants if two licensed physicians, one of whom is the Principal's attending physician, have personally examined the Principal and the Principal's attending physician has noted in the Principal's medical records that the Principal's condition is terminal and irreversible.

6.2 Nourishment. Refuse or discontinue intravenous or parenteral feeding, hydration, misting and endotracheal or nasogastric tubes, if advised that no undue pain will be caused to the Principal.

DECLARATION

7. Contemplating that the Principal's medical care may be rendered in Louisiana, or that state law might apply, the Principal has executed a Declaration Concerning Life-Sustaining Procedures ("Declaration") pursuant to State Revised Statues 40:1299.58.1 and following as amended, a copy of which is attached. The Principal declares that by executing that Declaration the Principal does not intend to limit or reduce the powers over the Principal's person elsewhere granted to the Agent in this agency, but rather to convey to the Agent any additional powers as are necessary to make or carry out the terms of that Declaration.

8. THUS DONE AND PASSED in multiple originals on the date first above written in the presence of the undersigned competent witnesses, who signed their names with the Principal and me Notary, after reading of the whole.

WITNESSES:

____________________________ ____________________________

Print Name:____________________ Principal

____

Print Name:____________________

____

Notary Public

APPENDIX 17.5: LIVING WILL

LIVING WILL DECLARATION

This Declaration is made on the _______ day of ______________, 2000, pursuant to the Louisiana Natural Death Act, La. R.S. 40:1299.58.1 *et seq.*

I,__________________________, being of sound mind, willfully and voluntarily make known my desire that my dying shall not be artificially prolonged under the circumstances set forth below and do hereby declare:

If at any time I should have an incurable injury, disease or illness certified to be a terminal and irreversible condition or a continual profound comatose state with no reasonable chance of recovery by two physicians who have personally examined me, one of whom shall be my attending physician, and the physicians have determined that my death will occur whether or not life-sustaining procedures are utilized and where the application of life-sustaining procedures would only serve to prolong artificially the dying process, I direct that such procedures (including but not limited to artificial means of respiration, hydration and/or nutrition) be withheld or withdrawn and that I be permitted to die naturally with only the administration of medication or the performance of any medical procedure deemed necessary to provide me with comfort care.

In the absence of my ability to give direction regarding the use of such life-sustaining procedures, it is my intention that this Declaration shall be honored by my family and physician(s) as the final expression of my legal right to refuse medical or surgical treatment and accept the consequences from such refusal.

I understand the full import of this Declaration, and I am emotionally and mentally competent to make this Declaration. Terms used in this Declaration shall have the meanings prescribed in the Louisiana Natural Death Act, La. R.S. 40:1299.58 *et seq.*, as amended now or hereafter.

____

Declarant

Metairie, Jefferson Parish, Louisiana

The declarant has been personally known to me, and I believe the declarant to be of sound mind. Both witnesses are competent adults who are not entitled to any portion of the estate of the declarant upon declarant's decease. The declarant signed this Declaration in our presence on the date set forth above.

____

Witnesses

____

Witnesses

Financial Planning Profession

in BRIEF

- Financial planning institutions
- Financial planning professionals
- The Code of Ethics
- Disciplinary Rules and Procedures
- The Practice Standards
- State laws
- Civil liability

↓

- Developing a financial planning practice
- Maintaining competence
- Developing clients

↓

- Practice competently, ethically, and legally
- Procedures regarding discipline
- Civil liability

SECTION V

The Financial Planning Profession

CHAPTER 18 The Practice of Financial Planning
CHAPTER 19 Regulatory and Ethical Responsibilities

Risks

- Incompentence of planner
- Improper practice
- Unethical practice
- Illegal practice
- Professional discipline
- Civil liabilty

Data Collection

- Financial planning institutions
- Financial planning professionals
- The Code of Ethics
- Practice Standards
- Laws regarding malpractice
- Disciplinary rules
- Civil liability

Goals

- The competent, legal, and ethical practice of financial planning

Data Analysis

- Maintaining professional competence
- Continuing education
- Practicing lawfully and ethically
- How to build a practice

CHAPTER 18

The Practice of Financial Planning

LEARNING OBJECTIVES:

After learning the material in this chapter, you will be able to:

1. Describe various types of financial planning institutions.
2. Identify the types of services that are provided by the various types of financial planning institutions.
3. List some of the common credentials associated with the financial planning industry.
4. Discuss common compensation methods for professional financial planners.
5. Identify some important aspects of building a financial planning practice and maintaining clients.
6. Discuss why continuing education is important for financial planners.

INTRODUCTION

The professional financial planner understands that the overall purpose of personal financial planning is to assist the client in achieving goals and objectives. While most of those goals are finance related, many are more qualitative than quantitative. The planner realizes that personal financial planning is about the adaptation of the individual client's strengths and weaknesses in an environment characterized by opportunities and threats. Generally throughout the text, we have referred to these threats as risks.

The planner must possess a wide variety of skills and knowledge and must be able to apply those skills in any given client situation to assess the client's current financial situation, to help the client establish realistic financial goals, and to develop a plan or strategy for accomplishing those goals.

To be successful as a financial planner, the professional should have a working knowledge of the concepts within the financial planning pyramid.

EXHIBIT 18.1: FINANCIAL PLANNER'S PYRAMID OF KNOWLEDGE

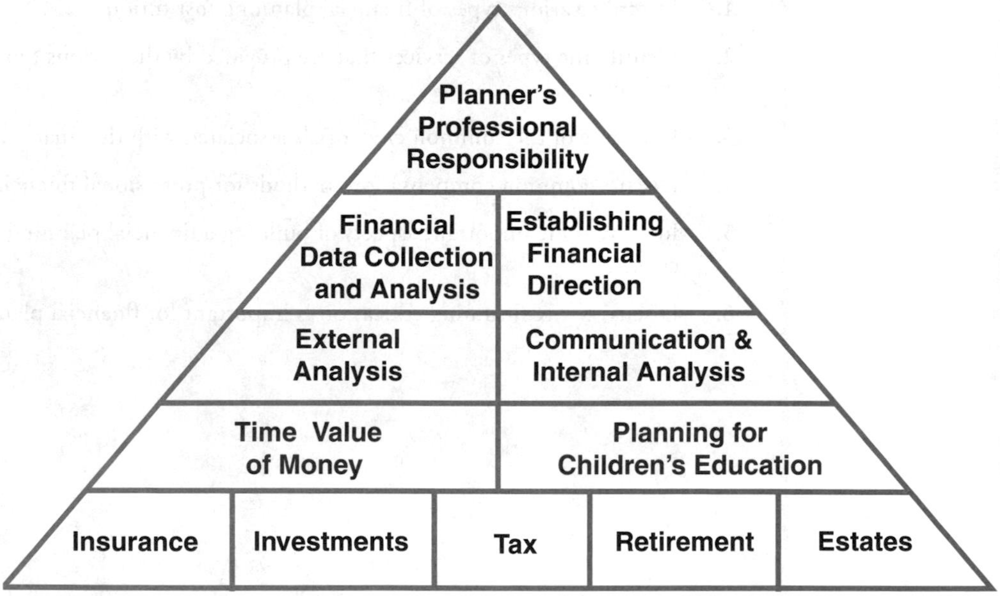

Planner's Professional Responsibility

Financial Data Collection and Analysis | Establishing Financial Direction

External Analysis | Communication & Internal Analysis

Time Value of Money | Planning for Children's Education

Insurance | Investments | Tax | Retirement | Estates

THE FINANCIAL PLANNING PROFESSION

The financial planning profession is practiced by a diverse group of individuals and institutions. Many practitioners have individual private practices. However, most financial planners work for accounting firms, law firms, insurance companies, personal financial planning firms, brokerage houses, banks and other financial institutions that provide financial planning-related services.

Financial Planning Institutions

Accounting Firms

Accounting firms have traditionally provided accounting, tax, and auditing-related services. From an individual's perspective, these services were limited to preparing tax returns, preparing financial statements, business consulting, and business and individual tax planning. Today, however, accounting firms are providing even more services related to financial planning. These services include assistance in investment planning, retirement planning, and estate planning.

The American Institute of Certified Public Accountants (AICPA) has been actively assisting CPAs in the development of financial planning practices in recent years. They provide training for members at national conferences and have instituted a designation devoted solely to financial planning. The AICPA has also been able to establish relationships with other financial services firms that allow CPAs to deliver more financial planning services to their new and existing clients.

Law Firms

Attorneys have always been an integral part of developing and implementing financial and estate plans. Since attorneys are the ones who draft legal documents, they are in a perfect position to provide additional services to their clients. Law firms have always drafted such documents as wills, powers of attorney, trusts, qualified plan documents, partnership agreements and other similar documents. Their traditional services include tax planning, estate planning, and retirement and benefit planning.

Insurance Companies

Insurance companies primarily sell life, health and/or property and casualty insurance products. Many insurance companies are expanding their services to include other areas of financial planning, particularly estate planning and retirement planning. Some have their own proprietary mutual funds.

Personal Financial Planning Firms (PFP Firms)

These firms are generally small and specialize in a particular market niche. Some PFP firms manage assets, while others provide comprehensive financial planning or sell products.

Brokerage Houses

Many brokerage houses provide global financial management and advisory services, including financial planning, securities underwriting, and trading and brokering. Some brokerage firms provide research, banking and insurance services, and investment banking. Brokerage houses are currently in the process of changing the nature of their business from transaction oriented to more service-and-planning related. These new services include retirement and estate planning.

Mutual Funds

Many mutual fund companies now provide financial planning assistance to their customers to better serve their clients and differentiate themselves from their competition. Some have established personal counselors for some of their large customers while providing generic planning on the Internet for all customers.

Banks

Banks offer a wide range of financial planning services. Banks generally offer checking and savings, mortgages, loans, and other credit products. Most banks now offer comprehensive brokerage services, including stocks, bonds, mutual funds, investments and retirement planning. Estate planning services are also offered through their trust departments.

EXHIBIT 18.2: SUMMARY OF FINANCIAL PLANNING INSTITUTIONS

Common Practice Areas	Accounting Firms	Law Firms	Insurance Companies	PFP Firms	Brokerage Houses	Mutual Funds	Banks
Insurance			✔	✔	✔		✔
Investments	✔		✔	✔	✔	✔	✔
Tax	✔	✔		✔			
Retirement	✔	✔	✔	✔	✔	✔	✔
Estate Planning	✔	✔	✔	✔	✔		✔

As competition for clients increases, and as more firms and individual practices attempt to attract more clients in an effort to increase the assets under management, many firms are expanding their services to include all aspects of financial planning. Such diversification allows the client the opportunity for one-stop shopping. Firms have accomplished this change and expansion by keeping their traditional expertise, such as tax planning for accounting firms and investment advice for brokerage houses, and hiring "office specialists" in the other areas. Thus, the institutions continue to have a dominance of service and training in one specific area, but have the capacity, through company experts, to cover all aspects of financial planning. In addition, the institutions themselves continue to expand as the competition increases, in order to spread the costs of experts and additional services over the greatest number of clients and the amount of assets under management.

The consolidation of the various practice areas will likely provide an opportunity for lower-to-middle-income clients to receive better financial planning services. Those services may become less personal, however, with computerized planning being offered over the Internet. Meanwhile, the wealthiest clients will likely continue to seek the service of a team of professionals, generally from more than one institution. Individuals with a large amount of investments generally seek independence of thought and appreciate reasonable differences of opinion, which may be unlikely from a single institution.

Financial Planning Professionals

The public perceives, and has a reasonable expectation, that those who "practice" financial planning are competent and ethical. Many financial professionals are licensed at the state and federal levels in specific areas such as insurance or securities. They are not specifically regulated, however, for their financial planning activities, with the exception of the CERTIFIED FINANCIAL PLANNER™ practitioner, who is certified by Certified Financial Planner Board of Standards, Inc. (CFP Board). Persons who have only an elementary understanding of one or two functional areas are not prepared to assist clients faced with complex choices in a changing environment. While there are many competent, highly trained, and highly credentialed persons practicing financial planning, there are many more persons holding themselves out as financial planners who are not trained, competent, or credentialed. Unfortunately, therefore, the practice of financial planning is currently characterized by a lack of uniform educational standards, a lack of professional competence standards, and a lack of commitment to one profession with a self-regulating set of ethical standards.

There is, of course, hope. The professionalism in personal financial planning is changing, albeit slowly. As the planners themselves recognize that they need to become competent to distinguish themselves, the consuming public is becoming more sophisticated when choosing financial planning professionals.

Many financial planning professionals attempt to distinguish themselves by earning financial planning designations. The following three sections briefly describe some of the more common credentials for individuals who work in the financial planning area.

Financial Planning Designations

Certified Financial Planner (CFP®)

CFP® certification is perhaps the most recognized and respected financial planning certification and is awarded by CFP Board. CFP® certificants are individuals who have met CFP Board's education, examination, experience, and ethics requirements. These individuals are committed to high standards of ethical conduct and must complete biennial certification requirements. Additional information about CFP Board and its Code of Ethics is provided in the next chapter.

Chartered Financial Consultant (ChFC)

The ChFC credential is a financial planning designation awarded by The American College to those individuals who complete the required education program, meet the experience requirements, and agree to adhere to the code of ethics.

Personal Financial Specialist (PFS)

The PFS designation is granted exclusively to CPAs who wish to specialize in personal financial planning. The PFS credential is a financial planning designation awarded by the AICPA to those candidates who have met the CPA education requirements, have the minimum hours of financial planning experience, and successfully complete a six-hour exam.

EXHIBIT 18.3: SUMMARY OF FINANCIAL PLANNING DESIGNATIONS

	Education/ Experience	Exam	Ethics	Continuing Education	Designating Organization	Number of Designees
CFP®	Three years (with bachelors degree) of financial planning-related experience; five years without degree*	10 hrs over two days.	Yes	30 hrs every 2 years	CFP Board	45,755 (as of 2004)
ChFC	8-course financial planning curriculum from The American College and 3 years of business experience	Two-hour exam for each of the 8 courses	Adherence to The American College's Code of Ethics	30 hours every two years (mandatory for certain designees who matriculated after 6/30/89; voluntary for others)	The American College	40,000 (as of 2004)
PFS	Candidates must be a CPA and practice in the area of financial planning for a minimum number of hours per year.	Comprehensive six-hour exam covering six financial planning topic areas	Adherence to the AICPA's Code of Professional Conduct	60 points every three years - earned through classes, research, and work experience	AICPA, only to members who meet its requirements	3,300 (as of 2004)

* Starting in 2007, individuals will be required to posses at least a bachelor's degree in order to qualify for the CFP® designation.

Other Designations Held by Financial Services Professionals

Chartered Life Underwriter (CLU)

The CLU designation is awarded by The American College to insurance and financial services professionals who have met the College's three-year business experience requirement, passed its 10 college-level education courses, and agreed to abide by its code of ethics.

Chartered Financial Analyst (CFA)

This designation is awarded by The CFA Institute (formerly the Association for Investment Management and Research (AIMR)) to experienced financial analysts who successfully complete a CFA study course and pass three examinations covering economics, financial accounting, portfolio management, securities analysis, and ethics.

Certified Public Accountant (CPA)

The CPA designation is awarded by the American Institute of Certified Public Accountants (AICPA) to accountants who pass the AICPA's Uniform CPA Examination and satisfy the work experience and statutory and licensing requirements of the state(s) in which they practice.

Other Licenses Held by Financial Services Professionals

Attorney (JD)

As mentioned in the previous section, a small percentage of attorneys provide financial planning services. Generally, those who provide such services, specialize in estate and/or tax planning. The attorney is typically part of a financial planning team and may provide specific legal advice to a client, prepare legal documents, and consult on estate and tax planning issues.

Insurance Agent

Insurance agents are individuals licensed by a state or states to sell or give advice on insurance products, including life, health, property, and casualty insurance. Financial planning services will vary based on the type of agent. Independent insurance agents sell products for more than one insurance company, where exclusive insurance agents represent only one company.

Securities Analyst

These professionals are usually employed by investment brokers, banks, mutual fund managers, or other investment institutions to conduct investment research and analyze the value of securities and financial condition of a company, group of companies, or industry sector. Based on their analysis, securities analysts will make investment recommendations.

Registered Investment Adviser (RIA)

Registered Investment Advisors are individuals (or firms) providing securities advice for compensation. They must be registered with the Securities and Exchange Commission (SEC) and/or appropriate state securities agencies. Financial planning services provided by RIAs include recommendations of stocks, bonds, mutual funds, and other investments.

Real Estate Broker

Real estate brokers are licensed by a state or states in which they practice. These individuals arrange the purchase or sale of property in return for a commission. Financial planning services provided by real estate brokers are limited and may include helping customers finance a real estate purchase through their contacts with banks, savings and loans, and mortgage bankers.

Compensation Methods

The methods of compensation for professional financial planners are as diverse as the planners themselves, and include fee-only planners, fee-based planners, commission-based, and those receiving fees for assets under management. In recent years, there has been a move toward fee-only and fee-based planners due to the perception on the part of the public of a conflict of interest for commission-based planners.

Fee-Only Planners

Fee-only planners typically charge an hourly rate for advice or a fixed fee for a defined engagement. These planners do not receive commissions and, therefore, their compensation is not contingent on the purchase or sale of a product. Many attorneys, CPAs, and CFP® practitioners are compensated as fee-only financial planners.

Fee-Based Planners

Fee-based planners are compensated by both fees and commissions that are contingent on the purchase or sale of financial products.

Commission-Based Planners

Commission-based planners are compensated solely by commissions that are contingent on the purchase or sale of financial products. These products are used in the implementation of the financial plan.

Fees for Assets under Management

Some planners are fee-only for advice, and then, if they take investment assets under management will charge a monthly, quarterly, or annual fee of some percent of the overall portfolio value. Fees charged for the management of assets are predominantly based on a percentage of assets. The percentage charged will generally be lower as the size of the asset pool increases.

COMPLIANCE ISSUES

The financial planning profession has few standards set by state and federal agencies regarding the regulation of financial planners as a group. However, most financial planners render some sort of advice in specific areas that are regulated by the federal or state government. Planners selling stocks and bonds, insurance products, real estate, or providing legal or tax advice are all required to have licenses for the specific services they provide. In addition, most planners providing investment advice must register with their state as well as with the Securities Exchange Commission (SEC) in accordance with the Investment Advisors Act of 1940. In the absence of government regulation of financial planners, those planners who are CFP® certificants have voluntarily chosen to be regulated by a professional regulatory organization, CFP Board.

Financial planners who work in the securities industry may need to register with the National Association of Securities Dealers, Inc. (NASD). NASD is a self-regulatory agency overseen by the SEC that enforces standards of practice upon its members for the protection of investors. Member firms of NASD are entitled to participate in investment banking and securities sales sponsored by NASD members. Employees of member firms who engage in securities transactions must register with NASD as a registered representative which includes passing a qualification examination that tests the employee's understanding of securities products.

EXHIBIT 18.4: REQUIRED NASD EXAMS

Securities Transaction	Qualification Exam Required
Mutual Funds (open-end) Variable Annuities Variable Life Insurance Unit Investment Trusts	Series 6
Corporate Securities Mutual Funds Money Market Funds REITs Asset-backed Securities Mortgage-backed Securities Options Government Securities Venture Capital	Series 7
Limited Partnership Programs	Series 22
Municipal Securities	Series 52
Equity Traders	Series 55
Corporate Securities Closed-end Funds Money Market Funds REITs Venture Capital	Series 62
Unsolicited securities orders from firm's clients (excludes municipal securities and limited partnerships)	Series 11
Government Securities Government Agency Securities Mortgage-backed Securities	Series 72
Investment Advice	Series 65/66

Many financial planners are investment advisers under the SEC definition and are required to register as such. According to SEC regulations an investment adviser is a person who:

- Provides advice or issues reports or analyses regarding securities
- Is in the business of providing such services
- Provides such services for compensation.

Where on the Web

American Bar Association Network *www.abanet.org*
American Institute of Certified Public Accountants (CPA/PFS) *www.aicpa.org*
Certified Financial Planner Board of Standards *www.cfp.net*
CFA Institute (CFA designation) *www.cfainstitute.org*
Financial Planning Association *www.fpanet.org*
Financial Planning Magazine Online *www.financial-planning.com*
National Association of Insurance Commissioners *www.naic.org*
National Association of Personal Financial Advisors *www.napfa.org*
National Association of Securities Dealers, Inc. *www.nasd.com*
National Association of State Boards of Accountancy *www.nasba.org*
North American Securities Administrators Association *www.nasaa.org*
Securities and Exchange Commission *www.sec.gov*
Small Business Administration *www.sba.gov*
Society of Financial Service Professionals *www.financialpro.org*
U.S. Chamber of Commerce *www.uschamber.org*

Exceptions include:

- Banks and bank holding companies
- Lawyers, accountants, engineers, or teachers, if their performance of advisory services is solely incidental to their professions
- Brokers or dealers, if their performance of advisory services is solely incidental to their business as brokers or dealers
- Publishers of newspapers, newsmagazines, or business or financial publications of general and regular circulation
- Persons whose advice is related only to securities that are direct obligations of or guaranteed by the United States.

SEC prohibits misstatements or misleading omissions in connection with purchases or sales of securities or investment advice. An investment adviser owes his clients undivided loyalty and may not engage in activity that conflicts with a client's interest.

DEVELOPING A PROFESSIONAL PRACTICE

BUILDING A PRACTICE

Like any other service-oriented professional practice, the growth and development of a personal financial planning practice will occur slowly. The professional developing a practice generally begins by writing a business or strategic plan that identifies the exact market niche of clients to be targeted and establishes goals and objectives for the practice. The planner assesses the competition for that market niche, the external environment, and his or her internal strengths and weaknesses. The planner then selects from alternative strategies and begins to implement the strategies to begin the development of the practice. Finally, the planner must monitor and adjust the practice on a continuing basis.

Choosing a market niche is perhaps the most important strategic decision a professional can make regarding the development of a long lasting, viable practice. An individual planner cannot be all things to all clients. Therefore, a professional must direct attention to the niches that he can penetrate and that will allow him to prosper. An appropriate approach to developing a practice is to scan the environment for a market niche that is currently not being well served or for a newly developing market need that is underserved or will soon be underserved.

Once a market niche is selected, the planner must promote the professional services that are relevant to that particular niche in such a way as to be effective. Finding the best form of promotion depends on the market niche, the external environment, and the professional's strengths and weaknesses.

Clients typically feel insecure, skeptical, and somewhat threatened when buying professional services. Therefore, the client must not only have confidence in the planner's technical abilities, but must also feel that they can trust the planner. After all, the client is not just buying a product, but entering into a relationship. With that in mind, a successful marketing plan generally begins with promoting to an already existing client base. Such client-centered marketing is a good start because the planner and client have already developed a relationship. In addition, the planner is already familiar with the client's concerns and needs. If the planner is developing a new practice, an alternative option may be to partner with other professionals who do not provide the same services that the planner expects to provide.

The pursuit of new clients is more of a challenge, as the ability to win the client's trust and confidence is a substantial obstacle in the sale of professional services. Clients of "less than competent" practitioners do not leave those practitioners just because a more competent professional becomes available. Many clients lack the ability to assess a practitioner's competence and, even if they can assess competence, they fear and resist changing practitioners. Thus, many clients stay with poor practitioners because the relationship is "comfortable." An understanding of this phenomenon should lead the developing professional to understand that they must be creative, aggressive, and patient in developing a practice. Marketing to new clients may take the form of referrals, networking, educational and professional seminars, teaching courses, and direct advertising. The development of a successful practice will require a variety of promotional tools used in combination, consistent with an overall marketing and development plan.

MAINTAINING CLIENTS

As mentioned, a high level of interpersonal trust is the key to long-term planner-client relationships. Regular contact and effective communication help to develop the personal relationships that are essential in maintaining clients. Regular contact with clients, such as written communications, telephone conversations, lunch meetings, and other social activities help to develop the personal relationships.

Although regular contact is important, perhaps the most essential key to good planner-client relationships is the ability of the planner to listen. Clients should feel that the planner listens to their concerns and respects them. According to researchers at the University of Minnesota, on average, people spend nearly half of their communication time listening. Good listening is an active and complex process that requires knowledge of a few basic skills and lots of practice. Many professionals are so used to selling that they do not stop to listen. Some tips to demonstrate that the planner is listening to the client include taking notes during client meetings; restating what the client has just said and getting acknowledgement from the client; and speaking up when an issue is unclear. Such active listening improves interpersonal skills, human relations, and personal selling capabilities.

Nurturing client relationships takes time, but will greatly benefit the planner in the long run and may result in additional business.

EDUCATION AND CONTINUING EDUCATION

Although a financial planner does not have to be an expert in all areas, it is critical for the planner to be familiar with the various life stages and the kinds of planning issues with which their clients are faced. The professional financial planner must obtain an initial education, followed by a lifetime of continuing professional monitoring and education.

The external environment is complex and constantly changing, as are some of the functional areas of financial planning. The risks to life, health, disability, property, and liability change. The tax laws are complex and change so frequently that the average client has no understanding of them. While investment information is more readily available today, discerning what is relevant and useful requires more than an elementary understanding. Competent financial planning professionals will make staying abreast of these changes a major priority throughout their professional careers.

TECHNOLOGY

A substantial part of the financial planning profession involves data collection and analysis. Fortunately with the advanced computer software available today, planners can harness vast amounts of financial and economic data. Financial planners who are setting-up practice or upgrading their software and network system should consider the following:

- Planning software for creation of financial statements
- Software for evaluating recommendations and alternatives—budgeting, estate-planning
- Monte Carlo simulation software to evaluate effects of various economic conditions on financial goals
- Data management tools for collecting, storing, and protecting client data
- Data mining/sorting tools to identify clients affected by legal or economic changes.

DISCUSSION QUESTIONS

1. What are the primary differences in services provided by accounting firms and law firms?
2. Generally, which types of financial planning firms specialize in investment planning?
3. Generally, which types of financial planning firms specialize in estate planning?
4. How is the Internet changing the financial planning industry?
5. Which is the most recognized and respected financial planning certification?
6. What are the differences between CFP® certification and the CFA charter?
7. Describe the fee-only compensation method.
8. What is one of the most important strategic decisions that must be made when developing a financial planning practice?
9. What can the planner do to improve the planner-client relationship?

CHAPTER 19

Ethical Responsibilities

LEARNING OBJECTIVES:

After learning the material in this chapter, you will be able to:

1. Differentiate among ethics, law, and an ethics code giving similarities and differences.
2. Define Certified Financial Planner Board of Standards, Inc. (CFP Board).
3. Define the Code of Ethics and Professional Responsibility (the Code).
4. Explain the role of CFP Board's Practice Standards in relation to the Code.
5. Explain the role of the Board of Professional Review (BOPR), the Board of Practice Standards, and the Board of Governors in relation to the Code.
6. Explain the role of the Disciplinary Rules and Procedures (the Procedures) and the Financial Planning Practice Standards (the Standards) in relation to the Code.
7. Describe the structure of the Code and give the role of each of its parts.
8. List the seven Principles of the Code and give a rule that relates to each Principle.
9. Explain how the "commingling of funds" and the "fiduciary relationship" relate to the Code's Principle of Integrity.
10. Compare the three distinct standards or "burdens" of proof to illustrate different treatment of a CFP Board designee at various stages of disciplinary proceedings.
11. Differentiate among the four forms of discipline that can be applied by the BOPR to a CFP Board designee.

CFP Board's Code of Ethics and Professional Responsibility - the set of principles of conduct that regulates behavior of CFP Board designees

Certified Financial Planner Board of Standards, Inc. - an independent professional regulatory organization that regulates financial planners

ethics - the discipline of dealing with the moral principles or values that guide oneself

law - rules of conduct that are established by a government or other authority that command and encourage behavior considered right and prohibit behavior considered wrong

code of ethics - a set of principles of conduct that governs a group of individuals and usually requires conformity to professional standards of conduct

ETHICS, LAW, AND CODES OF ETHICS

This chapter identifies, describes, and explains ethical rules for those involved in the financial planning industry through an analysis of the **Code of Ethics and Professional Responsibility (the "Code")** established by **Certified Financial Planner Board of Standards, Inc. (the "CFP Board")** for CFP Board designees. Analyzing the Code as it pertains to CFP Board designees, including its rules, principles, and procedures of professional ethics and responsibility, proves to be an excellent guide for all of those involved in the financial planning field. Before delving into the Code, however, it is important to distinguish between ethics, law, and ethics codes.

Ethics is the discipline of dealing with the moral principles or values that guide one's self. In situations where a decision must be made about a certain act, ethics aids us in deciding what is good and bad. In other words, ethics is doing or not doing what one feels is right. This feeling comes from within ourselves. Morals relate to one's conscience, character, and social relations. Morals form one's behavior and basically dictate whether one engages in conduct that is considered to be right or wrong. Thus, each individual's set of morals and values forms the ethics or ethical behavior of that individual.

Law is defined as rules of conduct that are established by a government or other authority that command and encourage behavior considered right and prohibit behavior considered wrong. Law and ethics differ in that laws apply to everyone, under certain authority, and compliance with laws is mandatory for those individuals. If the law is broken, that person is subject to punishment by governmental authorities. A violation of or deviation from one's own ethics, on the other hand, does not necessarily subject that person to punishment.

A **code of ethics** is a set of principles of conduct that governs a group of individuals and usually requires conformity to professional standards of conduct. Although the Code provides rules for ethical behavior, the Code itself is more closely aligned with law. The same goes for attorneys concerning State Bar Ethics Codes, for example. The Code is considered to be a set of laws or rules for CFP Board designees because compliance is mandatory, and failure to abide by these ethics rules may result in discipline, such as revocation or suspension of one's CFP® certification. These ethics rules must be followed. The ethics rules are, therefore, law as far as the CFP Board designee is concerned.

Many professions have codes of ethics or sets of laws of conduct for that particular profession designed to promote ethical behavior on the part of all such professionals. No finite set of ethical rules, however, can anticipate all situations or future developments in the industry. To truly satisfy the goal of ethics codes, the applicable professional must do more than merely fulfill ethics codes' minimum requirements. To reach the ideals of these codes, there must be a conscientious, good faith commitment by the professional to the spirit of the standards of the code under any circumstance.

Ethical behavior, which conforms to moral principles, is the aim of CFP Board's Code. If financial planners abide by the highest standards of ethical behavior, the financial services industry will maintain or gain public trust. There is a need for a common, accepted set of ethical principles to ensure fair representation and full disclosure in financial planning services. The Code basically seeks to regulate behavior of CFP Board designees with the intent to provide fairness to clients, maintain and increase public trust, and foster accountability on the CFP Board designee's behalf. Public trust in the profession is crucial because opportunities for unethical behavior arise frequently in the financial planning services industry. It is imperative for the profession to maintain and increase the public trust because people place their money, trust, and financial well-being into the hands of the CFP Board designee. Without that trust, people will not seek the advice of CFP Board designees, but will instead consult other professionals, or simply not seek services in financial planning. Hence, the importance of an ethics code, and of compliance with it, is clear.

In short, although an ethics code is a set of laws or rules for the professional that must be followed, CFP Board, through the adoption of its ethics code, attempts to instill in the professional a set of internal morals and values that will hopefully guide the professional in all situations.

Aside from the mandatory nature of the Code, the principles and rules embodied in the Code comprise a framework for ethical practices that will serve clients and CFP Board designees well in the long run. CFP Board's Practice Standards further seek to add to the quality of those ethical practices by requiring excellence, not minimum effort, from CFP Board designees. In a time when the public is yearning for quality services from financial planners, virtually every member of the public can benefit from ethical and competent advice from those who follow the rules and principles found in the Code. For these reasons, a closer look at the Code and the standards and principles it discusses is appropriate.

CFP BOARD AND THE CODE OF ETHICS

CFP Board is an independent professional regulatory organization that owns the federally registered "CFP®" and "CERTIFIED FINANCIAL PLANNER™" marks (the "marks") in the U.S. CFP Board regulates financial planners through trademark law by licensing individuals who meet CFP Board's certification requirements to use these federally registered marks. CFP Board has four subsidiary boards, one of which is the **Board of Professional Review ("BOPR")** which interprets and applies the Code, and further investigates, reviews, and takes appropriate action in connection with alleged violations of the Code by CFP Board designees. The Board of Practice Standards (another subsidiary board) develops and promulgates standards for the practice of personal financial planning for CFP Board designees.

CFP Board's Board of Professional Review ("BOPR") - a subsidiary board of CFP Board that interprets and applies the Code

CFP Board's Board of Governors requires compliance with this Code by all those who have been recognized and certified to use the CFP® mark, as well as those who seek certification. The Code represents the minimum standards of acceptable professional conduct for CFP Board designees. Violations of the Code may result in a letter of admonition, private censure, suspension, or revocation of the right to use the CFP® mark. These forms of discipline are established in the Disciplinary Rules and Procedures (the "Procedures") to enforce the Code.

CFP Board's Board of Governors - the governing board for the certified financial planning profession

The Procedures also explain the disciplinary process. The final area of rules established by CFP Board are the Financial Planning Practice Standards (the "Practice Standards"). The final authority for CFP Board designees in all disciplinary matters rests solely with CFP Board and BOPR under the limitations of the Code.

Principles - one of two main parts of the Code that addresses the profession's recognition of the responsibilities of its members to the public, clients, colleagues, and employers, and provides statements of ideals to members during the performance of their professional duties

CFP Board designee - an individual who uses the CFP® certification mark

CFP Board requires adherence to the Code by all those recognized and certified to use the marks, as well as those candidates who seek to obtain the marks. Compliance with the Code on an individual basis and by the profession as a whole depends upon each CFP Board designee's knowledge and voluntary compliance with the applicable Rules and Principles. Compliance also depends on the influence of fellow professionals and public opinion. The effectiveness of the Code and the success of the profession depend on the appropriate application of disciplinary proceedings involving CFP Board designees who fail to comply with the Code.

The Code is divided into two main parts, Principles and Rules. The **Principles** of the Code address the profession's recognition of the responsibilities of its members to the public, clients, colleagues, and employers, and provide statement of ideals to members during the performance of their professional duties. The Principles apply to all those who have been recognized and allowed to use the CFP® mark or those seeking certification. Throughout this chapter, reference will be made to one who uses the CFP® mark as a "*CFP Board designee.*" For purposes of the Code, the term **CFP Board designee** is deemed to include candidates for the marks.

The Principles apply to all CFP Board designees and provide guidance to CFP Board designees in the performance of their duties. The seven separate Principles are: Integrity, Objectivity, Competence, Fairness, Confidentiality, Professionalism, and Diligence. These seven Principles form the framework of the Code. Each Principle has a set of corresponding Rules that are examined below. Although the Principles apply to all CFP Board designees, certain Rules may not apply to a particular CFP Board designee's activities because of the nature of the CFP Board designee's particular field. CFP Board designees provide diverse services, and as a result, a CFP Board designee must recognize what specific services he or she is rendering and determine whether a given Rule applies to those services. The following is an evaluation of each Principle and the accompanying Rules relating to that Principle. All text below within quotation marks in *italicized type* is a direct quote from the Code.

Rules - one of two main parts of the Code that is derived from the doctrine expressed in the Principles and helps to establish a foundation for complying with the Principles of the Code

The **Rules** are derived from the doctrine expressed in the Principles and help to establish a foundation for complying with the Principles of the Code. The Rules apply only in certain specific professional instances. The Rules tend to be somewhat situation-specific to a particular service being offered.

NOTE ON CIVIL LIABILITY

The Code does not define standards of professional conduct of CFP Board designees for purposes of civil liability. Nonetheless, there are various areas where a violation of the Code could likely result in civil liability for malpractice or professional negligence on the part of the CFP Board designee if the client sustains "damages" resulting from the CFP Board designee's action or inaction. For instance, if a CFP Board designee violates the Rules regarding Competence, the CFP Board designee is probably susceptible to a lawsuit for professional negligence or malpractice if the client sustained losses or damages because of the CFP Board designee's incompetence. The CFP Board designee can avoid such a situation if he or she seeks the advice of, or refers his or her client to, another CFP Board designee or qualified individual who is competent in the areas where the CFP Board designee was not professionally competent, as stated by Rule 302 of the Code.

PRINCIPLE 1: INTEGRITY

The Code provides that *"[a] CFP Board designee shall offer and provide professional services with integrity." See Code of Ethics and Prof. Resp., Part I, Principle 1.* Clients often place CFP Board designees in positions of trust and confidence. A client denotes a person, persons, or entity for whom professional services are rendered. A practitioner is engaged when an individual, based on the relevant facts and circumstances, reasonably relies upon information or service provided by that practitioner. For the field of financial planning to prosper, there must be a foundation of trust in the CFP Board designee. The ultimate source of such public trust is personal integrity. In determining what is right and just, a CFP Board designee should rely on his or her integrity as the appropriate touchstone. Integrity demands honesty and candor that must not be subordinated to personal gain and advantage. The CFP Board designee must be incorruptible.

Although there is some room for innocent error and legitimate difference of opinion, integrity cannot coexist with deceit or subordination of one's principles. Indeed, the interests of the client must come before the interests of the CFP Board designee. Integrity requires a CFP Board designee to observe not simply the letter of the Code, but also the spirit of the Code. In other words, the CFP Board designee must not merely follow the specific rules outlined in the Code. Instead, the CFP Board designee must strive to conduct himself or herself in a manner that the CFP Board designee believes is consistent with the Principles and Rules when situations arise that are not specified or outlined in the Code. This is the essence of integrity.

RULES THAT RELATE TO THE PRINCIPLE OF INTEGRITY

Rule 101 of the Code prohibits the solicitation of clients through "*false or misleading communications or advertisements.*" *See Code of Ethics and Prof. Resp., Part II, Rule 101.* Rule 101 emphasizes (a) misleading advertising, (b) promotional activities, and (c) representation of authority.

Rule 101(a) prohibits a CFP Board designee from making false or misleading communications about the size, scope, or areas of competence of the CFP Board designee's practice. In other words, a CFP Board designee cannot try to lure in clients by stating that the CFP Board designee's practice is larger than it really is or that the CFP Board designee specializes in a certain area when he or she in fact does not.

Under Rule 101(b), a CFP Board designee shall not "*create unjustified expectations*" in promotional activities regarding financial planning or the CFP Board designee's professional activities and competence. *See Code of Ethics and Prof. Resp., Part II, Rule 101(b).* Promotional activities include, but are not limited to, speeches, interviews, books, printed publications, seminars, radio shows, television shows, and videocassettes. For example, Fred, a CFP Board designee, promotes his services in an ad in a trade magazine. One of Fred's clients, Julia, states in the ad: "I was almost bankrupt when I consulted Fred. Six months after our consultation, I had a net worth of half a million dollars." The ad also stated: "If I can achieve these results for Julia, just imagine the results I can achieve for you." Fred is subject to discipline for this promotional activity because Julia's statement concerning her financial resurrection would likely be construed as creating unjustified expectations regarding Fred's services.

Rule 101(c) prohibits a CFP Board designee from giving the impression that he or she represents the views of the CFP Board or any other group without authorization. Personal opinions must be clearly identified as such.

Under Rule 102, a CFP Board designee must not, in the course of professional activities, "*engage in conduct involving dishonesty, fraud, deceit or misrepresentation, or knowingly make a false or misleading statement to a client, employer, employee, professional colleague, governmental or other regulatory body or official, or any other person or entity.*" *See Code of Ethics and Prof. Resp., Part II, Rule 102.* Rule 102 is very clear and self-explanatory. Even though several rules deal with integrity, none are more important than Rule 102's simple prohibition of "*conduct involving dishonesty, fraud, deceit or misrepresentation, or knowingly making a false or misleading statement.*" Although Rule 102 only prohibits dishonesty or deceit in the course of professional activities, integrity would require the CFP Board designee to refrain from dishonesty or deceit in the course of all activities, whether the CFP Board designee has clients or only carries the CFP® mark. This furthers the spirit of the Code and will increase the public's trust in the profession.

Fraudulent or deceitful conduct on the part of the CFP Board designee outside the course of the CFP Board designee's professional activities would likely have an adverse effect on the CFP Board designee's fitness as a CFP Board designee or upon the profession as a whole. Accordingly, fraudulent or deceitful conduct outside the course of professional activities would be a direct violation of Rule 607, which relates to the principle of Professionalism.

Rule 103 establishes responsibilities for a CFP Board designee regarding funds and property of clients. First, a CFP Board designee must act only according to the authority set forth in the legal instrument governing the relationship between the CFP Board designee and client when the CFP Board designee exercises custody or discretionary authority over client funds or property. *See Code of Ethics and Prof. Resp., Part II, Rule 103(a).* For instance, if the CFP Board designee is acting as trustee for a client who is the beneficiary of a trust, the CFP Board designee must not exceed his or her authority as delineated within the trust documents. Other such legal instruments include special powers of attorney.

Second, a CFP Board designee must keep complete records of all property or funds of a client which are under the custody of the CFP Board designee. *See Code of Ethics and Prof. Resp., Part II, Rule 103(b).* If a client or third party is entitled to receive funds or property of a client, the CFP Board designee must deliver the funds or property promptly to the client or third party. Also, upon the client's request, the CFP Board designee must "*render a full accounting*" of such property and funds while in the custody of the CFP Board designee. *Rule 103(c).*

Commingling of Funds

Under Rule 103(d), a "*CFP Board designee shall not commingle client funds or other property with a CFP Board designee's personal funds and/or other property or the funds and/or other property of a CFP Board designee's firm. Commingling one or more clients' funds or other property together is permitted, subject to compliance with applicable legal requirements and provided accurate records are maintained for each client's funds or other property." See Code of Ethics and Prof. Resp., Part II, Rule 103(d).* In other words, under Rule 103(d) a CFP Board designee shall not **commingle client funds** with the CFP Board designee's funds, whereas commingling one or more clients' funds is permissible if accurate records are maintained.

commingle client funds - Rules specifically prohibit the combining (or commingling) of client funds or other property with a CFP Board designee's personal funds and/or other property or the funds and/or other property of a CFP Board designee's firm

Even if a CFP Board designee deposits a nominal amount of money of his own funds into a holding account for a client's funds just to ensure that the account is never overdrawn and to avoid unnecessary account charges for minimum balances, such action is improper because a CFP Board designee may commingle one or more clients' funds if accurate records are maintained, but is prohibited from commingling the CFP Board designee's funds with the client's funds. Thus, even if the CFP Board designee has no "negative" intent, the Code simply restricts such behavior that gives the appearance of impropriety.

Fiduciary Relationship

Rule 103(e) of the Code provides that CFP Board designees who take custody of clients' assets for investment purposes must *"do so with the care required of a fiduciary." Code of Ethics and Prof. Resp., Part II, Rule 103(e).* The Code uses the word *"fiduciary"* in Rule 103(e), but does not provide a definition of the word fiduciary. Although its definition is subject to various interpretations and standards in different state jurisdictions, the term fiduciary generally describes a person that holds the character similar in nature to that of a trustee who is placed in a position of trust and confidence based on that character and the scrupulous good faith and candor it requires. By virtue of his or her engagement or undertaking, the fiduciary has a duty to act primarily for another's benefit in matters concerning the undertaking.

More particularly, a fiduciary is a person who manages money or property for another and who must exercise a standard of care in such management activity imposed by law or by contract, such as an executor of an estate, a receiver in bankruptcy, or a trustee of a trust. A trustee, for example, possesses a fiduciary responsibility to the beneficiary of the trust to follow the terms of the trust and the requirements of applicable state law. Out of this fiduciary relationship where one places special confidence in another, the law recognizes the rule that neither party may exert influence or pressure upon the other, take selfish advantage of his or her trust, or deal with the subject matter of the undertaking in such a way as to benefit himself or herself. Accordingly, the status of being a fiduciary for another gives rise to certain legal obligations, including the prohibition against investing money or property in investments that are imprudent or inappropriately speculative. See Rule 103(e) of the Code, which requires the CFP Board designee who takes custody of a client's assets for investment purposes to do so with the care required of a fiduciary.

fiduciary relationship - relationship between a CFP Board designee and a client where the client places special trust and confidence in the CFP Board designee. This relationship places a higher burden on the CFP Board designee, which is warranted, because the CFP Board designee is dealing with the client's funds or property for investment purposes

A **fiduciary relationship** is thus a relationship where a person places special trust and confidence in another. The fiduciary must abide by a heightened standard of care during the engagement. In the circumstance described in Rule 103(e), the CFP Board designee is charged with the obligation to act with the same care required of a fiduciary. This places a higher burden on the CFP Board designee, which is warranted because the CFP Board designee is dealing with the clients' funds or property for investment purposes.

PRINCIPLE 2: OBJECTIVITY

The Code provides that a "*CFP Board designee shall be objective in providing professional services to clients.*" *Code of Ethics and Prof. Resp., Part I, Principle 2.* Objectivity requires intellectual honesty and impartiality. Irrespective of the CFP Board designee's capacity or function, a CFP Board designee should protect the integrity of his or her work, maintain objectivity, and avoid subordination of his or her judgment that would be a violation of this Code.

There is obviously some overlap between Integrity and Objectivity. However, Objectivity focuses on the interests of the client, while Integrity focuses on the actions of the CFP Board designee. With regard to Objectivity, a CFP Board designee must not let the enticement of profit sway his or her professional judgment. The decision made by the CFP Board designee and accompanying advice given should instead be driven by what is best for the client. Objectivity also focuses on CFP® practitioners because they provide professional services to clients, whereas some CFP Board designees may not be CFP® practitioners.

RULES THAT RELATE TO THE PRINCIPLE OF OBJECTIVITY

Rule 201 states as follows: "*A CFP Board designee shall exercise reasonable and prudent professional judgment in providing professional services.*" *Code of Ethics and Prof. Resp., Part II, Rule 201.* Here, the CFP Board designee is held to a standard of a reasonable, prudent person. In other words, the CFP Board designee must act as an ordinary, reasonably prudent CFP Board designee would act when faced with similar facts and circumstances.

financial planning practitioners - individuals who are capable and qualified to offer objective, integrated, and comprehensive financial advice to, or for the benefit of, clients; help clients achieve their financial objectives and by using the financial planning process

Rule 202 provides as follows: "*A financial planning practitioner shall act in the interest of the client.*" *Code of Ethics and Prof. Resp., Part II, Rule 202.* Rule 202 does not speak to CFP Board designees in general, but to the "*financial planning practitioner*" because **financial planning practitioners** are those CFP Board designees who have clients. A financial planning practitioner denotes a person who is capable and qualified to offer objective, integrated, and comprehensive financial advice to or for the benefit of clients to help them achieve their financial objectives and who engage in financial planning using the financial planning process in working with clients. The financial planning process denotes the process which typically includes, but is not limited to, the six elements of establishing and defining the client-planner relationship, gathering data including goals, analyzing and evaluating the client's financial status, developing and presenting financial planning recommendations and/or alternatives, implementing the financial planning recommendations and monitoring the financial planning recommendations.

In an actual disciplinary case before the CFP Board, a CFP Board designee reported on his Annual CFP® License Renewal form that a former client filed a civil lawsuit against him, alleging fraud, breach of fiduciary duty, negligent misrepresentation and "churning" in connection with investments he recommended. Of the $394,765 the client invested through the CFP Board designee, the client lost $382,240. The CFP Board designee settled the case for $26,500. The CFP Board designee was disciplined through private censure. One mitigating factor in the CFP Board designee's favor was that the CFP Board designee disclosed the matter to the CFP Board and cooperated with the CFP Board's investigation.

PRINCIPLE 3: COMPETENCE

The Code provides that CFP Board designees *"shall provide services to clients competently and maintain the necessary knowledge and skill to continue to do so in those areas in which the certificant is engaged." Code of Ethics and Prof. Resp., Part I, Principle 3.* Competence can be described as that point where a CFP Board designee has acquired and maintained an adequate level of knowledge and skill, and the CFP Board designee applies that knowledge effectively in providing services to clients. Along these same lines, competence also includes the wisdom and insight to recognize the limitations of one's knowledge. In those instances where the CFP Board designee realizes his or her knowledge is limited, consultation with another professional for guidance in those areas where the CFP Board designee's knowledge is limited is appropriate. Referral of the client to another CFP Board designee or other professional may also be appropriate.

By virtue of having earned CFP® certification, a CFP Board designee is deemed to be qualified to practice in the field of financial planning and is deemed to be knowledgeable in the field of financial planning. However, it is not sufficient to simply assimilate and absorb the common body of knowledge required to obtain CFP® certification, nor is it sufficient to simply acquire the necessary experience. Rather, a CFP Board designee must make a continuing commitment to learn and improve professionally. The CFP Board thus requires that the CFP Board designee satisfy minimum continuing education requirements. Nonetheless, the CFP Board designee's commitment to continue to learn and to improve professionally should not stop there.

The two areas of competence are knowledge and the application of that knowledge. One can avoid incompetence pertaining to lack of knowledge by consulting or associating with, or by referring a client to, qualified individuals with the appropriate knowledge. Indeed, this is a situation where the CFP Board designee recognizes that he or she is not competent or is inexperienced in a certain area of financial planning. However, issues of competence regarding one's application of knowledge normally arise after the application has been undertaken. Therefore, it is this area, the misapplication of one's knowledge, where most violations of the rules of Competence occur because the CFP Board designee unwittingly fails in applying knowledge and cannot necessarily recognize such incompetence.

On a related note, the principle of Competence is closely aligned with the standard for malpractice or professional negligence in the field of financial planning. Although malpractice or professional negligence is determined by the standards and rules of each individual state, generally a CFP Board designee can be held liable for malpractice or professional negligence if the plaintiff demonstrates the ordinary standard of knowledge or skills for CFP Board designees, that the CFP Board designee did not possess that standard of knowledge or failed in applying that knowledge, and that the CFP Board designee's breach of that standard caused injury or loss to the plaintiff. All three items must be present.

It is important to note that the principle of Competence generally involves CFP Board designee-client relationships. The Code specifically refers to clients in defining the principle of Competence and the rules relating to Competence. The driving force behind this is that the financial planning "client" or consumer must be protected from incompetence. In CFP Board designee-client relationships, a CFP Board designee's incompetence can result in damage or loss to the client, not simply a disappointment or disciplinary action for the individual CFP Board designee. Thus, Competence requires the CFP Board designee to continue to educate himself or herself and maintain a high level of standards. Competence also prohibits a CFP Board designee from failing to acquire or properly apply knowledge, as such failure on the CFP Board designee's behalf may reflect poorly upon the profession and/or result in loss or damage to the client. Still, a CFP Board designee who is purely an educator and does not have clients can violate the principle of Competence, for example, by failing to satisfy minimum continuing education requirements established for CFP Board designees by the CFP Board.

RULES THAT RELATE TO THE PRINCIPLE OF COMPETENCE

Rule 301 states as follows: "*A CFP Board designee shall keep informed of developments in the field of financial planning and participate in continuing education throughout the CFP Board designee's professional career in order to improve professional competence in all areas in which the CFP Board designee is engaged. As a distinct part of this requirement, a CFP Board designee shall satisfy all minimum continuing education requirements established for CFP Board designees by CFP Board.*" *Code of Ethics and Prof. Resp., Part II, Rule 301.* Under Rule 301, CFP Board designees must keep informed of developments in financial planning and must participate in minimum continuing education requirements established for CFP Board designees by CFP Board. The aim of Rule 301 is to improve the CFP Board designee's professional competence in all areas in which the CFP Board designee is engaged. CFP Board requires thirty (30) hours of continuing education bi-annually; of these 30 hours, at least 2 hours must cover ethics.

Under Rule 302, a CFP Board designee must offer advice "*only in those areas in which the CFP Board designee has competence. In areas where the CFP Board designee is not professionally competent, the CFP Board designee shall seek the counsel of qualified individuals and/or refer clients to such parties.*" *Code of Ethics and Prof. Resp., Part II, Rule 302.* Rule 302 is very clear in dealing with areas of financial planning not thoroughly understood by the CFP Board designee. The first sentence provides that the CFP Board designee must offer advice only in those areas in which the CFP Board designee has competence. This permits a CFP Board designee to offer advice only in those areas where the CFP Board designee is competent. Conversely, this means that a CFP Board designee is prohibited from extending any advice to a client in an area where the CFP Board designee does not have an adequate level of knowledge. Keep in mind that financial planning is very broad, and a CFP Board designee may be knowledgeable in many areas but deficient in others. This is particularly true today because financial services are quite complicated, and few people can be experts in all areas due to the vast diversity and scope of financial services.

The second sentence of Rule 302 requires a CFP Board designee to seek advice of qualified individuals or to refer clients to qualified individuals in those areas in which the CFP Board designee is not professionally competent. Here, the CFP Board designee must be able to recognize his or her deficiencies in areas of financial planning and seek advice of others or refer clients when necessary.

PRINCIPLE 4: FAIRNESS

The Code provides that a CFP Board designee "*shall perform professional services in a manner that is fair and reasonable to clients, principals, partners, and employers and shall disclose conflict(s) of interest in providing such services.*" *Code of Ethics and Prof. Resp., Part I, Principle 4.* Fairness is an essential trait for any professional in any profession. The principle of Fairness is basically a culmination or combination of the first three principles of the Code: Integrity, Objectivity, and Competence.

Like Objectivity, Fairness requires impartiality and intellectual honesty. The CFP Board's reason for including Fairness as one of the principles in the Code is to guide the CFP Board designee in achieving a proper balance of conflicting interests. Similar to Integrity, Fairness demands that CFP Board designees put the interests of the client first. Fairness also involves a subordination of a CFP Board designee's own feelings, prejudices, desires, and personal gain. Like Competence, CFP Board designees must under the principle of Fairness provide fair and reasonable professional services.

Further, a major obligation on the part of CFP Board designees with respect to Fairness is disclosure of conflicts of interests. A **conflict of interest** denotes circumstances, relationships or other facts about the CFP Board designee's own financial, business, property, and/or personal interests which will, or reasonably may, impair the CFP Board designee's rendering of disinterested advice, recommendations, or services. Fairness is also treating others in the same fashion that you would want to be treated.

conflict of interest - denotes circumstances, relationships or other facts about a CFP Board designee's own financial, business, property, and/or personal interests which will, or reasonably may, impair the CFP Board certificant's rendering of disinterested advice, recommendations, or services

Under the principle of Fairness, CFP Board designees are required to disclose conflicts of interest and sources of compensation. Because of the disclosure requirements of the Code, it is necessary to call attention to the inherent conflicts of interests that frequently arise in CFP Board designee-client relationships. The very nature of providing financial services as a financial planning practitioner is to provide the client with the best possible financial advice for the specific needs of the client that will maximize the financial well-being of the client. On the other hand, the CFP Board designee is engaged in the provision of financial planning services to earn money—it is an occupation. In order for the CFP Board designee to earn money, the CFP Board designee must be compensated for his or her services. This compensation comes from the client, the same client that has engaged the CFP Board designee to improve the client's financial status. Theoretically speaking, this is a conflict of interest in and of itself.

Compare the CFP Board designee-client relationship with a physician-patient relationship. When an individual seeks the advice of a physician regarding his or her physical health, the patient seeks to improve his or her health or to solve a physical problem. However, when an individual seeks the advice of a CFP Board designee to improve his or her financial status, the client compensates the CFP Board designee with money, the same object that the client seeks to keep or maximize. Although this analysis may seem somewhat absurd, it becomes more apparent when identifying certain situations that all too often arise during the normal course of activities of the CFP Board designee.

For example, many CFP Board designees sell stocks, bonds, mutual funds, life insurance, or annuities and earn commissions from the sale of these products to their clients. A commission is

the compensation received by an agent or broker when the compensation is calculated as a percentage on the amount of his or her sales or purchase transactions. If this is the only source of compensation for the CFP Board designee, then the CFP Board designee is considered a "commission-only" financial planner. The commission-only financial planner thus receives a commission for the products that he or she sells to the client. This arguably creates an incentive for the CFP Board designee to recommend products that provide the CFP Board designee with higher commissions, like annuities or life insurance, instead of products with lower or no commissions, such as bonds. This "incentive" is the foundation for the conflict of interest. There may also exist an incentive to sway the CFP Board designee from recommending another course of action for the client that may be in the client's best interest, but would not provide the CFP Board designee with any compensation through commissions. Even though the CFP Board designee may not in fact be swayed in this scenario, there is simply an appearance that the CFP Board designee would be swayed or that the interests of the CFP Board designee and the client are in conflict. Indeed, when a conflict of interest exists, unfortunately there is an assumption that the CFP Board designee will act in his or her interest, instead of in the client's interests.

In such a situation where a conflict exists, it would be impractical for the CFP Board designee to disqualify or disengage himself or herself from the relationship with the client because there would basically be no circumstance in which a CFP Board designee could earn a commission from a client for the sale of a product. Instead of disqualification or disengagement, the Code requires that a CFP Board designee in a financial planning engagement shall disclose all conflicts of interests to the client in writing. See Rule 402, for example. Also, the CFP Board designee must disclose in writing to the client sources of compensation and a statement of compensation "*that in reasonable detail discloses (as applicable) conflict(s) of interests and source(s) of and any contingencies or other aspects material to, the CFP Board designee's compensation. Code of Ethics and Prof. Resp., Part II, Rule 402.* Such disclosure in situations where there may be a conflict helps to diffuse or negate public distrust or suspicion.

In short, although conflicts of interests may arise in the CFP Board designee-client relationship, these conflicts can be minimized or dealt with through disclosure by the CFP Board designee to the client. The assumption is that, if the CFP Board designee discloses the information to the client, the client will feel as if the CFP Board designee has nothing to hide, while at the same time, the CFP Board designee is reminding himself or herself to be objective. Nonetheless, even though the CFP Board designee has disclosed the "conflict" and arguably set aside the appearance of impropriety, it is conceivable that the credibility of the financial planner is tainted when the compensation of the financial planner is directly related to the purchase of recommended investments. However, some if not all credibility can be restored through disclosure. Moreover, the appearance of impropriety is diminished because the CFP Board designee and the client at the inception of the relationship choose the compensation structure on an individual basis according to their comfort level.

Rules that Relate to the Principle of Fairness

Under Rule 401, when rendering professional services, a CFP Board designee shall "*disclose to the client:*

> "*Material information relevant to the professional relationship, including conflict(s) of interest,*

changes in the CFP Board designee's business affiliation, address, telephone number, credentials, qualifications, licenses, compensation structure, and any agency relationships, and the scope of the CFP Board designee's authority in that capacity; and the information required by all laws applicable to the relationship in a manner complying with such laws." Code of Ethics and Prof. Resp., Part II, Rule 401.

As seen, Rule 401 applies to all CFP Board designees who render "*professional services.*" Rule 401 states the general rule that CFP Board designees must disclose conflicts of interest and any other material information relevant to the relationship. Rule 401 does not, however, provide for the method (that is, written or otherwise) that the CFP Board designee should use to satisfy the disclosure requirements of Rule 401.

Rule 402 requires the financial planning practitioner to make "*timely written disclosure of all material information relative to the professional relationship.*" *Code of Ethics and Prof. Resp., Part II, Rule 402.* This written disclosure must "*include conflict(s) of interest and sources of compensation.*" Such disclosure regarding sources of compensation must be made annually for ongoing clients according to Rule 404. Rule 405 permits, but does not require, this annual disclosure to be satisfied by offering to provide clients with the current copy of SEC Form ADV, part 2 or the CFP Board Disclosure Form.

The following information is permitted and encouraged with respect to the written disclosure under Rule 402:

- ▲ A statement disclosing the CFP Board designee's basic philosophy, theory, and principles of financial planning.
- ▲ Resumés of employees who are expected to provide financial planning services to the client. These resumés must include educational background, professional history, employment history, professional designations or licenses, and areas of competence and specialization (if applicable).
- ▲ A statement of compensation disclosing in reasonable detail conflict(s) of interest aspects material to the fee.
- ▲ A statement describing material agency or employment relationships between the CFP Board designee and third parties and any fees or commissions resulting from those relationships.
- ▲ A statement identifying conflicts of interest. This is the fourth instance in which the Code requires disclosure of conflicts of interest. However, written disclosure of conflicts of interest is only required of the financial planning practitioner. Meanwhile, a CFP Board designee who is "*engaged solely in the sale of securities as a registered representative*" is not subject to the written disclosure requirements of Rule 402. Rule 402 as stated is only applicable to CFP Board designees engaged in personal financial planning, although the CFP Board designee may have disclosure responsibilities under Rule 401. A CFP Board designee is thus obligated to determine what responsibilities the CFP Board designee has in each professional relationship including, for instance, duties that arise in particular circumstances from a position of trust or confidence that a CFP Board designee may have. A CFP Board designee is obligated to meet those responsibilities in accordance with the rules of Fairness.
- ▲ A statement informing the client of his or her right to obtain compensation information related to the CFP Board designee's services.

Rule 403 requires a CFP Board designee providing financial planning services to disclose upon request of the client or prospective client the details of the financial planner's compensation as it relates to his or her engagement. *Code of Ethics and Prof. Resp., Part II, Rule 403.* Estimates provided shall be designated as such. If at any time the CFP Board designee realizes that information provided pursuant to this rule has become inaccurate, the designee will provide updated information to client or prospective clients.

Rule 404 mandates CFP Board designees to offer the disclosures described in Rule 402 at least annually to the client or other necessary parties after commencement of the relationship but before services are completed. *Code of Ethics and Prof. Resp., Part II, Rule 404.* Rule 404 is thus an extension of Rule 402. Rule 404 does not require the disclosure to be in writing. Nonetheless, it would be wise to do so in writing because, in disciplinary procedures and even litigation dealing with malpractice or professional negligence, the CFP Board designee can more easily prove that disclosure was made if it was done in writing.

Rule 405 provides as follows: "*A CFP Board designee's compensation shall be fair and reasonable.*" *See Code of Ethics and Prof. Resp., Part II, Rule 405.* The "reasonableness" test of Rule 405 is both objective and subjective.

An objective test means that the disciplinary board, or a court, would ask whether the compensation received was reasonable under similar or like circumstances based on the industry and generally accepted norms. A subjective test, as opposed to an objective test, seeks to determine that the compensation was reasonable considering various factors such as the CFP Board designee's experience and knowledge, the time and labor required by the CFP Board designee, the compensation normally charged in the locality for similar financial planning services, the nature and length of the professional relationship with the client, whether the compensation is fee-based or commission-based or both, and the client's financial position. Obviously, there is no clear test as to what is fair and reasonable. However, the CFP Board designee must be careful not to charge an excessive fee because the CFP Board designee may subject himself or herself to disciplinary proceedings.

Rule 406 requires all CFP Board designees to adhere to the same standards of disclosure and service whether the CFP Board designee is employed by a financial planning firm, an investment institution, or serves as an agent for such an organization. The test of Rule 406 provides: "*A CFP Board designee who is an employee shall perform professional services with dedication to the lawful objectives of the employer and in accordance with this Code.*" *Code of Ethics and Prof. Resp., Part II, Rule 406.* Rule 406 was drafted to address the problem of violations of the Code by employees who are CFP Board designees. There are some unfortunate situations where a CFP Board designee is forced to act in violation of the Code or other laws by an employer or superior. Rule 406 basically prevents CFP Board designees from asserting a defense or justification for unethical conduct by stating that they were ordered to do so by their superiors or employers. Rule 406 hence expressly requires employees to perform services in accordance with the Code and in compliance with lawful objectives of employers.

Rule 407 deals with CFP Board designees' obligations to their employers. Under Rule 407, a CFP Board designee must "*advise the CFP Board designee's employer of outside affiliations which reasonably may compromise service to an employer and provide timely notice to the employer and clients, unless precluded by contractual obligation, in the event of change of employment or CFP®*

certification status." *Code of Ethics and Prof. Resp., Part II, Rule 407.* Rule 407 requires a CFP Board designee to advise his or her employer of outside affiliations of the CFP Board designee that may compromise the CFP Board designee's service to an employer. Rule 407 also requires timely notice to employers and to clients of any change of employment or CFP Board licensing status. Rule 407 places responsibilities on CFP Board designees to give pertinent information to their employers, thus providing added safeguards to employers. Of course, this ultimately benefits clients and the public because the CFP Board designee is required to advise employers of affiliations that would compromise the CFP Board designee's service to an employer, that very service which is normally provided to clients.

Rule 408 requires CFP Board designees to inform employers or partners of compensation in connection with their services to clients that are in addition to compensation from the employers or partners from such services. Although the CFP Board designee's duty to inform employers or partners of other compensation is broad, Rule 408 has a limitation. This duty to inform applies only when the services performed by the CFP Board designee for the client will be compensated by the employer or partner. If the CFP Board designee advises individual clients (not clients of the CFP Board designee's employer) in his spare time, then Rule 408 does not require the CFP Board designees to inform his or her employer of the hourly fee received.

The final rule pertaining to the principal of Fairness is Rule 409, which mandates CFP Board designees entering into personal business transactions with clients to be "*fair and reasonable*" and to disclose risks, conflicts of interest, and other relevant information in writing.

PRINCIPLE 5: CONFIDENTIALITY

A CFP Board designee "*shall not disclose any confidential client information without the specific consent of the client unless in response to proper legal process, to defend against charges of wrongdoing by the CFP Board designee or in connection with a civil dispute between the CFP Board designee and client.*" *Code of Ethics and Prof. Resp., Principle 5.* When a client consults or seeks the services of a CFP Board designee, the client is typically interested in creating a relationship of personal trust and confidence with the CFP Board designee. Indeed, the client is placing his or her financial well-being into the hands of the CFP Board designee. The CFP Board designee-client relationship can only be built upon the client's understanding that the information supplied to the CFP Board designee will be held in confidence by the CFP Board designee. This understanding will promote candor and productive consultation with the CFP Board designee, which will benefit the client.

As in any profession where a client seeks advice of a professional, the CFP Board designee must safeguard the confidentiality of all information gained from the relationship in order to provide the contemplated services effectively. This will also help the CFP Board designee protect the client's privacy.

RULES THAT RELATE TO THE PRINCIPLE OF CONFIDENTIALITY

Rule 501 of the Code provides that a CFP Board designee is prohibited from revealing "*or use for his or her own benefit—without the client's consent, any personally identifiable information relating to the client relationship or the affairs of the client, except and to the extent disclosure or use is reasonably necessary:*

- To establish an advisory or brokerage account, to effect a transaction for the client, or as otherwise impliedly authorized in order to carry out the client engagement; or
- To comply with legal requirements or legal process; or
- To defend the CFP Board designee against charges of wrongdoing; or
- In connection with a civil dispute between the CFP Board designee and the client."

Code of Ethics and Prof. Resp., Rule 501. The use of client information is improper whether or not it actually causes harm to the client.

Rule 501 characterizes confidential information as any personally identifiable information relating to the client relationship or the affairs of the client. This means that a CFP Board designee could probably describe the basic facts of a client's affairs to another but in no way reveal information that would identify that client either by name or by other detectable means.

There are a few narrow exceptions to the rule of confidentiality.

1. Consent. A CFP Board designee can reveal confidential information if the client consents to the revelation. In cases where the client expressly consents, the CFP Board designee's authorization is clear. It would be wise for the CFP Board designee to reduce the express consent to writing, but there are situations where consent is implied although not expressly given by the client.
2. Implied authorization. There are situations where consent, although not expressly given by the client, is implied or tacitly given. Rule 501(a) lists those situations. The basic question to ask is whether the CFP Board designee was impliedly authorized to divulge the information in order to carry out the client engagement. For instance, Mike, a client, consults Patty, a CFP Board designee, about a trust and ultimately asks Patty to draft a trust. Patty indicates that she uses an attorney to help her draft the necessary documents that she will revise accordingly. Here, although Mike did not expressly authorize Patty to divulge confidential information, Mike implicitly authorized Patty to consult with the attorney. Patty will need to tell the attorney certain confidential information. Also, there will be others at the attorney's office who will need to hear the information as well like a paralegal or secretary. Such situations are not violations of the Principle of Confidentiality.
3. Compliance with legal requirements. Under Rule 501(b), a CFP Board designee may reveal confidential information to comply with legal requirements or legal process (that is, a subpoena or court order).
4. CFP Board designee's defense. Under Rule 501(c), a CFP Board designee may reveal confidential information to defend the CFP Board designee against charges of wrongdoing.
5. CFP Board/Client disputes. Rule 501(d) allows a CFP Board designee to divulge confidential information in connection with a civil dispute between the CFP Board designee and the client. It would be absurd to allow a client to divulge information pertaining to the CFP Board designee-client relationship against a CFP Board designee while prohibiting the CFP Board designee from defending against those claims. In situations where the client claims wrongdoing on the part of the CFP Board designee, the client is said to have "opened the door" to rebuttal by the CFP Board designee.

Except for those instances where the client expressly consents to the CFP Board designee's unbridled use of confidential information, the CFP Board designee is not free to disclose all confidential information even though one of the previous exceptions apply. Instead, it is important to note that Rule 501 allows disclosure by the CFP Board designee of confidential information only to the extent "*reasonably necessary*" to comply with the exception. In other words, when an exception to the rule of Confidentiality applies, the CFP Board designee's right to divulge confidential information is not absolute; rather, the CFP Board designee is limited to remain within the scope of the exception and can go no further.

Finally, the CFP Board designee is subject to discipline for violation of Rule 501 whether or not the CFP Board designee's breach of confidentiality causes harm to the client. Thus, the old adage of "no harm - no foul" is not an available defense to the CFP Board designee. In a professional negligence or malpractice case against the CFP Board designee, the client must prove (1) that the CFP Board designee was somehow negligent or acted below the standard of care for ordinary CFP Board designees, (2) that the client sustained damage (this is referred to as "proof of damages"), and (3) that the CFP Board designee's misconduct caused damage to the client (this is referred to as proof of "causation"). However, Rule 501 prohibits improper disclosure of confidential information without regard for causation or damages. Accordingly, Rule 501 goes far beyond professional negligence standards, as it should, and goes to the heart of ethics. Even though the client may not have been damaged or harmed financially due to the CFP Board designee's improper disclosure of confidential information, the client's trust in the CFP Board designee and the profession as a whole are damaged. Thus, the CFP Board designee should be subjected to discipline.

Rule 502 requires a CFP Board designee to "*maintain the same standards of confidentiality to employers as to clients.*" *Code of Ethics and Prof. Resp., Part II, Rule 502.* These are the same standards discussed above regarding Rule 501. Accordingly, those standards should apply to employers as well.

Rule 503 states that a CFP Board designee doing business as a partner of a financial services firm "*owes to the CFP Board designee's partners or co-owners a responsibility to act in good faith. This includes, but is not limited to, adherence to reasonable expectations of confidentiality both while in business together and thereafter.*" *Code of Ethics and Prof. Resp., Part II, Rule 503.* This duty of good faith specifically includes disclosure of relevant and material financial information. Good faith is not defined in the Code. Good faith generally encompasses, among other things, an honest belief, the absence of malice, and the absence of an intention to mislead or obtain an unfair advantage. Good faith is also an honest intention to abstain from taking conscious advantage of another. This term is ordinarily used to describe an intention indicating faithfulness, duty, or obligation to another. As utilized in Rule 503, good faith entails being honest and faithful to other co-owners or partners in a financial planning services firm. Rule 503 expressly requires CFP Board designees as partners to adhere to reasonable expectations of confidentiality during and after the partnership.

For example, two CFP Board designees are partners in a financial services firm, and during the partnership, one learns of the other's debt problems. Even if the partnership later dissolves, the partner should be able to reasonably rely on the other to keep that information confidential despite dissolution of the partnership because CFP Board designees who are partners must adhere to reasonable expectations of confidentiality during the partnership and after its dissolution.

PRINCIPLE 6: PROFESSIONALISM

"*A CFP Board designee's conduct in all matters shall reflect credit upon the profession.*" *Code of Ethics and Prof. Resp., Part I, Principle 6.* In order to better the CFP® profession and foster significant growth, the profession and its individuals must be held to a standard of professionalism and accountability. Because of the importance and magnitude of the professional services rendered by CFP Board designees, CFP Board designees must have attendant responsibilities to behave with dignity and courtesy to all of those who seek or use those services. CFP Board designees also have responsibilities to behave with dignity and courtesy to fellow professionals and to those in related professions (that is, CPAs and attorneys).

A CFP Board designee is further obligated to cooperate with fellow CFP Board designees to maintain and enhance the public image of the profession. The CFP Board designee also has an obligation to cooperate and work jointly with other CFP Board designees to improve the quality of services. The vision of maintaining and enhancing the public image of the profession can only be realized through the combined efforts of all CFP Board designees in cooperation with other professionals.

RULES THAT RELATE TO THE PRINCIPLE OF PROFESSIONALISM

CFP Board designees must "*use the marks in compliance with the rules and regulations of the CFP Board.*" *Code of Ethics and Prof. Resp., Part II, Rule 601.* Under Rule 602, CFP Board designees must show respect for, and engage in fair and honorable competitive practices with other financial planning professionals and related occupational groups. "Financial planning professional" denotes a person who is capable and qualified to offer objective, integrated, and comprehensive financial advice to, or for the benefit of, individuals to help them achieve their financial objectives. A financial planning professional must have the ability to provide financial planning services to clients, using the financial planning process covering the basic financial planning subjects. Of course, Rule 602 should not prevent CFP Board designees from engaging in competition with each other as long as the competition is fair and honorable.

The text of Rule 603 requires a CFP Board designee who has knowledge that is not confidential that another CFP Board designee violated the Code which "*raises substantial questions as to the designee's honesty, trustworthiness or fitness as a CFP Board designee in other respects, shall promptly inform the CFP Board . . .*" *Code of Ethics and Prof. Resp., Part II, Rule 603.* Under Rule 603, a CFP Board designee who has knowledge (that is, no substantial doubt) that another CFP Board designee has violated the Code raising substantial questions as to the CFP Board designee's honesty or fitness as a CFP Board designee, must promptly inform CFP Board. Rule 603 thus requires a CFP Board designee to inform CFP Board of violations of the Code by another CFP Board designee. There are two (2) stated exceptions to this rule. First, a CFP Board designee does not have to inform CFP Board if the CFP Board designee is required to keep the information confidential under the Code. Second, Rule 603 does not require disclosure based on knowledge gained as a consultant or expert witness in anticipation of, or relating to, litigation.

Under Rule 604, a CFP Board designee with knowledge that raises a substantial question of unprofessional, fraudulent, or illegal conduct by a CFP Board designee or other financial professional must promptly inform the appropriate regulatory body. *Code of Ethics and Prof. Resp., Part II, Rule 604.* Rule 604 is similar to Rule 603, except that Rule 604 requires the CFP Board designee to report improper conduct by other CFP Board designees or by other financial professionals. The same two (2) exceptions to Rule 603 apply to Rule 604.

If a CFP Board designee has reason to suspect illegal conduct within a CFP Board designee's organization, the CFP Board designee must timely inform his or her immediate supervisor or partner. If appropriate measures are not taken to remedy the situation and the CFP Board designee is convinced that the illegal conduct exists, the CFP Board designee is required by Rule 605 to alert the appropriate authorities including CFP Board.

Rule 605 requires a CFP Board designee to inform his or her organization if the CFP Board designee has "*reason to suspect*" illegal conduct. However, a CFP Board designee is not required to report to the authorities or CFP Board unless no remedial measures were taken and the CFP Board designee is "*convinced*" illegal conduct still exists. "*Convinced*" is much stronger than "*reason to suspect.*" Rule 605 is drafted this way to promote internal investigation when one becomes suspicious of illegal conduct, but to require something more than suspicion when contacting third party regulatory bodies.

When rendering professional activities, a CFP Board designee must perform services according to applicable laws, rules, and regulations of governmental agencies or authorities or rules or policies of CFP Board. *Code of Ethics and Prof. Resp., Part II, Rule 606.* A CFP Board designee must provide services in compliance with applicable laws, rules, regulations, and policies of governmental agencies and of CFP Board. Failure to do so would damage the public image of the profession.

Rule 607 of the Code prohibits CFP Board designees from engaging in any conduct that reflects adversely (1) on his or her integrity or fitness as a CFP Board designee, (2) upon the CFP® mark, or (3) upon the profession. The scope of Rule 607 is broader than the other rules pertaining to Professionalism. Rule 607 applies to any conduct that has an adverse effect on the CFP Board designee or the profession. In short, the principle of Professionalism is essentially embodied into Rule 607. Also, as is done on several occasions throughout the Code, there is some overlap between Rule 607 and the principle of Integrity.

Actions Reflecting Upon the Profession

In the case of *Ibanez v. Florida Department of Business and Professional Regulation, Board of Accountancy*, 512 U.S. 136, 114 S. Ct. 2084, 129 L. Ed. 2d 118 (1994), Ibanez, an attorney, licensed CPA, and CFP® certificant, was reprimanded by the Florida Board of Accountancy for engaging in "false, deceptive, and misleading" advertising. Ibanez referred to her credentials as an attorney, a CPA, and CFP Board designee in her advertising and other communications with the public concerning her law practice, placing CPA and CFP Board designee next to her name in her yellow pages listing and in her business cards and law office stationery.

The Florida Board of Accountancy argued that the term "certified" in the phrase "*Certified Financial Planner*" was inherently misleading by causing the public to infer state approval and recognition, when in fact the CFP Board designation is not given by the state. The United States Supreme Court rejected this argument and instead ruled that Ibanez had a constitutional right to promote herself as an attorney/CPA that was also a CFP Board designee. The Court then approvingly stated: "Noteworthy in this connection, 'Certified Financial Planner' and 'CFP®' are well-established, protected federal trademarks that have been described as the most recognized designation(s) in the planning field. Approximately 27,000 persons have qualified for the designation nationwide. Over 50 accredited universities and colleges have established courses of study in financial planning approved by the Certified Financial Planner Board of Standards, Inc. and standards for licensure include satisfaction of certain core educational requirements, a passing score on a certification examination similar in concept to the Bar or CPA examinations, completion of a planning-related work experience requirement, agreement to abide by the CFP Board's Code of Ethics and Professional Responsibility, and an annual continuing education requirement." The Court concluded that Ibanez could use all three credentials in her advertising because it was not misleading or false and because she had a constitutional right to commercial speech.

The *Ibanez* case shows that CFP Board designees who have other credentials can promote those credentials without engaging in misleading, deceptive, or false communications with the public. The case also casts the CFP® mark in a favorable light, recognizing the credibility that accompanies the CFP® mark. Thus, Ibanez's actions did not mislead the public with respect to Rule 101(b) and did not adversely affect the profession with respect to Rule 607.

Registered Investment Advisor (RIA) - a person or company that offers ongoing portfolio management or advice and charges money for it

Meanwhile, Rule 608 of the Code deals with **registered investment advisers**, or RIAs. A registered investment advisor is a person or company that offers ongoing portfolio management or investment advice and charges money for it. Rule 608 requires CFP Board designees to disclose to clients their firm's status as Registered Investment Advisors. Use of the letters RIA or R.I.A. following a CFP Board designee's name in advertising, letterhead, stationery, and business cards can be misleading and is prohibited by Rule 608 and by SEC regulations because this tends to indicate that the CFP Board designee has a higher level of competency or skill, which may create unjustified expectations on the part of the client.

Rule 609 forbids CFP Board designees from practicing any other profession unless the CFP Board designee is qualified and licensed (if applicable) to practice in that field: *"A CFP Board designee shall not practice any other profession or offer to provide such services unless the CFP Board designee is qualified to practice in those fields and is licensed as required by state law." Code of Ethics and Prof. Resp., Part II, Rule 609.* Rule 609 was implemented because a CFP Board designee's failure to service others competently in another profession would adversely affect the public image of CFP Board designees.

Rule 610 mandates that CFP Board designees return clients' original records timely upon request. *"A CFP Board designee shall return the client's original records in a timely manner after their return has been requested by a client." Code of Ethics and Prof. Resp., Part II, Rule 610.* Procrastination or outright refusal to return the client's original records is unprofessional and inappropriate. A CFP Board designee is thus bound by Rule 610 to return the client's original records promptly upon request even though he or she has not been paid. For instance, a financial plan developed and drafted by a CFP Board designee is not considered the client's original records, but the proformas, budgets and bank statements of the client provided to the CFP Board designee to draft a plan are original records.

A CFP Board designee is required to report information to the CFP Board under Rule 603 and 604. However, under Rule 611, a CFP Board designee is prohibited from bringing or threatening to bring disciplinary proceedings *"for no substantial purpose other than to harass, maliciously injure, embarrass, and/or unfairly burden another CFP Board designee." Code of Ethics and Prof. Resp., Part II, Rule 611.*

Rule 612 commands CFP Board designees to comply with the CFP Board's postcertification requirements which include continuing education, payment of annual CFP Board designee fees, certification renewal requirements, and compliance with the Code.

PRINCIPLE 7: DILIGENCE

"A CFP Board designee shall act diligently in providing professional services." Code of Ethics and Prof. Resp., Part I, Principle 7. Diligence means the CFP Board designee provides services in a reasonably prompt and thorough manner. Diligence also includes proper planning for the provision of professional services, as well as proper supervision of the provision of professional services.

RULES THAT RELATE TO THE PRINCIPLE OF DILIGENCE

Under Rule 701, a CFP Board designee *"shall provide services diligently."* CFP Board designees are bound to ensure that the services are diligently provided to the client under the circumstances. Failure to properly supervise other CFP Board designees working for others could potentially result in disciplinary action under Rule 701.

A financial planning practitioner shall enter into an engagement by a client only after determining that the relationship is warranted by the client's needs and objectives and that the CFP Board designee can provide competent services or involve other professionals who can provide competent services. *Code of Ethics and Prof. Resp., Part II, Rule 702.* There is some common ground between Rule 702 and Rule 302, which relates to the principle of Competence. However, if the CFP Board designee complies with Rule 702 and determines that he or she is not competent regarding the individual's objectives, the CFP Board designee will not enter into the engagement and will ultimately avoid a potential situation where the CFP Board designee would violate the rules of Competence. This could also prevent a professional negligence case against the CFP Board designee.

Rule 703 directs a CFP Board designee to *"make and/or implement only recommendations which are suitable for the client." Code of Ethics and Prof. Resp., Part II, Rule 703.* The key word in Rule 703 is "suitable." What is suitable for the client obviously depends upon the facts and circumstances of the client's situation. Again, one can detect some common ground between the Diligence requirement of Rule 703 and Competence in Rule 302.

For instance, if the CFP Board designee recommends a course of action that is not suitable for the client, the question then becomes, for purposes of this Code, whether the CFP Board designee attempted to determine if the recommendation was suitable for the client. If there is evidence that the CFP Board designee determined that the recommended course of action was suitable for the client, when in fact it clearly was not, then the CFP Board designee is probably subject to discipline under Rule 302 for incompetence. However, if there is evidence that the CFP Board designee failed to even attempt to determine if the recommended course of action was suitable for the client, the CFP Board designee is probably subject to discipline under Rule 703 for lack of Diligence.

Under Rule 704, the CFP Board designee is required to "*make a reasonable investigation regarding the financial products recommended to clients.*" *Code of Ethics and Prof. Resp., Part II, Rule 704.* This does not mean, however, that the CFP Board designee must make the investigation. Although the Code permits the CFP Board designee to do the actual investigation, Rule 704 adds the provision that the investigation "may" be done by others if the CFP Board designee acts reasonably in relying upon such investigation. For example, a CFP Board designee who recommends a small cap stock to a client may rely on a report about that stock from Barron's financial newspaper that the stock was recommended by several mutual fund managers and had good ratings from ratings companies. The CFP Board designee need not necessarily investigate the stock on his own. It is reasonable for the CFP Board designee to rely on the investigation of Barron's, mutual fund managers, and ratings companies.

A CFP Board designee must properly "*supervise subordinates with regard to their delivery of financial planning services, and shall not accept or condone conduct in violation of this Code.*" *Code of Ethics and Prof. Resp., Part II, Rule 705.* Rule 705 requires CFP Board designees to properly supervise subordinates regarding their delivery of financial planning services. Rule 705 also prohibits CFP Board designees from accepting or condoning conduct in violation of the Code. Thus, Rule 705 adds the requirement of diligence to CFP Board designees who supervise subordinates. This is yet another safeguard that ultimately benefits the client and should strengthen the public's trust in the profession. Also, Rule 705 is the converse of Rule 410. You will recall that Rule 410 prohibits employees from violating the Code, which includes situations where a superior orders a CFP Board designee to engage in unethical conduct. Rule 705 forbids CFP Board designees from accepting or condoning unethical conduct which could occur when an employer or superior discovers unethical conduct by an employee and either conceals the conduct or fails to report the conduct to the proper parties.

Disciplinary Rules and Procedures - the rules and regulations for disciplinary proceedings against CFP Board designees

DISCIPLINARY RULES AND PROCEDURES

The Code also provides the rules and regulations for disciplinary proceedings against CFP Board designees. The enforcement of the Code is accomplished through the CFP Board's **Disciplinary Rules and Procedures** (the "Procedures"). Adherence to the Code is mandatory for all CFP Board designees. The CFP Board strictly enforces the provisions of the Code through the Procedures.

burden of proof - the requirement of proving facts to a certain degree of probability. With regard to disciplinary rules and procedures, there are three distinct burdens of proof: (1) preponderance of the evidence; (2) clear and convincing evidence; and (3) evidence beyond a reasonable doubt.

NOTES ON BURDENS OF PROOF

It is important to understand the various standards of proof that are involved with litigation in general and in disciplinary procedures (including subjecting a CFP Board designee to discipline). A standard of proof, or "**burden of proof,**" is the requirement of proving facts to a certain degree of probability. Basically, there are three distinct burdens of proof: (1) preponderance of the evidence; (2) clear and convincing evidence; and (3) evidence beyond a reasonable doubt. A comparison of these burdens of proof illustrates different treatment of the CFP Board designee at various stages of disciplinary proceedings. Note that burden of proof in

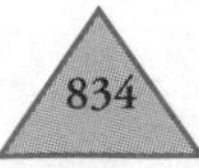

disciplinary proceedings is upon CFP Board. The CFP Board designee is presumed to be free from ethical violations until proven otherwise.

The "Preponderance of the Evidence" Standard

"**Preponderance of the evidence**" means that the evidence as a whole shows what it was intended to prove with a probability of 51 percent or better. To say it another way, the evidence tends to prove that the existence of a fact is more likely than not. For example, proof of misconduct by a CFP Board designee must be "*established by a preponderance of the evidence.*" In other words, it must be shown that a CFP Board designee more likely than not violated the Code. In professional negligence or malpractice cases, the standard of proof is generally by a preponderance of the evidence.

preponderance of the evidence standard - a measure or degree of proof. With regard to disciplinary rules and procedures, "preponderance of the evidence" means the evidence as a whole shows what it was intended to prove with a probability of

The "Clear and Convincing Evidence" Standard

"*Clear and convincing evidence*" requires more proof or more certainty in the eyes of the fact finder than a preponderance of the evidence. **Clear and convincing evidence** is the measure or degree of proof that will produce in the mind of the finder of fact a firm belief or conviction as to allegations sought to be established. It is loosely described as a 75 percent certainty that a fact has been proven. Under the Procedures, a CFP Board designee who has been suspended for over a year must petition the Board of Professional Review (BOPR) for reinstatement and prove by clear and convincing evidence that he or she has been rehabilitated, has met continuing education requirements, and is fit to use the marks. In other words, the CFP Board designee must clearly and convincingly prove that he or she is worthy of reinstatement, with more certainty than by a preponderance of the evidence, but less than that beyond a reasonable doubt.

clear and convincing evidence - a measure or degree of proof. With regard to disciplinary rules and procedures, "clear and convincing evidence" means the evidence as a whole shows what it was intended to prove with a probability of 75 percent or better.

In litigation involving fraud, usually the party alleging fraud must prove fraud by clear and convincing evidence.

The "Beyond a Reasonable Doubt" Standard

"***Beyond a reasonable doubt***" in evidence means that the finder of fact is fully satisfied, entirely convinced, and satisfied to a moral certainty that a fact has been established. The fact finder can have no doubt as to the existence of a fact unless that doubt is unreasonable or irrational. Some define the term as a 99 percent certainty that the evidence shows as a whole the fact sought to be proved. For example, this standard of proof comes into play in the Procedures under Article 12.1 where a CFP Board designee who has been convicted of a crime is subject to discipline, and the conviction is conclusive proof of the commission of the crime. In criminal proceedings, the burden of proof is beyond a reasonable doubt.

GROUNDS FOR AND FORMS OF DISCIPLINE

The grounds for discipline of a CFP Board designee under the Procedures are:

- Any act which violates the Code.
- Any act which fails to comply with the Practice Standards.

private censure - an unpublished written reproach that is mailed to the censured CFP Board certificant by the BOPR

public letter of admonition - written reproach of the CFP Board designee's behavior that will normally be published in a press release or other form of publicity selected by the BOPR.

suspension - may be ordered by the BOPR for a specified period of time, not to exceed five (5) years, for individuals it deems can be rehabilitated

revocation - the BOPR may order permanent revocation of a CFP Board designee's right to use the mark, and publish the revocation in a press release or other form of

Hearing Panel - panel that establishes the rules of procedures and evidence to be observed at a complaint hearing seeking disciplinary action against a CFP Board designee

- Any act which violates any criminal laws, whether the CFP Board designee is convicted or acquitted.
- Any act which is the proper basis for professional suspension.
- Any act which violates these Procedures or an order of discipline.
- Failure to respond to a request of the CFP Board without good cause, or obstruction of the CFP Board or staff in the performance of their duties.
- Any false or misleading statement made to CFP Board.
- Other acts amounting to unprofessional conduct.

If grounds for discipline are established, the BOPR has discretion to use any of the following forms of discipline:

- **Private Censure** - an unpublished written reproach that is mailed to the censured CFP Board designee by the BOPR.
- **Public Letter of Admonition** - a publishable written reproach of the CFP Board designee's behavior that will normally be published in a press release or other form of publicity selected by the BOPR.
- **Suspension** - may be ordered by the BOPR for a specified period of time, not to exceed five (5) years, for individuals it deems can be rehabilitated. The suspension will normally be published in a press release or other form of publicity, unless extreme mitigating circumstances exist. CFP Board designees who are suspended may qualify for reinstatement.
- **Revocation** - The BOPR may order permanent revocation of a CFP Board designee's right to use the mark. All revocations are "*permanent.*" It is standard procedure to publish the revocation in a press release or other form of publicity.

Disciplinary proceedings under the Procedures are commenced upon a written request by any person. After commencement, the matter is referred to the BOPR. If the BOPR in its discretion determines to proceed with the investigation, the CFP Board provides written notice to the CFP Board designee of the investigation and of the allegations made, and the CFP Board designee has thirty (30) calendar days from the date of notice of the investigation to file a written response to the allegations. If a timely response is received, CFP Board Staff Counsel shall compile all documents and materials and commerce probable cause determination procedures as soon thereafter as is reasonably practicable.

The Staff Counsel, determines if there is "probable cause" for disciplinary action and then does one of the following: dismiss the allegations as being without merit; dismiss the allegations with a letter of caution; or issue a formal Complaint, stating the grounds for discipline and the alleged wrongful conduct of the CFP Board designee. Within 20 days, the CFP Board designee must admit or deny all allegations and set forth any affirmative defenses. If the CFP Board designee fails to file an answer within 20 days of service, the CFP Board designee will be in default and the allegations of the Complaints will be deemed admitted. Staff Counsel must serve the CFP Board designee with an Order of Revocation, stating clearly and with reasonable particularity the grounds for revocation of the CFP Board designee's right to use the CFP® marks.

All hearings on Complaints seeking disciplinary action against a CFP Board designee are required to be conducted by a **Hearing Panel**. The Hearing Panel must establish the rules of procedures and evidence to be observed at the hearing. Proof of misconduct is established by a "preponderance of the evidence." A CFP Board designee may not be required to testify or to produce records over the objection of the CFP Board designee if it would violate the CFP Board designee's constitutional privilege against self-incrimination in a court of law. Staff Counsel or the CFP Board designee may request written discovery or depositions. A deposition is an examination of a person whereby that person answers questions while under oath or affirmation with a court reporter present. The Hearing Panel must rule on such requests and may order the party to comply with the request. All testimony at hearings before the Hearing Panel must be transcribed.

beyond a reasonable doubt - a measure or degree of proof. With regard to disciplinary rules and procedures, "beyond a reasonable doubt" means the evidence as a whole shows what it was intended to prove with a probability of 99 percent or better.

Self-incrimination

Self-incrimination is the process whereby acts or declarations either as testimony at trial or prior to trial implicate oneself in a crime. The Fifth Amendment to the United States Constitution, as well as provisions in many state constitutions, prohibits the government from requiring a person to be a witness or furnish evidence against himself or herself involuntarily. This privilege against self-incrimination requires the government to prove a criminal case against defendants without the aid of defendants as witnesses against themselves. However, this privilege against self-incrimination is waived when the witness voluntarily testifies. Interestingly, the Fifth Amendment privilege against self-incrimination protects a witness not only from the requirement of answering questions which might call for directly incriminating answers, but also from answers which might tie or link oneself to criminal activity in the chain of evidence.

Rather than coerce the CFP Board designee into a confession or admission or require the CFP Board designee to provide a link in the chain of evidence of criminal activity, the BOPR must turn to other evidence to prove that a CFP Board designee violated the Code in the event that the CFP Board designee objects to testifying or to producing records.

Report, Findings of Fact, and Recommendation

After the hearing, the Hearing Panel records its findings of fact and recommendations and submits them to the BOPR for consideration. The report must dismiss the Complaint as not proven or refer the matter to the BOPR with the recommendation of discipline, stating which form of discipline the Hearing Panel deems appropriate. The Hearing Panel may also recommend that the BOPR enter other appropriate orders.

The BOPR has the power to review any determination made during disciplinary proceedings or practice standards proceedings. The BOPR may, in its discretion, approve or modify the report. However, the BOPR must accept the Hearing Panel's findings of fact unless it determines that such findings are "clearly erroneous" based on a review of the record. The BOPR may modify the Hearing Panel's recommendation without reviewing the record, whether or not the recommendation is clearly erroneous.

The "Clearly Erroneous" Standard – Explanation

When the Hearing Panel makes findings of fact, these findings are based on the broad discretion and judgment of those serving on the panel. Their findings should not be taken lightly because the panel members were present during the hearing and were able to see firsthand the evidence, to hear the live witnesses, if any, and to evaluate the CFP Board designee and the CFP Board designee's demeanor. Under these circumstances, the Hearing Panel should be given vast

clearly erroneous standard - asks the basic question: could a reasonable finder of fact have ruled in a certain way, based on the entire record?

discretion as to factual findings. Accordingly, these findings should only be set aside or altered by the BOPR if the findings are clearly erroneous or clearly wrong. Many appellate courts of law utilize this clearly erroneous standard. The **clearly erroneous standard** boils down to this basic question: Could a reasonable finder of fact have possibly ruled this way, based on the entire record? Only when review of the entire record reveals that a reasonable person could not have ruled that way will the findings be considered clearly erroneous.

The factual findings of the Hearing Panel are given much discretion and deference by the BOPR. If the Hearing Panel makes unfavorable factual findings for the CFP Board designee, these factual findings will be binding upon the CFP Board designee and are not taken lightly. The Hearing Panel's factual findings normally will not be overturned or disturbed by the BOPR or the Board of Appeals, much like litigation during the appellate process.

In contrast to findings of fact, however, the recommendations of the Hearing Panel are subject to modification as the BOPR deems appropriate. The BOPR must, however, state the reasons for modification. All appeals from orders of the BOPR shall be submitted to the Board of Appeals within thirty (30) calendar days after notice of the order is sent to the CFP Board designee. If no appeal is lodged with the Board of Appeals within that time frame, the order shall become final and binding.

Conviction of a Crime or Professional Suspension

Conviction of a crime or an order of professional suspension is conclusive evidence and proof of the commission of the act for purposes of disciplinary proceedings. The CFP Board designee has a duty to report convictions or professional suspension to the CFP Board within ten (10) days after the date on which the CFP Board designee is notified of the conviction or suspension. After receiving notice that a CFP Board designee has been convicted of a crime other than a serious crime, the CFP Board Staff Counsel shall commence an investigation. If a CFP Board designee is convicted of a serious crime or is the subject of a professional suspension, the CFP Board shall obtain the record of the conviction or suspension and file a Complaint against the CFP Board designee. The CFP Board Staff Counsel may report the name of any CFP Board designee who is convicted of a serious crime or is the subject of a professional suspension to the BOPR and may issue a notice to the convicted CFP Board designee to show cause why the CFP Board designee's right to use the marks should not be immediately suspended.

offer of settlement - a CFP Board designee may tender an Offer of Settlement in exchange for a stipulated form of disciplinary action by the BOPR

Settlement Procedure

A CFP Board designee may tender an **Offer of Settlement** in exchange for a stipulated form of action by the BOPR. The Offer of Settlement may be made where the public interests and CFP Board permit. A CFP Board designee is allowed only one Offer of Settlement during the course of a disciplinary proceeding. If an Offer of Settlement is accepted by the Hearing Panel, it must propose an **Order of Acceptance** containing findings of fact. The Order of Acceptance must be reviewed by the BOPR. If the Offer of Settlement is rejected by the Hearing Panel, the Offer is deemed withdrawn. The CFP Board designee shall not be prejudiced in any way by a rejection.

order of acceptance - if an Offer of Settlement is accepted by the Hearing Panel during a disciplinary review, it must propose an Order of Acceptance containing findings of fact to be reviewed by the Board of Professional Review

Required Action after Revocation or Suspension

When an order of revocation or suspension becomes final, the CFP Board designee *"shall promptly terminate"* any use of the CFP® mark. If one's right to use the CFP® mark is revoked, there is no opportunity for reinstatement. Revocation is *"permanent."* A CFP Board designee who has been suspended for less than one year shall be automatically reinstated after expiration of the suspension, provided that the CFP Board designee complies with the order of suspension and files an affidavit verifying such compliance. A CFP Board designee who has been suspended over one year must petition the BOPR for reinstatement within six months of the end of the suspension, or else reinstatement is relinquished or waived. If the CFP Board designee petitions the BOPR within six months of possible reinstatement, the CFP Board designee has the burden of proving by *"clear and convincing evidence"* that the CFP Board designee has been rehabilitated; has complied with all applicable disciplinary Procedures; has met all CFP Board designee continuing education requirements; and is fit to use the marks.

If the CFP Board designee petitions for reinstatement, Staff Counsel will initiate an investigation. The CFP Board designee must cooperate with the investigation, and Staff Counsel shall submit a report of the investigation that shall report on the CFP Board designee's past disciplinary record and any recommendation regarding reinstatement. If the CFP Board designee is denied reinstatement, the CFP Board designee must wait two years to petition again for reinstatement. If the second petition is denied, the CFP Board designee's right to use the marks is relinquished.

All proceedings and records conducted in accordance with the Procedures are confidential. They will not be made public, unless otherwise provided in the Procedures. The Procedures allow disclosure of disciplinary proceedings if the proceeding is based on criminal conviction or professional suspension; the CFP Board designee has waived confidentiality; or disclosure is required by legal process.

THE PRACTICE STANDARDS

The CFP Board established the Board of Practice Standards to draft **Practice Standards** to assure that the financial planning practice by CFP Board designees is based on agreed-upon norms of practice. The Practice Standards are also in place to advance professionalism in the practice of financial planning and to enhance the value of the personal financial planning process. A Practice Standard establishes the level of professional practice that is expected of CFP Board designees engaged in personal financial planning. The facts and circumstances of each particular situation determine the services to be provided.

practice standards - the set of standards that: (1) establish the level of professional practice that is expected of CFP Board designees engaged in personal financial planning, (2) advance professionalism in the practice of financial planning, and (3) enhance the value of the personal financial planning process

Currently, there are six sections of Practice Standards in effect: the "100 Series," the "200 Series," the "300 Series," the "400 Series," the "500 Series," and the "600 series."

The 100 Series

Practice Standard 100-1

Establishing and defining the relationship with the client—Defining the scope of the engagement. The scope of the engagement shall be mutually defined by the financial planning practitioner and the client prior to providing any financial planning service.

The 200 Series

Practice Standard 200-1

Gathering client data—Determining a client's personal and financial goals, needs and priorities. A client's personal financial goals, needs, and priorities that are relevant to the scope of the engagement and the service(s) being provided shall be mutually defined by the financial planning practitioner and the client prior to making and/or implementing any recommendation.

Practice Standards 200-2

Gathering client data—Obtaining quantitative information and documents. A financial planning practitioner shall obtain sufficient and relevant quantitative information and documents about a client applicable to the scope of the engagement and the services being provided prior to making and/or implementing any recommendation.

The 300 Series

Practice Standard 300-1

Analyzing and evaluating the client's financial status—Analyzing and evaluating the client's information. A financial planning practitioner must analyze the client's information in order to gain a full understanding of the client's financial situation; then evaluate and assess to what extent the client's goals, needs and priorities can be met by the client's resources and current course of action. Analysis and evaluation are critical to the process of financial planning. After this analysis and evaluation, it may even be appropriate to amend the scope of the engagement and/or to obtain additional information.

The 400 Series

Practice Standard 400-1

Developing and presenting the financial planning recommendation(s)—Identifying and evaluating financial planning alternatives. A financial planning practitioner shall consider sufficient and relevant alternatives to the client's current course of action in an effort to reasonably meet the client's goals, needs and priorities. This evaluation, which is done prior to any recommendations, may involve multiple reasonable assumptions, research or consultation with other competent professionals. This process may result in one alternative, no alternatives, multiple alternatives or various combinations in relation to the client's current course of action.

Practice Standard 400-2

Developing and presenting the financial planning recommendation(s)—Developing the financial planning recommendation(s). A financial planning practitioner must develop recommendations based on the selected alternatives and the current course of action in order to reasonably achieve the client's goals, needs and priorities. A recommendation may be an independent action, continuation of the current course of action, inaction or a combination of actions that may need to be implemented collectively.

Practice Standard 400-3

Developing and presenting the financial planning recommendation(s)—Presenting the financial planning recommendation(s). A financial planning practitioner shall communicate the recommendations to the client in a manner and to an extent reasonably necessary to assist the client in making an informed decision. The practitioner is charged with the responsibility of assisting the client in understanding (i) the client's current situation, (ii) the recommendation itself, and (iii) the impact of the recommendation on the ability to achieve the client's goals, needs and priorities. If the client possesses an understanding of these items, the client can make the truly informed decision. Presenting recommendations also provides the practitioner an opportunity to further assess whether the recommendations meet the client's expectations, the client's willingness to act on the recommendations and whether modifications are in order.

THE 500 SERIES

Practice Standard 500-1

Implementing the financial planning recommendation(s) - Agreeing on implementation responsibilities. The client and the financial planning practitioner must mutually agree on the implementation responsibilities consistent with the scope of the engagement. The client is responsible for accepting or rejecting recommendations and for retaining or delegating implementation responsibilities. The responsibilities of the financial planning practitioner may include: (i) identifying activities necessary for implementation; (ii) determining division of activities between the client and practitioner; (iii) referral to and/or coordination with other professionals; (iv) sharing of information as authorized; and (v) selecting and securing products or services.

Practice Standard 500-2

Implementing the financial planning recommendation(s) - Selecting products and services for implementation. The financial planning practitioner shall select appropriate products and services consistent with the goals, needs and priorities of the client. The financial planning practitioner has the duty to use his or her judgment in investigating products or services that reasonably address the client's needs and are suitable to the client's financial situation. Professional judgment incorporates information that is both qualitative and quantitative and, of course, may differ from those of other practitioners or advisers.

THE 600 SERIES

Practice Standard 600-1

Monitoring - Defining monitoring responsibilities. The financial planning practitioner and client shall mutually define monitoring responsibilities. This Practice Standard clarifies the role, if any, of the practitioner so that the client's expectations are more likely to be in alignment with the level of monitoring services that the practitioner intends to provide. When monitoring services are engaged, the financial planning practitioner must make a reasonable effort to define and communicate to the client those monitoring activities that the practitioner is able and willing to provide, including an explanation of what is to be monitored, the frequency of monitoring and the communication method.

These Practice Standards are excellent ways to promote sound practices and basically good business for CFP Board designees when rendering financial planning services. Similar to an ethics code, such standards can only add to the value of services of the financial planning industry as a whole. Even though these standards are applicable only to CFP Board designees, these standards (and the ensuing Practice Standards) are admirable guides for those in the financial world in general.

THE IMPORTANCE OF ETHICS

While learning the fundamentals of financial planning is vital to those who aspire to work and interact in the world of business and finance, equally important is understanding and being able to handle ethical issues that accompany interaction in the finance industry and that accompany the provision of financial services. The negative effects of unethical practices and actions of a few not only damage the individual engaging in unethical behavior and the victim of such behavior, but damage the image and the productivity of the entire industry. Ethics codes and practice standards can help significantly in reducing the incidence of unethical and damaging conduct, while providing much needed counsel, tutelage, guidance, and direction to the individual professional.

DISCUSSION QUESTIONS

1. How do ethics, law, and an ethics code differ, and how are they similar?
2. What is Certified Financial Planner Board of Standards, Inc.?
3. What is the Code of Ethics and Professional Responsibility (the Code)?
4. What is the role of the CFP Board's Practice Standards in relation to the Code?
5. What is the role of the Board of Professional Review (BOPR), the Board of Practice Standards, and the Board of Governors in relation to the Code?
6. What is the role of the Disciplinary Rules and Procedures (the Procedures) and the Financial Planning Practice Standards (the Standards) in relation to the Code?
7. How is the Code structured, and what is the role of each of its parts?
8. What are the seven Principles of the Code? Give a rule that relates to each Principle?
9. How does the "commingling of funds" and the "fiduciary relationship" relate to the Code's Principle of Integrity?
10. How do the three distinct standards or "burdens" of proof affect the treatment of the CFP Board designee at various stages of disciplinary proceedings?
11. What four forms of discipline can be applied by the BOPR to a CFP Board designee?

SECTION VI

Appendices

APPENDIX A Comprehensive Financial Planning Case
APPENDIX B Time Value of Money Tables
APPENDIX C Regulatory Requirements - Federal Securities Regulation
APPENDIX D CFP Board's Topic List

Appendix A

Comprehensive Case

Today is January 1, 2006. Mark and Ava Lane have come to you, a financial planner, for help in developing a plan to accomplish their financial goals. From your initial meeting together, you have gathered the following information:

PERSONAL BACKGROUND AND INFORMATION

Mark Lane (Age 30)

Mark is an assistant in the marketing department for Gas & Electric, Inc. His annual salary is $26,000.

Ava Lane (Age 30)

Ava is a legal research assistant with the law firm of Sabrio, Johnson & Williams, L.L.C. Her annual salary is $20,000.

The Children

Mark and Ava have no children from this marriage. Mark has two children, Shawn (Age 4) and Ronald (Age 3), from a former marriage. Shawn and Ronald live with their mother, Kimberly.

The Lanes

Mark and Ava have been married for two years.

Mark must pay $325 per month in child support until both Shawn and Ronald reach age 18. The divorce decree also requires Mark to create an insurance trust for the benefit of the children and contribute $175 per month to the trustee. The trustee is Kimberly's father. There are no withdrawal powers on the part of the beneficiaries. The trust is to be used for the education and/or maintenance of the children in the event of Mark's death. The trustee has the power to invade any trust principal for the beneficiaries at the earlier of the death of Mark or when Ronald reaches age 18.

ECONOMIC INFORMATION

- Inflation is expected to be 4.0% annually.
- Their salaries should increase 5.0% for the next five to ten years.
- No state income tax.
- Slow growth economy; stocks are expected to grow at 9.5%.

Bank Lending Rates are as Follows:

- 15-year mortgage 7.5%.
- 30-year mortgage 8.0%.
- Secured personal loan 10.0%.

INSURANCE INFORMATION

LIFE INSURANCE

	Policy A	Policy B	Policy C
Insured	Mark	Mark	Ava
Face Amount	$300,000	$78,000[2]	$20,000
Type	Whole Life	Group Term	Group Term
Cash Value	$2,000	$0	$0
Annual Premium	$2,100	$178	$50
Who pays premium	Trustee	Employer	Employer
Beneficiary	Trustee[1]	Kimberly	Mark
Policy Owner	Trust	Mark	Ava
Settlement options clause selected	None	None	None

[1] *Shawn and Ronald are beneficiaries of the trust.*
[2] *This was increased from $50,000 to $78,000 January 1, 2006.*

HEALTH INSURANCE

- Mark and Ava are covered under Mark's employer plan which is an indemnity plan with a $200 deductible per person per year and an 80/20 major medical coinsurance clause with a family annual stop loss of $1,500.

LONG-TERM DISABILITY INSURANCE

- Mark is covered by an "own occupation" policy with premiums paid by his employer. The benefits equal 60% of his gross pay after an elimination period of 180 days. The policy covers both sickness and accidents and is guaranteed renewable.
- Ava is not covered by disability insurance.

RENTERS INSURANCE

- The Lanes have an HO4 renters policy without endorsements.
- Content Coverage $25,000; Liability $100,000.

AUTOMOBILE INSURANCE

- Both Car and Truck
- They do not have any additional insurance on Mark's motorcycle.

Type	PAP
Bodily Injury	$25,000/$50,000
Property Damage	$10,000
Medical Payments	$5,000 per person
Physical Damage	Actual Cash Value
Uninsured Motorist	$25,000/$50,000
Comprehensive Deductible	$200
Collision Deductible	$500
Premium (annual)	$3,300

INVESTMENT INFORMATION

The Lanes think that they need six months of cash flow net of all taxes, savings, vacation, and discretionary cash flow in an emergency fund. They are willing to include in the emergency fund the savings account and Mark's 401(k) balance because it has borrowing provisions.

The Amazon.com stock was a gift to Mark from his Uncle Bill. At the date of the gift (July 1, 2003), the fair market value of the stock was $3,500. Uncle Bill's tax basis was $2,500, and Uncle Bill paid gift tax of $1,400 on the gift. Uncle Bill had already used up both his unified credit and annual exclusion to Mark.

The K&B stock was a gift to Ava of 100 shares from her Uncle Mike. At the date of the gift (December 25, 2003) the fair market value was $8,000 and Mike had paid $10,000 for the stock in 1996 (his tax basis).

The Growth Mutual Fund (currently valued at $13,900) had been acquired by Mark over the years 2000, 2001, 2002, 2003, 2004 and 2005 with deposits of $1,000, $1,000, $2,000, $2,000, $2,500 and $3,000. The earnings were all reinvested and Mark received 1099s for the income and capital gains during the years of earnings ($0/2000, $200/2001, $400/2002, $400/2003, $650/2004, $750/2005).

INCOME TAX INFORMATION

The filing status of the Lanes for federal income tax is married filing jointly. Both the children (Shawn and Ronald) are claimed as dependents on the Lane's tax return as part of the divorce agreement. The Lanes live in a state that does not have state income tax.

Section 79 Limit on Premium Schedule
Age 29 and under $0.06 per month/per $1,000.

RETIREMENT INFORMATION

Mark currently contributes 3% of his salary to his 401(k). The employer matches each $1 contributed with $0.50 up to a total employer contribution of 3% of salary.

GIFTS, ESTATES, TRUSTS, AND WILL INFORMATION

- Mark has a will leaving all of his probate estate to his children.
- Ava does not have a will.
- The Lanes live in a common law state that has adopted the Uniform Probate Code.

STATEMENT OF CASH FLOWS

Mark and Ava Lane
Statement of Cash Flows (Expected to be similar in 2006)
January 1, 2005 - December 31, 2005

CASH INFLOWS		
Salaries		
Mark-Salary	$26,000	
Ava-Salary	20,000	
Investment Income*	1,090	
Total Inflows		$47,090
CASH OUTFLOWS		
Savings-House down payment	$ 1,200	
Reinvestment of Investment Income	1,090	
401(k) Contribution	780	
Total Savings		$ 3,070
FIXED OUTFLOWS		
Child Support	$ 3,900	
Life Insurance Payment (To Trustee)	2,100	
Rent	6,600	
Renters Insurance	480	
Utilities	720	
Telephone	360	
Auto down payment 12/31/05**	3,699	
Auto Insurance	3,300	
Gas, Oil, Maintenance	2,400	
Student loans	3,600	
Credit Card Debt	1,800	
Furniture payments	1,302	
Total Fixed Outflows		$30,261
VARIABLE OUTFLOWS		
Taxes-Mark FICA	$ 1,989	
Taxes-Ava FICA	1,530	
Taxes-Federal Tax Withheld	4,316	
Food	3,600	
Clothing	1,000	
Entertainment/Vacation	1,500	
Total Variable Outflows		$13,935
Total Cash Outflows		$47,266
Discretionary Cash Flows (negative)		$ (176)
TOTAL CASH OUTFLOWS		$47,090

**$340 from dividends and $750 from other investment sources.*

*** P&I next year will total $3,600*

STATEMENT OF FINANCIAL POSITION

Mark and Ava Lane
Balance Sheet
As of January 1, 2006

ASSETS[1]		LIABILITIES & NET WORTH	
Cash and Equivalents		Liabilities[2]	
Cash	$ 500	Credit Card balance VISA	$ 9,000
Savings Account	1,000	Credit Card balance M/C	0
Total Cash and Equivalents	$1,500	Student Loan-Mark[4]	45,061
		Auto Loan-Ava	14,796
Invested Assets		Furniture Loan	1,533
Amazon.com Stock (100 Shares)[3]	$ 5,000	Total Liabilities	$70,390
K&B Stock (100 shares)	7,200		
Growth Mutual Fund	13,900		
401(k) Account	1,500	Net Worth	(46)
Total Invested Assets	$27,600		
Use Assets			
Auto-Ava	$18,494		
Truck-Mark	4,000		
Motorcycle – Mark	1,000		
Personal Property & Furniture	17,750		
Total Use Of Assets	$41,244		
Total Assets	$70,344	Total Liabilities & Net Worth	$70,344

Notes to Financial Statements:

1. *Assets are stated at fair market value.*
2. *Liabilities are stated at principal only as of January 1, 2006 before January payments.*
3. *Amazon.com's current dividend is $3.40.*
4. *Mark's parents took out the student loans, but he is repaying them.*

INFORMATION REGARDING ASSETS AND LIABILITIES

HOME FURNISHINGS

The furniture was purchased with 20% down and 18% interest over 36 months. The monthly payment is $108.46.

AUTOMOBILE

The automobile was purchased December 31, 2005 for $18,494 with 20% down and 80% financed over 60 months with payments of $300 per month.

STEREO SYSTEM

The Lanes have a fabulous stereo system (FMV $10,000). They asked and received permission to alter the apartment to build speakers into every room. The agreement with the landlord requires the Lanes to leave the speakers if they move because the speakers are permanently installed and affixed to the property. The replacement value of the installed speakers is $4,500, and the non-installed components are valued at $5,500. The cost of the system was $10,000, and it was purchased in late 2004.

REQUIREMENTS:

- ▲ Complete an Engagement Letter to the Lanes to advise them on financial planning.
- ▲ Complete a Client Planner Worksheet.
- ▲ Calculate financial ratios for the Lanes.
- ▲ Identify the financial strengths and weaknesses of the Lanes.
- ▲ Identify the likely appropriate mission, goals, and objectives of the Lanes.
- ▲ Make recommendations based on the goals and risks of the Lanes in all areas of their financial situation.

Appendix B-1

Present Value of a Dollar

Present Value of $1

$$\left[\frac{1}{(1+i)^n}\right]$$

Period	1%	2%	3%	4%	5%	6%	7%	8%	9%	10%	11%	12%	13%
1	0.9901	0.9804	0.9709	0.9615	0.9524	0.9434	0.9346	0.9259	0.9174	0.9091	0.9009	0.8929	0.8850
2	0.9803	0.9612	0.9426	0.9246	0.9070	0.8900	0.8734	0.8573	0.8417	0.8264	0.8116	0.7972	0.7831
3	0.9706	0.9423	0.9151	0.8890	0.8638	0.8396	0.8163	0.7938	0.7722	0.7513	0.7312	0.7118	0.6931
4	0.9610	0.9238	0.8885	0.8548	0.8227	0.7921	0.7629	0.7350	0.7084	0.6830	0.6587	0.6355	0.6133
5	0.9515	0.9057	0.8626	0.8219	0.7835	0.7473	0.7130	0.6806	0.6499	0.6209	0.5935	0.5674	0.5428
6	0.9420	0.8880	0.8375	0.7903	0.7462	0.7050	0.6663	0.6302	0.5963	0.5645	0.5346	0.5066	0.4803
7	0.9327	0.8706	0.8131	0.7599	0.7107	0.6651	0.6227	0.5835	0.5470	0.5132	0.4817	0.4523	0.4251
8	0.9235	0.8535	0.7894	0.7307	0.6768	0.6274	0.5820	0.5403	0.5019	0.4665	0.4339	0.4039	0.3762
9	0.9143	0.8368	0.7664	0.7026	0.6446	0.5919	0.5439	0.5002	0.4604	0.4241	0.3909	0.3606	0.3329
10	0.9053	0.8203	0.7441	0.6756	0.6139	0.5584	0.5083	0.4632	0.4224	0.3855	0.3522	0.3220	0.2946
11	0.8963	0.8043	0.7224	0.6496	0.5847	0.5268	0.4751	0.4289	0.3875	0.3505	0.3173	0.2875	0.2607
12	0.8874	0.7885	0.7014	0.6246	0.5568	0.4970	0.4440	0.3971	0.3555	0.3186	0.2858	0.2567	0.2307
13	0.8787	0.7730	0.6810	0.6006	0.5303	0.4688	0.4150	0.3677	0.3262	0.2897	0.2575	0.2292	0.2042
14	0.8700	0.7579	0.6611	0.5775	0.5051	0.4423	0.3878	0.3405	0.2992	0.2633	0.2320	0.2046	0.1807
15	0.8613	0.7430	0.6419	0.5553	0.4810	0.4173	0.3624	0.3152	0.2745	0.2394	0.2090	0.1827	0.1599
16	0.8528	0.7284	0.6232	0.5339	0.4581	0.3936	0.3387	0.2919	0.2519	0.2176	0.1883	0.1631	0.1415
17	0.8444	0.7142	0.6050	0.5134	0.4363	0.3714	0.3166	0.2703	0.2311	0.1978	0.1696	0.1456	0.1252
18	0.8360	0.7002	0.5874	0.4936	0.4155	0.3503	0.2959	0.2502	0.2120	0.1799	0.1528	0.1300	0.1108
19	0.8277	0.6864	0.5703	0.4746	0.3957	0.3305	0.2765	0.2317	0.1945	0.1635	0.1377	0.1161	0.0981
20	0.8195	0.6730	0.5537	0.4564	0.3769	0.3118	0.2584	0.2145	0.1784	0.1486	0.1240	0.1037	0.0868
25	0.7798	0.6095	0.4776	0.3751	0.2953	0.2330	0.1842	0.1460	0.1160	0.0923	0.0736	0.0588	0.0471
30	0.7419	0.5521	0.4120	0.3083	0.2314	0.1741	0.1314	0.0994	0.0754	0.0573	0.0437	0.0334	0.0256
35	0.7059	0.5000	0.3554	0.2534	0.1813	0.1301	0.0937	0.0676	0.0490	0.0356	0.0259	0.0189	0.0139
40	0.6717	0.4529	0.3066	0.2083	0.1420	0.0972	0.0668	0.0460	0.0318	0.0221	0.0154	0.0107	0.0075
45	0.6391	0.4102	0.2644	0.1712	0.1113	0.0727	0.0476	0.0313	0.0207	0.0137	0.0091	0.0061	0.0041
50	0.6080	0.3715	0.2281	0.1407	0.0872	0.0543	0.0339	0.0213	0.0134	0.0085	0.0054	0.0035	0.0022

Appendix B-1

Present Value of a Dollar (continued)

Present Value of $1

$$\left[\frac{1}{(1+i)^n}\right]$$

Period	14%	15%	16%	17%	18%	19%	20%	25%	30%	35%	40%	45%	50%
1	0.8772	0.8696	0.8621	0.8547	0.8475	0.8403	0.8333	0.8000	0.7692	0.7407	0.7143	0.6897	0.6667
2	0.7695	0.7561	0.7432	0.7305	0.7182	0.7062	0.6944	0.6400	0.5917	0.5487	0.5102	0.4756	0.4444
3	0.6750	0.6575	0.6407	0.6244	0.6086	0.5934	0.5787	0.5120	0.4552	0.4064	0.3644	0.3280	0.2963
4	0.5921	0.5718	0.5523	0.5337	0.5158	0.4987	0.4823	0.4096	0.3501	0.3011	0.2603	0.2262	0.1975
5	0.5194	0.4972	0.4761	0.4561	0.4371	0.4190	0.4019	0.3277	0.2693	0.2230	0.1859	0.1560	0.1317
6	0.4556	0.4323	0.4104	0.3898	0.3704	0.3521	0.3349	0.2621	0.2072	0.1652	0.1328	0.1076	0.0878
7	0.3996	0.3759	0.3538	0.3332	0.3139	0.2959	0.2791	0.2097	0.1594	0.1224	0.0949	0.0742	0.0585
8	0.3506	0.3269	0.3050	0.2848	0.2660	0.2487	0.2326	0.1678	0.1226	0.0906	0.0678	0.0512	0.0390
9	0.3075	0.2843	0.2630	0.2434	0.2255	0.2090	0.1938	0.1342	0.0943	0.0671	0.0484	0.0353	0.0260
10	0.2697	0.2472	0.2267	0.2080	0.1911	0.1756	0.1615	0.1074	0.0725	0.0497	0.0346	0.0243	0.0173
11	0.2366	0.2149	0.1954	0.1778	0.1619	0.1476	0.1346	0.0859	0.0558	0.0368	0.0247	0.0168	0.0116
12	0.2076	0.1869	0.1685	0.1520	0.1372	0.1240	0.1122	0.0687	0.0429	0.0273	0.0176	0.0116	0.0077
13	0.1821	0.1625	0.1452	0.1299	0.1163	0.1042	0.0935	0.0550	0.0330	0.0202	0.0126	0.0080	0.0051
14	0.1597	0.1413	0.1252	0.1110	0.0985	0.0876	0.0779	0.0440	0.0254	0.0150	0.0090	0.0055	0.0034
15	0.1401	0.1229	0.1079	0.0949	0.0835	0.0736	0.0649	0.0352	0.0195	0.0111	0.0064	0.0038	0.0023
16	0.1229	0.1069	0.0930	0.0811	0.0708	0.0618	0.0541	0.0281	0.0150	0.0082	0.0046	0.0026	0.0015
17	0.1078	0.0929	0.0802	0.0693	0.0600	0.0520	0.0451	0.0225	0.0116	0.0061	0.0033	0.0018	0.0010
18	0.0946	0.0808	0.0691	0.0592	0.0508	0.0437	0.0376	0.0180	0.0089	0.0045	0.0023	0.0012	0.0007
19	0.0829	0.0703	0.0596	0.0506	0.0431	0.0367	0.0313	0.0144	0.0068	0.0033	0.0017	0.0009	0.0005
20	0.0728	0.0611	0.0514	0.0433	0.0365	0.0308	0.0261	0.0115	0.0053	0.0025	0.0012	0.0006	0.0003
25	0.0378	0.0304	0.0245	0.0197	0.0160	0.0129	0.0105	0.0038	0.0014	0.0006	0.0002	0.0001	0.0000
30	0.0196	0.0151	0.0116	0.0090	0.0070	0.0054	0.0042	0.0012	0.0004	0.0001	0.0000	0.0000	0.0000
35	0.0102	0.0075	0.0055	0.0041	0.0030	0.0023	0.0017	0.0004	0.0001	0.0000	0.0000	0.0000	0.0000
40	0.0053	0.0037	0.0026	0.0019	0.0013	0.0010	0.0007	0.0001	0.0000	0.0000	0.0000	0.0000	0.0000
45	0.0027	0.0019	0.0013	0.0009	0.0006	0.0004	0.0003	0.0000	0.0000	0.0000	0.0000	0.0000	0.0000
50	0.0014	0.0009	0.0006	0.0004	0.0003	0.0002	0.0001	0.0000	0.0000	0.0000	0.0000	0.0000	0.0000

Appendix B-2

Future Value of a Dollar

Future Value of $1

$$\left[(1+i)^n\right]$$

Period	1%	2%	3%	4%	5%	6%	7%	8%	9%	10%	11%	12%	13%
1	1.0100	1.0200	1.0300	1.0400	1.0500	1.0600	1.0700	1.0800	1.0900	1.1000	1.1100	1.1200	1.1300
2	1.0201	1.0404	1.0609	1.0816	1.1025	1.1236	1.1449	1.1664	1.1881	1.2100	1.2321	1.2544	1.2769
3	1.0303	1.0612	1.0927	1.1249	1.1576	1.1910	1.2250	1.2597	1.2950	1.3310	1.3676	1.4049	1.4429
4	1.0406	1.0824	1.1255	1.1699	1.2155	1.2625	1.3108	1.3605	1.4116	1.4641	1.5181	1.5735	1.6305
5	1.0510	1.1041	1.1593	1.2167	1.2763	1.3382	1.4026	1.4693	1.5386	1.6105	1.6851	1.7623	1.8424
6	1.0615	1.1262	1.1941	1.2653	1.3401	1.4185	1.5007	1.5869	1.6771	1.7716	1.8704	1.9738	2.0820
7	1.0721	1.1487	1.2299	1.3159	1.4071	1.5036	1.6058	1.7138	1.8280	1.9487	2.0762	2.2107	2.3526
8	1.0829	1.1717	1.2668	1.3686	1.4775	1.5938	1.7182	1.8509	1.9926	2.1436	2.3045	2.4760	2.6584
9	1.0937	1.1951	1.3048	1.4233	1.5513	1.6895	1.8385	1.9990	2.1719	2.3579	2.5580	2.7731	3.0040
10	1.1046	1.2190	1.3439	1.4802	1.6289	1.7908	1.9672	2.1589	2.3674	2.5937	2.8394	3.1058	3.3946
11	1.1157	1.2434	1.3842	1.5395	1.7103	1.8983	2.1049	2.3316	2.5804	2.8531	3.1518	3.4785	3.8359
12	1.1268	1.2682	1.4258	1.6010	1.7959	2.0122	2.2522	2.5182	2.8127	3.1384	3.4985	3.8960	4.3345
13	1.1381	1.2936	1.4685	1.6651	1.8856	2.1329	2.4098	2.7196	3.0658	3.4523	3.8833	4.3635	4.8980
14	1.1495	1.3195	1.5126	1.7317	1.9799	2.2609	2.5785	2.9372	3.3417	3.7975	4.3104	4.8871	5.5348
15	1.1610	1.3459	1.5580	1.8009	2.0789	2.3966	2.7590	3.1722	3.6425	4.1772	4.7846	5.4736	6.2543
16	1.1726	1.3728	1.6047	1.8730	2.1829	2.5404	2.9522	3.4259	3.9703	4.5950	5.3109	6.1304	7.0673
17	1.1843	1.4002	1.6528	1.9479	2.2920	2.6928	3.1588	3.7000	4.3276	5.0545	5.8951	6.8660	7.9861
18	1.1961	1.4282	1.7024	2.0258	2.4066	2.8543	3.3799	3.9960	4.7171	5.5599	6.5436	7.6900	9.0243
19	1.2081	1.4568	1.7535	2.1068	2.5270	3.0256	3.6165	4.3157	5.1417	6.1159	7.2633	8.6128	10.1974
20	1.2202	1.4859	1.8061	2.1911	2.6533	3.2071	3.8697	4.6610	5.6044	6.7275	8.0623	9.6463	11.5231
25	1.2824	1.6406	2.0938	2.6658	3.3864	4.2919	5.4274	6.8485	8.6231	10.8347	13.5855	17.0001	21.2305
30	1.3478	1.8114	2.4273	3.2434	4.3219	5.7435	7.6123	10.0627	13.2677	17.4494	22.8923	29.9599	39.1159
35	1.4166	1.9999	2.8139	3.9461	5.5160	7.6861	10.6766	14.7853	20.4140	28.1024	38.5749	52.7996	72.0685
40	1.4889	2.2080	3.2620	4.8010	7.0400	10.2857	14.9745	21.7245	31.4094	45.2593	65.0009	93.0510	132.7816
45	1.5648	2.4379	3.7816	5.8412	8.9850	13.7646	21.0025	31.9204	48.3273	72.8905	109.5302	163.9876	244.6414
50	1.6446	2.6916	4.3839	7.1067	11.4674	18.4202	29.4570	46.9016	74.3575	117.3909	184.5648	289.0022	450.7359

Appendix B-2

Future Value of a Dollar (continued)

Future Value of $1

$$\left[(1+i)^n \right]$$

Period	14%	15%	16%	17%	18%	19%	20%	25%	30%	35%	40%	45%	50%
1	1.1400	1.1500	1.1600	1.1700	1.1800	1.1900	1.2000	1.2500	1.3000	1.3500	1.4000	1.4500	1.5000
2	1.2996	1.3225	1.3456	1.3689	1.3924	1.4161	1.4400	1.5625	1.6900	1.8225	1.9600	2.1025	2.2500
3	1.4815	1.5209	1.5609	1.6016	1.6430	1.6852	1.7280	1.9531	2.1970	2.4604	2.7440	3.0486	3.3750
4	1.6890	1.7490	1.8106	1.8739	1.9388	2.0053	2.0736	2.4414	2.8561	3.3215	3.8416	4.4205	5.0625
5	1.9254	2.0114	2.1003	2.1924	2.2878	2.3864	2.4883	3.0518	3.7129	4.4840	5.3782	6.4097	7.5938
6	2.1950	2.3131	2.4364	2.5652	2.6996	2.8398	2.9860	3.8147	4.8268	6.0534	7.5295	9.2941	11.3906
7	2.5023	2.6600	2.8262	3.0012	3.1855	3.3793	3.5832	4.7684	6.2749	8.1722	10.5414	13.4765	17.0859
8	2.8526	3.0590	3.2784	3.5115	3.7589	4.0214	4.2998	5.9605	8.1573	11.0324	14.7579	19.5409	25.6289
9	3.2519	3.5179	3.8030	4.1084	4.4355	4.7854	5.1598	7.4506	10.6045	14.8937	20.6610	28.3343	38.4434
10	3.7072	4.0456	4.4114	4.8068	5.2338	5.6947	6.1917	9.3132	13.7858	20.1066	28.9255	41.0847	57.6650
11	4.2262	4.6524	5.1173	5.6240	6.1759	6.7767	7.4301	11.6415	17.9216	27.1439	40.4957	59.5728	86.4976
12	4.8179	5.3503	5.9360	6.5801	7.2876	8.0642	8.9161	14.5519	23.2981	36.6442	56.6939	86.3806	129.7463
13	5.4924	6.1528	6.8858	7.6987	8.5994	9.5964	10.6993	18.1899	30.2875	49.4697	79.3715	125.2518	194.6195
14	6.2613	7.0757	7.9875	9.0075	10.1472	11.4198	12.8392	22.7374	39.3738	66.7841	111.1201	181.6151	291.9293
15	7.1379	8.1371	9.2655	10.5387	11.9737	13.5895	15.4070	28.4217	51.1859	90.1585	155.5681	263.3419	437.8939
16	8.1372	9.3576	10.7480	12.3303	14.1290	16.1715	18.4884	35.5271	66.5417	121.7139	217.7953	381.8458	656.8408
17	9.2765	10.7613	12.4677	14.4265	16.6722	19.2441	22.1861	44.4089	86.5042	164.3138	304.9135	553.6764	985.2613
18	10.5752	12.3755	14.4625	16.8790	19.6733	22.9005	26.6233	55.5112	112.4554	221.8236	426.8789	802.8308	1477.892
19	12.0557	14.2318	16.7765	19.7484	23.2144	27.2516	31.9480	69.3889	146.1920	299.4619	597.6304	1164.105	2216.838
20	13.7435	16.3665	19.4608	23.1056	27.3930	32.4294	38.3376	86.7362	190.0496	404.2736	836.6826	1687.952	3325.257
25	26.4619	32.9190	40.8742	50.6578	62.6686	77.3881	95.3962	264.6978	705.6410	1812.776	4499.880	10819.32	25251.17
30	50.9502	66.2118	85.8499	111.0647	143.3706	184.6753	237.3763	807.7936	2619.996	8128.550	24201.43	69348.98	191751.1
35	98.1002	133.1755	180.3141	243.5035	327.9973	440.7006	590.6682	2465.190	9727.860	36448.69	130161.1	444509	1456110
40	188.8835	267.8635	378.7212	533.8687	750.3783	1051.668	1469.772	7523.164	36118.86	163437.1	700037.7	2849181	11057332
45	363.6791	538.7693	795.4438	1170.479	1716.684	2509.651	3657.262	22958.87	134106.8	732857.6	3764971	18262495	83966617
50	700.2330	1083.657	1670.704	2566.215	3927.357	5988.914	9100.438	70064.92	497929.2	3286158	20248916	117057734	637621500

Appendix B-3

Present Value of an Ordinary Annuity

Present Value of Ordinary Annuity

$$\left[\frac{1-\frac{1}{(1+i)^n}}{i}\right]$$

Period	1%	2%	3%	4%	5%	6%	7%	8%	9%	10%	11%	12%	13%
1	0.9901	0.9804	0.9709	0.9615	0.9524	0.9434	0.9346	0.9259	0.9174	0.9091	0.9009	0.8929	0.8850
2	1.9704	1.9416	1.9135	1.8861	1.8594	1.8334	1.8080	1.7833	1.7591	1.7355	1.7125	1.6901	1.6681
3	2.9410	2.8839	2.8286	2.7751	2.7232	2.6730	2.6243	2.5771	2.5313	2.4869	2.4437	2.4018	2.3612
4	3.9020	3.8077	3.7171	3.6299	3.5460	3.4651	3.3872	3.3121	3.2397	3.1699	3.1024	3.0373	2.9745
5	4.8534	4.7135	4.5797	4.4518	4.3295	4.2124	4.1002	3.9927	3.8897	3.7908	3.6959	3.6048	3.5172
6	5.7955	5.6014	5.4172	5.2421	5.0757	4.9173	4.7665	4.6229	4.4859	4.3553	4.2305	4.1114	3.9975
7	6.7282	6.4720	6.2303	6.0021	5.7864	5.5824	5.3893	5.2064	5.0330	4.8684	4.7122	4.5638	4.4226
8	7.6517	7.3255	7.0197	6.7327	6.4632	6.2098	5.9713	5.7466	5.5348	5.3349	5.1461	4.9676	4.7988
9	8.5660	8.1622	7.7861	7.4353	7.1078	6.8017	6.5152	6.2469	5.9952	5.7590	5.5370	5.3282	5.1317
10	9.4713	8.9826	8.5302	8.1109	7.7217	7.3601	7.0236	6.7101	6.4177	6.1446	5.8892	5.6502	5.4262
11	10.3676	9.7868	9.2526	8.7605	8.3064	7.8869	7.4987	7.1390	6.8052	6.4951	6.2065	5.9377	5.6869
12	11.2551	10.5753	9.9540	9.3851	8.8633	8.3838	7.9427	7.5361	7.1607	6.8137	6.4924	6.1944	5.9176
13	12.1337	11.3484	10.6350	9.9856	9.3936	8.8527	8.3577	7.9038	7.4869	7.1034	6.7499	6.4235	6.1218
14	13.0037	12.1062	11.2961	10.5631	9.8986	9.2950	8.7455	8.2442	7.7862	7.3667	6.9819	6.6282	6.3025
15	13.8651	12.8493	11.9379	11.1184	10.3797	9.7122	9.1079	8.5595	8.0607	7.6061	7.1909	6.8109	6.4624
16	14.7179	13.5777	12.5611	11.6523	10.8378	10.1059	9.4466	8.8514	8.3126	7.8237	7.3792	6.9740	6.6039
17	15.5623	14.2919	13.1661	12.1657	11.2741	10.4773	9.7632	9.1216	8.5436	8.0216	7.5488	7.1196	6.7291
18	16.3983	14.9920	13.7535	12.6593	11.6896	10.8276	10.0591	9.3719	8.7556	8.2014	7.7016	7.2497	6.8399
19	17.2260	15.6785	14.3238	13.1339	12.0853	11.1581	10.3356	9.6036	8.9501	8.3649	7.8393	7.3658	6.9380
20	18.0456	16.3514	14.8775	13.5903	12.4622	11.4699	10.5940	9.8181	9.1285	8.5136	7.9633	7.4694	7.0248
25	22.0232	19.5235	17.4131	15.6221	14.0939	12.7834	11.6536	10.6748	9.8226	9.0770	8.4217	7.8431	7.3300
30	25.8077	22.3965	19.6004	17.2920	15.3725	13.7648	12.4090	11.2578	10.2737	9.4269	8.6938	8.0552	7.4957
35	29.4086	24.9986	21.4872	18.6646	16.3742	14.4982	12.9477	11.6546	10.5668	9.6442	8.8552	8.1755	7.5856
40	32.8347	27.3555	23.1148	19.7928	17.1591	15.0463	13.3317	11.9246	10.7574	9.7791	8.9511	8.2438	7.6344
45	36.0945	29.4902	24.5187	20.7200	17.7741	15.4558	13.6055	12.1084	10.8812	9.8628	9.0079	8.2825	7.6609
50	39.1961	31.4236	25.7298	21.4822	18.2559	15.7619	13.8007	12.2335	10.9617	9.9148	9.0417	8.3045	7.6752

Appendix B-3

Present Value of an Ordinary Annuity (continued)

Present Value of Ordinary Annuity

$$\left[\frac{1-\frac{1}{(1+i)^n}}{i}\right]$$

Period	14%	15%	16%	17%	18%	19%	20%	25%	30%	35%	40%	45%	50%
1	0.8772	0.8696	0.8621	0.8547	0.8475	0.8403	0.8333	0.8000	0.7692	0.7407	0.7143	0.6897	0.6667
2	1.6467	1.6257	1.6052	1.5852	1.5656	1.5465	1.5278	1.4400	1.3609	1.2894	1.2245	1.1653	1.1111
3	2.3216	2.2832	2.2459	2.2096	2.1743	2.1399	2.1065	1.9520	1.8161	1.6959	1.5889	1.4933	1.4074
4	2.9137	2.8550	2.7982	2.7432	2.6901	2.6386	2.5887	2.3616	2.1662	1.9969	1.8492	1.7195	1.6049
5	3.4331	3.3522	3.2743	3.1993	3.1272	3.0576	2.9906	2.6893	2.4356	2.2200	2.0352	1.8755	1.7366
6	3.8887	3.7845	3.6847	3.5892	3.4976	3.4098	3.3255	2.9514	2.6427	2.3852	2.1680	1.9831	1.8244
7	4.2883	4.1604	4.0386	3.9224	3.8115	3.7057	3.6046	3.1611	2.8021	2.5075	2.2628	2.0573	1.8829
8	4.6389	4.4873	4.3436	4.2072	4.0776	3.9544	3.8372	3.3289	2.9247	2.5982	2.3306	2.1085	1.9220
9	4.9464	4.7716	4.6065	4.4506	4.3030	4.1633	4.0310	3.4631	3.0190	2.6653	2.3790	2.1438	1.9480
10	5.2161	5.0188	4.8332	4.6586	4.4941	4.3389	4.1925	3.5705	3.0915	2.7150	2.4136	2.1681	1.9653
11	5.4527	5.2337	5.0286	4.8364	4.6560	4.4865	4.3271	3.6564	3.1473	2.7519	2.4383	2.1849	1.9769
12	5.6603	5.4206	5.1971	4.9884	4.7932	4.6105	4.4392	3.7251	3.1903	2.7792	2.4559	2.1965	1.9846
13	5.8424	5.5831	5.3423	5.1183	4.9095	4.7147	4.5327	3.7801	3.2233	2.7994	2.4685	2.2045	1.9897
14	6.0021	5.7245	5.4675	5.2293	5.0081	4.8023	4.6106	3.8241	3.2487	2.8144	2.4775	2.2100	1.9931
15	6.1422	5.8474	5.5755	5.3242	5.0916	4.8759	4.6755	3.8593	3.2682	2.8255	2.4839	2.2138	1.9954
16	6.2651	5.9542	5.6685	5.4053	5.1624	4.9377	4.7296	3.8874	3.2832	2.8337	2.4885	2.2164	1.9970
17	6.3729	6.0472	5.7487	5.4746	5.2223	4.9897	4.7746	3.9099	3.2948	2.8398	2.4918	2.2182	1.9980
18	6.4674	6.1280	5.8178	5.5339	5.2732	5.0333	4.8122	3.9279	3.3037	2.8443	2.4941	2.2195	1.9986
19	6.5504	6.1982	5.8775	5.5845	5.3162	5.0700	4.8435	3.9424	3.3105	2.8476	2.4958	2.2203	1.9991
20	6.6231	6.2593	5.9288	5.6278	5.3527	5.1009	4.8696	3.9539	3.3158	2.8501	2.4970	2.2209	1.9994
25	6.8729	6.4641	6.0971	5.7662	5.4669	5.1951	4.9476	3.9849	3.3286	2.8556	2.4994	2.2220	1.9999
30	7.0027	6.5660	6.1772	5.8294	5.5168	5.2347	4.9789	3.9950	3.3321	2.8568	2.4999	2.2222	2.0000
35	7.0700	6.6166	6.2153	5.8582	5.5386	5.2512	4.9915	3.9984	3.3330	2.8571	2.5000	2.2222	2.0000
40	7.1050	6.6418	6.2335	5.8713	5.5482	5.2582	4.9966	3.9995	3.3332	2.8571	2.5000	2.2222	2.0000
45	7.1232	6.6543	6.2421	5.8773	5.5523	5.2611	4.9986	3.9998	3.3333	2.8571	2.5000	2.2222	2.0000
50	7.1327	6.6605	6.2463	5.8801	5.5541	5.2623	4.9995	3.9999	3.3333	2.8571	2.5000	2.2222	2.0000

Appendix B-4

Future Value of an Ordinary Annuity

Future Value of Ordinary Annuity

$$\left[\frac{(1+i)^n - 1}{i}\right]$$

Period	1%	2%	3%	4%	5%	6%	7%	8%	9%	10%	11%	12%	13%
1	1.0000	1.0000	1.0000	1.0000	1.0000	1.0000	1.0000	1.0000	1.0000	1.0000	1.0000	1.0000	1.0000
2	2.0100	2.0200	2.0300	2.0400	2.0500	2.0600	2.0700	2.0800	2.0900	2.1000	2.1100	2.1200	2.1300
3	3.0301	3.0604	3.0909	3.1216	3.1525	3.1836	3.2149	3.2464	3.2781	3.3100	3.3421	3.3744	3.4069
4	4.0604	4.1216	4.1836	4.2465	4.3101	4.3746	4.4399	4.5061	4.5731	4.6410	4.7097	4.7793	4.8498
5	5.1010	5.2040	5.3091	5.4163	5.5256	5.6371	5.7507	5.8666	5.9847	6.1051	6.2278	6.3528	6.4803
6	6.1520	6.3081	6.4684	6.6330	6.8019	6.9753	7.1533	7.3359	7.5233	7.7156	7.9129	8.1152	8.3227
7	7.2135	7.4343	7.6625	7.8983	8.1420	8.3938	8.6540	8.9228	9.2004	9.4872	9.7833	10.0890	10.4047
8	8.2857	8.5830	8.8923	9.2142	9.5491	9.8975	10.2598	10.6366	11.0285	11.4359	11.8594	12.2997	12.7573
9	9.3685	9.7546	10.1591	10.5828	11.0266	11.4913	11.9780	12.4876	13.0210	13.5795	14.1640	14.7757	15.4157
10	10.4622	10.9497	11.4639	12.0061	12.5779	13.1808	13.8164	14.4866	15.1929	15.9374	16.7220	17.5487	18.4197
11	11.5668	12.1687	12.8078	13.4864	14.2068	14.9716	15.7836	16.6455	17.5603	18.5312	19.5614	20.6546	21.8143
12	12.6825	13.4121	14.1920	15.0258	15.9171	16.8699	17.8885	18.9771	20.1407	21.3843	22.7132	24.1331	25.6502
13	13.8093	14.6803	15.6178	16.6268	17.7130	18.8821	20.1406	21.4953	22.9534	24.5227	26.2116	28.0291	29.9847
14	14.9474	15.9739	17.0863	18.2919	19.5986	21.0151	22.5505	24.2149	26.0192	27.9750	30.0949	32.3926	34.8827
15	16.0969	17.2934	18.5989	20.0236	21.5786	23.2760	25.1290	27.1521	29.3609	31.7725	34.4054	37.2797	40.4175
16	17.2579	18.6393	20.1569	21.8245	23.6575	25.6725	27.8881	30.3243	33.0034	35.9497	39.1899	42.7533	46.6717
17	18.4304	20.0121	21.7616	23.6975	25.8404	28.2129	30.8402	33.7502	36.9737	40.5447	44.5008	48.8837	53.7391
18	19.6147	21.4123	23.4144	25.6454	28.1324	30.9057	33.9990	37.4502	41.3013	45.5992	50.3959	55.7497	61.7251
19	20.8109	22.8406	25.1169	27.6712	30.5390	33.7600	37.3790	41.4463	46.0185	51.1591	56.9395	63.4397	70.7494
20	22.0190	24.2974	26.8704	29.7781	33.0660	36.7856	40.9955	45.7620	51.1601	57.2750	64.2028	72.0524	80.9468
25	28.2432	32.0303	36.4593	41.6459	47.7271	54.8645	63.2490	73.1059	84.7009	98.3471	114.4133	133.3339	155.6196
30	34.7849	40.5681	47.5754	56.0849	66.4388	79.0582	94.4608	113.2832	136.3075	164.4940	199.0209	241.3327	293.1992
35	41.6603	49.9945	60.4621	73.6522	90.3203	111.4348	138.2369	172.3168	215.7108	271.0244	341.5896	431.6635	546.6808
40	48.8864	60.4020	75.4013	95.0255	120.7998	154.7620	199.6351	259.0565	337.8824	442.5926	581.8261	767.0914	1013.704
45	56.4811	71.8927	92.7199	121.0294	159.7002	212.7435	285.7493	386.5056	525.8587	718.9048	986.6386	1358.230	1874.165
50	64.4632	84.5794	112.7969	152.6671	209.3480	290.3359	406.5289	573.7702	815.0836	1163.909	1668.771	2400.018	3459.507

Appendix B-4

Future Value of an Ordinary Annuity (continued)

Future Value of Ordinary Annuity

$$\left[\frac{(1+i)^n - 1}{i}\right]$$

Period	14%	15%	16%	17%	18%	19%	20%	25%	30%	35%	40%	45%	50%
1	1.0000	1.0000	1.0000	1.0000	1.0000	1.0000	1.0000	1.0000	1.0000	1.0000	1.0000	1.0000	1.0000
2	2.1400	2.1500	2.1600	2.1700	2.1800	2.1900	2.2000	2.2500	2.3000	2.3500	2.4000	2.4500	2.5000
3	3.4396	3.4725	3.5056	3.5389	3.5724	3.6061	3.6400	3.8125	3.9900	4.1725	4.3600	4.5525	4.7500
4	4.9211	4.9934	5.0665	5.1405	5.2154	5.2913	5.3680	5.7656	6.1870	6.6329	7.1040	7.6011	8.1250
5	6.6101	6.7424	6.8771	7.0144	7.1542	7.2966	7.4416	8.2070	9.0431	9.9544	10.9456	12.0216	13.1875
6	8.5355	8.7537	8.9775	9.2068	9.4420	9.6830	9.9299	11.2588	12.7560	14.4384	16.3238	18.4314	20.7813
7	10.7305	11.0668	11.4139	11.7720	12.1415	12.5227	12.9159	15.0735	17.5828	20.4919	23.8534	27.7255	32.1719
8	13.2328	13.7268	14.2401	14.7733	15.3270	15.9020	16.4991	19.8419	23.8577	28.6640	34.3947	41.2019	49.2578
9	16.0853	16.7858	17.5185	18.2847	19.0859	19.9234	20.7989	25.8023	32.0150	39.6964	49.1526	60.7428	74.8867
10	19.3373	20.3037	21.3215	22.3931	23.5213	24.7089	25.9587	33.2529	42.6195	54.5902	69.8137	89.0771	113.3301
11	23.0445	24.3493	25.7329	27.1999	28.7551	30.4035	32.1504	42.5661	56.4053	74.6967	98.7391	130.1618	170.9951
12	27.2707	29.0017	30.8502	32.8239	34.9311	37.1802	39.5805	54.2077	74.3270	101.8406	139.2348	189.7346	257.4927
13	32.0887	34.3519	36.7862	39.4040	42.2187	45.2445	48.4966	68.7596	97.6250	138.4848	195.9287	276.1151	387.2390
14	37.5811	40.5047	43.6720	47.1027	50.8180	54.8409	59.1959	86.9495	127.9125	187.9544	275.3002	401.3670	581.8585
15	43.8424	47.5804	51.6595	56.1101	60.9653	66.2607	72.0351	109.6868	167.2863	254.7385	386.4202	582.9821	873.7878
16	50.9804	55.7175	60.9250	66.6488	72.9390	79.8502	87.4421	138.1085	218.4722	344.8970	541.9883	846.3240	1311.682
17	59.1176	65.0751	71.6730	78.9792	87.0680	96.0218	105.9306	173.6357	285.0139	466.6109	759.7837	1228.170	1968.523
18	68.3941	75.8364	84.1407	93.4056	103.7403	115.2659	128.1167	218.0446	371.5180	630.9247	1064.697	1781.846	2953.784
19	78.9692	88.2118	98.6032	110.2846	123.4135	138.1664	154.7400	273.5558	483.9734	852.7483	1491.576	2584.677	4431.676
20	91.0249	102.4436	115.3797	130.0329	146.6280	165.4180	186.6880	342.9447	630.1655	1152.210	2089.206	3748.782	6648.513
25	181.8708	212.7930	249.2140	292.1049	342.6035	402.0425	471.9811	1054.791	2348.803	5176.504	11247.20	24040.72	50500.34
30	356.7868	434.7451	530.3117	647.4391	790.9480	966.7122	1181.882	3227.174	8729.985	23221.57	60501.08	154106.6	383500.1
35	693.5727	881.1702	1120.713	1426.491	1816.652	2314.214	2948.341	9856.761	32422.87	104136.3	325400.3	987794.5	2912217
40	1342.025	1779.090	2360.757	3134.522	4163.213	5529.829	7343.858	30088.66	120392.9	466960.4	1750092	6331512	22114663
45	2590.565	3585.128	4965.274	6879.291	9531.577	13203.42	18281.31	91831.50	447019.4	2093876	9412424	40583319	167933233
50	4994.521	7217.716	10435.65	15089.50	21813.09	31515.34	45497.19	280255.7	1659761	9389020	50622288	260128295	1275242998

Appendix B-5

Present Value of an Annuity Due

Present Value of Annuity Due

$$\left[\frac{1-\frac{1}{(1+i)^{n-1}}}{i}+1\right]$$

Period	1%	2%	3%	4%	5%	6%	7%	8%	9%	10%	11%	12%	13%
1	1.0000	1.0000	1.0000	1.0000	1.0000	1.0000	1.0000	1.0000	1.0000	1.0000	1.0000	1.0000	1.0000
2	1.9901	1.9804	1.9709	1.9615	1.9524	1.9434	1.9346	1.9259	1.9174	1.9091	1.9009	1.8929	1.8850
3	2.9704	2.9416	2.9135	2.8861	2.8594	2.8334	2.8080	2.7833	2.7591	2.7355	2.7125	2.6901	2.6681
4	3.9410	3.8839	3.8286	3.7751	3.7232	3.6730	3.6243	3.5771	3.5313	3.4869	3.4437	3.4018	3.3612
5	4.9020	4.8077	4.7171	4.6299	4.5460	4.4651	4.3872	4.3121	4.2397	4.1699	4.1024	4.0373	3.9745
6	5.8534	5.7135	5.5797	5.4518	5.3295	5.2124	5.1002	4.9927	4.8897	4.7908	4.6959	4.6048	4.5172
7	6.7955	6.6014	6.4172	6.2421	6.0757	5.9173	5.7665	5.6229	5.4859	5.3553	5.2305	5.1114	4.9975
8	7.7282	7.4720	7.2303	7.0021	6.7864	6.5824	6.3893	6.2064	6.0330	5.8684	5.7122	5.5638	5.4226
9	8.6517	8.3255	8.0197	7.7327	7.4632	7.2098	6.9713	6.7466	6.5348	6.3349	6.1461	5.9676	5.7988
10	9.5660	9.1622	8.7861	8.4353	8.1078	7.8017	7.5152	7.2469	6.9952	6.7590	6.5370	6.3282	6.1317
11	10.4713	9.9826	9.5302	9.1109	8.7217	8.3601	8.0236	7.7101	7.4177	7.1446	6.8892	6.6502	6.4262
12	11.3676	10.7868	10.2526	9.7605	9.3064	8.8869	8.4987	8.1390	7.8052	7.4951	7.2065	6.9377	6.6869
13	12.2551	11.5753	10.9540	10.3851	9.8633	9.3838	8.9427	8.5361	8.1607	7.8137	7.4924	7.1944	6.9176
14	13.1337	12.3484	11.6350	10.9856	10.3936	9.8527	9.3577	8.9038	8.4869	8.1034	7.7499	7.4235	7.1218
15	14.0037	13.1062	12.2961	11.5631	10.8986	10.2950	9.7455	9.2442	8.7862	8.3667	7.9819	7.6282	7.3025
16	14.8651	13.8493	12.9379	12.1184	11.3797	10.7122	10.1079	9.5595	9.0607	8.6061	8.1909	7.8109	7.4624
17	15.7179	14.5777	13.5611	12.6523	11.8378	11.1059	10.4466	9.8514	9.3126	8.8237	8.3792	7.9740	7.6039
18	16.5623	15.2919	14.1661	13.1657	12.2741	11.4773	10.7632	10.1216	9.5436	9.0216	8.5488	8.1196	7.7291
19	17.3983	15.9920	14.7535	13.6593	12.6896	11.8276	11.0591	10.3719	9.7556	9.2014	8.7016	8.2497	7.8399
20	18.2260	16.6785	15.3238	14.1339	13.0853	12.1581	11.3356	10.6036	9.9501	9.3649	8.8393	8.3658	7.9380
25	22.2434	19.9139	17.9355	16.2470	14.7986	13.5504	12.4693	11.5288	10.7066	9.9847	9.3481	8.7843	8.2829
30	26.0658	22.8444	20.1885	17.9837	16.1411	14.5907	13.2777	12.1584	11.1983	10.3696	9.6501	9.0218	8.4701
35	29.7027	25.4986	22.1318	19.4112	17.1929	15.3681	13.8540	12.5869	11.5178	10.6086	9.8293	9.1566	8.5717
40	33.1630	27.9026	23.8082	20.5845	18.0170	15.9491	14.2649	12.8786	11.7255	10.7570	9.9357	9.2330	8.6268
45	36.4555	30.0800	25.2543	21.5488	18.6628	16.3832	14.5579	13.0771	11.8605	10.8491	9.9988	9.2764	8.6568
50	39.5881	32.0521	26.5017	22.3415	19.1687	16.7076	14.7668	13.2122	11.9482	10.9063	10.0362	9.3010	8.6730

Appendix B-5

Present Value of an Annuity Due (continued)

Present Value of Annuity Due

$$\left[\frac{1-\frac{1}{(1+i)^{n-1}}}{i}+1\right]$$

Period	14%	15%	16%	17%	18%	19%	20%	25%	30%	35%	40%	45%	50%
1	1.0000	1.0000	1.0000	1.0000	1.0000	1.0000	1.0000	1.0000	1.0000	1.0000	1.0000	1.0000	1.0000
2	1.8772	1.8696	1.8621	1.8547	1.8475	1.8403	1.8333	1.8000	1.7692	1.7407	1.7143	1.6897	1.6667
3	2.6467	2.6257	2.6052	2.5852	2.5656	2.5465	2.5278	2.4400	2.3609	2.2894	2.2245	2.1653	2.1111
4	3.3216	3.2832	3.2459	3.2096	3.1743	3.1399	3.1065	2.9520	2.8161	2.6959	2.5889	2.4933	2.4074
5	3.9137	3.8550	3.7982	3.7432	3.6901	3.6386	3.5887	3.3616	3.1662	2.9969	2.8492	2.7195	2.6049
6	4.4331	4.3522	4.2743	4.1993	4.1272	4.0576	3.9906	3.6893	3.4356	3.2200	3.0352	2.8755	2.7366
7	4.8887	4.7845	4.6847	4.5892	4.4976	4.4098	4.3255	3.9514	3.6427	3.3852	3.1680	2.9831	2.8244
8	5.2883	5.1604	5.0386	4.9224	4.8115	4.7057	4.6046	4.1611	3.8021	3.5075	3.2628	3.0573	2.8829
9	5.6389	5.4873	5.3436	5.2072	5.0776	4.9544	4.8372	4.3289	3.9247	3.5982	3.3306	3.1085	2.9220
10	5.9464	5.7716	5.6065	5.4506	5.3030	5.1633	5.0310	4.4631	4.0190	3.6653	3.3790	3.1438	2.9480
11	6.2161	6.0188	5.8332	5.6586	5.4941	5.3389	5.1925	4.5705	4.0915	3.7150	3.4136	3.1681	2.9653
12	6.4527	6.2337	6.0286	5.8364	5.6560	5.4865	5.3271	4.6564	4.1473	3.7519	3.4383	3.1849	2.9769
13	6.6603	6.4206	6.1971	5.9884	5.7932	5.6105	5.4392	4.7251	4.1903	3.7792	3.4559	3.1965	2.9846
14	6.8424	6.5831	6.3423	6.1183	5.9095	5.7147	5.5327	4.7801	4.2233	3.7994	3.4685	3.2045	2.9897
15	7.0021	6.7245	6.4675	6.2293	6.0081	5.8023	5.6106	4.8241	4.2487	3.8144	3.4775	3.2100	2.9931
16	7.1422	6.8474	6.5755	6.3242	6.0916	5.8759	5.6755	4.8593	4.2682	3.8255	3.4839	3.2138	2.9954
17	7.2651	6.9542	6.6685	6.4053	6.1624	5.9377	5.7296	4.8874	4.2832	3.8337	3.4885	3.2164	2.9970
18	7.3729	7.0472	6.7487	6.4746	6.2223	5.9897	5.7746	4.9099	4.2948	3.8398	3.4918	3.2182	2.9980
19	7.4674	7.1280	6.8178	6.5339	6.2732	6.0333	5.8122	4.9279	4.3037	3.8443	3.4941	3.2195	2.9986
20	7.5504	7.1982	6.8775	6.5845	6.3162	6.0700	5.8435	4.9424	4.3105	3.8476	3.4958	3.2203	2.9991
25	7.8351	7.4338	7.0726	6.7465	6.4509	6.1822	5.9371	4.9811	4.3272	3.8550	3.4992	3.2219	2.9999
30	7.9830	7.5509	7.1656	6.8204	6.5098	6.2292	5.9747	4.9938	4.3317	3.8567	3.4999	3.2222	3.0000
35	8.0599	7.6091	7.2098	6.8541	6.5356	6.2489	5.9898	4.9980	4.3329	3.8570	3.5000	3.2222	3.0000
40	8.0997	7.6380	7.2309	6.8695	6.5468	6.2572	5.9959	4.9993	4.3332	3.8571	3.5000	3.2222	3.0000
45	8.1205	7.6524	7.2409	6.8765	6.5517	6.2607	5.9984	4.9998	4.3333	3.8571	3.5000	3.2222	3.0000
50	8.1312	7.6596	7.2457	6.8797	6.5539	6.2621	5.9993	4.9999	4.3333	3.8571	3.5000	3.2222	3.0000

Appendix B-6

Future Value of an Annuity Due

Future Value of Annuity Due

$$\left[\frac{(1+i)^n - 1}{i}\right] \times \left[1+i\right]$$

Period	1%	2%	3%	4%	5%	6%	7%	8%	9%	10%	11%	12%	13%
1	1.0100	1.0200	1.0300	1.0400	1.0500	1.0600	1.0700	1.0800	1.0900	1.1000	1.1100	1.1200	1.1300
2	2.0301	2.0604	2.0909	2.1216	2.1525	2.1836	2.2149	2.2464	2.2781	2.3100	2.3421	2.3744	2.4069
3	3.0604	3.1216	3.1836	3.2465	3.3101	3.3746	3.4399	3.5061	3.5731	3.6410	3.7097	3.7793	3.8498
4	4.1010	4.2040	4.3091	4.4163	4.5256	4.6371	4.7507	4.8666	4.9847	5.1051	5.2278	5.3528	5.4803
5	5.1520	5.3081	5.4684	5.6330	5.8019	5.9753	6.1533	6.3359	6.5233	6.7156	6.9129	7.1152	7.3227
6	6.2135	6.4343	6.6625	6.8983	7.1420	7.3938	7.6540	7.9228	8.2004	8.4872	8.7833	9.0890	9.4047
7	7.2857	7.5830	7.8923	8.2142	8.5491	8.8975	9.2598	9.6366	10.0285	10.4359	10.8594	11.2997	11.7573
8	8.3685	8.7546	9.1591	9.5828	10.0266	10.4913	10.9780	11.4876	12.0210	12.5795	13.1640	13.7757	14.4157
9	9.4622	9.9497	10.4639	11.0061	11.5779	12.1808	12.8164	13.4866	14.1929	14.9374	15.7220	16.5487	17.4197
10	10.5668	11.1687	11.8078	12.4864	13.2068	13.9716	14.7836	15.6455	16.5603	17.5312	18.5614	19.6546	20.8143
11	11.6825	12.4121	13.1920	14.0258	14.9171	15.8699	16.8885	17.9771	19.1407	20.3843	21.7132	23.1331	24.6502
12	12.8093	13.6803	14.6178	15.6268	16.7130	17.8821	19.1406	20.4953	21.9534	23.5227	25.2116	27.0291	28.9847
13	13.9474	14.9739	16.0863	17.2919	18.5986	20.0151	21.5505	23.2149	25.0192	26.9750	29.0949	31.3926	33.8827
14	15.0969	16.2934	17.5989	19.0236	20.5786	22.2760	24.1290	26.1521	28.3609	30.7725	33.4054	36.2797	39.4175
15	16.2579	17.6393	19.1569	20.8245	22.6575	24.6725	26.8881	29.3243	32.0034	34.9497	38.1899	41.7533	45.6717
16	17.4304	19.0121	20.7616	22.6975	24.8404	27.2129	29.8402	32.7502	35.9737	39.5447	43.5008	47.8837	52.7391
17	18.6147	20.4123	22.4144	24.6454	27.1324	29.9057	32.9990	36.4502	40.3013	44.5992	49.3959	54.7497	60.7251
18	19.8109	21.8406	24.1169	26.6712	29.5390	32.7600	36.3790	40.4463	45.0185	50.1591	55.9395	62.4397	69.7494
19	21.0190	23.2974	25.8704	28.7781	32.0660	35.7856	39.9955	44.7620	50.1601	56.2750	63.2028	71.0524	79.9468
20	22.2392	24.7833	27.6765	30.9692	34.7193	38.9927	43.8652	49.4229	55.7645	63.0025	71.2651	80.6987	91.4699
25	28.5256	32.6709	37.5530	43.3117	50.1135	58.1564	67.6765	78.9544	92.3240	108.1818	126.9988	149.3339	175.8501
30	35.1327	41.3794	49.0027	58.3283	69.7608	83.8017	101.0730	122.3459	148.5752	180.9434	220.9132	270.2926	331.3151
35	42.0769	50.9944	62.2759	76.5983	94.8363	118.1209	147.9135	186.1021	235.1247	298.1268	379.1644	483.4631	617.7493
40	49.3752	61.6100	77.6633	98.8265	126.8398	164.0477	213.6096	279.7810	368.2919	486.8518	645.8269	859.1424	1145.486
45	57.0459	73.3306	95.5015	125.8706	167.6852	225.5081	305.7518	417.4261	573.1860	790.7953	1095.169	1521.218	2117.806
50	65.1078	86.2710	116.1808	158.7738	219.8154	307.7561	434.9860	619.6718	888.4411	1280.299	1852.336	2688.020	3909.243

Appendix B-6

Future Value of an Annuity Due (Continued)

Future Value of Annuity Due

$$\left[\frac{(1+i)^n - 1}{i}\right] \times \left[1+i\right]$$

Period	14%	15%	16%	17%	18%	19%	20%	25%	30%	35%	40%	45%	50%
1	1.1400	1.1500	1.1600	1.1700	1.1800	1.1900	1.2000	1.2500	1.3000	1.3500	1.4000	1.4500	1.5000
2	2.4396	2.4725	2.5056	2.5389	2.5724	2.6061	2.6400	2.8125	2.9900	3.1725	3.3600	3.5525	3.7500
3	3.9211	3.9934	4.0665	4.1405	4.2154	4.2913	4.3680	4.7656	5.1870	5.6329	6.1040	6.6011	7.1250
4	5.6101	5.7424	5.8771	6.0144	6.1542	6.2966	6.4416	7.2070	8.0431	8.9544	9.9456	11.0216	12.1875
5	7.5355	7.7537	7.9775	8.2068	8.4420	8.6830	8.9299	10.2588	11.7560	13.4384	15.3238	17.4314	19.7813
6	9.7305	10.0668	10.4139	10.7720	11.1415	11.5227	11.9159	14.0735	16.5828	19.4919	22.8534	26.7255	31.1719
7	12.2328	12.7268	13.2401	13.7733	14.3270	14.9020	15.4991	18.8419	22.8577	27.6640	33.3947	40.2019	48.2578
8	15.0853	15.7858	16.5185	17.2847	18.0859	18.9234	19.7989	24.8023	31.0150	38.6964	48.1526	59.7428	73.8867
9	18.3373	19.3037	20.3215	21.3931	22.5213	23.7089	24.9587	32.2529	41.6195	53.5902	68.8137	88.0771	112.3301
10	22.0445	23.3493	24.7329	26.1999	27.7551	29.4035	31.1504	41.5661	55.4053	73.6967	97.7391	129.1618	169.9951
11	26.2707	28.0017	29.8502	31.8239	33.9311	36.1802	38.5805	53.2077	73.3270	100.8406	138.2348	188.7346	256.4927
12	31.0887	33.3519	35.7862	38.4040	41.2187	44.2445	47.4966	67.7596	96.6250	137.4848	194.9287	275.1151	386.2390
13	36.5811	39.5047	42.6720	46.1027	49.8180	53.8409	58.1959	85.9495	126.9125	186.9544	274.3002	400.3670	580.8585
14	42.8424	46.5804	50.6595	55.1101	59.9653	65.2607	71.0351	108.6868	166.2863	253.7385	385.4202	581.9821	872.7878
15	49.9804	54.7175	59.9250	65.6488	71.9390	78.8502	86.4421	137.1085	217.4722	343.8970	540.9883	845.3240	1310.6817
16	58.1176	64.0751	70.6730	77.9792	86.0680	95.0218	104.9306	172.6357	284.0139	465.6109	758.7837	1227.1699	1967.5225
17	67.3941	74.8364	83.1407	92.4056	102.7403	114.2659	127.1167	217.0446	370.5180	629.9247	1063.697	1780.8463	2952.7838
18	77.9692	87.2118	97.6032	109.2846	122.4135	137.1664	153.7400	272.5558	482.9734	851.7483	1490.576	2583.6771	4430.6756
19	90.0249	101.4436	114.3797	129.0329	145.6280	164.4180	185.6880	341.9447	629.1655	1151.210	2088.206	3747.7818	6647.5135
20	103.7684	117.8101	133.8405	152.1385	173.0210	196.8474	224.0256	428.6809	819.2151	1555.484	2924.889	5435.7336	9972.7702
25	207.3327	244.7120	289.0883	341.7627	404.2721	478.4306	566.3773	1318.489	3053.444	6988.280	15746.08	34859.038	75750.5049
30	406.7370	499.9569	615.1616	757.5038	933.3186	1150.387	1418.258	4033.968	11348.98	31349.12	84701.51	223454.60	575250.178
35	790.6729	1013.346	1300.027	1668.994	2143.649	2753.914	3538.009	12320.95	42149.73	140583.9	455560.4	1432302.0	4368325.82
40	1529.909	2045.954	2738.478	3667.391	4912.591	6580.496	8812.629	37610.82	156510.7	630396.5	2450128	9180692.2	33171994.0
45	2953.244	4122.898	5759.718	8048.770	11247.26	15712.07	21937.57	114789.4	581125.2	2826733	13177394	58845813	251899849
50	5693.75	8300.37	12105.35	17654.72	25739.45	37503.25	54596.63	350319.6	2157689	12675177	70871203	377186028	1912864498

Appendix C

Regulatory Requirements

REGULATORY REQUIREMENTS—FEDERAL SECURITIES REGULATION

INTRODUCTION

The issuance and sale of corporate securities are extensively regulated by the Securities and Exchange Commission (SEC), a federal agency that administers the Securities Act of 1933, the Securities Exchange Act of 1934, and other federal statutes. A major objective of securities regulation is to protect the investing public by requiring full and correct disclosure of relevant information. Both the federal and state governments require a substantial amount of regulation; however, most is from the federal government because the majority of trading is across state borders.

THE SECURITIES ACT OF 1933

This securities act is primarily concerned with new issues of securities or issues in the primary market. The term investment security is broadly defined as:

"Any note, stock, treasury stock, bond, debenture, evidence of indebtedness, certificate of interest or participation in any profit-sharing agreement ... investment contract… or, in general, any interest or instrument commonly known as a 'security' or any certificate of interest or participation in ... receipt for ... or right to subscribe to or purchase, any of the foregoing".

Any transaction in which a person invests money or property in a common enterprise or venture or an investor who reasonably expects to make a profit primarily or substantially as a result of the managerial efforts of others is regulated by this act.

The 1933 Act requires full disclosure of material information that is relevant to investment decisions, and prohibits fraud and misstatements when securities are offered to the public through the mail and/or interstate commerce. Registration statements, including financial statements, must be filed with the Securities and Exchange Commission (SEC) before investment securities can be offered for sale by an issuer. A registration statement contains a thorough description of the securities, the financial structure, condition and management personnel of the issuing corporation, and a description of material pending litigation against the issuing corporation. This statement is filed with the SEC. The 1933 Act also requires that a prospectus, based upon the information in the registration statement, be given to any prospective investor or purchaser.

Securities that are exempt from registration requirements include:

- ▲ Intrastate offerings where all offerees and issuers are residents of the state in which issuer performs substantially all of its operations.
- ▲ The issuer is a governmental body or nonprofit organization.
- ▲ The issuer is a bank, savings institution, common carrier, or farmers' cooperative and is subject to other regulatory legislation.
- ▲ Commercial paper having a maturity date of less than 9 months (270 days).
- ▲ Stock dividends, stock splits, and securities issued in connection with corporate reorganizations.
- ▲ Insurance, endowment, and annuity contracts.

Regulation A requires less demanding disclosures and registration for small issues of less than $1,500,000. Regulation D lists those transactions that are exempt from registration requirement:

- ▲ Private, noninvestment company sales of less than $500,000 worth of securities in a twelve-month period to investors who will not resell the securities within two years.
- ▲ Private, noninvestment company sales of less than $5,000,000 worth of securities in a twelve-month period to:
  - ▲ Accredited investors - Natural persons with annual income of more than $200,000 or whose net worth exceeds $1,000,000; or
  - ▲ Investors who are furnished with purchaser representatives who are knowledgeable and experienced regarding finance and business; or
  - ▲ Up to 35 unaccredited investors that have financial and business knowledge and experience, who are furnished with the same information as would be contained in a full registration statement prospectus.
  - ▲ Sales of any amount of securities to accredited investors or those furnished with independent purchaser representatives (private placement).

The Securities Exchange Act of 1934 (SEA)

While the Securities Act of 1933 was limited to new issues, the 1934 Securities Act extended the regulation to securities sold in the secondary markets. The Act provided the following provisions:

- ▲ Establishment of the SEC - The SEC's primary function is to regulate the securities markets.
- ▲ Disclosure requirements for Secondary Market - Annual reports and other financial reports are required to be filed with the SEC prior to listing on the organized exchanges. These reports include the annual 10K Report, which must be audited, and the quarterly 10Q Report, which is not required to be audited.
- ▲ Registration of organized exchanges - All organized exchanges must register with the SEC and provide copies of their rules and bylaws.
- ▲ Credit regulation - Congress gave the Federal Reserve Board the power to set margin requirements for credit purchases of securities. Securities dealers' indebtedness was also limited to 20 times their owners' equity capital by this act.
- ▲ Proxy solicitation - Specific rules governing solicitation of proxies were established.
- ▲ Exemptions - Securities of federal, state, and local governments, securities that are not traded across state lines, and any other securities specified by the SEC are exempt from registering with the SEC. This includes Treasury bonds and municipal bonds.
- ▲ Insider activities - A public report, called an insider report, must be filed with the SEC in every month that a change in the holding of a firm's securities occurs for an officer, director, or 10% or more shareholder. The 1934 SEA forbids insiders profiting from securities held less than 6 months and requires these profits be returned to the organization. In addition, short sales are not permitted by individuals considered to be insiders.
- ▲ Price manipulation - The SEA of 1934 forbids price manipulation schemes such as wash sales, pools, circulation of manipulative information, and false and misleading statements about securities.

Liability under the Securities Exchange Act of 1934

The Securities Exchange Act of 1934 relates to the purchase and sale of investment securities in the market (i.e., being public). Section 18 states that a financial planner is liable for false and/or misleading statements of material facts that are made in applications, reports, documents, and registration statements, which are prepared by the financial planner and filed with the SEC. Liability is imposed upon those (including financial planners) who, because of their inside positions, have access to material information (which is not available to the public and which may affect the value of securities) and trade in the securities without making a disclosure.

A financial planner may be liable to a person who purchased or sold securities when it can be established that:

- The statement or omission was material.
- The financial planner intended to deceive or defraud others.
- As a result of his or her reasonable reliance upon the misrepresentation, the purchaser or seller incurred a loss.

Criminal liability for willful conduct is imposed by the Securities Act of 1933, the Securities Exchange Act of 1934, the Internal Revenue Act, and other Federal statutes as well as state criminal codes.

NASD

Note: The following excerpts from "An Explanation of the NASD Regulations and Qualification Requirements – February 1998" have been reprinted with the permission of the NASD.

The National Association of Securities Dealers, Inc. (NASD) is a self-regulatory organization of the securities industry that was established under the 1938 Maloney Act Amendments and is subject to oversight by the Securities and Exchange Commission. The NASD is responsible for the regulation of the NASDAQ Stock Market as well as the over-the-counter securities market. Through its subsidiaries, NASD Regulation Inc. and the NASDAQ Stock Market, Inc., the NASD develops rules and regulations, conducts regulatory reviews of members' business activities, and designs and operates marketplace services and facilities. The NASD helps establish and coordinate the policies for its two subsidiaries and oversees their effectiveness.

NASD Regulation, Inc. (NASDR) was established in 1996 as a separate, independent subsidiary of the National Association of Securities Dealers, Inc. to separate the regulation of the broker/dealer professional from the operation of the NASDAQ Stock Market. The purpose of NASDR is to regulate the securities markets for the benefit and protection of investors.

Membership in the NASD entitles a firm to participate in the investment banking and over-the-counter securities business, to distribute new issues underwritten by NASD members and to distribute shares of investment companies sponsored by NASD members.

The Investment Advisors Act of 1940

Any individual or firm who provides investment advice to 15 or more interstate clients during a twelve-month period is required to register with the SEC and file educational and background information for all Registered Investment Advisors (RIAs). This act also forbids RIAs from assigning investment advisory contracts to other advisors without permission from the client, entering into profit-sharing agreements with clients, and advertising with selected testimonials. An investment adviser is a person who meets the following three tests:

- Provides advice, or issues reports or analyses, regarding securities;
- Is in the business of providing such services; and
- Provides such services for compensation (compensation is "the receipt of any economic benefit" including commissions on the sale of products).

Certain organizations and individuals are excluded, including:

- Banks and bank holding companies (except as amended by the Gramm-Leach-Bliley Act of 1999).
- Lawyers, accountants, engineers, or teachers, if their performance of advisory services is solely incidental to their professions.
- Brokers or dealers, if their performance of advisory services is solely incidental to the conduct of their business as

brokers or dealers, and they do not receive any special compensation for their advisory services.

- Publishers of bona fide newspapers, news magazines, or business or financial publications of general and regular circulation.
- Those persons whose advice is related only to securities, which are, direct obligations of, or guaranteed by, the United States.
- Incidental practice exception is not available to individuals who hold themselves out to the public as providing financial planning, pension consulting, or other financial advisory services.

The Act provides limited exemptions. Investment advisers who, during the course of the preceding 12 months, had fewer than 15 clients and do not hold themselves out generally to the public as investment advisers. The Act generally requires investment advisers entering into an advisory contract with a client to deliver a written disclosure statement on their background and business practices. Form ADV Part II must be given to a client under Rule 204-3, known as the "brochure" rule. The 1940 Adviser's Act and the SEC's rules require that advisers maintain and preserve specified books and records and make them available for inspection.

In accordance with the Investment Adviser Brochure Rule, an investment adviser shall furnish each advisory client and prospective client with a written disclosure statement which may be a copy of Part II of Form ADV, or written documents containing at least the information required by Part II of Form ADV, or such other information as the administrator may require.

Disclosure should be delivered not less than 48 hours prior to entering into any investment advisory contract with such client or prospective client, or at the time of entering into any contract, if the advisory client has a right to terminate the contract without penalty within five business days after entering into the contract.

If an investment adviser renders substantially different types of investment advisory services to different advisory clients, any information required by Part II of Form ADV may be omitted from the statement furnished to an advisory client or prospective advisory client if such information is applicable only to a type of investment advisory service or fee which is not rendered or charged, or proposed to be rendered or charged, to that client or prospective client.

Restriction on the use of the term Investment Counsel - A registered investment adviser may not use the term investment counsel unless its principal business is acting as an investment adviser and a substantial portion of its business is providing "investment supervisory services."

Anti-Fraud Provisions - Section 206 of the Act, Section 17 of the Securities Act of 1933, Section 10(b) of the Securities Exchange Act of 1934, and Rule 10b-5 prohibit misstatements or misleading omissions of material facts, fraudulent acts, and practices in connection with the purchase or sale of securities or the conduct of an investment advisory business. An investment adviser owes his or her clients undivided loyalty and may not engage in activity that conflicts with a client's interest.

- ▲ Registration - Form ADV is kept current by filing periodic amendments. Form ADV-W is used to withdraw as an investment adviser.
- ▲ Filing Requirements.
- ▲ Forms - ADV and ADV-W can be obtained from the SEC's Office of Consumer Affairs and Information Services in Washington, DC, or from the Commission office in your area (www.sec.gov/divisions/investment.shtml).
- ▲ Copies - All advisers' filings must be submitted in triplicate and typewritten. Copies can be filed, but each must be signed manually.
- ▲ Fees - Must include a registration fee of $150 (for assets under management of less than $25 million), by check or money order payable to the Securities and Exchange Commission, with your initial application of Form ADV. No part of this fee can be refunded.
- ▲ Name and Signatures - Full names are required. Each copy of an execution page must contain an original manual signature.

REGISTRATION

In the Fall of 1996, Congress amended the Advisors Act to reallocate regulatory responsibility for investment advisers between the Commission and state authorities. Congress did this by prohibiting certain advisers from registering with the Commission. As a result, for the most part, larger advisers will be regulated by the Commission, and smaller advisers will be regulated by state securities authorities. Only certain types of advisers are permitted to register with the Commission (and, therefore, must register with the Commission, unless exempt under a specific rule). Following is a list of advisers who are permitted to register with the Commission:

- ▲ Advisers having "assets under management" of $25 million or more. The $25 million threshold has been increased to $30 million. However, advisers with assets under management between $25 million and $30 million may still register with the Commission. Advisers with assets under management less than $25 million are generally required to register at the state level.
- ▲ Advisers to registered investment companies.
- ▲ Advisers who have their principal office and place of business in a state that has not enacted an investment adviser statute or that have their principal office and place of business outside the United States.
- ▲ Advisers are required to report their eligibility for Commission registration on Schedule I to Form ADV upon initial registration. Schedule I must be filed every year to establish and report their continuing eligibility for Commission registrations.

Investment Adviser Registration Depository

Note: The following excerpts from "What is IARD?" have been reprinted with the permission of the NASD.

The Investment Adviser Registration Depository (IARD) is an electronic filing system for Investment Advisers sponsored by the Securities and Exchange Commission (SEC) and North American Securities Administrators Association (NASAA), with NASD Regulation, Inc. serving as the developer and operator of the system. The IARD system collects and maintains the registration and disclosure information for Investment Advisers and their associated persons. The new IARD system supports electronic filing of the revised Forms ADV and ADV-W, centralized fee and form processing, regulatory review, the annual registration renewal process, and public disclosure of Investment Adviser information (www.iard.com).

NASD Regulation does not have regulatory authority over Investment Advisers; however, it was chosen to develop, operate, and maintain the system because of its regulatory business and technical expertise and the success of its Web-based licensing and regulation system, Web CRD℠, deployed in 1999. Web CRD is a state-of-the-art Web application for the registration of broker/dealers and their representatives. IARD provides regulators with the ability to monitor and process Investment Adviser information via a single, centralized system.

The SEC has mandated its Investment Adviser registrants use the system to make all filings with the Commission beginning January 1, 2001. The IARD system satisfies the requirements of the National Securities Markets Improvement Act (NSMIA,1996), which authorized electronic system registration of Investment Advisers.

IARD provides a mechanism that allows federal Investment Advisers to satisfy the SEC mandate for electronic filing and related public disclosure. The system also offers states similar benefits by facilitating "Notice Filing" requirements for federal filers and registration requirements of state-regulated Investment Advisers. In the near future, IARD will provide for the registration of Investment Adviser Representatives (IARs).

IARD is composed of four critical components: IA Firm Registration, IA Firm Public Disclosure, IAR Registration, which is registration of individual investment advisers, and IAR Public Disclosure. The Firm Registration component was released into production on January 1, 2001. This allows Investment Adviser firms to file a Form ADV and/or Form ADV-W electronically with the SEC and states. This release also provides the ability to view the information contained on the filings, collect and disburse fees associated with these filings, request reports, and allow firms that are both broker/dealers and Investment Advisers to share filing information between Web CRD and IARD.

Due Diligence

Due diligence requires that investment advisers investigate any security prior to offering it for sale to a client. Additionally, the security must be "suited" to the client's needs and objectives.

Due diligence is addressed in the Securities Act of 1933.

REFORM OF PREVIOUS ACTS

The Glass-Steagall Act (1933) prohibited commercial banks from acting as investment bankers, established the Federal Deposit Insurance Corporation (FDIC), and prohibited commercial banks from paying interest on demand deposits. This was one of the first of many securities regulation laws that impacted the investment markets. However, the Gramm-Leach-Bliley Act, passed by Congress in November 1999, eliminated many of the restrictions against affiliations among banks, securities firms, and insurance companies.

The Act repealed the affiliation sections of the Glass-Steagall Act that prohibited a bank holding company and a securities firm that underwrites and deals in ineligible securities from owning and controlling each other.

It also amended the Bank Holding Company Act (1956) to permit cross-ownership and control among bank holding companies, securities firms and insurance companies, provided that such cross-ownership and control is effected through a financial holding company that engages in activities that conform to the Act.

A bank must register as an investment adviser if it provides investment advice to a registered investment company, provided that, if the bank provides such advice through a "separately identified department or division," that department or division shall be deemed to be the investment adviser.

INVESTMENT COMPANY ACT OF 1940

Investment Company Act of 1940 requires registration with the SEC and restricts activities of investment companies (including mutual funds). The Investment Company Act of 1940 governs the management of investment companies. This act requires that investment companies register with the SEC, provide prospectuses to investors prior to the sale of shares, disclose the investment goals of the company, have outside members on the board of directors, use uniform accounting practices, and gain approval by shareholders for changes in management.

Appendix D

Topic List for the CFP® Certification Examination

General Principles of Financial Planning	Investment Planning	Retirement Planning
1. Financial planning process 2. CFP Board's Code of Ethics and Professional Responsibility and Disciplinary Rules and Procedures 3. CFP Board's Financial Planning Practice Standards 4. Financial statements 5. Cash flow management 6. Financing strategies 7. Function, purpose, and regulation of financial institutions 8. Educational planning 9. Financial planning for special circumstances 10. Economic concepts 11. Time value of money concepts and calculations 12. Financial services industry regulation requirements 13. Business Law 14. Consumer protection laws	34. Characteristics, uses and taxation of investment vehicles 35. Types of investment risk 36. Quantitative investment concepts 37. Measures of investment returns 38. Bond and stock valuation concepts 39. Investment theory 40. Portfolio development and analysis 41. Investment strategies 42. Asset allocation and portfolio diversification 43. Asset pricing models	59. Retirement needs analysis 60. Social Security [Old Age, Survivor, and Disability Insurance (OASDI)] 61. Types of retirement plans 62. Qualified plan rules and options 63. Other tax-advantaged retirement plans 64. Regulatory considerations 65. Key factors affecting plan selection for businesses 66. Investment considerations for retirement plans 67. Distribution rules, alternatives, and taxation
Insurance Planning and Risk Management	**Income Tax Planning**	**Estate Planning**
15. Principles of insurance 16. Analysis and evaluation of risk exposures 17. Property casualty and liability insurance 18. Health insurance and health care cost management (individual) 19. Disability income insurance (individual) 20. Long-term care insurance (individual) 21. Life insurance (individual) 22. Income taxation of life insurance 23. Business uses of insurance 24. Insurance needs analysis 25. Insurance policy and company selection 26. Annuities **Employee Benefits Planning** 27. Group life insurance 28. Group disability insurance 29. Group medical insurance 30. Other employee benefits 31. Employee stock options 32. Stock plans 33. Nonqualified deferred compensation	44. Income tax law fundamentals 45. Tax compliance 46. Income tax fundamentals and calculations 47. Tax accounting 48. Characteristics and income taxation of business entities 49. Income taxation of trusts and estates 50. Basis 51. Depreciation/cost-recovery concepts 52. Tax consequences of like-kind exchanges 53. Tax consequences of disposition of property 54. Alternative Minimum Tax (AMT) 55. Tax reduction/management techniques 56. Passive activity and at-risk rules 57. Tax implications of special circumstances 58. Charitable contributions and deductions	68. Characteristics and consequences of property titling 69. Methods of property transfer at death 70. Estate planning documents 71. Gifting strategies 72. Gift tax compliance and tax calculation 73. Incapacity planning 74. Estate tax compliance and tax calculation 75. Sources for estate liquidity 76. Powers of appointment 77. Types, features, and taxation of trusts 78. Qualified interest trusts 79. Charitable transfers 80. Use of life insurance in estate planning 81. Valuation issues 82. Marital deduction 83. Deferral and minimization of estate taxes 84. Intra-family and other business transfer techniques 85. Generation-Skipping Transfer Tax (GSTT) 86. Fiduciaries 87. Income in Respect of Decedent (IRD) 88. Postmortem estate planning techniques 89. Estate planning for nontraditional relationships

Addendum: The topics, "Client and planner attitudes, values, biases and behavioral characteristics and the impact on financial planning" and "Principles of communication and counseling," are an addendum to the *Topic List for CFP® Certification Examination*. Although individuals taking the CFP® Certification Examination will not be tested directly over these topics, CFP Board registered programs are strongly encouraged to teach them in their curricula. Continuing education (CE) programs and materials that address these topics will be eligible for CFP Board CE credit.

Glossary

12b-1 fee - a fee that pays for the services of brokers who sell mutual funds and who maintain the client relationship.

401(k) profit-sharing plan - a defined-contribution profit-sharing plan that gives participants the option of reducing their taxable salary and contributing the salary reduction on a tax-deferred basis to an individual account for retirement purposes.

529 plan - see *qualified tuition plan.*

A trust - see *power-of-appointment trust.*

"above-the-line" deductions - an above-the-line deduction (also known as a deduction *for* AGI) is one that reduces gross income directly.

absolute assignment - transference of all life insurance policy ownership rights to a designated assignee.

absolute liability - see *strict and absolute liability.*

abstract thinking - the third phase of a client's thinking process in establishing financial direction, where a client becomes aware of the consequences of financial actions and understands how day-to-day savings and consumption decisions impact a financial plan.

accelerated death benefit rider - life insurance rider that permits the policyowner to receive a portion of the death benefit during the insured's lifetime if the insured is diagnosed with a terminal illness.

accidental bodily injury - the injury incurred is accidental.

accidental death benefit rider - life insurance rider that increases the death benefit if the insured dies as a result of an accident.

accuracy-related penalty - a penalty of 20% of the portion of the tax underpayment attributable to negligence, substantial understatement of tax, or substantial valuation misstatement without intent to defraud.

activities of daily living (ADLs) - eating, bathing, dressing, transferring from bed to chair, using the toilet, and continence.

actual cash value (ACV) - one of three ways in which losses are valued in most insurance policies. Actual cash value (ACV) is calculated as replacement cost minus functional depreciation.

ACV - see *actual cash value.*

additional living expenses - the difference between the cost of living in temporary arrangements and the normal costs that would have been incurred had there been no loss.

adhesion - a characteristic of insurance meaning that insurance is "a take it or leave it contract." The insured must accept (or adhere to) the contract as written, without any bargaining over its terms and conditions.

adjusted gross estate - gross estate less deductions provided for by law in recognition that the entire value of the gross estate will not be transferred to the heirs due to costs, debts, and certain other deductions.

adjusted gross income (AGI) - a determination peculiar to individual taxpayers that represents gross income less business expenses, expenses attributable to the production of rent or royalty income, the allowed capital loss deduction, and certain personal expenses.

ADLs - see *activities of daily living.*

administrator - in the event a decedent dies intestate (without a valid will), or where an executor cannot be appointed by the probate court, the court appoints an administrator with powers called letters of administration which enable the administrator to carry out duties set down in the laws of intestacy.

ADRs - see *American Depositary Receipts.*

adult day care - basic assistance and supervision provided outside the home usually during the primary caregiver's working hours.

adverse selection - the tendency of higher-than-average risks (people who need insurance the most) to purchase or renew insurance policies.

age-based profit-sharing plan - a profit-sharing plan with an age-weighted factor in the allocation formula.

agent - a legal representative of the insurer with authority to enter into agreements on its behalf.

AGI - see *adjusted gross income.*

AIME - see *average indexed monthly earnings.*

aleatory - a characteristic of insurance meaning that monetary values exchanged by each party in an insurance agreement are unequal.

alpha - see *Jensen's Alpha.*

American Depositary Receipts (ADRs) - certificates of ownership issued by U.S. banks representing ownership in shares of stock of a foreign company that are held on deposit in a bank in the firm's home country.

amortization table - a time value of money tool used primarily to illustrate the amortization, or extinguishments, of debt. The table presents the number of years of indebtedness, the beginning balance, level payments, interest amount, principal reduction, and ending balance of indebtedness.

annual exclusion - a result of a de minimis rule by Congress to help reduce income tax reporting by eliminating the need for taxpayers to keep an account of, or report, small gifts. All individuals are allowed to gift, tax free, up to $10,000 per donee per year.

annual renewable term (ART) - term insurance issued for one year; renewable for subsequent periods up to a stated age without evidence of insurability.

anomalies - occurrences in the stock market that are not supported by the concept of the Efficient Market Hypothesis.

antitrust legislation - laws passed to protect consumers from monopolistic price practices and to protect investors by promoting fair competition.

any occupation- a definition of disability in which an insured is considered totally disabled if duties of any occupation cannot be performed.

APL - see *automatic premium loan.*

apparent authority - the insured is led to believe that the agent has authority, either express or implied, where no such authority actually exists.

arithmetic mean- a measure of investment return that is the result of averaging periodic returns.

ART - see *annual renewable term.*

articles of organization - document filed in compliance with state law to create a limited liability company (LLC).

Asset Accumulation Phase - life cycle phase through which clients pass. Usually begins somewhere between the ages of 20 and 25 and lasts until about age 50, characterized by limited excess funds for investing, high degree of debt and low net worth.

asset allocation - the distribution of investments in a portfolio by asset class.

asset-backed securities - securities issued against some type of asset-linked debts bundled together, such as credit card receivables or mortgages.

assets - property owned completely or partially by the client.

assisted living - apartment-style housing combined with support services and basic health.

attorney-in-fact- the person designated by the principal in a power of attorney to act in place of the principal on the principal's behalf.

audits - correspondence, office, and field inspections and verification of a taxpayer's return or other transactions possessing tax consequences. Correspondence audits are conducted by mail; office audits are conducted in the tax agent's office; field audits are conducted on the business premises of the taxpayer or in the office of the tax practitioner representing the taxpayer.

automatic premium loan (APL) **provision** - life insurance contract provision that directs the insurer to pay an overdue premium by making an interest-bearing loan against the policy's cash value.

average indexed monthly earnings (AIME) - amount that adjusts, or indexes, a worker's actual earnings to current dollars.

B trust - see *bypass trust.*

back-end load - a sales charge incurred upon the ultimate sale or redemption of mutual fund shares rather than at the time of purchase.

bailee - a party that holds the property of another.

balance sheet - a listing of assets, liabilities, and net worth.

bankruptcy- the financial condition when a debtor is determined by the court to be unable to pay creditors.

barbell strategy - portfolio immunization strategy that uses a portfolio of short-term and long-term bonds.

"below-the-line" deductions - (also known as a deduction from AGI) is one that is subtracted from AGI in arriving at taxable income.

bend points- the three separate percentages of portions of the AIME that are summed to arrive at the PIA.

benefit periods- the number of days that Medicare covers care in hospitals and skilled nursing facilities.

best-efforts agreement - equity underwriting in which the issuing firm agrees to repurchase any securities remaining after the initial offering is made by the underwriter.

beta - a commonly used measure of systematic risk that is derived from regression analysis.

beyond a reasonable doubt - a measure or degree of proof – with regard to CFP Board's Disciplinary Rules and Procedures, "beyond a reasonable doubt" means the evidence as a whole shows what it was intended to prove with a probability of 99 percent or better.

black-out period - the period from when Social Security benefits for the surviving caretaker spouse are discounted (usually when child reaches age 16) to when the spouse begins to receive Social Security benefits at retirement age.

blue chip stocks - stock issued by older, well-established companies that maintain the ability to pay dividends both in years the company has income and in years the company has losses.

board of directors - the governing body of a corporation whose members are elected by shareholders.

bodily injury by accidental means - accidental injury by accidental means.

bond indenture agreement - the legal document that sets forth the repayment schedules, restrictions, and promises between the issuer of a corporate bond and the borrower.

bond mutual funds - see *fixed-income mutual funds.*

BOPR - see *Certified Financial Planner Board's Board of Professional Review.*

boot - property (other than like-kind property) that qualifies as a tax gain when received in a property exchange.

broad coverage - homeowners insurance coverage that includes eighteen named perils.

brokers - legal representatives of the insured who offer products from many insurers.

budgeting - a process of projecting, monitoring, adjusting, and controlling future income and expenditures.

bullet strategy - portfolio immunization strategy that uses a portfolio of bonds with similar maturities.

burden of proof -the requirement of proving facts to a certain degree of probability. With regard to CFP Board's Disciplinary Rules and Procedures, there are three distinct burdens of proof: (1) preponderance of the evidence; (2) clear and convincing evidence; and (3) evidence beyond a reasonable doubt.

business cycles - swings in total national output, income, and employment marked by widespread expansion or contraction in many sectors of the economy.

business risk - an unsystematic risk based on predictability of operating income for a specific business; dependent upon management and industry characteristics.

bypass trust - avoids inclusion in, or bypasses, the surviving spouse's gross estate—the assets transfer to a future generation free of estate taxes. The purpose of a bypass trust (known as a "B" trust) is to take advantage of the applicable credit amount.

C corporation - a business entity created by state law that is separate and distinct from its shareholders/owners.

C trust - see *qualified terminable interest property trust.*

call options - a derivative that gives the holder the right to purchase the underlying asset, generally stock, at a specified price within a specified period of time.

call provision - right to redeem the bond issue prior to maturity.

capital appreciation - when a company chooses to retain the earnings to invest in additional projects, the investor receives his return in the form of appreciation of the stock.

capital asset - broadly speaking, all assets are capital except those specifically excluded by the Internal Revenue Code. Excluded assets include property held for resale in the normal course of business (inventory), trade accounts and notes receivable, and depreciable property and real estate used in a trade or business.

Capital Asset Pricing Model (CAPM) - an asset-pricing model that developed from the Markowitz efficient frontier and the introduction of a risk-free asset.

capital formation - production of buildings, machinery, tools, and other equipment that will assist in the ability of economic participants to produce in the future.

capital gain - see *long-term capital gain* and *short-term capital gain*.

capital loss - the loss from the sale or exchange of a capital asset.

capital needs analysis - the process of calculating the amount of investment capital needed at retirement to maintain the preretirement lifestyle and mitigate the impact of inflation during the retirement years.

capital preservation model - a capital needs analysis method that assumes that at life expectancy, the client has exactly the same account balance as he did at retirement.

capital retention approach - method for determining the required amount of life insurance; provides a death benefit amount that is sufficient to provide investment income that will cover the projected needs of the family.

capital stock insurance company - operated for profit, owned by stockholders.

CAPM - see *Capital Asset Pricing Model.*

cash accounts - a type of brokerage account that requires that all securities purchased by the investor be paid for in full without any indebtedness.

cash flow timeline - a time value of money analysis tool that graphically depicts cash inflows (cash received) and cash outflows (cash deposited or invested) over a certain period (the term).

cash flows from financing - cash inflows from the issuance of additional debt and cash outflows for the repayment of debt.

cash flows from investing - cash receipts or expenditures for the sale or purchase of assets.

cash flows from operations - net cash generated or used due to normal work and living.

Certified Financial Planner (CFP®) - designation conferred upon individuals who successfully complete the education and experience outlined by the Certified Financial Planner Board of Standards, Inc. General requirements include completion of core personal financial planning coursework, three-years of financial planning experience and a passing score on the Certified Financial Planner Examination.

Certified Financial Planner Board of Standards, Inc. - an independent professional regulatory organization that regulates financial planners.

Certified Financial Planner Board's Board of Governors - the governing board for the certified financial planning profession.

Certified Financial Planner Board's Board of Professional Review (BOPR) - a subsidiary board of CFP Board that interprets and applies the Code of Ethics and Professional Responsibility.

Certified Financial Planner Board's Code of Ethics and Professional Responsibility - the set of principles of conduct that regulates behavior of CFP® certificants.

Certified Public Accountant (CPA) - license/certificate conferred upon individuals who successfully complete the education and experience requirements outlined by the licensing state/jurisdiction. General requirements include two-years of public accounting experience, a bachelor's degree and a passing score on the CPA examination.

CFA - see *Chartered Financial Analyst.*

CFP®- see *Certified Financial Planner.*

CFP Board - see *Certified Financial Planner Board of Standards, Inc.*

CFP Board designee - an individual who uses the CFP® certification marks.

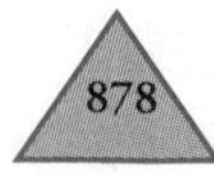

change in demand - occurs when the entire demand curve shifts to the right or left.

changes in quantity demanded - the movements along the demand curve in response to a change in price.

charitable deduction - a charitable contribution made as a gift to a qualified organization.

charitable lead trust (CLT) - a split-interest trust where a charity is the income beneficiary and there is a noncharitable remainderman.

charitable remainder trust (CRT) - a split interest trust. If created during life, the income goes to one or more parties, usually the grantor, or grantor and spouse for life, and upon the income beneficiary's death, the principal (remainder) is transferred to a charity. If the CRT is created testamentary, the usual income beneficiary is the spouse for life.

Chartered Financial Analyst (CFA) - designation conferred upon individuals who successfully complete the education and experience requirements outlined by the CFA Institute. General requirements include a bachelor's degree, three-years of experience in financial analysis, and passing scores on the three CFA examinations.

Chartered Financial Consultant (ChFC) - designation conferred upon individuals who successfully complete required coursework offered by the American College.

Chartered Life Underwriter (CLU) - designation conferred upon individuals who successfully complete required coursework offered by the American College.

ChFC - see *Chartered Financial Consultant.*

child insurance rider - see *spouse and child insurance riders.*

chronically ill - illness or injury resulting in the inability to perform, without substantial assistance, at least two of six activities of daily living for at least 90 days.

clean-up fund - amount of money needed immediately by survivors to cover final expenses and debts of the decedent.

clear and convincing evidence - a measure or degree of proof—with regard to CFP Board's Disciplinary Rules and Procedures, "clear and convincing evidence" means the evidence as a whole shows what it was intended to prove with a probability of 75 percent or better.

clearly erroneous standard - asks the basic question: could a reasonable finder of fact have ruled in a certain way, based on the entire record?

Client Data Collection Questionnaire - a survey used by financial planners to gather internal data from clients, such as their tolerance for risk and their personal perception of their financial situation, as well as tax-related data, Social Security numbers, information relating to their dependents, and so on.

closed-end fund - a type of investment company whose shares trade in the same manner that publicly traded stocks trade in the secondary market.

CLT - see *charitable lead trust.*

CLU - see *Chartered Life Underwriter.*

CMOs - see *collateralized mortgage obligations.*

COBRA - see *Consolidated Omnibus Budget Reconciliation Act.*

code of ethics - a set of principles of conduct that governs a group of individuals and usually requires conformity to professional standards of conduct.

coefficient of determination (R^2) - percentage of variability in the dependent variable that is explained by variability in the independent variable.

coinsurance - the percentage of financial responsibility that the insured and the insurer must uphold in order to achieve equity in rating.

COLA - see *cost-of-living adjustment.*

collateral assignment - transference of a life insurance policy to a creditor as security for a loan or debt.

collateral trust bonds - bonds secured by securities issued by other companies.

collateralized mortgage obligations (CMOs) - mortgage-backed securities that are divided into principal repayment tranches.

collision - auto insurance coverage that protects the insured against upset and collision damages, such as those sustained in an accident involving other vehicles, or those sustained when an auto runs off the road and into a lake.

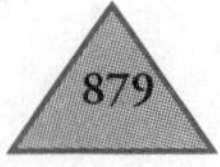

commercial package policy (CPP) - business property and liability coverage combined into a single policy.

commingle client funds - CFP Board Rules specifically prohibit the combining (or commingling) of client funds or other property with a CFP Board designee's personal funds and/or other property or the funds and/or other property of a CFP Board designee's firm.

common law liability - liability based on breach of contract, tort, or fraud.

common stock - ownership interest in a company.

community property - a regime where married individuals own an equal undivided interest in all wealth accumulated during the marriage.

compound interest - interest earned on interest.

comprehensive - auto insurance coverage that protects the insured's auto against perils out of the insured's control, such as missiles or falling objects, fire, theft, earthquake, hail, flood, and vandalism.

comprehensive major medical - stand-alone medical insurance that provides for a broad range of medical services and has high limits on coverage.

concealment - occurs when the insured is silent about a fact that is material to the risk.

conditionally renewable - type of insurance that cannot be cancelled by the insurer during the policy term but which is renewable under certain conditions.

conflict of interest - denotes circumstances, relationships or other facts about a CFP Board designee's own financial, business, property, and/or personal interests which will, or reasonably may, impair the CFP Board designee's rendering of disinterested advice, recommendations, or services.

Conservation/Protection Phase - life cycle phase through which clients pass characterized by an increase in cash flow, assets, and net worth with some decrease in the proportional use of debt.

Consolidated Omnibus Budget Reconciliation Act (COBRA) - a federal law that requires certain employers to provide the previously covered persons (including dependents and spouses) with the same insurance coverage he or she received prior to unemployment.

consolidation loan - a loan that provides borrowers with a way to consolidate various types of federal student loans that have separate repayment schedules into one loan.

Consumer Price Index (CPI) - a price index that measures the cost of a "market basket" of consumer goods and services purchased for day-to-day living.

consumption movements - an economic variable that fluctuates during the business cycle, usually lags behind trends, and seems to be the effect of a business cycle phase rather than its cause.

contingent beneficiary - an individual, group or entity designated to receive the policy proceeds if the primary beneficiary should die before the insured dies.

contraction phase - one of the two general business cycle phases characterized by a fall in business sales, decreased growth of Gross Domestic Product, and increased unemployment.

convertible - in term life insurance, ability to exchange the policy for a cash value life insurance policy without evidence of insurability.

convertible bonds - hybrid securities that permit the holder to acquire shares of common stock from the issuing company by exchanging the currently held debt security for a specific number of common stock shares.

convertible preferred stock - preferred stock that includes the right to convert the preferred stock into a specific number of common shares at the option of the stockholder.

coordination of benefits clause - an insurance contract clause that prevents an insured from receiving greater than 100% of the cost of health care received when covered by multiple policies.

copayment - a loss-sharing arrangement in which the insured pays a percentage of the loss in excess of the deductible.

corporation - see *C corporation* or *S corporation*.

correlation coefficient (R) - a statistical measure of the direction and strength of the relationship between two sets of data. Correlation coefficients close to +1.0 are strongly positively correlated and those close to -1.0 are strongly negatively correlated.

cost-of-living adjustment (COLA) - annual increase in Social Security benefits related to increases in inflation based on changes in the Consumer Price Index.

cost-of-living rider - disability insurance rider that increases the benefits received by the policyowner each year based on an inflation index.

country risk - an unsystematic risk where changes in a country's laws or political situation will have an adverse effect on an investment.

coupon payments - interest payments paid to the bondholder on a semiannual basis and based on a percentage of the face value or par value of the bond.

Coverdell Education Savings Account (Coverdell ESA) - an investment account established with cash contributions that grow tax free within the account. Money withdrawn from the account remains free from tax or penalty if the funds are used for higher educational expenses. If not, the earnings are subject to income tax and a 10 percent penalty.

Coverdell ESA - see *Coverdell Education Savings Account.*

CPA - see *Certified Public Accountant.*

CPI - see *Consumer Price Index.*

CPP - see *commercial package policy.*

CRT - see *charitable remainder trust.*

cumulative preferred stock - preferred stock that requires receipt of previously unpaid preferred dividends before common shareholders receive dividend payments.

cumulative voting - number of votes per share equal to number of seats on the board of directors.

current assets - assets expected to be converted to cash within one year.

current assumption whole life - whole life insurance policy that uses new-money interest rates and current mortality assumptions to determine cash values.

current liability - debt owed by the client that is expected to be paid off within the year (current $\leq$ 12 months).

current yield - a bond's annual coupon divided by the current market price.

custodial care - assistance provided for tasks of daily life, such as eating, dressing, bathing, and taking medications.

cyclical stocks - stocks of companies that tend to prosper in expanding economies and do poorly during down business cycles.

date of declaration - date on which a corporation's board of directors declares a dividend payment creating an obligation on the company to make a dividend payment to shareholders.

date of payment - the date that the dividend will actually be paid.

date of record - the date at which an owner of the common stock of a corporation is entitled to receive the dividend payment.

debentures - unsecured corporate bonds whose holders have no claim to specific assets of the issuing corporation.

decreasing term - term life insurance that has a level premium with a decreasing death benefit.

deductible - a stated amount of money the insured is required to pay on a loss before the insurer will make any payments under the policy conditions.

default risk - an unsystematic risk where a business will be unable to service its debt.

defensive stocks - stock companies that are relatively unaffected by general fluctuations in the economy.

deferred annuity - annuity that provides income at some date in the future.

deferred compensation plan - a nonqualified plan that is a contractual agreement between the employer and selected employees; takes the form of either salary reduction or salary continuation. Compensation is deferred until retirement, disability, death, or termination of employment, but usually only at normal retirement age.

deficit spending - occurs when governmental expenditures exceed the government's tax collections.

defined-benefit plan - a retirement plan that specifies the benefits that each employee receives at retirement. Defined-benefit plans actuarially determine the benefit to be paid at normal retirement age.

defined-contribution plan - a retirement plan that specifies the annual employer current contribution. The amount of benefit received by an employee depends on the account balance at retirement.

defined-period approach - long-term care benefit approach in which coverage is provided for a specific period of time following an elimination period.

deflation - the opposite of inflation, it occurs when the general level of prices is falling.

demand - the quantity of a particular good that people are willing to buy. Demand is heavily dependent on price.

demand curve - the graphic depiction that illustrates the relationship between a particular good's price and the quantity demanded.

dependency period - period in which others would have been dependent on the deceased had he survived.

dependent - an individual who can be claimed by a taxpayer for an exemption on an income tax return.

depression - a persistent recession that brings a severe decline in economic activity.

derivatives - securities whose value is based on the value of some other security or proxy.

determination letter - a written statement issued by an IRS district director that applies the principles and precedents announced by the National Office to a given set of facts.

direct bequest (to a spouse) - the first spouse who dies, leaves everything outright to the surviving spouse.

direct investing - a process of investing where investors purchase actual securities.

direct negligence - negligence that involves acts or omissions directly attributable to an individual.

Direct Stafford Loan - federal financial aid funds provided by the U.S. Dept. of Education directly to the student.

directors - individuals who, acting as a group known as the board of directors, manage the business affairs of a corporation.

disability benefit - Social Security benefit available to recipients who have a severe physical or mental impairment that is expected to prevent them from performing substantial work for at least a year or result in death, and who have the sufficient amount of Social Security credits.

disability income insurance - a type of insurance that provides a regular income while the insured is unable to work because of illness or injury.

Disciplinary Rules and Procedures - rules and procedures that enforce the CFP Board's Code of Ethics and regulate disciplinary proceedings against CFP Board designees.

disclaimer - the refusal of the receipt of an estate. The use of disclaimers allows an individual to disclaim or renounce receiving any part of an estate.

disclaimer clause - a common clause in a decedent's will that allows property to pass from one party to another without gift tax consequences.

discretionary cash flow - money available after all expenses are accounted for.

discretionary expenses - luxuries or expenses over which the client has complete control.

disinflation - the term used to denote a decline in the rate of inflation.

Distribution/Gifting Phase - life cycle phase through which clients pass characterized by excess relative cash flows, low debt, and high relative net worth.

dividend yield - the measure of a security's annual dividend payment as a percent of the current market price.

dividends - distributions of cash or additional shares of stock paid to the shareholders of a corporation.

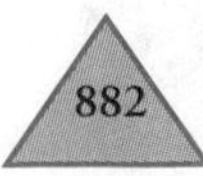

dividends-received deduction - a deduction for dividends received by one corporation from another corporation. The amount of the deduction is based on the percentage owned by the corporation receiving the dividend.

DJIA - see *Dow Jones Industrial Average.*

dollar-weighted returns - a method of determining the internal rate of return that an individual investor earned based on the investor's particular cash flow into and out of the portfolio.

double taxation of dividends - the taxation of income at the corporate level and the subsequent taxation of dividend distributions at the individual shareholder's level.

Dow Jones Industrial Average (DJIA) - a financial index that is a price weighted average of thirty leading industrial stocks used to measure the status of the equity market.

durable feature - the power survives incapacity and disability of the principal.

durable goods - products that are not consumed or quickly disposed of, and can be used for several years.

durable power of attorney for health care or property - a written document enabling the principal to designate another person or persons to act as his or her "attorney-in-fact."

duration - a concept developed by Fred Macaulay in 1938 that provides a time-weighted measure of a security's cash flows in terms of payback.

dwelling - residential structure covered under a homeowners insurance policy.

dynamic risk – a risk that results from changes in society or the economy (i.e., inflation).

EAFE Index - see *Europe, Australia, and Far East (EAFE) index.*

EE bonds - see *Series EE United States Savings Bonds.*

EFC - see *expected family contribution.*

efficient frontier - consists of investment portfolios with the highest expected return for a given level of risk.

Efficient Market Hypothesis (EMH) - a theory that suggests that securities are priced fairly and efficiently by the market, and investors are unable to consistently outperform the market on a risk-adjusted basis.

elimination period - the amount of time that must pass before benefits are paid.

EMH - see *Efficient Market Hypothesis.*

Employers' Educational Assistance Program - under this program, an employer can pay for an employee's undergraduate tuition, enrollment fees, books, supplies, and equipment while these employer benefits are excluded from the employee's income up to $5,250.

endorsement - see *riders.*

engagement letter - a tool of communication between client and financial planner that sets down in writing information about any agreements or understandings obtained at client/planner meetings including the plan of action for developing a financial plan, the expected outcome of the engagement, and the method of compensation.

entire contract clause - insurance contract clause that maintains that the policy and the policyowner's application comprise the complete life insurance contract.

equilibrium - the state of the market where quantity demanded equals quantity supplied

equity mutual funds - a mutual fund that invests primarily in equity securities, such as preferred stock and common stock.

error and omissions insurance coverage - insurance that provides protection against loss from negligent acts, errors, and omissions by the insured.

ETF - see *exchange-traded fund.*

ethics - the discipline of dealing with the moral principles or values that guide oneself.

Europe, Australia, and Far East (EAFE) index - index created as a measure of the international securities markets.

exchange-rate risk - a systematic risk associated with a change in the relationship between the value of the dollar (or investor's currency) and the value of the foreign currency during the period of investment.

exchange-traded fund (ETF) - a type of investment company whose investment objective is to achieve the same return as a particular market index.

exclusion - income exempt from tax and not included in a taxpayer's gross income.

ex-dividend date - the date on which the market reflects the dividend payment.

exemptions - a basic deduction to which a taxpayer is entitled for self support (personal exemption) or for the support of a spouse and/or dependent (dependency exemption).

exercise price - the price at which an underlying stock will either be sold (put) or purchased (call) by the holder of an option.

expansion phase - one of the two general business cycle phases characterized by a rise in business sales, growth of Gross Domestic Product, and a decline in unemployment.

expected family contribution (EFC) - a formula that indicates how much of a student's family resources ought to be available to assist in paying for the student's college education. Some of the factors used in this calculation include taxable and nontaxable income, assets, retirement funds, and benefits, such as unemployment and Social Security.

expense ratio - disclosed by all mutual funds in their fund prospectuses as an indication of the annual fund expenses that are stated as a percentage of total assets.

expenses - recurring obligations.

express authority - powers explicitly given or denied to the agent by the insurer.

external environment - the whole complex of factors that influence the financial planning process, including economic, legal, social, technological, political, and taxation factors.

FAFSA - see *Free Application for Federal Student Aid.*

failure-to-file penalty - a civil penalty imposed on taxpayers and tax return preparers who fail to file tax returns according to the requirements of tax law.

failure-to-pay-tax penalty - a civil penalty imposed on taxpayers who, without reasonable cause, fail to pay the tax shown on their return.

fair market value (FMV) - the price at which an exchange will take place between a willing buyer and a willing seller.

fair rental value, loss of - see *loss of fair rental value.*

family benefit - Social Security benefit available to certain family members of workers eligible for retirement or disability benefits.

FASB - see *Financial Accounting Standards Board.*

Fed - see *Federal Reserve.*

federal agency securities - public debt issued by agencies of the U.S. government as a means of raising funds for operations of the respective agency.

federal estate tax - an excise tax on the right to transfer assets by a decedent.

Federal Insurance Contributions Act (FICA) - the law allowing Social Security taxes, including Medicare, to be deducted from paychecks.

Federal Perkins Loan - federally funded, campus-based, low-interest student loan that is provided to undergraduate and graduate students that have exceptional financial need, that is, very low EFCs.

Federal Reserve (the Fed) - the banking and financial system developed under the Federal Reserve Act of 1913 that makes the basic policy decisions that regulate our money and banking systems.

Federal Reserve discount rate - the rate at which Federal Reserve member banks can borrow funds to meet reserve requirements. The Fed will lower the discount rate when it wants to increase the money supply.

Federal Supplemental Education Opportunity Grant (FSEOG) - campus-based student financial aid grant awarded to undergraduate students with low EFCs that gives priority to students who receive federal Pell Grants.

Federal Trade Commission (FTC) - the federal organization created in 1914 to keep competition free and fair and to protect U. S. consumers.

Federal Work-Study Program - campus-based student financial aid program that enables undergraduate and graduate students to earn money for education expenses through jobs that pay at least current minimum wages but do not exceed the award received through the program.

fee simple - the complete individual ownership of property with all rights associated with outright ownership, such as the right to use, sell, gift, alienate, or convey.

FFEL Stafford Loan - see Stafford Loan

FICA - see *Federal Insurance Contributions Act.*

fiduciary relationship - relationship between a CFP® practitioner and a client where the client places special trust and confidence in the CFP® practitioner. This relationship places a higher burden on the CFP Board designee, which is warranted, because the CFP Board designee is dealing with the client's funds or property for investment purposes.

Financial Accounting Standards Board (FASB) - nongovernmental board that sets standards for financial statements and generally accepted accounting principals (GAAP).

financial goals - high-level statements of financial desire that may be for the short run or the long run.

financial mission - a broad and enduring statement that identifies the client's long-term purpose for wanting a financial plan.

financial needs approach - method of determining required amount of life insurance; evaluates the income replacement needs of one's survivors in the event of an untimely death.

financial objectives - statements of financial desire that contain time and measurement attributes, making them more specific than financial goals.

financial phases - accumulation, conservation/protection, and distribution/gifting.

financial planning practitioners - individuals who are capable and qualified to offer objective, integrated, and comprehensive financial advice to, or for the benefit of, clients; help clients achieve their financial objectives and by using the financial planning process.

financial risk - an unsystematic risk based on the inclusion of debt in the capital structure of a firm which affects the return on equity (ROE) for a company.

financial success - for most individuals, financial success means accomplishing one's financial goals.

firm commitment - equity underwriting in which the underwriter purchases the entire issue at a specific price from the firm and resells it on the open market.

first-to-die policy - life insurance policy that pays the face amount to the beneficiaries upon the first death of two or more insureds.

fiscal policy - taxation, expenditures, and debt management of the federal government.

fixed annuity - an annuity in which the insurer agrees to credit a specified interest rate over a stated period of time.

fixed expenses - expenses that remain constant over a period of time and over which the client has little control.

fixed-amount option - life insurance settlement option that specifies that a designated amount of income will be provided to the beneficiary on a regular basis until the proceeds and accumulated interest are depleted.

fixed-income mutual funds - a mutual fund that invests in fixed-income securities ranging in maturity of several months to thirty years or longer. Bond funds invest in numerous bond issues to diversify the investment portfolio from default risk.

fixed-income securities - securities with specified payment dates and amounts, primarily bonds.

fixed-period option - life insurance settlement option in which the beneficiary will receive the maximum periodic payments that the death benefit proceeds will purchase for a specified time period.

flexible premium annuity - annuity that allows the insured the option to vary premium deposits.

flow-through entity - A type of business entity where the results of business operations are reported directly on the owner's income tax return.

FMV - see *fair market value.*

foreign closed-end funds - closed-end funds that invest in foreign firms.

foreign currency risk - a systematic risk due to the potential change in the relationship between the value of the dollar (or investor's currency) and the value of the foreign currency during the period of investment; also known as exchange rate risk.

foreign mutual funds - securities that provide investors with the easiest method of investing in foreign markets in the context of a diversified portfolio.

foreign securities - securities issued by non-U.S. firms.

forfeitures - employer contributions that are not fully vested and thus revert to the employer in the event that an employee terminates service.

fourth market - comprised of institutional traders that trade without the help of brokers.

fraud penalty - a penalty levied against a taxpayer by the IRS after it has proven an underpayment of tax by the taxpayer and proven that the underpayment was attributable to a willful attempt to evade tax.

Free Application for Federal Student Aid (FAFSA) - an application form that must be submitted by a college student to become eligible for federal financial aid.

free cash flow to equity - term that describes the available cash after meeting all of a firm's operating and financial needs; used to calculate the value a company.

front-end load - a sales charge based on the initial investment into a mutual fund.

FSEOG - see *Federal Supplemental Education Opportunity Grant.*

FTC - see *Federal Trade Commission.*

fundamental analysis - the analysis of a stock's value using basic, publicly available data such as the stock's earnings, sales, risk, and industry analysis.

fundamental risk – an impersonal risk that involves a possible loss for a large group.

future value - the future amount to which $1 today will increase based on a defined interest rate and a period of time.

future value of an annuity due - the future amount to which a series of deposits of equal size will increase when deposited over a definite number of equal interval time periods, based on a defined interest rate, and the deposits are made at the beginning of each time period.

future value of an ordinary annuity - the future amount to which a series of deposits of equal size will increase when deposited over a definite number of equal interval time periods, based on a defined interest rate, and the deposits are made at the end of each time period.

futures contract - an agreement to do something in the future—generally, purchasing/selling a futures contract obligates the buyer to take delivery/ make delivery of a specific commodity at a specific time in the future.

galloping inflation - inflation that occurs when money loses its value very quickly and when real interest rates can be minus 50 or 100 percent per year.

GDP - see *Gross Domestic Product.*

general agent - an independent businessperson who represents one insurer for a designated territory.

general partnership - a type of business entity owned entirely by general partners, each of whom can act on behalf of the partnership.

general power of attorney/appointment (POA) - gives the appointee the power to do anything the principal could do.

generation-skipping transfer tax (GSTT) - a tax that is in addition to the unified gift and estate tax and is designed to tax large transfers that skip a generation (that is, from grandparent to grandchild).

geometric mean - a method of calculating the internal rate of return based on periodic rates of return.

gift - in estate planning, a direct transfer of property or cash made during life.

grace period - period of time during which a policyowner may convert a group term policy, upon termination from a company, to a regular cash value policy at a rate that is commensurate with his or her attained age.

green fund - a fund that invests in environmentally friendly companies.

Gross Domestic Product (GDP) - the value of all goods and services produced in the country; GDP is the broadest measure of the general state of the economy.

gross estate - all assets included in a decedent's estate including, but not limited to, cash, stocks, bonds, annuities, retirement accounts, notes receivable, personal residences, automobiles, art collections, life insurance proceeds, and income tax refunds due.

gross income - income subject to the federal income tax. Gross income does not include income for which the IRC permits exclusion treatment.

group supplemental plans - insurance plans often attached to basic medical expense policies that allow the employer to use more than one provider for coverage, offer first-dollar coverage, or use different contribution rates for basic and supplemental coverages.

growth stocks - stock issued by companies whose sales, earnings, and market share are growing at higher rates than average or the general economy.

GSTT - see *generation-skipping transfer tax.*

guaranteed renewable option - medical and disability insurance option in which the insurer must renew the policy for a specified period of time regardless of changes to the insured's health.

hazard - a condition that creates or increases the likelihood of a loss occurring.

head of household - the filing status that identifies a taxpayer as an unmarried individual who maintains a household for another and satisfies certain conditions set forth in the Internal Revenue Code.

health maintenance organization (HMO) - organized system of health care that provides comprehensive health services to its members for a fixed prepaid fee.

Hearing Panel - panel that establishes the rules of procedures and evidence to be observed at a complaint hearing seeking disciplinary action against a CFP Board designee.

heir - one who inherits; beneficiary.

HMO - see *health maintenance organization.*

holding period return (HPR) - measures the total return an investor receives over a specific time period.

holographic will - handwritten will dated and signed by the testator.

home health care - part-time skilled nursing care and rehabilitative therapy provided at the patient's home.

homeowners insurance - a package insurance policy that provides both property and liability coverage for the insured's dwelling, other structures, personal property, and loss of use.

Hope Scholarship Credit - a tax credit available for qualified tuition and enrollment fees incurred and paid after 1997 in the first two years of postsecondary education for the taxpayer, spouse, or dependent.

hospice care - care that provides dignity and comfort to terminally ill patients and their families.

hospital expense insurance - provides payment for expenses incurred by the insured while in the hospital.

housing costs - principal and interest to pay the mortgage loan, real estate taxes, and homeowners insurance.

HPR - see *holding period return.*

human life value approach - method used to determine required amount of life insurance; uses an individual's income-earning ability as the basis for risk measurement.

hybrid mutual funds - a mutual fund that invests in a combination of cash, fixed-income securities, and equity securities.

immediate annuity - an annuity in which the first annuity payment is due one payment interval from its purchase date.

immunization - the concept of minimizing the impact of changes in interest rates on the value of investments.

implied authority - power to perform any incidental act required in fulfillment of obligations designated in the agency agreement.

income - all monies received from employment, investments, and other sources.

income and expense statement - summary of the client's income and expenses during an interval of time, usually one year.

income stock - stock issued by companies in the maturity phase of the industry life cycle and payout the majority of their earnings in the form of dividends.

incontestability clause - insurance contract clause that prevents the insurer from canceling the policy after it has been in force for two years in the event material misrepresentations or concealments are discovered.

indemnity - see *principle of indemnity.*

independent agents - property and casualty agents that represent multiple unrelated insurers through the American agency system.

indirect investing - a process of investing where investors invest in companies that invest directly.

information return - a written statement provided to the taxpayer after the end of each tax year detailing the amount of income (as well as unearned income such as interest or dividends) earned by the taxpayer. The most common information return is the Form W-2.

inflation - an increase in the price level of goods and services.

initial public offering (IPO) - first offering of equity securities to the general public.

installment payment method - life insurance surrender method in which the policyowner receives the cash value and accrued interest over a period of time, usually in fixed amounts.

installment refund annuity - an annuity in which the insurer continues periodic payments after the annuitant has died until the sum of all annuity payments equals the purchase price of the annuity or, with the cash refund option, the balance is paid in cash to a beneficiary at the annuitant's death.

insurable interest - see *principle of insurable interest.*

insurance - pooling of fortuitous losses by transfer of risks to insurers who agree to indemnify insureds for such losses, to provide other pecuniary benefits on their occurrence, or to render services connected with the risk.

intentional interference - intentional act committed against another that causes injury.

interest payment method - life insurance surrender method in which the policyowner may choose to leave the cash value proceeds with the insurer and receive only interest payments on the cash value.

interest-only option - life insurance settlement option in which the insurance company retains the death benefit and pays the primary beneficiary interest on that sum.

interest-rate risk - a systematic risk where changes in interest rates will affect the value of securities.

interest-sensitive stock - stock issued by companies whose performance is largely affected by changes in interest rates.

intermediate nursing care - occasional nursing and rehabilitative care ordered and monitored by a physician.

internal rate of return (IRR) - a measure of return that equates discounted future cash flows to the present value of an asset.

intestacy laws - state laws that direct how a decedent's property will be distributed when the decedent dies without a valid will.

intestate - to die without a valid will.

investment companies - financial services companies that sell shares of stock to the public and use the proceeds to invest in a portfolio of securities.

IPO - see *initial public offering.*

IRR - see *internal rate of return.*

irrevocable beneficiary - a beneficiary who cannot be changed without the beneficiary's consent.

iShares - passively managed international index funds.

itemized deductions - deductions that are in excess of the standard deduction and are used in lieu of the standard deduction.

Jensen's Alpha - an absolute measure of performance that indicates how the actual performance of an investment compares with the expected performance.

joint and last survivor income option - life insurance settlement option that provides joint beneficiaries a stated amount of income during their lives and a continuation of the original or reduced amount for the remaining beneficiary's life.

joint and survivor annuity - an annuity based on the lives of two or more annuitants, usually husband and wife. Annuity payments are made until the last annuitant dies.

joint life - life insurance policy that covers two or more lives under one policy at a cost lower than the total premium for multiple separate policies.

joint tenancy - two or more persons, called equal owners, hold the same fractional interest in a property.

Keogh plan - a qualified plan for unincorporated businesses.

ladder strategy - portfolio immunization strategy that uses a portfolio of bonds with staggered maturities.

last-to-die policy - life insurance policy that pays a death benefit upon the last death of multiple insureds.

law - rules of conduct that are established by a government or other authority that command and encourage behavior considered right and prohibit behavior considered wrong.

law of large numbers- concept that the greater the number of exposures, the more closely will actual results approach the probable results expected from an indefinite number of exposures.

learning styles (auditory, visual, kinetic or tactile) - the conditions under which people learn best—clients whose preferred learning style is auditory learn best by hearing information; clients who prefer a visual learning style learn best by reading and viewing; those who prefer a kinetic, or tactile, style learn best through manipulation and testing information.

legal reserve - a fund, maintained by the insurer, used to meet future obligations, such as administrative expenses and mortality charges.

lending securities - securities where an investor of bonds lends funds to the issuer in exchange for a promise of a stream of periodic interest payments and a repayment of the loaned principal at the maturity of the bond.

letter ruling - a written statement issued by the National Office of the IRS that gives guidance on the way the IRS will treat a prospective or contemplated transaction for tax purposes.

liability - money owed by the client.

libel - written statement that causes harm to another.

life cycle phase - an interval in a client's life cycle that tends to give a planner insight into the client's financial objectives and concerns—the Asset Accumulation phase, the Conservation/Protection phase, the Distribution/Gifting phase.

life cycle positioning - using information about a client's age, marital status, dependents, income level, and net worth to help determine goals and risks.

life income option - life insurance settlement option which allows the beneficiary to receive a specified monthly payment for his or her lifetime.

life income with period certain option - life insurance settlement option that provides an income to the beneficiary for his or her lifetime or a specified period, if greater.

life income with refund option - life insurance settlement option that refunds to the contingent beneficiary the difference between the proceeds of the policy and the amount paid-out to the primary beneficiary under the life income option.

Lifetime Learning Credit - a tax credit available to pay for tuition and enrollment fees for undergraduate, graduate, or professional degree programs paid after June 30, 1998.

limit order - type of securities order that requires the trade be made at a specified price or better.

limited liability company (LLC) - a relatively new and versatile form of business entity created under state law by filing articles of organization—versatile because it can be taxed as a sole proprietorship, partnership, C corporation, or S corporation.

limited liability partnership (LLP) - a form of business entity similar to a general partnership, except that an LLP provides additional liability protection to the partners.

limited partnership - a type of business entity formed under the limited partnership laws of a state. In a limited partnership, limited partners are not allowed to participate in the management of operations, but generally are allowed to vote on major changes affecting the structure of the partnership.

limited power of attorney - see *special power of attorney.*

limited-payment policy - permanent life insurance for which premiums are payable for a limited number of years, after which the policy becomes paid up for its stated face amount.

linear thinking - the initial phase of a client's thinking process when setting financial direction in which a client focuses on accomplishing one particular goal or narrow objective using a very compartmentalized, simplistic, self-designed financial plan.

liquidity - the ability to sell an investment quickly and at a competitive price, with no loss of principal and little price concession.

liquidity preference theory - yield curve theory that assets that long-term bonds have greater yields to compensate investors for increased interest-rate risk.

living benefits rider - see *accelerated death benefit rider.*

LLC - see *limited liability company.*

LLP - see *limited liability partnership.*

load funds - mutual funds that charge either a front-end load or back-end load.

long position - the purchase of a stock in hopes that it will appreciate over time.

long-term capital gain - a gain from a sale or exchange of a capital asset that has been held for more than one year.

long-term care insurance - provides coverage for nursing home stays and other types of routine care that are not covered by health insurance. There are five levels of coverage: skilled nursing care, intermediate nursing care, custodial care, home health care, and adult day care.

long-term disability - provides coverage for specified term, until specified age, or until death.

long-term liability - debt extending beyond one year.

loss frequency - the expected number of losses that will occur within a given period of time.

loss of fair rental value - gross rental value less charges and expenses that do not continue during the period in which the property is uninhabitable.

loss of use - homeowners insurance coverage that provides reimbursement to an insured homeowner for additional living expenses or loss of fair rental value.

loss severity - refers to the potential size or damage of a loss.

lump-sum payment method - life insurance surrender method in which the total cash value of the life insurance policy is paid to the policyowner.

major medical insurance - health insurance that provides broad coverage of all reasonable and necessary expenses associated with an illness or injury, whether incurred at a doctor's office, a hospital, or the insured's home.

management fee - a fee charged by an investment adviser for the management of a mutual fund's assets.

managers - individuals who are responsible for the maintenance, administration and management of the affairs of a limited liability company.

MAGI - see *modified adjusted gross income.*

marital deduction - deduction of an unlimited amount for transfers to spouse of property during life (gifts) or at death.

market capitalization - the product of the number of outstanding common stock shares and the current stock price.

market orders - type of securities order that requires the trade be made at the best current market price.

market risk - a systematic risk where securities tend to move with the market.

market segmentation theory - yield curve theory that asserts that yields are determined by the laws of supply and demand for specific bond maturities.

marketability - the ability of an investor to find a ready market where the investor may sell his or her investment.

Markowitz's Three Rules - 1. Same return, choose lower risk. 2. Same risk, choose higher return. 3. Choose higher return with lower risk.

maturity - the period of time through which the issuer has control over the bond proceeds and the period of time it must continue to pay coupon payments.

maximum family benefit - the limit on the amount of monthly Social Security benefits that may be paid to a family.

MBS - see *mortgage-backed securities.*

mean-variance optimization model - used to determine the highest level of return (based on combinations of asset classes and different weightings of asset classes) for a specified level of risk tolerance.

MECs - see *modified endowment contracts.*

Medicaid - provides medical assistance for persons with low incomes and resources.

medical payments - a no-fault, first-party insurance coverage designed to pay for bodily injuries sustained in an auto accident.

medical savings account (MSA) - an account used to pay the out-of-pocket medical expenses of an insured enrolled in a high-deductible health insurance plan.

Medicare - a federal health insurance plan for those who have attained full retirement age or have been disabled, whether retired or still working.

Medicare Advantage - a managed care plan that uses a network of doctors, hospitals, and health care providers approved by Medicare.

members - the owners of a limited liability company (LLC) who can be individuals, partnerships, trusts, corporations, or other LLCs.

misstatement of age or gender provision - insurance contract provision that allows the insurer to adjust the face amount of the policy to what the premiums paid would have purchased had the age and gender been stated correctly.

moderate inflation - inflation characterized by slowly rising prices.

Modern Portfolio Theory (MPT) - theory created by Harry Markowitz that describes portfolio diversification gained by combining securities with varying characteristics

modified adjusted gross income (MAGI) - on the 1040 federal tax return, modified adjusted gross income is the sum of adjusted gross income, nontaxable interest, and foreign-earned income.

modified endowment contracts (MECs) - whole life policies that fail the IRS's 7-pay test; distributions receive LIFO tax treatment and are subject to a 10% penalty if policyowner is under age 59 1/2.

modified whole life - whole life insurance policy where premiums are lower for the first few years after the policy issue, typically three to five years, and increase thereafter.

money market - consists of debt securities that have the following characteristics: short-term maturity, low credit risk, and high liquidity.

money market mutual funds - a mutual fund that invests in money market instruments, such as Treasury bills and negotiable CDs.

monopoly - a single seller of a well-defined product with no valid substitutes.

moral hazard - a character flaw or level of dishonesty an individual possesses that causes or increases the chance for loss.

morale hazard - indifference to a loss based on the existence of insurance.

morbidity - relates to the probability of becoming disabled.

mortality charge - the amount of money the insurance company charges for providing a death benefit.

mortgage bond - bond secured by real property.

mortgage-backed securities (MBSs) - ownership claims on a pool of mortgages.

MPT - see *Modern Portfolio Theory.*

MSA - see *medical savings account.*

municipal bonds - debt instruments issued by municipalities (states, counties, parishes, cities, towns) as general obligation bonds or revenue bonds.

mutual funds - open-end investment companies that sell shares of stock to the public and use the proceeds to invest in a portfolio of securities on behalf of their shareholders.

mutual insurance company - owned by policyholders; distributes profit in the form of dividends.

named perils - perils specifically listed in an insurance policy.

named-perils policy - a policy which provides protection against losses caused only by the perils specifically listed in the policy.

NAV - see *net asset value.*

negligence - tort caused by acting without reasonable care.

Nasdaq - the first electronic trading system made up of leading technology and internet-related companies.

net asset value (NAV) - the price at which shares of an open-end investment company are sold. The NAV of a fund is determined by subtracting total liabilities from total assets of the fund and dividing the difference by the outstanding shares.

net present value (NPV) - the difference between the initial cash outflow (investment) and the present value of discounted cash inflows.

net worth - the amount of wealth or equity the client has in owned assets.

new comparability plan - a defined-contribution plan that maximizes the age-weighting discrepancy permitted under the cross-testing provisions of proposed non-discrimination regulations.

new economy stocks - stocks within the technology industry that are expected to benefit greatly from the popularity and mainstreaming of the Internet.

no-fault insurance - automobile insurance that places limits on the insured's ability to sue other drivers for damages.

no-load funds - mutual funds purchased directly through the mutual fund family without the assistance of a broker.

nominal return - the stated return from an investment.

noncancellable - type of insurance in which the insurer guarantees renewal of the policy for a given period or to a stated age without an increase in premium.

nonfinancial risk – a risk that involves a non-monetary loss.

nonparticipating - in life insurance, a policy that does not pay dividends.

NPV - see *net present value.*

nuncupative/oral will - dying declarations made before sufficient witnesses.

OASDI - see *Old Age and Survivor Disability Insurance.*

objectivity - relating to facts without distortion by personal feelings or prejudices.

occurrence - an accident, including exposure to conditions, which results in bodily injury or property damage during the homeowners insurance policy period.

offer of settlement - a CFP Board designee may tender an Offer of Settlement in exchange for a stipulated form of disciplinary action by the CFP Board's Board of Professional Review.

officers - individuals appointed by a corporation's board of directors to carry out the board's policies and make day-to-day operating decisions.

OI - see *ordinary income.*

Old Age and Survivor Disability Insurance (OASDI) - Social Security.

oligopoly - small number of rival seller firms; incentive to collude; high barrier to entry.

online trading - a method of buying and selling securities over the internet without the use of a broker.

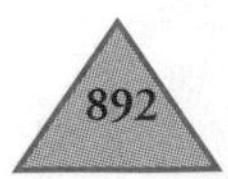

open market operations - the process by which the Federal Reserve purchases and sells government securities in the open market.

open-end investment company - an investment company whose capitalization constantly changes as new shares are sold and outstanding shares are redeemed.

open-perils policy - a policy in which all perils or causes of loss are covered, unless they are specifically listed under the exclusions section.

opportunity cost - when faced with investment alternatives, it is the highest-valued alternative *not* chosen and represents what is forgone by choosing another alternative. When discounting a future sum or series of payments back to present value, it is the composite rate of return on the client's assets with similar risk to the assets being examined.

options - derivatives that give the holder or buyer the right to do something.

oral will - see *nuncupative will.*

order of acceptance - if an Offer of Settlement is accepted by the Hearing Panel during a disciplinary review, it must propose an Order of Acceptance containing findings of fact to be reviewed by the CFP Board's Board of Professional Review.

ordinary income (OI) - any income that arises from services or from property that is not classified as a capital asset.

ordinary (straight) life - a continuous-premium whole life policy in which premiums are paid regularly until either the date of death or age 100.

other insured rider - see *spouse and child insurance riders.*

other structures - small detached structures on insured's property in addition to the main house, such as garages, greenhouses, or storage buildings.

own occupation - a definition of disability in which an insured is considered totally disabled if he cannot perform each and every duty of his own occupation.

paid-up additions, option to purchase - life insurance options that increase the whole life death benefit protection; builds additional cash value.

paid-up policy - characteristic of a life insurance policy in which no future premiums payments are due and the policy remains in effect.

PAP - see *personal automobile policy.*

paradoxical thinking - the second phase of a client's thinking process when setting financial direction in which a client tries to focus on several simultaneous objectives, causing confusion, goal conflict, and ambiguity. The paradoxical thinking phase is where a client often seeks the advice of a financial planner.

Parent Loans for Undergraduate Students (PLUS) - loans available through the Direct Loan and FFEL programs that allow parents with good credit histories to borrow funds for a child's educational expenses.

partial disability - definition of disability in which the insured cannot perform all of the substantial and material duties of the job or is prevented from working at least 80% of his normal work schedule.

participating - in life insurance, a policy that pays dividends.

participating preferred stock - preferred stock that receives dividends based on the performance of the firm in addition to the specified preferred stock dividend.

particular risk – personal risk that involves a possible loss for an individual or a small group.

partner - an individual, corporation, trust, estate, or other partnership that has an ownership interest in a partnership.

partnership - an association of two or more entities that carry on as co-owners of a business for the purpose of making a profit..

payments for legal support - transfers to children that are essentially legal support obligations; exempt from gift tax rules.

P/E ratio - see *price-to-earnings ratio.*

peak - the point in the business cycle that appears at the end of the expansion phase when most businesses are operating at full capacity and Gross Domestic Product is increasing rapidly.

Pell Grant - a grant from the federal government awarded to undergraduate students who have not earned bachelors or professional degrees. A student's EFC is used to determine the student's eligibility for a Pell Grant and how much is awarded to the student.

pension plan - a qualified plan structured to provide a regularly paid, fixed sum at retirement.

peril - the proximate, or actual, cause of a loss.

Perkins Loan - see *Federal Perkins Loan.*

personal automobile policy (PAP) - insurance policy that covers liability for injuries and damages to persons inside and outside the vehicle and covers the cost to repair/replace a damaged or stolen vehicle.

personal financial planning - the process, both art and science, of formulating, implementing, and monitoring multifunctional decisions that enable an individual or family to achieve financial goals.

Personal Financial Specialist (PFS) - designation conferred upon CPAs who successfully complete the education and experience requirements outlined by the American Institute of Certified Public Accountants (AICPA). General requirements include three years of financial planning experience and a passing score on AICPA's personal financial planning examination.

personal instruction letter - see *side instruction letter.*

personal service corporation (PSC) - a C corporation in which substantially all of the activities involve the performance of services in the fields of health, law, engineering, architecture, accounting, actuarial science, or consulting.

personal umbrella policy (PUP) - coverage designed to provide a catastrophic layer of liability coverage on top of the individual's homeowners and automobile insurance policies.

personal utility curves - economic curves that describe the satisfaction that an individual receives from a selected item and/or additional units of that item.

PFS - see *Personal Financial Specialist.*

physical hazard - a tangible condition or circumstance that increases the probability of a peril occurring and/or the severity of damages that result from a peril.

physician's expense insurance - pays for fees charged by physicians who provide the insured with nonsurgical care.

PIA - see *primary insurance amount.*

PLRs - see *private letter rulings.*

PLUS - see *Parent Loans for Undergraduate Students.*

POA - see *general power of attorney.*

policy loan provision - life insurance contract provision that allows the policyowner to borrow against the cash surrender value of a permanent insurance policy.

pool-of-money concept - long-term care coverage that provides coverage up to a specific dollar amount regardless of time period.

power-of-appointment trust - allows a terminable interest to be passed to a surviving spouse and the property to still qualify for the marital deduction. Unlike a QTIP Trust, no election is required.

PPI - see *Producer Price Index.*

PPO - see *preferred provider organization.*

practice standards - the set of standards that: (1) establish the level of professional practice that is expected of CFP Board designees engaged in personal financial planning, (2) advance professionalism in the practice of financial planning, and (3) enhance the value of the personal financial planning process.

preemptive right - allows shareholder to maintain ownership percentage by requiring new issues of stock to be offered first to current shareholders.

pre-existing condition - a medical condition that required treatment during a specified period of time prior to the insured's effective date of coverage.

pre-existing conditions clause - an insurance contract clause that excludes coverage for pre-existing conditions for a specified period time after the effective date of coverage.

preferred habitat theory - yield curve theory that asserts that financial institutions prefer to match asset maturities to liability maturities.

preferred provider organization (PPO) - a contractual arrangement between the insured, the insurer, and the health care provider that allows the insurer to receive discounted rates from service providers.

preferred stock - a type of stock that has characteristics of both fixed-income investments and of common stock in that dividend payments must be paid each year before paying a dividend to the common shareholders.

premium - the cost of an option contract.

prepaid tuition plans - plans where prepayment of college tuition is allowed at current prices for enrollment in the future; in other words, a parent can "lock in" future tuition at current rates.

prepayment risk - the risk that homeowners will pay off their loans before the scheduled loan maturity date.

preponderance of the evidence standard - a measure or degree of proof – with regard to CFP Board's Disciplinary Rules and Procedures, "preponderance of the evidence" means the evidence as a whole shows what it was intended to prove with a probability of 51 percent or better.

present value (PV) - what a sum of money to be received in a future year is worth in today's dollars based on a specific discount rate.

present value of an annuity due (PVAD) - the value today of a series of equal payments made at the *beginning* of each period for a finite number of periods.

present value of an ordinary annuity (PVOA) - the value today of a series of equal payments made at the *end* of each period for a finite number of periods.

price elasticity - the quantity demanded of a good in response to changes in that good's price. A good is *elastic* when its quantity demanded responds greatly to price changes (luxuries). A good is *inelastic* when its quantity demanded responds little to price changes (necessities).

price index - a weighted average of the prices of numerous goods and services, (for example, the consumer price index, the gross national product deflator, and the producer price index).

price-to-earnings (P/E) ratio - a measure of how much the market is willing to pay for each dollar of earnings of a company.

primary beneficiary - the party designated by the policyowner to receive death benefits.

primary insurance amount (PIA) - amount on which a worker's retirement benefit is based, the PIA determines the amount the applicant will receive at his or her full retirement age, based on the year in which the retiree turns 62. The PIA is indexed to the consumer price index (CPI) annually.

primary market - the market where new issues of securities are first offered to the public.

principal (**re: power of attorney**) - in a power of attorney document, the person (power giver) who designates another person or persons to act as his attorney-in-fact.

principle of indemnity - states that a person is entitled to compensation only to the extent that financial loss has been suffered.

principle of insurable interest - to have an insurable interest, an insured must be subject to emotional or financial hardship resulting from damage, loss, or destruction.

principle of utmost good faith - also known as the principle of fair dealing, the principle of utmost good faith requires that the insured and the insurer both be forthcoming with all relevant facts about the insured risk and the coverage provided for that risk.

Principles - one of two main parts of the CFP Board's Code of Ethics that addresses the profession's recognition of the responsibilities of its members to the public, clients, colleagues, and employers, and provides statements of ideals to members during the performance of their professional duties.

private censure - an unpublished written reproach that is mailed to the censured CFP Board designee by the CFP Board's Board of Professional Review.

private letter rulings (PLRs) - statements issued for a fee upon a taxpayer's request that describe how the IRS will treat a proposed transaction for tax purposes.

private placement - equity underwriting in which the underwriter assists in identifying private purchasers of an issue.

probate process - serves to prove the validity of any will, supervise the orderly distribution of assets to the heirs, and protect creditors by insuring that valid debts of the estate are paid. Probate is also the legal process that performs the function of changing property title from a decedent's name to an heir's name.

Producer Price Index (PPI) - the oldest continuous statistical series published by the Labor Department that measures the level of prices at the wholesale or producer stage.

profit-sharing plan - a qualified defined-contribution plan featuring a flexible (discretionary) employer-contribution provision. Profit-sharing plans are structured to offer employees participation in company profits that they may use for retirement purposes.

proprietor - the owner of a sole proprietorship.

proxy voting - authorizing an agent to cast the vote for the shareholder.

PSC - see *personal service corporation.*

public letter of admonition - a written reproach of the CFP Board designee's behavior that will normally be published in a press release or other form of publicity selected by the CFP Board's Board of Professional Review (BOPR).

PUP - see *personal umbrella policy.*

purchasing power preservation model - a capital needs analysis method that assumes that the client will have a capital balance of equal purchasing power at life expectancy as he did at retirement.

purchasing-power risk - a systematic risk where inflation will erode the real value of the investor's assets.

pure annuity concept - the basic capital needs analysis approach that is generally prepared on a pretax basis.

pure expectations theory - yield curve theory that assets that long-term interest rates are based on expectations about future short-term interest rates.

pure risk - a risk that creates a financial loss when it occurs.

put option - a derivative that gives the holder the right to sell the underlying asset, generally stock, at a specified price within a specified period.

PV - see *present value.*

PVAD - see *present value of an annuity due.*

PVOA - see *present value of an ordinary annuity.*

QDOT - see *qualified domestic trust.*

QTIP Trust- see *qualified terminable interest property trust.*

QTP - see *qualified tuition plans.*

qualified domestic trust (QDOT) - for a noncitizen spouse who was a U.S. resident at the time of the decedent's death, the marital deduction is allowed if the property is placed in a QDOT that passes to a noncitizen surviving spouse.

qualified long-term care services - as defined by HIPAA—necessary diagnostic, preventative, therapeutic, caring, treating, rehabilitative services, and maintenance or personal care services required by a chronically ill or cognitively impaired person and provided by a plan prescribed by a licensed health care practitioner.

qualified tuition plans (QTPs) - also known as 529 plans, QTPs allow individuals to either participate in prepaid tuition plans in which tuition credits are purchased for a designated beneficiary for payment or waiver of higher education expenses, or participate in savings plans in which contributions of money are made to an account to eventually pay for higher education expenses of a designated beneficiary.

qualified terminable interest property (QTIP) **trust** - allows a terminable interest to be passed to a surviving spouse and the property to still qualify for the unlimited marital deduction. The executor makes the election on IRS Form 706.

qualified transfer - a payment made directly to an educational institution for tuition and fees or to a medical institution for medical expenses for the benefit of someone else.

R - see *correlation coefficient.*

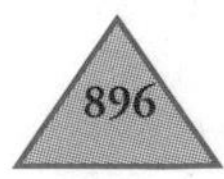

R^2 - see *coefficient of determination.*

random walk - an unpredictable pattern that describes the movement of security prices over time.

ratio analysis - the relationship or relative value of two characteristics used to analyze an individual's financial health and to conduct comparison and trend analysis.

readjustment period - period lasting one to two years following the death of a breadwinner.

real interest rate adjustment - the rate of interest expressed in dollars of constant value (adjusted for inflation); and equal to the nominal interest rate less the rate of inflation.

real rate of return - the nominal return adjusted for inflation.

recession - a decline in real Gross Domestic Product for two or more successive quarters.

reentry term - term life insurance that allows for renewal coverage at a lower premium if the insured provides satisfactory evidence of insurability.

Registered Investment Adviser (RIA) - a person or company that offers ongoing portfolio management or investment advice and charges money for it.

reinstatement clause - life insurance contract clause that outlines the conditions under which a lapsed policy may be reinstated.

reinvestment risk - a systematic risk where earnings (cash flows) distributed from current investments cannot be reinvested at a rate of return equal to the expected yield of the current investments.

remaining work-life expectancy (RWLE) - work period remaining at a certain point in time before retirement.

renewable - in term life insurance products, may be renewed without evidence of insurability at a premium determined by the current age of the insured.

renewable at the insurer's option - type of insurance which may not be canceled during the policy's term but may only be renewed at the insurer's option.

replacement cost - the amount necessary to purchase, repair, or replace the dwelling with materials of the same or similar quality at current prices.

representations - statements made by the insured to the insurer in the application process.

reserve requirement - for a member bank of the Federal Reserve, it is the percent of deposit liabilities that must be held in reserve. As the reserve requirement is increased, less money is available to be loaned, resulting in a restriction of the money supply.

residual benefits provision - disability insurance provision in which the policyowner receives a percentage of the disability benefit based on the percentage of income loss due to sickness or injury.

residuary clause - a general provision in a will that provides for the transfer of the balance of any assets not specifically mentioned in the will to a person or institution named by the testator.

retirement benefit - the most familiar Social Security benefit, full retirement benefits are payable at full retirement age with reduced benefits as early as age 62, to anyone who has obtained at least a minimum amount of Social Security credits.

retirement earnings limitations test - one of the ways in which Social Security benefits are reduced based on earnings.

retirement life expectancy (RLE) - the time period beginning at retirement and extending until death; the RLE is the period of retirement that must be funded.

return of premium rider - life insurance rider that returns the premiums paid for a policy, less administrative charges and rider premiums, at the end of the insurance term.

revenue procedures- statements reflecting the internal management practices of the IRS that affect the rights and duties of taxpayers.

revenue rulings- official pronouncements of the National Office of the IRS.

revocable beneficiary - a beneficiary who can be changed by the policyowner at any time.

revocation - the CFP Board's Board of Professional Review (BOPR) may order permanent revocation of a CFP Board designee's right to use the mark, and publish the revocation in a press release or other form of publicity.

RIA - see *Registered Investment Adviser.*

riders/endorsements - written additions to an insurance contract that modify its original provisions.

risk - the chance of loss, possibility of loss, uncertainty, or a variation of actual from expected results.

risk assumption - bearing all or part of the financial burden in the event of a loss.

risk avoidance - the avoidance of any chance of loss.

risk reduction – activities that reduce the frequency or severity of losses.

risk tolerance - the level of risk exposure with which an individual is comfortable; an estimate of the level of risk an investor is willing to accept in his or her investment portfolio.

risk transfer - shifting the probability of loss to another party, such as an insurance company.

RLE - see *retirement life expectancy.*

Roth IRA - an IRA created by the Taxpayer Relief Act of 1997. Contributions to a Roth IRA are nondeductible; qualified distributions are excluded from an individuals taxable income. Distributions used for qualified educational expenses can also avoid the 10 percent penalty.

Rule of 72 - a method of approximation that estimates the time that it takes to double the value of an investment where the earnings (interest) rate is known (by dividing 72 by the interest rate). Alternatively, it can also estimate the earnings (interest) rate necessary to double an investment value if the time is known (by dividing 72 by the period of investment).

Rules - one of two main parts of the CFP Board's Code of Ethics that is derived from the doctrine expressed in the Principles and helps to establish a foundation for complying with the Principles of the Code.

Russell Indexes - a collection of financial indexes made up of over 24 U.S. stock indexes, as well as foreign indexes in Australia, Canada, Japan, and the United Kingdom, maintained by the Frank Russell Company.

RWLE - see *remaining work-life expectancy.*

S&P 500 Index - see *Standard & Poor's 500 Index.*

S corporation - a special type of corporation formed under state law like a regular corporation; however, for income tax purposes, is treated similar to a partnership.

savings - deferred consumption.

Savings Plan - a type of Qualified State Tuition Plan similar to a Coverdell Education Savings Account where the owner of the account, (the parent or grandparent of the student) contributes cash to the account so that the contributions can grow tax deferred and, hopefully, realize a higher return on the investment than could be achieved outside of the plan.

scheduled personal property endorsement - homeowners insurance policy endorsement that provides open-peril coverage under the same terms as if separate contracts were purchased for each type of property. The amount for which an item is insured is considered the value of the item if a loss is incurred.

secondary market - the market where investors can buy and sell securities with other investors.

Securities Act of 1933 - federal law that provides rules and regulations related to new issues of investment securities.

Securities Exchange Act of 1934 - federal law that provides rules and regulations related to the purchase and sale of investment securities in the market.

securitization - the process of transforming nonnegotiable securities into negotiable securities.

self-employment tax - tax paid by self-employed individuals that is based on net earnings, not on the individual's wages. Since the self-employed must bear the burden of both the employer and employee portion of FICA, the self-employment tax rate is 15.3%—double the employee's rate of 7.65%.

self-insured retention - a payment similar to a deductible that an insured is usually required to pay for each loss under a personal umbrella policy.

Separate Trading of Registered Interest and Principal of Securities (STRIPS) - a program that permits investors to hold and trade the individual interest and principal components of eligible Treasury notes and bonds as separate securities.

serial payment - a payment that increases at a constant rate (usually, the rate of inflation) on an annual (ordinary) basis.

Series EE United States Savings Bonds (EE bonds) - if used to pay for qualified higher education expenses at an eligible institution or state tuition plan, EE bonds bestow significant tax savings; that is, no federal income tax on the interest.

settlement options - life insurance policy options that allow the policyowner or beneficiary to choose either cash or one of several alternatives to how the death benefit will be paid.

shareholders - the owners of a corporation who elect the corporation's board of directors.

Sharpe ratio - a measure of risk-adjusted portfolio performance that uses standard deviation as the risk measure.

short position - a type of position investors take by selling borrowed shares in hopes that the stock price will decline over time.

short-term capital gain - a gain from sale or exchange of a capital asset that has been held for one year or less

short-term disability - provides coverage for up to 2 years.

side instruction letter - also known as a personal instruction letter, separate from a will; details the testator's wishes regarding the disposition of tangible possessions (household goods), the disposition of the decedent's body, and funeral arrangements.

simultaneous death clause - in the event that both spouses die simultaneously, this clause provides an assumption that one spouse (predetermined) predeceased the other spouse.

single premium annuity - an annuity purchased with a single lump sum.

sinking funds - funds usually held by trustee to ensure repayment of borrowed principal.

skilled nursing care - daily nursing care and rehabilitation services ordered and monitored by a physician.

slander - verbal statement that causes harm to another.

Social Security statement, Form SSA-7005 - a written report mailed by the Social Security Administration to all workers age 25 and over who are not yet receiving Social Security benefits that provides an estimate of the worker's eventual Social Security benefits and instructions on how to qualify for those benefits.

sole proprietorship - a business owned and controlled by one person who is personally liable for all debts and claims against the business.

special power of attorney/appointment - limits the appointee to specific standards such as health, education, maintenance, and support (HEMS), or nearly as broad as a general power, except no appointments to one's self, one's creditors, one's estate or one's estate's creditors.

speculative risk - a risk where profit, loss or no loss may occur.

split gift - a joint gift made by spouses which has the effect of doubling the annual exclusion of gifts to the donee. Requires the consent of the spouse and spouse's signature on Form 709.

split limits - three separate liability coverage limits covering per person bodily injury, per occurrence bodily injury, and property damage.

spouse and child insurance riders - life insurance riders that provide life insurance coverage on the insured's spouse and children.

SSA-7005 - see *Social Security statement.*

SSI - see *Supplemental Security Income.*

Stafford Loan - the primary type of financial aid provided by the United States Department of Education. There are two types of Stafford Loans: Direct Stafford Loans ("Direct Loans") provided directly to the student, and Federal Family Education Stafford Loans ("FFEL Loans") made to the student through a lender (such as a bank or other approved financial institution) that participates in the FFEL program.

Standard & Poor's 500 Index (S&P 500) - a financial index of 500 U.S. equities chosen for market size, liquidity, and industry group representation.

standard deviation - measures a portfolio's total volatility and its total risk (that is, systematic and unsystematic risk).

standard deduction - the deduction allowed to taxpayers who do not itemize deductions.

stand-by underwriting - equity underwriting in which the underwriter purchases any securities remaining after an initial offering.

statement of cash flows - summary of the client's changes to the cash account.

statement of changes in net worth - summary of changes from one balance sheet to the next.

static risk – a risk dependent on factors other than a change in economy (e.g., natural disaster - earthquake/flood).

statutory will - generally drawn by an attorney, signed in the presence of witnesses, complying with the statutes for wills of the domiciliary state.

stock bonus plan - a defined-contribution profit-sharing plan in which all employer contributions are in the form of employer stock; distributions to participants can be made in the form of employer stock.

stop limit orders - a type of securities order that becomes a limit order when the security's price reaches a specific level.

stop loss orders - a type of securities order that becomes a market order when the security's price reaches a specific level.

straight life - see *ordinary life.*

straight life annuity - an annuity that provides a lifetime income to the annuitant regardless of how long he or she lives.

straight voting - one vote per share of common stock.

strengths, weaknesses, opportunities and threats (SWOT) analysis - an analysis that helps the financial planner understand how internal and external environmental factors affects the client's financial situation.

strict and absolute liability - liability resulting from law; strict liability allows for defense, absolute liability does not.

STRIPS - see Separate Trading of Registered Interest and Principal of Securities.

subjective risk - a particular person's perception of risk, varying greatly among individuals.

subjectivity - relating to the client's perception of reality.

subrogation clause - states that the insured cannot indemnify himself or herself from both the insurance company and a negligent third party for the same claim.

substitution effect - the phenomenon in which consumers substitute less expensive goods for similar, expensive goods. This is one of two reasons why the demand curve slopes downward.

suicide clause - life insurance contract clause that voids the policy and refunds premiums to the beneficiaries if the insured commits suicide within a specified period of time.

Supplemental Security Income (SSI) - program administered by the Social Security Administration and funded by the general Treasury that is available to those at full retirement age, or those who are disabled and have a low income and few assets.

supply - that quantity of a particular good which businesses are willing to produce or sell.

supply curve - the graphic depiction that shows the relationship between the market price of a particular good and the quantity supplied.

surgical expense insurance - insurance that may be added to a hospital expense insurance policy to provide for the payment of the surgeon's fees, even when surgery is not performed in a hospital.

surplus-line agents - agents with authority to place business with unadmitted insurers.

survivors benefit - Social Security benefit available to surviving family members of a deceased, eligible worker.

survivorship clause - provides that the beneficiary must survive the decedent for a specified period in order to receive the inheritance or bequest.

suspension - a form of discipline that the CFP Board's Board of Professional Review (BOPR) may order for a specified period, not to exceed five (5) years, for individuals it deems can be rehabilitated.

SWOT analysis - see *strengths, weaknesses, opportunities, and threats analysis.*

investment risks impacted by broad macroeconomic factors that influence all securities.

memoranda.

899

target plan - an age-weighted money-purchase pension plan; a hybrid between a defined-contribution plan and a defined-benefit plan.

taxable bond market - one of two markets that make up the United States bond market, and that consists of U.S. Treasury bonds, U.S. government agency bonds, and corporate bonds.

tax-exempt bond market - one of the two markets that make up the United States bond market, and that consists of municipal bonds.

technical advice memoranda (TAM)- advice or guidance in memorandum form furnished by the National Office of the IRS to IRS agents who request such advice or guidance during an audit. Technical advice memoranda help to close cases and maintain consistent holdings throughout the IRS.

technical analysis - the search for identifiable and recurring stock price patterns.

tenancy by the entirety - a joint tenancy with right of survivorship (JTWROS) that can only occur between a husband and wife.

tenancy in common - two or more persons hold an undivided interest in a whole property.

term insurance - type of life insurance that provides temporary protection for a specified number of years.

term insurance rider - rider for a whole life policy that offers additional, affordable term life insurance on the insured.

term to age 65 or 70 - a term life insurance policy that provides protection until the insured reaches age 65 or 70.

terminable interest - an interest that ends upon an event or contingency

testamentary capacity - having the mental capability to make a will to transfer assets; being of sound mind.

third market - over-the-counter trading of equity shares that are listed on an exchange.

time value of money (TVM) - the concept that money received today is worth more than the same amount of money received sometime in the future.

time-weighted returns - a method of determining an internal rate of return by evaluating the performance of portfolio managers without the influence of additional investor deposits to or withdrawals from the portfolio.

Treynor ratio - a measure of a risk-adjusted portfolio performance that uses beta as the risk measure.

trough - the point in the business cycle that appears at the end of the contraction phase when most businesses are operating at their lowest capacity levels and Gross Domestic Product is at its lowest or is negative.

trust - a legal arrangement, usually provided for under state law, in which a grantor transfers property to a trustee for the management and conservation of the property for the benefit of the named beneficiaries.

TVM - see *time value of money.*

UGMA - see *Uniform Gift to Minors Act.*

UIT - see *unit investment trust.*

UL - see *universal life.*

underwriting - the process by which investment bankers purchase an issue of securities from a firm and resell it to the public.

unemployment rider - life insurance rider that waives policy premiums for a limited period of time if the insured becomes unemployed.

uneven cash flows - investment returns or deposits that may not be single interval deposits or equal payments.

unified gift and estate transfer tax system - unified tax transfer system created by Congress to ensure that at the time of transfer of property, either during life (gifts) or at death (bequests), the transferor will pay the same tax rate or amount for the transfer, regardless of when the transfer is made.

Uniform Gift to Minors Act (UGMA) - allows parents the option to put assets in a custodial account for a child, for example, to pay for college tuition.

Uniform Transfer to Minors Act (UTMA) - allows parents to put cash, securities, and real property in a custodial account for a child.

uninsured/underinsured motorist - motorist without liability coverage or whose insurer can/will not pay claim, hit-and-run driver, or motorist with insufficient liability coverage according to state law.

unit investment trust (UIT) - a registered investment company that is passively managed and may invest in stocks, bonds, or other securities.

universal life (UL) - life insurance that gives policyowners the ability to adjust the premiums, death benefit, and cash values to meet their individual needs.

unsystematic risks - types of investment risks unique to a single company, industry, or country that can be eliminated by portfolio diversification.

UTMA - see *Uniform Transfer to Minors Act.*

utmost good faith - see *principle of utmost good faith.*

value stocks - stock trading at prices that are low given the stock's historical earnings and current asset value.

variable annuity - an annuity that does not guarantee specific payments.

variable expenses - expenses that fluctuate from time to time over which the client has some control.

variable life - a fixed-premium whole life policy in which the death benefit and cash values fluctuate based on the investment performance of a separate account maintained by the insurer.

variable universal life (VUL) - combines the investment direction of variable life and the premium, death benefit, and cash value flexibility of universal life.

vesting - an employee's nonforfeitable right to receive a present or future pension benefit.

viatical agreement - sale of life insurance contract by the insured when terminally ill or when chronically ill and proceeds are used for long-term care.

vicarious acts - negligent acts performed by someone else for which the individual is held at least partially responsible.

VUL - see *variable universal life.*

wage replacement ratio (WRR) - an estimate of the percent of income needed at retirement compared to earnings prior to retirement.

waiver of premium rider - life insurance rider that waives premium payments during a period of disability for the insured; disability insurance rider that waives the premium payments after the insured has been disabled for the lesser of 90 days or the elimination period.

war exclusion - life insurance policy exclusion that allows the insurer to deny the death claim if the insured's death is related to war or military service.

whole life insurance - life insurance that provides coverage for the lifetime of the insured.

will - a legal document used in estate planning that provides the testator, or will maker, the opportunity to control the distribution of property and avoid the state's intestacy law distribution scheme.

Wilshire 5000 Index - a financial index consisting of over 5,000 U.S. based companies that is often used as a measure of the overall market within the U.S.

WLE - see *work-life expectancy.*

work-life expectancy (WLE) - the years that a person spends in the work force, generally 30-40 years.

WRR - see *wage replacement ratio.*

yield curves - graphical representations that reflect current market interest rates for various bond maturities.

yield-to-call (YTC) - the expected return on a bond from the purchase date to the date that the bond may be called.

yield-to-maturity (YTM) - the compounded rate of return on a bond purchased at the current market price and held to maturity.

ld-to-call.

l that does not pay periodic coupon or interest payments.

Index

Numerics

401(k) plan. *See Retirement plan*
403(b) plan. *See Retirement plan*
529 Plan. *See QTP*

A

Accumulation schedule, 181
Active investment, 469
Active participant, 716
Active approach to. *See Investment*, 469
Actual cash value, 274, 360
Adhesion, 270
Adjustable Rate Mortgage (ARM), 135–136
Administrator, 733
  Duties, 736
Adult day care. *See Long-term care insurance*
Advanced medical directive, 736
Adverse selection, 263
Advisors Act, 869
Age-banding, 246
Age-weighted plan, 712
Aging parent. *See Special needs*
Agreed-upon value, 273–274
Aleatory, 270
Allocation formula, 712
Alpha, 585
Alternative minimum tax. *See Income tax*
American Depositary Receipts (ADRs), 523
Amortization table, 209–211
AMT. *See Income tax - Alternative minimum tax*
Annual exclusion. *See Estate transfer tax*
Annuity
  Annuity due, 182
  Joint and survivor annuity, 324
  Pure life annuity, 322
  Taxation of, 327
  Types of, 322
Anomaly. *See Efficient market hypothesis*
Anti-Fraud Provisions, 868
Antitrust, 40
Any occupation disability definition. See Disability insurance, 335
Apparent authority, 272
Applicable credit amount. *See Estate transfer tax*
Arithmetic mean. *See Return*
ARM, 135–136
Armed Forces aid, 232
Articles of organization. *See Limited liability company (LLC)*
Asset
  Asset allocation, 465
  Cash and cash equivalents, 94–95, 102
  Classes of, 461
  Expected returns for, 461
  Historical performance of, 454
  Investment asset, 94–95, 102, 123–124, 128
  Personal-use asset, 95–96, 100–102, 108, 129
  Standard deviation of, 455
Asset allocation, 576–578, 584
Asset allocation. *See Asset*
Asset-backed securities *See securities*
Assisted living. *See Long-term care insurance*
Assumption of the risk, 36
Audit
  Correspondence, 660
  Field, 660
  Office, 660
  Outcomes of, 660
  Types of, 660
Average indexed monthly earnings (AIME), 408

B

Back-end load. *See Mutual fund - Fees*
Balance sheet. *See Financial statement*
Bank Insurance Fund (BIF), 42
Banker's acceptances, 485
Bankruptcy, 39
  Federal bankruptcy laws, 39
Banks, 42
Barbell strategy, 513
Belth model, 316
Belth, Joseph, 316
Benchmark, 533
Bend points, 410
Beneficiary designation, 319
Best-Efforts, 529
Beta, 455, 584
Beyond a reasonable doubt, 835
BIF, 42
Board of directors, 633
Board of Professional Review (BOPR), 815
Bond fund. *See Fixed-income fund*
Bond indenture agreement, 492

Bonds, 43
    Call provisions of, 492
    Collateral provisions of, 493
    Convertible bonds, 493
    Corporate bonds, 492
    Coupon payments, 476
    Maturity, 476
    Methods of immunizing portfolios, 512
    Savings bonds, 488
    Sinking fund provisions of, 493
    Taxable bond Market, 482
    Tax-exempt bond Market, 483
    Tax-treasury bonds, 486
bonds, 449
Boot, 610
    See also Like-kind exchange
Budgeting, 129, 442
    Steps, 129
Built-in gain. *See Mutual fund - Disadvantages of*
Bullet strategy, 513
Burden of proof, 36, 834
Business and professional insurance
    Summary of policies, 388
Business cycle, 24–26, 33
    Contraction, 25
    Depression, 26
    Expansion, 25–26, 32–34
    External business cycle theory, 26
    Peak, 25
    Recession, 25–26, 33–34
Business liability insurance, 627
Business risk. *See Risk*
Bypass trust. *See Trust*

C

Capital appreciation, 517
Capital asset, 594
Capital Asset Pricing Model (CAPM), 549
Capital formation, 26
Capital gain, 595
    See also Income tax
Capital market line, 549
Capital needs analysis, 685
    Annuity method, 685
    Capital preservation model, 688
    Purchasing power preservation model, 689
Capital preservation model, 688
...l retention approach. See Life insurance, 298
...cial needs*

Cash flow capacity, 135
Cash flow timeline. *See Timeline*
Cash value build-up, 304, 310–311
Certificate of deposit, 48
Certificates of deposit (CD), 485
Certified Financial Planner (CFP "), 803
Certified Financial Planner (CFP) Board of Standards, Inc.(CFP Board), 814
Certified Public Accountant (CPA), 804
CFP Board of Governors, 815
CFP Board of Practice Standards, 815
CFP Board of Professional Review, 836
CFP Code of Ethics and Professional Responsibility, 816
Charitable bequest
    Direct bequest, 765
    Trust, 765
    Types of, 765
    See also Trust
Charitable deduction, 765
Charitable lead trust. *See Trust*
Charitable Remainder Trust, 747
Charitable remainder trust. *See Trust*
Chartered Financial Analyst (CFA), 804
Chartered Financial Consultant (ChFC), 803
Chartered Life Underwriter (CLU), 804
Check, 42–43, 47, 129
Citizenship test, 602
Clayton Act, 41
Clear and convincing evidence, 835
Clearly erroneous standard, 837
Client data collection questionnaire, 72
Client questionnaire, 656
Client/Planner worksheet, 147
Closed-end fund, 556–557, 559
    Foreign closed-end fund, 524
Code of ethics, 814
Codicil, 735
Coefficient of determination, 463, 584
Coinsurance, 275, 359
COLA. *See Cost-of-living adjustment*
Collateralized mortgage obligations (CMOs), 496
College expenses, 221, 223, 246
Collision. *See Personal auto policy*
Commercial paper, 485
Common size analysis. *See Financial statement analysis*
Common stock. *See Stock*
Communication techniques, 59
Community property, 740
Compensation method
    Commission-based, 806
    Fee-based, 806
    Fee-only, 805

Fees for assets under management, 806
Complements, 22
Compliance, 806
NASD exam, 807
Compound interest. *See Interest*
Comprehensive. *See Personal auto policy*
Condominium insurance. *See Homeowners insurance - HO-6, 366*
Conflict of interest, 823
Consolidated Omnibus Budget Reconciliation Act of 1986 (COBRA), 42
Consumer, 42–43
Consumer Price Index (CPI), 29, 205–206, 402
Consumer protection, 37
Consumption movement, 26
Contract
Elements of, 266
Formal contract, 869
Insurance contract
Distinguishing characteristics of, 270
Exclusion, 273
Important features of, 273
Legal principles of, 267
Contraction. *See Business cycle*
Contracts
Form, 869
Convertible bonds *See bonds*
Coordination of benefits. *See Health insurance*
Copayment, 275
Corporate bonds *See bonds*
Corporation, 42, 626, 632–635, 641–643, 664–665
Corporation income tax, 635
Personal service corporation (PSC), 635
Correlation coefficient, 462
Cost-of-living adjustment (COLA), 402
Cost-of-living insurance rider, 336
Country risk. *See Risk*
Coupon payments, 476
Coupon rate, 502
Courts of original jurisdiction, 662
Coverdell ESA, 233–238
Credit Equivalency Trust, 747
Credit rating
Definition, 497
Rating agencies, 496
Credit unions, 43
Current yield *See yield*
Custodial care. *See Long-term care insurance*

D

Date of declaration. *See Dividend*
Date of record. *See Dividend*
Debentures, 493
Debt, 133
Types of, 120
Debt securities, 43, 865–868
Deductible, 275
Deductions for income tax. *See Income tax - Adjusted gross income*
Default risk. *See Risk*
Deficit spending, 32
Defined-benefit plan. *See Retirement plan*
Defined-contribution plan. *See Retirement plan*
Defined-contribution plans, 712
Deflation. *See Inflation*
Demand, 20
Change in demand, 21
Change in quantity demanded, 22
Demand curve, 20
Dental insurance, 341
Department of Housing and Urban Development (HUD), 495
Dependent, 601
Depreciation, 451
Depression. *See Business cycle*
Derivative, 452
Call options, 452
Derivatives, 452
Future, 453
Option, 452
Call option, 452
Exercise price, 452
Premium, 452
Put option, 452
Derivative. *See Derivatives*
Derivatives
Put options, 452
Determination letter, 603
Direct investing, 454
Director. *See Board of directors*
Disability, 275, 277
Long-term disability insurance checklist, 338
Disability insurance
Characteristics of, 336
Definition of disability, 335
Group insurance, 341
Integration with Social Security, 337
Residual benefits, 337
Taxation of, 337
Disabled dependent. *See Special needs*
Disciplinary rules and procedures, 834
Disclaimer, 771
Discount rate, 188
Discount rate. *See Interest rate or Monetary policy*
Discretionary cash flow, 103, 159
Discriminant index function system (DIF), 659

Disinflation. *See Inflation*
Dividend, 516–518, 540
Date of declaration, 516
Date of record, 516
Double taxation of, 635
Ex-dividend date, 517
Taxation of, 596
Dividend, 450
Dividend discount model. *See Valuation of equities*
Dividend reinvestment plans (DRIPs), 444
Dividend yield. *See Return*
Dividends
Stock dividends, 865
Dividends-received deduction (DRD), 634
Divorce. *See Special needs*
Dollar-weighted return. *See Return*
Dow Jones Industrial Average (DJIA), 530
Due Diligence., 870
Durable good, 26
Durable power of attorney *See Power of attorney*
Duration, 506
As a measure of volatility, 508

E

EAFE Index, 533
Earned income, 657
Earnings rate. *See Rate of return*
Economic environment. *See Environment*
Economic Growth and Tax Relief Reconciliation Act of 2001, 700–701, 705, 717, 730
Economy, 20, 25, 33
Education funding, 9, 220
Educational IRA. *See Coverdell ESA*
Educational loans. *See Student loan*
EFC, 224–227, 230–231
Efficient frontier, 460
Efficient market hypothesis, 468–469
Anomaly, 468
EGTRRA 2001, 730
Elasticity, 22
Price elasticity, 22
Elimination period, 336
Emergency Home Finance Act, 495
EMH
Semistrong form, 468
Strong form, 468
weak form, 468
Employee Retirement Income Security Act (ERISA), 42, 700
Employee stock option plan (ESOP), 722
Employer's educational assistance program, 240
Endorsement, 273, 368
Engagement letter, 60
Environment
Economic environment, 19
External environment, 4, 150
Internal environment, 4, 67, 150–151
Legal environment, 18
Political environment, 51
Social environment, 49
Taxation environment, 51
Technological environment, 50
Equal Credit Opportunity Act of 1975, 38
Equilibrium, 20, 24
Equity mutual fund. *See Mutual fund*
Errors and omissions insurance, 387
Estate planning
Definition, 730
Process, 732
Team, 731
Estate transfer tax, 752
Annual exclusion, 755
Applicable credit amount, 758
Charitable deduction, 765
Estate tax formula, 762
Gift splitting, 756
Gift tax return, 755, 761
Marital deduction, 766
Payments for support, 759
Purpose of, 754
Qualified transfer, 758
Strategies for transferring wealth through gifting, 760
Unified tax rate schedule, 753
ETF. *See Exchange traded fund*
Ethics, 814
Exchange traded fund, 556–557
Ex-dividend. *See Dividend*
Executor
Duties, 736
Expansion. *See Business cycle*
Expected Family Contribution. *See EFC*
Expense ratio. *See Mutual fund - Fees*
Express authority, 272
Extended term insurance, 308
Extension of credit, 47
External business cycle theory. *See Business cycle*
External environment. *See Environment*

F

FAFSA, 224, 227
Fair Credit Billing Act (FCBA), 39
Fair Credit Reporting Act, 38
Fair Debt Collections Practice Act (FDCPA), 39

Fair market value, 97
Family limited partnership (FLP), 663–664
FDIC, 42
Federal agency securities *See securities*
Federal bankruptcy laws. *See Bankruptcy*
Federal Deposit Insurance Corporation (FDIC), 42
Federal Deposit Insurance Corporation (FDIC), 870
Federal Home Loan Mortgage Corporation (Freddie Mac), 495
Federal Insurance Contributions Act (FICA), 403
Federal National Mortgage Association (Fannie Mae), 495
Federal Reserve, 31
Federal Trade Commission (FTC), 37
Federal Unemployment Tax Act (FUTA), 608
Federal Work-Study program. *See Work-study*
Fee simple, 740
Fellowships, 232
FICA. *See Federal Insurance Contributions Act*
Fiduciary relationship, 819
Financial Accounting Standards Board (FASB), 93
Financial aid, 220, 223–224, 243, 247
Financial goal, 9, 151–153, 440–441, 465
Financial independence, 8
    Risks to, 684
Financial institutions, 42, 44
Financial mission, 9, 149
Financial objective, 9, 154, 156
Financial planner
    Role in retirement planning, 723
Financial planning institution
    Accounting, 801
    Bank, 802
    Brokerage, 801
    Law, 801
    Personal Financial Planning (PFP), 801
Financial planning practitioner, 820
Financial ratio
    Current ratio, 117
    Debt ratio, 118
    Discretionary cash flow plus savings to gross income ratio, 122
    Emergency fund ratio, 116
    Income on investments ratio, 123
    Investment assets to gross income, 124
    Liquidity ratio, 116
    Long-term debt to net worth, 119
    Long-term debt to total assets, 119
    Monthly housing costs to monthly gross income, 121
    Performance ratio, 123
    Return on investment (ROI), 123
    Savings ratio, 122
    Total debt to net worth, 118
    Total debt to total assets, 119
Financial risk. *See Risk*
Financial services companies, 43
Financial statement
    Balance sheet, 93
    Current liability, 96
    Income and expense statement, 103
    Long-term liability, 96
    Statement of cash flows, 107
    Statement of changes in net worth, 111
    Types of cash flows, 108–109
    Types of expenses, 104
    Types of income, 104
    Valuation of assets and liabilities, 97
Financial statement analysis
    Common size analysis, 125
    Growth analysis, 92, 115, 128
    Limitations of, 128
    Ratio analysis, 115
    Risk analysis, 129
    Sensitivity analysis, 129
    Vertical analysis, 125
Fiscal policy, 32
Fixed income securities
    Volatility of, 502
Fixed income securities *See securities*
Fixed-income mutual fund. *See Mutual fund*
Fixed-income securities
    Risk, 498
Fixed-to-fixed rates, 135
Fixed-to-variable rates, 135
Flow-through entity. *See Partnership or S corporation*
Foreign currency risk. *See Risk*
Foreign securities, 523
Form 1040, 607
Form 1065 Schedule K-1, 631
Form 1098, 657
Form 1099-DIV, 657
Form 1099-G, 657
Form 1099-INT, 657
Form 1099-MISC, 657
Form 1099-R, 657
Form 1120, 634
Form 1120S, 636
Form 2553, 637
Form 709, 755, 761
Fourth market, 529
Fraud, 372, 605
fraud, 865, 867–868
Free cash flow to equity. *See Valuation of equities*
Fundamental analysis, 468, 545
Future value, 176–179, 181–182, 188–189, 205–206, 213
    Future value of an annuity due, 185–186, 208
    Future value of an ordinary annuity, 182–184

- Uneven cash flows, 197–198

Future. *See Derivative*

G

General damages, 36
General partnership. *See Partnership*
General powers of appointment, 732
Generation-skipping transfer tax (GSTT), 772
- Form 709, 755, 761

Geometric mean. *See Return*
Gift tax. *See Estate transfer tax*
Good faith, 268
- Concealment, 268–269
- Representation, 268–269
- Warranty, 268

Government National Mortgage Association (Ginnie Mae), 495
Grace period, 315
Gramm-Leach-Bliley Act, 870
Grant, 225–227, 230, 232, 247
- FSEOG, 226–227, 230
- Pell grant, 225–227, 230, 247

Grantor trust, 746
Gross domestic product (GDP), 29
Gross estate, 762–763
- Deductions from, 764

Gross income test, 602
Gross national product (GNP), 29
Group life insurance. See Life insurance, 315
Growth analysis. *See Financial statement analysis*

H

Hazard, 262
- Moral hazard, 263
- Morale hazard, 263
- Physical hazard, 262

Head of household. *See Income tax - Filing status*
Health insurance
- Coordination of benefits, 343
- Group health insurance
  - Taxation of, 345
- Health maintenance organization (HM0), 342
- Hospital expense insurance, 328
- Indemnity plan, 342
- Major medical insurance, 329
- Medical expense insurance, 328
- Noncancellable option, 339
- Physician's expense insurance, 329
- Preferred provider organization (PPO), 342
- Surgical expense insurance, 328

Health Insurance Portability and Accountability Act (HIPAA), 346
Health Maintenance Organization (HMO), 421
Health maintenance organization (HMO), 342
Hearing panel, 836
Hedging, 446
Heir, 731
Holding period return. *See Return*
Holding period return. *See Return*
Home equity, 241
Home health care. *See Long-term care insurance*
Home mortgage
- Adjustable-rate mortgage (ARM), 134–135
- Balloon mortgage, 135
- Fixed-rate mortgage, 134
- Variable-rate mortgage, 134–135

Home mortgages, 134
Homeowners checklist, 362
Homeowners insurance
- Coinsurance, 359
- Coverage A - Dwelling, 359
- Coverage B - Other structures, 360
- Coverage D - Loss of use, 361
- Coverage E - Personal liability, 362
- Endorsement, 368
- HO-2 - Broad form, 366
- HO-3 - Special form, 366
- HO-4 - Contents broad form, 366
- HO-5 - Comprehensive form, 366
- HO-6 - Unit owners form, 366
- HO-8 - Modified form, 367
- Homeowners checklist, 362
- Section I coverage, 358
- Section II coverage, 362
- Summary of, 374

HOPE credit, 238–239, 241
Hospice care. *See Long-term care insurance*
Hybrid mutual fund. *See Mutual fund*

I

IARD, 869
Immunization, 511
Implied authority, 272
Incentive stock option (ISO), 723
Income and expense statement. *See Financial statement*
Income tax
- Adjusted gross income, 599
  - Deductions for, 599
  - Deductions from, 599
  - Itemized deductions, 600
  - Standard deduction, 600
- Alternative minimum tax, 596
- Appeal procedure, 662
- Audit. *See Audit*

Capital loss, 596
Dependency exemption, 602
Dependent, 601
Dividends, 596
Filing status, 594
Gross income, 598
Exclusion, 598
Individual income tax rates, 593
Long-term capital gains, 595
Ordinary income, 593
Penalty
Accuracy-related, 604
Failure-to-file, 604
Failure-to-pay, 604
Fraud, 605
Personal exemption, 601
Tax credit, 602
Taxable income, 598, 602
Indemnity, 267
Subrogation, 267
Independent activity, 46
Index of leading economic indicators, 33
Indirect investing, 454
Individual retirement account (IRA), 715
Inflation, 17–19, 27–29, 31, 33, 674
Deflation, 27
Disinflation, 27
Galloping inflation, 27
Moderate inflation, 27
Information returns, 657
Initial public offering, 528
Initial public offering (IPO), 528
Inland marine policy, 386
Insurable interest, 267
Insurable loss, 264
Insurable risk
Requisites for, 264
Insurance, 256, 260
Agent, 271
Company ownership, 280
Federal and state regulation, 281
Underwriting, 281
Valuation of a loss, 273
Insurance agent, 805
Insurance company, 805
Insurance contract. *See Contract*
Integration of benefits. See Social Security or Disability insurance, 337
Interest, 176
Compound interest, 177
Interest for term, 741
Interest rate, 29, 32, 176
Discount rate, 32
Real interest rate, 33
Real interest rate adjustment, 29
Interest rate risk. *See Risk*
Internal environment. *See Environment*
Internal rate of return (IRR), 202–203
Internal rate of return (IRR). *See Return*
Internal Revenue Code, 592
Intestacy Laws, 733
Investment
Active approach to, 469
In business, 450
In real estate, 451
Indexing, 469–470
Lending investment, 449
Tax issues for, 465
Time horizon for, 464
Investment, 123
Investment adviser, 807–808
Investment adviser, 867
Investment Adviser Registration Depository, 869
Investment Advisors Act of 1940, 556, 867
investment companies, 871
Investment company
Internal Revenue Code criteria, 555
Investment Company Act of 1940, 556, 871
Investment Company Act of 1940., 871
investment counsel, 868
Investment goal, 441
investment security, 865
IRA, 716

J

JD, 805
Jensen's alpha. *See Alpha*
Jobs and Growth Tax Relief Reconciliation Act of 2003, 600
Joint accounts, 45
Joint and survivor annuity. See Annuity, 324
Joint return test, 602
Joint tenancy, 740

K

Keogh plan. *See Retirement plan*

L

Ladder strategy, 513
Law, 814
Law of large numbers, 258
Learning styles, 64
Legal environment. *See Environment*
Lending investment. *See Investment*

909

Lending securities, 476
Letter ruling, 603
Life insurance
- Group whole life, 315

Liability, 277, 518
- Business, 260
- Business and professional insurance, 386
- Business liability insurance, 387
- Business owner's policy, 386
- Civil liability, 816
- Commercial package policy, 386
- Errors and omissions insurance, 387
- For injuries inflicted upon others, 277
- Libel, 384
- Malpractice insurance, 387
- Negligence, 385
- Personal auto policy, 376
- Personal liability, 362
- Product liability insurance, 388
- Professional liability, 35, 62–63
- Slander, 384
- Strict and absolute, 384
- Torts, 384
- Workers' compensation, 387
- *See also Financial statement*
- *See also Personal liability policy*, 385

Libel, 384
Life cycle position, 67–68, 71
- Asset accumulation phase, 69
- Conservation/protection phase, 69
- Distribution/gifting phase, 70

Life estate, 741
Life insurance, 319
- Belth model, 316
- Capital retention approach, 298
- Feature comparison, 314
- Group term insurance, 315
- Incontestability clause, 317
- Individual life insurance, 300
- Modified life, 306
- NAIC criteria, 279
- Needs approach, 295
- Policy loan provision, 319
- Policy replacement, 317
- Split-dollar life insurance, 722
- Taxation of, 326
- Term insurance
  - Limitations of, 303
  - Types of, 302
- Transfer of policy, 325
- Variable life, 306
- Variable universal life, 311
- Whole life insurance
  - Cash value build-up, 304, 310–311
  - Characteristics of, 305
  - Dividend option, 307
  - Nonforfeiture option, 307
  - Settlement option, 308
  - Types of, 305–306

Lifetime learning credit, 238–239, 241
Like-kind exchange
- Boot, 610

Limit order, 542
Limited liability company (LLC), 638–642
- Articles of organization, 638

Limited partnership. *See Partnership*
Liquidity, 94, 449
Liquidity preference theory, 505
Liquidity. *See Risk*
Living trust, 746
Living will, 736
Loans, 42
Long position, 539
Long-term care insurance
- Adult day care, 331
- Assisted living, 331
- Custodial care, 331
- Defined benefit approach, 331
- Home health care, 331
- Hospice care, 331
- Intermediate nursing care, 330
- Pool of money concept, 331
- Skilled nursing care, 330
- Tax deduction of premiums, 334

Loss control, 259

M

Magnuson-Moss Warranty Act, 39
Malpractice insurance, 387
Managed care, 341
Manager, 638
Margin account, 540–542
Margin call, 541
Marginal utility, 22
Market order, 542
Market risk. *See Risk*
Market segmentation theory, 506
Marketability, 449
Marketability. *See Risk*
Markowitz, Harry, 459–460
Maturity, 476, 502
Mean-variance optimization model, 577
Medicaid, 327, 402

Medical insurance. *See Health insurance*
Medicare, 327, 401–404, 408, 419–423
Modern portfolio theory, 459, 584
    Efficient frontier, 459
Modified adjusted gross income, 415
Monetary policy, 31
    Open market operations, 32
    Reserve requirement, 32
Money market, 484
Money market mutual fund. *See Mutual fund*
Money market mutual funds, 43
Monopoly, 40–41
Moral hazard. *See Hazard*
Morale hazard *See Hazard*
Morbidity, 334
Morningstar analysis, 582–583
Mortality charge, 305
Mortgage-backed securities, 494
Municipal bonds, 491
Mutual fund, 43, 559–560
    Advantages of, 565–568
    Classes of, 563
    Disadvantages of, 568–570
    Equity mutual fund, 575
    Fees, 562–563
    Fixed-income mutual fund, 573
    Foreign mutual fund, 523
    Hybrid (or balanced) mutual fund, 575
    Load fund, 563
    Money market mutual fund, 572
    No load fund, 563
    Objectives of, 570
    Performance measures of, 584
    Prospectus, 578–579, 581
    Selection of, 578
    Types of, 571
Mutual savings banks, 42

N

NASD, 867
NASD exam. *See Compliance*
Nasdaq, 531–532
National Association of Securities Dealers, 867
National Credit Union Administration (NCUA), 43
National Credit Union Share Insurance Fund (NCUSSIF), 43
National Housing Act of 1934, 495
NCUA, 43
NCUSSIF, 43
Needs approach. See Life insurance, 295
Negligence, 36, 385, 604
    Contributory, 36
Negligence per se, 35
Negotiable, 47
Net asset value (NAV), 560
Net present value (NPV), 197, 201–202
Net unrealized appreciation, 700, 720
Net worth, 94
No load fund. *See Mutual fund*
Nominal return. *See Return*
Noncancellable option, 339
Nonqualified stock option (NQSO), 722
Nontraditional family. *See Special needs*

O

OASDI (Old Age and Survivor Disability Insurance), 403
Objective risk. *See Risk*
Occupational Safety and Health Act, 41
Officer, 633
Oligopoly, 40
Online trading, 543
Open market operations. *See Monetary policy*
Open-end investment company. *See Mutual fund*
Opportunity cost, 6, 205
Option. *See Derivative*
Ordinary income. *See Income tax*
Over the counter trading, 529
Own occupation disability definition. See Disability insurance, 335

P

P&I payments, 135
P/E ratio, 547
Parent Loans for Undergraduate Students. *See Student loan*
Partner. *See Partnership*
Partnership, 628–631, 640–643, 662–663
    General partnership, 629
    Limited partnership, 629, 631–632
    Partner, 628
Passive investing. *See Investment - Indexing*
Pay-on-death, 741
Peak. *See Business cycle*
Pension plan. *See Retirement plan*
Peril, 262
    General exclusions, 358
    Open peril, 262
Perpetuity, 197, 208–209
Personal auto policy
    Collision, 383
    Comprehensive, 383
    Part A - Liability coverage, 376
    Part C - Uninsured motorist, 381
    Part D - Coverage for damage to your auto, 382
    Part E - Duties after an accident or loss, 384

Part F - General provisions, 384
Split limits, 379
Personal exemption, 601
Personal Financial Specialist (PFS), 803
Personal instruction letter, 736
Personal liability policy
Characteristics of, 385
Personal umbrella policy, 385
Self-insured retention, 385
Personal savings
Qualitative factors in, 682
Personal savings, 443
Personal service corporation (PSC). *See Corporation*
Personal utility curve, 6
Physical hazard. *See Hazard*
Political environment. *See Environment*
Power of Appointment Trust, 747
Power of appointment trust. *See Trust*
Power of attorney, 732
Attorney-in-fact, 735
Principal, 735
Practice standards, 839
Preemptive right, 518
Preemptive right
Stock, 518
Preferred habitat theory, 505
Preferred Provider Organization (PPO), 421
Preferred provider organization (PPO), 342
Preferred stock. *See Stock*
Prepaid tuition, 223, 233–234
Prepayment risk *See risk*
Preponderance of evidence, 835
Present value, 176–177, 188–191, 194, 199, 201–202, 205–206
Present value of an annuity due, 194–196
Present value of an ordinary annuity, 191–193
Uneven cash flows, 198
Price elasticity. *See Elasticity*
Price index, 29
Primary insurance amount (PIA), 409
Primary market, 484, 528
Principal, 42, 133, 135–136
principal, 868–869
Principal and interest payments, 135
Private censure, 836
Private letter ruling, 603
Private pension plans, 681
Private Placement, 529
Probate, 736
Producer Price Index (PPI), 30
Product liability insurance, 388
Professional liability. *See Liability*
Profit-sharing plan, 712
Profit-sharing plan. *See Retirement plan*
Promissory note, 47
Property damage, 36
Property insurance
Inland marine policy, 386
Property interests, 740
Community property, 740
Fee simple, 740
Interest for term, 741
Joint Tenancy With Right of Survivorship, 740
Life estate, 741
Pay-on-death, 741
Tenancy by the entirety, 740
Tenancy in common, 740
Transfer-on-Death, 741
Usufruct, 741
Proprietor. *See Sole proprietorship*
Prospectus, 865
Prospectus. *See Mutual fund*
Provider Sponsored Organization (PSO), 421
Public letter of admonition, 836
Punitive damages, 36
Purchasing power preservation model (PPP), 689
Purchasing power risk. *See Risk*
Pure annuity concept, 688
Pure expectations theory, 504
Pure risk. See Risk, 260
Put options. *See Derivatives*
Pyramid of knowledge, 8, 58, 800

Q

QDOT. *See Trust*
QTIP. *See Trust*
QTP, 233–236, 246
Qualified domestic trust. *See Trust*
Qualified higher education expense, 235, 239, 241
Qualified retirement plan. *See Retirement plan*
Qualified Terminable Interest Property Trust, 747
Qualified terminable interest property trust. *See Trust*
Qualified transfer. *See Estate transfer tax*
Qualified Tuition Plan *See QTP*
Quantitative analysis comparison, 135

R

R2. *See Coefficient of determination*
Random walk, 468
Rate of return
Earnings rate, 178
Real rate of return, 205–207
Rating agency
Insurer, 279

Ratio analysis. *See Financial statement analysis*
Ratios. *See Financial ratio*
Real Estate, 451
Real estate broker, 805
Real interest rate adjustment. *See Interest rate*
Real rate of return. *See Rate of return*
Real rate of return. *See Return*
Recession. *See Business cycle*
Reduced paid-up insurance, 308
Registered investment adviser, 832
Registered Investment Adviser (RIA), 805
Registration, 865, 869
Registration statement, 865
Regulation, 866–867
Regulation risk. *See Risk*
Reinsurance, 281
Reinvestment risk. *See Risk*
Relationship test, 602
Remaining work life expectancy (RWLE), 668
Remarriage. *See Special needs*
Replacement cost, 273–275, 359
Repurchase agreements, 486
Res ipsa loquitur, 36
Reserve requirement. *See Monetary policy*
Residual benefits. *See Disability insurance, 337*
Retirement goal, 675
Retirement income
- Sources of income, 680

Retirement life expectancy (RLE), 669
- relationship with (WLE), 670

Retirement Plan
- 401(k) plan, 708
- Defined-contribution plan, 711
- Simplified employee pension (SEP), 717

Retirement plan
- 403(b) plan, 718
- Characteristics of qualified plans, 697, 700–701, 712
- Contributory plan, 713
- Deferred-compensation plan, 721
- Defined-benefit plan, 710
- Disadvantages of qualified plans, 701–705
- Keogh plan, 713
- Noncontributory plan, 713
- Nonqualified plan, 720
- Pension plan, 707–708, 710, 712–713
  - Money-purchase pension plan, 708
- Profit-sharing plan, 707–708, 710, 713
- SIMPLE plan, 717
- Stock bonus plan, 708
- Thrift plan, 698
- Types of qualified plans, 696, 707

Retirement planning
- Basic factors affecting, 668
- Investment decisions, 673
- Summary of factors affecting, 685

Return, 534
- Arithmetic mean, 534–535
- Dividend yield, 539
- Dollar-weighted return, 536–538
- Geometric mean, 457, 535
- Holding period return, 456, 534
- Internal rate of return (IRR), 458
- Nominal return, 459
- Real rate of return, 459
- return on equity, 885
- Time-weighted return, 536–537

Return, 866, 883, 885, 897
Return on investment (ROI). *See Financial ratio*
Revenue procedure, 603
Revenue ruling, 603
Revocation, 836
Rider, 273
Risk, 525
- Avoidance of, 259
- Business risk, 447, 527
- Country risk, 448, 528
- Credit risk, 500
- Default risk, 450, 500
- Exchange rate risk, 501, 526
- Financial risk, 448, 527
- Foreign currency risk, 446
- Interest rate risk, 446, 498, 526
- Investment risks, 444
- Liquidity, 449
- Liquidity risk, 501
- Market risk, 446, 525
- Marketability, 449
- Objective risk, 257
- Prepayment risk, 494
- Purchasing power risk, 445
- Pure risk, 260
  - Identifying and evaluating, 282
- Regulation risk, 445
- Reinvestment rate risk, 500
- Reinvestment risk, 445
- Retention or assumption of, 260
- Risk management, 282
  - Selecting an appropriate tool, 283
- Speculative risk, 256
- Subjective risk, 257
- Systematic risk, 445, 525
- Total risk, 447, 455
- Transfer of, 256, 259–261, 264, 284
- Types of, 276

Unsystematic risk, 447, 527
Risk analysis. *See Financial statement analysis*
Risk management. *See Risk*
Risk tolerance, 72, 464
Roth IRA, 233, 237–238, 716
Rule of 72, 209
Russell Index, 533

S

S corporation, 636–638, 640–643, 665
SAIF, 42
Saving and consumption habits, 133
Savings, 104, 449
Rate, 672
Timing, 672
Savings accounts, 449
Savings Association Insurance Fund (SAIF), 42
Savings bond, 239, 241
Series EE Bonds, 239
Savings bonds
Series EE, 488
Series HH, 488
Series I, 489
Schedule C, 626
Scholarships, 221, 231–232, 247
Section I coverage. *See Homeowners insurance,* 358
Secondary market, 484, 529
Section 457 plans, 721–722
Section II coverage. *See Homeowners insurance,* 362
Securities
Asset-backed securities, 478
Federal agency securities, 491
Fixed income securities, 476
Securities Act of 1933, 48, 63, 556, 865, 867
Securities analyst, 805
Securities Exchange Act of 1934, 48, 63, 556, 865–868
Securities Exchange Act of 1934., 866
Securities Exchange Commission (SEC), 556
Securities market line, 550
Securitization, 494
Security Act of 1933, 865
Self-employment tax, 606
Self-employment taxes, 627
Semivariance, 455–456
Sensitivity analysis. *See Financial statement analysis*
Serial payment, 197, 207–208
Settlement procedure, 838
Shareholder, 632
Sharpe ratio, 585–586
Sherman Act, 40
Short position, 539
Side instruction letter, 736
SIMPLE plan. *See Retirement plan*
Simplified employee pension (SEP). *See Retirement plan*
Single ownership accounts, 45
Skilled nursing care. *See Long-term care insurance*
Slander, 384
Social environment. *See Environment*
Social Security
Beneficiaries of, 406
Benefits of, 400
Changes for 2004, 424
Currently insured, 418
Disability benefit, 401
Disability insured, 416, 418
Earnings limitations test, 414
Family benefit, 401
Federal Insurance Contributions Act (FICA), 606
Filing for, 423
Fully insured, 405–406, 412, 416, 418
Integration of benefits, 337
Maximum family benefit, 418
Retirement benefit, 400, 411
Statement of, 407
Survivors benefit, 401
Taxation of benefits, 415
Social security, 680
Social Security Act, 402
Social Security Administration, 400
Social Security tax, 605
Social Security tax. *See Federal Insurance Contributions Act*
Sole proprietorship, 45–46, 626, 641–642
Proprietor, 626
Special damages, 36
Special needs, 73
Aging parent, 74
Career change, 76
Disabled dependent, 75
Divorce, 73
Nontraditional family, 75
Remarriage, 74
Terminal illness, 75
Speculative risk. *See Risk*
SSI (Supplemental Security Income), 423
Standard and Poor's 500 Index (S&P 500), 525, 531
Standard deviation, 455
Standard of proof, 36
Stand-by underwriting, 529
Statement of cash flows. *See Financial statement*
Statement of changes in net worth. *See Financial statement*
Stock
Blue chip stock, 520
Common stock, 450–451, 454, 519

Cyclical stock, 519
Defensive stock, 519
Growth stock, 520
Interest sensitive stock, 521
New economy stock, 522
Preferred stock, 451, 522, 546–548
Value stock, 521
Stock, 518
Stock bonus plan. *See Retirement plan*
Stock brokerage firms, 43
Stock See Voting, 518
Stock.
Preemptive right, 518
Stop limit order, 543
Stop loss order, 543
Strategy formulation, 159
Strategy selection, 164
Student loan, 222, 224, 229, 240–241
Consolidation loan, 226, 229
Direct loan, 227, 229
FFEL loan, 227
Perkins loan, 226–227, 230–231
PLUS loan, 224, 226, 229, 231
Stafford loan, 226–229
Student loan deferment, 228–229, 231
Subjective risk. *See Risk*
Subrogation, 373
Subrogation. *See Indemnity*
Substitute for money, 47
Substitutes, 22
Substitution effect, 20
Suicide, 318
Supply, 21
Supply curve, 21
Support test, 602
Suspension, 836
SWOT analysis, 157–158
Systematic risk. *See Risk*

T

Target-benefit plan, 712
Tax avoidance, 658
Tax credit. *See Income tax*
Tax deferral
Benefits of, 705
Tax evasion, 658
Tax rates. *See Income tax, Estate transfer tax, or Generation-skipping transfer tax*
Tax Reform Act of 1986, 495
Tax Relief Act of 2001, 236, 240–241
Tax shelter, 609
Taxable bond Market *See bonds*
Taxation environment. *See Environment*
Tax-exempt bond Market *See bonds*
Tax-exempt security, 609
Technical advice memoranda, 603
Technical analysis, 468, 544
Technological environment. *See Environment*
Tenancy by the entirety, 740
Tenancy in common, 740
Term, 176
Term insurance. *See Life insurance*, 302
Terminal illness. *See Special needs*
Thinking phase, 64–66, 149, 151, 162
Third market, 529
Thrift plan. *See Retirement plan*
Time horizon. *See Investment*
Time value of money, 8, 176–177, 179–183, 185–186, 188–191, 193–194, 196–197, 201, 205, 209
Timelines, 179
Time-weighted return. *See Return*
Tolerance for risk, 135
Top-heavy, 705
Tort, 35
Damages, 36
Defenses, 36
Negligence, 35–36
Strict liability, 35
Unintentional torts, 35
Vicarious liability, 36
Transfer-on-Death, 741
Treasury bills, 484
Treasury bonds *See bonds*
Treasury notes, 486
Inflation Indexed Treasury Notes and Bonds, 486
Treasury STRIPS, 486
Treynor ratio, 587
Trust, 743
Bypass trust, 768–769, 771
Charitable lead trust (CLT), 766
Charitable Remainder Trust, 747
Charitable remainder trust (CRT), 765
Credit Equivalency Trust, 747
Grantor trust, 746
Living trust, 746
Power of Appointment Trust, 747
Power of appointment trust, 768
Qualified domestic trust (QDOT), 771
Qualified Terminable Interest Property Trust, 747
Qualified terminable interest property trust (QTIP), 767
Truth in Lending Act, 39
TVM, 176

U

UGMA, 239
Unaccredited investor, 529
Underwriting, 528–529
    Firm commitment, 528
    Insurance, 281
    Stock, 528
Underwriting, stock
    Underwriting, 528
Unearned income, 657
Unemployment, 76
Unemployment compensation, 41
Uneven cash flows, 197
Unified credit. *See Estate transfer tax - Applicable credit amount*
Unified tax rate, 753
Uniform Gift to Minor's Act *See UGMA*
Uniform Transfer to Minor's Act *See UTMA*
Unilateral, 270
Uninsured motorist. *See Personal auto policy*
Unit investment trust (UIT), 556
Unsystematic risk. *See Risk*
Usufruct, 741
UTMA, 239

V

Valuation of equities, 544
    Dividend discount model, 546
    Free cash flow to equity, 548
Variable life. See Life insurance, 306
Veritcal analysis. *See Financial statement analysis*
Viatical agreement, 326
Vision insurance, 341
Volatility. *See Standard deviation or Beta*
Voting
    Stock, 518
    Straight voting
        Cumulative voting
        Proxy voting, 518

W

Wage replacement ratio (WRR), 676
    Calculation of, 677
    The budgeting approach, 677
    The top-down approach, 677
Whole life insurance. *See Life insurance,* 306
Will, 733
    Clauses
        Appointment and powers clause, 734
        Attestation clause, 734
        Disclaimer clause, 735
        No-contest clause, 735
        Residuary clause, 734
        Self-proving clause, 734
        Simultaneous death clause, 734
        Survivorship clause, 734
    Type
        Holographic, 734
        Oral (Nuncupative), 734
        Statutory, 734
Wilshire 5000 Index, 533
Work life expectancy (WLE), 668
    relationship with (RLE), 670
Workers' compensation, 41
Work-study, 223, 226, 230

Y

Yield
    Current yield, 479
Yield curves, 503
Yield to call (YTC), 482
Yield to maturity (YTM), 197, 203–204, 480

Z

Zero-coupon bond, 479